P9-CCE-672

LET TV MOVIES
ENTERTAIN YOU!

Tonight's the night to enjoy a movie on TV. Today's the day to consult the indispensable book to help you pick the best of the best.

All the legendary films are here—hundreds of great new super releases, thousands of golden oldies, all of your all-time favorites. Shoot 'em up westerns. Tuneful musicals. War sagas. Science fiction. Comedies. Foreign films. Enjoy them more with this handy, alphabetized guide. It will let you know in advance which stars are appearing, what the story is about—and whether the picture is worth watching.

1) Check your daily newspaper for time and channel.
2) Consult MOVIES ON TV to help you select the movie to entertain you—tonight.

ENJOY!

MOVIES ON TV

1978-79 Edition

Formerly Published
as

TV KEY MOVIE GUIDE

Edited by Steven H. Scheuer

MOVIES ON TV

Original Bantam edition / November 1958
under the title TV MOVIE ALMANAC & RATINGS 1958 & 1959
2nd printing .. November 1958
Second (revised) edition / December 1961
under the title TV KEY MOVIE REVIEWS & RATINGS
Third (revised) edition / December 1966
under the title TV KEY MOVIE GUIDE
2nd printing . December 1966   3rd printing . November 1967
under the title MOVIES ON TV
4th printing ...... March 1968
Fourth (revised) edition / October 1968
Fifth (revised) edition / September 1969
Sixth (revised) edition / November 1971
2nd printing . November 1971   4th printing .. February 1972
3rd printing . December 1971   5th printing ...... May 1972
Seventh (revised) edition / October 1974
2nd printing ... October 1974   3rd printing .. December 1974
4th printing .... April 1975
Eighth (revised) edition / November 1977

Cover photo courtesy of
Paramount Pictures Corporation.

Library of Congress Catalog Card Number: 66-28552

All rights reserved.
Copyright © 1958, 1961, 1966, 1968, 1969, 1971, 1974, 1977
by Bantam Books, Inc.
Cover photo Copyright © 1974 by Paramount Pictures
Corporation and The Coppola Company.
This book may not be reproduced in whole or in part, by
mimeograph or any other means, without permission.
For information address: Bantam Books, Inc.

ISBN 0-553-11451-4

Published simultaneously in the United States and Canada

Bantam Books are published by Bantam Books, Inc. Its trade-
mark, consisting of the words "Bantam Books" and the por-
trayal of a bantam, is registered in the United States Patent
Office and in other countries. Marca Registrada. Bantam
Books, Inc., 666 Fifth Avenue, New York, New York 10019.

PRINTED IN THE UNITED STATES OF AMERICA

For Nikki—more than ever,
my most perceptive and beloved critic.

Special thanks are due to John Goudas, Don Miller, James Steinberg, Joel Altschuler, and Linda Sandahl.

Preface

This is the eighth edition of *Movies on TV,* and it is substantially larger and more comprehensive than any of the earlier editions. This updated, revised and expanded publication includes over 1000 films that were not included in the last edition—the overwhelming percentage of them now available to TV for the first time. As always, we have one principal objective in mind—to make the viewing of feature films on TV easier and more enjoyable by enabling movie enthusiasts to be better informed and more selective in their choice of film fare.

In the past few years, virtually every good film—and thousands of poor ones—made during the 1960s and early '70s has become available for telecasting. These outstanding films are made available when a network, sponsor or advertiser pays the distributor's asking price for a TV showcasing. "The Sound of Music," "My Fair Lady," "Bonnie and Clyde," "The Graduate," and "Love Story" have already been shown on TV. "Gone With the Wind" and "The Godfather," two of the all-time box-office champions, have been on. "The Godfather" fetched a record price for TV showcasing—10 million dollars for one airing.

Most of the broadcast time that local TV stations now devote to feature films is filled by movies of comparatively recent vintage, primarily products of the 1960s and early '70s. Until the early 1960s, many TV stations regularly telecast dreary black and white features produced during the '30s and '40s. This is no longer true, especially if the films in question do not boast any big-name stars. I have consequently included in this edition fewer reviews of the undistinguished films of the '30s and '40s than were found in the first two editions of this work, published in 1958 and 1961. The films of the '30s and '40s have had their hours of glory on TV and, with the exception of the greats and near greats, are gradually being returned for good to the film vaults by their licensees. However, most of the enduring and worthwhile films of these two decades are reviewed here because of their continuing popularity and exposure. (There are, unhappily, a substantial number of "lost films" —movies which have disappeared without leaving a single known complete print. I have not reviewed such films here even though some of these "lost films" were seen years ago by me and members of my reviewing staff.)

Both serious cinema scholars and casual fans of the art of motion pictures are still indebted to television for one continuing blessing. TV continues to provide a previously undreamed of opportunity to examine at one's leisure, and with little expense, most of the history of a major American and international art form—an art form, furthermore, that has had a profound impact on the habits and attitudes of audiences throughout the world. In the middle of the 1970s it is, I think, unquestionably true that motion pictures are the dominant and most popular art form of our time, both here and abroad.

Today's American college students have grown up with TV. Millions of American school children, in today's "post-linear generation," are *visually* literate and perceptive at a time when they, and their peers, seem to be encountering increasing difficulties with traditional reading and writing skills. It is not surprising that the impact of the visual arts, primarily motion pictures and television, increases every year.

With a little advance planning, movie devotees can now sample on TV the work of the most noteworthy talents and personalities since movies first learned to walk and talk. Social anthropologists concerned with changing sex symbols can scrutinize Rudolph Valentino's early silent films. They can dispassionately assess the on-screen love-making techniques of such celebrated past practitioners as Garbo, Gable, Harlow, and Flynn; and such standard bearers as Marilyn Monroe, Sophia Loren, Elizabeth Taylor, Elvis Presley, Sean Connery, Paul Newman, and Robert Redford. Future film critics can analyze the directorial accomplishments of such early titans as D. W. Griffith, Lubitsch, Eisenstein, Chaplin, and Vidor; the refinements of such later but still contemporary masters as John Ford, Hitchcock, Renoir, Capra, Kazan, Billy Wilder, William Wyler, and Kurosawa; and the recent films of such remarkable directors, of a still younger generation, as

Fellini, Ingmar Bergman, Kubrick, Antonioni, Truffaut, Godard, Altman, Coppola, and Scorcese.

Today's movie feast is becoming ever more varied thanks partially to the developments, however slow, of pay TV; and, more particularly, cable TV, which offers the possibility of additional TV channels; and the future role of TV cartridges, cassettes, and home video tape recorders and playback units, which will allow film buffs the opportunity to build home movie libraries of books and records. In the 1972–73 season, public TV stations throughout the country broadcast full-length classic foreign films with new English subtitles which were telecast, happily, without interruptions for commercials or station breaks. One of the many lamentable policies of the former Nixon administration was their ongoing policy of intimidating public TV while simultaneously starving the public TV stations for programming funds. With a one-billion-dollar annual budget, which American public TV needs and deserves, public TV could broadcast many superior films ignored by the commercial networks, and could show them without the mood-destroying commercials. But even a billion dollars won't improve the quality of the picture and the sound on a 21-inch screen, a viewing area much less than one percent of the size of the theater screens for which the films were originally designed and conceived.

Careful planning, a carefree schedule, and the luck to live in a community within reception range of a TV station whose program manager or film buyer is a knowledgeable film fan will permit today's movie buff to trace the careers of their favorite performers. You can watch most of the movie roles played by such current box-office stars as Sidney Poitier, Paul Newman, Robert Redford, and Barbra Streisand. You can also follow the careers of older stars who are still headliners like John Wayne or Katharine Hepburn. Admirers of the inimitable Hepburn style can see her in dozens of films: with John Barrymore in the vintage 1932 "Bill of Divorcement," with Cary Grant in "The Philadelphia Story," boating with Bogart in "The African Queen," dallying in the canals of Venice in "Summertime," in her triumphant performance in the 1963 version of O'Neill's "Long Day's Journey into Night," with her beloved Spencer Tracy in many films, including his last film "Guess Who's Coming to Dinner," "The Madwoman of Chaillot," "A Delicate Balance" with Paul Scofield, the 1973 TV-movie remake of "The Glass Menagerie," plus her co-starring vehicle with Laurence Olivier, "Love Among the Ruins." Her performance in Tennessee Williams' "The Glass Menagerie" post-dates the great Kate's film debut by nearly half a century.

Those viewers who prefer a familiar story line while gazing at the Hollywood idols may still treat themselves to the no-doubt edifying spectacle of Doris Day in modern-day versions of "The Perils of Pauline." Most of these serialized feature-length thrillers—in blushing color, not the black and white of the old cliffhangers—reveal the freckled over-thirtyish Doris maintaining a precarious hold on her chastity while being romanced, though never seduced, by such dapper worthies as Rock Hudson, and the ageless Cary Grant. Depending on your tastes you can see Buster Keaton, Bette Davis, or, if you hunt long and hard enough, assorted creaky whodunnits with such second feature stalwarts of the '40s as Sheila Ryan, Kane Richmond, and Stephanie Bachelor.

In the mid-1950s the release to TV of some of the best films from the major studios coincided with a particularly rapid, and as yet unchecked, deterioration in commercial network TV programming. The numerous rewarding "live" dramas starting around 1950 developed an audience with an increasing appreciation of spirited, if often flawed, drama coupled with the comforts of home. But the qualities of immediacy, honesty, and literacy which distinguished much of the "live" drama in TV's formative years were increasingly disregarded in favor of the innocuous, banal, and frequently inexcusably violent TV series. Current programming by the three commercial networks, with altogether few exceptions, is still a case of the "bland leading the bland," and the reprehensible quality of most children's programming is a national scandal. The drama-oriented viewer of the mid-1950s understandably turned to the good old films, which were suddenly available in large numbers on the small home screen. He/she was not disappointed. Many millions of moviegoers were then exposed to this vast body of Americana for the first time, and were given a unique insight into the feelings and fashions of the 1930s and '40s. High school students of the '70s, and film buffs young or old, now have a similar opportunity with regard to the films of the 1950s and '60s, both foreign and domestic.

The enormous interest in movies on TV exhibits few signs of abating. One of the landmark dates in TV's history is a Saturday night in the fall of 1961. In September of that year NBC introduced a brand-new concept, indeed a revolutionary notion, in network programming. They simply telecast a recent Hollywood movie, in its entirety, in prime evening time. It was just as simple as that! Born out of desperation, and conceived as yet another effort to win respectable ratings against CBS in the crucial Saturday evening time slot, two blondes named Monroe and Grable showed gray-haired NBC executives how to win high ratings. The movie that started a fundamental change in the pattern of TV programming was "How to Marry a Millionaire." Since then, network broadcasts of feature films originally made for theatrical exhibition have usually shot down their opposition in a fight decided by the most cold-blooded sheriff of them all—A. C. Nielsen and his quick-draw ratings.

There were several important developments concerning the presentation of movies on TV in the late 1960s. One of the notable and inevitable developments is that a feature-length film is now shown as a prime-time network presentation every single night of the week. Some of these feature presentations are in reality nothing more than two-hour TV shows, sometimes with high budgets, that are first seen on TV. The general quality of these films, such as the NBC "World Premiere" series, is quite low, and few of them are ever released to the theaters for paying customers *after* being shown on TV. Another comparatively recent development is the short time between the release of a film in movie theaters and its later broadcast on network or local TV. Some legitimate movies now show up on TV little more than a year after being seen in movie houses throughout the country.

The 1977–78 season marks the inauguration of still another innovation for movies on TV. NBC will devote no less than four nights to the showing of "The Godfather Saga," which will consist of the entire "Godfather" and "Godfather II," plus added footage which was shot but never used. Director Francis Ford Coppola will personally re-edit the nine hours worth of film. There's also the possibility that Robert Altman will eventually do the same with "Nashville," also using never-before-seen footage. Undoubtedly, the success of the mini-series, such as "Rich Man, Poor Man" and "Roots," has paved the way for "The Godfather Saga" and more of the same.

One final bit of advice. The film reviews in this book are all written by myself and my associates, and are based upon the original, uncut versions usually seen in movie theaters where they were *intended* to be watched. I regret to say that all three commercial networks continue to unconscionably butcher movies in the guise of censorship or "good taste." Your enjoyment of certain films seen over your local TV stations will sometimes depend upon what time you tune in. You're much more likely to see a full-length, non-censored version of a superior film during the late evening hours than if you watch during the day or early evening. It doesn't matter much whether a station concludes a feature showing at 12:51 A.M. or 1:07 A.M., but it is imperative that shows end at a precise pre-determined time during the rest of the broadcast day. Lengthy films have sometimes been chopped to fit into a one hour period, and viewers in all too many cities have been subjected to such outrages as seeing movies from which some indolent film editor simply chopped off the first 15 minutes, the middle 18, or snipped a similar chunk out toward the close of the once-upon-a-time intelligible film. So if your local station perpetrates any of these indignities for reasons of time, taste, or lack of talent, complain to *them*, or the Federal Communications Commission in Washington, D. C.

And finally, in response to the question often asked, here is a categorical reply we'll stand by for several years to come. There are no plans for network TV showings of "Deep Throat."

Steven H. Scheuer
New York City

Key to ratings:

**** Excellent
***   Good
**   Fair
*   Poor

All "A's" and "The's" are filed under the second word:

("A Night at the Opera" under "Night at the Opera, A")

TV Movie Reviews and Ratings

Aaron Slick from Punkin Crick (1952)** Alan Young, Robert Merrill, Dinah Shore, Guy Mitchell. Stylized satirization of the old tent show plot about the city slicker who tries to fleece the poor widow out West. Attempt at novelty doesn't come off and becomes just a rather tedious musical comedy. (Dir: Claude Binyon, 95 mins.)

Abandon Ship (1957)*** Tyrone Power, Mai Zetterling, Lloyd Nolan. Tense and terrifying drama about the fate of 26 survivors of a luxury liner disaster all crammed into a life boat that can only hold 12 safely. Tyrone Power is fine as the officer who has to decide who is to live or die. The lovely Mai Zetterling is now a gifted movie director. (Dir: Richard Sale, 100 mins.)

Abandoned (1949)**½ Dennis O'Keefe, Jeff Chandler. Somewhat sensationalized drama centering around the baby-adoption rackets and how a determined girl and a newspaper man help to crack them. (Dir: Joe Newman, 79 mins.)

Abbott and Costello Go to Mars (1953)** Bud Abbott, Lou Costello, Mari Blanchard. Strictly for the comedy duo fans. All their slapstick and double talk routines are evident in this silly space comedy about an accidental trip to Mars. (Dir: Charles Lamont, 77 mins.)

Abbott and Costello in the Foreign Legion (1950)** Bud Abbott, Lou Costello, Patricia Medina. The comedy duo dons Foreign Legionnaires' duds in this moderately funny farce about intrigue and the sand dunes of Algiers. A & C fans will get their quota of laughs. (Dir: Charles Lamont, 80 mins.)

Abbott and Costello in the Navy (1941)**½ Abbott and Costello, Dick Powell. The youngsters should enjoy this crazy film about a radio singer who seeks refuge in the Navy. (Dir: Arthur Lubin, 85 mins.)

Abbott and Costello Meet Captain Kidd (1952)** Charles Laughton, Fran Warren. Standard A & C nonsense, as the boys go after Captain Kidd's treasure with the bold pirate in hot pursuit. Laughton seems to be having a good time in his role. (Dir: Charles Lamont, 70 mins.)

Abbott and Costello Meet Dr. Jekyll and Mr. Hyde (1953)**½ Bud Abbott, Lou Costello, Boris Karloff. Abbott and Costello fans will enjoy this comedy-horror film which has them playing a couple of American detectives in London during the late 1800's. Boris Karloff, who has played most of the screen's well-known monsters, plays the dual role of Jekyll and Hyde. (Dir: Charles Lamont, 76 mins.)

Abbott and Costello Meet Frankenstein (1948)*** Abbott and Costello, Lon Chaney. A plot by the horror boys to put Lou's harmless brain in a monster makes for an entertaining film for fans of the comedy team. (Dir: Charles T. Barton, 92 mins.)

Abbott and Costello Meet the Invisible Man (1951)** Abbott and Costello, Nancy Guild. A light-weight farce in which Abbott and Costello play a couple of detectives who are hired by a unique client—an invisible man. Gimmicks galore in this wacky comedy in the usual Abbott and Costello style. (Dir: Charles Lamont, 82 mins.)

Abbott and Costello Meet the Keystone Kops (1955)*** Abbott and Costello, Fred Clark, Lynn Bari. They're in the movie business circa 1912 this time out. In between pies in the face, there's a wild chase complete with the famous Keystone Kops. (Dir: Charles Lamont, 80 mins.)

Abbott and Costello Meet the Killer (1949)** Abbott and Costello, Boris Karloff. A silly excursion into murder and mirth with the comedy team as a pair of amateur sleuths who almost get themselves killed in order to solve a murder. Karloff has some funny moments as an Indian fakir with a ghoulish look. (Dir: Charles Barton, 94 mins.)

Abbott and Costello Meet the Mummy (1955)** Abbott and Costello, Marie Windsor. They meet the mummy, not your mummy. Bud and Lou are treasure hunters in this yarn about Egyptian tombs and the many crooks who want to get their hands on a valuable hoard of gold and jewels. Usual slapstick antics. (Dir: Charles Lamont, 90 mins.)

1

Abdication, The (Great Britain, 1974)*½ Liv Ullmann, Peter Finch, Cyril Cusack. Ponderous historical drama—but full of absurd inaccuracies—about Christina, the Queen of Sweden who renounced her Protestant kingdom, circa 1655, to become a convert to the Catholic Church. A lot of normally good actors can't save this turgid entry, which reveals the shocking truth that the saintly souls wearing religious robes have sexual drives and hangups just like other earthlings. (Dir: Anthony Harvey, 102 mins.)

Abduction of Saint Anne, The (1975)**½ E. G. Marshall, Robert Wagner, Lloyd Nelson. Don't be put off by the title . . . this story (screenplay by Edward Hume) is original and not bad. A young girl is reputed to have healing powers, and the Catholic Church wants to have her miracles certified. But there's a hitch . . . she's being held a virtual prisoner in her gangland father's estate. Enter the Bishop and the private detective (Marshall and Wagner respectively). Made-for-TV. (Dir: Harry Falk, 72 mins.)

Abductors, The (1957)**½ Victor McLaglen, Fay Spain. Fairly well done crime tale supposedly based on true story. Concerns attempt to rob Lincoln's grave and is reasonably interesting. (Dir: Andrew McLaglen, 80 mins.)

Abe Lincoln in Illinois (1940)**** Raymond Massey and Ruth Gordon star in this moving, wonderfully acted version of Robert E. Sherwood's Broadway play. The 16th President's life, his ill-fated love for Ann Rutledge, and his marriage to Mary Todd. Massey, in subsequent performances on stage and screen, has proved to be a generally routine actor of limited range; but he was deeply moving as Lincoln and has made a good living, thanks largely to Lincoln, ever since. (Dir: John Cromwell, 110 mins.)

Abie's Irish Rose (1946)* From the stage play that's been kicking around for ages, as Jewish Richard Norris marries Irish Joanne Dru, and the families bicker and bicker. Bing Crosby produced this, if that means anything. Out of date, often offensive comedy. (Dir: A. Edward Sutherland, 96 mins.)

Abilene Town (1945)*** Randolph Scott, Ann Dvorak, Rhonda Fleming. The marshal of Abilene has his hands full separating the cattlemen from the homesteaders in 1870. Fast, well-produced western. (Dir: Edwin Marin, 89 mins.)

Abominable Dr. Phibes (U.S.-British, 1971)*** Vincent Price, Joseph Cotten, Terry-Thomas. The king of camp horror, Vincent Price, is at it again with great style. Stalking amid gothic backdrops, he plays a mad doctor out to polish off a surgical team who he believes did in his wife. There's a marvelous ending, with Price climbing into his grave as "Over the Rainbow" swells on the soundtrack. (Dir: Robert Fuest, 93 mins.)

Abominable Snowman of the Himalayas, The (1957)**½ Forrest Tucker, Peter Cushing, Maureen Connell. Better than average horror/science fiction yarn about the legendary Snowman of the Himalayas. Forrest Tucker and a British cast adequately play members of an expedition. Very high altitudes seem to help Tucker's acting. (Dir: Val Guest, 85 mins.)

About Face (1952)** Gordon MacRae, Eddie Bracken, Phyllis Kirk. Cadet musical with lavish, over-produced production numbers. This is remake of "Brother Rat" with tunes added for good measure. (Dir: Roy Del Ruth, 94 mins.)

About Mrs. Leslie (1954)**½ Shirley Booth, Robert Ryan. When a tycoon dies and leaves a boarding house owner some money, her secret love affair is recalled. Follow-up to Booth's award-winning performance in "Come Back, Little Sheba" is unadorned soap opera, partly compensated for by acting of the leads. (Dir: Daniel Mann, 104 mins.)

Above and Beyond (1953)*** Robert Taylor, Eleanor Parker. An absorbing subject well handled, in this screenplay about Colonel Tibbets, the officer who piloted the plane which dropped the atom bomb on Hiroshima. Robert Taylor gives a nicely etched performance as the conscience-stricken Tibbets, and gets good support from Eleanor Parker as his wife. (Dirs: Melvin Frank, Norman Panama, 122 mins.)

Above Suspicion (1943)**½ Joan Crawford, Fred MacMurray, Basil Rathbone. Fast moving chase melodrama with Fred and Joan trying to aid the British secret service while they honeymoon in Paris. Confusing at times but fairly entertaining film. (Dir: Richard Thorpe, 90 mins.)

Above Us the Waves (British, 1956) *** John Mills, John Gregson. High tension war drama of midget submarines and the stalking of German battleships. Fine acting and excellent photography. (Dir: Ralph Thomas, 99 mins.)

Abraham Lincoln (1930)*** Walter Huston, Una Merkel, Kay Hammond. Screenplay by Stephen St. Vincent Benet. A biographical drama about the great president, directed by D. W. Griffith. Outdated by now, but still frequently interesting. (Dir: D. W. Griffith, 97 mins.)

Abroad with Two Yanks (1944)*** Dennis O'Keefe, William Bendix, John Loder, Helen Walker. Two whacky Marines turn Australia inside out in their escapades over a girl. Wild, frequently hilarious comedy. (Dir: Alan Owan, 80 mins.)

Accattone! (Italian, 1961)*** The life and fate of a young Roman parasite, told in grimly neo-realistic style by director Pasolini (his first feature, before "The Gospel According to St. Matthew"). Somewhat remote emotionally, but the squalor of the locale is graphically captured. Well-acted by Franco Citti as the wastrel, and a nonprofessional cast. (Dir: Pier Paolo Pasolini, 120 mins.)

Accident, The (Italian, 1962)* Magali Noel, Georges Riviere. Familiar claptrap concerning a schoolteacher who falls in love with a shapely colleague, despite his wife's anger. Consternation causes him to attempt to do away with his wife. The plan goes wrong, and so does the plot. (85 mins.)

Accident (1967)***½ Dirk Bogarde, Stanley Baker, Jacqueline Sassard. Another fascinating film directed by Joseph Losey working with screenwriter Pinter and actor Bogarde—the same two responsible for "The Servant." Harold Pinter has fashioned a fascinating, if uneven, study of a married college professor who becomes involved with one of his attractive female students. It's not as simple as it sounds. The complexities are many, and the shadings of Dirk Bogarde's characterization as the professor are superbly etched. The entire cast is top drawer. (Dir: Joseph Losey, 105 mins.)

Accidental Death (British, 1964)**

John Carson, Jacqueline Ellis. Former intelligence agents set death traps for each other. Average suspense drama. (Dir: Geoffrey Nethercott, 57 mins.)

Accursed, The (1958)**½ Donald Wolfitt, Robert Bray. A fairly interesting mystery involving the guests of a onetime colonel of the Resistance forces at the annual reunion held at his home. The tale unfolds at the last reunion. (Dir: Michael McCarthy, 78 mins.)

Accused, The (1948)*** Loretta Young, Robert Cummings, Wendell Corey. Schoolteacher accidentally kills an amorous student, tries to cover her crime. Well-made drama keeps the attention pretty much throughout. (Dir: William Dieterle, 101 mins.)

Accused of Murder (1957)** Vera Ralston, David Brian. Homicide officer falls for a night club singer suspected of killing a gangland lawyer. Ordinary mystery. (Dir: Joseph Kane, 80 mins.)

Ace Eli and Rodger of the Skies (1973)*½ Cliff Robertson, Pamela Franklin, Eric Shea, Bernadette Peters. Nostalgia for the 1920's pervades this otherwise dismally confused melodrama. Eli, dreadfully played by Robertson, is a barnstorming pilot in rural Kansas, who flies with son Rodger, 11 years old and the more mature of the duo. Fine aerial photography. Based on a story by "Jaws" director Steven Spielberg. Such a bad story that those who produced it used different names on the screen. (Dir: Bill Sampson [John Erman], 92 mins.)

Ace High (Italian, 1968)**½ Eli Wallach, Brock Peters, Kevin McCarthy. Occasionally interesting spaghetti western which spoofs the genre. Wallach plays a sly bandit in Mexico, who gets the loot no matter what obstacles are in his way. Fine supporting cast makes this an above-average adventure. (Dir: Giuseppe Colizzi, 120 mins.)

Ace in the Hole—See: **Big Carnival, The**

Across 110th Street (1972)** Anthony Quinn, Anthony Franciosa, Yaphet Kotto. Violent crime drama shot in Harlem where the story, about in-fighting among the Mafia and small-time hoods regarding a theft of syndicate cash amounting to close to a half a million, takes place. There's an attempt to keep the dialogue natural, but most of the performances seem arch and contrived, except for Yaphet Kotto's policeman-sidekick of Quinn's veteran cop. Director Barry Shear keeps things moving at such a fast clip, you won't know the film is as bad as it is until it's over. (Dir: Barry Shear, 102 mins.)

Across the Bridge (1957)*** Rod Steiger, David Knight. Crooked tycoon on the lam from Scotland Yard is cornered in Mexico. Considerable suspense in this drama; good performances, especially Steiger's. (Dir: Ken Annakin, 103 mins.)

Across The Great Divide (1976)***½ Robert Logan, George Flower, Heather Rattray, Mark Edward Hall. An unusually well done children's film with no objectionable violence or language. Two spunky orphans have plenty of adventures and hardships en route to their new home in Oregon in the old West. A charming fugitive meets and helps the children in the wilderness of the West. There are some remarkably good scenes with trained animals, and the glories of the American West serve as a permanent backdrop for "Divide," filmed on location. (Dir: Stuart Raffill, 89 mins.)

Across the Pacific (1942)***½ Humphrey Bogart, Mary Astor, Sydney Greenstreet. John Huston's directing magic and a fine cast make this a taut spy melodrama. (Dir: John Huston, 97 mins.)

Across the Wide Missouri (1951)** Clark Gable, Ricardo Montalban, John Hodiak. A slow-moving outdoor adventure saga about the trail blazers of the Rockies. Gable fits his role of fur trapper nicely, but has little to do other than look strong and brave. Supporting cast is adequate.

Act of Love (1955)***½ Kirk Douglas, Dany Robin. American soldier has a tragic affair with a poor girl in occupied Paris. Powerful love story, excellently acted, filmed in France. (Dir: Anatole Litvak, 105 mins.)

Act of Murder, An (1948)***½ Fredric March, Edmond O'Brien, Florence Eldridge. Judge is tried for the mercy killing of his wife. Grim and unrelenting, but finely done drama

deserves praise. (Dir: Michael Gordon, 91 mins.)

Act of Reprisal, An (1965)*½ Ina Balin, Jeremy Brett. A romance is broken up between a British official and a Greek girl when the Greek-Cypriot civil war erupts. It couldn't happen to two duller characters. (87 mins.)

Act of the Heart (Canada, 1970)*** Genevieve Bujold, Donald Sutherland, Bill Mitchell. An often moving, superbly acted, independently made low-budget entry that is profoundly marred by a preposterous, unbelievable ending. Young former farm girl arrives in Montreal and falls in love with a priest while developing what turns out to be a fatal case of religious hysteria. Bujold is touching and radiant playing Martha, the pious novice choir singer. Skillfully directed and written for Bujold by her husband, Paul Almond. But oh that finale! (Dir: Paul Almond, 103 mins.)

Act of Violence (1948)**½ Van Heflin, Janet Leigh, Robert Ryan. Well acted and directed but routine chase melodrama about a guy who betrayed his buddies in a Nazi prison camp. (Dir: Fred Zinnemann, 82 mins.)

Act One (1963)*** George Hamilton, Jason Robards, Eli Wallach. If you have never read Moss Hart's sentimental, best-selling novel about his youthful love affair with the Broadway theater, this watered-down film version will entertain you. The supporting cast is good, but George Hamilton as Hart is a bit too good looking and polished to convey the innocence and dedication of a poor Jewish boy who became a major playwright-author-director. (Dir: Dore Schary, 110 mins.)

Action in the North Atlantic (1943)***½ Humphrey Bogart, Raymond Massey. Forget that it was originally war propaganda, relax and enjoy this exciting dramatic tribute to the Merchant Marine. (Dir: Lloyd Bacon, 127 mins.)

Action Man (French, 1967)** Jean Gabin, Robert Stack. Confused tale of a criminal and an American adventurer out to rob a bank. The plot goes well until the criminal's wife is kidnapped by some dope smugglers. Saved by the always watchable Jean Gabin. Low-budget entry. (Dir: Jean Delannoy, 95 mins.)

Action of the Tiger (1957)**½ Van Johnson, Martine Carol, Herbert Lom. Routine adventure yarn with all the cliches intact—an American adventurer on foreign soil (Van Johnson); a glamorous lady with dangerous plans (M. Carol); and a clever underworld figure with a good heart (H. Lom). Nothing new here, but action fans might enjoy it. (Dir: Terence Young, 92 mins.)

Actors and Sin (1952)*** Edward G. Robinson, Eddie Albert, Marsha Hunt. Two stories by Ben Hecht: "Woman of Sin," hilarious Hollywood burlesque about a child who writes a great screenplay, and "Actor's Blood," trite, overdrawn drama of a beautiful actress whose strange death implicates many people. All in all, an entertaining package. (Dir: Ben Hecht, 86 mins.)

Actor's Holiday (1969)** James Franciscus and his family take a vacation in Puerto Rico, in the Dominican Republic, and on other islands. A few picturesque sights along the way. (60 mins.)

Actress, The (1953)*** Spencer Tracy, Jean Simmons, Teresa Wright, Anthony Perkins. Thoroughly enjoyable screen version of Ruth Gordon's delightful play, "Years Ago." Tracy and Jean Simmons shine brilliantly as father and daughter. Anthony Perkins has a brief role as Jean's boyfriend. (Dir: George Cukor, 90 mins.)

Ada (1961)** Susan Hayward, Dean Martin. Guitar-playing sheriff is persuaded to run for governor, but his attraction to a good-time girl threatens his political career. Unconvincing drama of Southern politics. (Dir: Daniel Mann, 109 mins.)

Adalen 31 (Swedish, 1969)**** Peter Schildt, Roland Hedlund, Martin Widerberg, Marie de Geer. Director Bo (Elvira Madigan) Widerberg's beautiful, perceptive drama played out against the background of a real event in Swedish history—the 1931 strike in the town of Adalen. Five workers were killed when soldiers fired on the peaceful protesters. Focuses on one family, whose working father is one of the leaders of the strike. Makes its social comment, but Widerberg has also captured one of the most exquisite and touching scenes of young love ever seen on film, as Kjell, the son of a striker, has an idyllic affair with the daughter

of the factory manager. Visually breathtaking film about politics, love, and lots more. Widerberg also wrote the screenplay. English subtitles. (115 mins.)

Adam and Evalyn (British, 1949)**½ Stewart Granger, Jean Simmons. Handsome gambler adopts the daughter of a deceased friend, finds she's pretty enough to fall for. Mildly entertaining romance. (Dir: Harold French, 90 mins.)

Adam and Eve (Mexican, 1956)** Carlos Baena, Christiane Martel. Unsuccessful adaptation of the Book of Genesis, brought to life occasionally by the camerawork of Alex Phillips, one of Mexico's finest cameramen. Acting is only fair. Miss Martel was Miss Universe 1953. (Dir: Albert Gout, 76 mins.)

Adam Had Four Sons (1941)*** Ingrid Bergman, Warner Baxter, Susan Hayward. Family governess looks after four children after the mistress of the house dies. Well acted drama. (Dir: Gregory Ratoff.)

Adam's Rib (1949)***½ Spencer Tracy, Katharine Hepburn, Judy Holliday, Tom Ewell, David Wayne, Jean Hagen. An uproarious, sophisticated comedy about the tribulations of a district attorney and a lady lawyer who happened to be married. (Dir: George Cukor, 101 mins.)

Adam's Woman (1968)* Beau Bridges, John Mills, Jane Merrow. Limp story of a wrongly imprisoned sailor (Bridges) and his attempts to escape from his jail in Sydney, Australia. The Governor (Mills) will release him if he can take a wife and so . . . Confusing and implausible. (Dir: Phillip Leacock, 95 mins.)

Adding Machine, The (Great Britain-U.S.A., 1969) Phyllis Diller, Milo O'Shea, Billie Whitelaw. Erratic film version of Elmer Rice's brilliant expressionist play of 1923. An overworked accountant murders his boss when he learns he is to be replaced by a machine. The employee, well played by Milo O'Shea, is electrocuted, and finds himself in the next world, one of hundreds who are forced to punch endless rows of buttons. The play has been softened, but the impact remains. (Dir: Jerome Epstein, 100 mins.)

Address Unknown (1944)*** Paul Lukas, Carl Esmond. Businessman in Germany embraces the Nazi cause, but his partner in America has his revenge. Interestingly produced drama. (Dir: D. William Menzies, 72 mins.)

Adios Gringo (Italian, 1965)* Montgomery Wood (i.e., Giuliano Gemma), Evelyn Stewart, Pierre Cressoy. More spaghetti-western shenanigans; cattleman braves death to get revenge on the swine who doublecrossed him. Nicely photographed in Spain, which still doesn't make it authentic. (Dir: Giorgio Stegani, 98 mins.)

Adios Sabata (Italian, 1971)* Yul Brynner. Another violent, grotesque spaghetti western. Brynner plays the tough hombre, out to get a bag of $1 million gold dust from a villainous Austrian colonel. Carnage instead of plot. Sequel to the 1970 entry "Sabata." (Dir: Frank Kramer, 106 mins.)

Admiral Was a Lady, The (1950)** Four ex-GI's living on their wits meet an ex-Wave, vie for her hand. Edmond O'Brien, Wanda Hendrix, Rudy Vallee. Mild, amusing comedy.

Adorable Creatures (French, 1956) *** Danielle Darrieux, Martine Carol. Delightful romance taking a young man through many affairs with a variety of beauties and finally to the proverbial "girl next door." Well acted by a top French cast. (Dir: Christian-Jaque, 108 mins.)

Adorable Julia (French, 1962)** Lilli Palmer, Charles Boyer, Jean Sorel. Glamorous actress of the London stage embarks on one last fling with a younger man, soon regrets it. Based on a Somerset Maugham play, this sophisticated comedy dubbed in English is rather flat when it should have bubbled. Palmer is charming, livens things up somewhat. (Dir: Alfred Heidenmann, 94 mins.)

Adorable Menteuse (French, 1962)* Marina Vlady, Macha Meril. Two sisters romping around Paris playing with romance and hurting everyone but themselves, until they fall in love and find out how much such real love can hurt. Plodding and cliched. (110 mins.)

Adulteress, The (French, 1958)**½ Simone Signoret, Raf Vallone, Sylvie. Somewhat simple story of a woman who kills her husband for her lover, and the ensuing blackmail by a young sailor. Marcel Carne directed and adapted the screenplay from the Emile Zola story "Therese Raquin." Saved by the acting of Miss Signoret. (106 mins.)

Advance to the Rear (1964)**½ Glenn Ford, Stella Stevens, Melvyn Douglas. Civil War comedy about a band of Union Army goldbricks who are transferred to the wild and wooly West. Though it plays like three or four segments of a weekly TV situation comedy all rolled into one and relies heavily on slapstick, its professional cast, led by Glenn Ford, Melvyn Douglas, Jim Backus, and Joan Blondell, deliver their lines in a spirit of fun. (Dir: George Marshall, 97 mins.)

Adventure (1945)*½ Clark Gable, Greer Garson, Joan Blondell. Much publicized post-war film is one big fizzle. Romance of a sea going bum and a shy librarian is as bad a film as either of its stars ever appeared in. (Dir: Victor Fleming, 125 mins.)

Adventure in Baltimore (1948)** Robert Young, Shirley Temple. Minister's daughter has modern views for the 1900 period, keeps her father in hot water by sticking by them. Mild, slow little comedydrama. (Dir: Richard Wallace, 89 mins.)

Adventure Island (1947)** Rory Calhoun, Rhonda Fleming. Pitiful version of the story about shipwrecked sailors on an island ruled by a madman. (Dir: Peter Stewart, 66 mins.)

Adventure of Sherlock Holmes' Smarter Brother, The (1975)***½ Gene Wilder, Leo McKern, Madeline Kahn, Marty Feldman, Dom DeLuise. Gene Wilder strikes out on his own as a writer-director of the Mel Brooks school in this often hilarious period farce. Slapstick is rampant as Sigerson Holmes (Wilder), Sherlock's younger (and sillier) brother, tries to solve a mystery involving international spies, a secret document, a beautiful young woman in distress (Madeline Kahn), and the ubiquitous Professor Moriarty (Leo McKern). Along with the comedy, there are some heroics from Sigi as he fights off Moriarty and his minions, winning the day, of course, in an exciting sequence. The atmospheric sets by Peter Howett and the deliciously funny score by John Morris deserve special mention, as do the performances by Wilder, Kahn, Marty Feldman as Sigi's Watson, and Dom DeLuise as a larcenous opera singer. (Dir: Gene Wilder, 91 mins.)

Adventurer of Seville, The (1954)*½ Luis Mariano, Lolita Sevilla. Spanish-made, English-dubbed costumer about a young barber used by thieves as a bait to waylay travelers. Some singing, some good scenery, not much else.

Adventurer of Tortuga (Italian, 1964) * Guy Madison, Nadia Gray. Romance on the high seas as a pirate and a provincial governor vie for the hand of a gorgeous Indian girl in the New World. The pirate wins and the governor is annihilated. Intolerable. Low-budget entry. (100 mins.)

Adventurers, The (1970)* Bekim Fehmiu, Candice Bergen, Olivia de Havilland, Anna Moffo. Harold Robbins' sex-filled saga of a poor boy who grew up to be an international playboy reaches the screen with all its soap-opera ingredients intact. Yugoslav actor Fehmiu plays the leading role in an eye-drooping, pantherlike manner, but he can't rise above the impossible character he has to try to breathe life into. The cast includes Candice Bergen as a wealthy girl who dallies with Fehmiu. (Dir: Lewis Gilbert, 171 mins.)

Adventures in Indo-China (French, 1961)* Jean Gaven, Dominique Wilms. Five men and a beautiful girl search for hidden gold nuggets in the Oriental wilderness. Melodrama dubbed in English is as tedious as the trek.

Adventures in Silverado (1948)** William Bishop, Forrest Tucker. A stage driver captures a hooded holdup man in the Old West, thereby clearing himself. Based on a Robert Louis Stevenson true story. Routine western. (Dir: Phil Karlsen, 75 mins.)

Adventures of a Young Man (1962) ** Richard Beymer, Paul Newman, Dan Dailey, Arthur Kennedy, Susan Strasberg. Devotees of Ernest Hemingway's works will find a great deal wrong with this film based on a number of his short stories on the life of his fictional hero, Nick Adams. This saga of a young man's experiences around the time of World War I boasts some fine acting. Richard Beymer is awful in the title role. Paul Newman as a scarred, punchy ex-boxer is excellent. (Dir: Martin Ritt, 145 mins.)

Adventures of Arsene Lupin (1957) ** Robert Lamoureux, Lilo Pulver, O. E. Hasse. The gentleman thief after the gems again, and after a wealthy princess too. French-made, English-dubbed romantic adventure has pleasant period (1912) atmosphere but a slow-moving story, not much excitement.

Adventures of Captain Fabian (1951) *½ Errol Flynn, Micheline Prell, Vincent Price. Sea captain saves a servant girl from a murder charge, but she is bent only on revenge. Slipshod costume adventure, wooden and dull. Produced in France. (Dir: William Marshall, 100 mins.)

Adventures of Casanova (1947)*½ Arturo de Cordova, Turhan Bey, John Sutton, Lucille Bremer, Noreen Nash. The dashing rogue and lover comes to the aid of his country when it is in the grip of tyrants. Opulent but otherwise undistinguished costume melodrama, produced in Mexico. (Dir: Roberto Galuadon, 83 mins.)

Adventures of Don Juan (1948)** Errol Flynn, Viveca Lindfors. Title notwithstanding, this is just another Errol Flynn "swashbuckler" with Errol as the great Don Juan. (Dir: Vincent Sherman, 110 mins.)

Adventures of Freddie (1977)** Michael Burns, Harry Morgan, Tom Poston. This pilot is a throwback to the situation comedies of the early sixties, with an updated energy crisis plot thrown in. Likeable Michael Burns plays the second-generation inventor who comes up with a fabulous "energy disk" which could save the world. As expected, his bosses can only see the "profit motive" of his invention, and thereby hangs the thin premise. Made-for-TV. (Dir: Hy Averback, 83 mins.)

Adventures of Frontier Freemont, The (1976)**½ Dan Haggerty, Denver Pyle. Remember "The Life and Times of Grizzly Adams"? Well, here's a sort of sequel with different character names but the same leading man, Dan Haggerty. Haggerty plays a farmer and tinsmith in the 1830's who gets tired of his lot in St. Louis and decides to head for the hills and the simple bucolic life. He then encounters bears, rattlesnakes, and cougars. (Dir: Richard Freidenberg, 106 mins.)

Adventures of Gallant Bess (1948)** Cameron Mitchell, Audrey Long.

Rodeo performer captures a wild mare, enters it for prize money. Ordinary outdoor drama. (Dir: Lew Landers, 73 mins.)

Adventures of Gil Blas, The (French, 1955)* Georges Marchal, Susana Canales. Young Spaniard is forced to join a band of thieves, falls for a beauty whom they hold captive. Draggy costume drama dubbed in English.

Adventures of Hajji Baba, The (1954) *½ John Derek, Elaine Stewart. How a barber longing for adventure finds it when he rescues the daughter of the caliph. It's played straight which should have made this Arabian Nights tale even funnier. But it's merely dull. (Dir: Don Weis, 110 mins.)

Adventures of Huckleberry Finn (1938)** Mickey Rooney, William Frawley, Walter Connolly. Strictly for the youngsters is this flavorless adaptation of the Mark Twain story. (Dir: Richard Thorpe, 110 mins.)

Adventures of Huckleberry Finn, The (1960)**½ Tony Randall, Eddie Hodges. Although this most recent version of the Mark Twain classic is far from the best, the photography is splendid and the Twain atmosphere is occasionally captured. A good cast including Eddie Hodges as Huck, Tony Randall, Judy Canova, Andy Devine, and former champ Archie Moore help to overcome the deficiencies of the adaptation. (Dir: Michael Curtiz, 107 mins.)

Adventures of Mandrin, The (Italian, 1960)** Raf Vallone, Silvana Pampanini. Soldier of fortune organizes a band of outlaws to fight oppression in a Spanish dukedom. Usual swashbuckler with a better than usual cast. English-dubbed. Alternate title: "Captain Adventure."

Adventures of Marco Polo (1938)** ½ Gary Cooper, Sigrid Gurie, Basil Rathbone. Sprawling adventure film with extravagant production detail, but still somewhat of a miss as entertainment. Cooper does fairly well but hardly seems the right choice for the adventurer whose travels brought him to China, long before we or Cooper had to worry about whether to recognize it. (Dir: Archie Mayo, 101 mins.)

Adventures of Mark Twain (1944)*** Fredric March, Alexis Smith. Biographical sketch of America's great

humorist falls short of its goal and cannot be ranked with the great screen biographies. More informative than entertaining. (Dir: Irving Rapper, 130 mins.)

Adventures of Martin Eden (1942) *** Glenn Ford, Evelyn Keyes, Claire Trevor. A seaman struggles to become a successful author. Well done drama based on Jack London's novel. Well acted. (Dir: Sidney Sulkow, 87 mins.)

Adventures of Michael Strogoff (1937)*** Anton Walbrook, Akim Tamiroff. In 1870, a messenger of the Czar imperils his life to warn of invading hordes. Crammed full of action, this Jules Verne story should satisfy the most demanding adventure fan. (Also called "Soldier and the Lady.") (Dir: George Nicholls, Jr., 90 mins.)

Adventures of Mr. Wonderbird (1959) *** Animated cartoon feature tells the tales of a princess and a handsome chimneysweep. Ideal for the children. Voices of Claire Bloom and Peter Ustinov are heard.

Adventures of Nick Carter, The (1972)** Robert Conrad, Shelley Winters, Broderick Crawford, Dean Stockwell. Robert Conrad, a TV-series perennial, plays the famous private eye of the early 1900's in this pilot film for a series. Flavor of the era is nicely captured in this glossy production, but it's familiar gangster stuff. Made-for-TV. (Dir: Paul Krasny, 72 mins.)

Adventures of Robin Hood (1938) *** Errol Flynn, Basil Rathbone. Slick, entertaining saga of the hero of Sherwood Forest. (Dir: Michael Curtiz, 106 mins.)

Adventures of Robinson Crusoe (Mexican, 1952)***½ Dan O'Herlihy, James Fernandez. The fact that the great Luis Bunuel directed this faithful adaptation of the classic tale by Daniel Defoe is reason enough for watching this version of "Crusoe," even though there is little dialogue, only narrative, for most of the film. O'Herlihy plays the 17th-century English squire shipwrecked on a deserted island off the coast of South America. The kids will enjoy it, and the adults will delight in the beautiful color shots of the Mexican coast, while watching one of the world's most famous campers and outdoorsmen plying his trade. (100 mins.)

Adventures of Sadie (British, 1955)

*** Joan Collins, Kenneth More. Curvaceous and beautiful Joan Collins is stranded on a tropic island with three males and the situation becomes hilarious. Well done comedy. Hermione Gingold is seen briefly, and she's funny. (Dir: Noel Langley, 88 mins.)

Adventures of Scaramouche, The (French, 1963)** Gerard Barray, Gianna Maria Canale, Michele Girardon. Traveling clown learns he is really a nobleman, goes after the wicked duke trying to usurp his title. Standard swashbuckling melodramatics, enough swordplay to satisfy the action fans, if not enthrall them. Dubbed in English. (Dir: Antonio Isomendi, 98 mins.)

Adventures of Sherlock Holmes (1939)*** Basil Rathbone, Nigel Bruce, Ida Lupino. Holmes stops the attempt to steal the Crown Jewels of England. Good Holmes mystery, well made and exciting. (Dir: Alfred Wesker, 85 mins.)

Adventures of Tartu, The (1943)**½ Robert Donat, Valerie Hobson. Illogical story of a British spy's adventures in Czechoslovakia during World War II. Thanks to Mr. Donat, you'll enjoy the "Perils of Pauline" escapes, and unbelievable heroism. (Dir: Harold Bucqnet, 102 mins.)

Adventures of the Queen (1975)** Robert Stack, Ralph Bellamy, David Hedison, Bradford Dillman. A mini-holocaust by special-effects king Irwin ("Poseidon Adventure," "Towering Inferno") Allen. It's the old bomb plot, set on a cruise ship, to which Allen adds a whiz-bang explosion, dazzling fire-and-rescue number. Special effects crew deserves top billing, along with the ship Queen Mary. Made-for-TV. (Dir: David Lowell Rich, 100 mins.)

Adventures of the Wilderness Family (1975)*** Robert Logan, Susan Damante Shaw. Photogenic fauna and a wholesome family with wild pets who are devoted enough to protect them from animals of prey, team together for a convincing piece of family fare. Shot in the Utah mountains, a beleaguered family, led by a disillusioned construction worker, jettisons their urban existence for life on the land. Goodnatured. (Dir: Stewart Raffill, 101 mins.)

Adventures of Tom Sawyer (1938) ***½ Tommy Kelly, Ann Gillis. The famous Mark Twain tale of a mischievous boy in a small Missouri town receives a splendid production. (Dir: Norman Taurog, 100 mins.)

Adventuress, The (British, 1947)**** Deborah Kerr, Trevor Howard. An Irish lassie, traditionally hating the English, unwittingly becomes the tool of Nazi agents. Thoroughly delightful comic espionage thriller, with Miss Kerr giving an utterly charming performance. Excellent. (Dir: Frank Launder, 98 mins.)

Advise and Consent (1962)**** Henry Fonda, Walter Pidgeon, Charles Laughton, Don Murray, Lew Ayres, Gene Tierney, Franchot Tone, Burgess Meredith. Absorbing, excellently acted drama of Washington politics; slick and glossy, in the better sense of the words. Taken from Allen Drury's prize-winning novel, it concerns the appointment of a controversial figure as Secretary of State by the President, and the various machinations for and against this appointment. Fascinating background of political infighting; Burgess Meredith, in a bit role, makes it stand out, but the entire cast is fine. (Dir: Otto Preminger, 139 mins.)

Affair, The (1973)**½ Natalie Wood, Robert Wagner, Bruce Davison. An old-fashioned love story with some modern twists serves as a vehicle for Natalie Wood and husband Robert Wagner. Miss Wood, as beautiful as ever, plays an insulated lyricist of 30-plus who had polio as a kid, and walks with the aid of canes. The dialogue doesn't always ring true, but the sentimental theme is not without interest. Made-for-TV. (Dir: Gilbert Cates.)

Affair at Ischia (Italian, 1964)* Tony Sailer, Eva Astor. Fanciful adventures of a middle-aged vagabond and his old flame who get involved in the suspicious business deals of a yacht-sailing millionaire. None of it believable. (90 mins.)

Affair in Havana (1957)**½ John Cassavetes, Raymond Burr, Sara Shane. The actors are better than their material in this outing, and they make this somewhat melodramatic opus palatable. It's a love story, triangular-fashion, and the setting adds to the mood of the film. (Dir: Laslo Benedek, 80 mins.)

Affair in Monte Carlo (1953)** Merle Oberon, Richard Todd. British-made

9

drama of a wealthy young widow attempting to reform a gambler. Nice backgrounds, but with the sluggish story it's all bets off. (Dir: Victor Saville, 75 mins.)

Affair in Reno (1957)**½ John Lund, Doris Singleton. Public relations man falls for a lady detective hired as his bodyguard. Pleasant little comedy. (Dir: R. G. Springsteen, 80 mins.)

Affair in Trinidad (1952)**½ Glenn Ford, Rita Hayworth, Valerie Bettis. Intrigue and romance in the tropics with Rita Hayworth cast as a valuable pawn in the deadly game of espionage. Rita also has a dance number. (Dir: Vincent Sherman, 98 mins.)

Affair of State, An (W. German, 1966)* Curt Jurgens, Lilli Palmer. Dull spy spoof which rode the wave of James Bond imitations—but this one sank. Low-budget entry. (95 mins.)

Affair of Susan, The (1935)** Zasu Pitts, Hugh O'Connell. Humorous yarn about two depressed people who journey to Coney Island in search of soul mates. They land in jail in a most unusual manner. (Dir: Kurt Neuman, 70 mins.)

Affair to Remember, An (1957)**½ Cary Grant, Deborah Kerr. Cary Grant's romantic image and the four handkerchief soap opera plot make this a must for the female audience. The story casts Deborah Kerr as a lovely woman who falls for Cary but doesn't get him until she's gone through a series of unfortunate events. This is a remake of an old Irene Dunne-Charles Boyer film. (Dir: Leo McCarey, 119 mins.)

Affair with a Killer (Canadian, 1967)** Stephen Young, Austin Willis. Mediocre suspense as two investigators looking into U.S.-Canadian smuggling reopen a challenging case when their prime suspect is murdered. Low-budget entry. (90 mins.)

Affair with a Stranger (1953)*** Jean Simmons, Victor Mature. Successful playwright and wife plan to divorce, but later manage to solve their problems. Well acted romantic drama. (Dir: Ray Rowland, 89 mins.)

Affairs in Versailles (French, 1954)**½ Claudette Colbert, Gerard Philippe, Orson Welles. Sacha Guitry's colorful and ambitious film about the court affairs and naughty intrigues during the time of Louis XIV. Good cast but film is overdone

and lacks continuity. (Dir: Sacha Guitry, 152 mins.)

Affairs of Dobie Gillis (1953)**½ Debbie Reynolds, Bobby Van, Bob Fosse. Light comedy with musical numbers about the young and their carefree antics. Bobby Van dances well and is competent as "Dobie." Debbie is bouncy as ever as his special girl. (Dir: Don Weis, 73 mins.)

Affairs of Dr. Holl (German, 1954)** Maria Schell, Dieter Borsche. Young doctor finds a millionaire's daughter has fallen for him. Undistinguished drama.

Affairs of Julie, The (W. German, 1957)*½ Lilo Pulver, Paul Hubschmid. Innocent fluff about a young girl's romances. She's had a fight with her fiance, and wants to leave Hamburg. Miss Pulver, as the young girl, looks like Germany's answer to Debbie Reynolds. (Dir: Helmut Kautner, 88 mins.)

Affairs of Martha, The (1942)**½ Marsha Hunt, Richard Carlson, Spring Byington. A maid turns a small town upside down when she writes a book about her employers. Diverting comedy.

Affairs of Messalina (Italian, 1953)**½ Maria Felix, Georges Marchal. Ornate, but overproduced, overacted, and over-long spectacle about the evil temptress of the Ancient Roman Empire. (120 mins.)

Affairs of Susan, The (1945)**½ Joan Fontaine, Dennis O'Keefe, George Brent. Occasionally amusing, but overdone, romantic comedy about an actress who changes character to match the requirements of her suitors. (Dir: William A. Seiter, 110 mins.)

Affectionately Yours (1941)** Rita Hayworth, Merle Oberon, Dennis Morgan. Forced, weak little comedy about a man trying to woo back his ex-wife. (Dir: Lloyd Bacon, 90 mins.)

Africa Addio (Italian, 1966)** Inflammatory, provocative feature-length documentary about African culture and history, written, directed, conceived, and edited by Gualtiero Jacopetti. Packed with violent scenes including the mass carnage that ravaged various African countries during the late '50's and early '60's. Scenes of violence juxtaposed with lurid sex scenes, animal slaughter, etc. Some question about the authenticity of various scenes. (122 mins.)

Africa Screams (1949)*½ Bud Abbott, Lou Costello, Frank Buck. Bud and Lou on safari for diamonds in darkest Africa. Pretty weak slapstick. (Dir: Charles Burton, 80 mins.)

Africa—Texas Style (1966)**½ Hugh O'Brian, John Mills, Tom Nardini. Authentic African locales add to this otherwise slow-moving adventure about a cowboy who hunts and tames wild game. There are two or three subplots, none too exciting. However, the photography is splendid, and the youngsters will enjoy a lot of the wildlife footage lensed in Kenya. (Dir: Andrew Burton, 106 mins.)

African Manhunt (1955)* Myron Healey, Karen Booth. A gent is assigned to bring back a killer hiding out in the Congo. Poor jungle melodrama. (80 mins.)

African Queen (1952)**** Humphrey Bogart, Katharine Hepburn. Wonderful tale of a voyage down African rivers and the romance of the rough and sloppy captain and the prim, refined lady. Bogey and Katie playing a missionary are both marvelous, and so is John Huston's direction. (Dir: John Huston, 106 mins.)

After the Ball (British, 1957)** Pat Kirkwood, Laurence Harvey. Biography of English music hall girl Vesta Tilley, who became the toast of two continents. Plodding, old-fashioned musical, pretty mild.

After the Fox (1966)**½ Peter Sellers, Britt Eklund, Victor Mature. Considering all the talent working on this comedy, both behind and in front of the cameras, it should have been much better. It's only a mildly funny tale about an ingenious convict (Peter Sellers) who gets involved in moviemaking in order to cover a big caper. Victor Mature plays an American has-been movie star and he hams it up all the way for the film's biggest laughs. Neil Simon wrote the script and Vittorio De Sica directed. (103 mins.)

After the Thin Man (1936)*** William Powell, Myrna Loy, James Stewart. Second in the series is again a delight thanks to smooth acting, glib dialogue and top production. Detective story is incidental to the fun. (Dir: W. S. Van Dyke, 110 mins.)

After Tonight (1935)*½ Constance Bennett, Gilbert Roland. The perils of a female secret-service agent operating in the dangerous Vienna during World War I. Heavy on atmosphere; short on plot. (80 mins.)

After You, Comrade (South African, 1966)** Jamie Uys, Bob Courtney. At a world conference in Athens, a small utopian country proposes that the United States and Russian delegates hold a footrace in order to avoid World War III. Good comedy idea with no substantial development. Written and directed by Jamie Uys. (84 mins.)

Against a Crooked Sky (1975)*½ Richard Boone, Stewart Peterson. Still another old-fashioned Western in which a young boy enlists the aid of a craggy, crusty old codger to find his sister kidnapped by hostile redskins. Richard Boone chews his words as well as the scenery as the hard-drinking trapper. (Dir: Earl Bellamy, 89 mins.)

Against All Flags (1953)** Errol Flynn, Maureen O'Hara, Anthony Quinn. Flynn the dauntless officer vs. Quinn the brazen Caribbean pirate in a thoroughly routine adventure yarn. (Dir: George Sherman, 84 mins.)

Against the Wind (British, 1949)***½ Simone Signoret, Jack Warner. British agents parachute into occupied France to aid the resistance movement in their fight against the Nazis. Tense, exciting war melodrama, well done.

Age of Infidelity (Spanish, 1955)*** Lucia Bose, Alberto Closas. Flawed, complex morality play which concerns two lovers who accidentally injure a man on a motorcycle and leave him to die, fearing publicity about their love affair. (Dir: Juan Bardum, 86 mins.)

Age of the Medici (Italian, 1973)***½ One of the longest and most ambitious of Roberto Rossellini's historical films for Italian TV. Focuses on two distinguished Renaissance figures, Cosimo de Medici, a banker and merchant, and Leon Battista Alberti, architect, humanist, and patron, and through them shows what took place in Florence during one of the greatest periods in the history of art (1430-50). Deals with the whole development of Italian culture. Superb color photography captures look and texture of period.

11

English subtitles. (Dir: Roberto Rossellini, 252 mins.)

Agent 8¾ (Great Britain, 1964)** Dirk Bogarde, Sylva Koscina, Robert Morley. Promising idea—Bogarde plays a rather witless guy, out of a job, who's sent to Czechoslovakia on U.S. "business." Finds himself embroiled in international espionage, and involved with a very sexy "Red." The parody is saccharine! (Dir: Ralph Thomas, 98 mins.)

Agent for H.A.R.M. (1965)** Mark Richman, Wendell Corey. Secret agent is assigned to protect the life of a defecting scientist. Routine Iron Curtain cloak-and-dagger melodrama. (Dir: Gerd Oswald, 84 mins.)

Agent for Panic (W. German, 1964)*½ Brad Newman, Eric Douglas. A Western agent tries to get in touch with an old contact in Czechoslovakia in order to transmit highly important information. Routine. (86 mins.)

Agent for the Plaintiff (1968)** Gene Barry, Susan Saint James, Honor Blackman, Brian Bedford. A segment of the television series "The Name of the Game" has publisher Glenn Howard framed by an unethical woman lawyer trying to gain money for her boyfriend. Nothing new or exciting. (74 mins.)

Agent of Doom (French, 1963)**½ Annette Stroyberg, Michel le Royer, Jean Servais, Pierre Brasseur. Scientist recovers from an accident in a strange house where unexplainable things occur, discovers it's part of a plot against him. Involved spy thriller begins well, soon becomes routine. Dubbed in English.

Agent 383/Passport to Hell (Italian, 1964)* George Ardisson, Georges Riviere. Secret Agent 383 tracking down the leader of the Black Scorpion, a nefarious group of villains with branch offices all over the world. A black scorpion should have bitten the scriptwriter and director. (101 mins.)

Agent 255/Desperate Mission (Japanese, 1964)* Jerry Cobb, Yoko Tani. Tough American agent goes to Hong Kong in quest of a nuclear physicist who is running from the Red Chinese. Desperate is right. (112 mins.)

Agony and the Ecstasy, The (1965) **½ Charlton Heston, Rex Harrison. The agony refers to Michelangelo's troubles during the painting of the Sistine Chapel, but there's a lot of irritations and historical inaccuracies along the way in this over blown and finally tiresome accoun of the Italian artistic genius. Base on Irving Stone's best-selling nov and a Hollywood writer's idea of th way the Vatican and other patron of the arts functioned hundreds years ago. If you're a devotee films about marble quarries, by a means tune in! (Dir: Carol Ree 140 mins.)

Ah Wilderness (1935)***½ Lion Barrymore, Mickey Rooney, Wa lace Beery. O'Neill's poignant, y warm story of a boy breakin through the shackles of adolescenc receives an excellent screen trea ment. May appear dated but onl because adolescents have change since 1906 when film takes plac (Dir: Clarence Brown, 100 mins.)

Aida (Italian, 1955)**½ Sophia L ren, Lois Maxwell. If you can ove come your reaction to the humorou sight of Miss Loren pretending sing, you will enjoy this first col version of Verdi's excellent oper The voices include Tebaldi and Ca pora. (96 mins.)

Ain't Misbehavin' (1955)**½ Ro Calhoun, Piper Laurie, Jack Carson Mildly amusing comedy about a sex chorine (Miss Laurie) who marrie a millionaire tycoon and then ha to learn how to get along in hig society. Every girl should hav Piper's problems! (Dir: Edwa Buzzell, 82 mins.)

Ain't No Time for Glory (1957)* Barry Sullivan, Gene Barry. Amer can officer tries to take a German held fortress. Talky World War drama, originally produced as "Playhouse 90" TV feature.

Air Cadet (1951)** Stephen McNally Gail Russell. Another routine dram about the training of a group of j air cadets, and how they finally tur into flying aces. (Dir: Joseph Pe ney, 94 mins.)

Air Patrol (1962)* Willard Parke Merry Anders. Predictable mel drama about the theft of a paintin ransom, and the tracking down the enigmatic criminal by the A Patrol in a cheap helicopter. (7 mins.)

Air Strike (1955)** Richard Dennin Gloria Jean. A navy commande tries to mold a jet fighting unit in an efficient fighting machine. Cheap

12

ly-made service melodrama, about average. (63 mins.)

Airborne (1962)* Bobby Diamond, Robert Christan. Story of the 82d Airborne Division and the rigorous training they subject themselves to. Another machismo marine story. (80 mins.)

Airforce (1942)*** John Garfield, Arthur Kennedy, Faye Emerson. Another exciting war story about an army plane which takes off for the Pacific, December 6, 1941. Again, forget the propaganda, and watch an exciting film. (Dir: Howard Hawks, 124 mins.)

Airport (1970)*** Burt Lancaster, Dean Martin, Helen Hayes, Jacqueline Bisset, Jean Seberg, Van Heflin. Entertaining film and a big box-office hit. Miss Hayes is so memorable as an unlikely stowaway of 70 who manages to visit her daughter whenever the spirit moves her, she's worth the film. Add to her performance the scene of a busy bustling metropolitan airport, beset not only with tracking her down, but by the tragic madness of a passenger whose attache case holds a bomb. Lancaster's unflappable airport manager; Martin's sturdy yet sensitive pilot; and Miss Bisset's charm as his stewardess mistress are other ingredients in this Ross Hunter gloss. (Dir: George Seaton, 137 mins.)

Airport 1975 (1974)** Charlton Heston, Karen Black, George Kennedy, Efrem Zimbalist, Jr., Helen Reddy, Sid Caesar. A tacky successor to the commercially successful potboiler "Airport." In this particular crippled airline saga, Heston plays an airline troubleshooter whose derring-do involves transferring from a helicopter to the cockpit of a disabled 747 being flown by stewardess Karen Black. Most of the acting and all of the writing is terrible, but the cinematography and special effects are well done. (Dir: Jack Smight, 106 mins.)

Airport '77 (1977)** Jack Lemmon, Lee Grant, Brenda Vaccaro, George Kennedy, James Stewart, Joseph Cotten, Olivia de Havilland, Darren McGavin, Christopher Lee. More mindless diversion starring that triumph of technology, the Boeing 747. For this flight, art-magnate Stewart has converted a jumbo jet to transport his friends and his art treasures to the opening of his Palm Beach museum. Disaster strikes when hijackers take over the plane and crash it into the ocean. The plane is watertight. The script is not. Though the special effects (involving the undersea rescue by the navy) are the equal of the original "Airport," adapted from Arthur Hailey's best-selling book, this airborne soap opera literally and figuratively flops! (Dir: Jerry Jameson, 113 mins.)

Aku Aku (1959)*** Generally interesting documentary despite the amateurish camerawork, as Thor Heyerdahl, of "Kon Tiki" fame, explores Easter Island and makes some fascinating discoveries. (60 mins.)

Al Capone (1959)***½ Rod Steiger, Fay Spain, Martin Balsam. An excellent performance by Rod Steiger, as the biggest gangster of all time, aided by a hand-picked cast of good supporting performers raises this crime drama several notches above the average fare. The setting is the Prohibition area in Chicago when Capone controlled everything. (Dir: Richard Wilson, 104 mins.)

Alakazam the Great (1961)*** Nice little cartoon feature for the younger set. About a smart monkey who fancies himself brighter than humans until he learns otherwise. Originally Japanese-made; voices heard include Jonathan Winters, Frankie Avalon, Dodie Stevens. (84 mins.)

Alamo, The (1960)*½ John Wayne, Richard Widmark, Laurence Harvey. John Wayne not only plays Colonel David Crockett in this splashy, simple-minded reenactment of the famous clash between our outnumbered soldiers and the Mexican army, but he also produced and directed—with help from his friend John Ford. You can see where Wayne spent most of the 12 million bucks for this long, boring western running over three hours. There is little excuse however, for the outrageous historical inaccuracies found everywhere throughout this irritating cliché-ridden script. The "Siege" itself, towards the end of the film, is a rousin' battle, if that's what you're pining for, and you don't fall asleep during the two-hour buildup. (Dir: John Wayne, 192 mins.)

Alarm on 83rd Street (1965)*½ George Nader, Sylvia Pascal. Unsolved murders and robberies call for special FBI agent Nader who

13

solves the whole thing by infiltrating the gang and ruining the planned robbery of some ritzy jewelry. Boring. (91 mins.)

Alaska Passage (1959)*½ Bill Williams, Nora Hayden. Partners in a trucking outfit fight when the wife of one makes a play for the other. Poor action melodrama. (72 mins.)

Alaska Seas (1954)** Robert Ryan, Gene Barry, Jan Sterling, Brian Keith. Ex-jailbird is given a chance by his former partner in an Alaskan salmon cannery, but joins a gang of robbers. Lukewarm remake of "Spawn of the North." (Dir: Jerry Hepper, 78 mins.)

Albert Schweitzer (1957)*** Documentary story of the famed doctor and his African medical work. Continually interesting, good narration spoken by Fredric March.

Alcatraz Express (1962)**½ Robert Stack, Neville Brand. Pasted together from a two-part entry in TV's "The Untouchables" series, this tells of Al Capone's ride to Atlanta Penitentiary after a conviction for income-tax evasion, and of Eliot Ness making sure he gets there. It still looks like a TV show, but manages to whip up a good amount of suspense.

Alex and the Gypsy (1976)½ Jack Lemmon, Genevieve Bujold, James Woods. Clichéd characters copulate, cinema suffers! That's not the best line I ever wrote but it's better than the junk you'll hear if you make the mistake of joining "Gypsy." Lemmon is too old to play romantic leads these days, but there he is, a middle-aged, cynical bailbondsman who falls in love with Maritza, an aggressive, nubile gypsy. He bails her out of the slammer and . . . Wretchedly adapted by Lawrence B. Marcus from Stanley Elkin's not uninteresting novella, "The Bailbondsman." First major directorial effort by John Korty who directed the acclaimed TV drama, "The Autobiography of Miss Jane Pittman." Korty should have chosen a better script. (Dir: John Korty, 99 mins.)

Alexander Nevsky (Russian, 1938)**** Nikolai Cherkassov. Sergei Eisenstein, Russia's greatest director, used all his cinematic magic to tell the epic tale of Prince Nevsky and his heroic stand against German invaders during the 13th century. When the film was released in 1938,

audiences and critics alike couldn't help but draw a parallel between the history depicted in the film and the real-life situation in Russia, with German Nazism raising its menacing head. (Dir: Sergei Eisenstein)

Alexander the Great (1956)***½ Richard Burton, Fredric March, Claire Bloom. Lavish spectacle that just misses being a truly good film. Burton and March are effective as the Greek Father and Son but Claire Bloom is largely wasted as the love interest. A lot of money went into this production and it shows in the magnificent sets and costumes. Burton is brilliant in several of his major scenes. (Dir: Robert Rossen, 141 mins.)

Alexander the Great (1964)*½ William Shatner, John Cassavetes, Joseph Cotten, Simon Oakland. A pilot film for a television series which was never sold. A pint-size epic about the Battle of Issus in 333 B.C. Alexander's army fights the Persians with limited interest for the viewer. (60 mins.)

Alexander: The Other Side of Dawn (1977)**½ Eve Plumb, Leigh McCloskey. Here's a sequel to "Dawn: Portrait of a Teenage Runaway," with young Eve Plumb as a Hollywood Boulevard hooker. This time around, cameras follow Dawn's part-time roomie, good looking Alexander (Leigh McCloskey), as he hustles women and men on Hollywood Boulevard because he can't land a job. The homosexual aspect is treated with relative care. Made-for-TV. (Dir: John Erman, 106 mins.)

Alexander's Ragtime Band (1938)***½ Tyrone Power, Alice Faye, Don Ameche, Ethel Merman. Sentimental story of some performers taking them from 1911-1938, serves as a nice excuse for 26 Irving Berlin all-time hits. (Dir: Henry King, 105 mins.)

Alfie (1966)**** Michael Caine, Shelley Winters, Millicent Martin. This is the film which catapulted Michael Caine to stardom and his performance as an unscrupulous womanizing male is excellent. Alfie is a lecher and he lets you know it right from the start (Caine's talking to the audience really works). The romantic excursions are consistently and honestly portrayed. Shelley Winters registers as a blowsy American who takes some of the wind out of Alfie's sails. Vivien Merchant, as a drab housewife who becomes one of Alfie's conquests and submits to an abortion, is electrifying in her big scene. (Dir: Lewis Gilbert, 114 mins.)

Alfred Nobel Story, The (German, 1955)**½ Dieter Borsche, Hilde Krahl. English-dubbed biography of the discoverer of dynamite and initiator of the Peace Prize. Fairly well done. Alternative title: **No Greater Love.**

Alfred the Great (1969)* David Hemmings, Michael York, Prunella Ransome. Idiotic treatment of the saga of the 9th-century King Alfred of Wessex, who, according to this text, tried valiantly and nobly to unite all of England by warring both physically and intellectually with the Danes. The Danes' leader is played by Michael York and he has been used to better advantage. Miss Ransome, as plain a girl as ever starred in a film, is the hot-blooded Queen Aelhswith (don't even try to pronounce it). Boring! (Dir: Clive Donner, 122 mins.)

Algiers (1938)*** Charles Boyer, Hedy Lamarr, Sigrid Gurie. The story of Pepe LeMoko the crook who sought refuge from the police in the Casbah of North Africa, but who came out to meet his fate for the love of a beautiful woman. Familiar story to movie-goers, perhaps Boyer's most famous role. (Dir: John Cromwell, 100 mins.)

Ali-Baba (French, 1950)** Fernandel, Samia Gamal. The Gallic funny-faced comic seems out of place romping around in this Arabian Nights tale. Some amusing moments, not enough.

Ali Baba and the Forty Thieves (1943)**½ Maria Montez, Jon Hall. Lad brought up by outlaws fights a Mongol tyrant to regain his rightful place on the throne. Juvenile but lively costume fantasy; pretty good fun. (Dir: Arthur Lubin, 87 mins.)

Ali Baba and the Sacred Crown (1960)*½ Rod Flash, Celia Cortez. One of the many Italian epics made on a small budget by small talents. This one depicts the tale of the desert hero and his adventures against a sinister boy and his henchmen.

Ali Baba and the Seven Saracens (Italian, 1964)* Dan Harrison, Bella Cortez. Ali Baba returns from the sea to match brawn and wits with a tyrant king. Same old childish stuff, weak Arabian Nights spectacle. Dubbed in English.

Alias a Gentleman (1948)** Wallace Beery, Tom Drake. Reformed crook's ex-partner hires a girl to pose as his former confederate's daughter. Ordinary film. (Dir: Henry Beaumont, 76 mins.)

Alias Jesse James (1959)*** Bob Hope, Rhonda Fleming, Wendell Corey. Eastern insurance company sends its worst agent out West to protect a client, who turns out to be the notorious outlaw. Diverting Hope spoof of Westerns; some gags miss the mark, but most land on the funnybone. Particularly funny ending. (Dir: Norman McLeod, 92 mins.)

Alias John Preston (British, 1955)** Betta St. John, Alexander Knox, Christopher Lee. Mysterious young man becomes the pillar of a small-town community, but begins to be bothered by strange dreams. Unexceptional, psychological drama.

Alias Nick Beal (1949)***½ Ray Milland, Thomas Mitchell, Audrey Totter. Honest district attorney is side-tracked in his crime crusade by a mysterious stranger with Satanlike ideas. Absorbing fantasy with fine performances. (Dir: John Farrow, 93 mins.)

Alias Smith & Jones (1971)*½ Pete Duel, Ben Murphy. The made-for-TV feature which was turned into a TV series. The best thing about this tale of two young outlaws seeking amnesty from the Governor is the free-wheeling performance by Pete Duel as Hannibal Heyes, alias Smith. The Kid is played by Ben Murphy, who looks like a young Paul Newman at times. The film has its share of bungled bank robbery attempts, jail breaks, and other slapstick situations, plus guest stars Forrest Tucker, Earl Holliman, Susan Saint James, and James Drury. (Dir: Gene Levitt)

Alibi for Death, An (W. German, 1964)** Peter Van Eyck, Ruth Leuwerik. Interesting if unlikely saga of a man accused of a hit-and-run killing. He claims the dead man was pushed in front of his truck. While most of the movie is routine, the ending is rather original. (97 mins.)

Alice Adams (1935)***½ Katharine Hepburn, Fred MacMurray. Lonely girl in a small American town finally finds the man she loves. Well done drama ; fine atmosphere, direction, splendid performances. (Dir: George Stevens, 99 mins.)

Alice Doesn't Live Here Anymore (1974)**** Ellen Burstyn, Kris Kristofferson, Alfred Lutter, Jodie Foster. Memorable, poignant and often funny comedy-drama about a 35-year-old widow who finds her own identity while being obliged to cope with the sometimes harsh reality of economic survival. Ellen Burstyn is wonderful playing Alice and, deservedly, won the Academy Award for her many-shaded portrait of this itinerant ex-housewife turned waitress-singer trying to support herself and her 12-year-old son, winningly played by Alfred Lutter. Shot on location throughout New Mexico and the Southwest, "Alice"'s impact is based largely on uniformly fine acting, on good direction from Martin Scorsese and an unusually deft, original screenplay by Robert Getchell. (Dir: Martin Scorsese, 113 mins.)

Alice in the Navy (Greek, 1963)* Aliki Vouyouclaki, Dimitri Papamichael. Sailor on a weekend pass has met the admiral's daughter. She's decided to stow away on his ship as it sails off for maneuvers. The film sinks—or stinks, if you prefer. (90 mins.)

Alice In Wonderland (1933)*** W. C. Fields, All-Star Cast. Disappointing but ambitious film version of the classic fantasy. A must for the young in heart but lovers of the book will not find the film satisfactory. (Dir: Norman McLeod, 80 mins.)

Alice In Wonderland (British, 1950) **½ Carole Marsh, Pamela Brown, Bunin Puppets. The Lewis Carroll tale of the little girl in a land of fantasy. Combination of live action and puppets is interesting, faithful to the book, but the film is rather disjointed. (Dir: Dallas Bowers, 83 mins.)

Alice's Restaurant (1969)**** Arlo Guthrie. Director Arthur Penn, using a novel source for movie material—a hit song—has triumphantly managed to take the original slim story outline, and produce an original film of substance and charm. Based of course on Arlo Guthrie's best-selling l.p. which recounted his adventures and subsequent arrest for littering.

This scene and several others, especially a remarkably funny scene where Arlo is momentarily inducted into the U.S. Army, sustain this striking film, which is a unique commentary on how some of our youth felt about our society in the late 60's. Arlo is quite appealing in his movie debut. (Dir: Arthur Penn, 111 mins.)

Alive and Kicking (British, 1958)*** Sybil Thorndike, Kathleen Harrison, Estelle Winwood, Stanley Holloway. Genial comedy about three cronies at an old ladies' home who run away when they learn they are to be moved. Good cast, pleasant fun.

All About Eve (1950)**** Bette Davis, Anne Baxter, George Sanders, Celeste Holm, Gary Merrill, Thelma Ritter, Marilyn Monroe. One of the best comedy-dramas of all time. Witty, sophisticated and thoroughly entertaining film dealing with the theatre and those who toil in it. Writer-director Joseph L. Mankiewicz has assembled a great cast and gets top performances, especially from the femme performers. Multiprize winner including 7 Oscars. Don't miss this one. (Dir: Joseph L. Mankiewicz, 138 mins.)

All American, The (1953)** Tony Curtis, Lori Nelson, Mamie Van Doren. This drama about college football heroes and their problems, on the field and off, is a bit stilted. Curtis fits the requirements of the football hero who carries a chip on his shoulder, but some of the supporting cast seem out of place. (Dir: Jesse Hibbs, 80 mins.)

All American Boy, The (1973)** Jon Voight, Carol Androsky, Anne Archer. Though completed in 1970, this clumsy tale of a small town boy's hope to make good by becoming a boxer was not released until some three years later. Voight skillfully plays the alienated boxer who desperately wants to leave his town, but does not want to commit himself to anything or anyone. Some nice touches scattered along the way. Written and directed by Charles Erdman. (118 mins.)

All Ashore (1953)** Mickey Rooney, Dick Haymes, Peggy Ryan. Same old musical about three sailors on leave and their adventures. Dick Haymes sings some ballads in his usual fine style. (Dir: Richard Quine, 80 mins.)

All at Sea (1958)★★★½ Alec Guinness, Irene Browne. An often hilarious comedy about a seasick skipper, who finds himself in charge of one of the most unusual vessels ever seen. There's small-town politics, British fashion, and some delightfully zany characters popping in and out of the film. (Dir: Charles Frend, 83 mins.)

All at Sea (British, 1970)★ Early Smith, Steven Mallett. Trite adventures of some children on a school cruise to Portugal and North Africa. (60 mins.)

All Fall Down (1962)★★½ Eva Marie Saint, Warren Beatty, Karl Malden, Angela Lansbury. Wild lad with a way with women is attracted to a girl in town for a visit, and an affair results. Drama often sacrifices plausibility for theatricality; generally well acted. (Dir: John Frankenheimer, 110 mins.)

All for Mary (British, 1956)★★ Nigel Patrick, Kathleen Harrison. Old woman straightens out a romance at a Swiss hotel. Dull comedy doesn't do right by the players.

All Hands on Deck (1961)★½ Pat Boone, Buddy Hackett, Barbara Eden, Dennis O'Keefe. A predictable service comedy with songs, long on corny dialogue and a ridiculous plot. Buddy Hackett (of all people) plays a wealthy American Indian in the U. S. Navy whose juvenile and outlandish antics are geared for laughs that aren't in the script. Pat Boone sings between Hackett's antics. (Dir: Norman Taurog, 98 mins.)

All I Desire (1953)★★½ Barbara Stanwyck, Richard Carlson. A woman's film with all the sentimental stops pulled! B. Stanwyck plays a woman who deserted her husband and family, and returns ten years later to try to pick up the pieces of her broken life. The ladies will have a 2½ hankie cry. (Dir: Douglas Sirk, 79 mins.)

All in a Night's Work (1961)★★★ Shirley MacLaine, Dean Martin, Cliff Robertson. When a tycoon dies under mysterious circumstances, his nephew inherits the empire and the headaches surrounding the demise. Sophisticated comedy with some well-timed laughs, a bright pace, pleasant performances. (Dir: Joseph Anthony, 94 mins.)

All Mine to Give (1956)★★½ Glynis Johns, Cameron Mitchell. Long, sad saga of a brave pioneer family and their hardships in early Wisconsin. Good performances give some spark to the tale. (Dir: Allen Reisner, 102 mins.)

All My Darling Daughters (1972)★★½ Robert Young. Enjoyable family holiday fare finds Robert Young playing the kindly father, watching his four daughters marry in a single ceremony. Actually, Young's liberal judge is an unusual parent. He listens, never shouts or indicates disapproval with his offspring, and says a daughter living with her man before nuptials is none of his business. Star Young has Raymond Massey as a caustic father-in-law for grownup company. Made-for-TV. (Dir: David Lowell Rich.)

All My Sons (1948)★★★½ Edward G. Robinson, Burt Lancaster, Howard Duff. Wealthy man's son accuses him of selling defective airplane parts to the government during the war. Frequently gripping, based on Broadway play by Arthur Miller. Well acted. (Dir: Irving Reis, 94 mins.)

All Night Long (British, 1962)★★★ Patrick McGoohan, Betsy Blair, Paul Harris, Richard Attenborough. Novel transference of the "Othello" theme to a modern jazz background, as an ambitious drummer sets out to discredit a top jazzman by compromising his wife. Plot gets a bit thick at times, but there's some fine swingin' music by top British and American players such as Brubeck, Dankworth, Mingus, etc. (Dir: Michael Relph, 95 mins.)

All Nudity Shall Be Punished (Brazilian, 1973)★★★★ Darlene Gloria, Paulo Porto, Paulo Sacks. Wonderful, bawdy, satiric, and imaginative comedy about an unlikely love affair between a middle-aged bourgeois, rich businessman and a spunky prostitute gloriously acted by Darlene Gloria. Her performance is reminiscent in some ways of Melina Mercouri's in "Never on Sunday," though the comparison has nothing whatever to do with the fact that they both play whores. Directed at a brisk pace by Arnaldo Jabor, this is one of the most inventive and telling comedies in years, and there's one closing payoff scene involving the businessman's son that you won't possibly guess. Screenplay written

17

by Jabor. English subtitles. (97 mins.)

All Over the Town (British, 1949) ***½ Sarah Churchill, Norman Wooland. Young newspaper editor battles a powerful advertiser trying to promote a crooked housing deal. Mildly pleasant romantic comedy-drama, helped by Sir Winston's daughter and Wooland.

All Quiet on the Western Front (1930) **** Lew Ayres, Louis Wolheim. The reactions of young German soldiers to the utter calamity of warfare. A film classic, its dated technique doesn't interfere with its great power. (Dir: Lewis Milestone, 140 mins.)

All That Heaven Allows (1956) ** Jane Wyman, Rock Hudson. Corny soap opera that should appeal to the ladies about a widow who falls in love with a younger man. (Dir: Douglas Sirk, 89 mins.)

All the Brothers Were Valiant (1953) **½ Robert Taylor, Stewart Granger, Ann Blyth. The valiant brothers of the title, two strong-willed New England whaling captains, come to grips when one decides to go after lost treasure rather than blubber. Ann Blyth co-stars as Taylor's new bride, whose presence on the vessel adds to the trouble. Plenty of action in this poor man's "Mutiny on the Bounty." (Dir: Richard Thorpe, 95 mins.)

All the Fine Young Cannibals (1960) ** Natalie Wood, Robert Wagner, Susan Kohner, George Hamilton. Muddled soap opera that capitalizes on the attractiveness of four principals, as a headstrong girl is loved by one lad but marries another. Also thrown in are such topics as babies, broken-down singers, nasty sisters and a bit of religion—i.e. something for everybody. (Dir: Michael Anderson, 112 mins.)

All the Kind Strangers (1974) **½ Stacy Keach, Samantha Eggar, John Savage, Robby Benson. Unusual entry maintains interest most of the way. The tale of quiet terror begins with photographer-journalist Keach giving a young boy a ride to his secluded farmhouse . . . There, he meets the rest of the kids and a young woman (Eggar) whom they call mother. Keach realizes he and Miss Eggar are prisoners of the brood of kids. Made-for-TV. (Dir: Burt Kennedy, 72 mins.)

All the King's Horses (1935) *½ Carl Brisson, Mary Ellis. In one of those mythical kingdoms, a visiting film star is mistaken for a husband of a noblewoman. Tired operetta.

All the King's Men (1950) **** Broderick Crawford, Mercedes McCambridge, John Ireland, Joanne Dru, John Derek. One of the all-time best films on the rise and fall of a politician. Broderick Crawford won the Oscar as Best Actor, while Mercedes McCambridge won in the Supporting Actress category. Pic also was Oscar winner as Best Film of 1950. (Dir: Robert Rossen, 109 mins.)

All The President's Men (1976) **** Dustin Hoffman, Robert Redford, Jason Robards Jr, Jane Alexander, Martin Balsam, Jack Warden. One of the many triumphs of this award-winning, understated, spellbinding political thriller about the Watergate-related events leading to the resignation of President Nixon is that the audience is constantly fascinated and involved. All this, of course, despite the fact that we already know, to use a metaphor of the Old West, who the villain is, and that he will be captured by the posse but never brought fully to justice. Thanks to all concerned, especially to director Alan J. Pakula, there is nary a false note in this entire real-life melodrama. American movies have made some superlative newspaper stories in their day including "Citizen Kane." This updated variation of "The Front Page" is more tantalizing than any of them, but no contemporary Ben Hecht or novelist would dare dream up such a preposterous, farfetched plot line. (After all who would believe a yarn about such a mendacious knave living in the White House, for God's sake, while posing as the President Of The United States). The astonishingly high level of the ensemble acting is extraordinary. Jason Robards Jr, giving his best film performance in years, won and deserved the Academy Award for supporting actor. Hoffman and Redford come across like dogged professional newspapermen, not Hollywood superstars imitating political reporters. There's one special moment for those who treasure ironic understatement—Hoffman and Redford pecking away at their typewriters while a small

18

TV set, on a nearby desk, shows a real news clip of Richard M. Nixon being nominated for a second term by a faceless party hack, who turns out to be Gerald R. Ford. Expertly adapted from the Woodward and Bernstein book by William Goldman. (Dir: Alan J. Pakula, 136 mins.)

All the Way Home (1963)***½ Jean Simmons, Robert Preston, Pat Hingle, Michael Kearney. Adapted from Tad Mosel's prize-winning play, which in turn was based on James Agee's Pulitzer Prize-winning novel about the death of the head of a family in rural America during the early 1900's and its effects upon his small son. Acting is uneven, but much of it is poignant and moving. (Dir: Alex Segal, 103 mins.)

All the Young Men (1960)**½ Alan Ladd, Sidney Poitier, James Darren. There's nothing new in this war story set in Korea. All the young men are types you met in so many other war films. They include the bitter career man; the Negro who has to fight prejudice when he's thrown into a position of authority; the young, frightened idealist; and the miscellaneous members of the platoon—(which includes Mort Sahl, Ingemar Johansson & Glenn Corbett). (Dir: Hal Bartlett, 87 mins.)

All These Women (Sweden, 1964)**½ Bibi Andersson, Carl Billquist. Director Ingmar Bergman's first film in color is a disappointing first attempt at farcical comedy. A critic makes a deal with a concert cellist to write his autobiography if the cellist will play the critic's compositions. The pacing is slow, even for Bergman, but all the actors deliver excellent performances. (Dir: Ingmar Bergman, 80 mins.)

All This and Heaven Too (1940)*** Bette Davis, Charles Boyer. Overlong, but moving film based on the Rachel Field novel. Story of an infamous romance which led to murder, suicide and scandal is told skilfully enough to wring tears from the frigid. A bit too much for modern taste but a good film. (Dir: Anatole Litvak, 143 mins.)

All Through the Night (1942)*** Humphrey Bogart, Peter Lorre, Phil Silvers. American crook against Nazi spies in this exciting melodrama. The propaganda value is dated but the picture is good fun.

One of TV's Sgt. Bilko's early movie efforts. (Dir: Vincent Sherman, 107 mins.)

All Together Now (1975)**½ Bill Macy, Jane Withers, John Rubinstein, Glynnis O'Connor. Family movie that blends tears and joy in predictable fashion. A family of four orphans decides to go it alone with their older brother at the head of the household, and they have to convince their relatives they can make it. Bill Macy and Jane Withers play the children's skeptical aunt and uncle. Made-for-TV. (Dir: Randall Kleiser, 72 mins.)

All Women Have Secrets (1940)*½ Jean Cagney, Joseph Allen. Frail little B film dealing with the now familiar problem of married college students.

Alligator Named Daisy, An (British, 1955)**½ Diana Dors, Donald Sinden. Young man gets saddled with a pet alligator, meets a girl who loves 'em both. Fairly pleasant comedy. (Dir: J. Lee Thompson, 88 mins.)

Alligator People, The (1959)*½ Beverly Garland, Lon Chaney, Bruce Bennett. Scientist gives a wounded man serum taken from an alligator, and the poor guy starts turning into one. Unpleasant horror thriller is unfair to nice alligators. (Dir: Roy Del Ruth, 74 mins.)

Aloha, Bobby and Rose (1975)* Paul Le Mat, Diane Hull, Martine Bertlett. Sappy love story about two losers. Bobby's a garage mechanic. Rose works in a car-wash office. He kills a liquor store clerk in a hold-up that was meant to be a joke. The rotten screenplay is on a par with the direction—both by Floyd Mutrix. One critic correctly described Le Mat, saying he "often resembles Warren Beatty imitating James Dean imitating Marlon Brando imitating John Garfield." (Dir: Floyd Mutrix, 89 mins.)

Aloha Means Goodbye (1974)* Sally Struthers, James Franciscus, Joanna Miles, Henry Darrow. Boring, unending suspense yarn geared for Sally Struthers. Sally plays a teacher singled out to become a heart-transplant donor because of her rare blood type. Hawaiian island background. Made-for-TV. (Dir: David Lowell Rich, 104 mins.)

Aloma of the South Seas (1941)*½ Dorothy Lamour, Jon Hall. Native king goes to American college and returns in time to stop rebellion in this trashy sarong saga. (Dir: Alfred Santell, 77 mins.)

Alone Against Rome (Italian, 1961) *½ Jeffrey Lang, Rossana Podesta, Philippe Leroy. English-dubbed. Cruel invading captain makes it rough for a couple of young lovers in ancient Rome.

Along Came a Spider (1970)**½ Suzanne Pleshette, Ed Nelson. For about two-thirds of the way, this made-for-TV mystery film is intriguing but it dissolves into predictable melodrama. Miss Pleshette's a young widow who goes to incredible lengths to prove that Prof. Ed Nelson was responsible for her scientist-husband's death. Her ingenious scheme of revenge is almost foolproof. The two attractive stars are very good in their roles. (Dir: Lee Katzin.)

Along Came Jones (1945)***½ Gary Cooper, Loretta Young, Dan Duryea. A mild-mannered cowpoke is mistaken for a notorious killer, nearly gets killed by both sides of the law. Humorous, enjoyable western, a good show. (Dir: Stuart Heisler, 90 mins.)

Along Came Youth (1931)* Buddy Rogers, Frances Dee, Stuart Erwin. Young sportsman finds romance in London. Outdated. (Dirs: Lloyd Corrigan, Norman McLeod.)

Along the Great Divide (1951)**½ Kirk Douglas, Virginia Mayo, Walter Brennan. Slow paced but interesting western drama about the capture and return to justice of an escaped criminal. Excellent desert photography. (Dir: Raoul Walsh, 88 mins.)

Along the Mohawk Trail (1956)*½ John Hart, Lon Chaney. Frontiersman and his faithful Indian companion battle a man who has set himself up as tyrannical ruler of a town. Weak outdoor drama edited from "The Last of the Mohicans"-"Hawkeye" TV series.

Alpha Beta (British, 1973)***½ Albert Finney, Rachel Roberts. Lacerating drama, based on the British hit play by E. A. Whitehead. A virtual duplication of the stage version, it packs a wallop because of the superb performances of the two stars as they torment and torture each other during the course of a rotting marriage. Some passages reminiscent of

20

"Who's Afraid Of Virginia Woolf" as the hapless couple verbally assault each other. Finney is magnificent, whether taunting his wife or contemplating his bleak future. (Dir: Anthony Page, 67 mins.)

Alpha Caper, The (1973)**½ Henry Fonda, Larry Hagman, Leonard Nimoy, James McEachin. An old plot surfaces in this moderately entertaining thriller. A knowledgeable probation officer, forced to retire, uses ex-cons to heist a huge shipment of gold ingots. Hagman, Nimoy, and McEachin, as the heisting team, do an adequate job in support. Made-for-TV. (Dir: Robert Lewis, 90 mins.)

Alphabet Murders, The (British, 1966) ** Tony Randall, Anita Ekberg, Robert Morley. An overly coy attempt to bring Agatha Christie's shrewd master sleuth, Hercule Poirot, to the screen in the person of Tony Randall. It misses all the way. The usually competent Randall, complete with extensive makeup, is lost in a series of silly plot developments involving a group of murders which are linked to the alphabet. Even a cameo appearance by Margaret Rutherford, as Miss Christie's Miss Marple, doesn't help. (Dir: Frank Tashlin, 90 mins.)

Alphaville (French, 1965)**½ Eddie Constantine, Anna Karina, Akim Tamiroff. Pretentious juvenile fantasy about a trouble shooter sent to a distant planet where the dictator has a race of robots doing his bidding. Typically Gallic idea of American sci-fi tough-guy style. Dubbed English. Some critics took this film much more seriously! (Dir: Jean-Luc Godard, 100 mins.)

Alvarez Kelly (1966)*** William Holden, Richard Widmark, Janice Rule. Two-fisted acting by Richard Widmark and William Holden, and the colorful setting of the Civil War make this western yarn a good bet for devotees of the genre. Includes all the basic ingredients of heroic horse operas, plus a well-staged stampede at the climax, which puts the cap on all the action which comes before. Southern guerrilla officer Widmark decides to rustle some 2500 head of cattle for his side and meets up with adventurer, Alvarez Kelly (William Holden). (Dir: Edward Dmytryk, 116 mins.)

Always a Bride (British, 1953)***

Peggy Cummins, Terence Morgan. Stuffy Treasury official gets mixed up with a confidence ring, including an attractive blonde. Light, laughable romantic comedy. (Dir: Ralph Smart, 83 mins.)

Always In My Heart (1942)**½ Walter Huston, Kay Francis. Huston tries desperately to overcome the plot, but it's impossible. The old tear jerker about a man who comes home after a long, unjust prison stretch and wins his daughter's love although she does not know his true identity. (Dir: Joe Graham, 92 mins.)

Always Leave Them Laughing (1949)**½ Milton Berle, Virginia Mayo. Milton is well cast as a comedian who rides to the top on everybody's jokes and by hamming but the film does not follow its own title. Bert Lahr is wonderful in some old sketches. (Dir: Roy Del Ruth, 116 mins.)

Amarcord (Italy-France, 1973)**** Magali Noel, Bruno Zanin, Luigi Rossi. A joyous, beautiful film. Fellini's semi-autobiographical look back at life in the Italian provinces in the 1930's. Set in the seaside town of Rimini, Fellini is concerned with Italian fascism of the 30's under Mussolini. The screen is filled with an unending succession of dazzling, remarkable images which few other living directors can match. Screenplay by Fellini and Tonino Guerra. (Dir: Federico Fellini, 127 mins.)

Amazing Colossal Man (1956)** Glen Langan, Cathy Downs. Atomic effects make a guy grow and grow and grow. Science-fiction script drags. (Dir: Bert Gordon, 80 mins.)

Amazing Dr. Clitterhouse (1938)***½ Edward G. Robinson, Claire Trevor, Humphrey Bogart. Entertaining, amusing story of a psychiatrist who becomes a crook to study the criminal mind. (Dir: Anatole Litvak, 90 mins.)

Amazing Dr. G., The (Italian, 1965)** Franco Franchi, Gloria Paul. A creaky takeoff on the James Bond movies with Italy's Franco Franchi playing the debonair Mr. B. Goldfinger pops up in this one, too.

Amazing Grace (1974)* Moms Mabley, Slappy White, Stepin Fetchit, Butterfly McQueen. The only amazing thing about this supposed comedy, aimed at black audiences, is

the absurd "vehicle" selected to display the talents of Moms Mabley. She's a venerable, raunchy, off-color nightclub comedienne long popular with black audiences. She can be quite funny using her own material, throwing barbs and slurs at blacks and whites alike. But she's absurdly cast as a pious, God-fearing, harmless old lady. Too bad, because Mabley died soon after "Amazing" was finished. Two old-time black performers have supporting bits. Stepin Fetchit embarrasses himself and the audience. (Dir: Stan Lathan, 99 mins.)

Amazing Howard Hughes, The (1977)*** Tommy Lee Jones, Ed Flanders, James Hampton, Tovah Feldshuh, Lee Purcell. Originally shown in two parts, this is an engrossing study of the puzzling eccentric who had an eye for Hollywood beauties but really preferred airplanes and gadgets to people. Jones portrays Hughes as a young, cold fish out of Texas, determined to be the best at flying, movie-making and even golf. Flanders is accountant Noah Dietrich, the confidant to Hughes who takes his orders and shakes his head in wonderment. First-rate flying and air-crash sequences; Hughes bossing people around on movie sets; Hughes' sense of remoteness even with women, and his belief that everyone has a price. Scenes of Congressional hearings where Hughes displays his contempt mark the turning point. After that, the movie becomes an account of a deteriorating human in need of psychiatric help, and rich enough to indulge in his eccentricities. The behind-the-scenes drama, supposedly authentic, offers a revealing portrait of a fascinating psychotic. Made-for-TV. (Dir: William Graham, 210 mins.)

Amazing Mrs. Holliday, The (1943)**½ Deanna Durbin, Edmond O'Brien, Barry Fitzgerald. A silly comedy with dramatic overtones about an American schoolteacher and a group of refugee children who go through many adventures from evacuating a torpedoed ship to masquerading as a family. (Dir: Bruce Manning, 96 mins.)

Amazing Transparent Man, The (1960)** Marguerite Chapman, Douglas Kennedy. Fair science fiction yarn coupled with a crime story.

21

A scientist tries his serum, which makes men transparent, on an ex-con who is dispatched to rob a bank. A neat trick that doesn't quite come off. (Dir: Edgar Ulmer, 59 mins.)

Ambassador's Daughter (1956)**½ Olivia de Havilland, John Forsythe, Myrna Loy. GI in Paris falls for ambassador's daughter. Strained comedy isn't as funny as it might have been. (Dir: Norman Krasna, 102 mins.)

Ambush (1950)** Robert Taylor, Arlene Dahl, John Hodiak. Routine western fare. An Indian scout draws a special mission which makes him a hero and allows him to win the heart of a long time love. Some good action sequences. (Dir: Sam Wood, 88 mins.)

Ambush at Cimarron Pass (1958)** Scott Brady, Margia Deane. The title tells the story of this typical juvenile western, about an attempt by the Apaches to ambush a patrol. (Dir: Jackie Copelon, 73 mins.)

Ambush at Tomahawk Gap (1953)*** John Hodiak, John Derek, David Brian. Offbeat Western with a good story about four ex-convicts who band together to find some buried stolen money. Exciting climax. Good performances by all. (Dir: Fred Sears, 73 mins.)

Ambush Bay (1966)**½ Hugh O'Brian, Mickey Rooney, James Mitchum. A familiar WW II drama about two-fisted Marines in the Philippines on a special mission. You've seen it all before, but if you don't mind another sampling, it's done in a fairly straightforward manner and the leads are well played by O'Brian and Rooney. Filmed on location, adding to the realism. (Dir: Ron Winston, 109 mins.)

Ambush In Leopard Street (British, 1959)*½ James Kenney, Michael Brennan. Hoodlums plan a big diamond robbery, but internal troubles interfere. Hackneyed crime drama. (Dir: J. Henry Piperno, 60 mins.)

Ambushers, The (1967)* Dean Martin, Senta Berger. The first two of Dino's "Matt Helm" epics were "The Silencers" and "Murderer's Row." This is the worst of the lot, with the obligatory number of fist fights and tasty, available femmes. As a gumshoe star, Dean's a fine crooner! (Dir: Henry Levin, 102 mins.)

Amelie (French, 1960)** Jean Sorel, Marie-Jose Nat. Girl returns to her childhood home, a desolated islet, after ten years to find romance and tragedy. Brooding drama gets the arty treatment. Occasionally interesting, mostly slow, confused. English-dubbed. Alternate title: "A Time to Die."

America, America (1963)**** Stathis Giallelis, Lou Antonio, John Marley. Written, produced and directed by Elia Kazan, this is an eloquent tribute to Kazan's forebears, and to generations of immigrants from many countries that struggled to get to America, and pursue their vision of the American dream. Kazan himself came to the U.S. from Turkey when he was a young child, and much of this story is based on his own family. Filmed in Greece, "America" focuses on one young Greek boy who works his way to the U.S. in the late 1890's. Using both professional and non-professional actors, Kazan captures much of the anguish and hope that drove millions of Americans to these shores. Giallelis's innocent face matures through each harrowing adventure from his Turkish dominated homeland to the jammed steerage ship which brings him to New York's Ellis Island. Fine cast features John Marley as a waterfront philosopher-laborer; Lou Antonio as a thieving Arab. Enduring cinema valentine to all immigrants. (Dir: Elia Kazan, 174 mins.)

American Dream, An (1966)**½ Stuart Whitman, Janet Leigh, Eleanor Parker. Norman Mailer's offbeat novel served as the basis for this film adaptation which fluctuates between good and mediocre. Eleanor Parker, as the hero's bitter, drunken ex-wife, makes the first few scenes memorable, and Stuart Whitman just looks numb throughout as the tough TV commentator whose attacks on the Mafia have bought him a death warrant. (Dir: Robert Gist, 103 mins.)

American Graffiti (1973)**** Ronny Howard, Cindy Williams, Charlie Martin Smith, Richard Dreyfuss, Mackenzie Phillips, Candy Clark. A remarkable film about the American car-culture and what it was like to be a high-school teen-ager in a small town in northern California in the fall of '62. The gifted director George Lucas (who also had a hand in the screenplay) was himself a teenager in 1962, and has turned out by far the best film that the movie nostalgia craze of the '70's has yet produced. This perceptive, painfully funny, and accurate study of adolescence was produced on a low budget with high marks for all the talent including the contribution, from the outset, of producer Francis Ford Coppola. Received several Academy Award nominations for best picture, director, and for Miss Clark's memorable portrayal of a blond kewpie doll. (Dir: George Lucas, 110 mins.)

American Guerilla in the Philippines (1950)** Tyrone Power, Micheline Presle. American Naval officer joins forces with Filipino patriots in WWII. Usual adventure story, slowed down by love angle. Filmed in the South Pacific. (Dir: Fritz Lang, 105 mins.)

American in Paris, An (1951)**** Gene Kelly, Leslie Caron, Oscar Levant. This Oscar-winning film musical written by Alan Jay Lerner, with a George & Ira Gershwin score, and Gene Kelly's brilliant, ambitious choreography, is a must. Leslie Caron made her film debut in this story about an American ex-G.I. (Kelly) who stays in Paris after WW II to make it as an artist, but the mood of the city comes across with considerable charm. The musical numbers are the main attraction, especially a marvelous ballet sequence near the end, accompanied by Gershwin's music for "An American in Paris." One of the finest American musicals ever made, directed by Vincente Minnelli. (Dir: Vincente Minnelli, 113 mins.)

American Tragedy, An (1931)*** Sylvia Sidney, Frances Dee, Phillips Holmes. The first and remarkably faithful adaptation of Theodore Dreiser's enduring, sprawling novel, filmed twenty years later as "A Place in the Sun." The trial scenes at the end are not as effective as the first part of this striking film, which compares favorably to Sternberg's best filmmaking and deserves to be seen for that reason alone. (Dir: Josef von Sternberg, 95 mins.)

Americanization of Emily, The (1964)*** James Garner, Julie Andrews, Melvyn Douglas. An anti-war film which chooses comedy to make its point. Paddy Chayefsky's skillful screenplay is adapted from William Bradford Huie's book about a Navy officer whose main job during WW II is to supply his superiors with a variety of the creature comforts, including girls. Garner plays the military procurer without burlesquing it and he's matched all the way by Julie Andrews' beguiling portrayal of a British war widow who despises Garner's non-heroic attitude, but can't help falling in love with him. The ending is a bit trumped up considering what has come before, but it's all entertaining, and if you listen, the film actually has something pertinent to say. (Dir: Arthur Hiller, 117 mins.)

Americano, The (1954)**½ Glenn Ford, Frank Lovejoy. Texas cowboy gets mixed up with bandits in Brazil. Good cast helps this below-the-equator western over the familiar road. (Dir: William Castle, 85 mins.)

Among the Headhunters (British, 1955)*** Documentary of the Armand and Michaela Denis expedition to the island of New Guinea. Well done for armchair adventurers.

Among the Living (1941)**½ Albert Dekker, Susan Hayward. Man is wrongfully accused when his insane twin brother escapes and commits murder. Strong thriller had good direction and performance. (Dir: Stuart Heisler, 68 mins.)

Amorous Adventures of Moll Flanders, The (1965)*** Kim Novak, Richard Johnson, George Sanders. Daniel Defoe's classic tale about a gorgeous 18th-century female who stops at nothing to achieve money and social position comes off as a poor man's "Tom Jones" but it's fun all the same. Kim Novak physically fits the title role, and her performance is acceptable. Many of the scenes are "bawdy," and editing for TV may alter some of the intended satirical bits, but the superb costumes and atmospheric settings remain intact. (Dir: Terence Young, 126 mins.)

Amorous Mr. Prawn, The (British, 1962)**½ Joan Greenwood, Cecil Parker, Ian Carmichael, Dennis Price. General about to retire hasn't enough money, so while he's away his wife converts his HQ into a vacation spot for salmon fishermen. Mildly amusing comedy with some agreeable performers, some amusing scenes. (Dir: Anthony Kimmins, 89 mins.)

Amphibian Man, The (Russian, 1964) * William Koren, Anastasia Virten. English-dubbed. Inept, sci-fi thriller about a scientist who plans to make use of a lad who can swim like a fish.

Amy Prentiss: Baptism of Fire (1974) ** Jessica Walter, William Shatner, Peter Haskell. The pilot for a mini-series about a woman chief of detectives played by Jessica Walter. She takes on two cases involving industrial espionage, and a mad bomber about to blow up San Francisco. The action is standard, but with a little less violence than usual, and the script well-paced. Made-for-TV. (Dir: Jeffrey Hayden, 72 mins.)

Anastasia (1956)***½ Ingrid Bergman, Yul Brynner, Helen Hayes. Absorbing drama of an amnesiac girl in Germany who may or may not be the daughter of Czar Nicholas II of Russia. Excellently acted, won Miss Bergman her second Oscar award. (Dir: Anatole Litvak, 105 mins.)

Anatomist, The (British, 1961)**½ Alastair Sim, George Cole. Gruesome story of a Scots doctor who procures bodies for his medical experiments. Good cast, good fare for thriller fans. (Dir: Leonard William, 73 mins.)

Anatomy of a Marriage (France/ Italy, 1964)** Marie-Jose Nat, Jacques Charrier. Released in Europe as two films, each running 112 minutes, examining a failed marriage from two points of view. The version released in America included just the first film, "My Days With Jean-Marc." Over-long, superficial, but intermittently interesting. (Dir: Andre Cayatte, 112 mins.)

Anatomy of a Murder (1959)***½ James Stewart, Lee Remick, Ben Gazzara, Joseph Welch. Plenty of adult excitement in Otto Preminger's adaptation of the best-seller about a Michigan lawyer who defends an Army Lieutenant on a murder charge after the man's wife had been attacked. Dialogue is explicit, performances fine without exception. Engrossing fare for the mature. (Dir: Otto Preminger, 160 mins.)

Anatomy of a Psycho (1963)* Ronnie Burns, Pamela Lincoln. Terrible crime drama about a guy out to avenge his brother's death. Bad performances.

Anatomy of the Syndicate—See: **Big Operator, The**

Anchors Aweigh (1944)***½ Frank Sinatra, Gene Kelly, Kathryn Grayson. Tuneful, gay, lively musical about two sailors on leave in Hollywood. The cast is great and you'll love it. (Dir: George Sidney, 140 mins.)

And Baby Makes Three (1949)** Robert Young, Barbara Hale. Foolish comedy about a recently divorced couple who discover that they are to be parents and their bumpy and "slapsticky" road to reconciliation. Good performances. (Dir: Henry Lewis, 83 mins.)

And God Created Woman (1957)**½ Brigitte Bardot, Curt Jurgens, Jean-Louis Trintignant. Director Roger Vadim's enormously successful introduction of curvacious Brigitte Bardot to American film audiences! B.B. was an immediate hit in this tale of a family of sexually preoccupied men who openly and understandably lust after her. Director and cameraman primarily concerned with Brigitte's shape in various states of dress and undress. (Dir: Roger Vadim, 92 mins.)

And Hope to Die (French, 1972)* Robert Ryan, Jean-Louis Trintignant, Aldo Ray. Director Rene Clement has seen better days than this muddled mess. Two fine actors are wasted in this garbage about a million-dollar robbery. Trintignant is being pursued by gypsies when he meets Ryan, who is a father figure for a gang of mental misfits. (Dir: Rene Clement, 99 mins.)

And No One Could Save Her (1973)** Lee Remick, Milo O'Shea. Dublin locations and attractive Lee Remick, plus a colorful performance by character actor Milo O'Shea as an unorthodox attorney, make up for the shortcomings in this mystery. A wealthy American woman comes to Ireland looking for her husband, who has disappeared. Frank Grimes, talented Irish actor, registers in the brief role of Miss Remick's elusive spouse. Made-for-TV. (Dir: Kevin Billington, 74 mins.)

And Now Miguel (1966)*** Pat Cardi, Michael Ansara, Guy Stockwell. Young son of a sheepherder tries to prove that he's old enough to go along on grazing treks. Refreshing entry, especially for the youngsters. Pleasant entertainment for all the family. (Dir: James Clark, 95 mins.)

And Now the Screaming Starts (Great Britain, 1973)**½ Peter Cushing, Herbert Lom, Patrick Magee, Stephanie Beacham. A curse involving a severed hand hangs heavy over the pregnant bride of the lord of a British manor house. Cushing lends his high cheekbones to a doctor with the wisdom of Freud. Lom is dour as the ⁎ late grandfather, who brought the curse down on the clan. Veteran horror director Roy Ward Baker slackens his usual chill-a-minute pace to create a suitable Gothic mood. (Dir: Roy Ward Baker, 91 mins.)

And Now Tomorrow (1944)**½ Loretta Young, Alan Ladd. The ladies may enjoy this corny story about a romance between a deaf girl and her doctor. (Dir: Irving Pichel, 85 mins.)

And So They Were Married (1944)*** Simone Simon, James Ellison. Screwball comedy about a girl who gives out too many keys to her apartment during wartime, the romantic complications that ensue. Cute, sometimes highly original. Watch for Robert Mitchum in a bit role. (Dir: Elliott Nugent, 74 mins.)

And Soon the Darkness (British, 1970)** Pamela Franklin, Michele Dotrice. Fine terror—for a while. Two British girls are alone on a bicycle holiday in France. When one girl is missing, with intimations of a sexual assault, the other girl panics. The buildup is breathtaking, but with no definitive denouement the film fizzles into disappointment. (Dir: Robert Fuest, 98 mins.)

And Sudden Death (1936)*½ Randolph Scott, Frances Drake. Grade B melodrama is supposed to be a crusade for safe and sober driving, but it is merely a flat tire. (Dir: Charles Burton, 70 mins.)

And the Angels Sing (1944)**½ Betty Hutton, Fred MacMurray. Story of some singing sisters and the band leader who discovers them. Routine musical but Betty sings one of her biggest hits, "My Rocking Horse Ran Away." (Dir: George Marshall, 96 mins.)

And the Wild, Wild Women (1962)*** Anna Magnani, Giulietta Masina. This Italian film drama about a women's prison is altered a great deal for this dubbed version but it still has two of Italy's great film stars—Anna Magnani and Giulietta Massina—to make it worthwhile.

And Then There Were None (1945)**** Barry Fitzgerald, Walter Huston, Louis Hayward, Judith Anderson. Ten people are invited to a remote, deserted island. There, they are killed off mysteriously, one by one. Excellent thriller, with Rene Clair's direction mixing humor and mystery with skillful touches. Fine performances from a grand cast. (Dir: Rene Clair, 98 mins.)

Anderson Tapes, The (1971)*** Sean Connery, Dyan Cannon, Martin Balsam, Alan King. Lively, suspenseful crime caper with a gimmick. Connery plays thief John Anderson, who plans to rob an entire Fifth Avenue apartment house. The gimmick is that all his plans are inadvertently on tapes made to check on other matters. The robbery is exciting, and the acting is uniformly good. Director Sidney Lumet uses New York well. (98 mins.)

Andrea Chenier (Italian, 1960)** Antonella Lualdi, Raf Vallone. So-so English-dubbed costume tale of the French Revolution, the love of a patriot and the daughter of a Count.

Andrei Rublev (Russian, 1966)***½ Anatoli Solonitzine, Ivan Lapikov. Ambitious film about the famous Russian monk of the 15th century who developed new forms of icon painting. Clumsily cut and edited for its American release (the full film runs over three hours) so the abridged version seems curiously fragmented. There are individual sequences throughout that are extremely well done. Important political parable filmed on an epochal scale. English subtitles. (Dir: Andrei Tarkovsky, 146 mins.)

Andrews' Raiders—See: Great Locomotive Chase, The

Androcles and the Lion (1952)** Jean Simmons, Alan Young, Victor Mature. George Bernard Shaw's satiric comedy about a meek little tailor and the friendly lion during the days of the Roman Empire. It misses; the Shavian wit is blunted, the performances range from fair to terrible. (Dir: Chester Erskine, 98 mins.)

Andromeda Strain, The (1971)***½ James Olson, Arthur Hill. Excellent sci-fi tale based on the popular novel by Michael Crichton. A remote spot in New Mexico is contaminated when a satellite crashes there and a team of four top scientists fight the clock trying to analyze the lethal organism and discover a solution. Interesting throughout. Excellent cast. (Dir: Robert Wise, 130 mins.)

Andy (1965)**½ Norman Alden, Ann Wedgeworth. Mentally retarded son of Greek immigrants struggles to communicate with people. Attempt at realism of the "Marty" variety too often is self-conscious artiness. Some powerful moments, deserves credit for trying. (Dir: Richard Sarafian, 86 mins.)

Andy Hardy Comes Home (1958)**½ Mickey Rooney, Pat Breslin. Andy Hardy is all grown up and a successful lawyer when he returns to his home town. Andy Hardy film fans will get a kick out of seeing Fay Holden (mother), Sara Haden (Aunt) and Cecilia Parker (sister) once again. (Dir: Howard Koch, 80 mins.)

Andy Hardy Meets a Debutante (1939)**½ Mickey Rooney, Judy Garland. Mickey is still chasing attractive MGM starlets in this one. Good Andy Hardy comedy. (Dir: George Seitz, 86 mins.)

Andy Hardy's Blonde Trouble (1943)** Mickey Rooney, Lewis Stone. Andy's college days are complicated by a pair of luscious blonde co-eds who happen to be twins. (Dir: George Seitz, 107 mins.)

Andy Hardy's Double Life (1942)** Mickey Rooney, Lewis Stone. Andy goes to college in this one. The series has lost all its charm and the only important thing about this one is that one of Andy's flirtations is a screen newcomer, Esther Williams. (Dir: George Seitz, 92 mins.)

Andy Hardy's Private Secretary (1940)**½ Mickey Rooney, Lewis Stone. Andy gets out of high school in this one and his secretary is played by a lovely newcomer with a delightful voice named Kathryn Grayson. (Dir: George Seitz, 101 mins.)

Angel (1937)** Marlene Dietrich, Herbert Marshall, Melvyn Douglas. Poorly done, dated story of a diplomat's wife who has an affair with a stranger and then meets him again through her husband. This one will disappoint you. (Dir: Ernst Lubitsch, 90 mins.)

Angel and the Badman (1946)***½ John Wayne, Gail Russell. A notorious gun-slinger is reformed by the love of a Quaker girl. Western has action, fine scenery, and a good plot; superior entertainment of its type. (Dir: James Edward Grant, 100 mins.)

Angel Baby (1961)*** Salome Jens, George Hamilton, Mercedes McCambridge. Effective drama about the tent-circuit evangelists who travel through small towns preaching salvation for sinners. Miss Jens makes an impressive film debut in the title role. She plays a mute who miraculously gets her voice back and falls in love with the young preacher who she thinks is responsible for her recovery. Hamilton is less wooden than usual but Miss McCambridge overacts outrageously as Hamilton's wife. (Dir: Paul Wendkos, 97 mins.)

Angel Face (1952)**½ Jean Simmons, Robert Mitchum. Spoiled heiress lets nothing stand in her way, becomes a murderess. Slow-paced melodrama, occasionally interesting. (Dir: Otto Preminger, 91 mins.)

Angel from Texas, An (1940)**½ Jane Wyman, Ronald Reagan, Eddie Albert. Occasionally cute, Grade B comedy about the yokels who take the city slickers.

Angel in Exile (1949)*** John Carroll, Adele Mara. Crooks plan to hide stolen gold in a small town and then "discover" it, but the townspeople look upon the gold as a miracle. Good melodrama.

Angel in My Pocket (1969)**½ Andy Griffith, Lee Meriwether. If you're an Andy Griffith fan, you'll enjoy this homespun bit of corn in which he plays the new minister in a midwestern town. The town's many problems become Reverend Andy's personal responsibilities. TV faces in the supporting cast including Jerry Van Dyke, Kay Medford, and Edgar Buchanan. (Dir: Alan Rufkin, 105 mins.)

Angel Levine, The (1970)** Zero Mostel, Harry Belafonte. Bernard Malamud's simple story about a black angel with a Jewish last name (Belafonte) who comes to earth to redeem an aging Jew (Mostel) who has lost his faith when everything went down the drain. However, there's nothing simple about the dialogue, the overdrawn performances, and the abundance of supersentimentality. (Dir: Jan Kadar, 104 mins.)

Angel on Earth (French, 1961)** Romy Schneider, Jean-Paul Belmondo, Henri Vidal. Wispy fantasy about a beautiful angel who comes to earth to keep an eye on a racing driver who's contemplating suicide. Some amusement, not enough. Dubbed in English.

Angel on My Shoulder (1946)*** Paul Muni, Claude Rains, Anne Baxter. A deceased gangster makes a deal with the Devil to return to earth and pose as a respected judge. Enjoyable fantasy, keeps the light touch throughout. (Dir: Archie Mayo, 101 mins.)

Angel on the Amazon (1948)*½ George Brent, Vera Ralston, Brian Aherne. A pilot falls in love with a beautiful girl with a mysterious past. Far-fetched, improbable melodrama, badly acted. (Dir: John Auer, 86 mins.)

Angel Who Pawned Her Harp (British, 1956)*** Diane Cilento, Felix Aylmer. Romantic fantasy with lovely and talented Diane Cilento cast as an angel. Excellent performances by all.

Angel with a Trumpet, The (British, 1949)***½ Eileen Herlie, Basil Sydney. The panoramic story of a Viennese family, from the last century to Hitler's time. Carefully produced, fine performances. (110 mins.)

Angel Wore Red, The (1960)** Ava Gardner, Dirk Bogarde, Joseph Cotten. A serious attempt to mount a love story against the turmoil of the Spanish Civil War of the 1930's, is ultimately disappointing despite a fairly literate script and earnest performances by the attractive stars. Perhaps the heavy accent on religious overtones (Bogarde plays a Catholic priest who gives up his beliefs and returns to the everyday world) is the film's weakest point. (Dir: Nunnally Johnson, 99 mins.)

Angela—Portrait of a Revolutionary (1971)*** Enlightening if technically primitive documentary about political revolutionary Angela Davis. Film follows Angela beginning 1969, before she went to prison in late 1970, and then picks her up again after the trial where she was acquitted. Scenes find Davis lecturing on campus with students at UCLA, in her own apartment, and later at a protest rally for the Soledad Brothers. Davis' philosophy is articulated throughout the film and is the best film record to date of this young charismatic black woman. Filmmaker was student of Davis' at college. (Dir: Yolande du Luart, 80 mins.)

Angels in the Outfield (1951)***½ Paul Douglas, Janet Leigh, Keenan Wynn. Enjoyable comedy fantasy about a baseball team, their manager, a newspaper woman and an orphan who sees angels. There's a delightful performance by moppet Donna Corcoran, as the orphan. (Dir: Clarence Brown, 99 mins.)

Angels of Darkness (Italian, 1957) **½ Linda Darnell, Anthony Quinn, Giulietta Masina. Frank adult film of "loose" women in Rome and their attempts to find true love and happiness. Morbid and rather on the dull side. (Dir: Giuseppe Amato, 84 mins.)

Angels One Five (British, 1952)*** Jack Hawkins, Michael Denison. Story of the Royal Air Force and its brave pilots in the dark days of 1940. Authentic, well-made war drama. (Dir: George O'Ferrall, 98 mins.)

Angels Over Broadway (1940)***½ Rita Hayworth, Douglas Fairbanks Jr. and Thomas Mitchell. Good performances and top notch Ben Hecht screenplay make this story, about a group of oddballs in a Broadway cafe, fascinating viewing. Fairbanks is a con artist, Rita's his tasty assistant, and Mitchell's a drunken playwright. (Dir: Ben Hecht, 80 mins.)

Angels Wash Their Faces (1939)**½ Ann Sheridan, Dead End Kids. Mildly entertaining drama featuring the Dead End Kids, forerunners and ancestors of the Bowery Boys and the East Side Kids, depending on which studio was grinding out their misadventures. (Dir: Ray Enright, 90 mins.)

Angels With Dirty Faces (1938)***½ James Cagney, Pat O'Brien. Exciting story of two men whose roots were in the same gutter. One becomes a priest. The other, a killer. (Dir: Michael Curtiz, 97 mins.)

Angry Breed, The (1969)* Jan Sterling, James MacArthur, William Windom. Incredible plot concerning a returned Vietnam veteran who wants to be an actor. Badly written, produced and directed by the overly-ambitious David Commons. (89 mins.)

Angry Hills, The (1959)**½ Robert Mitchum, Gia Scala, Stanley Baker. Based on a lesser-known Leon (Exodus) Uris novel, this tale concerns the Greek Resistance work during WWII and the various people who became involved. The adventure is predictable but a good international cast keeps things moving. (Dir: Robert Aldrich, 105 mins.)

Angry Red Planet, The (1960)*½ Gerald Mohr, Les Tremayne, Nora Hayden. Spaceship returning from Mars meets with disaster. Sci-fi thriller has some occasionally clever trick camerawork but very little else.

Angry Silence, The (British, 1960) **** Pier Angeli, Richard Attenborough, Michael Craig. Hard-hitting, absorbing drama beautifully played by Miss Angeli and Mr. Attenborough. Story deals with one man's stand against a labor union's strike and the "silent" but "violent" treatment he's accorded. (Dir: Guy Green, 95 mins.)

Animal Crackers (1931)**** The Four Marx Brothers, Margaret Dumont. It's **four** Marx brothers because Zeppo's in this knockout romp, which is worth watching just to see Groucho strut his way through one of his great numbers, "Hooray for Captain Spaulding." There are lots of other scenes that deserve a hooray, as well as the wacky screenplay by Morrie Ryskind, based on the hit Broadway musical he wrote with George S. Kaufman. (Dir: Victor Heerman, 98 mins.)

Animal Farm (1955)**** Excellent cartoon based on George Orwell's famous book. For all age groups. (Dir: John Hakas, 75 mins.)

Animals, The (1972)**½ Henry Silva, Keenan Wynn, Michele Carey. Interesting vengeance tale of the old West features Carey as an abducted lady left to die, who teams with Apache Silva to track down the criminals and elude the sheriff's posse. Excessive carnage and profane language detract from the finely crafted story written by producer Richard Bakalyan. (Dir: Ron Joy, 86 mins.)

Anna (Italian, 1951)** Silvana Mangano, Raf Vallone, Vittorio Gassman. Night-club singer who has become a nun thinks over the reason for her doing so, and the man in her life. Glum, rather shoddy drama, dubbed-in English. (Dir: Alberto Lattunda, 95 mins.)

Anna and the King of Siam (1948) **** Rex Harrison, Irene Dunne. Even without the music the story of the English teacher and the King of Siam is a wonderful, heartwarming, et cetera, et cetera, et cetera. (Dir: John Cromwell, 128 mins.)

Anna Christie (1930)**** Greta Garbo, Charles Bickford, Marie Dressler. O'Neill's drama of a waterfront tramp who seeks happiness with a young sea captain. Garbo's first talkie and a film that is still brilliant in spite of its age. (Dir: Clarence Brown, 86 mins.)

Anna Karenina (1935)***½ Greta Garbo, Fredric March. Tolstoy's story of an illicit romance in the imperial court of Russia is splendidly acted and emerges as good screen fare. A bit heavy in dialogue for modern taste but Garbo compensates for a lot of things. (Dir: Clarence Brown, 95 mins.)

Anna Karenina (British, 1948)*** Vivien Leigh, Ralph Richardson. Tolstoy's immortal classic of the life and loves of a lady in old Russia. Elaborately produced, well acted drama. (Dir: Julien Duvivier, 110 mins.)

Anna Lucasta (1958)**½ Eartha Kitt, Sammy Davis, Jr. This is the second time around for the filming of the hit Broadway show about a loose woman who tries to go straight when she falls for a sailor. The play starred an all-Negro cast as does this film version but the first time, the characters were made Polish and Paulette Goddard played the role of Anna. This version is an improvement. (Dir: Arnold Luven, 97 mins.)

Annapolis Story (1955)** John Derek, Diana Lynn. Two brothers, both midshipmen at Annapolis, vie for the same girl, in this familiar story. You've seen it before at West Point. (Dir: Don Siegel, 81 mins.)

Annapurna (British, 1953)**** Fascinating documentary account of the Herzog expedition's ascent of the Himalayan peak. Ideal for armchair adventurers.

Anne of the Indies (1951)**½ Jean Peters, Louis Jourdan, Debra Paget. Lady pirate comes to the aid of an ex-French naval officer and finds herself battling her own kind. A lady swashbuckler, yet—but smart direction and some fast action makes the nonsense easier to swallow. Good fare for adventure devotees. (Dir: Jacques Tourneur, 81 mins.)

Anne of the Thousand Days (Great Britain, 1969)*** Richard Burton, Geneviève Bujold, Irene Papas, Anthony Quayle. An often effective historical drama about England's King Henry the Eighth and his legendary romance with Anne Boleyn, quite wonderfully acted by Geneviève Bujold. This is a lavish, civilized and rather genteel depiction of one of history's great romances. Benefits from one of Richard Burton's best performances playing Henry. Burton, who has squandered his remarkable gifts on a lot of cinematic trash, is excellent throughout and his scenes with Bujold are noteworthy. Adapted by Bridget Boland and John Hale from the 1948 play by Maxwell Anderson. Produced by Hal Wallis. (Dir: Charles Jarrott, 146 mins.)

Annie Get Your Gun (1950)*** Betty Hutton, Howard Keel, Keenan Wynn. Film version of the hit Broadway musical, relating the story of sharpshooter Annie Oakley and her rise to fame and fortune. The Irving Berlin tunes are great, the production lavish—and if the leading roles leave something to be desired, the displays of song and dance largely atone for it. (Dir: George Sidney, 107 mins.)

Annie Hall (1977)**** Woody Allen, Diane Keaton, Shelley Duvall. This is an absolutely marvelous film, directed and co-authored by the extravagantly talented Woody Allen. "Annie" is not only one of the funniest and wisest film comedies ever made, it's also a courageous, poignant, perceptive and perfectly acted film. This is more of an autobiographical film than any of Allen's earlier entries. Our red-headed hero Alvy Singer has been in analysis for fifteen years, loves New York with a passion and, understandably, falls head over heels in love with a beguiling lass played to perfection by Diane Keaton. Some of their scenes together are amongst the wittiest, tenderest and most romantic scenes ever captured on film. Woody and co-author Marshall Brickman

fire off an enormous number of comic salvos, and an astonishingly high percentage of the one-liners and the sight gags pay off brilliantly. "Annie" has minor flaws, but it's Allen's most ambitious, demanding effort to date and marks him clearly—as of 1977 anyway—as America's most inventive, creative comic artist. A joy from start to finish! (Dir: Woody Allen, 94 mins.)

Annie Oakley (1935)*** Barbara Stanwyck, Preston Foster, Melvyn Douglas. Frontier girl becomes a great celebrity as a circus sharpshooter. Entertaining biographical drama. (Dir: George Stevens, 100 mins.)

Anniversary, The (British, 1968)*½ Bette Davis, Sheila Hancock. Inferior horror stuff with Bette Davis playing (or overplaying) the macabre head of a household, fraught with neurotic people. Mama Davis (with an eyepatch, no less) celebrates her anniversary, even though her husband has been dead for 10 years. During the latest celebration, the family of three sons (one married, one about to become an unwed father, and the third a transvestite) try to find their independence, but Mama is just too strong for all of them. (Dir: Roy Ward Baker, 95 mins.)

Anonymous Venetian, The (Italian, 1970)* Tony Musante, Florinda Bolkan. Soapy melodrama about an estranged couple who spend a day together in Venice talking about their marriage and rekindling their love. But it is too late, the man is dying of a brain tumor. Only asset is the beautiful setting of Venice in winter. (Dir: Enrico Maria Salerno, 91 mins.)

Another Man's Poison (British, 1952)*** Bette Davis, Gary Merrill. A blackmailer enters the scene with proof that a woman has murdered her husband, and forces her to do his bidding. Fairly interesting melodrama, good cast. Emlyn Williams. (Dir: Irving Rapper, 89 mins.)

Another Part of the Forest (1948)*** Fredric March, Ann Blyth, Dan Duryea. Lillian Hellman's absorbing story of the fabulous Hubbard family, a band of ruthless Southern industrialists who hated each other but loved money. This story takes place before Miss Hellman's "The Little Foxes." (Dir: Michael Gordon, 107 mins.)

Another Thin Man (1939)******* William Powell, Myrna Loy. Not as sharp as the earlier efforts but Powell and Loy are still (including the present) the most delightful screen sleuths around. It's a guy who prophetically dreams of deaths before they happen who's causing the trouble in this one. (Dir: W. S. Van Dyke, 105 mins.)

Another Time, Another Place (British, 1958)****** Lana Turner, Barry Sullivan, Sean Connery. Soapy stuff about a lady correspondent during World War II who engages in a hopeless love affair with a married man, suffers a breakdown when he's killed. Turner's fans like her this way, so there's no use fighting it. Film "introduced" Sean Connery, now James Bond, to movie audiences. (Dir: Lewis Allen, 98 mins.)

Antarctic Crossing (British, 1958)****** Documentary recounting the crossing of the Antarctic by Sir Vivian Fuchs, and his intense rivalry with fellow explorer Sir Edmund Hillary. Creates enough personal tension to relieve the endless parade of panning shots of the snowy wilderness. (50 mins.)

Anthony Adverse (1936)*****½** Fredric March, Olivia de Havilland, Claude Rains. Adaptation of Hervey Allen's best seller is a mammoth achievement by 1936 standards. Characterization was sacrificed to make room for the story, but even on TV it should prove entertaining. (Dir: Mervyn Le Roy, 136 mins.)

Antonia: A Portrait of the Woman (1974)******** Antonia Brico, Judy Collins. Excellent, moving documentary about a gifted symphony orchestra conductor, ignored by her colleagues for almost 40 years because of her sex. Brico's brilliant early successes, abroad and in the U.S., are traced in still photographs, newspaper headlines and some rare film footage. There is joy and sorrow here—Brico's first triumphs and then obscurity as Brico is confined to irregular performances with a semi-professional orchestra in Denver. Singer Judy Collins talks with her former teacher, Brico, and manages to get below the surface to give us a portrait of a complex woman who, as a result of the film, got many offers

to conduct. (Dirs: Judy Collins and Jill Godmilow, 58 mins.)

Antonio and the Mayor (1975)******* Diego Gonzales, Gregory Sierra. Howard Rodman's offbeat, touching little drama of the 1920's, filmed in Mexico, is the story of a bright Mexican boy who infuriates the Mayor of his village because of his ability to handle a bicycle that the Mayor can't manage. This simple morality tale takes its time in the telling, capturing the flavor of village life and building slowly to an emotional, tear-jerking finale. Neophyte Gonzales may appear a shade too cute for the leading role, but his charm grows on you as he plays the village genius who can't read. Made-for-TV. (Dir: Jerry Thorpe, 72 mins.)

Any Gun Can Play (Italian, 1967)***½** Bold bandito (Gilbert Roland) and brawny banker (Edd Byrnes) both searching for hidden treasure. And both act as if they wish they were back in Palm Springs. Another transplanted oats opera with the customary sub-par results.

Any Number Can Play (1949)******* Clark Gable, Alexis Smith, Wendell Corey. Well done drama about a gambler who faces a series of crises in the matter of a few hours. Good cast supports Gable in this fast-moving story. (Dir: Mervyn Le Roy, 112 mins.)

Any Number Can Win (French, 1963)****½** Jean Gabin, Alain Delon. Big plans to rob the Cannes gambling casino. Crime caper benefits from the presence of venerable Jean Gabin and debonair Alain Delon. Elaborate but overlong. With Viviane Romance (merely a bit part, but welcome back) and Jose de Villalonga. (Dir: Henri Verneuil.)

Any Second Now (1969)***½** Stewart Granger, Lois Nettleton, Joseph Campanella. Contrived suspense as photographer Granger attempts to do away with wife Nettleton—unsuccessfully. Unconvincing acting by all, especially Campanella as a Mexican doctor who helps Miss Nettleton over her amnesia. Made-for-TV. (Dir: Gene Levitt, 100 mins.)

Any Wednesday (1966)*****½** Jane Fonda, Jason Robards, Jr., Dean Jones. The successful Broadway comedy about a kept girl, her married lover, his wife, and an out-of-town salesman who acts as a catalyst, comes to the screen improved, thanks to Miss Fonda's bright performance. The comedy has good dialogue and the cast delivers it well. (Dir: Robert Miller, 109 mins.)

Anyone Can Play (Italian, 1957)** Ursula Andress, Virna Lisi, Marisa Mell, Claudine Auger. Mediocre comedy about four women trying to solve their varied problems. Blackmail, bad marriages, and even worse nightmares all come into play. The real highlight of the film is not the plot, but the beauty of the four fabulous leading ladies. (Dir: Luigi Zampa, 88 mins.)

Anything Can Happen (1952)***½ Jose Ferrer, Kim Hunter. Delightfully played comedy about an immigrant who accustoms himself to America and finds himself a wife. Script has great warmth, humorous dialogue and situations. Cast is excellent. (Dir: George Seaton, 107 mins.)

Anything Goes (1936)**½ Bing Crosby, Ethel Merman. Not enough of the original Porter score makes this watered down production moderately entertaining. "You're the Top" number with Ethel is the limit. (Dir: Lewis Milestone, 100 mins.)

Anything Goes (1956)**½ Bing Crosby, Donald O'Connor, Jeanmaire, Mitzi Gaynor. Complicated situations arise when musical comedy co-stars in Europe try to sign a leading lady for their show. Performers take the fun in stride, but the film needs more sparkle. Crosby and O'Connor fans won't mind. (Dir: Robert Lewis, 106 mins.)

Anzio (1968)** Fabricated account of the decisive World War II battle of the Italian campaign. Even the location filming doesn't raise it above the commonplace. Good cast: Robert Mitchum (struggling in a bad role as a war correspondent), Peter Falk, Arthur Kennedy, Robert Ryan (once again, a general). (Dir: Edward Dmytryk.)

Apache (1954)** Burt Lancaster, Jean Peters. Burt Lancaster bares his chest and gnashes his teeth in the title role as a peace-seeking Indian forced to turn renegade in this action-filled western. Jean Peters has little else to do but look worried as his faithful squaw. (Dir: Robert Aldrich, 91 mins.)

Apache Ambush (1955)** Bill Wil-

liams, Richard Jaeckel. Action filled but routine Western—hero fights unreconstructed Confederate soldiers, Mexican banditos, and, of course, the Apaches. (Dir: Fred Sears, 70 mins.)

Apache Drums (1951)** Stephen McNally, Coleen Gray. Familiar western fare with McNally playing a gambler with a bad reputation who shows he's made of sterner stuff when the chips are down. (Dir: Hugo Fragonse, 75 mins.)

Apache Fury (Spanish, 1965)*½ Frank Latimore, George Gordon, Liza Moreno. Inexperienced youth kills a friendly Indian, whose tribe joins the Apaches in an attack on a fort. Rambling, tedious dubbed-English "western."

Apache Rifles (1964)** Audie Murphy, Michael Dante, Linda Lawson. Competent Western; cavalry captain struggles to bring peace when the Apaches go on the warpath. Some good action sequences. (Dir: William Witney, 92 mins.)

Apache Territory (1958)** Rory Calhoun, Barbara Bates. Routine western about a group of survivors of an Indian attack led to safety by a brave cowboy. There's some action for adventure fans. (Dir: Ray Nazarro, 75 mins.)

Apache Uprising (1966)*½ Rory Calhoun, Corinne Calvet. Routine western. Rory Calhoun is adequate as the yarn's hero, but the films's best performance is by crusty Arthur Hunnicut as a salty old western character. Oh yes, there are a handful of Indians causing some trouble along the way. (Dir: R. G. Springsteen, 90 mins.)

Apache War Smoke (1952)** Gilbert Roland, Robert Horton. Sprawling Western spectacle with all the necessary ingredients—Indians, cavalry, stagecoaches, and romance. Familiar. (Dir: Harold Kress, 65 mins.)

Apache Warrior (1957)** Keith Larsen, Jim Davis. Routine Indian adventure about the mean Apache and his battles with the white man. (Dir: Elmo Williams, 74 mins.)

Apache Woman (1955)** Joan Taylor, Lloyd Bridges. Crimes are being blamed on the Apaches—government investigator looks into it, falls for a halfbreed girl. Unexceptional low-budget western. (83 mins.)

Aparajito (The Unvanquished) (Indian, 1958)**** An Indian cast brilliantly performs this artistic masterpiece of a boy's growth to manhood, the second in a trilogy of features made by Satyajit Ray. For the discriminating viewer, a must-see.

Apartment, The (1960)******** Jack Lemmon, Shirley MacLaine, Fred MacMurray. Billy Wilder's bitterly funny view of modern urban morality won the Oscar as the best film of its year. The laughs and the cynicisms are still intact, and Jack Lemmon's expert performance is a grand job. He plays a young wheeler-dealer who "lends" his apartment to his senior executives who wish to do a bit of cheating on the side. Shirley MacLaine is equally expert in her role as the girl who changes his *modus operandi*, and Fred MacMurray is Lemmon's boss. Witty adult fare. (Dir: Billy Wilder, 125 mins.)

Apartment for Peggy (1948)******* Jeanne Crain, William Holden, Edmund Gwenn. Dated story about married vets struggling to get through college, have families and straighten out their lives. However, it's still warm, humorous and charming. (Dirs: Henry Koster, George Seaton, 98 mins.)

Ape Man of the Jungle (Italian, 1962)***** Silly English-dubbed nonsense, peopled by an apelike creature who holes up in a jungle lair.

Ape Woman, The (Italian, 1964)****** Ugo Tognazzi, Annie Girardot. Fastbuck operator encounters a woman covered with hair, exploits her as a freak attraction. Commentary on human greed emerges as merely grotesque, despite some touching scenes. Dubbed in English.

Aphrodite, Goddess of Love (Italian, 1962)***½** Isabel Cory, Ivo Garrani. More spear-and-sandal shenanigans, dubbed in English; a sculptor calls for a beautiful Christian girl in pagan Rome, and that spells trouble. Usual thing of its kind.

Appaloosa, The (1966)****** Marlon Brando, Anjanette Comer, John Saxon. A pretentious western yarn which suffers from too much talk, arty camerawork, and a stilted performance by Marlon Brando as a wronged buffalo hunter who meets with adversity at every turn. The story has Brando pitted against a Mexican bandit, played with spewing intensity by John Saxon, and their many confrontations becoming tiresome long

before the shoot-out at the finale. Once again, Brando has squandered his prodigious talent on meretricious material. (Dir: Sidney J. Furie, 98 mins.)

Applause (1929)****** Helen Morgan, Joan Peers. Early talkie about a burlesque star who almost forsakes her daughter's life for success. Technically primitive, but Morgan's work may still be of interest to old-film buffs. (Dir: Rouben Mamoulian, 87 mins.)

Apple Dumpling Gang, The (1975)****** Bill Bixby, Susan Clark. Another "wholesome" Disney entry which is so syrupy it may give adults a stomach ache. A story for kids about a trio of orphans who find a huge gold nugget in a seemingly tapped-out mine during the 1870's. The kids are adorable, of course. Bill Bixby is a gambler with a heart as big as the gold nugget and his girl friend is Susan Clark, a stagecoach driver! (Dir: Norman Tokar, 104 mins.)

Appointment, The (1969)***** Omar Sharif, Anouk Aimee. A love story, elaborately mounted, peopled by sophisticated, continental stars, and amounting to nothing. Mawkish and melodramatic yarn with the stolid Sharif marrying model Aimee, against his friend's advice that she's been a lady of the night. (Dir: Sidney Lumet, 100 mins.)

Appointment for Love (1941)******* Charles Boyer, Margaret Sullavan, Reginald Denny. Marital mix-ups get a big play in this sometimes clever, sometimes silly comedy-romance. Stars make the movie worthwhile. (Dir: William Seiter, 89 mins.)

Appointment In Honduras (1953)****** Glenn Ford, Ann Sheridan, Zachary Scott. Adventurer goes on a dangerous trek through the jungles to deliver funds for the president of Honduras. Melodrama moves slowly and has banal plot. (Dir: Jacques Tourneur, 79 mins.)

Appointment in London (British, 1953)*****½** Dirk Bogarde, Ian Hunter, Dinah Sheridan. Life among an RAF bomber command during the dark days of 1943, climaxing with a raid over Germany. Intelligent, well acted and directed drama, worth-while.

Appointment with a Shadow (1958)****** George Nader, Joanna Moore,

Brian Keith. Alcoholic reporter is given a chance at a big story, finds himself target for a killer. Undistinguished crime melodrama. (Dir: Joseph Penney, 72 mins.)

Appointment with Danger (1951)*** Alan Ladd, Phyllis Calvert, Jack Webb. Post Office investigator gets some aid from unexpected sources while foiling a mail robbery. Good crime melodrama benefits from a sharp writing job, good performances, especially by Webb as a killer. (Dir: Lewis Allen, 88 mins.)

Apprenticeship of Duddy Kravitz, The (Canada, 1974)**** Richard Dreyfuss, Randy Quaid, Joseph Wiseman, Jack Warden, Denholm Elliot, Micheline Lanctot. An exuberant, hilarious, sometimes sad film about a mid-forties Canadian version of "What Makes Sammy Run." Richard Dreyfuss is excellent playing a hustling Jewish teenager on the make in Montreal. One of the many strengths of "Duddy" is the near perfect screenplay by Mordecai Richler, nominated for an Academy Award, based on his own novel and adapted by Lionel Chetwynd. There is one paralyzingly funny scene of a Bar Mitzvah movie made by a pretentious 'intellectual' blacklisted documentary filmmaker who is constantly worried about having his artistic integrity compromised. There seem to have been no unfortunate compromises made during the course of this joyous, poignant winner. (Dir: Ted Kotcheff, 121 mins.)

April Fools, The (1969)**½ Jack Lemmon, Catherine Deneuve, Sally Kellerman, Jack Weston. A good idea for a romantic romp with comedy as its base—but, alas, it doesn't really come off. Jack Lemmon is the much-married Madison Avenue exec. Once again, schnook Lemmon falls in love with his boss' beautiful wife (Miss Deneuve), and gets in and out of improbable messes until the final scene, when true love triumphs. (Dir: Stuart Rosenberg, 95 mins.)

April in Paris (1953)**½ Doris Day, Ray Bolger, Claude Dauphin. Take a chorus girl named "Dynamite" (Doris, of course) and get her invited to Paris Arts Festival (by mistake) as the representative of the American Theatre; add a bumbling State Dept. official (how about Ray Bolger?) and a' suave Frenchman (on the order of Claude Dauphin) ; garnish with songs and dances and you have an "April in Paris" technicolor "parfait." It's still a routine dessert. (Dir: David Butler, 101 mins.)

April Love (1957)**½ Pat Boone, Shirley Jones. Strictly for Pat Boone fans. Pat plays a young man who arrives on a farm in Kentucky and immediately is up to his blue jeans in romance and song. Shirley Jones is the sweet, young love interest. Happily she's improved a great deal since this film. The songs are routine and the plot is incidental. (Dir: Henry Levin, 99 mins.)

April Showers (1948)**½ Jack Carson, Ann Sothern. The old vaudeville backstage theme receives an undistinguished treatment in this musical. (Dir: James Kern, 94 mins.)

Aquarians, The (1970)**½ Ricardo Montalban, Jose Ferrer, Tom Simcox, Kate Woodville. This Ivan Tors made-for-TV feature is so technically fine, just forget the monosyllabic dialogue and scientific jargon, and enjoy it for its pure adventure elements. (Of course, it will help if you are under 12 years old.) A team of deep sea laboratory scientists, headed by no-nonsense boss Ricardo Montalban, stumble upon a group of opportunists bent on salvaging a wrecked vessel with a cargo of poison nerve gas. The underwater photography is superb and there's a breath-taking (pardon the pun) aquatic chase between Montalban and a specially rigged one-man submarine. (Dir: Don McDougall.)

Arabella (Italy, 1967)**½ Virna Lisi, Margaret Rutherford, James Fox, Terry-Thomas. Mild romantic comedy set in Italy in the 1920's. Virna Lisi tries to extract money from men in order to help her aunt pay off taxes dating back to 1895. Terry-Thomas appears in three small roles, an Italian hotel manager, an Italian duke and a British general, all delivered in broad English splutter. James Fox is excellent as the scoundrel Miss Lisi keeps falling in love with, but even these good performances can't save the weak script. (Dir: Mauro Bolognini, 105 mins.)

Arabesque (1966)**½ Gregory Peck, Sophia Loren. A contrived, not altogether successful chase melodrama with handsome Greg Peck and beautiful Sophia Loren amid lavish international settings. Director Stanley Donen ("Charade") keeps the film bouncing around, but the camera tricks can't disguise the thin plot about secret documents and a language expert (Peck) who unwillingly gets involved in all the intrigue. The sights are more absorbing than any dialogue you'll hear. (Dir: Stanley Donen, 104 mins.)

Arabian Nights (1942)** Maria Montez, Jon Hall, Sabu. Corny but elaborately produced spectacle about the days of dancing slave girls, tent cities, and the Caliph of Baghdad. (Dir: John Rawling, 86 mins.)

Arch of Triumph (1948)**½ Charles Boyer, Ingrid Bergman, Charles Laughton. Story of a refugee doctor and a girl with a past in Paris, just before the Nazis take over. From Remarque's novel, but something is missing; the result, a long, rather emotionless drama that fans of Boyer and Bergman will enjoy. (Dir: Lewis Milestone, 120 mins.)

Archangels, The (Italian, 1965)** Roberto Bisacco, Virginia Onorato. Girl in Rome to seek her brother's aid in getting family acceptance for her fiancé is caught up in the life led by him and his city friends. Attempt at realism that meanders too much, giving it a slow pace. Dubbed in English.

Arctic Flight (1952)**½ Wayne Morris, Lola Albright. Bush pilot battles foreign agents way up North. Not bad little action melodrama—good location scenes. (75 mins.)

Are Husbands Necessary (1942)** Ray Milland, Betty Field. Contrived, forced farce about the problems of newlyweds. Rarely funny, often embarrassing. (Dir: Norman Taurog, 75 mins.)

Are You There? (British, 1930)**** Beatrice Lillie. A comic masterpiece (also released as "Exit Laughing") that contains one of the most excruciatingly funny scenes ever recorded on film—the great Lady Peel (Lillie) wooing a recalcitrant suitor while swirling a huge chain of beads, jumping over and around couches, and trying, all the while, to be seductive. A sad reminder of the shameful way the movie industry neglected this extraordinary comedienne throughout virtually all of her long and brilliant stage career. If you ever get a chance to see this comedy gem do so. Your sides will hurt from laughing. (Dir: Hamilton MacFadden.)

Are You With It? (1948)*** Donald O'Connor, Olga San Juan. Mathematician leaves his job and joins a traveling carnival. Cute and pleasant musical, with some good work by O'Connor. (Dir: Jack Hively, 90 mins.)

Arena (1953)** Gig Young, Polly Bergen. Story of cowboys competing for prizes in the Tucson rodeo—but there's not much story. Originally this had 3-D to help promote it in theatres, but here it's just ordinary stuff. (Dir: Richard Fleischer, 70 mins.)

Arise My Love (1940)** Claudette Colbert, Ray Milland. A confused melange of love and war set against the Spanish Civil War and the second World War. Weak film. (Dir: Mitchell Leisen, 113 mins.)

Aristocats, The (1970)***½ A grand-style Walt Disney full-length cartoon. Full of invention and character, which has always distinguished Disney products. This one's about a mama cat and three of her babies who are kidnapped and left in the country by a mean butler. Everything is set magnificently in Paris in 1910. Especially distinctive are the stellar voices, which include Eva Gabor, Phil Harris, Sterling Holloway, Ruth Buzzi—and Maurice Chevalier singing the title tune. Pleasant family fare. (Dir: Wolfgang Reitherman, 78 mins.)

Arizona (1940)**½ William Holden, Jean Arthur. Western gal has trouble when her rivals have her wagon trains attached. This is big, sprawling, with some fine action scenes; but it's just too darn long. Result: pleasing but otherwise unexceptional western.

Arizona Bushwhackers (1968)** Standard western has a gunslinger-spy (Howard Keel) town-taming during the Civil War. Typical A. C. Lyles-produced action; weak plot, good cast of veterans including Yvonne DeCarlo, Scott Brady, John Ireland, Marilyn Maxwell, Barton MacLane, Brian Donlevy, James Craig, Roy Rogers Jr. (Junior??? ! ! !) In case you think the voice of the narrator sounds familiar, you're right. It's James Cagney! (Dir: Lesley Selander, 86 mins.)

Arizona Mission (1956)** James Ar-

34

ness, Angie Dickinson, Harry Carey, Jr. The stars give good performances in an otherwise run of the mill western drama. You've seen it a thousand times before and can see it any night of the week on "series" westerns. (Dir: Andrew V. McLaglen, 78 mins.)

Armored Attack (1943)**½ Anne Baxter, Walter Huston, Dana Andrews. Russian villagers defend their land when the Nazis invade. Wartime drama has been given a political face-lifting, but still remains, as originally, only occasionally effective. (Dir: Lewis Milestone, 105 mins.)

Armored Car Robbery (1950)***½ Charles McGraw, William Talman. Four participants in an armored car robbery are brought to justice when they kill a cop. Tough, exciting, extremely well-made melodrama. (Dir: Richard Fleischer, 67 mins.)

Armored Command (1961)** Howard Keel, Tina Louise, Earl Holliman. Routine war film with a large amount of romance thrown in for good measure. The stars do what they can, which isn't much, with a very predictable script. (Dir: Byron Haskin, 99 mins.)

Arms and the Man (West Germany, 1958)*** O. W. Fischer, Lisa Pulver. Nicely executed German version of Shaw's memorable play about a Swiss mercenary, fleeing the enemy in the Balkans, who takes refuge in a girl's bedroom. The bite of Shaw's irony toward war and heroism is somehow lost, but otherwise the movie is good entertainment. The two leads are perfectly cast. (Dir: Franz Peter Wirth, 96 mins.)

Around the World (1943)**½ Kay Kyser, Joan Davis. Kyser's orchestra takes a round-the-world tour to cheer up fighting men in battle areas. Dull musical.

Around the World in 80 Days (1958) **** David Niven, Shirley MacLaine, Cantinflas. Delightful rendition of the Jules Verne tale. In 1872 traveling around the world took a bit longer than it takes to jet around today. Phileas Fogg (Niven) bets his London club that he can do it in 80 days, and away we go. His valet's (Cantinflas') historic confrontation in a Spanish bullring, the defiant rescue of an Indian princess (Shirley MacLaine) from a funeral pyre, and a hysterical balloon flight over France are all part of the bet. An odds-on favorite all the way. (Dir: Michael Anderson, 170 mins.)

Around the World Under the Sea (1966)** David McCallum, Brian Kelly. TV fans may like seeing some familiar faces of series stars in a different type of role in this scientific sea saga. David McCallum, Marshall Thompson, Brian Kelly, and Lloyd Bridges costar as scientists exploring the ocean deep to determine the course of tidal waves and such. It's played strictly for the juvenile trade. (Dir: Andrew Marton, 117 mins.)

Arrangement, The (1968)**½ Kirk Douglas, Faye Dunaway, Deborah Kerr. Uneven treatment of Elia Kazan's thinly veiled autobiographical novel about the search for meaning in his life by a successful ad agency exec, and the resistance he encounters from those closest to him. Douglas misses all the subtleties of the character, and the two female leads, Misses Kerr and Dunaway, have little better than one-dimensional characters to portray. However, Richard Boone as Douglas' Greek-immigrant father scores in a fully realized performance. Director Kazan allowed himself to wax poetic too often in this weakly constructed self-analysis. (Dir: Elia Kazan, 127 mins.)

Arrivederci, Baby! (1966)*** Tony Curtis, Rosanna Schiaffino. An amusing comedy about a money-hungry young man (Curtis) who keeps discarding guardians and wives for their fortunes. He meets his match in Rosanna Schiaffino, the widow of a nobleman, and their stormy marriage provides many laughs. Curtis is well suited to the role of playboy-conniver and Miss Schiaffino also registers. (Dir: Ken Hughes, 105 mins.)

Arrow in the Dust (1954)** Sterling Hayden, Coleen Gray. Another Western with the safety of an entire wagon train dependent on one strong man—this time it's Sterling Hayden and he's a cavalry trooper who impersonates a major in order to have authority. (Dir: Lesley Selander, 80 mins.)

Arrowhead (1953)**½ Charlton Heston, Jack Palance, Katy Jurado. Trouble in the Southwest when a Cavalry unit attempts to sign a peace treaty with the Apaches. Heston and Palance are worth watching in this otherwise well-made but routine western. (Dir: Charles Warren, 105 mins.)

Arsene Lupin (1932)***½ John Barrymore, Lionel Barrymore, Karen Morley. Master burglar is continually hounded by a wily police inspector. (Guess who's who.) Well-acted, entertaining melodrama. (Dir: Jack Conway, 85 mins.)

Arsenic and Old Lace (1944)***½ Cary Grant, Josephine Hull, Raymond Massey. Plenty of fun with corpses in the adaptation of the Broadway hit. Josephine Hull is magnificent as the pixilated poisoner but a lot of the intimacy of the original is lost on the screen. (Dir: Frank Capra, 118 mins.)

Arson for Hire (1959)*½ Steve Brodie, Tom Hubbard. A rash of unexplained fires sends Steve Brodie out to investigate the arson gang racket. Grade "C" melodrama with grade "D" performances. (67 mins.)

Art of Crime, The (1975)**½ Ron Leibman, Jose Ferrer, David Hedison, Jill Clayburgh. Clever gypsy forced to play detective to save a friend. Leibman gives a polished, winning performance as Roman Grey, a cool gypsy who inhabits two worlds. Writers Martin Smith and Bill Davidson, basing their material on the novel "Gypsy in Amber," dip into gypsy culture and reveal interesting tidbits on the art of fooling the antique-buying public. A slick and slightly different product. Made-for-TV. (Dir: Richard Irving, 72 mins.)

Art of Love, The (1965)**½ James Garner, Dick Van Dyke, Elke Sommer, Angie Dickinson. Deciding that dead artists are the only ones who sell well, a painter and his buddy decide to fake a suicide. Good cast helps this mild comedy, which should have been better. (Dir: Norman Jewison, 98 mins.)

Artists and Models (1937)*** Jack Benny, Ida Lupino, Gail Patrick. A smash hit in 1937 and fairly entertaining today. Jack runs a down-and-out advertising agency, and if he can find the right model, he lands a big account. Plenty of specialty numbers performed by Martha Raye, Connee Boswell, and Louis Armstrong. (Dir: Raoul Walsh, 97 mins.)

Artists and Models (1955)**½ Dean Martin, Jerry Lewis, Shirley MacLaine, Dorothy Malone. Artist lands a big job doing comic strips, inspired by his goofy partner's dreams. Garish musical comedy chiefly for M & L devotees. Pretty girls, gorgeous sets and costumes, some fun, but it goes on too long. (Dir: Frank Tashlin, 109 mins.)

Arturo's Island (Italy, 1963)**½ Yanni de Maigret, Kay Meersman, Reginald Kernan. Somber tale of a boy who's left alone in a huge house on his father's island. Offbeat treatment of a young boy's emergence into manhood. (Dir: Damiano Damiani, 93 mins.)

As If It Were Raining (French, 1960)*½ Eddie Constantine, Elisa Montes. Novelist framed for murder goes after the real killer. Hackneyed imitation-American detective story, dubbed in English. (Dir: Jose Monter, 85 mins.)

As Long as They're Happy (British, 1955)**½ Jack Buchanan, Janette Scott. Englishman's daughter swoons for a visiting American crooner, invites him to her home. Amusing comedy. (Dir: J. Lee Thompson, 76 mins.)

As Long as You're Near Me (German, 1956)** Maria Schell, O. W. Fischer. Turgid love story of a girl who lived her love life twice. Excellent performances by two of Germany's leading actors, Miss Schell and Mr. Fischer. (101 mins.)

As the Sea Rages (1960)*½ Maria Schell, Cliff Robertson. Crude plot mars this story of Yugoslavian refugees. (Dir: Horst Haechler, 74 mins.)

As You Desire Me (1932)*** Greta Garbo, Melvyn Douglas, Erich Von Stroheim. From the play by Luigi Pirandello. Exotic nightclub singer has many lovers. Excellently acted drama. (Dir: George Fitzmaurice, 71 mins.)

As Young as We Are (1958)** Pippa Scott, Robert Harland. School teacher falls in love with one of her pupils. Kind of drama usually found in confession magazines given a lift by sincere performances. (76 mins.)

As Young as You Feel (1951)** Monty Woolley, Thelma Ritter, David Wayne, Jean Peters, Marilyn Monroe, Constance Bennett. Screwy attempt to conjure the spirits of the zany family and their madcap shenanigans which proved so successful in "You Can't Take It with You." It doesn't come off despite the starring line-up. Woolley adopts a caustic attitude, but the lines aren't there. (77 mins.)

Ashes and Diamonds (Poland, 1958) **** Zbigniew Cybulski. One of the first and best of some extraordinary Polish films that examined Poland's role in World War II and the reaction of Poles to the war and its aftermath. This film, based on a controversial post-war Polish novel, is about the last day of war and the first day of peace in Warsaw, and the mixed-up loyalties and emotions of a young Polish partisan. Zbigniew Cybulski, who acted the young Pole, achieved superstar stature as a result of this role; his early death in 1967 was mourned by the whole country. Director Wajda gained almost equal fame: the subjective camera-work in this film, which captures the visual richness of Polish Romantic paintings and poetry, has come to be his trademark. (Dir: Andrzej Wajda, 104 mins.)

Ask Any Girl (1959)**½ David Niven, Shirley MacLaine, Gig Young. An attractive cast of expert screen comics adds stature to this feather-weight story about the plight of the single girl in the big city. David Niven almost does a takeoff of his own sophisticated style. (Dir: Charles Walters, 98 mins.)

Asphalt Jungle, The (1950)**** Sterling Hayden, Sam Jaffe, Louis Calhern, James Whitmore, Marilyn Monroe. Director John Huston's narrative of a gang of robbers, their "perfect" crime's disastrous outcome was THE big gangster story of the '50's. Absorbing story of what is called "a left-handed form of human endeavor"; superb performances by all, tough action. Brilliantly directed. (Dir: John Huston, 112 mins.)

Assassin, The (British, 1953)**½ Richard Todd, Eva Bartok. Good European backgrounds, but just a routine chase story as detective tracks down a man who is supposed to be dead. (Dir: Elio Petr, 94 mins.)

Assassination Bureau, The (British, 1969)*** Diana Rigg, Oliver Reed, Telly Savalas, Curt Jurgens. Adventures of a lady journalist (Diana Rigg) on the trail of an organization

specializing in timely eliminations. Neat costumed fun, played tongue-in-cheek. (Dir: Basil Dearden, 110 mins.)

Assassination of Trotsky, The (French-Italian-British, 1972)*** Richard Burton, Alain Delon, Romy Schneider. Like watching an earth-shattering bullfight . . . a matador, intense with purpose, toying with a defenseless bull. This is the fatalism with which the killing of Trotsky, the famous Russian revolutionary leader, is documented. Delon plays the murderer, whose only purpose is to kill Trotsky (Richard Burton). Trotsky lives in a total fortress but is still defenseless because of his humanitarian ideology. Laced with symbolism and psychological insight. The acting is good, and the direction is intense and atmospheric. You may either hate or love this film, but you will react. (Dir: Joseph Losey, 103 mins.)

Assault on a Queen (1966)* Frank Sinatra, Virna Lisi, Tony Franciosa. Boring assault on your senses. Not even Sinatra could breathe life into this foolish story about a group of con men who get together to pull the biggest caper of them all, robbing the Queen Mary on the high seas by using a reconverted German U-boat. The screenplay by Rod Serling is embarrassingly bad, and Miss Lisi's accent makes it even worse. (Dir: Jack Donohue, 106 mins.)

Assault on the Wayne (1971)*½ Leonard Nimoy, Lloyd Haynes, William Windom. Routine made-for-TV espionage yarn, set aboard a nuclear sub. The set is more interesting than the actors. Nimoy is all stiffness and orders as the commander who discovers some of his submarine crew members are working for a foreign power. The climax plays like a Hardy Boys adventure. But action fans won't complain. (Dir: Marvin Chomsky.)

Assignment Abroad (1955)* Robert Alda. Ace secret agent tackles three cases during World War II. Trashy heroics clipped together from the TV series "Secret File USA."

Assignment in Paris (1952)**½ Dana Andrews, Marta Toren, George Sanders. Interesting but never exciting spy story concerning a reporter who is captured and imprisoned when he comes into possession of some important microfilm. Marta

Toren plays a female spy in the great Mata Hari tradition. (Dir: Robert Parrish, 85 mins.)

Assignment K (British, 1968)★★ Stephen Boyd, Camilla Sparv, Michael Redgrave (good in a thankless bit), Leo McKern, Jeremy Kemp. Spies and counterspies all over Europe, with an intrepid British intelligence agent once more played for a patsy. Good scenery, but the plot doesn't begin until it's half over, when it's too late. (Dir: Val Guest, 97 mins.)

Assignment Outer Space (German, 1952)★½ Archie Savage, Rik Von Nutter. A spaceship gets out of control and threatens to destroy earth. Gimmicky English-dubbed science fiction may bore the non-believer.

Assignment Redhead (British, 1957) ★½ Paul Carpenter, Kay Callard. Reporter investigates his brother-in-law's death, exposes a dope ring. Tedious crime melodrama.

Assignment to Kill (1968)★½ Patrick O'Neal, Joan Hackett, Herbert Lom. Contrived, boring melodrama written and directed by Sheldon Reynolds, whose "Foreign Intrigue" TV series is still fondly remembered. Private eye is hired to investigate possible big time corporate fraud in Switzerland. Assets like the glorious Swiss countryside and great actors like John Gielgud wasted in this bungled effort. (Dir: Sheldon Reynolds.)

Astonished Heart (British, 1948)★★½ Noel Coward, Margaret Leighton, Celia Johnson. Married psychiatrist falls for an old friend, the affair leading to tragedy. Overdone drama, but elaborately produced and well acted. (Dir: Terence Fisher, 92 mins.)

Astounding She Monster (1957)★ Robert Clarke, Marilyn Harvey. Dull, inept science fiction yarn about a very tall female creature from another star, or planet if you will, who wanders in the mountains.

Astronaut, The (1972)★★½ Monte Markham, Susan Clark. The title is misleading, for the show is really a love story with moving performances by the leads. After an astronaut dies during a Mars landing, space officials use the old masquerade trick, hoping to deceive the world with a double. The deception succeeds in public but backfires in private. Miss Clark's portrayal of the duped wife —livid with anger over the stunt—

keys the show, and she's supported nicely by Monte Markham. Jackie Cooper also earns a vote as the tough-minded space exec intent on covering up the truth. Made-for-TV. (Dir: Robert Michael Lewis.)

Asylum (1972)★★★★ Involving documentary about mentally disturbed patients living in a "community" under the guiding aegis of the distinguished British psychiatrist R. D. Laing. You'll discover in this honest, troubling film how the individually oriented Laingian approach is upset by an individual who threatens to destroy the functioning of the entire community. Several of the patients are clearly psychotic, but director-producer Peter Robinson never exploits them, and the resulting film is a moving prohuman statement showing how Laing's theories often work to save these troubled souls. Filmed in London at Laing's "community" clinic. (Dir: Peter Robinson, 95 mins.)

Asylum (British, 1972)★★½ Peter Cushing, Herbert Lom, Richard Todd, Barbara Parkins. A chilling quartet of tales—"Frozen Fear," "The Weird Tailor," "Lucy Comes to Stay," and "Mannikins of Horror" —are told to a visiting doctor at an asylum and the results are very entertaining. A good cast and a surprise ending bolster the proceedings. Written by Robert Bloch. (Dir: Roy Ward Baker, 88 mins.)

Asylum for a Spy (1967)★½ Robert Stack, Felicia Farr, Martin Milner. Familiar tale of a U.S. agent who suffers a mental breakdown, and the foreign agent who's sent to pry secrets from him. Made-for-TV. (Dir: Stuart Rosenberg, 90 mins.)

At Dawn We Die (Great Britain, 1943)★★ John Clements, Godfrey Tearle, Greta Gynt. Another version of French Underground versus Nazis. Action-packed anti-Nazi entry. (Dir: George King, 78 mins.)

At Gunpoint (1955)★★½ Fred MacMurray, Dorothy Malone. A good cast and good production makes this western drama an entertaining one. Plot concerns a peaceful man who does his duty as a citizen and ends up being stalked by a band of outlaws. Veteran actor Walter Brennan has a featured role. (Dir: Alfred Werker, 81 mins.)

At Long Last Love (1975)★ Burt Reynolds, Cybill Shepherd, Madeline

Kahn, Eileen Brennan, Duilio Del Prete, John Hillerman. It's disgraceful, it's deplorable, it's disastrous! Cole Porter would spin in his grave if he knew how his sophisticated songs were used in this inane musical, clumsily directed, written and produced by Peter Bogdanovich. Intending to make a valentine to the thirties, Bogdanovich has instead fashioned a poison-pen letter. Burt Reynolds, miscast as a wealthy playboy of the Art Deco set, sings poorly, and Cybill Shepherd as his warbling vis-a-vis proves that a little talent is just that. Madeline Kahn and Eileen Brennan at least can sing, but they are lost in the silly plot muddle. Skip this one and look for the genuine item, an Astaire-Rogers film. (Dir: Peter Bogdanovich, 115 mins.)

At Sword's Point (1952)*** Cornel Wilde, Maureen O'Hara. The sons of the Three Musketeers save their queen from intrigue of enemies. Lively costume melodrama; some fast action. (Dir: Lewis Allen, 81 mins.)

At the Circus (1939)**½ Marx Brothers. People who adore the Marx Brothers will, of course, laugh but even they will be disappointed at this forced effort. The boys are trying to save a circus in this epic which can only be recommended to their many fans. (Dir: Edward Buzzell, 90 mins.)

At the Earth's Core (Great Britain, 1976)**½ Doug McClure, Peter Cushing, Cy Grant. A sequel to the 1974 "The Land that Time Forgot." Occasionally entertaining blend of fantasy, humor and chills based on the 1923 novel by Edgar Rice Burroughs. Sci-fi entry as Cushing bores through to the center of the earth and meets some strange creatures including a "rhamphorhynchus of the Middle Eolithic." (Dir: Kevin Connor, 90 mins.)

At the Stroke of Nine (British, 1957)** Patricia Dainton, Stephen Murray. A slow paced but interesting "meller" drama about the kidnapping of a newspaper woman by a madman.

At War with the Army (1950)**½ Dean Martin, Jerry Lewis, Polly Bergen. Sergeant tries to get a dumb PFC to help him out of some girl trouble. Despite the fact that this farce shot Martin & Lewis to fame

as a screen comedy team, it doesn't happen to be terribly funny. (Dir: Hal Walker, 93 mins.)

Athena (1954)** Jane Powell, Debbie Reynolds, Edmund Purdom, Vic Damone. Lawyer falls for a pretty miss, meets her family, a bunch of health nuts. Musical tried for a different angle and missed. (Dir. Richard Thorpe, 96 mins.)

Atlantic City (1944)** Constance Moore, Brad Taylor, Jerry Colonna. Musical panorama of the famous joy pier, told via the romantic story of an idea man and his girl, who build an enterprise out of some useless swampland. Just fair.

Atlantic Convoy (1942)**½ Bruce Bennett, Virginia Field, John Beal. Good Grade "B" wartime spy film. A man is suspected of aiding the Nazis and must redeem himself.

Atlantis, the Lost Continent (1961)** Anthony Hall, Joyce Taylor. The young set will enjoy this costume adventure tale about a mythical lost continent in the days of the Roman Empire. The acting is wooden as is often the case in these films and much of the footage is left over from "Quo Vadis," M-G-M's spectacle of a few years earlier. (Dir: George Pal, 90 mins.)

Atlas (1960)** Michael Forrest, Frank Wolff. Cheaply made costume catastrophe—hardly any extras are used and the producers even scrimped on the lighting.

Atlas Against the Cyclops (Italian, 1961)* Mitchell Gordon, Chelo Alonso. Muscleman accepts a challenge to rescue prisoners from a monstrous beast. English-dubbed. Avoid the challenge of sitting through this junk.

Atlas Against the Czar (Italian, 1964)* Kirk Morris, Gloria Milland. Muscleman pits his brawn, if not brains, against Tartar hordes. Dull spectacle dubbed in English.

Atom Age Vampire (Italian, 1961)*½ Alberto Lupo, Susanne Loret. Scientist restores beauty to a scarred entertainer with serum taken from dead women, which means he has to kill more to keep her that way. Slow, dull horror thriller.

Atomic Agent (French, 1959)* Martine Carol, Felix Marten, Dany Saval. Cute but screwball model outwits the police in trapping a spy ring after an atomic motor. Pert Miss Carol is good to look at; otherwise just a routine comedy-adventure. Dubbed in English.

Atomic City (1952)*** Gene Barry, Lydia Clarke, Milburn Stone. Son of a physicist working in Los Alamos is kidnapped by foreign agents. Suspenseful melodrama with an unusual locale, thoughtful script, nice performances. Underrated entry. (Dir: Jerry Hopper, 85 mins.)

Atomic Kid (1954)** Mickey Rooney, Robert Straus, Elaine Davis. Guy survives an atomic blast but becomes radioactive, mixed up with spies. Fair comedy. (Dir: Leslie Martinson, 86 mins.)

Atomic Man, The (1956)** Gene Nelson, Faith Domergue. British-made thriller about a reporter and his girl who stumble on a mystery concerning a shady scientist. Just about average for shady scientist flicks. (Dir: Ken Hughes, 78 mins.)

Atomic Rulers of the World (Japanese, 1964)* English-dubbed sci-fi about a daring detective and some orphan children joining forces to thwart an atom-bomb smuggling plot. Nippon's feeble parody of the old serial technique, only played straight. Only audience gets thrown a curve.

Atomic Submarine (1960)*½ Arthur Franz, Dick Foran. Something from outer space has been messing with subs in the Arctic. Science-fiction leaves one cold. (Dir: Spencer Bennet, 72 mins.)

Atomic War Bride (1966)* Anton Voldak, Eva Krewskan. Inane story about two lovers whose romance is momentarily interrupted by an atomic war. They live through the atomic war, but it's hardly worth the bother. Low-budget entry, (77 mins.)

Atragon (Japanese, 1964)*½ Creatures from a submerged continent rise to the surface to cause all kinds of mischief. Some clever trick effects, otherwise the usual silly sci-fi nonsense.

Attack (1956)**** Jack Palance, Eddie Albert. Enormously moving drama of cowardice and heroism during the Battle of the Bulge in WWII. Excellent cast and good script. One of the finest anti-war movies ever made and a much underrated effort of director Robert Aldrich. (107 mins.)

Attack and Retreat (Russ.-Italian, 1964)**½ Arthur Kennedy, Peter Falk, Tatiana Samilova. Sprawling World War II story of Italian soldiers and their experiences on the Russian front. Lavishly produced and reminds us again that war is hell. (Dir: Giuseppe De Santis, 156 mins.)

Attack of the Crab Monsters (1957)*½ Richard Garland, Pamela Duncan. Another one of those sci-fi films which tells of monsters unearthed by the H-Bomb tests, fallout in the Pacific. Should please sci-fi fans who don't make too many demands from films of this type. (Dir: Roger Corman, 70 mins.)

Attack of the 50-Foot Woman (1958)** Allison Hayes, William Hudson. This science-fictioner could be amusing if you just don't take it seriously. The giantess of the title manages to create quite a fuss. (Dir: Nathan Juran, 65 mins.)

Attack of the Giant Leeches (1959)** Ken Clark, Yvette Vickers. Routine horror-science fiction tale about outsized leeches which take over a Florida swamp.

Attack of the Mayan Mummy (Mexican, 1963)* Nina Knight, Richard Webb. Girl is regressed into past life by a scientist, describes ancient Mayan civilization, which leads to an expedition seeking a lost tomb. Below-par horror thriller, ineptly produced.

Attack of the Moors (Italian, 1960)* Rik Bataglia, Chelo Alonso. Count captures Moorish chief's daughter as a safeguard to insure the safe return home of Spanish royal children. Seedy costume adventure, dubbed in English.

Attack of the Mushroom People (Japanese, 1964)*½ Group on holiday land on a mysterious island, run afoul of a strange funguslike growth which spells disaster for them. Some fair special effects, otherwise farfetched horror thriller dubbed in English.

Attack of the Normans (Italian, 1961)*½ Cameron Mitchell. A count is falsely accused of kidnapping England's king, during the 9th Century. Mediocre costume adventure, dubbed in English.

Attack of the Puppet People (1958)*½ John Agar, June Kenny. Silly horror film about a doll manufacturer who makes some rather unique products—humans turned into puppets. (Dir: Bert Gordon, 79 mins.)

Attack of the Robots (French-Spanish, 1967)* Eddie Constantine, Fernando Rey. Far-fetched tale about an Interpol agent tracking down an organization which has control over people with O-type blood. (Dir: J. Franco, 85 mins.)

Attack on Terror: The FBI Versus the Ku Klux Klan (1975)**½ Rip Torn, George Grizzard. Compelling recreation of the 1964 murder of three civil-rights workers in the piney woods of Mississippi that works because of the obvious care taken with the story, acting and research. The build-up to the impending tragedy provides insight into the main characters, especially Rip Torn's Ku Klux Klan Imperial Wizard, a villain of menacing proportions, brought to life by a blockbuster performance. The movie romanticizes the real performance of the FBI in the Deep South during the 50's and 60's, but it's still worth seeing. One of the few films that deals with any area of the civil-rights struggle in the South. Originally shown in two parts as a four-hour drama. Made-for-TV. (Dir: Marvin Chomsky.)

Attack on the Iron Coast (British, 1968)**½ Lloyd Bridges, Andrew Keir, Sue Lloyd, Mark Eden. Commandos attempt a daring raid on German installations during World War II. The same old war story, but competently handled.

Attack Squadron (Japanese, 1963)** Toshiro Mifune. English-dubbed. The war from enemy viewpoint, as a Japanese officer fights in vain to replace an Air Attack unit in 1944. Crude production and badly dubbed in English, nevertheless has novelty interest.

Attempt to Kill (British, 1962)* Derek Farr, Freda Jackson. Former employee and wife are suspects when a businessman is murdered. Poor, cheaply-made mystery. (Dir: Royston Morley, 57 mins.)

Attica (1973)***½ A powerful documentary recreating the events leading up to and including the famous showdown and inexcusable shootout at Attica State Prison in New York in September 1971. This valuable historical record of the slaughter of many prison inmates during the Governorship of Nelson Rockefeller utilizes existing newsreel and TV footage, together with some new interviews, to create a chilling story of bureaucratic bungling, intransigence and lack of compassion. Conceived, edited and directed by Cinda Firestone, an impressive debut effort. (79 mins.)

Attila (French-Italian, 1955)*½ Anthony Quinn, Sophia Loren, Irene Papas. Pint-sized epic as Quinn plays Attila the Hun, scourge of the Roman Empire. He takes over Europe with a hunting party, and piously does an about-face when met by Pope Leo I and his tabernacle choir. Schmaltz. (Dir: Pietro Francisci, 83 mins.)

Audrey Rose (1977)* Marsha Mason, Anthony Hopkins. My beloved Central Park West has been defamed by this unscary drivel about reincarnation, ploddingly directed by Robert Wise who has made some good films in his day. Another ripoff of "The Exorcist" gambit and it fails, as another teenaged girl has nightmares and is seized by forces of the devil, tra la la . . . Adapted by Frank De Felitta from his novel. (In an earlier reincarnation, author De Felitta was an extremely talented documentary producer for NBC-TV.) (Dir: Robert Wise, 113 mins.)

Augustine of Hippo (Italian, 1973)**½ About St. Augustine and the history of the fall of the Roman Empire. Concerned with showing Augustine as a man of action in his younger years promulgating Christianity. English subtitles. (Dir: Roberto Rossellini for Italian TV, 120 mins.)

Auntie Mame (1958)**½ Rosalind Russell, Forrest Tucker, Peggy Cass, Coral Browne. All of the raucous incidents from the best seller and the hit play are repeated in the screen version but, somehow, they seem less funny on the screen. Roz Russell works like a dynamo in a role that seems tailor-made for her talents. Peggy Cass, repeating her stage role of "Miss Gooch," gets her share of belly laughs. (Dir: Morton DaCosta, 143 mins.)

Autobiography of Miss Jane Pittman, The (1974)**** Cicely Tyson, Odetta, Michael Murphy, Collin Wilcox. This is one of the three or four best movies ever made for American TV, and that is not meant to be a patronizing remark, for "Pittman" is a deeply moving film whatever its origin. Cicely Tyson won a richly deserved Emmy award for her triumphant performance in the role of a

110-year-old woman who was an ex-slave, and lived to take part in a civil rights demonstration in 1962. Extensive use of flashbacks depicting various episodes in the life of Miss Jane, a fictional character; but the incidents are based on real incidents that happened throughout the South after the Civil War. Adapted from Ernest J. Gaines' novel, the movie has been superbly done by, among others, director John Korty, screenwriter Tracy Keenan Wynn (both of whom also won Emmy awards), and makeup men Stan Winston and Rick Baker for their astonishing work on Tyson's face as she becomes a spirited 110-year-old storyteller. The meaning of the civil rights movement in the early and mid-'60's has seldom been shown with greater dramatic impact than when Miss Jane, haltingly but proudly, walks to and drinks from a water fountain previously reserved "For Whites Only." (Dir: John Korty)

Autopsy of a Criminal (Spanish, 1964)*½ Daniele Godet, Francisco Rabal. Gambler tries to retrieve a necklace, gets involved in murder. Dull crime melodrama dubbed in English.

Autumn Leaves (1956)**½ Joan Crawford, Cliff Robertson, Vera Miles. A woman's picture! Miss Crawford once more goes through hell for the love of a man she believes in. She marries young and handsome Cliff Robertson only to discover he is on the verge of a mental breakdown. La Crawford suffers valiantly and Robertson is very good as her mixed-up husband. (Dir: Robert Aldrich, 110 mins.)

Avanti! (1972)*** Jack Lemmon, Juliet Mills. Not one of director Billy Wilder's best, but entertaining nevertheless. Lemmon's deft comedic style is in perfect harmony with his role of a successful businessman who goes to Italy to arrange for the return of his tycoon-father's body only to discover dad died with his mistress of long standing. Enter Mills' delightful British miss with a similar objective—to bring mum back—and the comedy rolls laughingly along. Escapist fare? Yes. Overlong? Yes. A better time waster than most? Yes. (Dir: Billy Wilder, 144 mins.)

Avenger, The (German, 1961)*½

Heinz Drache, Ingrid Bergen. Mysterious murders are traced to a motive of revenge. English-dubbed; trite Edgar Wallace mystery. (Dir: Karl Anton, 102 mins.)

Avenger of the Seven Seas (Italian, 1960)* Richard Harrison, Walter Barnes. English-dubbed adventure about a young seaman getting his revenge on a cruel captain in the 17th Century. Everyone connected with movie seems to be bent on revenge.

Avenger of Venice (Italian, 1963)* Brett Halsey. Greedy lords plot the overthrow of a nobleman in 16th Century Venice. Weak costume adventure, dubbed in English.

Avengers, The (1950)*½ John Carroll, Adele Mara, Fernando Lamas. Hero battles a gang terrorizing the settlers of South America. Zorro-type swashbuckler was filmed down Argentine way but is still the same old thing. (90 mins.)

Awakening (Italian, 1956)***½ Anna Magnani, Eleonora Rossi-Drago. A heartwarming and touching film about a nun who becomes attached to a little boy who has run away from his mother. A superb performance by Anna Magnani.

Away All Boats (1956)**½ Jeff Chandler, George Nader, Julia Adams. Overproduced naval war drama with an abundance of outrageous displays of heroics. Action fans who like their war movies paced at breakneck speed will go for this one. The cast is serviceable. (Dir: Joseph Pevney, 114 mins.)

Awful Dr. Orlof, The (Spanish, 1962)* Howard Vernon, Conrado Sammartin, Diana Lorys. Mad doctor aided by a robotlike creature kidnaps beautiful women to try to restore beauty to his disfigured wife. Orlof is awful. (Dir: Jess Franco, 95 mins.)

Awful Truth, The (1937)***½ Cary Grant, Irene Dunne, Ralph Bellamy. No script, dated, silly—but very entertaining. A couple on the verge of divorce discover they love each other, but not until they hand you a nice share of chuckles. (Dir: Leo McCarey, 90 mins.)

Babbitt (1934)*** Guy Kibbee, Aline MacMahon, Claire Dodd. They lost the bite of the Sinclair Lewis novel, out the performances, especially Mr. Kibbee's, help you forget the weak adaptation. (Dir: William Keighley, 74 mins.)

abe (1975)*** Susan Clark, Alex Karras. Babe Didrikson Zaharias was one of the greatest female athletes of all time, and it was inevitable that a movie would be made about her life. The surprise here is that it is a good one, with two solid performances by Clark, as Babe, and Karras, as her husband George Zaharias. Clark might seem too beautiful to play the less-than-gorgeous Babe, but her energy and drive in the role make you forget Ms. Clark's innate sophisticated glamour. Unlikely love story between the two athletes is believable throughout, and worth watching. Made-for-TV. (Dir: Buzz Kulik, 106 mins.)

abe Ruth Story, The (1948)** William Bendix, Claire Trevor, Charles Bickford. Sentimental, mediocre biography of the mighty Babe. Should have been a great film, but the writing makes it run-of-the-mill. (Dir: Roy Del Ruth, 106 mins.)

abes in Arms (1939)*** Mickey Rooney, Judy Garland. Delightful though doctored version of the Rodgers and Hart musical hit about children of vaudeville parents who grow up to see vaudeville die. It's all Mickey and Judy so if you like them, cancel all plans. (Dir: Busby Berkeley, 97 mins.)

abes in Bagdad (1952)* Paulette Goddard, Gypsy Rose Lee. A beautiful new addition to a sultan's harem fights for freedom and justice for her sex. Ridiculous burlesque of Arabian Nights epics; weak all around. (Dir: Edgar Ulmer, 79 mins.)

abes on Broadway (1941)**½ Mickey Rooney, Judy Garland. Grade B musical story about young hopefuls on Broadway. Receives an A production but only the musical numbers merit any attention. (Dir: Busby Berkeley, 118 mins.)

abette Goes to War (1960)**½ Brigitte Bardot, Jacques Charrier. Okay attempt to give Brigitte Bardot a chance to display her comedy prowess and she's not half bad. It's a WW II spy yarn with lovely B.B. assigned to prowl behind enemy lines for the French army. Jacques Charrier, one of B.B.'s real life husbands,

plays her French officer love. (Dir: Christian-Jaque, 103 mins.)

Baby and the Battleship, The (British, 1955)**½ John Mills, Richard Attenborough. Fast and rowdy comedy about a couple of sailors smuggling a baby aboard their ship and the hilarious consequences. (Dir: Jay Lewis, 96 mins.)

Baby Blue Marine (1976)*½ Jan-Michael Vincent, Glynnis O'Connor, Katherine Helmond. Sentimental, nostalgic story of a young man washed out of boot camp who returns to his small California home town claiming to be a war hero who has been to Guadalcanal. Idealized characters, vacuously played. (Dir: John Hancock, 89 mins.)

Baby Doll (1956)***½ Carroll Baker, Eli Wallach, Karl Malden. Tennessee Williams' tale about a child bride, her possessive but foolish husband, and a stranger who dupes them both is a mood piece which works most of the time, thanks to Elia Kazan's direction and a good cast, particularly Eli Wallach as the manipulator of the plot. Carroll Baker is quite striking in a swing—she's never been as good since in all the trashy films she's made. (Dir: Elia Kazan, 114 mins.)

Baby Face Nelson (1957)*** Mickey Rooney, Carolyn Jones, Cedric Hardwicke. Mickey Rooney gives a good performance as "Baby Face Nelson" in this action-crammed story of stickups, bank robberies, ruthless killings, and prison breaks. (Dir: Don Siegel, 85 mins.)

Baby Love (1969)** Linda Hayden, Keith Barron. A sleazy tale about a young, teenage nymphet who uses her wiles and body to sexually enslave a household, including the master, his wife, and their son. It's claptrap most of the way, but nymphet Hayden is not without talent.

Baby, the Rain Must Fall (1965)** Lee Remick, Steve McQueen, Don Murray. Soggy drama of a noble wife who tries to live with her moody, guitar-twanging, hotheaded husband. A stab at Texas realism that becomes merely regional boredom as a result of pretentious, heavy-handed treatment. (Dir: Robert Mulligan, 100 mins.)

Babymaker, The (1972)**½ Barbara Hershey, Sam Groom, Collin Wilcox-Horne. Barbara Hershey's the whole show. She's luminous as a young, free-spirited girl who agrees to a rather unconventional arrangement to bear a child, fathered by the husband of a childless couple. The beginning scenes work best as Miss Hershey is screened by the couple and then moves in. Offbeat drama, successful most of the way. (Dir: James Bridges, 107 mins.)

Bacchantes, The (1961)** Taina Elg, Akim Tamiroff. One step, that of ballerina Elg, above the run-of-the-mill fare of this kind (Italian-made, English dubbed) thanks to Akim Tamiroff's showy thesping.

Bachelor and the Bobby-Soxer (1947) ***½ Cary Grant, Myrna Loy, Shirley Temple. Dashing eligible male is plagued by a teen-ager who has a crush on him. Sprightly, often hilarious comedy. (Dir: Irving Reis, 95 mins.)

Bachelor Flat (1962)**½ Terry-Thomas, Tuesday Weld, Richard Beymer. A shy professor of archeology is caught in a romantic complication with a forthright teenager. Dizzy comedy has some moments of mad fun, but not a little of it misfires. Anyway, Terry-Thomas is amusing, as are the situations. (Dir: Frank Tashlin, 91 mins.)

Bachelor in Paradise (1961)*** Bob Hope, Lana Turner, Paula Prentiss, Jim Hutton. Author upsets a suburban community when he moves in to write about life there. Pleasing comedy gives Hope some clever situations, while the glamor of Turner is a definite asset. Relaxing entertainment. (Dir: Jack Arnold, 109 mins.)

Bachelor Mother (1939)**** Ginger Rogers, David Niven. Salesgirl finds herself the "adopted" mother of an abandoned baby on the day she is fired. Fine romantic comedy, with hilarious situations, excellent cast. (Dir: Garson Kanin, 82 mins.)

Bachelor of Hearts (British, 1958) **½ Hardy Kruger, Sylvia Syms. Pleasant comedy about a romantic undergraduate student and his escapades in preparing for the May Ball.

Bachelor Party (1957)***½ Don Murray, E. G. Marshall, Larry Blyden, Carolyn Jones, Philip Abbott, Jack Warden. Paddy Chayefsky's TV play is expanded and embellished in this entertaining film about a quintet of accountants who indulge in one of our society's tribal rituals, the bachelor party. The act-

ing is top-notch, with E. G. Marshall, the older member of the group, who is suffering from asthma, and Carolyn Jones as an emancipated Greenwich Village inhabitant who picks up Don Murray, the standouts. (Dir: Delbert Mann, 9? mins.)

Back at the Front (1952)**½ Tom Ewell, Harvey Lembeck, Mari Blanchard. Bill Mauldin's wacky G.I. creations—Willie and Joe—find themselves back in uniform and in trouble with the M.P.'s. Plenty of laughs as these two misfits become involved in a smuggling operation based in Tokyo. (Dir: George Sherman, 87 mins.)

Back from Eternity (1956) **½ Robert Ryan, Anita Ekberg, Rod Steiger. Plane forced down in the jungle can return to safety with only five passengers. Well produced but otherwise routine melodrama, a remake of a successful "B" film of years ago. (Dir: John Farrow, 97 mins.)

Back Street (1941)***½ Charles Boyer, Margaret Sullavan, Richard Carlson. Soap opera by today's standards, but still a well-acted film about a married man and his "back street" wife. Based on Fannie Hurst's novel. (Dir: Robert Stevenson, 89 mins.)

Back Street (1961)** Susan Hayward, John Gavin, Vera Miles. Third version of Fannie Hurst's tearful tale of love on the sly, somewhat modernized but still the old plot about a woman sacrificing all for love of a married man. A big yawn, not up to the standards of the previous versions. (Dir: David Miller, 107 mins.)

Back to Bataan (1945)*** John Wayne, Anthony Quinn. American colonel forms a guerrilla army in the Philippines to fight the Japanese. Well made, exciting war drama. (Dir: Edward Dmytryk, 95 mins.)

Back to God's Country (1954)** Rock Hudson, Marcia Henderson, Steve Cochran. Adventure yarn about a couple who face tremendous obstacles (most contrived, too) before they can be free to go on living to say nothing of being happy and carefree. Takes place in Canada during the cold spell. (Dir: Joseph Pevney, 78 mins.)

Back to the Wall (French, 1957) ***½ Jeanne Moreau, Gerard Oury. Excellent suspense film dealing with a jealous husband's clever plan for revenge on his faithless wife. Top French cast. (Dir: Edward Molinaro)

Backfire (1950)** Virginia Mayo, Gordon MacRae, Dane Clark. Routine drama placing Virginia Mayo in a series of confusing events. Poor script but cast gives it a good try. (Dir: Vincent Sherman, 91 mins.)

Backfire (British, 1962)*½ Alfred Burke, Zena Marshall. Partner in a cosmetics firm arranges arson and murder to extricate himself from financial difficulty. Trite mystery melodrama.

Backfire (French, 1965)**½ Jean-Paul Belmondo, Jean Seberg, Gert Frobe. Good comedy and action is derived from a simple plot that has free-lance smuggler Belmondo trying to transport a car to Lebanon where the gold hidden under the paint job will be stripped. Miss Seberg is along to make sure he doesn't try a double-cross. (Dir: Jean Becker, 97 mins.)

Background to Danger. (1943)**½ George Brent, Brenda Marshall. A lot of intrigue but nothing really jells in this spy story set in Turkey. You will enjoy the two menaces, Lorre and Greenstreet, working against each other. (Dir: Raoul Walsh, 80 mins.)

Backlash (1956)**½ Richard Widmark, Donna Reed. Moderately interesting western adventure in which two people set out to solve the mystery surrounding an Apache massacre of five people—two of whom were never identified. Widmark and Miss Reed go through their paces in a professional manner. (Dir: John Sturges, 84 mins.)

Backtrack (1969)* Neville Brand, James Drury, Doug McClure, Ida Lupino. If this looks familiar and seems confusing, it's because part of this film was originally aired on TV as an episode of "The Virginian," and part as a segment of "Laredo." The plot has McClure being sent by Drury to pick up a bull in Mexico. On the way he runs into mucho mean hombres. (Dir: Earl Bellamy, 95 mins.)

Bad and the Beautiful, The (1953) **** Kirk Douglas, Lana Turner, Dick Powell, Gloria Grahame, Walter Pidgeon, Barry Sullivan. Excellent drama about ambition and success in the movie capital of the world, Hollywood. One ruthless producer, superbly played by Kirk Douglas, touches and affects the lives of many people. Gloria Grahame won an Oscar for her portrayal of a Southern belle, and Lana Turner gives one of her finest dramatic performances in this memorable film. (Dir: Vincente Minnelli, 118 mins.)

Bad Bascomb (1945)** Wallace Beery, Margaret O'Brien. Run-of-the-mill western which is only good in the scenes where little Margaret tames outlaw Beery. (Dir: Sylvan Simon, 110 mins.)

Bad Boy (1949)***½ Audie Murphy, Lloyd Nolan. The head of a boys' rehabilitation ranch makes a man of a youth considered to be a hopeless criminal. Good melodrama, well done in every department. (Dir: Kurt Neumann, 86 mins.)

Bad Company (1972)***½ Jeff Bridges, Barry Brown. Brown plays a youth on the run in the Civil War West. He meets Bridges who is more experienced than Brown, and joins Bridges' gang. Their misadventures form the basis of the film. Fine script meshes humor, action, and insight to give a picture of an immature generation forced to grow up to survive. Written by Robert Benton and David Newman of "Bonnie and Clyde." Benton also doubled quite credibly as director. (91 mins.)

Bad Day at Black Rock (1954)**** Spencer Tracy, Robert Ryan, Anne Francis, Ernest Borgnine, Lee Marvin, John Ericson, Walter Brennan. An excellent cast enhances this powerful story about a well guarded town secret and the stranger who uncovers it. Director John Sturges pulls all the stops in building the suspense and there's "edge of the sofa" excitement by the time the climax arrives. A near perfect western. (Dir: John Sturges, 81 mins.)

Bad for Each Other (1954)** Charlton Heston, Lizabeth Scott, Dianne Foster. Wealthy socialite, Lizabeth Scott, tries to convince young doctor, Charlton Heston, to practice among the town's exclusive clientele; while nurse Dianne Foster points out the coal miners' needs for his services. Dull soap opera about artificial people. (Dir: Irving Rapper, 80 mins.)

Bad Lord Byron (British, 1949)*½ Dennis Price, Joan Greenwood, Mai

Zetterling. The life and many loves of the poet-sinner-soldier. Over-stuffed historical biography, wordy and dull. (Dir: David Macdonald, 85 mins.)

Bad News Bears, The (1976)**** Walter Matthau, Tatum O'Neal, Vic Morrow, Joyce Van Patten, Brandon Cruz, Jackie Earle Haley. Sparkling comedy about the whipping into shape of a little-league team by an alcoholic coach. Morris Buttermaker, a a former minor-league ballplayer who presently cleans swimming pools, signs on to coach a team with lots of enthusiasm, but little skill. His solution is to recruit the meanest spitball pitcher in the state, an 11-year-old girl anxious to shed her tomboy image, and a chain-smoking motorcycle-riding 12-year-old slugger. The Bears' rise is inevitable, but the screenplay is endearing for its unsentimental approach—Matthau doesn't really like kids, and the kids aren't too fond of their abrasive coach either. Screenplay by Bill Lancaster (Burt's son). (Dir: Michael Ritchie, 105 mins.)

Bad Ronald (1974)**½ Scott Jacoby, Kim Hunter, Pippa Scott. Once the exposition in this macabre little tale is taken care of, the story about a young boy living in a secret room in an old Victorian house and slowly going mad is interesting. One of the better young actors in TV, Scott Jacoby, plays Ronald, a mother-dominated boy who accidentally kills a girl. Made-for-TV. (Dir: Buzz Kulik, 72 mins.)

Bad Seed, The (1956)*** Nancy Kelly, Patty McCormack, Eileen Heckart. The macabre stage hit is faithfully brought to the screen, chills intact, except for a trumped-up Hollywood ending. Nancy Kelly once more goes through a series of hysterical scenes as the mother of a six year old murderess, excellently portrayed by Patty McCormack. Able support is registered by Eileen Heckart and Henry Jones. (Dir: Mervyn Le Roy, 129 mins.)

Bad Sister (British, 1947)** Margaret Lockwood, Joan Greenwood, Ian Hunter. The warden of a home for delinquent girls takes one of them under her wing, tries to straighten her out. Long, talky, trite drama.

Badlanders, The (1958)**½ Alan Ladd, Ernest Borgnine, Katy Ju-rado. Fast-paced western, a sort of "Asphalt Jungle" on horseback as Ladd and Borgnine plan a big gold robbery. Good action. (Dir: Delmer Daves, 83 mins.)

Badlands (1974)**** Sissy Spacek, Martin Sheen, Warren Oates. A remarkable directorial debut by Terrence Malick, who also wrote and produced this perceptive, beautifully observed film about two young, vapid lovers who go on a killing spree in the 1950's before being apprehended. This is an homage to "Bonnie & Clyde" but it is not a derivative, imitative film; it is based on the real-life killing spree of Charles Starkweather and Carol Fugate. The two leads are very convincingly played by Sheen and Spacek, here playing her first starring role devastatingly—a bored 15-year-old whose dim mind is filled with the trivia of movie magazines. Malick, a Rhodes scholar, Harvard graduate and philosophy lecturer, had only one previous movie credit, the screenplay for the tedious 1972 entry "Pocket Money." "Badlands" is one of the most impressive directorial debuts of the decade. (Dir: Terrence Malick, 95 mins.)

Badman's Country (1958)** George Montgomery, Neville Brand, Buster Crabbe. Pat Garrett (Montgomery) forsakes retirement to team with Wyatt Earp (Crabbe) and Buffalo Bill (Malcolm Atterbury) to snare outlaws led by Butch Cassidy (Brand)—and there you have another routine western. (Dir: Fred Sears, 68 mins.)

Badman's Territory (1946)*** Randolph Scott, Ann Richards. Marshal has to put up with the most notorious outlaws in the west in a territory outside the control of the government. Good western. (Dir: Tim Whelan, 97 mins.)

Badmen of Missouri (1941)*** Dennis Morgan, Jane Wyman, Arthur Kennedy. Pity the western fan who doesn't know all about the distorted, "based on fact" exploits of the infamous Younger brothers. This is the picture that started the outlaws on their way to Hollywood immortality.

Bagdad (1950)** Maureen O'Hara, Paul Christian, Vincent Price. Another sand and sex epic with Miss O'Hara cast as the British-educated daughter of a tribal leader of the desert who returns to her people after her father is murdered. (Dir: Charles Lamont, 82 mins.)

Bahama Passage (1942)*½ Madeleine Carroll, Sterling Hayden. "A" picture offers "C" entertainment in this hack tale of a lady who tames a bronze he-man in the Bahamas. Film designed to show off Hayden's physique accomplishes nothing else. (Dir: Edward Griffith, 83 mins.)

Bail Out at 43,000 (1957)** John Payne, Karen Steele, Paul Kelly. Routine flying film about pilots and their affairs in the sky and on the ground. Performances are adequate considering the material. (Dir: Francis Lyon, 73 mins.)

Bait (1954)** Hugo Haas, Cleo Moore, John Agar. This time, Haas is an old prospector married to a sexy blonde, trying to kill his partner. Cornball dramatics. (Dir: Hugo Haas, 80 mins.)

Bait, The (1973)** Donna Mills. Another routine police-show pilot with a slight twist—Miss Mills plays a policewoman acting as bait to catch a demented murderer. She specializes in wide-eyed looks of terror. Michael Constantine, William Devane, and Arlene Golonka in supporting roles. Made-for-TV. (Dir: Leonard Horn.)

Baker's Wife, The (French, 1938) **** Raimu. There are no camera tricks to dazzle the eye, no tricky flashbacks or pioneering editing techniques. Just a truly great actor (Raimu) in a superb story that makes, for this reviewer, a quite perfect and profoundly poignant movie. The story is simplicity itself—about cuckoldry in rural France. There's not a false note in director Marcel Pagnol's adaptation. Raimu is sad, funny, and altogether wonderful. (Dir: Marcel Pagnol.)

Bal Tabarin (1952)*½ Muriel Lawrence, William Ching. Singer implicated in a murder flees to Paris. Some interesting scenes actually lensed inside the famed Parisian club, but otherwise poor melodrama.

Balalaika (1939)** Nelson Eddy, Ilona Massey. Pretentious, dull operetta set in Russia during World War I and about the time of the Revolution. The only things in its favor are Miss Massey's beauty, Mr. Eddy's voice. (Dir: Reinhold Schunzel, 102 mins.)

Balcony, The (1963)*** Shelley Winters, Peter Falk, Lee Grant, Leonard Nimoy. Uneven but frequently interesting adaptation by screenwriter Ben Maddow of French author Jean Genet's difficult, disturbing symbolic play about life in a Parisian brothel. The ending of the play has been changed, but director Joseph Strick provides a few striking visual images, and occasional glimpses of Genet's tormented, macabre genius. Shelley plays a coarse madam, and Peter Falk provides a few light touches as the police chief of the mythical state. Maddow-Strick have a more sophisticated approach to matters of sex than most American films. "Balcony" does offer a good part to actress Lee Grant, who is enormously talented, and has been scandalously wasted and neglected by Hollywood for a long time. (Dir: Joseph Strick.)

Ball of Fire (1941)***½ Gary Cooper, Barbara Stanwyck, Dana Andrews. Comedy hit about a group of professors who get entangled in the world of gangsters and burlesque girls during their study of slang in the English language. Cooper is very effective in this comedy role. (Dir: Howard Hawks, 111 mins.)

Ballad in Blue—See: **Blues for Lovers**

Ballad of a Gunfighter (1963)* Marty Robbins, Joyce Redd. Two outlaws are attracted to the same girl. Film itself has no attraction.

Ballad of a Soldier (Russian, 1960) **** This is a hauntingly beautiful and tender story of a young Russian soldier's attempts to get home to see his mother during a leave from the Army during World War II. This honest and magnificently acted film is unspoiled by any propaganda whatever and could have been made anywhere. The soldier's falling in love with a young girl en route is nicely handled. It is wonderfully directed and photographed and is, by any standard, a superb and deeply moving film. (Dir: Grigori Chukhrai, 89 mins.)

Ballad of Andy Crocker, The (1969) *** Lee Majors, Joey Heatherton. One of the better-made-for-TV movies. Lee Majors does a very good job as Andy Crocker, a Vietnam war hero who comes home to find nothing but disappointment and despair. Andy is one of those quiet, nice guys and you'll feel for him as he discovers his sweetheart, played by sexy Joey Heatherton, has married another guy and that his motorcycle repair business has been run to the ground by his lazy partner (Jimmy Dean). Circumstances defeat our hero and the final scene is jolting. (Dir: George McCowan.)

Ballad of Cable Hogue, The (1970) ***½ Jason Robards, Stella Stevens, David Warner. Director Sam Peckinpah's ambitious, romantic elegy about capitalism and the Old West. Droll, offbeat screenplay written by John Crawford and Edmund Penney, gives Jason Robards, one of our greatest stage actors, his best and most demanding movie role to date, including his Academy Award-winning performance in "All the President's Men." Robards is a worn-out prospector who talks to God, and is quite marvelous for mere mortals in the audience. Stevens plays a prostitute who takes up with Robards, and Warner plays a disturbed preacher with style and detachment. A gentle, funny, touching film. (Dir: Sam Peckinpah, 121 mins.)

Ballad of Josie, The (1968) *½ Doris Day, Peter Graves. For a change, Doris' virginity is not threatened, but otherwise it's a tiresome balad indeed. Day cavorts as a frontier widow in trouble with her neighboring ranchers when she tries to raise sheep. It's not all serious. There are several raucous, unfunny comedy scenes thrown in, including a suffragette free-for-all. (Dir: Andrew McLaglen, 102 mins.)

Ballerina (French, 1953) ** Violette Verdy, Henry Guisol. Young dancer's sleep is interrupted by three telephone calls, bringing on a trio of dreams. Fairish drama, dubbed in English.

Ballerina (W. German, 1958) ** Willy Birgel, Elisabeth Mueller. Limp melodrama put together by some of Germany's top film talent. Polio strikes a prima ballerina who is heartbroken she can't dance. Best scenes are of the ballet, but alas, there are too few. (Dir: G. W. Pabst, 91 mins.)

Bambole (France-Italy, 1965) ** Monica Vitti, Elke Sommer, Franco Rossi, Gina Lollobrigida. Mundane quartet of stories on Italian life. "Monsignor Cupid" episode based on a Boccaccio story directed by Mauro Bolognini. "The Soup" directed by Franco Rossi. "Treatise in Eugenics" directed by Luigi Comencini. "The

Telephone Call" directed by Dino Risi.

Bamboo Prison, The (1955) *** Robert Francis, Brian Keith, Dianne Foster. A young Sergeant is accused of collaborating with the Communists during the Korean War, but he is, in actuality, a U. S. Intelligence Officer. Well-handled subject with a minimum of amateur heroics. (Dir: Lewis Seiler, 80 mins.)

Bamboo Saucer, The (1968) * Dan Duryea, John Ericson, Lois Nettleton. Unsuccessful attempt to merge the cold-war and sci-fi genres. American and Russian team band together to hunt a flying saucer in Red China. Duryea is lethargic in his last role, and Nettleton tries in vain to affect a Russian accent. (Dir: Frank Telford, 100 mins.)

Banacek (1972) **½ George Peppard. The pilot for the series with a Polish-American hero. Peppard fills the bill as T. Banacek, a wily, resourceful, and thoroughly civilized insurance investigator who operates solo. Has a first-rate production to its credit as well as slick action touches by director Jack Smight. The plot revolves around the disappearance, between Oklahoma and Texas borders, of an armored truck with a million-dollar-plus gold cargo. Enter Banacek. Made-for-TV. (Dir: Jack Smight)

Banacek: Horse of a Slightly Different Color (1974) *½ George Peppard, Anne Francis. Nothing fazes Peppard's super-investigator, Banacek, not even when a champion race horse, worth millions, disappears on one lap of a workout, in full view except for five seconds during which another horse has been substituted in his place. Anne Francis is the strong owner who had just sold her horse to a millionaire. Nothing special. Made-for-TV. (Dir: Herschel Daugherty, 72 mins.)

Banacek: No Sign of the Cross (1972) ** George Peppard, Broderick Crawford. Entertaining where-is-it? Once you accept the contrivances of this former series, the plots are sometimes fun. Peppard must recover a jeweled cross valued at a million bucks. Made-for-TV. (Dir: Daryl Duke, 72 mins.)

Banacek: No Stone Unturned (1973) ** George Peppard, Christine Belford. More of the Polish supersleuth. Banacek is faced with another case involving the disappearance of an art treasure. Christine Belford, as an insurance investigator, provides some interest as Banacek's sparring partner. Made-for-TV. (Dir: Dick Heffron, 72 mins.)

Banacek: Now You See Me—Now You Don't (1974)*½ George Peppard, Ralph Manza. Another old series episode with Peppard as the Polish private eye who solves cases that nobody, including the viewer, can begin to figure out. This one involves an embezzling banker who disappears in a magic act with lots of ill-gotten loot. Made-for-TV. (Dir: Bernard McEveety, 72 mins.)

Banacek: Project Phoenix (1972)** George Peppard. The old NBC series. George Peppard is the dapper private eye. This one involves a missing experimental automobile valued at five million dollars. Banacek "brilliantly" solves the case at the very end, of course. Made-for-TV. (73 mins.)

Banacek: The Greatest Collection of Them All (1973)*½ George Peppard, Penny Fuller. The heist of a collection of great French Impressionist paintings, worth $23 million, is just the kind of challenge that Peppard's Banacek, super-insurance sleuth that he is, thrives on. How he coolly goes about solving the case of the theft of the paintings, while they're being transported by truck from New York to Boston under heavy security guard may interest mystery fans. Made-for-TV. (Dir: George McCowan, 72 mins.)

Banacek: The Two Million Clams of Cap'n Jack (1973)* George Peppard, Andrew Duggan, Jessica Walter. The "heist" this time is engraved plates worth a few million. Peppard is the slick private eye, the script is nonsense! Made-for-TV. (Dir: Dick Heffron, 72 mins.)

Banacek: The Vanishing Chalice (1974)*½ George Peppard, Cesar Romero, John Saxon. Another old series episode with Peppard as the super-cool insurance investigator. This time he's after an irreplaceable Greek chalice, worth a million and a half, stolen from a museum while it was under heavy guard. Made-for-TV. (Dir: Bernie Kowalski, 72 mins.)

Banacek: To Steal a King (1972)*½ George Peppard as the Polish private eye again. A coin collection of inestimable value is stolen from a high-security hotel vault hours before it

is set to be auctioned off. Solution is, as always, complicated and slick. Made-for-TV. (73 mins.)

Banana Peel (France-Italy, 1964)**½ Jeanne Moreau, Jean-Paul Belmondo, Gert Frobe. Frequently entertaining comedy as a pair of scoundrels cheat a millionaire out of a large bankroll an the French Riviera. Ophuls co-scripted with Claude Sautet. (Dir: Marcel Ophuls, 97 mins.)

Bananas (1971)**** Woody Allen, Louise Lasser, Howard Cosell, Carlos Montalban. Allen is an inspired lunatic. So many of the jokes and sight gags are hilarious it doesn't matter—and probably can't be helped—that a few of them bomb out. All-purpose filmmaker and director Woody plays the role of frustrated inventor working on such needed amenities for a civilized society as an electric warmer for toilet seats (for cold days). Woody runs off to South America and becomes a revolutionary leader, and it's the only American film within memory that makes clear that J. Edgar Hoover really was a black woman. The spirit of the Marx Brothers is alive and well and living in Woody Allen. (Dir: Woody Allen, 82 mins.)

Band of Angels (1957)**½ Clark Gable, Yvonne DeCarlo, Sidney Poitier. The producers of this Civil War epic thought that by casting Gable in the role of a New Orleans gentleman with a past, lightning might strike twice at the box office (shades of "Gone with the Wind"). The only thing however that the two films have in common is the Civil War. Sidney Poitier easily walks off with the acting honors as an educated slave. (Dir: Raoul Walsh, 127 mins.)

Band Wagon, The (1953)***½ Fred Astaire, Cyd Charisse, Jack Buchanan, Nanette Fabray, Oscar Levant. A delightful musical with a wealth of familiar (Howard) Dietz and (Arthur) Schwartz tunes, and the nimble-footed master Astaire in top form. The plot on which the musical numbers are conveniently hung involves the trials and tribulations of a Broadway show. (Dir: Vincente Minnelli, 112 mins.)

Bandido (1956)**½ Robert Mitchum, Ursula Thiess, Zachary Scott. American adventurers cross the border into Mexico during the revolt of 1916 to sell weapons to the highest

49

bidders. Involved action story with love triangle to spice the proceedings. (Dir: Richard Fleischer, 92 mins.)

Bandit and the Princess, The (German, 1964)*½ Helmut Lohner, Peter Weck. Tailor decides the life of a bandit is more profitable and pleasurable, and sets off to become a highwayman. Attempt at spoofing the costume adventures misfires for the most part, not helped by English dubbing.

Bandit of Sherwood Forest (1946)** Cornel Wilde, Anita Louise, Jill Esmond, Henry Daniell. The son of Robin Hood comes to the aid of the Queen and saves her from a cruel regent. Elaborate but uninspired costumer. (Dirs: George Sherman, Clifford Sanforth, 86 mins.)

Bandit of Zhobe, The (1959)** Victor Mature, Anne Aubrey. Routine desert adventure with Victor Mature flexing his muscles all over the place. Biceps fans will enjoy it. (Dir: John Gilling, 80 mins.)

Bandits of Corsica (1953)** Richard Greene, Paula Raymond, Raymond Burr. Siamese twins separated at birth overthrow a villainous tyrant in Corsica. Humdrum costume melodrama, based on Dumas' "Corsican Brothers." (Dir: Ray Nazarro, 82 mins.)

Bandolero! (1968)*½ James Stewart, Dean Martin, Raquel Welch. Offbeat casting, with James Stewart and Dean Martin as two robbers, doesn't overcome the familiarity of this big-scale western. Good support by George Kennedy. The contemptible characters don't help much either, and the violence is excessive. Blame for the direction falls on Andrew V. McLaglen. (106 mins.)

Bang, Bang Kid, The (US-Spain-Italy, 1968)*** Guy Madison, Sandra Milo, Tom Bosley. Underrated European-made western. Tight comedy approach to absurd tale of a feudal Westerner who gets his comeuppance when a robot incites his people to insurgency. Written by Howard Berk. (Dir: Stanley Praeger, 90 mins.)

Bang, Bang, You're Dead (1966)** Tony Randall, Senta Berger, Terry-Thomas. The cast of expert comedy players can't save this muddled farce involving the spy-game set in Marrakech. There are more villains here than you can keep straight, and everyone works very hard for laughs,

which are few and far between. Filmed in Morocco. (Dir: Don Sharp, 92 mins.)

Bang the Drum Slowly (1973)**** Robert De Niro, Michael Moriarty. Mark Harris' poignant 1956 novel is splendidly translated to the screen and serves as a good vehicle for these two wonderful actors. De Niro is touching as an average baseball player dying of Hodgkin's Disease, who wants to play just one more season. Moriarty, in the more difficult role, shines as his friend and teammate who makes the final season possible. The tale never becomes maudlin and there's a goodly number of surprising comedy touches. Harris wrote his own screenplay. This is one of the rare times when a superior novel is turned into an even better film. (Dir: John Hancock, 98 mins.)

Bang! You're Dead (Great Britain, 1954)**½ Jack Warner, Derek Farr, Veronica Hurst, Anthony Richmond. Young boy shoots a man in rural England and is tracked down by police. Slow suspense tale aided by the good performance of Richmond as the boy. (Dir: Lance Comfort, 88 mins.)

Banjo Hackett (1976)**½ Don Meredith, Ike Eisenmann, Jennifer Warren, Chuck Connors. Meredith, the former Dallas Cowboys quarterback and sportscaster, becomes an 1880's horse trader with a good heart, whisking his nephew out of an orphanage with the intention of giving the boy a prize mare along the way. Don's warmth helps in the early stages, but the ex-athlete's lack of acting training shows before long. Made-for-TV. (Dir: Andrew McLaglen, 103 mins.)

Banjo on My Knee (1936)**½ Joel McCrea, Barbara Stanwyck, Walter Brennan. Story of the folks who live along the banks of the Mississippi has a little of everything and not much of anything. (Dir: John Cromwell, 80 mins.)

Bank Dick, The (1940)**** W. C. Fields. One of the handful of the genuinely great movie comedians has a field day in this still wonderfully funny romp. As a reward for accidentally capturing a bank robber, Egbert Souse (Fields) is made a bank guard. (Dir: Eddie Cline, 74 mins.)

Bank Holiday (Great Britain, 1938)

*** John Lodge, Margaret Lockwood. Good, low-key British drama; nurse flees her lover to save the suicidally distraught husband of a dead patient. Rich characterizations, varied locales. Dated, but interesting. (Dir: Carol Reed, 86 mins.)

Bank Raiders, The (British, 1958) **½ Honor Blackman, Patrick Holt. An above average British cops and bank robbers yarn which reaches its dramatic high point a little too early.

Bank Shot, The (1974)* George C. Scott, Joanna Cassidy, Clifton James. A limp crime-caper comedy which strains for laughs. Why George C. Scott got involved with this yarn about a collection of losers who execute a bank heist (they actually uproot a small bank and drive it away) remains a mystery. He's boring as the mastermind behind the "bank shot," and the supporting cast is no better. Based on the novel by Donald E. Westlake. (Dir: Gower Champion, 83 mins.)

Bannerline (1951)** Keefe Brasselle, Sally Forrest, Lionel Barrymore. Routine newspaper story about an aggressive small town reporter who tries to launch a one-man campaign against corruption. Too many cliches pop up too frequently in this drama. (Dir: Don Weis, 86 mins.)

Banning (1967)*½ Robert Wagner, Jill St. John, James Farentino, Anjanette Comer. Heavy-handed attempt to capture the slick attitude of the country club set and the young men who earn their living as golf pros. Watching a few reels is as tiring as walking eighteen holes around Banning's course. (Dir: Ron Winston, 102 mins.)

Banyon (1971)**½ Robert Forster, Anjanette Comer. TV pilot film echoing the nostalgic craze for the thirties, starring a tough John Garfield-type private-eye hero (Robert Forster) who drinks tea instead of booze, tinkers with an erector set, and plays it cool with the ladies. Sleuth Banyon can hardly keep up with the killings after a hood is released from prison, and he runs into a maze of plot twists. There's a little of everything for fans of the era—Jose Ferrer as a Walter Winchell type, Nazi followers, vintage cars and songs, and a fight scene that conjures up the memory of the old TV series "Untouchables." The cast, which includes Jose Ferrer, Herb Edelman and Darren McGavin, plays it straight. (Dir: Robert Daly.)

Barabbas (Italian, 1962)***½ Anthony Quinn, Silvana Mangano, Arthur Kennedy, Jack Palance, Ernest Borgnine. Lavish Biblical spectacle concerning the thief whom Jesus replaced on the cross of crucifixion, his life in the mines, his victories as a gladiator. Far superior to the usual run of its kind, it is graced with literate dialogue by Christopher Fry, excellent performances by a large cast, distinguished direction. A creditable film. (Dir: Richard Fleischer, 134 mins.)

Barbarella (French-Italian, 1968)*** Jane Fonda, Milo O'Shea, Marcel Marceau. Far-out science fiction comic strip about a 41st Century astronaut—Fonda—and her assorted interplanetary escapades. When Charles Bluhdorn, the president of Paramount Pictures, first screened "Barbarella," he said it was an absurd piece of trash and ordered his underlings not to release the film and to write it off as a disaster. There will be some who agree with him, and others—obviously prexy Bluhdorn had second thoughts about this opus —who'll be amused by this yarn. You can't help but be impressed by the resourcefulness of the special-effects crew and the various ways that were found to tear off what few clothes Jane seemed to possess. (Dir: Roger Vadim, 98 mins.)

Barbarian and the Geisha (1958)** John Wayne, Sam Jaffe. Confused historical drama about Townsend Harris, first U.S. Ambassador to Japan and his adventures in the East. The film's chief liability is the casting of John Wayne in the leading role. With ruffled shirts and stilted dialogue, Wayne looks lost in most scenes. Famed Director John Huston laid an Oriental egg with this one. (105 mins.)

Barbarian King, The (Bulgarian, 1964)*½ Victor Stoichev, Ginka Stancheva. Barbarian hordes battle the Knights of the Crusades in a rather naive historical spectacle with some well-done battle scenes. Dubbed in English.

Barbarians, The (Italian, 1957)*½ Helene Remy, Pierre Cressoy. Italy, 1527—family feuds are forgotten as the country is threatened by Spain. Combination of Romeo and Juliet plus lots of blood-letting, resulting in near-tedium. Alternate title: "The Pagans."

Barbary Coast (1935)** Joel McCrea, Edward G. Robinson, Miriam Hopkins. Hokey drama about the tough Barbary Coast during the late 1800's. Robinson is good as the man who runs the show and there are two fine supporting performances by Walter Brennan and Brian Donlevy. (Dir: Howard Hawks, 100 mins.)

Barbary Coast, The (1975)**½ William Shatner, Dennis Cole, Lynda Day George, John Vernon. Shatner plays an undercover agent skulking about San Francisco's muddy streets of iniquity, back in the days before the great earthquake. Shatner's Jeff Cable is a flamboyant type who dons disguises, taking his time to defrock a vigilante's committee. Hokum amidst fairly gaudy surroundings. Made-for-TV. (Dir: Bill Bixby, 100 mins.)

Barber of Seville (Italian, 1955)** Tito Gobbi, Irene Genna. Another version of Rossini's comic opera. For the dedicated!

Barefoot Battalion (Greek, 1954)** Maria Costi, Nicos Fermas. Orphans band together to fight the invading Nazis during World War II. Greek film suffers from choppy cutting—indications that it would be much better in its original length. English-dubbed. (89 mins.)

Barefoot Contessa, The (1954)*** Humphrey Bogart, Ava Gardner, Rossano Brazzi, Edmond O'Brien. Bogart recalls the life and times of an unhappy glamour girl at her funeral: her beginnings, her rise to stardom, her loneliness, her tragedy. Splendid production and cast, occasional witty dialogue—but it still misses the mark. Too talky, often obscure drama. O'Brien won an Oscar for his role as a loud-mouthed press agent, and he deserved it. (Dir: Joseph L. Mankiewicz, 128 mins.)

Barefoot Executive, The (1971)*** Kurt Russell, Joe Flynn, Harry Morgan, Wally Cox. Walt Disney spoofs TV ratings with an amiable comedy for kids about a chimpanzee who is able to predict programs with good ratings. The chimp's reaction to TV pilots proves superior to the opinions of network executives. The simian's unusual talents turn an enterprising studio page (Russell) into a company program director. (Dir: Robert Butler, 96 mins.)

Barefoot in the Park (1967)***½ Robert Redford, Jane Fonda, Charles Boyer. Neil Simon's romantic, funny froth was a Broadway smash hit, and has survived the transfer to the big screen reasonably well. Benefits from the charm of the newlyweds—Robert Redford who repeats his Broadway role and Jane Fonda who does not. They're setting up Manhattan housekeeping with more ideas than money, and mother-in-law Mildred Natwick is on hand to lend her special daffy quality to this engaging romp. (Dir: Gene Saks, 104 mins.)

Barefoot Mailman, The (1951)**½ Robert Cummings, Terry Moore. Robert Cummings' comic artistry saves this film from becoming ridiculous. Genial confidence man and a young school girl try to swindle some yokels with shady railroad stock. (Dir: Earl McEvoy, 83 mins.)

Barefoot Savage, The (formerly "Sensualita") (Italian, 1954)** Eleonora Rossi-Drago, Amadeo Nazzari. Female without morals sets two brothers against each other, with the expected tragic results. Steamy English-dubbed drama, overdone. (Dir: Clemente Fracassi, 72 mins.)

Barkleys of Broadway, The (1948)***½ Fred Astaire, Ginger Rogers, Oscar Levant. Fred and Ginger are together again in this delightful, though not first rate, film about the battles of a theatrical couple when one wants to abandon musicals for drama. Their dancing together is as marvelous as always! (Dir: Charles Walters, 109 mins.)

Barnacle Bill (1940)** Wallace Beery, Marjorie Main. They're a good team for those that are entertained by their type of characters. He's a no good fisherman and she's the widow out to get him. (Dir: Richard Thorpe, 98 mins.)

Baron Blood (Italy, 1972)½ Joseph Cotten, Elke Sommer, Massimo Girotti. Cotten cavorts as a reincarnation of an evil nobleman, returning to his ancestral castle in hopes of redecorating. Sommer tries to get rid of him. She should have dispensed with this trash. Ghastly ghost story, many gruesome murders. (Dir: Mario Bava, 90 mins.)

Baron of Arizona, The (1949)** Vincent Price, Ellen Drew. The story of James Addison Reavis, who once tried to swindle the government out of Arizona Territory by means of a fantastic scheme. Based on fact. Theatrically performed, but interesting. Beulah Bondi. (Dir: Samuel Fuller, 97 mins.)

Baron's African War, The (1943-66) **½ Rod Cameron, Joan Marsh, Duncan Renaldo. Feature version of serial "Secret Service in Darkest Africa." Nazi poses as Arab leader to influence tribesmen during World War II, is battled by an American agent working with the French. One of the most action-packed serials ever made, turned into an equally speedy feature. Dated and lowbrow, but well done for what it is. (Dir: Spencer Bennet, 100 mins.)

Barren Lives (Brazil 1963)***½ Athila Iorio, Maria Riberio. Small budget film about the lives of Brazil's peasant farmers packs a powerful punch. Sensitively written and directed by Nelson Pereira dos Santos, it documents the lives of poverty and despair typical of millions of peasants throughout Latin America. Particularly moving sequence shows the protagonist victimized by the police in his desolate village in the 1940's. One of the first and best films from Brazil's Cinema Novo movement. Subtitles.

Barretts of Wimpole Street, The (1934) ***½ Norma Shearer, Fredric March, Charles Laughton, Maureen O'Sullivan. Romance of Elizabeth Barrett and Robert Browning. You'll still love this splendid screen version. (Dir: Sidney Franklin, 110 mins.)

Barretts of Wimpole Street, The (1957)**½ Jennifer Jones, William Travers, John Gielgud. Sensitive but occasionally dull remake of the luminous love story between Elizabeth Barrett and Robert Browning. Jennifer Jones and Bill Travers are very good as the poets in love and John Gielgud is properly tyrannical as her domineering father. (Dir: Sidney Franklin, 105 mins.)

Barricade (1950)** Ruth Roman, Dane Clark. Routine Western drama with a mining camp setting. Acting is uninspired. (Dir: Peter Godfrey, 75 mins.)

Barrier of the Law (Italian, 1950)*½ Rossano Brazzi, Jacques Sernas, Lea Padovani. Girl whose brother is a member of a gang of smugglers and counterfeiters falls for a cop trying to bring them to justice. Mediocre melodrama dubbed in English.

Barry Lyndon (Great Britain, 1975) ***½ Ryan O'Neal, Marisa Berenson, Patrick Magee, Hardy Kruger, Michael Hordern. Stanley Kubrick's tenth feature film is a lavish, visually ravishing, elegant adaptation of the William Makepeace Thackeray novel. Rarely has the 18th century been so painstakingly depicted—from from the rich Irish landscapes to the lush interiors of European castles. The texture of the film, however, is one of cold detachment. Lyndon rises from a passive but likeable Irish lad to a socially fashionable peer after his marriage to a rich widow (Marisa Berenson), who is exquisitely photographed at every turn. Ryan O'Neal's brand of unemotional stoicism lends itself well to the role of the naive fledgling who learns very quickly and adroitly how to become a successful opportunist. Kubrick also did the adaptation. Some critics called it boring, some a masterpiece. "Barry Lyndon" is one of those few films that will be greatly diminished when seen on the tiny TV screen. (Dir: Stanley Kubrick, 185 mins.)

Bartleby (British, 1970)***½ Paul Scofield, John McEnery. Slow-moving, brilliantly acted updating of Herman Melville's novella, redefines the main character of Bartleby as a symbol of modern, alienated man who is slowly giving up. Paul Scofield plays the boss who has empathy with Bartleby, but must fire him. Bartleby won't go and once taken away he no longer has the will to live. The acting is superb. McEnery has resisted the temptation to imply feeling as Bartleby. A rare chance to watch Scofield, always an outstanding actor, who conveys the perfect mixture of sympathy, bewilderment, and finally humor. (Dir: Anthony Friedman, 79 mins.)

Bashful Elephant, The (1962)** Molly McGowan, Kai Fischer. Story about a little girl and her elephant. Circus background offers good scenery, but the so-so plot still offers the best film of the day about a shy elephant. (Dir: Darrell McGovern, 82 mins.)

Basic Training (1971)***½ Documentary by American filmmaker Frederick Wiseman about the induction procedure in the American army, the tension between obedience and resistance, etc. Virtually all of Wiseman's films, in recent years made primarily for American public television, deal with institutions. This arresting film provides numerous insights about the experience of basic training while simultaneously reinforcing many existing movie clichés about army life and personnel. (Dir: Frederick Wiseman, 80 mins.)

Bat, The (1958)*½ Vincent Price, Agnes Moorehead. The old chiller about the smart dowager who foils a killer in a spooky mansion—it's time to put it to celluloid pasture, for it's ineffective and out-of-date. (Dir: Crane Wilbur, 80 mins.)

Bat People, The (1974)* Stewart Moss, Marianne McAndrew. A low-budget sci-fi thriller. Dr. Beck is bitten by a bat on his honeymoon, starts acting strangely, and finally turns into a bat! (Dir: Jerry Jameson)

Bataan (1942)*** Robert Taylor, Thomas Mitchell. Good story of the heroes who endured one of our early World War II defeats. A grim reminder and a realistic melodrama. (Dir: Tay Garnett, 114 mins.)

Bathing Beauty (1943)** Red Skelton, Esther Williams. Pleasant musical comedy with Esther as a swimming teacher and Red a student in a girl's school. (Dir: George Sidney, 101 mins.)

Batmen of Africa (1936-66)*½ Clyde Beatty, Elaine Shepard. Feature version of serial "Darkest Africa." Famous lion tamer undertakes to save a girl from a hidden city, meets plenty of opposition there. Beyond-the-fringe thriller makes "Flash Gordon" look like "The Bobbsey Twins." Serial devotees may still care, but others beware. (Dir: B. Reeves Eason, 100 mins.)

Battle at Apache Pass (1952)**½ John Lund, Jeff Chandler. Jeff Chandler repeats his characterization of the Indian Chieftain Cochise, which he originated in the film "Broken Arrow," in this rousing western adventure. There are several action sequences for sagebrush fans. (Dir: George Sherman, 85 mins.)

Battle at Bloody Beach (1961)** Audie Murphy, Dolores Michaels, Gary Crosby. American joins guerrillas in holding off Japanese forces on an island in the Pacific during World War II. Action drama on the dull side until the bullet-riddled conclusion. (Dir: Herbert Coleman, 83 mins.)

Battle Beneath the Earth (British, 1968)** Kerwin Mathews, Viviane Ventura. Absurd yarn about a planned invasion of the U.S. by Red China. It is discovered that the Chinese plan to accomplish this by virtue of a maze of underground tunnels dug beneath the major cities and defense centers of the U.S. (Dir: Montgomery Tully, 92 mins.)

Battle Beyond the Sun (German, 1963)*½ Arla Powell, Andy Stewart. Spaceship trying for Mars is defective and lands on a star in orbit. Tedious science fiction dubbed in English. Special effects occasionally interesting.

Battle Circus (1953)** Humphrey Bogart, June Allyson. Love amid the holocaust of war serves as the plot line in this maudlin drama. Bogart plays a doctor in the service and June Allyson his nurse and love. Poor script and uninspired performances. (Dir: Richard Brooks, 90 mins.)

Battle Cry (1954)**½ Van Heflin, Aldo Ray, Nancy Olson, Tab Hunter, Mona Freeman, Dorothy Malone. A star filled picturization of Leon Uris' adventure-packed tale of a bunch of marines during WW II. There are multiple sub plots, all involving romance. Dorothy Malone manages to create a good portrait of a desperate woman, over thirty, who is attracted to young men. (Dir: Raoul Walsh, 149 mins.)

Battle Flame (1959)** Scott Brady, Elaine Edwards. Romantic drama played against the background of war. Brady plays a Lt. who meets his former love when he is wounded —you guessed it—she's a nurse. If you don't expect "A Farewell to Arms," you just might enjoy it. (Dir. R. G. Springsteen, 78 mins.)

Battle for the Planet of the Apes (1973)** Roddy McDowall, Claude Akins, John Huston. The fifth in the "Apes" films is just too much of a good thing. Whereas the first few were reasonably inventive and interesting in plot and characterization, this one just allows the chimps to dart their eyes and mouth inanities through much makeup. The plot, for those who still care, is another case of crass human beings vs. the more intelligent simians. (Dir: J. Lee Thompson, 86 mins.)

Battle Hell (1956)*** Richard Todd, Akim Tamiroff. A fine film about the daring escape of a British ship which has run aground in the Yangtze river during the Chinese Civil War. Excellent performances, notably by Akim Tamiroff.

Battle Hymn (1957)*** Rock Hudson, Martha Hyer. Good combination of sentiment and war makes this a must for the ladies who like to cry a bit during a film. Hudson plays a chaplain during World War II whose adventures earn him many honors. Based on a true story. (Dir: Douglas Sirk, 108 mins.)

Battle in Outer Space (1960)*½ Japanese made science-fiction film. The same old story—unexplainable happenings around the world lead scientists to suspect "outer space" destruction forces. (Dir: Inoshiro Honda, 74 mins.)

Battle of Algiers (Italian-Algerian, 1967)**** Brahim Haggiag, Jean Martin. One of the most brilliant and moving films of modern times, thanks largely to the extraordinary talents of director Gillo Pontecorvo. He recreated and staged the events leading up to the Algerians winning their independence from France without using any actual newsreel footage, but imparting to the entire film a quality of astonishing realism. The viewer truly believes he is watching a documentary record of the proceedings. The nonprofessional actors are superb, as is the technical work on the film including the texture of the film itself. Pontecorvo's triumph includes his sympathetic handling of both sides of this agonizing, brutal struggle for independence. Quite simply a movie masterpiece. (Dir: Gillo Pontecorvo, 123 mins.)

Battle of Austerlitz (French, 1960)** Leslie Caron, Jack Palance, Vittorio De Sica, Claudia Cardinale. Lavishly produced story of Napoleon and his ambitions as ruler. Badly marred by excessive cutting from original length, inept dubbing into English.

Battle of Blood Island (1960)**½ Ron Kennedy, Richard Devon. Two GIs, survivors of a Japanese attack, endeavor to stay alive on a Pacific island during World War II. Offbeat war story doesn't quite make it but deserves credit for trying with a two-man cast.

Battle of Britain (British, 1969)** Michael Caine, Laurence Olivier, Trevor Howard. $12 million was shot down making this historical tribute, but the producers seem to have spent nothing on a scenario. All the cliche characters from the war movies of the '40's are back to haunt you, ruthless German generals and young British fliers shot down on their first mission. As for the actual fighting of the Battle of Britain, it's squeezed in as a break from the melodrama of the one-dimensional story line. Strategies are displayed by having model airplanes pushed around war rooms. Fine cast wasted. (Dir: Guy Hamilton, 130 mins.)

Battle of Culloden, The (1964)**** Peter Watkins' brilliant documentary about the battle waged by the pretender to the British throne, Bonnie Prince Charlie, against George II in 1746. Although this is set in the past, Watkins uses a present-tense, documentary approach not unlike the method employed by TV's "You Are There" and this technique works to great advantage, stressing the personal rather than the epic proportions of the battle. Among the better cinematic antiwar statements. (Dir: Peter Watkins.)

Battle of Neretva, The (Yugoslavia-U.S.-Italy-Germany, 1969)** Yul Brynner, Sergei Bondarchuk, Curt Jurgens, Sylva Koscina, Hardy Kruger, Orson Welles. Tale of Yugoslavians facing a 1943 invasion by the Germans and Italians was originally nominated in 1969 for an Oscar for Best Foreign Film. However, when this spectacle was cut for American release, it lost much of its impact and coherence. (Dir: Veljko Bulajic, 102 mins.)

Battle of Rogue River (1954)** George Montgomery, Martha Hyer. The struggle for peace with the Indians and the admittance of Oregon as a state are the topics of interest in this average western drama. (Dir: William Castle, 70 mins.)

Battle of the Bulge (1965)** Henry Fonda, Robert Ryan, Pier Angeli. Muddled WW II film, supposedly depicting the events of the epic battle which gave the Germans an edge during the European campaign. The performances are secondary to the battle scenes, and they're nothing special. (Dir: Ken Annakin, 162 mins.)

Battle of the Coral Sea (1959)** Cliff Robertson, Gia Scala. Highly improbable tale of daring heroics on the part of one man during WW II. Robertson is a submarine officer who is captured by the Japanese and escapes from an island with the aid of a curvaceous would-be Japanese agent. (Dir: Paul Wendkos, 100 mins.)

Battle of the Sexes (British, 1960)*** Peter Sellers, Constance Cummings. The old retainer of a plodding Scottish firm is aghast when a girl efficiency expert starts nosing around. Is murder the answer? Diverting comedy, with Sellers in good form, some hilarious sequences. (Dir: Charles Crichton, 88 mins.)

Battle of the Villa Florita, The (1965)** Maureen O'Hara, Richard Todd, Rossano Brazzi. When their mother (Maureen) runs off with her lover (Rossano) her children try to get her back with pater (Richard Todd). The Italian waters and your tearducts are filled with soapsuds. Filmed in Italy with Phyllis Calvert, Olivia Hussey. (Dir: Delmer Daves, 111 mins.)

Battle of the Worlds (Italian, 1961) *½ Claude Rains, Bill Carter. Scientist races to explode a hostile planet as it hurtles toward earth. Rains is hopelessly lost in this dull sci-fi thriller dubbed in English.

Battle Stations (1956)** William Bendix, Richard Boone, John Lund. Life aboard a naval aircraft carrier during WWII is once more the subject of an uninspired war movie. (Dir: Lewis Seiler, 90 mins.)

Battle Taxi (1954)** Sterling Hayden, Arthur Franz. Young officer learns the value of the helicopter rescue service in Korea, after disliking it. Uninspired war drama, nothing new. (Dir: Herbert Strock, 80 mins.)

Battle Zone (1952)** John Hodiak, Stephen McNally. If war stories about buddies and their exploits suit your tastes, this will do. (Dir: Lesley Selander, 82 mins.)

Battleaxe, The (British, 1961)** Jill Ireland, Francis Matthews. Man is accused of owning a lock company which employs ex-cons who are safecracking experts. Mildly amusing low-budget comedy. (Dir: Godfrey Grayson, 66 mins.)

Battleground (1949)***½ Van Johnson, John Hodiak, Denise Darcel. One of the better World War II film

dramas turned out by Hollywood. The action takes place in France during 1944 and the fighting sequences are excellent. The cast is very good. (Dir: William Wellman, 118 mins.)

Bawdy Adventures of Tom Jones, The (Great Britain, 1975)* Nicky Henson, Trevor Howard, Georgia Brown. The rollicking Henry Fielding novel, so gloriously adapted for the screen in 1962, is smothered with a witless series of sight gags and untitillating scenes of bawdy, no doubt lusty folks jumping in and out of bed—all about as exciting as coitus interruptus for someone else. Read the book instead. (Dir: Cliff Owen, 94 mins.)

Baxter (Great Britain, 1972)**½ Patricia Neal, Jean-Pierre Cassell, Britt Ekland, Scott Jacoby, Lynn Carlin. Often moving drama of a boy's breakdown after his parents divorce and he is forced to move with his mother to London. Based on the novel "The Boy Who Could Make Himself Disappear," and adapted by Reginald Rose. The acting is remarkably sensitive. Miss Neal as the boy's speech therapist, Miss Carlin as the mother who ignores Baxter while pursuing her pleasures, Cassell and Miss Ekland as lovers who befriend the boy, and especially Scott Jacoby in the title role, animate their roles. (Dir: Lionel Jeffries, 105 mins.)

Bay of Angels (France, 1963)** Jeanne Moreau, Claude Mann. Barely skin-deep examination of compulsive gamblers, but worth seeing for the wonderfully seedy, overdone performance by Moreau. Written and directed by Jacques Demy. B & W. (85 mins.)

Be Beautiful But Shut Up (French, 1958)*½ Mylene Demongeot, Henri Vidal. English-dubbed crime story of a pretty juvenile delinquent who gets mixed up with a gang of smugglers. Junky plot played more for comedy than drama. (Dir: Henri Verneuil, 94 mins.)

Beach Blanket Bingo (1965)**½ Frankie Avalon, Annette Funicello, Deborah Walley, Paul Lynde. Another harmless teen-ager slanted beach adventure with the typical muscle-bound boys and the bikiniclad girls. Romances happen fast and furious, and you really need a score card to keep up. Paul Lynde, as a press agent, has some funny moments. (Dir: William Asher, 98 mins.)

Beach Casanova (Italian, 1965)**½ Curt Jurgens, Martine Carol, Capucine. Don't let the title fool you. This is an Italian soap opera about the goings-on of the rich and the not-so-rich on the Riviera. Some of the plot is different, but it doesn't really jell.

Beach Party (1963)** Dorothy Malone, Robert Cummings, Frankie Avalon. For the teenage crowd. Robert Cummings has some good moments as a professor spying on the beach-partying kids for research data. There's a funny lampoon of a delinquent motorcycle gang leader named Eric Von Zipper by Harvey Lembeck. (Dir: William Asher, 101 mins.)

Beach Party—Italian Style (Italian, 1963)*½ Catherine Spaak, Luisa Mattoli, Lisa Gastoni. Youngsters on the Riviera engage in some romantic entanglements. Mild, undistinguished romantic comedy dubbed in English.

Beach Red (1967)*** Cornel Wilde, Rip Torn, Burr De Benning. A WW II film, produced and directed by Cornel Wilde, that is really a sincere and frequently moving anti-war plea. Concerns a group of Marines who try to capture a Japanese held island near the Philippines. Shot on location in the Philippines and Japan, based on the well-known novel by Peter Bowman, this is better and more thoughtful than most American films about WW II in the Pacific. (Dir: Cornel Wilde, 105 mins.)

Beachcomber, The (British, 1938)***½ Charles Laughton, Elsa Lanchester. A tropical island man of a shiftless and lazy disposition becomes respectable when a lady missionary sets out to reform him. Delightful comedy-drama based on Somerset Maugham's story, with the two stars superb in their roles. (Dir: Erich Pommer, 90 mins.)

Beachcomber, The (1955)**½ Robert Newton, Glynis Johns. Bum meets missionary's sister on a tropical island and his life is changed. A bit over-acted, but absorbing film. (Dir: Muriel Box, 82 mins.)

Beachhead (1954)**½ Tony Curtis, Frank Lovejoy, Mary Murphy. Four Marines are assigned, during the war, to locate Jap mine fields off Bougainville. Routine tale, but they do find luscious Mary Murphy on the island. (Dir: Stuart Heisler, 89 mins.)

Bear, The (French, 1963)*** Renato Rascel, Francis Blanche. English-dubbed comedy about a talking bear and his keeper who raise havoc in Paris Zoo. Different, well acted, good fun.

Beast from the Haunted Cave, The (1960)*½ Sheila Carol, Michael Forrest, Frank Wolff. A combination gangster/horror film if you can imagine such a thing. The kids may go for the "beast" in the cave gimmick. The performances of the actors are better than the script, but not as good as the beasts.

Beast from 20,000 Fathoms (1953)**½ Paul Christian, Paula Raymond, Cecil Kellaway. Better than average "science fiction meller" with stress on scenic effects. Screenplay by top SF writer Ray Bradbury. (Dir: Eugene Laurie, 80 mins.)

Beast of Babylon Against the Son of Hercules—See: Hero of Babylon

Beast of Budapest, The (1958)** Gerald Milton, Greta Thyssen. Mildly effective drama about a father and son who conflict in their beliefs as to Hungary's fight for freedom from the Communists. (Dir: Harmon Jones, 74 mins.)

Beast of Hollow Mountain (1956)**½ Guy Madison, Patricia Medina. Somewhat of a novelty in that this film incorporates a routine western with a bit of science fiction. Interesting idea as a gimmick but that's all it is. (Dir: Edward Nassons, 79 mins.)

Beast of Morocco (1967)* William Sylvester, Diane Clare, Alizia Gur. Drivel about a man obsessed with a woman who turns out to be a vampire. Low-budget entry. (86 mins.)

Beast with Five Fingers (1946)*½ Robert Alda, Andrea King. Nonsense about a hand that's running around loose fails to generate any excitement. (Dir: Robert Florey, 88 mins.)

Beasts of Marseilles (1957)*** Stephen Boyd, Anna Gaylor. Two English soldiers hide from the Nazis in Occupied France. Well-made melodrama shows good direction and performances.

Beat Generation, The (1959)*½ Mamie Van Doren, Steve Cochran,

Ray Denton. Psychopath gets his kicks assaulting housewives, does same to a detective's spouse, and the manhunt is on in earnest. Bunch of capable performers enmeshed in trashy material; pretty sick stuff. Alternate title: "This Rebel Age." (93 mins.)

Beat Girl (British, 1960)* David Farrar, Noelle Adam, Christopher Lee, Gillian Hills. Teenager resents her new young stepmother, descends into the world of beatniks. Tawdry little juvenile-delinquency drama adds nothing to the subject.

Beat the Devil (1954)***½ Humphrey Bogart, Jennifer Jones, Gina Lollobrigida, Peter Lorre. John Huston's grab-bag of international crooks and swindlers all trying to doublecross and outwit each other in a money hunt. They say everybody was kidding when they made this adventure; anyway, it's fun. Delicious acting. (Dir: John Huston, 92 mins.)

Beatniks, The (1958)*½ Peter Breck, Tony Travis. Bunch of over-age juvenile delinquents make things tough for a young singer, and anyone else who happens to be watching. (73 mins.)

Beau Brummell (1954)*** Elizabeth Taylor, Stewart Granger, Peter Ustinov. Superbly photographed and excellently played adventure-drama about the exploits of one of England's most colorful figures, Beau Brummell. Miss Taylor has never been more beautiful. (Dir: Curtis Bernhardt, 111 mins.)

Beau Geste (1939)***½ Gary Cooper, Ray Milland, Brian Donlevy. Exciting tale of the Foreign Legion which undoubtedly has lost some of its punch through age, but can still stand up to most modern adventure films. (Dir: William Wellman, 120 mins.)

Beau Geste (1966)**½ Doug McClure, Guy Stockwell, Telly Savalas. Another go-round for this plot of brothers in the Foreign Legion, the despotic commandant, etc. Pretty slack retelling of a familiar tale. (Dir: Douglas Heyes, 103 mins.)

Beau James (1957)*** Bob Hope, Vera Miles, Paul Douglas, Alexis Smith. Hope as the dapper Mayor James Walker, in the life and times of New York's favorite politician and gay blade of the dizzy decade of the 1920s. Nostalgic, some sharp humor in the dialogue, a general air of

good feeling prevailing—good entertainment. (Dir: Melville Shavelson, 105 mins.)

Beauties of the Night (French, 1952)***½ Gina Lollobrigida, Gerard Philippe, Martine Carol. French director Rene Clair fashions a whimsical and charming fantasy in which a struggling young composer takes refuge in a dream world where he is very successful with his work and with women. A very bright performance by Gerard Philippe. (Dir: Rene Clair, 84 mins.)

Beautiful Blonde from Bashful Bend, The (1950)** Betty Grable, Cesar Romero. Couple of chorines try their luck out west. Made by great comedy talent Preston Sturges, but something went wrong—more silly than funny. (Dir: Preston Sturges, 77 mins.)

Beautiful But Dangerous (Italian, (1958)*½ Gina Lollobrigida, Vittorio Gassman, Robert Alda. Operatic hijinks of 1900. Gina Lollobrigida plays a soprano forced to separate from her Russian lover when she suspects he is a murderer. Cliches come and go, but Miss Lollobrigida looks ravishing in her turn-of-the-century gowns. (Dir: Robert Z. Leonard, 103 mins.)

Beauty and the Beast (1946)**** Josette Day, Jean Marais. French director Jean Cocteau took the familiar fairy-tale romance and turned it into a lavish, surrealistic film of great interest. The fantasy mood is established from the opening scenes, and Cocteau's wild imagination never lets up as he follows the heroine (Miss Day) through her unconventional love story with the Beast (Marais). The photography is brilliant and Cocteau, the artist, treats the whole film like a painting, creating memorable images that will stay with you long after it is over. (Dir: Jean Cocteau, 90 mins.)

Bebo's Girl (Italian, 1964)**½ Claudia Cardinale, George Chakiris. Fairly entertaining romance about a village girl and a former war hero who is now wanted by the police. Takes its time in getting to the point, but offers some interest along the way. Dubbed in English. (Dir: Luigi Comencini, 106 mins.)

Because of Him (1946)*** Deanna Durbin, Franchot Tone, Charles Laughton. A rather false impression of the theatre and how to succeed in show business; but, nevertheless, an innocent and delightful comedy-romance. Charles Laughton does his usual best. (Dir: Richard Wallace, 88 mins.)

Because of You (1952)**½ Loretta Young, Jeff Chandler. Loretta Young fans will relish this melodrama about a woman who serves a prison term for being an accessory to a crime and is determined to pick up the pieces of her life when she is paroled. Complications keep the plot boiling up to the last reel and Loretta sheds many a tear between start and finish. (Dir. Joseph Pevney, 95 mins.)

Because They're Young (1960)**½ Dick Clark, Tuesday Weld. New high school teacher asks for trouble when he takes an active interest in the destinies of his pupils. Popular disc jockey acquits himself well in his first starring role; film rates slightly above the usual run of teenage problem dramas. (Dir: Robert Paterson, 102 mins.)

Because You're Mine (1952)*** Mario Lanza, James Whitmore, Doretta Morrow. Mario's a drafted opera singer who falls for the sister (Morrow) of his tough Army sergeant (Whitmore). One of Lanza's pleasanter vehicles; good entertainment for Mario's devotees. With Paula Corday, Dean Miller. (103 mins.)

Becket (1964)**** Richard Burton, Peter O'Toole. A rare spectacle film, one that is as satisfying to the mind and the ear as it is to the eye. About the remarkable 12th century Englishman, Thomas Becket, and his turbulent relationship with King Henry II of England. Based on the wonderful play by Frenchman Jean Anouilh and acted to the hilt by the two stars, whose scenes together are a particular joy to watch, this is a thrilling pageant and a valuable history lesson. Sumptuously costumed (you certainly should see this film in color) and flawlessly acted by the supporting players. One of Peter Glenville's finest movie directing jobs. (148 mins.)

Becket Affair, The (Italian, 1966)* Lang Jeffries, Ivan Desny. More sub-dubbed spy stuff, as a crack agent investigates spies in Paris.

Bed and Board (French-Italian, 1970) **** Jean-Pierre Leaud, Claude Jade, Hiroko Berghauer. One of director Francois Truffaut's most glowing commentaries on life and love, and the fourth in his partly autobiographical series which began with Antoine Doinel (Leaud) in "The 400 Blows." (Then came "Love at Twenty" and "Stolen Kisses.") His true love (Jade) has now become Antoine's wife and the film covers the first few years of their marriage. To add a further note of authenticity the interior shots were filmed in Truffaut's own apartment in Paris, not in a movie studio. Touching scene where Antoine telephones his wife while dining in a restaurant with a Japanese girl with whom he is having a brief affair. English subtitles. (Dir: Francois Truffaut, 95 mins.)

Bed of Roses (1933)*** Constance Bennett, Joel McCrea, Pert Kelton, Franklin Pangborn. Little-known, acerbic comedy about the early years of the Depression. Pert Kelton gets laughs mimicking Mae West and Constance Bennett gives one of her best performances. Much of the credit goes to director Gregory La Cava who also contributed to the script. (67 mins.)

Bed Sitting Room, The (British, 1969)*** Rita Tushingham, Ralph Richardson, Spike Milligan, Sandy Nichols. Surreal comedy about the survivors of an atomic war which has wiped out most of the world. Though episodic, it remains wickedly inventive, successfully pointing out the prejudices of the middle and upper classes. The acting, surprisingly, is not good enough. Even the masterly Ralph Richardson, playing a bigoted aristocrat who is slowly mutating into a bed sitting room, cannot handle his part successfully. (Dir: Richard Lester, 91 mins.)

Bedazzled (British, 1967)***½ Peter Cook, Dudley Moore, Eleanor Bron, Raquel Welch. Trying to concoct a comedy based on the Faustian legend is a challenging notion indeed, and Messrs. Cook and Moore have pulled off this caper remarkably well. It doesn't all work, but the jokes, both visual and verbal—are hurled at a rapid nonstop pace, and enough of them are sufficiently inventive and outrageous to reward any enterprising viewer. The men in the audience will be bedazzled by the scantily clad Raquel, and there's a closing scene on a trampoline that is one of the funniest sequences in many years. A stimulating comedy directed by Stanley Donen. (107 mins.)

Bedelia (British, 1946)**½ Margaret Lockwood, Ian Hunter. Engineer weds a previously married woman, suspects her to be a notorious poisoner. Well acted, leisurely mystery melodrama.

Bedevilled (1955)** Anne Baxter, Steve Forrest. Muddled melodrama about a young American preparing for the clergy and his encounter with a femme fatale in Paris. Miss Baxter overacts in an effort to be sexy.

Bedford Incident, The (1965)*** Richard Widmark, Sidney Poitier. The best thing about this slow-moving naval drama is Richard Widmark's fine portrayal of an officer obsessed with his duty. The film details the dilemma which arises aboard a U.S. Navy destroyer after an unidentified submarine is discovered in the North Atlantic. There's a melodramatic finish, but Widmark's performance plus a fine production should hold your attention. (Dir: James Harris, 102 mins.)

Bedlam (1946)*** Boris Karloff, Anna Lee. A girl risks her life to reform the notorious mental institutions in England in the 17th century. Well made, strong horror thriller. (Dir: Mark Robson.)

Bedtime for Bonzo (1951)** Ronald Reagan, Diana Lynn, Walter Slezak. Silly comedy that has some appeal for kids and grownups who want something very light. Professor Reagan experiments with a chimp to prove that early environment plays an important part in how a child turns out. (Dir: Frederick de Cordova, 83 mins.)

Bedtime Story (1941)***½ Fredric March, Loretta Young. Actress wants to retire, but her playwright-husband has other ideas, so a marital rift develops. Sparkling comedy, aided by fine performances. (Dir: Alexander Hall, 85 mins.)

Bedtime Story (1964)**½ Marlon Brando, David Niven, Shirley Jones. Wolfish GI and a smooth con man vie for the affections of a visiting soap queen in Europe. Change of pace for Brando in a comedy that often substitutes leers for laughs. Niven is more adept in his tailored role. Provides some moments of fun. (Dir: Ralph Levy, 99 mins.)

Before the Revolution (France, 1964)

***½ Adriana Asti, Francesco Barilli. An absorbing, astonishing film about European politics and Marxism. One of the most surprising things about "Before the Revolution" is that Bertolucci was only twenty-two when he made this richly textured, excellently acted drama. Asti is outstanding playing a neurotic young aunt suffering from guilt complexes. Original screenplay by Bertolucci. (Dir: Bernardo Bertolucci, 112 mins.)

Before Winter Comes (Great Britain, 1969)**½ David Niven, Topol, Anna Karina. A promising frame—P.O.W. comedy about the use of democratic or autocratic means in dispatching prisoners East and West after WWII; the language conflict is resolved when a multi-lingual con man gets into the action—but the situation wears thin, the biting humor begins to meander. The acting is excellent, Niven is his old, upright self, Karina is as sensual as always, while showing she can act. But top honors go to the droll Israeli, Topol, as the linguist. Based on a New Yorker magazine short story by Frederick I. Keefe called "The Interpreter." (Dir: J. Lee Thompson, 108 mins.)

Beg, Borrow or Steal (1973)**½ Michael Cole, Michael Connors, Kent McCord. Offbeat heist film. Handicapped buddies find it rough staying legit, and decide to execute a robbery of a valuable museum treasure. Made-for-TV. (Dir: David Lowell Rich, 72 mins.)

Beggar Student, The (W. German, 1958)** Gerhard Riedmann, Waltraut Haas. Melodic lighthearted operetta with a familiar book. Students protest against the King in turn-of-the-century Germany, and after being arrested, one of them is forced to woo a countess. Close your eyes, and open your ears. (Dir: Werner Jacobs, 97 mins.)

Beginning of the End, The (1946) **½ Brian Donlevy, Robert Walker. Ambitious film which strives to tell the story of the first A-Bomb. Becomes ensnared by too many Hollywood cliches to be truly effective.

Beginning of the End (1957)*½ Peter Graves, Peggie Castle. Giant grasshoppers menace the world this time in this all too drab and phony science fiction "thriller." (Dir: Bert Gordon, 74 mins.)

Beguiled, The (1971)**½ Clint Eastwood, Geraldine Page, Elizabeth Hartman. A macabre yarn set during the Civil War. Eastwood is a wounded Union soldier who stumbles on a girls' school run by sex-starved Geraldine Page and the meek Miss Hartman. Before you can say "libido," the gals are having their go at Eastwood, and the gothic aspects of the sinister story come to light. Some sexy and brutal scenes have been cut for TV but it still packs a punch. (Dir: Don Siegel, 109 mins.)

Behave Yourself (1951)**½ Shelley Winters, Farley Granger. Young couple find a dog that's wanted by crooks, suddenly find dead bodies dropping all around them. A few amusing moments in this comedy of murders, which would have been even better with different leads. (Dir: George Beck, 81 mins.)

Behind Locked Doors (1948)*** Richard Carlson, Lucille Bremer. Investigator goes to a sanitarium where a missing judge is being held captive. Suspenseful, well-acted thriller.

Behind the High Wall (1956)*½ Tom Tully, Sylvia Sidney. Worn-out prison escape plot is warmed up once more. Many people are involved in this chase melodrama and it's hard to keep the guilty separated from the innocent without a scorecard. (Dir: Abner Biberman, 85 mins.)

Behind the Mask (British, 1959)*** Michael Redgrave, Tony Britton. Behind the scenes drama of a London hospital, highlighting the conflict between two surgeons. Fine performances lift this medical drama from the realm of soap opera into something worthwhile. (Dir: John Francis Dillon, 70 mins.)

Behind the Mask of Zorro (Italian, 1964)*½ Tony Russel. Masked rider fights the tyranny of an unscrupulous tyrant. Juvenile swashbuckling actioner dubbed in English.

Behind the Rising Sun (1943)*** Tom Neal, Margo, Robert Ryan. Japanese publisher alienates his son with his extreme political views in Japan. Well acted war drama. (Dir: Edward Dmytryk, 89 mins.)

Behind the Wall (Polish, 1971)**** Maja Komorowska, Zbigniew Zapasiewicz. Deeply moving personal story of loneliness and our need for reassurance. Young female chemist, on the edge of a nervous breakdown, tries to confide in a neighbor in her apartment, while simultaneously asking him for a job. Beautifully acted by Miss Komorowska. (70 mins.)

Behold a Pale Horse (1964)**½ Gregory Peck, Anthony Quinn, Omar Sharif. Renegade Loyalist continues to harass the Spanish regime, police captain finally sees a chance to trap him. Drama directed by Fred Zinnemann misfires—vague, cloudy in treatment, slow in action, and Peck is miscast. (Dir: Fred Zinnemann, 118 mins.)

Bel Antonio (1963)*** Marcello Mastroianni. Moderately funny comedy about a man-about-town—Italian made, English dubbed. Mastroianni is very good. Claudia Cardinale is the object of Marcello's affections. You may not agree with all the Italian sexual mores but parts of the film are both funny and heartfelt.

Belated Flowers (Russia, 1972)*** Olga Zhizneva, Irina Lavrentyeva, Alexander Lazarev. Charming, romantic story based on Chekhov's novella, "Late-Blooming Flowers," published in 1882, and directed by a filmmaker born in 1894 (Abram Room). A royal family is on its uppers, the money's run out, and the young princess dreams of love while dying of consumption. It sounds corny but it's all quite pleasant and entirely non-political. (Dir: Abram Room, 100 mins.)

Believe in Me (1971)* Michael Sarrazin, Jacqueline Bisset, Allen Garfield. Botched drama about a drug addict whose girl friend also becomes hooked on speed. Production problems encountered in shooting film show up in muddled story. Originally called "Speed Is of the Essence," based on an article by Gail Sheehy, most of the film was directed by Stuart Hagmann who gets screen credit. But John G. Avildsen, who later directed "Rocky," was brought in. Several scenes, including those in a hospital and the final sequence, were directed by Avildsen. Screenplay credited to playwright Israel Horovitz, but he did not write most of the Avildsen-directed sequences. (90 mins.)

Bell, Book & Candle (1959)*** James Stewart, Kim Novak, Jack Lemmon, Ernie Kovacs. Despite the miscasting of the inept Miss Novak as a modern day witch, this wacky B'way play is delightfully brought to the screen. The supporting cast of zany characters include Jack Lemmon as a whimsical warlock, Elsa Lanchester as a high priestess of magic, Hermione Gingold as a "spell" expert, and Ernie Kovacs as a eccentric author. It's fun all the way! (Dir: Richard Quine, 106 mins.)

Bell for Adano, A (1947)*******½ John Hodiak, William Bendix, Gene Tierney. John Hersey's story of the American occupation of a small Italian town is beautifully brought to life on the screen. The character sketches are believable and the simplicity of the subject is sensitively handled. (Dir: Henry King, 103 mins.)

Bellboy, The (1960)****** Jerry Lewis, Alex Gerry. Madcap misadventures of a bungling bellboy at a posh Florida hotel, and that's it—no plot, just a series of Lewis-oriented gags. Matter of taste; fans will collapse with hilarity, others apt to sit there straight-faced. (Dir: Jerry Lewis, 72 mins.)

Belle de Jour (French-Italian, 1967) ******** Catherine Deneuve, Jean Sorel, Genevieve Page, Michel Piccoli. A remarkably beautiful film by Luis Bunuel and his first comedy. About a frigid young housewife (Deneuve) who decides to spend her midweek afternoons as a prostitute. Bunuel's familiar obsessions with anticlericism and hypocritical society, and a preoccupation with erotica, are all here. In lesser hands this story line might have been a sleazy exploitation film. But Bunuel's comments on our sexual fantasies and hang-ups are humorous and perceptive, and his masterful use of color, after so many films shot in black and white, further enhances this elegant fantasy, based on Joseph Kessel's novel. Deneuve, who by the age of 24 had made almost two dozen films, is marvelous in her role of the hooker, initially detached, who gets increasingly involved with her clients. (Dir: Luis Bunuel, 100 mins.)

Belle Le Grand (1951)*****½ Vera Ralston, John Carroll. Gambling queen is plagued by her rascally ex-husband. Dull, corny costume melodrama, badly acted. (90 mins.)

Belle of New York, The (1952)****** Fred Astaire, Vera-Ellen. This musical is remembered as the one in which Fred Astaire danced on the ceiling. There's little else to recommend the turn-of-the-century comedy about a stage door Johnny who falls in love. The dancing's the thing and Astaire and Vera-Ellen make a good team. (Dir: Charles Walters, 80 mins.)

Belle of Old Mexico (1949)****** Estelita Rodriguez, Robert Rockwell. Ex-GI promises to take care of a buddy's sister, finds her to be a grown-up glamorous senorita. Mild comedy with music.

Belle of the Nineties (1934)******½ Mae West, Roger Pryor, John Mack Brown, Katherine De Mille; Duke Ellington and his Orchestra. The censors took the bite out of this one. It's a mildly amusing satire on life in the Gay Nineties. Song: "My Old Flame," by Arthur Johnston and Sam Coslow. (Dir: Leo McCarey, 75 mins.)

Belle of the Yukon (1944)****** Gypsy Rose Lee, Randolph Scott, Dinah Shore. Dance hall boss in the Yukon country finally turns over a new leaf and becomes an honest man, as his sweetie wishes. Mild Alaskan melodrama with music. (Dir: William Seiter, 84 mins.)

Belle Sommers (1962)****** Polly Bergen, David Janssen. Press agent takes on as a client a former recording star, now in dutch with the mobs. Uninspired drama looks like a TV pilot rather than a feature film.

Belle Starr (1941)******½ Gene Tierney, Randolph Scott, Dana Andrews. Occasionally exciting, generally tedious western about a female Jesse James. Picture the sophisticated Miss Tierney in the title role and you have a good imagination. (Dir: Irving Cummings, 87 mins.)

Belles and Ballets (French, 1960) ******½ Members of the Paris Ballet De L'Etoile perform varied numbers. For balletomaniacs worthy fare, well done.

Belles of St. Trinian's, The (British, 1954)******* Alastair Sim, Joyce Grenfell. The headmistress of a girls' school has her problems with the girls, a bunch of hoodlums if ever there was one, and her brother, a crooked bookmaker. Wild and woolly farce, many laughs. (Dir: Lesley Selander, 86 mins.)

Belles on Their Toes (1952)******½ Jeanne Crain, Myrna Loy, Debra

Paget, Jeffrey Hunter. In this sequel to "Cheaper By the Dozen," Clifton Webb's presence (he died in "Dozen") is sorely needed. But, there are some funny scenes involving the further adventures of the large Gilbreth family. (Dir: Frank Launder, 89 mins.)

Bellissima (Italian, 1952)**½ Anna Magnani, Tina Apicella, Walter Chiari. Ambitious mother pushes her plain-looking young daughter without mercy in an effort to turn her into an Italian Shirley Temple. What could have been a biting tragedy of stage-motherhood becomes a rambling, only occasionally effective drama through unduly heavy treatment. Dubbed in English. (Dir: Luchino Vicenti, 95 mins.)

Bells Are Ringing (1960)*** Judy Holliday, Dean Martin. Musical stage success tailored for the talents of Judy Holliday, and she repeats that success in the screen version, as she plays a lovestruck operator of a telephone-answering service, fallen for the voice of a young show writer. Some nice tunes by Jule Styne, and if the script has weaknesses, Holliday makes it all worthwhile. (Dir: Vincente Minnelli, 127 mins.)

Bells of St. Mary's (1946)***½ Bing Crosby, Ingrid Bergman. Young priest and a Mother Superior make plans to entice a wealthy skinflint to build them new surroundings. Enjoyable sequel to the famous "Going My Way," not up to its predecessor, but still entertaining. (Dir: Leo McCarey, 126 mins.)

Beloved Enemy (1936)*** David Niven, Brian Aherne, Merle Oberon. Rather well done drama about the people caught in the Irish Rebellion. A love story combined with some action—benefits from a good cast. (Dir: H. C. Potter, 90 mins.)

Beloved Infidel (1959)**½ Gregory Peck, Deborah Kerr, Eddie Albert. The story of writer F. Scott Fitzgerald, his last years as a Hollywood scenarist, and the inspiration given him by his love for columnist Sheilah Graham. Tearful drama comes perilously close to true-confessions style, but should give the ladies a good cry. Excellent performance by Miss Kerr. (Dir: Henry King, 123 mins.)

Ben (1972)* Lee Harcourt Montgomery. Tasteless sequel to "Willard," the box-office success about killer rats. This opus has a young boy, who has a heart condition, befriending the rampaging rodent and his friends. Disney it ain't! (Dir: Phil Karlson, 75 mins.)

Ben Hur (1959)**** Charlton Heston, Stephen Boyd. A movie special in the truest sense of the word. The entire family will enjoy this spectacular screen version of the celebrated novel about the conflict of power between the Jews of Judea and the Romans in Jerusalem during the lifetime of Jesus. Directed by William Wyler. Charlton Heston is excellent in his Academy Award-winning role as Ben Hur, an aristocratic Jew who suffers grievously at the hands of the Romans for his defense of his people, and is drawn to Jesus in scenes before and during the Crucifixion. The film is meticulously produced and there are numerous sequences of awesome proportions, capped by the marvelous chariot race in which Heston and the villain, Stephen Boyd, vie for honors in the mammoth arena. If you've never seen this motion picture classic in its initial or subsequent theatrical releases, by all means tune in and see how well Heston looks after years in the galley. When this film was made in the late 50's, it cost about $15 million and was the most expensive movie ever made until that time. Special credit due to second unit directors Andrew Marton and Yakima Canutt who directed the spectacular chariot-race sequence. (Dir: William Wyler, 217 mins.)

Bend of the River (1952)*** James Stewart, Rock Hudson, Arthur Kennedy. Large, sprawling western adventure with a top-name cast and excellent photography to recommend it. Stewart and Kennedy are pitted against each other in this tale of big men in the big country. Rock Hudson has a small featured role. (Dir: Anthony Mann, 91 mins.)

Beneath the Planet of the Apes (1970)**½ James Franciscus, Charlton Heston, Kim Hunter, Roddy McDowall. Those who went bananas over the original ape opus will probably want to monkey around with this sequel. No one can leave Chuck Heston in the lurch for long, so astronaut Franciscus is sent on a rescue mission, and things really get hairy when the special-effects virtuosos are let loose! A race of mutated humans living "beneath" the planet and the continuing presence of Hunter's Zira character are featured. (Dir: Ted Post, 108 mins.)

Beneath the Twelve-Mile Reef (1953) **½ Robert Wagner, Terry Moore, Gilbert Roland. The stars take a back seat to the fine underwater photography (even more beautiful in color) in this adventure about Greek sponge divers, their rivalry in business, and their special code of ethics. Shot on location off the coast of Florida. (Dir: Robert Webb, 101 mins.)

Bengal Brigade (1954)** Rock Hudson, Arlene Dahl, Ursula Thiess. Another adventure epic which juggles historical facts in order to keep the action hopping. Hudson plays a wronged British officer in the Bengal troops in India who sets out to clear his reputation and averts an all out war in the process. Miss Dahl is exquisite as Hudson's romantic interest. (Dir: Laslo Benedek, 87 mins.)

Ben-Gurion Remembers (Israeli, 1972)***½ Absorbing feature-length documentary about one of the most remarkable political leaders of the 20th century—David Ben-Gurion. If the interviews with the longtime Prime Minister are occasionally worshipful, it's compensated for by extensive documentary footage dealing with Jews in Eastern Europe, the founding of the state of Israel, and the fascinating personal reminiscences of this dynamic octogenarian who died soon after the shooting of this feature was completed. (Dir: Simon Hesera, 82 mins.)

Benjamin (French, 1968)*** Michele Morgan, Catherine Deneuve, Pierre Clementi. A graceful, rather old-fashioned French film. Elegantly photographed adventures of a dashing young rake and his conquests in 18th-century France. Dubbed.

Benji (1974)*** Patsy Garrett, Allen Fiuzat, Cynthia Smith, Peter Breck. Frisky family fare which toplines a lovable mutt of a dog, played by Higgins (already familiar to TV audiences who have seen "Petticoat Junction"). Benji outshines his human supporting players, showing a range of emotion unparalleled in the history of animal movie-acting. Simple story has the hound saving two kids from kidnappers and earn-

ing a place in their grateful parents' home. (Dir: Joe Camp, 89 mins.)

Benny and Barney: Las Vegas Undercover (1977)*½ Jack Cassidy, Terry Kiser, Timothy Thomerson. This smacks of a pilot that didn't make it. The Las Vegas location adds some glitter to the show but not enough to perk up this routine cops-and-kidnappers yarn. Benny and Barney are two ex-cops performing as singers in a duo known as the Aristocrats. The late Jack Cassidy plays a theatrical agent with flair. (Dir: Ron Stalof, 86 mins.)

Benny Goodman Story, The (1956) **½ Steve Allen, Donna Reed. Typical Hollywood version of a bandleader's life and loves. Steve Allen seems miscast but he does fairly well as the famed Goodman. Harry James, Gene Krupa and others make guest appearances. (Dir: Valentine Davies, 140 mins.)

Berkeley Square (British, 1933)**** Leslie Howard, Heather Angel, Irene Browne. One of the best romantic fantasies of the '30's, greatly aided by a gloriously stylish performance from Howard, who plays a dapper transatlantic commuter who hobnobs with persons dead for more than a century. Picture has pathos, warmth, humor, and Peter Standish (Howard) is also present. Whether Howard is wearing clothes of the 18th or the 20th century he's a joy. (Dir: Frank "Cavalcade" Lloyd, 87 mins.)

Berlin Affair (1970)**½ Darren McGavin, Claude Dauphin, Brian Kelly. This might easily be subtitled "Shake Well and Mix" because it is a neat combination of all the ingredients needed for a two-hour made-for-TV intrigue film. Take an honest, durable hero (Darren McGavin), set him out looking for an old friend (Brian Kelly) suspected of countless things, throw in a girl to advance the story, provide a love interest (Pascale Petite) and let the audience in on one secret in the plot maze every 21½ minutes. Then, just in case the viewers like the idea, have Darren working for a Geneva-based manhunt organization (run by Fritz Weaver) so you can make a series out of the thing if there's a demand. (Dir: David Lowell Rich.)

Berlin Express (1948)***½ Merle Oberon, Robert Ryan. Allied group in Europe battle a band of Nazi fanatics seeking to prevent the unification of Germany. Exciting, well written spy thriller. (Dir: Jacques Tourneur, 86 mins.)

Bermuda Affair (1956)**½ Kim Hunter, Gary Merrill. Grim but interesting film about the disintegration of a marriage. Kim Hunter gives a good performance despite the spotty script.

Bernadette of Lourdes (French, 1961) *** Daniele Ajoret, Robert Arnoux. English-dubbed. The story of the simple peasant girl who became a Saint. For the devout, quite good. Miss Ajoret is excellent in the main role. (Dir: Robert Darene, 90 mins.)

Bernadine (1957)*½ Pat Boone, Terry Moore, Janet Gaynor. Mediocre movie version of B'way play about the trials and tribulations of the younger set. Pat Boone, complete with white shoes and teeth, grins, sings and makes a stab at acting. Janet Gaynor, a star of silent films and the early thirties' talkies, came out of retirement to do a featured part in this opus and she's unbelievably bad. (Dir: Henry Levin, 97 mins.)

Berserk! (1968)** Joan Crawford, Ty Hardin, Judy Geeson. Circus nonsense as Joan Crawford takes to the big top in a murder yarn with practically no surprises, just unintended laughs. There are gory murders every 20 minutes or so, the best thing that can be said about Miss Crawford is she's got better legs than any other 60-year-old female ringmaster we've ever seen! (Dir: Jim O'Connolly, 96 mins.)

Best Foot Forward (1943)*** Lucille Ball, June Allyson, William Gaxton. Lively, entertaining adaptation of the musical about a boy who induces a screen star to be his date at the school prom. Production may strike you as slightly stilted but you'll enjoy it anyway. (Dir: Edward Buzzell, 95 mins.)

Best House in London, The (British, 1969)*½ David Hemmings, Joanna Pettet, George Sanders, Dany Robin. Or, the Problems with Prostitutes, as Victorian England tries to cope with the bawdy-house situation. When risque farce is ineptly handled, it becomes very boring indeed. As happens here. (Dir: Philip Saville, 105 mins.)

Best Man, The (1964)**** Cliff Robertson, Henry Fonda, Lee Tracy.

Based on Gore Vidal's perceptive and outspoken play, it deals with the hot-and-heavy fight between two leading contenders for the Presidential nomination of their party. The film boasts excellent performances from Cliff Robertson and Henry Fonda as the political rivals, and a grand tour de force by Lee Tracy in the role of an ex-President. The jargon of the political arena and the lengths to which each presidential aspirant will go to achieve his goal make for interesting and literate drama. One of the best American movies about politics. (Dir: Franklin Schaffner, 102 mins.)

Best of Enemies, The (1962)*** David Niven, Alberto Sordi, Michael Wilding. Comedy drama about the grudging respect that develops between a British and an Italian Captain in North Africa during World War II. Indecisive handling often blunts the point, although performances are rewarding and help carry the film. (Dir: Guy Hamilton, 104 mins.)

Best of Everything, The (1959)**½ Hope Lange, Suzy Parker, Joan Crawford, Louis Jourdan. Inside darkest Madison Avenue, an exploration of the loves of office workers and the higher-ups. Unabashedly trashy, taken from a trashy novel. Production gloss, star performers slant this drama toward the ladies. (Dir: Jean Negulesco, 127 mins.)

Best of the Bad Men (1948)**½ Randolph Scott, Robert Ryan. Marshal goes after the Sundance Kid, who heads a murderous band of outlaws. Fairly good western. (Dir: William Russell.)

Best Things in Life Are Free, The (1956)**½ Gordon MacRae, Sheree North, Dan Dailey, Ernest Borgnine. Another of those musical biographies about song writers. MacRae, Borgnine and Dailey portray the hit song-smiths DeSylva, Brown and Henderson, who were the rage of the Broadway stage during the twenties. The plot doesn't really matter—it's the tunes that make up the best part of the film. Songs include: "Good News," "Sonny Boy," "Sunnyside Up," and "Birth of the Blues." (Dir: Michael Curtiz, 104 mins.)

Best Years of Our Lives, The (1946) **** Fredric March, Myrna Loy, Teresa Wright, Dana Andrews, Harold Russell, Cathy O'Donnell. One of

Hollywood's best. A beautifully acted story about three soldiers who come home after WWII and the time each has making his adjustment. Funny, sad, touching and entertaining fare. Film won and deserved many Oscars. (Dir: William Wyler, 172 mins.)

Betrayal, The (1958)**½ Phillip Friend, Diana Decker. Blind Canadian ex-officer hears the voice of the one who betrayed him in prison camp during the war. Neat melodrama.

Betrayal (1974)**½ Amanda Blake, Tisha Sterling. A fairly suspenseful drama brings Amanda Blake back to the contemporary scene after all those years as Kitty on "Gunsmoke." She's attractive as a wealthy widow who falls into the manipulative hands of a pair of con artists. The girl in the duo, played by Tisha Sterling, has second thoughts about preying on kindly Amanda Blake. Dick Haymes, popular singer of the 40's, makes a rare dramatic TV appearance. Made-for-TV. (Dir: Gordon Hessler.)

Betrayed (formerly "When Strangers Marry," 1944)***½ One of the best "surprise" films ever made. Suspenseful melodrama of a wife whose husband of a few days is suspected of murder. Kim Hunter, Dean Jagger and Bob Mitchum are in the leads.

Betrayed (1954)** Clark Gable, Lana Turner, Victor Mature. Routine spy meller with more than its share of contrivances has big names to bolster its appeal. Gable & Mature handle the he-man aspects of their roles in true heroic fashion and Miss Turner supplies the necessary curves. (Dir: Gottfried Reinhardt, 108 mins.)

Betrayed Women (1950)*½ Tom Drake, Beverly Michaels. Lawyer exposes cruelties inflicted upon the inmates of a women's reformatory. Unnecessary cruelty inflicted upon any audience. (Dir: Edward Cahn, 70 mins.)

Better a Widow (Italian-French, 1968)*½ Peter McEnery, Virna Lisi. Unimaginative comedy pokes fun at the Sicilian Mafia. English engineer (P. McEnery) arrives on the scene to set up plans for building an oil refining plant. Enter Virna Lisi and numerous romantic entangle-ments. Empty-headed frivolity. (Dir: Duccio Tessar, 105 mins.)

Between Heaven and Hell (1956)**½ Robert Wagner, Terry Moore, Broderick Crawford. Another war tale about a group of less than exemplary soldiers and how they achieve title of "Hell Fighters of the Pacific." Wagner plays a spoiled Southerner who learns things the hard way. The war sequences should please action fans. (Dir: Richard Fleischer, 93 mins.)

Between Midnight and Dawn (1950)** Edmond O'Brien, Gale Storm, Mark Stevens. Two cops love the same gal but the gal doesn't have to choose because a mobster kills one off and makes the decision for her. Routine cops and robbers yarn with uninspired acting. (Dir: Gordon Douglas, 90 mins.)

Between the Lines (1977)***½ John Heard, Lindsay Crouse, Jeff Goldblum, Jill Eikenberry, Gwen Welles. Another winner from the husband and wife team that made "Hester Street." "Between the Lines" is an enormously appealing, perceptive comedy about the problems and pressures of publishing a youth-oriented anti-establishment weekly newspaper. Benefits greatly from the marvelous ensemble acting from the non-star cast, some of who will be big stars. There's one remarkably funny scene of a crazed conceptual artist invading the Boston premises of the paper and busting up the joint, if not the staff, before departing. Sardonic, skillful screenplay by Fred Barron. (Dir: Joan Micklin Silver, 101 mins.)

Between Time and Eternity (German, 1960)** Lilli Palmer, Carlos Thompson. Woman with an incurable disease decides to have one last fling, becomes involved with a petty thief. Sudsy English-dubbed drama for the handkerchief trade. (Dir: Arthur Maria Rabenalt, 98 mins.)

Between Two Women (1944)** Van Johnson, Gloria De Haven. Another in the Dr. Gillespie series with Johnson still following in Lew Ayres' footsteps. Lionel Barrymore is the same as ever. (Dir: Willis Goldback, 83 mins.)

Between Two Worlds (1944)**½ John Garfield, Edmund Gwenn, Eleanor Parker. Second and weaker version of Sutton Vane's play "Outward Bound" which has been released for TV. Story of people who don't know they're dead, sailing to meet their destiny. Gwenn is excellent as the ship's steward. (Dir: Edward Blatt, 112 mins.)

Beware, My Lovely (1952)**½ Ida Lupino, Robert Ryan. Young war widow is menaced by a sinister handyman. Fairly suspenseful melodrama. (Dir: Harry Horner, 77 mins.)

Beware of Blondie (1950)** Penny Singleton, Arthur Lake, Adele Jergens, Douglas Fowley. Dagwood is left in charge of his boss' construction company, is a target for confidence tricksters. Fair comedy in the series. (Dir: Edward Bernds, 66 mins.)

Beware of Children (British, 1961)** Leslie Phillips, Julia Lockwood, Geraldine McEwan. Young couple decide to turn property left them into a holiday home for disturbed children. Mild little comedy-drama. (Dir: Gerald Thomas, 80 mins.)

Beware! The Blob (1972)*½ Robert Walker, Godfrey Cambridge, Shelley Berman. An update of the 1958 "The Blob," this science-fiction thriller plays better for laughs than terror. A frozen, shapeless mass thaws, grows and goes on a rampage. Godfrey Cambridge and Shelley Berman, of all people, are among those trying to stop the destruction. (Dir: Larry Hagman, 88 mins.)

Bewitched (1944)**½ Phyllis Thaxter, Edmund Gwenn. Occasionally illogical but generally interesting psychological melodrama about a girl with a split personality. (Dir: Arch Oboler, 65 mins.)

Beyond a Reasonable Doubt (1956)** Dana Andrews, Joan Fontaine. Man agrees to serve as a guinea pig in a scheme proving the fallibility of circumstantial evidence. Sluggish mystery melodrama. (Dir: Fritz Lang, 80 mins.)

Beyond All Limits (1960)* Jack Palance, Maria Felix, Pedro Armendariz. Rather skimpy tale of a shrimp fisherman who discovers his wife's child was fathered by a gringo partner. Slimness of plot partially compensated for by picturesque photography, capable performances. Produced in Mexico.

Beyond Glory (1948)**½ Alan Ladd, Donna Reed. West Point drama has some good moments but many of its scenes away from the Academy are boring. (Dir: John Farrow, 82 mins.)

Beyond Mombasa (1957)** Cornel Wilde, Donna Reed, Leo Genn. Mediocre adventure film set in Africa with all the clichés—dangerous safaris, murderous tribes, uranium mines, etc. (Dir: George Marshall, 100 mins.)

Beyond the Bermuda Triangle (1975)* Fred MacMurray, Sam Groom, Donna Mills. Good old Fred MacMurray can't do much with this flat-footed yarn about people mysteriously disappearing off the Florida coast. He's wealthy, retired and more than a little curious about his friends who have vanished in the legendary area of the Caribbean known as the Bermuda Triangle. Made-for-TV. (Dir: William A. Graham)

Beyond the Blue Horizon (1942)*½ Dorothy Lamour, Richard Denning. Childish sarong saga has Dotty out to prove she is the rightful heir to something. A good film is definitely not her legacy. (Dir: Alfred Santell, 76 mins.)

Beyond the Curtain (British, 1961)**½ Richard Greene, Eva Bartok, Marius Goring. Stewardess eludes East German police while searching for her brother. Entertaining espionage melodrama with good performances.

Beyond the Forest (1949)** Bette Davis, Joseph Cotten. Ridiculous melodrama heavy in corny histrionics with Bette Davis playing a character who defies description. (Dir: King Vidor, 96 mins.)

Beyond the Law (1968)***½ Rip Torn, George Plimpton, Norman Mailer, Jose Torres, Beverly Bentley. Anything that the gifted writer Norman Mailer is likely to be involved in is worth your attention. This tough, frequently absorbing Mailer-directed film is off-beat, original movie-making and a huge improvement on his earlier film "Wild 90." It's Mailer's version, and vision, of a modern big city police lieutenant (Mailer) and his interrogations in the course of a single evening. Script improvised by members of the cast based on an idea of Mailer's. Low-budget, high-interest offering, if you forgive the poor technical quality of the production.

Beyond the Time Barrier (1960)*½ Robert Clarke, Darlene Tompkins. Air Force pilot crashes through the time barrier into the future, finds the earth in a pretty sad state. Undistinguished sci-fi story, cheaply produced. (Dir: Edgar Ulmer, 75 mins.)

Beyond the Valley of the Dolls (1970) * Edy Williams, Dolly Reed. Vulgar, tawdry, laughable exploitation film directed by the porno king of the '60's, Russ Meyer. The story about an all-girl rock-combo and their search for stardom in Hollywood defies description. Every girl in the cast looks like a playboy bunny-reject, and the men run a close second. Incidentally this has little to do with Jacqueline Susann's trashy novel. (Dir: Russ Meyer, 93 mins.)

B. F.'s Daughter (1947) *½ Barbara Stanwyck, Van Heflin, Charles Coburn. J. B. Marquand's novel about an heiress's marriage to an economics professor is boring, poorly paced and uninteresting in this screen adaptation.

Bhowani Junction (1956) **½ Ava Gardner, Stewart Granger, Bill Travers. The pictorial beauty of on-location filming in Pakistan is the best feature of this turbulent drama mixing love with political intrigue. Ava Gardner plays an Anglo-Indian girl who is torn between her loyalty for the British and the Indians. Her ardent lovers are played by Granger, Travers, and Francis Matthews. (Dir: George Cukor, 110 mins.)

Bible, The . . . In the Beginning (U.S.-Italy, 1966) *** George C. Scott, Ava Gardner, Peter O'Toole, Franco Nero. Elaborate production trappings and some good acting spark this otherwise predictable Hollywood retelling of the Bible stories. The beginning in the Garden of Eden is beautifully photographed, and the Noah's Ark sequence with the technicians giving viewers an awesome flood is also visually brilliant. The story of Abraham and Sarah (Scott and Gardner) is the best-acted section of the film, and comes closest to intimate human drama in an otherwise spectacular film of enormous proportions. (Dir: John Huston, 174 mins.)

Bicycle Thief, The (Italian, 1949) **** Enzo Stajola, Lamberto Maggiorani. Tragic story of a poor man whose needed bicycle is stolen, his search through Rome with his small son to find the thief. Superbly directed by Vittorio De Sica, a touch-

ing, heart-gripping drama. (90 mins.)

Big Bad Mamma (1974) * Angie Dickinson, William Shatner, Tom Skerritt. Break-neck pacing and several sexy bedroom romps can't disguise this vulgar attempt to create another "Bonnie and Clyde" yarn about a Depression-era gang of bank robbers. Angie Dickinson tries valiantly to breathe life into the one-dimensional character of a mother of two turgid "sexpots" who turn to a life of crime in order to escape the dire poverty she has known all her life. (Dir: Steve Carver, 85 mins.)

Big Beat, The (1958) ** William Reynolds, Gogi Grant. Musical with pop tunes and a thin background story about the record business makes thin movie. (85 mins.)

Big Bluff, The (1959) *½ John Bromfield, Martha Vickers. Inept melodrama about a fortune hunter who marries a girl with a short time to live, decides to hurry her demise. (Dir: W. Lee Wilder, 70 mins.)

Big Boodle, The (1957) ** Errol Flynn, Pedro Armendariz, Gia Scala. Counterfeiters pass phony bills in casino in Havana, Cuba which leads Errol Flynn on a merry chase. Slim film fare. Big Boodle is a routine bungle. (Dir: Richard Wilson, 83 mins.)

Big Bounce, The (1969) * Ryan O'Neal, Leigh Taylor-Young, Lee Grant, James Daly, Van Heflin. Muddled crime melodrama made when O'Neal and Miss Taylor-Young were married. The film resembles a poor made-for-TV entry with action for action's sake, and virtually non-existent character motivation. A fine supporting cast is wasted. (Dir: Alex March, 102 mins.)

Big Broadcast of 1938, The (1938) *** W. C. Fields, Dorothy Lamour, Bob Hope, Shirley Ross. Fields' golf and billiards routines plus Bob and Shirley singing "Thanks for the Memory" are all this film offers—but it's enough. (Dir: Mitchell Leisen, 100 mins.)

Big Broadcast of 1937, The (1936) **½ Jack Benny, George Burns, Gracie Allen, Martha Raye, Shirley Ross; Benny Goodman and his Orchestra, Leopold Stokowski and his Symphony Orchestra. Entertaining variety show which provides a fair satire on the radio industry. Songs: "La Bomba," "Here's Love in Your Eye" by Leo Robin and Ralph Rainger. (Dir: Mitchell Leisen, 100 mins.)

Big Bus, The (1976)** Joseph Bologna, Stockard Channing, Rene Auberjonois, Lynn Redgrave, Ruth Gordon. This parody of disaster pics, involving a runaway nuclear-powered bus, is so self-conscious of the clichés of the genre that it misses the comic mark, disintegrating into absurdity. The usual nuts sign on for the first nuclear-powered bus trip from New York to Denver, but most of the action centers on the romance between driver Bologna and bus-designer Channing. Good satiric jabs are awash in a sea of crude humor and contrivance. (Dir: James Frawley, 88 mins.)

Big Caper, The (1957)** Rory Calhoun, Mary Costa. Crooked couple decide to mend their ways after a taste of small town friendliness, but the gang has other ideas. It all sounds familiar, and it is. (Dir: Robert Stevens, 84 mins.)

Big Carnival, The (1951)**** Kirk Douglas, Jan Sterling. Terrific drama packs a king-sized wallop. Grim tale of a nasty big city reporter stuck in the sticks who capitalizes on a disaster to gain attention and ride himself back to the big time. Unrelenting in its cynicism, superb performances, direction by Billy Wilder. (112 mins.)

Big Cat, The (1948)*** Preston Foster, Lon McCallister, Forrest Tucker. City lad in the mountain country aids in the tracking down of a killer cougar. Exciting outdoor story, loaded with action of the more virile sort.

Big Chance, The (British, 1957)** Adrienne Corri. A man gives in just once to temptation, thinking it's his big chance for the big time, and gets nothing but trouble. Grade "C" film.

Big Circus, The (1959)**½ Victor Mature, Red Buttons, Rhonda Fleming. A sort of "Grand Hotel" of the big top. Many subplots are unfolded in this sprawling film about behind-the-scenes activities of the clowns, aerialists, bareback riders, etc. Victor Mature plays the tough circus boss who has his hands full with his performers and their problems. (Dir: Joseph Neuman, 109 mins.)

Big City (1947)*½ Margaret O'Brien, Danny Thomas, Robert Preston. This film about an orphan who is jointly adopted by a Catholic, Protestant and Jew left its good intentions somewhere along the road and comes out talky, sentimental hokum. (Dir: Norman Taurog, 103 mins.)

Big Clock, The (1948)***½ Ray Milland, Charles Laughton. Contrived, but exciting, suspenseful drama about a man who follows a murderer's clues and finds they lead directly to him. Top mystery entertainment. (Dir: John Farrow, 75 mins.)

Big Combo, The (1955)**½ Cornel Wilde, Richard Conte, Jean Wallace. A good crime drama about policemen and their battle with the syndicate. A good cast manages to make the drama believable. (Dir: Joseph Lewis, 89 mins.)

Big Country, The (1958)*** Gregory Peck, Carroll Baker, Jean Simmons, Burl Ives, Charlton Heston. Producer-Director William Wyler believes in scope and spectacle, and he has embellished this above average story of cattle barons and their fight for control with panoramic photography and a big cast. All the stars fare well in their roles with Ives and Heston coming out on top. (Dir: William Wyler, 165 mins.)

Big Cube, The (Mexican-U.S., 1969)** Lana Turner, George Chakiris, Dan O'Herlihy. Uninspired melodrama confused by bad direction. A stepdaughter resents her stepmother and tries to do away with her by putting LSD in her nightly sedative. Ho-hum. (Dir: Tito Davison, 91 mins.)

Big Deal on Madonna Street, The (Italian, 1956)**** An incredibly funny film with Vittorio Gassman and a superb collection of Italian character actors including Toto and Renato Salvatori. A motley gang of bungling crooks make a mess of trying to rob a pawn shop. Delightful comedy about an intended crime was made as a takeoff on the superb French crime meller "Rififi," directed by Jules Dassin. Many ardent film buffs think this is among the funniest films made in the last twenty years and they're dead right. (Dir: Maria Monicelli, 91 mins.)

Big Frame, The (British, 1953)** Mark Stevens, Jean Kent. American pilot attends an RAF reunion, gets a mickey, wakes up to find he's a murder suspect. Routine whodunit. (67 mins.)

Big Gamble, The (1961)** Stephen

Boyd, Juliette Greco, David Wayne. An Irishman, his bride and a meek cousin seek their fortune on the Ivory Coast. Intended as an "African Queen" sort of comedy-adventure, this mishmash misses the mark. Pretty mild stuff from wild Africa. (Dir: Richard Fleischer, 100 mins.)

Big Gundown, The (Italian, 1967)** Gunman (Lee Van Cleef) chases after an elusive bandit (Tomas Milian), catches him, loses him, etc. etc. Western import mighty like the rest; only Van Cleef's steely presence is worthwhile.

Big Gusher, The (1951)** Preston Foster, Wayne Morris. Against all odds, two buddies strike it rich with black gold. Routine adventure pic. (Dir: Lew Landers, 68 mins.)

Big Hand for the Little Lady, A (1966)***½ Joanne Woodward, Henry Fonda, Jason Robards Jr. Clever, well-played yarn about a poker game which will keep you on the edge of your seat. Fonda and his wife arrive in Laredo during an annual big-stakes poker game, and before you can shuffle a deck, Fonda is in the game, losing his homestead money, and has a heart attack. Wife Joanne takes his hand and there's a surprise ending. Don't miss it. (Dir: Fielder Cook, 95 mins.)

Big Hangover, The (1950)**½ Elizabeth Taylor, Van Johnson. Generally wacky, sometimes funny, sometimes not so funny comedy about a young lawyer who has a peculiar drinking problem. Johnson tends to mug more than is necessary as the junior advocate and Miss Taylor relies on her handsome appearance rather than on comedic flair in her role of a rich girl studying psychiatry. (Dir: Norman Krasna, 82 mins.)

Big Heat, The (1953)***½ Glenn Ford, Gloria Grahame, Lee Marvin. Excellent police drama with top performances. Glenn Ford, as an ex-cop, cracks the underworld hold on a city with the help of a mobster's moll played by Gloria Grahame. Lee Marvin excels as a sadistic killer. (Dir: Fritz Lang, 90 mins.)

Big House, The (1930)*** Robert Montgomery, Chester Morris, Wallace Beery, Lewis Stone. Desperate convicts try prison break. This early example of prison melodrama is still

entertaining. (Dir: George Hill, 88 mins.)

Big House, USA (1955)*** Broderick Crawford, Ralph Meeker. The FBI is called in to track down a brutal kidnap gang. Strong, often too much so, but better than most crime melodramas. (Dir: Howard Koch, 82 mins.)

Big Jack (1949)**½ Wallace Beery, Marjorie Main, Richard Conte. Fast moving comedy-drama about a renegade bandit and his misadventures with a young doctor he saves from being hanged by an angry mob for stealing cadavers for his scientific experiments. Wallace Beery and Marjorie Main have marvelous scenes together. (Dir: Jack Thorpe, 85 mins.)

Big Jake (1971)**½ John Wayne, Richard Boone, Maureen O'Hara. Tall-in-the-saddle John Wayne rides to the rescue of his kidnapped grandson. The conniving Boone is holding the boy for $1 million, but the Duke will have none of it. The fight finale is fine. Wayne's trouble is he's given some very unfunny lines, in a western that tries to be a comedy. (Dir: George Sherman, 110 mins.)

Big Jim McLain (1952)** John Wayne, Nancy Olson, James Arness. Juvenile adventure story with Wayne playing his usual two-fisted character. The setting is Hawaii and Wayne, as a special agent, arrives on the scene to investigate a report about a ring of terrorists. (Dir: Edward Ludwig, 90 mins.)

Big Job, The (Great Britain, 1965)** Sidney James, Sylvia Syms. Bungling ex-cons try to retrieve the cached cash—hidden in a tree now situated in the front yard of a police station. Made by the "Carry On" folks, with their standard antics, though the usual coarse humor is somewhat subdued. (Dir: Gerald Thomas, 88 mins.)

Big Knife, The (1955)***½ Jack Palance, Ida Lupino, Wendell Corey. A Hollywood star tries to break with a grasping producer and causes tragedy. Indictment of Hollywood is perceptive, and it's uniformly well acted. (Dir: Robert Aldrich, 111 mins.)

Big Land, The (1957)**½ Alan Ladd, Virginia Mayo, Edmond O'Brien. Cattleman and wheat growers combine to have a railroad built near their land and thwart the high-handed buyers. Post-Civil War adventure doesn't blaze any new trails but is well enough done. (Dir: Gordon Douglas, 92 mins.)

Big Leaguer (1953)** Edward G. Robinson, Vera-Ellen, Jeff Richards. Routine baseball film centering on the bush leagues and the potential stars of the diamond. Both Edward G. Robinson and dancer Vera-Ellen seem very much out of place in this movie. (Dir: Robert Aldrich, 70 mins.)

Big Lift, The (1950)** Montgomery Clift, Paul Douglas. Factual story of the Berlin Airlift filmed on the spot, marred by an uneven romantic line. Excellent aerial photography. (Dir: George Seaton, 120 mins.)

Big Money (British, 1958)** Ian Carmichael, Belinda Lee. Offspring of a family of thieves tries his wings, filches a suitcase full of dough—but it's all counterfeit. Mild comedy.

Big Mouth, The (1967)** Jerry Lewis, Harold J. Stone, Susan Bay. The big mouth (Jerry) is after diamonds and the gangsters are after Jerry. Usual quota of slapstick farce and gags directed by Lewis, primarily of interest to French film critics and pre-teenagers.

Big Night, The (1951)*** John Barrymore, Jr., Preston Foster. A young kid goes looking for the man who mercilessly beat his father, intending to kill him. Moody, grim drama has a lot to recommend it; fine direction, performances, good atmosphere. (Dir: Joseph Losey, 75 mins.)

Big Night, The (1960)**½ Randy Sparks, Venetia Stevenson, Dick Foran. Young couple come upon money stolen in a holdup, hide it, become the targets for crooks. Above average melodrama made on a low budget.

Big Operator, The (1959)*½ Mickey Rooney, Steve Cochran, Mamie Van Doren. A crooked union boss terrorizes an upstanding worker who threatens to expose his racket; little Mickey is the tough crooked leader. Ridiculous? So's the film. Alternate title: **Anatomy of the Syndicate.** (Dir: Charles Haas, 91 mins.)

Big Parade of Comedy (1964)***½ Selected clips from silent and sound features compiled by Robert Youngson, ranging from Laurel & Hardy to Garbo and Gable. There's a lot of funny material in this nostalgic mix,

even though this combination of silent and talkie clips doesn't jell quite as well as other Youngson laughfests.

Big Red (1962)**½ Walter Pidgeon, Gilles Payant. Shades of "Lassie, Come Home," this is a Disney tale about a boy and his dog, well, not exactly his dog, but a dog. Walter Pidgeon owns Big Red and little Gilles Payant exercises him. Filmed against the vast backdrop of the Canadian wilderness in Quebec. Naturally, Big Red escapes while on his way to be sold, goes in search of the little boy he loves. O.K. fare for the kids. (Dir: Norman Tokar, 89 mins.)

Big Ripoff, The (1975)**½ Tony Curtis, Brenda Vaccaro, Larry Hagman, Roscoe Lee Browne. Curtis stars as a stylish con man hired by a millionaire to recover a huge ransom paid to kidnappers. It's calculated but fairly interesting. Supporting cast boasts such talents as Vaccaro as a newspaper reporter, Hagman as a high-priced lawyer, and Browne as a nightclub performer. Made-for-TV. (Dir: Dean Hargrove, 72 mins.)

Big Rose (1974)** Shelley Winters, Barry Primus. A TV pilot with Miss Winters and Primus teaming up as a pair of detectives, hired by a wealthy contractor (Michael Constantine) to find out who is out to do him in. Constantine is very good in his role, but the Winters-Primus pairing doesn't really get off the ground. Made-for-TV. (Dir: Paul Krasny)

Big Shot, The (1942)**½ Humphrey Bogart, Irene Manning. Bogart is fine in the title role but the cut and dried gangster picture plot leaves much to be desired. (Dir: Lewis Seiler, 82 mins.)

Big Show, The (1961)** Esther Williams, Cliff Robertson, Nehemiah Persoff, Robert Vaughn. Son takes the rap for domineering circus father's negligence, returns from prison to find forces working against him. Hashed-up circus drama remade from "House of Strangers" and "Broken Lance," and is not an improvement on either. (Dir: James Clark, 113 mins.)

Big Sky (1952)*** Kirk Douglas, Dewey Martin. Adventures of a keelboat expedition to establish a new trading post in 1830. Lengthy, rather tame frontier melodrama. Well acted. (Dir: Howard Hawks, 122 mins.)

Big Sleep, The (1946)*** Humphrey Bogart, Lauren Bacall. Raymond Chandler detective story emerges as a confused drama, but keeps its head above water thanks to good performances and racy dialogue. Bogey and Baby had already been united in matrimony when this was made. (Dir: Howard Hawks, 114 mins.)

Big Store, The (1940)*** Marx Brothers, Tony Martin. They're store detectives in this one and their legion of fans will have a picnic watching it. (Dir: Charles Reisner, 80 mins.)

Big Street (1942)**½ Henry Fonda, Lucille Ball. Busboy falls for a crippled nitery singer, becomes her servant. Maudlin Damon Runyon drama; some good moments. (Dir: Irving Reis, 88 mins.)

Big Tip Off (1955)** Richard Conte, Constance Smith. Newsman exposes a charity fund racket. Slow-moving crime melodrama. (70 mins.)

Big Trees, The (1952)** Kirk Douglas, Patrice Wymore. Kirk Douglas matches his strength against the "Big Trees" in this dull logging epic. Patrice Wymore adds a touch of glamour to the proceedings. (Dir: Felix Feist, 89 mins.)

Big Wave, The (1961)**½ Sessue Hayakawa, Mickey Curtis. Pearl Buck's story of a Japanese fishing village hit by a tidal wave, and of a lad's growing up. Spoken in English, filmed in Japan, this has an unusual background, in addition to a slow moving plot. Well acted. (Dir: Tad Danielowski, 60 mins.)

Big Wheel, The (1949)**½ Mickey Rooney, Thomas Mitchell. Hot-shot auto racer becomes inflicted with an enlarged cranium, nearly causes tragedy before righting himself. Usual plot, excellent Indianapolis racing scenes. (Dir: Edward Ludwig, 92 mins.)

Bigamist, The (1953)*** Edmond O'Brien, Joan Fontaine, Ida Lupino. Businessman married to a career woman is discovered to have another wife in another city. Good production values and performances carry this drama along nicely. (Dir: Ida Lupino, 80 mins.)

Bigfoot, The Mysterious Monsters (1975)* Clumsy compilation of so-called eyewitness reports about legendary creatures such as the Loch Ness Monster, the Abominable Snowman, the Kyoto Lizard, and various Bigfoot monsters. Peter Graves is the host-narrator. (Dir: Robert Guenette, 76 mins.)

Bigger Than Life (1956)***½ James Mason, Barbara Rush, Walter Matthau. A frightening tale about a man who is given a new wonder drug (cortisone) to relieve the pain of an arteries condition and becomes a veritable madman when he starts taking overdoses. James Mason is superb as the school teacher turned tyrant in his home. Barbara Rush as his frightened wife and Walter Matthau as his friend give Mason solid support. (Dir: Nicholas Ray, 95 mins.)

Biggest Bundle of Them All, The (U.S.-Italian, 1967)** Robert Wagner, Raquel Welch, Edward G. Robinson. A gangster film which is supposed to be funny but isn't. A group of bumbling kidnappers abduct an exiled American hood living in Italy. The elegant gangster comes up with a plan to rob a $5 million platinum reserve. (Dir: Ken Annakin, 110 mins.)

Bikini Beach (1964)**½ Frankie Avalon, Annette Funicello, Martha Hyer. The familiar beach-movie cast in another romp. For good measure some drag strip racing is thrown in. Usual quota of songs and bikinis. (Dir: William Aster, 100 mins.)

Bill of Divorcement, A (1932)***½ John Barrymore, Katharine Hepburn. A father who has been in a mental institution returns to his home and his daughter, who feels a strong bond for him. Superlatively acted drama. (Dir: George Cukor, 76 mins.)

Billie (1965)** Patty Duke, Jim Backus, Warren Berlinger. Fans who enjoyed Patty Duke's TV series will accept her in this family comedy about a young miss who's a wizard in all athletic endeavors. Her prowess on the track field makes her unpopular with the boys, her dad and a variety of other stereotyped small-town types. If you didn't see Patty's TV series . . . (Dir: Don Weis, 87 mins.)

Billion Dollar Brain (British, 1967)** Michael Caine, Karl Malden, Ed Begley. The third of the films featuring Caine as sleuth Harry Palmer, and not as good as the first two. This time out it's secret agent Palmer crossing and doublecrossing the enemy in Finland. With Francoise Dorleac and Oscar Homolka. (Dir: Diken Russell, 111 mins.)

Billy Budd (1962)***½ Peter Ustinov, Robert Ryan, Terence Stamp. Well-produced film based on Herman Melville's classic allegorical tale of treachery in the 18th century British navy. The cast is uniformly first rate, with Ustinov as the weak captain taking a slight edge. The photography keeps interest throughout in this stimulating film which versatile Ustinov directed and adapted from the Broadway play. (Dir: Peter Ustinov, 112 mins.)

Billy Jack (1971)***½ Tom Laughlin, Delores Taylor, Clark Howat, Bert Freed. Interesting drama about youth vs. the establishment had a unique distribution history. When first released in 1971 it got lackluster reviews but was developing a growing audience response. Rereleased in 1973 it became a huge grosser, mostly among the young, and it's not hard to see why. Laughlin stars as Billy Jack, a loner, an idealistic young Indian who is committed to aiding a "freedom school" after the young students are harassed by small-town western bigots. Laughlin's real-life wife Delores Taylor is genuinely appealing in the role of the school head. Laughlin himself directed, using the pseudonym T. C. Frank, the same pseudonym he used when he directed "Born Losers" in '67. Filmed on location in Arizona and New Mexico. Some of it is fairly simplistic, but it's involving anyway. Also written and produced by Mr. and Mrs. Laughlin. (Dir: T. C. Frank, 112 mins.)

Billy Jack Goes to Washington (1977)** Tom Laughlin, Delores Taylor, Sam Wanamaker, Lucie Arnaz. Clumsy remake of Frank Capra's 1939 classic, "Mr. Smith Goes to Washington." (Just to keep it all in the family, this entry was produced by Frank Capra, Jr.) Some of the updating seems simple-minded indeed, thanks to the screenplay written by Laughlin and his wife using pseudonyms. Billy Jack is fighting political corruption, but it's all too vacuous and is overlong. (Dir: Tom Laughlin, 155 mins.)

Billy Liar (British, 1963)***½ Tom Courtenay, Julie Christie. Generally delightful story of a young clerk who takes refuge in daydreams as a relief from his dreary life, and of the free-roving girl he meets who encourages him to go to London and seek a career. Adept direction blends the fantasies with realities of everyday existence expertly, performances are excellent. Miss Christie in a supporting role is a radiant delight. (Dir: John Schlesinger, 96 mins.)

Billy Rose's Diamond Horseshoe (1945)*** Betty Grable, Phil Silvers, Dick Haymes. An abundance of the Grable gams, good clowning by Phil, tongue-in-cheek writing and a fair production almost compensate for a mediocre score and a backstage plot built around Rose's once popular club. (Dir: George Seaton, 104 mins.)

Billy Rose's Jumbo (1962)**½ Doris Day, Stephen Boyd, Jimmy Durante, Martha Raye. Elaborate musical about a circus and the efforts of its owners to save it, but the elaborateness doesn't necessarily mean top quality. Rodgers & Hart songs are the best thing about it—the rest is rather empty in a glittering sort of way. (Dir: Charles Walters, 125 mins.)

Billy the Kid (1940)**½ Robert Taylor, Brian Donlevy. Good western adventure based on the life of the famous outlaw. Picture's main asset is its technicolor backgrounds. (Dir: David Miller, 95 mins.)

Billy the Kid Vs. Dracula (1966)* Chuck Courtney, John Carradine, Melinda Plowman. Outlandish combo of western and horror thriller as the gunslinger wants to reform and settle down, only to find his gal's uncle is old vampire Drac himself. Spare us! (Dir: Harold Philipp, 96 mins.)

Bimbo the Great (1960)** A foreign film about the circus, sentimental and corny at times. English dubbed. (Dir: Harold Philipp, 96 mins.)

Bingo Long Traveling All-Stars and Motor Kings (1976)*** Billy Dee Williams, James Earl Jones, Richard Pryor. High-spirited, charming tale of a barnstorming black baseball team of 1939, who have abandoned the Negro National League in favor of lighting out on their own, playing white teams in the midwest and South. The team must not only play well but clown and cakewalk to attract fans. So Bingo pitches in a gorilla suit, and the team parades as if they were in the circus. Standout comic performance is Pryor's ballplayer who impersonates a Cuban, and then an American Indian, to break into the big leagues. Good blend of show business and the struggle for survival. (Dir: John Badham, 111 mins.)

Bird of Paradise (1951)** Debra Paget, Louis Jourdan, Jeff Chandler. South Sea island yarn about a superstitious tribe of natives who have big sacrificial rituals and offer a virgin to an angry volcano. Reminiscent of the early Dorothy Lamour epics, but minus the music and happy ending. (Dir: Delmer Daves, 100 mins.)

Bird with the Crystal Plumage, The (1970)**½ Tony Musante, Suzy Kendall. Forget the title and enjoy this slick murder mystery story shot in Italy. Musante witnesses a near-murder and becomes obsessed in his amateur sleuthing as a series of gorgeous young ladies are killed. (Dir: Dario Argento, 98 mins.)

Birdman of Alcatraz (1962)**** Burt Lancaster, Karl Malden, Thelma Ritter, Betty Field, Neville Brand. Gripping true story of convict Robert Stroud, who became an expert on birdlife while serving time for murder. Complex personality is explored fascinatingly under John Frankenheimer's direction, and Lancaster is excellent in the role. Superior adult drama. (Dir: John Frankenheimer, 147 mins.)

Birds, The (1963)**½ Tippi Hedren, Rod Taylor, Suzanne Pleshette. Alfred Hitchcock thriller about the bird-world turning on humans, creating death and terror. Some fine trick camerawork, but the suspense master fizzles out in the obscure plotting, unsympathetic characters —both human and birdlike—so it's all largely a matter of how fond one is of the Hitchcock touch. (Dir: Alfred Hitchcock, 120 mins.)

Birds and the Bees, The (1956)** George Gobel, Mitzi Gaynor, David Niven. Millionaire innocent is snared by a lady card sharp, finds out all, calls off the romance, but she gets him anyway. Mild remake of "The Lady Eve" doesn't do right by Gobel, or the birds and bees for that matter. (Dir: Norman Taurog, 94 mins.)

Birds, Bees and the Italians, The (Italy-France, 1966)***½ Virna Lisi, Gastone Moschin, Nora Ricci. Extremely humorous sex farce involving a local café set, and a lot of mate-swapping. Based on original story co-authored by director Pietro Germi, who gave us earlier "Divorce —Italian Style." (Dir: Pietro Germi, 115 mins.)

Birds Do It (1966)** Soupy Sales, Tab Hunter, Arthur O'Connell. A Cape Kennedy janitor enters an off-limits room and finds after coming out that he is irresistible to women and that he can fly. Soupy's feature debut and he gets some laughs but it all peters out. (Dir: Andrew Marton, 95 mins.)

Birds in Peru (French, 1968)* The problems, rather restricted, of an oh-so-unhappy nymphomaniac, played with glacial inexpressiveness by Jean Seberg and onanistically directed by her husband, writer Romain Gary. Cinematic balderdash masquerading as Art. Maurice Ronet, Pierre Brasseur and Danielle Darrieux are unfortunately involved.

Birds of Prey (1973)** David Janssen stars as an airwatch pilot who chases bank robbers. Unusual aerial footage has Janssen's chopper flying at rooftop level, and then engaging in a wild aerial chase when the bad guys use a big copter as their getaway vehicle. Made-for-TV. (Dir: William Graham.)

Birth of the Blues (1941)***½ Bing Crosby, Mary Martin. Minor little story of a trumpet player who supposedly organized the first Dixieland jazz band is trimmed with pleasant dialogue, a delightful score and good performances. (Dir: Victor Schertzinger, 85 mins.)

Birthday Party, The (1968)**** Robert Shaw, Dandy Nichols. Visually uninteresting but stimulating, well acted version of Harold Pinter's enigmatic play. Brought to the screen with all its allegorical complexities intact, with gratifying results. About a boarder in a British seaside dwelling who is taken away by two strangers, who've come to give him a birthday party, demands your undivided attention in order to absorb Pinter's many moods, subtleties and inferences. (Dir: William Friedkin, 127 mins.)

Birthday Present (British, 1957)*** Tony Britton, Sylvia Syms. Salesman tries to smuggle a German watch through customs, suffers the consequences when caught. Well-made drama holds the attention.

Biscuit Eater, The (1972)** Johnny Whitaker, Lew Ayres, Godfrey Cambridge. Formula family film from Disney. Another story about a boy and his dog. In post-World War II Tennessee two youngsters (one black and one white) try to train a mutt into a champion bird dog. Honesty, friendship, and fair play predictably conquer all. (Dir: Vincent McEveety, 90 mins.)

Bishop's Wife, The (1947)*** Cary Grant, Loretta Young, David Niven, Monty Woolley. Amusing comedy fantasy which has Grant cast as an angel who comes to earth to aid in the lives of some pleasant people including Monty Woolley, who steals each scene he's in. Family fare. (Dir: Henry Koster, 108 mins.)

Bite the Bullet (1975)*** Gene Hackman, James Coburn, Candice Bergen. Written, directed and produced by Richard Brooks, "Bullet" is, in many ways, reminiscent of Brooks' superb "The Professionals," his 1966 triumph. This is an unconventional, entertaining western about the cruel endurance horseraces that were customary in the West between 1880 and 1910. This 1906 race is sponsored by a big newspaper and offers a $2,000 prize. Hackman, a cowboy who cares for animals, is angered by the whole spectacle. He meets his old Army pal Coburn, now a gambler and drifter. Bergen is a "bad" girl who needs the prize money. Coburn and Hackman are marvelous and there's a happy, believable ending. (Dir: Richard Brooks, 131 mins.)

Bitter Creek (1956)*½ Wild Bill Elliot, Carlton Young. Strictly for "Wild" Bill Elliot fans! A grade "B" western that doesn't aspire to be anything else. All the expected shoot-outs, bar-room brawls and the inevitable ride into the sunset. (Dir: Thomas Carr, 74 mins.)

Bitter Harvest (British, 1963)** Janet Munro, John Stride, Alan Badel. Moth-eaten plot about the village girl who goes to the big city and is soon caught in a web of vice and corruption. Fine performance by Miss Munro, but the drama was old in grandma's day.

Bitter Reunion (French, 1959)*** Gerard Blain, Jean-Claude Brialy.

France's new-wave director Claude Chabrol etches a fine drama about a reunion of two childhood friends after ten years of separation. Excellent performances by Gerard Blain and Jean-Claude Brialy, stars of "The Cousins."

Bitter Rice (1950)*** Silvana Mangano. Italian film, with English dialogue very poorly dubbed in, about workers in the rice fields who toil for grain. Better in Italian but still earthy, shocking drama. Adults only. (Dir: Giuseppe De Santis, 107 mins.)

Bitter Springs (Australian, 1950)***½ Tommy Trinder, Chips Rafferty. Pioneer attempts to settle the Australian wilderness, meets with opposition from the natives. Different, exciting historical melodrama, with fine photography, thrilling scenes.

Bitter Tears of Petra von Kant, The (West Germany, 1972)**½ Margit Carstensen, Hanna Schygulla. A morose, elegant film about unrequited love between two lesbians. The protagonist is a top fashion designer who brutalizes her worker-slave, Marlene, and talks of why her two marriages failed. Overlong, occasionally interesting from the prolific young director. Written and directed by Rainer Werner Fassbinder. (124 mins.)

Bitter Victory (1958)**½ Richard Burton, Curt Jurgens, Ruth Roman. An interesting personal drama played out against a background of the African campaign during WW II. Jurgens is quite effective as a commander who fears he is losing his nerve and Burton, in the less colorful role of a young captain under Jurgens' command, adds to the drama. (Dir: Nicholas Ray, 83 mins.)

Bittersweet (1940)**½ Jeanette MacDonald, Nelson Eddy. This is a rather flimsy version of the Noel Coward original. Score is not too distinguished and Jeanette and Nelson starving in Vienna are not too exciting either.

Black Arrow, The (1948)*** Louis Hayward, Janet Blair. Above average swashbuckler which should keep the kids glued to the set. Adventure tale is set around England's famous Wars of the Roses.

Black Bird, The (1975)**½ George Segal, Stephane Audran, Lionel Stander, Signe Hasso, Elisha Cook,

A very uneven but occasionally funny updated parody of John Huston's 1941 classic private-eye film "The Maltese Falcon." Some of the jokes are very "inside" and will only mean anything to trivia buffs who know the Dashiell Hammett novel and the Huston film in their sleep. (E.g., do you know who Floyd Thursby is?) Segal plays Sam Spade Jr. and serves as his own producer, while the writing and directing chores are handled, with varying degrees of skill, by David Giler. Sam Spade is still a grumpy, second-rate detective. Film-trivia buffs please note that Elisha Cook Jr., the professional perspirer of the '41 film, is back playing the same role. He has added a few years and lost the Jr. Lee Patrick again plays Spade's secretary. (Dir: David Giler, 98 mins.)

Black Book, The (1949)*** Robert Cummings, Arlene Dahl. Both forces during the French Revolution are after possession of a secret diary containing vital information. Lively, exciting costume adventure; good cast, crammed full of action.

Black Castle, The (1953)** Richard Greene, Boris Karloff, Stephen McNally. Another moderately chilling horror tale about sinister castles, unscrupulous counts, and strange happenings. Boris Karloff is not the heavy this time out. (81 mins.)

Black Cat, The (1934)** Boris Karloff, Bela Lugosi. In this one, Lugosi is on the side of law and order, Karloff is a practitioner of black rites. Some of the nonsense is palatable, but the film is designed mainly for all-out horror fans. (Dir: Edgar G. Ulmer, 70 mins.)

Black Cat, The (1941) **½ Broderick Crawford, Hugh Herbert, Basil Rathbone. A real estate promoter and a goofy antique collector intrude upon the reading of a will in a gloomy old mansion, with murder following. Pretty neat mixture of comedy and shudders; some creepy scenes. Alan Ladd has a small role. (Dir: Albert Rogell, 70 mins.)

Black Chapel (French, 1962)** Peter Van Eyck, Dawn Addams. A journalist is given a document—containing proof of anti-Hitler German generals' wish for peace—to deliver to an agent in Rome, but finds the agent murdered. Fair suspense melodrama dubbed in English; the edge

is taken off because the end is already known, thanks to history.

Black Cobra, The (German, 1961)*½ Adrian Hoven, Ann Smyrner. Mysterious criminal remains at large until sleuth gets on the case. No mystery about this being a bore.

Black Dakotas, The (1954)** Gary Merrill, Wanda Hendrix. The peace that exists with the Sioux Nation is endangered by a couple of ruthless hi-jackers. Plenty of shooting and riding for action fans. (Dir: Ray Nazarro, 81 mins.)

Black Devils of Kali (1955)* Lex Barker, Jane Maxwell. Hunter in India attempts to rescue a girl from a group of murdering fanatics. Poorly made action melodrama.

Black Dragon of Manzanar (1942-66) **½ Rod Cameron, Constance Worth. Feature version of serial "G-Men vs. the Black Dragon." G-Man extraordinary goes after a ring of Black Dragon agents bent on destroying America's war effort. Wild and woolly action opus, enjoyable if not taken seriously. (Dir: William Witney, 100 mins.)

Black Duke, The (Italian, 1961)*½ Cameron Mitchell, Gloria Milland. One of the Borgias falls for a gal who was out to assassinate him, overcomes a conspiracy against him. Limp costume drama dubbed in English.

Black Flowers for the Bride—See: Something for Everyone

Black Fox, The (1963)*** Unusually interesting documentary of Hitler and his rise to power, paralleled by the Goethe fable of Reynard the fox, symbol of political ruthlessness. Different approach to the by-now familiar horror saga of WWII; good narration by Marlene Dietrich. (Dir: Louis Clyde Stoumen, 89 mins.)

Black Fury (1935)***½ Paul Muni, William Gargan, Akim Tamiroff. Paul Muni is great in this drama of life in the coal mines which may appear dated today but should serve as a reminder of how our workers have progressed in the last 40 years. (Dir: Michael Curtiz, 100 mins.)

Black Girl (Senegalese-French, 1969) ***½ Mbissine Therese Diop, Anne-Marie Jelinck. A remarkable and moving first directorial effort by the talented young African novelist Ousmane Sembene, who also wrote the screenplay based on his book. Story concerns a young black girl from Dakar, hired to be a maid for a French family living in France. Filmed in both Africa and France this perceptive drama might be called an African "400 Blows," as it chronicles the unhappy life of an unsophisticated, lonely girl trying to cope with an alien culture. Dubbed. (Dir: Ossie Davis, 97 mins.)

Black Glove, The (British, 1954)**½ Alex Nicol, Eleanor Summerfield. An American musician in London becomes involved in the murder of a singer. Fair mystery ; good jazz music background. (84 mins.)

Black Gold (1947)*** Anthony Quinn, Katherine De Mille. An Indian gives permission to drill for oil on his property to obtain money enough to raise horses. Excellent performances turn this into an interesting drama.

Black Gold (1963)** Philip Carey, Diane McBain, James Best, Fay Spain. Thoroughly routine melodrama of an adventurer betting all on a big oil strike, his troubles in hitting paydirt. Nothing wrong with it except that it's so familiar. (Dir: Leslie Martinson, 98 mins.)

Black Hand (1950)**½ Gene Kelly, J. Carrol Naish, Teresa Celli. Moderately interesting drama about the activities in the Italian neighborhoods in N. Y. of the Mafia or Black Hand as it was known at the turn of the century. Kelly is not cast to advantage as a young man bent on revenge for his "Papa's" death. (Dir: Richard Thorpe, 93 mins.)

Black Holiday (Italian, 1973)**** Adalberto Maria Merli, Adolfo Celi, John Steiner, Milena Vukotic. A penetrating, chilling film about Fascism or, in the words of the director "about the white shirt variety of fascism, that courteous, moderate, polite fascism that has survived much longer than black-shirt Fascism. It is the story of a moral holiday during which, then as now, there are enough alibis to convince one to give up the struggle. There are no political choices which are not at the same time moral choices." About a college professor during the early years of Mussolini's dictatorship who refused to cooperate with the Fascists and was sent to a detention center on a small island in the Mediterranean. Superb understated performance from Merli as the idealistic professor. Directed by Marco Leto who also contributed to the screenplay based

on a story idea of his. English subtitles. (110 mins.)

Black Horse Canyon (1954)**½ Joel McCrea, Mari Blanchard. Interesting western yarn about a group of people who try to recapture a wild stallion who has taken to the hills. Joel McCrea's easy style sets the pace for the film. (Dir: Jesse Hibbs, 81 mins.)

Black Ice (British, 1957)** Paul Carpenter, Kim Parker. Submarine rushed to save sinking trawler. Routine melodrama.

Black Invaders, The (Italian, 1960)* Daniele de Metz. Officer becomes a masked pirate to avenge a massacre of settlers. Hey, officer, ever think about the Italian producers of this nonsense?

Black Jack Ketchum, Desperado (1956)** Victor Jory, Howard Duff. Moderately entertaining western about a one time gunslinger's efforts to restore peace in Oxhorn.

Black Knight, The (1954)** Alan Ladd, Patricia Medina. Fast but disappointing tale of knighthood in the days of King Arthur. Alan Ladd plays the Black Knight as if he were still on the Texas range. (Dir: Tay Garnett, 90 mins.)

Black Lancers, The (Italian, 1961)** Mel Ferrer, Yvonne Furneaux. Wicked queen will stop at nothing to keep a kingdom under her control. English-dubbed costume adventure is helped by better than usual performances for this sort of thing.

Black Legion (1936)**½ Humphrey Bogart, Ann Sheridan, Dick Foran, Erin O'Brien Moore. Honest worker is duped into joining a terrorist Ku Klux Klan-type organization. Fair melodrama, based on fact. (Dir: Archie Mayo, 83 mins.)

Black Like Me (1964)**½ James Whitmore, Clifton James, Roscoe Lee Browne. Based on fact, the story of a writer who poses as a Negro by chemically changing the color of his skin, the injustices he meets in the South. Sincere attempt but rambling, ineffective too much of the time. (Dir: Carl Lerner, 107 mins.)

Black Magic (1949)** Orson Welles, Nancy Guild. The evil plans of Cagliostro the magician are thwarted when he seeks to take over an empire. Heavy, hammily acted costume melodrama. Produced in Italy. (Dir: Gregory Ratoff, 105 mins.)

Black Monocle, The (French, 1961)

*½ Paul Meurisse, Elga Anderson. Suave agent goes after a neo-Nazi organization. Far-fetched melodrama dubbed in English.

Black Moon (France-West Germany, 1975)**½ Cathryn Harrison, Therese Giese, Alexandra Stewart, Joe Dallesandro. Challenging, uneven, sometimes pretentious and then dazzling —Louis Malle's surrealistic dream film with Alice in Wonderland-like characters. Young girl flees from a civil war in which the men are battling the women. Bizarre, self-indulgent, difficult. Directed by Louis Malle, who co-authored the screenplay with Ghislain Uhry and Joyce Bunuel. Wonderful photography by Sven Nykvist, Ingmar Bergman's longtime cinematographer. (Dir: Louis Malle, 92 mins.)

Black Narcissus (British, 1947)***½ Deborah Kerr, David Farrar, Jean Simmons. A group of nuns doing missionary work in the Himalayas find worldly temptations a difficult handicap to surmount. Unusual, beautifully made drama. Deborah Kerr is particularly striking. (Dir: Michael Powell, 99 mins.)

Black Orchid, The (1959)**½ Sophia Loren, Anthony Quinn, Ina Balin. Gangster's widow tries to overcome barriers when she falls in love again. Weepy drama has good performances, especially by Quinn, to help it over the slippery soap-spots. (Dir: Martin Ritt, 95 mins.)

Black Orpheus (1959)**** Breno Mello, Marpessa Dawn. Excellent Portuguese language film based on the Orpheus-Eurydice legend. Updated and played against the colorful background of carnival time in Brazil, complete with dancing, love-making, and black witchcraft. The two leads are very attractive and handle their roles as the star-crossed lovers effectively. A hauntingly beautiful score is also an asset. (Dir: Marcel Camus, 98 mins.)

Black Panther of Ratana (German, 1962)* Brad Harris, Marianne Cook, Heinz Drache. Undercover man searches for robbers of a precious ruby, runs into plenty of murder and intrigue in Thailand. Laughably inept thriller; even youngsters won't take it seriously. Dubbed in English.

Black Patch (1957)** George Montgomery, Diane Brewster. Horses and wholesome folk have their problems in this adventure yarn. The young-

sters might enjoy this more than their parents. (Dir: Allen Miner, 83 mins.)

Black Peter (Czech, 1964)***½ Ladislav Jakim, Pavla Martinkova. Charming story of a virginal Czech teen-ager who isn't making much headway with his girl friend or his new job of store detective in a supermarket. Directed and coauthored by Milos Forman, who went on to direct the even better "Loves of a Blonde" and "The Fireman's Ball." Forman has a keen eye for the hesitancies and insecurity of adolescents, and there's a lovely scene when the young man, Peter, goes to a local dance. Black and white. (Dir: Milos Forman, 85 mins.)

Black Pit of Dr. M (Mexican, 1959) * Gaston Santos, Mapita Cortes. The spirit of an insane scientist returns from the dead to enter another's body, seeking vengeance. Poor horror thriller, dubbed in English.

Black Rodeo (1972)**½ Muhammad Ali, Woody Strode. Documentary of black rodeo held in New York. Simplistic, but made relevant by commentary concerning the role of the black in winning the West. Ali and Strode clown with the participants, with an excellent soundtrack of black music in the background. (Dir: Jeff Kanew, 87 mins.)

Black Roots (1970)*** Rev. Frederick Douglass Kirkpatrick, Rev. Gary Davis, Florynce Kennedy. This is not an early version of the historic 8-part 1977 TV drama, "Roots." But it is a generally interesting, straight-forward documentary about the black experience in America. Mostly interviews with different black spokesmen, some of it is very moving indeed and aided by some wonderful music. (Dir: Lionel Rogosin, 60 mins.)

Black Rose, The (1950)**½ Tyrone Power, Orson Welles, Cecile Aubrey. Ornate but a slow-moving adventure costume drama with Power once more the hero who must triumph over the evil rulers. Familiar? French actress Cecile Aubrey (Manon) made her American debut in this one but returned to France when she failed to excite the American moviegoers. (Dir: Henry Hathaway, 120 mins.)

Black Sabbath (Italian, 1964)*** Boris Karloff, Mark Damon, Susy Andersen. Boris acts as m.c. and performs in the third of a trio of terror tales. His one, "The Wurdalak," is shuddery; the others, "A Drop of Water" and "The Telephone," are similarly above average for horror fans. English dialogue. (Dir: Mario Bava, 99 mins.)

Black Scorpion (1957)* Richard Denning, Mara Corday. This time it's giant scorpions who have come to destroy the world. The acting, writing and direction do destroy the film. (Dir: Edward Ludwig, 88 mins.)

Black Shield of Falworth, The (1954)**½ Tony Curtis, Janet Leigh. Tony Curtis fans might get a kick out of this swashbuckling adventure set in medieval times. Janet Leigh wears a series of lovely costumes and spends most of her time waiting for Curtis to finish off his assailants in drafty castle halls. (Dir: Rudolph Mate, 99 mins.)

Black Star (Italian, 1966)* Robert Woods, Elga Anderson. A beautiful girl and her father are aided by a western Robin Hood when they are threatened with murder charges. Mundane, badly dubbed. (93 mins.)

Black Sun (French, 1967)** Michele Mercier, Daniel Gelin. Rich girl pursues her brother, who has been condemned to death for cooperating with the Nazis. She never finds him, but she does get a husband. (90 mins.)

Black Sunday (Italian, 1961)** Barbara Steele, John Richardson, Andrea Checchi. Witch returns from her grave to seek revenge after being burned at the stake. Atmospheric horror thriller, better than the usual run. Good photography, assortment of chills. Dubbed in English. (Dir: Mario Bava, 83 mins.)

Black Sunday (1977)***½ Robert Shaw, Bruce Dern, Martha Keller, Fritz Weaver. The best of the plethora of lavishly produced crisis-caper melodramas. Members of the Arab guerrilla terrorist organization Black September plan to intimidate America by blowing up the championship Super Bowl football game while the President is in attendance. Builds to an exciting climax over Miami's Orange Bowl, via the final save-the-citizens shootout between some F.B.I.-manned police helicopters who've stolen the fantastic Goodyear blimp following a murderous shooting spree. Based on the best-selling suspense novel by Thomas Harris. Director Frankenheimer does a Hitchcock bit by appearing momentarily as the CBS-TV director in the control room adjoining the stadium. (Dir: John Frankenheimer, 145 mins.)

Black Swan, The (1942)*** Tyrone Power, Maureen O'Hara, George Sanders. Swashbuckling pirate tale adapted from Sabatini's novel. Great for the kids and plenty for adventure minded adults. (Dir: Henry King, 85 mins.)

Black Thirteen (1954)** Peter Reynolds, Rona Anderson. A fugitive on the run—this time he's the son of a college professor who has gotten involved with some petty thieves. Nothing original, but well paced. (75 mins.)

Black Tide (British, 1956)*½ John Ireland, Joy Webster. Who killed the channel swimmer? Sleuth investigates, almost becomes a victim himself. Mediocre mystery.

Black Torment, The (British, 1964)**½ Heather Sears, John Turner, Ann Lynn. Nobleman returns with his second wife to his estate to find ghostly goings-on and accusations of witchcraft against him. Spooky costume thriller whips up its share of suspense.

Black Tuesday (1955)*** Edward G. Robinson. Condemned killer masterminds his escape from the death house. Good gangster film, plenty of tension. (80 mins.)

Black Veil for Lisa, A (Italy-West Germany, 1968)** John Mills, Luciana Paluzzi, Robert Hoffman. Slim thriller has Mills playing a narcotics agent who spends more time tailing his flirtatious wife than a gang of suspected drug smugglers. Hamburg locations add vitality. (Dir: Massimo Dallamano, 88 mins.)

Black Water Gold (1970)** Keir Dullea, Ricardo Montalban, Bradford Dillman. This made-for-TV feature is actually an unsold pilot film for an underwater adventure series. The only thing to recommend is the beautiful Bahama locations—the story is a mish-mash about sunken treasure, etc. The acting is waterlogged, too! (Dir: Alan Landsburg, 75 mins.)

Black Widow (1954)**½ Van Heflin, Ginger Rogers, Gene Tierney, Peggy Ann Garner. An interesting whodunit with many plot gimmicks plus an attractive cast of professionals make this a good bet for murder mystery fans. Peggy Ann Garner plays an ambitious girl who comes to the big city to cash in on her dreams of position and wealth and ends up being murdered. Through a series of flashbacks, the pieces are fitted into the puzzling murder case by detective George Raft. (Dir: Nunnally Johnson, 94 mins.)

Black Windmill, The (1974)** Michael Caine, Janet Suzman, Donald Pleasence, Delphine Seyrig. Espionage potboiler starts out slickly, but loses steam midway. Michael Caine is a British agent whose son is kidnapped as part of a bigger plan to discredit him. The rest of the cast do what they can, but they too seem bored before long. A bright spot is Clive Revill's caustic Scotland Yard inspector. Based on the novel "Seven Days to a Killing." (Dir: Don Siegel, 106 mins.)

Black Zoo (1963)** Michael Gough, Jeanne Cooper, Virginia Grey. Proprietor of a private zoo turns murderer when anyone stands in his way. Horror thriller is average.

Blackbeard, The Pirate (1952)**½ Robert Newton, Maureen O'Hara, William Bendix. The notorious pirate with a price on his head holds a girl captive as he seeks a fortune. Overdone pirate melodrama, but some good moments. (Dir: Raoul Walsh, 99 mins.)

Blackboard Jungle (1955)**** Glenn Ford, Anne Francis, Richard Kiley, Sidney Poitier, Vic Morrow, Margaret Hayes. Based on Evan Hunter's best selling novel about the terror a young teacher encounters in his job in a New York vocational school. Excellent script and direction by Richard Brooks. Acting honors are shared by Ford as the teacher, Poitier as a problem pupil who shows some signs of sensitivity and Vic Morrow as a knife-wielding delinquent. One of the more honest American films. (Dir: Richard Brooks, 101 mins.)

Blackmail (Great Britain, 1929)***½ Sara Allgood, Anny Ondra, Cyril Ritchard. A Scotland Yard-London detective story that is Alfred Hitchcock's first sound film, and marks the brilliant young Hitchcock as a major talent based on this one film alone. Many of the techniques used and refined by Hitch in later films are glimpsed in this early, critically acclaimed black and white entry.

Based on a play by Charles Bennett. (Dir: Alfred Hitchcock, 78 mins.)

Blackmailers, The (Spanish, 1960) *½ Manuel Benitez, Alberto de Mendoza. Matador becomes involved with criminals, pays the penalty. English-dubbed trivia.

Blackout (British, 1954)** Dane Clark, Belinda Lee. A man awakens from a drunk with blood on his clothes, finds he may have committed murder. So-so melodrama. (Dir: Terence Fisher, 87 mins.)

Blackwell Story, The (1957)***½ Joanne Dru, Dan O'Herlihy. Story of the early career of Elizabeth Blackwell, the first woman in America to be accepted into medical school in 1856 and finally become a doctor. Depicts an intelligent, committed woman. Accurate portrayal of the prejudice and obstacles male-oriented-and-dominated society of the time imposed on women who tried to break the professional sex barrier. One of the first American films to have a heroine defined by her professional competence rather than her role as a romantic object. (74 mins.)

Blacula (1972)**½ William Marshall, Vonetta McGee, Emily Yancy, Thalmus Rasalala. This film has a certain style to it if you like horror films. It tells the story of an African prince who is turned into a vampire by the original Count Dracula. Two hundred years later he turns up in Los Angeles. At first he rampages freely among the unsuspecting populace. Naturally he must meet the end of all vampires, and be vanquished eventually by the forces of good! Quite a lot of blood is spilled along the way, along with a few campy laughs. William Marshall is scary as the black vampire, Mamuwalde. (Dir: William Crain, 92 mins.)

Blaise Pascal (Italian, 1972)*** Another in the series of historical films made for Italian television by Roberto Rossellini. About the 17th-century French scientist and writer on religious and philosophical subjects. Shows how his Catholic faith was in conflict with his scientific findings and interest. Not on the level with "Rise of Louis XIV" but interesting on its own terms. (120 mins.)

Blanche Fury (British, 1948)**½ Valerie Hobson, Stewart Granger. Grasping girl about to marry her uncle's son carries on an affair with a steward, resulting in murder.

Hard-breathing costume drama is heavy, but nicely acted, tastefully produced. (Dir: Marc Allegret, 93 mins.)

Blancheville Monster (Italian, 1960) ****½** Joan Hills, Richard Davis. Young girl is terrorized in a spooky castle as an ancient family legend says her life must be sacrificed. Fairly effective English-dubbed horror thriller.

Blast of Silence (1961)****** Allen Baron, Molly McCarthy. Professional assassin works himself up to get in the mood for bumping off a racketeer. New York-made, low-budget drama has some effective moments, but mostly comes off as a pretentious try for artiness. Produced by unknowns, it's a better-luck-next-time sort of film.

Blaze of Noon (1947)****½** William Holden, Anne Baxter. Drama about a pilot in love with the sky who gets married. Plays like a corny "B" movie, but the kids may like its air scenes. (Dir: John Farrow, 91 mins.)

Blazing Forest, The (1952)****** John Payne, Susan Morrow, William Demarest. A dull story of the big men who fell the big trees for big stakes. As the title implies, there is a big forest fire sequence. (Dir: Edward Ludwig, 90 mins.)

Blazing Saddles (1974)******** Mel Brooks, Cleavon Little, Gene Wilder, Madeline Kahn. Director Brooks' maniacal, uneven, but often wildly funny spoof of westerns that was accurately described in a promotional ad for the pic: "Ridin', Ropin', Wranglin', and all that Western Bullshit pulled together by Mel Brooks in his new Comedy Classic Blazing Saddles, brought to you by Warner Bros.—the people that gave you 'The Jazz Singer.' " Some of the jokes are hysterical, some sophomoric, but they keep coming so fast you'll forgive the clinkers. There's a spectacularly funny sequence featuring Kahn in a devastating takeoff of Marlene Dietrich while playing the character of Lili Von Shtupp. There are takeoffs on other western film classics including "High Noon." The ending peters out, but it's often lunacy of a high order with some great sight gags. (Dir: Mel Brooks, 93 mins.)

Blazing Sand (Israeli, 1960)****** Daliah Lavi, Gert Guenter Hoffman. Selfish girl tries to persuade four men to undertake a perilous mission to save her lover, lying trapped and helpless in a tomb. Unusual locale is far superior to the trite melodramatic story. Dubbed in English.

Bless the Beasts and Children (1971) ****½** Billy Mumy, Barry Robbins. Glendon Swarthout's novel serves as the basis for this interesting if not totally successful story about a group of problem boys from an expensive ranch-camp who set out to free some captive buffalo earmarked to be shot for sport. To get the message across and still be entertaining is a tall order, and director Stanley Kramer almost pulls it off. Mumy, known to TV fans from "Lost in Space," is quite good as the true rebel of the group, and the western locations add greatly to the atmosphere. (Dir: Stanley Kramer, 106 mins.)

Blind Goddess (British, 1949)****½** Eric Portman, Anne Crawford. A young diplomat is involved in a romantic affair that eventually brings on a nasty courtroom trial. Occasionally interesting but extremely verbose drama; well acted.

Blind Justice (German, 1961)****½** Peter Van Eyck. A somewhat complicated multiple murder drama in which Peter Van Eyck plays a prosecuting attorney who almost destroys himself in his relentless search for the facts in a closed case. Good shots of German night life adds interest when the story gets too heavy-handed.

Blind Man's Bluff—See: **Cauldron of Blood**

Blind Spot (1947)******* Chester Morris, Constance Dowling. Writer on a drunk is accused of the murder of his publisher. Well done mystery. (Dir: Robert Gordon, 73 mins.)

Blind Spot (British, 1958)****** Robert Mackenzie, Delphi Lawrence. Blinded officer becomes involved in a smuggling ring. Ordinary melodrama.

Blindfold (1966)******* Rock Hudson, Claudia Cardinale, Jack Warden. Psychologist is contacted by a security officer to treat a mentally disturbed scientist, which involves the headshrinker in an international plot. One of the more enjoyable secret-agent suspense thrillers, never takes itself too seriously, has good performances and direction. (Dir: Philip Dunne, 102 mins.)

Bliss of Mrs. Blossom, The (British,

1968)*** Far-out farce about a bored wife (Shirley MacLaine) of a brassière manufacturer (Richard Attenborough) who stashes away a lover (James Booth) in the attic. Slyly amusing, once the spirit of the thing makes itself evident; amazingly, it's based on fact. Good fun. (Dir: Joe McGrath, 93 mins.)

Blitz on Britain (British, 1962)**½ Documentary narrated by Alistair Cooke of the Nazi air attack of World War II. Has been seen before, but still interesting.

Blitzkrieg—The War for Russia (1960)**½ Documentary, German war film showing the Nazi attack on Russia, the ultimate defeat of the German forces. Familiar, but absorbing for war buffs of WWII.

Blob, The (1958)*½ Steve McQueen, Anita Corseaut. Gooey glob of ooze flops down from outer space and devours people. Adolescent sci-fi thriller doesn't have much except young McQueen's performance. (Dir: Irvin Yeaworth, 85 mins.)

Blockade (1938)***½ Henry Fonda, Madeleine Carroll. An adventuress meets and loves a member of the Loyalist forces in Civil War-torn Spain. Well-made, excellently acted. (Dir: William Dieterle, 90 mins.)

Blonde Bait (British, 1956)*½ Beverly Michaels, Jim Davis. Night-club girl is allowed to escape from prison, so she will lead police to her murderer boy friend. Mediocre melodrama. (71 mins.)

Blonde Blackmailer (British, 1958)* Richard Arlen, Constance Leigh. After serving a rap for murder, an innocent man is released and sets out to prove his innocence. Poor mystery, Arlen wasted on shoddy material. (Dir: Charles Deane, 58 mins.)

Blonde In a White Car—See: **Nude in a White Car**

Blonde Ransom (1946)*½ Donald Cook, Virginia Grey. Girl pretends to be kidnapped so she can raise money for her gambling boy friend. Thoroughly mediocre comedy-drama.

Blondie (1938)**½ Penny Singleton, Arthur Lake, Larry Simms, Jonathan Hale. Snappy comedy, first one in the series based on the popular comic strip. Blondie and Dagwood have problems paying off their furniture installments when he gets stuck with a loan shark's note. Pleasing introduction to the Bumstead family. (Dir: Frank R. Strayer, 80 mins.)

Blondie Brings Up Baby (1939)**½ Penny Singleton, Arthur Lake, Larry Simms. A salesman tells Blondie that Baby Dumpling has a high IQ, so he's enrolled in school. Good share of laughs in this series comedy. Well done. (Dir: Frank R. Strayer, 70 mins.)

Blondie Goes Latin (1941)**½ Penny Singleton, Arthur Lake, Tito Guizar, Ruth Terry. The Bumsteads are on the way to South America for a business deal, with some frantic byplay on shipboard. Singleton has a chance to sing and dance here—it's a good musical as well as an up-to-standard entry in the series. (Dir: Frank Strayer, 69 mins.)

Blondie Goes to College (1942)** Penny Singleton, Arthur Lake, Janet Blair, Larry Parks. Blondie and Dagwood decide to go to college, concealing their marriage. Series comedy moves more slowly than some others but is still fair fun. At the end of this one Dagwood learns he's to become a father again. (Dir: Frank Strayer, 74 mins.)

Blondie in Society (1941)*** Penny Singleton, Arthur Lake, William Frawley. Dagwood's in the dog house when he accepts a Great Dane as payment for a loan and Blondie enters it in a dog show. Series comedy has more laughs than many higher-budgeted shows. Good fun. (Dir. Frank Strayer, 75 mins.)

Blondie Knows Best (1946)**½ Penny Singleton, Arthur Lake, Shemp Howard. Dagwood gets himself in hot water when he has to impersonate his boss to corner a client. Amusing series comedy, with a funny bit by Shemp Howard as a process server. (Dir: Abby Berlin, 69 mins.)

Blondie Meets the Boss (1939)**½ Penny Singleton, Arthur Lake, Jonathan Hale. Dagwood loses his job and Blondie takes his place at the office. Second in the series, keeps up the fast moving amusement set by its predecessor. (Dir: Frank Strayer, 80 mins.)

Blondie on a Budget (1940)*** Penny Singleton, Arthur Lake, Rita Hayworth. Blondie wants a fur coat, Dagwood wants to join the Trout Club; complications become even more clouded when Dagwood's ex-girl enters the picture. Enjoyable series comedy has good gags, the presence of Hayworth at her most glamorous. (Dir: Frank Strayer, 73 mins.)

Blondie Plays Cupid (1940)**½ Penny Singleton, Arthur Lake, Glenn Ford. En route to a vacation, Blondie and Dagwood help out an eloping couple. Pleasant comedy in the series, with the added attraction of Ford in his salad days. (Dir: Frank Strayer, 68 mins.)

Blondie Takes a Vacation (1939)**½ Penny Singleton, Arthur Lake, Donald MacBride. The Bumsteads take over a rundown resort hotel and try to put it on a paying basis. Chucklesome comedy in the series, some good laughs. (Dir: Frank Strayer, 70 mins.)

Blondie's Anniversary (1947)** Penny Singleton, Arthur Lake, Adele Jergens, William Frawley. Dagwood inadvertently gives Blondie the wrong package for her anniversary present, which means more trouble. (Dir: Abby Berlin, 75 mins.)

Blondie's Blessed Event (1942)*** Penny Singleton, Arthur Lake, Hans Conried. When the strain of Blondie's expectant motherhood begins to show on Dagwood, he's sent to a Chicago convention, where he encounters an impoverished arty playwright. Many laughs in this series comedy, largely due to a gem of a performance by Conried. (Dir: Frank Strayer, 75 mins.)

Blondie's Reward (1948)** Penny Singleton, Arthur Lake, Chick Chandler, Frank Jenks. Dagwood buys a swamp instead of the property he was supposed to purchase. Mild comedy in the series. (Dir: Abby Berlin, 67 mins.)

Blondie's Secret (1948)** Penny Singleton, Arthur Lake, Thurston Hall. While waiting for Dagwood so they can start their postponed vacation, Blondie chances upon some counterfeit money. Mild comedy in the series. (Dir: Edward Bernds, 68 mins.)

Blood Alley (1955)** John Wayne, Lauren Bacall, Anita Ekberg. He-man adventurer John Wayne fights off Chinese Communists single handed and still finds time for Lauren Bacall. Anita Ekberg is disguised in this one, plays refugee clad in burlap. Strictly for the undiscriminating. (Dir: William Wellman, 115 mins.)

Blood and Black Lace (Italian, 1965) ** Cameron Mitchell, Eva Bartok. Grisly shocker concerning some mysterious murders of fashion models. Not for the squeamish, with its multitude of gruesome sequences. Horror fans should give it a passing mark. English-dubbed. (Dir: Mario Buva, 88 mins.)

Blood and Defiance (Italian, 1966)* Gerard Landry, Jose Greci. Hero seeks to uproot a tyrannical dictator from his small country. Another in the never-ending line of stilted English-dubbed adventures, weak stuff.

Blood and Roses (French, 1961)** Mel Ferrer, Annette Vadim, Elsa Martinelli. English dialogue; jealous girl's body becomes possessed, commits murders as a vampire. Colorful backgrounds and photography can't overcome a hazy plot—just fair horror thriller. (Dir: Roger Vadim, 74 mins.)

Blood and Sand (1941)** Tyrone Power, Linda Darnell, Rita Hayworth. A big cast is wasted in this elaborate but dull story of the life and love of a bull fighter. Does not hold a candle to later films on the same subject. (Dir: Rouben Mamoulian, 123 mins.)

Blood and Steel (1959)** John Lupton, Brett Halsey, Ziva Rodann. Navy Seabees under fire on an enemy-held island are helped by a native girl. Unimportant but competent World War II drama, with its briefness an asset. (Dir: Bernard Kowalski, 63 mins.)

Blood Fiend—See: Theatre of Death

Blood of a Poet, The (France, 1920) **½ Enrico Ribero, Lee Miller, Jean Desbordes. A landmark film, Cocteau's first, written and narrated by him. "Poet" is constructed as a series of episodic, enigmatic, frequently autobiographical imaginary events, revelations and transformations. From the opening scene when the poet, while drawing, creates a real mouth to the final scene when the poet shoots himself, Cocteau fills the screen with an unending collage of remarkable allegories and images including some fantastic masks. (Dir: Jean Cocteau, 53 mins.)

Blood of Dracula (1957)* Sandra Harrison, Louise Lewis. Wicked girls' school teacher puts one of her students under a vampire's curse. Curse, is right. (69 mins.)

Blood of Nostradamus, The (Mexican, 1960)* Jermon Robles, Julio Aleman. Vampire returned from the dead marks a police inspector for one of his victims. Childish horror thriller dubbed in English.

Blood of the Condor (Bolivian, 1969) **** Marcelino Yanahuaya, Benedicta Mendoza Huanca, Vicente Salinas. Extremely moving film, totally without artifice, concerning the plight of the impoverished Quechua Indians, who are cheated and dehumanized at every turn by whites and mestizos of mixed blood. Fictional story about the "Progress Corps" (the American Peace Corps) and efforts to sterilize the Indian women. The story line doesn't matter here. What does come through is the overwhelming commitment of the director to use this film as a consciousness-raising tool among suffering Bolivian peasants. The film has a naked power, raw power that is undeniable even for educated urbanites from other cultures. Banned in Bolivia, and its talented director exiled, but you should see this cinematic plea for justice if you have an opportunity. (Dir: Jorge Sanjines, 74 mins.)

Blood on His Sword (French, 1961)** Jean Marais, Rosanna Schiaffino. Dashing hero saves the King's goddaughter from charges of witchcraft. Lavishly produced, rather naive costume adventure. Some good action. English-dubbed.

Blood on Satan's Claw (British, 1970) **½ Patrick Wymark, Linda Hayden, Barry Andrews. Rural England circa 1670 is the setting for witch trials and an atmosphere of suspense. Better-than-average horror, complete with a girl who grows claws. Not for the squeamish. Hayden gives best performance. (Dir: Piers Haggard, 93 mins.)

Blood on the Arrow (1964)** Dale Robertson, Martha Hyer, Wendell Corey. Lone survivor of an Indian attack is taken care of by the wife of a trader who is involved with outlaws. Typical western. (Dir: Sidney Salkow, 91 mins.)

Blood on the Moon (1948)*** Robert Mitchum, Barbara Bel Geddes, Robert Preston. Cowpoke fights a girl and her father, realizes it was an underhanded trick by his friend, and reverses his actions. Good western. (Dir: Robert Wise, 88 mins.)

Blood on the Sun (1945)*** James Cagney, Sylvia Sidney. In pre-war Japan, an American newspaperman foresees the threat to democracy posed by the ruling warlords, who try to silence him. Fast-paced, suspenseful melodrama. Plenty of Cagney action.

Blood Sisters—See: **Sisters**

Blood Suckers, The—See: **Dr. Terror's House of Horrors**

Bloodhounds of Broadway (1952)**½ Mitzi Gaynor, Scott Brady. A comedy with music in the "Guys & Dolls" tradition, but not nearly as effective. Miss Gaynor plays a hillbilly who comes to the city and turns into a curvaceous Broadway babe. The plot revolves around a crime investigating committee and the various sharpies who spend most of their time dodging the law. (Dir: Harmon Jones, 90 mins.)

Bloodlust (1962)* Wilton Graff, Robert Reed, Lilyan Chauvin. Madman makes a sport of hunting humans. He should have included the producer, director and author of this crude horror dud. Film's only distinguishing characteristic is that it contains one of the few movie appearances to date of Miss Chauvin, a gifted actress seldom used to best advantage by American TV or motion pictures.

Bloodsport (1973)*** Ben Johnson, Larry Hagman, Gary Busey. Johnson charges this drama with tension and appeal in the role of a small-town worker who sees nothing but big-time gridiron glory for his hot-shot high-school-star son. The father pushes and pushes and the son is strained and pulled taut, and the confrontation-climax, as well as the entire attitude of the film, is truthful and direct. Made-for-TV. (Dir: Jerold Freedman.)

Bloody Mama (1970)*** Shelley Winters, Pat Hingle. Tough crime saga about Ma Barker and her brood of disturbed sons will be appreciated by some, dismissed by others. It's a brutal, machine-gun-paced account of the criminal rise and fall of the Barker brood. Miss Winters' blatant vulgarity as the dominant Ma Barker is perfectly suited to this movie treatment of the legendary public enemy of the Depression era, while Don Stroud, as her bad-tempered son Herman, and Pat Hingle, as a kidnapped banker, also register with strong performances. The bloody finale is virtually choreographed, and is a stunner. (Dir: Roger Corman, 92 mins.)

Bloody Vampire, The (Mexican, 1963)* Carlos Agosti, Adrias Roel. The evil Count Frankenhausen turns into a vampire and causes a reign of terror. Dreadful horror thriller dubbed in English. (Dir: Edward Dmytryk, 107 mins.)

Blossoms in the Dust (1940)*** Greer Garson, Walter Pidgeon. Story of a dedicated woman who founded a Texas children's home is top drawer fare for the ladies in the audience. Men will find it a bit too sweet and sentimental.

Blow-Up (British-Italian, 1966)**** David Hemmings, Vanessa Redgrave. Director Michelangelo Antonioni's fascinating psychological puzzler of the young photographer (David Hemmings) who believes he's an accidental witness to a murder. (The small screen won't help clarify the filmmaker's intent.) Viewers may find the story baffling, but should hold on and catch incandescent Vanessa Redgrave, and assorted models who fill the photographer's nightmarish world. (111 mins.)

Blowing Wild (1953)**½ Barbara Stanwyck, Gary Cooper. Power-crazy gal tries to gain control in Mexican oil fields. Well done but hardly worth the trouble. (Dir: Hugo Fregonse, 90 mins.)

Blue (1968)* Terence Stamp, Joanna Pettet. It took many celebrated names on both sides of the camera to botch up this western drama. The tale about a blond boy adopted and reared by the Mexicans, who finds himself in the position of fighting against his childhood protectors, should have been more fascinating than it turns out. The supporting cast includes such stars as Karl Malden, Ricardo Montalban, and Stathis Giallelis (the lead in "America, America"). Director Silvio Narizzano was responsible for the lovely "Georgy Girl" so we can't blame him entirely for this no-color no-flavor western. (Dir: Silvio Narizzano, 113 mins.)

Blue Angel, The (German, 1930) **** Marlene Dietrich, Emil Jannings. The story of a professor who falls for a cheap nitery singer, and his eventual downfall therefrom.

Fine old film classic hasn't lost any of its power. Excellent. (Dir: Josef von Sternberg, 90 mins.)

Blue Angel, The (1959)**½ May Britt, Curt Jurgens. Remake of the 1930 classic which made Marlene Dietrich an international star. Nowhere near as good as the original, but those who aren't familiar with the Dietrich opus will probably enjoy it. Curt Jurgens is very good as a German school teacher who succumbs to the slinky nightclub singer named Lola-Lola. Miss Britt is physically attractive, but she's not convincing as the temptress who leads the professor to near destruction.

Blue Bird, The (1940)**½ Shirley Temple, Spring Byington. Maeterlinck's classical fantasy about a little girl's search for true happiness receives an elaborate but, unfortunately, dreary screen treatment. Only for the kids. (Dir: Walter Lang, 88 mins.)

Blue Blood (1951)**½ Bill Williams, Jane Nigh. Veteran horse trainer persuades a wealthy girl to let him train a former winner headed for oblivion. Refreshing racing story, pleasantly handled. (Dir: Lew Landers, 72 mins.)

Blue Continent (Italian, 1954)** Documentary of an expedition to the depths of the Red Sea to explore marine life. Average amount of interest in a subject which has been covered more thoroughly and better by Cousteau and others. Narration in English.

Blue Dahlia, The (1946)*** Alan Ladd, Veronica Lake, William Bendix. Fairly exciting melodrama about an ex-serviceman who must clear himself of suspicion in the murder of his unfaithful wife. Good entertainment. (Dir: George Marshall, 96 mins.)

Blue Denim (1959)**½ Carol Lynley, Brandon de Wilde. Another one about misunderstood youth and the consequences of premature love. Well acted but says nothing especially profound. (Dir: Philip Dunne, 89 mins.)

Blue Gardenia (1953)**½ Anne Baxter, Richard Conte, Ann Sothern. Slick, but slow moving mystery-drama about a girl wrongly accused of murder and her efforts to prove her innocence. Good performances. (Dir: Fritz Lang, 90 mins.)

Blue Grass of Kentucky (1950)**½
Bill Williams, Jane Nigh. Daughter
of a rival race horse owner allows
breeding with her boyfriend's nag,
with a fine-running colt the result.
Horseflesh fanciers should enjoy
this. Well done. (Dir: William Beaudine, 71 mins.)

Blue Hawaii (1962)** Elvis Presley,
Joan Blackman, Angela Lansbury.
Returning soldier takes a job with a
tourist agency against his parent's
wishes, makes good. As goes Elvis,
so goes this mild musical. Pretty
pictures do not always a movie make
—and this one has little else except
Presley. (Dir: Norman Taurog, 101
mins.)

Blue Knight, The (1975)**½ George
Kennedy, Alex Rocco. George Kennedy plays Joseph Wambaugh's
Bumper Morgan (a role beautifully
acted by William Holden in the previous TV mini-series), with his big-
bear warmth. Shootouts, chases, and
all that Hollywood jazz are missing,
as Bumper tracks down a cop-killer
while making human contact on the
street. There's a feeling of reality
to this pilot film. Made-for-TV.
(Dir: J. Lee Thompson, 73 mins.)

Blue Lagoon, The (British, 1948)**
Jean Simmons, Donald Houston.
Boy and girl are shipwrecked on a
tropic isle, grow to maturity and
love each other. Picturesque scenery doesn't overcome the weakness
of the tale; moderate adventure
drama. (Dir: Frank Launder, 101
mins.)

Blue Lamp, The (British, 1950)***
Jack Warner, Dirk Bogarde. A
young recruit nabs a robber after
he has killed a fellow-policeman.
Glorifying the British bobby, this
is exciting as well as having an
authentic documentary-like flavor.
(Dir: Basil Dearden, 84 mins.)

Blue Max, The (1966)**½ George
Peppard, Ursula Andress, James
Mason. Overblown World War I
flying epic that is at its best during
some superbly photographed and
staged aerial battle sequences featuring vintage planes. George Peppard is well cast as a fastidious German pilot who is eager to become a
war ace, and James Mason delivers
one of his familiar German-officer
performances. For added interest
there's Ursula Andress in the role
of a glamorous countess. (Dir: John
Guillerman, 156 mins.)

Blue Murder at St. Trinians (British,
1958)**½ Alastair Sim, Joyce Grenfell, Terry-Thomas. Foolish comedy
about a jewel thief hiding from the
law in a girls' school. The events
leading to his eventual capture are
pure slapstick. The delightful cast
of performers are at the poor
script's mercy, but Sim still gets
his share of laughs. (Dir: Frank
Launder, 88 mins.)

Blue Skies (1946)*** Bing Crosby,
Fred Astaire, Joan Caulfield. Bing,
Fred and 20 Irving Berlin tunes add
up to pleasant entertainment. Plot is
corny, but it doesn't get in the way.
(Dir: Stuart Heisler, 104 mins.)

Blue Veil, The (1951)**½ Jane Wyman, Charles Laughton, Joan Blondell. Young woman thwarted by love
finds happiness in being a children's
nurse. Long, tearful drama, mainly
for the ladies. (Dir: Curtis Bernhardt, 114 mins.)

Blue Water, White Death (1971)
***½ Underwater-photography buffs
and adventurers of all ages will not
want to miss this exciting odyssey in
search of a Great White Shark, also
known as White Death. Peter Gimbel, adventurer, underwater-photography expert and documentary filmmaker, assembled a crew of ten
divers and photographers and set
out to find the White Shark in a
journey which took them from South
Africa to Ceylon, India and finally
to the coast of Australia. Builds to
an unforgettable crescendo. The last
15 or 20 minutes showing the elusive
and terrifying Great White Shark
battering the aluminum cage in a
frenzied attempt to destroy any people and cameras in its path, is one
of the most thrilling, awesome sequences ever captured on film. (Dir:
Peter Gimbel, 100 mins.)

Blue, White and Perfect (1942)**½
Lloyd Nolan, Mary Beth Hughes.
Detective Michael Shayne gets in
the war effort by chasing foreign
agents who've been stealing industrial diamonds. Good B film.

Bluebeard (1944)*** John Carradine,
Jean Parker. A puppeteer who
strangles girls as a sideline falls for
a beautiful dress shopowner, which
is his downfall. Suspenseful thriller.
Carradine is restrained, very good.
(Dir: Edgar Ulmer, 73 mins.)

Bluebeard (French-Italian-W. German, 1972)*½ Richard Burton, Raquel Welch, Joey Heatherton. Burton

portrays Bluebeard and tries to make this junk a bit of high camp. Update of the legendary woman killer; Burton picks beauties to do away with. The scriptwriters get credit for imagining so many varied ways to commit carnage. (Dir: Edward Dmytryk, 124 mins.)

Bluebeard's Ten Honeymoons (British, 1959)**½ George Sanders, Corinne Calvet. George Sanders is so suave that he could probably get away with multiple murders as he does in this modern version of Bluebeard. The women fall under George's charming spell and end up done in. (Dir: D. Lee Wilder, 93 mins.)

Bluebird, The (U.S.-Russian, 1976)* Elizabeth Taylor, Jane Fonda, Cicely Tyson, Ava Gardner, Robert Morley, Todd Lookinland, Patsy Kensit. This Soviet-American co-production was heralded as the greatest movie marriage since Hepburn and Tracy, but it turned out to be "amateur night in Siberia." Maeterlinck's simple story about two kids who venture into a fantasy world in search of that proverbial bluebird of happiness has been given such a heavy-handed mounting, it sinks under its own velvet trappings. The cast, made up of top names, is terrible—everyone overacts and Liz Taylor's makeup for the witch looks as if it were done for a grammar-school production of "Hansel and Gretel." A loser all the way. (Dir: George Cukor, 100 mins.)

Blueprint for Murder, A (1953)** Joseph Cotten, Jean Peters. Contrived "perfect crime" melodrama which may keep some viewers guessing as to whether the beautiful Miss Peters is guilty or not. The clues are plentiful and the action predictable for most mystery fans. (Dir: Andrew Stone, 76 mins.)

Blueprint for Robbery (1961)** J. Pat O'Malley, Robert Wilkie, Robert Gist. Fair suspense drama as a gang of thieves attempt to rob a Brink's truck of $2 million. Character actor O'Malley is the main attraction, playing the head of the bandits. (Dir. Jerry Hopper, 87 mins.)

Blues for Lovers (Great Britain, 1965)** Ray Charles, Tom Bell, Mary Peach, Dawn Addams. Dull, restrained melodrama about a blind boy's friendship with a blind American jazz musician. Jazz-pianist Ray Charles performs well enough in his screen debut, but the music is best—an attractive mixture of American jazz and English-ballad blues. Charles' songs include "Cry," "Talking about You," and "Lucky Old Sun." (Dir: Paul Henreid, 89 mins.)

Blues in the Night (1941)*** Priscilla Lane, Richard Whorf. A wonderful score by Harold Arlen and Johnny Mercer, plus an occasionally moving plot combine for good entertainment. With a little more work this could have been a great motion picture. (Dir: Anatole Litvak, 88 mins.)

Blume in Love (1973)***½ George Segal, Susan Anspach, Kris Kristofferson, Marsha Mason, Shelley Winters. Wry, affecting comedy-drama about a husband lamenting the loss of his ex-wife. Segal will capture your affection as the husband who has been divorced because of infidelity (an affair with a secretary), though he's still quite passionate for his kooky mate (charmingly played by Anspach). Writer-director Paul Mazursky is on target in capturing the middle class facing the breakdown of their institutions. Supporting acting gleams, especially Shelley Winters as a plump matron whose husband has run off with a stewardess. (115 mins.)

Bob and Carol and Ted and Alice (1969)**** Natalie Wood, Robert Culp, Dyan Cannon, Elliott Gould. Funny contemporary comedy which toys with many foibles of the late 60's, such as pot smoking, wife swapping, extramarital affairs, and psychiatry. The standouts in the film are Elliott Gould and Dyan Cannon (Ted and Alice), a married couple who have a rocky marriage at best, and secretly envy their best friends' seemingly happy marriage. Funny dialogue and wacky situations keep this film entertaining throughout. Skillfully directed by Paul Mazursky, who also wrote the droll screenplay with Larry Tucker.

Bob Mathias Story, The (1954)**½ Bob Mathias, Ann Doran. Low budget, entertaining biography of the decathlon champ of the 1948 and 1952 Olympics. Good for the youngsters. (Dir: Francis Lyon, 80 mins.)

Bobikins (British, 1960)**½ Max Bygraves, Shirley Jones. Young couple are amazed to discover their

14-month-old baby talking like an adult, and giving stock market tips too. Pleasant fantasy has some chuckles, clever manipulating of baby to give the effect of speech. (Dir: Robert Day, 89 mins.)

Bobby Ware Is Missing (1955)**½ Neville Brand, Arthur Franz. An offbeat drama about the search for a young teen age boy who has an accident and doesn't come home. The performances are better than average for a Grade "B" film. (Dir: Thomas Carr, 66 mins.)

Bobo, The (British, 1967)** Peter Sellers, Britt Ekland, Rossano Brazzi. Sellers as an inept matador who can land a singing job, providing he's able to seduce a courtesan (Ekland). Once in a while Sellers gets a few chuckles, but the script of "The Bobo" is surfeited with boo-boos! (Dir: Robert Parrish, 105 mins.)

Boccaccio '70 (Italian, 1962) ***½ Sophia Loren, Anita Ekberg, Romy Schneider. Three naughty tales— "The Temptation of Dr. Antonio," with Ekberg as a poster come to life in a satire on prudishness; "The Job," with Schneider as a discontented wife; and "The Raffle," with Loren as the big prize in a love lottery. One's liking for the stories will vary; Sophia is ravishing in "The Raffle," and this segment is extremely funny; all are well acted. Directors: Fellini, Visconti, De Sica. Dubbed in English.

Body and Soul (1947)**** John Garfield, Lilli Palmer. A guy from the slums battles his way to the top of the fight racket, only to learn that the crooked way isn't necessarily the best. Hard-hitting melodrama, crisp and rugged, with some excellent prizefight sequences. Recommended. Lilli Palmer is near perfect in one of the best films ever made about boxing. (Dir: Robert Rossen, 104 mins.)

Body Disappeared, The (1941)** Jane Wyman, Jeffrey Lynn. Daffy little forced comedy in the "Topper" tradition but not in the same league. Disappearing people as a comedy device is old hat. (Dir: Ross Lederman, 72 mins.)

Body Is Missing, The (German, 1962) *½ Elke Sommer. Two house salesmen have a crime on their hands when the owner of a mansion is found dead. Mediocre comedy-mystery dubbed in English.

Body Snatcher (1944)***½ Boris Karloff, Bela Lugosi, Henry Daniell. A doctor is blackmailed by a villainous coachman when he wishes to stop securing bodies for medical research in Scotland of the 19th century. For horror fans, this is one of the best; for others, a good and chilling version of Robert Louis Stevenson's tale. (Dir: Robert Wise, 77 mins.)

Body Stealers, The—See: **Thin Air**

Bodyhold (1950)** Willard Parker, Lola Albright. The wrestling game is exposed in this dull story of the sport's managers and flunkies. (63 mins.)

Boeing-Boeing (1965)** Tony Curtis, Jerry Lewis. The London stage success is Americanized for the screen, hypoed by casting Curtis and Lewis as a pair of calculating Romeos who figure out an elaborate plan involving a bachelor pad with airline stewardesses coming and going. It still comes out, as you might expect, loud and unfunny. (Dir: John Rich, 102 mins.)

Bofors Gun, The (British, 1968)***½ Grim sessions at a British army camp in postwar Germany, with a superb performance by Nicol Williamson as a tragically misfit Irish soldier. Builds to a poignant climax. Well directed (Jack Gold), excellent cast. Ian Holm, David Warner. Inexcusably, the salty dialogue has been toned down on the TV prints. (Dir: Jack Gold, 106 mins.)

Bold Adventure, The (Franco-German, 1956)** Gerard Philippe, Jean Vilar. Lavish, colorful, but drowsy costume adventure about a frivolous Robin Hood battling the Spanish Inquisition in Flemish Belgium. Based on the "Till Eulenspiegel" legend, directed by the star—could have had more dash, pace. Dubbed in English.

Bold and the Brave (1956)***½ Mickey Rooney, Wendell Corey, Don Taylor. Better than average war film with many touches of comedy, the best being a "crap game" sequence in which Mickey Rooney is marvelously funny. (Dir: Lewis Foster, 87 mins.)

Bomb at 10:10 (1967)** George Montgomery. Routine war drama about an escape from a concentration camp and the heroics of the escapees in their bouts with the Nazis. George Montgomery and a European cast do well, but it's all too familiar. (Dir: Charles Damic, 86 mins.)

Bomb for a Dictator, A (French, 1960)** Pierre Fresnay, Michel Auclair. Revolutionists plan to eliminate a dictator via an elaborate plan, which backfires. Talky drama dubbed in English—good performers struggle with the material.

Bomb in High Street, The (British, 1963)*½ Ronald Howard, Terry Palmer. Crooks plan to rob bank by creating a bomb scare. Slipshod crime melodrama, cheaply-made. (Dir: Terence Bishop, 60 mins.)

Bombardier (1943)*** Pat O'Brien, Randolph Scott. Men are trained for missions in the flying fortresses in raids over Japan. Good war melodrama, well done. (Dir: Richard Wallace, 99 mins.)

Bombers B-52 (1957)** Natalie Wood, Karl Malden, Efrem Zimbalist, Jr. So-so romance and airplane drama. Malden plays Natalie's father who opposes her seeing Col. Zimbalist. After almost 2 hours running time, all, no one will be surprised to learn, ends well. (Dir: Gordon Douglas, 106 mins.)

Bonjour Tristesse (1958)**½ Deborah Kerr, David Niven, Jean Seberg. Lavishly produced film romance based on Francoise Sagan's first novel. The setting is the exquisite countryside of France and Italy, but the script overstates the more melodramatic aspects of the story about a young girl who hero-worships her father and resents his mistress. (Dir: Otto Preminger, 94 mins.)

Bonnie and Clyde (1967)**** Warren Beatty, Faye Dunaway, Estelle Parsons, Gene Hackman, Michael J. Pollard. Another film version of the story of Prim Bonnie Parker and Clyde Barrow, the tough, psychotic young bankrobbers who terrorized the Midwest in the early 1930's. A stunning, perceptive film essay, quite brilliantly directed by Arthur Penn, and deservedly one of the biggest-grossing films in the history of American cinema. Warren Beatty, who also produced this exciting, well-written "gangster" classic, turns in his best movie performance to date playing the lead role of the impotent —at least as written by David Newman and Robert Benton—hoodlum Barrow. The film established Faye Dunaway as a major screen personality, and Estelle Parsons won an Academy Award for her supporting role as Clyde's sister-in-law. Don't hold your breath waiting for this remarkable film to show up on TV— it won't be released to TV for a long time! Besides, you'll appreciate it much more on the big theater screen. Earlier version of this same story was the mediocre "Bonnie Parker Story," a 1958 release starring Dorothy Provine and Jack Hogan, which is on TV. (Dir: Arthur Penn, 111 mins.)

Bonnie Parker Story (1958)** Dorothy Provine, Richard Bakalyan. Blood-spattered story of the infamous gal desperado of the public enemy era of the 1930s. Some fast action, otherwise second rate. (Dir: William Witney, 80 mins.)

Bonzo Goes to College (1952)** Maureen O'Sullivan, Edmund Gwenn. Sequel to "Bedtime for Bonzo," the zany comedy that introduced the misadventures of the mischievous chimp known as Bonzo. This was Universal's attempt to repeat the box-office jingle set by the "Francis" films. The human actors can't help but appear ridiculous. (Dir: Frederick de Cordova, 80 mins.)

Booby Trap (British, 1957)**½ Sydney Tafler, Patti Morgan. A fountain pen "bomb" is stolen, and passes from hand to hand. Wildly plotted comedy is fairly amusing fun.

Boom! (U.S.-British, 1968)** Elizabeth Taylor, Richard Burton, Noel Coward. Considering all the major talents involved in this opulent opus based on Tennessee Williams' play "The Milk Train Doesn't Stop Here Anymore," it's a big disappointment. However, if you're in the mood for a "campy" exercise dominated by Miss Taylor's beauty, clothes, jewelry and overacting, you might enjoy this story about a coarse, dying millionairess who forms an unholy alliance with a stranger known as the "Angel of Death" (Burton). Miss Taylor is miscast—she's much too young and beautiful to be believable. (Dir: Joseph Losey, 113 mins.)

Boom Town (1939)*** Clark Gable, Spencer Tracy, Hedy Lamarr, Claudette Colbert. A good cast in a rousing tale about a pair of roughnecks who strike it rich in the oil fields. Entertaining and exciting although not a first rate film. (Dir: Jack Conway, 116 mins.)

Boomerang (1947)**** Dana Andrews, Jane Wyatt, Lee J. Cobb. Elia Kazan's brilliant direction, an outstanding cast and a fascinating story of a prosecuting attorney who didn't believe the state's case. This semi-documentary based on an actual case is top flight screen entertainment. (88 mins.)

Boots Malone (1952)*** William Holden, Johnny Stewart. Fast paced racetrack story with good performances. William Holden plays a somewhat shady character with a good heart. (Dir: William Dieterle, 103 mins.)

Border Incident (1949)**½ Ricardo Montalban, George Murphy, Howard Da Silva. Interesting drama about "wetbacks" and murder. Montalban effectively plays an immigration agent who is used as a decoy to break up a large "slave trading" market. (Dir: Anthony Mann, 92 mins.)

Borderline (1950)** Fred MacMurray, Claire Trevor. A policewoman is sent to get the goods on dope smugglers working from Los Angeles to Mexico. Uncertain melodrama wavers between seriousness and farce, is successful at neither. (88 mins.)

Bordertown (1935)***½ Paul Muni, Bette Davis. Exciting, realistic drama about an ambitious Mexican who is hungry for power. Beautifully acted and produced. (Dir: Archie L. Mayo, 100 mins.)

Borgia Stick, The (1966)** Don Murray, Inger Stevens, Barry Nelson, Fritz Weaver. Far-fetched story of two pawns in a super-crime syndicate who try to break with the organization. First half is interesting, giving a unique interpretation of modern-day gangsterism; made for TV feature. (Dir: David Lowell Rich)

Born Free (1966)**** Bill Travers, Virginia McKenna. A treat for the whole family. Even if you don't particularly care for films about animals, you'll be won over by the touching tale of Elsa, the lion cub raised in captivity, who then must learn to fend for herself in the jungle wilds of Kenya. Bill Travers and Virginia McKenna play a game warden and his wife who supervise the retraining of Elsa when they find out she's too big to remain a pet and might be shipped to the confinement

of a zoo. The scenes of Elsa's efforts to return to the jungle are memorable. (Dir: James Hill, 96 mins.)

Born Innocent (1974)**½ Linda Blair, Joanna Miles, Kim Hunter. Capitalizing on her notoriety from "The Exorcist," 15-year-old Linda Blair is cast as a runaway teenager facing the cruelties of a juvenile detention home. Though the subject matter may put many people off, the hardy should find merit in Joanna Miles' portrayal of the home's understanding teacher and Miss Blair's capable handling of the unfortunate youngster. Filmed on location in Albuquerque, New Mexico. A vivid rape sequence showing Blair being raped by a broomstick was inexplicably included for its first TV showing and has now been toned down for this re-edited version. Made-for-TV. (Dir: Donald Wrye, 100 mins.)

Born Losers, The (1967)*½ Elizabeth James, Jane Russell, Tom Laughlin. A California town is overrun by young ruffians out to pillage everything (and everyone) in sight. This quickie film shows signs of talent obscured by exploitative, inane story. Tom Laughlin, who went on to direct "Billy Jack," started by directing these cheap pictures. (112 mins.)

Born Reckless (1959)*½ Mamie Van Doren, Jeff Richards. Blonde sexpot mixes among rodeo performers. Plot is strictly side saddle. (Dir: Howard Koch, 79 mins.)

Born to Be Bad (1950)*** Joan Fontaine, Robert Ryan, Zachary Scott. Ruthless female hides behind an innocent exterior, but eventually reveals her true self. Fashionable romantic drama, good for the ladies.

Born to Be Loved (1959)** Carol Morris, Hugo Haas. Leisurely, mild little drama finds elderly music teacher taking a plain-looking seamstress in hand and making her popular and wanted. We're happy Hugo was so kind to Carol in this particular situation, but the long range implications of this kind of thoughtfulness are worrisome—the decimation of the drab spinster population would put a further and perhaps intolerable strain on this nation's already overburdened maternity wards and public schools system. (Dir: Hugo Haas, 82 mins.)

Born to Dance (1936)*** Eleanor Powell, James Stewart. Eleanor's dancing and a Cole Porter score which included "I've Got You Under My Skin," and "Easy to Love." Need we say more? To add to the prize plot is fairly good and comedy is funny.

Born to Kill (1947)*½ Claire Trevor, Walter Slezak, Lawrence Tierney. Ruthless killer marries a girl for her money, then makes passes at her sister. Grim, unpleasant melodrama. (Dir: Robert Wise, 92 mins.)

Born to Sing (1941)** Virginia Weidler, Leo Gorcey, Ray McDonald. Juvenile cast is surrounded by juvenile plot in this Grade B nonsense with music thrown in. Picture's one fine moment is a rendition of "Ballad for Americans."

Born Yesterday (1951)**** Judy Holliday, William Holden, Broderick Crawford. Excellent movie version of the B'way success. Judy Holliday copped an Oscar for her hilarious performance as Billie, the dumb blonde to end all dumb blondes. Witty dialogue and top performances by all. (Dir: George Cukor, 103 mins.)

Borsalino (France-Italy, 1970)*** Jean-Paul Belmondo, Alain Delon, Mireille Darc. A French tribute to the gangster films of the Hollywood 1930's! But the setting has been shifted from Beverly Hills to Marseilles in the 30's. Belmondo and Delon, teamed together for the first time, play two small-time hoodlums on the make. The main virtue of the film is not the familiar story, but the costumes, settings and musical backdrop which really do capture the look and mood of the period. The obligatory cars of the period are on display, as are some garish whores. Engaging period piece if you don't take it too seriously. Based on the book "Bandits of Marseilles." (Dir: Jacques Deray, 126 mins.)

Boss, The (1956)*** John Payne, William Bishop, Doe Avedon. A power-hungry politician takes over a city in the U. S. with frightening results. He joins forces with the rackets and is responsible for the murder of 4 federal agents and innocent bystanders. John Payne gives one of the best performances of his career. (Dir: Byron Haskin, 89 mins.)

Boston Strangler, The (1968)**½ Tony Curtis, Henry Fonda. Despite its lapses, this is a reasonably absorbing screen treatment of Gerold Frank's best-selling account of the Boston murders of a group of women, allegedly committed by a schizophrenic plumber named Albert De Salvo. Tony Curtis is convincing as the deranged De Salvo and Henry Fonda, with mustache, adds to the credibility of director Richard Fleischer's direct, documentary-like approach. (120 mins.)

Botany Bay (1953)** Alan Ladd, James Mason, Patricia Medina. Unjustly convicted man suffers aboard a convict ship bound for Australia, under the wheel of a cruel captain. Fancy but undistinguished costume melodrama. Ladd and Mason in stereotyped roles. (Dir: John Farrow, 94 mins.)

Both Sides of the Law (British, 1953)*** Anne Crawford, Peggy Cummins. Details the work of a London policewoman who takes on a multitude of cases daily. Good episodic melodrama, holds the interest. (Dir: Muriel Box, 94 mins.)

Bottom of the Bottle (1956)**½ Van Johnson, Joseph Cotten, Ruth Roman, Jack Carson. Melodrama all the way—Van Johnson is an escaped convict. He invades his brother's (Joseph Cotten) comfortable world and asks for help. Old tensions arise while confused wife (Ruth Roman) looks on. A fairly exciting climax puts things in order. (Dir: Henry Hathaway, 88 mins.)

Bottoms Up (British, 1960)** Jimmy Edwards, Martita Hunt. Headmaster of a school for boys has his hands full when his charges try to take over the place. Some farcical fun here, but not as much as intended.

Bound for Glory (1976)**** David Carradine, Ronny Cox, Melinda Dillon. A generally excellent biography of Woody Guthrie, one of America's greatest folksingers. Woody's left-wing politics have been toned down somewhat in this, the first major screen story of how Woody left his dust-devastated Texas home in the 30's to find work, and discovered the oppression, suffering and strength of the working people of America during the Great Depression. Carradine gives a superb, intelligent performance as Guthrie, and the supporting cast is excellent. Photography by Haskell Wexler is outstanding and deservedly won an Academy Award. Screenplay by Robert Getchell based on Guthrie's autobiography. (Dir: Hal Ashby, 147 mins.)

Bounty Hunter, The (1954)** Randolph Scott, Dolores Dorn. For Randolph Scott fans—he's a bounty hunter this time, out to capture three criminals. (Dir: Andre de Toth, 79 mins.)

Bounty Killer, The (1965)*½ Dan Duryea, Rod Cameron, Audrey Dalton. Easterner arrives in the Wild West, soon learns the law of the gun, becomes a conscienceless bounty hunter without friends or hopes. Good to see oldtimers such as Richard Arlen, Buster Crabbe, John Mack Brown, Bob Steele and others, but as a western it suffers from subpar production work. (Dir: Spencer G. Bennet, 92 mins.)

Bounty Man, The (1972)** Clint Walker, Richard Basehart, Margot Kidder. Granite-like Clint Walker rides the vengeance trail once again in this western yarn. It's the same old story—a man sets out to find the varmint who caused his wife's death, and falls in love in the process. Made-for-TV. (Dir: John Llewelyn-Moxey, 72 mins.)

Bowery, The (1933)**½ George Raft, Wallace Beery. Robust tale of the Gay Nineties, with Raft as the legendary Steve Brodie who supposedly made the jump from the Brooklyn Bridge. (Dir: Raoul Walsh, 110 mins.)

Boxcar Bertha (1972)*** David Carradine, Barbara Hershey, Barry Primus. Often interesting drama, based on a book, "Sister of the Road." About a woman labor organizer in Arkansas during the violence-filled Depression era of the early '30's. Rabble-rousing union man (Carradine) fights this railroad establishment aided by the remarkable real-life character Boxcar Bertha (Hershey). Well directed by Martin Scorsese before his '73 hit "Mean Streets." (88 mins.)

Boy (Japan, 1969)*** Tetsuo Abe, Fumio Watanabe, Akiko Koyama. Director Nagisa Oshima got his inspiration for this story from a newspaper account of a family that staged auto accidents. Using their young boy as a decoy, the family then extorted money from the frightened drivers. The examination of a family engaged in this treacherous con game is graphic, probing and

disturbing in its morbid fascination. (Dir: Nagisa Oshima, 97 mins.)

Boy and the Pirates (1960)** Charles Herbert, Susan Gordon, Murvyn Vye. Strictly for the young tots. A long dream sequence in which a boy imagines he's involved with pirates and buried treasure. (Dir: Bert Gordon, 82 mins.)

Boy Cried Murder, The (1966)**½ Veronica Hurst, Phil Brown, Fraser MacIntosh. Boy with a vivid imagination witnesses a murder, but nobody will believe him. Remake of "The Window" still carries some effective suspense. (Dir: George Breakston, 86 mins.)

Boy, Did I Get a Wrong Number (1966)* Bob Hope, Elke Sommer, Phyllis Diller. Poor Bob Hope entry. In this outing, Hope is a small-town real estate agent who gets involved with a visiting movie sex queen (Miss Sommer). Phyllis Diller is wasted as Hope's silly domestic and the script offers little in the way of funny lines. (Dir: George Marshall, 99 mins.)

Boy from Oklahoma, The (1954)*** Will Rogers, Jr., Nancy Olson. Will Rogers, Jr. has more acting ability than his famous father displayed in his early films. In this charming western comedy-drama, he is cast as a quiet, peace loving sheriff of a town called Bluerock, which is run by a group of desperadoes. (Dir: Michael Curtiz, 88 mins.)

Boy in the Plastic Bubble, The (1976)**½ John Travolta, Robert Reed, Diana Hyland. A fascinating, disturbing subject is given a sensitive airing in this provocative story about a boy, born with immunity deficiencies, who grows up in a special plastic-bound controlled environment. Popular TV teen idol John Travolta (Barbarino in "Welcome Back, Kotter") discards his wiseguy image and comes up with a believable portrait of a lad on the brink of manhood, who suddenly finds his germ-free plastic home a prison. The TV film is interesting throughout. The ending will draw a tear or two. Diana Hyland and Robert Reed, as the boy's parents, are good in smaller roles, and Glynnis O'Connor registers as the blossoming, slightly selfish teenager who lives next door. Made-for-TV. (Dir: Randal Kleiser, 106 mins.)

Boy Meets Girl (1938)*** Pat

O'Brien, Marie Wilson, James Cagney. Slightly antiquated today but still a delightful spoof of the movie business. Forerunner of hundreds of imitations. (Dir: Lloyd Bacon, 90 mins.)

Boy Named Charlie Brown, A (1970) ****½** The famous comic strip, "Peanuts," which has inspired endless TV specials, serves as the basis for this full-blown, animated theatrical feature. While charming in its own way, the film merely becomes a series of vignettes played with gusto by the familiar cast of characters, including the winsome Charlie Brown and the abrasive Lucy. Voices fit the drawings for the most part, but the Rod McKuen score doesn't. The film seemed too small for the big screen when it was theatrically released. Now, it's right where it belongs—on television. (Dir: Bill Melendez, 85 mins.)

Boy Next Door, The—See: To Find a Man

Boy on a Dolphin (1957) ****½** Alan Ladd, Sophia Loren, Clifton Webb. The best things about this adventure film are visual—great on location photographic splendor of the blue Aegean, the Greek islands, the majestic city of Athens, plus the physical beauty of the amply endowed Sophia Loren. The plot about the discovery of a sunken work of art is on an elementary level and offers no surprises. (Dir: Jean Negulesco, 113 mins.)

Boy Ten Feet Tall, A (British, 1963) *****½** Edward G. Robinson, Fergus McClelland, Constance Cummings, Harry H. Corbett. Nice family entertainment, thanks to the exotic locale and a good human interest story of a young lad (Fergus M.) trying to cross Africa alone to reach his aunt. Old pro Robinson is first rate, and the youngster is charmingly played. (Dir: Alexander Mackendrick, 88 mins.)

Boy Who Caught a Crook, The (1961) ***½** Wanda Hendrix, Roger Mobley, Don Beddoe. Newsboy and his hobo friend stumble across a briefcase full of stolen money. Trite little drama makes little impression. (Dir: Edward Cahn, 72 mins.)

Boy Who Stole a Million (British, 1960) ****** Maurice Reyna, Virgilio Texera. Boy steals from a bank to help his father pay some bills, becomes object in a search by the police and the underworld. Good Spanish locations, rambling story that never quite makes its point. Mild drama. (Dir: Charles Crichton, 64 mins.)

Boy Who Talked to Badgers, The (1975) ****½** Christian Juttner, Carl Betz, Salome Jens. Lovely Alberta, Canada, scenery is a help to this Disney adventure about a lost 6-year-old boy who survives out on the prairie thanks to a friendly badger. Scenes in which the animal provides food for the boy should please the youngsters. Betz portrays the boy's stiff, unyielding Dad. Made-for-TV. (Dir: Gary Nelson)

Boy with Green Hair (1948) ******* Pat O'Brien, Dean Stockwell. War orphan becomes an outcast when he finds his hair has suddenly turned green. Fanciful drama has a message, delivered not too well, but impressive nevertheless. (Dir: Joseph Losey, 82 mins.)

Boys, The (British, 1962) ****½** Richard Todd, Robert Morley, Jess Conrad. Four teenagers go on trial for murder and robbery. Juvenile-delinquency courtroom drama adds little to the subject that is not familiar but is well enough done. Todd and Morley are good as the opposing counsels. (Dir: Sidney Furie, 82 mins.)

Boys from Syracuse, The (1940) ******* Joe Penner, Allan Jones, Martha Raye. Two sets of twins cause confusion and havoc in ancient Greece. Entertaining musical comedy based on the Broadway show. Fine Rodgers and Hart songs. (Dir: A. Edward Sutherland, 73 mins.)

Boys in the Band, The (1970) ******** Cliff Gorman, Laurence Luckinbill, Kenneth Nelson, Leonard Frey. It doesn't sound like much to say that "Boys in the Band" is the most honest, revealing and poignant American film made about homosexuality up until 1970, but it is intended to be a genuine, admiring compliment. Mart Crowley has adapted his own acclaimed award-winning play, retaining much of the qualities of pathos, bitchiness, loneliness and jealousy that so enriched the play. Remarkably well acted, incidentally, by the leading players, some of whom are heterosexuals in real life. Under William Friedkin's generally sensitive guiding hand, "Boys" is often hilarious and builds to a powerful climax. The TV commercial networks have, in recent years, exploited the theme of homosexuality along with many other subjects, so see this moving film in its original version if you get a chance. (Dir: William Friedkin, 118 mins.)

Boys' Night Out (1962)*** Kim Novak, James Garner, Tony Randall, Howard Duff, Howard Morris. Entertaining comedy about a quartet of executives who want a little fun and scheme to lease an apartment for their shenanigans. Kim Novak, if you can imagine, is a college student doing research in s-e-x who is their prime target. Generally harmless, some good chuckles. (Dir: Michael Gordon, 115 mins.)

Boys of Paul Street, The (U. S.-Hungarian, 1968)*** Anthony Kemp, William Burleigh. War's futility is examined in this story of boys squabbling over rights to a vacant lot. Points a moral, is well acted by the lads. (Dir: Zoltan Fabri, 108 mins.)

Boy's Ranch (1945)**½ Butch Jenkins, James Craig. Highly recommended for the youngsters is this cute story about delinquents who are given a chance to reform by working on a cattle ranch.

Boys Town (1938)*** Spencer Tracy, Mickey Rooney. Punk Rooney and Spencer Tracy make this film good entertainment. Story of Father Flanagan's Boys Town and how his motto, "There is no such thing as a bad boy," is almost destroyed by an incorrigible youngster is too sentimental but is still rewarding film fare. (Dir: Norman Taurog, 90 mins.)

Brain, The (British, 1964)**½ Anne Heywood, Peter Van Eyck, Cecil Parker, Bernard Lee. Scientist keeps alive the brain of a dead tycoon, which hypnotically compels him to find the murderer. Another version of Siodmak's "Donovan's Brain," filmed twice before, but still effective as a suspenseful horror thriller. (Dir: Freddie Francis, 85 mins.)

Brain, The (France, Italy 1969)*½ David Niven, Jean-Paul Belmondo, Bourvil, Eli Wallach. Everyone overplays in this international comedy that requires the actors to caricature their nationalities. Niven is the epitome of English cool as "the brain" who masterminded the Great Train Robbery and is now eyeing $12 million in NATO funds. Slim

94

jokes defeated by broad playing. (Dir: Gerard Oury, 100 mins.)

Brain Eaters (1958)** Edwin Nelson. Another thing from outer space terrorizes a town. Well, it's better than some of these sci-fi time-wasters.

Brain from the Planet Arous *½ John Agar, Joyce Meadows. Outer space being captures the body of a young scientist, takes over his will. No brains necessary to skip this one. (Dir: Nathan Juran, 71 mins.)

Brain That Wouldn't Die (1963)*½ Jason Evers, Virginia Leith. Surgeon manages to keep his fiancee's head alive after she has been decapitated in an accident, searches for a body to go with it. Grisly thriller suffers from below-average production, farfetched plot. (Dir: Jason Evers, 81 mins.)

Brainiac, The (Mexican, 1963)* Abel Salazar, Carmen Montejo. English-dubbed. Hokey horror thriller about an evil baron who returns from the dead to seek revenge.

Brainsnatchers, The—See: Man Who Changed His Mind, The

Brainstorm (1965)**½ Jeffrey Hunter, Anne Francis, Viveca Lindfors. Nicely played suspense yarn about a pair of lovers who work out a plan to get rid of the lady's husband. It's old hat, as far as plot goes, but a good cast breathes new life into it. (Dir: William Conrad, 114 mins.)

Brainwashed (German, 1961)** Curt Jurgens, Claire Bloom. A German aristocrat is imprisoned by the Nazis and struggles to keep his sanity in this English-dialogued drama. Good performances cannot overcome the static nature of the tale. (Dir: Gerd Oswald, 102 mins.)

Bramble Bush, The (1960)** Richard Burton, Barbara Rush, Jack Carson, Angie Dickinson. Small-town sinful dramatics reminiscent of "Peyton Place" as a doctor returns home to find all sorts of physical, mental, and moral complications. It's all quite distasteful, but soap opera fans will probably sit enthralled. (Dir: Daniel Petrie, 105 mins.)

Brand New Life, A (1973)***½ Cloris Leachman, Martin Balsam. Among the best made-for-TV films. Honest, touching, thoroughly human story about a couple, married for 18 years (she's going to be 41 and he'll be 46), who discover they are about to become parents for the first time. The drama examines various reactions to the situation, especially in two candidly outspoken scenes—one with star Cloris Leachman and her worldly friend, beautifully played by Marge Redmond, and another with Miss Leachman and her brutally honest mother (Mildred Dunnock). Cloris Leachman has never been better, and her performance earned her an Emmy. (Director: Sam O. Steen.)

Branded (1950)**½ Alan Ladd, Mona Freeman, Charles Bickford. Crooks pick a wanderer to pose as heir to a wealthy rancher. Leisurely western needs more pace, but has a story that holds the interest. (Dir: Rudolph Mate, 104 mins.)

Brandy for the Parson (British, 1952) ***½ James Donald, Jean Lodge. Young couple on a boating trip become involved with some whiskey smuggling. Refreshing comedy, good fun.

Brannigan (Great Britain, 1975)**½ John Wayne, Richard Attenborough. John Wayne in London town! He's an Irish cop from Chicago who journeys to London to bring back a criminal who has fled there. Wayne's American tactics clash with Scotland Yard's Richard Attenborough and the two actors work well together in counterpoint. Action includes the old Wayne staples, a barroom brawl and plenty of fisticuffs. (Dir: Douglas Hickox, 111 mins.)

Brass Bottle, The (1964)** Tony Randall, Burl Ives, Barbara Eden. Oops! The one about the inferior man who finds an old lamp with a genie in it. Although Barbara Eden of "I Dream of Jeannie" is in the cast, it's Burl Ives who plays the helpful spirit. Familiar stuff by now, and pretty mild at that. (Dir: Harvey Keller, 89 mins.)

Brass Legend, The (1956)** Hugh O'Brian, Raymond Burr, Nancy Gates. Sheriff Hugh O'Brian tracks down and `shoots it out with desperado Raymond Burr. Involved western drama. (Dir: Gerd Oswald, 79 mins.)

Bravados, The (1958)** Gregory Peck, Joan Collins, Stephen Boyd. Rambling western about a man bent on revenge for his wife's murder. More than half of the film is dedicated to the tracking down of the quartet of despicable murderers and it becomes tedious. Peck is as stoic

as ever and Joan Collins is beautiful but rides a horse badly. (Dir: Henry King, 98 mins.)

Brave Bulls, The (1951)**** Mel Ferrer, Anthony Quinn, Miroslava. Superb screenplay about the life, both private and public, of a famed matador. Probing photography makes it a penetrating study. Performances are top caliber, except for Mel Ferrer—even Ferrer is not as dull as usual. (Dir: Robert Rossen, 108 mins.)

Brave Don't Cry, The (British, 1952) *** John Gregson, Meg Buchanan. Sober, attention-holding story of a mine cave-in, the rescue attempts. Done almost documentary-style; good acting.

Brave One, The (1956)*** Michael Ray, Rodolfo Hoyos. Young boy is attached to his pet bull, runs away to Mexico City to find the beast when he's sold. Charming drama won an Oscar for original story—and original it is. Good entertainment. Written by Dalton Trumbo. (100 mins.)

Brave Warrior (1952)** Jon Hall, Michael Ansara. History gets in the way of the action in this western set in the time of the War of 1812. (Dir: Spencer Bennet, 73 mins.)

Bravos, The (1971)* George Peppard, Peter Duel, Pernell Roberts. Dull Western concerning an Army officer sent to command a small fort after the Civil War. Made-for-TV. (Dir: Ted Post, 100 mins.)

Bread, Love and Dreams (Italian, 1954)*** Vittorio De Sica, Gina Lollobrigida. English dubbing detracts a bit from this amusing comedy about a small town law officer and his troubles with a spirited girl, but the fun still maintains a pretty high level. (Dir: Luigi Comencini, 90 mins.)

Bread Peddler, The (French, 1963)** Suzanne Flon. Woman escapes prison, finds a job as bread deliverer, eventually proves her innocence. Long-drawn-out drama has some occasionally stirring moments. Dubbed in English.

Break in the Circle (1957)*½ Forrest Tucker, Eva Bartok. An espionage yarn that has enough kidnappings, muggings, double-crosses, gunfire, and heroics for at least five more films. Badly written and poorly played.

Break of Hearts (1935)*** Katharine

Hepburn, Charles Boyer. Female musician falls in love with an orchestra leader. Good romantic drama.

Break to Freedom (1955)*** Anthony Steel, Jack Warner. British prisoners in a German camp construct a life-size dummy to cover an escape. Intriguing war drama, good suspense.

Breakdown (British, 1953)*½ Michael Conrad, Lila Graham. Poorly done mystery about a mad man and his dastardly deeds.

Breakfast at Tiffany's (1961)***½ Audrey Hepburn, George Peppard, Patricia Neal. Truman Capote's wispily wistful story of a young writer who becomes involved with a madcap New York playgirl. All-out attempt at whacky sophistication should please the cosmopolite, but others may wonder if they didn't go too far over the edge. Nevertheless some fine performances, with the exception of a badly miscast Mickey Rooney, and some hilarious sequences.

Breakfast in Bed (German, 1963)** Lilo Pulver, O. W. Fischer, Lex Barker. Busy editor neglects his wife, who takes a handsome yoga teacher in retaliation. Then he makes passes at an attractive authoress, and it's off to the divorce court. English-dubbed comedy is reminiscent of the U. S. farces of the 1930s, without their charm.

Breakheart Pass (1976)*** Charles Bronson, Richard Crenna. A nice, action-packed (but **not** violent) Charles Bronson film for all ages. It involves a train crossing the Rockies in the 1870's, carrying territorial Governor Fairchild (Richard Crenna), Marshal Nathan Pearce (Ben Johnson), his mysterious prisoner John Deakin (Charles Bronson), Major Claremont (Ed Lauter), and a beautiful lady, Marcia Scoville (Jill Ireland). The train is bringing relief from a diphtheria epidemic when some unnatural deaths occur. There are some real surprises, and the acting keeps you guessing. Like train wrecks? There's a good one here. Screenplay by Alistair MacLean from his own novel. And Miss Ireland and Mr. Bronson get together at the end! (Dir: Tom Gries, 95 mins.)

Breaking Point, The (1950)**½ John Garfield, Patricia Neal. Despite an insipid script, the stars give good performances in this tale of crime and love. Based on a story by Ernest Hemingway.

Breaking the Sound Barrier (British, 1952)**** Ralph Richardson, Ann Todd, Nigel Patrick. An aircraft manufacturer endures personal grief in his quest to produce a plane that can travel faster than the speed of sound. Truly marvelous aerial drama with a stirring story, superb performances, breathtaking photography.

Breakout (British, 1959)**½ Richard Todd, Richard Attenborough. British soldiers about to break out of an Italian POW camp realize there's a traitor among them. Well done war thriller, in a familiar sort of way. (Dir: Don Chaffey, 99 mins.)

Breakout (British, 1961)** Lee Patterson, Billie Whitelaw, Hazel Court. Unassuming office worker is contacted by a gang to devise a daring escape from prison. Standard crime melodrama.

Breakout (1971)** James Drury, Kathryn Hays. Prison drama takes a different twist as bank robber James Drury becomes thwarted in various escape plans. Wooden dialogue and character follow predictable turns with comic support from Red Buttons as Pipes, the pickpocket con. But the show, at least, breaks out of Folsom prison, with much of the action taking place in the High Sierras near Reno. Woody Strode, Red Buttons, and Sean Garrison add little to cliché material. (Dir: Richard Irving, made-for-TV.)

Breakout (1975)* Charles Bronson, Robert Duvall, Jill Ireland, John Huston. Charles Bronson is, as usual, a stoic, squinting superhero, playing a helicopter pilot who engineers the escape of a falsely accused prisoner from a Mexican prison. Wooden acting teamed with a laughable script. (Dir: Tom Gries, 96 mins.)

Breakthrough (1950)** David Brian, Frank Lovejoy, John Agar. Run of the mill glory-drenched war story with time out for occasional romance. Competent performances. (Dir: Lewis Seiler, 91 mins.)

Breakaway (British, 1957)** Tom Conway, Honor Blackman. An average mystery dealing with racketeer's attempt to obtain a secret formula used to eliminate fatigue in jet flying.

Breath of Scandal, A (1959)** Sophia Loren, Maurice Chevalier, John Gavin. Young American in Vienna rescues a princess, falls for her, is hampered by court protocol. Stale romance despite pretty costumes, production. Loren and Chevalier the sole assets otherwise. (Dir: Michael Curtiz, 98 mins.)

Breezy (1973)** William Holden, Kay Lenz, Roger C. Carmel, Marj Dusay. Sudsy, romantic film about a weary, middle-aged man (Holden) who regains his lust for life through an affair with a "flower child" (Lenz). The scene is sun-drenched California; the obligatory cute dog completes the menage a trois; the villains are the ex-wife and other nasty adults. Of interest only to romanticists and film freaks following Clint Eastwood's dreary directorial career. (Dir: Clint Eastwood, 108 mins.)

Brenda Starr (1976)*½ Jill St. John, Jed Allan, Victor Buono. Lightweight spoof features Jill St. John as a comic-strip newspaper reporter Brenda Starr. She tracks down a group of voodoo extortionists from Los Angeles to the jungles of Brazil. Made-for-TV. (Dir: Mel Stuart, 72 mins.)

Brennus, Enemy of Rome (Italian, 1960)* Gordon Mitchell, Tony Kendall. Invader captures the defender of Rome, forces a pretty lass into marriage to save the city. English-dubbed. Don't force yourself into wasting your time.

Brewster McCloud (1970)*** Bud Cort, Sally Kellerman, Shelley Duvall, Stacy Keach, Michael Murphy, Jennifer Salt. The running pictorial image in Brewster is bird crap, and the "hero" of this slapstick is a retarded young gent who thinks he can fly. Obviously not for every genteel taste, but there are some funny, gross, inventive scenes and Cort (remember him from "Harold and Maude"?) is appropriately spacey. We all get our rocks off in various and surprising ways, Altman tells us, and pretty Jennifer Salt, e.g., has an orgasmic response to just watching our crazed hero do pushups. Written by Doran William Cannon. (Dir: Robert Altman, 104 mins.)

Brewster's Millions (1945)**½ Dennis O'Keefe, June Havoc. Young man inherits a million dollars, but has to spend it in two months in order to claim an even larger fortune. Amusing comedy. (Dir: Allan Dwan, 79 mins.)

Brian's Song (1971)**** James Caan, Billy Dee Williams. Beautifully adapted true story about Brian Piccolo, the Chicago Bears football player who shared a unique friendship with teammate Gale Sayers before cancer claimed Piccolo's life at the age of 26. For a tale dealing with death, this film is bursting with life, particularly in the impeccable, perfectly matched performances of Caan, as the warm and witty Piccolo, and Williams, as the more serious Sayers. William Blinn's thoughtful screenplay is at its best in presenting the growing friendship between the first black-and-white roommates on the Chicago team. You may choke up in the final scenes. Made-for-TV. (Dir: Buzz Kulik.)

Bribe, The (1948)** Robert Taylor, Ava Gardner. Corny, cheap melodrama about the government agent chasing crooks in the Caribbean who falls in love with the seductive wife of one of the bad men.

Bridal Path, The (British, 1959)**½ Bill Travers, Bernadette O'Farrell, George Cole. Young and innocent Scotsman goes on the hunt for a suitable wife in a leisurely but amusing comedy, full of local atmosphere.

Bride and the Beast, The (1960)* Charlotte Austin, Lance Fuller. Young groom finds his bride reverting to her prehistoric past. Darwin was right.

Bride by Mistake (1944)**½ Laraine Day, Alan Marshall. Millionaire's daughter falls for a dashing Air Force pilot. Amusing comedy.

Bride Came C.O.D. (1941)*** James Cagney, Bette Davis. Cagney and Davis dig all the laughs possible out of the script and succeed in making it funny. Plot is all in the title with Cagney as the flying delivery boy and Bette as the bride. Jimmy is better than his co-star but it was Miss Davis' first attempt at comedy, a field where she later proved her skill.

Bride Comes Home, The (1935)**½ Claudette Colbert, Fred MacMurray, Robert Young. Routine romantic triangle comedy, well played by its stars.

Bride for Frank, A (Italian, 1958)** Walter Chiari, Gino Cervi. Rich man returns from America and proceeds to try to marry his son off to a local belle. Fair comedy, English-dubbed.

Bride for Sale (1949)**½ Claudette Colbert, Robert Young, George Brent. Head of an accounting firm finds his ace female tax expert is marriage-minded, so he persuades his handsome friend to go to work on her. Romantic comedy acted by old masters, even if the material is thin.

Bride Goes Wild, The (1947)**½ Van Johnson, June Allyson, Hume Cronyn. Van, who hates kids, has to get Butch Jenkins to pose as his son and the result is an occasionally amusing farce. (Dir: Norman Taurog, 98 mins.)

Bride Is Much Too Beautiful, The (French, 1957)** Brigitte Bardot, Louis Jourdan, Micheline Presle. Cover girl (Brigitte, who else?) is publicized into a fake romance, but she really loves a photographer. Mild for Bardot—or anyone else. (Dir: Fred Surin, 90 mins.)

Bride of Frankenstein, The (1935)*** Boris Karloff, Elsa Lanchester. An "offbeat" boy-meets-girl story, and probably the best of the "Frankenstein" series as the monster finds a mate. Karloff and Lanchester are excellent and her make-up in the final scene is marvelous. Way above average for this kind of trash. (Dir: James Whale, 80 mins.)

Bride of the Monster (1956)* Bela Lugosi, Tony McCoy. Mad scientist experiments with increasing the size of men. Extremely poor horror thriller.

Bride Wore Black, The (France, 1967)***½ Jeanne Moreau, Jean-Claude Brialy, Charles Denner. An entertaining murder melodrama, dedicated to Alfred Hitchcock, whom Truffaut so enormously admires and about whom Truffaut has written so knowledgeably. Moreau is out to revenge the death of her bridegroom. Screenplay by Truffaut and Jean Louis Richard based on a 1940 novel by William Irish (Cornell Woolrich). (Dir: Francois Truffaut, 107 mins.)

Bride Wore Red, The (1937)** Joan Crawford, Franchot Tone, Robert Young. This rags to riches romance offers nothing but Miss Crawford in

a parade of what the well-dressed lady wore in 1937. (Dir: Dorothy Arzner, 110 mins.)

Brides of Fu Manchu, The (Great Britain, 1966)* Christopher Lee, Douglas Wilner, Marie Versini. Lee, king of Hammer horror productions, is back playing the ominous Fu Manchu, once again bent on taking over the world. This time his plan has scientists working feverishly on a monster ray gun. Comic-strip adventure, written by "Peter Welbeck," a pseudonym for the untalented producer Harry Alan Towers. (Dir: Don Sharp, 94 mins.)

Bridge, The (German, 1959)**** Fritz Wepper, Volker Bohnet. Among the most powerful antiwar films ever made. Taut direction by Swiss director Bernhard Wicki. Based on a true story about a group of German youths killed two days before the end of WW II in Europe, in a hopeless attempt to stall the Allied advance before the Nazi regime surrendered. English subtitles. (Dir: Bernhard Wicki, 100 mins.)

Bridge at Remagen, The (1969)**½ George Segal, Robert Vaughn, Ben Gazzara, Bradford Dillman, E. G. Marshall. Based on fact, an account of the efforts by Allied soldiers to commandeer an important tactical bridge from German hands before it's destroyed. Familiar war plot; excellent camera work in the action scenes. (Dir: John Guillermin)

Bridge of San Luis Rey (1944)** Lynn Bari, Francis Lederer. A priest looks into the reason behind a bridge collapsing with five souls upon it, hurtling them to their doom. Long, slow drama based on Thornton Wilder's novel. (Dir: Rowland Lee, 85 mins.)

Bridge on the River Kwai, The (British, 1957)**** William Holden, Alec Guinness, Jack Hawkins, Sessue Hayakawa. Mammoth, magnificent war drama directed by David Lean, a superb motion picture; about a hardened, resolute British officer, captive of the Japanese, who drives his men to build a bridge as therapy, and the attempt of an escaped prisoner to demolish it. Performances, production, script, all deserve the highest praise. Not to be missed. (Dir: David Lean, 161 mins.)

Bridge to the Sun (1961)***½ Carroll Baker, James Shigeta. Based on Gwen Terasaki's autobiography, this compelling drama relates the difficulties of a young woman married to a Japanese diplomat during World War II, victim of suspicion and animosity from her husband's government. Capable performances add to the interest, as do the actual location sequences. (Dir: Etienne Perier, 113 mins.)

Bridges at Toko-Ri, The (1954)***½ William Holden, Grace Kelly, Fredric March, Mickey Rooney. Jet pilot takes off on a dangerous mission during the Korean conflict, while his wife waits patiently for his return. Based on James Michener's book, filmed professionally, powerfully, with fine performances. Superior of its kind. (Dir: Mark Robson, 110 mins.)

Brief Encounter (British, 1946)**** Celia Johnson, Trevor Howard. Superb transcription of Noel Coward's drama; a mature married woman suddenly finds the beginnings of an affair with a chance acquaintanceship, unknown to her husband. Sensitively directed, finely acted. The love scenes between Johnson and Howard are among the most touching and sensitive ever filmed. (Dir: David Lean, 85 mins.)

Brigadoon (1945)***½ Gene Kelly, Cyd Charisse, Van Johnson. Lerner and Loewe's charming, imaginative Broadway musical gets a fine mounting with Gene Kelly & Cyd Charisse dancing like a dream. In fact, the story is a dream—two friends stumble upon Brigadoon, a village which comes to life for a day every hundred years. The music has charm and the cast does it justice. (Dir: Vincente Minnelli)

Brigand, The (1962)**½ Anthony Dexter, Jody Lawrence, Anthony Quinn. Anthony Dexter plays a dual role in this predictable adventure film about intrigue in the Spanish royal court. Anthony Quinn's talents are completely wasted. (Dir: Phil Karlson, 94 mins.)

Brigand of Kandahar, The (British, 1965)*½ Ronald Lewis, Oliver Reed, Yvonne Romain. Adventure and courtroom drama in India, 1850. A half-caste British officer is falsely accused of cowardice and faces dishonorable discharge. A waste of Reed's talent. (Director: John Gilling, 81 mins.)

Brigham Young, Frontiersman (1940)*** Dean Jagger, Tyrone Power,

Linda Darnell. Interesting, but not particularly exciting, story of the Mormons and Brigham Young's struggle to find a place to live. (Dir: Henry Hathaway, 114 mins.)

Bright Leaf (1950)**½ Gary Cooper, Lauren Bacall, Patricia Neal. A fine cast tells the story of one man's rise to wealth in the early days of tobacco growing. Well acted but a bit overlong. (Dir: Michael Curtiz, 110 mins.)

Bright Road (1953)** Dorothy Dandridge, Robert Horton, Harry Belafonte. New fourth-grade teacher takes an interest in a lad who is antagonistic. Story of a Negro boy and his teacher has sincerity but lacks that necessary spark. (Dir: Gerald Mayer, 68 mins.)

Bright Victory (1952)***½ Arthur Kennedy, Peggy Dow. Touching film about the crisis-laden rehabilitation of a WW II soldier who is blinded in battle. Arthur Kennedy gives one of the best performances of his career as the victim and Peggy Dow is perfect as the understanding girl who finally gives him the courage he needs to go on. Excellent direction by Mark Robson. (Dir: Mark Robson, 97 mins.)

Brighthaven Express (British, 1950) *½ John Bentley, Carol Marsh. Sleuth on vacation becomes involved with a lady in distress and some criminals. Film is in distress too.

Brighty of the Grand Canyon (1967) ** Joseph Cotten, Dick Foran. Brighty is a mule who befriends an old prospector (Foran) who has discovered a mother lode of gold. The Grand Canyon steals the film from the mule. (Director: Norman Foster, 89 mins.)

Brimstone (1949)*** Rod Cameron, Adrian Booth, Walter Brennan. Undercover marshal tangles with a cattleman who has turned outlaw with his sons. Good performances and some rugged action lift this western above the usual run.

Bring Me the Vampire (Mexican, 1965)* Charles Riquelme, Mary Eugenia St. Martin. Heirs to a fortune must spend time together in a creepy castle. Combination comedy-thriller furnishes neither laughs nor thrills. Dubbed in English.

Bring Your Smile Along (1955)**½ Keefe Brasselle, Frankie Laine, Constance Towers. Frankie Laine fans will enjoy this musical romance in which he sings many songs. The lightweight story is about a female high school teacher who writes lyrics for her composer boy friend's music.

Bringing Up Baby (1938)*** Katharine Hepburn, Cary Grant. Archaeologist tries to promote a million dollars for his museum, gets mixed up with a dizzy society girl and a baby leopard. Very funny screwball comedy, good fun. (Dir: Howard Hawks, 102 mins.)

Brink's: The Great Robbery (1976)** Darren McGavin, Cliff Gorman, Jenny O'Hara, Leslie Nielsen, Carl Betz. Lengthy recreation of the famous 1950 Boston robbery which took years to solve. First half-hour centers on Boston's small-time crooks wrangling over the best approach to the job, while the remainder deals with the FBI's patient efforts to make some member of the gang sing. The drama of law versus crooks feuding among themselves sounds more exciting than it really is. Darren McGavin's lock expert and his girl Maggie (O'Hara) dominate. Made-for-TV. (Dir: Marvin Chomsky, 102 mins.)

Broadway (1942)*** George Raft, Janet Blair, Broderick Crawford. George Raft plays himself in this entertaining period piece of the speakeasy era, gangsters, and bootleggers. A highlight of the film is Raft's dancing. (Dir: William Seiter, 91 mins.)

Broadway Bad (1933)**½ Joan Blondell, Ricardo Cortez, Ginger Rogers. Blondell effective as a chorus girl who, when slandered by her husband, uses the publicity to get ahead. Stylish melodrama. (Dir: Sidney Lanfield, 61 mins.)

Broadway Melody of 1936, The (1935)*** Jack Benny, Robert Taylor, Eleanor Powell, Una Merkel, Frances Langford. Original story by Moss Hart. A top-rate score, Miss Powell's dancing, and the old reliable showbiz plot are perfectly blended and create an entertaining musical. Songs: "Broadway Rhythm," "You Are My Lucky Star," "I Gotta Feelin' You're Foolin'," by Arthur Freed and Nacio Herb Brown. (Dir: Roy Del Ruth, 103 mins.)

Broadway Rhythm (1943)**½ Gloria De Haven, Ginny Simms, Ben Blue, George Murphy. Some good individual numbers by people like Lena Horne but generally just a lavish

100

piece of nothing. (Dir: Roy Del Ruth, 114 mins.)

Broadway Thru a Keyhole (1933)** Constance Cummings, Paul Kelly. Very dated musical comedy but a rare chance to see and hear the late Russ Columbo, the famous crooner of the 30's. (Dir: Lowell Sherman, 100 mins.)

Brock's Last Case (1973)**½ Richard Widmark. This pilot film about a New York detective quitting the force to raise oranges in California led to Widmark's brief "Madigan" series. Brock (or Madigan, out West) is entertaining. Everything goes wrong for the retired cop; still he manfully springs his Indian foreman loose from a murder rap. Overlong plot, but the dialogue is above average; and Widmark, Henry Darrow, and the whole cast add a nice touch. Made-for-TV. (Dir: David Lowell Rich.)

Broken Arrow (1950)*** James Stewart, Debra Paget, Jeff Chandler. Engrossing western drama about a scout and his personal relationship with the Indians. Debra Paget is quite good as an Indian maiden whom Stewart marries. The late Jeff Chandler won an Oscar nomination for his portrayal of Cochise. (Dir: Delmer Daves.)

Broken Blossoms (1919)*** Lillian Gish, Richard Barthelmess, Donald Crisp. The celebrated D.W. Griffith classic love story of a young woman and a Chinese gentleman can still tug at the heartstrings and draw a tear or two from even the most callous. Griffith allowed his stars, Gish and Barthelmess, to play the romantic duo with realistic enthusiasm. The result is very moving when the tragic aspects of the story take over. Donald Crisp, whose career as one of Hollywood's most distinguished character actors lasted 45 years after this production, is hateful and menacing as Miss Gish's horrible, vicious ex-prizefighter father. (Dir: D. W. Griffith, 80 mins.)

Broken Horseshoe, The (British, 1952)*** Robert Beatty, Elizabeth Sellars. A hit-and-run accident victim puts police on the trail of a narcotics ring. Good melodrama, well acted. (Dir: Joseph Kane, 90 mins.)

Broken Journey (British, 1948)*** Phyllis Calvert, James Donald. Survivors of a plane crash in the Alps attempt to reach safety. Tense, well acted melodrama. (89 mins.)

Broken Lance (1954)******* Spencer Tracy, Richard Widmark, Robert Wagner, Jean Peters. Spencer Tracy gives another of his fine performances in this western drama about a strong willed head of a ranch empire and the eruptive conflicts in his family. Richard Widmark is as villainous as only he can be in the role of the oldest son. Robert Wagner and Jean Peters supply the love interest and there's a fine supporting cast. The story, except for the setting, was originally used in the movie "House of Strangers." (Dir: Edward Dmytryk, 96 mins.)

Broken Wings, The (Lebanese, 1964)****½** Pierre Bordey, Saladin Nader, Philip Akiki. The first film from Lebanon ever released in this country, made in black and white. It's based on the world-famous book by Kahlil Gibran, **The Prophet.** It may strike you as moving and profound, or pretentious and silly. We won't guess which! If you like old-fashioned romantic melodramatic love stories, you'll be in Arabic heaven with this one. Subtitles.

Bronco Buster (1952)****½** Scott Brady, John Lund, Joyce Holden. Some good touches in this unassuming yarn about a champ rodeo rider who takes a young hopeful in hand and trains him. Frequently quite amusing, good performances. (Dir: Budd Boetticher, 90 mins.)

Broth of a Boy (British, 1959)******* Barry Fitzgerald, Tony Wright, June Thorburn. Entertaining comedy about a TV producer who discovers the oldest man in the world, tries to get him on his video show. Top honors to Fitzgerald for his crusty Irish portrayal. (Dir: George Polleck, 77 mins.)

Brother, Can You Spare a Dime? (British, 1975)******* An unusual documentary collage about the Depression Era in America, using contemporary film and newsreel footage, made by Australian Philippe Mora. There are some remarkable clips rarely seen anywhere else, of FDR, film stars, bread lines, strikes, gangsters, etc., and the soundtrack is equally interesting. Definitely worth seeing. (Dir: Philippe Mora, 103 mins.)

Brother John (1971)****** Sidney Poitier, Beverly Todd, Will Geer, Bradford Dillman. Here's a lesser Poitier effort. He plays an angel (that's right) who returns to his hometown in Alabama to see how the folk are faring in this day and age of hate and violence. It's not a bad idea, but before you can say "Gabriel," the clichés are flying and the southern stereotypes are parading in front of the camera. The plot revolves around a strike at the town's big plant but it really doesn't matter. (Dir: James Goldstone, 94 mins.)

Brother Orchid (1940)*****½** Edward G. Robinson, Ann Sothern, Humphrey Bogart, Donald Crisp. Hysterically funny film about a gangster who takes refuge in a monastery and learns some things about life. You'll have a lot of fun with this one especially if you happen to catch it after exposure to some of the rough gangster pictures of the era. (Dir: Lloyd Bacon, 91 mins.)

Brother Rat (1938)*****½** Eddie Albert, Wayne Morris, Priscilla Lane, Ronald Reagan. Side-splitting comedy about life in a military school. A tremendous hit on Broadway and equally good in this screen version. (Dir: William Keighley, 90 mins.)

Brother Rat and a Baby (1940)****** Eddie Albert, Jane Wyman, Ronald Reagan. Good performances don't help this weak script cash in on the success of "Brother Rat." (Dir: Ray Enright, 87 mins.)

Brotherhood, The (1968)****½** Kirk Douglas, Alex Cord, Irene Papas, Susan Strasberg. Highly charged drama about the passions and intrigues of an Italian family connected with the Mafia. K. Douglas, complete with dark hair and handlebar moustache, gives a very strong performance as a syndicate leader who has to run away to Sicily after killing his younger brother's father-in-law. Alex Cord is also effective as Douglas' brother, who, years later, is dispatched to Sicily with a contract on his brother's life. The supporting cast is top-notch, with Luther Adler a standout as Cord's double-crossing father-in-law. (Dir: Martin Ritt, 96 mins.)

Brotherhood of the Bell, The (1970)****½** Glenn Ford. Interesting made-for-TV feature film. Professor Glenn Ford loses his young wife, father, all his possessions and his reputation in a one-sided battle aimed at exposing a secret college fraternity whose members apparently control the business world. The idea of a secret Mafia-like organization originating in a Catholic college may be hard to swallow at first, but David Karp's script gains plausibility over the distance. Ford plays the harassed professor displaying wild, frustrated anger fighting an invisible force, but he can't cover up the tale's weak point—the professor's obvious naïveté in waging an amateur counterattack. (Dir: Paul Wendkos)

Brotherhood of Satan (1971)** Strother Martin, L. Q. Jones. Martin has a field day in this devil-go-round horror movie set in the Southwest. A local coven needs only one more possessed child to continue their Satan-filled activities . . . and thereby hangs the tale. Some surprising bits of horror, at least enough to get you shivering. (Dir: Bernard Mc-Eveety, 92 mins.)

Brothers-in-Law (British, 1957)**½ Ian Carmichael, Terry-Thomas. Zany but only occasionally funny comedy about big business and love. Two lawyers vie for the same girl but both lose out to a third party.

Brothers Karamazov, The (1958)*** Yul Brynner, Maria Schell, Lee J. Cobb, Claire Bloom. Handsomely mounted drama, based on Dostoyevsky's classic. The cast is very good, particularly Lee Cobb. Film is overlong and episodic. Fans of the book will probably find fault with Richard Brooks' screenplay, but still better than most. (Dir: Richard Brooks, 146 mins.)

Brothers Rico, The (1957)**½ Richard Conte, Dianne Foster. Fairly well done crime drama with good performances by the principals. Plenty of action. (Dir: Phil Karlson, 100 mins.)

Browning Version, The (British, 1951)**** Michael Redgrave, Jean Kent. An extraordinarily brilliant and moving performance by Michael Redgrave in the title role makes this Terence Rattigan story a touching and memorable film. About a stuffy professor of English at a boys' school who learns of his wife's affair with another teacher as he prepares to leave the school for another teaching post. Supporting roles uniformly well handled (Dir: Anthony Asquith, 90 mins.)

Brute Force (1947)***½ Burt Lan-

caster, Yvonne DeCarlo, Howard Duff, Ann Blyth, Hume Cronyn. Prisoners plan a daring break, and to get even with a sadistic guard captain. Prison drama offers nothing new, but is well done within its own limits. Fine cast. (Dir: Jules Dassin, 98 mins.)

B.S. I Love You (1971)**½ Peter Kastner, Jo Anna Cameron, Louise Sorel, Gary Burghoff. Saucy little flick spotlighting an ad man (Kastner) lost among the spice of life —a fiancee, an 18-year-old temptress and her mother, his boss (Joanna Barnes). Revolving-door sex but always rather proper. Cast is attractive, but labors with Canadian director Steven Stern's screenplay. (99 mins.)

Buccaneer, The (1958)*** Yul Brynner, Inger Stevens, Charlton Heston, Charles Boyer, Claire Bloom. Jean LaFitte the pirate comes to the aid of Andy Jackson during the War of 1812. Remake of De Mille's early version with Fredric March as LaFitte, this swashbuckler could have used more movement and action. However, the big cast, generally good performances and lavish production make it good big-scale adventure stuff. This was directed by Anthony Quinn, produced by Cecil B. De Mille—his last such.

Buccaneer's Girl (1950)** Yvonne DeCarlo, Philip Friend. Typical pirate yarn with dashing buccaneers and the women who love and chase them. Action fans will enjoy the battle scenes. (Dir: Frederick de Cordova, 77 mins.)

Buchanan Rides Alone (1958)*** Randolph Scott, Craig Stevens, Jennifer Holden. Rugged western with strong plot, good cast and generally far more entertaining than usual western film fare. (Dir: Budd Boetticher, 78 mins.)

Buck and the Preacher (1972)*** Sidney Poitier, Harry Belafonte, Ruby Dee. Poitier and Belafonte work well together, but the mood is odd. Starts as drama, mood lightens, and becomes more entertaining. The duo play escaped slaves heading West, and Cameron Mitchell plays the sly villain. Well acted, but the plot has as many holes as Swiss cheese. Poitier's first directional effort. (102 mins.)

Buck Benny Rides Again (1940)**½ Jack Benny, Ellen Drew. Routine comedy that employed Jack's radio character Buck Benny. Film is loosely put together and only occasionally funny. (Dir: Mark Sandrich, 82 mins.)

Buck Privates (1941)***½ Abbott & Costello. First of a parade of comedies about army life, but one of the best. Even if you're not A & C fans you'll get a kick out of their escapades as G.I.'s. (Dir: Arthur Lubin, 84 mins.)

Buck Privates Come Home (1947)** Abbott & Costello, Tom Brown. Ex-GIs take care of a French war orphan. Typical A & C slapstick. (Dir: Charles Barton, 77 mins.)

Bucket of Blood, A (1960)**½ Dick Miller, Barboura Morris. Far-out sculptor gets a macabre idea on how to improve his art-work. Sick, sick, sick horror-comedy that's interesting, in a repulsive way. (Dir: Roger Corman, 66 mins.)

Buckskin (1968)*½ Marshal (Barry Sullivan) vs. greedy landowner (Wendell Corey) in old Montana. Familiar faces (Joan Caulfield, Lon Chaney, John Russell, Bill Williams, Barbara Hale, Barton MacLane, Richard Arlen) abound in an even more familiar outdoor saga. (Dir: Anthony Quinn, 121 mins.)

Buddenbrooks (German, 1964)**½ Liselotte Pulver, Nadja Tiller, Hansjorg Felmy. Rather compressed version of Thomas Mann's novel about the dynasty of a mercantile family and its problems. Moves slowly, with occasional good scenes, able performances. Dubbed-in English.

Buffalo Bill (1944)**½ Joel McCrea, Linda Darnell, Maureen O'Hara. Big budget western makes some noise but biography of famous hero is generally routine. (Dir: William Wellman, 90 mins.)

Buffalo Bill and the Indians or Sitting Bull's History Lesson (1976)***½ Paul Newman, Joel Grey, Shelley Duvall, Geraldine Chaplin, Burt Lancaster, Kevin McCarthy, E. L. Doctorow. Robert Altman's eccentric, ambitious, flawed but invariably interesting Bicentennial offering, a visually stunning celebration of his understandable conviction that the business of America is and has been, for a long time, show business! Virtually nothing is left of playwright Arthur Kopit's Broadway play, "Indians," about Buffalo Bill, played here with style and

flourish by Paul Newman. Screenplay by Altman and Alan Rudolph presents a different version of William F. Cody's exploits during the Presidency of Grover Cleveland than you have seen in Hollywood films before. (Dir: Robert Altman, 125 mins.)

Buffalo Gun (1962)* Marty Robbins, Wayne Morris, Mary Ellen Kay. Government agents investigate raids on shipments to the Indians. Poor western with hillbilly music added, makes it even worse.

Bugles in the Afternoon (1952)*** Ray Milland, Helena Carter. Fast moving cavalry western about an officer who is demoted but rejoins the service as a private and goes on to become a hero. Good performances. (Dir: Roy Rowland, 85 mins.)

Bugs Bunny, Superstar (1975)*** Fine collection of the best works of the immortal rabbit. Even those who have never been fans of Warner Brothers' classic cartoons made between 1940-1948 will be entranced by the artistry of the "old-fashioned," realistic animation technique, as well as the ageless wisecracking humor. They don't make them like this anymore. Too bad they could only fit in ten cartoons. Narrated by Orson Welles. Brief appearances by famed animation directors Tex Avery, Bob Clampett, Friz Freleng. (Dir: Larry Jackson, 90 mins.)

Bulldog Breed (1960)**½ Norman Wisdom, Ian Hunter. Slapstick-comedian Wisdom up to his ears in catastrophes, as he stubbornly bungles his way through life—from the Navy into Outer Space. Fun if you like this style. (Dir: Robert Asher, 97 mins.)

Bulldog Drummond Strikes Back (1934)**** Ronald Colman, Loretta Young, C. Aubrey Smith, Warner Oland. An excellent comedy-suspense film that holds up well today. One of the best of the "Drummond" series that started in 1930; based on the novel entitled (I kid you not) "Bulldog Drummond: The Adventures of a Demobilized Officer Who Found Peace Dull." You won't find this detective yarn at all dull. (Dir: Roy Del Ruth.)

Bulldog Jack (Great Britain, 1935)*** Jack Hulbert, Ralph Richardson, Claude Hulbert. "Bulldog Drummond"'s sidekick Jack Hulbert is on his own, in this entertaining comedy-thriller, about an attempted jewel heist from the British Museum via the London Tube (subway). Stylishly mounted, well-acted. (Dir: Walter Forde, 73 mins.)

Bullet for a Badman (1964)** Audie Murphy, Darren McGavin, Ruta Lee. Ex-ranger is menaced by an outlaw who threatens to kill him for marrying his ex-wife. Passable western has the standard ingredients of action and suspense. (Dir: R. G. Springsteen, 80 mins.)

Bullet for Joey, A (1955)** Edward G. Robinson, George Raft. Ex-gangster is hired to kidnap a scientist. Routine melodrama. (Dir: Lewis Allen, 85 mins.)

Bullet for Pretty Boy, A (1970)* Fabian Forte, Jocelyn Lane. A beach-blanket biography of gangster Pretty Boy Floyd. Former pop star Fabian plays Floyd as if he was just a nice guy who found himself in an unfortunate situation. Ludicrous. (Dir: Larry Buchanan, 88 mins.)

Bullet for the General, A (Italian, 1967)* Giana Maria Volonte, Klaus Kinski. Italians playing Pancho Villa action in the Mexican Revolution as an American agent infiltrates the Mexican Army in an attempt to arrest the notorious bandit El Chuncho. Pedestrian but not a bad ending as El Chuncho temporarily gets the upper hand. (Dir: Damiano Damiani, 115 mins.)

Bullet Is Waiting, A (1954)**½ Rory Calhoun, Jean Simmons, Stephen McNally, Brian Aherne. Suspense when a lawman and his prisoner are marooned with an old man and his daughter. Melodrama begins well, falls off as it progresses. Performances by the small cast help. (Dir: John Farrow, 90 mins.)

Bullets or Ballots (1936)*** Edward G. Robinson, Joan Blondell. Good racketeering story with customary top drawer, tough guy performance by Mr. Robinson. (Dir: William Keighley, 77 mins.)

Bullfight (French, 1956)***½ Documentary story of bullfighting, from pre-Christian days up to the present. Highly interesting, includes many scenes of modern matadors, plus some fascinating older material.

Bullfighter and the Lady (1951)***½ Robert Stack, Joy Page, Gilbert Roland. American sportsman visiting in Mexico is intrigued by bullfight-

ing, gets a matador to help him become one. Absorbing drama of the bullring, with suspenseful ring scenes, fine performances. (Dir: Budd Boetticher, 87 mins.)

Bullitt (1968)**** Steve McQueen, Robert Vaughn, Jacqueline Bisset. Excellent chase finale would make this film worthwhile by itself but it has more to recommend it . . . not the least being Steve McQueen's aggressive performance as a tough, modern-day police detective involved in the middle of Mafia dealings and political intervention. If fast-paced crime dramas-plus are your preference, here's one to savor. Well directed by Peter Yates. (113 mins.)

Bullwhip (1958)**½ Guy Madison, Rhonda Fleming. Guy Madison accepts a shotgun wedding to avoid the gallows in this western, which seems a fair exchange, especially when the bride is lovely Rhonda Fleming. (Dir: Harmon Jones, 80 mins.)

Bundle of Joy (1956)**½ Debbie Reynolds, Eddie Fisher. Love and songs amid a big department store setting in this light and occasionally amusing comedy. Debbie's cute and Eddie sings. Remake of old Ginger Rogers comedy "Bachelor Mother." (Dir: Norman Taurog, 98 mins.)

Bunny Lake Is Missing (1965)*** Carol Lynley, Keir Dullea, Laurence Olivier, Noel Coward. A first-class mystery drama with an excellent cast. Miss Lynley goes through one nightmare after another as a harried young mother who enlists the aid of Scotland Yard to find her missing daughter. Miss Lynley's brother, fascinatingly played by Keir Dullea, joins his sister in her search, despite the fact that Inspector Olivier begins to doubt that Bunny Lake ever existed. The surprise ending is played for chills. (Dir: Otto Preminger, 107 mins.)

Bunny O'Hare (1971)*½ Bette Davis, Ernest Borgnine, Jack Cassidy. It's embarrassing to watch Miss Davis and Borgnine playing aging bank robbers who make up to look like hippies to stage their holdup and make their getaway on a motorcycle. Juvenile fare; the less said about it the better. (Director: Gerd Oswald, 92 mins.)

Buona Sera, Mrs. Campbell (1969)**½ Gina Lollobrigida, Peter Lawford, Shelley Winters, Phil Silvers. A diverting comedy premise, well handled by old pro Melvin Frank. Gina, an Italian mother of a lovely young daughter, has been getting checks from 3 former WW II American romances who each think they are the father of her child. Some twenty years later, the Air Force veterans come back for a squadron reunion and the fun starts. Good performances all the way around. (Dir: Melvin Frank, 111 mins.)

Bureau of Missing Persons (1933) **½ Bette Davis, Pat O'Brien. Supposed inside story of Missing Persons Bureau never stays in one direction and gets lost itself. Comedy portion is much more entertaining than dramatic segment. (Dir: Roy Del Ruth)

Burglar, The (1957)*½ Dan Duryea, Jayne Mansfield. A grade "C" meller about a couple of thieves who try to get away with some "hot ice" but are double-crossed at every turn. Miss Mansfield tries to play it straight and misses the boat. (Dir: Paul Wendkos, 90 mins.)

Burglars, The (France-Italy, 1971) **½ Jean-Paul Belmondo, Omar Sharif, Dyan Cannon. Above-average heist film with an attractive cast of stars, a lush Greek setting, and exciting work from the stuntmen in a car chase. Belmondo is the head crook, who steals a fortune in emeralds; Sharif is the dishonest and sadistic policeman out to get the jewels for himself; and Cannon is a woman whose loyalties waver between the two of them. (Dir: Henri Verneuil, 120 mins.)

Burn (1970)*** Marlon Brando. Ambitious film about an island in the Caribbean during the mid-19th century, but made in Italy by the Italian director Gillo Pontecorvo, who directed the remarkable "Battle of Algiers." Story concerns the troubled course of a slave revolt and a small island's battle for nationhood while brutalized and exploited by a succession of colonial powers. Brando plays a manipulative Britisher who betrays the islanders. Timely and important subject, marred by inconsistencies in the script, but gifted director Pontecorvo maintains interest.

Burn, Witch, Burn (British, 1962) **½ Janet Blair, Peter Wyngarde. Professor's wife becomes obsessed with witchcraft, is convinced she must die in his place. Well-made

supernatural thriller gets good direction helping the plot through its more far-fetched phases. (Dir: Sidney Hayers, 90 mins.)

Burning Court, The (France-Italy-West Germany, 1962)** Nadja Tiller, Jean-Claude Brialy. John Dickson Carr's suspense novel of mystery and the occult about an eccentric man awaiting inevitable death, peters out into this unconvincing, badly dubbed screen rendition, occasionally sparked by fantastic effects. (Dir: Julien Duvivier, 102 mins.)

Burning Hills (1956)*½ Natalie Wood, Tab Hunter. Trite western drama aimed towards the juvenile set by casting Tab & Natalie as a pair of young lovers who fight for their chance for happiness against a ruthless cattle baron's young son and his band of murderers. (Dir: Stuart Heisler, 94 mins.)

Burnt Offerings (1976)* Oliver Reed, Karen Black, Burgess Meredith, Eileen Heckart, Bette Davis. Is it possible to create terror with an inanimate villain? Not if this trite, talky attempt at horror is an example. When Miss Black and hubby Reed rent a summer house, they're faced with a number of surprises, none of which seems credible. Red herrings abound! Wonderful performers are wasted. Based on the novel by Robert Morasco, produced and directed by Dan Curtis. (106 mins.)

Bus Riley's Back in Town (1965)** Ann-Margret, Michael Parks, Janet Margolin. Youth returns to his home from the Navy determined to make good, resumes an affair with an old flame from the high-rent district. Plodding drama made of artificialities—Parks tries to act like James Dean, the script sounds like William Inge (who did write it, but refused credit), the direction imitation Kazan. The result: mild. (Dir: Harvey Hart, 93 mins.)

Bus Stop—See: **Wrong Kind of Girl, The**

Bush Christmas (Australian, 1947) *** Chips Rafferty. Some school kids run afoul of a couple of thieves on Christmas Day. Highly unusual drama, depicting Yuletide life Down Under. Recommended.

Buster and Billie (1974)**½ Jan-Michael Vincent, Joan Goodfellow. An uneven, occasionally perceptive story about a gang-bang among high-school students in rural Georgia, circa 1948, long before most Americans ever heard of Plains. Sometimes poignant screenplay by Ron Turbeville who based the story on his own high-school days. Joan Goodfellow is quite touching as the acquiescent but disinterested town tramp who finally falls for Buster, played with strength and charm by Jan-Michael Vincent. (Dir: Daniel Petrie, 100 mins.)

Buster Keaton Story, The (1957)** Donald O'Connor, Ann Blyth, Rhonda Fleming, Peter Lorre. Screen biography of the brilliant movie comedian disregards facts flagrantly, presents an almost totally false impression of Hollywood and its brilliant subject. O'Connor tries hard, is responsible for what little success the film has. (Dir: Sidney Sheldon, 91 mins.)

Busting (1973)*** Elliott Gould, Robert Blake, Allen Garfield. Commendable attempt to realistically portray the seamy lives of two Los Angeles vice-squad cops. Gould and Blake are the cynical detectives, forced to arrest (or "bust") the small-time addicts and hookers instead of the real kingpins of organized crime because their police department superiors are getting paid off by the big guys. Well acted by Gould and Blake who go their merry way, flaunting all the rules, seeking revenge on everybody. Peter Hyams, a TV director and screenwriter, makes his feature film debut both directing and writing this one. (92 mins.)

Busy Body, The (1967)**½ Sid Caesar, Robert Ryan, Anne Baxter. This fairly funny comedy about bumbling gangsters has Sid Caesar in a role which seems tailored for Jerry Lewis. In fact, the whole thing seems like a Jerry Lewis film, which means heavy slapstick antics and joke-filled dialogue. Some clever moments, a good supporting cast. Once again, Caesar's superb talents have been wasted by Hollywood. (Dir: William Castle, 90 mins.)

But, I Don't Want to Get Married (1970)**½ Herschel Bernardi, Shirley Jones, Nanette Fabray. This made-for-TV comedy has two things going for it . . . Herschel Bernardi as a recent widower who is thrust once again into the world of eager women looking for husbands, and a fairly good script. Bernardi's perplexed face in dealing with various ladies (including a brash Shirley Jones, an impossible Nanette Fabray, and an obvious Sue Lyon, among others) keeps the film funny most of the way. The ending at a PTA meeting at which Bernardi encounters a handsome widow (June Lockhart) has a great deal of charm. (Dir: Jerry Paris)

But Not for Me (1959)**½ Clark Gable, Carroll Baker, Lilli Palmer. Middle-aged Broadway producer is chased by a young secretary, who doesn't think the difference in age matters. Remake of "Accent on Youth" starts promisingly, loses steam as it progresses. Gable is good, as usual, the net result mildly amusing. (Dir: Walter Lang, 105 mins.)

But Where Is Daniel Vax? (Israeli, 1972)*** Some funny and ironic scenes in this insightful story about an Israeli pop singer, with an American wife, who returns to Israel to visit some of his old schoolmates, and unexpectedly becomes involved in the difficult task of trying to locate one of them. English subtitles. (Dir: Avram Heffner, 95 mins.)

Butch Cassidy and the Sundance Kid (1969)**** Paul Newman, Robert Redford, Katharine Ross. An enormously appealing anti-western directed with great flair by George Roy Hill. Newman and Redford give such ingratiating performances that it's easy to overlook some shortcomings in the original screenplay by William Goldman based on two legendary bank and train robbers who clowned their way through much of the 1890's before fleeing to South America. These are certainly the drollest and most sophisticated gunmen you've seen in any American western in a long time. The movie starts out promisingly with Katharine Ross taking her clothes off, but does not lose interest after that. Graced with a catchy musical score including the award-winning tune "Raindrops Keep Fallin' on My Head." (Dir: George Roy Hill, 112 mins.)

Butch Minds the Baby (1942)**½ Brod Crawford, Virginia Bruce. A softhearted mug helps out a mother and her baby when rough times approach. Damon Runyon story has some good moments, some laughs, some tears.

Butley (Great Britain, 1973)******** Alan Bates, Jessica Tandy, Richard O'Callaghan. Alan Bates is absolutely marvelous in this filmed version of Simon Gray's witty, award-winning play about a masochistic, joyfully malicious English university professor dealing rather badly with his onrushing male menopause. Bates is an actor of great range and technical virtuosity, and this is a valuable permanent record of one of the best acting performances of the decade. The brilliant playwright Harold Pinter, incidentally, makes an extremely auspicious directorial debut, skillfully guiding Gray's own screenplay. Bates' bitchy, witty, slashing tirades are a joy to behold. (127 mins.)

Butterfield 8 (1960)****½** Elizabeth Taylor, Laurence Harvey, Eddie Fisher. Elizabeth Taylor won her first Oscar for her portrayal in this melodrama. (Some say she received the award for sentimental reasons. She'd been so sick.) Based on John O'Hara's best seller about a misguided gal who lets herself go whenever a man enters the scene. Miss Taylor has given far better performances in better films, but there's a glamorous aura about the slick yarn and Laurence Harvey cuts a good romantic figure as Liz's once-in-a-lifetime, deep love. The supporting cast boasts such stalwarts as Dina Merrill, Mildred Dunnock, Betty Field, and George Voskovec. (Dir: Daniel Mann, 109 mins.)

Butterflies Are Free (1972)******* Goldie Hawn, Edward Albert, Eileen Heckart. The funny and credible Broadway play has been turned into a top-entertainment film. Goldie Hawn is perfectly cast as a fledgling actress who stumbles into the life of self-sufficient blind boy Edward Albert. Enter the boy's over-protective but genuinely loving mother, brilliantly played by Eileen Heckart (she won an Oscar for this role), and doubts creep into the relationship. (Dir: Milton Katselas, 109 mins.)

By Love Possessed (1961)****½** Lana Turner, Efrem Zimbalist Jr., Thomas Mitchell, Jason Robards Jr., George Hamilton. Wealthy attorney realizes his domestic life is not all it should be, is drawn into an affair with the equally lonely and discontented wife of his crippled partner. Controversial novel made into a lackluster film suffering mainly from script trouble. Performances as good as can be expected. (Dir: John Sturges, 115 mins.)

By the Light of the Silvery Moon (1953)******* Doris Day, Gordon MacRae. Songs, dances, and a good amount of nostalgia in this turn of the century musical comedy. Doris and Gordon are a likeable team and make sweet music together. (Dir: David Butler, 102 mins.)

Bye Bye Birdie (1963)*****½** Dick Van Dyke, Janet Leigh, Ann-Margret. What happens when a teenage singing idol about to be drafted gives his final TV performance. Musical based on the Broadway stage success. Some tuneful songs, sharp performances by Van Dyke as a songwriter, Paul Lynde as a small-town father, Maureen Stapleton as a domineering mom. Sprightly fun. (Dir: George Sidney, 111 mins.)

Bye Bye Braverman (1968)******* George Segal, Jack Warden, Alan King, Godfrey Cambridge. Interesting if not completely successful attempt by director Sidney Lumet to create a comedy on the mores of would-be Jewish intellectuals in New York City. Focuses on one day when a group of friends attend the funeral of a deceased comrade. Filmed partially in Brooklyn. Lumet gets what humor there may be from the funeral itself; some of the brightest moments of the film are vignettes contributed by such character actors as Joseph Wiseman and Sorrell Booke. (Dir: Sidney Lumet, 94 mins.)

Cabaret (1972)******** Liza Minnelli, Joel Grey, Michael York. A knockout. One of the most brilliant musicals ever made and certainly the definitive version of Sally Bowles, the original character in Christopher Isherwood's 1939 book about life in pre-World War Two Berlin. Far better than the Broadway musical, thanks largely to the bravura performance of Liza Minnelli playing Sally. Liza can act better than her mother (Judy Garland) and already seems equally accomplished with the songs. Joel Grey won an Academy Award for his dazzling decadence playing a nightclub m.c., the same role he created on Broadway. It's handling of the political material during the time of Hitler's rise to power is done with style and integrity. Bob Fosse's direction is inspired throughout. (124 mins.)

Cabin in the Sky (1942)*** Ethel Waters, Rochester, Lena Horne. This spiritual fable of a fight between heaven and the Devil is in such capable hands on the screen that it is a delight to watch. Not nearly as good as the play but must be recommended as off-beat entertainment.

Cable Car Murder, The (1971)**½ Robert Hooks. Well-made San Francisco cops-and-robbers film features a '70's style murder story. Will interest action fans. Unusual camera views of the city give the show an extra edge as black Inspector Louis Van Alsdale (Hooks) takes on the Establishment over the murder of a shipping magnate's son. Of particular interest is the menacing atmosphere created in a confrontation between the black cop and black bad guys. Cool and strong, Hooks' character shows courage throughout. Made-for-TV. (Dir: Jerry Thorpe.)

Cactus Flower (1969)**½ Walter Matthau, Ingrid Bergman, Goldie Hawn. Disappointing adaptation of the Broadway hit comedy of Abe Burrows, despite an enchanting debut by Goldie Hawn for which she won the Academy Award for best supporting actress. Matthau plays a dentist who is having an affair with Goldie, while not admitting to himself that he really loves his nurse played by Ingrid. Bergman is too mature for this kind of role. Could use more of Quincy Jones' musical score, and less stilted dialogue. (Dir: Gene Saks, 103 mins.)

Caddy, The (1953)**½ Dean Martin, Jerry Lewis, Donna Reed. Jerry's a golf hopeful who's afraid of crowds in this one. Not the team's best, but should please the partisans. (Dir: Norman Taurog, 95 mins.)

Cadet Girl (1941)* Carole Landis, George Montgomery. Should a young West Pointer stay at the Point or romance the lovely blonde? This is a movie so you know what he does. On brave old Army team. Awful film.

Cadets on Parade (1942)** Freddie Bartholomew, Jimmy Lydon. Boy runs away from a military academy,

108

is befriended by a poor newsboy. Fair melodrama.

Caesar Against the Pirates (1960)*½ Gordon Mitchell, Abbe Lane. Routine Italian produced adventure epic dubbed in English. (Dir: Gabriel Pascal, 127 mins.)

Caesar and Cleopatra (British, 1945) *** Vivien Leigh, Claude Rains, Stewart Granger. Bernard Shaw's intellectual joke about the aging Roman conquerer and the beautiful but slightly addle-brained beauty of the Nile. Some of the Shavian wit has been preserved, but there are dull stretches.

Caesar, the Conquerer (1961)*½ Cameron Mitchell. Familiar, Italianmade, English-dubbed, heroic adventure for the action fan in the postmongoloid category. (Dir: Edward H. Griffith)

Café Metropole (1937)*** Tyrone Power, Loretta Young. Amusing comedy about a young man who is forced to pose as a prince in order to make good on a gambling debt. The phony prince, played by Tyrone, is ordered by his creditor to woo and win an heiress, played by Loretta.

Cage of Gold (British, 1950) **½ Jean Simmons, David Farrar. An old flame, who's a scoundrel, returns to blackmail a girl now happily married. Good performances manage to overcome a familiar plot to make this acceptable melodrama.

Cage Without a Key (1975)**½ Susan Dey, Michael Brandon, Sam Bottoms. The theme of this film—how a poorly run juvenile detention home can turn teenagers into hardened criminals—is placed in director Buzz Kulik's careful hands, and his treatment of the material and the cast keeps this shocker from going awry. Sweet ingenue Susan Dey plays a naive youngster, making the transition into a tough little monkey, thanks to her fellow inmates. Made-for-TV. (Dir: Buzz Kulik, 100 mins.)

Caged (1950)***½ Eleanor Parker, Hope Emerson, Jan Sterling. Gripping drama of women's prison. Eleanor Parker runs the gamut from young innocent bystander sentenced for the theft to hard and bitter convict. Hope Emerson, as the cruel police matron, equals Parker's great performance. (Dir: John Cromwell, 91 mins.)

Cahill: U.S. Marshal (1973)*½ John

Wayne, Gary Grimes, George Kennedy, Neville Brand. Tiresome attempt to flesh out the usual Wayne-Western plots by saddling him—and there are a lot of saddle-sore jokes —with two sons who get involved with bank robbers and murders because Daddy isn't home enough to guide their moral upbringing. Wayne's films often have a morally repellent theme, and this one is no exception. The kids, you see, can get away with anything including murder, if their father is the U.S. Marshal and they just say they're sorry. (Richard Nixon said he was sorry, too—not wrong, just sorry!) (Dir: Andrew V. McLaglen, 102 mins.)

Caine Mutiny, The (1954)***½ Humphrey Bogart, Jose Ferrer, Van Johnson, Fred MacMurray, Robert Francis. An all star cast effectively brings this tale of a modern day mutiny to the screen. Humphrey Bogart is a standout as Captain Queeg, the skipper of the Caine. Based on Herman Wouk's novel. (Dir: Edward Dmytryk, 125 mins.)

Cairo (U.S./Great Britain, 1963)* George Sanders, Richard Johnson, Faten Hamama. Stale remake of "The Asphalt Jungle"—British major robs Egyptian museum of ancient jewels. Good acting wasted. (Dir: Wolf Rilla, 91 mins.)

Calamity Jane (1953)**½ Doris Day, Howard Keel. Miss Day gives a robust performance in this tuneful musical. Howard Keel is well cast as the tough cowboy who sets out to tame "Jane." (Dir: David Butler, 101 mins.)

Calamity Jane & Sam Bass (1949)*½ Yvonne DeCarlo, Howard Duff. Mediocre western about the two celebrated figures of the wild and woolly. Miss DeCarlo overacts throughout and the rest of the cast underplays as if they were afraid of her. (Dir: George Sherman, 85 mins.)

California (1947)*** Ray Milland, Barbara Stanwyck. Rip-roaring western set in early California when greedy men did not want the territory to become a state. (Dir: John Farrow, 97 mins.)

California (1963)*½ Jock Mahoney, Faith Domergue, Michael Pate. Collaborator leads Mexican troops in terrorizing the territory while his half-brother heads the revolutionists

trying to break away from Mexico. Trite tale of Old California.

California Conquest (1952)**½ Cornel Wilde, Teresa Wright, Alphonso Bedoya. Spanish Californians, under Mexican rule, almost end up in the hands of the Russians in this fast paced but not too exciting western drama. (Dir: Lew Landers, 79 mins.)

California Kid, The (1974)**½ Martin Sheen, Vic Morrow, Michelle Phillips, Stuart Margolin. Sheen and Morrow are pitted against each other throughout this tense drama about a sheriff who is a one-man judge, jury, and executioner in dealing with speeders on the highway. Morrow plays the small-town lawman, and Sheen is the brother of one of the dead speeders. The action of the duel-race-to-the-death at the end is worth waiting for. Made-for-TV. (Dir: Richard Heffron, 72 mins.)

California Split (1974)**** Elliott Gould, George Segal, Ann Prentiss, Gwen Welles. California Split is western-slang jargon for cutthroat high-low poker, and Robert Altman has fashioned here one of his most entertaining, compelling and powerful films. Taut original screenplay by Joseph Walsh about a pair of parasitical California gamblers, who become pals after getting mugged. Gould and Segal work beautifully together, and the scenes in the poker parlor capture the compulsive quality of the frenzied, possessed souls down on their luck, hoping for a reprieve, but obliged to bet on virtually everything including the names of the Seven Dwarfs. There's a funny, touching scene where two amiable semi-hookers, wonderfully played by Ann Prentiss and Gwen Welles, serve the stars breakfast consisting of beer and Froot Loops cereal. Altman's unique vision and his sense of character, pacing and detail combine to produce a multi-textured essay that is funny, and genuinely moving. (Dir: Robert Altman, 111 mins.)

Call Her Mom (1972)*½ Connie Stevens, Van Johnson. College campus show played strictly on the "camp" side, with Miss Stevens cast as a peppery fraternity housemother. Mixing 1970 college problems with early '50's atmosphere, the show attempts a spoof but only succeeds half the time. Made-for-TV. (Dir: Jerry Paris, 73 mins.)

Call Her Savage (1932)* Clara Bow, Gilbert Roland, Monroe Owsley, Thelma Todd. Minor Clara Bow film gives the actress a chance to play everything from comedy to melodrama. Only for her fans. (Dir: John Francis Dillon, 88 mins.)

Call Me Bwana (British, 1963)**½ Bob Hope, Anita Ekberg, Edie Adams. Hope chased by foreign agents once more as he tries to recover a lost capsule. It all has the ring of familiarity, but Hope springs eternal and he has some good gags. (Dir: Gordon Douglas, 103 mins.)

Call Me Genius (British, 1961)**½ Tony Hancock, George Sanders. London office clerk becomes a mad painter in the Paris artists' quarter. Hancock is a popular English clown —his comedy is a matter of taste. For those who may take to him, there are some funny moments here.

Call Me Madam (1959)***½ Ethel Merman, Donald O'Connor, George Sanders, Vera-Ellen. It's Merman and Irving Berlin all the way in this picturization of the snappy stage musical about the free-wheeling Washington "hostess with the mostess." The tunes are fine, the production colorful; Merman fans will be in heaven, of course. (Dir: Walter Lang, 117 mins.)

Call Me Mister (1951)**½ Betty Grable, Dan Dailey, Danny Thomas, Dale Robertson. A sparkling stage success turned into a watery movie musical with a plot about a soldier in post-war Japan following his entainer wife while AWOL. (Dir: Lloyd Bacon, 95 mins.)

Call of the Wild (1935)*** Clark Gable, Loretta Young, Jack Oakie. Adaptation of Jack London's story of a man and his dog's adventures in the Klondike hasn't got too much of the dog. But there's enough love and adventure to please most audiences. (Dir: William Wellman, 100 mins.)

Call of the Yukon (1938)** Richard Arlen, Beverly Roberts, Lyle Talbot. James Oliver Curwood's novel "Swift Lightning," about parallel romances in Northern Alaska—one canine, the other human—watered down for the Hollywood version, is an antique by now, but harmless enough. (Dir: B. Reeves Eason, 70 mins.)

Call Out the Marines (1942)**½ Edmund Lowe, Victor McLaglen. Two thickheads round up foreign agents. Funny comedy, boisterous and bawdy.

Call to Danger (1973)**½ Peter Graves. Slick outing by "Mission: Impossible" writer-producer Laurence Heath, featuring "Mission" star Peter Graves as a Justice Department sleuth. Diving out of windows and kissing sexy models, Graves retrieves a mobster kidnapped by thugs during crime hearings held in Washington. Made-for-TV. (Dir: Tom Gries, 73 mins.)

Calling Bulldog Drummond (British, 1951)**½ Walter Pidgeon, Margaret Leighton. Drummond comes out of retirement and with the aid of a policewoman smashes a crime ring. Pretty fair detective story given better production than the usual run. (Dir: Victor Saville, 80 mins.)

Calling Doctor Death (1943)*** Lon Chaney, Patricia Morison. Effective little thriller, with Chaney as a distinguished doctor whose wife has a yen for other fellows. When the cheating wife is murdered, there are suspects a-plenty. (Dir: Reginald Le Borg, 63 mins.)

Calling Homicide (1956)**½ William Elliott, Kathleen Case. Cop investigating the death of a fellow policeman uncovers blackmail in a modeling school. Neat little mystery merits praise for achievement on a small budget. (Dir: Edward Bernds, 61 mins.)

Calling Northside 777 (1947)***½ James Stewart, Lee J. Cobb, Richard Conte. Exciting, fast-paced story of a newspaperman who proves a man innocent by probing an eleven-year-old case history. A bit implausible towards the end but you'll like it. (Dir: Henry Hathaway, 111 mins.)

Calloway Went That Away (1951)*** Fred MacMurray, Dorothy McGuire, Howard Keel. Funny film about a western hero whose career is revitalized by TV showings of his early films. This has been done before but the cast of pros make it work. (Dir: Norman Panama, 81 mins.)

Caltiki, the Immortal Monster (Italian, 1960)** John Merivale. This time it's archeologists and corpses of Mayans from the seventh century who come to grips. The kids who like their chills on the wild side might enjoy this one. (Dir: Robert Hampton, 76 mins.)

Calypso Heat Wave (1957)*½ Johnny Desmond, Merry Anders. Tiresome musical with a gangster plot thrown in for good measure. Plenty of calypso songs scattered amid some ineffective drama sequences, but they don't relieve the tedium. (90 mins.)

Calypso Joe (1957)*½ Angie Dickinson, Edward Kemmer, Herb Jeffries. Airline hostess plans to marry a South American millionaire, but her ex-boyfriend and his musical chums dissuade her. Nothing musical comedy aside from a dozen or so Calypso numbers. (76 mins.)

Camelot (1967)*** Richard Harris, Vanessa Redgrave, David Hemmings. Opulent, generally well-acted version of the Broadway Lerner & Loewe musical. About the Knights of the Round Table in Hollywood's—and author T. H. White's—version of life in the Middle Ages. Joshua Logan's plodding direction of this $15 million epic is relieved by the magnetic performances of the two British stars Harris and Redgrave, with the latter displaying her special magical brand of beauty, femininity, and strength. Harris, incidentally, really does sing his own songs. The costume designer John Truscott deserves a special accolade for his ravishing creations. (Dir: Joshua Logan, 179 mins.)

Cameraman, The (1928)**** Buster Keaton. A marvelously funny and inventive comedy, one of Buster's last and greatest efforts. He plays a still photographer hoping to win both his fortune and a pretty girl while learning the intricacies of being a news cameraman. You'll see an inspired pantomime sequence as Buster journeys to what was then an empty and newly built Yankee Stadium. This is another movie treasure which was thought to be lost forever, but has been found thanks to the work of the American Film Institute. Directed, for the benefit of real movie buffs, by Edward Sedgwick. (80 mins.)

Camille (1936)***½ Greta Garbo, Robert Taylor. For Garbo's performance alone this beautiful production of Dumas' classic romance is a must. Taylor is good too and although the story is beginning to creak it did make a good vehicle for Garbo. (Dir: George Cukor, 108 mins.)

Campbells' Kingdom (British, 1957) *** Dirk Bogarde, Stanley Baker. Young landowner battles a crooked contractor who wants to build a dam across it. Typical western plot transplanted to Canada—still plenty of action, elaborate production values. (Dir: Ralph Thomas, 102 mins.)

Can-Can (1960)**½ Frank Sinatra, Shirley MacLaine, Maurice Chevalier, Louis Jourdan. Lawyer protects a cafe owner when she's accused of presenting the Can-Can, a supposedly lewd dance. Cole Porter musical lumbers across the screen with emphasis upon the dazzle, but the score isn't one of his best and the script lacks true wit. Sinatra fans and lovers of musicals will approve, even though it really isn't up to par. (Dir: Walter Lang, 131 mins.)

Can Ellen Be Saved? (1974)**½ Kathy Cannon, Michael Parks. Based on a spate of newspaper articles about kids who become "Jesus freaks" and have to be literally kidnapped by their parents and deprogrammed by experts. Young girl gets caught up with a religious group who live and work on a commune until her worried parents enlist help. The script is a bit talky, especially in the commune scenes. Parks is seen as the self-appointed guru of the pack. Made-for-TV. (Dir: Harvey Hart, 72 mins.)

Can Hieronymus Merkin Ever Forget Mercy Humppe and Find True Happiness? (British, 1969)* Anthony Newley, Milton Berle, Joan Collins, George Jessel, Bruce Forsyth. An awful ego trip by Anthony Newley (produced, directed, co-written, composed and is responsible for) in the role of a star who reviews his tawdry life. In roaring bad taste generally. One or two non-dirty laughs. (Dir: Anthony Newley, 106 mins.)

Canadian Pacific (1949)**½ Randolph Scott, Jane Wyatt. A surveyor fights all odds to get the railroad through the wilderness. Outdoor melodrama has enough action to receive a passing grade.

Canadians, The (British, 1961)*½ Robert Ryan, John Dehner, Teresa Stratas. The mounties have a tough job on their hands trying to keep peace among the Indians responsible for the Custer massacre. Authentic detail and actual Canadian location sites go for naught in a slow adventure drama which needs much more

111

action. (Dir: Burt Kennedy, 85 mins.)

Cancel My Reservation (1972) ½ Bob Hope, Eva Marie Saint. This stinker wasn't planned as a disaster film—it just turned out that way. NBC, incidentally, co-produced this relentlessly unfunny mishmosh about murder and mayhem on a Phoenix ranch. Saint is miscast and the 69-year-old Hope is embarrassing pretending to be a 42-year-old in this, his 54th film. Based on the novel "The Broken Gun" by Louis L'Amour. (Dir: Paul Bogart, 99 mins.)

Candidate, The (1972)**** Robert Redford, Peter Boyle, Melvyn Douglas. The best and most honest movie about American politics to have hit the screen in years. Many of those involved including director Michael Ritchie and screenwriter Jeremy Larner were in real political campaigns during the late 60's and they've captured some of the look and feel of a political campaign. Redford plays a young liberal lawyer in California who runs for the U.S. Senate and tries to avoid selling out or resorting to demagoguery. He turns in one of his best performances to date. (110 mins.)

Candidate for Murder (British, 1960) ** Michael Gough, Erica Remberg, John Justin. Professional killer is hired to do away with a man's wife but fears he will be the victim of a doublecross. Minor but compact melodrama from an Edgar Wallace story—well acted. (Dir: David Villiers, 60 mins.)

Candide (France, 1960)**½ Jean-Pierre Cassel, Dahlia Lavi, Pierre Brasseur, Nadia Gray, Michel Simon. Inconsistent updating of Voltaire's classic satire on optimism in the face of worldly strife, which places the brightly positive hero Candide in a world threatened by atomic holocaust. Ironies fail to jell, though there are some fine grotesque moments. (Dir: Norbert Carbonnaux, 90 mins.)

Candy (U.S.-Italian-French, 1968)* Ewa Aulin, Marlon Brando, Richard Burton. Dreary, sophomoric film version of amusing bestseller by Terry Southern and Mason Hoffenberg. The adventures of a young lady named Candy include a visit to a men's lavatory, and the overstated satire throws in a bloody operating sequence in a medical amphitheater. Miss Aulin is blonde, pert and completely unbelievable in the lead . . . her respected co-stars (Marlon Brando, Richard Burton, Walter Matthau, John Huston, James Coburn, and Ringo Starr) all should have known better. This trash, incidentally, was financed by the American Broadcasting Company—but don't wait up hoping to see it uncut on the ABC-TV network.

Candy Man, The (1969)* George Sanders, Leslie Parrish. Drug dealer in Mexico, known as the Candy Man, engineers kidnapping. Wooden drama, acting likewise. Poorly written and directed by Herbert J. Leder. (97 mins.)

Cangaciero—the Story of an Outlaw Bandit (Brazil, 1953)*** Marisa Prado, Alberto Ruschel. Interesting for its novelty alone, this rugged tale of an outlaw and his downfall has been dubbed into English in okay fashion. Plot gets rather bloody at times. Generally well done.

Cannibal Attack (1954)*½ Johnny Weissmuller, David Bruce. Jungle Jim (Johnny Weissmuller) cracks a cobalt-thieving operation with the aid of a chimp. Need we say more? (Dir: Lee Sholem, 69 mins.)

Cannon (1971)**½ William Conrad, Vera Miles, Barry Sullivan. Made-for-TV feature. Stocky William Conrad with those hard blue eyes stars as a private investigator who travels to New Mexico to solve a war buddy's murder. Playing for realism, producer Quinn Martin often uses hand-held cameras while filming near Las Cruces, New Mexico, where his hero Cannon, a stranger, faces small-town antagonism. When plot complications tend to wear the viewer down, Martin shores it up with fine location work, Conrad's imposing presence, and a supporting cast featuring Vera Miles, Barry Sullivan, J.D. Cannon, Keenan Wynn, and Earl Holliman. (Dir: George McCowan, 99 mins.)

Cannon: He Who Digs a Grave (1973)** William Conrad, Anne Baxter, Barry Sullivan, David Janssen. Sniper bullets, a horse stampede and a fire don't deter our rotund hero, Frank Cannon, from helping an old war buddy who's been arrested on two counts of murder in a small cattle town. The location scenes in Grass Valley, California, and the performances by the guest stars add gloss to this routine tale. Made-for-TV. (Dir: Richard Donner, 106 mins.)

Canon City (1948)*** Scott Brady, Jeff Corby, Whit Bissell. True story of an escape from the Colorado prison told in semi-documentary style and filmed where it happened. Not as good as top prison fiction—but exciting.

Can't Help Singing (1944)**½ Deanna Durbin, Robert Paige. Strongwilled girl trails her sweetheart west. Pleasant but uneven costume musical. Jerome Kern tunes help. (Dir: Frank Ryan, 89 mins.)

Canterville Ghost, The (1943)*** Charles Laughton, Robert Young. Amusing little whimsy about a cowardly ghost who can only be released from his haunting chores when a descendant performs a deed of bravery. Laughton is wonderful as the ghost. (Dir: Jules Dassin, 96 mins.)

Canyon Crossroads (1955)**½ Richard Basehart, Phyllis Kirk. Uranium prospectors are beset by crooks when they make a strike. Interesting western with a modern touch. (Dir: Alfred L. Werker, 84 mins.)

Canyon Passage (1946)*** Dana Andrews, Susan Hayward, Brian Donlevy. Good western. Dana loves Susan who is his buddy Brian's fiancee. Brian gets into trouble, is almost hanged. There's an Indian battle and, of course, Donlevy obligingly dies to let Dana kiss Susan. Lots of action. (Dir: Jacques Tourneur, 99 mins.)

Canyon River (1958)*½ George Montgomery, Marcia Henderson. Rancher takes on the perils of a cattle drive. Routine oats opera. (Dir: Harmon Jones, 80 mins.)

Cape Canaveral Monsters (1960)* Scott Peters, Linda Connell. Still another "invaders from space" science-fiction yarn with all the expected turns. In view of serious missile efforts these days, this may be silly to most.

Cape Fear (1962)*** Gregory Peck, Robert Mitchum, Polly Bergen. Brutal tale of a revenge-seeking convict preying upon the sensibilities of the lawyer who sent him to prison. Excellent performances, with a brilliant study in sadism by Mitchum as the meanie. Not for the kiddies, but this is often very power-

ful. (Dir: J. Lee Thompson, 105 mins.)

Caper of the Golden Bulls, The (1967)**½ Stephen Boyd, Yvette Mimieux, Giovanna Ralli. The familiar plot of having a group of professional crooks combine their talents to pull a big caper is trotted out again for this handsomely mounted production. The Spanish setting is beautifully photographed, and some suspense is generated. (Dir: Russell Rouse, 104 mins.)

Capetown Affair, The (1967)*½ Claire Trevor, James Brolin, Jacqueline Bisset. South African secret agents attempt to save confidential microfilm before it falls into the hands of Communists. Early, unmemorable roles for Bisset and Brolin. (90 mins.)

Caprice (1967)** Doris Day, Richard Harris. Pure escapist film fare. Doris Day is the same bouncy blonde she plays in all her films, but her leading man in this one is none other than Richard Harris, and he manages to inject some life into the generally witless proceedings. The plot involves espionage, complete with double agents, undercover men, and a lineup of international villains. (Dir: Frank Tashlin, 98 mins.)

Caprice of "Dear Caroline" (French, 1953)** Martine Carol. Continuing the romantic escapades of the "Forever Amber" of the French Court. English-dubbed costume drama, overstuffed as usual.

Capricious Summer (Czechoslovakian, 1968)*** Rudolf Hrusinsky, Mila Myslikova. A gentle, visually lovely film, written and directed by Jiri Menzel, the director of "Closely Watched Trains." The slight but perceptive story concerns three middle-aged Czech men on a summer vacation, interrupted by the arrival in a small town of a circus tightrope walker (Menzel) and his fetching young female assistant. A touching, beautifully acted fable for those of you who don't demand constant action. English subtitles.

Captain Adventure—See: Adventures of Mandrin, The

Captain Blood (1935)***½ Errol Flynn, Olivia de Havilland. Exciting adaptation of the Sabatini adventure story. This was Mr. Flynn's first picture and he was happily welcomed by critics and fans. It's a top drawer pirate tale. (Dir: Michael Curtiz, 119 mins.)

Captain Boycott (British, 1947)***½ Stewart Granger, Kathleen Ryan, Cecil Parker. When a wealthy landowner in Ireland threatens his tenants with eviction, the farmers decide to fight. Lusty historical melodrama moves with speed, has fine performances. (Dir: Frank Launder, 92 mins.)

Captain Carey, U.S.A. (1950)**½ Alan Ladd, Wanda Hendrix, Francis Lederer. OSS agent returns to Italy after World War II to track down the man who had betrayed him to the Nazis. Unexceptional suspense drama has a typical Ladd action look. Fairly competent; also includes the hit song "Mona Lisa." (Dir: Mitchell Leisen, 85 mins.)

Captain Caution (1940)** Victor Mature, Louise Platt, Bruce Cabot. A girl takes over her father's ship and battles the British during the War of 1812. Lots of action here, and if you don't blink you'll see Alan Ladd in a small role. (Dir: Richard Wallace, 85 mins.)

Captain Eddie (1945)**½ Fred MacMurray, Lynn Bari. Famous aviator's life is used as an excuse for a routine sentimental comedy-drama covering most of this century. Don't expect Rickenbacker's story and film is pleasant enough. (Dir: Lloyd Bacon, 107 mins.)

Captain Falcon (Italian, 1964)*½ Lex Barker, Rosanna Rory. Patriot in thirteenth-century Italy fights to free a kingdom from an evil baron in the same manner as a hundred other movie heroes have—dubbed-English drag. (Dir: Carlo Campogalliani, 97 mins.)

Captain from Castile (1947)**½ Tyrone Power, Jean Peters, Cesar Romero. Action but nothing else in this confused tale of Spain during the Inquisition and the conquest of Mexico. Those that like duels won't be too disappointed. (Dir: Henry King, 140 mins.)

Captain from Koepenick (German, 1956)***½ Heinz Ruhmann. Criminal poses as an officer in order to get the one thing he wants most. It's a perceptive satire and commentary on civilian reaction to the military any time or place and features an extraordinarily moving performance as the would-be officer by Ruhmann.

This is a frequently poignant though episodic film.

Captain Fury (1939)*** Brian Aherne, Paul Lukas, Victor McLaglen. A brave soldier of fortune fights the villainous heads of early Australia's penal colony. Rousing action film, highly enjoyable. (Dir: Hal Roach, 90 mins.)

Captain Horatio Hornblower (1951)***½ Gregory Peck, Virginia Mayo. Sprawling sea saga about the British captain of the Napoleonic wars —his naval victories and his loves. From the novel by C. S. Forester. Robust, exciting, colorful. (Dir: Raoul Walsh, 117 mins.)

Captain Is a Lady, The (1939)** Charles Coburn, Beulah Bondi. Well acted but minor comedy about an old man who insists on being with his wife in an old ladies' home. (Dir: Robert B. Sinclair, 63 mins.)

Captain January (1936)** Shirley Temple, Guy Kibbee. Shirley is an orphan again and the mean old law is trying to take her away from her wonderful guardian. Real junk but Shirley is cute. (Dir: David Butler, 75 mins.)

Captain John Smith and Pocahontas (1953)*½ Anthony Dexter, Jody Lawrence. The one about the settler who was saved by an Injun gal from losing his head. Feeble adventure drama. (Dir: Lew Landers, 76 mins.)

Captain Kidd (1945)*½ Charles Laughton, Randolph Scott. The notorious pirate of the Seven Seas is finally captured through the trickery of one of his own men. Slow, dull costume melodrama. (Dir: Rowland V. Lee, 89 mins.)

Captain Kidd and the Slave Girl (1954)* Anthony Dexter, Eva Gabor. Pirate crew helps Captain Kidd escape execution to try and find the hiding place of his treasure. Action opus is funny in the wrong places. (Dir: Lew Landers, 85 mins.)

Captain Lightfoot (1955)**½ Rock Hudson, Barbara Rush. Beautifully filmed period adventure about rebellion in Old Ireland of the 1800's. Rock Hudson fits his adventurer's role to a T and Miss Rush offers fine feminine support. (Dir: Douglas Sirk, 90 mins.)

Captain Mephisto and the Transformation Machine (1945-66)**½ Richard Bailey, Linda Stirling, Roy Barcroft. Feature version of serial

"Manhunt of Mystery Island." Unknown villain poses as a pirate of old while holding a scientist prisoner in seeking radium deposits. Way, way out serial turned into a kookie feature—lots of action, good camp enjoyment. (Dir: Spencer Bennet, 100 mins.)

Captain Nemo and the Underwater City (1970)** Robert Ryan, Chuck Connors, Nanette Newman. The underwater special effects of this movie may seem a bit dull, but there are enough spurts of action, wondrous sights, and music to keep this nautical children's tale fairly entertaining. Ryan is Captain Nemo, whose underwater empire is visited by shipwrecked people, including a U.S. Senator (Connors) and a feminist (Miss Newman). (Dir: James Hill, 106 mins.)

Captain Newman, M.D. (1963)*** Gregory Peck, Tony Curtis, Angie Dickinson, Eddie Albert. Interesting drama of an air-force psychiatrist whose duty is to his patients first, the military brass second. Well-done vignettes are used as a substitute for any strong plot line, with some good performances helping considerably. (Dir: David Miller, 126 mins.)

Captain Sinbad (1962)* Guy Williams, Pedro Armendariz. The hero (Williams) sets out to save the princess (Heidi Bruhl) from the villain. The kids might be amused. Filmed in Germany, with Bernie Hamilton, Abraham Sofaer. (Dir: Byron Haskin, 85 mins.)

Captains Courageous (1936)***½ Spencer Tracy, Freddie Bartholomew, Lionel Barrymore. The kids will love this adaptation of Kipling's story. Parents also will find a lot to like in this adventurous tale of a young brat who spends three months on a rough fishing vessel. (Dir: Victor Fleming, 116 mins.)

Captains of the Clouds (1942)*** James Cagney, Dennis Morgan. Some good moments in this fairly exciting melodramatic salute to the RCAF. Cagney may be a bum for the first few reels but he literally comes through with flying colors at the end. (Dir: Michael Curtiz, 113 mins.)

Captain's Paradise, The (British, 1953)**** Alec Guinness, Celia Johnson, Yvonne DeCarlo. A ferryboat captain between Gibraltar and Algiers establishes the perfect formula for living by having two wives, one in each port, of opposite personalities. Another merry Guinness romp; delightful comedy, adult, witty, grand fun. (Dir: Anthony Kimmins, 80 mins.)

Captain's Table, The (British, 1959)**½ John Gregson, Peggy Cummins. Captain of a cargo vessel is given a trial command of a luxury liner, with the expected comic complications resulting. Pleasing little comedy gets a fair share of grins. (Dir: Jack Lee, 90 mins.)

Captive City, The (1952)***½ John Forsythe, Joan Camden. A fearless newspaper editor and his wife are threatened when they intend to expose a gangland syndicate. Suspenseful, intelligent crime melodrama, well above average.

Captive Heart, The (British, 1946)**** Michael Redgrave, Rachel Kempson. Czech officer posing as a British officer killed in action writes to his wife from a concentration camp, and they fall in love with each other through the letters. Finely done war drama, excellent in every way. (Dir: Basil Dearden, 86 mins.)

Captive Wild Woman (1943)** Acquanetta, John Carradine, Milburn Stone. Mad doctor transforms an orang-utang into a beautiful girl. Horror thriller isn't as bad as it sounds, but is cheaply made. (Dir: Edward Dmytryk, 61 mins.)

Capture, The (1951)***½ Lew Ayres, Teresa Wright. In Mexico a man unjustly becomes a fugitive. Good melodrama, well acted.

Capture That Capsule—See: Spy Squad

Caravan (British, 1946)**½ Stewart Granger, Jean Kent. Adventurer sent to deliver a valuable necklace in Spain is waylaid by enemies, found and cared for by a gypsy girl. Costume melodrama has moments of excitement, as well as some warm love scenes.

Carbine Williams (1952)*** James Stewart, Jean Hagen, Wendell Corey. Based on fact, this is an engrossing personal drama of the man who invented and improved the Carbine Rifle for use by the Armed Forces. Stewart is effective in the lead role. (Dir: Richard Thorpe, 92 mins.)

Cardinal, The (1963)*** Tom Tryon, Carol Lynley, John Huston, Romy Schneider. Handsomely produced, if overlong and episodic saga about the personal life and religious career of a dedicated young Catholic priest who rises to the lofty position of cardinal. Tom Tryon is very attractive as the young cleric, but he plays his role in too stoic a fashion for a person who believed in and cared for people as much as the film indicates. The large supporting cast is uniformly good with the best performances delivered by John Huston as a rather gruff and outspoken cardinal, and Burgess Meredith as the priest of a very poor parish. (Dir: Otto Preminger, 175 mins.)

Career (1959) ***½ Dean Martin, Anthony Franciosa, Shirley MacLaine, Carolyn Jones. Strong drama about an actor whose ambition and unwillingness to quit enables him to surmount obstacles in getting to the top of his profession. Story stacks the cards against him a bit too much, but the film is continually absorbing, has fine performances by Franciosa and Martin. (Dir: Joseph Anthony, 105 mins.)

Carefree (1938) *** Fred Astaire, Ginger Rogers. Psychiatrist attempts to help a young lawyer and his fiancee, falls for her. Not up to the Astaire-Rogers standard, but still a good musical. (Dir: Mark Sandrich, 83 mins.)

Careful—Soft Shoulder (1942) **½ Virginia Bruce, James Ellison. Nitwit Washington society girl gets involved with a Nazi spy. Surprisingly entertaining comedy, only the wartime background dating it. Pleasing fun.

Caretaker, The (Great Britain, 1964) ***½ Robert Shaw, Donald Pleasence, Alan Bates. Harold Pinter's shatteringly absurd play about the confrontation of two mentally unbalanced brothers and a tramp they take in, adapted by Pinter for the screen, and filmed with care on a low budget. Remains too 'staged' in appearance, but the superb acting, and sharp, witty dialogue give it punch. Alternate title: "The Guest." (Dir: Clive Donner, 105 mins.)

Caretaker, The—See: **The Guest**

Caretakers, The (1963) *½ Robert Stack, Joan Crawford, Polly Bergen, Janis Paige. The plight of a young woman who suffers a nervous breakdown, is treated at a mental hospital. Touchy subject needs careful handling, which it doesn't get here.

116

Aside from a good performance by Janis Paige as an inmate, this crude and insensitive drama has nothing. (Dir: Hall Bartlett, 97 mins.)

Carey Treatment, The (1972) *½ James Coburn, Jennifer O'Neill. Slipshod but stylish-looking mystery yarn. A Boston pathologist sets out to solve an abortion-murder. James Coburn is the slick, impeccably groomed and sexy doctor-detective. Jennifer O'Neill is beautiful, but she's window-dressing. Director Edwards complained about the final cut of the film. The screenplay credit for James P. Bonner is a pseudonym for the three writers who disavowed the final work. Based on the novel "A Case of Need" written by Michael Crichton, though credited to the non-existent Jeffrey Hudson. (Dir: Blake Edwards, 100 mins.)

Cargo to Capetown (1950) **½ Broderick Crawford, Ellen Drew, John Ireland. Personal drama gets in the way of the action in this adventure film about two tanker tramps in love with the same girl. (Dir: Earl McEvoy, 80 mins.)

Carib Gold (1957) ** Ethel Waters, Coley Wallace, Geoffrey Holder. The things that happen when a shrimp boat discovers a sunken treasure. Miss Waters and the Negro cast enhance matters considerably, although the production often has an amateur look. (97 mins.)

Caribbean (1952) ** John Payne, Arlene Dahl, Cedric Hardwicke. Mild adventure yarn about the days of pirates, land grants, and the slave trade in the Caribbean. John Payne is heroic and Arlene Dahl serenely beautiful. (Dir: Edward Ludwig, 97 mins.)

Caribbean Hawk (Spanish, 1964) *½ Johnny Desmond, Yvonne Monlaur. Escaped slaves hold a Spanish blockhouse, but are influenced to throw in with the Spaniards to fight England. Undistinguished adventure melodrama, dubbed-in English.

Cariboo Trail, The (1950) **½ Randolph Scott, "Gabby" Hayes, Bill Williams. Up in Canada in the 1890's, a cattleman turns to gold prospecting accidentally while searching for land. Above average western has a good story, performances. (Dir: Edward L. Marlin, 90 mins.)

Carmen Jones (1955) ***½ Dorothy Dandridge, Harry Belafonte, Pearl

Bailey. The story of the femme fatale "Carmen," adapted by Oscar Hammerstein II updating the Bizet music, and directed by Otto Preminger. Despite some faults, it packs quite a bit of power. Well sung by dubbed voices for the principals. The late Miss Dandridge is a spectacularly beautiful dish in this entry. (Dir: Otto Preminger, 105 mins.)

Carnaby, M.D. (Great Britain, 1966) ** Leslie Phillips, James Robertson Justice, Shirley Ann Field. Sixth entry in the "doctor" series has Justice once again playing Sir Lancelot Spratt trying to train a young doctor. Phillips is hardly as effective as other young apprentices in the series, who include Dirk Bogarde and Kenneth More. Also released as "Doctor in Clover." (Dir: Ralph Thomas, 95 mins.)

Carnal Knowledge (1971)***½ Jack Nicholson, Arthur Garfunkel, Ann-Margret, Candice Bergen. Two enormously gifted artists, writer Jules Feiffer and director Mike Nichols, have combined to create a funny, perceptive, and sometimes painfully accurate account of the sexual mores and hang-ups of the American male over a period of two decades. Nicholson and Garfunkel play Amherst college students in the late '40's, who share the same dormitory room and a blond virgin from nearby Smith (Candice Bergen). There are problems with the film, including the fact that Nicholson is such a reprehensible louse that it's hard to give a damn about him. But so much of the movie is fresh and revealing that you'll overlook its defects. Ann-Margret is surprisingly effective as a 30-ish TV model, as is Garfunkel in his debut, costarring role. (97 mins.)

Carnation Frank (German, 1961)* Chris Howland, Dagmar Hanks. Private eye exposes a counterfeiting ring while on vacation in Yugoslavia. Poorly done crime melodrama dubbed in English.

Carnival (British, 1946)*** Sally Gray, Michael Wilding. The tragic story of a ballerina whose romantic escapades eventually prove to be her downfall. Elaborately produced romantic drama, well acted; women should enjoy it.

Carnival of Souls (1960)**½ Candance Hilligoss, Frances Feist. Victim of auto accident has her spirit continue to live. Made in Lawrence, Kansas. Despite some crudities, it's pretty good for Lawrence—it's good for Kansas City while we're at it.

Carnival Story (1954)**½ Anne Baxter, Steve Cochran, George Nader. Tragedy ensues when two men love a beautiful carnival high-diving star. Heavy-handed drama; good performances. (Dir: Kurt Neumann, 95 mins.)

Carolina Cannonball (1955)*½ Judy Canova, Andy Clyde. Hillbilly girl runs afoul of foreign agents after control of an atomic-powered missile. For corn-lovers exclusively. (Dir: Charles Lamont, 80 mins.)

Carousel (1956)***½ Gordon MacRae, Shirley Jones. Tastefully produced version of the fantasy "Liliom," with the Rodgers & Hammerstein evergreen score. Concerns the marriage of a swaggering carnival barker and a shy girl, and the tragic consequences when he takes drastic steps to provide for their child. Nicely sung, beautiful Maine locale. (Dir: Henry King, 128 mins.)

Carpet of Horror, The (German, 1962)*½ Joachim Berger, Eleonora Rossi-Drago. It's a case of who's-got-the-documents as a special agent carrying information about an international crime syndicate is murdered. Plenty of running around, little finesse in this Edgar Wallace mystery dubbed in English.

Carpetbaggers, The (1964)*½ Carroll Baker, George Peppard, Alan Ladd. There are some laughs in this sleazy, badly acted soap opera based on the best-selling rubbish of Harold Robbins, but they're the kind of laughs that come when you laugh at a film rather than with it. The implausible plot concerns a disagreeable rich young man on the corporate make, with some subplots about booze, Hollywood, and broads. Even in a negligee, Carroll Baker manages the not-inconsiderable feat of coming across as utterly sexless. For those who care, this was Alan Ladd's last film. (Dir: Edward Dmytryk, 150 mins.)

Carrie (1952)***½ Jennifer Jones, Laurence Olivier, Miriam Hopkins. Grim, powerful drama based on Dreiser's novel about a girl who runs off with a married man, goes on to become a noted actress while he sinks to the depths. Good performance by Jones, a fine one by Olivier, with William Wyler's direction cogent. Superior dramatic fare. (Dir: William Wyler, 118 mins.)

Carry On Again, Doctor (Great Britain, 1969)*½ Kenneth Williams, Jim Dale. Unlike most "Carry On" entries, this item has the semblance of a plot, but otherwise the puns fly thick and fast and occasionally funny. The alternative opening title, "The Bowels are Ringing," sets the tone, such as it is. (Dir: Gerald Thomas, 89 mins.)

Carry On Cabby (British, 1967)** Sidney James, Hattie Jacques. Another in the long line of English "Carry On" films. A taxicab company competes against a rival that's owned by the boss's neglected wife. Doesn't export too well. (Director: Gerald Thomas, 91 mins.)

Carry On Cleo (British, 1965)**½ Amanda Barrie, Sidney James, Kenneth Connor. Corned-up take-off on the Cleopatra legend, with some comics scampering around, like an old blackout skit prolonged. Despite the crudity, it's reasonably amusing. (Dir: Gerald Thomas, 92 mins.)

Carry On Constable (British, 1960)** Sidney James, Eric Barker, Kenneth Connor. Group of bungling police rookies manage to gum up the works but redeem themselves. Broad comedy depends on a bunch of old wheezes for laughs, sometimes hits the mark.

Carry On Cruising (British, 1962)** Sidney James, Kenneth Williams, Kenneth Connor, Liz Fraser. Skipper of a Mediterranean cruising ship is inflicted with a group of inept crewmen gumming up the works. One moth-eaten slapstick gag after another, but this lowbrow comedy manages to keep afloat.

Carry On Nurse (British, 1959)**½ Kenneth Connor, Shirley Eaton, Wilfrid Hyde-White. Fun and games in an English hospital—and that's all there is to it. No plot, just a string of farcical sight gags, some of them very funny. (Dir: Gerald Thomas, 90 mins.)

Carry On Regardless (British, 1961)** Sidney James, Kenneth Connor, Joan Sims, Liz Fraser. Head of an employment agency assigns various bunglers to jobs. Sheer persistence makes some of the ancient gags in this broad farce seem occasionally amusing.

Carry On Sergeant (British, 1958)

118

**½ William Hartnell, Bob Monkhouse, Shirley Eaton. Tough sergeant about to retire wants his last platoon to be a crack one—but the members are mostly cracked. All the old army routines are crammed into this low-brow comedy. Some of it is funny. (Dir: Gerald Thomas, 88 mins.)

Carry On Spying (British, 1964)**½ Kenneth Williams, Barbara Windsor, Bernard Cribbins. B.O.S.H. Security Headquarters sends some inept agents to Vienna to combat the villainous activities of S.T.E.N.C.H. —which gives you the idea of the subtle humor involved here. Nevertheless, frequent hearty chuckles are provided. (Dir: Gerald Thomas, 88 mins.)

Carry On Teacher (British, 1961)**½ Ted Ray, Kenneth Connor, Joan Sims. Dean of a private school wants a better position, but his students and classmates wish him to stay, so they sabotage a scheduled inspection to make him look bad. Practically a textbook of ancient gags, some of which are still funny.

Carry On TV (British, 1963)*½ Bob Monkhouse, Kenneth Connor. Lackluster farce, not really one of the "Carry On" series. Ambitious advertising huckster goes to wild lengths to promote a new toothpaste.

Carry On Venus (British, 1964)**½ Bernard Cribbins, Juliet Mills, Kenneth Williams. More royal messing up as a bunch of deadheads nearly manage to upset the Royal Navy. Burlesque of all those sea dramas manages to shape up a nice covey of chuckles.

Carson City (1952)**½ Randolph Scott, Raymond Massey, Lucille Norman. Railroad engineer fights those who don't want the thing built. Well made western. (Dir: Andre de Toth, 87 mins.)

Carter's Army (1970)**½ Stephen Boyd, Robert Hooks, Susan Oliver. Often interesting made-for-TV feature which benefits greatly from the fine performance by Robert Hooks as the lieutenant in charge of an all black outfit during WW II. Stephen Boyd plays a white southern officer who clashes with Hooks and his men while trying to carry off a dangerous mission behind enemy lines involving a strategic bridge marked for demolition by the Nazis. Richard Pryor, as a terrified G.I., and Moses

Gunn, as a college professor turned foot soldier, are the standouts in a uniformly fine supporting cast.

Carthage in Flames (Italian, 1961)** Anne Heywood, Jose Suarez, Pierre Brasseur, Daniel Gelin. Carthaginian warrior rescues a young slave girl during the Third Punic War, and she eventually is instrumental in avenging his death. Elaborate costume spectacle dubbed in English has the advantage of a better-than-average cast, some impressive mass scenes. (Dir: Carmine Gallone, 96 mins.)

Cartouche (1957)** Richard Basehart, Patricia Roc. Nobleman's son returns to France to clear himself of a crime. Average costume adventure, nothing new.

Cartouche (French, 1964)*** Jean-Paul Belmondo, Claudia Cardinale. Generally amusing swashbuckling spoof, with the athletic Mr. Belmondo as a sort of Gallic Robin Hood. Cardinale is pretty, the pace is fast, so . . . (Dir: Philippe de Broca, 115 mins.)

Carve Her Name With Pride (British, 1958)**** Virginia McKenna, Paul Scofield. Inspiring true story of Violette Szabo, who braved death while working for the French Resistance in World War II. Excellent performances from McKenna and Scofield. Also noteworthy because this is one of the few films to date made by Scofield, who happens to be second only to Laurence Olivier, about the greatest actor alive.

Casa Ricordi (Italian, 1954)** Roland Alexandre, Marta Toren. Long, draggy saga of the famous Italian publishing house. Lots of operatic arias, dubbed English dialogue. (Dir: Carmine Gallone, 117 mins.)

Casablanca (1942)***½ Humphrey Bogart, Ingrid Bergman, Paul Henreid. This one is famous for the song, "As Time Goes By," plus a wonderful cast but try not to forget that overall it's a very dull melodrama of intrigue. You'll enjoy it if you can overlook its faults and keep track (between commercials) of its stream of characters. (Dir: Michael Curtiz, 102 mins.)

Casanova (French, 1958)*½ Georges Marchal, Corinne Calvet, Marina Vlady. Romantic life and loves of the famous ladies' man, done floridly, without much style. Dubbed in English.

Casanova Brown (1944)**½ Gary Cooper, Teresa Wright. College professor, whose marriage has been annulled, finds that he's a father as he is about to marry again. Fairly amusing comedy, but could have been better. (Dir: Sam Wood, 94 mins.)

Casanova '70 (Italian, 1965)*** Marcello Mastroianni, Virna Lisi, Michele Mercier, Marisa Mell. Attractive wolf has psychological difficulty with his love affairs, becoming even more complicated when he meets the real love for him. The best of Mastroianni's films but still has some good laughs, and he's always a joy to behold.

Casanova's Big Night (1954)** Bob Hope, Joan Fontaine, Basil Rathbone, Vincent Price. Hope as a tailor's apprentice who poses as the great lover and finds himself in the middle of court intrigue. Not on a par with other Hope farces—some laughs, but too much tedium in between. (Dir: Norman Z. McLeod, 86 mins.)

Casbah (1948)**½ Yvonne DeCarlo, Tony Martin, Peter Lorre. Another version of the saga of Pepe LeMoko, the criminal who hides from the law in the Casbah section of Algiers, until the love of a woman forces him to the outside world and his doom. Not bad; Martin is convincing as an actor, and the production is good. (Dir: John Berry, 94 mins.)

Case Against Brooklyn, The (1958)** Darren McGavin, Maggie Hayes. A hard hitting, forceful but highly fictionalized account of one rookie cop's attempt to single-handedly break a big gambling syndicate in Brooklyn. McGavin is a good actor but is totally wasted in this overdone police story. (Dir: Paul Wendkos, 82 mins.)

Case of Dr. Laurent, The (1959)**** Jean Gabin, Nicole Courcel. An excellent French film (dubbed) about a country doctor who is a dedicated man with an abundance of compassion for his patients. There is a superb birth sequence which is both educational and dramatic, though it may not be intact by the time the TV butchers with the editing scissors get finished. (92 mins.)

Case of Mrs. Loring (British, 1959)** Julie London, Anthony Steele. Provocative theme poorly handled. Wife realizing her husband is ster-

119

ile submits to artificial insemination and thereby loses her husband in the process. This theme deserves better acting and writing. Julie London is so luscious it makes things even more confusing. (Dir: Don Chaffey, 86 mins.)

Case of Patty Smith, The (1962)** Dani Lynn, Merry Anders, J. Edward McKinley. Controversial movie when it appeared, because it was a plea for legalized abortion. Impregnated rape victim, rebuffed by all, seeks a criminal abortion. Overly dramatic, suffers also from Miss Lynn's poor acting. Written, produced and directed by Leo Handel. (93 mins.)

Case of Rape, A (1974)***½ Elizabeth Montgomery. A provocative, controversial subject is treated with candor in this fine dramatization about a married woman who is raped twice by the same young man, and then suffers indignities and personal loss when she goes to court. Miss Montgomery buries her "Bewitched" cuteness and gives a thoughtful, believable performance as the lovely woman subjected to the nightmare of rape. The script introduces little-publicized legal facts about rape cases which will surprise you, and the ending does not make any compromises. Worthwhile. Made-for-TV. (Dir: Boris Sagal.)

Case of the Red Monkey (British, 1953)*½ Richard Conte, Rona Anderson. Investigator attacks a series of baffling murders of atomic scientists. You might try a good book instead. (Dir: Ken Hughes, 73 mins.)

Case 33: Antwerp (German, 1965)*½ Adrian Hoven, Corny Collins. Sleuth aids the Antwerp police in solving a series of knife murders. Low-grade whodunit, dubbed in English.

Cash McCall (1960)**½ Natalie Wood, James Garner. The best selling novel about big business and the people who play at it. Glossily produced. The attractive stars go through the motions but the script defeats any true development of characters. This film is reminiscent of the 1940's product which has since come to be known as "the typical Hollywood film." (Dir: Joseph Pevney, 102 mins.)

Cash on Demand (Great Britain, 1963)* Peter Cushing, Andre Morell. Dull crime drama. Man poses as

an insurance investigator in an attempt to rob a bank. (Dir: Quentin Lawrence, 66 mins.)

Casino de Paris (German, 1960)** Caterina Valente, Vittorio De Sica. Lothario-playwright has designs on a glamorous star, invites her to his villa. She arrives with her family. Mild musical comedy provides only fair fun. Dubbed in English.

Casino Royale (British, 1967)**½ Peter Sellers, Ursula Andress, David Niven. An overblown, lavish production and an array of big-name guest stars such as William Holden, Charles Boyer, Deborah Kerr, Orson Welles, Jean-Paul Belmondo and Woody Allen in the leads are the come-ons for this one. It's a spoof of all the James Bond spy adventures and there are more Bonds than you can keep track of—but what the picture really needs is Sean Connery and he's conspicuously missing. The special effects are stunning and the gambling casino finale is well staged. No less than five directors had a hand in this not so royale romp. (Dirs: John Huston, Ken Hughes, Robert Parrish, Joe McGrath, Val Guest, 100 mins.)

Cass Timberlane (1947)**½ Spencer Tracy, Lana Turner, Zachary Scott. One of Sinclair Lewis' weakest novels receives a sincere adaptation and is fairly good commercial screen fare. Story is about a respectable midwestern judge who marries a beautiful immature bride and has trouble keeping pace with her youth. (Dir: George Sidney, 119 mins.)

Cast a Dark Shadow (British, 1957)**½ Dirk Bogarde, Margaret Lockwood. Scoundrel after cash marries a woman—object: matrimony, then murder. Unevenly paced thriller has some good suspense, sturdy performances. (Dir: Lewis Gilbert, 84 mins.)

Cast a Giant Shadow (1966)**½ Kirk Douglas, Senta Berger, Angie Dickinson, Topol. Highly romanticized but interesting tale about the Israeli-Arab conflict in the days when Israel first became a state. Kirk Douglas is cast as Col. Marcus, the legendary American soldier who helps shape up Israel's fighting force in 1948. There's action galore, and even a love story for the ladies, plus cameo roles played by none other than John Wayne, Frank Sinatra and Yul Brynner. (Topol is fine playing a Bedouin partial to the Israeli cause. Topol's a major star with his glorious lead performance in "Fiddler on the Roof.") (Dir: Melville Shavelson, 142 mins.)

Cast a Long Shadow (1959)*½ Audie Murphy, Terry Moore. Drifter rides back to his former ranch home to renew old feuds and settle some scores. It's a slow ride. (Dir: Thomas Carr, 82 mins.)

Casta Diva (Italian, 1954)** Maurice Ronet, Nadia Gray. Another musical biography, this time it's operatic composer Bellini. Dubbed in English, only the music hath charms.

Castaway Cowboy, The (1974)*** James Garner, Vera Miles. Amiable family fare which bears the authentic stamp of Disney quality. James Garner is a Texan who finds himself in Hawaii in 1850 where he gives in to the pleadings of a widow and her charming son to turn their farm into a cattle ranch. The Hawaiian locale and the Western yarn work well in tandem and the cast is fine, notably James Garner, young Eric Shea, and capable Vera Miles. (Dir: Vincent McEveety, 91 mins.)

Castilian, The (Spanish, 1963)** Cesar Romero, Broderick Crawford, Alida Valli. Castilian nobleman comes out of exile to lead his people against the Moors. Some fine scenery, big action scenes, but the usual ragged scripting and some inferior performances defeat this European-made spectacle. (Dir: Javier Seto, 129 mins.)

Castle, The (West German, 1968) ***½ Maximilian Schell, Cordula Trantow. Generally absorbing adaptation of Franz Kafka's uncompleted novel about a land surveyor who comes to a village, and can't make contact with the people in "the castle" who control the town. Beautiful photography by Rudolf Noelte and fine acting by Schell playing K, the surveyor, make this a graphic study of man in hopeless conflict with bureaucracy. (Dir: Rudolf Noelte, 90 mins.)

Castle in the Air (British, 1955)**½ David Tomlinson, Margaret Rutherford. Scottish earl without funds tries to sell his castle. Amusing comedy. (89 mins.)

Castle Keep (1969)**½ Burt Lancaster, Peter Falk, Patrick O'Neal. Uneven, ambitious film directed by Sydney Pollack. Offbeat, well-produced WW II story set in a Belgian castle where a great many art treasures are kept. Lancaster is the Major who has to hold off a German attack from the castle, and he comes to grips with the Count (Jean-Pierre Aumont), who can't stand by and see the priceless art be destroyed. Too talky at times but good performances keep your attention. (Dir: Sydney Pollack, 105 mins.)

Castle of Evil (1966)* Scott Brady, Virginia Mayo, David Brian. Hokum. A group of heirs gather on a chemist's island for the reading of his will, only to have his robot go berserk and begin a murder spree! (Dir: Francis D. Lyon, 81 mins.)

Castle of Purity (Mexican, 1972)**** Claudio Brook, Rita Macedo, Arturo Beristain, Diana Braco. An extraordinary, powerful drama based on a real incident. A psychotic man kept his family locked in their home for 18 years while he went about his daily chores in the outside world, selling homemade rat poison. Fascinating study of human weakness, alternating love and hate, and the emergence of sexuality on the part of the children and a will to resist among the children and the mother. Brilliantly directed by Arturo Ripstein, who has managed to capture the quality of being trapped in an enclosed space, and uses his camera to illuminate the characters. Screenplay by Ripstein and Jose Emileo Pacheco. Superb photography by Alex Phillips, Sr. English subtitles. (114 mins.)

Castle of Terror (Italian, 1963)** Barbara Steele, Georges Rivière. Man makes a bet that he can spend the night in a castle from which no living soul has ever returned. Dubbed-English horror thriller has its share of creepy moments, along with some ridiculous ones. (Dir: Anthony Dawson, 77 mins.)

Castle of the Living Dead (Italian, 1964)*½ Christopher Lee, Rossana Podesta, Georges Rivière. Wife of a German nobleman finds terror when she spends her first night at his ancestral home. Generally ineffective shocker has all the familiar gimmicks. Dubbed in English.

Castle on the Hudson (1940)**½ John Garfield, Ann Sheridan, Pat O'Brien, Burgess Meredith. Of course the acting is top drawer, but you've seen this tired old prison movie plot a million times. (Dir: Anatole Litvak, 77 mins.)

Castles in Spain (French, 1954)** Danielle Darrieux, Maurice Ronet. Soggy story of a bullfighter's love for a French belle, English-dubbed. Attractive cast, but the plot's a lot of bull.

Cat, The (French, 1958)**½ Francoise Arnoul, Bernard Blier. Love and intrigue in the French underground during the Second World War. Sexy Francoise Arnoul makes a good impression as Cora.

Cat! (1966)**½ Roger Perry, Peggy Ann Garner, Barry Coe. Youngsters may like this outdoor tale of a boy who makes friends with a wildcat who eventually saves him from a rustler. Pleasantly done.

Cat Ballou (1965)**** Lee Marvin, Jane Fonda, Michael Callan. A very funny offbeat western yarn with a magnificent comedy performance by Lee Marvin as a grizzly, has-been gunslinger who is called back into duty to do away with a look-alike villain. Marvin won an Oscar for this role. His performance is the major interest in the film, but the funny screenplay deserves a good deal of the credit, too. Well directed by Elliot Silverstein. (Dir: Elliot Silverstein, 96 mins.)

Cat Creature, The (1973)** Stuart Whitman, Meredith Baxter. When you subtract tension and discovery from a thriller, there isn't much left. So it is with this tale of prowling cats, Egyptian curses, and reincarnation. Pack these elements tightly around Whitman as a detective and you're in for nothing more than you expect. Made-for-TV. (Dir: Curtis Harrington, 73 mins.)

Cat Girl (1958)** Barbara Shelley, Kay Callard. Beauty suddenly turns feline, murders result. British-made and cheap, but Shelley is a good actress, better than the material. (Dir: Alfred Shaunessy, 69 mins.)

Cat o' Nine Tails (U.S.-Italian, 1971)* Karl Malden, James Franciscus, Catherine Spaak. A grisly, repellent and altogether distasteful mystery shocker. "Cat" is loaded with gratuitous, gruesome stranglings and assorted violence. One of the most outrageous things about this offensive film is that it received a GP rating from the Motion Picture Industry Code Association. Don't let your children see this rubbish, and you shouldn't bother either with this drivel about a blind Karl Malden helping a newspaperman track down a mad killer. Catherine Spaak must certainly be about the dullest young leading woman now working in films —even her breasts are boring when she reveals them for the edification of Franciscus!

Cat on a Hot Tin Roof (1958)**** Elizabeth Taylor, Paul Newman, Burl Ives. One of Tennessee Williams' most powerful studies of a southern family is successfully filmed by adaptor-director Richard Brooks. Elizabeth Taylor gives a very fine performance as the wife of a former hero (Paul Newman), who is dominated by his father and has taken to drink. Newman is very good, and Ives masterfully recreates his stage portrayal of massive "Big Daddy." Potent drama. (Dir: Richard Brooks, 108 mins.)

Cat People (1942)***½ Simone Simon, Kent Smith, Tom Conway. Man marries a strange girl possessed with a dreadful spell. Superior horror thriller, intelligently written and directed, well acted, suspenseful. (Dir: Jacques Tourneur, 73 mins.)

Catch As Catch Can (Italy, 1967)** Vittorio Gassman, Martha Hyer. Moderately bawdy satire features Gassman as a billboard advertising model being harassed by every sort of beast and bug. Improbable 'bugging' is overdone—satire of advertising/political idolization is better —but Gassman is finally overcome by the endless situations. (Dir: Franco Indovina, 95 mins.)

Catch-22 (1970)***½ Alan Arkin, Martin Balsam, Richard Benjamin, Arthur Garfunkel, Jack Gilford, Bob Newhart, Anthony Perkins, Jon Voight. Joseph Heller's black comedy about war and all it really means to the common man has been turned into a flawed masterpiece by director Mike Nichols and the adapter-writer Buck Henry. The setting for Heller's anti-war crusade against the war profiteers is a bombardier group stationed in Italy during WW I, and his gallery of lunatic characters are vividly brought to life, for the most part, by a wonderful cast headed by Alan Arkin as the very sane Yossarian who tried desperately to be certified mad so that he can stop flying missions. The film starts off brilliantly but the various sequences, no matter how well played, come off as isolated anecdotes that don't fully pay off. But it's well worth seeing and Arkin is wonderful. (Dir: Mike Nichols, 120 mins.)

Catcher, The (1972)*½ Michael Whitney. Former policeman turns to contemporary bounty hunting, i.e., looking for lost persons for cash rewards. Whitney, who stars as the stoic, solid, almost humorless ex-cop, lacks the talent necessary to make the character more palatable. Made-for-TV. (Director: Allen H. Miner, 99 mins.)

Catered Affair, The (1956)*** Bette Davis, Debbie Reynolds, Ernest Borgnine. Paddy Chayefsky's TV drama turned into a fairly absorbing film which suffers a bit from the miscasting of Bette Davis as a middle-class Bronx housewife who wants to give her only daughter a big "catered affair" for her wedding. Miss Reynolds comes off nicely and E. Borgnine plays an older married "Marty." (Dir: Richard Brooks, 93 mins.)

Catherine of Russia (German, 1962)** Hildegarde Neff, Sergio Fantoni. Empress Catherine and how she got that way—by overthrowing Peter of Russia and taking the throne. Over-stuffed costume drama dubbed in English.

Catherine the Great (British, 1934)**½ Elisabeth Bergner, Douglas Fairbanks Jr. The Empress of Russia is forced into a marriage that she does not wish, with resulting unhappiness. Elaborate but heavy, slow historical drama. (Dir: Paul Czinner, 100 mins.)

Catholics (1973)***½ Trevor Howard, Cyril Cusack, Martin Sheen. Splendid adaptation of Brian Moore's novel about simple worship in an ancient Irish monastery, threatened by increasing permissiveness in the Mother Church. Filmed against the rugged Irish coast, the striking opening scene of this provocative, brooding drama offers the melodic sound of the Latin Mass being offered by an old Irish monk (Cusack) before a tremendous crowd of worshippers, held spellbound by the experience. A memorable performance by Trevor Howard, as the wise, wistful abbot of the institution. Superior made-for-TV entry. (Dir: Jack Gold, 100 mins.)

Catlow (British, 1971)**½ Yul Brynner, Richard Crenna, Leonard Nimoy. Unpretentious action western as Brynner plays a post-Civil War outlaw-drifter hunted down by friend and marshal Crenna. The Spanish desert looks as fine as ever. (Dir: Sam Wanamaker, 101 mins.)

Cattle Drive (1951)**½ Joel McCrea, Dean Stockwell. Interesting western with good performances by McCrea and Stockwell as a saddle worn cowhand and a young upstart, respectively, who team up on a cattle drive and become fast friends. (Dir: Kurt Neumann, 77 mins.)

Cattle Empire (1958)**½ Joel McCrea, Gloria Talbott. Another western tale in which the hero is believed to be a renegade but turns out all right after all, but done with finesse. Better than average. (Dir: Charles Marquis Warren, 83 mins.)

Cattle Queen of Montana (1954)** Barbara Stanwyck, Ronald Reagan. When her pop is murdered, a lone gal fights an unscrupulous land grabber. Slow; not very believable western. (Dir: Allan Dwan, 88 mins.)

Caught (1949)*** James Mason, Barbara Bel Geddes, Robert Ryan. Model marries neurotic millionaire, is unhappy until a young doctor comes to her aid. Good melodrama, well acted. (Dir: Max Ophuls, 88 mins.)

Caught in the Draft (1941)***½ Bob Hope, Dorothy Lamour. The Army may have changed since 1941, but this picture about a draft-dodging movie star who is finally caught and placed in the Army is grand fun. (Dir: David Butler, 82 mins.)

Cauldron of Blood (Spain-U.S., 1968)* Jean-Pierre Aumont, Boris Karloff, Viveca Lindfors. Drab horror tale, Karloff's last major role. Blind sculptor is provided with skeletons for his work by his obliging murderess-wife. The devices creak. Karloff manages to sit through it all . . . you need not bother. Alternate title: "Blind Man's Bluff." (Dir: Edward Mann, 101 mins.)

Cause for Alarm (1951)** Loretta Young, Barry Sullivan. This over dramatic story about a woman being terrorized by her husband who suspects her of infidelity is like an expanded TV show. (Dir: Tay Garnett, 74 mins.)

Cavalcade (1933)*** Diana Wynyard, Clive Brook, Una O'Connor, Margaret Lindsay. Elegant adaptation of Noel Coward's play traces the Marryot family from 1899 to 1932. Rich characterizations bring alive the sorrows and triumphs which befall the family during World War I and the Depression. Coward's wonderful songs are left intact. An Oscar-winner for best direction. (Dir: Frank Lloyd, 110 mins.)

Cavalier In Devil's Castle (Italian, 1962)*½ Massimo Serato, Irene Tunc. Heir to a castle is imprisoned by a dastardly nobleman but turns the tables with the aid of a mysterious Black Knight. Stilted swashbuckler dubbed in English.

Cavalleria Rusticana (Italian, 1952)** Mario Del Monico, Rina Telli. Mascagni's opera, sung in Italian with English narration. For opera lovers.

Cavalry Command (1963)*½ John Agar, Richard Arlen. Soldiers try to restore order to a Philippine village during the Spanish-American War. Filmed on the spot, this "western" has a novel locale and plenty of action but is ineptly produced.

Cave of Outlaws (1952)** MacDonald Carey, Alexis Smith. Routine western about hidden gold and the lengths men go to uncover the secret hiding place. (Dir: William Castle, 75 mins.)

Cavern, The (1965)** John Saxon, Brian Aherne, Rosanna Schiaffino. World War II adventure about six men and a woman trapped in a German munitions dump—the cavern of the title. Tensions are high, death is near and escape remote—you can fill in the rest. Directed by veteran Hollywood director Edgar G. Ulmer ("The Black Cat"). (100 mins.)

C.C. and Company (1970)* Ann-Margret, Joe Namath. Pop art, motorcycles, sexy Ann-Margret and sex-symbol Joe Namath meld into a perfectly awful film. Joe belongs to one of those burly motorcycle gangs, and Ann-Margret is a fashion magazine writer. Namath is embarrassing. (Dir: Seymour Robbie, 94 mins.)

Cease Fire (1953)*** Different sort of war film, using a cast of non-professionals, showing the activities of an infantry company in Korea prior to the peace talks. Filmed

there by Owen Crump with real GIs, it has the stamp of authenticity, should still be of interest. (75 mins.)

Ceiling Zero (1935)***½ James Cagney, Pat O'Brien. The planes may look like antiques but this is still as exciting an aviation story as today's film makers can produce at supersonic speeds. (Dir: Howard Hawks, 95 mins.)

Cell 2455, Death Row (1955)**½ William Campbell, Kathryn Grant. Based on Caryl Chessman's book about his life in prison and the events leading up to it. Frank and sometimes effective. (Dir: Fred F. Sears, 80 mins.)

Centennial Summer (1946)** Jeanne Crain, Linda Darnell, Cornel Wilde. Jerome Kern music, and two attractive female stars make up the credit side of the ledger in this slow, corny, contrived nonsense about a family in 1876 Philadelphia at the time of the Exposition. (Dir: Otto Preminger, 102 mins.)

Centurion, The (Italian, 1963)*½ John Drew Barrymore, Jacques Sernas. Centurion is placed in a tight spot when he's tricked by a jealous adversary. Dull spectacle dubbed in English has some action near the end, little else.

Ceremony, The (British, 1964)** Sarah Miles, Laurence Harvey, Robert Walker, John Ireland. A try for suspense, detailing efforts to spring a criminal from a Tangier prison. Harvey stars and directs—one task too many, for this cinema ceremony. Good moments offset by uneven treatment. (Dir: Laurence Harvey, 105 mins.)

Certain Smile, A (1958)**½ Rossano Brazzi, Joan Fontaine, Bradford Dillman, Christene Carere. Romantic melodrama for the ladies. Francoise Sagan's novel about a young girl's adventures in affairs of the heart with a suave, middle-aged Frenchman (played by Brazzi as if he were remembering all the early Boyer films) and a rebellious youth (played by Dillman as if he never saw an early Boyer film) is given a sumptuous production that spills all over with the beauty of the French Riviera. (Dir: Jean Negulesco, 104 mins.)

Chadwick Family, The (1974)**½ Fred MacMurray, Kathleen Maguire. MacMurray stars in a family-oriented film. He's the editor and publisher of a newspaper, thinking of moving to Chicago to head a new national magazine. Crises in his family call for a last-minute change of plans. Cast is good, with Barry Bostwick, playing MacMurray's colorful son-in-law, coming off best. Made for TV. (Dir: David Lowell Rich, 78 mins.)

Chain Lightning (1950)**½ Humphrey Bogart, Eleanor Parker, Raymond Massey. Good shots of jet planes and air action but unfortunately pilot Bogart lands and fights a losing battle with a hackneyed script. (Dir: Stuart Heisler, 94 mins.)

Chain of Evidence (1957)** William Elliott, James Lydon. An amnesia victim is arrested for murder, but a clever cop proves otherwise. Average "B" mystery. (Dir: Paul Landres, 63 mins.)

Chained (1934)** Joan Crawford, Clark Gable, Stuart Erwin. Trite little love triangle. And you'll know before the first reel that Joan will end up with the dashing Gable. (Dir: Clarence Brown, 71 mins.)

Chairman, The (British, 1969)** Gregory Peck, Anne Heywood, Arthur Hill. Picture if you will Gregory Peck behind the Chinese bamboo curtain on a spy mission, with an explosive device sewn into his head ready to be detonated. Far-fetched? Yes, indeed. In this one the Russians are our friends! Title refers to Chairman Mao. (Dir: J. Lee Thompson, 102 mins.)

Chalk Garden, The (1964)***½ Deborah Kerr, Hayley Mills, John Mills, Edith Evans. Tender story of a governess who tries to provide the love her charge, a disturbed 16-year-old girl, needs so badly. Sensitively written and directed, with fine performances by all. It's a superior drama for discriminating audiences, and Edith Evans is superb. (Dir: Ronald Neame, 106 mins.)

Challenge, The (1960)—See: **It Takes a Thief**

Challenge, The (1970)* Darren McGavin, Broderick Crawford, Mako, James Whitmore. Far-fetched silliness, as a United States spacecraft crashes far from target site and is claimed by a small Communist country. Will nuclear war ensue? Made-for-TV. (Dir: Allen Smithee, 73 mins.)

Challenge for Robin Hood, A (British, 1968)*** Barrie Ingham, Leon Greene. Yet another recounting of the fun and games in Sherwood Forest, but this retelling is better than most, and recommended for the kids who haven't seen it all many times before. There are some songs thrown in for good measure and director C. M. Pennington-Richards for those who treasure such monickers has kept things moving at a lively clip.

Challenge of the Gladiator (Italian, 1964)*½ Rock Stevens, Gloria Milland. The rebel slave Spartacus leads a revolt against the corrupt Nero. Usual splashy simpleminded English-dubbed spectacle.

Challenge to Be Free (1972)* Mike Mazurki. Crude hodgepodge, with a lot of natural footage of animals in the Yukon. The first half is basically a wildlife travelogue. The second half has the real action as trapper "accidentally" kills a state trooper. (Dirs: Tay Garnett and Ford Beebe, 88 mins.)

Challenge to Lassie (1949)**½ Edmund Gwenn, Donald Crisp, Lassie. Good family picture starring the famous collie. Veteran actors Edmund Gwenn and Donald Crisp make the somewhat sentimental story ring true. (Dir: Richard Thorpe, 76 mins.)

Challengers, The (1969)**½ Darren McGavin, Sean Garrison, Nico Minardos, Susan Clark. A car-racing drama with all the pat characters and situations. The racing sequences are excitingly photographed, but the triangular love story between racer Garrison, heiress Susan Clark, and playboy-racer Minardos gets a bit too obvious to sustain interest. Originally produced as a possible TV series pilot film, it has a "guest star" lineup including Anne Baxter, Farley Granger, Richard Conte and Juliet Mills. (Dir: Leslie Martinson, 99 mins.)

Chamber of Horrors (1966)** Patrick O'Neal, Suzy Parker. Horror film fans may enjoy this opus about a mass killer loose in Baltimore of the 1880's. All others will probably laugh at the wrong places. Patrick O'Neal rolls his eyes a great deal as the notorious madman. (Dir: Hy Averback, 99 mins.)

Champ, The (1931)*** Wallace Beery, Jackie Cooper, Irene Rich. A down and out former boxing champ

(Beery) tries to lick his addiction to booze to get in shape for a comeback. Beery won the Academy Award for his role and he repeated variations of this performance in many of his later films throughout his career. Jackie Cooper was an up and coming child star at the time, and the Beery-Cooper relationship is nicely developed by director King Vidor. (87 mins.)

Champ for a Day (1953)*** Alex Nicol, Audrey Trotter. Prize fighter investigates the disappearance of his manager. Good melodrama has some unusual plot twists. (Dir: William Seiter, 90 mins.)

Champagne for Caesar (1950)***½ Ronald Colman, Celeste Holm, Vincent Price. An unemployed genius gets on a quiz show and proceeds to take the sponsor for all he's worth. Rollicking comedy never lets up for a minute! And Vincent Price as a mad soap tycoon is just about the funniest thing in ages. (Dir: Richard Whorf, 99 mins.)

Champagne Murders, The (French, 1967)** Is the eccentric playboy (Anthony Perkins) a murderer as well? Seems that way, but you never know. Too many other things are unclear in this Gallic-made whodunit, wherein director Claude Chabrol dallies by the wayside too long. Maurice Ronet, Yvonne Furneaux, Stephane Audran, and a particularly silly, unresolved ending. (Dir: Claude Chabrol, 98 mins.)

Champagne Waltz (1937)*** Fred MacMurray, Gladys Swarthout. Jazz musician incurs the wrath of a Viennese waltz enthusiast, but all is well at the end because of the old man's pretty daughter. Good musical. (Dir: A. Edward Sutherland, 100 mins.)

Champion (1949)**** Kirk Douglas, Arthur Kennedy, Ruth Roman. One of the early films produced by Stanley Kramer, and this is still one of the handful of great movies about the fight game. Boxer slams his way to the championship by alienating his brother, wife and friends. Perceptive portrait of a totally unscrupulous human being, faultlessly acted and directed. (Dir: Stanley Kramer, 99 mins.)

Chance Meeting (British, 1958)**½ David Knight, Odile Versois, Theodore Bikel. American Embassy worker falls for the daughter of an Iron Curtain diplomat. Good idea marred by inconclusive, fence-straddling treatment. Some tender, romantic moments, well acted by Bikel. (Dir: Joseph Losey, 95 mins.)

Chance Meeting (British, 1960)**½ Hardy Kruger, Stanley Baker, Micheline Presle. It looks bad for a painter who is arrested for a girl's murder although he insists he's innocent. Good performances in a mystery that never grips as it should.

Chandler (1971)* Warren Oates, Leslie Caron. Muddled detective story. Oates drags his way through as a security guard setting out to trail Miss Caron, who is linked to an important underworld figure. Footage of the Monterey (Calif.) Peninsula helps to relieve the boredom of the yarn. Caron wasted, alas. (Dir: Paul Magwood, 95 mins.)

Change of Habit (1970)** Elvis Presley, Mary Tyler Moore. Presley plays a doctor, no less, who heads a clinic in a poor section of town, and Miss Moore plays one of a trio of nuns who offer their services to help out Presley's cause in this mild film. Oh yes, Presley does sing a song or two along the way, in this his 31st film. (Dir: William Graham, 93 mins.)

Change of Mind (1969)** Raymond St. Jacques, Susan Oliver. Absurd premise—the brain of a prominent white DA, dying of cancer, is transplanted into the body of a black listed as virtually DOA after an auto accident—gets a mounting here. The problems the transplant generate are numerous, of course, and they are not uninteresting . . . but you have to be ready to accept the idea and that's asking too much to begin with. Music by Duke Ellington. (Dir: Robert Stevens, 103 mins.)

Change Partners (British, 1966)*½ Zena Walker, Kenneth Cope, Basil Henson. Businessman does away with a blackmailer, but finds the same thing happening when a witness to the crime approaches him. So-so crime melodrama, too many clichés.

Chapman Report, The (1962)**½ Jane Fonda, Efrem Zimbalist, Jr., Claire Bloom, Glynis Johns, Shelley Winters. The best-selling novel inspired by the Kinsey Report on the sexual mores of suburban women is brought to the screen as a glossy soap opera. Zimbalist is all cool authority as a research psychologist who becomes entangled with Jane Fonda, a young woman suffering from emotional frigidity. Of the group, Glynis Johns delivers the best performance as a scatterbrained housewife with a secret. (Dir: George Cukor, 125 mins.)

Chappaqua (1967)***½ Jean-Louis Barrault, Allen Ginsberg. Ambitious, underrated vision of what a drug addict feels and sees. Accomplished first directorial effort by Conrad Rooks, who wrote and produced this film over a four-year period, in addition to playing the role of Russell Harwick. (Rooks is himself a drug user who quit.) Through stunning photographic effects he manages to suggest the eerie, dazzling, dangerous world of drug takers; includes LSD. Not completely successful, but it's a memorable psychedelic tour with scenes shot in France and India, and boasting a marvelous score by Ravi Shankar.

Charade (1963)***½ Cary Grant, Audrey Hepburn. Slick and sophisticated as its two charming stars. It seems Miss Hepburn's late husband swindled his cronies out of a quarter of a million dollars in gold coins, and they think Audrey knows where it's stashed. Enter the suave Mr. Grant, as an undercover C.I.A. agent, and they're off on a wild chase amid the marvelous European settings. After all is said and done, it's a lightweight affair, but the stars and the stylish direction by Stanley Donen keep it alive. (Dir: Stanley Donen, 114 mins.)

Charades (1952)*½ James Mason, Pamela Mason, Scott Forbes. Three unrelated episodes combined to make a feature. Suspiciously resembles TV pilot castoffs.

Charge at Feather River (1953)** Guy Madison, Vera Miles, Frank Lovejoy. Just another western adventure—originally made in 3-D but without the optical effects the gimmicks misfire. (Dir: Gordon Douglas, 96 mins.)

Charge of the Lancers (1954)** Paulette Goddard, Jean-Pierre Aumont. Mediocre adventure pic about a gypsy girl and an officer who fight a major portion of the Crimean War. (Dir: William Castle, 80 mins.)

Charge of the Light Brigade (1936)

***½ Errol Flynn, Olivia de Havilland, David Niven. Exciting, fast moving adventure story suggested by Tennyson's poem. Good performances by all concerned. (Dir: Michael Curtiz, 115 mins.)

Charge of the Light Brigade (British, 1968)***½ Trevor Howard, Vanessa Redgrave, David Hemmings, John Gielgud. Director Tony Richardson's withering, stimulating polemic about the stupidity and brutality of the military mind, and societies that not only condone but glorify war. This fifth movie version—the last was the 1936 entry starring Errol Flynn—of the historic 1854 battle at Balaclava, Turkey, when the English Brigade was decimated by the Russian army, is superlatively acted by an all-star cast in this "thinking man's" spectacle film. No false heroics here, and there's excellent use made of special animated sequences done by Richard Williams. (Dir: Tony Richardson, 116 mins.)

Chariots of the Gods (West Germany, 1971)*½ A "documentary" based on the best-selling books of Swiss writer Erich von Daniken, speculating on whether or not WE are the Martians in our midst. Film is part travelogue, part bunkum, with a dabble of scientific speculation, including ruminations about "Are There Ancient Astronauts?" The cameras touch down at such arresting sights as the Egyptian pyramids, Mayan temples, Baghdad. Von Daniken considers earthlings as children in need of fatherly advice. My fatherly advice is to treat this with a huge grain of extra-terrestrial salt. The film was a box-office surprise hit all over the world. (Dir: Harald Reinl, 97 mins.)

Charles Dead or Alive (Swiss, 1972) ***½ Francois Simon, Marcel Robert. Absorbing drama of a rich watch manufacturer who is fed up with the materialism that encases his emptiness. He runs off to live with a young married couple, but society and his family find him and commit him to a mental hospital. Francois Simon (Marcel Simon's son) is touching as the manufacturer, his life very relevant to our time. (Dir: Alain Tanner, 110 mins.)

Charley Varrick (1973)***½ Walter Matthau, Joe Don Baker. Very slick, entertaining crime yarn sparked by Matthau's deft performance as a crop-duster pilot who dabbles in bank robbing on the side. Director Don Siegel is right on the beam with the action, and his casting in the smaller supporting roles is perfect—Andy Robinson as a greedy sidekick of Matthau's; Sheree North as an accommodating photographer; Joe Don Baker as a Mafia man; and John Vernon as a banker. Matthau specializes in small bank heists until he accidentally steals some Mafia funds and thereby hangs the story line—a good one that will keep you going until the end. (111 mins.)

Charley's Aunt (1941)*** Jack Benny, Kay Francis. Perennial comedy about the man who poses as a girl to help his roommate out of a jam is a good vehicle for Jack. (Dir: Archie Mayo, 81 mins.)

Charlie Bubbles (1968)***½ Albert Finney, Liza Minnelli. Tantalizing, uneven, offbeat movie finds the celebrated British actor Albert Finney doing double duty. As director of the film, as well as its star, Mr. Finney is wonderfully resourceful in creating the image of a young man of very modest circumstances who is catapulted out of his station and into fame, fortune, and an excessive boredom he simply cannot bear. The emptiness of his life is beautifully reflected in scenes of his electronically gadget-filled house, making robots of everyone within. Actually, however, the novelty of the atmosphere wears thin even before he leaves it in a vain effort to go home again to his wife and son. As for the ending, it's either an imaginative cop-out or an irritating one, depending on your point of view. (Dir: Albert Finney, 91 mins.)

Charlie Chan (Happiness Is a Warm Clue) (1971)* Ross Martin, Rocky Gunn, Virginia Ann Lee. Misguided, campy revival, brings the Oriental detective out of retirement to solve some less-than-inscrutable mysteries on board a yacht. Martin rarely evokes the mystique created by former Chans, Warner Oland and Sidney Toler. Made-for-TV. (Dir: Leslie Martinson, 97 mins.)

Charlie Chan in Egypt (1935)** Warner Oland, Pat Paterson, Rita Cansino. Chan uncovers murder on an archeological expedition. Standard Chan whodunit—some scary scenes. (Dir: Louis King)

Charlie Chaplin Carnival (1916-17)

**** Four Chaplin shorts: "Behind the Screen," "The Count," "The Vagabond," "The Fireman." Good old-fashioned slapstick from one of cinema's authentic geniuses. (75 mins.)

Charlie Chaplin Cavalcade (1916-17) **** Four Chaplin comedies: "One A.M.," "The Rink," "The Pawnshop," "The Floorwalker." Still stupendous. (75 mins.)

Charlie Chaplin Festival (1916-17) **** Four Chaplin comedies: "The Immigrant," "The Adventurer," "The Cure," "Easy Street." As funny as ever. (75 mins.)

Charlie Cobb: Nice Night for a Hanging (1977)** Clu Gulager, Ralph Bellamy, Blair Brown, Stella Stevens. Gulager, an ingratiating actor who seems to get better with age, is an 1880's Western private eye named Charlie Cobb, who is taken for a greenhorn by everyone when he turns up with a rancher's daughter. The prodigal daughter isn't exactly welcomed by the rancher's second wife, a lady with a murderous scheme. Good cast, fair story. Made-for-TV. (Dir: Richard Michaels, 100 mins.)

Charlie Moon (British, 1956)** Max Bygraves, Dennis Price. Old army buddy starts his friend on a show-business career. Hackneyed backstage story that doesn't come off.

Charlotte's Web (1973)***½ Heartwarming animated version of children's classic by E. B. White about a pig who's afraid he's going to be turned into bacon, and a spider who saves him through her magic web. The voices, all marvelous, include Debbie Reynolds, Paul Lynde, Henry Gibson, and Agnes Moorehead. Well animated with an excellently constructed narrative and good climax. For the whole family. (Dirs: Charles Nichols and Iwao Takamoto, 93 mins.)

Charly (1968)*** Cliff Robertson, Claire Bloom, Lilia Skala. The superlative Academy Award-winning performance of Cliff Robertson playing a mentally retarded bakery worker is reason enough to see this one. The rest of the film is appreciably less successful, including a questionable romance between Charly (Robertson) and a bright, beautiful woman (Bloom) after surgery has drastically improved Charly's I.Q. Director Ralph Nelson includes some attractive shots of Boston, a welter of split screens and other "new" camera techniques, but it's Robertson's sensitive handling of the title role, first performed by him on TV, that makes this worth your time. (Dir: Ralph Nelson, 103 mins.)

Charro! (1969)* Elvis Presley, Ina Balin, Victor French. Elvis takes to the saddle in this western which casts him as a one-time outlaw who decides to go straight. Ina Balin is awful as a saloon hostess who takes to Elvis, and Elvis runs her a close second. Produced, written and directed by Charles Marquis Warren. (98 mins.)

Chartroose Caboose (1960)** Molly Bee, Ben Cooper, Edgar Buchanan. A sugary and sentimental tale (with musical numbers added) about an old railroader who takes in stray people in trouble and is rewarded handsomely for his kindness in the end. You will not be equally rewarded. (Dir: William 'Red' Reynolds, 75 mins.)

Chase, The (1966)** Marlon Brando, Jane Fonda, Robert Redford, E. G. Marshall, Angie Dickinson. Despite a fine cast, a screenplay that bears Lillian Hellman's name, though others were involved, and the directorial talents of Arthur Penn, this story about sex and sin in a small Texas town is an unending compendium of film clichés! Producer Sam Spiegel kept interfering with and overruling Penn during production, and the final jumbled film is evidence of various unresolved points of view. Dickinson and Brando are both as convincing as possible under the trying circumstances. (Dir: Arthur Penn, 135 mins.)

Chase a Crooked Shadow (British, 1958)**½ Anne Baxter, Richard Todd. Performances make up for many of the inconsistencies in the plot of this drama. Miss Baxter becomes the victim of a diabolical plot that is set up to do her out of her wealthy inheritance. (Dir: Michael Anderson, 87 mins.)

Chase Me Charlie (1914-32)*** Charlie Chaplin, Edna Purviance, Ben Turpin. Old Chaplin short subjects strung together to form a thin narrative about Charlie's quest for work to win his girl. Antiquated in technique and presentation. The Chaplin comedy genius breaks through occasionally. (61 mins.)

Chasers, The (France, 1959)**½ Jacques Charrier, Charles Aznavour. A not very profound but occasionally interesting look at rootless youths in Paris, their search for love, partners, company. First film for director Jean-Pierre Mocky is disappointing. (75 mins.)

Chastity (1969)* Cher, Barbara London. Of interest only because it marks Cher's second film appearance (first was "Good Times" in '67) and this sophomoric nonsense about a forlorn girl trying to find both her own identity and a little love and affection in the bargain. Banal script written and produced by Sonny Bono for his then-wife. (Dir: Alessio De Paola, 85 mins.)

Chato's Land (1972)*½ Charles Bronson, Jack Palance. Diehard Bronson fans will be the only ones to stick with this violence-ridden western in which a half-breed Apache stays one step ahead of a bloodthirsty posse in New Mexico, circa 1873. Filmed in Spain. No winner here. (Dir: Michael Winner, 108 mins.)

Chatterbox (1942)**½ Judy Canova, Joe E. Brown. A timid radio cowboy goes to a dude ranch, where he becomes a hero with the aid of the ranch's handy girl. Amusing comedy. (Dir: Joseph Santley, 76 mins.)

Che! (1969)* Omar Sharif, Jack Palance. A notably asinine bit of Hollywood claptrap, allegedly depicting the Cuban Revolution, with a focus on Che Guevara. Played by Omar Sharif with almost no real emotion. It's a stupid, offensive film about an interesting, important subject. Everyone connected with it deserves censure. (Dir: Richard Fleischer, 96 mins.)

Cheaper by the Dozen (1959)*** Clifton Webb, Jeanne Crain, Myrna Loy. Heartwarming and funny comedy drama about a very large family ruled by Papa Webb. Nostalgic and corny at the same time. One of Webb's best performances. Based on the best-selling novel of the same name. There was a sequel to this film a few years later entitled "Belles on Their Toes" but it wasn't half as good due to the fact that Webb died in the original. (Dir: Walter Lang, 85 mins.)

Cheaters, The (1945)*** Joseph Schildkraut, Billie Burke. A broken-down ham actor comes to a household of snobs at Christmastime, makes human beings of them. Delightful comedy-drama, excellently acted. (Dir: Joseph Kane, 87 mins.)

Cheaters, The (French, 1961)** Pascale Petit, Jacques Charrier. English-dubbed drama of teenagers on the loose, as a university student becomes involved with the fast-living set. Long and tiresome. A few good moments.

Cheers for Miss Bishop (1941)*** Martha Scott, William Gargan. The story of the long life span of a midwest schoolteacher, her loves, sorrows. Heartwarming drama, excellently acted, written. Marsha Hunt. (Dir: Tay Garnett, 95 mins.)

Cheyenne—See: **Wyoming Kid, The**

Cheyenne Autumn (1964)***½ Richard Widmark, Carroll Baker, Karl Malden, James Stewart. Director John Ford, one of Hollywood's best western film makers, really came up with a winner in this epic retelling of a true incident in frontier history. It's about the migration of a tribe of half-starved Cheyenne Indians from their barren reservation in Oklahoma to their home ground in Wyoming. The treacherous journey tests the Cheyenne's courage and stamina, and their trek is further endangered as the Cavalry sets out to prevent their exodus. The cast is a large one, and they are all good, including Richard Widmark, Karl Malden, Carroll Baker, Dolores Del Rio, and, in cameo appearances, James Stewart and Edward G. Robinson. (Dir: John Ford, 160 mins.)

Cheyenne Social Club, The (1970)*½ James Stewart, Henry Fonda, Shirley Jones. The only lure here is the names of James Stewart and Henry Fonda playing a couple of middle-aged cowboys who take up residence at the "Cheyenne Social Club," which is, in reality, a frontier bordello run by Shirley Jones. It's not bawdy in the least despite some childish stabs at humor in this vein. (Dir: Gene Kelly, 103 mins.)

Chicago Calling (1952)** Dan Duryea, Mary Anderson. A man hears that his estranged wife and daughter have been injured in a motor accident, is unable to contact them via telephone. Slim story, but plenty of human interest in this drama, practically a one-man show by

130

Duryea. (Dir: John Reinhardt, 74 mins.)

Chicago Confidential (1957)**½ Brian Keith, Beverly Garland. Hollywood seems to think that there should be a motion picture about every city in the United States with the tag "confidential" after it. This is one of them. Crime exposés, gangster war lords, etc. (Dir: Sidney Salkow, 74 mins.)

Chicago Deadline (1949)**½ Alan Ladd, Donna Reed, Arthur Kennedy. Routine newspaper yarn about crusading reporter who gets involved with murder and the underworld. Alan Ladd plays it in his usual wooden style. (Dir: Lewis Allen, 87 mins.)

Chicago Syndicate (1955)** Dennis O'Keefe, Abbe Lane, Paul Stewart. Unbelievable drama about one man's attempt to smash the ten billion dollar crime network of the "Chicago Syndicate." Abbe Lane sings to a mambo beat supplied by Xavier Cugat's orchestra. (Dir: Fred F. Sears, 90 mins.)

Chicken Every Sunday (1949)**½ Dan Dailey, Celeste Holm, Alan Young. As homespun as a sampler and as nostalgic as blueberry pie cooling off on the window sill. Plot involves a small town dreamer (Dailey) who's always going to strike it big and always ends up losing his shirt. Celeste Holm is good as his patient wife. Good turn of the century music is played behind the action. (Dir. George Seaton, 91 mins.)

Chief Crazy Horse (1955)**½ Victor Mature, Suzan Ball, John Lund. An interesting yarn about one of the greatest Indian chiefs of all time— Crazy Horse, well played by athletic Victor Mature. The plot concerns his alliance with a cavalry major and their eventually necessary parting.

Child and the Killer (British, 1959)** Pat Driscoll, Robert Arden. GI murderer escapes to the backwoods, is helped by an unknowing child. Average melodrama. (Dir: George Sherman, 100 mins.)

Child in the House (British, 1959) *** Phyllis Calvert, Eric Portman, Mandy Miller, Stanley Baker. Intelligent drama of a youngster from a broken home and the change she brings into the lives of her aunt and uncle. Could have been soap opera but the treatment saves it.

Child Is Born, A (1940)**½ Jeffrey Lynn, Geraldine Fitzgerald. Remake of "Life Begins" is well done but the maternity hospital drama is still too morbid and heavy to be called entertaining. (Dir: Lloyd Bacon, 79 mins.)

Child Is Waiting, A (1963)*** Burt Lancaster, Judy Garland. Frequently gripping story of a music teacher and a psychologist on the staff of a school for retarded children. Strong stuff, not for the sensitive, the film uses actual retarded youngsters in the cast, develops a great deal of poignancy despite some weak spots in script and direction. (Dir: John Cassavetes, 102 mins.)

Children of Paradise (French, 1946)**** Jean-Louis Barrault, Arletty, Pierre Brasseur. Brilliant costume allegory, the story of a clown who falls in love with a beautiful woman and experiences tragedy. First postwar French film success, its excellence manifests itself throughout its length. English-dubbed. Barrault's famous mime sequence is breathtaking and perfection itself. (Dir: Marcel Carné, 161 mins.)

Children of the Damned (1964)**½ Ian Hendry, Barbara Ferris. Here's the sequel to the infinitely superior "Village of the Damned" horror film. The menacing children with the strange luminous eyes are back in another sci-fi excursion. The children are really feeling their power in this outing . . . they set their target as the destruction of the world. (Dir: Anton M. Leader, 90 mins.)

Children's Hour, The (1961)**½ Audrey Hepburn, Shirley MacLaine, James Garner. Lillian Hellman's drama of malicious gossip about two teachers bringing ruin and tragedy. This was filmed before, as "These Three" (1936), by the same director, William Wyler. The present version is more daring in theme, but somehow less effective, partly because lesbianism is no longer such a verboten subject. (Dir: William Wyler, 107 mins.)

Child's Play (British, 1957)** Mona Washburne, Peter Martyn. A comedy sparked with some drama concerning the escapades of a group of quiz kids and their experiments in an atomic plant.

Child's Play (1972)***½ James Mason, Robert Preston, Beau Bridges. Is Mr. Malley (James Mason) paranoid? Is there really a conspiracy against him by the boys of St. Charles boarding school? Dynamite ending. Direction is atmospheric to create the obligatory demonic and suspenseful mood. Acting is exemplary, led by Preston as the teacher suspected of leading the conspiracy. (Dir: Sidney Lumet, 100 mins.)

China Clipper (1936)*** Pat O'Brien, Beverly Roberts. Well acted and written story of the first flight of Pan American's China Clipper. Sticks to the facts and avoids the wornout cliches of air stories. If you want to see how far we've come, take a look at what was considered amazing in 1936. (Dir: Raymond Enright, 100 mins.)

China Corsair (1951)* Jon Hall, Lisa Ferraday. For pirate-action film fans only—a pirate queen and her lover protect a treasure of antiques. (Dir: Ray Nazarro, 67 mins.)

China Doll (1958)*½ Victor Mature, Lili Hua. Tragic romance between a Flying Tiger and a Chinese girl. Confucius say skip tiger and rest eyeballs. (Dir: Frank Borzage, 88 mins.)

China Gate (1957)** Gene Barry, Angie Dickinson. TV's Bat Masterson in a contrived bit of action concerning France's troubles in Indo-China. If you'd like to believe that the Foreign Legion is still glamorous, take a look. Nat King Cole throws in a song or two, and even does a nice job as a Legionnaire. (Dir: Samuel Fuller, 97 mins.)

China Is Near (Italian, 1967)*** Elda Tattoli, Glauco Mauri. An uneven, yet occasionally brilliant film from the talented young Italian director Marco Bellochio. (Bellochio's first film was "Fist in His Pocket.") Story concerns the affairs of an Italian politician's family, and most of it is a satire on left-wing Italian politics, with a few darts thrown at Italian sexual mores. English subtitles.

China Seas (1935)*** Clark Gable, Jean Harlow. A rousing melodrama about pirates in the China Seas trying to defeat Captain Gable. The stars give a good account of themselves, although the film is an undistinguished, entertaining adventure story. (Dir: Tay Garnett, 89 mins.)

China Venture (1953)**½ Edmond O'Brien, Barry Sullivan, Jocelyn

Brando. WW II adventure story about two officers and a navy nurse who try to rescue an Admiral held captive by Chinese Guerrillas. Some exciting sequences. (Dir: Don Siegel, 83 mins.)

Chinatown (1974)**** Jack Nicholson, Faye Dunaway. Excellent crime drama, set in the Los Angeles of the thirties, which evokes those wonderful Bogart films while remaining true to its own spirit and energy. Jack Nicholson is superb as a small-time private eye who stumbles on a big case which involves graft over valuable land and water rights, murder, incest and other attention-getting devices. They're all put in their proper place by writer Robert Towne in an intricate, entertaining screenplay. Director Roman Polanski (he's seen in a bit part as a sadistic, knife-wielding hood) has kept a keen and knowing eye on his cast, including Faye Dunaway as a highly dramatic femme fatale and John Huston as a despicable villain. (Dir: Roman Polanski, 130 mins.)

Chip Off the Old Block (1944)*** Donald O'Connor, Ann Blyth. Teenager goes through misunderstandings with the young daughter of a musical comedy star. Neat, breezy comedy with music. (Dir: Charles Lamont, 82 mins.)

Chisum (1970)**½ John Wayne, Forrest Tucker, Christopher George, Ben Johnson. Slam-bang action westerns ride again with tall-in-the-saddle John Wayne as a cattle baron fighting off the treacherous land barons. He's helped by a fine cast who follow the golden rule, "Actions speak louder than words." (Dir: Andrew V. McLaglen, 118 mins.)

Chitty, Chitty, Bang, Bang (British, 1968)**½ Dick Van Dyke, Sally Ann Howes, Anna Quayle. Intended by the director to repeat the artistic triumph and financial bonanza of "Those Magnificent Men in Their Flying Machines," he flops on both counts. This $10-million production does provide a few laughs for the kids, but it's pretty sophomoric most of the way and bogged down by some really terrible songs. The car-star does eventually get airborne, though the picture itself never takes off. (Dir: Ken Hughes, 142 mins.)

Chloe in the Afternoon (France, 1972)**** Bernard Verley, Zouzou, Francoise Verley, Francoise Fabian,

Beatrice Romand. The fourth of Rohmer's feature-length films and the concluding part of his cycle of romantic comedies he calls "Six Moral Fables." A featherweight, beautifully crafted look at monogamous marriage and the foibles of imperfect man. Valery struggles to avoid being unfaithful with "Chloe," charmingly played by singer-actress Zouzou. Written and directed by Eric Rohmer. (97 mins.)

Chocolate Soldier, The (1941)*** Nelson Eddy, Rise Stevens. Score from "The Chocolate Soldier," plus plot of Molnar's "The Guardsman," tempered with good debut performance of Miss Stevens adds up to a nice package for operetta fans. (Dir: Roy Del Ruth, 102 mins.)

Choppers, The (1962)*½ Arch Hall Jr., Tom Brown, Marianne Gaba. Teenager makes a crime career by operating a car-stripping racket. Lurid and unconvincing juvenile-delinquency drama.

Christine (1955)**½ Romy Schneider, Alain Delon. A terribly romantic French language film based on a Schnitzler play about a pair of star-crossed lovers, the dashing young officer and the beautiful opera singer. Miss Schneider and Mr. Delon make a perfect pair of lovers, but the dubbing detracts from their performances.

Christmas Carol, A (1938)*** Reginald Owen, Gene Lockhart. Sincere, well-acted adaptation of the Dickens classic. (Dir: Edwin L. Marin, 70 mins.)

Christmas Carol, A (British, 1951)***½ Alastair Sim, Kathleen Harrison. Another version of the classic Dickens tale of miser Scrooge who was turned into a human being by the spirit of Yuletide. Well done. (Dir: Brian Desmond Hurst, 86 mins.)

Christmas Holiday (1944)*** Deanna Durbin, Gene Kelly. Nice girl marries a ne'er-do-well whose weakness turns him to crime. Sordid tale receives classy direction, good performances to make it above average. (Dir: Robert Siodmak, 92 mins.)

Christmas In Connecticut (1945)**½ Barbara Stanwyck, Dennis Morgan. Occasionally funny farce about a newspaper columnist who is instructed by her boss to have a war hero as her family's guest for Christmas dinner. Of course, she has no family . . . and by that thread the film hangs. (Dir: Peter Godfrey, 101 mins.)

Christmas in July (1940)******** Dick Powell, Ellen Drew. Guy mistakenly thinks he has won a coffee slogan contest, starts buying everything on credit. Often hilarious comedy, written and directed by Preston Sturges with an unerring hand. Great fun. (Dir: Preston Sturges, 70 mins.)

Christmas Tree, The (1969)****** William Holden, Virna Lisi, Brook Fuller, Bourvil. A strained lunge for the tear ducts, in a tale of a father's attempt to make the last days happy for his son, dying of leukemia. Too obvious to be effective. Filmed in France. (Dir: Terence Young, 110 mins.)

Christopher Columbus (British, 1949) ****½** Fredric March, Florence Eldridge. Lavish but empty production concerning the attempts of the explorer to get permission from the Spanish court to sail to the New World. Very slow, talky, dull. (Dir: David MacDonald, 104 mins.)

Chronicle of Anna Magdalena Bach (Italian-West German, 1968)****½** Gustav Leonhardt, Christiana Lang. A somber account of the final years of the great composer Johann Sebastian Bach, of particular interest to serious music students, as the bulk of "Chronicle" is devoted to performances of Bach works including several cantatas. Film details Bach's poverty prior to his death in 1750. Unfortunately the acting, and much of the direction, is poverty-stricken as well. Subtitles.

Chubasco (1968)***½** Richard Egan, Susan Strasberg, Christopher Jones. Poor generation-gap drama set in San Diego. A wayward youth is eventually reformed after joining a tuna fishing fleet. Jones' first feature role. A few interesting scenes showing workings of a tuna boat. (Dir: Allen H. Miner, 99 mins.)

Chuka (1967)***½** Rod Taylor, Ernest Borgnine, John Mills. Predictable western, with rugged Rod Taylor handling the hero stuff and good character actors, such as Ernest Borgnine, John Mills, James Whitmore and Louis Hayward, giving him able support. Climax comes when Taylor and his lady love (Luciana Paluzzi) are holed up in a fort waiting for the Indians to attack. You may not wait that long! (Dir: Gordon Douglas, 105 mins.)

Cigarettes, Whiskey and Wild Women (French, 1958)***½** Nadine Tellier, Annie Cordy. Girls discover a cache of black market goods, get tangled up with smugglers when they try to sell the loot. Weak English-dubbed comedy, ruins promising elements in title.

Cimarron (1961)****½** Glenn Ford, Maria Schell, Anne Baxter. Long, sprawling remake of Edna Ferber's famous novel about Oklahoma pioneers, in particular the marriage of an immigrant girl and a compulsive wanderer. Big landrush at the beginning is superbly photographed, but action and interest both go downhill from there. Undistinguished in performance. (Dir: Anthony Mann, 140 mins.)

Cimarron Kid, The (1952)****** Audie Murphy, Yvette Dugay. Routine western fare with Audie Murphy playing the "Cimarron Kid," an ex-con who tries to go straight against tremendous odds. (Dir: Budd Boetticher, 84 mins.)

Cincinnati Kid, The (1965)******* Steve McQueen, Edward G. Robinson, Ann-Margret, Tuesday Weld. Fine performances by McQueen and Robinson. Their confrontation in a superbly staged card game finale is a highlight in this adventure based on Richard Jessup's novel. McQueen, in the title role, is an itinerant card shark who travels from one big game to the next, stopping along the way up with various girls, including Ann-Margret and Tuesday Weld. Director Norman Jewison has a good eye for detail and the technical end of the film evokes the depression period, in which the story is laid. (Dir: Norman Jewison, 113 mins.)

Cinderella Jones (1946)****** Joan Leslie, Robert Alda. Silly triviality about a dumb but pretty little scatterbrain who must marry an intelligent man to be eligible for a milliondollar legacy. (Dir: Busby Berkeley, 88 mins.)

Cinderella Liberty (1973)******* James Caan, Marsha Mason. The best things about this film are the performances by James Caan, as an offbeat sailor with a sense of responsibility, and Marsha Mason, as an unorthodox bar girl with a street-toughened 11-year-old, whose black-sailor father ran away before his birth. The story, which deals with their volatile love-hate relationship, offers nothing new, but the two actors manage to keep interest. Credit also to director Mark Rydell. (117 mins.)

Cinderfella (1960)** Jerry Lewis, Anna Maria Alberghetti, Ed Wynn. The fairytale adapted to suit the talents of Lewis. A misguided venture—tasteless, ornately dull musical fantasy should appeal to fans of the comic, but no one else. (Dir: Frank Tashlin, 91 mins.)

Circle of Children, A (1977)***½ Jane Alexander, Rachel Roberts, David Ogden Stiers, Nan Martin. Luminous adaptation of Mary Mc-Cracken's novel about a financially poor, spiritually rich private school for emotionally disturbed children. The most talented of the understanding teachers is Helga, a woman with a marked German accent, unschooled, but a "therapeutic genius," who inspires an affluent suburban woman to volunteer at the school. Rachel Roberts is wonderful as Helga and Jane Alexander is moving in her worship of this incomparable teacher. You'll be especially dazzled by the children with whom Jane Alexander must prove her worth. Made-for-TV. (Dir: Don Taylor, 100 mins.)

Circle of Danger (British, 1951)*** Ray Milland, Patricia Roc. American returns to Europe to investigate the mysterious death of his brother during World War II. Interesting melodrama keeps the viewer in suspense. (Dir: Jacques Tourneur, 86 mins.)

Circle of Death (Mexican, 1960)** Sarita Montiel, Raul Remirez. Businessman stoops to murder to gain control of his wife's fortune. Undistinguished melodrama dubbed in English.

Circle of Deception (British, 1961)**½ Bradford Dillman, Suzy Parker. Intelligence agent is assigned a dangerous mission in Germany, is captured and spills the beans. War melodrama has a suspenseful twist but doesn't bring it off too well. However, it has its moments. (Dir: Jack Lee, 100 mins.)

Circle of Love (France-Italy, 1964) *½ Marie Dubois, Claude Giroud, Jean-Claude Brialy, Jane Fonda. Poor remake of Max Ophuls' classic movie, based on Arthur Schnitzler's play, about the chainlike link of love and sex through various social strata—and partners. Director Roger Vadim and scriptwriter Jean Anouilh have produced a tired charade. The actors try hard but are uniformly miscast. The dubbing is painfully apparent. (Dir: Roger Vadim, 105 mins.)

Circular Triangle (German, 1964)** Lilli Palmer, Sylva Koscina. Battle for industrial power brings on three murders. Fair drama saved by some good acting. Dubbed in English.

Circumstantial Evidence (British, 1954)** Patrick Holt, Rona Anderson. Doctor is placed on trial for murder when his fiancée's ex-husband is found dead. Average courtroom drama. (Dir: John Larkin, 68 mins.)

Circus, The (1928)***½ Charles Chaplin, Merna Kennedy, Betty Morrissey. Some marvelous sight gags and other glimpses of the Chaplin genius in this little-known early film made in 1926, re-issued in this version with music and a theme song written by Chaplin himself. There is one notable sequence of Chaplin playing a circus tramp, being chased by a policeman through a hall of mirrors. A circus setting all right, played for laughs, but the characters are right out of all the melodramas of the time, including a wicked father, an ailing daughter, etc. Original story also written by Chaplin. (Dir: Charles Chaplin, 71 mins.)

Circus of Fear (British, 1967)** Leo Genn, Christopher Lee, Suzy Kendall, Cecil Parker, Eddi Arent. Robbery clues lead to a circus, where the bodies and the film begin to pile up. Involved plot, but enough red herrings strewn along the way to interest mystery fans. (Dir: John Moxey, 65 mins.)

Circus of Horrors (1960)**½ Anton Diffring, Erica Remberg. Well done, British-made horror film about a plastic surgeon who finds temporary shelter from flight in a traveling circus. The circus background serves well for the surgeon's experiments. Good cast adds to the film. (Dir: Sidney Hayers, 89 mins.)

Circus of Love (West German, 1954)** Eva Bartok, Curt Jurgens. Mediocre carnival melodrama as a woman is caught between emotions for two men. An English-language version ("Carnival Story") was made simultaneously, and some of the stars of the American version (Anne Baxter, Steve Cochran) appear here as extras. English subtitles. (Dir: Kurt Neumann, 93 mins.)

Circus World (1964)**½ John Wayne, Claudia Cardinale, Rita Hayworth. The large-scale excitement of the big top, the presence of John Wayne, Rita Hayworth and Claudia Cardinale in starring roles, plus excellent Spanish locations help to overcome the shortcomings of the script. Wayne is the head of a combination wild west and circus show which is in financial straits, and if that isn't enough plot, there are two or three romantic involvements thrown in. Don't expect another "Trapeze" and you'll enjoy it. (Dir: Henry Hathaway, 135 mins.)

Cisco Pike (1972)**½ Gene Hackman, Kris Kristofferson. Narcotics agent (Hackman) blackmails a washed-up rock star (Kristofferson) into dealing off $10,000 worth of Acapulco Gold. The plot's predictable but Kristofferson is fascinating to watch in a role which seems to be an extension of himself. (Dir: Bill L. Norton, 94 mins.)

Citadel, The (1938)**** Robert Donat, Rosalind Russell. Cronin's novel about a young dedicated Scots physician who almost loses his way in life is a brilliantly acted gem which almost improves on the wonderful book. (Dir: King Vidor, 110 mins.)

Citizen Kane (1941)**** Orson Welles, Joseph Cotten. This story of a brilliant tyrant who built up a vast chain of newspapers, sacrificing his personal happiness along the way, was directed by the youthful Orson Welles over three decades ago and it still stands up as one of the most remarkable films ever made. Welles was a slim and a wonderful actor. As a director he opened up, in this brilliantly edited and photographed film, whole new vistas for the motion picture industry. (Dir: Orson Welles, 119 mins.)

City, The (1977)* Robert Forster, Don Johnson, Jimmy Dean. Another tedious Quinn Martin pilot for a series starring Robert Forster and Don Johnson as a pair of Los Angeles policemen. Their assignment has them tracking down a psychotic killer (are there any other kinds in TV series?) who is out to kill a popular country-western singing star, charmingly played by Jimmy Dean. Made-for-TV. (Dir: Harvey Hart, 72 mins.)

City Across the River (1949)**½ Stephen McNally, Peter Fernendez, Thelma Ritter. Irving Shulman's explosive book on juvenile delinquency in Brooklyn, "The Amboy Dukes," makes a tough movie. The "kids" of the streets are depicted in melodramatic terms, but there's enough bite left to retain your interest. (Dir: Maxwell Shane, 90 mins.)

City After Midnight—See: That Woman Opposite

City Beneath the Sea (1953)**½ Robert Ryan, Anthony Quinn, Mala Powers. Two-fisted adventure about big men in the big business of treasure hunting beneath the sea. The plot's predictable but Quinn and Ryan are convincing leads and carry the show. (Dir: Budd Boetticher, 87 mins.)

City Beneath the Sea (1971)**½ Stuart Whitman, Robert Wagner, Richard Basehart. Science-fiction fans take note—futuristic underwater storyteller Irwin Allen is at it again. His made-for-TV film is a scenic-effects wonder starring Stuart Whitman and Robert Wagner. Tells of an undersea city, Pacifica, in the year 2053. When its co-creator Mathews (Whitman) returns under Presidential orders, he faces a fistful of crises during shipments of gold and nuclear H-128 from Fort Knox. (Dir: Irwin Allen, 99 mins.)

City for Conquest (1940)*** James Cagney, Ann Sheridan. Sentimental story of a boxer who goes blind making sacrifices for his brother. There's a lot of corn here but it's well seasoned and expertly served. A newcomer named Arthur Kennedy does a nice job as Cagney's brother and you'll also see Elia Kazan, one of America's most talented directors, in a minor role. (Dir: Anatole Litvak, 101 mins.)

City Lights (1931)**** Charlie Chaplin, Virginia Cherrill, Florence Lee. Perhaps Chaplin's greatest comedy, which means that it is one of the great works in the history of cinema. The last of Chaplin's silent films, thanks to Chaplin's refusal to make this a talkie after he had been preparing it for two years. Touching and hilarious tale of the "Little Tramp" who falls in love with a blind flower girl and gets money for her to have an operation to restore her sight. The sequence when Chaplin becomes a boxer to get money for his beloved is one of his most remarkable. If the ending of this classic doesn't move you, when the Little Tramp peers through the window of a flower shop and sees the hitherto blind girl, you'd better have your heart and your head examined. Written and directed by Chaplin. (Dir: Charles Chaplin, 90 mins.)

City of Bad Men (1953)**½ Dale Robertson, Jeanne Crain, Richard Boone, Lloyd Bridges. Outlaws ride into Carson City and plan to rob the proceeds from the Corbett-Fitzsimmons prizefight. Pleasant western with a slightly different twist. (Dir: Harmon Jones, 82 mins.)

City of Fear (1959)**½ Vince Edwards. One of the many "B" films Vince Edwards made before he became famous as TV's sullen medic "Ben Casey." This one has him cast as an escaped convict who steals a metal container he believes is filled with heroin but actually contains a dangerous, radioactive powder called cobalt 60. Neatly made on a small budget. (Dir: Irving Lerner, 81 mins.)

City of Fear (1965)*½ Paul Maxwell, Terry Moore. Reporter is involved in a plot to smuggle a scientist from behind the Iron Curtain. Which is where they should have left the script of this shaky espionage thriller filmed in Europe. (Dir: Peter Bezencenet, 90 mins.)

City on a Hunt (1953)** Lew Ayres, Sonny Tufts. Routine mystery, innocent victim of a murder charge uncovering the real culprit. San Francisco background. Cast superior to material. Alternate title: "No Escape." (Dir: Charles Bennett, 76 mins.)

City Stands Trial, The (Italian, 1954)**½ Silvana Pampanini, Eduardo Cianelli. Police investigate a double murder, combat an underworld syndicate controlling the city. Period crime story of Naples at the turn of the century has a documentary-like atmosphere, some good moments. English-dubbed.

City Streets (1931)** Gary Cooper, Sylvia Sidney, Paul Lukas, William Boyd, Guy Kibbee. Story by Dashiell Hammett. No need to comment on this routine gangster film, as the curious will want to see a 1931 Gary Cooper playing "the Kid." (Dir: Rouben Mamoulian, 82 mins.)

City That Never Sleeps (1953)*** Gig Young, Mala Powers. Policeman nearly strays off the straight and narrow because of a cafe entertainer. Well made crime melodrama with some good performances. (Dir: John H. Auer, 90 mins.)

Claire's Knee (France, 1970)**** Jean-Claude Brialy, Aurora Cornu, Laurence De Monaghan, Beatrice Romand. A sophisticated, literate, joyous gem, one of Eric Rohmer's "Six Moral Fables," preceded by "My Night At Maud's" and followed by "Chloe in the Afternoon." Brialy plays a 35-year-old Frenchman who has the enormous good fortune to spend a summer dallying with three enchanting women, including two nubile sisters, on the shores of Lake Geneva. The Frenchman turns out to be at least as much interested in their minds as he is in their bodies. A film full of grace and gossamer joys, one to be savored frame by frame. Quite perfectly written and directed by Eric Rohmer. (103 mins.)

Clambake (1967)* Elvis Presley, Shelley Fabares, Bill Bixby. Elvis as a millionaire incognito who gets involved in boat racing. A dull clambake indeed.

Clarence, the Cross-Eyed Lion (1965)**½ Marshall Thompson, Betty Drake. Another in the string of nature movies resembling "Born Free." Clarence can't focus on his prey when hunting, and he is taken to the Study Center for Animal Behavior in Africa, where he is taken as a pet by the daughter of a doctor. Clarence also aids in capturing ape poachers. The television series "Daktari" was based on this film. (Dir: Andrew Marton, 98 mins.)

Clash by Night (1952)**½ Barbara Stanwyck, Robert Ryan, Paul Douglas, Marilyn Monroe. Stark early Odets drama of a lonely woman married to a fishing boat skipper who becomes involved in an affair with his best friend. Good performances, some good scenes, but never quite makes it. (Dir: Fritz Lang, 105 mins.)

Clash of Steel (French, 1964) *½ Gerard Barray, Gianna Maria Canale. Bold cavalier comes to the aid of a dancer who is really the daughter of a count. Humdrum swash-buckling melodrama dubbed in English. (Dir: Benard Borderie, 79 mins.)

Class of '44 (1973)** Gary Grimes, Jerry Houser, Oliver Conant, William Atherton. A disappointing sequel to the much better "Summer of '42," with the same three boys—Hermie, Oscy and Benjie—now a little older and graduating from high school. It's also less well acted than "Summer of '42." Benjie disappears early, off to war, while the others go on to college—fraternity hazings, cheating on exams, proms, etc. The whole thing seems terribly contrived, with a serious climax that comes out of nowhere. Fails to generate much emotional impact. Screenplay by Herman Raucher. (Dir: Paul Bogart, 95 mins.)

Class of '63 (1973)***½ Joan Hackett, James Brolin. This class-reunion story turns a surprisingly effective emotional drama. Talented actress Joan Hackett delivers a stunning performance as the unhappy wife who meets her old campus flame. What could be soap-opera material about a jealous husband and a wandering wife becomes an absorbing conflict played against fraternity foolishness. Miss Hackett is worth seeing, and so is Cliff Gorman as her husband. Made-for-TV. (Dir: John Korty, 73 mins.)

Claudelle Inglish (1961)** Diane McBain, Arthur Kennedy, Will Hutchins. Novel by Erskine Caldwell about a teenager, a sharecropper's daughter, who drives men mad, eventually comes to a sad end. Miss McBain and her director try to make something of it, to little avail—pretty drab. (Dir: Gordon Douglas, 99 mins.)

Claudia (1943)***½ Dorothy McGuire, Robert Young. If you've never seen Rose Franken's almost classical story of a child bride who grows up, you're in for treat. Funny but not hilarious, sentimental but not corny. A delightful story. (Dir: Edmund Goulding, 91 mins.)

Claudia and David (1946)*** Dorothy McGuire, Robert Young. Not as delightful as "Claudia," but this sequel about their baby and life in suburban Connecticut is easy to take and should please the ladies. (Dir: Walter Lang, 78 mins.)

Claw Monsters, The (1955-66)** Phyllis Coates, Myron Healey. Feature version of serial "Panther Girl of the Kongo." Jungle girl combats a scientist using a monster to scare the natives away from his diamond mine. Serial fans might go for this lowbrow but actionful adventure. (Dir: Franklin Adreon, 100 mins.)

Clear and Present Danger, A (1970)**½ Hal Holbrook, E. G. Marshall, Joseph Campanella. The pilot film for "The Senator" TV series starring Hal Holbrook. His performance, plus a thoughtful script about air pollution, should keep your interest. Holbrook is a candidate for the U.S. Senate who sacrifices his political aspirations in order to combat a smog crisis and its repercussions. (Dir: James Goldstone, 99 mins.)

Cleo From 5 to 7 (French, 1962)**½ Corinne Marchand, Dorothea Blanck. Two hours in the life of a beautiful but spiritually empty singer who anxiously awaits a doctor's report on her health. Some critics found this artistic, others will think it merely arty. Some good informal camerawork on the streets of Paris. (Dir: Agnes Varda, 90 mins.)

Cleopatra (1934)**½ Claudette Colbert, Warren William. Lavish film tale of the famous queen has little to offer besides a "big" production. Those who don't like Shaw's or Shakespeare's versions may enjoy this. (Dir: Cecil B. De Mille, 101 mins.)

Cleopatra (1963)*** Elizabeth Taylor, Richard Burton, Rex Harrison. As a spectacle, this elaborate production has few equals, but as historical drama it leaves something to be desired. The acting ranges from brilliant (Rex Harrison as Caesar) to uneven (Elizabeth Taylor as Cleopatra). Richard Burton fluctuates between being good and bad. Miss Taylor is a feast for the eyes and some of the drama is interesting. Although the film is overlong, most viewers will probably stay with it to the end. Whatever impact spactacles like this have when seen on a big theater screen, much of it is lost during the transfer to a tiny TV screen. (Dir: Joseph Mankiewicz, 243 mins.)

Cleopatra's Daughter (Italian, 1961)*½ Debra Paget, Robert Alda. Familiar Hollywood names join an international group of actors in this quickie, foreign production (English-dubbed). Adventure is the key-note and everyone plays it that way. (Dir: Richard MacNamara, 102 mins.)

Climats (French, 1962)****½** Marina Vlady, Jean-Pierre Marielle, Emmanuela Riva. Leisurely drama of an ill-matched married couple who divorce, and their eventual emotional entanglements thereafter. Sensitive performances, but the delicate theme needed more understanding treatment. Dubbed in English.

Climb an Angry Mountain (1972)****** Barry Nelson, Fess Parker. Since so many TV heroes pack guns it seemed logical for Fess Parker to become a low-keyed country sheriff. Filmed around Mount Shasta country, lawman Parker, a widower who raises his kids on a ranch, reluctantly goes after a local Indian on the run for a murder rap. The real star is the Shasta scenery, aided by an assist from football's Joe Kapp as the running Indian. Made-for-TV. (Dir: Leonard Horn, 97 mins.)

Climbers, The (1964)***** Edmond O'Brien, Richard Basehart. The two fine actors, O'Brien and Basehart, are wasted in this trivial drama about a love triangle that leads to murder.

Cloak and Dagger (1946)******* Gary Cooper, Lilli Palmer, Robert Alda. University professor works on a secret mission for the OSS inside Germany. Loosely constructed but tense espionage melodrama, well acted. (Dir: Fritz Lang, 106 mins.)

Clock, The (1944)****½** Judy Garland, Robert Walker, Keenan Wynn. Fair romantic drama about a soldier who meets, woos and weds a girl during his last 48-hour leave before shipping out. It's too "gooey" for some tastes, but the ladies will love it. Judy, incidentally, does not sing. (Dir: Vincente Minnelli, 90 mins.)

Clockmaker, The (France, 1974)*****½** Philippe Noiret. An astonishing, perceptive first feature film directed by former film critic Bertrand Tavernier and based on a novel by Georges Simenon. Protagonist is a watchmaker in Lyon who is mortified to learn that his grown-up son has committed a political murder, though the son is not politically involved. Philippe Noiret is remarkable playing the watchmaker, inspecting and analyzing the developments as if he were looking through

his magnifying glass. A complex, beautifully observed film directed with great restraint, uniformly well acted. The character of the young killer is never adequately dealt with, but "Clockmaker" does finally understand. (Dir: Bertrand Tavernier, 100 mins.)

Clockwork Orange, A (Great Britain, 1971)******** Malcolm McDowell, Patrick Magee, Adrienne Corri. A shattering political allegory about a loathsome, violent anti-hero in a modern society where gangs of young punks run amok and peaceful citizens are imprisoned in their own homes. Produced, written and directed by Stanley Kubrick, based on the novel by Anthony Burgess. (The novel is partially autobiographical, as Burgess' own wife was robbed, raped and severely beaten by three G.I. deserters during a London WW2 blackout, and subsequently died of these injuries.) "Clockwork" is loaded with fascinating cinematic images, including some of the most repellent scenes ever, but in Kubrick's masterful hands it builds to a devastating finale. Nominated for Academy Awards for best picture, best direction, and best screenplay. Malcolm McDowell is altogether chilling playing a pathological toughie. After the initial release, Kubrick re-edited "Clockwork" slightly to make it less violent. An unforgettable cinema masterpiece with an appalling message of immorality. (Dir: Stanley Kubrick, 135 mins.)

Clones, The (1973)****** Michael Greene, Gregory Sierra. A strange sci-fi thriller that tries, without much luck, for laughs. There's this scientist, see, who wants to kill this doctor, so he makes a clone (duplicate) to replace the doctor, but the clone . . . Woody Allen did it far better in his sketch in "Sleeper." (Dirs: Paul Hunt and Lamar Card, 94 mins.)

Close to My Heart (1951)****½** Gene Tierney, Ray Milland, Fay Bainter. Soap opera plot about a couple who adopt the baby of a convicted murderer and prove there's nothing in heredity. Well acted by a good cast. (Dir: William Keighley, 90 mins.)

Close-Up (1948)****½** Alan Baxter, Virginia Gilmore. Newsreel photographer finds plenty of trouble when he accidentally catches a picture of a wanted Nazi criminal. Fairly good melodrama moves at a fast clip.

Closely Watched Trains (Czechoslovak, 1966)***½ Vaclav Neckar, Jitka Bendova. Gentle, touching film directed by Jiri Menzel, about a shy sexually inexperienced train dispatcher during the period of the German occupation during World War II. Made during a period of increasing artistic freedom in Czechoslovakia, this comedy-drama shows how the decent instincts in people can survive during difficult times, and there is one delicious scene showing a novel use for the posterior of an obliging country wench. Menzel's perceptive hand is evident throughout as this slight story builds to the unhappy finale. Dubbed.

Cloudburst (British, 1952)** Robert Preston, Elizabeth Sellars. An inoffensive little item from England with good actor Robert Preston completely wasted as an adventurer who can't seem to stay away from trouble. (Dir: Francis Searle, 83 mins.)

Clouded Yellow (British, 1951)*** Jean Simmons, Trevor Howard. Secret service agent demoted to cataloguing butterflies aids a girl wrongly accused of murder. Mystery begins slowly but picks up as it progresses to a suspenseful climax. (Dir: Ralph Thomas, 96 mins.)

Clouds Over Europe—See: **Q Planes**

Clouds Over Israel (Israel, 1962)**½ Yiftach Spector, Shimon Israeli, Dina Doronne. Compelling, unpretentious picture about a human confrontation between Israeli military men and an Arab family during the 1956 hostilities. The growth of mutual respect and friendship is nicely told, technical shortcomings and awkward script notwithstanding. (Dir: Ivan Lengyel, 85 mins.)

Clown, The (1953)*** Red Skelton, Jane Greer, Tim Considine. If you're a Red Skelton fan, you might be surprised to see him act in this one-A drama about a comedy performer who loses his wife through divorce and almost loses his son's love. (Dir: Robert Z. Leonard, 89 mins.)

Clowns, The (Italian-French, 1971)***½ Mayo Morin, Lima Alberti, Alvaro Vitali, Gasparmo. Three rings of spectacle, slapstick, and sensation invade the screen in this piece from the master Italian director

Federico Fellini. Clowns race to and fro in a fantasy circus world of Fellini's youth which is approached as a documentary-within-a-film. Fellini appears in the film as the head of the camera crew and if you ask what it all means you may be hit with the same bucket of water as the journalist who asked the question in the film. Without Fellini's usually amazing substance, but the surface glows with spirit throughout. English subtitles. (90 mins.)

Clue of the New Pin, The (British, 1962)** Paul Daneman, Bernard Archard. Sleuth investigates the murder of a millionaire whose body is found in a locked vault. Old-fashioned-style whodunit based on an Edgar Wallace story. Should satisfy mystery fans. (Dir: Allan Davis, 58 mins.)

Clue of the Silver Key, The (British, 1962)** Bernard Lee, Finlay Currie. Scotland Yard investigates the murder of a wealthy moneylender. Typical Edgar Wallace mystery for the sleuthing devotees. (Dir: Gerald Glaister, 59 mins.)

Clue of the Twisted Candle, The (British, 1962)** Bernard Lee, David Knight. Wealthy man who fears for his life is implicated in murder. Okay Edgar Wallace mystery.

Cluny Brown (1946)***½ Jennifer Jones, Charles Boyer. Pleasant comedy, superbly acted and directed, about the turbulent career of a plumber's niece and a Czech refugee in England during the war. A satirical spoof of the first order directed by Ernst Lubitsch. (Dir: Ernst Lubitsch, 100 mins.)

Coast of Skeletons (Great Britain, 1965)* Richard Todd, Dale Robertson, Heinz Drache. Dull. Africa is the setting as an ex-British officer investigates a heavily insured diamond miner. Based on the Edgar Wallace story "Sanders of the River." See instead "Sanders of the River," 1935 film with Paul Robeson. (Dir: Robert Lynn, 90 mins.)

Cobweb, The (1955)***½ Richard Widmark, Lauren Bacall, Charles Boyer, Gloria Grahame, Susan Strasberg, John Kerr, Lillian Gish. A stellar cast brings William Gibson's dramatic novel about a modern mental institution to the screen with conviction. Miss Gish and Mr. Boyer are standouts as the institution's business manager and head administrator respectively. (Dir: Vincente Minnelli, 124 mins.)

Cockeyed Miracle, The (1946)** Frank Morgan, Keenan Wynn, Audrey Totter. Cockeyed little fantasy about a couple of ghosts trying to straighten out those they left behind is completely dependent on the cast. (Dir: Sylvan Simon, 81 mins.)

Cockleshell Heroes (British, 1956)***½ Jose Ferrer, Trevor Howard. Tense suspense tale about one of the most dangerous missions of WW II. "Operation Cockleshell" is the name given to the canoe invasion by a handful of volunteers of an enemy-held French port in order to destroy a group of battleships. Good invasion sequence with "edge-of-sofa" excitement. (Dir: Jose Ferrer, 110 mins.)

Cocoanuts, The (1929)*** Four Marx Brothers, Oscar Shaw. Early sound effort, first film made by the mad Marxes. They're still funny, but the dated sound and technique hurts. (Dir: Robert Florey, 96 mins.)

Code Name: Diamond Head (1977)* Roy Thinnes, France Nuyen. This dull "Hawaii Five-O"-type mystery show has Roy Thinnes instead of Jack Lord chasing around the islands after a master of disguises, who's about to steal a toxic gas formula. Agent Thinnes pretends to be a gambler and a pool shark. Even Don Knight, a favorite Five-O villain, appears to make "Hawaii"-series fans feel right at home. Made-for-TV. (Dir: Jeannot Szwarc, 79 mins.)

Code Name: Tiger (French, 1964)*½ Roger Hanin, Daniela Bianchi. Two-fisted secret agent has his hands full guarding the wife and daughter of a Turkish diplomat. Arty "new Wave" director Claude Chabrol did this espionage melodrama and provided plenty of scurrying around but little sense. Action scenes are overdone.

Code of Silence—See: Killer's Cage

Code 7, Victim 5! (British, 1964)*½ Lex Barker, Ronald Fraser. An American private eye tracks down the killer of a prominent man's butler. Paper-thin mystery, but at least it's not dubbed. (Dir: Robert Lynn, 88 mins.)

Code 645 (1947-66)*½ Clayton Moore, Ramsay Ames, Roy Barcroft. Feature version of serial "G-Men Never Forget." Notorious es-caped criminal has a face lift, poses as the police commissioner he has kidnaped; FBI agent gets on the job. Humdrum serial heroics; action, that's all. (Dir: Fred Brannon, 100 mins.)

Coffee, Tea or Me? (1973)**½ Karen Valentine, John Davidson, Michael Anderson. This lighthearted comedy leans heavily on the perkiness of Karen Valentine. Karen is an airline stewardess with a weakness for strays which leads to a double life, commuting between two husbands in Los Angeles and London. Alec Guinness charmed movie fans in a similar plot in "Captain's Paradise," and it works fairly well in this revamped format. Davidson and Anderson supply the right measure of charm as the young cuckolds. Made-for-TV. (Dir: Norman Panama, 90 mins.)

Coffin From Hong Kong, A (German, 1964)*½ Heinz Drache, Elga Andersen. Private eye finds a dead girl in his room, takes off for Hong Kong, where he risks his life smashing a smuggling ring. Atmospheric-locale scenes are the only highlights of this low-grade adventure dubbed in English.

Cold Night's Death (1973)*** Eli Wallach, Robert Culp. Culp, Wallach, and a supporting cast of monkeys! Strange forces disrupt experiments being made on monkeys in a snowbound mountain lab. Working in isolation with the animals, scientists blame each other for weird acts of vandalism. Could the culprit be the Abominable Snowman? Takes its time building up the dilemma, scattering occasional clues, but it's worth hanging on for the unpredictable solution. Made-for-TV. (Dir: Jerrold Freedman, 73 mins.)

Cold Sweat (1974)* Liv Ullmann, Charles Bronson, James Mason. Top stars in this routine crime story can't overcome the banality of its script. Mason arrives to collect a favor from his old friend Bronson, which entails smuggling illegal drugs in his fishing boat . . . and the intrigue (yawn) is on. Based on the novel "Ride the Nightmare." (Dir: Terence Young, 94 mins.)

Cold Turkey (1971)*** Dick Van Dyke, Pippa Scott, Tom Poston. Uneven but often funny comedy about a small Mid-western town trying to win a 25 million dollar reward if everyone in the town will go "cold turkey" for thirty days, i.e. give up smoking cigarettes. Van Dyke plays a preacher urging his flock to avoid the weed. Produced, directed and co-authored by Norman Lear, responsible for the hit TV series "All In The Family." (102 mins.)

Cold Wind in August, A (1961)***½ Lola Albright, Scott Marlowe, Herschel Bernardi. A very moving drama of a lonely burlesque stripper in her thirties and her friendship, which turns into a love affair, with a 17-year-old boy. Lola Albright, under the sensitive directorial hand of Alexander Singer, gives a beautifully shaded, poignant, convincing performance playing the stripper searching for affection. Albright, who conclusively proves here that she's a most gifted actress, has never been seen to such good advantage in films since. Scott Marlowe impresses as the young boy. Screenplay by Burton Wohl based on his novel "Cold Wind in August." One of the best American films dealing with adolescent love, especially that of a young boy for an older woman. (Dir: Alexander Singer, 80 mins.)

Colditz Story (British, 1957)*** John Mills, Eric Portman. Offbeat comedy-drama about British prisoners of war in a German castle fortress (WW II). Excellent performance by Eric Portman. (Dir: Guy Hamilton, 97 mins.)

Cole Younger, Gunfighter (1958)** Frank Lovejoy, James Best. The young cowboy fans will go for this rough and tough western about the notorious gunslinger, Cole Younger, and a couple of men who cross his path. (Dir: R. G. Springsteen, 79 mins.)

Collector, The (1965)***½ Samantha Eggar, Terrence Stamp. Veteran director William Wyler has fashioned an interesting psychological drama of John Fowles' best selling novel about a maniacal plan executed by a psychotic young Englishman. The young man, well acted by Terrence Stamp, kidnaps beautiful art student (Miss Eggar) and keeps her captive in the cellar of his country home. The film builds considerable tension, and the two stars are helpful throughout. (Dir: William Wyler, 119 mins.)

Colleen (1936)**½ Ruby Keeler, Dick Powell, Jack Oakie. Typical 1936 Dick Powell musical. Hugh Herbert's portrayal of an eccentric millionaire is the only redeeming feature. (Dir: Alfred E. Green, 100 mins.)

College Confidential (1960)*½ Steve Allen, Jayne Meadows, Mamie Van Doren. Another of producer-director Albert Zugsmith's crude commercial opuses spiced with sex, violence. This time the action takes place in a small college town where Prof. Steve Allen's classroom is filled with such typical college types as Mamie Van Doren, Conway Twitty and Ziva Rodman. (Dir: Albert Zugsmith, 91 mins.)

Collision Course (1969)—See: **Bamboo Saucer, The**

Colonel Effingham's Raid (1946)*** Charles Coburn, Joan Bennett. A retired Southern colonel decides to use his military background to straighten out a town. Good comedy thanks to Coburn. (Dir: Irving Pichel, 70 mins.)

Color Me Dead (Australia, 1969) *½ Tom Tryon, Carolyn Jones. Ineffective remake of 1949 flick "D.O.A." Sluggish crime story has poisoned man searching for his own killer. Carolyn Jones stands out among otherwise tepid performers. Filmed in Sydney. (Dir: Eddie Davis, 97 mins.)

Colorado Territory (1949)*** Joel McCrea, Virginia Mayo. Good western with plenty of action. About a bad man who gets out of jail only to find himself trapped in a valley. (Dir: Raoul Walsh, 94 mins.)

Colossus and the Amazon Queen (Italian, 1960)* Ed Fury, Rod Taylor. Two gladiators are captured by Amazon women, fall in love, save the gals from pirates. Ridiculous English-dubbed action thriller—one of its major crimes is wasting Taylor in a comedy-relief role.

Colossus and the Headhunters (Italian, 1960)* Kirk Morris, Laura Brown. Muscleman aids a dethroned queen in fighting off a ferocious tribe. Poor English-dubbed action thriller.

Colossus and the Huns (Italian, 1960) *½ Jerome Courtland, Lisa Gastoni. Adventurer comes to the aid of a king whose land is terrorized by barbarian hordes. Slapdash swashbuckler dubbed in English.

Colossus of New York, The (1958)** John Baragrey, Otto Kruger, Mala Powers, Ross Martin. Surgeon transfers the brain of his son into a huge robot, which promptly goes on the rampage. Far-fetched sci-fi thriller has the advantage of good production effects. (Dir: Eugene Lourie, 70 mins.)

Colossus of Rhodes, The (Italian, 1960)** Rory Calhoun, Lea Massari. Better than usual spear-and-sandal effort. Lots of action as heroes try to destroy a huge statue guarding the port of Rhodes.

Colossus of the Arena (Italian, 1960)*½ Mark Forrest, Scilla Gabel. Gladiator saves a princess from the schemes of a duke. Typically low-brow English-dubbed action spectacle.

Colt .45—See: Thunder Cloud

Columbo: An Exercise in Fatality (1974)**½ Peter Falk, Robert Conrad. Features a complicated duel of wits between Peter Falk's sloppy Columbo and a nasty physical fitness character (Robert Conrad), an expert at manipulating taped telephone conversations as an alibi for murder. Columbo takes out a 30-day introductory membership to one of the health spas the guy owns. Made-for-TV. (Dir: Bernard Kowalski, 98 mins.)

Columbo: Death Lends a Hand (1971)**½ Peter Falk, Robert Culp. Peter Falk's characterization of the seemingly clumsy detective with the brain of a Sherlock Holmes is a joy to watch, and he's provided here with a fine adversary in the person of Robert Culp. Culp, who heads up a super-investigative agency, accidentally kills the wife of a client who, in turn, hires Culp's firm to augment the regular police force. The cat-and-mouse game is great fun. Made-for-TV. (Dir: Bernard Kowalski, 72 mins.)

Columbo: Double Shock (1973)**½ Peter Falk, Jeanette Nolan, Julie Newmar, Martin Landau. Peter Falk's usually unflappable Columbo has a hard time making the grade with Jeanette Nolan's officious housekeeper, while trying to determine how and by whom her aging, wealthy physical-fitness addict of an employer was murdered. Made-for-TV. (Dir: Robert Butler, 72 mins.)

Columbo: Swan Song (1974)**½ Peter Falk, Johnny Cash, Ida Lupino. This can be called a flying musical-murder story. It gains interest from the casting of gravel-

throated, country-western star Johnny Cash. He plays a former convict-turned-pop-star with the help of his wife, well played by Ida Lupino. Made-for-TV. (Dir: Nicholas Colasanto, 106 mins.)

Columbo: Troubled Waters (1975)** Peter Falk, Robert Vaughn, Dean Stockwell. Even when Peter Falk's Columbo goes on a much-needed vacation he's confronted with murder, blackmail and the usual quota of guest-starring suspects. The sleuth boards the "Sun Princess," a cruise ship en route to Mexico. Shortly after they raise anchor, the exotic band singer is found dead. The director is a better actor. Made-for-TV. (Dir: Ben Gazzara, 98 mins.)

Column South (1953)** Audie Murphy, Joan Evans, Robert Sterling. Slow moving Civil War yarn with Murphy playing a young cavalry officer who averts an all out Navajo uprising. Miss Evans supplies the necessary romance. (Dir: Frederick de Cordova, 85 mins.)

Comanche (1956)** Dana Andrews, Linda Cristal, Kent Smith. Indians raid a Mexican town and kidnap the daughter of a Spanish aristocrat among others. Cavalry Scout Andrews has a rough time before he convinces chief that he is on a peace mission. Some good battle scenes. (Dir: George Sherman, 87 mins.)

Comanche Station (1960)*** Randolph Scott, Nancy Gates. Lawman guides a woman and three desperadoes through hostile Indian country. These Scott westerns are usually better than average, and this one is no exception; well-made and exciting.

Comanche Territory (1950)** Maureen O'Hara, Macdonald Carey. Another retelling of the adventures of famed Jim Bowie and his encounter with the Apaches. Macdonald Carey isn't quite to the image of Bowie but he gives it the old college try. Maureen O'Hara is, as always, Maureen O'Hara. (Dir: George Sherman, 76 mins.)

Comancheros, The (1961)*** John Wayne, Stuart Whitman, Ina Balin, Lee Marvin, Nehemiah Persoff. Generally enjoyable big-scale western about a ranger who infiltrates a gang supplying guns and firewater to the Indians. Played for fun by Wayne, Whitman, Marvin and others; some good action at the end. (Dir: Michael Curtiz, 107 mins.)

Combat Squad (1953)** John Ireland, Lon McCallister, Hal March. During the Korean War, a young, frightened boy finds the courage to become a man in the eyes of his buddies. Familiar war story. (Dir: Cy Roth, 72 mins.)

Come and Get It (1936)*** Joel McCrea, Frances Farmer, Walter Brennan. Good drama based on Edna Ferber's tale of the lumber country and the people who toil in it. The cast does well with Walter Brennan the standout (he won a supporting Oscar for his performance in this film). Director buffs might be interested to know that William Wyler took over the direction from Howard Hawks for the last part of the film. (Dirs: William Wyler, Howard Hawks, 99 mins.)

Come Back, Africa (1960)***½ Zachariah Mgabi. Semi-documentary, surreptitiously filmed in South Africa, describes the stifling, often violent lives of blacks in that divided society. Unprofessional cast is mostly awkward but Mgabi, the lead, is extraordinary, his performance evoking the helpless despair of being perpetually harassed. Squalid settings evoke the reality best. (Dir: Lionel Rogosin, 90 mins.)

Come Back Charleston Blue (1972)** Godfrey Cambridge, Raymond St. Jacques, Jonelle Allen. Coffin Ed Johnson and Grave Digger Jones return in this sequel to the amusing "Cotton Comes to Harlem." Unfortunately, the gritty frivolity that made "Cotton" a joy is missing in this opus concerning the fight between the black and white gangs that hope to control the Harlem heroin trade. Many may find the hip lingo incomprehensible, and everyone will notice the lack of continuity in the plot. Based on the novel, "The Heat's On," by Chester Himes. The co-author of the screenplay is listed as "Bontche Schweig." It's a Sholom Aleichem charactername used by the gifted TV writer Ernest Kinoy, though this is certainly not a sample of the award-winning Kinoy's best work. (Dir: Mark Warren, 100 mins.)

Come Back, Little Sheba (1952)**** Shirley Booth, Burt Lancaster, Terry Moore. Splendid performance by Shirley Booth as a slatternly middle-aged housewife, an equally effective one by Lancaster as her alcoholic husband in this absorbing adaptation of the hit play by William Inge. Emotionally searing drama of an unhappy marriage for those who insist on top-quality filmmaking. TV's Hazel fans will be reminded what a moving actress Miss Booth can be. (Dir: Daniel Mann, 99 mins.)

Come Blow Your Horn (1963)*** Frank Sinatra, Lee J. Cobb, Barbara Rush. Neil Simon's Broadway comedy about a Jewish family in New York City is successfully brought to the screen with Sinatra well cast as a playboy and Tony Bill as his hero-worshipping younger brother. Lee J. Cobb and Molly Picon, as the parents, supply the humor of the original script. (Dir: Bud Yorkin, 112 mins.)

Come Dance With Me (France, 1959)*½ Brigitte Bardot, Henri Vidal. When husband Vidal is framed, Bardot turns sleuth. Some well-handled comedy touches, but weak plot never jells. Vidal's last movie. (Dir: Michel Boisrond, 91 mins.)

Come Fill the Cup (1951)*** James Cagney, Phyllis Thaxter, Gig Young. James Cagney in another fine performance as an alcoholic ex-newspaper reporter and his struggle to reconstruct his shattered life. Fine performances throughout. (Dir: Gordon Douglas, 112 mins.)

Come Fly with Me (1963)** Dolores Hart, Hugh O'Brian, Karl Malden, Pamela Tiffin, Lois Nettleton. Typical empty romantic yarn about a trio of attractive girls who share secrets and troubles—this time they're three overseas airline hostesses, and the objects of their affection are a pilot, a titled jewel thief and a Texas millionaire (what else)! (Dir: Henry Levin, 109 mins.)

Come Live with Me (1940)** James Stewart, Hedy Lamarr. Hedy marries Jimmy to avoid being deported and if you can't guess how it ends you haven't seen many movies. (Dir: Clarence Brown, 86 mins.)

Come Next Spring (1956)***½ Ann Sheridan, Steve Cochran, Walter Brennan, Sonny Tufts. Arkansas man returns home to his wife and family after eight years of wandering. Touching drama with excellent performances, a good script. (Dir: R. G. Springsteen, 92 mins.)

Come September (1961)**½ Rock Hudson, Gina Lollobrigida, Sandra Dee, Bobby Darin. Splendid Italian scenery grafted to a frothy little comedy plot about a millionaire who discovers his caretaker is using his villa as a hotel when he's away. None of the starring players are exactly comedy whizzes, but it's all pleasant enough and Lollo is yummy to look at. (Dir: Robert Mulligan, 112 mins.)

Come to the Stable (1949)*** Loretta Young, Celeste Holm. Warm, human story about two French nuns and their efforts to build a children's hospital in America. Loretta Young and Celeste Holm, both nominated for Oscars, play the nuns with taste and charm. (Dir: Henry Koster, 94 mins.)

Comedians, The (1967)**½ Richard Burton, Elizabeth Taylor, Peter Ustinov, Alec Guinness. Graham Greene's novel of unrest in Haiti transferred to the screen as a vehicle for Mr. & Mrs. Burton. The basic material of the novel is interesting but the splendid cast is hampered by Peter Glenville's sluggish direction, and a script that dwells too long on unnecessary detail. Fine supporting performances from Lillian Gish and Paul Ford. (Dir: Peter Glenville, 160 mins.)

Comedy Man, The (British, 1964)**** Kenneth More, Cecil Parker, Billie Whitelaw, Dennis Price. Soundly sketched portrait of a small-time actor trying to make the big-time London stage before age catches up with him. Some racy adult sequences, realistically backstage atmosphere, excellent performances.

Comedy of Terrors, The (1964)*** Vincent Price, Peter Lorre, Boris Karloff, Basil Rathbone. An outstanding cast of masters of the horror-film genre have fun spoofing the type of film they used to work in with nary a smile on their faces. The whole thing concerns a funeral home and a unique scheme for garnering more business. (Dir: Jacques Tourneur, 111 mins.)

Comic, The (1969)***½ Dick Van Dyke, Mickey Rooney, Michele Lee, Cornel Wilde. Those of you who revere the comedy greats of silent films will particularly enjoy this fine, incisive portrait by Dick Van Dyke of a silent-film comedian. Authentic Hollywood atmosphere, hilarious

144

scenes blended with pathos; youngsters will also delight in this worthy entry, somewhat underrated at the time of its release. Special high praise to writer-producer-director Carl Reiner who also plays a bit part. Pert Kelton is seen to good advantage in a cameo role. (Dir: Carl Reiner, 94 mins.)

Comin' Round the Mountain (1951)** Bud Abbott, Lou Costello, Dorothy Shay. The feudin', fussin' and a-fightin' gets an added slapstick touch as A & C head for them there hills in this cornball comedy about hillbilly hostility. The kids will find it painless. (Dir: Charles Lamont, 77 mins.)

Coming Out Party, A (British, 1962)*** James Robertson Justice, Leslie Phillips. Crusty radar expert is captured and imprisoned by the Germans incognito, devises a daring escape from prison camp. World War II story played for comedy, it succeeds because of witty bits of business and the performance etched in acid by Justice. (Dir: Ken Annakin, 90 mins.)

Command, The (1953)** Guy Madison, Joan Weldon, James Whitmore. The first CinemaScope western—which calls for a big "So What?" for TV. Generally formula Cavalry vs Indians plot about a medic who takes over a fighting outfit. (Dir: David Butler, 120 mins.)

Command Decision (1948)***½ Clark Gable, Walter Pidgeon, Van Johnson. Interesting insight into the emotions of military brass who must send men to their deaths to win battles. A fine cast does very well in this adaptation of the Broadway hit. (Dir: Sam Wood, 112 mins.)

Commando (Italian, 1963)**½ Stewart Granger, Dorian Grey. Foreign Legionnaires embark on a dangerous mission to capture the leader of an Algerian resistance movement. Fairly well-done action drama has some good moments. Dubbed in English. (Dir: Frank Wisbar, 90 mins.)

Commandos (Italy, 1972)* Lee Van Cleef, Jack Kelly. A spaghetti war film. This Italian-produced World War II yarn about Allied commandos stars Lee Van Cleef, who has made his reputation in Italian westerns. He trades his six-guns for combat weapons but the plot is basically the same! (Dir: Armando Crispino, 89 mins.)

Commandos Strike at Dawn (1943) ★★★ Paul Muni, Anna Lee. When the Nazis invade Norway, partisans resist and pave the way for a Commando raid. Occasionally exciting war drama. (Dir: John Farrow, 98 mins.)

Committee, The (1968) ★★ The San Francisco improvisational comedy group in a straight performance of sketches. Almost a TV variety show in concept, but some very amusing bits. Cast includes Peter Bonerz, Barbara Bosson, Gary Goodrow.

Companions in Nightmare (1968) ★★½ Melvyn Douglas, Gig Young, Anne Baxter, Dana Wynter, Patrick O'Neal. An interesting made-for-TV feature which starts out promisingly, but reverts to melodrama. Various types undergoing group therapy become suspects when one of their kind is murdered. Douglas is very good as a leading psychiatrist who takes things into his own hands to uncover the culprit. (Dir: Norman Lloyd, 99 mins.)

Company of Killers (1970) ★★½ Van Johnson, Ray Milland, John Saxon, Diana Lynn. Above-average thriller about a man being harassed by a newspaperman and later the police, after having muttered in a fit of delirium that he is a hired killer. Some suspense and lots of plot. Notable primarily as Diana Lynn's last film, as she died not long after this film was completed. Made-for-TV. (Dir: Jerry Thorpe, 86 mins.)

Compulsion (1959) ★★★ Dean Stockwell, Bradford Dillman, Orson Welles. Unrelenting account of the murder trial of two twisted youths for a "thrill" murder, based on the Loeb-Leopold case of the 20's. Has a certain horrific fascination, a bravura performance by Welles as the defense lawyer; but remains a rather cold, detached film. (Dir: Richard Fleischer, 103 mins.)

Comrade X (1940) ★★★ Clark Gable, Hedy Lamarr. Cute, slapstick anti-Russian comedy in the "Ninotchka" vein but not half as good. Hedy's a Russian street car conductor and Clark's an American newspaperman. (Dir: King Vidor, 90 mins.)

Concert for Bangladesh (1972) ★★★ Bob Dylan, Ravi Shankar, George Harrison, Eric Clapton, Leon Russell. Straightforward film record of the historic benefit concert at Madison Square Garden in August 1971.

Ravi Shankar opens with a series of pieces which are likely to seem overlong to many movie watchers. But there are glorious renditions of Dylan standards, including "Blowing in the Wind," and the concert builds to a powerful close with ex-Beatle Harrison playing his own tunes, "Something" and "Bangladesh." Few trick camera shots here, or unending "crowd" shots—just a faithful rendition of the driving, spirited music. (Dir: Saul Swimmer, 99 mins.)

Concert of Intrigue (Italian, 1954) ★½ Brigitte Bardot, Lucia Bose, Pierre Cressoy. Early BB effort; she plays a minor role in a turgid drama of wartime underground activities. Pass up this concert.

Concrete Jungle, The (British, 1960) ★★ Stanley Baker, Sam Wanamaker, Margit Saad. Hoodlum pulls a racetrack robbery and goes to prison after burying the loot. His attempts to retrieve it fail due to some double-crossing. Crime drama has evidence of careful production but is disjointed, severely abrupt in its storytelling. Good performances. (Dir: Joseph Losey, 86 mins.)

Condemned (1929) ★★ Ronald Colman, Ann Harding. Early talkie which is very dated today. The stars aren't able to make much of this routine Devil's Island yarn. (Dir: Wesley Ruggles, 100 mins.)

Condemned of Altona, The (1963) ★★★ Sophia Loren, Maximilian Schell, Fredric March, Robert Wagner. Confused, but often interesting drama based on a play by Jean-Paul Sartre, which tells the story of a strange family living in postwar Germany. March builds ships, and his son (Schell) is a madman living in the attic rooms of their estate wearing his Nazi officer's uniform. (Dir: Vittorio De Sica, 114 mins.)

Condemned to Life (Great Britain, 1962)—See: **Walk in the Shadow**

Conduct Unbecoming (1975) ★★★ Michael York, Richard Attenborough, Trevor Howard, Stacy Keach, Susannah York. Really quite setbound, but the acting is so good and the plot so intricate that you don't really notice the lack of action. The film is an actor's holiday and the cast is uniformly excellent. About a scandal in a British officers' mess in Northwest India circa 1878, and their notions about honor, women and civility. Unfortunately, once the mystery is revealed it seems rather silly, but up until that time you've enjoyed the suspense. Based on the hit play by Barry England. (Dir: Michael Anderson, 107 mins.)

Coney Island (1943)*** Betty Grable. Cesar Romero, George Montgomery. Betty is at her leggy best in this gay, though routine, musical set in Coney Island at the turn of the century. George and Cesar fight over Betty's affections and who can blame them. (Dir: Walter Lang, 96 mins.)

Confess Dr. Corda (German, 1961) Hardy Kruger, Elizabeth Muller. Doctor has a blackout, finds he's suspect in a girl's murder. Kruger is too stodgy for this occasionally interesting whodunit. (Dir: Joseph Von Baky, 81 mins.)

Confession, The (French, 1970)**** Yves Montand, Simone Signoret. Emotionally shattering drama about contemporary politics, brilliantly directed by Costa-Gavras. Stands as one of the most powerful and intellectually compelling anti-Communist films ever made. Based on a book by a survivor of the 1952 purges in Czechoslovakia. Montand, giving one of the most restrained and moving performances of his distinguished career, depicts a top party bureaucrat tortured and dehumanized by his beloved Communist party leaders into giving a false confession. You'll not find any of the puerile sloganeering or oversimplifications found in most American movies, "anti-Communist films" such as John Wayne's drivel "The Green Berets." With this searing essay following upon "Z," Costa-Gavras emerges as one of the most important new directors in world cinema. (Dir: Costa-Gavras, 138 mins.)

Confessions of a Nazi Spy (1939)*** Edward G. Robinson. Francis Lederer. Well done propaganda melodrama about a weak link in the Nazi spy network. Dated but for all its flag waving speeches, still a grim reminder. (Dir: Anatole Litvak, 102 mins.)

Confessions of a Police Captain (Italy, 1971)**1/2 Martin Balsam, Franco Nero, Marilu Tolo. Martin Balsam gives a fine performance in this film detailing a policeman's fight to bring in criminals who seem above the reach of the law. Franco

Nero is equally fine as the D.A. who is first suspected of corruption, and then leads the investigation. (Dir: Damiano Damiani, 92 mins.)

Confessions of an Opium Eater (1962) * Vincent Price, Linda Ho, Richard Loo, Philip Ahn. Soldier of fortune saves some slave girls in San Francisco when a Tong war breaks out. Dreadful costume adventure makes everyone concerned look bad. (Dir: Albert Zugsmith, 85 mins.)

Confessions of Felix Krull (German, 1958)**1/2 Horst Buchholz, Lisa Pulver. The amours and experiences of a young opportunist. Better things could have been done with Mann's novel, but the results are satisfactory. (Dir: Kurt Hoffman, 107 mins.)

Confidential Agent (1945)*** Charles Boyer, Lauren Bacall. Exciting intrigue adventure with the Spanish Civil War as background in this slick adaptation of a Graham Greene story. (Dir: Herman Shumlin, 118 mins.)

Confidentially Connie (1953)** Van Johnson, Janet Leigh, Walter Slezak. Teacher in a small Maine college is thrown into the middle of a terrific uproar, all because his wife loves steaks, which come high. Skinny little story. (Dir: Edward Buzzell, 71 mins.)

Confirm or Deny (1941)**1/2 Don Ameche, Joan Bennett. War correspondent finds love in a London blackout and it mixes up his whole life. Some excitement but a bit dated. (Dir: Archie Mayo, 73 mins.)

Conflict (1945)*** Humphrey Bogart, Alexis Smith, Sydney Greenstreet. Humphrey kills his wife in this one and spends most of the film in a battle of wits with Greenstreet who tries to break the perfect alibi. Without the fine cast it would be a routine melodrama. (Dir: Curtis Bernhardt, 86 mins.)

Conflict of Wings (British, 1954)*** John Gregson, Muriel Pavlow, Kieron Moore. The RAF wants to use a small island as a site for testing rockets, but the townspeople prefer to let the birds which have nested there for generations remain. Pleasant comedy-drama.

Conformist, The (Italy-France-West Germany, 1970)**** Jean-Louis Trintignant, Stefania Sandrelli, Dominique Sanda. A fascinating study of decadence and Fascism during Mussolini's reign in Italy in 1938, based on the novel by Alberto Moravia, and written and directed by Bernardo Bertolucci. Brilliantly captures the mood, texture and look of the 1930's, and it's extraordinarily well acted by Trintignant, Sandrelli and Sandra. Trintignant plays a philosophy professor reflecting on his past life. Nominated for major awards for best screenplay and director, Sanda for best actress, and for the stunning cinematography by Vittorio Storaro. (Dir: Bernardo Bertolucci, 115 mins.)

Confrontation, The (Hungarian, 1971)** Andrea Drahota, Kati Kovacs. Occasionally interesting story about the political and ideological fighting occurring amongst a group of college-age students in Hungary in 1947, after the assumption of power by the Communists. Westerners, lacking an intimate knowledge of Hungarian politics, will be puzzled by some of the political plot twists. Directed by Miklos Jancso, who made the superior "Red Psalm."

Congo Crossing (1956)** Virginia Mayo, George Nader, Peter Lorre. A predictable tale of fugitives from the law who congregate in a West African city where extradition laws are not practiced. Peter Lorre is the best thing in the film. (Dir: Joseph Pevney, 85 mins.)

Conjugal Bed, The (Italian, 1963) **** Ugo Tognazzi, Marina Vlady. The original title translation for this was "The Queen Bee," which explains all. It's about a 40-year-old bachelor who marries a virtuous young girl who—literally—loves him to death. Taken seriously, it could be a fine horror story; taken in the manner intended, it's a funny, ribald comedy-drama. Dubbed in English. For adults only. (Dir: Marco Ferreri, 90 mins.)

Connecticut Yankee in King Arthur's Court, A (1949)*** Bing Crosby, Rhonda Fleming, Cedric Hardwicke. The Mark Twain tale of a blacksmith who is transported back to the time of King Arthur, uses modern methods to overcome obstacles. Lavish musical fits Crosby like a glove; good fun. (Dir: Tay Garnett, 107 mins.)

Connection, The (1973)**½ Charles Durning. If you like tough, hard-boiled New York characters who have hearts of gold you'll enjoy the lead in this film. Durning's casual acting style fits his character in a tale concerning a daring hotel robbery, and a deal between the crooks and the insurance companies. Made-for-TV. (Dir: Tom Gries, 73 mins.)

Conquered City (1963)**½ David Niven, Ben Gazzara, Martin Balsam, Michael Craig. After the Nazis are chased from Athens, a British major is ordered to hold a hotel at all costs to prevent a cache of arms from falling into the hands of Greek rebels. A passably interesting melodrama filmed in Europe. (Dir: Joseph Anthony, 91 mins.)

Conqueror of Atlantis (Italian, 1963) * Kirk Morris, Luciana Gilli. Muscleman pits his wits, if that's the word, against the Shadow People. Silly action spectacle, dubbed in English.

Conqueror of Maracaibo (Italian, 1960)*½ Hans Barsody, Brigit Corey. Buccaneer and his men sail and fight on the Caribbean in the days of Spanish colonization. Juvenile English-dubbed adventure.

Conqueror of the Orient (Italian, 1962)*½ Rik Battaglia, Gianna Maria Canale. Sultan's son saves dad's throne by overthrowing a traitorous villain. Usual low-grade action, Italian-style. English-dubbed.

Conqueror Worm, The (British, 1968) * Ian Ogilvy, Hilary Dwyer, Vincent Price. Vincent Price as a nasty 17th-century tyrant holds the people in slavery while posing as a witchhunter. Gruesome sequences may be trimmed for the tube. There isn't much else. (Dir: Michael Reeves, 98 mins.)

Conquest (1937)*** Greta Garbo, Charles Boyer. Romance of Napoleon and his Polish mistress, Countess Valewska, is told here in one of 1937's top budgeted films. It is a good film but, in spite of the expense and the cast, not on a par with Garbo's or Boyer's best. (Dir: Clarence Brown, 112 mins.)

Conquest of Cochise (1953)** John Hodiak, Robert Stack, Joy Page. Mediocre Cowboys and Indians yarn hampered greatly by miscasting of John Hodiak as Cochise. (Dir: William Castle, 80 mins.)

Conquest of Mycene (Italian, 1963) *½ Gordon Scott, Genevieve Grad. Muscleman battles a cult which demands human sacrifices. Corny English-dubbed spectacle.

Conquest of Space (1955)**✱✱½** Eric Fleming, Walter Brooke, Phil Foster. Army space explorers set out to make a landing on Mars. Clever production effects by George Pal, along with a rather bloodless narrative. (Dir: Byron Haskin, 80 mins.)

Conquest of the Air (British, 1935) **✱✱** Laurence Olivier, Valentine Dyall. Documentary story of aviation from man's early struggles to his final triumph. Scrappy—could have been better.

Conquest of the Planet of the Apes (1972)**✱✱✱** Roddy McDowall, Don Murray, Ricardo Montalban. The fourth of the big box-office "ape" films. Roddy McDowall once again plays an ape with leadership qualities, and he's comfortable in the mask as well as the role by now. The time is 1990 and the apes are being used as slaves. One of the best ape entries. Once again, screenwriter Paul Dehn has concocted an absorbing sci-fi tale. (Dir: J. Lee Thompson, 86 mins.)

Conrack (1974)**✱✱✱** Jon Voight, Paul Winfield, Madge Sinclair, Hume Cronyn. A gentle, moving story about a young white schoolteacher who goes to help a group of culturally deprived black youngsters on an island off the coast of South Carolina. This is a particularly appealing film for children, and has many of the same qualities as "Sounder," which was also directed by Martin Ritt. Set in 1969, and based on the non-fiction book "The Water Is Wide." Jon Voight is convincing as he gradually reaches the children with his stories and activities. The last part of the film doesn't quite come together, but there are moments of tenderness and decency, rare commodities in the mid-70's filmmaking world. (Dir: Martin Ritt, 106 mins.)

Conspiracy of Hearts (British, 1961) **✱✱✱** Lilli Palmer, Sylvia Syms. Group of nuns hide Jewish children from the Nazis. Well done drama, keeps the suspense pretty much on high throughout. (Dir: Ralph Thomas, 116 mins.)

Conspiracy of the Borgias (Italian, 1965)**✱½** Frank Latimore, Constance Smith. Cesare and Lucretia Borgia devise means to come into possession of valuable documents in this Eng-

lish-dubbed costume drama. Overstuffed, frequently dull.

Conspirator (1950)**✱✱½** Elizabeth Taylor, Robert Taylor. Interesting but not altogether engrossing drama about a beautiful girl who discovers the alarming fact that her new husband, a British army officer, is working with the Communists. Robert Taylor is properly sober as the agent and Elizabeth Taylor is more decorative than dramatic. Remember, this was Miss Taylor's first grown-up role in films ; she was seventeen at the time. (Dir: Victor Saville, 85 mins.)

Conspirators, The (1944)**✱** Hedy Lamarr, Paul Henreid. Routine intrigue melodrama which is bogged down by gimmicks and contrivances. Greenstreet and Lorre are almost so embarrassed by the script that they play it for comedy. (Dir: Jean Negulesco, 101 mins.)

Constant Husband (British, 1955)**✱✱✱** Rex Harrison, Margaret Leighton. Man about to be wed discovers he has already been married—seven times. Amusing, well-acted comedy. (88 mins.)

Constantine and the Cross (1960)**✱½** Cornel Wilde, Christine Kaufman. Routine Italian-made, English dubbed adventure epic. (Dir: Lionello de Felice, 120 mins.)

Contempt (France-Italy, 1963)**✱✱✱✱** Brigitte Bardot, Michel Piccoli, Jack Palance, Fritz Lang, Jean-Luc Godard. Godard's complex, alternately subtle and expansive contemporary tragedy. Concerns an Italian filming of "The Odyssey," with Piccoli as scriptwriter, Palance as an American producer, and Lang as the director, each interpreting the classic Greek tale in his own way. Action centers on the breakup of dramatist Piccoli's marriage to Bardot—her "contempt" for him is only one of the involved causes. As intricate, bitter, and wrenching a movie as Godard has done, this one more personal than political. Based on a novel by Alberto Moravia. (Dir: Jean-Luc Godard, 103 mins.)

Contest Girl (British, 1965)**✱✱✱** Janette Scott, Ian Hendry, Edmund Purdom. Nicely acted and directed exposé of the beauty-contest racket, as a pretty typist enters a contest, and finds herself caught up in a whirl of deceit and disappointments. Makes its point cleanly, holds interest throughout. (Dir: Val Guest, 82 mins.)

Contraband Spain (British, 1958)** Richard Greene, Anouk Aimee. Greene discards his "Robin Hood" garb but not his "Robin Hood" attitude in this adventure crammed story of smugglers and intrigue in Barcelona. Usual plot twists with predictable outcome. (82 mins.)

Conversation, The (1974)**** Gene Hackman, John Cazale, Allen Garfield, Cindy Williams. A shattering mystery-drama shot in San Francisco about surveillance and wiretapping in America, produced, written, and directed by Francis Ford Coppola. Bugging expert (Hackman) becomes uneasy about the contents of a tape he made, and what it will be used for. Coppola began writing the screenplay in 1966, but it now relates directly to some pivotal Watergate themes as one wiretapper boasts about the way he illegally got information on a top presidential political candidate. There is murder at the end, but Coppola's theme is the much larger one of our whole eroding system of values and civil liberties, and the ease with which new technologies, if unchecked, can destroy our democratic heritage. Hackman is marvelous—displaying little emotion most of the time as the guilt-ridden Catholic bugger trying to keep his sanity. Extraordinary scene at the end: Hackman destroys his own apartment as the bugger becomes the bugged. Not a false note in this disciplined, chilling knockout. (113 mins.)

Convicted (1950)*** Glenn Ford, Broderick Crawford, Dorothy Malone. Prison life gets a candid look in this good screen play about a prisoner and his personal relationship with a warden's daughter. The cast is fine. (Dir: Henry Levin, 91 mins.)

Convicts Four (1963)**½ Ben Gazzara, Stuart Whitman, Sammy Davis Jr., Vincent Price. Based on fact —the story of a prisoner who is rehabilitated through his love for painting. Starts off well, soon becomes cloudy in motivation, uncertain in treatment. Good cast, including bits by Broderick Crawford, Rod Steiger, others. (Dir: Millard Kaufman, 105 mins.)

Coogan's Bluff (1968)** Clint Eastwood, Lee J. Cobb, Susan Clark.

Fast-paced, familiar detective story with big, boring Clint Eastwood playing a western sheriff who arrives in New York City to nab a hood convicted of murder. Eastwood doesn't really act—he just stands there! Of the good supporting cast, Don Stroud registers strongly as the hood. (Dir: Don Siegel, 100 mins.)

Cool and the Crazy (1958)** Scott Marlowe, Gigi Perreau. Reform school graduate goes to high school —to hook students on dope. Some good acting here. Subject matter has by now become quite routine, alas! (Dir: William Witney, 78 mins.)

Cool Hand Luke (1967)**** Paul Newman, George Kennedy, Dennis Hopper. Taut, honest drama greatly aided by Stuart Rosenberg's direction and a marvelously controlled and artful performance by Paul Newman as a gutsy prisoner on a chain gang. Matching Newman's stunning acting is George Kennedy's Academy Award winning performance as the brutal leader of the chain-gang crew, a notable musical score by Lalo Schifrin, and the spare screenplay written by Donn Pearce and Frank R. Pierson. Newman's loner-hero with an insatiable appetite for freedom and the ability to do "his own thing" with or without the approval of society is one of the most memorable screen portraits in years. "Cool Hand Luke" deals you a winner. (Dir: Stuart Rosenberg, 126 mins.)

Cool Million: Assault on Gravaloni (1972)**½ A puzzler that keeps crackling along at a swift pace. Jefferson Keyes (James Farentino) invades the almost impregnable world of a Greek multi-millionaire in order to replace a valuable painting with a copy. This dexterous sleight-of-hand takes every bit of finesse Keyes possesses. The cast includes Ilka Chase as a terribly chatty member of the jet set. Made-for-TV. (Dir: John Badham, 72 mins.)

Cool Ones, The (1967)* Roddy McDowall, Debbie Watson, Phil Harris. Junior-grade tale about a show biz talent manager (Roddy McDowall) who tries to get two of his clients, a rock singer and cute dancer, to the top. Romantic aspects of the plot are silly, and the music loud and undistinguished. Look for Glen Campbell in a cameo spot. (Dir: Gene Nelson, 95 mins.)

Cool World, The (1964)***½ Gloria Foster, Hampton Clanton, Carl Lee, Georgia Burke. A powerful, no-punches-pulled film with outstanding direction by Shirley Clarke. She has gotten remarkable performances from the cast, virtually all of whom were chosen from students in the junior high schools of Harlem. A stark semidocumentary look at the horrors of ghetto slum life filled with drugs, violence, human misery, and a sense of despair due to the racial prejudices of American society. No patronizing of the blacks in this cinematic cry for justice. Interesting that this pioneering cinema verite entry was produced by Frederick Wiseman, who, a decade later, has proven to be the most gifted documentary filmmaker in America. (105 mins.)

Cooley High (1975)***½ Glynn Turman, Lawrence-Hilton Jacobs, Garrett Morris. Described as a black companion piece to "American Graffiti," but "Cooley" does not suffer from the comparison. It's a perceptive, funny account of what it meant to be a black adolescent in Chicago in the mid-60's. Cooley Vocational High's kids are street-wise, numbed by some of life's injustices, but still hopeful. They talk, laugh, get into trouble and pay for being what they are. Glynn Turman is wonderful as Preacher, who dreams of becoming a Hollywood screenwriter, and Lawrence-Hilton Jacobs ("Welcome Back, Kotter") is equally good as a high-school basketball player. Fine original screenplay by Eric Monte makes this good history and sociology, and extremely entertaining as well. Impressive directorial debut by Michael Schultz. (107 mins.)

Cop Hater (1958)**½ Robert Loggia, Gerald O'Loughlin. Mild meller about a cop killer. Based on an Ed McBain novel. Routine acting and direction, but the finale is fine. New York locations are used to good advantage. (Dir: William Berke, 75 mins.)

Copper Canyon (1950)** Ray Milland, Hedy Lamarr, Macdonald Carey. Gunman helps Civil War vets build new homes in the untamed west. Mild western never achieves the lively pace it needs. (83 mins.)

Cops and Robbers (1973)***½ Cliff Gorman, Joe Bologna. A cleverly plotted, adroitly executed comedy caper film which boasts a pair of excellent perfomances by Gorman and Bologna as two utterly convincing cops who decide to pull one big robbery and retire to the exotic locales of their dreams. The robbery itself, in a fortresslike security-bond Wall Street firm, becomes a tense comedy of errors and you'll find yourself rooting for the cops-turned-crooks. The workable, funny script by Donald Westlake and Aram Avakian's unerring direction help make this a delightful outing. (89 mins.)

Corky (1971)*½ Charlotte Rampling, Robert Blake, Partick O'Neal. Robert Blake almost manages to save this film, but he gets bogged down before too long. A routine version of the country boy who wants to make it big as a stock-car racer. Texas and Georgia locations help a little. (Dir: Leonard Horn, 88 mins.)

Corn Is Green, The (1945)***½ Bette Davis, John Dall, Joan Loring. There's a lot to like in this faithful adaptation of the Emlyn Williams play about the problems of education in a Welsh town. It's a moving, human story which you should enjoy. (Dir: Irving Rapper, 114 mins.)

Cornered (1945)**** Dick Powell, Micheleine Cheirel, Walter Slezak. Airman goes seeking those responsible for the death of his French wife during the war. Excellent melodrama, fast, tough, fine performances. (Dir: Edward Dmytryk, 102 mins.)

Corpse Came C.O.D. (1947)** George Brent, Joan Blondell. Grade B mystery about a couple of Hollywood reporters out to solve some movieland murders. (Dir: Henry Levin, 87 mins.)

Corridor of Mirrors (British, 1947) *** Edana Romney, Eric Portman. A girl meets a mysterious man who lives in the past, and marries him, but their happiness is shattered by murder. Well done melodrama holds the attention.

Corridors of Blood (British, 1962)** Boris Karloff, Betta St. John. Surgeon in 19th Century London seeks the key to an anesthetic, but becomes a narcotics addict in doing so. Passable horror thriller, with

Karloff giving a good performance. (Dir: Robert Day, 87 mins.)

Corrupt Ones, The (1966)** Robert Stack, Nancy Kwan, Elke Sommer. Everybody hustles after a Chinese medallion holding the key to the treasure. Exotic but familiar adventure tale, aided by interesting location shots of Macao and Hong Kong. (Dir: James Hill, 92 mins.)

Corruption (Great Britain, 1968)** Peter Cushing, Sue Lloyd, Kate O'Mara. Intriguing but one-dimensional story of plastic surgeon who atones for his guilt in causing his fiancée to be permanently scarred in an auto accident. The catch—he has to steal glands from strangers! Another psycho doctor on the loose! (Dir: Robert Hartford-Davis, 91 mins.)

Corsican Brothers, The (1941)**½ Doug Fairbanks Jr., Akim Tamiroff. The classic tale of Siamese twin brothers separated at birth but still joined by a mental bond. Lively costume melodrama. (Dir: Gregory Ratoff, 112 mins.)

Corsican Brothers, The (French, 1960)** Geoffrey Horne, Jean Servais. The Dumas novel of twins who are reunited to avenge the murder of their family. Not too successfully done, just passable costume melodrama dubbed in English.

Corvette K-225 (1943)***½ Randolph Scott, Ella Raines. Canadian Naval officer's courage and fighting spirit prevents destruction of a convoy. Excellent war drama, with many scenes actually photographed in combat. (Dir: Richard Rossen, 99 mins.)

Cosh Boy (Great Britain, 1953)** James Kenney, Joan Collins, Hermione Gingold. Sensationalized London street life, with the accent on violence—delivered in thick Cockney brogue. About a "cosh" youth who goes around molesting ladies of all ages. Kenney, effectively cocky and uninhibited as the boy, and Gingold, outstanding in a small supporting role as a street-walker. (Dir: Lewis Gilbert, 75 mins.)

Cosmic Man, The (1958)* Bruce Bennett, John Carradine. Visitor from another planet lands on earth to try to reconcile world differences. Peace will never break out here when the spacemen bring such pitiful movies. (Dir: Herbert Greene, 72 mins.)

Cosmic Monsters (British, 1958)** Forrest Tucker, Gaby Andre. Muddled science fiction thriller with the mad scientist and the giant insects and the world in constant danger of complete annihilation.

Cotton Comes to Harlem (1970)**** Godfrey Cambridge, Raymond St. Jacques, Calvin Lockhart, Redd Foxx. Raucous, racy, funny treatment of Chester Himes' fictional black detectives, Grave Digger Jones and Coffin Ed Johnson, and their exploits in Harlem. Cambridge and St. Jacques give perfectly matched performances as Grave Digger and Coffin Ed hot on the trail of a bogus Reverend and his scheme to milk his people out of money. The collected bundle of cash disappears and it's a free-for-all search from then on. (Director: Ossie Davis, 92 mins.)

Couch, The (1962)** Grant Williams, Shirley Knight. Psychotic is released from prison, undergoes treatment, but commits crimes while doing so. Plodding suspense melodrama has been done before in more capable fashion. Strictly routine. (Dir: Owen Crump, 100 mins.)

Count Five and Die (British, 1958)**½ Jeffrey Hunter, Annemarie Dueringer, Nigel Patrick. American undercover agent works with the British to convince the Germans the Allied landing will be in Holland, thus misleading them. Pretty fair spy thriller is well worked out, has some suspenseful moments. (Dir: Victor Vicas, 100 mins.)

Count of Monte Cristo, The (1933)***½ Robert Donat, Elissa Landi. The classic adventure tale of Dumas about the unjustly imprisoned patriot who makes a spectacular escape during the Napoleonic era. A notable film achievement. (Dir: Rowland V. Lee, 113 mins.)

Count of Monte Cristo, The (French, 1955)*½ Pierre-Richard Wilm, Michele Alfa. Another version of Dumas' adventure of unjust imprisonment and escape. The French seem to produce this annually, but this isn't one of the better attempts. English-dubbed. (Dir: Robert Vernay, 97 mins.)

Count of Monte Cristo (1961)—See: **Story of the Count of Monte Cristo, The**

Count the Hours (1953)** Teresa Wright, Macdonald Carey. Ranch worker and wife are accused of murdering ranchowners; he confesses to spare his pregnant wife. Muddled melodrama. (Dir: Don Siegel, 74 mins.)

Count Three and Pray (1955)***½ Van Heflin, Joanne Woodward, Raymond Burr. First rate western drama about a Civil War veteran and his influence on a small town when he becomes a self ordained minister. Joanne Woodward is excellent in her first major role. (Dir: George Sherman, 120 mins.)

Count Yorga, Vampire (1970)* Robert Quarry, Roger Perry. A homegrown, corny version of the vampire legend laid in Los Angeles. The sets are appropriately gothic. Clumsily written and directed by Robert Kelljan. (92 mins.)

Count Your Blessings (1959)**½ Deborah Kerr, Rossano Brazzi, Maurice Chevalier. A slight comedy which totally relies on the trio of stars' charm and attractiveness to carry it off. The plot has a British Miss Kerr sharing a civilized long-distance marriage arrangement with Brazzi until she decides to shorten the gap. M. Chevalier plays his usual role of romantic mentor. (Dir: Jean Negulesco, 120 mins.)

Countdown (1968)**½ James Caan, Robert Duvall. Drama about space shots to the moon may be dated by now, but it has some good moments. If you can be patient through the soap opera of the spacemen's private lives, the finale delivers the goods. Caan and Duvall lead years before their costarring assignments in "The Godfather." (Dir: Robert Altman, 101 mins.)

Counter-Attack (1945)**½ Paul Muni, Marguerite Chapman, Larry Parks. Russian paratroopers land behind enemy lines and attack German headquarters. Passing fair war melodrama, a bit too slow. (Dir: Zoltan Korda, 90 mins.)

Counterfeit Killer, The (1968)* Jack Lord, Shirley Knight, Mercedes McCambridge, Jack Weston. Undercover agent after counterfeit cash. Its TV origins (NBC-Chrysler Theatre, 1966) painfully apparent, with inferior footage added to stretch the plot. (Dir: Joseph Leytes, 95 mins.)

Counterfeit Traitor, The (1962)***½ William Holden, Lilli Palmer, Hugh Griffith. Suspenseful tale based on fact of a businessman approached by the British to pose as sympathetic to the Nazis, in reality spying for England. Fascinating details of espionage, some tense situations, excellent performances by Holden and Palmer. (Dir: George Seaton, 140 mins.)

Counterplot (1959)*½ Forrest Tucker, Allison Hayes. Fugitive from the law tries to clear himself of a murder charge in Puerto Rico. Trite melodrama, thoroughly undistinguished. (Dir: Kurt Neumann, 76 mins.)

Counterpoint (1968)* Charlton Heston, Kathryn Hays, Maximilian Schell. Idiotic drama set in Belgium during 1944. Charlton Heston plays a symphony conductor on a USO tour who is captured by the Nazis, headed by General Maximilian Schell. Schell loves music and hopes Heston will accommodate with a private concert. A total waste of talented actors. Director Ralph Nelsen strikes a sour note with this clinker. (107 mins.)

Countess from Hong Kong, A (1967)**½ Marlon Brando, Sophia Loren. Although this film boasts the talents of Sophia Loren and Marlon Brando in the leading roles and the direction of Charlie Chaplin, it's just another romantic comedy, worth watching but very disappointing. Most of the action takes place aboard a luxury liner with Sophia as an immigrant stowaway in U.S. diplomat Brando's cabin and there's a fair amount of boudoir fun and games before the finale in which true love triumphs. A bonus for Chaplin fans is a brief silent appearance by the master himself as a very seasick steward. First major feature directed by Chaplin in years. (108 mins.)

Country Girl, The (1954)**** Bing Crosby, Grace Kelly, William Holden. Superlative performances in a dynamic drama about a performer wallowing in self-pity who has a chance to make a comeback. Kelly won the Oscar for her portrayal, but Crosby is no less effective, gives the acting effort of his long career. Fine film. (Dir: George Seaton, 104 mins.)

Country Music Holiday (1958)*½ Ferlin Husky, Zsa Zsa Gabor, Rocky Graziano. Cornball musical about a young ex-GI who is built up as a recording star. Lots of hillbilly music, little else. (81 mins.)

County Fair (1950)**½ Jane High, Rory Calhoun. Generally pleasant, if uneventful tale of romance and racing. (76 mins.)

Couple Takes a Wife, The (1972)*** Bill Bixby, Paula Prentiss. Entertaining, brittle. Concerns a modern married couple who reach an impasse after nine years of wedded bliss, and try to assert their individuality with the aid of a hired "wife." The "wife" turns out to be a young supercombination governess-cook-housekeeper-confidante. Writer Susan Silver has given her characters good dialogue, wisely avoiding the obvious pitfalls. Cast is first-rate, especially Miss Prentiss as the bright wife-mother who wants to get back into the swing of life; and sexy Valerie Perrine as the offbeat young Ms. who takes on the unique job. Made-for-TV. (Dir: Jerry Paris, 73 mins.)

Courage of Lassie (1945)**½ Elizabeth Taylor, Frank Morgan. Good Lassie adventure with the famous collie becoming a war hero and then, after discharge, he's as confused as any veteran. (Dir: Fred Wilcox, 92 mins.)

Courageous Mr. Penn (British, 1942) *** Clifford Evans, Deborah Kerr. The story of William Penn the Quaker, and how he pioneered the American wilderness while seeking religious freedom. Thoughtful, well acted drama. Also called "Penn of Pennsylvania."

Court Jester, The (1956)*** Danny Kaye, Glynis Johns, Basil Rathbone. Circus clown gets involved with a band of outlaws trying to overthrow the king. Kaye's comedy is an asset in this pleasing spoof of costume epics. (Dir: Norman Panama, 101 mins.)

Court Martial (British, 1955)***½ David Niven, Margaret Leighton. Army major is court-martialed for taking company funds and being AWOL, and he fights against unjust treatment. Finely acted, tightly directed drama maintains interest on high. (Dir: Anthony Asquith, 105 mins.)

Court Martial of Billy Mitchell (1955) ***½ Gary Cooper, Rod Steiger. Excellent, true story of one of the most controversial American military leaders of this country. Film concentrates on Billy Mitchell's defiance of military brass when they called him a crackpot for ideas that might have cut World War II in half. A fascinat-

ing film. (Dir: Otto Preminger, 100 mins.)

Courtmartial of Major Keller, The (British, 1963)**½ Laurence Payne, Susan Stephen. Army has to prove that an officer was incompetent and a coward during battle. Passable service drama; well acted.

Courtney Affair, The (British, 1947) **½ Anna Neagle, Michael Wilding. The son of a rich family falls for the scullery maid. Sugary romantic drama.

Courtship of Eddie's Father, The 1963)*** Glenn Ford, Shirley Jones, Stella Stevens, Ronny Howard. Frequently charming comedy drama about a widower who tries to bring up his motherless son—and vice versa. Nice balance between humor and poignancy, well acted by a superior cast, with Stella Stevens standing out—literally—with an excellent comedy job. Good fun. (Dir: Vincente Minnelli, 117 mins.)

Cousins, The (French, 1959)***½ Jean-Claude Brialy, Gerard Blain. Director Claude Chabrol has fashioned a marvelous study of the contrasting personalities of two young male cousins, both law students at the Sorbonne. Blain is a country lad with an unsophisticated manner who comes to stay with his egomaniacal and decadent cousin, brilliantly played by Jean-Claude Brialy. It's not so much what happens in the way of plot, but more in the almost hypnotic way the story unfolds. Dubbing works very well here. (Dir: Claude Chabrol, 112 mins.)

Covenant with Death, A (1967)** George Maharis, Laura Devon, Katy Jurado. Muddled, often silly dramatization of the best-selling book by Stephen Becker about a condemned murderer who is instrumental in another man's death while awaiting execution. George Maharis is better than the script as a young Mexican-American judge faced with a sticky decision. Promising material never delivers real impact. (Dir: Lamont Johnson, 97 mins.)

Cover Girl (1944)***½ Gene Kelly, Rita Hayworth. Chorus girl achieves fame and glory when she becomes a top cover girl. Lavish musical with some swell Jerome Kern tunes, spectacular dances by Kelly. It was more effective in color, unfortunately. (Dir: Charles Vidor, 107 mins.)

Cover Girls (1977)* Jayne Kennedy,

Cornelia Sharpe. Silly, improbable pilot film which tries to imitate "Charlie's Angels" and falls flat. Two gorgeous actresses, Cornelia Sharpe and Jayne Kennedy, play models who work undercover as espionage agents. Made-for-TV. (Dir: Jerry London, 79 mins.)

Cover Up (1949)*** William Bendix, Dennis O'Keefe. An insurance investigator comes to a small town to check on a doctor's death, and finds that nobody wants to talk about it; hence, foul play is suspected. Nicely-turned mystery. O'Keefe helped write this one, and a good job it is.

Cow and I, The (French, 1961)*** Fernandel. One of Fernandel's better films. The story concerns a French prisoner of war who escapes from a German labor farm and encounters a series of adventures en route to France. There are many charming sequences in this off-beat comedy. (Dir: Henri Verneuil, 98 mins.)

Cowboy, The (1954)***½ Documentary feature of the way of life of our American cowboys, their work, recreations, day-to-day happenings. Made by Elmo Williams, who worked on "High Noon." Narrated by William Conrad, Tex Ritter, John Dehner, Larry Dobkin. Authentic, sincere, a true picture of the west today. Recommended. (69 mins.)

Cowboy (1958)*** Glenn Ford, Jack Lemmon. Refreshing, generally entertaining western story, based on the experiences of a young Frank Harris —a dude goes west and learns the ways of the range. (Dir: Delmer Daves, 92 mins.)

Cowboy and the Lady, The (1939)** Gary Cooper, Merle Oberon, Walter Brennan. Just exactly what the title suggests—a routine romance between a cowpoke and a rich city girl. Some of the comedy falls flat by today's standards. (Dir: H. C. Potter, 90 mins.)

Cowboys, The (1972)* John Wayne, Slim Pickens, Roscoe Lee Browne, Colleen Dewhurst. Another "morality" tale about the Old West in the 1870's seen through the warped vision of star John Wayne. This repellent entry glorifies the turning of young schoolboys into conscienceless killers. Wayne's own performance isn't bad, but on balance, it's another mindless ode to violence. (Dir: Mark Rydell, 120 mins.)

Crack in the Mirror (1960)** Orson Welles, Juliette Greco, Bradford Dillman. Unpalatable involvements about a team of lawyers defending two plaintiffs in a murder trial, whose lives parallel those of their clients. Not helped by the three main actors playing dual roles, a trick that doesn't come off. (Dir: Richard Fleischer, 97 mins.)

Crack In the World (1965)**½ Dana Andrews, Janette Scott. A science-fiction tale that seems very credible and registers a good amount of suspense. A group of scientists are attempting to reach the earth's core and in their efforts, they explode some nuclear bombs causing "a crack in the world." (Dir: Andrew Marton, 96 mins.)

Crack-Up (1946)*** Pat O'Brien, Claire Trevor. Art museum curator is framed into thinking he was in a train wreck by art forgers. Involved but successful mystery. (Dir: Irving Reis, 93 mins.)

Cracked Nuts (1941)*½ Stuart Erwin, Una Merkel, Mischa Auer. Con men try to fleece a small town lad out of his dough by promoting a mechanical robot . . . who must have produced this mechanically unamusing comedy.

Cracksman, The (British, 1963)** Charlie Drake, George Sanders. Innocent locksmith gets mixed up with two rival gangs of crooks. Drake is a local slapstick comedian and may be too far out for most tastes; the comedy is wild, but not particularly inspired.

Craig's Wife (1936)*** Rosalind Russell, John Boles. This one has been done to death, but it's still a good story. About a woman who lives only for worldly possessions and loses sight of human values. Creaks at the seams—but worthwhile. (Dir: Dorothy Arzner, 80 mins.)

Crash Dive (1943)**½ Tyrone Power, Dana Andrews, Anne Baxter. Routine war story of a submarine in the North Atlantic and the officers who love the same girl. Why aren't there ever enough girls to go around? (Dir: Archie Mayo, 105 mins.)

Crash Landing (1958)*½ Gary Merrill, Nancy Davis, Roger Smith. A sort of poor man's "High and the Mighty." A troubled captain of an airliner informs his passengers that they may have to crash land in mid ocean when the engines fail. (Dir: Fred F. Sears, 77 mins.)

Crashout (1955)*** William Bendix, Arthur Kennedy. Six convicts make a break for freedom. Familiar but fast, gutsy melodrama, better than usual for this sort of thing. (Dir: Lewis R. Foster, 91 mins.)

Crawling Eye (British, 1957)** Forrest Tucker, Janet Munro. Once more we are confronted with oversized deadly menaces, this time a "crawling eye" and once more a group of scientists save the world.

Crawling Hand, The (1963)* Peter Breck, Kent Taylor, Arlene Judge. Unbelievable horror epic with a collection of equally unbelievable performances. Crawl to bed and forget it.

Crawlspace (1972)**½ Arthur Kennedy, Teresa Wright, Tom Happer. Interesting, if not altogether successful drama, about a middle-aged couple who take in a strange young man prone to violence. Fine performances by the trio of actors, including newcomer Tom Happer as the weird youth, keep the story from falling apart earlier than it does. Made-for-TV. (Dir: John Newland, 72 mins.)

Crazy Desire (Italian, 1964)*** Ugo Tognazzi, Catherine Spaak. Charming comedy-drama about a middle-aged man trying momentarily to recapture his youth, as an engineer encounters some teenagers on the road and tries to keep abreast of their fast pace. Many amusing as well as poignant moments, although a trifle overlong. Dubbed in English. (Dir: Luciano Salce, 108 mins.)

Crazy for Love (French, 1955)*½ Bourvil, Brigitte Bardot. Village simpleton will inherit the town inn if he can get a diploma within a year. No diplomas for this inane English-dubbed farce—Bardot has a minor role.

Crazy House (1943)**½ Olsen and Johnson, Cass Dailey. The two comics arrive in Hollywood to make a movie, form their own company and all hell breaks loose. Amusing nonsensical comedy. (Dir: Edward F. Cline, 80 mins.)

Crazy Joe (1974)** Peter Boyle, Paula Prentiss, Rip Torn. The ads for this gangster saga about real-life hood Joey Gallo read "Who was Crazy Joe?" Well, after seeing this film, you might be prompted to an-

swer, "He's one-third imitation Edward G. Robinson, one-third bogus Humphrey Bogart, and one-third warmed-over James Cagney." Nothing about this film is original . . . it's cliched all the way and Boyle, a good actor, fails to give his character any conviction. (Dir: Carlo Lizzani, 100 mins.)

Crazy Quilt (1966)***½ Tom Rosqui, Ina Mela. Surprisingly sophisticated and sensitive first film written, produced, directed, photographed and edited by multi-talented John Korty, on an ambitious subject—the 50-year span of a marriage. Fresh, witty treatment, beautifully acted interpretations make this seemingly pat tale—a pragmatic man marrying a romantic dreamer—a meaningful contemporary fable. San Francisco locales are nicely used. Filmed on a tiny budget of $70,000. Director Korty has gone on to make several other fine films. (75 mins.)

Crazy World of Julius Vrooder, The (1974)** Timothy Bottoms, Barbara Seagull, Lawrence Pressman, George Marshall. Attempt to make a comedy about hospitalized Vietnam war veterans misfires. Timothy Bottoms gives an attractive performance but it's not enough. Film-trivia buffs, please note the appearance of veteran director George Marshall playing Corky, a wizened veteran of WWI. (Dir: Arthur Hiller, 100 mins.)

Crazylegs (1953)*** Elroy Hirsch, Lloyd Nolan. Biography of the famous football star has two advantages—"Crazylegs" plays himself, and he's a pretty good actor. Sports fans should love it, while others will find it a pleasant film. (Dir: Francis D. Lyon, 88 mins.)

Creation of the Humanoids (1962)* Don Megowan, Erica Elliot. Endlessly talky, inept sci-fi film about a future race of robots gaily nicknamed "clickers." Flick fails to click.

Creature from the Black Lagoon (1954)**½ Richard Carlson, Julia Adams. Originally produced in 3-D, this better-than-average science fiction tale has more than its share of visual gimmicks. The plot, complete with bewildered scientists and love interest, appears no innovation, but fans of this genre will enjoy it. (Dir: Jack Arnold, 79 mins.)

Creature from the Haunted Sea

(1960)**½ Anthony Carbone, Betsy Jones-Moreland. Low-budget item turns out to be a spoof of horror thrillers mixing gangsters, fleeing revolutionaries and a sea beast. Some good hip dialogue, good-natured kidding of the genre.

Creature of the Walking Dead (1963) *½ Rock Madison, Ann Wells. Descendant of a scientist who sought lasting life finds his grandfather in an ancient laboratory, brings him back to life. Far-fetched horror thriller.

Creature Walks Among Us, A (1956) *½ Jeff Morrow, Rex Reason. Low budget science fiction meller—this time the expedition sets out to capture and study a monster known as "The Gill Man." (Dir: John Sherwood, 80 mins.)

Creature with the Atom Brain (1955) ** Richard Denning, Angela Stevens. Overdone science fiction story about a deported mobster who "bumps off" the people who testified against him with the aid of a mad scientist. The method by which the victims meet their end has something to do with "atomic brains." (Dir: Edward L. Cahn, 70 mins.)

Creatures of Darkness (1969)* Bill Williams, Aaron Kincaid. Silly hocus-pocus! A hypnotist predicts murders at a famous lodge and the guests panic. Beware of the hypnotist's assistant—and beware of this trash. (Dir: Bill Williams, 83 mins.)

Creeping Flesh, The (British, 1970) **½ Peter Cushing, Christopher Lee, Lorna Heilbron. Here's still another "scientist tampering with unknown forces," starring the deadly duo of British horror flicks, Lee and Cushing. It's slickly produced and might even provoke a chill or two if you care for this sort of thing. The plot, if it can be defined at all, concerns a scientist absolutely obsessed with harnessing the "essence of evil"—an ambitious and lofty dedication. (Dir: Freddie Francis, 89 mins.)

Cremator, The (Czech, 1968)***½ Rudolph Hrusinsky, Vlasta Chramostova. Ghoulish, gripping, grotesque horror tale. Protagonist is the director of a crematorium who comes to believe in his work (1937) and turns Nazi sympathizer. When Hitler's armies invade and take over Czechoslovakia he is promoted. Subtly, scary performance from Hrusinsky as the crazed mass killer, and you won't soon forget the scenes of him chasing his relatives in the huge crematorium, his place of "business." (Dir: Juraj Herz, 90 mins.)

Crest of the Wave (1954)**½ Gene Kelly, Jeff Richards, John Justin. Interesting but slow moving war film made in England. Gene Kelly seems miscast in a straight non-dancing role. (Dirs: John & Roy Boulting, 90 mins.)

Cries and Whispers (Sweden, 1972) **** Liv Ullmann, Ingrid Thulin, Harriet Andersson. A searing, devastating masterpiece written, directed and produced by Ingmar Bergman. This shattering drama about the relationships of three sisters in a Swedish manor house was voted the best film of the year by the New York Film Critics. It is, quite simply, one of the great films of the decade. Agnes (Andersson) is dying of cancer, circa 1900, and her older and younger sister come to her home for the deathwatch. The sense of pain and suffering is portrayed so realistically as to become almost unendurable, and the acting throughout is faultless. The great cinematographer Sven Nykvist is at the top of his form. Some of the closeup images are as powerful and beautifully composed as anything in modern cinema. Only Bergman, of today's filmmakers, could, successfully, hold a closeup for such a long period of time. A work of genius. (Dir: Ingmar Bergman, 94 mins.)

Crime Against Joe (1956)*** John Bromfield, Julie London. Painter is accused of a girl's murder. Compact mystery has some surprises; nice pace. (Dir: Lee Sholem, 69 mins.)

Crime and Punishment (1935)**½ Edward Arnold, Peter Lorre, Marian Marsh. Hollywood's version of Dostoyevsky's classic novel casts a subtly neurotic Peter Lorre as the haunted student-murderer. Arnold's portrayal of the inspector, who doggedly tracks him down, is overblown. Sternberg's direction is full of flavor and invention. (Dir: Josef von Sternberg, 88 mins.)

Crime and Punishment (French, 1958) *** Jean Gabin, Robert Hossein. Inspector breaks down the will of a murderer. One of the many versions of this crime tale, and rather well done. (Dir: George Lampin, 108 mins.)

Crime and Punishment, USA (1959) ** George Hamilton, Mary Murphy. A good idea that never quite jells and a good deal of blame can be attributed to George Hamilton's stoic performance. As the title suggests, this is an updated version of the classic "Crime and Punishment." (Dir: Denis Sanders, 95 mins.)

Crime by Night (1944)**½ Jane Wyman, Faye Emerson, Eleanor Parker. Private eye on vacation suddenly finds himself investigating an axe murder. Satisfying mystery with Jerome Cowan as the detective. (Dir: Geoffrey Homes, 72 mins.)

Crime Club (1973)**½ Lloyd Bridges, Victor Buono. Fairly interesting mystery story. Bridges and Buono play vigilantes, and a wide range of suspects are played by guest stars Cloris Leachman, Paul Burke, Martin Sheen, and David Hedison. Made-for-TV. (Dir: David Lowell Rich)

Crime in the Streets (1956)*** John Cassavetes, James Whitmore, Sal Mineo. A good cast help make this Reginald Rose TV drama about juvenile gangs in a big city an interesting film. Cassavetes plays the leader of a street gang who meets strong opposition from a determined social worker with a special understanding of their problems. (Dir: Don Siegel, 91 mins.)

Crime of Passion (1957)**½ Barbara Stanwyck, Sterling Hayden, Raymond Burr. A wife's ambition for her husband leads to murder. Barbara Stanwyck tends to over-act. (Dir: Gerd Oswald, 84 mins.)

Crime School (1938)**½ Humphrey Bogart, and the "Dead End Kids." Warden Bogart reforms the "kids" in this tired melodrama. (Dir: Lewis Seiler, 90 mins.)

Crime Wave (1954)** Sterling Hayden, Gene Nelson. Dancer Gene Nelson plays a straight dramatic role in this average cops and crooks "meller." Not too effective on all counts. (Dir: Andre de Toth, 74 mins.)

Crime Without Passion (1934)***½ Claude Rains, Margo. Story of a lawyer who gets involved in crime and tries to clear himself by criminal methods. Rains is superb as the sadistic lawyer and Margo scores in the role of the girl he thinks he's

murdered. (Dirs: Ben Hecht, Charles MacArthur, 80 mins.)

Crimson Affair, The—See: **Crimson Cult, The**

Crimson Blade, The (Great Britain, 1963)** Lionel Jeffries, Oliver Reed, Jack Hedley. Swashbuckler concerning a love affair between the daughter of one of Cromwell's strongest supporters and a Royalist. The emphasis is on character and the cast is uniformly good. Oliver Reed is especially effective as the young Royalist. Written and directed by John Gilling. (83 mins.)

Crimson Canary (1945)**½ Noah Beery Jr., John Litel, Lois Collier. Members of a jazz combo are suspected when a singer is murdered. Neat little mystery with a good jazz background. (Dir: John Hoffman, 64 mins.)

Crimson Cult, The (1968)* Boris Karloff, Christopher Lee, Barbara Steele. Veteran cast of horror stalwarts does little to enliven this black-magic tale. Boris Karloff's last role shows remarkable patience with such nonsensical dialogue. (Dir: Vernon Sewell, 81 mins.)

Crimson Kimono, The (1959)** Victoria Shaw, Glenn Corbett, James Shigeta. Muddled detective story about a pair of super-sleuths and their adventures hunting for a killer who specialized in beautiful girls. The two detectives wage a battle of their own when they both fall in love with the same girl. (Dir: Samuel Fuller, 82 mins.)

Crimson Pirate, The (1952)*** Burt Lancaster, Eva Bartok. Adventure on the high seas with Lancaster buckling every swash in sight. Lancaster and circus acrobat Nick Cravat execute some tricky gymnastics in their effort to overthrow tyranny. (Dir: Robert Siodmak, 104 mins.)

Cripple Creek (1952)** George Montgomery, Jerome Courtland, Karin Booth. Two government agents join a band of gold mine thieves to crack a case in this familiar plot. (Dir: Ray Nazarro, 78 mins.)

Crisis (1950)**½ Cary Grant, Jose Ferrer, Paula Raymond. Suspense yarn about the kidnapping of an American doctor and his wife by a Latin American government in order to have the doctor perform a delicate operation on the country's dictator. Well acted but much of the action is telegraphed from the beginning. (Dir: Richard Brooks, 96 mins.)

Criss Cross (1948)*** Burt Lancaster, Yvonne DeCarlo, Dan Duryea. Burt Lancaster gets double-crossed by everyone in this good cops and robbers story about an armored car robbery. Dan Duryea is as villainous as they come. (Dir: Robert Siodmak, 87 mins.)

Critic's Choice (1963)**½ Bob Hope, Lucille Ball. Even the expert comedy talents of Hope and Ball can't save this contrived tale about a New York drama critic whose wife writes a play. Based on the Broadway play with the same title, the screen adaptation was altered to suit the talents of the leads but it doesn't really help. (Dir: Don Weis, 100 mins.)

Cromwell (Great Britain, 1970)**½ Richard Harris, Alec Guinness, Robert Morley, Dorothy Tutin, Frank Finlay, Timothy Dalton, Patrick Magee. Straightforward narrative about the 17th-century civil war which divided England and brought Oliver Cromwell to prominence as a revolutionary. Richard Harris' Cromwell is beautifully realized, as he changes from the quiet country squire to a national leader and, eventually, a dictator figure caught up in political intrigues. Alec Guinness as King Charles I gives a dignified, restrained performance as the doomed monarch. His execution scene is memorable. Not everyone's beheading, of course, but . . . Written and directed by Ken Hughes, responsible for "The Trials of Oscar Wilde." (Dir: Ken Hughes, 139 mins.)

Crook, The (French-Italian, 1970)***½ Jean-Louis Trintignant, Christine Lelouch. Claude Lelouch, director of "A Man and a Woman," casts his romantic eye on crime. Trintignant plays a criminal out to commit an elaborate kidnapping of a bank employee's son and collect ransom from the bank, which would then profit from the publicity. The plan works until a subtle plot twist. Slick, and cynical. First-rate entertainment, and Trintignant is splendid. (Dir: Claude Lelouch, 73 mins.)

Crooked Hearts, The (1972)**½ Rosalind Russell, Douglas Fairbanks, Jr. The stars add class to this tale about flim-flam amid the geriatric set. Miss Russell corresponds with the elegant Mr. Fairbanks via a

158

lonely hearts club and they strike up a romance—each thinking the other is enormously wealthy. Predictable story, but Miss Russell is always interesting to watch. Made-for-TV. (Dir: Jay Sandrich)

Crooked Road, The (British, 1964) * Robert Ryan, Stewart Granger, Nadia Gray. Third-rate melodrama, made in Yugoslavia on an obviously small budget. Ryan plays a newspaperman who almost gets the goods on a Balkan dictator. But there's so much muddled plot before the fadeout, you'll probably root for the dictator, over-played by Stewart Granger. (Dir: Don Chaffey, 86 mins.)

Crooked Sky, The (British, 1957)*½ Wayne Morris, Karin Booth. American joins Scotland Yard to break up a ring of counterfeiters. Same old thing.

Crooked Web, The (1955)** Frank Lovejoy, Mari Blanchard. Undercover agents go to great lengths to trap a wartime criminal into a confession. A slow moving film. (Dir: Nathan Juran, 80 mins.)

Crooks and Coronets—See: **Sophie's Place**

Crooks Anonymous (British, 1962)** Julie Christie, Leslie Phillips, Wilfred Hyde-White. Petty thief tries to mend his ways, joins an organization dedicated to the reformation of criminals. Cute idea, mediocre handling.

Cross My Heart (1946)** Betty Hutton, Sonny Tufts. Silly comedy about a girl who rarely tells the truth. The young lady confesses to a murder thinking it will help her boy friend, but the scheme backfires.

Cross of Lorraine, The (1943)*** Jean-Pierre Aumont, Gene Kelly, Sir Cedric Hardwicke. An exceptionally good anti-Nazi film about a group of Frenchmen who surrender too easily, go to a prison camp and learn how the Nazis really operate. Grim, but a picture that may remind you of things you have no right to forget. (Dir: Tay Garnett, 90 mins.)

Cross Winds (1951)** John Payne, Rhonda Fleming, Forrest Tucker. John Payne is the victim of a double cross and other villainous deeds in this average tale of island intrigues. Rhonda Fleming almost loses her head (literally) when a band of head-hunters capture her. (93 mins.)

Crossed Swords (1954)*½ Errol Flynn, Gina Lollobrigida. Gay adventurer foils a wicked counselor in medieval Italy. Made in Italy, dubbed-in English, and badly produced costume melodrama. (Dir: Nato de Angelis, 84 mins.)

Crossfire (1947)**** Robert Young, Robert Mitchum, Robert Ryan. Crazed intolerant becomes a killer, is trapped by his own anti-Semitism. Tense, excellently done hard-hitting melodrama. (Dir: Edward Dmytryk, 86 mins.)

Crossfire (1975)½ James Farentino, John Saxon, Patrick O'Neal, Pamela Franklin. Another clichéd TV film about an undercover cop. Made-for-TV. (Dir: William Hale, 72 mins.)

Crossroads (1941)** William Powell, Hedy Lamarr. Suspense film about an amnesia victim who is uncertain of his former life is well played. Has some good moments but, overall, is not effective drama. (Dir: Jack Conway, 84 mins.)

Crossroads to Crime (British, 1964)** Anthony Oliver, Patricia Henegan. Policeman on his own goes after a gang of hijackers. Passable Edgar Wallace mystery.

Crosstrap (British, 1960)** Laurence Payne, Jill Adams. Writer and his wife on honeymoon in a bungalow run across murder. Average mystery. (Dir: Robert Hartford-Davis, 62 mins.)

Crossup—See: **Tiger by the Tail**

Crowd, The (1928)***½ Eleanor Boardman, James Murray. Silent film classic. The life together of a man and a woman in a large, impersonal metropolis, their hopes, struggles and downfall beautifully captured. (Dir: King Vidor, 90 mins.)

Crowded Day, The—See: **Shop Soiled**

Crowded Paradise (1955)**½ Hume Cronyn. Janitor has a crazy hatred for his Puerto Rican tenants. Low-budget film has some good scenes.

Crowded Sky, The (1960)**½ Dana Andrews, Rhonda Fleming, Efrem Zimbalist, Troy Donahue. This airplane drama will strike you as a bit familiar and rightly so—it is a slightly altered re-telling of "The High and the Mighty" with some new characters thrown in. The large cast does what it can with the episodic script. (Dir: Joseph Pevney, 105 mins.)

Crowhaven Farm (1970) **½ Hope Lange, Paul Burke, Lloyd Bochner.

Made-for-TV thriller dealing with witchcraft and the supernatural. Hope Lange and Paul Burke inherit a farm, which becomes the setting for some very strange happenings. Although most of the plot becomes transparent before too long, you'll probably stay with it to the end. (Dir: Walter Gravman, 73 mins.)

Crowning Experience, The (1960)** Muriel Smith, Ann Buckles. Religious film made for Moral Rearmament—the biography of educator Mary McLeod Bethune. Good performance by Muriel Smith in the role. As a drama, not as effective as it should be—simplistic approach detracts from the power of the narrative.

Crucible, The (French, 1958)***½ Simone Signoret, Yves Montand, Mylene Demongeot. A gripping version of Arthur Miller's memorable play about the Salem witch trials and how a young girl's jealousy caused innocent people to be condemned to death. Miller's play, based on events in Massachusetts almost three hundred years ago, was written as a searing commentary on the evils of McCarthyism in America in the 1950's. This movie was ultimately made in France because the prize-winning playwright was blacklisted in America and blackballed by Hollywood at that time. (Dir: Raymond Rouleau, 120 mins.)

Crucible of Horror (U.S.-Great Britain, 1970)*** Michael Gough, Yvonne Mitchell, Sharon Gurney. Tight, chilling tingler. Mother and daughter plan murder of sadistic father. Top-flight suspense, biting and original. Well-acted by a small cast. Ending disappoints. (Dir: Viktors Ritelis, 91 mins.)

Cruel Sea, The (British, 1953)**** Jack Hawkins, Donald Sinden. Story of the officers and men of the Compass Rose, who faced the dangers of the Nazi subs during World War II. Superbly produced war drama, deserves praise in all departments. (Dir: Charles Frend, 140 mins.)

Cruel Swamp (1956)*½ Beverly Garland, Marie Windsor, Carole Matthews. Three tough babes trudge through a swamp in quest of their hidden stolen loot after they break out of prison. Some lively but contrived action. (Dir: Roger Corman, 73 mins.)

Cruel Tower (1957)*** John Ericson,

Mari Blanchard. Drifter takes a job as a steeplejack, incurs jealousy over a girl. Suspenseful melodrama with some hair-raising scenes showing the steeplejacks at their work. (80 mins.)

Cruisin' Down the River (1953)** Dick Haymes, Audrey Totter, Billy Daniels. Dick Haymes' singing makes this otherwise dull musical comedy worthwhile. Story is about a riverboat that's turned into a floating nightclub by enterprising ancestors of the original owners. (90 mins.)

Crusades, The (1935)**½ Loretta Young, Henry Wilcoxon. De Mille epic about the third crusade is lavish, exciting and fairly entertaining. History is twisted a bit too much in favor of romance. (Dir: C. B. De Mille, 123 mins.)

Cry Baby Killer (1958)**½ Jack Nicholson, Brett Halsey. Teenager thinks he has killed, holds up in a storeroom with hostages, holding police at bay. Not much to this grim little tale of juvenile delinquents, but what there is is well done. Alert direction, capable acting. (62 mins.)

Cry Danger (1951)***½ Dick Powell, Rhonda Fleming. Released from prison, a man attempts to prove he was innocent of robbery. Fast, tough melodrama, very good. (Dir: Richard Parrish, 79 mins.)

Cry for Happy (1961)**½ Glenn Ford, Donald O'Connor, Miyoshi Umecki. Through a misunderstanding a group of Navy men living it up in a geisha house is forced to turn its paradise into an orphanage to cool the brass. Mildly amusing service comedy is pleasant enough despite a few misfires on the laugh situations. (Dir: George Marshall, 110 mins.)

Cry for Help, A (1975)**½ Robert Culp, Elayne Heilveil, Chuck McCann. Follows a sardonic, ex-drunk radio phone-show host (Culp) as he starts a normal day of putting down the parade of kooks who call his early AM show. When an 18-year-old girl indicates she's about to pack it in and do away with herself, he sloughs her off, and a barrage of calls starts a race with the clock to find the mystery girl. Well done. Made-for-TV. (Dir: Daryl Duke, 72 mins.)

Cry Freedom (Philippines, 1959)** Pancho Magalona, Rosa Rosal. Out-

160

of-the-ordinary World War II movie views war from the Philippine perspective—a disparate group of commandos, led by a bus driver, battle the Japanese occupiers. Technically crude, amateurish in other respects. (Dir: Lamberto V. Avellana.)

Cry from the Streets, A (British, 1959)*** Max Bygraves, Barbara Murray. Often effective drama of homeless children and the welfare workers who try to give them a reason for living. Miss Murray is most effective. (Dir: Lewis Gilbert, 100 mins.)

Cry Havoc (1943)**½ Margaret Sullavan, Ann Sothern. All-female cast in this occasionally moving war melodrama about women who served tirelessly as nurses during our defeat on Bataan. (Dir: Richard Thorpe, 97 mins.)

Cry in the Night, A (1956)** Edmond O'Brien, Natalie Wood, Brian Donlevy, Raymond Burr. A mentally unbalanced man kidnaps the daughter of a policeman, and police try to track them down before it's too late. Only fair melodrama misses on the suspense. (Dir: Frank Tuttle, 75 mins.)

Cry in the Wilderness, A (1974)* George Kennedy, Paul Sorenson, Irene Tedrow. A nonsensical "crisis upon crisis" mishmash that starts off with an absurd premise. Kennedy plays an Oregon farmer who gets bitten by a skunk and then locks himself in the barn for fear that he will go mad from rabies. You're mad to bother. Made-for-TV. (Dir: Gordon Hessler, 90 mins.)

Cry of Battle (1963)** Van Heflin, Rita Moreno, James MacArthur. Wealthy lad earns his mettle when he joins a guerilla unit in the Philippines during World War II. War drama never gets out of the routine rut despite local color, fairly effective performances. (Dir: Irving Lerner, 99 mins.)

Cry of the Banshee (1970)**½ Vincent Price rolls his eyes and snarls in his inimitable fashion in still another chiller-diller horror film. In this one, he's a British magistrate who dabbles in heinous deeds during his off-hours. (Dir: Gordon Hessler, 87 mins.)

Cry of the Bewitched (Mexican, 1957)*½ Ninon Sevilla, Ramon Gay. Voodoo on a sugar plantation of a hundred years ago. Dull melodrama dubbed in English.

Cry of the City (1948)*** Victor Mature, Richard Conte. Rough, brutal melodrama about a killer and a cop who came from the same neighborhood. Goes off the deep end at times but still a good film. (Dir: Robert Siodmak, 95 mins.)

Cry of the Hunted (1953)**½ Vittorio Gassman, Polly Bergen, Barry Sullivan. Gassman's performance as an escaped convict trudging through the swamps gives some credulity to this otherwise melodramatic yarn about the hunter and the hunted. (Dir: Joseph H. Lewis, 79 mins.)

Cry of the Wild (Canadian, 1972)***½ A superior animal documentary about Canadian wolves. The best parts of the film are those in the middle made by the National Film Board of Canada. Some of the wolves are captured and tamed while living in with the director-photographer Bill Mason. Good scenes in the Canadian Arctic and some truly remarkable shots at the end, filmed in a large enclosure where the wolves do not run wild, of the courtship of two wolves and the following scenes of the female wolf with her litter. (90 mins.)

Cry Panic (1974)*** John Forsythe, Anne Francis, Earl Holliman. Good mystery which will have you rooting for the poor hero, played by Forsythe. He accidentally hits and kills a man on a highway, but when he leaves the scene of the accident to call the police, the body disappears and he's thrown into a complicated web of events. The audience is let in on the reasons for the strange happenings in the small town where Forsythe is detained, but it subtracts from your sustained interest in the proceedings. Made-for-TV. (Dir: James Goldstone)

Cry Rape! (1973)** Andrea Marcovicci, Peter Coffield. A worthy theme, the indignities a rape victim has to endure at the police station, is mishandled. Based on a true story, it veers away from the rape problem to the innocent man wrongly identified in the lineup, and simply becomes a variation on the old plot about a look-alike with the added twist that the suspect is also saddled with the wrong kind of lawyer. Made-for-TV. (Dir: Corey Allen, 90 mins.)

Cry Terror! (1958)**½ James Mason, Inger Stevens, Rod Steiger, Angie Dickinson. Crafty criminal forces an electronics expert to aid him in an elaborate extortion plot. Occasionally suspenseful crime drama stretches things too far at times but has a good share of thrills. Aided by interesting New York locations. (Dir: Andrew L. Stone, 96 mins.)

Cry the Beloved Country (British, 1951)***½ Canada Lee, Charles Carson. Negro Reverend in the back country of South Africa journeys to the city, only to find his people living in squalor, and his son a criminal. Powerful drama of Africa has many gripping moments. (Dir: Zoltan Korda, 105 mins.)

Cry Tough (1959)**½ John Saxon, Linda Cristal. Only moderately interesting drama about the young juvenile delinquent element which springs up in minority groups due to racial hatred. The performances are better than the material. (Dir: Paul Stanley, 83 mins.)

Cry Vengeance (1954)*** Mark Stevens, Martha Hyer. Detective seeks revenge for the murder of his wife and child. Tense, well-directed (by Stevens) crime drama with some new plot twists. (Dir: Mark Stevens, 83 mins.)

Cry Wolf (1947)** Errol Flynn, Barbara Stanwyck. Woman has a creepy time when she goes to her late husband's estate to claim her inheritance. Hackneyed thriller. (Dir: Peter Godfrey, 83 mins.)

Cry Wolf (Great Britain, 1968)**½ Anthony Kemp, Judy Cornwall. Good adventure yarn for the kids— the old fable about the boy who cried wolf once too often is set in contemporary Britain, among diplomats instead of sheep. Resourcefulness of the young hero makes for a happier ending. (Dir: John Davis, 58 mins.)

Crystal Ball (1943)** Paulette Goddard, Ray Milland. A gal from Texas takes a job as a fortune-teller's assistant, where she snags her man. Just passable comedy, with the players better than the script. (Dir: Elliott Nugent, 81 mins.)

Cuban Rebel Girls (1959)*½ Errol Flynn, Beverly Aadland. Filmed in Cuba with the assistance of Fidel Castro's army. An aging Errol Flynn and some beautiful girls join Castro's forces to fight against Batista. Amateurish efforts, interesting only as Flynn's last film, plus the Castro twist. (Dir: Barry Mahon.)

Culpepper Cattle Company, The (1972)**½ Gary Grimes, Billy "Green" Bush, Luke Askew, Bo Hopkins. A great deal of effort on the part of the cameramen and art directors has been expended to give this Western an authentic look, even though it isn't much more than a routine yarn about the "coming of age," in post-Civil War Texas, of a young man who signs on as a cook's helper on a huge cattle drive. Gary Grimes is properly green as the kid who is forced to become a man when he is confronted by killing and rustling. Directorial debut by Dick Richards, who had been a director of TV commercials, and sometimes it shows. Screenplay by Eric Bercovici and Gregory Prentiss, based on a story by Richards. (Dir: Dick Richards, 92 mins.)

Cult of the Cobra (1955)** Faith Domergue, Richard Long. Combination murder mystery-horror film about superstitions and curses. Faith Domergue plays a mysterious woman who has the power to change into a snake. (Dir: Francis D. Lyon, 90 mins.)

Cure for Love (British, 1949)**½ Robert Donat, Renée Asherson. A returning soldier finds romantic complications in his home town. Pleasant comedy.

Curse of Dracula, The (1959)** Francis Lederer, Ray Stricklyn. Still another film about the most famous vampire of them all. This tale takes place in the U.S., but the stock characters are all intact.

Curse of Frankenstein, The (British, 1957)** Peter Cushing, Christopher Lee. The dynamic duo of British horror films, Cushing and Lee, join forces in another installment in the saga of a certain mad scientist and his creature, who both often go under the same name—Frankenstein. (Dir: Freddie Francis, 93 mins.)

Curse of Nostradamus, The (Mexican, 1962)* Domingo Soler, Jermon Robles. Vampire threatens death unless a professor helps him establish a cult. Ridiculously poor horror thriller, dubbed in English.

Curse of the Cat People (1944)*** Simone Simon, Kent Smith. Child whose mother was cursed is regarded as strange by her playmates and parents. Odd little drama has mo-

162

ments of genuine quality. (Dirs: Gunther Fritsch & Robert Wise, 70 mins.)

Curse of the Crimson Altar—See: Crimson Cult, The

Curse of the Crying Woman, The (Mexican, 1960)* Rosita Arenas, Abel Salazar. Young bride finds she has inherited a legacy of terror when she visits the home of her aunt. Ridiculous horror thriller complete with mummies, curses, bodies, all ineffective. Dubbed in English.

Curse of the Demon (British, 1957) **½ Dana Andrews, Peggy Cummins. Fearsome monster from the past returns to wreak havoc in London. Uneven shocker; some shuddery scenes. (Dir: Jacques Tourneur, 95 mins.)

Curse of the Doll People (Mexican, 1961)* Elvira Quintana, Ramon Gay. Scientist's daughter insists a series of tragedies are the work of black magic and voodoo. Silly horror thriller dubbed in English.

Curse of the Faceless Man (1958)* Richard Anderson, Elaine Edwards. Horror-science-fiction story with completely implausible plot twists and amateur acting. (Dir: Edward L. Cahn, 66 mins.)

Curse of the Fly, The (1965)* Rusty thriller finds Brian Donlevy struggling with the intricacies of the fourth dimension and assorted weirdos. Best to avoid. (Dir: Don Sharp, 85 mins.)

Curse of the Hidden Vault, The (German, 1964)*½ Judith Dornys, Harald Lieb. Gangland tries to trace the hidden treasure of a deceased gambler. Edgar Wallace mystery is hokum-filled, slow moving. Dubbed in English.

Curse of the Mummy's Tomb, The (British, 1964)** Terence Morgan, Ronald Howard. Mummy returns to life to commence a reign of terror. Undistinguished horror thriller. (Dir: Michael Carreras, 80 mins.)

Curse of the Stone Hand (1964)* John Carradine, Sheila Bon. Inept horror yarn. Carradine, as usual, is terrible.

Curse of the Undead (1956)** Eric Fleming, Kathleen Crowley, Michael Pate. Intriguing mixture of western and "Dracula"-type horror yarn as a vampire stalks the west. Not too successful in execution but deserves credit for trying something different. (Dir: Edward Dein, 79 mins.)

Curse of the Voodoo (1965)** Bryant Halliday, Dennis Price, Lisa Daniely. White hunter is the recipient of a curse when he ventures into forbidden territory. Fairish thriller has the asset of some well-constructed suspense scenes. (Dir: Lindsay Shontoff, 77 mins.)

Curse of the Werewolf (British, 1961)*** Clifford Evans, Oliver Reed. Young lad with questionable antecedents is discovered to be a werewolf. Superior shocker, with more adult ramifications than usual in the plotting. Gruesome, but good. (Dir: Terence Fisher, 91 mins.)

Curse of the Yellow Snake (German, 1963)*½ Joachim Berger, Pinkas Braun. English lad is entrusted with a Chinese symbol of death, uncovers a ring of fanatics. Farfetched and hokey Edgar Wallace thriller, for the unsophisticates. Dubbed in English. (Dir: Frank Gottlieb, 99 mins.)

Curtain Call at Cactus Creek (1950)**½ Donald O'Connor, Gale Storm, Eve Arden, Vincent Price. Amusing romp about a traveling troupe of actors who run into trouble wherever they set up to perform. The melodramas staged by the troupe are the funniest things in the movie. The cast plays it broadly and that's how it should be done. (Dir: Charles Lamont, 86 mins.)

Curtain Up (British, 1952)**½ Robert Morley, Margaret Rutherford. Small theatre group is plagued by an old lady, aunt of the backer, who has written a very bad play. Pleasing comedy that doesn't come off as it should. (Dir: Ralph Smart, 81 mins.)

Curucu, Beast of the Amazon (1956)** John Bromfield, Beverly Garland. Plantation foreman sets out to track down a legendary monster who is killing and terrorizing the natives. Routine thriller yarn is picturesque. (Dir: Curt Siodmak, 76 mins.)

Custer of the West (1967)**½ Robert Shaw, Mary Ure, Robert Ryan, Jeffrey Hunter, Ty Hardin. Story of the 7th Cavalry general who ran afoul of all those Indians at the Little Big Horn. Made in Spain and falls mainly all over the plains; sprawling narrative redeemed somewhat by Robert Shaw's thespic capabilities as Custer. Some good big-scale action scenes.

Customs Agent (1950)** William Eythe, Marjorie Reynolds. A U. S. Customs Agent poses as a dope peddler in order to crack a drug smuggling outfit. Plenty of action. (80 mins.)

Cyborg 2087 (1966)* Michael Rennie, Wendell Corey. Cyborgs, beings that are half man and half machine, revolt in the year 2087 and travel back to 1966 to prevent their own creation. The creation of "Cyborg" should have been prevented. (Dir: Franklin Andreon, 86 mins.)

Cyclops (1957)*½ Gloria Talbott, James Craig. Searching party finds their subject turned into a one-eyed monster. Humdrum thriller. (Dir: Bert I. Gordon, 75 mins.)

Cyclotrode "X" (1946-66)**½ Charles Quigley, Linda Stirling, Clayton Moore. Feature version of serial "The Crimson Ghost." Masked villain is out to steal an atomic device, and the hero is out to stop him. Good action sequences give this feature cliffhanger a lift. (Dir: William Witney, 100 mins.)

Cynara (1932)**½ Ronald Colman, Kay Francis. Dated romantic drama based on a play has Ronald Colman's excellent performance to recommend it. (Dir: King Vidor, 90 mins.)

Cynthia (1946)** Elizabeth Taylor, Gene Lockhart, George Murphy. Syrupy tale of a sickly girl who proves she's normal and, by so doing, solves everybody's problems. (Dir: Robert Z. Leonard, 99 mins.)

Cyrano de Bergerac (1950)***½ Jose Ferrer, Mala Powers. The classic play about the soldier of fortune with the oversize proboscis, and of his unrequited love for the beautiful Roxanne. Ferrer won the Academy Award for this, but production shortcomings and uninspired casting of other roles mitigate against its effectiveness. Ferrer's performance is properly flamboyant and very moving, and makes this perennial well worth seeing. (Dir: Michael Gordon, 112 mins.)

D-Day, the Sixth of June (1956)*** Robert Taylor, Dana Wynter, Richard Todd. The usual plot of two officers loving one girl, but presented with a bit more credibility then is customary. Good production values, including WW II scenes. With Edmond O'Brien, John Williams, Jerry Paris. (Dir: Henry Koster, 106 mins.)

D.A.—Conspiracy to Kill, The (1970)
★½ Robert Conrad, William Conrad, Belinda Montgomery. TV feature. Robert Conrad joins producer Jack Webb's law-and order staff to play a deputy district attorney working on cases from Los Angeles police files. Conrad teams with chief prosecutor William Conrad, a big candy eater, to unravel murders involving a meek druggist. One murder is hardly enough to fill out the time, but three fit the requirements nicely. It's just-the-facts approach, a typical Webb oversimplified view of law and order. (Dir: Jack Webb, 99 mins.)

D.A.: Murder One, The (1969)★★½ Howard Duff, Robert Conrad, Diane Baker. A made-for-TV murder mystery produced by Jack Webb which should appeal to fans of the "Dragnet" TV series. The two hours are filled with painstaking detective work as the D.A.'s office tries to trap an attractive nurse (Diane Baker) suspected of multiple murders. The D.A.s are Robert Conrad and Howard Duff, and the capable supporting cast includes J. D. Cannon, David Opatoshu, and Alfred Ryder. (Dir: Jack Webb, 99 mins.)

Daddy Long Legs (1955)★★★½ Fred Astaire, Leslie Caron. Delightful musical romance. Debonair Fred Astaire has seldom had a better dancing partner than charming and graceful Leslie Caron—their numbers are the film's highlights. The plot borders on modern fairy tale—a French orphan (Miss Caron) is subsidized by a wealthy bachelor with the stipulation that his identity be kept secret. (Dir: Jean Negulesco, 126 mins.)

Daddy-O (1959)★ Dick Contino, Sandra Giles. Crooks hire a truck driver to drive a getaway car, but he's really an undercover agent. Trashy crime film should have stayed undercover too ; poorly done.

Daddy's Gone A-Hunting (1969)★★½ Carol White, Paul Burke, Scott Hylands. A pretty lively suspense tale. Carol White has her hands full when her ex-lover shows up bent on revenge because she had an abortion during their time together. The mad young man (Scott Hylands) kidnaps the now happily married Miss White's new baby and the chase is on. Exciting photography during the final moments of the chase adds to the tension. (Dir: Mark Robson, 108 mins.)

Daggers Drawn (French, 1964)★★½ Françoise Arnoul, Pierre Mondy, Petula Clark. Ragged adventure tale about the quest for some of Hitler's sunken treasure, and the misery it causes. Miss Clark is in for a song or two, otherwise nil. Dubbed in English.

Dagora, the Space Monster (Japanese, 1965)★ Another monster from outer space job, sukiyaki style. This time the thing even interferes with some gangland operations. Pretty silly. Dubbed in English.

Daisy Kenyon (1947)★★½ Joan Crawford, Henry Fonda, Dana Andrews. A woman must choose between her lover, who has a wife and family, and the man she married on the rebound. Well done film but a bore. (Dir: Otto Preminger, 99 mins.)

Daisy Miller (1974)★★★ Cybill Shepherd, Barry Brown, Mildred Natwick, Cloris Leachman, Eileen Brennan. An intelligent, visually stunning but curiously uninvolving adaptation of Henry Miller's superb novella about expatriate Americans in Europe and a nouveau riche American girl from Schenectady, colliding with European high society circa 1879. Part of the problem is that Shepherd is simply not a talented enough actress with sufficient range to develop a fully rounded portrait of Daisy. But she does look exquisite, and exactly right—a Renoir vision as captured by cinematographer Alberto Spagnoli. Screenplay by Frederic Raphael. (Dir: Peter Bogdanovich, 91 mins.)

Dakota Incident (1956)★★½ Linda Darnell, Dale Robertson, John Lund. Stagecoach wards off Indian attacks. Fairly good western ; good performances. (Dir: Lewis R. Foster, 88 mins.)

Dakota Lil (1950)★★½ George Montgomery, Rod Cameron, Marie Windsor. Secret agent poses as an outlaw, enlists the aid of a beautiful lady forger to trap a bandit gang. Lively western has the stuff to attract the oats fanciers. (Dir: Lesley Selander, 88 mins.)

Daleks—Invasion Earth 2150 A.D.— See : **Invasion Earth 2150 A.D.**

Dallas (1950)★★½ Gary Cooper, Ruth Roman, Steve Cochran. Cooper plays a man who comes to Dallas for revenge, in this moderately entertaining western drama. Ruth Roman supplies the necessary love interest and Steve Cochran does very well as one of Cooper's intended victims. (Dir: Stuart Heisler, 94 mins.)

Dalton Girls (1957)*½ John Russell, Merry Anders. The distaff side takes over in this uninteresting western drama. John Russell is the lucky man involved with the gals. (Dir: Reginald LeBorg, 71 mins.)

Dambusters, The (British, 1955)**** Richard Todd, Michael Redgrave. Excellent war drama about one of the most dangerous missions of WW II. Effective cast and fine script make this one worth your while. (Dir: Michael Anderson, 102 mins.)

Damn Citizen (1958)**½ Keith Andes, Maggie Hayes, Gene Evans. Story based on fact of a World War II vet who is given a free hand to clean up crime and corruption in a state police organization. Done in documentary fashion, has a fairly good share of interest. (Dir: Robert Gordon, 88 mins.)

Damn the Defiant! (British, 1962)*** Alec Guinness, Dirk Bogarde, Anthony Quayle. Commander of a fighting vessel faces the opposition of his second in command, a sadistic and cruel officer hated by the crew. Salty maritime costume drama with performances of high standard, interest maintained throughout. (Dir: Lewis Gilbert, 101 mins.)

Damn Yankees (1958)**½ Gwen Verdon, Tab Hunter, Ray Walston. The hit B'dway musical reaches the screen with one big change—Tab Hunter is cast in one of the leads. It's a mistake. He seems out of his element dancing and singing with pro Gwen Verdon. Miss Verdon is best when dancing and she dances most of the time. Ray Walston as the "Devil" has some funny moments. (Dir: George Abbott, 110 mins.)

Damned, The (Italian-West German, 1969)*** Helmut Berger, Ingrid Thulin, Dirk Bogarde. Italian director Luchino Visconti has fashioned a fascinating portrait of a powerful, wealthy, twisted German family, whose steel-business profits helped to back Hitler's rise to power in the 1930's. The personal dramas of various members of the family are woven into the larger fabric of the Nazi-dominated era, and a good cast adds to the film's overall impact. (155 mins.)

Damned Don't Cry, The (1950)**½ Joan Crawford, David Brian, Steve Cochran. Joan Crawford finds herself up to her mink in crime and corruption. Heavy David Brian makes the going rougher for her but she knows the "damned don't cry." You might, though. (Dir: Vincent Sherman, 103 mins.)

Dance, Girl, Dance (1940)*** Maureen O'Hara, Lucille Ball, Ralph Bellamy. An interesting film in light of today's "women's lib" movement. It's based on an original screen story by Vicki Baum, and directed by Dorothy Arzner,—probably the most gifted of the tiny number of women directors who were working in Hollywood during the '30's and early '40's. Two girls are rivals in their careers, and in love with the same man. (Dir: Dorothy Arzner, 90 mins.)

Dance Hall (British, 1950)**½ Natasha Perry, Jane Hylton, Diana Dors. Four factory girls break away from their squalid lives at night when they hang out at the local dance hall. Loosely told melodrama manages some good moments, but is too rambling in structure.

Dance Little Lady (British, 1955)**½ Mai Zetterling, Terence Morgan. Ballerina's career is halted by an accident, but she sees her daughter take up where she left off. Slightly tedious drama is aided by good performances. (87 mins.)

Dance of Death (French, 1960)*½ Felix Marten, Michele Mercier. Private eye is hired to protect a playboy, solves a murder. Dreary mystery, dubbed-in English, no style.

Dance with Me, Henry (1956)*½ Bud Abbott, Lou Costello, Gigi Perreau. Gangsters, orphans, cops, and comics find themselves in "Kiddyland," an amusement park owned by Lou Costello. In true but trying slapstick style. (Dir: Charles Barton, 79 mins.)

Dancing Co-ed (1939)** Lana Turner, Richard Carlson. Nothing here but Lana Turner in dancing clothes back in 1939 and that should be enough to stir memories in many a red-blooded American male. (Dir: S. Sylvan Simon, 80 mins.)

Dancing Heart, The (W. German, 1958)*½ Gertrud Kueckelmann, Herta Staal. Musical fantasy set in an Austrian village where a puppet maker is designing a puppet to look like his daughter. Isn't OK for the children. (Dir: Wolfgang Liebeneiner, 91 mins.)

Dancing in Manhattan (1944)**½ Fred Brady, Jeff Donnell. Garbage man finds $5,000, doesn't know the bills are marked to trap blackmailers. Amusing little comedy.

Dancing in the Dark (1950)*** William Powell, Betsy Drake, Mark Stevens. Powell's delightfully droll performance as an ex-ham turned talent scout gives this musical a big lift. Betsy Drake, as his discovery, is hardly a song-and-dance girl, but no matter—Powell steals the show. (Dir: Irving Reis, 92 mins.)

Dancing on a Dime (1940) **½ Grace McDonald, Robert Paige, Peter Lind Hayes. Out-of-work performers live in an abandoned theatre, try to put on their big show. Likable musical is pleasing fun. (Dir: Joseph Santley, 74 mins.)

Dandy in Aspic, A (British, 1968)* Laurence Harvey, Mia Farrow. Soggy spy stuff, as a Soviet agent (Laurence Harvey) working undercover gets tangled in an inextricable web. Sometimes one wishes that Spy had never come in from the Cold. Mia Farrow (inept), Tom Courtenay, Harry Andrews (what would espionage be without him?), Lionel Stander, Peter Cook, Per Oscarsson. Good cast wasted! (Dirs: Anthony Mann, Laurence Harvey, 107 mins.)

Danger: Diabolik (Italian, 1968)* John Philip Law, Marisa Mell, Michel Piccoli, Terry-Thomas. The escapades of an infernally clever thief who continually thwarts the law. Tries for sophistication, succeeds in being merely sappy.

Danger in Paradise (1977)*½ John Dehner, Ina Balin, Cliff Potts. Hawaii serves as a handsome background for this ordinary family dynasty drama. While Big Daddy (John Dehner) lies dying of a stroke, his young bride (Ina Balin) schemes to sell off choice land to the Mafia. The film, however, is a vehicle for Cliff Potts cast as a hellraising son. Pilot for the subsequent TV series. Made-for-TV. (Dir: Marvin Chomsky, 106 mins.)

Danger in the Middle East (French, 1959)*½ Françoise Arnoul, Michel Piccoli. Criminal is rubbed out before he can go after a fortune, so his wife takes up the hunt, matching wits against a rival gang. Sluggish crime melodrama dubbed in English.

Danger on My Side (British, 1961) *½ Maureen Connell, Anthony Oliver. Sister of murdered policeman sets out to avenge his death. Mediocre crime melodrama.

Danger Route (British, 1968)** Richard Johnson, Carol Lynley. British secret agent ordered to kill a Russian scientist who has defected to the Americans. The agent gets his man (his 31st), but a chase ensues with more double crosses than a game of tick tack toe. (Dir: Seth Holt, 91 mins.)

Danger Signal (1945)** Faye Emerson, Zachary Scott. Corny, Grade B melodrama about a fortune-hunting heel, his women and murder. (Dir: Robert Florey, 78 mins.)

Danger Tomorrow (British, 1957)** Zena Walker, Robert Urquhart. Strange occurrences threaten a woman's sanity. Fair mystery.

Dangerous (1935)**½ Bette Davis, Franchot Tone. A young architect tries to bring a great actress back from the gutter to stardom and falls in love with her. Very soapy, especially at the end, but Bette's Oscar-winning performance is worth a look. (Dir: Alfred E. Green, 78 mins.)

Dangerous Age, A (Canadian, 1959) ** Ben Piazza, Anne Pearson. Young couple in love have difficulty adjusting to the world and its demands. Sincere problem drama adds little to the case, becomes just another picture.

Dangerous Agent (French, 1954)*½ Eddie Constantine, Colette Dereal. Undercover agent tracks down and cracks a gang of international racketeers. Inferior imitation of American action melodrama. Dubbed in English.

Dangerous Assignment (British, 1957)*½ Lionel Murton, Pamela Deeming. Ace reporter goes to London, breaks up a gang of car thieves. Trite crime drama.

Dangerous Blondes (1943)*** Allyn Joslyn, Evelyn Keyes. Mystery writer helps his wife solve the murder of a wealthy matron. More laughs than thrills in this comedy-mystery; well done.

Dangerous Charter (1962)*½ Chris Warfield, Sally Fraser. Weak melodrama, heroes vs. dope smugglers. Good actor Warfield tries hard against script odds.

Dangerous Crossing (1953)**½ Jeanne Crain, Michael Rennie. Mystery drama which takes place on an ocean liner. Miss Crain is cast as a bride whose husband disappears during the first few hours after they set sail. Some suspense and the acting's good. (Dir: Joseph M. Newman, 75 mins.)

Dangerous Days of Kiowa Jones, The (1966)** Robert Horton, Diane Baker, Sal Mineo, Nehemiah Persoff. Draggy western about a wandering cowpoke who accedes to the request of a dying lawman to take in two killers. (Dir: Alex March, 83 mins.)

Dangerous Exile (British, 1957)**½ Louis Jourdan, Belinda Lee. During the Revolution, the small son of Marie Antoinette is secretly smuggled into Wales. Typical overblown costume drama. (Dir: Brian Desmond Hurst, 90 mins.)

Dangerous Female (1931)** Bebe Daniels, Ricardo Cortez. Earliest version of "The Maltese Falcon," with Cortez as private eye Sam Spade after the mysterious black bird and avenging the death of his partner. Despite antiquated technique Hammett's original plot is strong enough to hold it up. Alternate title: "The Maltese Falcon." (Dir: Roy Del Ruth, 90 mins.)

Dangerous Games (French, 1958)** Jean Servais, Pascale Audret. Teenagers get involved in kidnapping and murder. Fair English-dubbed melodrama.

Dangerous Mission (1953)** Victor Mature, Piper Laurie, William Bendix. Girl witnesses a gangland killing, flees to Glacier National Park, with both the crooks and the law after her. Good scenery, otherwise mild melodrama. (75 mins.)

Dangerous Moonlight (British, 1941) **** Anton Walbrook, Sally Gray. Polish pianist flies for the RAF, is implored by his loved one to stick to music. Superb war drama, finely acted, with excellent music sequences ("Warsaw Concerto"). (Dir: Brian Desmond Hurst, 83 mins.)

Dangerous Partners (1945)**½ James Craig, Signe Hasso. Fairly good Grade B chase melodrama with the object in question a mere four million dollars worth of bonds. (Dir: Edward L. Cahn, 74 mins.)

Dangerous Profession, A (1949)** George Raft, Ella Raines, Pat O'Brien. Bail bondsman clashes with the underworld after a killing. Confused, slow crime melodrama. (Dir: Ted Tetzlaff, 79 mins.)

Dangerous When Wet (1953)** Esther Williams, Fernando Lamas. Dairy farm family agrees to a promotion scheme to swim the English Channel together. Choppy musical on the lightweight side. (Dir: Charles Waters, 95 mins.)

Dangerous Years (1947)** Juvenile delinquent William Halop is on trial for murder, learns that he's really the D.A.'s son. In a very small role can be seen Marilyn Monroe, if one watches closely. Fair juvenile delinquency drama.

Dangerous Youth (British, 1958)* Frankie Vaughan, George Baker. Unbelievably bad musical-drama about a rock n' roll singer who is drafted into the service and gets into more trouble in one week than most people would in a lifetime. Incredible script with an appalling performance by Frankie Vaughan in the lead.

Daniel Boone, Trail Blazer (1956)*½ Bruce Bennett, Lon Chaney. Frontiersman leads a wagon train of settlers from the dangers of marauding Indians and other treachery. Humdrum outdoor action drama. (Dir: Albert C. Gannaway, 90 mins.)

Darby O'Gill and the Little People (1959)**½ Albert Sharpe, Janet Munro, Sean Connery, Jimmy O'Dea. Disney presents Irish folklore. Estate caretaker-storyteller Darby O'Gill (Sharpe) is involved in sundry adventures with the leprechauns. Kids might not catch all the dialogue because of the rolling brogue, but the color and attractive decors should hold their interest. (Dir: Robert Stevenson, 93 mins.)

Darby's Rangers (1958)** James Garner, Etchika Choureau. Uneven war drama about a band of heroes led by the hero of them all, Major Wm. Darby, played by James Garner. The supporting cast includes the entire Warner Bros. TV talent roster at that time. (Dir: William Wellman, 121 mins.)

Daring Game (1968)** Lloyd Bridges underwater again, and in the air too, as he messes in a Caribbean political plot. Kids will like it best. With Michael Ansara, Joan Blackman, and Nico Minardos. (Dir: Laslo Benedek, 100 mins.)

Daring Young Man (1943)** Joe E. Brown, Marguerite Chapman. Joe E., rejected for military service, becomes a hero by outwitting Nazi spies. O.K. for kids and Joe E. Brown's many fans. (Dir: Frank Strayer, 73 mins.)

Dark Angel, The (1935)*** Fredric March, Merle Oberon. Remake of a silent film drama about a pair of lovers whose lives are all but destroyed by blindness. Good performances by the cast. (Dir: Sidney Franklin, 110 mins.)

Dark at the Top of the Stairs (1960) *** Robert Preston, Dorothy McGuire, Eve Arden. William Inge's play about a mid-Western family is brought to the screen with all the dramatic moments intact. Preston bellows his way through the film as the head of the family and Dorothy McGuire lends a quiet dignity to the proceedings as his wife. Eve Arden has some moments in the flashy role of Miss McGuire's older and unhappily married sister. (Dir: Delbert Mann, 123 mins.)

Dark City (1950)**½ Charlton Heston, Lizabeth Scott, Viveca Lindfors, Jack Webb. Overblown melodrama about a gambler who becomes a target for murder. Good performances by Heston (his first film) and Jack Webb lift it above routine. (Dir: William Dieterle, 110 mins.)

Dark Command, The (1940)***½ John Wayne, Claire Trevor, Walter Pidgeon, Roy Rogers. After the Civil War, the Southwest is terrorized by Quantrill's raiders, until one man puts a stop to it. Big, actionful western drama, colorful, fine cast. (Dir: Raoul Walsh, 94 mins.)

Dark Corner, The (1946)*** Mark Stevens, Lucille Ball, Clifton Webb. A detective is neatly framed for murder in this well played and generally interesting melodrama. Lucy has some good comedy lines as the detective's secretary. (Dir: Henry Hathaway, 99 mins.)

Dark Delusion (1947)**½ Lionel Barrymore, James Craig. One of Dr. Gillespie's assistants cures a girl of mental disorder. Likeable medical drama. (Dir: Willis Goldbeck, 90 mins.)

Dark Horse, The (1946)**½ Philip Terry, Ann Savage. War vet innocently becomes a political contender, makes it rough for the big boss. Pleasant comedy with a fine comedy

performance by Donald MacBride as the big shot.

Dark Intruder (1965)** Leslie Nielsen, Judi Meredith. Sleuth steps in to aid the police in solving a mysterious series of murders. Okay vest-pocket mystery, short in running time, looks as if it was made for a TV series. (Dir: Harvey Hart, 59 mins.)

Dark Man, The (British, 1951)**½ Maxwell Reed, Natasha Perry. A witness to a murder committed during a robbery is chased by the killer, since she is the only one alive who can identify him. Okay thriller has its share of suspense.

Dark Mirror, The (1946)***½ Olivia de Havilland, Lew Ayres. A doctor has to figure out which twin sister is normal, and which is a demented murderess. Tight, suspenseful mystery, excellent. (Dir: Robert Siodmak, 85 mins.)

Dark of the Sun (British, 1968)** Congo mercenary (Rod Taylor) undertakes a dangerous mission: rescue citizens of a besieged town, and bring back valuable diamonds. Plenty of action helps a threadbare script. With Jim Brown, Yvette Mimieux, Kenneth More. (Dir: Jack Cardiff, 101 mins.)

Dark Passage (1947)**½ Humphrey Bogart, Lauren Bacall. Man escapes from San Quentin to prove himself innocent of murdering his wife. Occasionally good, but uneven melodrama. (Dir: Delmer Daves, 106 mins.)

Dark Past (1949)*** William Holden, Lee J. Cobb, Nina Foch. Psychiatrist breaks down the resistance of a desperate killer holding him captive. Remake of "Blind Alley" has plenty of suspense, good performances. (Dir: Rudolph Mate, 75 mins.)

Dark Purpose (Italian-French, 1963)* Shirley Jones, Rossano Brazzi, George Sanders, Micheline Presle. Dark question is why "Dark Purpose" is so boring despite the attractive cast. There's an easy answer but it doesn't really matter. The nice Italian scenery includes Georgia Moll, in this what evil awaits the pretty secretary (Jones) when she visits an Italian villa. From the "had-I-but-known" school of movie mysteries.

Dark Side of Innocence, The (1976)* Joanna Pettet, Anne Archer, John Anderson, Lawrence Casey, Kim Hunter. Tedious soap opera, focusing on the daughters of an affluent lumber company man. Made-for-TV. (Dir: Jerry Thorpe, 72 mins.)

Dark Victory (1939)***½ Bette Davis, George Brent. Tragic melodrama about a woman who is dying is tastefully spiced with some light comic overtones. It's corny and a real tear jerker but Miss Davis' superb acting makes this one of the best handkerchief soakers. (Dir: Edmund Goulding, 106 mins.)

Dark Victory (1976)*** Elizabeth Montgomery, Anthony Hopkins. Elizabeth Montgomery chose the role of the doomed heroine in Bette Davis's weepy 1939 melodrama as a vehicle for her talents. It's been dusted off, brought up to date and given a handsome production. Concerns a successful, beautiful television executive who discovers she has a short time to live and falls in love with her doctor (British actor Anthony Hopkins). Don't be misled, the film isn't all that downbeat. Ms. Montgomery has seldom been better, and the script avoids making too many excursions into mawkish sentimentality. Made-for-TV. (Dir: Robert Butler, 144 mins.)

Dark Waters (1944)**½ Merle Oberon, Franchot Tone, Thomas Mitchell. A girl returns to her Southern mansion after a shipboard disaster, where she becomes convinced someone is trying to drive her insane. Occasionally suspenseful, generally undistinguished thriller. (Dir: Andre de Toth, 90 mins.)

Darker Than Amber (1970)***½ Rod Taylor, Suzy Kendall, Theodore Bikel. Tough mystery action with more brawn than brain as Taylor plays author John D. MacDonald's character Travis McGee, who lives on a houseboat in Florida and only comes out to play detective or gain revenge on a criminal. Travis falls in love with a girl whose life is endangered by some mobsters, and in true form takes off after them. Well directed by Robert Clouse. Colorful location filming in Florida and the Caribbean add extra flavor. (Dir: Robert Clouse, 97 mins.)

Darling (British, 1965)**** Julie Christie, Dirk Bogarde, Laurence Harvey. A quite remarkable film commenting on the manners, morals and mores of our time and richly deserving of all the awards it got, including the Academy Award for Julie Christie's stunning performance which was given, and the Academy Award for best film which it did not receive. Perceptive, cynical, deftly written portrait of a young London model who decides to climb the social ladder quickly by jumping, in rather unceremonious fashion, in and out of assorted beds. Brilliantly directed by John Schlesinger, imaginatively edited, and featuring the radiant performance of the ravishing Miss Christie, this is a moving, often amusing and invariably honest film. (Dir: John Schlesinger, 122 mins.)

Darling, How Could You (1951)** Joan Fontaine, John Lund, Mona Freeman. Sentimental drama of an imaginative girl whose fantasies nearly wreck her parents' domestic life. Inoffensive but overly sweet, slow-moving. (Dir: Mitchell Leisen, 96 mins.)

Darling Lili (1970)½ Julie Andrews, Rock Hudson, Jeremy Kemp, Lance Percival. Some twenty million dollars was invested in this glamorous dinosaur that quickly degenerates into self-parody. WW I, that musical comedy natural, is the setting for what might have been a charming spoof of the Mata Hari legend. Miss Andrews, who projects the sex appeal of an angry nun, plays the English music hall star alias German spy who must coax secrets from flyboy Hudson. Musical interludes blend with romantic interludes which give way to battle interludes which blend into ennui. Produced, directed and co-written by Blake Edwards. A box-office and artistic disaster. (Dir: Blake Edwards, 136 mins.)

Date at Midnight (British, 1959)** Paul Carpenter, Jean Aubrey. Man with a past is suspected of foul play when a tragedy occurs. Ordinary melodrama.

Date Bait (1960)* Gary Clark, Marlo Ryan. Youngsters planning to marry secretly find trouble in the form of her former boyfriend, now a dope addict. Low grade—a good blanket title for these things could be "Teen Trash."

Date with Death (1959)* Robert Clarke, Liz Renay, Gerald Mohr. Wanderer is mistaken for a New York cop, is sworn in as police chief of a town, and proceeds to clean up the rackets. Weak crime melodrama suffers from amateurish performances, bad direction.

Date with Judy, A (1947)**½ Elizabeth Taylor, Jane Powell, Wallace Beery. The youngsters may enjoy this juvenile comedy but outside of some good musical numbers and the sight of Elizabeth Taylor as she reached physical maturity, it's not much of a film. (Dir: Richard Thorpe, 113 mins.)

Daughter of Dr. Jekyll (1957)* Gloria Talbott, Arthur Shields. Girl thinks she turns into a monster at night. Ghastly. (Dir: Edgar Ulmer, 69 mins.)

Daughter of Rosie O'Grady, The (1950)**½ June Haver, Gordon MacRae, James Barton. A gay, tuneful turn of the century musical comedy film. Miss Haver and Mr. MacRae sing and dance delightfully and take care of the romance department. James Barton plays June Haver's father, who forbids her to seek a career on the stage. Look for Debbie Reynolds in a small role as June's sister. (Dir: David Butler, 104 mins.)

Daughter of the Mind (1969)**½ Gene Tierney, Ray Milland, Don Murray. Made-for-TV feature based on Paul Gallico's book "The Hand of Mary Constable." Ray Milland is cast as a professor of cybernetics who claims he is visited by his recently killed young daughter's spirit. The plot thickens when government officials become involved and a professor of parapsychology (Don Murray) also enters the picture. (Dir: Walter Grauman, 73 mins.)

Daughters Courageous (1939)*** John Garfield, Claude Rains, Lane Sisters. Trying to cash in on the box office success of "Four Daughters," they assembled the same cast and put them through their paces again. They would have made a sequel but they killed Garfield in the original. Good acting still makes it passable. (Dir: Michael Curtiz, 120 mins.)

Daughters of Destiny (French, 1955)** Claudette Colbert, Michele Morgan, Martine Carol. Triple tale of three women of history and how their fortunes are changed—Queen Elizabeth, Joan of Arc, and Lysistrata. Elaborate production negated by plodding script, sluggish movement. (Dir: Marcel Dagliero, 94 mins.)

Daughters of Joshua Cabe (1972)** Buddy Ebsen, Sandra Dee, Lesley Warren, Karen Valentine, Jack Elam. Moderately entertaining Western comedy-drama, with Ebsen as a rancher-trapper who has to come up with three long-lost daughters in order to keep his land when a new homesteaders' law is passed. Elam, as a grizzled sidekick of Ebsen's, steals the show. Made-for-TV. (Dir: Philip Leacock, 72 mins.)

Daughters of Joshua Cabe Return, The (1975)** Dan Dailey, Dub Taylor, Ronne Troup, Carl Betz. If you enjoyed the antics of the three less-than-respectable girls who are hired to portray the daughters of a wily rancher in the first film, here's the follow-up with a complete cast change. Dan Dailey heads the cast in the role of the rancher, created by Buddy Ebsen the first time around. Made-for-TV. (Dir: David Lowell Rich, 72 mins.)

Daughters of Satan (1972)*½ Tom Selleck, Barra Grant. A stupid witch story. An alleged intellectual is enticed by a painting of three witches being burned, because one of the witches resembles his wife. Set in Manila, the story is as contrived as the characters are false. (Dir: Hollingsworth Morse, 90 mins.)

David and Bathsheba (1952)**½ Gregory Peck, Susan Hayward. Typical Biblical epic with all the stops pulled—lavish sets, sumptuous costumes, posing actors and wooden dialogue. Women will buy the love story aspects of the tale of King David (Greg Peck) and the ravishing Bathsheba (Susan Hayward) and the adventure-seeking males have a few battle scenes to keep their attention. (Dir: Henry King, 116 mins.)

David and Goliath (1961)** Orson Welles, Ivo Payer. Italian-made version of the Biblical tale. Usual stuff. (Dir: Richard Potter, 95 mins.)

David and Lisa (1962)**** Keir Dullea, Janet Margolin. Sensitively written, beautifully acted and altogether touching story of two mentally disturbed youngsters finding happiness and faith. Low budget "sleeper" was Academy Award nominee for first time director Frank Perry. (Dir: Frank Perry, 94 mins.)

David Copperfield (1935)**** W. C. Fields, Lionel Barrymore, Maureen O'Sullivan. If TV doesn't cut it to ribbons, you'll love this fine, sensitive and sincere adaptation of the Dickens novel. It originally ran 2 hours and thirteen minutes so you'll be able to check and see how much has been snipped for commercials. (Dir: George Cukor, 133 mins.)

David Copperfield (1970)*** Ralph Richardson, Michael Redgrave, Edith Evans. Marvelous TV film. Charles Dickens' novel comes to life with inspired casting in a first-class production. (W. C. Fields fans may even forget the master's Mr. Micawber in the old MGM picture.) There are flaws in this adaptation, and Dickens purists may object to some of it, but most viewers—young and old alike—will be enthralled. The cast of British stalwarts are almost all superb. Made-for-TV. (Dir: Delbert Mann, 100 mins.)

David Holzman's Diary (1968)*** David Holzman, Eileen Dietz, Louise Levine. An imaginative low-budget black and white independently made feature about movie-making and movie-makers. There's one perceptive street-corner interview with a tart, and inventive touches throughout. Written, produced and directed by Jim McBride on location in New York. (74 mins.)

Davy Crockett, Indian Scout (1950)** George Montgomery, Ellen Drew. Army scout looks into a series of wagon train attacks. Average outdoor action drama, those marauding Injuns again. (Dir: Lew Landers, 71 mins.)

Dawn at Socorro (1954)**½ Piper Laurie, Rory Calhoun, David Brian. A good cast and a better than average western plot make this one entertaining. Calhoun plays a gunfighter who's forced to think about his life when his health, if not his trigger finger, starts to slip. (Dir: George Sherman, 81 mins.)

Dawn Patrol (1938)***½ Errol Flynn, Basil Rathbone, David Niven. Exciting tale of the men of Britain's Royal Flying Corps during World War I. Conflict concerns the torment of making command decisions and sending your comrades to certain death just to gain an objective. (Dir: Edmund Goulding, 120 mins.)

Day and the Hour, The (French, 1963)*** Simone Signoret, Stuart Whitman, Genevieve Page. Old-fashioned, uneven, but frequently absorbing thanks to veteran director Rene Clement. Melodrama set in Nazi-occupied France during World War II. Signoret's husband has been nailed by the Nazis and she befriends Whitman. Exciting scene aboard the train to Toulouse. Film buffs please note—one of the two assistant directors on this film was the brilliant Costa-Gavras who went on to helm "Z" and "The Conformist." Partially dubbed.

Day at the Races, A (1937)***½ Marx Brothers, Allan Jones. The boys are turned loose at a race track and when Chico, as a tout, tries to give Groucho a tip you'll choke with laughter. Not their best but still hilarious. (Dir: Sam Wood, 111 mins.)

Day For Night (France, 1972)**** Francois Truffaut, Jacqueline Bisset, Jean-Pierre Léaud, Valentina Cortesa. Francois Truffaut's joyous, exhilarating comedy, an affectionate satire on the art and madness of making movies. Truffaut himself plays a film director named Ferrand and he tells his crew, "Before starting I hope to make a fine movie. Halfway through, I hope to make a movie." Well, the movie in a movie is called "Meet Pamela," and we don't ever see the finished version. But the complete "Day For Night" is a lighthearted, charming beauty, faultlessly acted by Truffaut himself and the rest of a carefully chosen cast. Truffaut co-authored the screenplay. (Dir: Francois Truffaut, 116 mins.)

Day of Fury, A (1956)** Dale Robertson, Jock Mahoney. The old plot gimmick of the marshal and an outlaw being friends from the past gets more mileage in this slow moving opus. Robertson is well cast as a charming villain who finally gets his comeuppance. (Dir: Harmon Jones, 80 mins.)

Day of the Bad Man (1958)** Fred MacMurray, Joan Weldon, John Ericson. Circuit judge has to sentence a convicted killer to death and face the rage of the man's brothers. Western goes in for suspense, succeeds in being merely routine. (Dir: Harry Keller, 81 mins.)

Day of the Dolphin, The (1973)**½ George C. Scott, Trish Van Devere, Paul Sorvino, Fritz Weaver. Misguided fable about the efforts of a dedicated scientist (Scott) trying to train a dolphin to talk, while simultaneously participating in a counter-intelligence scheme involving political assassination. Buck Henry's screenplay touches a number of genres without securing a firm foothold in any particular one—the result is occasional comedy or suspense but never genuine audience involvement. Some extraordinary scenes give the real life sounds made by dolphins swimming and playing and "communicating with each other." (Dir: Mike Nichols, 104 mins.)

Day of the Evil Gun (1968)**½ Glenn Ford, Arthur Kennedy, Dean Jagger, Nico Minardos. Reasonably suspenseful western about a search for women kidnaped by Apaches. Good performances. A made-for-TV pic, although this was actually released to theaters first. (Dir: Jerry Thorpe, 93 mins.)

Day of the Jackal, The (British-French, 1973)***½ Edward Fox, Cyril Cusack, Delphine Seyrig. High suspense as an assassin (Fox) is hired by French generals to kill Charles de Gaulle. Intensive manhunt is juxtaposed with Fox's preparation for the killing. Acting and the fine European locations are the highpoints. Fox's portrait of the ruthless, anonymous killer is necessarily unemotional, and he's backed by a strong international cast. (Dir: Fred Zinnemann, 141 mins.)

Day of the Locust, The (1975)***½ Donald Sutherland, Karen Black, Burgess Meredith, William Atherton, Geraldine Page. Memorable, harrowing, long-awaited adaptation of Nathanael West's 1939 novel, a crystalization of his long Hollywood experience as a screen writer. There are shortcomings in "Locust"—Karen Black is far too old, e.g., to play the vulnerable, 17-year-old heroine of West's novel. William Atherton is impressive in his debut in a major role playing an impressionable "civilized" young Yale screen writer trying to cope and succeed in Hollywood circa '38. Schlesinger builds to an unforgettable climax of a movie premiere which becomes a riotous nightmare. Burgess Meredith won an Academy nomination for his endearing performance as a washed-up vaudevillian still selling dreams. Cinematographer Conrad Hall deserves special credit, and got an Academy Award

nomination for his work. Screenplay by Waldo Salt. (Dir: John Schlesinger, 140 mins.)

Day of the Outlaw (1959)** Robert Ryan, Burl Ives, Tina Louise. Outlaws, with their leader seriously wounded and the Cavalry in hot pursuit, take over a western community and terrorize the townspeople. Gloomy western, some good blizzard scenes, adequate performances. (Dir: Andre de Toth, 90 mins.)

Day of the Triffids (British, 1963)*** Howard Keel, Nicole Maurey. A shower of meteorites strikes most of the earth blind, then comes a hail of seeds blossoming into fast-growing, killing plants. Eerie sci-fi thriller rates with the better efforts of its type; suspenseful, good special effects. (Dir: Steve Sekely, 93 mins.)

Day that Shook the World, The (Italy-Yugoslavia, 1976)*½ Christopher Plummer, Florinda Bolkan, Maximilian Schell. Inept drama of one of the most important and dramatic events of this century, the assassination of Archduke Ferdinand in Sarajevo on June 28, 1914, that led inexorably to the outbreak of World War I. The backgrounds of the Serbian nationalists who were responsible for the politically-motivated killing are never adequately explained, to say nothing of the real melodramatic events leading up to the momentous slaying. (Dir: Veljko Bulajic.)

Day the Earth Caught Fire, The (British, 1962)***½ Edward Judd, Janet Munro, Leo McKern. In the front rank of sci-fi thrillers, this one is almost too realistic for comfort. Nuclear tests at the North and South Poles shift the earth's orbit, send the planet plummeting toward the sun. The tension runs high throughout, thanks to expert scripting and direction. (Dir: Val Guest, 90 mins.)

Day the Earth Moved, The (1974)** Jackie Cooper, Cleavon Little, William Windom, Beverly Garland. Another crisis film about a series of unexplained earthquakes. Jackie Cooper and Cleavon Little are a pair of aerial photographers who notice some suspicious blurs in photos they have taken. Moderately engrossing. Made-for-TV. (Dir: Robert Michael Lewis, 72 mins.)

Day the Earth Stood Still, The (1951) *** Michael Rennie, Patricia Neal. Better than average science-fiction

172

film with top stars and a good script. Rennie plays the man from another planet but not with the obvious gimmicks that space travelers in cheaper films always employ. Good for adults as well as the younger set. (Dir: Robert Wise, 92 mins.)

Day the Fish Came Out, The (Greek-British, 1967)* Tom Courtenay, Candice Bergen, Sam Wanamaker, Colin Blakely. Normally talented writer-producer-director Michael Cacoyannis (responsible for "Zorba the Greek") lays an egg-plant with this limp Greek serving about the military trying to retrieve secret material dropped off a Greek island. Effetely awful throughout, including the costumes which Cacoyannis got around to designing himself. (Dir: Michael Cacoyannis, 109 mins.)

Day the Sky Exploded, The (German, 1958)*½ Paul Hubschmid, Madeleine Fischer. Exploded missile in outer space spells potential disaster for Earth. Gadgety sci-fi, occasional interesting special effects floating in a welter of wordage. English-dubbed. (Dir: Paolo Heusch, 80 mins.)

Day the World Ended, The (1956)*½ Richard Denning, Lori Nelson. Survivors of an atomic war find a valley with a house still uncontaminated, battle among themselves. Sci-fi thriller tries to say something profound and doesn't. (Dir: Roger Corman, 81 mins.)

Day They Robbed the Bank of England, The (British, 1960)*** Peter O'Toole, Hugh Griffith, Elizabeth Sellars, Aldo Ray. "They" are Irish dissidents, who try the big heist in 1901. Considerable suspense in this crime yarn. O'Toole shows the promise fulfilled later, portraying the arm of the law.

Day to Remember, A (British, 1955) **½ Joan Rice, Donald Sinden. The part-time owner of an English pub prepares for an outing to France. Very British, mild comedy. (100 mins.)

Daybreak (British, 1946)** Ann Todd, Eric Portman. The life and loves of an executioner are on exhibition in this melodrama. Dull film fare.

Daydreamer, The (1966)*** Cyril Ritchard, Paul O'Keefe, Ray Bolger. A very entertaining animated and live musical adventure. Paul O'Keefe plays a young Hans Christian Andersen who has many adventures with a series of wonderful characters from the Andersen fairy tales. Voices are supplied by such stars as Tallulah Bankhead, Victor Borge, Burl Ives, and Terry-Thomas. (Dir: Jules Bass, 98 mins.)

Days of Glory (1943)**½ Gregory Peck, Tamara Toumanova. Russian guerrillas beat back the Nazi enemy. Slow moving war drama. Well acted. (Dir: Jacques Tourneur, 86 mins.)

Days of 36 (Greek, 1972)** George Kiritsis, Tharos Grammenos. Tries, without much success, to repeat the techniques of "Z" in this story of a political episode in Athens in 1936 at the beginning of the dictatorship. Does create some feeling of how a mood of terror and neo-fascism is created in a populace. Written and directed by Theo Angelopoulos. English subtitles. (110 mins.)

Days of Thrills and Laughter (1961) ***½ Third compilation film made by Robert Youngson featuring silent movie clips, and some of it is fabulous. Scenes of comedy and excitement, ranging from Charlie Chaplin, Laurel and Hardy, the Keystone Kops and Fatty Arbuckle to Douglas Fairbanks and Pearl White. Some little-seen gems in this collection of early movie chuckles and thrills. (Dir: Robert Youngson, 93 mins.)

Days of Wine and Roses (1962) ***½ Jack Lemmon, Lee Remick, J. P. Miller's memorable "Playhouse 90" drama about a young couple's desperate bout with alcoholism, expanded to the screen, loses some of its bite in the process, but remains pretty strong stuff. The startling realism of the story of two seemingly normal people whose lives are shattered by drink, fine acting by the two stars. Jack Lemmon is a quite marvelous lush. (Dir: Blake Edwards, 117 mins.)

Dayton's Devils (1968)** Leslie Nielsen, Lainie Kazan, Rory Calhoun. Action and romantic interest. An ex-Army colonel trains a team of experts in order to pull a $1.5 million heist at a Strategic Air Command base. Routine. This was, unfortunately, Lainie Kazan's film debut, but she comes off well singing "Sunny." (Dir: Jack Shea, 103 mins.)

De L'Amour (France, 1965)**½ Anna Karina, Michel Piccoli, Elsa

Martinelli, Jean Sorel. Free adaptation of Stendhal's book to a modern-day setting: a series of vignettes on love and seduction. Amusing fluff. (Dir: Jean Aurel, 90 mins.)

Dead Don't Die, The (1975) ½ George Hamilton, Ray Milland, Joan Blondell, Linda Cristal, Ralph Meeker. Hamilton goes sleuthing in this 30's action yarn. Supposedly a scare piece! Made-for-TV. (Dir: Curtis Harrington, 72 mins.)

Dead End (1937)***½ Humphrey Bogart, Joel McCrea, Sylvia Sidney, Claire Trevor. A film classic. Based on the successful Broadway play about the slums and the youngsters who fight for survival against their environment with the aid of social workers. A fine mixture of comedy and social drama, excellently played by a choice cast. (Dir: William Wyler, 93 mins.)

Dead Eyes of London (German, 1961) *½ Karin Baal, Joachim Fuchsberger. Scotland Yard investigates some gruesome insurance murders. Overdone Edgar Wallace mystery with a Teutonic touch.

Dead Heat on a Merry-Go-Round (1966)***½ James Coburn, Camilla Sparv. James Coburn is well cast as one of the great con artists of all time. After he manages to win a parole from prison, Coburn sets up an ingenious bank heist, marries a gorgeous girl, impersonates about half-a-dozen characters, robs some wealthy dames, pulls off the bank job and, of course, gets away with it all. It's entertaining from start to finish, thanks to Coburn's flip, charming performance, and to writer-director Bernard Girard. (104 mins.)

Dead Man on the Run (1975)** Peter Graves, Tom Rosqui, Mills Watson. Graves stars in this violent action series pilot, filmed in New Orleans. The personable Mr. Graves gives chase around the old, colorful river city. Made-for-TV. (Dir: Bruce Bilson, 72 mins.)

Dead Man's Chest (British, 1966)** John Thaw, Ann Firbank, John Meillon. Two young journalists devise a publicity stunt wherein one is to play dead in a trunk. But the trunk is stolen, leading to a charge of murder. Competent mystery melodrama provides enough twists in its short running time.

Dead Men Tell No Tales (1971)** Christopher George, Judy Carne. As an attractive young couple, George and Miss Carne play hide-and-seek with hoods in this moderately entertaining film. Made-for-TV. (Dir: Walter Grauman, 73 mins.)

Dead of Night (British, 1946)**** Michael Redgrave, Googie Withers, Mervyn Johns. A man who has had a strange dream visits in the country, where other guests relate how some dream of theirs has had basis in fact. Fine spine-tingling episodic thriller, a true suspense-rouser. The sequence with Redgrave is especially spellbinding. (102 mins.)

Dead Reckoning (1947)*** Humphrey Bogart, Lizabeth Scott. Occasionally exciting chase melodrama about a veteran investigating the disappearance of his hero buddy. Bogart is excellent, as usual. (Dir: John Cromwell, 100 mins.)

Dead Ringer (1964)**½ Bette Davis, Karl Malden, Peter Lawford. Bette Davis fans will adore her histrionics in this typical B.D. film. Bette, the proprietress of a saloon, kills her look-alike sister and takes over her home and jewels. It's a cushy position until dead sister's boyfriend catches on, and the plot thickens and thickens. (Dir: Paul Henreid, 115 mins.)

Dead Run (French-Italian, 1969)**½ Peter Lawford, Ira Furstenberg. There's enough plot in this superspy versus spy versus CIA agent yarn for a dozen films. Peter Lawford is the topcoat-clad agent who is hot on the trail of an international crime organization which steals top U.S. documents for resale to an enemy power. The on-location filming in Berlin, Munich, and Paris at least offers a vicarious scenic tour for home viewers. (Director: Christian-Jaque, 97 mins.)

Dead to the World (1962)* Reedy Talton, Jana Pearce. Political boss pushing the investigation of a State Department employee for treason is murdered—the employee finds the killer and clears his name. Awful mystery, amateurish throughout.

Deadfall (British, 1968)*½ Michael Caine, Giovanna Ralli. Turgid tale of a jewel thief (Michael Caine) whose love affair proves his undoing. Lamentably pretentious script and direction by the usually capable Bryan Forbes buries a lot of good performers. With Eric Portman,

Nanette Newman. (Dir: Bryan Forbes, 120 mins.)

Deadlier Than the Male (French, 1957)**½ Jean Gabin, Daniele Delorme. Well acted (mainly by Gabin) drama about a young girl who plots to marry and murder her mother's ex-husband. Sounds provocative but not in the league of top French suspense shockers. (Dir: Julien Duvivier, 104 mins.)

Deadlier Than the Male (British, 1967)**½ Richard Johnson, Elke Sommer, Sylva Koscina. The return of Bulldog Drummond (Johnson) as the hardy sleuth comes up against a pair of beautiful but deadly assassins (Sommer & Koscina). Amusing in a lowbrow bulldog way. (Ronald Colman first played Bulldog in the 1929 opus "Bulldog Drummond"). With Suzanna Leigh, Steve Carlson. (Dir: Ralph Thomas, 101 mins.)

Deadliest Season, The (1977)**½ Michael Moriarty, Kevin Conway, Meryl Streep, Andrew Duggan, Patrick O'Neal, Sully Boyer. Provocative drama, extremely well written by Ernest Kinoy, about the world of professional ice hockey and the bloodthirsty, violent sport it has become to attract paying audiences and TV watchers. Moriarty gives a well-rounded performance as the run-of-the-mill hockey player who decides to become a "goon"—someone who incites mayhem and violence during a game. When he accidentally kills another player during a game, he is arrested and tried. One of the few dramas to deal with the way TV is brutalizing our sports and our society. Made-for-TV. (Dir: Robert Markowitz, 110 mins.)

Deadliest Sin (British, 1955)** Sydney Chaplin, Audrey Dalton. A man is marked for death when he attempts to confess an accidental shooting. Grim, slow melodrama. (Dir: Ken Hughes, 75 mins.)

Deadline, U.S.A. (1952)*** Humphrey Bogart, Kim Hunter, Ethel Barrymore. Engrossing newspaper drama without the usual "city room" phoniness. Bogart is excellent as the editor of a large city paper who has to fight the underworld and keep the paper's publisher, superbly portrayed by the late Miss Barrymore, from throwing in the towel and selling out. The scenes between these two stars are standouts. Kim Hunter is wasted in a small role as Bogart's ex-wife. (Dir: Richard Brooks, 87 mins.)

Deadlock (1969)*** Leslie Nielsen, Hari Rhodes. Better-than-average, hard-hitting police drama about racial tensions in the ghetto of a large west coast city. Well produced action yarn with a good feel for earthy jargon and strong performances by Leslie Nielsen as a fair but firm police lieutenant, and Hari Rhodes as the ambitious Negro district attorney with his eye on the Senate. The scenes between Rhodes and Nielsen are the meatiest of the film, but watch for talented Ruby Dee in one scene playing a prostitute being questioned about the murder. Made as a pilot film for a TV series. (Dir: Lamont Johnson, 99 mins.)

Deadly Affair (1967)*** James Mason, Simone Signoret, Maximilian Schell, Lynn Redgrave. Engrossing detective drama set amid the world of espionage and agents. James Mason is excellent as a British agent who sets out to uncover the hidden facts behind a British government employee's suicide. The plot twists and turns and, although you may be a bit ahead of the action at times, the film sustains interest. In addition to Mason, other top performances include Simone Signoret as a deeply troubled woman and Harry Andrews as a detective. Sidney Lumet directed the yarn based on the John le Carré novel "Call for the Dead." (Dir: Sidney Lumet, 107 mins.)

Deadly Bees, The (1967)**½ Frank Finlay, Suzanna Leigh. This British film, based on H. F. Heard's horror classic "A Taste for Honey," starts off well, but disintegrates into stark melodrama before the finale. It's all about a beekeeper who trains a swarm of giant killer bees, and a young lady who almost becomes a victim. (Dir: Freddie Francis, 85 mins.)

Deadly Companions, The (1962)*** Maureen O'Hara, Brian Keith, Steve Cochran. A gunslinger escorts a dance hall hostess through Apache territory on a perilous journey. Good western with a script above the usual run, expert direction, capable performances. (Dir: Sam Peckinpah, 90 mins.)

Deadly Decision (German, 1957)**½ O. E. Hasse, Adrian Hoven. Well-made film telling the remarkable true story of Canaris, a top spy who had the Nazis fooled. O. E. Hasse and a fine German cast make the film tense and exciting.

Deadly Decoy, The (French, 1962)*½ Roger Hanin, Roger Dumas. Ace secret agent looks into a planned political assassination. Low grade action melodrama; plenty of action, little sense. Dubbed in English.

Deadly Dream, The (1971)**½ Lloyd Bridges, Janet Leigh, Carl Betz, Leif Erickson. Bridges wanders through a nightmare world and his own seemingly real one . . . but the question posed here is "which world is the real one?" The strange film builds interest following Bridges, a brilliant scientist, as he goes slowly mad. Leigh, as his wife, looks sensational. Made-for-TV. (Dir: Alf Kjellin, 72 mins.)

Deadly Game, The (1976)**½ David Birney, Allen Garfield, Walter McGinn, Lane Bradbury. A pilot for a TV series with Birney taking over the role of Serpico, the famous New York cop who had the nerve to finger corruption within the Police Department. Birney is no Al Pacino, but he's no slouch here either, working from the inside on a drug smuggling racket among dock workers! Made-for-TV. (Dir: Robert Collins, 98 mins.)

Deadly Harvest (1972)*** Richard Boone, Patty Duke. Interesting chase drama filmed in California's Napa Valley benefits greatly from good performances by Boone and Miss Duke. Boone supplies the tang, playing a taciturn, suspicious old wine-grower who defected from an Iron Curtain country years ago, and is now marked for assassination. Duke is a wandering songwriter who sticks with the old winegrower during the murder attempts, and their growing relationship merits attention. Made-for-TV. (Dir: Michael O'Herlihy, 73 mins.)

Deadly Mantis, The (1957)**½ Craig Stevens, William Hopper. Scientist works feverishly to stop a giant mantis heading south from the polar regions. As these thrillers go, it's a fairly good one—clever special effects, should please the horror fans.

Deadly Record (British, 1960)** Lee Patterson, Barbara Shelley. Pilot is accused of murdering his estranged wife, escapes and sets out to clear himself. Routine whodunit, no sur-prises. (Dir: Nathan Juran, 78 mins).

Deadly Tower, The (1975)* Kurt Russell, Ned Beatty, John Forsythe, Richard Yniguez, Pernell Roberts. Another irresponsible film from TV-land. Based on fact, this is the dramatization of a young sniper who climbed up the tower at the University of Texas and fired upon innocent passersby, killing 13 people and wounding 33 others. The film is technically well done and the actors, including Kurt Russell in the leading role, do well. A tragic footnote: a newspaper account, a few days after this film was first shown on TV in 1975, reported on a man who saw this film on TV and went out with his shotgun and killed a few innocent people. Made-for-TV. (Dir: Jerry Jamesson, 105 mins.)

Deadly Trackers, The (1973)½ Richard Harris, Rod Taylor, Isela Varga. Director Samuel Fuller tried to turn his short story, "Riata," into a film but was fired from the project. Without his guiding hand, this turns into a terrible, violent revenge drama with Harris on the trail of his wife's murderers. (Dir: Barry Shear, 104 mins.)

Deadly Triangle, The (1977)** Dale Robinette, Diana Muldaur, Robert Lansing. Another pilot film which has one advantage over most of the others—the gorgeous location scenery of Sun Valley, Idaho. Dale Robinette stars as a former Olympic downhill skiing champion who takes to the slopes as the sheriff of Sun Valley. A member of a ski team training in the area is killed, and Sheriff Robinette is called in to investigate. (Dir: Charles S. Dubin, 79 mins.)

Deadwood '76 (1964)* Arch Hall Jr., Robert Dix. Shoddy western about a Civil War vet who's mistaken for Billy the Kid, and the resulting consequences. Poor all around.

Dealing: Or the Berkeley-to-Boston-Forty-Bricks-Lost-Bag-Blues (1972) ** Richard Lyons, Barbara Hershey, John Lithgrow. Based on the novel by Michael and Douglas Crichton dealing with Peter, a bored Harvard Law student (Lyons) who moves grass from Berkeley to Boston for dealer John (Lithgrow). Underwearless girl friend Susan (Hershey) gets busted helping and Peter attempts to blackmail a crooked detective to free her. No assertion of values makes for little drama. Lyons' dreary performance doesn't help matters. (Dir: Paul Williams, 88 mins.)

Dear Brigitte (1965)**½ James Stewart, Glynis Johns. Homey family comedy that doesn't come off as successfully as it should have. Papa Stewart tries to cope with his young son's problem—it seems that he has developed a big .crush on Brigitte Bardot and keeps sending her fan letters. Finally Stewart and his little boy go to Paris and visit the celebrated French star. (Dir: Henry Koster, 100 mins.)

Dear Caroline (French, 1951)** Martine Carol, Jacques Dacqmine. Romantic adventures of a nobleman's daughter in finding love and excitement at the time of the French Revolution. The novel "Caroline Cherie" was a big-seller, the film version is elaborate but on the level of a dime novel. English-dubbed.

Dear Heart (1965)*** Glenn Ford, Geraldine Page, Angela Lansbury. This is the type of sentimental romance which earns the label of "heartwarming" without even trying too hard. Ford is a salesman who meets and woos spinster postmistress Geraldine Page in New York City during a convention. There's more gushing sentiment than need be, but the good cast keeps things under control. Page is customarily expert. (Dir: Delbert Mann, 114 mins.)

Dear Murderer (British, 1948)** Eric Portman, Greta Gynt. A businessman murders his unfaithful wife's lover, but finds that the solution isn't as simple as all that. Passable melodrama, definitely not for Junior. Dennis Price.

Dear Ruth (1947)**½ Joan Caulfield, William Holden. Topical farce of 1947 is now rather obvious comedy about a youngster who has a hot correspondence with a soldier while posing as her older, attractive sister. (Dir: William D. Russell, 95 mins.)

Dear Wife (1949)*** William Holden, Joan Caulfield, Mona Freeman, Billy DeWolfe. "Dear Ruth" is now married, and her teenage sister launches a campaign to get her husband to the State Senate, which disrupts things. Some good laughs in this cleverly directed domestic comedy. (Dir: Richard Haydn, 88 mins.)

Death Among Friends (1975)* Kate Reid, Martin Balsam, Jack Cassidy, Paul Henreid. Reid plays a lady sleuth, working out of the Los Angeles homicide office, investigating a Bel Air murder. The suspects are portrayed by pros like Balsam, Cassidy and Henreid in hopes of stifling audience yawns, but high-life in Bel Air turns out to be a bore. Made-for-TV. (Dir: Paul Wendkos, 72 mins.)

Death at Love House (1976)*½ Robert Wagner, Kate Jackson, Sylvia Sidney, Joan Blondell. Clumsy "high-camp." A big Hollywood mansion almost steals the attention from the cast in this tale about a big movie star of the thirties who still has a mysterious hold on the son of one of her lovers. Veteran stars like the Misses Blondell, Sidney, Dorothy Lamour and John Carradine have some fun with their cameo roles. Made-for-TV. (Dir: E. W. Swackhamer, 72 mins.)

Death Be Not Proud (1975)***½ Arthur Hill, Jane Alexander, Robby Benson. A moving film based on a memoir by John Gunther, in which he wrote about his teenaged son's valiant bout with cancer and the effect the boy's unflagging efforts to beat the unbeatable had on his divorced parents. Although this is a story dealing with death, it is not downbeat. The scenes in which Arthur Hill, as Gunther, and Jane Alexander, as the boy's mother, do their best to cope with the daily agony of their lives, watching their son holding on to hope, are poignant. Robby Benson, in the pivotal, difficult role of Johnny Gunther, is excellent, and the scene in which he comes forth to accept his diploma at his high school graduation will leave you limp. Made-for-TV. (Dir: Donald Wrye, 100 mins.)

Death Cruise (1974)*½ Richard Long, Polly Bergen, Edward Albert, Kate Jackson, Celeste Holm. Yarn about a luxury cruise that turns out to be a death ship for five out of six passengers, who all won the trip in a contest. It's well cast, with a surprise ending. Made-for-TV. (Dir: Ralph Senensky, 72 mins.)

Death in Small Doses (1957)** Peter Graves, Mala Powers, Chuck Conners. When "pep" pills cause accidents among truck drivers, an investigation is started. Pep pill yarn

177

may put you to sleep. (Dir: Joseph M. Newman, 79 mins.)

Death in Venice (Italy, 1971)*** Dirk Bogarde, Bjorn Andresen, Silvana Mangano, Marisa Berenson. It may not simply be possible to really do full cinematic justice to Thomas Mann's classic, complicated, richly textured novella published in 1913. But Visconti has assuredly captured the visual quality, the look and feel of Venice circa 1911, a city dying of a secret pestilence. Bogarde plays, with great restraint, an aging, world-famous homosexual writer who has developed an uncontrollable passion for a ravishing young boy (Andresen). Andresen is ravishing, so is Visconti's cinematic eye. Directed and co-authored by Luchino Visconti. Venice has never looked more beautiful or decadent. (130 mins.)

Death Is a Woman (1965)** Mark Burns, William Dexter. Mediocre undercover-agent story set in the Mediterranean. There are no name stars in this one, and the plot is merely serviceable.

Death of a Cyclist—See: Age of Infidelity

Death of a Gunfighter (1969)**½ Richard Widmark, Lena Horne. Don't let the title fool you if you're a western action fan—this is a slow-moving character study of a small-town marshal (R. Widmark) who is no longer needed by the townspeople. Widmark is effective in the leading role. Lena Horne, neglected by Hollywood during the 1960's, is cast in the non-singing role of his long-standing mistress. Offbeat, quiet western. Movie buffs please note that this is one of the few films in recent years to have been directed by two people—Robert Totten, who shot the first part of the movie, and Don Siegel, responsible for the last section. (100 mins.)

Death of a Salesman (1952)**** Fredric March, Mildred Dunnock, Kevin McCarthy. A very moving and forceful filmization of Arthur Miller's Pulitzer Prize winning play about fading salesman Willy Loman and his emotionally charged relationships with his family. Superb performances and interesting film technique add to its appeal. March, one of our handful of genuinely distinguished stage actors, is at the top

of his charm. (Dir: Laslo Benedek, 115 mins.)

Death of a Scoundrel (1956)** George Sanders, Zsa Zsa Gabor, Yvonne DeCarlo. A silly and obvious drama about a suave scoundrel who lives by his charm. Zsa Zsa Gabor plays one of the victims which certainly is a switch. (Dir: Charles Martin, 119 mins.)

Death of Innocence (1971)**½ Shelley Winters, Tish Sterling. Playing a Utah mother, Miss Winters arrives in New York with husband to attend daughter's murder trial, certain it's all a mistake. Mom slowly faces the idea her daughter might be guilty. Filmed partly in New York, with scenes in the old Women's Detention Home and city streets, the show delivers solid performances from cast. Good support from Tish Sterling, Arthur Kennedy, Ann Sothern, and newcomer Richard Bright. Made-for-TV. (Dir: Paul Wendkos, 73 mins.)

Death of Ritchie, The (1977)***½ Ben Gazzara, Robby Benson, Eileen Brennan. Here's a sleeper—a well-made emotional drama about a teen-aged drug addict who can't give up the habit. Robby Benson is quite believable as the kid on drugs, needing help from his parents and from group therapy, since he can't cope on his own. Gazzara plays the father, a man too busy to take the time to really deal with his son's addiction, but one who attempts too late to reach out to the hooked teenager. Watch this show because it spells out the horrors of drugs. Based on a real case history. Made-for-TV. (Dir: Paul Wendkos, 103 mins.)

Death of Tarzan, The (Czechoslovakia, 1962)*** Rudolph Hrusinsky, Jana Stepankova. Don't be put off by the title. This deft Czech satire has nothing whatever to do with the moronic "Tarzan" films based on the Edgar Rice Burroughs character. An odd, winning combination of farce and drama generated by yet another (Jaroslav Balik) director of the ill-fated Czech film renaissance. Modern morality play, about a half-man, half-gorilla introduced into modern Czech aristocracy. Beautifully acted with some stunning visual sequences. Subtitles.

Death of the Ape-Man—See: Death of Tarzan, The

Death Race (1973)**½ Lloyd Bridges, Doug McClure, Roy Thinnes, Eric

Braeden. A good cast fight it out in the dust and sand of this WW II story about Rommel's retreat from El Alamein. A Nazi tank commander (Bridges) stalks American fighter pilots caught in a crippled P-40 plane that is unable to take off. Desert chase scenes filmed among the sand dunes of El Centro, Calif., with stunt segments by Frank Tallman in his old P-40. Made-for-TV. (Dir: David Lowell Rich, 90 mins.)

Death Race 2000 (1975)*** David Carradine, Simone Griffith, Sylvester Stallone. Like "Rollerball," this film offers a vision of an ultra-violent sport in a futuristic society, in this case an annual cross-country road race with drivers scoring points for running over pedestrians. Black humor savages violent sports effectively. Carradine, as one of the drivers who secretly opposes the race, is challenged by four other drivers, including gangster-like Sylvester Stallone (before "Rocky"). Despite a small budget, this uneven film offers taut action, together with some alternately funny and banal political satire. Based on a 1956 short story by Ib Melchior. (Dir: Paul Bartel, 80 mins.)

Death Rides a Horse (Italian, 1968) *½ Lee Van Cleef, John Phillip Law. Overlong spaghetti western with Van Cleef and Law tracking down a gang of killers for revenge. Trouble brews when Law finds out steely-eyed Van Cleef was part of the gang who killed his parents. (Dir: Giulio Petroni, 114 mins.)

Death Scream (1975)**½ Raul Julia, Tina Louise, Cloris Leachman, Art Carney. Effective, updated version of the real-life Kitty Genovese murder on a Brooklyn street years ago, in which the victim screamed for help for close to half an hour, fighting off her attacker while no one came to her aid. This story makes the victim a lesbian, adding some depth to the investigation, headed by Raul Julia as Lt. Rodriguez. Uses TV stars as witnesses. Tina Louise shines in the brief interrogation scene, playing a former lover of the victim. The subject is involving and the script doesn't cheat. Made-for-TV. (Dir: Richard T. Heffron, 100 mins.)

Death Sentence (1974)**½ Cloris Leachman, Laurence Luckinbill. Cloris Leachman has made a spe-

cialty out of playing women driven to the brink of disaster by circumstances out of her control, and here's another. This gifted actress tries to overcome some of the plot's more obvious loopholes in this story which has her playing a juror who realizes halfway through a murder trial that her own husband may be the real culprit. Laurence Luckinbill is well cast as Miss Leachman's suspected spouse. Made-for-TV. (Dir: E. W. Swackhamer, 72 mins.)

Death Squad, The (1973)**½ Robert Forster, Melvyn Douglas. Strong police yarn about a group of vigilante cops who secretly take the law into their own hands and murder criminals. Forster crisply plays a poor man's "Serpico," a cop who was kicked off the force but is brought back to get to the bottom of the rash of killings. A fine supporting cast helps the action. Made-for-TV. (Director: Harry Falk.)

Death Stalk (1975)** Vic Morrow, Vince Edwards, Anjanette Comer, Carol Lynley, Robert Webber. Crisis drama borrows liberally from the movie "Deliverance" for its plot. Focuses on two couples enjoying an outdoors vacation riding the rapids in rafts, when they are pounced upon by four escaped convicts who abduct the wives and leave the two husbands behind. Vic Morrow, leading the pack of escaped convicts, generates a bit of heat in his scenes with Anjanette Comer. Made-for-TV. (Dir: Robert Day, 72 mins.)

Death Takes a Holiday (1934)***½ Fredric March, Evelyn Venable. Fascinating drama. Mr. March, as Death, decides to assume human form and take a vacation. Interesting, well played and worth seeing. (Dir: Mitchell Leisen, 90 mins.)

Death Trap (British, 1960)** Albert Lieven, Barbara Shelley. Girl learns her deceased sister drew some money from the bank before her death, but it seems to have disappeared. Fairly interesting Edgar Wallace mystery.

Decameron Nights (1953)*** Joan Fontaine, Louis Jourdan, Joan Collins. Author Boccaccio follows his lady-love, tries to win her affection by telling her two spicy tales. Good-natured costume adventure, made in Italy. Pleasant fun. (Dir: Hugo Fregonese, 85 mins.)

Deception (1946)**½ Bette Davis, Claude Rains, Paul Henreid. Claude

179

is Bette's lover but she marries Paul and soon someone is full of lead in this extremely slow-moving but well acted melodrama. (Dir: Irving Rapper, 112 mins.)

Decision Against Time (British, 1957) **½ Jack Hawkins, Elizabeth Sellars. Test pilot is determined to bring his troubled ship in for a safe landing. Fairly suspenseful drama, well-made. (87 mins.)

Decision at Sundown (1957)***½ Randolph Scott, Karen Steele, John Carroll. Exceptionally good, adult-slanted Scott western manages to break most of the accepted hoss-opera rules advantageously. Randy is out for revenge again—but the plot gets a novel twist this time. (Dir: Budd Boetticher, 80 mins.)

Decision Before Dawn (1951)**½ Oskar Werner, Richard Basehart, Gary Merrill. A very fine performance by German actor Oskar Werner as "Happy" makes up for some of the shortcomings of the script of this World War II espionage drama. Good on-location photography and a capable supporting cast including Basehart, Merrill and Hildegarde Neff also make this worthwhile but it's Werner's show. (Dir: Anatole Litvak, 119 mins.)

Decision of Christopher Blake (1948) **½ Alexis Smith, Robert Douglas. Good play about the effect a divorce trial has on a small boy becomes an episodic, meaningless story in this screen treatment. (Dir: Peter Godfrey, 75 mins.)

Decks Ran Red, The (1958)** James Mason, Dorothy Dandridge, Broderick Crawford, Stuart Whitman. Foolish film about a captain endeavoring to thwart a mutiny engineered by two nasty seamen. The dialogue is hollow, the suspense isn't, and the acting only occasionally effective. (Dir: Andrew L. Stone, 84 mins.)

Decline and Fall of a Bird Watcher (British, 1968)** Genevieve Page, Colin Blakely, Leo McKern, Donald Wolfit, Robert Harris, Evelyn Waugh's biting satire on English manners and mores begins well as the callow hero (Robin Phillips) gets a position at a weirdly run school for boys. Thereafter, the fun becomes cumbersome, off-target, and runs downhill quickly.

Deep Blue Sea, The (British, 1955)** Vivien Leigh, Kenneth More. Terence Rattigan's stage success of an emotionally unstable woman's affair with a man beneath her station, rather cumbersomely adapted for the screen. Defects in direction, performances detract from the drama. (Dir: Anatole Litvak, 99 mins.)

Deep End (West Germany-U.S., 1970)***½ Jane Asher, John Moulder-Brown, Diana Dors. Intelligent, powerful fable of a young boy's first love. Moulder-Brown epitomizes the adolescent who will not be deterred by the obstacles he faces in courting a nubile bathhouse attendant. His dedicated pursuit sees him overcoming the girl's indifference, as well as triumphing over her fiancé and lover. The affectionately subdued directing conveys all of the high spirits and aspirations of a building passion. Skolomowsky also helped write the screenplay. (Dir: Jerzy Skolomowsky, 87 mins.)

Deep In My Heart (1954)*** Jose Ferrer, Merle Oberon, Walter Pidgeon. Story of composer Sigmund Romberg serves as a peg on which to hand a host of fancy musical numbers with specialties by Astaire, Kelly, Tony Martin, Rosemary Clooney, Ann Miller, et al. Top-heavy, but good musical entertainment. (Dir: Stanley Donen, 132 mins.)

Deep Six, The (1958)** Alan Ladd, William Bendix, Joey Bishop, Dianne Foster, James Whitmore. Naval lieutenant whose religious beliefs are Quaker loses the respect of his men but regains it through an act of heroism. World War II drama is thoroughly routine, runs far too long. (Dir: Rudolph Mate, 108 mins.)

Deep Valley (1947)*** Ida Lupino, Dane Clark. Girl living an unhappy life on a farm is attracted to a convict working on a construction job. Excellently acted drama—grim but good. (Dir: Jean Negulesco, 104 mins.)

Deep Waters (1948)** Dana Andrews, Jean Peters. This one may remind you of a dull one-hour TV play. Maine fishing village girl wants man to work on shore. Man likes fishing. An orphan taken care of by girl but likes to fish with man. Familiar? (Dir: Henry King, 85 mins.)

Deerslayer, The (1957)*½ Lex Barker, Forrest Tucker, Rita Moreno. Passable adaptation of James Fenimore Cooper's exciting tale of adventure in the frontiers of colonial America. Somewhere in this story there may still be a good film. (78 mins.)

Defeat of Hannibal, The (Italian, 1937)* Annibale Ninchi, Isa Miranda, Francesca Braggiotti. Opulent hangover from the days of Mussolini; story of Scipio outsmarting the attacking legions of Hannibal during the second Punic War was intended as Il Duce's gift to the cinema world. It's lavish, but dull. English dubbed.

Defector, The (German-French, 1966) ***½ Montgomery Clift, Hardy Kruger. A fairly engrossing espionage yarn which benefits from good on-location atmosphere in Berlin, and a fine performance by Montgomery Clift as an American professor of physics who gets involved with cold-war intrigues. Hardy Kruger, as the German working for the communists, is constantly in opposition to Clift, the amateur spy on a dangerous mission involving the defection of Russian scientist to the West. The story gets a bit muddled towards the end, but fans of this sort of film will not be disappointed. Incidentally, this was the last film Clift made before his death, and that is the brilliant French film director Jean-Luc Godard playing the small role of a tourist spy. (Dir: Raoul Levy, 106 mins.)

Defiant Daughters (Swiss, 1962)** Barbara Rutting, Luise Ulrich. Housemistress of a girls' reformatory tries to save a young rebellious girl from a life of misery. Sometimes interesting, mostly heavy-handed delinquency drama dubbed in English.

Defiant Ones, The (1958)**** Tony Curtis, Sidney Poitier, Theodore Bikel, Cara Williams. Provocative, honest racial drama of two escaping chain-gang convicts, white and Negro, whose differences make their flight more difficult because they are literally chained together. Still packs quite a punch, has superb performances, potent Stanley Kramer direction. Fine mature fare. (Dir: Stanley Kramer, 97 mins.)

Delancey Street: The Crisis Within (1975)**½ Walter McGinn, Lou Gossett. Fairly interesting dramatic version of San Francisco's successful rehabilitation center, Delancey Street, in which ex-cons, junkies and dropouts live together and learn new skills. McGinn exudes force and energy as Delancey's free-wheeling innovator, while action focuses on inmates battling problems. Positive, earthy upbeat! Made-for-TV. (Dir: James Frawley, 72 mins.)

Delicate Balance, A (U.S.-Great Britain, 1974)***½ Katharine Hepburn, Paul Scofield, Lee Remick, Joseph Cotten, Betsy Blair. A virtual filmed record of Albee's 1966 Broadway play, a bitter distillation of lost dreams and loves as an aging, civilized couple—Hepburn and Scofield —try to make living together tolerable. "A Delicate Balance," a talky, occasionally poetic and witty play, is not among Albee's best works, but this version does present the opportunity of seeing one of the half-dozen greatest actors in the world—Scofield—making one of his all-too-rare film appearances in a leading role. Scofield, playing the urbane head of the household, builds to a terrifying final outburst. (Dir: Tony Richardson, 134 mins.)

Delicate Delinquent, The (1957)*** Jerry Lewis, Darren McGavin, Martha Hyer. Scapegoat Jerry joins the police force and has a hard time proving himself as a rookie cop. One of the better Lewis offerings. He's restrained, the story is logical, the laughs come frequently. (Dir: Don McGuire, 101 mins.)

Deliver Us from Evil (1973)*** George Kennedy, Jan-Michael Vincent, Bradford Dillman. Mount Hood, Oregon, which stands over 11,000 feet high, is the real star of this adventure drama filmed on location. Spectacular photography adds to the tale of five men who set out, with the aid of a guide, to spend three days in the Oregon wilderness (shades of "Deliverance") but end up trying to survive the rugged terrain when their guide is killed. Tension builds as the men come across a skyjacker with his fortune in ransom money. The cast, especially Jim Davis in a brief role, is very good. Made-for-TV. (Dir: Boris Sagal, 90 mins.)

Deliverance (1972)**** Jon Voight, Burt Reynolds, Ned Beatty, Ronny Cox. James Dickey's novel has been excitingly brought to the screen by director John Boorman, earning Academy Award nominations for best picture, direction and editing. Four businessmen—Voight, Reynolds, Beatty and Cox—set out on a canoe trip down a wild Georgia river and look forward to nothing more hazardous than riding the rapids, but their adventure becomes a nightmare of survival. They encounter two demented hillbillies, one of whom physically violates Beatty, and the innocent nature trek turns into a struggle laced with killing. Strong stuff, superbly acted by the entire cast, particularly Voight as the sensitive man who finds he wants to release his primitive instincts when his own life is at stake. (Dir : John Boorman, 109 mins.)

Delphi Bureau, The (1972)*½ Laurence Luckinbill, Joanna Pettet, Celeste Holm. Luckinbill is an agent for the government with a photographic memory. He searches for a stockpile of weapons, with the usual unforeseen consequences. Trivial. Made-for-TV. (Dir: Paul Wendkos, 72 mins.)

Delta County (1977)*½ Peter Donat, Joanna Miles, Jeff Conway. An old Southern family locks horns with a real-estate development corporation which wants to move in and build a large shopping mall. You've seen it all before, but this time it's helped by the acting of Donat and Miles. Made-for-TV. (Dir : Glenn Jordan, 106 mins.)

Delta Factor, The (1971)½ Christopher George, Yvette Mimieux, Diane McBain. A trashy bore, based on Mickey Spillane's novel. Wrongly-accused international privateer forced to help a top scientist escape from the clutches of an evil dictator. Badly written, directed and produced by Tay Garnett. (91 mins.)

Dementia 13 (1963)*** William Campbell, Luana Anders, Bart Patton. Terror sweeps through an Irish castle, all wound up in the memory of a dead girl, which brings on murder by axe. Creepy horror thriller really delivers the goods for the fans of blood and gore; direction is most efficient, performances good. Superior of its kind.

Demetrius and the Gladiators (1954)**½ Susan Hayward, Victor Mature, Richard Egan. A sequel to TC Fox's successful film "The Robe." Not as good in any department. Probably the only reason it was made was to utilize the very expensive sets and

182

costumes left over from "The Robe." Action fans might like the scenes in the arena where the gladiators do their stuff. (Dir : Delmer Daves, 101 mins.)

Demon Planet, The (Italian, 1965) *½ Barry Sullivan, Norma Bengell. After its sister ship, a spacecraft lands on a strange planet and its crew encounters some bloodthirsty creatures there. Low-grade science-fiction thriller with a bunch of dubbed Italian actors giving it their all, while Sullivan frequently looks embarrassed. (Dir : Mario Bava, 86 mins.)

Demon Seed, The (1977)*½ Julie Christie, Fritz Weaver, Gerrit Graham. What if there was a computer that could think? Would its first thought be how to create offspring? The premise has a super-computer named "Proteus" trying to mate with the alluring wife of scientist and computer-creator Weaver. Miss Christie faces the unfortunate job of acting opposite the gadget-happy, deep-voiced computer terminal that locks her in her home and woos her in sadistic fashion. The technically minded might find solace in the interminable parade of 21st-century inventions, but the writing is prehistoric gibberish. (Dir : Donald Cammell, 94 mins.)

Demoniac (French, 1957)***½ Jeanne Moreau, Micheline Presle, Francois Perier. Taut and baffling mystery drama of mistaken identities during W.W. II in France. Fascinating and suspenseful throughout. (Dir : Luis Saslavsky, 97 mins.)

Dentist in the Chair (British, 1961) *½ Bob Monkhouse, Peggy Cummins. Slapstick comedy about the trials and tribulations of dental students. More silly than funny. (Dir: Don Chaffey, 84 mins.)

Denver and Rio Grande, The (1952) **½ Edmond O'Brien, Sterling Hayden, Dean Jagger. Plenty of roughhouse action in this western about two rival railroads battling to see who gets through the Royal Gorge first. Outdoor fans should find it routinely entertaining. (89 mins.)

Deported (1951)**½ Marta Toren, Jeff Chandler, Claude Dauphin. Over-sentimentalized tale of a deported American gangster and his reformation in the hands of a beautiful Italian Countess. Chandler does very well as the gangster who's deported to Italy and gets involved with the black market. (Dir: Robert Siodmak, 89 mins.)

Derby (1971)***½ Mike Snell, Butch Snell, Janet Earp, Eddie Krebs. Enlightening, entertaining documentary about the great American pastime, the Roller Derby. Some of the scenes are stage-managed, while the film pretends to be a cinema-verité report of what happens to the generally sad, dispirited characters trying to make their dream come true in this tacky, tawdry "sport." Directed and photographed by Robert Kaylor. (91 mins.)

Derby Day (British, 1952)*** Anna Neagle, Michael Wilding. Four stories revolving about the big horse race at Epsom, where the various spectators all have their little plots to unfold. Mildly entertaining package of comedy and drama. (Dir: Herbert Wilcox, 84 mins.)

Dersu Uzala (Russia-Japan, 1974) ***½ Maxim Munzuk, Yuri Solomin. A fascinating, overlong epic about the struggles of hardy souls to chart the wilderness of Siberia around 1900. The second part of this absorbing survival picture is directed by Japan's wonderful Akira Kurosawa, and is appreciably better than the balance of the film, directed by a Russian colleague. Based on the journals of a Russian, Vladmir Arseniev, "Dersu" 's remarkable photography and the performance of Munzuk as an old native hunter carry this most of the way. (Dir: Akira Kurosawa, 140 mins.)

Desert Attack (British, 1959)*** John Mills, Sylvia Syms, Anthony Quayle. Tank commander has his hands full in North Africa carrying two nurses to safety and combating a German spy. Originally, a rattling good war story; American version is severely cut, obscuring some of the sense. However, good performances, exciting scenes still make it worthwhile. Alternative title: **Ice Cold In Alex** (Dir: J. Lee Thompson, 80 mins.)

Desert Desperadoes (Italian, 1956)*½ Ruth Roman, Otello Toso, Akim Tamiroff. Caravan guarded by Roman soldiers picks up a beautiful woman in the desert; she causes jealousy and disaster. Ponderous drama of ancient times has only the principal players to recommend it,

and it's not enough. (Dir: Steve Sekely, 73 mins.)

Desert Fighters (French, 1960)*½ Michel Auclair, Emma Panella, Dalio. Engineer seeks a lost gold mine in the Sahara, but the price is high. Sluggish adventure melodrama dubbed in English.

Desert Fox (1951)***½ James Mason, Jessica Tandy. Exciting war drama about the African campaign of Rommel. James Mason is nothing short of great as the Nazi general. Good desert photography. Mason repeated his characterization of Rommel in another film, "The Desert Rats," which showed the other side of the coin regarding the German military tactics under Rommel's command. (Dir: Henry Hathaway, 88 mins.)

Desert Fury (1947)** John Hodiak, Burt Lancaster. Good cast in confusing melodrama about gambling. Everybody in the film has a shady past, and the result is a shady motion picture. (Dir: Lewis Allen, 75 mins.)

Desert Hawk, The (1950)** Yvonne DeCarlo, Richard Greene. The only interesting thing about this stale tale of an Arabian Nights adventure is Jackie Gleason in the supporting role of Aladdin. No one really takes the film seriously, especially the pre-rich Gleason. (Dir: Frederick de Cordova, 78 mins.)

Desert Hell (1958)*½ Brian Keith, Barbara Hale, Richard Denning. Legionnaires on a dangerous trek are menaced by tribesmen on the warpath. Drama of the burning sands substitutes talk for action. (Dir: Charles Marquis Warren, 82 mins.)

Desert Legion (1953)** Alan Ladd, Arlene Dahl, Richard Conte. Can you imagine Alan Ladd as a French Foreign Legionnaire? This adventure yarn has super heroics and beautiful desert princesses. (Dir: Joseph Pevney, 86 mins.)

Desert Mice (Great Britain, 1960) **½ Alfred Marks, Sidney James, Dora Bryan. Engaging comedy about British vaudevillian entertainers who performed for British troops during World War II. Non-stellar cast is uniformly fine, especially James as an unfunny boss comic. (Dir: Michael Ralph, 83 mins.)

Desert Pursuit (1952)** Wayne Morris, Virginia Grey. Prospector and a lady gambler are chased by a murderous gang after gold. Western with a gimmick—the baddies are Arabs and use camels instead of horses. Twist makes this one okay. (71 mins.)

Desert Raiders (Italian, 1963)* Kirk Morris, Helene Chanel. Hero saves the beautiful daughter of a village notable from the clutches of a tyrant. Hero's name is Nadir, which aptly describes this desert action melodrama dubbed in English.

Desert Rats, The (1953)*** James Mason, Richard Burton, Robert Newton. Good war drama about the turbulent siege at Tobruk during World War II. James Mason once again effectively portrays Gen. Rommel, "The Desert Fox," leader of the Nazi troops. Richard Burton is fine as the commander of the Australian forces; and Robert Newton gives a standout performance as a professor turned soldier. (Dir: Robert Wise, 88 mins.)

Desert Song, The (1953)** Kathryn Grayson, Gordon MacRae. Still another version of the "never say die" operetta. Kathryn Grayson and Gordon MacRae play the duetting stars this time around and they're no better nor worse than any of their predecessors. The score contains the familiar "Riff Song," among others. (Dir: H. Bruce Humberstone, 110 mins.)

Desert War (Italian, 1960)*½ Peter Baldwin, Chelo Alonso. Hackneyed war melodrama about a Libyan patrol who find a beautiful girl in the desert and suspect her of being a spy. Dubbed in English.

Desert Warrior, The (1960)** Ricardo Montalban, Carmen Sevilla. Spanish-made, English-dubbed Arabian adventure yarn that benefits somewhat from Ricardo Montalban's ability to perform heroic feats without seeming ridiculous.

Deserter, The (Italy-Yugoslavia-U.S., 1970)** John Huston, Richard Crenna, Ricardo Montalban, Bekim Fehmiu. A fair Western yarn set in 1886. Army officer is out for revenge after the Apaches mutilated his wife—but a good cast of pros, including John Huston, Richard Crenna, Ricardo Montalban and Bekim Fehmiu (remember him as Dax in "The Adventurers"?) help it along. (Dir: Burt Kennedy, 99 mins.)

Design For Living (1933)**½ Gary Cooper, Fredric March, Miriam

184

Hopkins. Noel Coward's delightful comedy receives an unsuccessful screen treatment. Story of three "sensible" people involved in a love triangle was too sophisticated for a movie. The stars are very attractive, though. (Dir: Ernst Lubitsch, 90 mins.)

Design for Loving (British, 1960)*½ June Thorburn, Pete Murray. Fashion artist gets involved in scandal. You won't get involved at all.

Design for Scandal (1941)**½ Rosalind Russell, Walter Pidgeon, Edward Arnold. Some good fun in this comedy about an upstanding lady judge and the scoundrel who sets out to smear her good name. (Dir: Norman Taurog, 85 mins.)

Designing Woman (1957)*** Gregory Peck, Lauren Bacall, Dolores Gray. A sophisticated comedy graced by Mr. Peck and Miss Bacall's presence. Miss B. plays a successful dress designer who meets and marries sportswriter Peck and the fun comes as each tries to adapt to the other's friends and habits. (Dir: Vincente Minnelli, 117 mins.)

Desire (1936)*** Marlene Dietrich, Gary Cooper. Familiar but delightful. Lovely jewel thief takes advantage of innocent young man and he becomes her unwitting accomplice in smuggling a stolen necklace. She must now seduce him to regain her prize. (Dir: Frank Borzage, 100 mins.)

Desire in the Dust (1960)** Raymond Burr, Martha Hyer, Joan Bennett. Tyrannical landowner with plenty of skeletons in his closet sees his political ambitions in jeopardy, tries unscrupulous means to rid himself of his troubles. A dose of lust and desire in a southern town, but it's a long way from Faulkner. Burr does well, better than his material. (Dir: William F. Claxton, 102 mins.)

Desire Under the Elms (1958)**½ Sophia Loren, Anthony Perkins, Burl Ives. O'Neill's play concerning the passions of a farmer's young son and the wife of the elderly man misses something in its transference to the screen. Some powerful dramatic moments, mostly unrelieved gloom, meandering pace. (Dir: Delbert Mann, 111 mins.)

Desiree (1954)**½ Marlon Brando, Jean Simmons, Merle Oberon. With this elaborately produced historical drama, Mr. Brando adds Napoleon to his list of screen portrayals, but it does not rank with his best. Jean Simmons is vividly beautiful and, as always, competent in the title role as Napoleon's love before he becomes Emperor. Merle Oberon as Josephine has few scenes, but she makes them count. Michael Rennie completes the starring lineup in this adventure film which sacrifices historical accuracy in favor of romantic flair. (Dir: Henry Koster, 110 mins.)

Desk Set (1957)***½ Spencer Tracy, Katharine Hepburn, Gig Young. Loosely based on the Broadway hit which starred Shirley Booth, this sophisticated comedy is jauntily performed by that delectable pair of pros, Hepburn and Tracy. The plot revolves around the possibility of replacing the reference department of a major broadcasting company with automation. Plenty of laughs. (Dir: Walter Lang, 103 mins.)

Desperadoes, The (1969)* Jack Palance, Vince Edwards, George Maharis, Neville Brand. Violence-drenched tale of a young son trying to break away from his outlaw family in the post-Civil War West. Palance is laughable as the father whose iron rule dictates that the renegade son must die. (Dir: Henry Levin, 90 mins.)

Desperate (1947)*** Steve Brodie, Nan Leslie. Truckdriver becomes a fugitive when his vehicle is used in a robbery. Above average melodrama.

Desperate Characters (1971)*** Shirley MacLaine, Kenneth Mars, Gerald O'Laughlin, Sada Thompson. Well-written character study of a day in the life of an urban couple who face a decaying New York that they are helpless to change. Features fine performances by Miss MacLaine and Mars as the white middle-class pair insulated against their crumbling city in a renovated brownstone. Shares some of the same vision as "Little Murders," but without the humor. Novel by Paula Fox was adapted by Pulitzer Prize-winning author Frank Gilroy, who made an impressive directorial debut as well! (88 mins.)

Desperate Hours, The (1955)***½ Humphrey Bogart, Fredric March, Martha Scott, Gig Young. The suspense runs high in this taut drama of three escaped convicts who hole up in the home of a respected family and use them as hostages. Bogart's last hoodlum role, which fits him like a glove. Others in the cast measure up. (Dir: William Wyler, 112 mins.)

Desperate Journey (1942)**½ Errol Flynn, Ronald Reagan. One of the pictures made when Errol was winning the war single-handed. Today, stripped of its propaganda value, it's just a good action story. (Dir: Raoul Walsh, 107 mins.)

Desperate Miles, The (1975)½ Tony Musante, Joanna Pettet, Jeanette Nolan. Made-for-TV movie is so embarrassingly bad that it finally becomes funny. Simplistic drivel about a serious subject—wounded Vietnam veteran trying to adjust to the new realities of life—is further burdened by the wooden acting of Tony Musante. (Dir: Dan Haller, 72 mins.)

Desperate Mission (French, 1964)* German Cobos, Yoko Tani. American secret agent is sent to Hong Kong to search for a nuclear physicist who escaped from the Red Chinese. Try blaming the Chinese Reds for this dubbed stinker.

Desperate Mission (1971)* Ricardo Montalban, Slim Pickens, Earl Holliman. Bland tale of a victimized man forced to protect wife of wealthy landowner on her journey. Made-for-TV. (Dir: Earl Bellamy, 100 mins.)

Desperate Moment (British, 1953)***½ Dirk Bogarde, Mai Zetterling. Displaced person in Europe is tricked into confessing to a murder he didn't commit, and his girl tries to help track down the guilty party. Exciting, tense melodrama; excellent performances. (Dir: Compton Bennett, 88 mins.)

Desperate Ones, The (Spain-U.S., 1967)** Maximilian Schell, Raf Vallone, Irene Papas, Theodore Bikel, Maria Perschy. O.K. World War II melodrama. Two Polish brothers escape a Siberian labor camp. Along the way to the Afghanistan border, Schell and Vallone meet Papas and Perschy, and a weak romantic subplot ensues. Alexander Romati authored the original novel, "Beyond the Mountains," as well as producing, scripting and directing. (104 mins.)

Desperate Search (1953)**½ Howard Keel, Jane Greer, Patricia Medina.

Moderately interesting drama about the efforts of a search party to bring back two young survivors of a plane crash in the Canadian mountains. Personal drama enters the picture as Keel's ex-wife (Miss Medina) shows up to complicate matters. (Dir: Joseph H. Lewis, 71 mins.)

Desperate Siege (1951)**½ Tyrone Power, Susan Hayward. This routine western drama is sparked by the acting of Tyrone Power and Susan Hayward. The two stars find themselves in the desperate position of being held prisoners in a remote stagecoach station by a band of outlaws. Most of the action unfolds slowly except for one or two tense gun-play sequences. (Dir: Henry Hathaway, 86 mins.)

Destination Death (German, 1963)** Hannes Messemer, Armin Dahlen. German sergeant saves 40 military prisoners who are being transported to their doom during the final days of World War II. Occasionally suspenseful war drama dubbed in English.

Destination Fury (Italian, 1964)** Eddie Constantine, Renato Rascel, Dorian Grey. Police inspector appointed to Interpol in Rome is ordered to Paris to bring back a notorious gangster, gets involved in an illegal drug operation. Mild gangster story mixes laughs with thrills in fair fashion. Dubbed in English. (Dir: Giorgio Bianchi, 85 mins.)

Destination Gobi (1953)**½ Richard Widmark, Don Taylor. A notch or two above the average heroic war story. Good photography and some solid acting make up for some of the shortcomings of the script. (Dir: Robert Wise, 89 mins.)

Destination Inner Space (1966)*½ Scott Brady, Sheree North, Gary Merrill. Lame science fiction as deep-sea divers remove exotic devices from a weird craft they have salvaged from the ocean's floor. A strange creature arrives for the finale. Kids may enjoy the underwater photography—it's the above-the-water stuff that's so boring. (Dir: Francis D. Lyon, 82 mins.)

Destination Moon (1950)*** Warner Anderson, John Archer. An American space ship takes off to reach the moon. Science-fiction drama is not as fantastic as when it was first released; good detail, imaginative

special effects. (Dir: Irving Pichel, 91 mins.)

Destination 60,000 (1957)*½ Preston Foster, Coleen Gray, Pat Conway. Here come the brave pilots again, trying out jets, risking their lives, boring the audience. Air technology progresses, but the plot is World War I vintage. (Dir: George Waggner, 65 mins.)

Destination Tokyo (1943)***½ Cary Grant, John Garfield. Great adventure story of a submarine which goes into Tokyo harbor. Again, forget it's dated. Relax and enjoy it. (Dir: Delmer Daves, 135 mins.)

Destiny (1944)** Alan Curtis, Gloria Jean. Escaped prisoner takes refuge in a farm owned by a man with a blind daughter. Uneven drama, with some sequences much better than others. (Dir: Reginald Le Borg, 65 mins.)

Destiny of a Spy (1969)**½ Lorne Greene, Rachel Roberts. This made-for-TV feature film has two things going for it—an excellent British supporting cast and the fine on-location photography of London. Lorne Greene's fans will probably have some trouble accepting him as a Russian spy who is taken out of mothballs to complete just one more dangerous mission involving a frightened British scientist, a German informer, and the development of a sophisticated counter-radar system. The yarn spins along with few surprises but is richly enhanced by Patrick Magee as a demented witness, Harry Andrews as a compassionate but efficient intelligence officer and Anthony Quayle as Greene's superior. (Dir: Boris Sagal, 99 mins.)

Destroy All Monsters (Japanese, 1969)* Akira Kubo, Jun Tazaki. The Kilaaks want to take over the Earth. To do it Mothra, Manda, Rodan, and even the dreaded Godzilla break their cages and go on the rampage. Godzilla gives the best performance. (Dir: Ishiro Honda, 87 mins.)

Destry (1955)**½ Audie Murphy, Mari Blanchard. Not altogether successful remake of the Stewart-Dietrich vehicle made 15 years earlier. Murphy is very good as the gunless Sheriff, but Mari Blanchard is a bust as a replacement for marvelous Marlene. The plot still holds a certain fascination. (Dir: George Marshall, 95 mins.)

Destry Rides Again (1939)**** James

Stewart, Marlene Dietrich, Brian Donlevy. One of the best westerns ever made with an equal mixture of comedy and drama. Has been often copied but never matched. Stewart and Dietrich are great. (Dir: George Marshall, 94 mins.)

Detective, The (British, 1955)*** Alec Guinness, Joan Greenwood. Guinness is delightful as a priest who fancies himself a top flight amateur detective. The picture is not among his best but has some pleasant moments as Father Brown tries to trap an art thief. (Dir: Robert Hamer, 100 mins.)

Detective, The (1968)*** Frank Sinatra, Lee Remick, Jack Klugman. Screenwriter Abby Mann has written some pungent, realistic dialogue for this well above-average drama about a hard-bitten New York City police detective investigating a messy murder of a young homosexual. It's your only chance of the night, perhaps, to see Horace McMahon playing a police officer, and there's an attractive performance from Jacqueline Bisset. (When Frankie leaves the environs of New York for a short drive and shows up at a beach house that looks suspiciously like California, don't trade in your glasses! It really was California used in the location sequences by the lazy producer.) (Dir: Gordon Douglas, 114 mins.)

Detective Story (1951)**** Kirk Douglas, Eleanor Parker, William Bendix. Sidney Kingsley's Broadway play is excellently adapted to the screen by director William Wyler. Kirk Douglas gives one of his finest screen performances as a detective whose personal code becomes twisted from dealing with criminals over a number of years. Most of the action takes place in a New York precinct on one day with assorted "supporting" thieves getting some good scenes, particularly Joseph Wiseman as a burglar, and Lee Grant as a shoplifter. (Dir: William Wyler, 103 mins.)

Detour (1945)*** Tom Neal, Ann Savage. While hitchhiking cross country, a piano player meets a scheming blonde and is innocently involved in sudden death. Well above average, ironic melodrama. Deserves praise for screenplay by Martin Goldsmith, direction by Edgar Ulmer. (Dir: Edgar G. Ulmer, 69 mins.)

Devil, The—See: To Bed or Not to Bed

Devil and Daniel Webster, The (1941)**** Walter Huston, Edward Arnold, James Craig, Ann Shirley. One of the best films ever made. Superb fantasy set in early New England, as a man sells his soul to the devil in return for riches.

Devil and Miss Jones (1941)*** Jean Arthur, Robert Cummings, Charles Coburn. Pleasant comedy about a department store tycoon who takes a job, incognito, in his own store. Dated but fun. (Dir: Sam Wood, 92 mins.)

Devil and Miss Sarah (1971)* Gene Barry, James Drury, Janice Rule, Slim Pickens. Satanist outlaw takes possession of the mind of his tormentor's wife. Plodding Western. Made-for-TV. (Dir: Michael Caffey, 72 mins.)

Devil at 4 O'Clock, The (1961)**½ Spencer Tracy, Frank Sinatra, Kerwin Mathews, Jean-Pierre Aumont. Aging priest and three convicts undertake a perilous rescue mission when a tropic island is threatened by a volcano eruption. Uneven drama has the two stars lending their talents to a weak script, occasionally overcoming the routine situations, direction. (Dir: Mervyn Le Roy, 126 mins.)

Devil at My Heels (French, 1966)*½ Sami Frey, Francoise Hardy, Spiros Focas. Young aristocrat is victimized in a swindle, sets out to seek revenge. Plodding dubbed drama.

Devil Doll (1936)***½ Lionel Barrymore. Director Tod Browning's terrific horror thriller about the revenge of a man framed for murder by three business rivals. Marvelous, scary special effects. (Dir: Tod Browning, 80 mins.)

Devil Doll (British, 1964)** Bryant Haliday, William Sylvester, Yvonne Romain. Hypnotist who uses a wooden dummy in his act is suspected by an investigating reporter of having some dire secret. Adequate thriller has some slightly offbeat angles to keep the interest.

Devil in Love, The (Italy, 1966)**½ Vittorio Gassman, Mickey Rooney, Claudine Auger. Surprisingly entertaining film. Gassman and Rooney are sent as envoys from Archdevil Beelzebub circa 1478 to foment war between Rome and Florence during the Renaissance. Refreshing approach to period farce, exuberant cast make this an amusing outing. (Dir: Ettore Scola, 72 mins.)

Devil in the Flesh (French, 1949) ***½ Gerard Philippe, Micheline Presle. English-dubbed. Beautifully acted tragic tale of a young student's affair with a mature married woman during World War I. Dubbed dialogue detracts a bit from the drama, but it's still well worthwhile adult drama. (Dir: Claude Autant-Lara, 110 mins.)

Devil Is a Sissy, The (1936)**½ Mickey Rooney, Jackie Cooper, Freddie Bartholomew. Occasionally entertaining juvenile delinquency story featuring the top three young male stars of the era. (Dir: W. S. Van Dyke, 92 mins.)

Devil Is a Woman, The (1935)** Marlene Dietrich, Cesar Romero, Lionel Atwill. Story of an older man who permits himself to be destroyed by the demands of a lovely woman. A bit stilted for modern tastes and you may find it boring. (Dir: Joseph von Sternberg, 85 mins.)

Devil Makes Three, The (1952)**½ Gene Kelly, Pier Angeli. American GI in post-war Germany becomes involved in black market smuggling after meeting a night club girl. Familiar melodrama given a lift by on-the-spot locations in Germany. (Dir: Andrew Marton, 90 mins.)

Devil of the Desert Against the Son of Hercules (Italian, 1964)*½ Kirk Morris, Michele Girardon. Heroic strongman saves a princess from a villain who has assassinated the king and sold her into slavery. Far-fetched English-dubbed action adventure, strictly for the kiddies.

Devil on Horseback (British, 1954)** Googie Withers, John McCallum, Jeremy Spenser. A young miner's son becomes a winning jockey, but is responsible for the death of a horse when he fouls another jockey in a race. Slow-moving racing melodrama.

Devil Pays Off, The (1941)*** J. Edward Bromberg, Osa Massen. A civilian agent exposes a shipping magnate about to sell his fleet to a foreign power. Well-made, exciting melodrama; noteworthy are John Auer's direction, John Alton's photography. (Dir: John H. Auer, 56 mins.)

Devil Rides Out, The—See: **Devil's Bride, The**

Devil Strikes at Night (German, 1958)*** Mario Adorf, Claus Holm. Penetrating study of a psychopathic murderer during the war in Germany. Gestapo enters the case with fascinating results. Mario Adorf is magnificent as the homicidal maniac.

Devil to Pay, The (1931)** Ronald Colman, Loretta Young, Myrna Loy. A not too successful adaptation of a Lonsdale comedy of manners. A bit too stiff and artificial for today's audiences. (Dir: George Fitzmaurice, 80 mins.)

Devil's Agent (British, 1964)** Macdonald Carey, Peter Van Eyck, Christopher Lee. Wine merchant used as an informer by both sides of the Iron Curtain is shot down in Vienna. Average spy thriller with a better than average cast.

Devil's Bedroom, The (1963)* John Lupton, Dick Jones, Valerie Allen. Simple-minded country lad is accused of murder, escapes with a posse in hot pursuit. Inept drama looks like it was shot with a Brownie camera.

Devil's Bride, The (Great Britain, 1968)**½ Christopher Lee, Charles Gray, Nike Arrighi. Above average horror chiller, with Lee razor-sharp in a switch to the good-guy role—fending off the gathering powers of evil aroused by a group of Satanists. Alternate title: "The Devil Rides Out." (Dir: Terence Fisher, 95 mins.)

Devil's Brigade, The (1968)**½ William Holden, Cliff Robertson, Vince Edwards, Michael Rennie, Dana Andrews. Misfit American GIs join efficient Canadian troops for commando tactics during World War II. Competent if familiar heroics. (Dir: Andrew McLaglen, 130 mins.)

Devil's Canyon (1953)**½ Virginia Mayo, Dale Robertson. Ex-marshal is sent to prison where he becomes involved with mutineers against his will. Passable combination of western and prison melodrama. (Dir: Alfred L. Werker, 91 mins.)

Devil's Daughter, The (1972)* Shelley Winters, Belinda Montgomery. The devil's going to get you no matter how you fight back—that's the premise of this occult hokum about a sweet young girl whose soul has been sold to Satan. Belinda Montgomery plays the girl who tries to buck the odds and avert a marriage to the Prince of Doom. Occult hokum! Made-for-TV. (Dir: Jeannot Szwarc, 74 mins.)

Devil's Disciple (1959)***½ Kirk Douglas, Burt Lancaster, Laurence Olivier. Not the best screen translation of a George Bernard Shaw work, but a rousing good try. Kirk Douglas energetically portrays "Dick Dudgeon," the rebellious and romantic rogue; Burt Lancaster, miscast once again, pompously plays a New English pastor; and Olivier makes the most of his few scenes as the very grand and very opinionated British General Burgoyne. (Dir: Guy Hamilton, 82 mins.)

Devil's Doorway, (1950)*** Robert Taylor, Louis Calhern. An Indian veteran of the Civil War returns to find injustice and tragedy for his people, fights to aid them. Well-done western drama takes the Indian's point of view, does a good job of it. Direction and photography especially noteworthy, performances good. (Dir: Anthony Mann, 84 mins.)

Devil's Eight, The (1969)** Christopher George, Ralph Meeker, Fabian. Action meller which turns out to be a poor man's "Dirty Dozen." George is a federal agent who enlists the services of a motley crew of prisoners to bust a big moonshining syndicate. (Dir: Burt Topper, 97 mins.)

Devil's Eye, The (Swedish, 1960)*** Jarl Kulle, Bibi Andersson. Bits of the Bergman elegance and insight, snips of humor and captivating paradoxical detail. Story is reminiscent of G. B. Shaw's "Don Juan in Hell": the Devil gets a sty in his eye and resurrects his captive, Don Juan, to deal with its cause—the irritating chastity of a young woman up on earth. One of Bergman's few comedies. Written and directed by Ingmar Bergman. (90 mins.)

Devil's General (German, 1956)***½ Curt Jurgens, Marianne Cook. Famous wartime flyer gradually becomes disgusted with the Nazis, and the hopelessness of World War II. Talkative, but engrossing drama, with superb performances, direction.

Devil's Hairpin, The (1957)**½ Cornel Wilde, Jean Wallace, Mary Astor. Champion sports-car racer's disregard of safety is responsible for the crippling of his brother—he tries to reform. As usual, the racing scenes are the main attraction—

story line holds up fairly well. (Dir: Cornel Wilde, 82 mins.)

Devil's Hand, The (1962)* Robert Alda, Linda Christian. Horror film with all the obvious cliches used once again. Serves Linda Christian right.

Devil's Messenger, The (1962)*½ Lon Chaney, Karen Kadler. Satan assigns an attractive girl to perform tasks for him in order that she be admitted to the Dark World. Episodic thriller, some of which apparently was filmed in Sweden; cheap production detracts from what would ordinarily be a fairly interesting idea. (Dir: Curt Siodmak, 72 mins.)

Devil's Own, The (British 1966)**½ Joan Fontaine, Kay Walsh, Ingrid Brett. Teacher (Fontaine) at an English private school comes across witchcraft and voodoo rites. Suspense fans will come across a few chills. Marvelous actor Alec McCowen wasted.

Devil's Partner, The (1960)** Edwin Nelson, Jean Allison. Stranger shows up in a small town, then weird things begin to happen. Unbelievable thriller has good acting to help it.

Devil's Rain, The (1975)* Ernest Borgnine, Eddie Albert, Ida Lupino, William Shatner, Keenan Wynn, John Travolta. Satanic shenanigans. Garbled attempt at horror, sports Borgnine as a coven leader back to haunt New England. Finale which features the coven turning into wax and melting in a storm is the only sequence that doesn't dissolve on the spot. Excellent makeup and special effects. Your only chance of the day to see Borgnine transformed into a goat-like version of the devil. (Dir: Robert Fuest, 85 mins.)

Devil's Wanton, The (Swedish, 1949)**½ Doris Svedlund, Birger Malmsten. Director Ingmar Bergman's theory of Hell on earth, told from the viewpoint of a girl who tries to find happiness with a man deserted by his wife after her lover has had their baby killed. Often more artiness than art; gloomy drama for devotees of the Swedish director. English-dubbed. (Dir: Ingmar Bergman, 72 mins.)

Devil's Widow, The—See: Tam Lin

Devotion (1946)**½ Ida Lupino, Paul Henreid, Olivia de Havilland. The genius of the Bronte sisters receives a Hollywood treatment in this photoplay. Excellent acting rescues the film but they should have called it "Distortion." (Dir: Curtis Bernhardt, 107 mins.)

D.I., The (1957)** Jack Webb, Don Dubbins, Monica Lewis. Webb portrays a very tough drill instructor in the marines. We see him take a group through the rigorous routines and it gets a little boring. In addition to starring, Webb produced and directed this opus. (Dir: Jack Webb, 106 mins.)

Diabolically Yours (French, 1968)** Senta Berger, Alain Delon. Middling mystery about an amnesiac (Delon) who attempts to unravel the secret of his forgotten memory. Miss Berger is a mysterious woman who helps treat him. Never sustains its suspense. (Dir: Ralph Baum, 101 mins.)

Diabolique (1955)**** Simone Signoret, Vera Clouzot. Excellent, scary murder mystery, as the mistress of a schoolmaster and her lover plan an elaborate murder. One of Simone Signoret's finest performances, the film contains scenes that will leave you on the edge of your seat. Superb direction by Henri-Georges Clouzot. (107 mins.)

Dial Hot Line (1969)* Vince Edwards, Chelsea Brown, Kim Hunter. Pilot film for the television series "Matt Lincoln" had Vince Edwards heading a "Hot Line," a telephone service for people who need psychiatric aid. Problems in this film include a suicide who threatens the hot line's existence and two young girls in trouble. Other problems of "Dial" include the acting, writing and directing. Made-for-TV. (Dir: Jerry Thorpe, 100 mins.)

Dial M for Murder (1954)***½ Grace Kelly, Ray Milland, Robert Cummings. Alfred Hitchcock directed this exciting screen version of the famed Broadway mystery drama. Robert Cummings and Ray Milland make Princess Grace's life a very hectic one up to the surprising climax. (Dir: Alfred Hitchcock, 105 mins.)

Dial 1119 (1950)**½ Marshall Thompson, Keefe Brasselle. Good suspense thriller that keeps your interest. The cast is primarily made up of no name stars but do very nicely. The setting is a bar where a killer keeps a group trapped. (Dir: Gerald Mayer, 74 mins.)

Dial Red O (1955)**½ William Elli-

ott, Keith Larsen. Smart detective proves the innocence of a disturbed war vet accused of murder. Neat little detective story made on a small budget. (62 mins.)

Diamond Earrings, The (French, 1953)** Charles Boyer, Danielle Darrieux, Vittorio De Sica. A sometimes tragic and most times confusing "merry-go-round" giving and receiving of a pair of diamond earrings. Stars cannot rise above the script. (Dir: Max Ophuls, 105 mins.)

Diamond Head (1962)** Charlton Heston, Yvette Mimieux, George Chakiris. Strictly for fans who like their soap opera lavishly mounted and star-studded with Hollywood names. Charlton Heston is a bigger-than-life plantation owner in Hawaii who wants everything his way. His sister (Yvette Mimieux) is equally independent and announces she is going to marry a Hawaiian native (James Darren). The conflict rages on to the finale with Heston baring his chest and teeth at the entire supporting cast. The Hawaiian locations are more interesting than the cardboard characters. (Dir: Guy Green, 107 mins.)

Diamond Jim (1935)*** Edward Arnold, Binnie Barnes, Jean Arthur. Story of "Diamond Jim" Brady, the millionaire sportsman and man-about-town of the gay nineties. Well done period drama. (Dir: A. Edward Sutherland, 100 mins.)

Diamond Queen, The (1953)**½ Fernando Lamas, Arlene Dahl, Gilbert Roland. Two soldiers of fortune in India bargain with a treacherous Mogul for a fabulous blue diamond. Routine adventure. (Dir: John Brahm, 80 mins.)

Diamond Safari (1958)*½ Kevin McCarthy, Andre Morell. Private eye gets involved in murder and diamond smuggling. Filming in South Africa doesn't help this mediocre melodrama, which looks like two unsold TV pilot films strung togther. (67 mins.)

Diamond Wizard, The (British, 1954)**½ Dennis O'Keefe, Margaret Sheridan. T-Man traces a stolen million to England, ties it in with diamond thievery. Okay crime melodrama. (Dir: Dennis O'Keefe, 83 mins.)

Diamonds (U.S.-Israel, 1976)*½ Robert Shaw, Richard Roundtree, Barbara Seagull. One droll critic accurately noted, "Diamonds are a goy's best friend." Maybe, but Jews and gentiles alike will find this Israeli crime caper pretty thin fare, enlivened by location shooting in Bethlehem, Jerusalem and Tel Aviv. Robert Shaw plays a dual role—the mastermind behind a gem heist as well as his rival brother. Roundtree and Seagull on hand for an interracial romance. Based on a story by Menahem Golan who also produced and directed. (106 mins.)

Diamonds Are Forever (Great Britain, 1971)***½ Sean Connery, Jill St. John, Charles Gray, Bruce Cabot. Terrific escapist James Bond fun. This is the eighth 007 entry, the sixth to star Connery, and the first to utilize American locations—Los Angeles, Palm Springs, Reno, etc. The basic setting is Las Vegas, the quarry is another evil villain willing and eager to rule the world. Maestro Bond's libido, drollery, and extensive gadgetry foil the rascals, of course. Connery returns to the role of Bond after an absence of four years and he's wonderful—far better than George Lazenby or Roger Moore. Deft screenplay by Richard Maibaum and Tom Mankiewicz, based, of course, on the novel by Ian Fleming. (Dir: Guy Hamilton, 119 mins.)

Diane (1956)** Lana Turner, Pedro Armendariz, Roger Moore. King's son about to be married to an Italian princess is enamoured of a glamorous French countess. Overstuffed costume drama. (Dir: David Miller, 102 mins.)

Diary of a Bad Girl (French, 1958) *½ Anne Vernon, Denik Patisson. Offensive morality tale about a "bad girl" who is lovingly taken care of by a crusading welfare worker. Patronizing. Drivel. (Dir: Leonide Moguy, 87 mins.)

Diary of a Chambermaid (1946)**½ Paulette Goddard, Burgess Meredith. A bewitching chambermaid is hired by a family of eccentrics, where she is involved in amorous byplay and finally murder. Odd, uneven comedy-drama. Some interesting moments, but all rather uncertain. Jean Renoir directed. (Dir: Jean Renoir, 86 mins.)

Diary of a High School Bride (1959)** Anita Sands, Ronald Foster. When a teenager marries a young law student, her mother and ex-boyfriend do all they can to break it up. Sin-

cerely done despite the lurid title, but doesn't quite succeed. Some good moments.

Diary of a Mad Housewife (1970)**** Richard Benjamin, Carrie Snodgrass. Entertaining, perceptive drama boasts marvelous performance by Carrie Snodgrass as a bored New York housewife-mother, and Frank Langella as a dashing, successful, and thoroughly selfish writer with whom she has an affair. Richard Benjamin is less interesting in the role of Miss Snodgrass's fastidious lawyer-husband who wants to be part of the New York chic scene. Excellent dissection of a modern urban marriage. (Dir: Frank Perry, 94 mins.)

Diary of a Madman (1963)**½ Vincent Price, Nancy Kovack. More of Vincent Price's flamboyant overacting. He plays a French judge who finds he's possessed by a demon, decides life's not worth living. Based on a story by Guy de Maupassant. (Dir: Reginald Le Borg, 96 mins.)

Diary of a Teacher (Italian, 1972) ***½ Bruno Cirino, Marisa Fabbri, Mico Cundari. Ambitious and lengthy —over 4½ hours—documentary drama written and directed by Vittorio De Seta and produced by RAI, Italian TV. Frequently moving and perceptive story based on the book "A Year in Petralata," chronicling the attempts of a young, committed teacher and his attempts to involve and intellectually stimulate "problem" youngsters born of impoverished, poorly educated parents. Director decided to "reconstruct, relive, and film from reality, from the authentic teaching experience." Italian dialogue with frequent English narration. Example of imaginative innovative TV, so seldom undertaken by the American TV industry. "Diary" is TV debut for De Seta, responsible for the 1960 "Bandits of Orgosolo." (272 mins.)

Diary of Anne Frank, The (1959) ***½ Joseph Schildkraut, Millie Perkins, Shelley Winters. Faithful screen translation of the hit Broadway play about the true, harrowing experiences of the Jewish Frank family and their friends when they are forced to hide from the Nazis in a factory attic in Amsterdam for two long years. Millie Perkins is visually perfect as the young Anne Frank whose spirit gives the group the courage to go on when they lose all hope, but her thesping leaves much to be desired. Of the good supporting cast, Joseph Schildkraut as Anne's strong father and Shelley Winters, as the terrified Mrs. Van Daan, are standouts. (Dir: George Stevens, 170 mins.)

Dick Tracy (1945)** Morgan Conway, Anne Jeffreys, Mike Mazurki, Jane Greer. Sleuth tracks down Splitface, a maniacal killer bent on revenge. Acceptable comic-strip heroics. (Dir: William Berke, 62 mins.)

Dick Tracy Meets Gruesome (1947) **½ Ralph Byrd, Boris Karloff, Anne Gwynne, Edward Ashley. Sleuth goes after a quartet of bank robbers, using a new kind of paralyzing gas. Fast moving comic-strip melodrama, with Karloff giving it added allure. (Dir: John Rawlins, 65 mins.)

Dictator's Guns, The (Italian, 1965) *½ Sylva Koscina, Leo Gordon, Lino Ventura. Miss Koscina's yacht seems to have disappeared with a prospective buyer in the Caribbean, and when she goes to find it she gets more than she bargained for. Routine in every department. (105 mins.)

Did You Hear the One About the Traveling Saleslady? (1968)* Phyllis Diller. We'd rather not. If you care, it's about how Phyllis Diller invades a Kansas town. For Diller devotees only. With Bob Denver, Joe Flynn. (Dir: Don Weis, 97 mins.)

Die! Die! My Darling (British, 1965) **½ Tallulah Bankhead, Stefanie Powers. Demented woman keeps a young American girl prisoner because she was the fiancée of her dead son. Standard shocker, with Bankhead giving a ripe performance. Thriller fans should give it a passing shudder. Miss Powers was TV's "Girl from U.N.C.L.E." (Dir: Silvio Narizzano, 97 mins.)

Die, Monster, Die (British, 1965)** Boris Karloff, Nick Adams, Suzi Farmer. Young American arrives in Britain to visit his fiancée, finds her living in a house of horror. Slow-moving thriller can boast of Karloff's customary fine performance, a certain air of suspense. (Dir: Daniel Haller, 80 mins.)

Dillinger (1945)**½ Lawrence Tierney, Anne Jeffreys. Story of the 20th Century's most notorious public enemy hardly does his career justice

but is an above average gangster film. (Dir: Max Nosseck, 89 mins.)

Dillinger (1973)**½ Warren Oates, Ben Johnson, Cloris Leachman, Richard Dreyfuss. Hard-driving rhythm of this narrative, supposedly the truth about John Dillinger, Public Enemy No. 1 of the Depression years, keeps interest, but the gratuitous violence finally overwhelms the film. Warren Oates gives a fine performance as Dillinger, but the script leaves no room for insight into the character and thus makes him merely a cartoon book villain. Written and directed by John Milius, then 29 years old. Impressive debut in some ways. (107 mins.)

Dime with a Halo (1963) *½ Barbara Luna, Robert Mobley. Five Mexican street kids steal a dime from the church collection plate so they can bet a tip at the local racetrack. The humor is thin as the kids have trouble cashing their winning tickets. (Dir: Boris Sagal, 97 mins.)

Dimples (1936)**½ Shirley Temple, Frank Morgan. Set right before the Civil War on New York's Bowery, this one has Shirley practically selling herself to a rich lady to save her poor daddy. There's a happy, tearful ending for the faithful. (Dir: William A. Seiter, 78 mins.)

Dingaka (British, 1965)**½ Stanley Baker, Juliet Prowse, Ken Gampu. Attorney takes the case of a tribesman up for murdering a rival whom he believes killed his daughter. Fairly interesting drama filmed in Africa, with the local color partially compensating for a rather sketchy plot. (Dir: Jamie Uys, 98 mins.)

Dinner at Eight (1933)***½ John Barrymore, Wallace Beery, Lionel Barrymore. Delightful adaptation of the Kaufman-Ferber comedy about the incidents leading up to a dinner party. Flawlessly played by an all-star cast. (Dir: George Cukor, 113 mins.)

Dinner at the Ritz (British, 1937) **½ Annabella, Paul Lukas, David Niven. A girl sets out to find her father's murderer, runs into a swindling gang in her quest. Good melodrama keeps the interest. (Dir: Harold D. Schuster, 80 mins.)

Dino (1957)*** Sal Mineo, Susan Kohner, Brian Keith. Sometimes moving drama about a young hood with a chip on his shoulder. Played with a sneer by Sal Mineo. Brian

Keith gives a good performance as a social worker who tries to help the hostile youth. Based on a TV play by Reginald Rose. (Dir: Thomas Carr, 96 mins.)

Dinosaurus (1960)**½ Ward Ramsey, Paul Lukather, Gregg Martell. A caveman and assorted prehistoric beasts are brought back to life on a tropic island. Intended as a horror thriller, this is more fun, intentional or otherwise, than you'd expect. Some good laughs involving the caveman's groping attempts to cope with civilization. (Dir: Irvin S. Yeaworth, 85 mins.)

Diplomatic Courier (1952)**½ Tyrone Power, Patricia Neal, Hildegarde Neff. Cloak-and-dagger yarn with good performances by Power and Hildegarde Neff. Plot offers no new twists but keeps the pace fast and suspenseful. (Dir: Henry Hathaway, 97 mins.)

Dirty Dingus Magee (1970)* Frank Sinatra, George Kennedy, Anne Jackson. Western in which the jokes are all simple-minded double-entendres and the script (for lack of a better word) merely allows Sinatra, as a runaway renegade, to make lamentable wisecracks. (Dir: Burt Kennedy, 91 mins.)

Dirty Dozen, The (1967)***½ Lee Marvin, Jim Brown, Ernest Borgnine, John Cassavetes. If you're a devotee of rugged wartime adventure stories filled with lots of tough guys and fights, this is your dream picture. Director Robert Aldrich may have filmed this in Britain, but what's on the screen is an unmistakably American vision of authority and army life, and the nature of the violence in the soldiers is dealt with on some interesting levels. Concerns a gang of convicted G.I.s who are reprieved, only to be trained and turned into more efficient killers. (Dir: Robert Aldrich, 149 mins.)

Dirty Game, The (France-Italy-West Germany, 1965)* Henry Fonda, Vittorio Gassman, Robert Ryan, Annie Girardot. Trio of tales concerning the spy trade has a cast of major stars wasting their talents. Will U.S. nuclear subs be blown up? Will an Italian scientist with a new jet fuel tell of his discovery? Will anyone care? (Dirs: Terence Young, Christian-Jaque, Carlo Lizzani, Werner Klingler, 91 mins.)

Dirty Game, The (1967)**½ Robert Ryan, Henry Fonda, Vittorio Gassman. Robert Ryan plays an American intelligence chief who remembers three of his most difficult cases. The trio of tales are familiar spy fare, but the one with Gassman playing a double agent in Rome who has a tricky assignment involving a Russian scientist, is the most interesting. Originally produced as a pilot for a TV series, and it looks like it. (Dir: Terence Young, 91 mins.)

Dirty Harry (1971)* Clint Eastwood, Harry Guardino. Shallow, bloody police thriller. Eastwood plays a San Francisco cop out to capture a long-haired mass murderer. The conservative cliches are intolerable, made even worse by the discontinuity of the plot. Eastwood is as nondescript a policeman as he was a cowboy in all those unmemorable Italian westerns. (Director: Don Siegel, 102 mins.)

Dirty Mary, Crazy Larry (1974)** Peter Fonda, Vic Morrow, Susan George. If your tastes run to multiple car crashes, high-speed car chases and race car heroes-turned-thieves, this is for you. Peter Fonda is a small-time car racer with dreams for the big time. He and his buddy rob a supermarket, and spend the rest of the film running from the law. A perky, sexy, thrill-crazy girl joins them and it's full throttle from start to finish. (Dir: John Hough, 93 mins.)

Disappearance of Flight 412, The (1974)**½ Glenn Ford, Bradford Dillman, Guy Stockwell. For sci-fi fans. Air Force personnel become involved with a missing aircraft which might have tangled with UFO's. It's played straight and the production values are good. Made-for-TV. (Dir: Jud Taylor, 72 mins.)

Discreet Charm of the Bourgeoisie, The (France, 1972)**** Delphine Seyrig, Fernando Rey, Stephane Audran, Jean-Pierre Cassel. The great master-writer-director Luis Bunuel, at age 72 helming his 29th film, has produced one of his most dazzling films ever—wry, stylish, serious, ebullient, funny and profound—all at different times in the same delicious film. Bunuel here savages the upper and middle classes with better humor than usual, but no less brilliance. About some South American diplomats from a tiny country, posted to Paris.

Bunuel thrusts at many of his usual targets—politics, the church, the army and the foibles of all mankind. Co-authored by Bunuel and Jean Claude Carriere. (Dir: Luis Bunuel, 100 mins.)

Disembodied, The (1957)** Paul Burke, Allison Hayes. Combination horror-mystery film with some sci-fi phenomena thrown in. The kids may go for this tale set in the jungle. If you're not in the jungle, you can do better. (Dir: Walter Grauman, 65 mins.)

Dishonorable Discharge (French, 1958)** Eddie Constantine. Another Eddie Constantine Grade B drama with the keynote on action. He plays a wrongly accused ex-Navy officer who manages to clear his name after some action-filled complications. English-dubbed. (Dir: Bernard Borderie, 105 mins.)

Dishonored (1931)*** Marlene Dietrich, Victor McLaglen, Warner Oland. Story by Josef von Sternberg. Dated spy drama but you'll enjoy secret agent Marlene's encounter with General Oland. As usual, La Dietrich is gorgeous. (Dir: Josef von Sternberg, 91 mins.)

Disobedient (British, 1955)*½ Marian Spencer, Russell Enoch. Weirdie translation of a Cocteau play about the disruption of a family when father and son love the same girl. Depressing, clumsily done. Alternative title: **Intimate Relations.**

Disorder (Italian, 1962)*½ Louis Jourdan, Susan Strasberg, Curt Jurgens, Alida Valli. All the critics said the title describes the film, so there's a little use in trying to synopsize the plot, which has to do with a party, the return of a daughter to her home, and a servant. Hopelessly jumbled, makes no sense. Good cast seems lost in the obscurity. English-dubbed.

Disorderly Orderly, The (1964)** Jerry Lewis, Susan Oliver. Routine Jerry Lewis fun fare. In this excursion, Jerry works as a hospital orderly, the setting for his frenzied slapstick. Familiar faces in the supporting cast include veterans Alice Pearce, Kathleen Freeman and Glenda Farrell. If only Lewis had had the discipline and sense to have a gifted director, and then listen to him! (Dir: Frank Tashlin, 90 mins.)

Disraeli (1929)*** George Arliss, Joan Bennett. The wily and brilliant Prime Minister of England paves the way for the Suez Canal. Despite its primitive movie technique, this historical drama contains a still gripping, authoritative performance by Arliss. (Dir: Alfred E. Green, 90 mins.)

Dispatch from Reuters (1940)*** Edward G. Robinson, Eddie Albert. Story of the founder of the world-famous British news agency is informative, well produced and acted but sorely lacking in dramatic content. (Dir: William Dieterle, 89 mins.)

Distant Drums (1953)*** Gary Cooper. Drama of Seminole Indian uprising in Florida is loaded with action and must be classified as good entertainment for adventure fans. (Dir: Raoul Walsh, 101 mins.)

Distant Trumpet, A (1964)** Troy Donahue, Suzanne Pleshette. A dull cavalry western with every cliché about the personal problems of those stationed at a frontier outpost. The scenery is fine. Oh, yes, there are Indians waiting in the wings. (Dir. Raoul Walsh, 117 mins.)

Dive Bomber (1941)*** Errol Flynn, Fred MacMurray, Alexis Smith, Ralph Bellamy. Interesting, well played story about medical problems concerning flying in 1941. Even though it's dated today, there's still a certain amount of historical interest. (Dir: Michael Curtiz, 133 mins.)

Divided Heart, The (British, 1954)***½ Theodore Bikel, Alexander Knox. An absorbing drama about the story of a boy torn between two mothers who love and want him. Good performances. Set in Europe after World War II. (Dir: Charles Crichton, 100 mins.)

Divorce American Style (1967)***½ Dick Van Dyke, Debbie Reynolds, Jason Robards, Jean Simmons. One of the very few deft satires produced by the American film industry in recent years. Stylish script by producer Norman Lear casts a perceptive and jaundiced eye on the American institution of marriage in suburbia. Dick and Debbie are splitting up after many years, and friend Robards, divorced from Jean Simmons, comes up with a far-fetched scheme to fix everything. Director Bud Yorkin gets good performances from all concerned. (Dir: Bud Yorkin, 109 mins.)

Divorce His; Divorce Hers (1973)** Richard Burton, Elizabeth Taylor. Weak vehicle for Taylor and Burton. Intended to be a brittle analysis of the events leading up to the disintegration of a marriage, holds interest when the break-up is viewed from both sides. Movie's first half is the story as seen by Burton; second half has Miss Taylor's Jane as the focal point. Made-for-TV. (Dir: Warris Hussein, 144 mins.)

Divorce—Italian Style (Italian, 1962) **** Marcello Mastroianni, Daniela Rocca. One of the most brilliant modern film comedies. Tremendous performance by Mastroianni as a decadent Sicilian nobleman who wants to get rid of his wife, but can't—the law, you know. Excellent satire on modern Italian manners and mores. Expertly directed, a biting satiric joy throughout. Don't miss it. (Dir: Pietro Germi, 104 mins.)

Divorce of Lady X, The (British, 1938)*** Merle Oberon, Laurence Olivier. A London barrister allows a pretty miss to spend the night (innocently) in his flat, then discovers he may be named corespondent in a divorce action. Pleasant sophisticated comedy, some good laughs. (Dir: Tim Whelan, 91 mins.)

Dixie (1943)**½ Bing Crosby, Dorothy Lamour. Some good minstrel numbers in this fictitious biography of a famous minstrel man, but story is weak and tiresome. (Dir: A. Edward Sutherland, 89 mins.)

Do Not Disturb (1965)** Doris Day, Rod Taylor. Another Doris Day romantic comedy which her immediate family will no doubt enjoy. All others, be forewarned—it's overly cute. In this one, Miss Day is married to Rod Taylor. They go to England where a series of madcap adventures threaten their marital bliss. Script gives no indication of whether Doris is or is not a virgin in this opus. (Dir: Ralph Levy, 102 mins.)

Do You Know This Voice? (British, (1964)**½ Dan Duryea, Isa Miranda, Gwen Watford. Fair enough suspense item about a couple who find their son has been kidnaped, with tragic consequences. Some good performances.

Do You Love Me? (1946)**½ Maureen O'Hara, Dick Haymes, Harry James. Harmless musical about a prudish girl's romance with a crooner. Plenty of swing music for those who want to see what was the rage in '46. (Dir: Gregory Ratoff, 91 mins.)

Do You Take This Stranger? (1970)* Gene Barry, Lloyd Bridges, Diane Baker. Made for TV features. This entry is supposed to entrance the ladies. It probably won't. Middle-aged loser Lloyd Bridges, dying of cancer, agrees to impersonate a no-goodnik (Gene Barry), and accompany Barry's lovely wife (Diane Baker) on a world tour before death strikes. (Dir: Richard Heffron, 100 mins.)

D.O.A. (1949)***½ Edmond O'Brien, Pamela Britton. When he is slipped a dose of slow-acting poison, a man sets out to find his own murderer. Terrifically taut melodrama with suspense on high throughout. (Dir: Rudolph Mate, 83 mins.)

Doberman Gang, The (1972)* Byron Mabe, Julie Parrish. Ridiculous story about a gang of trained Doberman Pinschers who rob banks, under the command of a novel criminal and an animal trainer. (Dir: Ron Chudgow, 87 mins.)

Doc (1971)**½ Stacy Keach, Faye Dunaway, Harris Yulin. Disappointing, offbeat western. Wyatt Earp gets his face smashed in and Doc Holliday is incapacitated by coughing spasms in this shake-up-the-myth reworking of OK Corral. Wyatt (Yulin) is small and droopy-eyed and Doc (Keach) is self-conscious and brooding. Collectively they will manage to remain standing after the shooting, which takes only seven seconds in what is otherwise a slickly paced character study. If you're looking for a slambanger, this isn't it. (Director: Frank Perry, 122 mins.)

Doctor—See also **Dr.**

Doctor and the Girl, The (1949)**½ Glenn Ford, Janet Leigh, Gloria De Haven, Charles Coburn. Pure soap opera but well done. Glenn Ford plays the doctor son of Park Ave. doctor who decides he wants to earn his way in the medical life and sets up his own practice on the Lower East side of N. Y. The cast does well with the crisis-ridden script. (Dir: Curtis Bernhardt, 98 mins.)

Doctor at Large (British, 1957)**½ Dirk Bogarde, James Robertson Justice. Amusing comedy about a young

195

doctor's efforts to get into a hospital on staff, over the protest of the superintendent. One of a series, up to the standard of its predecessors. (Dir: Ralph Thomas, 98 mins.)

Doctor at Sea (British, 1956)*** Dirk Bogarde, Brigitte Bardot. Another in the film series about the adventures of a young doctor. Brigitte Bardot is aboard for this amusing trip. (Dir: Ralph Thomas, 93 mins.)

Doctor Dolittle (1967)*** Rex Harrison, Anthony Newley, Samantha Eggar. A somewhat disappointing version of the classic children's stories of Hugh Lofting, but the youngsters will undoubtedly enjoy it, and believe that the magical Rex really does talk to the animals. Harrison seems to be more Prof. Higgins than Dr. John Dolittle from Puddleby-on-the-Marsh, but he is so ingratiating that young and old will find this no-expense-spared fable a diverting few hours. Several of Leslie Bricusse's melodies are good fun and there's a delicious supporting performance from Richard Attenborough playing Mr. Blossom. All in all, pleasant entertainment for the whole family. (Dir: Richard Fleischer, 152 mins.)

Doctor Faustus (British, 1967)*½ Richard Burton, Elizabeth Taylor. Richard Burton stars and co-directs a flaccid version of Christopher Marlowe's play about a man who sells his soul to the Devil. Elizabeth Taylor appears as the silent Helen of Troy, looking like an 8 x 10 glossy. Well, a great play has been preserved on film . . . so what else is new? (Dir: Richard Burton, 93 mins.)

Doctor in Clover—See: **Carnaby, M.D.**

Doctor in Distress (British, 1964)*** Dirk Bogarde, Samantha Eggar, James Robertson Justice. Continuing the medical shenanigans in this series, the grumpy head of a hospital becomes a changed man when he falls in love, and his young aide has his own problems with a glamorous model. Good performers and some amusing situations make this comedy a good entry.

Doctor in Love (British, 1962)** Michael Craig, Virginia Maskell. Young doctor romances a nurse who disappears only to return at a most inopportune moment. Mild comedy doesn't hit the laugh mark set by others in this series. (Dir: Ralph Thomas, 93 mins.)

Doctor in the House (British, 1955) *** Kay Kendall, Dirk Bogarde. Highly amusing comedy about the hectic and hilarious life of a medical student. Stars shine. (Dir: Ralph Thomas, 92 mins.)

Doctor of Doom (Mexican, 1960)* Armando Silvestre, Lorena Velasquez. Mad doctor carries out fiendish experiments with brain transplants. Brainless horror thriller dubbed in English.

Doctor Paul Joseph Goebbels (1962) **½ Documentary study of Hitler's propaganda chief. Well-compiled material, should interest World War II historians.

Doctor Rhythm (1938)**½ Bing Crosby, Beatrice Lillie. Forced, unfunny comedy about a doctor who pinch-hits for a policeman friend on a "routine" bodyguard job. The Lady Peel's many fans will enjoy watching several of her delightful routines. (Dir: Frank Tuttle, 80 mins.)

Doctor Satan's Robot (1940-66)**½ Eduardo Ciannelli, Robert Wilcox, Ella Neal. Feature version of serial "Mysterious Doctor Satan." Mad doctor plans an army of robots, is thwarted by a masked hero. Juvenile nonsense, but has a lickety-split pace, plenty of action. Good fun. (Dir: William Witney, 100 mins.)

Doctor Socrates (1935)*** Paul Muni, Ann Dvorak. Mr. Muni raises this ordinary story of a doctor who patches up a criminal at gunpoint out of the commonplace. (Dir: William Dieterle, 80 mins.)

Doctor Takes a Wife (1940)*** Loretta Young, Ray Milland. Professor and authoress are forced to make the best of it when people get the impression they're married. Entertaining romantic comedy. (Dir: Alexander Hall, 89 mins.)

Doctor Without Scruples (German, 1960)** Barbara Rutting. Doctor successfully experimenting in heart surgery is placed under a cloud of suspicion when his assistant proves to be a former Nazi. Mildly interesting drama dubbed in English.

Doctor, You've Got to Be Kidding (1967)* George Hamilton, Sandra Dee. The producers of this stinker must be kidding! Tasteless comedy dealing with a perky young lady, played with wide-eyed blondness by Miss Dee, and her arrogant boss, played with dark-haired blandness by Hamilton and their on-again, off-again romantic hijinks. The finale finds a pregnant Miss Dee marrying Hamilton moments before she's taken over to the delivery room. We tell you this for the benefit of those who tune out long before Sandra gets to the hospital. (Dir: Peter Tewksbury, 94 mins.)

Doctor Zhivago (British, 1965)***½ Julie Christie, Omar Sharif, Tom Courtenay. The prize-winning novel of Boris Pasternak about life in Russia before and during the Russian Revolution. Directed by the master David Lean, this mammoth spectacle, filmed partially on location in Spain, not Russia, is too long and episodic, but it's still an impressive and pretty consistently absorbing account of one of the most fascinating and important periods in human history. The screenplay by Robert Bolt is much superior to the screenwriting normally found in such historical dramas, and it takes fewer liberties with the facts of history. Courtenay is an impoverished revolutionary, and he gives one of his best performances to date. (Dir: David Lean, 197 mins.)

Doctors, The (French, 1956)*** Jeanne Moreau, Raymond Pellegrin. Well made French drama about the growth of a young doctor. Excellently acted by a top French cast.

Doctor's Dilemma, The (British, 1959)***½ Leslie Caron, Dirk Bogarde, Robert Morley. George Bernard Shaw's thoroughly delightful comedy is excellently brought to the screen with an almost perfect cast. The adventures of a young devoted wife who consults a number of physicians regarding her husband's failing health makes fascinating entertainment. (Dir: Anthony Asquith, 99 mins.)

Doctor's Wives (1971)* Gene Hackman, Richard Crenna, Carroll O'Connor, Diana Sands. There's enough phony melodrama in this opus for a month's worth of afternoon soap opera. Lots of blood and surgery. Notables are Cara Williams as a divorcee who likes to drink; Dyan Cannon in a brief, flash appearance as a blatantly immoral spouse; and Janice Rule as a troubled wife who has taken to drugs. (Dir: George Schaefer, 100 mins.)

Dodge City (1939)*** Errol Flynn, Olivia de Havilland, Ann Sheridan. Fairly good 1939 version of today's CinemaScope outdoor epics. No underplaying like today but plenty of action in this story of Kansas in the days when the railroads were slowly heading west. (Dir: Michael Curtiz, 105 mins.)

Dodsworth (1936)**** Walter Huston, Ruth Chatterton, David Niven, Paul Lukas. Outstanding film based on Sinclair Lewis' classic novel. Dodsworth, excellently portrayed by Walter Huston, is an archetype of the American self-made man. After a long trip to Europe he finds he is in danger of losing his wife and the peace he thought he had secured. Excellent supporting cast. (Dir: William Wyler, 101 mins.)

Dog Day Afternoon (1975)**** Al Pacino, John Cazale, Charles Durning, Carol Kane. Gripping, funny, sometimes grotesque true story about a Brooklyn bank robbery on August 22, 1972. Robbery ringleader, with a wife and two children, sticks up the joint to get money for a sex-change operation for his drag-queen lover. Al Pacino is stunning playing the bossy hoodlum who revels in being an "instant TV news celebrity" while he negotiates the release of his hostages. There's a wonderful phone conversation between Pacino and his male lover (Chris Sarandon). Sidney Lumet has accurately and perceptively captured part of New York's life-giving frenzy and the diversity of its street people. (Dir: Sidney Lumet, 130 mins.)

Dog of Flanders, A (1960)**** David Ladd, Donald Crisp, Theodore Bikel. One of the loveliest children's films ever made, the third film version of the famous novel by Ouida written in 1872. About a young Dutch boy, his grandfather, and the stray dog they adopt. Beautifully photographed in color against the Dutch and Belgian countryside with fine performances from all the humans, plus the dog scene stealer Patrasche. (Moviedog buffs may remember that this is the same foxy mutt that got such good reviews in the '58 film "Old Yeller.") Tastefully produced by Robert Radnitz. (Dir: James B. Clark, 96 mins.)

Doll Face (1946)**½ Vivian Blaine, Dennis O'Keefe, Perry Como. Story of a burlesque girl and her boy friend is routine. But Perry is around and Vivian looks good. (Dir: Lewis Seiler, 80 mins.)

Doll That Took the Town, The (Italian, 1957)*½ Virna Lisi, Haya Harareet, Serge Reggiani. Girl wanting to make it big in show business fakes an attack to get some publicity, but the stunt gets out of hand and she is forced to name her attackers. Threadbare drama.

$ (Dollars) (1971)**½ Warren Beatty, Goldie Hawn. Bank robbery in Germany masterminded by Beatty, a bank employee out to steal $1.5 million. Hawn plays a "dippy hooker" and his accessory to the crime. The pacing is slow, but there are a few brief moments of suspense and humor. Good chase as a climax. Casting is odd; Beatty is too subtle an actor for this part and he has difficulty working with Miss Hawn. (Dir: Richard Brooks, 120 mins.)

Doll's House, A (1973)*** Jane Fonda, Trevor Howard, David Warner, Edward Fox. Women's lib, 19th-century style. Ms. Fonda gives an uneven performance as Nora, Ibsen's doll-like wife and mother who suddenly and dramatically asserts her independence when she is confronted with her husband's arrogant male immorality. The rest of the cast fare much better under director Joseph Losey's steady hand. Interesting note: although the film was produced for theatrical release, it made its debut on TV. (87 mins.)

Dolly Sisters, The (1945)**½ Betty Grable, John Payne, June Haver. Some nice legs and a good score are the only assets of this fictionalized story of the famous sister act. (Dir: Irving Cummings, 114 mins.)

Don Is Dead, The (1973)**½ Anthony Quinn, Robert Forster, Frederic Forrest, Al Lettieri. "Godfather" imitation but well acted. Once again, the Mafiosi families are fighting for control of their interests in Las Vegas, and their code of honor among thieves gets a workout here. Anthony Quinn is perfect as the older Mafia boss and Frederic Forrest scores as a modern-day member of a Mafia family who wants out but can't manage the feat. The dialogue seems natural and the story, though familiar from all those other Mafia movies, still works. (Dir: Richard Fleischer, 115 mins.)

Don Juan Quilligan (1945)**½ William Bendix, Joan Blondell, Phil Silvers. Comedy about a bigamist is similar to "Captain's Paradise" only it lacks the wit of the Guinness film. Bendix is married to a girl in Brooklyn and one in upstate New York. Some laughs but not enough. (Dir: Frank Tuttle, 75 mins.)

Dondi (1960)*½ David Janssen, Patti Page, David Korey. Insipid little comedy based on the exploits of the cartoon character "Dondi," who is an Italian waif who's adopted by a group of G.I.'s and brought to this country. Dondi is played by one of the most untalented child performers ever to appear on the screen, David Korey, and he's about as Italian as the 4th of July. (Dir: Albert Zugsmith, 100 mins.)

Donovan's Brain (1953)*** Lew Ayres, Gene Evans, Nancy Davis. Scientist keeps the brain tissue of a dead millionaire alive, but the brain overcomes him and causes him to do its bidding. Suspenseful, well-made melodrama. (Dir: Felix Feist, 83 mins.)

Donovan's Reef (1963)*** John Wayne, Elizabeth Allen, Lee Marvin, Dorothy Lamour, Jack Warden. What happens when a stuffy Boston girl arrives on a South Pacific isle in search of her father forms the basis of this light-hearted, frequently light-headed comedy directed by John Ford as if he was enjoying a vacation. Art it isn't, but there's lots of fun, outrageously played in broad style by the entire cast. Scenic values are superb. (Dir: John Ford, 109 mins.)

Don't Be Afraid of the Dark (1973)** Kim Darby, Jim Hutton, Barbara Anderson. A film for fans of horror stories laced with the supernatural. Miss Darby and Hutton play a young couple whose house seems to be inhabited by little demons intent on drawing Kim into their web. Made-for-TV. (Dir: John Newland, 74 mins.)

Don't Blame the Stork (British, 1958)** Ian Hunter, Veronica Hurst. Famous actor finds himself an unexpected father when a baby is left on his doorstep. Fairly amusing comedy with a good cast.

Don't Bother to Knock (1952)** Marilyn Monroe, Richard Widmark, Anne Bancroft. This was the first dramatic part Marilyn did after her sensational sex-queen build-up and she didn't come off too well. It isn't entirely her fault—the script about a mentally disturbed girl who takes a job as a baby sitter in a large hotel is very weak and often laughable. Widmark, in a familiar role as a tough guy with a good heart, tries to overcome the script but can't. Anne Bancroft, in the thankless role of Widmark's girl, is entirely wasted. (Dir: Robert Baker, 76 mins.)

Don't Cry With Your Mouth Full (French, 1973)**** Annie Cole, Bernard Menez, Frederic Duru. Charming, perceptive comedy about a nubile young girl in provincial France, reminiscent of the early work of Jean Renoir, but not quite as good. You'll see three generations of one French family and their differing manners, mores and morals. Affecting portrayal from Annie Cole as the 15-year-old teenager before and after her first affair. Skillful performance by Menez. (Dir: Pascal Thomas, 116 mins.)

Don't Drink the Water (1969)**½ Jackie Gleason, Estelle Parsons. A Jewish caterer being accused of spying in a Communist country and taking refuge with his family in the American embassy formed the premise of Woody Allen's hilarious but uneven stage play. The timing, pace, and direction of the work have been altered to fit the frame of Jackie Gleason as the caterer. The results may delight Gleason fans, but they will surely outrage Allen fans. Fortunately Allen's comic genius will out, so there are a few chuckles and guffaws for all. (Dir: Howard Morris, 97 mins.)

Don't Give Up the Ship (1959)** Jerry Lewis, Dina Merrill. Jerry in the Navy accomplishes the amazing feat of losing a destroyer, and the big brass would sincerely like to know where he misplaced it. Mild service comedy; some laughs, but Jerry's done better. (Dir: Norman Taurog, 85 mins.)

Don't Go Near the Water (1957)**½ Glenn Ford, Anne Francis, Gia Scala, Earl Holliman, Eva Gabor. Fast paced, amusing service comedy about the goings-on in a naval installation on a South Pacific tropical paradise complete with friendly, curvaceous natives. Ford gets a good share of the laughs and is ably supported by an excellent cast of actors. Based on novel by William Brinkley. (Dir: Charles Walters, 107 mins.)

Don't Just Stand There (1968)** Robert Wagner, Mary Tyler Moore, Glynis Johns. Not too funny comedy about a group of sophisticated would-be novelist-adventurers who can't seem to stay out of trouble. If you don't look too closely at the plot, you might enjoy some of the shenanigans. One good thing, the ladies—Mary Tyler Moore, Glynis Johns and statuesque Barbara Rhoades—are nice to look at. (Dir: Ron Winston, 100 mins.)

Don't Knock the Rock (1957)*½ Bill Haley and His Comets, Alan Dale. Strictly for kids who don't care about plot—just music, music and more music, rock style. We can and do, knock the rock. (90 mins.)

Don't Knock the Twist (1962)*½ Chubby Checker, Linda Scott. TV idea man tries to stage a big spectacular, against some rivalry. Innocuous musical, for twisters only, and whatever happened to the dance?

Don't Look Back (1967)***½ Bob Dylan, Joan Baez, Donovan. Unique documentary about folk-singer Bob Dylan's tour of England in 1965, and a rare opportunity to watch this remarkable young musician on stage and off. You'll see Dylan toying with some simple-minded newspapermen, shots of Dylan's manager, generally get a better idea of what this guarded young artist cares about. Much of the credit for the film goes to the director-editor D. A. Pennebaker.

Don't Look Now (Great Britain-Italy, 1973)***½ Julie Christie, Donald Sutherland, Hilary Mason, Clelia Matania. Stylistically beautiful thriller about psychic phenomenon that works, thanks partially to the haunting visual quality of Venice as photographed by director Nicolas Roeg. The baroque images dominate what could be a straightforward suspense story about a young British married couple who, shortly after their daughter's accidental death, make contact with the child through a blind medium. The eeriness of Venice in winter magnificently captured, and Christie and Sutherland are extremely good. Based on a short story by Daphne du Maurier. (Dir: Nicolas Roeg, 110 mins.)

Don't Make Waves (1967)* Tony Curtis, Claudia Cardinale, Sharon Tate. Don't make the effort to tune in. Based on Ira Wallach's book "Muscle Beach," this musclebound nonsense finds Tony as a tourist who finds love on the beach at Malibu. Claudia looks ravishing but they forgot the script. With Mort Sahl, Edgar Bergen, Joanna Barnes. Mort Sahl is a funny man, but you'd never know it from "Waves." (Dir: Alexander Mackendrick, 97 mins.)

Don't Push, I'll Charge When I'm Ready (1969)* Sue Lyon, Cesar Romero, Soupy Sales. Weak World War II comedy of an Italian P.O.W. who gets drafted into the American army. Made-for-TV. (Dir: Nathaniel Lande, 100 mins.)

Don't Raise the Bridge, Lower the River (1968)** Jerry Lewis, Terry-Thomas, Jacqueline Pearce, Patricia Routledge. Jerry Lewis plays it more or less straight as an American in England trying to hold on to his wife. Soft-pedaling of Lewis rates praise under any conditions, but otherwise it's only mild amusement. Screenplay by Max Wilk is better than most of Jerry's scripts. (Dir: Jerry Paris, 99 mins.)

Don't Take It to Heart (British, 1945)***½ Richard Greene, Patricia Medina. Young lawyer falls for the daughter of the owner of a run-down castle, stays in the small town to help out the victims of a wealthy skinflint. Exceptionally ingenious romantic comedy, has those little clever touches that mean so much.

Don't Tempt the Devil (France-Italy, 1963)** Marina Vlady, Virna Lisi, Bourvil, Pierre Brasseur. Ironic, mystery-suspense tale features Vlady as a cool, calculating widow and Lisi as the tearful nurse of a murdered man. A few suspenseful moments! (Dir: Christian-Jaque, 106 mins.)

Don't Trust Your Husband (1948)** Fred MacMurray, Madeleine Carroll. The wife of an ad agency exec. doesn't like his after-office hours dealings with a glamorous client, so she decides to make him jealous. Fair comedy which doesn't do right by the players. (Dir: Lloyd Bacon, 90 mins.)

Don't Turn 'Em Loose (1936)**½ Lewis Stone, Bruce Cabot, Betty Grable. Parole board member sees his own son turn out to be a criminal. Interesting crime melodrama. (Dir: Ben Stoloff, 65 mins.)

Doomsday Flight, The (1966)**½ Van Johnson, Jack Lord, Edmond O'Brien, John Saxon. Familiar but suspenseful melodrama — frantic search for a bomb placed aboard a passenger airliner, to find it before it goes off. Nicely written (Rod Serling), competently acted. Another made-for-TV feature. (Dir: William Graham, 100 mins.)

Doomsday Voyage (1972)* Joseph Cotten, John Gabriel, Ann Randall. About a political assassin who stows away on a ship by locking himself into a stateroom with the captain's daughter. Inept nonsense stuffed with stock footage of ships and shuffleboard. (Dir: John Vidette, 88 mins.)

Door with Seven Locks (German, 1962)*½ Heinz Drache, Sabina Sesselman. Villain with a love of torture instruments imperils the life of a young heiress. Implausible Edgar Wallace mystery dubbed in English. (Dir: Alfred Vohrer, 96 mins.)

Dorian Gray (Italy-Liechtenstein-West Germany, 1970)** Helmut Berger, Herbert Lom, Richard Todd. The second, definitely inferior filming of Oscar Wilde's classic novel about late 19th-century perversions and mores and a painting which ages, updated to London, 1970. Most of the terror, ghastliness and artistry of the original is lost. (Dir: Massimo Dallamano, 93 mins.)

Double, The (British, 1960)** Jeanette Sterke, Jane Griffiths, Robert Brown. Scoundrel returns to England to assume his partner's identity to claim an inheritance, but his plot runs into a snag. Fair Edgar Wallace mystery melodrama produced on a low budget. (Dir: Lionel Harris, 56 mins.)

Double Agents, The (French, 1962)** Marina Vlady, Robert Hossein. It's a case of whose spy is whose as a young man and a girl suspect each other of being enemy agents. Involved and verbose melodrama dubbed in English.

Double Bunk (British, 1960)**½ Ian Carmichael, Janette Scott. Amusing comedy about newlyweds who buy a broken-down houseboat. Some clever comedy moments. (Dir: C. M. Pennington-Richards, 92 mins.)

Double Con, The (1973)** Mel Stewart, Kiel Martin. Originally released to theaters as "Trick Baby," this was a black-exploitation film that didn't overdo the sex and violence. You might call it a black "Sting," as two con men, one a light-skinned black passing for white, the other his slick black buddy, work their game in an inner-city land deal. However, the pair makes the fatal mistake of involving the relative of a Mafia boss in one of their cons and they in turn become victims. Martin and Stewart are fine in the leading roles and the script makes some interesting comments about race relations. (Dir: Larry Yust, 89 mins.)

Double Confession (British, 1951)** Derek Farr, Peter Lorre, William Hartnell. A seaside resort is disrupted by murder and blackmail. Sluggish crime drama has only the performances to recommend it. (Dir: Harry Reynolds, 86 mins.)

Double Cross (British, 1956)** Donald Houston, Fay Compton. Boatman accepts plenty of trouble when he agrees to take some people across the channel. Fair. (Dir: Anthony Squire, 71 mins.)

Double Crossbones (1951)**½ Donald O'Connor, Helena Carter. The kids will probably get many laughs out of this comedy tale of would-be pirates and their misadventures. O'Connor is very agile and funny as the bumpkin turned buccaneer. Hope Emerson stands out in the supporting cast in the role of a colorful lady captain. (Dir: Charles Barton, 76 mins.)

Double Deception (French, 1960)** Jacques Riberolles, Alice and Ellen Kessler. Young man becomes involved with twin entertainers; one of them is murdered; which one? Whodunit takes too long to get to the point.

Double Dynamite (1951)**½ Jane Russell, Groucho Marx, Frank Sinatra. Bank clerk saves a gangster's life, is suspected of being in on a theft. Fairly amusing comedy. (Dir: Irving Cummings, 80 mins.)

Double Exposure (British, 1954)**½ John Bentley, Rona Anderson. Private eye looking for a missing girl runs into murder. Standard mystery is competently done.

Double Indemnity (1944)**** Fred MacMurray, Barbara Stanwyck, Edward G. Robinson. Deliberate murder receives a microscopic examina-

tion in this tense, exciting, well-acted adaptation of the James Cain novel. (Dir: Billy Wilder, 106 mins.)

Double Indemnity (1973)**½ Richard Crenna, Samantha Eggar, Lee J. Cobb. This remake of Fred MacMurray's film classic hasn't the old oomph, but James Cain's clever story will hold one's interest. Crenna plays the uncertain insurance man, conned into murder by a calculating wife who wants to polish off her husband. As for Miss Eggar's Phyllis, the troublemaker, she somehow doesn't seem worth the big risks. Made-for-TV. (Dir: Jack Smight, 73 mins.)

Double Life, A (1947)**** Ronald Colman, Signe Hasso, Edmond O'Brien, Shelley Winters. A noted actor finds the role of "Othello" taking over his off-stage life. Superb melodrama, suspenseful, excellently written, directed, acted. Highly recommended. (Dir: George Cukor, 104 mins.)

Double Man, The (British, 1967)*** Yul Brynner, Britt Ekland, Clive Revill, Anton Diffring, Lloyd Nolan. A CIA agent meets danger when he investigates the death of his son in a skiing accident. Novel twists in this spy thriller, well-played and directed. (Dir: Franklin Schaffner, 105 mins.)

Double Suicide (Japanese, 1969)*** Kichiemon Nakamura, Shima Iwashita. Absorbing black and white drama from a play written in the early 18th century. The plot involves a married man, his wife, and the prostitute he is in love with. It is almost impossible for an Occidental to understand the emotional progress leading to the end, the "Double Suicide," yet the enduring play is one of the most popular in Japan. The acting is superb—especially Shima Iwashita, who plays both the plain wife and the gorgeous prostitute. There are some strong sexual scenes, and the ending is not for the squeamish. (Dir: Masahiro Shinoda, 104 mins.)

Double Trouble (1967)** Elvis Presley, Anette Day. Typical Presley fare for his fans, but better than most of his earlier vehicles. This time he's a rock singer (what a surprise) who finds love with an English heiress whose life is threatened at every turn. The songs interrupt the action on the average of every ten minutes or so. (Dir: Norman Taurog, 90 mins.)

Double Verdict (French, 1961)** Serge Sauvion, Paul Frankeur, Magli de Vendeuil. Man acquitted of murdering his wife marries the daughter of the jury foreman, and history nearly repeats itself. Fairly interesting drama gets some good performances. Dubbed in English.

Double Wedding (1937)**½ William Powell, Myrna Loy. If daffy slapstick is your cup of tea, you'll get plenty of laughs out of this screwball romance which, in spite of severe script trouble, is expertly played by its stars. (Dir: Richard Thorpe, 90 mins.)

Doughgirls, The (1944)*** Ann Sheridan, Jane Wyman, Jack Carson. Fair screen adaptation of the excellent Broadway play about wartime Washington. Eve Arden is wonderful as a lady Russian guerrilla. (Dir: James V. Kern, 102 mins.)

Down Among the Sheltering Palms (1953)** Mitzi Gaynor, Gloria De Haven, David Wayne, William Lundigan, Jane Greer, and Jack Paar. Palm trees, Army officers (post WW II), beautiful native girls, beautiful American girls, songs, comedy (well, almost) and Jack Paar in a small role—who would ask for anything more? Pure escapist fare—entertaining in spots. (Dir: Edmund Goulding, 87 mins.)

Down Argentine Way (1940)** Betty Grable, Don Ameche, Carmen Miranda. A lot of talent is wasted in this silly musical about the romance of an American heiress and a South American cowboy. Ends with a big horse race and you'll be glad to see it end. (Dir: Irving Cummings, 94 mins.)

Down 3 Dark Streets (1954)*** Brod Crawford, Ruth Roman. FBI man works on three cases at the same time and, naturally, they all come out together at the end. Well-done, entertaining cops-and-robbers tale. (Dir: Arnold Laven, 85 mins.)

Down to Earth (1947)*** Rita Hayworth, Larry Parks. Miss Hayworth, 1947 vintage, appropriately plays the goddess of dance. She takes a part in Producer Parks' musical posing as a mortal. Pleasant, uninspired musical. (Dir: Alexander Hall, 101 mins.)

Down to the Sea in Ships (1949)*** Richard Widmark, Lionel Barry-

more, Dean Stockwell. Life on the New England whaling boats seen through the eyes of a very young Dean Stockwell. It's overlong, but Lionel Barrymore creates an exceptional portrait of the salty sea captain. (Dir: Henry Hathaway, 120 mins.)

Downfall (British, 1963)** Maurice Denham, Nadja Regin. Lawyer wins acquittal for a pathological murderer then hires him as a chauffeur, having his own reasons. Adequate crime melodrama with a good performance by Denham.

Downhill Racer (1969)**** Robert Redford, Gene Hackman, Camilla Sparv. All the skiing enthusiasts in the audience will thrill to the superb sequences, filmed in famous European ski locations, which make up a goodly portion of this movie. It's a quiet drama about a ski champion, played with understated passion by Redford, who finds himself part of an American team competing for the honor of going to the Olympics. He's aloof and arrogant. His coach, well played by Hackman, warns him that he will never be a true champion if all he wants to do is break records. Sparv is around for romantic window dressing, but it's Redford and the skiing sequences that fascinate. (Dir: Michael Ritchie, 101 mins.)

Dr.—See also Doctor

Dr. Broadway (1942)*** Macdonald Carey, Jean Phillips. Broadway doctor becomes involved in the slaying of a reformed gangster. Good melodrama has a script containing bright dialogue, a fast pace.

Dr. Cook's Garden (1971)*** Bing Crosby, Frank Converse, Blythe Danner. Better than average made-for-TV film. Bing Crosby is very good as the venerable small-town New England doctor who has worked out a unique and frightening plan to keep the town's population as perfect as his beautiful prize-winning garden. Frank Converse is also effective as a young doctor who comes back home and uncovers Dr. Cook's diabolical plot. Although the action unfolds slowly, stay with it for Crosby's restrained performance, the splendid New England photography, and the surprise ending. Robert Markell, one of TV drama's finest producers, makes this better than most of the junk made for TV. (Dir: Ted Post, 73 mins.)

Dr. Crippen (British, 1963)**½ Donald Pleasence, Samantha Eggar, Donald Wolfit. For those who prefer their thriller-killers based on fact. About the 1910 crime case of an accused wife murderer (Pleasence) and his mistress (Samantha). There's a new invention in this one —London 1910—as the suspect is apprehended thanks to a new invention called the wireless. Donald Pleasence is an extraordinary actor, and he's effective in this English why-did-he-dun-it.

Dr. Ehrlich's Magic Bullet (1940)**** Edward G. Robinson, Ruth Gordon. Another one of those great biographical films which Hollywood occasionally makes. Story of the man who discovered the first cure for syphilis and forced the medical profession to take notice of it as a disease is beautifully told. Robinson is wonderful as the doctor and Ruth Gordon matches him every step of the way as his wife. (Dir: William Dieterle, 103 mins.)

Dr. Gillespie's Assistant (1942)** Lionel Barrymore, Van Johnson, Susan Peters. Usual run-of-the-mill medical drama but MGM introduced a newcomer named Van Johnson in the title role. (Dir: Willis Goldbeck, 87 mins.)

Dr. Gillespie's Criminal Case (1943)** Lionel Barrymore, Van Johnson. Same old formula medical melodrama with Mr. Barrymore bellowing and Van Johnson struggling to learn how to act in a film.

Dr. Goldfoot and the Bikini Machine (1965)* Vincent Price, Frankie Avalon, Dwayne Hickman, Annette Funicello. Mad scientist plans to rob rich men by creating robots who can pass as sexy females. For robots. (Dir: Norman Taurog, 90 mins.)

Dr. Goldfoot and the Girl Bombs (U.S.-Italy, 1966)*½ Vincent Price, Fabian, Franco Franchi. Treacherous Dr. Goldfoot creates robots who appear to be sexy females—and uses them to eliminate the top generals in NATO! Sequel to "Dr. Goldfoot and the Bikini Machine." (Dir: Marco Bava, 85 mins.)

Dr. Jekyll and Mr. Hyde (1920)***½ John Barrymore, Nita Naldi, Louis Wolheim. Worth watching just to see a truly great actor at work, before alcohol finally destroyed his prodigious gifts. This version of the famous Robert Louis Stevenson story "The Strange Case of Dr. Jekyll and Mr. Hyde" was based on a New York play version and adapted by Clara S. Beranger. A fascinating bravura performance by Barrymore, and you will see the 'great profile' as he gazes at Nita Naldi when visiting a London music hall. Forget about the film's shortcomings and revel in this charismatic actor pulling out all the stops. (Dir: John S. Robertson, 63 mins.)

Dr. Jekyll and Mr. Hyde (1932)***½ Fredric March, Miriam Hopkins, Rose Hobart. Fredric March's Oscar-winning portrayal of Robert Louis Stevenson's doctor with a split personality induced by his experimental potions. Worth seeing because of March. (Dir: Rouben Mamoulian, 93 mins.)

Dr. Jekyll and Mr. Hyde (1941)*** Spencer Tracy, Ingrid Bergman, Lana Turner. Stevenson's classic horror story is brought to life by a fine cast. Not for the kids or the squeamish. (Dir: Victor Fleming, 127 mins.)

Dr. Kildare Goes Home (1940)** Lew Ayres, Lionel Barrymore, Laraine Day. Sure he's got a family other than kindly old Doctor Gillespie. This one was made to appease those who thought Kildare was born in the hospital. (Dir: Harold S. Bucquet, 78 mins.)

Dr. Kildare's Victory (1941)** Lionel Barrymore, Lew Ayres. Kildare performs his usual astounding medical feats on a beautiful debutante and comes up with a new heart throb. (Dir: W. S. Van Dyke, 92 mins.)

Dr. Kildare's Wedding Day (1940)** Lew Ayres, Lionel Barrymore, Laraine Day. He's finally going to marry nurse Laraine in this one but, as she doesn't want to make any more Kildare pictures, she gracefully dies. (Dir: Harold S. Bucquet, 82 mins.)

Dr. Mabuse vs. Scotland Yard (German, 1964)*½ Peter Van Eyck, Dieter Borsche. Crazed criminal genius inflicts his will upon a mental specialist, and a Scotland Yard man enters the case to stop him. Another in the never-ending series of "Mabuse" thrillers, dubbed in English. Once they were good, but they've been done to death.

Dr. Maniac—See: Man Who Changed His Mind, The

203

Dr. Max (1974)**½ Lee J. Cobb, Janet Ward. Another medical drama, but Lee J. Cobb deserves your attention as Dr. Max, a Baltimore doctor and weary fighter who takes one day at a time, and doesn't try to play the hero in his authentic on-location surroundings. Dr. Max battles death, and applies a sense of naturalness and anger to the standard moments of crisis that come his way. Made-for-TV. (Dir: James Goldstone, 72 mins.)

Dr. No (British, 1962)**** Sean Connery, Ursula Andress. First of the James Bond extravaganzas, with Sean Connery as the super-agent combating a fiend (Joseph Wiseman) out to control the world. Wildly flamboyant, this still possesses the novelty values that made the series so popular. Great tongue-in-cheek fun. With Jack Lord, Bernard Lee, Lois Maxwell, Anthony Dayson. (Dir: Terence Young, 111 mins.)

Dr. Phibes Rises Again (Great Britain, 1972)**½ Vincent Price, Peter Cushing, Beryl Reid, Terry-Thomas. As campy a horror film as you are likely to see. Vincent Price is back from the dead and off to Egypt to do his thing—murder and mayhem. It's all ridiculous, entertaining and better than the first "Phibes." (Dir: Robert Fuest, 89 mins.)

Dr. Strangelove: Or, How I Learned to Stop Worrying and Love the Bomb (1964)**** Peter Sellers, Sterling Hayden, George C. Scott, Keenan Wynn. This masterpiece was produced and directed by Stanley Kubrick, who, along with Terry Southern and Peter George, also had a hand in the screenplay. It is quite simply one of the greatest, funniest, and most shattering motion pictures ever made. Kubrick casts a jaundiced and perceptive eye on a crazed U.S. Air Force general who is determined to save the free world personally from an imagined Communist takeover and nearly starts WW III in the process. Kubrick comments unsparingly — and hilariously — on our alienated, self-righteous society, and supplies bitter humor, great excitement, and a number of marvelous acting performances. Peter Sellers plays three roles brilliantly, and even Sellers has never been more ludicrous or amusing. Sterling Hayden, portraying the general, gives the best performance of his career,

and reminds us how foolishly this actor has been wasted in most of his other films. A cinema classic that makes a personal, pertinent, and devastating statement about our troubled society. (Dir: Stanley Kubrick, 93 mins.)

Dr. Terror's House of Horrs (U.S.-Great Britain, 1965)*** Peter Cushing, Christopher Lee, Donald Sutherland. Five creepy tales of the macabre are dealt out in the Tarot cards of a mysterious doctor who reads the fortunes of his companions in a railway car. Veterans Cushing and Lee deliver the chills and thrills under the able direction of Francis. Gruesome fun. (Dir: Freddie Francis, 98 mins.)

Dr. Who and the Daleks (British, 1965)**½ Peter Cushing, Roy Castle. Kids are the likeliest audience for this science-fiction yarn about a planet of the future with good guys (Thals) and bad guys (Daleks who live in metal shields to protect them against radiation). A scientist, the Dr. Who of the title, gets himself, his two daughters and a friend transported to the planet when his time machine goes berserk. (Dir: Gordon Flemyng, 85 mins.)

Dracula (1931)**½ Bela Lugosi, Edward Van Sloan, Helen Chandler. This shocker is somewhat dated, but horror fans will get a kick out of it, anyway. Count Dracula (Lugosi) comes to London looking for fresh blood, and puts a sweet young girl under his spell. Most frightening scenes are at the beginning when you visit Dracula's castle. (Dir: Tod Browning, 84 mins.)

Dracula (1973)** Jack Palance, Simon Ward, Nigel Davenport, Pamela Brown. The premise of the original Bram Stoker novel forms the basis and the strength of this gothic tale of the "nosferatu" (undead). Palance, as the terrifying Count, captures both the sensitivity and the aristocratic evil of the character, and the on-location filming in Yugoslavia and England supports the mood and atmosphere of eerie ritual. The supporting cast contributes to this entertaining effort. Made-for-TV. (Dir: Dan Curtis.)

Dracula A.D. 1972 (Great Britain, 1972)* Christopher Lee, Peter Cushing, Stephanie Beacham. Dracula is recalled on the centennial of his death by a descendant of his former assistant, a now-modish Mr. Alucard. (Dir: Alan Gibson, 95 mins.)

Dracula Has Risen from the Grave (British, 1969)* Christopher Lee. Believe it or not—Vincent Price isn't in this one, but Christopher Lee, king of the British horror films, is. He's up to some new campfire hijinks, but the title is about the best thing in the picture. (Dir: Freddie Francis, 92 mins.)

Dracula—Prince of Darkness (British, 1968)** Christopher Lee, Barbara Shelley. If your tastes run toward tales of vampires and helpless victims being scared out of their wits, this is for you. The British do this sort of thing best and Lee, one of the veterans of British horror films, is on hand as Dracula. (Dir: Terence Fisher, 90 mins.)

Dracula's Daughter (1936)*** Otto Kruger, Gloria Holden. This vampire yarn benefits from a logical script and good acting by Gloria Holden in the title role. Dracula's daughter falls in love, and tries to hold her man by putting a spell on his fiancee. (Dir: Lambert Hillyer, 80 mins.)

Dragnet (1954)**½ Jack Webb, Richard Boone, Ben Alexander. Feature version of the old TV success. Cops Friday (Webb) and Smith (Alexander) are after a crafty killer. The by-now-standardized technique works satisfactorily. Virginia Gregg is excellent in a poignant bit part. (Dir: Jack Webb, 89 mins.)

Dragnet (1969)**½ Jack Webb, Harry Morgan. Full-length feature film based on popular TV series. Fans of the series will enjoy watching Sgt. Friday and Officer Gannon take more time solving the mysterious murders of beautiful young models. There's an especially suspense-filled climax. (Dir: Jack Webb, 97 mins.)

Dragon Seed (1944)*** Katharine Hepburn, Walter Huston, Agnes Moorehead, Akim Tamiroff. Occasionally gripping adaptation of Pearl Buck's novel about the impact of the Japanese invasion on a small Chinese community. The subject matter and the production make up for many of the film's shortcomings. Miss Hepburn has done better work. (Dirs: Jack Conway, Harold S. Bucquet, 145 mins.)

Dragonfly Squadron (1954)**½ John Hodiak, Barbara Britton. Air Force major is sent to train the South Koreans. Satisfactory war drama. (Dir: Lesley Selander, 83 mins.)

Dragon's Blood, The (Italian, 1963) *½ Rolf Tasna, Katharina Mayberg. The legend of Siegfried, who slays the dragon with his magic sword. Needed an epic concept, didn't attain it—just another far-fetched spectacle dubbed in English.

Dragonwyck (1946)** Gene Tierney, Walter Huston, Vincent Price. This film, set about 1850 in a gloomy, mysterious mansion on the Hudson river, is one big bore. Story of a girl from Connecticut who comes to this house of horrors. (Dir: Joseph L. Mankiewicz, 103 mins.)

Dragoon Wells Massacre (1957)*** Barry Sullivan, Dennis O'Keefe, Mona Freeman. An ill-assorted group finds itself stranded in the desert with Apaches on the prowl. Above-average western with fine performances and direction. (Dir: Harold Schuster, 88 mins.)

Dragstrip Girl (1957)*½ Fay Spain, Steve Terrell. Car-crazy gal takes her boyfriend's place in a race when he's unable to drive. Brainless low-gear melodrama. (69 mins.)

Dragstrip Riot (1958)*½ Gary Clarke, Yvonne Lime, Fay Wray. Teenage sports car racer battles a motorcycle gang, saves the day. Are these our children? It's certainly not our film.

Drama of Jealousy (1970)** Marcello Mastroianni, Monica Vitti. Despite the high-powered stars of this Italian film, it is merely a labored comedy-drama about the obvious repercussions involving a love triangle. Dubbed in English, the film loses most of its original flavor, little as it has to begin with. (Dir: Ettore Scola.)

Drango (1957)**½ Jeff Chandler, Joanne Dru, Julie London. Top budgeted but otherwise routine western with plenty of two-fisted action to keep viewers awake. Good performances by the cast. (Dir: Hall Bartlett, 96 mins.)

Dream for Christmas, A (1973)*** Hari Rhodes, Beah Richards, George Spell. Earl Hamner, creator of the TV hit "The Waltons," has created a moving film about a black minister's family rebuilding a rundown Los Angeles pastorate in the early 1950's. Drama emphasizes family togetherness under duress, as the kids go to new schools; wife and grandmother do day work; and the college-trained minister looks for a job to keep going. Author Hamner, who likes sentiment and happy endings, says be good, be kind, be strong, and everything will work out. His Christmas finale is a rouser and should make everyone feel teary and warm inside. The cast does well, but young George Spell is particularly effective as son Joey. Made-for-TV. (Dir: Ralph Senensky.)

Dream Girl (1948)** Betty Hutton, Macdonald Carey. Pitiful screen treatment of the delightful Elmer Rice play about a girl who daydreams too much. (Dir: Mitchell Leisen, 85 mins.)

Dream Maker, The (British, 1963)*½ Tommy Steele, Michael Medwin. Talent scout arranges a rock concert for orphans. Skinny plot, lots of rock musical artists, all hoping to be the next Beatles.

Dream Makers, The (1975)**½ James Franciscus, Diane Baker, John Astin. Franciscus reveals unexpected emotional flair, playing a hot-shot executive in a topsy-turvy record business. He's most effective turning on the melodramatic valves when his record biggie is fired and he discovers that he himself is out of favor. Offers an interesting exposé of the seamy side of the pop music industry. Made-for-TV. (Dir: Boris Sagal, 72 mins.)

Dream Wife (1953)**½ Cary Grant, Deborah Kerr, Walter Pidgeon. A happy merry-go-round of a comedy about the capers of a very eligible bachelor who is involved with a modern career woman and a Middle-Eastern beauty. Performances by the stars are in the right groove. Dir: Sidney Sheldon, 99 mins.)

Dreamboat (1952)**½ Clifton Webb, Ginger Rogers, Anne Francis, Jeffrey Hunter. A silent film matinee idol (Webb) becomes a sensation all over again when his old films are released to TV. Now retired and with a grown daughter, this presents somewhat of a crisis in his peaceful life. Basically a funny idea that somehow never reaches its potential. (Dir: Claude Binyon, 83 mins.)

Dressed to Kill (1941)**½ Lloyd Nolan, Mary Beth Hughes. Michael Shayne private eye adventure is well paced thanks to glib dialogue and Lloyd Nolan.

Drive a Crooked Road (1954)***½ Mickey Rooney, Dianne Foster, Kevin McCarthy. A little runt of a guy who races cars gets involved with a bank robbery and murder all because of a girl. Mickey Rooney gives a fine account of himself as the pint-sized Eddie, and the film itself is in the "sleeper" class. (Dir: Richard Quine, 90 mins.)

Drive Hard, Drive Fast (1973)**½ Joan Collins, Brian Kelly, Henry Silva, and Joseph Campanella play handsome murder targets in an auto drama geared to scare. Racing pilot Kelly drives a lady home to New Orleans from Mexico City in her husband's sports car, and is tailed all the way. Silva, glowering with satisfaction, is the menacing pursuer who listens to all of the couple's car conversations through a hidden bugging device. Made-for-TV. (Dir: Douglas Heyes, 73 mins.)

Drum Beat (1954)**½ Alan Ladd, Marisa Pavan, Charles Bronson. Alan Ladd tries to make peace with the Modoc Indians. Slightly more meat than the average Indian tale, thanks to writer-director Delmer Daves ("Broken Arrow"). With Audrey Dalton, Robert Keith. (111 mins.)

Drums (British, 1938)*** Sabu, Raymond Massey. A lad saves the British regiment in India from being slaughtered by a tyrant. Picturesque, colorful, action-packed melodrama, highly enjoyable. (Dir: Zoltan Korda, 100 mins.)

Drums Along the Mohawk (1939)***½ Claudette Colbert, Henry Fonda. John Ford's direction holds this rambling narrative together and it emerges as an exciting film. Story of a group of farmers in upstate New York who were caught in the middle of the Revolutionary War although they didn't understand its meaning. (Dir: John Ford, 103 mins.)

Drums in the Deep South (1951)**½ James Craig, Guy Madison. Buddies at West Point find themselves on opposite sides when the Civil War breaks out. Fairly exciting historical drama. (Dir: William Cameron Menzies, 87 mins.)

Drums of Tahiti (1954)** Dennis O'Keefe, Patricia Medina. Tahiti is about to become a French possession in 1877 but an American adventurer and a show girl smuggle guns to be used in the fight for independence.

Fast moving but nothing new. (Dir: William Castle, 80 mins.)

Du Barry Was a Lady (1942)***½ Lucille Ball, Gene Kelly, Red Skelton. An expert cast has done such a great job on the Broadway smash about a bartender who, after being slipped a mickey finn, imagines himself Louis XV consorting with the luscious Madame Du Barry. The Cole Porter score, although not his best, is a big help. (Dir: Roy Del Ruth, 101 mins.)

Duchess and the Dirtwater Fox, The (1976)* George Segal, Goldie Hawn. Goldie sings a heavy-handed song called "Please Don't Touch My Plums." Please don't bother with this tedious drivel about a hooker (Hawn) in the Wild, Wild West trying to get off her ass and onto her feet. The numbing "comedy" story patched together by Melvin Frank, Barry Sandler and Jack Rose. Clumsily directed by Melvin Frank. (104 mins.)

Duchess of Idaho (1950)** Esther Williams, Van Johnson, John Lund. Swimming star (who else?) has romantic complications with a playboy and a band leader in Sun Valley. If you like Williams in the water, okay; otherwise, pretty tedious romantic comedy. Couple of good musical specialties by Lena Horne and Eleanor Powell thrown in. (Dir: Robert Z. Leonard, 98 mins.)

Duck Soup (1933)***½ Marx Bros. Groucho is the dictator of a mythical kingdom and the other two are spies. Crazy, stupid and hilarious. Not their best but their legion of fans will love it. (Dir: Leo McCarey, 70 mins.)

Duel (1971)*** Dennis Weaver. A highway game of death between a salesman in a compact car and a gasoline truck sustains its suspense for the full 90 minutes. Salesman Weaver, rolling along on California backroads, can't shake the menacing truck intent on bagging the compact. All attempts to call for help from police and bystanders prove fruitless, and the duel between machine and man reaches a showdown. Young director Steve Spielberg's camera work gives Richard Matheson's story a fine sense of reality, and he has achieved a nerve-racking driver's bad dream in color. Made-for-TV. (Dir: Steven Spielberg, 73 mins.)

Duel at Apache Wells (1957)** Anna Maria Alberghetti, Ben Cooper. Lad returns home to save his father's ranch from crooks. Slow western. (Dir: Joe Kane, 70 mins.)

Duel at Diablo (1966)*** James Garner, Sidney Poitier. A tough, sometimes effective western, not for the squeamish. About a fight between the plainsmen and the Apaches. The subplots are plentiful and they're all presented in realistic terms, making for some bloody sequences. Garner is very good as an Indian scout who seeks revenge for his wife's death and Poitier is equally as good in an offbeat role of an ex-Army sergeant. Film also benefits by fine musical score of jazz composer Neal Hefti. (Dir: Ralph Nelson, 103 mins.)

Duel in Durango (1957)** George Montgomery, Ann Robinson. Average "horse opera" with the law pitted against the lawless. Montgomery is comfortable in this type of role and he sets the tone for the rest of the gun-toters. (Dir: Sidney Salkow, 73 mins.)

Duel in the Forest (1959)**½ Curt Jurgens, Maria Schell. A well-photographed costume drama set in Germany during the feudal era. Jurgens cuts a dashing figure as the Hessian Robin Hood and Miss Schell adequately fills the bill as his love.

Duel in the Jungle (British, 1954)*½ Dana Andrews, Jeanne Crain, David Farrar. Insurance investigator looks into the supposed death of the head of a diamond concern, uncovers a swindling plot. Ludicrous jungle adventure has a bunch of good actors standing around looking silly. (Dir: George Marshall, 102 mins.)

Duel in the Sun (1946)***½ Jennifer Jones, Gregory Peck, Joseph Cotten, Lionel Barrymore, Walter Huston, Lillian Gish. Big, sprawling Western epic-romance, based on the Nevil Shute novel about the adventures of a half-breed Indian girl (Miss Jones) who comes to live in the home of a wealthy cattle baron and falls in love with both of his sons. Supporting performances, particularly Lionel Barrymore, and Lillian Gish, overshadow the acting contributions of the stars, but there's plenty of scope, romance and action to satisfy almost everyone. (Dir: King Vidor, 138 mins.)

Duel of Fire (Italian, 1960)*½ Fernando Lamas, Liana Orfei. Avenger discovers the murderer of his sister by joining a gang of robbers. Shaky English-dubbed costume adventure.

Duel of the Champions (Italian, 1960) ** Alan Ladd, Robert Keith. Dull Italian production done in the epic groove—English dubbed. Alan Ladd appears rather foolish in this adventure. (Dir: Ferdinando Baldi, 105 mins.)

Duel of the Titans (1963)* Steve Reeves, Gordon Scott, Virna Lisi. Overproduced Italian costume epic dubbed-in English. Muscle men Reeves and Scott play Romulus and Remus, respectively, and they are very athletic in their founding of Rome. Virna Lisi is featured as a Sabine princess. (Dir: Sergio Cobucci, 88 mins.)

Duel on the Mississippi (1955)** Lex Barker, Patricia Medina. Tempers flare and passions are unleashed in this cliched adventure pic about Louisiana plantations and river pirates. (80 mins.)

Duel With Death (German, 1960)** Gert Frobe, Mai-Britt Nilsson. Proud man knows only his own law but is forced to come to grips with the world. Fair drama located in Norway, dubbed in English.

Duffy (1968)** James Coburn, James Mason, Susannah York. Another "heist-caper-escapade" film, peopled with handsome men, a beautiful girl, and played against a sumptuous Spanish beach setting . . . all of which amounts to very little. The cast is better than average for this type of chic adventure but they can't seem to rise above the plodding script. (Dir: Robert Parrish, 101 mins.)

Duffy's Tavern (1945)*** All-Star Cast. Popular 1945 radio show is used as a frame that permits every star on the Paramount lot to perform. Some of it is excellent and the balance, routine. (Dir: Hal Walker, 97 mins.)

Duke Wore Jeans, The (Great Britain, 1958)** Tommy Steele, June Laverick, Michael Medwin. British rock star Tommy Steele, in his second picture, plays a look-alike twosome—an uppercrust noble and a brazen Cockney lad! Breezy comedy with fun and music. (Dir: Gerald Thomas, 90 mins.)

Dulcimer Street (British, 1947)**** Alastair Sim, Richard Attenborough. Tenants of a boarding house get signatures on a petition to save a boy from paying the murder penalty. Elaborate, at once comic and dramatic tale of London; excellent. (Dir: Sidney Gilliat, 112 mins.)

Dungeons of Horror (1962)* Russ Harvey, Helen Hogan. Weak thriller about a couple of castaways trapped by an evil count and made prisoner in the 1870's.

Dunkirk (British, 1958)***½ John Mills, Richard Attenborough. Story of the gallant British rescue operation in early World War II. Graphically done, almost documentary-fashion; excellent performances by a fine cast, authentic recreation of the event. (Dir: Leslie Norman, 115 mins.)

Dunwich Horror, The (1970)*½ Sandra Dee, Dean Stockwell. Film about the supernatural. It's all about "black masses" and "demonic rituals" with Miss Dee as the young, pretty thing being drawn into it all by the outwardly attractive, but inwardly deadly, Dean Stockwell. (Dir: Daniel Haller, 90 mins.)

Durant Affair, The (British, 1962)** Jane Griffiths, Conrad Phillips. Young woman becomes enmeshed in a legal battle. Good performances help this rather slow drama. (Dir: Godfrey Grayson, 73 mins.)

Dust Be My Destiny (1939)**½ John Garfield, Priscilla Lane. John and Priscilla have plenty of trouble in this saga of a man trying to find his destiny but the smooth acting and production should entertain you. (Dir: Lewis Seiler, 100 mins.)

Dying Room Only (1973)**½ Cloris Leachman, Ross Martin. The first 15 minutes or so of this made-for-TV suspense film will fascinate. Miss Leachman goes through a harrowing experience at a deserted roadside cafe where her husband disappers when he goes to the men's room. You will probably figure out what's going on before long, but Leachman has a good opportunity to emote in a highly charged drama. Made-for-TV. (Dir: Philip Leacock.)

Dynamiters, The (British, 1954)** Wayne Morris, Patrick Holt. Sleuth tracks down a gang of safe-crackers and killers. Crime melodrama without a bang.

Each Dawn I Die (1939)**½ James Cagney, George Raft. The boys are tough and they give this cliche-loaded prison epic a big lift but it's still sentenced to nothingness. (Dir: William Keighley, 100 mins.)

Eagle and the Hawk, The (1933)*** Fredric March, Cary Grant, Carole Lombard. Grim, realistic story of World War I air fighting. A bit dated by our standards but well ahead of its time. Comparable in many ways to "Dawn Patrol." (Dir: Stuart Walker, 68 mins.)

Eagle in a Cage (U.S.-Yugoslavia, 1970)**½ John Gielgud, Ralph Richardson, Kenneth Haigh. The exiled Napoleon's escapades on the island of St. Helena. Adapted from the TV production, an uninspired look at the private man behind the emperor. However, Gielgud and Richardson offer superb, complementary performances as two highly placed officials. (Dir: Fielder Cook, 92 mins.)

Eagle Squadron (1942)*** Robert Stack, Jon Hall, Eddie Albert. In 1940, a handful of Americans join the RAF to fight the Nazis. Good war melodrama with some exciting action scenes. (Dir: Arthur Lubin, 109 mins.)

Earl Carroll Vanities (1945)**½ Dennis O'Keefe, Constance Moore. A princess traveling incognito accidentally becomes a hit in a show, falls for a young song writer. Typical musical, nothing important, but fair enough. (Dir: Joseph Santley, 91 mins.)

Earl of Chicago, The (1940)***½ Robert Montgomery, Edward Arnold. Plenty of fun in this story of a Chicago beer baron who becomes an English lord after the death of a long-lost relative. Cast is excellent. (Dir: Richard Thorpe, 85 mins.)

Early Bird, The (Great Britain, 1965) *½ Norman Wisdom, Edward Chapman, Jerry Desmonde. Another slapstick entry from comedian Norman Wisdom has a minimal plot with Wisdom as a milkman for a small dairy being taken over by a monopoly. Much comedic destruction ensues (a garden, a golf course) and pratfalls abound. (Dir: Robert Asher, 98 mins.)

Early Summer (Japan, 1951)**½ Ichiro Sugai, Chishu Ryu. Yasujiro Ozu is one of Japan's top directors, and this is a good example of his

work. Movie concentrates on the emotional problems of a family trying to hold on to the ancient traditions despite the overwhelming tide of changes that sweep their lives. For some, the action may seem too slow, but the drama builds nicely. (Dir: Yasujiro Ozu, 150 mins.)

Earth Cries Out, The (Italian, 1949) ** Marina Berti, Andrea Checchi. When fighting in Palestine breaks out, former wartime buddies choose different paths—one a British officer, one an immigrant, one a terrorist. Slow-moving drama originally had topicality as an asset. English-dubbed.

Earth II (1971)** Gary Lockwood, Anthony Franciosa. Science-fiction fans may enjoy this mini-sized "space odyssey" about the adventures of the first manned orbiting space station, known as "Earth II." The technical effects are excellent but the drama played out in the futuristic sets seems dwarfed by comparison. Note the dialogue which says that Communist China doesn't have to abide by interspace rules because it is not a member of the United Nations! Made-for-TV. (Dir: Tom Gries, 100 mins.)

Earthquake (1974)** Charlton Heston, Ava Gardner, George Kennedy, Lorne Greene, Genevieve Bujold, Richard Roundtree, Marjoe Gortner, Barry Sullivan, Walter Matthau. Stilted "disaster" adventure about the destruction of Los Angeles by an earthquake. The all-star cast is secondary to the marvelous special-effects crew which makes highways buckle, buildings crash, streets split and dams burst, amid extras fleeing and screaming on cue. For its theatrical release, the film introduced "Sensurround," a soundtrack device which was supposed to make the viewer feel the tremors. You'll get a few chills even from the small screen. (Dir: Mark Robson, 122 mins.)

East of Eden (1955)**** James Dean, Julie Harris, Raymond Massey, Jo Van Fleet. A superb film! James Dean delivers a great performance as the sensitive youth who feels unloved and unwanted by his father. The cast is top notch, notably Jo Van Fleet who won an Oscar for her portrayal of Kate. Directed with taste and skill by Elia Kazan. Based on just a portion of John Steinbeck's novel of the same name. (Dir: Elia Kazan, 115 mins.)

East of Kilimanjaro (1962)*½ Marshall Thompson, Gaby Andre. An adventure tale set in Africa about big game hunting. Fair action sequences, little else.

East of Sudan (British, 1964)**½ Anthony Quayle, Sylvia Syms. Action drama which doesn't aspire to be anything else. Adventure fans will go along with the treacherous journey taken by a small group of British and Moslem survivors of a brutal Moslem attack on a British outpost located a couple of hundred miles from Khartoum. The time is the latter part of the nineteenth century and the party includes Anthony Quayle as a seasoned soldier and Sylvia Syms as a very proper governess. (Dir: Nathan Juran, 84 mins.)

East of Sumatra (1953)**½ Jeff Chandler, Marilyn Maxwell, Anthony Quinn. Two-fisted adventure film bolstered by performances of Chandler and Quinn as opponents in an effort to set up a tin mining project. Plenty of action and romance. (Dir: Budd Boetticher, 90 mins.)

East of the River (1940)**½ John Garfield, Brenda Marshall. Typical Garfield yarn about the ex-con who, when put to the test, is a nice guy. It's a pity that a talent like Garfield's had to be wasted in so many of these cliche films. (Dir: Alfred E. Green, 73 mins.)

East Side of Heaven (1938)*** Bing Crosby, Joan Blondell. Singing taxi driver finds himself custodian of a baby left by a young mother. Tuneful light comedy, pleasingly done. (Dir: David Butler, 100 mins.)

East Side, West Side (1950)**½ James Mason, Barbara Stanwyck, Ava Gardner, Van Heflin, and Cyd Charisse. Slickly mounted soap opera set in the chic world of the wealthy social set of New York. Miss Stanwyck overacts in her role of a wife who stops pretending her husband still loves her and Ava slinks in and out of the proceedings as a femme fatale. (Dir: Mervyn Le Roy, 108 mins.)

Easter Parade (1948)***½ Judy Garland, Fred Astaire, Ann Miller. Forget the plot and enjoy the talented cast performing 17 Irving Berlin tunes and you have more than

enough. (Dir: Charles Walters, 103 mins.)

Easy Come, Easy Go (1947)**½ Barry Fitzgerald, Diana Lynn. Barry is wonderful, but the picture is so bad it weighs him down. Story of a lazy, horse-playing Irishman whose sole occupation is stopping his daughter from getting married. (Dir: John Farrow, 77 mins.)

Easy Come, Easy Go (1967)** Elvis Presley, Dodie Marshall. Elvis' fans may enjoy this aimless musical adventure yarn which has the singer playing a Navy frogman who thinks he may have stumbled upon a sunken treasure. Naturally, there are songs and girls galore. Elvis' acting, incidentally, is better than the dopey script. (Dir: John Rich, 95 mins.)

Easy Life, The (Italian, 1963)**** Vittorio Gassman, Jean-Louis Trintignant, Catherine Spaak. Offbeat, absorbing drama of a happy-go-lucky extrovert who has an effect on a serious young law student when they are thrown together by chance. Sharp observation of contrasting personalities, story holds the attention tightly all the way. Fine performances. English-dubbed. (Dir: Dino Risi, 105 mins.)

Easy Living (1937)*** Jean Arthur, Edward Arnold, Ray Milland. Amusing little farce about a man who throws his wife's fur coat out the window. Silly, but well done in all departments. (Dir: Mitchell Leisen, 90 mins.)

Easy Money (British, 1948)**½ Dennis Price, Edward Rigby. Episodic stories about the effects of sudden riches upon the winners of a football pool. Amusing, with the last episode a comedy gem.

Easy Rider (1969)**** Dennis Hopper, Peter Fonda, Jack Nicholson, Karen Black, Robert Walker. A devastating, original film that has something truthful and compelling to say about what one critic aptly called "our trigger-happy, hate-ridden nation in which increasing numbers of morons bear increasing numbers of arms." The story line of this box-office smash—made for less than $400,000 and expected to gross more than 100 times that figure—is straightforward enough. Two young "hippie" motorcyclists sell some dope in Southern California, stash their grubstake away in their gas tank, and take off for a jaunt across the

Southwest destined for New Orleans. It doesn't matter, finally, that much of the dialogue is vapid banalities, spoken by inarticulate people. What does matter is that Dennis Hopper has made a stunning directorial debut, especially considering he played a leading role—and plays it better than Fonda—and had a hand in the screenplay along with Fonda and writer Terry Southern. Acting honors go to Jack Nicholson's marvelous, virtuoso portrayal of an alcoholic small-town Southern lawyer. The photography of Laszlo Kovacs captures much of the beauty of the Southwest that we haven't yet destroyed. It'll be a long time before this remarkable film shows up on your home screen, so take a night off and go out to see this dazzler on a big screen. (Dir: Dennis Hopper, 94 mins.)

Easy to Love (1953)** Esther Williams, Van Johnson, Tony Martin. Swimming show star wants to quit and settle down, but her boss won't let her—'cause he loves her too, and if you've seen any Esther Williams films before, you can guess how this will end. (Dir: Charles Walters, 96 mins.)

Easy to Wed (1945)*** Esther Williams, Van Johnson, Lucille Ball. Entertaining, well played remake of "Libeled Lady." Keenan Wynn and Lucille Ball are exceptionally good with the comedy. (Dir: Edward Buzzell, 110 mins.)

Easy Way, The—See: **Room For One More**

Eddie Cantor Story, The (1954)** Keefe Brasselle, Marilyn Erskine. Disappointing biography of the famed "Banjo Eyes" rise to fame and fortune. All the stops are pulled to inject pathos and sympathy for the obstacles which befell Cantor in this retelling of his life. Keefe Brasselle goes at it tooth and nail but fails to make an impression. (Dir: Alfred E. Green, 116 mins.)

Eddy Duchin Story, The (1956)**½ Tyrone Power, Kim Novak. Oversentimentalized account of pianist Eddy Duchin's early career and two marriages. Tyrone Power is good as the eager pianist who wants to make it big and does. (Dir: George Sidney, 123 mins.)

Edge, The (1968)*** Jack Rader, Tom Griffin. Visually static, but a maddening, stimulating tract about contemporary American politics and society. Written and directed by Robert Kramer, one of the most gifted of the film world's "underground" directors. Technically sloppy film due to a minuscule budget-film shot for less than $15,000—"Edge" is noteworthy because it's one of the few times that the convictions of the radical young left in our country have been captured on film. Much of the dialogue may strike political sophisticates as puerile, but if you pay more attention to what you hear rather than what you see, you'll find Kramer's film disturbing and involving. Kramer later directed the searing blueprint for a revolution called "Ice."

Edge of Darkness (1943)*** Errol Flynn, Ann Sheridan, Walter Huston. Errol tries to liberate Norway in this but all he manages to do is assist a good cast in making another top flight war drama. (Dir: Lewis Milestone, 120 mins.)

Edge of Divorce—See: **Background**

Edge of Eternity (1959)*** Cornel Wilde, Victoria Shaw. Frequently suspenseful "cops and robbers" stuff with Cornel Wilde as a deputy sheriff who's hot on the trail of a murderer who operates around the Grand Canyon resort area. (Dir: Don Siegel, 80 mins.)

Edge of Fear (Spanish, 1964)*½ May Heatherly, Virgilio Teixeira. Witness to a murder is hunted by the killer, even though she can't identify him. Prolonged suspense melodrama, nothing novel. English dialogue.

Edge of Fury (1958)* Michael Higgins, Lois Holmes. Bungled story of a young psychopathic beachcomber who is out to plunder a family. Futile attempt to handle the story clinically adds to the confusion. (Dir: Robert Gurney, 77 mins.)

Edge of Hell (1956)* Hugo Haas, Francesca de Scaffa. An embarrassingly bad attempt at Silent Film pathos fails in the hands of Hugo Haas who wrote, directed and stars in this story of a beggar who befriends a little lonely boy. (Dir: Hugo Haas, 78 mins.)

Edge of the City (1957)***½ John Cassavetes, Sidney Poitier, Jack Warden. Based on Robert Alan Aurthur's memorable TV play "A Man Is Ten Feet Tall," this filmed-on-location along the dock fronts in New York is an exciting, moving film about two longshoremen whose growing friendship is threatened by a bullying bigot. Poitier and Warden, playing a notably repellent punk, are terrific and there's a rousing "claw" fight toward the end of the film. First directorial effort, and a good one, of Martin Ritt, now one of Hollywood's best. Also first feature produced by David Susskind. (Dir: Martin Ritt, 85 mins.)

Edison the Man (1939)*** Spencer Tracy, Charles Coburn. Tracy is perfect as the most famous of all American inventors. His portrayal compensates for certain shortcomings in the script and makes the film a fine tribute to Edison's genius. (See: "Young Tom Edison") (Dir: Clarence Brown, 107 mins.)

Edvard Munch (Sweden-Norway, 1975)**** Geir Westby, Gro Fraas. An extraordinary film, originally made for Scandinavian TV, about the great Norwegian artist whose work is so little known in the United States. At the time of his death in 1944, the maverick Munch had become one of the most influential figures in European expressionism. This ambitious film, a labor of love by British filmmaker Peter Watkins, chronicles his turbulent early years, starting in Norway in 1884. Geir Westby is consistently interesting playing the neurotic artist. "Munch" is among the very best films ever made dealing, not only with painters but attempting to explain the creative process in artists of all kinds, be they painters, poets, writers, dancers, etc. Imaginative photography of virtually all of Munch's major canvases. This docu-drama is too long perhaps, but it is almost always rewarding. A hugely skillful film, produced on a tiny budget. (Dir: Peter Watkins, 167 mins.)

Edward My Son (1948)*** Spencer Tracy, Deborah Kerr. Story of a man who builds a fortune for his son through some shady deeds. Is a compelling film but lacks the superb stage acting of Robert Morley. (Dir: George Cukor, 112 mins.)

Eegah! (1962)* Arch Hall Jr., Richard Kiel, Marilyn Manning. Couple of teenagers come upon a prehistoric caveman, who follows them to the city. Ridiculous thriller.

Effect of Gamma Rays on Man-in-the-Moon Marigolds, The (1972)*** Joanne Woodward, Nell Potts, Roberta Wallach, Judith Lowry. Adapted from Paul Zindel's Pulitzer Prize-winning play, this tale of Beatrice Hunsdorfer, the gallant loser whose dreams are unfulfilled, gets an adequate expansion onto the screen. Highlight of the tale is Miss Woodward's performance, which captures all of the desperate dreams of a widow with two children who has not resigned herself to obscurity. The daughter's winning of the science prize, and the ensuing household tension, evoke shock and sympathy. Roberta Wallach is also excellent. At its best in capturing the seemingly chance encounters and dialogues that shape destinies. (Nell Potts is Woodward's real daughter.) (Dir: Paul Newman, 101 mins.)

Egg and I, The (1947)*** Claudette Colbert, Fred MacMurray, Marjorie Main. A memorably funny comedy about trials and tribulations on a chicken farm. This picture introduced the characters of Ma and Pa Kettle (Marjorie Main and Percy Kilbride). Claudette Colbert is excellent. Based on Betty McDonald's best seller. (Dir: Chester Erskine, 108 mins.)

Egyptian, The (1954)** Edmund Purdom, Jean Simmons, Gene Tierney, Victor Mature, Peter Ustinov, Michael Wilding, Bella Darvi. The best things about this film are the lavish sets and costumes which manage to gloss over the flatness of the Biblical epic and the posing performances of most of the stars. Purdom in the title role of Sinhue, the court physician, does fairly well as does Michael Wilding as the Pharaoh. Such performers as Miss Simmons and Mr. Ustinov are wasted in thankless parts; Gene Tierney and Bella Darvi give sharply overdrawn performances. (Dir: Michael Curtiz, 140 mins.)

Eiger Sanction, The (1975)**½ Clint Eastwood, George Kennedy, Jack Cassidy. The Eiger is a Swiss mountain peak, and if you wait long enough there is an exciting sequence involving climbers in the Swiss peaks. But there are a lot of lows along the way, thanks to the rambling story based on the best-selling novel by Trevanian. Eastwood plays a college art professor who also happens to be an assassin for a secret

U.S. government agency known in this film as CII. Eastwood directs himself for the third time and he allegedly did his own mountain climbing as well. It took three writers to turn out the jumbled, sophomoric screenplay. (Dir: Clint Eastwood, 128 mins.)

8½ (Italian, 1963)**** Marcello Mastroianni, Claudia Cardinale, Sandra Milo, Anouk Aimee. A stupendous, brilliant and sometimes baffling film, properly deemed one of the truly great films of modern times. Is a stunningly edited semi-autobiographical filmic psychoanalysis by director Federico Fellini as he records the fantasies and real life happenings of a noted filmmaker who is having artistic difficulties completing his new project. Boasts superb performances not only from Mastroianni but right down to the smallest bit parts. Technically dazzling as Fellini's complete mastery of the film medium seems to make him start his films on a creative level where other directors end up. A complex, stimulating adventurous masterpiece. (Dir: Federico Fellini, 135 mins.)

800 Leagues Over the Amazon (Mexican, 1960)*½ Carlos Moctezuma, Elvira Quintana. Woman attempting to save an innocent man has all kinds of problems with the villainous crew of a tramp steamer. Hokey adventure tale dubbed in English.

Eight Iron Men (1952)***½ Bonar Colleano, Lee Marvin, Arthur Franz. Absorbing drama of the war in Italy, and a squad of soldiers tied down by heavy enemy fire. Good character sketches, some welcome moments of grim humor. Fine performances. (Dir: Edward Dmytryk, 80 mins.)

Eight O'Clock Walk (British, 1954)*** Richard Attenborough, Cathy O'Donnell. An innocent young taxi driver is placed on trial for the murder of an eight-year-old girl. Tense mystery, above average. (Dir: Lance Comfort, 87 mins.)

Eight on the Lam (1967)* Bob Hope, Jonathan Winters, Jill St. John, Phyllis Diller. Bob Hope as a bank teller finds a lot of cash, but nobody steals any laughs in this stinker. All concerned with this clinker should be on the lam, but many of them have reappeared and worked since this was made. (Dir: George Marshall, 106 mins.)

Eighteen and Anxious (1957)** Martha Scott, Jackie Coogan. A girl has a wild fling despite her mother's overprotective ways and almost winds up dead. Pure soap opera all the way. (Dir: Joe Parker, 93 mins.)

8th Day of the Week, The (Polish, 1959)**** Sonja Ziemann, Zbigniew Cybulski. A prize-winning Polish film, sensitively acted and superbly directed. A young pair of lovers try to fight against the bitterness and sordidness left by the war. Powerful stuff.

Eighty Steps to Jonah (1969)** Wayne Newton. Overly sentimental tale about a young man (Newton) who is on the run from the police and comes across a camp for blind children. A chorus of violins in the background, and you can take it from there. . . . (Dir: Gerd Oswald, 107 mins.)

80,000 Suspects (British, 1963)*** Claire Bloom, Richard Johnson. Occasionally gripping drama showing the attempts to track down smallpox carriers when an epidemic hits a town. Realistic atmosphere sometimes marred by intrusion of a sideplot about a doctor trying to save his marriage, but the medical suspense elements are well handled. Good performance. (Dir: Val Guest, 113 mins.)

El Cid (1961)**½ Charlton Heston, Sophia Loren. This film spectacle is about as opulent as they come and fans of this type of adventure get a full quota of great battle scenes, superb Spanish settings, magnificent costumes and the attractive presence of stars Charlton Heston and Sophia Loren. The saga of the hero, El Cid, who became a legend in Spanish history, is more for the eye than the ear and the final scenes of the film, in which a mortally wounded El Cid is strapped to his mount and sent to ride against his adversaries is a splashy bit of derring do. Much of the visual splendor of this kind of pageant film is lost on your small home screen. (Dir: Anthony Mann, 184 mins.)

El Condor (1970)½ Jim Brown, Lee Van Cleef. Mindless, violent western set in Mexico starring Brown and Van Cleef as a pair who join forces to get at a fortune supposedly stored in a fortress known as El Condor. Stilted performances, inept dialogue! (Dir: Jim Guillermin, 102 mins.)

213

El Dorado (1967)★★★½ John Wayne, Robert Mitchum, Christopher George (very good), Arthur Hunnicutt, Michele Carey, Charlene Holt. Rip-snortin' old-fashioned Howard Hawks-directed western fun. Gun-fighter (Wayne) helps a whiskey-sodden sheriff (Mitchum) redeem himself and clean up the baddies. Good-natured shenanigans with lots of old pros showing how it's done. (Dir: Howard Hawks, 127 mins.)

El Greco (Italian-French, 1964)★★ Mel Ferrer, Rosanna Schiaffino, Adolfo Celi. When you wake up after watching Mel Ferrer's soporific performance, you may be hard to convince that good films about great artistic geniuses have been and will be made. (Laughton as Rembrandt and Kirk Douglas in "Lust for Life" among others.) But here Mel's in an Italian-French co-production made in Spain about a Greek who speaks English. Theoretically it's about the legendary painter, but there actually are some lovely sequences filmed in Toledo—Spain, not Ohio! (Dir: Luciano Salce, 95 mins.)

El Topo (Mexican, 1971)★★★★ Alexandro Jodorowsky, Mara Lorenzio, David Silva. An ambitious, fascinating, violence-filled allegorical western, the second film made by Jodorowsky, a Chilean-Russian stage director who once worked for Marcel Marceau. It's also a filmed homage to director Luis Bunuel, as writer-director-editor Jodorowsky sums up the Old Testament and man's search for meaning in his life—all the while filling the screen with a dazzling, decadent panorama of flagellation, assorted grotesqueries, and an altogether remarkable visual style. It doesn't all work but you won't soon forget this cinematic assault on all your senses. Not for the squeamish. Early in the film Jodorowsky explains the title by noting the parable of the mole, which spends its whole life digging toward the light, only to be blinded, in the end, by the sun. English subtitles. (123 mins.)

Eleanor and Franklin (1976)★★★★ Jane Alexander, Edward Herrmann, Ed Flanders, Rosemary Murphy. Screenwriter James Costigan has adapted Joseph P. Lash's Pulitzer Prize-winning book illuminating the special relationship between plain Eleanor and her more dynamic, dashing cousin, Franklin Delano

214

Roosevelt. Since Eleanor is the focal point of the show, the opening is devoted to her painful, lonely childhood, her adolescent years at school, and her eventual proper courtship with Franklin. The title roles are brilliantly realized by Jane Alexander, who never resorts to parody either in voice or mannerism; and Edward Herrmann, a relative newcomer, who all but steals the film with his portrayal of FDR. In supporting roles, Miss Murphy as FDR's mother and Flanders as Louis Howe, FDR's political manager, are both excellent. Ms. Alexander will break your heart when she discovers a love letter to her husband written by her personal secretary. All in all, a fine personal drama about famous historical figures. Originally shown in two parts. Made-for-TV. (Dir: Dan Petrie, 208 mins.)

Eleanor and Franklin: The White House Years (1977)★★★★ Jane Alexander, Edward Herrmann, Priscilla Pointer. More of the public and personal history of Eleanor and Franklin Roosevelt, dramatizing sections of Joseph Lash's book. The best scenes are those dealing with WW II, particularly a scene in which Eleanor visits a hospital ward in the South Pacific and shares a touching moment with a Marine amputee. Miss Alexander and Herrmann are even better than they were in the original "Eleanor and Franklin," having honed their portrayals to perfection. In the large supporting cast, Walter McGinn, taking over the role of Louis Howe from Ed Flanders, comes off best. Made-for-TV. (Dir: Daniel Petrie, 144 mins.)

Eleanor Roosevelt Story, The (1965) ★★★★ Eloquent, truly inspiring documentary biography of Mrs. FDR, graphically portrayed in newsreel and still pictures and especially in the words of Archibald MacLeish's brilliant narrative. Beautifully done, deserves the lavish praise bestowed upon it. (Dir: Richard Kaplan, 91 mins.)

Electra Glide in Blue (1973)★★½ Robert Blake, Billy Bush. Some of this updated homage to the spirit of "Easy Rider" works well, thanks to the pacing of directorial newcomer James William Guercio. Parts of the rest are heavy-handed, but there are interesting sequences throughout, and Robert Blake, playing a pint-sized Arizona motorcycle cop who wants to become a detective, helps sustain interest. (Dir: James William Guercio, 106 mins.)

Electronic Monster, The (British, 1960)** Rod Cameron, Mary Murphy. Interesting science-fiction yarn about a group of experimenting scientists who work with dream-inducing devices. (Dir: Montgomery Tully, 72 mins.)

Elephant Boy (British, 1937)*** Sabu, Walter Hudd. Kipling's "Toomai, of the Elephants"; a small native lad claims he knows the congregating place of the elephant hordes. Fine jungle scenes, made on location. Interesting, often poetic story. (Dirs: Robert Flaherty, Zoltan Korda, 100 mins.)

Elephant Called Slowly, An (Great Britain, 1969)** Virginia McKenna, Bill Travers, George Adamson. McKenna and Travers return to Africa, in a dramatized travelogue to the scene of their previous "Born Free," for a vacation, and to house-sit in the African bush. They make some elephant friends, visit former lion friends. Nice pictures of the animals. (Dir: James Hill, 91 mins.)

Elephant Walk (1954)**½ Elizabeth Taylor, Peter Finch, Dana Andrews. A muddled soap opera played out against the splendor of Ceylon. Miss Taylor is ravishingly beautiful as the young English bride who comes to her new husband's (Peter Finch) tea plantation in Ceylon and finds the adjustment to a new life difficult. Action fans will enjoy the large elephant stampede which comes at the film's climax. (Dir: William Dieterle, 103 mins.)

Elevator, The (1974)** James Farentino, Roddy McDowall, Craig Stevens, Carol Lynley, Myrna Loy. Still another familiar "trapped" melodrama. An elevator stalls following a robbery in a high-rise office building, trapping the thief and seven passengers. Thief James Farentino carries the brunt of the soap opera with an interesting cast supplying the range of expected histrionics. Made-for-TV. (Dir: Jerry Jameson.)

11 Harrowhouse (1974)** Charles Grodin, Candice Bergen, John Gielgud, James Mason. Muddled, contrived robbery caper. Grodin is a diamond salesman enlisted by a mad millionaire (Trevor Howard) to steal millions of dollars' worth of diamonds. Candice Bergen is one of those flighty, bored heiresses who crave adventure with a capital A. The great supporting cast—John Gielgud, James Mason, Howard—is largely wasted. Also, a flip voice-over narration by Grodin seems jarringly out of place with what is going on in the film. Occasional nice touches, but this is not as rewarding as Avakian's "Cops and Robbers." (Dir: Aram Avakian, 95 mins.)

Elizabeth the Queen—See: **Private Lives of Elizabeth and Essex**

Ellery Queen (1975)** Jim Hutton, David Wayne, Ray Milland, Kim Hunter, Monte Markham. The popular mystery writer-sleuth again. Boyish, lanky Jim Hutton plays an absent-minded, bumbling "Ellery" in an investigation of the murder of a man's mistress. Hutton, Wayne, and supporting actors all work hard, unsuccessfully trying for a light touch. Made-for-TV. (Dir: David Greene, 100 mins.)

Ellery Queen: Don't Look Behind You (1971)**½ Peter Lawford. The sophisticated finesse of Lawford is compatible with the character of Ellery Queen, the worldly American criminologist-author. In this film, Lawford and his American uncle, played with a staccato delivery by Harry Morgan, team up to crack an ominous multiple-murder case. Mystery fans will enjoy following Queen's clever analysis of the hidden clues. Credit director Barry Shear with a stylish production, particularly the New York City location shots. Made-for-TV. (Dir: Barry Shear, 100 mins.)

Elmer Gantry (1960)**** Burt Lancaster, Jean Simmons, Shirley Jones, Arthur Kennedy. The Sinclair Lewis novel about an unscrupulous salesman who becomes a fire-eating preacher under the tent of a lady evangelist is screened with terrific impact. Award-winning performances by Lancaster and Shirley Jones. Superb dramatic fare for adults. Lancaster at his best, and here that's very good indeed. (Dir: Richard Brooks, 146 mins.)

Elopement (1951)** Clifton Webb, Anne Francis, William Lundigan. Crusty individual gets involved with young love. Another sneering Webb portrayal, if you like 'em. (Dir: Henry Koster, 82 mins.)

Elusive Corporal, The (France, 1962)***½ Jean-Pierre Cassel, Claude Brasseur. Jean Renoir's memorable, bittersweet film about freedom and a Frenchman in a WW II POW camp. Similar in subjects to his masterpiece about WW I, "Grand Illusions." In "Corporal," we learn that men's dreams are often more elusive than grand. Renoir adapted from a French novel. Well cast. (Dir: Jean Renoir, 108 mins.)

Elvira Madigan (Swedish, 1967)**** Pia Degermark, Thommy Berggren. One of the most exquisite, romantic movies ever made. It is exquisite in a quite literal sense, as the color photography provides some of the most ravishing, beautiful scenes ever filmed, thanks to cinematographer Jorgen Persson and the multi-talented Bo Widerberg who wrote, directed and edited this remarkable love story. Based on a true story about a young Swedish army officer around 1900 who runs off with Elvira, a lovely young circus artist. The leads are most attractive, but most of all it is Widerberg's triumph as he offers some of the most glorious images and tones ever seen. English dubbed. (Dir: Bo Widerberg, 89 mins.)

Elvis on Tour (1972)** Elvis Presley. For Presley fans. A documentary of an Elvis road tour—lots of performance footage with some backstage glimpses, intercut with old movie and television appearances. (Dirs: Pierre Adidge and Robert Abel, 92 mins.)

Elvis: That's the Way It Is (1970)** Elvis Presley fans will enjoy every frantic frame of this documentary about Elvis in a 1970 Las Vegas stint. Elvis is seen in rehearsal, in performance, backstage and in his dressing room . . . while fans, friends, promoters, publicists and all his entourage discuss the rock-and-roll king. Elvis' songs include "Bridge Over Troubled Water," "Sweet Carolina." (Dir: Denis Sanders, 108 mins.)

Embezzled Heaven (Austrian, 1959) ** Annie Rosar, Hans Holt. Mawkish drama about a cook who tries to buy a seat in Heaven, by helping a nephew to become a priest. Good in-

216

tentions, weak execution. English-dubbed.

Emergency (1972)** Robert Fuller, Julie London. Fire trucks race through Los Angeles streets as the rescue squad covers a barrage of accidents——auto crashes, a tunnel cave-in, and even a high-wire accident victim. This is director Jack Webb's two-hour pilot for the TV series. Made-for-TV. (Dir: Christian Nyby, 100 mins.)

Emergency Ward—See: **Carey Treatment, The**

Emergency Wedding (1950)** Larry Parks, Barbara Hale. Silly little comedy about a couple who love each other but don't like each other enough to make a go of their marriage. (Dir: Edward Buzzell, 78 mins.)

Emigrants, The (Swedish, 1970)**** Max von Sydow, Liv Ullmann. Profoundly touching story about the hardships of a Swedish peasant family who came to America's Midwest in the middle of the 19th century. Pace is slow and lyrical. Acting by everyone is subtle and emotional. A stirring reaffirmation of man's faith, bravery, and inner strength. Directed, photographed, and coscripted by Jan Troell. (151 mins.)

Emperor of the North (1973)*½ Lee Marvin, Ernest Borgnine, Keith Carradine. A sadistic, violent film with a pretentious script. The setting is Oregon in 1933. Marvin is a train-riding hobo; Carradine is his would-be protégé; Borgnine is the brutal conductor who threatens to kill any freeloaders who want to hop his freight. The duel of wits and axes between Marvin and Borgnine is, at times, engrossing. The best scenes are those between Marvin and Carradine, where Marvin tries to pass on a little of his lore. (Dir: Robert Aldrich, 120 mins.)

Emperor Waltz, The (1948)*** Bing Crosby, Joan Fontaine. Pleasing operetta finds Bing as a phonograph salesman trying to sell one to Emperor Franz Joseph of Austria, and wooing a countess on the side. (Dir: Billy Wilder, 106 mins.)

Empire in the Sun (Italian, 1956)*** Engrossing documentary exploring the life and habits of the Peruvian Indians. Fascinating scenes of unfamiliar peoples, should interest all.

Empty Canvas, The (1964)*½ Bette

Davis, Horst Buchholz, Catherine Spaak. The book by the Italian novelist on which this film is based was called "Boredom." That's a deft description of the film, too. It's another Bette Davis opus in which she overacts in a ludicrously overwritten story, based on an Alberto Moravia novel. Mama Bette tries to keep a tight rein on her son (Buchholz) who's absolutely obsessed with young and spicy Catherine Spaak. There's a great deal of silly dialogue and some graphic sex scenes (for 1964).

Enchanted Cottage (1945)***½ Robert Young, Dorothy McGuire. Two people are thrown together and find love in their mutual unhappiness. Sensitive, touching romantic drama. (Dir: John Cromwell, 91 mins.)

Enchanted Island (1958)*½ Jane Powell, Dana Andrews. Herman Melville's "Typee" badly brought to the screen. About two runaway sailors who live among a tribe of cannibals. If one can accept Jane Powell as a blue-eyed native girl, this will suffice. (Dir: Allan Dwan, 94 mins.)

Enchantment (1948)*** David Niven, Teresa Wright, Evelyn Keyes, Farley Granger. Occasionally interesting story about a doddering old colonel (Niven) who relives his romantic past via the reverie route. Vintage World War I. The flashbacks are triggered by Niven's grandson's romantic problems. The ladies will love this one. (Dir: Irving Reis, 102 mins.)

Encore (British, 1952)**** Glynis Johns, Kay Walsh, Nigel Patrick. Three Somerset Maugham stories—a playboy tries to get money from his brother; a spinster makes things rough on ship passengers; and a high-dive artist who has a fear of an accident. Excellent entertainment. (Dir: Pat Jackson, 90 mins.)

End of Desire (French, 1959)**½ Maria Schell, Christian Marquand. Wealthy girl discovers her husband has married her to pay off his debts and is carrying on with a servant girl. Slow, occasionally interesting costume drama based on a story by De Maupassant. English-dubbed. (Dir: Alexander Astruc, 86 mins.)

End of the Affair, The (1955)*** Deborah Kerr, Van Johnson, John Mills. Well acted, although overlong story of a love affair between an American and the wife of a British civil servant. Based on a Graham Greene novel. (Dir: Edward Dmytryk, 106 mins.)

End of the Dialogue (South African, 1970)**** A devastating short documentary, secretly filmed in South Africa, showing how the practice of apartheid affects and degrades the black population of the country. The list of horrors shown is endless—the appalling conditions under which blacks live and work, their denial of basic amenities, and the general hopelessness of their condition without a profound change—most unlikely at the time the film was made—in the whole structure of the oppressive government. Ends with a crawl of blacks murdered or imprisoned for long terms by the government. (Dir: Nana Mahomo, 50 mins.)

End of the Line (British, 1958)** Alan Baxter, Barbara Shelley. Evil woman induces a man to commit murder for her. Performances help this crime melodrama.

End of the Road (British, 1957)**½ Finlay Currie. Veteran British character actor Finlay Currie gives an excellent performance as "Mick-Mack" in this well made, heart-warming story of an old man and his grandson.

Endless Summer, The (1966)***½ This lovely feature-length documentary about the joys of surfing around the world is a good one. Director, cinematographer, writer Bruce Brown is largely responsible for the glorious, lyrical footage which captures the exhilaration and the danger of this increasingly popular sport among youngsters. A charming musical score and a disarming narrative nicely complement the scenes of two carefree surfers looking for the perfect wave. If you're already a fan of surfing, or are still wondering what all the excitement is about, "The Endless Summer" is a treat! (Dir: Bruce Brown, 95 mins.)

Enemy Below, The (1957)*** Robert Mitchum, Curt Jurgens. Interesting WWII drama in which an American destroyer and a German U-boat play cat and mouse in the Atlantic ocean. Good photography heightens the action. Superior performances. (Dir: Dick Powell, 98 mins.)

Enemy from Space (British, 1957)* Brian Donlevy, Vera Day. The title explains the plot thoroughly. Veter-

217

an actor Donlevy understandably looks as if he was ashamed of the whole business. (Dir: Val Guest, 84 mins.)

Enemy General, The (1960)** Van Johnson, Jean-Pierre Aumont. Fair World War II drama set on the European Front. Good performances by the principals. (Dir: George Sherman, 74 mins.)

Enforcer, The (1951)*** Humphrey Bogart. Violent, well-done semi documentary about the smashing of Murder Inc. by an assistant district attorney. (Dir: Bretaigne Windust, 87 mins.)

Enforcer, The (1976) ½ Clint Eastwood, Harry Guardino, Bradford Dillman, Tyne Daly. We thought the first of the "Dirty Harry" adventures was a mindless police adventure, but we never reckoned that Harry would return in this third piece of cardboard-celluloid. In this outing, Eastwood is joined by a female partner, Miss Daly, ruffling Harry's male-chauvinist mien until . . . The mindless violence, here, follows from the mayor's being kidnapped by some homicidal maniacs. (Dir: James Fargo, 96 mins.)

England Made Me (Great Britain, 1972)*** Peter Finch, Michael York, Hildegard Neil, Michael Hordern. Graham Greene's prescient, ironic first novel, published in 1935, has received an intelligent treatment on the screen. Richly evocative of pre-WW II Berlin, the film focuses on the moral conflict between an innocent British idealist (York) and the decadent Germany he visits in 1935, especially as personified in a corrupt industrialist (Finch). Though most every detail echoes the theme of disaster just around the corner, the acting, especially Hordern's washed-up newspaper reporter, keeps the film from being too ponderous. (Dir: Peter Duffell, 100 mins.)

Ensign Pulver (1964)** Robert Walker, Burl Ives, Millie Perkins. Director Joshua Logan, who guided "Mr. Roberts" to success, hoped to repeat the feat but failed. It's slapstick comedy all the way, and even pros like Burl Ives, Walter Matthau, and Kay Medford can't rise above the sinking material. (Dir: Joshua Logan, 104 mins.)

Enter Inspector Maigret (French-W. German, 1967)** ½ Heinz Ruh-

218

mann, Eddi Arent. Georges Simenon's famous detective Inspector Maigret investigates the case of a Van Gogh painting stolen from a Paris art museum. Mild suspense, tricky dubbing. (90 mins.)

Enter Laughing (1961)*** Shelley Winters, Elaine May, Jose Ferrer, Rene Santoni. Carl Reiner's funny Broadway lark about a young Jewish boy from the Bronx who wants to be a star of stage 'n screen made a star out of Alan Arkin, but it didn't do the same for Rene Santoni who plays the young would-be actor here. And that's the principal shortcoming of this picture, because newcomer Santoni has neither the range nor the warmth to do justice to this meaty role. But Reiner's romp is still a funny vehicle and there are a lot of laughs along the way, especially from such proven laugh getters as Elaine May and Jack Gilford. (Dir: Carl Reiner, 112 mins.)

Entertainer, The (British, 1960)**** Laurence Olivier, Joan Plowright, Brenda de Banzie. Story concerns an unpleasant, third-rate British music-hall performer on the skids, but the bravura performance of Laurence Olivier is one of the most brilliant and exciting acting performances ever filmed. Olivier captures all the shabbiness, banality, pathos, and false hope of this fatuous man, and it is photographed against the backdrop of a depressing English seaside resort. Miss de Banzie playing his comforting wife is outstanding in a fine supporting cast, which includes Albert Finney in a small part. John Osborne wrote the screenplay from his play which also starred Olivier, and the perceptive direction is the work of Tony Richardson. Olivier's technical virtuosity is quite breathtaking in this definitive portrait of a show-business louse. (Dir: Tony Richardson, 97 mins.)

Entertainer, The (1976)** ½ Jack Lemmon, Sada Thompson, Ray Bolger. It's easy to understand why Jack Lemmon would be drawn to the role of Archie Rice in John Osborne's play, a role so brilliantly created on stage and film by Laurence Olivier. Lemmon gives a quite moving and varied performance, which is reason enough to see this version. The overall effect is curiously diminished, partly due to some lacklustre performances, notably Sada Thompson as Archie's harassed, embittered wife. The locale has been foolishly changed from Brighton, England, to Santa Cruz, California; Ray Bolger is effective playing Archie's showbiz dad; but it's Jack Lemmon's performance that's the main attraction. Made-for-TV. (Dir: Donald Wrye, 98 mins.)

Entertaining Mr. Sloane (British, 1970)***½ Beryl Reid, Harry Andrews, Peter McEnery. Fine, literate black comedy based on Joe Orton's play. McEnery plays Mr. Sloane, a young hustler who is boarded by the blowsy, kittenish Kate. But complications arise when Ed, Kate's latently homosexual brother, also lusts for the young boy. Nontype casting of Andrews as Ed and Miss Reid as Kate make the farce shine. Some devastating social insight. (Dir: Douglas Hickox, 94 mins.)

Eric (1975)*** John Savage, Patricia Neal, Claude Akins, Mark Hamill, Eileen McDonough. Doris Lund's best-selling book about her son Eric's brave struggle with cancer becomes a sound and emotional drama. Miss Neal plays the boy's mother with restraint and dignity, allowing her son to set up his own ground rules in his bout with leukemia. Savage, as Eric, maintains that fine line between optimism and resignation with remarkable credibility, continuing his studies and even playing soccer as long as he is able to. The brief but touching scene in which Eric's little sister gives him her babysitting earnings for his birthday is just one of several that build to a compelling finale. Made-for-TV. (Dir: James Goldstone, 100 mins.)

Erik the Conqueror (Italian, 1963)*½ Cameron Mitchell, Alice and Ellen Kessler, Francoise Christophe. Viking swears to avenge a massacre occurring in his youth. Some action, mostly hokey, in this English-dubbed adventure spectacle. (Dir: Mario Bava, 81 mins.)

Errand Boy, The (1962)**½ Jerry Lewis. Strictly for fans of Lewis. He's a goofy paper hanger who gets involved in a Hollywood studio management mix-up. The Hollywood setting triggers many sight gags. (Dir: Jerry Lewis, 92 mins.)

Escapade (British, 1957)** John Mills, Yvonne Mitchell, Alastair Sim. Three boys run away from school and endeavor to show the adults how to make the world peaceful. Verbose comedy-drama moves too leisurely. (Dir: Philip Leacock, 87 mins.)

Escapade in Japan (1957)*** Teresa Wright, Cameron Mitchell, Jon Provost. American boy's plane is forced down, so he joins with a Japanese lad to reach his parents. Attention-holding benefits from fascinating Japan locations, good performances. (Dir: Arthur Lubin, 92 mins.)

Escape (1940)*** Norma Shearer, Robert Taylor. Good exciting melodrama based on a best selling novel. Story is about an American trying to get his mother out of a concentration camp in pre-war Nazi Germany. (Dir: Mervyn Le Roy, 104 mins.)

Escape (1948)*** Rex Harrison, Peggy Cummins. Fascinating, deep study of a man who is sentenced to jail for what he considers a just act. His defiance of the law, escape and eventual surrender make this an intriguing film. (Dir: Joseph Mankiewicz, 78 mins.)

Escape (1971)*½ Christopher George, Marilyn Mason. Slick, empty made-for-TV feature which doubled as a pilot for a proposed series. Chris George is a former escape artist who employs his unique skills to uncover a sinister plot involving a supposedly dead scientist and his guilt-ridden brother. An amusement park chase at the end is terribly familiar. (Dir: John Llewellyn Moxley, 73 mins.)

Escape by Night (Italian, 1960)**½ Leo Genn, Peter Baldwin. Three escaped prisoners of war, an American, an Englishman, and a Russian, are befriended and helped by an Italian girl during World War II. Drama directed by Roberto Rossellini lacks his usual flair, becomes a mildly interesting, somewhat choppy war drama dubbed in English.

Escape from East Berlin (1962)**½ Don Murray, Christine Kaufmann. Based on a true story, this drama generates a good deal of suspense. Don Murray plays a man who engineers an escape tunnel leading to the western sector of Berlin and safety. Miss Kaufmann plays a determined young girl in on the plan. (Dir: Robert Siodmak, 94 mins.)

Escape From Fort Bravo (1953)*** Eleanor Parker, William Holden, John Forsythe. Good western film set during the Civil War. The plot concerns the relationship between the Union Captain (Holden) and the people in Fort Bravo. There's a very exciting sequence towards the end of the film in which a large group of hostile Indians pin down a party, escaping from the fort. (Dir: John Sturges, 98 mins.)

Escape from Hell Island (1964)** Mark Stevens, Jack Donner, Linda Scott. Captain of a charter boat saves a pretty refugee from Castro's Cuba, but becomes a target for death. Stevens is actor and director of this melier; also has some nice Florida location scenes.

Escape from Red Rock (1958)** Brian Donlevy, Eilene Janssen. Run-of-the-treadmill western with Donlevy leading a gang of no-goods. Nothing new, but good action and average acting. (Dir: Edward Bernds, 75 mins.)

Escape from Sahara (German, 1963)** Hildegarde Neff, Harry Meyer. Three legionnaires decide to desert, force the pilot to change course; the plane crash-lands. Passable desert drama gets a good performance from Neff as a nurse. English-dubbed.

Escape from Saigon (French, 1960)*** Jean Chevrier, Barbara Laage. Occasionally suspenseful, lively melodrama about an engineer who rescues his wife from a ruthless trader and flees to safety. Dubbed in English.

Escape from Terror (1959)* Jackie Coogan, Mona Knox. Awful film about Americans trying to escape from behind the Iron Curtain. Poor performances.

Escape from the Planet of the Apes (1971)*** Roddy McDowall, Kim Hunter, Bradford Dillman, Sal Mineo. The third in the simian cycle of films and a fairly good sci-fi story. Hunter and McDowall, in ape makeup, escape from their planet in the very spaceship that brought Charlton Heston to their world two films before . . . but they go back in time to the present, the 1970's. Needless to say their arrival in California causes an uproar, and their adventure in our society is both entertaining and, at times, surprisingly

220

meaningful. (Dir: Don Taylor, 98 mins.)

Escape from Zahrain (1962)**½ Yul Brynner, Sal Mineo, Jack Warden, Madlyn Rhue. Rebel leader in an Arab oil state escapes along with some fellow-convicts, and they make a dash for the border. Typical action opus. (Dir: Ronald Neame, 93 mins.)

Escape in the Desert (1945)**½ Helmut Dantine, Jean Sullivan, Philip Dorn. If you want to see what is meant by the Hollywood touch, take a look at this hopped up version of "The Petrified Forest." They removed the original's depth, added some Nazis for timeliness and come up with a mediocre adventure tale. (Dir: Edward A. Blatt, 81 mins.)

Escape to Burma (1955)*½ Barbara Stanwyck, Robert Ryan. Fugitive finds refuge and romance in an isolated jungle home. Threadbare melodrama, nothing new. (86 mins.)

Escape to Mindanao (1968)**½ George Maharis, Willi Koopman, Nehemiah Persoff, James Shigeta. Good adventure. George Maharis stars in a drama about a prisoner-of-war back in 1942, who's perfectly happy to spend the rest of the war simply staying alive in the camp. A good setup—a reluctant anti-hero, a chase via train, car and ship, a pretty girl, and some absorbing if standard characters—combine to make this better-than-average entertainment. (Dir: Don McDougall, 95 mins.)

Escape to the Sun (Israel, 1972)* Laurence Harvey, Joseph Chaplin, John Ireland, Jack Hawkins. An important, timely subject—the plight of Russian Jews who wish to emigrate—is insultingly handled and loaded with clichés. Harvey evokes little menace as the villainous Russian intelligence man on the trail of a motley group of dissidents. Clumsily, directed and co-authored by Menahem Golan. (105 mins.)

Escort for Hire (British, 1962)** June Thorburn, Pete Murray. Man hired as an escort gets mixed up in a murder case. Average mystery melodrama. (Dir: Godfrey Grayson, 66 mins.)

Esther and the King (1960)*½ Joan Collings, Richard Egan, Daniella Rocca. When his queen is murdered, a Persian king chooses a Judean maiden to replace her. She intends to influence him in ceasing persecution of the Jews. Long, rambling, inept Biblical drama, filmed in Italy —no better than the rest. (Dir: Raoul Walsh, 109 mins.)

Essene (1972)*** Documentary by Frederick Wiseman about an Anglican monastery in the Middle West. The members of the monastery are very reserved in their quest for a meaningful group relationship to counter the loneliness of their personal lives. Some of the footage is purely drab and unemotional. In many ways, "Essene" is Wiseman's least accessible, and in some other ways, least interesting essay on American institutions. But you do learn a lot of recondite data about the austere life of these members of a sect which began in the second century B.C. (Dir: Frederick Wiseman, 86 mins.)

Eternal Chains (1958)** Marcello Mastroianni and Gianna Maria Canale. An Italian soap opera. Mastroianni plays the leading role of a man who falls in love with his brother's wife. The plot takes on typical melodramatic overtones.

Eternal Sea (1955)**½ Sterling Hayden, Alexis Smith, Dean Jagger. True story of a Navy officer who continues to serve, despite an artificial limb. Factual but overlong war drama. (Dir: John H. Auer, 110 mins.)

Eternal Waltz (German, 1959)** Bernhard Wicki, Hilde Krahl. Ponderous biography of the waltz king. Johann Strauss. For the musicminded, okay. Dubbed-English dialogue.

Eternally Yours (1939)** Ladies, if you ever plan to marry a magician, watch what happens to Loretta Young when she falls for trickster David Niven. Broderick Crawford is also on hand in this romantic comedy. Good cast wasted on trite material. (Dir: Tay Garnett, 110 mins.)

Eureka Stockade (Australian, 1949) *** Chips Rafferty, Jane Barrett. Four gold-seekers in early Australia band together to fight a despotic governor, get public sentiment on their side. Impressive historical drama contains plenty of action.

Eve (British, 1969)*½ Herbert Lom, Celeste Yarnall, Robert Walker, Fred Clark, Christopher Lee. The search is on for a blonde jungle goddess. The gal (Celeste Yarnall) is sexy, the plot's silly. (Dir: Jeremy Summers, 94 mins.)

Eve of St. Mark, The (1944)*** Anne Baxter, William Eythe. Maxwell Anderson's poetic commentary on war is an often moving, occasionally stilted film. (Dir: John M. Stahl, 96 mins.)

Evel Knievel (1971)*** George Hamilton, Sue Lyon. There's a certain inherent interest in watching a story about an egomaniac who flirts with death, and makes a fortune doing it. Evel Knievel is an American folk hero who's performed some of the most daring death-defying stunts ever executed on a motorcycle. How accurate a portrait of his personal life this film presents is open to question, but Hamilton evokes the cocksure flamboyance necessary to play the spectacular daredevil who dresses like a rock star and basks in the adoration of his fans. (Dir: Marvin Chomsky, 90 mins.)

Event, An (Yugoslav, 1969)***½ Deeply moving story set in Yugoslavia during World War II, loosely based on a story by Anton Chekhov. Directed by Vatroslav Mimica, story concerns an old peasant and his grandson who set out to sell their decrepit horse. One of the numerous rewarding features made in recent years by the increasingly impressive film industry of this small country.

Every Girl Should Be Married (1947) **½ Cary Grant, Betsy Drake. A shopgirl uses her wiles to land a bachelor doctor. Disappointingly mild, undistinguished comedy. (Dir: Don Hartman, 85 mins.)

Every Little Crook and Nanny (1972) *½ Victor Mature, Lynn Redgrave, Paul Sand, Maggie Blye, Austin Pendleton, John Astin, Dom De-Luise. Farcical entertainment about a "lighthearted kidnapping," played for laughs and doesn't get 'em. After Miss Redgrave's dancing school is taken over by the mob as a bookie joint, she kidnaps a mob leader's son. Broad playing, especially by Mature as the amiably vulgar mob chieftain, can't inflate the unfunny script. Mature's first film in six years. Based on the novel by Evan Hunter. (Dir: Cy Howard, 92 mins.)

Every Man Needs One (1972)* Ken Berry, Connie Stevens. Boring comedy fare. Architect hires an assistant who is big on Women's Lib. Made-for-TV. (Dir: Jerry Paris, 88 mins.)

Every Man's Woman—See: Rose for Everyone, A

Every Minute Counts (French, 1960) *½ Dominique Wilms, Jean Lara. English-dubbed. Paris police go into action when a girl is kidnapped. Every minute does not count in this tedious entry.

Everybody Does It (1949)***½ Paul Douglas, Linda Darnell, Celeste Holm. A businessman takes up singing, discovers he really has a voice —with Douglas in the role, it's a howl from beginning to end. Sharp dialogue helps, too. (Dir: Edmund Goulding, 98 mins.)

Everything Happens at Night (1939) *** Ray Milland, Robert Cummings, Sonja Henie. Thanks to good playing by its leading men, this film about two reporters trying to find a Nobel Prize winner is good entertainment. Sonja does some skating between scenes. (Dir: Irving Cummings, 77 mins.)

Everything I Have Is Yours (1952) **½ Marge & Gower Champion, Dennis O'Keefe. Wedded song and dance team find married life interfering with their stage careers. Aside from the dancing of the Champions, nothing particularly novel about this routine musical. (Dir: Robert Z. Leonard, 92 mins.)

Everything You Always Wanted to Know About Sex, But Were Afraid to Ask (1972)**** Woody Allen, Lou Jacobi, Anthony Quayle, Gene Wilder, Burt Reynolds, Tony Randall. The most important and inventive comedy talent in American film has borrowed the title of Dr. David Reuben's best-selling rip-off book about sex, and transformed it into a series of lunatic, hysterical sketches. They don't all work, but it doesn't matter because ordinary Allen is funnier than virtually anything else around. A number of sketches (Woody does not appear in all of them, though he has conceived of and directed the whole mad lot) are excruciatingly funny. Gene Wilder plays a mild-mannered doctor falling head over heels in love with one of his patients—an Armenian sheep named Daisy. Besides that it's your only other chance of the filmic week to see a 40-feet-high female breast, Lynn Redgrave wearing a chastity belt, and a wondrous bit of madness which finds Woody playing a sperm. (87 mins.)

Everything's Ducky (1961)** Mickey Rooney, Buddy Hackett, Jackie Cooper, Joanie Sommers. Two sailors and a talking duck—fill in the rest. Rooney and Hackett try hard for laughs, which aren't there. (Dir: Don Taylor, 81 mins.)

Evil Eye, The (1964)**½ John Saxon, Leticia Roman, Valentina Cortesa. Young doctor and a frightened girl uncover a series of unsolved murders when she fears the worst has happened to her aunt. Suspenseful thriller made in Italy serves up the shudders in interesting fashion. (Dir: Mario Bava, 92 mins.)

Evil of Frankenstein, The (British, 1964)** Peter Cushing, Peter Woodthorpe. Baron Frankenstein returns to his castle, finds his homemade creature encased in ice, and starts all over again. He shouldn't have bothered. (Dir: Freddie Francis, 87 mins.)

Evil Roy Slade (1972)** John Astin. A crazy, offbeat comedy that might amuse the youngsters. Astin plays the title role of a mean, unremorseful outlaw who has never been loved. While robbing a bank he meets and kisses curvy but pure Pamela Austin, and love hits Evil Roy. Some scenes are quite funny. The film was apparently intended as a pilot for a TV series. Other funny performances are delivered by Dick Shawn as a singing marshal and Dom DeLuise as a psychiatrist trying to help Slade reform. (Dir: Jerry Paris, 100 mins.)

Ex-Champ (1939)**½ Victor McLaglen, Constance Moore, Tom Brown. Former champ turned doorman undertakes to train a young boxer. Fairly interesting melodrama. (Dir: Phil Rosen, 64 mins.)

Ex-Mrs. Bradford, The (1936)***½ William Powell, Jean Arthur. Amateur sleuth with the aid of his ex-wife solves some race track murders. Delightful comedy-mystery, smooth and sophisticated. (Dir: Stephen Roberts, 100 mins.)

Excuse My Dust (1951)**½ Red Skelton, Macdonald Carey. Amusing Skelton comedy about the days of the "Horseless Carriage." Some good gags, pleasant performers. (Dir: Roy Rowland, 82 mins.)

Execution of Private Slovik, The (1974)**** Martin Sheen, Mariclare

Costello. Sheen's riveting performance as WW II soldier Eddie Slovik, the first serviceman to be executed for desertion since the Civil War, is a profoundly moving experience. His portrait of Eddie is one of a man who walks through life as if it were a lost continent, saved only by his love for the girl who becomes his wife (Miss Costello). Slovik's battle experience makes firing a rifle an impossible duty and leads to his desertion and execution. A drama about a soul in agony which will haunt you. Made-for-TV. (Dir: Lamont Johnson.)

Executioner, The (1970)**½ George Peppard, Joan Collins, Nigel Patrick. Enjoyable spy-chase-adventure thriller, which uses plot turns to advantage. Suave George Peppard is an American-trained British agent who, along with the necessary quota of sidekicks, must track down the traitor involved in a massacre at a country estate. The landscape from London to Athens is lush, and the action remains tense throughout. Well directed by actor-director Sam Wanamaker. (107 mins.)

Executioners, The (1958)**½ Documentary showing the reign of Nazi terror, its eventual downfall. It's been compiled before and better done, but still worth seeing. Alternate title: Hitler's Executioners.

Executive Suite (1954)*** William Holden, June Allyson, Fredric March, Barbara Stanwyck, Shelley Winters, Paul Douglas, Walter Pidgeon. A big cast effectively brings this best-selling novel about big business to the screen. There are many subplots which tend to get in the way of the main theme (the struggle of a group of V.P.s to take over control of a major furniture-manufacturing firm). The best performances are delivered by William Holden, Fredric March, Dean Jagger and Nina Foch. (Dir: Robert Wise, 104 mins.)

Exit Laughing—See: **Are You There?**

Exit Smiling (1926)**** Bea Lillie. A wonderfully funny comedy, presumed lost but happily recovered recently by the American Film Institute. Bea Lillie can do more riotously funny things with a string of pearls than most performers can do with ten pages of dialogue and 100 props. If you don't laugh hysterically at the great Lady Peel's seducing a reluc-

tant gent, you'd better rush to your doctor and check your eyesight and funnybone. Directed by Sam Taylor, this film reminds us how tragically the motion picture industry wasted Lillie's superb talents over the years. The plot doesn't matter. Just tune in, young and old.

Exodus (1960)***½ Paul Newman, Eva Marie Saint, Lee J. Cobb, Sal Mineo. Producer-director Otto Preminger put considerable stress on scope and pictorial splendor in bringing Leon Uris' bestselling novel about the hardships of Jewish refugees in the new Israel to the screen. Shows perils of getting to Israel and running the British blockade, and there's an exciting post-Cyprus scene in Israel toward the end of the film. Episodic but generally exciting, well acted and of considerable historic interest about a fascinating and exasperating period in post-war Europe. (Dir: Otto Preminger, 213 mins.)

Exorcist, The (1973)***½ Ellen Burstyn, Max von Sydow, Lee J. Cobb, Jason Miller, Linda Blair. Welcome back from Mars if you haven't heard about this one yet. It's devilishly clever and involving, and virtually impossible to summarize adequately in a few lines. The story of a 12-year-old girl in a prosperous home in Georgetown, Washington, D.C., who becomes possessed by demons and is finally saved when the vile spirits are exorcised and driven from her body. The implications may not be encouraging for American sociologists but it's easy to understand why this drama had such staggering audience appeal, making it one of the very top grossing films in the history of cinema. Based on author William Peter Blatty's best-selling novel, the film takes itself quite seriously, even though its primary purpose is to scare hell out of the audience, and it certainly succeeds. It succeeds partly because it sometimes is more repellent than scary—when the afflicted girl spews vomit in the Jesuit priests' faces, for example. In some ways it's a familiar blood-and-thunder horror film, but it's undeniably more compelling than almost any other of this genre because it is remarkably well made by the talented director William Friedkin. You momentarily believe the levita-

223

tions and the swiveling heads, and it's uniformly well acted throughout. Miss Blair is convincing as the deranged child and playwright Jason Miller is effective as the supportive priest. Mercedes McCambridge provides the Voice of the Demon. (122 mins.)

Exorcist II: The Heretic (1977) ½ Linda Blair, Richard Burton, Louise Fletcher, James Earl Jones. This may just well be the worst sequel in the history of films—a stupefying, boring, vapid and NON-SCARY follow-up to the box-office champ of 1973 that spawned a new cycle of Devil films. "Exorcist II" is a disaster on virtually every level— a sophomoric script, terrible editing, worst direction from John "Deliverance" Boorman, inevitably coupled with silly acting. In one scene that typifies this lamentable sci-fi horror pic, Burton and Jones, two splendid actors, are spouting inane dialogue while Jones is outfitted like a witch doctor. Abominable screenplay by William Goodheart. (Dir: John Boorman, 117 mins.)

Experiment in Terror (1962)*** Glenn Ford, Lee Remick, Stefanie Powers, Ross Martin. High-tension thriller about a girl and her sister terrorized by a criminal with a plan to pull a robbery, while the FBI frantically tries to prevent tragedy. Director Blake Edwards uses unusual camerawork, San Francisco backgrounds to full effect. Excellent suspense. (Dir: Blake Edwards, 123 mins.)

Experiment Perilous (1944)*** Hedy Lamarr, George Brent, Paul Lukas. Doctor investigates the death of a wealthy philanthropist's sister, suspects foul play. Well done mystery. (Dir: Jacques Tourneur, 91 mins.)

Explosive Generation, The (1961)*** Patty McCormick, William Shatner. When a high-school teacher is expelled for teaching sex education, his students rush to his defense. Give this one credit—it tries to say something important and does so in an efficient manner, despite production failings. Unusual adult drama. (Dir: Buzz Kulik, 89 mins.)

Expresso Bongo (British, 1960)**** Laurence Harvey, Sylvia Syms, Cliff Richard. Delightful mixture of fantasy and realism, as a small-time agent uses any means to push a teenage singer into the big time.

224

Great stylish performance by Harvey as the agent; excellent script with witty dialogue. For adults, fine entertainment. (Dir: Val Guest, 109 mins.)

Extra Day, The (British, 1956)*** Richard Basehart, Simone Simon. Adventures and aspirations of a bit player in a film studio. Well acted, different comedy-drama.

Extraordinary Seaman, The (1969) ** David Niven, Faye Dunaway, Alan Alda, Mickey Rooney. This film, directed by John Frankenheimer ("The Manchurian Candidate" and "Grand Prix"), was released without any publicity and died at the box office. It's a supposedly whimsical, nautical tale set in the Pacific of WW II. Take a look and see if Hollywood made the correct decision in scuttling the hoopla for this film. P.S. We would have done the same. (Dir: John Frankenheimer, 80 mins.)

Eye for an Eye, An (1966)**½ Robert Lansing, Pat Wayne. An offbeat western yarn which benefits from a good performance by Robert Lansing. Revenge is the keynote of this tale, which has Lansing teaming up with the blinded Pat Wayne as the two prepare for a shootout with villains. (Dir: Michael Moore, 92 mins.)

Eye of the Cat (1969)**½ Eleanor Parker, Michael Sarrazin, Gayle Hunnicutt. A macabre outing manages some frightening visual effects involving cats. Tale revolves around wealthy invalid Eleanor Parker (who has numerous cats as pets) and her nephew's (Sarrazin) scheme to get her money. It's both predictable, and implausible, straight through, but Miss Parker and her feline protectors may interest you. (Dir: David Lowell Rich, 102 mins.)

Eye of the Devil (British, 1967)*½ Deborah Kerr, David Niven, Emlyn Williams, Donald Pleasence. Save eyesight and your time. Many good actors, including Flora Robson and David Hemmings, wasted in not-so-spooky doings and terror at a French chateau. (Dir: J. Lee Thompson, 92 mins.)

Eye of the Monocle, The (French, 1962)*½ Paul Meurisse, Elga Anderson. Effete French agent vies with the British and Russians in a hunt for Himmler's hidden treasure. Overdone espionage thriller dubbed in English.

Eye of the Needle, The (Italy-France, 1963)*** Vittorio Gassman, Annette Stroyberg, Gerard Blain. Broad, on-target satire of everything Sicilian, from marriage mores to Mafioso tactics. Follows the legal acrobatics necessary to restore tranquillity to a small town when two local youths deflower a local innocent. (Dir: Marcello Andrei, 97 mins.)

Eye Witness (British, 1949)*** Robert Montgomery, Patricia Wayne. An American lawyer goes to England to save a friend from a murder charge. Neat melodrama, well played nicely directed by Montgomery himself. (Dir: Robert Montgomery, 104 mins.)

Eyes of Annie Jones, The (U.S.-British, 1964)* Richard Conte, Joyce Carey. Bad picture about an orphan girl believed to possess ESP. The girl, Francesca Annis, does possess some acting talent, but the film is a blank otherwise.

Eyes of Charles Sand, The (1972)**½ Peter Haskell, Sharon Farrell, Barbara Rush, Brad Dillman. Splashy melodrama about the rich has the characters working at a highly emotional pitch acting demented and running about brandishing butcher knives. Young business success Charles Sand (Haskell) inherits a gift of visionary sight—seeing quick flashes of old hags and bodies behind crumbling walls —and is soon besieged by a babbling redhead crying for help. Escapist fare, with the actors having more fun than the audience. Made-for-TV. (Dir: Reza Badiyi, 75 mins.)

Eyes of the Sahara (French, 1957)** Curt Jurgens, Lea Padovani, Folco Lulli. Arab native seeks revenge upon a neglectful doctor who was responsible for the death of his wife. Grim, well-acted drama becomes too involved with vague symbolism for complete success. Dubbed-in English.

F. Scott Fitzgerald and "The Last of the Belles" (1974)**½ Richard Chamberlain, Blythe Danner, Susan Sarandon, David Huffman. Interesting, uneven attempt to dramatize a portion of Fitzgerald's life and his short story, "The Last of the Belles." The action is intercut between two separate dramas, with the short story, about a small-town flirt who keeps a steady flow of WW I Army officers buzzing around her, coming off best. Chamberlain and Danner, as Scott and Zelda, are one-dimensional, but Susan Sarandon as the wide-eyed, drawling darling, and Huffman, as the love-struck soldier, keep things moving. Made-for-TV. (Dir: George Schaefer, 98 mins.)

F. Scott Fitzgerald in Hollywood (1976)** Jason Miller, Tuesday Weld, Julia Foster. Hollywood has always been intrigued with the legend that was F. Scott Fitzgerald, and this is still another chapter in the saga of Zelda and Scott, those enduring icons of the Jazz Age. Miller's humorless performance as the writing genius gone sour is strictly one-note, but Tuesday Weld, in an all-too-brief appearance as the moth-like Zelda, teetering on the brink of madness, fares much better. Julia Foster, as the young Sheilah Graham, also scores in a confessional scene in which she pours her heart out to Scott about her upbringing in the poverty of London slums. The character of Dorothy Parker keeps popping in and out, uttering quotable one-liners. Writer James Costigan has fashioned an ordinary script, and British director Anthony Page has done little to enhance the material. Made-for-TV. (98 mins.)

Fabulous Dorseys, The (1947)** Tommy and Jimmy Dorsey, Janet Blair. The biography of the famous bandleaders who fought each other as they fought to the top. Mild musical; good tunes, not much on plot. (Dir: Alfred E. Green, 88 mins.)

Fabulous World of Jules Verne, The (1961)*** An adventure yarn, a puppet show, and a cartoon festival all rolled into one. In a process called Mystimation (using live actors, animation and puppets) the younger set will be treated to a fabulous journey beneath the sea and above the clouds in true Jules Verne fashion. Czech-made, dubbed in English. (Dir: Karel Zeman, 83 mins.)

Face in the Crowd, A (1957)***½ Andy Griffith, Patricia Neal, Anthony Franciosa. An excellent screenplay by Budd Schulberg is well directed by Elia Kazan and gives Andy Griffith the best role of his career, as a backwoods, guitar playing bum who becomes a national TV personality. Patricia Neal is equally as good as a reporter who discovers and protects and finally destroys the big man. A considerably under-rated film when first released. (Dir: Elia Kazan, 125 mins.)

Face in the Rain, A (1963)******* Rory Calhoun, Marina Berti. During World War II an American boy is sheltered from the enemy by the mistress of a German commandant. Suspenseful melodrama, made in Italy. Better than average of its type. (Dir: Irvin Kershner, 91 mins.)

Face in the Sky (1933)****½** Spencer Tracy, Marion Nixon, Lila Lee. The hard-working Tracy made six films that were released in 1933, including "20,000 Years in Sing Sing." An unusual but consistently enjoyable outing that changes from romance down on the farm to life, love, and music in the big city. (Dir: Harry Lachman.)

Face of a Fugitive (1959)****½** Fred MacMurray, Lin McCarthy. Good western with better than average performances by MacMurray and a good supporting cast. MacMurray, falsely accused of murder, changes his identity when he decides to settle in a town, but trouble follows his trail. (Dir: Paul Wendkos, 81 mins.)

Face of Eve, The—See: Eve

Face of Fear—See: Peeping Tom

Face of Fire (1959)****½** Cameron Mitchell, James Whitmore, Bettye Ackerman. Disfigured in a fire, a well-liked local handyman becomes a social outcast. Odd little drama produced in Sweden; but well-acted, often photographically beautiful. (Dir: Albert Band, 83 mins.)

Face of War, A (1968)******** A memorable documentary directed and photographed by Eugene S. Jones in Vietnam during 1966. Jones, who was wounded twice during the filming, captures the particular horror of the war as seen by the front line troops—in this case foot soldiers of the Seventh Marine Regiment. It is a compassionate, searing account of this and most other wars fought by the front-line troops, and it is mercifully devoid of the chauvinism that was such a standard ingredient for a long period of many American

226

TV documentaries and coverage about the Vietnam War. A chilling, unforgettable document.

Face to Face (1952)*****½** Package of two stories: "The Secret Sharer" (James Mason), a shipboard drama, and "Bride Comes to Yellow Sky" (Robert Preston, Marjorie Steele), a tale of a sheriff in a small western town. Both tastefully produced, literate, well acted. (Dirs: John Brahm, Bretaigne Windust, 90 mins.)

Face to Face (Sweden, 1975)******** Liv Ullmann, Erland Josephson. A devastating masterpiece, Bergman's 39th film, featuring one of the most remarkable acting performances (Ullmann's) in modern cinema. This award-winning drama is about a psychiatrist (Ullmann) who goes through a nervous breakdown on camera. There are very few other contemporary actresses who could be so convincing and convey so many varied emotions and passions. She is remarkable, and so is virtually everything else about "Face to Face." Original screenplay by Bergman himself. Originally made as a four-part series for Swedish TV. (Dir: Ingmar Bergman, 136 mins.)

Faces (1968)******** John Marley, Gena Rowlands, Lynn Carlin, Seymour Cassell. John Cassavetes' brilliant moving drama is one of the most important American films in years, and richly deserves all the awards it got including three Academy Award nominations. (One for Cassavetes' screenplay, one for supporting actress Lynn Carlin, one for supporting actor Seymour Cassell.) Concerns the disintegration of the marriage, after a fourteen-year period, of a middle-class couple in California. What is unique about this document is not the plot line, which is familiar enough, but the revelatory nature of the experience, watching the actors who suggest an improvisatory quality about their work that almost makes the audience feel you are improperly eavesdropping on the most personal of conversations. A stunning, perceptive study of American manners and morals. (Dir: John Cassavetes, 130 mins.)

Facts of Life, The (1960)******* Lucille Ball, Bob Hope. Two of show business' funniest comics are teamed in this laugh filled comedy about the many sides of marriage. Many scenes border on slapstick but they're skillfully carried off by the two old pros. (Dir: Melvin Frank, 103 mins.)

Facts of Murder, The (Italian, 1960) *** Claudia Cardinale, Pietro Germi, Franco Fabrizi, Eleanora Rossi-Drago. Absorbing story of a humanistic police inspector investigating an ugly murder case, his reactions to the people he meets during its course. Good as whodunit or straight drama, well acted, English dubbed.

Fade In (1968)** Burt Reynolds, Barbara Loden. Of some note. Reynolds and Miss Loden appeared in this drama about the movie business and the people involved in an on-location film shooting, but it never was released theatrically in the U.S. Tune in and judge for yourself.

Fahrenheit 451 (British, 1966)*** Oskar Werner, Julie Christie. Based on Ray Bradbury's fascinating science-fiction yarn about the near future, in which firemen go around burning books. Film only partially succeeds in this adaptation directed by François Truffaut. The stars (Miss Christie in a dual role) do what they can, but the screenplay never delves into the psychological overtones of Bradbury's tale. Despite its flaws, this sci-fi film is more absorbing than most and worth seeing. (Dir: François Truffaut, 111 mins.)

Failing of Raymond, The (1971)**½ Jane Wyman, Dean Stockwell. It's Miss Wyman in a role which suits her dignified style. She plays a schoolteacher who is thinking of retiring when an old student who failed an important test a few years past shows up with vengeance on his mind. Made-for-TV. (Dir: Boris Sagal.)

Failsafe (1964)***½ Henry Fonda, Dan O'Herlihy, Walter Matthau. Nightmarish problem drama of what might happen when, through an error, a SAC plane is ordered to bomb Moscow. This develops into a gripping, suspenseful tale of something that could possibly happen. Excellent performances, Sidney Lumet direction, no punches spared. (Dir: Sidney Lumet, 111 mins.)

Fair Wind to Java (1953)*** Fred MacMurray, Vera Ralston. Sea captain battles a pirate chief on the high seas. Well made adventure melodrama contains a lot of action, plenty of excitement. (Dir: Joseph Kane, 92 mins.)

Faithful City (Israeli, 1952)*** Jamie Smith, Rachel Markus. Frequently effective drama of the rehabilitation of wartime youngsters in Israel. English dialogue. Sometimes crude technically, but generally interesting. (86 mins.)

Faithful in My Fashion (1946)*** Donna Reed, Tom Drake. Sergeant returns to his shoe-clerking job after the war and falls for a pretty salesgirl. Modest but light, ingratiating comedy, good fun. (Dir: Sidney Salkow, 81 mins.)

Fake, The (British, 1954)**½ Dennis O'Keefe, Coleen Gray. Private eye in London cracks down on art forgers. Fairly good mystery. (Dir: Godfrey Grayson, 80 mins.)

Falcon and the Co-Eds (1943)*** Tom Conway, Jean Brooks. The Falcon goes to a girls' school to look into the death of an instructress. Above average mystery, well done. (Dir: William Clemens, 68 mins.)

Falcon in Mexico (1944)**½ Tom Conway, Mona Maris. The Falcon trails a killer from New York to Mexico. Pleasant mystery with good backgrounds. (Dir: William Beike, 70 mins.)

Falcon Out West (1944)**½ Tom Conway, Barbara Hale. A cowboy is murdered in an eastern night club, causing the Falcon to head west to find the killer. Okay mystery. (Dir: William Clemens, 64 mins.)

Falcon Strikes Back (1943)**½ Tom Conway, Harriet Hilliard. The Falcon avoids a trap set for him by a gang of criminals. Neat mystery with a surprise solution. (Dir: Edward Dmytryk, 66 mins.)

Falcon Takes Over (1942)**½ George Sanders, Lynn Bari. The Falcon mixes with a fake fortune-telling racket. Pleasing mystery. (Dir: Irving Reis, 63 mins.)

Fall of Rome, The (Italian, 1960)** Carl Mohner, Jim Dolen. Brave centurion comes to the aid of Christians when they're persecuted. A notch above the usual Italian spear-and-sandal spectacle. English-dubbed.

Fall of the Roman Empire (1964)*½ Alec Guinness, Sophia Loren, Christopher Plummer, James Mason, Anthony Quayle, Omar Sharif. Overlong, poorly written and generally inept spectacle, theoretically depicting the events leading up to the crumbling of the mighty Roman Empire. The action sequences are impressive, if by now familiar, but the superb cast is constantly defeated by the idiotic things they are asked to do and say. So excuse the divine Sophia for looking so uncomfortable. Strictly for those who prefer their adventure and history on a comic book level. Incidentally, producer Samuel Bronston's movie empire also fell apart after the release of this nonsense, so there is some justice in the world. (Dir: Anthony Mann, 149 mins.)

Fallen Angel (1946)**½** Alice Faye, Dana Andrews, Linda Darnell. Dana marries Alice for her money, hoping to latch on to Linda after he gets some dough. But, alas, Linda is murdered and he's a suspect. Fair drama but not too effective. (Dir: Otto Preminger, 97 mins.)

Fallen Idol, The (British, 1949)**** Ralph Richardson, Michele Morgan, Bobby Henrey. An ambassador's small son idolizes a servant, who has a nagging wife but loves an embassy clerk. When the wife is accidentally killed, the boy innocently points suspicion toward the servant. Superb drama of an adult world seen through the eyes of a child; merits praise in every respect. Directed by Carol Reed written by Graham Greene. (94 mins.)

Fallen Sparrow (1943)***½** John Garfield, Maureen O'Hara. Survivor of a Spanish Brigade returns to America to tangle with Nazi spies. Smooth, excellently produced melodrama. (Dir: Richard Wallace, 94 mins.)

Fame is the Name of the Game (1966)** Tony Franciosa, Jill St. John, Jack Klugman, Susan Saint James. Involved melodrama about a magazine writer who gets his lumps when he investigates the supposed suicide of a girl. Slick production, but scripting and performances seldom rise above the routine. Incidentally, this is a remake of 1949's "Chicago Deadline," with Alan Ladd. Made-for-TV feature. (Dir: Stuart Rosenberg, 100 mins.)

Fame Is the Spur (British, 1949)***½** Michael Redgrave, Rosamund John. The saga of a liberal English statesman who refuses to sacrifice his ideals. Thoughtful, finely performed and directed drama. (Dirs: John and Roy Boulting, 116 mins.)

Family, The (1973)½ Charles Bronson, Telly Savalas. A cheap, claptrap version of the workings of the Mafia . . . This is no "Godfather," and Bronson is once again the hired assassin for the mob and Savalas the syndicate boss. Gratuitous violence, little characterization! (Dir: Sergio Sollima)

Family Affair, A (1937)**½** Lionel Barrymore, Spring Byington, Mickey Rooney. This mild little comedy was the start of the Hardy series. Mr. Barrymore gave way to Lewis Stone in the later editions, however. Catch this one and see if you could have seen its box office potential. (Dir: George B. Seitz, 80 mins.)

Family Diary (Italy, 1962)** Marcello Mastroianni, Sylvie, Jacques Perrin. Saga of two brothers who are separated at birth. One lives in poverty (Mastroianni), the other (Perrin) in comfort. They are reunited, but inevitably split. Outstanding cast helps breathe some life into plodding script. (Dir: Valerio Zurlini, 115 mins.)

Family Flight (1972)**½** Rod Taylor, Dina Merrill. Out of the old desert plane-crash plot comes a pretty fair flying show. A strained San Diego, Calif., family develops togetherness and maturity when they work their way out of a tight spot. Taylor pulls the family through and straightens out his defeatist son. The flying sequences, particularly in the last act crisis, are good. Made-for-TV. (Dir: Marvin Chomsky.)

Family Honeymoon (1948)**½** Claudette Colbert, Fred MacMurray, Gigi Perreau. One joke is stretched too far in this thin comedy. A widow with three children takes her brood with her on her second honeymoon. Some funny scenes. (Dir: Claude Binyon, 80 mins.)

Family Jewels, The (1965)** Jerry Lewis, Donna Butterworth. This film can be described as a Jerry Lewis film festival! He produced, directed, co-authored and plays seven (count 'em) parts. Little Donna Butterworth plays an orphaned heiress who has to decide which of her six uncles (all Lewis) she wants to be her guardian. In case you're counting, Lewis also plays the family chauffeur. (Dir: Jerry Lewis, 100 mins.)

Family Life—See: Wednesday's Child

Family Nobody Wanted, The (1975) **½ Shirley Jones, James Olson, Catherine Helmond. Heartwarming, sentimental story of a minister and his loving wife, and the brood of kids they adopt. The twist is that the bids are of mixed ethnic background. Shirley Jones strikes the right note as the minister's wife and James Olson adds his customary authority as the patient husband. A true story, based on Helen Doss' book about her family. Made-for-TV. (Dir: Ralph Senensky, 72 mins.)

Family Plot (1976) ***½ Karen Black, Bruce Dern, Barbara Harris, Ed Lauter. A return to the tongue-in-cheek, pre-war Hitchcock. It is closer to "The Lady Vanishes" than to "Psycho." Of course, there's plenty of suspense and a whiz of a plot. Kidnapping, robbery, arson and murder, are involved, along with a little petty larceny. Bruce Dern and Barbara Harris are the almost-good guys; William Devane, Karen Black, and a chilling Ed Lauter are the villains. There isn't any on-screen violence, but a great chase provides some spine-tingling moments. Based on the novel "The Rainbird Pattern" by Victor Canning. "Family Plot" was made by the masterly Hitchcock when he was 75, and it was his 53rd film. Not one of his best but better than most thrillers. (120 mins.)

Family Rico, The (1972) **½ Ben Gazzara, James Farentino. Adaptation of a Georges Simenon novel avoids gangland shooting and gore in "The Godfather" style, and focuses on a character study of a crime syndicate chief instead. Gazzara stars as a big-time hood, brought up in the old school. Good supporting cast includes Jo Van Fleet, Dane Clark, John Marley, and James Farentino. Made-for-TV. (Dir: Paul Wendkos, 73 mins.)

Family Secret, The (1951) **½ John Derek, Lee J. Cobb, Jody Lawrence. A young man accidentally kills his best friend and doesn't report it to the police. Strange circumstances keep the suspense mounting until the climax. Some interesting moments. (Dir: Henry Levin, 85 mins.)

Family Way, The (British, 1967) ***½ Hayley Mills, John Mills, Hywel Bennett. Compassionate look at the troubles of young newlyweds (Miss Mills and Bennett). Fine performances by all. John Mills and Marjorie Rhodes are the parents. (Dirs: John and Roy Boulting, 115 mins.)

Fan, The (1949) **½ Jeanne Crain, Madeleine Carroll, George Sanders. Oscar Wilde's comedy of manners, about a lady with a past who uses her daughter to crash society. Attractive production enhances the slightly old-fashioned sentiments of the story. (Dir: Otto Preminger, 89 mins.)

Fanatics, The (British, 1963) ** Craig Stevens, Eugene Deckers. Correspondent matches wits with a gang bent on assassination. Average melodrama based on "Man of the World" TV series.

Fancy Pants (1950) *** Bob Hope, Lucille Ball. Bob poses as a gentlemen's gentleman in this hyped-up version of "Ruggles of Red Gap." Could have been funnier, but the stars help it over the rough spots. (Dir: George Marshall, 92 mins.)

Fangs of the Arctic (1953) * Kirby Grant, Lorna Hansen. Mountie and his dog go after a gang of fur trappers. Best acting comes from the dog. (62 mins.)

Fanny (France, 1938) ***½ Raimu, Pierre Fresnay, Orane Demazis, Charpin. Another of French writer-producer Marcel Pagnol's ironic tales about a lady "compromised," has unwed Mme. Demazis expecting, the father gone off to sea, and two men who want the offspring a-knocking at her door. Raimu is lovely. (Dir: Marc Allegret, 125 mins.)

Fanny (1961) *** Leslie Caron, Horst Buchholz, Maurice Chevalier, Charles Boyer. The earthy magnificence of Marseilles, the personal charm of Charles Boyer and Maurice Chevalier, and the attractiveness of Leslie Caron and Horst Buchholz all help to make this love story entertaining. The tale about young lovers parting, a marriage of convenience, and a reunion which almost destroys everyone's life is a bit overlong but works fairly well most of the time. Director Joshua Logan chose to eliminate the songs from this straight film version based on the Broadway musical, but he uses the familiar score as background music. (Dir: Joshua Logan, 133 mins.)

Fanny by Gaslight (Great Britain, 1945)—See: **Man of Evil**

Fantastic Voyage (1966)**** Stephen Boyd, Arthur Kennedy, Raquel Welch. The title is absolutely accurate for a change and this is a fantastic voyage, and one of the best science-fiction films made in a long time. The cinematography and special effects are fabulous as you see a team of surgeons and scientists shrunk to bacteria size in order to enter the human body to perform a delicate brain operation. The color work and the animation are first rate, and the kids will enjoy this striking, exciting, futuristic journey. Dad will too, even if Raquel does have all her clothes on. Producer Saul David, director Richard Fleischer and director of photography Ernest Laszlo all deserve special credit for the superb production work. (Dir: Richard Fleischer, 100 mins.)

Fantasy Island (1977)**½ Bill Bixby, Sandra Dee, Peter Lawford, Hugh O'Brian, Loretta Swit. Pure escapist fare which usually works on some level. Remember "Westworld" and "Futureworld"? Well, here's ABC's made-for-TV answer to those films. A group of adventurous souls come to a private island where they have been promised they can live out their wildest fantasies. Their dreams soon turn into nightmares. Made-for-TV. (Dir: Richard Lang, 98 mins.)

Far Country, The (1955)*** James Stewart, Ruth Roman, Corinne Calvet. Lively adventure about cattle rustling, Alaska-style. Stewart plays all the stops as a peaceful cowpoke who gets trampled on at every turn until he just explodes. Walter Brennan, as Stewart's sidekick, gives another good performance. (Dir: Anthony Mann, 97 mins.)

Far from the Madding Crowd (British, 1967)*** Julie Christie, Alan Bates, Terence Stamp, Peter Finch. Thomas Hardy's novel about a beautiful girl who manages to make a shambles out of three men's lives is not completely successful as brought to the big screen by director John Schlesinger ("Midnight Cowboy" & "Darling"). Julie Christie never finds quite the right beat as the willful farm girl

who betters her station in life but can't seem to find love. Of the three male stars, only Alan Bates emerges with a definite character. There is some glorious color photography in this long saga which runs almost three hours. (Dir: John Schlesinger, 169 mins.)

Far from Vietnam (French, 1967)***½ Ambitious, very uneven anti-war documentary made by many members of the French film industry who contributed their time and talent. This intellectualized propaganda film condemning the American action and presence in Vietnam includes 12 different sequences directed by Alain Resnais, Jean-Luc Godard, Agnes Varda, and others. The various sequences differ in quality and content and they are moving, maddening, unfair, accurate, etc., depending, to some degree, on your own political convictions. However, it's well worth seeing, as the subject of the Vietnam War has been with few exceptions, studiously avoided by the American film industry.

Far Horizons, The (1955)**½ Charlton Heston, Fred MacMurray, Donna Reed. Hollywood's version of the historical Lewis & Clark Expedition with a stress on the romance between Clark and the Indian maiden guide. Good photography. (Dir: Rudolph Mate, 108 mins.)

Farewell Again (British, 1937)*** Leslie Banks, Flora Robson. Following the events that befall men who are given six hours' leave before their troopship sails. Interesting, frequently absorbing drama, well acted. (Dir: Tim Whelan, 90 mins.)

Farewell Friend (1968)**½ Alain Delon, Charles Bronson. Seen-it-all-before saga of former mercenaries who chum up to rob company vaults. Delon's handsome and Bronson's tough, so together there's romance and action. (Dir: Jean Herman, 119 mins.)

Farewell To Arms, A (1932)***½ Helen Hayes, Gary Cooper. Miss Hayes is magnificent as the English nurse in Hemingway's tragic romance. Film is fairly good, but it's all Miss Hayes. Parts of the story dealing with war are not as effective as the romance. One of Miss Hayes' few film efforts. (Dir: Frank Borzage, 78 mins.)

Farewell To Arms, A (1957)**½ Jennifer Jones, Rock Hudson,

Vittorio De Sica. Hemingway's novel of the love affair between a soldier and a nurse in WW I has been given a huge production with spectacular scenery, big-name cast; but the delicate love story threatens to collapse under all the tonnage. Faulty performance by Jennifer Jones, an earnest one by Hudson. (Dir: Charles Vidor, 150 mins.)

Farewell to Manzanar (1976)***½ Yuki Shimoda, Nobu McCarthy, Akemi Kikumura, Clyde Kusatsu, Mako. A superb TV drama. The time is California in World War II, and the government is edgy about all those Japanese in coastal areas. Will the Japanese blow up everything in the name of the Rising Sun? To prevent such an occurrence, all Japanese, American-born or not, were sent to detention camps, families split up, and property confiscated. It's a sorry chapter in American history, and it comes to life as we watch a peaceful fisherman's family being incarcerated in Camp Manzanar. An Oriental cast plays the Wakatsuki family in this true story, and they will arouse sympathy and guilt in abundance. Director John Korty ("The Autobiography of Miss Jane Pittman") helped to write this tale of bitterness and sorrow, and turned it into one of the better TV movies. Made-for-TV. (98 mins.)

Farmer Takes a Wife, The (1953)** Betty Grable, Dale Robertson. Canal boat girl runs away and is aided by a young farmer in refurbishing her father's barge. Musical version of an earlier film doesn't come off. Fair, at best. (Dir : Henry Levin, 90 mins.)

Farmer's Daughter, The (1947)**** Loretta Young, Joseph Cotten, Ethel Barrymore. Fiery Swedish servant girl makes a fight for a Congressional seat, soon has everyone rooting for her. Fine comedy-drama combines patriotism and good humor in an expert blend. Wonderfully acted.

Farrebique (France, 1947)*** Enthralling, intimate documentary look at the life of a provincial French farming family, culled from a year of living with and photographing three generations, and the sprawling acreage, vineyards, livestock that comprise the farm, "Farrebique." Sensitive view of nature

and traditions. (Dir: George Rouquier, 100 mins.)

Fascist, The (Italian, 1965)*** Ugo Tognazzi, Georges Wilson. A hardcore Fascist is ordered to capture a famous professor who's a thorn in the side of the enemy, and he does—but the tables are turned before the professor can be brought back. Mildly amusing comedy-drama has some clever sequences, nice performances. Dubbed in English.

Fast and Loose (British, 1954)**½ Kay Kendall, Brian Reece. Husband is stranded in the country with a glamor girl, wife becomes suspicious. Pleasant comedy.

Fast and Sexy (Italian, 1960)** Gina Lollobrigida, Dale Robertson. A good comedy idea that gets bogged down with sentiment. Gina is a joy to behold but Dale Robertson as an Italian is a little much. (Dir: Vittorio De Sica, 98 mins.)

Fast Company (1953)**½ Howard Keel, Polly Bergen. Trainer has a knack of making a certain horse win, goes into partnership with a pretty owner. Amusing racing comedy. (Dir: John Sturges, 67 mins.)

Fastest Guitar Alive, The (1967)** Roy Orbison, Sammy Jackson, Maggie Pierce, Lyle Bettger, Joan Freeman. Misadventures of a couple of Confederate operators (Roy Orbison, Sammy Jackson) out to rob a mint. Simple Civil War comedy with songs; harmless enough. (Dir: Michael Moore, 87 mins.)

Fastest Gun Alive, The (1956)**½ Glenn Ford, Broderick Crawford, Jeanne Crain. Storekeeper gets a reputation as a fast gun, is challenged by a gunman to a duel. Fairly suspenseful western flamboyantly acted by Ford and Crawford. (Dir: Russell Rouse, 92 mins.)

Fat City (1972)**** Stacy Keach, Jeff Bridges, Susan Tyrell. Director John Huston's deeply moving drama about a washed-up 31-year-old boxer (Keach)—his best film in many years. Filmed on location in and around Stockton, Calif. Benefits greatly from the superb, lean, compassionate screenplay of Leonard Gardner, based on his novel. The protagonist is a boxer but this heartbreaking film is not essentially about boxing—it's about the lonely, empty life of some of the urban poor and their limited expectations. "Before you get rollin', your life makes a beeline for the drain" sums up Keach's attitude. Bridges is fine, and there's a really remarkable supporting performance by Susan Tyrell that earned her an Oscar nomination for her portrayal of a sherry-drinking, alcoholic floozie. She's convincing and heartbreaking. Keach is one of our most gifted young actors and he's memorable. No false bravado in this one as he takes his place among the most affecting losers in recent films. (96 mins.)

Fat Man, The (1951)** J. Scott Smart, Julie London, Rock Hudson. Radio's famed serial reaches the screen and plays like a radio show; that is, heavy on exposition and slow on action. It's interesting to note that the love interest is supplied by Rock Hudson and Julie London, who have since increased their marquee value somewhat. Emmett Kelly, the famous clown, plays a dramatic role in the film. (Dir: William Castle, 77 mins.)

Fate Is the Hunter (1964)**½ Glenn Ford, Nancy Kwan, Rod Taylor, Suzanne Pleshette. A sometimes exciting drama which has Ford playing an airlines investigator who leaves no stone unturned in trying to piece together the why and wherefores of a fatal crash which took more than fifty lives. The flashback technique works well, and the cast is competent. There's an excellent climax which maintains the tension. (Dir: Ralph Nelson, 106 mins.)

Fate Takes a Hand (British, 1962) *½ Ronald Howard, Christina Gregg. Five lost letters hold the key to people's lives in the 15 ensuing years. Muddled drama. (Dir: Max Varnel, 72 mins.)

Father (Hungary, 1966)***½ Andras Balint, Miklos Gabor, Kati Solyom. Post-Stalin Hungarian films are distinguished by a certain philosophical quality, intelligence, and a rich suggestiveness that assails on both political and personal fronts. Istvan Szabo's second film displays these qualities, arguing the overriding need of a true conception of one's history and heritage, as a boy finally accepts the realities of his father's past. Movie is both a parable of Stalinism, and a tale of human error and growth. Lightly told, sensitively acted. Written and directed by Istvan Szabo. (95 mins.)

Father Goose (1964)**½ Cary Grant, Leslie Caron. Cary Grant is always worth seeing, even in a lukewarm comedy effort such as this. Grant forgoes his customary polish and trim wardrobe for the role of a genial, fun-loving drifter named Walter who assists the Australian Navy during World War II by becoming a plane spotter on a remote atoll in the South Seas. Leslie Caron, as a French schoolteacher with a group of her young pupils in tow, descends upon the island, and Grant's peaceful mission turns into a free-for-all. (Dir: Ralph Nelson, 115 mins.)

Father Is a Bachelor (1950)** William Holden, Coleen Gray, Charles Winninger. Lightweight comedy about a roustabout bachelor and his involvement with five orphans, a lovable old medicine showman, and a judge's daughter. (Dir: Norman Foster, 84 mins.)

Father of the Bride (1950)**** Spencer Tracy, Elizabeth Taylor, Joan Bennett. One of the best comedies ever made about the many "very" important and "utterly" unimportant things that make a young bride's wedding day a success. Tracy, as the bride's father and/or financial backer, has a field day in the role and there seldom has been a more beautiful bride than Elizabeth. (Dir: Vincente Minnelli, 93 mins.)

Father Was a Fullback (1949)** Fred MacMurray, Maureen O'Hara, Thelma Ritter. Football coach's efforts to win the Big Game and solve his family problems simultaneously. Bright comic touches by Thelma Ritter. (Dir: John M. Stahl, 84 mins.)

Father's Dilemma (Italian, 1952)**** Aldo Fabrizi, Gaby Morlay. A very funny comedy revolving around a communion dress and a father's efforts to find it after he has lost it. Hilarious situations arise. The father is superbly played by Aldo Fabrizi.

Father's Little Dividend (1951)***½ Elizabeth Taylor, Spencer Tracy, Joan Bennett. Refreshing sequel to "Father of the Bride," all the characters are present and the laughs come fast and furious. What an excellent farceur Spencer Tracy is— see this one if you like well done family comedies. (Dir: Vincente Minnelli, 82 mins.)

Fathom (1967)**½ Raquel Welch, Tony Franciosa. Entertaining, mindless spy spoof with the title role being bikinied rather than acted by the truly ravishing Raquel Welch. She's a superwoman who can do almost anything, and she gets a chance to try skin diving, sky diving, swimming (bikini-clad, of course) and other vigorous stunts. The plot is as busy as Miss Welch, involving a stolen figurine and the parade of villains who are after it. The coastline of Spain is glorious to behold if the males in the audience can keep their eyes off Raquel. (Dir: Leslie H. Martinson, 90 mins.)

FBI Code 98 (1964)** Jack Kelley, Ray Danton, Andrew Duggan. Philip Carey, Peggy McCay, Jack Cassidy. Hoover's heroes investigate an unexploded bomb — sabotage, or some other motive? Routine FBI story.

F.B.I. Story, The (1959)** James Stewart, Vera Miles. Action and sentiment are ineffectually mixed in this story of the operations of the Federal Bureau of Investigation. Isolated cases solved by the F.B.I. are touched upon. James Stewart is his usual competent self in the leading role of an agent and Vera Miles offers loyal support as his wife. (Dir: Mervyn Le Roy, 149 mins.)

FBI Story: The FBI Versus Alvin Karpis, Public Enemy Number One, The (1974)** Robert Foxworth, Harris Yulin, Eileen Heckart. Submachine gun blasts fill the screen as 30's killer Alvin Karpis and his gang run rampant, kidnapping and robbing banks and trains. It takes J. Edgar Hoover, the new head of the FBI, to nail the cold-eyed hoodlum, but not before Karpis and his following shoot at innocents as easily as shooting at birds. Takes pains not to glamorize Karpis, effectively portrayed by Robert Foxworth. Eileen Heckart is Ma Barker, a lady hood with a weakness for white gloves. Made-for-TV. (Dir: Marvin Chomsky, 100 mins.)

Fear (German, 1955)** Ingrid Bergman, Mathias Wieman, Kurt Kreuger. English-dubbed. An indiscreet woman is blackmailed by her lover's ex-girl, then worries that her husband will find out. Names of Bergman and director Roberto Rossellini should have meant a better film than this dull drama.

Fear in the Night (1947)*** Paul Kelly, De Forest Kelley. An innocent dupe is made to think he has murdered by use of hypnosis. Tense mystery, well above average. (Dir: Maxwell Shane, 72 mins.)

Fear Is the Key (Great Britain, 1972)* Barry Newman, Suzy Kenwall. Alistair MacLean's heavily plotted novel about a deep-sea treasure-recovery expert and his run-in with an international group of thieves, plays like a cartoon-book adventure. Barry Newman, TV's "Petrocelli," is the escaped would-be convict and lovely Suzy Kendall is his hostage. "Fear" is the seventh of MacLean's novels turned into films. Filmed on location off Louisiana. (Dir: Michael Tuchner, 103 mins.)

Fear No Evil (1969)*** Louis Jourdan, Lynda Day, Bradford Dillman. Fans of the supernatural will enjoy this well produced chiller about a young lady (Lynda Day) who keeps a nightly rendezvous with her dead fiancé (Bradford Dillman). Louis Jourdan is very effective as the handsome psychiatrist who becomes interested in the girl's strange plight, and Miss Day makes an attractive, convincing heroine. The absorbing story delves into the macabre world of the occult which worships evil demons, and the finale involving an enchanted full-length mirror may jolt you. (Dir: Paul Wendkos, 98 mins.)

Fear No More (1961)** Mala Powers, Jacques Bergerac. Girl accused of murder escapes the law and with help from a good samaritan finds the real killer. Passable mystery: enough plot twists to keep it going.

Fear on Trial (1975)***½ William Devane, George C. Scott. John Henry Faulk's book about the infamous blacklisting in TV in the 50's and how it ruined his most promising radio and TV career finally has been made into a film, and a surprisingly good one at that. Devane plays the homespun radio personality whose name appears on the powerful AWARE bulletin, a publication created by two vicious businessmen who took it upon themselves to "safeguard" the entertainment industry from infiltration by leftwingers in the McCarthy era. The facts are all here, with some names changed to protect the guilty. The screenplay pays attention to details of the time. Scott enhances every scene he's in, playing the successful lawyer, Louis Nizer, who took on Faulk's case, dedicating over five years to the project. A film to be seen. Made-for-TV. (Dir: Lamont Johnson, 100 mins.)

Fear Strikes Out (1957)**** Anthony Perkins, Karl Malden, Norma Moore. Don't miss this fine drama with Anthony Perkins giving his best screen performance to date as baseball player Jim Piersall. The film deals mostly with Piersall's personal problems which contributed to his nervous breakdown. Karl Malden is excellent as Piersall's pushy father. (Dir: Robert Mulligan, 100 mins.)

Fearless Frank (1969)* Jon Voight, Monique Van Vooren, Severn Darden. Urban morality tale casts Voight as a country boy turned mechanized evil-fighter in the big city, counterpointed by his reforming replica, "False Frank." The antics are thoroughly confusing—only Darden, playing two mad scientists, is at home in the ridiculous. Shot on location in Chicago. (Dir: Philip Kaufman, 78 mins.)

Fearless Vampire Killers, The (1967) ** Roman Polanski, Sharon Tate. Polanski, who scored with "Rosemary's Baby" a couple of years after this film, not only directed this meandering comedy-horror story but also played one of the leads. He is the familiar assistant to the equally familiar mad professor who come to Transylvania to obliterate the local vampires. Sharon Tate is the sexy lass who has been kidnapped by the bloodthirsty throng and she supplies the only diverting moments in the film. Don't expect much. (110 mins.)

Fearmakers (1959)** Dana Andrews, Mel Torme, Dick Foran. A mixed-up drama about crime and violence tied in with political intrigue. Some action but mostly talk. The cast is adequate. (Dir: Jacques Tourneur, 83 mins.)

Fellini's Casanova (Italy, 1976)**½ Donald Sutherland, Tina Aumont, Cicely Browne. An enormously disappointing, overlong narrative about the celebrated 18th-century Venetian rake, Giovanni Jacopo Casanova de Seingat. Starting with the very first frame of the picture, Fellini provides the eye with some spectacular, bizarre pictorial images— but alas, there is little reward for the mind or the ear! Donald Sutherland plays the fornicating, elegant dandy who is reduced eventually to a whining librarian. He's as good as possible, but it's not enough. (Dir: Federico Fellini, 166 mins.)

Fellini's Roma (Italian-French, 1972) ***½ Peter Gonzales, Stefano Majore, Anna Magnani, Gore Vidal. Fellini is the first important director to insert his own name into the title of a film, and he certainly hasn't chosen his best film to memorialize himself for the first time. But mediocre Fellini is more involving and inventive filmmaking than the best efforts of most other directors, so this "nostalgic, carefree diary," as Fellini describes it, is worth seeing. It is a grab bag of comedy, drama, fantasy moving from childhood to the present day, intended to be a sardonic commentary on the collapse of Rome and of Western Europe. If you're a devotee of film whores this film is the promised land—fat whores, skinny ones, beautiful ones, grotesques ones, old harlots, young ones, black ones, white ones. There is a wonderful sequence recreating a World War II music hall. Fellini has offered us many of these dazzling, baroque images before but some of the new ones are worth seeing. (113 mins.)

Fellini's Satyricon (Italy-France, 1969)***½ Martin Potter, Hiram Keller, Capucine, Donyale Luna, Lucia Bose, Gordon Mitchell, Alain Cuny. Flawed Fellini is, of course, more interesting than the best work of virtually all other directors. Once again, Fellini dazzles the eye with a series of ghastly, picaresque, beautiful, freaky, ravishing, bestial images as he turns his attention to recreating the world of Petronius Arbiter, Rome circa 50-66 A.D. But movie math finds that in this "Satyricon" the whole adds up to less than the sum of its parts. One film reference book provides an illuminating list of subjects dealt with in "Fellini's Satyricon." They include, among others, freaks, royalty, hedonism, sorcerers, dwarfs, male homosexuality, perfidy, impotence, priapism, nymphomania, hermaphroditism, mutilation, cannibalism, slavery, suicide, flagellation, orgies, tombs, theater, deserts, ships, Lupercalia and Rome. A fantasmagorical, grotesque dream, a Pagan Dolce Vita. Fellini co-authored the screenplay. (120 mins.)

Female Animal, The (1958)** Hedy Lamarr, Jane Powell, Jan Sterling, George Nader. Romantic melodrama. A Hollywood star, Miss Lamarr, is saved from death by a handsome extra, Nader. Fouled up by the wooden acting of Nader and the trite, storybook ending. Jan Sterling is best as a has-been actress. (Dir: Harry Keeler, 83 mins.)

Female Artillery (1973)**½ Dennis Weaver, Ida Lupino. Western yarn, shot on location in Antelope Valley, Calif. A group of unescorted women and children traveling West by wagon train meet up with a stranger on the run, played by Weaver. On the distaff side, there's Ida Lupino, Nina Foch, Sally Anne Howes, and Linda Evans. Made-for-TV. (Dir: Marvin Chomsky, 73 mins.)

Female on the Beach (1955)**½ Joan Crawford, Jeff Chandler, Jan Sterling. Widow falls for a mysterious man who may be out to do away with her for her money. Drama would be suspenseful if it weren't so obvious. However, Crawford handles a tailor-made role with aplomb, so the ladies should like it. (Dir: Joseph Pevney, 97 mins.)

Female Trap—See: The Name of the Game Is Kill!

Feminine Touch, The (1941)**½ Rosalind Russell, Don Ameche, Van Heflin. Miss Russell enjoys a romp in this occasionally funny comedy about a professor who brings his wife to New York and discovers the woman in her. (Dir: W. S. Van Dyke, 97 mins.)

Fer-de-Lance (1974)½ David Janssen, Hope Lange. Ridiculous submarine drama played in tight-lipped fashion by the cast submerged in this TV clinker. Crawling, poisonous snakes, demented crewmen and a diver pinned by falling rocks. Made-for-TV. (Dir: Russ Mayberry, 100 mins.)

Ferry To Hong Kong (British, 1960)** Curt Jurgens, Orson Welles, Sylvia Syms. Slow-moving, outdated melodrama about a drifter who winds up aboard a ferryboat and turns hero when the ship is attacked. Welles overacts as the skipper. (Dir: Lewis Gilbert, 103 mins.)

Festival (1967)*** Feature-length documentary of various performers playing at the Newport Folk Festival in 1963-66. Uneven, but there are some magical moments, including Bob Dylan's first appearance singing a rock version of "Maggie's Farm." Other performers include Joan Baez, Johnny Cash, Judy Collins, Odetta, and Peter, Paul, and Mary. Important historical record of this period in the development of American "folk" music. (Dir: Murray Lerner, 98 mins.)

Feudin' Fussin' and A-fightin' (1948)** Donald O'Connor, Marjorie Main, Penny Edwards. Take a little of "Hatfield and McCoy Feud" and a lot of "Li'l Abner," add plenty of corn and you have "Feudin' Fussin' and a-Fightin'." (Dir: George Sherman, 78 mins.)

Fever Heat (1968)** Nick Adams, Jeannine Riley. Race driver Ace Jones wants to work his way into the life of a widow of a dead driver so that he can use her inherited garage. Ace is as crooked as a pretzel, but that doesn't make the movie any more interesting. Spiced with subplots of the lives of the other drivers. (Dir: Russell Doughton, Jr., 109 mins.)

Fever in the Blood, A (1961)**½ Efrem Zimbalist, Jr., Angie Dickinson, Jack Kelly, Don Ameche. A judge, a D.A., and a senator all have their eye on the governor's chair, and a murder trial is used to further their political ambitions. Drama of political maneuvering is salty enough to hold the attention, although the casting and the script could have been better. (Dir: Vincent Sherman, 117 mins.)

Fiction-Makers, The *½ Roger Moore, Sylvia Syms. An outgrowth of the old "The Saint" English television series, with Moore as detective Simon Templar. Standard mystery co-starring Syms as a novelist who fears for her life. (Dir: Roy Baker, 102 mins.)

Fiddler On The Roof (1971)**** Topol, Molly Picon, Norma Crane, Leonard Frey. The long-running, prize-winning Broadway musical hit based on the stories of Sholem Aleichem survives the transfer to the big screen quite well. Set in a small Ukranian village in 1905,

"Fiddler" is carried by a splendid score including such rousing songs as "If I Were A Rich Man" and "Tevye's Dream." Director Norman Jewison is fairly literal minded about transferring this stage property to the wide screen but, perhaps surprisingly, it works quite well. Topol does not have the brilliance of Zero Mostel's Broadway "Topol" but he is engaging enough. The rooftop violin solo you see and hear is played by Isaac Stern. (180 mins.)

Fidel (1970) *****½** Continuously interesting, frequently amusing feature-length documentary about Cuban leader Fidel Castro. Made in Cuba in 1968, it records some of the changes in Cuban life since Castro came to power in 1959. Written, produced, and directed by Saul Landau, this is an unusually revealing study of this charismatic political figure. It shows Castro speaking to crowds, playing baseball, chatting with peasants, discussing farm policies, etc. Some of the footage was used in a TV documentary broadcast in June '69. (Dir: Saul Landau.)

5th Day of Peace, The (1972)****** Richard Johnson, Franco Nero. Prisoner-of-war story which starts out interesting but soon falters into obvious plot twists. Johnson adds some dignity to the proceedings and Nero supplies the necessary he-man gloss. (Dir: Giuliano Montaldo.)

Fifth Horseman Is Fear, The (Czech, 1966)******** Powerfully presented story of a Jewish doctor (Miroslav Machacek) harboring a fugitive in Nazi-occupied Prague. Grim, strong sequences stay in the memory. An excellent example of the capabilities of the heretofore neglected Czechoslovakian filmmakers. Fine direction by Zbynek Brynych, superb performances. Subtitles.

Fifty-Five Days at Peking (1963)****½** Charlton Heston, Ava Gardner, David Niven. Big, sprawling adventure epic about the Boxer Rebellion of 1900 which threatened all foreign citizens in Peking. The cast of principals congregate at the American Embassy in Peking as they await their fate. Action is on the grand scale, but no believable characterizations emerge from the story. (Dir: Nicolas Ray, 150 mins.)

Fighter, The (1952)*****½** Richard Conte, Vanessa Brown, Lee J. Cobb.

236

In revolution-torn Mexico of 1910, a young patriot offers his services as a boxer to raise money for the cause. Good fight melodrama, well done throughout. (Dir: Herbert Kline, 78 mins.)

Fighter Attack (1953)****½** Sterling Hayden, Joy Page. Another war yarn with Sterling Hayden cast as a heroic Major who leads an important mission before the film runs its course. Action fans might find this too slow for their tastes but if you stick it out, there's a bang-up climax. (Dir: Lesley Selander, 80 mins.)

Fighting Father Dunne (1948)*****½** Pat O'Brien, Darryl Hickman. A St. Louis priest establishes a home for orphan newsboys. Sincere, well-made drama, good entertainment. (Dir: Ted Tetzlaff, 93 mins.)

Fighting Kentuckian (1949)****½** John Wayne, Vera Ralston. Frontiersman courting an aristocrat's daughter foils a plot to steal land from French settlers. Action melodrama is a big production with some good action, but this only partially compensates for script and directorial shortcomings. (Dir: George Waggoner, 100 mins.)

Fighting Lawman, The (1953)****** Wayne Morris, Virginia Grey. Routine western fare about a lawman who comes under a wicked woman's influence but everything turns out for the best. (Dir: Thomas Carr, 71 mins.)

Fighting Rats of Tobruk (Australian, 1945)****½** Chips Rafferty, Grant Taylor. Story of the dramatic siege during World War II, when the Anzacs held the Nazi hordes off for months under cruel fire. A bit ragged production-wise, but sincere, occasionally exciting.

Fighting Seabees, The (1944)****½** John Wayne, Susan Hayward, Dennis O'Keefe. Tough construction foreman and a Navy man organize a work battalion to repair installations close to Japanese lines. Rousing war melodrama, loaded with action. (Dir: Edward Ludwig, 100 mins.)

Fighting 69th (1949)*****½** James Cagney, Pat O'Brien. This picture is as corny as they come but is one of the most stirring war pictures you'll ever see. It lacks the dignity of an "All Quiet on the Western Front" but what it lacks in dignity and sensitivity it makes up for in spirit.

Top-flight entertainment. (Dir: William Keighley, 89 mins.)

Fighting Sullivans, The—See: Sullivans, The

Fighting Wildcats (British, 1957)** Keefe Brasselle, Kay Callard. Dynamite expert is hired to plant a time bomb to kill an Arab leader. Passable melodrama. (Dir: Arthur Crabtree, 74 mins.)

File of the Golden Goose, The (Great Britain, 1969)** Yul Brynner, Charles Gray, Edward Woodward. American secret agent, played in an obvious manner by Brynner, infiltrates a counterfeiting ring with the help of Scotland Yard. No-nonsense script sticks to the story which is plodding and clichéd. London locations add color, and there's a good sequence of assassination in the Burlington shopping arcade. Well acted by Woodward, in particular, and Gray. (Dir: Sam Wanamaker, 105 mins.)

File on Thelma Jordan, The (1949) *** Barbara Stanwyck, Wendell Corey. Assistant D.A. with an unhappy married life meets the niece of a wealthy eccentric, falls for her, suddenly finds himself defending her for murder. Grim drama is heavy going, but excellently played, sharply directed. (Dir: Robert Siodmak, 100 mins.)

Fillmore (1972)***½ Last days of the Fillmore West in San Francisco are documented, mainly focusing on the great acts that appeared there and their music. Included are Santana, the Grateful Dead, the New Riders of the Purple Sage, the Jefferson Airplane, Hot Tuna, and the Quicksilver Messenger Service. Most fascinating are the shots of Bill Graham, owner of the Fillmore, which reveal him as a dedicated man with a fine sense of ironic humor. (Dir: Richard T. Heffron, 105 mins.)

Final Test, The (British, 1953)***½ Jack Warner, Robert Morley. Star cricket batsman is dismayed when he finds his son wants to be a poet. Witty, finely written comedy-drama. Recommended. (Dir: Anthony Asquith, 84 mins.)

Find the Lady (British, 1956)** Donald Houston. A lady disappears and this starts a merry chase for a young doctor and a pretty model. Uneven but brief British film.

Finders Keepers (1952)**½ Tom Ewell, Julia Adams. Tom Ewell makes this wacky comedy seem better than it really is. He plays an ex-con who wants to go legit but his two year old son's innocent habits almost land him back in stir. Broad comedy played for belly laughs. (Dir: Frederick de Cordova, 74 mins.)

Fine Madness, A (1966)***½ Sean Connery, Joanne Woodward, Jean Seberg. Sean Connery gives a very fine performance as a bold, outspoken, radical poet who gets caught up in his own momentum. Joanne Woodward as his waitress-wife is brash and funny, and the rest of the cast, mostly made up of Broadway actors, adds greatly to the inventive screwball comedy. Unconventional fun. (Dir: Irving Kershner, 104 mins.)

Fine Pair, A (Italy, 1968)* Rock Hudson, Claudia Cardinale, Thomas Milian. Stars Cardinale and Hudson were neatly teamed in "Blindfold," and this film, made three years later, again capitalizes on their talent but fails miserably. Complicated caper as police-captain Hudson is tricked by Miss Cardinale into aiding in a heist. Cardinale's hair gives the best performance—wet, dry or blowing in the wind! (Dir: Francesco Maselli, 89 mins.)

Finest Hours, The (Great Britain, 1964)***½ An exhilarating history lesson about Winston Spencer Churchill. This prize-winning documentary is stunning on several counts—scenes of Churchill's childhood, his early adventures in India and South Africa, followed by his remarkable career which thrust him into the heart of most of the great events of this century. F.D.R., Hitler, Mussolini, Stalin, Chamberlain et al appear in vignettes. Churchill's own memorable speeches are heard, as well as the glories of Orson Welles' voice as narrator. Young and old should enjoy this wondrous saga together. (Dir: Peter Baylis, 114 mins.)

Finger Man (1955)**½ Frank Lovejoy, Forrest Tucker. Criminal is released from prison to get the goods on an underworld boss. Fast moving crime melodrama. (Dir: Harold Schuster, 82 mins.)

Finger of Guilt (British, 1956) Richard Basehart, Mary Murphy. Film director in England is haunted by the constant arrival of mysterious letters. Suspense thriller manages to build up some interest. (Dir: Joseph Walton, 84 mins.)

Fire!—See: **Irwin Allen's Production of Fire!**

Fire and Ice (French, 1963)*** Romy Schneider, Jean-Louis Trintignant. Unbalanced young would-be assassin swears revenge upon the organization leader who has made a fool of him. Uneven, rambling melodrama dubbed in English. Good performances, but lacks the necessary tension.

Fire Down Below (1957)*** Rita Hayworth, Robert Mitchum, Jack Lemmon. Mitchum and Lemmon are two adventurers who meet and fall for Rita, a shady lady. A ship's explosion traps Lemmon in the debris and Mitchum risks his life to save him. Lemmon is excellent but Hayworth fares less successfully. (Dir: Robert Parrish, 110 mins.)

Fire Over Africa (1954)** Maureen O'Hara, Macdonald Carey. Undercover agents work against great odds to smash a smuggling ring operating in Tangier. Mild melodrama. (Dir: Richard Sale, 84 mins.)

Fire Under Her Skin (French, 1954) * Giselle Pascal, Raymond Pellegrin. Postwar France is the setting for this boring melodrama about life on a farm inhabited by two brothers and their wives or girl friends. (Dir: Marcel Blistene, 90 mins.)

Fire Within, The (France-Italy, 1963) *** Maurice Ronet, Lena Skerla. Absorbing study of a man (Maurice Ronet) contemplating suicide. Ronet cavorts among friends and lovers. To him, perceptions fall in shades of gray and compromise is mediocrity: neither is satisfying. Writer-director Louis Malle got mixed notices for this early work. (110 mins.)

Fireball, The (1950)** Mickey Rooney, Pat O'Brien, Marilyn Monroe. An orphan kid becomes a hot-shot roller skater, but his ego gets the best of him. Typical Rooney plot; good roller derby scenes; and The Monroe! (Dir: Tay Garnett, 84 mins.)

Fireball 500 (1966)*½ Frankie Avalon, Annette Funicello, Fabian, Chill Wills. An action-drama set against the world of stock-car racing. The only conceivable reason you might want to watch this movie smashup is to catch a few pop-cultural antiques in action, namely Frankie Avalon and his fellow beach-bikini comrades. (Dir: William Asher, 92 mins.)

Fireball Forward (1972)**½ Ben Gazzara, Eddie Albert, Edward Binns, Ricardo Montalban. World War II drama, by the "Patton" writing-producing team, actually uses excess battle footage taken while shooting that movie. Story focuses on command problems after a major general takes charge of a division plagued by bad luck and poor morale. The "Patton" battle sequences are cleverly inserted, but the main interest in the film is Gazzara's major general, a tough dogface up from the ranks. Sporting a close-clipped haircut, Gazzara uses his strong presence to turn his short cigar-smoking general into a believable authority figure. Made-for-TV. (Dir: Marvin Chomsky, 100 mins.)

Firechasers, The (British, 1970)*½ Chad Everett, Anjanette Comer. Everett as a fire-insurance investigator trying to track down an arsonist in London, with some help from Miss Comer. Plays like a TV show. (Dir: Sidney Hayers, 101 mins.)

Firecreek (1968)**½ Henry Fonda, James Stewart. It's the timid sheriff (James Stewart) against the gang-leader (Henry Fonda), whose men are terrorizing the town. Traditional western tale gets the heavy treatment. Unduly protracted, but some good performances. With Inger Stevens, Gary Lockwood, Dean Jagger, Ed Begley, Jay C. Flippen, Jack Elam. (Dir: Vincent McEveety, 104 mins.)

Firefly, The (1937)**½ Jeanette Mac-Donald, Allan Jones. Rudolf Friml's score is the only redeeming feature in this pretentious operetta about Napoleon's Spanish battles. This is the film where Allan Jones first sang "Donkey Serenade." (Dir: Robert Z. Leonard, 138 mins.)

Firehouse (1972)**½ Richard Round-tree, Vince Edwards. Drama about racism in an all-white fire-engine company. Benefits from a decent script, realistic surroundings, and good performances by the stars. An Archie Bunker-type blue-collar fireman (Edwards) leads his close-knit company in the hazing of a new black recruit (Roundtree). The duel between Edwards' hard-eyed station leader and Roundtree's smoldering black man is generally effective, thanks to Frank Cucci's script. Made-for-TV. (Dir: Alex March, 73 mins.)

Fireman, Save My Child (1954)** Spike Jones, Buddy Hackett. A turn of the century comedy-musical about a group of misfit firemen who are more trouble than a four alarmer. If your tastes lean towards slaphappy slapstick, this is right up your hook and ladder. (Dir: Leslie Goodwins, 80 mins.)

Fireman's Ball, The (Czechoslovak, 1967)**** Vaclav Stockel, Josef Svet. Director Milos Forman has directed and helped write a wonderfully funny, touching, and observant study of petty bureaucratic minds and people in a small Czechoslovakian town. Simple story concerns the effort to honor a fire chief who is retiring at the ripe old age of 86. The ceremony is turned into a shambles and the film makes its points about politics, life and art in understated but unerringly accurate terms. No big-name stars here—just superb actors portraying recognizable people and constantly offering both humor and insight. Dubbed. (73 mins.)

First Legion, The (1951)**** Charles Boyer, William Demarest, Barbara Rush. A Jesuit seminary in a small town is the center of attraction when a miracle seemingly occurs, but it is disbelieved by one of the priests. This is a really fine, sensitive drama, wonderfully well acted, directed, written. (Dir: Douglas Sirk, 86 mins.)

First Love (1939)***½ Deanna Durbin, Robert Stack, Eugene Pallette. A Cinderella story complete with the big ball at the end and Prince Charming (none other than Robert Stack). Young Deanna Durbin got her first screen kiss by Stack in this film. (Dir: Henry Koster, 90 mins.)

First Man into Space (British, 1959)** Marshall Thompson, Marla Landi. Considering all the factual and advanced information compiled since this science-fiction film was made, the science details are dated. The fiction part is taken care of by the introduction of a monster-creature from out-of-space. Strictly for the kiddies and very young kiddies at that. (Dir: Robert Day, 77 mins.)

First Men in the Moon (British,

1964)*** Edward Judd, Lionel Jeffries, Martha Hyer. Fanciful science-fiction tale of a trip to the moon made by a scientist and his companions in 1899, based on the H. G. Wells work. Clever, entertaining, superb trick photography. (Dir: Nathan Juran, 103 mins.)

First Space Ship on Venus (1962)* Yoko Tani, Oldrick Lukes. Science fiction film made in Germany with poor production values. (Dir: Kurt Maetzig, 78 mins.)

First Texan, The (1956)** Joel McCrea, Felicia Farr. Lively western about the days when Texas fought for and gained independence from Mexico. History may be altered a bit here and there but it's all for entertainment's sake. (Dir: Byron Haskin, 82 mins.)

First 36 Hours of Dr. Durant, The (1975)**½ Scott Hylands, Katherine Helmond, Lawrence Pressman, Peter Donat, Dana Andrews. Stirling Silliphant ("Route 66," "Naked City," "Longstreet"), turned out this medical pilot film on hospital life seen through the eyes of a young resident. Except for a nurse suing the hospital for discrimination, and hero Durant battling against "ghost surgery," it's not radically different from its predecessors. Made-for-TV. (Dir: Alexander Singer, 72 mins.)

First Time, The (1956)*** Robert Cummings, Barbara Hale. Fast and funny comedy dealing with the financial woes of a newly married couple. Cummings is excellent as the male in the middle. (Dir: Frank Tashlin, 89 mins.)

First to Fight (1967)*½ Chad Everett, Marilyn Devin. Grade "C" drama with Chad Everett cast as a Marine who wins the Congressional Medal of Honor, returns to the States, trains troops, and then returns to combat and freezes under fire. Familiar tale, stuffed with the usual clichés of WW-II war films. (Dir: Christian Nyby, 97 mins.)

First Traveling Saleslady, The (1956)** Ginger Rogers, Carol Channing, James Arness. Ginger Rogers takes to the West selling corsets during the turn-of-the-century in this light comedy. Some funny situations but most is labored visual jokes. (Dir: Arthur Lubin, 92 mins.)

Fist in His Pocket (Italian, 1965)***½ Lou Castel, Paola Pitagora, Marino Mase. A young director

(Marco Bellochio) made his first film about a decaying family into a grim, frequently grotesque study of rampant psychopathology. A morbidly fascinating drama, well acted. English subtitles.

Fistful of Dollars, A (Italian, 1967) ** Clint Eastwood. Eastwood made his name in a long line of Italian-made spaghetti westerns. This was the first imported to the United States. He plays a role he was to repeat several times, a stranger—ruthless, mysterious, and nameless! Gets involved in a feud between two powerful families, deceiving both, taking money from each. Large doses of violence. (Dir: Sergio Leone, 95 mins.)

Fitzwilly (1967)**½ Dick Van Dyke, Edith Evans, Barbara Feldon, John McGiver, Harry Townes. Van Dyke plays a butler whose stuffy exterior hides a heart of pure larceny, culminating in a try for a heist of Gimbel's department store. Amusing bit of whimsy, helped by a fine cast. (Dir: Delbert Mann, 102 mins.)

Five (1951)**½ Susan Douglas, William Phipps. After an attack, the world is almost completely dead except for five survivors. They argue, hate, love, and finally there are two left. Well acted despite the tired plot. (93 mins.)

Five Against the House (1955)***½ Kim Novak, Guy Madison, Brian Keith. Engrossing drama about four college students and a glamorous night club singer who plan to hold up a large gambling casino in Reno. merely as an experiment. Good performance by Brian Keith as Brick.

Five Bloody Graves (1971)* Robert Dix, John Carradine. Repulsive western written by and starring Robert Dix, son of the late actor Richard Dix. Derelicts, Indians, and stagecoach passengers all wander aimlessly, before everyone is done away with. Carradine plays a lecherous preacher. (Dir: Al Adamson, 88 mins.)

Five Bold Women (1959)*½ Jeff Morrow, Merry Anders, Irish McCalla. Marshall escorting five women to prison has troubles with the outlaw husband of one of them and some marauding Indians. So-so western whose photography is the main asset.

Five Branded Women (1960)** Silvana Mangano, Van Heflin, Barbara Bel Geddes, Vera Miles. Five girls suffer the wrath of the people when they are found to be friendly to the Nazis, but redeem themselves in the Underground. Clumsy WW II drama set in Yugoslavia, never arouses complete sympathy for the characters. (Dir: Martin Ritt, 106 mins.)

Five Came Back (1939)*** Chester Morris, Wendy Barrie. Plane crashes in the jungle, and is able to take off with only five passengers. Suspenseful melodrama. (Dir: John Farrow, 75 mins.)

Five Card Stud (1968)**½ Dean Martin, Robert Mitchum. Somebody's been eliminating the participants in a poker session that ended in violence. Dean Martin attempts the western whodunit. Obvious tale has people like Robert Mitchum, Inger Stevens, Roddy McDowell, and John Anderson around to help it over the bumpy spots, of which there are more than a few. (Dir: Henry Hathaway, 103 mins.)

Five Easy Pieces (1970)**** Jack Nicholson, Karen Black, Susan Anspach, Fannie Flagg. An impressive, beautifully observed film about a dropout from middle-class America (Nicholson) who picks up work along the way on oil-rigs when his life isn't spent in a squalid succession of bars, motels, and other points along the way in northwest America. Inspired in some ways by "Easy Rider," Nicholson gives a bravura performance. . . . He's in virtually every scene. This is one of the best-acted American films in years. Karen Black playing Nicholson's waitress-girl friend is gauche, vulnerable, and altogether winning. Miss Anspach is equally fine playing the sympathetic, cultivated fiancee of Nicholson's brother. And Helena Kallianotes is devastating in one scene as a butch hitchhiker complaining about the air and moral pollution of America. Perceptive screenplay by Adrien Joyce. Outstanding direction from Bob Rafelson. The title incidentally refers not to the five women Nicholson has affairs with along the way, but to five musical compositions played at his family's gracious home. (Dir: Bob Rafelson, 98 mins.)

Five Finger Exercise (1962)** Rosalind Russell, Jack Hawkins, Maximilian Schell. Another domineering woman role for Russell, in a sluggish drama about a silly demanding wife who nearly wrecks her family's existence. Based on a Broadway play, which was far better, film emerges as talky, unconvincing. (Dir: Daniel Mann, 109 mins.)

Five Fingers (Operation Cicero) (1952)**** James Mason, Danielle Darrieux. A superb film in the class of "39 Steps" and "Saboteur." One of the most daring espionage agents' deeds are shown with an almost documentary reality. James Mason excels in a fine cast. Suspenseful and engrossing all the way. Don't miss. (Dir: Joseph L. Mankiewicz, 108 mins.)

Five Gates to Hell (1959)* Neville Brand, Patricia Owens, Dolores Michaels. Ridiculous plot has a band of glamorous Red Cross nurses (who ever heard of an ugly nurse in a Hollywood War film?) who go through a series of adventures after being captured by hostile guerillas in the Far East, that would make "The Perils of Pauline" seem like child's play. Dialogue meant to be serious often gets laughs instead. (Dir: James Clavell, 98 mins.)

Five Golden Dragons (Great Britain, 1967)* Bob Cummings, Rupert Davies. Intrigue in Hong Kong is not intriguing. Dan Duryea, Brian Donlevy, Christopher Lee and George Raft appear briefly as four of the villainous Golden Dragons. (Dir: Jeremy Summers, 70 mins.)

Five Golden Hours (British, 1961) **½ Ernie Kovacs, Cyd Charisse, George Sanders. Professional "mourner" who consoles widows and is not above a bit of crookery, teams with a beautiful baroness in a swindling scheme, which backfires. Attempt at offbeat comedy misses for the most part; a few humorous scenes offset by unsteady treatment. (Dir: Mario Zampi, 90 mins.)

500-Pound Jerk, The (1973)** James Franciscus, Alex Karras. Perhaps the only way the U.S. can win an Olympic gold medal in heavyweight weightlifting is to make a light comedy like this on the subject. Starts out in terribly hokey fashion with a hillbilly being groomed as an Olympic hopeful, but picks up steam when the scene shifts to Munich and Olympic action blends into the story. The Olympics footage is worth catching, and old Detroit

Lions tackle Karras slowly turns into an ingratiating strong man, after a rocky beginning. Made-for-TV. (Dir: William Kronick, 73 mins.)

Five Man Army, The (1970)*½ Peter Graves, James Daly. Predictable adventure tale set in north Mexico in 1914, involving a band of Americans fighting Mexican revolutionaries. (Dir: Don Taylor, 105 mins.)

Five Miles to Midnight (1962)** Sophia Loren, Anthony Perkins, Gig Young. Young scoundrel survives a plane crash and goes into hiding, forcing his wife to carry out his plan to collect from the insurance company. Even Loren's looks and the Parisian locale can't save this one.

Five Million Years to Earth (British, 1967)*** James Donald, Andrew Keir, Barbara Shelley. Are creatures from outer space menacing modern London? The old sci-fi question is suspensefully examined in a good one for the buffs. (Dir: Raymond Baker, 98 mins.)

Five Pennies, The (1959)*** Danny Kaye, Barbara Bel Geddes, Tuesday Weld. The music's the thing here—pleasant biography of jazzman Red Nichols, a good change of pace for Kaye. But the sound track glistens with solos by Nichols himself, Bob Crosby, and notably Louis Armstrong. A treat for the jazz buffs, entertaining for others. (Dir: Melville Shavelson, 117 mins.)

5,000 Fingers of Dr. T., The (1953) **** Peter Lind Hayes, Mary Healy, Hans Conried. Excellent fantasy about a young boy who hates his piano teacher and dreams of being held captive, along with 500 other little boys, in a large castle with the largest piano in the world. Fun for adults as well as the youngsters. (Dir: Roy Rowland, 89 mins.)

Five Weeks in a Balloon (1962)** Red Buttons, Fabian, Barbara Eden, Cedric Hardwicke, Peter Lorre. Lightweight, heavy-handed adaptation of an early Jules Verne novel; a balloon-propelled gondola is dispatched by the British government to lay claim to some East African territory. Meant to parody balloon adventures, but is itself a series of well-worn clichés. (Dir: Irwin Allen, 101 mins.)

Fixed Bayonets (1951)**½ Richard Basehart, Gene Evans, Richard Hylton. Interesting and often graphic account of a group of American soldiers in Korea during the hard winter of 1951. Many scenes have a documentary flavor and Basehart is very good as a Cpl. who has a chance to be a hero. (Dir: Samuel Fuller, 92 mins.)

Fixer, The (1968)******** Alan Bates, Dirk Bogarde, Georgia Brown. A deeply moving drama about anti-Semitism in tsarist Russia around 1911, based on Bernard Malamud's Pulitzer Prize-winning novel. As directed by John Frankenheimer, this is one of the better novel-to-screen adaptations of recent years. Based on a true story of a Russian Jewish peasant (Bates) who was wrongly imprisoned for a most unlikely crime—the "ritual murder" of a Gentile child in Kiev. Much of the film, detailing the protagonist's life in prison, is unrelenting, but it pays off as we see the peasant-handyman gain indignity as the efforts to humiliate him and make him confess fail. Bates is impressive in the title role, and Bogarde is exceptionally good playing a sympathetic tsarist defense attorney. Screenplay by Dalton Trumbo. Photographed on location in rural Hungary. (Dir: John Frankenheimer, 132 mins.)

Flame, The (1948)******* John Carroll, Vera Ralston, Broderick Crawford. Penniless playboy hits upon an elaborate plan of getting rid of his brother so he will inherit a fortune. Capable melodrama keeps the interest. (Dir: John H. Auer, 97 mins.)

Flame and the Arrow, The (1950)******* Burt Lancaster, Virginia Mayo. Lots of lusty bravado as Lancaster pits himself against the forces of evil in this costume drama. (Dir: Jacques Tourneur.)

Flame and the Flesh, The (1954)****** Lana Turner, Pier Angeli, Carlos Thompson. A corny, over-done tale of an unfortunate woman whose luck has just about run out. Filmed in Europe, the background is about the best thing in the film. Lana Turner is sorely miscast and is almost unrecognizable under a black wig. (Dir: Richard Thorpe, 104 mins.)

Flame Barrier, The (1958)****** Arthur Franz, Kathleen Crowley. Scientist disappears in the Yucatan jungles while searching for a lost satellite, so his wife hires two adventurers to locate him. Passable science-fiction,

some suspenseful moments. (Dir: Paul Landres, 70 mins.)

Flame in the Streets (Great Britain, 1961)****** John Mills, Sylvia Syms, Johnny Sekka. Sober drama of racial conflict in Britain. A white girl announces her plans to marry a black West Indian. Presents a real problem honestly. Well-acted, but the direction is uninteresting. (Dir: Roy Ward Baker, 93 mins.)

Flame of Araby (1952)***½** Maureen O'Hara, Jeff Chandler. Rudolph Valentino lives again—well, not quite—as Jeff Chandler dons the trappings of a desert sheik who woos and wins the not-so-fiery princess Maureen O'Hara. (Dir: Charles Lamont, 77 mins.)

Flame of Calcutta (1953)***** Denise Darcel, Patric Knowles. Downright foolish film about a French beauty who disguises herself as "The Flame" to dethrone a tyrant. Denise Darcel is laughable in the leading role. (Dir: Seyhour Friedman, 70 mins.)

Flame of New Orleans, The (1941)******* Marlene Dietrich, Bruce Cabot. Glamorous doll chooses wealthy suitor rather than the adventurous rogue she loves. Romantic tale is not among Dietrich's best but it's still Dietrich. (Dir: Rene Clair, 78 mins.)

Flame of the Barbary Coast (1945)****½** John Wayne, Ann Dvorak. Montana cattleman falls for a San Francisco saloon singer and opens his own gambling hall. Standard period melodrama, not much action but holds the interest fairly well. (Dir: Joseph Kane, 91 mins.)

Flame of the Islands (1955)****½** Yvonne DeCarlo, Howard Duff, Zachary Scott, James Arness. Many men fight for the love of a beautiful but dangerous night club singer. Overly involved but interesting melodrama; good Bahama locations. (Dir: Edward Ludwig, 90 mins.)

Flame Over India (British, 1959)*****½** Kenneth More, Lauren Bacall, Herbert Lom. Exciting adventure melodrama about a soldier assigned to rescue a Hindu prince and his American governess when rebellion breaks out. Practically the entire film is one big, rousing chase aboard a train, with action aplenty. Superior escapist fare. (Dir: J. Lee Thompson, 130 mins.)

Flaming Frontier (German, 1965)***½** Stewart Granger, Pierre Brice, Larry

Pennell, Leticia Roman, Mario Girotti. Old Surehand (Stewart Granger) and faithful Indian friend Winnetou (Pierre Brice) match wits with a nasty bandito (Larry Pennell) in this Teutonic version of the Old West. Anachronisms abound, but it might provide some chuckles.

Flaming Fury (1949)**½ Roy Roberts, George Cooper. Head of the Arson Bureau looks into a mysterious series of fires, uncovers dirty work. Neat little melodrama, speedy and well made.

Flaming Star (1960)*** Elvis Presley, Steve Forrest, Barbara Eden, Dolores Del Rio. Grim, well-done outdoor drama gives Presley a good role, and he makes the most of it. He's a part-Kiowa lad who tries to put a halt to bloodshed between Indians and settlers. Script makes some cogent points concerning peace among men, and the direction and performances are better than you might expect. (Dir: Don Siegel, 101 mins.)

Flamingo Road (1949)**½ Joan Crawford, Zachary Scott, David Brian. Crawford fans only will enjoy this vehicle about a woman's contact with men and the world. Others will find it unbelievable. (Dir: Michael Curtiz, 94 mins.)

Flap (1970)½ Anthony Quinn, Shelley Winters, Tony Bill. A really grotesque, despicable film pretending to deal with the many ways the United States government has cheated the American Indian tribes. This is exploitative drivel, written by Clair Huffaker from his novel, "Nobody Loves a Drunken Indian." Nobody loves Anthony Quinn either, still playing Zorba the Greek as a redskin. A disaster for everyone, including the gifted English director Sir Carol Reed. (106 mins.)

Flareup (1969)* Raquel Welch, James Stacy. Miss Welch portrays a go-go dancer on the run from a psychopath killer as if she was trying for a self-parody. No acting, no directing, no nothing. (Dir: James Nelson, 100 mins.)

Flea in Her Ear, A (U.S.-French, 1968)** Rex Harrison, Rosemary Harris, Louis Jourdan, Rachel Roberts, John Williams. Flatfooted French farce, with the philandering spouse (Rex Harrison), the vengeful wife (Rosemary Harris), numerous misunderstandings, much running

around. Superb cast wasted. Dir: Jacques Charon, 94 mins.)

Fleet's In, The (1942)**½ Dorothy Lamour, William Holden, Betty Hutton. Some good specialty numbers and lively direction make this silly film passable entertainment. Story concerns the "lover" of the Navy's attempts to score with a virtuous gal. (Dir: Victor Schertzinger, 93 mins.)

Flesh and Blood (British, 1949)** Richard Todd, Glynis Johns. Love, death and medicine in the generations of a turbulent family. Hard to follow, but interesting drama. (Dir: Anthony Kimmins, 102 mins.)

Flesh and Fantasy (1943)***½ Charles Boyer, Edward G. Robinson, Barbara Stanwyck. Three exciting and mysterious tales all well acted and gripping. The one starring Robinson as a man told by a fortune teller that his palm says "Murder" is the best but they're all quite good. (Dir: Julien Duvivier, 93 mins.)

Flesh and Flame—See: Night of the Quarter Moon

Flesh and Fury (1952)**½ Tony Curtis, Jan Sterling, Mona Freeman. Tony Curtis shows the first signs of acting talent in this prize fighting yarn. He plays a deaf mute who stumbles into the boxing game and winds up a champion. The Misses Sterling and Freeman play the women in his life. (Dir: Joseph Pevney, 82 mins.)

Flesh and the Fiends (British, 1960)*** Peter Cushing, Donald Pleasence, George Rose. Dastardly grave robbers supply bodies for medical experiments in old Scotland. Horror thriller has some fine performances, should satisfy the fans—too gruesome for the timid!

Flesh and the Woman (Italian, 1958)** Gina Lollobrigida. "Lollo" is cast as a "lady of easy virtue" once again in this mild story of Foreign Legionnaires and their loves. (Dir: Robert Siodmak, 102 mins.)

Flight from Ashiya (1964)** Yul Brynner, Richard Widmark, George Chakiris, Suzy Parker, Shirley Knight. With the Air Rescue Service, looking for survivors and recalling their pasts. Airborne soap opera. Sags. (Dir: Michael Anderson, 100 mins.)

Flight from Destiny (1941)*** Thomas Mitchell, Geraldine Fitzgerald.

An off-beat story of a man with only six months to live. Thomas Mitchell's superb acting gives this story a tremendous wallop if you're willing to accept his actions. (Dir: Vincent Sherman, 73 mins.)

Flight from Singapore (English, 1965)* Patrick Allen, Patrick Holt, Jane Rodgers. Two former RAF flyers start an airline with flights from Singapore to Hong Kong. Their first flight crashes in the jungle and thin suspense is created when it is learned a special blood serum needed to save a life will not arrive. Unconvincing. (80 mins.)

Flight from Treason (British, 1960)** John Gregson, Robert Brown. Man is blackmailed by spies into stealing atomic plans, fights treason charges. Fair spy melodrama.

Flight from Vienna (British, 1958)*½ John Bentley, Theodore Bikel. Hungarian official seeks asylum in Vienna, aids the British. Slow-moving espionage melodrama photographed in Vienna.

Flight Nurse (1953)** Joan Leslie, Forrest Tucker. Two pilots both love the same nurse, and if this sounds familiar don't blame us. (Dir: Allan Dwan, 90 mins.)

Flight of the Doves (British, 1971)*** Ron Moody, Jack Wild, Dorothy McGuire, Stanley Holloway. Fun film for the kids as Moody has a virtuoso role playing a detective of many disguises trying to track down two young orphans who have been given a large inheritance. Good Irish scenery, but the plot is slowed by some sentimental songs. (Dir: Ralph Nelson, 105 mins.)

Flight of the Lost Balloon, The (1960)*½ Marshall Thompson, Mala Powers. A little science fiction—a little jungle adventure—a little plot—and you have it. And you can keep it. (Dir: Bernard Woolner, 91 mins.)

Flight of the Phoenix, The (1966)***½ James Stewart, Richard Attenborough, Peter Finch, Hardy Kruger. An exciting old-fashioned adventure about a group of plane crash survivors who fight the desert and other awesome odds in order to rebuild their plane and save themselves. The characters are mostly stereotyped, but an excellent cast overcomes the shortcomings of the script. Director Robert Aldrich stages a fantastic finale which generates

edge-of-the-seat suspense. (Dir: Robert Aldrich, 147 mins.)

Flight to Hong Kong (1956)** Rory Calhoun, Barbara Rush, Dolores Donlon. Hollywood once more uses Hong Kong as the background for adventure. This tale of intrigue is no more nor less successful than any of its predecessors. Two attractive girls, the Misses Rush and Donlon, are very pleasing to the eyes. (Dir: Joseph Newman, 88 mins.)

Flight to the Holocaust (1977)*½ Patrick Wayne, Chris Mitchum, Desi Arnaz, Jr. Familiar "crisis" item. When private plane rams into skyscraper, rescue squad works feverishly to get victims out in time. Pat Wayne, Chris Mitchum, sons of movie stars, and newcomer Fawne Harriman head cast of guest stars ranging from Sid Caesar to Lloyd Nolan, actors who deserve better. Made-for-TV. (Dir: Bernard Kowalski, 106 mins.)

Flim Flam Man, The (1967)**½ George C. Scott, Michael Sarrazin. A robust ingratiating performance by George C. Scott as a rural con artist makes this picture seem better than it really is. Scott, made up to look old, obviously enjoys himself as he winks, chortles and exudes charm and rascality. Tale about the adventures of a con man and his protégé, a young Army deserter, winningly played by Michael Sarrazin. There is a terrific automobile chase scene that should be noted by those who cherish this kind of cinema hijinks. (Dir: Irvin Kershner, 115 mins.)

Flipper (1963)**½ Chuck Connors, Luke Halpin, Flipper. Youthful fans of the TV series will get a bang out of this film on which it was based. As everybody knows, Flipper is the remarkable dolphin whose relationship with young Luke blossoms into a real friendship when he saves the wounded dolphin's life. (Dir: James Clark, 90 mins.)

Flipper's New Adventure (1964)**½ Luke Halpin, Flipper, Pamela Franklin. Second "Flipper" feature is again nice kiddie fare, as boy and dolphin head out to sea rather than be separated. They wind up combatting extortionists on a deserted isle to help out a marooned mother and daughters. Tale isn't water-tight, but Flipper is gurglingly delightful. (Dir: Leon Benson, 92 mins.)

Flirtation Walk (1934)**½ Ruby Keeler, Dick Powell, Pat O'Brien. Dick goes to West Point for this one and it is fair entertainment. A little bit too long, it still comes out an interesting West Point story with some pleasant music for diversion. (Dir: Frank Borzage, 97 mins.)

Flood! (1976)**½ Robert Culp, Richard Basehart, Teresa Wright, Irwin Allen, the producer who brought movie audiences big-budgeted disaster films such as "Poseidon Adventure" and "Towering Inferno," turns his attention to the small screen with a yarn about a collapsing dam which destroys a small town. The vignettes which show people in peril as the flood rises range from predictable to well done. Made-for-TV. (Dir: Earl Bellamy, 106 mins.)

Flood Tide (1958)** George Nader, Cornell Borchers. Man tries to convince authorities that a crippled youngster whose testimony has convicted a man of murder is a habitual liar. Undistinguished melodrama. (Dir: Abner Biberman, 82 mins.)

Floods of Fear (British, 1958)**½ Howard Keel, Anne Heywood. Wrongly convicted of murder, a man escapes during a flood and proves his innocence. Frequently exciting melodrama—an English film located in the U.S., and atmospherically well done. (Dir: Charles Crichton, 82 mins.)

Flower Drum Song (1961)*** Nancy Kwan, James Shigeta, Miyoshi Umeki. The Rodgers & Hammerstein musical play about a Chinese picture-bride in San Francisco falling for another is colorfully decked out on film, with some capable players and good song numbers. It runs too long and may pall before it's over, but all in all it's worthwhile. (Dir: Henry Koster, 133 mins.)

Fluffy (1965)** Tony Randall, Shirley Jones. Professor gets into a lot of trouble when he escorts a tame lion around. Mild comedy on the silly side; the lion gets most of the laughs. (Dir: Earl Bellamy, 92 mins.)

Fly, The (1958)*** Vincent Price, Al Hedison, Herbert Marshall. During a scientific experiment a miscalculation causes a man to turn into a mutation. Superior science-fiction

thriller with a literate script for a change, plus good production effects and capable performances. (Dir: Kurt Neumann, 94 mins.)

Fly by Night (1943)**½ Nancy Kelly, Richard Carlson. Slick little Grade "B" spy story about an interne who becomes involved in espionage.

Flying Down to Rio (1933)*** Dolores Del Rio, Fred Astaire, Ginger Rogers. Beautiful girl has to choose between two men down in Rio. Pretty corny, but Astaire-Rogers dancing is still tops. (Dir: Thornton Freeland, 89 mins.)

Flying Irishman (1939)*** Doug Corrigan, Paul Kelly. Story of "Wrong Way" Corrigan, who made a spectacular flight—in reverse. Entertaining, amusing comedy-drama. (Dir: Leigh Jason, 72 mins.)

Flying Leathernecks (1951)** John Wayne, Robert Ryan. Strict Marine officer is disliked by his squadron, but in wartime all is forgotten. Badly written, slow war drama; some good actual battle scenes. (Dir: Nicholas Ray, 102 mins.)

Flying Missile, The (1951)** Glenn Ford, Viveca Lindfors. Grim and superficial drama about guided missiles and the men who build and test them. Cliché script prevents actors from doing anything with their roles. (Dir: Henry Levin, 93 mins.)

Flying Saucer (Italian, 1965)** Alberto Sordi, Monica Vitti, Silvana Mangano. An account of what happens when an invasion from Mars is threatened. Science-fiction opus is a field day for Sordi, playing four separate roles; but the fun is relatively sparse. Dubbed in English.

Flying Tigers (1942)***½ John Wayne, John Carroll, Anna Lee. Squadron leader and his reckless buddy vie for the affections of a pretty nurse while fighting the Japanese. Familiar but lively, well-produced war melodrama; fine special effects. (Dir: David Millar, 102 mins.)

Folies Bergere (French, 1957)** Jeanmaire, Eddie Constantine. Ex-GI remains in Paris to seek a singing career, romances a gorgeous folies girl. American-style musical done the French way, not too well. Some nice numbers, otherwise tepid. English-dubbed. (Dir: Henri Decoin, 90 mins.)

Follow a Star (British, 1961)**½

Norman Wisdom, June Laverick. Cleaning store employee who wants a stage career is duped by a scheming popular singer into using his voice. Slapstick comedy has some amusing scenes, but Wisdom for non-British audiences is a matter of taste. (Dir: Robert Asher, 93 mins.)

Follow Me Quietly (1950)*** William Lundigan, Dorothy Patrick. Detective traps a psychopathic killer. Well made, exciting melodrama.

Follow That Camel (Great Britain, 1967)** Phil Silvers, Kenneth William, Jim Dale. Fun in the Foreign Legion as Sergeant Phil Silvers is forced to aid a friend in a whacky plan. Vaudeville in the desert. (Dir: Gerald Thomas, 95 mins.)

Follow That Dream (1962)**½ Elvis Presley, Arthur O'Connell, Joanna Moore. Strictly for Presley fans! He sings, drawls and gets into plenty of trouble in this comedy about a group of hillbilly homesteaders who settle in a small Florida town which turns into a fairly thriving community. (Dir: Gordon Douglas, 110 mins.)

Follow the Boys (1944)*** George Raft, Vera Zorina, Guest Stars. A hoofer does his bit for the war effort by entertaining with the USO. Slender story is helped by many stars making brief appearances, best of which is a routine by W. C. Fields. (Dir: A. Edward Sutherland, 122 mins.)

Follow the Fleet (1936)**** Fred Astaire, Ginger Rogers, Randolph Scott. Song and dance man joins the Navy when his girl turns him down. Fine musical, Astaire and Rogers in top form, as are Berlin tunes. (Dir: Mark Sandrica, 110 mins.)

Follow the Sun (1951)**½ Glenn Ford, Anne Baxter, Dennis O'Keefe. The biography of golfer Ben Hogan, his ups and downs. Golf fans will vote it great—others, the usual sports saga. (Dir: Sidney Lanfield, 93 mins.)

Folly to Be Wise (British, 1953)***½ Alastair Sim, Roland Culver. The trials and tribulations of an Army chaplain make a delightfully witty comedy. (Dir: Frank Launder, 91 mins.)

Fool Killer, The (1965)**½ Anthony Perkins, Salome Jens, Dana Elcar, Edward Albert. Runaway boy teams with a tormented Civil War veteran who has lost his memory, and together they are involved in a mysterious murder. A try for a mood piece that becomes simply moody, this arty drama nevertheless has its moments. Good performances. (Dir: Servando Gonzalez, 103 mins.)

Fools (1970)* Jason Robards, Jr., Katharine Ross, Scott Hylands. Trite December-May romance as 50-year-old horror-film-star Robards falls in love with the anxiety-ridden wife of a millionaire. Robards imitates the outrage at society he so tenderly expressed in "A Thousand Clowns," but the cliched script defeats him. (Dir: Tom Gries, 93 mins.)

Fool's Parade (1971)**½ James Stewart, George Kennedy. Stewart is very good in this tale about a man who is released from prison after serving 40 years and has plans to open a business with the $25,000 he earned while behind bars. However, bad guy George Kennedy, who plays a guard at the prison, has other plans for the money. Anne Baxter also offers a colorful, brief appearance as a flashy madam. (Dir: Andrew McLaglen, 98 mins.)

Footlight Serenade (1942)**½ John Payne, Betty Grable, Victor Mature. Routine backstage musical with uninspired score. TV's Phil Silvers is in there to hold up the comedy. (Dir: Gregory Ratoff, 80 mins.)

Footsteps (1972)**½ Richard Crenna, Joanna Pettet. Better-than-average football yarn with Crenna as the hero-villain, a skillful defense coach who cuts corners to win. Saddled with a shady past, Crenna's character aims for the big time, coldly using players, ladies, and friends to climb up the ladder. Action clips, well-staged practice sessions, and knowledgeable football talk blend with the character study, and Miss Pettet, Clu Gulager, Florence Tucker, and Bill Overton back up Crenna. Made-for-TV. (Director: Paul Wendkos, 73 mins.)

Footsteps in the Dark (1941)**½ Errol Flynn, Brenda Marshall. Occasionally amusing comedy-drama with Errol as a slick detective. One of the amusing scenes is contributed by William Frawley. (Dir: Lloyd Bacon, 96 mins.)

Footsteps in the Fog (British, 1955)** Stewart Granger, Jean Simmons. Mediocre costume melodrama about an ambitious servant girl and her

246

diabolical employer. Well played by the cast. (Dir: Arthur Lubin, 90 mins.)

Footsteps in the Night (1957)**½ Bill Elliott, Don Haggerty, Douglas Dick. Policeman investigates a motel murder, saves an innocent man. Good low-budget mystery developed logically and interestingly. (Dir: Jean Yarbrough, 62 mins.)

For a Few Dollars More (Italian, 1967)* Clint Eastwood, Lee Van Cleef. Resembling its predecessor, "A Fistful of Dollars," this spaghetti western has Eastwood playing the stranger with no name, and the expected overdose of violence. Eastwood plays a bounty hunter like a zombie, pairing with Van Cleef to hunt Mexican bandits. (Dir: Sergio Leone, 131 mins.)

For Heaven's Sake (1950)**½ Clifton Webb, Joan Bennett, Robert Cummings, Joan Blondell, Edmund Gwenn, Gigi Perreau. Whimsical comedy about a couple of aging angels (Webb & Edmund Gwenn) who come to earth to save a marriage. They manage to create quite a fuss during their visit. Webb & Gwenn are a good team and the rest of the star-filled cast do their best. (Dir: George Seaton, 92 mins.)

For Love or Money (1963)**½ Kirk Douglas, Mitzi Gaynor, Gig Young, Thelma Ritter. Attorney is hired by a wealthy widow to act as matchmaker for her three gorgeous daughters and the men she has selected for their mates. Douglas tries comedy for a change of pace, which may be good for him, if not the audience. He gets by, and so does the film, in a routine sort of way. (Dir: Michael Gordon, 108 mins.)

For Me and My Gal (1942)*** Judy Garland, Gene Kelly. Story of the romance of two vaudevillians around World War I is moderately entertaining but musically wonderful thanks to its stars. (Dir: Busby Berkeley, 104 mins.)

For Pete's Sake (1974)**½ Barbra Streisand, Michael Sarrazin, Estelle Parsons. An uneven attempt at screwball comedy. Streisand is a young Brooklyn matron who manages to dress and live exquisitely, although her husband is making no money driving a cab. But never mind; she gets mixed up with the Mafia, goofs miserably as a call girl, and winds up in the middle of

a rampaging herd of rustled cattle in downtown Brooklyn. Some good laughs along the way. (Dir: Peter Yates, 90 mins.)

For Singles Only (1968)* John Saxon, Mary Ann Mobley, Lana Wood. One of those simple-minded comedies about life in a California "swingles" apartment complex inhabited by assorted buxom ladies and beefcake men. Milton Berle plays the hotel manager, and a group of nondescript rock bands provide some forgettable music. (Dir: Arthur Dreifuss, 91 mins.)

For the First Time (1959)** Mario Lanza, Johanna von Kosnian, Zsa Zsa Gabor. Opera star (Lanza) finds romance with a deaf girl (von Kosnian). Mario sings plenty, and that's about it! Filmed in Europe. (Dir: Rudy Mate, 97 mins.)

For the Love of Ivy (1968)**½ Sidney Poitier, Abbey Lincoln, Beau Bridges. A promising story idea conceived by Sidney Poitier—to place him in a romantic situation with a black girl and to show a young Negro woman with some pride and dignity—has gone astray, thanks to a well-meaning if muddled screenplay and some pedestrian direction. Story concerns a young domestic who decides to quit being a maid and go to secretarial school. Principal virtue of "Ivy" is the engaging performance of Abbey Lincoln in the title role.

For the Love of Mary (1948)**½ Deanna Durbin, Edmond O'Brien, Don Taylor. Deanna Durbin is a switchboard operator at the White House and meets many men not solely involved with politics. Charming little comedy. (Dir: Frederick de Cordova, 90 mins.)

For Those Who Think Young (1964)* James Darren, Pamela Tiffin, Tina Louise. For those who think stupid! About a college where surfing and romancing seem to be the major subjects. Paul Lynde manages a few chuckles in a supporting role. (Dir: Leslie Martinson, 96 mins.)

For Whom the Bell Tolls (1943)**** Gary Cooper, Ingrid Bergman. Hemingway's brilliant novel of the Spanish Civil War and people pledged to destroy a bridge is exciting, gripping drama and the screen at its suspenseful best. Bergman is marvelous and Cooper here gives one of his best screen performances. (Dir: Sam Wood, 170 mins.)

Forbidden (1954)✶✶ Tony Curtis, Joanne Dru. Adventure set in Macao (where else?) where two old flames (Curtis and Dru) rekindle their passion only to have their love and lives threatened by big time racketeers. Good actors at the mercy of the gangsters and the script. (Dir: Rudolph Maté, 85 mins.)

Forbidden (Italian, 1956)✶✶ Mel Ferrer, Lea Massari. A young priest comes home to assume his new post as parish priest and gets involved with feudal hostilities. Second-rate Italian-made film.

Forbidden Cargo (British, 1954)✶✶✶ Nigel Patrick, Elizabeth Sellars. Complaints send a private investigator to a coastal town, where he uncovers a smuggling racket. Well-done melodrama, at once amusing and suspenseful. (Dir: Harold French, 83 mins.)

Forbidden Fruit (French, 1958)✶✶½ Fernandel, Francoise Arnoul. Fernandel is cast in a dramatic role as middle-aged married man who has an affair with a pretty young girl. He doesn't quite come off as a dramatic actor, you wait for him to do something funny.

Forbidden Games (French, 1952)✶✶✶✶ Brigitte Fossey, Georges Poujouly. Superb, poignant film about a poor family who take in a little girl whose parents are killed in an air raid. The youngest son and the little girl become great friends and learn to rely on one another for understanding. Many comic touches are supplied by the noisy neighbors. This film contains one of the most shatteringly dramatic climaxes ever filmed. (Dir: René Clement, 87 mins.)

Forbidden Planet (1956)✶✶½ Walter Pidgeon, Anne Francis, Leslie Nielsen. Better than average science fiction pic. The year is 2200 A.D. and the Planet is Altair-4. Good use of visual gimmicks, and sound effects. (Dir: Fred McLeod Wilcox, 98 mins.)

Forbidden Street, The (1949)✶✶ Dana Andrews, Maureen O'Hara. Melodrama set in London slums with soap opera tendencies. Nice performance by Dame Sybil Thorndike as a crusty old witch. (Dir: Jean Negulesco, 91 mins.)

Force Five (1975)✶ Gerald Gordon,
248

Nick Pryor, William Lucking. Predictable TV pilot about a group of ex-cons forming a police undercover unit. They zero in on thugs who beat up a basketball star. Made-for-TV. (Dir: Walter Grauman, 72 mins.)

Force of Arms (1951)✶✶½ William Holden, Nancy Olson, Frank Lovejoy. An Army officer and a young WAC meet and fall in love in the midst of war (WW II). Very reminiscent of "A Farewell to Arms" but not as effective. Good performances by the stars. (Dir: Michael Curtiz, 100 mins.)

Force of Evil (1949)✶✶✶ John Garfield, Beatrice Pearson. The "numbers" racket is broken wide open when one of its hirelings refuses to play ball any longer. Fairly competent crime melodrama; occasional good dialogue. (Dir: Abraham Polonsky, 78 mins.)

Foreign Affair, A (1948)✶✶✶ Jean Arthur, Marlene Dietrich, John Lund. No longer topical but still amusing comedy about life among our troops in post-war Berlin, around airlift time. (Dir: Billy Wilder, 116 mins.)

Foreign Correspondent (1949)✶✶✶ Joel McCrea, Laraine Day, George Sanders. Young American newsman chases all over Europe after international spies. Directed by Alfred Hitchcock, with many of the suspenseful master's touches in evidence, this should have one busily biting nails for a couple of hours. (Dir: Alfred Hitchcock, 119 mins.)

Foreign Exchange (1970)✶✶ Robert Horton, Sebastian Cabot, Jill St. John. One of two made-for-TV features starring Robert Horton as former British agent John Smith, adventurer and fatalist. Horton is customarily expressionless as the put-upon ex-agent who gets involved in a prisoner-exchange plot which backfires.

Foreign Intrigue (1956)✶✶✶ Robert Mitchum and Genevieve Page. Overlong but sometimes exciting melodrama written and directed by Sheldon Reynolds who created the TV series. Press agent finds plenty of surprises when he checks into the past of his deceased employer. Filmed in Europe. (Dir: Sheldon Reynolds, 100 mins.)

Foreman Went to France, The (British, 1942)✶✶✶½ Tommy Trinder, Clifford Evans, Constance Cummings, Robert Morley. A factory foreman is trapped in France by the onrush of the Nazis, joins with two Tommies and a girl to escape across the channel. One of the best of its kind, a fast, thrilling "chase" melodrama. Recommended. (Dir: Charles Frend, 88 mins.)

Forest Rangers (1942)**½ Fred MacMurray, Susan Hayward, Paulette Goddard. When a forest ranger marries a socialite, his former girl tries to show her up. Mildly pleasant comedy-drama, but the cast is better than the material. (Dir: George Marshall, 87 mins.)

Forever Amber (1947)**½ Linda Darnell, Cornel Wilde, Richard Greene. Kathleen Winsor's novel of a 17th Century tramp loses what appeal the book had by the very just limitations of the motion picture. A long, elaborate bore with one or two passable sequences. (Dir: Otto Preminger, 138 mins.)

Forever and a Day (1943)**** Ida Lupino, Charles Laughton, Merle Oberon, Brian Aherne, Ray Milland, all-star cast. The saga of a house in London, and of the generations who lived in it. Each sequence shows care, fine casting, direction, writing. (Dirs: René Clair, Edmund Goulding, Cedric Hardwicke, Frank Lloyd, Victor Saville, Robert Stevenson, Herbert Wilcox, 104 mins.)

Forever Darling (1956)** Lucille Ball, Desi Arnaz, James Mason. Silliness about a guardian angel who comes to earth to save a marriage, isn't worthy of the talents of the cast. For Lucy addicts primarily. (Dir: Alexander Hall, 96 mins.)

Forever My Love (Austrian, 1955) ** Romy Schneider, Karl Boehm. Three films compressed into one, recounting the life and love of Elizabeth of Bavaria (Schneider) and Franz Josef (Boehm). Like Viennese pastry, nice and sweet, but a lot of it makes you sick. (Dir: Ernst Marischka, 147 mins.)

Forgiven Sinner, The (French, 1962) ***½ Jean-Paul Belmondo, Emmanuele Riva. Disillusioned, bitter war widow is helped by the understanding of a kindly priest during World War II. Meticulously detailed, well-acted drama, sober and thoughtful. Slow pace may bother some, but the film is well worthwhile. Dubbed in English. (Dir: Jean-Pierre Melville, 101 mins.)

Fort Apache (1948)*** John Wayne, Henry Fonda, Shirley Temple. Brass-bound Army colonel sticks to the book and invites an Indian massacre. Large-scale John Ford western, big but lacks action. (Dir: John Ford, 127 mins.)

Fort Defiance (1951)*** Dane Clark, Ben Johnson. Above average Grade "B" western with Johnson out to avenge against Clark for deserting during the Civil War. Plenty of action and a passable production. (Dir: John Rawlins, 81 mins.)

Fort Dobbs (1958)** Clint Walker, Virginia Mayo, Brian Keith. An average western epic with the cowboys and Indians fighting it out. Walker, of TV cowboy fame, fits well into the hero groove. (Dir: Gordon Douglas, 90 mins.)

Fort Massacre (1958)** Joel McCrea, Forrest Tucker, Susan Cabot. Joel McCrea's in the saddle again and trouble's not far from his behind. Good action scenes with plenty of gun smoke and Indian warfare. The kids will enjoy this more than their parents. (Dir: Joseph Newman, 80 mins.)

Fort Ti (1953)** George Montgomery, Joan Vohs. An Indian scout joins with the English forces to capture the French-held Fort Ticonderoga. Routine western. (Dir: William Castle, 73 mins.)

Fort Utah (1967)* John Ireland, Virginia Mayo, Robert Strauss. Weary, beat tale of reformed gunfighter (Ireland) and Indian agent (Strauss) hot on the trail of an Indian-massacring Army deserter (Scott Brady). The horses look plastic, the rocks papier-mache, Fort Utah itself appears to have been constructed from popsicle sticks. (Dir: Lesley Selander, 84 mins.)

Fortress of the Dead (1965)**½ John Hackett, Conrad Parkham. Man returning to the Philippines after 20 years cannot shake his guilty actions which began at Corregidor during the Japanese invasion. On-the-spot shooting gives this drama a realistic air, which aids it considerably.

Fortune, The (1975)*** Warren Beatty, Jack Nicholson, Stockard Channing. Some very good moments of farce. Mike Nichols obviously loved the screwball comedies of the thirties and tried to create a 1970's valentine to them. Beatty and Nicholson are a pair of bumbling con artists who lure an heiress, Channing, from her father's home and plan to wed, bed and kill her—not necessarily in that order. The laughs keep flowing and Stockard Channing makes an auspicious debut in a major role. (Dir: Mike Nichols, 86 mins.)

Fortune Cookie (1966)***½ Jack Lemmon, Walter Matthau. Walter Matthau's Academy Award-winning performance as best supporting actor is a joy, and carries this uneven Billy Wilder comedy. Jack Lemmon takes a back seat, or more literally a wheel chair, to Matthau's portrayal as his money-hungry brother-in-law, who sees a chance to score big when Lemmon is knocked down by a football player while performing his job as a TV cameraman during a Cleveland Browns game. Billy Wilder gets his satiric licks in, but Matthau's is the only completely successful characterization that emerges. Matthau's windup harangue when he touches on a number of things including some variations on the theme of civil rights and civil liberties is one of the funniest individual scenes in recent years. (Dir: Billy Wilder, 125 mins.)

Fortune in Diamonds (British, 1951) **½ Jack Hawkins, Dennis Price. Four men trek into the South African jungle to retrieve a cache of diamonds hidden away. Slow-moving adventure melodrama, bolstered by good location scenes. (Dir: David MacDonald, 74 mins.)

Fortunes of Captain Blood (1950)**½ Louis Hayward, Patricia Medina. The dashing Captain Peter Blood, the Spanish Main's most feared buccaneer, is with us once more, this time in the guise of Louis Hayward. Same plot and outcome as in Errol Flynn's swashbuckling days. (Dir: Gordon Douglas, 91 mins.)

Forty Carats (1973)**½ Liv Ullmann, Edward Albert, Gene Kelly, Binnie Barnes, Nancy Walker. The Broadway success about an older woman and a young lover plays like glossy soap opera on the screen. However, if charm can suffice, this film is loaded with it. Liv Ullmann uses only about ⅓ of her acting talent as the 40-year-old divorcée who falls under the spell of a 22-year-old (Albert) while vacationing in Greece.

250

Gene Kelly is quite adroit with his Noel Coward lines as her ex-husband, and Binnie Barnes, in a return to the screen after many years, scores as Liv's sophisticated mother. Escapist fare! (Dir: Milton Katselas, 110 mins.)

48 Hours to Live (Swedish, 1960)*½ Anthony Steel, Marlies Behrens. Reporter saves a nuclear scientist from a ring of international thieves after his secret. Weak spy melodrama, with boxer Ingemar Johannson playing himself briefly, if that still means anything.

Forty-eighth Mile, The (1970)** Darren McGavin, William Windom, Kathy Brown, Carrie Snodgress. McGavin plays yet another private eye, this time on an assignment involving two women in love with the same man. Good acting helps. Made-for-TV. (Dir: Gene Levitt, 97 mins.)

Forty Guns (1957)** Barbara Stanwyck, Barry Sullivan. The Forty Guns of the title must go off forty times each in this literal "shoot 'em up" Western. It seems the entire cast is either shooting or being shot at during every scene in this Western about the Tombstone territory of Arizona and the men who tamed it. (Dir: Sameul Fuller, 80 mins.)

Forty-Niners, The (1954)**½ Bill Elliott, Virginia Grey. Marshal makes friends with a gambler in order to track down some killers. Well-done western.

49th Man, The (1953)**½ John Ireland, Suzanne Dalbert. Fast moving spy film about U. S. Security Investigators' tracking down of an A-Bomb parts smuggling outfit. Tense climax. (Dir: Fred F. Sears, 73 mins.)

49th Parallel, The (British, 1942) ***½ Laurence Olivier, Leslie Howard, Raymond Massey, Eric Portman, Glynis Johns. Gripping war drama of a German U-Boat sunk off Canada, its survivors trying to reach safety in neutral territory. Superb cast, with Olivier, Howard, and Massey in for "guest" appearances. The manhunt is exciting, picturesque, with actual background shooting. Alternate title: Invaders, The. (Dir: Michael Powell, 105 mins.)

40 Pounds of Trouble (1963)** Tony Curtis, Phil Silvers, Suzanne Pleshette, Claire Wilcox. Limp reworking of Shirley Temple's "Little Miss Marker," the one about the woman-hating gambler who takes a tyke under his wing and softens up. The cast tries hard, but the results are often cloying, saccharine. (Dir: Norman Jewison, 106 mins.)

Forty-Second Street (1933)***½ Dick Powell, Ruby Keeler, Ginger Rogers. One of the best screen musicals of that era and one that should still entertain you. Two of the numbers in the delightful score have become standards and even the usual backstage plot is neatly done. (Dir: Lloyd Bacon, 98 mins.)

Forty Thousand Horsemen (Australian, 1941)*** Grant Taylor, Betty Bryant. Saga of the Anzacs in Jerusalem, fighting the Germans during World War I. Lusty, rip-roaring action drama, featuring truly spectacular battle scenes.

42:6 (Ben Gurion) (Swiss, 1969)* Arieh Mandelblit, David Muchtar, Rolf Brin. Irritating pseudo-documentary about the legendary founder and longtime Prime Minister of Israel, David Ben-Gurion. Three different actors play Ben-Gurion—who is not interviewed by the filmmaker—and there are reconstructed scenes of events in Palestine, before and after the First World War. The title is a reference to the Covenant (in the Book of Isaiah). English subtitles. (Dir: David Perlov, 103 mins.)

Foster and Laurie (1975)*** Perry King, Dorian Harewood. Excellently produced, well-acted police film based on the true life slaying of two cops, Gregory Foster and Rocco Laurie, in New York City, 1972. Begins with the street ambush of the patrolmen and, through flashbacks, the lives of the two men are played out. Effective cross-cutting between the personal married lives of the black Foster and the Italian-American Laurie. On-the-job vignettes help make the men real people and, by the time the brutal killing is shown again, we've grown to care about them. Perry King, as Rocco Laurie, and Dorian Harewood, as Gregory Foster, couldn't be better in the leading roles. Director John Llewelyn Moxey also deserves a share of the credit for this hard-hitting police drama. Made-for-TV. (98 mins.)

Fountainhead, The (1949)**½ Raymond Massey, Gary Cooper, Patricia Neal. The year's best seller gets carved up and destroyed by the Hollywood knife. Brilliant book about a modern architect turns into a confusing screen play. (Dir: King Vidor, 114 mins.)

Four Bags Full (French, 1957)*** Jean Gabin, Bourvil. Award winning French film combining comedy with a good dramatic plot about two men who take great risks during the Nazi occupation in Paris. Excellent performances. (Dir: Claude Autant-Lara, 84 mins.)

Four Daughters (1938)**** Claude Rains, John Garfield, Gale Page, 3 Lane Sisters. Beautifully acted adaptation of the Fannie Hurst story. One of the year's best, this made the late John Garfield a star. A tragic, moving drama. (Dir: Michael Curtiz, 90 mins.)

Four Days' Leave (Swiss, 1951)**½ Cornel Wilde, Josette Day. A sailor on tour in Switzerland falls for the girl in the watch shop, enters in a skiing contest, wins both. Highly amusing, pleasant comedy with beautiful scenery. (Dir: Leopold Lindtberg, 98 mins.)

Four Days of Naples, The (U.S.-Italy, 1962)***½ Regina Bianchi, Jean Sorel, Lea Massari. Epic re-enactment chronicling the spontaneous anti-Nazi uprising in Naples, which liberated the city after WW II. Reminiscent of the early Soviet revolutionary opuses, film has a biting intensity and power. Mostly nonprofessional cast performs admirably. Nominated for an Academy Award for a foreign language film. (Dir: Nanni Loy, 116 mins.)

Four Desperate Men (Australian, 1960)*** Aldo Ray, Heather Sears. Cornered criminals hole up on an island off Sydney, Australia, and threaten to blow up the entire town if they're not permitted to escape. Tense drama with the on-scene shooting (both varieties) adding to the suspense. Well acted. (Dir: Harry Watt, 104 mins.)

Four Feathers (British, 1939)***½ Ralph Richardson, C. Aubrey Smith, June Duprez, John Clements. An Army officer "branded a coward" redeems himself by foiling a native uprising. Lavish spectacularly staged melodrama. Good acting, good action. Recommended. (Dir: Zoltan Korda, 140 mins.)

Four for Texas (1963)*½ Frank Sinatra, Dean Martin, Anita Ekberg,

Ursula Andress. "Four for Texas" struggles to provide three laughs. Another private in-joke for Frank and his buddies. Western comedy-drama pits the two stars against each other until they join forces against a third party. Martin comes off best as an adventurer who gets romantically involved with Miss Andress and Anita Ekberg is Sinatra's love interest. Director Robert Aldrich doesn't help his own cause with the sophomoric script which he co-authored.

Four Girls in Town (1957)***½ Julia Adams, Elsa Martinelli, Sydney Chaplin, George Nader. Hollywood story about four hopeful misses who arrive to make good in the flicks. Offbeat handling of the usual success story makes this one stand out; pleasant surprise twists, nice insight into the cinema capital. (Dir: Jack Sher, 85 mins.)

Four Guns to the Border (1954)** Rory Calhoun, Colleen Miller, George Nader. Western fare served with all the necessary ingredients intact. Action fans will enjoy the Apache raids and the gun duels. (Dir: Richard Carlson, 82 mins.)

Four Horsemen of the Apocalypse, The (1962)**½ Glenn Ford, Ingrid Thulin, Charles Boyer, Lee J. Cobb, Paul Henreid. Elephantine drama of an Argentine family and their involvements in World War II, updated but hardly improved from the old silent version, which made a star of Valentino. In this one, Ford's no Rudy, but in fairness he receives little help from script or director. Some of the other performances are okay, but the film runs too long to maintain interest. (Dir: Vincente Minnelli, 153 mins.)

400 Blows, The (French, 1959)**** Jean-Pierre Leaud. Memorable study of an adolescent boy, neglected by his selfish parents, who discovers some unpleasant facts about life. The boy is played with great sensitivity by Jean-Pierre Leaud. The excellent photography and superb editing set the mood for this touching film. (Dir: Francois Truffaut, 99 mins.)

Four in a Jeep (Swiss, 1951)**** Ralph Meeker, Viveca Lindfors. Dramatic story of the international MP patrol in Vienna, and of a girl who needs their help. Excellently done, actually filmed on the spot, with

252

many fine scenes. (Dir: Leopold Lindtberg, 97 mins.)

Four Jills and a Jeep (1944)** Kay Francis, Carole Landis, Martha Raye, Phil Silvers. A big cast in a boring, inept musical about the experiences of its female stars when they went overseas for the USO. Ignore the name performers. This is a below-average "B." (Dir: William Seiter, 89 mins.)

Four Kinds of Love (Italy, 1965)— See: **Bambole**

Four Musketeers, The (1975)**** Raquel Welch, Oliver Reed, Richard Chamberlain, Faye Dunaway, Michael York, Charlton Heston, Simon Ward, Geraldine Chaplin. This is not a sequel to the delightful "Three Musketeers" of director Richard Lester, released in 1973. "The Four Musketeers" was always planned by Lester as a two-part romp and was lensed at the same time as "Three Musketeers" by an unsuspecting cast. (The complexities of international film financing being what they are, one film reference source cites Panama as the producing nation.) On screen, however, it's more joyous escapades of rogues, gallant damsels, derring-do and swordplay. Loaded with more marvelous sight gags. Huge fun for all. (Dir: Richard Lester, 107 mins.)

Four Skulls of Jonathan Drake (1959) * Edward Franz, Valerie French, Grant Richards. One of the worst of the science-fiction horror films. Granted they're mostly pretty bad but this one is ghastly! (Dir: Edward L. Cahn, 70 mins.)

Four Sons (1940)**½ Don Ameche, Eugenie Leontovich. Drama of a Czech family ripped apart by the Nazi invasion is almost a fine film but reaches for more than it is able to give. Still worth seeing as an anti-war story. (Dir: Archie Mayo, 89 mins.)

Four Ways Out (Italian, 1954)** Gina Lollobrigida, Renato Baldini. Four men who have held up a cashier's office are tracked down. Ordinary crime melodrama, not helped by English dubbing. (Dir: Pietro Germi, 77 mins.)

Four Wives (1939)**½ Lane Sisters, Claude Rains. The four daughters ride again, this time as wives and mothers. But this time they ran out of breath and came up with a very ordinary movie. (Dir: Michael Curtiz, 110 mins.)

Fourposter, The (1953)*** Rex Harrison, Lilli Palmer. Fine screen treatment of hilarious Broadway comedy about a married couple who go through their lives in scenes played in and around their four-poster bed. Excellent performances by the stars. (Dir: Irving Reis, 103 mins.)

Four's a Crowd (1938)**½ Errol Flynn, Olivia de Havilland, Rosalind Russell. A lot of funny situations help this not-so-funny comedy about a wealthy heiress and her beaus. (Dir: Michael Curtiz, 100 mins.)

Fourteen Hours (1951)*** Richard Basehart, Barbara Bel Geddes, Paul Douglas. Director Henry Hathaway keeps the suspense sharply in focus in this drama about a mentally disturbed man who stands on a ledge of a Manhattan hotel threatening to jump for a period of 14 hours. A few subplots are interwoven into the action involving various spectators (Grace Kelly, Jeffrey Hunter, Debra Paget). Basehart is very effective as the troubled man and Barbara Bel Geddes has some touching moments as his girl friend. This drama is based on a true life incident. (Dir: Henry Hathaway, 92 mins.)

Fourth for Marriage, A (1964)* Tommy Holden, Marilyn Manning. Country boy becomes a brassiere salesman and outwits city slickers. Very bad comedy on the amateur level. Alternate title: **What's Up Front.**

Fourth Square, The (British, 1961)** Conrad Phillips, Natasha Perry. Lawyer turns sleuth when his client is involved in robbery and murder. Adequate mystery based on an Edgar Wallace story.

Fox, The (1968)*** Sandy Dennis, Keir Dullea, Anne Heywood. Sensitive dramatization of D. H. Lawrence's novella about a relationship between two young lesbians. For those of you who care there is a heterosexual liaison between Dullea and Miss Heywood, but the brooding story, filmed largely in rural Canada, benefits greatly from the restrained, moving performances from the three leads. Britain's Anne Heywood is seen to particularly good advantage, and TV-director-actor Mark Rydell has done a commendable job in directing his first feature, tackling this challenging material which could so easily have been vulgarized and distorted. (Dir: Mark Rydell, 110 mins.)

Fox Fire (1955)**½ Jane Russell, Jeff Chandler. Anya Seton's novel is brought to the screen as a glossy love story with overtones of adventure. Jeff Chandler is well cast as the dedicated mining engineer who has to learn to understand his new socialite wife (Jane Russell in the casting error of many years). (Dir: Joseph Pevney, 92 mins.)

Foxes of Harrow, The (1947)*** Rex Harrison, Maureen O'Hara. Fans of historical fiction will be disappointed with this dime novel tale but there's enough excitement in some of the episodes to please less discerning viewers. Tells of the rise to fame and fortune of an adventurer in 1820 New Orleans. (Dir: John M. Stahl, 117 mins.)

Foxhole in Cairo (British, 1961)** Peter Van Eyck, James Robertson Justice, Adrian Hoven. British Intelligence trails a German agent sent to Cairo by Rommel to determine the Allied line of defense. Routinely interesting World War II espionage thriller; nothing new, but fairly well done. (Dir: John Moxey, 79 mins.)

Foxiest Girl in Paris, The (French, 1957)**½ Martine Carol, Mischa Auer. French fashion model gets involved with jewel thieves and murder and sets out to crack the case with little or no assistance from the gendarmes. Some laughs. (Dir: Roger De Broin, 100 mins.)

Fragment of Fear (Great Britain, 1970)**½ David Hemmings, Gayle Hunnicutt, Flora Robson, Wilfred Hyde White. Suspense as former drug addict Hemmings goes through a slow emotional breakdown. Strange, unexplainable events lead him to question his own sanity. O.K. whodunit! (Dir: Richard C. Sarafian, 95 mins.)

Framed (1947)*** Glenn Ford, Janis Carter, Barry Sullivan. Man is marked for death by two crooks who wish to steal money from a bank. Suspenseful melodrama with a good cast. (Dir: Richard Wallace, 82 mins.)

Francis (1950)**½ Donald O'Connor, Patricia Medina. This was the first of a series of films which featured the box-office-winning gimmick, Francis, The Talking Mule. Donald

O'Connor takes a back seat to the bellowing burro (Chill Wills supplies Francis's voice). (Dir: Arthur Lubin, 91 mins.)

Francis Covers the Big Town (1953) **½ Donald O'Connor, Nancy Guild. It's inevitable that Francis, The Talking Mule should become involved with detective work and this is the film in which he does it. He and sidekick Donald O'Connor go through a series of narrow escapes as they get a scoop for the papers on underworld activities. (Dir: Arthur Lubin, 86 mins.)

Francis Goes to the Races (1951) **½ Donald O'Connor, Piper Laurie. The Talking Mule gets information from his equine relatives and causes his innocent master, O'Connor, a great deal of trouble. Piper Laurie is wasted as the love interest. (Dir: Arthur Lubin, 88 mins.)

Francis Goes to West Point (1952) **½ Donald O'Connor, Lori Nelson. O'Connor and his talking-mule sidekick end up at West Point after they become heroes in a sabotage plot. The usual shenanigans prevail as O'Connor gets in and out of trouble because of his four-legged "pal." (Dir: Arthur Lubin, 81 mins.)

Francis in the Haunted House (1956) ** Mickey Rooney, Virginia Welles. When Donald O'Connor screamed "no" to any more Francis epics, Universal tried once again with Mickey Rooney as the mule's confidant but without much success. Only moderately funny acting with Rooney mugging his way as a bumpkin nobody believes. (Dir: Charles Lamont, 80 mins.)

Francis in the Navy (1955)** Donald O'Connor, Martha Hyer. The last "Francis" film starring Donald O'Connor and not the funniest. After a go at West Point and the Wacs in previous films, Francis makes some choice comments about the nautical division of our armed services. Martha Hyer supplies the obligatory love interest. (Dir: Arthur Lubin, 80 mins.)

Francis Joins the Wacs (1954)**½ Donald O'Connor, Julie Adams. Silly, but Francis' fans will enjoy the hijinks that he and Donald O'Connor go through when a mistake sends Don back into the service—as a Wac recruit! (Dir: Arthur Lubin, 94 mins.)

Francis of Assisi (1961)** Bradford Dillman, Dolores Hart, Stuart Whitman. Cumbersome, frequently inept narrative of St. Francis and the founding of his order in the 13th century. Lavish production should have meant a far better film. (Dir: Michael Curtiz, 111 mins.)

Frankenstein (1932)*** Boris Karloff, Colin Clive. A scientist creates artificial life, only to have his monster run amok. Karloff's impressive portrayal of the monster, and some fascinating technical effects, make this one worth seeing again. (Dir: James Whale, 71 mins.)

Frankenstein Conquers the World (1966)*½ Nick Adams. A confused science-fiction film with shock elements. A monsterlike boy grows up wild in Japan, and Dr. Nick Adams, tries to find a connection between the lost heart of the Frankenstein monster and the giant growing monster. (Dir: Inoshiro Honda, 87 mins.)

Frankenstein Created Woman (1967) * Peter Cushing, Susan Denberg. This one dwells on the Baron's attempt to create a gorgeous woman from a deformed creature. Strictly for fans who relish another visit to the Baron's laboratory. (Dir: Terence Fisher, 92 mins.)

Frankenstein Meets the Space Monster (1965)* James Karen, Nancy Marshall. Man-like robot saves his inventors from outer space creatures bent on invading earth. Outlandish science-fiction horror. (Dir: Robert Gaffney, 78 mins.)

Frankenstein Meets the Wolf Man (1943)**½ Bela Lugosi, Lon Chaney. It's only natural that these two cutups should get to know each other, and when they do meet, the countryside is crowded with corpses. Pretty lively horror film. (Dir: Roy William Neill, 72 mins.)

Frankenstein Must Be Destroyed (Great Britain, 1969) ½ Peter Cushing, Simon Ward, Veronica Carlson. Another bad imitation! This time Peter Cushing stars as the insane doctor who is very busy transplanting brains. (Dir: Terence Fisher, 97 mins.)

Frankenstein—1970 (1958)** Boris Karloff, Charlotte Austin. The real Baron Von Frankenstein would turn in his crypt if he saw what they're doing to his castle in this film—A TV troupe is using it as the locale of a horror show. Is nothing sacred? If you take your horror films seriously you can skip this one.—However, it's good for a few laughs. (Dir: Howard W. Koch, 83 mins.)

Frankenstein: The True Story (1973)*** James Mason, David McCallum, Michael Sarrazin, John Gielgud. Despite its over three-hour length, the quality of performance is so uniformly high in this version of the Frankenstein tale, based on Mary Shelley's gothic novel, that it holds your interest and casts a tantalizing spell of horror, mixed with wonder and suspense. Most convincing are Leonard Whiting's Dr. Frankenstein and Sarrazin's compelling figure of the Creature. Made-for-TV. (Dir: Jack Smight.)

Frankenstein's Daughter (1959)* John Ashley, Sandra Knight. Pretty awful horror yarn with modern setting. The title suggests fun for horror-film fans but doesn't deliver. Cheaply made and it shows. (Dir: Richard Cunha, 85 mins.)

Frankie and Johnny (1966)* Elvis Presley, Donna Douglas. Shoddy Elvis Presley musical loosely based on the folk ballad. Elvis is a riverboat singer who is big on gambling and girls. His Frankie, played by Donna ("The Beverly Hillbillies") Douglas, is always after him—in between musical numbers—that is. (Dir: Frederick de Cordova, 87 mins.)

Frank's Greatest Adventure—See: Fearless Frank

Frantic (1958)**½ Jeanne Moreau, Maurice Ronet. A suspense tale (French-English dubbed) that just misses being very good. A couple of people plan what appears to be an almost perfect crime but as it always happens, things don't turn out that way. The first half is better than the windup. Moreau carries film anyway. (Dir: Serge Friedman, 94 mins.)

Fraulein (1958)*½ Dana Wynter, Mel Ferrer. Ridiculous drama which traces a young German girl's hard times during the last days of World War II. Miss Wynter appears well-groomed throughout the many harrowing adventures she encounters—an accomplishment in itself. Mel Ferrer is customarily tall, thin and tedious. (Dir: Henry Koster, 98 mins.)

Fraulein Doktor (Italian-Yugoslav, 1968)*½ Suzy Kendall, Kenneth More, Capucine. Silly espionage film which ends up unintentionally funny in spots. Suzy Kendall plays a World War I Mata Hari-type spy, based on the real-life exploits of Anna Maria Lesser, a notorious German spy during World War I. Only saving grace is the fine period reconstruction. (Dir: Alberto Lattuada, 102 mins.)

Freaks (1932)***½ Leila Hyams, Olga Baclanova, Harry Earles. A cult classic, this unusual picture is a terrifying vision of life among the weird inhabitants of the sideshow world. The performers are real freaks, and this film is not for the squeamish. (Dir: Tod Browning, 64 mins.)

Freckles (1960)** Martin West, Carol Christensen. Lad gets a job in a lumber camp, proves the lack of one hand doesn't mean a total handicap. Unexceptional outdoor drama might get by with juvenile audiences. (Dir: Andrew V. McLaglen, 84 mins.)

Free for All (1949)** Ann Blyth, Robert Cummings. An innocent bit of nonsense about an inventor who comes up with a tablet that supposedly turns water into gasoline. Cummings mugs his way through the proceedings and Miss Blyth looks startled and wide-eyed which she mistakenly thinks is the only way to play comedy. (Dir: Charles Barton, 83 mins.)

Freebie and the Bean (1974)* Alan Arkin, James Caan, Valerie Harper, Loretta Swit. The keystone cops plus mayhem and sado-masochism in San Francisco. Ugh. Arkin is saddled with playing a Chicano worried about his wife's infidelity. Action includes auto stunts. Caan and Arkin should work together some other time in a decent script. (Dir: Richard Rush, 113 mins.)

French Connection, The (1971)**** Gene Hackman, Fernando Rey, Roy Scheider, Eddie Egan, Sonny Grosso. Marvelously exciting yarn about a New York cop (Hackman) busting a huge international narcotics ring smuggling vast quantities of heroin into the U.S. Based on the book by Robin Moore; the real narcotics squad officers who broke the case in 1961 (Egan & Grosso) play bit parts in the film. Action takes place in Marseilles, Washington, and New York, and there's one of the best chase sequences in the history of film as Hackman tries to catch his prey on a subway and then follows by auto. It's an exciting zinger all the way. (Dir: William Friedkin, 104 mins.)

French Connection II (1975)***½ Gene Hackman, Fernando Rey. The sequel to the Academy Award-winning film about New York cop Popeye Doyle and his adventures with the international narcotics ring doesn't pack the punch of the original, but it's still exciting. Gene Hackman is Popeye once again, on the trail of the elusive Kingpin of the French narcotics syndicate (Fernando Rey also repeats his role from the original), and the action set in Marseilles adds to the chase drama. Less complex, more brutal than "F.C." #1—there's a rousing finale in the harbor in Marseille. Frankenheimer back in stride. (Dir: John Frankenheimer, 118 mins.)

French Key, The (1946)*** Albert Dekker, Mike Mazurki. Smart-talking amateur sleuth and his brawny assistant find a corpse in their hotel room. Good, well-paced mystery, above average. (Dir: Walter Colmes, 64 mins.)

French Line (1954)** Gilbert Roland, Jane Russell. Multi-millionairess travels to Paris posing as a model, falls in love with a dashing Frenchman. Boring musical. (Dir: Lloyd Bacon, 102 mins.)

French Mistress, A (Great Britain, 1960)** Cecil Parker, James Robertson Justice, Agnes Laurent, Ian Bannen. Droll fluff. An alluring woman gets teaching post at a British boys' school. Inoffensive, mild comedy! (Dir: Roy Boulting, 98 mins.)

French, They Are a Funny Race, The (French, 1957)**½ Martine Carol, Jack Buchanan. Fast and funny spoof on the French people as seen through the eyes of an English novelist, retired from the British Army and residing in Paris with his glamorous French wife. (Dir: Preston Sturges, 83 mins.)

French Without Tears (1940)*½ Ray Milland, Ellen Drew. Title should be "Comedy Without Laughs" in this boring film about some Englishman fighting for the attentions of a French lass. (Dir: Anthony Asquith, 67 mins.)

Frenchie (1951)** Joel McCrea, Shel-

ley Winters. Comedy and drama are juggled in this awkward western about a gal who comes back to the town which sent her away to settle a few scores. McCrea is the town's easygoing sheriff and Miss Winters is Frenchie, of course. (Dir: Louis King, 81 mins.)

Frenchman's Creek (1944)**½ Joan Fontaine, Basil Rathbone, Arturo de Cordova, Nigel Bruce. Costume film about an unholy alliance between an English lady and a French pirate. Swashbuckling and romantic! (Dir: Mitchell Leisen, 113 mins.)

Frenzy (British, 1972)**** Jon Finch, Alec McCowen, Vivien Merchant, Barry Foster, Barbara Leigh-Hunt. A marvelous suspense film directed by that master of the genre, Alfred Hitchcock. Taut screenplay by Anthony Shaffer based on the novel "Goodbye Piccadilly, Farewell Leicester Square." Hitchcock's best effort in years, with a faultless cast of nonstars. The wrong man becomes the chief suspect when his wife is murdered—we've seen this plot before but Hitchcock, the old magician, keeps the pace spinning with humor and invention. (116 mins.)

Freud (1962)*** Montgomery Clift, Susannah York, Larry Parks. The early struggle for recognition and the general work of Sigmund Freud, the founder of modern psychiatry, are depicted in often interesting fashion in this drama directed by John Huston. Some inventive montage sequences used to show meaning of dreams, etc. Main storyline involved Freud's treatment of a young patient, well played by Miss York. (Dir: John Huston, 139 mins.)

Frieda (British, 1947)***½ Mai Zetterling, David Farrar, Glynis Johns. RAF officer brings his German war bride to his home town, where she is looked upon with suspicion and hatred. Powerful drama, intelligently handled, excellently acted. (Dir: Basil Dearden, 97 mins.)

Friendly Persuasion (1956)**** Gary Cooper, Dorothy McGuire, Tony Perkins. Touching and often amusing story about a family of Quakers who live in peace and contentment on their land in Indiana until the Civil War breaks out and disrupts their lives. Dorothy McGuire and Gary Cooper are perfectly cast in their roles as the parents. The standout performance in the film is delivered by Tony Perkins as their son who is faced with the realities of war. Well-produced and directed by William Wyler. (Dir: William Wyler, 139 mins.)

Friends (1971)* Sean Bury, Anicee Alvina. Sappy tale of 14-year-old French orphan and neglected 15-year-old English child who steal off to a beach cottage and play house for a year. This could have been passably sentimental, especially the finale where the two deliver a child into the world, if not for the exploitative directing by Lewis Gilbert, and the rip-off rock score by Elton John and Bernie Taupin. (101 mins.)

Friends of Eddie Coyle, The (1973) **** Robert Mitchum, Peter Boyle, Richard Jordan. A tough, unsentimental, first-rate drama about a Boston hoodlum, which boasts Mitchum giving perhaps the best performance of his career. Mitchum plays Eddie Coyle, a small-time mobster who winds up turning stoolie. Well adapted by Paul Monash based on the novel by George V. Higgins. Skillfully directed by Peter Yates. (102 mins.)

Fright (1956)*½ Eric Fleming, Nancy Malone. Psychiatrist investigates a young woman who has taken on the personality of the mistress of Crown Prince Rudolph of Austria in 1889, attempts to save her from self-destruction. Meandering psycho-drama plays around with the "Bridey Murphy" theme ineptly. Filmed in New York on a low budget. Alternate title: Spell of the Hypnotist.

Frightened Bride, The (British, 1952) **½ Mai Zetterling, Michael Denison. A family tries to escape the past when one of the sons is convicted of murdering a girl, sees it start all over again with the younger son. Occasionally interesting but unconvincing melodrama. Some good moments. (Dir: Terence Young, 75 mins.)

Frightened City, The (British, 1962) *½ Herbert Lom, John Gregson, Sean Connery. Accountant is really the mastermind of a large London gang specializing in a protection racket, meets his downfall when he becomes too greedy. Unpleasant, trite imitation-American gangster story. (Dir: John Lemont, 97 mins.)

Frisco Kid (1935)*** James Cagney, Margaret Lindsay. Typical, fast moving Cagney melodrama. Plenty of fighting in this tale of revenge on the Barbary Coast. (Dir: Lloyd Bacon, 80 mins.)

Frisco Sal (1945)**½ Susanna Foster, Turhan Bey, Alan Curtis. Girl gets a job as a singer in a Barbary Coast saloon while seeking the killers of her brother. Oft-told but nicely produced costume melodrama with music. (Dir: George Waggoner, 63 mins.)

Frisky (Italian, 1954)**½ Gina Lollobrigida, Vittorio De Sica. Gossipy small towners concoct an affair between an official and a gorgeous local belle. Mildly amusing comedy, pleasantly performed. Dubbed-in English. (Dir: Luigi Comencini, 98 mins.)

Fritz the Cat (1972)***½ Perhaps the first X-rated animated feature, based on the successful "underground" comic strip by social satirist Robert Crumb. Director, designer, writer Ralph Bakshi has done appreciably more than make a "dirty" cartoon—he and his raunchy on-screen characters puncture just about every myth and sacred cow they swing at. Reminds one of comic Mort Sahl's ingenuous query "Is there anyone I haven't offended?" There are anti-Jewish, anti-black jibes and a wide variety of other generally funny slams and put-downs. It doesn't all work and it seems like a one-note joke before the end, but if you've got an open mind, it's worth seeing. (77 mins.)

Frogman (1951)**½ Richard Widmark, Dana Andrews, Jeffrey Hunter. Slow-paced story of the Navy's heroes of the deep and their dangerous exploits during the war. Interesting underwater photography.

Frogs (1972)** Ray Milland, Sam Elliot, Joan Van Ark. This film has a certain inane appeal. It is a straightforward rip-off of "Willard," using amphibians instead of rodents. There is a nice, swampy atmosphere, and some cheerful, tongue-in-cheek acting. If you don't like monster movies, stay away. (Dir: George McCowan, 91 mins.)

From Hell It Came (1957)* Tod Andrews, Tina Carver. Science-fiction-horror film with witch doctors and walking dead. To hell with it. (Dir: Dan Miller, 71 mins.)

From Hell to Borneo (1964)✱✱ George Montgomery, Torin Thatcher, Julie Gregg. Soldier of fortune fights to keep control of his private island when he's menaced by pirates and a notorious gangster. Lively Philippine-made actioner makes up in movement what it lacks in finesse. (Dir: George Montgomery, 96 mins.)

From Hell to Texas (1958)✱✱½ Don Murray, Diane Varsi. Interesting Western drama about a young cowboy, nicely played by Murray, who tries to mind his own business and avoid trouble during a time when gunmen ruled the territory. (Dir: Henry Hathaway, 100 mins.)

From Here to Eternity (1954)✱✱✱✱ Burt Lancaster, Montgomery Clift, Deborah Kerr, Frank Sinatra, and Donna Reed. An excellent drama taken from James Jones' superb novel about the few days before the bombing of Pearl Harbor, in the lives of five people. This film won the Oscar for best film and Sinatra and Reed won supporting Oscars for their performances. One of the best American films made in the fifties. (Dir: Fred Zinnemann, 118 mins.)

From Istanbul—Orders to Kill (European, 1965)✱½ Christopher Logan, Geraldine Pearsall. FBI persuades the look-alike of a drug-smuggling chief to take his place, which brings on danger in the Middle East. Hokey dubbed-English crime melodrama.

From Russia, with Love (1964)✱✱✱½ Sean Connery, Lotte Lenya, Daniela Bianchi. High class, diverting hokum. Perhaps the best of the James Bond adventures, so far. Agent 007 is on a tricky mission and he executes more narrow escapes than you can count. There's a dandy encounter with a muscular blond enemy agent (played by Robert Shaw) on a European train. Lotte Lenya is an evil spy out to get Bond. Of course, Sean Connery is, as always, suave, indestructible, and a wow with the ladies. (Dir: Terence Young, 118 mins.)

From the Earth to the Moon (1958)✱✱½ Joseph Cotten, George Sanders, Debra Paget. Scientist discovering a new source of energy plans to send a rocket to the moon. Jules Verne sci-fi adventure; predictably, the special effects take top honors. (Dir: Byron Haskin, 100 mins.)

From the Mixed-Up Files of Mrs. Basil E. Frankweiler (1973)✱½ Ingrid Bergman, Sally Prager, George Rose, Johnny Doran, Madeline Kahn. The delightful children's book by E. L. Konigsburg has been made into a film too sentimental and drippy even for most children. Two suburban youngsters run away to live in New York's Metropolitan Museum for a week. Miss Bergman, who is fine as Mrs. Frankweiler, does not appear until 70 minutes into this ramshackle affair. Madeline Kahn engagingly plays a teacher who brings her class on a trip through the museum, which is the real star. (Dir: Fielder Cook, 105 mins.)

From the Terrace (1960)✱✱✱ Paul Newman, Joanne Woodward, Myrna Loy. John O'Hara's mammoth novel about big business, social strata, and marriage problems turned into an overlength but well-acted film drama, helped by steady performances, good production. (Dir: Mark Robson, 144 mins.)

From This Day Forward (1946)✱✱✱ Joan Fontaine, Mark Stevens. Young couple tries hard to adjust to the post-war world. Well-acted, interesting drama. (Dir: John Berry, 95 mins.)

Front, The (1976)✱✱✱½ Woody Allen, Zero Mostel, Andrea Marcovicci, Joshua Shelley, Georgann Johnson. Woody Allen did not invent this bizarre horror story—the blacklisting in films and TV of the 1950's—he just plays the leading role, and very well, too, of a pal fronting for a blacklisted writer. (For the newborn, blacklisting was the abhorrent practice of denying actors, directors, writers, etc., the right to work because of their alleged leftwing political views. The top executives of the TV industry in the early 50's could have quickly ended this loathsome industry-wide practice, but they did not have the elementary decency to do so.) Walter Bernstein's original screenplay, which was nominated for an Academy Award, doesn't hold up all the way, but it does bring some humor to a nightmare-real situation full of anguish and suffering. There is a lot of expertise on the subject of blacklisting involved with "The Front." Performers Mostel and Shelley were blackballed for a long time, as were writer Bernstein and director Ritt. This is not the definitive film of the squalid, demoralizing McCarthy days, but it's the only major movie that deals honestly with the aberration of blacklisting, and we must be grateful for that. (Dir: Martin Ritt, 94 mins.)

Front Page, The (1931)***½ Pat O'Brien, Adolphe Menjou, Frank McHugh, Edward Everett Horton. A film classic. Fast and furious action and dialogue, as reporter O'Brien and editor Menjou battle corruption (and each other). Fascinatingly filmed by director Lewis Milestone, with a cast of Warner Bros. stalwarts. (Dir: Lewis Milestone, 101 mins.)

Front Page, The (1974)**½ Jack Lemmon, Walter Matthau, Carol Burnett, Susan Sarandon, David Wayne. Here's the third movie version of the Ben Hecht-Charles MacArthur hit play of the late '20s about the Chicago newspaper world and the city-room gang. Billy Wilder manages to get some steam out of the love-hate relationship between unscrupulous editor Matthau and ace reporter Lemmon. As a nostalgic romp, this film can be enjoyed on its own level, but much of the humor is awfully dated and everyone, except the flawless Mr. Matthau, punches across their lines with an urgency that seems misplaced. Even Carol Burnett in a juicy cameo role as a hooker is surprisingly bad. (Dir: Billy Wilder, 105 mins.)

Front Page Story (British, 1954) ***½ Jack Hawkins, Elizabeth Allan, Eva Bartok. A day in the life of a daily newspaper, pointing up a woman on trial for murder, a mother killed in an accident, etc. Dramatic, absorbing, well acted. (Dir: Gordon Parry, 95 mins.)

Frontier Gal (1945)*** Yvonne De-Carlo, Rod Cameron, Andy Devine. Fast, brawling Western with many comic touches. Yvonne DeCarlo, as a saloon operator, marries Rod Cameron, a fugitive wanted by the law, and the trouble begins. (Dir: Charles Lamont, 84 mins.)

Frontier Uprising (1961)*½ Jim Davis, Nancy Hadley. Fearless frontier scout leads a wagon train into Mexican-owned California, unaware that Indians are ready to attack. Cheap western uses plot and plenty of stock footage from the 1940 "Kit Carson." (Dir: Edward L. Cahn, 68 mins.)

Frozen Alive (1964)*½ Scientist attempts some experiments in deep-freezing humans, which leads to complications. Sluggish German-made sci-fi thriller.

Frozen Dead, The (British, 1967)** Dana Andrews. Gruesome experiments involving resuscitation of frozen bodies lead to murder. Routine thriller. (Dir: Herbert J. Leder, 95 mins.)

Frozen Ghost, The (1945)** Lon Chaney. A hypnotist, working in a wax museum, uncovers a murder plot. Typical melodramatics, with a harried performance by Chaney. (Dir: Harold Young, 61 mins.)

Fugitive, The (1947)**** Henry Fonda, Pedro Armendariz. In Mexico, a priest refuses to support the anticleric government. Gripping, superbly directed by John Ford. Fine drama. (Dir: John Ford, 104 mins.)

Fugitive in Belgrade (1966)*½ Jose Laurence, Sven Belik. Cliched adventures of a resistance fighter hiding refugees during World War II. Short on plot, logic, and good acting. (80 mins.)

Fugitive in Saigon (French, 1957)** Daniel Gelin, Anh Mechard. Frenchman escapes, lands in Saigon, redeems himself by aiding villagers and a native girl with whom he has fallen in love. English-dubbed drama has good location scenes but the plot dawdles.

Fugitive Kind, The (1959)*** Marlon Brando, Anna Magnani, Joanne Woodward. Despite the impressive star lineup, this Southern drama is still second rate Tennessee Williams' fare. However, second rate T.W. is still appreciably better than most of his imitators' major efforts. Brando is just a few years too old for the part of a wandering "stud" who wants to plant roots and Miss Magnani has been better. Joanne Woodward, as one of T.W.'s "Kookiest" females, takes the top acting honors. Based on "Orpheus Descending." (Dir: Sidney Lumet, 135 mins.)

Full Confession (1939)*** Victor McLaglen, Joseph Calleia, Sally Eilers. A priest hears a murderer's confession, cannot divulge the information. Gripping, well-done drama. (Dir: John Farrow, 73 mins.)

Full Hearts and Empty Pockets (German, 1964)**½ Thomas Fritsch,

Senta Berger, Linda Christian. Opportunistic young man uses blackmail and double-dealing as a means of succeeding in business (he really tries). Pretty fair drama in the spirit of "Room at the Top," not as good, but it holds the interest. English-dubbed.

Full of Life (1957)***½ Judy Holliday, Richard Conte, Salvatore Baccaloni. Charming and heartwarming comedy-drama about a young couple of newlyweds who move in with the husband's father when the wife announces she's going to have a baby. Miss Holliday is perfect as the perplexed mother-to-be and Conte matches her performance but Salvatore Baccaloni almost steals the picture with his magnificent portrait of Judy's Italian father-in-law. (Dir: Richard Quine, 91 mins.)

Fuller Brush Girl, The (1950)*** Lucille Ball, Eddie Albert. Lovable Lucy is a Fuller Brush salesgirl in this farcical comedy with smugglers, murderers, and plenty of laughs. (Dir: Lloyd Bacon, 85 mins.)

Fuller Brush Man (1948)*** Red Skelton, Janet Blair. Salesman stumbles into a murder mystery, traps the hoodlums. Wild and woolly slapstick, well done. (Dir: S. Sylvan Simon, 93 mins.)

Fun in Acapulco (1963)** Elvis Presley, Ursula Andress. What distinguishes this one from the myriad of other Presley films is some nifty scenery. Scenic beauty of a different kind is amply provided as the cameras explore the topographies of Ursula Andress and Elsa Cardenas. (Dir: Richard Thorpe, 97 mins.)

Fun with Dick and Jane (1977)*** Jane Fonda, George Segal, Ed McMahon. Parts of this comedy about contemporary life are quite funny and zany, others are serious and contemptible. The writers and director never seem to have quite made up their minds whether they wanted to produce a satire or an apologia for some of the more repellent values of American middle-class life. Segal plays an unemployed aerospace executive who, quite casually, turns to armed robbery to maintain his luxurious life-style. There are numerous writing credits in this erratic caper which evidently started out as a serious statement, then was turned into a jape, and finally given to the splendid Canadian

writer Mordecai Richler for polishing. (Richler worked with director Kotcheff on "The Apprenticeship of Duddy Kravitz.") Fonda and Segal help over the rough spots in this wacky, irritating comedy-drama. Deft, surprising ending finds Segal again back in the corporate driver's seat. (Dir: Ted Kotcheff, 95 mins.)

Funeral in Berlin (1967)**½ Michael Caine, Oscar Homolka. This sequel to the highly successful film "The Ipcress File" again stars Michael Caine as Harry Palmer, spy. Though it's not quite up to the original, it's still good adventure. Shot on location in Berlin, the authentic footage—showing the Berlin Wall—adds to the suspense of the story about the possible defection of the head of Russian security (Homolka). (Dir: Guy Hamilton, 102 mins.)

Funniest Man in the World (1969)* Charles Chaplin. Disgraceful collage of clips from Chaplin's early films which belies the title. Cues for laughter are provided by Douglas Fairbanks, Jr. All concerned should be ashamed of this project which desecrates the Tramp. The genius of Chaplin is not seen here. (Dir: Vernon P. Becker, 95 mins.)

Funny Face (1957)**** Fred Astaire, Audrey Hepburn, Kay Thompson. Astaire at his best, top George Gershwin tunes, colorful Parisian scenics, all combine to make a sprightly musical about a fashion photographer who turns a girl working in a bookstore into a high-fashion model. Top entertainment. (Dir: Stanley Donen, 103 mins.)

Funny Girl (1968)**** Barbra Streisand, Omar Sharif, Walter Pidgeon, Kay Medford. The nifty musical in which Barbra plays the famous Broadway star, Fanny Brice. Barbra is quite simply fabulous, giving one of the most triumphant and brilliant performances in the long history of musical films. If you've ever wondered what constitutes "star" quality in motion pictures, just tune in and watch this magical performer provide a definitive answer. Several of the supporting performances are fine, particularly Kay Medford playing Barbra's Jewish momma, who deserved the Oscar nomination she received. Barbra belts out some good songs and she makes them sound great, especially the most recorded song in the show, the Styne-

Merrill hit "People." Director William Wyler deserves credit for having handled Barbra's film debut so superbly. (155 mins.)

Funny Lady (1975)***½ Barbra Streisand, James Caan, Omar Sharif, Ben Vereen. This is "Funny Girl 2," but not quite as good overall, though when Barbra's singing it's magic all the way. The talking scenes get in the way and slow things down. Barbra is Fanny Brice, a big star on Broadway in the 30's, but a luckless lady in the offstage happiness department. James Caan playing the pushy Billy Rose works nicely with Barbra, and her spiffy songs include "It's Gonna Be A Great Day," which is a great number, and the enduring ballad, "Me and My Shadow." Ben Vereen is dynamite in a big, flashy dance routine. Screenplay by Jay Presson Allan and Arnold Schulman. (Dir: Herbert Ross, 140 mins.)

Funny Thing Happened on the Way to the Forum, A (1966)**** Zero Mostel, Phil Silvers, Jack Gilford. The mad, bawdy, Broadway musical set in Ancient Rome with Zero Mostel playing a sly and eager-to-be-free slave is tranferred to the screen with zest and style. It's burlesque at its best, and director Richard Lester keeps the cast working at a break-neck pace for laughs. The musical numbers are fun, but many have been deleted from the original score by Stephen Sondheim. It's a joy to see Messrs. Mostel, Silvers and Gilford romping through this farce, and it reminds us again of the unfortunate way in which the movies have neglected and wasted the enormous talents of these three comics. Mostel is much more than a comic—he is, simply, one of the very greatest actors alive. (Dir: Richard Lester, 99 mins.)

Further Perils of Laurel and Hardy, The (1967)***½ Expert Robert Youngson's compilation of some hilarious sequences from Stan and Ollie's silent film period. Contains the kind of bellylaughs one experiences all too seldom these days. (Dir: Robert Youngson, 99 mins.)

Fury (1936)**** Spencer Tracy, Sylvia Sidney. Excellent drama of mob violence and a miscarriage of justice. Similar to the "Ox Bow Incident" but a fine motion picture and forerunner of many modern social drama type films. Cast, direction and production are tops. (Dir: Fritz Lang, 90 mins.)

Fury at Showdown (1957)*½ John Derek, John Smith, Nick Adams. Another Western with handsome Derek cast as the former gunfighter who returns to his hometown to face the anger of the townspeople. Even though it is a little less than 90 minutes in length, it seems like 3 hours. (Dir: Gerd Oswald, 75 mins.)

Fury at Smugglers' Bay (British, 1962)** Peter Cushing, Bernard Lee, Michele Mercier. Head of a cutthroat band of ship wreckers holds a community in the grip of terror. Swashbuckler is on the lengthy side, with a good cast saving inferior material from seeming even worse. (Dir: John Gilling, 92 mins.)

Fury in Paradise (Mexican, 1955)* Peter Thompson, Rea Iturbide, Carlos Rivas. Tourist gets involved in a revolutionary plot. "Revolutionary" is hardly the word for the plot of this inept adventure drama.

Fury of Achilles (Italian, 1962)*½ Jacques Bergerac, Gordon Mitchell. Achilles is persuaded to lead his soldiers in battle when the Trojans war on the Greeks. Usual sort of action spectacle dubbed in English; for the indiscriminate.

Fury of Hercules (Italian, 1960)*½ Brad Harris, Alan Steel. More muscle stuff as ol' Herc leads a rebellion for the good guys. Take our word for it. Herc wins. (Dir: V. Scega, 95 mins.)

Fury of the Pagans (Italian, 1962) *½ Edmund Purdom, Rossana Podesta. Tribal chief battles the villainous rival who had slain his betrothed, finally challenges him to hand-to-hand combat. Usual type of imported spectacle dubbed in English, this time in Old Italy. Lots of action, no sense. (Dir: Guido Malatesta, 86 mins.)

Future Cop (1976)*½ Ernest Borgnine, Michael Shannon, John Amos. This unsold pilot follows the adventures of two cops on the beat—Borgnine as the old-timer and Shannon as the rookie. Uneven mix of comic and dramatic elements. Made-for-TV. (Dir: Jud Taylor, 72 mins.)

Futz (1969)*** Seth Allen, John Bakos, Mari-Claire Charba. You won't be seeing this far-out allegory on prime-time commercial TV. Ever wanted to see a film about an Appalachian farmer who likes making love to a pig? This is your only chance! It's director Tom O'Horgan's surrealistic vision of Rochelle Owens' award-winning Off-Broadway play. Grotesque, demanding, sometimes rewarding. A film for special tastes for cable TV audiences. "Futz" may be smuts to some. (Dir: Tom O'Horgan, 92 mins.)

Fuzz (1972)**½ Burt Reynolds, Yul Brynner, Raquel Welch. Uneven and scatterbrained police yarn which relies on the easygoing style and charm of Reynolds, as a police detective, and the under-played villainy of Brynner as a culprit with a penchant for bombings. Miss Welch is also on hand as a policewoman who has trouble getting the guys to treat her as just one of the fellas. The cops tend to play each situation for laughs but there are enough serious moments to satisfy crime-story fans. In the fine supporting cast, Tom Skerritt registers strongest as Reynolds' cop-buddy. (Dir: Richard Colla, 92 mins.)

Fuzzy Pink Nightgown, The (1957)** Jane Russell, Ralph Meeker, Keenan Wynn. Jane Russell, as a movie star with blonde hair, is kidnapped by two clumsy but nice guys and the fun begins. Good for a few chuckles. (Dir: Norman Taurog, 87 mins.)

FX 18, Secret Agent (French, 1964)* Ken Clark, Jany Clair. Agent is sent to investigate a spy ring, and the bodies begin to fall with a thud. Poor English-dubbed espionage thriller.

G-Men (1935)*** James Cagney, Lloyd Nolan. Exciting crime-busting story with Cagney on the side of the law for a change. (Dir: William Keighley, 85 mins.)

Gable and Lombard (1976)½ Jill Clayburgh, James Brolin, Red Buttons. A really bad picture about the love affair of the two great stars. It is not entirely the actors' fault—this is one of the worst scripts ever. It is inaccurate, shallow, slick, and totally lacking in real feeling. In fact, one sometimes gets the feeling that Jill Clayburgh and James Brolin might have been effective with decent material to work with. The

262

1930's clothes and cars function best. (Dir: Sidney J. Furie, 131 mins.)

Gaby (1956)**½ Leslie Caron, John Kerr. A somewhat weak remake of the romantic tale "Waterloo Bridge." The story is about a young soldier who falls in love with a ballerina before he's shipped to the front during WWII. Miss Caron is wistful in the title role but the melodramatic script doesn't help. (Dir: Curtis Bernhardt, 97 mins.)

Gaily, Gaily (1969)***½ Beau Bridges, Melina Mercouri, Brian Keith, George Kennedy, Margot Kidder, Wilfred Hyde-White, Hume Cronyn. Norman Jewison produced and directed this uneven but generally appealing comedy based on Ben Hecht's autobiographical reminiscences of his days as a youthful cub reporter on a Chicago paper. The period is 1910, and the corruption in Chicago is second to none when young bumpkin Ben Harvey, engagingly played by Beau Bridges, comes to town and lands at the jolliest bordello in town. Mercouri is well cast in another of her lovable madam roles and the rest of the supporting cast is good. Bridges is charming, conveying a quality of manly innocence and vulnerability. (Dir: Norman Jewison, 117 mins.)

Gal Who Took the West, The (1949)** Yvonne DeCarlo, Charles Coburn, Scott Brady. Amusing comedy-drama set in the wild and woolly west. Miss DeCarlo plays an entertainer who takes the Arizona frontier by storm. (Dir: Frederick de Cordova, 84 mins.)

Galileo (Great Britain-Canada, 1974)*** Topol, Edward Fox, John Gielgud, Clive Revill. Uneven but often absorbing version of Bertolt Brecht's stimulating play as adapted by, and earlier played on the stage by, Charles Laughton. Opens in 1609 in Padua with an impoverished Galileo seeking funds both to support his family and his scientific research, which scandalized the intellectual and political establishment of the time. Director Joseph Losey had wanted to direct this project for years, and rounded up an illustrious supporting cast with generally fine performances. But Topol playing Galileo is simply not an actor of enough range and power to play such a demanding role, and the film suffers finally because somehow the events of Galileo do not seem as important as they should. But there is enough of interest to hold thoughtful viewers. (Dir: Joseph Losey, 145 mins.)

Gallant Hours, The (1960)**½ James Cagney. Cagney's restrained performance as "Admiral Halsey" is a far cry from his raucous "Captain" in "Mr. Roberts," but it is the only worthwhile thing about this otherwise routine war film, based on actual events in the South Pacific Campaign during World War II. Robert Montgomery directed. (111 mins.)

Gallant Journey (1946)**½ Glenn Ford, Janet Blair. Biography of the man who contributed to aviation by experimenting with glider planes. Factual but not very exciting drama. (Dir: William Wellman, 85 mins.)

Gallant Lady (1934)*** Ann Harding, Clive Brook, Otto Kruger, Dickie Moore. Predictable but beguiling tale of a purposeful mother who contrives to regain her son born out of wedlock. Sentimental, though less so than was customary then, and stylish. (Dir: Gregory La Cava, 81 mins.)

Gallant Legion, The (1948)*** William Elliott, Adrian Booth, Bruce Cabot. Texas Ranger fights the leader of a powerful group desiring to split Texas into sections. Exciting western, well done.

Gallant Sons (1940)** Jackie Cooper, Bonita Granville. Good juvenile mystery for the kids as three youngsters turn detectives and solve a crime.

Galloping Major, The (British, 1951) *** Basil Radford, Jimmy Hanley. A retired major has his eye on a race horse, but when bidding time comes he buys a broken-down temperamental nag by mistake. This one gets very funny at times; one of the better comedies. (Dir: Henry Cornelius, 82 mins.)

Gambit (1966)*** Shirley MacLaine, Michael Caine. Shirley MacLaine as a Eurasian lady of intrigue, Michael Caine as an ambitious, but not very effective crook, and a jaunty story about a proposed theft of a valuable art treasure add up to fun. However, be forewarned, the plot fluctuates between subtle comedy, out-and-out spoofing, and serious business. With a little more care, this film could have been very good indeed but it's still entertaining as

is. Directed by Ronald Neame, it may remind you occasionally of some of Jules Dassin's spiffy crime films. (108 mins.)

Gambler, The (1974)*** James Caan, Paul Sorvino, Lauren Hutton. James Caan is very good in this story of a compulsive gambler who eventually gets what he seems to be striving for, humiliation and a brutal beating. Along the way, the educated college professor with the double life cons and uses everyone from his bewildered mother to a girl who cares for him. You can't help but feel exasperation as the antihero keeps taking risk after risk, never knowing when to call it quits. Director Karel Reisz keeps it all sharply in focus. (Dir: Karel Reisz, 111 mins.)

Gambler from Natchez, The (1954) ** Dale Robertson, Debra Paget. Adventurer goes after the varmint who killed his pa. Churns a well-worn path down that old celluloid river. (Dir: Henry Levin, 88 mins.)

Game for Three Losers (British, 1964)** Michael Gough, Mark Eden. Prominent politician becomes enmeshed in an extortion plot. Routine but competent crime melodrama.

Game of Danger (British, 1954)**½ Jack Warner, Veronica Hurst. Two little boys playing cops 'n' robbers accidentally kill a man. Out of the ordinary melodrama, but routine handling prevents it from being anything more. (Dir: Lance Comfort, 88 mins.)

Game of Death, A (1945)**½ John Loder, Audrey Long, Edgar Barrier. Big-game hunter is shipwrecked on an island owned by a madman who makes sport of hunting human prey. Exciting version of famous story, "The Most Dangerous Game"; thriller fans should like. (Dir: Robert Wise, 72 mins.)

Games (1967)*** Simone Signoret, Katharine Ross, James Caan. Offbeat, macabre drama which won't be everyone's cup of tea, but there certainly are novel and ghoulish plot turns along the way. The attractive Katharine Ross, who played Dustin Hoffman's young girlfriend in "The Graduate," is convincing playing a young wife, quite rightfully worried about her well being. Newcomer James Caan, playing her husband, is about as animated as a totem pole. Curtis Harrington directed from a story of his own creation. You've got to pay attention to this intellectual chiller-diller about a warped, rich young couple who indulge in way out "games" of a kind not condoned by civilized society. (100 mins.)

Games, The (Great Britain, 1969) **½ Ryan O'Neal, Michael Crawford, Charles Aznavour. Hugh Atkinson's novel "The Games," about the grueling preparation of long-distance runners preparing for the Olympic marathon race, makes an episodic drama enlivened by the great race itself at the end of the film. Erich ("Love Story") Segal, who is himself an enthusiastic and quite good marathon runner, wrote the screenplay. The character of Vendek, played by Aznavour, is clearly based on the great Czech long-distance runner, Emil Zatopek, who won this race in the 1950's. (Dir: Michael Winner, 96 mins.)

Gamma People, The (British, 1956) ** Paul Douglas, Eva Bartok. Moderate drama with science-fiction and political overtones concerning a gamma ray invention by which people are transformed into either geniuses or imbeciles. (Dir: John Gilling, 79 mins.)

Gammera the Invincible (U.S.-Japan, 1966)* Brian Donlevy, Albert Dekker, John Baragrey. Atomic explosion releases monster-sized turtle who terrorizes the world! Papier-mâché plot does not mask transparency of special effects. Baragrey, incidentally, a journeyman actor, was a much-seen performer in the early 50s during the period of "live" TV drama. (Dir: Noriaki Yuasi, 88 mins.)

Gang That Couldn't Shoot Straight, The (1971)½ Jerry Orbach, Leigh Taylor-Young, Jo Van Fleet, Robert De Niro, Lionel Stander. Ethnic humor at its most offensive. You don't have to be Italian to hate this strained adaptation of Jimmy Breslin's quite funny novel. The dimwits who comprise the mob are involved in assassinating a rival gang boss, broadly played by Lionel Stander. Only Robert De Niro as an emigrant who quickly adapts to the dishonest shenanigans emerges credibly. Badly directed by James Goldstone. (96 mins.)

Gang War (1958) **½ Charles Bronson, Kent Taylor. Teacher's wife is slain by hoodlums, he becomes a one-man vengeance committee. Good performances lift this from the gangster rut. (Dir: Gene Fowler, Jr., 75 mins.)

Gang's All Here, The (1943) **½ Alice Faye, Carmen Miranda. Routine musical but has a lifeless plot. You'll enjoy some of the musical numbers. (Dir: Busby Berkeley, 103 mins.)

Gangster, The (1947) *** Barry Sullivan, Belita, John Ireland. The leader of a mob lets his inner fear and insecurity get the best of him, loses his gang; is finally mowed down by a rival outfit. Interesting psychological study of a hoodlum, strong, well acted. (Dir: Gordon Wiles, 84 mins.)

Gangster Boss (French, 1961) ** Fernandel. Timid professor unwittingly carries a bag stuffed with money, becomes involved with criminals. Typical Fernandel comedy, with the horse-faced comedian supplying some mild chuckles. Dubbed in English. (Dir: Henri Verneuil, 100 mins.)

Gangster Story (1960)* Walter Matthau, Carol Grace. Notorious killer-robber tries to break away from a crime syndicate when he falls in love, but it's too late. A normally capable performer, Matthau also directed this trashy crime melodrama, presumably on a dare. Pretty bad. (Dir: Walter Matthau, 65 mins.)

Garden of Allah, The (1936) *** Marlene Dietrich, Charles Boyer. Seductive temptress has men at her feet, until she meets a man of destiny. Picturesque, opulent romantic drama; dated story, but plush production. (Dir: Richard Boleslawski, 90 mins.)

Garden of Evil (1954) **½ Gary Cooper, Susan Hayward, Richard Widmark. Sprawling western drama filmed on location in Mexico. Cooper is once more the quiet hero, Widmark the conniving villain, and Miss Hayward the tempestuous heroine. Plenty of action and a good musical background score. (Dir: Henry Hathaway, 100 mins.)

Garden of the Finzi Continis, The (Italy-West Germany, 1970) **** Dominique Sanda, Lino Capolicchio, Helmut Berger, Fabio Testi. The late director Vittorio De Sica's finest film since the post-war years is a melancholy, slowly-paced rendering of an aristocratic Jewish family's downfall in Mussolini's Italy. As patricians living in a walled estate, the family is impervious to the political events that will engulf them. The acting is flawless—Dominique Sanda's enigmatic portrayal of Micol, the eldest daughter involved in an affair with a gentile, and Helmut Berger's moving performance as her sickly brother, are the two standouts in a uniformly superb cast. De Sica directs in hazy colors which give an air of sentimentality, but in combining personal tragedy with the rising political fervor that will provide the "final solution," De Sica has achieved a rare subtlety. Based on Giorgio Bassani's autobiographical novel. (Dir: Vittorio De Sica, 95 mins.)

Gargoyles (1972)* Cornel Wilde. Laughs rather than thrills accompany this lousy "horror" film. Anthropologist Wilde faces legendary gargoyles, busy hatching 500-year-old eggs in the Carlsbad Caverns. Made-for-TV. (Dir: B. W. L. Norton, 74 mins.)

Garibaldi (Italian, 1961)** Renzo Ricci, Paolo Stoppa. Biography of patriotic Italian leader, soldier, and statesman who fought forces of oppression and saved the country. Elaborately produced, filmed by Roberto Rossellini, but quite lengthy, leisurely in movement. Dubbed in English.

Garment Jungle, The (1957)*** Lee J. Cobb, Kerwin Mathews, Gia Scala. Forceful drama about the control by the rackets of the garment industry in a big city. Performances are good with a standout bit by Robert Loggia as a brave union organizer who meets with opposition by the thugs. (Dir: Vincent Sherman, 88 mins.)

Gas-Oil (French, 1957)** Jean Gabin, Jeanne Moreau. A truck driver becomes involved in a killing, clears himself. The above rating is solely for the talents of the principal players, who don't deserve this tired old crime story. English-dubbed. Alternate title: **Hi-Jack Highway.**

Gaslight (1943)*** Charles Boyer, Ingrid Bergman, Joseph Cotten. Exciting psychological melodrama about a man who is trying to drive his wife to insanity. Not as good as the Broadway hit "Angel Street" but still good entertainment. (Dir: George Cukor, 114 mins.)

Gaslight Follies (1945)** Nostalgic roundup of films of yesteryear includes glimpses of such luminaries as Mary Pickford, Tom Mix, Chaplin, etc. As well as some old newsreel clips. Narrated by Milton Cross. Passable as a novelty. This was the first production effort of Joe ("Hercules") Levine, who's gone on to bigger and richer productions. (Dir: Joseph E. Levine, 110 mins.)

Gas-s-s. . . . Or It May Be Necessary to Destroy The World In Order to Save It! (1970)**½ Robert Corff, Elaine Giftos, Ben Vereen, Bud Cort, Cindy Williams, Talia Coppola. Some effective scenes in this end-of-the-world youth survival tale, that had a cult following for a while at the time of its release. Country Joe and the Fish supply most of the music. The screenplay, written by George Armitage, tries to be hip and cool! Story line about a defense plant in Alaska which springs a gas main, and everyone over their twenties perishes. Survivors have some spacey experiences back in the U.S. of A. Director Roger Corman has elicited deft performances from a number of troupers who went on to achieve substantial recognition later. Note Talia "Rocky" Shire playing Coralie, and still using the name Coppola. (Dir: Roger Corman, 79 mins.)

Gate of Hell (Japanese, 1954)***½ Machiko Kyo, Kazuo Hasegawa. A treat for color TV sets! Pictorially beautiful, exotic drama of 12th Century Japan and of a good soldier's love for a married woman that ends in tragedy. While the story and performances are interesting and unusual in themselves, it is the color photography and the settings commanding major attention. (Dir: Teinosuke Kinugasa, 89 mins.)

Gates of Paris (French, 1957)***½ Pierre Brasseur, Henri Vidal. Loafer hides a hunted criminal. Beautiful performances and fine direction of Rene Clair make this comedy drama a standout import that packs a wallop in its own quiet way. (103 mins.)

Gathering of Eagles, A (1963)**½ Rock Hudson, Mary Peach, Rod Taylor. It's the Strategic Air Command this time, with the stern officer whose devotion to duty causes complications in his home life. Some fine aerial camerawork and good performances, along with a story that suffers from slowness when it's on the ground. (Dir: Delbert Mann, 115 mins.)

Gay Deceivers, The (1969)* Kevin Coughlin, Larry Casey, Brooke Bundy. Someday someone may make a funny film about two "straight" guys posing as homosexuals in order to avoid the draft—but this isn't it. The pace, dialogue and performances are too obvious, and go for and don't get laughs at every turn. The scenes of "gay" life in California may cause some to be slightly shocked but it's actually a cheap try to expose the "gay" set for comedy purposes.

Gay Divorcee (1934)**** Ginger Rogers, Fred Astaire. Love-sick dancer pursues his light-o-love until she gives in. Fine musical, one of the best. (Dir: Mark Sandrich, 107 mins.)

Gay Lady (British, 1949)*** Jean Kent, James Donald. A music hall entertainer makes the grade when she marries a young duke. Pleasant turn-of-the-century romance, well acted. (Dir: Brian Desmond Hurst, 91 mins.)

Gay Purr-ee (1962)**½ Pleasant animated cartoon about a pussycat who goes to Paris, is saved from the villain, etc. Voices of Judy Garland and Robert Goulet and the songs of Harold Arlen are assets; there are some cute moments, for the younger set. (Dir: Abe Levitow, 86 mins.)

Gay Sisters (1942)** Barbara Stanwyck, George Brent. Long, dull, tiresome melodrama about one of Hollywood's favorite topics, the bad apple in a fine family. (Dir: Irving Rapper, 108 mins.)

Gazebo, The (1959)*** Glenn Ford, Debbie Reynolds, Carl Reiner, John McGiver. When a TV mystery writer is blackmailed, he decides on murder as the way out, takes a shot at a shadowy figure in his home, later discovers the real blackmailer has been murdered—so who did he kill? Whacky comedy gets the laughs—Ford works hard, and there's an adroit performance by McGiver. (Dir: George Marshall, 100 mins.)

Geisha Boy, The (1958)**½ Jerry Lewis, Marie McDonald, Suzanne Pleshette. Jerry as an inept magician who joins a USO unit touring the Orient works mightily to produce some laughs in this comedy and succeeds to a fair degree. Some clever gags stand out, while the film has nice visual backgrounds. (Dir: Frank Tashlin, 98 mins.)

Gemini Man (1976)* Ben Murphy, Katherine Crawford, Richard Dysart, Dana Elcar. This TV series pilot was NBC's second try at the invisible-man gimmick after the first version, starring David McCallum, failed. Ben Murphy is the special agent for a think-tank outfit, who can disappear at will. Boring! Made-for-TV. (Dir: Alan Levi, 98 mins.)

Gene Krupa Story, The (1960)** Sal Mineo, Susan Kohner, James Darren. Corny, highly fictionalized account of the rise to fame by drummer Gene Krupa. One of the worst scenes is a bit of hokum which describes how Krupa got in with a fast crowd and started smoking marijuana. The casting of Sal Mineo as Krupa is another stroke of idiocy. (Dir: Don Weis, 101 mins.)

General Della Rovere (Italian, 1960) ***½ Vittorio De Sica, Hannes Messmer. Rewarding though lengthy tale of a petty swindler who impersonates an Italian military officer, and in doing so becomes a hero. Excellent acting by De Sica. The plot rambles a bit too much, but holds interest for the most part. English-dubbed. (Dir: Roberto Rossellini, 129 mins.)

General Died at Dawn, The (1936) ***½ Gary Cooper, Madeleine Carroll, Akim Tamiroff. Exciting adventure story. An American soldier of fortune in China tries to save a community from a cruel war lord. (Dir: Lewis Milestone, 100 mins.)

Generation (1969)** David Janssen, Kim Darby, Carl Reiner. Unsuccessful filming of the moderately entertaining play about the relationship between a rebellious young couple and her establishment father. Henry Fonda gave a fine, low-key performance on stage, but David Janssen seems totally out of touch with the role, a dogmatic dad determined to have his pregnant daughter deliver his grandchild as he sees fit. Even Kim Darby's usually beguiling manner gets tiresome here. (Dir: George Schaefer, 104 mins.)

Genesis II (1973)**½ Alex Cord. Fans of Gene Roddenberry's imaginative science-fiction series "Star Trek" might enjoy this science-fiction film. Alex Cord stars as a 20th-century space scientist who is discovered almost two centuries later in a natural catastrophe. Sci-fi hocus-pocus, served up with a straight face as warring tribes seek to pick the scientist's brain. Made-for-TV. (Dir: John Llewellyn Moxey, 97 mins.)

Genevieve (British, 1953)****** John Gregson, Kenneth More, Dinah Sheridan, Kay Kendall. A divinely funny romp about two English couples who are old-car buffs and enter their trophies in a cross-country race. In addition to the glories of the old four-wheeled beauties, a large number of which were collected for this race, you also see Kay Kendall, who was not only sublimely pretty but also a high comedy farceur of enormous skill. There are numerous delicious sequences in this consistently inventive comedy and if you don't enjoy it immensely you should have your sense of humor checked under Medicare. (Dir: Henry Cornelius, 86 mins.)

Genghis Khan (Philippine, 1953)*** Manuel Conde, Elvira Reyes. A Mongol tribesman rises to be a powerful ruler by overcoming all opposition. Unusual novelty offering has plenty of well-staged action scenes to compensate for some technical weaknesses.

Genghis Khan (1965)** Omar Sharif, Stephen Boyd, James Mason, Eli Wallach. Mongol youth grows up to be the mighty Genghis Khan, seeking vengeance upon the rival chieftain who killed his father. Large-scale spectacle has the action, but the story and acting are little better than the usual for this type of film. (Dir: Henry Levin, 124 mins.)

Gentle Annie (1944) **½ James Craig, Donna Reed, Marjorie Main. Entertaining little western with Miss Main playing the part of a lovable train robber. Based on a MacKinlay Kantor novel, this offers slightly different types of bad men. (Dir: Andrew Martin, 80 mins.)

Gentle Art of Murder, The—See: Crime Does Not Pay

Gentle Giant (1967)**½ Dennis Weaver, Vera Miles, Ralph Meeker, Clint Howard, Huntz Hall. Youngsters may go for this uncomplicated tale of a boy and a bear which led to the TV series "Gentle Ben." Adults may sit through it without flinching. (Dir: James Neilson, 93 mins.)

Gentle Gunman, The (British, 1952) *** John Mills, Dirk Bogarde. A gunman for the Irish rebels believes in more peaceful means for obtaining their goal. Good melodrama. (Dir: Basil Dearden, 86 mins.)

Gentle Rain, The (U.S.-Brazil, 1966) *½ Christopher George, Lynda Day, Fay Spain. Two social outcasts, a frigid upper-class girl and a disturbed mute architect, meet in Rio de Janeiro and fall in love. Awkwardly done and mawkish. (Dir: Burt Balaban, 94 mins.)

Gentle Sex, The (British, 1943)**½ Lilli Palmer, Jean Gillie. Dramatic story of women in wartime in Britain doing their bit for the eventual victory. Nicely done, some good moments.

Gentleman after Dark, A (1942)*½ Brian Donlevy, Miriam Hopkins, Preston Foster. A reformed thief struggles to bring up his daughter properly, despite the efforts of his wife. Sentimental, old-hat drama, hammily acted. (Dir: Edward L. Marin, 77 mins.)

Gentleman at Heart, A (1942)**½ Cesar Romero, Carole Landis, Milton Berle. Fairly amusing comedy about a racketeer who goes into the art business. Berle and Romero are partners in crime and when the material is passable, they'll make you laugh. (Dir: Ray McCarey, 66 mins.)

Gentleman Jim (1942)***½ Errol Flynn, Jack Carson, Alexis Smith. Errol took time out from winning the war to play Jim Corbett in this exciting biography of the suave boxer which also presents an interesting panorama of boxing's early years as an outlawed sport. (Dir: Raoul Walsh, 104 mins.)

Gentlemen Marry Brunettes (1955) **½ Jane Russell, Jeanne Crain. Beautiful sisters on the loose in Paris is the inviting theme of this dull musical. The girls are fun to look at, but the picture doesn't match their charms. (Dir: Richard Sale, 97 mins.)

Gentlemen of the Night (1963)*½ Guy Madison, Lisa Gastoni. Italian-made, English-dubbed epic about Venetian intrigue during the revolt against the Doge. Guy Madison has made a series of this type of action film and seems at home in them.

Gentlemen Prefer Blondes (1953)*** Marilyn Monroe, Jane Russell,

Charles Coburn. An elaborate, updated screen version of the popular B'dway musical about 2 show business beauties on the prowl enroute to Paris. Miss Monroe is well cast as the blonde bombshell who really believes "diamonds are a girl's best friend" and Jane Russell is also around for decorative purposes. The two stars sing many songs of the "bumps and grind" variety and there's a fine comedy assist by Charles Coburn. (Dir: Howard Hawks, 91 mins.)

Gentlemen's Agreement (1947)******** Gregory Peck, Dorothy McGuire, John Garfield. Laura Hobson's brilliant novel becomes a screen masterpiece. Story of a writer who poses as a Jew to find out what it feels like to be a Jew in a Christian world packs an emotional punch you'll not soon forget. (Dir: Elia Kazan, 118 mins.)

George Raft Story, The (1961)****½** Ray Danton, Julie London, Jayne Mansfield. Biography of the screen badman, his rise from hoofer to movie star. Not as bad as might be expected; doesn't stick too close to facts, but Danton delivers well in the title role, while the story is continually attention-holding. (Dir: Joseph M. Newman, 106 mins.)

George Washington Slept Here (1942) ******* Jack Benny, Ann Sheridan. Jack has fun in this screen adaptation of the Broadway hit about a city dwelling family which buys a Pennsylvania farmhouse—not in Gettysburg. Ending is weary but there's a lot of fun before it. (Dir: William Keighley, 93 mins.)

Georgy Girl (1966)******** Lynn Redgrave, Alan Bates, James Mason. A very touching, charming, and thoroughly entertaining comedy-drama with top-notch characterizations played superbly by the cast. Lynn Redgrave, in the title role of the frumpy British lass who's satisfied with living life vicariously with her swinging London roommate, is quite marvelous and deeply moving. Many things happen to Georgy before she makes a final compromise. Sensitive direction by Silvio Narizzano. Miss Redgrave makes her first starring role a memorable one, that richly deserved all the honors it received, and a few that she didn't receive as well. (100 mins.)

Geronimo (1940)****** Preston Foster,

Ellen Drew. The kids may like this childish dramatization of the white man's scrapes with the Apaches, but it's not particularly good for a top budget western. (Dir: Paul H. Sloane, 89 mins.)

Gervaise (French, 1957)******* Maria Schell, Francois Perier. Zola's tale of a woman's misfortunes as she tries to provide for her family, care for her alcoholic husband. Excellent performances, direction. English-dubbed. (Dir: Rene Clement, 116 mins.)

Get Carter (British, 1971)******* Michael Caine, Britt Ekland, Ian Hendry. British gangster film set in the north of England in the '70's. The inspiration is Hollywood 1940's. Compelling entry written and directed by English TV director Michael Hodges, making a promising switch to the big screen. Caine is a cheap hood who returns home to investigate his brother's death. One of Caine's best performances, and Hodges captures the dreary quality of life in the industrial towns. (111 mins.)

Get Christie Love! (1974)****½** Teresa Graves, Harry Guardino. Even TV films get remade. Here's a reworking of an earlier pilot ("Bait") about a lady special investigator dedicated to her job. The sexy and resourceful police detective is played by Miss Graves. The plot keeps her busy, her major target being a large drug-dealing operation connected with the underworld. (Dir: William Graham.)

Get Out of Town (1959)***½** Douglas Wilson, Jeanne Baird. Man comes to town determined to avenge the death of his brother, which was claimed to be an accident. Crime melodrama is cheaply produced, has some good unknown players battling a losing script. (Dir: Charles Davis, 62 mins.)

Get Yourself a College Girl (1964)½ Mary Ann Mobley, Chad Everett, Nancy Sinatra, Stan Getz. Thin plot has Miss Mobley facing expulsion for writing some sexy songs. Story is periodically interrupted by dated, badly dubbed-in tunes from the Animals, the Dave Clark Five, and Stan Getz. Junk. (Dir: Sidney Miller, 87 mins.)

Getaway, The (1972)****½** Steve McQueen, Ali MacGraw, Ben Johnson, Sally Struthers. Bank robbers, shotguns, beauty, all slowed down, distorted, and re-sorted by director Sam Peckinpah to smash out a brand of adventurous excitement that is commercially successful. McQueen and MacGraw look so fine together that we can easily ignore their "roles" as an ex-con and his wife frolicking through money and cops. MacGraw's acting is nonexistent. In a fine, excruciatingly explicit moment, McQueen levels a police car with a shotgun—slowly, with impact—Peckinpah-style. (122 mins.)

Getting Away from It All (1972)** Larry Hagman, Barbara Feldon, Gary Collins, E. J. Peaker. Light-hearted comedy about two New York couples who buy a small island in Maine. Thanks to Hagman's charm, and bits by town justice Burgess Meredith and Paul Hartman, the movie bounces along, overcoming the slight story line. Made-for-TV. (Dir: Lee Philips.)

Getting Gertie's Garter (1945)**½ The efforts of Dennis O'Keefe to retrieve a garter from Marie McDonald that would get him in trouble with sweetie Sheila Ryan. Comedy has many good chuckles. (Dir: Allan Dwan, 72 mins.)

Getting Straight (1970)** Elliott Gould, Candice Bergen, Robert F. Lyons. Hippiedom alienation at its shallowest except when Gould, as Harry Baily—an ex-vet finishing his master's in education—asserts himself. Baily, trying to tiptoe between the administration and radical students at Everywhere University, succeeds only in reducing deeply felt principles to melodramatic pap. The campus riot is perverse in its slapstick appearance with police looking like Keystone cops and the students throwing pies. The script and Gould take hold only once, at Harry's oral exam where obscene limericks meet a professor's claim that F. Scott Fitzgerald was a homosexual. Oh, and Candice Bergen is quite beautiful. (Dir: Richard Rush, 124 mins.)

Geundalina (Italian, 1957)**½ Jacqueline Sassard. A teenager is awakened to life and love. Diverting little drama.

Ghidrah, The Three-Headed Monster (Japanese, 1965)*½ Each Nippon-produced science-fiction thriller seems more ridiculous than the last.

This time, a triple-domed destroyer from another planet meets its match. Special effects are okay. (Dir: Inoshiro Honda, 85 mins.)

Ghost and Mr. Chicken, The (1966) ** Don Knotts, Joan Staley. Typesetter who wants to be a reporter stumbles into a murder case. As a vehicle for Knotts, this comedy should please his fans; for others, it's pretty silly. (Dir: Alan Rafkin, 90 mins.)

Ghost and Mrs. Muir, The (1947)*** Rex Harrison, Gene Tierney. Comedy about a widow's friendship with the ghost of a sea captain has charm and humor, but fails to sustain an entire film. (Dir: Joseph L. Mankiewicz, 104 mins.)

Ghost Breakers (1940)*** Bob Hope, Paulette Goddard. Good Hope comedy, which combines chills with laughs. Bob goes along to Cuba to help Paulette claim a haunted castle. (Dir: George Marshall, 82 mins.)

Ghost Catchers (1944)**½ Olsen and Johnson, Gloria Jean. Ole and Chic run a night club next door to a house hired by a southern colonel in town to produce a show, and the house is said to be haunted. Entertaining zany comedy-mystery. (Dir: Edward F. Cline, 67 mins.)

Ghost Goes West, The (British, 1935) ***½ Robert Donat, Jean Parker. The spirit of a Scottish rogue returns to modern times to help a young member of the family. Charming fantasy-comedy, written by Robert E. Sherwood, directed by Rene Clair. (100 mins.)

Ghost in the Invisible Bikini (1966) *½ Tommy Kirk, Deborah Walley, Susan Hart. A ridiculous combination of horror stories and scantily clad beauties. It's intended as a spoof, but the laughs come few and far between. (Dir: Don Weis, 82 mins.)

Ghost of Cypress Swamp, The (1977) **½ Vic Morrow, Jeff East. The Disney camp's first made-for-TV effort. Expertly utilizes all the ingredients which make the Disney features a family affair. Young Lenny, played by Jeff East, tracks a wounded black panther through the interior of the forbidden Great Cypress Swamp and finds a hermit. Made-for-TV. (Dir: Vincent McEveety, 106 mins.)

Ghost Ship (1943)*** Richard Dix,

Russell Wade. A mad sea captain makes life unbearable for his crew. Brutally violent, but extremely well done film; fine performances.

Ghosts—Italian Style (1969)** Sophia Loren, Vittorio Gassman, Mario Adorf. Loren and Gassman, two very capable actors who can switch from comedy to drama, fail to ignite this silly, empty Italian farce about a married couple down on their luck who move into a cavernous palazzo at the request of the owner to dispel the rumors that the place is haunted. The supporting cast consists of a leering old man and a colorful prostitute, and alas, they're more interesting than the stars. (Dir: Renato Castellani, 92 mins.)

Ghosts of Rome (Italian, 1961)*** Marcello Mastroianni, Sandro Milo, Vittorio Gassman. Spirits "living" in an old house with an eccentric prince seek to right things when the old boy dies and the house is to be sold by his nephew. Fantasy has a fine cast in its favor, although the whimsy becomes a bit repetitious after awhile. Dubbed in English. (Dir: Antonio Pietrangeli, 105 mins.)

GI Blues (1960)**½ Elvis Presley, Juliet Prowse. Tank sergeant becomes the number-one contender to break down the resistance of an iceberg night-club dancer. Pleasant Presley musical should satisfy his fans, while others should find some fun along the way. (Dir: Norman Taurog, 104 mins.)

Giant (1956)***½ Elizabeth Taylor, Rock Hudson, James Dean. Sprawling epic detailing the growth of the Texas cattle and oil empires of two fascinating men—Rock Hudson and James Dean—and their mutual love for the beautiful Elizabeth Taylor. George Stevens has directed this large-scale drama, based on Edna Ferber's novel, with a sure hand and he evokes a sense of the people who struck it rich in Texas. The personal drama and love stories are kept in check and sentiment is kept at a minimum. Dean is seen to good advantage. (198 mins.)

Giant Behemoth, The (British, 1959)** Gene Evans, Andre Morell. Another prehistoric monster epic and again it rises from the sea and flips its giant lid before it is itself destroyed. Par for the course. (Dir: Eugene Lourie, 80 mins.)

Giant From the Unknown (1958)** Buddy Baer, Sally Fraser. Low-budget shocker with few surprises. Superstitious Spanish villagers think a spirit from the past is seeking revenge and thereby hangs the yarn.

Giant of Metropolis, The (Italian, 1962)*½ Gordon Mitchell, Bella Cortez. Muscleman is subjected to tests by a mad king so that he may become the first immortal man. Futuristic combination sci-fi and spectacle really reaches for a plot. Kids may dig the serial-type technique. Dubbed in English. (Dir: Umberto Scarpelli, 82 mins.)

Giant of the Evil Island (Italian, 1964)* Rock Stevens, Dina De Santis. Pirate plundering Spanish ships meets his match in a brave galleon commander. Dull swashbuckler, dubbed in English.

Gideon of Scotland Yard (British, 1959)*** Jack Hawkins. Police inspector has a multitude of assorted crimes on his hands, all part of police routine. Done in leisurely John Ford style, a pleasing addition to the ranks of genteel crime stories. Hawkins is very English and very good. (91 mins.)

Gidget (1959)** Sandra Dee, Cliff Robertson. The original in the "Gidget" films—strictly for the teen set. Miss Dee is pert and Robertson is wasted. (Dir: Paul Wendkos, 95 mins.)

Gidget Gets Married (1971)*½ Monie Ellis, Michael Burns, Don Ameche. For all those who have followed the adventures of teen-heroine Gidget, here's the ultimate adventure—Gidget is led down the aisle to the waiting arms of her long-time boyfriend. Now all we have to look forward to is "Gidget Has a Baby" or, perish the thought, "Gidget Gets Divorced." Made-for-TV. (Dir: James Sheldon, 72 mins.)

Gidget Goes Hawaiian (1961)** Deborah Walley, James Darren, Michael Callan, Carl Reiner. Further adventures of the little surfer—this time she's on a vacation in Hawaii and pursued by a brash young TV performer. Cute for the teenagers; adults know what to expect. (Dir: Paul Wendkos, 102 mins.)

Gidget Goes to Rome (1963)** Cindy Carol, James Darren. The teenager does as it says in the title, gets involved in some romantic complications. Comedy mainly for the pre-adult set; others can look at the scenery. (Dir: Paul Wendkos, 101 mins.)

Gidget Grows Up (1969)**½ Karen Valentine, Robert Cummings, Edward Mulhare. Gidget just keeps going on and on! A made-for-TV feature which shows the all-American teenager grown up, having an innocent affair with an older man (Mulhare). Karen Valentine supplies the energy for Gidget but the script doesn't help her much. The best thing about the film is a high-camp performance by Paul Lynde as a Greenwich Village landlord whose avocation is the films of the thirties. (Dir: James Sheldon, 75 mins.)

Gift for Heidi, A (1959)*½ Sandy Descher, Douglas Fowley. Based on the characters created by Johanna Spyri, further adventures of the little Swiss girl in the mountains. Mawkish and dull, a gift only for the very young.

Gift of Love (1958)** Lauren Bacall, Robert Stack, Evelyn Rudie. A remake of the four-handkerchiefer "Sentimental Journey." Unlike its predecessor, this version doesn't even come up with a hit tune. Overly sentimental and sticky plot concerns a childless couple who adopt a strange little girl. Pure soap opera that should appeal to the ladies—gentlemen, beware! (Dir: Jean Negulesco, 105 mins.)

Gigantis, the Fire Monster (1959)** Japanese made science-fiction saga about two giant, prehistoric monsters who try to gobble the world. The kids may find it exciting. (78 mins.)

Gigi (1958)**** Leslie Caron, Louis Jourdan, Maurice Chevalier, Hermione Gingold. Lerner and Loewe's sumptious original musical for the screen is a complete delight—a feast for your eyes and ears. Louis Jourdan is the epitome of the French man-about-town who suddenly realizes that little Gigi (beautifully played by Leslie Caron) has grown up into a lovely young lady. Maurice Chevalier is perfectly cast as Gigi's guardian and the musical numbers are brilliantly staged. Musical numbers include "Thank Heaven For Little Girls." Elegantly directed by Vincente Minnelli. (116 mins.)

Gigot (1962)**½ Jackie Gleason, Katherine Kath. A somewhat moving performance by Jackie Gleason as a Chaplinesque mute in Paris who becomes the protector of a French streetwalker and her little daughter, is the best feature of this maudlin entry. The plot is steeped in obvious attempts to tug at your heart, and only about half of it works. Gene Kelly directed with a wavering hand. (104 mins.)

Gilda (1946)**½ Rita Hayworth, Glenn Ford. Gambler meets the new wife of his boss, and it turns out to be the gal he once loved. This one was big stuff when it first came out, with the Hayworth-Ford combination very successful. It may still be, but it doesn't hide the fact this is merely a routine melodrama, not particularly well done. (Dir: Charles Vidor, 110 mins.)

Gilded Lily, The (1935)*** Claudette Colbert, Fred MacMurray, Ray Milland. Amusing romantic comedy about a girl who achieves fame and notoriety by turning down a titled suitor. Fred came into his own with this one. (Dir: Wesley Ruggles, 90 mins.)

Gimme Shelter (1970)**** Mick Jagger, Charlie Watts, Melvin Belli. A stunning documentary by Albert and David Maysles about the rock star Mick Jagger and his Rolling Stones group, including the climactic concert in December 1969 at Altamont which wound up with an on-camera real-life knife slaying. The final concert took place at the Altamont Speedway in California before a crowd of 300,000. There are lots of bad vibes captured by the cinema verite-style filmmakers coming from the huge throng responding to Jagger's bisexual performing style, and the feeling of spiritual and emotional malignancy is pervasive. Disturbing, powerful essay on one aspect of the rock and drug culture at the end of the 1960's. (Dirs: David Maysles, Albert Maysles, and Charlotte Swerin, 91 mins.)

Gina (French, 1959)** Simone Signoret, Charles Vanel. Six ill-assorted seekers of a lost diamond mine face the jungle and greed. Grim, unpleasant drama, although it's well acted. Dubbed in English.

Ginger in the Morning (1973)*½ Monte Markham, Sissy Spacek, Susan Oliver. After the break-up of his marriage, an advertising executive falls in love with a young hitchhiker. Chaotic melodrama. (Dir: Gordon Wiles, 93 mins.)

Girl, a Guy and a Gob, A (1941)**★★★** Lucille Ball, Edmond O'Brien, George Murphy. Secretary is in love with her boss, but is engaged to a sailor. Cute comedy produced by Harold Lloyd, has some good laughs. (Dir: Richard Jones, 91 mins.)

Girl Against Napoleon, A (Spanish, 1960)**★★** Sarita Montiel. A mixture of historical misinformation and adventure served up for the action fan. Miss Montiel is a looker and makes the viewing palatable. English-dubbed.

Girl and the Legend, The (German, 1962)**★★** Romy Schneider, Horst Buchholz. Author of the famous "Robinson Crusoe" helps to make some youths happy before his death. Slow-moving, rather saccharine costume drama dubbed in English.

Girl and the Palio, The (Italy, 1958)**★★½** Diana Dors, Vittorio Gassman. American girl wins trip to Italy, and the romantic adventures begin. Played against background pageantry of the colorful Sienese "Palio," a traditional, biennial horse race, film offers a fast-paced plot, plenty of excitement. Alternate title: "The Love Specialist." (Dir: Luigi Zampa, 104 mins.)

Girl Can't Help It, The (1956)**★★½** Tom Ewell, Joyce Mansfield, Edmond O'Brien. An amusing and often quite funny comedy about an average press agent (Ewell) and his association with a mobster and his singer-girl friend. Some songs help to spark the proceedings and Ewell's expert clowning adds greatly. (Dir: Frank Tashlin, 99 mins.)

Girl Crazy (1943)**★★★½** Mickey Rooney, Judy Garland, June Allyson, Nancy Walker. Mickey and Judy have it all to themselves and they make the Gershwin score a pure delight. Story of the rich young Easterner whose dad exiles him to a small school out west, never gets in the way of the Rooney-Garland talent. (Dir: Norman Taurog, 99 mins.)

Girl from Flanders, The (German, 1963)**★★** Nicole Berger, Maximilian Schell. Orphan girl is wrongly accused of stealing arms during World War I, escapes to work in a night club, is finally rescued by a soldier. Leisurely, rather mild drama dubbed in English—some good detail, performances help it.

Girl From Hong Kong, The (German, 1963)**★½** Akiko, Helmut Greim. Red China refugee working as a dance-hall girl falls for a sailor. Boy meets-loses-gets girl drama with a "Suzie Wong" background, not a palatable mixture. Dubbed in English.

Girl from Jones Beach (1949)**★★½** Virginia Mayo, Eddie Bracken, Ronald Reagan. Mild comedy about an artist's amusing search for the perfect female model. Miss Mayo in a bathing suit is certainly a worth-while attraction for male viewers. (Dir: Peter Godfrey, 78 mins.)

Girl from Missouri, The (1933)**★★½** Jean Harlow, Lionel Barrymore. Cute, harmless comedy about a young lady from Missouri who by use of her physical assets achieves success in the big city. (Dir: Jack Conway, 80 mins.)

Girl from Petrovka (1974)**★½** Goldie Hawn, Hal Holbrook, Anthony Hopkins. Goldie's never convinced me that she's a Russian girl living by her wits without working papers, but American-newspaperman Holbrook must know something that the rest of us don't know because he falls in love with Hawn. There isn't much for the rest of us to love in this clumsy, bittersweet romance which says—surprise! surprise! (and just about as wittily)—that capitalism is much better than communism. Based on the book by George Feifer. (Dir: Robert Ellis Miller, 104 mins.)

Girl-Getters, The (British, 1964)**★★★** Oliver Reed, Jane Merrow. Girl-chasing photographer has phenomenal success in his conquests, but the tables are turned when he meets a glamor girl one summer. Well-done drama of life and love among the younger set. Thick dialect may cause some confusion, but performances are very good, the story interesting. (Dir: Michael Winner, 79 mins.)

Girl Happy (1965)**★★** Elvis Presley, Shelley Fabares. Typical Presley film for his fans. Elvis is a night-club entertainer who finds love in Fort Lauderdale during those raucous college Easter vacations. For the record, there are twelve songs delivered by Elvis and cast. (Dir: Boris Sagal, 96 mins.)

Girl He Left Behind (1956)**★★** Tab Hunter, Natalie Wood, Jim Backus. Silly comedy about a young boy who is drafted into the peacetime army. The events depicted are artificial and what's worse, not very funny. Natalie Wood, as the girl in the title, also gets left behind when it comes to a part. (Dir: David Butler, 103 mins.)

Girl Hunters, The (British, 1963)** Mickey Spillane, Shirley Eaton, Lloyd Nolan. Mike Hammer beats his way through assorted mayhem while trying to locate his missing secretary. Unique in a trashy sort of way—Spillane plays his own fictional creation, not too badly; British-made American backgrounds are accurate; when it comes, the action is fast and bloody. (Dir: Roy Rowland, 103 mins.)

Girl in Black Stockings, The (1957) **½ Anne Bancroft, Mamie Van Doren, Lex Barker. Some gorgeous suspects in a double murder. Passable whodunit, with nicely filled stockings. (Dir: Howard W. Koch, 73 mins.)

Girl in Every Port, A (1952)** Groucho Marx, William Bendix, Marie Wilson. Navy pals acquire two race horses and try to conceal them on board ship. Tame comedy isn't what one would expect of the talent involved. (Dir: Chester Erskine, 86 mins.)

Girl in His Pocket (1958)** Jean Marais, Genevieve Page. A wacky French language film about a handsome scientist whose experiments lead to wild results—he concocts a solution which reduces people to 3" in size. More silly than funny. (Dir: Pierre Kast, 82 mins.)

Girl in Lovers Lane, The (1960)* Joyce Meadows, Brett Halsey. Youngster on the loose spurns a local belle, later is accused of her murder. Cheap, lurid melodrama.

Girl in Room 13, The (1960)*½ Brian Donlevy, Andrea Bayard. Private eye in Brazil searching for a girl murder suspect runs into a ring of counterfeiters. Mediocre melodrama, the location photography the sole asset. (Dir: Richard Cunha, 97 mins.)

Girl in the Bikini, The (French, 1952) *½ Brigitte Bardot, Jean-Francois Calvé. Lighthousekeeper's daughter aids a student searching for treasure. BB's physique is the only excuse for watching this tedious melodrama dubbed in English. One of her early efforts, she has little to do.

Girl in the Kremlin, The (1957)*½ Lex Barker, Zsa Zsa Gabor. Into darkest Communist Russia with an ex-OSS agent who learns of a plot to overthrow Stalin. History has taken the edge off this espionage drama, which wasn't any great shakes anyway. (Dir: Russell Birdwell, 81 mins.)

Girl in the Painting, The (British, 1948)*** Mai Zetterling, Guy Rolfe, Robert Beatty. Army major runs into a spy plot when he tries to help a girl regain her memory. Good melodrama. (Dir: Terence Fisher, 89 mins.)

Girl in the Red Velvet Swing, The (1955)**½ Ray Milland, Joan Collins, Farley Granger. One of the most sensational murders of the early 1900's was millionaire Harry K. Thaw's killing of famed architect Stanford White over his wife Evelyn Nesbitt Thaw. Their story is brought to the screen in an elaborate production and a good cast who do very nicely despite the soap opera overtones of the script. (Dir: Richard Fleischer, 109 mins.)

Girl in White (1952)** June Allyson, Gary Merrill, Arthur Kennedy. A soap opera about one of the first women doctors to invade a man's world. Miss Allyson weeps, smiles, and looks bewildered throughout the "sudsy" drama. (Dir: John Sturges, 93 mins.)

Girl Most Likely, The (1957)*** Jane Powell, Cliff Robertson, Kaye Ballard. Girl has a tough time choosing her dream man, for she has three from which to choose. Musical version of a successful Ginger Rogers film ("Tom, Dick and Harry") is helped considerably by ingenious production numbers staged by Gower Champion. Good entertainment. (Dir: Mitchell Leisen, 98 mins.)

Girl Most Likely to . . . The (1973) **½ Stockard Channing, Edward Asner, Joe Flynn, Jim Backus, Chuck McCann. Bizarre comedy about a homely, dumpy college girl who is transformed into a lovely, sexy dish after a car accident and plastic surgery. The twist here is the new Miriam harbors the old Miriam's hate and goes about seeking revenge in no uncertain terms. Talented Miss Channing has a plum leading role, and the makeup men responsible for Miriam's "before-and-after transformation" deserve

273

a special nod. Comic Joan Rivers, with an assist from Agnes Gallin, wrote the script. Made-for-TV. (Dir: Lee Philips, 74 mins.)

Girl Named Sooner, A (1975)*** Cloris Leachman, Richard Crenna, Lee Remick, Susan Deer. Cloris Leachman is superb as a mean, unwashed, brittle, shabby, old and shrewd hill-country woman, knowing where a dollar can be turned from her illegally made whiskey. Concerns her neglected, mistreated 8-year-old granddaughter (Sooner), but it's Cloris who dominates, with her plan to disown the child in exchange for a government handout. Made-for-TV. (Dir: Delbert Mann, 98 mins.)

Girl Named Tamiko, A (1962)**½ Laurence Harvey, France Nuyen. Moderately interesting drama which has Harvey playing a Eurasian who is a bitter expatriate from Tokyo eager to gain admission to the United States. Harvey is good but he gets little help from the script. (Dir: John Sturges, 110 mins.)

Girl Next Door, The (1953)** Dan Dailey, June Haver, Dennis Day. Night club star falls for a cartoonist, whose offspring complicates matters. Nothing to sing or draw about. (Dir: Richard Sale, 92 mins.)

Girl of the Golden West (1937)** Jeanette MacDonald, Nelson Eddy. Perennial western tale of the sweet young thing who loves the outlaw is dusted off here and turned into an operetta. Score is pretty good but the old story has withered with age. (Dir: Robert Z. Leonard, 120 mins.)

Girl of the Night (1960)*½ Anne Francis, Lloyd Nolan, Kay Medford, Julius Monk. Embarrassing study of a prostitute who tries to run away from her profession. (Dir: Joseph Cates, 93 mins.)

Girl on a Motorcycle, The (British-French, 1968)* Marianne Faithfull, Alain Delon, Roger Mutton, Marius Goring. Artiness slick and sick, as a girl speeds through the countryside to meet her lover and reminisces up a bunch of erotic flashbacks. Glossy junk, with the beautiful photography and reprehensible direction, both by Jack Cardiff.

Girl on Approval (1962)** Rachel Roberts, James Maxwell. Even Rachel Roberts' good performance can't save this well-worn soap opera about a woman who defies her family

and friends in her efforts to help a young orphan.

Girl Rush, The (1955)** Rosalind Russell, Fernando Lamas, Eddie Albert, Gloria De Haven. Museum employee arrives in Las Vegas to claim partnership in a hotel left by her gambler-father. Try for musical gaiety that fizzles for the most part. Musical numbers below par, the comedy rather tired. (Dir: Robert Pirosh, 85 mins.)

Girl Who Came Gift Wrapped, The (1974)**½ Karen Valentine, Richard Long, Dave Madden. Harmless comedy casting Miss Valentine as a young lady who is thrust upon a successful man-about-town publisher of a sophisticated girlie magazine. Count the possibilities, and then see how many are trotted out. Made-for-TV. (Dir: Bruce Bilson.)

Girl Who Had Everything, The (1953) ** Elizabeth Taylor, Fernando Lamas, William Powell, Gig Young. Criminal lawyer's daughter becomes infatuated with a suave crook. Old-hat melodrama with very little. (Dir: Richard Thorpe, 69 mins.)

Girl Who Knew Too Much, The (1969)* Nancy Kwan, Adam West, Robert Alda. Adventurer hired by the CIA tracks down the assassin who killed a syndicate boss, only to find that the Communists are trying to take over his mob. Far-fetched fiction, takes itself too seriously. (Dir: Francis D. Lyon, 95 mins.)

Girl With a Suitcase (Italian, 1960) ***½ Claudia Cardinale, Jacques Perrin. A thoroughly absorbing and sensitively played Italian language drama about a 16-year-old boy and his innocent and brief romance with a beautiful, sensual girl who lives by her wits. Director Valerie Zurini captures the mood of the poignant episode and uses his camera to the best advantage in the location shooting of Parma and the Italian Riviera. (96 mins.)

Girls' Dormitory (1936)**½ Simone Simon, Herbert Marshall. Simone is outstanding in her first American film. Story of a girl in love with the headmaster of her school isn't too well written. (Dir: Irving Cummings, 66 mins.)

Girls! Girls! Girls! (1962)** Elvis Presley, Stella Stevens. This Presley opus finds him playing a fishing-boat captain with shapely Stella Stevens on hand. Elvis sings and swings his way through this harmless bit of fluff. (Dir: Norman Taurog, 105 mins.)

Girls of Huntington House, The (1973)**½ Sweet Shirley Jones proves she can handle a dramatic role as the new teacher in a small school for unwed mothers. Shirley and Mercedes McCambridge provide the grownup histrionics. Sparked by good performances from Sissy Spacek and Pamela Sue Martin. Made-for-TV. (Dir: Alf Kjellin, 73 mins.)

Girls on the Beach (1964)** Lana Wood, The Beach Boys, Noreen Corcoran. "Sally Sorority" (Miss Corcoran) promises her sisters the Beatles at a benefit performance to pay off the mortgage on their boardinghouse. The Beach Boys, the Crickets, and Lesley Gore do nicely. Humor and acting on a low level. (Dir: William N. Witney, 80 mins.)

Girls' Town (1959)* Mamie Van Doren, Mel Torme, Paul Anka. Sleazy bit of trash about a "girl" (Van Doren) sent to a correctional school unjustly, who manages to uncover the real culprit. Bad for movies and TV both. Alternate title: Innocent and the Damned. (Dir: Charles Haas, 92 mins.)

Git! (1965)** Jack Chaplain, Heather North. Runaway orphan trains an English setter to become a fine hunting dog. Harmless little boy-and-dog drama; children will like it best. (Dir: Ellis Kadison, 90 mins.)

Giuseppe Verdi (Italian, 1953)** Pierre Cressoy, Anna Maria Ferraro. Biography of the composer and patriot. Some good operatic selections sung by Del Monico, Gobbi, etc. Otherwise competent.

Give a Girl a Break (1953)**½ Marge & Gower Champion, Debbie Reynolds. Three girls compete for a top spot in a new Broadway musical. Tuneful comedy with some engaging routines by the dancing Champions. (Dir: Stanley Donen, 82 mins.)

Give 'Em Hell, Harry (1975)***½ This is basically a photographed stage play, but James Whitmore is so splendid impersonating Harry Truman (without makeup), and Truman's words and personality are so rousing, that "Give 'Em Hell" is a joy. Whitmore dares a great deal, undertaking a one-man show

with no help from film technique, makeup or props, and he succeeds. A compelling tribute to a President more and more Americans think was rough, honest, perceptive, and responsible. (Dir: Peter H. Hunt, 104 mins.)

Give My Regards to Broadway (1948)** Dan Dailey, Charles Winninger. A father who is waiting for vaudeville to come back and the romances of his kids make up the ingredients for this pitiful film. Some good standard songs, well done by Dailey, are the only redeeming features. (Dir: Lloyd Bacon, 89 mins.)

Glass Alibi, The (1946)**½ Paul Kelly, Anne Gwynne, Douglas Fowley. An unscrupulous reporter sees a chance to commit a perfect crime, but fate trips him up. Sturdy crime drama, showing what brains can do with a small budget. (Dir: W. Lee Wilder, 70 mins.)

Glass Bottom Boat, The (1966)*½ Doris Day, Rod Taylor, Arthur Godfrey. A relentlessly unfunny outing finding Doris up to her pretty blonde hair in an espionage ring. After what seems like weeks of sleuthing, and a barrage of lame gags, our heroine turns out to be a true-blue patriot after all. Godfrey's film debut playing Doris' papa is quite painless, and there's a small role by Dick Martin before he hit big with "Laugh-In." (Dir: Frank Tashlin, 109 mins.)

Glass Cage, The (1963)** John Hoyt, Arline Sax, Robert Kelljan. Detective becomes involved with a strange girl who has a dominating elder sister and a sinister father. Fair psychological melodrama makes an attempt to be different. (Dir: Antonio Santean, 78 mins.)

Glass House, The (1972)***½ Vic Morrow, Alan Alda, Clu Gulager. As a deterrent to crime, this Truman Capote prison drama is hard to beat—a shocker to the core, besides being a savage indictment of our penal system. In filming it at Utah State Prison in semidocumentary style, director Tom Gries trains his cameras on a new guard, a college professor up for manslaughter, and a kid doing time on a drug rap. Their initiation into the system, with guards looking the other way as a con boss runs "The Glass House," turns into a reign of terror. Bucking the con leader means death by stabbing, going along means homosexual attacks. Raw and gutsy by TV standards. The cast is splendid. Made-for-TV. (73 mins.)

Glass Key, The (1935)*** Edward Arnold, George Raft. Good, exciting Dashiell Hammett melodrama about crime, murder and politics. Characters are superbly drawn and overshadow the routine plot. (Dir: Frank Tuttle, 80 mins.)

Glass Key, The (1942)*** Alan Ladd, Brian Donlevy, Veronica Lake. Fast, slick but complicated story of a politician wrongly accused of murder. Ladd is perfect as the politician's henchman who sets out to clear him. (Dir: Stuart Heisler, 85 mins.)

Glass Menagerie, The (1950)*** Gertrude Lawrence, Kirk Douglas, Jane Wyman. The Tennessee Williams play about a woman living in the past and her plain daughter, whose lives are changed for the better by a stranger. Alternately tender and dramatic, with fine performances. Something different, for those who desire class fare. (Dir: Irving Rapper, 107 mins.)

Glass Menagerie, The (1973)**** Katharine Hepburn, Sam Waterston, Joanne Miles, Michael Moriarty. A generally wonderful production of Tennessee Williams' early masterwork, in many ways superior to the original 1950 version starring Gertrude Lawrence. The cast infuses the play with real human beings you come to care about in this classic of the American theater. Katharine Hepburn shines as Amanda Wingfield, the fading, domineering southern belle desperately trying to instill confidence in her sad crippled daughter (Miles) while steering her poetry-writing son toward a more remunerative career. Actually Hepburn is such a strong, charismatic presence on screen that you occasionally doubt her stated inability to straighten out and improve their lives, but it's a moving portrait nonetheless. Waterston scores as Tom, the tortured son, torn between love for his mother and sister and a strong desire to simply pick up and leave; Miles is touching as the fragile and frightened Laura, who collects equally delicate glass animals; and Moriarty, who may be the best young actor in America, is

276

a wonderfully refreshing and convincing "gentleman caller" who serves as the catalyst in the play. Anthony Harvey directed with unerring taste and skill, and mercifully few cuts have been made in the original full-length play. Made-for-TV.

Glass Mountain, The (British, 1950) ***½ Michael Denison, Dulcie Gray, Valentina Cortesa. A composer writes an opera inspired by a beautiful Italian girl, but finds he has lost interest in his wife in doing so. Well done romantic drama with fine musical score, performances. (Dir: Henry Cass, 94 mins.)

Glass Slipper, The (1955)*** Leslie Caron, Michael Wilding. Lovely Leslie Caron is perfectly cast as Cinderella in this musical fantasy which works most of the way. Don't look for anything but a fairy tale, exquisitely mounted, and you'll be entertained. Michael Wilding is the Prince Charming in this opus. (Dir: Charles Walters, 94 mins.)

Glass Sphinx, The (Egypt-Italy-Spain, 1967)* Robert Taylor, Anita Ekberg. International intrigue and romance centers around excavation of an ancient Egyptian tomb. You've seen it all before, in more attractive packaging! (Dir: Luigi Scattini, 91 mins.)

Glass Tomb, The (British, 1955)**½ John Ireland, Honor Blackman. Carnival people are suspected when a murder is committed there. Neat mystery. (Dir: Montgomery Tully, 59 mins.)

Glass Tower, The (German, 1957)** Lilli Palmer, O. E. Hasse, Peter Van Eyck. German-made soap opera about an actress who is virtually kept a prisoner by her wealthy husband in a specially built glass palace. (Dir: Harold Braun, 93 mins.)

Glass Wall, The (1953)*** Vittorio Gassman, Gloria Grahame. Interesting off-beat story about a foreigner who jumps ship in New York after he is refused entry. His exploits in the big city lead him to the U. N. building—the glass wall—where he almost kills himself. Vittorio Gassman is fine as the desperate Peter. (Dir: Maxwell Shane, 80 mins.)

Glass Web, The (1954)**½ Edward G. Robinson, John Forsythe. Strictly for the whodunit fans. A murder mystery involving members of the staff of a weekly TV show titled "Crime-of-the-Week." Get the picture? A good cast keeps it from becoming silly. (Dir: Jack Arnold, 81 mins.)

Glen and Randa (1971)*** Steven Curry, Shelley Plimpton. An ambitious, seriously flawed, but often provocative apocalyptic vision of two survivors of an atomic holocaust. Third film, but first commercial release for the talented but undisciplined writer-director Jim McBride, who also co-authored the biting screenplay. Chambliss, a little-known British character actor, is excellent playing an old man who befriends Plimpton and Curry. (McBride's first two films were the experimental "David Holzman's Diary" and "My Girlfriend's Wedding." Cuts were made in "Glen and Randa," not approved by McBride. (Dir: Jim McBride, 94 mins.)

Glenn Miller Story, The (1954)*** James Stewart, June Allyson. Highly romanticized biography of the famed band leader who was lost during World War II. Immensely successful when first released, the personal charm of James Stewart as Glenn Miller, and June Allyson, as his loving wife, did a great deal to carry the film's more sentimental sequences. Plenty of music in the tradition of the big band sound. (Dir: Anthony Mann, 116 mins.)

Global Affair, A (1964)** Bob Hope, Lilo Pulver, Yvonne DeCarlo. A featherweight comedy not worthy of Hope's talents. He's a United Nations staff member who becomes the temporary guardian of an abandoned baby left at the U.N. A cast of international females try to convince Hope their various countries should adopt the infant. Thereby hangs the thin diaper. (Dir: Jack Arnold, 84 mins.)

Glory (1956)*½ Margaret O'Brien, Walter Brennan, Charlotte Greenwood. Another in the endless line of stories about a girl (or boy) and a horse. No glory for anyone involved. (Dir: David Butler, 100 mins.)

Glory Alley (1952)**½ Leslie Caron, Ralph Meeker. An entertaining yarn about a soldier who comes home to New Orleans and tries to pick up where he left off with his girl. A great deal of jazz is played throughout the film by such stars as Louis Armstrong, Jack Teagarden, and others. (Dir: Raoul Walsh, 79 mins.)

Glory at Sea (British, 1952)*** Trevor Howard, Richard Attenborough, Sonny Tufts. Captain of a lend-lease ship during World War II earns the respect of his crew after committing some errors. Good war melodrama has excitement, compactness, fine performances.

Glory Brigade, The (1953)*** Victor Mature, Lee Marvin, Richard Egan. Unpretentious but well made, fast moving story of Greek UN forces in war-torn Korea. Different sort of war plot, above average. (Dir: Robert D. Webb, 82 mins.)

Glory Guys, The (1965)** Tom Tryon, Senta Berger, Andrew Duggan, James Caan. Soldier Tom Tryon is forced by an order from his commanding officer to send raw recruits into action against the Sioux. One-dimensional plot gives way to better action. Screenplay by director Sam Peckinpah. Based on the novel "Dice of God." (Dir: Arnold Laven, 112 mins.)

Glory Stompers, The (1968)* Dennis Hooper, Jody McCrea, Chris Noel, Jock Mahoney. Rival motorcycle gangs battle it out in another noisy zoom-zoom saga. Feeding time at the zoo.

Go Ask Alice (1973)*** Jamie Smith Jackson. Provocative fare. The disturbing subject of the indiscriminate use of drugs by high-school kids has seldom been portrayed with more honesty and validity than in this made-for-TV film. Based on the real-life diary of a young girl caught up in addiction from the age of 15, and adapted with sensitivity and restraint by Ellen Violett, the story of Alice, an average teen-ager with a craving for popularity that starts her on the road to severe drug addiction, should be seen by high-school students and their parents. Newcomer Jackson registers in the difficult title role. (Dir: John Korty, 73 mins.)

Go-Between, The (1971)**** Julie Christie, Alan Bates, Dominic Guard. A movie gem of extraordinary beauty. Set in turn-of-the-century England, it tells the story of a little boy who unwittingly becomes the go-between for the daughter of a wealthy family he is visiting and the lower-class neighboring farmer she loves. Its consequences unfold with rare sensitivity and passion. The screenplay by Harold Pinter,

Joseph Losey's direction, and the cast, led by Bates and Christie as the furtive lovers, and Guard as the boy, add up to perfection. (116 mins.)

Go for Broke (1951)******* Van Johnson. The exploits of the 442nd Regimental Combat Team which was comprised of Nisei (Americans of Japanese ancestry) are graphically portrayed in this above average drama set in Italy and France during WW-II. Johnson is joined by a competent cast. (Dir: Robert Pirosh, 92 mins.)

Go Go Mania (British, 1965)***½** A mulligan stew of group acts, including Herman's Hermits, Matt Munro, the Animals, even the Beatles. Paste-up job, no plot. For the teens okay, provided they turn down the sound.

Go, Man, Go (1954)****½** Dane Clark, Sidney Poitier, Pat Breslin. Promoter gets an idea for an all-Negro basketball team, which becomes the Harlem Globetrotters. Sports fans should get a boot out of the fast court scenes; for others, an interesting drama. (Dir: James Wong Howe, 82 mins.)

Go Naked in the World (1961)***½** Gina Lollobrigida, Anthony Franciosa, Ernest Borgnine. Histrionics dominate in this tale of a high-class prostitute who comes between (not literally) father and son. Gina is attractive, but all that yelling . . . ! (Dir: Ronald MacDougall, 103 mins.)

Go West (1940)******* Marx Brothers Weak comedy about the easterners who head west and meet the bad men. Riotous ending and plenty of good lines but disappointing when you realize it's a Marx Brothers' film. (Dir: Edward Buzzell, 81 mins.)

Go West, Young Man (1936)****½** Mae West, Warren William. Moderately entertaining comedy about what happens when a screen star makes a personal appearance and is forced to mingle with the common folk. (Dir: Henry Hathaway, 90 mins.)

Goat Horn, The (Bulgarian, 1972) ******** Anton Gortchev, Milene Penev, Katia Paskaleva. Powerful drama set in the Balkans of the 17th century when what is now Bulgaria was part of the Ottoman Empire and under the brutal reign of the Turks. A shepherd's wife is raped and murdered by swaggering local Turkish officials and the shepherd methodically gets his revenge by killing each of them. Little dialogue but the action builds to a compelling climax aided by the lyrical cinematography of Dimo Lolarov and the taut direction of Metodi Andonov. Uses some of the techniques from the best dramas of the silent days, but the film is convincing and modern in every detail. English subtitles. (95 mins.)

God Is My Co-Pilot (1945)****½** Dennis Morgan, Dane Clark, Raymond Massey. Tribute to the famous Flying Tigers is very trite and only occasionally exciting. (Dir: Robert Florey, 90 mins.)

Godchild, The (1974)****½** Jack Palance, Jack Warden, Jose Perez. Rousing remake of the 1948 John Ford-John Wayne film, "Three Godfathers," which told the story of three Civil War prisoners who are running from the Confederates and Apaches, and come across a dying woman about to give birth. Made-for-TV. (Dir: John Badham, 72 mins.)

Goddess, The (1958)*****½** Kim Stanley, Lloyd Bridges, Steven Hill. An original screenplay by TV's Paddy Chayefsky about a lonely girl who becomes "a love goddess of the silver screen," just like you read about in the fan magazines. Except in this case the lady finds phonies and misses happiness, but it lasts long enough to unwind a striking and powerful performance by Kim Stanley, certainly one of the half dozen most gifted American actresses of today, and one largely ignored by Hollywood before and since this film. Parts of the film may be high-class soap opera, but it's an infrequent opportunity to watch the splendid Miss Stanley at work. (Dir: John Cromwell, 105 mins.)

Godfather, The (1972)******** Marlon Brando, Al Pacino, James Caan, Sterling Hayden, Robert Duvall. One of the most riveting American movies of the decade which also happens to be a superlative gangster film. An absolutely superb performance by Brando as the aging head of a powerful Mafia clan, with fine performances from the supporting cast especially Al Pacino playing Brando's youngest son. Set in 1945 on Long Island with other sequences shot on location in Sicily. Based on the best selling novel by Mario Puzo, this is one of the few times where the film is an improvement on the book. Francis Ford Coppola co-authored the screenplay with Puzo and brilliantly directed this exciting drama. (175 mins.)

Godfather, The, Part II (1974)****
Al Pacino, Robert De Niro, Robert Duvall, Diane Keaton, Talia Shire, Lee Strasberg, Michael V. Gazzo. Won the Academy Award for best picture and is even better in many ways, than Godfather I, as this blockbuster, which begins where Godfather I ended, completes what is surely the greatest gangster saga ever filmed. Michael Corleone (Pacino) has consolidated the power handed to him by his father (Brando) while Godfather II flashes back and forth between the early life of the late Don Vito, and the ongoing story of his embattled family after his death. Pacino and De Niro are customarily excellent, and there's an effective supporting performance by the great method-acting teacher Lee Strasberg playing a Meyer-Lansky type of Jewish, brainy Mafioso. Again written by Coppola and Mario Puzo and marvelously directed by Coppola, who won the Academy Award for best direction. De Niro won an Oscar for best supporting actor and Pacino and Shire got nominated.

God's Little Acre (1958)**½ Robert Ryan, Aldo Ray, Tina Louise. Erskine Caldwell's famous novel about the Walden family of dirt farmers in Georgia and their endless earthy conflicts reaches the screen with some of the passion diluted. Robert Ryan is most effective as the head of the Walden clan, whose mad obsession that there's gold on his land leads him to near tragedy. Tina Louise is properly seductive as Jack Lord's cheating wife, and Aldo Ray, Buddy Hackett, Vic Morrow and Fay Spain deliver good performances. (Dir: Anthony Mann, 110 mins.)

Godson, The (French, 1972)***½ Alain Delon, Nathalie Delon. Don't be put off by the title, which stems from the distributors' hope to cash in on the huge success of "The Godfather" in 1972. Alain Delon plays a contract killer caught between the police and the syndicate. His isolation is poignantly brought out by the distinguished French director Jean-Pierre Melville. The dubbing is inane (everyone sounds like a Brooklyn cab driver) ; Alain Delon is perfect, always impassive and fatalistic. The chase in the subway is terrifically exciting. (103 mins.)

Godspell (1973)*** Victor Garber, David Haskell. Jesus as a hermaphroditic circus clown. The long-running American rock musical, an international hit, comes to the screen as a stimulating if rather long vaudeville turn . . . based on the gospel according to St. Matthew, book writer John-Michael Tebelak, and composer-lyricist Stephen Schwartz. Tells the story of Jesus and his disciples in one musical number after another, imaginatively filmed against the fabulous backdrop of New York City. It starts out very interestingly but soon gets somewhat monotonous. The cast of young singers-dancers-actors does very well and the Schwartz score is always listenable. Special credit to cinematographer Richard G. Heimann for his glorious paean to the magic of New York. (Dir: David Greene, 103 mins.)

Godzilla vs. the Sea Monster (Japanese, 1966)** Akira Takarada, Toru Watanabe. The kids will enjoy this tale of the giant prehistoric monster who goes around doing good. In this one he and the special effects men wage a battle with an evil sea monster. Technically good science-fiction fare on a juvenile level.

Going Home (1971)** Robert Mitchum, Brenda Vaccaro, Jan-Michael Vincent. Ineffective drama tries to analyze the effect on a boy of seeing his mother die after being stabbed by his father. Performances by Mitchum, Vaccaro and Vincent help but can't save this entry, the first directorial effort by producer Herbert B. Leonard. (At the time of release Leonard complained the film had been mutilated by the then-President of MGM, James Aubrey, who chopped 12 minutes out of the completed film.) (Dir: Herbert B. Leonard, 97 mins.)

Going My Way (1944)**** Bing Crosby, Barry Fitzgerald. Rivalry between an old priest and his new young assistant supplies enough plot for one of the most beautiful, sentimental and delightful films ever made. Performances are perfect. Fitzgerald is an absolute joy. (Dir: Leo McCarey, 130 mins.)

Going Places (French, 1974)***½ Jeanne Moreau, Gerard Depardieu, Patrick Dewaere, Miou-Miou, Brigitte Fossey. A compelling, maddening comedy-drama about two Rabelaisian louts who steal, fornicate, and generally act like swine all over France. But somehow director Bertrand Blier has managed to combine many disparate elements into a disturbing, provocative tapestry. With a screenplay by Blier and Philippe Dumarcay based on Blier's famous novel (in France) "Les Valseuses," "Places" is alternately tender and brutal, compassionate and misogynistic, crude, lyrical, sexy, and enraging. One of the two hoodlums is shot in the groin, but they both worry about their virility. Miss Moreau, looking quite beautiful playing a woman back in circulation after a ten-year prison stint, appears briefly in the middle of the film and gives it a performing authority it lacks elsewhere. It's an antiestablishment film about the alienation of the young, and the bankruptcy of their lives and goals. English subtitles. (117 mins.)

Going Steady (1958)**½ Molly Bee, Alan Reed Jr. High school seniors keep their marriage a secret until the bride becomes pregnant. Cute comedy-drama, nothing sensational but entertaining. (Dir: Fred F. Sears, 79 mins.)

Gold (Great Britain, 1974)* Roger Moore, Susannah York, Bradford Dillman, Ray Milland, John Gielgud. A ridiculous thriller. The writing and plotting are ludicrous. Moore is the hero, dragged unwittingly into a nefarious plot to boost prices on the world gold market. It all takes place in the mines of South Africa (filmed entirely on location). The phony moralizing doesn't help, and all the ole blacks seem ever so happy. (Dir: Peter Hunt, 120 mins.)

Gold Diggers of 1933 (1933)*** Joan Blondell, Warren William, Ruby Keeler, Dick Powell, Guy Kibbee. Another good film musical about how a couple of good-looking dolls can fleece a few chaps from out of town who come to New York to really live. (Dir: Mervyn Le Roy, 96 mins.)

Gold of Naples (Italian, 1955)***½ Sophia Loren, Vittorio De Sica. Four generally well done stories about life in Naples. The luscious Sophia should hold male viewers throughout. Dubbed in English. (Dir: Vittorio De Sica, 107 mins.)

Gold Rush, The (1925)**** Charlie Chaplin, Mack Swain, Tom Murray. Written and directed by Chaplin. One of the greatest comedies in the history of cinema. Using the backdrop of the Klondike, Chaplin combines a touching love scene with some of the most inventive and funniest scenes ever filmed including a dance utilizing two bread rolls and his pantomime sequence where he eats an old shoe. (100 mins.)

Golden Age of Comedy, The (1957)**** A welcome nostalgic glimpse of some of the screen's funniest scenes featuring the all-time great clowns of Hollywood—Charlie Chaplin, Laurel & Hardy, Keystone Kops, Will Rogers, plus others. What makes this collection of film clips better than most movies of this kind is a superb editing job and the excellent choice of scenes. (Dir: Robert Youngson, 79 mins.)

Golden Arrow, The (Italy, 1964)* Tab Hunter, Rossana Podesta. Romantic fantasy with Tab Hunter as the handsome young prince who disguises himself as a beggar to try to gain the hand of a voluptuous princess. Another dull cinema trip to "Damascus." (Dir: Antonio Margheriti, 91 mins.)

Golden Blade, The (1953)** Rock Hudson, Piper Laurie. Costume nonsense in old Bagdad with Rock seeking to avenge the death of his father and meeting Princess Piper—all this and a magic sword, yet. (Dir: Nathan Juran, 81 mins.)

Golden Boy (1939)*** William Holden, Barbara Stanwyck. Clifford Odets' brilliant fight drama has lost some of its wallop in 40 years. Still worth seeing for direction and performances, particularly from the supporting cast. This was Holden's first big break. (Dir: Rouben Mamoulian, 100 mins.)

Golden Breed (1968)*** Dale Davis, Butch Van Artsdalen, Mickey Dova. Vivid documentary about surfing, full of towering waves and the glinting, "golden breed" of surfers. Filmed in Hawaii, California and Mexico. (Dir: Dale Davis, 88 mins.)

Golden Coach, The (1953)***½ Anna Magnani, Duncan Lamont. Adventures of a traveling troupe of actors on a swing through South America. Splendidly produced costume comedy drama with a fine performance from Magnani, who also sings. Highbrow fun. Made in Italy, English dialogue. (Dir: Jean Renoir, 105 mins.)

Golden Demon (Japanese, 1956)**½ A young girl loves a poor student but is forced into marrying a rich man. Soap opera, Japanese style, but done rather well. English-dubbed.

Golden Earrings (1947)**½ Ray Milland, Marlene Dietrich. A British spy is hidden by a gypsy girl in this aimless comedy which was quite successful when it was released. (Dir: Mitchell Leisen, 95 mins.)

Golden Girl (1951)**½ Mitzi Gaynor, Dale Robertson, Dennis Day, James Barton. If you disregard the cornball plot about the ups and downs a dancer named Lotta Crabtree (Miss Gaynor) has during the Civil War and just watch Mitzi dance and listen to Dennis Day sing, this film can be fun. (Dir: Lloyd Bacon, 108 mins.)

Golden Goddess of Rio Beni (German, 1964)*½ Pierre Brice, Harald Juhnke. A search party is formed to hunt for a missing airline pilot. Tedious dubbed-English adventure.

Golden Horde, The (1951)** Ann Blyth, David Farrar. Overproduced epic about the barbaric sweep of Genghis Khan out of Asia. Miss Blyth is sorely miscast as a voluptuous princess of Samarkand who falls in love with a visiting crusader named Sir Guy (David Farrar). (Dir: George Sherman, 77 mins.)

Golden Madonna, The (British, 1949)*** Phyllis Calvert, Michael Rennie. Artist and a girl attempt to retrieve a valuable painting that was accidentally sold in Italy. Pleasant romantic comedy-drama. (Dir: Ladislas Vajda, 88 mins.)

Golden Mask (British, 1955)**½ Van Heflin, Wanda Hendrix, Eric Portman. Reporter accompanies an expedition seeking buried treasure in North Africa. Fairly exciting melodrama with fine location backgrounds. (Dir: Jack Lee, 88 mins.)

Golden Mistress (1954)**½ John Agar, Rosemarie Bowe. Treasure hunters incur voodoo vengeance when they steal an idol. Frequently exciting melodrama takes advantage of Haiti locations. (Dir: Joel Judge, 83 mins.)

Golden Needles (1974)* Elizabeth Ashley, Burgess Meredith, Joe Don Baker, Ann Sothern. The "needles" refer to acupuncture and the opening setting is Hong Kong, for this absurd combination of karate and Fu Manchu. One hopes this is the third and last in a dreary series preceded by "Enter the Dragon" and "Black Belt Jones." Some wonderful actors wasted. Now if they'd only made a film called "Golden Noodles" about the great restaurants of Hong Kong . . . (Dir: Robert Clouse, 92 mins.)

Golden Patsy, The (German, 1962)** Gert Frobe. Family man teaches his clan the meaning of money when he announces everything's been lost and they'll have to live like paupers. Mild comedy-drama with a capable performance by Frobe. Dubbed in English.

Golden Salamander, The (British, 1950)*** Trevor Howard, Anouk. British archaeologist goes to North Africa to collect valuable antiques, gets mixed up in gun running. Exciting, well made melodrama. (Dir: Ronald Neame, 96 mins.)

Goldenrod (1977)**½ Tony Lo Bianco, Gloria Carlin. Story about a rodeo star on the Canadian circuit, circa 1950's, whose career experiences ups, downs, and ups. Tony Lo Bianco is good as the champion who takes his wife for granted. Made-for-TV. (Dir: Harvey Hart, 106 mins.)

Goldfinger (1964)*** Sean Connery, Gert Frobe, Honor Blackman. This is the third in the James Bond superadventures and it's a big, splashy gimmicked film which should appeal to fans of Agent 007, and of films of this genre. The plot revolves around a spectacular planned heist of the gold deposits in none other than Fort Knox. A smashing finale takes place during the big robbery. Honor Blackman is "Pussy Galore." (Dir: Guy Hamilton, 108 mins.)

Goldstein (1965)**½ Lou Gilbert, Ellen Madison, Nelson Algren. The most interesting thing about this offbeat entry is that it is based on an unidentified story by Martin Buber. Symbolic comedy about a bedraggled modern-day prophet who rises out of a lake near Chicago to wander the city streets. Episodic, at times very witty (Dirs: Benjamin

Manaster, Philip Kaufman, 85 mins.)

Goldwyn Follies, The (1938)** Zorina, Ritz Brothers, Adolphe Menjou, Phil Baker, Ella Logan. Top-heavy variety revue featuring some of the 1930's biggest attractions. There's a plot but who needs it? A plus factor is a Gershwin score. (Dir: George Marshall, 115 mins.)

Goliath and the Barbarians (Italian, 1960)*½ Steve Reeves, Chelo Alonso, Bruce Cabot. Rebels led by muscleman Reeves battle savage hordes who have been terrorizing the land. Typical spectacle with the usual assortment of battles. Dubbed in English. (Dir: Carlo Campogalliani, 86 mins.)

Goliath and the Dragon (Italian, 1960)*½ Mark Forrest, Broderick Crawford, Eleanora Ruffo. Muscleman goes through a variety of supertests to save the land from an evil ruler. Outlandish English-dubbed spectacle—amusing novelty seeing Brod Crawford playing a corrupt politician in costume. (Dir: Vittorio Cottafavi, 87 mins.)

Goliath at the Conquest of Damascus (Italian, 1964)* Rock Stevens, Helga Line. Muscleman leads an army against savage marauders, no differently than a thousand other inept dubbed-English spectacles.

Goliath, the Rebel Slave (Italian, 1963)*½ Gordon Scott, Massimo Serrato. Once again the musclebender rights wrongs and brings peace in his time. English-dubbed, a bore in any language.

Gone Are the Days (1963)***½ Ossie Davis, Ruby Dee, Godfrey Cambridge, Alan Alda. Screen version by Ossie Davis of his Broadway hit, "Purlie Victorious"; a brash, satiric swipe at racism and Uncle Tomism in the South by updating Negro folk tales to contemporary struggles. Farcical lampoon, topicality, and energetic acting make for good entertainment. "Amos 'n' Andy" with a potent, civilizing message. (Dir: Nicholas Webster, 100 mins.)

Gone with the Wind (1939)**** Clark Gable, Vivien Leigh, Leslie Howard, Olivia de Havilland, Hattie McDaniel, Butterfly McQueen, Thomas Mitchell. This landmark film got eight Academy Awards in 1939, and $5 million for one TV showing in 1976. The siege of Atlanta and the

hardships of the South during the Civil War are masterfully unfolded in this terrific spectacle, probably the most ambitious film Hollywood had ever attempted at the time. Vivien Leigh deservedly won an Academy Award for her fetching performance as Scarlett O'Hara, based on Margaret Mitchell's mammoth novel of 1,037 pages. Producer David Selznick spared no expense (the budget exceeded $4 million), whether building the magnificent home Tara, or hiring a perfect cast. Gable still makes the ladies' hearts flutter as Rhett Butler, and there was an Academy Award-winning supporting performance (Gable was just nominated) from Miss McDaniel, along with awards for director Victor Fleming, screenwriter Sidney Howard, and best film. This all-time box-office champion is part spectacle, part history, a dash of biography, and all smashing entertainment. Much of the sweep of the film will be lost on the tiny home screen, but if you've never seen it before, don't miss it. (219 mins.)

Good Against Evil (1977)* Dack Rambo, Elyssa Davalos, Dan O'Herlihy. An exorcist yarn in which a young lady (Elyssa Davalos) has been selected for the devil, the prince of darkness. Exorcist scenes with Dan O'Herlihy battling the powers of evil are supposed to scare fans! Made-for-TV. (Dir: Paul Wendkos, 79 mins.)

Good Day for a Hanging (1959)** Fred MacMurray, Maggie Hayes, Robert Vaughn. Ex-lawman captures a charming killer, but the townspeople refuse to believe him guilty. Offbeat western moves too slowly, but tries to be different. (Dir: Nathan Juran, 85 mins.)

Good Die Young (British, 1954)**½ Richard Basehart, John Ireland, Gloria Grahame, Margaret Leighton, Laurence Harvey. Four men from assorted backgrounds plan a daring robbery. Rambling melodrama is benefited by a fine cast, some suspense. (Dir: Lewis Gilbert, 100 mins.)

Good Earth, The (1936)**** Paul Muni, Luise Rainer. Pearl Buck's great novel of famine, plague and the fight for survival in China is one of the greatest films Hollywood ever made. Both Muni and Rainer give faultless portrayals in this still wonderful film. (Dir: Sidney Franklin, 138 mins.)

Good Girls Go to Paris (1939)**½ Joan Blondell, Melvyn Douglas. Waitress with a yen to see Paris tries her wiles on the scion of a social family. Amusing comedy. (Dir: Alexander Hall, 80 mins.)

Good Guys and the Bad Guys, The (1969)**½ Robert Mitchum, George Kennedy. Entertaining Western fare with Mitchum as an aging sheriff who teams with his old enemy Kennedy to ward off a planned train robbery. There's more attention paid to characterization than action, and Mitchum and Kennedy are good in the leading roles, while David Carradine scores as a young outlaw in an energetic performance. The supporting cast is also top-notch, including Lois Nettleton, Marie Windsor and the wily Douglas V. Fowley as a hermit-of-sorts. (Dir: Burt Kennedy, 90 mins.)

Good Humor Man, The (1950)*** Jack Carson, Lola Albright. Slapstick all the way—but many funny moments as Jack Carson gets involved with murderers and blondes and the police. (Dir: Lloyd Bacon, 79 mins.)

Good Morning and Goodbye! (1967)* Zoftig wife of an elderly farmer goes male hunting when the old boy can't cut the mustard. A profound message from sexploiteer Russ Meyer: "sex is good for you and me, especially me, in the pocketbook." Alaina Capri, Stuart Lancaster and other famous (?) names. Sexploitation junk.

Good Morning, Miss Dove (1955)**½ Jennifer Jones, Robert Stack. A nostalgic film about a dearly beloved middle-aged school teacher and her effect on her former pupils. The ladies will have two or three good cries during the movie. Miss Jones, with the aid of old-age makeup, is adequate in the title role. (Dir: Henry Koster, 107 mins.)

Good Neighbor Sam (1964)** Jack Lemmon, Romy Schneider, Dorothy Provine. Seemingly endless comedy about an ad man who has to pose as another woman's husband, the consequences therefrom, etc. Lemmon is funny, but he can't do it without help from the writers, which he doesn't receive here. Edward G. Robinson is in for a guest role, to

little avail. (Dir: David Swift, 130 mins.)

Good News (1947)*** Peter Lawford, June Allyson. One of the liveliest musical scores aids the cast in making this flimsy college story a tuneful pleasure. (Dir: Charles Walters, 95 mins.)

Good, the Bad and the Ugly, The (Italian, 1966)** Clint Eastwood, Eli Wallach, Lee Van Cleef. The third of the Clint Eastwood westerns made in Italy (ergo the term spaghetti westerns came into being) which racked up huge box-office receipts in the U.S. as well as Europe. The first two were "A Fistful of Dollars" and "For a Few Dollars." It's a bloody, four-fisted tale of stolen loot, double-crossing partners, endless fights and indestructible cowboys. Strictly for fans of the genre. Clint will never get wrinkles on his face from this kind of acting. He's quite expressionless from beginning to end. (Dir: Sergio Leone, 161 mins.)

Good Times (1967)*** Sonny and Cher, George Sanders. Much better than expected. Sonny and Cher, popular recording team, star in their first film, and it's a mad romp in which they play themselves. Sonny wants them to become movie stars, and his fantasies about their would-be films are quite funny. Breezy direction by William Friedkin. (91 mins.)

Goodbye Again (1961)** Ingrid Bergman, Yves Montand, Anthony Perkins. Ingrid as a "mature" interior decorator who enters into an affair with "young American boy" Tony. Romantic drama on the tedious side, based on Françoise Sagan's novel. The Paris locale is aptly captured, but the emotional conflicts border on soap opera. (Dir: Anatole Litvak, 120 mins.)

Goodbye Charlie (1964)* Debbie Reynolds, Tony Curtis, Walter Matthau, Pat Boone. This was a stupefyingly awful comedy when it flopped on Broadway in 1959. George Axelrod's sleazy play seems even worse when transferred to the big screen. Debbie is the reincarnation of a woman-chasing Casanova named Charlie. Even Walter Matthau can't save this turkey! (Dir: Vincente Minnelli, 117 mins.)

Goodbye Columbus (1969)**** Richard Benjamin, Ali MacGraw, Jack Klugman. Unusually successful adaptation of Philip Roth's acclaimed novella about Jewish life in the Bronx in the 1950's. So much of the film is charming, observant, and accurate that one can forgive the lapses from director Larry Peerce. "Columbus" is the first of Roth's work to be filmed and marked the screen debut for Benjamin and Mac-Graw. Benjamin deftly plays a college dropout who meets the stylish, stunning Ali at a country club. Excellent screenplay written by Arnold Schulman. Peerce's father, famed opera singer Jan, has a bit part as one of the wedding guests. (Dir: Larry Peerce, 105 mins.)

Goodbye Mr. Chips (1938)**** Robert Donat, Greer Garson. Story of the life of an English schoolteacher taken from the James Hilton novel is brilliant screen entertainment. Donat's award-winning portrayal of the lovable Mr. Chips is an acting masterpiece. (Dir: Sam Wood, 114 mins.)

Goodbye, Mr. Chips (1969)** Peter O'Toole, Petula Clark, Michael Redgrave. Mundane musical remake of the original, which starred Robert Donat and Greer Garson. O'Toole plays the shy professor who falls in love with a young girl, Miss Clark. In this version, the young girl is a musical-comedy actress, complete with outlandish friends and a racy past. O'Toole carries the film and even he isn't up to par. The songs are laughable. (Dir: Herbert Ross, 151 mins.)

Goodbye My Fancy (1951)**½ Joan Crawford, Robert Young, Eve Arden. Bright comedy-drama about a lady politician who returns to her alma mater to receive an honorary degree and digs up a lot of old scandals. Based on the Broadway success. (Dir: Vincent Sherman, 107 mins.)

Goodbye, My Lady (1956)**½ Walter Brennan, Brandon de Wilde, Phil Harris. A family movie about an old man, a young boy and a dog. These three live through adventures that would make Huck Finn's mouth water. (Dir: William Wellman, 94 mins.)

Goodnight, My Love (1972)**½ Richard Boone, Barbara Bain. The nostalgia craze reaches back to the '40's, and all those thrillers with Barbara Bain doubling for Miss Bacall (blond '40's hairdo, shoulder pads, and red, red lipstick); Richard Boone playing an older, more tired, and much heavier version of Bogey's gumshoe; and Michael Dunn cast as his wisecracking dwarf sidekick. Everyone goes around spouting tight-lipped jargon, and even the sinister fat man (Victor Buono) is on hand to complete the picture. Made-for-TV. (Dir: Peter Hyams, 73 mins.)

Gorath (Japan, 1962)** Ryo Ikebe, Akihiko Hirata. Average sci-fi about an enormous planetary body ("Gorath") hurtling toward the earth. More "scientific" than most of this genre. (Dir: Inoshiro Hônda, 83 mins.)

Gorgeous Hussy, The (1936)** Joan Crawford, Franchot Tone, Robert Taylor. Fictionalized biography of Peggy Eaton, the notorious belle of Washington during Jackson's administration. Picture tells little of her notoriety and emerges as a dull, overly long love story. (Dir: Clarence Brown, 102 mins.)

Gorgo (British, 1961)*** Bill Travers, William Sylvester, Vincent Winter. Sea monster is captured and put on display in London, but its parent comes after it to wreak havoc on the city. If all those terrible horror thrillers haven't taken the edge off, here's a good one—well-made and exciting. (Dir: Eugene Lourie, 78 mins.)

Gorgon, The (British, 1964)**½ Peter Cushing, Christopher Lee. Village terrorized when murders occur, the victims turned to stone. Well-made horror thriller has its share of suspenseful sequences. (Dir: Terence Fisher, 83 mins.)

Gorilla at Large (1954)** Anne Bancroft, Cameron Mitchell, Lee J. Cobb. A murder mystery unfolded amid the gaudy atmosphere of a cheap carnival. Good actors are totally wasted in this routine meller. (Dir: Harmon Jones, 84 mins.)

Gospel According to St. Matthew, The (Italy-France, 1964)**** Enrique Irazoqui, Margherita Caruso. Graphic, rough, fiercely realistic filming of the story of Christ, using only the words and scenes described by Matthew. Director Pasolini, an avowed Marxist and atheist, portrays Christ as a determined revolutionary. The cast, composed only of non-professionals, including Pasolini's own mother, is persuasive, visually affecting. (Dir: Pier Paolo Pasolini, 136 mins.)

Graduate, The (1967)******** Dustin Hoffman, Anne Bancroft, Katharine Ross. A brilliant, funny, and touching film directed by Mike Nichols, who won an Academy Award for this box-office smash, one of the most successful films of all time. Based on the novel by Charles Webb. In his first major role Hoffman is both hilarious and deeply moving. His first hotel-room tryst with Mrs. Robinson (Bancroft) is one of the most paralyzingly funny scenes ever captured on film. Script by Calder Willingham and Buck Henry concerns a young college graduate who returns to his parents' affluent California swimming-pool world which he despises, and tries to find his own values. (105 mins.)

Grand Central Murder (1942)******* Van Heflin, Cecelia Parker. Private eye solves the murder of an actress in Grand Central Station. Good compact mystery.

Grand Hotel (1932)******** Greta Garbo, John Barrymore, Joan Crawford. Award-winning version of Vicki Baum's story has become a screen classic and a must for all. (Dir: Edmund Goulding, 115 mins.)

Grand Illusion (French, 1938)******** Jean Gabin, Erich Von Stroheim, Pierre Fresnay. One of the all-time great films about the men of the First World War. Superb performances by the entire cast from the stars down to the extras. A movie masterpiece. (Dir: Jean Renoir.)

Grand Prix (1967)****½** James Garner, Eva Marie Saint, Yves Montand. Sappy story about the European auto racing circuit, greatly aided by some magnificent shots of the racing itself, and what it feels like to be traveling well over 100 miles an hour going around sharp turns. The racing scenes are among the best ever to hit the screen. (Dir: John Frankenheimer, 179 mins.)

Grand Slam (Italian-French-German, 1967)******* Edward G. Robinson, Adolfo Celi, Janet Leigh, Robert Hoffman. A professor and a gangster embark on a split-second scheme to heist some diamonds. Perfect-crime capers demand ingenuity and suspense for success, and this has both. (Dir: Giuliano Montaldo, 120 mins.)

Grapes of Wrath (1940)******** Henry Fonda, Jane Darwell, John Carradine. John Steinbeck's novel of impoverished migratory workers and their struggle to get to California and find work is one of the all-time great films. John Ford's direction and a superb cast make this story of a group of people who were almost destroyed by the depression, a "must." (128 mins.)

Grass Is Greener, The (1961)******* Cary Grant, Deborah Kerr, Jean Simmons, Robert Mitchum. Martini-dry comedy about an American millionaire who complicates the wedded bliss of an English couple. Overdose of brittle Noel Coward-ish dialogue makes the pace slow but the cast is good, the production attractive. (Dir: Stanley Donen, 105 mins.)

Grasshopper, The (1970)****½** Jacqueline Bisset, Jim Brown, Joseph Cotten. The slow decline of a 19-year-old girl is adequately rendered by Miss Bisset, who marries ex-football star Brown and is kept by sugar daddy Cotten. There are a few flashes of insight, but the movie flounders in its own ordinary ambitions and wooden acting. (Dir: Jerry Paris, 95 mins.)

Greaser's Palace (1972)****** Albert Henderson, Michael Sullivan. Robert Downey, gifted director of "Putney Swope," has become self-indulgent. Allegorical story of Jesus. Full of parody and bright ideas which never conquer or compete with the dreariness of the symbolism. The few bright moments are rooted in irreverence: a zoot-suited Jesus, the Holy Ghost running around in a white sheet, and a constipated God who hates his son for being a "homo." The production is glossier than any of Downey's previous productions. (Dir: Robert Downey, 91 mins.)

Great American Beauty Contest, The (1973)****½** Louis Jourdan, Eleanor Parker, Robert Cummings. Behind-the-scenes drama about the beauty-contest business complete with proposed hanky-panky between judge and contestant. Bob Cummings plays the emcee and show director, anxious to avoid any murmur of scandal, and Miss Parker is the elegant hostess who must deal with Jourdan's Hollywood producer, the troublemaking judge. It's slick soap-opera fare with pretty girls to look at. Made-for-TV. (Dir: Robert Day, 73 mins.)

Great American Broadcast, The (1941)******* Alice Faye, Jack Oakie.

History of radio (?) is used as a background for a tuneful film, loaded with specialty acts. Jack Oakie is at his best and this one is grand entertainment. (Dir: Archie Mayo, 92 mins.)

Great American Cowboy, The (1974) ***½ Larry Mahan, Phil Lyne. Academy Award-winning documentary about the hardships and rewards of the rodeo circuit, follows two stars as they prepare for competition. Rodeo footage well blended with other sequences detailing the off-bronco lives of the two circuit-winning cowboys. Narrated by Joel McCrea. Most of the credit goes to producer, director, editor Keith Merrill. (90 mins.)

Great American Pastime, The (1956) ** Tom Ewell, Anne Francis, Ann Miller, Dean Jones. Moderately entertaining comedy about a suburban lawyer who becomes manager of his son's little-league team. For the kids. (Dir: Herman Hoffman, 89 mins.)

Great American Tragedy, A (1972) *** George Kennedy, Vera Miles. Story about a successful aerospace engineer whose life undergoes a complete reversal when he's fired from the job he has held for 20 years. This modern-day dilemma has been explored in documentaries, but the dramatic treatment it receives here drives the facts home. Kennedy and Miles are excellent as the couple who face unexpected struggles and challenges when their affluent world crumbles, and the script by Caryl Ledner is adult, believable, and affecting. An above-average made-for-TV feature. (Dir: J. Lee Thompson, 73 mins.)

Great Bank Robbery, The (1969) ** Kim Novak, Clint Walker, Zero Mostel. Although this comedy western boasts the presence of Mostel as a wily would-be bank robber and a plot that sounds like it can't miss, it peters out long before it gets up a full head of steam. The yarn is about three separate plans to rob a top-security bank in the western town of Friendly, circa 1880. (Dir: Hy Averback, 98 mins.)

Great British Train Robbery, The (West Germany, 1965) *** Horst Tappert, Hans Cossy. Despite the improbable idea of having Germans recreate the famous British train robbery of 1963, the attempt comes

off. The German actors could pass for Britons; action is crisp, realistic, well-paced—and non-violent. Horst Tappert is tops as the dispassionate criminal mastermind. Made-for-West German-TV in three ninety-minute segments. (Dirs: John Olden, Claus Peter Witt, 104 mins.)

Great Caruso, The (1950) ***½ Mario Lanza, Ann Blyth. Screen biography of the noted opera tenor was a fitting vehicle for Lanza and his powerful voice. Music devotees should revel in the many songs, arias presented. Others should find it a well-made, consistently interesting drama. (Dir: Richard Thorpe, 109 mins.)

Great Catherine (Great Britain, 1968) *** Peter O'Toole, Jeanne Moreau, Zero Mostel, Jack Hawkins. Mostel is marvelously funny in this entertaining adaptation of George Bernard Shaw's one-act play, "Whom Glory Still Adores." Moreau playing Catherine is overshadowed by the maniacal Mostel, but she does join an illustrious list of screen actresses who have portrayed the notorious mother of all the Russians, including Pola Negri, Elisabeth Bergner, Marlene Dietrich, Tallulah Bankhead, and Bette Davis. It's not all Shavian gems, but there is a reenactment of the Battle of Bunker Hill and Voltaire is denounced, so . . . (Dir: Gordon Flemyng, 98 mins.)

Great Chase, The (1962) **½ Compilation of old films stressing the action elements; scenes of Fairbanks, William S. Hart, Lillian Gish, many others. Lengthy sequence from Buster Keaton's "The General." Pleasant if uninspired nostalgia. (77 mins.)

Great Dan Patch, The (1949) ** Dennis O'Keefe, Gail Russell. The story of the greatest trotting horse of them all, told through the family who owned him. Mild, slow, but of some interest to horse lovers. (Dir: Joseph M. Newman, 94 mins.)

Great Day (British, 1946) ** Eric Portman, Flora Robson. English village makes preparations for a visit from Mrs. Roosevelt during World War II. Mild drama. (Dir: Lance Comfort, 94 mins.)

Great Day in the Morning (1956) **½ Virginia Mayo, Robert Stack, Ruth Roman, Raymond Burr. The loyalties of an assortment of townspeople are tested when the Civil War breaks out. Slightly offbeat western drama with good performances, some above-average touches in the direction. (Dir: Jacques Tourneur, 92 mins.)

Great Escape, The (1963)******** Steve McQueen, James Garner, Richard Attenborough. A fine, big block buster of a movie about Allied prisoners attempting a daring escape from a POW camp during World War II. The entire cast is top-notch, and the action builds from the very beginning to the exciting climax. Watch for Steve McQueen's mad motorcycle dash for safety, one of the most hair-raising action sequences ever filmed. Mighty exciting war drama. (Dir: James Clavell, 168 mins.)

Great Expectations (British, 1946) ******** John Mills, Valerie Hobson, Finlay Currie, Alec Guinness, Martita Hunt. The Dickens classic of the young orphan lad whose path crosses that of an escaped convict who aids him in the world. Faithfully transcribed, painstakingly produced, superlatively directed, acted, photographed. A film great. (Dir: David Lean, 115 mins.)

Great Flamarion, The (1945)****½** Erich Von Stroheim, Mary Beth Hughes, Dan Duryea. A vaudeville trick-shot artist is tricked by a woman into murdering her husband, while she beats it with another man. Standard melodrama, made palatable by Von Stroheim's fine acting. (Dir: Anthony Mann, 78 mins.)

Great Gabbo, The (1929)******* Erich Von Stroheim, Betty Compson. This is Von Stroheim's first talking film, and he gives a fascinating performance as a disgruntled ventriloquist. The musical numbers from the burlesque stage are forgettable, but several scenes of Von Stroheim talking to his dummy are memorable. Screenplay by Hugh Herbert based on a story by Ben Hecht. Von Stroheim tried and failed, incidentally, to get the rights for a remake of "Gabbo." (Dir: James Cruze, 96 mins.)

Great Garrick, The (1937)******* Brian Aherne, Olivia de Havilland. Ponderous, moderately entertaining biography of famous actor, David Garrick. (Dir: Elliott Nugent, 92 mins.)

Great Gatsby (1949)******* Alan Ladd, Betty Field, Macdonald Carey. Racketeer buys a fabulous estate to be near the woman he loved and lost. Not completely successful but interesting picturization of Fitzgerald's saga of the roaring twenties.

Great Gatsby, The (1974)******* Robert Redford, Mia Farrow, Karen Black, Sam Waterston, Bruce Dern. This is Paramount's third film version of F. Scott Fitzgerald's enduring novel about the Beautiful People of rich WASP society in New York and Long Island of the 1920's. To capture the lavish, extravagant look of the palatial estates of the period, director Jack Clayton and David Merrick took their camera crews to one of the great mansions in Newport, R.I., and it works just fine. In this go-around Redford plays Gatsby (ne Gatz), the same part played by Alan Ladd in 1949 and Warner Baxter in '26. Redford is such a skillful actor that you tend to overlook the fact that he's a mite too genteel and civilized, given his modest background and hustling business career with bootlegging connections. Critical opinion was sharply divided re Mia Farrow's performance, but the rest of the cast, especially Waterston playing Nick Carraway, is excellent. There are numerous flaws in the film but director Clayton has caught the look and sometimes the feel of this rich if emotionally impoverished crowd, and there are other virtues besides the glorious clothes. Screenplay by Francis Ford Coppola. (144 mins.)

Great Gilbert & Sullivan, The (British, 1953)*****½** Maurice Evans, Robert Morley. The biography of the leading exponents of light operetta who established a legion of worshipers. Elaborately produced, finely portrayed, with many scenes of their most famous works well represented. (Dir: Sidney Gilliat, 105 mins.)

Great Houdinis, The (1976)****½** Paul Michael Glaser, Sally Struthers. Paul Michael Glaser (half of "Starsky and Hutch") makes his TV-feature debut as Harry Houdini, and he's well cast as the arrogant performer who rose from a third-rate vaudevillian to the ranks of internationally famous escape artist. Sally Struthers, cast as his long-suffering wife, gives a good account of the Catholic girl who married the Jewish magician, and never won acceptance by her husband's unpleasantly stubborn mother (overplayed by Ruth Gordon). A good deal of the film is devoted to Houdini's relentless efforts to contact his dead mother through mediums, and the epilogue has us believe that he himself made contact with his own wife after death. Who can say if this is a definitive biography? It is entertaining. Made-for-TV. (Dir: Melville Shavelson, 108 mins.)

Great Ice Rip-Off, The (1974)**½ Lee J. Cobb, Gig Young. Here's a caper film that pits one great actor, Cobb, and one good actor, Young, against each other. Young plays a leader of a small gang of jewel thieves. Cobb is a retired cop. Made-for-TV. (Dir: Dan Curtis, 72 mins.)

Great Impostor, The (1961)**½ Tony Curtis, Edmond O'Brien, Arthur O'Connell. Based on the life story of Fred Demara, con artist supreme, who takes on different professions and personalities. Curtis has a field day in this uneven but generally satisfying tale. (Dir: Robert Mulligan, 112 mins.)

Great John L., The (1945)*** Greg McClure, Linda Darnell, Barbara Britton. The biography of the great heavyweight champ, as he rises to the top and falls from the heights to drunkenness and disgrace. Nicely done, with exciting, often hilarious ring sequences. (Dir: Frank Tuttle, 96 mins.)

Great Lie, The (1941)**½ Bette Davis, George Brent, Mary Astor. Mary has a child by George, who is Bette's husband and Bette raises the child as her own which is the great lie. Very talky, never compelling but some of the ladies may like it. (Dir: Edmund Goulding, 107 mins.)

Great Locomotive Chase, The (1956) ** Fess Parker. Theatrically released under the title of "Andrews' Raiders." Big Fess Parker cuts an imposing figure playing a Union soldier who leads a dangerous mission behind the Confederate lines in order to destroy strategic railroad bridges. Fair Civil War outing. (Dir: Francis D. Lyon.)

Great Lover, The (1949)*** Bob Hope, Rhonda Fleming, Roland Young. Another of Hope's smooth comic performances in this typical funny Hope film filled with intrigue, beautiful women (there are few more gorgeous than luscious Miss Fleming), and enough plot twists to make

you dizzy. (Dir: Alexander Hall, 80 mins.)

Great Man, The (1957)*** Jose Ferrer, Dean Jagger, Julie London. Fairly honest treatment of Al Morgan novel about a ruthless TV personality who was loved by his public and despised by the people who really knew him. Ferrer plays a reporter who sets out to find out about "The Great Man" after his untimely death. Good performances by the entire cast. (Dir: Jose Ferrer, 92 mins.)

Great Man Votes (1939)**** John Barrymore, Virginia Weidler. Scholar who has turned to drink reforms when the Children's Society threatens to take away his offspring. Superb drama, with moments of high comedy; fine performances, a gem of a movie. (Dir: Garson Kanin, 70 mins.)

Great Man's Whiskers, The (1973) **½ Dean Jones, Dennis Weaver. Old-fashioned drama loosely based on a young girl's letter to President Lincoln suggesting he grow whiskers to hide his look of sadness. The best part—an ingratiating meeting between Lincoln and the youngster—comes in the last act. Jones as an earnest teacher dominates the show while Weaver surprises as Lincoln, giving a brief, appealing performance. Made-for-TV. (Dir: Philip Leacock, 99 mins.)

Great McGinty, The (1940)**** Brian Donlevy, Akim Tamiroff. Fable about the rise of a dumb guy to the Governor's mansion is delightful entertainment and Donlevy is superb in the title role. (Dir: Preston Sturges, 81 mins.)

Great Moment, The (1944)**½ Joel McCrea, Betty Field. Story of the Boston dentist who was the first to use ether is well done, but not a particularly outstanding biography. (Dir: Preston Sturges, 83 mins.)

Great Niagara, The (1974)**½ Richard Boone, Michael Sacks, Randy Quaid. Adventure yarn benefits from the on-location filming at Niagara Falls, Canada. Make no mistake, this is no honeymoon comedy . . . it's a tale, set in the Depression era, of a prideful old man (Richard Boone) and his dominance over his two sons who don't want to follow in their father's footsteps and conquer the great Falls. Exciting rescue scenes! Made-for-TV. (Dir: William Hale, 72 mins.)

Great Northfield Minnesota Raid (1972)**½ Cliff Robertson, Robert Duvall. Slow-building but somewhat satisfying western tale in which Jesse James (Duvall) and Cole Younger (Robertson) team up to rob the Northfield, Minn., bank. The leads provide offbeat portrayals of two famed outlaws, and this, along with the thundering climax, provides the main focus of the film. (Dir: Philip Kaufman, 104 mins.)

Great Profile, The (1940)** John Barrymore, Mary Beth Hughes. Sad to see the greatest of them all in a Grade B comedy, supposedly about his own backstage shenanigans. If you remember Barrymore, avoid it —if you've never seen him, don't let the opportunity escape. (Dir: Walter Lang, 82 mins.)

Great Race, The (1965)**½ Tony Curtis, Jack Lemmon, Natalie Wood. The cast plus an extravagant production are the stars of this farce, which chronicles the first New York-to-Paris car race in the early 1900s. What happens enroute is always implausible and only occasionally amusing. Lemmon starts off nicely as the most dastardly screen villain ever to hide behind a cape but he soon becomes tiresome. However, there is plenty to look at, including Natalie Wood, and the race itself provides laughs. (Dir: Blake Edwards, 150 mins.)

Great Rupert, The (1950)**½ Jimmy Durante, Terry Moore. Jimmy and a friendly squirrel combine talents to make happiness. Slim story tied to Durante antics. Amusing. (Dir: Irving Pichel, 86 mins.)

Great Sinner (1949)**½ Gregory Peck, Ava Gardner, Melvyn Douglas, Walter Huston, Ethel Barrymore, Frank Morgan. An impressive cast of stars tells the story of a collection of people whose gambling fever almost ruins their lives. Peck and Gardner make a good love team. (Dir: Robert Siodmak, 110 mins.)

Great Sioux Massacre, The (1965)** Joseph Cotten, Darren McGavin, Philip Carey. A low-budget western which attempts, once again, to tell the story behind Custer's last stand. Strictly for dyed-in-the-wool western movie fans. (Dir: Sidney Salkow, 91 mins:)

Great St. Louis Bank Robbery, The

(1959)** An early Steve McQueen effort—he's a football hero who goes wrong and becomes involved in the plot of the title. Filmed on location, it has a gritty realism, along with slack pacing. David Clarke, Molly McCarthy, Crahan Denton.

Great Victor Herbert, The (1939)*** Allan Jones, Mary Martin. Inaccurate and bad film biography of the famous composer, but 28 of his songs well performed compensate for the rest of the picture. (Dir: Andrew L. Stone, 84 mins.)

Great Waldo Pepper, The (1975) ***½ Robert Redford, Bo Svenson, Susan Sarandon, Bo Brundin. An appealing homage, conceived and directed by George Roy Hill, to the boy-men aerial barnstorming pilots of the early 1920's. Redford plays Waldo Pepper, a daredevil who regrets having missed the opportunity to trade shoot-outs with the great German aces of WW I, and senses that America of the mad 20's doesn't share his passions for stunting and aerial acrobatics. Redford gives one of his most winning, unselfish performances, and his charisma, along with some marvelous dogfights using the venerable antique planes, help make this period piece so appealing to non-flyers who do not worship speed and risk. Screenplay by William Goldman. Director Hill's avocation is flying just such vintage planes, and his love for the planes and the pilots of the period is abundantly clear. If you liked even parts of "Hell's Angels" and "The Red Baron," you'll be entranced by "Waldo." (Dir: George Roy Hill, 106 mins.)

Great Waltz, The (1938)** Luise Rainer, Fernand Gravet. Lavish but not too entertaining screen biography of Johann Strauss. The music, however, is sheer delight. (Dir: Julien Duvivier, 100 mins.)

Great War, The (Italian, 1961)***½ Vittorio Gassman, Silvana Mangano, Alberto Sordi. Unusual, fascinating mixture of low comedy and high drama, as a couple of stiffs find themselves becoming heroes in World War I. Gassman is particularly good. (Dir: Mario Monicelli, 118 mins.)

Great White Hope, The (1970)***½ James Earl Jones, Jane Alexander, Chester Morris, Hal Holbrook. Film captures much of the passion of the original Broadway play and, most important of all, the dazzling, virtuoso performance of James Earl Jones portraying Jack Johnson, the first black heavyweight boxing champion crowned in 1908. (Many of the issues "White Hope" deals with are the same ones Muhammad Ali was punished for fifty years later, but Hollywood hasn't had the courage to make a meaningful, topical film about Cassius Clay.) Playwright Howard Sackler and director Martin Ritt show the way Johnson (Jones) was victimized and humiliated by a racist, white society, and subjected to, what for Johnson, must have been the ultimate degradation—being forced to take a dive in a fixed championship fight and lose to a white opponent whom he could easily have beaten. Both Jones, and Miss Alexander, playing his white mistress, garnered richly deserved Academy Award nominations for their performances. Jones has been thrilling theater audiences for years. Watch his bravura screen acting as Jack Jefferson and see why. (101 mins.)

Great Ziegfeld, The (1936)**** William Powell, Luise Rainer, Myrna Loy. Story of great American showman is superbly told and the production is in the Ziegfeld manner. It runs three hours and we hope your TV station doesn't cut it. (Dir: Robert Z. Leonard, 184 mins.)

Greatest Gift, The (1974)*** Glenn Ford, Julie Harris, Lance Kerwin. Don't let the sanctimonious title put you off, this is a lovely made-for-TV movie almost in the same league with "To Kill a Mockingbird." It's all about life in the South back in 1940, as seen through the eyes of a 13-year-old boy who thinks his preacher father is the greatest man in the world. Filmed in Georgia and based on Jack Farris' novel, "Ramey," the film captures the feeling of a boy growing up and being lucky enough to have a wise and understanding father. Glenn Ford, Julie Harris, Harris Yulin, and especially Lance Kerwin, are splendid, thanks in part to a good script and Boris Sagal's astute direction. Made-for-TV. (Dir: Boris Sagal, 100 mins.)

Greatest Show on Earth, The (1953) **** James Stewart, Charlton Heston, Betty Hutton, Cornel Wilde, Dorothy Lamour. . . . Or, Cecil B. De Mille visits the circus, resulting

in the Big Top show to end 'em all. Splendiferous production of circus life captures all the thrills and excitement, plus a story line that holds it all together capably. Many amusing "guest" appearances by top stars in bit roles, dazzling camerawork. Entertainment plus. (153 mins.)

Greatest Story Ever Told, The (1965) *** Max von Sydow, John Wayne, Charlton Heston. Earnest but overlong depiction of the story of Christ's life on earth. Max von Sydow is well cast as Jesus Christ, but there is the unnecessary casting of name stars in minor roles—a practice which is always distracting in epics such as these. For example, there's Wayne as the Centurion, Heston as John the Baptist, Carroll Baker as Veronica, Jose Ferrer as Herod, and Shelley Winters as a woman of no name (as the credits list her). Impeccably mounted by director George Stevens but rambling, and just too long. 195 mins.)

Greed in the Sun (France-Italy, 1964) ** Jean-Paul Belmondo, Lino Ventura, Reginald Kernan. French truck drivers in Northern Africa. Parched scenery, ancient Moroccan villages form stark backgrounds for disjointed tale. Filmed in Morocco. (Dir: Henri Verneuil, 122 mins.)

Green Berets, The (1968)* John Wayne, David Janssen, Raymond St. Jacques. This is not just a bad film, which incidentally was co-directed by John Wayne . . . it is more than two hours' worth of relentlessly simple-minded, chauvinistic claptrap about a complex and profoundly important question—the American role and presence in the Vietnam War. It is a depressing commentary on the American movie industry that this insulting film, which of course reflects Duke's attitude and glorifies America's part in the holocaust of Vietnam, is the only film specifically dealing with the Vietnam War that has been financed (Warner Bros.) by a major Hollywood film company. Wayne offers his "Sands of Iwo Jima" characterization, though this time he's playing a Col. (Kirby) not a Sgt. (141 mins.)

Green Dolphin Street (1947)** Lana Turner, Van Heflin, Donna Reed. A girl sails to New Zealand to marry her sister's fellow and sets off a feature-length series of clichés and outlandish gimmicks. It's not the actors' fault, but this one is pretty bad. (Dir: Victor Saville, 141 mins.)

Green Eyes (1977)*** Paul Winfield, Rita Tushingham. Lemi. Strong, emotional drama about a black American Vietnam-war veteran who returns to Saigon in 1973 to find his son, born to a Vietnamese bar girl. The only clue he has is that his son has green eyes. His relentless odyssey, filmed in Manila, puts him in contact with an ingratiating, street-wise urchin played with beguiling naturalness by a young actor named Lemi. The scenes of overcrowded orphanages and street kids rummaging through garbage for scraps of food are compelling. You'll not easily forget the tender, tragic reunion scene between the ex-soldier and his Vietnamese lover, in which she tells him of the heartbreaking fate of their son. Paul Winfield gives his best performance since "Sounder" as the haunted man with a mission. Made-for-TV. (Dir: John Erman, 96 mins.)

Green Fingers (British, 1948)*** Robert Beatty, Nova Pilbeam, Carol Raye. A fisherman who has talent as a bone-setter refuses to study for a degree and goes into practice for society patients. Well-acted drama, with a slightly new plot twist.

Green Fire (1955)**½ Stewart Granger, Grace Kelly, Paul Douglas, John Ericson. Colorful drama about love adventure, and emerald mining in South America. Princess Grace and Granger have some torrid love scenes in this one. (Dir: Andrew Marton, 100 mins.)

Green for Danger (British, 1947)***½ Sally Gray, Trevor Howard, Alastair Sim. Droll police inspector wades through suspects and solves murder at a hospital. Tightly-knit mystery, helped immeasurably by Sim's witty performance as the sleuth. (Dir: Sidney Gilliat, 93 mins.)

Green Glove, The (1952)**½ Glenn Ford, Geraldine Brooks. Minor little chase drama concerning wartime treasures. European backgrounds are more exciting than the film. (Dir: Rudolph Maté, 88 mins.)

Green Goddess, The (1930)**½ George Arliss, H.B. Warner, Alice Joyce, Ralph Forbes. An early talkie, remake of a 1923 silent film based on the successful stage play, both of which also starred Arliss as an insidious far-Eastern potentate who takes three Britishers hostage when they crash-land in his kingdom. An antique melodrama that reeks with atmosphere, even when it clunks. The crafty Arliss shines. (Dir: Alfred E. Green, 74 mins.)

Green Grass of Wyoming (1948)*** Peggy Cummins, Charles Coburn. Another pleasant horse story for the youngsters. All about wild stallions, frisky mares and even some trotting races. (Dir: Louis King, 89 mins.)

Green Grow the Rushes (British, 1952)***½ Richard Burton, Honor Blackman. When the government comes snooping around a small village, the natives are afraid their whiskey-smuggling business is in danger. Extremely pleasant, humorous comedy. (Dir: Derek Twist, 77 mins.)

Green Helmet, The (British, 1961)** Bill Travers, Nancy Walters, Ed Begley, Jack Brabham. Aging race-car driver (Travers) falls in love with a girl who fears for his life. Sentimentality avoided by the cast, who act straight-faced. Some racing scenes shot at Le Mans and Sebring. B & W. (Dir: Michael Forlong, 88 mins.)

Green Man, The (British, 1957)*** Alastair Sim, George Cole, Jill Adams. Comedy about a professional assassin who schemes to knock off an obnoxious diplomat. Fast, bright and breezy farce. (Dir: Robert Day, 80 mins.)

Green Mansions (1959)**½ Audrey Hepburn, Anthony Perkins, Lee J. Cobb. Young man in the jungles of Venezuela meets a strange girl of the forest, falls in love with her. Based on a novel that would be difficult for anyone to film adequately, this fantasy tries hard, manages some affecting scenes, pretty scenery. (Dir: Mel Ferrer, 101 mins.)

Green Pastures (1936)**** Rex Ingram, Eddie Anderson. The Scriptures, as seen by Marc Connolly, with an all-Negro cast. Something different, superbly produced, highly entertaining. (Dirs: Marc Connolly, Wm. Keighley, 93 mins.)

Green Scarf, The (British, 1954)***½ Ann Todd, Michael Redgrave, Leo Genn. A deaf and blind mute who confesses to an apparently motiveless murder is defended by a wily lawyer. Excellent melodrama; a fine cast, tight direction and a good script all add to the drama. (Dir: George More O'Ferrell, 96 mins.)

Green Slime, The (U.S.-Japanese, 1969)* Robert Horton, Luciana Paluzzi. If the title doesn't turn you off, maybe the plot will . . . the earth is going to collide with an asteroid gone wild and Horton is dispatched to blow it up from the space station called Gamma III. (Dir: Kenji Fukasaku, 90 mins.)

Green Years, The (1945) *** Charles Coburn, Tom Drake, Beverly Tyler. Occasionally moving and generally interesting adaptation of A. J. Cronin's novel about an Irish lad who goes to live with his grandparents in Scotland. Coburn as the boy's great-grandfather is a treat. (Dir: Victor Saville, 127 mins.)

Greetings (1968)***½ Robert De Niro, Janathan Warden, Gerritt Graham, Allen Garfield, Roz Kelly. Publicity material described "Greetings" as "an overground sex-protest film that takes a look at the needs and problems of contemporary American youth." That's accurate enough, but it's got a zesty, irreverent, satirical quality that is infectious most of the time. Directed and co-authored by the then 28-year-old Brian De Palma, whose style matured in later directorial efforts. Also a chance to glimpse an early low-budget effort of De Niro's before his current fame and critical acclaim. Filmed on location in Manhattan. (Dir: Brian De Palma, 88 mins.)

Greyfriar's Bobby (U.S.-Great Britain, 1961)*** Donald Crisp, Laurence Naismith. Appealing Disney entry for children about a shepherd's faithful Skye terrier who wins the affection of the city of Edinburgh. (Dir: Don Chaffey, 91 mins.)

Griffin and Phoenix: A Love Story (1976)**½ Peter Falk, Jill Clayburgh. The personal charisma of Falk and Clayburgh carries this predictable, calculated heart-tugger. Falk, estranged from his wife and two boys, discovers he is dying of cancer and splits the scene. Meanwhile, Clayburgh, a young and vital woman, is told she too has a short time to live, and the two doomed individuals meet. The writers would have us believe that the way to get through a terminal ill-

292

ness is to sneak into a movie, try hang-gliding, and steal cars—in other words, do all the things you always wanted to do without regard for the consequences. The movie runs out of sentimental steam long before the fadeout, but the two stars give it a good try. Made-for-TV. (Dir: Daryl Duke, 98 mins.)

Grisbi (French, 1953)*** Jean Gabin, Rene Dary, Jeanne Moreau. Fast paced story of the Paris underworld and the men who take the big risks for big stakes. Jean Gabin registers strongly as Max. (Dir: Jacques Becker, 94 mins.)

Grissly's Millions (1945)*** Paul Kelly, Virginia Grey. Murder strikes when a group of relatives gather together waiting for a wealthy old man to die so they can receive his fortune. Above-average mystery, well written. (Dir: John English, 54 mins.)

Grissom Gang, The (1971)** Kim Darby, Scott Wilson, Tony Musante, Connie Stevens. Excessive action doesn't help an inane premise that has Kim Darby abducted by a bunch of small-time hoods in Depression era Kansas City. The juvenile kidnapper (who giggles when he shoots his best friend) eventually finds love with his victim. The actors sweat a lot. (Dir: Robert Aldrich, 127 mins.)

Groom Wore Spurs, The (1951)* Ginger Rogers, Jack Carson, Joan Davis. A pretty woman attorney is hired to keep a high-flying cowboy movie star out of trouble. Dull, badly played, unfunny comedy. (Dir: Richard Whorf, 80 mins.)

Groove Tube, The (1974)***½ Chevy Chase, Ken Shapiro, Richard Belzer, Buzzy Linhart. A wacky, satirical, scatological series of maniacal sketches that started out life in an off-off Broadway showcase where the sketches were seen on TV screens. Television itself is the target of much of the humor, some of it sophomoric, some excruciatingly funny, including a ribald takeoff of Howard Cosell and the Sexual Olympics. Written by Ken Shapiro and Lane Sarasohn. One of several reasons to tune in is the chance to see Chevy Chase carry on, well before his success and fame on "Saturday Night Live." (Dir: Ken Shapiro, 75 mins.)

Grounds for Marriage (1951)**½ Van

Johnson, Kathryn Grayson. Somewhat silly but amusing tale about an opera singer who decides to make a play for her doctor who just so happens to be her ex-husband. Miss Grayson sings a few arias in addition to being cute and coy. (Dir: Robert Z. Leonard, 91 mins.)

Groundstar Conspiracy, The (1972) ***½ George Peppard, Michael Sarrazin, Christine Belford. A topflight thriller. Peppard plays a government agent assigned to uncover a conspiracy which caused the destruction of a vital secret space unit, and left behind a lone survivor (Sarrazin) who's been badly burned. Before this suspense-charged adventure is over, Peppard has him undergo plastic surgery and brainwashing, so he can be set free and trailed. (Dir: Lamont Johnson, 103 mins.)

Group, The (1966)*** Candice Bergen, Joan Hackett, Joanna Pettet, Shirley Knight. Mary McCarthy's best selling novel about eight girls who graduate from Vassar but keep in touch while living their separate lives comes to the screen half soap-opera and half valid drama. The cast is excellent with Joan Hackett (Dottie), Joanna Pettet (Kay), Jessica Walter (Libby) and Shirley Knight (Polly) delivering the best performances. Sidney Lumet directed. (150 mins.)

Groupies (1970)***½ Joe Cocker and the Grease Band, Ten Years After, Cry Creek Road. Fascinating, honest and profoundly sad documentary showing the loves and lives of assorted "groupies," that special subculture of the rock music scene. The girls'—and a few homosexual boys' —fondest dream is to smoke the best dope, meet all the most "far-out people." To the over-40 set, the hapless groupies may seem pretty far out, as directors Ron Dorman and Peter Nevard capture the squalid, itinerant life-style of these teenaged hangers-on. The directors artfully avoid any feeling of voyeurism, or exploitation of their young subjects. (92 mins.)

Guadalcanal Diary (1943)***½ William Bendix, Lloyd Nolan, Preston Foster. A worthy tribute to the men who fought on Guadalcanal is this stirring action film. Of course it has the mock heroics but it's still one of the best war films. (Dir: Lewis Seiler, 93 mins.)

Guardsman, The (1931)**** Alfred Lunt, Lynn Fontanne, Roland Young, Zasu Pitts. A superior film adaptation of Ferenc Molnar's Broadway hit about the conceited Austrian actor (Lunt) who goes to elaborate lengths to test his wife's (Fontanne's) marital fidelity. This is, alas, the only film ever made by Lunt and Fontanne, who were enduring glories of the American theater for nearly half a century. Lunt was one of the truly great actors of his time (matched among theater actors during the '40's and '50's only by Fredric March and Lee J. Cobb), and in this delightful continental conceit you'll see his dazzling range and technical virtuosity. Fontanne was as gifted as her husband but this is essentially his picture. Watch it for the only film record of their brilliance. (Dir: Sidney Franklin, 83 mins.)

Guendalina (France-Italy, 1957)**½ Jacqueline Sassard, Raffaele Mattioli. Guendalina (Sassard) befriends a young student on the Italian Riviera while her parents are planning a divorce. A gentle, sensitive movie looks at adolescence and the awakening to love of both parents and children. Sassard's first starring role is a skillful, unforced etching of the awkwardness of growing up. (Dir: Alberto Lattuada, 95 mins.)

Guerillas in Pink Lace (1964)** George Montgomery, Joan Shawlee, Valerie Varda. Five showgirls and an adventurer disguised as a priest make an unlikely combination to escape from enemy-held Manila, but they do—only to wind up on an island also held by the enemy. Juvenile but fast-moving wartime adventure, made in the Philippines. (Dir: George Montgomery, 96 mins.)

Guerrilla Girl (1953)*½ Helmut Dantine, Marianne. Partisan girl risks her life for the Greek underground during World War II. Shoddy production detracts from this routine war melodrama.

Guess Who's Coming to Dinner (1967) ***½ Spencer Tracy, Katharine Hepburn, Sidney Poitier, Katharine Houghton. Sidney comes to woo Katie's and Spencer's daughter. Result: one frequently sophomoric sentimental screenplay, buoyed up by a glorious bow-out performance by the deservedly legendary screen team.

(The Academy Awards went berserk in 1967, nominating Hepburn and Tracy, which made sense, but also nominating the film for best picture, which was silly, and voting the award for best screenplay to William Rose, which was idiotic.) Poitier's role was inspired equally by Superman and Horatio Alger, and why he wanted to marry the vapid virgin, portrayed by Hepburn's niece Katharine Houghton, is one of the many things about the film, including Stanley Kramer's direction, that you shouldn't quibble about. Just sit back and watch that great artist Tracy at work for the last time. (112 mins.)

Guess Who's Sleeping in My Bed? (1973)**½ Dean Jones, Barbara Eden, Ken Mars. Fairly good comedy is extracted from a rather ridiculous situation. Ex-husband Jones barges in on his ex-wife, Miss Eden, with his new wife and infant child, and asks to be put up awhile. Made-for-TV. (Dir: Theodore J. Flicker, 90 mins.)

Guest, The (Great Britain, 1964)*** Donald Pleasence, Alan Bates, Robert Shaw. "The Caretaker," absorbing early play of Harold Pinter, filmed with three superlative actors. About an old derelict (Pleasence) invited to spend the night in a run-down London house, who becomes involved with two neurotic brothers. Screenplay by Harold Pinter. This not very commercially promising entry was financed by a group including Noel Coward, Richard Burton, Peter Sellers, Leslie Caron and Elizabeth Taylor. (Dir: Clive Donner, 105 mins.)

Guest, The—See: The Caretaker

Guest in the House (1942)**½ Anne Baxter, Ralph Bellamy, Marie McDonald. A young girl taken in by an average household sets to poisoning their minds against each other. Psychological melodrama has its moments. (Dir: John Brahm, 121 mins.)

Guest Wife (1945)*** Claudette Colbert, Don Ameche. Married woman is persuaded to pose as a war correspondent's wife to fool his boss. Amusing romantic comedy. (Dir: Sam Wood, 90 mins.)

Guide for the Married Man, A (1967) *** Walter Matthau, Robert Morse, Inger Stevens. Walter Matthau's comedic talents are put to good use in this broad comedy about phi-

landering husbands, and the efforts they expend to keep the news from reaching their wives. Some spirited bedroom chatter, helps move things along. Robert Morse comes off well as an operator with the ladies who advises friend Walter. A shrewd selection of guest stars (Art Carney, Joey Bishop, Terry-Thomas, Jayne Mansfield, Carl Reiner, Lucille Ball and others) adds to the fun. (Dir: Gene Kelly, 89 mins.)

Guilt of Janet Ames (1947)*** Rosalind Russell, Melvyn Douglas. Woman embittered by the death of her husband in the war is shown the light by a journalist. Interesting drama. (Dir: Henry Levin, 83 mins.)

Guilty, The (1947)**½ Don Castle, Bonita Granville. Two friends are in love with the same girl, and she has a twin sister. One of them is murdered, and from there it's anybody's guess as to who, what and why. Complicated mystery, but nevertheless attention-holding. (Dir: John Reinhardt, 70 mins.)

Guilty (British, 1956)** John Justin, Barbara Laage. French girl is placed on trial for murdering her lover. Slow-moving courtroom drama.

Guilty Bystander (1950)*** Zachary Scott, Faye Emerson. A private eye down on his luck snaps out of the fog when he finds his little child has been kidnapped. Generally well done mystery, made in New York. Good musical score by Dimitri Tiomkin. (Dir: Joseph Lerner, 92 mins.)

Guilty or Innocent: The Sam Sheppard Murder Case (1975)**½ George Peppard, Barnard Hughes, Walter McGinn. Lengthy recreation of the bizarre 1954 Cleveland murder case where osteopath Sam Sheppard was accused of murdering his wife. Two trials, circus-like courtroom proceedings, the emergence of defense attorney F. Lee Bailey (McGinn) as a national figure, and the puzzling personality of Sheppard—a ladies' man, a drinker, a professional wrestler—offer melodramatic grist but supply precious few insights as to what actually happened. Good performances, especially by Peppard as Sheppard and Hughes as a defense attorney, key the drama, and the production gives the right feeling for the tempo and the thinking in 1954. Made-for-TV. (Dir: Robert Michael Lewis, 144 mins.)

Guitars of Love (West German, 1954)
* Vico Torriani, Elma Karlowa. Silly drivel. Young girl wants to leave the Mantovani orchestra. In order to break her contract she needs to find a replacement. Romance is thrown in, but to no avail. (Dir: Werner Jacobs, 90 mins.)

Gulliver's Travels (1939)*** Full-length cartoon is strictly for the youngsters and, although not up to Disney's level, is enchanting fun. (Dir: Dave Fleischer, 74 mins.)

Gulliver's Travels Beyond the Moon (1966)***½. Good animated science-fiction feature loosely based on the celebrated Jonathan Swift fantasy tale. The updating has Gulliver and his cohorts traveling in a spaceship and involved with a number of adventures which should delight the young audience. An additional treat is a good score by Milton Delugg. (Dir: Yoshio Kuroda, 78 mins.)

Gumshoe (British, 1971)** Albert Finney, Billie Whitelaw, Janice Rule. Finney's homage and that of his screenwriter go to the detective stories of Dashiell Hammett, Raymond Chandler, etc., and the screen image of Humphrey Bogart. The British writer and crew can't quite pull off this most American genre—the private-eye films of the '40's—even though Finney gives his all to playing and living Sam Spade from Liverpool. (Dir: Stephen Frears, 88 mins.)

Gun, The (1974)**½ Stephen Elliott, Jean Le Bouvier, Wallace Rooney. Ambitious attempt to show the life of a gun from the day it comes off the assembly line at the weapons factory through its various owners. Ironically, the gun is fired only twice . . . at the factory for testing purposes and at the very end. The semi-documentary approach, which works well at the start of the film, soon gives in to melodrama, especially in a rather long segment involving a Spanish car-wash worker who finds the gun and brings it home. A good try! Made-for-TV. (Dir: John Badham, 72 mins.)

Gun and the Pulpit, The (1974)*** Marjoe Gortner, Estelle Parsons, Slim Pickens. Marjoe Gortner (who was so compelling in "Marjoe") is well suited for this colorful role of a gunslinger who finds himself in the garb and guise of a small-town preacher while running hard from a

posse. The script is full of clever comedy touches in the dialogue. A supporting cast of pros adds to the yarn. Made-for-TV. (Dir: Dan Petrie.)

Gun Crazy (1949)*** Peggy Cummins, John Dall. Ex-carnival girl persuades her husband to join her in a series of robberies, and they become wanted criminals. Excellently done gangster film, reminiscent of 1930s; fast, tough and vicious.

Gun Fever (1958)*½ Mark Stevens, John Lupton. Revenge drama as a rancher goes after the killer of his parents. Unknown to the boy, the criminal is the father of his best friend. Cliched plot plays like a western soap opera. (Dir: Lynn Stalmaster, 81 mins.)

Gun for a Coward (1957)** Fred MacMurray, Jeffrey Hunter, Dean Stockwell, Janice Rule. Rancher faces trouble trying to raise two younger brothers, one a hothead, the other accused of cowardice. Good cast in a standard western. (Dir: Abner Biberman, 72 mins.)

Gun Fury (1953)**½ Rock Hudson, Donna Reed. Rock Hudson's beautiful fiancee (Donna Reed) is kidnapped by a lustful gunslinger and the search for revenge is on. Slow paced but interesting Western drama. (Dir: Raoul Walsh, 83 mins.)

Gun Hawk, The (1963)** Rory Calhoun, Rod Cameron, Ruta Lee, Rod Lauren. Outlaw gunman tracked by the sheriff dissuades a youngster from following the same crooked trail. Formula hoss opera for the western devotees. (Dir: Edward Ludwig, 92 mins.)

Gun of Zangara (1959)**½ Robert Stack, Robert Middleton. Eliot Ness and the "Untouchables" strive to prevent an assassination attempt on President Roosevelt in 1933. Originally seen as a two-part presentation on TV, the feature version carries a fairly good amount of suspense.

Gun Runners (1958)**½ Audie Murphy, Eddie Albert, Everett Sloane. Interesting adventure story about a man who risks his life for a big share of profit for illegal gun-running. Murphy is believable in the role of an adventurer and it's a welcome change from his western parts. Based-again-on Hemingway's

*"To Have and Have Not." (Dir: Don Siegel, 83 mins.)

Gunbelt (1953)**½ Tab Hunter, George Montgomery, William Bishop. Fairly entertaining, low budget western about an outlaw who wants to go straight and his old "buddies" who have different plans.

Gunfight, A (1970)**½ Kirk Douglas, Johnny Cash. There's lots of talk before this offbeat western justifies its title, but a good part of the dialogue is crisp. Also the stars are interesting as a couple of has-been gunfighters who decide to face each other in one last duel—staged in a bullring and attended by a ticket-buying audience. (Dir: Lamont Johnson, 90 mins.)

Gunfight at Dodge City, The (1959) ** Joel McCrea, Julie Adams, John McIntire. Bat Masterson is elected Sheriff and proceeds to clean up the town. Should sound familiar, and it is. (Dir: Joseph M. Newman, 81 mins.)

Gunfight at Red Sands (Spanish, 1965)** Richard Harrison, Mikaela, Giacomo Rossi Stuart. When a miner is killed and his gold stolen, his adopted son swears vengeance and sets out to find the outlaws. Spanish locations substituting for Mexico add a note of novelty to this English-dubbed western, which compares in passable fashion with our local product.

Gunfight at the OK Corral (1957) ***½ Burt Lancaster, Kirk Douglas, Rhonda Fleming. Wyatt Earp and Doc Holliday join forces to battle the notorious Clanton gang. Very good big-budgeted western. A bit too long, but when the action comes, it's with a bang. Preceding scenes are well acted, carry much suspense. (Dir: John Sturges, 122 mins.)

Gunfight in Abilene (1967)*½ Bobby Darin, Emily Banks, Leslie Nielsen. Even the title of this routine western seems familiar. Bobby Darin is the ex-confederate soldier returned to his home town to find everything at odds and ends. You've seen it all at least fifty times this season alone if you're a TV western series fan. (Dir: William Hale, 86 mins.)

Gunfighter, The (1950)**** Gregory Peck, Jean Parker, Karl Malden. One of Peck's best performances as the would-be-retired gunslinger Johnny Ringo. Skip Homeier, determined to grab the "Fastest Gun"

title for himself, forces Ringo into one more shoot-out. Very off-beat Western for its time. (Dir: Henry King, 84 mins.)

Gunfighters (1947)*** Randolph Scott, Barbara Britton, Forrest Tucker. Gunslinger wants to hang up his pistols, but lands in the middle of a range war. Well-made western with some rugged action. (Dir: George Waggner, 87 mins.)

Gunga Din (1939)**** Cary Grant, Douglas Fairbanks Jr., Victor McLaglen, Sam Jaffe, Joan Fontaine. Three members of Her Majesty's Indian Regiment foil a native uprising with the aid of a loyal water boy. Crammed with spectacle, action, comedy, this is one of the most enjoyable adventure films ever made. Great fun. (Dir: George Stevens, 117 mins.)

Gunman's Walk (1958)*** Van Heflin, Tab Hunter, Kathryn Grant. Rancher tries to bring his sons up properly, but the black sheep of the family causes tragedy for all. Superior western, especially in the acting and directing departments—good for outdoor fans. (Dir: Phil Karlson, 97 mins.)

Gunn (1967)**½ Laura Devon, Edward Asner, Sherry Jackson. TV's private eye (Craig Stevens) matches wits and fists with gangland and murderers in an actionful mystery feature. Elements are the same, and fans of the video series should enjoy. (Dir: Blake Edwards, 94 mins.)

Guns at Batasi (British, 1964)***½ Richard Attenborough, Jack Hawkins, Flora Robson. A provocative drama of substance dealing with the strife-ridden climate prevalent in Africa of the early 1960's. Richard Attenborough, as an old school British sergeant major stationed right in the middle of the upheaval, gives a splendid performance, and he's matched by a distinguished supporting cast including Jack Hawkins, Flora Robson and Cecil Parker. The conflict builds to a tense climax in which the natives plan violent action against the British subjects and their supporters. Incidentally, Mia Farrow is cast as the young love interest in the film. (Dir: John Guillermin, 103 mins.)

Guns for San Sebastian (French-Mexican-Italian, 1967)** Anthony Quinn, Anjanette Comer, Charles Bronson. Plodding adventure yarn set and filmed in a Mexican village during the 1750's. Quinn plays a renegade who is thrust into the unlikely position of impersonating a priest of a poor mission. The pace is a bit slow, but it picks up when Quinn steps into action against a gang of invading outlaws, led by Charles Bronson. (Dir: Henri Verneuil, 110 mins.)

Guns of August, The (1964)***½ Documentary based on Barbara Tuchman's Pulitzer Prize winning book about the causes and effects of World War I. Old newsreel footage compiled in a capable manner. Good for historians, students and WW I buffs.

Guns of Darkness (British, 1962)** David Niven, Leslie Caron. Businessman and his wife are caught in the turmoil of a South American revolution, find themselves helping the overthrown president escape to the border. Drama gets itself tangled in deeper meanings, never quite makes itself clear. Cast tries hard, but the result is no better than fair. (Dir: Anthony Asquith, 95 mins.)

Guns of Fort Petticoat (1957)**½ Audie Murphy, Kathryn Grant. This is a good story idea that could have made a better film if more attention had been paid to the script. Murphy is a deserter during the Civil War who doesn't agree with his power-hungry colonel's ideas about pointless attacks on the Indians. He assembles the women whose men are fighting in the war and trains them so they can be prepared for Indian attacks which would come as a result of the colonel's senseless campaign against the Indian tribes. (Dir: George Marshall, 82 mins.)

Guns of Navarone, The (1961)**** Gregory Peck, David Niven, Anthony Quinn, Anthony Quayle, Irene Papas. One of the best World War II adventure films. A great cast bolsters this superb tension-filled tale involving a group of heterogeneous soldiers and green guerrilla fighters who must destroy one of the most heavily guarded German fortresses in the Aegean. The suspense builds throughout as the yarn unfolds in excellent scenes shot on location in the Greek Isles. Don't miss this marvelous movie. (Dir: J. Lee Thompson, 159 mins.)

Guns of the Black Witch (Italian, 1962)*½ Don Megowan, Silvana

Pampanini. Two boys escape Spanish tyranny and join a band of pirates. Weak English-dubbed costume adventure. (Dir: Domenico Paolella, 83 mins.)

Guns of the Magnificent Seven (1969)**½ George Kennedy, James Whitmore, Monte Markham. Third "Magnificent Seven" film, with Kennedy's character being the only survivor from the original 1960 film. The action and gunplay are just as fast, but the plot has become routine. Set in Mexico in the 1890's, the group attempt to rescue a Mexican Robin Hood who has been caught by the government. Thrilling conclusion. (Dir: Paul Wendkos, 106 mins.)

Guns of the Timberland (1960)** Alan Ladd, Jeanne Crain, Gilbert Roland, Frankie Avalon. Routine action melodrama about a fight between lumbermen and townspeople who don't want the trees cut down. Moves slowly. (Dir: Robert D. Webb, 91 mins.)

Gunslinger (1956)*½ Beverly Garland, John Ireland. When her husband is ambushed, his wife takes over as town marshal; a killer is brought in to get her, too. Western goes off in all directions, gets laughably far-fetched by the end. (Dir: Roger Corman, 83 mins.)

Gunsmoke (1953)** Audie Murphy, Susan Cabot. Not to be confused with the long running TV series of the same name. Just another Audie Murphy starrer in which he plays the stranger in town who has to prove his worth before he's accepted. (Dir: Nathan Juran, 79 mins.)

Guru, The (U.S.-India, 1969)*** Michael York, Uptal Dutt, Rita Tushingham. A strange, generally rewarding and magnificently photographed film made in India and directed by James Ivory. One of the themes of the film is the conflict of Eastern & Western cultures. British pop singer (Michael York) arrives in India to study the sitar with an Indian guru. A silly love story is thrown in, but the music is worth listening to. If you're in the mood for a visually stunning, if somewhat slow-moving film pay attention to this "Guru." The best performance is turned in by Mr. Dutt. (112 mins.)

Guy Named Joe, A (1943)**½ Spencer Tracy, Irene Dunne, Van Johnson. Spencer comes back from the dead to try and make Van a better Air Corps pilot in this often entertaining but occasionally stupid fantasy. Tracy is excellent but he is often up against too much script trouble. (Dir: Victor Fleming, 118 mins.)

Guy Who Came Back, The (1951)** Paul Douglas, Linda Darnell, Joan Bennett. Soap opera about a former football star who can't seem to make it after his career comes to a standstill due to an injury. Douglas is better than his material in this one. (Dir: Joseph M. Newman, 91 mins.)

Guys and Dolls (1955)*** Marlon Brando, Jean Simmons, Frank Sinatra, Vivian Blaine. The musical success concerning a gambler who meets a Salvation Army girl, a floating crap game, and an assortment of Damon Runyon's colorful characters. The Frank Loesser songs are marvelous, but Brando's miscast. Production lavish. A big movie, an entertaining one—but no smash. (Dir: Joseph L. Mankiewicz, 138 mins.)

Gypsy (1962)*** Natalie Wood, Rosalind Russell, Karl Malden. Not as good as the Broadway original, but an interesting backstage musical all the same. An excellent score by Jule Styne and Stephen Sondheim enhances the gay film about the stage mother of them all, Rose Hovick, whose daughters grew up to be Gypsy Rose Lee and June Havoc. The dubbed-in singing detracts from the effectiveness of the musical numbers. Miss Russell is a poor substitute indeed for Ethel Merman who created Gypsy's mother on Broadway. (Dir: Mervyn Le Roy, 149 mins.)

Gypsy and the Gentleman (British, 1958)** Melina Mercouri, Keith Mitchell. Villain tries to cheat his sister out of her inheritance to keep his gypsy lady friend in a proper manner. Wildly theatrical costume drama, may be fun if not taken seriously. (Dir: Joseph Losey, 89 mins.)

Gypsy Colt (1954)**½ Donna Corcoran, Ward Bond, Frances Dee. Appealing tale for the kids, as wonderful-colt Gypsy proves that she and her small mistress can't be kept apart. (Dir: Andrew Marton, 72 mins.)

Gypsy Girl (1966)*** Hayley Mills, Ian McShane. A poignant drama

which benefits from good English location sites and a sensitive performance by Hayley Mills as a retiring young girl who is looked upon by her village as a trouble maker. A very attractive young actor named Ian McShane also registers as a gypsy lad who saves Hayley from being sent to a home. It's all a bit old hat, but the charm with which it's presented keeps it interesting. (Dir: John Mills, 102 mins.)

Gypsy Moths, The (1969)**½ Deborah Kerr, Burt Lancaster, Gene Hackman. The story about a trio of barnstorming free-fall parachutists and the turmoil they cause when they hit a small Kansas town during the 4th of July holiday is wonderful at times, and unendurably slow-moving at others. Miss Kerr is quite good as·an average housewife who falls for the flashy charms of Lancaster's free spirits, and the flying scenes are marvelous. (Dir: John Frankenheimer, 110 mins.)

H-Man, The (1959)* Japanese science fiction film obviously made on a low budget. The effects are routine and the dubbing is annoying. The H-Man of the title refers to creatures created by hydrogen bomb explosions. (Dir: Inoshiro Honda, 79 mins.)

Hagbard and Signe (Danish-Swedish-Icelandic, 1967)***½ Eva Dahlbeck, Gunnar Bjornstrand, Gitte Haenning, Oleg Vidov. A stark, beautiful color film, shot in Iceland. Almost primitive in its technique, it is, in its own way, startling in its simplicity. A Scandinavian Romeo-Juliet story about young love in the Middle Ages, marred only by some excessive violence in its battle scenes. The love scenes between the two youngsters are sensitively handled. The "Romeo" of this film is Russian.

Hail the Conquering Hero (1944)**** Eddie Bracken, William Demarest, Ella Raines. Riotous satire about wartime hero worship, and what happens in a small American town when a young man contrives a Marine-hero history for himself. (Dir: Preston Sturges, 101 mins.)

Hairy Ape, The (1944)*** William Bendix, Susan Hayward. A rough ship's stoker falls for a red-headed wench who uses him as a pawn in her conquest of other men. From the play by Eugene O'Neill, a good production, well acted. (Dir: Alfred Santell, 90 mins.)

Half a Hero (1953)** Red Skelton, Jean Hagen. Writer gets in over his head when he buys a modern home in the country to please the wife. Very mild for Skelton, this comedy has a few chuckles. (Dir: Don Weis, 71 mins.)

Half a Sixpence (Great Britain-U.S., 1967)**½ Tommy Steele, Cyril Ritchard, Julia Foster, Penelope Horner. English star Tommy Steele plays the orphan in Edwardian England who inherits a fortune in this musical adaptation of the 1905 H. G. Wells novel, "Kipps: The Story of a Simple Soul." Occasionally sprightly, with some diverting musical numbers. Kids will enjoy. Ritchard, an enormously talented performer, appears here in his first film since Alfred Hitchcock's 1929 "Blackmail." (Dir: George Sidney, 148 mins.)

Half Angel (1951)** Loretta Young, Joseph Cotten. For those who've enjoyed Loretta for lo, these many years. The versatile Miss Young plays a nurse who's suffering from split personality and the whole thing's played for comedy. (Dir: Richard Sale, 77 mins.)

Half Naked Truth, The (1932)*** Lee Tracy, Lupe Velez, Franklin Pangborn. Some vintage laughs in this lighthearted romp about show business in a carnival and along the Great White Way. Often funny screenplay by director La Cava and humorist Corey Ford based on other material. Franklin Pangborn does his set piece in this one, playing a fawning hotel manager. (Dir: Gregory La Cava, 77 mins.)

Hallelujah Trail, The (1965)* Burt Lancaster, Lee Remick. Very little to cheer about in this muddled western saga, as director John Sturges and the stars stumble down a long—almost three hours—and banal path that has been explored much more satisfactorily by countless film makers in the past. The clumsy plot finds Lancaster assigned to protect a valuable liquor shipment destined for Denver which attracts a band of thirsty Hollywood-caricature Indians, and an itinerant chapter of a ladies temperance league. Lancaster looks understandably bored to death, and Lee Remick is miscast and wasted. (165 mins.)

Halliday Brand (1957)**½ Joseph Cotten, Viveca Lindfors, Betsy Blair, Ward Bond. A talented cast makes most of this western drama bearable but for the most part, the script defeats them. (Dir: Joseph H. Lewis, 77 mins.)

Halls of Anger (1969)**½ Calvin Lockhart, Rob Reiner, Jeff Bridges, Edward Asner. A second helping of "To Sir, With Love." Handsome Calvin Lockhart plays a black high-school vice-principal, who is the focal point of bussed-in white students. The resulting tensions erupt all over the place in episodic fashion. (Dir: Paul Bogart, 103 mins.)

Halls of Montezuma (1951)**½ Richard Widmark, Jack Palance, Robert Wagner. The Marines are once more graphically displayed by Hollywood as the roughest, toughest, brawliest, brawniest, and bravest of all the military who ever fought for the preservation of liberty. Glory drenched heroics played to the accompaniment of the "The Marine Hymn." Widmark is effective as are the other players. (Dir: Lewis Milestone, 113 mins.)

Hamlet (British, 1948)**** Laurence Olivier, Jean Simmons, Basil Sydney, Eileen Herlie. Shakespeare's tragedy of the Danish prince brought to life by Olivier; film-making at its finest, should be seen by all. The greatest play in all literature superbly directed and performed by the greatest actor of his era—a perfect combination. (153 mins.)

Hamlet (British, 1969)***½ Nicol Williamson, Judy Parfitt, Anthony Hopkins, Marianne Faithfull. A filmed version of Wiliamson's riveting performance of this classic on the stage. This film, directed by Tony Richardson, has serious flaws —the supporting cast ranges from adequate to terrible, and the text has been unnecessarily trimmed, even diluting most of the famous Hamlet soliloquies. But it does give us a permanent record of the Scotsman (Williamson) playing Hamlet with a broad Yorkshire accent. Nearly 40 minutes shorter than Olivier's 1948 version, but parts of it —especially the close-ups of Williamson—are remarkable. Williamson is one of the English-speaking world's finest actors, and he assuredly is a great Hamlet. (114 mins.)

Hammerhead (British, 1968)* Vince

Edwards, Judy Geeson. Poor spy yarn with Vince Edwards (TV's Ben Casey) playing a secret agent out to crack an international plot involving plans to a nuclear defense system (what else!). (Dir: David Miller, 99 mins.)

Hammersmith Is Out (1972)**½** Richard Burton, Elizabeth Taylor, Peter Ustinov, Beau Bridges. Uneven, sometimes funny attempt at making the legend of Faust a timely theme. Burton plays Hammersmith, a lunatic, who promises Bridges he can have anything if he frees Hammersmith. Bridges obliges and receives wealth and Miss Taylor before his inevitable destruction. Occasional inventive satirical touches. (Dir: Peter Ustinov, 108 mins.)

Hand, The (British, 1961)**½** Derek Bond, Ronald Leigh Hunt. Series of one-arm murders grips London, and the motive seems to date back to a World War II prison camp. Gruesome little thriller is well made, should please horror fans. (Dir: Henry Cass, 60 mins.)

Hand in Hand (Great Britain, 1961)***½** Philip Needs, Loretta Parry, Sybil Thorndike. A poignant drama featuring two wonderful performances by child troupers Philip Needs and Loretta Parry. They, together with the deft direction of Philip Leacock, make this a charming, moving story about the evils of religious bigotry and intolerance. An eight-year-old Roman Catholic boy and a Jewish girl of the same age meet in school and become chums. They start hitchhiking to London to meet the Queen, but their friendship is soon tested, and they are taunted by the cruelties of other children. Has some of the same charm of Leacock's enchanting "The Little Kidnappers." A wonderful film, especially for children. (Dir: Philip Leacock, 73 mins.)

Handle with Care (1958)** Dean Jones, Joan O'Brien, Thomas Mitchell. Young law student persuades his classmates to investigate unethical practices in a small town. Dry little drama tries to put across a message but takes too many words. (Dir: David Friedkin, 82 mins.)

Hands of a Stranger (1960)** Paul Lukather, Joan Harvey. Concert pianist is in accident, has the hands of a killer grafted on him. Wildly

implausible—some good moments. (Dir: Newton Arnold, 86 mins.)

Hands of a Strangler (French, 1961) *½ Mel Ferrer, Dany Carel. Pianist has the hands of a murderer grafted on when he is mutilated in an accident. Mediocre thriller, dubbed in English. Alternate title: **Hands of Orlac, The.**

Hands of the Ripper (Great Britain, 1971)**½** Eric Porter, Angharad Rees, Jane Morrow. Intriguing, if far-fetched, treatment of the Jack the Ripper tale. The novel premise features the daughter of the famous criminal seeking psychiatric help from Porter (a disciple of Freud) when she claims to inherit her father's murderous tendencies. Victorian London subtly hued, with a stunning finale in St. Paul's Cathedral. (Dir: Peter Sasdy, 85 mins.)

Hang 'Em High (1968)**½** Clint Eastwood, Inger Stevens. Steely avenger sets out to take care of those varmints who strung him up and left him for dead. Played in Clint Eastwood's usual flinty manner, should please nondiscriminating western buffs. With Ed Begley, Pat Hingle, Charles McGraw. (Dir: Ted Post, 114 mins.)

Hanged Man, The (1964)** Robert Culp, Edmond O'Brien, Vera Miles. Gunman out to avenge the murder of a friend traces his quarry to New Orleans during Mardi Gras time. Originally made as a feature-length film for TV; a revamping of "Ride the Pink Horse" that has little of the Robert Montgomery film's finesse. Just a routine crime drama. (Dir: Don Siegel, 87 mins.)

Hanged Man, The (1974)**½** Steve Forrest, Cameron Mitchell, Sharon Acker. A western-mystical adventure which casts Forrest as James Devlin, a gunslinger who fantastically survives a hanging, and then dedicates himself to truth and justice. A troupe of solid supporting actors contribute to this far-fetched tale. Made-for-TV. (Dir: Michael Caffey, 90 mins.)

Hanging Tree, The (1959)***½** Gary Cooper, Maria Schell, Karl Malden. An under-rated Western drama when it was first released. Gary Cooper gives a fine performance as a man torn between law and order. The photography helps to sustain the sober mood of the film. Two Broadway actors (George C. Scott and

Ben Piazza) who have since made names for themselves are featured in the supporting cast. (Dir: Delmer Daves, 106 mins.)

Hangman, The (1959)** Robert Taylor, Fess Parker, Tina Louise. Grim U.S. marshal is determined to track down a wanted man but finds himself pitted against an entire town. Draggy western doesn't do right by the cast. (Dir: Michael Curtiz, 86 mins.)

Hangman's Knot (1952)*** Randolph Scott, Donna Reed, Lee Marvin. Action filled western with hero Randolph Scott fighting off vigilantes and winning Donna Reed. More carefully made than most. (Dir: Roy Huggins, 81 mins.)

Hangmen Also Die (1943)*** Brian Donlevy, Walter Brennan, Dennis O'Keefe. A doctor assassinates the notorious Nazi Heydrich, the Hangman, and as a result a wave of terror sweeps occupied Czechoslovakia. Tense, gripping underground melodrama. (Dir: Fritz Lang, 131 mins.)

Hangover Square (1945)***½ George Sanders, Laird Cregar. Police inspector, played by a youthful Sanders, tries to discover if a decent, talented composer, who suffers from amnesia, is a psychotic killer. Exciting murder melodrama with Jack the Ripper overtones that handles its subject with sensitivity. Fine musical score by Bernard Herman, excellent atmospheric camerawork, including a sweeping crane shot during the climactic concert scene. (Dir: John Brahm, 77 mins.)

Hannibal (1960)** Victor Mature, Rita Gam. An Italian made epic starring Victor Mature as the Carthaginian General, Hannibal. Splendor and spectacle but nothing else. One cliche upon another. Action fans might enjoy the great battle scenes provided they have at least a 30 inch set. (Dir: Edgar G. Ulmer, 103 mins.)

Hannibal Brooks (British, 1969)* Oliver Reed, Michael Pollard, James Donald. The climax of this stupefying entry is an effort by a British soldier to lead a pet elephant named Lucy across the Alps to safety in Switzerland during World War II. Lucy also turns in the best acting performance. (Dir: Michael Winner, 101 mins.)

Hannie Caulder (Great Britain, 1971)** Raquel Welch, Robert Culp, Ernest Borgnine, Strother Martin, Jack Elam. If you want to look at Raquel in a poncho riding the trail of revenge, here's your chance. The story starts as a trio of vermin-ridden villains—Borgnine, Martin and Elam—rape Ms. Welch after killing her husband and setting fire to her home. The resilient Raquel bounces back, learns how to shoot a gun like Jesse James and sets out to get those varmints. Culp is the man who teaches Hannie how to handle the firing iron. Raquel is more beautiful than talented. Director Burt Kennedy co-authored the pedestrian screenplay with David Haft, using the pseudonym Z. X. Jones. I don't blame them for not wanting credit. (Dir: Burt Kennedy, 85 mins.)

Hans Christian Andersen (1952)*** Danny Kaye, Jeanmaire, Farley Granger. Kaye as the teller of fairytales, who falls in love with a beautiful ballerina. Ideal children's entertainment with some spectacular fantasy scenes—adults may become impatient with the excessive amount of sweetness and light. (Dir: Charles Vidor, 120 mins.)

Happening, The (1967)**½ Anthony Quinn, Faye Dunaway, George Maharis, Michael Parks, Milton Berle. A superb idea which isn't fully realized. A group of young beach-type vagrants (Miss Dunaway, Maharis, Parks and Robert Walker) accidentally kidnap former big-time mafia hood Quinn and the plot takes off. However, the scripters and director Elliot ("Cat Ballou") Silverstein can't make up their minds between a way-out comedy, or an off-beat comedy-drama and the emphasis is juggled back and forth. A maddening offbeat entry. (101 mins.)

Happiest Days of Your Life, The (British, 1950)**** Alastair Sim, Margaret Rutherford. Merry mixups when a group of schoolgirls are billeted at a boys' school by mistake. Hilarious madcap comedy, a laugh a minute! (Dir: Frank Launder, 81 mins.)

Happy Anniversary (1959)*** David Niven, Mitzi Gaynor. The hit B'way show about a couple celebrating their 13th (for good luck) anniversary makes a perfect screen comedy and David Niven couldn't be better, as the spouse. Patty Duke is seen in a typical youngster role. (Dir: David Miller, 81 mins.)

Happy Birthday, Wanda June (1971) *** Rod Steiger, Susannah York, George Grizzard, Don Murray. Literal rendering of Kurt Vonnegut's maniacal play onto the screen finds plenty of funny lines plunked in front of a static camera. The satire of the Hemingway macho myth works sometimes. Steiger plays a modern Ulysses, back from an eight-year search for diamonds in Africa, returning to a perky car-hop who has collected a handful of college degrees in his absence. The ensuing re-education of a devout male chauvinist creates the laughs. (Dir: Mark Robson, 105 mins.)

Happy End (Czech, 1967)***½ Give this one a pat for trying something different—the story of a love affair with tragic consequences, told backwards from beginning to end (or is it end to beginning?). Little more than a trick, but amusing as directed by Oldrich Lipsky. Vladimir Mensik and Czech cast. English subtitles.

Happy Go Lovely (British, 1950)*** Vera-Ellen, David Niven, Cesar Romero. American producer in Edinburgh tries to produce a big musical show, and a chorus girl and a millionaire are enticed into the plot. Diverting musical comedy moves along pleasantly. (Dir: H. Bruce Humberstone, 87 mins.)

Happy Go Lucky (1943)**½ Mary Martin, Dick Powell, Betty Hutton. Pleasant, undistinguished musical about a stenographer who saves her money for a big husband-hunting cruise. (Dir: Curtis Bernhardt, 81 mins.)

Happy Hooker, The (1975)** Lynn Redgrave, Jean-Pierre Aumont, Lovelady Powell, Nicholas Powell, Tom Posten. Xaviera Hollander's experiences as a madam have been turned into a light comedy which ignores the raunchy specifics of the profession in favor of recounting a businesswoman's rise to success. Ms. Redgrave, looking quite lithe, dispenses puns as she's called on to make Hollander seem an amiable professional catering to such clients as industry-magnate Posten with a table-top striptease. New York locations and a variety of New York stage actors colorfully flavor the unlikely script. Hollander was a tart who could type. Remember, she was voted "secretary of the year" in

Holland. (Dir: Nicholas Sgarro, 96 mins.)

Happy Is the Bride (British, 1959) *** Ian Carmichael, Janette Scott. The strain of going through with their wedding almost causes the betrothed couple to call the whole thing off. Amusing little domestic comedy, nicely played. (Dir: Roy Boulting, 84 mins.)

Happy Landing (1938)**½ Sonja Henie, Don Ameche, Cesar Romero. Entertaining, though not outstanding is this little musical about a plane that makes a forced landing in Norway near "you know whose" home. (Dir: Roy Del Ruth, 102 mins.)

Happy Mother's Day, Love George— See: Run, Stranger, Run

Happy Road, The (1957)*** Gene Kelly, Barbara Laage, Bobby Clark, Brigitte Fossey, Michael Redgrave. Engaging escapades of two youngsters who become fugitives in the French countryside when they run away from their Swiss school, and of their respective parents, a U.S. businessman widower and a French divorcée, in pursuit. The sight gags are fun—and there are some delicious scenes with Michael Redgrave as a NATO commander hot on their trail. Kelly produced and directed, as well as starred, his first such effort. (Dir: Gene Kelly, 100 mins.)

Happy Thieves, The (1962)** Rita Hayworth, Rex Harrison. The attractiveness of the two stars compensates somewhat for this mediocre comedy about sophisticated art thieves. The plot twists are predictable and the supporting cast mugs outrageously. (Dir: George Marshall, 88 mins.)

Happy Time, The (1952)***½ Charles Boyer, Louis Jourdan, Linda Christian. A fine comedy about the ups and downs in the daily lives of an eccentric family headed by Charles Boyer. There's a French maid (Linda Christian) and a roué uncle (Louis Jourdan) and many others to make you laugh. (Dir: Richard Fleischer, 94 mins.)

Happy Years, The (1950)**** Dean Stockwell, Darryl Hickman, Leon Ames, Leo G. Carroll. Delightful tale of a mischievous boy and his adventures at a boys' school in the 1890's. Often hilariously funny, with Stockwell giving a superb performance. Fine fare for the entire family.

(Dir: William Wellman, 110 mins.)

Harakiri (Japan, 1962)**½ Tatsuya Nakadai. Another Samurai film which examines the code of the wandering warriors who often used the ploy of pretending they would commit "harakiri" (suicide in the traditional manner) on some lord's estate if they weren't subsidized by the rich man. Beautifully photographed as usual, but slow-moving. (Dir: Masaki Kobayashi, 150 mins.)

Hard Contract (1969)**½ James Coburn, Lee Remick, Sterling Hayden, Karen Black. Interesting but flawed effort of writer-director S. Lee Pogostin to comment on the way in which Americans so readily accept or explain away murder. Coburn, sleek and rugged, portrays an international hit man who has a contract to kill three men—one in Brussels, one in Spain, and the third (Hayden) he must locate. Miss Remick delivers an attractive performance as a jet-set chick who breaks down Coburn's cool and shakes his calm hand as he stalks his triple prey. Violent in spots, awkward in others. (Dir: S. Lee Pogostin, 106 mins.)

Hard Day's Night (British, 1964)**** The Beatles. During the peak of their popularity the Beatles made their first movie, and to everyone's surprise and delight it turned out to be a stylishly inventive and thoroughly made contemporary comedy classic. There are a good share of laughs, interspersed with a dozen or so of the Beatles' best songs, plus the astonishing range of talent of these four captivating personalities—John Lennon, Ringo Starr, Paul McCartney, and George Harrison. Director Richard Lester filmed the story about the Beatles on tour in England with a sense of frenzy and unabashed humor, much in the style of the early Marx Brothers' Hollywood comedies, and it works from start to finish. (85 mins.)

Hard Driver (1973)**** Jeff Bridges, Valerie Perrine, Art Lund, Geraldine Fitzgerald, Ed Lauter, Gary Busey. (Theatrically released as "The Last American Hero.") Perceptive, involving examination of a real slice of Americana—stock-car racing—in North Carolina that features outstanding performances and a literate script by William Roberts, based on articles by Tom Wolfe.

Bridges is marvelous as a young moonshiner, running whiskey past the revenuers, who turns to racing to help his father (Lund) who has been jailed. Perrine is lovely as a tender, amoral, romantic interest. It's more than a standard action yarn: the movie explores the compromises needed to succeed and the vapid car-racing groupies that follow the circuit. Some expert racing footage (all filmed on location in Virginia and the Carolinas) and healthy doses of humor and pathos. Skillfully directed by Lamont Johnson. (95 mins.)

Hard Man, The (1957)**½ Guy Madison, Valerie French. Interesting enough for a western plot. Madison is a strong-willed cowboy who comes into a town which is run by one man (indirectly by the man's greedy wife). He gets involved with the woman and almost pays for this mistake with his life. (Dir: George Sherman, 80 mins.)

Hard Times (1975)***½ Charles Bronson, James Coburn, Jill Ireland, Strother Martin. A tough, lean, remarkably effective fable about a bare-knuckle street fighter slugging his way to a couple of paydays in New Orleans during the Depression era of the 1930's. Charles Bronson, as usual, is a laconic stranger, in this case arriving and departing by train as a hobo. Bronson's sullen power works to good advantage. There are three main fights, one in Bayou country, and two in the piers and warehouses of New Orleans. They are surprisingly exciting despite the obvious fact that neither Bronson nor his opponents seems visibly scarred after a pounding that would break knuckles as well as skin on any mortal. But that carping aside, this marks an auspicious directorial debut for screenwriter Walter Hill. Screenplay, written by Hill, Bryan Gindorff and Bruce Henstell, captures the aura and the hard times of the early 1930's. To say that this is Bronson's best screen acting is not much of a compliment, but he does energize this no-nonsense melodrama, and plays well with Coburn portraying an on-the-make small-time hustler and boxing promoter. (Dir: Walter Hill, 97 mins.)

Hard Way, The (1942)**½ Ida Lupino, Dennis Morgan, Joan Leslie.

It's an old ambitious girl stepping on everyone in her way plot but Miss Lupino gives it some dignity. The first half is well done but producer's luck runs out in the final reels. (Dir: Vincent Sherman, 109 mins.)

Hardcase (1971)** Clint Walker, Stefanie Powers, Alex Karras. Offbeat Western has Walker playing a soldier of fortune who helps Mexican revolutionaries, and finds his wife among them. Occasionally credible, but badly paced. Made-for-TV. (Dir: John Llewellyn Moxey, 74 mins.)

Harder They Come, The (Jamaica, 1972)***½ Jimmy Cliff, Carl Bradshaw, Janet Bartley. Though Jamaica has often appeared as the background for Hollywood films, this is the first film to get a major release that has been made by indigenous Jamaicans. Raggae music-star Jimmy Cliff makes impressive film debut playing a country boy who comes to downtown Kingston (quite different from what tourists see), becomes a pop hero, and is forced into a life of crime. Cliff's own rhythmic, sinuous music makes this mock-heroic tale appealing. This has understandably become a film with substantial cult appeal. Directed and co-authored by Perry Henzell. (93 mins.)

Harder They Fall, The (1956)***½ Humphrey Bogart, Jan Sterling, Rod Steiger. Excellent fight game movie based on the Budd Schulberg novel. Bogart gives his usual great performance with Rod Steiger matching him. (Dir: Mark Robson, 109 mins.)

Harlem Globetrotters, The (1951)**½ Thomas Gomez, Dorothy Dandridge. A dull story about one of the members of the famous Negro basketball team. The basketball game scenes are the best things in the film, and they're terrific! Dorothy Dandridge has a small non-singing part. (Dir: Phil Brown, 80 mins.)

Harlow (1964)** Carroll Baker, Mike Connors, Peter Lawford. If you're looking for a definitive biography of the late movie queen of the thirties, skip this one. It's strictly for those who prefer to believe what they read in the movie fan magazines. Carroll Baker is unconvincing as the glamorous sex symbol. The best performance in the film is one by Angela Lansbury in the un-

palatable role of Mama Jean. (Dir: Gordon Douglas, 125 mins.)

Harness, The (1971)***½ Lorne Greene, Julie Sommars. A lovely movie version of John Steinbeck's Salinas Valley tale about a withdrawn farmer and his ailing wife. A bearded Greene is most believable as the grumpy, close-mouthed Californian, who endures his wife's illness until a red-haired hippie and her little boy come along and alter his ideas about living. Greene's farmer isn't converted overnight. Literate script plus Boris Sagal's careful direction convey the man's torment in trying to find out who he is. Miss Sommars is a free soul, the farmer's mentor on life: she never makes a false move, handling Greene gently and lightly. Made-for-TV. (99 mins.)

Harold and Maude (1971)**** Ruth Gordon, Bud Cort, Vivian Pickles, Ellen Geer. An often wildly funny and original "black comedy" that was largely ignored at the time of its original release, and panned by most of the tiny number of perceptive critics who should have known better. It's a wry lyrical ode to controlled lunacy, boasting an imaginative, stylish screenplay by young writer Colin Higgins, and an equally fine directorial job from Hal Ashby. (This is not your standard love story, so don't wait for it to ever show up on prime-time network TV.) Young man of 20 (Cort) is a necrophiliac of considerable promise, and he's got a great flair for inspired sight gags, all relating to death. His companion in love and adventures is a wacky 79-year-old gloriously played by Ruth Gordon, who'd be a formidable foe in automobile demolition derbies. Special credit too to Vivian Pickles playing Cort's beleaguered mother—her arch comments on her son's demented behavior are superbly written and masterfully acted. It's a sick comedy all right—but if you go along with the spirit of this farce, it's one of the most inventive American comedy films in years. (91 mins.)

Harp of Burma (1956)*** Director Kon Ichikawa has fashioned a poetic anti-war film which has impact. A Japanese Army private (Shoji Yasui) takes on a personal crusade to bury all the dead soldiers he finds after the end of World War II.

Along his journey's trail, the soldier dons the robes of a Buddhist monk. (Dir: Kon Ichikawa)

Harper (1966)***½ Paul Newman, Janet Leigh, Robert Wagner, Lauren Bacall. Fast paced private eye yarn with Paul Newman playing a Bogart-type detective who gets beaten up as much as he dishes it out. No super tough-guy but a cool operator, Newman is excellent as Harper, a cool private investigator hired to see who's causing a prominent wealthy California family a great deal of trouble. A better than average cast of pros—Julie Harris and Arthur Hill—adds to the film's appeal. (Dir: Jack Smight, 121 mins.)

Harpy (1971)* Hugh O'Brian, Elizabeth Ashley. Dreary made-for-TV feature about an impossible woman (Miss Ashley) who'll stop at nothing to win and woo her ex-husband, who's about to remarry. There's shouting, rather than acting, and a silly "harpy eagle" figures into the plot, if you're a bird fancier. (Dir: Jerrold Freedman, 99 mins.)

Harriet Craig (1950)*** Joan Crawford, Wendell Corey, Lucile Watson. Remake of "Craig's Wife" which was based on George Kelly's Broadway play. Crawford plays a domineering wife whose meanness backfires in the end. (Dir: Vincent Sherman, 94 mins.)

Harry and Tonto (1974)***½ Art Carney, Ellen Burstyn, Larry Hagman, Geraldine Fitzgerald. Art Carney's Academy Award-winning performance as a New York-based septuagenarian who decides to pack his beloved cat Tonto and head across the United States on his last odyssey. It's a lovely trip, filled with adventures, love, disappointment, people, and death. Director Paul Mazursky doesn't shy away from sentiment but, just when it might get too sticky, his camera picks up something else. Carney doesn't look 72, but let's not quibble —it's a splendid performance worthy of the Oscar he received. O.K. for kids, too. (Dir: Paul Mazursky, 115 mins.)

Harry and Walter Go to New York (1976)*½ James Caan, Elliott Gould, Michael Caine, Diane Keaton, Charles Durning. If sets and costumes and energy were enough, this would be a four-star movie. But, alas, the script about two bumbling fifth-rate vaudevillians (they seem to have only one song number in their repertoire) turned reluctant safe-crackers is incredibly boring. No amount of overplaying can save this farce, circa 1892, but Diane Keaton manages some funny moments as a zealous editor of an anarchist newspaper and, in all fairness, Mr. Caine stays aloof of most of the mugging, providing a sort of serious relief. (Dir: Mark Rydell, 123 mins.)

Harry Black and the Tiger (1958)** Stewart Granger, Barbara Rush. Talky, only occasionally interesting tale about a man who stalks dangerous jungle beasts for profit and thrills. Photography during hunts surpasses the drama's plot. (Dir: Hugo Fregonese, 107 mins.)

Harry In Your Pocket (1973)**½ James Coburn, Michael Sarrazin, Walter Pidgeon, Trish Van Devere. A slick crime film which explores, at length, the "art" of pickpockets. The Harry of the title is the superdip of them all, and he's played with icy detachment by Coburn. Sarrazin and Miss Van Devere are two new recruits to the world of pickpockets and Walter Pidgeon is a veteran. Pidgeon gives a good account of himself as an aged con man with contemporary habits (coke sniffing, for instance). The script takes its time as the group travels from one big city to another, plying their "trade." Slow-moving but not uninteresting. If you want to see a good film on this subject try Robert Bresson's "Pickpocket" (1963). (Dir: Bruce Geller, 103 mins.)

Harry Never Holds—See: Harry In Your Pocket

Harum Scarum (1965)* Elvis Presley, Mary Ann Mobley. Even for Elvis's nubile fans, this one is a little much. Elvis is a movie star who is kidnapped while he's on a personal appearance tour in the Middle East. What follows would make Rudolph Valentino's "The Sheik" blush. (Dir: Gene Nelson, 95 mins.)

Harvey (1950)**** James Stewart, Josephine Hull, Peggy Dow. Delightful fable of a gentle tippler and the six-foot invisible "rabbit" he has adopted for a friend. Stewart is excellent as the whimsical Elwood P. Dowd, while Miss Hull is a joy as his straight-laced sister who is continually embarrassed by his actions. Only those not sympathetic to fantasy will not enjoy it—others will find it a treat. (Dir: Henry Koster, 104 mins.)

Harvey Girls, The (1945)*** Judy Garland, John Hodiak, Ray Bolger. Good score, nice performers and an ordinary story add up to a fairly good musical. Tale of a group of young ladies who go to the wild west to become waitresses in a Fred Harvey restaurant is a good background for some nice production numbers. (Dir: George Sidney, 104 mins.)

Harvey Middleman, Fireman (1965)** Gene Troobnick, Hermione Gingold, Charles Durning. Writer-director Ernest Pintoff is a talented, inventive maker of short animated films such as "The Critic." But he comes a cropper here with this juvenile, semi-fairy-tale version of a theme dealt with better in Axelrod's "The Seven Year Itch"—the arrested adolescence of many American adult males. Has a nice scene at the New York World's Fair. Most of the best sequences are without dialogue. (Dir: Ernest Pintoff, 90 mins.)

Has Anybody Seen My Gal (1952)**½ Piper Laurie, Rock Hudson, Charles Coburn. Mildly entertaining package of fads, songs and silly antics of the twenties. The Blaisdells come into a large amount of money and it changes their life drastically. Some laughs and the cast is attractive. (Dir: Douglas Sirk, 89 mins.)

Hasty Heart, The (1950)***½ Richard Todd, Patricia Neal, Ronald Reagan. Heartwarming story of a stubborn Scottish soldier who has a short time to live and the friends he makes in an Army hospital. A beautiful performance by Richard Todd as the kilted "Lochy." Based on the Broadway play. (Dir: Vincent Sherman, 99 mins.)

Hatari (1962)*** John Wayne, Hardy Kruger, Red Buttons. A well-produced comedy-adventure about a group of he-men who round up African animals for shipment to zoos around the world. The animal sequences, filmed on location in Africa, add immensely to the film's appeal, and Wayne is at home in his role of the top man of the adventure-loving crew. (Dir: Howard Hawks, 159 mins.)

Hatchet Man, The (1932)*½ Edward G. Robinson, Loretta Young, Dudley

Digges. Oriental tong wars and the hatchet of a Chinese avenger are involved in Robinson's romancing of Young in San Francisco's Chinatown. Early effort by all involved. (Dir: William Wellman, 74 mins.)

Hatfields and the McCoys, The (1975)*½ Jack Palance, Steve Forrest, John Calvin, Robert Harch. The old Hatfield-McCoy feud is trotted out again. Competent cast of strong faces brings a he-man vitality to the tale of feuding Kentucky clans. Made-for-TV. (Dir: Clyde Ware, 72 mins.)

Hatful of Rain, A (1957)**** Eva Marie Saint, Anthony Franciosa, Don Murray, Lloyd Nolan. An excellent film version of Michael Gazzo's hard-hitting B'way play about a junkie and the people who love him and therefore suffer with him. The performances are of a high level from the stars to the supporting cast, with Anthony Franciosa (repeating his stage role as the junkie's brother) a standout. The last scene which has Miss Saint calling the authorities' help is memorable. (Dir: Fred Zinnemann, 109 mins.)

Hatter's Castle (British, 1941)** James Mason, Emlyn Williams, Deborah Kerr, Robert Newton. A hatter stops at nothing to attain a higher place in society, drives his family mercilessly. Old-fashioned, wheezing costume drama with a fine cast. (Dir: Lance Comfort, 90 mins.)

Haunted Palace, The (1963)** Vincent Price, Debra Paget. It's Price sent to chill and thrill. He's a warlock returned from the grave in the person of his descendant, to seek revenge against the villagers who burned him at the stake a century ago. You can't keep a good bogeyman down. (Dir: Roger Corman, 85 mins.)

Haunted Strangler, The (British, 1958)** Boris Karloff, Anthony Dawson. Silly, far-fetched thriller in which Boris is cast as a novelist who does some research on a "grisly" murder case and becomes so immersed, he starts duplicating some of the "violent" acts. (Dir: Robert Day, 81 mins.)

Haunting, The (1963)*** Julie Harris, Claire Bloom, Richard Johnson. Tingly ghost story about a believer in the supernatural who brings together a group in a supposedly haunted house, where weird things begin to happen. Guaranteed to raise the hackles, definitely should not be seen in a darkened room. Well acted. (Dir: Robert Wise, 112 mins.)

Haunts of the Very Rich (1972)**½ Lloyd Bridges, Cloris Leachman, Anne Francis, Moses Gunn. Remember "Outward Bound" and "No Exit"? Here's a variation of their themes, placing a group of strangers together in a remote spot, which may or may not be hell. Setting is a sumptuous resort on a plush island where the guests trot out their personal hang-ups before too long. Attractive cast. Made-for-TV. (Dir: Paul Wendkos, 72 mins.)

Hauser's Memory (1970)**½ David McCallum, Susan Strasberg, Lilli Palmer. Above average made-for-TV-feature. Fairly absorbing drama about the risky business of attempting to use a scientific experiment involving a human memory transplant, before the nature of its result has been tested. David McCallum is particularly effective as the young scientist who boldly takes the injection himself in order to prevent his Nobel Prize-winning superior from being subjected to its hazzards. Cold, impersonal espionage is at the root of the emergency transplant, as well as of the personal drama that follows. (Dir: Boris Sagal, 99 mins.)

Have Rocket, Will Travel (1959)*½ The Three Stooges. Strictly for 3 Stooges' fans and children under 7 years old! All the usual slapstick shenanigans played within an outrageous science fiction plot. (Dir: David Lowell Rich, 76 mins.)

Have You Heard of the San Francisco Mime Troupe? (1968)***½ A generally well-done hour report on the politically oriented, original "guerrilla theater" group in this country. Funny, satirically incisive, this film should look better on TV than it did in theatres. Director of this refreshing American "commedia dell'arte" group is Ronnie Davis. Rewarding, provocative documentary produced and directed by Don Lenzer and Fred Wardenburg.

Having a Wild Weekend (1965)**½ Dave Clark Five. The English pop group's first film, and although it doesn't measure up to the Beatles' "A Hard Day's Night," it has a similar kooky appeal. The plot is best not outlined, but the charm of Dave Clark and his group registers nicely. (Dir: John Boorman, 91 mins.)

Having Babies (1976)**½ Jessica Walter, Vicki Lawrence, Karen Valentine, Desi Arnaz, Jr. A good cast and fine production values help bolster this story about the personal lives of four expectant mothers (three with husbands) who come together while attending classes in the Lamaze method of natural childbirth. Episodic, but you finally come to care about all of them. Jessica Walter is quite good as a not-so-young woman having her first child. The rest of the cast is competent. A graphic birth sequence at the end is handled with taste. Made-for-TV. (Dir: Robert Day, 98 mins.)

Having Wonderful Crime (1945)*** Pat O'Brien, George Murphy, Carole Landis. A shady lawyer and his two friends turn sleuths and look into the murder of a magician. Fast paced, breezy comedy-mystery. (Dir: A. Edward Sutherland, 70 mins.)

Having Wonderful Time (1938)**½ Ginger Rogers, Douglas Fairbanks Jr., Red Skelton, Lucille Ball. City girl goes to the mountains for a vacation and falls in love there. Pretty mild comedy has some good scenes but isn't what it should have been. (Dir: Alfred Santell, 70 mins.)

Hawaii (1966)*** Julie Andrews, Richard Harris, Max von Sydow. This epic film based on James Michener's rambling narrative about the early (1820) settlers of Hawaii amounts to pure escapist adventure fare rather than historical drama, but it's lavishly produced, well acted, and reasonably entertaining. Sit back and share the exploits of the strict missionary (von Sydow), his friendly, outgoing wife (Andrews), and the dashing sea captain (Harris) who loves the preacher's wife. The scenery is gorgeous, the spectacle impressive. Von Sydow is miscast in the leading role of a young graduate of Yale Divinity School. (Dir: George Roy Hill, 186 mins.)

Hawaii Five-O (1968)* Jack Lord, Nancy Kwan, Leslie Nielsen, Lew Ayres. McGarrett's first case (pilot for the TV series) finds him leading his special investigative force on the trail of a deadly weapon that has been killing American secret agents. Played with typical one-dimensional intensity. Made-for-TV. (Dir: Leonard Freeman, 96 mins.)

Hawaii Five-O: V for Vashon (1972) **½ Jack Lord, Luther Adler, Harold Gould. Originally seen as a three-parter on "Hawaii Five-O," it's a fairly interesting story about three generations of an island underworld family. Made-for-TV. (Dir: Charles S. Dubin, 159 mins.)

Hawaiians, The (1970) **½ Charlton Heston, Geraldine Chaplin. Spectacle, Charlton Heston, Hawaiian history (Hollywood-style, of course), and a cast of thousands (or so it seems) still can't make this old-fashioned saga really work. Based on a portion of James Michener's rambling novel, the story has so much plot and so many big scenes that the actors are dwarfed by the surroundings. However, a pair of Oriental actors, Mako and Tina Chen, register in the secondary leads. For the record, Charlton Heston's name is Whip and Geraldine Chaplin plays his wife, Purity. Sequel to "Hawaii," covering period 1870-1900. (Dir: Tom Gries, 134 mins.)

Hawkins on Murder (1973) **½ James Stewart. Given a good script by David Karp to work with, Stewart plays a shrewd murder trial lawyer. Stewart is Hawkins, a country boy in city clothes, who defends a poor little rich girl—the sensitive, withdrawn type—accused of slaying daddy, stepmother, and stepsister. Stewart combines gentleness with probing queries. Occasionally, the pace of the film is sacrificed for the development of character, but the gamble usually pays off. Bonnie Bedelia, as the accused, leads the supporting cast. Made-for-TV. (Dir: Jud Taylor, 73 mins.)

He Ran All the Way (1951) *** John Garfield, Shelley Winters. Exciting, contrived melodrama about a killer who holds a decent family at bay and hides out in their home. Excellent performance by Garfield. (Dir: John Berry, 77 mins.)

He Rides Tall (1964) ** Tony Young, Dan Duryea, Jo Morrow. Marshal finds dirty work on the ranch of his foster-father, instigated by a no-good foreman. Routine western. (Dir: R. G. Springsteen, 84 mins.)

He Stayed for Breakfast (1940) ** Melvyn Douglas, Loretta Young.

Communist man learns about life, love and capitalist luxury from a beautiful American girl. Comedy employing "Ninotchka" theme is forced and only occasionally funny. (Dir: Alexander Hall, 89 mins.)

He Walked by Night (1949) ***½ Richard Basehart, Scott Brady. Semi-documentary chase drama showing how the police stalk a killer is an exciting, tense and absorbing film. Basehart is superb as the killer. (Dir: Alfred L. Werker, 79 mins.)

He Who Must Die (France, 1957) **** Melina Mercouri, Pierre Vaneck, Jean Servais, Gert Frobe. A great film about the Passion Play, set in a small Cretan village in 1921, based on the riveting novel, "The Greek Passion," by Nikos Kazantzakis. A Greek village, still under Turkish control following World War I, re-enacts the Passion Play for Holy Week, and finds that the roles of Christ, Mary Magdalene and the Apostles still have great meaning for their modern society. A powerful, searing film that won many awards. Mercouri and Vaneck are perfect, as is the rest of the company. (Gert "Goldfinger" Frobe is seen in a small part.) This was Dassin's second film made in France after being blacklisted in Hollywood during the 1950's. An enduring masterpiece. Dassin co-authored the screenplay with Ben Barzman. Filmed in black and white. (Dir: Jules Dassin, 122 mins.)

He Who Rides a Tiger (British, 1966) ***½ Tom Bell, Judi Dench, Paul Rogers, Kay Walsh, Jeremy Spenser. The unlikely love affair between a burglar (Tom Bell) and a young mother (Judi Dench) is compellingly unreeled in this well-directed (Charles Crichton) drama. Good performances. (103 mins.)

Head, The (1962) ** Horst Frank, Michel Simon. A German made (dubbed in English) horror film and a somewhat gruesome affair. Scientists are working on a way to keep a head alive after it has been removed from the rest of the body. (Dir: Victor Trivas, 92 mins.)

Head (1968) ** The Monkees cavorting through a harebrained series of plotless incidents. They camp it up to please their devotees. In '68, this was "in." By now, it may be just in-ane. Matter of taste. Includes appearances by Victor Mature, Annette Funicello, Timothy Carey, Vito Scotti, female impersonator T. C. Jones. Interesting to note this was "written" by director Bob Rafelson and actor Jack Nicholson. Rafelson later directed the splendid "Five Easy Pieces." (86 mins.)

Headlines of Destruction (French, 1959)** Eddie Constantine, Bella Darvi. Newsman is convinced a man is innocent of murder, sets out to nab the real culprit. Adequate imitation American whodunit, dubbed-in English. (Dir: John Berry)

Headquarters State Secret (German, 1962)** Gert Frobe, Peter Carsten. German agent receives a plan for the construction of a mine, but his brother thwarts him and aids the Allies. Fairly interesting WW II spy melodrama, dubbed-in English.

Healers, The (1974)**½ John Forsythe, Season Hubley, Pat Harrington. Fairly absorbing pilot film for a proposed series with Forsythe playing the chief of staff of one of those massive medical research complexes where problems abound. Forsythe's Dr. Kier comes face-to-face with money problems, defecting research men, and a decision on the use of an untested drug in a crisis case. Director Tom Gries manages to give the familiar material some freshness. Made-for-TV.

Hear Me Good (1957)*** Hal March, Joe E. Ross, Merry Anders. Fast-talking promoter finds he has to rig a beauty contest to satisfy a racketeer and his moll. Minor but breezy, fun-filled Runyonesque comedy with frequently sparkling dialogue, wisecracks. Good fun. (Dir: Don McGuire, 80 mins.)

Heart Is a Lonely Hunter, The (1968) **** Alan Arkin, Sondra Locke, Stacy Keach Jr., Cicely Tyson. Carson McCullers' beautiful novel about the life of a deaf-mute in a small Southern town is brought to the screen with admirable sensitivity by all those involved. Moving story of loneliness, human boorishness and cruelty never strikes a false note, and features a remarkable prize-winning performance by Alan Arkin in the role of the deaf-mute. Thomas C. Ryan adapted the McCullers novel with special grace and insight, and the performances are fine throughout, including newcomer Sondra Locke as a young girl who befriends

the deaf-mute, and the gifted young actor Stacy Keach portraying a town drunk. Filmed largely on location in Alabama. (Dir: Robert Ellis Miller, 125 mins.)

Heart of a Child (British, 1958)*** Jean Anderson, Richard Williams. Small boy tries to save his St. Bernard during the food shortage in World War I. Corny, but entertaining drama, especially for the younger fry.

Heart of a Man, The (British, 1959) *½ Frankie Vaughan, Anne Heywood. Young sailor launches a singing career, finds all isn't happiness at the top. Trite musical drama; Vaughan sings well but doesn't come across on-screen.

Heart of the Matter, The (British, 1953)***½ Trevor Howard, Elizabeth Allan. From Graham Greene's novel, about a police commissioner in South Africa who falls in love with an Austrian girl, and is threatened with blackmail. Not always effective drama, but fine performances. (Dir: George More O'Ferrall, 100 mins.)

Heartbeat (1946)*** Ginger Rogers, Jean-Pierre Aumont. Lady pickpocket falls for a dancing diplomat, attains her place in society. Pleasant comedy with a good cast, elaborate production. (Dir: Sam Wood, 102 mins.)

Heartbreak Kid, The (1972)**** Cybill Shepherd, Charles Grodin, Jeannie Berlin, Eddie Albert. A unique American comedy, directed by Elaine May, that is alternately hilarious, poignant, and irritating. (Why do the three main parts have to be such vacuous saps, e.g.?) The story is the chronicle of a young New York Jewish couple whose marriage disintegrates on the Florida turnpike, while they head south, just days after the wedding. Miss Berlin, who is Elaine May's daughter and looks and acts like mama, steals the film playing a gross, nagging young-married. She's quite remarkable in a restaurant scene where she's in the process of being ill. Miss Shepherd is the titillating blond wasp love interest from chilly Minnesota. (105 mins.)

Hearts and Minds (1974)**** A shattering Academy Award-winning documentary about the agony, lies and moral squalor of the Vietnam War, and America's nightmarish involvement in that faraway Civil War. Conceived and directed by Peter Davis, "Hearts and Minds" brilliantly intertwines interviews shot for this cinematic essay, newsreel footage, and parts of old movies. One veteran reminds us, "We've all tried very hard to resist what we've learned from our experience in Vietnam." Director Davis confronts us with the harsh, bitter truth in this searing, invaluable history lesson. Should be obligatory viewing for every political office-holder, now and for all times. "Hearts and Minds" is a further reminder that the American movie industry virtually never dealt with the Vietnam War, the dominant story in all our lives during the late 60's and early 70's. (Dir: Peter Davis, 112 mins.)

Hearts of the West (1975)**** Jeff Bridges, Alan Arkin, Blythe Danner, Andy Griffith. A charming lark paying homage to the myths of the Old West as seen by an aspiring young writer from Iowa in the early 1930's who heads for Titan, Nevada, and winds up in Hollywood. Deft screenplay is stylishly handled by director Howard Zieff, who gets uncommonly good performances from all the cast. Bridges is delightful as the eager, innocent Iowan, and Blythe Danner provides kisses for Bridges and joy for the rest of us. Alan Arkin plays an excitable no-talent director, jerks his director's chair across an office floor, and gets one of many laughs. Andy Griffith is likeable as a durable stuntman in this eccentric, perceptive love letter to Hollywood and Western films. Nice touches throughout, including Bridges asking to get his hair cut exactly like Zane Grey's. (Dir: Howard Zieff, 103 mins.)

Heat of Anger (1972)** Susan Hayward, James Stacy, Lee J. Cobb. Ordinary courtroom drama about a clever lady lawyer. Legal beagle Hayward defends establishment contractor Cobb on a murder rap. Made-for-TV. (Dir: Don Taylor, 74 mins.)

Heatwave (1974)** Ben Murphy, Bonnie Bedelia, Lew Ayres. Yet another crisis drama which uses the premise of a heatwave hitting a town not prepared to cope with it. Naturally a leader comes forth from the panicked crowd and helps to create some order out of the chaos. Made-for-TV. (Dir: Jerry Jameson.)

Heaven Can Wait (1943)*** Charles Coburn, Don Ameche, Gene Tierney. This film reaches for greatness but just falls short. Comedy about a late 19th Century lover trying to explain to the Devil why he thinks he belongs in Hades. Entertaining, but unfortunately, does not hold up all the way. (Dir: Ernst Lubitsch, 113 mins.)

Heaven Knows, Mr. Allison (1957) *** Deborah Kerr, Robert Mitchum. A somewhat incredible story, which places a rugged U.S. Marine corporal and a gentle Roman Catholic nun on a South Pacific island during WW II, is made palatable by the two good performances of its stars, Miss Kerr and Mr. Mitchum. Directed with his customary skill by John Huston. (107 mins.)

Heaven on Earth (Italian, 1960)** Barbara Florian, Charles Fawcett. Count overcomes his resentment of Americans when he guides an Army major and his daughter on a tour of the beauties of Rome. Scenes of the city are an armchair sightseer's delight, some of them filmed for the first time—but the thin plot is a bore. English dialogue.

Heaven Only Knows—See: **Montana Mike**

Heaven with a Barbed Wire Fence (1939)**½ Glenn Ford, Nicholas Conte, Jean Rogers. Two drifters team up with a refugee girl and try to make a living. Ford's first role, also (Richard) Conte's; pleasing little drama. (Dir: Ricardo Cortez, 62 mins.)

Heaven with a Gun (1969)**½ Glenn Ford, Carolyn Jones. Predictable western yarn. Glenn Ford playing a preacher who tries to bring peace (inner and outer) to a small town. There's the usual collection of citizenry and John Anderson makes a good bad guy. (Dir: Lee H. Katzin, 101 mins.)

Heavenly Body (1943)** William Powell, Hedy Lamarr. Bedroom farce is forced comedy and falls short of its goal. Story of an astronomer's wife who believes a fortune teller and almost runs off with a handsome stranger. (Dir: Alexander Hall, 95 mins.)

Heavens Above (British, 1963)***½ Peter Sellers, Cecil Parker, Isabel Jeans. Sharp, biting satire about a do-gooder clergyman who always manages to make things difficult for his parishioners. For most it will prove to be a wealth of laughs backgrounded by some thoughtful comment. Sellers is superb as the well-meaning reverend. (Dirs: John & Roy Boulting, 105 mins.)

Hec Ramsey: Scar Tissue (1974)*½ Richard Boone, Kurt Russell, Harry Morgan. Another familiar episode from the old TV series, with Boone as the humanitarian Western lawman. This time he's out to help a confused young man (Russell) who keeps getting into trouble while furiously searching for the father he never saw. Made-for-TV. (Dir: Andrew V. McLaglen)

Hec Ramsey: The Mystery of the Green Feather (1972)*½ Richard Boone. Another episode in the tales of the turn-of-the-century Western criminologist. Not as well plotted as some, but Ramsey's inquiring eye is appropriately alert in dealing with the railroaders, land-grabbers, and Indian scapegoats. Made-for-TV. (Dir: Herschel Daugherty, 72 mins.)

Hec Ramsey: The Mystery of the Yellow Rose (1973)*½ Richard Boone, Diana Muldaur, Claude Akins. Stars provide the chief interest in this story of old Hec's attempt to rescue an old love from a murder charge. Made-for-TV. (Dir: Douglas Benton, 72 mins.)

Hedda (Great Britain, 1975)***½ Glenda Jackson, Timothy West, Jennie Linden. Glenda Jackson dominates this powerful film version of a critically acclaimed London stage production, starring Jackson, of Henrik Ibsen's enduring drama about a Nordic femme fatale—a neurotic, controlling, strong-willed woman who is nonetheless alluring to the males in her town. Jackson is an actress of extraordinary range, and this classic stage role is ideally suited to her. The Ibsen text has been trimmed considerably, which eliminates some of the shadings in Hedda's character, but this is a welcome, absorbing production of a fascinating 19th-century play which is very relevant indeed in the mid-20th century. (Dir: Trevor Nunn, 100 mins.)

Heidi (1937)** Shirley Temple, Jean Hersholt. The youngsters should love this adaptation of Johanna Spyri's juvenile classic. Story of a little Swiss girl's adventures as everybody seems to conspire to take her from her grandfather has warmth and charm. (Dir: Allan Dwan, 88 mins.)

Heidi (Swiss, 1953)*** Elsbeth Sigmund, Heinrich Gretler. The children's classic of the little girl whose grandfather ends his feud with the village so she can receive an education. Well made, especially for children. English dubbed. (Dir: Luigi Comencini)

Heidi (Austria, 1965)*** Eva-Maria Singhammer, Gertraud Mittermayr. Generally well-acted filming of the beloved children's story about a little mountain girl who is taken to the city but cannot survive there. Straightforward, far better than the 1937 Shirley Temple schmaltz; benefits notably from its authentic Alpine settings. (Dir: Werner Jacobs, 95 mins.)

Heidi and Peter (Swiss, 1955)** Elspeth Sigmund, Heinrich Gretler. Sugary sequel to "Heidi" continuing the adventures of the Swiss girl and her family. (Dir: Franz Schnyder, 89 mins.)

Heiress, The (1949)**** Olivia de Havilland, Montgomery Clift. The celebrated B'way play based on Henry James' "Washington Square" is brought to the screen with uncommon taste and skill. Miss de Havilland offers a brilliantly penetrating portrayal as the very plain and unloved spinster who falls under the cunning spell of a handsome fortune hunter, well played by Montgomery Clift. Sir Ralph Richardson is equally brilliant as the heiress' arrogant father. (Dir: William Wyler, 115 mins.)

Heist, The (1972)** Christopher George. Serviceable action piece about the amateur who must prove his innocence. Accused of being in on a truck robbery, a harried armored guard goes sleuthing on his own, and does nothing right. Made-for-TV. (Dir: Don McDougall, 73 mins.)

Helen Morgan Story (1957)**½ Ann Blyth, Paul Newman, Richard Carlson. Highly fictionalized life story of the famed singer of blues who was very popular during the twenties and early thirties. Ann Blyth is miscast as the torch singer but she has a few believable dramatic moments. Paul Newman, as the man she loves, does very well with a badly written character. Comedian Alan King, as Newman's buddy, gives a good performance. Gogi Grant sings while Miss Blyth mouths the words. (Dir: Michael Curtiz, 118 mins.)

Helen of Troy (1956)** Rossana Podesta, Jack Sernas, Sir Cedric Hardwicke. No expense was spared in bringing this tale of Paris and Helen to the screen. Lavish sets and a cast of thousands are evident but the drama is sorely missing. Miss Podesta is well endowed physically but her Helen leaves much to be desired histrionically and Jack Sernas is as wooden as the horse employed in the great final battle. Brigitte Bardot plays a hand maiden to Helen in a small role. (Dir: Robert Wise, 118 mins.)

Helga (German, 1967)** Sex-education film, tracing a woman's pregnancy from conception to birth. Fairly instructive; could be advertised as something else.

Hell and High Water (1954)**½ Richard Widmark, David Wayne, Bella Darvi. Although the plot is somewhat far fetched, this high adventure tale about the efforts of a hand picked group of sailors who are assigned the task of breaking up an enemy plan to trigger another major war, has some tense moments and good underwater photographic effects to recommend it. (Dir: Samuel Fuller, 103 mins.)

Hell Below Zero (1954)** Alan Ladd, Joan Tetzel. Inept drama of erupting emotions and conflicts aboard an Antarctic ice-breaker. (Dir: Mark Robson, 91 mins.)

Hell Bent for Leather (1960)**½ Audie Murphy, Stephen McNally, Felicia Farr. Not bad western—Murphy is a wandering cowpoke who is framed by a glory-seeking marshal for a crime he didn't commit. McNally is particularly good. (Dir: George Sherman, 82 mins.)

Hell Cats of the Navy (1957)** Ronald Reagan, Nancy Davis. So-so drama with a naval setting. Some action, but mostly painfully familiar.

Hell in Korea (British, 1956)*** Ronald Lewis, Stephen Boyd. War drama about conflict, courage, and cowardice in Korea. Good performances and action-filled battle scenes.

Hell Is a City (Great Britain, 1960)**½ Stanley Baker, John Crawford, Donald Pleasence. Absorbing British crime chase. Police inspector tracks down escaped criminal he has caught once before. Thoroughly English in its pace and use of bleak locales of city rooftops and desolate moors. Well acted. (Dir: Val Guest, 93 mins.)

Hell Is for Heroes (1962)*** Steve McQueen, Bobby Darin, Fess Parker, Nick Adams. World War II drama that benefits greatly from the fine ensemble acting by McQueen, Darin, Adams, and in lesser roles James Coburn, Harry Guardino and Bob Newhart. The action centers around a single maneuver by a squad of GI's in retaliation against the force of the German Siegfried line. (Dir: Don Siegel, 90 mins.)

Hell on Frisco Bay (1956)**½ Alan Ladd, Edward G. Robinson, Joanne Dru. Waterfront cop out of prison goes after the gangland big shot who was responsible for framing him. Hard-boiled crime melodrama is reminiscent of the gangster films of the 30's. Okay for the action fans. (Dir: Frank Tuttle, 98 mins.)

Hell Raiders (1965)* Bum pow l-pow l story of demolition squad in World War II asked to blow up an American headquarters containing valuable records which could fall into enemy hands. Run for cover. (80 mins.)

Hell Squad (1957)**½ Wally Campo, Brenden Carroll. Better than average war story of the "Lost Patrol" variety; GIs vs Nazis in North Africa. At times, surprisingly good, considering the low budget.

Hell to Eternity (1960)*** Jeff Hunter, David Janssen, Vic Damone. Effective drama about true-life Marine hero Guy Gabaladan and his war time (WW II) story. Jeff Hunter is well cast as the handsome and tough marine who became a hero in the South Pacific. David Janssen delivers the film's best acting job as Guy's smooth talking and smooth operating buddy. Vic Damone, in a non-singing role, also comes across nicely. The battle scenes are first rate. (Dir: Phil Karlson, 132 mins.)

Hell with Heroes, The (1968)** Rod Taylor, Claudia Cardinale, Harry Guardino. Routine smuggling yarn with a competent cast who can't save it. Taylor runs a small air cargo service and he gets into trouble with the authorities when he accepts a deal to fly some loot for smuggler Guardino. The only good thing to come out of Taylor's trouble is

312

meeting Guardino's girl Claudia Cardinale. (Dir: Joseph Sargent, 95 mins.)

Hellbenders, The (1967)** Joseph Cotten, Norma Bengell. This Civil War tale was produced in Spain. Except for Joseph Cotten, the entire cast is European, and the dubbing is apparent. The plot involves a Confederate major and his family who steal Union money to rebuild the Confederacy.

Heller in Pink Tights (1960)**½ Sophia Loren, Anthony Quinn. Fairly entertaining western drama about a theatrical troupe touring the untamed frontier in the 1880's. Slightly different plot, some amusing scenes dealing with the backstage life of the era. (Dir: George Cukor, 100 mins.)

Hellfighters (1969)* John Wayne, Katharine Ross, Vera Miles. Typical juvenile John Wayne adventure yarn about oil fire fighters, and worse than most. "Duke" is the head of the "hellfighters" and Miss Ross is his long-lost daughter. The film mixes a sentimental soap opera plot with action shots, and some customarily dim-witted political philosophizing. (Dir: Andrew V. McLaglen, 121 mins.)

Hellfire Club, The (British, 1963)*½ Keith Mitchell, Adrienne Corri. Returning home to claim his inheritance, a man learns his cousin has taken the estate, is carrying on all sorts of degradations. Lurid costume melodrama with extraneous sensationalism.

Hellgate (1953)**½ Sterling Hayden, Joan Leslie, Ward Bond. An innocent man is convicted of consorting with Civil War guerrillas and sent to suffer the tortures of Hellgate Prison, in barren New Mexico. Strong western drama, unpleasant for women and children, but well made. (Dir: Charles Marquis Warren, 87 mins.)

Hellions, The (British, 1962)** Richard Todd, Anne Aubrey. Five outlaws ride into a frontier town, and the lone lawman is hard put to find help to curtail them. Sounds like a western, sounds like "High Noon"; despite the South African setting, that's about what it is—an imitation, competently made but familiar. (Dir: Ken Annakin, 87 mins.)

Hello, Dolly (1969)***½ Barbra Streisand, Walter Matthau, Louis Armstrong. Huge, lavish, Gene Kelly directed "spectacle" based, of course, on the long running hit Broadway musical. The Broadway success was undeserved, and this transfer to the screen depends almost entirely on Barbra's special magic. She is, of course, quite up to the challenge, even though she is miscast—Barbra is much too young and obviously marriageable while portraying a marriage broker to make the story have much sense—but all these legitimate objections, including a generally routine score, are forgotten when Barbra takes over—as take over she does, especially in a big splashy parade sequence. Barbra overpowers everyone in the cast with the exception of the indomitable "Satchmo" Armstrong making a brief appearance with la Belle Streisand to sing the title song "Hello, Dolly!" which Armstrong helped popularize via his own hit recording of the tune. The story, set in Yonkers, New York, circa 1900, was borrowed from Thornton Wilder, who borrowed the basic plot himself. (118 mins.)

Hello Down There (1969)*½ Tony Randall, Janet Leigh, Ken Berry. Witless underwater shenanigans as Tony Randall convinces his family to test an ocean-floor home by living under the sea for a month. His comic talent can't overcome a silly script. Acting honors go to the dolphins. (Dir: Jack Arnold, 98 mins.)

Hello, Frisco, Hello (1943)*½ John Payne, Alice Faye, Jack Oakie. Story of a Barbary Coast saloon keeper who longs for Nob Hill is a long, boring, undistinguished musical. (Dir: H. Bruce Humberstone, 98 mins.)

Hell's Angels on Wheels (1967)½ Jack Nicholson, Adam Roarke, Sabina Scharf, Sonny Barger. Infamous gang of California motorcycle creeps, out for laughs, terrorizes a small town, indulges in orgies and has a rollicking good time, until their leader gets his come-uppance in the end. Yes, that is THE Jack Nicholson, pre-"Easy Rider," playing a put-upon gas-station attendant who joins the boys. The only thing that redeems this rubbish is some good color cinematography by Leslie Kovacs. (Dir: Richard Rush, 95 mins.)

Hell's Five Hours (1958)*½ Stephen McNally, Coleen Gray, Vic Morrow.

An ex-employee of a rocket fuel company is out to blow up the plant, along with his boss's wife and child. Some suspense, but gets bogged down. (Dir: Jack L. Copeland, 73 mins.)

Hell's Half Acre (1954)**½ Wendell Corey, Evelyn Keyes. Woman goes to Honolulu when she suspects a night club owner of being her husband, believed killed at Pearl Harbor. Involved melodrama has interesting Honolulu locations. (Dir: John H. Auer, 91 mins.)

Hell's Island (1955)*** John Payne, Mary Murphy, Francis L. Sullivan. The whereabouts of a stolen ruby sends John Payne on a wild goose chase with murders and plot twists all along the way. Good for action-melodrama fans. (Dir: Phil Karlson, 84 mins.)

Hell's Kitchen (1939)**½ Ronald Reagan, Dead End Kids. Pretty good Dead End Kids melodrama with the boys involved in blackmail, torture and straightening out the rather unsavory situation in Hell's Kitchen. (Dirs: Lewis Seiler, C.E.A. Dupont, 90 mins.)

Hellstrom Chronicle, The (1971)***½ Lawrence Pressman. Fascinating documentary film on insects, marred only by some inane and inadvertently funny narration by Dr. Hellstrom (Pressman). He tries to make us believe that the creatures will one day conquer the human race. Contains spectacular photography of insects, using varied and new techniques. So ignore the sensationalism of the phony doctor and sit back and watch a remarkable film. (Dir: Walon Green, 90 mins.)

Hellzapoppin (1941)***½ Olsen and Johnson, Mischa Auer, Martha Raye. The two screwballs unfold their own plot when their director tells them they can't make a movie without a story. It depends upon your own particular taste, but for some this hodge-podge will be screamingly funny; as such, recommended. (Dir: H. C. Potter, 84 mins.)

Help! (1965)*** The Beatles. Some funny moments, but much of it is obvious and protracted, and a distinct disappointment to those movie buffs and Beatle fans for whom "A Hard Day's Night" was such a wondrous surprise. Take our word for it that the plot doesn't matter much

in this Richard Lester effort. John, Paul, Ringo, and George are still extraordinarily talented, but their scripters let them down in this frenetic farce. (Dir: Richard Lester, 90 mins.)

Helter Skelter (1976)* George Di Cenzo, Steve Railsback, Nancy Wolfe, Sondra Blake, Skip Homeier. A repellent, irresponsible dramatization of the loathsome Manson mass murders produced for and broadcast by CBS. We are spared the sight of buckets of blood when the hapless victims are stabbed, but otherwise this long—over three-hour—adaptation of the book by prosecuting attorney Vincent Bugliosi and Curt Gentry recounts the orgies, the "thrill" of stabbing some innocent, and the other gruesome details associated with Manson and his demented, psychopathic followers. Some of the acting is quite good, including Di Cenzo as the crazed Manson and Sondra Blake in a brief prison scene. Adapted by James P. Miller who complained at the time about the liberties taken with his original script. (Dir: Tom Gries, 175 mins.)

Hemingway's Adventure of a Young Man—See: Adventures of a Young Man

Hennessy (Great Britain, 1975)**½ Rod Steiger, Lee Remick, Richard Johnson, Trevor Howard, Eric Porter. The Queen of England was enraged. You'll find some suspense. Irish-demolitions-expert Hennessy, who has resigned from the I.R.A., witnesses his wife and daughter killed in a street riot by a British soldier. So he plans to take revenge by single-handedly blowing up Parliament with the Queen in attendance. Scotland Yard is duly alarmed, while the I.R.A. are afraid of the bad publicity. News footage of the Queen is well edited with Hennessy's fictional appearance as a human bomb, but generally this is an apolitical yawn. Story by Richard Johnson, who appears as an impassive Yard man. On-location scenes shot in Belfast. (Dir: Don Sharp, 103 mins.)

Henry V (British, 1945)**** Laurence Olivier, Robert Newton, Leslie Banks, Leo Genn. Olivier's performance is one of the most brilliant ever captured on film, in this, the first film version of Shakespeare's great drama. The entire film is superb in every detail. The distinguished American movie critic James Agee noted, "The one great glory of the film is the language. The seductive power of pacing alone and its shifts and contrasts, in scene after scene, has seldom been equaled in a movie; the adjustments and relationships of tone are just as good. Olivier does many beautiful pieces of reading and playing. There are dozens of large and hundreds of small excellences which Sir Laurence and his associates have developed to sustain Shakespeare's poem." The battle scenes are brilliantly directed by Olivier, the color photography is breathtaking. All in all one of the greatest films ever made.

Her Cardboard Lover (1941)*½ Norma Shearer, Robert Taylor. Not too funny sophisticated comedy about a girl, her male secretary and a "wolf" who's out to get her. Forced, stiff and boring. (Dir: George Cukor, 93 mins.)

Her First Romance (1951)** Margaret O'Brien, Allen Martin, Jr. Margaret O'Brien's first teen-ager film in which she received her first screen kiss. Routine story about adolescence. (Dir: Seymour Friedman, 73 mins.)

Her Husband's Affairs (1948)*½ Franchot Tone, Lucille Ball. In spite of the stars, this is a meaningless farce about a man, his wife and some crazy invention. (Dir: S. Sylvan Simon, 83 mins.)

Her Panelled Door (British, 1952) *** Phyllis Calvert, Edward Underdown. A woman found suffering from amnesia tries to retrace her past. Fairly good psychological melodrama. (Dir: Ladislas Vajda, 84 mins.)

Her Twelve Men (1954)**½ Greer Garson, Robert Ryan, Barry Sullivan. An attempt to make a humorous "Mr. Chips" out of Greer Garson, as a school teacher in a boys' boarding school, just doesn't come off. Greer works hard but the script lets her down. (Dir: Robert Z. Leonard, 91 mins.)

Hercule (French, 1960)*½ Fernandel. Country boy blunders into the newspaper business after being mistaken for a publisher's son. Slow English-dubbed comedy for Fernandel fans only.

Hercules (1960)** Steve Reeves. Successful Italian epic, English dubbed, starring muscleman Steve Reeves as Hercules. Kids will love it. Box office click "Biblical" Tarzan film cued many later imitations. (Dir: Pietro Francisci, 107 mins.)

Hercules Against the Moon Men (Italian, 1965)* Alan Steel. Muscleman comes to the rescue of a country whose inhabitants are forced to undergo a sacrificial ritual imposed on them by invaders from the moon. Wildly fantastic English-dubbed spectacle, just too much. (Dir: Giacomo Gentilomo, 88 mins.)

Hercules Against the Sons of the Sun (Italian, 1963)* Mark Forrest, Anna Maria Pace. Muscleman pits himself against the King of the Incas and some Sun God worshipers in another silly English-dubbed spectacle. (Dir: Osvaldo Civirani, 91 mins.)

Hercules and the Black Pirates (Italian, 1960)* Alan Steel, Rosalina Neri. Captain foils a plot to kidnap the daughter of the governor. Silly swashbuckling adventure, dubbed in English.

Hercules and the Captive Women (Italian, 1962)** Reg Park, Fay Spain. The muscleman matches wits with a wicked queen of Atlantis, escapes from the lost city. More fanciful than many of these other English-dubbed spectacles. Some fair moments of action. (Dir: Vittorio Cottafavi, 87 mins.)

Hercules and the Masked Rider (Italian, 1960)* Alan Steel, Ettore Manni. Spanish soldier becomes the leader of a gypsy band and fights the oppressors. Weak swashbuckler dubbed in English.

Hercules and the Ten Avengers (Italian, 1964)* Dan Vadis. Muscleman fights for the Greeks, has to best ten giant warriors sent by the enemy. Poor spectacle, English-dubbed —quo, Vadis? Whoa, Vadis!

Hercules and the Treasure of the Incas (Italian, 1960)* Alan Steel. Muscleman battles a hostile tribe in quest of a secret treasure. Ridiculous spectacle dubbed in English.

Hercules and the Tyrants of Babylon (Italian, 1964)* Rock Stevens, Helga Line. Muscleman pits his strength against three wicked rulers. Childish English-dubbed spectacle.

Hercules in the Haunted World (Italian, 1961)* Reg Park, Christopher Lee. Hercules literally goes to Hell, taking the advice of his nonfans. He's looking for a plant that will break a mysterious spell. Unfortunately he finds it. Dubbed in English, of course. (Dir: Mario Bava, 83 mins.)

Hercules in the Vale of Woe (Italian, 1964)*½ Kirk Morris, Frank Gordon. Couple of con men find themselves back in Caesar's time ready to do battle with Hercules and Maciste. Burlesque of the spear-and-sandal epics the Italians do so badly, but the originals are funnier, even if unintentionally so. Dubbed in English.

Hercules of the Desert (Italian, 1964)* Kirk Morris, Helene Chanel. Muscleman comes to the aid of nomads under the thumb of a ruthless princess. Brainless English-dubbed action spectacle.

Hercules, Prisoner of Evil (Italian, 1964)* Reg Park, Mireille Granelli. Nasty prince frames the muscleman so it seems like he's in cahoots with a monster terrorizing the territory. English-dubbed spectacle.

Hercules Unchained (1961)** Sequel to Hercules—juvenile adventure epic starring muscleman Steve Reeves and an Italian cast, English dubbed. (Dir: Pietro Francisci, 101 mins.)

Hercules vs Ulysses (Italian, 1962)*½ Georges Marchal, Michael Lane. Mighty men of muscle meet in a mishmash of mediocre malarkey. English-dubbed.

Here Come the Girls (1953)**½ Bob Hope, Tony Martin, Arlene Dahl. Chorus boy is shoved into the limelight as leading man of a show when the star is threatened by a killer. Fairly amusing Hope comedy, the comedian up to his usual bag of tricks. (Dir: Claude Binyon, 78 mins.)

Here Come the Waves (1944)*** Bing Crosby, Betty Hutton. Fairly cute nautical musical about a successful crooner who joins the Navy. Best song is "Accentuate the Positive." (Dir: Mark Sandrich, 99 mins.)

Here Comes Mr. Jordan (1941)**** Robert Montgomery, Claude Rains, Evelyn Keyes. Boxer in a plane crash discovers his time isn't up as yet, so the celestial powers have to find him a new body. One of the most unusual, original fantasies ever made; fine entertainment all

around. (Dir: Alexander Hall, 93 mins.)

Here Comes the Groom (1951)*** Bing Crosby, Jane Wyman, Franchot Tone, Alexis Smith. Likable Frank Capra comedy with songs about a happy-go-lucky reporter who competes with a real-estate dealer for the hand of a girl. Nice songs, general air of good fun. (Dir: Frank Capra, 113 mins.)

Here We Go Round the Mulberry Bush (British, 1968)*½ Barry Evans, Judy Geeson, Angela Scoular, Denholm Elliott. A stupefyingly awful script which offers a barrage of relentlessly unfunny jokes and situations, smothers whatever merit there is in the directorial touches of Clive Donner and a not unattractive cast of English players. Seventeen-year-old student determines to do something about his virginity—i.e., lose it at the first possible opportunity. Filmed with several attractive flourishes, in and around London. (Dir: Clive Donner, 96 mins.)

Here's Your Life (Swedish, 1967)**½ Gunnar Bjornstrand, Per Oscarsson, Ulla Sjoberg. How a boy (Eddie Axberg) comes of age during World War I. Slow-paced, but catches some of the real yearnings and frustrations of youth. Well acted. Impressive first feature by young director Jan Troell, who also collaborated on the screenplay.

Hero, The (British, 1969)* Richard Harris, Romy Schneider. Forty-year-old Eitan Bloomfield (Harris) is headed for his last game as a soccer superstar. (Also his last directorial assignment, perhaps.) But he won't go without using up every movie cliche he can think of. Harris made his directorial debut, and his direction is more excessive than his acting! He even hired his cousin to write the music. (97 mins.)

Hero of Babylon (Italian, 1963)*½ Gordon Scott, Michael Lane. More sandal-and-spear stuff, as the former "Tarzan" looks out of place amid a bunch of English-dubbed actors.

Hero of Rome (Italian, 1963)*½ Gordon Scott, Gabriella Pallotta. Brave warrior battles the forces of a tyrant who acquires a powerful army to regain Rome. Usual sort of historical action spectacle dubbed in English—big battles, little sense.

Herod the Great (1960)** Edmund Purdom, Sylvia Lopez. One of many

Italian made spectacles with sumptuous sets (used over and over again), cliched scripts and confusing dubbed-in-English performances by a mixture of British, American and Italian actors. Also, some scenes may be considered too sexy for family viewing and will probably be snipped for early evening showings. (Dir: Arnaldo Genoino, 93 mins.)

Heroes of Telemark (1965)**½ Kirk Douglas, Richard Harris, Ulla Jacobsson. A true-life WW II incident is turned into a moderately interesting adventure drama. Kirk Douglas heads a group of brave Norwegians who stop at nothing to destroy a Nazi plant producing essential matter for the development of the atomic bomb. The colorful Norwegian locations help make some of the heroics more believable. (Dir: Anthony Mann, 131 mins.)

Hero's Island (1962)*½ James Mason, Neville Brand, Rip Torn. A pirate comes to the aid of a man to save his Carolina island from marauders who consider it their own. Inept historical drama handles a good idea badly. Cast does what they can with it. (Dir: Leslie Stevens, 94 mins.)

Herostratus (British, 1967)**** Michael Gothard, Gabriella Licudi, Malcolm Muggeridge. Despite its occasional obvious faults, this is a remarkable, chilling, and provocative film which never got the American commercial release it so richly deserved. An impoverished, disillusioned young poet who sees a plastic, uncaring, and unfeeling society all around him decides to commit suicide. But he's anxious to get as much publicity as possible for the "event," so he offers his death to the head of an advertising agency to capitalize on. Written, directed, and edited by Don Levy, a young American director working on a miniscule budget of less than $50,000. Much of the dialogue was improvised by the actors as they went along. Some resourceful shots and technical effects. Filmed mostly in black and white. For those of you who have forgotten, Herostratus was the man who burned down the temple at Ephesus to guarantee himself eternal fame. (142 mins.)

Hey, I'm Alive (1975)**½ Sally Struthers, Edward Asner. In 1963, young Helen Klaban and middle-aged Ralph Flores crashed in the frozen Yukon wilderness and, somehow, managed to survive for 49 days. This harrowing true-life ordeal is a natural for dramatization, and the TV film starring Struthers and Asner is a fairly good one. Since the action is limited and the scenes repetitive, the middle section bogs down a bit. The performances of the stars, especially Asner, keep things interesting. The ending is well handled, and you'll probably find yourself cheering for their rescue. Made-for-TV. (Dir: Lawrence Schiller, 72 mins.)

Hey, Let's Twist (1961)* Joey Dee, The Starliters, Teddy Randazzo. The height of the twist era spawned this songfest, with minimal plot about sons inheriting a nightclub to keep things moving. Twist the dial elsewhere. (Dir: Greg Garrison, 80 mins.)

Hey, Pineapple! (Japanese, 1963)*½ Dubbed in English—story of Hawaiian Japanese-Americans who fought in the Korean conflict, infiltrating enemy lines. Offbeat war story marred by dull treatment, English dubbing. Japanese cast.

Hey, Rookie (1944)**½ Ann Miller, Larry Parks. Big producer is drafted, stages a big Army show. Pleasant comedy musical with some above average material. (Dir: Charles Barton, 77 mins.)

Hey There, It's Yogi Bear (1964)*½ First movie-length appearance for TV's animated cartoon, Yogi Bear. A series of escapades lands him far from Jellystone National Park, in the Chizzling Brothers Circus. For tiny kiddies. (Dirs: William Hanna, Joseph Barbera, 89 mins.)

Hi-Jack Highway—See: Gas-Oil

Hiawatha (1952)** Vincent Edwards, Keith Larsen, Yvette Dugay. Indian brave tries to prevent a war among tribes perpetrated by a hot-headed warrior. Mildly entertaining adventure based on Longfellow's poem. (Dir: Kurt Neumann, 80 mins.)

Hickey and Boggs (1972)**½ Robert Culp, Bill Cosby. Everyone's chasing $400,000 of stolen bank loot including detectives Al Hickey (Cosby) and Frank Boggs (Culp). The "I Spy" team work with the same understatement that made them super to watch on TV, but there isn't enough character development in Walter Hill's script to merit their glancing at each other with so much familiarity. Culp's direction paces the film well with shoot-outs and destruction on the streets of LA. (111 mins.)

Hidden Eye, The (1945)*** Edward Arnold, Frances Rafferty. Blind detective uses his powers to save an innocent man and uncover a murder plot. Tightly knit, suspenseful mystery, above average. (Dir: Richard Whorf, 69 mins.)

Hidden Fear (1957)** John Payne, Alexander Knox. Routine crime meller set in Copenhagen has American (Payne) arriving on the scene to investigate his young sister's involvement with a group of "intrigue-soaked" characters. You've seen it all before at least a hundred times. (Dir: Andre de Toth, 83 mins.)

Hidden Room, The (British, 1949) ***½ Robert Newton, Sally Gray, Phil Brown. A madly jealous doctor captures his wife's paramour and imprisons him in a deserted bomb-site cellar, where he intends to slowly kill him. Tense, excellently acted and directed melodrama. (Dir: Edward Dmytryk, 98 mins.)

Hide and Seek (British, 1963)**½ Ian Carmichael, Janet Munro, Curt Jurgens. Professor involved in government work becomes a target for spies who want to kidnap him. Agreeable melodrama, played not too seriously, does well with the familiar material.

Hideout, The (British, 1949)*** Howard Keel, Valerie Hobson. An escaped criminal forces a young couple to hide him out while the law pursues him. Tense melodrama, Keel does a good acting job in a non-singing role.

High and Dry (British, 1953)*** Paul Douglas, Alex Mackenzie, Hubert Gregg. An American businessman runs afoul of a rickety cargo vessel in Scotland in this wryly amusing comedy with the crafty Ealing Studios touch. (Dir: Alexander Mackendrick, 93 mins.)

High and Low (Japanese, 1963)**** Toshiro Mifune, Kyoko Kagawa. Long but grippingly filmed crime story adapted by the Japanese from an American novel by Ed "87th Precinct" McBain. Fascinatingly detailed plot about a kidnaping attempt that backfires and turns into a murder case for the hard-working police. Something different for those who prefer the unusual. Dubbed-in English. (Dir: Akira Kurosawa, 142 mins.)

High and the Mighty, The (1954) ***½ John Wayne, Claire Trevor, Robert Stack, Jan Sterling, Laraine Day, David Brian. Passengers on a crippled airplane feel compelled to review their lives and in doing so come to a new awareness. Overlong and episodic but successful in its suspense. (Dir: William Wellman, 147 mins.)

High Barbaree (1946)*½ Van Johnson, June Allyson, Thomas Mitchell. Two airmen are floating on a raft in the Pacific and while one moans the other bores him to death with the story of his life. (Dir: Jack Conway, 91 mins.)

High Bright Sun, The—See: McGuire Go Home

High Commissioner, The (British, 1968)**½ Rod Taylor, Christopher Plummer, Lilli Palmer, Franchot Tone, Camilla Sparv, Daliah Lavi, Leo McKern, Clive Revill. Dogged Australian sleuth (Rod Taylor) arrives in London to arrest a political bigwig for murder. Mystery never quite achieves the mark intended, despite a fine cast. (Dir: Ralph Thomas, 93 mins.)

High Cost of Loving, The (1958)*** Jose Ferrer, Gena Rowlands, Jim Backus. Fine, if somewhat thin, satire of a white-collar worker's insecure job. Ferrer directs and plays Jim Fry, who fears he is going to be fired at the same time he learns his wife is pregnant. Entertaining, but the ending is too predictable. (87 mins.)

High Flight (British, 1958)**½ Ray Milland, Kenneth Haigh. Well acted (particularly by Kenneth Haigh as an arrogant young R.A.F. flyer) drama about the training of R.A.F. jet flying cadets. Personal drama revolves around the relationship of instructor Milland and his most brilliant but stubbornly undisciplined pupil. (Dir. John Gilling, 89 mins.)

High Infidelity (France-Italy, 1964) *** Nino Manfredi, Charles Aznavour, Claire Bloom, Monica Vitti, Jean-Pierre Cassel, Ugo Tognazzi. Four tales of marital "infidelity," minor infractions. Pleasant, often witty quartet, complemented by the performances of some appealing stars. Directors, in order: Mario Monicelli, Elio Petri, Franco Rossi, Luciano Salce. (120 mins.)

High Lonesome (1950)*** John Barrymore Jr., Chill Wills. A mysterious young man wanders into a ranch and sets into motion a series of weird happenings. Expert combination of western and mystery, well above average. (Dir: Alan LeMay, 81 mins.)

High Noon (1952)**** Gary Cooper, Grace Kelly. Well on its way to becoming a western classic; story of a brave lawman who has to face outlaws sworn to kill him on his wedding day. As fine an outdoor drama as one could wish, as witness its numerous awards. (Dir: Fred Zinnemann, 85 mins.)

High Plains Drifter (1973)** Clint Eastwood, Verna Bloom. For bloodthirsty fans of the tough, silent, and sexy sado-superheroics of Clint Eastwood as a cowboy to reckon with. You could swear Sergio Leone directed this ambling, violence-ridden western but it is Clint himself who called the directorial shots. The stranger (Clint) rides into the town of Lago, killing three varmints, raping a willing wench, and taking over in anticipation of standing up to three other culprits just released from prison. (105 mins.)

High-Powered Rifle, The (1960)* Willard Parker, Allison Hayes. Private-eye adventure. Shot at by hired thugs, detective Parker sets out to find the killer who employed them. Nothing new. (Dir: Maury Dexter, 62 mins.)

High Risk (Made-for-TV—1976)** Victor Buono, Joseph Sirola, Don Stroud. Another pilot for an adventure series which starts off well but dissipates before long. A group of former circus performers exercise their penchant for larceny by executing an elaborate plan to steal a jewel-encrusted mask from a foreign embassy in Washington, D.C. The planning is more fun than the actual robbery sequences and besides, it was all done so much better in "Topkapi." (Dir: Sam O'Steen, 72 mins.)

High School (1969)**** A brilliant documentary about a middle-class American high school in Philadelphia and the way in which it—and thousands of other schools all over the country—kills the creative spirit in students and graduates uniformed robots. Produced and directed by Frederick Wiseman, the most important and gifted documentary filmmaker at work in America today. This is a chilling statement about the intellectual and moral bankruptcy of so much contemporary education. Should be seen by all adults and students in or above the junior-high-school level. No famous paid actors here—just typical students in joyless classrooms, where banality is encouraged by the generally pitiful, brutalizing faculty. (75 mins.)

High School Confidential (1958)* Russ Tamblyn, Mamie Van Doren, Jan Sterling. New student gets in with the high school dope-taking crowd. Proves to be an undercover agent. Like, man, this is ghastly! Alternate title: **Young Hellions.** (Dir: Jack Arnold, 85 mins.)

High School Hellcats (1959)*½ Yvonne Lime, Jana Lund. High school girl falls in with a cruel sorority. Immature drama.

High Sierra (1941)***½ Humphrey Bogart, Ida Lupino, Arthur Kennedy. Tired old killer on the loose theme receives an exciting rejuvenation from this superb cast aided by an excellent script and production. (Dir: Raoul Walsh, 100 mins.)

High Society (1956)*** Bing Crosby, Grace Kelly, Frank Sinatra. Musical version of "The Philadelphia Story," about the efforts of a wealthy man to win back his ex-wife who's about to be remarried, and the reporters who become entangled in the romantic complications. With a stellar cast and a Cole Porter score, it should have been better than it is, but somehow it lacks the sparkle of the original. Nevertheless, pleasant fun. (Dir: Charles Walters, 107 mins.)

High Time (1960)*** Bing Crosby, Fabian, Tuesday Weld. What happens when a wealthy widower returns to college to complete his education. Episodic comedy starts excellently but wears thin before the conclusion. Generally good fun. (Dir: Blake Edwards, 130 mins.)

High Treason (British, 1952)***½ Liam Redmond. Thrilling spy drama with plot twists that keep the pace fast and tense. Good script. (Dir: Roy Boulting, 93 mins.)

High Wall (1947)*** Robert Taylor, Audrey Totter, Herbert Marshall. Lady doctor helps a man regain his memory, then proves he didn't kill his wife. Suspenseful, well acted mystery melodrama. (Dir: Curtis Bernhardt, 99 mins.)

High, Wide and Handsome (1937)*** Irene Dunne, Randolph Scott, Dorothy Lamour. Musical tale of the robust adventure which surrounded the discovery of oil in Pennsylvania around 1860. Music by Jerome Kern and Oscar Hammerstein II. Not as good as it seems when you study the credits, but enterprising. (Dir: Rouben Mamoulian, 110 mins.)

High Wind in Jamaica (1965)***½ Anthony Quinn, James Coburn. Good adventure drama with fine acting by the cast headed by Quinn as the captain of a pirate vessel. There's a great deal of action when Captain Quinn's ship encounters another vessel and takes some children and the crew. It turns into a stark drama before the climax and never lets up until the tragic ending. Based on the famous novel. (Dir: Alexander Mackendrick, 104 mins.)

Higher and Higher (1943)*** Michele Morgan, Jack Haley, Frank Sinatra, Victor Borge. Man unable to pay his servants forms a corporation with them. Entertaining musical comedy. (Dir: Tim Whelan, 90 mins.)

Highly Dangerous (British, 1951)*** Margaret Lockwood, Dane Clark. Pretty lady scientist and an American reporter risk their necks obtaining vital information behind the Iron Curtain. Exciting, entertaining spy thriller. (Dir: Roy Baker, 88 mins.)

Highway Dragnet (1954)** Joan Bennett, Richard Conte. A routine chase film of an ex-marine, accused of murdering a girl he has just met. Richard Conte gives a good performance despite the weak script. (Dir: Nathan Juran, 71 mins.)

Highway to Battle (British, 1960)** Gerald Heinz, Margaret Tyzack. Enemy agents search for a political refugee. Standard espionage drama. (Dir: Ernest Morris, 71 mins.)

Hijack (1973)** David Janssen and Keenan Wynn are the stars of this suspenseful film about two truck drivers, down on their luck, who take on the job of driving a secret cargo from Los Angeles to Houston. On-location footage in the Antelope Valley, near the Mojave Desert, and a number of gripping auto scenes spark the show. Made-for-TV. (Dir: Leonard Horn, 90 mins.)

Hilda Crane (1956)*½ Jean Simmons,

Guy Madison, Jean-Pierre Aumont. Big-budget soap opera—can a woman with a past still find happiness? Does any one still care? (Dir: Philip Dunne, 87 mins.)

Hill, The (1965)***½ Sean Connery, Harry Andrews, Ossie Davis. Director Sidney Lumet has etched a chilling study of a British military prison in Africa during WW II. The hitch here is that the inmates are British soldiers. Their almost inhuman treatment makes an absorbing and memorable drama. Sean Connery has never been better as an outspoken, tough prisoner and the supporting cast is flawless, especially Harry Andrews as the sinister head of the detention camp. You won't soon forget the scenes of Connery assaulting the ever crumbling "Hill." (122 mins.)

Hill 24 Doesn't Answer (1955)***½ Edward Mulhare, Haya Hararit. First feature made in Israel. Story of four Israeli volunteers who defended their homeland at the cost of their lives. Grim drama with numerous moving scenes. (Dir: Thorold Dickinson, 100 mins.)

Hills of Home (1948)*** Lassie, Donald Crisp, Janet Leigh, Edmund Gwenn. Sentimental warm tale of a Scottish doctor (Gwenn) and his beloved collie. Certainly the best dog loves man film since "Lassie Come Home." Big difference here is that Gwenn steals the honors from Lassie. (Dir: Fred M. Wilcox, 97 mins.)

Hillsboro Story, The—See: **Divorce**

Hindenburg, The (1975)*½ George C. Scott, Anne Bancroft, William Atherton, Burgess Meredith, Charles Durning. Another disaster film which turns out to be not only boring but unintentionally funny. Based on the book by Michael M. Mooney about the legendary dirigible disaster of May 6, 1937, and featuring George C. Scott as a troubled German officer. A fictional view, of course, of what really happened on that fateful day, as the mean Nazis are alerted to the possibility of sabotage. The script, however, sabotaged this film, and the best acting is from the exploding dirigible. (Dir: Robert Wise, 125 mins.)

Hippodrome (German, 1961) Gerhard Reidmann, Willy Birgel, Margit Nunke. Adventures, romantic and otherwise, of a girl performer in a circus. Ponderous. (Dir: Herbert Gruber, 96 mins.)

Hired Gun, The (1957)** Rory Calhoun, Anne Francis, Vince Edwards, Chuck Connors. Professional gunfighter is offered a large reward to bring back an escaped murderess. Average western with a better than average cast. (Dir: Ray Nazarro, 63 mins.)

Hired Hand, The (1971)**½ Peter Fonda, Verna Bloom, Warren Oates. Uneven, but often sensitive drama set in New Mexico in 1880, and directed by Peter Fonda. Verna Bloom takes the acting honors with a moving performance as the patient wife of Fonda, an itinerant cowhand. Aided by excellent cinematography and an unobtrusive but helpful musical score. (93 mins.)

Hired Wife (1940)*** Rosalind Russell, Brian Aherne. Super-secretary marries her boss for business reasons, finds domesticity more difficult than work. Entertaining comedy. (Dir: William A. Seiter, 93 mins.)

Hiroshima, Mon Amour (French, 1959)**** Emmanuele Riva, Eliji Okada. The international film hit is slightly hampered by the English language dubbing for its TV showing, but it is still one of the greatest films of all time. French Director Alain Resnais has created a magnificent mood piece in his telling of the unique love story of a French cinema actress and a Japanese architect who meet in Hiroshima years after the war. Emmanuele Riva and Eliji Okada give memorable performances as the lovers. (88 mins.)

His Butler's Sister (1943)*** Deanna Durbin, Franchot Tone, Pat O'Brien. A pleasant romantic comedy that has Deanna Durbin's singing to bolster the proceedings. Deanna, as a maid, gets her employer to fall in love with her. (Dir: Frank Borzage, 94 mins.)

His Girl Friday (1940)**** Cary Grant, Rosalind Russell. Screamingly funny farce about a crafty editor trying to lure his ace reporter (and ex-wife) back on the job. Hilarious, frantic film. (Dir: Howard Hawks, 92 mins.)

His Kind of Woman (1951)*** Robert Mitchum, Jane Russell, Vincent Price. Fall guy in a plot to bring an expatriated racketeer back to the U. S. gets wise and rounds up the crooks. Long but lively, entertaining melodrama. (Dir: John Farrow, 120 mins.)

His Majesty O'Keefe (1954)*** Burt Lancaster. Action packed pirate story about the derring-do of a brave adventurer, Burt Lancaster. Fun for the younger set. (Dir: Byron Haskin, 92 mins.)

History Is Made at Night (1937)**½ Charles Boyer, Jean Arthur. The eternal triangle of wife, husband and other man in a curious mixture of comedy and melodrama. Some bright moments, including a finely portrayed shipwreck sequence. (Dir: Frank Borzage, 110 mins.)

History of Mr. Polly, The (British, 1949)***½ John Mills, Sally Ann Howes. A young draper carries a dream of adventure replacing his placid life, finally achieves the dream. Witty, tastefully done period comedy-drama. Excellent performances. (Dir: Anthony Pelissier, 96 mins.)

Hit and Run (1957)* Hugo Haas, Cleo Moore, Vince Edwards. Drivel about a middle-aged man married to a showgirl, who plans an accident to eliminate her young boyfriend. Run! (Dir: Hugo Haas, 84 mins.)

Hit Lady (1974)**½ Yvette Mimieux. Yvette Mimieux wrote the screenplay for this predictable but slick gangster drama in which she stars as the beauty playing a cool, collected and deadly hired assassin. The best scenes involve the "hit lady's" setting up of her victims and, for those who don't catch on earlier, there's a twist ending. Made-for-TV. (Dir: Tracy Keenan Wynn, 72 mins.)

Hitched (1971)* Tim Matheson, Sally Field, Neville Brand. Western-comedy, as a pair of newlyweds overcome mishaps in the early West. "Hitched" falls apart quickly. Made-for-TV. (Dir: Boris Sagal, 100 mins.)

Hitchhike (1974)** Cloris Leachman, Richard Brandon, Sherry Jackson. Miss Leachman plays Los Angeles motorist Claire Stephens, who picks up a hitchhiker on her way to San Francisco. Her passenger is on the run after murdering his stepmother. Routine stuff. Made-for-TV. (Dir: Gordon Hessler.)

Hitchhiker, The (1953)***½ Frank Lovejoy, Edmond O'Brien, William Talman. Two men on a camping trip are waylaid and held by a desperate fugitive. Excellent, spellbinding melodrama, tense and exciting; directed by Ida Lupino. (71 mins).

Hitler (1962)** Richard Basehart, Maria Emo. Story of the rise to power of the infamous Nazi dictator. Despite the good intentions it has nothing unseen before—and doesn't have the production values necessary for the scope of the tale. Basehart tries, but misses as Adolf. (Dir: Stuart Heisler, 107 mins.)

Hitler: The Last Ten Days (Great Britain-Italy, 1973)* Alec Guinness, Simon Ward, Diane Cilento, Adolfo Celi. A shameful film. The fascination with the Hitler legend seems to be endless, but that still doesn't justify this production, which is a rehash of known facts about Hitler's last days in his bunker fortress and his stormy relationships with his love, Eva Braun, and his military henchmen. Alec Guinness, a peculiar choice to play the Führer, is too cerebral and misses out on the madness of the man. There's an unintended laugh when Eva refers to Adolf's art work and laments, "Why didn't he turn his energies to art rather than war . . ." Amen to that! Narrated by Alistair Cooke. (Dir: Ennio de Concini, 106 mins.)

Hitler's Children (1943)*** Tim Holt, Bonita Granville. Two youngsters are caught in the relentless gears of the Nazi war machine. Good drama of wartime Germany. (Dir: Edward Dmytryk, 83 mins.)

Hitler's Executioners—See: Executioners, The

H. M. Pulham, Esq. (1941)***½ Hedy Lamarr, Robert Young, Ruth Hussey, Van Heflin. The life of a stuffy Bostonian who is momentarily uprooted from his life by a love affair. Tastefully produced, superbly directed drama, with Young giving a superb performance. (Dir: King Vidor, 120 mins.)

Hobson's Choice (British, 1954)**** Charles Laughton, John Mills, Brenda de Banzie. A spinster picks out a shy young man, and literally drags him to the altar. Wonderfully bright, clever comedy, with a masterful performance by Laughton as old Mr. Hobson, who likes his spot of whiskey now and then. A comic delight. (Dir: David Lean, 107 mins.)

Hoffman (Great Britain, 1969)**½ Peter Sellers, Sinead Cusack. Certainly not one of Sellers' best entries, but there are some off-beat laughs along the way in this story about a lonely middle-aged man who blackmails a young female typist into spending a week in his apartment. Sellers' character is a little like an aged Benjamin Braddock from "The Graduate." Screenplay by Ernest Gebler from his novel. (Dir: Alvin Rakoff, 113 mins.)

Hold Back the Dawn (1941)***½ Charles Boyer, Olivia de Havilland, Paulette Goddard. Beautiful, moving story of a refugee from the Nazis who woos and weds an American girl in Mexico merely to gain admittance to the U. S. Excellent script, direction and acting. One of Boyer's best. (Dir: Mitchell Leisen, 115 mins.)

Hold Back the Night (1956)**½ John Payne, Mona Freeman. Nothing exceptional but fairly entertaining Korean War story. (Dir: Allan Dwan, 80 mins.)

Hold Back Tomorrow (1956)* Cleo Moore, John Agar. Embarrassingly bad film with two incredibly inept performances by the stars. Story concerns a condemned prisoner and a town prostitute who find love just before the death toll. If you enjoy really terrible acting, tune in. (Dir: Hugo Haas, 75 mins.)

Hold On! (1966)*½ Peter Noone, Shelley Fabares, Herman's Hermits. A juvenile opus geared to spotlight the talents of the popular recording group, Herman's Hermits. The plot, if you can label it that, manages to involve the U.S. Air Space program, a publicity-hungry starlet, a rich girl's romantic attentions and the ever present mobs of screaming female fans. (Dir: Arthur Lubin, 85 mins.)

Hold That Co-ed (1938)***½ John Barrymore, George Murphy, Joan Davis. Barrymore in a hilarious musical comedy about politics and football. The great man appears as a caricature of all political demagogues and he's magnificent. Good fun. Murphy has since added some comedy to non-Hollywood politics. (Dir: George Marshall, 80 mins.)

Hole in the Head, A (1959)*** Frank Sinatra, Edward G. Robinson, Eleanor Parker. Fairly funny film with a good measure of sentimental jazz thrown in. Sinatra plays a good-time Charlie who comes to the end of his financial rope and has to re-evaluate his place in life. Edward G. Robinson is a standout as Sinatra's older brother who bails him out time and again. (Dir: Frank Capra, 120 mins.)

Holiday (1938)***½ Katharine Hepburn, Cary Grant, Lew Ayres. Society girl falls for her sister's fiance, sees that the family is going to run his life for him. Sophisticated comedy has plenty of class, expert performances. (Dir: George Cukor, 100 mins.)

Holiday Affair (1947)**½ Robert Mitchum, Janet Leigh, Wendell Corey. War widow with a small son is faced with having to choose between two suitors. Mildly amusing comedy-drama. (Dir: Don Hartman, 87 mins.)

Holiday Camp (British, 1947)**½ Flora Robson, Dennis Price, Jack Warner. Typical family has many varied adventures at a vacation resort. Loosely written, uneven comedy-drama. (Dir: Ken Annakin, 97 mins.)

Holiday for Henrietta (France, 1954)***½ Hildegarde Neff, Michel Auclair, Dany Robin. Captivating comedy about the making of a movie, and the participants' inability to distinguish fact from fiction. Plot summary doesn't do justice to the inventive, stylish quality of the film. (Dir: Julien Duvivier)

Holiday for Lovers (1959)** Clifton Webb, Jane Wyman, Carol Lynley, Gary Crosby. Psychiatrist and his wife face the difficulties of keeping their daughters from romance while on a tour of South America. Lightweight romantic comedy has all been done before. (Dir: Henry Levin, 103 mins.)

Holiday for Sinners (1952)*** Gig Young, Janice Rule, Keenan Wynn. The future and plans of a young doctor are changed when a broken-down prizefighter commits murder. Offbeat drama taking place in New Orleans during the Mardi Gras. Unusual in plotting, presentation—fine performance by Wynn as the fighter. (Dir: Gerald Mayer, 72 mins.)

Holiday in Havana (1949)** Desi Arnaz, Mary Hatcher. A Cuban beat, Desi Arnaz, and you have this mild musical comedy about carnival time in Havana.

Holiday in Mexico (1946)*** Walter Pidgeon, Jane Powell, Xavier Cugat. Semi-classical music is spiced with some Latin American melodies in this musical treat. Plot about a widowed ambassador to Mexico and his teen-age daughter who tries to run his house doesn't interfere with Miss Powell's singing, Cugat's rhumbas and Jose Iturbi's piano. (Dir: George Sidney, 127 mins.)

Holiday Inn (1942)***½ Fred Astaire, Bing Crosby. Irving Berlin's finest music ("White Christmas," "Easter Parade," "Be Careful, It's My Heart"), plus Bing and Fred add up to a screen delight. (Dir: Mark Sandrich, 101 mins.)

Holly and the Ivy, The (British, 1953)***½ Ralph Richardson, Celia Johnson, Margaret Leighton. A country parson gathers his family together at Christmas, discovers that because of him they are unhappy. Superlatively acted drama, slowly paced but always absorbing. (Dir: George More O'Ferrall, 80 mins.)

Hollywood Canteen (1944)**½ Bette Davis, Joan Crawford, Jack Carson, Dane Clark. Just about everybody makes a guest appearance in this piece of Hollywood propaganda. Everybody likes names so you'll enjoy it. But outside of some good musical numbers, it's an awful movie. (Dir: Delmer Daves, 124 mins.)

Hollywood Cavalcade (1939)*** Don Ameche, Alice Faye. Film which traces the history of the motion-picture industry (through 1939) has some wonderful moments. It eventually gets lost in the cliche mill but its earlier scenes are worth catching. (Dir: Irving Cummings, 96 mins.)

Hollywood Cowboy—See: **Hearts of the West**

Hollywood or Bust (1956)*** Dean Martin, Jerry Lewis, Anita Ekberg. A movie nut journeys west to meet his favorite star, picks up a gambler along the way. One of the whackier Martin-Lewis farces has some inventive gags, a fast pace. Good fun. (Dir: Frank Tashlin, 95 mins.)

Holy Matrimony (1943)***½ Monty Woolley, Gracie Fields. Superbly acted tale of a great artist who poses as his dead valet, gets married and involved in scandal when his wife innocently sells some of his paintings. Wonderful fun. (Dir: John M. Stahl, 87 mins.)

Homage to Chagall—The Colours of Love (Canada, 1976)***½ A visual-

323

ly stunning, understandably admiring tribute to the great 20th-century artist Marc Chagall, written, produced and directed by Canadian documentary filmmaker Harry Rasky. Produced originally for the CBC television, the focus is almost entirely on the paintings and other work of the great Russian-born artist. The luminous paintings, photographed imaginatively in many parts of the world and from many collections, are enough reason to watch and be dazzled. (Dir: Harry Rasky, 88 mins.)

Hombre (1967)***½ Paul Newman, Fredric March, Diane Cilento. Thoughtful, generally absorbing western, starring Paul Newman as a white man raised by Indians. The plot begins to resemble the John Wayne classic "Stagecoach" when Newman boards a stage on which Fredric March and the rest of the principals are passengers, and there is a final shoot out between the good guys (Newman and pals), and the outlaws. However, the screenplay by Irving Ravetch and Harriet Frank, Jr. raises some interesting human and moral issues along the way, and it's all held together by Martin Ritt's taut direction. (111 mins.)

Home at Seven (British, 1952)*** Ralph Richardson, Margaret Leighton, Jack Hawkins. A bank clerk returns home to discover he has been missing one day, due to amnesia, and that he is suspect in a murder. Clever mystery melodrama, well acted and directed (by Richardson) and with several twists. (85 mins.)

Home Before Dark (1958)**½ Jean Simmons, Dan O'Herlihy, Rhonda Fleming, Efrem Zimbalist, Jr. Jean Simmons gives a fine performance in this drama about a young woman who comes home after being hospitalized for a nervous breakdown. Her struggle to pick up the pieces of her broken life is touchingly portrayed. The film loses its initial punch about halfway through and settles into soap opera. (Dir: Mervyn Le Roy, 136 mins.)

Home for the Holidays (1972)** Eleanor Parker, Sally Field, Julie Harris, Walter Brennan. Murder melodrama uses all the standard tricks to convey terror. Unhappy daughter returning to their father's bedside for a family get-together,

only to become the target of a deranged killer. Made-for-TV. (Dir: John Llewellyn Moxey, 73 mins.)

Home from the Hill (1960)**** Robert Mitchum, Eleanor Parker, George Peppard, George Hamilton. Powerful yarn of a southern town, a roistering landowner, his son, and the youth whose relationship to the family causes tragedy. Fine characterization builds in interest, makes the drama absorbing throughout its length. Excellent performances, especially by Mitchum and Peppard. Recommended. (Dir: Vincente Minnelli, 150 mins.)

Home in Indiana (1944)*** Walter Brennan, Lon McCallister, Jeanne Crain, June Haver. A routine plot but delightful performances and photography make this film about harness racing a pleasure to see. Lon drives a blind filly in the big race and you'll find yourself cheering. (Dir: Henry Hathaway, 103 mins.)

Home Is the Hero (Irish, 1961)*** Arthur Kennedy, Walter Macken. Based on a well-known play by Macken, this is a leisurely drama about a violent-tempered man who returns to his household after serving a prison sentence for manslaughter, the changes he finds, he tries to make within himself. Some fine acting by the Abbey Players, authentic atmosphere helps the slow pace. (Dir: Fielder Cook, 83 mins.)

Home of the Brave (1949)***½ Lloyd Bridges, Frank Lovejoy, James Edwards. Negro soldier on a dangerous Pacific patrol is made a mental case by the intolerance of his white cohorts. Hard-hitting drama makes its point well, is excellently acted, especially by Edwards. (Dir: Mark Robson, 85 mins.)

Homecoming (1947)** Clark Gable, Lana Turner, Anne Baxter, John Hodiak. Clark is married to Anne in this one but through flashbacks he manages to have his torrid box-office dynamite romance with Lana. It has a war background but it's nothing to shout about. (Dir: Mervyn Le Roy, 113 mins.)

Homecoming, The (1973)**** Cyril Cusack, Ian Holm, Vivien Merchant, Paul Rogers, Michael Jayston. A marvelous adaptation of Harold Pinter's lacerating, fascinating play about the interpersonal relationships of a British working-class family.

Peter Hall, who directed the triumphant stage production, repeats the assignment and it's even more savage, if possible, than on stage. The poignant Pinter pauses and exchanges are stunningly acted by many of the original cast members. Paul Robers, playing Max, a retired butcher who taunts and competes with his three grown sons, is a standout along with Merchant, the playwright's talented ex-wife. Pinter adapted for the screen. (Dir: Peter Hall, 116 mins.)

Homestretch, The (1947)** Cornel Wilde, Maureen O'Hara. Some wonderful horse racing shots from Ascot to Churchill Downs but the story makes you wish they had eliminated the actors and just shown the races. Fancy-free horse owner and disapproving wife is the worn frame. (Dir: H. Bruce Humberstone, 96 mins.)

Hondo (1954)***½ John Wayne, Geraldine Page, James Arness, Ward Bond. One of Hollywood's best adult westerns. Strong in human relationships with a minimum of violence. Broadway actress Geraldine Page makes her film debut in this much underrated western. (Dir: John Farrow, 83 mins.)

Honey Pot, The (British-U.S.-Italian, 1967)*** Rex Harrison, Susan Hayward, Cliff Robertson, Capucine, Edie Adams, Maggie Smith. Even a second-rate Joseph L. Mankiewicz film is better than most high-style comedies. Here Mankiewicz takes his turn at updating Ben Jonson's "Volpone." Rex Harrison is a wealthy scoundrel who invites three of his former amours (the Misses Hayward, Adams and Capucine) to share his last days in his Venetian showplace and the intrigues begin. It's all a big fraud, as are most of the characters, but Mankiewicz' brittle, sophisticated dialogue, expertly handled by Harrison and company, is worth savoring, and Maggie Smith is a special delight. For those film buffs who care about such matters, Mankiewicz's screenplay was based partially on a play "Mr. Fox of Venice," a novel called "The Evil of the Day," and the aforementioned Ben Jonson, who is not a member of the Screenwriters Guild. (131 mins.)

Honeymoon (1947)** Shirley Temple, Guy Madison, Franchot Tone. GI has trouble marrying his fiancee, since he only has a three-day pass. Uninspired comedy. (Dir: William Keighley, 74 mins.)

Honeymoon Hotel (1964)** Robert Goulet, Nancy Kwan, Robert Morse. When a guy's wedding breaks up at the altar, his wolfish buddy joins him on the honeymoon trip, and they check in at a hotel—for honeymooners only. Flimsy farce defeats the hard-working players. (Dir: Henry Levin, 89 mins.)

Honeymoon In Bali (1939)*** Fred MacMurray, Madeleine Carroll. Witty romantic comedy about a cold, calculating career girl who is conquered by a man. Silly and out of hand in spots, but very entertaining. (Dir: Edward H. Griffith, 100 mins.)

Honeymoon Killers, The (1970)**½ Tony Lo Bianco, Shirley Stoler, Doris Roberts, Mary Jane Higby. Based on the multiple murderers, Martha Beck and Raymond Fernandez, who were executed in 1951. This low-budgeted drama succeeds in many departments where other more ambitiously produced films fail. Tony Lo Bianco and Shirley Stoler portray a pair of ruthless killers who pose as a nurse and her brother, and seek out wealthy women who fall prey to their murderous schemes. Although the plot is rather direct and straightforward, it's the playing, especially by Lo Bianco in his starring debut, which impresses. Photographed in black and white. Written and skillfully directed by Leonard Kastle. (107 mins.)

Honeymoon Machine, The (1961)*** Steve McQueen, Brigid Bazlen, Jim Hutton, Paula Prentiss. Navy officer gets an idea to use an electronic brain on board his vessel to beat the roulette wheel at the Venice casino. Entertaining comedy, with some youthful players getting the chance to show their stuff. Good fun. (Dir: Richard Thorpe, 87 mins.)

Honeymoon with a Stranger (1969)**½ Janet Leigh, Rossano Brazzi. This is the type of melodramatic opus Joan Crawford and Greer Garson used to suffer through during the forties. This time out, the troubled gal is Janet Leigh, who spends her honeymoon in Spain looking for her husband, who has disappeared, and trying to convince the local police that the man who claims to be her spouse really isn't. It's all complicated and terribly contrived but the scenery, including Miss Leigh, is nice to look at, and for some, the twist at the end will come as a surprise. Made-for-TV. (Dir: John Peyser, 73 mins.)

Honeymoons Will Kill You (Italian, 1964)*½ Tony Russell. A silly bedroom farce with playboys, honeymoon couples, house detectives, and crooks running around a very wacky hotel.

Hong Kong (1951)** Ronald Reagan, Rhonda Fleming. A W.W. II veteran and a mission schoolteacher tangle with jewel thieves and murderers in this average adventure story. (Dir: Lewis R. Foster, 92 mins.)

Hong Kong Affair (1958)* Jack Kelly, May Wynn. Messed up and downright boring tale of a G.I. in Hong Kong who finds trouble at every turn in his attempt to investigate mysterious happenings on his tea plantation. Filmed in Hong Kong, if it matters. (Dir: Paul F. Heard, 79 mins.)

Hong Kong Confidential (1958)**½ Gene Barry, Beverly Tyler. Another in the expose series of the criminal machines of famous cities. This one is set in the orient in the port of Hong Kong, where crime runs rampant until our hero, Gene Barry, enters the picture. Fast moving crime drama. (Dir: Edward L. Cahn, 67 mins.)

Hong Kong Hot Harbor (German, 1962)* Brad Harris, Marianne Cook, Horst Frank. Newspaperman uncovers plenty of crookedness during his stay in Hong Kong, at the risk of his life. Inept adventure actioner dubbed in English.

Honkers, The (1972)** James Coburn, Lois Nettleton, Slim Pickens. "Honkers" refers to wild bulls and available women in this erratic rodeo tale. Coburn tries hard to overcome a plodding script playing a self-centered, second-rate rodeo performer. "Honkers" was the second and last film directed by Canadian actor Steve "Fuzz" Ihnat, who died after "Honkers" was finished. Some good rodeo action by cinematographer James Crabe. (Dir: Steve Ihnat, 103 mins.)

Honky (1971)** Brenda Sykes, John Nielson, William Marshall. Highschool romance between black girl and white youth leads to violence from peers and parents in the mid-

West. Overdone; adds nothing to theme of interracial love problem. But Brenda Sykes is most attractive playing the black girl. Based on the novel "Sheila." (Dir: William A. Graham, 89 mins.)

Honky Tonk (1941)**½ Clark Gable, Lana Turner, Frank Morgan, Claire Trevor. First screen meeting of Gable and Turner has no originality other than the teaming. He's a gambler, she's a good girl and you know all along where they're headed. Enough action and loving though, to please most of their fans. (Dir: Jack Conway, 105 mins.)

Honor Thy Father (1973)*** Joseph Bologna, Raf Vallone. Interesting, well-cast television adaptation of Gay Talese's book about an underworld family. Moral is that educated sons seldom matched their father's toughness during the questioning '60's, even in the Mafia. The best thing about this true-life account of New York gangland's infighting is the look and performance of playwright-actor Bologna as heir to his father's Cosa Nostra gang. Brought up as a gentleman, the young man can't hold thugs together while questioning old Sicilian feuds. Bologna's performance is effectively supported by Brenda Vaccaro, Richard Castellano, Raf Vallone. Made-for-TV. (Dir: Paul Wendkos, 99 mins.)

Hoodlum Priest, The (1961)***½ Don Murray, Keir Dullea. Murray stars as Father Charles Dismas Clark, the Jesuit priest who befriended young criminal offenders and tried to help them help themselves. The film centers on one case in particular, that of a young hotheaded and arrogant ex-con who almost makes it with Father Clark's help and friendship. Murray delivers a fine portrait of a determined man with a mission and Keir Dullea makes a deep impression as the youth he befriends. (Dir: Irvin Kershner, 101 mins.)

Hook, The (1963)*** Kirk Douglas, Robert Walker, Nick Adams. Korean war drama poses a problem—what does a man do when he's ordered to kill a prisoner of war, even if it will insure his own safety? The development is somewhat sketchily presented, but it's food for thought. Well acted. (Dir: George Seaton, 98 mins.)

Hook, Line and Sinker (1969)* Jerry

Lewis, Peter Lawford, Anne Francis. "Sinker" is a stinker, extremely poorly directed by George Marshall who, at the ripe old age of 77, seems not to give a damn any more. One almost forgets that Lewis IS a very gifted comedian, while he plods through this drivel about an insurance salesman who goes on a fishing trip around the world when told he has only two months to live. About two gags enliven the witless script concocted by Rod Amateau. (Dir: George Marshall, 92 mins.)

Hooked Generation, The (1969)½ Jeremy Slate, Willie Pastrano. Drug-crazed friends go on a murder spree, beginning with their Cuban heroin connections. Unrealistic, gory adventure. (Dir: William Grefe)

Horizons West (1952)**½ Robert Ryan, Rock Hudson. Familiar story of two brothers returning from the Civil War, one becoming a lawman and the other an outlaw. Better than usual cast and direction gives it a boost for the western fans. (Dir: Budd Boetticher, 81 mins.)

Horizontal Lieutenant, The (1962)**½ Paula Prentiss, Jim Hutton, Jack Carter. A moderately funny service comedy which benefits greatly from the able comedy team of Prentiss and Hutton as a pair of oddballs. There is a subplot involving a missing Japanese official, but Prentiss and Hutton remain in the focal point of the laughs. (Dir: Richard Thorpe, 90 mins.)

Hornets Nest (1970)** Rock Hudson, Sylva Koscina. Derring-do during World War II. Hudson plays a U.S. Army Captain who manages, with the aid of a group of Italian orphans and a sexy German lady doctor, to carry out his sabotage mission against incredible odds. (Dir: Phil Karlson, 109 mins.)

Horrible Dr. Hichcock, The (Italian, 1963)*½ Barbara Steele, Robert Flemyng. Mad professor tries to poison his second wife prior to a planned blood transfusion intended to restore beauty to his first wife. Ridiculous horror thriller with the efforts of capable players gone for naught. Dubbed in English. (Dir: Robert Hampton, 76 mins.)

Horror at 37,000 Feet, The (1973)* Buddy Ebsen, William Shatner. This is supposed to be a spine-tingling air thriller over the Atlantic, but the ghastly trauma disintegrates at the halfway point and so does the movie. Made-for-TV. (Dir: David Lowell Rich.)

Horror Chamber of Dr. Faustus (French, 1962)** Pierre Brasseur, Alida Valli. Doctor procures young girls for skin-grafting operations on his daughter's face, injured in an accident. Grisly horror thriller dubbed in English, has some effective moments but moves too slowly. (Dir: Georges Franju, 84 mins.)

Horror Hotel (British, 1962)**½ Christopher Lee, Betta St. John, Venetia Stevenson. College student doing research in witchcraft stumbles upon a cult in a Massachusetts village. Shuddery little shocker works up some scary moments. Well done of its kind. (Dir: John Moxey, 76 mins.)

Horror of Dracula (British, 1958)*** Peter Cushing, Christopher Lee, Michael Gough. A return to the original "Dracula" tale, of how the fiendish count arises from the dead to seek his victims. Fine fare for horror fans, produced with care, well acted. (Dir: Terence Fisher, 82 mins.)

Horror of Frankenstein, The (Great Britain, 1970)½ Ralph Bates, Kate O'Mara, Dennis Price. Lamentable remake finds our old friend the Baron transformed into a horny anti-hero of the mod 70's (Dir: Jimmy Sangster, 95 mins.)

Horror of Party Beach, The (1964)½ John Scott, Alice Lyon. Musical science-fiction horror, as the ooze at the bottom of the sea comes to life and attacks partying teenagers on the California coast. Pity the ooze didn't drown the filmmakers. (Dir: Del Tenney, 82 mins.)

Horrors of the Black Museum (British, 1959)** Michael Gough, Geoffrey Keen. Gruesome thriller about a famous crime writer with a do-it-yourself technique, providing himself with his own material. Script is one on the silly side, but performances and production are effective. For strong stomachs. (Dir: Arthur Crabtree, 95 mins.)

Horse and Carriage (Greek, 1957)** Orestis Makris. Simple, sentimental tale of a father who disowns his no-good son, and the son's repentance upon his father's death. Avoids being saccharine until the 400-violin ending. (Dir: Dino Dimopoulos, 104 mins.)

Horse Feathers (1932)***½ Marx Brothers. Their fans will love this one. Groucho takes over a college and the gags fly fast and free. (Dir: Norman McLeod, 80 mins.)

Horse in the Gray Flannel Suit, The (1968)** Dean Jones, Diane Baker, Fred Clark. Walt Disney comedy about an advertising exec who comes up with a clever scheme to promote his client's upset-stomach remedy and get his young daughter the horse she dreams about. The horse is named Aspercel after the patent medicine! Flimsy material gets a long ride. (Dir: Norman Tokar, 113 mins.)

Horse Named Comanche, A (1958)** Sal Mineo, Phillip Carey, Jerome Cortland, Rafael Campos. For youngsters. Sal Mineo turns up as a young Indian, White Bull, who will do almost anything to own a certain wild stallion. Tribal customs prevent White Bull from such ownership. Interest centers on scenes between the boy and the horse. (Dir: Lewis R. Foster)

Horse Soldiers, The (1959)** John Wayne, William Holden. Sprawling action film set during the Civil War benefits little from its potent casting of Wayne and Holden in the leading roles. They play union officers who have contrasting viewpoints on war. John Ford directed and not very well at that, but his producers and screenwriters are more to blame. (Dir: John Ford, 119 mins.)

Horseman, The (1971)**½ Jack Palance, Omar Sharif, Leigh Taylor-Young. Action, adventure, and romance on a superficial level but still entertaining. Sharif in still another death-defying desert role—he's the son of an Afghanistan lord's stablemaster, played by Palance. The beautiful cinematography could pass as a travelogue on Afghanistan and Spain! Stilted screenplay from ace scripter Dalton Trumbo. (Dir: John Frankenheimer, 105 mins.)

Horse's Mouth (British, 1959)**** Alec Guinness, Kay Walsh. Mad misadventures of an eccentric artist and his companions. Written and deftly performed by Guinness, a real comedy treat. (Dir: Ronald Neame, 93 mins.)

Hospital (1971)*** Magnificent, deeply moving documentary directed by Frederick Wiseman, about the workings of Metropolitan Hospital in New York City, and the over-burdened compassionate staff who try to bring some grace and dignity to their task of dealing with the sick and mostly poor people who flood in to the hospital with all kinds of ailments—victims of razor fights, junkies, etc. There is one absolutely heartbreaking scene showing a concerned psychiatrist doing everything he possibly can to make the laborious city bureaucracy respond to the ongoing needs of a disturbed black homosexual. Wiseman's enormous sympathy for the onscreen characters is evident throughout. Another penetrating study of an American institution from this pioneering documentary filmmaker. (90 mins.)

Hospital, The (1971)**** George C. Scott, Diana Rigg, Richard Dysart, Bernard Hughes. An original screenplay by Paddy Chayefsky got the Academy Award for this funny and devastating, if slightly exaggerated, account of the incompetence and slothfulness in a typical American hospital, in this case Metropolitan Hospital in New York City. Chayefsky's dialogue and the flamboyant performance of Scott, nominated for an Academy Award, are the two choice ingredients. Hughes is scary and very funny playing a mad impostor doctor. Miss Rigg's unquestionable allure handily solves Scott's fear of impotence. (Dir: Arthur Hiller, 103 mins.)

Hostage, The (1968)**½ Danny Martins, Don O'Kelley, John Carradine. A low-budget surprise drama about a runaway boy features unorthodox editing and plenty of character conviction. (Dir: Russell S. Doughton, Jr., 84 mins.)

Hostages (1943)** Luise Rainer, William Bendix, Arturo de Cordova. Fair action film pays tribute to the Czech underground. A group of people are held as hostages after a Nazi is murdered. (Dir: Frank Tuttle, 88 mins.)

Hostile Guns (1967)** George Montgomery, Yvonne DeCarlo. Poor western about a U.S. marshal who has to transport a wagonful of prisoners to the state pen. The only interest is the familiar faces of some of the supporting players—Brian Donlevy, Richard Arlen, Don Barry and Fuzzy Knight. (Dir: R. G. Springsteen, 91 mins.)

Hot Angel, The (1958)** Jackie Loughery, Edward Kemmer. Aerial surveyor for a uranium prospector fights off crooks. Routine action melodrama. Good flying scenes.

Hot Blood (1956)*½ Jane Russell, Cornel Wilde. Hot Blood makes cold movie. A ridiculous tale about a band of gypsies and their fiery adventures. Miss Russell is miscast and shows it. (Dir: Nicholas Ray, 85 mins.)

Hot Enough for June—See: **Agent 8¾**

Hot Ice (British, 1953)*** Barbara Murray, John Justin. Laughs and thrills evenly divided in one of those spooky mansion-type mysteries. Better than average.

Hot Millions (British, 1968)***½ Peter Ustinov, Maggie Smith. Amusing comedy about a high-class swindling operation, with some of the action set in London and South America. Ustinov is at his roguish best and there's a delightful performance from the versatile British star Maggie Smith, who seems to have a virtually unlimited acting range. (Dir: Eric Till, 105 mins.)

Hot Pepper (1933)**½ Victor McLaglen, Edmund Lowe, Lupe Velez. Sequel to "What Price Glory?" follows Flagg (McLaglen) and Quirt (Lowe) into civilian life as co-owners of a nightclub who fight over the love of Ms. Velez. Old rivalry keeps plot interesting. (Dir: John G. Blystone, 76 mins.)

Hot Rock, The (1972)*** Robert Redford, George Segal, Ron Liebman, Zero Mostel. The picture combines comedy and suspense in a delightful mixture, nicely balanced by director Peter Yates. Redford and Segal are hired to steal a diamond. Most of the picture concerns not the robbery but the bungling of the burglars in losing the gem, and trying to get it back. Uneven script and Mostel are wasted, but there's much fun along the way, especially Liebman as Murch, who claims he can drive anything. (Dir: Peter Yates, 101 mins.)

Hot Rods to Hell (1967)** Dana Andrews, Jeanne Crain, Mimsy Farmer. Family on the road terrorized by a teenage gang. Usual delinquency theme, nothing new. (Dir: John Brahm, 92 mins.)

Hot Spell (1958)*** Shirley Booth, Anthony Quinn, Shirley MacLaine, Earl Holliman. Family drama set in the South with some good acting to recommend it. Miss Booth plays a disillusioned housewife whose family has grown away from her but refuses to face the brutal truth. Marred by phony ending, well directed by Daniel Mann. (85 mins.)

Hotel (1967)*** Rod Taylor, Catherine Spaak, Karl Malden, Melvyn Douglas, Merle Oberon, Richard Conte, Michael Rennie, Kevin McCarthy, Carmen McRae. Trials and tribulations at a posh New Orleans hotel, mainly the efforts made to keep it from falling into the wrong hands. Many stars, many plots; familiar, but something cooking all the time. Suspenseful conclusion. (Dir: Richard Quine, 124 mins.)

Hotel Berlin (1945)*** Faye Emerson, Helmut Dantine. Occasionally interesting adaptation of Vicki Baum's novel centered in a Berlin hotel as Hitler's Germany is collapsing. Most of the characters and situations are contrived but there's some good excitement. (Dir: Peter Godfrey, 98 mins.)

Hotel Paradiso (British, 1966)**½ Gina Lollobrigida, Alec Guinness, Robert Morley. If your tastes lean towards French farce, peppered with British players (Guinness and Morley) and featuring that Italian eyeful Lollobrigida, this amiable and frothy comedy set in Paris during the early 1900's will entertain you. The plot is much too complicated to go into, but most of the action takes place in a fashionable hotel where secret rendezvous and misunderstandings run rampant. The production directed by Peter Glenville is handsomely mounted, and the cast goes through the standard paces with a sense of style and period. (Dir: Peter Glenville, 96 mins.)

Hotel Sahara (1952)**½ Yvonne DeCarlo, Peter Ustinov. Occasionally amusing satire on the changing attitudes of civilians occupied during a war. Miss DeCarlo is prepared to accept any current winner. English-made film. Not for American taste. (Dir: Ken Annakin, 87 mins.)

Houdini (1953)*** Tony Curtis, Janet Leigh. Colorful film based on the life and loves of the world's most famous magician. Tony Curtis brings a great deal of energy to the title role and he gets good support from Janet Leigh, as his faithful wife and Torin Thatcher, as his mentor. The kids will enjoy magic acts. (Dir: George Marshall, 106 mins.)

Hound-Dog Man (1959)*** Carol Lynley, Arthur O'Connell, Betty Field, Dodie Stevens. Fabian's first film. On the credit side, it's a nice, homey tale of a scalawag (Stuart Whitman) who is hero-worshiped by two lads (Fabian, Dennis Holmes). Very relaxing, and neglected when shown in theaters. Try it.

Hound of the Baskervilles (1939)*** Basil Rathbone, Nigel Bruce, Richard Greene. Young man who has inherited an estate from his uncle suspects foul play, calls on Sherlock Holmes. Good mystery, well produced and suspenseful. (Dir: Sidney Lanfield, 80 mins.)

Hound of the Baskervilles (British, 1959)*** Peter Cushing, Christopher Lee. Frightening mystery yarn based on the famous Sherlock Holmes novel reaches the screen in all its macabre fascination with every terror-filled moment intact. Far superior to many horror films. (Dir: Terence Fisher, 84 mins.)

Hound of the Baskervilles, The (1972)** Stewart Granger, Bernard Fox. Know-it-all Sherlock Holmes emerges once again, baffling follower Dr. Watson with canny insights as the two investigate Baskerville deaths by the legendary hound. Much is made of Holmes' deductive brilliance, spoken crisply by Granger, and Fox plays the stodgy Watson for chuckles. Producer Stan Kallis gave this relic the old college try. Made-for-TV. (Dir: Barry Crane, 73 mins.)

Hour of Decision (British, 1955)** Jeff Morrow, Hazel Court. A writer becomes involved in the murder of a gossip columnist. Usual sort of whodunit aided by good performances. (Dir: Pennington Richards, 74 mins.)

Hour of the Furnaces, The (Argentinian, 1966-68)**** A propaganda masterpiece, secretly made by underground Argentine filmmakers. A devastating indictment of American and British "imperialism" in Argentina and the rest of South America. This remarkable film, directed by Fernando Solanas, is one of the most powerful and effective propaganda films ever made. Part one deals with neocolonialism and violence, and the final shot, over four hours later in the full version, is a close-up held for well over two minutes of Che Guevara. In between you'll find a variety of searing images that you'll not soon forget, together with factual material documenting the filmmakers' belief in the inevitability and desirability of violent revolution to achieve justice for South American working masses. Made to be shown to peasants, factory workers, etc., as a "consciousness-raising tool," it is an unforgettable cinematic experience. (250 mins.)

Hour of the Gun (1967)**½ James Garner, Jason Robards, Robert Ryan. Mediocre western drama with Garner as Wyatt Earp and Robards as "Doc" Holliday. This tale might be said to be part two of the 1957 film "Gun Fight at the O.K. Corral." Garner and Robards are quite good in their roles and a better-than-average supporting cast gives the film an added boost. (Dir: John Sturges, 100 mins.)

Hour of 13, The (1952)**½ Peter Lawford, Dawn Addams. Satisfactory thriller about a gentleman crook who tracks down a mad killer specializing in policemen. British-made, good atmosphere. (Dir: Harold French, 79 mins.)

Hour of Truth (France-Israel, 1966)**½ Corrine Marchand, Karl Boehm, Brett Halsey, Daniel Gelin, Mischa Azeroff. Controversial film about a disguised ex-Nazi concentration-camp commander who is virtually adopted by an Israeli family. When his real history becomes known, the family must deal with a figure at once hated and beloved, and the issue of whether a Nazi criminal can "reform." A difficult, sensitive situation, fairly well handled. (Dir: Henri Calef, 93 mins.)

Hours of Love, The (Italy, 1963)** Ugo Tognazzi, Barbara Steele, Emmanuele Riva. Ecstatic lovers decide on marriage, and then become disillusioned about each other's interests. Slow comedy, clinched with a happy ending. (Dir: Luciano Salce, 89 mins.)

House Across the Bay (1940)**½ Joan Bennett, George Raft, Walter Pidgeon, Lloyd Nolan. While waiting for her jailbird husband to come out, a singer falls for an aircraft designer; hubby hears of this, seeks revenge. Fair melodrama; Nolan is fine as a shady lawyer. (Dir: Archie Mayo, 72 mins.)

House by the River (1950)** Louis Hayward, Lee Bowman, Jane Wyatt. Philanderer strangles his maid, implicates his brother in the crime. Well made but otherwise undistinguished costume thriller. (Dir: Fritz Lang, 88 mins.)

House I Live In, The (U.S.S.R., 1958)**½ Vladimir Zemlyanikin, Valentina Telegina. Sensitive Russian film follows a family and their neighbors through troubles, marriages, war, by focusing on their apartment. An interesting film, gracefully performed, which stays clear of sentimentality. (Dirs: Lev Kulidjanov, Yakov Segel, 100 mins.)

House Is Not a Home, A (1964)* Shelley Winters, Robert Taylor, Cesar Romero, Ralph Taeger, Broderick Crawford, Kaye Ballard. One of Polly's "girls"—Raquel Welch. Based on the life of Polly Adler—call her "Madam." Whorehouse story unrelieved by finesse.

House of Bamboo (1955)**½ Robert Stack, Robert Ryan, Shirley Yamaguchi. Off-beat drama about a group of Americans in Tokyo who set up a protection racket operation for some easy money. Robert Stack stoically plays the undercover agent assigned to crack the case. On-location photography adds to the atmosphere of the adventure tale. (Dir: Samuel Fuller, 102 mins.)

House of Cards (1968)**½ George Peppard, Inger Stevens, Orson Welles. Action and lush European locations keep this tale of intrigue crackling from beginning to end. George Peppard plays an unlikely tutor in Paris who gets enmeshed in a right-wing operation made up of French aristocrats headed by arch-villain Orson Welles. There's a suspenseful chase at the end and the production values are first-rate. (Dir: John Guillermin, 105 mins.)

House of Dark Shadows (1970)** Joan Bennett, Jonathan Frid, Grayson Hall. Fans of the horror-soap "Dark Shadows" will enjoy this theatrical version of the vampire saga. Bloodsucker Jonathan Frid overplays in the accepted grand style of a junior-league Vincent Price, and there are familiar faces from the long-gone but fondly remembered gothic TV soaper. (Dir: Dan Curtis, 98 mins.)

House of Dracula (1945)*½ Lon Chaney, John Carradine, Lionel Atwill. Scientist is tricked into helping Count Dracula, also meets up with the Wolf Man and the Frankenstein monster. Too many ghouls spoil the brew. (Dir: Erle C. Kenton, 67 mins.)

House of Intrigue (1959)** Dawn Addams, Curt Jurgens. Beautiful spy bewitches a German officer, who eventually helps her out of a tight situation. Good European backgrounds from Barcelona to Holland, but the espionage plot rambles. (Dir: Dullio Coletti, 94 mins.)

House of Numbers (1957)** Jack Palance, Barbara Lang. Strictly for Jack Palance fans. He plays the dual role of a murderer and his lookalike brother. The story concerns a clever plan for the murderer's escape from prison and manages to generate some suspense along the way. (Dir: Russell Rouse, 92 mins.)

House of 1000 Dolls (Spain-West Germany, 1967)½ Vincent Price, Martha Hyer, George Nader. Price and Hyer team together as illusionists who lure girls into working at their bordello. Barely 20 "dolls" are visible in this low-budget exploitation melodrama. Screenplay, such as it is, written by producer Harry Alan Towers, again under a pseudonym. (Dir: Jeremy Summers, 87 mins.)

House of Rothschild (1934)**** George Arliss, Boris Karloff, Loretta Young, Robert Young. Story of the Jewish banking family that saved Europe from Napoleon is magnificently acted and directed, intelligently written. A slice of history which is a must. (Dir: Alfred L. Werker, 86 mins.)

House of Secrets (Great Britain, 1956)½ Michael Craig, Brenda de Banzie. Low-class, high-decibel thriller about a gang of crooks planning to inundate the world with counterfeit currencies. (Dir: Guy Green, 97 mins.)

House of Seven Gables (1940)***½ George Sanders, Margaret Lindsay, Vincent Price. Scheming lawyer falsely accuses his sister's sweetheart of murder, but she waits for him for twenty years to be released from prison. Superbly acted; well made drama, version of Hawthorne's classic novel. (Dir: Joe May, 89 mins.)

House of Strangers (1949)**★★★½** Susan Hayward, Edward G. Robinson, Richard Conte. A powerful drama of family conflicts, filled with hatred and revenge. One of the older sons, Richard Conte, has sworn vengeance on his brothers, whom he blames for his father's death. Superb performance by Robinson as the father. (Dir: Joseph L. Mankiewicz, 101 mins.)

House of the Damned (1963)½ Ron Foster, Merry Anders. Absurd tale about a castle inhabited by freaks who terrorize its new owners. (Dir: Maury Dexter, 62 mins.)

House of the Seven Hawks, The (1959)**★★½** Robert Taylor, Nicole Maurey, Linda Christian. A straightforward espionage adventure yarn with touches of legitimate suspense. Robert Taylor plays a charter boat captain who gets involved with international thieves and the Dutch police when a mysterious man dies on his vessel. Taylor discovers an important-looking map on the dead man and spends the rest of the film trying to solve its mystery. Nicole Maurey and Linda Christian are the two females in the case, and the British and Dutch locations add necessary atmosphere. (Dir: Richard Thorpe, 92 mins.)

House of Usher (1960)**★★** Vincent Price, Mark Damon. Price is keeping company with Edgar Allen Poe again. Horror tale about the talented Ushers and how brother Roderick (Price) executes a plan to end the long line of madness that gallops in their family. (Dir: Roger Corman, 79 mins.)

House of Wax (1953)**★★½** Vincent Price, Phyllis Kirk, Carolyn Jones. Originally made as a 3-D movie, it is loaded with visual gimmicks which were specifically tailored for the process. Nevertheless, there's sinister Vincent Price lurking in the shadows of a wax museum of horrors. Phyllis Kirk and Carolyn Jones add to the proceedings by alternately screaming and looking terrified. (Dir: Andre de Toth, 88 mins.)

House of Women (1962)**★★** Shirley Knight, Andrew Duggan, Constance Ford. Innocent expectant mother is convicted of robbery and sent to prison, where she undergoes many trials. Remake of "Caged" doesn't

measure up—just a formula prison drama. (Dir: Walter Doniger, 85 mins.)

House on Green Apple Road, The (1970)**★★½** Janet Leigh, Christopher George, Julie Harris, Barry Sullivan. Suspenseful made-for-TV feature which uses flashbacks to fairly good advantage to tell the story of a woman (Miss Leigh) whose extramarital activities lead to murder. The police believe Miss Leigh's been murdered by her distraught husband but they can't come up with a corpse and thereby hangs the mystery. The supporting cast includes many familiar TV guest-star personalities. (Dir: Robert Day, 113 mins.)

House on Haunted Hill (1959)**★★½** Vincent Price, Carol Ohmart. A horror film with some laughs if you don't take it too seriously. Host Vincent Price rents a haunted house and offers a select group a large reward if they spend the night. Many strange goings-on liven up their stay. The effects are startling enough for the younger set, if they aren't prone to nightmares. (Dir: William Castle, 75 mins.)

House on 92nd Street (1945)**★★★½** William Eythe, Lloyd Nolan, Signe Hasso. The FBI's battle against the fifth column in a fast paced, exciting film. This was the first picture to effectively combine documentary techniques with the dramatic and none of its imitators have topped it. (Dir: Henry Hathaway, 88 mins.)

House on Telegraph Hill (1951)**★★** Richard Basehart, Valentina Cortesa, William Lundigan. Predictable melodrama with a good performance by Richard Basehart to recommend it. Basehart plays a convincing charmer who marries Miss Cortesa, thinking she is someone else. (Dir: Robert Wise, 93 mins.)

House That Dripped Blood, The (British, 1970)**★★★** Peter Cushing, Christopher Lee, Nyree Dawn Porter, Ingrid Pitt. A series of four British vignettes set in an appropriately eerie estate, centering on the line of consecutive owners. Much better done than most of this genre—some scary, the last amusing. The first yarn involves a hack murder-mystery writer who sees his fictional character, a wild strangler, wandering all around the house. In other segments, the house has been turned into a wax museum with a striking statue of Salome; witches roam the place pitted against an ample serving of young innocence; and a film star puts on a genuine Transylvanian cloak for his vampire role . . . and suddenly . . . The cast, all battle-scarred horror movie veterans, provide satisfying chills but no full-blown terror. (Dir: Peter Duffell, 101 mins.)

House That Wouldn't Die, The (1970) **½** Barbara Stanwyck, Richard Egan, Katharine Winn. Made-for-TV feature, old-fashioned haunted house yarn provides some chills. Miss Stanwyck inherits an old house and goes there with her niece. Almost at once, strange goings-on begin occurring and it takes a seance to uncover some macabre facts. The cast is very serious, and plays it straight. (Dir: John Llewellyn Moxey, 73 mins.)

Houseboat (1958)***½ Cary Grant, Sophia Loren, Harry Guardino. Widower on a houseboat hires a maid for his children, little realizing she's the daughter of a noted Italian symphony conductor. Amusing sophisticated comedy benefits from the presence of Grant and Loren. (Dir: Melville Shavelson, 110 mins.)

Housekeeper's Daughter, The (1939) **½** Joan Bennett, Adolphe Menjou, John Hubbard, Victor Mature. A pretty miss helps a mild-mannered man get rid of some racketeers. Mildly amusing comedy with a hilarious finish. (Dir: Hal Roach, 80 mins.)

Houston Story, The (1956)** Gene Barry, Barbara Hale, Edward Arnold. Predictable gangster plot has Gene Barry striving for a top position in the syndicate centered in Houston, Texas. There's plenty of action for fans of this type of story. (Dir: William Castle, 79 mins.)

Houston, We've Got a Problem (1974)** Robert Culp, Clu Gulager, Gary Collins, Sandra Dee. A melodramatic "current events" story is in store for viewers tuning in to this "suspense" saga based on the near-fatal Apollo 13 mission. In this fictionalized version, the astronauts dangle in space after a crippling explosion in their spacecraft, while Mission Control's staff—Culp, Gulager, and Collins—alternate between attempting to get them back down and dealing with their soap-opera prob-

lems. Made-for-TV. (Dir: Lawrence Doheny.)

How Awful About Allan (1970)**½ Anthony Perkins, Julie Harris, Joan Hackett. Made-for-TV feature. A run-of-the-mill horror story aimed, hopefully, at sending chills up your spine. Anthony Perkins plays a young man recently returned from a mental institution who is a victim of psychosomatic blindness resulting from a fire which killed his father and scarred his sister (Julie Harris). We won't give away the plot but mystery fans will have little trouble figuring out the eerie goings-on. (Dir: Curtis Harrington, 73 mins.)

How Green Was My Valley (1941) **** Walter Pidgeon, Maureen O'Hara, Donald Crisp, Roddy McDowall. Beautiful, poignant, moving story of a coal mining family in Wales. Nothing alarming in the plot but loaded with incidents that pluck at your heartstrings. A "must" film. (Dir: John Ford, 118 mins.)

How I Spent My Summer Vacation (1966)** Robert Wagner, Peter Lawford, Jill St. John, Lola Albright, Walter Pidgeon. Cluttered adventure tale about a young ne'er-do-well who thinks he has the goods on a millionaire. It begins well, with some sharply directed scenes played tongue-in-cheek, but soon falls into utter confusion. Made-for-TV. (Dir: William Hale, 99 mins.)

How I Won the War (British, 1967) **½ Stumbling attempt to satirize World War II by director Richard Lester, as he tells of a doltish officer who manages to remain alive while his comrades die grisly deaths. Supposed to be funny, and is occasionally. A further deterrent is sometimes unintelligible dialogue. Michael Crawford, (Beatle) John Lennon, Jack MacGowran, Michael Hordern. (Dir: Richard Lester, 109 mins.)

How Sweet It Is! (1968)**½ Debbie Reynolds, James Garner. Mishaps galore dog the steps of a couple on a European vacation. Some genuinely funny sequences in this amiable laughgetter, with Maurice Ronet, Terry-Thomas, Paul Lynde, Elena Verdugo and Vito Scotti (superb in a bit as a cook). (Dir: Jerry Paris, 99 mins.)

How the West Was Won (1963)*½ Gregory Peck, Henry Fonda, James Stewart, Debbie Reynolds. This over-long, mammoth Hollywood spectacle purporting to show "How the West Was Won" contains virtually every known Hollywood cliché about the Old West and the great American spirit. It also contains a huge, stalwart cast and enough incidents, if you don't take it all very seriously, to help while away what seems like a whole day. A family of New England farmers heads West in the 1830's on land and river. Narrated by Spencer Tracy. What little impact this sophomoric "epic" had was due to the vast "Cinerama" screen when shown in movie theaters. Most of that impact is lost on the tiny home screen. Based on a seven-lively-arts Life magazine series. Directors include Henry Hathaway, John Ford, and George Marshall. (155 mins.)

How to Be Very, Very Popular (1955) *** Betty Grable, Sheree North, Robert Cummings. Two chorus kids on the lam find refuge in a college fraternity whose members hide them. Comedy on the frantic side has some funny lines, pleasant players. (Dir: Nunnally Johnson, 89 mins.)

How to Break Up a Happy Divorce (1976) ½ Barbara Eden, Hal Linden. Dismal comedy. Barbara Eden is too coy for her own good as the energetic ex-wife who campaigns all too vigorously and obviously to win her ex back. Hal Linden is wasted as a guy who is used by the enterprising Ms. Eden to make her ex-husband jealous. Made-for-TV. (Dir: Jerry Paris, 72 mins.)

How to Commit Marriage (1969)* Jackie Gleason, Bob Hope, Jane Wyman. A terrible comedy about the foibles of modern marriage and divorce, wasting top comics Gleason and Hope. The script is as clumsy as Norman Panama's direction. (104 mins.)

How to Make a Monster (1960)* ½ Robert H. Harris, Gary Conway. Good idea, bad execution; Hollywood makeup man creates his own monsters. (Dir: Herbert L. Strock, 74 mins.)

How to Marry a Millionaire (1953)*** Marilyn Monroe, Lauren Bacall, Betty Grable, David Wayne, William Powell, Rory Calhoun, Cameron Mitchell. Slick comedy about three fortune huntresses and their adventures in the big city. Bacall is the brains of the trio; Monroe, the sexy

mantrap who takes off her glasses when a man is around even though she can't see without them; and Betty Grable seems to be along just for the ride. Some funny situations that lead to a happy fadeout with the three girls settling for love but winding up with both love and cash. (Dir: Jean Negulesco, 95 mins.)

How to Murder a Rich Uncle (British, 1958)** ½ Charles Coburn, Nigel Patrick, Wendy Hiller. Only moderately amusing entry in the British "How To" comedy films. Coburn is the wealthy relation in the title and the manipulators of the plot include sly and suave Mr. Patrick and his family. Miss Hiller is totally wasted in this mild fare. (Dir: Nigel Patrick, 80 mins.)

How to Murder Your Wife (1965)*** Jack Lemmon, Virna Lisi, Terry-Thomas. A frantic, often funny farce-comedy tailored to the talents of Jack Lemmon, who is in top form here. He plays a bachelor about town who wakes up one A.M. to find gorgeous Virna Lisi in his bed with a wedding ring on her left hand. The rest of the action is devoted to Lemmon's frantic efforts to get rid of his Italian spouse, even to the point of contemplating murder. The supporting cast matches Lemmon's energy and offer bright performances, particularly Eddie Mayehoff as an accommodating lawyer and Terry-Thomas as a quipping valet. Written and produced by George Axelrod. (Dir: Richard Quine, 118 mins.)

How to Save a Marriage—And Ruin Your Life (1968)** ½ Dean Martin, Stella Stevens, Eli Wallach. A bachelor friend tries to save the marriage of an unfaithful husband, with unexpected results. Strains for laughs at times, but generally amusing. With Anne Jackson, Betty Field, Jack Albertson. (Dir: Fielder Cook, 108 mins.)

How to Seduce a Playboy (Austrian, 1966)* Peter Alexander, Renato Salvatori, Antonella Lualdi. A computer mistake turns a meek clerk into a Playboy of the Year, and the gals appear in droves. Even location scenes in Paris, Rome and Tokyo can't save this sleazy farce.

How to Steal a Million (1966)*** ½ Audrey Hepburn, Peter O'Toole, Charles Boyer. The grace and charm of the two stars, and William

Wyler's deft direction are displayed in this sophisticated suspense story about the heist of a valuable piece of sculpture from a Paris museum. The theft itself is ingenious, on a par with such memorable scenes in "Rififi" and "Topkapi," and there's a particularly good supporting company including Eli Wallach and the always triumphant Welsh actor Hugh Griffith. Also assorted mouth-watering scenes in and around Paris for the benefit of those of you who can't visit the fabled city in person this season. (Dir: William Wyler, 127 mins.)

How to Steal an Airplane (1971)*½ Peter Duel, Clinton Greyn, Sal Mineo, Claudine Longet. Action as an American and a Welshman pose as tourists in Latin America in order to steal a jet from a dictator's son. Fly away! Made-for-TV. (Dir: Leslie Martinson)

How to Stuff a Wild Bikini (1965)*½ Frankie Avalon, Annette Funicello, Dwayne Hickman, Mickey Rooney. Another "Beach Party" opus for fans. This time, an advertising man is looking for a typical girl next door type and Frankie Avalon gets competition in the romance department with Annette from Dwayne Hickman. (Dir: William Asher, 90 mins.)

How to Succeed in Business Without Really Trying (1967)**** Robert Morse, Michele Lee, Rudy Vallee, Sammy Smith. The whole family will have a lot of fun without really trying to watch this long-running Broadway smash transferred to the big screen by David Swift who wrote, directed and produced this adaptation. Robert Morse, playing a Protestant what-makes-Sammy-run with a captivating charm, repeats his Broadway triumph. Rudy Vallee, who was a stiff in the Broadway production, repeats his wooden performance. Morse, who offers an instructive lesson in how to rise quickly up the corporate ladder, sings "The Company Way" and other tunes written by the late Frank Loesser. Cartoonist Virgil Partch is responsible for many of the funny visual sight gags that are to be found in this good-natured romp. (Dir: David Swift, 119 mins.)

How Yukong Moved the Mountains (France, 1976)**** A very extraordinary, almost definitive cinematic essay on contemporary mainland China, directed by the remarkable European filmmaker Joris Ivens, together with Marceline Loridan. The total body of work presented runs over twelve hours, and the filmmakers feel strongly that it be considered as a single work. Space precludes our going into any great detail. It is not enough, of course, to say that it is by far the finest film Westerners have recently been permitted to see about so many aspects of contemporary Chinese civilization, culture and society. Ivens has made numerous trips to China since 1938, and shot over 120 hours of film. Different parts of this truly epic film include sequences on a woman and her family, a pharmacy in Shanghai, a factory worker, etc. English commentary dubbed over the questions asked in French and answered in Chinese. See this, if you ever get a chance, in its entirety. (Dirs: Joris Ivens, Marceline Loridan, 763 mins.)

Howards of Virginia, The (1940)***½ Cary Grant, Martha Scott, Sir Cedric Hardwicke. Spirited backwoodsman is married to an aristocratic Virginia girl at the time of the American Revolution. Their story is a fine example of "flag waving"—with taste. (Dir: Frank Lloyd, 122 mins.)

Huckleberry Finn (1974)*½ Paul Winfield, Harvey Korman, David Wayne, Jeff East. Twain's durable classic gets a beating in this lumbering "musical adaptation"—some of the many problems with the picture are that the adaptation is clumsy and the direction poor, and it sags throughout with several of the most forgettable songs that have plopped from the screen in many years. The only note of levity is that provided by Korman posing as a phony king and clergyman. East is a wooden Huck and Winfield is trapped playing his sidekick, Jim. (Dir: J. Lee Thompson, 113 mins.)

Hucksters, The (1946)*** Clark Gable, Ava Gardner, Deborah Kerr, Sydney Greenstreet. Adaptation of the novel about advertising which set the style for cheap modern novels is not nearly as pungent as the book. You'll still enjoy Ava Gardner in the role that really boosted her Hollywood stock. (Dir: Jack Conway, 115 mins.)

Hud (1963)**** Paul Newman, Patricia Neal, Melvyn Douglas. A must for movie-drama fans. A superb cast makes this story, about a ruthless young man who tarnishes everything and everyone he touches, ring true from the start to finish. Newman is the perfect embodiment of alienated youth, out for kicks with no regard for the consequences. The drama is deepened by the bitter conflict between the callous Hud and his stern and highly principled father (Douglas). Patricia Neal makes all her scenes count in her Oscar-winning portrayal, as their world-weary housekeeper. Taut direction from Martin Ritt and excellent on-location Texas photography. (112 mins.)

Hudson's Bay (1941)**½ Paul Muni, Gene Tierney. Story of the founding of the famed Hudson Bay Company is a drawn out story, lacking action or motivation. A disappointing film. (Dir: Irving Pichel, 95 mins.)

Hue and Cry (British, 1948)*** Alastair Sim, Valerie White. A meek detective story writer and a group of kids crack a gang of thieves. Highly enjoyable romp, from the same men who made "The Lavender Hill Mob." Sim, as usual, is grand. (Dir: Charles Crichton, 82 mins.)

Hugs and Kisses (Swedish, 1967) **½ Agneta Ekmanner, Sven-Bertil Taube, Hakan Serner. What happens when a married couple invite a carefree bachelor to stay with them. Domestic comedy with spice never reaches great heights, but is mildly entertaining.

Huk (1956)*** George Montgomery, Mona Freeman. Huks were marauding fanatic guerrillas terrorizing and plundering plantations in Manila. American, Montgomery, arrives to sell his inherited plantation and stays to fight. Exciting action scenes, and plenty of them. (Dir: John Barnwell, 84 mins.)

Humain, Trop Humain—See: Human, Too Human

Human Comedy, The (1942)**** Mickey Rooney, Frank Morgan, Marsha Hunt, Van Johnson. If you don't like top drawer sentimental hokum, forget this one. William Saroyan's optimistic philosophy on the human race is beautifully expressed in this story which is almost plotless but deep in characterization and sensitivity. It just tells about a

336

small town in California during World War II but see it and reaffirm your faith in people. (Dir: Clarence Brown, 118 mins.)

Human Desire (1954)** Glenn Ford, Gloria Grahame, Broderick Crawford. Updated, sex-filled version of Emile Zola's "Human Beast" about an unfaithful wife and a railroad engineer's blind love for her. Ponderous. (Dir: Fritz Lang, 90 mins.)

Human Duplicators, The (1964)** George Nader, Barbara Nichols, George MacCready. Special agent investigates, find superior beings from another world creating a race of robots who will infiltrate key positions paving the way for invasion. Way-out science fiction, not really as bad as it sounds; should entertain the fans. (Dir: Hugo Grimaldi, 82 mins.)

Human Factor, The (1975)½ George Kennedy, John Mills, Raf Vallone, Rita Tushingham, Barry Sullivan. Distasteful rubbish about an American computer expert stationed in Italy. Returns home to find his family brutally slain. Using available technology, he tracks down the terrorists responsible and exacts revenge. Vigilante violence resulting from the vendetta is illogical and repugnant. (Dir: Edward Dmytryk, 96 mins.)

Human Jungle, The (1954)**½ Gary Merrill, Jan Sterling. Exciting cops and robbers yarn with more action than most similar type films. Merrill plays a police Capt. who comes face to face with some very shady characters of the underworld. (Dir: Joseph M. Newman, 82 mins.)

Human Monster (1940)—See: **Dark Eyes of London**

Human, Too Human (France, 1972) ***½ Penetrating and provocative work. Director Louis Malle ("Lacombe Lucien") takes a documentary look at the problems of technology at a Citroen plant and the Paris auto show. Stunning images show the factory workers actually deriving comfort from the repetition of their tasks, the public fanatically trusting the manufacturers. Like Malle's other documentary, "Phantom India," this work shows concern with the environmental factors that shape people's lives. A remarkable feat—an absorbing film about boredom. (Dir: Louis Malle, 77 mins.)

Human Vapor, The (Japan, 1960)**✶✶½** Yoshio Tsuchiya, Kaoru Yachigusa. Well-handled Japanese sci-fi about a man who can make himself into vapor at will—variation on the "Invisible Man" theme. His true love, a classical Japanese dancer, provides some attractive side action. (Dir: Inoshiro Honda, 79 mins.)

Humoresque (1947)**✶✶✶** Joan Crawford, John Garfield, Oscar Levant. Lengthy Fannie Hurst drama of a talented musician from the slums who meets, is sponsored and loved by a wealthy society woman, with the inevitable tragic finale. Spiced up with some Clifford Odets dialogue, good (classical) music sequences, capable performances. (Dir: Jean Negulesco, 125 mins.)

Hunchback of Notre Dame, The (1923)**✶✶✶½** Lon Chaney, Patsy Ruth Miller, Ernest Torrence. Lon Chaney's "Hunchback" is one of the most extraordinary characters anyone has ever gazed on in the history of motion pictures. Not only was his makeup fantastic, including forty pounds of rubber and putty, but Chaney's acting beneath all those layers was very inventive and believable. Chaney, with his darting tongue and single eye, looks grotesque, but his movements in the bell tower and elsewhere are remarkably nimble. First major film version of "Hunchback" and based, of course, on Victor Hugo's novel "Notre Dame de Paris." This was a mammoth production for the period, employing, not to very good advantage, thousands of extras. But Chaney dominates throughout, and worth seeing because of him. (Dir: Wallace Worsley, 108 mins.)

Hunchback of Notre Dame (1939) **✶✶✶½** Charles Laughton, Maureen O'Hara, Edmond O'Brien. Victor Hugo's classic tale of the hunchback who saves a gypsy girl from a Paris mob. Fine production values, well acted. (Dir: William Dieterle, 117 min.)

Hunchback of Notre Dame (French, 1957)**✶✶✶** Anthony Quinn, Gina Lollobrigida. The latest screen version of the classic tale about the deformed bell ringer of Notre Dame and his love for Esmeralda. Quinn's makeup job is grotesque but he has a field day in the role. Gina's "Esmeralda" is the sexiest so far. (Dir: Jean Delannoy, 104 mins.)

Hundred Hour Hunt (British, 1953) **✶✶✶** Anthony Steel, Jack Warner. A little girl who is an accident victim needs blood plasma that can only be supplied by a sailor, a boxer and a fugitive. Suspenseful melodrama.

Hungry Hill (British, 1947)**✶✶½** Margaret Lockwood, Dennis Price. Two Irish families feud with each other through the years, bringing despair and poverty. Rambling, drawn out melodrama, has some good moments, some trite ones. (Dir: Brian Desmond Hurst, 92 mins.)

Huns, The (Italian, 1963)**✶½** Chelo Alonso, Jacques Sernas. Queen of the Tartars falls for a warrior of the opposition, they eventually unite in battle and romance. Some big battle scenes save this English-dubbed costume spectacle from complete boredom.

Hunt, The (Spain, 1966)**✶✶✶✶** Ismael Merlo, Alfred Mayo. Powerful, brutal, haunting film, superbly directed by young Spaniard Carlos Saura. Three middle-aged men, out on a rabbit-hunting party-picnic, are themselves brutalized by the hunt in this searing drama. Depicts how the well-intentioned hunt disintegrates into a setting for an unexpected kind of violence. Memorable film which never got the attention or the distribution it deserves. English subtitles.

Hunt the Man Down (1951)**✶✶✶** Gig Young, Lynne Roberts. Public defender is asked to solve a killing for which an innocent man is charged. Above average mystery with a good plot. (Dir: George Archainbaud, 68 mins.)

Hunter (1971)**✶✶** John Vernon, Steve Ihnat. Slick, cold, concise bit of hanky-panky, produced by "Mission: Impossible" 's executive producer, Bruce Geller. Involves a government man who assumes the identity of a brainwashed agent, programmed to release a shipment of deadly virus. Made-for-TV. (Dir: Leonard Horn, 73 mins.)

Hunters, The (1958)**✶✶½** Robert Mitchum, Robert Wagner, May Britt, Lee Philips. Jet pilots in Korea. More melodrama than action, but the pace picks up when "the boys" are aloft, due to some first-rate aerial photography. Robert Wagner's first substantial role, and he's on target as a hotshot pilot. (Dir: Dick Powell, 108 mins.)

Hunters Are for Killing (1970)**½
Burt Reynolds, Melvyn Douglas.
This made-for-TV feature is a well-
done drama with a small-town setting
which uses its Napa Valley, California, scenery to full advantage.
Lead Burt Reynolds, a man of few
words, returns to the wine country
aiming to prove his innocence on a
murder rap. He is promptly pushed
around by the police and adopted
dad (Melvyn Douglas), who orders
cops about like servants. Reynolds'
strong point is the silent treatment,
and he's quite believable as the ex-
high school hero with a chip on his
shoulder, sore at the Establishment
and his father. (Dir: Bernard
Kowalski, 99 mins.)

Hunting Party, The (Great Britain,
1971)½ Candice Bergen, Oliver
Reed, Gene Hackman. Violence-
filled western trash, set in Texas in
the 1890's. Bergen is married to a
sadistic, impotent husband. The
audience is about as well off as
Candice! Extremely badly directed
by Don Medford. (108 mins.)

Hurricane, The (1937)***½ Dorothy
Lamour, Jon Hall, Raymond Massey,
Mary Astor. The actors take second
billing to the special effects in this
film. There's a rousing, frightening
hurricane sequence that makes the
film worth sitting through. John
Ford directed. (Dir: John Ford, 120
mins.)

Hurricane (1974)*½ Jessica Walter,
Larry Hagman, Frank Sutton, Barry Sullivan. The sound effects of a
hurricane in progress are easily
the best elements of this entry.
Frank Sutton's insufferable assur-
ance that he and his friends will
ride out the storm helps a drop or
two. Made-for-TV. (Dir: Jerry
Jameson, 72 mins.)

Hurry Sundown (1967)* Michael
Caine, Jane Fonda, Robert Hooks,
John Phillip Law. A good cast of
pros, expensive mounting and a not
uninteresting story based on the
novel can't save this muddled screen
treatment of the best-selling novel
on which it is based. The tale of
passions and predicaments of the
black and white inhabitants of a
Georgia town loses its interest before the halfway mark. Once again
producer Otto Preminger has mutilated and cheapened potentially
rewarding screen material, in this

case the novel by K. B. Gilden. (142
mins.)

Husbands (1970)**** John Cassavetes, Peter Falk, Ben Gazzara. A
poignant film about three middle-
aged men who go on a drinking binge
when a mutual friend dies. The sadness and despair of their lives pour
out as they even go to England to
try to escape themselves. Cassavetes,
Falk, and Gazzara are all perfect,
and much of their dialogue is improvised. Cassavetes directed and as
always, his style is personal and
intense. (138 mins.)

Hush, Hush, Sweet Charlotte (1965)
*** Bette Davis, Olivia de Havilland.
A macabre, absorbing drama about
the conniving plan by cousin Olivia
and her old beau Joseph Cotten to
do pitiful Charlotte (Miss Davis)
out of her valuable property. Agnes
Moorehead scores as a slovenly
housekeeper who catches onto Miss
Olivia's ominous plan. (Dir: Robert
Aldrich, 133 mins.)

Hustle (1975)*** Burt Reynolds,
Catherine Deneuve, Paul Winfield,
Ben Johnson, Eileen Brennan, Eddie Albert. Involving police drama,
unusually well acted and directed in
crisp, professional fashion by veteran Robert Aldrich. Burt Reynolds
is well cast as a police detective in
love with a high-priced call girl,
played with too much class by
France's beauty, Catherine Deneuve.
The subplot, about a teenage girl's
murder, keeps the detective work
bouncing along. The soundtrack recording from "A Man and a Woman" played by Deneuve over and
over again. Heavy-handed screenplay by Steve Shagan. (Dir: Robert
Aldrich, 120 mins.)

Hustler, The (1961)**** Paul Newman, Jackie Gleason, Piper Laurie,
George C. Scott. Gripping portrait of
a pool shark who challenges the top
man at the game, risking all. An
achievement in that it makes a game
of pool exciting on film, it also possesses superb performances from all
concerned, incisive characterizations, fine direction by Robert Rossen. Excellent. (135 mins.)

Hustling (1975)*** Lee Remick, Jill
Clayburgh, Monte Markham. Effective drama about the streetwalkers
of New York. Fay Kanin's gutsy,
seamy sad tale, based on Gail
Sheehy's book, portrays the prostitutes as victims, pushed around by

just about everybody, including their pimps. Lee Remick is well cast as the straight woman, a reporter digging into all facets of the shabby business by following a scrappy hooker and her pals around. Jill Clayburgh plays the hooker extremely well. Made-for-TV. (Dir: Joseph Sargent, 100 mins.)

Hypnotic Eye, The (1960)*½ Jacques Bergerac. A silly mystery about a professional hypnotist whose victims are beautiful women whom he instructs to destroy their beauty while under his spell. The laughs are unintentional. (Dir: George Blair, 79 mins.)

I **Accuse** (1958)**½ Jose Ferrer, Viveca Lindfors, Emlyn Williams, Leo Genn, Anton Walbrook. The famous Capt. Dreyfus trial and conviction as the basis for this drama. Ferrer plays Dreyfus with a commendable restraint and an excellent supporting cast backs him up. However, this is not as effective as "The Life of Emile Zola" which starred Paul Muni and dealt with the same story line. (Dir: Jose Ferrer, 99 mins.)

I **Aim at the Stars** (British, 1960)*** Curt Jurgens, Victoria Shaw. Gripping semi-documentary styled account of how Wernher von Braun, missile expert, came to work for the U.S. after his close association with the Nazis during WW II. Jurgens is ideally cast as von Braun. Proof that some of our Nazis are better than the Nazis the Russians grabbed. (Dir: J. Lee Thompson, 107 mins.)

I **Am a Camera** (British, 1955)*** Julie Harris, Laurence Harvey, Shelley Winters. The record of a young author and a hard-living, carefree girl in pre-war Berlin. Literate, excellently acted comedy-drama. (Dir: Henry Cornelius, 98 mins.)

I **Am a Fugitive** (1932)***½ Paul Muni. A scathing indictment of life in a Southern chain gang which has become a film classic. The movie and the book on which it was based caused quite a stir at the time and even led to some investigations. Muni is magnificent in the lead and he's ably assisted by a fine cast. (Dir: Mervyn Le Roy, 100 mins.)

I **Am Curious Yellow** (Sweden, 1967)**½ Lena Nyman, Borje Ahlstedt, Peter Lindgren. It's hard to believe that this Swedish import about a female sociologist could have created such a storm of moral outrage at the time of its release. Our heroine is concerned with questions of class structure, but the director is equally concerned with ass structure. People are tumbling, not only in and out of bed, but fornicating in trees, in public buildings, in the water, etc. It's good natured enough and not very erotic. Blessedly lacking any of the accoutrements of sado-masochism, violence and drugs found in films made a decade later. (Dir: Vilgot Sjoman, 121 mins.)

I **Am the Law** (1938)*** Edward G. Robinson, Wendy Barrie. Law professor wages a one-man war against protection racketeers. Well acted, well done crime melodrama. (Dir: Alexander Hall, 90 mins.)

I **Became a Criminal** (British, 1947)*** Trevor Howard, Sally Gray. An ex-pilot framed into prison escapes to square the double cross. Tense, exciting melodrama; well acted. (Dir: Alberto Cavalcanti, 80 mins.)

I **Believe in You** (British, 1952)*** Cecil Parker, Celia Johnson. A wayward young girl and a hoodlum are looked after by a kindly probation officer. Interesting drama is well thought out. (Dir: Michael Relph, 93 mins.)

I **Bombed Pearl Harbor** (1961)** Toshiro Mifune. A Japanese made film about the Japanese outlook of the war. Moderately interesting.

I **Bury the Living** (1958)**½ Richard Boone, Theodore Bikel. Each time a manager sticks a black pin on a community cemetery chart, somebody dies. Three-fourths of a good thriller; falls apart at the end, but prior to that has some very effective moments. (Dir: Albert Band, 76 mins.)

I **Can Get It for You Wholesale** (1951)**½ Susan Hayward, Dan Dailey, George Sanders. Story of a heel in the garment industry. Well acted, but somehow unsympathetic, at times rather nasty. (Dir: Michael Gordon, 90 mins.)

I **Can't Give You Anything But Love, Baby** (1940)**½ Broderick Crawford, Johnny Downs. Snappy little musical about a hoodlum who kidnaps a young song writer to compose a love song for his moll. Some good laughs.

I Confess (1953)**½ Montgomery Clift, Anne Baxter, Karl Malden. Even Alfred Hitchcock has to strike out some time and this is one of those times—a priest, well played by Clift, will not violate the sanctity of the confessional even at his own expense. (Dir: Alfred Hitchcock, 95 mins.)

I Could Go on Singing (British, 1963)** Judy Garland, Dirk Bogarde. The singing star is far from her best in this sudsy drama about an entertainer who meets an old love in London. Garland fans will relish her vocalistics no matter what, but she is not seen to advantage here, either dramatically or musically. (Dir: Ronald Neame, 99 mins.)

I Deal in Danger (1966)½ Robert Goulet, Christine Carere. American goes undercover as a traitor to try to infiltrate controlling leaders of the Third Reich. Made from the first three episodes of the 1966 TV series "The Blue Light." Clumsy action picture, is not helped by the acting. (Dir: Walter Grauman, 89 mins.)

I Died a Thousand Times (1955)** Jack Palance, Shelley Winters, Lee Marvin. Fair remake of a Humphrey Bogart-Ida Lupino film called "High Sierra." Palance plays a gangster who loves only two things in the whole world, a dog and a clubfooted girl. After he pays for an operation to correct the girl's foot, he is rejected by her and goes almost mad. Palance overacts. (Dir: Stuart Heisler, 109 mins.)

"I Don't Care" Girl, The (1953)**½ Mitzi Gaynor, David Wayne. George Jessel produced this musical biography of Eva Tanguay and the film is about George Jessel's work in getting the facts about Miss Tanguay. If you disregard the extraneous plot gimmicks, you may enjoy the musical numbers executed by Miss Gaynor and Mr. Wayne and singer Bob Graham. (Dir: Lloyd Bacon, 78 mins.)

I Dood It (1943)**½ Red Skelton, Eleanor Powell. Red's many fans may like this zany slapstick but it's not one of his best. Romance of a pants presser and a movie star is loaded with trite situations and forced humor. (Dir: Vincente Minnelli, 102 mins.)

I Dream of Jeannie (1952)** Ray Middleton, Bill Shielry. Story of how Stephen Foster came to write many of his famous tunes. Corny plot, but plenty of ditties for those who care. (Dir: Allan Dwan, 90 mins.)

I Dream Too Much (1935)*** Lily Pons, Henry Fonda. Two young music students are happily married until the wife wins success as a singer. Superb vocalizing by Miss Pons is the feature of this pleasant romantic comedy-drama. (Dir: John Cromwell, 110 mins.)

I Even Met Happy Gypsies (Yugoslavian, 1967)*** Gypsy life, far from happy, surveyed with an ingenious eye by director Aleksandar Petrovic. Principal role played by Bekim Fehmiu, later seen to disadvantage in "The Adventurers." Subtitles.

I. F. Stone's Weekly (1973)**** A remarkable, low-budget documentary paying rightful tribute to one of the greatest and, for a long time, most ignored newspapermen of our age—the award-winning investigative journalist I. F. Stone. Filmmaker Jerry Bruck has not made an obsequious film about Stone—he captures the flavor of what Stone himself calls his "maniacal zest and idiot zeal." There was no single momentous Watergate-type story uncovered by Izzy Stone, just many scoops, decade after decade, thanks to a first-rate journalist concerned only with truth, not power. (Dir: Jerry Bruck Jr., 62 mins.)

I Know Where I'm Going (British, 1946)**** Wendy Hiller, Roger Livesey. An enchanting, touching romance about a rich girl on her way to marry an unwanted suitor, who runs away and finds true love on a picturesque island off the coast of Scotland. Wendy Hiller, an astonishing actress of seemingly limitless range, often wasted in motion pictures, is an irresistible delight in this sensitively directed film that is an enduring treat. (Dir: Michael Powell, 91 mins.)

I Like Money (British, 1961)** Peter Sellers, Nadia Gray, Herbert Lom. Sellers as an honest schoolteacher who learns that dishonesty pays off. A version of Pagnol's "Topaze." Sellers makes the mistake of directing himself, resulting in a slow, stiff ironic comedy, done much better in the past by such as Barrymore and Fernandel. (Dir: Peter Sellers, 97 mins.)

I Love a Mystery (1973)* Ida Lupino, David Hartman, Les Crane, Terry-

Thomas, Don Knotts. Moldy revival of the old Carlton E. Morse radio series. Three detectives fly to a private island to flush out missing billionaire. Made-for-TV. (Dir: Leslie Stevens, 99 mins.)

▌ **Love Melvin** (1953)**½ Donald O'Connor, Debbie Reynolds. A happy musical with the accent on youth in song and dance. The plot, which serves as an excuse for the many musical numbers, has O'Connor cast as a top magazine photographer and Miss Reynolds as a Broadway chorus girl. (Dir: Don Weis, 76 mins.)

▌ **Love My Wife** (1970)**½ Elliott Gould, Brenda Vaccaro. Funny but uneven comedy dealing with modern marriage. It's all about what happens to Gould and Vaccaro's matrimonial bliss when hubby starts to roam and rove. The film gets into trouble with its sudden changes from satirical to serious moments, but the performances are all topnotch. (Dir: Mel Stuart, 95 mins.)

▌ **Love Trouble** (1948)*** Franchot Tone, Janet Blair. Tough private eye runs into foul play while searching for a missing girl. Smooth, speedy, well done mystery. (Dir: S. Sylvan Simon, 94 mins.)

▌ **Love You Again** (1939)*** Myrna Loy, William Powell. Lots of fun in this silly comedy about a nice, dull husband who, after a bump on the head, recovers from amnesia and becomes his true self, a slick con man. (Dir: W. S. Van Dyke, 99 mins.)

▌ **Love You, Alice B. Toklas** (1968)*** Peter Sellers, Leigh Taylor-Young, Jo Van Fleet. A frequently amusing original comedy by Paul Mazursky and Larry Tucker, with a message, believe it or not. Peter Sellers is at his best as a mother-dominated Los Angeles lawyer who leaves his fiancee at the altar not once but twice to seek "the better things in life," as he puts it. One of those better things is lovely Leigh Taylor-Young as a liberated young lady who turns on Peter and turns him into a hippie, complete with crash pad and long hair. There's more here than the frivolity outlined in this capsule synopsis. Worthwhile and funny, too. (Dir: Hy Averback, 93 mins.)

▌ **Love You, Goodbye** (1974)**½ Hope Lange, Earl Holliman. Muddled story about a housewife and mother of 18 years who suddenly craves more meaning in her life and leaves the whole kit and kaboodle to find herself. The dialogue often reverts to cliches associated with the early preachments of the women's lib movement and minimizes the dramatic moments of the story. Patricia Smith has the best written role as a divorcee who seems content with her new life-style and helps friend Hope Lange. Made-for-TV. (Dir: Sam O'Steen.)

▌ **Married a Monster From Outer Space** (1958)** Tom Tryon, Gloria Talbott. The title tells all, as a young bride discovers her husband is really a being from another planet intent on conquering earth. As these sci-fi thrillers go, not bad; has a certain amount of style. (Dir: Gene Fowler, Jr., 78 mins.)

▌ **Married a Witch** (1942)*** Fredric March, Veronica Lake, Susan Hayward. The candidate for governor is in quite a stew when a beautiful witch is released from her three-hundred-year hiding place and goes after him with romance in mind. Clever fantasy has a good share of chuckles. (Dir: Rene Clair, 76 mins.)

▌ **Married a Woman** (1956)*½ George Gobel, Jessie Royce Landis, Diana Dors. Lonesome George Gobel plays an advertising man perplexed by the problems of coming up with an ad campaign, and keeping his wife (a beauty-contest winner) happy. Breezy comedy? Not quite. (Dir: Hal Kanter, 84 mins.)

▌ **Met a Murderer** (British, 1939)*** James Mason, Pamela Kellino. Goaded into murdering his shrewish wife, a farmer flees from the police, is sheltered by a young girl. Brooding, suspenseful melodrama, artistically done.

▌ **Mobster** (1959)**½ Steve Cochran, Lita Milan. A criminal tells his story —from a young punk to a big time mobster. Effective only at times due to script limitations. Cochran is good. (Dir: Roger Corman, 80 mins.)

▌ **Never Sang for My Father** (1970) ***½ Melvyn Douglas, Gene Hackman, Estelle Parsons. Deeply moving drama. Hackman as a 40-year-old still trying to play son to Melvyn Douglas as the father. Based on Robert Anderson's stage play about an 80-year-old father, former mayor of a Long Island suburb, who is tyrannically obsessed with concepts of strength and pride. Douglas and Hackman are profoundly moving. (Dir: Gilbert Cates, 90 mins.)

I **Passed for White** (1960)*½ James Franciscus, Sonya Wilde. Sloppily made drama about a light-skinned Negro girl who passes for white and marries an upper class white man. The characters are poorly motivated and the result is often heavy handed. Franciscus is totally wasted in the role of the girl's husband. (Dir: Fred M. Wilcox, 93 mins.)

I **Remember Mama** (1948)**** Irene Dunne, Barbara Bel Geddes. Story of a mother who runs a Norwegian family as they attempt to establish a home in San Francisco. Superb drama tugs the heartstrings in fine fashion. (Dir: George Stevens, 134 mins.)

I **Sailed to Tahiti with an All Girl Crew** (1968)* Gardner McKay, Fred Clark, Diane McBain. Young man reacts to jokes made about his ability to be a sailor, says he can win a race to Tahiti using an all-girl crew. Male chauvinist antique. (Dir: Richard Bore, 95 mins.)

I **Saw What You Did** (1965)** Joan Crawford, John Ireland. Couple of teen-age girls play a telephone prank, which upsets a murderer and makes them candidate for his next crime. Okay suspense drama with Crawford wasted in a minor role. (Dir: William Castle, 82 mins.)

I **Shot Jesse James** (1949)*** Preston Foster, John Ireland, Barbara Britton. The story of Bob Ford, and the guilty conscience that plagues him after drilling the famous outlaw. Above average western drama, well done. (Dir: Samuel Fuller, 81 mins.)

I **Spy, You Spy** (British, 1965)**½ Tony Randall, Senta Berger, Herbert Lom. American in Morocco suddenly finds himself enmeshed in the sinister deeds of a spy ring and a disappearing corpse. Good performers add zest to an otherwise familiar, routine comedy thriller.

I **Thank a Fool** (1962)*½ Susan Hayward, Peter Finch. Ridiculous melodrama. Susan Hayward is all stiff upper lip and nobility as an ex-doctor who was charged with euthanasia and served a prison term only to end up as companion-nurse to the wife of the man who prosecuted her (Finch). The ladies who

follow the daily crises of the soap operas will pull for Miss Hayward's plight. (Dir: Robert Stevens, 100 mins.)

I **Wake Up Screaming** (1942)*** Betty Grable, Victor Mature, Carole Landis, Laird Cregar. What there is of this melodrama belongs to Mr. Cregar as a psychopathic cop with an insane love for a dead girl. If you've never seen this in any of its forms, you may like it. (Dir: H. Bruce Humberstone, 82 mins.)

I **Walk Alone** (1948)** Burt Lancaster, Kirk Douglas, Lizabeth Scott. Man returns from prison to find that things have changed in this grim, weak melodrama. (Dir: Byron Haskin, 98 mins.)

I **Walk the Line** (1970)*** Gregory Peck, Tuesday Weld. Interesting drama set in the moonshine country of Tennessee. Miss Weld's performance as a young girl who captivates married Sheriff Peck is the main inducement for watching this story about bootlegging moonshiners and their constant bouts with the local law. (Dir: John Frankenheimer, 96 mins.)

I **Walked with a Zombie** (1943)*** Frances Dee, Tom Conway. Canadian nurse goes to the West Indies to attend a patient, finds voodooism involved. Suspenseful, well made thriller. (Dir: Jacques Tourneur, 69 mins.)

I **Want to Keep My Baby** (1976)*** Mariel Hemingway, Susan Anspach, Jack Rader. This is a strong, poignant, if lengthy film about a fifteen-year-old girl who becomes pregnant, is abandoned by her teenage lover, decides to have her baby, and is persuaded by various forces to keep the infant and care for it. Mariel Hemingway is so tantalizingly gripping in the role of the girl, she rivets your attention to the screen even in repetitious scenes. In addition to the fascination of watching the very young Miss Hemingway, a number of serious questions are raised. Most important, perhaps, is whether a teenager with little experience in living is capable of bringing up her baby alone; or whether it would be preferable both for her and the child if the infant were given up for adoption. Made-for-TV. (Dir: Jerry Thorpe, 106 mins.)

I **Want To Live** (1958)**** Susan Hayward. Susan Hayward's Academy Award winning performance directed by Robert Wise is the main attraction in this film based on the sensational and controversial murder trial of vice girl Barbara Graham. Miss Graham's past prison record and other incriminating evidence worked against her and resulted in her conviction. The final segment dealing with her execution in the gas chamber packs a real wallop. A powerful indictment of capital punishment. (Dir: Robert Wise, 120 mins.)

I **Want You** (1951)** Dana Andrews, Dorothy McGuire, Farley Granger, Peggy Dow. Samuel Goldwyn's effort to have box office lightning strike twice ("Best Years of Our Lives") via this slow moving drama about the effect of the Korean War on a typical American family. Talky, artificial and often boring. (Dir: Mark Robson, 102 mins.)

I **Wanted Wings** (1941)**½ Ray Milland, Bill Holden, Wayne Morris. Story of three young men taking our pre-war Air Cadet training is nothing more than dated propaganda today. (Dir: Mitchell Leisen, 131 mins.)

I **Was a Communist for the F.B.I.** (1951)** Frank Lovejoy, Dorothy Hart. The title tells the whole story. Lovejoy plays Matt Cvetic, a real life F.B.I. agent who posed as a Communist in order to inform on the Reds' activities in the U.S. (Dir: Gordon Douglas, 83 mins.)

I **Was a Male War Bride** (1949)*** Cary Grant, Ann Sheridan. Cary Grant, as an ex-French Army officer, disguises himself as a WAC in order to accompany his American WAC bride (Ann Sheridan) to the U. S. on troop ship. Doesn't sound very funny but it is; stars and script are hilarious. (Dir: Howard Hawks, 105 mins.)

I **Was a Parish Priest** (Franco-Spanish, 1957)*** Claude Laydu, Francisco Rabal. Well-made drama of the trials and tribulations of a young priest in his first parish assignment. Capable performances, sincere in treatment. English-dubbed.

I **Was a Teenage Frankenstein** (1957) *½ Whit Bissell, Phyllis Coates. Mad doctor creates his own superbeing. Script made of rags, snails, dog-tails, etc. (Dir: Herbert L. Strock, 72 mins.)

I **Was Monty's Double** (British, 1959) ***½ John Mills, Cecil Parker. Well done British war drama about a great plot involving an actor impersonating a General to confuse the Germans in the North African campaign. Top performances by a good cast. (Dir: John Guillerman, 100 mins.)

I **Wonder Who's Kissing Her Now** (1947)*** June Haver, Mark Stevens. Highly fictionalized career of song writer Joe Howard has such a delightful score and so many talented people that we can overlook its childish plot. (Dir: Lloyd Bacon, 104 mins.)

Ice (1970)***½ Provocative, powerful, maddening drama directed in semidocumentary form by radical writer-filmmaker Robert Kramer. Virtually a blueprint-textbook of how the American urban guerrilla revolution will proceed. A motley collection of earnest but intellectually vapid young political activists talk, commit acts of sabotage, and finally blow up part of New York. Because this is virtually the only American-made feature that deals candidly with the question of political revolution in America, it is especially disappointing that the film is so detached, and that the audience learns little about, and cares nothing for, any of the characters. The young rebels in "Ice" are, incidentally, just as repellent and dehumanized as the system they seek to overthrow. Mostly nonprofessional cast, which eats and makes love without humor or joy. Despite its shortcomings, "Ice" is an absorbing, disturbing document. (132 mins.)

Ice Cold In Alex—See: Desert Attack

Ice Palace (1960)**½ Richard Burton, Robert Ryan, Carolyn Jones. Edna Ferber's sprawling novel about the formation of Alaska as a state makes a long episodic film with some good performers trying their best to overcome the soap opera tendencies of the script. Burton and Ryan clash in business, private life and finally politics. Miss Jones goes from a young girl in love with Burton to a gray-haired old lady watching out for Burton's granddaughter. (Dir: Vincent Sherman, 143 mins.)

Ice Station Zebra (1968)**½ Rock Hudson, Ernest Borgnine, Patrick McGoohan. Sprawling submarine adventure produced on a grand scale.

Rock Hudson is the commander of an elaborate sub sent to the North Pole on a secret mission involving missile data recorded by a Russian space satellite. Enough plot , . . tune in and enjoy the many intrigues and excellent photography. Some of the film crawls at a snail's pace, but the overall action clips along. Kids are probably the best audience for this submarine yarn. (Dir: John Sturges, 148 mins.)

Iceland (1942)**½ Sonja Henie, John Payne. A fair score, Sonja's skating and that's it for this film. Plot and dialogue about romance of an Iceland girl and a Marine are a disgrace. (Dir: H. B. Humberstone, 79 mins.)

Iceman Cometh, The (1973)**** Fredric March, Lee Marvin, Robert Ryan, Jeff Bridges, Tom Pedi. This may not be the definitive "Iceman" we may have hoped for, or may yet be blessed with, at some future date. But no matter. "Iceman" is an O'Neill masterpiece, not quite as devastating as "Long Day's Journey into Night," perhaps, but it's a fascinating play with several marvelous roles. Fredric March, one of the greatest American actors since the beginning of motion pictures, is extraordinary playing Harry Hope, which is more than can be said for the performance of Lee Marvin in the pivotal role of Hickey, the "iceman," the shill, the destroyer of his hapless pals' drunken dreams. Set in a 1912 waterfront saloon, a combination of a bar and flophouse. This towering play, not perfectly served, emerges as a powerful, harrowing film. (Dir: John Frankenheimer, 239 mins.)

I'd Climb the Highest Mountain (1951)**½ Susan Hayward, William Lundigan. Backwoods drama aimed toward the female audience. Story centers about a hill-country minister's wife's adjustment to her new life and responsibilities. There are some colorful characters scattered throughout the screenplay, well acted by Alexander Knox, Barbara Bates and Gene Lockhart. (Dir: Henry King, 88 mins.)

I'd Rather Be Rich (1964)**½ Sandra Dee, Robert Goulet, Andy Williams, Maurice Chevalier. Millionaire's granddaughter asks a stranger to pose as her fiancé to please the old man, who is ill.

Amusing romantic comedy, thanks largely to Chevalier. It's a remake of an old Deanna Durbin movie, but lacks the charm of the original. (Dir: Jack Smight, 96 mins.)

Ideal Husband, An (British, 1948)**½ Paulette Goddard, Michael Wilding, Glynis Johns. Oscar Wilde's comedy of manners and morals in Victorian England, elaborately produced, but stuffy, dull. (Dir: Alexander Korda, 96 mins.)

Idiot, The (U.S.S.R., 1958)** Yuri Yakovlev, Julia Borisova. Dostoyevsky's novel of introspection, about a sensitive nobleman who arrives in the harried, corrupt world of 19th-century Moscow and falls in love with a worldly woman, becomes an almost raucous affair in this screen version, full of emoting and sweeping operatic gesture. (Dir: Ivan Pyriev, 95 mins.)

Idiot's Delight (1938)***½ Clark Gable, Norma Shearer. Robert Sherwood's Pulitzer Prize play loses in the screen-version but enough is left to make it worthwhile. Written prior to World War II it is worth seeing today because it expresses one of America's great playwright's views on war. Story has enough comedy to keep it going as pure entertainment. (Dir: Clarence Brown, 120 mins.)

If (British, 1969)**** Malcolm McDowell, David Wood, Richard Warwick, Peter Jeffrey, Christine Noonan. A striking, enormously powerful if episodic drama about life in a repressive boys' boarding school in England. Distinguished documentary film maker Lindsay Anderson, who directed the memorable "This Sporting Life," has skillfully used both professional and non-professional actors to build this ultimately shattering account of how the students finally react to what they believe is senseless discipline and authoritarianism, both from the faculty and the upper-class prefects. (Don't spend any time worrying about the symbolism and meaning of why the film alternates from time to time from color to black-and-white sequences. The producer simply ran out of money while finishing the movie, and black-and-white processing was cheaper than finishing the film completely in color.) (111 mins.)

If a Man Answers (1962)** Sandra

344

Dee, Bobby Darin, John Lund, Stefanie Powers. Playgirl marries a carefree photographer, resorts to extreme measures to keep him in line after they're married. Lightweight romantic comedy comes along about 26 years too late—they did them better in those days. (Dir: Henry Levin, 102 mins.)

If All the Guys in the World . . . (French, 1956)**½ André Valmy, Jean Gaven. Amateur radio operators all over Europe come to the aid of the crew of a French fishing trawler when they become ill and signal for help. Based on an actual incident in the North Sea, this drama attempting to depict the "brotherhood of man" nevertheless seems often contrived. Dubbed in English.

If He Hollers, Let Him Go! (1968)*½ Escaped black convict (Raymond St. Jacques) is caught in a murder scheme devised by a no-good playboy (Kevin McCarthy) after his wife's (Dana Wynter) money. Purple passions and race relations in a chintzy ill-mixture. Pity the performers. Charles Martin takes the blame for producing, writing and directing this claptrap. (106 mins.)

If I Had a Million (1932)***½ W. C. Fields, George Raft, Gary Cooper, Charles Laughton. Eccentric millionaire decides to will his dough to people picked at random from the phone book, and this is about them. Enjoyable multi-storied film, with the Fields and Laughton episodes screamingly funny. (Dirs: Ernst Lubitsch, Norman Taurog, 90 mins.)

If I Were King (1938)*** Ronald Colman, Basil Rathbone, Frances Dee. You'll love Colman as the swashbuckling, romantic Francois Villon, who, in real life, was a rogue but, in reel life is a lovable hero. One might call him the French Robin Hood. Good costume drama, loaded with action. (Dir: Frank Lloyd, 110 mins.)

If It's Tuesday, This Must Be Belgium (1969)*** Suzanne Pleshette, Mildred Natwick, Norman Fell. If you've ever been on a package European tour (and even if you haven't) you'll find plenty of laughs in this saga about a group of travelers who race through seven countries in 18 days. The mixture of the vacationers is delightful, including Pleshette as a young miss who finds time for

some romance with handsome Britisher Ian McShane; Miss Natwick as an old lady with energy to spare; Fell and Reva Rose as a married couple who get separated; and Sandy Baron as an Italian-American who almost gets married off while visiting relatives in Venice. Deft screenplay by David Shaw. (Dir: Mel Stuart, 98 mins.)

If Tomorrow Comes (1971)** Patty Duke, Frank Liu. A tearjerker for the ladies. Miss Duke plays a young lady who falls for, and secretly marries, a Japanese-American in southern California a few days before Pearl Harbor. Liu as Patty's husband gives a sincere performance, and James Whitmore as Patty's bigoted father, and Anne Baxter as an understanding schoolteacher, are effective. Made-for-TV. (Dir: George McGowan, 73 mins.)

If Winter Comes (1947)* Walter Pidgeon, Deborah Kerr. Terrible, confused soap opera story which is an insult to its cast. (Dir: Victor Saville, 97 mins.)

If You Could Only Cook (1935)**½ Jean Arthur, Herbert Marshall. Dated, but mildly entertaining "depression era" comedy, poor girl meets sad millionaire, thinks he's unemployed, helps him get a job. Result: love. (Dir: William A. Seiter, 70 mins.)

If You Knew Susie (1947)** Eddie Cantor, Joan Davis. Vaudeville team discover a famous ancestor and go to Washington to collect seven billion dollars the government owes them. Mild comedy with music. (Dir: Gordon Douglas, 90 mins.)

Ikiru (Japan, 1952)**** Akira Kurosawa has fashioned a haunting portrait of a lonely man who has spent his life working as a civil servant, seen his wife die, alienated his son, and discovers he is dying of cancer. Determined to give his last days over to enjoying himself, he finds it is not enough, and pours his remaining energy into getting a playground built on the site of a sewage dump. Told in flashback, Kurosawa's intense portrait of a man searching for fulfillment is brilliantly fashioned, capped by a memorable, touching final scene. (Dir: Akira Kurosawa, 150 mins.)

I'll Be Seeing You (1944)**½ Ginger Rogers, Joseph Cotten, Shirley Temple. Lady convict gets a Christmas furlough, meets a soldier undergoing psychiatric treatment, and love blossoms. Sentimental drama, uneven, some good moments. (Dir: William Dieterle, 85 mins.)

I'll Be Yours (1947)**½ Deanna Durbin, Tom Drake, Adolphe Menjou. Another light and gay Deanna Durbin comedy about a nice girl searching for a niche in the big city. Tom Drake supplies the love interest opposite Deanna. (Dir: William A. Seiter, 93 mins.)

I'll Cry Tomorrow (1956)**** Susan Hayward, Richard Conte, Jo Van Fleet, Eddie Albert. Superb drama based on Lillian Roth's bold and frank story of her days as an alcoholic and her fight to conquer the dreaded disease. Miss Hayward has never been better and she's matched every step of the way by Jo Van Fleet as her bewildered mother. Conte, Albert and Don Taylor play her various husbands. (Dir: Daniel Mann, 117 mins.)

I'll Get By (1950)**½ June Haver, Gloria De Haven, Dennis Day, William Lundigan. Pleasant musical about a couple of song pluggers and a singing sister act. Many songs and dances and some surprise guest stars (Victor Mature, Jeanne Crain, and Dan Dailey). Gloria De Haven comes off the best in the singing department. (Dir: Richard Sale, 83 mins.)

I'll Get You (British, 1953)** George Raft, Sally Gray. An FBI man, assisted by a pretty MI operator, tracking down foreign agents who smuggle atomic scientists to the Commies. Slow, not very convincing. (Dir: Seymour Friedman, 79 mins.)

I'll Never Forget What's 'Is Name (British, 1967)***½ Oliver Reed, Orson Welles, Carol White. Incisive portrait of a man disillusioned with his shallow life, and the failure of his efforts to change. Alternately witty and uncomfortably real, generally nicely balanced by director Michael Winner. Fine job by Oliver Reed in the main role. Good work by Orson Welles and Harry Andrews. (99 mins.)

I'll Never Forget You (British, 1951)**½ Tyrone Power, Ann Blyth, Michael Rennie. Based on the play "Berkeley Square," this charming romantic adventure concerns a scientist who goes back to the 18th Century and relives one of his ancestors' adventures. Women will especially enjoy this film. The cast is perfectly suited to their roles. (Dir: Roy Baker, 90 mins.)

I'll See You In Hell (Italian, 1963) *½ John Drew Barrymore, Eva Bartok. Three jewel thieves make their way across a swamp eluding the police—one kills another, who later seemingly returns to haunt the killer. Grim, brutal drama dubbed in English leaves an unpleasant taste.

I'll See You In My Dreams (1952)*** Doris Day, Danny Thomas. A romantic biopic on the rise and success of song writer Gus Kahn. Many good standards are heard done by Doris Day, who plays Mrs. Kahn. Danny Thomas is quite believable as the songsmith. (Dir: Michael Curtiz, 110 mins.)

I'll Take Sweden (1965)**½ Bob Hope, Tuesday Weld, Frankie Avalon. If Bob Hope's brand of film comedy is to your liking, you'll have fun watching his antics in this one. Bob is Tuesday Weld's Daddy, and he whisks her off to Sweden when her romance with Frankie Avalon reaches the serious stage. However, things get hotter in Sweden when Jeremy Slate pops into Tuesday's life and Dina Merrill becomes interested in Hope. The pace is fast but the plot doesn't bear too close an examination. (Dir: Frederick de Cordova, 96 mins.)

Illegal (1955)** Edward G. Robinson, Nina Foch. Well acted but poorly scripted story of the rackets and one couple's involvement. Jayne Mansfield has a brief scene. (Dir: Lewis Allen, 88 mins.)

Illegal Cargo (French, 1958)*½ Francoise Arnoul, Jean-Claude Michel. English-dubbed. Newspaperman is murdered while investigating white slavery, but his girl friend takes over to avenge him. Trashy expose melodrama.

Illegal Entry (1949)**½ Howard Duff, Marta Toren, George Brent. Fast-paced action drama about the undercover agents who crack open a large scale smuggling operation which deals with illicit border traffic between Mexico and the United States. The cast is more than competent. (Dir: Frederick de Cordova, 84 mins.)

Illustrated Man, The (1969)***½ Rod Steiger, Claire Bloom, Robert Drivas. Interesting allegorical morality play based on a story by sci-fi writer Ray Bradbury. Scene is a rural camping ground in 1933, where a young man (Drivas) meets a completely tattooed fellow (Steiger). The tattoos each represents a story and as Drivas looks at them, they come to life. (Dir: Jack Smight, 103 mins.)

I'm All Right Jack (British, 1960)**** Ian Carmichael, Peter Sellers, Terry-Thomas. Screamingly funny satire on labor-management relations in England, as an inept young man finds himself caught between the two in trying to run a factory. Sellers is priceless as an oafish labor leader, and the entire cast catches the spirit of the fun. Recommended. (Dirs: John & Roy Boulting, 104 mins.)

I'm from Missouri (1939)*** Bob Burns, Gladys George. Amusing folksy comedy about a small town Missouri man who goes to England on business and turns the peerage upside down and inspires the English war industry. (Dir: Theodore Reed, 90 mins.)

I'm No Angel (1933)***½ Mae West, Cary Grant, Edward Arnold. Even within the limitations of the screen, Mae is not for the kids. Typical Mae West story of a female (what else?) circus performer who conquers all with her wit, daring, and physical assets. There's a courtroom scene that's priceless. (Dir: Wesley Ruggles, 87 mins.)

Images (1972)**½ Susannah York, Rene Auberjonois. Odd film which attempts to explore the schizophrenia of a young woman. Director-author Robert Altman tried to create suspense by not identifying the woman's images as rooted in either illusion or fact. It doesn't work. Miss York is passable in an impossible role. Compensations include the camerawork by Vilmos Zsigmond and the background of beautiful Ireland. (101 mins.)

Imitation General (1958)*** Glenn Ford, Red Buttons, Taina Elg. Fast-paced service comedy that treats the subject of war lightly and makes heroes of buffoons. Red Buttons steals every scene he's in with his very funny portrayal of a corporal who is on a military stratagem which has M/Sgt. Glenn Ford masquerading as a general. (Dir: George Marshall, 120 mins.)

Imitation of Life (1959)**½ Lana Turner, Sandra Dee, John Gavin, Susan Kohner, Juanita Moore. A four handkerchief tear-jerker—aimed at the ladies, remake of earlier version with Claudette Colbert and Hattie McDaniel, gets a bit over-sentimental at times. Lavish production. (Dir: Douglas Sirk, 124 mins.)

Immortal, The (1969)**½ Christopher George, Carol Lynley. The fairly original story was the pilot film for a TV series. Christopher George is cast as a young-looking fortyish test-driver-mechanic who discovers he has a unique blood type which slows down his aging process almost to a halt and keeps him from contracting diseases. The whole thing comes out when his aged boss, millionaire tycoon Barry Sullivan, receives a transfusion of George's blood and temporarily feels rejuvenated. Naturally, George becomes a hunted man. The production is first rate and the acting standout is Barry Sullivan as the wealthy old man who can't face dying at any cost. (Dir: Joseph Sargent, 75 mins.)

Immortal Garden, The (Russian, 1956)*** V. Makarov, V. Emelyanov. Grim, effective WW II film, designed to glorify the Russian soldiers' valor. Follows the defenders of the Brest fortress, where the initial Nazi invasion of Russia occurred, throughout the war, making liberal use of documentary footage. Co-director and cameraman Tisse is best known for his camera work in Eisenstein's movies. (Dirs: Z. Agnanenko, Edward Tisse, 90 mins.)

Immortal Story, The (French, 1968)***½ Orson Welles, Jeanne Moreau, Roger Coggio. Based on the story by Isak Dinesen, this has been adapted and directed by Orson Welles who also plays the role of an elderly merchant in the Portuguese colony of Macao on the coast of China during the end of the 19th century. This is not top drawer Welles, but lesser Welles is still better than most other film-making, and this is well worth seeing. There's a sailor lucky enough to get paid to sleep with Jeanne Moreau, in this curious tale, originally commissioned by French television. (It runs just over one hour.) English dialogue. The color shots of the Orient by cameraman Willy Kurant are a major help in bringing off this bizarre story. (63 mins.)

Impasse (1969)**½ Burt Reynolds,

347

Anne Francis. An adventure film of the sort in which fearless heroes deal with both women and danger at about the same emotional level . . . two steps above stoicism. Burt Reynolds (before he took off as a sex symbol of the '70s in films) plays the organizer of a caper involving buried World War II treasure in the Philippines. (Dir: Richard Benedict)

Imperfect Angel (German, 1964)*½ Peter Van Eyck, Corny Collins. Spoiled teenager with a crush on a handsome professor accuses him of assaulting her. Predictable English-dubbed drama, it's all been done before.

Imperfect Lady, The (1947)**½ Ray Milland, Teresa Wright. In order to aid a gentleman who shielded her, a woman must admit an indiscretion and risk exposing her husband to shame and ruin. If that interests you, maybe you'll like this film. (Dir: Lewis Allen, 97 mins.)

Impersonator, The (British, 1963)** John Crawford, Jane Griffiths. American soldier in London is a suspected molester of women and murderer, but his innocence is proven. Fairly interesting whodunit with a rather unusual plot twist. (Dir: Alfred Shaughnessy, 64 mins.)

Importance of Being Earnest, The (British, 1952)*** Michael Redgrave, Joan Greenwood. Bachelor leads a double life, but love finally catches up with him. Oscar Wilde's Victorian comedy remains a photographed stage play, but is well acted by a stellar cast. (Dir: Anthony Asquith, 95 mins.)

Impossible Years, The (1968)*½ David Niven, Lola Albright. Stage hit about a psychiatrist who has his problems with his offspring turned into a leering, unattractive vehicle for David Niven and a cast deserving of better things. With Chad Everett, Ozzie Nelson, Christina Ferrare. (Dir: Michael Gordon, 91 mins.)

Impostor, The (1944)**½ Jean Gabin, Ellen Drew. Criminal escapes during an air raid, assumes a new identity and becomes a soldier during World War II. Slow and talky drama, nevertheless has a certain interest. Well acted. Alternate title: **Strange Confession.** (Dir: Julien Duvivier, 95 mins.)

Impostor, The (1975)* Paul Hecht, Edward Asner, Meredith Baxter.

Hecht stars in another version of the old impersonation story, surfacing as an investigator for a development company who assumes many disguises. Don't bother to investigate. Made-for-TV. (Dir: Edward M. Abrams)

In a Lonely Place (1950)***½ Humphrey Bogart, Gloria Grahame, Frank Lovejoy. Gripping story of a Hollywood writer who is under suspicion of murder and his strange romance with his female alibi. Good script with Hollywood background raises the film above the average murder yarn. Bogart great as always. (Dir: Nicholas Ray, 91 mins.)

In Celebration (Great Britain-Canada, 1974)**** Alan Bates, James Bolam, Brian Cox, Bill Owen. The marvelous combination of director Lindsay Anderson and writer David Storey that produced the memorable "This Sporting Life" is reunited in this powerful adaptation of Storey's play about a coalminer's family in a drab town in northern England. Three grown sons return to the village to celebrate their parents' fortieth wedding anniversary. The sons, whose jobs are distasteful to them, mock their father about the "significance" of his mining career. Storey has skillfully delineated his major characters, and there's not a false acting note anywhere. Bates is superb in the leading role of Andrew, a failed painter. (Dir: Lindsay Anderson, 131 mins.)

In Cold Blood (1967)**** Robert Blake, Scott Wilson, John Forsythe. Writer - producer - director Richard Brooks' skillful adaptation of Truman Capote's searing novel about two young ex-cons who slaughtered a Kansas farmer and his family in cold blood. Gripping scenes, played in stark documentary style, build up to the actual multiple murders. This is obviously not for the squeamish or the children, but if you can take it, you'll be rewarded with an unforgettable reenactment of a real-life incident, horrifying as it was. (134 mins.)

In Enemy Country (1968)**½ Tony Franciosa, Anjanette Comer, Paul Hubschmidt. Old-fashioned espionage yarn set during WW II. It's the kind of film in which the heroic action never lets up so you're not too bothered by the holes in the script. Tony Franciosa is properly

348

stoic as a French agent who leads a mission into Nazi Germany and manages to carry it off. The finale in a munitions factory generates excitement and the supporting cast, particularly Paul Hubschmidt as Miss Gomer's Nazi officer husband, is good. (Dir: Harry Keller, 107 mins.)

In Harm's Way (1965)**½ John Wayne, Kirk Douglas, Patrick Neal, Brandon de Wilde. Despite an impressive all-star cast and a fairly interesting WW II setting, this film fails to register a strong impact. There are too many sub-plots and the Japanese attack of Pearl Harbor merely serves as a backdrop to the love stories of the principals. Of the large cast, Burgess Meredith and Patrick O'Neal come across best. (Dir: Otto Preminger, 165 mins.)

In Like Flint (1967)*** James Coburn, Lee J. Cobb, Jean Hale. Fun and games, spy-spoof style! This sequel to "Our Man Flint" chronicles the further outrageous adventures of the "coolest" super-spy of them all, Derek Flint, stylishly played by James Coburn. The plot, merely an excuse for displays at Coburn's gymnastic and romantic skills, centers on a diabolical scheme by a group of women to take control of the world. (Dir: Gordon Douglas, 114 mins.)

In Love and War (1958)**½ Robert Wagner, Bradford Dillman, Jeffrey Hunter, Hope Lange, Sheree North, Dana Wynter, France Nuyen. Episodic but entertaining drama about three young marines' adventures "in love and war." The most interesting character is Brad Dillman as a bright, well read, young man who questions life and tries to find some answers. Dana Wynter, as a beautiful mixed-up socialite in love with Dillman has a couple of good scenes. (Dir: Philip Dunne, 111 mins.)

In Name Only (1939)*** Carole Lombard, Cary Grant, Kay Francis. Heartless woman marries for social prestige and keeps her husband from being with the girl he really loves. Interesting, well acted drama. (Dir: John Cromwell, 94 mins.)

In Name Only (1969)* Michael Callan, Ann Prentiss, Eve Arden. Absurd made-for-TV feature. The warmed over premise has Callan and Prentiss as marriage consultants discovering three couples whose marriages they arranged are not legally hitched. (Dir: E. W. Swackhamer, 75 mins.)

In Old California (1942)** John Wayne, Binnie Barnes, Albert Dekker. Young pharmacist sets up shop in Sacramento, bucks the outlaw boss of the town. In modern California they can make some dull oaters. (Dir: William McGann, 88 mins.)

In Old Chicago (1938)***½ Tyrone Power, Alice Faye, Don Ameche. Story of the O'Leary family whose cow is credited with starting the great Chicago fire. Fictional story is interesting and builds neatly into the fire spectacle. Good drama of an era. (Dir: Henry King, 115 mins.)

In Old Vienna (Austrian, 1956)* Heina Roettinger, Robert Killich. Stories of great composers Schubert, Strauss and Beethoven in Vienna. Lots of music, badly strung-together otherwise. English-dubbed.

In Search of America (1971)**½ Carl Betz, Vera Miles, Jeff Bridges. Don't let the grandiose title of this offbeat pilot film for a proposed series put you off . . . it's an entertaining tale with a charming family that takes to the road en masse to experience the land and its variety of people. Jeff Bridges (Lloyd Bridges' younger son) is very good in the leading role of the catalyst of the venture. He convinces his father (Carl Betz), mother (Vera Miles), and grandmother (Ruth McDevitt) to accompany him on a trek around the country in a reconverted vintage passenger bus. The production is first-rate, but the tale goes a bit stale with the introduction of too many fringe characters in a rock festival setting. In any case, it's worth watching. (Dir: Paul Bogart, 72 mins.)

In Search of Gregory (1970)** Julie Christie, Michael Sarrazin. A forgettable adventure which largely wastes the lovely Miss Christie. Confused story about a young girl (Christie) living in Rome, who goes to Geneva to find romance at her father's wedding. Julie's disturbed younger brother isn't much help in her quest. (Dir: Peter Wood, 90 mins.)

In Search of Noah's Ark (1976)* This film should be subtitled "Amateur Night in Mount Ararat." The biblical legend of Noah's Ark and the great flood is given a boring Sunday

School rendering here with lots of scientific gibberish thrown in. Brad Crandall narrates the film, which looks suspiciously like a syndicated TV documentary that somehow made it to theaters. The reenactment of Noah and his family is hokum on a grade-school level. The one-star rating is for the animated monkey who makes it onto the ark. Boring! (Dir: James L. Conway, 95 mins.)

In Tandem (1974)** Claude Akins, Frank Converse. Truckers side with an orange rancher, pressured to sell his land to an amusement-park group. It may be predictable fare, but Akins and Converse carry it off with their attractive, energetic performances. Pilot for the subsequent series. Made-for-TV. (Dir: Bernard Kowalski.)

In the Cool of the Day (1963)**½ Peter Finch, Jane Fonda, Angela Lansbury. It's the performances by a trio of stars that saves this film from being just another soap opera geared for the ladies. Jane Fonda, Peter Finch and Angela Lansbury form a strange triangle amid the landscape of Greece in this tale about a young, bored wife (Miss Fonda) who falls hopelessly in love with the very married Mr. Finch. Miss Lansbury is Finch's emotionally and physically scarred wife. It's all very old fashioned movie drama, but the acting at least keeps you interested. (Dir: Robert Stevens, 89 mins.)

In the Doghouse (British, 1964)** Leslie Phillips, James Booth, Peggy Cummins. Forced farce about two veterinarians fresh out of college who set up quarters in the same area. Some laughs but thin going.

In the French Style (1963)*** Jean Seberg, Stanley Baker. Frequently fascinating study of the post-World War II female expatriate, embodied in a young art student who comes to Paris, remains to become involved in a series of passionate, usually brief, ultimately meaningless love affairs. Incisive Irwin Shaw script, Robert Parrish direction; very good performance by Seberg. Flavorsome Parisian location scenes. (105 mins.)

In the Glitter Palace (1977)**½ Chad Everett, David Wayne, Barbara Hershey. Here's a murder mystery with lesbian overtones that turns out to be better than expected. "Medical Center" 's Chad Everett is more than

competent as a lawyer digging into a seamy case involving lesbians. The women's side is told with taste and understanding. Robert Butler deserves a plug for his direction, and the supporting cast, from Barbara Hershey to David Wayne, is effective. Made-for-TV. (Dir: Robert Butler, 106 mins.)

In the Good Old Summertime (1949) *** Judy Garland, Van Johnson. A must for Judy Garland fans. Warm hearted comedy-romance about two clerks in a music shop who have a mutual secret, without knowing it. Judy sings "I Don't Care" and other delightful tunes. Based on James Stewart-Margaret Sullavan film "The Shop Around the Corner." (Dir: Robert Z. Leonard, 102 mins.)

In the Heat of the Night (1967)**** Sidney Poitier, Rod Steiger, Lee Grant, Warren Oates. Exciting, superbly acted and directed film about prejudice, manners and morals in a small Mississippi town. Poitier, portraying a Philadelphia detective who becomes accidentally involved in trying to solve a murder case, teams with Steiger to create one of the most fascinating duels of wits the screen has offered in a long time. Steiger won a richly deserved Academy Award, as did Stirling Silliphant's adaptation of the novel by John Ball. Director Norman Jewison does an outstanding job in creating the subsurface tension of life in a "sleepy" Southern town, and the supporting performances are uniformly fine. A first-rate film in all respects. The location scenes of Mississippi, incidentally, were filmed in Southern Illinois. (110 mins.)

In the Year of the Pig (1969)**** A riveting, informative, and ultimately moving documentary about American involvement in the Vietnam War. Produced and directed by Emile de Antonio, who was responsible for the remarkable '64 documentary "Point of Order." "Pig" is a shattering indictment of American policy in Vietnam and Southeast Asia. Shows through a series of brilliantly edited sequences of stock footage our lying politicians, and the way in which we devastated the land and the people all the while talking about "peace." Probably the finest film yet made about the Vietnam War, and a reminder that the timid American movie industry never honestly dealt with this momentous event in American society. (101 mins.)

In This Our Life (1942)**½ Bette Davis, George Brent, Olivia de Havilland. Another good and bad sister mix-up in this ponderous adaptation of the Pulitzer Prize novel. John Huston directed and this is one of the thorns in a great career although it's the script which causes the trouble. (97 mins.)

In Which We Serve (British, 1942) **** Noel Coward, John Mills. Drama of the men of a British destroyer during World War II, from the captain to the crew. Coward wrote, co-directed, composed the music, and plays the leading role, and does a great job in all departments. Stirring, poignant, a great film. (Dirs: Noel Coward, David Lean, 115 mins.)

Inadmissible Evidence (British, 1968) **** Nicol Williamson, Eleanor Fazan, Jill Bennett, Gillian Hills. John Osborne's searing stage play about a middle-aged English barrister whose emotional disintegration is unsparingly depicted. If the title role of Bill Maitland was poorly or even just competently acted, this could be an exasperating and embarrassing experience. In the hands of British film and stage star Nicol Williamson, it is one of the most overwhelming and moving experiences that films have offered in many years. Williamson is an actor of staggering energy, technical virtuosity, and sheer theatrical magnetism. This film must be seen by anyone who appreciates great acting, and his enormous talents keep the viewer absorbed, even though you may seldom identify with or care about the manic solicitor Williamson portrays. (Dir: Anthony Page, 96 mins.)

Incendiary Blonde (1945)*** Betty Hutton, Arturo de Cordova. Entertaining musical framed in a fictitious screen biography of famous speakeasy hostess, Texas Guinan. Good music from the prohibition era well done by Miss Hutton. (Dir: George Marshall, 113 mins.)

Incident, The (1967)**½ Tony Musante, Martin Sheen, Beau Bridges, Jack Gilford, Thelma Ritter, Ed McMahon, Ruby Dee, Brock Peters. Terror on the New York subway, as two hoodlums molest an assorted group of passengers. May seem overdone to non-New Yorkers, and it is to a considerable extent, but the basic premise—the passivity of people in times of danger—is disturbingly true. If this all sounds familiar to some of you it's because you may have seen the original 1963 TV production of this drama, which was then entitled "Ride With Terror." (Dir: Larry Peerce, 107 mins.)

Incident at Midnight (British, 1961) ** Anton Diffring, William Sylvester. A former Nazi is spotted in a druggist's shop by an undercover member of the narcotics squad. Okay Edgar Wallace mystery. (Dir: Norman Harrison, 58 mins.)

Incident at Phantom Hill (1966)** Robert Fuller, Jocelyn Lane, Dan Duryea. Assorted group engages in a perilous trek to reclaim gold which had been stolen and hidden years before. Undistinguished western. (Dir: Earl Bellamy, 88 mins.)

Incident in Saigon (French, 1960)*½ Odile Versois, Pierre Massima. Young girl aids an architect wrongly suspected of being a dope smuggler. Ragged melodrama dubbed in English.

Incident in San Francisco (1971)** Christopher Connelly, Richard Kiley. Here's another slick pilot film for a proposed big city newspaper TV series, and as these stories go, it's fair. Christopher Connelly has the leading role of the brash young reporter on the San Francisco Times who gets deeply involved in the plight of a man (Richard Kiley) who accidentally causes the death of a young punk while coming to the aid of an old man. Familiar yarn about the honest samaritan who has his good deed turn into a nightmare. Cast, especially Kiley as the victim, is more than competent. (Dir: Don Medford, 98 mins.)

Incident on a Dark Street (1973)** James Olson, Robert Pine. Fair entry on U.S. attorneys who try court cases on dope peddling, and mobsters in the building contracting business. Good legal guys (Olson, David Canary, Pine) are overshadowed by the colorful baddies (Richard Castellano, Gilbert Roland, William Shatner), with Castellano's small-time Italian hood stealing the show. Made-for-TV. (Dir: Buzz Kulik, 73 mins.)

Incredible Mr. Limpet, The (1964)**

Don Knotts, Carole Cook, Jack Weston. Mr. Knotts as Mr. Limpet, the man who wished he was a fish—and got his wish, becoming the Navy's secret weapon during World War II. Fantasy may provide some moments of amusement, but the viewer has to be either a Knotts fan or pretty fish-happy. (Dir: Arthur Lubin, 102 mins.)

Incredible Petrified World, The (1958)*½ John Carradine, Robert Clarke. Scientists attempt to explore the ocean depths and find themselves trapped beneath the sea. Dull sci-fi thriller will petrify audiences. (Dir: Jerry Warren, 78 mins.)

Incredible Shrinking Man, The (1957) *** Grant Williams, Randy Stuart. Man is exposed to a mysterious fog, begins to grow smaller and smaller. In the better class of sci-fi thrillers —expert trick photography brings much suspense to scenes of a tiny man pitted against nature. Script also makes it seem believable. (Dir: Jack Arnold, 81 mins.)

Incredibly Strange Creatures Who Stopped Living And Became Mixed-Up Zombies, The (1962)* Cash Flagg, Carolyn Brandt. Incredible is right—repulsive horror film about monsters on the loose murdering carnival dancing girls.

Indestructible Man, The (1956)* Lon Chaney, Marian Carr. Executed killer is brought back to life, lights up like a Christmas tree. Whole film short circuits. (Dir: Jack Pollexfen, 70 mins.)

Indian Fighter (1955)**½ Kirk Douglas. Douglas is the whole show in this western drama about Sioux uprisings in the Oregon Territory circa 1870. Army Scout Douglas is sent on a peace mission deep into Sioux country. Plenty of action. (Dir: Andre de Toth, 88 mins.)

Indian Paint (1963)** Johnny Crawford, Jay Silverheels. Oft-told story of an Indian boy's love for a wild colt, but done pleasantly enough.

Indian Scarf, The (German, 1963)*½ Heinz Drache, Corny Collins. Heirs gathered in an isolated castle to hear the reading of the will start dropping like flies when a strangler strikes. Old-hat Edgar Wallace mystery— high mortality rate, low interest. Dubbed in English. (Dir: Alfred Vohrer, 85 mins.)

Indict and Convict (1974)**½ George Grizzard, Eli Wallach, William Shat-

ner, Myrna Loy. A sensational case of a seamy Los Angeles double murder. When the wife of a deputy district attorney and her lover are found shot, the chief suspect, the D.A., claims to have been miles away at the time. Made-for-TV. (Dir: Boris Sagal, 100 mins.)

Indiscreet (1958)***½ Cary Grant, Ingrid Bergman. Delightfully sophisticated comedy about the on-again, off-again romance between a handsome and wealthy American diplomat and a ravishing European actress. Good lines and magnificent sets. Grant and Bergman are perfect as the urbane pair of lovers. Produced and directed by Stanley Donen on location in London. (100 mins.)

Indiscretion of an American Wife (1954)** Jennifer Jones, Montgomery Clift. American woman tries to part from her Italian lover in Rome's Terminal Station. Skimpy, unconvincing drama, not worthy of the talent involved. (Dir: Vittorio De Sica, 63 mins.)

Inferno (1953)*** Robert Ryan, Rhonda Fleming, William Lundigan. Suspenseful drama about a pair of ruthless lovers who plot the abandonment of the woman's husband in the Mojave Desert. Robert Ryan plays the abandoned millionaire who manages to survive his plotters' deed. Keeps your interest throughout. (Dir: Roy Baker, 83 mins.)

Infiltrator, The (French, 1964)** Henry Vidal, Monique Van Vooren, Erich Von Stroheim. Slim story of a police agent who penetrates a drug ring and is threatened by the release from prison of a former underworld czar (played by Stroheim in an appearance that briefly enlivens the proceedings). (110 mins.)

Informer, The (1935)**** Victor McLaglen, Preston Foster. A brilliant, deeply moving film directed superbly by John Ford, that has, in the four decades since the film was made, become a true cinema classic. Set in Ireland during the time of the Irish rebellion, it concerns a slow-witted traitor who turns in a compatriot and suffers the pangs of conscience. Victor McLaglen will be long remembered for this portrayal, and the film also benefits from a fine musical score. (Dir: John Ford, 100 mins.)

Informers, The (British, 1964)**½ Nigel Patrick, Catherine Woodville,

Margaret Whiting. Police Inspector's informer is killed by a gang of robbers, so he carries on to nab the ring despite orders to leave it alone. Capable crime melodrama breaks no new ground but is well done. (Dir: Ken Annakin, 105 mins.)

Inga (Swedish, 1968)* Sexploitation about a virginal miss (Marie Liljedahl) victimized by her grasping aunt (Monica Strommerstedt). For the male overcoat-across-the-lap crowd.

Inherit the Wind (1960)**** Spencer Tracy, Fredric March, Gene Kelly. The powerful B'dway play dealing with the famous trial in the twenties in which a school teacher was arrested for teaching Darwin's theory of evolution makes exciting screen entertainment. Tracy and March are excellent as defender and prosecutor respectively. Kelly is surprisingly good as the newspaper man who is instrumental in focusing national attention on the court proceedings. (Dir: Stanley Kramer, 127 mins.)

Inheritance, The (British, 1948)*** Jean Simmons, Derrick DeMarney. Girl attempts to foil a wicked uncle's effort to have her put out of the way so he can claim her inheritance. Theatrical Victorian thriller manages to generate considerable suspense. (Dir: Charles Frank, 90 mins.)

Inn of the Sixth Happiness, The (1958)***½ Ingrid Bergman, Curt Jurgens, Robert Donat. Excellently acted drama of a missionary woman in China and her attempts to lead some children to safety on a perilous trek through enemy territory. Runs to excessive length, but has top work by Bergman and Robert Donat as a mandarin, a compelling finale. (Dir: Mark Robson, 158 mins.)

Inn on Dartmoor, The (German, 1964)*½ Heinz Drache, Paul Klinger. Young artist and a policeman uncover a criminal scheme behind the escape of several convicts from prison. So-so Edgar Wallace mystery dubbed in English.

Innocent and the Damned—See: **Girls' Town** (1959, Mamie Van Doren)

Innocent Bystanders (1973)** Stanley Baker, Geraldine Chaplin, Donald Pleasence, Dana Andrews. Muddled espionage film which looks and sounds a great deal like Richard Burton's infinitely superior film, "The Spy Who Came in From the Cold." Stanley Baker is the aging agent who is sent on his last assignment to bring back a Russian scientist named Kaplan from his exile in Turkey. (Dir: Peter Collinson, 111 mins.)

Innocent Sinners (Great Britain, 1958)**½ June Archer, Christopher Hey, Brian Hammond, Flora Robson, David Kossoff. Sentimental but often touching screening of Rumer Godden's novel, "An Episode of Sparrows," about a neglected, tough little girl and two street youths, who try to make a garden out of a bombed-out London lot. Fairy-tale motifs in a barren reality are not as fully exploited as in the novel. Ms. Godden co-scripted. (Dir: Philip Leacock, 95 mins.)

Innocents, The (1961)**** Deborah Kerr, Martin Stephens, Pamela Franklin. Henry James' classic tale dealing with the supernatural, "The Turn of the Screw," becomes a brilliant suspense film. Deborah Kerr is magnificent as the governess who becomes enmeshed in the eerie household in which the two young children appear to be possessed by ghosts. The youngsters, Pamela Franklin and Martin Stephens, complement Miss Kerr's performance and the entire film is flawless in building to the shattering climax. By all means, don't miss this one, directed by Jack Clayton. (100 mins.)

Innocents in Paris (British, 1953)**½ Alastair Sim, Margaret Rutherford. Londoners take off to see Paris for the first time. Lengthy but amusing film. (Dir: Gordon Parry, 93 mins.)

Inside a Girls' Dormitory (French, 1953)** Jean Marais, Francoise Arnoul. A young, handsome detective arrives at a French girls' boarding school to solve a murder. A choice assignment but a dull movie.

Inside Daisy Clover (1965)**½ Natalie Wood, Christopher Plummer, Robert Redford. Although the story about a young film star in the Hollywood of the '30s is mostly glossy soap opera, some good performances make it palatable. Christopher Plummer comes off best as a tyrannical studio head, and Robert Redford is effective in the complex role of a deeply troubled motion-picture matinee idol. Natalie Wood is only half as successful as her co-stars in the title role, the waif-turned-star-turned-neurotic. (Dir: Robert Mulligan, 128 mins.)

Inside Detroit (1956)** Dennis O'Keefe, Pat O'Brien. The war for control by the rackets of the unions in the automobile industry comes into focus in this overdone drama. O'Keefe and O'Brien (sounds like a vaudeville team) are competent in their roles as foes. (Dir: Fred F. Sears, 82 mins.)

Inside North Vietnam (1967)*** Documentary report photographed in North Vietnam by film-maker Felix Greene, which is of interest, among other reasons, because American audiences have seen so little footage taken in North Vietnam itself. Greene is admittedly hostile to the American presence in Vietnam, and his documentary must be viewed in that light, but there are numerous scenes of village life, and life in the capital of Hanoi, which will interest any thoughtful viewer.

Inside Out (Great Britain-West Germany, 1975)*½ Telly Savalas, Robert Culp, James Mason. Telly's first starring part in a feature film. He forgot to pick a decent script. Not very exciting, far-fetched caper film about Telly and his pals who are after some really big stakes—buried Nazi loot—and want to break into a prison to drug a prisoner with truth serum and find out where the loot is stashed. About as interesting as the hair on Telly's head. (Dir: Peter Duffell, 97 mins.)

Inside Story, The (1948)** William Lundigan, Marsha Hunt. During a bank holiday in the depression days of 1933, a thousand dollars is suddenly in circulation, with startling consequences. Mild little comedy-drama. Dir: Allan Dwan, 87 mins.)

Inside Straight (1951)** David Brian, Arlene Dahl, Mercedes McCambridge. Ruthless man out to make money lets nothing stand in his way. Slow-paced costume melodrama, stereotyped role for Brian as the big tycoon. (Dir: Gerald Mayer, 89 mins.)

Inside the Mafia (1959)** Cameron Mitchell, Elaine Edwards, Robert Strauss. Rival hoods set up a plot to bump off a ganglord arriving for a big power meeting. Obvious crime melodrama relies upon the action to get it over. (Dir: Edward L. Cahn, 72 mins.)

Inspector Calls, An (British, 1954)

*** Alastair Sim, Eileen Moore. A mysterious policeman investigates the family of a girl who has died of poisoning. From J. B. Priestley's mystical drama, this is rather vague, but occasionally interesting. (Dir: Guy Hamilton, 80 mins.)

Inspector Clouseau (British, 1968)* Alan Arkin, Frank Finlay, Beryl Reid. Our British allies shouldn't have to bear the blame for this incredibly witless comedy. The director and the financing both hail from America. The character of Inspector Clouseau, as created by Peter Sellers in "The Pink Panther" and later in "A Shot in the Dark," was a hilarious bungler, and the films themselves were great fun. I won't bother you with the plot here. Just take our word for it that even the talented Alan Arkin fails badly in this lame entry. (Dir: Bud Yorkin, 94 mins.)

Inspector General (1949)**** Danny Kaye, Walter Slezak. Delightful period farce about an illiterate who's mistaken for a friend of Napoleon's. It's a Danny Kaye romp and one of those rare times when the story comes close to matching his artistry. (Dir: Henry Koster, 102 mins.)

Inspector Maigret (French, 1958)**½ Jean Gabin, Annie Girardot. Wily policeman investigates a brutal murder case. They do such things better over here, despite Gabin's fine acting job. (Dir: Jean Delannoy, 110 mins.)

Interlude (1957)**½ June Allyson, Rossano Brazzi. Hankies out, ladies ... here's a plot about an American librarian in Germany who falls for a married conductor, etc. Soap opera, as such, competent. (Dir: Douglas Sirk, 90 mins.)

Interlude (British, 1968)** Oskar Werner, Barbara Ferris, Virginia Maskell, Donald Sutherland. The slick tale of an impossible love between a symphony conductor (Oskar Werner) and a newspaperwoman (Barbara Ferris). All gush and nonsense, but shrewdly catered toward the impressionable ladies in the audience. Some good classical music. (Dir: Kevin Billington, 113 mins.)

Intermezzo (1939)*** Leslie Howard, Ingrid Bergman. Great violinist has his happy marriage imperiled when he falls in love with his daughter's piano teacher. Emotional love story is well-acted, will appeal to the ladies. (Bergman's first American film.) (Dir: Gregory Ratoff, 80 mins.)

International House (1933)*** W. C. Fields, Burns & Allen, Stuart Erwin. Foolish but occasionally hilarious comedy about an invention. A fine assortment of characters in this film and, in spite of its age, comedy lovers should enjoy it. (Dir: A. Edward Sutherland.)

International Squadron (1941)**½ Ronald Reagan. Mr. Reagan ends up in the RAF changing from an irresponsible bum to a great hero. Trouble is the script makes the change unbelievable. (Dir: Lothar Mendes, 87 mins.)

Interns, The (1962)** Michael Callan, Cliff Robertson, Nick Adams, James MacArthur, Stefanie Powers. A workout for several of the younger performers is the only discernible reason for this melange of medical clichés about the problems faced by assorted young interns during their year of apprenticeship. For all the care lavished upon it, it still looks like a daytime TV serial. (Dir: David Swift, 129 mins.)

Interpol Code 8 (Japanese, 1965)* Undercover agent is sent to Saigon and battles a spy ring there. Dubbed-English spy thriller Japanese style, no better than any of the others.

Interrupted Journey (British, 1950) **½ Richard Todd, Valerie Hobson. After a spat with his wife, a man takes a train where he is suddenly involved in the murder of a woman. Fair thriller is marred by weak ending. (Dir: Daniel Birt, 80 mins.)

Interrupted Melody (1955)*** Eleanor Parker, Glenn Ford. Story of Australian soprano Marjorie Lawrence, her operatic successes, her bout with polio and return. Biographical details interesting, singing sequences well done by Miss Lawrence, while Miss Parker goes through the vocalizing motions. Well done. (Dir: Curtis Bernhardt, 106 mins.)

Interval (U.S.-Mexico, 1973)½ Merle Oberon, Robert Wolders. The only prize this excruciating drama will receive is for the International Film Vanity Competition. "Producer" Oberon has cast herself as a woman "well over 40" who falls in love with a young American painter. Her young, real-life boy friend Robert Wolders presumably has some talent, but it certainly isn't acting in front

of movie cameras. Clumsily written by Gavin Lambert, and directed with a heavy hand indeed by Daniel Mann. The Mayan ruins of Mexico are far more interesting than anything moving and talking on the screen. (Dir: Daniel Mann, 84 mins.)

Intimacy (1966)* Jack Ging, Joan Blackman, Barry Sullivan. Businessman spies on politician only to discover that his own wife is having an affair with him. Screenplay by Eva Wolas. (Dir: Victor Stoloff, 87 mins.)

Intimate Relations—See: **Disobedient**

Intruder, The (British, 1953)*** Jack Hawkins, Michael Medwin, George Cole. An army colonel discovers one of his former regiment men rifling his house, decides to contact the old wartime crew to find out what made the lad turn thief. Interesting drama, well done. (Dir: Guy Hamilton, 84 mins.)

Intruder in the Dust (1949)**** David Brian, Claude Jarman Jr., Juano Hernandez. Based on William Faulkner's novel—a lawyer and a lad come to the aid of a Negro when he's accused of murder. Fine dramatic film for the more discriminating; successful both as a straight whodunit, and as more immediate topical fare. Performances and direction are first rate and Hernandez is marvelous. (Dir: Clarence Brown, 87 mins.)

Intruders, The (1970)**½ Don Murray, Anne Francis, John Saxon. Moderately absorbing made-for-TV western film with a couple of good performances to recommend it— Don Murray as an ex-gunslinger turned marshal and John Saxon as a half-breed Indian trying to cope with prejudice. The action is centered around a small town's preparation for the reported arrival of the notorious Younger Brothers and Jesse James. (Dir: William Graham, 95 mins.)

Invaders, The—See: **49th Parallel, The**

Invasion (British, 1965)** Edward Judd, Yoko Tani, Valerie Gearon. Creatures from another planet crash on earth, perpetrate murders and havoc until outwitted by a doctor. Farfetched but occasionally tense sci-fi thriller. Good cast helps. (Dir: Alan Bridges, 82 mins.)

Invasion Earth 2150 A.D. (Great Britain, 1966)**½ Peter Cushing, Bernard Cribbins, Andrew Keir.

Fast-paced science fiction pits a small band of freedom fighters against maniacal, super-intelligent robots from outer space, who have been turning humans into programmed slaves. Based on the BBC-TV serial, "Dr. Who," sequel to "Dr. Who and the Daleks." (Dir: Gordon Flemyng, 84 mins.)

Invasion of Johnson County, The (1976) **½ Bill Bixby, Bo Hopkins, John Hillerman, Billy Green Bush. Bixby and Hopkins are well cast in this offbeat Western adventure yarn. Bixby is a dapper Bostonian Brahmin who finds himself in the wild and wooly West without any funds. He teams up with cowpoke Hopkins, who confesses he has been hired by a private army of men who plan to take the law into their own hands. Made-for-TV. (Dir: Jerry Jameson, 98 mins.)

Invasion of the Animal People (1962) * Barbara Wilson, John Carradine. Awful horror film. Another monster from space landing on earth. They should know better by now.

Invasion of the Body Snatchers (1956)***½ Dana Wynter, Kevin McCarthy. Space invaders overcome townspeople, inhabit their bodies. One of the better thrillers; lively, imaginative, suspenseful. (Dir: Don Siegel, 80 mins.)

Invasion of the Body Stealers—See: **Thin Air**

Invasion of the Neptune Men (1963)* Corny science fiction meller—Japanese made.

Invasion of the Saucer Men (1957)** Steve Terrell, Gloria Castillo. Cool kids spot some invaders from outer space. Script kids the horror films, only it isn't as funny as the ones on the level. (Dir: Edward L. Cahn, 69 mins.)

Invasion of the Star Creatures (1963) *½ Bob Ball, Dolores Reed. Comedy mixed with mild sci-fi effects. A couple of soldiers discover plant-like creatures who are in control of a group of sexy Amazons. The plot goes haywire from here on but the kids will probably get a laugh or two out of it.

Invasion of the Vampires, The (Mexican, 1962)* Tito Junco, Rena-Martha Bauman. A doctor suspects a vampire behind a series of mysterious deaths. Laughable horror thriller badly dubbed in English.

Invasion U.S.A. (1953)*½ Dan O'Her-

lihy, Peggy Castle, Gerald Mohr. Ridiculous science-fiction melodrama about the end of the world via atomic destruction as told by a famous forecaster and hypnotist. If you're confused now, wait until you see the film. (Dir: Alfred E. Green, 74 mins.)

Investigation of a Citizen Above Suspicion (Italian, 1970)***½ Florinda Balkan, Gianni Santuccio. Complex satirical parable about politics and Fascist ideology. Smug, mentally unbalanced police chief plants evidence against himself to test his underlings, his own status, and his moral and social superiority. Absorbing throughout and stylishly directed by Elio Petri, who happens to be a Communist. (Dir: Elio Petri, 112 mins.)

Investigation of Murder, An—See: **Laughing Policeman, The**

Invincible Brothers Maciste, The (Italian, 1964)* Richard Lloyd, Claudia Lange. Wicked queen uses her leopard-men to kidnap fiancée of the Prince, but two heroic avengers thwart her evil plans. Silly English-dubbed spectacle.

Invincible Gladiator, The (Italian, 1962)** Richard Harrison, Isabel Corey. Roman warrior is put to the test as he tries to save the oppressed of the city. Lack of finesse partially atoned for by some fast action scenes in this passable spectacle dubbed in English. (Dir: Anthony Momplet, 96 mins.)

Invincible Six (U.S.-Iran, 1968)*½ Stuart Whitman, Elke Sommer, Curt Jurgens, James Mitchum. Leaky, confused crime thriller pits international criminals against local bandits in Iran. Authentic Persian locales add some exoticism, but otherwise humdrum. (Dir: Jean Negulesco, 96 mins.)

Invisible Avenger (1958)**½ Richard Derr, Mark Daniels. Lamont Cranston (the Shadow) travels to New Orleans to find mystery and adventure. A plot to kill the President of Santa Cruz is foiled, and Lamont learns to be invisible from an Indian sage. OK make-believe. (Dirs: James Wong Howe and John Sledge, 60 mins.)

Invisible Boy, The (1957)**½ Richard Eyer, Philip Abbott. A science-fiction yarn about a young boy and his robot. The kids might enjoy this adventure which incorporates smuggled cargoes of bombs, rocket ships, spies, scientists and hokum. (Dir: Herman Hoffman, 85 mins.)

Invisible Creature (British, 1960)** Sandra Dorne, Tony Wright. Moderate supernatural story about an unfaithful husband with murder on his mind and his wife, who seems to have a protective ghost on her side. (Dir: Montgomery Tully, 70 mins.)

Invisible Dr. Mabuse, The (German, 1960)*½ Lex Barker, Alan Dijon. FBI agent battles a mad doctor out to conquer the world. Farfetched crime thriller in what was originally an intriguing series. English-dubbed. (Dir: Harald Reinl, 89 mins.)

Invisible Man, The (1933)***½ Claude Rains, Henry Travers. Despite its age, this horror classic still captures the imagination. Raines turns in a first-rate performance as the hero of H. G. Wells' tale, a demented scientist who has successfully made himself transparent and now wants to rule the world. Slow-moving but worth-while. (Dir: James Whale, 80 mins.)

Invisible Man, The (1975)**½ David McCallum, Melinda Fee, Jackie Cooper. A successful pilot film for the subsequent NBC series. David McCallum assumes the title role (played by Claude Rains in the 1933 classic) of the invisible researcher (clad in a blue body-stocking), a man who discovers how to make animals invisible, then plays guinea-pig himself. Made-for-TV. (Dir: Robert Michael Lewis, 72 mins.)

Invisible Man Returns, The (1940)*** Sir Cedric Hardwicke, Vincent Price, Nan Grey. A sequel to "The Invisible Man," and almost as good in its own way as the original. Technical effects are excellent and the dialogue crisp. Concerns a man who uses invisibility to hunt for his brother's murderer. (Dir: Joe May, 81 mins.)

Invisible Ray, The (1936)** Boris Karloff, Bela Lugosi. Shudder story about a scientist whose touch is deadly. Karloff and Lugosi keep the yarn perking, but it comes off as familiar stuff for horror fans. (Dir: Lambert Hillyer, 90 mins.)

Invisible Terror, The (German, 1963)*½ Hanaes Hauser, Ellen Schwiers. Scientist invents a serum that will cause invisibility, then he disappears. Could have used some on the script of this Edgar Wallace mystery

dubbed in English, which is strictly for the indiscriminate.

Invitation (1952)*** Dorothy McGuire, Van Johnson, Ruth Roman, Louis Calhern. Dorothy McGuire gives a glowing performance as an invalid who makes a stab for happiness despite the constant presence of death. The plot often slips to "soap opera" level but Miss McGuire is worth your attention. (Dir: Gottfried Reinhardt, 84 mins.)

Invitation, The (Switzerland-France, 1973)*** Michel Robin, François Simon, Jean-Luc Bideau, Cecille Vassort. Office workers are invited for the afternoon to the home of fellow-worker Remy Placet (Robin), and are surprised to find him ensconced in almost palatial surroundings. It is a sultry summer day: the sprinklers are running constantly and the liquor poured as freely by a cooly capable butler (played by François Simon, son of the late Michel Simon). By the end of the afternoon, in this subtly crafted film, in-office façades and barriers have come dislodged. The wily, expressionless butler Simon, who concocts the brews, is demonic, and an edge of mystery develops. Acting is good, and Miss Vassort is outstanding as a red-haired, flighty, flirty innocent. Impressive work from director Claude Goretta in this, his third feature.

Invitation to a Gunfighter (1964)** Yul Brynner, Janice Rule, George Segal. Western fans should be forewarned that there's more Freud than Zane Grey in this story of renegades and revenge. The supporting cast doesn't get much of a chance to rise above their stereotyped roles. (Dir: Richard Wilson, 92 mins.)

Invitation to Happiness (1939) **½ Irene Dunne, Fred MacMurray. Well made but minor little tale of an ambitious fighter who neglects his family while rising to the top. The comedy is fairly good, but the drama is routine. (Dir: Wesley Ruggles, 100 mins.)

Invitation to Murder (British, 1962)** Robert Beatty, Lisa Daniely. American adventurer goes to the French Riviera to check on beneficiaries of a millionaire's will, finds murder. Standard whodunit.

Ipcress File, The (1965)**** Michael Caine, Nigel Green. First-rate espionage yarn which will keep you

357

fascinated from start to finish. Michael Caine's British agent Harry Palmer is a magnificent example of role and star fitting like a glove and director Sidney J. Furie's exciting camera work heightens the action at every plot twist. Based on Len Deighton's bestseller, the tense and complex spy story has Palmer investigating the kidnaping of scientists detained behind the Iron Curtain and he comes up with information that threatens his life. (108 mins.)

Irish Eyes Are Smiling (1944)**✦½** June Haver, Dick Haymes, Monty Woolley. Routine musical supposedly about the chap who wrote the title song. Some fine Irish melodies but little else. (Dir: Gregory Ratoff, 90 mins.)

Irma La Douce (1963)***½ Jack Lemmon, Shirley MacLaine. Talented producer-director-writer Billy Wilder took the hit Broadway musical, extracted the musical numbers, and came up with a delightfully raucous comedy about Paris prostitutes and their procurers. Lemmon is forced into leading a double life in order to keep his love, streetwalker MacLaine, and his energetic performance is among his best. Miss MacLaine is perfect as the sweet tart named Irma, and director Wilder has punched up the proceedings with style and a spirit of fun. (120 mins.)

Iron Curtain, The (1948)**✦½** Dana Andrews, Gene Tierney. First major anti-Communist film is based on the Igor Gouzenko incident. He's the Russian who helped round up a Canadian spy ring. Film is confused, episodic and only has a few exciting scenes. (Dir: William Wellman, 87 mins.)

Iron Major (1948)*** Pat O'Brien, Robert Ryan. Life story of Frank Cavanaugh, famous football coach and World War I hero. Well done biographical drama. (Dir: Ray Enright, 85 mins.)

Iron Man (1951)**✦½** Jeff Chandler, Evelyn Keyes, Stephen McNally. A notch or two above the run of the mill boxing yarns. Jeff Chandler is good as the peace loving coal miner turned boxing champ. The whole cast keeps up with the competent pace set by Chandler. Look for Rock Hudson and James Arness in small roles. (Dir: Joseph Pevney, 82 mins.)

Iron Mistress, The (1952)**✦½** Alan Ladd, Virginia Mayo. Action filled, colorful adventure yarn about Jim Bowie, whose primary claim to fame was a special knife he had made which came to be known as the "Bowie Knife." Ladd is as stoic as always but fits well into the hero adventurer mold. (Dir: Gordon Douglas, 110 mins.)

Iron Petticoat, The (British, 1956)*✦½ Bob Hope, Katharine Hepburn, Noelle Middleton. Hope as a pilot acting as bodyguard to frigid Russian Air Force Captain (Hepburn). Both seem understandably embarrassed to be caught in this sub-"Ninotchka" attempt at humor. A miss-ky. With James Robertson-Justice, Robert Helpmann.

Ironside (1967)**✦½** Raymond Burr, Geraldine Brooks, Wally Cox, Kim Darby, Don Galloway, Donald Mitchell. Pilot movie for the TV series stars Burr as a gruff, blunt, cantankerous sleuth confined to a wheelchair, crippled by a sniper's bullet. Don Mankiewicz's script provides pungent dialogue, incisive characterizations, and their staccato direction. Made-for-TV. (Dir: James Goldstone, 104 mins.)

Iroquois Trail (1950)**✦½** George Montgomery, Brenda Marshall. Hunter avenging his brother's death uncovers traitors on the frontier. Plenty of action in this outdoor action drama. (Dir: Phil Karlson, 85 mins.)

Irwin Allen's Production of Fire! (1977)**✦½** Ernest Borgnine, Vera Miles, Patty Duke Astin, Alex Cord, Donna Mills, Lloyd Nolan, Neville Brand, Ty Hardin. Yet another one on devastating forest fires, but this Irwin Allen edition filmed around Portland, Oregon, benefits from multiple story lines, a better than average cast, and excellent fire sequences. Stock footage has been held down to a minimum, and various characters face the threat of cremation throughout, creating some suspense. Made-for-TV. (Dir: Earl Bellamy, 144 mins.)

Is Everybody Happy (1943)**✦½** Ted Lewis, Michael Duane, Larry Parks. Based on the career of bandleader Ted Lewis, this tells of the ups and downs of a jazz band. For Lewis fans, good; for others, fairly pleasant.

Is Paris Burning? (1966)** Leslie

Caron, Yves Montand, Simone Signoret, Orson Welles, Gert Frobe. The best-selling novel about the efforts to save Paris from Hitler's torch is turned into a dull, episodic drama with a series of cameo roles played by an international roster of film names. The epic story gets lost as each vignette is highlighted to give its star or stars their moment before the camera. (And each vignette may have been scripted by a different writer, considering the half-dozen scribblers involved.) (Dir: Rene Clement, 173 mins.)

Is There Sex After Death? (1971) ***½ Buck Henry, Alan Abel, Marshall Efron, Holly Woodlawn. A raunchy, outrageous, but often wildly funny satire that mocks all the other films that take themselves seriously and try to capitalize on the recent "sexual revolution." It's directed, written, and produced by two hoaxers with a flair—Alan and Jeanne Abel. It's a series of not so serious sketches with Earle Doud as a pornographic magician. "Sex" won't show up on network TV Sunday evening following Walt Disney, but it's a funny outing for the non-prudish. (97 mins.)

Isabel (Canadian, 1968) ***½ Fine actress Genevieve Bujold and her husband, writer - producer - director Paul Almond, join talents to spin an effective weird tale of a girl who returns home to find mystery and fear. Atmospheric Canadian coastal backgrounds, and an eerie, otherworldly quality. Interesting and offbeat. With Mark Strange, Elton Hayes.

Isadora—See: Loves of Isadora

Island, The (Japanese, 1962) ***½ Powerful Japanese film about a family struggling for existence on a remote and barren island. No dialogue, story told through the camera, actions of the principals. Unusual, engrossing drama. (Dir: Kaneto Shindo, 96 mins.)

Island Affair (1964) * Dorian Grey, Daniela Rocca, Elaine Stewart. Melodramatic mishmash flows all over a villa-filled island among rich industrialists, lovers, husbands, and strangers. (85 mins.)

Island In the Sky (1953) *** John Wayne, Lloyd Nolan, James Arness. Wayne exchanges the plains for planes in this adventure film about a pilot and a dangerous rescue mis-

sion. Photography is a plus factor here. (Dir: William Wellman, 109 mins.)

Island in the Sun (1957) **½ James Mason, John Fontaine, Harry Belafonte, Dorothy Dandridge. Alec Waugh's best-seller is watered-down in this screen translation. Revolves around an assorted group of blacks and whites living in the British West Indies, and their political and personal lives. The fact that this film was made in the late fifties limits the portrayal of inter-racial romances (Harry Belafonte and Joan Fontaine—Dorothy Dandridge and John Justin) and the film loses some of its intended impact as a result. (Dir: Robert Rossen, 119 mins.)

Island of Desire (1953) ** Linda Darnell, Tab Hunter. Poorly acted film about a woman and a young Marine shipwrecked on an island during the war. A mature Englishman joins them to complete the triangle. Your desire may be to tune out. (Dir: Gordon Douglas, 103 mins.)

Island of Lost Souls (1932) *** Charles Laughton. For horror fans only is this film version of an H. G. Wells story. Laughton will chill you as the mad scientist who converts animals into human beings. Need we add—not for the kids. (Dir: Erle C. Kenton, 80 mins.)

Island of Lost Women (1959) *½ Jeff Richards, Venetia Stevenson, John Smith. Balderdash about a reporter and pilot forced down on an island inhabited by a scientist and his pretty daughters. Dreary comic strip stuff. (Dir: Frank Tuttle, 71 mins.)

Island of Love (1963) *** Robert Preston, Tony Randall, Walter Matthau. Bright comedy about a fast-talking promoter who cons a gangster into financing a movie stinker, then promotes a Greek island as a paradise spot. The fun lets down before the end, but there's some funny, crackling dialogue, a wow comedy performance from gangster Matthau. (Dir: Morton Da Costa, 101 mins.)

Island of Terror (British, 1967) *** Peter Cushing, Edward Judd, Carole Gray. Medical experts journey to an island where they discover shell-like creatures that show a penchant for devouring the bones of victims. Well-done science-fiction thriller summons up a good share of shudders for the addicts. (Dir: Terence Fisher, 90 mins.)

Island of the Blue Dolphins (1964) **½ Celia Kaye, Larry Domasin. Youngsters are left alone on an island, and the girl befriends a wild dog who becomes her protector. The kids should particularly enjoy this pleasant adventure story, with colorful scenery and an adequate amount of interest.

Island Princess, The (Italian, 1955) *½ Marcello Mastroianni, Silvana Pampanini. Spanish captain stationed in the Canary Islands falls for a beautiful princess but becomes embroiled in revolt. Childish costume adventure made before Marcello became internationally recognized. Dubbed in English. (Dir: Paolo Moffa, 98 mins.)

Island Rescue (British, 1952)**½ David Niven, Glynis Johns. A major is assigned the task of rescuing a prize cow from a British island occupied by the Nazis. Uneven adventure falls midway between comedy and melodrama, never seems to make up its mind which way to turn. (Dir: Ralph Thomas, 87 mins.)

Isle of the Dead (1945)*** Boris Karloff, Ellen Drew. Greek general on a small island is enmeshed with vampires and witchcraft. Eerie thriller has some good effects. (Dir: Mark Robson, 72 mins.)

Isn't It Shocking (1973)**½ Alan Alda, Edmond O'Brien, Will Geer, Lloyd Nolan, Ruth Gordon. Alda and a cast of veteran character actors manage to convey the right mood in this offbeat made-for-TV murder mystery. In the rural New England town of Mount Angel, the elderly are dying but not from old age, and thereby hangs the tale. Louise Lasser and Pat Quinn costar as the ladies in Sheriff Alda's life. (Dir: John Badham, 90 mins.)

Israel Why (French, 1973)***½ Provocative, lengthy (three hours) documentary about the dream of Israel. Director Claude Lanzmann has clearly been inspired by the techniques and film form of Marcel Ophuls' "The Sorrow and the Pity." This work, though not as brilliantly handled as Ophuls' landmark documentary, is an enlightening, probing study of the dynamics of contemporary Israel. Interviews some of the early settlers, along with the young sabras. Edited in terms of various themes, with the filmmaker's point of view sometimes obtrusive. On balance it is a stimulating, if uneven, feature that will hold your interest if you want to learn more about this historic embattled land. (180 mins.)

Istanbul (1957)** Errol Flynn, Cornell Borchers. Adventurer returns to recover a fortune in diamonds, finds his old flame, presumed dead, alive and an amnesia victim. Shopworn melodrama for Flynn fans, who may take to it—but the accent is on the last syllable of the title. (Dir: Joseph Pevney, 84 mins.)

Istanbul Express (1968)**½ Gene Barry, Senta Berger, John Saxon. An entertaining film on two totally different levels. Viewers who've enjoyed previous made-for-television adventure movies will find this tale of intrigue exciting. It follows art dealer Gene Barry aboard a train, journeying to Turkey to buy certain valuable papers for the U.S. government at an international auction. Old-time movie buffs however, weaned on the trains of Alfred Hitchcock and Carol Reed, may find this all rather droll and a bit of cinematic high camp. (Dir: Richard Irving, 94 mins.)

It (Great Britain, 1967)* Roddy McDowall, Jill Haworth, Ernest Clark. Silly horror thriller. Roddy McDowall plays a mad assistant museum curator who uncovers a statue with a curse, and takes possession of its power. McDowall overacts shamefully, and the primarily British cast follows suit. Produced, directed and written by Herbert J. Leder. (95 mins.)

It All Came True (1940)**½ Humphrey Bogart, Ann Sheridan. Humphrey goes soft in this occasionally entertaining story of a gangster whose spirit is captured by some old-time vaudevillians. (Dir: Lewis Seiler, 97 mins.)

It Always Rains on Sunday (British, 1948)*** Googie Withers, John McCallum. Story of a family in the slums of London torn apart by crime. Well-made, but grim, unpleasant. (Dir: Robert Hamer, 92 mins.)

It Came from Beneath the Sea (1956) ** Donald Curtis, Faith Domergue. A U.S. submarine tangles with a giant octopus which has come from the lower depths of the sea due to the many H-bomb experiments. Fair science-fiction meller — good for younger audience. (Dir: Robert Gordon, 80 mins.)

It Came from Outer Space (1953)**½ Richard Carlson, Barbara Rush. Good photography and a large budget help to make this first-grade sci-fi entertainment. Richard Carlson, an old hand at fighting visitors from beneath the sea and above the stars, is stalwart once again in the face of faceless creatures. (Dir: Jack Arnold, 81 mins.)

It Comes Up Murder—See: Honey Pot, The

It Conquered the World (1956)** Peter Graves, Beverly Garland. Thing from another planet communicates with a scientist who is to help him conquer earth. Science-fiction thriller is average as these things go, with some occasional good moments. (Dir: Roger Corman, 68 mins.)

It Couldn't Happen to a Nicer Guy (1974)**½ Paul Sorvino, Michael Learned. A silly premise gets a lot of mileage in this comedy, which boasts a better than average cast, including Michael Learned, mother of TV's "The Waltons." Paul Sorvino can't convince anyone that he was forced, at gunpoint, to make love to a very glamorous young lady who picked him up while he was hitchhiking. Try explaining that to your wife? Made-for-TV. (Dir: Cy Howard, 72 mins.)

It Grows on Trees (1952)**½ Irene Dunne, Dean Jagger, Joan Evans. An amusing idea which doesn't quite live up to its expectations. The Baxter family discover two trees in their yard which sprout money (5 and 10 dollar bills) rather than leaves. Naturally, the situation becomes hectic. (Dir: Arthur Lubin, 84 mins.)

It Had to Be You (1947)**½ Ginger Rogers, Cornel Wilde. Socialite always fails to marry at the last moment, until she meets the right man. Amusing comedy. (Dir: Don Hartman, 98 mins.)

It Happened at the World's Fair (1963)** Elvis Presley, Joan O'Brien, Gary Lockwood. Mix Elvis, the Seattle World's Fair, some romance, and a cute Chinese girl together, and out comes a musical tailored for the fans. Hardly inspired, it should serve its purpose with the undiscriminating. (Dir: Norman Taurog, 105 mins.)

It Happened in Athens (1962)* Jayne Mansfield, Trax Colton, Nico Minardos, Bob Mathias. Drab, often distasteful comedy-drama of the 1896 Greek Olympic Games, when a young shepherd wins the marathon, gaining the unwanted hand of an actress (Miss Mansfield). Does have some footage of the actual '96 games incorporated in the film. (Dir: Andrew Marton, 92 mins.)

It Happened in Broad Daylight (Swiss, 1960)**½ Heinz Ruhmann, Michel Simon. When a little girl is brutally murdered, a wily police inspector gets on the case and nails the culprit. Uneven mystery drama moves too slowly, but has a fine performance by cop Ruhmann, documentary-like police detail. English-dubbed.

It Happened In Brooklyn (1946)**½ Frank Sinatra, Kathryn Grayson, Peter Lawford, Jimmy Durante. Pleasant, inconsequential musical about an ex-sailor (Frank) who moves in with a janitor in Brooklyn (Durante) and tries to make the grade in the music business. Uninspired score hurts this film. (Dir: Richard Whorf, 105 mins.)

It Happened One Night (1934)**** Clark Gable, Claudette Colbert, Dizzy society girl flees from her father, finds romance with a reporter on a cross-country bus. The granddaddy of all sophisticated comedy romances still packs a lot of entertainment. Great fun. (Dir: Frank Capra, 110 mins.)

It Happened One Summer (1945)*** Jeanne Crain, Dana Andrews, Dick Haymes, Charles Winninger, Vivian Blaine. The story of an Iowa farm family who encounter love and adventure while at the state fair, graced by the Rodgers & Hammerstein tunes, which are still a delight. Plot's slightness is still evident, but this version is superior to the later remakes. Alternate title: **State Fair.** (Dir: Walter Lang, 100 mins.)

It Happened to Jane (1959)**½ Doris Day, Jack Lemmon, Ernie Kovacs. Silly but pleasant comedy about a New England business woman dealing in lobsters who manages to throw a wrench into the big-time operations of a railroad. Kovacs all but steals the show as the cigar-chewing, bald-pated railroad tycoon. (Dir: Richard Quine, 98 mins.)

It Happened Tomorrow (1944)***½

Dick Powell, Linda Darnell. A reporter manages to get tomorrow's newspaper from a strange little man; then one day he reads his own obituary. Charming fantasy-comedy, with Rene Clair's splendid direction making it a grand show. (84 mins.)

It Happens Every Spring (1949)*** Ray Milland, Jean Peters, Paul Douglas. Funny film about a chemistry professor who discovers a compound which makes baseballs react strangely to bats. His discovery takes him from the lab to the baseball diamond where he quickly becomes a great strike-out pitcher. Ray Milland is good as the prof and gets able support from Paul Douglas as a catcher and Jean Peters as his sweetheart. (Dir: Lloyd Bacon, 80 mins.)

It Happens Every Thursday (1953) **½ Loretta Young, John Forsythe. Simple little comedy-drama about a couple of city dwellers who move to a small California community and try to run the town's weekly newspaper. The comedy stems from the outrageous schemes Forsythe dreams up to bolster circulation. (Dir: Joseph Pevney, 80 mins.)

It Happens in Roma (Italian, 1956) *** Vittorio De Sica, Linda Darnell, Rossano Brazzi. A good comedy idea that doesn't quite materialize—a married couple agrees to allow each other extramarital activities but eventually end up in each other's arms.

It Means That to Me (French, 1962) *½ Eddie Constantine, Bernadette Lafont. Reporter is sent on a special mission to see if he can qualify as a crack agent. Another in the multitude of haphazard Constantine action adventures, with the same naivete. Dubbed in English.

It Should Happen to You (1953) ***½ Judy Holliday, Jack Lemmon, Peter Lawford. Very funny comedy about a model who rents a billboard overlooking a busy section of New York City and becomes a celebrity sight unseen. Judy Holliday is delightful as Gladys Glover, the unemployed model. (Dir: George Cukor, 81 mins.)

It Started in Naples (1960)*** Clark Gable, Sophia Loren, Vittorio De Sica. Lawyer resists the efforts of an Italian waif to take him back to America, until love takes a hand in the shape of the lad's sexy aunt. Good-humored comedy drama has beautiful Italian scenery, Gable and Loren in good form. (Dir: Melville Shavelson, 100 mins.)

It Started in Paradise (British, 1952) *** Jane Hylton, Ian Hunter. Young dress designer will stop at nothing to achieve success, makes enemies by the score. Elaborately produced, well acted drama, especially enticing for the ladies.

It Started with a Kiss (1959)**½ Glenn Ford, Debbie Reynolds, Fred Clark. Flimsy but mildly amusing comedy about an Air Force sergeant, his new bride and a fabulous car, highlighted by splendid scenic backgrounds shot in Spain. Nothing wildly hilarious, but entertaining. (Dir: George Marshall, 104 mins.)

It Started with Eve (1941)***½ Deanna Durbin, Charles Laughton, Robert Cummings. Deanna Durbin's best film. Very funny comedy about mistaken identity and its effect on a zany family. Laughton is very good. (Dir: Henry Koster, 90 mins.)

It Takes a Thief (British, 1960)*½ Jayne Mansfield, Anthony Quayle. Innocent dupe joins in a bullion robbery, is caught and sent to prison; the old gang terrorizes him when he's released. Pretty weak dime-novel gangster melodrama, with a good cast doing nothing with the material provided. (Dir: John Gilling, 90 mins.)

It Takes All Kinds (U.S.-Australia, 1969)* Vera Miles, Robert Lansing, Barry Sullivan. Unremarkable blackmail drama, as Vera Miles enlists Lansing's aid in a daring theft. Some Australian scenery, not enough to matter. (Dir: Eddie Davis, 100 mins.)

It Won't Rub Off, Baby!—See: Sweet Love, Bitter

Italian Job, The (British, 1969)***½ Michael Caine, Noel Coward, Rossano Brazzi. Caine shines as a criminal who inherits the plans for a $4 million gold robbery in Turin, Italy. Fast and entertaining with a wonderful car chase rivaling "Bullitt" and "Otley." Coward plays a master criminal who has complete control of the prison he's been placed in. Caine and Coward together are a delight. (Dir: Peter Collinson, 101 mins.)

It's a Big Country (1952)**½ Gene Kelly, Janet Leigh, Fredric March.

An octet of stories, some better than others, comprise the framework of this film which is a big valentine to America. One of the best episodes stars Kelly as the son of a Greek immigrant who falls in love with the daughter, played by Miss Leigh, of a Hungarian farmer charmingly played by S. Z. Sakall. Among the many stars who appear in the various segments are Van Johnson, James Whitmore, Gary Cooper and Ethel Barrymore. (Dirs: Charles Vidor, Richard Thorpe, John Sturges, Don Hartman, Don Weis, Clarence Brown, William Wellman, 89 mins.)

It's a Bikini World (1965)** Tommy Kirk, Deborah Walley. A silly "bikini" movie in which Tommy Kirk doubles as a shy bespectacled guy when in truth he's quite a ladies' man. Girl watchers will enjoy this one. (Dir: Stephanie Rothman, 86 mins.)

It's a Dog's Life (1955)***½ Jeff Richards, Dean Jagger, Edmund Gwenn. The saga of a dog—a bull terrier from the Bowery who ultimately is entered in a classy dog show. Charming dog story, thanks mainly to a witty, offbeat screenplay and intelligent direction. Plenty of fun, heart-tugs.

It's a Gift (1935)*** W. C. Fields. The "Master" is a family man in this one and he gets the usual share of laughs from his bouts with his shrewish wife. Plenty of fun as Fields holds the film together. (Dir: Norman McLeod, 70 mins.)

It's a Great Feeling (1949)*** Dennis Morgan, Jack Carson, Doris Day. A lot of fun in this off-beat satire about what a ham Carson is and how nobody at the studio wants to direct him. Lot of stars come on for comic bits. (Dir: David Butler, 85 mins.)

It's a Great Life (1943)**½ Penny Singleton, Arthur Lake, Hugh Herbert. Blondie and Dagwood have a horse on their hands, which pleases an eccentric millionaire client of Dagwood's boss. Amusing comedy in the "Blondie" series, with some capable clowning by Herbert. (Dir: Frank Strayer, 75 mins.)

It's a Mad, Mad, Mad, Mad World (1963)**½ Spencer Tracy, Milton Berle, Mickey Rooney. Here's director Stanley Kramer's tribute to those screen comedy chases of old. He's assembled an all-star cast headed by Tracy. It's a wild, occasionally funny romp about a robbery and the multiple double crosses that follow. The gags are pretty feeble, but there's a rousing car-chase scene. Here's just a partial list of names you'll see on screen in bit parts: Jimmy Durante, Sid Caesar, Edie Adams, Milton Berle, Dick Shawn, Ethel Merman, Phil Silvers, Buddy Hackett, Mickey Rooney, Terry-Thomas, Jonathan Winters, Peter Falk, and even the Three Stooges. (190 mins.)

It's a Wonderful Life (1946)***½ James Stewart, Donna Reed, Lionel Barrymore. A man facing ruin, who has had a hard time of it all his life, is sent help from above in the guise of a guardian angel. Charming comedy-drama has scenes of great warmth, humor. Excellent performances. (Dir: Frank Capra, 129 mins.)

It's Alive (1964)* Tommy Kirk, Shirley Bonne. Motorists break down in the Ozarks and are imprisoned along with a geologist in the cave of a demented man. If this is alive, kill it, or at least bury it somewhere. (80 mins.)

It's Always Fair Weather (1955)*** Gene Kelly, Dan Dailey, Cyd Charisse, Dolores Gray, Michael Kidd. Tuneful romp of a musical about three ex-soldiers who meet 10 years after V-J day in New York City to paint the town the proverbial bright hue. Plenty of songs and some expert group dancing by Kelly, Dailey and choreographer Michael Kidd. (Dirs: Gene Kelly, Stanley Donen, 102 mins.)

It's Good to Be Alive (1974)*** Paul Winfield, Ruby Dee, Lou Gossett. Winfield delivers a moving portrait of Brooklyn Dodger-catcher Roy Campanella, facing life as a quadraplegic following his tragic 1958 auto accident. Though Winfield bears no resemblance to the squat, boyish "Campy," the actor's luminous face carries this venture. Battling deep depression, a crumbling marriage and the alienation of his son, David, the ballplayer undergoes treatment with therapist Sam Brockington before he learns to survive. The finale is most effective as he tells 80,000 fans in the Los Angeles Coliseum, "It's good to be alive." Michael Landon directed with taste; Ruby Dee is wonderful as Ruthe Campanella, and Lou Gossett scores as the patient Sam Brockington. But it's Winfield's performance and the story itself that are the winners here. Made-for-TV. (Dir: Michael Landon, 98 mins.)

It's in the Bag (1945)*** Fred Allen, Jack Benny. Owner of a flea circus sells chairs he has inherited, little realizing that a fortune is hidden in one of them. Amusing comedy has some biting Allen wit.

It's Never Too Late (1961)** Phyllis Calvert, Guy Rolfe. Moderately amusing British comedy about a large household who discover that one of its female members is the authoress of a best-selling novel which has been sold to the movies. The idea is better than the resulting film. (Dir: Michael McCarthy, 95 mins.)

It's Only Money (1962)**½ Jerry Lewis, Zachary Scott, Joan O'Brien. Jerry in an amusing role, as a TV repairman who becomes heir to a fortune—that is, if an unscrupulous lawyer doesn't put him out of the way permanently. Mildly funny slapstick situations. (Dir: Frank Tashlin, 84 mins.)

It's Your Move (Italy-Spain, 1968) *½ Edward G. Robinson, Adolfo Celi, Terry-Thomas. Mildly humorous tale of an Englishman who plans a bank heist on the island of Majorca.

Ivailo the Great (Bulgarian, 1963)*½ Bogomil Simenov, Lona Davidova. Shepherd leads his people to freedom against tyrants. Some spectacular battle scenes, otherwise technically ragged historical drama dubbed in English.

Ivan, Son of the White Devil (1954)** Nadia Gray, Paul Campbell. Love and adventure set in mysterious Turkey are the ingredients in this costume epic.

Ivanhoe (1953)*** Robert Taylor, Elizabeth Taylor, Joan Fontaine. Elaborate production based on Sir Walter Scott's tale of the days of knights and jousts and fair maidens in distress. R. Taylor is the dashing Ivanhoe and his loves are E. Taylor, as Rebecca, and J. Fontaine, as Rowena. Well-done. (Dir: Richard Thorpe, 106 mins.)

I've Lived Before (1956)** Jock Mahoney, Leigh Snowden. An interesting idea rather amateurishly handled—this film deals with the mystery of reincarnation. Jock Mahoney plays a man who believes he has lived before in another time.

Ivory Hunter (British, 1951)***½ Anthony Steel, Dinah Sheridan. A game warden in East Africa tries to preserve wild life, foils some poachers making away with ivory. Authentic African scenes together with a suspenseful story make this adventure rate high. (Dir: Harry Watt, 97 mins.)

Ivy (1947)*** Joan Fontaine, Herbert Marshall, Sir Cedric Hardwicke. Diabolical drama about a ruthless woman and her evil deeds in her attempt to find personal happiness. Joan Fontaine is excellent as the poisonous Ivy. (Dir: Sam Wood, 99 mins.)

Ivy League Killers (Canadian, 1962) *½ Don Borisenko, Barbara Bricker. Rich teenagers clash with a motorcycle gang, culminating in robbery and murder. Sincere but weakly made juvenile delinquency drama.

Jack and the Beanstalk (1952)*½ Bud Abbott, Lou Costello, Buddy Baer. Costello falls asleep and dreams himself into the fairy tale of Jack and the Beanstalk. For the very young, and Abbott and Costello fans only. (87 mins.)

Jack Johnson (1971)**** Fascinating documentary biography of the legendary black heavyweight boxing champion. Uses remarkable vintage clips, most of them never seen before, compiled and edited with skill by boxing aficionados Jim Jacobs and William Clayton. Scenes of his great fights against Jess Willard and others, but there's unique footage of Johnson out of the ring as well—with his white brides, in Russia meeting Rasputin, an auto race with Barney Oldfield, etc. Johnson's pride and drive come through in the narration spoken by Brock Peters. (Dir: William Clayton, 90 mins.)

Jack London (1943)*** Michael O'Shea, Susan Hayward, Virginia Mayo, Frank Craven. Biographical adventure story of the illustrious career of Jack London. Strong cast and exciting sequences make for good entertainment. (Dir: Albert Santell, 94 mins.)

Jack of Diamonds (U.S.-German, 1967)** George Hamilton, Joseph Cotten, Marie Laforet. Ordinary adventure about a sophisticated cat-burglar (George Hamilton) and his capers, both at work and at play. Curvaceous Marie Laforet is also cast as a cat-burglar which should give you an idea of the extent of the seriousness of the plot. (Dir: Don Taylor, 105 mins.)

Jack the Ripper (1959)** Lee Patterson. British made meller with many shock gimmicks—moderately well done. Producer Joseph E. Levine exploited this Grade B film into a big box office grosser. (Dir: Robert Baker, 88 mins.)

Jackie Robinson Story (1950)*** Jackie Robinson, Ruby Lee. Interesting biographical film about Jackie's years as the first Negro in organized baseball. Corny, but recommended for the youngsters. (Dir: Alfred E. Green, 76 mins.)

Jackpot, The (1950)***½ James Stewart, Barbara Hale. Average man wins a fabulous radio-quiz jackpot (in pre-scandal days) and finds his life and wife radically changed, but not for the better. Very funny. (Dir: Walter Lang, 85 mins.)

Jackpot (British, 1962)*½ William Hartnell, Betty McDowall. Scotland Yard investigates robbery and the murder of a policeman, involving an ex-convict. No filmic jackpot here!

Jackson County Jail (1976)*** Yvette Mimieux, Tommy Lee Jones, Robert Carradine, Severn Darden. Surprisingly good drama from the Roger Corman film factory about a young, attractive woman (Mimieux) who stumbles into a nightmare land of hijacking, rape, and other indignities while driving cross-country from California to New York. There's a very explicit, powerful rape scene when Mimieux is assaulted by her jailer after she is thrown in jail on a bum rap in a dinky Western town. Jones plays a fugitive on the lam who escapes from the jail with Mimieux, who soon faces some important moral questions. Written by Donald Stewart. (Dir: Michael Miller, 84 mins.)

Jacob the Liar (East Germany, 1975) *** Vlastimil Brodsky, Manuela Simon. A haunting, heartwarming, poignant drama—with some comic touches—about life in a Jewish ghetto in Poland during the Nazi occupation of World War II. A Jewish prisoner invents lies to keep hope alive among his doomed co-

religionists. Magnificently acted by Czech actor Brodsky and unerringly directed by Frank Beyer, with a gentle, perceptive screenplay by Jurek Becker. One particularly notable scene when the protagonist pretends to be playing a radio for his wide-eyed young niece.

Jacqueline (British, 1956)*** John Gregson, Kathleen Ryan. His small daughter helps an Irish dock worker obtain work on a farm. Well-made, nicely acted comedy-drama has charm. (Dir: Roy Baker, 92 mins.)

Jacqueline Susann's Once Is Not Enough—See: Once Is Not Enough

Jailbreakers, The (1960)* Robert Hutton, Mary Castle. Innocent couple are held hostage by a trio of escaped convicts in a ghost town where loot is buried. Weak crime melodrama.

Jailhouse Rock (1957)** Elvis Presley, Judy Tyler. While serving a term for manslaughter, a young convict learns to play the guitar, becomes a top pop singer. For Presley fans—he shivers and shakes with gusto, much more than is provided by the script. (Dir: Richard Thorpe, 96 mins.)

Jam Session (1944)** Ann Miller, Louis Armstrong. Not much plot but plenty of swing (remember?) performed by top performers including the Pied Pipers, Charlie Barnet and, of course, Ann and Louis. (Dir: Charles Barton, 77 mins.)

Jamaica Run (1958)** Ray Milland, Arlene Dahl, Wendell Corey. Jumbled drama with family skeletons in every closet of a large mansion in Jamaica inhabited by a strange crew including beautiful Arlene Dahl. Ray Milland is a skipper of a schooner who helps things back to normalcy. (Dir: Lewis R. Foster, 92 mins.)

Jamboree (1957)*½ Kay Medford, Robert Pastine. Nothing plot about a boy-girl music team and their agents tied to a lot of numbers by Connie Francis, Frankie Avalon, Jerry Lee Lewis, Fats Domino, etc. There it is, kiddies, if you want it.

James Dean (1976)**½ Stephen McHattie, Michael Brandon, Meg Foster, Candy Clark. Recollection of the 50's actor's early days by his best friend, Bill Bast (played by Brandon), when the two met at UCLA and struggled together in New York. The show becomes a curiosity piece, therefore, with McHattie striving to capture the essence of the young rebel, refusing to attempt an all-out imitation. Directed with care and feeling, which James Dean's fans will appreciate. Made-for-TV. (Dir: Robert Butler, 98 mins.)

James Dean Story, The (1957)** Documentary compilation recounts the life of the controversial film star who was killed in an auto crash. Made up of stills, home movies, scenes from his films, interviews with those who knew him. Dean's fans will like it—others will find it scrappy, inconclusive. (Dir: George W. George, 82 mins.)

James Michener's Dynasty (1976) **½ Sarah Miles, Stacy Keach, Harris Yulin. James Michener outlines the saga of an American epoch, the beginning of a family dynasty in Ohio back in the 1820's. It's Michener's contention that the temptation to move West was not the correct one in most cases, and he sets out to prove this in the tale of a threesome—two brothers and a small, bright, ambitious woman, played by Harris Yulin, Stacy Keach and England's Sarah Miles as Yulin's wife. The acting juices up this TV "epic" with Miles' Jennifer, wife of a good, solid farmer, leading the way as a fighter and a shrewd businesswoman. Made-for-TV. (Dir: Lee Philips, 98 mins.)

Jamilya (Russian, 1970)***½ Natalya Arinbasarova, Suimenkul Chkmorov. A lovely, gentle story about love, beautifully directed by Irina Poplavskaya and making wonderful use of a novel setting—a village in eastern Russia near the Chinese border. Story line is simplicity itself—a young boy, a budding painter, watches the developing love of two adults he adores. Shot in both black and white and color, the color used when we see the lad's painting. (78 mins.)

Jan Hus (Czech, 1964)**½ Zdenek Stepanek, Jan Pivec. Occasionally impressive historical drama dubbed in English, about a simple man persecuted for his religious beliefs. Overlong and leisurely in pace, it nevertheless has some impressive sequences.

Jane Eyre (1944)*** Joan Fontaine, Orson Welles. Charlotte Bronte's novel receives a fine production but Mr. Welles' performance as Rochester makes it a good horror film and overshadows most of the original's substance. (Dir: Robert Stevenson, 96 mins.)

Jason and the Argonauts (British, 1963)**½ Todd Armstrong, Nancy Kovack, Gary Raymond. The tale of Jason and his search for the golden fleece in his endeavors to rescue his land from the rule of a tyrant. Magical special effects should delight the kiddies, and the elders should have a fairly entertaining time of it. (Dir: Don Chaffey, 104 mins.)

Jaws (1975)**** Roy Scheider, Robert Shaw, Richard Dreyfuss. In case you were on Mars in the mid-70's, there's this nasty shark off the coast of Martha's Vineyard, see . . . . "Jaws" was one of the great box-office hits of all time, and it's easy to understand why! Young director Steven Spielberg (he was 27 when he directed "Jaws," his only other feature credit being "The Sugarland Express") builds the tension methodically, and unerringly. It pays off with one of the scariest movie finales ever. Special credit, too, to the special-effects crew who created the great mechanical man-eater. Real-live shark footage filmed off the Australian coast is cleverly integrated with the movie marvel. A rousing, fantastic adventure, and I don't give a damn if Peter Benchley's original novel was good, bad or indifferent. "Jaws" is a fabulous finner! (Dir: Steven Spielberg, 124 mins.)

Jayhawkers, The (1959)**½ Jeff Chandler, Fess Parker. Fast-paced western about ruthless men who try to take over control of an entire state after the Civil War. (Dir: Melvin Frank, 100 mins.)

Jazz Ball (1956)** Compilation of musical acts culled from old Paramount short subjects, featuring Betty Hutton, Mills Brothers, Louis Armstrong, etc. No story line. Occasionally interesting memento of what the greats were doing decades ago.

Jazz Boat (1960)** Anthony Newley, Anne Aubrey. A British rock 'n roll musical with a good cast but a tiresome script and an equally boring score. (Dir: Ken Hughes, 90 mins.)

Jazz on a Summer's Day (1960)**** The best filmed records of a jazz concert. The Newport Jazz Festival of 1958 is the setting for Bert Stern's superbly edited account of the exciting, festive air generated by a host of talents who held a crew-cut, long-skirted audience spellbound with their artistry. The roster reads like a who's who of pop jazz . . . the immortal Louis Armstrong, Dinah Washington, Thelonious Monk, Gerry Mulligan, Chuck Berry, Bib Maybelle, Anita O'Day and Mahalia Jackson, with Miss Jackson bringing the whole thing to a rousing close with her gospel song. (Dir: Bert Stern, 85 mins.)

Jazz Singer, The (1927)*** Al Jolson, Warner Oland, May McAvoy. The film that brought sound to the movies to stay. Story of a cantor's son who becomes a stage star. As a film, not so good, and never was; as movie history, of interest and Al Jolson's overpowering stage personality does come through and is still worth seeing for the first time. (Dir: Alan Crosland, 90 mins.)

Jazz Singer (1953)*** Danny Thomas, Peggy Lee. Updated version of the old Al Jolson film which revolutionized the motion picture business. This version did not make history but is nevertheless an entertaining story about a Jewish boy who prefers show business to becoming a cantor like his father before him. Danny Thomas is quite good in the title role. (Dir: Michael Curtiz, 107 mins.)

Jeanne Eagels (1957)**½ Kim Novak, Jeff Chandler, Agnes Moorehead. A glorified yet watered down depiction of the rise and fall of actress Jeanne Eagels. Kim Novak is sorely miscast and overacts throughout. (109 mins.)

Jenny (1970)**½ Marlo Thomas, Alan Alda, Vincent Gardenia, Marian Hailey, Elizabeth Wilson. There are a number of good things about this movie, including the performances of Thomas and Alda, but they don't compensate for the overall mushiness of the plot and script. Thomas is an unwed, pregnant girl who leaves her conservative Connecticut home for New York City, where she meets hip young filmmaker Alda, who's looking for a way to beat the draft. Bingo! A "marriage of convenience!" The story progresses emotionally from there. Individual vignettes—city street scenes, Alda directing a TV commercial, a talk with her father —are worth waiting for. Includes scenes from "A Place in the Sun." (Dir: George Bloomfield, 86 mins.)

Jeopardy (1953)**½ Barbara Stanwyck, Barry Sullivan, Ralph Meeker. Woman trying to find help for her injured husband is captured by an escaped killer. Modest little thriller is well made, but remains a minor drama. (Dir: John Sturges, 69 mins.)

Jeremiah Johnson (1972)*** Robert Redford, Will Geer, Stefan Gierasch. Offbeat, visually beautiful western about a loner in the mountain country of Utah shortly after the Mexican-American War. Redford hunts bear, fishes, and acquires an Indian wife during the course of his picaresque adventures. He's on camera virtually throughout the film in this man vs. nature saga. The Indians are not caricatured, and there are scenes of interest throughout, although the film is ultimately too long and somewhat disappointing, thanks partly to Redford's monotonous portrayal. (Dir: Sydney Pollack, 107 mins.)

Jeremy (1973)***½ Robby Benson, Glynis O'Connor, Leonardo Cimino, Pat Wheel. A love story about two New York high-school teenagers, without the usual overlay of drugs, violence, rape, etc. A tender, often quite sensitive portrayal of first love and sexual awakenings. Robby Benson is enormously appealing as a Jewish would-be cellist, meeting and wooing a Gentile lass who loves the dance. Written by Arthur Barron, a distinguished TV documentary filmmaker, who makes an impressive feature film directorial debut with this sensitive, low-budget entry. "Jeremy" never got the attention it deserved. (Dir: Arthur Barron, 90 mins.)

Jerusalem File, The (U.S.-Israeli, 1972)**½ Bruce Davison, Zeev Revah, Donald Pleasence, Nicol Williamson. Naive story of student idealism working to solve the Arab-Israeli turmoil. An American archaeology student (Davison), studying in Israel, attempts to continue and expand his Yale-based friendship with an Arab student leader (Revah) amid a background of militarism and strife. Pleasence and Williamson offer well-drawn characterizations, but the real star is Raoul Coutard's cinematograhy (he also did "Z"), which breathes a sense of time and place into this simplistic tale. (Dir: John Flynn, 96 mins.)

Jesse James (1939)***½ Tyrone Power, Henry Fonda, Nancy Kelly. A superb cast in a highly fictionalized account of the life of America's most famous outlaw. Glorifies him too much but is real exciting screen entertainment. (Dir: Henry King.)

Jesse James Meets Frankenstein's Daughter (1966)* John Lupton, Cal Bolder, Narda Onyx. Lady scientist, descendant of you-know-who, turns the outlaw's wounded friend into a monster. Monstrous western-horror thriller. (Dir: William Beaudine, 88 mins.)

Jessica (1962)** Angie Dickinson, Maurice Chevalier. When a glamorous midwife turns men's heads in a small Italian village, the women of the town pull a "Lysistrata" and go on "strike." Filmed in Italy, the scenics are the main attraction in this slow-moving comedy. (Dir: Jean Negulesco, 112 mins.)

Jesus Christ, Superstar (1973)**½ Ted Neeley, Carl Anderson, Yvonne Elliman. The famous rock-opera recording which spawned a Broadway production is turned into an ambitious but, in the final analysis, unsuccessful movie. The story of Jesus, told in musical terms, was filmed on location in Israel, and director Norman Jewison cleverly used the device of having a troupe of actors arriving by bus on the desert location to film the biblical play within the play. Those familiar with the score will probably be more tolerant of the song-saga of Jesus at the mercy of the Romans, but don't expect Cecil B. De Mille. There are sprinklings of anti-war statements made by Jewison's use of jet fighters and tanks chasing Judas during his big production number. The cast performs ably, and the film comes off as an interesting curiosity. (Dir: Norman Jewison, 107 mins.)

Jet Over the Atlantic (1959)**½ Guy Madison, Virginia Mayo, George Raft. Fairly interesting drama about a plane which is in danger when a bomb is discovered aboard during the flight from Spain to New York. (Dir: Byron Haskin, 95 mins.)

Jet Storm (Great Britain, 1959)**½ Stanley Baker, Richard Attenborough, Diane Cilento. Interesting psychological drama as a demented father tries to gain revenge on the man who killed his child. Will he explode the bomb in his suitcase or will he be persuaded by jet-plane passengers to give himself up? (Dir: C. Raker Endfield, 99 mins.)

Jezebel (1938)*** Bette Davis, George Brent. Miss Davis is at her best as a vicious Southern belle and succeeds in making this a good film.

Jigsaw (British, 1961)**½ Jack Warner, Ronald Lewis, Yolande Donlan. Capable whodunit about police investigating a murder, painstakingly putting the clues together. Done efficiently, semidocumentary style; mystery fans should enjoy.

Jigsaw (1968)**½ Harry Guardino, Hope Lange, Bradford Dillman, Pat Hingle. Fairly engrossing tale about a scientist (Dillman) who thinks he has committed a murder, and hires a private detective to fill in the missing pieces. No real surprises in this mystery but most of it works. (Dir: James Goldstone, 97 mins.)

Jigsaw (1972)**½ James Wainwright, an offbeat, rugged actor in the Lee Marvin groove, plays the leading role of a police detective in this well-paced pilot for a TV series. When Wainwright follows a suspicious-looking character to a hotel, he becomes involved in a mystery. There's an exciting two-car chase across dirt roads, and the supporting cast, including Vera Miles, Richard Kiley, and Irene Dailey, helps Wainwright's earnest, convincing performance. (Dir: William Graham, 99 mins.)

Jim Thorpe, All American (1951)*** Burt Lancaster, Phyllis Thaxter. Burt Lancaster portrays the All-American athlete who rose from an obscure beginning to international fame. Sport fans will enjoy this one. (Dir: Michael Curtiz, 107 mins.)

Jivaro (1954)**½ Fernando Lamas, Rhonda Fleming, Brian Keith. Into the land of head-hunters come the fearless treasure seeking adventurers with Fernando Lamas at the helm and beautiful Rhonda Fleming not far behind. Action filled jungle film. (Dir: Edward Ludwig, 91 mins.)

Joan of Arc (1948)**½ Ingrid Bergman, Jose Ferrer, Ward Bond. Mammoth, lavish production based on the life of the French farm girl who led the French armies against England and was later tried as a heretic. Despite the pretensions, the film is top-heavy, wallows in its own opulence. Performances, including Bergman's, are adequate, no more. May hold the attention, but a classic it isn't. (Dir: Victor Fleming, 145 mins.)

Joan of Paris (1942)***½ Michele Morgan, Paul Henreid. French girl sacrifices her life so that English flyers may escape the Gestapo in occupied France. Gripping suspenseful war drama, excellently acted, well produced. (Dir: Robert Stevenson, 95 mins.)

Joe (1970)***½ Peter Boyle, Dennis Patrick. Savage, powerful, but imperfect film, which benefits greatly from an astonishingly bravura performance by Peter Boyle. Joe is a foul-mouthed, unashamed, reactionary bigot, who hates "niggers" and "hippies" with equal rage. Boyle somehow manages to find some humor in the role. His monologue in a neighborhood bar, where he meets and befriends an affluent advertising executive who is also a murderer, is one of the most compelling scenes in years. The other acting is not on a par with Boyle's and the generally perceptive script by Norman Wexler flounders at the end, but you'll be mesmerized by "Joe" long before this low-budget entry, shot on location in New York, comes to its flawed conclusion. (Dir: John G. Avildsen, 107 mins.)

Joe Butterfly (1957)** Audie Murphy, George Nader, Burgess Meredith. GIs in Japan encounter a shrewd native operator who helps them get out the first edition of "Yank." Disappointing service comedy takes an amusing idea and almost completely botches it. Mild, at best. (Dir: Jesse Hibbs, 90 mins.)

Joe Dakota (1957)**½ Jock Mahoney, Luana Patten. Stranger rides into town and finds the populace agog with oil fever, uncovers skullduggery behind the drilling. Pleasant little western carries a good amount of entertainment. (Dir: Richard Bartlett, 79 mins.)

Joe Kidd (1972)**½ Clint Eastwood, Robert Duvall. Moderately interesting Eastwood western with the star giving still another of his "quiet cowboy with a quick gun" portrayals. The setting is New Mexico at the turn of the century. The plot centers on the Spanish-Americans fighting the land barons for what they believe to be their property. In steps Joe Kidd (Eastwood) to aid the Spaniards and the sparks fly in a flashy, violent finale. The on-location photography of the High Sierras is a spectacular bonus. (Dir: John Sturges, 88 mins.)

Joe Macbeth (British, 1956)**½ Paul Douglas, Ruth Roman. Egged on by his grasping wife, a gangster kills his way to the top of the mob. Modernized Shakespeare, a noble experiment that doesn't quite succeed. Made in England, but the American locale is fairly accurate. (Dir: Ken Hughes, 90 mins.)

John and Julie (British, 1957)**½ Moira Lister, Constance Cummings, Noelle Middleton. Warm-hearted British comedy about two children and their adventures in the splendor-filled world of royalty.

John and Mary (1969)**½ Dustin Hoffman, Mia Farrow. Gentle if sometimes tedious study which treads lightly on a resigned affair between two singles who pick each other up at a bar but don't really swing. Hoffman is "John" and Farrow is "Mary," names revealed only after the night's lovemaking has turned into the morning after's falling in love. The action is painfully confined to an apartment interior (with some flashes of the outdoors) and the acting is constricted by the screenplay which prefers social commentary to humanism. But it is a "star vehicle" and Hoffman and Farrow are alternately quarrelsome and lovable. (Dir: Peter Yates, 92 mins.)

John F. Kennedy: Years of Lightning, Day of Drums (1964)**** Excellent U.S. Government documentary on the Presidential life, and death, of John F. Kennedy, guarantees to stir up all the old emotions. Memorial tribute, also a propaganda effort, the film was intended for showing abroad and only made available in the U.S. by an act of Congress. It does not attempt a sober reassessment of Kennedy's brief term in office. The narration by Gregory Peck is unobtrusive, yet adds to the compelling, emotional mood. (Dir: Bruce Herschenson, 88 mins.)

John Goldfarb, Please Come Home (1965)*½ Shirley MacLaine, Peter Ustinov, Richard Crenna. This offbeat comedy set in a mythical Arabian principality doesn't work at all. Peter Ustinov manages a few chuckles as the ruler. (Dir: J. Lee Thompson, 96 mins.)

John Loves Mary (1949)****½** Ronald Reagan, Patricia Neal, Jack Carson. Stage comedy about a returning soldier trying to sneak a war bride into this country, while his fiancee wants to get married. Loses a lot of its spontaneity. (Dir: David Butler, 96 mins.)

John Paul Jones (1959)****½** Robert Stack, Marisa Pavan, Charles Coburn, Bette Davis. Rambling biography of America's first naval hero, moderately well played by Stack against stacked odds—talky script, static direction. Miss Davis makes a token appearance as Empress Catherine of Russia. Battle scenes lend some maritime excitement. (Dir: John Farrow, 126 mins.)

Johnny Allegro (1949)****½** George Raft, Nina Foch. Raft is once again the shady hoodlum who squares himself with the cops by acting as an undercover agent to expose an international smuggling outfit. Plenty of two-fisted action. (Dir: Ted Tetzlaff, 81 mins.)

Johnny Angel (1945)******* George Raft, Claire Trevor. Merchant marine officer unravels the murder of his father, smashes a ring of enemy agents. Well done melodrama with good production values. (Dir: Edward L. Marin, 79 mins.)

Johnny Apollo (1940)******* Tyrone Power, Dorothy Lamour. Fast paced gangster melodrama with college grad Power choosing a life of crime out of bitterness over his dad's conviction as a fraud. Mostly routine but good entertainment. (Dir: Henry Hathaway, 93 mins.)

Johnny Belinda (1948)*****½** Jane Wyman, Lew Ayres. Jane Wyman gives an award-winning performance as a deaf mute in this sensitive and moving story of a person living in a world of silence. (Dir: Jean Negulesco, 103 mins.)

Johnny Cash: The Man, His World, His Music (1970)******* Johnny Cash, June Carter, Bob Dylan, Don Reed. Quite interesting feature about the famous country-music star. We hear a lot of good Cash tunes, also learn something about Cash himself as we travel with Johnny to his hometown in rural Arkansas where he grew up in poverty. This is a longer version of material first seen as a television

documentary. Cash joins Dylan on "One Too Many Mornings" and there's a couple of fine tunes from a young man named Don Reed who auditions for Cash. (Dir: Robert Elfstrom, 94 mins.)

Johnny Come Lately (1943)****½** James Cagney, Grace George. A wandering vagabond stops in a small town and helps an old lady run her newspaper. Mild for Cagney, but generally entertaining comedy-drama. (Dir: William K. Howard, 97 mins.)

Johnny Concho (1956)****** Frank Sinatra, Keenan Wynn, Phyllis Kirk. Sinatra as a cowboy is very hard to take! The plot centers around a coward who must face up to a fast gun. Some good scenes but slow moving and, to be truthful, rather boring. (Dir: Don McGuire, 84 mins.)

Johnny Cool (1963)****** Henry Silva. Violent, familiar tale of a mafioso (Silva) seeking revenge in gangsterdom. Studded with guest bit parts including Sammy Davis, Jr., Mort Sahl, Joey Bishop, Telly Savalas, Elizabeth Montgomery. (Dir: William Asher, 101 mins.)

Johnny Dark (1954)***½** Tony Curtis, Piper Laurie, Don Taylor. Predictable sports-car dramatics, hyped a little by a good cast and burning-rubber road shots. (Dir: George Sherman, 85 mins.)

Johnny Eager (1941)*****½** Robert Taylor, Lana Turner, Van Heflin. Top rate gangster melodrama about a good-looking, egotistical hood. Van Heflin's performance as Taylor's confidante and Greek chorus won him awards and stardom. (Dir: Mervyn Le Roy, 107 mins.)

Johnny Guitar (1954)******* Joan Crawford, Sterling Hayden, Scott Brady, Mercedes McCambridge. Gambling house proprietress has built her establishment on a railroad site, earns the resentment of the town. Unusual western tries to be different, which is something to commend, anyway. (Dir: Nicholas Ray, 110 mins.)

Johnny Holiday (1949)*****½** William Bendix, Stanley Clements. Delinquent boy is reformed at the Indiana Boys' School. Authentic, forceful drama has a good air of sincerity. (Dir: Willis Goldbeck, 92 mins.)

Johnny in the Clouds (British, 1944) *****½** Douglas Montgomery, John Mills, Michael Redgrave. Story of a flying field in England during

World War II, and the various emotional entanglements of the airmen. Stirring war drama with praiseworthy performance, direction. (Dir: Anthony Asquith, 87 mins.)

Johnny Nobody (British, 1964)*** Nigel Patrick, Aldo Ray, William Bendix, Yvonne Mitchell. When a disliked writer is killed by a mysterious stranger soon known as "Johnny Nobody," the local priest suspects a plot; the villagers are claiming the deed to be a miracle. Offbeat drama has a decidedly unusual story, interesting performances and direction to back it up. Good fare. (Dir: Nigel Patrick, 88 mins.)

Johnny O'Clock (1947)**½ Dick Powell, Evelyn Keyes. Confused, tough tale of an honest gambler who gets accused of murder. Good, rough dialogue but without a purpose. (Dir: Robert Rossen, 95 mins.)

Johnny Stool Pigeon (1949)**½ Howard Duff, Shelley Winters, Dan Duryea. Routine but well played crime drama about an ex-con who serves as a "stoolie" for the police in order to uncover a dope ring. Good gangland scenes. (Dir: William Castle, 76 mins.)

Johnny Tiger (1966)**½ Robert Taylor, Geraldine Brooks, Chad Everett, Brenda Scott. Teacher comes to the Seminole Reservation in Florida to instruct the Indian children, finds his task is harder than he bargained for. Different sort of drama makes good use of location scenery, Indian customs. Runs a bit too long, but worth seeing. (Dir: Paul Wendkos, 102 mins.)

Johnny Trouble (1957)** Stuart Whitman, Ethel Barrymore. Guy on the road turns a new leaf when he meets a woman who has never given up hope of her long-lost son's returning. Drama leans toward the maudlin, was done better years ago as "Someone To Remember." (Dir: John H. Auer, 80 mins.)

Johnny You're Wanted (British, 1956) *½ John Slater, Alfred Marks. Truck driver picks up a blonde on the road, later finds her murdered. Weak mystery.

Johnny Yuma (Italian, 1966)* Mark Damon, Lawrence Dobkin, Rosalba Neri. Muscleman Damon as Johnny Yuma, the inheritor of a rich dead uncle's fortune, monkeys his way around this slightly sick western. (Dir: Romolo Guorri, 99 mins.)

Joker Is Wild, The (1957)*** Frank Sinatra, Jeanne Crain, Mitzi Gaynor. The story of nightclub entertainer Joe E. Lewis, who conquered problems with the gang lords of the roaring 20's, and the bottle of today. Played by Sinatra in his standard hipster style, the story has moments of dramatic force, some good nostalgic tunes. (Dir: Charles Vidor, 123 mins.)

Jokers, The (1967)***½ Michael Crawford, Oliver Reed. A sparkling British comedy that doesn't go for big laughs but keeps you smiling throughout. An attractive pair of well-to-do brothers, charmingly played by Oliver Reed and Michael Crawford, come up with a wild plot to snatch the Crown Jewels and then give them back. They figure all the odds and go through with it. The actual theft is a brilliantly staged sequence, and viewers will find the suspense almost unbearable. There's a twist to the ending which adds to the film's bite, and credit must be paid to the superb photography which heightens the action at all times. Director Michael Winner also thought up this engaging yarn! (94 mins.)

Jolly Bad Fellow, A (British, 1964) ***½ Leo McKern, Janet Munro, Maxine Audley. Wildly amusing comedy about a scoundrelly professor who discovers a poison which will cause painless and untraceable death, decides to use it for his own devices. Anyone who can mix murder and mirth successfully deserves credit, and the participants here have done it. (Dir: Don Chaffey, 94 mins.)

Jolson Sings Again (1950)**** Larry Parks, Barbara Hale. The rest of the Al Jolson Story and as good as its predecessor. Parks once again mouths the songs that made the "Minstrel of Broadway" famous. (Dir: Henry Levin, 96 mins.)

Jolson Story, The (1947)**** Larry Parks, Evelyn Keyes. The film biography of the popular singer from his boyhood to his success on the stage and in talkies. Grand show with Jolson singing his numbers perfectly to Parks' miming. (Dir: Alfred E. Green, 128 mins.)

Joseph and His Brethren (1960)*½ Geoffrey Horne, Robert Morley. Poor Italian produced adventure epic dubbed in English. Even Robert

371

Morley doesn't help much. (Dir: Irving Rapper, 103 mins.)

Josephine and Men (British, 1955)** Glynis Johns, Jack Buchanan. Girl's mother instincts gets her into plenty of trouble with men. Comedy is never as funny as it should be.

Journey, The (1959)**½ Deborah Kerr, Yul Brynner, Jason Robards, Jr. Brynner parades around as a Russian officer who mixes business (detaining the evacuation of neutral citizens from revolution-torn Hungary circa 1956) and pleasure (putting the make on pale Deborah Kerr). A good cast, including Robert Morley, E. G. Marshall and Anne Jackson, are at the mercy of a mediocre script. Some mild suspense at the end. (Dir: Anatole Litvak, 125 mins.)

Journey Beneath the Desert (1963)*½ Haya Harareet, Rod Fulton. Dull Italian produced adventure epic dubbed in English. Some lost flyers find Atlantis, and a wicked, wicked queen.

Journey for Margaret (1942)***½ Robert Young, Laraine Day, Margaret O'Brien. Story of the small, innocent victims of the blitz is splendidly acted, warm melodrama. If this doesn't make you cry, then you simply don't like children. (Dir: W. S. Van Dyke, 81 mins.)

Journey from Darkness (1975)**½ Marc Singer, Kay Lenz, Joseph Campanella, William Windom. Marc Singer is effective in this adptation of a true story about a blind student who doggedly battles his way into medical school, when everyone says that's impossible. The parents don't want to see their boy hurt, college professors spell out the difficulties, and only the student and his girl, well played by Kay Lenz, remain undaunted. Made-for-TV. (Dir: James Goldstone, 100 mins.)

Journey Into Fear (1942)***½ Orson Welles, Joseph Cotten, Dolores Del Rio. American armaments expert is sought by Axis agents, but a Turkish police inspector aids him. Complicated but expertly made spy melodrama in the Welles manner. (Dir: Norman Foster, 69 mins.)

Journey into Fear (1975)** Sam Waterston, Yvette Mimieux, Zero Mostel. An unsuccessful attempt to remake Orson Welles' 1942 film based on Eric Ambler's novel. Sam Waterston is no Welles, and the up-

dating of the espionage yarn set in Turkey and the U.S. to the 70's dilutes the suspense of the original tale. Yvette Mimieux offers something to look at during the dull movie. (Dir: Daniel Mann, 103 mins.)

Journey Into Light (1952)**½ Sterling Hayden, Viveca Lindfors. A minister loses faith, becomes a derelict, is reformed by a blind girl in a Skid Row mission. Slow, well acted drama. (Dir: Stuart Heisler, 87 mins.)

Journey Into Nowhere (1963) **½ Tony Wright, Sonja Ziemann. Odd little suspense drama made in South Africa; man on the lam from hoodlums meets a woman about to go blind, they devise a double indemnity insurance plan, the survivor collecting. Unpolished, but with good acting by the leads.

Journey of Robert F. Kennedy, The (1970)***½ An engrossing, perceptive and touching portrait of the late Senator Robert F. Kennedy, the man, the politician, the husband and father, and the inspired spokesman for the blacks and the poor. The 90-minute documentary benefits from the narration written by Arthur Schlesinger, Jr., which presents views from both supporters and opponents of Kennedy, and gives a clear picture of RFK's strong sense of dedication to his work and family as well as his ambition. Through a series of well edited film clips, RFK's political career is traced from the days he managed his brother John F. Kennedy's 1960 Presidential campaign to his own strenuous campaign for the Presidential nomination in 1968, which ended abruptly when he was killed by an assassin. A highlight, among many others, is an interview with civil rights leader Charles Evers, who sums up Robert F. Kennedy as a man who really cared about people. (Dir: Mel Stuart, 75 mins.)

Journey to Freedom (1957)* Jacques Scott, Genevieve Aumont. Communist agents trail an escapee from Bulgaria. Poor melodrama. (Dir: Robert C. Dertano, 60 mins.)

Journey to Jerusalem (1968)*** A documentary record of a concert given by violinist Isaac Stern and conducted by Leonard Bernstein. Filmed in Jerusalem several weeks after the end of the Six Day War

In 1967. The music, including selections from Mahler and Mendelssohn, is glorious. The filmmaking itself, partially because the film was organized and shot so hurriedly, is less well done. But "Journey" is a moving record of an emotion-filled event, the reunification of Jerusalem.

Journey to Shiloh (1968)** Michael Sarrazin, Brenda Scott. A cast of young players, including Michael Sarrazin, James Caan, Michael Burns and Brenda Scott, is featured in this western yarn set during the Civil War. Fans get a good amount of action in this tale about a group of green young men who set out for Virginia to join up and fight for the Confederacy. Routine but played with youthful energy. (Dir: William Hale, 101 mins.)

Journey to the Beginning of Time (Czechoslovakia, 1960)**½ Victor Betral, James Lukas, Peter Herman, Charles Goldsmith. Nice kiddie fare. Four youngsters explore a cave in New York's Central Park after a museum visit, find themselves in prehistoric times. (Dir: Karel Zeman, 87 mins.)

Journey to the Center of the Earth (1960)*** Pat Boone, James Mason, Arlene Dahl. The real star of this fanciful Jules Verne tale of an expedition to the earth's center is the 20th Century-Fox special-effects department, who have developed some fascinating trick camera work and sets. Otherwise, the story's a frequently exciting one, with some welcome comedy relief. Good performances. (Dir: Henry Levin, 132 mins.)

Journey to the Center of Time (1967) *½ Scott Brady, Gigi Perreau, Anthony Eisley. Travelers caught in a time mix-up are forced to battle in prehistoric jungles and the world of the year 5000. Mildly entertaining. (Dir: D. L. Hewitt, 82 mins.)

Journey to the Far Side of the Sun (Great Britain, 1969)*½ Roy Thinnes, Lynn Loring, Herbert Lom. Astronaut Thinnes discovers and explores a planet behind the sun. His melodramatic social life causes complications. (Dir: Robert Parrish.)

Journey to the Lost City (German, 1960)*½ Debra Paget, Paul Christian. Architect in India falls for a beautiful dancing girl, foils a revolt. Hashed-up fantastic adventure, dubbed in English. Far below what is normally expected of director Fritz Lang. (94 mins.)

Journey to the 7th Planet (1962)** John Agar, Greta Thyssen. A group of earthmen come to grips with beautiful women and strange forces on the planet number 7 in this predictable sci-fi entry. (Dir: Sidney Pink, 83 mins.)

Joy House (1965)**½ Jane Fonda, Alain Delon, Lola Albright. French director Rene Clement is only half successful in making this macabre suspense yarn work—but the half that does is worthwhile. Lola Albright is hiding her lover (a criminal) in a chamber in her Riviera villa, while cousin Jane Fonda is trying to seduce chauffeur Alain Delon. They all clash before the surprise ending. (Dir: Rene Clement, 98 mins.)

Joy in the Morning (1965)**½ Richard Chamberlain, Yvette Mimieux. The two attractive stars are earnest in this uneven love story about a young couple who face many of every day's problems during the early days of their marriage. Set in the early 1900's in a college town, the plot reads like a monthly installment in a ladies' magazine, but it's harmless stuff, and the stars are decorative. (Dir: Alex Segal, 103 mins.)

Joy of Living (1938)***½ Irene Dunne, Douglas Fairbanks Jr. Happy-go-lucky globe trotter romances a career-minded stage star. Delightful romantic comedy, with some good Jerome Kern tunes. (Dir: Tay Garnett, 100 mins.)

Joy Ride (1958)*** Regis Toomey, Ann Doran. Punch-packed little suspense drama about an "average man" who is terrorized by a bunch of young punks, turns the tables on them. Nothing big, but within its own framework quite good, including the performances and script. (Dir: Edward Bernds, 60 mins.)

Juarez (1949)**** Paul Muni, Brian Aherne, Bette Davis. Brilliantly acted, moving, dramatic story of the great Mexican hero. Muni adds another notch to his record of screen portrayals. (Dir: William Dieterle, 132 mins.)

Jubal (1956)***½ Glenn Ford, Ernest Borgnine, Rod Steiger, Felicia Farr. Superior western. Ford plays a drifter named Jubal Troop who is given a job by rancher (Borgnine)

373

and immediately starts off a chain reaction of jealousy, hate and violence. Rod Steiger's portrayal of a sadistic cowhand named "Pinky" is outstanding. (Dir: Delmer Daves, 101 mins.)

Jubilee Trail (1953)**½ Vera Ralston, Joan Leslie, Forrest Tucker, Pat O'Brien. Singer helps a young wife overcome skulduggery in old California. Costume drama has plenty of lavish scenes, but a rambling story. (Dir: Joseph Kane, 103 mins.)

Judex (France-Italy, 1964)**½ Channing Pollock, Francine Berge, Michel Vitold. Slow-moving refilming of a 1916 French silent serial about master-criminal Judex, whose main weapons are magic and style (he is portrayed by American magician Channing Pollock), and his arch-enemy, a beautiful woman who strips down to black for her nefarious deeds. Director Franju has aimed for the unabashed melodrama of the original, and overdoes it. But it's intermittently inventive and absorbing. (Dir: Georges Franju, 96 mins.)

Judge and Jake Wyler, The (1972)**½ Bette Davis, Doug McClure. Although Miss Davis is top-lined in this pilot film for an unsold TV series, it's really McClure's show. He plays an ex-con working for ex-Judge Davis, who runs a detective agency from her fortresslike home. (Dir: David Lowell Rich, 100 mins.)

Judge Dee and the Monastery Murders (1974)* Khigh Dhiegh. Chinese detective in the—ready for this?—seventh century. After a storm prompts Judge Dee (Khigh Dhiegh) and his entourage to stop at a monastery, the murder and mayhem begin. It's not Agatha Christie! Made-for-TV. (Dir: Jeremy Kagan, 72 mins.)

Judge Hardy's Children (1937)**½ Mickey Rooney, Lewis Stone. Andy and the judge are in Washington for this one and Andy saves the day for his dad. Good family entertainment. (Dir: George B. Seitz, 80 mins.)

Judge Horton and the Scottsboro Boys (1976)*** Arthur Hill, Vera Miles, Lewis J. Stadlin, Ken Kercheval, Ellen Barber. A drama about one of the most shameful miscarriages of justice in American history, the famous case of the "Scottsboro Boys." In Alabama back in 1931, nine poor, young and virtually illiterate black men were arrested and tried for the alleged rape of two promiscuous white women. Despite compelling evidence proving their innocence, they were convicted by several all-white, male juries, and some of them remained incarcerated for almost 20 years—their lives destroyed. This disturbing, absorbing history lesson about racial bigotry in the South at that time focuses on one courageous white judge, who reversed the jury's verdict and may well have saved the young men from being hanged. Hill plays the embattled Judge Horton, heading a generally good cast, skillfully directed by Fielder Cook. Based on the book "The Scottsboro Boys," by Professor Dan T. Carter. Made-for-TV. (Dir: Fielder Cook, 98 mins.)

Judge Steps Out (1949)**½ Alexander Knox, Ann Sothern. Probate judge leaves home and finds happiness as a cook in a roadside stand. Occasionally good, generally rather mild comedy-drama. (Dir: Boris Ingster, 91 mins.)

Judgment At Nuremberg (1961)**** Spencer Tracy, Burt Lancaster, Judy Garland, Richard Widmark, Montgomery Clift, Maximilian Schell, Marlene Dietrich. A searing, thoughtful film from producer Stanley Kramer, based on Abby Mann's memorable TV drama of the same name. Concerns the proceedings at the Nazi War Crimes Trials in Nuremberg and explores, among other things, the degree to which an individual or a nation can be held responsible for carrying out the orders of their leaders, however heinous the commands may be. Uniformly well acted with Schell winning, and deservedly so, an Academy Award for his portrayal. Several of the stars appeared for a fraction of their normal salaries and some in small roles, just because they wanted to be in this distinguished, disturbing movie. (Dir: Stanley Kramer, 178 mins.)

Judith (U.S.-British, 1966)* Sophia Loren, Peter Finch, Jack Hawkins. A mundane melodrama partially filmed in Israel. Sophia Loren struggles against the conflicts of the Middle East, and a trite script. Judith (Miss Loren) is suffering from the memory of her past, including a a tormented stay in a concentration camp, and her trail is motivated by revenge. Peter Finch does what he can as a dedicated Jewish freedom fighter. (Dir: Daniel Mann, 109 mins.)

Juggernaut (1974)****½** Omar Sharif, Richard Harris, David Hemmings, Shirley Knight, Ian Holm. Director Richard Lester must be given credit right off for whatever suspense this familiar tale generates. A cumbersome script and some bland performances, especially by Omar Sharif as a luxury liner's captain, don't help the yarn about a ship which has received threats of being blown up if a million dollar-plus ransom isn't paid. The excitement comes from a team of demolition experts. Richard Harris gives the film's best portrayal as the head of the demolition crew, but it's really a supporting role. (Dir: Richard Lester, 110 mins.)

Juggler, The (1953)******* Kirk Douglas, Milly Vitale. An absorbing drama about the Jewish refugee camps and the fight for rehabilitation; Kirk Douglas gives a powerful performance as a one-time circus juggler. (Dir: Edward Dmytryk, 86 mins.)

Juke Box Rhythm (1959)***** Jo Morrow, Brian Donlevy, Jack Jones. Inept musical film which has a plot reminiscent of the 1930 Ruby Keeler-Dick Powell films. A princess arrives in the U.S. for a shopping spree and falls in love (almost immediately) with a young singer whose father is a B'dway producer who's looking for an angel to back his show—an opus called "Juke Box Jamboree." (Dir: Arthur Dreifuss, 81 mins.)

Juke Girl (1942)****½** Ann Sheridan, Ronald Reagan. This was supposed to be the sordid tale of conditions among Florida's migratory workers but it emerges as a well-acted, tiresome melodrama. (Dir: Curtis Bernhardt, 90 mins.)

Jules and Jim (1962)******* Jeanne Moreau, Oskar Werner, Henry Serre. The story of two good friends and their alternatingly joyful, wayward, and tragic love for the same woman. In the hands of director Francois Truffaut, their saga becomes a touching and tender love story, which aroused the kind of controversy in 1962 that would be unlikely in the movie climate today. (Dir: Francois Truffaut, 104 mins.)

Julia Misbehaves (1948)****½** Greer Garson, Walter Pidgeon, Elizabeth Taylor. Farce about an ex-chorus girl who is her estranged husband's guest after an 18-year separation is ridiculous and lowers Miss Garson's dignity. She does manage to squeeze some laughs out of the proceedings, however. (Dir: Jack Conway, 99 mins.)

Julie (1956)****** Doris Day, Louis Jourdan, Barry Sullivan. Thoroughly unbelievable melodrama about an airline stewardess who is terrorized by her insane husband, menacingly overplayed by Jourdan. There's an almost laughable climactic sequence in which Miss Day single-handedly brings in an airliner. (Dir: Andrew L. Stone, 99 mins.)

Julie, the Redhead (French, 1962)****½** Pascale Petit, Daniel Gelin. Factory tycoon leaves a share to his former mistress; his son and her niece try to iron things out, love blossoms. Mildly amusing, mildly spicy comedy—some clever scenes, attractive performance by Petit. Dubbed in English.

Julius Caesar (1953)******** Marlon Brando, James Mason, John Gielgud, Edmond O'Brien. Shakespeare's tragedy of evil doings in Rome excellently done. Faithful rendition of the Bard by fine cast, filmed with taste and imagination, by Joseph Mankiewicz. Mason and Gielgud are especially good. (120 mins.)

Julius Caesar (British, 1970)****½** John Gielgud, Jason Robards, Charlton Heston, Richard Chamberlain, Robert Vaughn, Richard Johnson, Diana Rigg. There have been at least five earlier film versions of Shakespeare's political drama, the most recent being the '53 version starring Marlon Brando as Caesar. This version is curiously uneven, despite a generally superior cast. There are some excellent performances, particularly Gielgud playing Caesar and Richard Johnson as Cassius, but Jason Robards playing Brutus is embarrassingly bad. There still are scenes where you will enjoy the glories of Shakespeare's play. (Dir: Stuart Burge, 117 mins.)

Jumping Jacks (1952)****½** Dean Martin, Jerry Lewis, Mona Freeman. The boys join up for paratroop training, with the predictable gags coming thick and fast. Should provide

375

some pleasant moments. (Dir: Norman Taurog, 96 mins.)

June Bride (1948)*** Bette Davis, Robert Montgomery. Good sophisticated comedy-drama expertly played and chock full of excitement. Not fast and hilarious but enough chuckles to satisfy as Bob plays a magazine writer and Bette his boss. They're doing a June bride feature but the wedding takes place in March so it can make the June issue. (Dir: Bretaigne Windust, 97 mins.)

Jungle Book (1942)** Sabu, Joseph Calleia. Kipling's tale of a boy who grew up with the animals, learned their language, habits. Colorful, occasionally exciting, but sometimes pretty hard to swallow. (Dir: Zoltan Korda, 109 mins.)

Jungle Cat (1960)**½ Disney documentary on the feline jaguar, its natural life in the Amazon rain forest fully detailed. Unusual footage includes mating of yellow and black jaguar cats. (Dir: James Agar, 70 mins.)

Jungle Fighters (British, 1961)***½ Laurence Harvey, Richard Todd. Rugged war drama about a British patrol in Burma, a nasty private who breaks all the rules, and a dangerous trap set by the Japanese. Grim, mainly for the male audience; excellent performances. Alternate title: Long, the Short and the Tall, The. (Dir: Leslie Norman, 105 mins.)

Jungle Gold (1944-66)**½ Linda Stirling, Allan Lane, Duncan Renaldo. Feature version of serial "The Tiger Woman." Outlandish nonsense about a girl Tarzan type who helps the hero battle some wicked oil seekers. Good action for kids; adults may get a kick out of it too. Miss Stirling looks fetching in abbreviated garb. (Dirs: Spencer Bennet, Wallace Grissell, 100 mins.)

Jungle Headhunters (1951)**½ Interesting documentary travelogue, Cotlow expedition into headhunter territory on the Amazon. Good for armchair adventurers.

Junior Bonner (1972)*** Steve McQueen, Robert Preston, Ida Lupino. Junior Bonner (McQueen), onetime rodeo star, returns home to dazzle hometown fans with the skills he no longer has. McQueen is superb in this film, which begins as a reaching for lost frontiers and transforms into a family saga. Preston is out-

rageous as the father with one hand on the bottle and the other on someone's shoulder. (Dir: Sam Peckinpah, 100 mins.)

Junior Miss (1945)*** Peggy Ann Garner, Allyn Joslyn. Cute little teen-age comedy which should remind us of how our youngsters behaved during the '40's. Based on the hit Broadway play. (Dir: George Seaton, 94 mins.)

Jupiter's Darling (1955)** Esther Williams, Howard Keel, Marge & Gower Champion, George Sanders. Gay doings in old Rome, as Hannibal Keel captures gorgeous Esther and stops the battle while they romance. Historical spoof doesn't quite make it, so except for the Champions' dancing it's pretty much of a drag. (Dir: George Sidney, 96 mins.)

Just Across the Street (1952)**½ Ann Sheridan, John Lund. An often amusing comedy about mistaken identity and the incidents leading up to the final confrontation and happy conclusion. Miss Sheridan is an old hand at comedy dialogue and a good supporting cast, add to the film's appeal. (Dir: Joseph Pevney, 78 mins.)

Just Around the Corner (1938)** Shirley Temple, Joan Davis, Bill Robinson. Shirley dances with "Bojangles" but close your eyes for the rest of this silly film. It's a depression story and it will depress you. (Dir: Irving Cummings, 70 mins.)

Just for You (1952)**½ Bing Crosby, Jane Wyman, Ethel Barrymore. Pleasant comedy-drama with many musical moments thrown in for good measure. Bing plays a successful B'dway producer who sets out to win his son and daughter's affection after a long period of concentrating only on his career. Miss Wyman plays the woman in Bing's life and young Natalie Wood (age 14) plays Bing's daughter. (Dir: Elliott Nugent, 104 mins.)

Just Great—See: Tout Va Bien

Just Imagine (1930)*** John Garrick, El Brendel, Maureen O'Sullivan, Marjorie White, Hobart Bosworth, Kenneth Thomson. Beguiling bit of antique musical frumpery, about New York City past, present, future—e.g., 1880, 1930 and 1980. New Yorkers of the 1980's all have numbers instead of names, their own airplanes to get around in, with landing pads all over the many-tiered city. A bizarre trip to Mars is also included, where everything comes double or upside-down. Songs by B. G. De Sylva, Lew Brown, and others. (Dir: David Butler, 102 mins.)

Just Like a Woman (Great Britain, 1968)**½** Wendy Craig, Francis Matthews. Bright, witty dialogue paces this situation comedy about a TV producer and his somewhat eccentric wife as their marriage breaks up. Flimsy plot, but the gags, particularly in-jokes about British TV, abound. Written and directed by Robert Fuest. (89 mins.)

Just Off Broadway (1942)** Lloyd Nolan, Phil Silvers, Marjorie Weaver. Weak Michael Shayne adventure with the great detective serving on a murder jury but solving the case on the side. (Dir: Herbert I. Leeds, 66 mins.)

Just This Once (1952)**½** Janet Leigh, Peter Lawford. Pleasant comedy about the ins and outs of romance. The attractive stars go through their paces as if they really enjoy their work.

Juvenile Court (1973)**** A remarkable study of a juvenile court in Memphis, Tennessee. You'll see the frightened children, worried about their punishment as well as their crimes, and you'll see a number of the generally sympathetic counselors who take up their cases with gratifying dedication—cases ranging from prostitution, to child abuse, drug addiction and armed robbery. One of the many things you will remember from this insightful look at an American institution is the character of the judge of the court, Kenneth A. Turner. Wiseman clearly believes that the juvenile offender is the victim of society and therefore its ward, and that children in such courts are the results of institutional neglect and abuse, and of misunderstanding and mis-education on the part of the responsible parents and schools. (Dir: Frederick Wiseman, 135 mins.)

Juvenile Jungle (1958)*½** Corey Allen, Rebecca Welles. Teenage beach party turns into violence, and crime. Painfully familiar delinquency drama.

J. W. Coop (1972)**** Cliff Robertson, Geraldine Page, Christina Ferrare. Accurate, honest, often touching story about an ex-con (Robert-

son) who becomes a star of the small-time western rodeo circuit after a ten-year hitch in the pen. Robertson produced, directed, and co-authored this appealing film. One of his accomplishments, and that of his cameraman, Frank Stanley, is some extraordinary rodeo footage that captures the challenge and beauty of bronco riding. Miss Ferrare is lovely playing Robertson's funny, candid girl friend. Shot on location in Oklahoma and other towns in the West and Midwest. (113 mins.)

Kaleidoscope (British, 1966)** Warren Beatty, Susannah York, Clive Revill, Eric Porter. A playboy (Beatty) tries a cleverly crooked way to beat the European gambling casinos in this visually pretty but placid caper. (Dir: Jack Smight, 103 mins.)

Kanal (Polish, 1957)**** Grim and powerful drama of Polish patriots using the sewers of Warsaw in an attempt to escape from the Nazis during the uprising of 1944. Excellent in direction and performance, unrelieved in its intensity. English-dubbed. (Dir: Andrzej Wajda, 91 mins.)

Kangaroo (1952)** Peter Lawford, Maureen O'Hara. The beautiful on-location photography (Australia) is the best feature of this adventure drama. Lawford is miscast as a sailor who becomes involved in a muddled mistaken identity plot. Miss O'Hara thinks the Australian landscape is the County Cork and plays it accordingly. (Dir: Lewis Milestone, 84 mins.)

Kansas City Bomber (1972)*½** Raquel Welch, Kevin McCarthy. Miss Welch in a numbered jersey and all the phony slam-bang excitement of the roller derby might interest a few diehard derby devotees, but those who also expect a plot or decent writing will look and listen in vain. It's the "All About Eve" of the roller rinks — the up-and-coming skater (Welch) ready and willing to replace the boozing and aging former queen of the track, Helena Kallianiotes, who gives the film's best performance. ("All About Eve" we remind you was a marvelous film —this is a sleazy one.) (Dir: Jerrold Freedman, 99 mins.)

Kansas City Confidential (1952)****½** John Payne, Coleen Gray, Preston Foster, Neville Brand. Sharply done crime story of bank robbers. Suspense chase from Kansas City to Guatemala maintains interest and pace. A graphic tale that chickens out for a "nice" ending. (Dir: Phil Karlson, 98 mins.)

Kansas City Massacre, The (1975)****½** Dale Robertson, Bo Hopkins, Lynn Loring, Scott Brady. Robertson is back playing Melvin Purvis, G-Man, in this tough gangster saga set during the Depression. Has the high production values of the previous made-for-TV film. Follows the events leading up to the infamous Kansas City massacre at the Union Plaza Railroad Station, in which two gunmen and five officers were killed and twelve innocent bystanders were wounded. Robertson is all quiet swagger and authority as the G-Man who's out to nail Pretty Boy Floyd, John Dillinger and Baby Face Nelson. Made-for-TV. (Dir: Dan Curtis, 100 mins.)

Kansas Raiders (1951)****½** Audie Murphy, Brian Donlevy, Marguerite Chapman. Exciting Western adventure that benefits greatly from an assorted group of young actors playing famous outlaws who joined Quantrill's Raiders and destroyed Lawrence, Kansas. Audie Murphy plays Jesse James, Tony Curtis is Kit Dalton, Dewey Martin and James Best are the Younger Brothers and Richard Long is Frank James. (Dir: Ray Enright, 80 mins.)

Kapo (France-Italy-Yugoslavia, 1960)****½** Susan Strasberg, Emmanuele Riva. Disguised Jewish girl in Nazi prison camps becomes hardened, murderously intent on her own survival. Movie begins well, is effectively graphic about the horrors of the holocaust and imprisonment, with Strasberg apt as a wide-eyed Jewish innocent (reminiscent of the starring Broadway role of Anne Frank that rocketed her to fame); but the subsequent melodramatics prove too much for Strasberg, and the film is not worthy of the momentous realities involved. (Dir: Gillo Pontecorvo, 116 mins.)

Karate (1961)***** Joel Holt, Reiko Okada. In Japan, an adventurer comes into possession of a mysterious coin holding the key to the location of a fortune in platinum. This melodrama was filmed in Japan in a slipshod manner.

Kate McShane (1975)****½** Anne Meara, Christine Belford, Cal Bellini. Comedienne Anne Meara plays a pugnacious Denver, Colorado, lawyer, defending a blueblood in the stabbing of a no-good husband. It's all Kate McShane as she, backed by her Irish dad, battles a pompous D.A., throws snowballs at her Jesuit brother. Despite her efforts, this predictable lady-lawyer pilot never really takes off, although it did result in a TV series. Made-for-TV. (Dir: Martin Chomsky, 72 mins.)

Katerina Izmailova (Russian, 1967)*****½** Galina Vishnevskaya, N. Boyarsky. Good version of the dramatic opera by Russian composer Dimitri Shostakovich. First performed in 1934, the opera is about a woman whose illicit affair leads to murder and tragedy in Siberia. Bolshoi Opera company star Vishnevskaya is excellent in the title role. (Dir: Mikhail Shapiro, 118 mins.)

Kathleen (1941)***½** Shirley Temple, Herbert Marshall, Laraine Day. Corny bit of hokum about a widower who neglects his daughter then sends for Laraine Day to straighten the child out and you know the rest. (Dir: Harold S. Bucquet, 88 mins.)

Kathy O' (1958)*****½** Patty McCormack, Dan Duryea, Jan Sterling. Publicity man is assigned to a brat of a child movie star, gets involved when she runs away. Plenty of fun in this Hollywood-behind-the-scenes comedy drama. Well played, highly enjoyable. (Dir: Jack Sher, 99 mins.)

Katie Did It (1951)***½** Ann Blyth, Mark Stevens. Moderately entertaining comedy about a small town girl who runs into a New York City slicker who just won't take no for a final answer. Miss Blyth is cute and Stevens has an abundance of persuasive charm. (Dir: Frederick de Cordova, 81 mins.)

Keegans, The (1976)***½** Adam Roarke, Spencer Milligan, Paul Shenar, Judd Hirsch, Heather Menzies, Tom Clancy, Joan Leslie. New York Irish family solidarity is the pitch. Pro football-player Pat Keegan (Milligan) takes revenge when his sister (Menzies) is beaten up, only to be held for murder. The complicated plotting on the sordid underworld is familiar stuff, overshadowing the Irish family bond. Made-for-TV. (Dir: John Badham, 72 mins.)

Keep 'Em Flying (1941)**½ Bud Abbott and Lou Costello, Martha Raye. Early Abbott & Costello comedy with all the slapstick antics that made the pair famous. Martha Raye plays twin sisters. (Dir: Arthur Lubin, 86 mins.)

Keep It Clean (British, 1959)*½ Ronald Shiner, Diane Hart. Unsubtle comedy about a promoter trying to push a new cleaning detergent.

Keep Talking, Baby (French, 1961) * Eddie Constantine, Mariella Lozzi. Eddie's framed for murder again, but escapes prison to round up the gang who put him there. Ridiculously familiar hard-boiled mystery dubbed in English.

Keeper of the Flame (1942)*** Spencer Tracy, Katharine Hepburn. Good drama, superbly acted by one of our better screen teams. Tracy is doing an article on the death of a great American and the excitement mounts when the widow, Miss Hepburn, finally admits that the great American was a fascist. (Dir: George Cukor, 100 mins.)

Kelly and Me (1957)**½ Van Johnson, Piper Laurie, Martha Hyer. Song-and-dance man hits the big time when he teams up with a smart police dog. Fairly pleasing show-biz drama. (Dir: Robert Z. Leonard, 86 mins.)

Kelly's Heroes (1970)** Clint Eastwood, Don Rickles, Donald Sutherland. Clumsy copy of "The Dirty Dozen." Soldiers, turned plunderers under the command of Eastwood, march into German-occupied town to rob the bank during World War II. Sutherland creates an anachronistic role of a spaced-out hippie tank commander which is beautiful to watch, despite the rest of the film. (Dir: Brian Hutton, 149 mins.)

Kenner (1969)** Jim Brown, Madlyn Rhue, Robert Coote. Brown is a two-fisted adventurer in this predictable yarn about a man out to avenge his partner's murder amid the teeming background of Bombay, India. You've seen it a thousand times before. (Dir: Steve Sekely, 87 mins.)

Kentuckian, The (1955)**½ Burt Lancaster. Lancaster stars as a two-fisted frontiersman in this adventure

tale set in the early 1800's. The plot is filled with rugged action, romance, and an ample amount of comedy. Diana Lynn, as a shy and proper "School Marm," stands out in a good supporting cast which includes Dianne Foster, John McIntire, and Una Merkel. (Dir: Burt Lancaster, 104 mins.)

Kentucky (1938)*** Loretta Young, Richard Greene, Walter Brennan. Horse racing story has nothing new to contribute but it's pleasant entertainment and very well done. (Dir: David Butler, 94 mins.)

Kentucky Moonshine (1938)*** Ritz Brothers. If you don't like the Ritzes, run for the hills because the boys disguised as Kentucky hillbillies have this all to themselves. (Dir: David Butler, 85 mins.)

Kenya—Country of Treasure (1964)* William Sylvester, June Ritchie. Syndicate prospecting for uranium in East Africa detoured by gang of crooks. No claim on excitement for this strikeout. (85 mins.)

Kes (British, 1970)**** David Bradley, Colin Welland, Lynne Perrie. A beautiful, tender story about a 15-year-old Yorkshire boy who tames and trains his pet—a kestrel hawk. Shooting entirely on location in northern England, with a largely nonprofessional cast, director Ken Loach coaxed some glorious natural performances from these adept scene stealers. Bradley is particularly marvelous while training his beloved "Kes," or listening to various boorish adults including a frustrated athletic coach at his school. Only drawback to this luminous tale is the heavy Yorkshire accents, which are not always intelligible to American audiences. One of the first English-language films where you sometimes yearn for subtitles. A delicate, haunting film with pathos and humor. (110 mins.)

Kettles in the Ozarks, The (1956)** Marjorie Main, Arthur Hunnicutt. This one is without the benefit of Percy Kilbride's (Pa Kettle) special participation. Ma Kettle visits Pa's lazy brother, played in the screen hillbilly tradition by Arthur Hunnicutt, and gets in the middle of a heap of trouble with bootleggers and the law. (Dir: Charles Lamont, 81 mins.)

Kettles on Old MacDonald's Farm, The (1957)** Marjorie Main, Parker

Fennelly. Last Kettle epic (without Pa Kettle as played by Percy Kilbride) and the least effective. Some sight gags still work but Percy is sorely missed. (Dir: Virgil Vogel, 80 mins.)

Key, The (1958)*** Sophia Loren, William Holden, Trevor Howard. A stellar lineup, but this drama doesn't quite deliver the dramatic impact it sets out to. The premise involves a man (Howard) who gives a duplicate key to his friend (Holden) to Sophia Loren's apartment, with the instructions that he must do the same when and if Howard is killed in enemy action during WW II. Trevor Howard is first rate as always and there are enough interesting scenes and issues raised to make this worth seeing. (Dir: Carol Reed, 125 mins.)

Key Largo (1948)*** Humphrey Bogart, Lauren Bacall, Edward G. Robinson, Claire Trevor. Not a great movie but John Huston manages to get so much out of his wonderful cast that you're bound to be entertained by this gangster melodrama set in Key West, Florida. (Dir: John Huston, 101 mins.)

Key Man, The (British, 1957)*½ Lee Patterson, Hy Hazell. Radio reporter solves a murder and robbery. Remember radio? Otherwise there's nothing to remember. (Dir: Montgomery Tully, 78 mins.)

Key to the City (1950)**½ Clark Gable, Loretta Young. A light comedy romance for indiscriminating film fans, as small town mayors meet and fall in love during a mayors' convention in San Francisco. The action is predictable but fast paced. (Dir: George Sidney, 99 mins.)

Key West (1973)*½ Stephen Boyd, Ford Rainey, Tiffany Bolling, Sheree North. Yawning, predictable, and lazy detective yarn that doesn't work too hard for originality. Boyd is a CIA agent floating around in Florida when he becomes the victim of revenge-seeking maniac Rainey. Beautiful girls adorn this tale of upper-class evil. Made-for-TV. (Dir: Anthony Martin, 100 mins.)

Key Witness (1960)**½ Jeffrey Hunter, Pat Crowley. Hard-hitting drama about a man who is a witness to a crime and the terror he and his family face because of it. Some brutal scenes make this strong stuff,

not for the squeamish. (Dir: Phil Karlson, 82 mins.)

Keys of the Kingdom, The (1944)*** Gregory Peck, Thomas Mitchell, Roddy McDowall. Slow, rambling, occasionally moving adaptation of A. J. Cronin's novel about the life of a missionary. Peck's first major film and he does a nice job. (Dir: John M. Stahl, 137 mins.)

Khartoum (1966)***½ Charlton Heston, Laurence Olivier. Some well-directed gigantic battle scenes and Olivier's splendid performance are two of the best features in this better-than-most spectacle film. Major scenes filmed in the desert along the Nile, as historical fact and Hollywood fiction are combined to tell the tale of confrontation in 1883 between British General Charles Gordon (Heston) and the Arab leader named Mahdi (Olivier) involved in the siege of Khartoum in the Sudan. Scene between Heston and Olivier is excellently handled by director Basil Dearden. (134 mins.)

Khyber Patrol (1954)**½ Richard Egan, Dawn Addams. The Empire vs. The Rebels in this familiar English adventure film. O.K. for the kids and action fans. (Dir: Seymour Friedman, 71 mins.)

Kid for Two Farthings (British, 1956)**** Celia Johnson, Diana Dors, Jonathan Ashmore. Lad in the London slums believes a one-horned goat is a magic unicorn that will bring him luck. Something different; touching, superbly directed (Carol Reed) comedy-drama, a fine film. (113 mins.)

Kid from Brooklyn, The (1946)*** Danny Kaye, Virginia Mayo, Vera-Ellen. Remake of Harold Lloyd's comedy "The Milky Way" and although not as good, Kaye manages to make it fun. Story concerns a milkman who is turned into a prize fighter. Leo McCarey directed.

Kid from Left Field, The (1953)**½ Dan Dailey, Anne Bancroft, Lloyd Bridges. Peanut vendor used his son, operating as batboy, to break a baseball team's slump. Pleasant, but doesn't exactly burn up the league. (Dir: Harmon Jones, 80 mins.)

Kid from Spain, The (1932)*** Eddie Cantor, Robert Young. Eddie Cantor at the top of his movie form—he's a bullfighter in this song and jokes epic. Cantor fans will eat it up. (Dir: Leo McCarey, 110 mins.)

Kid Galahad (1962)**½ Elvis Presley, Lola Albright, Gig Young. Another vehicle which shows off Elvis' singing, gyrating, and limited acting talents. The tale is a boxing yarn and all the stereotypes found in such films are present. Elvis sings many songs which should please his followers. (Dir: Phil Karlson, 95 mins.)

Kid Glove Killer (1941)*** Van Heflin, Marsha Hunt. A superior Grade B crime film which uses police labs instead of chases and other contrivances. Many of our modern, adult crime stories stem from the type of thinking that went into this film.

Kid Millions (1934)*** Eddie Cantor, Ann Sothern, Ethel Merman, George Murphy. Another of Cantor's extravagant, song filled comedies made under the Sam Goldwyn banner. Cantor's a millionaire this time around and he has a good supporting cast including the raucous Ethel Merman. (Dir: Roy Del Ruth, 100 mins.)

Kid Rodelo (1966)** Don Murray, Janet Leigh, Broderick Crawford. Dull western made in Spain. Don Murray's very brave as he tries to fight off the greedy crooks after a cache of stolen gold, and keep an eye on fetching Janet Leigh at the same time. Not worth keeping an eye on this oater. (Dir: Richard Carlson, 91 mins.)

Kidnaped (1938)**½ Freddie Bartholomew, Warner Baxter. Robert Louis Stevenson's classic altered for the screen with just the title and character names maintained. Good juvenile adventure tale. (Dir: Alfred Werker, 90 mins.)

Kidnapped (1960)**½ Peter Finch, James MacArthur. Straightforward, restrained Disney production of Robert Louis Stevenson's classic about a young heir whose scheming uncle arranges for his kidnapping, and his adventures at sea with a stalwart Jacobite (anti-King George) Scotsman. Movie lacks vigor, excitement of book's previous filmings. It's well acted. The director is not related to the author. (Dir: Robert Stevenson)

Kidnapped (British, 1971)*** Michael Caine, Trevor Howard, Jack Hawkins, Donald Pleasence. The fourth cinematization of the famous classic by Robert Louis Stevenson,

and a lesser-known sequel, "David Balfour." The film deals with the fighting between the English and the Scottish during the end of the 18th century. The main character is the swashbuckling Alan Breck, played with flair by Caine. David Balfour has been nicely woven into the story as an aid in Breck's fight for Scotland. The Scottish highlands steal the show. (Dir: Delbert Mann, 100 mins.)

Kill Her Gently (British, 1958)** Marc Lawrence, Maureen Connell, Griffith Jones. Two escaped convicts are talked into bumping off the wife of an ex-mental patient. Cheaply made but adequate crime drama. (Dir: Charles Saunders, 73 mins.)

Kill Me Tomorrow (British, 1957)** Pat O'Brien, Lois Maxwell. Crime reporter needing money for his son's operation smashes a diamond smuggling ring. "Kill Me Tomorrow" is a bore today. (Dir: Terence Fisher, 80 mins.)

Kill or Cure (British, 1962)** Terry-Thomas, Dennis Price, Lionel Jeffries, Moira Redmond. Terry-Thomas as a private sleuth investigating murder at a health resort. The gap-toothed comic finds it difficult to carry a film on his shoulders alone, and gets little help from the script.

Kill the Umpire (1950)**½ William Bendix, Una Merkel. Pretty funny film about an umpire's life—his training, his job and his love of baseball.

Killdozer (1974)** Clint Walker, Carl Betz, Neville Brand, and James Wainwright all play construction workers on a desolate island, but stunt man Carey Loftin is the real star of the film. Loftin manages a battle between an unmanned bulldozer and a power shovel in the main act, so if you dig machine duels, tune in. Made-for-TV. (Dir: Jerry London.)

Killer Bees (1974)** Gloria Swanson, Kate Jackson, Edward Albert, Craig Stevens. Old-time movie fans will be curious to see the indomitable Swanson once again in this predictable chiller about a strange family of winegrowers who keep killer bees on the premises. Albert is the prodigal grandson returned with his pregnant fiancee (Miss Jackson), and their visit triggers the macabre finale. It's Miss Swanson's and the bees' show. Made-for-

381

TV. (Dir: Curtis Harrington, 90 mins.)

Killer by Night (1971)** Robert Wagner, Diane Baker. One of TV's favorite plots—about the highly communicable disease which invades the city, requiring doctors to find the carrier before an epidemic breaks out—gets a new twist. This time the carrier is an armed, dangerous cop killer, all of which sets up a contrived film peopled by familiar, competent performers. Made-for-TV. (Dir: Bernard Mc-Eveety, 100 mins.)

Killer Elite, The (1975)** James Caan, Robert Duvall, Arthur Hill, Bo Hopkins, Gig Young, Helmut Dantine. Double-crosses abound in this confused action picture that centers on the operations of the fictional company, Communications Integrity Associates, specializing in political assassination. Caan and Duvall are the opposing agents whose struggle decides the fate of a Chinese political activist visiting San Francisco. Fast editing makes the surfeit of carnage less offensive than many of director Sam Peckinpah's previous efforts. Story much like "Three Days of the Condor." (123 mins.)

Killer Force (1975)*½ Telly Savalas, Peter Fonda, Hugh O'Brian, O. J. Simpson. Action melodrama about a diamond heist in South Africa which doesn't tax your brain. It's the same old stuff! Telly Savalas as a security officer at the diamond mine, and Peter Fonda as his seemingly innocent sidekick add a little bite to the proceedings. (Dir: Michael Winner, 100 mins.)

Killer Is Loose (1956)*** Joseph Cotten, Rhonda Fleming. Bank robber vows vengeance upon the detective who nabbed him. Suspenseful, exciting drama. (Dir: Budd Boetticher, 73 mins.)

Killer Shrews, The (1959)* James Best, Ingrid Goude. Scientist on an island creates giant flesh-eating mammals which break loose during a storm. Slapdash sci-fi thriller, with shrews that . . . . ugh.

Killer Spy (French, 1963)** Jean Marais, Nadja Tiller. Retired secret agent stumbles across a body and goes to work once again trapping a spy ring. Routine but fairly actionful espionage thriller, with Marais

in good form. Dubbed in English. (Dir: Georges Lampik, 82 mins.)

Killer That Stalked New York, The (1950)**½ Evelyn Keyes, Charles Korvin. A diamond smuggler enters the U. S. carrying a contagious disease and the fuse is set in a wild search to save the city from death. Some tense moments. (Dir: Earl McEvory, 79 mins.)

Killer Who Wouldn't Die, The (1976)*½ Mike Connors, Gregoire Aslan, Mariette Hartley. Connors plays a former homicide detective who runs a charter-boat service, but just can't stay away from intrigue and trouble. Before you can reel in a marlin, Connors is hot on the trail of a killer of an undercover agent. Supporting cast is impressive—Samantha Eggar, Patrick O'Neal, Clu Gulager, Robert Hooks. The Hawaii location shots add to the lacklustre production. Made-for-TV. (Dir: William Hale, 98 mins.)

Killers, The (1946)**** Burt Lancaster, Ava Gardner, Edmond O'Brien. Insurance detective unravels the killing of a washed up boxer. Suspenseful, excellently produced and directed crime drama, extending Hemingway's taut tale. (Dir: Robert Siodmak, 105 mins.)

Killers, The (1964)**½ Lee Marvin, John Cassavetes, Angie Dickinson, Ronald Reagan. Two gunmen search for a mechanic who has double-crossed a crime boss. Remake of Hemingway's story was originally scheduled for TV first, but wound up in theaters. Some good touches in the direction, but it still looks like a TV show. (Dir: Don Siegel, 95 mins.)

Killers Are Challenged (Italian, 1965)** Richard Harrison, Wandisa Guida. Undercover agent has a task to recover some important plans. Routine spy thriller dubbed in English, lots of action, little sense. (Dir: Martin Donan, 89 mins.)

Killers' Cage (1958)*½ Terry Becker, Elisa Loti, Ed Nelson. The FBI wants a former crime syndicate member to return to the U.S. and testify—the mob wants him rubbed out. So-so suspense melodrama made in Mexico. Alternate title: **Code of Silence.**

Killer's Carnival (1965)** Stewart Granger, Lex Barker. Viennese narcotics smuggling, Roman secret agents, and Brazilian political assassination are on this bland menu of three plodding adventure stories. Low-budget entry. (Dirs: Albert Cardiff, Robert Lynn, and Sheldon Reynolds, 95 mins.)

Killer's Kiss (1955)** Jamie Smith, Irene Kane. Pug saves a girl from a lecherous dance hall owner. Over-arty crime melodrama is hindered by adolescent treatment.

Killers of Kilimanjaro (British, 1960) ** Robert Taylor, Anne Aubrey. An adventure story set in deepest Africa has Taylor cast as an engineer who is surveying the territory for the eventual building of the first African railway. There are the compulsory shots of wildlife and the close calls on each principal in the cast. (Dir: Richard Thorpe, 91 mins.)

Killers of the East (Italian, 1958)* Lex Barker, Florence Mari, Paul Muller. Girl is rescued from tribesmen as she is about to be sacrificed. Poor jungle melodrama, ineptly produced. Dubbed in English.

Killers Three (1969)*½ Robert Walker, Diane Varsi, Dick Clark. Unconvincing saga of a moonshiner who wants to quit the profession by stealing $200,000 from his boss. Robert Walker, son of the late actor and Jennifer Jones, is lousy, and the supporting cast is even more frightening, especially disk jockey Dick Clark—who produced this crap—wearing glasses and a moustache. (Dir: Bruce Kessler, 88 mins.)

Killing, The (1956)*** Sterling Hayden, Coleen Gray. Crooks plan a daring racetrack robbery. Some thrills in this crime meller plus a fine performance by Marie Windsor. Direction by Stanley Kubrick, a newcomer at that time, is unnecessarily arty but interesting. (83 mins.)

Killing Game, The (French, 1967)**½ Jean-Pierre Cassel, Claudine Auger. An often lovely, yet overly tricky film done in an almost pop-art style. A young couple drive a rich young man to distraction. There are some good scenes, but the overall effect is strained. (Dir: Alain Jessua, 94 mins.)

Killing Urge—See: Jet Storm

Kim (1951)*** Errol Flynn, Dean Stockwell, Paul Lukas. Rudyard Kipling's exciting tale of a little white boy who grew up as a Hindu in India during the 19th Century becomes a colorful screen adventure for young and old alike. Young Dean Stockwell registers just the right spirit as the lucky lad caught up in a world of suspense and intrigue. (Dir: Victor Saville, 113 mins.)

Kimberley Jim (South African, 1965) ** Jim Reeves, Madeleine Usher, Clive Parnell. Two American con men win a diamond claim and become involved in the conflicts between the town tyrant and everybody else. Naive action drama with plenty of rough edges, but for all that rather pleasant. (Dir: Emil Nofal, 82 mins.)

Kind Hearts and Coronets (British, 1949)**** Alec Guinness, Dennis Price, Valerie Hobson, Joan Greenwood. Devilishly clever young man intends to claim a legacy by eliminating the remaining heirs. Fiendishly funny satiric comedy, handling murder as a joke and getting away with it. Guinness has a tour de farce in eight distinct roles. (Dir: Robert Hamer, 104 mins.)

Kind Lady (1935)*** Aline MacMahon, Basil Rathbone. Murdering criminals take over the house of a recluse, intending to rob and kill her. Suspenseful melodrama. (Dir: George E. Seitz, 80 mins.)

Kind Lady (1951)**½ Ethel Barrymore, Maurice Evans, Angela Lansbury. A chilling mystery about a sinister retinue of servants who invade an old lady's home and terrorize her. Top rate performance by the talented cast. (Dir: John Sturges, 78 mins.)

Kind of Loving, A (British, 1962)*** Alan Bates, June Ritchie, Thora Hird, Bert Palmer. Young love, realistic style. Nicely played by Bates and Ritchie. Interestingly directed by John Schlesinger, his first feature. (112 mins.)

Kindar the Invulnerable (Italian, 1964)* Mark Forest, Rosalba Neri. Once again a muscular hero fights to free his countrymen against all odds. Silly English-dubbed adventure.

King: A Filmed Record . . . Montgomery to Memphis (1970)**** Brilliant, eloquent documentary, recording the remarkable life of Rev. Martin Luther King, Jr. It traces King's leadership from the beginnings of the civil rights movement in 1955 to his tragic assassination in 1968. Packs a terrific emotional wallop including his historic "I have a dream" speech at the Washington Monument, "Bull" Connor the racist sheriff shouting orders to jail "that blind nigger" (singer Al Hibbler), and finally the scenes of Sen. Robert Kennedy at King's funeral. The readings by a variety of cinema stars are superfluous, but the film is one of the important and most moving historical documents of this or any age. Produced originally by Ely Landau as a fund raiser for the Martin Luther King Special Fund. Longer versions run over four hours. Sequences supervised by directors Joseph L. Mankiewicz and Sidney Lumet. (153 mins.)

King and Country (British, 1964) ***½ Dirk Bogarde, Tom Courtenay, Leo McKern. Sensitive private is placed on trial for desertion during World War I, is defended by a Captain convinced of his innocence. Brutal study of the injustices of war may prove too strong for the more delicate viewers; but it packs quite a punch, is excellently acted. (Dir: Joseph Losey, 90 mins.)

King and Four Queens, The (1957) ** Clark Gable, Eleanor Parker, Jo Van Fleet. King Gable locks horns with four beautiful would-be-widows and their gun-toting mother-in-law for a prize of $100,000 in gold. Picture jumps from comedy to drama without much conviction. (Dir: Raoul Walsh, 86 mins.)

King and I, The (1956) **** Yul Brynner, Deborah Kerr. Rodgers and Hammerstein's magnificent Broadway musical makes a memorable film, enhanced by sumptuous settings and other superb production values, Brynner struts about creating the perfect picture of the absolute monarch as the King of Siam, and Miss Kerr matches his sharply defined performance as the spirited British schoolteacher who is hired to tutor the royal offspring. The familiar Rodgers and Hammerstein score, one of the celebrated team's better efforts, includes such showstoppers as "Hello, Young Lovers," "Getting to Know You," and "Shall We Dance." (Dir: Walter Lang, 133 mins.)

King and the Chorus Girl (1937) ***½ Fernand Gravet, Joan Blondell. Excellent comedy about a king who falls in love with a commoner. Very popular subject in 1937. Screen play by Norman Krasna and Groucho Marx. (100 mins.)

King Creole (1959) **½ Elvis Presley, Carolyn Jones, Walter Matthau. Young bus boy on the verge of delinquency gets his break when he is forced to sing at a nightclub, makes a hit. Presley goes dramatic in this tale of New Orleans, and does pretty well. Fairly good melodrama. (Dir: Michael Curtiz, 116 mins.)

King in New York, A (British, 1957) **** Charles Chaplin, Dawn Addams, Michael Chaplin, Phil Brown. A remarkable, uneven political satire, written and directed by Chaplin. He plays the title role, a deposed European monarch, who visits America in the mid-'50's during the hysteria of McCarthyism and neo-fascism. Hilarious scene as the King is tricked into appearing on live TV by a sultry pitch-lady (Addams). Serious statements from the mouth of a young "radical" schoolboy, played by Chaplin's son Michael, who informs on his parents' friends, thereby saving his parents' teaching job. This during a period when teachers were, in fact, being blacklisted. Ironic that this film about political repression was itself banned from theaters in America for more than 15 years.

King in Shadow (German, 1957) ** O. W. Fischer, Horst Buchholz, Odile Versois. Brain specialist determines that a young king is not mad, but extremely sensitive; his efforts to help him lead to triumph, then tragedy. Heavy English-dubbed historical drama, glum going. (Dir: Harold Braun, 87 mins.)

King Kong (1933) **** Fay Wray, Robert Armstrong, Bruce Cabot. The famous shocker about the giant ape captured and displayed in New York, only to escape and wreak havoc in the city. Years after release, it remains a marvel of technical achievement as well as a thrilling, actionful experience. (Dirs: Merian C. Cooper, Earnest Schroedsack, 110 mins.)

King Kong Escapes (Japan, 1967) * Rhodes Reason, Mie Hama. Again King Kong's eye for a beautiful woman lands him in trouble. He gets involved in international plots, and comes face-to-face with a mechanical replica of himself. As usual, Kong fares better than the small-minded humans. Escape! (Dir: Inoshira Honda, 96 mins.)

384

King Kong vs. Godzilla (Japan, 1962) *½ Michael Keith, James Yagi. Typical Japanese sci-fi shenanigans provide a field day for special-effects crews and a day off for script writers. It's all-out war between the two monsters. (Dir: Thomas Montgomery, 90 mins.)

King Lear (British-Danish, 1970) ***½ Paul Scofield, Irene Worth, Alan Webb, Jack MacGowran, Cyril Cusack. Exciting production of the Shakespeare classic about the aging, raging king who becomes senile before his death. Two of the greatest theater artists in the world, director Peter Brook and actor Paul Scofield playing Lear, have left their indelible mark on this imaginative version. Shot on location in the cold climate of Denmark's Jutland Peninsula with a uniformly stellar ensemble. Curiously enough, Lear's "storm" scene is not, to this critic at least, the high point of the film. Scofield is restrained, eloquent, and deeply moving. Major shortcoming of the work is that so many cuts have been made in the text that those who do not know the play extremely well will occasionally be unable to follow the narrative. (Dir: Peter Brook, 137 mins.)

King of Burlesque (1936) *** Warner Baxter, Alice Faye, Jack Oakie. A nice score and good performances make this musical entertaining. Story of a burlesque producer who loses his shirt in the arts offers nothing to the film. (Dir: Sidney Lanfield, 83 mins.)

King of Hearts (French-Italian, 1966) **** Alan Bates, Pierre Brasseur, Genevieve Bujold, Jean-Claude Brialy. A beautiful antiwar film, with underplayed satire. Toward the end of World War I a Scottish private (Bates) comes to a French town to investigate a bomb threat. The only residents he finds are the residents of the local insane asylum. You will find a funny, touching parable, wonderfully well acted, especially by Bates and by Bujold playing an enchanting acrobat. English subtitles. (Dir: Philippe de Broca, 102 mins.)

King of Jazz (1930) **½ Bing Crosby, Paul Whiteman. Musical revue in two-color technicolor, blackout gags, vaudeville turns, Gershwin's "Rhapsody in Blue," assorted production numbers and—to be sure

not to miss anything in this early musical—a brief animated cartoon sequence. Lively musical fun with early '30's flavor. (Dir: John Murray Anderson, 120 mins.)

King of Kings (1962) ***½ Jeffrey Hunter, Robert Ryan, Siobhan McKenna, Viveca Lindfors. Excellently produced story of Jesus Christ. Told simply yet with great emotional power, generally well acted. Some may quibble with variations in story, but the overall result is one of a difficult task successfully carried out. (Dir: Nicholas Ray, 168 mins.)

King of Marvin Gardens, The (1972) ** Jack Nicholson, Bruce Dern, Ellen Burstyn, Julia Anne Robinson. A major disappointment because this could have been a superior film. Nicholson and Dern are brothers—as unlike each other as night and day—but bound together by a childhood dream about retiring to an island paradise where they will both be kings. Ellen Burstyn is wonderful as a wigged-out woman who shares Dern's bed with him and her daughter; Dern is all swagger as the small-time entrepreneur with big ideas; and Nicholson is effective as the bewildered man in the middle. The best part of the movie is the beginning—a long, late-night radio monologue by Nicholson, who has his own FM talk series in Philadelphia. (Dir: Bob Rafelson, 103 mins.)

King of the Coral Sea (Australian, 1953) ** Charles Tingwell, Chips Rafferty, Rod Taylor. Smugglers use a pearl diving operation as a front to get aliens into Australia. Crude but fast moving adventure yarn with nice local backgrounds. (Dir: Lee Robinson, 74 mins.)

King of the Khyber Rifles (1954) ** Tyrone Power, Terry Moore, Michael Rennie. Only occasionally interesting adventure epic set in India during a minor revolution. Power is cast as a half-caste (pun intended) British Captain in the Khyber patrol. Miss Moore is miscast as a young lady caught in the turbulent proceedings. (Dir: Henry King, 100 mins.)

King of the Mongols (Japanese, 1960) ** Hashizo Okawa, Yoshio Yoshida. Samurai soldier comes to the aid of an emperor besieged by a rebel lord. Childish but spectacular, in the true sense of the word, costume adventure. Fun if not taken seriously. Dubbed in English; bears a suspicious resemblance to the Jules Verne adventure "Michael Strogoff."

King of the Roaring Twenties (1961) **½ David Janssen, Mickey Rooney. David Janssen carrys the cumbersome lead of an uneven script and some glaring miscasting and still comes off rather well in the role of racketeer Arnold Rothstein. The film traces his climb to the top of "gangdom." (Dir: Joseph M. Newman, 106 mins.)

King of the Underworld (1939) **½ Humphrey Bogart, Kay Francis. Kay Francis is a lady doctor again in this one but she succeeds in outwitting Bogie who is of course the character in the title. (Dir: Lewis Seiler, 80 mins.)

King of the Vikings (Spanish, 1964) * Antonio Vilar, Marie Mahor. Fighting Norseman bests all adversaries to save his love from danger. Hokey costume spectacle dubbed in English.

King on Horseback (French, 1958) ** Jean Marais, Nadja Tiller, Eleonora Rossi-Drago. English-dubbed costume adventure about some traveling players who aid the French in their war against Austria. Passable, thanks to the cast.

King Rat (1965) **** George Segal, Tom Courtenay, James Fox. An excellent World War II prisoner-of-war story graphically depicts the everyday existence of British and American POWs confined in a Japanese war camp. The interest of the film lies in the character of a thoroughly unscrupulous opportunist, skillfully played by George Segal, and a standout performance as a young British soldier by James Fox who manages to emerge as an individualist, despite Segal's influence on his survival. Well-paced and directed by Bryan Forbes. (133 mins.)

King Richard and the Crusaders (1954) **½ Rex Harrison, Virginia Mayo, Laurence Harvey. Elaborate costume epic based on Sir Walter Scott's tale of the Crusaders, "The Talisman." Many battle scenes keep the action lively for adventure fans. (Dir: David Butler, 114 mins.)

King Solomon's Mines (1950) **** Stewart Granger, Deborah Kerr, Richard Carlson, Hugo Haas. Rousing adventure tale of a white hunter guiding a party through darkest Africa in search of a lady's missing husband. Authentic jungle sites filmed magnificently; enough action, suspense for all. Excellent entertainment. (Dirs: Compton Bennett, Andrew Marton, 102 mins.)

Kings Go Forth (1958) **½ Frank Sinatra, Tony Curtis, Natalie Wood. Implausible tale mixing war action and racial problems, as a heelish GI romances a beautiful gal with questionable antecedents. Well acted, with Sinatra his usual self, Curtis as the heel, Miss Wood nice to look at—but the story has holes. (Dir: Delmer Daves, 109 mins.)

Kings of the Sun (1963) **½ Yul Brynner, George Chakiris, Shirley Ann Field. Impressively mounted, but empty historical drama about the ancient Mayan civilization. Yul Brynner, wearing little but a loincloth, plays an Indian chief. Production gradually disintegrates into melodrama. (Dir: J. Lee Thompson, 108 mins.)

King's Pirate (1967) ** Doug McClure, Jill St. John, Guy Stockwell, Mary Ann Mobley. Silly costume comedy-drama about pirates and their adventures, circa eighteenth century. The absurd goings-on set in Madagascar involve a pirate queen (Miss St. John), a British naval officer (McClure), a pirate leader (Stockwell), and an Indian princess a long way from home (Miss Mobley). Nonsense like this made stars thirty years ago, of people like Turhan Bey—to say nothing of exciting personalities like Errol Flynn—but it all seems pretty dated and stilted for audiences of the 1970's. (Dir: Don Weis, 100 mins.)

King's Rhapsody (British, 1956) *½ Anna Neagle, Errol Flynn, Patrice Wymore. Stilted and out of date operetta type of story—heir to the throne has to forsake his true love and marry a princess. Sad reminder of Flynn's declining years.

King's Row (1941) **** Ann Sheridan, Robert Cummings, Ronald Reagan. Young doctor sees a small town in all its pettiness and squalor at the turn of the century. Splendid drama, superbly done in all respects. (Dir: Sam Wood, 127 mins.)

King's Story, A (Great Britain, 1965) *** Over-long, absorbing documentary about the early life of the former Edward VIII of Britain, who abdicated his throne in 1936 to marry the woman he loved. Narrated by Orson Welles, the film uses old clips from the late Duke of Windsor's personal records, closes with a moving re-reading, by him, of his abdication speech. (Dir: Harry Booth, 100 mins.)

King's Thief, The (1955)** Edmund Purdom, Ann Blyth, David Niven. Lively but routine costume thriller, dastardly nobleman tries to steal the Crown Jewels. Purdom foils him. David Niven deserves better. (Dir: Robert Z. Leonard, 78 mins.)

Kismet (1944)*** Ronald Colman, Marlene Dietrich. If you still care to see this perennial fable of poets and caliphs and poets' daughters this is as good a version as any. (Dir: William Dieterle, 100 mins.)

Kismet (1955)** Ann Blyth, Howard Keel, Vic Damone. Stilted version of Broadway stage success, about the wise beggar and his beautiful daughter in old Bagdad. For those who like songs and razzle-dazzle, okay. Otherwise, a bore. (Dir: Vincente Minnelli, 113 mins.)

Kiss and Tell (1945)*** Shirley Temple, Jerome Courtland. Corliss Archer is in more hot water when she is suspected of being a future mother. Pleasant, humorous teenage comedy. (Dir: Richard Wallace, 90 mins.)

Kiss Before Dying, A (1956)***½ Robert Wagner, Jeffrey Hunter, Virginia Leith, Joanne Woodward. Nicely knit murder story about a young psychopath who cold-bloodedly murders his pregnant girl friend. Good suspense as the police start to close in on the killer. Joanne Woodward, in one of her first big roles, is excellent as the victim. (Dir: Gerd Oswald, 94 mins.)

Kiss in the Dark, A (1949)** David Niven, Jane Wyman, Broderick Crawford. Silly nonsense about a stuffed shirt who takes over an apartment house and comes face to face with life. (Dir: Delmer Daves, 87 mins.)

Kiss Me Deadly (1955)** Ralph Meeker, Albert Dekker. Mike Hammer runs into secret formula and plenty of murder. Brutal, unconvincing Mickey Spillane mystery. (Dir: Robert Aldrich, 105 mins.)

Kiss Me Kate (1953)**** Kathryn Grayson, Howard Keel, Ann Miller.

Cole Porter's delightful Broadway play is turned into a bright entertainment package with songs, dances, and comedy. The score includes the familiar "Wunderbar," "So in Love," and "Always True to You in My Fashion." The stars are perfectly cast with Ann Miller a standout in what may be her best screen role. A truly great score makes this a musical treat. (Dir: George Sidney, 109 mins.)

Kiss Me, Kill Me (1976)*½ Stella Stevens, Claude Akins, Pat O'Brien, Robert Vaughn. Average thriller that benefits from the complexity of its characters. Stella Stevens is fine as the young D.A. tracking down the killer of a young schoolteacher. Made-for-TV. (Dir: Michael O'Herlihy, 72 mins.)

Kiss of Death (1947)***½ Victor Mature, Richard Widmark, Coleen Gray. A routine story, perfectly written, acted and directed combine for one of the best underworld films in years. Story of an ex-con who wants to go straight and his war with his old pals will have you gripping your chair. Mature is excellent and Widmark even better. (Dir: Henry Hathaway, 98 mins.)

Kiss of Evil (British, 1963)**½ Clifford Evans, Noel Williams. Honeymooning couple are ensnared by the owner of a chateau who turns out to be a vampire. Effective horror thriller, well done for those who like 'em. (Alt. title: Kiss of the Vampire.) (Dir: Don Sharp, 88 mins.)

Kiss of Fire (1955)**½ Jack Palance, Barbara Rush, Martha Hyer. Adventure with a capital A! All the ingredients of adventure are present in this fast-paced yarn about Spanish traitors, hostile Indians, rebels, renegades, and a Spanish Robin Hood named El Tigre. The cast is uniformly good. (Dir: Joseph Newman, 87 mins.)

Kiss the Blood Off My Hands (1948)** Burt Lancaster, Joan Fontaine, Robert Newton. Muddled melodrama about two ill-fated lovers who each commits an accidental murder for the sake of their love. Weak script and fair performances. (Dir: Norman Foster, 79 mins.)

Kiss the Girls and Make Them Die (Italian, 1966)*½ Mike Connors, Dorothy Provine, Terry-Thomas, Raf Vallone. CIA agent (Connors) after an industrialist (Vallone) with a deadly secret weapon. Tongue-in-cheek secret-agent stuff doesn't come off: a yawn. (Dir: Henry Levin, 106 mins.)

Kiss Them For Me (1959)****** Cary Grant, Jayne Mansfield, Suzy Parker. Even suave Cary Grant can't save this belabored farce about a trio of Navy war heroes who arrive in San Francisco for some rest and recreation, with the accent on the latter. Jayne Mansfield giggles and wiggles appropriately while Suzy Parker proves, once again, she's breathtakingly beautiful, but no actress. (Dir: Stanley Donen, 105 mins.)

Kiss Tomorrow Goodbye (1950)****½** James Cagney, Barbara Payton. Cagney is the whole show in a familiar role of an escaped convict who gets his comeuppance in the last scenes of the fast paced drama. (Dir: Gordon Douglas, 102 mins.)

Kisses for My President (1964)****** Fred MacMurray, Polly Bergen, Arlene Dahl. Lightweight, silly comedy about the trials and tribulations of the first lady President of the U.S. Polly Bergen is all crooked-raised-eyebrows as the Commanderess-in-Chief, and Fred MacMurray is bewilderment personified as her spouse. (Dir: Curtis Bernhardt, 113 mins.)

Kissin' Cousins (1964)****** Elvis Presley, Arthur O'Connell, Pam Austin. Elvis in a dual role, which is either too much or not enough, depending on one's outlook. Here he plays an Air Force officer trying to persuade a mountaineer to allow a missile base on his land, and also his distant cousin who always wants to fight him. Strictly for Presleyites. (Dir: Gene Nelson, 96 mins.)

Kissing Bandit, The (1948)****** Frank Sinatra, Kathryn Grayson. No wonder Frank had to make a come-back after pictures like this. Story of a nice chap who is forced to go out West and enter Dad's business. Dad was an outlaw and, in spite of the potential, the picture is a bore. (Dir: Laslo Benedek, 102 mins.)

Kitten with a Whip (1964)****** Ann-Margret, John Forsythe, Peter Brown. Juvenile delinquent gal breaks into the home of an aspiring political figure and nearly ruins his career. Sleazy bit of sensationalism not helped by Ann-Margret's in-

ability to project; direction and the rest of the cast better than the material. (Dir: Douglas Heyes, 83 mins.)

Kitty (1946)****½** Paulette Goddard, Ray Milland. Costume drama about a girl who rises from poverty to fame, fortune and title (set in England) by indiscreet use of her charms. Moderate entertainment. (Dir: Mitchell Leisen, 104 mins.)

Kitty Foyle (1940)******** Ginger Rogers, Dennis Morgan, James Craig. Girl from the wrong side of the tracks loves a Philadelphia socialite, but finds true happiness elsewhere. Excellent drama from Christopher Morley's novel, with fine performances. (Dir: Sam Wood, 107 mins.)

Klansman, The (1974)***½** Lee Marvin, Richard Burton, Lola Falana, O. J. Simpson. William Bradford Huie's reasonably interesting novel about today's deep South and the operations of the Ku Klux Klan turned into mawkish melodrama. Marvin isn't bad playing a sheriff who wants to be fair to both blacks and whites, but it's election time, remember, and . . . Burton plays an embittered, alcoholic, Southern aristocrat. Burton was allegedly drunk throughout most of the shooting of the film, and it shows in this inept, over-acted performance. But he's still sane enough to want to dally around with ravishing Falana. (Dir: Terence Young, 112 mins.)

Klute (1971)******** Jane Fonda, Donald Sutherland. An absolutely brilliant performance by Jane Fonda, for which she quite deservedly won the Academy Award, carries the day in this psychological thriller. Fonda plays a would-be actress-model. She is a vulnerable, self-aware, articulate, hustling middle-class call girl. Story concerns Klute (Sutherland), a small-town policeman. He comes to New York in search of a missing friend, meets Fonda, and falls in love with her—sort of! But it's Jane's picture all the way under the sure hand of director Alan J. Pakula. Fonda is believable and heartbreaking — whether she is pretending to be interested while turning tricks with her paying clients, or talking to her psychiatrist. (Dir: Alan J. Pakula, 114 mins.)

Knickerbocker Holiday (1944)****** Nelson Eddy, Charles Coburn. The famous play of Old New York, and of

Peter Stuyvesant the governor, and of how love makes a fool out of him. Fine Maxwell Anderson-Kurt Weill songs—including "September Song" —but otherwise, dull, stiffly acted. (Dir: Harry Brown, 85 mins.)

Knife in the Water (1962)**** Leon Niemczyk, Julanta Umeoka, Zygmunt Malanowicz. This was the first feature film directed by the brilliant Roman Polanski, and it put the world on notice that a major new talent had arrived. The film is a taut, tight character study of three people on a sailboat—a successful, middle-aged sportswriter, his young and sexy wife, and a wandering young student they picked up hitchhiking. Polanski very successfully creates an atmosphere of suspense, tension, and potential violence as the two men compete for the lady's attention and approval. The conclusion is particularly effective and the film is a literal tour de force. (Dir: Roman Polanski, 95 mins.)

Knight without Armor (British, 1937) *** Robert Donat, Marlene Dietrich. Suspense tale of couple fleeing from the Russian Revolution. Gripping, well made. Alexander Korda production. (Dir: Jacques Feyder, 107 mins.)

Knights of the Black Cross (1958)*** Ursula Modrynska. Sprawling adventure made in Poland, directed by Alexander Ford. In its original form, this was a very fine film about the Crusaders, but it's been edited here. Nevertheless, impressive.

Knights of the Round Table (1954)** Ava Gardner, Robert Taylor, Mel Ferrer. This pre-dates the musical "Camelot" by many years, but it's the same story (more or less)— Queen Guinevere (Ava Gardner) being taken with Lancelot (Robert Taylor) while King Arthur (Mel Ferrer) looks on with long suffering glances. In between, we have jousts, battle scenes, court magicians, and the expected. History, M-G-M style. But Ava is ravishing. (Dir: Richard Thorpe, 115 mins.)

Knives of the Avenger (Italy, 1967)** Cameron Mitchell, Fausto Tozzi. Well-done adventure story set among the Vikings. When their king is away, a tribal people are threatened by marauders, until a strange warrior intervenes. Dramatic lighting, tight direction, keep this story jumping. Poor dubbing. (Dir: Mario Bava, 86 mins.)

Knock on Any Door (1949)**½ Humphrey Bogart, John Derek, Allene Roberts. Willard Motley's frank novel about a young hood in the slums of Chicago makes a powerful motion picture. Bogart plays an attorney who defends the boy when he is charged with murder. Derek is fine in his first major role as Nick Romano. (Dir: Nicholas Ray, 100 mins.)

Knock on Wood (1954)*** Danny Kaye, Mai Zetterling. Another treat for Danny Kaye fans. Danny's up to his neck in international adventures as a night club puppeteer with a penchant for getting into trouble. Lovely Mai Zetterling adds to the fun. (Dir: Norman Panama, 103 mins.)

Knockout (1941)** Arthur Kennedy, Cornel Wilde, Anthony Quinn. Stereotyped fight picture characters combine to knock out good acting and directing. (Dir: William Clemens, 73 mins.)

Knute Rockne—All American (1940) ***½ Pat O'Brien, Ronald Reagan. Good biography of the famous Notre Dame football coach, and contains that now immortal movie line, "Go in there and win it for the Gipper." Fact is mixed in with the corn, but it's still one of the best football films glorifying the old college try. Reagan shows off his shifty movements in this one, long before he started to run for elective office. (Dir: Lloyd Bacon, 98 mins.)

Kojak: The Chinatown Murders (1974) *½ Telly Savalas, Dan Frazer, Kevin Dobson, Demosthenes. Violent action-packed drama. Down in New York City's Chinatown, an alien on foreign turf, Telly Savalas as Kojak has precious few allies, but he must prevent a blood bath which youth gangs are about to unleash. Too long. Made-for-TV. (Dir: Jeannot Szwarc, 98 mins.)

Kona Coast (1968)**½ Richard Boone as a seaman investigating the death of his teenaged daughter. Ordinary plot highlighted by exotic Hawaiian locations, a superior cast. Joan Blondell, Vera Miles, Steve Inhat, Chips Rafferty, Kent Smith. (Dir: Lamont Johnson, 93 mins.)

Konga (British, 1961)** Michael Gough, Margo Johns. The one about the mad scientist who turns a small chimp into a murdering huge gorilla monster. Thriller diehards may take to it, but it reminds one how really good "King Kong" still is. (Dir: John Lemont, 90 mins.)

Kon-Tiki (1951)***½ Documentary of the Thor Heyerdahl expedition, covering 4,300 miles in a raft to the Polynesian Islands. Despite crude photography, an absorbing filmic record of an amazing achievement. Narrated by Ben Grauer. (73 mins.)

Koroshi (1966)** Patrick McGoohan, Yoko Tani. Actually a two-part adventure based on the TV series "Secret Agent," which has been strung together for theatrical release. Drake, the agent from British Security, is dispatched to Tokyo to get to the bottom of a mystery involving a planned assassination of a U.N. dignitary. (Dirs: Peter Yates, Michael Truman, 93 mins.)

Krakatoa, East of Java—See: Volcano

Kremlin Letter, The (1970)**½ Richard Boone, Patrick O'Neal, Bibi Andersson, Orson Welles. Confusing espionage meller with a cast of international stars, who can do very little to save it from floundering. John Huston directed (and not very well) the tale concerning a volatile letter dispatched by a U.S. official to Russia, proposing the annihilation of China. It's a shrieking chase yarn, with O'Neal as the hero and the assorted villains and victims played by Orson Welles, Richard Boone, George Sanders, Max von Sydow, Barbara Parkins, Nigel Green, Bibi Andersson, and the director (Huston) himself. (116 mins.)

Kronos (1957)*½ Jeff Morrow, Barbara Lawrence. Poorly made science-fiction thriller featuring the usual interplanetary monster destroyed in time for the kiddies to go to bed and have nightmares. (Dir: Kurt Neumann, 78 mins.)

Kung Fu (1972)**½ David Carradine. The pilot film for the popular oriental western TV series. David Carradine stars as a Chinese-American priest trained in discipline, humility, perception, and the art of karate-judo. Hunted for the murder of Chinese royalty, the priest finds work with a railroad crew and he humbles the white villain bosses with his superior ways. Flashbacks to the priest's boyhood training allow the film to avoid using the usual western claptrap. Carradine is very good in the lead and gets fine support from Barry Sullivan and Albert Salmi as the bad guys. (Dir: Jerry Thorpe, 75 mins.)

L-Shaped Room, The (British, 1963) **** Leslie Caron, Tom Bell, Brock Peters. Beautifully done drama of a pregnant girl taking lodgings in a rundown boarding house, and the struggling young writer who meets, helps, loves her. Leslie Caron never better; rest of the cast excellent, with the script and direction by Bryan Forbes superb. Fine adult fare. (125 mins.)

La Belle Americaine (French, 1960) *** Robert Dhery, Colette Brosset. Enjoyable comedy about an American automobile, and its meaning to an average Frenchman. Some hilarious moments.

La Chinoise (French, 1967)**** Anne Wiazemsky, Jean-Pierre Leaud, Francis Jeanson. Continuing some of the themes dealt with in "Masculine-Feminine" (1966), the brilliant Jean-Luc Godard turns out one of his most stimulating films—one of the times when his genius for movie making meshes perfectly with the ideas he is expressing. This is a film about ideas, mostly those of a group of anarchic Maoist students in Paris. Subtitles.

La Dolce Vita (Italian, 1961)**** Marcello Mastroianni, Anita Ekberg, Anouk Aimee. Staggering portrayal of decadence, hopelessness among the upper crust of Rome. Masterfully directed by Federico Fellini in a series of episodic images literally battering the eye, brain. Strictly for adults, it is absorbing throughout its length, has the elements of greatness. Dubbed in English. (Dir: Federico Fellini, 175 mins.)

La Favorita (Italian, 1952)*½ Gino Sinemberghi, Paolo Silveri, Sophia Loren. Turgid tale of a young monastery probate who falls for a courtesan, based on Donizetti's opera. Curiosity seekers might be interested in Sophia Loren early in her career.

La Guerre Est Finie (French-Swiss, 1966)**** Yves Montand, Ingrid Thulin, Genevieve Bujold. A marvelous film about political idealism, superbly directed by Alain Resnais and exquisitely acted by Montand and Thulin. Montand plays, to quiet perfection, the role of an aging revolutionary who fought against Franco in the Spanish Civil War but now knows, and reluctantly understands, that he and his cause will not win. Intelligent, perceptive script from screenwriter Jorge Semprun. Miss Thulin plays Montand's sensual, political mistress, and their scenes together are quiet magic. (121 mins.)

La Maternelle (French, 1932)*** Madeleine Renaud, Alice Tissot. Early French sound classic about the love of a woman for the children in a day nursery. Poignant, superb scenes of children caught by the camera. But its age, poor print condition limit it to specialized audiences. Otherwise, it would merit top rating.

La Parisienne (French, 1959)***½ Brigitte Bardot, Charles Boyer. Diplomat's daughter goes to great lengths to make her husband pay attention to her. One of the best Bardot films; a sly, sophisticated comedy that is pleasant all the way. (Dir: Michel Boisrond, 85 mins.)

La Religieuse—See: The Nun

La Sonnambula (Italian, 1952)*½ Gino Sinemberghi, Paola Bertini. Musty version of Bellini's opera. It's been done better. Florid production presentation.

La Strada (Italian, 1955)**** Anthony Quinn, Giulietta Masina, Richard Basehart. An altogether beautiful movie, both touching and amusing, magnificently acted by Masina and Quinn. A brutal, itinerant performer takes in a pathetic slow-witted waif, and her devotion to him is repaid with insults and indifference. English dubbed. A basically simple story has been turned into one of the most memorable films available on TV. (Dir: Federico Fellini, 115 mins.)

La Traviata (Italian, 1966)**½ Gino Bechi, Franco Bonisolli. Verdi's opera, starring Anna Moffo as the ill-fated Violetta. Dignified attempt, but remains staged opera . . . and, to an amateur music critic's ear, not especially well sung.

Lad: A Dog (1962)** Peter Breck, Peggy McCay, Angela Cartwright. How a collie brings love to a crippled girl, and various other saccharrine ingredients. For canine lovers

and impressionable youngsters exclusively. (Dirs: Leslie H. Martinson, Avram Avakian, 98 mins.)

Ladies First (French, 1963)*½ Eddie Constantine, Christiane Minazzoli, Mischa Auer. Adventurer helps a girl in distress, runs into murder, and flees from crooks during a Paris transportation strike. Attempt at tongue-in-cheek humor leaves just a lump; mostly boring comedy-crime combo dubbed in English. (Dir: Bernard Borderie, 93 mins.)

Ladies in Love (1936)**½ Janet Gaynor, Loretta Young, Simone Simon. Strictly for the ladies is this overly romantic tale of the affairs of four beautiful girls in Budapest. A load of familiar faces in the cast. (Dir: Edward H. Griffith, 97 mins.)

Ladies in Retirement (1941)***½ Ida Lupino, Louis Hayward, Evelyn Keyes. Housekeeper kills her employer to save her sisters from being put in an asylum. Gripping suspense drama, excellently acted. (Dir: Charles Vidor, 92 mins.)

Ladies' Man, The (1961)**½ Jerry Lewis, Helen Traubel, Pat Stanley. Jerry as a confirmed bachelor who gets a job as an assistant in a girls' boarding house. This comedy begins like a riot, but soon slows down considerably. Uneven, with some funny scenes—Lewis fans will like it. (Dir: Jerry Lewis, 106 mins.)

Ladies' Man (French, 1962)** Eddie Constantine. Another French-made Grade B crime film with Eddie Constantine playing FBI Agent Lemmy Caution. This time, the action is based on the French Riviera.

Ladies Who Do (British, 1963)** Robert Morley, Peggy Mount, Harry H. Corbett. Rather dawdling comedy about a cleaning woman who begins to make her mark on the Stock Exchange, quite by chance. Amusing, thanks to the players, but seldom rises to any great heights. (Dir: C. M. Pennington-Richards, 85 mins.)

Lady and the Mob (1939)*** Ida Lupino, Fay Bainter, Lee Bowman. Wealthy old eccentric takes harsh steps to rid her town of racketeers. Frequently funny comedy. (Dir: Ben Stoloff, 70 mins.)

Lady Be Good (1941)*** Eleanor Powell, Robert Young, Ann Sothern. Gershwin score, a fine cast and a good production add up to better-than-average screen entertainment.

Story of a boy and girl songwriting team isn't much but thanks to Miss Sothern and Mr. Young it doesn't hurt the picture. (Dir: Norman Z. McLeod, 111 mins.)

Lady Caroline Lamb (British-Italian, 1972)*½ Sarah Miles, Jon Finch, Richard Chamberlain, Laurence Olivier. Misguided, melodramatic attempt at portraying the story of Caroline Lamb, who had a brief, two-month affair with the poet Lord Byron. Played as soap opera, with wooden actors, Lady Lamb's story is depicted as possible fiction for "Cosmopolitan." Not for discriminating audiences. Robert Bolt wrote and directed. (123 mins.)

Lady Dances, The—See: Merry Widow, The (1934)

Lady Doctor (Italian, 1958)** The lady doctor is none other than Abbe Lane in this feather-weight comedy about love's bout with the Hippocratic oath. Vittorio De Sica plays a baffled suitor. (Dir: Camillo Mastrocinque, 97 mins.)

Lady Eve, The (1941)**** Barbara Stanwyck, Henry Fonda, Charles Coburn. Preston Sturges' delightful, witty and hilarious treatment of the much abused plot about the bad girl who makes a sucker out of a nice boy. Perfect screen comedy. (Dir: Preston Sturges, 97 mins.)

Lady for a Night (1942)** John Wayne, Joan Blondell. The lady owner of a Mississippi gambling boat is accused of murdering a wealthy socialite. Slow, rather corny costume drama. Wayne looks out of place. (Dir: Leigh Jason, 87 mins.)

Lady from Shanghai (1948)*** Rita Hayworth, Orson Welles. Irish sailor accompanies a beautiful woman and her lawyer husband on a cruise, becomes a pawn in murder. Melodrama is saved by Welles touches in direction, turning it into a good thriller. (Dir: Orson Welles, 87 mins.)

Lady From Texas (1951)**½ Josephine Hull, Howard Duff, Mona Freeman. Universal had to come up with a follow up vehicle for Josephine Hull, who won an Oscar the year before for her brilliant performance in "Harvey," and this lightweight Western comedy is it. Miss Hull's special brand of whimsy is wasted on this yarn about an eccentric old lady who turns a whole town upside down, but the film itself is pleasant. (Dir: Joseph Pevney, 77 mins.)

Lady Gambles, The (1949)**½ Barbara Stanwyck, Robert Preston, Stephen McNally. Miss Stanwyck gives a good performance in this melodrama about a woman deeply caught in a compulsive trap of gambling. Preston is also fine in the role of her patient husband. (Dir: Michael Gordon, 99 mins.)

Lady Godiva (1956)** Maureen O'Hara, George Nader. Normans and Saxons are at each other's throats while history gets a bit of a reshuffling in this familiar tale of adventure. Don't expect too much from Lady Godiva's famous ride. (Dir: Arthur Lubin, 89 mins.)

Lady Has Plans, The (1942)** Paulette Goddard, Ray Milland. Spy story is comedy-drama and not outstanding in either department. Paulette is mistaken for a tattooed woman spy when she comes to neutral Lisbon and is immediately pursued by all sides. (Dir: Sidney Lanfield, 77 mins.)

Lady Ice (1973)*½ Donald Sutherland, Jennifer O'Neill, Robert Duvall, Patrick Magee. Thinly plotted diamond caper with trendy "cool" characters. O'Neill is the stylish mastermind who must fence the million-dollar jewels, while Sutherland listlessly pursues her as a private eye. In fine but unnecessary cameos are Duvall as a federal agent and Magee as Miss O'Neill's malevolent father. (Dir: Tom Gries, 93 mins.)

Lady in a Cage (1964)** Olivia de Havilland, James Caan, Ann Sothern, Jennifer Billingsley. Unpleasant drama about young toughs who keep a woman (Miss de Havilland) trapped in an elevator while they ransack her home. Some good scenes, but generally overplayed. (Dir: Luther Davis, 93 mins.)

Lady in a Jam (1942)** Irene Dunne, Ralph Bellamy, Patric Knowles. Daffy comedy about a crazy mixed-up heiress and her love life, especially her love for her psychiatrist. (Dir: Gregory La Cava, 78 mins.)

Lady In Cement (1968)*½ Frank Sinatra, Raquel Welch, Dan Blocker, Richard Conte, Lainie Kazan, Martin Gabel. Frank Sinatra returns as private eye Tony Rome, sleuthing out the mystery of the pretty gal discovered lodged at the bottom of the sea. The snappy-gag hipster formula doesn't work this time. Ring-a-ding-dull. (Dir: Gordon Douglas, 93 mins.)

Lady in Distress (British, 1939)*** Paul Lukas, Michael Redgrave, Sally Gray. Happily married man brings on trouble when he meets a magican's lovely assistant. Fine performances bolster this mild little dramatic tale, turn it into superior entertainment. (Dir: Herbert Mason, 76 mins.)

Lady in the Car with Glasses and a Gun, The (U.S.-France, 1970)*** Samantha Eggar, Oliver Reed, John McEnery, Stephane Audran. Better than average suspense as secretary Samantha Eggar takes her boss's car for the holiday in the Mediterranean, oddly retracing a journey she has not taken, and is recognized by people she has not met before. When a body turns up in her trunk, things get serious. Miss Eggar delivers an outstanding performance, but the mystery of the film is limited by its premise. (Dir: Anatole Litvak, 105 mins.)

Lady in the Dark (1944)***½ Ginger Rogers, Ray Milland. This wonderful Broadway musical of Moss Hart's was a pioneering production at the time, and if you never saw Gertrude Lawrence in the original you won't have to make any invidious comparisons with Ginger's trouping in this splendid tuneful fantasy about a successful career woman under psychoanalysis. If you've got a color set the dream sequences are especially worth seeing and there are several good tunes. (Dir: Mitchell Leisen, 100 mins.)

Lady in the Iron Mask (1952)** Louis Hayward, Patricia Medina, John Sutton, Steve Brodie, Alan Hale Jr. Princess is kept a prisoner locked in an iron mask, so her twin sister will inherit the throne. Usual sort of costume melodrama. (Dir: Ralph Murphy, 78 mins.)

Lady in the Lake (1946)***½ Robert Montgomery, Audrey Trotter, Lloyd Nolan. Just a routine Phillip Marlowe mystery but Montgomery as director experimented by having the audience follow the picture with the hero and the result is good off-beat entertainment. (Dir: Robert Montgomery, 103 mins.)

Lady in the Morgue (1938)*** Preston Foster, Frank Jenks. The body of a beautiful woman disappears from the morgue, and private eye

Bill Crane has a heck of a time with gals and gangsters before solving the case. High-rating mystery has many clever touches above average. (Dir: Otis Garrett, 80 mins.)

Lady Is Willing (1942)*** Marlene Dietrich, Fred MacMurray. Broadway star arranges a marriage of convenience with a baby doctor so she can adopt a child. Nicely done drama. (Dir: Mitchell Leisen, 92 mins.)

Lady Killers, The (British, 1956)**** Alec Guinness, Peter Sellers. Two of Britain's best actors team in this uproariously funny comedy about a strange crew of bank robbers whose plans are thwarted by a nice old lady. (Dir: Alexander Mackendrick, 99 mins.)

Lady L (U.S.-Italian-French, 1965)*** Sophia Loren, Paul Newman, David Niven. Sumptuous settings and Sophia Loren and her male co-stars help shore up this lightweight saga of a laundress who works her way up to a title through a series of wacky misadventures. The tale of Lady L offers Miss Loren the chance to age some fifty or so years and she manages quite nicely, but we prefer her in the early sequences, where she romps about turn-of-the-century Paris with revolutionist Newman and Lord Niven. For those film historians who care about details, Peter Ustinov directed, wrote the screenplay and plays a cameo role. Ustinov took over this project after many other writers and millions of dollars had already been spent on the pre-production required to turn the Romain Gary novel into a workable screenplay. (Dir: Peter Ustinov, 107 mins.)

Lady Liberty (Italy-France, 1971)* Sophia Loren, William Devane, Luigi Proietti. Terrible comedy, would have been even worse in the hands of less capable players than Sophia Loren and William Devane. She's an Italian bride-to-be who arrives in New York with a mortadella sausage for her bridegroom, but cannot get clearance from customs. A rancid sausage! (Dir: Mario Monicelli, 95 mins.)

Lady Luck (1946)*** Robert Young, Barbara Hale. Nice girl tries to tame a high-rolling gambler by marrying him. Good comedy-drama, well made and satisfying. (Dir: Edwin L. Marin, 97 mins.)

Lady of Burlesque (1943)*** Barbara Stanwyck, Michael O'Shea. Strippers are strangled backstage, with one of the cuties eventually figuring out the solution. Entertaining, boisterous mystery; good fun. Based on Gypsy Rose Lee's "The G-String Murders." (Dir: William Wellman, 91 mins.)

Lady of Lebanon Castle—See: Lebanese Mission

Lady of the Tropics (1939)**½ Robert Taylor, Hedy Lamarr. The ladies may like this torrid romance between the half-native girl and the American millionaire. It's a tragic story which you'll find dated by our standards. (Dir: Jack Conway, 100 mins.)

Lady on a Train (1945)*** Deanna Durbin, Ralph Bellamy. Fairly exciting mystery. A girl sees a man murdered but nobody believes her. Not content to leave well enough alone she follows up what she has seen and becomes involved in an absorbing adventure. (Dir: Charles David, 93 mins.)

Lady Says No, The (1951)** Joan Caulfield, David Niven. Magazine photographer interviews a gal who's written an anti-men book, breaks down her romantic resistance. Ordinary comedy has a good cast that deserves better. (Dir: Frank Ross, 80 mins.)

Lady Sings the Blues (1972)*** Diana Ross, Billy Dee Williams, Richard Pryor. Fictionalized story of great singer Billie Holiday employs enough clichés for a dozen films of this genre, but comes out a winner solely due to the truly luminous performance by Diana Ross as Lady Day, which earned her an Academy Award-nomination. Not only does the beautiful Diana recreate the songs of Miss Holiday, duplicating the style without reverting to mimicking, but her dramatic power is surprising and convincing. The story takes many liberties with the facts surrounding the hapless singer's life, such as her being raped as a teenager, her working in a brothel, her severe addiction to heroin, and her tumultuous love life. Ignoring the script superficialities, you will be rewarded by La Ross's bigger than life portrayal of a musical giant. (Dir: Sidney J. Furie, 144 mins.)

Lady Takes a Chance, A (1943)**** Jean Arthur, John Wayne. New York

working girl takes a western tour, falls for a brawny cowpoke who doesn't want to be tied down. Fine fun; delightful romantic comedy with some hilarious sequences, capable players. (Dir: William A. Seiter, 86 mins.)

Lady Takes a Flyer, The (1958)** Lana Turner, Jeff Chandler. Attractive stars in a very predictable yarn about a beautiful lady who falls for an aviation ace and the trouble they have reconciling their lives. (Dir: Jack Arnold, 94 mins.)

Lady Takes a Sailor (1949)*** Jane Wyman, Dennis Morgan. Slapstick comedy about an efficient girl who always tells the truth has a lot of laughs in its contrived and comic plot. (Dir: Michael Curtiz, 99 mins.)

Lady Vanishes, The (British, 1938)**** Margaret Lockwood, Paul Lukas, Michael Redgrave, Dame May Whitty. Playgirl befriends an old lady on a train, finds she's involved in a spy plot when the lady disappears. Top-notch thriller, directed by Alfred Hitchcock; a classic of its kind. (97 mins.)

Lady Wants Mink (1953)*** Dennis O'Keefe, Ruth Hussey, Eve Arden. Accountant's wife causes trouble when she starts a mink farm. Breezy comedy has some good laughs. (Dir: William A. Seiter, 92 mins.)

Lady Windermere's Fan (1925)*** Irene Rich, Ronald Colman. Silent film directed by Ernst Lubitsch based on an Oscar Wilde play. For specialized showings only. (Dir: Ernst Lubitsch, 80 mins.)

Lady with a Lamp (British, 1950)*** Anna Neagle, Michael Wilding. Story of courageous nurse Florence Nightingale. Lavishly produced biography, well acted. (Dir: Herbert Wilcox, 85 mins.)

Lady with Red Hair (1940)**½ Miriam Hopkins, Claude Rains. Inaccurate, occasionally interesting story of the great actress Mrs. Leslie Carter and the famous producer David Belasco. Film is uneven, stodgy and only occasionally entertaining. (Dir: Curtis Bernhardt, 81 mins.)

Lady With the Dog, The (Russia, 1960)**** Iya Savvina, Aleksey Batalov. A magnificently acted and directed story based on a Chekhov short story. Set in Yalta around 1900, a middle-aged married banker from Moscow meets the unhappy, beautiful young wife of a local petty official. Very low-key, and straightforward. Sensitively directed without a lot of extraneous flourishes by director Iosif Kheyfits, who also wrote the adaptation. (90 mins.)

Lady Without a Passport (1950)**½ Hedy Lamarr, John Hodiak. Intrigue and romance in an exotic locale serves as the basis once again for an adventure film starring the beautiful Hedy Lamarr. (Dir: Joseph H. Lewis, 72 mins.)

Lady Without Camellias, The (Italy, 1953)*** Lucia Bose, Andrea Cecchi, Alain Cuny. A little-known, impressive early film directed by Michelangelo Antonioni. About a former Milanese shop girl who has a small part in a low-budget quickie movie, and then dreams of becoming a serious, recognized movie star. Bose's quality of distant, detached glamour is used to good advantage by the fledgling Antonioni, and there are evidences throughout of the striking cinematic techniques that earned him world-wide recognition a decade later.

Lafayette (French, 1960)** Orson Welles, Jack Hawkins, Edmund Purdom. Muddled historical drama about the French patriot Lafayette. Some action scenes come off nicely, but it moves sluggishly, despite the international cast. (Dir: Jean Dreville, 110 mins.)

Lafayette Escadrille (1958)*½ Tab Hunter, Etchika Choureau, David Janssen. Corny and melodramatic story about an American boy (Hunter) who runs away to France and joins the Foreign Legion. He goes through a series of adventures that include prison, marriage, etc. (Dir: William Wellman, 93 mins.)

Land of Fury (British, 1954)**½ Jack Hawkins, Glynis Johns, Noel Purcell. Danger and hardships pioneering in old New Zealand. Well cast, fine outdoor locale, but the plot lacks pace.

Land of the Pharaohs (1955)*** Jack Hawkins, Joan Collins, Dewey Martin. Egyptian drama about the building of the great pyramids with elaborate sets, lavish costumes and millions of extras. William Faulkner had a hand in the screenplay and Joan Collins is beautiful. (Dir: Howard Hawks, 106 mins.)

Land Raiders (1970)** Telly Savalas, George Maharis, Arlene Dahl. Ordinary western about a feud between two brothers, and the woman they both love. The feud is broken up by rampaging Apaches, and not a moment too soon. George Maharis has a part-time Spanish accent. (Dir: Nathan Juran, 100 mins.)

Land That Time Forgot, The (Great Britain, 1974)**½ Doug McClure, Susan Penhaligon, John McEnery. An old-fashioned adventure yarn based on the 1918 novel by Edgar Rice Burroughs which never lets logic get in the way of the action. The time is World War I. A group from a German sub and the survivors of an Allied ship come together and find themselves in a lost world where prehistoric animals still rule the roost! This is the type of movie which had kids screaming and shouting at Saturday matinees during the 40's—BTV (Before TV). There's even a volcano eruption at the film's finale. (Dir: Kevin Connor, 91 mins.)

Landlord, The (1970)**** Beau Bridges, Lee Grant, Pearl Bailey, Diana Sands, Lou Gossett. Alternately hilarious and serious satire on our fouled-up race relations. The entire cast is superb in this story of a young, rich white man (Bridges) who buys a tenement in Brooklyn, with dreams of converting it to a showplace home for himself. But he hasn't bargained on the militant black tenants who have no intention of conveniently moving out. The confrontations are very funny, and the satire is devastating. Director Hal Ashby, in his first effort, and writer William Gunn have produced a gem. Based on the novel by Kristin Hunter. (Dir: Hal Ashby, 114 mins.)

Landru (1962)**½ Charles Denner, Michele Morgan, Danielle Darrieux. Men who've dreamed of having numerous wives and getting rid of them without the bother of a divorce will love this entry. The macabre tale of Bluebeard, the husband who did away with many wives, is told again via this fairly well done French film, dubbed in English. (Dir: Claude Chabrol, 114 mins.)

Lannigan's Rabbi (1976)**½ Art Carney, Stuart Margolin, Janis Paige, Janet Margolin. Character is the key here. A mildly diverting comedy with Carney as a sympathetic police chief who refuses to believe the town Rabbi (Stuart Margolin) is a real murder suspect. Based on the best-seller "Friday the Rabbi Slept Late," the show takes a different tack from the usual cop format, with the detective and the suspect becoming close friends. Carney shoulders the load, and that's good enough part of the time. Made-for-TV. (Dir: Louis Antonio, 98 mins.)

Larceny (1948)****½** John Payne, Shelley Winters, Dan Duryea. Routine crime pic with bad guy turning good guy and the gangster's moll who wants to go legit. Dan Duryea plays Silky, an arch villain, to the hilt. (Dir: George Sherman, 89 mins.)

Larceny, Inc. (1942)******* Edward G. Robinson, Jane Wyman, Broderick Crawford. Entertaining story about an ex-con who does his best to go straight. This is a fairly amusing little farce which is well played by an expert cast. (Dir: Lloyd Bacon, 95 mins.)

Las Vegas Hillbillies (1966)***** Ferlin Husky, Jayne Mansfield, Mamie Van Doren. Country boy inherits a broken-down saloon, turns it into a success by bringing hillbilly music to Las Vegas. If one cares for country music, okay. Those who don't will have to decide which is worse—the music, the plot, or the acting!

Las Vegas Lady (1976)***** Stella Stevens, Stuart Whitman, George Di Cenzo. Heist in a Nevada amusement park offers no surprises. Motivation is to satisfy the dreams of Miss Stevens who hopes to leave her seamy past behind, and Whitman is the casino security guard who hopes to whisk her off to Montana. (Dir: Noel Nosseck, 87 mins.)

Las Vegas Shakedown (1955)****** Dennis O'Keefe, Coleen Gray. Ex-convict swears to kill a gambling house owner who testified against him. Fair melodrama tries to tell too much story. (Dir: Sidney Salkow, 79 mins.)

Las Vegas Story (1952)****** Jane Russell, Victor Mature, Vincent Price. Married woman meets an old flame in Las Vegas, who saves her husband from a murder charge. Undistinguished melodrama. (Dir: Robert Stevenson, 88 mins.)

Lassie Come Home (1943)*****½** Roddy McDowall, Donald Crisp, Lassie.

Story of an impoverished family which sells a prize collie is warm, sentimental and beautifully done. Lassie is, of course, the star but the rest of the fine cast contributes more than their share. (Dir: Fred M. Wilcox, 88 mins.)

Last Adventure, The (France-Italy, 1967)****** Alain Delon, Lino Venturi, Joanna Shimkus. A stunt flyer, a racing mechanic and a girl who's in love with both of them set out on a treasure hunt in the Congo. No riches for the audience. (Dir: Robert Enrico, 102 mins.)

Last American Hero, The—See: **Hard Driver**

Last Angry Man, The (1959)******* Paul Muni, David Wayne, Betsy Palmer. Even Paul Muni can't always raise this story of a dedicated general practitioner in Brooklyn above the level of soap opera. A very uneven script hampers the talented cast. There's a great performance by Luther Adler in the role of a longtime doctor friend of Muni's who became a specialist to raise his standard of living. (Dir: Daniel Mann, 100 mins.)

Last Angry Man, The (1974)****½** Pat Hingle, Lynn Carlin. Gerald Green's best-selling novel about a lovable old general practitioner was turned into a fairly successful film in 1959 with Paul Muni. In this version, only the title and the central characters remain . . . the setting is the Brooklyn of 1936 and Hingle brings a dignity and quiet force to the role of Dr. Abelman. Nostalgia and sentiment are the mainstays but the pace is too lethargic at times to sustain involvement. Michael Margotta shines in the role of Frankie, a young tough with a serious illness. Made-for-TV. (Dir: Jerrold Freedman.)

Last Blitzkrieg, The (1959)****** Van Johnson, Kerwin Matthews. Routine war film with some good action shots. The performances are of no help. (Dir: Arthur Dreifuss, 84 mins.)

Last Bridge (German, 1954)******** Maria Schell. This is the beautiful, profoundly moving film that marked Maria Schell as one of the finest new screen actresses of her generation. A tender story about a nurse during the war (WWII) who has loyalties and affections for individuals on both sides—German and Yugoslav. It's one of the most stirring anti-war arguments you'll ever see or hear.

Expertly directed on location in Yugoslavia by Helmut Kautner. (90 mins.)

Last Challenge, The (1967)**½ Glenn Ford, Angie Dickinson. Western fans will not be cheated by this routine but well-played horse opera. Glenn Ford is the former gunslinger turned marshal who has to keep an eager young gun (Chad Everett) from shooting up the town. The tension builds to the inevitable shootout and the supporting cast includes such good actors as Angie Dickinson, Jack Elam and Gary Merrill. (Dir: Richard Thorpe, 105 mins.)

Last Chance, The (Swiss, 1945)**** E. G. Morrison, John Hoy. American and RAF pilot downed in enemy territory attempt to make their way to Switzerland and freedom. Stirring war drama, superbly written and directed, acted by a nonprofessional cast.

Last Charge, The (Italian, 1964)* Tony Russell, Haya Harareet. Inept costume adventure, patriot goes into action when the forces of Napoleon invade Italy. Dubbed in English, alternate title: Fra Diavolo.

Last Command (1955)***½ Sterling Hayden, Anna Maria Alberghetti, Ernest Borgnine, Richard Carlson. Story of Jim Bowie, and the historic battle of the Alamo. Historical action drama has fine battle scenes, a good cast, and holds the interest. (Dir: Frank Lloyd, 110 mins.)

Last Day, The (1975)½ Richard Widmark, Barbara Rush, Robert Conrad, Loretta Swit. You've seen this Western a hundred times before. The fact that it's based on the true story of the end of the Dalton gang doesn't make it any more interesting. The script uses every cliché in the book. Boredom leads to a hideous, bloody climax. Made-for-TV. (Dir: Vincent McEveety, 100 mins.)

Last Days of Pompeii (1935)*** Preston Foster, Basil Rathbone, Alan Hale. Peace-loving blacksmith strives for wealth by becoming a champion gladiator. Average story bolstered by spectacular scenes of the destruction of Pompeii, a technical tour de force. (Dir: Ernest B. Schoedsack, 100 mins.)

Last Days of Pompeii, The (1959)**½ Steve Reeves, Christine Kaufmann. Italian made, English dubbed, spectacle produced for the adventure

fans. There's some good photographic effects during the climactic eruption of the volcano, Vesuvius. (Dir: Mario Bonnard, 105 mins.)

Last Detail, The (1973)***½ Jack Nicholson, Otis Young, Randy Quaid. With some careful editing of dialogue and pruning of scenes for TV exposure, this tough story about two sailors escorting a third one to a military prison comes off as an effective drama. Nicholson, as the honcho of the detail, is marvelous as an alternately brawling and sensitive swabbie who has found a home in the Navy. The other two major roles are well played by Young, as the other Shore Patrol non-com, and Quaid, as the hapless young prisoner. The "detail" turns into a sort of last-celebration-of-life for Quaid when his two jailers take pity on him and show him a good time, sailor-liberty-style. For those who saw the film in theaters, the harsh language is gone, but it doesn't really detract greatly from the film's cumulative impact. (Dir: Hal Ashby, 104 mins.)

Last Escape, The (1969)* Stuart Whitman, John Collin. Whitman is a spy out to capture a German rocket scientist from both the Germans and the advancing Russians. Most of the boring film is one long, repetitive escape of the two men. (Dir: Walter Grauman, 90 mins.)

Last Frontier, The (1956)** Victor Mature, Anne Bancroft, Robert Preston. A frontier outpost is almost destroyed due to the arrogant stubbornness of ruthless colonel. Routine western heroics with plenty of battle scenes. (Dir: Anthony Mann, 98 mins.)

Last Gangster, The (1937)*** Edward G. Robinson, James Stewart. Robinson is released after ten years on the rock and finds his world has changed. His futile fight to regain power makes this an interesting, although not superior, film. (Dir: Edmund Ludwig, 80 mins.)

Last Glory of Troy, The (Italian, 1961)*½ Steve Reeves. Muscleman Reeves wins out over the oppressors again in a typically juvenile English-dubbed spear-and-sandal epic.

Last Grenade, The (Great Britain, 1969)* Stanley Baker, Honor Blackman, Richard Attenborough, Rafer Johnson, Alex Cord. Fine acting talent can't help this predictable melodrama. Confused plot concerns war and revenge in the Far East, intertwined with domestic entanglements centering on an unbelievable love affair between Baker's gruff soldier and Miss Blackman's willowy wife of General Attenborough. Based on the novel "The Ordeal of Major Grigsby," musical score by John Dankworth. (Dir: Gordon Flemyng, 93 mins.)

Last Gun, The (Spanish, 1964)* Cameron Mitchell. Gunfighter has to prove himself one more time. Inept "western" made overseas, dubbed in English.

Last Gunfight, The (Japanese, 1964)*** Toshiro Mifune. Demoted detective is transferred from Tokyo to a city ruled by criminals. Gangster story, Nipponese style—as a novelty, not without interest. Dubbed in English.

Last Holiday (British, 1950)**** Alec Guinness, Beatrice Campbell. Man decides to make the time count when he is told he has a short time to live. Excellent comedy-drama with the usual impeccable Guinness performance. (Dir: Henry Cass, 89 mins.)

Last Hours Before Morning (1975)*½ Ed Lauter, Rhonda Fleming, Robert Alda, Peter Donat. Lauter stars as a 1946 ex-cop, now a private eye working on a hotel murder. You've seen it all before! Made-for-TV. (Dir: Joe Hardy)

Last Hunt, The (1956)*** Stewart Granger, Robert Taylor, Debra Paget. Engrossing action drama about the last of the big buffalo hunters in the Dakotas during the 1880's. The on-location photography is the film's main asset and the actors are secondary to the action sequences. (Dir: Richard Brooks, 108 mins.)

Last Hurrah, The (1958)**** Spencer Tracy, Jeffrey Hunter, Pat O'Brien, Dianne Foster. Superb film version of best seller concerning the heyday of the last of the big time politicians. Spencer Tracy gives one of his finest portrayals and is matched by a great hand-picked cast. (Dir: John Ford, 121 mins.)

Last Laugh, The (Germany, 1924)***½ Emil Jannings, Maly Delschaft. One of the most unusual and interesting of Murnau's films, which shows directorial techniques imitated half a century later by lesser European directors. Jannings

plays an elderly hotel doorman forced to retire and surrender his precious uniform, which gave him status in his neighborhood. Jannings is excellent, and there's interesting imagery throughout. (Dir: F. W. Murnau, 72 mins.)

Last Man on Earth, The (1964)** Vincent Price, Franca Bettoia. Scientist finds himself the sole survivor of a plague that has either killed the earth's population or turned them into subhuman zombies. Adequate sci-fi horror thriller filmed in Italy. Some scary sequences. (Dir: Sidney Salkow, 86 mins.)

Last Mile (1958)**½ Mickey Rooney, Frank Conroy. A good attempt at remaking the famous movie that starred Preston Foster. The years have taken some of the bite of this hard-hitting prison drama. Mickey Rooney tries but never quite comes off. (Dir: Howard W. Koch, 81 mins.)

Last Movie, The (1971)* Dennis Hopper, Julie Adams, Sam Fuller. Bungled, confusing parable of film crew shooting an American western in a Peruvian village high in the Andes. Hopper, extending the spirituality of "Easy Rider" to this tale, is both the director and the hero—a wrangler named Kansas who beats on people. Reality and illusion fuse in flashbacks, flashaheads, and flasharounds which race throughout, burying significance in abstraction. (110 mins.)

Last Musketeer, The (French, 1955)*½ Georges Marchal, Dawn Addams. Once more D'Artagnan fights the villainous forces of Louis XIV and saves the fair lady. Overly familiar, undistinguished swashbuckler dubbed in English. (Dir: Fernando Cerchio, 95 mins.)

Last of Sheila, The (1973)*** James Coburn, Dyan Cannon, Richard Benjamin, James Mason, Joan Hackett, Raquel Welch, Ian McShane. A nifty, intricate, campy parlor game, set on a yacht on the Riviera, which should keep you absorbed watching for clues. The plot concerns conniving Hollywood-producer Coburn who invites six friends for a cruise, during which he plans to discover which one killed his wife at a party a year ago. The personalities are outrageously colorful: the brash agent, the has-been director, the failed screenwriter, the sex-pot starlet, etc.

The script, by Stephen Sondheim and actor Anthony Perkins, is a full-fledged mystery, full of bitchy Hollywood in-jokes. Song "Friends" sung by Bette Midler. (Dir: Herbert Ross, 120 mins.)

Last of the Comanches (1953)**½ Broderick Crawford, Barbara Hale. A group of courageous men and women are trekking across a desert to Fort Macklin when Indians attack. The cavalry and a young Indian save the day in this fair Western drama. (Dir: Andre de Toth, 85 mins.)

Last of the Fast Guns (1958)**½ Jock Mahoney, Gilbert Roland, Linda Cristal. Gunslinger is hired to find a man's missing brother in Mexico, finds danger in the quest. Neat western moves at a speedy clip. (Dir: George Sherman, 82 mins.)

Last of the Mobile Hot Shots (1970)*½ James Coburn, Lynn Redgrave, Robert Hooks. Muddled interpretation of Tennessee Williams' "Seven Descents of Myrtle" by director Sidney Lumet, who replaces poetry with parody. Jeb (Coburn), the last of the Thoringtons, marries a hooker, Myrtle (Redgrave), on a game show so he can return to his decaying Mississippi plantation and try to germinate an heir before his terminal cancer kills him. Chicken, his black half-brother (Hooks), waits in the kitchen for his death, while Myrtle tries making love to anything. A flood floats away everyone's dreams, but the film was caught in a deluge from the beginning. (108 mins.)

Last of the Mohicans, The (1936)*** Randolph Scott, Binnie Barnes. The famous story of the French-Indian wars, and of the noble redmen who helped turn the tide against their brothers. Exciting, elaborately produced, good action. (Dir: George B. Seitz, 100 mins.)

Last of the Red Hot Lovers (1972)**½ Alan Arkin, Sally Kellerman, Paula Prentiss, Renee Taylor. Neil Simon's hit play arrives on the screen jazzed up with fewer laughs and Simon's own screen treatment of his play. Story of Jewish, middle-class Barney Fishman's hopes for an extramarital affair. Arkin plays the Don Juan owner of a seafood restaurant who can't remove the smell of fish from his hands as he tries three assignations using his mother's apartment.

Arkin's physical mannerisms are funny and fine in conveying the erotic urge and its accompanying guilt. (Dir: Gene Saks, 98 mins.)

Last of the Secret Agents (1966)** Nancy Sinatra, Marty Allen, Steve Rossi. Comedy team of Allen and Rossi play American tourists mixed up in espionage. Familiar pattern, but a few surprisingly funny moments. (Dir: Norman Abbott, 92 mins.)

Last of the Ski Bums (1969)*** A snow skier's version of "The Endless Summer," except that this world-wide search for perfect powder instead of the perfect wave isn't quite as skillfully done. Several ski bums are shown schussing their favorite mountains in various parts of the world including the Western U.S., Europe and New Zealand. There is some first-rate photography, and the film does capture some of the joy of skiing, and the special nature of the world-wide breed of "ski bum." Dir: Dick Barrymore, 86 mins.)

Last of the Vikings (Italian, 1962)*½ Cameron Mitchell, Edmund Purdom, Isabelle Corey. Son of murdered Viking chieftain battles a wicked overlord. Tasteless adventure epic with gruesome battle scenes, with flagrant overacting by villain Purdom. (Dir: Giacomo Gentilomo, 102 mins.)

Last Outpost, The (1951)** Ronald Reagan, Rhonda Fleming, Bruce Bennett. Brothers are pitted against each other in this story of the West during the Civil War. Indians add to the confusion. (Dir: Lewis R. Foster, 88 mins.)

Last Picture Show, The (1971)**** Timothy Bottoms, Jeff Bridges, Cybill Shepherd, Ben Johnson, Cloris Leachman. A poignant and deeply moving drama about a young boy growing up in a small town (Archer City) in Texas during the early 1950's. Part of the remarkable quality of director Peter Bogdanovich's masterpiece is that the camera is, quite purposely, not the star, and Bogdanovich has further enhanced the simplicity of the story by shooting the film in black and white. Based on the novel by Larry McMurtry, the performances from both established veterans—Leachman, Johnson—and assorted newcomers like Bottoms are uniformly and unerringly perfect. (Both

Leachman, playing the vulnerable neglected wife of a high-school football coach, and Johnson, a pool-hall owner, deservedly won Academy Awards for their performances.) Only Bogdanovich's second feature, this won an Academy Award nomination for best picture. One of the finest American films in 20 years. (118 mins.)

Last Posse, The (1953)*** Broderick Crawford, John Derek, Charles Bickford. Good western about a ruthless cattle baron who forms a posse to regain $100,000 stolen from him. Performances and script better than average. (Dir: Alfred L. Werker, 73 mins.)

Last Rebel, The (1971)* Joe Namath, Jack Elam, Victoria George. A dull excuse to put Joe Namath on the screen, though his followers will enjoy seeing him as a two-fisted western hero who goes around busting heads and saving black men from being lynched. It's set in post-Civil War time. As an actor, Joe's a helluva football player. (Dir: Denys McCoy, 88 mins.)

Last Ride, The (1944)** Richard Travis, Eleanor Parker. Remember the black market in tires? Well, it's the background for this Class "B" melodrama. (Dir: Ross Lederman, 56 mins.)

Last Ride to Santa Cruz, The (German, 1964)*½ Edmund Purdom, Marion Cook, Mario Adorf. Ex-lawman rides again, after an outlaw who has captured his wife and son in revenge. Teutonic idea of American western gets rather amusing at times, but wasn't meant to be. Dubbed in English.

Last Run, The (1971)** George C. Scott, Trish Van Devere, Tony Musante. Scott's screen presence is the only decent thing in this chase entry about a retired getaway driver (Scott) who comes back to help a hot-shot hood escape from the police in Spain. John Huston, who was the original director, escaped after a brief spell behind the cameras, and was replaced by the plodding Richard Fleischer. (100 mins.)

Last Safari, The (British, 1967)**½ Gabriella Licudd, Johnny Sekka, Stewart Granger, Kaz Garas. Safari guide (Stewart Granger) antagonized by a playboy (Kaz Garas), with thrilling African scenery atoning for the lack of plot and a subpar performance from Garas. (Dir: Henry Hathaway, 110 mins.)

Last Summer (1969)**** Barbara Hershey, Richard Thomas, Bruce Davison, Cathy Burns. Perceptive, beautifully acted drama about the experiences of four teen-agers during a summer on Long Island's Fire Island. Beautiful, restrained screenplay by Eleanor Perry based on the novel by Evan Hunter. The performances are uniformly fine, and Cathy Burns in particular is marvelous. Alternately funny, poignant, and chilling, it's been sensitively directed by Frank Perry. Powerful finale. (97 mins.)

Last Sunset, The (1961)** Kirk Douglas, Rock Hudson, Dorothy Malone, Joseph Cotten, Carol Lynley. Drifter pursued by a lawman arrives at the ranch of an old sweetheart. Combination of "Rawhide" and "Peyton Place," really gets the emotional relationships a-churning; more silly than dramatic, overwritten, overdirected, overacted. (Dir: Robert Aldrich, 112 mins.)

Last Survivors, The (1975)* Martin Sheen, Diane Baker, Christopher George, Anne Francis. Senior-officer Sheen decides who must be dumped from an overcrowded lifeboat—subject trivialized. Made-for-TV. (Dir: Lee H. Katzin, 89 mins.)

Last Tango in Paris (Italy-France, 1972)**** Marlon Brando, Maria Schneider, Jean-Pierre Leaud. This is, in many ways, a remarkable film, but you won't know why unless you manage to see this much-publicized pioneering work unedited on pay cable or some late-evening non-network broadcast. Brando plays a middle-aged American who meets Schneider, a young French girl, while he's apartment hunting. Quickly and silently, they make love. There are other surprises and many revealing moments throughout the rest of the film. (One of the few widely distributed films, incidentally, that clearly depicts anal intercourse.) One critic called "Tango" not a sex film; yet it is the first sex film. Brando gives one of his most moving performances of the decade, which, considering how many terrible films he's appeared in, doesn't sound like much of a compliment, but he remains a very great actor. Director Bernardo Bertolucci also collaborated on the original screenplay. (Dir: Bernardo Berto-lucci, 129 mins.)

Last Ten Days, The (German), 1956) ***½ Oskar Werner, Albin Skoda. A right, gripping, detailed depiction of the last ten days of Adolph Hitler. Excellent portrayal by Oskar Werner. (Dir: G. W. Pabst, 113 mins.)

Last Time I Saw Archie, The (1961) ** Robert Mitchum, Jack Webb, Martha Hyer, France Nuyen. Weak service comedy about a fast-talking "gold brick" and his less confident side-kick, played by Robert Mitchum and Jack Webb, respectively, (Dir: Jack Webb, 98 mins.)

Last Time I Saw Paris, The (1954) **½ Elizabeth Taylor, Van Johnson, Donna Reed, Walter Pidgeon. F. Scott Fitzgerald's short story "Babylon Revisited" is expanded and glossed over in this sumptuous but overly dramatic film. Miss Taylor is as gorgeous as always as Johnson's true love and Donna Reed registers strongly in a climactic scene with Johnson. (Dir: Richard Brooks, 116 mins.)

Last Train from Bombay (1952) ** Jon Hall, Lisa Ferraday. An American diplomat gets involved with the intrigues of Bombay. Nothing new in this tired plot. (Dir: Fred F. Sears, 72 mins.)

Last Train from Gun Hill (1959) **½ Kirk Douglas, Anthony Quinn, Earl Holliman, Carolyn Jones. All the action comes at the end of this deliberately paced western drama about a law officer who tries to bring the young killer of his wife to justice. The hitch is the young killer's father and the lawman were the best of friends at one time. Builds to okay payoff. (Dir: John Sturges, 94 mins.)

Last Tycoon, The (1976) ***½ Robert De Niro, Jeanne Moreau, Robert Mitchum, Ingrid Boulting, Jack Nicholson. A generally rewarding, remarkably faithful adaptation of F. Scott Fitzgerald's unfinished tragedy about Hollywood and its movie moguls of the late 20's and 30's. The character of Monroe Stahr is clearly based on the legendary movie producer Irving Thalberg. Robert De Niro is remarkably effective, capturing Stahr's power and influence in a low-key, restrained, subtly shaded performance. The main weakness of the film, however —and it's a serious one—is the lack-

lustre performance by young English actress Ingrid Boulting playing Kathleen, who consummates a love affair with Stahr in a half-finished open beach house Stahr is building on Malibu. Kazan contributes his best directorial work in a decade, and gets fine supporting performances from Moreau and from Nicholson, who is seen in a brief but deft turn as a labor organizer. Faithful, skillful screenplay by Harold Pinter. (Dir: Elia Kazan, 125 mins.)

Last Valley, The (Great Britain, 1971)** Michael Caine, Omar Sharif, Florinda Bolkan, Nigel Davenport, Arthur O'Connell. Scenery steals the show in this misguided but not altogether uninteresting allegorical adventure epic. The tail end of the Thirty Years War, circa 1641, is the setting for a group of strangers meeting in a hidden valley, where life is tranquil and untouched by the chaos of war. Captain Michael Caine brings his troops into the Eden and meets runaway philosophy professor Omar Sharif. Confusing accents, sophomoric dialogue and a confused plot sabotage the promising premise. Produced, directed and written by James Clavell, based on the novel by J. B. Pick. (127 mins.)

Last Voyage, The (1960) **½ Robert Stack, Dorothy Malone, Edmond O'Brien, George Sanders. Suspense drama about a liner ripped by an explosion, the efforts of the passengers and crew to abandon ship. Stretches things a bit too far at times, but the sinking scenes are the real thing, quite fascinating. (Dir: Andrew L. Stone, 91 mins.)

Last Wagon, The (1956) **½ Richard Widmark, Felicia Farr, Nick Adams. Tough leader brings a wagon train through perilous country. Okay western, but good cast deserves better. (Dir: Delmer Daves, 99 mins.)

Last Waltz, The (West German, 1958) *½ Eva Bartok, Curt Jurgens. Silly story of the ill-fated romance of a Polish officer, Jurgens, and his love, a nightclub singer who is really a Baroness. They're cute, but the movie can't match the Strauss waltzes. (Dir: Arthur Maria Rabenalt, 92 mins.)

Last Warning, The (1939) *** Preston Foster, Frances Robinson. Above average mystery with amusing dialogue. Private detective is hired to catch a kidnapper who calls himself

"The Eye." (Dir: Al Rogell, 70 mins.)

Last Woman on Earth, The (1960)** Antony Carbone, Betsy Jones-Moreland. Moderately entertaining film about the last 3 people left on earth after fallout does everyone else in. The actors are better than the script and the on-location photography in Puerto Rico enhances the film. (Dir: Roger Corman, 71 mins.)

Last Year at Marienbad (French, 1962)***½ Delphine Seyrig, Giorgio Albertazzi. This is a fascinating, elusive film that was hailed by international critics when it first appeared and has been puzzling and satisfying audiences since that time. Well photographed symbolic, allegorical drama of a trio at a forlorn spa, and the attempts of a man to lure a mysterious woman away with him. A difficult multi-leveled arty entry that is worth the attention of serious discriminating film enthusiasts. (Dir: Alain Resnais, 93 mins.)

Late George Apley, The (1947)*** Ronald Colman, Peggy Cummins. J. P. Marquand's pungent satire on stuffy Boston society emerges on the screen as a pleasing family comedy, milder than "Life With Father" and not half as good. (Dir: Joseph L. Mankiewicz, 98 mins.)

Late Show, The (1977)**** Art Carney, Lily Tomlin, Howard Duff, Bill Macy. A sardonic, affectionate paean to the private-eye genre flicks of the 40's and 50's. It benefits greatly from a touching, nicely underplayed stint by Art Carney playing a washed-up, aging private eye determined to solve one tantalizing biggie. The major credit for the success of the film goes to Robert Benton who not only wrote the wise, knowing original screenplay but makes a most impressive directorial debut as well. Tomlin starts out as Carney's client but soon turns into a dizzy sidekick. They are delicious together. If this occasionally seems like a Robert Altman film, it's because it almost is— he produced this deft winner. (Dir: Robert Benton, 94 mins.)

Latin Lovers (1953)** Lana Turner, Ricardo Montalban, John Lund. Lana, a very rich girl, arrives in Brazil for a rest and ends up being chased by a dashing rancher, Ricardo. Lana and Ricardo make a torrid pair of "Latin Lovers," but

the rest is tepid. (Dir: Mervyn Le Roy, 104 mins.)

Laughing Policeman, The (1973)**½ Walter Matthau, Bruce Dern, Lou Gossett. Intended as a documentary reworking of "Dirty Harry." Matthau and Dern are much better than the story about a pair of policemen who try diligently to piece together the clues after a violent mass murder takes place on a San Francisco bus. Those questioned come on for interesting but all too brief vignettes, and the plot has too many disjointed facts. Gossett gives another solid characterization. This time he's a detective who is both streetwise and fair. (Dir: Stuart Rosenberg, 111 mins.)

Laughter in Paradise (British, 1951) **** Alastair Sim, George Cole, Guy Middleton. Four relatives have to perform impossible stunts if they are to collect an inheritance. Screamingly funny comedy has some great comic moments. Grand fun! (Dir: Mario Zampi, 95 mins.)

Laura (1944)***½ Dana Andrews, Clifton Webb, Gene Tierney. Fascinating, witty, suspenseful melodrama about the investigation of a death and the avalanche of surprise that follows. If you've never seen this—it's particularly a "must." (Dir: Otto Preminger, 88 mins.)

Lavender Hill Mob, The (British, 1952)**** Alec Guinness, Stanley Holloway. A mild-mannered bank employee evolves a fool-proof plan, he thinks, to make away with an armored car gold shipment. Hilarious comedy, fun all the way, another triumph for Guinness. (Dir: Charles Crichton, 82 mins.)

L'Avventura (Italian, 1959)**** Monica Vitti, Bagriele Ferzetti, Lea Massari. Director Michelangelo Antonioni's studied, enormously perceptive film about empty relationships in an unfeeling world. Story superficially concerns the disappearance of a girl, and the search for her by her lover and her best friend. This is one of Miss Vitti's best performances. The slow pace of the film contributes to its overall impact. (Dir: Michelangelo Antonioni, 145 mins.)

Law, The (1974)**** Judd Hirsch, John Beck. Here's a rarity . . . an excellent TV film which graphically depicts the everyday workings of the public defender's role in Los Angeles.

This is not an ordinary cops-and-crooks yarn with pat conclusions built into the script, but a true-to-life look at a deputy public defender who accidentally latches on to some vital information which could crack a bizarre, unsolved murder case. The first third sets up the job of the public defender, and Judd Hirsch, as Murray Stone, creates a full-blown character who never lets up in his intensity, giving the film its chief interest and appeal. Other performances are also first-rate and the story keeps you riveted from start to finish. Made-for-TV. (Dir: John Badham, 124 mins.)

Law and Disorder (British, 1958)******* Michael Redgrave, Robert Morley. Two of England's top theatrical and movie names make this comedy worth your attention. Plot concerns a retired crook who can't seem to stay far enough away from trouble. (Dir: Charles Crichton, 76 mins.)

Law and Disorder (1974)****½** Carroll O'Connor, Ernest Borgnine, Karen Black, Alan Arbus. Urban decay blights the neighborhood, so O'Connor, a cabbie, and Borgnine, a chauffeur, pair off as auxiliary cops. The middle-aged duo project outrage at being victimized city dwellers as well. This episodic satire alternates between drama and laughs and fails on both levels, despite some effective scenes. (Dir: Ivan Passer, 99 mins.)

Law and Jake Wade, The (1958)****½** Robert Taylor, Richard Widmark, Patricia Owens. Good western. Taylor is well cast as a former outlaw turned marshal in a town in New Mexico. His old buddy, played with all the stops pulled, by Richard Widmark, pops up and things change. The action sequences are excitingly staged. (Dir: John Sturges, 86 mins.)

Law and Order (1953)****** Ronald Reagan, Dorothy Malone. Customary western story about the retired U. S. Marshal who couldn't hang up his holster for any length of time. Rather ponderously paced.

Law and Order (1969)*****½** Documentary essay by Frederick Wiseman about the police force in Kansas City is a compassionate statement about the sometimes dangerous and always delicate task of being a policeman, and the fact that policemen, like the rest of us, are sometimes humane, sometimes cruel, impatient, etc.

There's one particularly notable sequence as a truculent, black male teenager is manacled after creating a commotion in an apartment house and how he tries, successfully, to antagonize his white captors while waiting to be taken to the police station. Many viewers will understand why filmmaker Wiseman feels that being a policeman is a difficult and often undesirable job. Also several vivid sequences where ordinary citizens brutalize each other. Another valuable Wiseman study of American institutions.

Law and Order (1976)****½** Darren McGavin, Keir Dullea, Robert Reed, James Olson, Teri Garr. Excessively long TV drama based on Dorothy Uhnak's best-seller about a New York Irish family of cops. With abundant use of flashbacks, the capable McGavin displays authority and stubbornness portraying the young and middle-aged cop, Brian O'Malley, warts and all, as he rises in the ranks. While the film concentrates on corruption within the force, its aim is to show policemen as human beings with normal weaknesses, such as an inability to communicate with their kids. Made-for-TV. (Dir: Marvin J. Chomsky, 144 mins.)

Law Is the Law, The (French, 1959)****½** Fernandel, Toto. A broad comedy tailored to the talents of France's top comedian, Fernandel, and Italy's top clown, Toto. Each represents opposite sides of the law and it's a tug-of-war all the way. (Dir: Christian-Jaque, 103 mins.)

Law of the Land, The (1976)***** Jim Davis, Barbara Parkins, Glenn Corbett, Andrew Prine, Moses Gunn, Don Johnson, Cal Bellini, Charlie Martin Smith, Nicholas Hammond. Utterly predictable Western made as a pilot, unbought, for a TV series. Leathery Jim Davis stars as a tough old Denver sheriff saddled with a group of eager-beaver deputies who are tracing a psychopathic killer of prostitutes. Made-for-TV. (Dir: Virgil Vogel, 98 mins.)

Law of the Lawless (1964)***½** Dale Robertson, Yvonne DeCarlo, William Bendix, Bruce Cabot, Richard Arlen. A Kansas judge in 1889, trying a murder case in a town full of his enemies, is seemingly in more danger than the defendant. Sparked by presence of Bendix and a retinue of other old familiars, who add a bit of nostalgia to the proceedings. (Dir: William F. Claxton.)

Law vs. Billy the Kid, The (1954)** Scott Brady, Betta St. John. Another version on the notorious career of Billy the Kid and his good friend Pat Garrett. Nothing new about this Western. (Dir: William Castle, 73 mins.)

Law West of Tombstone (1938)*** Harry Carey, Tim Holt. Ex-outlaw moves into a new town and establishes law and order. Above-average western has a good cast, better story than usual. (Dir: Glenn Tyron, 80 mins.)

Lawless, The (1950)***½ Macdonald Carey, Gail Russell, John Sands. A hard hitting and gripping story of bigotry against the Mexican-American fruit pickers in California and a crusading newspaperman's fight against it. Well acted. (Dir: Joseph Losey, 83 mins.)

Lawless Breed, The (1953)** Rock Hudson, Julia Adams. Ordinary western fare with Hudson playing a marked man who finally stops running and serves a long prison term so that he can end his days a free man. Some action but mostly talk. (Dir: Raoul Walsh, 83 mins.)

Lawless Street, A (1955)*** Randolph Scott, Angela Lansbury. Randolph Scott as the marshal has a hard job cleaning up the town of Medicine Bend. Gunplay wins the day. (Dir: Joseph L. Lewis, 78 mins.)

Lawman (1971)**½ Burt Lancaster, Robert Ryan, Lee J. Cobb, Robert Duvall, Ralph Waite. Familiar premise has "lawman" Lancaster riding into town to arrest cowman Cobb and his boys for the accidental shooting of an old man. In the middle stands the town's sheriff Ryan, who weakly sides with Lancaster. Stars better than their material. (Dir: Michael Winner, 99 mins.)

Lawrence of Arabia (British, 1962) **** Peter O'Toole, Omar Sharif. Director David Lean's marvelous Academy Award-winning spectacle about the legendary British officer and his exploits, military and nonmilitary, in Palestine circa WW I. A remarkable film on many counts: screenwriter Robert Bolt's intelligent screenplay, Peter O'Toole portraying Lawrence making a stunning film debut and capturing many of the nuances and character subtleties of

this complex homosexual hero; Lean's directorial work and certainly the cinematography. Try if you can to see this film in a theater before you watch it on TV. Lean and his colleagues capture the awsome beauty of the desert as it has never been shown before in this kind of a dramatic film. Even on your small-screen TV, however, this is a treat for the eye and ear, and the supporting cast is flawless. (222 mins.)

Lawyer, The (1970)**½ Barry Newman, Diana Muldaur. A brash, no-holds-barred performance by Newman as a small-town lawyer trying to make it to the top with a local murder case that gets a lot of national attention is the main lure of this film. Loosely based on the true-life murder trial of Dr. Sam Sheppard, the drama focuses more on the attorney than the defendant. In addition, Miss Muldaur has some good scenes as the young lawyer's lovely wife. (Dir: Sidney J. Furie, 103 mins.)

Lay that Rifle Down (1955)*½ Judy Canova, Robert Lowery. Canova working in a small-town hotel secretly takes a charm course. Country-style version of the Cinderella tale, for Canova fans only. (Dir: Charles Lamont, 70 mins.)

Le Mans (1971)** Steve McQueen. Racing fans will appreciate this excitingly photographed account of the famous 24-hour Le Mans endurance race and the participants of the annual event. Steve McQueen, who races in real life, looks right at home in the role of a determined American out to win the big one despite some near-fatal mishaps in his other attempts. There's virtually no plot or dialogue other than in the time-out sequences, but the racing footage is the thing here. Incorporates real footage from the 1969 and 1970 Le Mans races. Repetitive for non-racing freaks. (Dir: Lee H. Katzin, 106 mins.)

Leadbelly (1976)**½ Roger E. Mosley, Paul Benjamin, Madge Sinclair. Smooth, sanitized life of the legendary black folk-singer Huddie Ledbetter reveals a good-natured man unaware of the social forces that made his life hard and violent. Rather than concentrating on the mean temper and predilection for drunkenness that caused the real Leadbelly to be jailed twice for murder, screenwriter Ernest Kinoy and director Gordon Parks focus on the indomitable spirit that allowed Leadbelly's music to flower despite his personal troubles. The songs performed by Hi Tide Harris are well integrated with the melodrama. Bruce Surtees' photography makes the on-location shooting in Texas so lushly beautiful that even prison seems like a pleasant place. Listen to the still marvelous Leadbelly records after you've seen this "wholesome" version. (Dir: Gordon Parks, 126 mins.)

League of Gentlemen, The (British, 1961)**** Jack Hawkins, Richard Attenborough, Nigel Patrick. Fine blend of comedy and suspense, as a retired ex-army officer recruits some of his former men to pull off a big robbery. Writing shows much wit, style—performances excellent, direction perceptive. (Dir: Basil Dearden, 114 mins.)

Learning Tree, The (1969)***½ Kyle Johnson, Alex Clarke. This is the first film directed by famed still photographer Gordon Parks, who went on to direct "Shaft." He not only directed, but also produced and wrote the sensitive screenplay for this film, based on his autobiographical novel about growing up as a black youth in the Kansas of the mid-1920's. Provides most viewers with a fresh and new perspective on being black in America. It's also the first major Hollywood-financed film directed by a black. (107 mins.)

Lease of Life (British, 1955)***½ Robert Donat, Kay Walsh. Moving drama, superbly acted, as always, by the late Robert Donat. About a dying vicar in a small parish. (Dir: Charles French, 93 mins.)

Leather Boys (Great Britain, 1964)***½ Rita Tushingham, Dudley Sutton. Moving drama of teenager who marries a serious auto mechanic and then begins to cheat on him. The plot is minor, but the characters are touching. (Dir: Sidney J. Furie.)

Leather Saint, The (1956)** John Derek, Paul Douglas, Cesar Romero. Young minister becomes a fighter to aid polio victims. Undistinguished boxing drama has all the familiar plot ingredients. (Dir: Alvin Ganzer, 86 mins.)

Leave Her To Heaven (1945)**½ Gene Tierney, Cornel Wilde, Jeanne Crain. A fine novel about a psychopathic bitch becomes a poor film because of an unconvincing performance of Ms. Tierney and a generally ordinary script. (Dir: John M. Stahl, 111 mins.)

Leave It to Blondie (1945)**½ Penny Singleton, Arthur Lake, Chick Chandler, Marjorie Weaver. Dagwood finds himself among the finalists in a song-writing contest, although he didn't write it. Entertaining comedy in the "Blondie" series. (Dir: Abby Berlin, 75 mins.)

Lebanese Mission, The (French, 1956)**½ Jean-Claude Fascal, Jean Servais, Gianna Maria Canale. English-dubbed. Countess becomes involved with two prospectors who have discovered a uranium lode. Occasionally interesting melodrama. Well acted.

Leda—See: Web of Passion

Leech Woman, The (1960)** Coleen Gray, Grant Williams. Scientist's wife discovers the secret of perpetual youth and begins to bump off unsuspecting males for their hormones. Well, that's one way to get them. (Dir: Edward Dein, 77 mins.)

Left Hand of God, The (1955)**½ Humphrey Bogart, Gene Tierney, Lee J. Cobb. Slow-moving adventure yarn made interesting by the performances of the male stars. Bogart is an American who gets caught up in the private wars of a renegade Chinese warlord, played with much bravado by Cobb. (Dir: Edward Dmytryk, 87 mins.)

Left-Handed Gun, The (1958)*** Paul Newman, Lita Milan, John Dehner. An underrated film which tells the story of the west's legendary desperado, Billy the Kid. Paul Newman, as Billy, is superb. This screenplay sheds some light on Billy's reasons for his infamy and treats the Pat Garrett-Billy friendship with insight. TV's Fred Coe produced and Arthur Penn directed. (This was the duo's first film.) (102 mins.)

Left, Right and Center (British, 1960)**½ Alastair Sim, Ian Carmichael, Patricia Bredin. Television personality runs for office on the Conservative ticket and is opposed by a pretty young Laborite—love blossoms. Satire on British politics has its moments, but some of the punch may be lost outside the Commonwealth. (Dir: Sidney Gilliant, 100 mins.)

Legend of Boggy Creek, The (1973)* Hoary trash about a hairy monster. Inept mixture of fiction and documentary styles, allegedly based on the true experiences of the residents of Fouke, Ark., terrorized for years by the hairy monster that lived in the woods. The monster, it seems, turns out to be some clown in a gorilla suit. Writer-director-producer Charles B. Pierce should find some other line of work. (90 mins.)

Legend of Custer (1968) ½ Wayne Maunder, Slim Pickens, Michael Danter. Weak effort, relates the early Army career of the famous general. Originally aired as two episodes of the TV series "Custer." Made-for-TV. (Dir: William Graham, 100 mins.)

Legend of Lizzie Borden, The (1975) *** Elizabeth Montgomery, Ed Flanders, Fritz Weaver. Carefully handled version of the famous Lizzie Borden murders, casts no new light on the Massachusetts legend, but entertains, in its fashion. Montgomery gives a tour-de-force performance playing the celebrated ax-murderess, and capable Ed Flanders scores in the chief supporting role of the prosecuting district attorney. The sets and background detail are worthy of a theatrical feature, and the pacing is tight. Made-for-TV. (Dir: Paul Wendkos, 100 mins.)

Legend of Lylah Clare, The (1968) **½ Kim Novak, Peter Finch, Ernest Borgnine. Uneven but interesting old-fashioned melodrama about the movies and those by-now-familiar stereotypes who live, eat and breathe film-making. Kim Novak is the sexy starlet who resembles a flamboyant star of the thirties, Lylah Clare (who died mysteriously and tragically on her wedding night) and gets a crack at playing Lylah in a biographical film. Peter Finch is Lylah's real-life director-husband and history repeats itself as he falls for her reincarnation. A great deal of this is pure pap, but there are glimpses of good film-making and Peter Finch's wonderfully tormented characterization. Based on a 1963 TV drama of the same name, directed by Franklin ("Patton") J. Schaffner, which starred Tuesday Weld and Alfred Drake. (Dir: Robert Aldrich, 130 mins.)

Legend of the Lost (1957) **½ John Wayne, Sophia Loren, Rossano Brazzi. A powerhouse trio of stars and some excellent photography are the only plus factors of this sprawl-

ing, over-produced adventure epic. By the way, Miss Loren has come a long way in the acting department since this opus. (Dir: Henry Hathaway, 109 mins.)

Legend of Valentino, The (1975)** Franco Nero, Suzanne Pleshette, Judd Hirsch, Yvette Mimieux. Highly romanticized version of the life and loves of Rudolph Valentino, the legendary silent film star! Nero plays the Italian emigrant who rose to Hollywood stardom, and the best thing that can be said about his performance in this cliché-ridden script is that at least he's authentically Italian. According to writer-director Melville Shavelson, Valentino was an unhappy man who never enjoyed his success and became the victim of a line of heartless women, ruthless producers and over-sexed fans. Can be enjoyed on the same level as a fan magazine. Made-for-TV. (Dir: Melville Shavelson, 98 mins.)

Legendary Champions, The (1968) ***½ Documentary of heavyweight boxing champs from John L. Sullivan to Gene Tunney. A natural for ring devotees; others will find it absorbing too. (Dir: Henry Chapin, 77 mins.)

Legion of the Doomed (1958)* Bill Williams, Dawn Richard. If you've ever wanted to join the French Foreign Legion, this dull film will certainly cure you. (Dir: Thor Brooks, 75 mins.)

Legions of the Nile (Italy, 1960)** Linda Cristal, Georges Marchal. Fast-paced, superficial treatment of Antony and Cleopatra features two-dimensional plot of action and amour. (Dir: Vittorio Cattafavi, 90 mins.)

Lemon Drop Kid, The (1951)*** Bob Hope, Marilyn Maxwell. Hope's delivery makes a natural for this role of a fast talking race track bum who has to come up with a bundle he owes the syndicate or else. The laughs are all there. (Dir: Sidney Lanfield, 91 mins.)

Lemonade Joe (Czech, 1964)*** Carl Fialam, Olga Schoberova. Wild spoof of Yank westerns with the usual pure hero, purer heroine, dirty varmints. At first it's frantically funny, then the hoke palls; but it's certainly a novelty and good fun. Dubbed-in English. (Dir: Oldrich Lipsky, 84 mins.)

Lenny (1974)**** Dustin Hoffman,

Valerie Perrine, Jan Miner. Dustin Hoffman's bravura portrayal of the tortured, self-destructive, brilliantly inventive comic Lenny Bruce is enough of a reason to see "Lenny," which garnered several Academy Award nominations, including one for Hoffman, Perrine and director Bob Fosse. Drug-addict Lenny Bruce, who died in 1966 after being harassed by the police and courts for years, has been the subject of plays, books and films. This film has the advantage of using material from Bruce's trials which are "performed" by Hoffman as part of his nightclub act. Valerie Perrine is sexy, sad and funny as Lenny's suffering wife. Hoffman is a marvel—overlook some of the weak points and watch dazzling Dustin. (Dir: Bob Fosse, 111 mins.)

Lenny Bruce (1967)**** A valuable icon of the 1960's, and this brilliant, visionary, self-destructive, put-upon comedy genius. This is the only film Bruce ever made, an unedited filmed record of a San Francisco nightclub performance in August of 1965. The photography is uneven, as are some of Bruce's routines, but the best of it is astonishing, and it remains the best record of this tormented soul's inspired, bizarre, irreverent and sometimes grotesque humor. Bruce discusses savagely and inventively his trial in New York State for having performed obscene material.

Lenny Bruce Performance Film, The —See: Lenny Bruce

Lenny Bruce Without Tears (1975)*** A documentary about the comedian Lenny Bruce, who died in 1966, written and directed by Fred Baker. It contains clips from kinescopes of old Bruce TV appearances, interviews with Bruce himself, and people like Kenneth Tynan and Mort Sahl talking about Bruce and his influence on American comedy and society. Valuable sociological record provides a few insights and some Bruce-generated laughs. (Dir: Fred Baker, 78 mins.)

Leopard, The (Italian, 1963)**½ Burt Lancaster, Claudia Cardinale, Alain Delon. Giant epic film based on the novel by Giovanni di Lampedusa. This slow-moving film is exquisitely photographed, and tells the story of the aristocracy in Italy during the 1860's. Burt Lancaster looks great as the noble patriarch of a leading family of Sicily, but he is miscast. Another irritation is the poor dubbing into English. (Dir: Luchino Visconti, 165 mins.)

Leopard Man (1943)***½ Dennis O'Keefe, Margo. Black leopard used as a stunt by an actress escapes in a small New Mexican town, and a wave of murders begins. Terrifically thrilling, suspenseful melodrama, a very good job. (Dir: Jacques Tourneur, 66 mins.)

Lepke (1974)*½ Tony Curtis, Anjanette Comer, Michael Callan, Warren Berlinger, Milton Berle. Clumsy "kosher" version of "The Godfather." Mediocre amalgam of gangster clichés assembled to immortalize Jewish gangster Louis "Lepke" Buchalter of the 1920's. Curtis acts tough and talks from the side of his mouth as the anti-hero. Supporting roles are cardboard. Berle plays Lepke's disapproving father-in-law. Direction reinforces the clichés. (Dir: Menahem Golan, 109 mins.)

Les Belles-de-Nuit (French, 1952) ***½ Gerard Philippe, Martine Carol. Director Rene Clair was inspired to some degree by Griffith's "Intolerance," but the Frenchman decided to make a humorous version, while letting his hero act out his dreams, set in different countries in varying historical periods. Outstanding sequence toward the end when Philippe, during the course of a hilarious comic chase, advances from the Neanderthal age to the 1950's. (84 mins.)

Les Carabiniers (French, 1967)***½ Genevieve Gaela, Marino Nase. Ironic, difficult allegory on war which is ultimately worth the trouble necessary to understand it. An important work by one of the masters of movies in the period before he gave up films for polemics. (Dir: Jean-Luc Godard, 80 mins.)

Les Girls (1957)**** Gene Kelly, Kay Kendall, Mitzi Gaynor, Taina Elg. Very entertaining musical with a talented cast plus a sparkling Cole Porter score. Kelly plays an American hoofer in Paris with three beautiful girls in his act. In between musical numbers, he falls in love with his gorgeous co-workers. Kay Kendall steals every scene she's in. A joyous film. (Dir: George Cukor, 114 mins.)

Les Miserables (1935)**** Fredric March, Charles Laughton. Victor

Hugo's classic story of a man who went to prison for stealing a loaf of bread is brought to life by a faithful adaptation, good production and fine performances by March as the tormented Jean Valjean and Laughton as the cop who plagues him. (Dir: Richard Boleslawski, 108 mins.)

Les Miserables (1952)**½** Michael Rennie, Debra Paget, Robert Newton. Victor Hugo's classic story of an escaped convict and the detective who trails him for a lifetime. Well acted, well enough produced, but there are just too many versions around now, though this isn't a bad one. (Dir: Lewis Milestone, 104 mins.)

Les Miserables (French, 1957)***** Jean Gabin, Bernard Hlier, Bourvil. Faithful adaptation of Victor Hugo's novel of an escaped convict and his relentless police pursuer—so faithful, in fact, that the nearly four-hour version is available in two separate parts. Generally commendable, but doesn't alter the fact that too many versions of this story are already around. This happens to be one of the better ones though. English-dubbing.

Let George Do It (Great Britain, 1940)****** George Formby, Phyllis Calvert, Bernard Lee. Several good comic turns in a light spy spoof, as vaudevillian Fromby jokes and sings his way past agents of the Third Reich. (Dir: Marcel Varnel, 72 mins.)

Let It Be (1970)****½** The Beatles. Whenever a myth is explored there are always a myriad of folks willing to go on the expedition. The journey here is to the roof of the Beatles-Apple building where we are allowed to peek in on a recording session. The songs are lilting, poetic, and, yes, they can do them live! But you have to be in on the myth to flow with this documentary. (Dir: Michael Lindsay-Hogg, 88 mins.)

Let No Man Write My Epitaph (1960)****** Burl Ives, Shelley Winters, James Darren. Badly done sequel to "Knock on Any Door." The performances are on the amateurish side, particularly Shelley Winters, who overacts throughout in the role of a junkie. (Dir: Philip Leacock, 106 mins.)

Let the Good Times Roll (1973)****½** Little Richard, Bo Diddley, The Shirelles, The Five Satins, Chuck Berry.

If you grew up in the 50's with its music blaring in your ear and stacks of 45's spinning in your brain, this nostalgic trip down memory lane, via two filmed concerts of oldies but goodies, will give you a high. Split-screen devices showing the performers as they were when you were sporting a D.A., upturned collars, pointed shoes, and teased hair, and as they are now (some drastically different), bolsters the endless parade of rock and roll. The lineup of performers includes Little Richard, The Shirelles, The Five Satins, Chuck Berry, Chubby Checkers, Fats Domino, Bill Haley and the Comets, and Bo Diddley, among others. (Dirs: Sid Levin, Robert Abel, 99 mins.)

Let Us Live (1939)****½** Henry Fonda, Maureen O'Sullivan. Fiancee of an innocent man about to be executed fights to save his life. Grim, overdone but well-acted drama. (Dir: John Brahm, 70 mins.)

Let's Be Happy (1957)****½** Tony Martin, Vera-Ellen. Vera-Ellen inherits some money and travels to Scotland dancing in the heather all the way. Tony Martin sings. Some lovely on the spot photography. (Dir: Henry Levin, 93 mins.)

Let's Dance (1950)****** Fred Astaire, Betty Hutton. Ex-actress and her former partner fight her wealthy mother-in-law when she tries to take away her son. Astaire's superlative dancing gets lost in a sugary, dull plot, and Hutton is hardly his best vis-à-vis in the terpsichore department. (Dir: Norman Z. McLeod, 112 mins.)

Let's Do It Again (1953)****½** Jane Wyman, Ray Milland, Aldo Ray. Footloose comedy about an almost divorced couple and their escapades to make each jealous. Wyman is very funny as the wife. (Dir: Alexander Hall, 95 mins.)

Let's Do It Again (1975)******* Sidney Poitier, Bill Cosby, Calvin Lockhart, John Amos, Jimmie Walker, Ossie Davis, Denise Nicholas, George Foreman. Sequel which is funnier than the original "Uptown Saturday Night." Poitier and Cosby are once again two pals who are involved in shenanigans to raise money for their ailing lodge. This time, Poitier has hypnotic skills which are trained on a puny boxer (hilariously played by Walker) to turn him into a champ.

Trouble comes when they confound two gangsters with opposite life-styles, Amos and Lockhart. High-spirited fun, that might be called a black, lower-middle class version of "The Sting." (Dir: Sidney Poitier, 112 mins.)

Let's Face It (1943)** Bob Hope, Betty Hutton. Undistinguished, but occasionally amusing, Hope vehicle about soldiers who agree to help middle-aged married women avoid becoming lonesome. Complications are obvious, and so is much of the comedy. (Dir: Sidney Lanfield, 76 mins.)

Let's Kill Uncle (Great Britain, 1966) ½ Nigel Green, Mary Badham, Pat Cardi. Fun and games as a little boy and his uncle attempt to do away with each other—the prize being a five-million-dollar inheritance. The various tarantulas and sharks steal the picture. (Dir: William Castle, 92 mins.)

Let's Live a Little (1948)**½ Hedy Lamarr, Robert Cummings. A harassed ad man falls for a lady psychiatrist, and vice versa. Pleasant romantic comedy. (Dir: Richard Wallace, 85 mins.)

Let's Make It Legal (1951)**½ Claudette Colbert, Macdonald Carey, Marilyn Monroe, Robert Wagner, Zachary Scott. Mildly amusing comedy about a married couple who decide to get a divorce after 20 years of marriage. This throws their children and friends into a frenzy and everyone tries to do his small part in keeping the marriage intact. The cast does well. (Dir: Richard Sale, 77 mins.)

Let's Make Love (1960)**½ Marilyn Monroe, Yves Montand, Tony Randall. The personal appeal of the two stars—Monroe and Montand—should make up for the shortcomings of this lightweight comedy-romance played against a show-business background. Both stars sing a little, act a little and generate a lot of sex appeal. (Dir: George Cukor, 118 mins.)

Let's Make Up (British, 1955)*½ Anna Neagle, Errol Flynn, David Farrar. Actress can't choose between an actor and a businessman, has dreams of what life would be like with each at various periods of history. Plodding musical fantasy gives Flynn a chance to do a song-and-dance turn, badly. Alternate title:

Lilacs in the Spring. (Dir: Herbert Wilcox, 94 mins.)

Let's Rock (1958)** Julius La Rosa, Phyllis Newman. Phyllis Newman is the best and only worthwhile thing in this second rate rock 'n roll musical comedy.

Let's Scare Jessica to Death (1971) ** Zohra Lampert, Kevin O'Connor, Mariclaire Costello. Zohra Lampert, an interesting and talented actress, gives this horror yarn whatever allure it has, but alas, it's not enough. Ms. Lampert is Jessica, a former mental patient, who arrives at an old Connecticut house with her husband and their friend, supposedly for a rest. Enter a strange lady. (Dir: John Hancock, 89 mins.)

Let's Switch (1975)*½ Barbara Feldon, Barbara Eden, George Furth. Here's one of those silly premises which relies on the attractiveness of its two stars, in the roles of liberated women who put their theories to the test. Barbara Eden is the housewife who yearns for fulfillment of a different kind, like that enjoyed by her good friend, Barbara Feldon, editor of She Magazine. They decide to switch roles and thereby hangs the thin tale. Made-for-TV. (Dir: Alan Rafkin.)

Let's Talk About Women (Italy-France, 1964)**** Vittorio Gassman, Eleonora Rossi-Drago, Heidi Strop, Sylva Koscina. A series of sometimes excruciatingly funny vignettes, all of which star Gassman and involve his desire to get into or stay out of bed with some comely wench. The opener, about a gun-slinging stranger making a courtesy call to an isolated farmhouse, is hysterical, and so are a number of the other sketches in this delicious episodic entry. Just sit back and enjoy the almost unending laughs about manners, mores and amour! (Dir: Ettore Scola, 108 mins.)

Letter, The (1940)***½ Bette Davis, Herbert Marshall. Somerset Maugham's story receives a Class A treatment from a fine cast and magnificent direction from William Wyler. This combination of talents actually succeeds in breathing life into this tale of a woman who has incriminated herself in a letter and must retrieve it. (Dir: William Wyler, 95 mins.)

Letter for Evie, A (1945)**½ Marsha Hunt, John Carroll, Spring Byington. Fair Grade B film using the familiar plot about the man who sends his handsome friend's picture to the girl he has been courting by mail. Hume Cronyn is excellent as the deceiver. (Dir: Jules Dassin, 89 mins.)

Letter from an Unknown Woman (1948)***½ Joan Fontaine, Louis Jourdan. The tragic drama of a woman who continues to love a dashing pianist, although he doesn't sincerely love her. Well produced, a romance that will have the ladies drying their eyes, but the men may be bored. (Dir: Max Ophuls, 90 mins.)

Letter to Three Wives, A (1949)**** Ann Sothern, Kirk Douglas, Linda Darnell, Jeanne Crain, Paul Douglas, Thelma Ritter. "Letter" is addressed to 3 wives from their best friend, announcing that she is running away with one of their husbands—but she doesn't say which one. Each wife examines her marriage in flashbacks, wondering if the wandering husband is hers. Another fine film from director Joseph L. Mankiewicz. (103 mins.)

Letters, The (1973)**½ Barbara Stanwyck, Jane Powell, Dina Merrill, Ida Lupino, Leslie Nielsen. Three soap-operaish short stories are tied together by an old gimmick—a trio of letters that have been lost in the mail for a year, drastically altering the lives of the recipients when delivered. Made-for-TV. (Dirs: Gene Nelson and Paul Krasny, 73 mins.)

Letters from Three Lovers (1973)** June Allyson, Ken Berry, Juliet Mills. Undelivered letters find their way to the addressees a year after they were sent. June Allyson and Robert Sterling share a "brief encounter" and plan to make it a monthly thing, but his letter doesn't reach her in time, etc. Familiar fare! Made-for-TV. (Dir: John Erman, 72 mins.)

Liane, Jungle Goddess (West German, 1956)* Marion Michael, Hardy Kruger. Muddled mess from Germany, about a woman who grew up in the African jungle, even though she has millionaire relatives. (Dir: Eduard Borsody, 85 mins.)

Libel (British, 1959)**½ Olivia de Havilland, Dirk Bogarde, Paul Massie. A wealthy man is accused of being an impostor, sues for libel;

some doubt arises in his wife's mind whether or not he's telling the truth. Fairly interesting drama works up good suspense after a slow start. (Dir: Anthony Asquith, 100 mins.)

Libeled Lady (1936)***½ Jean Harlow, William Powell, Myrna Loy, Spencer Tracy. Screen comedy played by the experts is this offering about a paper, being justly sued for libel, which tries to convert the libel to truth. (Dir: Jack Conway, 98 mins.)

Liberation of L.B. Jones, The (1970) **½ Lee J. Cobb, Anthony Zerbe, Lola Falana, Lee Majors, Yaphet Kotto. The venerable William Wyler and writer Sterling ("In the Heat of the Night") Silliphant have combined to create a much gloomier vision of the possibility of decent relations between blacks and whites anywhere, including the South. L.B. Jones, the richest black man in his county of Tennessee, is divorcing his wife for infidelity with a white policeman. He takes a stand against racism and meets a grisly end. Script full of stereotypes, including policemen, "liberals from the North" and Southern bigots. Lola Falana glitters in her dramatic debut as the alluring Mrs. Jones. Irritating, occasionally interesting. (Dir: William Wyler, 101 mins.)

License to Kill (French, 1964)*½ Eddie Constantine, Daphne Dayle. Our old hero Nick Carter is called in when enemy agents try to swipe a new secret weapon. English-dubbed weak French imitation of American action story. (Dir: Henry Decoin, 95 mins.)

Lies My Father Told Me (Canada, 1975)***½ Yossi Yadin, Len Birman, Marilyn Lightstone, Jeffrey Lynas, Ted Allan. A charming, sentimental ethnic memoir about growing up in 1924 in a Jewish "ghetto" in Montreal. It's an autobiographical story of author Ted Allan who wrote the screenplay and also appears as Mr. Baumgarten. Focuses on the relationship of a young boy and his aged grandfather, a robust, free-spirited peddler. A gentle, tender tale suitable for children of all ages. Affectionately directed by Jan Kadar, remembered for his haunting "Shop on Main Street." (102 mins.)

Lieutenant Schuster's Wife (1972)** Lee Grant. Amateur detective, a New York cop's widow, is determined to clear her husband's good name. In the story, filmed for the most part on New York streets, sleuth Grant runs into the likes of Eartha Kitt at an uptown pool hall, and meets wily Nehemiah Persoff. Miss Grant deserves better. Made-for-TV. (Dir: David Lowell Rich, 73 mins.)

Lieutenant Wore Skirts, The (1956) **½ Tom Ewell, Sheree North. TV writer gets jealous when his wife is taken back into service. Funny at times, but never quite jells. (Dir: Frank Tashlin, 99 mins.)

Life and Assassination of the Kingfish, The (1977)*** Edward Asner, Nicholas Pryor, Diane Kagan, Fred Cook. The political saga of Huey P. Long, who rose from small-town lawyer to governor of Louisiana and U.S. Senator, is candidly presented in a well-produced TV feature starring Edward Asner. Asner's portrayal of the charming rogue who was labeled a demogogue by most of his critics is excellent. Wearing a dark wig and adopting a down-home accent, Asner creates a picture of a man driven by his lust for power, coupled with a strong desire to give the common man a fair shake. Long's personal life is sketchily treated; rather, the film favors the Huey Long who paraded among his puppet-politicians, bending rules and making deals. Though not totally accurate history, the film does spell out the relentless ambition of a man who might have made it to the White House if fate had not intervened in September, 1935, when he was gunned down in Louisiana. Written and directed by Robert Collins. Made-for-TV. (100 mins.)

Life and Loves of Mozart, The (German, 1956)**½ Oskar Werner, Nadja Tiller. The later years of Mozart, his work, and his love for a young singer. Well done but a bit too dramatic in performances.

Life and Times of Grizzly Adams, The (1974)*½ Dan Haggerty, Marjory Harper, Don Shanks, Lisa Jones. Mediocre "nature" tale of a mountain man, wrongly accused of a crime, who leaves civilization and his 8-year-old daughter for the rugged north country. For the kids. (Dir: Richard Friedenberg, 100 mins.)

Life and Times of Judge Roy Bean, The (1972)*½ Paul Newman, Ava Gardner, Stacy Keach, Victoria

Principal. Newman and director John Huston miss badly with this labored tale of Texas, circa 1880. There was a roguish Judge Roy Bean in Texas history, but fact is mixed with silly fantasy here as Newman plays a self-appointed judge. Best salaried performer is Keach playing an albino gunman. The best performance in the film is turned in by Bruno, a beer-guzzling grizzly. (124 mins.)

Life at Stake, A—See: **Key Man** (Keith Andes, Angela Lansbury)

Life at the Top (1965)**½ Laurence Harvey, Jean Simmons, Honor Blackman. Sequel to the successful "Room at the Top" but not as well done. Has Laurence Harvey repeating his characterization of the opportunist who married the boss' daughter and found true unhappiness. It's competently handled, but too familiar. However, the performances by Harvey and Jean Simmons, as his disappointed wife, are worth watching. (Dir: Ted Kotcheff, 117 mins.)

Life Begins at College (1937)*** Ritz Brothers, Joan Davis, Tony Martin. This zany film will only appeal to the youngsters and the many fans of the Ritz Brothers. It's a crazy football comedy played strictly for slapstick. (Dir: William A. Seiter, 110 mins.)

Life Begins at Eight-thirty (1942) **½ Monty Woolley, Ida Lupino, Cornel Wilde. Well acted but dreary drama of an alcoholic, broken-down actor and his daughter who gives up everything to help him. Too morbid in spite of Woolley's frequent attempts at humor. (Dir: Irving Pichel, 85 mins.)

Life Begins for Andy Hardy (1940) **½ Lewis Stone, Mickey Rooney, Judy Garland. Andy gives New York a fling and he almost misses out on starting college. Wait'll you see the troubles he gets into in the big city. (Dir: George B. Seitz, 100 mins.)

Life for Ruth—See: **Walk in the Shadow**

Life in Emergency Ward 10 (Great Britain, 1959)*½ Michael Craig, Wilfred Hyde White, Dorothy Alison. Melodrama of a little boy with a hole in his heart, played to the hilt. Subplots abound, as do the obligatory happy endings. (Dir: Robert Day, 86 mins.)

Life in the Balance, A (1955)** Ricardo Montalban, Anne Bancroft,

411

Lee Marvin. Despite the good cast, this cheaply made meller about a series of murders and the various suspects generates very little excitement. Mexican locations the chief asset. (Dir: Harry Horner, 74 mins.)

Life of Donizetti (Italian, 1951)** Amadeo Nazzari, Mariella Lotti. The film biography of the great composer of Italian opera. Good operatic sequences sung by Tito Schipa and others, a stilted story. English-dubbed.

Life of Emile Zola (1937)**** Paul Muni, Joseph Schildkraut, Donald Crisp. One of the greatest film biographies of all time. Story of Zola and the famous Dreyfus case are graphically and, at the same time, sensitively presented. Muni is magnificent. (Dir: William Dieterle, 130 mins.)

Life of Her Own, A (1950)** Lana Turner, Ray Milland, Tom Ewell. Sluggish soap opera—can a high-fashion model find happiness with the copper magnate who has a crippled wife? Turner wears the clothes, Milland suffers the emotions. One asset: good supporting job by Ann Dvorak. (Dir: George Cukor, 108 mins.)

Life Upside Down (French, 1965)*** Charles Denner, Anna Gaylor. Young Frenchman about to be married causes concern when he suddenly becomes withdrawn, living in another world. English-dubbed drama is a most intriguing study of a man on the verge of insanity but may not be appreciated by all viewers. For those who do, it will prove absorbing, excellently enacted and directed. (Dir: Alain Jessua, 93 mins.)

Life With Blondie (1945)**½ Penny Singleton, Arthur Lake, Ernest Truex. When Daisy becomes a pin-up dog, Blondie and Dagwood have to contend with many inconveniences, including some gangsters. Some good laughs in this entertaining entry in the "Blondie" series. (Dir: Michael Curtiz, 64 mins.)

Life with Father (1947)**** William Powell, Irene Dunne. A delightful, still charming screen adaptation of Broadway's long-running play by Howard Lindsay and Russel Crouse about the obstreperous Clarence Day and his wonderfully demanding presence as father of the Victorian household. William Powell is perfec-

tion itself as the vigorous patriarch of his red-headed brood and Irene Dunne is charming and graceful as his infinitely patient wife. Look for young Elizabeth Taylor as the oldest Day boy's girlfriend. (Dir: Michael Curtiz, 116 mins.)

Life With Henry (1941)**½ Jackie Cooper, Eddie Bracken. Good "Henry Aldrich" comedy as Henry tries to win a trip to Alaska and goes into the soap business. Bracken is a delight as Henry's sidekick. (Dir: Ted Reed, 80 mins.)

Lifeboat (1944)*** Tallulah Bankhead, John Hodiak, Walter Slezak, William Bendix. Alfred Hitchcock's drama of emotions under stress, developed within the confines of a lifeboat occupied by members of a torpedoed ship and by a U-boat commander. Experiment with a restricted setting comes off rather well, if not outstandingly. Some good performances. (96 mins.)

Lifeguard (1976)**½ Sam Elliott, Anne Archer, Stephen Young, Parker Stevenson. Aimless movie about a 30-plus-year-old lifeguard in California who thinks the time may have come for him to settle down and live a real life as a car salesman. Sam Elliott is handsome and well-built, but the role doesn't let him go much beyond his handsomeness. Anne Archer has a good scene as his high-school girl friend looking for a rekindling of sorts. A couple of involving sequences. (Dir: Daniel Petrie, 96 mins.)

Light Across the Street (French, 1956)** Brigitte Bardot, Raymond Pellegrin. An early BB movie before she became the "sex kitten." BB plays the wife of a trucker who switches her affections to a gas station jockey when her husband spends too much time trying to make money. (Dir: George Lacombe, 76 mins.)

Light at the Edge of the World, The (U.S.-Spanish-Liechtensteinian, 1971)* Kirk Douglas, Yul Brynner, Samantha Eggar. Douglas and Brynner are as hopeless as the movie itself. Loosely based on an adventure story concocted by Jules Verne, about a wayward lighthouse keeper who has witnessed the wrecking of a ship by pirates and therefore must die. (Dir: Kevin Billington, 101 mins.)

Light Fantastic, The (1963)*½ Dolores McDougal, Barry Bartle, Jean

Shepherd. Skinny little tale of love in the big city, as a young swinger realizes too late that his false sentiments have turned to real love. Tries hard to be offbeat, winds up being just off.

Light Fingers (British, 1958)** Guy Rolfe, Roland Culver, Eunice Gayson. Man suspects his wife of being a kleptomaniac, hires a bodyguard for her, who turns out to be a jewel thief. Comedy forces for laughs a bit too hard. (Dir: Terry Bishop, 90 mins.)

Light in the Forest, The (1958)**½ James MacArthur, Carol Lynley. Walt Disney's version of the Conrad Richter novel. Concerns an Indian who learns gradually that he must coexist with the whites. In time he falls in love with a white girl. Good outdoor locations. Bears the superficiality which is Disney's trademark. (Dir: Herschel Daugherty, 93 mins.)

Light in the Piazza (1962)*** Olivia de Havilland, Rossano Brazzi, Yvette Mimieux, George Hamilton. Woman and her childlike daughter travel to Italy, where the mother has fears when a nice young lad falls in love with the beautiful but retarded girl. Delicate and disturbing love story graced by beautiful Italian scenics, good performances. (Dir: Guy Green, 101 mins.)

Light That Failed, The (1939)***½ Ronald Colman, Ida Lupino, Walter Huston. Superb acting carries this sincere screen version of Kipling's first novel. Story of an artist who is losing his sight is romantic, heroic and often good drama. (Dir: William Wellman, 97 mins.)

Light Touch, The (1951)**½ Stewart Granger, Pier Angeli, George Sanders. Innocent young girl artist unwittingly provides a suave art thief with a copy of a masterpiece with which he plans a swindle. Flavorsome location scenes in Italy provide more interest than the flimsy romantic story. Good cast, pleasant innocuous entertainment. (Dir: Richard Brooks, 110 mins.)

Lightning Strikes Twice (1951)**½ Ruth Roman, Richard Todd, Mercedes McCambridge. Despite a hackneyed script about a man acquitted of his wife's murder, Richard Todd manages to create an interesting characterization and gets able sup-

port from the two ladies in the cast. (Dir: King Vidor, 91 mins.)

Likely Story, A (1947)***½ Bill Williams, Barbara Hale. Returned vet thinks he has only a short time to live and gets mixed up with racketeers. Surprisingly good little comedy has many laughs, extremely pleasant players. (Dir: H. C. Potter, 88 mins.)

Li'l Abner (1959)**½ Peter Palmer, Leslie Parrish, Stubby Kaye. The Broadway musical based on the famous cartoon characters of Dogpatch makes a mildly entertaining film. The humor seems forced but the musical numbers are fast paced and colorful. Peter Palmer fills the physical requirements of Li'l Abner and sings well. (Dir: Melvin Frank, 113 mins.)

Lili (1953)**** Leslie Caron, Mel Ferrer, Jean-Pierre Aumont. A thoroughly captivating film for youngsters and adults alike, beautifully scored, performed, and produced. Leslie Caron is utterly captivating in the title role of a French orphan who joins a small traveling carnival, and soon falls for the charms of a sophisticated magician (Jean-Pierre Aumont), very much the ladies' man although he's actually married. An unforgettable highlight of the film is a charming dream sequence in which Lili dances with the life-size replicas of the puppets who magically materialize on the road. (Dir: Charles Walters, 81 mins.)

Lilies of the Field (1963)**** Sidney Poitier, Lilia Skala. Heart-warming drama with an award-winning performance by Poitier as a handyman who encounters some nuns who have fled from East Germany, winds up building a chapel for them. Originally released with little fanfare, the film became a big hit, deservedly so. In addition to Poitier, there's a splendid job by Miss Skala, understanding direction by Ralph Nelson. See it. (Dir: Ralph Nelson, 93 mins.)

Lilith (1964)** Warren Beatty, Jean Seberg, Peter Fonda, Kim Hunter. Director Robert Rossen's study of searing passions at a mental home, and young therapist's (Beatty) involvement with a strange girl inmate (Seberg). Earnest effort becomes inordinately arty while reaching for effect. (114 mins.)

Lillian Russell (1940)**½ Alice Faye, Don Ameche, Henry Fonda. One of

America's fabled stage stars who reigned late in the 19th century deserved better screen treatment than she receives here. Old songs are good but her highly fictionalized romances are dreary. (Dir: Irving Cummings, 127 mins.)

Limbo Line, The (Great Britain, 1968) ½ Craig Stevens, Kate O'Mara, Eugene Deckers, Jean Marsh. Tedious Cold War espionage thriller. British-agent Stevens attempts to keep a ballerina away from those nasty Russians. (Dir: Samuel Gallu, 98 mins.)

Limelight (1952) **** Charles Chaplin, Claire Bloom, Sydney Chaplin. Beautiful, poignant love story, written, produced, and directed by the great man himself. Chaplin plays an over-the-hill British musichall comedian who nurses a ballet dancer (Bloom) back to health after she has attempted suicide. Some of the plot and camerawork are "old-fashioned" but the luminous qualities of Chaplin's genius and Bloom's enchanting performance make it all work. You're made out of stone if you're not moved by the clown's death at the end, or touched by the ballerina's tenderness and concern. A love story for all time and all generations.

Linda (1973) * Stella Stevens, Ed Nelson, John Saxon, John McIntire. John D. MacDonald's mystery yarn is better in book form. It's the old plot about a sexy blond wife and lover framing naive husband with a beach-front killing. Made-for-TV. (Dir: Jack Smight, 90 mins.)

Lindbergh Kidnapping Case, The (1976) *** Cliff De Young, Anthony Hopkins, Joseph Cotten, Walter Pidgeon, Sian Barbara Allen, Martin Balsam, David Spielberg. Well-made drama on the sensational 1932 tragedy is cast with care. The talented young De Young appears to be a dead ringer for the famous flyer, gallant Charles Lindbergh, but he finds it tough going trying to portray the stoic Lindy, who carefully masks his emotions during the kidnapping of his baby son and the subsequent trial of Bruno Richard Hauptmann. England's Anthony Hopkins is more effective as Hauptmann, and Spielberg outshines the principals in the role of prosecuting-attorney Wilentz. It's an earnest, sincere effort to depict an earlier

America that's only partly successful. Made-for-TV. (Dir: Buzz Kulik, 144 mins.)

Line Up, The (1958) **½ Eli Wallach, Robert Keith, Warner Anderson. "The Line Up" was a popular TV series in the fifties and this is merely an expanded version of the show using the two stars in their roles as Police Officers (Anderson and Tom Tully). Wallach has some good moments as a professional killer who takes pride in his work. (Dir: Don Siegel, 86 mins.)

Links of Justice (British, 1958) *½ Jack Watling, Sarah Lawson. Rotter sets up a plan to murder his wife, but it misfires, tragically for him. Dull thriller.

Lion, The (British, 1962) ** William Holden, Trevor Howard, Capucine, Pamela Franklin. Some mighty nice African backgrounds here—and some pretty unconvincing plot motivations. About an American lawyer who comes to Africa to see his remarried wife and their daughter. Fascinating locale offset by weak direction and the confused script. (Dir: Jack Cardiff, 96 mins.)

Lion in the Streets, A (1953) *** James Cagney, Barbara Hale, Anne Francis. The rise of a ruthless Southern politician is vividly portrayed by Jimmy Cagney. As a peddler he marries a local schoolteacher and begins his climb by exploiting the local townfolk. Familiar, but still stirring climax as exposed corruption causes the politician's downfall. (Dir: Raoul Walsh, 88 mins.)

Lion in Winter, The (British, 1968) **** Peter O'Toole, Katharine Hepburn, John Castle, Anthony Hopkins, Jane Merrow. Playwright James Goldman's excellent Broadway play, which was a financial flop despite good notices, is a superb historical drama, marvelously well acted by O'Toole and Hepburn. Katie tied for an Academy Award for her portrayal of the great medieval figure Eleanor of Aquitaine. Narrative starts in 1183 during the reign of King Henry II of England. The luminous Rosemary Harris dominated the Broadway play, but that is not the case in this wide screen version as Hepburn and O'Toole present one of film history's most fascinating pairs of embattled lovers. (Dir: Anthony Harvey, 135 mins.)

Lion of Thebes, The (Italian, 1964)✱ Mark Forest, Yvonne Furneaux. Would you believe that, after the fall of Troy, the beauteous Helen fled to Egypt, where she stirred up trouble once again? Another in the endless cycle of lame-brained spectacles.

Lions Are Loose, The (French, 1961)✱✱½ Claudia Cardinale, Michele Morgan, Danielle Darrieux, Lino Ventura. Good international cast can't do much with this labored comedy about a gal from the country who gets entangled in amours in Paris. Nice to look at, but that's all. Dubbed-in English.

Lipstick (1976)½ Margaux Hemingway, Chris Sarandon, Anne Bancroft, Mariel Hemingway. In a subheading for its review of this deplorable trash, Variety billed "Lipstick" as "Rape as exploitation material. Big openings." The movie is usually distasteful, but the Variety copy was an inadvertent vulgarity, while the movie is crammed with them, all on purpose. Margaux displays no talent whatever playing a successful model (which, of course, she is in real life) who is savagely molested by a sick composer and then humiliated in and out of court. Teenager Mariel Hemingway gives the least odious performance in this stinker. Produced by Freddie Fields. (Dir: Lamont Johnson, 89 mins.)

Liquidator, The (1966)✱✱ Rod Taylor, Trevor Howard, Jill St. John. If your tastes run toward secret missions and handsome spies messing with beautiful redheads on the Riviera and in London, this adventure yarn is definitely for you. Taylor is being trained by British Intelligence for a secret mission involving assassinations and such, but the plot doesn't really interfere with the two-fisted action and lovemaking. A big asset is the fine supporting cast of top-notch character actors. (Dir: Jack Cardiff, 104 mins.)

Lisa (1962)✱✱½ Stephen Boyd, Dolores Hart. If you like chase movies full of suspense and mystery, this one is definitely for you. The plot doesn't always make sense, with too many facts deliberately masked for the sake of building tension, but the excellent European locations, the performances of Dolores Hart and Stephen Boyd, and a better-than-average supporting cast compensate

for this flaw. The story concerns a flight across Europe by a disturbed young Jewish refugee right after World War II, and the aid she gets from a police officer who accidentally teams up with her. (Dir: Philip Dunne, 112 mins.)

Lisbon (1956)✱✱✱ Ray Milland, Maureen O'Hara, Claude Rains. Adventurer is hired by an international scoundrel to act as go-between in a kidnapping. Melodrama has a good bit of dash, pleasant players, and picturesque locale. (Dir: Ray Milland, 90 mins.)

Lisette (1961)✱½ John Agar, Greta Chi. Sexy Eurasian girl messes up plans of a newspaper editor to put his father-in-law in the Senate. Trashy melodrama.

List of Adrian Messenger, The (1963)✱✱✱ George C. Scott, Dana Wynter, "Guest Stars." John Huston directed this gimmicky whodunit about a crafty murderer who resorts to disguises to eliminate nearly a dozen people. The plot's routine in conception and execution, but the fun here is to see if you can spot some stellar names—Kirk Douglas, Robert Mitchum, Tony Curtis, Burt Lancaster, Frank Sinatra — all tricked out in funny faces. Should provide a good time for mystery buffs. (Dir: John Huston, 98 mins.)

Listen, Darling (1938)✱✱½ Judy Garland, Freddie Bartholomew, Walter Pidgeon, Mary Astor. Cute little tidbit about a couple of youngsters who try to marry off a widow so they can have a mother and father. (Dir: Edwin L. Marin, 80 mins.)

Little Big Horn (1951)✱✱✱ John Ireland, Lloyd Bridges. Saga of a small band of cavalry sent to warn Custer of impending Indian attack. Grim, gripping, excellently acted. (Dir: Charles Marquis Warren, 86 mins.)

Little Big Man (1970)✱✱✱✱ Dustin Hoffman, Faye Dunaway, Richard Mulligan, Chief Dan George. Powerful historical film about the development of the West, how the white man treated the Indians (in this case the Cheyennes), climaxing with General George A. Custer's famous last stand at Little Bighorn. This is one of the few American films, up till this time, that didn't patronize or caricature the Indians, and it benefits from a good screenplay by Calder Willingham based on Thomas Berger's novel. Much of the narrative unfolds in the form of flashbacks seen through the eyes of a 121-year-old white man, Jack Crabb (Hoffman), the sole white survivor of Custer's last stand. Custer is portrayed as the psychotic he clearly was. Special credit goes to makeup man Dick Smith for the extraordinary makeup he created for Hoffman. A complex, ambitious, rewarding "western," extremely well directed by Arthur Penn. (147 mins.)

Little Boy Lost (1953)***½ Bing Crosby, Claude Dauphin, Christian Fourcade. War correspondent returns to France in search of his son, born during World War II, whom he has never seen. Tender, touching drama, with Crosby carrying it off in fine style. Should cause the ladies to reach for the hankies. (Dir: George Seaton, 95 mins.)

Little Caesar (1930)***½ Edward G. Robinson, Douglas Fairbanks Jr. One of the all-time great gangster movies. By modern standards it's ordinary in many respects but Robinson's portrayal of a merciless killer is a masterpiece which has withstood years of mimicry. (Dir: Mervyn Le Roy, 80 mins.)

Little Egypt (1951)** Mark Stevens, Rhonda Fleming. Highly fictionalized account of the celebrated hootchy-kootch dancer who caused a near riot at the Chicago World's Fair in 1893. Miss Fleming is a decorative lass and her gyrations are worth waiting for. (Dir: Frederick de Cordova, 82 mins.)

Little Fauss and Big Halsy (1970)*½ Robert Redford, Michael Pollard, Lauren Hutton. Halsey is a suspended motorcycle racer looking for another name. Fauss is a Walter Mitty bike tuner waiting to give his name away. Together they race around the Southwest. The winner turns out to be a loser, and so is the film. Director Sidney Furie shows little sense of motorcycle motion and one wonders why not use cows . . . The title song by Johnny Cash, which pounces in and out of the film, is as moving as "Fat and Skinny had a race . . ." (97 mins.)

Little Foxes, The (1941)**** Bette Davis, Herbert Marshall, Teresa Wright, Dana Andrews, Dan Duryea. Superb film based on Lillian Hellman's strong play about the double dealings of a Southern family presided over by a vixen named Regina, a part tailor-made for Miss Davis' talents. A must for drama fans. Miss Davis is altogether bitchy and quite wonderful. (Dir: William Wyler, 116 mins.)

Little Fugitive, The (1953)***½ Richie Andrusco, Rickie Brewster. Mistakenly thinking he has killed his 12-year-old brother, a little boy runs away, lands at Coney Island. Human, often touching always amusing little comedy-drama, with a nonprofessional cast. The little boy Andrusco is amazing. (Dir: Ray Ashley, 75 mins.)

Little Game, A (1971)* Ed Nelson, Diane Baker, Katy Jurado, Howard Duff. Ed Nelson goes paranoid, wondering whether his 11-year-old stepson is a murderer and hiring a private detective to find out. Who cares. Made-for-TV. (Dir: Paul Wendkos, 72 mins.)

Little Giant (1956)** Bud Abbott & Lou Costello, Elena Verdugo. Costello plays a salesman who bilks the crooked manager (Abbott) of the firm he works for, and wins a prize for his effort. Plenty of slapstick. (Dir: William A. Seiter, 91 mins.)

Little House on the Prairie, The (1974)**½ Michael Landon, Karen Grassle. Landon returns to acting, as well as directing this simple story about a post-Civil War family trekking from Wisconsin to Kansas to open a new life as homesteaders. It's based on the book by Laura Ingalls Wilder, the real-life daughter of the pioneering family. Pilot for subsequent series, made-for-TV.

Little Hut, The (1957)*** Ava Gardner, Stewart Granger, David Niven. The French play about a wife, her husband and his best friend living a "civilized" existence while shipwrecked on an island makes a frothy, sophisticated film. The stars romp throughout and have at least as much fun as the audience. (Dir: Mark Robson, 78 mins.)

Little Kidnappers, The (1954)**** Adrienne Corri, Duncan MacRae. Two boys kidnap a baby because they can't have a dog. Brilliant, simple, moving and amusing film. That's all there is to it, but it's a gem.

Little Ladies of the Night (1977)**½ David Soul, Lou Gossett, Linda Purl, Clifton Davis, Carolyn Jones, Lana Wood, Dorothy Malone. Linda Purl is quite good playing the role of a very young teenager, around 14, forced into prostitution by some threatening pimps after running away from home and a pair of insensitive parents. David Soul, who became a TV star on "Starsky & Hutch," plays a sympathetic police officer. The squalid world of pimps, young hookers and their loveless clients is handled with reasonable restraint, though of course the language is greatly cleaned up, giving the whole proceeding an air of unreality. Made-for-TV. (Dir: Marvin Chomsky, 100 mins.)

Little Lord Fauntleroy (1936)*** Freddie Bartholomew, Mickey Rooney, C. Aubrey Smith. Warm, sentimental version of Frances Hodgson Burnett's mid-Victorian saga of a boy from Brooklyn in 1885 who becomes a lord. Memorable performances by a wonderful cast. (Dir: John Cromwell, 97 mins.)

Little Minister (1934)***½ Katharine Hepburn, John Beal. Barrie's tale of the romance of a pastor in Scotland. Very capably done, with fine performances. (Dir: Richard Wallace, 110 mins.)

Little Miss Broadway (1938)** Shirley Temple, Jimmy Durante. Routine Shirley Temple film carrying her from orphanage to success in her foster home. (Dir: Irving Cummings)

Little Miss Marker (1934)*** Adolphe Menjou, Charles Bickford, Shirley Temple. A little girl is left with gangsters as security for an IOU. Sentimental Damon Runyon tale was made when Miss Temple was at her cutest. Good entertainment. (Dir: Alexander Hall, 90 mins.)

Little Mr. Jim (1946)*** Butch Jenkins, James Craig, Frances Gifford. When tragedy strikes his family, a small lad turns to the Chinese cook for companionship. Touching, well done drama.

Little Murders (1971)***½ Elliott Gould, Marcia Rodd, Vincent Gardenia, Elizabeth Wilson. Jules Feiffer's devastating off-Broadway satire has been turned into an equally impressive movie. Under Alan Arkin's careful directorial eye for capturing the absurd moment without sacrificing the meat of the text, the film emerges as an important document of the violence-ridden New York scene, and what turns the average citizen from

apathy to militancy. The story of Alfred, the mild-mannered photographer, brilliantly played by Gould, and his romantic involvement with Patsy, the cockeyed optimist (Rodd) and her outrageous family, can't be summed up . . . it has to be seen and absorbed. The absurdities will keep you laughing until they hit home and make you stop and think in wide-eyed astonishment. Donald Sutherland's lunatic clergyman is extraordinarily funny. (110 mins.)

Little Nellie Kelly (1940)**½ Judy Garland, George Murphy. Granddaughter of a stubborn Irish cop tries to patch up a family feud that has lasted for years. Sentimentality reigns supreme in this Irish-laced comedy-drama. Garland's singing is always worthwhile, Murphy turns in a good job, helping to overcome the mawkishness of the plot; diverting for unsophisticates. (Dir: Norman Taurog, 100 mins.)

Little Nuns, The (Italian, 1965)*** Catherine Spaak, Sylva Koscina. Charming, tender comedy drama about the adventures of two nuns who go to the city to protest when the soundwaves of jets overhead threaten to destroy the ancient fresco of their convent. Good entertainment. Dubbed in English. (Dir: Luciano Salce, 101 mins.)

Little Old New York (1940)**½ Alice Faye, Fred MacMurray, Richard Greene. Don't take this story about Fulton and his steamboat too seriously and you may have some fun. It's long, slightly miscast but occasionally entertaining. (Dir: Henry King, 100 mins.)

Little Prince, The (1973)**½ Richard Kiley, Steven Warner, Gene Wilder, Bob Fosse, Clive Revill, Donna McKechnie. Disappointing musical version of the enduring book by Antoine de Saint-Exupery. The talent for this fable about a neurotic aviator and the little boy from outer space, who becomes his mentor about earthly matters like life and love, is impressive. Musical score by Lerner and Loewe, adaptation by Alan Jay Lerner. Director Stanley Donen has made several of the most stylish, charming musicals ever, but "Prince" remains too coy and pretentious. Multi-talented director Bob Fosse steals the show with his nifty Snake. (Dir: Stanley Donen, 88 mins.)

417

Little Princess, The (1939)***½ Shirley Temple, Richard Greene. The high rating is for Miss Temple's fans as this is probably her best film. Going from riches to rags in a Victorian drama she expertly runs the gamut of emotions. If you don't like Shirley or child stars in general, forget this one and forgive the rating. (Dir: Walter Lang)

Little Rebels, The (French, 1955)**½ Jean Gabin, Jacques Moulieres. Gabin gives another fine performance as an understanding judge who takes the time to care and love the young orphans who go the wrong way.

Little Savage, The (1959)** Pedro Armendariz, Terry Rango. Strictly for the junior set. A tale of piracy and island adventures seen through the eyes of a little boy.

Little Shepherd of Kingdom Come, The (1961)** Jimmy Rodgers, Luana Patten. Kentucky mountain boy is a wanderer until taken in by a loving family; but he takes the side of the North when the Civil War begins. Pleasing rural tale takes a bit too much time to tell its story. (Dir: Andrew V. McLaglen, 108 mins.)

Little Shop of Horrors, The (1960)*** Jonathan Haze, Jackie Joseph. Man, this is way out! Balmy plant-grower has a time feeding his creations—seems they like human food. Little quickie has a surprising amount of shuddery laughs.

Little Theatre of Jean Renoir, The (France-Italy-West Germany, 1969)*** Jeanne Moreau, Pierre Olaf. A valedictory from the great French director Jean Renoir—four short films of varying quality but full of Renoir's customary charm, grace and wisdom. Renoir made his first film in 1924, and this, his last, was commissioned and funded by French television. Renoir himself appears on camera at the outset, appearing for the first time in any of his films. The different sketches include "The Last Christmas Eve," "The Electric Waxer," and the last and finest sequence, "The King of Yvetot," a touching Pagnol-like beauty. (100 mins.)

Little Women (1933)**** Katharine Hepburn, Joan Bennett, Frances Dee, Jean Parker. The Alcott classic of four daughters growing up in a Civil War household, screened with great charm, fine production values, excellent performances. A timeless film, delightful for all ages. (Dir: George Cukor, 120 mins.)

Little Women (1948)**½ June Allyson, Peter Lawford, Margaret O'Brien, Elizabeth Taylor. Louisa May Alcott's girls Jo, Beth, Amy and Meg return in this re-make about life in Concord at the time of the Civil War. Entertaining when it's light and gay but when they turn on the tears, it's a mess. Those who like to cry at sentimental nonsense will have a good bath here. (Dir: Mervyn Le Roy, 121 mins.)

Little World of Don Camillo (Franco-Italian, 1953)*** Fernandel, Gino Cervi. Priest feuds with the Communist mayor of his town. Enjoyable comedy-drama with good performances. (Dir: Julien Duvivier, 96 mins.)

Littlest Hobo, The (1958)**½ Buddy Hart, Wendy Stuart. Nice story of a dog's adventures, especially for the kiddies. (Dir: Charles Rondeau, 77 mins.)

Littlest Rebel, The (1935)** Shirley Temple, John Boles, Bill Robinson. Another corny film featuring Shirley and Bill Robinson. Shirley is the heroine of the Civil War in this, and your kids will love it. (Dir: David Butler, 70 mins.)

Live a Little, Love a Little (1968)½ Elvis Presley, Michele Carey, Rudy Vallee. Elvis' 28th film and one of his dullest. Elvis tries to hold down two jobs, and stay out of the way of the ravishing Michelle Carey. (Dir: Norman Taurog, 89 mins.)

Live Again, Die Again (1974)**½ Walter Pidgeon, Donna Mills, Geraldine Page, Vera Miles. How a family reacts to the reemergence of a young mother (Miss Miles), frozen for 30 years. The family—husband Thomas (Pidgeon) in his 70's, middle-aged daughter Marcia (Miss Miles), and the housekeeper (Miss Page)—face a wrenching readjustment to Caroline's youthful 32, largely unprepared thanks to the wonders of cryogenics, the science of freezing which is actually still in the embryonic stage. Made-for-TV. (Dir: Richard A. Colla.)

Live and Let Die (1973)*** Roger Moore, Yaphet Kotto, Jane Seymour, Geoffrey Holder. If you're counting, this is number 8 in the James Bond films, and by now they all look and sound remarkably the same. This time out, Roger Moore as Agent 007

418

tries to unearth a large heroin operation in the Caribbean. Flashy photography, exotic locales, and an ample serving of sexy ladies keep things popping along at a nice clip. Personally, we miss Connery. (Dir: Guy Hamilton, 121 mins.)

Live Fast, Die Young (1958)** Mary Murphy, Michael Connors. Sister searches for a runaway teenager, finds her in time to prevent her from taking part in a robbery. Ordinary crime melodrama. (Dir: Paul Henreid, 82 mins.)

Live for Life (French, 1967)** Yves Montand, Candice Bergen, Annie Girardot. A TV reporter and his affairs, marital and extramarital, fancied up with pretty photography by the director of "A Man and a Woman," Claude Lelouch. Despite the frills, it never goes anywhere, not even when it tries for relevancy in a Vietnam sequence. (111 mins.)

Lively Set, The (1964)** James Darren, Pamela Tiffin, Doug McClure, Joanie Sommers. Lad shows more interest in racing engines than college, so he quits to devote his time to putt-putts. Teen-age fare exclusively with a lot of noise and a dull story. (Dir: Jack Arnold, 95 mins.)

Lives of a Bengal Lancer (1935)***½ Gary Cooper, Franchot Tone, C. Aubrey Smith. Solid action film which, in the Kipling tradition, glorifies the Empire's troops in India. It's history today. India no longer belongs to Britain. But this is still a whale of a yarn. (Dir: Henry Hathaway, 110 mins.)

Lives of Jenny Dolan, The (1975)** Shirley Jones, Dana Wynter, Lynn Carlin, George Grizzard, Ian McShane. Shirley Jones is starred in this slick murder-mystery drama, playing a retired investigative reporter who comes back to work for a crack at unearthing the sinister plot behind the governor's assassination, and three other deaths which occurred in the same night. Film producer Ross Hunter is billed as executive producer on this one and, as always, he makes sure his leading lady is dressed in an array of top fashions—Ms. Jones wears no less than a dozen chic costumes. Sewing better than the scripting. Made-for-TV. (Dir: Jerry Jameson, 98 mins.)

Living Coffin, The (Mexican, 1965)* Gaston Santos, Mary Duval. Members of a family are rumored to have been buried alive. Poor horror story in a western setting, dubbed in English.

Living Free (British, 1972)*** Susan Hampshire, Nigel Davenport. Exotic African scenery and three tiny lion cubs provide pleasant family entertainment in this sequel to "Born Free." Virginia McKenna and Bill Travers have been replaced as the keepers of lions held in captivity. In this picture, Elsa has died and left her young cubs to deal with the problem of learning to fend for themselves. This sequel is overly sentimental, and some of the scenes are patently phony, but the kids won't care. (Dir: Jack Couffer, 91 mins.)

Living It Up (1954)** Dean Martin, Jerry Lewis, Janet Leigh. Jerry as a railroad attendant whose sinus trouble is mistaken for radiation, becomes a human-interest story with New York at his feet. Martin and Lewis fans will approve, but the shadow of the original "Nothing Sacred" with March and Lombard makes this one shrivel in comparison. (Dir: Norman Taurog, 95 mins.)

Lizzie (1957)** Eleanor Parker, Richard Boone, Joan Blondell. Psychoshenanigans concerning a drab girl who seems to have another self lurking within her. Clumsy development loses the interest. (Dir: Hugo Haas, 81 mins.)

Lloyds of London (1936)***½ Tyrone Power, Madeleine Carroll, Freddie Bartholomew. Engrossing, often exciting story of the famous English insurance and banking firm. This picture tells of its early history and rise to prominence around the time of the battle of Trafalgar. (Dir: Henry King, 115 mins.)

Loan Shark (1952)**½ George Raft, Dorothy Hart, Paul Stewart. An ex-con smashes a vicious loan shark racket that has been plaguing workers in a tire plant. Fast-moving crime melodrama, with Raft at his best. (Dir: Seymour Friedman, 74 mins.)

Locker 69 (British, 1963)** Eddie Byrne, Paul Daneman. Private eye finds his employer dead, but when he tells the police, the body vanishes. Fair Edgar Wallace mystery. (Dir: Norman Harrison, 56 mins.)

Locusts (1974)** Ben Johnson, Ron Howard. Grasshoppers here, there and everywhere! A well-meaning but slow-moving account of a young man, washed out of Navy flight school and returned home to Montana farm country in 1943. Demanding father (Ben Johnson) is cutting down son (Ron Howard), and the boy finally gets a chance to win back his father's respect. A good, earnest cast gives the material a valiant try on location in Alberta, Canada. Made-for-TV. (Dir: Richard Heffron, 72 mins.)

Lodger, The (1944)**½ George Sanders, Merle Oberon, Laird Cregar. Story of Jack the Ripper is sometimes exciting but often laughable as the renowned killer walks through London knocking off young, beautiful girls. (Dir: John Brahm, 84 mins.)

Log of the Black Pearl, The (1974)**½ Ralph Bellamy, Keil Martin, Anne Archer. Here's a ripe old-fashioned sailing melodrama, filmed in Mexican waters and directed by outdoor expert Andy McLaglen, who learned his trade on "Have Gun Will Travel." A young stockbroker inherits a beautiful old sailing ship from his ailing grandfather and hunts for sunken treasure. The plot may not be exciting, but the boat and the scenery are put to good use by director McLaglen. Made-for-TV.

Logan's Run (1976)**½ Michael York, Richard Jordan, Jenny Agutter, Farrah Fawcett-Majors, Peter Ustinov, Roscoe Lee Browne. A science-fiction film that is less concerned with philosophizing about the future than providing some entertainment with dazzling sets and futuristic gadgets. Living in a domed-in hedonistic civilization, Logan (York) is a policeman who hunts down "runners" who attempt to escape the society's law that at 30 you must submit to "renewal," which is actually execution. Logan tries to flee the dome and encounters a lonely hermit, played by Ustinov. The technological gimmicks encountered in the year 2274 are enough to sustain interest, if the melodramatic plot is not to your liking. Jerry Goldsmith composed a rousing score to accompany the miles of glass used for sets. (Dir: Michael Anderson, 120 mins.)

Lola (1971)**½ Susan George, Charles Bronson. An adult drama about a May-September romance between a liberated 16-year-old and a close-to-40-year-old American writer who meet, have a tempestu-

ous affair, and make the mistake of marrying. (Dir: Richard Donner, 95 mins.)

Lola Montes—See: Sins of Lola Montes

Lolita (1962)*** James Mason, Peter Sellers, Shelley Winters, Sue Lyon. Controversial story of a man of the world suddenly if not inexplicably infatuated with a "nymphet." Satiric, many good sequences, but not a complete success. Decidedly unusual. Good performances, especially from Sellers. Worth seeing. (Dir: Stanley Kubrick, 152 mins.)

Lollipop Cover, The (1965)*** Don Gordon, Carol Seflinger. A thoughtful scenario brightens this low-budget production about a former prize-fighter and an abandoned child who are transformed by their experiences traveling together. (Dir: Everett Chambers, 85 mins.)

Lolly-Madonna XXX (1973)*½ Rod Steiger, Robert Ryan, Jeff Bridges. A family feud in Tennessee with little emotional or intellectual interest. Steiger and Ryan are the opposing fathers who let a small squabble over some disputed land escalate into a bloody war. Ill-fated allegory or poor entertainment, take your pick. (Dir: Richard C. Sarafian, 103 mins.)

London Town (British, 1946)** Sid Field, Greta Gynt, Kay Kendall. The rise of a comedian from the small-time to stardom. British imitation of an American musical had a lot of money spent on it but something went wrong somewhere. Mild at best.

Lone Ranger, The (1956)** Clayton Moore, Jay Silverheels, Lyle Bettger. The masked man and faithful Tonto uncover dirty work between Indians and whites. Feature version of popular perennial radio and TV show with a more elaborate production and well-known cast names, but it's still the same old Heigh-Yo, Silver. (Dir: Stuart Heisler, 86 mins.)

Lone Ranger and the Lost City of Gold, The (1958)*½ Clayton Moore, Jay Silverheels. The masked man and Tonto go after hooded riders murdering Indians, in order to find five medallions leading to a lost city. Juvenile western strictly for the kiddies. (Dir: Lesley Selander, 80 mins.)

Lone Star (1952)**½ Clark Gable, Ava Gardner, Broderick Crawford.

A big Western film with the stress on romance, but why complain when the romantic interest is supplied by Ava Gardner. (Dir: Vincent Sherman, 94 mins.)

Loneliness of the Long Distance Runner (1962)**** Tom Courtenay, Michael Redgrave. Continually absorbing British film about a rebellious school boy whose need for recognition prods him into trying out for the track team. Brilliantly directed by Tony Richardson, with near faultless performances from Tom Courtenay and the polished veteran Michael Redgrave. Richardson's camera work is dazzling, especially during the big race at the end. (103 mins.)

Lonely Are the Brave (1962)*** Kirk Douglas, Gena Rowlands. Offbeat western about a cowboy who escapes from jail and is hunted by a sheriff's posse; the big difference here is the well portrayed contrast between the old way of life and the modernization of today, with the cowboy as a man out of his time element. Excellent performance by Douglas; obvious symbolism in the script prevents this from being even better than it is. (Dir: David Miller, 107 mins.)

Lonely Hearts (1958)**½ Montgomery Clift, Robert Ryan, Myrna Loy, Dolores Hart, Maureen Stapleton. Overlong and brooding story about an "advice to the lovelorn" columnist who gets too involved with his job and ends up questioning himself about values in life and love. The subject matter doesn't come across in this badly written script based on the superb novel "Miss Lonelyhearts" by Nathanael West. The cast flounders with the material but Miss Stapleton fares the best as the wife of a cripple who hungers for a passionate love. (Dir: Vincent J. Donehue, 108 mins.)

Lonely Man, The (1957)**½ Jack Palance, Anthony Perkins, Neville Brand. Tried-and-true plot of a gunfighter's attempts to reform against all odds makes for a well-acted if unexceptional western drama. (Dir: Henry Levin, 87 mins.)

Lonely Profession, The (1969)*** Harry Guardino, Barbara McNair, Dina Merrill. Better-than-average, made-for-TV private eye film with a very good performance by Harry Guardino as a small-time detective who gets involved in a wild case.

After a frightened girl (Ina Balin) shows up in Guardino's office, he's plunged into a series of events and narrow escapes which keep the suspense mounting. A host of stars, including Dina Merrill, Dean Jagger, Jack Carter, Barbara McNair and Fernando Lamas, do very well in supporting roles, and the great San Francisco locales, slick dialogue and action, plus sharp editing keep this detective story moving at a fast clip. For those who don't catch on before the finale, there's a dandy surprise ending. (Dir: Douglas Heyes, 96 mins.)

Loners, The (1972)* Dean Stockwell, Pat Stich. Dreary tale of three teenagers on the run from police in the Southwest. Dean Stockwell plays the leader of the trio accused by the police of murder of a highway patrolman. (Dir: Sutton Roley, 79 mins.)

Long Ago Tomorrow (British, 1971) *** Malcolm McDowell, Nanette Newman, Georgia Brown. Though the story is somewhat cliched, the direction by Bryan Forbes and the powerful acting by a well-rounded cast overcome the difficulty. McDowell is impressive as a wheelchair victim who is strengthened by a love affair with another cripple, Miss Newman. She dies in true "Love Story" fashion, but he can overcome the tragedy because his life has been made meaningful. (111 mins.)

Long Dark Hall, The (British, 1951) **½ Rex Harrison, Lilli Palmer. A married man is accused of the murder of a showgirl, nearly is executed for the crime he didn't commit. Just average mystery melodrama; some good courtroom scenes. (Dir: Anthony Bushell, 86 mins.)

Long Day's Dying, The (British, 1968)** David Hemmings, Tom Bell, Tony Beckley, Alan Dobie. Grisly incident involving three privates and their German prisoner in no-man's land. War is hell; so is an overwrought war movie, despite laudable intentions. (Dir: Peter Collinson, 93 mins.)

Long Day's Journey Into Night (1963) **** Katharine Hepburn, Ralph Richardson, Jason Robards Jr., Dean Stockwell. An unrelenting, shattering film, magnificently directed by Sidney Lumet. Eugene O'Neill's triumphant tragedy, largely autobiographical, of a New England family and their relationships alternately wavering between love and hate, guilt and pride. Jason Robards Jr., who captured Broadway with his stunning portrayal of the oldest son, repeats his finely honed portrayal but is matched every step of the way by Katharine Hepburn, giving what must surely be one of the most devastating performances ever offered by an American actress. Ralph Richardson is also splendid but it is this landmark play by the great author and Hepburn's losing battle with drug addiction that will haunt any viewer for a long time. (108 mins.)

Long Duel, The (1967)*** Yul Brynner, Trevor Howard. Brynner and Howard star in this intelligent adventure epic which pits two men of honor against each other. Brynner plays an Indian leader who fights Howard, representing the British in India during the 1920's. Their personal integrity interferes with the call to duty in many instances. Good quota of action. (Dir: Ken Annakin, 115 mins.)

Long Goodbye, The (1973)**** Elliott Gould, Sterling Hayden, Mark Rydell, Nina van Pallandt. A gloriously entertaining and sophisticated detective yarn based on Raymond Chandler's novel about an indolent flatfoot, Philip Marlowe (Gould). Marlowe is hired to find a missing husband, is threatened by a Jewish hoodlum (hysterically played by Rydell), and journeys to Mexico. Style is more important in this Robert Altman-directed winner than plot. There's a slick opening sequence with Marlowe and his cat; nutty scenes where Marlowe, en route to visit his client, can only pass if he listens to the guard's imitations of old movie stars; and shots of Marlowe's neighbors—four luscious girls who are into nude yoga. Gould has a stylish slovenliness about him that is precisely right, as is the cinematography by Vilmos Zsigmond. The ending's been changed, along with some other details. But even Chandler purists will enjoy this one. (111 mins.)

Long Gray Line, The (1955)*** Tyrone Power, Maureen O'Hara. Tyrone Power gives one of his best performances as the Irish immigrant who finds a home and love at West

422

Point. John Ford directed with his usual skill. Film is extremely sentimental. (Dir: John Ford, 138 mins.)

Long Haul, The (British, 1957)*½ Victor Mature, Diana Dors. Mediocre drama about an American truck driver who settled in Liverpool, England after the war and falls prey to a beautiful girl who's working for a racketeer. Trashy love angle and overdramatic situations. (Dir: Ken Hughes, 88 mins.)

Long Hot Summer, The (1958)***½ Paul Newman, Joanne Woodward, Orson Welles, Lee Remick, Anthony Franciosa, and Angela Lansbury. Thanks to a good cast, William Faulkner's novel "The Hamlet," is brought to the screen with power and conviction. Welles is perfectly cast as the tyrannical head of a Southern family which includes a strong willed daughter (Miss Woodward), a weakling son (Franciosa) and his young, flighty wife (Miss Remick). A stranger (Paul Newman) shows up and things start crackling. Miss Lansbury gives another of her fine supporting performances as Welles' sometime mistress. Poor ending weakens film well directed by Martin Ritt. (117 mins.)

Long John Silver (Australian, 1953)**½ Robert Newton, Kit Taylor, Rod Taylor. The bold buccaneer battles a rival pirate for the spoils of Treasure Island. Entertaining swashbuckling saga, with Newton giving a broadly humorous portrayal. (Dir: Byron Haskin, 109 mins.)

Long, Long Trailer, The (1954)*** Lucille Ball, Desi Arnaz. Smoothly made, frequently charming comedy starring two popular TV veterans, all about how a trailer played a part in the honeymoon life of a couple of newlyweds, their difficulties in adjusting to the outdoor life. Good fun. (Dir: Vincente Minnelli, 103 mins.)

Long Memory, The (British, 1953)** John Mills, Eva Bergh, Elizabeth Sellars. Man wrongly imprisoned for murder is released full of bitterness, redeems himself through the love of a girl. Well acted, frequently exciting melodrama. (Dir: Robert Hamer, 91 mins.)

Long Night, The (1947)** Henry Fonda, Barbara Bel Geddes, Vincent Price. The killer of a shady magician hides out in a hotel room, while his girl pleads with him to give himself up. Dreary, ponderous drama;

some good moments. (Dir: Anatole Litvak, 101 mins.)

Long Ride from Hell, A (Italian, 1970)* Steve Reeves, Wayde Preston. Reeves has traded in his sandals on a sunny Roman Empire set for a six-gun and a role in a western which he helped write. Garbled plot has Steve playing a falsely imprisoned cowboy out to take revenge on his captors. Violence has been cut for TV version. (Dir: Alex Burks, 94 mins.)

Long Ride Home, The (1968)**½ Union officer (Glenn Ford) on the trail of escaped Confederate soldiers. Violent western carries an occasional punch. With George Hamilton, Inger Stevens, Paul Petersen, Max Baer. (Dir: Phil Karlson, 88 mins.)

Long Rope, The (British, 1955)*** Donald Houston, Susan Shaw. After serving a prison term, a man returns to his home town only to be implicated in a murder. Lengthy but well-done melodrama holds the interest.

Long Rope, The (1961)**½ Hugh Marlowe, Alan Hale, Chris Robinson. Circuit judge finds himself against an entire town when he tries a man for murder. Okay western drama made on a small budget—it's better than some of the more elaborate ones. (Dir: William Witney, 61 mins.)

Long Ships, The (1964)** Richard Widmark, Sidney Poitier. One of those epics about a brave Viking and his search for a golden bell, opposed by villainous Moors. Good actors usually look silly in these things, and this one is no exception. The two-star rating is for the scenery only. (Dir: Jack Cardiff, 125 mins.)

Long, the Short and the Tall, The —See: Jungle Fighters

Long Voyage Home, The (1940)**** John Wayne, Thomas Mitchell. Based on play of Eugene O'Neill. Tale of merchant seamen, their hopes, dreams, close comradeship. Superbly directed by John Ford, a gripping, dramatic, often beautiful film. (105 mins.)

Long Wait, The (1954)** Anthony Quinn. Dull Mickey Spillane adventure about an amnesia victim falsely accused of murder. Even Spillane fans will be disappointed. (Dir: Victor Saville, 93 mins.)

Longest Day, The (1962)**** Robert Mitchum, Richard Burton, Red Buttons, John Wayne, Irina Demick. Very little phony war heroics in this impressive handling of the preparation leading up to the historic WW II Normandy invasion by the Allied Forces, and the events of D-Day itself. Makes a fascinating war film you're not likely to forget for some time. An all-star cast plays various soldiers, generals, French resistance fighters, and Germans in short vignettes carefully woven into the larger fabric of the massive operation. Darryl F. Zanuck produced this gigantic war spectacle, and directed some of it, but you won't find his name among the directorial credits. (Dirs: Ken Annakin, Andrew Marton, Bernard Wicki, 108 mins.)

Longest Hundred Miles, The (1966)**½ Doug McClure, Katharine Ross, Ricardo Montalban. Young army corporal, a pretty lady lieutenant, a padre, and an assortment of children band together in an attempt to flee the Japanese occupation of the Philippines during World War II. Made-for-TV melodrama is paced swiftly but is cliché-filled, not particularly well acted. (Dir: Don Weis, 93 mins.)

Longest Night, The (1972)*** David Janssen, James Farentino. Good kidnap yarn based on a case that made headlines years ago. Daughter of a wealthy businessman is abducted by a meticulous, calculating, clever young man and his girl friend, and is subsequently buried alive in a specially constructed box with a battery-operated air supply for one week. Tension reaches nerve-racking stage. Well directed by Jack Smight. Cast, headed by Farentino as the kidnapper and Janssen as the girl's father, couldn't be better. Made-for-TV. (Dir: Jack Smight, 73 mins.)

Longest Yard, The (1974)*** Burt Reynolds, Eddie Albert, Jim Hampton, Ed Lauter. Clever, fiercely funny reworking of the plot of "The Dirty Dozen," features 12 convicts, murderers and other scalawags forming a football team to oppose a semi-pro group composed of their own guards. Ferocious gridiron action sees the prisoners take revenge for their captors' senseless brutality. Reynolds' portrayal of an imprisoned former football star who leads the cons in their pursuit of dignity, is only outshined by Albert's menacing characterization of the warden who has determined that the guards must humiliate the inmates in the big game. (Dir: Robert Aldrich, 123 mins.)

Longstreet (1971)*** James Franciscus, Jeanette Nolan. Good. Made-for-TV entry. Absorbing drama from start to finish. James Franciscus has seldom been better than he is in this excellently produced pilot film for a proposed series about a top-flight insurance investigator who is blinded in an explosion which kills his wife. Most of the film is taken up with Mike Longstreet's (Franciscus) specialized training program to cope with his blindness and it's interesting. In a uniformly fine cast, the standouts are Jeanette Nolan's as Longstreet's intelligent mother and John McIntire as the doctor who uses the human approach in dealing with Longstreet's blindness. (Dir: Joseph Sargent, 93 mins.)

Look Back in Anger (1959)**** Richard Burton, Claire Bloom, Mary Ure. Englishman John Osborne's famous and important play about an "angry young man" fighting against "the establishment" emerges as a powerful comment on the mood in England in the mid '50's. Richard Burton is a shade too mature for the part of "Jimmy Porter" but he's a glorious actor and has several excellent scenes. (Dir: Tony Richardson, 99 mins.)

Look for the Silver Lining (1949)**½ June Haver, Ray Bolger, Gordon MacRae. Story of how Marilyn Miller broke into show business and became the toast of the theatre world. Usual inaccurate musical biography, with lavish production numbers. (Dir: David Butler, 100 mins.)

Look in Any Window (1961)** Paul Anka, Ruth Roman, Alex Nicol. Paul Anka goes dramatic for the first time in this cheap, sensationalized story of parents who set bad examples for their teenage children and then are surprised when they get into trouble. Anka fans might like watching their singing idol play it straight on film. (Dir: William Alland, 87 mins.)

Look Who's Laughing (1941)**½ Lucille Ball, Bergen & McCarthy, Fibber McGee and Molly. Hectic happenings when the famous ventriloquist is forced down in the village of Wistful Vista. Pleasing comedy.

Lookin' Good—See: Corky

Looking for Love (1964)* Connie Francis, Jim Hutton, Susan Oliver. Few laughs, as Connie Francis spends most of the movie deciding to marry Jim Hutton. Distracting cameos by a number of semi-celebrities. (Dir: Don Weis)

Looking Glass War, The (1970)**½ Christopher Jones, Pia Degermark, Ralph Richardson. John le Carre's fine espionage novel has been turned into a mildly entertaining film. It begins with the usual spy jargon, this time in the expert hands of Richardson, Paul Rogers, and Anthony Hopkins . . . and they soon decide to send a Polish defector (Jones) into East Germany to gain information on a rocket operation. Jones' subsequent adventures, including a love scene or two with Degermark (less effective here than in the haunting "Elvira Madigan"), are predictable. (Dir: Frank R. Pierson, 106 mins.)

Loophole (1954)**½ Barry Sullivan, Dorothy Malone. Bank teller accused of theft clears himself by nabbing the real culprits. Tightly-knit crime melodrama. (Dir: Frank R. Pierson, 80 mins.)

Loot (1972)***½ Richard Attenborough, Lee Remick, Milo O'Shea. Black, funny farce, based on a play by Joe Orton. Its only fault lies in the failure by the director to open it up from a one-act play. The plot concerns money hidden in a coffin resting in a seedy British hotel. The acting is lively and Remick can be forgiven for her varying Irish brogue. It's rare to find a farce with sympathy for its characters. (Dir: Silvio Narizzano, 92 mins.)

Lord Jim (British, 1965)*** Peter O'Toole, Eli Wallach, James Mason, Daliah Lavi, Curt Jurgens. A lavish, magnificently photographed and unusually well acted story of a seaman in the Far East based on Joseph Conrad's famous novel written in 1900. You'll probably enjoy this more if you haven't read Conrad's rousing tale and you'll appreciate the stunning on-location sequences shot in many areas of the Orient, including Hong Kong, Cambodia and Singapore. Produced, written and directed by the multi-talented Richard Brooks. (154 mins.)

Lord Love a Duck (1966)*** Roddy McDowall, Tuesday Weld. George Axelrod's stinging, savagely funny portrait of teenage morals and mores is quite uneven, but there are numerous individual vignettes that have a bite seldom found in Hollywood films. Tuesday Weld again makes it clear that she can act. (104 mins.)

Lord of the Flies (1963)*** James Aubrey, Tom Chapin. Offbeat study of English schoolboys, stranded on an island, and their gradual reversion to savagery when left to their own devices. Adapted from William Golding's novel, which has become a sort of college classic, the film has numerous gripping moments, but is not quite the success it should have been. One of the few films directed to date by brilliant English stage director Peter Brook. (90 mins.)

Lords of Flatbush, The (1974)*** Perry King, Sylvester Stallone, Henry Winkler, Susan Blakely, Maria Smith, Renee Paris. Individual scenes will grab you in this accurately remembered comedy about high-school kids in Brooklyn in 1957. Parts seem a throwback to "Blackboard Jungle" or "On the Waterfront," but it's played mostly for laughs, and the scene where Smith and Paris force Stallone to buy an expensive engagement ring is a gem. Pre-"Rocky" for Stallone, and before "The Fonz" for Winkler. (Dirs: Stephen F. Verona, Martin Davidson, 85 mins.)

Los Tarantos (Spanish, 1963)*** Carmen Amaya, Antonio Gades. The Romeo and Juliet-West Side Story idea told to the tune of clicking heels and castanets in this decidedly unusual drama with some fine dancing, flamenco-style. For those who appreciate something different. Dubbed in English. (Dir: Rovira-Beleta, 81 mins.)

Loser Takes All (British, 1956)**½ Rossano Brazzi, Glynis Johns. Well acted comedy-drama about a young married couple who win at the tables in Monte Carlo but almost lose each other in the process. (Dir: Ken Annakin, 88 mins.)

Losers, The (1970)*½ William Smith, Bernie Hamilton. Ludicrous saga of five Hell's Angels who go to Cambodia complete with their Yamaha choppers. The first half hour is devoted to their wrecking a Cambodian

town, but after that the plot gets moving as the five cycle men are recruited to rescue a captured presidential adviser from the clutches of the Communists. (Dir: Jack Starrett, 96 mins.)

Loss of Innocence (British, 1961)**** Kenneth More, Danielle Darrieux, Susannah York. Exquisite drama of a young girl at a vacation hotel in France who becomes a woman through her involvement with a handsome jewel thief. Tender, touching, fine performances, colorful photography of the French countryside. (Dir: Lewis Gilbert, 99 mins.)

Lost (British, 1955)*** David Farrar. Exciting and tense British drama about a lost child and the clever police work involved in finding him. (Dir: Guy Green, 89 mins.)

Lost Battalion (1962)** Diane Jergens, Leopold Salcedo. Moderately interesting World War II yarn, filmed in the Philippines, about a group of Americans who go through the Japanese lines in order to rendezvous with a submarine. Some action sequences for adventure fans.

Lost Boundaries (1949)***½ Mel Ferrer, Beatrice Pearson. A light-skinned Negro doctor passes for white in a small New England town. Absorbing drama handles a touchy subject with taste, finesse. Based on fact. (Dir: Alfred L. Werker, 99 mins.)

Lost Command (1966)**½ Anthony Quinn, Alain Delon, George Segal, Claudia Cardinale, Michele Morgan. An all-star cast and well-staged war sequences help keep this action film interesting, despite the pretentious handling of the political and human aspects of the French-Algerian conflict. Best acting is contributed by Alain Delon, playing a dedicated military man whose clashes with the poor leadership and distaste for the endless killing eventually cause him to leave the French army. (Dir: Mark Robson, 130 mins.)

Lost Continent, The (British, 1968) ** Eric Porter, Hildegarde Knef (Neff), Suzanna Leigh, Tony Beckley. Balderdash about storm survivors landing on an uncharted land where weird things occur. Comic-strip stuff, played with grim determination. Some of it is inventive if you care for comic strip characters.

Lost Horizon (1937)***½ Ronald Colman, Jane Wyatt. Plane pas-

425

sengers forced down in Tibet discover the land of Shangri-La, the supreme paradise. Capra's version of the James Hilton story is lavish, well acted, still unusual and entertaining. (Dir: Frank Capra, 118 mins.)

Lost Horizon (1973)*½ Peter Finch, Liv Ullmann, John Gielgud, Olivia Hussey. Random, spontaneous singing and dancing in the midst of snowcapped mountains would produce a more exciting version of paradise than this Ross Hunter spectacle. Based on James Hilton's novel, this musical follows the book's shallower directions, and instead of discovering Shangri-La we are mired in an almost cartoonlike self-parody. The star-studded cast and Bacharach-David music are drawn into the snowbank. (Dir: Charles Jarrot, 151 mins.)

Lost In a Harem (1944)** Bud Abbott, Lou Costello, Marilyn Maxwell, John Conte. A slice of nothing about a couple of magicians and their adventure in an Oriental land. Strictly for the kids in spite of the misleading title. (Dir: Charles Reisner, 89 mins.)

Lost In Alaska (1952)**½ Bud Abbott, Lou Costello, Tom Ewell. The Klondike inherits the clowning duet in this fast paced comedy about gold, gambling and gals. Plenty of funny sight gags make this a notch or two above average A&C fares. (Dir: Jean Yarbrough, 76 mins.)

Lost In the Stars (1974)**½ Brock Peters, Melba Moore, Raymond St. Jacques, Paul Rogers. Occasionally interesting but ultimately disappointing adaptation of the Broadway musical of Kurt Weill and Maxwell Anderson which in turn was based on Alan Paton's famous novel "Cry the Beloved Country." (The 1951 film starred Canada Lee.) About racial prejudice in South Africa. Black clergyman (Peters) develops a relationship with a white painter (Rogers) after Rogers' son is killed in an attempted robbery. Neither the plodding direction of Daniel Mann nor the screenplay of Alfred Hayes manages to infuse the drama with much excitement, but the basic story of bigotry remains all too relevant and the performances are generally fine. (114 mins.)

Lost Island of Kioga (1938-66)** Herman Brix, Mala. Feature version

of serial "Hawk of the Wilderness." Survivors of shipwreck find a muscular ruler on an uncharted island. Farfetched adventure tale, but produced with some flair. (Dirs: William Witney, John English, 100 mins.)

Lost Lagoon (1958)** Jeffrey Lynn, Peter Donat. Castaway on a Caribbean isle begins a new life, but loses the audience. (Dir: John Rawlins, 79 mins.)

Lost Man, The (1969)**½ Sidney Poitier, Joanna Shimkus, Al Freeman, Jr. Sidney Poitier in the offbeat role of a hunted criminal, some interesting scenes involving the civil rights movement in this country, plus the excitement of a continuous chase, make this film palatable. Don't look beyond the surface story, which is loosely based on a far more successful film "Odd Man Out," and you'll probably enjoy it. Poitier is strong, and Miss Shimkus also registers as a social worker who falls in love with the fugitive. The film's best performance is by Al Freeman, Jr., as a questioning civil rights leader. Directed and written by author Robert Alan Aurthur. (122 mins.)

Lost Missile, The (1958)** Robert Loggia, Ellen Parker. As a runaway missile threatens New York, a young scientist works against time to stop its course of destruction. Fair cheaply-made science-fiction thriller manages to work up some suspense. (Dir: Lester Berke, 70 mins.)

Lost Moment, The (1947)***½ Robert Cummings, Susan Hayward, Agnes Moorehead. Young American publisher finds that love letters he has been seeking in Venice cause near-tragedy. Absorbing drama, taken from Henry James' novel; excellent in production and performance. (Dir: Martin Gasel, 88 mins.)

Lost One, The (Italian, 1948)*** Nelly Corradi, Tito Gobbi. Verdi's opera "La Traviata" sung in Italian with narrative portions in English. Nicely staged, well sung; good for opera devotees, interesting for others.

Lost One, The (West Germany, 1951) *** Peter Lorre, Karl John, Helmut Rudolph. Peter Lorre gives a fine performance portraying a resident doctor in a refugee camp in Germany shortly after the end of World War II. But in many ways the most interesting thing about this little-known film is that it was the only film directed by Lorre, and he turns in a more than creditable job. Lorre also had a hand in the involving screenplay which includes, among other things, commentary about the circumstances that fostered and permitted Nazism. An unusual film to have been made in Germany at that time. (Dir: Peter Lorre, 98 mins.)

Lost Patrol (1934)***½ Victor McLaglen, Boris Karloff, Wallace Ford. A British patrol is ambushed by hostile Arabs and picked off one by one. Gripping drama directed by John Ford. (80 mins.)

Lost People, The (British, 1949)*** Mai Zetterling, Dennis Price. Problems confronting a British Army captain in post-war Germany, trying to relocate displaced persons. Rambling, but frequently touching, well-acted topical drama.

Lost Planet Airmen (1949)*½ Tristram Coffin, Mae Clarke. Scientist combats a madman who seeks to rule the earth. Juvenile thriller, action and nothing else. Feature version of serial, "King of the Rocket Men." (Dir: Fred Bannon, 65 mins.)

Lost Squadron (1932)*** Joel McCrea, Richard Dix, Erich Von Stroheim, Mary Astor. Tyrannical film director makes his aerial stunt men do perilous tricks, so they band together to stop him. Unusual melodrama has plenty of suspense. (Dir: George Archainbaud, 90 mins.)

Lost Weekend, The (1945)**** Ray Milland, Jane Wyman. Grim, brutal, award-winning study of a dipsomaniac based on Charles Jackson's novel. Excellent film. (Dir: Billy Wilder, 101 mins.)

Lost World, The (1960)**½ Michael Rennie, Fernando Lamas, Jill St. John. Primarily for the youngsters who like their adventure yarns fast and colorful. Good screen version of Sir Arthur Conan Doyle's science-fiction story about an expedition into the deep regions of the Amazon. Visual tricks, such as prehistoric beasts doing battle with a modern helicopter are the film's best features. (Dir: Irwin Allen, 98 mins.)

Lost World of Sinbad, The (Japanese, 1964)*½ Toshiro Mifune, Makoto Satoh. Escaped adventurer is cast ashore on a mysterious island, saves the princess from the wicked tyrant. Pipe dream, Japanese style; exaggerated heroics become pretty weird in this dubbed-English opus.

Lotus for Miss Kwon, A (1967)*½ Lang Jefferies, Werner Peters. An American teacher and his girl friend inadvertently get involved with an espionage ring. Tepid.

Louis Armstrong—Chicago Style (1976)*** Ben Vereen, Red Buttons, Margaret Avery, Janet MacLachlan. Based on the early career of the great jazz trumpeter, this film zeroes in on Louis' struggle to avoid playing in a Chicago club run by the mob during the early 30's. Vereen is terrific in the title role, a musical genius who had to buck bigotry and shady characters before he could stand in front of an audience and share his genius with them. Vereen doesn't imitate "Satchmo," but captures the essence of Armstrong's individualistic singing style, and he's marvelous in the dramatic scenes. Also making an impression in supporting roles are Avery as Louis' true love, and Buttons as the trumpet player's opportunistic manager. Made-for-TV. (Dir: Lee Philips, 72 mins.)

Louisa (1950)**½ Ronald Reagan, Piper Laurie, Charles Coburn. Moderately entertaining film about the trials and tribulations of an average family which has to cope with the young daughter's romantic problems as well as Grandma's. A pleasant cast carries it off nicely. (Dir: Alexander Hall, 90 mins.)

Louisiana Purchase (1941)***½ Bob Hope, Victor Moore, Vera Zorina. Delightful comedy (plus 3 pleasant tunes) about an attempt to frame a senator down Louisiana way. Loads of laughs and Bob's filibuster is a classic. (Dir: Irving Cummings, 98 mins.)

Love (1927)*** Greta Garbo, John Gilbert. An early version of Tolstoy's "Anna Karenina" which has, among other things, a happy ending. Greta Garbo, who later starred in a talking version that struck closer to the original text, plays the harassed heroine who must choose between maternal love and passionate love. John Gilbert plays the handsome Count. The screen team of Garbo and Gilbert captured the fancy of the 1920's moviegoers. (Dir: Edmund Goulding, 135 mins.)

Love Affair (1939)**** Charles Boyer, Irene Dunne. One of the wittiest and most civilized of the romantic films of the '30's. Couple meet on shipboard, fall in love, but break their engagement and decide to meet again in six months. Touching, wry, and beautifully acted by the two leads; superior direction by Leo McCarey. (89 mins.)

Love Among the Ruins (1975)******** Katharine Hepburn, Laurence Olivier, Richard Pearson. One of the finest made-for-TV movies. Olivier and Hepburn star in this romantic comedy, written with style by James Costigan, and they're magical together. Olivier plays a prestigious London barrister—London circa 1911 —who is defending his client (Hepburn) from a suit brought by a younger man who claims she trifled with his affections and has reneged on her promise to marry him. It's the first time Olivier and Hepburn ever worked together, giving "Love" a touch of class that few, if any, other actors could provide. Made-for-TV. (Dir: George Cukor, 100 mins.)

Love and Anarchy (Italian, 1972)******** Giancarlo Giannini, Mariangela Melato, Lina Polito. Enormously powerful political drama about Italian fascism during the 1930's, brilliantly written and directed by Lina Wertmuller. Much of the action, before a shattering climax, takes place in a bordello. Anarchist peasant comes to Rome to assassinate Mussolini. There is one astonishing sequence where the assembled prostitutes are dining together and taunting each other, while Miss Wertmuller's sure hand indelibly captures the decadence and moral squalor of that society. Acting splendid throughout. Establishes Ms. Wertmuller as one of the most gifted directors, male or female, to emerge in years. (108 mins.)

Love and Death (1975)******** Woody Allen, Diane Keaton, Frank Adu, Olga Georges-Picot. One of Woody Allen's funniest, most consistent films. Woody plays a bumbling, to put it mildly, Russian, trying to avoid the draft in the Napoleonic War. Diane Keaton is the pretentious cousin he's loved from afar. Allen does take these dippy characters and parody 19th-century politics, philosophy, and war, and makes it funny. It's full of slapstick; and to movie buffs it's twice as funny, because it is full of mocking visual references to every film ever made from a Russian novel, from "The Brothers Karamazov" to "The Twelve Chairs." A treat. (Dir: Woody Allen, 85 mins.)

Love and Kisses (1965)****** Rick Nelson, Kristin Nelson, Jack Kelly. A spinoff of the Nelson family situations, this one has father Ozzie directing son Rick and daughter-in-law Kristin in a mild comedy about the problems occurring when a young couple elope. Very mild fare. (Dir: Ozzie Nelson, 87 mins.)

Love and Marriage (Italy, 1964)*****½** Lando Buzzanca, Maria Grazia Buccella, Renato Tagliani, Ingeborg Schoener. Uneven but highly amusing compendium of four episodes: lusty love stories with a twist. The first two are the best—beguiling, ribald, clever. The players are energetic, deliciously good-looking. (Dirs: Gianni Puccini, episodes 1 and 4; Mino Guerrini, episodes 2 and 3, 106 mins.)

Love and Pain and the Whole Damned Thing (1972)******* Maggie Smith, Timothy Bottoms, Charles Baxter. An eccentric, humorous love story notable for the glorious performance of lovely Maggie Smith. Smith is a superb actress, cast as a spinster in her late 30's who is running away from her two aunts in England, while Bottoms plays a college student, the son of a Pulitzer Prize-winning author, coming to Europe to flee his tyrannical dad. They meet in Spain, and quickly learn their neuroses complement one another. The affectionate comedy dissolves when Miss Smith reveals she is dying of "Love Story" disease. (Dir: Alan J. Pakula, 110 mins.)

Love and the Frenchwoman (French, 1961)******* Jean-Paul Belmondo, Annie Girardot, Martine Carol, Francois Perier. Seven separate stories detailing exactly what the title implies, dealing in aspects of love in all forms at all ages. As with most compilations, some scenes are better than others, but it all makes an entertaining if lengthy show. Narrated and dubbed in English.

Love at Twenty (1963)*****½** Jean-Pierre Leaud, Eleonora Rossi-Drago, Barbara Lass. Five vignettes of love among the young from youthful directors of France (Francois Truffaut), Italy, Japan, Germany, Poland. Varying in quality: French segment has a good deal of charm; the Italian is rather thin in plot; the Japanese is the most bizarre and dramatic; the German has the smoothest technique; and the Polish one is probably the best in all-around quality. English-dubbed. (113 mins.)

Love Bug, The (1969)*** Dean Jones, Michele Lee, Buddy Hackett, David Tomlinson. Many films produced by the Walt Disney organization, responsible for this comedy, have been sentimental tales about a young girl and her horse, or a freckle-faced boy and his favorite pooch. They were called "heart-warming" pictures for the youngsters. This is the same kind of film, intended for the same audience, but the "horse" happens to be a Volkswagen automobile. It's a long commercial for the German manufacturer, with a few mild chuckles provided along the way. This "family film" was a huge commercial success. Despite this parent's rather grumpy response to it, we suspect that the moppets will thoroughly enjoy it. Buddy Hackett provides most of the laughs, along with the cutesy car, as they tootle around San Francisco.

Love Crazy (1941)*** William Powell, Myrna Loy, Gail Patrick, Jack Carson. Myrna finds innocent Bill in a friendly situation with Gail Patrick. She sues for divorce and Bill fights to keep her in this zany comedy. (Dir: Jack Conway, 130 mins.)

Love Finds Andy Hardy (1938)*** Mickey Rooney, Judy Garland, Lewis Stone. Mickey is at his best here and so is Judge Lewis Stone as Andy gets involved with a bevy of young lovelies. Judy was being groomed for stardom by now and the Hardy pictures were so popular they were considered a good showcase for young talent. (Dir: George B. Seitz, 90 mins.)

Love from a Stranger (1947)**½ Sylvia Sidney, John Hodiak. After marriage, a woman suspects her husband to be a mad strangler with herself intended as his next victim. Acceptably exciting suspense melodrama. (Dir: Richard Whorf, 81 mins.)

Love From Paris (German, 1961)*** Romy Schneider, Horst Buchholz. Tender, tragic tale of the romance between a young painter and a girl

in Paris. Sensitively directed, well played; the ladies should particularly enjoy it. Dubbed in English.

Love God, The (1969)* Don Knotts, Anne Francis, Edmond O'Brien. Silly nonsense which should appeal to Don Knotts' fans. Don is the publisher of a bird-watchers' magazine which is converted into a girlie mag by an unscrupulous operator (Edmond O'Brien in a completely thankless role). (Dir: Nat Hiken, 101 mins.)

Love Happy (1949)**½ Marx Brothers, Ilona Massey, Vera-Ellen. Harpo befuddles some crooks who are after a precious diamond. The Marxian madness loses some of its magic in this spasmodically funny but uneven farce. (Dir: David Miller, 91 mins.)

Love Has Many Faces (1965)** Lana Turner, Cliff Robertson, Hugh O'Brian, Stefanie Powers. "Peyton Place" comes to Mexico, as a wealthy playgirl—"girl!"—fears she is losing her husband to a young girl. It's soap opera, with the suds a dirty gray. (Dir: Alexander Singer, 105 mins.)

Love Hate Love (1971)*** Ryan O'Neal, Peter Haskell, Lesley Warren. A good performance by Peter Haskell as a relentless rich man with sadistic tendencies is the main attraction of this made-for-TV suspense film. Haskell loses pretty Lesley Warren to handsome Ryan O'Neal and then makes their lives miserable by dogging their every move, even cross-country to California. The suspense builds nicely and Haskell's menacing presence will send chills up most lady viewers' backs. (Dir: George McGowan, 73 mins.)

Love in a Goldfish Bowl (1961)*** Tommy Sands, Fabian. Two students who are thought to be bad influences on each other get together anyway for a wild beach-house party. Nice chuckling adolescent comedy has quite a few bright touches. Watch especially for a hilarious bit by Elizabeth MacRae in a party scene. (Dir: Jack Sher, 88 mins.)

Love in a Hot Climate (French, 1959)*½ Daniel Gelin, Zsa Zsa Gabor. Famous matador wants to quit the bullring, but his greedy mistress and retinue lure him back. Trite, slow-moving, English-dubbed drama. Seems Zsa Zsa's a drag when the humidity's high.

Love In the Afternoon (1957)*** Audrey Hepburn, Gary Cooper, Maurice Chevalier. Director Billy Wilder, who usually hits a homer each time he is at bat, only manages to get to third base with this sophisticated comedy about the escapades of a middle-aged American playboy in Europe. Audrey Hepburn is, as always, winning as a young music student who falls under the playboy's spell, but Cooper is too old to fit the bill as the "champagne and violins" casanova. (Dir: Billy Wilder, 130 mins.)

Love In the City (Italian, 1953)**½ Five documentary stories illustrating typical Italian life. An exploration of a dance hall in Rome; interviews with women who have tried suicide; a survey of matrimonial agencies; story of a young mother; and (the best) male reaction to the female form divine walking the streets. Some moments of high interest, at other times aimless. English narration. (90 mins.)

Love Is a Ball (1963)** Glenn Ford, Hope Lange, Charles Boyer. Pure escapist fare. Glenn Ford plays a man of the world who gets involved in a scheme initiated by suave matchmaker Charles Boyer. The plot is predictable. Sumptuous French Riviera setting. (Dir: David Swift, 111 mins.)

Love Is a Many-Splendored Thing (1955)**½ Jennifer Jones, William Holden. Female fans will cry and just adore this romantic tale about the love affair between an American war correspondent and a glamorous Eurasian lady doctor. It's a modern "Madame Butterfly" yarn which is based on Han Suyin's autobiographical novel. (Dir: Henry King, 102 mins.)

Love Is Better Than Ever (1952)**½ Elizabeth Taylor, Larry Parks. Silly romantic comedy somewhat enhanced by the attractive stars. Miss Taylor plays a Conn. dancing teacher who meets a bachelor about town (Parks) and uses every trick in the book to nab him. (Dir: Stanley Donen, 81 mins.)

Love Is News (1937)** Loretta Young, Tyrone Power, Don Ameche. Forced, contrived comedy about an heiress who decides to marry a reporter because she hates newspapers. A poor film but agreeably played. (Dir: Tay Garnett, 78 mins.)

Love Laughs at Andy Hardy (1946)** Mickey Rooney, Lewis Stone, Sara Haden. Post-war Hardy film finds Andy getting out of service and going back to his romances with the same juvenile approach. (Dir: Willis Goldbeck, 93 mins.)

Love Letters (1945)** Jennifer Jones, Joseph Cotten. Contrived, confused and boring love story is only for soap opera fans. A girl develops amnesia when she learns that somebody other than her fellow has been sending her love letters. The real chap shows up, woos her, cures her, wins her. (Dir: William Dieterle, 101 mins.)

Love Lottery, The (British, 1954)** David Niven, Herbert Lom. David Niven is the lucky ticket holder who wins a movie star in a love lottery in this contrived and not so funny British film. (Dir: Charles Crichton, 89 mins.)

Love Machine, The (1971)½ John Phillip Law, Dyan Cannon, Robert Ryan, David Hemmings, Jackie Cooper. Jacqueline Susann's tacky best-seller has been further vulgarized in this adaptation with a screenplay by, alas, Samuel Taylor. Pretends to be about network television biggies at work. Ineptly handled—can't quite bring myself to use the word "directed"—by Jack Haley, Jr., and the acting is almost uniformly embarrassing. Susann, incidentally, got one and a half million dollars for the film rights to her hardcover rubbish. (Dir: Jack Haley, Jr., 108 mins.)

Love Makers, The (Italian, 1962)*** Jean-Paul Belmondo, Claudia Cardinale. Innocent farm boy goes to the big city where he meets and falls in love with a prostitute. Drama benefits from good performances and production. English-dubbed.

Love Match (British, 1955)** Arthur Askey, Thora Hird. Little man gets into trouble by disagreeing with a referee at a soccer match. Mild comedy, funnier on the other side of the pond than over here.

Love Me—Love Me Not (British, 1962)** Craig Stevens, Erica Rogers. Roving correspondent runs into plenty of trouble while vacationing on the Riviera. Okay melodrama adapted from "Man of the World" TV series.

Love Me or Leave Me (1955)***½ Doris Day, James Cagney. The highly dramatic and tune-filled career of singer Ruth Etting becomes the basis for a better than average film biography. Doris Day has seldom been shown to better advantage both vocally and dramatically. James Cagney, as Marty the Gimp, a racketeer who loves Ruth, steals every scene he is in. (Dir: Charles Vidor, 122 mins.)

Love Me Tender (1956)** Elvis Presley, Richard Egan, Debra Paget. This familiar Civil War western served to introduce Elvis Presley to film audiences. Except for this dubious distinction, the film has a predictable plot line involving robberies, double-crosses and assorted ingredients found in most westerns. Elvis sings a couple of tunes and has a death scene. (Dir: Robert D. Webb, 89 mins.)

Love Me Tonight (1932)*** Maurice Chevalier, Jeanette MacDonald. A Parisian tailor woos and wins a princess in this tuneful Rodgers and Hart film musical. Dated today but well-directed and a big step forward for its time. (Dir: Rouben Mamoulian, 100 mins.)

Love Nest (1951)** June Haver, William Lundigan, Marilyn Monroe, Jack Paar. Moderately funny comedy about an ex-GI and his wife and their adventures when they buy an apartment house. Among the zany tenants are shapely Marilyn Monroe as an ex-Wac and of all people, Jack Paar in one of his few movie appearances. Explains why Jack never did make the grade in motion pictures. (Dir: Joseph M. Newman, 85 mins.)

Love of Three Queens (Italian, 1953) *½ Hedy Lamarr. Stories concerning Helen of Troy, Genevieve of Brabant, and the Empress Josephine, all impersonated by Hedy. Her beauty is the sole asset in this weak costume compilation. Dubbed in English.

Love on a Pillow (France-Italy, 1962) * Brigitte Bardot, Robert Hossein, James Robertson-Justice. Have the men in the audience ever dreamed of watching Brigitte vacuum-cleaning in the nude? Her former husband, Roger Vadim, who directed and co-authored this drivel, gives us all the chance. Brigitte's been photographed from every conceivable angle. Hossein plays a drunkard who chooses a flat-chested prostitute when Brigitte

is available. Nuff said! (Dir: Roger Vadim, 102 mins.)

Love on the Dole (British, 1941)*** Deborah Kerr, Clifford Evans. The problems of a London slum family during the depression of the 1930s. Grim drama, but well made, well acted. From the novel and play by Walter Greenwood. (Dir: John Baxter, 89 mins.)

Love on the Run (1936)**½ Clark Gable, Joan Crawford, Franchot Tone. As the title indicates, Clark woos Joan from one end of the globe to the other. He and Tone are foreign correspondents so there's a spy plot too in this wild, cliche-heavy, romantic comedy. (Dir: W. S. Van Dyke, 80 mins.)

Love Story (British, 1946)**½ Margaret Lockwood, Stewart Granger, Patricia Roc. A concert pianist goes away for a rest, falls for a man who is loved by another girl, making a pretty triangle. Ladies should enjoy this overlong but otherwise interesting romance, with excellent piano, orchestral interludes. (Dir: Maurice Ostrer, 108 mins.)

Love Story (1970)**½ Ali MacGraw, Ryan O'Neal, Ray Milland. The box-office bonanza starring MacGraw and O'Neal as the star-crossed lovers who meet, fall in love, marry, struggle until they make it financially, only to be faced with the fact that the wife is dying. It's all high-gloss histrionics, written by Erich Segal, played out against a sentimental score by Francis Lai, and acted with quiet restraint by Miss MacGraw. Audiences loved it when it played in the movie theaters and TV viewers have followed suit. (Dir: Arthur Hiller, 100 mins.)

Love That Brute (1950)**½ Paul Douglas, Jean Peters, Cesar Romero. Gangster puts on a tough front but really has a heart of gold. Pleasant enough comedy, but original version —"Tall, Dark, and Handsome" was better. (Dir: Alexander Hall, 85 mins.)

Love Thy Neighbor (1940)*** Jack Benny, Fred Allen, Mary Martin. Film designed to cash in on the Benny-Allen gag feud of radio days is moderately entertaining. Mary has some good numbers while Jack and Fred trade insults. (Dir: Mark Sandrich, 82 mins.)

Love Under Fire (1937)**½ Loretta Young, Don Ameche. Some bright lines and a few good scenes but this comedy-drama about spies, which is set against the Spanish Civil War, never comes together as a unit. (Dir: George Marshall, 75 mins.)

Love War, The (1970) ½ Lloyd Bridges, Angie Dickinson, Harry Basch. Far-fetched fiction. Two planets fight over who will control the earth. A love affair cutting across interplanetary hostilities. Made-for-TV. (Dir: George McCowan, 72 mins.)

Love with the Proper Stranger (1963) *** Natalie Wood, Steve McQueen. Good performances by the two leads place this film a notch or two above the average fare. It's a contemporary love story set in New York City, and the on-location scenes add greatly to the film's appeal. McQueen is a musician, very much his own man, until he becomes involved with Miss Wood. (Dir: Robert Mulligan, 100 mins.)

Loveboat II (1977)* Bert Convy, Celeste Holm, Hope Lange, Craig Stevens, Robert Reed. Here's the sequel to last year's bummer about a cruise ship and the interplay between the wacky crew and the wackier passengers. Vignettes range from silly to unfunny. Made-for-TV. (Dir: Hy Averback, 106 mins.)

Loved One, The (1965)***½ Robert Morse, Jonathan Winters, Anjanette Comer, Milton Berle, John Gielgud, Rod Steiger, Liberace. Irreverent, uneven black comedy, based on the novel by Evelyn Waugh, concerns the sudden suicide of a Hollywood star and his nephew's problems in paying the exorbitant funeral bill. Macabre humor is well played by a large star-studded cast. Notable is Liberace's grinning portrayal of a funeral director. Deft, sometimes savage screenplay written by Terry Southern and Christopher Isherwood. Co-produced by award-winning cinematographer Haskell Wexler. (Dir: Tony Richardson, 116 mins.)

Love-ins, The (1967)* James MacArthur, Susan Oliver, Richard Todd. College professor becomes hippie hero, turns greedy, and that's all, Charlie. Meager fast-buck exploitation flick. (Dir: Arthur Dreifuss, 91 mins.)

Lovely to Look At (1952)**½ Kathryn Grayson, Howard Keel, Red Skelton. Entertaining remake of the musical "Roberta," with many of the lovely

Jerome Kern tunes, such as "Smoke Gets in Your Eyes." The songs take precedence over the thin plot, set in the haute-couture fashion world of Paris. Kathryn Grayson and Howard Keel are up to their musical assignments. Marge and Gower Champion offer some excellent dance turns.

Lovely Way To Die, A (1968)** Kirk Douglas, Sylva Koscina. Detective (Kirk Douglas) guards a woman accused of murder, sets out to prove her innocent. With Eli Wallach, Kenneth Haigh, Martyn Green, Sharon Farrell. Not such a lovely way to waste time. (Dir: David Lowell Rich, 103 mins.)

Lovemaker, The (1958)**½ Betsy Blair, Jose Suarez. Plain, unloved spinster is victimized by a cruel joke that ends tragically. Spanish-made drama is well acted but overlong.

Lover Boy (British, 1954)**½ Gerard Philippe, Valerie Hobson, Joan Greenwood. Opportunistic Frenchman in London has a talent for romancing the ladies, uses it—and them—to climb to success and wealth. Savagely bitter comedy packed quite a punch in its original form, but censorship has taken its toll. Nevertheless, there are still some splendid moments. Excellent direction by Rene Clement, performances by the entire cast. (105 mins.)

Lover Come Back (1946)**½ Lucille Ball, George Brent, Vera Zorina. George Brent is a war (WW-II) correspondent whose traveling keeps him away from his wife (Lucille Ball). Trouble comes in the shape of a war photographer (Vera Zorina) and Lucy heads for the divorce courts. Plenty of laughs for Lucy fans. (Dir: William A. Seiter, 90 mins.)

Lover Come Back (1962)*** Doris Day, Rock Hudson, Tony Randall, Edie Adams. Some good laughs in this Day-Hudson battle of the sexes. He's an advertising tycoon, she's on the make. Frequent bright dialogue, direction, clever situations, nice supporting performances. (Dir: Delbert Mann, 107 mins.)

Lovers, The (France, 1958)***½ Jeanne Moreau, Jean-Marc Bory, Alain Cuny. Louis Malle's second film, about a beautiful, bored housewife's thirst for a deeper love and a more meaningful life. Controversial at the time, due to some explicit lovemaking. Moving, poetic, vivid, and Moreau is simply superb in the starring role. There are boring stretches between the brilliant pivotal scenes, however. (Dir: Louis Malle, 90 mins.)

Lovers and Lollipops (1956)****½** Lori March, Cathy Dunn. Young widow worries if her daughter will accept a new suitor. Slender tale has some refreshing moments, but remains pretty lightweight. (Dir: Morris Engle, 80 mins.)

Lovers and Other Strangers (1970) *****½** Gig Young, Richard Castellano, Beatrice Arthur. A comedy winner! A raucously funny portrait of two families who come together when the daughter of one (Bonnie Bedelia) and the son of the other (Michael Brandon) announce wedding plans. Miss Arthur and Castellano play the first-generation Italian parents of the lad and they have the lion's share of the funny lines. Also scoring in individual scenes are Gig Young as the father of the bride; Anne Meara and Harry Guardino as a bickering couple; Anne Jackson as a cast-aside mistress; and Marian Hailey as a weepy, whining bridesmaid. (Dir: Cy Howard, 106 mins.)

Lovers and Thieves (French, 1957) *****½** Jean Poiret, Michel Serrault. Director Sacha Guitry's last picture maintained the laughing skepticism that was his trademark. This one concerns a thief and his victim who are coincidentally involved with each other in more than a simple robbery. Intelligent and impeccable. (81 mins.)

Lovers in Paris (French, 1958)****½** Gerard Philippe, Danielle Darrieux. A Frenchman finds that the easiest way to success entails a short-cut through the proprietress' boudoir. Sexy French bedroom comedy-drama, well acted. (Dir: Julien Duviver, 115 mins.)

Lovers on a Tightrope (French, 1960) ***½** Annie Girardot, Francois Perier. Businessman is a target for elimination by the brother of his business partner, who has been having an affair with his wife. Sluggish English-dubbed melodrama with an obvious plot.

Loves of a Blonde (Czechoslovakia, 1965)******** Hana Brejchova, Vladimir Pucholt. Milos Forman's touching, wry triumph about a shy girl in a small, male-depleted factory town, and her unconquerable romanticism. Uses humor, pathos, desire and sorrow in an original, touching way. The film seemingly moves of its own accord; most of the actors are non-professional and enact the situations honestly, often in wholly unexpected ways. Best is the dance scene, where some newly-arrived, middle-aged army reservists are faced by the man-hungry factory girls. (Dir: Milos Forman)

Loves of Carmen, The (1948)****½** Rita Hayworth, Glenn Ford. Familiar opera about the love of a soldier for a gypsy minus the music. Not a very impressive film, but Miss Hayworth should keep the men awake. (Dir: Charles Vidor, 99 mins.)

Loves of Edgar Allan Poe, The (1942) ****½** John Sheppard, Linda Darnell, Virginia Gilmore. Interesting but uninspired film biography of one of our greatest writers. Definitely one of the weakest biographical films to come from a major studio. (Dir: Harry Lachman, 67 mins.)

Loves of Isadora, The (British, 1969) *****½** Vanessa Redgrave, James Fox, Jason Robards. The long, rambling story of Isadora Duncan, the celebrated, tormented, passionate, and damned woman whose revolutionary work became the forerunner of modern dance. Flawed in many respects including a lack of continuity, but Vanessa Redgrave's no-holds-barred performance as Isadora is electrifying. (Dir: Karel Reisz, 131 mins.)

Loves of Joanna Godden, The (British, 1947)****½** Googie Withers, Jean Kent. Period melodrama, as a woman struggles to keep her home intact, despite the loss of her loved one and the interference of her sister. Leisurely, but commendably acted, directed. Fine music score by Vaughan Williams.

Lovin' Molly (1974)****½** Blythe Danner, Anthony Perkins, Beau Bridges, Susan Sarandon. Blythe Danner's luminous performance as a Texas lass who wouldn't let convention stand in the way of loving two men at the same time, for a period covering four decades, is the best thing about this strange little film. Based on Larry McMurtry's novel, "Leaving Cheyenne," the story starts out in 1925 and goes up to the mid-60's, but the earlier scenes are the best since the principals, Ms. Danner,

Bridges and Perkins, look silly in old-age makeup. (Dir: Sidney Lumet, 98 mins.)

Loving (1970)***½ George Segal, Eva Marie Saint. A quietly intense movie, humorous, human and insightful, about a New York illustrator whose suburban family, New York mistress and job prospects are veering toward unwanted routine. Movie's final scene is incongruous in its farcical mayhem, but otherwise the film is sensitive, restrained and, grounded in a peculiarly American reality, rings true. Segal gives a fine, multi-level performance as the harassed free-lance artist. Written by Don Devlin. (Dir: Irvin Kershner, 90 mins.)

Loving You (1957)** Elvis Presley, Lizabeth Scott, Wendell Corey. Small-town boy becomes an overnight sensation when he's signed by a lady press agent to sing with her ex-husband's country band. Tailormade for Presley and his tunes, the story matters little—too little, if one doesn't dig Elvis. (Dir: Hal Kanter, 101 mins.)

Lt. Robin Crusoe U.S.N. (1966)* Dick Van Dyke, Nancy Kwan. The screen credits say that this Disney comedy release was based on a story by one Retlaw Yensid. Heard of him before? I thought not. Retlaw is a pseudonym for Walt Disney, but the real Dick Van Dyke parachutes out of his disabled Navy plane and finds a lovely maiden (Nancy Kwan) whom he promptly dubs Wednesday. That'll give you a clue about the rest of the film. (Dir: Byron Paul, 110 mins.)

Lucan (1977)** Ned Beatty, Kevin Brophy, Stockard Channing. Here's another version of the old story about the boy raised in a forest with wild animals, attempting to understand modern civilization and the wickedness of man. Kevin Brophy plays the 20-year-old innocent, busy Ned Beatty is his deceitful boss, and Stockard Channing is the boss's friendly daughter, ready to initiate a shy Lucan. MGM production values help, but the story remains predictable. Try Truffaut's "The Wild Child." Made-for-TV. (Dir: David Greene, 79 mins.)

Lucas Tanner (1974)**½ David Hartman, Rosemary Murphy. In this pilot film for the TV series, lanky, personable David Hartman becomes a

434

midwestern high-school English teacher and his wholesome enthusiasm pays off. Tanner is that rarity, a good, open-minded teacher who understands kids, but battles suspicious parents and jealous cohorts. On-location footage in Webster Groves, Mo., and St. Louis provides a welcome change from the customary California scenery. (Dir: Richard Donner.)

Luck of Ginger Coffey, The (1964) **** Robert Shaw, Mary Ure. Fine drama of a young Irish immigrant in Montreal with his wife and daughter trying to better himself in the world against all odds, including his own attitude. Excellently acted and directed, with the actual locales adding to the authenticity. (Dir: Irvin Kershner, 100 mins.)

Luck of the Irish, The (1948)**½ Tyrone Power, Anne Baxter, Cecil Kellaway. While trying to choose between his newspaper boss' daughter and a sweet colleen, Tyrone has the invaluable aid of a leprechaun. Whimsical and ordinary film. (Dir: Henry Koster, 99 mins.)

Lucky Jordan (1943)**½ Alan Ladd, Helen Walker. Ladd carries this film about an AWOL soldier who inadvertently becomes a hero by defeating a gang of Nazi agents. (Dir: Frank Tuttle, 84 mins.)

Lucky Lady (1975)* Gene Hackman, Liza Minnelli, Burt Reynolds, Robby Benson, Michael Hordern. "Lucky Lady" is a big loser—it cost over twelve million dollars, and that works out to about six million dollars per joke. Hopeless script finds boring characters playing rum-runners off the California coast during Prohibition. One of the characters says, "It's so quiet around here you can hear a fish fart." Even that modest feat would have seemed like a notable triumph in this disaster, extremely poorly directed by Stanley Donen. The three stars look understandably embarrassed. (118 mins.)

Lucky Me (1954)** Doris Day, Bob Cummings, Phil Silvers, Nancy Walker. Disappointing musical comedy with only a few good things in the whole film. Chorus girl and friends out of jobs in Florida. A perfect example of Hollywood's wasting of talent. (Dir: Jack Donohue, 100 mins.)

Lucky Nick Cain (1950)*** George

Raft, Coleen Gray. A gambler on vacation on the Riviera is framed for the murder of a T-man, does some sleuthing on his own to break up an international counterfeiting ring. Good speedy melodrama for Raft fans. Made in Italy. (Dir: Joseph M. Newman, 87 mins.)

Lucky Night (1938)*½ Myrna Loy, Robert Taylor, Joseph Allen. Pitiful, contrived little nothing about an heiress who marries a poor poet. The cast is incapable of helping this film because the authors have failed to provide them with decent dialogue. (Dir: Norman Taurog, 80 mins.)

Lucky Partners (1940)**½ Ronald Colman, Ginger Rogers. Artist shares a sweepstakes ticket with a girl, which proves lucky. Occasionally amusing comedy, but could have been better. (Dir: Lewis Milestone, 102 mins.)

Lucky to Be a Woman (Italian, 1958) **½ Sophia Loren, Charles Boyer. Lightweight comedy bolstered by the stars' performances—plot centers around a model and her escapades in the international movie set. (Dir: Alessandro Blassetti, 94 mins.)

Lucy Gallant (1955)**½ Jane Wyman, Charlton Heston, Claire Trevor. Charlton Heston strikes oil and Jane Wyman builds the biggest fashion business in Texas but they find that marriage and careers don't mix. Claire Trevor adds another portrayal as the "heart of gold" saloon keeper to her list. (Dir: Robert Parrish, 104 mins.)

Ludwig (Italy, 1972)*½ Helmut Berger, Trevor Howard, Romy Schneider, Gert Frobe, Silvana Mangano. Overlong, poorly scripted historical drama about Ludwig, the Mad King of Bavaria, who misruled from age 19 in 1864 until his unlamented death in 1886. It's hard to believe that such a sophisticated filmmaker as Visconti could have labored so long to produce such a vapid, sterile work about the depraved lunatic with an edifice complex. (Dir: Luchino Visconti, 173 mins.)

Lullaby of Broadway (1951)** Doris Day, Gene Nelson, Gladys George. More backstage nonsense with music and plenty of dancing. Score includes standards by George Gershwin and Cole Porter which help. Gladys George registers as Doris' mother. Broadway was never like this! (Dir: David Butler, 92 mins.)

Lupo (Israeli, 1970)**½ Yuda Barkan, Gabi Amrani, Esther Greenberg. Sentimental, saccharine lightweight pastry about a middle-aged junk dealer in Tel Aviv. Leading role is played with charm by Barkan, a 25-year-old actor. Shot on location in Tel Aviv, and captures some of the infectious quality of the town's struggling tradesmen. Kids might enjoy. Written and directed by Menahem Golan, who made the lovely "Sallah." English subtitles. (100 mins.)

Lure of the Wilderness (1952)**½ Jean Peters, Jeffrey Hunter, Walter Brennan. Young man finds an escaped convict and his daughter hiding out in the swamp, helps him prove his innocence. Remake of 1941's "Swamp Water" has the benefit of color but doesn't have the interest of the original. Some good moments, however. (Dir: Jean Negulesco, 92 mins.)

Lured (1947)**½ A dance hall girl disappears in London, so friend Lucille Ball sets out to find her, nearly gets herself killed. With George Sanders, Boris Karloff. Fairly good mystery. (Also called "Personal Column.") (Dir: Douglas Sirk, 102 mins.)

Lust for a Vampire (Great Britain, 1970)**½ Michael Johnson, Suzanna Leigh, Yutte Stensgaard, Ralph Bates, Barbara Jefford. Ravishing young vampirette (Stensgaard) feels pangs of love for a novelist (Johnson) who has come to the old castle where she is a pupil in what is now an exclusive girls' school, to study the supernatural. Racy, high-humored, gory and full of female allures and perversions. Based on characters from J. Sheridan Le Fanu's 19th-century novel "Carmilla" (as were Roger Vadim's "Love and Roses" and Roy Ward Baker's "The Vampire Lovers"). (Dir: Jimmy Sangster, 95 mins.)

Lust for Gold (1949)**** Glenn Ford, Ida Lupino, Gig Young. Excellent film showing how greed and evil take over and ruin basically good people. Edge-of-seat suspense and fine performance by all. A real sleeper! (Dir: S. Sylvan Simon, 90 mins.)

Lust for Gold (Russian, 1957)** Ivan Pereverzev, Inna Kmit. Greed in the gold fields of prerevolutionary Russia. Several people are wiped out when they let their natural instincts get the better of them. As mundane a piece of anticapitalist propaganda as you'll ever see. (Dir: I. Pravov, 92 mins.)

Lust for Life (1956)******** Kirk Douglas, Anthony Quinn. Superb film about the turbulent, personal life of the tormented artist Vincent van Gogh, masterfully played by Kirk Douglas. Anthony Quinn won his second Oscar for his colorful performance as van Gogh's close friend and severest critic, artist Paul Gauguin. A special treat for viewers with color sets—all those marvelous van Gogh masterpieces. (Dir: Vincente Minnelli, 122 mins.)

Lusty Men (1952)*****½** Susan Hayward, Robert Mitchum, Arthur Kennedy. When a cowpoke becomes a rodeo star and lets it go to his head, his wife suffers. Very good drama with authentic rodeo atmosphere, solid performances and direction. (Dir: Nicholas Ray, 113 mins.)

Luther (1974)******* Stacy Keach, Patrick Magee, Alan Badel, Hugh Griffith. John Osborne's stunning play about the famous 16th-century cleric who changed the course of the world has been shortened and its impact reduced in the move to the screen. Albert Finney is not on hand to recreate his triumphant stage performance, but Stacy Keach, a fine but lesser actor, is increasingly effective as the film builds. Set in Germany in 1506-1533, Luther's actual early stamping grounds are now in East Germany, so this "Luther" was filmed on a "church" set in England. Rewarding historical drama. (Dir: Guy Green, 112 mins.)

Luv (1967)****½** Jack Lemmon, Peter Falk, Elaine May, Eddie Mayehoff. Heavy-handed rendering of Murray Schisgal's clever Broadway play about life and loves among a set of middle-class New Yorkers—part of a group much concerned with self-analysis and psychiatric jargon. Although the script and the performances have been cheapened, Elaine May is genuinely funny, and there's enough left to provide a few laughs along the way. If the whole picture had been as well handled as the scene with Elaine and Jack in a Ferris wheel . . . (Dir: Clive Donner, 95 mins.)

Luxury Liner (1948)****** George Brent, Jane Powell, Lauritz Melchior. Good

voices but nothing else in this musical about a ship's captain and his meddling teen-age daughter. (Dir: Richard Whorf, 98 mins.)

Lydia (1941)*****½** Merle Oberon, Joseph Cotten. An elderly lady has a reunion with four of her lost loves, relives the romantic past. Sensitive, poignant romantic drama, skillfully directed, acted. (Dir: Julien Duvivier, 144 mins.)

Lydia Bailey (1952)****½** Dale Robertson, Anne Francis. American lawyer goes to Haiti to get a girl's signature on a legal document. Becomes involved in a war with Napoleonic forces. Pleasant costume adventure moves at a good pace, has a colorful setting. (Dir: Jean Negulesco, 88 mins.)

M. (German, 1930)******** Peter Lorre, Ellen Widmann. Suspenseful, psychological crime drama, brilliantly directed by Fritz Lang—it was his first talking film—and played with subtle intensity by Peter Lorre, making his screen debut. Lorre plays a pitiable, disturbed child murderer in Berlin, and the film offers an intriguing delineation of the painstaking methods employed by both the police and the underworld to trap the killer. (Dir: Fritz Lang, 90 mins.)

Ma & Pa Kettle (1949)******* Marjorie Main, Percy Kilbride. The first of the "Ma and Pa Kettle" series and one of the funniest. These rural characters were first introduced in the Claudette Colbert-Fred MacMurray comedy "The Egg and I," and their fan appeal was so great that Universal starred them in their own vehicle. Marjorie Main and Percy Kilbride are a matchless pair as the Kettles. (Dir: Charles Lamont, 75 mins.)

Ma & Pa Kettle at Home (1954)****½** Marjorie Main, Percy Kilbride. "Ma & Pa Kettle" fans will get a kick out of this comedy in which Pa tries to make the dilapidated farm over into an efficient, prosperous operation. Just about everything turns out wrong and the results provide many laughs. (Dir: Charles Lamont, 81 mins.)

Ma & Pa Kettle at the Fair (1952)****½** Marjorie Main, Percy Kilbride. Cornball comedy with the Kettles getting into one impossible predicament after another. Pa buys a sick horse, Ma enters him in a race at the county fair by mistake, Rosie, the Kettles' oldest daughter, falls in love. (Dir: Charles Barton, 77 mins.)

Ma & Pa Kettle at Waikiki (1955) **½ Marjorie Main, Percy Kilbride. The Kettles find themselves in Hawaii in this outing. They are invited to that island paradise by another branch of the Kettle clan who has made millions in canned fruit. Many zany incidents occur during the Kettles' stay in Hawaii. (Dir: Lee Sholem, 79 mins.)

Ma & Pa Kettle Back on the Farm (1954)**½ Marjorie Main, Percy Kilbride. More fun as the Kettle clan gets involved with false uranium deposits on their property, in-law trouble via their oldest son's wife's parents, and gangsters who think their property is loaded with uranium. (Dir: Edward Sedgewick, 80 mins.)

Ma & Pa Kettle Go to Town (1950)** Marjorie Main, Percy Kilbride. Strictly for the Kettle-clan fans. Ma and Pa win a trip to New York City in a soft-drink-slogan contest and have a series of predictable but amusing adventures. There are gangsters, stolen money, kidnapings and zany chases galore. An added attraction is Marjorie Main's "beauty treatment" at a fashionable New York cosmetic mill. (Dir: Charles Lamont, 80 mins.)

Ma & Pa Kettle on Vacation (1953) **½ Marjorie Main, Percy Kilbride. The "Kettle" fans will have more fun with this broad comedy in which "Ma and Pa" go to Paris on vacation. Naturally, they don't confine their activities to sightseeing and get involved with an international espionage operation. (Dir: Charles Lamont, 75 mins.)

Macabre (1958)** William Prince, Jim Backus. This horror film doesn't rely on monsters for its impact—there are all sorts of fiendish things going on, such as burying people alive, for instance. The cast is better than the vehicle but they seem to enjoy playing at being terrorized. (Dir: William Castle, 72 mins.)

Macahans, The (1976)**½ James Arness, Eva Marie Saint, Richard Kiley, Bruce Boxleitner. Sprawling Western TV movie based on the theatrical feature "How the West Was Won," benefits from the cast and production. "Gunsmoke"'s Arness, backed up by Saint and young newcomer Boxleitner, returned to television playing scout Zeb Macahan, leading his brother's family west from Bull Run, Virginia, in time to avoid the Civil War. The trek west is interspersed with Civil War battle scenes involving Zeb's brother and nephew—sequences culled from other MGM pictures. Made-for-TV. (Dir: Bernard McEveety, 120 mins.)

Macao (1952)** Robert Mitchum, Jane Russell, William Bendix. Adventurer aids the police in capturing an underworld kingpin wanted in the States. Familiar, slow-moving melodrama. (Dir: Josef von Sternberg, 80 mins.)

Macbeth (1948)*** Orson Welles, Jeanette Nolan, Roddy McDowall. Welles' stylized version of the Shakespeare tragedy, in which he both plays the leading role and directs. In both departments it's an interesting if partially unrealized attempt to achieve the offbeat effect. Effectiveness and momentum of film impaired by the ludicrously incompetent performance of Jeanette Nolan playing Lady M. This appearance deservedly ended Miss Nolan's career in filmed versions of the Bard's plays. Welles' voice is still one of the great theater instruments around. (105 mins.)

Macbeth (U.S.-Great Britain, 1963) **½ Maurice Evans, Judith Anderson, Michael Hordern, Ian Bannen, Felix Aylmer. The Shakespeare play in a longer version of what was first seen on TV in 1960 in a shortened 80-minute form. Seems hard to believe, but there was a time when America took Maurice Evans very seriously as a Shakespearean actor. Chief value of this film is that it permanently records Judith Anderson, repeating her stage triumph as Lady Macbeth. Excellent British character actors including George Rose in support. But Evans is a mediocre Macbeth and the film disappoints because of that. Directed on location in Scotland by George Schaefer. (107 mins.)

Machine Gun Kelly (1958)** Charles Bronson, Susan Cabot. Small time hoodlum becomes a public enemy due to the goading of a dame. Bronson's good, the film less so. (Dir: Roger Corman, 80 mins.)

Machine Gun McCain (1970)** Peter Falk, John Cassavetes, Britt Ekland.

The stars are more interesting than this routine crime drama set in the U.S. but shot mostly in Europe. It involves a raid on a Las Vegas casino controlled by the Mafia, and it costs everyone concerned a large price. (Dir: Giuliano Montaldo, 94 mins.)

Machiste in King Solomon's Mines (Italian, 1963)* Reg Park, Wandisa Guida. Ancient African city is overthrown, but muscleman Machiste comes to the rescue to best the wicked rulers. Inane English-dubbed action spectacle.

Machiste in the Vale of Woe (Italian, 1960)*½ Kirk Norris, Frank Gordon. Routine Italian-produced adventure dubbed in English. Woe is you if you've got nothing better to do with your time.

Machiste, Strongest Man in the World (Italian, 1962)* Mark Forrest, Moira Orfei. Legendary musclepopping hero overcomes the oppressors despite the odds. Odds are overwhelming against your enjoying this lame brained nonsense.

Macho Callahan (1970)* David Janssen, Jean Seberg, Lee J. Cobb, David Carradine. Macho is mucho dull. Thin Western yarn features Janssen as an escaped convict from a Confederate prison seeking revenge against the man who put him behind bars. (Dir: Bernard L. Kowalski, 99 mins.)

MacKenna's Gold (1969)*½ Gregory Peck, Omar Sharif, Camilla Sparv. Overblown, over-produced, pretentious western, especially disappointing coming from producer Carl Foreman. Peck is cast as the marshal who knows where a fabulous fortune in gold is hidden and Sharif is the villain who wants to get his hands on it. For over 2 hours, the two, plus assorted supporting players, battle it out until all but a few remain for the final confrontation. Hard to believe, but this is the same producer-director (J. Lee Thompson) who was responsible for the marvelous "Guns of Navarone." Brilliant actors like Lee Cobb and Anthony Quayle are completely wasted. (128 mins.)

Mackintosh Man, The (Great Britain, 1973)**½ Paul Newman, Dominique Sanda, James Mason, Harry Andrews, Michael Horden. Thriller about cold-war espionage—the kind of plot that was quite popular in the 60's when spies were busy coming

in from the cold. Not only is the plot outdated, but the excellent supporting actors have been given lightweight roles badly cast. Miss Sanda's French accent belies her portraying a young Englishwoman. Newman affects a series of poses as he plays the agent out to trap Mason, a Communist who has infiltrated the top ranks of British intelligence. Enough car chases, escapes, captures and beatings as well as fine photography (by Oswald Morris) of England, Ireland and Malta, to keep fans of the genre occupied. Based on the novel "The Freedom Trap," by Desmond Bagley. (Dir: John Huston, 98 mins.)

Macomber Affair, The (1947)***½ Gregory Peck, Joan Bennett, Robert Preston. Hemingway's tale of the triangular difficulties of a husband, wife and guide on an African hunting expedition. Literate, well acted, recommended. (Dir: Zoltan Korda, 89 mins.)

Macon County Line (1974)**½ Alan Vint, Jesse Vint, Max Baer, Cheryl Waters. There is a great deal of violence and some effective drama in this supposedly factual story, about a vengeful Southern sheriff who is out for blood after his wife is brutally killed by a pair of drifters. The acting, by Alan and Jesse Vint (brothers in real life), and Max Baer (he also co-scripted and produced) as the sheriff, is very good. (Dir: Richard Compton, 89 mins.)

Macumba Love (1960)*½ Walter Reed, Ziva Rodann, June Wilkinson. Writer investigates a voodoo cult in South America, nearly loses his life. Filmed in Brazil, this thriller of the supernatural alternates between absorbing voodoo scenes and badly-acted story. (Dir: Douglas Fowley, 85 mins.)

Macunaima (Brazilian, 1970)**½ Grande Otelo, Paulo Jose. Daring Brazilian allegory of a black, born 45 years old, who turns white while prancing between the "jungle" and the "city." Wild and far-out fairy-tale sequences involving cannibalism and incest move the narrative. Sometimes interesting experiment. (Dir: Joaquim Pedro De Andrade, 95 mins.)

Mad About Men (British, 1955)** Glynis Johns, Donald Sinden. Girl who intends to do good keeps transferring her affections from her husband to her former fiance. Slow-moving comedy needs more sparkle.

Mad About Music (1938)*** Deanna Durbin, Herbert Marshall. Girl attending a swanky Swiss school invents a father to impress classmates. Fine Durbin film, well produced, acted and naturally featuring the lovely voice. (Dir: Norman Taurog, 100 mins.)

Mad Adventures of Rabbi Jacob (France, 1974)*** Louis De Funes, Suzy Delair, Marcel Dalio. French comedian Louis De Funes has made one of the best modern-day slapstick farces since Chaplin gave up the craft. De Funes plays a bigoted Catholic factory owner whose exasperation causes him to be chased by the police as a political assassin, dumped in a vat of green bubblegum, chased by Arab terrorists and finally to impersonate an American rabbi making a pilgrimage back to his birthplace. Truly jet-age humor. (Dir: Gerard Oury, 96 mins.)

Mad at the World (1955)**½ Frank Lovejoy, Keefe Brasselle, Cathy O'Donnell. When a gang of juvenile delinquents seriously injure a young father's baby, he decides to take the matter in his own hands and goes on the hunt for them. Grim drama, well made. (Dir: Harry Essex, 72 mins.)

Mad Dog Coll (1961)*½ John Chandler, Kay Doubleday, Brooke Hayward. Neighborhood hoodlum climbs to the top of the rackets by underhanded means, becomes hated by both police and the underworld. Unpleasant gangster melodrama without any redeeming qualities. (Dir: Burt Balaban, 85 mins.)

Mad Dogs and Englishmen (1971)*** Joe Cocker, Leon Russell. Filmed record of Cocker's tour of the United States during 1970. He is excellent and sings numbers like "Space Captain," "Something," and "Let It Be," adapting all to his unique gravelly voice. Leon Russell is his sideman, and occasionally sings. Shots of Cocker offstage are interesting, if you like Cocker. (Dir: Pierre Adidge, 114 mins.)

Mad Executioners, The (German, 1963)*½ Hansjorg Felmy, Maria Perschy, Dieter Borsche. Scotland Yard sleuth investigates two cases —a series of beheadings and a criminal band of executioners who've taken the law into their own hands. English-dubbed mystery takes on too much plotting, outdated theatrics. (Dir: Edwin Zbonek, 95 mins.)

Mad Ghoul, The (1943)**½ David Bruce, Evelyn Ankers. Wild thriller, with an excellent performance by David Bruce as a doctor kept in a state of living death. Grisly stuff which horror addicts should enjoy. (Dir: James Hogan, 65 mins.)

Mad Little Island (British, 1958)**½ Jeannie Carson, Donald Sinden. Scottish islanders are horrified to learn their home is to be turned into a rocket base. Sort of a sequel to "Tight Little Island," and not nearly as amusing. (Dir: Michael Relph, 95 mins.)

Mad Love (1935)**½ Peter Lorre, Frances Drake, Colin Clive. Mad doctor operates on a pianist mutilated in an accident, grafts the hands of a murderer to him. Overacted but atmospheric thriller. (Dir: Karl Freund, 70 mins.)

Mad Magician, The (1954)** Vincent Price, Eva Gabor. Vincent Price in a routine chore—the role he performs with relish. This time he is a deranged magician with a bent for murder. (Dir: John Brahm, 72 mins.)

Mad Miss Manton (1938)***½ Barbara Stanwyck, Henry Fonda. Society girl turns sleuth and investigates a murder. Fast, funny comedy-mystery, very good fun. (Dir: Leigh Jason, 80 mins.)

Mad Monster Party (1967)*½ Tame animated puppet film which includes the voices of Boris Karloff, Phyllis Diller and Gale Garnett, as monsters hold a reunion. Among the notables are Frankenstein, Dr. Jekyll and Mr. Hyde. For the kids. (Dir: Jules Bass, 94 mins.)

Mad Room, The (1969)*** Stella Stevens, Shelley Winters. Pretty good remake of 1941 "Ladies in Retirement"—a thriller full of suspense and plot twists to set you on the wrong track. Stella Stevens is quite good as the companion to a wealthy widow (Shelley Winters) who brings her brother and sister to live with her after they are released from an asylum. There are some gory scenes but fans of this type of horror story will be fascinated. Directed by Bernard Girard. (93 mins.)

Madame (French, 1963)** Sophia Loren, Robert Hossein. One of Sophia Loren's worst films—an in-

439

accurate account of France during Napoleon's reign. Loren is beautiful but the script defeats her efforts at comedy. Nothing however quite overcomes her good looks. (Dir: Christian-Jaque, 104 mins.)

Madame Bovary (1949)*** Jennifer Jones, Van Heflin, James Mason. Miss Jones gives a beautiful performance in the title role of Emma Bovary, an incurable romantic whose many loves led to her destruction. The female fans will swoon over Louis Jourdan as one of Emma's amours. Van Heflin plays Emma's respectable husband and James Mason portrays Gustave Flaubert. (Dir: Vincente Minnelli, 115 mins.)

Madame Curie (1943)***½ Greer Garson, Walter Pidgeon, Henry Travers. Occasionally too slow but generally brilliant screen biography of the discoverers of radium. Garson and Pidgeon are ideal in this informative and entertaining film. (Dir: Mervyn Le Roy, 124 mins.)

Madame Sin (1972)** Bette Davis, Robert Wagner. With silver-blue eyeshadow splashed over her famous lids, Miss Davis plays an oriental villainess in this handsomely mounted film made in England. The location footage taken on the Isle of Mull and the Scottish coast turns out to be the real star, backed by English supporting actors and Robert Wagner, with Miss Davis appearing content to remain in the background. The plot has Madame Sin kidnapping a U.S. intelligence agent. Made-for-TV. (Dir: David Greene, 73 mins.)

Madame X (1966)** Lana Turner, John Forsythe, Ricardo Montalban. The ancient tear-jerker about the tragic lady who sacrifices all for love and her son, given an updated but not improved treatment. Turner suffers and suffers; the Ross Hunter production is scrumptious, but it's all reminiscent of another day. (Dir: David Lowell Rich, 100 mins.)

Made for Each Other (1939)**** Carole Lombard, James Stewart. In-laws nearly bring about a smashup in the lives of a young married couple. Very good drama, at which the ladies should shed tears. (Dir: John Cromwell, 100 mins.)

Made for Each Other (1971)**** Renee Taylor, Joseph Bologna, Paul Sorvino. Delightful, joyous comedy about a pair of losers in New York who meet at an emergency group-therapy session. This original screenplay by Taylor and Bologna is a semi-autobiographical account of their real-life courtship before their marriage. It is full of revealing, poignant, sometimes noisy truths, and it's wonderfully well played by the two of them as an added bonus. Taylor's cabaret routine is one of the best good/bad performances you've ever seen. It's hilarious and touching at the same time. This frenetic love story was shot on location in the Big Apple, and it is surprisingly well directed by newcomer Robert B. Bean. (104 mins.)

Made in Heaven (British, 1952)**½ David Tomlinson, Petula Clark. Doubting young wife suspects her husband of flirting with an attractive maid. Pleasant little romantic comedy.

Made in Italy (Italy-France, 1965)***½ Anna Magnani, Nino Manfredi, Virna Lisi, Sylva Koscina. Thirty-two short vignettes about modern Italian life comprise this funny, often touching film. Anecdotes range from a tearful nun gazing at wedding gowns, to adulterous pursuits. Best is the final episode, starring the expressive Magnani as an imperious mother herding her brood across a crowded intersection. (Dir: Nanni Loy, 101 mins.)

Made in Paris (1966)*½ Ann-Margret, Louis Jourdan, Richard Crenna. Labored fare reminiscent of the M-G-M musicals of the forties. Ann-Margret is a fashion buyer in Paris on her first buying spree and designer Louis Jourdan gives her the big rush. The dialogue is totally unreal, but there are some snazzy hair styles and coiffures to look at. Talented performers like Edie Adams and Richard Crenna are wasted. (Dir: Boris Sagal, 101 mins.)

Madeleine (British, 1949)**** Ann Todd, Norman Wooland. The story of Madeleine Smith, who was tried for poisoning her lover in Scotland in 1857. Superbly directed and performed, absorbing drama from beginning to end. (Dir: David Lean, 101 mins.)

Madigan (1968)**½ Richard Widmark, Henry Fonda. This detective yarn is tougher both in dialogue and action than any TV series. On that basis it's worth catching, provided that hard-hitting police tales appeal to you. Widmark, playing a heel of a cop who gets the job done and doesn't care how he does it, gives a very fine performance. Henry Fonda is effective as Widmark's critical though not above-reproach superior, and all the secondary roles are well played with a special nod to Harry Guardino as Widmark's sidekick. (Dir: Don Siegel, 101 mins.)

Madigan: Park Avenue Beat (1973) *½ Richard Widmark, John Larch. Episode of the old "Madigan" series. Concerns a policeman (Larch) thrown off the force after killing a surrendering criminal he mistakenly believed had slain his partner. The plot may be contrived, but it's handled decently. Made-for-TV. (Dir: Alex March, 72 mins.)

Madigan: The Lisbon Beat (1973)*½ Richard Widmark. Somewhat off-beat episode of the old series; police-detective Madigan (Widmark) first loses a prisoner handcuffed to him, then spends most of his time enjoying the sights of spectacular Lisbon. Made-for-TV. (Dir: Boris Sagal)

Madigan: The Naples Beat (1973)** Richard Widmark, Rossano Brazzi, Raf Vallone. In addition to Widmark's skillful portrayal of that fearless New York City police detective, Madigan, this series episode features Rossano Brazzi and Raf Vallone as opposing mobsters. The setting is Naples, Italy, and the story concerns drug traffic and gang warfare. Made-for-TV. (Dir: Boris Sagal, 72 mins.)

Madigan's Millions (Spanish, Italian, 1967)*½ Dustin Hoffman, Cesar Romero, Elsa Martinelli. Hoffman's first screen performance, as an Internal Revenue Service agent, is a disaster. He goes to Rome to investigate the holding of a murdered mobster. There are a few bright spots, but Hoffman only gives glimpses of his real talent. (Dir: Stanley Prager, 76 mins.)

Madison Avenue (1962)** Dana Andrews, Eleanor Parker, Jeanne Crain, Eddie Albert. Routine drama supposedly revealing the naked truth about the cutthroat world of big time advertising. All the characters are caricatures, and the plot about the machinations involved in parlaying a small-time dairy into a national trademark is just a local

yawn. (Dir: H. Bruce Humberstone, 94 mins.)

Madness of the Heart (British, 1949) **½ Margaret Lockwood, Paul Dupuis. Beautiful blind girl marries a wealthy Frenchman, meets opposition from the family and friends. Slick romantic drama, familiar but competent.

Madonna of the Seven Moons (British, 1945)*** Phyllis Calvert, Stewart Granger. An early encounter with a gypsy leaves its mark upon a woman for life, endangers the safety of her daughter. Strong melodrama. Well done. (Dir: Arthur Crabtree, 88 mins.)

Madron (1970)**½ Richard Boone, Leslie Caron. Boone and Caron are far better than this routine western story about a nun and a gunman who team up in a dangerous trek across a desert, stalked by Apaches.

Madwoman of Chaillot (Great Britain, 1969)**½ Katharine Hepburn, Yul Brynner, Danny Kaye, Edith Evans, Charles Boyer, Claude Dauphin, Giulietta Masina, Richard Chamberlain, Margaret Leighton, Oscar Homolka, Donald Pleasence. John Huston left after shooting several weeks of this picture, but it was conceptually flawed from the outset. The producers foolishly tried to make a huge, opulent, star-studded spectacle out of Jean Giraudoux's bittersweet, small-scale morality fable. It couldn't and didn't work, but there are a few bright spots in this over-produced tale about a group of super-eccentrics who take it upon themselves to save Paris from corrupt promoters. Edith Evans, one of the very greatest modern actresses, scores in a trial scene, and the great Kate is stunning in her series of fantastic flowered bonnets. Adapted by Edward Anhalt and updated to 1969. (Dir: Bryan Forbes, 142 mins.)

Maedchen in Uniform (German, 1958) ** Lilli Palmer, Romy Schneider. Drama of life in a school for girls, and of the relationship between one emotionally sensitive girl and her teacher. Remake of a famous German film of the early talkie era, but not as potent—draggy, merely passable. Dubbed in English. (Dir: Geya Radvanyi, 91 mins.)

Mafia (Italy-France, 1968)*½ Claudia Cardinale, Lee J. Cobb, Franco Nero. Routine crime drama about the workings of the infamous Mafia didn't receive much theatrical release in this country. Didn't deserve it, either. (Dir: Damiano Damiani, 98 mins.)

Maggie, The (1954)*** Paul Douglas. The late Paul Douglas gives a robust performance in this diverting British comedy about a Scottish sea-captain and his shenanigans in outwitting big business. (Dir: Alexander Mackendrick, 93 mins.)

Magic Bow, The (British, 1947)**½ Classical music lovers have a treat in store for them, with this biography of famed violinist Paganini, as portrayed by Stewart Granger. With Phyllis Calvert, Jean Kent, Cecil Parker, Dennis Price. Offscreen violin solos played by concert artist Yehudi Menuhin. (Dir: Bernard Knowles, 105 mins.)

Magic Box, The (British, 1952)*** Robert Donat, Margaret Johnston, Maria Scheli, many others. The story of William Friese-Greene, the inventor of the motion picture camera, whose life was a tragedy through hardships and lack of recognition. The British industry collaborated to produce this biography, with practically every actor in English films making brief appearances. The result is interesting, but rather top-heavy, due to the number of hands involved. (Dir: John Boulting, 103 mins.)

Magic Carpet, The (1951)** Lucille Ball, Raymond Burr, John Agar. TV's Perry Mason (Raymond Burr) and Lucy (Lucille Ball) find themselves in the mystical time of Caliphs and Viziers in this corny Arabian Nights farce. (Dir: Lew Landers, 84 mins.)

Magic Carpet (1972)** Susan Saint James is the star of this scenic tour through Italy. She leads a group of Americans as a substitute tour guide. Supporting cast of disgruntled tourists includes Jim and Henry Backus, Abby Dalton, Wally Cox, Nanette Fabray, and Selma Diamond. Major interest is the footage of Rome, Venice, Florence, Ischia, and Naples. Made-for-TV. (Dir: William Graham, 99 mins.)

Magic Christian, The (1970)**½ Peter Sellers, Ringo Starr, Raquel Welch. Episodic version of Terry Southern's best novel. Sellers plays Guy Grand, a British business baronet, out to make life difficult for

everyone around him. Grand adopts Ringo, names him Youngman Grand, and off they go together to prove the corruptibility of the world. There are one or two good sequences, and the finale is better yet as the luxury vessel, the "Magic Christian," is destroyed. Sellers is fair, Ringo is better! (Dir: Joseph McGrath, 92 mins.)

Magic Face, The (1952)*** Luther Adler, Patricia Knight. Noted actor kills Hitler, then poses as Der Fuhrer, in order to halt Nazi tyranny. Well-done melodrama made in Europe holds the interest. (Dir: Frank Tuttle, 88 mins.)

Magic Fire (1956)** Yvonne DeCarlo, Rita Gam, Alan Badel. Tale of the romantic troubles of famed composer Wagner. Overdone drama is a victim of ham acting and plodding plot. (Dir: William Dieterle, 95 mins.)

Magic Flute, The (Sweden, 1973) **** Ulrik Gold, Josef Kostlinger. An exquisite adaptation by Ingmar Bergman of Mozart's opera "The Magic Flute," first performed in 1791. Most of the time, Bergman simply photographs the action unfolding during a stage production of the Mozart masterwork, but he does break out of it from time to time. There are also dashes of humor, but Bergman serves the genius of Mozart by trying to complement, not overwhelm, the opera itself. Primarily of interest to opera lovers, but it's a special treat for them. The singers, incidentally, pre-recorded their voices and then lip-synched the lyrics while filming was underway. Made for Swedish television. Photographed by Sven Nykvist. (Dir: Ingmar Bergman, 134 mins.)

Magic Fountain, The (1964)** Animated fairy tale about a hidden magic fountain, narrated by Sir Cedric Hardwicke. Okay for the small fry.

Magic Sword, The (1962)*½ Basil Rathbone, Anne Helm, Gary Lockwood. Young knight slays the evil dragon and bests the wicked sorcerer to win the hand of the fair princess. Mishmash of fantasy, played half straight, half kidding, successful at neither. (Dir: Bert I. Gordon, 80 mins.)

Magic Town (1947)**½ James Stewart, Jane Wyman. A public opinion pollster publicizes a small town as being statistically accurate in all polls, which only causes trouble for the town's mild way of life. Uneven comedy, misses fire most of the time; just fair. (Dir: William Wellman, 103 mins.)

Magic Voyage of Sinbad, The (1961)* Edward Stolar. No magic here. Hokum swashbuckling adventure.

Magic Weaver, The (Russian, 1965) *** Pleasant fairy tale about a returning soldier and his tall tales. Primarily for the youngsters. English-dubbed.

Magician, The (Sweden, 1958)**** Max von Sydow, Ingrid Thulin. An early Bergman film that will tingle your spine and stimulate your brain. The supernatural, comic, mystical and the human mingle in this imaginative tale of a magician and his troupe who are detained in a small Swedish community when their magical powers are disbelieved. Visually rich, gothic atmosphere. (Dir: Ingmar Bergman, 102 mins.)

Magnet, The (British, 1950)**** Stephen Murray, Kay Walsh, William Fox. An imaginative ten-year-old swindles a lad out of a magnet, is convinced the thing is some sort of charm. Delightful comedy, clean and refreshing, sparklingly written. (Dir: Charles Frend, 78 mins.)

Magnificent Ambersons (1942)**** Joseph Cotten, Dolores Del Rio, Tim Holt. Son of a wealthy midwestern family keeps his mother apart from the man she loves. Superb drama, written and directed by Orson Welles. Movie making at its best. (88 mins.)

Magnificent Cuckold, The (France-Italy, 1964)**½ Claudia Cardinale, Ugo Tognazzi, Bernard Blier. Racy comedy features Tognazzi as a suspicious husband who spies on his young wife, convinced she's having an affair. Naturally, he's outwitted by his sensual wife. Funny sequences along the way. (Dir: Antonio Pietrangeli, 117 mins.)

Magnificent Doll, The (1946)** Ginger Rogers, David Niven, Burgess Meredith. The story of Dolly Madison, the President's wife whose relationship with Aaron Burr nearly altered the course of American history. Elaborate but heavy, not too well acted drama. (Dir: Frank Borzage, 95 mins.)

Magnificent Dope, The (1942)*** Henry Fonda, Don Ameche, Lynne

Bari. Amusing comedy which has the country boy, as usual, outwitting the city slickers. Fonda and Ameche are a good contrast and the film has its share of laughs. (Dir: Walter Lang, 83 mins.)

Magnificent Fraud, The (1939)** Akim Tamiroff, Lloyd Nolan. Loud, yet boring, tale of an actor in a mythical South American country, who tries to impersonate an assassinated dictator. (Dir: Robert Florey, 80 mins.)

Magnificent Magical Magnet of Santa Mesa—See: Adventures of Freddie

Magnificent Matador (1955)**½ Anthony Quinn, Maureen O'Hara. Bullfighter runs away on the day of his protegee's entry into the ring. Good bullfight sequences atone somewhat for a hackneyed plot. (Dir: Budd Boetticher, 95 mins.)

Magnificent Obsession (1954)**½ Jane Wyman, Rock Hudson. Classily produced soap-opera which leans heavily on sentiment and turns out to be a four-handkerchief film for ladies. Lloyd C. Douglas' novel about one man's devotion and faith to a woman whose blindness he caused is handled well by the two stars and a good supporting cast. This is a remake of the 1935 version which starred Irene Dunne and Robert Taylor. (Dir: Douglas Sirk, 108 mins.)

Magnificent Roughnecks (1956)** Jack Carson, Mickey Rooney. Couple of oil men have trouble with rival drillers and rival gals. Two veteran performers in a plot that's seen even longer service. (Dir: Sherman A. Rose, 73 mins.)

Magnificent Seven, The (1960)*** Yul Brynner, Eli Wallach, Steve McQueen, Horst Buchholz, Robert Vaughn, James Coburn, Charles Bronson. An interesting western drama based on the marvelous Japanese film of the same name. A band of hired gunfighters, led by the bald pated Mr. Brynner, are enlisted to protect a small Mexican village from a group of thieving bandits. The acting is top notch, with James Coburn, Robert Vaughn and Horst Buchholz taking top honors. (Dir: John Sturges, 126 mins.)

Magnificent Sinner, The (German, 1961)**½ Romy Schneider, Curt Jurgens. Love story of a girl and the Czar of Russia, who is not free to marry her, ending tragically in assassination. Some tender scenes, good performances, but mostly murky, slow-moving historical drama. English-dubbed. (Dir: Robert Siodmak, 91 mins.)

Magnificent Yankee, The (1951)***½ Louis Calhern, Ann Harding. Superbly acted biographical drama, the story of Oliver Wendell Holmes, Supreme Court Justice and man of legal astuteness. Perhaps a bit too placid for some tastes, it is nevertheless a film of rare refinement, well worthwhile. (Dir: John Sturges, 80 mins.)

Magnum Force (1973)* Clint Eastwood, Hal Holbrook, David Soul, Tim Matheson. Sequel to "Dirty Harry," again putting unemotional Clint Eastwood in the role of homicide-detective "Dirty" Harry Callahan of the San Francisco P. D. The blood flows freely as Harry picks up the trail of a death squad of rookie cops, who are rubbing out the scum of the underworld. Off-beat casting of usually sweet Hal Holbrook as the leader of the heavies is the only interesting break with routine, excessive gunplay. (Dir: Ted Post, 124 mins.)

Magus, The (British, 1968)*** Anthony Quinn, Candice Bergen, Michael Caine, Anna Karina. John Fowles' complex, elliptical novel about a young English school teacher (Michael Caine) who arrives on a small Greek island is pretty heady material for a motion picture. But Fowles wrote the screenplay himself, and makes this bizarre story as intelligible as possible. If you're in the mood for a film that demands more of your attention and your intelligence than is usually the case, you'll be rewarded by this off-beat story. Quinn gives a restrained, effective performance. You may not completely understand Miss Bergen, but the men in the audience may be willing to settle for just looking at this lovely vision. (Dir: Guy Green, 117 mins.)

Mahogany (1975)* Diana Ross, Billy Dee Williams, Anthony Perkins. A stupefyingly inept yarn about a black girl from a Chicago ghetto who becomes an internationally famous model and dress designer. Diana Ross, who is enormously talented, has a few moments, but she's trapped by the ludicrous dialogue. Director Tony Richardson was fired

for "not capturing the black point of view," and was replaced by Berry Gordy, a record executive who clearly has no talent whatever as a filmmaker. Diana deserves far better. (110 mins.)

Maid in Paris (French, 1957)**½ Daniel Gelin, Dany Robin. Wacky French comedy about a young girl, whose father is a movie star, and her amours in Gay Paree. Dany Robin is delightful as the willing mademoiselle. (Dir: Gaspard-Hult, 84 mins.)

Mail Bag Robbery (British, 1957)** Lee Patterson, Kay Callard. Clever crooks plan a unique setup for robbing a train's gold shipment. Fairly well worked out low-budget crime melodrama. (Dir: Compton Bennett, 70 mins.)

Mail Order Bride (1964)**½ Buddy Ebsen, Keir Dullea, Lois Nettleton, Warren Oates. Early version of the western comedy as practiced by director-writer Burt Kennedy ("Support Your Local Sheriff"). In this one, Ebsen attempts to get Dullea to settle down by marrying him off to Nettleton. Fine supporting cast. (83 mins.)

Main Attraction, The (Great Britain, 1962)** Pat Boone, Nancy Kwan, Mai Zetterling. Picked up by an older circus woman, a mixed-up youth starts straying in his attentions, rouses ire and jealousy among the circus crowd. Boone's switch to playing a drifter finds him uncomfortable in a non-"All-American" role. Standard plot, corny ending. Zetterling is outstanding as the aging circus performer. (Dir: Daniel Petrie, 85 mins.)

Main Chance, The (British, 1965)** Gregoire Aslan, Tracy Reed, Edward De Souza. Mastermind organizes a diamond-smuggling scheme, picks an ex-RAF pilot to help him. Standard vest-pocket crime melodrama. (Dir: John Knight, 60 mins.)

Main Street to Broadway (1953)** Tom Morton, Mary Murphy. Young playwright refuses to be discouraged in trying to be a success on Broadway. Trite story of theatre life, with Broadway and Hollywood luminaries being dragged in briefly for name value. (Dir: Tay Garnett, 102 mins.)

Majin, the Monster of Terror (Japanese, 1965)* Another monster is set loose to terrorize and destroy. Feeble horror thriller dubbed in English.

Major and the Minor, The (1942) ***½ Ginger Rogers, Ray Milland. Not as fresh today as in 1942, but this delightful comedy about a girl who disguises herself as a child so she can travel at half fare is still riotous comedy. Often risque but never offensive as Major Milland tries to take care of little Ginger who's falling in love with him. (Dir: Billy Wilder, 100 mins.)

Major Barbara (British, 1940)**** George Bernard Shaw's biting wit evident in an ironic comedy of a rich girl who joins the Salvation Army. Wendy Hiller, Rex Harrison, Robert Newton, Robert Morley and a fine cast. Excellent adult entertainment. Hiller is heavenly. (Dir: Gabriel Pascal, 115 mins.)

Major Dundee (1965)**½ Charlton Heston, Richard Harris, Jim Hutton, Senta Berger. Cavalry major rounds up a motley crew of deserters and Confederate prisoners to go on a dangerous mission tracking down Apaches. Loosely knit western melodrama goes off in all directions after an excellent beginning; very uneven, but some occasional fine moments. (Dir: Sam Peckinpah, 134 mins.)

Majority of One, A (1961)**½ Rosalind Russell, Alec Guinness. Jewish widow meets a Japanese industrialist, resents him at first because her son was killed in the war, but soon finds they have many things in common. We don't know the Japanese word, but the Yiddish expression for this is "schmaltz"; some good moments, but it suffers from overlength, stiff direction. (Dir: Mervyn Le Roy, 153 mins.)

Make Haste to Live (1954)*** Dorothy McGuire, Stephen McNally. Husband returns from prison intending to kill his wife, after failing the first time. Suspenseful mystery melodrama with a good cast. (Dir: William A. Seiter, 90 mins.)

Make Me an Offer (British, 1956) **½ Peter Finch, Adrienne Corri. Amusing comedy about the buying and selling of antiques. Peter Finch gives a very entertaining performance and Adrienne Corri is a decorative side-kick. (Dir: Cyril Frankel, 89 mins.)

Make Mine Mink (British, 1960)***½ Terry-Thomas, Athene Seyler, Billie Whitelaw. Dowager and an ex-officer team to commit larceny, the proceeds going to charity. The British

have a knack for making these crazy comedies, and this is one of the better ones; often screamingly funny, with bright lines, situations.

Make Way For Lila (Swedish, 1962) **½ Erica Remberg, Joachim Hansen. Unusual locale adds interest to this slender tale of a girl, raised by Laplanders, who becomes the object of two men's affections. Picturesque scenery, pleasant performances. Dubbed in English.

Make Way for Tomorrow (1937) ***½ Victor Moore, Beulah Bondi. Beautifully told tale of an elderly couple who are forced by circumstance to appeal to their children for help. A real tear jerker, directed by Leo McCarey. (Dir: Leo McCarey, 100 mins.)

Make Your Own Bed (1944)*½ Jane Wyman, Jack Carson. Silly little comedy about a private eye and his girl who take jobs as butler and maid supposedly in line of duty. Most of the jokes are even old for 1944. (Dir: Peter Godfrey, 82 mins.)

Malaga (British, 1960)** Trevor Howard, Dorothy Dandridge, Edmund Purdom. Jewel thief heads for Spain after a partner who has doublecrossed him. Some good players trapped in a vague, cumbersome story, with only the location photography commendable. (Dir: Laslo Benedek, 97 mins.)

Malaya (1950)**½ Spencer Tracy, James Stewart, Valentina Cortesa. Good old-fashioned adventure tale about a pair of daring men of the world who combine their skills to smuggle raw rubber out of Jap-occupied Malaya. A good supporting cast includes such stalwarts as Sydney Greenstreet, John Hodiak, Lionel Barrymore and Gilbert Roland. (Dir: Richard Thorpe, 98 mins.)

Male Animal (1942)***½ Henry Fonda, Jack Carson, Olivia de Havilland. Clever, witty comedy about a dull but principled college professor, his wife and a former football hero friend from their college days who pays them a visit. Long live the memory of co-author James Thurber. (Dir: Elliott Nugent, 101 mins.)

Male Hunt (French, 1964)*** Jean-Paul Belmondo, Jean-Claude Brialy, Catherine Deneuve. Young man is determined to get married despite the efforts of assorted people to dissuade him. Sprightly comedy dubbed in English has a number of amusing twists and turns. (Dir: Edouard Molinaro, 92 mins.)

Malfas Mystery, The (British, 1962)** Maureen Swanson, Alan Cuthbertson. Girl released from prison works undercover for a detective agency, uncovers a crime ring. Okay Edgar Wallace mystery.

Malta Story, The (British, 1954)**½ Alec Guinness, Jack Hawkins. British pilot falls in love with a Maltese girl on that bomb stricken isle during war. Fair, but not up to Alec's later high standards. (Dir: Brian Desmond Hurst, 98 mins.)

Maltese Bippy, The (1969)*½ Dan Rowan, Dick Martin, Carol Lynley, Robert Reed. A "yawn-in" from the two stars of "Laugh-In" trying to capitalize on the success of their TV'er. Their previous film was a '58 clinker called "Once upon a Horse." Based on their impact on the big screen it may be another decade or so before they get a movie job. In case anyone cares, Dick imagines he's a werewolf, and Dan is a producer of cheaple pornographic nude films. (Dir: Norman Panama, 92 mins.)

Maltese Falcon, The (Ricardo Cortez, 1931)—See: **Dangerous Female**

Maltese Falcon (1941)**** Humphrey Bogart, Mary Astor, Peter Lorre, Sydney Greenstreet. Probably the finest "private eye" picture ever made. Film was initial effort of John Huston, one of the best directors Hollywood has ever had. John also did the adaptation of the Dashiell Hammett yarn about Sam Spade and it's a corker. (Dir: John Huston, 100 mins.)

Mambo (1955)** Silvana Mangano, Shelley Winters, Vittorio Gassman. Salesgirl rises to the heights as a glamorous dancer, becomes involved in complicated love affair. Romantic drama that never quite jells, overlong and sketchily developed. Produced in Italy, English dialogue. (Dir: Robert Rossen, 94 mins.)

Mame (1974)**½ Lucille Ball, Beatrice Arthur, Robert Preston. The wonderful Broadway musical based on the madcap misadventures of marvelous Auntie Mame has been diluted in this screen version starring Lucille Ball. The usually bright Ms. Ball doesn't measure up to the sophisticated grandness and exaggerated madness of the larger-than-life character, and it's a shame because she seems so right for the part. However, the film does have its moments and the music, particularly the big title tune, works well for the most part. Beatrice Arthur, TV's Maude, scores in a recreation of her Broadway part of Mame's best friend, Vera Charles, and the production values are first-class, if a little bit over-ambitious. (Dir: Gene Saks, 131 mins.)

Man, The (1972)**½ James Earl Jones, Martin Balsam, Lew Ayres, William Windom. Occasionally interesting drama about the first black President of the United States, played by Jones. Thrust into the job after the death of the President and Speaker of the House, and the incapacitating stroke of the Vice President, he finds himself not taken seriously by the Cabinet, so he attempts to assert his power. Script by Rod Serling, from the best seller by Irving Wallace. The dialogue and plot are brittle if somewhat amateur. Jones is fine. (Dir: Joseph Sargent, 93 mins.)

Man About the House, A (British, 1948)*** Margaret Johnston, Kieron Moore, Dulcie Gray. Spinsters take a villa in Italy, and one of them falls for a dashing young man who proves to be up to no good. Well done, frequently absorbing drama. (Dir: Leslie Arliss, 83 mins.)

Man About Town (1939)*** Jack Benny, Rochester, Dorothy Lamour. Jack is a great lover in this one (at least he thinks so) and when the routine musical numbers don't interfere, he and Rochester (Eddie Anderson) have a ball. (Dir: Mark Sandrich, 90 mins.)

Man About Town (French, 1947)**½ Maurice Chevalier, Francoise Perrier. Chevalier as a movie-maker in the old primitive silent days. Leisurely paced, but pleasant comedy dubbed in English. Some amusing insights into the days when movies were young. (Dir: René Clair, 89 mins.)

Man Alive (1945)**½ Pat O'Brien, Ellen Drew. Husband thought dead returns and plays "ghost" to haunt a suitor away from his wife. Amusing farce. (Dir: Ray Enright, 70 mins.)

Man Alone, A (1955)***½ Ray Milland, Mary Murphy, Raymond Burr, Ward Bond. Gunslinger exposes the leader of an outlaw band who massacred a stagecoach party. Different western has plenty of suspense, good direction by Milland. (Dir: Ray Milland, 95 mins.)

Man and a Woman, A (French, 1966) **** Anouk Aimee, Jean-Louis Trintignant. A visually stunning, superbly acted, and ultimately very moving contemporary love story. Anouk Aimee received international acclaim and an Academy Award nomination for her haunting, profoundly touching portrait of a young widow falling in love. Miss Aimee makes this seeming soap opera become art, not artifice, and she is aided by the direction and the inventive camera work of Claude Lelouch. Trintignant is also fine playing a racing-car driver wooing Miss Aimee, and there are two particularly expert performances by some scene-stealing children—his daughter and her son. The setting is various parts of France, but the emotional truths captured here are universal. (102 mins.)

Man and Child (French, 1957) ** Eddie Constantine, Juliette Greco, Jacqueline Ventura. When a girl is abducted by a dope ring, an innocent man's daughter is kidnaped by her family as an exchange. Passable crime drama, a bit better than the usual Constantine heroics. Dubbed in English.

Man and the Monster, The (Mexican, 1962) * Enrique Rambal, Marta Roth. Famous musician turns into a monster when the music affects him, becomes a killer. Farfetched horror thriller dubbed in English.

Man at the Carlton Tower (British, 1961) ** Maxine Audley, Lee Montague. Sleuth gets on the trail of a disappearing suspect in a jewel robbery. Mildly entertaining low-budget crime melodrama based on an Edgar Wallace mystery. (Dir: Robert Tronson, 57 mins.)

Man Bait (British, 1951) *** George Brent, Marguerite Chapman. An innocent moment off guard with a blonde gets a bookdealer into a mess of trouble, including murder. Nicely done melodrama. (Dir: Terence Fisher, 80 mins.)

Man Behind the Gun (1953) ** Randolph Scott. Depending on how you feel about the dubious charms of Los Angeles, you are either sore at Randolph Scott or beholden to him.

According to this hokey Western, he built the joint single-handed. (Dir: Felix E. Feist, 81 mins.)

Man Between, The (British, 1953) ***½ James Mason, Claire Bloom, Hildegarde Neff. A Berliner who makes a shady living risking his life to save a kidnapped girl from the Reds. Moody, topical melodrama has tenseness, atmosphere, a fine acting job from Mason. Directed by Carol Reed. (100 mins.)

Man Called Adam, A (1966) **½ Sammy Davis, Jr., Peter Lawford. Sammy Davis is excellent in the difficult role of a jazz musician who is filled with bitterness and self-pity. A tragic tale of the jazz world and a Negro striving for personal acceptance. (Dir: Leo Penn, 102 mins.)

Man Called Dagger, A (1967) * Terry Moore, Sue Ane Langdon, Eileen O'Neill (pretty, and merits better). Super secret agent (Paul Mantee) pitted against a nasty neo-Nazi (Jan Murray). Unrelievedly awful throughout. (Dir: Richard Rush, 86 mins.)

Man Called Gannon, A (1969) *** Tony Franciosa, Michael Sarrazin. A remake of the 1955 film "Man Without a Star." Well-paced western with a good performance by Tony Franciosa as a drifter who takes a young cowpoke (Michael Sarrazin) under his wing and ends up fighting against him in a small range war. There's not a wasted scene in this tale and the characterizations probe a little deeper than usual in this type of film fare. (Dir: James Goldstone, 105 mins.)

Man Called Horse, A (1970) *** Richard Harris, Dame Judith Anderson, Corinna Tsopei. An ambitious, serious film which sometimes gets laughs in the wrong places. Richard Harris convincingly plays a white man captured by the Sioux in 1825, tortured and finally converted to their way of life. He not only adopts their ways but becomes a Chief and leads them in battle. Judith Anderson, spouting in the role of his Indian mother-in-law, is ridiculous. "Horse" does try to recreate authentic Indian rituals. One of them, being suspended by his own mutilated skin, is harsh indeed, and not for children. Commendable attempt to deal with the Indian culture, doesn't always succeed for white man's

447

eyes. (Dir: Elliot Silverstein, 114 mins.)

Man Called Peter, A (1955)***½ Richard Todd, Jean Peters. A fine performance by Richard Todd as Peter Marshall, the Scotsman who became a minister in the U.S. and rose to the high position of U.S. Senate Chaplain, makes this film. Jean Peters capably handles her co-starring assignment as the girl Marshall weds. Todd's sermon scenes are standouts.

Man Could Get Killed, A (1966)**½ James Garner, Melina Mercouri, Sandra Dee, Tony Franciosa. Businessman in Portugal is mistaken for a secret agent, becomes involved with smugglers. Spoof of secret-agent stories isn't as funny as some of the supposedly serious ones, but it has some captivating scenery and a competent cast to atone for the plot deficiencies. (Dirs: Ronald Neame, Cliff Owen, 100 mins.)

Man Detained (British, 1962)** Bernard Archard, Elvi Hale. Owner of a company from which a large sum of money has been stolen is murdered, and a burglar is accused of the crime. Fair Edgar Wallace mystery. (Dir: Robert Tronson, 59 mins.)

Man Escaped (French, 1957)***½ Francois Leterrier, Charles Le Clainche. Taut and exciting film about a daring escape by a French Resistance leader who is captured by the Germans during WW II. This film is a multi-prize winner.

Man for All Seasons, A (British, 1966)**** Paul Scofield, Robert Shaw. Robert Bolt's literate and penetrating treatment of the conflict waged between Sir Thomas More and King Henry VIII makes a smooth transition to the screen, with excellent performances by Scofield as More, Shaw as Henry VIII, Wendy Hiller as Alice More, Orson Welles as Cardinal Wolsey, and, in a brief role, Vanessa Redgrave as Anne Boleyn. Director Fred Zinnemann has mounted the film with an eye for characterization rather than spectacle, and the result is superior drama. Scofield, one of the greatest actors in the world, richly deserved the Academy Award he won for his portrayal of the remarkable churchman. (120 mins.)

Man Friday (Great Britain, 1975)*½ Peter O'Toole, Richard Roundtree,

Peter Cellier. Literary purists may be put off by this transformation of Daniel Defoe's classic novel. All that remain from the original are the two principal characters, castaway and servant, but their relationship has been altered. O'Toole plays Crusoe as a conventionally repressive Englishman, teaching Friday English, Christian religion and guilt over sex. Roundtree's Friday offers an equally strong personality, free and instilled with a love of life. Amusing, occasionally moving, but generally clichéd version of the faults behind the master-servant relationship. (Dir: Jack Gold, 115 mins.)

Man From Atlantis: The Death Scouts (1977)** Patrick Duffy, Belinda Montgomery. Remember the water-breathing hero suspected to be the remaining survivor of the lost continent of Atlantis? No! Well, he's back anyway in this sequel for sci-fi fans. Encounters some alien beings reputed to be able to survive underwater, and teams up with the lady oceanographer who originally discovered him. Made-for-TV. (Dir: Marc Daniels, 106 mins.)

Man From Atlantis: The Disappearances (1977)**½ Patrick Duffy, Belinda Montgomery. The fourth 90-minute version of the series. Duffy shines as Mark Harris, the water-breathing humanoid thought to be the last survivor of the lost continent of Atlantis. Dr. Merrill (Miss Montgomery) is abducted and whisked to a mysterious island off South America, and Mark needs all his special powers to rescue her. For a change, the villain of the piece is a female mad scientist . . . Vincent Price beware. Made-for-TV. (Dir: Charles Dubin, 72 mins.)

Man From Atlantis: The Killer Spores (1977)** Patrick Duffy. Mark Harris' exploits as the Man From Atlantis—the humanoid with remarkable underwater-breathing capabilities. Patrick Duffy cuts a good stance as Harris in this venture, which finds him as a liaison between NASA and some deadly "ectoplasmic spores" capable of destroying the world. Made-for-TV. (Dir: Reza Badiyi, 106 mins.)

Man from Bitter Ridge, The (1955)** Lex Barker, Mara Corday, Stephen McNally. Ordinary western drama about cattle barons and those who oppose them. The cast just goes through the paces. Grade "B" movie fare. (Dir: Jack Arnold, 80 mins.)

Man from Button Willow, The (1965) ** Animated feature about the alleged adventures of the first government agent, Justin Eagle. The plot centers around Eagle's attempt to rescue a kidnapped senator in the old West. Voices include Dale Robertson, Howard Keel, and Edgar Buchanan. (Dir: David Detiege, 82 mins.)

Man From Cocody (French, 1965) ** Jean Marais, Liselotte Pulver. Diplomat becomes involved in tracking down a secret society and diamond smuggling in Africa. Pleasant players and some sharp direction overcome to some extent the rather silly melodramatic plot. Dubbed in English.

Man from Colorado (1948) *** William Holden, Glenn Ford, Ellen Drew. Sadist becomes a federal judge and runs things his way. Good western has an offbeat portrayal by Ford. (Dir: Henry Levin, 99 mins.)

Man From Del Rio (1956) ** Anthony Quinn, Katy Jurado. This western tale starts out well enough but slowly disintegrates into just another horse opera. Quinn is fine when the script isn't fighting him. (Dir: Harry Horner, 82 mins.)

Man from God's Country (1958) ** George Montgomery, Randy Stuart. Cattleman gets involved in a land grabbing scheme for a proposed railroad. Nothing new. (Dir: Paul Landres, 72 mins.)

Man from Laramie (1955) *** James Stewart, Arthur Kennedy, Cathy O'Donnell. Above average Western drama about a man who proves he is a tower of strength against the evil forces of a town. Stewart is good, as is the whole cast. (Dir: Anthony Mann, 104 mins.)

Man From Oklahoma, The (German, 1964) * Rich Horn, Sabine Bethmann. Sheriff gets the goods on a villainous rancher and his gunslingers. Embarrassing overseas version of "western" heroics. Dubbed in English.

Man From the Alamo, The (1953) **½ Glenn Ford, Julia Adams. Interesting western adventure about the only man to survive the Alamo massacre. Naturally, he's labeled a coward and has to keep silent until he finds out the truth about the mystery surrounding the massacre at Ox-Bow, a town near the Alamo. (Dir: Budd Boetticher, 79 mins.)

Man From the Diners' Club, The (1963) **½ Danny Kaye, Cara Williams, Martha Hyer. Employee of the Diners' Club makes out an application for a gangster trying to leave the country, and the troubles begin. Comedy on the silly side is not up to the star's talents but provides some mild amusement along the way. (Dir: Frank Tashlin, 95 mins.)

Man Hunt (1941) *** Walter Pidgeon, Joan Bennett, George Sanders. Exciting melodrama set just before the war about an English big game hunter who decides to stalk Hitler. A little choppy and hard to accept but good entertainment. (Dir: Fritz Lang, 105 mins.)

Man Hunter, The (1969) ½ Sandra Dee, Roy Thinnes, Al Hirt. Contrived plot concerning an American banker who hires an African hunter to avenge the killing of his son during a bank robbery. Made-for-TV. (Dir: Don Taylor, 100 mins.)

Man I Love, The (1946) **½ Ida Lupino, Robert Alda. Singer visiting her family catches the eye of a nitery owner. Good acting offsets a soapy opera. (Dir: Raoul Walsh, 96 mins.)

Man I Married, The (1940) *** Francis Lederer, Joan Bennett. Fascinating anti-Nazi film about an American girl married to a German-American. They visit Germany in 1938 and she sees her husband fall for Hitler's doctrines. (Dir: Irving Pichel, 77 mins.)

Man in a Cocked Hat (British, 1960) **½ Terry-Thomas, Peter Sellers. Inept clerk in the Foreign Office is sent to a small colony where he proceeds to gum up the works. Mildly amusing comedy. (Dirs: Jeffrey Dell, Roy Boulting, 88 mins.)

Man in Grey, The (British, 1945) *** James Mason, Stewart Granger, Margaret Lockwood. An evil marquis carries on with a hussy while married in name only to another. Purple-passioned costume melodrama is redeemed by good performances, particularly from James Mason. (Dir: Leslie Arliss, 116 mins.)

Man in Outer Space (Czech, 1964) ** Milos Kopecky, Radevan Lukavsky. Accidental space traveler lands on a far planet whose inhabitants help him back to earth, but centuries later; his greed affects the people of the future. Fanciful sci-fi saga is hard to swallow, but does have a slightly different plot, interesting effects. Dubbed in English.

Man in the Attic (1953)** Jack Palance, Constance Smith. Mysterious man takes a room in a lodging house when London is terrorized by Jack the Ripper. Remake of "The Lodger" passes muster, but doesn't add anything to the original. (Dir: Hugo Fregonese, 82 mins.)

Man in the Back Seat, The (British, 1962)**½ Darren Nesbitt, Carol White. Two young crooks attack a bookmaker carrying money from the racetrack chained to his wrist, are forced to make him a captive. Fairly suspenseful crime melodrama based on an Edgar Wallace story.

Man in the Dark (1953)**½ Edmond O'Brien, Audrey Totter. A somewhat novel approach to an old gangster story. A convict submits to a brain operation which is supposed to free him from his criminal tendencies but just makes him lose his memory instead. (Dir: Lew Landers, 70 mins.)

Man in the Gray Flannel Suit, The (1956)**½ Gregory Peck, Jennifer Jones, Fredric March, Marisa Pavan. Sloan Wilson's best seller is brought to the screen in typical Hollywood style—glossy and melodramatic. Peck is as wooden as ever as the Madison Ave. husband whose past comes back and makes him search for answers. Miss Jones is wasted and Fredric March, generally a superb actor, merely shouts his way through his scenes. (Dir: Nunnally Johnson, 153 mins.)

Man in the Iron Mask, The (1939)*** Louis Hayward, Joan Bennett. The classic tale of intrigue in France, and the twin brother of Louis XIV who was kept in an iron mask so that no one would see his face. Elaborate costume adventure. (Dir: James Whale, 120 mins.)

Man in the Middle, The (1964)**½ Robert Mitchum, France Nuyen, Trevor Howard, Keenan Wynn. This film starts off well, but before long, it turns into a muddled courtroom drama which can't make up its mind where to place the guilt. The story concerns an American sergeant stationed in India at the end of WW II, who shoots a British ser-

450

geant and causes a minor rift between His Majesty and Uncle Sam. The question whether the American soldier is sane or not becomes the crux of the case, but you may lose interest long before the end. (Dir: Guy Hamilton, 94 mins.)

Man in the Moon (1962)*** Kenneth More, Shirley Ann Field. British comedy with a good idea, satirizing the attempts to make a missile shot to the moon. Idea is superior to the execution; however, much of it is still quite droll. (Dir: Basil Dearden, 98 mins.)

Man in the Net, The (1959)*½ Alan Ladd, Carolyn Jones, Stan Moger, Tom Helmore. Suspense slips through the net in this melodrama with psychological overtones. TV-scripter Reginald Rose adapted the novel by Patrick Quentin. Ladd is involved in a murder, but can't clear up some of the facts. Moger, who has not been seen or heard from since, impresses in a cameo role. "Net" is one of the lesser efforts of veteran director Michael Curtiz. (97 mins.)

Man in the Raincoat (French, 1958)*** Fernandel, Bernard Blier. One of the better Fernandel movies—this time he is up to his neck in murder and bumbles his way to a hilarious climax.

Man in the Road, The (British, 1957)** Derek Farr, Ella Raines. Scientist becomes an amnesia victim after an accident, is a target for foreign agents after his secrets. Ordinary spy melodrama. (Dir: Lance Comfort, 83 mins.)

Man in the Saddle (1951)**½ Randolph Scott, Joan Leslie, Ellen Drew. We're asked to believe that two women are in love with Randolph Scott in this better-than-average R. S. Western. Don't misunderstand —there's still plenty of shooting and riding for devoted Scott fans. (Dir: Andre de Toth, 87 mins.)

Man in the Shadow (1957)**½ Jeff Chandler, Orson Welles, Ben Alexander. Sheriff engages in a battle with a tyrannical ranch owner who has ordered a Mexican laborer beaten badly enough to die. Top performers give this routine western drama more than it deserves. (Dir: Jack Arnold, 80 mins.)

Man in the Trunk, The (1942)* Lynne Roberts, George Holmes. Bookmaker's ghost comes back to find his murderer in this tasteless film.

Man in the White Suit, The (British, 1951)★★★★ Alec Guinness, Joan Greenwood. Furore in a textile plant when a young scientist invents a cloth material that will not tear or become dirty. One of the wittiest, most ingenious comedies in years! Top-flight fun. Miss Greenwood is particularly delicious. (Dir: Alexander Mackendrick, 84 mins.)

Man in the Wilderness (1971)★★★ Richard Harris, John Huston, John Bindon. Based on two actual incidents in the northwest, this adventure yarn of survival in the Dakotas of the 1820's is interesting, if flawed. Harris is an experienced guide who gets mauled by a bear and is left to die by his expedition companions, led by the menacing Huston. Extremely well photographed by Gerry Fisher. Several of the same people worked on "A Man Called Horse." The Spanish Pyrenees, incidentally, where it was shot, can pass for the U.S. northwest. (Dir: Richard C. Sarafian, 105 mins.)

Man Inside, The (British, 1958)★★½ Jack Palance, Anita Ekberg, Nigel Patrick. Fairly good drama about a group of international jewel thieves who really hit the jackpot when a very valuable diamond comes into their possession. Palance plays a detective who's on the group's trail. (Dir: John Gilling, 90 mins.)

Man Is Armed (1957)★★ Dane Clark, William Talman. Truck driver framed for murder leaves prison with revenge in mind. Fair melodrama. (Dir: Franklin Adreon, 70 mins.)

Man Made Monster (1941)★★ Lon Chaney, Lionel Atwill. After being used in a series of experiments, a young man finds that he's immune to electric shock. Familiar science-fiction yarn with plenty of technical mumbo-jumbo.

Man Named Rocca, A (French, 1961)★★ Jean-Paul Belmondo, Christine Kaufman. Two men imprisoned for a crime they didn't commit volunteer to dig mines in order to earn their freedom. Fair melodrama on the grim side. Dubbed-in English.

Man of Conquest (1938)★★½ Richard Dix, Joan Fontaine. The story of Sam Houston, soldier, statesman, hero of Texas. With fine, large scale battle scenes, good performances. (Dir: George Nicholls, Jr., 110 mins.)

Man of Evil (British, 1945)★½ James Mason, Phyllis Calvert, Stewart Granger. A wealthy but brutish lord and a young secretary both vie for the affections of a beautiful girl with a family secret, and treachery and murder follow. Flamboyant, hammy period drama, pretty labored. (Dir: Anthony Asquith, 90 mins.)

Man of La Mancha (Italy, 1962)★½ Sophia Loren, Peter O'Toole, James Coco. The international hit musical comes to the screen with a thud! Most of the action is in a dungeon! The musical numbers, which made the stage musical such memorable entertainment, bog down the film version. You can't help but wish this stellar cast would refrain from singing and play Cervantes' classic tale of Don Quixote straight. There are enough reprises to try anyone's patience. "The Impossible Dream," the big hit from the show, gets a reverent reading by Mr. O'Toole, which makes you think he's mistaken it for one of Shakespeare's soliloquies. The scenery is awesomely beautiful and the production values are first-rate, but you can't dress up this corpse and expect it to breathe life. Screenplay by Dale Wasserman never opens up the stage play. (Dir: Arthur Hiller, 140 mins.)

Man of 1000 Faces (1957)★★★½ James Cagney, Dorothy Malone, Jane Greer. Cagney is superb in this satisfying film biography of Lon Chaney, the silent screen star who was a make-up wizard and created a series of memorable screen characterizations. The introduction of too many sub-plots mars the film's pace, but Cagney is great and worth your tuning in. (Dir: Joseph Pevney, 122 mins.)

Man of the West (1958)★★½ Gary Cooper, Julie London, Lee J. Cobb. A good cast makes this otherwise routine western tale interesting. Screenplay by Reginald Rose has the hero, a reformed gunslinger, pitted predictably against his uncle, a notorious outlaw. (Dir: Anthony Mann, 100 mins.)

Man on a String (1960)★★½ Ernest Borgnine, Kerwin Mathews. Story of Boris Morros, who served as a double agent to expose Red tyranny. Documentary-type drama has some good moments but never quite hits the mark. (Dir: Andre de Toth, 92 mins.)

Man on a String (1972)*½ Christopher George. A government undercover man infiltrates gangland, setting up wars between rival mobsters. Standard action formula. Made-for-TV. (Dir: Joseph Sargent, 73 mins.)

Man on a Swing (1974)**½ Joel Grey, Cliff Robertson. Director Frank Perry almost pulled off this offbeat crime meller but it falls apart before the finale. Joel Grey, in a dramatic role as a clairvoyant, gives a solid performance, and Cliff Robertson is less stoic than usual as the cop trying to solve the sex slaying of a young woman. (Dir: Frank Perry, 109 mins.)

Man on a Tightrope (1953)*** Fredric March, Gloria Grahame, Terry Moore, Cameron Mitchell. Elia Kazan directed this story of a small German traveling circus troupe. March fares better than the other stars as a jealous husband who loves his unfaithful wife, unconvincingly portrayed by Gloria Grahame. Filmed on location in Europe. (Dir: Elia Kazan, 105 mins.)

Man on Fire (1957)**½ Bing Crosby, Inger Stevens, Mary Fickett. One of Bing Crosby's few non-musical films. The crooner plays a man with a custody problem concerning his son and his divorced wife and therefore, the film leans heavily towards melodramatic soap opera. (Dir: Ronald MacDougall, 95 mins.)

Man on the Eiffel Tower, The (1949)***½ Charles Laughton, Franchot Tone, Burgess Meredith. A wily police inspector craftily breaks down the resistance of a murderer when evidence is lacking. Intelligent, suspenseful melodrama, made in France. Performances of the principals are standout, as is the hair-raising conclusion. (Dir: Burgess Meredith, 97 mins.)

Man on the Outside (1975)½ Lorne Greene, Lorraine Gary, James Olsen. Pilot for Lorne Greene's old flop series, "Griff." He plays, much too soberly, a retired police lieutenant who goes back to action as a private eye when his son is murdered. Made-for-TV. (Dir: Boris Sagal, 100 mins.)

Man on the Run (1951)** Burgess Meredith, William Phipps. Small son

452

of an American living in Manila is kidnaped, he vainly tries to get the lad back. Fair suspense drama filmed in the Philippines.

Man or Gun (1957)*½ Macdonald Carey, Audrey Totter. Powerful family runs a town the way they wish until a cowpoke disrupts their reign. Below par western wastes good players. (Dir: Albert Gannaway, 79 mins.)

Man Outside, The (Great Britain, 1968)* Van Heflin, Heidelinde Weis, Pinkas Braun, Peter Vaughan. Uninspired espionage chase. Heflin cast as an ex-CIA agent, fed up with spying, who becomes involved in the defection of a top Soviet KGB man. (Dir: Sam Gallu, 98 mins.)

Man Proof (1937)**½ Myrna Loy, Rosalind Russell, Franchot Tone, Walter Pidgeon. Big cast plus little story equals ordinary film. Myrna loves Walter who marries wealthy Rosalind but would like to keep little Myrna in his closet. Franchot comes in to give Myrna that fadeout kiss. (Dir: Richard Thorpe, 80 mins.)

Man to Man Talk (French, 1958)**½ Yves Montand, Nicole Berger. Pleasant French comedy about a young lad who learns about the birds and the bees despite his over-protective and bumbling parents. Good performances. (Dir: Luis Saslavski, 89 mins.)

Man Upstairs, The (British, 1959)*** Richard Attenborough. Attenborough delivers a strong performance as a shattered human being who attempts to kill himself after a series of depressing events occur. Well made melodrama. (Dir: Don Chaffey, 88 mins.)

Man Who Came to Dinner (1941)**** Monty Woolley, Bette Davis, Ann Sheridan, Jimmy Durante. If you've never seen this Kaufman and Hart comedy make sure your doctor is nearby to sew you up when you split your sides laughing. Woolley will be cherished forever for this funny, acid performance. (Dir: William Keighley, 112 mins.)

Man Who Changed His Mind, The (British, 1936)*½ Boris Karloff, Anna Lee, John Loder. Boris as a mad scientist once more—this time he thinks he can transpose the human mind from one body to another. Typical mid-thirties thriller, English-style. Alternate titles: **The Man Who Lived Again, Dr. Maniac, The**

Brainsnatchers. (Dir: Robert Stevenson, 61 mins.)

Man Who Cheated Himself, The (1950)**½ Lee J. Cobb, Jane Wyatt, John Dall. An honest cop meets a cheating dame and forgets his honesty. Just fair crime melodrama; good cast better than the story. (Dir: Felix E. Feist, 81 mins.)

Man Who Could Cheat Death (British, 1959)**½ Anton Diffring, Hazel Court, Christopher Lee. Man becomes ageless through a gland operation, becomes a murderer when he learns the secret of eternal youth from the doctor. Occasionally effective thriller, remake of "Man in Half Moon Street." Good performances. (Dir: Terence Fisher, 83 mins.)

Man Who Could Talk to Kids, The (1973)**½ Peter Boyle, Scott Jacoby, Robert Reed, Tyne Daly. A touching subject gets dramatic treatment, but it never seems to fulfill the promise of the early scenes. Jacoby has the difficult role of a young teen-ager whose deep-rooted problems cause him to retreat into his own world except for occasional outbursts of violence. His troubled parents don't know how to cope, so they seek aid of an affable, honest, and unorthodox social worker, Boyle. Made-for-TV. (Dir: Donald Wrye, 73 mins.)

Man Who Could Work Miracles, The (British, 1937)*** Roland Young, Joan Gardner, Ralph Richardson. The gods above give an average citizen the power to perform any feat that he wishes. Amusing fantasy, written by H. G. Wells. (Dir: Lothar Mendes, 90 mins.)

Man Who Died Twice (1970)**½ Stuart Whitman, Brigitte Fossey, Jeremy Slate, Bernard Lee. Artist presumed dead, wanders in Spain and falls in love with a depressed French girl. Flashbacks of Whitman's previous life prove interesting, thanks to a good supporting cast. Made-for-TV. (Dir: Joseph Kane, 100 mins.)

Man Who Fell to Earth, The (1976)*** David Bowie, Buck Henry, Candy Clark, Rip Torn. A very strange film to those unfamiliar with science fiction. The enigmatic title at first refers to an extra-terrestrial, who comes to our planet from a distant galaxy, desperately seeking a water supply for his people. The ensuing plot is too complicated to describe—one of its charms is that it is never

simple-minded. Everything has ramifications. Has suspense, intrigue, romance of a sort, even humor. The sci-fi effects are absolutely beautiful. Several scenes show Newton's (Bowie) barren home and its people, and one lovely moment shows him slipping briefly and unobtrusively through a time warp. Leading actors are all good. (Dir: Nicolas Roeg, 140 mins.)

Man Who Finally Died, The (Great Britain, 1963)*½ Stanley Baker, Peter Cushing, Mai Zetterling. Good English Joe saves a scientist from being kidnapped to the "East" on a visit to the Bavarian town of his birth. Ordinary melodrama. (Dir: Quentin Lawrence, 100 mins.)

Man Who Haunted Himself (Great Britain, 1970)** Roger Moore, Olga Georges-Picot, Hildegard Neil. Venerable sci-fi gambit drama, as Roger Moore plays a businessman who finds that his double has been slowly taking his place in the office, at his club, and at home. Is Moore mad or is there sabotage afoot? Weak ending! (Dir: Basil Dearden, 94 mins.)

Man Who Knew Too Much, The (1955)***½ James Stewart, Doris Day. Alfred Hitchcock at his best. Stewart and Miss Day star in this exciting suspense yarn of intrigue complete with murder, assassination plots, kidnappings and a hair-raising climax. The stars do very nicely in their roles of an American couple vacationing in French Morocco who are accidentally drawn into a series of mysterious adventures. (Dir: Alfred Hitchcock, 120 mins.)

Man Who Liked Funerals, The (British, 1959)** Leslie Phillips. A British comedy with numerous unrealized possibilities thanks to the shoddy script. The acting doesn't salvage it either.

Man Who Lived Again, The—See: The Man Who Changed His Mind

Man Who Loved Cat Dancing, The (1973)* Burt Reynolds, Sarah Miles, George Hamilton. A dull Western! Reynolds is interesting as a train robber who kidnaps the prim Sarah Miles and begins a passionate love affair with her. The novel by Marilyn Durham on which Eleanor Perry has based her unsuccessful screenplay, was reputedly better than this film leads one to believe. (Dir: Richard C. Sarafian, 114 mins.)

Man Who Loved Redheads (British, 1955)***½ Moira Shearer, John Justin. Throughout his long life, a man seeks the redhead of his youthful dream, becoming enamored by many carrot-tops in the process. Charming romantic comedy graced by delightful performances, a good script. (Dir: Ronald Neame, 103 mins.)

Man Who Never Was, The (1956)**½ Clifton Webb, Gloria Grahame, Stephen Boyd. Based on an actual military case history, this is an account of a special mission known as "Operation Mincemeat," which was instrumental in paving the way for the Allied invasion of Europe. When the film sticks to the facts, it is engrossing.

Man Who Reclaimed His Head, The (1935)*** Claude Rains, Joan Bennett, Lionel Atwill. Effective antiwar picture, despite its improbable title, stars Rains as a brilliant journalist who sells his brains to an unscrupulous politician by ghostwriting for him. Upshot is war, adultery, misery, but Claude finally . . . well, you guessed it. Bitter picture doesn't pull its punches. (Dir: Edward Ludwig, 82 mins.)

Man Who Returned to Life, The (1942)**½ John Howard. Good "B" film about a man who leaves a town to get a fresh start and, some years later, learns that they're about to try a man for murdering him. Above average quickie.

Man Who Shot Liberty Valance, The (1962)*** James Stewart, John Wayne, Lee Marvin, Vera Miles. Standard John Ford western about a lawyer who becomes famous as the man who killed a notorious badman. "Standard Ford" means better than most westerns usually, although this time the vet director let his tale run too long for its content. But the cast is good, and fans should be satisfied. (Dir: John Ford, 122 mins.)

Man Who Turned to Stone (1957)* Victor Jory, Charlotte Austin. A ridiculous horror pic about a group of demented scientists who prey on young girls which are necessary for their experiments in longevity. Without the young girls, the group would turn to stone. (Dir: Leslie Kardos, 80 mins.)

Man Who Understood Women, The (1959)*** Henry Fonda, Leslie Caron. Hollywood genius make an aspiring actress a star, marries her, then finds he has no time for her. She looks elsewhere. Strange combination of sharp satire, heavy drama; unevenly balanced but with plenty to recommend it, including some biting dialogue, Fonda's fine performance. (Dir: Nunnally Johnson, 105 mins.)

Man Who Wagged His Tale, The (Spanish, 1961)**½ Peter Ustinov, Pablito Calvo. Disliked, miserly lawyer is changed by magic into an ugly dog and must find salvation before he can return to human form. Mild fantasy has some amusing moments but is loosely put together. English-dubbed.

Man Who Wanted to Live Forever, The (1970)**½ Burl Ives, Sandy Dennis, Stuart Whitman. Fairly gripping made-for-TV drama with a good performance by Ives as a multi-millionaire who built a fantastic medical heart-disease research center for his own sinister purpose. Whitman and Dennis costar as medical personnel at the remote research center who catch on to Ives' dark plans, and try to escape on skis down treacherous slopes. The escape sequence is beautifully filmed on location in the Canadian Rockies, and provides an exciting finale. (Dir: John Trent, 99 mins.)

Man Who Was Nobody, The (British, 1962)** Hazel Court, John Crawford. Lady detective joins forces with a sleuth to solve a murder. Fair low-budget Edgar Wallace mystery.

Man Who Would Be King (1975)**** Michael Caine, Sean Connery, Christopher Plummer. Excellent, rousing treatment of Rudyard Kipling's yarn of greed and ambition in India, circa 1880. Caine and Connery are fine as the pals who decide to resign from the Army and set themselves up as deities in Kafiristan—a land where no white man has set foot since Alexander. They succeed beyond their wildest dreams until the natives learn that they are indeed mortal. Given a grand treatment by John Huston, and quite reminiscent in plot and style to his wonderful "The Treasure of Sierra Madre." Huston co-authored the screenplay with Gladys Hill. (Dir: John Huston, 127 mins.)

Man Who Would Not Die, The (1975)

* Dorothy Malone, Keenan Wynn, Aldo Ray. Muddled melodrama about FBI agents, stolen bonds, Mafia henchmen, society women, and an adventurer who finds himself embroiled in the whole mess. Do not embroil! (Dir: Robert Arkless, 83 mins.)

Man Who Wouldn't Talk, The (British, 1959)****½** Anthony Quayle, Anna Neagle, Zsa Zsa Gabor. Man on trial for the murder of a beautiful secret agent refuses to help himself, is defended by a clever lady barrister. Mystery keeps the interest, moves at a fairly good pace.

Man With a Cloak, The (1951)****½** Joseph Cotten, Barbara Stanwyck, Leslie Caron. An interesting costume drama about a mysterious man who enters two women's lives. The stars do well with this suspense yarn. (Dir: Fletcher Markle, 81 mins.)

Man with a Million (1955)******* Gregory Peck. A man who's supposed to be rich becomes famous and powerful proving that money comes to money. Interesting, entertaining film based on a Mark Twain story. (Dir: Ronald Neame, 90 mins.)

Man with the Balloons, The (Italian, 1964)***½** Marcello Mastroianni trapped in a thing about a businessman obsessed with finding out how much air a balloon will hold. Script too holds a lot of hot air. Catherine Spaak, Ugo Tognazzi. (Dir: Marco Ferreri, 85 mins.)

Man With the Golden Arm, The (1955) ******* Frank Sinatra, Eleanor Parker, Kim Novak. Controversial drama of a narcotics addict and his efforts to kick the habit has good performances, along with a rather slow pace and some implausible dramatic aspects. Powerful, generally well-made, interestingly directed by Otto Preminger. Particularly good music score by Elmer Bernstein. (119 mins.)

Man With the Golden Gun, The (Great Britain, 1974)****½** Roger Moore, Christopher Lee. For those still counting, this is the ninth of the James Bond films, the second starring Roger Moore as Agent 007, and the fourth directed by Guy Hamilton. 007 has gone slightly stale. Oh yes, the plot this time around has Bond chasing after a solar energy capsule confiscated by a globe-hopping hit man, played with authority and villainy by Britain's Christopher Lee, of all those horror flicks. (Dir: Guy Hamilton, 125 mins.)

Man with the Golden Keys (French, 1956)****** Pierre Fresnay, Annie Girardot. College professor is framed by three students and dismissed in disgrace—he finally gets his revenge. Unexceptional but fairly interesting drama; dubbed-in English.

Man with the Gun (1955)****½** Robert Mitchum, Jan Sterling, Henry Hull. Absorbing but somewhat ponderous western drama. A good cast does more for the story than the story does for the stars. (Dir: Richard Wilson, 83 mins.)

Man With the Power, The (1977)***** Vic Morrow, Bob Neill. The invisible-man gimmick, focuses on a bodyguard for an Indian princess visiting America—a man who uses his eye concentration to manipulate things and people. Bodyguard loses his touch when it's most needed. Same for the filmmakers! Made-for-TV. (Dir: Nicholas Sgarro, 106 mins.)

Man With Two Faces (1964)***½** Tab Hunter, Zina Walter. Ex-prisoner tries to find respect and happiness in a hostile society. Dull drama.

Man Without a Star (1955)******* Kirk Douglas, Jeanne Crain, Claire Trevor. Two-fisted western with Kirk Douglas taking center stage and keeping it. He plays a loveable character who uses his fists and guns only when his charm fails to do the job. Jeanne Crain is properly stiff as the big land owner and Claire Trevor tosses off another of her bighearted saloon hostess portrayals. (Dir: King Vidor, 89 mins.)

Manchu Eagle Murder Caper Mystery, The (1975)***** Gabriel Dell, Barbara Harris, Will Geer. A relentlessly unfunny satire of Hollywood's private-eye films of the 1940's. Gabriel Dell, who plays a chicken breeder and an apprentice private eye, has only his director (Dean Hargrove) and himself to blame for the leaden dialogue, because Dell co-authored the screenplay with Hargrove. After the crack about the fourth hit-and-run chicken of the month, you'll want to hit the off-button and run screaming from the scene of the accident. (Dir: Dean Hargrove, 80 mins.)

Manchurian Candidate, The (1962) ******** Frank Sinatra, Laurence Harvey, Janet Leigh, Angela Lansbury.

Weird story of a soldier brainwashed by the Reds so that he becomes their pawn in an evil plot to take over the country. Can be viewed as a horror thriller, satire, or suspense-mystery drama; successful in all respects. Dazzling technique, excellent performances, an unusual film directed by TV graduate John Frankenheimer. (126 mins.)

Mandingo (1975)*½ James Mason, Ken Norton, Susan George, Perry King. Setting is a slave-breeding plantation in Louisiana circa 1840, based on the sprawling novel by Kyle Onstott and the play by Jack Kirkland. There are effective scenes in the first part of a film filled with racist brutality, with little sympathy shown for anyone, black or white. But the filmmakers seemed to have changed their point of view toward the material in the balance of the film, and most of the last half is full of absurd cinematic clichés and phony history. As an actor, Ken Norton has a beautiful physique, and Susan George gives a laughable imitation of Bette Davis. Perry King is effective as the limping heir to the plantation. (Dir: Richard Fleischer, 127 mins.)

Mandy (British, 1953)**** Phyllis Calvert, Jack Hawkins, Mandy Miller. Gripping story of a child born deaf and dumb, and of her efforts to adjust herself. Fine drama, superlatively acted by little Miss Miller.

Maneater (1973)** Ben Gazzara, Richard Basehart. Gazzara leads a band of hearty vacationers whose mobile home meets with mechanical difficulty, and accepts help from Basehart, who is a wild-animal trainer. Lions, and tigers, and bears, oh my! Predictable all the way as the animal trainer turns out to be quite "eccentric." Made-for-TV. (Dir: Vince Edwards.)

Maneater of Hydra (1969)* Cameron Mitchell, Kai Fischer. A weird baron wrecks havoc on a group of unknowing tourists who have come to his island. Clichés! Forgettable foreign-made entry. (Dir: Mel Welles, 85 mins.)

Man-eater of Kumaon (1948)**½ Sabu, Wendell Corey. Hunter wounds a tiger, then trails him when the beast terrorizes the community. Interesting jungle melodrama.

Manhattan Angel (1949)*½ Gloria

Jean, Ross Ford. Girl tries to save a Youth Center from being sold to a tycoon. Mediocre musical.

Manhattan Melodrama (1934)***½ Clark Gable, William Powell, Myrna Loy. Well acted, exciting story of a friendship which lasts from youth to a murder trial. Gable is a gangster and Powell a D.A. but their affection for each other is real. Good screen entertainment. (Dir: W. S. Van Dyke, 90 mins.)

Manhunt in Space (1954)* Richard Crane, Sally Mansfield, Rocky Jones. Space Ranger goes after interplanetary villains. Childish sci-fi story adapted from a TV series.

Manhunt in the Jungle (1958)** Robin Hughes. Fearless explorer journeys to the Amazon to search for a missing expedition. Locale provides film with only interest. (Dir: Tom McGowan, 79 mins.)

Manhunter (1974)* Ken Howard, Gary Lockwood, Stefanie Powers. Slight, inconsequential, slapped-together story of a returning Marine thrown into the midst of a bank robbery. Made-for-TV. (Dir: Walter Grauman, 100 mins.)

Mania—See: **Flesh and the Fiends**

Maniac, The (British, 1963)**½ Kerwin Mathews, Nadia Gray. American artist in France has his life placed in danger when the father of his sweetheart's stepdaughter escapes from a mental institution. Interesting thriller, with a wealth of plot complications keeping matters going at a good rate. (Dir: Michael Carreras, 86 mins.)

Mannequin (1937)** Joan Crawford, Spencer Tracy, Alan Curtis. Poor Joan lands rich Spencer but not until the audience has endured the usual parade of tired cliches and histrionics. (Dir: Frank Borzage, 90 mins.)

Manpower (1941)*** Marlene Dietrich, Edward G. Robinson, George Raft. Raft and Robinson want Dietrich and the sparks really fly in this rip roaring adventure about the hazards faced by the men who risk their lives daily repairing high tension lines. (Dir: Raoul Walsh, 105 mins.)

Man's Favorite Sport? (1964)**½ Rock Hudson, Paula Prentiss. Fishing expert who has never fished in his life has to become the real thing in a hurry to save his job and reputation. Some funny scenes, but a pretty thin little plot to be stretched out to two hours' running time. However, it's harmless, and mildly amusing. (Dir: Howard Hawks, 120 mins.)

Manster, The (1962)* Peter Dyneley, Jane Hylton. Reporter is injected with some serum and turns into a hairy two-headed monster. Made in Japan horror thriller disproves theory that two heads are better than one.

Man-Trap (1961)* Jeffrey Hunter, Stella Stevens, David Janssen. Young man with marital troubles accepts a friend's offer to recover half a million dollars, with tragic consequences for all. Based on the John D. MacDonald novel "Taint of the Tiger." Director Edmond O'Brien is a much better actor than director. (93 mins.)

Many Rivers to Cross (1955)*** Robert Taylor, Eleanor Parker, James Arness. Frontier girl goes to extreme lengths to land a marriage-shy adventurer. Outdoor setting, but the emphasis is on comedy rather than action—and it gets rib-tickling quite often. Good fun. (Dir: Roy Rowland, 92 mins.)

Mara of the Wilderness (1965)** Adam West, Linda Saunders. In a variation on Kipling's classic jungle tale, "Mowgli," a girl, Mara, is adopted and raised by Alaskan wolves after the death of her parents, and then rediscovered by civilization. Animal-adventure story for the kids; Adam West, in a pre-"Batman" role, does well as the anthropologist who befriends the young wolf-girl. (Dir: Frank McDonald, 90 mins.)

Mara Maru (1952)** Errol Flynn, Ruth Roman. He-man adventurer Flynn plays both sides against the middle in this rather dull story of sunken treasures. Ruth Roman stands around waiting to be embraced when Errol has a free moment. (Dir: Gordon Douglas, 98 mins.)

Maracaibo (1958)**½ Cornel Wilde, Jean Wallace, Abbe Lane. Top firefighter discovers an old flame while attempting to put out an oil-well blaze. Not much glow in the threadbare story, but occasional excitement in the action scenes, resulting in a mildly entertaining melodrama. (Dir: Cornel Wilde, 88 mins.)

Marat Sade (Great Britain, 1967) **** Patrick Magee, Glenda Jackson, Ian Richardson, Freddie Jones. A remarkable film, directed by Peter Brook of his own landmark, critically-acclaimed stage production of the play by Peter Weiss. Set in a 19th-century mental hospital in Paris, as fashionable "sane" Parisians attend the performances given by the inmates as a form of therapy. This riveting, erudite, complex, and chilling film never got the distribution it so richly deserved, recording as it did for posterity one of the greatest stage productions in the history of the modern theater. See it if you can—you'll not soon forget being plunged into the madness of the steam-bathhouse at the horrendous asylum Clarenton. The acting is only fabulous. (Dir: Peter Brook, 116 mins.)

Marathon Man (1976)*** Dustin Hoffman, Laurence Olivier, Marthe Keller, Roy Scheider. There is a lot of excitement in this thriller about double agents and elderly Nazis, but it's too heavily plotted and suffers finally from constant doses of gratuitous violence—whether it's plain, old-fashioned stabbings or Laurence Olivier playing a former dentist who puts his past calling to professional use by torturing Dustin Hoffman, drilling on the most sensitive nerves in captive Hoffman's mouth. There are two fast-paced chase sequences, including one around Central Park's reservoir, but one is left with the feeling that these gifted artists, including director John Schlesinger, should have spent the same time and money on something more substantial. Hoffman, looking almost as young as he did in "The Graduate," is customarily splendid, and I'm always glad to glimpse the genius of Olivier, but his Nazi role is really beneath him. Keller is attractive playing Hoffman's love interest. Screenplay by William Goldman from his own novel. (Dir: John Schlesinger, 120 mins.)

Marauders of the Sea (British, 1962) ** Terence Morgan, Jean Kent, Kieron Moore. Sir Francis Drake tries to rescue an English sailor who had hoped to establish himself as "King of America." Passing fair costume adventure edited from a good British TV series, "Sir Francis Drake."

Marco Polo (Italian, 1962)** Rory Calhoun, Yoko Tani. Nephew of the great Khan is rebelling against Uncle's wicked prime minister—along comes Marco Polo to help him out. Despite an attempt to treat things tongue in cheek, this costume adventure dubbed in English never manages to rise above the routine. (Dir : Hugo Fregonese, 90 mins.)

Marco, the Magnificent (1966)* Horst Buchholz, Anthony Quinn, Omar Sharif, Orson Welles. Despite a topnotch cast, this epic tale depicting the voyage of young Marco Polo (Buchholz) from Italy to China, is a dismal flop. Bad dubbing, comic strip-type characters, and a puerile script preclude the possibility of even good actors like Quinn and Welles making any difference or any real impact. Filmed in various parts of Yugoslavia, Africa and Asia but it doesn't really matter! (Dir : Denys De La Pateliere, 100 mins.)

Marcus-Nelson Murders, The (1973) ***½ Telly Savalas, Marjoe Gortner, Jose Ferrer, Gene Woodbury. It's a bit overlong, but Abby Mann's carefully researched drama is an indictment of backroom police methods and courtroom practices. Brooklyn detectives coerce a young black man into confessing to the grisly murder of two New York girls. Savalas' detective is the hero, blowing the whistle on fellow cops as he funnels information to the skilled defense attorney. Authentic New York locations and good performances by the cast, particularly Woodbury as the railroaded suspect, give this controversial material a sharp edge. Served as pilot for Savalas' TV series, "Kojak." (Dir : Joseph Sargent.)

Marcus Welby, M.D. (1969)**½ Robert Young, Anne Baxter, James Brolin. A two-hour pilot film for a TV series. Robert Young is cast as the last of a dying breed—the dedicated general medical practitioner who actually makes house calls. Young gets involved with his patients and neglects his private life and health in the process. Many familiar subplots interwoven, the most interesting of which involves Dr. Welby's taking on a young, enterprising assistant, played by tall, handsome James Brolin. (Dir : David Lowell Rich, 99 mins.)

Mardi Gras (1958)**½ Pat Boone, Christene Carere, Gary Crosby, Sheree North, Tommy Sands. Pure escapist fare, Pat Boone and company sing, dance, march, and act their way through this technicolor romance with a great deal of attractive energy. The setting is the Mardi Gras festival in New Orleans. (Dir : Edmund Goulding, 107 mins.)

Margie (1946)*** Jeanne Crain, Glenn Langan. Too cute, but still entertaining little comedy with music about high-school life in the late 20's. You'll fall in love with the stars in this one. (Dir : Henry King, 94 mins.)

Margin for Error (1943)**½ Joan Bennett, Milton Berle. Entertaining but dated comedy-drama about intrigues in the New York office of the German Consul before the war. (Dir : Otto Preminger, 74 mins.)

Marie Antoinette (1937)*** Norma Shearer, Tyrone Power, Robert Morley, John Barrymore. Lavish spectacle about the woman who said "Let them eat cake" is just that—too much cake and not enough bread. Picture lacks substance, character insight and meaning. It is rich in production and will suffer on a small TV screen. (Dir: W. S. Van Dyke, 170 mins.)

Marie Antoinette (French, 1958)** Michele Morgan, Richard Todd. Story of the girl who rises to power in the French court of Louis XVI and the stormy days of the Revolution is lavishly produced but frequently dull, moves at a slow pace. Cast is good but overwhelmed by the script. Dubbed in English. (Dir: Jean Delannoy, 108 mins.)

Marie of the Isles (Italian, 1961)*½ Belinda Lee, Alain Saury, Folco Lulli. Frenchman appointed governor of Martinique meets his former sweetheart, now the wife of the Minister General. Uninteresting and heavy-handed costume drama dubbed in English.

Marilyn (1963)**½ Marilyn Monroe. Film fans will be interested in this movie-magazine-type review of the life and career of Marilyn Monroe. Rock Hudson narrates the story of the girl who went from sexy starlet to super screen star in a short time. There are clips from 15 of Marilyn's films, including one from her last, uncompleted movie, "Something's Got to Give," which she was working on at the time of her tragic death in 1962. (83 mins.)

Marines Fly High (1940)*** Richard

Dix, Chester Morris, Lucille Ball. Marines foil a revolt in Central America. Fast moving action melodrama.

Marjoe (1972)**** A revealing cinema verité-style documentary about Marjoe Gartner, a charismatic former child prodigy on the evangelist revival circuit. This is "Elmer Gantry" for real as we see Gartner in action, hustling gullible "worshipers" in revival meetings filmed in California, Michigan, Texas and other states. Gartner is candid about his career on the religious circuit. He gave up his "ministry" when this film was released and widely publicized. It's frank, illuminating and a valuable record of an enduring part of the American religious experience. Gartner is a charismatic figure on screen, especially while performing and doing "God's work." Conceived and directed by Sarah Kernochan and Howard Smith. (92 mins.)

Marjorie Morningstar (1958)*** Natalie Wood, Gene Kelly, Ed Wynn. Well done adaptation of Herman Wouk's best seller about the trials and tribulations of a stage struck young girl. The film maintains the prime fault of the novel . . . some fine moments but the over-all story is lacking dramatic power. (Dir: Irving Rapper, 123 mins.)

Mark, The (British, 1961)**** Stuart Whitman, Rod Steiger, Maria Schell. One of the finest psychological dramas ever filmed, played with extraordinary distinction and excitement. It combines an honest awareness of the uses of psychiatric therapy as well as its limitations, as it follows the path of a highly disturbed parolee into the threatening world of reality. Wonderfully absorbing, memorable. (Dir: Guy Green, 127 mins.)

Mark of Cain (British, 1948)**½ Sally Gray, Eric Portman. A notorious crime passionel rocks Victorian London. Leisurely melodrama, but rather interesting. Well acted.

Mark of the Hawk (1958)** Sidney Poitier, Eartha Kitt, John McIntire. Well-intentioned but rambling, wordy topical drama of a young African politician who is swayed by his terrorist brother, but still adheres to nonviolence. Complex background of Africa's struggle for independence is attempted, but the good points are bogged down in an unsure scenario. (Dir: Michael Audley, 83 mins.)

Mark of the Phoenix (British, 1957) *½ Sheldon Lawrence, Julia Arnall. Jewel thief protects atomic secrets from a spy ring. Protect yourself from melodrama.

Mark of the Renegade (1952)**½ Ricardo Montalban, Cyd Charisse. Colorful adventure in Southern California during the middle nineteenth century. Montalban cuts a fine figure as a Spanish renegade and beautiful Cyd Charisse is ravishing as a Spanish noble woman. (Dir: Hugo Fregonese, 81 mins.)

Mark of the Vampire (1957)** John Beal, Coleen Gray. Doctor takes pills given him by a dying scientist; they turn him into a vampire. Passable horror thriller, thanks to Beal's good performance in the lead role. Alternate title: **Vampire, The.** (Dir: Paul Landres, 74 mins.)

Mark of the Whistler (1944)*** Richard Dix. Man manages to swindle an unclaimed bank account, but Justice triumphs. Neat, clever melodrama, above average "B." (Dir: William Castle, 61 mins.)

Mark of Zorro, The (1940)***½ Tyrone Power, Linda Darnell. Exciting tale of a swashbuckling swordsman who sought to avenge evil in the California of the 1820s. Great for those who love good screen duels. High rating is primarily for young adventure seekers. (Dir: Rouben Mamoulian, 93 mins.)

Mark of Zorro, The (1974)**½ Frank Langella, Gilbert Roland, Yvonne DeCarlo, Ricardo Montalban. Here's a zesty remake of the romantic adventures of Don Diego, a fop by day and the avenging bandit known as Zorro by night. Dashing, handsome Frank Langella is perfectly cast as the hero, and the hand-picked supporting cast includes Gilbert Roland, as Don Diego's aristocratic father; Yvonne DeCarlo as his loving mother; and Ricardo Montalban as the cruel Captain Esteban. Made-for-TV. (Dir: Don McDougall, 72 mins.)

Marked Woman (1937)***½ Bette Davis, Humphrey Bogart, Eduardo Ciannelli. Good drama about a gang czar and his underlings. Occasionally threatens to go off the deep end of melodrama but good direction and acting prevent this. (Dir: Lloyd Bacon, 100 mins.)

Marlowe (1969)*** James Garner, Gayle Hunnicutt, Carroll O'Connor. Garner plays Philip Marlowe, Raymond Chandler's legendary detective. He's caught under a pile of corpses when he's hired by a mysterious blond. Pace is fast and tough, but it's the bravura acting that carries the movie. O'Connor (pre-Archie Bunker) is a standout as a cop always two steps behind Marlowe. (Dir: Paul Bogart, 100 mins.)

Marnl (1964)** Tippi Hedren, Sean Connery, Diane Baker. Garbled tale of a girl kleptomaniac who is cured by love. Hitchcock made it, but it's definitely a lesser effort by the suspense master. Some tense moments the only saving graces. (Dir: Alfred Hitchcock, 129 mins.)

Maroc 7 (British, 1967)** Secret agent (Gene Barry) after clever jewel thieves. Slow chase, nothing exceptional. With Elsa Martinelli, Cyd Charisse, Denholm Elliott, Alexandra Stewart. (Dir: Gerry O'Hara, 91 mins.)

Marooned (1969)**½ Gregory Peck, Gene Hackman, James Franciscus, Richard Crenna, David Janssen. A lot of money went into making this space-adventure story about astronauts "marooned" out there, but it misfires. Peck plays the head of the ground-control center, but the personal stories about the stranded astronauts' wives get in the way. (Dir: John Sturges, 134 mins.)

Marriage-Go-Round, The (1961)** Susan Hayward, James Mason, Julie Newmar. Professor finds himself the target of a Swedish student who has selected him as her perfect mate—trouble is, he's married. Comedy tries for sophistication, becomes strained; actors not at home in their roles, which doesn't help.

Marriage Is a Private Affair (1944)** Lana Turner, James Craig, John Hodiak. Hasty war marriage, boy goes to fight, girl gets restless but all comes to a happy ending in this talky bore. (Dir: Robert Z. Leonard, 116 mins.)

Marriage Italian Style (Italian, 1964)***½ Sophia Loren, Marcello Mastroianni. Not quite as funny as "Divorce Italian Style," but the two wonderful stars carry off this caper in fine style. It's a comedy about a luscious, happy prostitute and her efforts to trick a wealthy business-

man into marriage, and then to hold on to the unwilling hubby. Some of the later scenes are quite touching and it again makes a meaningful comment on Italy's antiquated laws regarding marriage and divorce. Dubbed in English. (Dir: Vittorio De Sica, 102 mins.)

Marriage of a Young Stockbroker, The (1971)**½ Richard Benjamin, Joanna Shimkus, Elizabeth Ashley. Occasionally amusing but generally heavy-handed comedy about a young, married, bored stockbroker (Benjamin) who tries to improve his morale by going to porno flicks and ogling any passing young damsels. Based on the novel by Charles Webb, who wrote "The Graduate," and directed by Lawrence Turman, who produced "The Graduate." They tried to repeat the magic formula of that entry, but none of the participants happen to have Mike Nichols' talent. Tiffany Bolling is noteworthy in a supporting role. (Dir: Lawrence Turman, 95 mins.)

Marriage of Convenience, The (British, 1962)** Harry H. Corbett, John Cairney, Jennifer Daniel. Bank robber escapes prison, finds his girl has married the detective who arrested him. Passable crime drama based on an Edgar Wallace story.

Marriage on the Rocks (1965)**½ Frank Sinatra, Dean Martin, Deborah Kerr. One of those screwy comedies that almost works—but it's fun anyway. Frank and Deborah are Mr. and Mrs., but they get a Mexican divorce by mistake, and Miss Kerr marries Frank's best friend, Dean Martin. More complications, more switching, and a happy ending. (Dir: Jack Donohue, 109 mins.)

Marry Me (British, 1949)**½ Derek Bond, Susan Shaw. Couple of elderly spinsters run a marriage bureau, manage to tie together four couples. Pleasing little comedy.

Marry Me Again (1953)*** Robert Cummings, Marie Wilson. Girl tries to get her fella to marry her, even if she has more money than he. Enjoyable comedy has some clever gags. (Dir: Frank Tashlin, 73 mins.)

Marry Me, Marry Me (France, 1968)**** Claude Berri, Elizabeth Wiener, Betsy Blair, Regine. Charming romantic comedy, produced, directed and written by Claude Berri, who somehow also found time to play the role of Claude, a Jewish encyclopedia salesman in Paris who's inconveniently fallen in love with a pregnant Belgian girl. "Marry Me" is partly autobiographical, as was Berri's haunting "The Two of Us" about his childhood during WWII. There's a particularly engaging wedding scene in this gentle, perceptive story about European Jewish families. (Dir: Claude Berri)

Marrying Kind, The (1952)***½ Judy Holliday, Aldo Ray, Madge Kennedy. An excellent combination of comedy and pathos make this film of marital ups and downs a most entertaining one. Judy Holliday proves she can act in a serious dramatic vein as well as in her usual hilarious style; it's not much of a compliment but Aldo Ray gives the best performance of his career to date. (Dir: George Cukor, 93 mins.)

Mars Needs Women (1968)*½ Tommy Kirk, Yvonne Craig. Earth doesn't need this one. Supposedly high camp as Kirk and Miss Craig, stars of "bikini" movies, get involved in science fiction. Kirk plays the Martian "Dop" who has come to Earth to kidnap women for the men of his home planet. He falls in love with Miss Craig, an authority on space genetics. You can guess the rest, but don't bother. (Dir: Larry Buchanan, 80 mins.)

Marty (1955)**** Ernest Borgnine, Betsy Blair. Paddy Chayefsky's poignant TV drama is brought to the screen with taste and skill. It is a touching story about two lonely people who have almost resigned themselves to never being truly loved. The movie and Borgnine's performance were awarded Oscars. The excellent supporting cast includes Betsy Blair, Joe Montell, and Esther Minciotti. Director Delbert Mann, megging his first film, does a near faultless job. (90 mins.)

Mary, Mary (1963)**½ Debbie Reynolds, Barry Nelson, Michael Rennie, Diane McBain. A dashing movie star complicates matters when it appears that a book publisher still loves his ex-wife, and vice versa. Film version of long-running Broadway stage success isn't altered much, retains most of the witty lines—which is also a disadvantage, for it remains a photographed stage play. Should afford a fair amount of fun. (Dir: Mervyn Le Roy, 126 mins.)

Mary of Scotland (1936)***½ Katharine Hepburn, Fredric March. Story of the Queen of Scots who defies Queen Elizabeth and is sentenced to death. Elaborately produced, excellently acted historical drama. (Dir: John Ford, 140 mins.)

Mary Queen of Scots (British, 1971)*** Vanessa Redgrave, Glenda Jackson, Nigel Davenport, Trevor Howard. A lame script with plodding direction and not much concern for historical accuracy diffuses the excitement generated by Vanessa Redgrave's portrayal of Mary, Queen of Scots, a performance which earned Redgrave an Academy Award nomination. This is the second filming of the legendary confrontation between these two domineering women. First version was the 1936 "Mary of Scotland" with Katharine Hepburn playing Mary Stuart and Florence Eldridge playing Elizabeth. The picture really comes alive in the scenes between Jackson and Redgrave, marvelous actresses both. There are some lovely costumes and panoramas of the countryside, but it doesn't add up to much when Redgrave is not on screen. (Dir: Charles Jarrott, 128 mins.)

Maryjane (1968)* Fabian, Patty McCormack, Diane McBain. Marijuana, that is. Intended to be an indictment of pot-smoking and dope-peddling among high-schoolers, movie takes place in an average Hometown, U.S.A., and is long on talk, short on interest. Fabian, surprisingly, is cast as a high-school art teacher. Acting is wooden! (Dir: Maury Dexter, 95 mins.)

Maryland (1940)**½ Walter Brennan, Fay Bainter. Without Technicolor this film about a woman who sells all her horses after her husband is killed in an accident will lose much of its scenic splendor. It's still a fairly good horse story. (Dir: Henry King, 92 mins.)

M*A*S*H (1970)**** Donald Sutherland, Elliott Gould, Sally Kellerman. The two real stars of this extraordinarily funny film about an American Army medical unit during the Korean War are screenwriter Ring Lardner, Jr., who deservedly won an Academy Award, and director Robert Altman. Irreverent, perceptive screenplay superbly acted by all concerned, with director Altman pacing it brilliantly. One of the finest American comedies of the decade and a joy from start to finish. Nominated for an Academy Award for best picture. It's worth noting that this was the first big break for gifted screenwriter Lardner, who had been blacklisted in Hollywood for many years. (116 mins.)

Mask of Dimitrios (1944)**½ Zachary Scott, Sydney Greenstreet, Faye Emerson, Peter Lorre. Poorly told but occasionally exciting adaptation of the Eric Ambler novel about a Dutch mystery writer searching for a master crook whose exploits fascinate him. (Dir: Jean Negulesco, 95 mins.)

Mask of the Avenger (1951)** John Derek, Anthony Quinn, Jody Lawrence. The Count of Monte Cristo rides again but only in name. Young Renato Dimorna (John Derek) takes the guise of the Count to outwit the evil governor (Anthony Quinn) and win back his beloved Maria. You've seen it all before, and better done. (Dir: Phil Karlson, 83 mins.)

Mask of the Musketeers (Italian, 1960)*½ Gordon Scott, Jose Greci. The Musketeers aid a masked avenger in exposing a traitor. Costume adventure on the dull side. Dubbed in English.

Masked Conqueror, The (Italian, 1960)* Alberto Lupo, Giorgio Ardisson. Masked man on the side of justice battles the power-mad brother-in-law of the queen who plots against her. Trite costume adventure dubbed in English.

Masked Man Against the Pirates, The (Spanish, 1962)* George Hilton, Claude Dantes. Mysterious masked hero prevents pirates from harming a princess. Poor swashbuckling melodrama dubbed in English.

Masquerade (British, 1965)***½ Cliff Robertson, Jack Hawkins, Marizza Mell. A delightful spy spoof that works out better than you initially think it will. Cliff Robertson and Jack Hawkins are delightful as a pair of British Foreign Office emissaries who are assigned the challenging and highly dangerous task of kidnapping a young prince of a country that possesses vast oil deposits. The scheme creates the anticipated confusion, but director Basil Dearden keeps a firm hand on the proceedings, and we're spared much of the farcical mugging and hijinks so often found in this kind

of picture. A diverting masquerade. (Dir: Basil Dearden, 101 mins.)

Masquerade in Mexico (1945)*½ Dorothy Lamour, Arturo de Cordova. To earn some dough an American gal agrees to try and win a Mexican bullfighter's affections from a married woman. Poorly acted and written. (Dir: Mitchell Leisen, 96 mins.)

Masquerader, The (1933)**½ Ronald Colman, Elissa Landi. Colman plays two parts in this derring-do tale based on the popular novel of the time written by Katherine Cecil Thurston. (Dir: Richard Wallace, 78 mins.)

Massacre (1956)** Dane Clark, James Craig. Just another Western about the Indians massacring the good guys on our side by using guns sold to them by the bad guys. Set in Mexico. (Dir: Louis King, 76 mins.)

Massacre at Fort Perdition (Spanish, 1965)** Jerry Cobb, Martha May. Sole survivor of a bloody massacre tells the whole story when he's placed on trial. Slightly offbeat western—filmed abroad, and relatively fresh plot.

Massacre at Ft. Holman (1972)½ Telly Savalas, James Coburn, Bud Spencer. Atrocious spaghetti Western that wastes Coburn and Savalas as enemies in the Civil War. The plot, such as it is, revolves around control of a Missouri fort. Actually, it's a steal from "The Dirty Dozen," as Coburn enlists the aid of seven misfits to regain the battlements. Script, direction and acting are all terrible. (Dir: Tonino Valerii, 92 mins.)

Master of Ballantrae (British, 1953)**½ Errol Flynn, Yvonne Furneaux. Another swashbuckling role for Errol Flynn as he surmounts danger after danger. Plenty of adventure and romance in true Flynn cinema tradition. (Dir: William Keighley, 89 mins.)

Master of the World (1961)*** Vincent Price, Charles Bronson, Henry Hull. Back in the last century, a scientist uses a strange aircraft to try to persuade armament makers to cease and desist, to bring peace. Fanciful Jules Verne sci-fi tale given clever production effects, a steady pace. Good fun. (Dir: William Witney, 104 mins.)

Master Plan (British, 1954)*½ Wayne Morris, Tilda Thamar. Investigator nabs spies who have been sneaking out secret information from a combined military operation. Dull melodrama.

Master Race (1944)*** George Coulouris, Nancy Gates. German officer flees when the Nazi empire starts to collapse. Good war drama. (Dir: Herbert J. Biberman, 96 mins.)

Master Spy (British, 1964)**½ Stephen Murray, June Thorburn. Communist physicist visits England and asks for political asylum, but does he really mean it or is he in truth a Red spy? Good performances and several neat plot twists show to advantage in this interesting drama. (Dir: Montgomery Tully, 71 mins.)

Masterson of Kansas (1955)** George Montgomery, Nancy Gates. Some of the famous names of the West show up in this Western; Bat Masterson, Doc Holliday, Wyatt Earp. Now if only George Montgomery were that colorful! (Dir: William Castle, 73 mins.)

Mata Hari (1931)***½ Greta Garbo, Ramon Navarro, Lionel Barrymore. Story of World War I's famed spy has become a legend and this film, although not produced for modern tastes, is something of a classic. (Dir: George Fitzmaurice, 100 mins.)

Mata Hari's Daughter (Italian, 1955) ** Ludmilla Tcherina, Frank Latimore, Erno Crisa. Daughter of the famous spy follows in her mother's footsteps. Fairish espionage melodrama, cast and production better than the material. Dubbed in English. (Dir: Renzo Merius, 102 mins.)

Matchless (Italian, 1966)* Patrick O'Neal, Ira Furstenberg, Donald Pleasence. O'Neal as a comic-book version of James Bond working for American intelligence. Inane all around, especially O'Neal's magic ring. "Matchless" is worthless. (Dir: Alberto Lattuada, 103 mins.)

Matchmaker, The (1958)*** Shirley Booth, Tony Perkins, Shirley MacLaine, Robert Morse, Paul Ford. Well-meaning matchmaker assumes the responsibility of finding a wife for a wealthy skinflint of a merchant. Generally amusing version of Thornton Wilder's stage play, perhaps a bit too restricted in its technique to be completely successful—but good cast, some funny moments. Story was later turned into Broadway musical success "Hello Dolly." (Dir: Joseph Anthony, 101 mins.)

Mating Game, The (1959)*** Tony Randall, Debbie Reynolds, Paul Douglas. Randall steals the whole picture with his zany performance as an Internal Revenue investigator who comes to check on an unpredictable businessman who hasn't paid his taxes and ends up falling in love with the man's pretty daughter (Miss Reynolds). A lot of sight gags, a fast-paced script plus Randall's comedy timing add up to fun. (Dir: George Marshall, 96 mins.)

Mating of Millie (1948)**½ Glenn Ford, Evelyn Keyes. Career woman looks for a mate so she can legally adopt an orphan boy. Fairly amusing comedy-drama. (Dir: Henry Levin, 87 mins.)

Mating Season, The (1951)**½ Gene Tierney, John Lund, Thelma Ritter. Plain-spoken mother of a man who has married well poses as a servant without letting on her relationship to her social daughter-in-law. Amusing comedy hinges largely on Ritter's acid remarks, and she walks away with the show, making it better than it would otherwise normally be. (Dir: Mitchell Leisen, 101 mins.)

Matt Helm (1975)* Tony Franciosa, Laraine Stephens, Ann Turkel. Franciosa plays the TV-movie incarnation of the Dean Martin role, and does his best with dull private-eye scripting. His efforts to be the debonair ladies' man are forced, but Franciosa does it better than most. Made-for-TV. (Dir: Buzz Kulik, 72 mins.)

Matter of Innocence, A (British, 1968)** Hayley Mills, Trevor Howard, Shashi Kapoor. A sentimental, clumsily written tale in which a grown-up Hayley Mills actually has an affair with a dashing Indian gigolo, played with slick charm by Shashi Kapoor. The screenplay, based on a Noel Coward short story, follows the transformation of plain Polly (Hayley) to sexy Polly, thanks to the death of her wealthy aunt. Trevor Howard is totally wasted as Polly's ne'er-do-well uncle. The ladies may enjoy it. (Dir: Guy Green, 102 mins.)

Matter of Morals (U.S.-Sweden, 1960)**½ Patrick O'Neal, Maj-Britt Nilsson, Mogens Wieth, Eva Dahlbeck. In this U.S.-Swedish co-production, American businessman meets Swedish sex, discards his U.S. wife, his business and moral ethics. Alternately compelling and mediocre; the story is mainly mundane—acting, production, backgrounds more intriguing. (Dir: John Cromwell, 90 mins.)

Matter of Time, A (Italy-U.S., 1976) ½ Liza Minnelli, Ingrid Bergman, Charles Boyer, Tina Aumont. Disastrous mixture of Cinderella fantasy with a realistic rags-to-riches story. Director Vincente Minnelli had his footage recut by American International Pictures, with depressing results. Liza is a maid in a hotel, Rome, circa 1949, who quickly rises to become a film star. Based on the novel "The Film of Memory," by Maurice Druon. Liza sings two colorless tunes. Her first film, incidentally, with her illustrious director pappy. (99 mins.)

Matter of Who, A (British, 1961)**½ Terry-Thomas, Alex Nicol, Sonja Ziemann. When a man becomes ill aboard a plane, a conscientious investigator for the World Health Organization looks into the matter and becomes involved in an oil-swindle plot. Curious mixture of comedy and suspenseful drama, with a restrained performance by Terry-Thomas. Although it's never certain whether it should be taken seriously or for laughs, it manages to hold interest. (Dir: Don Chaffey, 90 mins.)

Matter of Wife . . . and Death, A (1975)* Rod Taylor, Dick Butkus, Anne Archer. A remake of "Shamus," the Burt Reynolds-Dyan Cannon 1972 movie, starring Taylor as the rough-and-tumble private eye. Shamus hangs out in a poolroom and nails the killer of a pal. Made-for-TV. (Dir: Marvin Chomsky, 72 mins.)

Maurie (1973)** Bernie Casey, Bo Swenson, Janet MacLachlan, Stephanie Edwards. A tear-jerker for men. Maurice Stokes, one of Cincinnati's finest basketball players, was mysteriously paralyzed soon after being named "Rookie of the Year" of the NBA. His teammate, Jack Twyman, spent 10 years trying to raise funds to rehabilitate his friend, who finally died. The results of this heroic struggle were quite depressing, and this drama which tells Maurie's story is not nearly so interesting as TV's own "Brian's Song," which related much the same tale. Char-

acter development is kept to a minimum. Instead we're given a soap opera with absolutely everyone being helpful to the disabled athlete. (Dir: Daniel Mann, 113 mins.)

Maurizius Case, The (French, 1953) **½ Daniel Gelin, Eleonora Rossi-Drago, Anton Walbrook. A young lawyer tries to investigate a murder case that sent a man to prison eighteen years before. It's talky, but still better than most—thanks to the original book.

Maverick Queen (1956)**½ Barbara Stanwyck, Barry Sullivan, Scott Brady. Bandit woman falls for a detective working undercover. Adequate western, with cast better than material. (Dir: Joseph Kane, 92 mins.)

Maxime (French, 1958)** Charles Boyer, Michele Morgan. Impoverished aristocrat is to arrange a romance for a boorish young millionaire, but falls for the lady himself. Costume romance tries for charm, but misses. Boyer and Morgan give the English-dubbed film what class it has. (Dir: Henri Verneuil, 93 mins.)

Maya (1965)**½ Clint Walker, Jay North, Sajid Kahn. Entertaining jungle-adventure tale, filmed on location in India. Two boys team up to deliver a small, sacred white elephant to a jungle temple in India. The two young stars are small but engaging. (Dir: John Berry, 91 mins.)

Maybe I'll Come Home in the Spring (1971)*** Sally Field, Eleanor Parker. A lovely little movie that doesn't try to take in too much. Searching, dreaming, confused daughters are unable to handle their own lives or get through for help to baffled, locked-in parents. It's another "generation gap" story —pathetic and touching—shot in California's middle-class San Fernando valley by talented director Joe Sargent. Sally Field and Lane Bradbury play the groping daughters, parents are Jackie Cooper and Eleanor Parker, and all give good performances. One of the best of the made-for-TV features. (Dir: Joseph Sargent, 73 mins.)

Mayday at 40,000 Feet (1976)*½ David Janssen, Lynda Day George, Christopher George. Still another in the slick, patented cliff-hanger films set in a disabled airliner with a killer aboard. The action begins at a stopover during which the killer comes aboard. Made-for-TV. (Dir: Robert Butler, 106 mins.)

Mayerling (Great Britain-France, 1968)* Omar Sharif, Catherine Deneuve, James Mason, Ava Gardner. Ponderous "romantic" reading of history, which ascribes the death of Austrian Crown Prince Rudolf and his mistress to a suicide pact on his hunting estate of Mayerling in 1889. The lovers may well have talked themselves to death, judging from this protracted picture. Authentic Austrian scenery, and the sets are lavish. The third filming of this historical episode; the best is still the genuinely moving 1936 French film starring Boyer and Danielle Darrieux. (Dir: Terence Young, 140 mins.)

Mayor of 44th Street (1942)**½ George Murphy, Anne Shirley. Reformed gangster becomes an agent for name bands, has trouble with another not-so-reformed hood. Pleasant musical comedy-drama.

Maytime (1937)*** Jeanette MacDonald, Nelson Eddy, John Barrymore. Lovely romance, set in Paris between (conveniently) a prima donna and a baritone is delightful screen entertainment, especially for music lovers. (Dir: Robert Z. Leonard, 140 mins.)

Maytime in Mayfair (British, 1949)** Anna Neagle, Michael Wilding. Gay sophisticated comedy about the rivalry between two fashionable dress salons. Elaborate, witty. (Dir: Herbert Wilcox, 94 mins.)

Maze, The (1954)*** Richard Carlson, Veronica Hurst. Originally produced as a 3D feature, this horror film has more than its share of visual gimmicks. The plot concerns a house where a mysterious mutation (an outsized frog) dominates the inhabitants. Weird and frightening at times. One of the better films of this genre. (Dir: William Cameron Menzies, 81 mins.)

McCabe & Mrs. Miller (1971)**** Warren Beatty, Julie Christie, Shelley Duvall, Keith Carradine. A stunning, inventively directed, droll yarn about life, whores and heroism —or the lack of it—in the bleak Northwest around 1902. Beatty gives one of his most affecting performances, playing a small-time gambler on the make who amuses himself, and sometimes the townspeople, by pretending that he's a former gunslinging outlaw, while setting up the town's first bordello in what used to be the Presbyterian Church. Julie Christie arrives to manage and increase the scope of the prosperous cathouse—and she's not above taking a fiver herself for services rendered for partner Beatty. Characters and conversations are not always fully developed or introduced—director Robert Altman's camera moves in and out making novel use of the soundtrack. Coauthored by Altman, based on the novel by McCabe. Christie was nominated for an Academy Award for her lovely performance. (Dir: Robert Altman, 120 mins.)

McCloud: Fifth Man In a String Quartet (1972)*½ Dennis Weaver, Lilia Skala, Avery Schreiber. Dennis Weaver probes a mystery with the help of a fascinating white-Russian refugee, and three kooky musicians. He's surrounded, if you care, by a supporting cast including Richard Haydn, Alex Hentelhoff, Rick Weaver (Dennis' son), plus Neville Brand, Gary Collins, Shelley Fabares and Joseph Wiseman. Made-for-TV. (Dir: Russ Mayberry, 79 mins.)

McCloud: Give My Regrets to Broadway (1972)*½ Dennis Weaver, Milton Berle, Barbara Rush. Dennis Weaver's displaced Western sheriff mingles with the theater crowd in this fair story about a cop who takes over for McCloud and is killed. Made-for-TV. (Dir: Lou Antonio, 78 mins.)

McCloud: Top of the World, Ma! (1971)** Dennis Weaver, Bo Svenson, Stefanie Powers, Robert Webber. Cast headed by Bo Svenson, Robert Webber and Stefanie Powers makes this unbelievable story almost believable while you're watching it. Bo plays a big, shy, semi-pro football player who steals his boss's car in Ohio, brings his mother to New York, checks her into the best hotel, and then sets out to collect a $10,000 debt. Made-for-TV. (Dir: Alex March, 76 mins.)

McCloud: Who Killed Miss U.S.A.? (1970)** Dennis Weaver, Craig Stevens, Diana Muldaur. Strictly for whodunit fans, this made-for-TV feature plays like a pilot film for a proposed TV series, which it is. Dennis Weaver plays the title role (McCloud, not Miss U.S.A.) of a New Mexico deputy marshal who finds himself in New York City on a murder case. Some topical references to the Puerto Rican minority, good on-location photography of New York City adds to the story about a young beauty queen's murder. (Dir: Richard Colla, 99 mins.)

McConnell Story, The (1955)**½** Alan Ladd, June Allyson, James Whitmore. The romanticized story of real life jet ace McConnell, acted as if he had lockjaw by Alan Ladd. As in many of her previous films, June Allyson winds up weeping in the window for her man. (Dir: Gordon Douglas, 107 mins.)

McGuire, Go Home (Great Britain, 1965)*½ Dirk Bogarde, Susan Strasberg, Denholm Elliott. Dull chase melodrama. Views of British presence in Cyprus, local resentments and terrorist activity. Meager plot pairs intelligencer-Bogarde and naive American student-Strasberg, after a decent interval of bombings and soul-searching. (Dir: Ralph Thomas, 114 mins.)

McHale's Navy (1964)** Ernest Borgnine, Tim Conway, Joe Flynn. Feature version of a once-popular TV series, this has the nutty PT crew involved in a horse race and some big betting. What was funny in 30 minutes becomes quite thin when protracted to feature length; however, the kids should get some laughs. (Dir: Edward J. Montagne, 93 mins.)

McHale's Navy Joins the Air Force (1965)** Joe Flynn, Tim Conway. TV series expanded to feature form again, this time without Ernest Borgnine. Tim Conway receives most of the attention, as he masquerades as an air-force looey. Pure slapstick, for the kiddies and fans of the TV series. (Dir: Edward J. Montagne, 90 mins.)

McKenzie Break, The (British, 1970) ***½ Brian Keith, Helmut Griem. Authentic, vivid World War II drama. Keith gives a tremendous performance as an Irish intelligence agent put in charge of a British prison in Scotland to prevent an escape by captured Germans. Griem plays his adversary, the leader of the POW's, and is also excellent. The screenplay is literate, the direction tough and tight, and the Germans

actually speak German. Watch for the suspenseful ending and Keith's last line. (Dir: Lamont Johnson, 108 mins.)

McLintock (1963)**½ John Wayne, Maureen O'Hara. Don't be fooled by the western setting and the presence of John Wayne in this film—it's primarily a comedy, amply supplied with slapstick. Wayne is a cattleman who literally pulls no punches in trying to win and woo his wife back. The pace is raucous and wild. (Dir: Andrew V. McLaglen, 127 mins.)

McMillan and Wife: Cop of the Year (1972)** Rock Hudson, Susan St. James, John Schuck. McMillan's sidekick Sgt. Enright is in a room arguing with his wife while plenty of people, including Mac, overhear the battle. The lady is then shot! You've seen it before . . . Made-for-TV. (Dir: Bob Lewis, 79 mins.)

McMillan and Wife: The Devil, You Say (1973)** Rock Hudson, Susan St. James, John Schuck. An early reminder that Hallowe'en is in the offing! Suspense builds when Commissioner McMillan discovers there's a cult of Satanists behind the mysterious Hallowe'en gifts. Chiller, thriller, meller! Made-for-TV. (Dir: Alex March, 72 mins.)

McNaughton's Daughter (1976)** Susan Clark, Vera Miles, Ralph Bellamy. A mediocre, somewhat different series pilot idea that was partially successful. Clark is a deputy district attorney assigned to prosecute a saintly missionary (Miles) accused of murder. Made-for-TV. (Dir: Jerry London, 98 mins.)

McQ (1974)** John Wayne, Eddie Albert, Diana Muldaur, Colleen Dewhurst, Clu Gulager. John Wayne just doesn't look comfortable in modern dress, as evidenced in "Brannigan" and now "McQ." Wayne is again a law enforcer whose theme song is "My Way." He quits the force when his buddy is killed in order to ride the vengeance trail, by car this time. Boring musical score by Elmer Bernstein. (Dir: John Sturges, 111 mins.)

Me and My Gal (1932)*** Spencer Tracy, Joan Bennett, George Walsh. A rather improbable but engaging concoction, teams burlesque and gangster genres, hard-nosed detective Tracy with fine-featured (but gum-chewing) cashieress Bennett.

A period piece, evocative and witty. (Dir: Raoul Walsh)

Me and the Colonel (1958)***½ Danny Kaye, Curt Jurgens, Nicole Maurey. A delightful serious comedy about military capers involved in the safe escape of fleeing refugees. Danny Kaye registers strongly a change of pace role as a Polish Jew pitted against an anti-semitic Colonel during the final days of World War II. Under Peter Glenville's sensitive direction Kaye's restrained performance is most affecting. (Dir: Peter Glenville, 109 mins.)

Mean Streets (1973)**** Robert De Niro, Harvey Keitel, Amy Robinson. Excellent portrait of the small-time hoods in New York City's Little Italy and their special code of ethics. This is director Martin Scorsese's third film and his first major success, before such later triumphs as "Alice Doesn't Live Here Anymore" and "Taxi Driver." Robert De Niro is wonderful as a hanger-on who is into a loan shark for a big sum, and tries to get his childhood friend, Charlie, a lower-echelon Mafioso, to intervene on his behalf. Harvey Keitel, as Charlie, is effective, and the film has a terrific impact. Scorsese grew up in the neighborhood and he reveals the brutality, competitiveness and strong family ties of the Italian families. Scorsese helped write the screenplay based on his own story. (Dir: Martin Scorsese, 110 mins.)

Meanest Man In the World, The (1943)**½ Jack Benny, Rochester. Jack rises above his material and makes something of this little one-hour comedy about an unsuccessful soft-hearted lawyer who gets rich by becoming mean. (Dir: Sidney Lanfield, 57 mins.)

Meat (1976)***½ A documentary about a meat-packing plant in Colorado, but it's really a film about—among other things—ecology, and some of the moral issues raised by the high meat consumption of affluent America. It's also about the process of death—a symphony of slaughter as the animals are stunned, killed, dressed and packaged in ways unfamiliar to most meat-eaters. One of Wiseman's most abstract, involved works. (Dir: Frederick Wiseman, 112 mins.)

Mechanic, The (1972)*½ Charles Bronson, Jan-Michael Vincent, Kee-

nan Wynn. Pretentious crime drama about a hired killer (mechanic) who uses complicated methods to annihilate his victims. The personal life of killer Arthur Bishop, played in arch style by Bronson, is trotted out and his Playboy-type pad and sex life only tend to confuse the audience even more. (Dir: Michael Winner, 100 mins.)

Medal for Benny, A (1945)***½ Dorothy Lamour, Arturo de Cordova, J. Carrol Naish. When news reaches a small California town that one of its sons has been killed in action, the town fathers see a chance for some publicity. Touching drama from a Steinbeck story, with fine performances, especially by Naish. (Dir: Irving Pichel, 77 mins.)

Medea (Italian, 1971)*** Maria Callas. Director Pier Paolo Pasolini's earnest interpretation of the classic Greek drama by Euripides. He has changed it greatly, and half the film is devoted to a prelude to Euripides, in which Jason grows up and Medea helps him steal the golden fleece. Medea's search for Jason, and her killing of her children, form the rest of this film. Miss Callas has made the transition from opera to cinema gracefully. For some purists, Pasolini's tampering may prove irritating. (100 mins.)

Medium, The (1954)***½ Anna Maria Alberghetti, Marie Powers. Menotti's strange, brooding opera, well sung. For specialized tastes, but there is a haunting score and Miss Powers' electric portrayal of a medium-spiritualist. (Dir: Gian-Carlo Menotti, 84 mins.)

Medium Cool (1969)**** Robert Forster, Verna Bloom, Harold Blankenship. The first film directed by the award-winning cinematographer Haskell Wexler, and a remarkably impressive debut it is, an amazingly realistic semi-documentary about the now-famous events at the 1968 Democratic National Convention in Chicago. "Medium Cool" is loosely based on the 1967 novel "The Concrete Wilderness" by Jack Couffer, written and photographed, of course, by Wexler. The title may be a punning reversal of Marshal McLuhan's celebrated definition of television, but multi-talented Wexler turns it into a major statement about the inter-relationship of life, love, TV news and the ever-increasing violence in American society to which we seem to have become inured. It's a probing, exploratory, important work by a major cinema artist. (Dir: Haskell Wexler, 110 mins.)

Medusa Against the Son of Hercules (Italian, 1963)* Richard Harrison, Anna Ranalli. All about how the son of Hercules kills a swamp monster and restores life to an army turned to stone. Strictly for the kiddies is this wildly ridiculous English-dubbed fantasy.

Meet Boston Blackie (1941)*** Chester Morris, Rochelle Hudson. First in series about reformed safecracker who aids police. Blackie breaks up a spy ring in this one. Better than average. (Dir: Robert Florey, 61 mins.)

Meet Danny Wilson (1952)**½ Frank Sinatra, Shelley Winters, Alex Nicol. Not a bad film but the story line about an entertainer and gangsters does get jumbled to say the least. A big bonus for Sinatra fans is the long list of standards he delivers. (Dir: Joseph Pevney, 86 mins.)

Meet John Doe (1941)*** Gary Cooper, Barbara Stanwyck. The search for the forgotten average man as a publicity stunt by a newspaper, and how it backfired. Elaborate Frank Capra production, often excellent but overlong. (Dir: Frank Capra, 123 mins.)

Meet Me After the Show (1951)** Betty Grable, Macdonald Carey, Rory Calhoun. Efforts of a producer to get his ex-wife, an amnesia case, back in his show. Grable gams its chief asset. (Dir: Richard Sale, 86 mins.)

Meet Me at the Fair (1953)*** Dan Dailey, Diana Lynn, Chet Allen. Charming film about a traveling medicine man who gets involved with a runaway orphan and the authorities. Dailey is charm personified as the fast talking con man with a heart of gold and young Chet Allen has a lovely voice. (Dir: Douglas Sirk, 87 mins.)

Meet Me in Las Vegas (1956)**½ Dan Dailey, Cyd Charisse. Wispy little story about a gambling rancher and the dancer who brings him luck doesn't mean a thing—the big news here is the terpsichore, including a "Frankie and Johnnie" ballet

that's a knockout, and the guest appearances of Lena Horne, Frankie Laine, Jerry Colonna, and others. (Dir: Roy Rowland, 112 mins.)

Meet Me in St. Louis (1944)***½ Judy Garland, Margaret O'Brien, Tom Drake, Mary Astor. To a charming, sentimental tale about a family in St. Louis and the turn of the century has been added a wonderful musical score and cast. (Dir: Vincente Minnelli, 113 mins.)

Meet Mr. Lucifer (British, 1954)*** Stanley Holloway, Peggy Cummins. The Devil introduces television into three homes to stir up trouble. Neat, amusing fantasy-comedy; some good laughs. (Dir: Anthony Pelissier, 83 mins.)

Meet Peter Foss (German, 1961)**½ O. W. Fischer, Walter Giller. Breezy crook melodrama featuring a likable scoundrel who outwits both hoodlums and the law in a chase after a fortune. Fischer is very dapper. Dubbed in English.

Meet the Stewarts (1942)*** William Holden, Frances Dee. Heiress marries a white-collar man, tries to get along on a budget. Pleasing, funny comedy. (Dir: Alfred E. Green, 73 mins.)

Mein Kampf (1961)***½ Grim documentation of the horrors of the Hitler regime. Technically rough, but the harrowing sequences eloquently speak for themselves. Should be seen. (121 mins.)

Melba (1953)*** Patrice Munsel, Robert Morley. Phony film biography of Nellie Melba is distinguished by Miss Munsel singing scores of areas. Opera fans only. (Dir: Lewis Milestone, 113 mins.)

Melody (British, 1972)*** Mark Lester, Jack Wild, Tracy Hyde. Appealing tale of an 11-year-old boy who wants to marry a 12-year-old girl so that they can always be together. Slightly silly premise saved by marvelous acting. Wild and Lester, who worked so well together in "Oliver," are a delight as Wild plays Lester's older friend. (Dir: Waris Hussein, 103 mins.)

Melvin Purvis, G-Man (1974)**½ Dale Robertson, Harris Yulin. A good script by John Milius and William F. Nolan graphically depicts the cat-and-mouse game employed by the notorious Machine Gun Kelly and colorful G-man Melvin Purvis. Robertson is right as Purvis and his casual manner adds to the tone of the piece. Kelly and his cohorts kidnap a wealthy playboy and the FBI steps in to crack the case, with Purvis in charge. Yulin also scores as Kelly and Margaret Blye has some good scenes as his pretty wife. Slick gangster fare. Made-for-TV. (Dir: Dan Curtis.)

Member of the Wedding, The (1953) ******** Julie Harris, Ethel Waters, Brandon de Wilde. Broadway's successful play by Carson McCullers delicately brought to the screen with great performances by the trio of stars. The theme of adolescence is beautifully treated. Stanley Kramer produced and Fred Zinnemann directed. You'll not soon forget Julie Harris' touching and beautifully realized growing pains. (Dir: Fred Zinnemann, 91 mins.)

Memories of Underdevelopment (Cuba, 1968)******** Sergio Corrieri, Daisy Granados, Eslinda Nunez. A remarkable film about alienation, virtually without any political rhetoric whatever, that was denied an American commercial release because of some cretinous bureaucrats in the Nixon administration. Captures the nuances of Cuban life in 1961, not long after Castro had come to power. Protagonist is a middle-class Cuban intellectual who voluntarily stays in Cuba after his parents and his wife have departed for America. The fifth film by Cuba's leading director, Tomas Gutierrez Alea, a director of enormous gifts and international stature. Starts out dramatically and builds audience involvement throughout. Based on the novel by Edmundo Desnoes. (104 mins.)

Men, The (1950)******** Marlon Brando, Teresa Wright, Jack Webb. Paralyzed war vet tries to adjust to society without the use of his limbs. Brando's first film, and a superb one. Dramatic, persuasive, with fine work in every department. (Dir: Fred Zinnemann, 85 mins.)

Men Against the Sun (British, 1954)****½** John Bentley, Zena Marshall. An engineer is persuaded to join the builders of a railroad across Darkest Africa. Good African backgrounds, but just an average plot.

Men and Wolves (Italian, 1957)****** Yves Montand, Silvana Mangano. Confused drama about a notorious lady killer who covets another lady killer's wife. Ably acted.

Men Are Not Gods (British, 1937)****** Miriam Hopkins, Gertrude Lawrence, Rex Harrison. A romantic triangle affair brings near-tragedy to three theatrical people. Rather stiff comedy-drama. Well acted. (Dir: Walter Reisch, 100 mins.)

Men in Her Diary (1945)****½** Peggy Ryan, Jon Hall, Louise Albritton. Unattractive secretary keeps a diary of imaginary romances, which gets her in plenty of hot water. Amusing comedy. (Dir: Charles Barton, 73 mins.)

Men in War (1957)******* Robert Ryan, Aldo Ray. Another in the grim, realistic war films about the Korean conflict. Good performances by Ryan and Ray make this tale about personal conflicts amid the hell of war palatable. Among the large supporting cast, Nehemiah Persoff, Scott Marlowe, and Vic Morrow stand out. (Dir: Anthony Mann, 104 mins.)

Men of Boys Town (1940)******* Spencer Tracy, Mickey Rooney. Sequel to "Boys Town" is just a sentimental rehash of a lot of B movies. Tracy is still good as Father Flanagan but, for the most part, film is awful. (Dir: Norman Taurog, 106 mins.)

Men of Sherwood Forest (British, 1954)****** Don Taylor, Eileen Moore. Robin Hood and his Merrie Men attempt to restore King Richard to the throne. It's all been done before on a much larger scale, but this costume adventure has enough action to get by. (Dir: Val Guest, 77 mins.)

Men of the Dragon (1974)****** Jared Martin, Robert Ito, Katie Saylor. In the wake of the popular feature films produced during the early '70's about martial arts, here's TV's belated answer. It's all fairly mild, with high-flying karate kicks and low-blow kung-fu thrusts, with a brother and sister martial-arts team, no less. Filmed in Hong Kong; the scenery is good enough but the story is silly. Character actor Joseph Wiseman has some fun with a delicious villain, a "white slaver" named Balashev. (Dir: Harry Falk.)

Men of the Fighting Lady (1954)****½** Van Johnson, Walter Pidgeon. Routine war film about an aircraft carrier and the men assigned to her who fought and died. There's the usual cast of stock characters, some exciting actual war footage. (Dir: Andrew Marton, 80 mins.)

Men of Two Worlds (British, 1945)

½ Eric Portman, Phyllis Calvert, Robert Adams. Educated native returns to his homeland of East Africa, realizes his people live literally in a different world, tries to persuade them to move from their highly-infested area. Carefully produced drama has picturesque scenes, a sincere attempt to cope with pressing problems—but the drama is loose, slow moving. Alternate title: **Witch Doctor. (Dir: Thorold Dickinson, 107 mins.)

Men With Wings (1938)*** Fred MacMurray, Ray Milland. Story of two air pioneers, one a stunt flier and war hero, the other a man who dreams of aviation's future. Ambitious film tries to chronicle the history of aviation (through 1938). Fair entertainment. (Dir: William A. Wellman, 110 mins.)

Menace, The (French, 1960)*½ Robert Hossein, Elsa Martinelli. Thrill-seeking girl joins a gang of motorcycling teenagers, becomes involved with a homicidal maniac. Weak drama, dubbed-in English.

Menace in the Night (British, 1958) ** Griffith Jones, Lisa Gastoni. Witness to a robbery and murder is threatened by the chief crook if she should go to the police. Ordinary crime melodrama, with a good performance by Miss Gastoni as the terrified witness. (Dir: Lance Comfort, 78 mins.)

Mephisto Waltz, The (1971)*** Alan Alda, Jacqueline Bisset, Curt Jurgens, Barbara Parkins. World-famous pianist Jurgens is dying of a rare blood disease when he grants journalist Alda a rare interview. Satanic possession is involved and Miss Bisset has the strange feeling that husband Alda is changing. Eerie music and subtlety are the chief assets of this West Coast "Rosemary's Baby." (Dir: Paul Wendkos, 108 mins.)

Merciless Trap, The (Japanese, 1964) *½ Makoto Sato. Detective helps an ex-con clear himself, exposes a gangland operation. Crime drama is reminiscent of the old American films, but not in quality. Dubbed in English.

Mermaids of Tiburon, The (1959)* George Rowe, Dianne Webber. Sexy type film about a guy who discovers underwater life. Pretty fishy, despite good camera work.

Merrill's Marauders (1962)**** Jeff Chandler, Ty Hardin, Will Hutchins, Claude Akins. Splendid war film—story of the famous outfit of war-hardened veterans who battled the enemy in Burma under excruciating conditions calling for the limit of human endurance. Rates with the best of them, realistic, tough, ultimately inspiring. Fine performance by Chandler, direction by Samuel Fuller. (98 mins.)

Merry Andrew (1958)**½ Danny Kaye, Pier Angeli. Pleasant, if not top drawer, Danny Kaye musical comedy vehicle. The setting is a small circus, with Danny cast as a schoolteacher who joins the troupe for a brief interval. There are songs, comedy, dances and, of course, a love story with pretty Pier Angeli as the object of Danny's affection. Mild, entertaining film, mostly for Kaye fans. (Dir: Michael Kidd, 103 mins.)

Merry-Go-Round (1923)**½ Norman Kerry, Dorothy Wallace. A romantic drama set in Vienna during the reign of Emperor Franz Josef. The story behind this film is more interesting than the film itself. Erich von Stroheim set up the film, devised the script, and intended to both direct the picture and play the leading role of the Count, who succumbs to the guiles of a commoner. Von Stroheim was first canned from his acting role and then, after about one month's work directing the film, was fired, and his friend Wallace Beery, playing Huber, also departed. Only a little of Stroheim's scenes survive, but his conception dominates the picture, largely directed by his replacement, Rupert Julian. (110 mins.)

Merry Monahans, The (1944)*** Donald O'Connor, Ann Blyth, Jack Oakie. Story of vaudevillians is so well played, including some cute musical numbers, that it rises above its commonplace plot. (Dir: Charles Lamont, 91 mins.)

Merry Widow, The (Lady Dances, The) (1934)***½ Maurice Chevalier, Jeanette MacDonald, Edward Everett Horton, Una Merkel. It's been done so often that it's lost a lot of its appeal but this Ernst Lubitsch version is a delight. (Dir: Ernst Lubitsch, 100 mins.)

Merry Widow, The (1956)**½ Lana Turner, Fernando Lamas. If you can accept Lana Turner as the "Merry

Widow" of Franz Lehar's operetta, you will probably enjoy this colorful, tune filled film. Fernando Lamas makes a dashing Count Danilo, and the familiar melodies are pleasant to the ear. (Dir: Curtis Bernhardt, 105 mins.)

Message to My Daughter, A (1973) ****½** Kitty Winn, Bonnie Bedelia. Everyone began to hop on the "dying woman" appeal when "Love Story" attracted record audiences; and the made-for-TV genre tries here for another, which ends up as mostly sentimental. Miss Winn is a daughter searching for "identity" against the background of her dead mother's tape-recorded words of wisdom. Miss Bedelia is the expired mom and she works well, as does Miss Winn. Solid production values, but not provoking enough. (Dir: Robert Michael Lewis.)

Messalina (Italian, 1960) ***½** Belinda Lee, Spyros Fokas. Unscrupulous woman marries an emperor and furthers her plan to become sole ruler, but love for a gladiator interferes. Cumbersome historical drama, not much aside from some lavish sets. Dubbed in English.

Messalina Against the Son of Hercules (Italian, 1963) ***½** Richard Harrison, Lisa Gastoni. Saxon warrior enslaved by Roman legions leads the oppressed against the rule of Messalina. Awkward historical adventure dubbed in English.

Meteor Monster (1958) ***** Anne Gwynne, Stuart Wade. Meteor from outer space turns a lad into a monster; he is shielded by his loving mother through the years. Trashy, unpleasant horror thriller. Alternate title: Teenage Monster.

Mexican Hayride (1948) ****½** Bud Abbott & Lou Costello, Luba Malina. Madcap antics South-of-the-Border as Abbott & Costello get involved with phony silver stock and a lady toreador. Luba Malina is funny as a Senorita named Dagmar. (Dir: Charles Barton, 77 mins.)

Mexican Spitfire (1939) ****½** Lupe Velez, Leon Errol. Senora's husband is aided by Uncle Matt in saving a big contract. Amusing comedy.

Mexican Spitfire at Sea (1940) ****** Lupe Velez, Leon Errol. The spitfire goes after an advertising contract for her husband en route to Honolulu. Mild comedy.

Mexican Spitfire's Baby (1941) ******

Lupe Velez, Leon Errol. The spitfire adopts a war orphan, who turns out to be a beautiful French girl. Mild comedy.

Mexican Spitfire's Blessed Event (1943) ****** Lupe Velez, Leon Errol. The success or failure of a big business deal depends upon a nonexistent baby, so the spitfire tries to get one. Mild comedy.

Mexican Spitfire's Elephant (1942) ****** Lupe Velez, Leon Errol. The spitfire gets tangled with crooks who try to smuggle a diamond through customs in a miniature elephant. Mild comedy.

Miami Exposé (1956) ****** Lee J. Cobb, Patricia Medina, Edward Arnold. A police lieutenant tracks down and cracks a vice operation in Florida. Fair cops and robbers. This is typical of how Lee J. Cobb, a really brilliant actor, was wasted by Hollywood film producers. (Dir: Fred F. Sears, 73 mins.)

Miami Story, The (1954) ****** Barry Sullivan, Luther Adler, Beverly Garland. Miami's big crime syndicate is cracked by an ex-gangster and his girl. Routine crime film. (Dir: Fred F. Sears, 75 mins.)

Michael Kohlhaas (1969) ***** David Warner, Anna Karina. Dull costume epic about a 16th-century horse trader who turns into a Robin Hood when he is mistreated by a rich landowner. It's talky and the stars are wasted. (Dir: Charles Parker, 97 mins.)

Michael Shayne, Private Detective (1940) ****½** Lloyd Nolan, Marjorie Weaver. In the capable hands of Mr. Nolan, this fast talking detective comes to life and is a welcome addition to the list of sleuths found in "B" films. (Dir. Eugene Forde, 77 mins.)

Mickey One (1965) *****½** Warren Beatty, Alexandra Stewart, Hurd Hatfield. An absorbing, imaginative film that was much underrated at the time of its original theatrical release. Collaboration of actor Beatty and director Arthur Penn, responsible in their next film for the smash hit "Bonnie and Clyde." Greatly aided by an electric performance from Beatty in the role of a struggling nightclub comic who's in a jam with the syndicate mobsters, and goes on the lam to get away from the hoods. Director Penn puts his personal, stylistic stamp on this film and makes good use of various Chicago locations. Supporting cast is unusually good. This is not the straightforward typical Hollywood narrative, and that's precisely why "Mickey One" will be rewarding for more discerning viewers. (Dir: Arthur Penn, 93 mins.)

Midas Run (1969)** Fred Astaire, Anne Heywood, Richard Crenna, Roddy McDowall, Ralph Richardson. A routine caper as Astaire organizes a plot to steal a gold shipment leaving England by air. His cronies become Crenna, a college professor fired for pacifism, and Miss Heywood, Crenna's eventual lover. Little credibility, but Astaire still retains his charm and Miss Heywood is ravishing. (Dir: Alf Kjellin, 106 mins.)

Middle of the Night (1959)**½ Fredric March, Kim Novak. A not altogether successful filmization of Paddy Chayefsky's hit play, primarily due to the miscasting of Kim Novak in the leading role of the girl who finds herself in love with an older man. March is good as the aging widower who finds a new meaning of life when he falls for a girl young enough to be his daughter. The supporting cast is top notch. (Dir: Delbert Mann, 118 mins.)

Midnight (1939)**½ Claudette Colbert, Don Ameche, John Barrymore. Well played but silly comedy about a chorus girl, stranded in Paris, who is "set-up" by a millionaire to break up his wife's flirtation by luring the lover away. Only occasionally funny. (Dir: Mitchell Leisen, 100 mins.)

Midnight Cowboy (1969****) Dustin Hoffman, Jon Voight, Sylvia Miles. A devastating, lacerating, superbly acted drama which deservedly won the Academy Award for best picture, best director and best screenplay by Waldo Salt. "Cowboy" received a total of seven nominations, including two for Hoffman and Voight, who are both stunning. Story of a male hustler (Voight) and his decrepit buddy (Hoffman) who dream of making it big in New York and retiring to Florida. Voight burst into stardom playing the Texas stud who comes to New York to bed the rich, horny ladies, relying on his athletic body and good looks. But he ends up as bait for the homosexual street prowlers. It's a re-

markable film on virtually every level, one of the best American films of the decade. Based on the novel by James Leo Herlihy. You won't soon forget the sordid, squalid, lost souls who populate New York's still-repellent 42nd St. area. (Dir: John Schlesinger, 113 mins.)

Midnight Lace (1960)**½ Doris Day, Rex Harrison, John Gavin. An overproduced mystery-thriller in which most of the footage finds lovely Doris Day being terrorized by an unknown phone caller. It's up to you to guess and you'll probably find it easy to figure out. (Dir: David Miller, 108 mins.)

Midnight Man, The (1974)** Burt Lancaster, Susan Clark, Cameron Mitchell. The title is literal—Lancaster plays a night watchman-turned-detective at a small Southern college. On parole from a murder conviction, Lancaster is doggedly persistent tracking down the killer of a campus coed. Clark provides the love interest as his parole officer. Plot is confusing, movie too slow. (Dirs: Roland Kibbee and Burt Lancaster, 119 mins.)

Midnight Story, The (1957)** Tony Curtis, Marisa Pavan, Gilbert Roland. Traffic cop investigates on his own when he is outraged by the murder of a parish priest. Strictly routine production graced by a good cast. (Dir: Joseph Pevney, 89 mins.)

Midsummer Night's Dream (1935)***½ James Cagney, Dick Powell, Olivia de Havilland, Joe E. Brown, Mickey Rooney. This was one of the first attempts to bring Shakespeare to the screen and it was, by and large, successful. Dwarfed by more recent films based on the Bard's work it is still a notable achievement. Mickey Rooney's Puck is the highlight of the film. (Dirs: Max Reinhardt, William Dieterle, 170 mins.)

Midsummer Night's Dream (Czech, 1961)*** Shakespeare's comedy fancifully done with animated puppets, well narrated by Richard Burton. Amusing novelty, interesting both for itself and technically.

Midsummer Night's Dream, A (1966)***½ Suzanne Farrell, Edward Villella, Patricia McBride, Arthur Mitchell. The enchanting ballet, based on Shakespeare's play about marital conflict in the royal fairy family, using George Ballanchine's direction and choreography, is brought to the screen unaltered, and complemented by skillful photography. The first feature-length filming of ballet in the U.S., this is one of the finest productions of the New York City Ballet. Close-ups reveal the extraordinary, delicate beauty of the company's youngest prima, Suzanne Farrell, who dances the fairy Queen, Tatiana. (Dir: Dan Erikson, 93 mins.)

Midway (1976)** Charlton Heston, Henry Fonda, Glenn Ford, James Coburn, Hal Holbrook, Toshiro Mifune, Robert Mitchum, Edward Albert, Cliff Robertson, Robert Wagner. The decisive air-sea battle off Midway Island in the Pacific during WW II, which turned the odds in favor of the U.S. over Japan, is painstakingly recreated via newsreel footage and expensively staged battle scenes. For WW II buffs, this is an interesting account of the historical event, but the personal drama, which is played out between the actual battle sequences, slows things up greatly. The all-star cast is uniformly fine. Henry Fonda is a spunky Admiral Chester Nimitz. (Dir: Jack Smight, 132 mins.)

Mighty Crusaders, The (Italian, 1961) *½ Francisco Rabal, Sylva Koscina, Gianna Maria Canale, Rik Battaglia. Crusader falls in love with a Saracen princess who fights with her army, while another is seduced and captured by the King's daughter—it all winds up in a big battle. Poorly done historical spectacle, dubbed-in English. (Dir: Carlo Ludovico Bragaglia, 87 mins.)

Mighty Joe Young (1949)*** Robert Armstrong, Ben Johnson, Terry Moore. Press agent finds a huge gorilla in Africa, brings it back as a night club act. Entertaining trick film, of the "King Kong'" school. (Dir: Ernest B. Schoedsack, 94 mins.)

Mighty Jungle, The (1964)*½ Marshall Thompson, Dave da Lie. Two explorers go their ways, one to the Amazon, the other to the Congo. Some interesting jungle scenes in a mishmash adventure that looks like it was originally two unrelated films strung together.

Mighty McGurk, The (1946)** Wallace Beery, Dean Stockwell, Edward Arnold, Cameron Mitchell. Contrived and confused drama about an ex-fighter who befriends an orphan boy. Don't think it will remind you of Beery's classic "The Champ" because it definitely won't. (Dir: John Waters, 85 mins.)

Mighty Ursus (Italian, 1962)*½ Ed Fury, Cristina Gajoni. Muscle man saves a kingdom, but not the film. (Dir: Carlo Campogalliani, 92 mins.)

Mikado, The (British, 1939)***½ Kenny Baker, Jean Colin, Martyn Green. The Gilbert and Sullivan operetta of shenanigans in the High Court of old Japan, with a wand'ring minstrel wooing a noble lady. Colorfully done, excellently sung. (Dir: Victor Schertzinger, 90 mins.)

Mildred Pierce (1945)*** Joan Crawford, Zachary Scott, Jack Carson. This adaptation of a James Cain novel was a big hit but it's not a great movie. Miss Crawford is superb but the characters are not too believable. Ann Blyth as Joan's vicious daughter is the character you must accept as real to enjoy the picture. If you can do that, you'll find it an engrossing melodrama. (Dir: Michael Curtiz, 111 mins.)

Milkman, The (1951)** Jimmy Durante, Donald O'Connor, Piper Laurie. A waste of talented people—this lightweight comedy with songs about a couple of milkmen and their escapades offers a few laughs. The stars work hard but the material is mediocre. Dir: Charles Barton, 87 mins.)

Mill of the Stone Women (Italian, 1963)*½ Pierre Brice, Scilla Gabel. Professor needs young girls to keep his daughter alive, turns their bodies into stone statues. Repulsive horror thriller dubbed in English.

Millhouse, a White Comedy (1971) ***½ A harsh satiric "documentary" about Richard Milhous Nixon released long before it became generally acceptable to display a clear, unashamed bias against Richard M. Nixon. (Nixon's flunkies harassed filmmaker de Antonio at the time of the release of this film, and did what they could to prevent its getting substantial distribution or TV coverage. The only TV exposure for the filmmaker and parts of "Millhouse" when first released came on a program called "All About TV," broadcast on the public TV station WNYC-TV in New York.) Filmmaker calls this a "comedy" in the tradition of the Marx

Brothers. "Millhouse" does offer a chance to see virtually all of Nixon's famous "Checkers" speech, and there are some other unflattering scenes of the ex-President for whom the filmmaker obviously has the most profound contempt. An incisive study, in its own terms, of the complex former President, and it deals harshly and mockingly with Nixon long before the TV network news ever began to report truthfully, and in depth, about Nixon's many swinish acts. (Dir: Emile de Antonio, 92 mins.)

Million Dollar Baby (1941)** Ronald Reagan, Priscilla Lane, Jeffrey Lynn. If you think girls who are poor and suddenly get a million dollars should give it up so their boy friend will still love them you may actually enjoy this Hollywood nonsense. (Dir: Curtis Bernhardt, 100 mins.)

Million Dollar Legs (1932)***½ W. C. Fields, Jack Oakie. Silly but funny political farce about a mythical kingdom. Never miss a chance to see Mr. Fields. (Dir: Edward Cline, 70 mins.)

Million Dollar Mermaid (1952)**½ Esther Williams, Victor Mature, Walter Pidgeon. At least the casting is most appropriate for this biography of swimmer Annette Kellerman, which is highly fictionized but good-spirited entertainment. (Dir: Mervyn Le Roy, 115 mins.)

Million Dollar Rip-Off, The (1976) *½ Freddie Prinze, Allen Garfield, Christine Belford, Brooke Mills. Caper with Freddie Prinze and four sexy broads, tells the story of a big payroll heist filled with characters double-crossing one another. The jazzy ending will be familiar to audiences who remember the movie "Ocean's 11." Made-for-TV. (Dir: Alexander Singer, 72 mins.)

Million Eyes of Su-Muru, The (Great Britain, 1967)*½ Shirley Eaton, Frankie Avalon, George Nader. The sultry, wily Su-Muru (Eaton) heads a gang of terrorist females plotting to conquer all mankind, beginning in Indonesia. The CIA and British Intelligence recruit Nader and Avalon to investigate. Tongue-in-cheek nonsense based on books and characters created by Sax Rohmer. (Dir: Lindsay Shonteff, 84 mins.)

Millionaire for Christy, A (1951)** Fred MacMurray, Eleanor Parker.

A secretary goes on the make for a millionaire, and lands him. Mild comedy. (Dir: George Marshall, 91 mins.)

Millionairess, The (British, 1960)**½ Sophia Loren, Peter Sellers, Vittorio De Sica. George Bernard Shaw's comedy about a millionairess and her pursuit of happiness and true love reaches the screen somewhat diluted but Sophia Loren and Peter Sellers keep things bouncing. Miss Loren plays the very rich lady of the title and Sellers is a dedicated Indian doctor who isn't interested in her or her money (silly boy). The supporting cast includes Alastair Sim, Vittorio De Sica, and Gary Raymond. It's not top-drawer Shaw but entertaining nevertheless. Directed by Anthony Asquith. (90 mins.)

Mind Benders, The (British, 1962) **½ Dirk Bogarde, Mary Ure, John Clements. Scientist engages in an experiment to test complete isolation from all the normal senses, emerges a psychological wreck, which imperils his domestic life. Drama begins well, slowly goes downhill as it progresses; good performances. (Dir: Basil Dearden, 101 mins.)

Mind of Mr. Soames, The (1970)**½ Terence Stamp, Robert Vaughn. Interesting situation marred by false characterizations. Mr. Soames (Stamp) is a 30-year-old man who has been in a coma since birth. He is to be operated on and brought to life by Dr. Bergen (Vaughn). Dir: Alan Cooke, 95 mins.)

Mine Own Executioner (British, 1949)***½ Burgess Meredith, Kieron Moore. A psychiatrist practicing without a medical degree finds trouble in his domestic life as well as with his patients. Well made drama, informative, with some tense situations. (Dir: Anthony Kimmens, 103 mins.)

Mini-Skirt Mob, The (1968)* Diane McBain, Jeremy Slate, Sherry Jackson, Patty McCormack. Female cyclists bent on revenge and terror. Puerile on all counts. (Dir: Maury Dexter, 82 mins.)

Ministry of Fear (1945)***½ Ray Milland, Marjorie Reynolds. Exciting, off-beat spy melodrama, set in wartime England and based on a Graham Greene novel. Good direction and an interesting, mysterious story. (Dir: Fritz Lang, 85 mins.)

Miniver Story, The (British, 1950)**

Greer Garson, Walter Pidgeon, John Hodiak. Peace comes to England after World War II, but not to the Miniver family—daughter's in the midst of a romantic attachment, while Mrs. Miniver discovers personal tragedy. Weepy drama, a travesty of the original "Mrs. Miniver" film. Dir: H. C. Potter, 104 mins.)

Minnesota Clay (Italy-France-Spain, 1966)½ Cameron Mitchell, Ethel Rojo, Georges Riviere. Following fad of spaghetti-western heroes, Mitchell plays "Minnesota Clay," an old gunfighter with faulty eyesight who has been unjustly imprisoned. Wooden acting. (Dir: Sergio Corbucci, 100 mins.)

Minnie and Moskowitz (1971)***½ Gena Rowlands, Seymour Cassel, Val Avery. Moving study of two dissimilar but lonely people whose unlikely romance illuminates the screen, thanks to the fine performances of Gena Rowlands and Seymour Cassel. Minnie is an art curator at the Los Angeles County Art Museum, with a duplex apartment and a large library. Moskowitz is a parking-lot attendant, and they meet when Minnie's blind date threatens her in Moskowitz's lot. The friendly animosity that builds into their romance forms the basis for a touching love story. (Dir: John Cassavetes, 114 mins.)

Minotaur, Wild Beast of Crete (Italian, 1961)** Bob Mathias, Rosanna Schiaffino. Muscleman faces the dangers brought on by a wicked queen. Schiaffino superstructure is solely responsible for rating. (Dir: Silvio Amadeo, 92 mins.)

Minute to Pray, a Second to Die, A (Italian, 1967)*½ Gunfighter takes on a town full of baddies. Alex Cord, Robert Ryan, Arthur Kennedy should have their passports revoked for taking part in this Mediterranean version of the Old West. (Dir: Franco Giraldi, 97 mins.)

Miracle, The (1959)**½ Carroll Baker, Roger Moore, Walter Slezak. An ambitious effort to bring Max Reinhardt's epic play about a girl and her rebellion with God to the screen. Carroll Baker is miscast and the overblown production values can't overcome the empty melodramatics. (Dir: Irving Rapper, 121 mins.)

Miracle in the Rain (1956)**½ Jane Wyman, Van Johnson. Sentimental women's picture about a lonely young woman (Wyman) who meets a young soldier (Johnson) and falls in love. Their joy is interrupted when he ships out but Jane holds on to the hope that he'll come back. The two stars do well and there's a good supporting performance by Eileen Heckart, as Jane's friend. (Dir: Rudolph Mate, 107 mins.)

Miracle of Marcelino, The (French, 1955)**** Pablito Calvo, Rafael Rivelles. A beautiful and heart warming film about a little orphan boy, who is raised by monks, and is visited by Christ in a miracle. Pablito Calvo gives a touching performance as Marcelino.

Miracle of Morgan's Creek (1944)**** Betty Hutton, Eddie Bracken, Diana Lynn, William Demarest. The real miracle here is director Preston Sturges, and the way in which he was able to deal, comically to be sure, with a theme that would not have been allowed by the censors at the time if it had been depicted solemnly. Small-town girl (Hutton) gets drunk and becomes pregnant, thanks to one of a variety of obliging GI's. The problem is that Betty can't remember which soldier is the daddy-to-be. The "miracle" concerns the way in which the problem is resolved. Thanks to a fine script and the director's deft touch this is one of the most perceptive and enduring American comedies of the 1940's. (Dir: Preston Sturges, 99 mins.)

Miracle of Our Lady of Fatima, The (1952)*** Gilbert Roland, Frank Silvera, Susan Whitney. An interesting treatment of the story of three peasant children who witnessed a vision in the small Portuguese village of Fatima in 1917. Well acted by a large cast. (Dir: John Brahm, 102 mins.)

Miracle of the Bells (1948)*½ Fred MacMurray, Valli, Frank Sinatra. A movie queen dies, and is taken to her home town to be buried, where a miracle takes place. Long, terribly trite and sentimental drama, badly acted, lumberingly presented. (Dir: Irving Pichel, 120 mins.)

Miracle of the Hills (1959)** Rex Reason, Nan Leslie. New minister meets plenty of opposition when he attempts to reactivate a parish in a wide-open mining town. Pleasing unsophisticated western drama. (Dir: Paul Landres, 73 mins.)

Miracle on 34th Street (1947)**** Edmund Gwenn, John Payne, Maureen O'Hara. Kris Kringle is hired to play Santa Claus at Macy's and that begins the most delightful combination of fantasy, whimsy, heart-warming humor and perfect screen entertainment. For young and old and all who want to believe in Santa. (Dir: George Seaton, 96 mins.)

Miracle Worker, The (1962)**** Anne Bancroft, Patty Duke. Superb film version of the brilliant Broadway play by William Gibson dealing with the early training period of Helen Keller. Miss Bancroft deserved the Oscar she won for the role of Miss Keller's teacher, Annie Sullivan. Patty Duke is equally effective in the role of young Miss Keller. Fine direction by Arthur Penn. (107 mins.)

Mirage (1965)*** Gregory Peck, Diane Baker, Walter Matthau. Man who believes he has amnesia starts to retrace his past, becomes involved in a murder plot. Suspense thriller starts off well. Mystery fans will like it, although it's never quite believable. Good production. (Dir: Edward Dmytryk, 109 mins.)

Miranda (British, 1948)**½ Glynis Johns, Griffith Jones. Physician on a holiday away from his wife snags an amorous mermaid while fishing. Mildly entertaining fantasy-comedy. (Dir: Ken Annakin, 80 mins.)

Mirror Has Two Faces, The (French, 1959)** Michele Morgan, Bourvil. Doctor performs plastic surgery on a plain-looking married woman, makes her a beauty and changes her life—not for the better. Slick treatment of an old soap opera idea. Well made and well acted, but still pretty hackneyed. English-dubbed. (Dir: Andre Cayette, 98 mins.)

Misfits, The (1961)*** Clark Gable, Marilyn Monroe, Montgomery Clift, Eli Wallach. Arthur Miller's original screenplay about a group of modern-day cowboys and a frightened divorcee turns out to be more a curiosity piece than good film drama. The best defined role is played by Montgomery Clift and he is the acting standout in the film. The dialogue often slows up the pace but there's a slam-bang wild horse roundup towards the end which compensates somewhat for the faulty

script. Gable's last film. (Dir: John Huston, 124 mins.)

Miss Grant Takes Richmond (1949)*** Lucille Ball, William Holden. Clever comedy about a secretarial school that is actually a front for a bookie syndicate. Lucy and William Holden make a good comedy team. (Dir: Lloyd Bacon, 87 mins.)

Miss Robin Hood (British, 1953)**½ Margaret Rutherford, Richard Hearne. The meek writer of girls' adventure stories aids a battle axe in repossessing her recipe for whisky which was stolen by a distiller. Screwball comedy isn't quite as funny as it was meant to be. Mild. (Dir: John Guillerman, 78 mins.)

Miss Sadie Thompson (1954)**½ Rita Hayworth, Jose Ferrer, Aldo Ray. The sultry saga of sinful Sadie Thompson is once more on view in this fair remake of Somerset Maugham's "Rain." Rita plays the island sinner this time while Jose Ferrer screams of fire and brimstone as "Mr." Davidson. (Dir: Curtis Bernhardt, 91 mins.)

Miss Susie Slagle's (1946) Sonny Tufts, Joan Caulfield. Leisurely, pleasant story about a boarding house for medical students in Baltimore around 1910. Inoffensive and generally entertaining. (Dir: John Berry, 88 mins.)

Miss Tatlock's Millions (1949)***½ John Lund, Wanda Hendrix. Movie stunt man agrees to pose as the feeble-minded heir to a fortune. Plenty of laughs in this sparkling comedy. (Dir: Richard Haydn, 100 mins.)

Missile Base at Taniak (1953-66)*½ Bill Henry, Susan Morrow, Arthur Space. Feature version of serial "Canadian Mounties vs. Atomic Invaders." Foreign agents plan to send atomic weapons at Canadian and American cities, but not while a mountie and a girl undercover agent are on the trail. Routine lowgrade adventure shows its serial origins. (Dir. Franklin Adreon, 100 mins.)

Missing Are Deadly, The (1975)*½ Ed Nelson, Leonard Nimoy, Jose Ferrer, Gary Morgan. A mini-crisis film! A disturbed 15-year-old boy takes a rat from his scientist-father's lab, not knowing it is carrying a deadly virus. The boy joins his brother and his brother's girl friend on a camping trip, and the epidemic begins. Some suspense!

Made-for-TV. (Dir: Don McDougall, 72 mins.)

Mission Batangas (1968)** Dennis Weaver, Vera Miles, Keith Larsen. Grade B adventure set during WW II in the Philippines. An American pilot stumbles upon a plan to commandeer the Philippine government's stock of gold bullion, but circumstances, both good and bad, interfere. (Dir: Keith Larsen, 100 mins.)

Mission Mars (1967)* Darren McGavin, Nick Adams, Heather Hewitt. The first manned rocket from Earth lands on Mars and finds some strange and rather uninteresting forces at work. The real star is a huge ball that swallows anything. Only for diehard sci-fi fans. (Dir: Nick Webster, 95 mins.)

Mission of the Sea Hawk (British, 1962)** Terence Morgan, Jean Kent. Sir Francis Drake journeys to France searching for a missing nobleman. Feature version of the TV series "Sir Francis Drake," better produced than the usual run—passable costume adventure.

Mission Over Korea (1953)** John Derek, John Hodiak, Audrey Totter. Typical war story with romantic sidelines. Two officers argue about their jobs in the Korean conflict and later show their true colors to one another. (Dir: Fred F. Sears, 85 mins.)

Mission Stardust (Italian, 1968)* Essy Persson, Lang Jeffries. Strange happenings in outer space as a space expedition from Earth is forced to land on the Moon by some robots who are after a cure for some strange disease affecting their race. Your brain has a strange disease if you like this spaghetti space yarn. (Dir: Primo Zeglio, 95 mins.)

Mission to Hell (German, 1964)* Paul Hubschmid, Marianne Hold, Horst Frank. Newshawk passes himself off as a diamond merchant, comes upon a smuggling operation in Bangkok. Trashy and inept adventure melodrama dubbed in English.

Mission to Morocco (1959)*½ Lex Barker, Julie Reding. Slow moving and inept yarn about an American oil business man who ties up some murders with a ruthless plot to take control of very important oil deposits.

Mission to Moscow (1943)***½ Walter Huston, Eleanor Parker. This is a fine, well-played movie adaptation from the book by former ambassador to Russia Joseph Davies but that is not why it's a must today. This film was widely applauded in 1943 and you might be interested in learning what a former diplomat to Russia thought of today's potential enemy in the early '40's. (Dir: Michael Curtiz, 123 mins.)

Mission to Venice (French, 1963)*½ Sean Flynn, Madeleine Robinson. Sleuth undertakes to find a missing husband in Venice, uncovers a ring of spies. Mediocre melodrama is dubbed in English.

Mississippi (1935)*** Bing Crosby, W. C. Fields, Joan Bennett. Pleasant musical about a young man who refuses to fight a duel and takes refuge as a singer on a show boat. A few good Rodgers and Hart tunes, plus Fields' work as the captain add up to nice entertainment. (Dir: A. Edward Sutherland, 80 mins.)

Mississippi Gambler (1953)*** Tyrone Power, Piper Laurie, Julie Adams. Colorful romantic-adventure with Tyrone Power perfectly cast as a dashing gambler who played for high stakes in matters of love, honor, and reputation. Piper Laurie is equally effective as a spirited, headstrong southern belle. Good escapist entertainment. (Dir: Rudolph Mate, 98 mins.)

Mississippi Gambler (Kent Taylor) —See: Danger on the River

Mississippi Summer (1968)½ J. A. Preston, Robert Earl Jones. A really terrible, clumsy, if well-intentioned film about a group of committed inter-racial civil rights workers, working in Mississippi in the summer of 1964. Embarrassingly badly written and directed by William Bayer, who made a tedious fiction film while trying to capture the look of a documentary. (Dir: William Bayer, 88 mins.)

Missouri Breaks, The (1976)**½ Marlon Brando, Jack Nicholson, Harry Dean Stanton, Kathleen Lloyd. An enormously disappointing, muddled Western set in Montana during the 1880's. The Missouri Breaks is the name of the headwaters of the Missouri river in Montana, but the audience doesn't get many breaks from this "Missouri." It may not be fair to criticize director Arthur Penn too harshly, because he reportedly had to cater to Brando's every whim, however absurd, including making inane alterations in the script. Brando's performance, as in so many of his other films, is maddening. He reminds you often enough of what a truly remarkable actor he is, and then you get angry watching him over-act in such a badly conceived part. Sometimes Marlon sports an Irish brogue, playing a Western lawman, sometimes not. Jack Nicholson gives the best acting performance in the film. Brando's and Nicholson's scenes together are curiously undramatic. Quirkish screenplay by Thomas McGuane. (Dir: Arthur Penn, 126 mins.)

Missouri Traveler, The (1958)**½ Brandon de Wilde, Lee Marvin, Gary Merrill. Exaggerated piece of Americana about a young runaway boy who provides for himself by training racing horses. Thinly plotted, but some good acting by Marvin, and de Wilde as the boy, save the picture. Paul Ford has a small humorous role. (Dir: Jerry Hopper, 103 mins.)

Mister—See also Mr.

Mister Buddwing (1966)** James Garner, Jean Simmons. One of those awful movies which you can sit back and enjoy provided you don't take the plot seriously for a minute. It has James Garner as an amnesiac running all over New York City (good on-location shots) trying to find out who he is, and why he can't remember anything. The ladies who help him along the way include Jean Simmons as a flighty rich lady, Angela Lansbury as a sympathetic woman, Katharine Ross as a pretty young thing and Suzanne Pleshette as an aspiring actress. (Dir: Delbert Mann, 100 mins.)

Mister Cory (1957)***½ Tony Curtis, Martha Hyer, Kathryn Grant. Fast, rowdy, fun-filled story of a lad from the Chicago slums who grows up to be a big-time gambler. Slick direction, well-written script, nice performance by Curtis and supporting players. (Dir: Blake Edwards, 92 mins.)

Mister Freedom (France, 1968)* Delphine Seyrig, Philippe Noiret, Donald Pleasence, Yves Montand, Daniel Cohn-Bendit, Simone Signoret. Muddled political diatribe written and directed by William Klein, a native American and long-time resident of Paris. A savage, witless cartoon about American foreign policy, is politically naive and visually tiresome. (Dir: William Klein, 95 mins.)

Mister Jericho (1970)**½ Patrick Macnee, Connie Stevens, Herbert Lom. If you go for jewel-thief capers all done up with slick production values, good on-location Riviera backgrounds and fast-paced gimmicks, this made-for-TV feature will fill the bill. Patrick Macnee plays the ingenious con artist with a definite flair and he's matched by Herbert Lom, as an eccentric millionaire. O.K. time-passer. (Dir: Sidney Hayers, 85 mins.)

Mister Moses (1965)** Robert Mitchum, Carroll Baker. Robert Mitchum and the blonde Miss Baker take a back seat to the glorious on-location African scenery in this mild adventure epic. Mitchum is involved in gem smuggling. (Dir: Ronald Neame, 113 mins.)

Mister Rock 'n Roll (1957)* Alan Freed, Rocky Graziano. Disc jockey persuades a newspaper editor that all rock-'n-roll addicts aren't juvenile delinquents. Tiresome melange of rock-'n-roll acts, which are a relief from that plot.

Mistress, The (Japanese, 1959)**½ English-dubbed drama of a girl who sells herself into slavery in order to support her ailing father. Japanese locale has novelty, but the movement is often extremely studied, slow moving.

Mistress of the World (German, 1959)** Martha Hyer, Carlos Thompson, Gino Cervi, Sabu. Wild sci-fi tale of a professor whose invention for controlling the world's magnetic fields is imperilled by Chinese agents. Lavishly produced, first-rate cast stuck in pure junk—but it's fun if not taken seriously.

Misty (1961)**½ David Ladd, Arthur O'Connell, Pam Smith. Good adventure story for the kids, as two young children try to tame "Misty," a wild horse. David Ladd (Alan Ladd's son) plays the wholesome young boy. Filmed on location on the islands of Chincoteague and Assateague off the coast of Maryland. (Dir: James B. Clark, 92 mins.)

Mix Me a Person (British, 1961)**½ Anne Baxter, Adam Faith, Donald Sinden. Teenage guitarist finds himself charged with murder when a policeman is killed. Uneven drama has some absorbing scenes, fairly good performances.

Mixed Company (1974)* Barbara Harris, Joseph Bologna. An objectionable, heavy-handed farce clumsily produced and directed by Melville Shavelson, who also directed this tasteless stew. The talented Barbara Harris, making one of her infrequent film appearances, is wasted in this simple-minded treatment of an important subject—an American couple with three children of their own adopting first a young black boy and then two more minority youngsters, including a Vietnamese girl. (Dir: Melville Shavelson, 109 mins.)

M.M.M. 83 (Italian, 1965)*½ Pier Angeli, Fred Beir, Gerard Bain. Secret agent investigates the murder of a professor who has invented a revolutionary new engine. Tiresome spy thriller; dubbed-in English, the same who's-got-the-papers routine.

Moana (1925)**** Ta'avale, Tama. One of the earliest feature-length documentaries and it remains one of the best ever made. (A new version has just been released with a new musical score added.) "Moana" is the name of a young Polynesian boy on the island of Samoa. This historic documentary directed by Robert Flaherty with the help of his wife, Frances Hubbard Flaherty, documents typical events in the life of a Samoan youth at that time. A beautiful lyrical film which had a profound impact, together with other Flaherty films, on the development of documentary and ethnographic filmmaking. Filmed on location in Samoa. (Dirs: Robert Flaherty, Frances Hubbard Flaherty, 77 mins.)

Mob, The (1951)*** Broderick Crawford, Ernest Borgnine. Good gangland film about a policeman's joining the "mob" in order to get to the big boys. Well acted, snappy dialogue. (Dir: Robert Parrish, 87 mins.)

Moby Dick (British, 1956)*** Gregory Peck, Orson Welles, Richard Basehart and Leo Genn. Director John Huston's filming of the classic Herman Melville symbolic story of Capt. Ahab and his maniacal chase to destroy the giant whale becomes a pretty good film instead of a great one

thanks to the leading role—Gregory Peck gives a notably dull and leaden performance. It's overlong but still well worth seeing. (116 mins.)

Model and the Marriage Broker, The (1952)*** Jeanne Crain, Thelma Ritter, Scott Brady. The marriage broker of the title is none other than wisecracking Thelma Ritter and the model for whom she performs her service is lovely Jeanne Crain. Scott Brady plays the handsome young swain whom cupid Ritter pigeonholes for Miss Crain and getting them together takes up most of the running time. Director George Cukor is a master at this type of sophisticated comedy. (Dir: George Cukor, 103 mins.)

Model for Murder (British, 1959)** Keith Andes, Hazel Court. Ordinary British murder mystery involving a search by an American officer for his dead brother's girl friend. (Dir: Terry Bishop, 75 mins.)

Modern Times (1936)**** Charles Chaplin, Paulette Goddard. One of the all-time greats, a sensational one-man show by Chaplin, writing, directing, producing, scoring, and starring in this eternal saga of everyman in all times. The Tramp moves from factory worker to department-store janitor to singing waiter, as modern times knock him cruelly about. Chaplin sums up his themes with the remarkable image of the assembly-line worker who only has to turn two screws, a job he performs whether or not he is on the line. An unbelievable exhibition of roller skating and Chaplin double-talking a song in French along the way as we follow the bouncing ball throughout—"Smile, though your heart is breaking . . . smile, smile, smile . . ." (Dir: Charles Chaplin, 100 mins.)

Modesty Blaise (British, 1966)*½ Monica Vitti, Terence Stamp, Dirk Bogarde. Modesty Blaise equals movie critic blasé! That's not much of a joke I admit, but it's about as droll and witty as anything you'll find in this lumbering film offering the comic-strip adventures of sexy super agent Modesty played by Vitti. It's all filled with beautiful sets and beautiful people in flimsy gowns—but it's so leaden you probably won't give a damn. Lots of talented people including director Joseph Losey bumbled on this one—maybe because of a costume supervisor named Bumble Dawson. (119 mins.)

Mogambo (1953)*** Clark Gable, Ava Gardner, Grace Kelly. This is a remake of "Red Dust" which starred Gable and Jean Harlow. Gable repeats his role of the white hunter whose life is complicated by two beautiful women—Ava and Princess Grace. Gardner gives one of the best performances of her career in a very colorful role. (Dir: John Ford, 115 mins.)

Mole Men Against the Son of Hercules (Italian, 1963)* Mark Forest, Moira Orfei. Muscleman saves a village from night-creeping monsters. Ridiculous English-dubbed adventure.

Molly (1951)**½ Gertrude Berg, Philip Loeb. Life with the Goldbergs, as Molly's former suitor pays the family a visit. Devotees of the long-running radio and TV show will like it—others will find it mildly amusing. (Dir: Walter Hart, 83 mins.)

Molly and Me (1945)*** Monty Woolley, Gracie Fields. Well played warm comedy about a maid who straightens out her employer's life. Not hilarious but a very pleasant diversion. (Dir: Lewis Seiler, 76 mins.)

Molly Maguires, The (1969)**½ Sean Connery, Richard Harris, Samantha Eggar. Often interesting but ultimately disappointing film about the hardships of coal miners in Pennsylvania during the 1870's, and focusing on the acts of the Molly Maguires, a real-life secret society trying to improve miners' conditions. Their terrorism, directed at mining officials and uncooperative members of their own community, intimidated western Pennsylvania coal-mining towns for two decades. James McParlan (Harris) is a Pinkerton detective and manages to infiltrate the Molly Maguires using an assumed name. One of the recurring themes of songwriter Walter Bernstein and director Martin Ritt—their ambivalent attitude toward the acts of violence committed by the Mollies—is, ironically, one of the weaknesses of the film in the end, because the audience finds it difficult to identify with either of the warring sides. (Shot on location in Eckley, Pa., which some civic boosters say is the ugliest town in America. Aided by the money Paramount spent to "uglify" the town, Eckley now considers itself a historical resource, and has a mining museum.) (125 mins.)

Moment of Truth, The (French, 1952) ** Michele Morgan, Jean Gabin, Daniel Gelin. An actress and her doctor husband are celebrating their tenth wedding anniversary when a stranger, who has attempted suicide, disrupts their life. Even the divine Michele Morgan can't triumph over the cumbersome plot. (Dir: Jean Delannoy, 90 mins.)

Moment to Moment (1966)**½ Jean Seberg, Sean Garrison, Honor Blackman. Wanting to end an illicit affair, a young wife accidentally shoots her paramour, then frantically tries to hide the body—which disappears. Creaky plot, with the audience always one step ahead—but the production's pretty and the players pleasant. (Dir: Mervyn Le Roy, 108 mins.)

Mona Kent (1961)* Sandra Donat, Johnny Olson. Farm girl tries to avoid the pitfalls of the big city as she becomes a Broadway star. Trashy, inept fast-buck drama.

Mondo Cane (Italian, 1963)**½ Documentary spoken in English—a look at the more sensational side of life, ranging from bizarre ceremonies to rather nauseating tastes in food throughout the world. Some sequences patently staged; despite the phoniness it holds the interest in a repelling sort of way. (105 mins.)

Money from Home (1953)** Dean Martin, Jerry Lewis, Pat Crowley. Dean and Jerry are on the spot when Dino's IOU's start showing up and a mobster tells him to pay up or else help throw a horse race. Strained comedy based on a Damon Runyon story is below the Martin-Lewis level. Strictly for their fans. (Dir: George Marshall, 99 mins.)

Money Talks (1972)**½ Allen Funt of TV's "Candid Camera" fame produced and directed this film, which puts people in situations where avarice might get the better of them. Using his hidden-camera technique, he photographs such scenes as bowls of free money on the street or girls dropping greenbacks. The movie only proves that the people he interviews and tests are not obsessed with money. Amusing diversion. (81 mins.)

Money to Burn (1973)**½ E. G. Marshall, Mildred Natwick, Alejandro Rey, Cleavon Little. Fun. A sympathetic cast portrays a counterfeiting group with a grand design to exchange their bogus bills for the real thing. The pace, the people, the plot and the dialogue all have a sense of humorous larceny, making you root for the gang! Made-for-TV. (Dir: Robert Michael Lewis, 72 mins.)

Money Trap, The (1965)** Glenn Ford, Elke Sommer, Rita Hayworth, Joseph Cotten, Ricardo Montalban. Familiar fare about an honest cop driven to dishonest deed by his sexy, money-hungry wife. Ford and Sommer fit their roles nicely, but it's Rita Hayworth who comes off best, in a supporting role as an embittered woman who has turned to alcohol for solace. (Dir: Burt Kennedy, 92 mins.)

Money, Women and Guns (1959)**½ Jock Mahoney, Kim Hunter, Tim Hovey. When an old prospector is bushwhacked, his will specifies four people as beneficiaries: a detective goes after the heirs and the killer. Offbeat western with an element of whodunit, nicely done. (Dir: Richard Bartlett, 80 mins.)

Mongols, The (1960)**½ Jack Palance, Anita Ekberg. Italian produced adventure epic, dubbed in English. Palance is tall and ugly, Anita is tall and pretty, the story just tall. (Dir: Andre de Toth, 102 mins.)

Mongo's Back in Town (1971)***½ Joe Don Baker. The author of the book on which this movie is based is a convict, and he understandably doesn't think TV crime shows have much to do with reality. His name is E. Richard Johnson and his unvarnished version is certainly different. Tough, rough, arresting Christmas yarn about a San Pedro killer who returns to help his brother out of a jam over counterfeit plates. The plot is complicated, but the characters and dialogue, and the acting of Baker as Mongo and of Sally Field are splendid. Reality, as Johnson sees it, may be hard on TV fans used to sugarcoating, but it proves to be fascinating material. Made-for-TV. (Dir: Marvin Chomsky, 73 mins.)

Monitors, The (1969)* Guy Stockwell, Keenan Wynn, Ed Begley. Confused tale about intelligent creatures from outer space who come to Earth to impose a rule of peace. Intelligent idea becomes muddled by an ineffectual point of view which switches between farce, satire, and seriousness. Inept direction. (Dir: Jack Shea, 90 mins.)

Monk, The (1969)*** George Maharis, Janet Leigh, Carl Betz, Jack Albertson, Raymond St. Jacques. Good made-for-TV yarn. This is one of those typical private-eye crime tales in which the hero spouts glib dialogue, the plot is totally incredible, and the writers manage to come up with a plot gimmick every 20 minutes or so. George Maharis is fine as the hero, Gus Monk, and he gets excellent support from the San Francisco backgrounds. We won't bore you with plot details because the story never interferes with the action. (Dir: George McCowan, 73 mins.)

Monkey Business (1931)**** Marx Brothers. Great comedy is never dated and even Groucho's depression puns will still make you laugh. The boys are stowaways on a ship and causing their usual amount of trouble. (Dir: Norman McLeod, 77 mins.)

Monkey Business (1952)*** Cary Grant, Ginger Rogers, Marilyn Monroe. Zany and often hilarious comedy about a scientist (Grant) who discovers a rejuvenation tonic and tries it out himself with surprising results. La Monroe has a small but funny part as a foil for Grant's comic shenanigans. (Dir: Howard Hawks, 97 mins.)

Monkey in Winter, A (France, 1962) *** Jean Gabin, Jean-Paul Belmondo. Two great male stars of French cinema discover they are kindred spirits, in this mild, unembellished, anecdotal tale of an old and young man who postpone reality for a day of drinking and dreams. (Dir: Henri Verneuil, 104 mins.)

Monkey on My Back (1957)*** Cameron Mitchell, Dianne Foster. Often interesting dramatized biography of boxer Barney Ross, his early rise to fame in the ring, his high spending days as a gambler, his heroic career in the Marines during WW II; and his eventual downfall to narcotics addiction and his struggle to "kick the habit." Brutal at times in its realism, with

481

helpful performance from Mitchell. (Dir: Andre de Toth, 93 mins.)

Monkeys, Go Home (1967)* Dean Jones, Maurice Chevalier, Yvette Mimieux. Bland Disney concoction for the kids. Dean Jones inherits an olive farm in France and hires some chimpanzees to help him pick the crop. Chevalier, as a local priest, has a cute song. Mimieux is charming, if badly used, as Jones' housekeeper. Lots of slapstick nonsense involving the chimps. (Dir: Andrew McLaglen, 101 mins.)

Monocle, The (French, 1964)* Paul Meurisse, Barbara Steele, Marcel Dalio. Secret agent battles terrorists in Hong Kong. Weak spy thriller dubbed in English, with an offensive characterization of the "hero."

Monolith Monsters, The (1957)** Grant Williams, Lois Albright. Strange deaths occur after a meteor shatters in the California desert. A geologist discovers why, at the risk of his life. Standard sci-fi thriller. (Dir: John Sherwood, 77 mins.)

Monpti (West Germany, 1957)*½ Romy Schneider, Horst Buchholz. Young lovers in Paris, in a story overwhelmed by cloying sentiment and morality. But the Parisian artists' quarter is nicely photographed, and Schneider and Buchholz make believable, attractive lovers. (Dir: Helmut Kautner, 97 mins.)

Monsieur Beaucaire (1946)***½ Bob Hope, Joan Caulfield. Zany Hope film about a timid barber in the court of France's Louis XV who by some accident is sent to Spain to marry a princess. Loads of fun, and the kids will love it. (Dir: George Marshall, 93 mins.)

Monsieur Gangster (French, 1960)**½ Lino Ventura, Sabine Sinjen, Bernard Blier. Small businessman takes over a deceased friend's interests, which prove to be on the shady side of the law, with discontent bubbling among members of his new "gang." Minor but fairly entertaining crime story dubbed in English.

Monsieur Robinson Crusoe (French, 1959)** Darry Cowl, Beatrice Altariba. Foolish French farce about an amorous street peddler who goes from one adventure to another.

Monsieur Verdoux (1947)**** Charles Chaplin, Martha Raye, Isobel Elsom. Chaplin's ironic masterpiece, a moral fable set in the Depression era period after the stock-market crash, complete with notations about the rise of European fascism and the beginning of World War II. Charlie's not the Tramp in this one—the character is closer to Bluebeard, a bank clerk who turns to murder to provide for his wife and child. "Verdoux" is one of Chaplin's most sublime performances, played off against the hilarious vulgarity of Miss Raye, who goes fishing in silver-fox furs. (Dir: Charles Chaplin.)

Monster From a Prehistoric Planet (Japanese, 1963)* It arrives, it terrorizes, and a lot of Japanese actors run around looking grim and frightened. Aside from the trick camera work, this stinker has nothing except English-dubbed dialogue.

Monster from Green Hell (1957)** Jim Davis, Barbara Turner. Dull horror filled science fiction story about huge monsters discovered in the jungles of Africa.

Monster from the Surf (1965)* Jen Hall, Sue Casey. Series of murders seem to have been committed by some sort of sea monster, but the truth finally comes to light. Bungling horror thriller mixes teenagers and terror ineptly.

Monster of Piedras Blancas, The (1961)*½ Les Tremayne, Jeanne Carmen. Lighthouse keeper is convinced a legendary monster lives in a cave near him. Farfetched, mediocre horror thriller. (Irvin Berwick, 71 mins.)

Monster on the Campus (1958)**½ Arthur Franz, Joanna Moore, Troy Donahue. Scientist injects himself with blood of an ancient fish, turns into a monster. Shocker that delivers the goods—enough eeriness to keep the nails bitten down. (Dir: Jack Arnold, 76 mins.)

Monster That Challenged the World, The (1957)** Tim Holt, Audrey Dalton. Atomic experiments uncover sea beasts who begin their reign of terror. Standard science fiction horror thriller—better than some, should please the fans. (Dir: Arnold Laven, 83 mins.)

Montana (1950)** Errol Flynn, Alexis Smith. Cowboys help to make a state of Montana; based on a novel by Ernest Haycox. Alexis Smith was almost as pretty as Errol in those days. (Dir: Ray Enright, 76 mins.)

Montana Belle (1952)** Jane Russell, George Brent, Scott Brady. Belle

Starr throws in with the Dalton gang, but is persuaded to reform and turn against the outlaws. So-so western, nothing new. (Dir: Allan Dwan, 81 mins.)

Montana Mike (1947)**½ Robert Cummings, Brian Donlevy, Marjorie Reynolds. An angel comes to earth to help reform a western badman. Different kind of western story, pleasant. (Dir: Albert S. Rogell, 95 mins.)

Monte Carlo Baby (French, 1962)*½ Audrey Hepburn, Cara Williams, Jules Munshin. Through a mistake, band drummer thinks he is grandfather to a baby, takes the tyke with him on tour. Comedy that mostly misfires. Hepburn made this when she was an unknown English actress.

Monte Carlo Story, The (1957)** Marlene Dietrich, Vittorio De Sica. A fortune hunter and huntress meet in Monte Carlo and foolishly choose love in lieu of wealth. Glamorous settings including Marlene, are the sole assets of this French Riviera trifle. (Dir: Samuel Taylor, 100 mins.)

Monterey Pop (1969)***½ Janis Joplin, Jimi Hendrix, Jefferson Airplane, Ravi Shankar. Terrific documentary film for fans of contemporary pop, rock, folk-rock music, etc. Many leading artists and recording groups are shown in action at the Monterey International Pop Festival. (88 mins.)

Monty Python and the Holy Grail (Great Britain, 1974)*** Graham Chapman, John Cleese, Terry Gilliam, Eric Idle. Made by the same talented zanies responsible for the wacky TV series "Monty Python's Flying Circus." It's a series of very uneven satiric sketches filmed amongst the castles, lochs and moors of Scotland. The best of them are funny, knockout routines of a high order. Eric Idle looks astonishingly like Tyrone Power when dressed in his medieval costume guarding Swamp Castle, and there's another excruciatingly funny sketch of a "courageous" knight who continues to be pugnacious while gradually being dismembered. Coconut shells provide the sound of horses' hoofs in this lunatic kingdom. (Dirs: Terry Gilliam, Terry Jones, 90 mins.)

Moon and Sixpence, The (1942)***½ Somerset Maugham's dramatic story of a man with the urge to paint, and how he discards his conventional life to follow his calling. With George Sanders and Herbert Marshall. Thoughtfully done, tastefully performed. (Dir: Albert Lewin, 89 mins.)

Moon is Blue, The (1953)** William Holden, Maggie McNamara, David Niven. When this comedy about a "virgin" and her determined gentlemen pursuers was first released, it caused quite a stir. Considered daring for its spicy dialogue, frank depiction of the sexual chase, the film, based on the F. Hugh Herbert Broadway success, is now just a mild fizzle, to say the most. It's hard to believe, twenty years later, that the use of the word "virgin" resulted in the film creating such a furor and being banned in many markets in the U.S. (Dir: Otto Preminger, 95 mins.)

Moon is Down, The (1943)***½ Sir Cedric Hardwicke, Lee J. Cobb. Dated but powerful version of the Steinbeck story of the Nazi occupation of Norway. There's still some great moral lessons to be learned from this story. (Dir: Irving Pichel, 90 mins.)

Moon of the Wolf (1972)** David Janssen, Barbara Rush. Modern-day werewolf tale rekindles some of the chills and menace of the old Frankenstein-Dracula monster flicks. After the badly torn body of a young lady is discovered, Sheriff Janssen has his work cut out for him. Scenes in which the werewolf appears are played for spine-tingling terror, and they work for the most part. The cast includes Bradford Dillman and John Beradino. Made-for-TV. (Dir: Daniel Petrie, 73 mins.)

Moon Over Miami (1941)*** Betty Grable, Don Ameche, Robert Cummings. Routine but entertaining musical with the old plot about pretty girls in search of millionaires. Supposed shots of Miami in 1941 should amuse those who have seen recent photos. (Dir: Walter Lang, 91 mins.)

Moon Spinners, The (1964)*** Hayley Mills, Joan Greenwood, Eli Wallach, Peter McEnery, Irene Papas. Pleasant Disney production tells the story of a young English girl (Mills) and her aunt (Greenwood), who visit Crete and receive an odd, chilly reception. Tale about thieves and stolen gems. The scenery and supporting cast make it entertaining for the youngsters. Keep an eye out for silent-screen star Pola Negri, appearing as Madame Habib, a shady buyer of stolen goods. Negri came out of a 20-year retirement. Hayley Mills was a grown-up 18 when "Spinners" was made. (Dir: James Neilson, 118 mins.)

Moon Wolf (Italian, 1964)** Carl Moehner, Ann Savo. Mildly interesting tale of a savage wolf captured in Alaska and trained to be used in space research. Dubbed in English.

Moon Zero Two (1970)** James Olson, Catharina Von Schell. Ordinary sci-fi yarn made on a restricted budget. The Moon is now a colonized community and spaceman James Olson is involved in transporting and harnessing a mammoth sapphire to the Moon, but the bad guys have other, nefarious plans. (Dir: Roy Ward Baker, 96 mins.)

Moonfleet (1955)** Stewart Granger, Viveca Lindfors, Joan Greenwood, George Sanders. A tale of smugglers and blackguards in 18th century England. Granger plays the dashing adventurer, Jeremy Fox, who's always irting with danger. Despite the good cast, the film is disappointing but should appeal to adventure fans. (Dir: Fritz Lang, 89 mins.)

Moonlighter, The (1953)½ Barbara Stanwyck, Fred MacMurray. Dreary Western, stars MacMurray as a reprehensible cattle rustler willing to be reformed by self-possessed Miss Stanwyck. They both should know better. (Dir: Roy Rowland, 77 mins.)

Moonraker, The (British, 1957)** George Baker, Sylvia Syms, Marius Goring. High adventure and court intrigues set in 17th century England. Mildly entertaining for swashbuckling fans. Good British cast go through the paces. (Dir: David MacDonald, 82 mins.)

Moonrise (1948)**½ Dane Clark, Lloyd Bridges, Ethel Barrymore. A man becomes a murderer during a brawl, flees, and his girl tries to persuade him to give himself up. Grim, moody drama of the backwoods country. (Dir: Frank Borzage, 90 mins.)

Moonshine War, The (1970)**½ Alan Alda, Patrick McGoohan, Richard Widmark, Melodie Johnson. The repeal of Prohibition is only a few months away, so revenue agent Mc-

Goohan is interested in getting the 150 bottles of aged moonshine hidden on Alda's property. He's not above bringing in gangster Widmark to try some violence. There's a neat twist for an ending, but little coherence in character motivation. (Dir: Richard Quine, 100 mins.)

Moontide (1942)**½ Jean Gabin, Ida Lupino, Thomas Mitchell. Beautifully acted but generally boring mood drama. A dock worker in a California fishing village prevents a waitress from committing suicide and then falls in love with her. (Dir: Archie Mayo, 94 mins.)

Moonwalk One (1972)***½ A unique documentary record of the Apollo 11 flight and man's first lunar landing on July 20, 1969. Pre-launch scenes from Cape Kennedy followed by truly awesome, dazzling films of the flight itself. The launch is shown in remarkable detail, and audiences can learn far more about this phenomenal feat and what it really looked like from this film than they ever could on TV. Valuable historical record of the momentous scientific feat, extremely well-produced by Francis Thompson. (Dir: Theo Kamecke, 96 mins.)

Moralist, The (Italian, 1957)** Vittorio De Sica, Alberto Sordi, Marina Perschy. The chief guardian of public morals turns out to be a scoundrel, a scamp and a swindler. Fair English-dubbed comedy never quite takes advantage of the good cast.

More (Luxembourg 1969)** Mimsy Farmer, Klaus Grunberg, Heinz Engelman. Before you get too smug thinking you can learn everything there is to know about movies from Luxembourg by watching "More," please note that this maddening, uneven tale about drug addiction was photographed entirely—and quite ravishingly, too—on the Spanish island of Ibiza in the Mediterrean. It's a kind of a "Days of Wine and Roses" about drug addiction, but these mindless flower-generation teenagers are glamorized as they proceed to kill themselves with heroin. Some very perverse sexual numbers in this convincingly-acted story, directed and co-scripted by Barbet Schroeder. (115 mins.)

More Dead Than Alive (1968)*½ Clint Walker, Vincent Price, Anne Francis. Clint Walker has taken over a role usually reserved for Clint Eastwood,

a gunslinger who lets his gun talk for him. It seems he's to be let out of prison, and wants to go straight, so he gets a job in Price's sideshow. His past won't leave him alone, however. Lots of violence. (Dir: Robert Sparr, 99 mins.)

More Than a Miracle (Italian-French, 1966)**½** Sophia Loren, Omar Sharif. Sumptuous fairy tale with the beautiful Sophia Loren and the dashing Omar Sharif managing to make the affair a diverting entertainment. The plot, or plots, are too fantastic and involved to go into. Suffice it to say, Sophia makes a gorgeous peasant girl who goes to any lengths to land her handsome prince. The lengths include the standard complement of plunging necklines. (Dir: Francesco Rosi, 105 mins.)

More Than a Secretary (1937)*** Jean Arthur, George Brent. Girl takes a job as secretary to the publisher of a health magazine, falls for him. Breezy, entertaining comedy. (Dir: Alfred E. Green, 77 mins.)

More the Merrier, The (1943)**** Jean Arthur, Joel McCrea, Charles Coburn. Wealthy philanthropist uses the crowded situation in wartime Washington as a means of furthering a young love affair. Fine comedy, one long laugh from beginning to end (Dir: George Stevens, 104 mins.)

Morgan (British, 1966)**** Vanessa Redgrave, David Warner, Robert Stephens. A daffy, dazzling bit of English black-comedy with a truly stunning debut in a major film role by David Warner. He plays a delightfully mad painter who goes about trying to win back the affections of his ex-wife (the gorgeous Vanessa) in decidedly novel fashion. He doesn't quite succeed, but director Karel Reisz does succeed in keeping the laughs flowing, delivering both pathos and truth along the way. Some superior camera work and editing are among the many virtues of this literate, sophisticated satire. (Dir: Karel Reisz, 97 mins.)

Morgan the Pirate (1960)** Steve Reeves, with his clothes on plus a beard, plays the legendary buccaneer. Action fans will enjoy this Italian produced action. (Dir: Andre de Toth, 95 mins.)

Morituri (1965)**½** Marlon Brando and Yul Brynner costar in a tangled tale of espionage on the high seas in World War II, aboard a German freighter bringing rubber from the Orient to Germany. Brando is a wealthy German pacifist working for the British and Brynner is the freighter's captain. (Dir: Bernhard Wicki, 123 mins.)

Morning After, The (1974)*** Dick Van Dyke, Lynn Carlin. Alcoholism has often been treated in dramatic terms, but for honesty, this TV feature is a first. Van Dyke valiantly attacks the difficult role of a successful public-relations writer who plunges deeper and deeper into the shattering world of alcoholism at the expense of his wife, kids, and job. Anyone familiar with this dreaded disease will recognize the man's lying promises to quit and the flashes of destructive acts. Effective acting, and Van Dyke may surprise you with his fine performance. (Dir: Richard Heffron.)

Morning Glory (1933)***½ Katharine Hepburn, Douglas Fairbanks Jr. Small-town girl struggles to become a great Broadway actress. Fine performance by Miss Hepburn is the highlight of this well done drama. (Dir: Lowell Sherman, 80 mins.)

Morocco (1930)** Marlene Dietrich, Gary Cooper. Sexy early talkie, as the glamorous one sacrifices all in her love for Legionnaire Coop. Shows the ravages of time, but should prove worthwhile to those who remember. (Dir: Joseph von Sternberg, 90 mins.)

Mortal Storm, The (1939)*** Margaret Sullavan, James Stewart, Robert Young, Robert Stack. This powerful dramatic story of Germany at the beginning of Hitler's rise to power should deliver an even more symbolic message today. Brilliantly acted. (Dir: Frank Borzage, 99 mins.)

Moses (Great Britain-Italy, 1975)*** Burt Lancaster, Anthony Quayle, Ingrid Thulin, Irene Papas, William Lancaster, A "new" version edited for theatrical release of the six-part television mini-series that includes elements of sex and violence not included in the original. The script by Anthony ("Clockwork Orange") Burgess provides a good mixture of epic spectacle and intimate narrative. Lancaster lends his usual steely presence to the role of "the lawgiver," but Quayle's talent is wasted as Aaron, and the rest of the international cast are not given much of a chance to develop their characters. (Dir: Gianfranco De Bosio, 141 mins.)

Mosquito Squadron (1969)** David McCallum, David Buck. McCallum heads RAF squadrons out to destroy a series of tunnels in France where the Nazis are building rockets. Complicating matters, McCallum is in love with the wife of a pilot held captive in the caves. Warmed-over treatment of some old cliches. (Dir: Boris Sagal, 90 mins.)

Moss Rose (1947)*** Ethel Barrymore, Peggy Cummins, Victor Mature. Slow moving but well played and interesting Victorian mystery drama. Story of a blackmailing chorus girl and an aristocratic family involved in murder. (Dir: Gregory Ratoff, 82 mins.)

Most Beautiful Woman in the World, The—See: Beautiful But Dangerous

Most Dangerous Man Alive (1961)* Ron Randell, Debra Paget, Elaine Stewart. Racketeer survives an explosion set off by a scientist doing experiments on mutation, but finds his body slowly turning to steel. Farfetched, inept sci-fi melodrama. (Dir: Allan Dwan, 82 mins.)

Most Wanted Man, The (British, 1962)*½ Zsa Zsa Gabor, David Opatoshu, Nicole Maurey. Timid soul suddenly finds himself the center of attention, because of a peculiar ability. Tasteless comedy wastes good talent. (Dir: Henri Verneuil, 85 mins.)

Most Wonderful Moment, The (Italian, 1955)**½ Marcello Mastroianni, Giovanna Rolli. A young doctor finds the way to love and peace of mind from the faith given him by a courageous girl. A realistic childbirth sequence is well-handled. (Dir: Luciano Enmer, 94 mins.)

Mother and the Whore, The (France, 1973)***½ Jean-Pierre Leaud, Bernadette Lafont, Francoise Lebrun. A fascinating, overlong psychodrama about a man and two women who brutalize each other, all in the name of love. This emotionally draining but rewarding marathon—it runs over three and a half hours —was written and directed by Jean Eustache. A narcissistic young man is involved with a nurse and an older woman with whom he shares an apartment. The three wind up

sharing the same bed in this maddening, perceptive, lyrical film which has an improvisatory quality about much of the writing. The last, lacerating scene with the three lead characters is quite shattering. Shot in black and white in Paris. (Dir: Jean Eustache, 215 mins.)

Mother Didn't Tell Me (1950)**½ Dorothy McGuire, William Lundigan. Dorothy McGuire has a flair for comedy which she seldom gets a chance to display in her film roles. However, this fast paced comedy gives her the opportunity to really cut loose in the role of a young bachelorette with a psychosomatic cough. Naturally the doctor turns out to be an eligible, handsome bachelor. Take it from there. (Dir: Claude Binyon, 88 mins.)

Mother Is a Freshman (1949)** Loretta Young, Van Johnson. Young widow joins daughter on campus and falls in love with English professor. Lightweight comedy, stretching one joke too far. (Dir: Lloyd Bacon, 81 mins.)

Mother, Jugs and Speed (1976)*½ Bill Cosby, Raquel Welch, Harvey Keitel, Allen Garfield, Dick Butkus. The easy camaraderie between three ambulance drivers (Cosby, Welch and Keitel) is not enough to sustain this forced blend of black farce and contrived melodrama, full of overlapping surprises. What could have been an urban version of "M*A*S*H" is marred by insensitive slapstick humor (a fat black woman falls from a stretcher and is nearly run over by a truck). Tragedy, such as the death of a pregnant woman, disconcertingly cuts through the often tasteless gags. (Dir: Peter Yates, 98 mins.)

Mother Wore Tights (1947)*** Betty Grable, Dan Dailey. Entertaining show biz cavalcade about a girl who marries and becomes part of a song-and-dance act. More plausible than the usual backstage musical; good cast, nice songs. (Dir: Walter Lang, 107 mins.)

Mothra (Japanese, 1962)** Giant monster threatens the earth. First-class trick work in this otherwise naive thriller. (Dir: Inoshiro Honda, 99 mins.)

Moulin Rouge (1953)***½ Jose Ferrer, Colette Marchand. Biography of the painter Toulouse-Lautrec, whose physical deformity caused his despair in love, and who frequented the more notorious quarters of Paris. Colorful drama with flash, dash and excellent performances. (Dir: John Huston, 123 mins.)

Mountain, The (1956)****½** Spencer Tracy, Robert Wagner. Two brothers climb an Alpine peak to reach the wreckage of a crashed airliner. Drama seems to be trying to say something on a lofty plane, doesn't make it—however, Tracy is always good to watch, the drama has occasionally suspenseful moments. (Dir: Edward Dmytryk, 105 mins.)

Mountain Road, The (1960)****** James Stewart, Glenn Corbett, Lisa Lu. Drab war drama of personal problems and stopping the enemy in China. Beneath the talents of Stewart and a good cast. (Dir: Daniel Mann, 102 mins.)

Mourning Becomes Electra (1947) ******* Rosalind Russell, Leo Genn, Raymond Massey, Kirk Douglas. Eugene O'Neill's tale of hatred and conflict in a New England family in the Civil War days. Long, powerful drama. (Dir. Dudley Nichols, 173 mins.)

Mouse on the Moon, The (Great Britain, 1963)****½** Margaret Rutherford, Ron Moody, David Kosoff. Sequel to the hilarious "The Mouse that Roared," again based on a novel by Leonard Wibberly, this pre-détente spoof of the race to space falls short of the rapid-fire satire of the first film. Margaret Rutherford is amusing as the graceless yet grand Duchess, and Kossoff repeats his captivating scientist role, here putting some explosive wine to imaginative use. An inventive spoof, eratically put together, has sluggish segments. (Dir: Richard Lester, 85 mins.)

Mouse That Roared, The (1958)*****½** Peter Sellers, Jean Seberg. Here's a comedy delight—an infinitesimal kingdom declares war on the U.S.—and wins! Loads of satiric fun, with Sellers doing a swell job in several assorted roles. (Dir: Jack Arnold, 83 mins.)

Mousey (1974)****** Kirk Douglas, Jean Seberg, John Vernon. Douglas makes his made-for-TV dramatic debut in this opus about a timid biology teacher in Canada who is driven to thoughts of murder by his callous wife (Seberg). It's complicated and not very interesting; there are many corpses before the fade-out, and Douglas' thirst for revenge remains unquenched. Kirk should have waited for a decent script. (Dir: Daniel Petrie.)

Move Over Darling (1963)****** Doris Day, James Garner, Polly Bergen, Chuck Connors. Returning from an airplane crash five years before, a wife discovers her husband about to remarry. Remake of "My Favorite Wife" somehow manages to drain all the fun from the situation, becomes a plodding, strained comedy. (Dir: Michael Gordon, 103 mins.)

Movie Maker, The (1967)****½** Rod Steiger, Robert Culp, Sally Kellerman. Battle for control of a film studio; Steiger, the last of the bigtime film moguls, takes on Culp, a young company man. Good acting highlights the Rod Serling script. Made-for-TV. (Dir: Josef Leytes, 91 mins.)

Movie Murderer, The (1970)****½** Arthur Kennedy, Warren Oates, Tom Selleck. Routine but interesting-in-spots made-for-TV feature. Arthur Kennedy is very good as an aging insurance company investigator who goes out on a limb to prove a series of fires involving the destruction of movie films are related. Warren Oates, as a hired arsonist, supplies the film's most interesting sequences as he goes about his business of setting blazes which look like accidents. (Dir: Boris Sagal, 99 mins.)

Mr.—See also Mister

Mr. and Mrs. Bo Jo Jones (1971)****** Desi Arnaz, Jr., Christopher Norris. This unpretentious little story about a teen-aged marriage comes up with some surprisingly effective moments and honest portrayals by Norris and Arnaz. In the film, set back in 1956 when our mores were different, a reluctant high-school boy marries his pregnant schoolmate, a blond snub-nosed youngster from a well-to-do family. The kids face disappointed parents on both sides and slowly grow as a unit, gaining strength as they push awkwardly through their problems. Miss Norris, who appeared in the movie "Summer of '42," gives the show a needed sense of reality as the child bride and young Arnaz backs her up nicely. Made-for-TV. (Dir: Robert Day, 73 mins.)

Mr. and Mrs. Smith (1941)******* Carole Lombard, Robert Montgomery.

Young couple discover their marriage has a legal hitch, which causes a rift. Entertaining romantic comedy with a good cast. (Dir: Alfred Hitchcock, 95 mins.)

Mr. Arkadin (1959)*** Orson Welles, Patricia Medina, Akim Tamiroff. Another of Orson Welles' cinema creations that falls short of being great due to ponderous theme. Plot concerns a wealthy man's past being reviewed and re-evaluated by those who loved and hated him. But Welles' work is still more stimulating and rewarding than most other directors around. (Dir: Orson Welles, 99 mins.)

Mr. Belvedere Goes to College (1949) ** Clifton Webb, Shirley Temple, Alan Young. Eccentric genius enrolls at a college to get a degree, finds life has its complications. Attempt to capitalize on Webb's success in "Sitting Pretty"—like most sequels, not up to the original. Mild comedy. (Dir: Elliott Nugent, 83 mins.)

Mr. Belvedere Rings the Bell (1951) *** Clifton Webb, Joanne Dru, Hugh Marlowe. Clifton Webb's "Belvedere" character fits perfectly into this screen adaptation of a B'way play about life in an old folks home titled "The Silver Whistle". When Belvedere decides to bring some merriment to the old folks home, the fun begins and hardly lets up throughout the entire film. (Dir: Henry Koster, 87 mins.)

Mr. Blandings Builds His Dream House (1947)***½ Cary Grant, Myrna Loy, Melvyn Douglas. Tired of city life, a married couple buys a run down country home. Some hilarious moments in this smoothly produced comedy. (Dir: H. C. Potter, 94 mins.)

Mr. Deeds Goes to Town (1936)**** Gary Cooper, Jean Arthur. Frank Capra comedy masterpiece about a millionaire and some New York con artists defies the years. (Dir: Frank Capra, 120 mins.)

Mr. Denning Drives North (British, 1951)*** John Mills, Phyllis Calvert. An aircraft manufacturer kills a blackmailer, suffers the consequences of conscience until an American lawyer-friend comes to his aid. Suspenseful melodrama, well acted. (Dir. Anthony Kimmins, 93 mins.)

Mr. Drake's Duck (British, 1951)***

Douglas Fairbanks Jr., Yolande Donlan. An American couple buys an English farm, where they encounter a duck that lays uranium eggs. Fast moving, sprightly comedy, pretty funny. (Dir: Val Guest, 76 mins.)

Mr. Dynamite (1941)**½ Lloyd Nolan, J. Carrol Naish, Irene Hervey. Baseball star visiting a carnival matches wits with a gang of enemy agents. Simple but fast-moving, exciting little melodrama gives a good hour's relaxation.

Mr. 880 (1950)***½ Burt Lancaster, Dorothy McGuire, Edmund Gwenn. Charming story about a T-man and a United Nations secretary who investigate a lovable old counterfeiter. Edmund Gwenn shines as the money-maker. (Dir: Edmund Goulding, 90 mins.)

Mr. Emmanuel (British, 1945)*** Felix Aylmer, Greta Gynt. A Jewish gentleman braves Nazi Germany in his quest for a lost friend. Well acted, frequently gripping drama.

Mr. Hobbs Takes a Vacation (1962) **½ James Stewart, Maureen O'Hara, Fabian. Family encounters plenty of trouble when they try to take a vacation in a run down beach house. Typical father-against-the-world domestic comedy, which Stewart can play in his sleep. Some funny scenes, in a familiar sort of way. (Dir: Henry Koster, 116 mins.)

Mr. Hulot's Holiday (French, 1953) **** Jacques Tati. Magnificently inventive comedy, mostly pantomime, about a well meaning but inept young vacationer at a French seaside resort. Reminiscent of some of the early Buster Keaton flicks. (Dir: Jacques Tati, 85 mins.)

Mr. Imperium (1951)** Lana Turner, Ezio Pinza. An improbable pair— Lana & Ezio—try to prove that May-December romances can work in this light romantic comedy. The film doesn't work but Ezio does sing. (Dir: Don Hartman, 87 mins.)

Mr. Inside/Mr. Outside (1973)**½ Hal Linden, Tony LoBianco. A number of factors lift this murder mystery above the usual thriller. It stars two capable actors, and is shot on location in New York City; the original fracas takes place inside a foreign embassy—off limits to the local police force because of diplomatic immunity. Made-for-TV. (Dir: William Graham, 73 mins.)

Mr. Lord Says No (British, 1952) *** Stanley Holloway, Kathleen Harrison. Mr. Lord defies the whole British government when they want to demolish his home to make way for a new highway. Highly amusing comedy.

Mr. Lucky (1943)***½ Cary Grant, Laraine Day. Professional gambler seeks to raise a fresh bankroll by operating at a war drive bazaar. Slickly made, well acted comedy-drama. (Dir: H. C. Potter, 100 mins.)

Mr. Majestyk (1974)* Charles Bronson, Al Lettieri, Linda Cristal, Alejandro Rey. Strictly for Bronson fans. Although the title suggests our hero may be a slick city detective, Bronson is cast as a simple dirt farmer who won't bow to the syndicate and hire pickers whom they choose. One of the more ludicrous scenes in the film has the gangsters machine-gunning a barn full of watermelons . . . yes, watermelons! (Dir: Richard Fleischer, 103 mins.)

Mr. Moto Takes a Chance (1938)** Peter Lorre, Rochelle Hudson. That almost too clever Japanese sleuth up against intrigue in Indo-China. Lorre is good, but the writing isn't as smooth as the Chan films. (Dir: Norman Foster, 70 mins.)

Mr. Music (1950)**½ Bing Crosby, Nancy Olson, Charles Coburn. Bing as a composer who would rather golf and loaf than work, and the attempts to get him into action. Mild story, below-par tunes, but Crosby carries the load well. (Dir: Richard Haydn, 113 mins.)

Mr. Peabody and the Mermaid (1948)**½ William Powell, Ann Blyth. A middle-aged gent has his life changed completely when he comes upon a amorous mermaid one day. Mildly amusing fantasy. (Dir: Irving Pichel, 89 mins.)

Mr. Peek-A-Boo (French, 1951)*** Bourvil, Joan Greenwood. Comedy about a man who has the power to walk through walls. Delightful, with Parisian comic Bourvil a riot.

Mr. Perrin and Mr. Traill (British, 1948)***½ David Farrar, Marius Goring. Bitterness develops between an old schoolmaster and a younger teacher, when the latter makes a better impression with his winning ways, over the stern attitude of the former. Excellent melodrama, with good performances, especially from Goring as the old schoolteacher. (Dir: Lawrence Huntington, 90 mins.)

Mr. Quilp (Great Britain, 1975)* Anthony Newley, David Hemmings, David Warner. Charles Dickens should sue from the grave. Reader's Digest should stick to the magazine business if this bumbling musical adaptation of Dickens' "The Old Curiosity Shop" is any indication. It boasts a spectacularly forgettable score by Anthony Newley, playing Mr. Quilp. If you remember the deathbed scene of Little Nell from the novel, you've got another good reason not to tune in. (Dir: Michael Tuchner, 120 mins.)

Mr. Reckless (1948)*½ William Eythe, Barbara Britton. Oil worker comes to town to find his sweetie about to marry another man. Dull melodrama lacks action, several other things too.

Mr. Ricco (1975)*½ Dean Martin, Eugene Roche, Denise Nicholas, Cindy Williams, Geraldine Brooks. Dean Martin is so laconic in his acting style that he seems to be playing in the wrong speed in this crime drama, which looks as if it was strung together from rejected TV scripts for a pilot about a middle-aged crusading lawyer trying to improve race relations. The dialogue is arch and tough. Supporting cast does better than Martin, which isn't saying much. (Dir: Paul Bogart, 98 mins.)

Mr. Roberts (1955)**** Henry Fonda, Jack Lemmon, James Cagney. A superb cast brings the rollicking B'way comedy to the screen. Henry Fonda repeats his solid, straight-forward characterization in the title role of Lt. Roberts, who is eager to be transferred to the fighting zone rather than serve on a cargo ship. Jack Lemmon steals the show in every scene in which he appears as the rambunctious and opportunistic Ensign Pulver. (Lemmon won the Oscar for this performance.) James Cagney was never better as the Captain of the cargo ship whose prize possession is a potted palm tree; and William Powell proves again to be a master of comedy timing as "Doc" the vessel's medic. (Dirs: John Ford, Mervyn Le Roy, 123 mins.)

Mr. Robinson Crusoe (1932)*** Douglas Fairbanks, Maria Alba.

Doug takes a bet that he cannot live on a deserted island for a year, and his athletic prowess overcomes all odds. Lively adventure is rather good fun. (Dir: A. Edward Sutherland, 80 mins.)

Mr. Sardonicus (1961)**½ Guy Rolfe, Oscar Homolka, Ronald Lewis, Audrey Dalton. Doctor is called by his former love to a castle to treat her husband, whose face is paralyzed. Thriller brings off the shudders in efficient fashion—good fare for the fans. (Dir: William Castle, 89 mins.)

Mr. Scoutmaster (1953)** Clifton Webb. Even Clifton Webb's aplomb at portraying the sophisticate caught in unsophisticated endeavors doesn't save this so-called comedy about a reluctant scoutmaster and his misadventures with a pack of future eagle scouts. (Dir: Henry Levin, 87 mins.)

Mr. Skeffington (1944)** Bette Davis, Claude Rains. Another "big" picture that laid a bigger egg. Story of a selfish woman whose loveless marriage to a Jewish financier fails, takes a long time to tell the obvious. (Dir: Vincent Sherman, 146 mins.)

Mr. Smith Goes to Washington (1939) **** James Stewart, Jean Arthur, Edward Arnold, Claude Rains. Naive man is elected to the U. S. Senate, but he doesn't conform to the pattern set for him by his backers. Fine production in every respect; superb comedy-drama. (Dir: Frank Capra, 130 mins.)

Mr. Soft Touch (1949)**½ Glenn Ford, Evelyn Keyes, John Ireland. A sentimental, corny comedy drama about a gambler who gets involved with a social worker of a local settlement house. Good performances despite the saccharine script. (Dirs: Henry Levin, Gordon Douglas, 93 mins.)

Mr. Steve (French, 1957)**½ Jeanne Moreau, Philippe Le Maire. Bank clerk is forced by a clever gangster to assist in a daring robbery, falls for the gangster's wife. English-dubbed crime melodrama unfolds fairly interestingly, with good performances.

Mr. Winkle Goes to War (1944)*** Edward G. Robinson, Ruth Warrick. Thirty-eight-year-old bank clerk is drafted, surprises everybody by becoming a hero. Entertaining, novel war melodrama. (Dir: Alfred E. Green, 80 mins.)

490

Mrs. Brown, You've Got a Lovely Daughter (British, 1968)** Herman's Hermits inherit a dog and try to make a racer of him. Inoffensive and mild. Stanley Holloway, Mona Washbourne. (Dir: Saul Swimmer, 110 mins.)

Mrs. Mike (1949)*** Dick Powell, Evelyn Keyes. Girl undergoes the hardships of rough living when she marries a Mountie. Entertaining drama. (Dir: Louis King, 100 mins.)

Mrs. Miniver (1942)**** Greer Garson, Walter Pidgeon, Richard Ney. Winner of 7 Academy Awards, this dramatic, yet simple story of the courage of the British people as the war crept into their backyard is a film masterpiece. (Dir: William Wyler, 134 mins.)

Mrs. O'Malley and Mr. Malone (1950) **½ Marjorie Main, James Whitmore. Marjorie Main, famous for her Ma Kettle characterization, plays a modified version of Ma in this comic murder mystery. The action takes place on a train and involves detectives, cached loot and chases. Good fun. (Dir: Norman Taurog, 69 mins.)

Mrs. Parkington (1944)*** Greer Garson, Walter Pidgeon, Edward Arnold, Peter Lawford. Fictitious story of the lives of a multi-millionaire and the poor girl he wed is well told although episodic and occasionally corny. (Dir: Tay Garnett, 124 mins.)

Mrs. Pollifax—Spy (1971)* Rosalind Russell, Darren McGavin. Rosalind Russell tries unsuccessfully to instill zany life into this brainless espionage comedy, but is overcome by the unctuous story, in which she plays a middle-aged matron who volunteers her services to the CIA. Dissolve . . . and she's off to Mexico with some microfilm. Dissolve . . . to another channel! (Dir: Leslie Martinson, 110 mins.)

Mrs. Sundance (1974)**½ Elizabeth Montgomery, Robert Foxworth, L. Q. Jones. Don't look for Robert Redford or Paul Newman in this TV sequel to the hit movie "Butch Cassidy and the Sundance Kid"—not even in flashbacks. As the title indicates, the focus is on Sundance's widow, played by Miss Montgomery. The lady has returned to the U.S. from South America, living a quiet life as a small-town teacher until word gets out that Sundance may be alive and waiting at his old hideout. The rumor is a ploy to get at Sundance's gang, but the plan backfires many times before the shoot-out finale. Routine. (Dir: Marvin Chomsky.)

Mudlark, The (1951)*** Irene Dunne, Alec Guinness, Andrew Ray. Interesting and charming story about a young orphan who manages to smuggle himself into Windsor Castle to meet Queen Victoria. Irene Dunne, with a good makeup job, is quite good as the Queen and Andrew Ray is perfect as the boy. Alec Guinness as Disraeli has a few well-played scenes with Miss Dunne, plus a long speech that's an actor's dream. (Dir: Jean Negulesco, 100 mins.)

Mugger, The (1958)*½ Kent Smith, James Franciscus. Detective story with two criminals, one a mugger, the other a killer. Film fails because it is unable to sustain both stories at the same time. Franciscus is fine in one of his first films. (Dir: William Berke, 74 mins.)

Mulligan's Stew (1977)**½ Lawrence Pressman, Elinor Donahue, Johnny Whitaker, Alex Karras. Warm tale of a high-school coach and his wife and three kids who take on the added responsibility of an additional four kids, when the coach's sister and brother-in-law die in a plane crash. The adjustment of the combined families to each other serves as an interesting plot, and the cast is quite good. Made-for-TV. (Dir: Noel Black, 72 mins.)

Mummy, The (1932)*** Boris Karloff, Zita Johann, David Manners. First of the "Mummy" films and the best. Karloff, as an ancient Egyptian prince brought to life, attempts to take pretty Zita Johann as his mate. Has some good shock scenes, although the production is dated. (Dir: Karl Freund, 80 mins.)

Mummy, The (British, 1959)** Christopher Lee, Peter Cushing. Lukewarm remake of the terrifying 1932 original with Boris Karloff. This version is slower on suspense, but its real treats lie in its stars, Lee and Cushing, the Rover Boys of the British horror films from Hammer Productions. Plot concerns an archaeological dig where a mummy comes back to life to deal with the scientists disturbing its rest. (Dir: Terence Fisher, 86 mins.)

Mummy's Ghost, The (1944)** Lon Chaney, John Carradine. The gauze-wrapped mummy of Prince Kharis is in America, searching for the reincarnation of his ancient love. Okay shudder story in this series. (Dir: Reginald Le Borg, 60 mins.)

Mummy's Tomb, The (1942)*½ Lon Chaney, Dick Foran, Turhan Bey. An Egyptian fanatic brings a mummy back to life, and sends it out to do his dirty work. Typical Grade "B" shocker. (Dir: Harold Young, 61 mins.)

Munster, Go Home (1966)** Fred Gwynne, Yvonne De Carlo, Al Lewis, Terry-Thomas. Herman Munster inherits a title, and the family goes to England, where they're involved in plenty of creepy doings. Feature based on the TV show will please the fans, but the noninitiated will find it on the silly side. (Dir: Earl Bellamy, 96 mins.)

Murder a la Mod (1968)**½ Jared Martin, Margo Norton, Jennifer Salt. A young filmmaker becomes involved in a brutal murder. Young director Brian De Palma, who also wrote and edited this offbeat try, creates some inventive sequences in this low-budget entry, even if the film as a whole is not completely successful.

Murder Ahoy (British, 1964)*** Margaret Rutherford, Lionel Jeffries. Once again Miss Rutherford is magnificent as Agatha Christie's Miss Marple, the geriatric set's counterpart to James Bond. In case you don't know, Miss Marple is an amateur detective in her 70's who solves many murders as a result of keen observations, cool logic, and a vast knowledge of the plots of detective stories. This time she's cast adrift with an unknown murderer on a British naval cadet training ship. (Dir: George Pollock, 93 mins.)

Murder at 45 RPM (French, 1961)** Danielle Darrieux, Georges Millot. Singing star and her husband are involved in a web of suspicion and murder. Fairish English-dubbed mystery builds up a lot of suspense to a weak letdown. (Dir: Etienne Perier, 105 mins.)

Murder at the Gallop (British, 1963)*** Margaret Rutherford, Robert Morley. Marvelous Miss Marple, Agatha Christie's 70-plus amateur sleuth brilliantly brought to life by Miss Rutherford, is at it again. Miss Marple manages to solve a double murder and turn down a proposal of marriage in the bargain. The droll Robert Morley is excellent. (Dir: Basil Rayburn, 81 mins.)

Murder at the World Series (1977)** Bruce Boxleitner, Hugh O'Brian, Michael Parks, Lynda Day George, Janet Leigh. It's the World Series, and the Houston Astros are pitted against the Oakland A's at the Houston Astrodome. Enter a young man, bent on revenge for a personal injustice (he didn't make the team in the tryouts), who executes a daring kidnapping of a top player's wife—but he gets the wrong girl. Routine story centers on the cops trying to find the young kidnapper, with the excitement of the World Series as a backdrop. Bruce Boxleitner is good as the demented kidnapper. Made-for-TV. (Dir: Andrew McLaglen, 106 mins.)

Murder by Contract (1958)**½ Vince Edwards. Good low budget film about a hired killer who painstakingly sets up his victim, a beautiful woman who is a government witness, for the kill. Tense and interesting. Edwards is coldly arrogant as the hired henchman. (Dir: Irving Lerner, 81 mins.)

Murder by Death (1976)**** Alec Guinness, Peter Falk, Peter Sellers, Maggie Smith, Nancy Walker, Truman Capote, Elsa Lanchester. A whimsical, breezy, enormously entertaining parody of murder mysteries by master comedy-marksman Neil Simon. It's based on a delicious conceit—invite five of the world's most legendary detectives to a weekend at an isolated country house—Sam Diamond, the San Francisco gumshoe (Falk), Milo Perrier, the greedy Belgian (Coco), the boisterous Englishwoman Jessica Marbles (Lanchester), dapper Dick Charleston (Niven) and Inspector Sidney Wang (Sellers) and watch them go through their paces concerning a murder at midnight. There are marvelous turns by Guinness as an unforgettable blind butler, and by Coco, Niven and Smith. The only really jarring note in this romp is the hopelessly clumsy pass at acting by Truman Capote. There's a triple-reverse, double-whammy ending that will leave you gasping and applauding. (Dir: Robert Moore, 95 mins.)

Murder, He Says (1945)*** Fred MacMurray, Helen Walker, Marjorie Main. Silly, confused but often hilarious mystery-comedy about a public opinion analyst who stumbles upon an insane family. (Dir: George Marshall, 91 mins.)

Murder in Reverse (British, 1947) *** William Hartnell, Dinah Sheridan. A man sent to prison for murder gets out to find that the supposed victim is still alive. Very good drama with an unusual twist.

Murder, Inc. (1960)*** Stuart Whitman, Mai Britt, Henry Morgan, Peter Falk. Relatively factual, unpleasant but fascinating story of the big crime syndicate, and how a young couple is caught in its web. Distinguished by a smashing portrayal by Peter Falk as Abe Reles. Should please crime story fanciers. (Dirs: Burt Balaban, Stuart Rosenberg, 103 mins.)

Murder Most Foul (British, 1965)*** Margaret Rutherford. The sight of Agatha Christie's engaging grand dame of detectives, Miss Marple, as played by Miss Rutherford, is cause for rejoicing. Tune in and watch Miss Marple saving the innocent and tracking down the guilty in her inimitable fashion. (Dir: · George Pollack, 90 mins.)

Murder, My Sweet (1944)***½ Dick Powell, Anne Shirley, Claire Trevor. Private eye takes a job finding a murder. Exciting, excellently produced mystery, emphasis on the hard-boiled. (Dir: Edward Dmytryk, 95 mins.)

Murder on Approval (British, 1956) ** Tom Conway, Delphi Lawrence. Average British crime "meller" dealing with the search for a rare stamp which leads to violence. (Dir: Bernard Knowles, 90 mins.)

Murder on Flight 502 (1975)**½ Robert Stack, Hugh O'Brian, Fernando Lamas, Walter Pidgeon, Polly Bergen, Molly Picon, Ralph Bellamy, George Maharis. Although airplane-crisis yarns may be formula drama, they usually work, and this one turns out to be pretty good. A 747 from New York to London reaches the "point of no return," when a letter is discovered that indicates a potential murderer is aboard. Sub-plots crop up without interfering with the suspense. Made-for-TV. (Dir: George McCowan, 98 mins.)

Murder on the Orient Express (Great Britain, 1974)*** Albert Finney, Lauren Bacall, Martin Balsam, Ingrid Bergman, Jacqueline Bisset, Sean Connery, John Gielgud, Wendy Hiller, Anthony Perkins, Vanessa Redgrave, Richard Widmark, Michael York. A terrific mystery for everyone, especially Christie fans. Sidney Lumet's direction and Paul Dehn's script stick close to Dame Agatha's suspenseful atmosphere in this deft whodunnit. Set in 1934, the complex plot involves a train—the Orient Express—full of exotic people traveling from Istanbul to Calais. In between they are snowbound, and one of the passengers is murdered. Fortunately, the Express also carries Hercule Poirot (Finney), famous Belgian detective, whose little gray cells are in splendid form. Soon it turns out that everyone aboard has something to hide, including the victim. Only the ingenious Poirot can solve this riddle. A delight, with a wonderful cast! (Dir: Sidney Lumet, 127 mins.)

Murder or Mercy (1974)**½ Melvyn Douglas, Bradford Dillman, Denver Pyle. This drama about a father-and-son law firm has two things going for it—a good story and that stalwart actor Melvyn Douglas. Mr. Douglas plays a doctor who is accused of practicing euthanasia by administering a lethal dose of morphine to his wife, who is dying of cancer. Good courtroom drama. Made-for-TV. (Dir: Harvey Hart.)

Murder Party (German, 1961)**½ Magali Noel, Harry Meyen. Fashion designer kills his mistress, goes with his friend to a party, intending to eliminate him too, because he was a witness at the scene of the crime. Nicely directed dubbed-English melodrama, some suspense and well-handled sequence.

Murder Reported (British, 1957)* Paul Carpenter, Melissa Stribling. A dead body in a trunk is the most convincing thing in this junky movie about a politician who has murdered a rival. (Dir: Peter Crowhurst, 58 mins.)

Murder She Said (Great Britain, 1961)*** Margaret Rutherford, James Robertson-Justice, Arthur Kennedy. Cheerily preposterous Margaret Rutherford, although 69 at the time, embodies Agatha Christie's matronly, home-style detective, Miss Jane Marple. Marple, as adroit and appealing as ever, poses as a housemaid in an estate full of nefarious goings-on. Based on the Christie novel "4:50 from Paddington." (Dir: George Pollock, 87 mins.)

Murder Will Out (British, 1952)***½ Valerie Hobson, James Robertson-Justice, Edward Underdown. The after-effects of the murder of a beautiful secretary involve an acid-tongued author, his wife, and a weak radio personality. Suspenseful mystery, intricately plotted, nicely done. (Dir: John Gilling, 83 mins.)

Murder Without Tears (1953)** Craig Stevens, Joyce Holden. A series of murders keeps detective Craig Stevens (pre-Peter Gunn days) on his toes in this mediocre crime movie.

Murderer's Row (1966)**½ Dean Martin, Ann-Margret, Camilla Sparv, Karl Malden. A sequel to Dean Martin's Matt Helm starrer "The Silencers"—but not as good. Martin handles his double-entendre lines well enough, but he just doesn't cut it in the super agent class. Ann-Margret is miscast once again—this time she's a kidnaped scientist's daughter and only Karl Malden, overplaying the villain of the piece, comes through with an interesting performance. (Dir: Henry Levin, 108 mins.)

Murders in the Rue Morgue (1932)*½ Bela Lugosi, Sidney Fox. Mad scientist Bela Lugosi, trying to create an ape-woman, kidnaps a toothsome girl for his experiments. The film was taken from an Edgar Allan Poe original, and John Huston wrote some of the dialogue—but the result is still Grade "B" shock stuff. (Dir: Robert Florey, 60 mins.)

Murders in the Rue Morgue (1973)*** Jason Robards, Herbert Lom, Michael Dunn. Fourth film version of Edgar Allan Poe's classic tale of murders at a Paris theater at the turn of the century. The only clue is that all the victims were business associates of the theater owner (Robards). The police suspect Lom. Lively chiller. (Dir: Gordon Hessler, 86 mins.)

Murdock's Gang (1973)** Alex Dreier, Janet Leigh. Premise is better than its realization. Revolves around a disbarred criminal attorney who decides to employ ex-cons to solve crimes. Dreier, as the attorney, operates out of an impressive office and dominates the proceedings.

493

Made-for-TV. (Dir: Charles Dubin, 73 mins.)

Murmur of the Heart (French-Italian-West German, 1971)**** Lea Massari, Daniel Gelin, Benoit Ferreux, Fabian Ferreux. A haunting, touching, humorous, and insightful study of a young boy's sexual awakening. Beautifully acted and unerringly directed by Louis Malle, who also wrote the original screenplay. Set in the town of Dijon in 1954. Malle captures the excitement, hesitancy, and sense of wonder of a 15-year-old who is taken by his older brothers for his sexual initiation with a prostitute. Malle's sense of restraint and tenderness is present throughout, so that when, after a slightly drunken evening, the son, perfectly played by Ferreux, has an incestuous relationship with his youthful mother (Massari) it seems tender and natural, leaving them without any regret or sense of shame. The comical ending is a perfect finale to this compassionate, tasteful film. (118 mins.)

Murph the Surf (1975)* Robert Conrad, Don Stroud, Donna Mills, Luther Adler. A bum ride, based loosely on the real-life adventures of jewel thieves Allan Kuhn and Jack Murphy (a.k.a. Murph the Surf). The two beach boys turned thieves are played by Don Stroud and Robert Conrad. Best part is the recreation of the theft of the Star of India sapphire from New York's American Museum of Natural History in 1964, and it's nowhere near enough. (Dir: Marvin Chomsky, 101 mins.)

Murphy's War (British, 1971)**½ Peter O'Toole, Sian Phillips, Philippe Noiret. Complex ideological effort concerning a World War II Irishman who, after the massacre of the crew of his ship by a German U-boat, seeks revenge at all costs. O'Toole, as the sole survivor of the attack, packs a ferocious wallop into his performance, as he moves from feelings of base brutality to noble vengeance, desperately trying to destroy the U-boat amid its hideout on a South American river. The photography is lush and the direction by Peter Yates adds flavor, yet the film tends to pull apart, never quite reaching the emotional involvement it strives for. (106 mins.)

Murrieta (Spain, 1965)* Jeffrey Hunter, Arthur Kennedy, Diana Lorys. About legendary California bandit of the 1849 Gold Rush days Joaquin Murrietta, and how anti-Mexican bigotry in the Old West forced him into his "Robin Hood" role. Bogs down under weight of its grim morality, and uninspired performances. (Dir: George Sherman, 108 mins.)

Muscle Beach Party (1964)** Frankie Avalon, Annette Funicello, Buddy Hackett. Strictly for the beach-party fans. In addition to the muscle men and the bathing beauties there are many songs. The plot is incidental. (Dir: William Asher, 94 mins.)

Music for Millions (1944)**½ Margaret O'Brien, Jose Iturbi, June Allyson, Jimmy Durante. Lovers of sentimental corn will adore this tearjerker but others are warned to steer clear. Girl cellist who worries about fighting hubby, with June and Margaret the great sob sisters working on your emotions. (Dir: Henry Koster, 120 mins.)

Music in Manhattan (1944)**½ Anne Shirley, Philip Terry, Dennis Day. Boy and girl are forced to pose as man and wife. Pleasant musical comedy.

Music in My Heart (1940)*** Tony Martin, Rita Hayworth. Singer about to be deported falls for a girl about to enter into an unhappy marriage with a millionaire. Entertaining comedy with music. (Dir: Joseph Stanley, 70 mins.)

Music Lovers, The (British, 1971)*** Richard Chamberlain, Glenda Jackson, Max Adrian. The critics both loved and hated this film-with-music about the great Russian composer Peter Tchaikovsky, and it's easy to see why. Flamboyant director Ken Russell mixes glorious visual images with patent nonsense, and pays scant attention to the historical facts concerning Tchaikovsky. Chamberlain plays the composer. If you're turned on by smashed champagne glasses you'll adore this bio. (122 mins.)

Music Man, The (1962)**** Robert Preston, Shirley Jones, Buddy Hackett. The saga of Harold Hill, who arrives in River City, Iowa, to organize a boys' band and falls for Marian, the librarian, etc. The Meredith Willson musical hit, filmed with most of its gaiety intact, including Preston's smashing performance, the well-whistled tunes. It's fun for the whole family, and what more could one ask? (Dir: Morton Da Costa, 151 mins.)

Musketeers of the Sea (Italian, 1960) *½ Pier Angeli, Robert Alda, Aldo Ray. Three well-known actors caught in a mishmash of sea heroics about a girl pirate who involves a crew of buccaneers in a plot to kill a wicked governor. Supporting cast dubbed in English. (Dir: Massimo Patrizi, 116 mins.)

Muss 'Em Up (1936)**½ Preston Foster, Margaret Callahan. Clever detective solves a kidnaping plot. Interesting mystery melodrama. (Dir: Charles Vidor, 80 mins.)

Mutations, The (Great Britain, 1973) ½ Donald Pleasence, Tom Baker, Brad Harris, Julie Ege. One part "Frankenstein," one part "Freaks," and one part soap opera, and you have this mutant of a movie. Pleasence is cast as the mad professor who has the stamina to teach biochemistry by day and wreck havoc on human subjects in bizarre experiments by night. The mutants are colorfully grotesque (Venus flytrap man, lizard woman, etc.) but the tale of their revenge is as stale as the cardboard characterizations. (Dir: Jack Cardiff, 92 mins.)

Mutiny (1952)*** Mark Stevens, Angela Lansbury. Patriots attempt to run the British blockade and get gold bullion from France during the War of 1812. Speedy maritime adventure maintains a no-nonsense attitude that helps the action. (Dir: Edward Dmytryk, 77 mins.)

Mutiny in Outer Space (1964)**½ William Leslie, Dolores Faith. Two astronauts return to a space station bearing a deadly fungus which, if brought back, would affect earth. Slightly better than the usual run of sci-fi adventures made on a low-budget; good effects. (Dir: Hugo Grimaldi, 81 mins.)

Mutiny on the Blackhawk (1939)*½ Richard Arlen, Andy Devine, Constance Moore. Captain breaks up slave running, then saves an army fort under attack. Cluttered action melodrama uses stock shots from other films for its story line. (Dir: Christy Cabanne, 80 mins.)

Mutiny on the Bounty (1935)**** Clark Gable, Charles Laughton, Franchot Tone. One of the great adventure movies of all time. Laughton's award-winning performance as the infamous Captain Bligh is worth canceling all plans, staying home to watch. Not as magnificent a story as its modern counterpart, "Caine Mutiny," but a much better film. (Dir: Frank Lloyd, 130 mins.)

Mutiny on the Bounty (1962)*** Marlon Brando, Trevor Howard, Richard Harris. If sheer length and opulence justifies the term "blockbuster," this movie remake of the famous Gable-Laughton epic of the midthirties qualifies. However, those who fondly recall its predecessor will find the comparisons unfavorable. The story of course concerns a seamen's mutiny aboard the H.M.S. Bounty. Marlon Brando's curiously erratic portrayal of Fletcher Christian throws the film off-balance. Trevor Howard is excellent as Captain Bligh. The scenic effects are frequently magnificent. (Dir: Lewis Milestone, 179 mins.)

My Blood Runs Cold (1965)*½ Troy Donahue, Joey Heatherton. An old-fashioned meller designed for the teen-age set who might gasp at watching Troy Donahue playing a psychopath who makes poor Joey Heatherton's life a nightmare. Donahue is predictably one-dimensional and tiresome, and Miss Heatherton offers little else but an attractive pair of gams. (Dir: William Conrad, 104 mins.)

My Blue Heaven (1950)**½ Betty Grable, Dan Dailey, David Wayne. Fast moving musical with Grable and Dailey tapping and singing their way through. The silly plot, which serves as stage waits between numbers, concerns a show business team and their efforts to adopt a family. (Dir: Henry Koster, 95 mins.)

My Brother Talks to Horses (1946) **½ Butch Jenkins, Peter Lawford, Edward Arnold. Butch Jenkins is adorable as the little chap who asks race horses if they're going to win but the charm of the film's basic theme is left at the post. (Dir: Fred Zinnemann, 93 mins.)

My Brother's Keeper (British, 1949) *** Jack Warner, George Cole. Two convicts escape prison, and the elder shows the young lad that it pays to go straight. Well done melodrama. (Dir: Alfred Roome, 96 mins.)

My Cousin Rachel (1953)***½ Olivia de Havilland, Richard Burton. The two stars are perfect in their roles in this fascinating suspense tale based on Daphne du Maurier's novel about a young man who sets out to prove that his cousin is a treacherous woman and ends up hopelessly in love with her. The low-key photography heightens the mood of this mysterious yarn set in 19th-century England. (Dir: Henry Koster, 98 mins.)

My Darling Clementine (1946)***½ Henry Fonda, Linda Darnell, Victor Mature. A super western about Wyatt Earp, and the doings in Tombstone, Ariz. Directed by John Ford who, along with a fine cast, makes up for an almost routine script. (97 mins.)

My Darling Daughters' Anniversary (1973)**½ Robert Young, Ruth Hussey, Raymond Massey. Here's a follow-up to the earlier TV film "All My Darling Daughters" in which Young, as a widower-judge, married off his four daughters on the same day. It's a year later and Young is planning his own nuptials to antique dealer Hussey, but the complications and obstacles pile up until they seem almost insurmountable. There's an ease and grace to the script and screen fans from the forties will relish the pairing of Young and Hussey. Made-for-TV. (Dir: Joseph Pevney, 73 mins.)

My Dear Secretary (1948)*** Laraine Day, Kirk Douglas, Keenan Wynn. A wolfish author meets a secretary who has written a scorching best seller. Cute comedy, with Wynn being especially amusing. (Dir: Charles Martin, 94 mins.)

My Dream Is Yours (1949)**½ Jack Carson, Doris Day. Ordinary, formula show business musical with Doris singing some standard tunes to at least make some pleasant moments. Highlight is a "Bugs Bunny" animated sequence. (Dir: Michael Curtiz, 101 mins.)

My Fair Lady (1964)**** Rex Harrison, Audrey Hepburn, Stanley Holloway, Wilfrid Hyde-White. The fabulous Broadway musical makes an entertaining film with most of its magnificent charm intact. Harrison deserved the Oscar he won for his superb performance as Prof. Henry Higgins, the British gentleman who turns the cockney flower seller, Eliza Doolittle, into a gracious lady. Miss Hepburn shines in the second half. The whole cast is a joy, and the sets and costumes resplendent, but it's the lyrics of Alan

496

Jay Lerner and the music of Frederick Loewe that make it all an unforgettable experience. (Dir: George Cukor, 170 mins.)

My Father's House (1975)** Cliff Robertson, Robert Preston. Muddled attempt at serious drama, bolstered by good performances. Cliff Robertson plays the 41-year-old successful businessman-husband-father who suffers a heart attack and does some heavy thinking about his own dad, via many flashbacks. Robert Preston's dominating performance as Robertson's father adds greatly to the sequences about the past. Made-for-TV. (Dir: Alex Segal, 100 mins.)

My Favorite Blonde (1942)***½ Bob Hope, Madeleine Carroll. Luscious British spy, Madeleine, is forced to enlist the aid of frightened Bob in carrying out her mission and the result is a barrel of laughs. (Dir: Sidney Lanfield, 78 mins.)

My Favorite Brunette (1947)*** Bob Hope, Dorothy Lamour, Peter Lorre. Photographer Bob turns detective to help Dotty out of a jam, and there you have all the ingredients for another romp for Hope fans. (Dir: Elliott Nugent, 87 mins.)

My Favorite Spy (1942)**½ Kay Kyser, Ellen Drew, Jane Wyman. Bandleader is a flop as a soldier, but is pressed into espionage duty. Pleasant comedy with music. (Dir: Tay Garnett, 86 mins.)

My Favorite Spy (1951)*** Bob Hope, Hedy Lamarr, Francis L. Sullivan. Bob's a small time burlesque performer who's a double for a spy, with the usual crossed identities. Typical Hope comedy, the sort of thing he does well; fast-paced, generally satisfying. (Dir: Norman Z. McLeod, 93 mins.)

My Favorite Wife (1940)**** Cary Grant, Irene Dunne, Randolph Scott. Wife believed dead returns after years on a desert island when the husband is about to rewed. Excellent comedy, a laugh a minute. (Dir: Garson Kanin, 88 mins.)

My Foolish Heart (1950)*** Susan Hayward, Dana Andrews. Good woman's film, heavy on sentiment and histrionics. Loosely based on one of J. D. Salinger's short stories, "Uncle Wiggly In Connecticut". The tale tells of a wartime romance between a lonely girl and a pilot. Miss Hayward is excellent in her role and Andrews plays it just at the right level to complement Miss Hayward. (Dir: Mark Robson, 98 mins.)

My Forbidden Past (1951)** Robert Mitchum, Ava Gardner, Melvyn Douglas. Girl from the wrong part of town inherits a fortune and plans to break up the marriage of the man she loves. Uneven, not-too-good costume melodrama. (Dir: Robert Stevenson, 81 mins.)

My Friend Flicka (1943)*** Roddy McDowall, Preston Foster. Devoid of hokum, this story of a boy's love for an outlaw horse is no "Lassie" or "The Yearling" but it's still a beautiful story and among the better animal films. (Dir: Harold Schuster, 89 mins.)

My Friend Irma (1949)** Marie Wilson, Diana Lynn, Dean Martin, Jerry Lewis, John Lund. Based on the once-popular radio series, this comedy concerns a girl dimwit whose boy friend discovers a potential singing talent at an orange-juice stand, the resulting complications. First film for Martin & Lewis. The gags are obvious, not too funny, but the film has a certain historical interest for fans. (Dir. George Marshall, 103 mins.)

My Friend Irma Goes West (1950)** Marie Wilson, John Lund, Dean Martin, Jerry Lewis, Diana Lynn, Corinne Calvet. Irma and company follow Dean and Jerry when they go to Hollywood to make their fortune. Comedy based on the radio show has some pretty low gags, one or two of them offensive. For fans only. (Dir: Hal Walker, 90 mins.)

My Gal Sal (1942)*** Rita Hayworth, Victor Mature, Carole Landis. Gay 90's musical about a song writer's love for a musical star is a harmless frame for some entertaining oldtime music and production numbers. (Dir: Irving Cummings, 103 mins.)

My Geisha (1962)** Shirley MacLaine, Yves Montand, Edward G. Robinson, Bob Cummings. Lengthy comedy about an actress who is so adept at posing as a geisha girl that her husband, not recognizing her, signs her to play the role of "Madame Butterfly." Assuming one can swallow this premise, there are some beautifully photographed scenes of Japan, but the tired plot and leaden direction keep interfering. (Dir: Jack Cardiff, 120 mins.)

My Girl Tisa (1948)**½ Lilli Palmer, Sam Wanamaker. Immigrant girl works to bring her father to New York, and to help her boy friend become a lawyer. Pleasant but leisurely costume comedy-drama. (Dir: Elliott Nugent, 95 mins.)

My Girlfriend's Wedding (1969)**½ Low-budget, experimental black and white film "diary" of a young Englishwoman talking about her life, her loves, her child and why, because she needs a visa, she's about to marry a willing anarchist. Interesting, off-beat effort, written and directed by Jim McBride. (60 mins.)

My Little Chickadee (1940)**** W. C. Fields, Mae West. The Fields-West combo was one of the funniest ever and this film is a permanent reminder. An effort was made to introduce a silly western plot. Forget it, and just listen to the great man's asides! (Dir: Edward Cline, 83 mins.)

My Love Comes Back (1941)*** Olivia de Havilland, Jeffrey Lynn. A lot of good music decorates this minor little tale of a girl violinist who wants a husband but if you like good music you should be able to tolerate the inoffensive plot. (Dir: Curtis Bernhardt, 81 mins.)

My Lucky Star (1938)*** Sonja Henie, Richard Greene, Cesar Romero. Typical Henie vehicle finds her in college, ice skating in a department store and just about everything else but it's good fun. (Dir: Roy Del Ruth, 84 mins.)

My Man and I (1952)**½ Shelley Winters, Ricardo Montalban, Claire Trevor, Wendell Corey. Mexican lad, a new citizen, has trouble with a stingy rancher and his wife. Uneven drama sometimes slips into second gear, occasionally comes up with a fine moment. Okay performances. (Dir: William Wellman, 100 mins.)

My Man Godfrey (1936)**** Carole Lombard, William Powell. Superb comedy film about a socialite and her amorous but proper butler. Carole Lombard & William Powell are brilliant as the pair. Far superior to the remake with June Allyson & David Niven. A comedy classic! (Dir: Gregory La Cava, 100 mins.)

My Man Godfrey (1958)**½ June Allyson, David Niven. Disappointing remake of the sophisticated comedy of the 1930's about a butler who competes for his mistress' romantic attentions. Niven is fine but Miss

Allyson is miscast and can't carry off the more subtle comedy aspects of the script. (Dir: Henry Koster, 92 mins.)

My Name Is Ivan—See: Youngest Spy, The

My Name Is Julia Ross (1945)***½ Nina Foch, Dame May Whitty, George Macready. Engrossing, fascinating and well played mystery. A girl reports for a job, is drugged and forced into a new identity. A sixty-five minute sleeper . . . worthwhile. (Dir: Joseph H. Lewis, 65 mins.)

My Name Is Nobody (Italy-France-Germany, 1974)*** Henry Fonda, Terence Hill, Jean Martin. Interesting study of an aging gunfighter (Fonda) and the young, up-and-coming cowboy (Hill) he teams with for one last shoot-'em-up before retiring. Fonda's portrait of the hero who must choose between becoming a dead legend or living in obscurity is well delineated, and his compromising solution shows an unusual intelligence at work in this action genre. Based on an idea by Sergio Leone. (Dir: Tonino Valerii, 115 mins.)

My Night at Maud's (France, 1969) **** Jean-Louis Trintignant, Francoise Fabian, Antoine Vitez, Christine Barrault. Of course you remember philosopher Pascal's famous "wager"—the proposition that it is worth betting on the existence of God because if He exists (even the French were not yet worrying about the possibility of She), then you gain eternity, but if you lose, you lose nothing. Well, in this marvelously witty and civilized comedy of manners, the leading man and woman are in bed together discussing such things—and they make reasoned arguments, not love. Maud, a divorced Protestant exquisitely acted by Francoise Fabian, invites a visiting Catholic engineer (Trintignant) to spend the night in her nonexistent spare room. Faultlessly written and directed by Eric Rohmer, photographed in black and white, this is one of the most beautifully realized films in years. (Dir: Eric Rohmer, 113 mins.)

My Outlaw Brother (1950)** Mickey Rooney, Robert Preston, Robert Stack. An Eastern kid comes West, and finds his brother to be the mysterious leader of an outlaw band. Rooney looks out of place in the

saddle, but then so does the rest of the cast. (Dir: Elliott Nugent, 82 mins.)

My Pal Gus (1952)*** Richard Widmark, Joanne Dru, George Winslow. Fay and Michael Kanin have fashioned a warm hearted comedy drama about a little boy who is the product of a divorced home. Little George Winslow (with the very deep voice) will capture your heart as Gus. Joanne Dru plays the proprietress of a school to which Gus is sent and it's with her help that everything turns out for the best. (Dir: Robert Parrish, 83 mins.)

My Pal Wolf (1944)**½ Sharyn Moffett, Jill Esmond. Little girl deserted by her parents and cared for by a cruel governess attaches herself to a stray dog. Nicely done little drama, entertaining.

My Reputation (1946)**½ Barbara Stanwyck, George Brent. Soap opera fans may like this story of a young widow who, in all innocence, dates an Army officer and is victimized by gossip and almost loses her sons' love. (Dir: Curtis Bernhardt, 95 mins.)

My Seven Little Sins (French, 1956) ** Maurice Chevalier, Paolo Stoppa. Harmless little comedy about an aging Casanova and his antics on the Riviera. For Maurice Chevalier fans only. (Dir: Jean Boyer, 98 mins.)

My Side of the Mountain (U.S.-Canadian, 1969)*** Ted Eccles, Theodore Bikel. Nice film for children about a Canadian boy who leaves his family to live in the mountains alone. He meets a retired folk singer, played by Bikel, who helps him get adjusted and saves him when he is trapped during the winter. Beautiful nature photography makes this fine family fare. (Dir: James B. Clark, 100 mins.)

My Sister Eileen (1942)***½ Rosalind Russell, Janet Blair, Brian Aherne. Two small-town sisters arrive in New York to pursue their careers, take a dingy Greenwich village apartment. Sparkling comedy has many laughs. (Dir: Alexander Hall, 96 mins.)

My Sister Eileen (1955)*** Janet Leigh, Jack Lemmon, Betty Garrett. Musical version of the famed Rosalind Russell movie of the same title (not to be confused with Rosalind Russell's Broadway musical "Wonderful Town" which was based on the same movie). Confused? Despite its origin, this film has songs, dances, and Jack Lemmon to recommend it. (Dir: Richard Quine, 108 mins.)

My Six Convicts (1952)***½ Millard Mitchell, Gilbert Roland, Marshall Thompson. Very, very funny film about prison life, unlike most films of this nature. Millard Mitchell is a standout in a great cast. Stanley Kramer produced. (Dir: Hugo Fregonese, 104 mins.)

My Six Loves (1963)*½ Debbie Reynolds, Cliff Robertson, David Janssen. Broadway star finds six abandoned kids living at her country home, decides to adopt them. Comedy-drama overloaded with cutesie-pooisms, sugary sentiment. Much too much. (Dir: Gower Champion, 100 mins.)

My Son John (1952)* Helen Hayes, Robert Walker, Van Heflin, Dean Jagger. Badly misguided drama of a mother's reactions when she learns her son is a Communist. Sincere attempt at patriotism becomes embarrassing in its lack of intellect, simple-minded solutions to problems, overstated dramatics. Could have the opposite effect of what was intended. (Dir: Leo McCarey, 122 mins.)

My Son, My Son (1940)*** Brian Aherne, Louis Hayward, Madeleine Carroll, Laraine Day. Good, though older vintage drama of a young wastrel who proves his father's faith in him by dying a hero. (Dir: Charles Vidor, 115 mins.)

My Sweet Charlie (1970)***½ Patty Duke, Al Freeman, Jr. Excellent made-for-TV feature. Though this drama is based on a highly contrived situation, its principal characters are so extremely well drawn and so superbly played by Al Freeman, Jr., and Patty Duke, you'll find yourself accepting the improbable situation willingly, and wanting to stay with it until the end. In a remote Louisiana resort area, closed up during the off-season, a young pregnant Southern girl, thrown out by her father, takes refuge in a cottage. Her solitary wait for the arrival of her child is broken when a young black lawyer, also on the run, decides to hide out in the same house. Based on the short-lived B'dway play. (Dir: Lamont Johnson, 97 mins.)

My Uncle (1958)**** Jacques Tati. In a memorable French comedy, Tati the inimitable runs afoul of the modern mechanized world, in some inspired pantomime reminiscent of the silent comedy days. Lots of fun, certainly worth seeing. (Dir: Jacques Tati, 110 mins.)

My Wife Is a Panther (French, 1960)** Jean Richard, Jean Poiret. Young man finds plenty of complications when a panther takes a shine to him. Mild, silly comedy dubbed in English.

My Wife's Best Friend (1952)**½ Anne Baxter, Macdonald Carey. Wife gets an inadvertent confession of philandering from her husband, and the upsets begin. Unimportant but cute romantic comedy. (Dir: Richard Sale, 87 mins.)

My Wild Irish Rose (1947)** Dennis Morgan, Arlene Dahl. Horrible musical supposedly based on the life of composer Chauncey Olcott. Only redeeming feature is a nice score of standard Irish tunes. (Dir: David Butler, 100 mins.)

Myra Breckinridge (1970)½ Mae West, Raquel Welch, John Huston, Rex Reed, Farrah Fawcett. In the press release for this malodorous garbage pile, oozed from Gore Vidal's book, 20th Century-Fox advises the reviewing press, "Do not look here for a synopsis of the story because it has been decided by producer and director that such would serve no good purpose." I fully understand their predicament, because there virtually is no story, and what little plot there is is excruciating—just like everything else about this grotesquery. Mae West, making one of her rare screen appearances these days, is wasted. The only good idea in the whole film was to typecast "critic" Rex Reed in the role of a tiny-talent homosexual. A macabre freak show about sexual perversity becomes not erotic or titillating—just numbingly bad. (Dir: Michael Sarne, 94 mins.)

Mysterians, The (Japanese, 1959)** English-dubbed science-fiction stuff about a race of intellects from outer space attempting to take over earth when their planet is destroyed. Dubbed dialogue is unintentionally funny, but the production is elaborate, often quite imaginative. (Dir: Inoshiro Honda, 85 mins.)

Mysterious Island (British, 1961)*** Michael Craig, Joan Greenwood, Gary Merrill, Herbert Lom. Exciting Jules Verne fantasy about escapees from a Confederate prison landing via balloon on an island where mammoth beasts roam. Special effects are fine, the fast pace seldom lets up. (Dir: Cy Enfield, 101 mins.)

Mysterious Lady, The (1928)**½ Greta Garbo, Conrad Nagel. A Garbo silent film in which she gets another chance to play the femme fatale. She's Tania, the Russian spy, and the setting is Berlin, 1915, where she uses and then falls for an Austrian Army officer. The plot doesn't miss a nuance of the early spy yarn genre, and Miss Garbo's fans will enjoy her portrayal of the amorous agent. (Dir: Fred Niblo, 90 mins.)

Mysterious Magician, The (German, 1965)*½ Joachim Berger, Heinz Drache. Phantomlike avenger seems to have returned to carry out a vendetta when his sister is found murdered. Old-hat mystery from an Edgar Wallace story, dubbed in English. (Dir: Alfred Vohrer, 95 mins.)

Mystery in Mexico (1948)**½ William Lundigan, Jacqueline White. American investigators look into a jewel robbery and hi-jacking in Mexico. Well made melodrama.

Mystery of Edwin Drood, The (1935) *** Claude Rains, Heather Angel. This is an adaptation of Charles Dickens' final—and uncompleted— novel. Concerns a choirmaster who leads a double life, giving choir lessons by day, smoking opium by night. Nicely played by Rains, and moderately interesting. (Dir: Stuart Walker, 90 mins.)

Mystery of Marie Roget (1942)**½ Maria Montez, Patric Knowles, John Litel. Crisp detective thriller, from the short story by Edgar Allan Poe. Medical examiner Paul Dupin tries to find out why a famous actress disappeared from home. (Dir: Phil Rosen, 91 mins.)

Mystery of the Wax Museum (1933) *** Lionel Atwill, Fay Wray, Glenda Farrell. Historic color-talkie suspense tale about a mad wax sculptor, whose London museum burns down leaving his fingers crippled, which prompts him to find an alternative sculpting method in New York. Disappearing bodies lead to the villain's unmasking. (During filming of this movie, the primitive color process produced such intense heat that some of the wax figures began to melt.) (Dir: Michael Curtiz, 77 mins.)

Mystery Street (1950)*** Ricardo Montalban, Sally Forrest, Jan Sterling. Neat mystery concerning police procedure in tracking down a killer in Boston. Emphasis on police lab work, absorbingly done, flavorsome location scenes, good acting. (Dir: John Sturges, 93 mins.)

Mystery Submarine (1951)* Macdonald Carey, Marta Toren, Robert Douglas. German U-boat commander refuses to surrender at the end of World War II, rampages in the South Atlantic until ferreted out by an undercover agent. The U.S. Navy gets on the ball, but "Mystery Submarine" sinks. (Dir: Douglas Sirk, 78 mins.)

Naked Africa (1957)**½ Documentary of tribal life in Africa narrated by Quentin Reynolds is interesting fare for travel buffs, should hold the attention of others as well.

Naked Alibi (1954)** Sterling Hayden, Gloria Grahame. Fast moving routine crime meller. Sterling Hayden plays an ex-cop who doggedly tracks down a murder suspect. The supporting cast needs a few alibis. (Dir: Jerry Hopper, 86 mins.)

Naked and the Dead, The (1958)** Aldo Ray, Cliff Robertson, Raymond Massey. Story of combat in the Pacific, and the war of resentment between officers and men, taken from Norman Mailer's best-selling novel. A botched job, unsteadily written and directed, not too well acted, it often becomes a parody of all war dramas. (Dir: Raoul Walsh, 131 mins.)

Naked Brigade, The (1965)*½ Shirley Eaton, Ken Scott. Girl joins up with Greek guerrillas when the country is overrun by Nazis in 1941. Mediocre war drama filmed on location in Greece. (Dir: Maury Dexter, 100 mins.)

Naked City (1948)***½ Barry Fitzgerald, Howard Duff. New York police investigate a girl's violent death. The "city" is the real star here; fine New York scenes in a conventional plot. This film served as the basis for the TV series of the same name. (Dir: Jules Dassin, 96 mins.)

Naked Dawn, The (1956)**½ Arthur Kennedy, Betta St. John. Slightly above average western about a bandit and his relationship with his young accomplice and the lad's wife. Not much action after the opening sequences but well played enough to maintain your interest. (Dir: Edgar G. Ulmer, 82 mins.)

Naked Earth (1959)** Richard Todd, Juliette Greco. Two lonely people are drawn together in the Africa of last century. Juliette's not naked; it's just the plot that gets exposed. (Dir: Vincent Sherman, 96 mins.)

Naked Edge, The (1961)**½ Gary Cooper, Deborah Kerr. Absorbing if not altogether successful film adaptation of the suspense novel "First Train to Babylon" by Max Ehrlich. Cooper, in his last film, plays a middle-aged business man whose wife begins to suspect him of murder after the arrival of a strange letter. The supporting cast is fine, including such names as Eric Portman, Diane Cilento, Hermione Gingold, and Michael Wilding. (Dir: Michael Anderson, 100 mins.)

Naked Heart (British, 1950)* Michele Morgan, Kieron Moore. In northern Canada, a girl returns from a convent to have three men pledge their love for her. Tiresome, plodding drama, badly acted. (Dir: Marc Allegret, 90 mins.)

Naked Hills, The (1956)** David Wayne, Marcia Henderson, James Barton. Uneven story about the men who caught the gold fever during the gold rush days in California way back in the 1800's. James Barton takes top acting honors as a dreamer who just won't give up. (Dir: Josef Shaftel, 73 mins.)

Naked Jungle, The (1954)**½ Charlton Heston, Eleanor Parker. Adventure fans will enjoy this taste of life on a South American jungle plantation. The finale is a large scale attack on the plantation by an army of ants. The ladies will enjoy the romantic interludes. (Dir: Byron Haskin, 95 mins.)

Naked Kiss, The (1964)* Constance Towers, Anthony Eisley. Prostitute runs away from her past and tries to begin life anew in a small town, but her dreams are suddenly blasted by murder. Vile little drama throws in every sleazy angle imaginable,

leaves a bad taste thereafter. (Dir: Samuel Fuller, 93 mins.)

Naked Maja, The (1959)** Ava Gardner, Anthony Franciosa. Elaborately mounted but intrinsically dull drama about the romance between Goya, the painter, and the Duchess of Alba. Miss Gardner is breathtakingly beautiful but the talky script and Franciosa's histrionics become tedious. (Dir: Henry Koster, 111 mins.)

Naked Prey, The (1966)*** Cornel Wilde. A striking adventure film which has some brutal scenes. A tale about man versus the jungle. Wilde plays an African safari guide who watches his party of three hunters brutally killed by a tribe who decide to give him a chance for survival. The jungle code allows Wilde, stripped of his clothing, weapons and food, to be hunted like a lion by the tribe's best hunters. Builds suspense. One of Wilde's best performances and he also directed this unusual entry with fine scenes filmed in Africa. (Dir: Cornel Wilde, 94 mins.)

Naked Runner, The (British, 1967)* Frank Sinatra, Peter Vaughan, Derren Nesbitt, Nadia Gray. Frank Sinatra conned into a dangerous mission behind the Iron Curtain. You should avoid being conned into watching this ineptly written, directed and acted film. Made when the spy film rage was slowing down after all the James Bond 007 imitations; the camera trickery tries to cover up for a hollow story and Sinatra's wooden acting. (Dir: Sidney J. Furie, 104 mins.)

Naked Spur, The (1953)*** James Stewart, Janet Leigh, Robert Ryan, Ralph Meeker. Good adventure film bolstered by a star cast. Filmed on location in the Rockies, the rugged tale follows a group of bounty hunters in pursuit of a killer with a price on his head. Excellent photography enhances the action. (Dir: Anthony Mann, 91 mins.)

Naked Street (1954)**½ Farley Granger, Anthony Quinn. Underworld leader gets a cheap hoodlum free from a murder rap so the hood can marry his sister. Satisfactory crime drama, well acted. (Dir: Maxwell Shane, 84 mins.)

Naked Truth, The (Great Britain, 1957)*** Terry-Thomas, Peter Sellers, Peggy Mount, Dennis Price,

Shirley Eaton. Fine farcical satire of scandal-sheet journalism, features a cast of top British comedians. Sellers delivers his usual set of funny improvisations as the leader of some 300 victims, who realize it would be in their best interest not to have blackmailer Price tell all at his trial. (Dir: Mario Zampi, 92 mins.)

Nakia (1974)** Robert Forster, Arthur Kennedy, Linda Evans. Forster strikes a heroic pose as an Indian deputy sheriff in this pilot film for the TV series. It combines action with a message about modern-day Indians. Although it is reasonably well written and well played, it still comes out old sombrero and totally familiar. Filmed on location in Albuquerque, N.M. (Dir: Leonard Horn.)

Name of the Game Is Kill, The (1968)* Jack Lord, Susan Strasberg, Collin Wilcox, T. C. Jones, Tisha Sterling. A violent horror movie, with pretensions of being a way-out parody-drama. About an innocent passerby waylaid by a rather odd and dangerous family. (Dir: Gunnar Hellstrom, 88 mins.)

Namu, the Killer Whale (1966)** Robert Lansing, Lee Meriwether. For the kiddies who find a killer whale adorable. This Ivan Tors production has a naturalist befriending a whale. Naturally, the fishermen in the vicinity object and cause trouble for both Namu and his master. (Dir: Laslo Benedek, 88 mins.)

Nancy Drew, Reporter (1939)**½ Bonita Granville, John Litel. In this one Nancy is putting in a month on a paper covering minor assignments but she manages to get her pretty nose on a murder and we're off again. The kids should enjoy this whole series. (Dir: William Clemens, 70 mins.)

Nancy Goes to Rio (1950)**½ Jane Powell, Ann Sothern, Barry Sullivan. The plot gets in the way of this otherwise charmingly played musical. Jane Powell and Ann Sothern play daughter and mother respectively. They both toil in the theatre. The film is at its best when Jane and company are singing. (Dir: Robert Z. Leonard, 99 mins.)

Nanny, The (British, 1965)**½ Bette Davis, William Dix. Bette Davis fans will enjoy still another of the star's growing gallery of sinister portraits in macabre yarns. This time out, Miss Davis is cast as an English nanny whose sense of reality is clouded due to some deep dark secret in her past. Her charge, a very disturbed young lad fresh out of a junior asylum and wonderfully well-acted by ten-year-old William Dix, is wise to her, but he has trouble making anyone else believe him. Despite the built-in melodrama, Miss Davis's performance is quite restrained and has touches of credibility and pathos. (Dir: Seth Holt)

Napoleon and Samantha (1972)**½ Michael Douglas, Will Geer, Jodie Foster, Johnny Whitaker. A pet lion, two good child actors—Foster and Whitaker—and TV names Douglas and Geer in an entertaining Disney item for kids. The kids want to keep the lion. They start out on an adventurous trek across the Oregon terrain to find their good friend Douglas. There are a few action scenes along the way, but Jodie Foster comes away with the lion's share of the good lines (pardon the pun). (Dir: Bernard McEveety, 92 mins.)

Napoleon II—L'Aiglon (French, 1964)** Jean Marais, Bernard Verley, Georges Marchal. Overstuffed historical drama about the efforts to prevent the son of Napoleon from fulfilling his destiny. Well produced but sluggish. Dubbed in English.

Narco Men, The (Spanish-Italian, 1967)*½ Tom Tryon, Ana Castor. Tryon as a former Interpol agent released from prison after serving a false narcotics rap. Now that he's out, he's hired to run with a large heroin shipment. Plenty of action, very little coherence. (Dir: Julio Coll, 95 mins.)

Narrow Margin (1951)*** Charles McGraw, Marie Windsor. Detective guards an important grand jury witness aboard a train. Suspenseful crime melodrama. (Dir: Richard Fleischer, 70 mins.)

Nashville (1975)**** Lily Tomlin, Shelley Duvall, Henry Gibson, Ronee Blakely, Karen Black, Geraldine Chaplin, Keenan Wynn, Keith Carradine. A stunning, bold work of art commenting on the American dream, while focusing on Nashville, the dream center and cultural capital of country music. Thanks to the audacity and prodigious talent of director Robert Altman, he expands the horizons of motion pictures with "Nashville." It's a collage, a series of stunning impressions and notes that does have an improvisatory quality—meant here in the best sense about this pioneering work. Extraordinary screenplay by Joan Tewksbury. The acting performances are uniformly remarkable, including impressive debuts from unknowns like Ronee Blakely. Lily Tomlin, in her movie debut, proves to any doubters that she is a tremendously gifted actress. Chosen as the best picture of the year by the New York Film Critics and the National Society of Film Critics. Won Academy Award nominations for best picture, best direction and for supporting performances by Tomlin and Blakely. Won the Academy Award for best original song, "I'm Easy." Movie buffs please note: this is not a sequel to the 1969 bummer "From Nashville with Music." (Dir: Robert Altman, 159 mins.)

Nasty Rabbit, The—See: **Spies A-Go-Go**

National Velvet (1944)***½ Mickey Rooney, Elizabeth Taylor, Donald Crisp. The whole family will love this enchanting story of a butcher's daughter and a bum kid who train a horse to win the Grand National. (Dir: Clarence Brown, 125 mins.)

Native Drums (Italian, 1955)* Pedro Armendariz, Kerima, Charles Vanel. A medical expedition treks through the African jungle to find a cure for sleeping sickness. You may be stricken by the same malady halfway through this film.

Naughty But Nice (1939)**½ Ann Sheridan, Dick Powell. Pleasant, diverting little musical which lampoons the popular music business and its relationship to the classics. Incidentally, this was near the beginning of Sheridan's "oomph" build-up and she does. (Dir: Lloyd Bacon, 108 mins.)

Naughty Girl (French, 1957)** Brigitte Bardot, Mischa Auer. Silly comedy about a young miss and her involvement with a band of counterfeiters. Bardot is sexy, as usual. (Dir. Michel Boisrond, 77 mins.)

Naughty Marietta (1934)***½ Jeanette MacDonald, Nelson Eddy. Mr. Eddy made his screen debut in this Victor Herbert operetta and the result was a new team which delighted audiences for many years. One of

Herbert's best scores expertly performed. (Dir: W. S. Van Dyke, 110 mins.)

Naughty Martine (French, 1953)** Claude Dauphin, Dany Robin, Henri Vidal. Saucy French comedy about the adventures of a beautiful young girl and her pursuit of l'amour, toujours l'amour. Loses a great deal in the dubbing, so brush up on your French.

Naughty Nineties, The (1945)** Bud Abbott & Lou Costello, Rita Johnson. Comics Abbott & Costello invade the old Southern world of showboats and card sharks on the Mississippi. Plenty of sight gags, even if the written jokes don't survive the trip downstream. (Dir: Jean Yarbrough, 76 mins.)

Navajo (1952)*** Documentary story of life among the Indians, as seen through the eyes of a small boy. Excellent; director Norman Foster, producer Hall Bartlett, cameraman Virgil Miller deserve plenty of credit for this warm, human drama.

Navajo Joe (Italian-Spanish, 1967)* Burt Reynolds, Aldo Sanbrell. It seems a fierce band of outlaws led by an Indian-hating half-breed have been slaughtering Navajos. Steely-eyed Burt Reynolds wants revenge for his tribe, so single-handedly he goes after the desperados. Even Reynolds had to start somewhere. (Dir: Sergio Corbucci, 89 mins.)

Navy Blue and Gold (1937)*** Robert Young, James Stewart, Lionel Barrymore. The old Annapolis story in the hands of a fine cast turns into an entertaining film. Stewart is exceptionally good in this one and began to display the charm which made him a star. (Dir: Sam Wood, 100 mins.)

Navy Blues (1941)*** Ann Sheridan, Martha Raye, Jack Oakie, Jack Haley. A lot of talented people, plenty of noise and a few good songs make this zany but not witty musical entertaining. A few surprises in the supporting cast. (Dir: Lloyd Bacon, 108 mins.)

Navy Comes Through (1942)*** Pat O'Brien, George Murphy, Jane Wyatt. The merchant marine keeps the sea lanes open during World War II. Exciting melodrama. (Dir: A. Edward Sutherland, 82 mins.)

Navy vs. the Night Monsters, The (1966)*½ Mamie Van Doren, Anthony Eisley, Pamela Mason. Now we know why Antarctica was uninhabited for so long. Man-eating plants, with mobile roots—yes indeedy! Sexy nurse and Navy man stand between the revived vegetation and disaster. Well-assembled bunk. Written and directed by Michael A. Hoey. (87 mins.)

Nebraskan, The (1953)** Phil Carey, Roberta Haynes. Routine Western about having Army Scout winning the trust of Indian War Chief of the Sioux tribe. Roberta Haynes, a good actress, deserves better, and so do you. (Dir: Fred F. Sears, 68 mins.)

Necromancy (1972)* Orson Welles, Pamela Franklin. Silly occult thriller. Saga of a strange town whose major business is a factory turning out occult items. Pamela Franklin is a young lady being groomed by a coven of witches as the object of a sacrifice. Necromancy involves witchcraft and offering one life in exchange for another. Suggest you exchange "Necromancy" for a better flick. (Dir: Bert I. Gordon, 82 mins.)

Negatives (British, 1968)*** Diane Cilento, Peter McEnery, Glenda Jackson. Macabre offbeat drama which is not everyone's cup of tea. It's a tale about a couple who thrive on charades for sexual stimulation (they usually play a famous wife-murderer and his victim). Enter a glamorous photographer (Diane Cilento) with an equally warped sense of bedroom play and the film goes off in mad, but interesting tangents. The three actors in the cast—Diane Cilento, Peter McEnery and Glenda Jackson—do very well. Promising directional debut by Peter Medak. (90 mins.)

Nelson Affair, The (1973)**½ Glenda Jackson, Peter Finch, Michael Jayston, Anthony Quayle, Margaret Leighton, Dominic Guard. The performances of the two leads almost make up for the shortcomings of the pedestrian script about the scandalous love affair between Admiral Lord Nelson (Finch) and Lady Hamilton (Jackson). The narrative moves along at a nice pace, but the inherent melodrama of the piece tends to detract from the actors' fine turns. Talky screenplay by Terence Rattigan from his play "A Bequest to the Nation." Glenda Jackson is a superb actress and an accomplished belcher. (Dir: James Cellan Jones, 115 mins.)

Neon Ceiling, The (1971)**½ Made-for-TV entry. Gig Young, Lee Grant, Denise Nickerson try their best to make this a moving drama but the script often defeats the talented trio. In any case, there are enough dramatic ingredients here to keep viewers interested for the two hours —an adolescent awakening to the ways of the world; a philosophical, beer-drinking loner; and a neurotic woman running away from an unsatisfactory marriage. The neon ceiling of the title refers to the collection of neon signs which Gig Young has assembled on the ceiling of his ramshackle, roadside combination restaurant-gas station. Lee Grant won an Emmy for her performance. (Dir: Frank R. Pierson, 100 mins.)

Neptune Disaster, The (1973)* Ben Gazzara, Yvette Mimieux, Ernest Borgnine, Walter Pidgeon. A disaster, all right. Ridiculous undersea adventure story! The special effects that turn ordinary sea creatures into threatening monsters are the only attraction. Originally released as "The Neptune Factor." (Dir: Daniel Petrie, 98 mins.)

Neptune's Daughter (1949)**½ Esther Williams, Ricardo Montalban, Red Skelton. Light and tuneful romantic comedy with Esther's swimming and Red Skelton's funny-man antics. Song "Baby, It's Cold Outside" is from this film. (Dir: Edward Buzzell, 93 mins.)

Nero and the Burning of Rome (Italian, 1955)** Gino Cervi, Steve Barclay, Milly Vitale. Story of the corrupt Roman Emperor whose degradation and degeneracy finally causes his overthrow. Cervi is good in the role, adding to what would otherwise be a typical English-dubbed historical spectacle.

Network (1976)**** Faye Dunaway, William Holden, Peter Finch, Robert Duvall, Beatrice Straight. Paddy Chayefsky's searing, perceptive satire of television network news— how grotesque it is, and what louts we all are to permit it! Chayefsky deservedly won the Academy Award for this trenchant, often terribly funny grotesque comedy about a network TV anchorman who's gone bananas, and the avaricious, immoral bastards in the executive suites that capitalize on his mad-

504

ness after initially firing him. The real theme of "Network," one which very few movie critics picked up at the time of release, is the question of ACCOUNTABILITY of network news or the lack thereof, and Chayefsky constructs a situation that is not as far-fetched and grotesque as network apologists would like to have us believe. It's a rousing, stimulating dilly served brilliantly by everyone involved. "Network" was nominated for a number of Academy Awards, including best picture and direction, and Peter Finch, playing the role of the maniacal newscaster, won—in this, his last starring role. Beatrice Straight also won for her lovely supporting role of Holden's embittered wife. Faye Dunaway is letter-perfect playing the wildly ambitious program executive who only cares about the ratings and doesn't care one iota for content. There's a remarkable scene where the network biggies are planning a new documentary-news-drama called the "Mao-Tse Tung Hour." Astonishingly enough, this is the first major film in years to use TV as its principal backdrop and theme. (Dir: Sidney Lumet, 121 mins.)

Nevada (1944)**½ Robert Mitchum, Anne Jeffreys. Cowpoke stops crooks after mining claims. Fast moving, well made western. (Dir: Edward Killy, 62 mins.)

Nevada Smith (1966)**½ Steve McQueen, Karl Malden, Suzanne Pleshette. The character who appeared in Harold Robbins' "The Carpetbaggers" (Nevada Smith) is given a film of his own. The tale of this half-breed rebel is episodic, but Steve McQueen makes him come alive and a fine supporting cast is helpful. It's primarily a tale of revenge in which Nevada tracks down the killers of his parents. (Dir: Henry Hathaway, 135 mins.)

Nevada Smith (1975)* Lorne Greene, Cliff Potts, Adam West. Lorne Greene sought another "Bonanza" in this remake of a Steve McQueen movie, and missed. Working in Durango, Mexico, Greene portrays a crusty old firearms hustler caught in a father-son, love-hate relationship with the half-Indian youth, Nevada Smith. (Dir: Gordon Douglas, 72 mins.)

Never a Dull Moment (1952)**½

Irene Dunne, Fred MacMurray. New York songwriter marries a rancher, tries to get used to open-air life. Mildly amusing comedy. (Dir: Edward Killy, 60 mins.)

Never Back Losers (British, 1963)** Jack Hedley, Jacqueline Ellis. Insurance investigator looks into case of a jockey injured in a car crash after taking out a large policy. Fair Edgar Wallace mystery.

Never Give a Sucker an Even Break (1941)***½ W. C. Fields, Gloria Jean, Margaret Dumont, Leon Errol. A Fields nightmare, as he relates a strange tale of romantic adventures in a mythical country to a skeptical movie producer. No use in describing it—plotless farce has some moments of Fields at his best, and a wild car chase at the end. (Dir: Edward Cline, 71 mins.)

Never Give an Inch (1971)*** Paul Newman, Michael Sarrazin, Henry Fonda, Lee Remick, Richard Jaeckel. Theatrically released under the title "Sometimes a Great Notion," this saga about a logging family in Oregon has good acting and glorious scenery going for it. The screenplay, based on Ken ("One Flew Over the Cuckoo's Nest") Kesey's novel, doesn't stay with the narrative closely enough to sustain interest completely. The Stampers—father Henry Fonda, and sons Paul Newman, Michael Sarrazin and Richard Jaeckel—are a tough group. They defy a local strike by most of the other loggers in the area, and pay dearly for their decision to keep their operation going. The performances are uniformly good, especially Jaeckel who was nominated for an Academy Award. (Dir: Paul Newman, 108 mins.)

Never Let Go (British, 1963)** Peter Sellers, Richard Todd. Unpleasant melodrama about car thieves and their bout with the police. Sellers plays it straight and it's a bad job —one of his few film misadventures. (Dir: John Guillermin, 90 mins.)

Never Let Me Go (1953)**½ Clark Gable, Gene Tierney. The two attractive stars make this drama worthwhile. Gable plays an American newspaper correspondent who takes tremendous risks to smuggle his wife out of Communist Russia. There are some exciting scenes involving the actual escape towards the end of the film. (Dir: Delmer Daves)

Never Love A Stranger (1958)** John Drew Barrymore, Lita Milan. John Drew Barrymore portrays a young man who chooses the "fast buck," "fast women" path to destruction in this drama based on Harold Robbins' best seller. If you got to go, Barrymore probably has the right idea, but the film is not much. (Dir: Robert Stevens, 91 mins.)

Never Mention Murder (British, 1965)** Maxine Audley, Dudley Foster. Surgeon discovers his wife loves another man, decides to eliminate him by bungling a cardiac operation. Ordinary crime drama whose main asset is its brevity.

Never on Sunday (1960)**** Melina Mercouri, Jules Dassin. Miss Mercouri delighted the movie audiences of the world with her inimitable performance of a carefree fille de joie in this film. A tourist named Homer tries to "reform" her, but his attempt to play Pygmalion has its setbacks. Director Dassin made an unfortunate choice in casting himself in the role of Homer, but the magnificent Melina is the stellar attraction here, and she's luminous throughout. Wonderful Greek musical score. (Dir: Jules Dassin, 91 mins.)

Never Put It in Writing (Great Britain, 1964)½ Pat Boone, Milo O'Shea, Fidelma Murphy. Weak comedy set in London, should never have been put on the screen! Boone is a young executive whose promotion is threatened by a fiery letter, which he attempts to retrieve. Poorly written and directed by Andrew L. Stone. (90 mins.)

Never Say Die (1939)**½ Bob Hope, Martha Raye. Bob tries but this is little more than juvenile slapstick about a hypochondriac millionaire who marries a Texas gal because he thinks he has but two weeks to live. (Dir: Elliott Nugent, 80 mins.)

Never Say Goodbye (1946)**½ Errol Flynn, Eleanor Parker. A few laughs in this familiar farce about a man trying to win back his ex-wife but too much of it is contrived and silly. (Dir: James V. Kern, 97 mins.)

Never Say Goodbye (1956)**½ Rock Hudson, Cornell Borchers, George Sanders. Satisfactory remake of a 1945 film, "This Love of Ours" which starred Merle Oberon in the role played by Cornell Borchers in this version. Story concerns a woman whose husband left her many years ago taking her only daughter with him and how they meet years later and try to pick up the pieces of their torn lives. (Dir: Jerry Hopper, 96 mins.)

Never So Few (1959)**½ Frank Sinatra, Gina Lollobrigida, Peter Lawford, Steve McQueen. Despite an all star cast, this turns out to be just another World War II adventure with heavy romantic overtones. Miss Lollobrigida is a vision and Steve McQueen comes off best among the male contingent. (Dir: John Sturges, 124 mins.)

Never Steal Anything Small (1959)**½ James Cagney, Shirley Jones, Roger Smith, Cara Wiiliams. Cagney as a crooked labor leader who will stop at nothing to become boss of the waterfront. Unlikely blend of satire, song, slapstick never jells, although the cast works hard. (Dir: Charles Lederer, 94 mins.)

Never Take No for an Answer (1951)*** Vittorio Manunta, Dennis O'Dea. Small boy tries to take his sick donkey to the crypt of St. Francis, where he is sure the animal will recover. Charming Italian story has plenty of good touches, human interest.

Never Too Late (1965)*** Paul Ford, Maureen O'Sullivan, Connie Stevens, Jim Hutton. Broadway comedy hit about a middle-aged couple with a grown, married daughter who discover they are to become parents. Transferred to the screen with all the funny situations intact. However, it becomes labored before the end, even with a truly wonderful performance by blustering Paul Ford as the old man thinking of retiring, and then hit with the news that he's to be a father. Maureen O'Sullivan, who appeared on Broadway along with Ford, is just right as the wife, and Connie Stevens and Jim Hutton supply the young romance of the subplot. (Dir: Bud Yorkin, 105 mins.)

Never Wave at a Wac (1952)**½ Rosalind Russell, Paul Douglas, Marie Wilson. Society hostess doesn't realize what she's in for when she joins the Women's Army Corp. Mildly amusing comedy, with a cast of seasoned laugh-getters helping it along. (Dir: Norman Z. McLeod, 87 mins.)

New Centurions, The (1972)**½ George C. Scott, Stacy Keach, Jane Alexander. Uneven police story, based on the novel by Sgt. Joseph Wambaugh, that falters despite a good acting turn by Scott as a veteran cop who winds up his years of duty and retires. Keach is the hotshot new cop with new ideas and he gets involved in a series of plot developments that play like separate TV cop shows. The best moment comes as Scott wars with the idleness of retirement and finally commits suicide in a scene that has an air of nobility only Scott can bring to it. Patronizing tone doesn't help. (Dir: Richard Fleischer, 103 mins.)

New Daughters of Joshua Cabe, The (1976)* John McIntire, Jack Elam, Liberty Williams, Renne Jarrett, Lezlie Dalton. The third time around for the "Cabe" property; maybe they'll get it right someday. Williams, Jarrett, and Dalton play a trio of city girls out in Wyoming doing their darndest to release their so-called Dad, Josh Cabe, from a murder rap! Made-for-TV. (Dir: Bruce Bilson, 72 mins.)

New Healers, The (1972)**½ Burgess Meredith, Leif Erickson. A pilot for a proposed series which isn't half bad. A trio of para-medics gravitates to a remote rural area which has one aging, ailing doctor. It takes a while for the populace to accept the new breed of "healers." Veteran actors Burgess Meredith and Leif Erickson shine in their supporting roles. Made-for-TV. (Dir: Bernard Kowalski, 54 mins.)

New Interns, The (1964)**½ Michael Callan, Barbara Eden, George Segal, Inger Stevens. Fairly interesting drama about hospitals and doctors. There are at least three major plots and as many subplots. Callan plays the wise-guy casanova who tries to interest nurse Barbara Eden in romance. (Dir: John Rich, 123 mins.)

New Kind of Love, A (1963)**½ Paul Newman, Joanne Woodward. The first quarter of this romantic comedy is quite funny, with an amusing opening scene of a department store rush. After that, the plot and the laughs go downhill. Mildly enjoyable fluff about how reporter Paul Newman meets and chases fashion designer Joanne Woodward.

(Dir: Melville Shavelson, 110 mins.)

New Land, The (Sweden, 1973)**** Liv Ullmann, Max von Sydow, Eddie Axberg. Superb sequel to deeply moving "The Emigrants," originally intended to be shown together as one film. The saga of the Oskar family documents their hardships in carving a new life in the growing U.S. Their grim experiences range from a fruitless search for gold in the Southwest to their eventual settlement in Minnesota. Ullmann and von Sydow provide a timeless example of the efficacy of married love. A remarkable filmed essay on foreign emigration to America. (Dir: Jan Troell, 161 mins.)

New Leaf, A (1971)***½ Walter Matthau, Elaine May. A large credit is due Miss May, the writer-actor-director whose inventiveness keeps you smiling throughout. Matthau plays a sly snob who's bankrupt and looking for a rich woman to marry within six weeks. He finds Miss May, a rich botanist and one of the world's clumsiest ladies. Laughs and love ensue! May's direction is perfect, never slick, always warm and slightly askew. Incidentally, if you have a feeling that you've heard the musical score before, it's because you have. It's lifted from Paramount's '67 release, "Oh Dad, Poor Dad, Mamma's Hung You in the Closet and I'm Feelin' So Sad." (102 mins.)

New Moon (1940)**½ Jeanette MacDonald, Nelson Eddy. Dated, though swashbuckling romantic operetta which has a delightful Romberg score and the excellent voices of the stars to its credit. (Dir: Robert Z. Leonard, 105 mins.)

New, Original Wonder Woman, The (1975)½ Lynda Carter, Lyle Waggoner. Spoofs are difficult to pull off—they require a light, deft touch . . . This TV cartoon has been mounted with a heavy hand. It is silly without being funny. Lynda Carter is a gorgeous, well-endowed woman who can't approximate acting, and Lyle Waggoner runs her a close second. Talents wasted in the misdirected mélange include Cloris Leachman, Stella Stevens, Kenneth Mars and Henry Gibson. Made-for-TV. (Dir: Leonard Horn, 72 mins.)

New Orleans (1947)** Jazz from Louis Armstrong, Woody Herman,

Billie Holiday and the like, in a story of the Basin Street town around 1917. Arturo de Cordova and Dorothy Patrick take care of the story, one of the those rich-girl poor-boy things. Dull story, good music.

New World, A (Mexican, 1960)*½ Arturo Arias, Lorena Velasquez. Deep-sea diver sets out to avenge the murder of his brother. Corny English-dubbed melodrama. (Dir: Arthur Lubin, 89 mins.)

New York Confidential (1955)**½ Broderick Crawford, Anne Bancroft, Richard Conte. Tense and exciting expose of the big crime syndicate working out of New York. Supposedly based on facts. Anne Bancroft took part in this before her Broadway successes. (Dir: Russell Rouse, 87 mins.)

New York Town (1941)**½ Fred MacMurray, Mary Martin. Occasionally amusing comedy about a sidewalk photographer who befriends a homeless lass in the big city. (Dir: Charles Vidor, 94 mins.)

Newman's Law (1974)*½ George Peppard, Roger Robinson, Abe Vigoda. Every cliché of the cop-movie genre has been retreaded here. Peppard plays the righteous cop accused of corruption and then suspended, who decides to pursue his case privately. (Dir: Richard Heffron, 98 mins.)

Next Man, The (1976)½ Sean Connery, Cornelia Sharpe, Albert Paulsen. One critic correctly summed up this fiasco by noting "The Next Man" is a suspense melodrama made by people whose talent for filmmaking and knowledge of international affairs would both fit comfortably into "the left nostril of a small bee." You'd also have ample room in the other nostril to shelter the acting talent of Cornelia Sharpe, who looks like Faye Dunaway, but Cornelia can't act at all. There's some attractive travelogue footage to distract you from the numbing talk and action about Saudi Arabian diplomats, and the effort to kill "The Next Man." (Dir: Richard Sarafian, 108 mins.)

Next of Kin (British, 1942)***½ Showing the effects of loose information, how it can lead to enemy ears. Excellent wartime drama, with Nova Pilbeam, Mervyn Johns.

Next Stop, Greenwich Village (1976)***½ Lenny Baker, Shelley Winters, Ellen Greene, Mike Kellin. Affectionate, engaging, autobiographical Valentine directed and written by Paul Mazursky about his own growing up in New York's Greenwich Village circa 1953. Two unusually winning performances by newcomers Baker and Greene combine to make this film alternately farcical, rueful and wistful. It doesn't all work, but it's an often lovely portrait of the joys and defeats of an aspiring adolescent comedian in the Big Apple! (109 mins.)

Next Time We Love (1936)**½ James Stewart, Margaret Sullavan, Ray Milland. Wife gives up her singing job to accompany her husband on a foreign assignment. Fairly good romantic drama. (Dir: Edward H. Griffith, 90 mins.)

Next to No Time (British, 1959)** Kenneth More, Betsy Drake. Shy factory employee tries to put his plan of automation into practice. Uneven comedy has some clever moments but never quite makes the top. Well acted. (Dir: Henry Cornelius, 93 mins.)

Next Voice You Hear, The (1950)*** James Whitmore, Nancy Davis, Gary Gray. Over-sentimentalized, but nevertheless engrossing drama about a group of people who hear the voice of God on the radio and the effect it has on their lives. (Dir: William Wellman, 82 mins.)

Niagara (1953)**½ Marilyn Monroe, Joseph Cotten, Jean Peters. This film boasts two scenic marvels, Niagara Falls and M.M. in various states of undress. The drama is heavy handed and pretty obvious but La Monroe's undulations and attempt at portraying a faithless wife make it worthwhile. (Primarily for the male viewers.) (Dir: Henry Hathaway, 89 mins.)

Nice Little Bank That Should Be Robbed, A (1958)** Tom Ewell, Mickey Rooney, Dina Merrill. Two amateur crooks bungle an elaborately planned bank robbery. Comedy with a clever idea that doesn't live up to its promise. Just middling fair fun. (Dir: Henry Levin, 87 mins.)

Nicholas and Alexandra (British, 1971)*** Michael Jayston, Janet Suzman, Laurence Olivier, Jack Hawkins. Huge sprawling, uneven, but often interesting historical film about the 14-year period leading up to the Russian Revolution. Film focuses on the royal couple, and there's some particularly good acting by Miss Suzman, whose performance earned her an Academy Award nomination. There are some ravishing costumes of the period, which deservedly did win the Academy Award. (Dir: Franklin J. Schaffner, 189 mins.)

Nicholas Nickleby (British, 1947)***
Derek Bond, Cedric Hardwicke. The Dickens classic tale of a lad who strives to save himself and his family from an evil, miserly uncle. Interesting, well-acted costume melodrama. The music score is also noteworthy. (Dir: Alberto Cavalcanti, 95 mins.)

Night Ambush (British, 1957)***
Dirk Bogarde, Marius Goring. British soldiers sneak into occupied Crete, capture a German general and make it to safety with him. Uneven but different war story has some moments. (Dir: Michael Powell, 93 mins.)

Night and Day (1946)***½ Cary Grant, Alexis Smith, Mary Martin. Biography of Cole Porter is effectively used to present some of the composer's fine music. Monty Woolley appears as himself when he knew Porter during earlier years. Grant is, as always, a pleasure to watch and the music is a delight. (Dir: Michael Curtiz, 128 mins.)

Night and the City (British, 1950)**
Richard Widmark, Gene Tierney. Widmark plays a sleazy, two-bit hood in this watered-down screenplay based on a rather fine crime novel by Gerald Kersh. There are many chases, tantrums, and unpleasant characters scattered throughout the proceedings. (Dir: Jules Dassin, 95 mins.)

Night at the Opera, A (1935)****
Marx Brothers. If you don't like the Marx Brothers, forget this four-star rating but, if you do, have plenty of adhesive handy because you'll laugh until your sides hurt. (Dir: Sam Wood, 100 mins.)

Night Caller, The (France-Italy, 1975)** Jean-Paul Belmondo, Charles Denner, Lea Massari. Clumsy French imitation of American crime films, which is badly dubbed to boot. Belmondo plays a police inspector tracking down a lunatic who calls up women on the telephone and then strangles them in person. Enlivened only by a chase

across the rooftops of Paris. The producer should have bought Belmondo rubber-soled shoes and a better script. (Dir: Henri Verneuil, 91 mins.)

Night Chase (1970)**½ David Janssen. Yaphet Kotto. TV-made-drama. David Janssen is on the run again. He's a world-weary gent taking an all-night cab ride along the California coast after shooting his wife's lover, and he gives cabbie Yaphet Kotto an exasperating time. Kotto's appealing character counters the familiar, tired, defeatist type Janssen specializes in. Even though the trip is much too long, location footage at Del Mar race track, along coastal highways, and at the San Diego Zoo help hold your attention. (Dir: Jack Starret, 99 mins.)

Night Club Scandal (1937)**½ John Barrymore, Lynne Overman. Well-acted, entertaining little mystery. Not a whodunit but interesting as you know who's guilty and watch the police make the mistakes. (Dir: Ralph Murphy, 80 mins.)

Night Creatures (British, 1962)**½ Peter Cushing, Yvonne Romain, Oliver Reed. Village vicar is in reality the head of a notorious smuggling ring. Lively, suspenseful costume thriller, some spooky scenes, some suspense, some action, all blended together ably. (Dir: Peter Graham Scott, 81 mins.)

Night Drum (Japanese, 1958)**½ Director Tadashi Imai chose a successful direct narrative approach for this somber tale set in feudal Japan —about a returning warrior who discovers his wife has committed adultery during his absence. According to the prescribed code, she must be killed to save his honor. (Dir: Tadashi Imai, 95 mins.)

Night Editor (1946)*** William Gargan, Janis Carter. Crooked cop gets involved with luscious but mean dame. Well scripted, well acted "B" melodrama. (Dir: Henry Levin, 68 mins.)

Night Fighters (1960)**½ Robert Mitchum, Anne Heywood, Dan O'Herlihy. The Irish rebellion is the setting of this adventure yarn which has a fine cast of players headed by Robert Mitchum. On-location photography is also an asset. (Dir: Tay Garnett, 85 mins.)

Night Flight From Moscow (France-Italy-West Germany, 1973)** Yul

Brynner, Henry Fonda, Dirk Bogarde, Virna Lisi, Philippe Noiret. An international cast of capable actors gets bogged down in a plot-heavy espionage tale about double agents and their intricate operations in Western Europe. Brynner has the biggest part as a Soviet KGB official who gives up names of his fellow agents to the CIA and British Intelligence. Originally released as "The Serpent." (Dir: Henri Verneuil, 121 mins.)

Night Freight (1955)**½ Forrest Tucker, Barbara Britton. Railroad operator battles ruthless trucking outfit. Action melodrama manages to whip up some excitement. (Dir: Jean Yarbrough, 79 mins.)

Night Gallery (1969)**½ Joan Crawford, Richard Kiley, Roddy McDowall. Strictly for those who found Rod Serling's "The Twilight Zone" TV series to their liking. This made-for-TV feature is divided into three separate mystery tales bridged together by a trio of portraits. None is really terribly original but a willing audience will probably stick with the suspenseful dramas of the macabre. Joan Crawford tears at the scenery in the second story about a wealthy blind woman who arranges to buy another person's sight and submit to an operation which may give her 10 or 11 hours of vision. The idea got bogged down in melodrama but Miss Crawford gives it her all. The other two tales have Roddy McDowall as an unscrupulous young man who meets his comeuppance, and Richard Kiley as a tortured ex-Nazi hiding out in South America. (Dir: Boris Sagal, 98 mins.)

Night Has a Thousand Eyes (1948)** Edward G. Robinson, Gail Russell. Ex-vaudeville magician seems to be able to predict the future, and the result is an uneven, overdone drama. (Dir: John Farrow, 80 mins.)

Night Heaven Fell, The (French, 1958)*½ Brigitte Bardot, Stephen Boyd, Alida Valli. Steamy passions rise as a countess and her niece both have designs on a handsome neighbor. One of those horrible films that plummeted sexpot Bardot to fame because of the vast amount of epidermis revealed. She's good to look at, but as a drama this is pretty much a strain. English-

dubbed. (Dir: Roger Vadim, 90 mins.)

Night Holds Terror, The (1955)**½ Jack Kelly, Hildy Parks. A trio of hitchhikers take over a man's home and terrorize his wife and children. Good performances spark the familiar plot line. (Dir: Andrew L. Stone, 86 mins.)

Night in Casablanca, A (1946)**½ Marx Brothers. The boys are involved in North African intrigue, but they get off enough humor to please their most ardent followers. Others beware. (Dir: Archie Mayo, 84 mins.)

Night in Paradise (1946)**½ Merle Oberon, Turhan Bey. In old Greece, dashing Aesop, disguised as an old man, falls for a beautiful princess. Romantic costume spectacle doesn't take itself seriously, which is all for the best. (Dir: Arthur Lubin, 84 mins.)

Night into Morning (1951)**½ Ray Milland, John Hodiak, Nancy Davis. The producers of this film probably thought lightning would strike twice if they cast Ray Milland as a man who turns to the bottle for solace (not unlike Milland's Oscar-winning "Lost Weekend") but it doesn't work. This time Milland is a college professor whose wife and son are killed in an explosion. Thereby triggering his battle with the bottle. (Dir: Fletcher Markle, 86 mins.)

Night Is My Future (Swedish, 1947)**½ Mai Zetterling, Birger Malmsten. Blinded young man meets a girl who tries to bring him happiness. Plodding drama directed by Ingmar Bergman is not up to his best work. English-dubbed. (Dir: Ingmar Bergman, 87 mins.)

Night Monster, The (1942)** Bela Lugosi, Lionel Atwill, Irene Hervey. A maniac is at work in a creepy mansion, and all of his victims are medical men. Typical horror yarn. (Dir: Ford Beebe, 73 mins.)

Night Moves (1975)**½ Gene Hackman, Susan Clark, Jennifer Warren. One character says, while talking about a local girl-chaser, "He'd fuck a woodpile on the chance there was a snake in it." Well, you won't find that line anywhere when "Night Moves" shows up on network TV, but you will find a disappointing, though sharply observed, melodrama shot on location in California and Florida. I say disappointing because it's the first film in five years from the talented Arthur Penn, but this melodrama about a private eye (Hackman) who goes to Florida to find a runaway girl-drifter never quite jells. Your stomach may curdle, though, at the violent end she meets—beheaded by a marauding seaplane while scuba diving. (Dir: Arthur Penn, 100 mins.)

Night Must Fall (1937)***½ Robert Montgomery, Rosalind Russell. Emlyn Williams' terrifying suspense drama is in good hands in this screen treatment. Montgomery as the outwardly charming homicidal maniac turns in an excellent job. (Dir: Richard Thorpe, 120 mins.)

Night Must Fall (British, 1964)**½ Albert Finney, Mona Washburne, Susan Hampshire. Inadequate remake of the 1937 classic film thriller of Emlyn Williams which starred Robert Montgomery. In this reincarnation, talented Albert Finney falls victim to gross overplaying as the psychotic killer who gets in the good graces of his aging invalid employer, only to turn around and do her in. The suspense falters before night falls. (Dir: Karel Reisz, 105 mins.)

Night My Number Came Up, The (British, 1956)***½ Michael Redgrave, Alexander Knox. Well acted British drama of an Air Force officer's troubled dreams and their effect on his work. (Dir: Leslie Norman, 94 mins.)

Night of Dark Shadows, (1971)*½ David Selby, Lara Parker, Kate Jackson, Grayson Hall. A sequel to "House of Dark Shadows," the TV gothic soap opera that spawned two feature films of dubious merit. This is the second one. Barnabas Collins, played with dangling teeth by Jonathan Frid in the TV series and the first film, is conspicuously missing. However, Grayson Hall tries to muster evil with every look, but she comes off looking like a poor woman's Gale Sondergaard. (Dir: Dan Curtis, 96 mins.)

Night of January 16th (1941)** Robert Preston, Ellen Drew. Fair little mystery about a sailor who is left a huge legacy but must solve a few mysteries before he can touch the dough. (Dir: William Clemens, 79 mins.)

Night of Nights, The (1939)** Pat O'Brien, Olympe Bradna. A broken down playwright makes a comeback after being reunited with his long-lost daughter. Corny, sentimental trash which is well acted. (Dir: Lewis Milestone, 90 mins.)

Night of San Juan, The (Bolivian, 1971)**** Federico Vallejio, Felicidad Coca. Powerful documentary recreation by gifted Bolivian director Jorge Sanjines, made after his memorable "Blood of the Condor." Reconstructs the 1967 massacre, by the Bolivian Army, of a group of striking, nonviolent, impoverished tin miners. Cast of nonprofessional actors, most of whom were participants in the '67 protest and witnesses to the massacre. Sanjines' passion about changing social and political institutions is evident throughout his earnest film. Financed and produced, interestingly enough, by RAI-TV, Italian television, as one of a series of six films commissioned by RAI and directed by young South American directors to examine today's society in various Latin-American countries.

Night of Terror (1972)** Donna Mills, Martin Balsam. Aims to scare, and often succeeds despite several contrived situations. Seeking a vital piece of information, a killer stalks two girls (Miss Mills and Catherine Burns) who share an apartment. Ex-New York cop Eddie Egan plays the police detective in the case. Made-for-TV. (Dir: Jeannot Szwarc, 73 mins.)

Night of the Following Day, The (1969)**½ Marlon Brando, Richard Boone, Rita Moreno. Complex, contrived, generally muddled melodrama. Once again Marlon Brando, looking very fit and lean, has squandered his remarkable talent on hokey material. Marlon is an accomplice in a kidnaping in France, but the only real quality in the film is found in a bathtub scene of Rita Moreno, and a few scenes where Brando displays that unique magnetism and acting brilliance that still set him apart from virtually all other actors of his generation. (Dir: Hubert Cornfield, 93 mins.)

Night of the Generals, The (1967)**½ Peter O'Toole, Omar Sharif, Joanna Pettet, Christopher Plummer. Despite an all-star cast of pros and careful production details, this film about the Nazi generals of Hitler's regime and the repercussions of a couple of prostitutes' murders, emerges as an overlong melodrama. Peter O'Toole is miscast as a sadistic Nazi general who covers his traces well until he's haunted by his past deeds twenty odd years later. The film is not without interest, but it only comes alive during individual scenes here and there, notably in some of the scenes filmed in Poland. (Dir: Anatole Litvak, 148 mins.)

Night of the Great Attack, The (Italian, 1964)*½ Agnes Laurent, Fausto Tozzi. Crafty Cesare Borgia schemes to acquire a dukedom, plans a night attack on an independent territory. Mediocre English-dubbed costume adventure.

Night of the Grizzly (1966)**½ Clint Walker, Martha Hyer. Predictable adventure about a former lawman who goes to Wyoming with his family in order to start a new life. He encounters a bear who threatens his existence, and he pursues it with a vengeance. The action is slow in starting, but the climax packs some excitement. (Dir: Joseph Pevney, 102 mins.)

Night of the Hunter (1955)**** Robert Mitchum, Shelley Winters, Lillian Gish. Religious fanatic marries a widow, murders her for her husband's loot. Brooding, artistic drama directed by Charles Laughton; superb mood, fine performances, plenty of suspense. Recommended. (90 mins.)

Night of the Iguana (1964)**** Richard Burton, Deborah Kerr, Ava Gardner. Tennessee Williams' plays have sometimes been diluted and sentimentalized when transferred to the screen. Thanks to John Huston's expert direction and a literate screenplay, which is largely faithful to the spirit of the original play, this searing study about genteel losers down on their luck in Mexico becomes a satisfying and moving film. Richard Burton is perfect as a defrocked clergyman bent on destruction; Deborah Kerr is superb playing an anguished spinster; and Ava Gardner, giving one of the best performances of her career, plays the proprietress of a seedy resort hotel with a remarkable quality of restrained sensuality. (Dir: John Huston, 125 mins.)

Night of the Lepus (1972)½ Stuart Whitman, Janet Leigh, Rory Calhoun. Lepus is the Latin word for rabbit! We've had giant ants, evil rats and killer roaches and now . . . it's marauding rabbits. When an Arizona ranch is overrun with rabbits reproducing at an alarming rate, a serum is sought to curtail the birth boom. Would have been thoughtful to curtail this bummer at birth. Based on the novel "Year of the Angry Rabbit," by Russell Braddon. (Dir: William Claxton, 90 mins.)

Night of the Living Dead (1968)* Judith O'Dea, Russell Streiner, Duane Jones. Group of people take refuge in a farmhouse and are menaced when the dead return to life. Made on a shoestring, often inept, frequently gruesome (Dir: George A. Romero, 90 mins.)

Night of the Quarter Moon (1959)* Julie London, John Drew Barrymore, Nat Cole. Social family backs a man who discovers his wife has Negro blood. Trashy drama handles a serious problem luridly. Alternate title: "Flesh and Flame." (Dir: Hugo Haas, 96 mins.)

Night Passage (1957)**½ James Stewart, Audie Murphy, Dan Duryea. Fairly interesting western about a railroad trouble shooter trying to recover a stolen payroll. Things get sticky when his brother turns up on the side of the outlaws. (Dir: James Neilson, 90 mins.)

Night People (1954)**½ Gregory Peck, Broderick Crawford, Rita Gam. Interesting cloak and dagger yarn set in Berlin concerning the efforts of the U.S. Army Intelligence Corps to get a young American soldier, who has been kidnapped, out of the Russian sector. (Dir: Nunnally Johnson, 93 mins.)

Night Plane from Chungking (1943)**½ Robert Preston, Ellen Drew. Well done, contrived little "B" action film about a plane downed in China containing one traitor on its passenger list.

Night Riders (Mexican, 1963)*½ Gaston Santos, Alma Rosa Aguirre. Lawman comes to the aid of a girl whose land is threatened by marauders. Thoroughly mediocre western dubbed in English.

Night Runner, The (1957)** Ray Danton, Merry Anders. Parolee from a mental hospital goes berserk, turns into a killer. Average suspense melodrama offers little novelty. (Dir: Abner Biberman, 79 mins.)

Night Slaves (1970)** James Franciscus, Lee Grant, Leslie Nielsen. Made-for-TV picture. A muddled sci-fi yarn which generates some suspense during the first few scenes but deteriorates into a somewhat silly plot, involving inhabitants from outer space and their take-over of a small town. Lee Grant deserves better.

Night Stalker, The (1972)**½ Darren McGavin. Exciting piece of foolishness involving a breezy reporter and a fanged vampire in Las Vegas, a perfect setting for the entertainment. In the old tradition of wise-cracking newsmen, McGavin shines as a nosy reporter sparring with the Vegas establishment over vampire killings. Result is a lively, violent, and irreverent murder show. Made-for-TV. (Dir: John Llewellyn Moxey, 73 mins.)

Night Strangler, The (1973)**½ Darren McGavin. Sequel to the thriller "The Night Stalker," which stands as one of the highest-rated made-for-TV films. McGavin repeats his newspaper reporter role tracking down a story to Seattle, Wash., where a nocturnal strangler is on the prowl. Made-for-TV. (Dir: Dan Curtis, 73 mins.)

Night Terror (1977)*½ Valerie Harper, Richard Romanus, Michael Tolan. Predictable melodrama which uses a time-worn device of having someone witness a killing and then have to flee for his life. Valerie Harper is on the road when she notices she needs gas and spots a highway patrolman giving a guy a ticket. When she approaches them, the patrolman is killed and the chase begins. Made-for-TV. (Dir: E. W. Swackhamer, 76 mins.)

Night That Panicked America, The (1975)*** Paul Shenar, Cliff De Young, Vic Morrow, Eileen Brennan. On October 30th, 1938, the now-famous Orson Welles radio broadcast of H. G. Wells' "War of the Worlds" struck a chord of panic in the hearts of millions of listeners, who mistook the dramatization about an invasion from Mars for the real thing. People actually fled from their homes in New Jersey, the locale of the radio drama. Film recreates the radio show in authentic detail, and speculates about what radio listeners did, in well-constructed fictional vignettes, brought to life by a hand-picked cast. The Mercury Radio players, led by Orson Welles (excellently played without resorting to mimicry by Shenar), are all fine, and the radio show sequences are fascinating. Joseph Sargent has directed with skill and taste. Made-for-TV. (98 mins.)

Night the World Exploded, The (1957)** Kathryn Grant, William Leslie. Pretentious science fiction "meller" dealing with the end of the world by destructive forces found deep in the Earth's crust. (Dir: Fred F. Sears, 94 mins.)

Night They Killed Rasputin, The (Italian-French, 1960)** Edmund Purdom, John Drew Barrymore, Gianna Maria Canale. Young aristocrat attempts to assassinate the power-loving mad monk Rasputin, who is running Russia his own way. Historical drama acted in the old wild-eyed style manages to drum up a fair amount of interest. English-dubbed.

Night They Raided Minsky's, The (1968)***½ Jason Robards, Bert Lahr, Britt Ekland, Norman Wisdom. Forget the silly story line about a pert, innocent Amish girl from the sticks of Pennsylvania (Ekland) who storms Broadway and ends up stripping—in burlesque. Just enjoy the many engaging things in the film, including some nostalgic scenes which capture the attractive, sleazy quality of old-time burlesque, and the comedians whose "racy" material filled out the stage waits between the strippers. (Dir: William Friedkin, 99 mins.)

Night Tide (1963)**½ Dennis Hopper, Linda Lawson, Launa Anders. A strange film that almost makes it. A young sailor meets a young carnival girl who believes she's really a mermaid transformed into an earthling and she fears her evil streak. The photography is arty but it works to establish mood. The acting is also better than average.

Night to Remember, A (1942)***½ Brian Aherne, Loretta Young. Mystery writer and wife turn detectives when they find a body in their Greenwich Village apartment. Bright comedy-mystery has some hilarious lines, smart performances. (Dir: Richard Wallace, 91 mins.)

Night to Remember, A (British, 1958) **** Kenneth More, Honor Blackman, David McCallum. Impressive achievement — documentarylike retelling of the ill-fated maiden voyage of the **Titanic**, magnificently detailed, authentic, stirring saga of heroism of "grace under pressure." Superb Eric Ambler script, Roy Baker direction, performances by the huge cast. (Dir: Roy Baker, 123 mins.)

Night Train (British, 1940)***½ Rex Harrison, Margaret Lockwood, Paul Henreid. With the help of the secret service, a scientist's daughter saves a valuable formula from the Nazis. Excellent suspense thriller, one of the best of its kind. Carol Reed directed.

Night Train for Inverness (British, 1959)** Norman Wooland, Jane Nylton. Diabetic is in great danger unless he's reached in time. Fairly suspenseful drama.

Night Train to Milan (Italian, 1965)**½ Jack Palance, Yvonne Furneaux. Passenger recognized as a wanted Nazi commits murder and holds a girl as hostage. Suspense thriller dubbed in English holds the attention pretty well.

Night Unto Night (1949)* Ronald Reagan, Broderick Crawford, Viveca Lindfors. Boring, tiresome melodrama about the romance of two characters who'd be better off dead. (Dir: Don Siegel, 92 mins.)

Night Visitor, The (1971)* Max von Sydow, Liv Ullmann, Trevor Howard. Despite a great cast, this is a stark, extremely boring mystery drama set in the Scandinavian wilderness. Max von Sydow plays a man incarcerated in a mental institution who escapes regularly in order to wreak revenge on those who have put him there. (Dir: Laslo Benedek, 102 mins.)

Night Walker, The (1964)**½ Barbara Stanwyck, Robert Taylor. Woman is terrorized by nightmares, which seem to be instigated by her husband who supposedly was killed in a fire. Suspense drama with some spooky moments, old pros Stanwyck and Taylor giving it a professional gloss. (Dir: William Castle, 86 mins.)

Night Watch (Great Britain, 1973)* Elizabeth Taylor, Laurence Harvey, Billie Whitelaw, Robert Lang. Is Elizabeth Taylor's husband really trying to do her in? Story reminiscent of the movie classic "Gaslight." Though employing all the usual hints to indicate Miss Taylor's oncoming insanity—squeaking stairs, evil looks and hysterical phone calls, they never create suspense. Based on Lucille Fletcher's stage play—fans of the genre would do better to view Miss Fletcher's classic "Sorry, Wrong Number." Seems like a dated 1940's item. (Dir: Brian G. Hutton, 98 mins.)

Night Without Sleep (1952)**½ Linda Darnell, Gary Merrill, Hildegarde Neff. Mentally disturbed man is driven to murder. Minor but well acted little psycho-thriller. (Dir: Roy Baker, 77 mins.)

Night Without Stars (British, 1953)**½ David Farrar, Nadia Gray. Blinded man in France becomes involved with black marketeers and murder, returns to England to have his sight restored, so he can solve the mystery. Interesting mystery melodrama.

Nightcomers, The (British, 1971)*** Marlon Brando, Stephanie Beacham, Harry Andrews. Atmosphere is the main ingredient in this cinematic prelude to Henry James' "The Turn of the Screw." (The James story was filmed in '61 as "The Innocents.") Worth seeing mainly for Brando's performance, which helps overcome the hardly believable story about children who plot to kill Brando and his lover. (Dir: Michael Winner, 95 mins.)

Nightfall (1957)**½ Aldo Ray, Brian Keith, Anne Bancroft. Fairly absorbing crime drama. Good performances. Suspenseful tale of an artist chased by robbers for their stolen loot. (Dir: Jacques Tourneur, 78 mins.)

Nightmare (1942)**½ Brian Donlevy, Diana Barrymore. Fairly exciting suspense tale. An American gambler stumbles into murder, and finds himself hot on the trail of foreign agents. Donlevy does nicely in the lead.

Nightmare (1973)**½ Richard Crenna, Patty Duke Astin, Vic Morrow. "Rear Window" type thriller. A New Yorker thinks he's witnessed a shooting, and decides to play sleuth when police display skepticism. Fair suspense yarn contains hokey segments along with a climactic chase scene. Crenna delivers a believable performance as the witness, Mrs. Astin handles the screaming bits, and Vic Morrow is the quizzical detective. Made-for-TV. (Dir: William Hale.)

Nightmare Alley (1947)***½ Tyrone Power, Coleen Gray, Joan Blondell. Strong drama about a carnival drifter who double-crosses everybody on his way to success. One of Power's best performances; absorbing film. (Dir: Edmund Goulding, 111 mins.)

Nightmare Castle (Italian, 1965)*½ Barbara Steele, Giorgio Ardisson. Eerie goings-on in a mysterious castle. Stilted costume thriller, some effective moments, mostly corn. English-dubbed. (Dir: Allan Grunewald, 90 mins.)

Nightmare In the Sun (1964)*½ Ursula Andress, John Derek, Arthur O'Connell, Aldo Ray. No-good wife of a rancher who's been playing around with the sheriff is the cause on an innocent hitchhiker's involvement in murder and terror. Drama of love and lust, played that way. Performances help some, not much. (Dir: Marc Lawrence, 80 mins.)

Nights of Cabiria (Italian, 1957)***½ Giulietta Masina. A simple minded prostitute is taken in by every man she meets. Intensely dramatic, grim tale. Finely acted and well directed by Federico Fellini. Very moving thanks to Mrs. Fellini's sensitive acting. (110 mins.)

Nina B. Affair, The (French, 1959)** Nadja Tiller, Pierre Brasseur. Millionaire's discontented wife plans his death. Slow-moving drama is stretched out past its proper length. Dubbed in English.

Nine Girls (1944)*** Evelyn Keyes, Jinx Falkenburg, Ann Harding. Hated sorority girl is murdered, and one of the girls turns sleuth to find the killer. Well written, nicely acted and directed mystery.

Nine Hours to Rama (1963)***½ Horst Buchholz, Jose Ferrer, Diane Baker. Absorbing, well-mounted political drama about the nine hours leading up to the assassination of India's Mahatma Gandhi, a significant and rarely treated subject in films. Buchholz plays the rebellious Indian youth who is assigned to kill Gandhi, and though his romantic entanglements slow the action, the pace picks up again before the shattering climax. The supporting cast is uniformly fine, and the superb on-location camera work in India adds greatly to the film. Memorable performance by nonprofessional actor J. S. Casshyap playing and looking remarkably like Mahatma Gandhi. (Dir: Mark Robson, 125 mins.)

Nine Lives (Norwegian, 1959)**½ Documentary reenactment of true story, as a brave resistance fighter braves the perils of the frozen wilderness in an attempt to disrupt Nazi operations during World War II. Fascinating tale suffers from stilted treatment, should have been much better. Native cast, with narration in English by March of Time voice Westbrook Van Voorhees, with Luis Van Rooten supplying additional commentary.

1984 (1956)***½ Edmond O'Brien, Michael Redgrave, Jan Sterling. Orwell's image of what our world will be like in '84 has been converted to an interesting if somewhat confused film. (Dir: Michael Anderson, 91 mins.)

90 Degrees in the Shade (Czech, 1964)***½ Anne Heywood, James Booth, Ann Todd, Donald Wolfit. Married food-store manager has an affair with a stock girl and has been stealing from the liquor supply; it spells tragedy. From Czechoslovakia, extremely well directed, acted by a cast that's partly British. Superior dramatic fare. (Dir: Jiri Weiss, 90 mins.)

99 River Street (1953)***½ John Payne, Evelyn Keyes. Taxi driver is aided by an ambitious actress in extricating him from a robbery in which his wife is involved. Sharp melodrama has superior acting, as well as excellent direction and camera work to make it above average. (Dir: Phil Karlson, 83 mins.)

99 Women (Italy-Spain-West Germany, 1969)½ Maria Schell, Mercedes McCambridge, Herbert Lom. The film treats women's prisons with as much brutality and exploitation as the prison abuse it purports to describe. Sexual assault and lesbianism are given center stage; a compassionate sociologist non-pervert (Schell), unsuccessful at introducing some leniency, just tries to keep smiling. You'll be so bored—or angry. Badly written by no-talent producer Harry Alan Towers. (Dir: Jesus Franco, 86 mins.)

Ninotchka (1939)***½ Greta Garbo, Melvyn Douglas. Delightful comedy about a female comrade who learns the meaning of life and love from an American in Paris. (Dir: Ernst Lubitsch, 120 mins.)

Nitwits, The (1935)*** Bert Wheeler, Robert Woolsey, Betty Grable. Proprietors of a cigar counter solve a murder in a department store. Pretty funny comedy-mystery, one of the better Wheeler-Woolseys. (Dir: George Stevens, 90 mins.)

No Down Payment (1957)**½ Joanne Woodward, Tony Randall, Jeffrey Hunter, Barbara Rush, Cameron Mitchell. Problems of four married couples living in a post-war housing project. Sort of a pre-fab Peyton Place, with as much underhand plotting going on. Good performances but the story often misses paying off. (Dir: Martin Ritt, 105 mins.)

No Escape (French, 1956)** Raf Vallone, Magali Noel. An escaped criminal enters the life of a lonely widow, who is dominated by her father-in-law and a mean servant. You've seen it before a hundred times.

No Greater Love—See: **Alfred Nobel Story, The**

No Highway in the Sky (British, 1951)***½ James Stewart, Marlene Dietrich, Glynis Johns. Absent-minded professor insists a new commercial airliner is not safe. Very good mixture of suspense and gentle comedy, excellently played by Stewart and Dietrich, a British cast. (Dir: Henry Koster, 98 mins.)

No Leave, No Love (1946)** Van Johnson, Keenan Wynn. Van's fans may be able to endure this long, forced comedy about a couple of Marines loose in the big city with plenty of money, thanks to a radio appearance. There's a romance, of course, but the picture never really moves. (Dir: Charles Martin, 119 mins.)

No Love for Johnnie (British, 1961)**** Peter Finch, Stanley Holloway, Mary Peach, Billie Whitelaw. Brilliantly acted drama about a member of parliament whose political and domestic affairs are both failures, and of his love for a young model. Incisive character portrait of a lonely man, frustrated in his attempt to cope with the world. Superior adult fare. (Dir: Ralph Thomas, 110 mins.)

No Man Is An Island (1962)**½ Jeffrey Hunter, Marshall Thompson. Story based on fact about a navy radioman who is trapped by the outbreak of World War II, becomes a guerrilla in the hills of Guam. Done in straightforward manner, with a good performance by Hunter. This nevertheless looks like all the other war films, although the location shooting in the Philippines is an added asset. (Dir: John Monks, Jr., 114 mins.)

No Man of Her Own (1933)**½ Clark Gable, Carole Lombard. A card shark is reformed by love. Not as potent as it used to be, but then Gable is Gable, and Lombard is pretty to look at. (Dir: Wesley Ruggles, 90 mins.)

No Man of Her Own (1950)** Barbara Stanwyck, John Lund, Lyle Bettger. Woman assumes the identity of a train-crash victim, begins a new life, but is blackmailed by her former boy friend. Stanwyck soap opera, similar to many of its kind, little better. (Dir: Mitchell Leisen, 98 mins.)

No Man's Land (1962)*½ Russ Harvey, Kim Lee. Corporal on night patrol in Korea establishes a friendship with a native girl. Weak war drama produced on a shoestring budget.

No Man's Woman (1955)** Marie Windsor, John Archer. Double-crossing dame is murdered. Ordinary mystery. (Dir: Franklin Adreon, 70 mins.)

No More Excuses (1968)***½ Robert Downey, Allen Abel, Paula Morris. The censorious prudes programming most TV stations probably won't run this sometimes inspired farce written and directed by Robert Downey, but we're going to review it anyway. One critic astutely noted "the whole experience was like watching and listening to a brilliant friend as he free associated with no thought of whether he was making a fool of himself." A collection of sight gags, scatological jokes, and one-liners running the gamut from the assassination of President Garfield to the Society for Indecency to Naked Animals. Downey, who also directed "Putney Swope," plays Private Steward Thompson. Low budget, big talent.

No, My Darling Daughter (British, 1964)**½ Michael Redgrave, Juliet Mills, Michael Craig, Roger Livesey. Tycoon realizes his daughter is at that grown-up age, entrusts her to a friend while on a business trip—and the trouble really begins. Performers such as Redgrave, Livesey, and Craig deserve better material than this mild comedy, but they troupe through it capably. (Dir: Betty Box, 97 mins.)

No Name on the Bullet (1959)**½ Audie Murphy, Joan Evans. When a hired killer rides into town, everybody wonders who his victim will be. Western keeps the secret well hidden until the end, should keep the fans in their seats. (Dir: Jack Arnold, 77 mins.)

No Ordinary Summer (Russian, 1956) *½ Viktor Korshunov. One-dimensional saga of several characters caught in the Russian Revolution. Mainly propaganda with little insight. (Dir: Vladimir Basov, 103 mins.)

No Place Like Homicide (British, 1962)** Kenneth Connor, Sidney James, Shirley Eaton. The one about all the relatives gathered in a spooky mansion to hear the reading of the will, done for laughs—only it might have been better played straight. Only a fair assortment of thrills and chuckles. (Dir: Pat Jackson, 87 mins.)

No Place to Hide (1956)*½ David Brian, Marsha Hunt, Keenan Wynn. The search is on for two boys who have innocently acquired pellets of deadly germs. Slow moving treatment robs this drama made in the Philippines of practically all its suspense. (Dir: Josef Shaftel, 71 mins.)

No Place to Run (1972)**½ Herschel Bernardi, Scott Jacoby. Touching old-man, young-boy drama, helped by the casting of Bernardi and Jacoby. Bernardi may be a shade underage for the over-70 grandfather part, and cameras avoid close-ups, but the skilled actor turns on the warmth and makes a credible character. Made-for-TV. (Dir: Delbert Mann, 73 mins.)

No Resting Place (British, 1951)**½ Michael Gough, Eithne Dunne. A drama of Irish vagrants, particularly of one who becomes a fugitive with his family when he accidentally kills a gamekeeper. Grim, beautifully photographed.

No Return Address (1961)*½ Harry Lovejoy, Alicia Hammond. Unscrupulous man causes his daughter to believe she is crippled so he can claim an insurance policy. Mediocre cheaply made drama.

No Room for the Groom (1952)**

Tony Curtis, Piper Laurie. Silly comedy about newlyweds who never get to enjoy a honeymoon has Tony Curtis mugging throughout and Piper Laurie looking perplexed. Obvious plot gimmicks often backfire. (Dir: Douglas Sirk, 82 mins.)

No Sad Songs for Me (1950)** Margaret Sullavan, Wendell Corey, Viveca Lindfors. Messy soap opera about a woman who starts setting her affairs straight, which includes promoting a love affair for her husband and her friend, when she finds she is dying of cancer. Good performances but limiting script. One of Sullavan's few film leads, and worth seeing largely for that reason. (Dir: Rudolph Mate, 89 mins.)

No Safety Ahead (British, 1957)*½ James Kennedy, Susan Beaumont. Another "perfect" bank robbery that doesn't turn out right—nor does the film. Mediocre.

No Sun in Venice (French-Italian, 1957)** Francoise Arnoul, Christian Marquand. Plodding, half-baked romance broken up by a villain who is in love with the girl. Good music is provided by the Modern Jazz Quartet. (Dir: Roger Vadim, 97 mins.)

No Survivors Please (German, 1963) *½ Marina Perschy, Robert Cunningham. Creatures from space cause accidents on earth so they can inhabit the bodies of the victims. Farfetched sci-fi thriller dubbed in English.

No Time for Comedy (1940)*** James Stewart, Rosalind Russell. Loose adaptation of the S. N. Behrman hit benefits from the cast but loses its satiric bite. As it now stands it's the story of a country boy who becomes a successful writer and must face the accompanying consequences. Stewart and Russell are at their best. (Dir: William Keighley, 93 mins.)

No Time for Flowers (1952)**½ Paul Christian, Viveca Lindfors. An actor is hired by the Communists to test the fidelity of an embassy clerk, but they both foil the Reds. Fairly amusing comedy made in Austria; no "Ninotchka," but pleasant enough. (Dir: Don Siegel, 83 mins.)

No Time for Love (1943)*** Claudette Colbert, Fred MacMurray. Amusing comedy about a lady photographer who falls for a sand-hog. Routine tale is superbly told and delightful viewing. (Dir: Mitchell Leisen, 83 mins.)

No Time for Sergeants (1958)******* Andy Griffith, Myron McCormick, Nick Adams. Andy Griffith is the whole show as the Georgia farm boy who gets drafted into the Army and creates mayhem among his superiors and colleagues. It's a virtuoso comedy performance. The supporting cast is fine. (Dir: Mervyn Le Roy, 111 mins.)

No Time for Tears (British, 1957)******* Anna Neagle, George Baker, Anthony Quayle, Sylvia Syms. Touching drama of the activities in a children's hospital, an unabashed tearjerker, but adeptly done. Fine performances.

No Time to Be Young (1957)****** Robert Vaughn, Roger Smith, Merry Anders. Slight drama about a trio of young men who find their backs are up against the wall and therefore plan a robbery. Cast is adequate considering the script. (Dir: David Lowell Rich, 82 mins.)

No Time to Kill (1962)***** John Ireland, Ellen Schwiers. Poor drama with an incredibly slow pace. An ex-con comes to Sweden seeking revenge because he was framed, as if we didn't know.

No Trees in the Street (British, 1958)****½** Stanley Holloway, Sylvia Syms, Herbert Lom. Director J. Lee Thompson makes a good attempt at showing the slum living conditions of pre-war London and the various personalities caught in them. With less stress on the personal dramas, this film could have been a good social commentary. (108 mins.)

No Vietnamese Ever Called Me Nigger (1968)****½** Low-budget black and white documentary about the anti-Vietnam War protests of the mid-60's is a powerful reminder of the moral outrage and passion of so many American citizens, young and old alike, during those embattled years. Has some memorable footage of an anti-war march, and some eloquent interviews with black veterans from "Nam." Made by a non-filmmaker, and did not get much attention or distribution at the time of its release. Produced and directed by David Loeb and Lois Weiss, a non-professional filmmaker. A valuable artifact for film historians. (76 mins.)

No Way Back (German, 1955)****** Ivan Desny, Ruth Niehaus. Russian Army officer in Berlin earns the suspicion of his superiors when he searches for a girl who had befriended him during the war. Problem drama doesn't make its point too well—leisurely and sometimes dull.

No Way Out (1950)*****½** Richard Widmark, Linda Darnell, Sidney Poitier. Biting drama about a Negro-hating, cop-hating hoodlum who incites a big race riot and almost ruins a Negro intern's chances of becoming a doctor. Director Joseph L. Mankiewicz gets top performances from his cast. (Dir: Joseph L. Mankiewicz, 106 mins.)

No Way to Treat a Lady (1968)*****½** Rod Steiger, Lee Remick, George Segal. Neat suspense yarn which affords Rod Steiger a tour-de-force as a psychotic killer who uses ingenious disguises to trick his victims. George Segal does very well as a harassed police detective who gets brief phone calls from the killer and builds a strange alliance as a result. A good show, primarily because it provides Steiger with a showcase to demonstrate his extraordinary acting range and talent. Alec Guinness played 8 roles in "Kind Hearts & Coronets." The versatile Steiger plays 7 roles in this one. (Dir: Jack Smight, 108 mins.)

Noah's Ark (1929-58)****** Dolores Costello, George O'Brien. Silent spectacle of Biblical times has been decked out with sound effects and narration. The spectacle is still effective, some scenes have tremendous scope—but the story dates badly. As a novelty, it will suffice. (Dir: Michael Curtiz, 75 mins.)

Nob Hill (1945)****** George Raft, Joan Bennett, Vivian Blaine. Saloon owner in the brawling San Francisco days breaks down the resistance of a blue-blooded socialite. Pleasant but unimportant drama with music. (Dir: Henry Hathaway, 95 mins.)

Nobody Lives Forever (1946)****½** John Garfield, Geraldine Fitzgerald. The acting is top drawer but this story of a hustler who comes back from the war and tries to swindle an innocent girl is very weak. Of course he falls for her—Oh, have you seen it too? (Dir: Jean Negulesco, 100 mins.)

Nobody Waved Goodbye (Canada, 1964)*****½** Peter Kastner, Julie Biggs, Claude Rae. Made on a small budget, this film beautifully documents the plight of a young 18-year-old who does not know what he stands for or cares about. Caught between the moral and material values of his parents and the boredom of high school, he steals a car and runs away with his girl friend. Compelling debut performance by Kastner gives the film real emotional impact. Underrated now, and at the time of release. Written, directed and produced by Don Owen.

Nobody's Perfect (1968)** Doug McClure, Nancy Kwan, James Whitmore. If you are devoted to scatter-brain service comedies in which the hero (Doug McClure, in this case) flits from one impossible situation to another and still manages to fall in love with a beautiful girl (Nancy Kwan in a nurse's uniform), tune in. The plot revolves around a missing Buddha statue, some crazy sailors and a jinxed village. Made for TV. (Dir: Alan Rafkin, 103 mins.)

Nocturne (1946)*** George Raft, Lynn Bari. Detective refuses to believe the death of a woman-chasing songwriter was suicide. Smooth mystery, interesting and suspenseful. (Dir: Edwin L. Marin, 88 mins.)

None But the Brave (1965)** Frank Sinatra, Clint Walker, Tommy Sands. Routine World War II action drama set in the Pacific, notable only because Sinatra also tried his hand at directing for the first time. Sinatra's platoon of Marines (he's the company medic) crash on an island occupied by a small band of Japanese soldiers and their many confrontations (some bloody . . . others peaceful) make up the bulk of the film's two-hour running time. (Dir: Frank Sinatra, 105 mins.)

None But the Lonely Heart (1944) ***½ Cary Grant, Ethel Barrymore. Cockney wanderer searches for some sort of spiritual fulfillment in the days before World War II. Excellently acted, powerfully written drama. (Dir: Clifford Odets, 113 mins.)

None But the Lonely Spy (Italian, 1964)* Ken Clark, Bella Cortez. Secret agent takes on the dangerous assignment of breaking up a dope-smuggling ring. Poor action melodrama dubbed in English.

None Shall Escape (1944)***½ Alexander Knox. Marsha Hunt. A Nazi officer is put on trial, and his crimes are reviewed. Gripping drama packs a punch. (Dir: Andre de Toth, 85 mins.)

Noose Hangs High, The (1948)** Abbott & Costello. Typical A & C film this time involving $50,000 stolen from the boys by some bad men. O.K. for kids. (Dir: Charles Barton, 77 mins.)

Nora Prentiss (1947)** Ann Sheridan, Kent Smith, Robert Alda. Meaningless, hackneyed melodrama about a doctor who almost loses everything just because he meets and falls for Miss Sheridan. (Dir: Vincent Sherman, 111 mins.)

Norliss Tapes, The (1973)** Roy Thinnes. Ghost story from horror-story specialist Dan Curtis. A serious Roy Thinnes plays an investigator of the occult involved in tracking down the mystery of a deceased sculptor who appears to be very much alive. Made-for-TV. (Dir: Dan Curtis.)

Norman, Is That You? (1976)* Redd Foxx, Pearl Bailey, Dennis Dugan, Michael Warren. Despite the potent casting of Redd Foxx and Pearlie May, this obvious, flimsy film remains a one-joke affair about parents discovering their strapping, handsome young son is sharing his digs with his gay lover. Most of the laughs are forced, but Foxx and Bailey try to punch their dialogue across. Dennis Dugan and Michael Warren are witless as the limp-wristed couple. Based on the Broadway flop play. (Dir: George Schlatter, 92 mins.)

North by Northwest (1959)***½ Cary Grant, Eva Marie Saint, James Mason. Master of suspense Alfred Hitchcock apparently had lots of fun directing this tongue-in-cheek spy thriller, and you'll have fun watching it. Grant, suave as ever, accidentally becomes entangled in one of those typically sinister Hitchcockian plots which never make much sense. Miss Saint looks marvelous and is a good leading lady for Grant. It's an adroit blend of laughter and excitement. (136 mins.)

North to Alaska (1960)***½ John Wayne, Stewart Granger, Ernie Kovacs, Capucine, Fabian. Big, brawling, lusty adventure about a couple of prospectors who have woman trouble in addition to their other problems. Lots of rugged action,

519

slapstick laughs played in fun. (Dir: Henry Hathaway, 122 mins.)

Northern Pursuit (1943)****½** Errol Flynn, Julie Bishop. Errol, still winning the war single-handed, is a Canadian Mountie in this one pursuing a Nazi aviator who's dashing through Canada bent on sabotage. (Dir: Raoul Walsh, 94 mins.)

Northwest Mounted Police (1940)******* Gary Cooper, Madeleine Carroll, Paulette Goddard. De Mille's tribute to the Mounties is a typical lavish, colorful, action-packed and shallow story. Will lose a lot in black and white, but if you like sagas, here it is. (Dir: Cecil B. De Mille, 125 mins.)

Northwest Outpost (1947)***½** Nelson Eddy, Ilona Massey. Historical melodrama of California's early days, when White Russian settlers populated the territory. Mostly dull, stiffly acted. (Dir: Allan Dwan, 91 mins.)

Northwest Passage (1939)*****½** Spencer Tracy, Robert Young, Walter Brennan. The kids will love it and so will most historical adventure fans as Spencer Tracy fights the Indians in his search for the Northwest Passage. (Dir: King Vidor, 125 mins.)

Norwood (1970)***** Glen Campbell, Kim Darby, Joe Namath. Insipid saga of a country boy, fresh from Vietnam, who sets out from Texas to New York to become a TV singer. Ten years earlier, Elvis Presley would have been the star, but in this opus it's Glen Campbell as Norwood. He's terrible whenever he's asked to do anything other than sing. Joe Namath is cast as his buddy Joe, and he's as good an actor as Campbell. Kim Darby, as a pregnant girl Norwood falls in love with en route, is the only decent thing about the film. (Dir: Jack Haley, Jr., 95 mins.)

Not as a Stranger (1955)******* Robert Mitchum, Frank Sinatra, Olivia de Havilland. This is a somewhat watered down version of Morton Thompson's best selling novel about doctors and their degrees of dedication to their chosen profession. The operating room scenes are far superior to the soap opera tendencies of the personal drama. Charles Bickford and Lon Chaney are outstanding in a large supporting cast. (Dir: Stanley Kramer, 125 mins.)

Not So Dusty (British, 1951)***½** Les-

lie Dwyer, Joy Nichols. Silliness about a couple of garbage men searching for a lost rare book.

Not with My Wife, You Don't (1966) ****½** Tony Curtis, Virna Lisi, George C. Scott, Carroll O'Connor. Occasionally diverting marital comedy which has George C. Scott playing a broad funny role for a change—and his fans might want to see this side of him. Also on hand, as handsome window dressing, is Tony Curtis, as a jealous husband-Air Force officer, and Virna Lisi, as his beautiful Italian wife. The plot is familiar fare but you'll get a few laughs out of it. (Dir: Norman Panama, 118 mins.)

Nothing But a Man (1964)******** Ivan Dixon, Abbey Lincoln. Moving, hardhitting film about a Negro couple who strive for dignity in an Alabama town. Ivan Dixon and Abbey Lincoln are excellent as the newlyweds who meet with more than their share of opposition as they try to make a life for themselves. Most of the film is simple in its narrative style which begins to haunt you even before the movie ends. Low-budget independent entry with a big wallop. (Dir: Michael Roemer, 92 mins.)

Nothing But the Best (1964)*****½** Alan Bates. A vastly underrated comedy gem, with a superb performance by Bates as a British workingclass stiff who wants to better his lot and uses his wiles, charm, and wit to reach the "top." Along the way, he encounters obstacles which he disposes of with alacrity and aplomb until he possibly has to resort to murder. Does he or doesn't he? Tune in (when it's on), find out, and have a good time along the way. (Dir: Clive Donner, 99 mins.)

Nothing But the Truth (1941)******* Bob Hope, Paulette Goddard. Bob is good, but much of the story is old hat in this tale of a man who bets that he can tell only the truth for 24 hours. Some laughs, of course, but not Bob's best.

Notorious (1946)*****½** Ingrid Bergman, Cary Grant, Claude Rains. Government agent and a refugee girl undertake a dangerous mission in Brazil, are suspected by a master spy chief. The Hitchcock brand of suspense, but doting heavily on the romantic angle. Nevertheless, some spine-tingling moments. (101 mins.)

Notorious Gentleman, The (British,

1947)***½ Rex Harrison, Lilli Palmer. The story of a charming but scoundrelly wastrel who goes through life without purpose until love redeems him. Absorbing ironic comedy-drama, with a fine performance from Harrison. (Dir: Frank Launder, 108 mins.)

Notorious Landlady, The (1962)*** Kim Novak, Jack Lemmon, Fred Astaire. Young American in London rents an apartment from a beautiful but mysterious girl whom the police suspect of having murdered her husband, and promptly gets involved. Generally entertaining comedy, thanks to Lemmon's droll antics; the proceedings occasionally become strained, but there's enough flash and dash to the production to satisfy. (Dir: Richard Quine, 123 mins.)

Notorious Mr. Monks (1958)*½ Vera Ralston, Don Kelly. Hitchhiker is picked up by a drunk and becomes involved in a murder. Pass this one by. (Dir: Joseph Kane, 70 mins.)

Novel Affair (British, 1957)*** Margaret Leighton, Ralph Richardson. Witty, sophisticated comedy about a respectably married authoress of a sexy novel and her over-amorous chauffeur. Cast is excellent. (Dir: Muriel Box, 83 mins.)

Now and Forever (1934)**½ Gary Cooper, Carole Lombard, Shirley Temple. Thief Gary sees the light thanks to adorable Shirley. Not a bad film. (Dir: Henry Hathaway, 90 mins.)

Now Voyager (1942)**½ Bette Davis, Paul Henreid. Strictly for the ladies is this Bette Davis romantic epic. Bette has as much trouble as the writers could contrive but the slick production and acting make it acceptable femme fare. (Dir: Irving Rapper, 117 mins.)

Now You See Him, Now You Don't (1972)** Kurt Russell, Joe Flynn, Jim Backus, Cesar Romero, William Windom. Sequel to the 1970 "The Computer Wore Tennis Shoes." Disney entry using the old gimmick of invisibility that's strictly for the kids. The stars all participate in a bit of hectic activity to save a nearly bankrupt college. Thanks to an invisible spray, everything disappears, even automobiles. Kids will chuckle. (Dir: Robert Butler, 88 mins.)

Now You See It, Now You Don't

(1968)*½ Jonathan Winters, Luciana Paluzzi. Inept, made-for-TV comedy which totally wastes Jonathan Winters' funny-man talents. The witless plot concerns a proposed theft of a Rembrandt which is thwarted by an art expert insurance man who performs above the call of duty: (Dir: Don Weis, 100 mins.)

Nowhere to Hide (1977)** Lee Van Cleef, Tony Musante, Edward Anhalt. Some suspense in this Edward Anhalt yarn about the problems of protecting a witness, a former hit man, against a syndicate boss who assures the law he will get the witness before trial. The casting of Tony Musante as the hit man, writer-producer Anhalt as the syndicate boss, and Lee Van Cleef as a U.S. Marshal, add points to a fair action script. Made-for-TV. (Dir: Jack Starrett, 79 mins.)

Nude in a White Car (1960)**½ Marina Vlady, Robert Hossein. Routine crime meller done by the French in an imitation-Hollywood fashion. Some excitement is generated by the stars but it's mostly familiar fare. (Dir: Robert Hossein, 87 mins.)

Number One (1969)* Charlton Heston, Jessica Walter, Diana Muldaur, Al Hirt, John Randolph. "Number One" delivers zero! An embarrassing, pretentious screenplay about the insecurity of an aging 40-year-old quarterback with gimpy knees is thrown for a final loss by Charlton Heston's hopeless try at making like Joe Willie Namath on the football field. About the only bright note in this fumbling football soap opera is an attractive performance by Diana Muldaur, who has an affair with Heston, no doubt to strengthen his weak knees! (Dir: Tom Gries, 105 mins.)

Number 17 (British, 1932)***½ John Stuart, Anne Casson, Donald Cathrop. Directed by the master, Alfred Hitchcock, before he started to work, within a couple of years, on bigger-budgeted films like "The 39 Steps." A classy entry throughout, with—of course—a splendid chase finale sequence.

Number Six (British, 1960)** Ivan Desny, Nadja Regin. Crook in London seeks the identity of a secret operative assigned by the police to keep an eye on him. Mildly entertaining Edgar Wallace crime melodrama. (Dir: Robert Tronson, 59 mins.)

Nun, The (French, 1965)**** Anna Karina, Liselotte Pulver, Micheline Presle. Masterful, subdued, intensely dramatic adaptation of French author Diderot's "La Religieuse." Set in a convent, it chronicles the anguish of a young and beautiful sister (Miss Karina) who refuses to take her vows, or Christ, quite seriously enough. First-rate direction from Jacques Rivette, who also coauthored the screenplay. You'll not soon forget this searing comment on religious life and training, and the problems Miss Karina encounters.

Nun and the Sergeant, The (1962)* Anna Sten, Robert Webber. During the Korean conflict, a Marine sergeant has his hands full with a nun and a group of schoolgirls in leading them to safety. Trashy, poorly done war drama. (Dir: Franklin Adreon, 73 mins.)

Nun's Story, The (1959)**** Audrey Hepburn, Peter Finch. The best selling novel is brought to the screen with taste and skill by a talented cast headed by Audrey Hepburn. The story follows a young girl through her early convent days, her taking of the vows and her work in Africa. Peter Finch gives a fine account of himself as a non-religious doctor working in the Congo. Director Fred Zinnemann gets excellent performances from the whole company. (149 mins.)

Nurse Edith Cavell (1939)**½ Anna Neagle, George Sanders. Story of the brave nurse who served the allies so gallantly during World War I. Impressive drama, well acted. (Dir: Herbert Wilcox, 98 mins.)

Nutty, Naughty Chateau (France-Italy, 1963)**½ Monica Vitti, Curt Jurgens, Jean-Claude Brialy, Jean-Louis Trintignant. Excellent cast of stars in slight comedy, concerning a young man who takes refuge in a strange chateau where everyone is dressed in 17th-century garb. Based on a Françoise Sagan play. (Dir: Roger Vadim, 102 mins.)

Nutty Professor, The (1963)** Jerry Lewis, Stella Stevens. Strictly for Lewis' legion of faithful fans. Employing a twist on the Jekyll-Hyde tale, Jerry plays a goofy college professor who turns into a campus hero with the aid of a concoction he devises in his lab. Miss Stevens is both decorative and skillful, playing a college cutie who gets the big rush from Jerry II. There are a few solid laughs, but as usual, Jerry never knows when or where to let a joke retire gracefully. (Dir: Jerry Lewis, 107 mins.)

Nylon Noose, The (German, 1963)*½ Richard Goodman, Laya Raki. Mysterious strangler terrorizes stockholders holding their annual meeting in a gloomy mansion. Mediocre whodunit dubbed in English.

Nyoka and the Lost Secrets of Hippocrates (1942-66)** Kay Aldridge, Clayton Moore. Feature version of serial "Perils of Nyoka." Jungle girl searching for her missing father competes with a villainous rival hand for some priceless tablets. Pretty farfetched stuff, but at least it moves fast. (Dir: William Witney, 100 mins.)

O. Henry's Full House (1952)*** Charles Laughton, David Wayne, Marilyn Monroe, Anne Baxter, Jeanne Crain, Jean Peters, Gregory Ratoff, Farley Granger. An all-star cast enacts a quintet of O. Henry's short stories, best of which is "The Last Leaf" with Anne Baxter and Gregory Ratoff sharing top acting honors. Each episode was directed by a different director with a different cast. This sort of film omnibus has never really been successfully done by Hollywood. The Italian and French film makers excel in this type of movie.

O Lucky Man! (British, 1973)**** Malcolm McDowell, Ralph Richardson, Rachel Roberts. Provocative, ambitious, complicated epic drama, brilliantly directed by Lindsay ("If") Anderson, with a superb cast, many of them playing a variety of roles throughout the long but always absorbing film. About a hustling young man making his way in the neo-fascist world of modern England where individuals, institutions, businesses, and governments are murderous and corrupt. Stimulating script by David Sherwin based on an original idea of star McDowell. (180 mins.)

Objective Burma (1945)***½ Errol Flynn, William Prince. Another superb war movie. This one is about paratroopers dropped in Burma with their objective being a Jap radar station. It's exciting, realistic entertainment. (Dir: Raoul Walsh, 142 mins.)

Obliging Young Lady (1941)***½ Joan Carroll, Edmond O'Brien, Ruth Warrick. Young girl involved in a court fight is sent to a mountain resort where complications arise over her parentage. Delightful comedy, many laughs. (Dir: Richard Wallace, 80 mins.)

Oblong Box, The (1969)** Vincent Price, Christopher Lee. Another in the seemingly endless Vincent Price-Edgar Allan Poe horror tales. (This is the eleventh Poe story produced by American International Pictures alone.) This time out, Price is a 19th-century Englishman who does his brother dirt, and lives to regret it. All the expected touches, including coffins, not-dead corpses, mutilations, etc., are present for fans of this genre. (Dir: Gordon Hessler, 91 mins.)

Obsession (French, 1954)**½ Michele Morgan, Raf Vallone. Slow paced well acted melodrama concerned chiefly with a woman's pain in facing the awful truth about the man she loves.

Ocean's Eleven (1960)**½ Frank Sinatra, Dean Martin, Sammy Davis, Jr., Joey Bishop, Peter Lawford. Ill-assorted group decides to pull a daring Las Vegas robbery, and it nearly comes off. Members of the so-called Sinatra "Clan" participated in this uneven comedy-crime drama, and it gives the uncomfortable impression of being a big inside joke. Some amusement, but they probably had more fun while making it. (Dir: Lewis Milestone, 127 mins.)

October Man, The (British, 1947)*** John Mills, Joan Greenwood. Man suffering from a head injury is suspected of murdering a model, proves his innocence. Good mystery has plenty of suspense. (Dir: Roy Baker, 89 mins.)

Odd Couple, The (1968)**** Jack Lemmon, Walter Matthau. A marvelously funny comedy. Neil Simon's hit play about two grumpy ex-marrieds (Lemmon and Matthau) who take up housekeeping together in New York. It's one of the few times in Hollywood history where the film version has improved on the Broadway original, and much of the credit for this happy state of affairs goes to

director Gene Saks, even though he does have a nearly foolproof screenplay and cast to work with. (Dir: Gene Saks, 105 mins.)

Odd Man Out (British, 1947)**** James Mason, Kathleen Ryan. Gripping story of the last hours of a wounded fugitive from a holdup during the Irish rebellion. Almost painful in its suspense, tragedy, a drama that is not soon forgotten. (Dir: Carol Reed, 113 mins.)

Odds Against Tomorrow (1959)*** Harry Belafonte, Robert Ryan, Shelley Winters. Tense story about a trio of bank robbers who plan the big job that will put them all on "easy street." Ryan is perfect as the excon who resents having Belafonte in the group. Harry's not very good in a straight acting role. (Dir: Robert Wise, 95 mins.)

Odessa File, The (Great Britain-West Germany, 1974)**½ Jon Voight, Maximilian Schell, Mary Tamm. Frederick Forsyth's novel about an earnest German journalist who stumbles upon the whereabouts of a Nazi war criminal and risks his life to get him, is only moderately successful in transition to the screen. A lugubrious screenplay, heavy on endless exposition, keeps the film from taking off. But Voight's wonderful performance (his German accent is very convincing), and the excellent confrontation scene between him and Maximilian Schell's evil SS officer, compensate for several lesser scenes. Not as good as "The Day of the Jackal," also by Forsyth. (Dir: Ronald Neame, 128 mins.)

Odette (British, 1950)***½ Anna Neagle, Trevor Howard. The true story of an heroic Frenchwoman who worked underground for the duration of the war fighting the Nazis. Excellent drama, all the more inspiring because it actually happened. (Dir: Herbert Wilcox, 100 mins.)

Odongo (1956)** Rhonda Fleming, Macdonald Carey. Passion, if little else, is set loose in the jungles of Africa when a Kenya white hunter and a woman doctor find themselves on the same safari. (Dir: John Gilling, 85 mins.)

Oedipus the King (British, 1967)*** Christopher Plummer, Orson Welles, Lilli Palmer, Richard Johnson, Donald Sutherland. In case you haven't heard, a playwright in ancient

523

Greece named Sophocles wrote a play about a plague-wracked city named Thebes, it's King Oedipus and his brother-in-law Creon. If you approach this all-star version of the classic play in terms of a stimulating history-drama class, you'll find this second modern rendering, filmed on location at a ruined Grecian amphitheater at Dodona, well worth your time. Plummer playing Oedipus gives a striking, if sometimes irritating performance. Notable supporting performances from Lilli Palmer playing Plummer's wife, and from Orson Welles portraying a blind seer, and looking very much like his Falstaff in "Chimes at Midnight." (Dir: Philip Saville, 97 mins.)

Of Human Bondage (British, 1964)** Kim Novak, Laurence Harvey. The classic Somerset Maugham novel of a young doctor and his obsessive infatuation with a frowzy waitress was memorably filmed before with Leslie Howard and Bette Davis. This time, everybody gives it the old try, but the results are scrappy. Harvey suffers nobly, Novak deserves credit for a performance that's ineffective but interesting. (Dir: Ken Hughes, 98 mins.)

Of Human Hearts (1937)***½ Walter Huston, James Stewart, Beulah Bondi. You'll like this sensitive, dramatic tale of a backwoods family in Ohio. Story tells of a young physician who is sent for by Lincoln during the Civil War because he has neglected writing to his mother. Picture tells the story of this boy and his family. (Dir: Clarence Brown, 110 mins.)

Of Life and Love (Italian, 1958)*** Anna Magnani. Several unrelated romantic plots, including Magnani as a famous screen actress. Skimpy tales, one of them pretty good and Magnani is customarily convincing. (Dir: Aldo Fabrizi, 103 mins.)

Of Love and Desire (1963)½ Merle Oberon, Steve Cochran, Curt Jurgens. Merle Oberon, absent from films for almost a decade, here returns in the embarrassing, unfulfilling role of a promiscuous Latin socialite drawn to Steve Cochran's macho good-guy. Miss Oberon allowed this seamy trash to be photographed in her Mexican homes, one of which was erected by Cortez 400 years ago. (Dir: Richard Rush, 97 mins.)

Of Mice and Men (1940)**** Burgess Meredith, Lon Chaney, Betty Field. Steinbeck's classic tale of a feebleminded soul and his protector, set on the migratory farms of the Salinas Valley. A film masterpiece! Excellent all around. (Dir: Lewis Milestone, 107 mins.)

Off Limits (1953)**½ Bob Hope, Mickey Rooney, Marilyn Maxwell. A fight manager is drafted and manages to break all the regulations when he tries to develop a new fighter. Mildly amusing Hope comedy with Rooney lending capable support. (Dir: George Marshall, 89 mins.)

Offense, The (1973)***½ Sean Connery, Trevor Howard, Vivien Merchant, Ian Bannen. In return for playing James Bond, United Artists allowed Connery to make two films of his choice—one was this powerful version of John Hopkins' stage play, which makes few compromises for its audience. Tale of a middle-class policeman's crackup is realistic and unsentimental. Connery is extremely moving as a cop who kills a child molester during an interrogation, because the criminal has forced the detective to face himself. Talky at times, betraying its theatrical origins, but one of the hardest hitting films financed by Hollywood in that period. Supporting roles wonderfully acted. (Dir: Sidney Lumet, 118 mins.)

Officer and the Lady (1941)**½ Bruce Bennett, Rochelle Hudson, Roger Pryor. Cop exposes two crooks who have pulled a robbery, even though his girl may be implicated. Fast moving crime melodrama.

Oh! Calcutta! (1972)** Bill Macy, Raina Barrett, Margo Sappington. At the end of "Calcutta," someone asks, "Who wrote this piece of shit anyway?" That's a good question under the circumstances, especially because this is a grainy, murky version of what was, in September of 1970, a closed-circuit videotape telecast of the long-running theatrical revue spoofing modern ideas of sex and sexuality. The voyeurs in the audience will be disappointed—there are some scenes photographed in the buff, but it's all pretty hazy, and seems rather tired and dated by now. A few clever sketches along the way written by such clever gents as Jules Feiffer, Dan Greenburg, David Newman and Robert Benton.

"Calcutta" was "devised" by the brilliant and audacious English theater critic Kenneth Tynan. Bill Macy seen before his starring days on "Maude." (Dir: Guillaume Martin Aucion, 108 mins.)

Oh Dad, Poor Dad, Mamma's Hung You in the Closet and I'm Feelin' So Sad (1967)* Rosalind Russell, Robert Morse, Jonathan Winters, Barbara Harris. Movie should have been left in the closet. Arthur Kopit's Broadway play was a fragile but funny satire that possessed a certain nightmarish quality—the ruinous cinema version directed by Richard Quine flattens out the dialogue to a quality of just-plain-folks and ruins what quality the original had. A black comedy about a mother (R.R.) who scoots around with a smothered son and her late husband's corpse. Some parts directed by Alexander Mackendrick, which he'd no doubt be pleased to forget. (Dir: Richard Quine, 86 mins.)

Oh Men! Oh Women! (1957)*** David Niven, Tony Randall, Ginger Rogers, Dan Dailey, Barbara Rush. Tony Randall steals the film from the other four stars in the role of a zany patient of psychoanalyst David Niven. As it turns out, they're both in love with the same woman, Barbara Rush. Based on the hit B'way play. Lots of laughs if you like your dialogue with gags about analysts. (Dir: Nunnally Johnson, 90 mins.)

Oh What a Lovely War (British, 1969) **** Laurence Olivier, Ralph Richardson, John Mills. Oh what a lovely film actor-producer-director Richard Attenborough has made from what was originally little more than a series of inspired sketches about man's continuing folly, and his endless appetite for war. (All directed brilliantly by Joan Littlewood in the theater in London, New York, etc.) Using real songs popular in Britain before and during World War I, Attenborough has skillfully given a cohesive form and narrative to this material, and employed in the process just about every great name in the British theater. (Paul Scofield is one of the few stars not in this remarkable movie.) The seaside town of Brighton is used to excellent advantage in several scenes. This stinging "comedy" has some intentional "laughs," but it is ultimately one of the most stirring anti-war films

ever made. (Dir: Richard Attenborough, 139 mins.)

O'Hara, United States Treasury (1971) ** David Janssen, Lana Wood. Jack Webb's latest movie stars customs agent David Janssen chasing narcotics smugglers around the country in this made-for-TV feature. This is a vintage blend of Webb and writer Jim Moser. The agents talk in code, using that efficient, manly, clipped, no-smiling technique which has become Webb's TV trademark; but in this pilot film, Treasury jargon is constant and fans may need a few subtitles. Location scenes in San Pedro, Chicago, and aboard a Marine jet fighter—Webb's closing ace for the climactic chase. (Dir: Jack Webb, 99 mins.)

Okinawa (1952)** Pat O'Brien, Cameron Mitchell. Action packed war drama about the heroic crew of the Destroyer U.S.S. Blake and their part in the invasion of Okinawa (WW II). (Dir: Georges Brooks, 67 mins.)

Oklahoma (1955)**** Gordon MacRae, Shirley Jones, Gloria Grahame. Rodgers and Hammerstein's classic Broadway musical reaches the screen with the memorable tunes intact, plus elaborate production trappings. From the opening "Oh, What a Beautiful Morning" to the rousing ensemble finale of "Oklahoma," you'll enjoy the many songs interwoven around the simple love story of cowboy Curly (Gordon MacRae) and farm girl Laurey (Shirley Jones). The leads are well cast which is more than can be said for Gloria Grahame as Ado Annie and Rod Steiger as the villain Jud. Fine, pleasant entertainment for the whole family, thanks largely to the memorable score. (Dir: Fred Zinnemann, 145 mins.)

Oklahoma Kid (1939)*** James Cagney, Humphrey Bogart. Hard-hitting western with the acting, mainly Cagney as a desperado, holding up a weak script. (Dir: Lloyd Bacon, 90 mins.)

Oklahoman, The (1956)** Joel McCrea, Barbara Hale. A quiet western with little action. Joel McCrea fans will enjoy watching the master film cowboy go through the paces as a widower who settles in a small town. (Dir: Francis D. Lyon, 80 mins.)

Old Acquaintance (1943)*** Bette

Davis, Miriam Hopkins. Occasionally moving story of a woman who is taken by a girlhood friend. A bit talky and hard to believe but still good entertainment. (Dir: Vincent Sherman, 110 mins.)

Old Dark House, The (British, 1962) ****½** Tom Poston, Robert Morley, Janette Scott. American salesman spends the night in a creepy mansion, where the heirs are bumped off one by one. Fairly effective spooky thriller, with a welcome note of lightness and a genuinely surprising ending. (Dir: William Castle, 86 mins.)

Old Dracula (1976)***** David Niven, Teresa Graves, Peter Bayliss. At the end of "Old Dracula," David Niven turns black. Film turns tedious long before that, as Niven plays an aged bloodsucker casually looking through Playboy for edible victims. (Dir: Clive Donner, 89 mins.)

Old Fashioned Way, The (1934)*****½** W. C. Fields. A "must" for students of comedy as are all of Fields' starring films. Here he's the head of an acting troupe that appropriately performs "The Drunkard." A one-man show. (Dir: William Beaudine, 80 mins.)

Old Los Angeles (1948)******* William Elliott, John Carroll, Catherine McLeod. Man finds that gold miners are being cheated and his brother murdered, tries to find the guilty one. Good western moves at a fast pace.

Old Maid, The (1939)*****½** Bette Davis, Miriam Hopkins. Send the men out to a poker game because this screen treatment of the Pulitzer Prize play is female from start to finish. Story of two sisters and their attempts to win from one another the love of one child is penetrating and often brilliant. (Dir: Edmund Goulding, 100 mins.)

Old Man and the Sea, The (1958)******* Spencer Tracy. Ernest Hemingway's story about the determined Cuban fisherman does not make a great film but it is a good try. Tracy is excellent in the leading role which amounts to virtually a monologue during the long passages out at sea. The fine camera work adds to the mood of the film. (Dir: John Sturges, 86 mins.)

Old Man Who Cried Wolf, The (1970) ******* Edward G. Robinson, Martin Balsam, Diane Baker. As movies

made-for-TV go, this one is better than most, thanks to the skillful performance by Edward G. Robinson as an old man who witnesses the murder of an old friend but can't convince anyone of it. Suspense builds as Robinson risks his life and sanity trying to prove he's right, and the production is first class all the way. The supporting cast is very good, with Percy Rodrigues a standout as a sinister murderer. (Dir: Walter Grauman, 73 mins.)

Old Testament, The (Italian, 1963) ***½** Susan Paget, Brad Harris. The Maccabees drive the unbelieving pagans from the temple of worship. Stilted Biblical drama dubbed in English.

Old Yeller (1957)******* Dorothy McGuire, Fess Parker, Tommy Kirk, Kevin Corcoran. An old Disney classic that the kids will adore. The title character is a terrific mongrel dog, redeemed from his bad ways by the love of a Texas ranch family. McGuire and Parker head the adoptive family, and Kirk and Corcoran are the two kids who get into and out of innumerable scrapes with the help of the faithful "Old Yeller." (Dir: Robert Stevenson)

Oldest Profession, The (France-Germany-Italy, 1967)****½** Jeanne Moreau, Jean-Claude Brialy, Raquel Welch, Jacques Charrier, Anna Karina. The prostitute traced from prehistory to future times, in six chronological chapters. The first five are mildly humorous, but sketchy. The final segment, "Anticipation," directed by Godard, is more polished and clever, a look at the future when a visitor from outer space arrives in Paris to discover an oddly programmed sort of lovemaking. (Dirs: in order: Franco Indovina, Mauro Bolognini, Philippe de Broca, Michel Pfleghar, Claude Autant-Lara, Jean-Luc Godard, 115 mins.)

Olive Trees of Justice, The (France, 1962)******* Pierre Prothon, Jean Pelegri. An Algerian-born Frenchman returns to Algeria where his father lies dying, and comes to grips with the Arab-French hostilities. Made by American James Blue as propaganda for the French government, but is far from pointed or heavyhanded. Film is a moving, lyrical, incisive document about war and humanitarian concerns, provides a fascinating retrospective on the colonization of Algeria by the French. Based on the book by Jean Pelegri. (Dir: James Blue)

Oliver (British, 1968)******** Ron Moody, Mark Lester, Shani Wallis, Oliver Reed, Jack Wild, Hugh Griffith. This superlative musical directed by Carol Reed won five Academy Awards including those for best picture and direction, and was nominated for several other categories it did not win. With an assist from Charles Dickens and some new dialogue and songs by Lionel Bart, taken from his smash hit theatrical musical, director Reed has given new life to Dickens' classic tale about the luckless orphan Oliver Twist. Mark Lester, playing Oliver, is one of the most appealing child actors to come along in a good while; the role of Fagin, acted with great relish by Ron Moody, has been sanitized so that virtually all of the anti-Semitic implications of the original story and earlier film renditions have been deleted. You'll be delighted by such songs as "Pick a Pocket or Two," and the magical re-creation of London in the 1830's. Shani Wallis and Jack Wild, playing Nancy and the Artful Dodger, respectively, are among the standouts in a fine supporting cast that even includes a bravura performance by Bill Sikes' scruffy-looking dog. (Dir: Carol Reed, 153 mins.)

Oliver Twist (British, 1948)******** Alec Guinness, John Howard Davies. The Dickens classic of an orphan boy and lower depths London, superbly done, reverently produced, fine performances. Guinness brings a touch of humor to his portrayal of mean old Fagin and his performance is a joy. You'll not soon forget this wonderful adaptation beautifully directed by David Lean. (Dir: David Lean, 105 mins.)

Olympic Visions—See: **Visions of Eight**

Omar Khayyam (1957)****** Cornel Wilde, Debra Paget, Raymond Massey, Michael Rennie. Adventurer and poet battles a gang of assassins who intend to take over Persia. Opulent production gracing the same old plot. (Dir: William Dieterle, 101 mins.)

Omega Man, The (1971)***½** Charlton Heston, Rosalind Cash, Tony Zerbe. Another reworking of the novel "I Am a Legend," on which the '64 release "The Last Man on Earth" was based. They shouldn't have bothered. Heston battles a group of robed zombies as he plays the lone human survivor of an atomic war. The zombies are the best actors around. (Dir: Boris Sagal, 98 mins.)

Omen, The (1976)******* Gregory Peck, Lee Remick, David Warner, Billie Whitelaw. About the best of the movies designed to imitate the success of "The Exorcist." The devil returns in another big screen performance—this time in the form of a five-year-old boy sired by the devil himself, and inadvertently adopted by a wealthy American couple. Some mystery derives from the boy's father (Peck) hunting for his son's true lineage. Clues include Scriptural quotes from the Book of Revelation and ominous hints from a dying priest. Enough carnage to convince any heathen something's askew. Earnest acting, especially by Billie Whitelaw as a maid sent by the devil to care for the boy, and David Warner as a photographer whose pictures reveal some disturbing "omens," enhance the chills. (Dir: Richard Donner, 110 mins.)

On a Clear Day You Can See Forever (1970)******* Barbra Streisand, Yves Montand. The combination of a perfectly cast Streisand and a melodic score by Alan Jay Lerner and Burton Lane adds up to pleasant fare if you're not too demanding. Barbra's a young woman who discovers acute ESP powers which send her to sexy psychiatrist Montand. He, in turn, puts her under hypnosis and off she goes to re-enact her past lives. Sounds silly; it's delicious. Director Vincente Minnelli is at the top of his form, especially when mounting the sequences taking place amid the pomp and pageantry of 19th-century English aristocracy. Film buffs should keep their eyes peeled for Jack Nicholson and Bob Newhart in minor supporting roles. Songs include title song, "He Wasn't You," "Come Back to Me," and "Go to Sleep." Barbra makes it worthwhile. (Dir: Vincente Minnelli, 129 mins.)

On an Island with You (1947)****½** Esther Williams, Peter Lawford, Jimmy Durante. A lot of Esther in bathing suits is what this romance of a Naval flyer and an actress of-

527

fers. If you like to watch Esther swim, this one is for you. (Dir: Richard Thorpe, 107 mins.)

On Approval (British, 1944)*** Clive Brook, Beatrice Lillie. Two couples spend a holiday on a deserted island home, to see if they are suited for each other. Highly amusing, often ingenious comedy. Good fun. (Dir: Clive Brook, 80 mins.)

On Borrowed Time (1939)***½ Lionel Barrymore, Sir Cedric Hardwicke, Beulah Bondi. Warm, sentimental fantasy about an old man who isn't ready to die so he chases "Death" up a tree. You'll laugh and cry at this good adaptation of the stage success. (Dir: Harold S. Bucquet, 100 mins.)

On Dangerous Ground (1951)***½ Ida Lupino, Robert Ryan. Detective on a murder case meets a blind girl whose brother committed the crime. Moody, but excellent melodrama, extremely well produced and acted. (Dir: Nicholas Ray, 82 mins.)

On Foot, on Horse and on Wheels (French, 1957)** Noel-Noel, Denise Grey. A muddled farce that makes a great deal of use out of the transportation problems in Paris. Most of the funnier episodes are too labored.

On Her Majesty's Secret Service (1969) *** George Lazenby, Diana Rigg. Agent 007 James Bond is back again, but Sean Connery has departed. His replacement, George Lazenby, is about as animated as Westminster Abbey, but there are enough exciting scenes in this hokum to keep most Bond fans entertained. Some splendid location scenes in Switzerland with a really thrilling ski chase, and our hero also being pursued by the meanies as he navigates down a toboggan course. It may be the longest toboggan race ever, but it's a short, exciting pursuit as handled by the director. Some tasty femmes, of course, are dished up to George, and the plot concerns the bad guys' plan to conquer England using a virus. (Dir: Peter Hunt, 140 mins.)

On Moonlight Bay (1951)**½ Doris Day, Gordon MacRae. Nostalgic musical set in the days preceding World War I. Doris and Gordon sing and romance and Leon Ames, as Doris' dad, takes care of the comedy department. (Dir: Roy Del Ruth, 95 mins.)

On Our Merry Way (1947)** Paul-

ette Goddard, Burgess Meredith, Dorothy Lamour, James Stewart, Henry Fonda. Questions asked by an inquiring reporter lead to a series of humorous stories. A good idea that doesn't come off, due to inept scripting. (Dirs: King Vidor, Leslie Fenton, 107 mins.)

On the Beach (1960)**** Gregory Peck, Ava Gardner, Fred Astaire, Anthony Perkins. Nevil Shute's searing novel about the last people on earth facing certain death by radioactive air pollution after the final World War, has tremendous impact in its screen translation. Marred somewhat by giving too much footage to the Peck-Gardner romantic interludes and in the miscasting of Fred Astaire as a scientist, the film manages to remain a powerful comment against war. (Dir: Stanley Kramer, 133 mins.)

On the Beat (British, 1963)*** Norman Wisdom, Jennifer Jayne. Stumbling car cleaner at Scotland Yard wants to be a policeman, gets his chance when he poses as a crook to trap jewel robbers. Amusing farce starring the popular English comic; some rib-tickling situations. (Dir: Robert Asher, 105 mins.)

On the Double (1961)**½ Danny Kaye, Dana Wynter, Margaret Rutherford, Wilfred Hyde-White. Danny's a GI whose impersonations land him in hot water during WW II. The talented Mr. Kaye doesn't get much help from the scriptwriters, but there are some nice moments. (Dir: Melville Shavelson, 92 mins.)

On the Fiddle—See: **Operation Snafu**

On the Riviera (1950)*** Danny Kaye, Gene Tierney, Corinne Calvet. Fast and funny comedy about the international set and their gay escapades on the Riviera, the playground of the rich. Kaye sings, dances, clowns and makes love to Gene Tierney. Watch for Gwen Verdon in a can-can number. (Dir: Walter Lang, 90 mins.)

On the Town (1950)**** Gene Kelly, Frank Sinatra, Betty Garrett, Ann Miller, Vera Ellen, Jules Munchin. The successful Broadway show by Leonard Bernstein, Betty Comden and Adolph Green receives the Hollywood treatment. The result is a notably entertaining, tuneful, well-cast musical about 3 sailors on liberty in N. Y. C. We'll never understand why only 2 songs from the brilliant original score were used by the Hollywood know-it-alls. (Dirs: Gene Kelly, Stanley Donen, 98 mins.)

On the Waterfront (1954) **** Marlon Brando, Eva Marie Saint, Karl Malden, Lee J. Cobb, Rod Steiger. Forceful, super-charged melodrama about the docks of New Jersey—the workers, the bosses, the criminals, and their families. Brilliantly acted by all with Marlon Brando a superb standout. Winner of many Oscars including "Best Film." Directed by Elia Kazan. Brando's shattering performance is among the finest ever recorded on film, and Rod Steiger got his start to stardom here. The scene between them in an auto is superbly played and directed. (108 mins.)

On Thin Ice (German, 1961) *½ Tony Sailer, Ina Bauer. Couple fall in love at the ice rink, eventually help put on the big ice show. Some good skating here, but little else of interest. Dubbed in English.

On Your Toes (1939) ** Vera Zorina, Eddie Albert. Screen treatment of the Rodgers and Hart musical which first introduced the ballet "Slaughter on Tenth Avenue." Terrible film and absolutely no music except for the ballet. (Dir: Ralph Enright, 110 mins.)

Once a Thief (1965) *** Ann-Margret, Alain Delon, Jack Palance. Absorbing crime yarn which benefits from Alain Delon's restrained performance as an ex-con who tries to go straight but has little luck. Ann-Margret is miscast as Delon's wife, but Jack Palance and Van Heflin are fine in the chief supporting roles. (Dir: Ralph Nelson, 107 mins.)

Once Before I Die (1966) *½ Actor John Derek produced and directed this routine opus, taking place in the Philippines in WW II, on a shoestring and it shows . . . it also displays an ample amount of Ursula Andress (who was married to Derek at the time) and that's a bonus by any man's standards. (97 mins.)

Once Is Not Enough (1975) **½ Kirk Douglas, Alexis Smith, David Janssen, Melina Mercouri, Brenda Vaccaro, Deborah Raffin, George Hamilton. Jacqueline Susann's highly readable and thoroughly superficial novel about the beautiful people and their sexual exploits reaches the screen with many changes in characters and plot—but sit back and let it roll over you. This is the kind of trashy movie that is fun because everyone looks so great, talks like soap opera heroes, and has such a sophisticated outlook that kinky becomes normal. This one has it all—father complexes, lesbianism, May-December romances, promiscuity on a grand scale, playboys, millionaires, burned-out writers, impotence, and even overt heterosexuality. Brenda Vaccaro, as a magazine editor who slept her way to the top, is marvelous and steals the show—no mean feat. (Dir: Guy Green, 121 mins.)

Once More, My Darling (1949) **½ Robert Montgomery, Ann Blyth. Suave and sophisticated comedy about a young lady who sets her cap for a somewhat older film matinee idol who is recalled to active duty in the Army. Silly in spots but still fun. (Dir: Robert Montgomery, 94 mins.)

Once More, with Feeling (1960) *** Yul Brynner, Kay Kendall. A bit of sophisticated fluff that relies on the charm of its two stars—and they are very winning. Brynner plays an egotistical symphony conductor who discovers he doesn't want his beautiful wife (played by the late Kay Kendall) to divorce him after all. Kendall, as always in her regrettably short career, is a comedic joy. (Dir: Stanley Donen, 92 mins.)

Once Upon a Honeymoon (1942) *** Cary Grant, Ginger Rogers. American reporter trails the wife of a Gestapo agent to follow Hitler's conquest, falls for her. Entertaining, if a bit long, comedy. (Dir: Leo McCarey, 117 mins.)

Once Upon a Horse (1958) ** Don Rowan, Dick Martin, Martha Hyer. Couple of dumb cowboys steal cattle and rob the bank of the beautiful owner of the town, but eventually wish they hadn't. Western satire doesn't come off most of the time, although there are a few funny moments. (Dir: Hal Kanter, 85 mins.)

Once Upon a Time (1944) **½ Cary Grant, Janet Blair, Ted Donaldson. Theatrical producer forms a "partnership" with a boy who has a dancing caterpillar. Mild comedy never quite hits the mark intended. (Dir: Alexander Hall, 89 mins.)

Once You Kiss a Stranger (1969) ** Carol Lynley, Paul Burke. Glossy

529

but empty melodrama about the country-club set and their intrigues. Burke suffers as the hero while Lynley, looking terrific, rolls her eyes as an unstable miss bent on using men. (Dir: Robert Sparr, 106 mins.)

One and Only, Genuine, Original Family Band, The (1968)* Buddy Ebsen, Lesley Warren, John Davidson. Walt Disney Studios has come up with a saccharine, enervating period costume musical about a family of singing, instrument-playing, and dancing members. It's all tied up with the presidential campaigns of Grover Cleveland and Benjamin Harrison, circa 1888. The songs are as rotten as the script.

One Day in the Life of Ivan Denisovich (Great Britain-Norway-U.S., 1971)**** Tom Courtenay, Alfred Burke. A remarkably moving, heartbreaking account, in very straightforward cinematic fashion, of the ongoing indignities and horrors of the Russian prison labor camps. The time is 1950, the setting the Siberian wilderness. Ivan (Courtenay) is in the 8th year of a 10-year sentence. His crime? Having escaped from a German prisoner-of-war camp! Based on the now-celebrated Alexander Solzhenitsyn's novel. (A different adaptation was seen on TV in '63 starring Jason Robards.) Filmed on location near the Arctic Circle in Norway. Courtenay is convincing in his unending struggle to survive. Memorable, underrated film. Screenplay by Ronald Harwood. (Dir: Casper Wrede, 100 mins.)

One Desire (1955)**½ Rock Hudson, Anne Baxter, Natalie Wood. A costume soap opera about a gal from the wrong side of the tracks who tries to cross over into the local social register. Based on novel "Tracey Cromwell." Anne Baxter works very hard to make the character more than just a soap opera heroine and she occasionally succeeds. (Dir: Jerry Hopper, 94 mins.)

One-Eyed Jacks (1961)*** Marlon Brando, Karl Malden, Katy Jurado. Outlaw out of prison goes hunting for the crony who betrayed him, finds him now a respected sheriff. Beautifully photographed western has some good scenes, interesting characterizations, but actor-director Brando lets it run nearly 2½ hours, which is too much. (Dir: Marlon Brando, 141 mins.)

One Eyed Soldiers, The (Italian, 1968)* Dale Robertson, Luciana Paluzzi. Muddled yarn concerning a missing treasure and the varied stereotypes in hot and heavy pursuit. Robertson plays an American journalist who teams with a young girl against such arch villains as the "Fat Man" and the "Dwarf." (80 mins.)

One Flew Over the Cuckoo's Nest (1975)**** Jack Nicholson, Louise Fletcher, Brad Dourif, William Redfield. A stunning adaptation of Ken Kesey's novel that deservedly won Academy Awards for best actor (Nicholson), best picture, best director (Forman) and best actress (Louise Fletcher). This is a far cry from the typical movieland version of mental hospitals—the "Snake Pit," etc. The acting is truly astonishing throughout, including supporting performances from Dourif as Billy Babbitt, and Will Sampson as the hapless strongman Chief Bromden. In the leading role of the unbalanced Randle P. McMurphy, Nicholson is really breathtaking, and shows an acting range that can be matched by few other movie actors in the world. He makes you alternately laugh, weep, and despair, but there's not a false note in this remarkable portrait. Louise Fletcher, playing Nurse Ratched, a constant irritant to Nicholson's deranged character, subtly manages to be almost always unpleasant, often insensitive, but never resorting to caricature. Flawlessly directed by Milos Forman, the brilliant Czech director who clearly understands all the nuances of this singularly American batch of tormented souls. Splendid screenplay by Laurence Haubman and Bo Goldman. A deeply moving, beautifully realized drama. (Dir: Milos Forman, 129 mins.)

One Foot in Heaven (1941)**** Fredric March, Martha Scott. With barely a plot of any consequence, this story of a minister's life is funny, sad, moving and interesting. Superbly acted by Mr. March as the minister and Martha Scott as his devoted wife. (Dir: Irving Rapper, 108 mins.)

One Foot in Hell (1960)**½ Alan Ladd, Don Murray, Dolores Michaels. Revenge-obsessed man takes job as deputy, intending to get even with townspeople responsible for the death of his wife. Fair-enough western with a plot slightly offbeat. (Dir: James B. Clark, 90 mins.)

One Girl's Confession (1953)** Cleo Moore, Hugo Haas, Glenn Langan. Tiresome melodrama about a young girl's predicament caused by her stealing $25,000 from her evil employer. Both of Cleo Moore's assets are well displayed. (Dir: Hugo Haas, 74 mins.)

One Heavenly Night (1931)** Evelyn Laye, John Boles, Leon Errol. One of many operetta-type films made during the early thirties. If you like this type of film stuff, here it is with all the sugar-coated ingredients intact. (Dir: George Fitzmaurice, 90 mins.)

100 Cries of Terror (Mexican, 1965) *½ Ariadne Welter, George Martinez. Two separate stories—husband and mistress plot to kill his wife but the plan backfires; man discovers a woman buried alive in a mausoleum. Weak horror duo, dubbed in English.

100 Men and a Girl (1937)*** Deanna Durbin, Leopold Stokowski, Adolphe Menjou. Light comedy drama about a poor violinist's daughter who sings at a great concert with maestro Leopold Stokowski conducting. Young Deanna Durbin is charming as the singing Patricia. (Dir: Henry Koster, 90 mins.)

100 Rifles (1969)* Jim Brown, Raquel Welch, Burt Reynolds. Nonsensical adventure which follows an American sheriff (Brown) as he joins an Indian revolt against the horrid Mexican oppressors. Miss Welch is dark and valiant as the Indian girl with whom Brown falls in with. Explosions, flames, and buckshot fly all around this bomb. (Dir: Tom Gries, 110 mins.)

One in a Million (1936)*** Sonja Henie, Don Ameche, Ritz Brothers. Sonja's first film and her skating is a treat to watch. Story isn't much but she's surrounded by a lot of good performers. Plot concerns a Swiss girl whose father is training her for the Olympics. (Dir: Sidney Lanfield)

One Is a Lonely Number (1972)**½ Trish Van Devere, Janet Leigh, Monte Markham, Melvyn Douglas. A women's-lib soap opera that turns out to be Hollywood glib. Trish Van Devere is a young woman who is thrust back into the world of men

on the make after her husband leaves her. Uneven, with a few believable scenes. Based on a New Yorker short story, "The Good Humor Man," by Rebecca Morris. Dir: Mel Stuart, 97 mins.)

One Man's China (Great Britain, 1972)***½ A fascinating pictorial essay by veteran journalist-filmmaker Felix Greene that presents the most comprehensive and up-to-date documentary on mainland China that was available at the time of release and for some years thereafter. Released as two separate feature-length films, covers among other things the ethnic minorities, visits to communes, the Chinese educational system, etc. Greene is virtually never critical of any aspect of Chinese society, but nonetheless this is an often visually stunning and rewarding documentary about a vast, important country so little understood by the rest of the world.

One Man's Way (1964)**½ Don Murray, Diana Hyland. Those who read Norman Vincent Peale's best-selling book **The Power of Positive Thinking** will want to tune in for this Hollywood version of the famed clergyman's life, despite its episodic treatment. Don Murray is very good in the leading role, as is Diana Hyland as his wife. (Dir: Denis Sanders, 105 mins.)

One Million B.C. (1940)** Carole Landis, Victor Mature. Story of the struggle of the cave men for survival in prehistoric times. Often rather ridiculous, sometimes fascinating; at least, it's different. (Dirs: Hal Roach, Hal Roach Jr., 80 mins.)

One Million Years B.C. (1967)*½ Raquel Welch, John Richardson. This is a remake of a 1940 opus called "One Million B.C." which starred Carole Landis, and, no doubt, a million years from now, some civic-minded movie producer will make a third version starring the then reigning sex queen. In the meantime, we have Raquel, who may well be the sexiest cave woman ever, but the movie is silly nonsense. John Richardson, sporting a furry loincloth, seems to have based his acting technique on the grunts and groans of pre-historic man before he learned to talk. (Dir: Don Chaffey, 100 mins.)

One Minute to Zero (1951)** Robert Mitchum, Ann Blyth. Colonel carries on a romance before leaving for the perils of Korea. Unconvincing war melodrama. (Dir: Tay Garnett, 105 mins.)

One More Time (British, 1969)* Peter Lawford, Sammy Davis, Jr., Esther Anderson. Lousy sequel to the first Lawford and Davis picture, "Salt and Pepper," which was also rotten. The duo play London bistro owners who go to the castle of Lawford's brother when he dies. The ensuing shenanigans are deadly dull. Direction by Jerry Lewis is typically inept. (93 mins.)

One More Tomorrow (1946)** Ann Sheridan, Dennis Morgan, Jane Wyman. They're trying to say something about war profiteering but it's poorly presented and emerges as a foolish twisting of Philip Barry's play "The Animal Kingdom." (Dir: Peter Godfrey, 88 mins.)

One More Train to Rob (1971)** George Peppard, Diana Muldaur. The attractiveness of the cast is the chief appeal of this western tale of vengeance set in California of the 1880's. After Peppard is framed for a train robbery and is released from prison, he seeks out his former double-crossing partners, now leading respectable lives, determined to get revenge. (Dir: Andrew McLaglen, 104 mins.)

One Night in Lisbon (1941)**½ Madeleine Carroll, Fred MacMurray. Romantic comedy about an American pilot and an aristocrat's English girl in wartime Britain has a few scattered laughs. (Dir: Edward H. Griffith, 97 mins.)

One Night of Love (1934)*** Grace Moore, Lyle Talbot, Tullio Carminati. Box-office musical hit at the time, about an American girl who goes to Italy to become an opera star, and promptly falls under the spell of her maestro. Grace Moore is very spirited and sings beautifully, with various tuneful sequences scattered throughout. (Dir: Victor Schertzinger, 90 mins.)

One of My Wives Is Missing (1976)**½ Jack Klugman, Elizabeth Ashley, James Franciscus. Although the story is terribly contrived, there are enough plot twists, admirably pulled out of a hat by a talented cast, to sustain interest. Klugman plays a resort-area police detective called by Franciscus to investigate the disappearance of his wife. If you're in the mood for a mystery with good performances, especially by Ms. Ashley, tune in. Made-for-TV. (Dir: Glen Jordan, 98 mins.)

One of Our Aircraft Is Missing (British, 1941)***½ Godfrey Tearle, Eric Portman, Hugh Williams, Pamela Brown, Joyce Redman, Googie Withers. The crew of a downed bomber tries to get back to England from its landing place in Holland. Excellent war melodrama, suspenseful, well acted. (Dirs: Michael Powell, Emeric Pressburger, 106 mins.)

One of Our Own (1975)**½ George Peppard, Zohra Lampert, William Daniels, Scott McKay, Oscar Homolka, Strother Martin. Peppard is into the surgery game as chief of services in a major hospital. Hospital crises are rampant. Good supporting cast gives pilot a touch of class. Made-for-TV. (Dir: Richard Sarafian)

One Potato, Two Potato (1964)**** Barbara Barrie, Bernie Hamilton. Vivid sensitive drama about an interracial courtship and marriage between a hesitant white divorcee and a strong, but mild-mannered black man. Barbara Barrie is magnificent as the woman who hesitates at first but then commits herself fully to the love she feels for the black man, well played by Bernie Hamilton. The climax is a shattering courtroom custody battle for the woman's daughter between Miss Barrie and her ex-husband. You'll probably disagree with the court's decision but tune in for an absorbing drama. Perceptive screenplay by Raphael Hayes and Orville Hampton; and impressively directed by Larry Peerce who went on to direct "Goodbye Columbus." The gifted Miss Barrie played a tiny part in the James Dean 1956 film "Giant." (Dir: Larry Peerce, 92 mins.)

One Spy Too Many (1968)** Robert Vaughn, David McCallum, Rip Torn. Culled from "The Man from UNCLE" series. Illya and Napoleon Solo employ their super-secret agent tactics to hunt down a mad scientist bent on brainwashing the world via a "will gas." Rip Torn gleefully plays the maniac. Made-for-TV. (Dir: Joseph Sargent, 100 mins.)

One Step to Eternity (French, 1954)**½ A French roue invites his first wife, his current wife, his mistress, and his fiancee to his apartment with the idea of committing murder. Some suspense is generated—however, a good premise doesn't go anywhere. It may give you an idea though for an off-beat party of your own. (Dir: Henri DeCoin, 94 mins.)

One Sunday Afternoon (1948)**½ Dennis Morgan, Janis Paige, Don Defore, Dorothy Malone. James Cagney carried this nostalgic gay-90's tale when it was called "Strawberry Blonde" (also released to TV) but he's not around to support this musical version. (Dir: Raoul Walsh, 90 mins.)

One That Got Away (British, 1957) **** Hardy Kruger, Colin Gordon. Cocky captured German pilot insists on trying to escape. Based on fact, this is a crack suspense drama, finely made and brilliantly acted by Kruger. (Dir: Roy Baker, 106 mins.)

1001 Arabian Nights (1960)**½ Color cartoon feature, with Mr. Magoo, and the voice of Jim Backus, back in old Baghdad. The nearsighted one is a lamp dealer whose nephew, Aladdin, gets the lamp with the genie, etc. Amusingly done, if not outstanding. Some songs, some cute moments —kiddies will like it. (Dir: Jack Kinney, 75 mins.)

One Touch of Venus (1948)**½ Ava Gardner, Robert Walker, Dick Haymes. A Greek statue of Venus comes to life in a department store, causes romance and misunderstandings. Mild musical comedy, never quite hits the mark intended. (Dir: William A. Seiter, 81 mins.)

One, Two Three (1961)***½ James Cagney, Horst Buchholz, Pamela Tiffin, Arlene Francis. Billy Wilder comes up with another of his glib sophisticated comedy romps which gives James Cagney the opportunity to overplay expertly in the role of a Coca-Cola executive in West Germany. The amusing plot examines the Cold War, East German beatniks, the internationality of Coca-Cola, and various other subjects. The pace is extremely fast, and you really have to listen to catch those often funny one-liners. (Dir: Billy Wilder, 108 mins.)

One Way Passage (1932)***½ William Powell, Kay Francis, Frank McHugh. Moving drama about the romance of an escaping convict and a girl dying of heart trouble, avoids being corny and emerges as an af-

fecting melodrama. (Dir: Tay Garnett, 69 mins.)

One Way Street (1950)**½ James Mason, Marta Toren, Dan Duryea. The charm of the stars make up for the inadequacies of the script in this chase melodrama about thieves, lovers and intrigue. (Dir: Hugo Fregonese, 79 mins.)

One Way Wahine (1965)*½ Anthony Eisley, Joy Harmon, Edgar Bergen. Silly story about gangsters hiding out in Hawaii with $100,000. Acting is wooden, and the film wastes Bergen, who plays a bearded beachcomber. (80 mins.)

One Woman's Story (British, 1948) ***½ Ann Todd, Trevor Howard, Claude Rains. Woman married to rich broker meets her former lover in Switzerland, and the affair begins once more. Poignant, sparklingly acted romantic drama. (Dir: David Lean, 86 mins.)

Onionhead (1958)**½ Andy Griffith, Felicia Farr, Walter Matthau. Not as funny as Griffith's army tour in "No Time for Sergeants" but this Coast Guard comedy has its moments. This time, Griffith is the ship's cook aboard a buoy tender. (Dir: Norman Taurog, 110 mins.)

Only a Woman (German, 1962)** Maria Schell, Paul Christian. Young man resents the advice of a lady head-shrinker, sets out to prove her wrong and winds up falling for her. Romantic comedy done with a too-heavy hand; dubbed in English.

Only Angels Have Wings (1939)*** Cary Grant, Jean Arthur, Richard Barthelmess. Dated, but fairly exciting melodrama about pilots trying to get a charter to fly mail in Central America. Plenty of crack-ups and aviation film cliches—but fun. (Dir: Howard Hawks, 120 mins.)

Only Game in Town, The (1970)*½ Elizabeth Taylor, Warren Beatty, Charles Braswell. Happily this is not the only movie in town. A two-character, one-set Broadway flop play has been turned into a boring eleven-million-dollar movie flop. Based on the play by Frank D. Gilroy. Taylor is absurdly cast as a 20-year-old (she does look lovely, but not 20, for God's sake), and piano player Beatty brings as much charm as humanly possible to some leaden dialogue before proposing marriage. (Dir: George Stevens, 113 mins.)

Only One New York (1964)**½

French-made, narrated in English; a roving camera-eye view of New York City, from Coney Island to Harlem and all stops in between. Interesting for what the foreign eye can discern about an American metropolis; also good for those natives who have never visited the place.

Only the Best—See: **I Can Get It for You Wholesale**

Only the French Can (French, 1954) ***½ Jean Gabin, Edith Piaf, Francoise Arnoul. Jean Renoir wrote and directed this thoroughly delightful and entertaining film dealing with the era when the Can-Can first shocked Parisians—long before the same dance upset Khrushchev. (93 mins.)

Only the Valiant (1951)** Gregory Peck, Barbara Payton. Peck stars as the misunderstood cavalry officer who must win his men's respect after having lost face in a previous skirmish with hostile Indians. Action galore for horse opera fans and little else in the way of character development or logical plot progression. (Dir: Gordon Douglas, 105 mins.)

Only Two Can Play (British, 1962) **** Peter Sellers, Mai Zetterling, Richard Attenborough. Comedy delight might be termed "The Best of Sellers." He's a frustrated Don Juan who tries a bit of extramarital maneuvering with disastrous results. Hilarious sequences dealing with his attempts at seduction turning into fiascoes, witty performance by Zetterling as the object of his desires. Fine adult fun. (Dir: Sidney Gilliat, 106 mins.)

Only When I Larf (British, 1968)** Richard Attenborough, David Hemmings, Alexandra Stewart. An innocuous caper about a trio of British con artists who try to fleece some African diplomats. Richard Attenborough gives a bravura performance, but the level of the humor explains the title. Man with a spear stuck in him repeatedly remarks it hurts "Only when I larf." (Dir: Basil Dearden, 104 mins.)

Only With Married Men (1974)*½ David Birney, Michele Lee, Dom DeLuise, Judy Carne. Silly premise, reminiscent of those frivolous '40s film comedies: Ms. Lee doesn't want to go through the hassle involved in dating single guys, so she goes out "only with married men." David Birney, on the other hand, is wary

of girls wanting to lead him to the altar, so he pretends to be married and starts dating Michele. Made-for-TV. (Dir: Jerry Paris, 72 mins.)

Open City (Italian, 1946)**** Aldo Fabrizi, Anna Magnani. Roberto Rossellini's picture of Rome during the occupation, as a priest aids the underground in routing the Nazis. Powerful, gripping, among the first of the superb post-war Italian films. Italian dialogue. English sub-titles. (105 mins.)

Open the Door and See All the People (1964)** Maybelle Nash, Alec Wilder. Conflict of two households run by elderly sisters, one a crab, the other open and generous. Offbeat whimsical comedy doesn't have the touch necessary for success. (Dir: Jerome Hill, 82 mins.)

Operation Abduction (French, 1957) *½ Frank Villard, Daniele Goedet. Secret agent goes after a ring of spies who have kidnaped the inventor of a new type of fuel. Hackneyed adventure melodrama dubbed in English.

Operation Amsterdam (British, 1959) ** Alexander Knox, Peter Finch, Eva Bartok. Exciting true-life incident emerges as routine suspense outing about a frantic attempt, in 1940, to smuggle out of Holland a fortune in industrial diamonds before the Nazis arrive. (Dir: Michael McCarthy, 105 mins.)

Operation Atlantis (Italian, 1965)*½ John Ericson, Berna Rock, Maria Granada. Secret agent is assigned to investigate acts of sabotage in Africa, runs into spies and counterspies. Shopworn espionage melodramatics dubbed in English.

Operation Bikini (1963)** Tab Hunter, Frankie Avalon, Scott Brady, Gary Crosby, Eva Six. Demolition squad seeks out an American sub held by the Japanese to destroy new radar equipment on it. War drama filled with the familiar plot clichés; okay for the action fans. (Dir: Anthony Carras, 83 mins.)

Operation Bottleneck (1961)*½ Ron Foster, Miko Taka. World War II, luckily for us, was never like this! GIs and some dames outwit the enemy in the Pacific. (Dir: Edward L. Cahn, 78 mins.)

Operation Bullshine (British, 1959)** Donald Sinden, Barbara Murray. Trouble when a horde of females in uniform descends on a woman-starved remote outpost. Some laughs in this military comedy, but there's little subtlety. All very obvious.

Operation Camel (Danish, 1961)* Lou Renard, Nora Hayden Danish UN soldiers in Gaza save a beautiful night club dancer from a dastardly villain. Spoken in English, this attempt at comedy is pitifully inept, despite the friendly personalities of actors speaking an unfamiliar language.

Operation Caviar (French, 1959)** O. W. Fischer, Eva Bartok. Bank clerk suddenly finds himself with plenty of complications when he becomes a spy. Mildly amusing wartime comedy-melodrama, dubbed in English.

Operation C.I.A. (1965)*½ Burt Reynolds, Danielle Aubry. Brave undercover agent foils an assassination plot in Saigon. This spy thriller was filmed in Thailand, and the authenticity of the locale is the sole asset. (Dir: Christian Nyey, 90 mins.)

Operation Conspiracy (British, 1957) ** Philip Friend, Mary Mackenzie. Undercover operator combats foreign agents after nuclear information, meets an old flame and murder along the way. Routine thriller. (Dir: Joseph Stirling, 69 mins.)

Operation Cross Eagles (1969)** Richard Conte, Rory Calhoun. Routine World War II thriller about a commando group behind German lines assigned to capture a German commandant and exchange him for an American captain. (Dir: Richard Conte, 90 mins.)

Operation Crossbow (1965)*** George Peppard, Tom Courtenay, Sophia Loren. Rip roaring WW II espionage adventure crammed with as much action as possible. Although Sophia Loren is top-billed, she has a brief role—it's really George Peppard, Tom Courtenay, and Jeremy Kemp as a trio of agents assigned to destroy a heavily guarded Nazi munitions installation who keep things buzzing. Exciting finale. (Dir: Michael Anderson, 116 mins.)

Operation Dames (1959)** Eve Meyer, Chuck Henderson. Entertainers in Korea are trapped behind enemy lines, take a perilous path to safety. War story made on a small budget has nothing new, but gets by.

Operation Delilah (1964)*½ Rory Calhoun, Gia Scala. Arrant nonsense about an electric shaver

salesman who plans to trim the beard of a Caribbean dictator. Played for laughs, but there aren't enough.

Operation Diplomat (British, 1953) **½ Guy Rolfe, Lisa Daniely. A doctor called in to perform an emergency operation at a deserted country house suspects his patient may be an important missing diplomat. Okay melodrama moves at a fast clip.

Operation Diplomatic Passport (French, 1962)*½ Roger Hanin, Christiane Minazzoli. French agent and a girl match wits with spies after a professor with a formula for synthetic oil. Patchy espionage melodrama substitutes running around for finesse. Dubbed in English.

Operation Disaster (British, 1950) ***½ John Mills, Nigel Patrick. A submarine on a routine cruise hits an old mine, and sinks to the bottom with twelve men still surviving. Tense, finely written and played story of rescue operations. (Dir: Roy Baker, 102 mins.)

Operation Eichmann (1962)** Werner Klemperer, Ruta Lee. Sensationalized account of the reign of terror in the German concentration and extermination camps presided over by Adolf Eichmann (played by Werner Klemperer). This film was made in a hurry to capitalize on Eichmann's trial and can hardly be taken seriously as a documentary of the time. (Dir: R. G. Springsteen, 93 mins.)

Operation Gold Ingot (French, 1963) ** Martine Carol, Felix Marten, Francis Blanche. Ex-secret service agent and his wife are asked to save a family friend from trouble, chase after gangsters in Barcelona. Average crime melodrama, with a fair pace and picturesque background aiding. Dubbed in English.

Operation Hong Kong (German, 1964) Horst Frank, Marina Perschy, Brad Harris. Two devil-may-care pilots become involved in a dope-smuggling plot. Terrible adventure melodrama dubbed in English.

Operation Kid Brother (1967)** The producers of this low-budget quickie tried to capitalize on Sean Connery's success in the Bond films and cast his real-life brother, Neil Connery, in the role of a cosmetic surgeon thrust into the world of espionage. The gimmick doesn't really work, and Neil doesn't generate the type of excitement his older brother does. A poor man's 003½! (Dir: Alberto De Maryino, 104 mins.)

Operation Mad Ball (1957)***½ Jack Lemmon, Ernie Kovacs, Mickey Rooney, Arthur O'Connell. Delightfully wacky Army comedy about an operator who upsets all rules and regulations in his search for fun for himself and his buddies. Kovacs is great as a bewildered officer and his scenes with Lemmon are gems. (Dir: Richard Quine, 105 mins.)

Operation Manhunt (1954)**½ Harry Townes, Jacques Aubuchon. The story of Igor Gouzenko, Russian code clerk who forsook the Communists and defected to the West. Okay melodrama made in Canada.

Operation Mermaid (British, 1963)*** Mai Zetterling, Keenan Wynn, Ronald Howard. American gathers together a crew of ex-Commandos to search for hidden Nazi treasure. Well-knit melodrama with a good cast, suspense.

Operation Pacific (1951)*½ John Wayne, Patricia Neal. Over-long and tedious story of a cautious and efficient skipper of a submarine. Patricia Neal is wasted and John Wayne is as dull as the script. (Dir: George Waggner, 111 mins.)

Operation Petticoat (1960)***½ Cary Grant, Tony Curtis. A big, big hit comedy highlighting Cary Grant's ageless appeal and Tony Curtis' energetic performing, about a sub and its mad, mad crew and their unbelievable exploits in the South Pacific. Fun for all. (Dir: Blake Edwards, 124 mins.)

Operation Secret (1952)*** Cornel Wilde, Phyllis Thaxter, Steve Cochran, Karl Malden. Good espionage thriller about the dangerous activities of the French underground, World War II. Many narrow escapes known as "The Maquis," during and tense situations in well acted adventure. (Dir: Lewis Seiler, 108 mins.)

Operation Snafu (Great Britain, 1961)** Alfred Lynch, Sean Connery, Stanley Holloway, Wilfred Hyde White. Lynch and Connery as a pair of cronies in the R.A.F., out to swindle fellow soldiers during WW II. Amiable pairing can't break through episodic script based on the R. F. Delderfield novel "Stop at a Winner." (Dir: Cyril Frankel, 97 mins.)

Operation Snatch (British, 1962)**½ Terry-Thomas, George Sanders. A bungling officer is sent to Gibraltar during World War II to make sure the Barbary apes stay there—legend has it that as long as they do, Gibraltar will remain in the British Empire. English comedy attempt that is only occasionally funny. (Dir: Robert Day, 83 mins.)

Operation St. Peter's (Italian, 1968)* Edward G. Robinson, Lando Buzzanca. Thirties hood (Robinson) on the comeback trail with an attempt to rob the Pieta from the Vatican. The script should have been stolen and then shredded. (Dir: Luccio Fulci, 100 mins.)

Operation Stogie (British, 1960)*½ John Hewer, Anton Rodgers, Susan Stephen. Two zany army sergeants try crashing society. Generally unfunny comedy.

Operation Warhead (British, 1961)** Sean Connery, Alan King, Cecil Parker. Misadventures of two Air Force misfits in WW II, brains (Alfred Lynch) and brawn (Connery). Traditional service antics, nothing special. This of course, was in Connery's pre-James Bond period.

Opposite Sex, The (1956)*** June Allyson, Joan Collins, Dolores Gray, Ann Sheridan, Ann Miller, Joan Blondell. Slickly produced, updated remake of the 1939 film classic "The Women," which was based on the celebrated Clare Boothe Luce B'way play. June Allyson plays the Norma Shearer role this time around and she has a few songs thrown in for good measure. The supporting cast is very good, particularly Joan Collins, who plays the feminine menace "Crystal" originally done by Joan Crawford. (Dir: David Miller, 117 mins.)

Optimists, The (British, 1973)*** Peter Sellers, Donna Mullane, John Chaffey. Sellers is marvelous in this often moving and charming if attenuated story about an ex-music hall performer (Sellers) who befriends two young children from a working-class family and helps them get a cherished dog. On-location scenes in London and various scenes throughout are well handled by director Anthony Simmons. Based on Simmons' novel "The Optimists of Nine Elms." (110 mins.)

Orchestra Wives (1942)*** Glenn Miller, Ann Rutherford. Silly story about girls married to musicians serves to give the Miller crew a chance to fill the screen with some wonderful arrangements. (Dir: Archie Mayo, 98 mins.)

Ordeal (1973)**½ Arthur Hill, Diana Muldaur, James Stacy. Hill is cast in the role of a man who is badly injured and left to fend for himself in the desert by a hateful wife and her lover, in this predictable man-versus-nature drama. Hill generates some interest. Made-for-TV. (Dir: Lee H. Katzin, 73 mins.)

Orders Are Orders (British, 1957)**½ Brian Reese, Margot Grahame, Peter Sellers. In his pre-stardom days, Peter Sellers has a small part in this confusing but funny British farce about a movie company descending on an Army camp to shoot a film on location. (Dir: David Paltenghi)

Orders to Kill (British, 1959)***½ Eddie Albert, Paul Massie, Lillian Gish, Irene Worth. Engrossing spy thriller concerning an American intelligence agent's mission to kill a supposedly French Nazi collaborator. Tight and tense. Acting is very good. (Dir: Anthony Asquith, 93 mins.)

Ordinary Tenderness (Canadian, 1973)**½ Esther Auger, Jocelyn Berube. Overlong, but well-photographed story about two young lovers waiting to get together after a lengthy separation. Little dialogue. Ambitious, but not altogether successful. English subtitles. (Dir: Jacques Leduc, 82 mins.)

Oregon Trail, The (1959)*½ Fred MacMurray, Gloria Talbott. Top star doesn't necessarily mean a top western. MacMurray is lost on the prairie. (Dir: Gene Fowler, Jr., 86 mins.)

Oregon Trail, The (1976)*½ Rod Taylor, Douglas V. Fowley, Blair Brown, Andrew Stevens. Western tale with the weatherbeaten Taylor heading a pioneer family en route to Oregon. Old, familiar odyssey of the wagon trains inching along while passengers face Indians, illness, and discouragement. No surprises! Made-for-TV. (Dir: Boris Sagal, 98 mins.)

Organization, The (1971)*** Sidney Poitier, Barbara McNair, Ron O'Neal. It's the third time round for Poitier's characterization of the low-key detective known as Virgil Tibbs, which he created in the memorable film "In the Heat of the Night," and subsequently played in "They Call Me Mr. Tibbs." In this tale, set in San Francisco, Tibbs reluctantly joins forces with a well-organized vigilante group determined to smash the drug traffic in their area. The action is swift, the performances slick. (Dir: Don Medford, 106 mins.)

Organizer, The (Italian, 1964)**** Marcello Mastroianni, Renato Salvatori, Annie Girardot. Absorbing drama of textile workers involved in a factory strike years ago. Tremendous performance by Mastroianni as a professor who leads them to fight for their rights. Excellent direction keeps the interest high throughout. Fine dramatic fare. Dubbed in English. (Dir: Mario Monicelli, 126 mins.)

Orientals, The (Italian, 1960)* Nagwa Fouad, Nick Kendall. Adventures in five oriental cities, none of them of much interest. Dubbed in English.

Orphans of the Storm (1922)*** Lillian Gish, Dorothy Gish, Joseph Schildkraut. A remarkable spectacle film directed by D. W. Griffith, based on a play called "Two Orphans" but transformed by Griffith to the period of the French Revolution. Griffith uses and improves upon the standard melodramatic tricks of his time so that Lillian Gish—searching for and finally finding an adopted blind sister—achieves a moving moment even in today's cinema. You name it, Griffith's got it—murder, orgies, kidnappings, hairbreath escapes, and Lillian Gish saved from the razor-sharp edge of the guillotine. A memorable landmark of the silent era. (Dir: D. W. Griffith, 120 mins.)

Oscar, The (1966)** Stephen Boyd, Elke Sommer, Eleanor Parker. A big splashy, sexy soap opera about an unscrupulous actor who uses everyone to further his career. There are many stars who do the best they can in their roles as Hollywood types but despite a first-class production, the film is corny and obvious. (Dir: Russel Rouse, 119 mins.)

Oscar Wilde (Great Britain, 1960)*** Robert Morley, John Neville, Ralph Richardson, Phyllis Calvert. One of two British films, made in

1960, about the tragic libel trial of the famed playwright in the 1890's, when he was accused of sodomy and sexual perversion. (Peter Finch starred in "The Trial of Oscar Wilde.") This filming is the harsher. Morley, physically close to the real Wilde, gustily exudes the wit and decay of the man; Richardson is masterful as the Queen's counsel. Some sequences are poorly conceived but, overall, a compelling portrait, in black and white. (Dir: Gregory Ratoff, 96 mins.)

O. S. S. (1946)*** Alan Ladd, Geraldine Fitzgerald. Fairly exciting drama about a mission by America's cloak and dagger heroes. A bit obvious, but interesting story.

Ossessione (Italy, 1942)*** Massimo Girotti, Clara Calamai. Excellent drama of love, passion and fate, based on the book "The Postman Always Rings Twice" by James M. Cain. Directed and co-authored by Luchino Visconti. (Because of the American version, Visconti's superior film was cleared for American release only in 1977.) Girotti plays a wandering lover who falls for the decorative young wife of a fat old restauranteur. The triangle proves awkward, but this fine Visconti work is graceful and involving. (Dir: Luchino Visconti, 135 mins.)

Othello (1955)*** Another of Welles' visually, and sometimes vocally exciting, assaults on a great Shakespearean drama. Welles' direction is often imaginative, and his performance rewarding, but the notably poor portrayal of Desdemona is a constant irritant. (Dir: Orson Welles, 92 mins.)

Othello (Great Britain, 1965)*** Laurence Olivier, Frank Finlay, Maggie Smith, Joyce Redman. The fourth filmed version of Shakespeare's masterpiece, and it's a towering achievement, largely due to the genius of Olivier. He is arguably the greatest stage actor of the century, and he does full justice to this most demanding role of the crazed Moor, Othello. There are some surprises here—Olivier plays Othello in blackface, but his interpretation is that of a modern man, sensitive to racial slurs, responsive to contemporary psychological nuances. This is a filmed version of Olivier's legendary stage portrayal, and generations to

538

come must be thankful this wondrous performance has been captured for all ages. Finlay, Smith and Redman, portraying Iago, Desdemona and Emilia, respectively, were all nominated for Academy Awards. Full Shakespeare text presented almost without cuts. (Dir: Stuart Burge, 166 mins.)

Other, The (1972)*** Chris Udvarnoky, Martin Udvarnoky, Uta Hagen, Diana Muldaur. Tom Tryon's best-selling gothic yarn about the eerie happenings in a Connecticut household during the 1930's, handsomely mounted, retaining much of the suspense of the novel. Twin boys have evolved a frightening game of identity change, causing everyone in their family to test their sanity. A fine twist to the story should shock those who aren't familiar with the book. (Dir: Robert Mulligan, 102 mins.)

Other Love, The (1947)**½ Barbara Stanwyck, David Niven, Richard Conte. A beautiful concert pianist finds she is ill, throws her life away before realizing a doctor is in love with her. Fair romantic drama. Good performances. (Dir: Andre de Toth, 95 mins.)

Other Man, The (1970)** Roy Thinnes, Joan Hackett, Arthur Hill. This made-for-TV feature goes back to the melodramas of the 1940's for its inspiration and the ladies may enjoy it. Joan Hackett plays a role once limned by Joan Crawford, Bette Davis, Greer Garson (take your pick). She's quite good as the rich married lady who falls hopelessly in love with a notorious playboy (Roy Thinnes). The plot sounds simple, but it's not. Thinnes makes an attractive mysterious mystery man, but it's Miss Hackett's vehicle, and she's up to the task. (Dir: Richard Colla, 99 mins.)

Other Side of the Mountain, The (1975)*½ Marilyn Hassett, Beau Bridges. True-life story of Jill Kinmont, a skier who might have made it to the 1956 Olympics if it hadn't been for an accident which left her paralyzed. Heavy-handed tearjerker, but there's a good performance by Beau Bridges, as a daredevil skier-racer who falls in love with her, to counteract sticky passages. If you want a good cry, this will provide it. Marilyn Hassett is attractive in debut role. (Dir: Larry Peerce, 103 mins.)

Other Voices (1969)*** Often interesting documentary about a small clinic in Pennsylvania dealing with mentally disturbed adolescents. Reminds us again of what an inexact science psychiatry is.

Other Woman, The (1955)** Cleo Moore, Hugo Haas. Girl trying to make good in Hollywood plans to blackmail a director. A little more time and effort would have made this drama of the movies much better—as it is, a fairly interesting story. (Dir: Hugo Haas, 81 mins.)

Otley (British, 1969)*** Tom Courtenay, Romy Schneider, Fiona Lewis, Alan Badel. Engaging secret-agent spoof, and it's a particular pleasure to be able to watch Tom Courtenay play a light role for a change, as he did so well in Billy Liar. (You can see the serious Tom Courtenay in films like "Dr. Zhivago" and "One Day in the Life of Ivan Denisovich.") Courtenay plays an affable drifter who picks up women and various inanimate objects that don't belong to him. (Dir: Dick Clement, 90 mins.)

Our Hearts Were Growing Up (1946) **½ Diana Lynn, Gail Russell. Silly story about two young girls on a weekend at Princeton University during the 1920's who get mixed up with bootleggers. A few laughs, but mostly forced comedy. (Dir: William D. Russell, 83 mins.)

Our Hearts Were Young and Gay (1944)*** Diana Lynn, Gail Patrick. Delightful little comedy about a trip abroad during the gay year of 1923 by two young, attractive girls. (Dir: Lewis Allen, 81 mins.)

Our Man Flint (1966)***½ James Coburn, Lee J. Cobb, Gila Golan. This super-gimmicked, high-style spoof of the James Bond superman, secret agent films benefits from the suave presence of James Coburn, as Flint. It's all tongue-in-cheek stuff kept bouncing along at a rapid clip by Director Daniel Mann. The plot, if you care, concerns an organization which plans to take over the world with their secret weapon—controlling the weather! There is the obligatory bevy of tasty, available damsels, but it's the unerringly right note of brains and bravado struck by Coburn that makes this such fun. Besides, we get a chance to root for the U.S.A. and against the meanies from abroad. (107 mins.)

Our Man Flint: Dead on Target (1976)** Ray Danton, Sharon Acker. Ray Danton takes over where James Coburn left off in this update of the old, flashy secret-agent spoofs. The action is predictably fast and ridiculous, and Sharon Acker adds a little luster to the production. Made-for-TV. (Dir: Joseph Scanlon, 72 mins.)

Our Man in Havana (1960)*** Alec Guinness, Burl Ives, Maureen O'Hara, Noel Coward, Ernie Kovacs. Graham Greene's novel is brought to the screen with many changes. The comedy is stressed in many scenes but the uneven picture fluctuates between out and out comedy and stark drama. The plot concerns a vacuum cleaner salesman who is recruited to become a spy but never receives any instructions about his duties as a spy. The best scenes are those between Alec Guinness (as the spy) and Ernie Kovacs, as a Cuban police officer. (Dir: Carol Reed, 107 mins.)

Our Man in Jamaica (European, 1965)*½ Larry Pennell, M. Scherr. American undercover man imperils his life looking for another agent, uncovers some smuggling. Our man in New York says forget it!

Our Man in the Caribbean (British, 1962)** Carlos Thompson, Shirley Eaton, Diana Rigg. Soldier of fortune finds himself the target for a swindle, manages to trick the tricksters. Passable melodrama based on a TV series.

Our Miss Brooks (1956)**½ Eve Arden, Gale Gordon, Richard Crenna. The popular radio and TV series is on the screen. Nothing new and if you were a fan of "Miss Brooks," you'll enjoy this visit with the old crew at Madison High. (Dir: Al Lewis, 85 mins.)

Our Mother's House (1967)*** Dirk Bogarde. Entertaining British entry concerns a group of children, the oldest being 13, who decide to conceal their invalid mother's death and carry on as a family unit. Enter wandering no-good dad (Bogarde) and the plot takes on shadings of the unexpected. (Dir: Jack Clayton, 105 mins.)

Our Town (1940)**** Martha Scott, William Holden. Thornton Wilder's study of life, love and death in a New England town at the turn of the century. Excellent film-making. (Dir: Sam Wood, 90 mins.)

Our Very Own (1950)** Ann Blyth, Farley Granger, Joan Evans, Donald Cook. Melodramatic yarn about a young girl who accidentally discovers she has been adopted. The stars do well but they can't escape the soap opera overtones of the script. There's a good scene between Miss Blyth and her legitimate mother, well played by Ann Dvorak. (Dir: David Miller, 93 mins.)

Our Vines Have Tender Grapes (1945)*** Edward G. Robinson, Margaret O'Brien, Agnes Moorehead. Warm, moving, well-played story about the love people have for each other in a small community. It's a touching theme and it's delivered with a minimum of corn. (Dir: Roy Rowland, 105 mins.)

Our Wife (1941)**½ Melvyn Douglas, Ruth Hussey. Trumpet player wants to marry a socialite, but his divorce isn't final. Lengthy comedy is too drawn out, but is nicely made. (Dir: John M. Stahl, 95 mins.)

Out of Sight (1966)*½ Jonathan Daly, Karen Jensen. Butler to a secret agent tries to emulate his employer. Insipid pop musical with a secret-agent yarn thrown in—which should have been thrown out. (Dir: Lennie Weinrib, 87 mins.)

Out of the Blue (1947)**½ George Brent, Virginia Mayo. A husband is in all sorts of hot water when a shady lady passes out in his apartment. Cute romantic comedy. (Dir: Leigh Jason, 84 mins.)

Out of the Fog (1941)*** Ida Lupino, John Garfield, Eddie Albert. Movie version of Irwin Shaw's "The Gentle People" benefits from wonderful acting by a top drawer cast and Anatole Litvak's skillful direction. Story of a gangster's preying on innocent people wavers between greatness and mediocrity. (Dir: Anatole Litvak, 93 mins.)

Out of the Past (1947)*** Robert Mitchum, Jane Greer, Kirk Douglas, Rhonda Fleming. Gas station owner with a past meets a desperate woman and winds up in murder. Complicated but intriguing mystery melodrama, well made. (Dir: Jacques Tourneur, 97 mins.)

Out of This World (1945)**½ Eddie Bracken, Diana Lynn. Good farce plot is poorly handled. Story of a crooner who makes the girls swoon has some funny moments, but is generally forced comedy. Bracken is the crooner, and he borrows a familiar voice for the occasion. (Dir: Hal Walker, 96 mins.)

Out-of-Towners, The (1970)*** Jack Lemmon, Sandy Dennis, Anthony Holland, Sandy Baron. The "Out-of-Towners" are non-New Yorkers in Neil Simon's uneven but frequently funny and sardonic notion of the perils that await the unwary who choose to visit the demilitarized zone of peacetime New York. Lemmon plays an obnoxious, dyspeptic executive from Ohio visiting "Fun City" for a job audition. "Out-of-Towners" is a discarded playlet from Simon's "Plaza Suite," but he's inserted some lacerating humor in this grim vision of New York, and Anthony Holland is a marvelously funny hotel clerk. (Dir: Arthur Hiller, 97 mins.)

Out West with the Hardys (1938)**½ Mickey Rooney, Lewis Stone. Just as many warm, human problems confront them out west as in their other films. Hardy pictures are always worthy of your attention if you like homespun humor, beautifully acted. (Dir: George B. Seitz, 90 mins.)

Outback (Australian, 1971)*** Gary Bond, Chips Rafferty, Donald Pleasence. Off-beat adventure. A young schoolteacher (Bond) in Australia's barren outback is scheduled to fly to Sydney during vacation. To get the plane, he goes to Yago, a small boomtown, and during the night he loses his money and joins several locals in a vicious hunt and some cheap sex leading to attempted suicide. Superbly played tale of the downfall of a civilized man when confronted with temptation. Pleasence is at his best as a grotesque alcoholic doctor. (Dir: Ted Kotcheff, 114 mins.)

Outcast, The (1954)*** John Derek, Joan Evans. Young man returns to Colorado intending to obtain a ranch from his uncle which he thinks is rightfully his. Fast, exciting western. (Dir: William Witney, 90 mins.)

Outcast of the Islands (British, 1952)**** Ralph Richardson, Trevor Howard, Robert Morley, Wendy Hiller. A clerk in the South Seas enters into a smuggling plot with the natives, betrays his employer, eventually becomes a broken man.

Fine study of moral corruption of man's character, based on Joseph Conrad's story. Directed by Carol Reed with finesse, superbly acted, photographed. (93 mins.)

Outcasts of Poker Flat, The (1952) **½ Anne Baxter, Dale Robertson, Cameron Mitchell. Four shady characters are run out of a mining town and marooned in a cabin during a snowstorm. Competent western drama based on a Bret Harte story, some nice performances by Baxter and Mitchell. (Dir: Joseph M. Newman, 81 mins.)

Outcry (Italian, 1959)** Steve Cochran, Alida Valli, Betsy Blair. Slow, muddled drama of a man and the women he loved and left. Arty effort by Antonioni leaves much to be desired. Dubbed in English. (Dir: Michelangelo Antonioni, 115 mins.)

Outer Space Connection, The (1975) **½ Fairly interesting documentary film probing the start of life on earth, with an accent on the possibility of outer-space visits from aliens from other planets, and their influence on ancient cultures. One of the most interesting sequences involves the Mayan and Inca civilizations. (Dir: Fred Warshofsky, 106 mins.)

Outfit, The (1973)* Robert Duvall, Karen Black, Sheree North, Robert Ryan, Joe Don Baker. Tacky, violent melodrama about criminals trying to outsmart each other. It's boring and trite. A total waste of a talented cast. Badly written and directed by John Flynn. (102 mins.)

Outlaw, The (1943)*½ Walter Huston, Thomas Mitchell, Jane Russell, Jack Beutel. The notorious sexy western about Billy the Kid, Doc Holliday his mentor, and the dame with the bulging blouse who loves him. Subtract all the publicity received by Jane's bosom, and you have left little but a bad western with some good work by Huston and Mitchell, who went along with the joke. (Dir: Howard Hughes, 123 mins.)

Outpost in Indo-China (French, 1964) ** Jacques Harden, Alain Saury. Captain faces the task of securing a fort and evacuating refugees during the Vietnamese fighting. Fairly interesting war drama dubbed in English.

Outpost in Malaya (1953)** Claudette Colbert, Jack Hawkins. Adventure and intrigue on a rubber plantation form the background for this mediocre, often dull, film. (Dir: Ken Annakin, 88 mins.)

Outrage (1964)***½ Paul Newman, Claire Bloom, Laurence Harvey, Edward G. Robinson. Conflicting stories are heard in the aftermath of a crime, as a bandit kidnaps a married couple, molests the wife, murders the husband. Story is taken from Japanese film "Rashomon" and set in our West. Intellectually interesting tale of the elusive nature of "truth" and how it changes in the eyes of the beholder. (Dir: Martin Ritt, 97 mins.)

Outrage (1973)**½ Robert Culp, Thomas Leopold, Marilyn Mason. Disturbing, thought-provoking story about a group of teen-age boys who menace a new family in an upper-middle-class neighborhood of a small California community. The kids begin with annoying pranks and graduate to real violence, until the man of the house (Culp) takes the law into his own hands. The finale, in which Culp goes on a hard-hitting no-holds-barred vengeance spree, packs a wallop. Incidentally, this story is based on a true-life incident. Made-for-TV. (Dir: Richard T. Heffron.)

Outriders, The (1950)*** Joel McCrea, Arlene Dahl, Barry Sullivan. Rousing, action filled western with the expert cowboy Joel McCrea at the helm. Good scenes focusing on the trek of a wagon train across treacherous Indian territory, and a better than usual script. (Dir: Roy Rowland, 93 mins.)

Outside Man, The (1973)** Jean-Louis Trintignant, Ann-Margret, Roy Scheider, and Angie Dickinson. Despite the star-studded cast, this crime melodrama suffers from a lack of cohesive continuity. Trintignant is a hired killer from France who arrives in Los Angeles to eliminate a syndicate biggie. What he doesn't know is that he too is earmarked for assassination by American hit-man Scheider. The chase is on and revenge is the name of the game. Too bad, this one had promise. (Dir: Jacques Deray, 104 mins.)

Outside the Law (1956)* Ray Danton, Leigh Snowden. Incredibly inept film about counterfeiters and how they are exposed by a determined ex-con with a chip on his shoulder. A brief jail term would be fitting penalty for everyone involved with this rubbish. (Dir: Jack Arnold, 81 mins.)

Outside the Wall (1950)** Richard Basehart, Marilyn Maxwell, Signe Hasso. Basehart's performance is the only recommendable feature of this tiresome tale of an ex-con who finds a job as a laboratory assistant at a sanitarium and encounters all sorts of evil people. (Dir: Crane Wilbur, 80 mins.)

Outsider, The (British, 1948)*** Richard Attenborough, Bernard Miles. An incorrigible youth is made into a decent citizen at a boys' school. Sensitively done drama of youth, merits praise in writing, direction, performances.

Outsider, The (1962) ***½ Tony Curtis, James Franciscus. An absorbing film which bogs down a bit in the last third but it doesn't detract from the overall impact of the true story of American-Indian Ira Hayes who was one of the Marines who helped hoist the flag on Iwo Jima. Tony Curtis gives one of his best screen performances. Good screenplay by Stewart Stern. (Dir: Delbert Mann, 108 mins.)

Outsider, The (1967)*½ Darren McGavin, Anna Hagan, Edmond O'Brien. McGavin is fine as David Ross, an ex-con who's hired as a private eye to learn if a young girl has been embezzling funds from a theatrical manager. Pilot for the defunct TV series. Made-for-TV. (Dir: William Graham, 98 mins.)

Over-exposed (1956)*½ Cleo Moore, Richard Crenna. Trite film about the expose of a vice ring by a crime photographer. Crenna's a better actor than you'd ever know from this stinker. (Dir: Lewis Seiler, 80 mins.)

Over My Dead Body (1942)** Milton Berle, Mary Beth Hughes. Milton as a writer who never finishes his mystery stories provides a fair amount of comedy in this "B" film. (Dir: Malcolm St. Clair, 68 mins.)

Over the Hill Gang, The (1969)*½ Edgar Buchanan, Andy Devine, Rick Nelson, Pat O'Brien. Old Texas rangers put themselves back into circulation to curtail the crime wave in their town. Routine, with a good cast of veteran old-timers. Made-for-TV. (Dir: Jean Yarbrough, 72 mins.)

Over the Hill Gang Rides Again, The (1970)** Walter Brennan, Fred As-
taire, Chill Wills, Edgar Buchanan. Sequel to "The Over the Hill Gang," a modest TV feature western which relied on a gimmick—the casting of Hollywood veteran actors in the role of ex-Texas rangers rallying once again. In this outing, Fred Astaire joins the group as a drunken, grizzled ex-lawman (he's really a sight with a five-day growth of whiskers and battered garb) who finds his way back thanks to aid from his old cronies. (Dir: George McCowan, 73 mins.)

Over There 1914-1918 (French, 1964) *** Compilation of old film showing the progress and effects of World War I. Well done, some powerful scenes from the past. Narrated in English.

Over 21 (1945)**½ Irene Dunne, Charles Coburn, Alexander Knox. Wartime comedy about a wife who stands by her "aging" hubby through the rigors of officers' candidate school. (Dir: Charles Vidor, 102 mins.)

Overland Pacific (1954)**½ Jock Mahoney, Peggie Castle. Undercover agent investigates Indian attacks on the railroad, discovers white men behind it all. Exciting western, with rugged action. (Dir: Fred F. Sears, 73 mins.)

Overlanders, The (Australian, 1946) ***½ Chips Rafferty, Daphne Campbell. When the Japanese threaten invasion of Australia, brave men undertake a great trek across the continent with precious cattle. Engrossing story of events that actually occurred has the ingredients of a western, war story, and documentary; an unusual film that is worth seeing.

Owen Marshall, Counsellor at Law (1971)* Arthur Hill, Vera Miles, Joseph Campanella, Dana Wynter. Poor legal drama. Hippie is charged with the murder of a rich socialite. Pilot for former TV series. Made-for-TV. (Dir: Buzz Kulik, 100 mins.)

Owl and the Pussycat, The (1970)*** Barbra Streisand, George Segal. Call girl (Streisand) hooks up with flunky bookstore clerk (Segal) in a raunchy, boisterous, often funny outing. The Streisand and Segal duet keep you involved even though the story's been done before. Let this one meow ya! (Dir: Herbert Ross, 95 mins.)

Ox Bow Incident, The (1943)****
Henry Fonda, Dana Andrews. A
powerful indictment of lynching
told with a simple force that leaves
you limp. A low budget film which
takes its place as a screen classic.
(Dir: William Wellman, 75 mins.)

Pacific Adventure (Australian, 1945)
*** Ron Randell, Muriel Steinbeck.
True story of Sir Charles Kingsford
Smith, pioneer aviator who conquered the Pacific. Factual, authentic atmosphere helps this interesting
biographical drama.

Pacific Liner (1939)*** Victor Mc-
Laglen, Chester Morris, Wendy Barrie. Ship's doctor tries to stem the
spread of cholera aboard an ocean
liner, but is hampered by the
engineer. Suspenseful melodrama.
(Dir: Lew Landers, 76 mins.)

Pack Up Your Troubles (1939)**
Ritz Brothers, Jane Withers. The
Ritzes provide a few laughs but
you'll have to be strong to tolerate
the sickly World War I plot about
spies and Jane Withers at the front.
(Dir: H. Bruce Humberstone, 68
mins.)

Pad (And How to Use It) The (1966)
**½ Brian Bedford, Julie Sommars,
James Farentino. Comedy about a
swinging bachelor and a shy one who
team up to woo an unsuspecting
young miss, provides a few laughs.
Brian Bedford playing the shy member of the duo is especially adroit
and amusing. Julie Sommars is adequate as the girl. This film is loosely
based on British playwright Peter
Shaffer's excellent one-act play "The
Private Ear," and those who may
have seen it on Broadway will probably want to skip this screen translation. Could have been much better
film if not entrusted to producer
Ross Hunter. (Dir: Brian Hutton, 68
mins.)

Paddy the Next Best Thing (1933)
*** Janet Gaynor, Warner Baxter,
Walter Connolly, Margaret Lindsay.
Delightful romantic romp, with
Gaynor particularly charming. (Dir:
Harry Lachman.)

Pagan, The—See: Barbarians, The

Pagan Love Song (1950)** Esther
Williams, Howard Keel. Strictly for
escapists—a tuneful and eye-filling
musical with the customary swimming sequences starring the "Queen

of the Surf," Miss Williams. Keel's
fine voice makes the songs worthwhile. (Dir: Robert Alton, 76 mins.)

Pagans, The (Italian, 1953)* Pierre
Cressoy, Helene Remy. Weak tale
about the ransacking of Rome in
1527 by the Spaniards. Shoddy battle scenes. (Dir: Ferruccio Cerio,
80 mins.)

Paid In Full (1950)*½ Robert Cummings, Lizabeth Scott, Diana Lynn.
Young executive marries a selfish
girl though he is loved by her older
sister. The dramatic consequences
that ensure are purest soap opera,
unrelieved by any distinguishing
elements. (Dir: William Dieterle,
105 mins.)

Paint Your Wagon (1969)*½ Lee
Marvin, Jean Seberg, Clint Eastwood. A boring, dated Broadway musical of the late 40's has been turned
into an enormously expensive, stupefyingly boring movie musical. About
life and romance in the California
boom towns during the gold rush in
the 1800's. Joshua Logan's direction
buries what little humor there is,
and Alan Jay Lerner's score is one
of his poorest. Any film with Lee
Marvin playing a drunk can't be all
bad, but this clinker comes pretty
close. Let this wagon roll by without
you. (166 mins.)

Painted Hills, The (1951)**½ Lassie,
Paul Kelly, Gary Gray. Typical Lassie adventure with the dog coming
out ahead of his human co-stars.
The kids will enjoy the villain who
is outsmarted by the crafty canine
and her young master. Pretty photography an asset. (Dir: Howard F.
Kress, 65 mins.)

Painted Veil, The (1934)*** Greta
Garbo, Herbert Marshall, George
Brent. Garbo pictures are always a
treat and this overly dramatic story
of a beautiful woman who is neglected by her husband while in
Hong Kong is passable entertainment. (Dir: Richard Boleslawski,
90 mins.)

Painting the Clouds with Sunshine
(1951)** Virginia Mayo, Dennis
Morgan, Gene Nelson. The chorines
have moved from Broadway to Las
Vegas in this re-make of "The
Golddiggers." Lively dances. (Dir:
David Butler, 87 mins.)

Paisan (1948)***½ The war in Italy,
as told through the directorial genius of Roberto Rossellini. Six
separate episodes, Italian and Eng-

lish dialogue, English subtitles. Well done. (90 mins.)

Pajama Game, The (1957)*** Doris Day, John Raitt, Carol Haney, Eddie Foy, Jr. All the fun, songs, dances, and laughs of the hit Broadway musical are brought to the screen with the added attraction being Doris Day. The plot, which serves as an excuse for all the musical numbers, revolves around a pajama factory union's efforts to get a seven and a-half-cent raise per hour. (Dirs: George Abbott, Stanley Donen, 101 mins.)

Pajama Party (1964)** Tommy Kirk, Annette Funicello, Donna Loren. This one is sillier than most beach-party films because it has a science-fiction bent. Would you believe Kirk as a Martian? (Dir: Don Weis, 85 mins.)

Pal Joey (1957)**½ Frank Sinatra, Rita Hayworth, Kim Novak. The saga of a heel, by Messrs. O'Hara, Rodgers & Hart. Film version of famed Broadway show is a disappointment. Sinatra sings the R & H tunes inimitably but somewhere along the way the bite of the original story has been lost. Novak is hopelessly bad. (Dir: George Sidney, 111 mins.)

Paleface, The (1948)*** Bob Hope, Jane Russell. Dentist becomes western hero because Calamity Jane is doing the shooting for him in this cute spoof of western films. (Dir: Norman Z. McLeod, 91 mins.)

Palm Beach Story (1942)**** Claudette Colbert, Joel McCrea, Rudy Vallee. Poor engineer's wife runs away to Florida, is romanced by a stuffy multi-millionaire. Frantic comedy is both sophisticated and slapstick, successful at both. A howling good time is guaranteed. (Dir: Preston Sturges, 90 mins.)

Palm Springs Weekend (1963)** Connie Stevens, Ty Hardin, Troy Donahue. Strictly for the teen-age audience, about the annual Easter Week invasion of Palm Springs by hordes of college kids and their friends out to have a good time. Hollywood's idea of typical "college types" may give the teen-agers an added chuckle. (Dir: Norman Taurog, 100 mins.)

Palmy Days (1931)**½ Eddie Cantor, George Raft, Charlotte Greenwood. Frantically paced comedy set in a health resort overrun by bath-

ing beauties, circa 1930, and gangsters. Many production numbers staged by Busby Berkely. Cantor is good and Charlotte Greenwood gets her share of laughs. (Dir: A. Edward Sutherland, 90 mins.)

Palomino, The (1956)** Jerome Courtland, Beverly Tyler. A prize palomino breeding stallion is stolen and as a result the heroine's ranch goes to pot. Fair outdoor adventure story for the youngsters.

Panache (1976)*½ Rene Auberjonois, David Healy, Charles Frank, Joseph Ruskin. Errol Flynn's old studio, Warner Brothers, revives the swashbuckling, sword-play costume show. This small-screen version of "The Three Musketeers" was at least a change from the then current crop of cops-and-robbers themes, as devil-may-care royal guards outwit France's wily Cardinal Richelieu. However, the pratfalls and comedy touches in between fencing scenes are old-hat and fail to amuse. Only bright spot is Harvey Solin's bright-eyed rendition of that foppish fool, Louis XIII. Made-for-TV. (Dir: Gary Nelson, 72 mins.)

Panama Hattie (1942)**½ Red Skelton, Ann Sothern, Marsha Hunt. Another Broadway musical hit is slaughtered in the screen transition. A fine cast does their best with the plot about blowing up the Canal but the film has no spark. Lena Horne makes her screen debut in this. (Dir: Norman Z. McLeod, 79 mins.)

Pandora and the Flying Dutchman (British, 1951)*** James Mason, Ava Gardner. A beautiful playgirl is the replica of the girl for whom the legendary Flying Dutchman was condemned to sail the seas forever; off the coast of Spain, she is visited by a mysterious stranger. Fanciful drama, not always successful, but extremely interesting. (Dir: Albert Lewin, 123 mins.)

Panhandle (1949)*** Rod Cameron, Cathy Downs. Brawny Cameron mops up a few western varmints, one a young gun played by Blake Edwards, who's now reformed and turned into a big time movie director. Actionful oats opera, one of the better ones.

Panic (British, 1963)** Janine Gray, Dyson Lovell, Glyn Houston. Girl working for a diamond merchant is hit during a robbery and loses her memory, is taken in by a friendly ex-boxer. Fair crime melodrama.

Panic Button (1963)** Maurice Chevalier, Michael Connors, Jayne Mansfield, Eleanor Parker. Gangster's son goes to Italy to make a pilot for a TV film, which must be a bad one so that the syndicate can take a tax loss. Mild comedy filmed in Europe stymies a cast of veteran performers. (Dir: George Sherman, 90 mins.)

Panic in Echo Park (1977)**½ Dorian Harewood, Robin Gammel, Catlin Adams. Good acting bolsters this routine pilot film for a proposed series about a dedicated black doctor who jeopardizes his career when he delves into a possible epidemic that has broken out in a ghetto community. Dorian Harewood is convincing as Dr. Stoner, a man who puts principles ahead of personal gain, and Robin Gammell, as his superior, opposed to his crusade, makes a good adversary. Made-for-TV. (Dir: John Llewellyn Moxey, 72 mins.)

Panic in Needle Park (1970)*** Al Pacino, Kitty Winn. Pacino in his first starring role. He's very effective as a drug addict who drags a young girl down into his world of hookers, pimps, thieves, and other low-life inhabitants of New York City's upper West Side area known as Needle Park. A somber sort of degenerate "Love Story." (Dir: Jerry Schatzberg, 110 mins.)

Panic in the City (1968)* Howard Duff, Linda Cristal, Nehemiah Persoff, Dennis Hopper. Los Angeles setting for a dull espionage thriller. A mad scientist runs amok, threatening to blow up the city. Yawn! (Dir: Eddie Davis, 97 mins.)

Panic in the Parlor (1957)** Peggy Mount, Shirley Eaton, Ronald Lewis. Raucous heavy handed British farce about a domineering mother (jarringly played by Peggy Mount) and a screwball family. (Dir: Gordon Parry, 81 mins.)

Panic in the Streets (1950)***½ Richard Widmark, Paul Douglas, Barbara Bel Geddes, Jack Palance. Dangers befall New Orleans when a dead body is found to be carrying the plague. A courageous doctor and the police try tracking down the source leading to an exciting climax. Directed by Elia Kazan with on-the-spot location realism, and good sup-

porting performance from Zero Mostel. (93 mins.)

Panic in Year Zero (1962)*** Ray Milland, Jean Hagen, Frankie Avalon. Forceful drama about a man trying to survive along with his family when the country is devastated by an atomic attack. Some of the drastic steps he takes may be questioned by the audience, but there's no doubt of the impact of the story. Milland acts well, directs even better. (95 mins.)

Pantaloons (French, 1956)*** Fernandel, Carmen Sevilla. Fernandel romps through this funny French farce as a valet masquerading as his master, Don Juan.

Papa's Delicate Condition (1963)** Jackie Gleason, Glynis Johns. Family comedy about a tippling, carefree railroad supervisor and his brood; not Gleason at his best. Infrequently amusing. (Dir: George Marshall, 98 mins.)

Paper Chase, The (1974)***½ Timothy Bottoms, Lindsay Wagner, John Houseman, James Naughton. Absorbing drama about trying to make it through Harvard Law School while going through other normal pains of growing up. Timothy Bottoms conveys all the passion, intelligence, wisdom, fear, and doubts which plague a bright student who really cares about his chosen field of endeavor—law. The classroom scenes, presided over by John Houseman as an awesome professor of contract law (he won an Oscar for his performance), are memorable, and better than the forced romance between Bottoms and the professor's daughter, well played by Ms. Wagner before she turned to TV bionics! (Dir: James Bridges, 112 mins.)

Paper Lion (1968)***½ Alan Alda. Engaging, observant, dramatization of George Plimpton's bestseller about his experiences in the world of pro football. Designed to capitalize on the huge audience that now sits transfixed, watching pro football every Sunday during the fall, producer Stuart Millar and his screenwriter have skillfully fashioned a believable plot line based on Plimpton's factual report. (Millar also directed much of the last part of the film skillfully, after the director who gets screen credit, Alex March, was fired.) Model-turned-actress Lauren

Hutton is both beautiful and charming playing Alda's girlfriend. The scenes of the Detroit Lions training scrimmages, and in the locker room capture the flavor of this tough, fascinating sport. (107 mins.)

Paper Man (1971)*** Dean Stockwell, James Stacy. Intriguing, imaginative drama about a computer. Group of bright college students, using the university computer, create a fictitious human and go off on a buying spree with the character's credit card. When bills come due, more data is put into the computer. Soon the paper man displays puzzling independent behavior which includes murder. Credit writers Tony Wilson, James D. Buchanan, and Ronald Austin with a sleeper! Made-for-TV. (Dir: Walter Grauman, 73 mins.)

Paper Moon (1973)**** Ryan O'Neal, Tatum O'Neal. Peter Bogdanovich is back with another lovely piece of yesterday in black and white. Finely engraved story of Kansas con man selling Bibles to women just turned widows, with the aid of an innocent nine-year-old determined to be corrupted. The interplay between the con man and his tiny sidekick (a real-life father and daughter) is irresistibly real and sweetly sentimental. Tatum O'Neal steals the movie from her dad while giving one of the most appealing performances by a child actor in many years. (Dir: Peter Bogdanovich, 101 mins.)

Paper Tiger (Great Britain, 1974)*½ David Niven, Toshiro Mifune, Ando, Hardy Kruger. Timely political kidnapping theme is misplaced in this sentimental minor comedy. Niven plays a tutor to the son of a Japanese ambassador to a fictitious Asian country. Claiming great war feats, the teacher is really a coward at heart. Filmed in Malaysia. (Dir: Ken Annakin, 99 mins.)

Papillon (1973)*** Steve McQueen, Dustin Hoffman, Victor Jory, William Smithers. A generally exciting film based on the best-selling novel about Henri "Papillon" Charriere's real-life escape from the indescribable horrors and brutality of the infamous French penal colony of Devil's Island, off the eastern coast of South America. In the 1930's, Papillon (Hoffman) is falsely convicted, he maintains, on a murder rap. Graphic depiction of the amenities

546

of prison life include cockroaches, brutal guards, marauding homosexual prisoners, and a rectal tube to store one's money. After several attempts, and long stretches in solitary, Papillon does escape on a raft, and the closing shot finds him screaming, "Hey, you bastards, I'm still here." You'll be rooting for him to escape long before that. Rousing escapist fare. (Dir: Franklin J. Schaffner, 150 mins.)

Parachute Battalion (1941)**½ Robert Preston, Nancy Kelly, Edmond O'Brien. Two trainees in the parachute corps go through the hazardous training and fall for the same girl. Typical but fairly interesting service melodrama. (Dir: Leslie Goodwins, 75 mins.)

Paradine Case, The (1948)**½ Gregory Peck, Ann Todd, Valli, Charles Laughton. Beautiful woman is accused of murdering her husband; young criminal lawyer takes the case, falls in love with her. Polished but empty, talkative melodrama, not up to par, for either Selznick or Hitchcock. (Dir: Alfred Hitchcock, 125 mins.)

Paradise, Hawaiian Style (1966)** Elvis Presley. Typical Presley musical for his fans. This time out, Presley is an airline pilot who returns to Hawaii to interest his buddy, played by James Shigeta, in setting up a shuttle-plane business. Songs, romance, and island cuties. (Dir: Michael Moore, 91 mins.)

Paradise Lagoon (British, 1958)*** Kenneth More, Sally Ann Howes, Diane Cilento. A funny comedy based on "The Admirable Crichton." The plot concerns a group of shipwrecked British families who come to rely on the resourcefulness of a butler. The young lady of a respectable family falls for the servant as does a flighty upstairs maid. (Dir: Lewis Gilbert, 94 mins.)

Parallax View, The (1974)***½ Warren Beatty, Paula Prentiss. Fascinating, disturbing story about a political assassination of a senator, not unlike the Kennedys, and one reporter's efforts to get to the bottom of the mystery surrounding the killing by a busboy who himself is killed. Suddenly witnesses at the assassination start dying off, and one of them goes to reporter Beatty who gets on the case. No answers to the Kennedy assassination offered, incidentally, in this intriguing, stimulating political chiller. Extremely well directed by Alan Pakula. Skillfully adapted by David Giler and Lorenzo Semple, Jr. from the novel by Loren Singer. (Dir: Alan Pakula, 102 mins.)

Paranoia (Italian, 1966)** Marcello Mastroianni, Virna Lisi, Pamela Tiffin. Three separate tales concerning man, romance, and mentality. Aside from Mastroianni's good looks, Tiffin's charm, and Lisi's glamour, little to recommend; tales never seem to come to a boil. Dubbed in English. (Dir: Umberto Lenzi, 91 mins.)

Paranoia (Italy-France, 1968)½ Carroll Baker, Lou Castel. Bereaved, bored widow is drawn into sexual perversion, blackmail. Poorly dubbed. (Dir: Umberto Lenzi, 91 mins.)

Paranoiac (Great Britain, 1963)**½ Janette Scott, Alexander Daviron, Oliver Reed. Elaborate, entertaining murder tale; plentiful gore, fanciful props, chilling atmosphere. (Dir: Freddie Francis, 80 mins.)

Paratrooper (British, 1954)** Alan Ladd, Leo Genn, Susan Stephen. A Canadian joins the paratroopers under an assumed name because he has a fear of responsibility due to an earlier service experience. Muddled action film with drab acting. (Dir: Terrence Hill, 87 mins.)

Pardners (1956)** Dean Martin, Jerry Lewis, Agnes Moorehead. Eccentric playboy and a ranch foreman head west with a prize bull, foil varmints bent on taking over the ranch. Dean and Jerry out west in a comedy which, after a good start, slows down to a canter. (Dir: Norman Taurog, 90 mins.)

Pardon My French (1951)** Merle Oberon, Paul Henreid. A Boston schoolteacher acquires a French chateau, finds it inhabited by miscellaneous squatters, including a dashing composer and five fatherless children. Slender little comedy, not much. Made in France. (Dir: Bernard Vorhaus, 81 mins.)

Pardon My Past (1945)***½ Fred MacMurray, Marguerite Chapman. Ex-soldier is mistaken for a wealthy playboy who owes money to some gamblers. Delightful comedy-drama, smoothly done and entertaining. (Dir: Leslie Fenton, 88 mins.)

Pardon My Sarong (1942)*** Bud Abbott, Lou Costello, Virginia Bruce. Two bus drivers on a playboy's yacht land on a tropic isle, where they thwart villains trying to steal the temple jewels. One of the better Abbott and Costello comedies, with some genuinely amusing bits of business. (Dir: Erle C. Kenton, 84 mins.)

Pardon My Trunk (Italian, 1953)** Vittorio De Sica, Sabu. Vittorio De Sica plays a school teacher who receives a real live elephant as a gift from an Indian Prince whom he has befriended. Sounds hilarious but isn't. On the strength of this film we feel De Sica is even a better actor than Sabu. (Dir: Gianni Franciolini, 78 mins.)

Parent Trap, The (1961)*** Hayley Mills, Maureen O'Hara, Brian Keith, Una Merkel, Joanna Barnes. Hayley Mills is simply wonderful playing twins in this family comedy-drama produced by the Walt Disney studio. Miss Mills meets her look-alike at a summer camp and, after some detective work, they discover they are twins. Adapted for the screen and directed by David Swift. (124 mins.)

Pariahs of Glory (French, 1964)**½ Curt Jurgens, Maurice Ronet. French soldier meets the German who killed his brother years ago, but the two fight together in Indo-China. War drama has some affecting scenes, but lacks the necessary punch. Dubbed in English.

Paris Blues (1961)***½ Paul Newman, Joanne Woodward, Sidney Poitier, Diahann Carroll. Directed on location in Paris by Martin Ritt. This is a frequently effective love story of "Two boys meet two girls." This quartet, however, consists of four supremely attractive performers who bolster the story line. Newman and Poitier play jazz musicians and there's a lot of good music thrown in as a bonus. (Dir: Martin Ritt, 98 mins.)

Paris Does Strange Things (1957)** Ingrid Bergman, Mel Ferrer, Jean Marais. Despite the talented female stars, this film is a slow moving romantic comedy about a lovely Princess who has a great desire to control everything around her. Considering the talents of the players and director Jean Renoir, it should have been much better. (86 mins.)

Paris Express (British, 1952)**½

Claude Rains, Marta Toren. Femme fatale plunges a bookkeeper into a web of murder and robbery. Well acted but complicated melodrama. (Dir: Harold French, 83 mins.)

Paris Holiday (1958)**½ Bob Hope, Fernandel, Anita Ekberg, Martha Hyer. Typical Bob Hope comedy with Bob sharing the clowning honors with France's Fernandel. Not all the jokes come off but there's Anita Ekberg to look at, so who can complain? (Dir: Gerd Oswald, 100 mins.)

Paris Honeymoon (1939)**½ Bing Crosby, Shirley Ross, Franciska Gaal. Pleasant, inconsequential Crosby film about the romance of an American with a French peasant girl. (Dir: Frank Tuttle, 90 mins.)

Paris in the Month of August (French, 1966)**½ Susan Hampshire, Michel De Re. A married clerk finds a bit of extra-marital romance with an English girl. Charles Aznavour as a lover, and it's pleasant.

Paris Model (1953)** Marilyn Maxwell, Paulette Goddard, Eva Gabor. Dull story but a parade of pulchritude to please men of all ages. The "Girls" racket is the thin theme. (Dir: Alfred E. Green, 81 mins.)

Paris Underground (1945)*** Constance Bennett, Gracie Fields. An American and her English companion are caught by the Nazi invasion of France, work for the underground throughout the war. Interesting melodrama, based on fact. (Dir: Gregory Ratoff, 97 mins.)

Paris When It Sizzles (1954)* William Holden, Audrey Hepburn, Noel Coward. Tepid remake of the delightful French film "Holiday for Henrietta." The blame falls on screenwriter George Axelrod, who also co-produced this leaden offering about moviemakers making a movie. Virtually all the charm and style of the original have been lost along the way, and lavish costumes, the streets of Paris, and cameo guest appearances from Marlene Dietrich and the voices of Sinatra and Astaire can't save it. (Dir: Richard Quine, 110 mins.)

Park Row (1952)*** Gene Evans, Mary Welch. The story of a crusading editor in old New York who tried to publish his paper despite opposition from a larger journal. Hard-hitting, vigorous melodrama,

548

well acted. (Dir: Samuel Fuller, 83 mins.)

Parnell (1936)** Clark Gable, Myrna Loy. One of Gable's worst prewar films. Story of the great Irish patriot is poorly written and terribly miscast. (Dir: John M. Stahl, 120 mins.)

Parrish (1961)**½ Claudette Colbert, Troy Donahue, Dean Jagger, Karl Malden, Connie Stevens. Long, drippy drama of a boy and his mother living on a tobacco plantation, with the lad soon learning the business and proving his worth in the battle to overcome his surroundings. Performances not so hot, plot too frequently goes to corn. But there's some interest, especially for the ladies. (Dir: Delmer Daves, 140 mins.)

Parson and the Outlaw, The (1957)* Anthony Dexter, Sonny Tufts. Another of the films about "Billy the Kid" and probably the worst one. Anthony Dexter, who played "Valentino" in the film about the famous screen lover, portrays the infamous gunslinger. It's easy to understand why Dexter has not been heard from recently. (Dir: Oliver Drake, 71 mins.)

Parson of Panamint, The (1941)*** Charles Ruggles, Ellen Drew. Offbeat western about a wild town that grew up with a gold strike and its young, hard hitting, yet gentle parson, who is almost executed as a murderer. (Dir: William McGann, 84 mins.)

Part-Time Wife (British, 1961)*½ Anton Rodgers, Nyree Dawn Porter. Young wife goes to extremes to help out her husband. Weak romantic comedy. (Dir: Max Varnel, 70 mins.)

Partner, The (British, 1961)** Yoko Tani, Guy Doleman. Movie producer gets involved in a swindling plot. Average mystery based on an Edgar Wallace story.

Partners in Crime (British, 1962)** Bernard Lee, John Van Eyssen. Police investigate the murder of a wealthy businessman and a burglary. Fair Edgar Wallace mystery.

Party, The (1968)**½ Peter Sellers, Claudine Longet, Marge Champion. Peter Sellers as an Indian actor who messes up a party to which he definitely wasn't invited. Some good laughs, but director Blake Edwards doesn't know when to cut off a gag, so it's mostly hit-and-miss.

Party Crashers, The (1958)** Mark Damon, Connie Stevens. Teenage gang gets into trouble when they intrude upon a party at a roadhouse. Routine juvenile delinquency drama. (Dir: Bernard Girard, 78 mins.)

Party Girl (1958)** Robert Taylor, Cyd Charisse, Lee J. Cobb. A gangster film about Chicago in the thirties which tries to copy the style of all those successful Robinson-Cagney-Bogart classics, but ends up a faded carbon copy. (Dir: Nicholas Ray, 99 mins.)

Passage to Marseille (1941)*** Humphrey Bogart, Claude Rains. Confused but often exciting story of convicts who escape from Devil's Island to join forces with the free French. When it finally gets down to adventure it's not a bad film. (Dir: Michael Curtiz, 110 mins.)

Passenger (Polish, 1963)***½ A remarkable if somewhat fragmented film about two women prisoners in Auschwitz, the infamous German concentration camp. Devastating sequences concerning life in the camp made by the gifted director Andrzej Munk, who died in 1961 before finishing the film. Later completed by film-industry colleagues. (60 mins.)

Passing Stranger, The (British, 1954)*** Lee Patterson, Diane Cilento. An American deserter becomes involved deeper and deeper in a smuggling racket, until he decides to take action. Above average, tense drama.

Passion of Anna, The (Swedish, 1970)**** Max von Sydow, Liv Ullmann, Bibi Andersson. Marvelous complex psychological drama about four people on an island in desolation and despair. Von Sydow is Andreas Winkelman, who has taken refuge in a hermit's existence. His actions are the catalyst for uncovering the others' self-deception. A masterwork from director Ingmar Bergman. Colors play a symbolic role and Sven Nykvist, the cameraman, has created amazing hues. (99 mins.)

Passion of Slow Fire, The (French, 1963)*** Jean DeSailly, Alexandra Stewart. Sleuth unravels a web of intrigue when a beautiful American girl is found murdered. Involved but intriguing Gallic mystery, done with style.

Passionate Sentry, The (British, 1953)*** Nigel Patrick, Peggy Cum-

mins. The romantic story of a palace guard and the girls who chase him. Pleasant comedy. (Dir: Anthony Kimmens, 84 mins.)

Passionate Summer (British, 1958)** Virginia McKenna, Bill Travers. Tropic schoolmaster's love starved wife makes a play for a young teacher. Overly dramatic story of the tropics; good cast, not much else.

Passionate Thief, The (Italian, 1962)**½ Anna Magnani, Ben Gazzara. Uneven comedy about a small time bit player who inadvertently keeps thwarting the attempts of a pickpocket on New Year's Eve. Some funny scenes, but it's too protracted. Dubbed in English. (Dir: Mario Monicelli, 105 mins.)

Passport for a Corpse (Italian, 1962)*½ Linda Christian, Albert Lupin. Criminal escaping after a payroll job tries to cross the Italian Alps to safety. Slow-moving crime drama dubbed in English.

Passport to China (British, 1961)** Richard Basehart, Lisa Gastoni. Adventurer attempts a rescue of an American secret agent and a Formosan pilot missing in Red China. Strictly routine melodrama, little new. (Dir: Michael Carreras, 75 mins.)

Passport to Destiny (1943)** Elsa Lancaster, Lloyd Corrigan. English scrubwoman believes she is guided by a "magic eye," goes to Germany to kill Hitler. Good idea, but routine in the telling; fair comedy-drama. (Dir: Ray McCarey, 64 mins.)

Passport to Hell (French, 1964)* George Ardisson, Georges Rivière. Undercover agent is assigned to track down the Black Scorpion, mysterious leader of a terrorist ring. Poor serial-style adventure melodrama dubbed in English.

Passport to Pimlico (British, 1949)**** Stanley Holloway, Hermione Baddeley, Margaret Rutherford. When an old charter is discovered in a small section of London claiming the land still belongs to the Duke of Burgundy, the inhabitants decide to secede from England. Hilarious comedy, highly original, witty. Excellent. (Dir: Henry Cornelius, 72 mins.)

Passport to Treason (British, 1955)** Rod Cameron, Lois Maxwell. Private detective called to help a friend finds him murdered, starts investigating. Average mystery on the complicated side. (Dir: Robert S. Baker, 70 mins.)

Password Is Courage, The (1963)**½ Dirk Bogarde, Maria Perschy. Reasonably interesting account of the WW II exploits of Charles Coward, a real-life hero who made many daring escapes from Nazi prison camps. Details many of the escapes, and a good cast of English actors adds to the flavor of the story. (Dir: Andrew L. Stone, 116 mins.)

Pastor Hall (British, 1940)**½ Wilfred Lawson, Nova Pilbeam. A courageous priest speaks out against the Nazis in Germany, is imprisoned, tortured. Strong drama, some gripping moments.

Pat and Mike (1952)***½ Spencer Tracy, Katharine Hepburn, Aldo Ray. Riotously funny comedy with the irresistible Tracy-Hepburn combination. Hepburn plays a golf pro and Tracy is a big time sports promoter and their business merger eventually turns to romance. Aldo Ray has some very funny moments as a pug with a good left hook and little else. (Dir: George Cukor, 95 mins.)

Pat Garrett and Billy the Kid (1973)*½ James Coburn, Kris Kristofferson, Bob Dylan. Director Sam Peckinpah has tackled the legend of Billy the Kid and his killer, Pat Garrett, a subject which has intrigued filmmakers for years. Disappointing, unnecessarily violent, but has some interest mainly due to Coburn's performance as the gunman-turned-sheriff who sets out to catch his one-time friend, Billy the Kid. Kristofferson looks perfect as Billy, but his role is poorly defined. Bob Dylan, the folksinger, scored the film and plays a small part—and fails on both counts. Peckinpah complained bitterly about the editing of the film's close by the then MGM studio chief, James Aubrey. (Dir: Sam Peckinpah, 106 mins.)

Patch of Blue, A (1965)***½ Sidney Poitier, Elizabeth Hartman, Shelley Winters. A moving, well-acted film about a sensitive relationship which develops between a blind white girl and a black man. The story is fairly predictable, but Sidney Poitier and Elizabeth Hartman bring a touching credibility to their roles which keeps you interested throughout. Shelley Winters is seen in her Oscar-winning

supporting role as the garish, vulgar, intolerable mother of the blind girl, and Wallace Ford offers a nice bit as Miss Hartman's alcoholic grandfather. (Dir: Guy Green, 105 mins.)

Path of Hope, The (Italian, 1950)**½ Raf Vallone, Elena Varzi. When their mine is closed down and there's no work, inhabitants of a small mining town trek from Italy to France to find a new life. Fairly well done social drama; won some awards when first released, but generally overrated.

Pather Panchali (Indian, 1956)**** First film in a mighty trilogy by Indian director Satyajit Ray. Beautifully done story of a poverty stricken family in a Bengali village. Although the locale is exotic, strange to the western eye, the situations should be familiar, as they relate to all of us. Superb performances, mostly by a non-professional cast. English-dubbed. (112 mins.)

Pathfinder and the Mohican, The (1956)*½ John Hart, Lon Chaney. Frontier scout and his Indian aide uncover false accusations of murder. Weak adventure melodrama edited from the old "Hawkeye" TV series.

Paths of Glory (1957)**** Kirk Douglas, Ralph Meeker, Adolphe Menjou, Wayne Morris. A superb film about a French Army division fighting in Verdun during World War I. Kirk Douglas is excellent as an officer who believes in treating his men as human beings as well as soldiers. Stanley Kubrick brilliantly directed a carefully chosen cast. Truly a great film! (86 mins.)

Patsy, The (1964)** Jerry Lewis, Ina Balin, Ed Wynn, Peter Lorre. Yet another Lewis starrer, directed and co-authored by Hollywood's self-appointed actor-producer-director-writer. This particular story line concerns a Hollywood bellboy tapped for movie stardom. The pace is frantic, the slapstick routines ever-present. Jerry did have the good sense to bolster the film with brief appearances from, among others, the late Ed Wynn and Peter Lorre. (101 mins.)

Pattern for Murder (German, 1964)* George Mather, Julie Reding. Maniacal killer commits murders until a sleuth gets the key to his identity. Poor mystery dubbed in English.

Patterns (1956)***½ Van Heflin, Everett Sloane. If you didn't see this compelling Rod Serling drama either time it was done on network TV, tune in. Executive becomes involved in power squeeze in large corporation. (Dir: Fielder Cook, 83 mins.)

Patton (1970)**** George C. Scott, Karl Malden. Scott's magnificent performance as General George S. Patton earned him an Oscar, and the film was selected as the best of 1970 by the Academy Award members. It's gutsy, tough, comparatively honest and fascinating portrait of the World War II general whose military bravado and love of war made him a hero, and also caused him to be relieved of his command in Sicily. In addition to Scott's monumental performance, the film boasts a series of brilliantly staged battle sequences, tracing Patton's career in the North African, Sicilian, and European campaigns. Recommended fare. (Dir: Franklin Schaffner, 170 mins.)

Paula (1952)*** Loretta Young, Kent Smith, Tommy Rettig. Paula (Loretta Young) takes a young boy, who is a mute as a result of a "hit and run" accident, into her home. Strange events come into focus as a result. Good acting despite the sometimes stilted script. (Dir: Rudolph Mate, 80 mins.)

Pawnbroker, The (1965)**** Rod Steiger, Geraldine Fitzgerald, Jaime Sanchez. One of the most shattering, powerful and honest films made in America in the sixties. Superbly directed by Sidney Lumet in New York's Harlem. Story concerns a Jewish pawnbroker, victim of Nazi persecution, who loses all faith in his fellow man until he realizes no man is an island. Uniformly fine performances down to the smallest bit part, but Steiger is quite spectacular in his own beautifully controlled performance. A rare experience for discerning adults. (Dir: Sidney Lumet, 116 mins.)

Pay or Die (1960)*** Ernest Borgnine, Zohra Lampert. Well acted and realistically brutal account of the Mafia's activities in New York City during the years preceding World War I, based on fact. Borgnine gives a strong performance as a detective and is backed by a good supporting cast. Miss Lampert is a remarkably versatile and talented performer. (Dir: Richard Wilson, 110 mins.)

Payday (1972)**** Rip Torn, Elayne Heilveil, Anna Capri. An absolutely marvelous, observant, and deeply moving film about a second-rate country and western singer (Torn) whose road to Mecca—in this case, Nashville, Tenn.—is littered with men and women used and abandoned when he no longer needs them. Honest, knowing screenplay by Don Carpenter; superbly directed by Daryl Duke. They have created in the title role of Maury Dann one of the most remarkably delineated portraits of an unmitigated louse seen in many years. Filled with illuminating sequences, alternately touching and gross, including Torn's making love to a new addition to his stable in the back seat of a traveling car while another girl friend snoozes beside him and his driver casts an envious glance through the rear-view mirror. Both the beauty and the poverty of the Alabama countryside are captured by cinematographer Richard C. Glouner and there's a particularly touching performance from Elayne Heilveil, playing a young, innocent groupie. An extraordinary film that never got the attention it deserved. (Dir: Daryl Duke, 103 mins.)

Payment in Blood (Italy, 1967)½ Edd Byrnes, Guy Madison. Spaghetti antics feature the usual excessive killing and plundering. Tale of Confederates looting around the Texas-Mexico border following the Civil War. Film is so terrible the director used a pseudonym for the screen credit. (Dir: Enzo Girolami [E. G. Rowland], 89 mins.)

Payment on Demand (1951)**½ Bette Davis, Barry Sullivan, Jane Cowl. For Bette Davis fans—here's a typical melodrama which makes full use of her "personal" acting style. Miss Davis' marriage to Barry Sullivan is on the rocks and headed toward divorce—but first, we have a series of flashbacks depicting the past and Bette really pours it on—crying, laughing, screaming, strutting, and generally chewing up the scenery. (Dir: Curtis Bernhardt, 90 mins.)

Payroll (British, 1963)**½ Michael Craig, Francoise Prevost, Billie Whitelaw. Wife of a murdered armored-car guard works with the police in trapping a gang of robbers. Tough, fast-paced crime melodrama, well acted. (Dir: Sidney Hayers, 94 mins.)

Pearl, The (1947)**** Pedro Armendariz, Maria Elena Marques. An excellent Mexican film about a poor fisherman who finds a luscious pearl which changes his life. Pedro Armendariz is superb as the bewildered fisherman who can't believe what is happening to him and his wife. (Dir: Emilio Fernandez, 77 mins.)

Peasants of the Second Fortress, The (Japanese, 1971)*** A unique documentary about Japanese farmers trying to block the building of a new airport near Tokyo. Directed over a five-year period by Shinsuke Ogawa, the unedited film runs almost nine hours. A small "war" erupted in Japan over this project, and the film chronicles the efforts—losing ones, ultimately—of farmers to fight the government and keep their land. (143 mins.)

Peeping Tom (British, 1961)* Carl Boehm, Moira Shearer, Anna Massey. Demented photographer kills models while making portraits of their reactions to death. Sick horror film; not even the well-made production values can cover the nastiness of the tale.

Peggy (1950)** Diana Lynn, Rock Hudson, Charles Coburn. Silly, unpretentious little comedy about college life, football heroes and the girls who scream over them, and the big Rose Bowl Tournament. (Dir: Frederick de Cordova, 77 mins.)

Peking Express (1951)** Joseph Cotten, Corinne Calvet, Edmund Gwenn. Romance and adventure aboard a speeding train, with a doctor and a wandering lady in the midst of it. Remake of a Dietrich film, "Shanghai Express," and as usual the original was better—routine melodrama. (Dir: William Dieterle, 95 mins.)

Pendulum (1969)*** George Peppard, Jean Seberg, Richard Kiley. Interesting action drama with George Peppard well cast as a Washington, D.C., police captain who becomes a chief suspect when his wife and her lover are murdered. There are many subplots, but TV director George Schaefer, making his film bow with this one, keeps the pace clipping along. Original screenplay by Stanley Niss is more intelligent than most, and raises some stimulating questions about civil liberties and

"law and order." (Dir: George Schaefer, 106 mins.)

Penelope (1966)** Natalie Wood, Ian Bannen, Dick Shawn, Peter Falk. Silly, occasionally entertaining comedy in which Natalie Wood plays a zany girl who befuddles even her psychiatrist, when she holds up her husband's bank. Peter Falk, as a detective, gives the film's best performance. (Dir: Arthur Hiller, 97 mins.)

Pennies from Heaven (1936)*** Bing Crosby, Madge Evans, Edith Fellows, Louis Armstrong. Wandering drifter befriends a homeless waif, soon has a pretty truant officer on their trail. Outdated but still amusing musical. (Dir: Norman Z. McLeod, 90 mins.)

Penny Serenade (1941)***½ Cary Grant, Irene Dunne. Childless couple plan to adopt one, but their happiness soon turns to tragedy. Fine emotional drama that the ladies will particularly enjoy. Excellent. (Dir: George Stevens, 125 mins.)

Pennywhistle Blues (British, 1952)***½ Something different—comedy about a thief who loses his stolen loot, as it passes from hand to hand. Made in South Africa, with a native cast. Utterly delightful, charming, funny. See it.

Penthouse, The (Great Britain, 1967)** Suzy Kendall, Terence Morgan. Excessively brutal drama about a day of sadism and terror when two intruders invade a penthouse shared by a married man and his young mistress. Based on the play "The Meter Man," by C. Scott Forbes. Written and directed by Peter Collinson. (97 mins.)

People, The (1972)*** Kim Darby, William Shatner, Diane Varsi, Dan O'Herlihy. Pleasant movie filmed in northern California's beautiful redwood country. Adapted from Zenna Henderson's science-fiction novel, the soft, gentle tale takes its time as Melodye (Kim Darby), a new, young schoolteacher, puzzles over an isolated community of stoic, shuffling parents and students who don't laugh, sing, or play games. Melodye's quiet probing into the community's past results in an unusual revelation, and the climactic scenes contain a Thoreaulike message. Made-for-TV. (Dir: John Korty, 73 mins.)

People Against O'Hara, The (1951),

*** Spencer Tracy, Diana Lynn, John Hodiak. Good film about lawyers—not merely their performance of duty but their personal involvements. Spencer Tracy is great as always and a competent supporting cast matches him. (Dir: John Sturges, 102 mins.)

People Next Door, The (1970)****** Eli Wallach, Julie Harris, Hal Holbrook, Cloris Leachman. When J. P. Miller's original drama was seen in 1968 as a made-for-TV drama, it was quite powerful and affecting. The movie version, released two years later, is much less rewarding, partially because there were so many more films dealing with suburbia and teenage drugs produced during this same period. Some remarkably talented people don't manage to convey much emotion or impact. Julie Harris, for example, is reduced to lighting lots of cigarettes in this occasionally involving story of suburban kids dealing and freaking out on drugs. (Dir: David Greene, 93 mins.)

People vs. Dr. Kildare, The (1940)****** Lew Ayres, Lionel Barrymore. It's not Kildare's fault that a leg he operated on is paralyzed but he has to go to court with Gillespie's help to clear himself. (Dir: Harold S. Bucquet, 78 mins.)

People Will Talk (1951)*******½ Cary Grant, Jeanne Crain, Walter Slezak, Hume Cronyn. An excellent comedy drama about a doctor whose past suddenly backfires and almost destroys his happy life. Grant is great as always and the supporting cast couldn't be better. Written and directed by Joseph L. Mankiewicz. (110 mins.)

Pepe (1960)******½ Cantinflas, Shirley Jones, Dan Dailey, guest stars. Shaky little plot doesn't do right by Mexico's great comedian in his Hollywood showcase, as he plays a ranch foreman who goes to the cinema city to try and get back his pet horse. It's all bloated with guest appearances by star personalities, some of whom seem embarrassed. Some amusing moments, not enough to subtantiate the length. (Dir: George Sidney, 195 mins.)

Pepote (Spanish, 1957)******* Pablito Calvo, Antonio Vico. A frequently touching film about an aging one-time toreador and his friendship with a young boy of seven. Acting is top-notch.

Perfect Friday (British, 1970)*******½ Stanley Baker, Ursula Andress, David Warner. Deft comedy thriller. Baker plays a British banker who, when faced with customer Andress, realizes he can steal a million dollars. Warner plays an artistocratic loafer, Miss Andress' husband, also involved in the caper. All three actors are marvelous, and Miss Andress, surprisingly, shows comic talent. (Dir: Peter Hall, 94 mins.)

Perfect Furlough, The (1959)******* Tony Curtis, Janet Leigh, Linda Cristal. Service comedy which borders on slapstick most of the way. Curtis works hard as a khaki-clad Lothario who gets into one insane predicament after another. Linda Cristal gets some of the film's best lines as a movie queen involved in a big publicity stunt that backfires. (Dir: Blake Edwards, 93 mins.)

Perfect Marriage, The (1947)****** Loretta Young, David Niven. Comedy about the problems of a couple who, after ten years of marriage, find they can't stand each other makes a labored, tedious film. (Dir: Lewis Allen, 87 mins.)

Perfect Strangers (1950)*****½ Ginger Rogers, Dennis Morgan, Thelma Ritter. Pure corn and soap opera. Story is about a couple of jurors at a murder trial who meet and fall in love amid the court proceedings. (Dir: Alexander Korda, 111 mins.)

Performance (1970)******½ James Fox, Mick Jagger. Fairly intriguing two-into-one identity exchange involving a fleeing gangster (Fox) renting a basement apartment in the spacious town house of a former rock star (Jagger). Fox and Jagger turn on and tune into each other, and their performances are the core of the film. (Dirs: Nicolas Roeg and Donald Cammell, 106 mins.)

Perilous Holiday (1946)******* Pat O'Brien, Ruth Warrick. Adventurer in Mexico City stumbles upon a counterfeiting ring that doesn't stop at murder. Good melodrama, breezily written, acted. (Dir: Edward H. Griffith, 89 mins.)

Perilous Voyage (1969)***** Michael Parks, William Shatner, Michael Tolan, Louise Sorel. Latin-American bandit holds a boat and its passengers hostage. Stereotyped characters, sunk by water-logged script.

Made-for-TV. (Dir: William Graham, 100 mins.)

Perils of Pauline, The (1967)*½ Pat Boone, Pamela Austin, Terry-Thomas. Originally made as a pilot for a proposed TV series that didn't sell, this forced farce is purely for those who find slapstick antics irresistible. Pamela Austin is all blonde innocence as the put-upon orphan who goes through a series of incredible adventures that would make Alice's wonderland excursion seem predictable. Movie buffs please note this bit of hokum has nothing to do with the 1947 Betty Hutton starrer bearing the same name. (Dir: George Marshall, 96 mins.)

Period of Adjustment (1962)*** Tony Franciosa, Jane Fonda, Jim Hutton. A rarity, a Tennessee Williams comedy—not his best work, but as transferred to the screen quite pleasant, refreshing entertainment, well played by a young cast. It's all about the problems of a young married couple in adjusting to the rigors of domestic life, and it has many amusing scenes. (Dir: George Roy Hill, 112 mins.)

Persecution (Great Britain, 1974)* Lana Turner, Ralph Bates, Trevor Howard, Olga Georges-Picot. Tawdry, gothic terror as Lana plays a very sick woman who does away with her husband. Deft, brief appearance by Howard as Lana's husband. Lana's first film since "The Big Cube" of '68. She's not much of a judge of scripts. (Dir: Don Chaffey, 96 mins.)

Persona (Swedish, 1967)**** Liv Ullmann, Bibi Andersson. One of director Ingmar Bergman's most remarkable pictures. A successful actress (Ullmann) withdraws into silence and is hospitalized. Her nurse Alma (Andersson) becomes her only companion and the two go to a secluded cottage for the summer. Slowly their roles reverse. A stunning psychological drama with heavy symbolism, and strong comment on the nature of women. (95 mins.)

Personal Affair (British, 1953)**½ Gene Tierney, Leo Genn, Glynis Johns. Teacher is implicated when a romantic schoolgirl suddenly disappears. Well-made but conventional drama. (Dir: Anthony Pelissier, 82 mins.)

Personal Column—See: **Lured**
Personal Property (1937)** Jean

554

Harlow, Robert Taylor. Bob does everything to win Jean in this one. He poses as a butler and a sheriff's deputy but before the first reel is over you know he'll win her. (Dir: W. S. Van Dyke, 80 mins.)

Pete Kelly's Blues (1955)**½ Jack Webb, Janet Leigh, Peggy Lee. Fairly successful reenactment of the people and sounds in the jazz world of the 20's. Jack Webb gives his usual wooden performance in the lead. Peggy Lee went dramatic in this one and surprisingly did very well. Ella Fitzgerald sings a couple of numbers. (Dir: Jack Webb, 95 mins.)

Pete 'n Tillie (1972)**½ Walter Matthau, Carol Burnett, Geraldine Page. An awkward but fairly interesting comedy-drama which relies heavily on the talents of its costars —Miss Burnett and Mr. Matthau. They are a pair of middle-aged realists who meet, have an affair, ultimately marry, have a child, and have to deal with the fact that the boy is dying. With less talented stars this could have been easily dismissed as soap-opera junk, but they keep it afloat in a sea of pathos. (Dir: Martin Ritt, 100 mins.)

Pete Seeger—a Song and a Stone (1972)**½ Pete Seeger, Johnny Cash, Lester Flatt. Seeger is a remarkable man, a talented musician and the star of this disappointing documentary; shows Seeger strummin', singin', and talkin' during a year and a half in various places throughout the U.S. Interesting sequence when Seeger talks about the many years when he was blacklisted by American television. (Dir: Robert Elfstrom, 85 mins.)

Peter Ibbetson (1935)** Gary Cooper, Ann Harding. For lovers of elaborate romances, who also put great stock in dramas. Story of a jailed killer who meets his love in the world of dreams. Dated. (Dir: Henry Hathaway, 100 mins.)

Petrified Forest (1936)**** Humphrey Bogart, Leslie Howard, Bette Davis. Excellent adaptation of the Robert E. Sherwood play. Of course it's been done live on TV but they didn't have Leslie Howard. (Dir: Archie L. Mayo, 80 mins.)

Petticoat Fever (1936)**½ Robert Montgomery, Myrna Loy. Perennial summer stock favorite fails to ring the bell as good movie comedy. Bob is all alone in Labrador when Myrna arrives, thanks to a plane crash, with her fiancé. Rest is pretty silly and forced. (Dir: George Fitzmaurice, 80 mins.)

Petty Girl, The (1950)*** Robert Cummings, Joan Caulfield. Bob Cummings plays an artist who specializes in glamour girls and his unlikely model is prim school teacher Joan Caulfield. Fun for all, and an early preview of a later TV series of the ageless Cummings. (Dir: Henry Levin, 87 mins.)

Petulia (1968)*** Julie Christie, George C. Scott, Joseph Cotten, Richard Chamberlain. Very uneven, but often interesting romantic drama about a kooky, disturbed wench (Christie) and her tempestuous fling with a doctor played by George Scott. Much of the interest in the film is due to Richard Lester's directing-editing techniques, and various good performances from not only Christie and Scott, but Richard Chamberlain playing Christie's weak-willed husband. Set in San Francisco, "Petulia" got very differing reviews, but enterprising viewers will find Lester & Co. worth your time and attention. (105 mins.)

Peyton Place (1957)*** Lana Turner, Diane Varsi, Hope Lange. Here's the original film which served as the basis for the popular TV soap opera. It's actually much better than you may expect. Lana Turner and a fine supporting cast bring to life all the shady secrets of the New England town which made Grace Metalious' book a best seller. Granted this is soap opera, but it's well played and the production is first rate, with excellent photography of a New England autumn adding greatly to the atmosphere. Diane Varsi as Allison and Hope Lange as Selena are the standouts among the young actors in the film. (Dir: Mark Robson, 162 mins.)

Phantom Horse, The (Japanese, 1956)**½ Pleasantly entertaining drama of a boy's love for a race horse. It's all been done many times before over here, but the different backgrounds make it refreshing.

Phantom India (French, 1969)**** Director Louis Malle's brilliant, staggering six-hour essay on India, an unending succession of dazzling imagery and cultural shock. From the opening scene of a flock of vul-

tures devouring the anus of a dead cow, Malle's cameras, as much as any movie possibly can, manage to capture the sense and smell of the Indian countryside. There are religious festivals in Madras, a malnourished village giving daily offerings of precious grain to feed rats, and scenes of urban life in Bombay and others. Malle completely avoids the customary device of endless interviews. He lets his camera tell everything in this vast, complex panorama of a fascinating country. Commissioned by French television, and shot with a small camera crew in 1967 and '68. A remarkable accomplishment by a sensitive filmmaker. (360 mins.)

Phantom Lady (1944)***½ Franchot Tone, Ella Raines, Thomas Gomez. A very intriguing mystery film. A man is convicted of murdering his wife and a few people who believe him innocent try to clear him. Typical plot, but handled so well that you forget you've seen it before. (Dir: Robert Siodmak, 87 mins.)

Phantom of Hollywood, The (1974)** Jack Cassidy, Broderick Crawford, Skye Aubrey, Jackie Coogan. High melodrama on the low hokey side. A disfigured actor goes amok when the movie studio back lot (the actor's secret home for 30 years) is torn down. A large name cast cavorts on the MGM studio premises. Made-for-TV. (Dir: Gene Levitt.)

Phantom of Liberty, The (France, 1974)**** Jean-Claude Brialy, Monica Vitti, Adolfo Celi, Michel Piccoli. An often brilliant, fragmented, episodic work about the frailties and enduring idiocies of the human race. The phrase "Phantom of Liberty" is from Karl Marx, but the genius on screen is all Bunuel. The first episode is set in Spain in the early 1800's and there are some memorable images—a fancy dinner party where guests sit on bathroom toilets and furtively ask permission to go to the dining room. As always, Bunuel is challenging the audience's conventional attitudes concerning sex, politics, and religion. There are dazzling visual images throughout. "Phantom" has its flaws, but Bunuel's lesser moments are far more interesting than the best efforts of most lesser mortals. Bunuel co-authored the screenplay with his longtime collaborator Jean-Claude Carrier. (Dir: Luis Bunuel, 104 mins.)

Phantom of the Opera, The (1925) **** Lon Chaney. Considered by many to be the best of the Lon Chaney silent films, and rightly so. Never before or since has this magnificent story, about a wronged musician who hides in the bowels of a cavernous opera house while weaving his diabolical plot of revenge after he's been disfigured, been more satisfactorily mounted. Chaney is fascinating as the crazed "phantom," and his makeup is a work of cinematic magic, especially for its day. (Dir: Rupert Julian, 90 mins.)

Phantom of the Opera (1943) *** Claude Rains, Nelson Eddy, Susanna Foster. A remake of the classic silent film which starred Lon Chaney. This version can stand on its own merit; it is expertly acted by Claude Rains. (Dir: Arthur Lubin, 92 mins.)

Phantom of the Opera, The (British, 1962) *** Herbert Lom, Heather Sears. Another version of the old Lon Chaney thriller about a hideously scarred creature terrorizing an opera house. This one is nicely produced, succeeds in its purpose of providing shudders. (Dir: Terence Fisher, 84 mins.)

Phantom of the Rue Morgue (1954) **½ Karl Malden, Patricia Medina. Eerie horror film about an insane murderer in Paris and his many coldblooded murders. Based on the story by Edgar Allan Poe. Well made, but pretty rough for the kiddies. (Dir: Roy Del Ruth, 84 mins.)

Phantom Planet (1962) ** Dean Fredericks, Coleen Gray. A fairly absorbing Grade B science fiction yarn about a planet of midget sized inhabitants who fight an enemy attack with the aid of an astronaut who lands there. The special photographic gimmicks are good and help the film. (Dir: William Marshall, 82 mins.)

Pharaoh's Curse (1957) ** Mark Dana, Ziva Rodann. Archeological expedition encounters a monster from thousands of years ago in Egypt. Fair horror thriller has some suspenseful scenes. (Dir: Lee Sholem, 66 mins.)

Phase IV (Great Britain, 1973) *½ Nigel Davenport, Lynne Frederick, Michael Murphy. Chilling images of destruction are wasted in this derivative script concerning the takeover of the earth by an ant population that has begun organizing itself for a coup against mankind. One-dimensional scientists to stop the antics prove the film's downfall. Some good graphics but little more. (Dir: Saul Bass, 93 mins.)

Phffft! (1954) ***½ Judy Holliday, Jack Lemmon, Kim Novak. Judy Holliday and Jack Lemmon make the most hilarious movie team since the days of Jean Arthur & James Stewart in this fast paced, sometimes funny, story of a marriage that almost goes PHFFFT! Kim Novak plays a small but decorative part. (Dir: Mark Robson, 91 mins.)

Philadelphia Story, The (1940) ***½ Katharine Hepburn, James Stewart, Cary Grant. Try and forget the miserable musical version released in 1956 and you'll adore this splendidly acted comedy of romance in Philadelphia. (Dir: George Cukor, 112 mins.)

Phoenix City Story, The (1955) *** Richard Kiley, John McIntire, Edward Andrews. Hard hitting drama dealing with the expose of one of the most corrupt "Sin-Cities" in the United States: Phoenix City, Alabama. Kiley and Andrews are standouts in a fine cast in this film based on actual news data.

Phone Call from a Stranger (1952) *** Shelley Winters, Gary Merrill, Michael Rennie, Bette Davis. Gary Merrill stars in this good episodic drama as the lone survivor of a plane crash who takes it upon himself to contact some of his traveling companions' relatives. Most of the action unfolds via flashbacks. Bette Davis, in a brief role as an invalid, gives the best performance in the film with Keenan Wynn, as her brash salesman of a husband, ranking a close second. (Dir: Jean Negulesco, 96 mins.)

Phone Rings Every Night, The (German, 1962) *½ Elke Sommer. When a plant manager has a fight with his new boss, his wife induces an assistant to pose as her husband so the boss won't get wise. Strained comedy dubbed in English.

Phony American, The (German, 1962) ** William Bendix, Ron Randell, Christine Kaufmann, Michael Hinz. War orphan is left with a German family by a U.S. Army officer, grows up and tries to enlist in our Air

Force. Drama has a certain amount of charm but moves quite slowly. (Dir: Akos Rathony, 72 mins.)

Picasso Summer, The (1969)**✶✶½** Albert Finney, Yvette Mimieux. Offbeat romantic tale just misses. It's a strange mixture of surrealism and reality, with Finney and Mimieux playing a couple who adore Picasso and form an alliance based on their mutual love for the great artist's work. When they try to visit the artist in the south of France, the film takes off on a wild tangent and never gets back on course. They never get to meet Pablo either. (Dir: Serge Bourguignon, 90 mins.)

Piccadilly Incident (British, 1946) **✶✶✶** Anna Neagle, Michael Wilding. In wartime England, a man thinks his wife has been killed, but she returns after he has married again. Blend of romance and drama is tailor-made for the feminine audience. (Dir: Herbert Wilcox, 88 mins.)

Piccadilly Jim (1936)**✶✶✶** Robert Montgomery, Madge Evans, Billie Burke. P. G. Wodehouse's story of a cartoonist and his bumbling father is turned into a delightful comedy. Eric Blore almost steals the picture playing, you guessed it, a gentleman's gentleman. (Dir: Robert Z. Leonard, 100 mins.)

Pickpocket (France, 1959)**✶✶✶** Martin LaSalle, Marika Green, Jean Pelegri. An austere meditation written and directed by Robert Bresson, about an educated thief who believes that the road to heaven is paved with bad intentions and that somehow God wants him to steal. Dryly acted by LaSalle, but, as in most of Bresson's other films, the cinematography is languid and exquisite. (Dir: Robert Bresson, 75 mins.)

Pickup (1951)**✶✶½** Beverly Michaels, Hugo Haas. Occasionally effective drama about an old man who marries a cheap girl he picks up and the complications that arise when a handsome younger man enters the picture. (Dir: Hugo Haas, 78 mins.)

Pickup Alley (British, 1957)**✶✶** Victor Mature, Anita Ekberg, Trevor Howard. Routine crime matter, Mature is a narcotics agent whose sleuthing takes him to London, Lisbon, Athens, Rome, etc. Miss Ekberg dresses up the picture with her presence. (Dir: John Gilling, 92 mins.)

Pickup on South Street (1953)**✶✶½** Richard Widmark, Jean Peters, Thelma Ritter. Pickpocket unwittingly lifts a message destined for enemy agents and becomes a target for a Communist spy ring. Brutal melodrama, but is well made and acted. (Dir: Samuel Fuller, 80 mins.)

Pickwick Papers, The (British, 1953) **✶✶✶½** James Hayter, Nigel Patrick, James Donald. A group of wealthy bachelors taking a country tour are exploited by an unscrupulous actor. Faithful adaptation of the Dickens classic is well-produced, finely acted, with much charm. (Dir: Noel Langley, 109 mins.)

Picnic (1956)**✶✶✶** William Holden, Kim Novak, Rosalind Russell. Unevenly acted film version of William Inge's moving Broadway play about a stranger who arrives in a small Kansas town and changes a number of lives. The acting ranges from good (William Holden, Arthur O'Connell, Cliff Robertson, Susan Strasberg) to fair (Rosalind Russell) to inept (Miss Novak). (Dir: Joshua Logan, 115 mins.)

Picture Mommy Dead (1966)**✶✶½** Don Ameche, Martha Hyer, Zsa Zsa Gabor. A complicated mystery which sustains its interest despite the hokey aspects of the script involving a young girl who loses her memory after the tragic death of her mother. It's all sinister, and a good deal of it works. (Dir: Bert I. Gordon, 88 mins.)

Picture of Dorian Gray, The (1944) **✶✶✶** George Sanders, Hurd Hatfield, Donna Reed. Not too faithful but still compelling adaptation of Oscar Wilde's tale about a good looking man whose face never ages or reflects the evil he has done but his portrait shows all. Fairly well acted and produced. (Dir: Albert Lewin, 110 mins.)

Pie in the Sky—See: Terror in the City

Pied Piper, The (1942)**✶✶✶½** Monty Woolley, Anne Baxter. Wartime story of a Monty Woolley type Englishman who hates kids and finds himself stuck with a pack of them and trying to escape the Nazis. Warm, amusing, and powerful film. (Dir: Jacques Demy, 90 mins.)

Pied Piper of Hamelin, The (1957)**✶✶** Van Johnson, Claude Rains, Kay Starr. Musical version of the fairy tale about the piper who rids the town of rats. Originally produced as a TV special, it suffers in comparison with motion picture feature technique; passable for the kiddies. (Dir: Bretaigne Windust, 87 mins.)

Pierrot le Fou (French, 1969)***½ Jean-Paul Belmondo, Anna Karina, Samuel Fuller. Diector Jean-Luc Godard produced this film in 1965 before his films became Marxist polemics. It deals with a young writer (Belmondo) and his love affair with Marianne (Miss Karina). Beautifully poignant, for as the two despair of each other they find they are both fed up. More Truffaut than Godard! Raoul Coutard's camerawork is exquisite. (110 mins.)

Pigeon, The (1969)** Sammy Davis, Jr., Pat Boone, Dorothy Malone. Although Sammy Davis, Jr., works very hard as a private detective, this weighty and clichéd made-for-TV feature falls short. Miss Malone is the widow of a former syndicate bigwig who kept a diary and the Mafia wants the little black book. Private eyes Davis and Boone get in on the case and it's fist fights and car chases, until the end. (Dir: Earl Bellamy, 94 mins.)

Pigeon That Took Rome, The (1962) **½ Charlton Heston, Elsa Martinelli. Tough infantry officer is sent behind Nazi lines into occupied Rome to see what's cooking, sends pigeons back with messages, finds time for some romance. Heston seems rather grimly determined to be a light comedian in this one, but the laughs come with fair frequency, aided by some good dialogue. (Dir: Melville Shavelson, 101 mins.)

Pillar of Fire (1963)*** Michael Shillo, Lawrence Montaigne. In 1948 an Israeli desert outpost sends out a patrol when the Arabs invade the area. Unusual locale aids this war drama filmed in Israel, compensating somewhat for sketchy production values. Spoken in English.

Pillars of the Sky (1956)**½ Jeff Chandler, Dorothy Malone, Ward Bond. Western fans will buy this tale of a no-account, hard drinking, woman chasin' Sgt. who finally sees the error of his ways after a series of action-packed scenes. Jeff Chandler makes a believable cavalry noncom and the supporting cast is more than competent.

Pillow of Death (1945)** Lon Chaney, Brenda Joyce. Lawyer commits a succession of murders to marry the girl he loves. Fair mys-

tery; the plot is old-hat. (Dir: Wallace Fox, 55 mins.)

Pillow Talk (1959)**** Doris Day, Rock Hudson, Tony Randall. Deft light comedy which may be labeled "a typical Doris Day vehicle," i.e. the thirtyish Miss Day has somehow managed to keep both her virginity and such attractive suitors as Rock Hudson. Tony Randall is very funny. Hudson is surprisingly skillful. Frothy dialogue makes this a fine film of its kind. (Dir: Michael Gordon, 105 mins.)

Pilot No. 5 (1942)*½ Franchot Tone, Marsha Hunt, Gene Kelly, Van Johnson. Don't be misled by the names because this story is so trite it's hardly worth your time. An episodic narrative about a man who inadvertently got mixed up with a Fascist politician and must now die for the country to redeem himself. (Dir: George Sidney, 70 mins.)

Pimpernel Smith (British, 1941)***½ Leslie Howard, Francis Sullivan, Mary Morris. A mild-mannered professor becomes an undercover leader against the Nazis. Delightfully witty, exciting melodrama, very good. (Dir: Leslie Howard, 122 mins.)

Pine Canyon Is Burning (1977)**½ Kent McCord, Diana Muldaur. Modest fire story attempts to emphasize people against a crisis background. It's a tale about a widowed fireman trying to raise two kids while working out of a lonely fire station. Happily, the characters are a bit more than wooden pieces set against the background of a canyon fire out of control. Made-for-TV. (Dir: Chris Nyby, III, 79 mins.)

Pink Jungle, The (1968)** James Garner, Eva Renzi, George Kennedy. Dull action drama set in a banana republic in South America. The mistaken identity gimmick is used to death in this one as James Garner, a photographer by trade, is taken for an espionage agent.

Pink Panther, The (1964)**** Peter Sellers, David Niven, Capucine, Claudia Cardinale, Robert Wagner. The high-voltage names of the cast is enough for fans to tune in, and Peter Sellers' bumbling French police inspector is a comic gem. Sellers is after a clever jewel thief known as the Phantom, and the Phantom is after a priceless gem. The skinny plot is played to a slapstick farethee-well with Sellers offering a definitive casebook of pratfalls, ineptitude, and sight gags. Inventive direction by Blake Edwards. (113 mins.)

Pink Panther Strikes Again, The (1976)******** Peter Sellers, Herbert Lom, Colin Blakely. Peter Sellers is so deliciously funny and inventive that this fourth farce about our slightly addle-brained Inspector Clouseau is funnier than entry number three, "The Return of the Pink Panther." The plot, as always, is almost incidental to the verbal puns and glorious sight gags. This time around, Clouseau is pitted against his own former chief, the villainous Dreyfus (Lom), who twitches as the Bondian rascal in control of a device that threatens to destroy the world. Sellers comes close to destroying your funnybone a few times. Expertly directed by Blake Edwards, who co-authored with Frank Waldman. (103 mins.)

Pink String and Sealing Wax (British, 1949)****½** Googie Withers, Gordon Jackson. Tavernkeeper's dissatisfied wife uses a chemist's son in her plan to murder her husband. Period melodrama is graced by good performances to help it along.

Pinky (1949)******* Jeanne Crain, Ethel Barrymore, Ethel Waters. Strong racial drama dealing with light-skinned Negro girl who comes home to the South. Director Elia Kazan gets excellent performances all around. (102 mins.)

Pin Up Girl (1944)****** Betty Grable, Martha Raye, Joe E. Brown. Promising title produces absolutely nothing. Story of the romance of a sailor and a girl has no comedy, not enough legs and a load of specialty numbers which don't help.

Pioneer Woman (1973)****½** William Shatner, Joanna Pettet. There's an old-fashioned quality of noble heroics against great odds in this well produced western adventure. A family uproots itself and sets out for the promised farmland in Nebraska, only to meet with hostility from the squatters and a seemingly endless line of personal defeats. Miss Pettet is well cast as the mother of the clan who must shoulder all the responsibility when her husband is killed. Made-for-TV. (Dir: Buzz Kulik.)

Pirate, The (1947)****½** Judy Garland, Gene Kelly. This may or may not appeal to you depending more on your mood than on your tastes. Period comedy about a man who poses as his rival to win his loved one hits every key from sheer delight to boredom. Cole Porter's score is not his best and the top number is "Be a Clown." (Dir: Vincente Minnelli, 102 mins.)

Pirate and the Slave Girl (Italian, 1962)***½** Lex Barker, Chelo Alonso. Pirate takes the daughter of the governor as prisoner, along with documents containing treaty negotiations. Swashbuckling melodramatics on the corny side. Dubbed in English.

Pirate of the Black Hawk (Italian, 1960)***½** Mijanou Bardot, Gerard Landry. More buccaneers, plus Brigitte's sister. Seems nothing helps this one. (Dir: Piero Pierotti, 87 mins.)

Pirates of the Coast (Italian, 1961) ***½** Lex Barker, Estella Blain. Spanish captain has a fulltime task escorting a load of silver to Madrid. Weak swashbuckling adventure dubbed in English.

Pirates of the Mississippi, The (German, 1964)***½** Hansjorg Felmy, Horst Frank, Sabine Sinjen. Lawman swears revenge on the leader of a gang of river pirates, brings the nasty crew to justice. Horse opera, German style—they all try hard, but it's more strudel than saddle. Dubbed in English.

Pirates of Tortuga (1961)***½** Ken Scott, Leticia Roman, Dave King. Captain of a British privateer is ordered to track down notorious pirate Sir Henry Morgan. Dull swashbuckling melodrama. (Dir: Robert D. Webb, 97 mins.)

Pit and the Pendulum, The (1961) ****½** Vincent Price, John Kerr. One of the first and probably still the best of the films based on Edgar Allan Poe tales starring Vincent Price. This thriller has all the stock ingredients inherent to horror yarns including the castle on the hill, a fantastic torture chamber, walled-up coffins and screams in the night. John Kerr plays the young innocent who comes to Price's Spanish castle to investigate his sister's mysterious death and falls prey to the spooky goings-on. (Dir: Roger Corman, 80 mins.)

Pitfall (1948)*****½** Dick Powell, Jane Wyatt, Lizabeth Scott. A momentary philandering with a glamorous charmer brings tragedy to a happily married man. Strong drama, tense, well acted. (Dir: Andre de Toth, 84 mins.)

Pittsburgh (1942)** John Wayne, Marlene Dietrich, Randolph Scott. Miner's drive for power costs him his friends and the woman he loves. Capable performers can't do much with this sluggish melodrama. (Dir: Lewis Seiler, 90 mins.)

P.J. (1968)**½ George Peppard, Gayle Hunnicutt, Raymond Burr. Intricate detective yarn starts on a tough note, and maintains a hardhitting approach up to the finale on a deserted island. Tale involves George Peppard as a small-time private eye hired by a wealthy tycoon Raymond Burr to watch over Burr's beautiful mistress Gayle Hunnicutt. There are enough villains around to cast at least five melodramas. (Dir: John Guillerman, 109 mins.)

Place for Lovers, A (Italian-French, 1968)* Faye Dunaway, Marcello Mastroianni. Not even the ladies will sit still for this trashy soap opera with the two beautiful stars playing sophisticated lovers amid the sumptuous setting of a Venetian villa. It's a disaster for all concerned, including the gifted director Vittorio De Sica. (88 mins.)

Place in the Sun, A (1951)**** Elizabeth Taylor, Montgomery Clift, Shelley Winters. Dreiser's "An American Tragedy" beautifully filmed. Story of a factory worker who loves a wealthy girl and has an affair with a working girl, with tragedy resulting. Superb direction by George Stevens, fine performances, dramatically powerful. (122 mins.)

Place of One's Own, A (British, 1945)*** Margaret Lockwood, James Mason. Elderly couple buy an old neglected house, take in a girl as companion, find she is influenced by spirits. Entertaining drama, well acted. (Dir: Bernard Knowles, 91 mins.)

Place to Go, A (British, 1964)** Bernard Lee, Rita Tushingham. Tiresome threadbare drama of an East End London family and their troubles. Miss Tushingham is wasted.

Plainsman, The (1937)***½ Gary Cooper, Jean Arthur. Rootin' shootin' western, loaded with story and action. A De Mille spectacle,

560

Plainsman, The (1966)** Don Murray, Guy Stockwell, Bradford Dillman, Abby Dalton. Wild Bill Hickok, Buffalo Bill, and Calamity Jane foiling Indians and gun runners. Imitation of the venerable old Gary Cooper-Jean Arthur epic, but nowhere near as good. (Dir: David Lowell Rich, 92 mins.)

Plan 9 from Outer Space (1956)* Bela Lugosi, Vampira. Ludicrous science fiction "thriller" pairing TV's Vampira and movies' Master of Horror, Bela Lugosi. Important for students of Vampira's mid-50's films. (Dir: Edward Wood, Jr., 79 mins.)

Planet Earth (1974)*** John Saxon, Diana Muldaur, Janet Margolin. Gene Roddenberry is back on the top-flight sci-fi track with this sociopolitical film incorporating the best elements of his former TV series ("Star Trek") plus an added bonus —it takes place on Earth. After the "Great Catastrophe," 22d-century Earth has been fragmented into isolated colonies, one of which is PAX, a lofty community of idealists dedicated to bringing the Earth into harmony with itself. The focus is on a PAX team of specialists who come into conflict with a female-dominated society where males are turned into cowering slaves called "dinks." Made-for-TV. (Dir: Marc Daniels)

Planet of Blood (1966)** Basil Rathbone, John Saxon, Judi Meredith, Dennis Hopper. Space ship is sent to Mars to investigate a mysterious missile; therein is found a survivor from another world with a passion for human blood. Set in 1990, this sci-fi thriller is way, way out. Fans might get a kick out of it. (Dir: Curtis Harrington, 80 mins.)

Planet of the Apes (1968)**** Charlton Heston, Kim Hunter, Maurice Evans, Roddy McDowall. Exciting science-fiction film based on Pierre Boulle's book "Monkey Planet." This sci-fi thriller even has some political and sociological comment on our troubled times. Four astronauts crash on a distant planet. Director Franklin Schaffner used desolate areas of Utah and Arizona to good advantage for his "planet" location scenes, and the makeup men who devised the fantastic ape masks rate a special bow. (Dir: Franklin J. Schaffner, 112 mins.)

Planets Against Us (French, 1960)* Jany Clair, Michel Lemoine. Badly made science fiction film, invaders from outer space again. Not the Gallic metier.

Platinum High School (1960)* Mickey Rooney, Terry Moore, Dan Duryea. Father visits an exclusive military school investigating the death of his son, finds it was no accident. Al Zugsmith's version of "Bad Day at Black Rock," pure junk. Alternative title: **Trouble at 16**. (Dir: Charles Haas, 93 mins.)

Play Dirty (British, 1969)*½ Michael Caine, Harry Andrews, Nigel Davenport. Still another World War II adventure which borrows the "Dirty Dozen" plotting, but with less successful results. Caine is the officer in charge of a group of mercenaries and misfits who set out to blow up that ever-present important enemy fuel depot. (Dir: Andre de Toth, 117 mins.)

Play It Again, Sam (1972)*** Woody Allen, Susan Anspach, Diane Keaton. Woody Allen fans (circa '78) may be slightly disappointed in this early effort—a one-joke affair that stretches on a little too long before the excellent fadeout, a faithful, funny recreation of the farewell scene between Bogart and Bergman in "Casablanca." Woody is a compulsive Bogart fantasizer and it drives his wife (Susan Anspach) out of his life, which drives him into the arms of his best friend's wife, Diane Keaton. Jerry Lacy, in an uncanny Bogart imitation, pops up every now and then as Bogart's spirit, and keeps things bubbling. Allen fans will love it. (Dir: Herbert Ross, 84 mins.)

Play It as It Lays (1972)*** Tuesday Weld, Anthony Perkins, Adam Roarke, Tammy Grimes. Joan Didion adapted her disturbing novel for the screen with her husband, John Gregory Dunne, and the result is a film that captures the meaningless void of Hollywood existence in a terse, unsentimental style. Tuesday Weld gives an extraordinarily accurate performance as Maria Wyeth, the actress who undergoes a psychic breakdown, whose memories from a sanatorium form the narrative, and Perkins subtly underplays her homosexual friend whose suicide undercuts Maria's slim grasp on reality. Stark, downbeat drama that

pulls no punches. (Dir: Frank Perry, 101 mins.)

Play It Cool (British, 1963)*½ Billy Fury, Helen Shapiro, Michael Anderson Jr., Dennis Price. Leader of a group of young swingers meets an heiress and saves her from running off with a heel. For the rock-and-rollers, maybe; for the rest, pretty deadly. (Dir: Michael Winner, 82 mins.)

Play Misty for Me (1971)*** Clint Eastwood, Jessica Walter, Donna Mills. Eastwood makes a surprisingly promising directorial debut while starring in this mystery. About a sexy disk jockey on a California radio station, and his involvement with a psychotic lady who keeps requesting that old standard "Misty." Miss Walter is first rate playing the dangerous listener who takes charge of Eastwood's life when he makes the mistake of entering into what he thinks is a casual affair. Roberta Flack's song "The First Time I Ever Saw Your Face" became a hit via this film. (102 mins.)

Playback (British, 1962)** Margit Saad, Barry Foster. Policeman falls for a married woman, agrees to kill her husband for the insurance. Fair example of "perfect crime" drama, based on an Edgar Wallace story.

Playboy of the Western World, The (Irish, 1962)**** Siobhan McKenna, Gary Raymond. Beautiful, lyrical, and long-overdue film of the classic Irish play of J. M. Synge. The actual plot about a young stranger who becomes the idol of a small village is less important than the soaring, poetic language of the play and the lovely performance of Siobhan McKenna, one of the truly great actresses of our time, seldom used to good advantage in films. Miss McKenna truthfully is a few years too old to play the role of Pegeen, but she and the playboy Gary Raymond are both fine, and the Irish brogue is a joy to hear.

Playgirl (1954)**½ Shelley Winters, Barry Sullivan. Moderately interesting drama about a woman's concern for her young sister's reputation. Miss Winters is fairly good in the role of the over-protective sister. (Dir: Joseph Pevney, 85 mins.)

Playmates (1972)**½ Alan Alda, Doug McClure. Surprisingly adult made-for-TV feature film about di-

561

vorce, California-style. Stars Alda and McClure as a pair of fathers who meet with their sons at an amusement park on their visitation days. Despite totally different backgrounds they become friends, and the complications begin. Sharp dialogue and realistic plot twist make it a cut above average. (Dir: Theodore Flicker, 93 mins.)

Playtime (French, 1968)**** Jacques Tati. A wonderful Tati triumph. Jacques Tati again plays the lovable Mr. Hulot, borrowing a walk from Chaplin and a face from Keaton. Hulot is placed in an ultramodern Paris, all skyscrapers, glass, and computers, only to find chaos, and tourists being led like sheep. Atmosphere emerges in the last third of the film—the breakdown of a nightclub and the return of people to an amiability previously lost among slick machines and buildings. Humor is mainly silent, and glorious. (Dir: Jacques Tati, 100 mins.)

Plaza Suite (1970)***½ Walter Matthau, Maureen Stapleton, Barbara Harris, Lee Grant. Matthau is supplied with three juicy comic roles by playwright Neil Simon in this film version of the hit play—and he's grand in all of them. In the first, he plays a businessman who agrees to try to find the old magic in his 20-year marriage by returning to the scene of the crime—the honeymoon suite at the Plaza—with his wife (Miss Stapleton). In number two, Miss Harris almost steals Matthau's thunder playing an old flame of a Hollywood producer who agrees to a meeting in a hotel room, but only to satisfy her hunger for tidbits about Hollywood. Miss Grant shares the honors in segment three, which has the duo playing the parents of a bride who won't come out of the bathroom in the hotel suite. (Dir: Arthur Hiller, 114 mins.)

Please Believe Me (1950)**½ Deborah Kerr, Robert Walker, Peter Lawford, Mark Stevens. A whacky comedy about a trio of bachelors who give a new heiress the rush. The cast, all pros, have some trouble making the script work. (Dir: Norman Taurog, 87 mins.)

Please Don't Eat the Daisies (1960) *** Doris Day, David Niven. Janis Paige. Friendly comedy about a drama critic, his wife and four children—the critic has problems with his work, the wife has problems with renovating an old house in the country, and things become quite hectic in general. Some good laughs, clever dialogue. (Dir: Charles Walters, 111 mins.)

Please Mr. Balzac (French, 1956)** Brigitte Bardot, Daniel Gelin. Routine comedy whose only asset is the now famous Bardot chassis. How much of it you'll see depends somewhat on the good nature of the film editor of your local station showing this dubbed import. About a girl who writes a scandalous novel, and lams out for Paris when her prudish family objects. (Dir: Marc Allegret, 99 mins.)

Please Murder Me (1955)** Raymond Burr, Angela Lansbury. A brilliant attorney sacrifices his career and scruples to defend a murderess with whom he is in love. Muddled melodrama. (Dir: Peter Godfrey, 78 mins.)

Please Turn Over (1960)** Ted Ray, Jean Kent. Silly comedy done in the British style. The actors are far better than their material. Plot concerns a girl who writes a sexy novel and causes a commotion. (Dir: Gerald Thomas, 86 mins.)

Pleasure of His Company, The (1961) **½ Fred Astaire, Debbie Reynolds, Lilli Palmer, Tab Hunter. Debonair charmer returns home for his daughter's wedding but tries to break up the couple when he finds her to be attractive. Good cast takes advantage of some witty lines to give this comedy a fair amount of fun. (Dir: George Seaton, 115 mins.)

Pleasure Seekers, The (1965)**½ Ann-Margret, Carol Lynley, Pamela Tiffin, Anthony Franciosa. A well-produced remake of "Three Coins in The Fountain" with the locale shifted from Rome to Spain. Three young girls looking for romance find it amid the Spanish architecture. The dialogue has a bite to it at times, but it's mainly a romantic excursion of the variety enjoyed most by the female audience. (Dir: Jean Negulesco, 107 mins.)

Plot to Assassinate Hitler, The (German, 1961)**½ Maximilian Schell. Story of the German officers' plan to eliminate the hated Nazi leader unfolds in documentary fashion, is frequently gripping despite the familiarity of the narrative. Dubbed in English.

Plunder In the Sun (1953)** Glenn Ford, Diana Lynn, Patricia Medina. An Aztec fortune is the prize in this involved modern day treasure hunt. Performances are good but the pace is slow and everybody talks too much. (Dir: John Farrow, 81 mins.)

Plunder Road (1958)***½ Gene Raymond, Wayne Morris. Make a thousand Grade "B" crime tales and you're bound to turn out one gem . . . this is it! Superior melodrama about an attempted ten million dollar theft. (Dir: Hubert Cornfield, 71 mins.)

Plunderers, The (1960)**½ Jeff Chandler, John Saxon, Dolores Hart. Sprawling western drama about a group of outlaws and their effect on a town. It's all familiar but played straight by a cast of actors who look comfortable in western garb. (Dir: Joseph Kane, 87 mins.)

Plunderers of Painted Flats (1959)*½ Corinne Calvet, John Carroll, Skip Homeir. Gunman comes across a lad who's searching for his father's killer. Mediocre western. (Dir: Albert C. Gannaway, 77 mins.)

Plymouth Adventure (1952)*** Spencer Tracy, Gene Tierney, Van Johnson. Good adventure epic about the Pilgrims' voyage on the Mayflower and the hardships they encounter when they land at Plymouth, Mass. Don't look for historical accuracy—just sit back and enjoy the fine acting of Spencer Tracy and his supporting players. For the record, Van Johnson plays John Alden to Dawn Addams' Priscilla Mullins. (Dir: Clarence Brown, 105 mins.)

Poacher's Daughter, The (Irish, 1960) **½ Julie Harris, Harry Brogan, Tim Selley. Irresponsible son with an eye on motor bikes and flashy ladies is finally straightened out by a sincere girl. Unlikely premise. Mildly amusing comedy has the Irish flavor for those who like it and the talented and wasted-by-films Miss Harris. (Dir: George Pollack, 74 mins.)

Pocket Money (1972)*** Naive Paul Newman and his alcoholic sidekick Lee Marvin go searching through Mexico to buy a herd of cattle for evil boss Strother Martin. The duo are suckers for every swindler with a bum steer, but their charming presence redeems the screenplay,

which is chock full of character development and short on plot. Written by Terry Malick, who went on to write and direct "Badlands." (Dir: Stuart Rosenberg, 102 mins.)

Pocketful of Miracles (1961)*** Glenn Ford, Bette Davis, Hope Lange. Veteran comedy director Frank Capra brings this Damon Runyon yarn to the screen with a liberal mixture of corn, sentiment, and broadly played performances. The plot revolves around a street vendor called Apple Annie (Bette Davis) and the lengths she and her "guys and dolls" friends go to help her masquerade as a society matron when her daughter pays a surprise visit. Not all of it works but there's Miss Davis giving it all she's got and a hilarious performance by Peter Falk as a Broadway type. (136 mins.)

Point, The (1971)***½ Charming animated TV feature musical fantasy that should fascinate the youngsters and keep the adults interested. It tells the story of Oblio, a little boy who is born without a point on his head in a kingdom where everything and everyone has a literal point. His uniqueness eventually causes him to be banished to the pointless forest, a veritable wonderland, where Oblio experiences one great adventure after another before returning home a hero. The images (especially in color) are superb, and the musical score by Harry Nilsson creates the appropriate mood. A welcome children's film, of substance, taste and imagination. (Dir: Fred Wolff, 73 mins.)

Point Blank (1967)**½ Lee Marvin, Angie Dickinson, Keenan Wynn. Brutal film about the underworld in Los Angeles. The story and much of the violence are familiar enough. What sets this nasty melodrama apart from most films of this genre is some striking direction by Britisher John Boorman and several imaginative visual sequences. Boorman clearly has the talent to make a first-rate film when he finds better material. (Dir: John Boorman, 92 mins.)

Point of Order (1964)**** Brilliant, deeply disturbing documentary about the Army-McCarthy hearings in the spring of 1954. Consists solely of kinescopes from the TV coverage, deftly edited by filmmaker Emile de

563

Antonio. The demagoguery and character assassination techniques of Wisconsin Sen. Joseph McCarthy seem even more chilling in light of the Watergate revelations two decades later. Others on screen include Robert Kennedy, Roy Cohn, Sens. Symington, Mundt, and McClellan, and the unforgettable Boston lawyer Joseph Welch, who, in his own civilized way, finally explodes with moral outrage at the reprehensible smear tactics of the Senator. An invaluable history lesson about one of the uglier aspects of American society in the early '50's. Black and white. (97 mins.)

Poison (French, 1957)**½ Michel Simon. Unhappily married couple each secretly plan to kill the other. Grim drama, well acted. English-dubbed.

Poison Ivy (French, 1953)** Eddie Constantine. Rousing French-made Grade B crime drama with Eddie Constantine playing a tough F.B.I. agent who's up to his badge in everything from gold smugglers to shark-infested waters. (Dir: Bernard Borderie, 90 mins.)

Police Story (1973)**½ Vic Morrow, Ed Asner, Chuck Connors, Sandy Baron, Harry Guardino. Gutsy, realistic police drama based on material written by Los Angeles lawman Joseph Wambaugh, who portrays police as human beings—this was a pilot for the anthology TV series. Not the idealized Hollywood version of police chasing bad guys. One cop can almost be compared to the cruel thief he's determined to nail, while an associate openly displays his racism only to be taught a humorous lesson by fellow officers. The characters, the story, and the realistic Los Angeles backgrounds are all first-rate. Good performances. (Dir: Billy Graham, 99 mins.)

Policeman, The (Israeli, 1971)**½ Shay K. Ophir, Zahariva Harifai. Pleasant lark about an Israeli policeman who is going to be retired from the force, after 20 years, unless he can make a big arrest and obtain a promotion. Ophir, a gifted pantomimist, plays the bungling cop well, but the film is too sentimental. Written and directed by leading Israeli humorist Ephraim Kishan. (87 mins.)

Pollyanna (1960)***½ Hayley Mills, Jane Wyman, Agnes Moorehead, Richard Egan, Adolphe Menjou. Enjoyable family fare. Nice, uncluttered tale about a young girl who changes the life of almost everyone she comes in contact with, due to her optimistic outlook on life. Thirteen-year-old Hayley Mills is perfect as Pollyanna, a role which lets her use her cute mannerisms naturally, and the supporting cast is absolutely right . . . Jane Wyman as Aunt Polly, Agnes Moorehead as a cured hypochondriac. (Dir: David Swift, 134 mins.)

Pony Express (1953)**½ Charlton Heston, Rhonda Fleming, Jan Sterling, Forrest Tucker. Buffalo Bill and Wild Bill Hickok team up to see that the mail goes through. Cast and production distinguish an ordinary western plot. (Dir: Jerry Hopper, 101 mins.)

Pony Soldier (1952)**½ Tyrone Power, Cameron Mitchell, Robert Horton. Mountie tries to stop a tribe of rebellious Indians from going on the warpath. Lively action melodrama goes through its familiar paces with speed and dispatch. (Dir: Joseph M. Newman, 82 mins.)

Pool of London (British, 1951)*** Bonar Colleano, Susan Shaw. A merchant sailor not above a little smuggling gets mixed up with stolen diamonds for which murder was committed. Suspenseful melodrama, well staged and acted.

Poor but Beautiful (1959)**½ Marisa Allasio, Renato Salvatori. An Italian film about love and triangles. Some funny scenes and the attractive cast make it worthwhile.

Poor Cow (British, 1957)**½ Carol White, Terence Stamp. Life in the Lower Depths, as a girl (Carol White) seeks happiness for her baby and contends with a husband in jail. Generally capable performances. Carol White is particularly impressive in this saga of the sexual mores of the English low-income worker.

Poor Little Rich Girl, The (1936)*** Shirley Temple, Alice Faye, Jack Haley. Shirley isn't an orphan in this one so she runs away from home and gets picked up by a vaudeville team. Typical Temple vehicle but pleasanter than most. (Dir: Irving Cummings, 72 mins.)

Popi (1969)**** Alan Arkin, Rita Moreno. Alan Arkin's flawless, luminous performance as the New York Puerto Rican widower who wants a better life for his two sons is the film's main attraction. He will win your heart as he comes up with an outrageous plan to set his boys adrift in a boat off the Florida coast in hopes of their finding a better home with some wealthy people after being rescued. The picture has charm and pathos in well-measured amounts, and Arkin is brilliant. Well directed by Arthur Hiller, and the lovely screenplay written by Tina and Lester Pine. (115 mins.)

Poppy (1936)*** W. C. Fields. When W. C. is on screen, this is a delight. Story of a carnival bum who tries to pass his daughter off as a missing heiress. (Dir: A. Edward Sutherland, 80 mins.)

Poppy Is Also a Flower, The (1966) **½ Trevor Howard, E. G. Marshall. First shown on TV as a special on behalf of the United Nations. A cast of all-stars (Yul Brynner, Omar Sharif, Marcello Mastroianni, Rita Hayworth, Angie Dickinson, and more) fill cameo roles in this dope-smuggling tale, and they weigh it down. However, Howard and Marshall, as agents assigned to follow the illegal operation right from its origin in the poppy fields, do well, and there's an exciting chase sequence in the action-packed last half hour. (Dir: Terence Young, 100 mins.)

Porgy and Bess (1959)***½ Sidney Poitier, Dorothy Dandridge, Sammy Davis Jr., Pearl Bailey. Gershwin's opera about the inhabitants of Catfish Row, and a crippled beggar who cares for a beautiful but reckless girl. Lavishly produced by Samuel Goldwyn, with the superb score brilliantly sung. However, the show is staged stiffly, unimaginatively—some of the performances are not on a par with the musical end. All in all, the score's the thing. (Dir: Otto Preminger, 138 mins.)

Pork Chop Hill (1959)*** Gregory Peck. Stark war drama about the last hours of the Korean War. It's hard-hitting and tough with an excellent supporting cast, which includes George Peppard, Harry Guardino, and Rip Torn. Superior war film directed by veteran Lewis Milestone. (97 mins.)

Port Afrique (1956)** Pier Angeli, Phil Carey. French Morocco is the setting for this dull story of revenge and murder. Lovely Pier Angeli plays a nightclub singer involved in the shady goings-on. (Dir: Rudolph Mate, 92 mins.)

Port of New York (1949)*** Scott Brady, Yul Brynner, K. T. Stevens. When a government agent is killed working on a narcotics case, his buddy crashes through to get the goods on the gang. Competent crime melodrama, made in New York. (Dir: Laslo Benedek, 96 mins.)

Port of Revenge (British, 1961)*½ Dan O'Herlihy, Maurice Teynac. Soldier of fortune matches wits with a narcotics smuggler. All yawn together, now.

Port of Seven Seas (1938)** Wallace Beery, Maureen O'Sullivan, John Beal. An earlier version of the oft-told tale of "Fanny," as a Marseilles girl loves a lad who goes to sea; when babytime is near, her father and an elderly suitor come to the rescue. The Gallic flavor just isn't there. (Dir: James Whale, 80 mins.)

Port Sinister (1953)*½ James Warren, Lynne Roberts. Insipid science fiction meller concerning an expedition which uncovers volcanic explosions which unearth giant man-eating crabs. "Port Sinister" is more stupid than sinister.

Portnoy's Complaint (1972)* Richard Benjamin, Karen Black, Lee Grant. Producer-screenwriter-director Ernest Lehman has pulled off, quite unintentionally, a remarkable and distressing feat. He's transformed Philip Roth's excruciatingly funny novel into a sniveling, ponderous film. Lehman's managed this reverse artistry by a rotten screenplay and terrible direction. Roth's best-selling novel, about the sexual hang-ups and fantasies of a Jewish boy growing up in New Jersey, is unrecognizable in this celluloid massacre, and normally talented performers like Black and Grant get trampled in the carnage. (101 mins.)

Portrait in Black (1960)**½ Lana Turner, Anthony Quinn, Sandra Dee. Typical example of slick Hollywood mystery-romance. Ingredients: bed-ridden tycoon, dissatisfied wife, weak-willed doctor in love with wife, mix well with murder, conscience pangs and revenge. It's all nicely garnished, but still hash. (Dir: Michael Gordon, 112 mins.)

Portrait of a Mobster (1961)**½ Vic Morrow, Leslie Parrish. Strictly for fans of gangster movies who like their action tough and the plot simple. Vic Morrow gives a tight-lipped performance as Dutch Schultz, the notorious hood of the Prohibition era. Lovely Leslie Parrish does quite well in a predictably written role. (Dir: Joseph Pevney, 108 mins.)

Portrait of a Sinner (British, 1959) ** Nadja Tiller, Tony Britton, William Bendix. Temptress keeps a young man and her elderly boss on a string, but really craves the man who did her dirt years before. Unsavory drama has a capable cast and director. (Dir: Robert Siodmak, 96 mins.)

Portrait of an Unknown Woman (W. German, 1954)**½ Ruth Leuwerik, O. W. Fischer. Tasteful treatment of a painter enchanted by a beautiful woman at the opera. When he molds her face on a sculpture, scandal is let loose. You've seen the rest. (Dir: Helmut Kautner, 86 mins.)

Portrait of Jason (1967)***½ Fascinating, haunting documentary portrait of a 33-year-old black male homosexual prostitute who is also a heroin addict. Filmmaker Shirley Clarke just turned her cameras on this charismatic, tortured soul as he tells about his past life, orgies, experiences in jail, and does a few pathetic impersonations, etc. You virtually feel Jason Halliday disintegrating right before your eyes. One of the most powerful anti-drug statements ever captured on film. (Dir: Shirley Clarke, 105 mins.)

Portrait of Jennie (1949)***½ Jennifer Jones, Joseph Cotten. Artist finds a strange girl in Central Park, successfully paints her, falls in love with her, even though he suspects she is a spirit. Beautifully photographed, haunting fantasy, unusual, hard to forget. (Dir: William Dieterle, 86 mins.)

Poseidon Adventure, The (1972)*** Gene Hackman, Ernest Borgnine, Shelley Winters, Stella Stevens. A gripping "Titaniclike" adventure that falls into the category of popular appeal films which score big at the box office, providing vicarious thrill after thrill. It's New Year's Eve on the "Poseidon" when a 90-foot tidal wave overturns the huge ocean liner and the stage is set for the survival of the fittest among the all-star passenger list . . . including resourceful leader-minister Gene Hackman; detective Ernest Borg-

nine and his ex-prostie-wife Stella Stevens; a middle-aged Jewish couple, Shelley Winters and Jack Albertson; terrified pop singer Carol Lynley; and amiable haberdasher-bachelor Red Buttons. Their plight and trek to possible survival is excellently photographed, if slightly on the incredible side. As it turns out, the special effects rank as the real star of the film. (Dir: Ronald Neame, 117 mins.)

Posse (1975)***½ Kirk Douglas, Bruce Dern. Offbeat, interesting western, part allegory, part political morality story. Douglas directed as well as playing the leading role, an affable Texas marshal circa 1890. Bruce Dern is very good as an outlaw whom Douglas is out to nab. Based on a story by Christopher Knopf. (Dir: Kirk Douglas, 94 mins.)

Posse from Hell (1961)** Audie Murphy, John Saxon, Zohra Lampert, Vic Morrow. Run-of-the-mill western with Audie Murphy riding and shooting once again in his usual brave fashion. No surprises, but action fans will probably stick with it, as a gunslinger goes after four escaped killers. (Dir: Herbert Coleman, 89 mins.)

Possessed (1947)**½ Joan Crawford, Van Heflin. Morbid story of a woman schizophrenic is occasionally interesting but generally too heavy and melodramatic to appeal to anyone but a loyal Joan Crowford fan. (Dir: Curtis Bernhardt, 108 mins.)

Possession of Joel Delaney, The (1972)** Shirley MacLaine, Perry King. OK thriller. New York divorcee MacLaine chases around her kid brother Joel (King) in a laughingly desperate attempt to make him her son. Poor Joel is possessed by the spirit of a deceased Puerto Rican friend who used to chop off girls' heads! The exorcism scene and the New York location shots can really shake you up, but the terror is in slow motion. (Dir: Waris Hussein, 105 mins.)

Possessors, The (1959)**½ Jean Gabin, Pierre Brasseur. Story of a family and their involvement with the stock exchange. Literate French drama, slow moving but well acted. (Dir: Denys De La Patelliere, 94 mins.)

Postman Always Rings Twice (1945) ***½ Lana Turner, John Garfield.

Exciting adaptation of the James M. Cain novel about a perfect crime and how the criminals are ironically punished. Lana is beautiful and seductive in this one and you can't blame Garfield for helping her kill her husband. (Dir: Tay Garnett, 113 mins.)

Pot o' Gold (1941)** James Stewart, Paulette Goddard. The gal's rich Pop hates dance bands, but nevertheless she lands Horace Heidt's orchestra on Pop's program. Pleasant musical comedy. (Dir: George Marshall, 86 mins.)

Potemkin (Russian, 1925)**** Antonov, Vladamir Barsky. This film has been labeled everything from "one of the best films ever made" to "the greatest film of all time." The Sergei Eisenstein masterpiece is a re-creation of the successful sailor revolt aboard the battleship "Potemkin" in Odessa harbor in 1905. The massacre of the civilian population that supported the mutiny, which takes place on the great steps of the city, is one of the most powerful sequences in the history of film. It is a thrilling, shocking, exciting, and overwhelming movie classic. (Dir: Sergei Eisenstein, 67 mins.)

Pound (1970)*** Lawrence Wolf, Elsie Downey, Marshall Efron. Rover and Feydeau hang loose in Robert Downey's erratically insane satire of impounded dogs (played by humans) awaiting an owner or the big sleep—the latter can only come when Con Edison fixes the gas lines. Not Downey's best but a lot of macabre humor, much of it funny. (Dir: Robert Downey, 92 mins.)

Poverty and Nobility (Italian, 1954)** Sophia Loren, Toto. Poor boy falls for a ballerina from a noble family, causing confusion. Dubbed-English comedy from Loren's salad days. She's good to look at, while the film itself is bearable.

Powder Keg (1971)** Rod Taylor, Dennis Cole. Railroad blowups, dirty bandits, rape, and a Stutz Bearcat roadster, circa 1914, keep the action barreling along in this made-for-TV film. Writer-producer-director Doug Heyes has thrown everything into the overlong story. Troubleshooters Taylor and Cole get around in the yellow roadster, and they're hired by the railroad to handle Mexican hijackers who hold a train and passengers hostage below the border. (100 mins.)

Powder River (1953)** Rory Calhoun, Corinne Calvet, Cameron Mitchell. Routine western about a gunman turned marshal and the collection of stock characters with whom he matches wits and/or guns. (Dir: Louis King, 78 mins.)

Power, The (1968)** George Hamilton, Suzanne Pleshette, Michael Rennie, Yvonne DeCarlo. Reasonably interesting, sci-fi yarn about a mind which has fantastic power to do almost anything as long as it's evil! Hamilton tries to oppose this "power" since he too possesses a "powerful" mind. It's a little confusing at times, but teen-agers with an historical bent might want to watch the "powerful mind" and blank countenance of a man who wooed Lyndon Johnson's daughter Lynda. (Dir: Byron Haskin, 109 mins.)

Power and the Glory, The (1933)**½ Spencer Tracy, Colleen Moore, Ralph Morgan. A railroad president commits suicide and his secretary reviews his employer's "rags to riches" life through a series of flash-backs. Some very good acting, primarily Tracy's. (Dir: Lawrence C. Windom)

Power and the Prize, The (1956)**½ Robert Taylor, Elisabeth Mueller, Burl Ives. Slick Hollywood version about the world of big business. Taylor adequately plays the ambitious executive who finds he fought too hard for things he really didn't want after he falls in love with an attractive refugee. Burl Ives is a stereotyped big tycoon. (Dir: Henry Koster, 98 mins.)

Power of the Whistler (1945)**½ Janis Carter, Richard Dix. Killer gets amnesia and girl amateur detective discovers his identity. Suspenseful thriller. (Dir: Lew Landers, 66 mins.)

Powers Girl, The (1942)** George Murphy, Anne Shirley, Carole Landis, Dennis Day, Benny Goodman. A fast-talking agent makes a Powers model out a dainty dish, but falls for her sister. Tolerable comedy (Dir: Norman Z. McLeod, 93 mins.)

Practically Yours (1945)** Fred MacMurray, Claudette Colbert. A pilot sends a message of love to a girl before he crashes into the Pacific.

This "comedy" is about all the confusion caused when a girl thinks he meant her and he turns up alive. Few laughs, silly situation. (Dir: Mitchell Leisen, 90 mins.)

Pray for the Wildcats (1974)★★★ Andy Griffith, William Shatner, Robert Reed, Marjoe Gortner, Angie Dickinson. An offbeat tale that should keep you engrossed throughout. Griffith, in a change-of-pace casting, plays an unscrupulous tycoon who gleefully manipulates three ad agency execs beyond the point of endurance. The four men go to the Baja California territory on a motorcycle trek, during which they discover their true strengths and inevitable weaknesses. The cast is first-rate and the story strives for originality. Made-for-TV. (Dir: Robert Michael Lewis.)

Prelude to Fame (British, 1950)★★★½ Guy Rolfe, Kathleen Byron, Jeremy Spenser. A boy is found to have musical talent, becomes a child prodigy conductor, but finds fame has its sadness too. Drama, well written and directed, finely acted.

Premature Burial, The (1962)★★ Ray Milland, Hazel Court. Edgar Allan Poe's intricate and engrossing suspense tale about a man who fears he will be buried alive is impoverished by this screen treatment, so packed with contrivances, clichés and gloomy decors as to be absurd, often funny, but not very scary. If you don't know the story and can stand the devices, see it. Better yet, read the original! (Dir: Roger Corman, 81 mins.)

Premeditated (French, 1960)★★ Jean-Claude Pascal, Pascale Roberts. Man goes on trial for the murder of his wife and her lover. Fair English-dubbed courtroom drama.

Prescription: Murder (1968)★★½ Peter Falk, Gene Barry. A familiar, old-fashioned murder yarn gets the glossy Universal mounting. Peter Falk plays the cigar-smoking, trenchcoat-carrying detective who just can't buy successful Hollywood psychiatrist Gene Barry's airtight alibi. Made-for-TV. (Dir: Richard Irving, 99 mins.)

Presenting Lily Mars (1942)★★ Judy Garland, Van Heflin. Judy's fans may like this syrupy distortion of a Booth Tarkington story but even they figure to be disappointed. The stage-struck girl looking for that old

568

break with nothing added to the familiar formula. (Dir: Norman Taurog, 104 mins.)

President's Analyst, The (1967)★★★½ James Coburn, Godfrey Cambridge. Wacky, rewarding satire written and directed by Theodore J. Flicker. Spy spoof which benefits greatly from the smoothness of James Coburn in the title role. The premise is tremendously original, and although it falters towards the end, the story offers some wild chases, and amusing sequences with analyst Coburn becoming more and more paranoid, thanks to his delicate assignment as secret headshrinker to the President. Even lampoons the F.B.I. (Dir: Theodore J. Flicker, 104 mins.)

President's Lady, The (1953)★★½ Susan Hayward, Charlton Heston. Charlton Heston's effective performance as Andrew Jackson makes this costume drama, based on Irving Stone's best seller about the romance between the young Jackson and a married woman, worthwhile. Miss Hayward is less effective in an overdrawn characterization. (Dir: Henry Levin, 96 mins.)

President's Plane Is Missing, The (1973)★★½ Buddy Ebsen, Peter Graves, Rip Torn, Raymond Massey, Arthur Kennedy. The premise—the threat of a nuclear attack by Red China—was devised before President Nixon journeyed to the Great Wall and visited with Mao Tse-tung. The fictional President boards Air Force One, which crashes soon thereafter. Cast brings the stock Washington characters to life in the midst of the ensuing international tension. Made-for-TV. (Dir: Daryl Duke, 100 mins.)

Pressure Point (1962)★★★ Sidney Poitier, Bobby Darin. A very interesting film with two good performances by its stars. Poitier plays, with quiet authority, a prison psychiatrist whose star patient is an anti-Semitic, Negro-hating American Nazi party member, portrayed with becoming arrogance by Bobby Darin. Their exchanges pave the way for some intriguing flashbacks into the prisoner's past which led to his being jailed for sedition. The plot is overloaded, but the stars carry it off. (Dir: Hubert Cornfield, 120 mins.)

Pretender, The (1947)★★★ Albert Dekker, Catherine Craig. Businessman marries for money, hires a gangster to eliminate his rival; through an error, he finds himself the intended victim. Tight, suspenseful melodrama, well above average. (Dir: Wilee Wilder, 69 mins.)

Pretty Baby (1950)**½ Dennis Morgan, Betsy Drake, Edmund Gwenn. Funny comedy about a resourceful working girl who uses gimmicks to get to the top in her career. Well acted by Betsy Drake & Edmund Gwenn. (Dir: Bretaigne Windust, 92 mins.)

Pretty Boy Floyd (1960)** John Ericson, Joan Harvey. Fictionalized account of one of the nation's big time killers. John Ericson has the physical attractiveness and acting ability to rise above some of the drama's cliched plot twists. Gangster-film fans will find all the familiar episodes to their liking. (Dir: Herbert J. Leder, 96 mins.)

Pretty Boy Floyd (1974)**½ Martin Sheen, Kim Darby, Michael Parks. Fine actor Martin Sheen gets a chance to portray the legendary criminal Pretty Boy Floyd in this low-key tale set in the '20's and early '30's, and it's his performance which makes the TV feature worthwhile. Credit must also go to writer-director Clyde Ware, whose careful attention to period detail adds greatly to the texture of the film.

Pretty Poison (1968)**** Anthony Perkins, Tuesday Weld, Beverly Garland. Absorbing, low-budget psychological drama about a paranoid young man (Perkins) and his girl friend (Weld), underrated critically at the time of its first release, "Poison" boasts first-rate performances from both Weld and Perkins. A notably adroit screenplay by Lorenzo Semple, Jr., and a promising debut from young director Noel Black. We are purposely not going to tell you any more of the story, but this tale of madness in Massachusetts will keep you guessing from beginning to end. (Dir: Noel Black, 89 mins.)

Price of Fear, The (1956)** Merle Oberon, Lex Barker. Muddled melodrama about a woman who is responsible for a hit and run accident and goes to extremes to keep it a secret. Miss Oberon has had better vehicles and better leading men too. (Dir: Abner Biberman, 79 mins.)

Price of Silence, The (British, 1959)** Gordon Jackson, June Thorburn. Ex-con takes a job with a real estate company intending to go straight, but a blackmailing former cellmate makes it tough. Routine crime melodrama.

Pride and Prejudice (1940)*** Greer Garson, Laurence Olivier. Faithful adaptation of the Jane Austen novel about five sisters in search of a husband in England at the turn of the century. Most surprising thing about this well acted comedy of manners is that it's witty but still dated. (Dir: Robert Z. Leonard, 118 mins.)

Pride and the Passion, The (1957)**½ Cary Grant, Sophia Loren, Frank Sinatra. Over-produced spectacle set during the Spanish Revolution against Napoleon. The real star of the overlong epic is an enormous cannon which is abandoned by the Spanish Army, and retrieved by the band of guerrillas with the aid of a British naval officer. Grant looks uncomfortable in his role of the naval officer; Sophia Loren is merely decorative as a fiery Spanish girl; and Frank Sinatra is badly miscast as the guerrilla leader, Miguel. (Dir: Stanley Kramer, 132 mins.)

Pride of St. Louis (1952)**½ Dan Dailey, Joanne Dru. Sentimentalized biography of Dizzy Dean, baseball pitcher extraordinary, character de luxe. Could have used more authenticity, but Dailey gives the role a good try. (Dir: Harmon Jones, 93 mins.)

Pride of the Blue Grass (1954)** Lloyd Bridges, Vera Miles. Routine race track story with some action on the turf for racing fans. The plot is all too familiar but the kids may enjoy the horses. (Dir: William Beaudine, 71 mins.)

Pride of the Marines (1945)***½ John Garfield, Eleanor Parker. Moving, human story of Al Schmid the Marine who was blinded by a grenade after killing 200 Japs. It's an account of his adjustment to blindness and it's told with simplicity and taste. Performances are excellent. (Dir: Delmer Daves, 119 mins.)

Pride of the Yankees (1942)**** Gary Cooper, Teresa Wright, Walter Brennan. The best baseball picture ever made. A touching, honest and interesting treatment of the life of one of baseball's greats—Lou Gehrig. Cooper is perfect as the Yankee first baseman and Teresa Wright gives a beautiful performance in the difficult role of the patient and loving wife.

569

Sam Wood directed with taste and skill. (127 mins.)

Priest Killer, The (1971)*½ George Kennedy, Raymond Burr, Don Galloway. Kennedy introduces his TV role of Sarge, the former cop-turned-priest, as he teams with Burr's Chief Ironside in this familiar hunt for a priest killer. Made-for-TV. (Dir: Richard Colla, 100 mins.)

Priest's Wife, The (Italian-French, 1970)** Marcello Mastroianni, Sophia Loren. Those stalwart Italian stars of many a tearjerker and comedy, Mastroianni and Miss Loren, team up once again for a piece of frothy nonsense about an earthy singer who falls in love with a man of the cloth. The plot fluctuates between outrageously staged scenes of blatant slapstick and melodrama. The stars have appeared to better advantage in other films. (Dir: Dino Risi, 106 mins.)

Primate (1974)*** Provocative, rewarding documentary by Frederick Wiseman but not for the squeamish. Shows in intimate closeup what will be, for some, the gruesome details of experiments being performed on animals, mostly monkeys, at the Yerkes Primate Research Center in Atlanta. One of the many questions raised by Wiseman in this probing documentary is what price progress, with regard to new scientific data and evidence that is relevant to the human condition? We see the primates copulating on cue, and being surgically operated on and dissected. Wiseman avoids the normal documentary pattern of offering the scientists involved the chance to explain in an interview what they are doing and why. For interested adults, not for children. (Dir: Frederick Wiseman, 105 mins.)

Prime Cut (1972)*½ Lee Marvin, Gene Hackman. Offensive gangland tale of Nick Devlin (Marvin) from Chicago, the old breed, trying to collect from "Mary Ann" (Hackman), the Kansas City Young Turk. Some gruesome scenes such as the opening where a dead man is meat-packed into a string of frankfurters, and the shoot-out in a field of sunflowers. Forget the dialogue. (Dir: Michael Ritchie, 91 mins.)

Prime of Miss Jean Brodie, The (British, 1969)**** Maggie Smith, Robert Stephens, Pamela Franklin, Celia Johnson. Don't miss Maggie

Smith's Academy Award-winning performance as the irrepressible, irresistible, melodramatic, and thoroughly mad teacher at an exclusive girls' school, circa late 1930's. Miss Smith's portrayal is one of those unique experiences in film which must be savored . . . she struts, poses, and mesmerizes you at every turn, as her wide-eyed charges (the "creme de la creme" as she labels them) raptly listen to her speak of her affairs, her misguided allegiances to Mussolini and Franco, and her dedication to love, art, and truth. The plot ends on an unhappy note, but Miss Brodie's contagious joie de vivre and final defeat, as interpreted by Miss Smith, remain long after the fade-out. (Dir: Ronald Neame, 116 mins.)

Prince and the Pauper (1937)***½ Errol Flynn, Claude Rains, Mauch Twins. Exciting, skillful adaptation of Mark Twain's story about a beggar who changes places with a prince. (Dir: William Keighley, 130 mins.)

Prince and the Showgirl, The (British, 1957)*** Marilyn Monroe, Laurence Olivier. Terence Rattigan's play about the affair of a nobleman and an American showgirl doesn't quite make it in its screen transition. But these two remarkable performers are still worth watching together. Olivier is deft in his haughty role. Miss Monroe manages to convey the flighty attitude of her character. (Dir: Laurence Olivier, 117 mins.)

Prince of Central Park, The, (1977) *** T. J. Hargrave, Ruth Gordon, Lisa Richard, Marc Vanhanian. A charming story, based loosely on the novel by Evan H. Rhodes, about a 12-year-old boy and his younger sister, who run away from their foster home and take refuge in a tree house in Central Park. The kids live hand-to-mouth until an old lady, who frequents the park each day, begins leaving them food and notes. Old lady wonderfully played by Ruth Gordon. T. J. Hargrave is so natural as the resourceful lad that he makes the fairy tale work. Made-for-TV. (Dir: Harvey Hart, 72 mins.)

Prince of Foxes (1949)** Tyrone Power, Orson Welles. Confused and ornate costume epic dealing with exploits of the Borgia regime. Even

Welles can't save this one. (Dir: Henry King, 107 mins.)

Prince of Pirates (1953)** John Derek, Barbara Rush. John Derek, Prince Roland of Hagen takes to the high seas of adventure to destroy the Spanish Armada. What's on the other channels? (Dir: Sidney Salkow, 80 mins.)

Prince of Players (1955)*** Richard Burton, Maggie McNamara, Raymond Massey. An excellent performance by Richard Burton in the role of famous Shakespearean actor Edwin Booth makes this uneven biography worthwhile. Within the framework of Booth's turbulent career and private life, Burton gets the chance to perform scenes from "Romeo & Juliet" with an assist by Eva Le Gallienne. (Dir: Philip Dunne, 102 mins.)

Prince Valiant (1954)**½ Robert Wagner, James Mason, Janet Leigh, Debra Paget. Colorful, elaborately mounted adventure tale about the dashing Viking Prince Valiant of cartoon fame. The youngsters will enjoy the spectacle and duels and there's enough plot to keep the adults interested, too. A good cast fit their roles nicely. (Dir: Henry Hathaway, 100 mins.)

Prince Who Was a Thief, The (1951)** Tony Curtis, Piper Laurie. Typical Hollywood film about the plush pageantry of the Arabian Nights and the colorful Princes and Paupers who lived on opposite sides of The Masques. (Dir: Rudolph Mate, 88 mins.)

Princess and the Pirate, The (1944)*** Bob Hope, Virginia Mayo, Walter Brennan. Typical Bob Hope film which should please his legions of fans. This time out, he's caught up in the sinister machinations of the scourge of the seas—buccaneers! Funny film. (Dir: David Butler, 94 mins.)

Princess Comes Across, The (1936)*** Carole Lombard, Fred MacMurray. Adventures of a bogus princess as she travels aboard a luxury liner and gets involved in some amusing incidents with a few zany characters. (Dir: William K. Howard, 76 mins.)

Princess O'Rourke (1943)***½ Robert Cummings, Olivia de Havilland, Jane Wyman. A pleasant, diverting comedy about a guy who discovers his fiancee is a queen. The Norman Krasna script is delightfully played

and a pleasure to watch. (Dir: Norman Krasna, 94 mins.)

Prisoner, The (British, 1955)**** Alec Guinness, Jack Hawkins. A cardinal is imprisoned and relentlessly questioned by the police of a communist state. An actor's show; and Guinness and Hawkins display superb performances in this gripping topical drama. (Dir: Peter Glenville, 91 mins.)

Prisoner of Shark Island, The (1936)*** Warner Baxter, Gloria Stuart. True story of the doctor who innocently set Booth's injured leg after the Lincoln assassination. The doctor was given a prejudiced trial and sent to Shark Island. Interesting film directed by John Ford. (95 mins.)

Prisoner of the Iron Mask (Italian, 1960)*½ Michel Lemoine, Wandisa Guida. Son of an Italian duke is imprisoned in an iron mask as the evil adviser plots to wed the duke's daughter, but an avenger puts a stop to all that. Tedious costume adventure, dubbed in English. (Dir: Francesco De Feo, 80 mins.)

Prisoner of the Jungle (French, 1958)*½ Georges Marchal, Francoise Rasquin. Five survivors of an airplane crash in the Congo try to reach civilization. Tedious jungle melodrama, dubbed-in-English.

Prisoner of the Volga (Italian, 1960)*½ John Derek, Elsa Martinelli, Dawn Addams. Cavalry officer is imprisoned by a corrupt general but escapes to right all wrongs. Lavish but theatrically ludicrous costume drama dubbed in English. (Dir: W. Tourjansky, 102 mins.)

Prisoner of War (1954)** Ronald Reagan, Steve Forrest. Volunteering to get information on how American prisoners are being treated, an undercover agent suffers in a Korean POW camp. Brutal, not too convincing war story. (Dir: Andrew Marton, 80 mins.)

Prisoner of Zenda, The (1937)***½ Ronald Colman, Madeleine Carroll, Douglas Fairbanks Jr., David Niven. The durable old melodrama of the king's double, who's called in to do an impersonation when the royal one is kidnapped. A swashbuckler to the core, done with great style, lavish production. Superior fun. (Dir: John Cromwell, 120 mins.)

Prisoner of Zenda, The (1952)**½ James Mason, Stewart Granger, Deborah Kerr. Technicolor remake of

571

the Ronald Colman starrer but not as good as the original. Action fans will enjoy the dueling sequences and there's romance for the ladies. (Dir: Richard Thorpe, 101 mins.)

Prisoners of the Casbah (1953)*½ Gloria Grahame, Cesar Romero. Ridiculous Arabian Nights tale about a "King of Thieves" and a princess hiding in the Casbah to escape the evil Grand Vizier. (Dir: Richard Bare, 78 mins.)

Private Affairs of Bel Ami, The (1947)**½ George Sanders, Angela Lansbury. An unscrupulous rake makes time with the women before his roguish ways finally do him in. Well acted but overlong drama. (Dir: Albert Lewin, 112 mins.)

Private Angelo (British, 1949)*** Peter Ustinov, Maria Denis. A cowardly private in the Italian army manages to pass himself off as a hero to his townspeople. Frequently delightful comedy, good fun.

Private Buckaroo (1942)*½ Andrews Sisters, Harry James, Joe E. Lewis. Bigtime band is drafted, and everyone gets together to put on a camp show. Wartime musical burdens the cast with terrible material; the music is the sole asset.

Private Hell 36 (1954)*** Ida Lupino, Howard Duff, Steve Cochran. Two detectives recover missing loot, turn greedy when they do. Suspenseful crime melodrama with some bright dialogue. (Dir: Don Siegel, 81 mins.)

Private Life of Don Juan, The (British, 1935)** The last film made by Douglas Fairbanks Sr., as he portrays the romantic rogue of legendary fame. Merle Oberon is featured. Slow, dull costume melodrama. (Dir: Alexander Korda, 100 mins.)

Private Life of Henry VIII (British, 1933)***½ Charles Laughton, Robert Donat, Merle Oberon. The hearty life and good times of England's colorful ruler. Fine robust historical pageant; excellent performances. (Dir: Alexander Korda, 97 mins.)

Private Lives of Adam and Eve, The (1960)* Mickey Rooney, Mamie Van Doren, Mel Torme. Silly, tasteless film combining dream sequences set in Eden and present day melodrama. The cast is a strange assortment of singers turned actors, actors turned comics and comics turned actors, etc. All the acting should have been kept private. (Dir: Albert Zugsmith, 87 mins.)

Private Lives of Elizabeth and Essex (1939)***½ Bette Davis, Errol Flynn. Good acting and writing combine to give this somewhat exaggerated story of an historical royal romance a true ring. (Dir: Michael Curtiz, 120 mins.)

Private Navy of Sergeant O'Farrell, The (1968)* Bob Hope bungling his way through World War II in the Pacific. Decades later, the idea doesn't seem so funny anymore, and the humor is old-fashioned. Phyllis Diller, Jeffrey Hunter, Gina Lollobrigida. (Dir: Frank Tashlin, 92 mins.)

Private Number (1936)**½ Robert Taylor, Loretta Young. Corny story of a secret marriage between a housemaid and her boss' son. O.K. for soap opera fans. (Dir: Roy Del Ruth, 80 mins.)

Private Parts (1972)*** Cheryl Stratton, Lucille Benson, Laurie Main. Teen-age girl runs away from home and goes to live with her neurotic aunt who runs a shabby hotel in a rundown part of Los Angeles. The lodgers are as gamey a bunch of perverts and nuts as you'll encounter in a dozen films. Made on a low budget as an independent feature by director Paul Bartel, there are some genuinely surprising twists and scares in this uneven, offbeat psychodrama. Some wild sexual hang-ups shown quickly for those of you who compile this kind of erotica. (87 mins.)

Private Property (1960)** Corey Allen, Warren Oates, Kate Manx. Two drifters step into the life of a beautiful, neglected housewife; slow-paced sex and seduction, which explodes in a violent finale. Despite the lurid story, Leslie Stevens' first film is occasionally interesting. (Dir: Leslie Stevens)

Private War of Major Benson, The (1955)*** Charlton Heston, Julie Adams, Tim Hovey, Sal Mineo. Hard-bitten army officer is forced to accept a transfer to a military school as commanding officer. Enjoyable if a big prolonged comedy is a welcome change of pace for Heston; good share of chuckles. (Dir: Jerry Hopper, 100 mins.)

Private Worlds (1935)**½ Claudette Colbert, Charles Boyer. Story of intrigue in a mental hospital is antiquated but might interest those who like modern psychiatric stories. Interesting for comparison. (Dir: Gregory La Cava, 90 mins.)

Private's Affair, A (1959)** Sal Mineo, Christine Carere, Barbara Eden, Gary Crosby. Four draftees and their girl friends are tapped for a big army show, but complications interfere. Threadbare comedy plot used as a showcase for some younger talent. Nothing much. (Dir: Raoul Walsh, 92 mins.)

Private's Progress (British, 1956)***½ Dennis Price, Ian Carmichael. An earnest but stumbling young man is called into the Army, where he makes a mess of things. Britain's answer to Private Hargrove is a rollicking comedy, often hilariously funny despite the thick dialect. (Dir: John Boulting, 99 mins.)

Prize, The (1963)**½ Paul Newman, Elke Sommer, Edward G. Robinson. Writer in Stockholm to accept the Nobel Prize becomes involved in a spy plot to kidnap a scientist. Overlong thriller tries for the Hitchcock touch, only occasionally succeeds. Some suspenseful moments, but the rest is padding. (Dir: Mark Robson, 136 mins.)

Prize of Arms, A (British, 1964)*** Stanley Baker, Tom Bell, Helmut Schmid. Another good example of the type of crime story the British do so well. A band of men attempt to rob an army payroll in a seemingly perfect crime that goes astray. Suspenseful, well acted. (Dir: Cliff Owen, 105 mins.)

Prize of Gold, A (1955)*** Richard Widmark, Mai Zetterling. An exciting drama set in occupied Berlin concerning a fabulous scheme to steal a shipment of gold bullion from the Berlin Air-Lift. Fine cast. Mai Zetterling is as talented as she is pretty. (Dir: Mark Robson, 98 mins.)

Prizefighter and the Lady (1933)**½ Max Baer, Myrna Loy, Jack Dempsey. This picture was made to cash in on Baer's popularity after he floored Max Schmeling. Surprise was that Baer could act and the film is reasonably entertaining. (Dir: W. S. Van Dyke, 110 mins.)

Probe (1971)*½ Hugh O'Brian, Elke Sommer, Burgess Meredith, Sir John Gielgud. Pilot for the defunct series has O'Brian playing a private eye backed by many modernistic devices. The gimmicks are novel, but they can't sustain a dismal plot.

Made-for-TV. (Dir: Russell Mayberry, 100 mins.)

Problem Girls (1953)*½ Susan Morrow, Helen Walker. Life in a reform school for rich girls. Cheap and tawdry film with obvious plot twists. Acting is stupid, and so are you if you can't find something better to do.

Prodigal, The (1955)*½ Lana Turner, Edmund Purdom. Draggy epic—it's 70 B.C. folks, and that wicked high priestess Lana is making it rough all over. If you must watch, concentrate on the elaborate scenery. (Dir: Richard Thorpe, 114 mins.)

Producers, The (1968)***½ Zero Mostel, Gene Wilder, Dick Shawn, Estelle Winwood. A preposterous, often wildly funny tale about an impoverished Broadway theater producer who stages a ghastly play in the hopes of making his fortune. Conceived, written and directed by Mel Brooks, an endearing, slightly mad comedy genius, this zany farce has moments of brilliance that are for some tastes—including mine—among the most hilarious scenes in recent years. There's a musical-comedy number called "Springtime for Hitler" to give you some idea of the spirit of this uneven, nutty outing, and there is a spate of supporting performances that are gems—Gene Wilder's flawless performance as Mostel's wily henchman earned him an Academy Award nomination. Dick Shawn playing Hitler is very funny too, once you accept the premise of this lunacy, which earned Brooks an Academy Award for his screenplay. (88 mins.)

Professional Soldier (1936)**½ Victor McLaglen, Freddie Bartholomew. The leads are delightful but the story isn't handled well. Tale of a retired colonel who is paid to kidnap the youthful king of a mythical European country had a lot of potential but it didn't come off. (Dir: Tay Garnett, 75 mins.)

Professionals, The (British, 1961)** William Lucas, Andrew Faulds. Safecracker is hired by a mob for a bank robbery. Passable low-budget crime melodrama.

Professionals, The (1966)**** Burt Lancaster, Lee Marvin, Claudia Cardinale, Jack Palance, Robert Ryan. Splendid, rip-snorting, old-fashioned adventure yarn, circa 1917, brilliantly brought to pulsating life by a cast of rugged leading men and sensuous

Claudia Cardinale. The plot has Ralph Bellamy hiring our he-men to fetch his allegedly kidnapped wife (Claudia) back from Mexico where she has been taken by bandito Jack Palance. The trail to and from Mexico is strewn with marvelously played sequences. Produced, written and directed by Richard Brooks, and he did a notable job in all three departments. (117 mins.)

Professor Beware (1938)**½ Harold Lloyd. It's all Mr. Lloyd and very little script in this silly comedy about a professor trying to unravel a 3,000-year-old love story who meets its modern counterpart. Plenty of typical Lloyd chase sequence. (Dir: Elliott Nugent, 100 mins.)

Project M-7 (British, 1953)*** Phyllis Calvert, James Donald. At a secret research station, an inventor is designing a plane that will fly at fantastic speeds. One of his colleagues is a spy. Interesting melodrama; good aerial scenes.

Project X (1968)* Christopher George, Greta Baldwin, Monte Markham, Henry Jones. In 2118, a secret agent tries to prevent world destruction. Involved sci-fi talks out most of the plot. (Dir: William Castle, 97 mins.)

Projectionist, The (1971)**** Chuck McCann, Ina Balin, Rodney Dangerfield. Wacky, appealing, low-budget winner written, directed, produced, and edited by Henry Hurwitz. Completed in 1968, this nutty farce will be especially appreciated by movie buffs. McCann plays Captain Flash, with impersonations along the way of Bogart, Beery, and Oliver Hardy. The projectionist works in a movie house and has difficulty separating the real world from the movie world. Some of the gags don't work, but Hurwitz has a high batting average and a lot of it is madcap movie farce, with novel editing effects. Fun for the whole family. (Dir: Henry Hurwitz, 88 mins.)

Promise Her Anything (British, 1966) **½ Warren Beatty, Lionel Stander, Robert Cummings, Hermione Gingold, Keenan Wynn, Leslie Caron. Pleasant romantic comedy set in New York's Greenwich Village, but shot in England. Beatty plays a destitute young filmmaker who sets out to woo and win a young widow (Caron). Beatty turns in a deft, charming performance, and Caron

574

always a delight. (Dir: Arthur Hiller, 98 mins.)

Promise Him Anything . . . (1975)* Frederic Forrest, Meg Foster, Eddie Albert, Tom Ewell. Inane story about computer-dating subject. The "twist" here is that the man sues the woman, in Small Claims Court yet, for breach of contract when she refuses to deliver the "anything goes" promised on her computer application card. Made-for-TV. (Dir: Edward Parone, 72 mins.)

Promised Land, The (Chilean, 1973) **½ Nelson Villagra, Marcelo Gaete, Rafael Benavente. Occasionally interesting political semidocumentary by the gifted Chilean filmmaker Miguel Littín. About the various ways in which the Chilean workers are degraded and kept in poverty. Some of the shooting began in rural Chile in 1972, but not finished as planned due to the overthrow of the Allende government. Written by Littín. English subtitles. (120 mins.)

Promised Lands (France, 1974)*** A complex, flawed, sometimes maddening, always stimulating docudrama about the cauldron of the Middle East and Israel after the 1973 Yom Kippur war. Conceived, written and directed by Susan Sontag, film utilizes newsreel footage, contemporary interviews, and "cinema-verite" footage to form this impressionistic collage of the embattled lands. Some cogent arguments advanced for the Israeli position by novelist-painter Yoram Kaniuk, and there's some lacerating footage of shell-shocked soldiers being forced to relive the horrors of battle as a therapeutic treatment. (Dir: Susan Sontag, 87 mins.)

Promoter, The (British, 1952)**** Alec Guinness, Valerie Hobson, Glynis Johns. Guinness romps his way through the tale of a lad from the slums who pushes his way to success. Witty, always intelligent, always entertaining. (Dir: Ronald Neame, 88 mins.)

Proud and the Beautiful (French, 1957)***½ Gerard Philippe, Michele Morgan. Her husband a victim of the plague in Mexico, a woman falls for and revitalizes a drunken doctor. Grim drama, well acted and directed. (Dir: Yves Allegret, 94 mins.)

Proud and the Profane, The (1956) *** William Holden, Deborah Kerr, Thelma Ritter. War and soap opera, but well mixed to form a reasonably entertaining film. It's the story of a war widow who meets and falls for a tough Marine colonel while serving in the Pacific during WW II. Good performances and superior treatment overcome the triteness of the yarn. (Dir: George Seaton, 111 mins.)

Proud Ones, The (1956)*** Robert Ryan, Virginia Mayo, Jeffrey Hunter. Good western bolstered by a better than average cast. The plot centers around a gun toting marshal and the men who tried to balk the law. (Dir: Robert D. Webb, 94 mins.)

Proud Rebel, The (1958)***½ Alan Ladd, Olivia de Havilland, David Ladd, Dean Jagger. Touching story of a Civil War veteran and his mute son who go to work for a farm woman as the father hopes to find a doctor who can cure the boy's affliction. Young David Ladd steals the show with a fine portrayal, while his father delivers one of his better performances. Superior family entertainment. (Dir: Michael Curtiz, 103 mins.)

Proud Stallion, The (Czech, 1964)**½ Jorga Kotrobova, Rudolph Pruncha. Girl attempts to save a beautiful wild stallion, marked for death. Pleasant English-dubbed outdoor story, especially for the kiddies.

Prowler, The (1951)***½ Van Heflin, Evelyn Keyes. Patrolman investigating a prowler falls for a disc jockey's wife, plans to do away with him. Strong, gripping melodrama, excellently acted. (Dir: Joseph Losey, 92 mins.)

Prudence and the Pill (1968)* David Niven, Deborah Kerr, Keith Mitchell. Sleazy, witless comedy about birth control which fizzles long before the fadeout. Even the attractive cast and seemingly adult theme can't sustain this shoddy affair about mistresses, girlfriends, and the pill. Director Fielder Cook understandably quit halfway through the filming. If you're prudent, avoid this pill (Dirs: Fielder Cook, Ronald Neame, 98 mins.)

Psych-Out (1968)*** Jack Nicholson, Susan Strasberg, Dean Stockwell. Above average drama about Haight-Ashbury hippie life (circa 1968) seen through the eyes of deaf Susan Strasberg, who arrives looking for her missing brother. Her adventures depict the world of the lost band experimenting with drugs and the supporting cast is pretty good all the way around. Flawed by a melodramatic ending.

Psyche 59 (1964)** Patricia Neal, Curt Jurgens, Samantha Eggar. Blind wife suspects there's something fishy between her husband and her sexy younger sister, and by golly, she's right. Lumbering drama seldom gets out of low gear. (Dir: Alexander Singer, 94 mins.)

Psychiatrist: God Bless the Children, The (1970)**½ Roy Thinnes, Pete Duel. Roy Thinnes stars as a psychiatrist who really cares about his patients. This made-for-TV movie belongs to Pete Duel, playing an uptight ex-junkie with a mad-on for the whole world. Duel's complex character is interesting, and his performance is effective. Duel and Thinnes, patient and doctor, respectively, join forces to combat the growing drug abuse in a small California community. One scene in which Duel confronts the leader of the kids (well played by John Rubinstein) and gets verbally shot down is the film's best. (Dir: Steven Spielberg, 100 mins.)

Psycho (1960)*** Anthony Perkins, Janet Leigh, Vera Miles, Martin Balsam. When a girl absconds with bank money, a nightmare of horror follows in this gruesome Alfred Hitchcock thriller. It's expertly done but may repel some viewers with its bloody violence. (Dir: Alfred Hitchcock, 109 mins.)

Psychomania (1963)*½ Lee Philips, Sheppard Strudwick. Contrived murder-mystery that tries to be arty and commercial at the same time and achieves neither one. Lee Philips is quite good as an artist with a problem. (Dir: Richard Hilliard, 90 mins.)

Psychopath, The (British, 1966)** Patrick Wymark, Margaret Johnston. Serves up all the expected bloody ingredients to satisfy chiller fans. Competent British cast goes through the paces in this tale about multiple murder and a strange German household. Written by Robert Bloch, who wrote the novel "Psycho," but it's not as good and director Freddie Francis isn't Alfred Hitchcock. (83 mins.)

PT 109 (1963)**½ Cliff Robertson, Ty Hardin, Robert Culp. The story of John F. Kennedy, naval hero of World War II, and his exploits in the Pacific. Minus the subject of the narrative, this would be a routine war story—as it is, it's still routine but with the added interest of the late President's name. Robertson does well in the role. (Dir: Leslie Martinson, 140 mins.)

Public Affair, A (1962)*** Myron McCormick, Edward Binns. Don't overlook this little story of a State Senator battling, with legal means, a crime syndicate. Rather strait-laced and leisurely, with the low budget showing through, but done with a sincerity that deserves commendation.

Public Enemy (1931)*** James Cagney, Jean Harlow. Another gangster film, so popular in the early 30's, but Cagney's acting lifts it from the commonplace. Today's audiences will probably get more laughs out of this than dramatic impact. (Dir: William A. Wellman, 90 mins.)

Public Eye, The (British, 1972) *½ Mia Farrow, Topol, Michael Jayston. Thinly plotted, poorly acted yarn about a stuffy English aristocrat (Jayston) who hires a Greek private detective (Topol) to see if his wife (Farrow) is having an affair. She isn't but Topol falls in love with her, and the rest is movie cliche. (Dir: Carol Reed, 95 mins.)

Public Hero No. 1 (1935)*** Lionel Barrymore, Jean Arthur, Chester Morris. Exciting, occasionally amusing drama of the destruction of a gang of outlaws by the then movie favorites, the G-Men. Best part of the picture is Joseph Calleia as the gangster. (Dir: J. Walter Rubin, 90 mins.)

Public Pigeon No. 1 (1956)** Red Skelton, Vivian Blaine, Janet Blair. Lunchroom counter man is taken in by a gang of crooks, but he turns the tables on them. Mild little comedy based on a TV show Skelton did; below average. (Dir: Norman Z. McLeod, 79 mins.)

Pueblo (1973)***½ Hal Holbrook. Absorbing dramatization of the seizure in 1968 by the North Koreans of the U.S.S. Pueblo, an American naval vessel equipped with sophisticated electronic devices used in spying missions. It re-enacts scenes from the court's questioning of Pueblo-commander Lloyd Bucher, intercut with the action of the seizure of the ship and the crew's subsequent torture in a North Korean camp, as well as the fact-finding sessions of a Congressional inquiry into the Pueblo incident. Hal Holbrook as Commander Bucher creates a whole human being out of his character, and his performance serves as the core of this literate drama. Made-for-TV. (Dir: Anthony Page, 108 mins.)

Pulp (British, 1972)**½ Michael Caine, Mickey Rooney, Lionel Stander. Occasionally amusing satire of the crime genre, with Caine as a writer of cheap detective thrillers caught up in the reality of one of his fantasies. Rooney is delightful as an over-the-hill gangster who hires Caine to ghostwrite a biography. (Dir: Mike Hodges, 95 mins.)

Pumping Iron (1977)**** Arnold Schwarzenegger, Louis Ferrigno, Mike Katz, Franco Colombu. A fascinating, surprisingly engaging documentary about world-champion body-builders. One of the many strengths of "Pumping Iron" is that the directors, George Butler and Robert Fiore, have avoided the considerable temptation of making body-building and those dedicated to it seem altogether grotesque. The world champion, Arnold Schwarzenegger turns out to have not only a miraculous body but a charming, sardonic sense of humor. Graphically shows the demanding, tortuous, constant weight-lifting regimen required of world champions in this sport. A mesmerizing film with moments of considerable beauty. Based on the book of the same name. (Dirs: George Butler and Robert Fiore, 85 mins.)

Pumpkin Eater, The (British, 1964) ***½ Anne Bancroft, Peter Finch, James Mason. Absorbing, brilliantly acted story of a woman's personal insecurity and her crumbling marriage. Leads to a breakdown and finally, a glimmer of understanding. Famed playwright Harold Pinter has written a stinging, perceptive screenplay based on the novel by Penelope Mortimer. Pinter has made Miss Bancroft's "Jo" a tremendously complex character, and Bancroft contributes a performance of truly dazzling range and power. Peter Finch's portrayal of her errant husband is equally impressive in a less volatile fashion, and there's a devastating scene in a beauty parlor with an actress named Yootha Joyce. This has all the ingredients of a Hollywood soap opera. But thanks to the talented artists involved, including director Jack Clayton, "The Pumpkin Eater" is a lacerating, often profoundly moving study of a sick, troubled soul. (110 mins.)

Punch and Judy (1974)** Glenn Ford, Ruth Roman, Pam Griffin. Sentiment is piled on with a trowel. Glenn Ford is a self-made, small-time circus boss who is suddenly made the guardian of a teenaged daughter he didn't know existed. Made-for-TV. (Dir: Barry Shear, 72 mins.)

Punishment Battalion (German, 1964) **½ Werner Peters, Georg Thomas. Doctor is banished to a battalion comprised of officers fallen from favor, experiences bloody battles at the Russian border. Grim World War II drama has some effective scenes, ably produced. Dubbed in English.

Punishment Park (1971)**½ Jim Bohan, Van Daniels, Harlan Greene. A maddeningly uneven, prescient drama about dissidents and the American political landscape in 1971, the middle of the Nixon years. Lensed by an angry, talented British filmmaker, Peter Watkins, who misunderstands a great deal about democracy and the political passions of American youth when confronted with a Neo-fascist government. Some of "Punishment Park" is simple-minded drivel, parts are chilling indeed, but Watkins' bitter vision is not so far-fetched in the post-Watergate era. Written and directed by Peter Watkins. (88 mins.)

Puppet on a Chain (British, 1970)** Sven-Bertil Taube, Barbara Parkins, Alexander Knox. Routine international smuggling entry, with Swedish actor Taube playing an American narcotics agent tracking down his prey in Amsterdam. Aided by exciting speedboat chase through the canals of glorious Amsterdam, which ends with a larcenous, murderous priest crashing into an impenetrable stone wall. Many shots of beautiful Amsterdam throughout this meller. (Dir: Geoffrey Reeve, 97 mins.)

Pure Hell of St. Trinian's, The (British, 1961)**½ Joyce Grenfell, Cecil Parker, George Cole. Girls' school full of mischievous lovelies receives a visit from an Eastern potentate with an eye out for harem wives. Free-wheeling nonsensical farce in this series churns up some laughs through its sheer wildness. (Dir: Frank Launder, 94 mins.)

Purple Gang, The (1959)** Barry Sullivan, Robert Blake. Average cops and gangsters yarn. Barry Sullivan represents the law and a group, known as the Purples, make his job a tough one. Robert Blake is very effective as a young hood with a taste for killing. (Dir: Frank McDonald, 85 mins.)

Purple Heart (1944)*** Dana Andrews, Richard Conte. Powerful, brutal story of the trial of the crew of a flying fortress shot down by the Japs during the Tokyo raid. (Dir: Lewis Milestone, 99 mins.)

Purple Hills, The (1961)** Gene Nelson, Kent Taylor, Joanna Barnes. Arizona cowboy kills an outlaw, but a gambler also puts in a claim for the reward; both are menaced by Indians friendly to the outlaw. Minor western just about gets by. (Dir: Maury Dexter, 60 mins.)

Purple Mask, The (1955)**½ Tony Curtis, Coleen Miller, Gene Barry. Tony Curtis is cast in an Errol Flynn-type role as a Count who puts on "the Purple Mask" and performs acts of derring-do which have Napoleon baffled. High adventure with some fun. (Dir: H. Bruce Humberstone, 82 mins.)

Purple Noon (French, 1963)***½ Alain Delon, Maurice Ronet, Marie Laforet. Director Rene Clement has fashioned a tightly paced mystery with an excellent performance by Alain Delon as a fun-loving loafer who gets into an almost unbelievable situation involving forgery, murder and impersonations. (Dir: René Clement, 115 mins.)

Purple Plain (1955)*** Gregory Peck. A flier crashes in the jungle, fights his way back to civilization. Good suspense story, a bit overlong, but well-acted by hero Peck. (Dir: Robert Parrish, 100 mins.)

Pursued (1947)*** Robert Mitchum, Teresa Wright. Spanish-American war vet seeks the man who killed his father years ago in a family feud. Offbeat western has a different story, good performances. (Dir: Raoul Walsh, 101 mins.)

Pursuers, The (British, 1961)*½ Cyril Sharpe, Francis Matthews.

Manhunt is on for a foreign agent. Below par melodramatics. (Dir: Godfrey Grayson, 63 mins.)

Pursuit (1972)*** Ben Gazzara, E. G. Marshall. Suspenseful thriller based on a novel by Michael Crichton (under the pen name of John Lange). Crichton also makes his directorial debut with this TV feature film, and he gets tension out of his tale. About a wealthy leader of an extremist group who plans to destroy a large number of people in a major city (San Diego) via lethal nerve gas. There's a revealing scene in which Gazzara has lunch with his psychiatrist, and the climax of the yarn will have your palms sweating. (Dir: Michael Crichton, 73 mins.)

Pursuit Across the Desert (Spanish, 1961)*½ Pedro Armendariz, Tere Velasquez. Man bent on revenge goes after his enemies. Mediocre English-dubbed adventure drama.

Pursuit of Happiness, The (1971) **½ Michael Sarrazin, Barbara Hershey, Arthur Hill, E. G. Marshall, Ruth White. Decent tale of a young man who accidentally runs over a jaywalker and, because of his rebellious attitude, faces long imprisonment. Sympathetic attempt to explain why a youth, with so many advantages, goes wrong. White's last film. (Dir: Robert Mulligan, 93 mins.)

Pursuit of the Graf Spee (British, 1956)*** John Gregson, Anthony Quayle, Peter Finch. True story of the German ship, and its scuttling off South America. Excellently produced war tale, good factual material. (Dirs: Michael Powell, Emeric Pressburger, 106 mins.)

Pushover (1954)***½ Kim Novak, Fred MacMurray, Dorothy Malone. Pretty good drama about a cop who is seduced into neglecting his duty by a blonde man-trap (Kim Novak). Kim Novak registered in this, her first major film assignment. Her lousy performances come later when she's richer and more famous. (Dir: Richard Quine, 88 mins.)

Putney Swope (1969)***½ Arnold Johnson, Laura Greene, Erik Krupnik, Allen Garfield, Alan Abel, Allan Arbus, Shelley Plimpton. An irreverent, manic, sometimes hysterically funny satire of various American sacred cows. Some wild put-downs and take-offs of TV commercials, scattered throughout this genuinely hip fable about the rise of a black, Madison Ave. advertising agency called Truth and Soul. Not for every taste, but this remains one of the most daring American comedies of the period. Credit due to the writer-director, Robert Downey, who was a ripe old 32 when he helmed "Putney." (84 mins.)

Puzzle of a Downfall Child (1971)* Faye Dunaway, Harry Primus, Viveca Lindfors, Barry Morse, Roy Scheider. Dreary soap opera. Former fashion model played by Faye Dunaway has retired to a secluded beach house to write the memoirs of her emotional breakdown. Fashion photographer Jerry Schatzberg has given a static, one-dimensional feeling to the heroine's inevitable defeat. Dunaway gives one of her few bad performances, but you can't really blame her. Scripter Adrian, "Five Easy Pieces," has done better. (Dir: Jerry Schatzberg, 104 mins.)

Pygmalion (British, 1938)**** Leslie Howard, Wendy Hiller. Bernard Shaw's sparkling comedy of a professor who picks up a guttersnipe and makes a lady of her. Witty, superbly acted, grand fun. In case you've been on Mars for 20 years, "My Fair Lady" was based on this lovely play. The original is great too, even without any songs! (Dirs: Anthony Asquith, Leslie Howard, 90 mins.)

Pyro (1963)** Barry Sullivan, Martha Hyer. Badly burned engineer vows vengeance upon the woman who jealously started the blaze in which his family perished. Grim melodrama made in Spain moves leisurely but does a fair job of keeping the attention. (Dir: Julio Coll, 99 mins.)

Q Planes (British, 1939)***½ Laurence Olivier, Ralph Richardson, Valerie Hobson. Spies are lurking around Britain's aircraft, but they are foiled by a young test pilot and a crafty Scotland Yard man. Good pre-war thriller, with Richardson's policeman's role being delightfully acted. (Dir: Tim Whelan, 78 mins.)

QB VII (Part I) (1974)*** Ben Gazzara, Anthony Hopkins, Leslie Caron, Lee Remick. Leon Uris' best seller becomes one of the most ambitious films ever produced for TV; it's nearly six hours long. Filmed on location in Israel, England, Belgium, and the U.S.A., it tells the story of a knighted Polish expatriate, Dr. Adam Kelno, living in England, and the libel suit he initiated against an American writer for accusing the doctor in his book of performing criminal medical practices in a concentration camp during WW II. In part I, Dr. Kelno's life from the close of the war to the present unfolds in fascinating flashbacks, centering particularly on the years he spent in Kuwait administering medical aid to the Arabs. Hopkins is absolutely superb as Kelno, and it is his portrayal of a difficult role which commands your attention. (Dir: Tom Gries.)

QB VII (Part II) (1974)*** Although the second half bogs down a little, concentrating on the post-WW II life of the author Abe Cady (Ben Gazzara), it leads to his father's death in the Holy Land, and triggers his interest in the struggle of the Jewish people and the writing of his major novel. The novel, of course, is the impetus for Dr. Kelno's libel suit, and the ensuing courtroom scenes pick up the pace considerably. Anthony Hopkins' final scenes in court, with Anthony Quayle matching him as Cady's lawyer, are shattering as the accuser turns accused.

Quality Street (1937)*** Katharine Hepburn, Franchot Tone. Girl assumes a dual identity to embarrass a suitor. Amusing, well acted costume comedy-drama. (Dir: George Stevens, 90 mins.)

Quantez (1957)**** Fred MacMurray, Dorothy Malone, Sydney Chaplin, John Gavin. Four men and a woman escape a posse after a bank robbery, hole up in a deserted Mexican town, where their emotions get the better of them. Western depends too much on conversation, slows down the pace. (Dir: Harry Keller, 80 mins.)

Quarantined (1970)½** John Dehner, Gary Collins, Sharon Farrell. Made-for-TV feature which also served as a pilot for a proposed medical series. John Dehner is the head of a family of doctors (three sons and a psychiatrist daughter-in-law) who run a modern clinic atop a hill near the sea. Just for the record, during the course of the film, there's a threat-

ened cholera epidemic. (Dir: Leo Penn, 73 mins.)

Quare Fellow, The (Great Britain-Ireland, 1962)**** Patrick McGoohan, Sylvia Syms, Walter Macken. A biting, intense prison drama, also packed with the Irish humor which characterized Brendan Behan's original play. Eloquent argument against capital punishment, on emotional rather than intellectual terms. Well acted. "Quare fellow" is Irish jargon for a condemned man. Written and directed by Arthur Dreifuss. (85 mins.)

Quartet (British, 1948)***** Mai Zetterling, Cecil Parker, George Cole. Somerset Maugham introduces four of his short stories, ranging from comic to dramatic. All tastefully done, something for every taste. (Dir: Ken Annakin, 120 mins.)

Quebec (1951)**** Corinne Calvet, Patric Knowles, John Barrymore Jr., Barbara Rush. When the Canadians rebel against England, fighting for freedom is the wife of the British forces' commander. Corny tale partially atoned for by spectacular battle scenes, plenty of action. (Dir: George Templeton, 85 mins.)

Queen, The (1968)***** Harlow, Jack Doroshow, Andy Warhol, Terry Southern. Not many TV station managers will have the courage to telecast "The Queen," but some might, somewhere—simply because it is a remarkable and tasteful documentary about one aspect of the subculture of American male homosexuals. "The Queen" refers to the winner of a beauty pageant quite unlike anything you've ever seen on TV before on all the other "beauty pageants." This is for the "drag" Queen, the loveliest transvestite of them all! But the beauty of this prize winner, directed by Frank Simon, is that it does not mock the hapless souls involved in the proceedings, or treat this beauty contest as a freak show.

Queen Bee (1955)**** Joan Crawford, Barry Sullivan, Betsy Palmer. Typical women's picture with the stress on melodrama. Joan Crawford plays a Southern socialite whose determination to dominate and rule everyone around her leads to destruction. TV star Betsy Palmer turns in a good job. (Dir: Ranald MacDougall, 95 mins.)

Queen Christina (1933)*½** Greta Garbo, John Gilbert. Garbo is at her best in this portrait of the inner conflicts of a Swedish queen of the 17th Century. It is a romantic story, beautifully told. (Dir: Rouben Mamoulian, 110 mins.)

Queen for a Day (1951)*** Phyllis Avery, Adam Williams, Edith Meiser. Stories of the contestants of the radio show are presented, some comic, some dramatic. Generally well-done episodic film.

Queen for Caesar, A (French, 1962)**½ Pascale Petit, Gordon Scott, Akim Tamiroff. Another Cleopatra tale as the beauteous princess challenges her brother for the throne. The alluring Miss Petit and some good production values rate this historical drama slightly better than the usual. Dubbed in English.

Queen of Babylon, The (Italian, 1956)* Rhonda Fleming, Ricardo Montalban. Beautiful girl saves a wounded leader, helps him lead a revolt against a wicked king. Lavish example of dreadful moviemaking on the spectacular plane, hilariously dubbed in inept English dialogue. (Dir: Carlo Bragaglia, 98 mins.)

Queen of Sheba, The (Italian, 1953)*½ Gino Cervi, Leonora Ruffo. Son of Solomon journeys to Sheba. Lots of crowds in costume, not much in the way of acting or script.

Queen of Spades (British, 1949)*** Anton Walbrook, Dame Edith Evans. Army captain learns the art of gambling at the expense of his soul. Fascinating version of Pushkin's famous tale. Some fine moments.

Queen of the Nile (Italian, 1962)** Jeanne Crain, Edmund Purdom, Vincent Price. Nefertiti's daughter is loved by a young sculptor who escapes execution and fights for her. Dubbed-English costume drama is a bit more logical than most. (Dir: Fernando Cerchio, 85 mins.)

Queen of the Seas (Italian, 1960)*½ Lisa Gastoni, Jerome Courtland. Beautiful girl poses as a man, takes over a pirate ship, is aided by a young nobleman. Hokey swashbuckler dubbed in English.

Queen of the Stardust Ballroom (1975)***½ Maureen Stapleton, Charles Durning, Michael Brandon, Michael Strong. Maureen Stapleton's lovely widow with grownup kids, meeting and falling in love with Charles Durning's shy, beer-barrel postman, evokes moments of warmth and sympathy. The over-

the-hill couple have much to offer, and their moments together, dancing old 30's steps in a ballroom jammed with lively, wrinkled peers, simply lift one's spirits. Early scenes miss the beat, particularly the use of a song sung by Stapleton, but the bravura performances overshadow any flaws. Made-for-TV. (Dir: Sam O'Steen, 100 mins.)

Queen's Guards, The (British, 1955) ** Raymond Massey, Robert Stephens. Story of the training and hard work that go into the making of an honored group of soldiers. Meticulous detail concerning aspects of soldier life slows up the pace too much. (Dir: Michael Powell, 110 mins.)

Quentin Durward (British, 1955)*** Robert Taylor, Kay Kendall, Robert Morley. If you're a devotee of costume spectacles, this is better than most. We have the requisite brave adventurer (Taylor) protecting the fair maiden (Kendall—and very fair she is too) from political intrigue. Exciting action scenes. With Alec Clunes.

Quest (1976)**½ Tim Matheson, Kurt Russell, Brian Keith, Keenan Wynn. Surprise—an enjoyable western TV-series pilot with a feeling for those rowdy, free-wheeling frontier times. Tracy Keenan Wynn, a careful writer, takes a shot at authenticity in this leisurely tale of brothers separated after an Indian raid—one a city boy training to be a doctor, and the other raised by Indians. As played by Matheson and Russell, the brothers are overshadowed by Brian Keith's Tank Logan, journeyman of the West—cattle thief, gunslinger, con artist, lover of language. Made-for-TV. (Dir: Lee H. Katzin, 98 mins.)

Questor Tapes, The (1974)*** Robert Foxworth, Mike Farrell, Lew Ayres, John Vernon. Well made science-fiction entry. Foxworth plays a very convincing android (computerized robot with human characteristics) who sets out on a mission to find his scientist-creator that takes him from California to London to Mount Ararat in Turkey. His exploits are never dull, and the fact that the leading character is a man-made machine with superior intelligence and highly sophisticated functioning parts paves the way for endless adventures. Made-for-TV. (Dir: Richard A. Colla.)

Quick and the Dead, The (1964)**
Larry Mann, Sandy Donigan. American patrol is captured but manages to escape. WW II drama made on an infinitesimal budget shows value for the dollar, but it's still just another war picture.

Quick, Before It Melts (1965)**
Robert Morse, George Maharis, Anjanette Comer. A silly comedy which doesn't come to life, despite some energetic playing by Robert Morse and Michael Constantine in a supporting role as a Russian. Morse and Maharis are a writer and photographer, respectively, who invade a military installation, Little America, and almost cause an international scandal. (Dir: Delbert Mann, 98 mins.)

Quick Gun, The (1964)*
Audie Murphy, Merry Anders, James Best. Minor Murphy Western. Hero redeems himself after he fights a gang of outlaws, saves a town from being overrun by the crooks. (Dir: Sidney Salkow, 87 mins.)

Quicksand (1950)**½
Mickey Rooney, Jean Cagney, Peter Lorre. A young man "borrows" twenty bucks from a cash register, intending to pay it back, but circumstances pile up to the point where his life is at stake. Neat little melodrama has suspense, a subdued Rooney. (Dir: Irving Pichel, 79 mins.)

Quiet American, The (1958)***
Audie Murphy, Michael Redgrave, Claude Dauphin, Giorgia Moll. Graham Greene's angry novel comes to the screen a bit watered down in its approach towards Americans. Audie Murphy is miscast as the hero but a good supporting cast makes up for it. (Dir: Joseph L. Mankiewicz, 120 mins.)

Quiet Man (1952)****
John Wayne, Maureen O'Hara, Barry Fitzgerald, Ward Bond. Boxer returns to his native Ireland to fall for a fiery colleen. Grand Eire idyll by John Ford has plenty of entertainment for everyone. (129 mins.)

Quiet Wedding (British, 1941)**
Margaret Lockwood, Derek Farr. Zany British comedy about a wedding that turns into a fracas. Some lively fun despite the excess talk.

Quiet Woman, The (British, 1949)***
Derek Bond, Jane Hylton. The owner of a seaside pub has her secret revealed when her jailbird husband returns. Good melodrama.

Quiller Memorandum, The (1966)**½
George Segal, Alec Guinness, Max von Sydow, Senta Berger. This uneven spy-drama will appeal to fans of espionage yarns who don't look to be surprised, just entertained. Segal is an American agent in Berlin looking for the head of a neo-Nazi party that is gaining momentum in present-day Germany. There is the usual quota of heavies plus the expected beautiful girl who tangles with our agent. Screenplay by Harold Pinter based on the novel "The Berlin Memorandum." (Dir: Michael Anderson, 105 mins.)

Quincannon, Frontier Scout (1956)**
Tony Martin, Peggie Castle, John Bromfield. Tony Martin as a cowboy. He seems very uncomfortable not being in a tux in front of a nightclub audience singing Neapolitan songs. Some lively action in this Grade "B" western. (Dir: Lesley Selander, 83 mins.)

Quo Vadis (1951)***½
Robert Taylor, Deborah Kerr, Leo Genn, Peter Ustinov. A really big one—the Christians are persecuted, Rome burns, Robert Taylor loves Deborah Kerr, and just about everything else happens in this splashy spectacle. Some weak moments, notably in the script, but some fine ones too, notably from Peter Ustinov. Lavishness throughout. (Dir: Mervyn Le Roy, 171 mins.)

Ra Expeditions, The (1974)***½
Engrossing documentary record of anthropologist Thor Heyerdahl's two ocean voyages aboard a small papyrus boat. Because he was fascinated by the similarity between Egyptian and Latin American pyramids, Heyerdahl set out to prove that pre-Columbian people were capable of crossing the Atlantic. So he sailed with a small crew of experts in a paper boat, identical to those of ancient times. The crew contends with the perils of the high seas—hurricanes, sharks, sickness and mechanical failures. Narrated by Roscoe Lee Browne with comments from Heyerdahl. (Dir: Lennart Ehrenborg, 93 mins.)

Rabbit, Run (1970)**½
James Caan, Carrie Snodgrass, Anjanette Comer. John Updike's grim best-selling novel

581

receives a less-than-successful screen treatment. The action reveals a desperately incompatible couple whose marriage in Reading, Pa., began to disintegrate the moment the ceremony was over. Caan and Snodgrass try to breathe life into their complex characters, but it doesn't work. Comer, as the other woman in Caan's life, has a better-written role and she comes off fairly well. Director Jack Smight tried to have his name removed from the credits, claiming the film had been butchered in the final editing. (94 mins.)

Rabbit Trap, The (1959)** Ernest Borgnine, Bethel Leslie, David Brian. Draftsman dominated by his job and boss is called back from a vacation, which proves to change his life. Based on a TV play, this sluggish little drama hoped to be another "Marty" but missed the mark. Mild, at best. (Dir: Philip Leacock, 72 mins.)

Race With the Devil (1975)*½ Peter Fonda, Loretta Swit, Warren Oates. Absurd, creepy yarn about two vacationing couples who encounter a cult of Satan worshippers engaging in a ritualistic sacrifice and have to flee for their lives. Flee! (Dir: Jack Starrett, 89 mins.)

Racers, The (1955)** Kirk Douglas, Gilbert Roland, Bella Darvi. The only redeeming feature of this film is the sports car racing sequences and they have a limited appeal to fans. The drama is contrived and woven out of the conflicts, both professional and personal, among the breed who thrive in the European sports car racing world. (Dir: Henry Hathaway, 112 mins.)

Rachel and the Stranger (1948)*** Loretta Young, William Holden, Robert Mitchum. Frontier wanderer stops at the cabin of a backwoodsman and wife and settles their problems. Entertaining frontier comedy-drama. (Dir: Norman Foster, 93 mins.)

Rachel, Rachel (1968)**** Joanne Woodward, James Olson, Estelle Parsons, Geraldine Fitzgerald. A beautiful, deeply moving story of a young spinster, thanks largely to a superb screenplay by Stewart Stern and contributions from various members of the Newman family, including producer-director Paul. The most thoughtful motion picture awards, those of the New York Film Critics Circle, were bestowed upon Newman for a truly remarkable directorial debut, and to wife Joanne for her restrained, poignant portrayal of the lonely, sexually inhibited mid-thirties schoolteacher living in a small town in Connecticut. (The Newmans' daughter lends a hand by acting Rachel as a child in the various flash-back sequences.) Plaudits also to editor Dede Allen, and the supporting performance of Estelle Parsons as Rachel's equally frustrated fellow-schoolmarm. Talented theater and opera director Frank Corsaro plays the town undertaker. One of the loveliest American films in years. (Dir: Paul Newman, 101 mins.)

Racing Blood (1954)** Bill Williams, Jean Porter, Jimmy Boyd. Colt born with a split hoof is supposed to be destroyed, but a stable boy and his uncle make him a winner. Usual turf story, pleasant in a familiar sort of way. If you have a split hoof in the family, take heart.

Racing Fever (1964)* Joe Morrison, Barbara Biggart. Poorly made melodrama combining teenagers, speedboat racing, and amorous activities among the jet set. Florida backgrounds attractive, nothing else. (Dir: William Grefe, 80 mins.)

Rack, The (1956)*** Paul Newman, Wendell Corey, Edmond O'Brien, Anne Francis. A war hero returns from a Korean prison camp and faces trial for treason. Well-acted courtroom drama grips the attention throughout. (Dir: Arnold Laven, 100 mins.)

Racket, The (1951)*** Robert Mitchum, Lizabeth Scott, Robert Ryan. Police captain opposes a big racketeer who stops at nothing. Nicely produced, exciting crime melodrama. (Dir: John Cromwell, 88 mins.)

Racket Man (1944)**½ Tom Neal, Larry Parks, Hugh Beaumont. Racketeer reformed by the Army becomes an undercover agent after black marketeers. Lively, well done action melodrama.

Rafferty and the Gold Dust Twins— See: **Rafferty and the Highway Hustlers**

Rafferty and the Highway Hustlers (1975)**½ Sally Kellerman, Mackenzie Phillips, Alan Arkin. Released as "Rafferty and the Gold Dust Twins," but given a more provocative title for TV. Familiar tale about a couple of footloose and fancy-free (and larcenous) females who get men to give them rides at gunpoint. The pair is made up of Sally Kellerman, who wants to be a singer, and Mackenzie Phillips, as a teenage runaway. Their victim is Alan Arkin, playing a not-too-bright driving-test inspector. Their escapades en route from Los Angeles to Arizona provide some laughs but the whole thing soon fizzles out. Screenplay by John Kaye has some nice moments. (Dir: Dick Richards, 91 mins.)

Raffles (1939)** Olivia de Havilland, David Niven. Weakly done film about the adventures of an amateur cracksman thief. Primarily a straight drama with obtrusive comedy overtones creeping in every now and then. (Dir: Sam Wood, 72 mins.)

Rage (1966)* Glenn Ford, Stella Stevens. Outrageous melodrama with heavy breathing substituting for acting. Glenn Ford plays a disillusioned doctor in a Mexican village who gets a second lease on life with the help of world-weary Stella Stevens. Except for the principals, the entire cast is Mexican, which adds to the authenticity of the absurd tale.

Rage (1972)*½ George C. Scott, Stella Stevens, Richard Basehart. Army helicopter accidentally sprays a rancher and his son with poison gas. His son dies and we find the father will die also. The picture's finale has the rancher blowing up a nerve-gas factory. Scott plays the rancher; this marked his directorial debut. (105 mins.)

Rage In Heaven (1940)** Robert Montgomery, Ingrid Bergman, George Sanders. Good performers suffer along with the audience in this dated, confused and pointless study of a paranoic. (Dir: W. S. Van Dyke, 83 mins.)

Rage of Paris, The (1938)**½ Danielle Darrieux, Douglas Fairbanks, Jr. Frothy comedy about a Parisian girl who sensibly campaigns vigorously to snare a wealthy husband but succumbs to true love. Dated but well played. (Dir: Henry Koster, 90 mins.)

Rage of the Buccaneers—See: **Black Pirate, The** (Ricardo Montalban)

Rage to Live, A (1965)*½ Suzanne Pleshette, Bradford Dillman, Ben Gazzara, Bethel Leslie. John O'Hara's novel of the life and loves of a near-nymphomaniac (Pleshette), flattened and vulgarized by Hollywood hacks. Good performances help a little. (Dir: Walter Grauman, 101 mins.)

Raggedy Ann and Andy (1977)*** Claire Williams. This full-length animated version of the classic children's book by Johnny Gruelle published more than half a century ago contains some superb animated sequences, in this musical adaptation supervised and directed by English animation wizard Richard Williams. The screenwriters—Patricia Thackray and author-TV comedy writer Max Wilk—have fashioned a plot of sorts: Babette the French doll is captured by pirates and Raggedy Ann and Andy set out to rescue her. The lacklustre musical score is by Joe Raposo. Do you, or your children, pine for a new old-time Disney animated flick? Well, tune in "Raggedy." (Dir: Richard Williams, 84 mins.)

Raging Tide, The (1952)** Richard Conte, Shelley Winters, Stephen McNally. Predictable crime melodrama which talks itself to death. Conte plays a murderer on the run who learns too late the value of honesty. Miss Winters drifts in and out of the film as Conte's moll. (Dir: George Sherman, 93 mins.)

Raid, The (1954)**½ Van Heflin, Anne Bancroft, Richard Boone. Interesting and well made western set after the Civil War. A small group of Confederate soldiers escape from a Union prison and plan the burning and sacking of a small Vermont town as partial payment for the destruction of Atlanta. Heflin is very good as the leader of the prisoners. (Dir: Hugo Fregonese, 83 mins.)

Raid on Entebbe (1976)***½ Peter Finch, Martin Balsam, Horst Bucholz, Jack Warden, Yaphet Kotto, Charles Bronson. Made as a hurried made-for-TV special in the race to be the first drama on the American TV screens to dramatize the heroic rescue at Entebbe by Israeli commandos. Considering the pressure under which this film was written, cast and produced, it emerges as the best of the initial batch, and is a quite accurate and dramatic recounting of the main events of this legendary raid. Starts with the capture of the plane by four terrorists on Sunday, June 27, 1976, and follows the main story through to the rescue one week later. Acting quite good throughout, as the movie stars play the leading characters in this historic drama. Finch is Itzhak Rabin, Yaphet Kotto is Idi Amin, and Bronson settles for General Dan Shomron. Written by Barry Beckerman; commendably directed by Irvin Kershner, considering the time restraints. Made-for-TV. (118 mins.)

Raid on Rommel (1971)*½ Richard Burton, John Colicos. Quickie filmed in Mexico, documenting the super human infiltration of the Germans in North Africa. Led by Richard Burton, the commando group weaves through enemy lines with the ease of Rommel himself. The action footage was left over from another production, the '67 "Tobruk," and the finale has Burton leading the attack on Tobruk like Errol Flynn leading the Charge of the Light Brigade. (Dir: Henry Hathaway, 99 mins.)

Raiders of Leyte Gulf (1963)**½ Michael Parsons, Leopold Salcedo. American paratrooper aids the Philippine guerrillas in harassing the Japanese forces. Filmed in the Philippines, this war drama contains plenty of rugged action, which compensates somewhat for the lack of production finesse. (Dir: Eddie Romero, 80 mins.)

Raiders of the Seven Seas (1953)**½ John Payne, Donna Reed. Bold pirate captures a countess, saves her from the rascal she is to marry. Lively costume adventure, plenty of action. (Dir: Sidney Salkow, 88 mins.)

Raiders of the Spanish Main (British, 1962)** Terence Morgan, Nanette Newman. En route back from the New World, Sir Francis Drake stops to rescue sailors held prisoner by the Spanish on an island. Adequate costume sea adventure taken from the "Sir Francis Drake" TV series.

Railroaded (1947)*** John Ireland, Hugh Beaumont. The law gets a desperate criminal who has involved an innocent youth. Tight, suspenseful crime opus, well above average.

Rails into Laramie (1954)** John Payne, Mari Blanchard, Dan Duryea. Another passable western about the pioneering group of he-men who tamed the lawless frontier in order to bring the "rails" into "Laramie." (Dir: Jesse Hibbs, 81 mins.)

Railway Children, The (British, 1970)**** Dinah Sheridan, Jenny Agutter, Sally Thomsett, Gary Warren. Family entertainment. An engaging and entertaining film version of the Edwardian children's classic story about three children who are relocated from London to a Yorkshire village on a railroad line with their mother. A vivid and heartwarming picture of British life at the turn of the century is evoked and the three young actors are superb. (Dir: Lionel Jeffries, 108 mins.)

Rain (1932)*** Joan Crawford, Walter Huston. The familiar tale of Sadie Thompson, the tropical man-killer. Dated, but still powerful drama based on Maugham's story. (Dir: Lewis Milestone, 110 mins.)

Rain People, The (1969)*** James Caan, Shirley Knight, Robert Duvall. A thoughtful, quiet film about losers, marred by, among other things, an abrupt, clumsy and obvious ending. Shirley Knight is the married, pregnant housewife who feels trapped in her Long Island home and therefore hops into her car one day and flees. Along her way, she picks up loser James Caan, a retarded ex-college football star who has a metal plate in his head. Original screenplay and direction by the talented young filmmaker Francis Ford Coppola. Imaginative use of location scenes from Colorado east to New York.

Rainbow Jacket, The (British, 1954)*** Robert Morley, Kay Walsh. Disbarred jockey takes a lad in hand and teaches him the tricks of the trade. Familiar but well constructed racing melodrama. (Dir: Basil Dearden, 99 mins.)

Rainbow 'Round My Shoulder (1952)**½ Frankie Laine, Charlotte Austin, Billy Daniels. Lively musical about a Hollywood studio messenger who gets a screen test and winds up in the movies. (Dir: Richard Quine, 78 mins.)

Rainmaker, The (1956)***½ Katharine Hepburn, Burt Lancaster. N. Richard Nash's hit play about a frightened spinster who's transformed into a woman ready for love by a visiting "con man" relies mainly on K. Hepburn's personal magnetism and is a success only in this area. Burt Lancaster blusters and bellows as "Starbuck," the rainmaker who has a drought-ridden town in the palm of his hand, but it's a surface performance with little emotional depth. The supporting cast is up to par. Hepburn makes it worth catching. (Dir: Joseph Anthony, 121 mins.)

Rains Came, The (1939)****½** Myrna Loy, Tyrone Power, George Brent. Louis Bromfield's brilliant novel about India comes to the screen as a long drawn out romance against the background of monsoons and earthquakes to prevent the audience from sleeping. (Dir: Clarence Brown, 104 mins.)

Rains of Ranchipur, The (1955)****½** Lana Turner, Richard Burton, Fred MacMurray, Michael Rennie, Joan Caulfield. Elaborately produced remake of the Myrna Loy-Tyrone Power film "The Rains Came," about the forbidden romance between the wife of an English nobleman (Miss Turner) and a progressive Hindu doctor (Richard Burton). The plot offers nothing new in the way of drama but the pace is smooth, the spectacle lavish and the stars attractive. (Dir: Jean Negulesco, 104 mins.)

Raintree County (1957)******* Elizabeth Taylor, Montgomery Clift, Eva Marie Saint, Lee Marvin, Rod Taylor. Sprawling story of a Southern belle who stops at nothing to get what she wants, including her man, and the Civil War that tears apart her family. Some stirring scenes, good acting in supporting roles; but rambling plot, defects in performances of the leads detract. (Dir: Edward Dmytryk, 187 mins.)

Raisin in the Sun, A (1961)******** Sidney Poitier, Ruby Dee, Claudia McNeil, Diana Sands. Lorraine Hansberry's Broadway play about a Negro family attempting to break away from their crowded Chicago apartment by moving into an all-white neighborhood. It's practically a photographed stage play, adhering closely to the original, but the dialogue is pungent and direct, the performances excellent, especially Dee, McNeil and Poitier. Worthwhile drama. (Dir: Daniel Petrie, 128 mins.)

Raising a Riot (British, 1957)******* Kenneth More, Mandy Miller. Delightful comedy about a sailor who comes home on leave and is left in charge of his three energetic children when his wife leaves to go to her mother's sick-bed. The Naval Commander tries to run his house like a tight ship, which results in laugh provoking situations. (Dir: Wendy Toye, 90 mins.)

Rally Round the Flag, Boys (1959) ****** Paul Newman, Joanne Woodward, Joan Collins. Max Shulman's funny novel about the citizens of Putnam's Landing and their reactions to an army missile base in their backyard gets the Hollywood treatment. The characters, hilarious in the book, appear somewhat ridiculous on the screen. Paul Newman lacks comedy timing and Miss Woodward is fighting the script all the way. (Dir: Leo McCarey, 106 mins.)

Rampage (British, 1963)****** Robert Mitchum, Elsa Martinelli, Jack Hawkins. Fans who like their adventure films with a minimum of plot twists might enjoy this action drama starring Mitchum as a big-game hunter. Mitchum's assignment is to bring back some rare examples of jungle cats from the Malayan wilds with the help of capable Jack Hawkins and lovely Elsa Martinelli. (Dir: Phil Karlson, 98 mins.)

Rampage at Apache Wells (West Germany-Yugoslavia, 1965)***** Stewart Granger, Pierre Brice, Marie Versini. Granger plays a white man whose Indian blood-brother convinces him to fight for the rights of his down-trodden Navajo tribe. Battles and adventure ensue, but are not enough to distract from the bad dubbing. (Dir: Harold Philipps, 90 mins.)

Ramparts of Clay (French-Algerian, 1970)******** Leila Schenna. A stunning, visually breathtaking masterpiece, a fictional documentary about the emancipation of a young woman who lives in a desolate, primitive mountain village in Tunisia. Produced and directed by a young (29) French filmmaker named Jean-Louis Bertucelli, this is one of the most eloquent and moving protest films ever made, all the more striking perhaps because there is virtually no dialogue. Shot on location in Tehouda, Algeria, "Ramparts" is based on a book by a sociology professor entitled "Change at Chebika." Miss Schenna, a handsome young actress, is the only professional in the cast. You'll learn more about poverty, ignorance, and religious superstition among these proud peasant peoples than you can find in most books.

The static, boring bleak life of the villagers becomes a poetic, totally involving experience. (87 mins.)

Ramsbottom Rides Again (British, 1957)* Arthur Askey, Sabrina. A British Western set in Canadian Rockies. Need we say more!

Rancho Deluxe (1974)***½ Jeff Bridges, Elizabeth Ashley, Sam Waterston, Clifton James, Slim Pickens, Helen Craig, Charlene Dallas. Thanks largely to a quirky, wry, picaresque screenplay by talented novelist Thomas McGuane, this Western spoof works quite well most of the time. Bridges and Waterston play two nonchalant cattle rustlers who finally do wind up in the pokey, but they and you will have some droll fun before the final fadeout. Slim Pickens, one of Hollywood's venerable character actors, finally has a nicely written role playing a supposedly inept cattle rustler. He's also got a most unusual "niece." (Dir: Frank Perry, 93 mins.)

Rancho Notorious (1952)***½ Marlene Dietrich, Arthur Kennedy, Mel Ferrer. Cowboy seeking the killer of his fiancee runs across a gambler and a dance hall queen who may hold the key. Western with a punch —excellently acted and directed, keeps the interest on high throughout. (Dir: Fritz Lang, 89 mins.)

Random Harvest (1942)*** Ronald Colman, Greer Garson. James Hilton novel of a romance which is interrupted by amnesia is beautifully acted and often compelling drama. Trouble here is that the acting is superior to the sometimes talky screenplay. (Dir: Mervyn Le Roy, 124 mins.)

Rangers, The (1974)* James G. Richardson, Colby Chester, Jim B. Smith. TV series pilot that aired after the show had already failed. Richardson, Chester and Smith are rangers coping with a laundry list of problems in a national park, from hungry bears to a deadly snow storm. "Rangers" is deadly, too! Made-for-TV. (Dir: Chris Nyby, Jr., 72 mins.)

Rangers of Fortune (1940)**½ Fred MacMurray, Albert Dekker. Off-beat western defies convention, but is a very confusing film. Story of three renegades who help an old man and a young girl. Ambitious try that just doesn't succeed in rising above average. (Dir: Sam Wood, 80 mins.)

Ransom! (1956)**½ Glenn Ford, Donna Reed, Leslie Nielsen. Somewhat hysterical drama of an industrialist who debates whether to pay the ransom when his son is kidnaped. Overwrought performance by Ford, but the story does contain some suspense. (Dir: Alex Segal, 109 mins.)

Ransom for a Dead Man (1971)**½ Peter Falk, Lee Grant. The idea of pairing Lee Grant and Peter Falk in a murder case is interesting, and it ended up as a Falk TV series. Miss Grant plays a brilliant lawyer who coolly murders her husband, then watches lawmen puzzle over her adroit kidnap-ransom, cover-up scheme. Falk is the bumbling local detective who gets in the way of the pros, but slowly zeroes in on the true picture. Falk's Lt. Columbo overdoes the dumb routine a bit in the early stages, but all is forgiven when the two stars play off each other. (Dir: Richard Irving, 100 mins.)

Ransom for Alice (1977)* Yvette Mimieux, Gil Gerard, Barnard Hughes. Yvette Mimieux and Gil Gerard play 1880's deputy marshals covering the Seattle waterfront in this pilot film for a series. While the unlikely pair search for a missing 19-year-old girl, unruly waterfront characters supply local color, but the hokey story doesn't amount to much. Made-for-TV. (Dir: David Lowell Rich, 79 mins.)

Rapture (1965)** Melvyn Douglas, Dean Stockwell. A romantic drama with pretensions toward art. Douglas plays a retired judge who keeps his beautiful daughter (Patricia Gozzi) isolated from the world; enter Stockwell as a handsome, intelligent fugitive. Have your hankies ready for the finale. (Dir: John Guillermin, 98 mins.)

Rashomon (1951)**** Superb film about a quartet of people involved in a rape-murder which takes place in the forest. Japan's leading filmmaker Akira Kurosawa combines pictorial beauty and poetic cinema techniques to achieve an exciting and memorable screen experience. Toshiro Mifune is outstanding as the bandit. (90 mins.)

Rasputin and the Empress (1932)***½ John, Ethel and Lionel Barrymore. Story of life at court in Russia prior to the murder of the czar and his family is exciting screen entertainment. Seeing the three Barrymores together is a treat in itself but the picture actually does their talent justice. (Dir: Richard Boleslawski, 130 mins.)

Rasputin—The Mad Monk (Great Britain, 1966)**½ Christopher Lee, Barbara Shelley. Putting historical inaccuracy aside, this is an effective, colorful shocker about Rasputin's insinuation of himself into the last of Russia's royal households, thanks to his uncanny hypnotic powers and sexuality. One of many "Rasputin" films. Lee plays the monk with compelling grossness. Written by the executive producer, Anthony Hinds. (Dir: Don Sharp, 92 mins.)

Rat Race, The (1960)*** Tony Curtis, Debbie Reynolds, Jack Oakie. Toughtender story of the Big City, of a love affair developing between a naive aspiring musician and a brittle-minded dancer. Nice N.Y. atmosphere, some good lines, insight into character. Entertaining. (Dir: Robert Mulligan, 105 mins.)

Raton Pass (1951)**½ Dennis Morgan, Patricia Neal, Steve Cochran. Exciting Western. Husband and wife fight tooth and nail for a cattle empire. (Dir: Edward L. Marin, 84 mins.)

Rattle of a Simple Man (Great Britain, 1964)**½ Harry H. Corbett, Diane Cilento, Thora Hird. Diverting sex comedy features Corbett as a shy bachelor who has to spend a night with entertainer Cilento to win a bet. Knowing of the wager, the girl graciously helps him. Adapted by Charles Dyer from his hit London play. (Dir: Muriel Box, 96 mins.)

Raven, The (1935)** Boris Karloff, Bela Lugosi. Lurid thriller about a plastic surgeon who adores the works of Edgar Allan Poe. Karloff is effective as a gangster who needs a facelift, but the film is just so-so. (Dir: Louis Friedlander, 70 mins.)

Ravishing Idiot, A (France-Italy, 1964)*½ Anthony Perkins, Brigitte Bardot. Allegedly a comedy, concerning Perkins' slapstick attempts to burgle NATO files with the help of the curvaceous Miss Bardot, but laughs lost in translation. (Dir: Edouard Molinaro, 110 mins.)

Raw Deal (1948)***½ Dennis O'Keefe, Claire Trevor, Marsha Hunt. Framed into prison by the mob, a gangster escapes and goes seeking vengeance. Excellent melodrama with fine direction, photography, good performances. (Dir: Anthony Mann, 79 mins.)

Raw Edge (1956)** Rory Calhoun, Yvonne DeCarlo. Just another western with Calhoun and Miss DeCarlo playing parts they could play in their sleep. Setting is Oregon at the time when land barons ruled the frontier. (Dir: John Sherwood, 76 mins.)

Raw Wind in Eden (1958)**½ Esther Williams, Jeff Chandler, Rossana Podesta. A mildly entertaining adventure yarn with an island setting and two-fisted men fighting over statuesque Miss Williams. The plot is predictable but things move fast so you won't get bored. (Dir: Richard Wilson, 89 mins.)

Rawhide (Tyrone Power)—See: Desperate Siege

Rawhide Years, The (1956)*** Tony Curtis, Colleen Miller, Arthur Kennedy. Fast, funny western yarn about double crosses and false accusations which cause Tony to become a hunted fugitive bent on clearing his name. Arthur Kennedy delivers the best acting job in the film. (Dir: Rudolph Mate, 85 mins.)

Raymie (1960)**½ David Ladd, Julie Adams. The charm of this film can be attributed mainly to David Ladd's completely believable performance as a boy who loves animals and fish, especially barracudas. Good family film fare. (Dir: Frank McDonald, 72 mins.)

Razor's Edge, The (1946)**½ Tyrone Power, Gene Tierney, Clifton Webb. Story of a man's search for faith, adapted from Maugham's novel, is a rambling, tedious film which has few high spots and fails to hold up. An "A" for effort but the book was too difficult to adapt. (Dir: Edmund Goulding, 146 mins.)

R.C.M.P. and the Treasure of Genghis Khan (1948-66)*½ Jim Bannon, Virginia Belmont. Feature version of serial "Dangers of the Canadian Mounted." Mountie battles a gang after a rediscovered secret treasure. Serial stuff on the silly side; for the faithful only.

Reach for Glory (Great Britain, 1962) ** Harry Andrews, Oliver Grimm, Michael Anderson, Jr., Martin Tomlinson. Well-meaning allegory that misses. Boys evacuated from London in World War II fashion their own war games. Similar idea to "Lord of the Flies," only much less coherent. Based on "The Custard Boys" by John Rae. (Dir: Philip Leacock, 89 mins.)

Reach for the Sky (British, 1956) ***½ Kenneth More, Muriel Pavlow. Story of a daring airman who never let the tragedy of amputated legs interfere with his success. Inspiring drama, based on fact. (Dir: Lewis Gilbert, 123 mins.)

Ready for the People (1964)* Simon Oakland, Richard Jordan, Everett Sloane, Anne Helm. Poor pilot for proposed TV series that didn't jell—man accused of murder after a barroom brawl, maintains his innocence; D.A. believes him. (Dir: Buzz Kulik, 54 mins.)

Real Glory, The (1939)*** Gary Cooper, David Niven, Andrea Leeds. Rousing action film about three soldiers who aid in trying to squelch the terrorist uprising in the Philippines. (Dir: Henry Hathaway, 100 mins.)

Reap the Wild Wind (1942)*** Ray Milland, John Wayne, Paulette Goddard. Lavish De Mille adventure tale of an 1840 love triangle off the Florida Keys where the most profitable thing a man could do was wreck ships. Lusty film, loses much of its value on small TV screen. (Dir: Cecil B. De Mille, 124 mins.)

Rear Window (1954)**** James Stewart, Grace Kelly, Raymond Burr, Wendell Corey. Alfred Hitchcock suspense treat—photographer is laid up in his apartment, takes to examining his neighbors through binoculars, witnesses a murder. Nail-biting tension laced with some scenes of sharp sophisticated comedy, a delight from beginning to end. (122 mins.)

Rebecca (1940)**** Laurence Olivier, Joan Fontaine, George Sanders. Sheltered girl marries a brooding man who is haunted by his mysteriously deceased first wife. Fine drama with brilliant Hitchcock direction, superb performances. (115 mins.)

Rebecca of Sunnybrook Farm (1938) **½ Shirley Temple, Randolph Scott. If you like Shirley you'll love her in this but if you want your kids to see a screen adaptation of the famous children's book—this is not it. (Dir: Allan Dwan, 80 mins.)

Rebel Flight to Cuba (German, 1962) *½ Peter Van Eyck, Linda Christian. Discredited airline pilot proves his mettle on a perilous flight as he is about to be expelled. Weak action melodrama dubbed in English.

Rebel Without a Cause (1955)***½ James Dean, Natalie Wood, Sal Mineo. Sensitively acted story of a teenager who is not satisfied with the world he never made. Dean's performance is both touching and exciting. In support, Natalie Wood and Sal Mineo are first-rate. Writer Stewart Stern later wrote the film biography of Dean after the actor's tragic but not surprising demise. (Dir: Nicholas Ray, 111 mins.)

Rebellion in Patagonia (Argentina, 1974)***½ Powerful drama by a gifted, little-recognized director, Hector Olivera. About a labor strike in Patagonia (Argentina) and the brutal way it was put down. Masterful recreation of the period. The political content is dealt with intelligently, including the changes in the character and attitude of the Army commander. (Dir: Hector Olivera)

Reckless (1934)** Jean Harlow, William Powell, Franchot Tone. Some good performers are wasted in this trashy chronicle of a chorus girl and her effect on people's lives. (Dir: Victor Fleming, 96 mins.)

Reckless Moment (1949)***½ James Mason, Joan Bennett. A woman who has killed a scoundrel to protect her family finds herself in the clutches of a blackmailer. Well acted and directed, this is a good melodrama. (Dir: Max Ophuls, 82 mins.)

Reckoning, The (British, 1969)*** Nicol Williamson, Rachel Roberts. Williamson stars as a ruthless businessman who has made a success in southern England but is forced to return to his home in the North to visit his dying father. Drama is frequently effective. Fine supporting cast. (Dir: Jack Gold, 109 mins.)

Red (Canadian, 1970)* Daniel Pilon, Genevieve Deloir. Jumbled, ultimately boring adventure-mystery. Leading character is a shoplifter and car stealer. None of the other characters are of any interest. (Dir: Gilles Carle, 101 mins.)

Red Alert (1977)*** William Devane, Ralph Waite, Michael Brandon. Gripping suspense drama about troubles within a nuclear power plant. The characters teeter on the edge of an atomic disaster, in a thriller that builds tension and never lets down. Although fiction, the drama provokes many questions about nuclear power-plant safety, and our growing dependence upon computer control. Given a strong story, the actors are effective, especially Ralph Waite playing a character 180 degrees removed from his portrayal of the father in "The Waltons." The film was photographed at Houston's giant Space Lab, and at the NASA Mission Control Center. Made-for-TV. (Dir: William Hale, 106 mins.)

Red and the Black, The (France, 1958)***½ Gerard Philipe, Danielle Darrieux, Antonella Lualdi. Stendhal's great work is given a sensitive and successful treatment on film, but don't expect all the novel's subtleties. A young man from provincial 19th-century France aspires to greatness, chooses first the Church, then gentleman's employment, and gentlewomen's seduction, to accomplish his ends. Philipe and Darrieux, in the leading roles, give truly splendid performances. (Dir: Claude Autant-Lara, 145 mins.)

Red Badge of Courage, The (1951) **** Audie Murphy, Bill Mauldin. Stephen Crane's novel about the Civil War as seen through the eyes of a young recruit who falters between cowardice and bravery throughout the many encounters. John Huston's masterful direction and impeccable casting in supporting roles make this an unforgettable film. (70 mins.)

Red Badge of Courage, The (1974) *** Richard Thomas, Warren Berlinger, Wendell Burton, Charles Aidman. This faithful adaptation of Stephen Crane's classic Civil War novel about fear under fire stars Richard ("The Waltons") Thomas as Henry Fleming, the youth who questions his courage in battle, runs away, and then fights again in a fit of madness with his tattered company of greenhorns. The braggart, the questioner and the solid man all have their moments before authentic, bloody battle scenes reveal a regiment learning how to be resolute, in this noble attempt at bringing a poignant story to life. Not as good as the '51 version, but worth seeing. Made-for-TV. (Dir: Lee Philips, 100 mins.)

Red Ball Express (1952)** Jeff Chandler, Alex Nicol. Routine World War II drama, played in the European combat zone, with all the cliched GI's. Jeff Chandler plays a tough but human leader of the truck division known as the Red Ball Express. (Dir: Budd Boetticher, 83 mins.)

Red Circle, The (German, 1960)*½ Karl Georg Saebisch, Renate Ewert. Mysterious blackmailer and murderer terrorizes London, leaving the mark of a red circle near his crimes. Edgar Wallace story has enough intrigue for ten films. Dubbed in English. (Dir: Jurgen Roland, 94 mins.)

Red Cloak, The (Italian, 1961)*½ Fausto Tozzi, Patricia Medina, Bruce Cabot, Domenico Modugno. Masked avenger comes to the aid of townspeople victimized by a villainous captain. English-dubbed. Hackneyed swashbuckling melodrama, Flynn used to do it better.

Red Culottes, The (French, 1963)** Bourvil, Laurent Terzieff. Story of French POWs trying to escape holds the interest fairly well, but the story has been done before, and better. Dubbed in English.

Red Danube, The (1949)**½ Walter Pidgeon, Janet Leigh, Peter Lawford, Ethel Barrymore, Angela Lansbury. Interesting but over-dramatic story of political intrigue and romance in Europe. A handsome British officer and a lovely ballerina are plagued by the Communists. (Dir: George Sidney, 119 mins.)

Red-Dragon (Italy-West Germany, 1965)* Stewart Granger, Rosanna Schiaffino, Horst Frank. FBI agents Granger and Schiaffino pursue a smuggling gang through Hong Kong. Predictable international intrigue. (Dir: Ernest Hofbauer, 89 mins.)

Red Dust (1932)*** Clark Gable, Jean Harlow, Mary Astor, Gene Raymond. Romance and intrigue on a rubber plantation in Indo-China are stretched beyond credibility. Strong, attractive star personalities make it. (Dir: Victor Fleming, 83 mins.)

Red Garters (1954)**½ Rosemary Clooney, Jack Carson, Gene Barry, Guy Mitchell. Satire of westerns uses all the standard plot ramifications: man seeks revenge for brother's death, falls for the purty town girl, etc. All done with stylized sets, costumes. It doesn't work but represents a try for something different. Some fair tunes warbled by Clooney, others. (Dir: George Marshall, 91 mins.)

Red Hand, The (German, 1960)*½ Eleonora Rossi-Drago, Paul Hubschmid, Hannes Messemer. Criminal leaving the imprint of a red hand at the scenes of his doings causes pandemonium in the munitions world. Well produced but ridiculously plotted Edgar Wallace mystery dubbed in English.

Red, Hot and Blue (1949) **½ Betty Hutton, Victor Mature, June Havoc, William Demarest. Girl ambitious to get ahead in the theater is helped by a director and a publicist but runs afoul of gangsters. Pleasant comedy is mainly a showcase for Hutton's brassy talents; songwriter Frank Loesser has a role as a hoodlum, in a bit of offbeat casting. (Dir: John Farrow, 84 mins.)

Red House, The (1947)***½ Edward G. Robinson, Lon McCallister. A farmer holds a terrifying secret concerning a sinister house in the woods. Excellent suspense thriller. (Dir: Delmer Daves, 100 mins.)

Red Inn, The (French, 1951)** Fernandel, Francoise Rosay. Monk discovers that travelers stopping at an inn are robbed and murdered by the proprietors, tries to save some potential new victims. Grotesque mixture of comedy and murder doesn't quite come off. Some amusing scenes, not enough. English-dubbed. (Dir: Claude Autant-Lara, 100 mins.)

Red Light (1949)** George Raft, Virginia Mayo, Raymond Burr. Another "innocent-man-sent-to-prison" mystery drama, with Raft playing his usual Great Stone Face. Virginia Mayo is pretty, in case you haven't heard. (Dir: Roy Del Ruth, 83 mins.)

Red Mountain (1951)**½ Alan Ladd, Lizabeth Scott, John Ireland, Arthur Kennedy. Confederate officer assigned to raider Quantrill discovers the leader is out for himself alone, goes on the hunt for him. Well-made western moves at a fast clip. (Dir: William Dieterle, 84 mins.)

Red Planet Mars (1952)**½ Peter Graves, Andrea King. Attempts to communicate with Mars set off a chain of events that threatens the safety of the entire world. Fanciful science-fiction melodrama, with a bit more meat to the plot than most of this type. (Dir: Harry Horner, 87 mins.)

Red Pony, The (1948)*** Robert Mitchum, Myrna Loy, Peter Miles. Ranch boy is gifted with a colt, grows to love him but the colt escapes. John Steinbeck story receives a good production, but moves rather leisurely. (Dir: Lewis Milestone, 89 mins.)

Red River (1952)**** John Wayne, Montgomery Clift. Story of a cattle baron and the empire he builds. Top-notch acting, direction and story make this a western film classic. (Dir: Howard Hawks, 125 mins.)

Red Sheik, The (Italian, 1961)* Channing Pollock, Mel Welles. Sheik overcomes invaders and recaptures his kingdom. Pollock is a magician by trade, but more than magic was needed to make this sappy spectacle palatable. Dubbed in English.

Red Shoes, The (British, 1948)*** Moira Shearer, Anton Walbrook. An impresario persuades a ballerina to give up her romance with a composer and sacrifice all for art. Beautiful design and superb dancing, but nevertheless a hackneyed, overdone dramatic plot. (Dir: Michael Powell, 133 mins.)

Red Skies of Montana (1952)** Richard Widmark, Jeffrey Hunter. Adventure yarn about the brave band of forest fire fighters known as "Smoke Jumpers." The fire fighting sequences will please action fans; but the plot involving Hunter's efforts to gain revenge for his father's accidental death in a mission led by Widmark merely serves as a stage wait between holocausts. (Dir: Joseph M. Newman, 89 mins.)

Red Sky at Morning (1971)**½ Richard Thomas, Claire Bloom, Desi Arnaz, Jr., Richard Crenna. Despite some flaws, this nostalgic excursion about a teen-age boy coming into his own in New Mexico in 1944 works fairly well, thanks largely to Thomas' performance in the leading role. Bloom tends to overact as Thomas' mother and Arnaz is surprisingly good as his buddy. The '40's flavor is there without being self-conscious. This film preceded Thomas' tenure as John-Boy in the TV series "The Waltons." (Dir: James Goldstone, 113 mins.)

Red Snow (1952)** Guy Madison, Carole Mathews. Twin adventure yarn about the Alaskan Air Command; their missions and their loves. Madison is incompetent once again.

Red Sun (French-Italian-Spanish,

1971)* Charles Bronson, Ursula Andress, Alain Delon, Toshiro Mifune, Capucine. International cast in a dull western about a falling-out between a pair of crooks, Bronson and Delon. Only interesting point is the absurdity of a Japanese samurai in full dress in the middle of the 1860's West. Filmed in Spain. (Dir: Terence Young, 112 mins.)

Red Sundown (1956)** Rory Calhoun, Martha Hyer, Dean Jagger. Usual western tale about the lawless renegade turned lawful deputy and the trouble he encounters before and after the transition. Calhoun at least looks believable in the role. (Dir: Jack Arnold, 81 mins.)

Red Tomahawk (1967)* Howard Keel, Joan Caulfield, Broderick Crawford. After Custer's defeat at Little Bighorn, the U.S. Cavalry takes on the Sioux and gamblers from the town of Deadwood. (Dir: R. G. Springsteen, 82 mins.)

Red Train, The (Swiss, 1973)** Pretentious pseudodocumentary which attempts not very successfully to combine, in supposed documentary form, scenes of emigrant Italian workers going home to vote with parables about the legend of William Tell. English subtitles. (Dir: Peter Ammann, 90 mins.)

Red, White and Black, The—See: Soul Soldier

Redhead and the Cowboy, The (1950)** Glenn Ford, Rhonda Fleming, Edmond O'Brien. At the close of the Civil War a cowhand is mistaken for a Confederate spy by a beautiful courier, gets himself tangled in espionage. Just fair western, doesn't have the necessary movement for a successful action film. (Dir: Leslie Fenton, 82 mins.)

Redhead from Manhattan (1943)** Lupe Velez, Michael Duane. Theatrical star agrees to impersonate her cousin until the cousin has her baby, which causes romantic mix-ups. Ordinary musical comedy.

Redhead from Wyoming, The (1953) *½ Maureen O'Hara, Alex Nicol. Even less interesting than usual— Maureen's a double-dealing dance-hall queen who can't choose between law and order. (Dir: Lee Sholem, 80 mins.)

Redline 7000 (1966)*** Laura Devon, James Caan. Fast-paced drama about the racing-car set in the United States. There are more sub-plots than you can keep up with, all involving the romances of the racers. The best thing about the film is the footage of the races. (Dir: Howard Hawks)

Redmen and the Renegades, The (1956)*½ John Hart, Lon Chaney. Frontiersman and his Indian aide battle to clear patriot Ethan Allen of treason charges. Weak historical action drama edited from an old TV series.

Redneck (Italy-Great Britain, 1972) *½ Franco Nero, Telly Savalas, Mark Lester. A grade C, low-budget, crime-chase thriller later exhumed for theatrical release starring Telly because of Savalas' "Kojak" drawing power. Mark "Oliver" Lester has "progressed" to playing an irritating psychopath. (Dir: Silvio Narizzano, 87 mins.)

Reflection of Fear, A (1973)*½ Robert Shaw, Sally Kellerman, Mary Ure, Sondra Locke. Thin "Psycho"-type mystery as a young girl's alter ego goes on a murderous rampage which is viewed with dismay by her parents and the local sheriff. The striking photography is hindered by the worn-out plot. (Dir: William A. Fraker, 90 mins.)

Reflections in a Golden Eye (1967) **½ Marlon Brando, Elizabeth Taylor, Brian Keith, Julie Harris, Robert Forster. Novelist Carson McCullers' perceptive novel has been cheapened and distorted in this film version directed by John Huston, but there are some splendid acting performances that give the movie more substance than it somehow deserves. Marlon Brando, playing a homosexual Southern army officer, has trouble with his Southern accent at times, but he does manage to convey, in a remarkable and deeply moving way, the personal anguish and indecision of the tortured officer. Other good performances from Robert Forster as the object of Marlon's affection—despite Brando having Liz Taylor in his bedroom each night—and from Brian Keith and Julie Harris. Brando's portrait makes this one worth seeing. (108 mins.)

Reflections of Murder (1974)*** Sam Waterston, Tuesday Weld, Joan Hackett. "Diabolique," classic French thriller with a surprise ending, has been remade with an American cast which is up to the demands of the tale. A schoolmaster,

591

who has been mistreating his ill wife, is murdered by her and his former mistress. They put his body in the private school's unused swimming pool, but when they drain the pool some days later, the body is gone and the suspense builds to the fascinating close. A far cry from the original, but it's still a chilling story. Made-for-TV. (Dir: John Badham, 100 mins.)

Reformer and the Redhead, The (1950)** June Allyson, Dick Powell, David Wayne. Zany comedy bordering on the ridiculous with June Allyson as an unpredictable redhead with a nose for trouble and Dick Powell as the patient reformer. (Dir: Norman Panama, 90 mins.)

Reivers, The (1969)**** Steve McQueen, Sharon Farrell, Mitch Vogel, Rupert Crosse. Not all of William Faulkner's novels have survived the transfer to film very well, but this charming tale about the adventures of a 12-year-old boy with some of his older buddies is a notable exception. The journey follows a northward route up to Memphis, and Steve McQueen, giving one of his most winning performances to date, is a big help. So is the direction of Mark Rydell, who can clearly deal with material as different as this and the 1968 film "The Fox." A particularly good film for teenagers, and a sure-fire hit for all the family. (Dir: Mark Rydell, 107 mins.)

Relations (Danish, 1972)* Bjorn Puggard Muller, Gertie Jung. Fat old man (Muller) fooling with slinky young slut (Jung), both of whom have bodies which cry out for clothing in this pseudopornographic Danish import. Most of the sex is a tease. The background rock music is pure jive. (Dir: Hans Abramson, 91 mins.)

Reluctant Astronaut, The (1967)*½ Don Knotts, Arthur O'Connell. You've got to be crazy about Don Knotts' brand of nervous acting to buy this juvenile tale about a silly, nervous nut who "reluctantly" becomes an astronaut. All the characters are unreal. Knotts manages to keep his twitching in control for the big climactic scene which takes place in a space capsule. (Dir: Edward Montagne, 101 mins.)

Reluctant Debutante, The (1958)**½ Rex Harrison, Kay Kendall, Sandra Dee. Lightweight comedy fluff

592

sparked considerably by the charm and attractiveness of its leading players—Rex Harrison, Kay Kendall. The story revolves around a zany British couple who choose to have their American-as-apple-pie daughter make her debut in England. (Dir: Vincente Minnelli, 94 mins.)

Reluctant Heroes, The (1971)** Ken Berry, Jim Hutton. Korean War service comedy-drama owes a lot to the picture "M*A*S*H" for its style and pace. Ken Berry is exceptionally adroit playing the role of Lt. Murphy, a war historian who finds himself heading a dangerous mission against the enemy. The dialogue among the men on the mission is brittle and often funny, providing the fine supporting cast, in which Hutton, Warren Oates, and Cameron Mitchell are standouts, with some good moments. Made-for-TV. (Dir: Robert Day, 73 mins.)

Reluctant Spy, The (French, 1963)** Jean Marais, Genevieve Page. Suave playboy works undercover for the French Secret Service, gets himself into plenty of scrapes. Mild, lightweight espionage thriller with comedy overtones; passable. Dubbed in English. (Dir: Jean-Charles Dudrumet, 93 mins.)

Remains to Be Seen (1953)**½ June Allyson, Van Johnson. Band vocalist and an apartment house manager who wants to be a drummer get tangled in a murder case. Mildly entertaining mystery-comedy, helped by a good supporting cast. (Dir: Don Weis, 89 mins.)

Remarkable Andrew, The (1942)**½ William Holden, Brian Donlevy. Ghosts of our founding fathers come to the aid of a timid young man fighting graft. Interesting, well played hokum. (Dir: Stuart Heisler, 80 mins.)

Remarkable Mr. Pennypacker, The (1959)** Clifton Webb, Dorothy McGuire, Charles Coburn. Scalawag specializes in large families and small talk—not much of it very amusing either. Misses capturing elusive charm of B'way play it's based on. (Dir: Henry Levin, 87 mins.)

Rembrandt (British, 1936)***½ Charles Laughton, Elsa Lanchester. The biographical drama of the great Dutch painter. Excellently written, performed. (Dir: Alexander Korda, 90 mins.)

Remember? (1939)** Robert Taylor, Greer Garson, Lew Ayres. Silly little comedy about a guy who elopes with his friend's fiancee, and then the friend instead of shooting his pal uses the couple for some nonsensical experiment. (Dir: Norman Z. McLeod, 80 mins.)

Remember the Day (1941)*** Claudette Colbert, John Payne. The ladies should like this sentimental story of a teacher's life, her guidance of one pupil and her unhappy romance. (Dir: Henry King, 85 mins.)

Remember the Night (1940)*** Fred MacMurray, Barbara Stanwyck. Warm, moving story of a DA who takes a shoplifter home with him when court recesses for the Xmas holidays. (Dir: Mitchell Leisen, 86 mins.)

Remember When? (1974)** Jack Warden, William Schallert, Jamie Smith Jackson. Writer Herman Raucher, who struck gold with the film "Summer of '42," is still on the '40's nostalgia trail. Here he wrote a pilot for a proposed TV series about the home front during WW II. The setting is Connecticut. (Dir: Buzz Kulik.)

Rendezvous with Annie (1946)**½ Eddie Albert, Faye Marlowe. Army pilot flies home secretly to spend a few hours with his wife, but this leads to complications. Light, frothy comedy has many amusing moments.

Renegade Gunfighter (1966)* Pier Angeli, Zachary Hatcher, Dick Palmer. Trite tidbit concerning boy turned hated gunfighter to avenge his parents' death. Ta, ta . . . (Dir: Silvio Amadio, 76 mins.)

Report to the Commissioner (1975)** Michael Moriarty, Susan Blakely. Some very good actors, writers and the director all seem to have been working at cross-purposes on this film version of James Mills' best-selling novel. Broadway's Michael Moriarty, in his starring debut in films, plays a puddin'-headed rookie cop who is used as a scapegoat by his superiors when he accidentally kills a sexy young lady who is actually an undercover cop, in the apartment of a big-time dope pusher she has been living with. Oh well, Susan Blakely is lovely to look at as the fearless lady cop. (Dir: Milton Katselas, 112 mins.)

Reprisal (1956)**½ Guy Madison, Felicia Farr. Good film with a novel approach to westerns—the plot concerns the racial issue. (Dir: George Sherman, 74 mins.)

Reptilicus (1962)*½ Carl Ottosen, Ann Smyrner. Prehistoric beast is dug up and sent to a Copenhagen laboratory, where it thaws out and escapes. Mediocre monster thriller made in Denmark.

Requiem for a Gunfighter (1965)*½ Rod Cameron, Stephen McNally, Tim McCoy. Gunslinger is mistaken for a judge, decides to play along with the impersonation and rids the town of the baddies. Threadbare western with a cast of veteran hands the only attractive point. (Dir: Spencer G. Bennet, 91 mins.)

Requiem for a Heavyweight (1962)***½ Anthony Quinn, Julie Harris, Jackie Gleason, Mickey Rooney. This drama of a washed-up pug and the employment counselor who tries to help him land a job is based on the highly successful TV presentation. As a film it hasn't been changed much, except for the cast, who contribute excellent performances. Familiar but well done. (Dir: Ralph Nelson, 95 mins.)

Rest Is Silence, The (German, 1960)**½ Hardy Kruger, Peter Van Eyck. Young man seeks to prove his father was murdered by his uncle. Or if you will, "Hamlet" modernized, with specific references to Shakespeare's work. Rather clever in adaptation, with some fairly good performances. Dubbed in English. (Dir: Helmut Kautner, 106 mins.)

Restless Breed (1957)** Scott Brady, Anne Bancroft. Routine western drama about a man bent on revenge for his father's murder. Anne Bancroft is wasted as an Indian girl. (Dir: Allan Dwan, 81 mins.)

Restless Years, The (1959)** John Saxon, Sandra Dee, Margaret Lindsay. Small town dressmaker tries to keep her daughter's illegitimacy a secret, but the secret's out. For ladies only, unadorned soap opera. (Dir: Helmut Kautner, 86 mins.)

Retik, the Moon Menace (1952-66)* George Wallace, Aline Towne. Feature version of serial "Radar Men from the Moon." Moon men seek to enslave earth but are foiled by "Commando Cody, Sky King of the Universe." Need we say more? Except that this was below par even as a cliffhanger. (Dir: Fred C. Brannon, 100 mins.)

Return from the Ashes (1965)***
Maximilian Schell, Ingrid Thulin
and Samantha Eggar plus some interesting plot twists make this weird
suspense film worthwhile. After
years in a Nazi concentration camp
which left her scarred, Miss Thulin
undergoes plastic surgery and returns to Paris eager to pick up her
life. In the interim, her husband and
stepdaughter have become lovers,
and a strange twist of fate unites the
trio in a diabolical game of wits.
(Dir: J. Lee Thompson, 105 mins.)

Return from the Past—See: Dr. Ter-
ror's Gallery of Horrors

Return From the Sea (1954)**½
Neville Brand, Jan Sterling. Pleasant
film about two lonely people who
meet in San Diego and fall in love.
Miss Sterling has some very good
moments as a plain waitress and
Neville Brand registers in a sympathetic role as a seaman. (Dir: Lesley Selander, 80 mins.)

Return of a Stranger (British, 1961)
**½ John Ireland, Susan Stephen.
Mysterious man causes plenty of
tense moments for a young couple.
Fairish suspense thriller, helped by
the performers. (Dir: Max Varnel,
63 mins.)

Return of Doctor X (1939)** Wayne
Morris, Rosemary Lane, Humphrey
Bogart. Typical horror movie made
from the old "bring back the dead"
formula. (Dir: Vincent Sherman, 70
mins.)

Return of Don Camillo, The (French,
1953)***½ Fernandel, Gino Cervi.
Fernandel once more delights all
as the hilariously unconventional
priest Don Camillo. A small village
is turned inside out and vastly
changed by the pixie padre's arrival.
Inventive writing and acting. (Dir:
Julien Duvivier, 115 mins.)

Return of Dracula, The (1958)*½
Francis Lederer, Norma Eberhardt.
Vampire shenanigans in California.
Victim rises from the grave and
takes the place of a traveler to
America. It's the same old death-of-
a-killer-bat story. (Dir: Paul Lan-
dres, 77 mins.)

Return of Frank James, The (1940)
*** Henry Fonda, Gene Tierney.
Jesse's brother sets out to get the
Ford boys in this interesting tale.
Not as exciting as Jesse's story but
plenty of warmth and humor mixed
in make up for the moderate pace.
(Dir: Fritz Lang, 92 mins.)

594

Return of Jesse James (1950)**½
John Ireland, Ann Dvorak. Small-
time outlaw is a dead ringer for the
late Jesse; he becomes a big-timer
by cashing in on the James name.
Above average western. (Dir: Arthur
Hilton, 75 mins.)

Return of Majin (Japanese, 1965) So,
he returns already! More havoc, until the world is saved in the nick.
As bad as its predecessor. English-
dubbed.

Return of Monte Cristo (1946)**½
Louis Hayward, Barbara Britton.
Nephew to Edmund Dantes is framed
to Devil's Island by enemies who
wish to prevent him from claiming
the Monte Cristo inheritance. Okay
costume melodrama. (Dir: Henry
Levin, 91 mins.)

Return of October, The (1949)**½
Glenn Ford, Terry Moore, James
Gleason. Girl buys a race horse be-
cause it reminds her of a dead
uncle. In spite of corny Kentucky
Derby finale, this has some laughs.
(Dir: Joseph H. Lewis, 98 mins.)

Return of Peter Grimm (1935)***
Lionel Barrymore, Helen Mack. Man
who dominated his household before
death returns from the Beyond to
find things changed. Interesting, well
acted drama. (Dir: George Nicholls,
Jr., 90 mins.)

Return of Sabata (Italian, 1971)* Lee
Van Cleef. Insanity out West, junk
on the screen. Van Cleef, who made
a reputation following in Clint Eastwood's spaghetti western boots,
produced his own series of films
playing an ex-Confederate officer. In
this, the third of the saga, he shoots
up most of the population of a town,
apparently for no good reason. (Dir:
Frank Kramer, 106 mins.)

Return of the Fly (1959)** Vincent
Price, Britt Halsey. Sequel to the
successful box-office thriller "The
Fly," this second attempt to construct another macabre tale about a
man who turns into a fly during an
experiment doesn't live up to its
predecessor's chilly sequences. (Dir:
Edward L. Bernds, 80 mins.)

Return of the Giant Monsters (Japanese, 1964)* Kojiro Hongo, Kichijiro
Ueda. Earthquakes erupt, lava turns
loose, and lo and behold, stick-figure
monsters Gammera versus Gaos, Go,
Go, Go-Away. (85 mins.)

Return of the Gunfighter (1966)**½
Robert Taylor, Chad Everett, Ana
Martin. Lively western about a gun-

slinger who goes looking for the murderers of an old friend. Routine plot but plenty of action, good production, rugged performance by Taylor. Produced for TV. (Dir: James Neilson, 100 mins.)

Return of the Pink Panther, The (Great Britain, 1974)*** Peter Sellers, Christopher Plummer, Herbert Lom. Imagine Peter Sellers as the immortal Inspector Clouseau, let loose with a vacuum cleaner, a steam bath, an organ grinder and his monkey, and a waxed dance floor, all in the same film. Series began with "The Pink Panther," and this is the third time out. Once again, the fabled Pink-Panther diamond is stolen, this time from a Topkapi-like museum in mythical Lugash (wait until you see Clouseau check out the museum's security system). Naturally, the Inspector takes the case. Herbert Lom returns, too, as Clouseau's harried boss, as does Burt Kwouk. Sellers is a great comic; some of this is very funny. (Dir: Blake Edwards, 113 mins.)

Return of the Seven (1966)* Yul Brynner, Robert Fuller, Jordan Christopher. Disappointing sequel to the 1960 John Sturges film "The Magnificent Seven" which was in turn based on the classic 1956 Japanese film of Kurosawa, "Seven Samurai." Only Yul Brynner repeats his role. Yul rides into a Mexican town—filmed in Spain—to free his buddy (Julian Mateos) being held captive by a band of outlaws. (Dir: Burt Kennedy, 96 mins.)

Return of the Texan (1952)** Dale Robertson, Joanne Dru, Walter Brennan. Talky drama about the obstacles faced by a handsome widower who comes back to the homestead where he grew up. Walter Brennan plays a role that may remind you of his "Grandpa McCoy" characterization. (Dir: Delmer Daves, 88 mins.)

Return of the World's Greatest Detective, The (1976)*½ Larry Hagman, Jenny O'Hara, Nicholas Colasanto, Woodrow Parfey. Based on the George C. Scott-Joanne Woodward movie "They Might Be Giants." Here, the adept Hagman makes the best of a comedy about a bumbling police officer who suffers a concussion only to believe he's Sherlock Holmes. Occasionally diverting. Made-for-TV. (Dir: Dean Hargrove, 72 mins.)

Return to Earth (1976)**½ Cliff Robertson, Shirley Knight, Ralph Bellamy, Stefanie Powers. Edwin "Buzz" Aldrin, the second man to walk on the moon, is the subject of this moderately engrossing TV movie. Robertson is excellent as Aldrin; his military carriage, clipped speech and low-key playing get inside the man, showing us how a national hero can suffer severe depression in the aftermath of what was, by his standards, the high point of his life. Knight is also good as Aldrin's wife, Joan, trying to help him but unable to break through his defenses. The main story itself is compelling, but it bogs down somewhat because the peripheral characters are too thinly drawn. (Dir: Jud Taylor, 72 mins.)

Return to Paradise (1953)**½ Gary Cooper, Roberta Haynes. Slow-moving story of the romance of a bum and a native girl in the South Seas. (Dir: Mark Robson, 100 mins.)

Return to Peyton Place (1961)* Carol Lynley, Jeff Chandler, Eleanor Parker, Mary Astor, Tuesday Weld. Trashy sequel to "Peyton Place" with some of the characters from the original novel. Carol Lynley is Allison in this version and she causes no small stir when she authors a book about her New England hometown. Soap opera all the way and poorly played at that! In "Peyton Place," screenwriter John Michael Hayes greatly improved upon the poorly written novel. No such luck this time around. (Dir: Jose Ferrer, 122 mins.)

Return to Sender (British, 1962)** Nigel Davenport, Yvonne Romain. Tycoon makes an agreement with the underworld to destroy the reputation of the prosecuting attorney who sent him to prison. Fair Edgar Wallace crime drama. (Dir: Gordon Hales, 63 mins.)

Returning Home (1975)**½ Dabney Coleman, Tom Selleck, James R. Miller, Whitney Blake, Joan Goodfellow. TV remake of the award-winning 1946 film "The Best Years of Our Lives." Tasteful retelling of the wonderful story of three returning World War II veterans, and their adjustment to civilian life. But it doesn't compare favorably with "Best Years." (Dir: Daniel Petrie, 72 mins.)

Reunion in France (1942)*½ Joan Crawford, John Wayne. Joan saves France, Wayne is an American flyer who needs her help and the whole thing adds up to nothing. (Dir: Jules Dassin, 104 mins.)

Reunion in Reno (1951)**½ Mark Stevens, Peggy Dow. Lightweight comedy-drama about a little girl who turns a Reno divorce lawyer's life into a merry-go-round when she decides to investigate the possibility of divorcing her parents. Gigi Perreau plays the nine year old with charm. (Dir: Kurt Neumann, 79 mins.)

Reveille with Beverly (1943)** Ann Miller, William Wright. Switchboard operator becomes a popular lady disk jockey. Appearances by Sinatra, Duke Ellington, Bob Crosby, etc., save this mild musical. (Dir: Charles Barton, 78 mins.)

Revenge at Daybreak (French, 1958)** Danielle Delorme, Henri Vidal. Ordinary melodrama set during the Irish revolution—young girl sets out to avenge her brother's death.

Revenge for a Rape (1976)½ Mike Connors, Robert Reed, Deanna Lund. Predictable, contrived, boring story about a nice-guy geologist who is turned into a marauding killer when his young, pregnant wife is brutally raped by three drunken hunters on a holiday. It's a clumsy combination of "Death Wish" and "Deliverance." Connors proves his wooden acting style is better suited to one-liners delivered on the phone as "Mannix." Made-for-TV. (Dir: Timothy Galfas, 106 mins.)

Revenge of Black Eagle (Italian, 1964)*½ Rossano Brazzi, Gianna Maria Canale. Prince vows vengeance for the death of his family, becomes a bandit. Lavish but ponderous dubbed-English swashbuckler.

Revenge of Frankenstein, The (British, 1958)**½ Peter Cushing, Francis Matthews. Another in the series of films made about the creation of the Frankenstein monster. Production is well mounted and very well acted. (Dir: Terence Fisher, 91 mins.)

Revenge of Ivanhoe, The (Italian, 1964)* Clyde Rogers, Gilda Lousak. Brave knight returns from the Crusades to free the Saxons. Dubbed-English costume adventure doesn't have much bounce to the ounce.

Revenge of the Barbarians (Italian, 1963)*½ Anthony Steel, Daniella Rocca, Robert Alda. Thwarted by the plan of the emperor's sister, two invading barbarian leaders reorganize their forces and attack again, taking the sister prisoner. Dull English-dubbed spectacle.

Revenge of the Conquered (Italian, 1964)* Burt Nelson, Wandisa Guida. Gypsy lad loves a princess, but she's turned against him by a swine who wants her for himself. Poor costume adventure dubbed in English.

Revenge of the Creature (1955)** John Agar, Lori Nelson. Another monster from the deep epic—this time a "gill man" is smitten with the leading lady, who happens to be an ichthyologist. For the juve audience. (Dir: Jack Arnold, 82 mins.)

Revenge of the Gladiators (Italian, 1964)* Mickey Hargitay, Jose Greci. Warrior fights the barbarian hordes and saves a princess from a fate worse than, etc. Depressingly familiar adventure spectacle dubbed in English.

Revenge of the Gladiators (Italian, 1965)** Roger Browne, Scilla Gabel, Gordon Mitchell. Suspense tale in post-Spartacus Rome as slave revolt turns out to be a plot by a Roman senator. Battle scenes are OK. (Dir: Michele Lupo, 100 mins.)

Revenge of the Musketeers (Italian, 1962)* Fernando Lamas, Gloria Milland. D'Artagnan and the musketeers aid a young king in escaping from the clutches of the cardinal. Hoky swashbuckling adventure dubbed in English.

Revenge of the Pirates (Italian, 1951) *½ Maria Montez, Jean-Pierre Aumont, Milly Vitale. Swashbuckling skullduggery in old Maracaibo, as the beautiful marquesa is saved from a fate worse than, etc. Dull and draggy. Dubbed in English. (Dir: Primo Zeglio, 95 mins.)

Revenge of Ursus (Italian, 1960)* Samson Burke. Another variation on the by now painfully familiar theme, strong man overcomes all odds and frees the village from oppression. Shoddy English-dubbed spectacle.

Revolt at Fort Laramie (1957)**½ John Dehner, Frances Helm. Army fort is split upon the outbreak of the Civil War, with the commander torn between loyalty to the South and duty as an officer. Pretty fair western, with a somewhat different plot and good acting by Dehner. (Dir: Lesley Selander, 73 mins.)

Revolt In the Big House (1958)**½ Gene Evans, Robert Blake. Cons plan a daring escape headed by a dramatics with a good performance by young Blake. (Dir: R. G. Springsteen, 79 mins.)

Revolt of Mamie Stover, The (1956) **½ Jane Russell, Richard Egan, Joan Leslie, Agnes Moorehead. Above-average melodrama of a beautiful young girl, forced to leave town, who goes to Hawaii and earns a small fortune as a dance-hall hostess during World War II. Based on a novel by William Bradford Huie. (Dir: Raoul Walsh, 93 mins.)

Revolt of the Barbarians (Italian, 1964)* Roland Caray, Grazia Maria Spina. Roman consul investigating gold raids unmasks the leader of the barbarian band causing all the trouble. Dull English-dubbed spectacle.

Revolt of the Mamalukes (Egyptian, 1960)*½ Omar Sharif. Emir is the last hope of a people seeking freedom from tyrant rule. Lavish spectacle is inept in every way but scope. Sharif has since become an international star. Dubbed in English.

Revolt of the Mercenaries (Italian, 1961)*½ Virginia Mayo, Conrad Sammartin. Dashing mercenary leader comes to the aid of a beautiful duchess who is feuding with a warlike neighbor. Tepid costume adventure English-dubbed, with the gorgeous Mayo lost amid the royal trappings.

Revolt of the Praetorians (Italian, 1963)* Richard Harrison, Moira Orfei. Heroic leader fights to overcome an evil Roman emperor. Boredom triumphs. English dubbed.

Revolt of the Tartars (Italian, 1960) ** Curt Jurgens, Genevieve Page. Emissary of the Czar undertakes a dangerous trek to deliver a message to the Grand Duke. Another version of "Michael Strogoff"; lavishly produced, somewhat slow moving. Fair spectacle stuff. English-dubbed.

Reward, The (1965)* Max von Sydow, Yvette Mimieux, Efrem Zimbalist, Jr., Gilbert Roland. Good cast, caught in a clichéd Western, about the greed that overcomes a five-man posse who begin eliminating one another. Little suspense. (Dir: Serge Bourguignon, 92 mins.)

Rhapsody (1954)**½ Elizabeth Taylor, Vittorio Gassman, John Ericson.

A romantic feast for the female viewers. Miss Taylor wears a succession of chic 1954 fashions and bounces from V. Gassman's to John Ericson's arms throughout this triangular love story involving a wealthy young woman, a continental violin virtuoso, and a sensitive promising pianist. (Dir: Charles Vidor, 115 mins.)

Rhapsody in Blue (1945)***½ Robert Alda, Oscar Levant, Alexis Smith. This is a trite, pedestrian film biography of the great George Gershwin but it's simply loaded with his magnificent music and the color of the years when he was on top. It's a treat to listen but it will make you feel cheated by his early death. (Dir: Irving Rapper, 139 mins.)

Rhino (1964)**½ Robert Culp, Shirley Eaton, Harry Guardino. An exciting show for the younger set. About a zoologist who goes after a rare white rhino. The animal footage is very interesting. The cast really has little to do, but the South African scenery is gorgeous. (Dir: Ivan Tors, 91 mins.)

Rhinoceros (1974)** Gene Wilder, Zero Mostel, Karen Black. Considering the fine cast and the at least semi-classic nature of Ionesco's play, this picture is a disappointment. Largely at fault are the senselessly updated screenplay and the trendy direction of Tom O'Horgan. The music, a sort of spineless rock, is unsuitable and unpleasant. Gene Wilder and Karen Black put up a really superhuman struggle against the director's inability to understand either his material or his medium. Mostel is a great actor, and it's your only chance of the day to see him turn into a "Rhinoceros." (Dir: Tom O'Horgan, 101 mins.)

Rhubarb (1951)***½ Ray Milland, Jan Sterling. When a millionaire who owns a baseball club passes on, a cat inherits the team; as a mascot the feline leads the club toward a pennant. Zany comedy has plenty of fun and an amazingly well-trained cat actor. (Dir: Arthur Lubin, 95 mins.)

Rhythm on the Range (1936)** Bing Crosby, Martha Raye, Bob Burns. Cowboy Bing romances an heiress and a prize cow in this forced comic offering. (Dir: Norman Taurog, 90 mins.)

Rhythm on the River (1940)*** Bing

Crosby, Mary Martin, Oscar Levant. Nothing turns into something when handled by experts. A couple of successful ghost song writers try and click on their own, but only succeed in falling in love. Pleasant musical. (Dir: Victor Schertzinger, 92 mins.)

Rice Girl (Italian, 1959)** Elsa Martinelli, Michel Auclair. Lust and love in the rice fields, as a girl finds promise of happiness after a hard past. After Mangano and Loren working in the same neighborhood, this drama is pretty mild. Dubbed-in English. (Dir: Raffaello Matarazzo, 90 mins.)

Rich and Strange (Great Britain, 1932)*** Henry Kendall, Joan Barry, Betty Amann. Alfred Hitchcock's sixth sound picture, treated somewhat more romantically than many of his other films. About a suburban English couple, tired of their humdrum life, who conveniently inherit money from a rich uncle and set off on a cruise around the world. "Rich and Strange" was neither a box-office nor commercial success at the time of its release, but it is interesting most of the time. (Dir: Alfred Hitchcock, 81 mins.)

Rich, Young and Pretty (1951)**½ Jane Powell, Vic Damone, Fernando Lamas, Wendell Corey, Danielle Darrieux. A typical M-G-M musical built around Jane Powell's soprano talents. She's a Texan's daughter who finds her long-lost mom in gay Paree. (Dir: Norman Taurog, 95 mins.)

Richard III (British, 1955)**** Laurence Olivier, Claire Bloom, John Gielgud, Ralph Richardson. The great actor at the top of his form in this marvelous film version of Shakespeare's powerful tale of the wicked deformed king and his conquests—on the battlefield, in the boudoir, etc. Olivier's definitive performance and his faultless direction combine to make this a model of how to film a great classic. (158 mins.)

Ricochet Romance (1955)** Marjorie Main, Chill Wills. Marjorie Main is back playing her "Ma Kettle" characterization in everything but name —her monicker in this comedy opus about life on a guest ranch is "Pansy Jones." Some funny moments. (Dir: Charles Lamont, 80 mins.)

Ride a Crooked Mile (1938)** Akim Tamiroff, Frances Farmer. Corny,

overdone drama about a boy who decides to help his growling thief of a father break out of Leavenworth. Some good acting, but the story is more confusing than entertaining. (Dir: Alfred E. Green, 80 mins.)

Ride Back, The (1957)*** Anthony Quinn, Lita Milan. Anthony Quinn makes more of this low key western than seems possible. The plot, about a U. S. law officer tracking a wanted murderer in Mexico, unfolds slowly but the actors bring honest characterizations. (Dir: Allen H. Miner, 79 mins.)

Ride Beyond Vengeance (1966)** Chuck Connors, Michael Rennie, Gloria Grahame. Familiar western drama told in flashback by a saloon keeper. Connors returns to his home after getting a stake and is robbed and branded by a band of outlaws. (Dir: Bernard McEveety, 101 mins.)

Ride 'Em Cowboy (1942)**½ Bud Abbott, Lou Costello, Dick Foran, Anne Gwynne. One of the better Abbott and Costello vehicles has them out West on a dude ranch. Features a great chase sequence and the usual antic humor. Songs by the Merry Macs and Ella Fitzgerald are a restful break. (Dir: Arthur Lubin, 82 mins.)

Ride in the Whirlwind (1967)*** Cameron Mitchell, Millie Perkins, Jack Nicholson. With a little bit more work, this western drama could have been memorable. As it is, it is a better-than-average tale of western justice and the men who fled from it and those who searched for it. The cast is good, with Cameron Mitchell delivering the film's best performance. (Dir: Monte Hellman, 82 mins.)

Ride Lonesome (1959)**½ Randolph Scott, Karen Steele, Pernell Roberts. Good Randy Scott western epic which should appeal to his fans. He plays a former sheriff who captures a young renegade and brings him to justice. (Dir: Budd Boetticher, 73 mins.)

Ride Out for Revenge (1957)**½ Rory Calhoun, Gloria Grahame, Lloyd Bridges. A bang up western with all the cliches nicely fitted into the brief running time of the film. Calhoun upholds the law and meets with a great deal of opposition from the bad guys. (Dir: Bernard Girard, 79 mins.)

Ride the High Country (1962)**** Joel McCrea, Randolph Scott, Mariette Hartley. An absolutely first-rate western, which gives Scott and McCrea, in their last performances as western heroes, the best roles of their lives, and they make the most of it. Directed by Sam Peckinpah in a controlled, subtle way—unlike much of his later violence-laden films. Written by N. B. Stone, Jr., and shot on location in the glorious Inyo National Forest in California. Two old-time lawmen sign on to escort gold from the goldfields to the bank, meeting trouble along the way. (Dir: Sam Peckinpah, 94 mins.)

Ride the High Iron (1957)*½ Don Taylor, Sally Forrest, Raymond Burr. Clumsy, romantic yarn about a young opportunist who meets a rich heiress through his contacts and falls in love with her. Some criminal intervention changes his plans. (Dir: Don Weis, 74 mins.)

Ride the High Wind (South African, 1966)** Bush pilot (Darren McGavin) sets out to recover long-lost gold. Unusual locale, familiar plot. Maria Perschy, Albert Lieven.

Ride the Man Down (1952)*** Rod Cameron, Brian Donlevy, Ella Raines. Ranch foreman keeps it from land grabbers while awaiting the new owners. Fast-paced, exciting western with a good cast. (Dir: Joseph Kane, 90 mins.)

Ride the Pink Horse (1947)**** Robert Montgomery, Wanda Hendrix, Thomas Gomez. Suspenseful tale of a hoodlum helped by a Mexican girl when he is crossed by his employers. Out of the ordinary crime drama with superb performances and direction by Montgomery. (Dir: Robert Montgomery, 101 mins.)

Ride the Wild Surf (1964)** Tab Hunter, Fabian, Barbara Eden. The kids are the best audience for this swinging film about the surfing craze in Hawaii. A group of young bronzed surfers engage in romantic interludes in between their riding the big waves. (Dir: Don Taylor, 101 mins.)

Ride to Hangman's Tree, The (1967)** Jack Lord, James Farentino, Melodie Johnson. A remake, for no discernible reason, of the '48 release "Black Bart." The original was a humdrum western, and so is this familiar tale about three partners in crime who decide to try and go straight. (Dir: Al Rafkin, 90 mins.)

Ride Vaquero (1953)** Robert Taylor, Ava Gardner, Howard Keel, Anthony Quinn. Sluggish western concerns a smouldering beauty who causes the downfall of some notorious outlaws. Melodramatic situations are too much, making the cast look silly at times. (Dir: John Farrow, 90 mins.)

Rider on a Dead Horse (1962)** John Vivyan, Lisa Lu, Bruce Gordon. Prospector seeks revenge when his partner murders a third and tries to pin it on him. Undistinguished western. (Dir: Herbert L. Strock, 72 mins.)

Rider on the Rain (France-Italy, 1969)*** Charles Bronson, Marlene Jobert, Jill Ireland. Satisfying thriller that suspends credulity and keeps you guessing through neat psychological twists. Mellie (Jobert) has been raped in her home but has dropped her attacker with a shotgun blast. Arrogant investigator Dobbs (Bronson) appears on the trail of an escaped inmate. Sharp dialogue, underplayed acting and deft directorial control blend for fine suspense. Taut screenplay by novelist Sebastien Japrisot. (Dir: Rene Clement, 119 mins.)

Riders to the Stars (1954)**½ William Lundigan, Herbert Marshall. Fair science-fiction thriller about three men sent into outer space to investigate certain meteor behavior. (Dir: Richard Carlson, 81 mins.)

Riding High (1943)*** Dorothy Lamour, Victor Moore, Dick Powell. Big budgeted musical with little entertainment value. Something about a silver mine, a young man who wants to save it, and some musical nothings. (Dir: George Marshall, 89 mins.)

Riding High (1950)**½ Bing Crosby, Coleen Gray, Charles Bickford. Mark Hellinger's story about a businessman who'd rather spend his time at the race track is turned into a pleasant Bing Crosby comedy with songs. Veteran comedy director Frank Capra keeps things snapping and a good supporting cast of pros, like Raymond Walburn, William Demarest and Charles Bickford, give the film an added charm. (Dir: Frank Capra, 112 mins.)

Riding Shotgun (1954)** Randolph Scott, Wayne Morris. Scott is riding and shooting in his usual manner. (Dir: Andre de Toth, 74 mins.)

Riff-Raff (French, 1961)** Robert Hossein, Marina Vlady. Inquest into a girl's death brings forth many surprising discoveries. Long, involved melodrama moves too slowly. English-dubbed.

Riffraff (1935)** Jean Harlow, Spencer Tracy. Cliche filled, melodramatic story of the tuna fishing industry in California. An insult to its excellent cast. (Dir: J. Walter Ruben, 100 mins.)

Riffraff (1947)*** Pat O'Brien, Anne Jeffreys. Crooks are after an oil field survey in Panama, but are foiled by the local jack-of-all-trades. Well done melodrama holds the interest. (Dir: Ted Tetzlaff, 80 mins.)

Rififi (French, 1954)**** Jean Servais, Carl Mohner. There's a classic robbery scene in this exciting story about some crooks whose mutual distrust traps them all. A superior film. Brilliantly directed by American Jules Dassin. (115 mins.)

Rififi in Amsterdam (1966)*½ Roger Browne, Aida Power, Evelyne Stewart. Jewel robbery along the Amsterdam Canal ends with four of the five thieves being murdered. Sounds more exciting than it is, and it doesn't sound like much! (Dir: Terence Hathaway, 83 mins.)

Right Cross (1950)**½ Dick Powell, June Allyson, Ricardo Montalban, Lionel Barrymore. Good prizefighting story about a Mexican boxer who desperately wants to become a champion. Montalban, as the pugilist, takes top acting honors with Dick Powell a close second as an easygoing sportswriter. (Dir: John Sturges, 90 mins.)

Right Hand of the Devil (1963)*½ Aram Katcher, Lisa McDonald. Girl seeks revenge upon a brutal gangster who has committed murder and robbery. Mediocre crime drama.

Right On (1971)***½ Powerful, independent low budget film. Director Herbert Danska focuses his cameras on three young, activist black poets. Their anger, dreams and concerns seem to burst thru the screen aided by some stunning visual images. Photographed largely in New York's Harlem. The poems, like the film itself, are of uneven quality, but this honest searing film captures the passion of the artists. A powerful political tract.

600

Ring, The (1952)**½ Gerald Mohr, Lalo Rios, Rita Moreno. Mexican lad from the Los Angeles slums is turned into a boxing prospect, gets too cocky as a result. Smoothly made drama of fighting and racial discrimination, nicely acted. (Dir: Kurt Neumann, 79 mins.)

Ring of Bright Water (Great Britain, 1969)*½ Bill Travers, Virginia McKenna, Peter Jeffrey. This "family" picture features the couple of "Born Free" fame, Bill Travers and Virginia McKenna. In this outing, the pair offers the same compassionate treatment to Mijbil, the otter, that they gave to Elsa, the lioness. Photographed against the background of the stunning wilds of Scotland. Acting honors to the otters. (Dir: Jack Couffer, 107 mins.)

Ring of Fear (1955)** Mickey Spillane, Pat O'Brien, Clyde Beatty. Cops and robbers in a circus tent performed mostly by non-actors—Beatty, Spillane, and tamed animals. (Dir: James Grant, 93 mins.)

Ring of Fire (1961)** David Janssen, Joyce Taylor, Frank Gorshin. A try for suspense as some hoodlums capture a lawman and hold him hostage in their flight for freedom. Some nice scenery and a spectacular explosion at the end, but it needs more; weak script, so-so performances. (Dir: Andrew L. Stone, 91 mins.)

Ring of Terror (German, 1962)*½ George Mather, Austin Green. Young premed student must open a crypt and remove a ring from the finger of a corpse as part of a fraternity initiation. Meandering horror thriller dubbed in English.

Ring of Treason (1964)**½ Bernard Lee, William Sylvester, Margaret Tyzack. Staccato suspense in this punctuated story of a Russian spy ring in London. Lee is an ex-Navy man taken to drink and mixing in with vile people. British in detail and design, and based on Britain's Portland spy case. Exciting finale. (Dir: Robert Tronson, 90 mins.)

Rings on Her Fingers (1942)**½ Henry Fonda, Gene Tierney, Laird Cregar. Well played but overdone tale of a girl who is conned into fronting for swindlers and falls for her first victim. (Dir: Rouben Mamoulian, 85 mins.)

Rio Bravo (1959)**½ John Wayne, Dean Martin, Ricky Nelson. An attempt at mixing humor and horse opera that doesn't quit come off. Wayne is his usual saddle worn self and Martin seems out of place in a wild west saloon. Ricky Nelson looks the most uncomfortable as a young cow-hand itching to prove that he's a man. Sexy Angie Dickinson supplies the love interest. (Dir: Howard Hawks, 141 mins.)

Rio Conchos (1964)** Richard Boone, Stuart Whitman, Tony Franciosa. For western action fans who can't get their fill of two-fisted he-men living by their own code in the old West. The cast is a good one, including Jim Brown and Edmond O'Brien. About a group who set out to recover some stolen rifles which are earmarked for sale to the Apaches. (Dir: Gordon Douglas, 107 mins.)

Rio Grande (1950)***½ John Wayne, Maureen O'Hara. Tough cavalry commander awaits orders to cross a river so he can clean up marauding Indians. John Ford epic western has beautiful scenery, some good action and plenty of human interest. (Dir: John Ford, 105 mins.)

Rio Lobo (1970)*½ John Wayne, Jorge Rivero, Jennifer O'Neill, Jack Elam. Director Hawks and star Wayne just aren't up to their old high standards in this Civil War-era western. The opening train robbery sequence is exciting, but the film then bogs down with slow, sadistic action, boring dialogue, wooden acting. (Dir: Howard Hawks, 114 mins.)

Rio Rita (1941)*** Kathryn Grayson, Abbott & Costello. Abbott & Costello fans and even a few others will enjoy this musical about a ranch which is infested with Nazi spies. (Dir: S. Sylvan Simon, 91 mins.)

Riot (1969)**½ This typical prison drama, in which some up-to-date violence has been thrown in, benefits from the strong acting personalities of Jim Brown and Gene Hackman. The story concerns a group of cons who take over a section of the prison, hold some guards as hostages, and the fireworks begin. (Dir: Buzz Kulik, 97 mins.)

Riot in Cell Block 11 (1954)*** Neville Brand. Exciting and well played prison drama. Neville Brand seems the perfect type to play a con who instigates a riot and plans an escape. (Dir: Don Siegel, 80 mins.)

Riot on Sunset Strip (1967)* Aldo Ray, Mimsy Farmer. Based on an actual riot of teenaged delinquents and connected incidents on California's Sunset Strip in 1966. Policeman must cope with events and his neglected daughter's involvement. The standard, noisy pap about mixed-up juveniles, parental shortcomings. (Dir: Arthur Dreifuss, 85 mins.)

Rise and Fall of Legs Diamond, The (1960)*** Ray Danton, Elaine Stewart. Fast-moving and impressive account of the career of a hoodlum who rose to national infamy. Ray Danton slickly portrays the racketeer and there's plenty of pulchritude for the male audience. (Dir: Budd Boetticher, 101 mins.)

Rise and Shine (1941)*** Jack Oakie, Linda Darnell. Occasionally hilarious comedy about a dumb football hero's adventures. Oakie is perfect and you should have some fun with this in spite of some uninspired music. (Dir: Allan Dwan, 93 mins.)

Rise of Louis XIV, The (Italian, 1965)**** Jean-Marie Patte, Raymond Jourdan Silvagni, Pierre Barrat. Roberto Rossellini's masterpiece on the consolidation of power by France's young king. This is one of a series of brilliant historical films made by Rossellini for Italian TV. It's an absorbing film and an invaluable history lesson. Begins with the last days and the death of Mazarin in 1661, and includes the building of Versailles and ends as Louis XIV forces his whole court to watch him devour a 14-course meal. This ravishing photography and the dazzling costumes are a feast for the eye thanks to cinematographer Georges LeClerc, and there's a lucid script from Philippe Erlanger and Jean Gruault. Most historical films treat the protagonists as cardboard cutouts, with little or no concern for accuracy and character delineation. The Sun King is presented as the complex, bizarre figure he surely was. Superb underplayed portrait of the King by Patte. (100 mins.)

Rising of the Moon (1957)*** Frank Lawton, Dennis O'Dea. Trio of Irish tales directed by John Ford. Full of the ould blarney but still charming. (81 mins.)

Risk, The (British, 1960)*** Peter Cushing, Tony Britton, Virginia Maskell. When a cure for plague is discovered then withheld, resentment causes a scientist to become prey for foreign agents after the formula. Tightly knit spy drama holds the attention throughout. (Dirs: Roy & John Boulting, 81 mins.)

Ritual of Evil (1970)**½ Louis Jourdan, Anne Baxter, Diana Hyland. Entertaining made-for-TV feature starring Louis Jourdan as a psychiatrist interested in the bizarre world of the occult. A young heiress' death brings about Jourdan's investigation of the events leading to the tragedy. A series of good supporting players come on for their scenes. (Dir: Robert Day, 100 mins.)

Ritz, The (1976)*** Jack Weston, Rita Moreno, Kaye Ballard, F. Murray Abraham, Jerry Stiller. A manic, fast-paced farce, set in a sleazy Manhattan homosexual bathhouse, that is, by turns, very funny, heavy-handed and repetitive. Adapted by Terrence McNally from his Broadway play. Director Richard Lester keeps things going along at a frantic pace. Rita Moreno, playing a hopelessly untalented but very determined pop singer, is hilarious. (Dir: Richard Lester, 91 mins.)

Rivals, The (British, 1961)** Jack Gwillin, Erica Rogers. Daughter of a wealthy industrialist is kidnaped. Okay Edgar Wallace crime melodrama. (Dir: Krishna Shah, 103 mins.)

River, The (1951)**** Nora Swinburne, Esmond Knight. Story of an English family living in India, and of the hardships and difficulties involved in their maturity. Off the beaten path; a pictorially beautiful fascinating drama, directed by Jean Renoir. (99 mins.)

River Changes, The (German, 1957)** Rossana Rory, Harold Maresch. A muddled drama about the inhabitants of a small village who are plagued by an army of ruthless men. Plenty of romance and some action.

River Gang (1945)**½ Gloria Jean, Keefe Brasselle, John Qualen. Waterfront girl who lives in a land of fantasy becomes involved in murder and a crime ring. Offbeat Grade B mystery has several above-average touches.

River of Evil (German, 1964)*½ Barbara Rutting, Harold Leipnitz. Girl braves the perils of the Amazon wilderness in search of the answer to her father's death. Lumbering English-dubbed jungle adventure.

River of Gold (1971)*½ Roger Davis, Suzanne Pleshette, Dick Rambo. Dull, made-for-TV adventure story about two free-wheeling buddies (Dick Rambo and Roger Davis) who get involved with a group of mysterious people—a rich man looking for hidden treasure (Ray Milland); a poet's widow (Suzanne Pleshette) and the poet's mistress (Melissa Newman). The best thing about the entire affair is the on-location Acapulco setting. (Dir: David Friedkin, 72 mins.)

River of No Return (1954)**½ Marilyn Monroe, Robert Mitchum. The potent casting of Marilyn Monroe and Robert Mitchum and some good location photography almost make up for the plot of this action-packed backwoods adventure yarn. La Monroe plays a saloon entertainer who enlists widower Mitchum's aid when her shiftless gambler husband deserts her. (Dir: Otto Preminger, 91 mins.)

River of Three Junks, The (French, 1957)*½ Dominique Wilms, Jean Gavin. Secret agent fights the arms traffic in Asia. Adventure is junk on the screen. Dubbed in English.

River's Edge, The (1957)*** Anthony Quinn, Ray Milland, Debra Paget. Better than average crime melodrama about a killer who menaces his old girl friend and her husband's life in an attempt to smuggle a stolen fortune into Mexico. Excitement for action fans. (Dir: Allan Dwan, 87 mins.)

Road House (1948)*** Ida Lupino, Richard Widmark, Cornel Wilde. A good cast lifts this routine melodrama out of the ranks of mediocrity. Widmark plays a sadistic road house owner who has his enemy paroled in his custody so he can torture him. (Dir: Jean Negulesco, 95 mins.)

Road Show (1940)**½ Adolphe Menjou, Carole Landis. A playboy and his screwy friend from an insane asylum join a traveling carnival. Completely mad, amusing farce. (Dirs: Hal Roach, Hal Roach, Jr., Gordon Douglas, 87 mins.)

Road to Bali (1953)*** Bing Crosby, Bob Hope, Dorothy Lamour. Another in the Hope-Crosby-Lamour road epics and a funny one. The boys play a couple of song-and-dance vaudevilians who end up on an island paradise complete with Lamour in a sarong and various and assorted savages. The laughs are fast and funny and there's music, too. (Dir: Hal Walker, 90 mins.)

Road to Denver (1955)**½ John Payne, Mona Freeman, Lee J. Cobb. Cowhand tries to keep his hot-headed brother out of trouble when the kid joins up with the outlaws. Pretty fair western. (Dir: Joseph Kane, 90 mins.)

Road to Glory, The (1936)*** Fredric March, Warner Baxter, Lionel Barrymore. Exciting World War I film which is episodic but superbly acted and directed. William Faulkner is credited as co-author of the script along with Joel Sayre. (Dir: Howard Hawks, 95 mins.)

Road to Hong Kong (1961)*** Bing Crosby, Bob Hope, Joan Collins, Dorothy Lamour. The latest and perhaps the last of the "Road" pictures with Hope, Crosby and a brief appearance by Dorothy Lamour. The plot centers around a couple of hustlers who find themselves up to their necks in international intrigue and interplanetary hokum. A good supporting cast includes Robert Morley, Joan Collins and last but not least, Peter Sellers. (Dir: Norman Panama, 91 mins.)

Road to Morocco (1942)*** Bob Hope, Bing Crosby, Dorothy Lamour. Zany Hope-Crosby comedy is a bit too silly, but still gets its share of laughs from their insults and encounters. A few good songs help out. (Dir: David Butler, 83 mins.)

Road to Rio (1948)*** Bob Hope, Bing Crosby, Dorothy Lamour. Crazy, delightful antics in Rio de Janeiro expertly handled by experts. Good fun. (Dir: Norman Z. McLeod, 100 mins.)

Road to Singapore (1940)*** Bob Hope, Bing Crosby. First of the "Road" films and not much to offer except for Bob and Bing's presence. Zany tale about two playboys who go to Singapore to forget women. (Dir: Victor Schertzinger, 92 mins.)

Road to Utopia (1946)***½ Bing Crosby, Bob Hope, Dorothy Lamour. Vaudeville team involved in search for Alaskan gold mine but—forget the plot—this one is funny. (Dir: Hal Walker, 90 mins.)

Road to Zanzibar (1941)***½ Bob Hope, Bing Crosby, Dorothy Lamour. Satire on all jungle pictures

is the funniest of the "Road" series. Bing and Bob tour Africa as a couple of carnival hustlers and it's really the greatest safari the movies have ever shown. (Dir: Victor Schertzinger, 92 mins.)

Roadblock (1951)**½ Charles McGraw, Joan Dixon. Insurance investigator turns crook to get enough money for his girl friend. Well acted, suspenseful crime melodrama.

Roaring Twenties, The (1939)*** James Cagney, Priscilla Lane. This saga of the "dry" years with its gang wars and speakeasies may, for nostalgic and historical reasons, look like a better film today than when it was originally presented. Cagney is wonderful in this adaptation of a Mark Hellinger story. (Dir: Raoul Walsh, 110 mins.)

Robber's Roost (1955)*½ George Montgomery, Richard Boone. Westerner manages to defeat two outlaw gangs. Below par western, ineptly handled. (Dir: Sidney Salkow, 82 mins.)

Robbery (British, 1967)**½ Stanley Baker, Joanna Pettet. This tense melodrama based on the hijacking of the London night mail train is only partially successful. The plans for the robbery and its actual execution are well handled, but the characterizations of those involved are overdrawn and get in the way. This is the second of two films based on the much publicized train robbery in England in 1963. The other film, which is better done, was made, curiously enough, by West German film makers and is entitled "The Great British Train Robbery." (Dir: Peter Yates, 114 mins.)

Robbery, Roman Style (Italian, 1964)** Claudio Mori, A. Celentano. Perfectly executed bank robbery goes awry when the crooks battle among themselves. Routine crime melodrama. Dubbed-in English.

Robbery Under Arms (British, 1957)**½ Peter Finch, Ronald Lewis. Two brothers join an outlaw on a cattle-stealing venture in Australia. Well made, but very similar to our westerns. (Dir: Jack Lee, 83 mins.)

Robe, The (1953)*** Richard Burton, Jean Simmons, Victor Mature, Michael Rennie, Richard Boone. Hailed as the first film to be made in the Cinemascope process—which means nothing for TV purposes. The Lloyd C. Douglas religious novel about a Roman tribune ordered to crucify the Messiah, and his conversion to Christianity when he dons the robe of Jesus, is reverent, stately, impressively produced. It is also slow-moving, rather stilted, and not especially well acted. (Dir: Henry Koster, 135 mins.)

Robin and Marian (1976)**** Audrey Hepburn, Sean Connery, Robert Shaw, Richard Harris, Nicol Williamson. After an absence from the screen of almost a decade (her last was the '67 "Wait Until Dark"), the sorely missed Audrey Hepburn returns in this historical romance—a revisionist view of medieval history and our friends from Sherwood Forest. But thanks largely to the two stars, this tale of Robin Hood, 20 years after he left Sherwood Forest to join Richard the Lion-Hearted on the Crusades, is a surprisingly affecting and genuinely touching love story. Connery, in case you're only used to seeing him in the 007 nonsense, is an astonishingly good actor. He and Hepburn are a magical pairing. Maid Marian is now the abbess of a nearby convent, and their love scenes, their simply being together as played by these two worthies, make "Robin and Marian" a rewarding film and one of the best love stories in years. Special credit to the photography of David Watkin. Screenplay by James Goldman. (Dir: Richard Lester, 106 mins.)

Robin and the Seven Hoods (1964)*** Frank Sinatra, Dean Martin, Bing Crosby, Sammy Davis, Jr., Barbara Rush, Peter Falk. Entertaining musical spoof of the prohibition days in Chicago. Sinatra and his cronies are well suited to their roles of small-time hoods who fleece the rich and give to the less affluent, like orphans and such. The original musical score is very good, including a couple of standout songs, "My Kind of Town" and "Style." The entire cast appears to be having a good time and so will you. (Dir: Gordon Douglas, 103 mins.)

Robin Hood and the Pirates (Italian, 1964)*½ Lex Barker. The Merrie Men led by Robin Hood go into action against invading buccaneers. Weak costume action adventure. Dubbed-In English.

Robinson Crusoe (1953)***½ Dan O'Herlihy. Daniel Defoe's classic story of a man marooned on a small island. O'Herlihy's performance is a stand-out, practically a one-man show.

Robinson Crusoe of Mystery Island (1936-66)*½ Ray Mala. Feature version of serial "Robinson Crusoe of Clipper Island." Native hero outwits crafty saboteurs. Ex-serial shows its age but may get by with the kiddies. (Dir: Mack J. Wright, 100 mins.)

Robinson Crusoe on Mars (1964)*** Adam West, Vic London, Paul Mantee. Despite its ridiculous title, this is a surprisingly imaginative and intelligent sci-fi film about the survival of an American spaceman marooned on Mars. (Dir: Byron Haskin, 109 mins.)

Robot Vs. the Aztec Mummy, The (Mexican, 1960)* Ramon Gay, Rosita Arenas. Mad scientist previously thwarted in his efforts to get a treasure buried in an Aztec tomb constructs a robot to do his dirty work. Ridiculously poor English-dubbed horror thriller.

Rocco and His Brothers (Italian, 1961)***½ Alain Delon, Renato Salvatori, Annie Girardot, Katina Paxinou. Drama of a woman and her sons who come to Milan to find livelihood and the various fates befalling the offspring. Many subplots meticulously woven together to make a broad canvas of contemporary Italy, absorbing despite the length. Review is based on the long version (152 minutes), although a shorter (95 minutes) one is available. Dubbed in English. (Dir: Luchino Visconti)

Rock-a-Bye Baby (1958)** Jerry Lewis, Marilyn Maxwell, Connie Stevens. Uneven farce with Jerry Lewis playing bachelor father to a Hollywood starlet's baby. Usual Lewis hijinks with only a pinch of originality. (Dir: Frank Tashlin, 103 mins.)

Rock Around the Clock (1956)** Bill Haley and His Comets, Johnny Johnston. Quickie musical produced to capitalize on the popularity of Bill Haley and His Comets, Johnston is around to further the plot—which is fairly non-existent. Rock 'n roll fans might like to compare this vintage film with the current musical trends. (Dir: Fred F. Sears, 77 mins.)

Rock Around the World (1957)** Tommy Steele. Story—fictional perhaps—of British singing idol Tommy

Steele. Lots of songs for Steele fans, nothing else.

Rock 'n Roll Revue (1956)** Duke Ellington, Dinah Washington and many others in a compilation of music acts. Hipsters may dig.

Rock, Pretty Baby (1957)** John Saxon, Luana Patten, Sal Mineo. Slight plot about a high-school band leader out to win the big contest tied to vast amount of r&r numbers. Teenagers should appreciate—for their elders it's at least bearable. (Dir: Richard Bartlett, 89 mins.)

Rocket from Calbuch (Spanish, 1958) **½ Edmund Gwenn, Valentina Cortesa. Silly comedy about an old scientist who decides to experiment in rockets. The flavor of the village setting comes through and enhances the otherwise lightweight comedy. Edmund Gwenn is funny in the role of the bearded scientist.

Rocket Man, The (1954)*½ Charles Coburn, Anne Francis, George Winslow. Adopted boy helps the town get rid of crooks by means of a mysterious gun. Childish fantasy; scripted by Lenny Bruce, but you'd never know it. (Dir: Oscar Rudolph, 79 mins.)

Rocketship X-M (1950)*** Lloyd Bridges, Osa Massen. Scientists begin their first rocket trip to the moon, but something goes wrong and they land on atomic-destroyed Mars instead. Good science-fiction thriller. Well done technically and dramatically. (Dir: Kurt Neumann, 77 mins.)

Rockford Files, The (1974)** James Garner, Lindsay Wagner. The pilot film for the subsequent TV series starring James Garner as a private eye who insists on a $200-a-day fee from his pretty client (Miss Wagner) for fingering the murderer of her wino father. The best thing about the film, involving such familiar ploys as a harrowing car chase, is Garner's performance—he uses his easygoing dry wit to advantage. (Dir: Dick Heffron.)

Rocking Horse Winner, The (British, 1949)***½ Valerie Hobson, John Howard Davies, John Mills. Youngster keeps picking winners while riding his rocking horse, bringing wealth to his family, but his gift soon brings tragedy. Gripping, superbly acted drama, with an un-

usual theme, treated carefully. (Dir: Anthony Pelissier, 91 mins.)

Rocky (1976)**** Sylvester Stallone, Talia Shire, Burgess Meredith, Burt Young, Carl Weathers. The low-budget smash-hit sleeper of the year that packs a powerful sentimental punch! The Academy Award-winner about a loutish lug who wants to become a boxing champ. In many ways, it's surprising that "Rocky" really does pay off emotionally, and that the audience does care about the "Italian Stumbler," a two-bit thumb-breaker working for the mob in seamy Philadelphia. John G. Avildsen won the Academy Award for his direction of "Rocky," which features a notable closing fight aided by a deft makeup man. It may be 30's make-believe, but Stallone does make you care for him in the screenplay written by him, and Talia Shire, playing his painfully shy girlfriend, is splendid. Uses the slums of Philadelphia to good advantage for much of the on-location scenes. (Dir: John G. Avildsen, 119 mins.)

Rocky Mountain (1950)** Errol Flynn, Patrice Wymore. Opposing forces unite to fight a common enemy, the attacking Indians. You've seen it before, though not always with Mr. & Mrs. Flynn. (Dir: William Keighley, 83 mins.)

Rodan (Japanese, 1957)** Kenji Sawara. Japanese made science fiction film about a huge flying monster. Technically inferior to American made films of the same insipid nature. (Dir: Inoshiro Honda, 70 mins.)

Rodeo (1952)**½ John Archer, Jan Nigh. Girl takes over a rodeo when the promoter skips with the loot, makes it a success. Pleasant melodrama doesn't try for any heights, manages to be pleasing in its own small way. (Dir: William Beaudine, 70 mins.)

Roger Touhy, Gangster (1944)**½ Preston Foster, Victor McLaglen. Fairly good crime film loosely based on Touhy's career. Maybe if he looked like Foster, he would have become an actor. (Dir: Robert Florey, 65 mins.)

Rogue Cop (1954)*** Robert Taylor, Janet Leigh, George Raft, Anne Francis. Better than usual cops and robbers yarn. Raft is a standout as a syndicate czar who is more than a

605

bit sadistic and ruthless. Taylor is effective as a detective who's on the take. Miss Francis has two excellent scenes as a young moll who drinks to forget her plight. (Dir: Roy Rowland, 92 mins.)

Rogue River (1950)***½ Rory Calhoun, Peter Graves. A state policeman and his ne'er-do-well cousin become involved in a bank robbery. Exceptionally well-written, lively melodrama, well above average. (Dir: John Rawlins, 81 mins.)

Rogue Song, The (1930)**½ Lawrence Tibbett, Catherine Dale Owen, Laurel and Hardy. Billed as the first "De-Luxe Screen Operetta," this was MGM's first technicolor film. Tibbett does a fine acting turn, highlighted by his operatic baritone in the role of a Robin Hood of Russia hunted by Cossacks. Lionel Barrymore is behind the cameras here. (Dir: Lionel Barrymore, 108 mins.)

Rogue's Gallery (1968)** Roger Smith, Dennis Morgan, Brian Donlevy. Private-eye yarn that started out as a TV pilot film and wound up getting a theatrical release. Smith is John Rogue (that's the title, folks) and he goes through a tussle trying to keep his client from killing himself. Movie buffs will spot various old-timers in the supporting cast, including Jackie Coogan, Morgan, Edgar Bergen, and Richard Arlen. (Dir: Leonard Horn, 88 mins.)

Rogue's March (1953)** Peter Lawford, Richard Greene, Janice Rule. Average costume drama about a British regiment stationed in India. Lawford and Greene make dashing soldiers of the Queen, lovely Janice Rule supplies love interest. (Dir: Allan Davies, 84 mins.)

Rogues of Sherwood Forest (1956)** John Derek, Diana Lynn. Robin Hood rides again! Lavish sets and costumes but the same tired plot.

Roland the Mighty (Italian, 1961)*½ Rik Battaglia. Conqueror leads his armies when the Saracens and the legions of Charlemagne battle. Tepid epic dubbed in English. (Dir: Gordon Douglas, 80 mins.)

Roll, Freddy, Roll (1974)** Tim Conway, Jan Murray, Ruta Lee. Tim Conway's adept comedy style adds a freshness to this silly plot about a man who accidentally finds himself a short-term celebrity as he tries to break a Guinness-book World Record for staying on roller skates for more than a week. Made-for-TV. (Dir: Bill Persky, 72 mins.)

Rollerball (1975)*½ James Caan, Ralph Richardson, John Houseman. A repellent, occasionally involving allegory which purports to be criticizing the violence of our society and our professional sports, but which winds up glorifying the singularly repellent sport of Rollerball —a futuristic combination of rugby, roller-skating and gladiator-fight-to-the-death spectacles. The setting of "Rollerball" may be thirty years in the future, but it's a sordid exploitation film appealing to the basest instincts of our sick 70's. Based on a short story, "Rollerball Murders," by William Harrison. (Dir: Norman Jewison, 123 mins.)

Rolling Man (1972)**½ Dennis Weaver. A born loser wanders about the country after serving a prison term, looking for his son and dreaming of becoming a successful racetrack driver. Uneven, but has a sense of reality. Prison sequences, sleazy bars, and small-town auto tracks form the sordid background for a colorful collection of characters Weaver encounters along the way. Weaver registers and so do Sheree North, Don Stroud, and Jimmy Dean as a fast-talking operator Weaver meets in jail. Made-for-TV. (Dir: Peter Hyams, 73 mins.)

Roman Holiday (1953)**** Gregory Peck, Audrey Hepburn, Eddie Albert. Comedy delight about a newspaperman in Rome who meets and falls for a lonely princess traveling incognito. Oscar-winning performance by Hepburn, smart William Wyler direction, a production with great charm, completely captivating. (119 mins.)

Roman Scandals (1933)**½ Eddie Cantor, Ruth Etting, Edward Arnold. Musical comedy set in Rome, during the time of the Caesars. (Dir: Frank Tuttle, 100 mins.)

Roman Spring of Mrs. Stone, The (1961)*** Vivien Leigh, Warren Beatty. Based on Tennessee Williams' novel. All the decadence of the takers and the taken along the Via Veneto in Rome is bared in this tale about an aging actress who succumbs to taking a young paid-for lover. Miss Leigh by now, has played this type of role often. Warren Beatty fills the physical requirements of the handsome Italian gigolo but his accent gets in the way. Lotte Lenya, in the role of a ruthless social procurer, adds a sinister note and her performance is, by far, the best in the film. (Dir: Jose Quintero, 104 mins.)

Romance of a Horsethief (1972)* Yul Brynner, Eli Wallach, Lainie Kazan. Comedy about Cossacks and Jews in turn-of-the-century Poland is hard to create, and there is none here. The devices are tired, and there's no variation in the characters. Everyone has a heart of gold (including Kazan as a madame) and is optimistic despite the worst persecution. Add to this that everyone has a different accent and you have a grotesque bit of claptrap. (Dir: Abraham Polonsky, 100 mins.)

Romance of Rosy Ridge, The (1947) *** Van Johnson, Thomas Mitchell, Janet Leigh. With tensions high after the Civil War, a mysterious stranger is looked upon with suspicion by a Southern-sympathizing Missouri farmer. Well made, charming drama. (Dir: Roy Rowland, 105 mins.)

Romance on the High Seas (1948) *** Doris Day, Jack Carson. This was Doris' first film and it made a lot more noise at the box office than with the critics. Light little romantic-comedy with a cruise background doesn't interfere too much with a delightful score. (Dir: Michael Curtiz, 99 mins.)

Romanoff and Juliet (1961)***½ Peter Ustinov, Sandra Dee, John Gavin. Peter Ustinov has written, directed and stars in this comedy spoof set in a mythical country in which the daughter of the American ambassador falls in love with the Russian ambassador's son. Some of the lines don't work but the premise is funny enough and there's always Ustinov as a jack-of-all-trades in the mythical country. (Dir: Peter Ustinov, 103 mins.)

Rome Adventure (1962)** Troy Donahue, Suzanne Pleshette, Angie Dickinson, Rossano Brazzi. Librarian out to see some fun and a young architectural student meet and romance in Italy. The usual complications ensue, but it all works out fine by the end—and predictably. Gorgeous scenery, but the actors get in front of it too often with the sappy plot. (Dir: Delmer Daves, 119 mins.)

Rome, 1585 (Italian, 1963)* Debra Paget, Daniella Rocca, Livio Lorenzon. Drab costume drama about an outlaw head who fears the return of the former leader, who has been imprisoned. Dubbed in English.

Romeo and Juliet (1936)**** Leslie Howard, John Barrymore, Norma Shearer. Brilliant screen production of Shakespeare's tragic romance. Cast is superb. (Dir: George Cukor, 104 mins.)

Romeo and Juliet (1954)***½ Laurence Harvey, Susan Shentall. Shakespeare's tragedy of star-crossed lovers, beautifully filmed (in color) in Italy. Pictorially splendid, but the performances leave something to be desired. (Dir: Renato Castelli, 140 mins.)

Romeo and Juliet (Great Britain, 1966)**** Margot Fonteyn, Rudolph Nureyev, David Blair. Margot Fonteyn belies her advancing age by her radiant, graceful dancing of the young, delicate Juliet, in this filming of the British Royal Ballet's interpretation of Prokofiev's ballet. Nureyev is moving as Romeo, and both he and Blair (Mercutio) make masterful use of mime in their roles, the ballet becoming a physically expressive blend of acting and dance. Not to be missed. (Dir: Paul Czinner, 126 mins.)

Romeo and Juliet (British-Italian, 1968)*** Leonard Whiting, Olivia Hussey, Milo O'Shea. Director Franco Zeffirelli's visually ravishing version of Shakespeare's tragic romance of tender young love. Romeo (17-year-old Whiting) and Juliet (15-year-old Hussey) are right in their youth but not good enough performers. The feel for 15th-century Verona is right and the Mercutio-Tybalt duel is sensational. For those who care, this is the 13th version of "R and J." (152 mins.)

Romulus and the Sabines (Italian, 1961)** Roger Moore, Mylene Demongeot. Romulus and his band raid the neighboring Sabines, carrying off their women, which, as you know, means war. English-dubbed costume spectacular at least has a better cast than customary, in addition to the usual gaucheries.

Roof, The (Italian, 1957)*** Gabriella Pallotta, Giorgio Liztuzzi. Poverty-stricken young couple overcome red tape in finding a new home and happiness. Gentle drama directed by Vittorio De Sica, some fine moments. English dubbing detracts somewhat. (98 mins.)

Rookie, The (1959)*½ Tommy Noonan, Pete Marshall, Julie Newmar. Leftover routines from all the World War II service comedies used in a generally strained farce about a dumb rookie, his sergeant, and a Hollywood blonde stranded on a desert island. (Dir: George O'Hanlon, 86 mins.)

Rookies, The (1972)** Darren McGavin, Paul Burke, Cameron Mitchell. TV pilot for the series of the same name, a police show focusing on the new breed of questioning, caring, college-trained recruits. The customary tough, skeptical sergeant puts rookies through training, grudgingly pays respect to the men when they perform well on the streets. Predictable, slickly produced. (Dir: Jud Taylor, 72 mins.)

Room at the Top (British, 1959)**** Laurence Harvey, Simone Signoret, Heather Sears. Powerful drama of an opportunist who stop at nothing to make a position for himself in life. Searing in its intensity, superbly acted—Oscar-winning job by Signoret. For adult audiences. This is a deeply moving film, with a first rate job by Harvey too and expertly directed by Jack Clayton. (115 mins.)

Room for One More (1952)***½ (Also called "The Easy Way"). Cary Grant, Betsy Drake. Warmhearted comedy-drama about an unselfish couple who open their home to problem foster children. Grant is perfect as the husband who occasionally blows his top when his wife, excellently played by Betsy Drake, tells him they're going to have another child come to live with them. (Dir: Norman Taurog, 98 mins.)

Room Service (1938)**½ Marx Brothers, Ann Miller. Broke producer and his aides stall from being kicked out of their hotel room. Amusing comedy, but not the Marxes at their best. (Dir: William A. Seiter, 78 mins.)

Room 13 (German, 1964)*½ Joachim Berger, Karin Dor, Walter Rilla. Crooks hole up in the London underworld while planning a train robbery. Mystery is involved, outdated in concept.

Rooney (1958)*** Barry Fitzgerald, John Gregson. Dublin dustman aids a bedridden man henpecked by his grasping relatives. Delightful little Irish comedy, good fun. (Dir: George Pollack, 88 mins.)

Rooster Cogburn (1975)**½ John Wayne, Katharine Hepburn, Anthony Zerbe, Strother Martin. Though not a good picture, this is enjoyable occasionally. The plot is not very interesting (to the writers, either, it seems). It concerns the murder of spinster Eula Goodnight's minister father (shades of "The African Queen"), and the theft by desperadoes of some nitroglycerin. Marshal Rooster Cogburn rides off to catch the miscreants. The star chemistry is the only thing of interest here; John Wayne and Katharine Hepburn are full of life and spark "Rooster" a little. (Dir: Stuart Millar, 107 mins.)

Roots, The (Mexican, 1957)**½ Beatriz Flores, Juan De La Cruz. Four assorted vignettes of the Mexican people, most of them fairly well done, but brevity of the plots doesn't give one time to become really interested. Dubbed in English.

Roots of Heaven, The (1958)*** Errol Flynn, Juliette Greco, Trevor Howard, Eddie Albert, and Orson Welles. Interesting ambitious film based on Romain Gary's prize winning novel about a group comprised of adventurers, opportunists, and one idealist who join forces in an effort to protect the African elephant (threatened with destruction and eventual extinction by ivory hunters). Trevor Howard is a standout as the idealist and there's a colorful contribution by Welles as TV news personality. (Dir: John Huston, 131 mins.)

Rope Around the Neck (French, 1964) ** Jean Richard, Dany Robin, Magali Noel. Man with an increasing desire to murder his wife finally attempts the deed, but finds himself involved in another crime. Tricky whodunit dubbed in English is developed too slowly.

Rope of Sand (1949)**½ Burt Lancaster, Corinne Calvet, Claude Rains, Peter Lorre, Sam Jaffe. Adventurer returns to claim a hidden fortune in diamonds, fights off the machinations of a police chief and a diamond-company executive after the cache. Hard-boiled melodrama heavy on the rough stuff; action fans should like it. (Dir: William Dieterle, 104 mins.)

Rose Bowl Story (1952)** Vera Miles, Marshall Thompson, Natalie Wood. Usual sort of football story, okay for those who love quarterbacks. Natalie plays the kid sister here. (Dir: William Beaudine, 73 mins.)

Rose Marie (1935)*** Jeanette MacDonald, Nelson Eddy, James Stewart. Loose adaptation of the original operetta of love and adventure with the Mounted Police is still good entertainment, thanks to the delightful score and top voices to do it justice. Look for a very young Jimmy Stewart as Jeanette's brother, and Allan Jones in a small role as her opera co-star. (Dir: W. S. Van Dyke II, 113 mins.)

Rose Marie (1954)**½ Ann Blyth, Howard Keel, Fernando Lamas, Bert Lahr. Orphan girl grows to be a beauty, and is loved by a Mountie and a trapper—that's the way this version of the venerable old operetta goes. Some colorful sequences, but has that old-fashioned quality that doesn't work to its advantage. (Dir: Mervyn Le Roy, 115 mins.)

Rose of Washington Square (1939)*** Al Jolson, Alice Faye, Tyrone Power. Alice and Al sing some of the most memorable songs of the twenties and it is, of course, the highlight of an otherwise ordinary film. Backstage plot about a follies girl who loves a bum is poorly written and not too well acted. (Dir: Gregory Ratoff, 86 mins.)

Rose Tattoo, The (1955)**** Anna Magnani, Burt Lancaster. Tennessee Williams play about an earthy dressmaker with a fond memory of her deceased husband finding love anew with a burly truck driver. Beautifully played by Magnani, who copped the Academy Award. Sensitively written, directed; first-rate dramatic fare. (Dir: Daniel Mann, 117 mins.)

Roseanna McCoy (1949)** Farley Granger, Joan Evans, Raymond Massey, Richard Basehart. Trite melodrama depicting the legendary feudin' hill families of the Hatfields and the McCoys. The performances range from fine (Richard Basehart) to very poor (Joan Evans in the title role). (Dir: Irving Reis, 100 mins.)

Rosebud (1974)½ Peter O'Toole, Richard Attenborough, Cliff Gorman, John V. Lindsay. Another stupefyingly inept film directed and produced by Otto Preminger, who

somehow manages to find financing for junk like this. Witless, badly directed, heavily plotted nonsense about politics, spying, and the C.I.A., the Israeli-Arab war of nerves and dozens of other subjects dealt with in a series of verbal and visual banalities. "Rosebud" marked the movie debut of New York's handsome former mayor, John V. Lindsay, who has the good looks to be a movie star, but clearly does not have the requisite talent. One of the characters in this stinker asks about Rosebud. "Something to do with a film, I think," is the answer. It's not a great joke, to be sure, but it's about the only intentional laugh. (Dir: Otto Preminger, 126 mins.)

Rosemary (1958)***½ Devastating German satire on its own middle-class morality, beautifully filmed and suspensefully performed by a superb cast of players. Based on the real-life story of a call girl whose social ambitions become a menace to her admirers, it keeps you glued to the screen from sophisticated beginning to cynical end. Nadja Tiller and Peter Van Eyck co-star. (Dir: Rolf Thiele, 99 mins.)

Rosemary's Baby (1968)**** Mia Farrow, Ruth Gordon, John Cassavetes, Ralph Bellamy, Sidney Blackmer. Double-threat Roman Polanski adapted Ira Levin's best seller about witchcraft as practiced on New York's Central Park West, and also directed this exciting horror film. (136 mins.)

Rosetti and Ryan: Men Who Love Women (1977)** Tony Roberts, Squire Fridell. The pilot film for the subsequent series. The light touch is the key when a pair of cocky lawyers defends a lady accused of doing in hubbie on the family yacht. Patty Duke Astin is the defendant, part of a classy supporting cast that includes Susan Anspach and Bill Dana. Made-for-TV. (Dir: John Astin, 106 mins.)

Rosie (1967)*½ Rosalind Russell, Sandra Dee, Brian Aherne. A tasteless drama with an ample dose of comedy hijinks by star Roz Russell. Roz plays Rosie, one of the world's richest women, and a bit of an eccentric, but definitely not mad. Her ungrateful daughters hope to prove she is. That's enough plot to let you you know what you're in for. (Dir: David Lowell Rich, 98 mins.)

Rotten to the Core (Great Britain, 1965) ****½** Charlotte Rampling, Ian Bannen, Anton Rogers, Eric Sykes. Sly comedy of a bumbling bunch of crooks who nearly make off with several million pounds. Rogers (who plays the brains behind the caper) highlights with his ingenious impersonations. (Dir: John Boulting, 87 mins.)

Rough Night in Jericho (1967) ***** Dean Martin, George Peppard, Jean Simmons. Violent, unnecessary brutality with Dean Martin as a sober heavy. George Peppard is the hero this time out, and the lady struggling to keep her stagecoach line out of crooked Martin's grasp is Jean Simmons. The three stars work hard. You needn't bother. (Dir: Arnold Laven, 104 mins.)

Roughly Speaking (1945) ******* Jack Carson, Rosalind Russell. Ambitious wife struggles to aid her ne'er-do-well husband in his business schemes, while raising a large family. Long but deftly acted, pleasantly done comedy drama. (Dir: Michael Curtiz, 117 mins.)

Rounders, The (1965) ******* Glenn Ford, Henry Fonda, Sue Ane Langdon, Chill Wills. Ford and Fonda are a very ingratiating pair of modern-day horse wranglers who share some comical adventures in this engaging tale, written and directed by Burt Kennedy. The two have their hands full when they attempt to break a stubborn horse and this becomes the film's funniest running gag. A good supporting cast of familiar faces—Chill Wills, Edgar Buchanan and Denver Pyle—keep the comedy rolling briskly along. (85 mins.)

Roustabout (1964) *****½** Elvis Presley, Barbara Stanwyck. Another Presley opus for his fans, with Barbara Stanwyck thrown in for good measure. Barbara runs a carnival, and Elvis is a vagabond youth who joins the show and sings in a honky-tonk on the midway. (Dir: John Rich, 101 mins.)

Roxie Hart (1943) ****½** Ginger Rogers, Adolphe Menjou. Story of a 1920 burlesque dancer who tries to use her murder trial for publicity purposes is fair comedy and poor drama. (Dir: William Wellman, 75 mins.)

Royal Scandal, A (1945) ****½** Tallulah Bankhead, William Eythe, Charles Coburn. Tallulah's fans will enjoy it but all others beware. Farce about Catherine the Great of Russia seems more like a succession of cleaned up burlesque skits than a film. (Dir: Ernst Lubitsch, 94 mins.)

Royal Wedding (1951) ******* Fred Astaire, Jane Powell, Peter Lawford. Merry musical romance with lovely dances by Astaire and good chirping by Jane Powell. A brother and sister act (Jane & Fred) are in London during the time of Queen Elizabeth's wedding. (Dir: Stanley Donen, 93 mins.)

"R.P.M." (Revolutions per Minute) (1970) ***½** Anthony Quinn, Ann-Margret, Gary Lockwood. What starts out as an interesting film about college unrest in the late '60's turns into driveling, simpleminded drama before long. Quinn tries his best to portray a college president who shares a rapport with the students, but this Zorbalike temperament gets in the way. Ann-Margret is miscast as his young mistress. Erich Segal wrote the vapid screenplay. (Dir: Stanley Kramer, 92 mins.)

Ruby Gentry (1953) ******* Jennifer Jones, Charlton Heston, Karl Malden. Jennifer Jones has never been more appealing on the screen than she is in this supercharged drama about a sexy wench who seeks revenge on an elaborate scale when her true love decides to marry a more respected female in the community. The love scenes are torrid and Miss Jones enacts the siren with all stops pulled. (Dir: King Vidor, 82 mins.)

Ruffians, The (French, 1960) ****** Marina Vlady, Robert Hossein. Man becomes involved with his boss's daughter, suspects she's leading a secret life. Fair drama dubbed in English.

Ruggles of Red Gap (1935) ******** Charles Laughton, Charles Ruggles, Mary Boland. Hilarious tale of the English butler who suddenly finds himself in the American west, when he is won by an American in a poker game. Laughton, at his best, and a superb cast make this one of the all-time great comedies. (Dir: Leo McCarey, 100 mins.)

Rulers of the Sea (1939) ******* Margaret Lockwood, Douglas Fairbanks Jr., Will Fyffe. Interesting drama of the first steam crossing of the Atlantic which led to the beginning of the luxury liner. Not a great epic, but Mr. Fyffe is superb and the tale well told. (Dir: Frank Lloyd, 110 mins.)

Rules of the Game (French, 1939) **** Dalio, Nora Gregor, Mila Parely, Jean Renoir, Roland Tourain. Written and directed by Jean Renoir (the son of the great impressionist painter), this is an altogether brilliant film, generally considered by critics to be among the greatest masterpieces in the history of world cinema. About the decaying social structure of France before the outbreak of World War II, and based on the play "Les Caprices de Marianne" by Alfred de Musset. A rich French aristocrat gives a lavish house party at his country chateau, where the hypocrisy and decadence of the French upper classes are superbly revealed. The title refers to the fact that no matter what happens, be it accidental murder or adultery, no one betrays his class, or loses his cool—in other words, they always play by the "Rules of the Game." There are several dazzling sequences including a rabbit hunt and later a skeleton dance at the masquerade ball. A work of genius. (110 mins.)

Ruling Class, The (British, 1971) **** Peter O'Toole, Alastair Sim, Harry Andrews. Biting satire, madcap farce about the English upper classes. O'Toole plays the mad 14th Earl of Gurney, who has inherited his father's huge estate. He thinks he's Jesus Christ and when his family tries to cure him, he becomes Jack the Ripper. Spiced with vaudeville songs and Arthur Lowe as a butler who has inherited $70,000. Wonderful fun, and O'Toole is marvelous in one of his best screen performances. (Dir: Peter Medak, 155 mins.)

Run a Crooked Mile (1969) **½ Louis Jourdan, Mary Tyler Moore. A muddled made-for-TV-feature, greatly enhanced by the charm of Louis Jourdan. Jourdan plays a school teacher who becomes an amnesia victim and lives the life of a wealthy playboy for a two-year period, marrying Mary Tyler Moore in the interim. However, it is not a comedy. (Dir: Gene Levitt, 100 mins.)

Run for Cover (1955) *** James Cagney, Viveca Lindfors, John Derek. Taut Western story about a duo of bandits and their reformation. Leads up to an exciting climax. Cagney fine as always with good support by John Derek and Viveca Lindfors. (Dir: Nicholas Ray, 93 mins.)

Run for Your Money, A (British, 1949) ***½ Donald Houston, Alec Guinness. Two Welsh coal miners have various misadventures when they visit London. Delightful comedy, raising many chuckles. Excellently acted. (Dir: Charles Frend, 83 mins.)

Run for Your Wife (Italy-France, 1965) **½ Ugo Tognazzi, Marina Vlady, Rhonda Fleming, Juliet Prowse. Nice, frothy comedy about an Italian bachelor visiting the U.S. on business, who decides to stay here by marrying a native. Only the "Native American Woman" turns out to be more formidable, less predictable, and less inclined to marry than he had expected. (Dir: Gian Luigi Polidoro, 97 mins.)

Run of the Arrow (1956) **½ Rod Steiger, Sarita Montiel, Brian Keith. Bitter ex-Confederate private joins the Sioux Indian nation in their fight against the country, then realizes where his heart really lies. Western drama has a thoughtful theme, different approach; not completely successful, however. (Dir: Samuel Fuller, 86 mins.)

Run Silent, Run Deep (1958) *** Clark Gable, Burt Lancaster. An interesting war drama about submarine warfare and the bitter conflict of the sub commander (Gable) and his lieutenant (Lancaster). Exciting photography adds to the suspense. Gable and Lancaster are realistic in their portrayals. (Dir: Robert Wise, 93 mins.)

Run, Simon, Run (1970) *** Burt Reynolds, Inger Stevens. Burt Reynolds gives a strong performance as a wronged American Indian who returns to the reservation after serving a long prison term for a murder he didn't commit. Reynolds is fascinating to watch as he patiently waits for his moment of revenge, falling in love with beautiful Inger Stevens in the meantime. Miss Stevens' character of a rich socialite-turned-social worker is a bit uneven in the writing, but it doesn't detract from the overall effect of the drama. The ending, although unexpected, is still jolting. Much better than most made-for-TV entries. (Dir: George McCowan, 73 mins.)

Run, Stranger, Run (1973)** Patricia Neal, Cloris Leachman, Bobby Darin, Ron Howard. Gothic horror set in Nova Scotia fails to live up to the beauty of the scenery. Everyone has a skeleton in the closet, and there are several corpses sunken by sub-plots. Interesting to watch is Tessa Dahl, Miss Neal's real-life daughter, as she plays a sexually infatuated youngster. (Dir: Darren McGavin, 90 mins.)

Runaround, The (1946)*** Broderick Crawford, Ella Raines, Rod Cameron. Fast moving comedy about two guys who are hired to trail a runaway heiress who is about to marry a deckhand. Good performances. (Dir: Charles Lamont, 86 mins.)

Runaway (1973)**½ Ben Johnson, Ed Nelson, Vera Miles, Martin Milner, Ben Murphy. A ski train roars down a mountainside when the brakes freeze in this "Airport"-type story which mixes scares with character bits. Realistic footage is the main ingredient, while the engineer and a trio of helpers struggle to prevent the almost certain crash. Made-for-TV. (Dir: David Lowell Rich, 73 mins.)

Runaway Barge, The (1975)*½ Tim Matheson, Bo Hopkins, Jim Davis. Scenes of life on the Mississippi River provide the only interest in this TV film, as boatmen get involved in a kidnapping and a hijacking. Made-for-TV. (Dir: Boris Sagal, 72 mins.)

Runaway Bus, The (British, 1954)** Frankie Howerd, Margaret Rutherford. A bus lost in a London fog commandeered by a screwy driver has an international thief aboard. Very mild comedy, misses fire often.

Runaways, The (1975)*½ Josh Albee, Dorothy McGuire, Van Williams. This drama about a runaway boy who becomes friendly with a runaway leopard often taxes credibility. However, young Josh Albee gives a low-keyed performance as the truant boy, and his scenes with the snarling, powerful leopard may hold the attention of the kids. Dorothy McGuire and Van Williams play friendly adults. Made-for-TV. (Dir: Harry Harris, 72 mins.)

Running Man, The (British, 1963)*** Laurence Harvey, Lee Remick, Alan Bates. Scoundrel fakes his death in a glider crash, joins with his wife

612

in a plan to defraud the insurance company, but while in Spain they are frightened by the appearance of an insurance investigator. Fairly ordinary story polished by fine performances, Carol Reed's suspenseful direction. Good melodrama. (103 mins.)

Running Target (1956)*** Arthur Franz, Doris Dowling. Different sort of outdoor drama, about a sheriff leading a posse after four escaped convicts. Exceptionally good photography, performances; tense chase scenes, good insight into human character. Above average. (Dir: Marvin Weinstein, 83 mins.)

Running Wild (1956)*½ William Campbell, Mamie Van Doren, Keenan Wynn. Cheaply made juvenile delinquency drama about a car-thieving operation and those involved with it. Keenan Wynn delivers the only valid characterization as an ex-con who's behind the whole thing. (Dir: Abner Biberman, 81 mins.)

Rush to Judgement (1967)**½ A documentary film about the assassination of President John F. Kennedy, conceived by producer Mark Lane as a "brief for the defense" of Lee Harvey Oswald. Film, condemned by most critics at the time of its release, remains a disturbing, if disjointed film, because many of the arguments raised in the film have never been answered satisfactorily—and maybe never will be. (Dir: Emile de Antonio, 122 mins.)

Russia (1972)**½ Earnest if uninspired documentary tour through a dozen of the 15 Soviet Republics. Filmed in 1969 in various parts of Siberia, the Baltic states, Moscow, the Ukraine, etc. Helpful narration written by Soviet expert Harrison Salisbury. Produced, directed, and photographed by Theodore Holcomb. (108 mins.)

Russians Are Coming, the Russians Are Coming, The (1966)***½ Alan Arkin, Paul Ford, Carl Reiner, Theo Bikel, Eva Marie Saint. Wacky amusing comedy about a Russian submarine which runs aground off the shore of Nantucket. Boasts a delightful performance by Alan Arkin as a befuddled Russian sailor. Satire has something to say on the subject of how we feel about the Russians, but does so in a deft manner which benefits from a number of laughs garnered along the way by such skilled scene stealers as Paul Ford, Doro Merande, and Carl Reiner. Director Norman Jewison, responsible for other winners, including "In the Heat of the Night," keeps things perking along, despite some holes in the script. (120 mins.)

Rx Murder (British, 1958)** Rick Jason, Marius Goring, Lisa Gastoni. American doctor arrives in a quiet English seaside resort and soon suspects the local practitioner, whose three previous wives have suddenly died. Passable mystery is well done in a familiar way.

Ryan's Daughter (1970)*** Robert Mitchum, Sarah Miles, John Mills, Christopher Jones. A wildly cinematic experience, featuring Oscar-winning camerawork roving over the land of Ireland. This David Lean claim to an epic was the center of much critical controversy as to its merit. The tale is unabashedly sentimental revolving around a pampered, indulged, romantic girl played with some intensity by Sarah Miles, and her desire for a British soldier (Christopher Jones) despite the fact that she is married. Soft, sultry Robert Mitchum plays her school teacher husband, a fallen image, with a sense of feeling and emotion which highlights the film even though John Mills won an Oscar for his portrayal of a crippled mute. (Dir: David Lean, 192 mins.)

Saadia (1954)*½ Cornel Wilde, Mel Ferrer, Rita Gam. Muddled costume epic set in Morocco where a young girl who believes she is a sorceress, a dashing leader of the Berber tribes, and a doctor engage in a war against plague and belief in black magic. (Dir: Albert Lewin, 82 mins.)

Saboteur (1942)***½ Robert Cummings, Priscilla Lane, Otto Kruger. The master of suspense, Alfred Hitchcock, uses all of the gimmicks in this WW II spy story set in Nevada and New York. Exciting climax takes place in the Statue of Liberty. (Dir: Alfred Hitchcock, 108 mins.)

Sabre Jet (1953)**½ Robert Stack, Coleen Gray. Wives wait for their husbands to return from Korean missions. Too few air action shots. (Dir: Louis King, 96 mins.)

Sabrina (1954)***½ Humphrey Bogart, Audrey Hepburn, William Holden. Hit play about the chauffeur's daughter and the two scions of wealth after her hand, filmed by Billy Wilder as a handsomely mounted production with three top stars in the leads. The fun is not always consistent, but the many delights more than atone for the occasional lapses. Superior comedy. (113 mins.)

Sabu and the Magic Ring (1957)** Sabu, Daria Massey. O K fantasy for the kiddies; it's played lightly for laughs, but could have used more. (Dir: George Blair, 61 mins.)

Sacco and Vanzetti (Italian, 1971) *** Gian Maria Volonte, Riccardo Cucciolla, Cyril Cusack. This documents the case of two Italian immigrants, admitted anarchists accused of robbery, but innocent of the crimes—in this film—they are being prosecuted for. Based on the world-famous 1920's court case in Massachusetts. It's still a powerful, sad indictment of American political hysteria. Meant to touch our prejudices, and it does! Well acted. (Dir: Giuliano Montaldo, 120 mins.)

Sad Horse, The (1959)** David Ladd, Patrice Wymore, Rex Reason. A boy and his horse—young Ladd is good, but one boy does not a picture make. (Dir: James B. Clark, 78 mins.)

Sad Sack, The (1957)*** Jerry Lewis, David Wayne, Phyllis Kirk, Peter Lorre. Jerry in the army again, as inept as ever, getting mixed up with spies and Arabian intrigue. Among his funnier efforts, with a fast pace and good gags. (Dir: George Marshall, 98 mins.)

Saddle the Wind (1958)**½ Robert Taylor, Julie London, John Cassavetes. Gunman turns in his weapons and becomes a rancher but is forced to return to them to face a showdown with his reckless younger brother. Nicely directed western breaks no new ground but is well done within its own framework. (Dir: Robert Parrish, 84 mins.)

Saddle Tramp (1950)*** Joel McCrea, Wanda Hendrix. McCrea plays a lovable "saddle tramp" who doesn't want any trouble but ends up right in the middle of a big scale range war. Entertaining, thanks to McCrea's casual way with a line and some clever dialogue. (Dir: Hugo Fregonese, 77 mins.)

Sadist, The—See: **Face of Terror, The** (Arch Hall Jr.)

Safari (1956)**½ Janet Leigh, Victor Mature, John Justin. Victor Mature as the brave white hunter heads a safari that meets with the savage tribes of the Mau Mau. Tense and action-filled adventure. (Dir: Hugo Fregonese, 80 mins.)

Safe at Home (1962)** Mickey Mantle, Roger Maris, Don Collier, Bryan Russell. Little Leaguer runs away to the Yankee spring-training camp to try to get Mantle and Maris to attend a banquet. Thin baseball story might get by with the youngsters. Mantle and Maris are better on the diamond than in front of a camera.

Safecracker, The (British, 1958)** Ray Milland, Barry Jones. Routine spy "meller" with a gimmick. Milland plays a respectable safe expert who turns thief and is imprisoned. During World War II his knowledge is put to use on a dangerous mission. Some suspense along the way. Incidentally, Milland also directed. (Dir: Ray Milland, 96 mins.)

Saga of Hemp Brown, The (1958)** Rory Calhoun, Beverly Garland, John Larch. Army lieutenant is dismissed from the service when he's framed for a payroll robbery; with the aid of a traveling show he goes after the true culprit. Standard western. (Dir: Richard Carlson, 80 mins.)

Sahara (1943)*** Humphrey Bogart, Dan Duryea. American tank with an assorted crew outwit the Nazis in the desert. Frequently exciting war drama, well done. (Dir: Zoltan Korda, 97 mins.)

Saigon (1948)** Alan Ladd, Veronica Lake. Routine adventure story set in Indochina involving a black marketeer and a half a million dollars. (Dir: Leslie Fenton, 94 mins.)

Sail a Crooked Ship (1962)** Robert Wagner, Dolores Hart, Ernie Kovacs. Young man gets tangled with a gang of crooks who intend to use an old Liberty ship to pull a bank robbery in Boston. Comedy huffs and puffs for laughs, achieves tedium instead—Kovacs, in his last film, strives mightily to hold it together. (Dir: Irving S. Brecher, 88 mins.)

Sail Into Danger (1957)** Dennis O'Keefe. Fast paced crime film about a skipper of a motor launch in Barcelona and his clever efforts to defeat a group of art treasure thieves. Poor script. (Dir: Kenneth Hume, 72 mins.)

Sailor Beware (1951)**½ Dean Martin, Jerry Lewis, Corinne Calvet, Robert Strauss, Marion Marshall. Martin and Lewis in the Navy, with Jerry getting a reputation as a ladykiller. More enjoyable when it was "The Fleet's In," but pleasant enough. (Dir: Hal Walker, 108 mins.)

Sailor of the King (British, 1953)**½ Jeffrey Hunter, Michael Rennie, Wendy Hiller. Another World War II drama. It's the British Navy against the Nazi U-Boats in this one. Rennie plays the British commander with commendable restraint while Hunter displays a bit too much energy as the novice who finally gets the chance to show the stuff of which heroes are made. (Dir: Roy Boulting, 83 mins.)

Sailor Who Fell From Grace With the Sea, The (1976)*** Sarah Miles, Kris Kristofferson, Jonathan Kahn, Margo Cunningham. The brooding, erotic story in Japanese writer Yukio Mishima's novella has been transferred from Japan to a coastal town in England. This is a very uneven but often striking, macabre piece about a group of five young schoolboys who ultimately commit a ritual murder upon a visiting sailor. There are some explicit, beautifully photographed lovemaking scenes between Kristofferson and Miles that further blur the narrow dividing line between exploitation films and more serious filmmaking. (Sarah Miles's son in the film may need an analyst when he grows up. He peeks through a keyhole into his mother's bedroom one night and sees her masturbating in front of a picture of her late husband.) Miles plays a lonely widow who meets and falls in love with Kristofferson before he meets an untimely end. Some arresting moments mark this directorial debut for writer Lewis John Carlino who also adapted the Mishima novel for the screen. (104 mins.)

Saint—See also **St.**

Saint in London (British, 1939)**½ George Sanders, Sally Gray. The Saint picks up a wounded man on a road and is plunged into crooked doings. Entertaining mystery. (Dir: John Paddy Carstairs, 72 mins.)

Saint in New York (1938)*** Kay

Sutton, Louis Hayward. The Saint helps a civic committee clean up a gang of racketeers. Good melodrama, well made and exciting. (Dir: Ben Holmes, 71 mins.)

Saint in Palm Springs (1941)**½ George Sanders, Wendy Barrie. The Saint is entrusted to deliver three valuable stamps to a girl for her inheritance. Entertaining mystery. (Dir: Jack Hively, 65 mins.)

Saint Joan (1957)**½ Richard Widmark, Richard Todd, John Gielgud, Kenneth Haigh and Jean Seberg. A poor filmization of Shaw's wondrous play "Saint Joan," marred by the performance of inexperienced actress Jean Seberg. Others in the cast range from good to superb, notably John Gielgud; will stand as a monument to the bad judgment of Otto Preminger in giving Jean Seberg the title role. (Seberg has since shown considerable ability in films.) (Dir: Otto Preminger, 110 mins.)

Saint Meets the Tiger (British, 1942)**½ Hugh Sinclair, Jean Gillie. The Saint gets on the trail of a gang that has stolen a fortune in gold. Lively detective story. (Dir: Paul Stein, 70 mins.)

Saint Strikes Back (1939)*** George Sanders, Wendy Barrie. The Saint helps a girl trap thieves who have framed her father. Good detective story, well made. (Dir: John Farrow, 64 mins.)

Saint Takes Over (1940)*** George Sanders, Wendy Barrie. The Saint arrives back in America to save a friend from a murder charge. Above average detective story, well done. (Dir: Jack Hively, 69 mins.)

Sainted Sisters, The (1948)**½ Joan Caulfield, Barry Fitzgerald. Barry reforms a couple of con girls in this film which completely depends on him for its appeal. (Dir: William Russell, 89 mins.)

Saints and Sinners (British, 1949)*** Kieron Moore, Christine Norden. A successful businessman returns to his native Irish village to find things changed. Warm comedy-drama with fine work by members of the famous Irish Abbey Theatre.

Saint's Double Trouble (1940)** George Sanders, Helene Whitney. The Saint traps a look-alike who has been engaging in diamond smuggling. Fair mystery. (Dir: Jack Hively, 68 mins.)

Saint's Girl Friday (British, 1953) ** Louis Hayward, Naomi Chance. The Saint investigates the murder of a socialite friend. Fair mystery. (Dir: Seymour Friedman, 68 mins.)

Sakima and the Masked Marvel (1943-66)**½ William Forrest, Louise Currie, Johnny Arthur. Feature version of serial "The Masked Marvel." Businessman is in league with a Japanese agent intending to sabotage the war effort; a masked crusader thwarts them at every turn. It may not be art, but it's entertaining; lively serial heroics for the kids and camps. (Dir: Spencer Bennet, 100 mins.)

Saladin and the Great Crusades (Egyptian, 1963)*½ Ahmed Mazhar, Nadia Lootfi. Oriental ruler clashes with King Richard the Lion-Hearted and his forces during the Crusades. Some big battle scenes in this spectacular, but little else. Dubbed in English.

Salesman (1969)**** Innovative, revealing; altogether shattering documentary, cinema-verite style, about the lives of several Bible salesmen in the South. Produced, directed, and photographed by the gifted brother team of Albert and David Maysles, this is one of the most extraordinarily honest glimpses of contemporary American life that you have ever seen captured on film. A real-life late 1960's sequel to Arthur Miller's creation of Willy Loman. There are no professional actors here —just real people going through their endless pitches and house calls. This is, in some ways, one of the saddest American films ever, but it is memorable on many counts, including the editing of Dede Allen. A towering film, made on a tiny budget.

Sally and Saint Anne (1952)**½ Ann Blyth, Edmund Gwenn, Gregg Palmer. Corny but heart warming story of a zany family and one member in particular, namely Sally (Ann Blyth), who really believes that Saint Anne is their patron saint. (Dir: Rudolph Mate, 90 mins.)

Salome (1953)**½ Rita Hayworth, Stewart Granger, Charles Laughton, Judith Anderson. Over-produced and over-long story of Salome and the events leading up to her famous dance of the seven veils. Rita sheds the veils while Charles Laughton leers and Judith Anderson flares her talented nostrils. (Dir: William Dieterle, 103 mins.)

Salome, Where She Danced (1945)* Yvonne DeCarlo, Rod Cameron, David Bruce. The sensuous dancer serves as an intelligence agent, and has many men tumbling after her. Ridiculous costume melodrama, often unintentionally funny. (Dir: Charles Lamont, 90 mins.)

Salt and Pepper (British, 1968)** Couple of carefree London club owners (Peter Lawford, Sammy Davis, Jr.) unwittingly become involved in international intrigue. Hipster comedy strains for fun. Made in England. Michael Bates, Ilona Rodgers. (Dir: Richard Donner, 101 mins.)

Salt of the Earth (1954)*** Will Geer, Mervin Williams. An interesting, seldom exhibited film about labor-management relations and the exploitation of the working class in America. Directed by Herbert Biberman, and partially financed and produced by the International Union of Mine, Mill & Smelter Workers. Shot on location in New Mexico, this film was never released by a national distributing company, but is well worth seeing if you get a chance to watch this 1950's version, and a more radical one at that, of some of the themes dealt with in "Grapes of Wrath." Cast is mostly nonprofessional.

Salty O'Rourke (1945)*** Alan Ladd, Gail Russell, Stanley Clements. Gambler hires a crooked jockey to ride for him. Racetrack story gets a good production, neat script. (Dir: Raoul Walsh, 97 mins.)

Salut l'Artiste (France-Italy, 1973)***½ Marcello Mastroianni, Francoise Fabian, Jean Rochefort. Mastroianni is marvelous in this charming, affectionate look at the struggles of an unsuccessful bit player. His personal life isn't so hot either. His mistress leaves him, so he tries going back to his wife and family—but it seems his wife is pregnant by another man. But Nicholas has one thing going for him: he believes in the elusive "glamour" of his profession, no matter how humiliating the acting role. Appealing, sardonic humor focusing on this naive oaf. (Dir: Yves Robert, 96 mins.)

Salzburg Connection, The (1972)** Barry Newman, Anna Karina, Karen Jensen. Inept treatment of Helen

616

MacInnes' spy thriller with so many plot twists you have to strain to make the story coherent. Every country in the world has an agent out to steal a box of incriminating Nazi war documents that has fallen into the hands of Anna Karina. Representing the United States and democracy is Barry Newman . . . democracy's in plenty of trouble . . . (Dir: Lee H. Katzin, 93 mins.)

Sam Hill—Who Killed the Mysterious Mr. Foster? (1971)**½ Ernest Borgnine, Judy Geeson. Here's a spirited comedy-western, a TV pilot starring Ernest Borgnine as a deputy sheriff who looks dumb but isn't. Borgnine teams up with a little tow-headed thief (Stephen Hudis) to find out who poisoned the local minister. Ernie plays his familiar lunkhead character and he's backed up smartly by a good cast including Will Geer, J. D. Cannon, Judy Geeson, and villain Bruce Dern. In lesser hands, the film might fall apart, but this bunch slips in a little fun. (Dir: Fielder Cook, 99 mins.)

Sam Whiskey (1969)* Burt Reynolds, Clint Walker, Ossie Davis, Angie Dickinson. Predictable western adventure yarn bolstered a bit by the tongue-in-cheek performance of Reynolds as a carefree guy who teams up with seductive Angie Dickinson to retrieve a sunken treasure in gold bars. You've seen it all before! (Dir: Arnold Laven, 96 mins.)

Samar (1962)*** George Montgomery, Gilbert Roland, Joan O'Brien, Ziva Rodann. Commandant of a penal colony refuses to bow to his strict superiors, breaks with the administration and leads his people through the jungles to freedom. Highly interesting, unusual story well done; rugged adventure fare. (Dir: George Montgomery, 89 mins.)

Samson (Italian, 1960)* Brad Harris, Brigitte Corey. Muscleman aids his king and restores law and order to the land. Another English-dubbed spectacle mishmash.

Samson Against the Sheik (Italian, 1960)* Ed Fury. Muscleman rescues a duke from a powerful sheik. But nothing can rescue the film.

Samson and Delilah (1951)***½ Victor Mature, Hedy Lamarr, George Sanders, Angela Lansbury. Biblical tale of the mighty Samson, whose power was curtailed by the scheming Delilah, given the high-powered

De Mille treatment. Some truly spectacular effects, action scenes—also the expected naiveté, hokey sequences. All in all, and when compared with some later imported spectacles, it comes off quite well. (Dir: Cecil B. De Mille, 128 mins.)

Samson and the Sea Beasts (Italian, 1963)* Kirk Morris, Margaret Lee. Hero battles a ferocious band of pirates, is taken prisoner, manages to escape and save the noblewoman who has aided him. Dreadful trash.

Samson and the Seven Challenges (Italian, 1964)* Dan Vadis. Muscleman faces all odds squarely and overthrows a wicked queen and her court. Brainless English-dubbed spectacle.

Samson and the Seven Miracles of the World (Italian, 1961)*½ Gordon Scott, Yoko Tani. Muscleman saves the royal children from the evil designs of a Tartar tyrant who wants to be emperor. Silly spectacle takes place in China but isn't very darned clever. Dubbed in English.

Samson and the Slave Queen (Italian, 1964)*½ Alan Steele, Pierre Brice, Moira Orfei, Maria Grazia Spina. Two heroic adventurers are off in search of the king's will, to see which of two sisters shall become queen. Farfetched costume adventure dubbed in English. (Dir: Umberto Lenzi, 92 mins.)

Samson and the Vampire Woman (Mexican, 1963)* Santo, Lorena Velasanez. Costumed do-gooder throws henchmen around like flies in combating an evil vampire queen. Terribly bad action adventure made by somebody who has been seeing too many old serials. Dubbed in English.

Samson in the Wax Museum (Mexican, 1963)* Santo, Norma Mora. Masked hero goes after a mad professor whose wish is to turn people into monsters. Very poor serial-style horror thriller dubbed in English.

San Antonio (1945)**½ Errol Flynn, Alexis Smith. Routine but lavish western with Errol as a rancher and Alexis as a night club singer who, of course, happens to work for the villain. (Dir: George Sherman, 111 mins.)

San Francisco (1936)***½ Clark Gable, Spencer Tracy, Jeanette MacDonald. Entertaining, well played drama of love and adventure as the notorious Barbary Coast comes to grips with snobbish Nob Hill. The famous earthquake is a perfect climax for the drama. (Dir: W. S. Van Dyke, 120 mins.)

San Francisco International Airport (1970)**½ Pernell Roberts, Clu Gulager, Van Johnson. Good TV film. Perhaps inspired by the extremely successful glossy feature film treatment of the best seller "Airport," the same studio (Universal) pieced together a film which borrows the setting and a few plots that were not used in the movie. If you liked "Airport," you'll like this film. The main plot—a big heist of a cargo plane carrying three million in cash—is well done, and a subplot climaxed by a 14-year-old boy taking a plane up on his own should delight air-minded small fry. The production overshadows the performance, but Pernell Roberts as the airport manager and Clu Gulager as the head airport security officer are excellent. (Dir: John Llewellyn Moxey, 100 mins.)

San Francisco Story (1952)** Joel McCrea, Yvonne DeCarlo. Miner is persuaded by a newspaper editor to help him fight vice in the city. Tale of the Gold Coast in the lusty days doesn't have anything new. (Dir: Robert Parrish, 80 mins.)

San Pedro Bums, The (1977)**½ Darryl McCullough, John Mark Robinson. The pilot for the series. Five newcomers (at the time) live a carefree existence on their rundown tuna boat. When their good friend, lovingly known as Pop, falls victim to a robbery by some local bullies, they attempt to right the wrong. The plot relies heavily on the appeal of the five male stars—Christopher Murney, Jeffry Druce, John Mark Robinson, Stuart Pankin, and Darryl McCullough. Made-for-TV. (Dir: Barry Shear, 79 mins.)

San Quentin (1937)*** Humphrey Bogart, Pat O'Brien, Ann Sheridan. Better than average prison drama about the rehabilitation of a criminal. As usual, Pat's the cop and Humphrey the bad boy. (Dir: Lloyd Bacon, 70 mins.)

Sanctuary (1961)** Lee Remick, Yves Montand, Odetta, Bradford Dillman. Governor's daughter is seduced by a Cajun, who returns after she's married, to cause her further trouble. It all ends in murder. Faulkner's seamy tale of the South in the 1920s given a distorted, choppy production treatment; even the talented cast is stymied. (Dir: Tony Richardson, 100 mins.)

Sand (1949)** Mark Stevens, Coleen Gray, Rory Calhoun. The trials and tribulations of a show horse named Jubilee. Some good photography. (Dir: Louis King, 78 mins.)

Sand Castle, The (1961)***½ Barry Cardwell, Alec Wilder. A diverting try for something away from the usual run, showing an afternoon in a boy's life at the seashore. Whimsical film is often quite charming, should be enjoyed by the discriminating who want something different. (Dir: Jerome Hill, 67 mins.)

Sand, Love and Salt (Italian, 1956) ** Marcello Mastroianni, Jester Naefe. A shipwrecked boat, a beautiful girl, a sunburned sailor, and love. Despite these ingredients, the film falls flat. Made before Mastroianni clicked big in later movies.

Sand Pebbles, The (1966)**½ Steve McQueen, Richard Attenborough, Candice Bergen. A sprawling, overlong adventure drama set in China during the 1920's. McQueen gives a commanding low-key performance as an independent sailor-engineer who clashes with his superiors after he becomes politically aware of the situation around him. The film is much too long, but not without interest. (Dir: Robert Wise, 195 mins.)

Sandcastles (1972)** Jan-Michael Vincent, Bonnie Bedelia. Good cast helps this trite ghost story. Vincent, Herschel Bernardi, and Bedelia try to bring off this love story about a man who dies in an auto crash, and returns to make amends for a previous act of thievery. If you can accept the idea that Miss Bedelia's character can fall in love with a ghost, the game is won. Miss Bedelia is an interesting actress, and she's backed up by Bernardi's understanding restauranteur. Made-for-TV. (Dir: Ted Post, 73 mins.)

Sanders (British, 1964)**½ Richard Todd, Marianne Koch, Albert Lieven. Young woman doctor arrives at a remote African outpost and finds a dedicated doctor involved in smuggling diamonds, with a policeman on his trail. Picturesque story of the Dark Continent moves at a fairly good rate.

Sanders of the River (British, 1935) ***½ Paul Robeson, Leslie Banks, Nina Mae McKinney. A proud tribal

chief helps the British Commissioner of Affairs in Africa to overcome the evil machinations of a greedy, warlike native king. Good melodrama, magnificent singing by Robeson. (Dir: Zoltan Korda, 90 mins.)

Sandokan Against the Leopard of Sarawak (Italian, 1964)*½ Ray Danton, Guy Madison. Brave ruler is celebrating the first anniversary of his return to power when an old enemy strikes again. Juvenile adventure dubbed in English. (Dir: Luigi Capuano, 94 mins.)

Sandokan Fights Back (Italian, 1964) *½ Guy Madison, Ray Danton. Brave ruler and his faithful aide fight to regain the throne taken by evil usurpers. Corny adventure dubbed in English will afford some fun if not taken seriously. (Dir: Luigi Capuano, 96 mins.)

Sandpiper, The (1965)** Elizabeth Taylor, Richard Burton. The presence of Elizabeth Taylor and Richard Burton and the grandeur of the great Big Sur location shots don't really make up for this limp and saccharine love story between a liberated artist (Miss Taylor) and a dedicated, married and confused minister (Burton). However, if you want to while away a couple of hours, this sophisticated soap opera peopled by beautiful people will fill the bill. (Dir: Vincente Minnelli, 116 mins.)

Sands of Beersheba (1965)**½ Diane Baker, David Opatoshu, Tom Bell. American girl in Israel meets the friend of her fiancé, who was killed in the 1948 fighting, soon finds herself caught between love and war. Filmed in Israel, this drama offers little that is new. (Dir: Alexander Ramati, 90 mins.)

Sands of Iwo Jima (1949)***½ John Wayne, John Agar, Forrest Tucker. Officer's son has no liking for the traditions of the Marine Corps, but a tough sergeant makes him see otherwise under stress of battle. Some of the best war scenes ever staged are here, together with a splendid performance by Wayne. (Dir: Allan Dwan, 110 mins.)

Sands of the Kalahari (1965)*** Stuart Whitman, Stanley Baker, Susannah York. A strange he-man adventure involving the survivors of a plane crash in Africa's dangerous Kalahari Desert. Stuart Whitman does very well in the role of an arrogant professional hunter whose desire to prove his strength leads to the destruction of most of his party and eventually himself. There's a fantastic finale in which Whitman pits his prowess against a tribe of wild baboons. (Dir: Cy Endfield, 119 mins.)

Sangaree (1953)** Fernando Lamas, Arlene Dahl, Francis L. Sullivan. Sangaree, a Georgia plantation, is the scene of this turbulent drama about pirates and family jealousies. Sangaree is sort of a poor man's Tara without the excitement of the Civil War to enhance it. Besides that Lamas is no Gable. (Dir: Edward Ludwig, 94 mins.)

Sansho the Bailiff (Japan, 1954)***½ This epic story about a brother and sister who fall into the hands of an unscrupulous slave owner is one of the finest films to come out of Japan. Director Kenji Mizoguchi heightens the inherent drama, the plight of the family being torn apart during 11th-century feudalism, by concentrating on the story and allowing the actors to emote with all stops out. May strike some as Japanese soap opera, but the setting and exquisite production details make it memorable. (Dir: Kenji Mizoguchi, 119 mins.)

Santa Fe Passage (1955)*** John Payne, Faith Domergue, Rod Cameron. Indian-hating scout takes a job with a wagon train. Actionful western, above average. (Dir: William Witney, 70 mins.)

Santa Fe Trail (1940)*** Errol Flynn, Olivia de Havilland, Van Heflin. Typical Class A 1940 western. A lot of action, plus an elaborate production was always sure to ring the bell at the box office. The formula hasn't changed much. (Dir: Michael Curtiz, 110 mins.)

Santee (1972)*½ Glenn Ford, Michael Burns, Dana Wynter. Uneven western which never got a general release but has some merit. Ford is a mean bounty hunter out for revenge who softens enough to take the homeless son of one of his victims under his wing. Poor songs are of no help whatever, but the script, by Brand Bell, is. (Dir: Gary Nelson, 91 mins.)

Santiago (1956)** Rossana Podesta, Alan Ladd, Lloyd Nolan. Action filled by cliched adventure yarn set in Cuba. Ladd is cast in the familiar role of opportunist who will sell guns to the highest bidder at the begin-

ning of the film but meets a patriotic, freedom fighting woman and switches allegiances. (Dir: Gordon Douglas, 93 mins.)

Sapphire (British, 1963)**** Nigel Patrick, Yvonne Mitchell. The murder of a good-time girl leads police to racial problems in untangling the mystery. A good whodunit further enhanced by some perceptive comments on current social problems; hits the mark either way. First rate screenplay and excellent performances, especially from Yvonne Mitchell, make this English entry a winner. (Dir: Basil Dearden, 92 mins.)

Sara T.—Portrait of a Teenaged Alcoholic (1975)*** Linda Blair, Verna Bloom, William Daniels, Larry Hagman. One of the better made-for-TV movies; Linda Blair is quite convincing as a mixed-up 15-year-old, hooked on secret drinking. It all begins when Sara must cope with a new school and surroundings after her mother remarries. Ends on an upbeat note, as Sara convinces her parents that she's an alcoholic ready for outside help. Made-for-TV. (Dir: Richard Donner, 100 mins.)

Saraband (British, 1948)*** Stewart Granger, Joan Greenwood. An unhappy girl married to a man in line for the English throne falls in love with an adventurer, but the affair ends tragically. Costume romance has a stylish presentation, especially in the direction. (Dir: Basil Dearden, 95 mins.)

Saracen Blade, The (1954)** Ricardo Montalban, Betta St. John. Not many cliches are omitted in this costume adventure about the Crusades and the days of knights and their valiant deeds. (Dir: William Castle, 76 mins.)

Saracens, The (Italian, 1960)*½ Richard Harrison, Ana Mori Obaldi. Adventurer returning from a journey finds pirates in possession of his castle, forms a guerilla band to rout them. Weak costume adventure dubbed in English.

Saratoga (1937)**½ Clark Gable, Jean Harlow. Gable is a bookie and Harlow is a racing man's daughter in this romantic comedy of the racing world. Miss Harlow died before completing this film. (Dir: Jack Conway, 100 mins.)

Saratoga Trunk (1945)**½ Ingrid Bergman, Gary Cooper. Though the movie is based on a novel by Pulitzer Prize-winning author Edna Ferber and has Ingrid Bergman and Gary Cooper in the leads, it's merely an overblown romantic adventure about the alliance of a Creole beauty of questionable reputation and a tall, handsome gambler. Miss Bergman is miscast, but she manages to bring some interest to the unscrupulous Clio, and Gary Cooper is Gary Cooper. (Dir: Sam Wood, 135 mins.)

Sarge—the Badge or the Cross (1971) *** George Kennedy, Ricardo Montalban. Thanks to writer Don Mankiewicz, director Richard Colla, and actor George Kennedy, this drama about a cop who turns priest after his wife is killed in a car bombing tragedy manages to avoid the clichés such a plot might trigger, and holds your interest throughout. George Kennedy plays the lead as a big laconic character, given to wearing tinted glasses, and he makes the man believable. Writer Don Mankiewicz keeps the sermonizing down, while priestly good deeds alternate with detective work on the bombing puzzle. Absorbing. Made-for-TV flick. (Dir: Richard Colla, 99 mins.)

Saskatchewan (1954) **½ Alan Ladd, Shelley Winters, J. Carrol Naish. Mountie needs all the help he can muster to drive the Sioux Indians back across the border. Fast-moving if familiar outdoor action tale. (Dir: Raoul Walsh, 87 mins.)

Satan Bug, The (1965) **½ George Maharis, Richard Basehart, Anne Francis. Science-fiction fans will buy this one without too many reservations, but drama fans will probably lose interest before the final fadeout. The suspense tale which starts out excitingly, has Richard Basehart playing a diabolical doctor bent on destroying mankind by unleashing stolen virus germs on an unsuspecting populace. Most of the action involves agent George Maharis' attempts to track down the stolen "satan bug" and avert total annihilation. (Dir: John Sturges, 114 mins.)

Satan Never Sleeps (1962) *½ William Holden, Clifton Webb, France Nuyen. Tasteless and banal drama about two priests who perilously oppose the Chinese Reds when they take over their mission. Intended as anti-Communist, it is so poorly developed it could have the opposite effect. Only the performances of Holden and Webb stand out in a lost cause. (Dir: Leo McCarey, 126 mins.)

Satan's Satellites (1958)* Judd Holdren, Aline Towne. Invaders from another planet land on earth to carry out their dirty work. Juvenile sci-fi thriller, cut down from serial "Zombies of the Stratosphere," which about tells all. (Dir: Fred Brannon, 70 mins.)

Satan's School for Girls (1973)**½ Roy Thinnes, Pamela Franklin, Jo Van Fleet, Lloyd Bochner. Thriller takes its time before getting to the mystery elements. Miss Franklin plays a young lady who enrolls in a private fine-arts school to get to the bottom of her younger sister's suicide. She's soon roaming into dark, hidden rooms. Made-for-TV. (Dir: David Lowell Rich, 73 mins.)

Satan's Triangle (1975)**½ Kim Novak, Doug McClure. Melodrama about the infamous "Devil's Triangle," an area where ships, planes and people just disappear off the face of the earth. Helicopter rescue pilots come to the aid of a distressed vessel and find a beautiful woman survivor. The surprise twist at the end is a good one. Made-for-TV. (Dir: Sutton Rolley, 72 mins.)

Satellite in the Sky (1956)**½ Kieron Moore, Lois Maxwell. A British made science-fiction tale of the earth satellite. Interesting but often too technical in the dialogue. (Dir: Paul Dickson, 85 mins.)

Saturday Night and Sunday Morning (British, 1961)**** Albert Finney, Shirley Ann Field. A wonderful, robust film, expertly directed by Tony Richardson, detailing the life and loves of a young working-class rascal from the English midlands. Incisive comment on certain mores of the English working class that captures the mood of such a dreary industrial community. Electric, vital performance of Finney deservedly shot him to stardom. An admirable piece of filmmaking in every detail. (Dir: Karel Reisz, 98 mins.)

Saturday Night Out (Great Britain, 1964)** Heather Sears, Bernard Lee, Nigel Green. Weak tale of a sailor's love has several unconnected episodes strung together. Solid acting, but wooden roles. Lee is the notable exception as a businessman involved with a blackmailing woman. (Dir: Robert Hartford-Davis, 96 mins.)

Saturday's Hero (1951)*** John Derek, Donna Reed, Sidney Blackmer. A handsome youth tries to rise above his immigrant family's background by going to college on a football scholarship. He finds things aren't all peaches and cream on the other side of the tracks. Better than usual performances from the actors involved. (Dir: David Miller, 111 mins.)

Savage, The (1960)**½ Charlton Heston, Susan Morrow. Man raised by the Sioux is torn between loyalties when war threatens between the Indians and the whites. Outdoor drama covers familiar ground, is done well enough to please the adventure fans. (Dir: George Marshall, 95 mins.)

Savage Bees, The (1976)** Ben Johnson, Michael Parks. Predictable New Orleans-based drama about the influx of African killer bees brought here by a visiting cargo ship. This is a "disaster" story with the sheriff's dog the initial victim. Do you thrill to the hum of buzzing critters? Made-for-TV. (Dir: Bruce Geller, 106 mins.)

Savage Eye, The (1961)**** Barbara Baxley. A dramatized documentary about a woman's lonely days following her recent divorce and the series of adventures she forces herself into in order to combat the feeling of desperation. Miss Baxley is excellent and the candid documentary technique works beautifully. An adult treatment of an adult subject. (Dir: Ben Maddow, 68 mins.)

Savage Gringo (Spanish, 1965)*½ Ken Clark, Yvonne Bastien, Alfonso Rojas. Rancher beset by trouble hires a young cowhand to protect him from his enemies. Cornball "western" made in Europe, dubbed in English.

Savage Innocents, The (1960)*** Anthony Quinn, Yoko Tani, Peter O'Toole. Unusual drama of Eskimo life, and the struggle of one family to keep alive in the barren wastes. Some spectacular photography, gripping scenes. Story line is uneven, occasionally confusing—but at least it's out of the ordinary fare. (Dir: Nicholas Ray, 110 mins.)

Savage Is Loose, The (1974)½ George C. Scott, Trish Van Devere, John David Carson. Embarrassing effort produced and directed by George C. Scott, as well as starring Scott and his wife. Playing a scientist, Scott is stranded on a desert island with his wife and their young son. The action centers on the boy's growing up without a proper mate upon whom to vent his lust. One wit referred to this as the "Swiss Family Oedipus," but the film's hardly as interesting as the appropriate subtitle. Witless screenplay by Max Ehrlich and Frank De Felitta. (Dir: George C. Scott, 114 mins.)

Savage Land, The (1968)**½ George C. Scott, Barry Sullivan. Film-feature version of Scott's guest appearance on the western TV series "The Road West." About the Pride family and their trials and tribulations in carving out a living in the post-Civil War West. Nothing special, but Scott adds stature.

Savage Pampas (1968)* Robert Taylor, Ron Randell. Dull, TV-made western set in Argentina during the late 1800's. Taylor portrays an army officer who tries to keep his military unit intact after interference from a band of Argentinian renegades. (Dir: Hugo Fregonese, 100 mins.)

Savage Seven, The (1968)* Robert Walker, Larry Bishop, Joanna Frank. Indians vs. motorcycle hoodlums in a desert town. Cro-Magnon in concept, dull-witted brutality. (Dir: Richard Rush, 96 mins.)

Savages (1974)**½ Andy Griffith, Sam Bottoms, Noah Beery. Andy Griffith takes a holiday from his usual nice-guy roles, to become a despicable menace. He's a New York lawyer who goes to a desert area to hunt bighorn sheep, with young Sam Bottoms as his guide. After Griffith kills an old prospector and pretends it was an animal, he and Sam begin a cat-and-mouse game of life and death in the desert. Suspenseful in parts. Made-for-TV. (Dir: Lee H. Katzin, 72 mins.)

Save the Tiger (1973)***½ Jack Lemmon, Jack Gilford. Jack Lemmon deservedly won an Oscar for his portrayal of Harry Stoner, a seamy one-time successful clothing manufacturer down on his luck and going through a mini-nervous breakdown. His performance and those of many in the supporting cast overcome many of the deficiencies in the talky script. Lemmon is seen on a long day during which he tries to convince his business partner (wonderful Jack Gilford) to set fire to their warehouse in order to collect the insurance money; puts up with the unpleasant business of supplying call girls for a prospective buyer. Thanks to Lemmon, "Tiger" is often quite moving. Written and produced by Steve Shagan. (Dir: John G. Avildsen, 100 mins.)

Saxon Charm, The (1948)***½ Robert Montgomery, Audrey Totter, Susan Hayward. Montgomery is good in this character study of a vicious Broadway producer. Story is at times hard to believe, but sustains interest throughout. (Dir: Claude Binyon, 88 mins.)

Say Goodbye, Maggie Cole (1972)**½ Susan Hayward, Darren McGavin. Strong performances by Hayward and McGavin give this one about doctors working in a slum area a boost. It's a tearjerker, with Hayward playing a recently widowed doctor who goes back into practice with McGavin, a gruff but dedicated ghetto G.P. There won't be a dry eye in your house when young leukemia patient Michele Nichols says goodbye to Dr. Maggie Cole. Made-for-TV. (Dir: Jud Taylor, 73 mins.)

Say Hello to Yesterday (Great Britain, 1970)**½ Leonard Whiting, Jean Simmons, Evelyn Laye. Modest, simply constructed romance of a suburban housewife, Simmons, and a young mod, played with exuberance by Whiting. They meet and part within the space of her ten-hour trip to London. A twist on "Brief Encounter." Jean Simmons is particularly touching, and Laye is funny as her mother. Written by Alvin Rakoff and Peter King. (Dir: Alvin Rakoff, 92 mins.)

Say One for Me (1959)** Bing Crosby, Debbie Reynolds, Robert Wagner. Bing back in priestly togs again, but this time he's almost defeated by a weak plot about a show-business parish, a chorus girl, and a night club manager with designs on her, all culminating in the Big Benefit Show. (Dir: Frank Tashlin, 119 mins.)

Sayonara (1957)***½ Marlon Brando, Red Buttons, Miiko Taka, Miyoshi Umeki, Ricardo Montalban. James Michener's novel about the romance between an American jet ace (Brando) and a Japanese performer. Brando is fine and Buttons

and Umeki give good performances (they won best supporting Oscars for this movie). (Dir: Joshua Logan, 147 mins.)

Scalphunters, The (1968)*** Burt Lancaster, Ossie Davis, Shelley Winters. Entertaining western which mixes excitement with an ample amount of comedy. Lancaster is at his athletic and charming best as a fur trapper whose pelts are stolen. Enter Ossie Davis as an educated runaway slave and the plot thickens. Telly Savalas and Shelley Winters are colorful as a renegade killer and his woman. Snappy direction by Sidney Pollack. (102 mins.)

Scalplock (1966)*½ Dale Robertson, Diana Hyland. Elongated pilot film for a TV series passed off as a feature—thoroughly routine, undistinguished western about a gambler who wins a railroad in a poker game, his efforts to make it a winning proposition. (Dir: James Goldstone, 100 mins.)

Scampolo (German, 1959)** Romy Schneider, Paul Christian, Carlos Thompson. Orphan girl finds happiness with a young architect. Sugary comedy, a bit too much sweetness and light. Dubbed in English.

Scandal at Scourie (1953)**½ Greer Garson, Walter Pidgeon. Another Garson-Pidgeon costume drama and not one of their best. The stars are more than adequate but the script is steeped in sentiment and affords little else, as it recounts the problems of a Canadian couple in adopting an orphan. (Dir: Jean Negulesco, 90 mins.)

Scandal in Paris, A (1946)*** George Sanders, Signe Hasso, Akim Tamiroff. The story of Vidocq, the thief and blackguard who cleverly talks his way into becoming Prefect of Police. Tasty costume melodrama, intelligently directed, well written and acted.

Scandal Sheet (1952)**½ Broderick Crawford, Donna Reed, John Derek. Over-done newspaper yarn about a couple of reporters who crack a murder case which involves their editor-friend. Energetically played by the principals. (Dir: Phil Karlson, 82 mins.)

Scapegoat, The (British, 1959)**½ Alec Guinness, Bette Davis, Nicole Maurey. Uneven comedy-drama about an English schoolteacher whose exact double, a French nobleman, offers him his family and responsibilities. Everything is done well, but it all doesn't seem to mesh. (Dir: Robert Hamer, 92 mins.)

Scapegoat, The (French, 1963)** Michele Morgan, Jacques Perrin. Not to be confused with Alec Guinness film with the same title. This one is a French made, English-dubbed adventure meller about madness, murder and injustice in 16th Century Venice. Miss Morgan, a fine actress who squandered her talents in too many of these costume films, is merely decorative once again.

Scar, The (1948)*** Paul Henreid, Joan Bennett. A gangster gets a new face, and a girl makes a new personality to go along with it, but too late, for he must pay the penalty. Suspenseful melodrama.

Scaramouche (1952)*** Stewart Granger, Eleanor Parker, Janet Leigh, Mel Ferrer. Exciting and colorful adventure drama set in 18th Century France. Granger handsomely fits the role of the swashbuckling and romancing hero and is surrounded by two beautiful ladies, the Misses Parker (sexier than she's ever been) and Leigh (as the patient noblewoman who secretly loves her "Scaramouche"). (Dir: George Sidney, 118 mins.)

Scarecrow (1973)*** Gene Hackman, Al Pacino, Dorothy Tristan, Ann Wedgeworth. In the rash of buddy films produced in the early 70's, this could have been the definitive one, except for a poor climax which robs the drama of lasting emotional impact. Hackman and Pacino are superb as a pair of drifter-losers who team up to travel from California to Philadelphia, where Hackman plans to open up a car wash. It's a foregone conclusion the pair will never make it to Philly. Their encounters along the way solidify their relationship. A kind of 70's version of Steinbeck's "Of Mice and Men." (Dir: Jerry Schatzberg, 112 mins.)

Scared Stiff (1953)*** Dean Martin, Jerry Lewis, Lizabeth Scott, Dorothy Malone. Singer and his busboy friend flee from a murder charge and land on a mysterious island to help an heiress in distress. Remake of Bob Hope's "The Ghost Breakers" works well with Dean and Jerry, blends laughs and chills expertly. (Dir: George Marshall, 108 mins.)

Scarface Mob, The (1962)**½ Robert Stack, Keenan Wynn, Neville Brand. Eliot Ness and a special force of lawmen band into "The Untouchables," out to get the goods on Al Capone and his mob. Originally the opening installments in the TV series, this crime drama of the Aspirin age still looks pretty good in feature form. (Dir: Phil Karlson, 90 mins.)

Scarlet Angel (1952)**½ Rock Hudson, Yvonne DeCarlo. Adventure yarn with Rock playing a sea captain who is constantly being used by vixen Yvonne. The plot gets very complicated but there are enough bar room brawls and love scenes to keep you awake. (Dir: Sidney Salkow, 80 mins.)

Scarlet Baroness, The (German, 1962) ** Dawn Addams, Joachim Fuchsberger. British secret agent is sent to wartime Germany to obtain information about the progress of production of atomic weapons by the Nazis. Passable cloak-and-dagger adventure dubbed in English.

Scarlet Buccaneer, The—See: Swashbuckler

Scarlet Coat, The (1955)** Cornel Wilde, Michael Wilding, Anne Francis. Heavy-handed historical costume drama about the American Revolution. Anne Francis is lovely as the lady caught in the web of espionage. (Dir: John Sturges, 101 mins.)

Scarlet Empress, The (1934)** Marlene Dietrich, Sam Jaffe. Dietrich is Catherine the Great in this stilted, corny, overacted story of the notorious woman. (Dir: Josef von Sternberg, 130 mins.)

Scarlet Pimpernel, The (British, 1935)**½ Leslie Howard, Merle Oberon, Raymond Massey. An underground hero masquerades as a fop in the familiar adventure story. (Dir: Harold Young, 110 mins.)

Scarlet Street (1945)*** Edward G. Robinson, Joan Bennett, Dan Duryea. Elderly cashier is attracted to a no-good woman. Grim drama has good performances, an ironic twist at the end. (Dir: Fritz Lang, 103 mins.)

Scars of Dracula, The (Great Britain, 1970)* Christopher Lee, Denis Waterman, Jenny Hanley. Dracula horrors pepped up with sex, violence and lots of gore . . . not for the kids. Jenny Hanley, daughter of actress Dinah Sheridan, makes her film debut as the female lead. Want to see Dracula creep up the wall of his castle face down? I thought not. (Dir: Roy Ward Baker, 94 mins.)

Scavengers, The (1959)**½ Vince Edwards, Carol Ohmart. In his pre-Ben Casey days. Edwards gets mixed up with shady women and shadier killers in the Orient. Quite mixed up, but some interest due to actual locales, John Cromwell's direction—and how did he get involved in all this???

Scenes From A Marriage (Sweden, 1973)**** Liv Ullmann, Erland Josephson, Bibi Andersson. Ingmar Bergman's stunning, telescopic examination of a crumbling marriage, originally made as six 50-minute TV programs for Swedish TV. Bergman shaped and edited the original footage into this remarkable drama running almost three hours. This superb film dissects different events, quarrels, lovemaking, misunderstandings, etc., over more than ten years of marriage, divorce and a new, more mature relationship. Ullmann is, to no one's surprise, astonishing, and Josephson is nearly as remarkable. A superb, demanding, profoundly rewarding character study. Written and directed by Ingmar Bergman. (168 mins.)

Scent of Mystery (1960)** Denholm Elliott, Peter Lorre, Beverly Bentley. Discovering that a young American heiress is about to be murdered, an Englishman and a sour-visaged cab driver (Lorre) set about to save her, sight unseen. Good cinematography in ordinary film released in theaters with an accompanying track of scents, such as perfume and tobacco odors, which were triggered mechanically at the right point in the film to serve as clues to the mystery. The process was labeled "Smell-o-vision." Some critics felt that described the film, too. (Dir: Jack Cardiff, 125 mins.)

Scheherazade (French, 1962)*½ Anna Karina, Fausto Tozzi, Gerard Barray. Crusader falls for the beautiful princess. Visually pretty production, otherwise it all adds up to just another Arabian Nights tale. Dubbed in English.

Schemer, The (French, 1959)** Michael Auclair, Annie Girardot. Art dealer is swindled by thieves, joins them in crime. Good perfor-

mances help this involved melodrama along. Dubbed-in English.

School for Love (French, 1955)*½ Brigitte Bardot, Jean Marais. Two sisters at a conservatory fall for the same music teacher. Trite little love story dubbed in English, displayed only for the Bardot personality. (Dir: Yves Allegret, 72 mins.)

School for Scoundrels (British, 1960)*** Ian Carmichael, Alastair Sim, Terry-Thomas. Innocent young man joins a school with an unusual course in successmanship. Enjoyable comedy has some pointed laughs, a cast of capable performers. (Dir: Robert Hamer, 94 mins.)

Scorpio (1973)**½ Burt Lancaster, Alain Delon, Paul Scofield. Adequate spy thriller which gives you the impression it should have been better. Lancaster, stoic and stolid, is the agent who is marked for extinction by fellow agent Scorpio (Delon), and the cat-and-mouse chase is on. You've seen it before but Lancaster gives it a slightly added dimension and a fine supporting cast, including Scofield as a Russian agent, John Colicos, and J. D. Cannon, provides substance to this rather flimsy affair. (Dir: Michael Winner, 114 mins.)

Scorpio Letters, The (1967)* Alex Cord, Shirley Eaton. Dull, obscure, and listless espionage "thriller" about two agents hired by the British to uncover a blackmailing ring. Complete lack of tension and suspense so necessary for this type of film. Made for TV. (Dir: Richard Thorpe, 98 mins.)

Scotch on the Rocks (British, 1954)*** Ronald Squire, Kathleen Ryan. Natives cause a Parliamentary investigation when they refuse to pay their taxes. Amusing comedy.

Scott Free (1976)*½ Michael Brandon, Susan Saint James, Michael Lerner. The trials of a professional gambler who wins a piece of desert land regarded by Indians as a sacred burial ground. Humdrum affair. Action counts more than character here, with the gambler being kidnapped three times. Made-for-TV. (Dir: William Wiard, 72 mins.)

Scott of the Antarctic (British, 1948)*** John Mills, Derek Bond. An account of the ill-fated British expedition to the South Pole, with stunning photographic effects (in color), authentic narrative, but as drama it's curiously remote, only occasionally affecting. (Dir: Charles Frend, 110 mins.)

Scream and Scream Again (1970) ****½** Vincent Price, Christopher Lee, Peter Cushing. An above-average, somewhat more sophisticated Vincent Price mad-scientist effort revolving around a series of psychotic murders in England. It seems Dr. Browning is gathering bits and pieces of people to build a perfect human being. Woven into this gruesome tale is a subplot of political intrigue. (Dir: Gordon Hessler, 94 mins.)

Scream of Fear (British, 1961) ******* Susan Strasberg, Ronald Lewis, Ann Todd, Christopher Lee. Girl poses as her paralyzed friend to investigate what has happened to her father, nearly loses her life in finding out. Sharply directed thriller works up good amount of suspense, shudders. (Dir: Seth Holt, 81 mins.)

Scream of the Wolf (1974) ****** Peter Graves, Clint Walker, Jo Ann Pflug. There's a creature which may or may not be a killer wolf, a rash of killings by an almost superhuman wolflike beast, so author Graves and hunter Walker are called in to solve the mystery. Made-for-TV. (Dir: Dan Curtis.)

Scream, Pretty Peggy (1973) ****½** Bette Davis, Ted Bessell, Sian Barbara Allen. This melodrama strains a bit to create a few scares, but fans of Miss Davis' horror-movie roles will enjoy watching her overact. An innocent college student plays part-time housekeeper for Bette's weird family in their creepy mansion. Made-for-TV. (Dir: Gordon Hessler, 90 mins.)

Screaming Mimi (1958) ***½** Anita Ekberg, Phil Carey, Gypsy Rose Lee. Inept mystery yarn with Ekberg as a bonus for male viewers. She's a dancer who thinks she's committed murder. Come to think of it, the script is murder. (Dir: Gerd Oswald, 79 mins.)

Screaming Skull, The (1958) ***½** John Hudson, Peggy Webber. Wife is terrorized by unexplainable happenings. Or is it inexplicable? Both describe the film.

Screaming Woman, The (1972) ****** Sweet Olivia de Havilland, as a wealthy lady recovering from a nervous breakdown, sees a woman buried alive, but nobody believes her. Ray Bradbury's short story will have viewers rooting for Olivia, frantically seeking help from the police, neighbors, little boys, and the killer. Filmed on a grand Santa Barbara estate by director Jack Smight; by and large, the suspenseful Bradbury plot holds up. Made-for-TV. (73 mins.)

Scrooge (Great Britain, 1970) ****½** Albert Finney, Sir Alec Guinness, Edith Evans. This musical version of Charles Dickens' timeless Christmas yarn about the flinty old miser-turned-philanthropist once he's shown the error of his ways, is as empty as a neglected Christmas stocking. Albert Finney, as Scrooge, plays the cantankerous, stingy businessman with great flair, and is the main bright spot. Music adds nothing and Sir Alec Guinness, painted a ghastly, ghostly gray from bandaged head to manacled foot, is a sight to behold as Marley. Unimaginatively directed by Ronald Neame. (118 mins.)

Scudda-Hoo! Scudda-Hay! (1948) ****** Lon McCallister, June Haver, Walter Brennan. Story of a farm boy who gets hold of a pair of mules and then trains them to be the best team around is mild fare. (Dir: F. Hugh Herbert, 95 mins.)

Sea Chase, The (1955) ****½** Lana Turner, John Wayne, Tab Hunter. Far-fetched tale of adventure and romance. Wayne skippers a renegade freighter which is bound for Valparaiso. On board is an assorted crew and Lana Turner, Wayne's woman. Curious to see Big John as a German officer. (Dir: John Farrow, 117 mins.)

Sea Devils (British, 1963) ****½** Rock Hudson, Yvonne DeCarlo. Fisherman turned smuggler gets involved with a beautiful spy during the Napoleonic era. Standard costume melodramatics get a lift from some action scenes. (Dir: Raoul Walsh, 91 mins.)

Sea Gull, The (1968) *****½** Vanessa Redgrave, Simone Signoret, David Warner, James Mason, Harry Andrews, Kathleen Widdoes. Let's start with the strengths of this adaptation of Anton Chekhov's story of life in rural Russia during the latter part of the 19th century. The play itself is an enduring, illuminating masterpiece, and director Sidney Lumet has rounded up a superlative cast of players. The no-doubt familiar story cannot be quickly summarized here. "Sea Gull" does seem static at times, but this is a generally absorbing rendition of a very great play, and we are thankful for that. (Dir: Sidney Lumet, 141 mins.)

Sea Hawk (1940)*** Errol Flynn, Claude Rains. Try and stop your youngsters from watching this salty tale of a sea-going Robin Hood. Don't leave the set too fast yourself because you're liable to enjoy this lusty sea story. Mike Curtiz gives it pace, Flynn gives it dash and Claude Rains and Flora Robson add dignity. (Dir: Michael Curtiz, 127 mins.)

Sea of Grass, The (1946)**½ Spencer Tracy, Katharine Hepburn, Robert Walker. The cast fights hard but this western about a man who sees New Mexico turning into a dust bowl and fights to save the grass is disappointing. It never stays with any of its many themes long enough to sustain interest and is certainly unworthy of the Tracy-Hepburn combo. (Dir: Elia Kazan, 131 mins.)

Sea Pirate, The (Italian, 1967)* Gerald Barray, Anbonella Lualdi, Genevieve Casile. Mealy mush as man turns pirate to collect a fortune so he may marry his lady. The swashbuckling keeps it moving between lovey-dovey lags. (Dir: Roy Rowland, 85 mins.)

Sea Shall Not Have Them (British, 1956)*** Michael Redgrave, Dirk Bogarde. Rescue launch attempts to save a crew of a downed plane, existing on a rubber raft in the North Sea. Good drama, well acted. (Dir: Lewis Gilbert, 91 mins.)

Sea Wife (British, 1957)*½ Richard Burton, Joan Collins. Impossible little drama about four survivors of a torpedoed boat and their struggle for survival in an island paradise. The quartet consists of a Negro purser, a hard-as-nails tycoon, an RAF officer, and a nun. (Dir: Bob McNaught, 82 mins.)

Sea Wolf (1941)*** Edward G. Robinson, John Garfield, Ida Lupino. Captain Queeg of "Caine Mutiny" was normal compared to Jack London's "Wolf" Larsen. This movie is too involved with the mental motivations of Larsen's action but the cast manages to make it a dynamic adventure of the sea. (Dir: Michael Curtiz, 100 mins.)

Sealed Cargo (1951)*** Dana Andrews, Carla Balenda, Claude Rains. Fishing vessel rescues the captain of a Danish ship, who is really the commander of a mother ship for Nazi subs. Exciting, suspenseful melodrama. (Dir: Alfred L. Werker, 90 mins.)

Seance on a Wet Afternoon (British, 1964)**** Kim Stanley, Richard Attenborough. Enthralling, brilliantly acted drama of a professional medium near the brink of insanity, who involves her weak husband in a kidnaping plot. Tremendous performances by Miss Stanley and Attenborough, backed by fine script and direction by Bryan Forbes. Top dramatic fare. (Dir: Bryan Forbes, 115 mins.)

Search, The (1947)**** Montgomery Clift, Aline MacMahon. Moving, sensitive story of a war orphan found in the ruins of post-war Europe. You're made of steel if this one doesn't move you. The cast is superb. (Dir: Fred Zinnemann, 105 mins.)

Search for Bridey Murphy, The (1956)** Louis Hayward, Teresa Wright. Based on M. Bernstein's freak best-seller about a housewife who when under hypnosis recalls a previous life. Quickly made to cash in on the then-current controversy, this drama has only fair entertainment values, except for a good performance by Wright. (Dir: Noel Langley, 84 mins.)

Search for the Gods (1975)*½ Stephen McHattie, Kurt Russell, Raymond St. Jacques, Ralph Bellamy. Plodding story about three young people who stumble upon a medallion purported to be more than 50,000 years old, which might have answers to the theory of space visitors to earth many, many years ago. Made-for-TV. (Dir: Jud Taylor, 100 mins.)

Searchers, The (1956)*** John Wayne, Jeffrey Hunter, Natalie Wood, Ward Bond. Director John Ford comes up with another fine Western drama. Wayne & Hunter play the searchers looking for a girl (Natalie Wood) who was kidnaped by Indians many years before. Suspenseful throughout. Excellent performances. (Dir: John Ford, 119 mins.)

Searching Wind, The (1946)*** Robert Young, Sylvia Sidney. Lillian Hellman's story of a career diplomat who has never taken a firm stand on anything is potentially good drama but never quite makes it. (Dir: William Dieterle, 108 mins.)

Seaside Swingers (British, 1965)****½** Freddie and the Dreamers, John Leyton, Mike Sarne, Liz Fraser. Zippy, hippy little musical about youngsters at a seaside resort and their problems with romance. Tunes aren't too bad, the players quite pleasant. Good fun for the teenagers. (Dir: James Hill, 94 mins.)

Season of Passion (Australian, 1961)******* Ernest Borgnine, John Mills, Anne Baxter, Angela Lansbury. Sugar-cane cutters find their annual on-the-town vacation in Sydney has changed, financially and romantically. Offbeat drama with a little-known locale, well acted, this drama should satisfy those in search of different fare. (Dir: Leslie Norman, 93 mins.)

Sebastian (British, 1968)****½** Dirk Bogarde, Susannah York, Lilli Palmer, John Gielgud. Fast faced espionage movie with talented cast members running all over the place deciphering codes, dodging double-agents, and falling in love. Dirk Bogarde sets the tone with his cool demeanor, and the supporting cast boasts such bright names as Lilli Palmer, Margaret Johnson and Nigel Davenport. (Dir: David Greene, 100 mins.)

Second Best Secret Agent, The (1965)***** Tom Adams, Veronica Hurst. A poor attempt at out-Bonding the great 007. Adams plays Charles Vine, a British secret agent who tries harder because he's number two, but it's still second-rate stuff. There's a formula which reverses the laws of gravity, but the ingredients for a good film are nowhere in sight. (Dir: Lindsay Shonteff, 96 mins.)

Second Chance (1953)****½** Robert Mitchum, Linda Darnell, Jack Palance. American in South America tries to forget an unfortunate experience in the ring, helps a lady in distress. Occasionally suspenseful melodrama. (Dir: Rudolph Mate, 82 mins.)

Second Chance (1972)****** Brian Keith, Elizabeth Ashley. Loosely woven, fairly pleasant comedy about a stockbroker who acquires a ghost town and fills it with assorted talent in need of another break. The experimental community works until the locals accuse their benefactor of becoming a dictator. Gentle humor and minor, low-key problems. Made-for-TV. (Dir: Peter Tewksbury, 73 mins.)

Second Chorus (1940)****** Fred Astaire, Paulette Goddard, Burgess Meredith. Two hot trumpeters try to keep their band together and vie for the affections of the same girl. Pleasant musical, but not Astaire's best. (Dir: H. C. Potter, 83 mins.)

Second Greatest Sex, The (1956)****** Jeanne Crain, George Nader, Kitty Kallen, Bert Lahr. "Lysistrata" gets another revamping in this western musical. The women are tired of the men fighting all the time, so they go on a love-strike. A lot of talent is wasted on this strained comedy effort, particularly Bert Lahr. (Dir: George Marshall, 87 mins.)

Second Time Around, The (1961)******* Debbie Reynolds, Andy Griffith, Steve Forrest, Juliet Prowse. Sprightly western comedy about a young widow and her children who find themselves stranded in an Arizona town—but she soon livens things up when she becomes sheriff. Good fun. (Dir: Vincent Sherman, 99 mins.)

Second Woman, The (1949)******* Robert Young, Betsy Drake. The whole community suspects a man of being responsible for the death of his fiancee, but his new love proves them wrong. Good psychological suspense melodrama. (Dir: James V. Kern, 91 mins.)

Seconds (1966)******* Rock Hudson, Salome Jens, John Randolph. Intriguing premise of this suspenseful drama should be enough to whet your appetite. Rock Hudson is a middle-aged businessman who discovers he can arrange for a secret organization to give him a "second" chance at life. After submitting to surgery, and psychiatric orientation, Rock emerges as a handsome young man with seemingly everything one could ask for. The nightmare begins at this point, and although some of the plot twists may seem excessive, the imaginative story holds your attention. Directed by John Frankenheimer. (106 mins.)

Secret Agent Superdragon (Italian-French-German, 1966)***** Ray Danton, Marisa Mell. An agent for the CIA vs. the Black Wolves, a fanatical group out to take over the world with help of Syncron 2, a drug that

turns people into robots! Who cares!
(Dir: Calvin Jackson Padget, 95 mins.)

Secret Agents, The (1964)**½ Henry Fonda, Robert Ryan, Vittorio Gassman. A message left by an espionage agent is the key to a kidnaping plot, with the trail winding through Europe and Africa. Rather muddled episodic spy thriller, shot on location. Despite some stellar cast names, the story never quite makes it.

Secret Ceremony (British, 1968)**½ Elizabeth Taylor, Mia Farrow, Robert Mitchum. A trio of stars—Taylor, Farrow & Mitchum—is the lure in this macabre, muddled but interesting melodrama. The plot, if it can be so simply stated, concerns a warped and wealthy Miss Farrow who brings a blowsy Miss Taylor home as a substitute mother, not counting on the sudden appearance of stepfather Mitchum. What goes on in this mad household cannot be described—you have to see and hear for yourself. New scenes have been added for this "edited-for-TV" version, and some of the more provocative ones were deleted. Directed by Joseph Losey. The butchered, watered-down TV print loses much of the film's quality. Peggy Ashcroft and Pamela Brown are marvelous in supporting roles. (109 mins.)

Secret Command (1943)*** Pat O'Brien, Carole Landis. A two-fisted gent puts a stop to sabotage in the California shipyards. Actionful melodrama, well above average. (Dir: A. Edward Sutherland, 82 mins.)

Secret Conclave, The (Italian, 1953)**½ Henri Vidon, Tullio Carminati. As Pope Pius X prays in time of World War I, recollections of his life are brought back to him—although he considers himself a simple country priest, he eventually becomes Pope at the meeting of the famed secret conclave. Recommended for Catholic audiences. Others should find this religious drama fairly interesting.

Secret Door, The (British, 1964)*½ Robert Hutton, Sandra Dorne. In the early World War II days, two American safecrackers are sent to Lisbon by Naval Intelligence to steal the Japanese naval code. Spy melodrama stymied by slipshod treatment. (Dir: Gilbert Kay, 72 mins.)

Secret File—Hollywood (1962)* Robert Clarke, Francine York. Corny detective yarn, badly done, about vice rackets and scandal magazines.

Secret Fury, The (1950)** Claudette Colbert, Robert Ryan. Bride is claimed to be already married, is sent to an asylum on what looks like a frameup. Just fair mystery moves too slowly. (Dir: Mel Ferrer, 86 mins.)

Secret Garden, The (1949)*** Margaret O'Brien, Dean Stockwell, Herbert Marshall. An eerie, suspenseful drama about two children, Margaret O'Brien and Dean Stockwell, and their discovery of a magical, secret garden. Well acted by the entire cast, including Miss O'Brien whose grown-up acting performances have been pretty awful. (Dir: Fred M. Wilcox, 92 mins.)

Secret Heart, The (1946)**½ Claudette Colbert, Walter Pidgeon, June Allyson. Cast helps but there's no spark to this dreary psychological study of a girl who worships her dead father and hates her lovely stepmother. Some of the ladies may like this. (Dir: Robert Z. Leonard, 97 mins.)

Secret Invasion (1964)**½ Stewart Granger, Raf Vallone, Edd Byrnes. Though this war film predates the popular film "Dirty Dozen" by a few years, it's basically the same story. A group of criminals are promised a pardon if they'll participate in a dangerous mission involving the infiltration of Nazi-held territory in Yugoslavia during World War II. Though the film has some exciting sequences, the cast isn't strong enough to give it a much-needed sense of adventure. Stewart Granger, as the major in charge of the mission, comes off best. (Dir: Roger Corman, 95 mins.)

Secret Life of an American Wife, The (1968)*½ Misfired comedy about a bored housewife (Anne Jackson) who tries dalliance with a sexy movie star (ineptly cast Walter Matthau). George Axelrod reverses his "The Seven Year Itch" with highly disappointing results. Patrick O'Neal, Edy Williams. (Dir: George Axelrod, 92 mins.)

Secret Life of John Chapman, The (1976)*** Ralph Waite, Susan Anspach, Brad Davis, Pat Hingle. A curiously affecting "real life" drama based on the notable book "Blue Collar Journal." It's a deft adaptation of the chronicle of the president of Pennsylvania's prestigious Haverford College, during his voluntary sojourn doing odd jobs of manual labor. Waite, familiar to TV viewers as the head of the Walton family, plays the adventurous college president with ease. The best performance, though, comes from Miss Anspach as a good-natured, harried and vulnerable waitress in a luncheonette. Made-for-TV. (Dir: David Lowell Rich, 72 mins.)

Secret Life of Walter Mitty, The (1947)***½ Danny Kaye, Virginia Mayo, Ann Rutherford. Thurber's story of a man who lived in two worlds—the real one and his own fantasy world—makes an entertaining vehicle for Danny Kaye. Some excellent song sequences and sharp comedy lines make this one above average. (Dir: Norman Z. McLeod, 105 mins.)

Secret Mark of D'Artagnan (Italian, 1960)*½ George Nader, Magali Noel. The fighting swordsman and musketeer thwarts the evil machinations of Cardinal Richelieu. English-dubbed swashbuckler doesn't have the necessary dash, or much else. (Dir: Siro Marcellini, 91 mins.)

Secret Mission (British, 1944)**½ James Mason, Stewart Granger, Michael Wilding. British spy drama with excellent actors making the most of the intrigue. (Dir: Harold French, 82 mins.)

Secret Night Caller, The (1975)*½ Robert Reed, Hope Lange, Elaine Giftos, Michael Constantine. Offbeat casting works fairly well here, as Robert ("The Brady Bunch") Reed plays a respectable family man with a weakness for making obscene phone calls. Tawdry melodrama, but Reed and the supporting cast are interesting. Made-for-TV. (Dir: Jerry Jameson, 72 mins.)

Secret of Convict Lake, The (1951)**½ Glenn Ford, Gene Tierney, Ethel Barrymore. Convicts invade a village inhabited only by women; complications arise. Ethel Barrymore, as matriarch of the village, is the only interesting feature. (Dir: Michael Gordon, 83 mins.)

Secret of Dr. Kildare, The (1939)** Lew Ayres, Lionel Barrymore, Laraine Day. Certainly not one of the best in this series. Kildare continues his long Hollywood internship, Barrymore is still the barking "heart of gold" Gillespie and Laraine continues as Kildare's pretty combination nurse-sweetheart. (Dir: Harold S. Bucquet, 90 mins.)

Secret of Dr. Mabuse (German, 1962) *½ Peter Van Eyck. Mad doctor steals a death-ray invention and proceeds in his plan to conquer the world. Farfetched fantastic thriller dubbed in English. (Dir: Fritz Lang, 90 mins.)

Secret of My Success, The (British, 1965)*½ Lionel Jeffries, James Booth, Honor Blackman, Stella Stevens, Shirley Jones. Onward and upward in the art of murder, as a constable (Booth) becomes wealthier and wealthier. Tries for comedy in the tradition of "Kind Hearts & Coronets" but "Secret" fails in nearly every respect. (Dir: Andrew L. Stone, 112 mins.)

Secret of Santa Vittoria, The (1969) **½ Anthony Quinn, Anna Magnani, Hardy Kruger, Virna Lisi. Ponderous direction by Stanley Kramer and a screenplay that savors little of the excellent dialogue found in Robert Crichton's novel dissipate most of the potential inherent in this story of Italian hill town at the end of WW II. Anna Magnani, back in a major picture after a lamentably long absence, is reason enough to see this comedy-drama, as she bullies husband Quinn and dominates every scene she is in. The German army never did find the big cache of wine, but you can content yourself with Magnani and a good supporting performance by Hardy Kruger as a German officer. (Dir: Stanley Kramer, 140 mins.)

Secret of the Black Trunk (German, 1962)*½ Joachim Hansen, Senta Berger. Detective unmasks the head of a notorious criminal ring. Farfetched Edgar Wallace mystery dubbed in English. (Dir: Werner Klingler, 96 mins.)

Secret of the Black Widow, The (German, 1964)*½ O. W. Fischer, Karin Dor, Werner Peters. London police investigate the deaths of three men killed with the venom of the black widow spider. Rambling mystery has good production, corny script. Dubbed.

Secret of the Chinese Carnation, The (German, 1965)* Brad Harris, Horst Frank. International crime ring are after a revolutionary new type of fuel, stop at nothing to get it. Naive

629

thriller dubbed in English; pretty weak.

Secret of the Incas (1954)**½ Charlton Heston, Robert Young, Nicole Maurey. Adventurer finds a map holding the location of a priceless gold sunburst, arrives to find an archeological expedition already there. Melodrama with enough intrigue and suspense to hold the action fans. (Dir: Jerry Hopper, 101 mins.)

Secret of the Purple Reef, The (1960)** Jeff Richards, Peter Falk, Richard Chamberlain. Two brothers arrive to investigate the mysterious sinking of their father's ship. Passable Grade B melodrama with a couple of TV names who meant less then. Colorful Caribbean location scenes. (Dir: William Witney, 80 mins.)

Secret of the Red Orchid (German, 1962)** Adrian Hoven, Christopher Lee, Marisa Mell. Scotland Yard teams with an FBI agent to nab a murdering blackmailer. Fair Edgar Wallace mystery dubbed in English —some moments of suspense. (Dir: Helmut Ashley, 94 mins.)

Secret of the Sphinx (French, 1964)*½ Tony Russell, Maria Perschy, Double-crosses and murder on an archaeological expedition, with a fortune in gold the prize. Haphazard adventure drama tries for dashing heroics. Achieves tedium. Dubbed-in English.

Secret of the Telegian, The (Japanese, 1963)*½ Reporter runs across a scientist who makes a monster from a living man by substituting electricity for blood. Farfetched and hokey dubbed-English thriller.

Secret of Treasure Mountain (1956)** Raymond Burr, Valerie French. A buried Indian treasure is mysteriously guarded by an old man and his attractive daughter. Routine adventure film. Burr in his pre-Perry Mason days. (Dir: Seymour Friedman, 68 mins.)

Secret Partner (British, 1961)** Stewart Granger, Haya Harareet. Routine meller with Stewart Granger cast as a man who must prove he is innocent of an embezzlement charge and win back his wife in the process. Haya Harareet woodenly plays Granger's wife. (Dir: Basil Dearden, 91 mins.)

Secret People, The (British, 1952)**½ Valentina Cortesa, Audrey Hepburn, Serge Reggiani. Refugee in London meets her former fiance who persuades her to enter into an espionage plot. Long, leisurely melodrama doesn't have enough spark to lift it much above the ordinary. (Dir: Thorold Dickinson, 87 mins.)

Secret War of Harry Frigg, The (1968)** Paul Newman, Sylva Koscina. In WW II, a rebellious private is called upon to try and free some captured Allied generals. Obvious attempt at service humor, with Paul Newman wasted. Andrew Duggan, Tom Bosley, John Williams. (Dir: Jack Smight, 110 mins.)

Secret Ways, The (1961)**½ Richard Widmark, Sonja Ziemann. Fast-paced but brainless chase thriller behind the Iron Curtain. Widmark tries to smuggle an anti-Communist leader out of Red Hungary. Some exciting narrow-escape sequences. (Dir: Phil Karlson, 112 mins.)

Secret World (1969)**½ Jacqueline Bisset, Jean-Francois Maurin. The combination of Miss Bisset's beauty and an offbeat tale makes this film interesting. A young French boy, scarred by his parents' death in a car crash, becomes deeply infatuated with a beautiful English lady visiting his aunt and uncle's chateau. When it comes time for Miss Bisset to go back to England, the boy is once again shattered and retreats into himself. (Dir: Robert Freeman, 94 mins.)

Secrets (1977)* Susan Blakely, Roy Thinnes. Pretentious, silly drama about a young married woman with a nice, handsome and good provider of a husband who starts compulsively sleeping around after her possessive mother dies. The camera work is archly "arty," the script cumbersome. Susan Blakely looks like a groomed sleepwalker most of the time. Made-for-TV. (Dir: Paul Wendkos, 106 mins.)

Seduced and Abandoned (Italian, 1964)**** Saro Urzi, Stefania Sandrelli. A wonderfully funny film that takes a sardonic, angry view of Sicilian family life and the hypocrisy which plays such an important part in their lives and mores. Pietro Germi, the same wizard responsible for "Divorce, Italian Style," wrote and directed this witty and bitter view of his countrymen. Story is about what happens in a Sicilian town when a young girl is seduced by the fiancé of her sister. English dubbed. (118 mins.)

See Here, Private Hargrove (1943) *** Robert Walker, Keenan Wynn. Many an ex-Army man will get plenty of laughs out of this fair adaptation of the famous best seller. (Dir: Wesley Ruggles.)

See How They Run (1964)** John Forsythe, Senta Berger, Jane Wyatt, Franchot Tone. Three orphaned children are pursued by their father's murderer when they take incriminating evidence with them to South America. Draggy suspense drama offers nothing unusual. Telefeature originally produced for TV. (Dir: David Lowell Rich, 99 mins.)

See My Lawyer (1945)**½ Olsen and Johnson, Grace McDonald. The two comics want to squirm out of a movie contract, hire three young lawyers to help them. Amusing musical nonsense.

See No Evil (British, 1971)**½ Mia Farrow, Robin Bailey. A suspense thriller which works only part of the way, but the chills are there if you're patient. Farrow plays a blind girl who comes home to her uncle's house after the accident which caused her blindness, and begins living a nightmare. (Dir: Richard Fleischer, 89 mins.)

See the Man Run (1971)**½ Robert Culp, Angie Dickinson, Eddie Albert, June Allyson. Stock kidnapping plot undergoes a wrenching, far-out twist here. Linked to a kidnapping through a wrong telephone number, an out-of-work actor decides to cut himself in. Culp carries off the idea quite well with a nice assist from Miss Dickinson. Made-for-TV. (Dir: Corey Allen, 73 mins.)

Seekers, The (British, 1954)**½ Jack Hawkins, Glynis Johns. Colorful story of struggling pioneers and their efforts to open new frontiers in New Zealand Stars are better than the story. (Dir: Ken Annakin, 90 mins.)

Sellout, The (1952)**½ Walter Pidgeon, John Hodiak, Audrey Totter. Okay crime yarn. Pidgeon plays a crusading newspaper editor who tries to overthrow the corrupt local law enforcement. (Dir: Gerald Mayer, 83 mins.)

Seminole (1953)**½ Rock Hudson, Barbara Hale, Anthony Quinn. A good cast makes this adventure movie seem better than it is. The story of Seminole Indians and their efforts to stay free takes up the bulk of the film and it's interestingly unfolded. (Dir: Budd Boetticher, 87 mins.)

Senator Was Indiscreet, The (1947) ***½ William Powell, Ella Raines, Peter Lind Hayes. A bird-brained senator lets a hot political diary get out of his hands, and it may spell doom to his machine. Side-splitting farce comedy. Some biting satire, hilarious dialogue. Don't miss it. (Dir: George S. Kaufman, 81 mins.)

Send Me No Flowers (1964)** Rock Hudson, Doris Day, Tony Randall. Hypochondriac thinks, mistakenly, he has a short time to live, starts getting his affairs in order, including a new husband for his wife. Some laughs here, but the subject matter really isn't as humorous as the scripters would like it to be. The usual Day-Hudson-Randall devotees shouldn't mind. (Dir: Norman Jewison, 100 mins.)

Senechal the Magnificent (French, 1958)** Fernandel, Nadia Gray. Actor is mistaken for an army officer, setting off a wave of misunderstandings and impersonations. Fernandel fans will like, others will merely tolerate this mild English-dubbed comedy. (Dir: Jacques Boyer, 78 mins.)

Senior Prom (1959)** Jill Cory, Jimmie Komack, Paul Hampton. Harmless little college musical about a young student who makes a hit recording and becomes "top man on campus." Guest appearances by Connie Boswell, Jose Melis, Louis Prima, Keely Smith and even Ed Sullivan. (Dir: David Lowell Rich, 82 mins.)

Senior Year (1974)* Gary Frank, Glynnis O'Connor. Pilot for a short-lived TV series. It's all about the traumas and growing pains of high-school seniors in the mid-50's. It quickly dissolves into histrionic melodrama with the emphasis placed on the extra-marital affair of one girl's mother. Made-for-TV. (Dir: Dick Donner, 72 mins.)

Sensations (1944)**½ Eleanor Powell, Dennis O'Keefe. Dancing star resorts to novel means to obtain publicity. Mild musical; some good moments. (Dir: Andrew L. Stone, 86 mins.)

Sense of Loss, A (1972)*** Enlightening but ultimately disappointing documentary about the fighting, bitterness and religious hatred in northern Ireland. (Directed by Marcel Ophuls, responsible for the documentary masterpiece "The Sorrow and the Pity.") Interviews with people closely involved bring out the mindless futility of the ongoing violence in that embittered land. Moving interview with Bernadette Devlin. Director Ophuls' concern and innate humanity are evident throughout. (135 mins.)

Sensitive, Passionate Man, A (1977) *½ Angie Dickinson, David Janssen. Sincere, depressing and occasionally moving soap opera about an alcoholic executive of an aerospace company who loses his job, his family, and eventually his life as the result of his obsession for alcohol. Based on a true story from the novel written by Barbara Mahoney. TV adaptation by Rita Larkin. Janssen is competent here as the doomed lush. Good intentions, but no artistry. Made-for-TV. (Dir: John Newland, 98 mins.)

Senso—See: Wanton Contessa, The

Sensualita—See: Barefoot Savage, The

Separate Tables (1957) **** Deborah Kerr, Burt Lancaster, David Niven, Rita Hayworth. Faithful film version of Terence Rattigan's two one-act plays about the guests of a British seaside resort and their individual dramas. Miss Kerr & Mr. Niven (he won an Oscar for this performance) come off with the top acting honors as a spinster and a charming ex-colonel who turns out to be a fraud. Wendy Hiller, also an Oscar winner for her work here, plays Mr. Lancaster's long suffering mistress and the proprietress of the establishment. (Dir: Delbert Mann, 98 mins.)

September Affair (1950) *** Joan Fontaine, Joseph Cotten, Jessica Tandy. Engineer and concert pianist miss their plane while sightseeing in Naples; when the plane is reported crashed, they find they have a chance to start life anew together. Romantic drama the ladies should enjoy—well made, generally avoids the maudlin. (Dir: William Dieterle, 104 mins.)

September Storm (1960) *½ Joanne Dru, Mark Stevens. Model joins adventurers in trying to recover a fortune in Spanish gold from a sunken ship. Mediocre melodrama—originally in CinemaScope and 3-D, but the plot is still transparent. (Dir: Byron Haskin, 99 mins.)

Serenade (1956) **½ Mario Lanza, Joan Fontaine, Vincent Price. One of Lanza's lesser efforts. He plays a street singer who is discovered by society playgirl (Miss Fontaine) and concert manager (Vincent Price). Over-dramatic plot but the opera arias are worthwhile. (Dir: Anthony Mann, 121 mins.)

Serengeti (1959) ***½ Absorbing documentary of two zoologists who take a census of wild animals facing extinction on the steppes of Serengeti in Tanganyika. Remarkable animal footage should fascinate everyone.

Sergeant, The (1968) *** Rod Steiger in a complex portrait of an army sergeant whose physical attraction to a handsome private (John Philip Law) proves his downfall. Filmed on location in France, has some dramatic moments. Promising directorial debut by John Flynn. (107 mins.)

Sergeant Deadhead (1965) ** Frankie Avalon, Deborah Walley, Cesar Romero, Fred Clark, Buster Keaton. Girl-shy GI (Avalon) turns into a wolf and disrupts a missile base. Silly, harmless antics that waste the great Keaton. (Dir: Norman Taurog, 89 mins.)

Sergeant Rutledge (1960) **½ Jeffrey Hunter, Constance Towers, Woody Strode. Director John Ford doesn't always come up with winners and this western film is one of his lesser efforts. There's rape, racial prejudice and courtroom dramatics thrown together in this muddled sagebrush drama. (118 mins.)

Sergeant Ryker (1968) ** Lee Marvin, Bradford Dillman, Vera Miles, Peter Graves, Lloyd Nolan. Lee Marvin as an army sergeant on trial for treason during the Korean conflict. Fleshed out from a 1963 TV show, this is of ordinary interest aside from Marvin's strong performance. (Dir: Buzz Kulik, 85 mins.)

Sergeant Was a Lady, The (1961) *½ Martin West, Venetia Stevenson, Bill Williams. Army corporal is sent by mistake to a missile installation site manned solely by WACs. Old-hat comedy with a lot of too-obvious humor.

Sergeant X of the Foreign Legion (French, 1960) *½ Christian Marquand, Noelle Adam, Paul Guers.

The old wheeze about the Legionnaire meeting up with his ex-girl friend, now married to another, at an oil site in the Sahara. It's all been done before, but better. Dubbed in English.

Sergeant York (1941)******** Gary Cooper, Walter Brennan. Story of World War I's greatest hero is told with simplicity and understanding and emerges as a poignant film. Gary Cooper is perfectly cast as the Tennessee hillbilly who captured over a hundred Germans single-handed. (Dir: Howard Hawks, 134 mins.)

Sergeants Three (1962)****** Frank Sinatra, Dean Martin, Sammy Davis, Jr. A supposedly high-camp remake of "Gunga Din" to accommodate Frank Sinatra and his buddies. Some of it is diverting, but you'll tire of the hijinks of the cavalry bunch, played by F. S. and group, long before Sammy Davis, Jr. gets his chance to be heroic in true Gunga-Din fashion. Other members of the Clan in attendance are Peter Lawford and Joey Bishop. (Dir: John Sturges, 112 mins.)

Serpent, The—See: **Night Flight from Moscow**

Serpent of the Nile (1953)****** Rhonda Fleming, Raymond Burr, William Lundigan. Foolish drama about the Roman Empire in the days of Cleopatra (Rhonda Fleming) and Mark Antony (Raymond Burr) and their eventual suicides. Rhonda looks ravishing. (Dir: William Castle, 80 mins.)

Serpico (1973)******** Al Pacino, John Randolph, Jack Kehoe. Peter Maas' book about real-life honest cop Frank Serpico, whose stories about corruption in the New York City police force led to the Knapp Commission investigations, is turned into an excellent film by director Sidney Lumet. Pacino is brilliant in the title role of the unorthodox cop, who couldn't keep his mouth shut after witnessing the blatant practice of cops on the take. Another plus is the sense of reality conveyed by the use of good New York location footage, focusing in on the habitués of street crime, which made up Serpico's world as a young, dedicated and eager patrolman. (Dir: Sidney Lumet, 130 mins.)

Servant, The (British, 1963)*****½** Dirk Bogarde, Sarah Miles, James Fox. Sinister servant completely encompasses the life of a spoiled rich youth, ultimately holding him in virtual bondage. Strong, absorbing drama has all the attributes of a good horror story in addition to some explosively powerful scenes, fine performances. For adults. Superbly directed by Joseph Losey. (115 mins.)

Session with the Committee, A—See: **Committee, The**

Set This Town on Fire (1972)****** Chuck Connors, Lynda Day. Drama about the pressures placed on a respected newspaper publisher sets a slow pace, but the theme is different and fairly interesting. A publisher (Carl Betz) goes along with close friends in having second thoughts over a local hero imprisoned for manslaughter, and then regrets his change of heart. Doesn't cop out with the expected ending. Made-for-TV. (Dir: David Lowell Rich, 99 mins.)

Set-Up, The (1949)******** Robert Ryan, Audrey Totter. Overaged fighter ignores the crooked gamblers and fights to win. Excellent boxing melodrama, superbly made. One of few outstanding films about the fight racket. Still a knockout. (Dir: Robert Wise, 72 mins.)

Set Up, The (British, 1961)****** Maurice Denham, John Carson. Thief is tricked into breaking into a wealthy businessman's home, becomes the target in a murder frame-up. Okay Edgar Wallace mystery.

Seven Alone (1975)****½** Dewey Martin, Aldo Ray, Anne Collings, Stewart Petersen. Adventure film for family viewing. Based on "On to Oregon" by Honore Morrow, it relates the crisis-filled journey of six young brothers and sisters led by a 13-year-old boy across the wild terrain of America during the 1840's. The Wyoming location adds to the film's appeal. Made-for-TV. (Dir: Earl Bellamy, 100 mins.)

Seven Angry Men (1955)******* Raymond Massey, Debra Paget, Jeffrey Hunter. Raymond Massey doesn't portray Lincoln in this film about the Civil War, instead he plays John Brown. Tense climax and fine acting throughout bolsters this Civil War Western. (Dir: Charles Marquis Warren, 90 mins.)

Seven Beauties (Italy, 1975)******** Giancarlo Giannini, Shirley Stoler, Fernando Rey, Elena Fiore. A remarkable, paradoxical, chilling masterpiece, one of the greatest films of this or any other decade. Written and directed altogether brilliantly by Lina Wertmuller, "Seven Beauties" firmly establishes Wertmuller in the very top rank of film directors. "Seven Beauties" is a nickname for a two-bit hoodlum known as the "monster of Naples" before World War II. Giannini's performance as Seven Beauties-Pasqualino is one of the most remarkable film acting stints in memory, as this squalid dandy stumbles ignominiously through peace and a stint in a German prisoner-of-war camp run by commandant Shirley Stoler. Giannini's scene in the loathsome prison camp where he tries to save his own wretched life by making love to the gross German commandant, superbly played by Shirley Stoler, is one of the most searing scenes in the history of modern cinema. "Seven Beauties" is an audacious film, full of risks for writer-director Wertmuller, but her vision is never blurred, and "Seven Beauties" is a statement full of stunning images about man's struggle in adversity for honor and survival. Won many international awards. (Dir: Lina Wertmuller, 115 mins.)

Seven Brides for Seven Brothers (1954)**** Jane Powell, Howard Keel. A rare treat—an original Hollywood musical which works in every department. Based loosely on a story by Stephen Vincent Benet, this tune-filled yarn tells of six fur-trapping brothers who come to town to find wives after their eldest brother (Keel) takes lovely Miss Powell as his bride. There's a kidnapping and a great many musical numbers before the happy conclusion. The dances by Michael Kidd are brilliant, and the entire cast is delightful. Credit must also go to director Stanley Donen for making the whole thing appear as fresh and bright as the accompanying musical score. (103 mins.)

Seven Capital Sins (1962)*** The sins as depicted by some notable French directors, in an episodic film. As expected, parts better than the whole—but some good sequences. (113 mins.)

Seven Cities of Gold (1955)** Anthony Quinn, Richard Egan, Jeffrey Hunter, Michael Rennie. Routine costume adventure tale about the Spanish Conquistadors' 18th century expedition to California in search of the legendary "7 cities of gold." Quinn is well cast as the hot blooded leader of the operation and the rest of the cast is adequate. (Dir: Robert D. Webb, 103 mins.)

Seven Days in May (1964)**** Burt Lancaster, Kirk Douglas, Ava Gardner, Fredric March. An exciting suspense drama concerned with politics and the problems of sanity and survival in a nuclear age. Benefits from taut screenplay by Rod Serling, and the direction of John Frankenheimer, which artfully builds interest leading to the finale. Fredric March is a standout in a uniformly fine cast. So many American-made films dealing with political subjects are so naive and simple-minded that the thoughtful and, in this case, the optimistic statement of the film is a welcome surprise. (118 mins.)

Seven Days' Leave (1942)**½ Victor Mature, Lucille Ball. Soldiers on leave discover that one of them will inherit a fortune if he can marry a girl who is already engaged. Mildly amusing musical comedy. (Dir: Tim Whelan)

Seven Days to Noon (British, 1951) **** Barry Jones, Olive Sloane. Tense melodrama about a deranged atomic scientist who threatens to blow up London if they fail to do his bidding. Excellent thriller; suspense on high throughout. (Dirs: John & Roy Boulting, 93 mins.)

Seven Deadly Sins (French, 1954) **** Gerard Philippe, Michele Morgan, Francoise Rosay. An episodic yet thoroughly enjoyable film dealing with each of the seven deadly sins. One of the best is the French episode dealing with "Pride," which is brilliantly acted by Michele Morgan. This has everything; comedy, drama, romance and adventure. Not to be missed. (120 mins.)

711 Ocean Drive (1950)**½ Edmond O'Brien, Joanne Dru. Interesting crime "meller" about an ingenious racketeer and the many tricks he employs to outwit the big gambling syndicate. Edmond O'Brien is fine in the leading role. (Dir: Joseph M. Newman, 102 mins.)

7 Faces of Dr. Lao (1964)*** Tony Randall, Barbara Eden, Arthur

O'Connell. Randall's performance is a tour-de-force affair, and it's the best thing about this fantasy set in the last century. He plays Dr. Lao, the mysterious magical Chinese proprietor of a circus that comes to town and generates a wave of good happenings. In addition to playing Dr. Lao, Randall plays six other roles with the aid of elaborate make-up and costumes—all performers in the one-man traveling show—he's great to watch. (Dir: George Pal, 100 mins.)

Seven Golden Men (Italian, 1967)** Philippe Leroy, Rossana Podesta. Familiar heist yarn with a foreign cast, including the attractive Miss Podesta for window dressing. The gold reserve of the Swiss National Bank in Geneva is the object of all the planning and executing by the seven criminals. (Dir: Marco Vicario, 87 mins.)

Seven Guns to Mesa (1956)** Lola Albright, Charles Quinlivan. The outlaws again hold stage-coach passengers as hostages while they wait to rob a gold shipment in this familiar story. Lola Albright is along for the bumpy ride.

Seven Hills of Rome, The (1957)**½ Mario Lanza, Peggie Castle. Mario singing and romancing a la Roma. Slight plot, with several attractive slices of female Italian pizza displaying some nice hills of their own. Lotsa Lanza lungwork and Renato Rascel ("Arrivederci Roma").

Seven in Darkness (1969)**½ Milton Berle, Dina Merrill, Sean Garrison. Highly melodramatic tale. Although its plane-crash-survivor theme is familiar, the fact that all the survivors are blind people on their way to a convention adds an interesting gimmick to the film. The on-location production is first-rate. Taking a cue from past films of this genre, the survivors are mostly well played stereotypes—Milton Berle as a gruff businessman not resigned to his blindness, Sean Garrison as the ex-Marine with a secret about an incident in Vietnam, Barry Nelson as a jealous group leader, Lesley Ann Warren as an overprotected blind folk singer, Dina Merrill as a woman blind from birth. Made-for-TV entry. (Dir: Michael Caffey, 73 mins.)

Seven in the Sun (Italian, 1964)*½ Frank Latimore, Saro Urzi, Gianna Maria Canale. Two brothers are re-united when danger threatens in Argentina. Mediocre adventure drama dubbed in English.

Seven Little Foys, The (1955)*** Bob Hope, Milly Vitale. Hope is a bit more reserved in this story about the real life vaudeville family known as the Singing and Dancing Foys. He plays a show business "ham" who has a large family and wants them all to love the stage as much as he does. When his wife dies, he's faced with more problems. Good production numbers and a guest appearance by James Cagney as George M. Cohan. (Dir: Melville Shavelson, 95 mins.)

Seven-Percent-Solution, The (1976) ***½ Nicol Williamson, Alan Arkin, Robert Duvall, Laurence Olivier, Joel Grey, Georgia Brown, Vanessa Redgrave, Samantha Eggar. An enjoyable lark! What would have happened if Sherlock Holmes had met with Sigmund Freud? According to Nicholas Meyer, who adapted his own novel for the screen, Freud could have cured the sleuth of his fondness for cocaine and Holmes could have solved the mystery of one of the psychiatrist's patients. An elegant plot, indeed, though perhaps too elementary in its textbook explanation of Holmes' fascination with crime. Splendid cast—Arkin as the droll Freud, Williamson as the drug-ridden Holmes, Duvall as a quite intelligent Watson, Olivier as an unjustly accused Moriarty and Redgrave as an abducted courtesan. A stylish exercise in whimsical speculation, (Dir: Herbert Ross, 113 mins.)

Seven Samurai, The (Japanese, 1956) **** Takashi Shimura, Toshiro Mifune. Superb Japanese film about a small village under constant attack by Civil war bandits (16th Century) and the intervention of seven samurai as its protectors. Magnificently photographed and directed, a visual treat throughout. (Dir: Akira Kurosawa.)

Seven Seas to Calais (Italy, 1962)** Rod Taylor, Keith Michell, Irene Worth. Admiral Drake, pirate galleons, and war on the high seas make "spaghetti" sea-going version of England's defeat of the Spanish Armada, and her laying claim to the New World, circa 1588. Some good actors in this swashbuckler. (Dirs:

Rudolph Mate, Primo Zeglio, 102 mins.)

Seven Sinners (1940)*** Marlene Dietrich, John Wayne, Broderick Crawford. Honky-tonk singer attracts a handsome lieutenant. Trashy tale atoned for by a fine cast, plenty of rugged action. (Dir: Tay Garnett, 87 mins.)

Seven Slaves Against the World (Italian, 1965)* Roger Browne, Gordon Mitchell, Scilla Gabel. Moronic "magnificent seven" in sandals and swords. Roman tribune, betrayed in an Asian prison camp, escapes with six gladiators. (Dir: Michele Lupo, 96 mins.)

Seven Surprises (Canadian, 1963)** Compilation of seven short films stressing the more fanciful aspects of life. Varying degree of interest, with some better than others. Might do as novelty, even though it adds up to little more than seven shorts in a row. (77 mins.)

Seven Sweethearts (1942)*** Kathryn Grayson, Van Heflin. Cute, occasionally entertaining musical about seven lovely girls of Dutch ancestry living in Michigan with their daddy, S. Z. (Cuddles) Sakall. A bit too cute. (Dir: Frank Borzage, 98 mins.)

Seven Thieves (1960)***½ Edward G. Robinson, Rod Steiger, Joan Collins, Eli Wallach. Tense melodrama about a plot to rob the Monte Carlo gambling vaults. High-gear suspense, fine performances; only drawback is a weak ending, which nevertheless won't hurt the preceding thrills. Well above average. (Dir: Henry Hathaway, 102 mins.)

Seven-Ups, The (1973)** Roy Scheider, Tony Lo Bianco, Richard Lynch. Producer Philip D'Antoni ("The French Connection," "Bullitt") made a shaky transition to director in this undercover cop story. Scheider leads the team of cops out to stop hoods from kidnapping one another, but with the exception of a thrilling car chase there is little that reminds you of D'Antoni's past successes. The ruthlessness of the cops is repulsive. (103 mins.)

Seven Ways from Sundown (1960) **½ Audie Murphy, Venetia Stevenson, Barry Sullivan. Well-made western starring Audie Murphy as a ranger with the strange name of Seven-Ways-from-Sundown Jones,

known as Seven for short. The action is plentiful and there's the inevitable shoot-out at the end. (Dir: Harry Keller, 87 mins.)

7 Women (1966)* Anne Bancroft, Margaret Leighton, Sue Lyon, Betty Field, Flora Robson. Director John Ford gets run over by an absurd Chinese-based western, where veteran Ford has substituted wily Mongols for the standard complement of Indians. Turgid tale of mission personnel in China circa 1935, trying to protect themselves from a barbaric warlord. It's easy to protect yourself from this drivel. (93 mins.)

Seven Year Itch, The (1955)**** Marilyn Monroe, Tom Ewell. This is probably Marilyn Monroe's best screen performance. She is ideally cast as a sexy model who lives in the same apartment building as a happily married man (Tom Ewell) who finds himself thinking and living like a bachelor when his wife goes on a prolonged summer vacation. Billy Wilder handles both his stars expertly and the result is high style comedy. Great fun. (105 mins.)

1776 (1972)*** Ken Howard, William Daniels, Blythe Danner, Howard da Silva. The hit Broadway musical has been reasonably, tastefully transferred to the screen. The efforts of our Founding Fathers and the Continental Congress to have the Declaration of Independence ratified by its members may sound like a dry history lesson, but it turns out to be an entertaining, sometimes touching film. The finale of the film, which recreates the actual signing of the Declaration of Independence, is quite a memorable moment. Overlook some of the absurdities, and you'll enjoy it. (Dir: Peter H. Hunt, 150 mins.)

7th Cavalry, The (1956)*** Randolph Scott, Barbara Hale. Above average Randolph Scott western. Good plot and action kept at a good level. Story concerns a cavalry unit returning to the scene of Custer's massacre.

Seventh Commandment (1962)* Jonathan Kidd, Lyn Statten. Poor drama with bad production values and stoic performances about a religious nut.

Seventh Cross, The (1944)***½ Spencer Tracy, Signe Hasso, Hume Cronyn. This is a truly exciting chase melodrama about an anti-Nazi who escapes from a concentration camp in 1936 and attempts to get out of the country. Beautifully acted. (Dir: Fred Zinnemann, 110 mins.)

Seventh Dawn, The (1964)* William Holden, Capucine, Susannah York. Insipid adventure set in Malaya right after World War II. Holden is a wealthy American planter who finds himself caught in the web of guerrilla warfare and romantic upheaval. Everyone suffers. The viewer suffers, too. (Dir: Lewis Gilbert, 123 mins.)

Seventh Heaven (1937)*½ Simone Simon, James Stewart. Corny, inept sound version of the 1927 silent classic. Story of love in a Paris garret is a complete bore. (Dir: Henry King, 102 mins.)

Seventh Seal, The (Swedish, 1957) **** Max von Sydow, Gunnar Bjornstrand, Bibi Andersson. Ingmar Bergman's masterpiece about the philosophical dilemmas of modern man. The setting is 14th-century Sweden. A knight (von Sydow) and his squire return from a crusade to find the black plague spreading death across their land. The knight confronts death incarnate to play a game of chess, with the knight's life at stake. Brilliantly directed and photographed. One of the greatest films of the era. (105 mins.)

Seventh Sin, The (1957)** Eleanor Parker, Bill Travers, George Sanders. Wife becomes bored while married to a doctor and begins an affair with a shipping tycoon. Remake of an old Garbo film, but not an improvement. Mostly soap opera. (Dir: Ronald Neame, 94 mins.)

Seventh Sword, The (1962)** Brett Halsey. Spanish-made, English-dubbed adventure epic with heroics running rampant in the person of Brett Halsey as a leader of a band of seven swordsmen. Kids will be pleased with fast-paced action. (Dir: Riccardo Freda, 84 mins.)

Seventh Veil, The (British, 1945) ***½ James Mason, Ann Todd. A girl runs away from her demanding uncle to experience many loves as she becomes a concert pianist. Fine romantic drama shows care in all departments. (Dir: Compton Bennett, 95 mins.)

Seventh Victim (1943)**½ Kim Hunter, Tom Conway. Girl in New York looking for her sister finds a mysterious cult of devil worshipers.

Suspenseful, eerie, but overly complicated thriller. (Dir: Mark Robson, 71 mins.)

7th Voyage of Sinbad, The (1958)*** Kerwin Mathews, Kathryn Grant. Well done children's film in the fantasy-adventure groove. It's fun all the way for the kids. (Dir: Nathan Juran, 87 mins.)

79 A.D. (Italian, 1961)*½ Brad Harris, Susan Paget, Mara Lane. Gladiator fights the oppressors of Rome, becomes innocently involved with a slave trader. Drab spectacle dubbed in English.

Severed Head, A (1971)**½ Lee Remick, Richard Attenborough, Claire Bloom. Talented cast works very hard to be sophisticated and chic in this faithful but awkward adaptation of Iris Murdoch's novel about multiple indiscretions among the British upper crust. The whole thing eventually acquires the taste of flat champagne. (Dir: Dick Clement, 96 mins.)

Sex and the Single Girl (1964)**½ Tony Curtis, Natalie Wood, Lauren Bacall, Henry Fonda. Helen Gurley Brown's best-seller has been turned into an innocent spoof of the sexual daydreams of Madison Avenue types and their female counterparts. The cast plays it for laughs that aren't always there. (Dir: Richard Quine, 114 mins.)

Sex and the Teenager—See: To Find A Man

Sex Kittens Go to College (1960)* Mamie Van Doren, Tuesday Weld, Louis Nye, Martin Milner. A stripper with a high IQ is picked by a computer to head the science department of a college. Computer that picked the plot for this one has a screw loose somewhere; ghastly attempt at farce has nothing. (Dir: Albert Zugsmith, 94 mins.)

Sex Symbol, The (1974)* Connie Stevens, Shelley Winters, Jack Carter. Sleazy story based on Marilyn Monroe's life. Connie Stevens shamelessly overplays the role of a blonde starlet who rises to international movie fame in the '50s. Script is pure soap opera. Made-for-TV. (Dir: David Lowell Rich, 72 mins.)

Shadow in the Sky (1951)**½ Ralph Meeker, Nancy Davis, James Whitmore. Trouble ensues when a war vet's brother-in-law comes to live with him, after being discharged from a hospital with a psychological disorder. Good writing makes this drama fairly gripping stuff. (Dir: Fred M. Wilcox, 78 mins.)

Shadow in the Steet (1975)**½ Tony Lo Bianco, Sheree North. Tony Lo Bianco stars as an ex-con struggling to survive as a sympathetic parole agent. He's dealing with a strict lady officer (Sheree North) and a desperate ex-con; and, though the situation may be predictable, John D. F. Black's script manages to create some suspense, and Lo Bianco gives it strength. Made-for-TV. (Dir: Richard D. Donner)

Shadow Man (1953)**½ Cesar Romero. Good direction sparks this British thriller which has been pretty tense moments as London gambling saloon owner, Romero, gets involved with murder, romance, jealousy and Scotland Yard. (Dir: Richard Vernon, 75 mins.)

Shadow of a Doubt (1942)**** Teresa Wright, Joseph Cotten. Gripping suspense film in the grand Alfred Hitchcock tradition. A niece suspects her uncle of being the Merry Widow murderer. Uniformly good performances. (Dir: Alfred Hitchcock, 108 mins.)

Shadow of Evil (France-Italy, 1964)** Kerwin Matthews, Robert Hossein, Pier Angeli. OSS 117, France's answer to Bond's 007, in his third recasting, here played by Kerwin Matthews. Flimsy plot concerns mad scientist, plague-contaminated rats in Bangkok. Elaborate production, incoherent yarn. (Dir: Andre Hunebelle, 92 mins.)

Shadow of Fear (British, 1956)**½ Mona Freeman, Jean Kent, Maxwell Reed. Melodrama with some suspense but no surprises. A good supporting cast fares better than the stars. (Dir: Albert S. Rogell, 76 mins.)

Shadow of the Thin Man (1941)**½ William Powell, Myrna Loy. Nick is solving a race track crime and, although it lacks the freshness of the others, it's still entertaining. (Dir: W. S. Van Dyke II, 97 mins.)

Shadow of Treason (British, 1964)* John Bentley, Faten Hamama, Anita West. Soldier of fortune aids a girl whose life has been threatened. Low-grade melodrama.

Shadow on the Land (1968)* Jackie Cooper, John Forsythe, Carol Lynley, Gene Hackman. Uninspiring account of American under totalitar-

ian rule, and the two men who seek to foment revolution. Sloppy, energyless production. Made, of course, before Hackman became a big star. Made-for-TV. (Dir: Richard Sarafian, 100 mins.)

Shadow on the Wall (1950)** Ann Sothern, Zachary Scott, Gigi Perreau. Unconvincing murder meller—a child is sole witness to a murder for which her father has been unjustly convicted. Change of pace role for Sothern as the murderess, otherwise not much. (Dir: Patrick Jackson, 84 mins.)

Shadow on the Window, The (1957)**½ Philip Carey, Betty Garrett, John Barrymore, Jr. An interesting crime drama about a group of young hoods led by a psychopath (played with a wild intensity by Barrymore, Jr.) who kill a businessman and take his secretary along as hostage. The secretary's ex-husband happens to be a detective and sets out to find her and apprehend the criminals. (Dir: William Asher, 73 mins.)

Shadow Over Elveron (1968)** James Franciscus, Shirley Knight, Leslie Nielsen. This predictable drama about a corrupt law officer in a small town and a dedicated young doctor who faces up to him and the town was made for TV, and it shows. The plot borrows from every other film about small-town tyranny and blackmail. (Dir: James Goldstone, 99 mins.)

Shaft (1971)*** Richard Roundtree, Moses Gunn, Charles Gioffi. Private eye John Shaft has it all, the Greenwich Village apartment, the girls, the ability to feel fine an hour after he's been shot in the chest with a machine gun. He's a typical Hollywood private eye, but he's black and relevant to the '70's. It seems there's been a kidnapping and Shaft has to take on most of the white hoods in New York. Good old-fashioned wish fulfillment; Hollywood was right on time. (Dir: Gordon Parks, 100 mins.)

Shaggy Dog, The (1959)**½ Fred MacMurray, Jean Hagen, Tommy Kirk, Annette Funicello. One of Disney's first plunges into real-life features. Cheerful tale of a boy's transformation into an old English sheep dog by way of a mystical antique ring. Will hold the attention of the youngsters. (Dir: Charles Barton, 104 mins.)

Shake Hands with the Devil (1959) *** James Cagney, Don Murray, Dana Wynter. An excellent cast, which also includes Michael Redgrave and Glynis Johns, make up for the shortcomings of the script in this rather grim tale of the Irish rebellion. (Dir: Michael Anderson, 100 mins.)

Shake, Rattle and Rock (1956)*½ Lisa Gaye, Michael Connors. A TV performer wants to open a rock-and-roll club for teenagers, but meets with opposition from snooty squares. Some numbers by Fats Domino and others for the youthful set—otherwise, nothing.

Shakedown, The (Great Britain, 1960)* Terence Morgan, Hazel Court. Bleak crime drama attempts to show tough underside of London back streets. Prostitutes are used to compromise amateur photographers. Sluggish, seamy. (Dir: John Lemont, 91 mins.)

Shakespeare Wallah (India, 1965) ***½ Geoffrey Kendal, Laura Liddell, Felicity Kendall, Shashi Kapoor. Set in India in 1947, a country in the throes of getting its independence. A family of Shakespearean actors tours the land, playing for increasingly indifferent Indian audiences. Finely acted scenes from the Bard's plays are interwoven with the family's personal dramas, notably the love affair between the daughter and a young, indolent Indian playboy. Their elusive relationship keeps the film alive and brooding. Filmed on location in India. (Dir: James Ivory, 115 mins.)

Shakiest Gun in the West, The (1968) *½ Don Knotts. Strictly for Knotts devotees. In this western opus (a remake of Bob Hope's "Paleface"), Don plays a cowardly salesman who has to stand up to a band of outlaws when he's mistaken for someone else. (Dir: Alan Rafkin, 101 mins.)

Shall We Dance (1937)**** Fred Astaire, Ginger Rogers. Revue artist and a ballet dancer are forced to pose as married. Fine musical comedy, with great dancing, tuneful Gershwin melodies. (Dir: Mark Sandrich, 120 mins.)

Shame (Swedish, 1968)**** Liv Ullmann, Max von Sydow, Gunnar Bjornstrand. The genius of director Ingmar Bergman focuses on the subject of war in modern society, and the way in which it degrades and humiliates us all. This overpowering vision of the apocalypse deservedly won many prizes including, from the National Society of Film Critics, the top award for movie, director and leading actress. Married concert violinists flee to a small island to escape the civil war raging on the mainland. Liv Ullmann is profoundly moving playing von Sydow's wife, trying to hang on to her own dignity while her husband and everyone around her lose theirs. Bergman also wrote this original screenplay, filmed in black and white. A numbing, unforgettable film, including at the end, when Ullmann finds herself in a small boat, one of the most haunting movie images ever. Dubbed.

Shameless Old Lady, The (French, 1965)**** Sylvie. Delightful, touching award-winning film about a 70-year-old widow who makes a late stab at putting a little fun in her life, after living a very quiet and sedate life. French character actress Sylvie gives one of the most luminous and endearing performances you'll ever hope to see, and her daily encounters as the "shameless" old lady are a delight. A gentle, honest, and altogether beautiful film. (Dir: Rene Allio, 94 mins.)

Shamus (1973)**½ Burt Reynolds, Dyan Cannon. Good sport and expert stunt man Reynolds plays a private eye in a confusing action film. All the characters are stock as shamus (detective, that is). Reynolds smiles, smacks, kisses, and belts his way through a series of thugs, mugs, broads, and cops while trying to get to the bottom of a large export deal involving government arms. Miss Cannon has little to do as one of Reynolds' women. (Dir: Buzz Kulik, 99 mins.)

Shane (1953)**** Alan Ladd, Jean Arthur, Van Heflin, Brandon de Wilde, Jack Palance. Truly epic western, among the best ever made. Simple story of a gunfighter coming to the aid of homesteaders has been filmed with amazing skill by George Stevens, with some of the finest scenic values ever put on film. There's action, drama, fine performances. A winner. (Dir: George Stevens, 118 mins.)

Shanghai Express (1932)***½ Marlene Dietrich, Clive Brook, Anna May Wong, Warner Oland. A film classic in many ways. Tale of intrigue among the passengers of an oriental train. Dietrich's sultry femme fatale sets the standard for all subsequent courtesans with hearts of gold. Stylish, starkly expressionistic direction makes the film hard to forget. (Dir: Josef von Sternberg, 84 mins.)

Shanghai Gesture, The (1941)** Gene Tierney, Walter Huston, Victor Mature. A tycoon is drawn into a web of evil in an Oriental gambling den, with his daughter as one of the lures. Arty, slow, far-fetched melodrama. (Dir: Josef von Sternberg, 106 mins.)

Shanghai Story (1954)**½ Ruth Roman, Edmond O'Brien. Americans in Shanghai are imprisoned by the Communists. Good cast and direction can't quite overcome a familiar plot. (Dir: Frank Lloyd, 99 mins.)

Sharad of Atlantis (1936-66)*½ Ray Corrigan, Lois Wilde, Monte Blue. Feature version of serial "Undersea Kingdom." Group of explorers find the lost continent of Atlantis. For the old-time serial buffs exclusively, this adventure is otherwise pretty hard to take. (Dir: B. Reeves Eason, 100 mins.)

Share Out, The (British, 1961)**½ Bernard Lee, Alexander Knox, Moira Redmond. Private eye works undercover to smash a blackmail racket. Good cast helps this standard Edgar Wallace mystery. (Dir: Gerard Glaister, 62 mins.)

Shark! (U.S.-Mexico, 1969)*½ Burt Reynolds, Barry Sullivan, Arthur Kennedy. Treasure-hunters in the Red Sea face peril, intrigue and the possibility of being split in two by a shark that never fails to attack at appropriate moments. Gets lost in clichés. "Jaws" was not a sequel to "Shark!" (Dir: Samuel Fuller, 92 mins.)

Shark Kill (1976)* Richard Yniguez, Phillip Clark, Jennifer Warren. A made-for-TV ripoff of the phenomenally successful "Jaws." It features a great white shark dining off divers until a macho marine biologist and an oil company consultant go fish hunting. Made-for-TV. (Dir: William A. Graham, 72 mins.)

Shark River (1954)** Steve Cochran, Carole Mathews, Warren Stevens, Brother accompanies a Civil War vet who has killed a man into the

Everglades. Good scenery, but otherwise so-so melodrama.

Sharkfighters, The (1956)** Victor Mature, Karen Steele. A naval research team of scientists headed by Victor Mature set out to find a repellent, which when dissolved around a man in water would keep sharks away. A bit too technical to be entertaining. (Dir: Jerry Hopper, 73 mins.)

Shark's Treasure (1974)*½ Cornel Wilde, Yaphet Kotto. A smarmy attempt to cash in with the "Jaws" crowd, and there isn't even all that much footage of sharks, though what there is is often exciting. Written, directed and produced by its star, Cornel Wilde, the movie concerns a fishing-boat captain and crew off to find some sunken treasure, but not without some interference from a band of escaped convicts. The whole thing is melodramatic to the point of parody. There are some scary scenes with real sharks, though. (Dir: Cornel Wilde, 95 mins.)

She Couldn't Say No (1954)*** Robert Mitchum, Jean Simmons. Oil heiress wishes to repay citizens of her home town for childhood kindnesses, disrupts the community in doing so. Pleasant, enjoyable comedy. (Dir: Lloyd Bacon, 89 mins.)

She Cried Murder! (1973)**½ Telly Savalas, Lynda Day George. Pretty widow witnesses a murder and has to face the killer, who turns out to be the inspector conducting the police investigations. Savalas plays the evil cop, and he's cold and forceful. Mrs. George registers suitable panic, on location in Toronto. Made-for-TV. (Dir: Herschel Daugherty, 73 mins.)

She Devil (1957)* Mari Blanchard, Jack Kelly, Albert Dekker. Unbelievably bad science-fiction tale about a she-monster. Only redeeming feature is that monster is quite sexy as monsters go. (Dir: Kurt Neumann, 77 mins.)

She Done Him Wrong (1933)*** Mae West, Cary Grant, Gilbert Roland, Rochelle Hudson. Screen version of Mae's "Diamond Lil" is bawdy entertainment. Slightly naughty even today, because Miss West manages to make anything suggestive. (Dir: Lowell Sherman, 66 mins.)

She Lives (1973)*** Desi Arnaz, Jr., Season Hubley, Anthony Zerbe. An excellent dramatic performance by a relative newcomer, Season Hubley, and a surprisingly sensitive turn by Desi Arnaz, Jr., make this a fine film. It's a "Love Story" theme about a young couple who discover the girl is dying, but unlike Ali MacGraw, Miss Hubley rages against that good night, refusing to go gently. She and her lover begin a determined search for a doctor who will give them hope. Made-for-TV. (Dir: Stuart Hagmann, 73 mins.)

She Played with Fire (British, 1958) **½ Jack Hawkins, Arlene Dahl. Arlene Dahl's attractive presence almost makes up for the inadequacies of this melodrama about a beautiful woman who has a bad influence on men. (Dir: Sidney Gilliat, 95 mins.)

She Waits (1972)** Patty Duke, David McCallum. Ghost-story enthusiasts get still another tale full of curtains rustling, and a mother-in-law warning that evil spirits are lurking about the family mansion. Delbert Mann produced and directed. Made-for-TV. (73 mins.)

She Wore a Yellow Ribbon (1949) ***½ John Wayne, Joanne Dru, John Agar. Rugged commander of a cavalry outpost although undermanned makes an attempt to drive invading Indians back North. John Ford western is his usual excellent production, with sweep, scope, entertainment. (103 mins.)

Sheep Has Five Legs, The (French, 1954)*** Fernandel, Francoise Arnoul. Fernandel plays no less than six different roles in this frequently amusing French comedy about an old wine-grower and his sons. (Dir: Henri Verneuil, 95 mins.)

Sheepman, The (1958)***½ Glenn Ford, Shirley MacLaine. Fast, lusty western with welcome comic overtones, about a stubborn sheepman who upsets things when he brings his herd into cattle country. Played mainly for laughs, and gets them. Plenty of fun. (Dir: George Marshall, 85 mins.)

Sheila Levine Is Dead and Living in New York (1975)*½ Jeannie Berlin, Roy Scheider, Rebecca Dianna Smith. Disappointing adaptation of Gail Parent's book of the familiar story of a spoiled Jewish girl from the suburbs who comes to New York in search of a husband and self-identity. Sheila is so naive in her pursuit of the doctor of her dreams, and Miss Berlin is so unbalanced in her characterization, that deft parody becomes mere mawkish melodrama laced with fatigued ethnic humor. Without intelligence or humor, the cast seems to cry for a script allowing them to act. (Dir: Sidney J. Furie, 112 mins.)

Shell Game (1975)** John Davidson, Tommy Atkins, Jack Kehoe, Robert Sampson. Singer John Davidson stars as a cheerful con man attempting to fleece a rat, in a film more interested in suspense and the light touch than in violence, which is a relief. Davidson performs with a certain ease. Made-for-TV. (Dir: Glenn Jordan, 72 mins.)

Shell Shock (1964)*½ Carl Crow, Frank Leo, Beach Dickerson. Weak war story about two separated brothers who meet again on the Italian front.

Shenandoah (1965)**½ James Stewart, Glenn Corbett, Doug McClure, Katharine Ross. Family entertainment with James Stewart playing the head of a household torn apart by the Civil War, and giving one of his best performances. It's a tear jerker and the ladies who dote on this type of film will have a good time, crying at every crisis. Director Andrew McLaglen makes the most of what is basically familiar material. (105 mins.)

Sheriff, The (1971)**½ Made-for-TV feature starring Ossie Davis as an elected black sheriff in a California town. Explosive situation develops when a black girl is raped and a white man is the chief suspect. Featured in the competent supporting cast are Ruby Dee, Moses Gunn, and Ross Martin. (Dir: David Lowell Rich, 73 mins.)

Sheriff of Fractured Jaw, The (English, 1958)** Kenneth More, Jayne Mansfield, Robert Morley, Henry Hull. Silly western comedy which benefits somewhat by the casting of English actor Kenneth More in the title role. "Ruggles Out West" or "How a British gentlman tries to establish his gunsmith business in the wild and woolly West of frontier days, and ends up sheriff of a lawless town" might be an appropriate subtitle. Miss Mansfield supplies window dressing as a saloon hostess. Connie Francis sings for

Mansfield in the musical numbers. (Dir: Raoul Walsh, 102 mins.)

Sheriff Was a Lady, The (German, 1964)* Mamie Van Doren, Rik Battaglia. Oh, boy—a German-made western about a guy who wants to avenge the murder of his parents by trapping the villains. It has an American director, which doesn't help a bit.

Sherlock Holmes (1932)*** Clive Brook, Reginald Owen, Ernest Torrence. The first of the many Holmes films based on the books of Conan Doyle. This debut is handsomely mounted; Torrence is especially appealing playing Moriarty. (Dir: William K. Howard.)

Sherlock Holmes and the Deadly Necklace (German, 1964)**½ Christopher Lee, Senta Berger, Thorley Walters. Holmes and Dr. Watson once again combat the evil Moriarty, who's after a valuable necklace. Interesting English-German effort, with Lee a perfectly adequate sleuth whom mystery fans, especially Holmes addicts, should appreciate.

She's Back on Broadway (1953)**½ Virginia Mayo, Gene Nelson, Steve Cochran, Frank Lovejoy. Backstage musical picture with singing, dancing and conflicts. Cochran plays the brilliant director at the helm of a Broadway bound musical that stars Miss Mayo, a former movie queen who is returning to the stage. Familiar. (Dir: Gordon Douglas, 95 mins.)

She's Working Her Way Through College (1952)** Virginia Mayo, Steve Cochran, Gene Nelson. A burlesque queen goes to college. That's right. The best thing about this movie is the dancing. (Dir: H. Bruce Humberstone, 101 mins.)

Shield for Murder (1954)*** Edmond O'Brien, Maria English, John Agar. Crooked cop kills a bookmaker and hides twenty-five grand. Brutal crime melodrama is well made, nicely acted. (Dirs: Howard Koch, Edmond O'Brien, 80 mins.)

Shine on Harvest Moon (1944)**½ Ann Sheridan, Dennis Morgan. Some good old songs but not much more in this ridiculously fictionalized biography of entertainers Nora Bayes and Jack Norworth. (Dir: David Butler, 112 mins.)

Shining Victory (1941)***½ Geraldine Fitzgerald, James Stephenson. Doctor doing psychiatry research in a Scotland sanitarium falls in love. Finely acted, powerful drama. (Dir: Irving Rapper, 80 mins.)

Ship Ahoy (1941)**½ Eleanor Powell, Red Skelton, Bert Lahr. Entertaining but trite little musical about a girl who is unwittingly helping enemy agents. Dancing and music (Tommy Dorsey) are worthwhile. (Dir: Edward Buzzell, 95 mins.)

Ship of Fools (1965)**** Vivien Leigh, Simone Signoret, Oskar Werner, Jose Ferrer, Lee Marvin, George Segal. A must-see film. Based on Katherine Anne Porter's best-selling novel, the film follows a group of passengers traveling on a ship enroute from South America to Berlin, just before the Nazi outbreak. The excellent cast is top flight with Simone Signoret and Oskar Werner as the stand-outs. Stanley Kramer ably directed as well as produced from a fine script by Abby Mann. (149 mins.)

Ship That Died of Shame, The (British, 1956)*** Richard Attenborough. Drama about the conversion of a one time heroic war ship into a smuggling vessel. Top performances. (Dirs: Michael Relph, Basil Dearden, 91 mins.)

Shipmates Forever (1935)**½ Dick Powell, Ruby Keeler. Musical about Annapolis has a nice score and a tired story. Interesting Annapolis setting and the music make it attractive entertainment. (Dir: Frank Borzage, 108 mins.)

Ships with Wings (British, 1941)*** John Clements, Michael Wilding, Michael Rennie, Ann Todd. A pilot cashiered from the service becomes a hero aboard an aircraft carrier when World War II breaks out. Good war melodrama, excellent combat scenes. (Dir: Sergei Nolbandov, 89 mins.)

Shipwreck Island (1961)**½ Pablito Calvo, Charito Maldonando. Spanish-made, English-dubbed adventure tale about a group of lads shipwrecked on a deserted island and their attempts to survive. Interesting premise, fairly well done.

Shirts/Skins (1973)***½ Bill Bixby, Doug McLure, McLean Stevenson, Leonard Frey. Fascinating, forthright story by writer Bruce Paltrow about a group of moderately successful men who turn a weekly basketball match into a hide-and-seek, win-or-lose contest in which two teams will hide basketballs somewhere in

Los Angeles and then retrieve them. The theme is fully explored—how men never really get over the phase of their lives when they excel in sports or at least have a fighting chance at being one of a team. The cast is uniformly first-rate in its believability. Made-for-TV. (Dir: William Graham, 73 mins.)

Shock Corridor (1963)*½ Peter Breck, Constance Towers, Gene Evans. Newsman enters a mental institution to unmask a murderer, becomes a victim of harrowing experiences. Grimy little sensationalized drama. (Dir: Samuel Fuller, 101 mins.)

Shock Treatment (1964)*½ Lauren Bacall, Stuart Whitman, Roddy McDowall, Carol Lynley. Objectionable film that starts off satisfactorily but soon disintegrates into melodramatic hysteria. Whitman is an actor who accepts a large sum of money to pretend he's looney. He has himself committed to an asylum, where he is to obtain information concerning the whereabouts of stolen money from a psychotic patient (Roddy McDowall). Once Whitman gets committed, it's hard to determine who's balmier, the patients, head psychiatrist Lauren Bacall, or any viewers still watching this sensationalized tripe. (Dir: Denis Sanders, 94 mins.)

Shocking Miss Pilgrim, The (1947) *½ Betty Grable, Dick Haymes. Tedious bore about women's suffrage and the first lady secretary set in 1874 Boston. Routine Gershwin score as uninspired as the film. (Dir: George Seaton, 85 mins.)

Shockproof (1949)*** Cornel Wilde, Patricia Knight. Female ex-con falls for her parole officer while trying to go straight. Well-made melodrama with a slightly different slant. (Dir: Douglas Sirk, 79 mins.)

Shoe Shine (Italian, 1947)**** Rinaldo Smordoni, Franco Interlenghi. Two youngsters who want to buy a horse become involved in black-market operations and are sent to reform school. Grim, gripping drama of post-war Italy, superbly directed, written. (Dir: Vittorio De Sica, 93 mins.)

Shoes of the Fisherman, The (1968)** Anthony Quinn, Laurence Olivier, John Gielgud, Barbara Jefford, Oskar Werner. A simple minded Pope opera—yes it does involve the Vatican—based upon Morris West's more thoughtful novel concerned, among other things, with liberalizing the Roman Catholic Church. Storyline of the bestseller concerns a Russian pope and his influence on world peace. Enormous production, loaded with brilliant actors, doesn't deal with the comparative subtleties of the novel, and it's overlong to boot. There is one fascinating quaint idea advanced in the film that is not in the book—in order to truly serve the needy, end war and malnutrition, etc., the Pope cedes all the church's riches to the poor, and continues the activities of the church in poverty. It's almost worth sitting through the first couple of confusing hours to catch this fanciful sequence. (Dir: Michael Anderson, 157 mins.)

Shoot, The (German, 1964)** Lex Barker, Ralf Wolter, Marie Versini. Hero and his friend pursue a notorious bandit. Good direction by Robert Siodmak keeps this costume adventure perking. English dubbed.

Shoot First (British, 1954)*** Joel McCrea, Evelyn Keyes. American officer thinks he has killed a man while hunting, but becomes involved in a spy plot while clearing himself. Well-knit thriller enlivened by good comedy sequences. (Dir: Robert Parrish, 88 mins.)

Shoot Loud, Louder I Don't Understand (1966)**½ Marcello Mastroianni, Raquel Welch. A zany, if not hilarious, comedy about the wild goings-on in a strange household inhabited by Marcello Mastroianni and his eccentric uncle. Add Raquel Welch, a murder, a disappearance, underworld hoods, and missing money—and you know what you're in for. (Dir: Eduardo De Filippo, 100 mins.)

Shoot Out (1971)** Gregory Peck, Dawn Lyn, Susan Tyrrell. Routine western bolstered by good acting turns by child actress Dawn Lyn and Gregory Peck, in that order. It's one of those trail-of-vengeance yarns, with Peck seeking his former double-crossing partner after serving time in prison. (Dir: Henry Hathaway, 95 mins.)

Shooting, The (1957)**½ Millie Perkins, Will Hutchins, Jack Nicholson. Offbeat Western which saves on sets by photographing a long trek with the trio of stars. The plot involves Miss Perkins, bent on revenge, getting two young cowpokes to help her in her deeds. Some good scenes add interest, and the film doesn't drag out the premise, which is another plus. (Dir: Monte Hellman, 82 mins.)

Shootout in a One Dog Town (1973) **½ Richard Crenna, Stefanie Powers, Jack Elam, Arthur O'Connell. Slick western yarn with a twist ending. Crenna is a small-town banker entrusted with a $200,000 deposit and must use all his resources to keep it from being stolen by a gang of desperadoes. Veteran actor Elam scores, as usual, in the role of the town's bartender, who also happens to be the makeshift law officer. Made-for-TV. (Dir: Burt Kennedy.)

Shop on High Street, The—See: Shop on Main Street, The

Shop on Main Street, The (Czech, 1965) **** Ida Kaminska, Josef Kroner. Not only one of the most stunning films ever made about racism and bigotry, it's simply one of the most heartrending and moving films ever. About anti-Semitism in Czechoslovakia during World War II. A Slovak (Kroner) befriends and protects an elderly Jewess (Kaminska) until he receives a deportation order. Miss Kaminska, playing the old lady, is altogether extraordinary and richly deserved the critical acclaim she received, including an Oscar nomination. Exquisitely directed by Jan Kadar and Elmar Klos. English subtitles by Lindsay ("O Lucky Man!") Anderson. (128 mins.)

Shopworn Angel, The (1938) ** Margaret Sullavan, James Stewart, Walter Pidgeon. Sentimental romance with a 1917 setting which is long on corn and short on sense. Another of those "waste of talent" films. (Dir: H. C. Potter, 90 mins.)

Short Cut to Hell (1957) **½ Robert Ivers, Georgann Johnson. Professional killer is doublecrossed after committing murder, seeks his revenge. Interesting for two reasons: it's a remake of "This Gun for Hire," and it was directed by James Cagney, who handles his task nicely. Film itself moves at a speedy clip, though not up to the original. (87 mins.)

Short Walk to Daylight (1972) ** James Brolin, Abbey Lincoln. Suspense adventure tale about seven passengers on a New York subway

train who try to find their way to safety after an earthquake destroys a good part of the city. If your tastes run to this brand of melodrama . . . Made-for-TV. (Dir: Barry Shear, 73 mins.)

Shortest Day, The (Italian, 1963) **½ F. Franchi, C. Ingrassia. Two zany soldiers accidentally destroy Germany's secret weapon during World War II. War comedy given a lift by an all-star cast supporting the two comics, a rather cheerful burlesque of "The Longest Day." Dubbed in English.

Shot in the Dark, A (1964) **** Peter Sellers, Elke Sommer. Free-wheeling often hysterically funny farce. Excellent comedy performance by Peter Sellers as the bumbling French inspector he created in the film "The Pink Panther." Elke Sommer is decorative icing on the cake. It's Sellers' film, and he has a field day investigating a pair of murders. Some wonderful sight gags. Sprightly direction by Blake Edwards. (101 mins.)

Shotgun (1955) **½ Sterling Hayden, Yvonne DeCarlo. Interesting western, hero out to avenge a brutal murder. Gets a bit bloody at times. (Dir: Lesley Selander, 81 mins.)

Show Boat (1951) *** Kathryn Grayson, Howard Keel, Ava Gardner, Marge & Gower Champion. The unforgettable Jerome Kern score is still a big asset to this version of the noted musical drama of love aboard a Mississippi show boat. Otherwise, the cast is highly capable, the song numbers put over with zest. All that's lacking is that certain something that distinguishes a great musical from a good one. (Dir: George Sidney, 107 mins.)

Showdown, The (1950) *** William Elliott, Walter Brennan. Former state trooper looking for his brother's killer finds suspects in a gambling house. Western with a slightly different twist is well handled throughout.

Showdown (1963) ** Audie Murphy, Kathleen Crowley, Charles Drake. Two drifters are imprisoned with some outlaws, who force them to hand over some stolen bonds. Fair western with a complicated plot, will satisfy the outdoor regulars. (Dir: R. G. Springsteen, 79 mins.)

Showdown (1972) **½ Rock Hudson, Dean Martin, Susan Clark. Above-average western, thanks to a screenplay by Theodore Taylor that has flashes of humor. Good-guy Rock is a sheriff who has to track down his old childhood buddy who has chosen the crooked path, played in a smirking, relaxed style by Dean, who again is a western wino. Susan Clark is cast as the woman who is fond of both men, naturally. (Dir: George Seaton, 99 mins.)

Shrike, The (1955)***½ Jose Ferrer, June Allyson. The impressive B'way play by Joseph Kramm is brought to the screen with some glaring defects which rob it of its total impact—the miscasting of June Allyson in the role of the domineering wife who nearly destroys her husband by her love turned to jealousy and a watered down script which reverts to a happy ending. Jose Ferrer repeats his B'way role as the husband and is very effective. He also directed the film. Still worth seeing. (88 mins.)

Shuttered Room, The (British, 1967) *½ Carol Lynley, Gig Young, Oliver Reed. Contrived mystery yarn which goes for the obvious at every turn. Little time is wasted on characterizations as Carol Lynley comes back to her New England home town with her husband, Gig Young, and learns some shocking things about her family tree. (The striking countryside incidentally is the Cornish coast of England.) The room in the title is the attic in and old mill where the climax takes place. Even the usually splendid Oliver Reed is unbelievable. (Dir: David Greene, 99 mins.)

Sicilian Clan, The (France, 1969)*** Jean Gabin, Alain Delon, Lino Ventura. Heist caper with style and restrained acting. Patriarch Gabin heads a family that lives over a pinball repair store and occasionally indulges in a spectacular crime. They spring an old friend, Delon, and embark on their biggest job yet —stealing a cache of diamonds from a DC-8 en route to New York. Beautifully photographed and directed, with a climax that's tops for a crime drama. (Dir: Henri Verneuil, 121 mins.)

Sicilians, The (British, 1964)*½ Robert Hutton, Reginald Marsh, Ursula Howells. Investigator takes on a dangerous mission when the mob kidnaps the son of a gangster who has turned state's evidence. Cheaply made, threadbare crime melodrama.

Side Street (1950)**½ Farley Granger, Cathy O'Donnell. Although the plot of this low budget gangster drama is old hat, the performances of Granger and Miss O'Donnell as a pair of newly-weds down on their luck give it added dimension. A good supporting cast includes Paul Kelly, James Craig and Jean Hagen. (Dir: Anthony Mann, 83 mins.)

Sidecar Racers (1974)*½ Ben Murphy, Wendy Hughes, John Clayton, Peter Graves. Exotic racing footage in a formula melodrama. Dangerous sport of two-man motorcycle racing finds Murphy, a visiting American, teaming with an Australian for the big race. Noisy! (Dir: Earl Bellamy, 100 mins.)

Sidekicks (1974)**½ Larry Hagman, Lou Gossett. Amiable feature stars Hagman as the white western hustler who keeps selling his black buddy Gossett as a slave. Mistaken for bank robbers by the law, as well as by a gang of silly thieves, the con men apply the light touch to the broad comedy. This is the TV version of the James Garner theatrical release "Skin Game." Made-for-TV. (Dir: Burt Kennedy, 72 mins.)

Sidewalks of London (British, 1938) **½ Charles Laughton, Vivien Leigh, Rex Harrison. A London street entertainer picks up a waif and sees her go to stardom, sacrificing his love for her to do so. Well acted, but brittle, unconvincing drama with music. Laughton is fine. (Dir: Tim Whelan, 84 mins.)

Siege at Red River, The (1954)**½ Van Johnson, Joanne Dru, Richard Boone. Interesting western with action and history combined to tell the story about the fore-runner of the machine gun, the Gatling gun, and how it served to revolutionize warfare. There's also a love story centering around Van Johnson and Joanne Dru. (Dir: Rudolph Mate, 81 mins.)

Siege of Fort Bismarck, The (Japanese, 1965)** World War I story based on fact, about the first aerial bombardment, as the Allies shatter a German stronghold. Japan was on our side then, remember? Interesting as a novelty. Dubbed in English.

Siege of Sidney Street, The (British, 1960)*** Donald Sinden, Nicole

Berger, Kieron Moore. Anarchist gang is trapped by police, which develops into one of the bloodiest battles in the annals of British crime. Historical melodrama should interest most viewers. Plenty of action; clever cameo of Winston Churchill played by the film's author. (Dirs: Robert Baker, Monty Berman, 94 mins.)

Siege of Syracuse (Italian, 1959)* Rossano Brazzi, Tina Louise, Sylva Koscina. History, movie-pasta style. Archimedes (Rossano) defends the Carthaginian city from the attacking Romans. The siege of the film is relieved occasionally by a glimpse of the tasty Tina. (Dir: Pietro Francisci, 97 mins.)

Siege of the Saxons (Great Britain, 1963)* Ronald Lewis, Janette Scott. Good King Arthur is knocked off by Saxon traitor; daughter Katherine finds a champion among the outlaws. Clanking, implausible adventure yarn. (Dir: Nathan Juran, 85 mins.)

Sigma III (1966)* Jack Taylor, Silvia Solar, Diana Martin. Lumbering CIA agent chases stolen laser-beam device. You need a laser beam to spot any talent in this junk. (Dir: Albert W. Whiteman, 90 mins.)

Sign of the Cross, The (1932)***½ Fredric March, Claudette Colbert, Charles Laughton. Not De Mille's best but a fine spectacle of decay in the Rome of Nero during the early days of Christianity. (Dir: C. B. De Mille, 140 mins.)

Sign of the Pagan (1955)** Jeff Chandler, Jack Palance, Rita Gam. Elaborately produced epic that doesn't come off. Chandler plays a Roman centurion who is captured by Attila's barbaric army and escapes to prepare for the large scale battle between the Christians and the Huns. Jack Palance overacts as Attila the Hun and the script becomes particularly muddled when it tries to explain the religious temper of the times. (Dir: Douglas Sirk, 92 mins.)

Sign of the Ram (1948)**½ Susan Peters, Alexander Knox. Invalided wife rules her family with iron hand, not wishing it to elude her grasp. Well acted but generally average drama. (Dir: John Sturges, 84 mins.)

Signed, Arsene Lupin (French, 1959) ** Robert Lamoureaux, Alida Valli. Gentleman cracksman gets involved in a case of missing paintings that's been baffling the Paris police. Well produced but sluggish period melodrama. Dubbed in English.

Signpost to Murder (1964)**½ Joanne Woodward, Stuart Whitman, Edward Mulhare. The cast is far better than the material in this obvious thriller about an escaped criminal who has been certified insane and his involvement with a lady he meets. The psychological delving into the man's past is pretty elementary and you'll probably have the whole thing figured out long before the end. (Dir: George Englund, 74 mins.)

Silence, The (Sweden, 1963)*** Ingrid Thulin, Gunnel Lindblom. Morbid, grim story of two sisters who must grapple with their lusts, personal isolation, degradation—the implications of their sordid lives are wider, the despair all-encompassing. A story of alienation made compelling by superb acting. The third part of a trilogy preceded by "Through a Glass Darkly," and "Winter Light." (Dir: Ingmar Bergman, 95 mins.)

Silence, The (1975)*** Richard Thomas, Cliff Gorman. In a superior production, Richard Thomas is most convincing as the real-life West Point cadet, James Pelosi, who was ostracized by the "silent treatment" by all the other cadets for two years, because of an alleged violation of the Academy's honor code. The excellent script by Stanley Greenberg is the result of his 70 hours of taped conversations with the actual cadet recalling the experience of his ordeal. (When originally shown, the film included a disclaimer by NBC for legal purposes, regarding Pelosi's real guilt or innocence, but author Greenberg objected to the disclaimer.) Made-for-TV. (Dir: Joseph Hardy, 72 mins.)

Silencers, The (1966)* Dean Martin, Stella Stevens, Victor Buono, Daliah Lavi. A dedicated attempt to capture the style and the box-office grosses of the socko 007 James Bond spy-spoofs falls completely flat, despite the many curved derrieres that decorate this limp effort. This was the first of Dean's appearances as suave cocksman Matt Helm, but there's nothing stylish about the film or Dino. (Dir: Phil Karlson, 102 mins.)

Silent Call, The (1961)**½ Gail

Russell, David McLean, Roger Mobley. Wispy little drama of a boy's dog, left behind when the family moves from Nevada to Los Angeles, who breaks away and follows the trail. Within its limits quite entertaining. Good script and direction. (Dir: John Bushelman, 63 mins.)

Silent Enemy, The (British, 1958)*** Laurence Harvey, Dawn Addams, John Clements. The story of Lionel Crabb, British frogman of World War II fame, whose underwater exploits in stopping the Italian fleet are recounted. Good suspense, absorbing submarine detail, capably performed. (Dir: William Fairchild, 92 mins.)

Silent Gun, The (1969)** Lloyd Bridges, John Beck, Ed Begley. Routine made-for-TV western about still another reformed gunman (Bridges) who helps to rid a small town of the bad guys. This 90-minute film was a pilot for a proposed TV series that didn't make it to the networks. (Dir: Michael Caffey.)

Silent Invasion, The (British, 1960)** Eric Flynn, Petra Davies. Girl loves an officer of the invading army, until her brother is killed. Average Grade B war drama.

Silent Movie (1976)**** Mel Brooks, Marty Feldman, Dom DeLuise, Harry Ritz, Bernadette Peters, Sid Caesar, Chuck McCann, Paul Newman. A joyous romp based on what would seem to lesser mortals than Mel Brooks a dubious notion around which to build a movie—a movie about a director trying to make a comeback in 1976 by making a silent movie. Well, as directed by Mel Brooks while also starring as Mel Funn, "Silent Movie" is wacky, consistently entertaining, inventive madness, including some boffo sight gags. (One surprise is to see Paul Newman careening about in a souped-up hospital chair. Newman gets laughs without dialogue.) The gags are written out in the form of subtitles, so you have to read as well as watch to savor all lunacy in "Silent Movie." Harry Ritz, one of Brooks' real-life comedy heroes, has a small part, but Mel wastes the prodigious talents of Sid Caesar in another unrewarding bit part. But "Silent Movie" is loud, boisterous fun. (Dir: Mel Brooks, 88 mins.)

Silent Night, Bloody Night (1973)**½ Patrick O'Neal, Astrid Heeren, John Carradine, Candy Darling. A pretty scary horror movie set in an old mansion in Massachusetts. Director Ted Gershuny keeps the audience right on the edge of its seat with the suspense, and adds some class in his deft handling of some flashback sequences. O'Neal is just right in the lead. (Dir: Ted Gershuny)

Silent Night, Lonely Night (1969)**½ Lloyd Bridges, Shirley Jones. Tale about a brief interlude shared by two lonely people during the Christmas holidays in a New England college town is the perfect example of what Hollywood calls a "woman's picture" and therefore it will appeal primarily to the ladies. Lloyd Bridges and Shirley Jones are the two strangers who come together while each is trying to cope with his own personal problem—Bridges' wife is a mental patient, and Miss Jones has found out her absent husband has had an affair. Naturally, there are many sentimental exchanges which tug at the heartstrings, but the two stars are effective in difficult parts and the winter location shots at Amherst, Massachusetts, add an authentic note. Made-for-TV feature. (Dir: Daniel Petrie, 98 mins.)

Silent Running (1972)*** Bruce Dern, Cliff Potts. Spectacular space effects highlights this skillful science-fiction speculation on the state of ecology in the year 2008. Dern plays the head of a rocket crew who have been sent to orbit Saturn with man's only remaining samples of vegetation. Dern is excellent and he is aided by two robots, Huey and Dewey, who have a marvelous scene playing poker. The director, Douglas Trumbull, served his apprenticeship as an assistant to Stanley Kubrick on "2001"—and it shows. (90 mins.)

Silent World, The (1957)**** Wonderful French documentary, Cousteau's exploration of the ocean's depths. Ideal in color, fascinating enough on ordinary sets. (86 mins.)

Silk Stockings (1957)*** Fred Astaire, Cyd Charisse, Janis Paige, Peter Lorre. Excellently mounted musical based on Cole Porter Broadway success which was based on Greta Garbo film "Ninotchka." Plot has Astaire, as a Hollywood producer, involved with a beautiful Russian agent (Miss Charisse) in Paris.

(Dir: Rouben Mamoulian, 117 mins.)

Silken Affair, The (British, 1957)****½**
David Niven, Genevieve Page. Funny
comedy that has David Niven playing
a somewhat sheepish accountant
who decides to take a fling. (Dir:
Roy Kellino, 96 mins.)

Silver Chalice, The (1955)****½** Paul
Newman, Pier Angeli, Jack Palance,
Virginia Mayo. Based on Thomas B.
Costain's novel. This is the story of
a Greek youth who makes the "Silver
Chalice" of the Last Supper. Many
subplots make the film much too
long. Paul Newman, one of our best
actors, gives one of his lesser performances here. (Dir: Victor Saville,
144 mins.)

Silver City (1951)****½** Yvonne De-
Carlo, Edmond O'Brien, Barry Fitzgerald. Assayer trying to escape his
past arrives in Silver City to help a
girl and her father mine a rich vein,
opposed by the owner of the land.
Actionful western with plenty of
movement for the fans. (Dir: Byron
Haskin, 90 mins.)

Silver River (1948)****½** Errol Flynn,
Ann Sheridan. Run-of-the-mill western which leans on its name actors
for support. Errol is a no-good
power-hungry louse in this one but
the ladies will still like him. (Dir:
Raoul Walsh, 110 mins.)

Silver Whip, The (1953)****** Dale
Robertson, Robert Wagner, Rory
Calhoun, Kathleen Crowley. If "action" speaks louder than "dialogue,"
this is a "noisy" picture. Wagner
plays an enthusiastic western youth
who wants to ape his two best
friends, Sheriff Calhoun and stage
guard Robertson, and ends up in
trouble. (Dir: Harmon Jones, 73
mins.)

Simba (British, 1955)*****½** Dirk Bogarde. Excellent drama dealing with
a man's revenge for his brother's
death against the hostile mau mau
tribes of Kenya. Some terrifying sequences graphically portrayed. (Dir:
Brian Desmond Hurst, 99 mins.)

Simon and Laura (British, 1956)
***½ Kay Kendall, Peter Finch.
Amusing British satirical comedy
about the "private lives" of a TV
husband and wife team. The late
Kay Kendall and Peter Finch are
excellent foils for each other as the
TV "ideal couple." (Dir: Muriel
Box, 91 mins.)

Simon of the Desert (Mexican, 1965)
***½ Claudio Brook, Silvia Pinal,
Hortensia Santovena. Short (45
minutes) savage examination by
famed director Luis Bunuel of man's
greed, frailties, and the deceptive
nature of religion. "Simon" has more
humor than is usually found in this
master's work. The protagonist is a
young ascetic who has gone to the
desert to commune with his God.
He finds some unexpected temptations in the wilderness.

Sinbad the Sailor (1947)******* Douglas Fairbanks Jr., Maureen O'Hara,
Anthony Quinn. The seafaring storyteller has adventurous experiences
with a secret amulet and a beautiful
princess. Ridiculous, but great fun
in this swashbuckling costume entertainment. (Dir: Richard Wallace,
117 mins.)

Since You Went Away (1944)*******
Claudette Colbert, Joseph Cotten,
Jennifer Jones, Shirley Temple. A
middle-class American family tries
to hold things together through the
arduous war and its sacrifices. Long,
sentimental, rather silly in these
days; but the women should still
love it. (Dir: John Cromwell, 172
mins.)

Sincerely Yours (1955)****** Liberace,
Joanne Dru, Dorothy Malone. It's
that man with the candelabra in a
heart-tugger full of corn and concerts. Liberace is just as obnoxious
in feature films as he was on his TV
show. (Dir: Gordon Douglas, 115
mins.)

Sing, Boy, Sing (1958)****** Tommy
Sands, Lili Gantle, Edmond O'Brien.
Rock-and-roll idol's religious training and the pressures of being a
star cause him to break under the
strain. The songs may hold the teenagers, but the plot is sluggishly
developed. (Dir: Henry Ephron, 90
mins.)

Sing You Sinners (1938)*****½** Bing
Crosby, Fred MacMurray, Donald
O'Connor. Solid entertainment as
Bing cavorts around as a wastrel
who strikes it rich at the track.
"I've Got a Pocket Full of Dreams"
is from this film and, although
there's not too much music, Crosby
fans should love it. (Dir: Wesley
Ruggles, 90 mins.)

Sing Your Worries Away (1942)****½**
Bert Lahr, June Havoc. Entertainers
get mixed up with some gangsters
trying to pull a swindle. Amusing
musical comedy. (Dir: A. Edward
Sutherland, 71 mins.)

Singapore (1947)** Fred MacMurray, Ava Gardner. Adventurer returns to Singapore to find his beloved a victim of amnesia, and married. Trite melodrama makes good actors look pretty silly. (Dir: John Brahm, 79 mins.)

Singer Not the Song, The (British, 1961)** John Mills, Dirk Bogarde. Long, glum drama of a priest and a bandit in Mexico, as one tries to reform the other to no avail. Miscast, overwritten, underdirected. (Dir: Roy Baker, 129 mins.)

Singin' in the Rain (1952)**** Gene Kelly, Debbie Reynolds, Donald O'Connor. One of the best musicals Hollywood has ever produced. Grand production numbers including a very lavish "Broadway Melody Ballet" with Kelly and Cyd Charisse. The story line deals with the transition period from silents to talkies in Hollywood films and gets a lot of comedy mileage out of the situation. Kelly and O'Connor are a great dancing team and Miss Reynolds keeps with their professional pace. Jean Hagen is a standout in the role of a silent film star with a speech problem. (Dirs: Gene Kelly, Stanley Donen, 103 mins.)

Singing Nun, The (1966)** Debbie Reynolds, Greer Garson, Ricardo Montalban. A fictionalized, mawkish account of the story behind the real-life nun who became an international celebrity when her recording of the song "Dominique" was released. Debbie Reynolds is bearable as the young nun whose energy becomes contagious when she arrives at a poor convent in Belgium. The plot switches frequently from light-hearted scenes to heavy handed pathos. The musical sequences are O.K., and Ed Sullivan is on hand displaying both of his facial expressions. (Dir: Henry Koster, 98 mins.)

Sinister Man, The (British, 1963)** John Bentley, Jacqueline Ellis. Oxford scholar is found dead and valuable archeological specimens missing. Fair Edgar Wallace mystery.

Sink the Bismarck! (British, 1960)*** Kenneth More, Dana Wynter. A maritime battle of wits as the British forces strive to conquer the pride of Hitler's Navy during World War II. Excellent special effects heighten this well done semidocumentary-style war story. (Dir: Lewis Gilbert, 97 mins.)

Sinners, The (Italian, 1956)*½ Ruth Roman, Akim Tamiroff. Wealthy merchant is attracted to a beautiful woman found stranded in the desert. Feeble melodrama of Biblical times. Dubbed.

Sinner's Holiday (1947)*½ George Raft, George Brent, Randolph Scott, Joan Blondell, Virginia Field. Three relatives answer the call of an aged lady to appear for Christmas dinner. Mish-mash of comedy, drama, hokum. (Formerly "Christmas Eve.") (Dir: Robert Siodmak, 92 mins.)

Sins of Babylon (Italian, 1963)* Mark Forrest, Jose Greci. Muscleman saves the people from a ruler who demands the sacrifice of virgin girls. Usual silly spectacle dubbed in English.

Sins of Lola Montes (French, 1955)*½ Martine Carol, Peter Ustinov, Anton Walbrook. Dull and foolish story of the famous dancer. The usually good performers get lost in the triteness of the script. Ustinov is amusing but it's hardly worth it, even to see him.

Sins of Rachel Cade, The (1961)**½ Angie Dickinson, Peter Finch, Roger Moore. Although this film is overlong and lapses into corny preaching, it has Angie Dickinson delivering a creditable acting job as an American nurse doing missionary work in the Belgian Congo. Peter Finch brings his usual quiet force to the role of a doctor who loves Miss Dickinson. (Dir: Gordon Douglas, 124 mins.)

Siren of Bagdad (1953)**½ Paul Henreid, Patricia Medina, Hans Conried. An Arabian Nights tale done with a flair for comedy—same old story but Hans Conried keeps things going at a bouncy pace. (Dir: Richard Quine, 77 mins.)

Sirocco (1951)** Humphrey Bogart, Marta Toren, Lee J. Cobb. Slow moving melodrama about sinister characters and their shady dealings. The stars are the picture's sole virtues. (Dir: Curtis Bernhardt, 98 mins.)

Sis Hopkins (1941)**½ Judy Canova, Susan Hayward. Country girl wins out over snooty cats at a girls' school. Amusing comedy. (Dir: Joseph Santley, 98 mins.)

Sister Angele's Secret (French, 1956)** Sophie Desmarets, Raf Vallone. Novice nun sees a murder committed, falls for the killer, tries to persuade him to surrender. Well acted but grim drama dubbed in English.

Sister Kenny (1946)***½ Rosalind Russell, Alexander Knox, Dean Jagger. Story of the famous nurse and her fight against infantile paralysis. Frequently stirring drama, excellently acted. (Dir: Dudley Nichols, 116 mins.)

Sisters, The (1938)*** Errol Flynn, Bette Davis. Good drama about a woman married to a newspaperman who can't seem to get going in spite of his talent. San Francisco background at the time of the earthquake gives hero and heroine even more trouble. (Dir: Anatole Litvak, 120 mins.)

Sisters (1973)*** Margot Kidder, Jennifer Salt, Charles Durning, Mary Davenport, Barnard Hughes, Dolph Sweet. An exceptionally gory and intelligent mystery-horror film that may be chopped up for the home screen. The plot is reminiscent of Hitchcock's "Rear Window"—a murder witnessed in a nearby apartment with no proof that it occurred. Kidder and Salt are excellent as the killer and the witness, and there are good supporting performances by all. Director Brian De Palma adds some nice touches, including a very funny satire of TV game shows. Screenplay by De Palma and Louisa Rose. Skillful homage by De Palma to the master of this genre—Alfred Hitchcock. (Dir: Brian De Palma, 92 mins.)

Sitting Bull (1954)**½ Dale Robertson, Mary Murphy. Ridiculous inaccurate tale of Sitting Bull and Custer is loaded with phony action and O.K. for the kids. (Dir: Sidney Salkow, 105 mins.)

Sitting Pretty (1948)***½ Clifton Webb, Maureen O'Hara, Robert Young. First and best of the hilarious Mr. Belvedere group. In this one, the amazing genius becomes a baby sitter in order to observe people and write a novel. (Dir: Walter Lang, 84 mins.)

Sitting Target (British, 1972)*½ Oliver Reed, Jill St. John, Ian McShane. A brutal British melodrama that verges on hysteria, starring Reed, who escapes from prison to take care of his unfaithful wife (St. John). Opening prison escape sequence is exciting but most of the rest is repulsive action for action's sake. (Dir: Douglas Hickox, 99 mins.)

Situation Hopeless—But Not Serious (1965)**½ Robert Redford, Alec Guinness, Michael Connors. An excellent idea that works only part of the way. A lonely German air-raid warden captures two American airmen (Redford and Connors) near the end of World War II, and keeps them prisoner in his cellar long after the war is over. Guinness manages to bring the suitable absurdity required by his character of the captor, but the pace of this satirical spoof is not as crisp as it should have been. (Dir: Gottfried Reinhardt, 97 mins.)

Six Black Horses (1962)** Audie Murphy, Dan Duryea, Joan O'Brien. A cowboy, a girl, and a killer are set upon by Indians in the desert. Ordinary western, with Duryea's familiar baddie performance worth noting; everything else's routine. (Dir: Harry Keller, 80 mins.)

Six Bridges to Cross (1955)*** Tony Curtis, George Nader, Julie Adams. Well made gangster film about a loser who keeps getting deeper and deeper into a life of crime until he masterminds a really big caper— knocking over an armored car and getting away with over 2½ million dollars. Loosely based on the Boston Brink's Robbery. Curtis is very good as the hood who couldn't go straight. (Dir: Joseph Pevney, 96 mins.)

633 Squadron (1964)*** George Chakiris, Cliff Robertson. A good action film which doesn't have to have a love story attached, but unfortunately, it has. However, it doesn't dominate the story, which becomes exciting. Chakiris and Robertson are assigned to destroy a very important Nazi stronghold in Norway, but complications set in, and an act of heroism above and beyond the call of duty gets the job done. (Dir: Walter Grauman, 101 mins.)

Six Million Dollar Man, The (1973)*½ Martin Balsam, Lee Majors. Majors stars as a Cyborg man, a "rebuilt" astronaut who learns to function with mechanical arms and legs before playing superhero on government missions. Pilot for subsequent TV series. (Dir: Richard Irving, 73 mins.)

Skezag (1971)**** Powerful, disturbing documentary about a black hustler-heroin addict in New York. Most of it is an interview with Vietnam veteran Wayne Shirley, including scenes of Shirley "shooting up." "Skezag" is a slang expression for heroin. In the beginning, Shirley comes on as a hip, ingratiating, wisecracking foul-mouthed con man. As time passes you see his bravado fading, as Shirley himself literally wastes away, and the viewer is left with a portrait of the hapless addict, fairly literally committing suicide in front of his eyes. Produced and directed by independent filmmakers Joel L. Freedman and Philip F. Messina. (73 mins.)

Ski Champ, The (German, 1962)** Olympic champ Tony Sailer. Lots of schussing around, little plot, about a skier preparing for a championship race. But Tony's a fabulous skier so. . . . Dubbed in English.

Ski Fever (U.S.-Austria-Czechoslovakia, 1967)* Martin Milner, Claudia Martin, Vivi Bach. Dreary tale of a ski instructor who falls in love with a pupil. Features lifeless performances (especially by Dean Martin's daughter, Claudia) and obligatory action ski sequences. (Dir: Curt Siodmak, 98 mins.)

Ski on the Wild Side (1967)*** Karl Schranz, Nancy Greene, Sue Chaffee, Roger Staub. A documentary for ski buffs shot on some of the great runs and mountains all over the world including the American Rockies, Europe, New Zealand and Japan. It's not as good as "The Endless Summer" about surfing, but skiers everywhere will enjoy this armchair travelogue. (Dir: Warren Miller, 104 mins.)

Ski Party (1965)** Frankie Avalon, Dwayne Hickman, Deborah Walley. A very poor man's "Some Like It Hot." Avalon and Hickman get into girls' costumes and go on a "ski party" to find out all about the opposite sex and the types of men they adore. The result is a film strictly for kids who probably can follow the plot and talk on the phone at the same time. (Dir: Alan Rafkin, 90 mins.)

Ski Troop Attack (1960)** Michael Forrest, Frank Wolff. American ski patrol is trapped behind enemy lines in Germany's Huertgen Forest. Modest but interesting World War II drama makes good use of icy locales, novel settings.

Skidoo (1969)½ Jackie Gleason, Groucho Marx, Peter Lawford, Mickey Rooney, George Raft. This is not just a "poor" movie as the half-star rating suggests. This is truly a ghastly film, a relentlessly unfunny collection of cinematic and comedy clichés compiled under the leaden direction of Otto Preminger. It's hard to believe that any film with Groucho could be all bad, but this monumental stinker is just that. The screenplay, if one can use that word to describe this tripe, concerns a bunch of petty hoodlums in California, and is just as terrible as the rest of this disaster. (Dir: Otto Preminger, 98 mins.)

Skin Game (1971)*** James Garner, Lou Gossett. James Garner's relaxed charm and winking good humor are put to fine use in this surprisingly agile comedy set in pre-Civil War days. Garner, a con artist, and his sidekick, runaway slave Lou Gossett—also excellent in his role, combine for some funny incidents including the unlikely subject of racism. Incidentally, a TV pilot starring Gossett and Larry Hagman in the leads didn't live up to this original. (Dir: Paul Bogart, 102 mins.)

Skirts Ahoy (1952)**½ Esther Williams, Vivian Blaine, Joan Evans. Typical musical about three sailors and their romances—only this time the sailors are Waves. The male side in the romance dept. is supplied by Barry Sullivan, Keefe Brasselle and Dean Miller. There are specialty numbers by the DeMarco Sisters and Billy Eckstine. (Dir: Sidney Lanfield, 109 mins.)

Skull, The (Great Britain, 1965)** Peter Cushing, Christopher Lee, Jill Bennett, Patrick Wymark. Acting vanguard of horror flicks peps up this improbable saga about the murderous powers of the notorious Marquis de Sade's skull. (Dir: Freddie Francis, 83 mins.)

Skullduggery (1970)* Burt Reynolds, Chips Rafferty, Edward Fox. Claptrap about an anthropological expedition in New Guinea which stumbles upon a band of blond apelike creatures who may be the missing link in evolution. Reynolds, playing a hunter, doesn't take anything too seriously, including the script. (Dir: Gordon Douglas, 103 mins.)

Sky Above and the Mud Below, The (1962)**** Absorbing, frequently harrowing documentary exploration of primitive peoples. Fascinating stuff. French-made and one of best of its kind. (Dir: Pierre-Dominique Gaisseau, 90 mins.)

Sky Above Heaven (French, 1965)*½ Andre Smagghe, Marcel Bozzufi. Mysterious flying object is sighted by an aircraft carrier, the world is thrown in turmoil. Sketchy, weak combination sci-fi thriller and French naval boost has an amateurish look. Dubbed in English.

Sky Full of Moon (1952)*** Carleton Carpenter, Jan Sterling, Keenan Wynn. Charming film about a young cowboy who comes to Las Vegas during Rodeo Week to strike it big. Carleton Carpenter gives remarkably accurate performance as the novice on-the-town and is aided by a professional supporting cast. (Dir: Norman Foster, 73 mins.)

Sky Hei$t (1975)*½ Don Meredith, Frank Gorshin, Stefanie Powers. Hollywood's pet action gimmick at the time was the ever-present helicopter, so someone dreamed up this pilot for a series on choppers. Crooks (Gorshin and Powers) plan to kidnap flying lawmen, led by Meredith, during a gold bullion theft. As expected, the flying machines upstage the actors at every turn. Made-for-TV. (Dir: Lee H. Katzin, 100 mins.)

Sky Riders (1976)** James Coburn, Susannah York, Robert Culp. Well above—several thousand feet above, as a matter of fact—the level of most mediocre melodramas, thanks entirely to some exciting, well-photographed scenes of the sport of hang-gliding. Here the sport is deftly employed to rescue some hostages held in an abandoned monastery on a high peak in Greece. The plot you've seen before—American industrialist (Culp) has his wife and children kidnapped by a terrorist group. Coburn and his derring-do glider gang ease down for the rescue. Filmed in Athens and the Greek countryside. (Dir: Douglas Hickox, 90 mins.)

Sky Terror (1972)**½ Charlton Heston, Jeanne Crain, Yvette Mimieux, Walter Pidgeon, James Brolin. Also known as "Son of Airport"! This tale about a bomb threat aboard an airplane flown by Heston, who was loved by stewardess Mimieux, is not a bomb. It's a straightforward thriller without any pretensions. Filled with fine ensemble character acting —including Pidgeon as a U.S. senator and Rosey Grier as a cellist. Don't let the subtle title change fool you—moviegoers saw this as "Skyjacked." Based on the novel "Hijacked" by David Harper. (Dir: John Guillermin, 100 mins.)

Sky Without Stars (Germany, 1955) *** Eva Kotthaus, Erik Schumann, Horst Buchholz. Post-war divided Berlin, from a West German view— and laudably done. (Dir: Helmut Kautner, 105 mins.)

Skydivers, The (1963)*½ Kevin Casey, Marcia Knight, Eric Tomlin. Ex-GI and his wife operate a sky-diving school, but the project is imperiled by a spoiled girl and an army buddy. Some fair aerial shots for those who care, otherwise a poorly done melodrama.

Skyjacked—See: **Sky Terror**

Skylark (1941)*** Claudette Colbert, Ray Milland, Brian Aherne. Amusing little comedy about a wife who gets the "seven-year itch" and has a brief and enlightening interlude with another man. (Dir: Mark Sandrich, 94 mins.)

Skylarks (British, 1965)** Eric Morecambe, Ernie Wise. British spy spoof which suffers in the trip across the Atlantic. The comedy team of Morecambe and Wise pull their antics all over the place as a pair of inept spies out to crack a sabotage scheme.

Sky's the Limit (1943)*** Fred Astaire, Joan Leslie. War hero spends his leave in New York and falls in love with a girl. Pleasing musical with great Astaire dancing. (Dir: Edward H. Griffith, 89 mins.)

Skywatch (1960)**½ Tommy Steele, Ian Carmichael. A routine service drama which benefits greatly from its fine British players. Song-and-dance man Steele does well as a renegade serviceman who has a yen for a good time during wartime.

Skyway to Death (1974)** Ross Martin, Stefanie Powers, Bobby Sherman, Nancy Malone. Another crisis drama with a host of TV names— Martin, Powers, Sherman, Malone, Joe Campanella, John Astin—coming together in an aerial tramway, kept there by a maniacal saboteur. Of course we get to know them and their hang-ups. It's obvious, to say the least. Made-for-TV. (Dir: Gordon Hessler.)

Slander (1957)** Van Johnson, Ann Blyth, Steve Cochran. TV star is victimized by the ruthless publisher of a scandal magazine. Weakly written drama misses out on a good idea with inferior treatment. (Dir: Roy Rowland, 81 mins.)

Slapshot (1977)**** Paul Newman, Strother Martin, Jennifer Warren, Lindsay Crouse, Melinda Dillon, Kathryn Walker, Michael Ontkean. There's an old adage in the movie business that says films about sports are box-office duds. Well, this foul-mouthed, funny, authentic, marvelously acted movie about a minor-league hockey team in a seedy Massachusetts mill town was a box-office winner. Young female screenwriter Nancy Dowd has a singular flair for the locker room patois, and the macho-bravado of professional athletes. In between the ribald asides and the on-ice violence, there's a morality tale lurking here about the pernicious spread of violence into our society and our sports. Newman plays an aging player-coach who's a clumsy romantic and a lousy, losing coach until he directs his simple-minded charges to act like crazed hoodlums on the ice. Dowd, incidentally, has written several juicy supporting parts for the women in "Slapshot," touchingly acted by Warren, Crouse, Dillon and Walker. Another fast-paced winner from savvy director George Roy Hill. (122 mins.)

Slattery's Hurricane (1949)**½ Richard Widmark, Linda Darnell, Veronica Lake. Personal drama amid a weather station's reporting of a hurricane. Herman Wouk penned the screenplay before his more successful efforts. Veronica Lake was a real dish in those days. (Dir: Andre de Toth, 83 mins.)

Slaughter on Tenth Avenue (1957) *** Richard Egan, Jan Sterling, Dan Duryea, Walter Matthau. Assistant D.A. runs into formidable obstacles when he tries to get the goods on waterfront hoodlums. Compact and informative crime drama, well done. (Dir: Arnold Laven, 103 mins.)

Slaughterhouse-Five (1972)***½ Michael Sacks, Ron Liebman, Sharon Gans. Ambitious film adaptation of Kurt Vonnegut's complex novel, a parable about Billy Pilgrim, an American Everyman. Director George Roy Hill and screenwriter Stephen Geller have a good feel for the fantasy in Vonnegut's work—World War II experiences and mental illness are mixed with other striking images in this demanding if flawed work. Newcomer Sacks is effective playing Billy. Filmed on location in Czechoslovakia and Minnesota. (104 mins.)

Slave Girl (1947)*** George Brent, Yvonne DeCarlo. Playboy is sent to Tripoli to rescue imprisoned American seamen. Often quite funny satire on adventure films; some good laughs. (Dir: Charles Lamont, 80 mins.)

Slave Girls of Sheba (Italian, 1961)* Linda Cristal, Jose Suarez. Saracen Sultan bests a tyrant controlling a narrow sea straight using slave girls. Mediocre English-dubbed costume spectacle.

Slave Queen of Babylon (Italian, 1962)*½ John Ericson, Yvonne Furneaux. Queen falls for a slave, and it's love against duty. Stilted costume drama dubbed in English.

Slave Trade in the World Today (France-Italy, 1964)*** A bizarre, not uninteresting semi-documentary concerning the plight of African and European women sold to rich Arabs for their harems. Filmed, often by hidden cameras, throughout Africa, India and the Middle East. Scenes include young boys and girls being openly traded, a slave market near Khartoum where old sheiks examine nude young girls, a caravan smuggling enslaved children from Chad to Saudi Arabia. Based partially on the book "The Slaves of Timbuktu" by Lord Robin Maugham. It's your only chance of the day to see giant land crabs dragging skeletons of escaped slaves on an island in the Red Sea. (Dirs: Roberto Melenotti and Folco Quilici.)

Slaves (1969)* Stephen Boyd, Ossie Davis, Barbara Ann Teer, Gale Sondergaard. One critic accurately noted, " 'Slaves' examines a monstrous institution with monstrous incompetence." Director and co-author Herbert J. Biberman, remembered for his provocative film "Salt of the Earth," serves up lust and villainy on the old plantation as a sensitive

653

slave (Ossie Davis) fights for freedom against the dastardly overseer (Stephen Boyd). Obviously sincere—but you and me, we sweat and strain while watching it. (110 mins.)

Slaves of Babylon (1953)** Richard Conte, Linda Christian, Maurice Schwartz. Biblical history suffers another setback with this romanticized nonsense relating how Nebuchadnezzar was defeated by an Israeli shepherd and his army. (Dir: William Castle, 82 mins.)

Slaves of the Invisible Monster (1950-66)* Richard Webb, Aline Towne. Feature version of serial "The Invisible Monster." Supercriminal uses a chemical to make himself invisible, the better to carry on his nefarious schemes. Pretty weak stuff, even for an ex-serial. (Dir: Fred Bannon, 100 mins.)

Sleep, My Love (1947)*** Claudette Colbert, Don Ameche, Robert Cummings. A husband who wants his wife out of the way tries to get rid of her by driving her insane. Familiar suspense melodrama; well done, but nothing new. (Dir: Douglas Sirk, 97 mins.)

Sleeper (1973)**** Woody Allen, Diane Keaton, John Beck, Don Keefer. A riotous film directed by the multitalented Allen. It's Woody's inspired, nutty vision of the future. After undergoing an operation Woody is frozen and awakens in 2173 to find himself in a police state, where the government has perfected its torture techniques to the point where hapless victims are forced to watch reruns of Howard Cosell on TV. There are marvelous sight gags, and an unending flow of one-liners, most of them funny. Woody also co-authored the screenplay with Marshall Brickman. Inventive lunacy of a high order, by the most gifted comedy mind working in films in the '70's. (88 mins.)

Sleeping Car Murder, The (France, 1965)***½ Yves Montand, Simone Signoret, Jean-Louis Trintignant, Jacques Perrin. An intriguing murder mystery mounted with class and taste by Costa-Gavras ("Z"). The cast are all perfect in this complex tale involving a multiple murderer. (Dir: Costa-Gavras, 95 mins.)

Sleeping Car to Trieste (British, 1948)*** Jean Kent, Albert Lieven. Some spies steal a valuable political diary and take off on the Trieste express, aboard which a famous detective outwits them. Neat spy thriller with some good comedy touches.

Sleeping City (1950)**½ Richard Conte, Coleen Gray, Peggy Dow. Moderately convincing drama about a detective who impersonates an intern in a hospital in order to crack a narcotics ring. Good performances by the cast. (Dir: George Sherman, 85 mins.)

Sleeping Tiger (British, 1954)***½ Alexis Smith, Dirk Bogarde, Alexander Knox. Psychiatrist brings a criminal to his home for study, but the doctor's wife falls for him. Excellently acted, suspenseful drama, well done throughout. (Dir: Joseph Losey, 89 mins.)

Sleepytime Gal (1942)**½ Judy Canova, Jerry Lester. A cake decorator in Miami enters singing competition, gets mixed up with gangsters. Amusing musical comedy.

Slender Thread, The (1965)*** Sidney Poitier, Anne Bancroft. The appeal of the two stars helps to overcome some of the strained dramatics in this story about a clinic whose sole purpose is to help desperate people via a phone call. Sidney Poitier plays a college student who volunteers his services at the "Crisis Clinic." The action of the film takes place during the time he tries to keep would-be suicide Anne Bancroft on the phone while police attempt to find her whereabouts. Miss Bancroft has the far showier role, but Poitier keeps his characterization crisp and interesting. (Dir: Sydney Pollack, 98 mins.)

Sleuth (1972)**** Laurence Olivier, Michael Caine. Marvelous inventive mystery based on the smash-hit play by Anthony Shaffer. It's a joy to see the great Olivier hamming it up, acting out his own special "games." Caine is equally skillful playing the butt of one of the "games," but it turns out that . . . well, we're not going to tell you the plot of this stylish thriller briskly directed by Joseph L. Mankiewicz. Just see and enjoy. (137 mins.)

Slight Case of Larceny, A (1953)*** Mickey Rooney, Elaine Stewart. A screwball comedy which almost makes it. Rooney and Eddie Bracken make a good team and it's their performances which are worth the whole film, as they play a couple of ex-GIs in trouble over a get-rich-quick scheme. (Dir: Don Weis, 71 mins.)

Slightly Dangerous (1942)*½ Lana Turner, Robert Young, Walter Brennan. "A" players in a poor "B" picture and the "B's" win. Pitiful nonsense. (Dir: Wesley Ruggles, 94 mins.)

Slightly French (1949)*** Dorothy Lamour, Don Ameche. Film director hires a carnival girl to pose as a new French import. Diverting comedy with good musical numbers, smooth direction. (Dir: Douglas Sirk, 81 mins.)

Slightly Honorable (1939)***½ Pat O'Brien, Broderick Crawford, Ruth Terry, Eve Arden, Edward Arnold, Evelyn Keyes. A murder mystery of the fast and whacky school, as a lawyer tangles with crooked politics and sinister killings. Rapid-paced, with bright dialogue and a great cast, how could it miss? (Dir: Tay Garnett, 83 mins.)

Slightly Scarlet (1956)*** John Payne, Arlene Dahl, Rhonda Fleming. Crook intends to turn the tables on his crime syndicate boss and muscle in himself. Unpleasant but well made, well acted melodrama. (Dir: Allan Dwan, 99 mins.)

Slim Carter (1957)*** Jock Mahoney, Julie Adams, Tim Hovey. Café entertainer becomes a western star and the idol of millions, but it all goes to his head—until an orphan boy takes a hand. Pleasant, slightly different behind-the-scenes comedy-drama, good entertainment. (Dir: Richard Bartlett, 82 mins.)

Slime People, The (1963)* Robert Hutton, Susan Hart. As ridiculous as its title—naturally a horror film about slimy things trying to take over. Hutton also directed this—for shame! (Dir: Robert Hutton, 76 mins.)

Slither (1973)***½ James Caan, Sally Kellerman, Peter Boyle, Louise Lasser. Very diverting first movie by director Howard Zieff. It's a wild and wooly chase in trailers and campers for a stash of loot, with lots of stops along the way for extravagantly detailed comic vignettes. Caan, Kellerman, Boyle and Lasser are the good guys—bumbling though they may be. Don't miss the American Legion Post party that introduced Boyle. Promising debut for Zieff, who was a TV commercials director. (Dir: Howard Zieff, 97 mins.)

Small Back Room, The (British, 1949)*** David Farrar, Kathleen Byron. A research scientist has problems both in his work and his home life. Expertly produced, interesting drama. Jack Hawkins. (Also called "Hour of Glory.") (Dir: Michael Powell, 106 mins.)

Small Change (France, 1976)**** Eva Truffaut, Tania Torrens, Jean-Francois Stevenin, Philippe Goldmann. A wise, beautiful, poetic comedy about children and a mistreated boy that also happens to be very funny. One of Truffaut's tenderest, most observant works. See it. Written and directed by Truffaut with Suzanne Schiffman. (104 mins.)

Small Town Girl (1953)**½ Jane Powell, Farley Granger, Ann Miller, Bobby Van. Plenty of songs and dances in this merry musical about a small town (Duck Creek, Connecticut?) and the change it goes through after a young and handsome millionaire playboy happens to get arrested while speeding through the one-horse "burg." (Dir: Leslie Kardos, 93 mins.)

Small World of Sammy Lee, The (Great Britain, 1963)*** Anthony Newley, Julia Foster. Sammy (Newley) is a minor Soho personality who must raise some money or face gang brutality; his reactions are a mixture of terror and his easygoing façade. Neatly crafted suspense, set in the unglamorous, tawdry locales of Soho. Movie is dominated by Newley's sterling performance. Original teleplay first seen on U.S. TV in 1958 entitled "Eddie." Written and directed by Ken Hughes. (105 mins.)

Smallest Show on Earth, The (1959)*** Peter Sellers, Margaret Rutherford, Bill Travers. Often amusing comedy about a young married couple who inherit a tacky movie theater along with its most improbable staff. The British cast expertly play it for laughs but the lines aren't all that funny. (Dir: Basil Dearden, 80 mins.)

Smart Woman (1948)*** Constance Bennett, Brian Aherne. A lady lawyer has a special prosecutor fall for her. Good melodrama. (Dir: Edward A. Blatt, 93 mins.)

Smash-Up (1947)*** Susan Hayward, Lee Bowman, Eddie Albert.

The wife of a successful songwriter finds home life unendurable with fame, takes to drink. Miss Hayward's excellent performance gives this drama distinction. (Dir: Stuart Heisler, 103 mins.)

Smash-Up Alley (1973)** Darren McGavin, Richard Petty, Noah Beery, Jr. For fans of stock-car racing, the "true" story of the king of the hill, Richard Petty, who plays himself, and his father, Lee, played by McGavin. The emphasis is on action—lots of racing footage—and the competition between father and son. Made-for-TV. (Dir: Edward J. Kakso, 72 mins.)

Smash-Up on Interstate 5 (1976)**½ David Groh, Vera Miles, Harriet Nelson. Another "disaster" film. This time it's with 39 cars involved, in which 14 people die and 62 are injured. The footage of the chain-reaction crack-up is superbly photographed, and the sequence both starts the movie and ends it (in slow motion the second time around). In between, flashbacks take viewers back 43 hours earlier and introduce all the characters. The vignettes are predictable and melodramatic, but Vera Miles manages to be quite good as a middle-aged divorcée who shares a brief romantic interlude with an unlikely truck driver (David Groh). Made-for-TV. (Dir: John Llewellyn Moxey, 106 mins.)

Smashing Time (British, 1967)*** Comic misadventures of two country girls (Lynn Redgrave, Rita Tushingham) in the mod world of London. Often harkens back to the old slapstick days; good-humored, enjoyable, knock-about farce with Michael York, Anna Quayle, Ian Carmichael. Directed with flair by Desmond Davis. (96 mins.)

Smile (1975)***½ Barbara Feldon, Bruce Dern. This could have been a great comedy. It isn't, but a lot of it is droll and satirical. It's a spoof on the biggest goof of all time, the American Beauty Pageant. This one is called the Young American Miss pageant, and all the expected participants are on hand for the event held in sunny California. There's the sponsor, Bruce Dern's used-car salesman; the den mother, well played by Barbara Feldon; Michael Kidd's sarcastic and bitter Hollywood choreographer down on his luck; and the parade of contestants

who give the picture its center. Fun most of the way. Biting screenplay by Jerry Belson. Fourth feature from the gifted director Michael Ritchie. (113 mins.)

Smile, Jenny, You're Dead (1974)*** David Janssen, Zalman King, Howard da Silva. Janssen plays private eye Harry O (for Orwell), a part created in a similar pilot film. Janssen is cool and collected as the sleuth who lives a relaxed life in a California beach community and only becomes involved when he chooses. The case which captures his attention involves a model who is being trailed, unbeknown to anyone, by a psychotic photographer. Tight pace, and Janssen's personal brand of laconic charm comes through nicely. Made-for-TV. (Dir: Jerry Thorpe.)

Smile When You Say "I Do" (1973)**½ Allen Funt uses his candid-camera technique to good advantage in this delightful series of vignettes focusing on the institution of marriage. There's a lot of fun in store in most of the wild and spontaneous situations. There's a segment about a nutty lady (who insists that her dogs be legally married before starting a family) that's a standout. Made-for-TV. (90 mins.)

Smiley (Australian, 1957)** Colin Peterson, Ralph Richardson, Chips Rafferty. Youngster trying to raise money for a bicycle gets involved with smugglers. Novel locale is the main asset of this mild little drama. The youngsters will like it best. (Dir: Anthony Kimmins, 97 mins.)

Smiley Gets a Gun (Australian, 1959) ** Keith Calvert, Chips Rafferty, Sybil Thorndike. Boy is promised a rifle by the local constabulary, provided he can earn it by doing good deeds. Mild comedy-drama, with the different locale helping somewhat. (Dir: Anthony Kimmins, 89 mins.)

Smoke (1970)*** Ronny Howard, Earl Holliman. Sensitive Disney production deals with a boy who distrusts his new stepfather and extends his love to a stray German shepherd dog. Howard and Holliman are acceptable in the leads of the drama, played at a slow pace. Nice children's fare. Made-for-TV. (Dir: Vincent McEveety, 98 mins.)

Smokey and the Bandit (1977)** Burt Reynolds, Sally Field, Jackie

Gleason, Jerry Reed, Paul Williams, Pat McCormick. Cars are the stars of this predictable race against time as two Texas millionaires commission trucker Reynolds to race from Georgia to Texas in 28 hours with a load of illegal Coors beer. Reynolds keeps cool as Bandit, a driver of legendary skill, Gleason fumes as Buford T. Justice, a Texas sheriff hot on Reynolds' trail, and Sally Field is charming as a runaway bride whom Reynolds picks up to complicate the comic-book plot with romance. CB radios augment the autos to prove this is a "modern" film. (Dir: Hal Needham, 97 mins.)

Smoky (1946)*** Fred MacMurray, Anne Baxter, Burl Ives. Story of a man's love for his horse is wonderful film fare for the youngsters and those who like sentimental outdoor drama. Smoother than '34 version. (Dir: Louis King, 87 mins.)

Smoky (1966)**½ Fess Parker, Diana Hyland. This is the third remake of the famous Will James sentimental story about a horse named Smoky and the events, both good and bad, which befall the animal. It's pretty old-fashioned fare by now, but this production is played straight, and therefore works. The kids will be pulling for Smoky from start to finish. (Dir: George Sherman, 103 mins.)

Smooth as Silk (1946)*** Kent Taylor, Virginia Grey. Attorney murders in a jealous rage, then schemes to cover his crime. Well-knit plot, good direction and performances put this "B" into the "A" class.

Smugglers, The (British, 1947)**½ Michael Redgrave, Richard Attenborough. A young lad is instrumental in rounding up a gang of smugglers, of which his guardian is the boss. Costume melodrama moves too slowly, and the net result is only fair.

Smugglers, The (1968)** Shirley Booth, Carol Lynley, Kurt Kasznar, David Opatoshu. A made-for-TV feature with good actors trying unsuccessfully to breathe some life into stereotyped roles in a predictable drama. About two American tourists in Europe (Miss Booth and Miss Lynley) who are used as decoys by an international smuggling operation. (Dir: Alfred Hayes, 97 mins.)

Snafu (1945)**½ Robert Benchley, Conrad Janis. Family is upset when "their boy" comes home a hardened teen-age soldier. Amusing comedy. (Dir: Jack Moss, 82 mins.)

Snake Pit, The (1949)***½ Olivia de Havilland, Mark Stevens, Leo Genn. Not for the squeamish. Adaptation of the best selling book about life in an overcrowded mental hospital. Olivia is wonderful in the lead. Slightly dated in the methods of treatment shown but an excellent film. (Dir: Anatole Litvak, 108 mins.)

Snatched (1973)**½ Howard Duff, Barbara Parkins. Fairly effective kidnapping film makes the grade with the help of a solid cast. A mastermind kidnaps the wives of three wealthy men and asks for a cool million for each. Made-for-TV. (Dir: Sutton Roley, 73 mins.)

Sniper, The (1952)*** Arthur Franz, Adolphe Menjou, Marie Windsor. Adult drama about a deranged sniper who baffles police on his trail. Exciting climax. Good performances, particularly by Arthur Franz. (Dir: Edward Dmytryk, 87 mins.)

Sniper's Ridge (1961)**½ Jack Ging, Stanley Clements. Captain orders a last raid before the Korea peace talks in an effort to grab glory for himself. Compact low-budget war drama is better than many bigger films of the same type. (Dir: John Bushelman, 61 mins.)

Snoop Sisters, The (1972)**½ Helen Hayes, Mildred Natwick. Thanks to the professional elan of its stars, Misses Hayes and Natwick, this comedy-murder mystery holds your interest despite some outrageous but amusing plot twists. The Snoop Sisters, who collaborate on writing mystery novels, get involved in solving the murder of a onetime movie star, played in a brief appearance by real-life onetime movie star Paulette Goddard. Art Carney also registers as the sisters' part-time bodyguard. This was the pilot for a TV series. (Dir: Leonard B. Stern, 99 mins.)

Snoopy, Come Home (1972)***½ Don't confuse this "Peanuts" theatrical release with the TV specials, even if they are similar. This was the second theatrical film based on Charles Schulz's wonderful collection of characters including Charlie Brown, Lucy, Linus, Schroeder and, of course, Snoopy, who is the star of this opus. It features a delightful musical score by the Sherman brothers (Robert B. and Richard M.), whose big credit is "Mary Poppins." Story is endearing, dealing with Snoopy's odyssey to find a place where there are no signs bearing the unwelcome greeting "No Dogs Allowed." We also liked the bird, "Woodstock." (Dir: Bill Melendez, 90 mins.)

Snorkel, The (British, 1958)*** Peter Van Eyck, Betta St. John, Mandy Miller. Clever murder mystery film with good acting by the principals about a "perfect crime" attempt that nearly succeeds. (Dir: Guy Green, 74 mins.)

Snow Job (1972)* Jean-Claude Killy, Daniele Gaubert, Vittorio De Sica. A couple of good ski scenes do not a picture make . . . Killy's acting, and that of most others, is as wooden as the Olympic ski champion's first skis. Killy dreams up a scheme to rob a local resort and make off with the loot on skis. Veteran De Sica hams it up in a supporting part. (Dir: George Englund, 90 mins.)

Snow Treasure (1968)*½ James Franciscus, Bente Nielsen. WW II adventure as underground resistance fighters try to smuggle gold out of German-occupied Norway. Some suspense scenes, but flimsy melodramatics mar any sustained effect. Franciscus is passable as a German officer who defects to the underground. (Dir: Irving Jacoby, 95 mins.)

Snow White and the Three Stooges (1961)**½ Carol Heiss, Three Stooges, Patricia Medina. The Snow White fairytale, with the heroine on ice skates and the team of Moe, Curley, and Larry substituting for the Seven Dwarfs. Not really as bad as it sounds—the small fry should love it, while grownups shouldn't have too bad a time. (Dir: Walter Lang, 107 mins.)

Snowbeast (1977)*½ Bo Svenson, Yvette Mimieux, Clint Walker. Scare film for the kiddies about a half-human who goes on a tear, frightening the wits out of vacationers at a ski resort. Bo Svenson and Yvette Mimieux are joined by big Clint Walker as the principals in this Grade-B thriller. (Dir: Herb Wallerstein, 106 mins.)

Snowbound (British, 1949)*** Robert Newton, Dennis Price. A movie director undertakes a dangerous mission to recover some gold bullion in the Italian Alps. Good cast, otherwise ordinary thriller.

Snowfire (1958)**½ Molly McGowan, Don Megowan, Claire Kelly. Family film about a little girl who befriends a wild stallion that is considered dangerous by ranchers who are hunting it down to destroy it. Kids and adults may be touched by the sentimental story.

Snows of Kilimanjaro, The (1953)*** Gregory Peck, Susan Hayward, Ava Gardner, Hildegarde Neff. Darryl F. Zanuck brings the late Ernest Hemingway's rambling novel to the screen with a powerhouse lineup of stars. The overall result, however, its a bit of a disappointment due to script limitations and uneven performances. There's a bit of melodramatic histrionics by Miss Gardner as she is being carried off a battlefield that is jarringly hammy. Neff does what she can with a skeleton of a part as a Contessa. (Dir: Henry King, 117 mins.)

So Big (1953)*** Jane Wyman, Sterling Hayden. Edna Ferber's sentimental novel, complete with every tearful scene and every sacrifice on the part of Miss Wyman's character. Nancy Olson registers strongly in a top supporting role and the two stars handle their roles expertly. A good family picture. (Dir: Robert Wise, 101 mins.)

So Dark the Night (1946)*** Steven Geray, Micheline Cheirel. Famous detective goes to the country for a rest, runs into a rash of murders. Unusual mystery, something different, and well done.

So Darling, So Deadly (1967)* Brad Harris, Barbara Frey, Jennie Kendall. A dull dubbed foreign film about two Americans hired to fight for a nuclear weapon.

So Ends Our Night (1941)**** Fredric March, Margaret Sullavan, Glenn Ford, Frances Dee, Erich Von Stroheim. Gripping drama of refugees from the Nazis traveling from country to country without passport. Excellent performances. A fine film. (Dir: John Cromwell, 117 mins.)

So Evil My Love (1948)**½ Ray Milland, Ann Todd. Well done, but strangely uninteresting drama of love, murder and blackmail in Victorian England. (Dir: Lewis Allen, 109 mins.)

So Long at the Fair (British, 1949) *** Jean Simmons, Dirk Bogarde. In Paris with her brother for the Exposition, a young girl is thrown in panic when he disappears, and everyone who has seen him denies his existence. Interesting melodrama keeps the attention. (Dirs: Terence Fisher, Anthony Darnborough, 90 mins.)

So Proudly We Hail (1943) **½ Claudette Colbert, Paulette Goddard. Picture dedicated to our brave army nurses on Bataan has some effective scenes, but is generally routine drama. In 1943, it was well received because of its timeliness. (Dir: Mark Sandrich, 126 mins.)

So This Is Love (1953) ** Kathryn Grayson, Merv Griffin. Contrived biography of opera singer Grace Moore, as artificial as these biographies usually are. Kathryn Grayson miscast as the diva. (Dir: Gordon Douglas, 101 mins.)

So This Is New York (1948) *** Henry Morgan, Rudy Vallee, Hugh Herbert. Small town family comes to the big city to find a man for sister, manages to turn the city on its ear. Extremely clever, funny comedy, with many original little touches, good performances. (Dir: Richard A. Fleischer, 79 mins.)

So This Is Paris (1955) *** Tony Curtis, Gloria De Haven, Gene Nelson. Entertaining musical comedy about three gobs on leave in Paris and their encounters with girls, orphans, Paris society, and the gendarmes. Many musical numbers with Curtis doing surprisingly well in the singing and dancing department. (Dir: Richard Quine, 96 mins.)

So Young, So Bad (1950) **½ Paul Henreid, Catherine McLeod. A doctor assigned to a girls' correctional school discovers inhuman conditions prevailing there, fights them. Fairly good melodrama. (Dir: Bernard Vorhaus, 91 mins.)

Socrates (Italian, 1970) ***½ Jean Sylvere, Anne Caprile, Richard Palacios. Another first-rate historical drama directed by Roberto Rossellini for Italian TV. Begins in Athens in 404 B.C. when the Spartan Lysander imposes the oligarchy of Thirty Tyrants, and Socrates refuses to carry out an order from Critias, one of his former students. Scenes from Socrates' trial; and his refusal to escape after being condemned to death. Concludes with Socrates drinking hemlock and dying among his friends. Enormously stimulating dialogue, thanks to the script by Rossellini and Marcella Mariani. Rossellini had wanted to film this story for 20 years and his dedication to the material and reverence for Socrates shine through. Some critics have suggested, properly I think, that there are similarities between Socrates and Rossellini, including "the same love of logic, the same independence and obstinacy; both have greatly influenced young people and both have awakened comparable religious and political hostility." English subtitles. (120 mins.)

Sodom and Gomorrah (1962) **½ Stewart Granger, Pier Angeli, Stanley Baker, Anouk Aimee. The story of Lot, who leads his people to Sodom, where a cruel queen reigns over a city of sin. Actually, it's all rather tame in structure, although it has the usual made-in-Italy trappings. Some fairly good performances make it a passable Biblical spectacle. (Dir: Robert Aldrich, 154 mins.)

Sol Madrid (1968) ** Narcotic agent (David McCallum) battles the Mafia in Mexico. Thoroughly routine. With Stella Stevens, Telly Savalas, Ricardo Montalban, Rip Torn, Pat Hingle. (Dir: Brian G. Hutton, 90 mins.)

Soldier Blue (1970) *** Candice Bergen, Peter Strauss, Donald Pleasence. Offbeat, violent, ultimately rewarding "western" about the U.S. Army's inhuman treatment of American Indians, based on the real Sand Creek Massacre of Cheyenne warriors and their families, including children. This may be one film where you'll be rooting for the U.S. Cavalry to be wiped out. Based on the novel "Arrow in the Sun" by Theodore V. Olsen, and adapted by John Gay. Bergen gives one of her best performances to date as the liberated young fiancée of an Army officer who sides with the Indians. (Dir: Ralph Nelson, 112 mins.)

Soldier in the Rain (1963) *** Steve McQueen, Jackie Gleason, Tuesday Weld. Uneven comedy-drama about the bond of friendship between a worldly-wise Master Sergeant and his naive worshiper. Always seems on the verge of something great without actually accomplishing it. However, there's a good share of laughs, some heart-tugs, fine performance by Gleason. (Dir: Ralph Nelson, 88 mins.)

Soldier of Fortune (1955)**½ Clark Gable, Susan Hayward. Just another routine adventure story set in Hong Kong. This production is handsomely mounted and has name stars but it can't disguise the commonplace plot. (Dir: Edward Dmytryk, 96 mins.)

Soldiers of Pancho Villa, The (Mexican, 1959)** Dolores Del Rio, Maria Felix, Emilio Fernandez. Elaborate, frequently colorful, often banal drama of Villa's fight to free Mexico from tyranny. Good cast, better than the material provided. Dubbed in English.

Soldiers Three (1951)** Stewart Granger, David Niven, Robert Newton, Walter Pidgeon. With the boys in India, 1890—a trio of army privates get into one mess after another. Try for a "Gunga Din" type of adventure misfires—some action, some amusement, but not enough. (Dir: Tay Garnett, 87 mins.)

Sole Survivor (1970)**½ Vince Edwards, Richard Basehart, William Shatner. A glossy production, excellent location photography of the Mojave Desert and a good male cast enhance this made-for-TV feature about a WW-II bomber discovered in the Libyan desert 17 years after it has crashed with the ghosts of the crew hovering over it. An investigation by the Inspector General's office reveals that the plane's navigator and only survivor, now an important General, might have bailed out and falsified his account of the plane's fate. The most interesting scenes find the ghosts watching while investigator Vince Edwards grills General Richard Basehart. (Dir: Paul Stanley, 100 mins.)

Solid Gold Cadillac, The (1956)***½ Judy Holliday, Paul Douglas. Very funny comedy about big business and the turmoil caused by one small stockholder, namely Judy Holliday The late Paul Douglas is a perfect match for Miss Holliday's comic genius. (Dir: Richard Quine, 99 mins.)

Solo for Sparrow (British, 1962)** Anthony Newlands, Nadja Regin. Policeman goes after robbers who have committed murder while pulling a heist. Okay crime drama based on an Edgar Wallace story.

Solomon and Sheba (1952)**½ Gina

Lollobrigida, Yul Brynner. Good escapist movie fare; lavish spectacle with the emphasis on pictorial splendor and not the script. Miss Lollobrigida is as appealing as ever as the voluptuous Queen of Sheba and Yul Brynner fits comfortably in the role of King Solomon. A large supporting cast includes George Sanders, Marisa Pavan and David Farrar. (Dir: King Vidor, 139 mins.)

Sombra, the Spider Woman (1947-66)*½ Bruce Edwards, Virginia Lindley, Carol Foreman. Feature version of serial "The Black Widow." Daughter of an Asian ruler helps pop form a plan for world conquest, plots to obtain atomic secrets. Pretty hokey far-out stuff. (Dirs: Spencer Bennet, Fred Brannon, 100 mins.)

Sombrero (1953)** Ricardo Montalban, Pier Angeli, Vittorio Gassman, Yvonne DeCarlo. Story of three bachelors in a small Mexican village and their adventures in love. Attempt at something different fails largely because the plots are inclined to wander all over. Some good moments, mostly confusion. (Dir: Norman Foster, 103 mins.)

Some Came Running (1958)**½ Frank Sinatra, Shirley MacLaine, Dean Martin, Martha Hyer, Arthur Kennedy. An all-star cast brings James Jones' novel about life in a small midwestern town after World War II to the screen. Most of the plot falls into the soap opera groove but the performances, especially Shirley MacLaine as a good time gal, should keep your interest. (Dir: Vincente Minnelli, 127 mins.)

Some Kind of a Nut (1969)* Dick Van Dyke, Angie Dickinson, Zohra Lampert. An inventive talented man named Garson Kanin has written and directed a hackneyed, unfunny, tale about a Manhattan bank teller played by Dick Van Dyke. You're a nut if you bother with this lemon! (89 mins.)

Some Like It Hot (1959)**** Tony Curtis, Marilyn Monroe, Jack Lemmon, Joe E. Brown, George Raft, Pat O'Brien. An incredibly funny imaginative farce that may well be the most hilarious American movie made in this generation. If you're mad at yourself, your spouse or the world in general, tune in for some free therapy provided by magician Billy Wilder putting a flawless cast through these improbable, riotous capers. Curtis and Lemmon play two musicians on the lam from Chicago mobsters after witnessing a gangland rubout. Marilyn is altogether edible and her scenes with Lemmon in a train's upper berth and one with Curtis aboard a yacht rank among the most excruciatingly funny sequences ever filmed. As if this weren't enough, Joe E. Brown delivers the last line as a classic topper. (120 mins.)

Some People (1964)* Kenneth More, David Hemmings, Annika Wills. Young English punks looking for kicks, reformed by church choirmaster. "Some People" is some lousy movie. (80 mins.)

Somebody Loves Me (1952)** Betty Hutton, Ralph Meeker. Biography of song-spinners Blossom Seeley and Benny Fields, their ups and downs in show biz. Thoroughly routine musical primarily for the nostalgically-minded.

Somebody Up There Likes Me (1956) ***½ Paul Newman, Pier Angeli, Everett Sloane. The true story of Rocky Graziano's rise from a small time hood to the middle-weight champ of the world. Newman is superb as "Rocky" and he gets top support from Miss Angeli as his wife, Joseph Buloff as a candy store philosopher, Eileen Heckart as his mother and Everett Sloane as a fight promoter. (Dir: Robert Wise, 113 mins.)

Someone Behind the Door (French, 1971)* Charles Bronson, Anthony Perkins, Jill Ireland. Unbalanced brain surgeon (Perkins) uses an amnesia victim (Bronson) to kill his wife's lover. This involves a personality transplant which Bronson is too dumb to reject. You need brain surgery if you like this trash. (Dir: Nicholas Gessner, 97 mins.)

Someone I Touched (1975)**½ Cloris Leachman, James Olson, Glynnis O'Connor, Kenneth Mars. Venereal disease, a provocative subject for TV, is explored in a fairly absorbing TV feature. Miss Leachman stars as an over-30 wife who finally becomes pregnant, only to discover that both her husband and a pretty young girl he has had a brief fling with have venereal disease. Handled rather well, except for occasional lapses into melodrama. Made-for-TV. (Dir: Sam O'Steen, 72 mins.)

Someone to Remember (1943)*** Mabel Paige, John Craven. Old woman whose son has disappeared years ago becomes a foster mother to some college boys. Touching, well acted drama, recommended.

Something Big (1971)* Dean Martin, Brian Keith, Carol White, Honor Blackman. I tried to resist making a pun on the title but . . . "Something Big" is something tiny in the writing and directing departments. Cartoon characters romp around a western town circa 1870 as Martin plays a naughty criminal. Dean delivers his lines as if he never read the script, which in this case would not have been a bad idea. (Dir: Andrew V. McLaglen, 108 mins.)

Something Evil (1972)**½ Sandy Dennis, Darren McGavin. Talented director Steven Spielberg turns to the devil here, and has a ball with scary visual effects. The devil occupies a Pennsylvania farmhouse, eager to assert his powers on new tenants. Spielberg's tricks with the camera make this entry better than the usual made-for-TV ghost-story film. (73 mins.)

Something for a Lonely Man (1968) *** Dan Blocker, Susan Clark. A very pleasant film. Dan Blocker stars as a man who convinces some settlers to locate in a spot he thinks the railroad will go through. When the train route turns out to be some twenty miles away, he becomes a subject of ridicule. Seeking redemption and satisfaction, he attempts to salvage a steam engine to prove that "a man is bigger than a town." Not fast moving or superslick, but charming, and well acted by Dan, Susan Clark as the girl who believes in him, and a good supporting cast. (Dir: Don Taylor, 99 mins.)

Something for Everyone (1970)*** Angela Lansbury, Michael York, Anthony Corlan. Bizarre black comedy with an occasional dash of sophistication and wit. It's Noel Coward cross-pollinated with Edgar Allan Poe, and sometimes it works. Michael York is a sexy opportunist in lederhosen who descends upon the castle of the Countess Von Ornstein, which has seen better days, and proceeds to infiltrate everyone's bedroom. York becomes a footman, but soon works his way up the household ladder until he's running things. A surprise ending is delicious, and the cast, especially York and Angela Lansbury as the flamboyant and outspoken countess, is excellent. Screenplay by Hugh Wheeler based on the novel "The Cook," by Harry Kressing. (Dir: Harold Prince, 110 mins.)

Something for Joey (1977)*** Geraldine Page, Marc Singer, Jeff Lynas. Heartwarming true-life story about Heisman Trophy-winner John Cappelletti and his special relationship with his young brother, Joey, a victim of leukemia. The script by Jerry McNeely can't avoid overt sentiment, but it's all so honestly portrayed that you will forgive the occasional lapses into pathos. Marc Singer as the college football star Cappelletti gives a sensitive performance, and he's matched by young Jeff Lynas as Joey. The scenes between the two brothers have an undercurrent of emotion which is kept in check until the final Heisman Trophy banquet scene, during which John breaks down during his acceptance speech and pays tribute to his courageous brother Joey. Be prepared to shed tears with a family that knows the meaning of love. Made-for-TV. (Dir: Lou Antonio, 108 mins.)

Something for the Birds (1952)**½ Victor Mature, Patricia Neal, Edmund Gwenn. Genial comedy about Washington society. Edmund Gwenn plays an aging engraver in a Washington printing plant who crashes many Washington social functions. The love story revolves around a lobbyist (Victor Mature) and a representative of an ornithology society (Patricia Neal). (Dir: Roger Wise, 81 mins.)

Something for the Boys (1944)*** Vivian Blaine, Phil Silvers, Carmen Miranda. Tuneful, loud musical loaded with feminine pulchritude and set in a home for war wives. Phil is at his best in this one and you'll hear a young newcomer named Perry Como sing "I Wish I Didn't Have To Say Good Night." (Dir: Lewis Seiler, 85 mins.)

Something in the Wind (1947)**½ Deanna Durbin, Donald O'Connor, John Dall. Girl disc jockey is mistaken for the amour of a late multimillionaire. Slight comedy has Durbin's fine singing to help it. (Dir: Irving Pichel, 89 mins.)

Something Money Can't Buy (British, 1952)**½ Patricia Roc, Anthony Steel. Discontented young man quits his job, and has his wife nearly beat him to breadwinning. Mildly amusing comedy.

Something of Value (1957)*** Rock Hudson, Dana Wynter, Sidney Poitier. Robert Ruark's overwritten but compelling novel about the Mau Mau uprising is transferred to the screen with many of the book's exciting highlights intact. The major conflict of the story centers around Rock Hudson and Sidney Poitier, childhood friends who find themselves on opposite sides of the law. Poitier gives an intense performance as the leader of a Mau Mau band and Hudson shows up to good advantage, too. (Dir: Richard Brooks, 113 mins.)

Something to Live For (1952)*** Ray Milland, Joan Fontaine, Teresa Wright. Deft direction by George Stevens gives added luster to this dramatic story of an alcoholic actress saved by an A.A. member who falls in love with her although he's married. Ladies should enjoy; men will find it interesting too. (89 mins.)

Something to Shout About (1943)**½ Don Ameche, Janet Blair, William Gaxton. Trite backstage plot receives a little support from some Cole Porter music. Best tune: "You'd Be So Nice to Come Home To." (Dir: Gregory Ratoff, 93 mins.)

Something Wild (1961)**½ Carroll Baker, Ralph Meeker. A strange film that weaves a hypnotic spell at the start but soon sinks into predictable melodrama. Carroll Baker plays an emotionally disturbed young girl who is saved from doing away with herself by a man who turns the incident to his advantage. Ralph Meeker's performance as the guy who brings the frightened girl to his apartment and keeps her prisoner is the best thing about the film. (Dir: Jack Garfein, 112 mins.)

Sometimes a Great Notion—See: Never Give An Inch

Somewhere I'll Find You (1942)**½ Clark Gable, Lana Turner. Clark and Lana burn up the screen in a mediocre adventure story which finds them as correspondents running all over the war-torn world. (Dir: Wesley Ruggles, 108 mins.)

Son of a Gunfighter (U.S.-Spain, 1965)*½ Russ Tamblyn, James Phil-brook, Fernando Rey, Maia Granada. Sandwiched among the 1877 shoot-outs, good-guy Tamblyn locates his father and his female. Flimsy plot, but has color, action! (Dir: Paul Landres, 92 mins.)

Son of Ali Baba (1952)** Tony Curtis, Piper Laurie. Typical Arabian nights adventure with Curtis cast as the son of Ali Baba and Princess Azura. Narrow escapes, colorful sets, and romance abounds in this Bagdad opus. (Dir: Kurt Neumann, 75 mins.)

Son of Captain Blood, The (U.S.-Italy-Spain, 1962)** Sean Flynn, Alessandra Panaro, Ann Todd. Back in 1935, Errol Flynn made his film debut as a young swashbuckler in "Captain Blood," a rousing tale that earned him instant fame. Son Sean here makes his screen debut, fittingly as the "Son of Blood," embroiled with his Pa's pirate friends in further sea adventures. Unfortunately, Flynn Jr., though as handsome as Dad, has none of his father's acting finesse and assertive charm. Movie itself is given slick production, but stultifying plot and dialogue. (Dir: Tullio Demichelli, 88 mins.)

Son of Dear Caroline, The (French, 1955)** Brigitte Bardot, Jean-Claude Pascal, Magali Noel. Adventures of an orphan boy fighting in Spain who learns he is of French parentage. Elaborate costume drama, novelettish in content. Bardot has a minor role. Dubbed in English.

Son of Dr. Jekyll (1951)** Louis Hayward, Jody Lawrance. Hollywood never lets a commercial gimmick die —so here's still another in the rash of "son of" films. Not so "horrific" as its predecessor, nor as well done. (Dir: Seymour Friedman, 77 mins.)

Son of Dracula (1943)**½ Lon Chaney, Louise Albritton. A strange fellow known as Count Alucard (that's Dracula spelled backwards) comes to stay at an American manse. Unbelievable horror yarn, but fun anyway. (Dir: Robert Siodmak, 78 mins.)

Son of Frankenstein (1939)*** Boris Karloff, Basil Rathbone, Bela Lugosi. The new Baron Von Frankenstein learns that his father's monster is running loose, and tries to catch up with the fiend. Lavishly produced, plenty of spine-tingling thrills. (Dir: Rowland V. Lee, 110 mins.)

Son of Fury (1942)*** Tyrone Power, George Sanders, Gene Tierney. No message in this 18th century drama but an abundance of action and romance. Ty, who's wronged by Uncle George, leaves England, goes to a Pacific island, finds Gene and a bucket of pearls. He goes back for his revenge. (Dir: John Cromwell, 98 mins.)

Son of Hercules in the Land of Darkness (Italian, 1963)* Dan Vadis, Carol Brown. Muscleman rescues captives of a cruel queen in a subterranean city. Ridiculous English-dubbed spectacle fantasy.

Son of Hercules in the Land of Fire (Italian, 1962)* Ed Fury, Claudia Mori. Muscleman plows his way through all obstacles in rescuing the king's daughter. Silly spectacle dubbed in English.

Son of Kong (1933)*** Robert Armstrong, Helen Mack. Adventurer returns to the island where the mighty King Kong used to dwell, finds another huge gorilla there. Fantastic adventure, a sequel to its famous predecessor, is good fun. (Dir: Ernest B. Schoedsack, 70 mins.)

Son of Lassie (1944)** Peter Lawford, June Lockhart, Donald Crisp. Unlike its magnificent predecessor ("Lassie Come Home") this is little more than a juvenile adventure which will, of course, also appeal to dog lovers. Collie and her master shot down over Germany during the war and so on to the fadeout. (Dir: S. Sylvan Simon, 102 mins.)

Son of Monte Cristo (1940)*** The offspring of Dumas' stalwart hero is portrayed by Louis Hayward, as he foils the dastardly plans of dictator George Sanders and wins the hand of Joan Bennett, whilst dueling all over the place. Entertaining swashbuckling melodrama. (Dir: Rowland V. Lee, 102 mins.)

Son of Paleface (1952)*** Bob Hope, Jane Russell, Roy Rogers. Enjoyable western story with Hope playing a dude who shows up in the wild and woolly west to collect his inheritance, left by his father who was a famous Indian fighter. Get the picture? Jane Russell, as a gun-toting gal, is perfect opposite Hope and even Roy Rogers comes in for his share of the laughs. (Dir: Frank Tashlin, 95 mins.)

Son of Robin Hood, The (British, 1959)*½ David Hedison, June Laverick, David Farrar. When a nasty duke stirs up trouble anew, the son of Robin Hood is sent for—only the son turns out to be a girl. Juvenile costume adventure. (Dir: George Sherman, 81 mins.)

Son of Sinbad (1954)*½ Dale Robertson, Sally Forrest, Vincent Price. Sinbad is captured by a wicked caliph, must perform arduous tasks to win his freedom. Dull fantasy had censor trouble when it was first released but looks tame today—and trite. (Dir: Ted Tetzlaff, 88 mins.)

Son of the Red Corsair (Italian, 1961) *½ Lex Barker, Sylvia Lopez. Lex Barker, who once played Tarzan in films, trades his loin cloth in for another costume but not his film courage as he tackles bad guy after bad guy. Foreign-made, English-dubbed.

Song and the Silence, The (1969)*** Harry Rubin, Anita Koutsouveli, Nana Austin. An unusual, surprisingly effective low-budget film about a group of Hasidic Jews in Poland in 1939, filmed by amateur actors in the Catskill Mountains of New York. Produced, directed, written, and photographed by Nathan Cohen, film does capture some of the love, humor and optimism of this sect little understood by the general public. An off-beat, often rewarding American entry.

Song Is Born, A (1948)** Danny Kaye, Virginia Mayo, Steve Cochran. Remake of Gary Cooper comedy titled "Ball of Fire" with music added for good measure. Not up to the original although Kaye tries very hard to rise above the material. (Dir: Howard Hawks, 113 mins.)

Song of Bernadette, The (1944)**** Jennifer Jones, Lee J. Cobb, Vincent Price. Story of a pious peasant girl who was almost destroyed because she saw a vision is a beautiful moving film. It's a bit too long but the message of faith is superbly told and Miss Jones is fine. (Dir: Henry King, 156 mins.)

Song of Love (1947)**½ Katharine Hepburn, Paul Henreid, Robert Walker. Story of Clara Schumann, who helped her composer-husband through his dark periods. Fine music, adequate story, weak performances. (Dir: Clarence Brown, 119 mins.)

Song of Scheherazade (1947)** Yvonne DeCarlo, Jean-Pierre Aumont, Brian Donlevy. Far fetched story of Rimsky-Korsakoff and his love for a dance girl named Cara. Elaborate settings and some of Rimsky-Korsakoff's music save the picture from being a stupefying bore. (Dir: Walter Reisch, 106 mins.)

Song of Sister Maria, The (Spanish, 1953)*** Dominique Blanchar, Maria Dulce. Sincere, well-made drama of a young singer who gives up her career to become a nun. Miss Blanchar is excellent in the role. Dubbed in English.

Song of the Islands (1942)*½ Victor Mature, Betty Grable. If you'd like to see Mature put his muscles in an assortment of sweaters and bathing suits or Betty in a grass skirt, you may watch this film. If you want entertainment, keep away. (Dir: Walter Lang, 75 mins.)

Song of the Open Road (1944)**½ Jane Powell, Edgar Bergen. Juvenile movie star runs away and joins youngsters who are saving farm crops. Fairly pleasant musical, with some comedy from Bergen and McCarthy, W. C. Fields. (Dir: S. Sylvan Simon, 93 mins.)

Son of the Sheik (1926)**½ Rudolph Valentino, Vilma Banky. A rousing, romantic melodrama, full of sandy fights, chases, and escapes. This was the legendary Italian's last film, and in it he played the dual role of father and son. In this sequel to Valentino's 1921 colossal hit, "The Sheik," Valentino remains a remarkable screen presence, and it's easy to understand why the ladies of the day made him the screen's earliest sex symbol. (Dir: George Fitzmaurice, 70 mins.)

Song of the Thin Man (1947)**½ William Powell, Myrna Loy. Nick and Nora move in jazz circles as they glibly track down a murderer in this one. Good dialogue but the series has become commonplace and obvious. (Dir: Edward Buzzell, 86 mins.)

Song to Remember, A (1945)**½ Paul Muni, Cornel Wilde, Merle Oberon. Story of composer Chopin, and of his tragic love for George Sand. Good piano selections played by Jose Iturbi help this lacklustre biographical drama. (Dir: Charles Vidor, 113 mins.)

Song Without End (1960)**½ Dirk

Bogarde, Capucine. If you can ignore the melodramatic aspects of this Hollywood version of Franz Liszt's life, you might be able to enjoy the musical selections. Dirk Bogarde makes a dashing Liszt but he's bogged down by the heavy handed script and the inept delivery of his co-star, Capucine. (Dirs: Charles Vidor, George Cukor, 141 mins.)

Sons and Lovers (U.S.-British, 1960) **** Trevor Howard, Dean Stockwell, Mary Ure, Wendy Hiller. Absorbing, successful dramatization of D. H. Lawrence's autobiographical novel, largely adapted by Gavin Lambert and T. E. B. Clarke. Trevor Howard is customarily splendid as the gruff coal-mining father of the sensitive, young, would-be artist (Dean Stockwell). Wendy Hiller, as the dominant mother, turns in a beautifully controlled and very moving performance, and Dean Stockwell keeps up with this high-powered cast. Extremely well directed by Jack Cardiff, and there's some outstanding cinematography from Freddie Francis. The stunning acting of Howard and Hiller make this a dramatic treat. (Dir: Jack Cardiff, 103 mins.)

Sons of Katie Elder, The (1965)**½ John Wayne, Dean Martin. John Wayne and Dean Martin may sound like strange co-stars but they work well together and make this otherwise standard western yarn entertaining. Wayne, Martin, Earl Holliman and Michael Anderson, Jr. are the sons of the title and they all show up at their Ma's funeral determined to make the name of Elder respectable once again. Some of the town bullies have other plans and this sets the stage for brawls-aplenty with Wayne and company right in the middle. (Dir: Henry Hathaway, 112 mins.)

Sophie's Place (U.S.-Great Britain, 1969)** Telly Savalas, Edith Evans, Warren Oates. A good cast is the main attraction of this crime spoof about a proposed heist at a stately British estate. Hoods Savalas and Oates work in cahoots with a British gang to rob Dame Evans' home. Written and directed by Jim O'Connolly. (106 mins.)

Sorceress, The (French, 1956)*** Marina Vlady, Maurice Ronet. The strange offbeat story of a beautiful girl who is believed to be a witch and her struggle to find happiness through love. Good turns by all concerned. (Dir: Andre Michel, 97 mins.)

Sorority Girl (1958)*½ Susan Cabot, Dick Miller. Young hussy makes sorority life hell for the innocent, and doesn't do much for the viewing audience either. Sordid nonsense. (Dir: Roger Corman, 60 mins.)

Sorrow and the Pity, The (French-Swiss-West German, 1970)**** Pierre Mendes-France, Louis Grave, Albert Speer, George Bidault, Jacques Duclos, Sir Anthony Eden. One of the most brilliant and shattering films ever made, a lengthy documentary directed by Marcel Ophuls about anti-Semitism and the Nazi occupation of France during the Vichy regime in World War II. French TV did not run the film for some time because, in the words of one spokesman, "the populace was not yet mature enough to accept the idea that during World War II most Frenchmen did not fight in the Resistance." They clearly didn't fight hard either against the virus of racial and religious bigotry, as filmmaker Ophuls makes devastatingly clear by interviewing dozens of people—some famous and powerful, some not—who lived through those dark days of Hitlerism. Focuses on the town of Clermont-Ferrand to serve as a microcosm for all of France. Richly deserved the many awards it received. Black and white. English subtitles and dubbing. (265 mins.)

Sorrowful Jones (1949)**½ Bob Hope, Lucille Ball. Bookie Bob Hope gets involved with racketeers and fixed races in this Damon Runyon story. Lucille Ball is more reserved than she is in her "Lucy" characterization. Surprisingly, this film is a remake on an old Shirley Temple movie, "Little Miss Marker." Hope and Lucy still deliver a goodly amount of laughs. (Dir: Sidney Lanfield, 88 mins.)

Sorry, Wrong Number (1948)*** Barbara Stanwyck, Burt Lancaster. Bedridden woman overhears a plot to murder her, frantically tries to summon help. Classic suspense radio show loses something on film, the effort to stretch things to the limit going too far. However, there's still a sufficient amount of tension to satisfy thriller addicts. (Dir: Anatole Litvak, 89 mins.)

Soul Soldier (1970)*½ Rafer Johnson, Cesar Romero, Janee Michelle. Worthless western tale concerning loyal but dangerous black soldier guarding the Mexican border in post-Civil War America. Ex-Olympics star Johnson has a certain amount of dignity, but the rest of the acting is rotten. Originally opened under the title "The Red, White and Black." (Dir: John Cardos, 84 mins.)

Soul to Soul (1971)*** This captivating musical documentary, filmed in cinema verité style, effectively captures the sights and sounds of a 1971 all-night concert by visiting black American soul and gospel artists, along with African musicians as part of the 14th annual Independence Celebration of Ghana, the first Black African nation. Director Denis Sanders manages to catch the excitement of the event on film. Stirring performances of such soul stars as Wilson Pickett, Ike and Tina Turner, Roberta Flack and Les McCann. Dir: Denis Sanders, 96 mins.)

Souls for Sale—See: **Confessions of an Opium Eater**

Sound and the Fury, The (1959)*** Yul Brynner, Joanne Woodward, Stuart Whitman, Ethel Waters. William Faulkner's novel of the decadent South, unevenly filmed—story of a young girl trying to find a life of her own away from the tyrannical rule of her uncle. Some fine moments, too often confused, static. Performances generally excellent. (Dir: Martin Ritt, 115 mins.)

Sound of Anger, The (1968)** Burl Ives, James Farentino, Guy Stockwell, Dorothy Provine. A made-for-TV feature which also served as a pilot for a series about two lawyer brothers and their partner. Courtroom case involves a pair of young lovers accused of doing away with the girl's wealthy papa. There's a fairly good surprise climax, but it's all familiar trial fare. (Dir: Michael Ritchie, 100 mins.)

Sound of Music, The (1965)** Julie Andrews, Christopher Plummer, Eleanor Parker. Don't send a lynching party at this late date to my publisher's office, but there were people in the movie business who referred to this bit of filmed treacle as "The Sound of Mucus." I agree! But most of the rest of the world did and does

not agree, and made this one of the most popular films in the history of cinema. Julie plays Maria Trapp escaping from Austria and the Nazis with her young children into the haven of Switzerland. Salzburg is a lovely town, and the Swiss Alps serve as a background for the lilting Rodgers and Hammerstein songs. (Dir: Robert Wise, 174 mins.)

Sound Off (1952)**½ Mickey Rooney, Anne James. A mild and often amusing comedy with music about a recruit who falls in love with a WAC officer. (Dir: Richard Quine, 83 mins.)

Sounder (1972)**** Cicely Tyson, Paul Winfield, Kevin Hooks, Carmen Mathews. One of the most moving and compassionate films in many years. About a Negro family of sharecroppers (it was Negroes then, not blacks) in rural Louisiana during the depression of the early '30's. (For impoverished blacks it was always a depression.) Based on the novel by William H. Armstrong, it has been expertly adapted for the screen by Lonne Elder III, and sensitively and lovingly directed by Martin Ritt. The father is imprisoned for stealing a ham, and injured at the prison work farm before he returns home. Miss Tyson is absolutely marvelous, a combination of warmth, strength, and tenderness as she carries her family through various crises. She was nominated for an Academy Award as was Winfield and the film itself. The entire cast is faultless. Another winner, for young and old alike, from producer Robert Radnitz. (105 mins.)

South of St. Louis (1949)**½ Joel McCrea, Alexis Smith, Zachary Scott, Dorothy Malone. Three ranch partners face post Civil War troubles, become involved in gun running. Adequately presented western. (Dir: Ray Enright, 88 mins.)

South of Tana River (Danish, 1964)** Paul Reichhardt, Axel Stroyby, Charlotte Ernst. Story of a girl, her father, and a game warden in the African wilderness. Interesting scenes of wild life, hokey story. Dubbed in English.

South Pacific (1958)***½ Mitzi Gaynor, Rossano Brazzi, France Nuyen, Ray Walston. Rodgers and Hammerstein's celebrated 1949 Broadway musical about the love story between a U.S. Navy nurse and a suave

French planter in the South Pacific during WW II is given a big, lavish production. Mitzi Gaynor, as the outspoken Nellie Forbush, is excellent in the leading role but Rossano Brazzi doesn't register quite as forcefully as he should. The supporting cast is wonderful and there are all those familiar and enduring songs—"Some Enchanted Evening," "Younger Than Springtime," "There Is Nothing Like a Dame," "Bali Ha'i." Josh Logan, who ruined numerous other films, did a splendid job with this one. (171 mins.)

South Sea Sinner (1950)** Shelley Winters, Macdonald Carey, Frank Lovejoy. This is so bad that, in a macabre way it's fun to sit through. Shelley Winters, complete with feather boa and bleached blonde hair, plays a small time "Sadie Thompson" on an island inhabited by various shady characters. Liberace is seen as "Maestro" the piano playing philosopher who accompanies Miss Winters in her nightclub scenes. (Dir: H. Bruce Humberstone, 88 mins.)

South Sea Woman (1953)*** Burt Lancaster, Virginia Mayo, Chuck Connors. Rollicking, free for all comedy with Lancaster and Connors playing a pair of brawling marines who end up fighting a large part of the Pacific War single-handed. Virgina Mayo comes between the two buddies and keeps things popping. (Dir: Arthur Lubin, 99 mins.)

South Seas Adventure (1958)**½ Diane Beardmore, Marlene Lizzio. Fifth feature film done in the Cinerama process loses most of its interest on the small screen. Basically a travelogue of the South Seas with an imposed plot about a budding romance. Narration is mundane. Real interest is in the foreign locations. (Dir: Francis Lyon, 120 mins.)

Southern Star, The (1969)**½ George Segal, Ursula Andress, Orson Welles. A mixed bag of tricks but an entertaining adventure based on a Jules Verne story about the ups and downs of jewel thieves in the wilds of Africa, circa 1900. Segal makes a capable hero-heel and Miss Andress adds visual interest as the lady in the proceedings. Welles has a brief part, but an African actor named Johnny Sekka and the scenery of Senegal are the most interesting ingredients. (Dir: Sidney Hayers, 105 mins.)

Southern Yankee, A (1948)*** Red Skelton, Arlene Dahl, Brian Donlevy. Red's fighting the Civil War in this one and his fans will eat it up. He crawls between the lines carrying a two-sided flag for protection in a really hysterical scene. (Dir: Edward Sedgwick, 90 mins.)

Southerner, The (1945)***½ Zachary Scott, Betty Field, J. Carrol Naish. A tenant farmer struggles to support his family, in spite of opposition from both man and nature. Directed by Jean Renoir, this is a fine study in movie making, with everything just right down to the smallest detail. (Dir: Jean Renoir, 91 mins.)

Southside 1-1000 (1950)**½ Don DeFore, Andrea King. A secret service agent tracks down a counterfeiting ring and its mysterious leader. Average crime melodrama. (Dir: Boris Ingster, 73 mins.)

Southwest Passage (1954)**½ John Ireland, Joanne Dru, Rod Cameron. Bank robber joins a caravan testing the value of camels in the desert. Fast moving western with some new plot angles. (Dir: Ray Nazarro, 82 mins.)

Soylent Green (1973)* Charlton Heston, Joseph Cotten, Edward G. Robinson. Insipid drama about New York in the year 2022, teeming with people (over 40 million) ; and with the erosion of everything. Enter granite-faced Heston as a detective investigating the murder of executive Cotten, and the pace almost comes to a halt. One historical note: Edward G. Robinson gives his last screen performance as a philosopher who remembers the good old days. Feminists be warned that women in the film are referred to as "furniture." (Dir: Richard Fleischer, 97 mins.)

Space Children, The (1958)* Adam Williams, Peggy Webber. Unconvincing, laughable science fiction concerning a giant gelatin monster who has come to Earth to disrupt a space launch. The gelatin is the sturdiest item in this clinker. (Dir: Jack Arnold, 69 mins.)

Spanish Affair (1957)**½ Richard Kiley, Carmen Sevilla. Practically nonexistent plot about an American architect falling for a secretary in Spain used as an excuse to show off some breathtaking scenery, places of historical interest in Spain. Lightweight but pleasant, especially for viewers planning a trip to Spain. (Dir: Don Siegel, 95 mins.)

Spanish Gardener (British, 1956)******* Dirk Bogarde, Jon Whiteley. Diplomat's boy makes friends with a gardener, who changes his outlook and way of living. Well acted, interesting drama. (Dir: Philip Leacock, 95 mins.)

Spanish Main, The (1945)****½** Maureen O'Hara, Paul Henreid, Walter Slezak. Dashing adventurer rescues the girl he loves from the clutches of a villainous nobleman. Colorful pirate melodrama has plenty of action. (Dir: Frank Borzage, 100 mins.)

Spare the Rod (British, 1961)****½** Max Bygraves, Donald Pleasence, Geoffrey Keen. New young teacher faces obstacles in trying to break through to a group of tough kids. English version of "Blackboard Jungle" type of story has some good supporting performances and a familiar plot. (Dir: Leslie Norman, 93 mins.)

Spartacus (1960)******** Kirk Douglas, Jean Simmons, Laurence Olivier, Tony Curtis, Charles Laughton. This star-studded, lavishly mounted spectacle about the slave revolt against the Romans approximately seventy-five years before Christ is a top-notch film for admirers of big spectacles. Director Stanley Kubrick deserves credit for his deft handling of the mammoth story without losing sight of the personal drama involved. Another plus is Dalton Trumbo's literate script which avoids the verbal banalities of comparable film epics. Kirk Douglas cuts a convincing figure as Spartacus, the Thracian slave whose thirst for freedom makes him a natural choice to lead the oppressed out of bondage. The film has some exciting and graphic scenes set in a gladiator school and a bloody encounter in the arena. Peter Ustinov and Laurence Olivier are both superb in major roles. This film suffers when seen on a small TV screen, but it's still wonderful entertainment and a thrilling ancient history lesson. (196 mins.)

Spartacus and the Ten Gladiators (Italian, 1964)***** Dan Vadis. Ten gladiators are sent to capture Spartacus but join him instead. Boring English-dubbed spectacle.

Spawn of the North (1938)******* Henry Fonda, Dorothy Lamour. Good, rousing adventure tale about the days when Russian pirates tried to take over our salmon industry. Well played and loaded with action. (Dir: Henry Hathaway, 130 mins.)

Speaking of Murder (French, 1957) ****** Jean Gabin, Annie Girardot. Gabin manages to rise above the weak script in this complex crime drama. Annie Girardot doesn't get a chance to show what she can do. (Dir: Gilles Grangier, 80 mins.)

Specialists, The (1975)***** Robert York, Jack Hogan, Maureen Reagan. Epidemiologists (workers investigating health problems which could lead to epidemics) deal with an unknown rash, venereal disease, typhoid, and accidents in a soap factory. Cast includes Maureen Reagan, daughter of actress Jane Wyman and former California governor Ronald Reagan. No specialists in filmmaking at work on this bummer. Made-for-TV. (Dir: Richard Quine, 72 mins.)

Specter of the Rose (1946)******* Judith Anderson, Ivan Kirov. Strange tale of a young ballet dancer who is slowly losing his mind, and of the girl who loves him. Written and directed by Ben Hecht, this is a wordy, theatrical, but often fascinating, offbeat drama. (Dir: Ben Hecht, 90 mins.)

Spectre (1977)****** Robert Culp, Gig Young. A slick film by "Star Trek"'s Gene Roddenberry, produced in England with stars Robert Culp and Gig Young, is regretfully mild fare. Roddenberry visualizes a modern Sherlock Holmes (Culp) and his medical associate (Young) confronted by murders at every turn as they delve into power plays by an English financier. Story, dealing with the supernatural, lacks polish. Made-for-TV. (Dir: Clive Donner, 106 mins.)

Spectre of Freedom, The—See: **Phantom of Liberty, The**

Speedway (1968)***½** Elvis Presley, Nancy Sinatra. Stock car racer (Elvis Presley) comes up against an Internal Revenue agent (Nancy Sinatra), and the results are taxing. If you like Elvis, okay. Otherwise . . . With Bill Bixby, Gale Gordon. (Dir: Norman Taurog, 94 mins.)

Spell, The (1977)****** Lee Grant, James Olson, Susan Myers. Shades of

"Carrie" ! Here's a TV movie which borrows liberally from the hit film "Carrie," and deals with an unhappy high-school girl, the brunt of jokes by her classmates, who starts willing bad things to happen to her enemies. In asking audiences to accept the effects of her concentration, the show inevitably runs into difficulties. Susan Myers, with her innocent face, is a good choice for the 15-year-old daughter. Made-for-TV. (Dir: Lee Philips, 76 mins.)

Spell of the Hypnotist—See: Fright

Spellbound (1945)*** Gregory Peck, Ingrid Bergman. Lady psychiatrist shields a doctor accused of murder, works to prove his innocence. Suspense drama has its moments, but is rather drawn out, unnecessarily tricky in its direction by Hitchcock. (111 mins.)

Spencer's Mountain (1963)** Henry Fonda, Maureen O'Hara, James MacArthur. A pastoral attempt about a land-loving valley dweller who keeps promising to build another home for his wife and family. Too much sweetness and light becomes quite cloying before long. Cast superior to the material provided. (Dir: Delmer Daves, 119 mins.)

Spider, The (1958)** Ed Kemmer, Gene Persson. A big one comes to life to terrorize a community. Special effects give this one a passing chill. (Dir: Robert D. Webb, 62 mins.)

Spider and the Fly, The (British, 1949)*** Guy Rolfe, Eric Portman, Nadia Gray. During World War I, the French espionage service enlists the aid of a safecracker in obtaining important documents from the enemy. Tense, suspenseful spy melodrama, well done. (Dir: Robert Hamer, 87 mins.)

Spider's Stratagem, The (Italy, 1969) ***½ Alida Valli, Giulio Brogi. Enormously interesting, convoluted film made by Bertolucci when he was 28 for Italian television, based on a short story, "Theme of the Traitor and Hero," by the Argentinian writer Jorge Luis Borges. A stylish, demanding political whodunit, set in the Po Valley of Italy during the middle 1930's, a time of Mussolini and Italian Fascism. Screenplay by the remarkable Bertolucci. (Dir: Bernardo Bertolucci, 97 mins.)

Spider's Web, The (British, 1960)*½

Glynis Johns, John Justin. Society wife is confronted with the corpse of a blackmailer in her home. Twittery mystery tries to play it lightly, becomes ponderous in doing so.

Spies (German, 1928)*** Take advantage of the opportunity to see this vintage spy thriller made by master director Fritz Lang. The silent film opens with a pair of hands stealing top secret documents from an Embassy safe and the intrigue never stops. The cast of characters includes : the master head of the spy ring, Haghi, who has many more identities ; Sonia, the sultry lady agent who is assigned to trap the hero but loses her heart to him ; and Agent 326, a suave, efficient superagent. Everyone indulges in the hair-pulling, eye-rolling style of silent screen acting, but the overall effect is mesmerizing and the finale in a vaudeville house is superb melodrama. (90 mins.)

Spies-A-Go-Go (1963)* Arch Hall Jr., Mischa Terr. Inane farce about Russian spies disguised as cowboys landing with an infected rabbit to be let loose to destroy the country. No laughs, no nothin'. Alternative title: Nasty Rabbit, The. (Dir: James Landis, 85 mins.)

Spin a Dark Web (1956)*½ Faith Domergue, Lee Patterson. Confused, badly played melodrama. Ex-GI gets involved with a bad crowd in London and when he tries to break loose they kidnap his girl friend. (Dir: Vernon Sewell, 76 mins.)

Spin Out (1966)* Elvis Presley, Shelley Fabares. Strictly for Elvis' fans. This time, he's the leader of a musical troupe and no less than four—count 'em—four pretty young things are after him. (Dir: Norman Taurog, 90 mins.)

Spiral Road, The (1962)*** Rock Hudson, Burl Ives, Gena Rowlands. Lengthy but interesting, well acted drama of a doctor in the remote jungles of Batavia and his discovery of both medical progress and faith. Grips the attention, although some sequences could have been shortened to advantage. (Dir: Robert Mulligan, 145 mins.)

Spiral Staircase, The (1946)***½ Dorothy McGuire, George Brent. Mute servant girl in a gloomy household is endangered by a mysterious killer. Breathlessly suspenseful mystery, superbly directed, a real thriller. (Dir: Robert Siodmak, 83 mins.)

Spirit Is Willing, The (1967)** Sid Caesar, Vera Miles, Harry Gordon, John McGiver. A couple rent a New England house by the sea, and summer vacation soon turns into a ghost-hunt. Mild farce. Once again, the talented Caesar is wasted by Hollywood. (Dir: William Castle, 100 mins.)

Spirit of Saint Louis, The (1957)**½ James Stewart, Murray Hamilton, Patricia Smith. Stewart stars as Charles Lindbergh in this sometimes absorbing, sometimes tedious account of his early life and his historic trans-atlantic solo flight. Stewart is good and the supporting cast gives him the necessary assistance. (Dir: Billy Wilder, 138 mins.)

Spirit of the Beehive (Spain, 1973)***½ Fernando Fernan Gomez, Teresa Gimpera, Ana Torrent. Time—1940 in a remote Castilian village in post-Civil War Spain. Two children watch a traveling film show of James Whale's Frankenstein and are traumatized by it, with alarming results for one of the children. A fascinating, underplayed drama which builds interest and tension. Expert use of some non-professional actors, all expertly directed by Victor Erice, who was also partially responsible for the original story. (98 mins.)

Spiritism (Mexican, 1965)* Joseph Louis Jiminez, Nora Veryan. Seance brings a monster back from the dead. Ridiculous horror thriller dubbed in English.

Spirits of the Dead (1969)*** Jane Fonda, Peter Fonda, Alain Delon, Brigitte Bardot, Terence Stamp. Based on three tales by Edgar Allan Poe, otherwise the film's three separately directed segments have little in common. Vadim's "Metzengerstein," starring the two Fondas, is a tale of medieval love and horror centering on a great black horse. Rather bad, but it has a sense of humor; Jane wears some flashy "neo-Barbarella" costumes, and Claude Renoir's photography is stunning. The final segment, "Never Bet the Devil Your Head" or "Toby Dammit," directed by Federico Fellini, is by far the best, self-contained and visually rich. An entrancing small girl with a large white ball lures alcoholic actor Terence Stamp to pursuit or escape. Fellini both absorbs and augments the Poe original in this fascinating study, and Stamp is superlative in a role which recalls Poe's own alcoholism and ignominious death in a gutter. (Dirs: Roger Vadim, Louis Malle, Federico Fellini, 117 mins.)

Spitfire (British, 1943)***½ Leslie Howard, David Niven. The story of the invention of the plane that served so well during World War II, and of its inventor. Fine biographical drama. (Dir: Leslie Howard, 90 mins.)

Splendor (1935)**½ Miriam Hopkins, Joel McCrea, David Niven. Dated romantic epic which seems a bit corny today but there's some good acting especially by Miriam Hopkins. (Dir: Elliott Nugent, 80 mins.)

Splendor in the Grass (1961)***½ Natalie Wood, Warren Beatty. This absorbing film produced and directed by Elia Kazan, just misses being a classic. Natalie Wood and Warren Beatty costar as two young people making the painful and beautiful discovery of love in a small Kansas town prior to the depression of the thirties. Their sensitive performances, along with good ones by Pat Hingle, Zohra Lampert, and Audrey Christie, make this a must for drama fans who're not above shedding a tear or two. The ending is unsatisfactory, but it doesn't ruin the movie. (124 mins.)

Split, The (1968)*½ Jim Brown, Diahann Carroll. Double- and triple-crosses abound in a plan to rob the Los Angeles Coliseum of football receipts. Fumbling crime yarn not helped by Jim Brown's wooden acting. Diahann Carroll, Ernest Borgnine, Julie Harris, Gene Hackman, Donald Sutherland, James Whitmore and others are trapped within the plot. Sutherland is particularly effective. (Dir: Gordon Flemyng, 91 mins.)

Split Second (1953)***½ Stephen McNally, Alexis Smith, Jan Sterling. Escaped prisoners hold hostages in a Nevada atom-bomb testing area. Terrifically suspenseful, taut melodrama, well done. Directed by Dick Powell. (85 mins.)

Spoilers, The (1942)*** Marlene Dietrich, John Wayne, Randolph Scott. John is out to protect his gold mine and his woman in this one. Loaded with action and a great hand-to-

hand fight by Wayne and Scott. (Dir: Ray Enright, 87 mins.)

Spoilers, The (1956)****½** Anne Baxter, Jeff Chandler, Rory Calhoun. Rex Beach's classic action yarn about the "spoilers" who turned the Yukon into a claim-jumper's paradise, remade with all the flair and flavor intact. Miss Baxter is very good as Cherry, the classy proprietress of the local saloon, and Chandler fulfills the requirements of western hero. (Dir: Jesse Hibbs, 84 mins.)

Spoilers of the Sea (1957)****** Jack Palance, Pedro Armendariz. Produced in Mexico; good troupers make this tale of a sea captain arriving home to his old hangouts looking for his lost love seem better than it really is.

Spring in Park Lane (British, 1948) ******* Anna Neagle, Michael Wilding. Delightful comedy concerning romantic complications and mistaken identity. Witty, fun. (Dir: Herbert Wilcox, 100 mins.)

Spring Reunion (1957)****** Betty Hutton, Dana Andrews. Betty Hutton goes dramatic as the spinster who attends her high school class reunion and finds true love at long last. Unbelievable script hampered by awkward acting of Hutton. (Dir: Robert Pirosh, 79 mins.)

Springfield Rifle (1952)****½** Gary Cooper, Phyllis Thaxter, David Brian. Cooper invents the rifle in this one. It's pretty conventional fare but still superior to most series westerns. (Dir: Andre de Toth, 93 mins.)

Sputnik (French, 1961)****** Noel Noel, Mischa Auer. Mildly amusing comedy about a henpecked Frenchman who discovers animals on his farm used by the Russians for rocket experiments, and they try to get them back. Dubbed in English. (Dir: Jean Dreville, 85 mins.)

Spy I Love, The (French, 1964)****** Jacques Balutin, Virna Lisi. Secret agents investigate the theft of an atomic device. Naive but actionful action thriller dubbed in English.

Spy In Your Eye (Italy, 1965)***** Brett Halsey, Pier Angeli, Dana Andrews. U.S.-Soviet tussle over a "death ray" is deadly dull; gimmick of hidden mini-camera in U.S. Intelligence Chief's false eye falls flat. (Dir: Vittorio Sala, 88 mins.)

Spy Killer, The (1969)****** Robert Horton, Sebastian Cabot, Jill St. John.

One of two made-for-TV features with Robert Horton cast as an ex-agent who now earns his living as a shady private eye. His old employer, British Security, enlists his aid for another assignment and he reluctantly agrees, for a stiff fee. Predictable espionage fare. (Dir: Roy Baker, 73 mins.)

Spy Smasher Returns (1942-66)****½** Kane Richmond, Marguerite Chapman. Feature version of serial "Spy Smasher." Comic-strip hero and his twin brother go after a master enemy agent, amid fistfights galore, some wild flamboyant action, making this good juvenile fun. (Dir: William Witney, 100 mins.)

Spy Squad (1962)***½** Dick O'Neil, Richard Jordahl. Government keep on the trail of foreign agents after an orbited capsule. Quickie spy thriller made in a hurry and looks it. Alternate title: "Capture That Capsule."

Spy Who Came In from the Cold, The (1965)******** Richard Burton, Claire Bloom, Oskar Werner. The best-selling novel about hypocrisy and betrayal in the world of espionage is brought to the screen with all its grim realities intact. Richard Burton is very effective as a disenchanted agent on his supposedly last assignment and Oskar Werner is a standout as a member of German intelligence. Tautly directed by Martin Ritt. (112 mins.)

Spy with a Cold Nose (1966)******* Laurence Harvey, Daliah Lavi. Funny, if uneven, spy spoof. Title refers to a dog equipped with a microphone-transmitter, which is given to the Russian prime minister by British intelligence. It's an offbeat idea for a film comedy. Laurence Harvey plays a veterinarian, and Lionel Jeffries is terribly amusing as a bumbling British counter spy. There's one riotous scene towards the end set in an embassy in Moscow. (Dir: Daniel Petrie, 93 mins.)

Spy With My Face, The (1966)***½** Robert Vaughn, Senta Berger, David McCallum. Here's a theatrical release of an episode from the 1964 "Man From U.N.C.L.E." series, which has added some footage and some seminudity to spark the proceedings. Familiar yarn—THRUSH agents kidnap Napoleon Solo (Robert Vaughn) and replace him with a double (also played by Vaughn). The intrigue mounts (mildly). (Dir: John Newland, 86 mins.)

Spylarks (Great Britain, 1965)** Eric Morecambe, Ernie Wise, William Franklyn. British spy spoof which suffers in the trip across the Atlantic. The comedy team of Morecambe and Wise pull their antics all over the place as a pair of inept spies out to crack a sabotage scheme. (Dir: Robert Asher, 104 mins.)

S*P*Y*S (Great Britain, 1974)** Elliott Gould, Donald Sutherland, Zou Zou, Joss Ackland. Misspelled and misguided attempt to pair that marvelous team from M*A*S*H together again for more comedy. "Gould and Sutherland" (as their names appear in the credits) are CIA agents whom their boss has decided are expendable. They are. Humor derives from their being shot at, beaten up and generally abused. Some funny asides from the two stars, but they're not worth waiting for. (Dir: Irvin Kershner, 87 mins.)

Squad Car (1960)* Paul Bryar, Vici Raaf. Police lieutenant investigating the murder of an airplane mechanic uncovers a smuggling racket. Poor crime melodrama. (Dir: Ed Leftwich, 60 mins.)

Square Jungle, The (1956)** Tony Curtis, Pat Crowley, Ernest Borgnine. Corny prizefight yarn with all the cliches. Tony plays a kid from the wrong side of the tracks who turns to boxing and becomes a temporary champion. The cast struggles with a trite script. (Dir: Jerry Hopper, 86 mins.)

Square of Violence (U.S.-Yugoslavia, 1961)**½ Broderick Crawford, Branko Plesa, Valentina Cortesa. When Yugoslav partisans in WW II kill 30 Nazi officers, 300 innocent men are taken hostage by the Germans. Crawford is the partisan responsible for the bombing, torn between his loyalty to the cause and his concern for the 300. A tense, little-known picture, director Leonardo Bercovici's first. (98 mins.)

Square Shooter, The (1951)**½ Maxie Rosenbloom, Max Baer. Two-gun "Skipalong" Rosenbloom tames feared outlaw "Butcher" Baer in this western burlesque. Crude slapstick, but funny at times.

Squeaker, The (German, 1965)** Heinz Drache, Barbara Rutting. Scotland Yard traces a robber-murderer who uses snake venom on his victims. Edgar Wallace mystery leaves a lot of loose ends dangling; some suspenseful scenes. (Dir: Alfred Vohrer, 95 mins.)

Squeeze A Flower (Australia, 1969)* Jack Albertson, Walter Chiari, Dave Allen. Dull comedy about a monk who conceals the secret ingredients for an exotic liquor, is bolstered slightly by Albertson's performance as the monk's business protegé! (Dir: Marc Daniels, 102 mins.)

SS Strikes at Dawn, The (1966)* Frederick Lake, Joseph Laurentz. World War II provides the background for this dull story about the German pursuit of Resistance fighters in the mountains of Europe. (79 mins.)

Sssssss (1973)*½ Strother Martin, Heather Menzies. From the producers who later gave us the blockbuster, "Jaws." Masterminds Zanuck and Brown must have thought a horror yarn about a demented snake expert (played with a combination of leering and sneering by Strother Martin) who decides to turn young healthy men into cobras would scare us out of our wits! But you'll probably laugh in all the wrong places. A gory ending may be too much for the youngsters. (Dir: Bernard L. Kowalski, 90 mins.)

SST-Death Flight (1977)** Lorne Greene, Susan Strasberg, Burgess Meredith. Formula TV fare. Tale about a planeload of passengers who suddenly are confronted with a life-and-death situation. The maiden trip of the first supersonic plane—and the invited guest list includes celebrities, contest winners, and a scientist carrying a deadly virus. Guess what happens! Made-for-TV. (Dir: David Lowell Rich, 106 mins.)

St.—See also Saint

St. Benny the Dip (1951)*** Dick Haymes, Nina Foch, Roland Young. Three con men hide from the police in a mission, where they are duly reformed. Rather pleasant comedy-drama, nice entertainment. (Dir: Edgar G. Ulmer, 80 mins.)

St. Louis Blues (1958)**½ Nat Cole, Eartha Kitt. The music's everything in this life story of composer W. C. Handy. Story line never really gets going, but the innumerable tunes are superbly performed by Cole, Kitt, Ella Fitzgerald, others. (Dir: Allen Reisner, 94 mins.)

St. Valentine's Day Massacre (1967) ** Jason Robards, George Segal, Jean Hale. Fans who adored the early Warner Bros. gangster films starring Raft, Cagney and Edward G. Robinson, might relish this warmed-over version of the Chicago gangland of the late 1920's. The famous "massacre" is the highlight of the film, and the cast is appropriately stern-faced and threatening. (Dir: Roger Corman, 150 mins.)

Stage Door (1937)***½ Katharine Hepburn, Ginger Rogers, Adolphe Menjou. The lives and ambitions of a group of stage aspirants who live in a theatrical boarding house. Polished, finely acted comedy-drama. (Dir: Gregory La Cava, 100 mins.)

Stage Door Canteen (1943)** William Terry, Cheryl Walker. Many "guest" stars. Romantic drama of a soldier boy and a canteen hostess, backgrounded by the famous servicemen's center of World War II. Sticky-sweet plot, with brief glimpses of stage and screen greats helping some. (Dir: Frank Borzage, 132 mins.)

Stage Fright (British, 1950)**½ Jane Wyman, Marlene Dietrich, Richard Todd, Michael Wilding. Even Alfred Hitchcock strikes out once in a while as he did with this story about a young man suspected of murdering an actress' husband. The best performance in this uneven mystery is given by Richard Todd, as the suspect. (110 mins.)

Stage Struck (1957)**½ Henry Fonda, Susan Strasberg, Christopher Plummer. Remake of Hepburn's "Morning Glory," relating the tale of a young girl whose ambitions spur her on to become a great actress. Strasberg doesn't live up to the role, which hurts the film; otherwise, some good New York atmosphere, other performances. First film by Plummer, one of our most brilliant stage actors and a movie name thanks to "Sound of Music." (Dir: Sidney Lumet, 95 mins.)

Stage to Thunder Rock (1964)** Barry Sullivan, Marilyn Maxwell, Scott Brady, Lon Chaney, Jr. Standard western item about gunslinger and his prisoner, padded with some pretentious comments on the mercenary side of justice, but tight action pacing, good acting helps. (Dir: William F. Claxton, 82 mins.)

Stage to Tucson (1951)**½ Rod Cameron, Wayne Morris, Sally Eilers. Two Civil War buddies are sent to Tucson to investigate the many stage coach hi-jackings and find more trouble than they bargained for. Action-crammed western.

Stagecoach (1939)**** Claire Trevor, John Wayne, Thomas Mitchell. The John Ford western classic about a group of assorted passengers on a stage going into Indian country, their reactions under stress. A fine, exciting, dramatic film, one of the best. (Dir: John Ford, 100 mins.)

Stagecoach (1966)**½ Ann-Margret, Alex Cord, Bing Crosby, Red Buttons. An all-star remake of the classic John Ford—John Wayne western about a handful of stagecoach passengers who go through a great deal before the final showdown. The Ford version was better, but the action is still pretty good the second time around. Gordon Douglas directed. (115 mins.)

Staircase (1969)**½ Richard Burton, Rex Harrison. The big lure here is the casting of Richard Burton and Rex Harrison as a pair of aging homosexuals who live over their barbershop business in London. The film is based on the moderately successful play by Charles Dyer and there's little in the way of plot. It's the cavorting by the stars, particularly Burton, which makes the film an interesting curiosity piece. (Dir: Stanley Donen)

Stairway to Heaven (British, 1946) ***½ David Niven, Kim Hunter, Roger Livesey, Raymond Massey. A pilot who miraculously escapes from a downed bomber soon finds himself in a battle with the Beyond. Touching allegorical drama often technically impressive and charmingly performed. (Dirs: Michael Powell, Emeric Pressburger, 104 mins.)

Stakeout (1962)*½ Bing Russell, Billy Hughes, Eve Brent. Ex-con and his son hit the road, and dad gets mixed in a kidnap plot. Slow, weak crime drama.

Stalag 17 (1953)**** William Holden, Don Taylor, Otto Preminger. Among the best of the prison-camp films; alternately suspenseful, dramatic, comic, brilliantly directed by Billy Wilder. Holden's performance as a cynical sergeant suspected of being a spy won him the Academy Award—rest of the cast is fine, especially Sig Ruman as a guard. Excellent World War II film. (120 mins.)

Stalking Moon, The (1968)**½ Gregory Peck, Eva Marie Saint. Peck and Miss Saint do well in this tightly paced western drama which requires some initial patience before getting into the story. Eva Marie Saint is released after being a prisoner of the Apaches for a number of years, with her nine-year-old half-breed son, but the boy's Indian father stalks them. Primarily a chase film. (Dir: Robert Mulligan, 109 mins.)

Stallion Road (1947)** Ronald Reagan, Alexis Smith. Ron is a veterinarian and Alexis a lovely rancher in this dull romantic drama which offers nothing more than some good looking horses.

Stand at Apache River (1953)**½ Stephen McNally, Julia Adams, Hugh Marlowe. Familiar western yarn about a group of strangers who find themselves stranded in a secluded trading post inn waiting for an inevitable Apache attack. Some suspense. (Dir: Lee Sholem, 77 mins.)

Stand By for Action (1942)**½ Robert Taylor, Brian Donlevy, Walter Brennan. The snooty wartime Naval officer in conflict with the regular Navy man, the sinking of a Jap ship, some salty humor create an occasionally entertaining but generally tiresome film. (Dir: Robert Z. Leonard, 109 mins.)

Stand In (1937)*** Leslie Howard, Joan Blondell, Humphrey Bogart. Screwball satire on Hollywood, as a stuffy banker takes over a movie company, is made into a man by a lady "stand in" for the temperamental star. Rather amusing comedy. (Dir: Tay Garnett, 100 mins.)

Stand Up and Be Counted (1972)**½ Jacqueline Bisset, Stella Stevens, Steve Lawrence, Gary Lockwood. Hollywood discovers women's lib, but insists on adding the usual bunch of stereotypes. Miss Bisset plays a fashion magazine journalist who covers the women's lib scene in Denver. The characters she meets are primarily used for old gags that lampoon the tenets of the movement. (Dir: Jackie Cooper, 99 mins.)

Standing Room Only (1944)**½ Fred MacMurray, Paulette Goddard. A secretary books herself and boss on as servants in a Washington home to avoid the hotel room shortage. Funny when it was topical but only

mildly amusing today. (Dir: Sidney Lanfield, 83 mins.)

Stanley and Livingstone (1939)***½ Spencer Tracy, Nancy Kelly, Walter Brennan. Interesting, well played story of a newsman's search through Africa for a missionary he believed to be alive. Tracy is, as usual, superb and the film is top entertainment. (Dir: Henry King, 101 mins.)

Star, The (1953)*** Bette Davis, Sterling Hayden. A fading movie queen finds love and marries, but still desires a come-back. Well-fashioned look at Hollywood backstage. Good performances. (Dir: Stuart Heisler, 89 mins.)

Star (1968)** Julie Andrews, Daniel Massey, Richard Crenna. Disappointing musical based on the life and career of the legendary Broadway theater star, English-born actress Gertrude Lawrence. Directed by Robert Wise and boasting songs by such greats as Cole Porter and Noel Coward, "Star" becomes overly sentimental and winds up depicting Miss Lawrence as a grown-up girl scout modeled on Mary Poppins. The best performance in the film is from Daniel Massey playing Noel Coward. (Dir: Robert Wise, 175 mins.)

Star Dust (1940)**½ Linda Darnell, John Payne, Roland Young. Story of young hopefuls trying to break through in Hollywood is mildly entertaining. (Dir: Walter Lang, 85 mins.)

Star Is Born, A (1937)***½ Fredric March, Janet Gaynor. Here's the original version of the poignant, dramatic story about a famous Hollywood star whose popularity declines as his young actress-wife reaches superstardom. March, as the matinee idol on the skids, and Gaynor, as his loyal wife, are perfectly cast and keep the story from slipping into cheap sentimentality. The direction by William Wellman hits the right note, and the fine screenplay by Dorothy Parker, Alan Campbell and Robert Carson reveals a great deal about Hollywood in the 30's. (Dir: William Wellman, 110 mins.)

Star Is Born, A (1954)**** Judy Garland, James Mason. The cliched Hollywood story of a husband forced into second place by his wife's career has been often told but it almost doesn't matter thanks to Judy's musical genius and a fine supporting cast. Judy's star was reborn with this film and James Mason adds another moving performance to his list. Garland's songs include "Born in a Trunk" and the sound of Judy's voice is certainly one of the enduring monuments of this century. (Dir: George Cukor, 154 mins.)

Star Is Born, A (1976)*½ Barbra Streisand, Kris Kristofferson. The third and worst film version of "Star," based on the original story by William Wellman and Robert Carson. (The original story, incidentally, shows up in the 1932 talkie "What Price Hollywood." The 1937 version starred Janet Gaynor and Fredric March, and the '54 version starred Judy Garland and James Mason.) This is an indulgent, insulting film in many ways, and Streisand deserves the blame because she had total control over every aspect of the picture. Director Jerry Schatzberg was fired after shooting parts of "Star," her boyfriend-producer Jon Peters helmed a few scenes before being replaced by journeyman Frank Pierson. Updating and transposing the story line from the Hollywood movie world to the 70's rock world was a fundamental mistake, and the film never recovers. "Star" is still supposed to be a "woman's picture," but the audience never cares about Esther Hoffman played by Barbra. Kristofferson sings well and does what he can with a lot of dumb, sentimental dialogue. Streisand is a charismatic presence on screen, especially while singing, so there are isolated parts of the film that work, but they're few and far between. Streisand got an Academy Award, incidentally, for her music—not for the film or her performance. Screenplay by John Gregory Dunne, Joan Didion, and Frank Pierson. (Dir: Frank Pierson, 140 mins.)

Star Spangled Girl, The (1971)*½ Sandy Duncan, Tony Roberts, Todd Susmann. Neil Simon's flop play (one of his few) becomes a flop movie. Casting Sandy Duncan as a patriotic lass from Texas who becomes the apple of her neighbor's eyes (the lads run an underground newspaper) doesn't work for a minute. The lightweight script defeats everyone before long, including expert farceur Tony Roberts as half of the newspaper's creative end.

Todd Susmann, as the other half, fares best in the smallest of starring roles. For the record, on Broadway the cast included Connie Stevens, Anthony Perkins and Richard Benjamin—it wasn't any funnier. (Dir: Jerry Paris, 93 mins.)

Star-Spangled Rhythm (1942)*** All-star cast. Gigantic variety is loaded with talent, but most of their ammunition is blank. Flimsy plot has little to do with film, but Victor Moore is good as the studio gate keeper who's supposed to be an executive.

Star Wars (1977)**** Alec Guinness, Peter Cushing, Mark Hamill, Harrison Ford, Carrie Fisher. Zowie! A "phantasmagorical space-opera," an intergalactic nine-million-dollar fairy tale, and to put it simply one of the most technically dazzling and enjoyable movies since the art form was invented in the last century. A miraculous film for children of all ages, "Star Wars" is a cross between Buck Rogers and Kubrick's "2001," and the heroes of this stunning achievement are not only the wondrous young George Lucas who conceived of, wrote and directed this knockout, but his entire crew of wizards responsible for the design and special effects seen throughout. Space only permits the mention of John Barry and John Dykstra. The plot really doesn't matter, and is confusing, anyway. Civil war is raging within a futuristic galactic empire and, as in all the westerns and cowboys-and-Indians flicks seen, there are good guys and bad guys, and "Star Wars" has you rooting for the good guys and hoping the beautiful young Princess will be rescued by two young Prince Charmings. There is one scene in a kind of spacey barsaloon where you'll meet as wild an assortment of ghouls, grotesques and charmers as you've ever encountered before on the silver screen. The masks, makeup and costumes are staggering, and so is everything else about this incredibly entertaining, huge commercial success. One special note: this is one film that DEMANDS to be seen in a movie theater if at all possible, and not on a tiny home screen. You'll enjoy it immensely on TV but "Star Wars" and the genius of its creators are greatly diminished on the tiny screen. Written and directed by George Lucas. (123 mins.)

Starfighters, The (1963)*½ Robert Dornan, Shirley Olmstead. Story of pilots being trained flying the F-104s goes overboard on the aerial scenics, which is good, but there's too much of it. Story's nothing.

Starlift (1951)** Doris Day, Gordon MacRae, Virginia Mayo, Gene Nelson, Janice Rule, Ruth Roman, and hosts of stars. All the Warner Brothers stars get together in this one to entertain the troops. Thin plot line serves merely as a wait between acts—and the acts are hardly worth it. (Dir: Roy Del Ruth, 103 mins.)

Stars Are Singing, The (1953)** Rosemary Clooney, Anna Maria Alberghetti, Lauritz Melchior. Singer shelters an escaped immigrant girl, finds she has a fine voice. Syrupy musical with the vocalistics far superior to the script. (Dir: Norman Taurog, 99 mins.)

Stars in My Crown (1950)**½ Joel McCrea, Ellen Drew, Dean Stockwell. There's a quiet charm about this film but it's not enough to overcome the soap-opera plot line about a self-made parson and his effect on a small Southern town. (Dir: Jacques Tourneur, 89 mins.)

Stars Look Down, The (British, 1940) **** Margaret Lockwood, Michael Redgrave. Dramatic tale of the life of Welsh coal miners, the ensuing tragedy. Grimly realistic, finely directed by Carol Reed, well acted. (110 mins.)

Starsky and Hutch (1975)**½ Paul Michael Glaser, David Soul, Michael Lerner. Another police yarn about undercover cops who face syndicate hit men, but creator William Blinn manages to hold interest because of his ability to develop believable characters. Starsky and Hutch (played by Glaser and Soul, respectively), portray two ingratiating, brave people. Made-for-TV. (Dir: Barry Shear, 72 mins.)

Start the Revolution Without Me (1970)**½ Donald Sutherland, Gene Wilder, Hugh Griffith, Orson Welles. Sometimes funny farce starts out promisingly. Sutherland and Wilder, two of the movies' better comedy actors, ham it up to the nth degree as a pair of twins (that's right, four of 'em) who are separated at birth (one from each set), with two lads

growing up in French aristocracy while the other pair are reared as peasants. The setting for this classic yarn of mistaken identity is the French Revolution, and the supporting cast includes Hugh Griffith as a bumbling King Louis XVI, Victor Spinetti as an oily Duke, and Orson Welles as a casual narrator. (Dir: Bud Yorkin, 90 mins.)

State Fair (1945, Jeanne Crain)—See: It Happened One Summer

State Fair (1962)** Pat Boone, Ann-Margret, Bobby Darin, Alice Faye, Tom Ewell. Third time around for this musical tale of a family attending the Iowa State Fair, and the various romantic mixups. This one lacks sparkle, freshness, lags well behind the other two in entertainment values. (Dir: Jose Ferrer, 118 mins.)

State of Siege (French, 1973)***½ Yves Montand, Renato Salvatori. Director Costa-Gavras ("Z") made this factually based story of a kidnapped and murdered American traffic adviser in South America. It raises many important questions about U.S. tactics. Brilliantly understated performance by Montand as the captured American. (115 mins.)

State of the Union (1948)*** Spencer Tracy, Katharine Hepburn, Van Johnson. Businessman is persuaded by a dynamic lady publisher to run for President. Age has withered some of the bite of this version of the popular stage hit; but Tracy and Hepburn click as usual, the Frank Capra direction still frequently effective. (124 mins.)

State Secret (British, 1951)**** Douglas Fairbanks Jr., Glynis Johns, Jack Hawkins. Noted surgeon is tricked into aiding the head of a European police state, flees with the secret police not far behind. Excellent suspense thriller played lightly; laughs, thrills and fun. (Dir: Sidney Gilliat, 97 mins.)

Station Six Sahara (British, 1964) *** Carroll Baker, Peter Van Eyck, Ian Bannen. Into a small group of men running an oil station in the Sahara comes a beautiful blonde who starts the emotions soaring. Lusty melodrama on the sizzling side with a well-written script describing the familiarity of the tale, and capable direction and performances adding to it. (Dir: Seth Holt, 99 mins.)

Station West (1948)*** Dick Powell,

Jane Greer. Army officer goes under-cover to trap a gang of hi-jackers and murderers. Good western has enough action, is well acted. (Dir: Sidney Lanfield, 92 mins.)

Statue, The (1971)** David Niven, Virna Lisi, Robert Vaughn. Prudish comedy as domestic bliss is threatened when Miss Lisi carves a nude 18-foot statue of her Nobel Peace Prize-winning husband Niven. The catch—Niven is mad because the bottom half does not resemble him. He searches for the real model thinking his wife has cheated on him. A mawkish, immature mess. (Dir: Ron Amateau, 92 mins.)

Stavisky (France-Italy, 1974)***½ Jean-Paul Belmondo, Charles Boyer, Anny Duperey. Director Alain Resnais' generally absorbing drama about corruption in France from 1936 until the outbreak of World War II. Focuses on the famous "Stavisky" case, a financial swindle conceived by a flamboyant con-man (Belmondo) and involving many top-level government officials. Referred to recently as the French "Watergate" of the 1930's, but it really bears little relation to the moral and legal horrors perpetrated by the Nixon Administration. Production, thanks partially to costumes by Yves St. Laurent, captures the look of rich, decadent France of that time. (Dir: Alain Resnais, 117 mins.)

Stay Away, Joe (1968)* Elvis Presley, Joan Blondell. Stay away, whatever your name is! Elvis as a rodeo champ upsetting the old Indian reservation. Tacky slapstick. (Dir: Peter Tewksbury, 102 mins.)

Stay Hungry (1976)**½ Jeff Bridges, Sally Field, Arnold Schwarzenegger, Scatman Crothers, Joe Santo. Promising premise of a young, privileged boy intent on his independence, and the spunky working girl he lives with, fizzles out due to unmanageable plot strands. Bridges is wonderful as the boy who occupies a Tara-like mansion, and Miss Field's first mature role shows her at her best. The gym club that Bridges invests in is authentically peopled by such brawny iron-pumpers as former Mr. Universe, Arnold Schwarzenegger. Well done fight sequence between Bridges and a weight-lifter who trains in a Batman costume. Based on the novel by

Charles Gaines. Some nice touches from director Bob Rafelson, who needs a firmer hand. (103 mins.)

Steagle, The (1971)**½ Richard Benjamin, Cloris Leachman, Chill Wills. Liberal college professor Benjamin is so entangled with politics that news of the Cuban missile crisis sends him daydreaming. He is propelled through Chicago, Las Vegas, and Hollywood only to recover when the Russians withdraw. Benjamin is a fine comedic actor, but the plot is too contrived for a full-length movie. (Dir: Paul Sylbert, 90 mins.)

Steel Bayonet (1958)** Leo Genn, Kieron Moore. Fairly well made British war drama. The performances outrank the film's rambling script about the exploits of a division of soldiers assigned a dangerous task. (Dir: Michael Carreras, 84 mins.)

Steel Claw, The (1961)**½ George Montgomery, Charito Luna. Marine about to be discharged because of the loss of a hand organizes guerrillas when the Japanese invade the Philippines. Fine photography, plenty of action compensate for a weak script in this frequently exciting war drama, very capably directed by Montgomery. (96 mins.)

Steel Fist, The (1952)** Roddy McDowall, Kristine Miller. Good try at serious drama about a U.S. Student who's trapped in an Iron Curtain country but it doesn't quite come off. The script is on the pedestrian side and even Roddy McDowall's earnest performance can't lift it out of the ordinary adventure groove. (Dir: Wesley Barry, 73 mins.)

Steel Helmet, The (1951)***½ Gene Evans, Robert Hutton. It's nip-and-tuck with the Reds for a UN platoon in the early days of Korea. War melodrama packs quite a punch; grim, hard-boiled, one of the better films of its type. (Dir: Samuel Fuller, 84 mins.)

Steel Key, The (British, 1952)*** Terence Morgan, Joan Rice. Two scientists working on a secret process for hardening steel die suddenly, and a private investigator tracks down the reason behind it all. Good melodrama moves at a fast pace. (Dir: Robert Baker, 74 mins.)

Steel Town (1952)** Ann Sheridan, John Lund, Howard Duff. Usual drama about two guys vieing for the same girl and a top spot in a large steel mill. (Dir: George Sherman, 85 mins.)

Steel Trap, The (1952)***½ Joseph Cotten, Teresa Wright. A banker steals five hundred thousand dollars on a Friday afternoon, and frantically tries to return it by Monday. Suspenseful melodrama, keeps one guessing, excited. (Dir: Andrew L. Stone, 85 mins.)

Steelyard Blues (1973)**½ Jane Fonda, Donald Sutherland, Peter Boyle. A fairly funny protest about three nonconformists who band together to steal an electrical circuit which will enable them to fly away. Sutherland plays the leader, whose dream is to have a demolition derby with mobile homes. Fonda plays an expensive prostitute, and Boyle is not up to the standards of the cast. (Dir: Alan Meyerson, 92 mins.)

Stella Dallas (1937)**½ Barbara Stanwyck, John Boles, Anne Shirley. As sudsy a melodrama as you're likely to see on the screen. Miss Stanwyck pulls all the stops as the woebegone heroine who suffers at every turn. The ladies who tune in on TV daytime serials will stay glued to the end of this opus. (Dir: King Vidor, 111 mins.)

Step Down to Terror (1959)** Colleen Miller, Charles Drake, Rod Taylor. So-so remake of "Shadow of a Doubt"—son returns home to his family, is eventually found to be a psychotic killer. Just fair suspense melodrama. (Dir: Harry Keller, 75 mins.)

Step Lively (1944)*** Frank Sinatra, George Murphy, Gloria De Haven. Fast-thinking theatrical producer gets his show on despite financial problems. Lively, enjoyable musical. (Dir: Tim Whelan, 88 mins.)

Step Out of Line, A (1971)*** Peter Falk, Peter Lawford, Vic Morrow. Easily one of the most interesting network films tailor-made for TV. It concerns three adults who consider a heist because they are badly in need of bread. The idea may be kid stuff, but once fans accept the premise, the show works. Amateurs that they are, they carry out the robbery of a San Francisco money exchange company in exciting fashion, goofing at crucial moments. Though the final result has to be what it is, you almost wish otherwise after you get to know the men. Peter Falk's role is the toughest, since he must change from a straight-as-an-arrow guy. (Dir: Bernard McEveety, 100 mins.)

Stepford Wives, The (1975)**½ Paula Prentiss, Tina Louise, Nanette Newman, Patrick O'Neal. Ira Levin's engrossing novel about a Connecticut community in which the housewife brigade consists of women who love to do housework, satisfy their husbands in every way and be absolute models of domesticity comes to the screen somewhat diluted. Katharine Ross is Joanne, who notices the strange behavior of her suburban colleagues and tries to get to the bottom of the mystery. You'll guess the outcome long before the final moments, but the cast keeps things boiling along. (Dir: Bryan Forbes, 115 mins.)

Sterile Cuckoo, The (1969)***½ Liza Minnelli, Wendell Burton. Touching romance of Pookie Adams (Minnelli), a kook who insists upon calling all those who won't participate in her world "weirdos," and the innocent straight (Burton) she captivates. Miss Minnelli is quite remarkable in her heartbreaking portrayal of a neurotic college girl creating obvious games to shut out dealing with the world. Liza was nominated for an Academy Award for this one. The film often plods due to the first directorial effort by Alan J. Pakula, but it finally gets where it was destined to go. Even, quiet, and touching. (107 mins.)

Sting, The (1973)**** Paul Newman, Robert Redford, Robert Shaw. A marvelously entertaining caper about two deft con men (Newman and Redford) operating in and around Chicago circa 1936. Has much of the same exuberant quality of the two stars' "Butch Cassidy and the Sundance Kid." Director George Roy Hill is on hand to give the film a fast pace and a glittering visual style. There are some rollicking Scott Joplin musical rags in this comedy which won the Academy Award for best picture. One of the best wrap-up scenes in many years as Newman and Redford swindle Shaw out of a big bundle in one of the most inventive schemes ever depicted on the big screen. A joy from beginning to end, and don't be upset if you miss some of the plot details along the way. It happens to the best of us. (129 mins.)

678

Stitch in Time, A (Great Britain, 1963)** Norman Wisdom, Edward Chapman, Jeanette Starke. Typical slapstick vehicle for Britain's most popular vaudeville star, Wisdom. Incidental plot keeps the clown cavorting around a hospital where his boss is having an operation for a swallowed watch. (Dir: Robert Asher, 94 mins.)

Stolen Face (British, 1952)*** Paul Henreid, Lizabeth Scott. A plastic surgeon molds the face of a convict into a replica of his lost love. Interesting drama.

Stolen Life (1946)**½ Bette Davis, Glenn Ford. Bette plays twins for part of this film. In the second half she has only one role thanks to a murder. She kills her sister over jealousy and then steals her twin's identity. If that sounds silly, it is! (Dir: Curtis Bernhardt, 107 mins.)

Stone Killer, The (1973)** Charles Bronson, Martin Balsam. Violent crime film, based on John Gardner's book "A Complete State of Death." Bronson plays a police officer, who stops at nothing to track down the plans of a crazed underworld figure out for revenge for the gangland assassinations of his cronies in 1931. Exciting finale set in a remote desert fortress, where Vietnam veterans are being trained to kill those remaining men who were responsible for the gangland killings. (Dir: Michael Winner, 120 mins.)

Stoolie, The (1974)**½ Jackie Mason, Dan Frazer, Marcia Jean Kurtz. Genial, sentimental treatment of a police informer who runs off to Miami Beach with $7,500 lent by the police department of N.Y. As a love story between two less than attractive people, this is quite touching, but as a tale of the underworld, the plotting is laughable. Cluttered by details like a parrot who roller skates. Mason's gritty performance is surprisingly skillful. Directed by John Avildsen ("Rocky") between two more ambitious efforts, "Joe" and "Save the Tiger." (90 mins.)

Stop! Look! and Laugh! (1960)** 3 Stooges, Paul Winchell. Half old footage of 3 Stooges comedies and half new stuff featuring Paul Winchell and his dummy Jerry Mahoney. Verdict: for half-pints. (Dir: Jules White, 78 mins.)

Stop Me Before I Kill (British, 1961)

**½ Claude Dauphin, Diane Cilento, Ronald Lewis. After a crash an auto racer recovers physically but finds himself trying to murder his wife. Fairly entertaining melodrama has enough twists and turns to keep the mystery fans guessing. Good performances. (Dir: Val Guest, 121 mins.)

Stop the World, I Want to Get Off (British, 1966)**½ Tony Tanner, Millicent Martin. Unfortunately, this literal screen version of the successful Broadway and London musical hit becomes boring before too long, although there are some standout songs including "What Kind of Fool Am I?" Tony Tanner makes a good Little Chap, a sort of everyday Everyman, who goes through his life in song, dance and mime. Music and lyrics by Anthony Newley and Leslie Bricuse. Newley starred in the theater and he's a more inventive performer than Tanner. (Dir: Philip Saville, 98 mins.)

Stop Train 349 (1964)** Sean Flynn, Jose Ferrer, Nicole Courcel. Young lieutenant faces the Russians who want to search a train for an East German defector. Merely passable suspense drama filmed in Germany suffers from overstated treatment, slowness of pace. (Dir: Rolf Haedrich, 95 mins.)

Stop, You're Killing Me (1953)** Broderick Crawford, Claire Trevor, Virginia Gibson, Bill Hayes. Remake of a gangster-comedy yarn which starred Edward G. Robinson. This updated version about a big time beer baron and his cronies just doesn't come off. Some tunes are added for good measure. (Dir: Roy Del Ruth, 86 mins.)

Stopover Tokyo (1957)** Robert Wagner, Joan Collins, Edmond O'Brien. The heroes of this spy thriller (Wagner and Ken Scott) behave like two TV series heroes. In other words, they manage to survive against extreme odds; show how brave they really are at the slightest provocation, and have all the beautiful women wish they would give up being Intelligence Agents and settle down. The Orient is the backdrop for murder, intrigues and occasional embraces. (Dir: Richard L. Breen, 100 mins.)

Stork Club, The (1945)**½ Barry Fitzgerald, Betty Hutton. Hat check girl befriends penniless bum who is, naturally, a billionaire. Silly fable is saved by some nice performances. (Dir: Hal Walker, 98 mins.)

Storm Center (1956)*** Bette Davis, Brian Keith, Kim Hunter. Intense drama about a librarian who refuses to remove a controversial book from the public library and meets with opposition from the town's politicians. There are too many tangents in this film which keep it from being great, but it has something important to say and is well worth seeing. (Dir: Daniel Taradash, 85 mins.)

Storm Fear (1955)**½ Cornel Wilde, Jean Wallace. Wounded bank robber shows up at his brother's house to seek shelter. Interesting drama, moves a bit too slowly but is well acted. (Dir: Cornel Wilde, 88 mins.)

Storm in a Teacup (British, 1937) *** Vivien Leigh, Rex Harrison. Candidate for election in a Scottish town is hurt by an accident with a dog, that is played upon by a young reporter into a national incident. Clever, amusing comedy. Cecil Parker is fine as the pompous politician. (Dirs: Victor Saville, Ian Dalrymple, 90 mins.)

Storm in Jamaica—See: Passionate Summer

Storm Over the Nile (British, 1956) **½ Anthony Steel, Laurence Harvey. Remake of a once great action film, "Four Feathers," is reasonably exciting. Englishman who resigns his army commission goes to the Sudan to prove he is not a coward. (Dir: Zoltan Korda, 113 mins.)

Storm Warning (1951)**½ Ginger Rogers, Ronald Reagan, Doris Day. Melodramatic story of a visiting in-law who witnesses a murder by the Ku-Klux-Klan. Good acting by Ginger Rogers. (Dir: Stuart Heisler, 93 mins.)

Stormy Weather (1943)*** Lena Horne, Bill Robinson, Fats Waller, Dooley Wilson. All-Negro musical has as silly a plot as most musicals but the individual performers do so well that the film provides some sock numbers. (Dir: Andrew L. Stone, 77 mins.)

Story of a Three Day Pass, The (French, 1967)***½ Harry Baird, Nicole Berger, Pierre Doris. The real star of this flawed but touching, honest and rewarding film is its young and talented black writer-director Melvin Van Peebles. (It is a shocking indictment of the American motion picture industry that until 1968 not a single American movie produced by a major movie company had been directed by a Negro.) Low-budget, independently made entry concerns a bittersweet romance of a Negro GI in peacetime Paris and a Parisian girl (Berger). The late Miss Berger, killed shortly after completing this film, is most attractive. (87 mins.)

Story of a Woman (1969)** Robert Stack, Bibi Andersson. An involved romance which should please the ladies. Swedish actress Bibi Andersson fluctuates between her American diplomat husband (Robert Stack) and her former flame (James Farentino) and there are many tears and love scenes before the fadeout. (Dir: Leonardo Bercovici, 90 mins.)

Story of Alexander Graham Bell, The (1939)***½ Don Ameche, Loretta Young, Henry Fonda. Warm, moving story of the man who gave us the telephone. The ending is a bit ridiculous but most of the film, which traces Bell's early disappointments and failures, is top entertainment. (Dir: Irving Pichel, 97 mins.)

Story of David, A (1960)** Jeff Chandler, Basil Sydney, Barbara Shelley. David is unjustly accused of seeking the throne of Israel. Biblical drama originally produced for TV, filmed in Israel. Better than usual production, but generally undistinguished, slow-moving.

Story of Dr. Wassell, The (1944)** Gary Cooper, Laraine Day, Signe Hasso. True story of an old doctor who rescued some men from the Japs in Java has been turned into a pulp fiction tale with few facts and little interest. (Dir: Cecil B. De Mille, 140 mins.)

Story of Esther Costello, The (1957) ** Joan Crawford, Rossano Brazzi, Heather Sears. Silly melodrama about a group of greedy promoters who exploit a mute girl as a front for a swindle. The script is cliched and reverts to outrageous melodramatics. (Dir: David Miller, 103 mins.)

Story of G.I. Joe, The (1944)***½ Burgess Meredith, Robert Mitchum. Incidents in the life of famed war correspondent Ernie Pyle, during the bloody Italian campaign. Fine performance, good drama. (Dir: William Wellman, 109 mins.)

Story of Louis Pasteur, The (1938) **** Paul Muni. Not as great as Muni's "Zola" but still a wonderful biographical tribute to the French scientist. Muni is, as usual, superb in this informative and moving film. (Dir: William Dieterle, 100 mins.)

Story of Mankind, The (1957)*½ Ronald Colman, Hedy Lamarr, Groucho Marx, Virginia Mayo, Peter Lorre, Agnes Moorehead, and others. Ridiculous excursion through the pages of history. A poor mixture of comedy and drama in an attempt to tell the so-called story of mankind. Segments range from Groucho playing "Peter Minuit" to Hedy Lamarr as an unbelievable "Joan of Arc." (Dir: Irving Allen, 100 mins.)

Story of Pretty Boy Floyd, The (1974)*** Martin Sheen, Kim Darby, Michael Parks. Fine actor Martin Sheen gets a chance to portray the legendary criminal Pretty Boy Floyd, in this low-key tale set in the 20's and early 30's, and it's his performance which makes the TV feature worthwhile. Credit must also go to writer-director Clyde Ware, whose careful attention to period detail adds greatly to the texture of the film. Made-for-TV. (72 mins.)

Story of Ruth, The (1960)**½ Elena Eden, Stuart Whitman, Tom Tryon, Viveca Lindfors. Biblical tale of a girl who renounces the worship of pagan gods when she finds the true religion. Stately, interesting drama, despite some dull stretches. (Dir: Henry Koster, 132 mins.)

Story of Seabiscuit (1949)**½ Lon McCallister, Shirley Temple, Barry Fitzgerald. Biography of famous horse is just an excuse for a run-of-the-mill racing picture. Fitzgerald is good as the trainer and there are a few fine racing scenes. (Dir: David Butler, 93 mins.)

Story of Three Loves, The (1953)*** Kirk Douglas, Leslie Caron, Pier Angeli, James Mason. Entertaining film for romantics. The stories of three love affairs are unfolded via flashback by three passengers on an ocean liner. (Dir: Vincente Minnelli, 122 mins.)

Story of Vernon and Irene Castle (1939)*** Fred Astaire, Ginger Rogers. The life and successes of the famous dance team early in the century. Not up to Astaire-Rogers standard, but still entertaining bio-

graphical musical. (Dir: H. C. Potter, 93 mins.)

Story of Will Rogers (1952)**½ Will Rogers Jr., Jane Wyman. Slow moving but well done bio-pic of the great humorist Will Rogers. His son, Will Rogers, Jr., looks a great deal like his father, but he inherited none of his dad's charm, talent or wit. (Dir: Michael Curtiz, 109 mins.)

Story on Page One, The (1959)*** Rita Hayworth, Anthony Franciosa, Gig Young. Lawyer agrees to defend two adulterers accused of murdering the lady's husband. Uneven but frequently gripping courtroom drama written and directed by Clifford Odets. Main performances quite good, the legal crossfires dramatically tense. (123 mins.)

Stowaway (1936)*** Shirley Temple, Alice Faye, Robert Young. One of Shirley's best is this tale of a slain Chinese missionary's daughter who stows away on a playboy's yacht and succeeds in solving all problems. (Dir: William A. Seiter, 85 mins.)

Strait-Jacket (1964)**½ Joan Crawford, Diane Baker. Released from a mental hospital years after having committed axe murders, a woman goes to live with her daughter and brother—then axe murders begin again. Unadorned shocker attempts the more flamboyant kind of thrills; mystery fans will see through it, after experiencing a few heart-jumps along the way. (Dir: William Castle, 89 mins.)

Strange Affair, The (British, 1968)* Michael York, Susan George, Jeremy Kemp. Naïve London copper is really taken in by a wild teenage girl. Vacillating mixture of melodrama and satire leaves a rather unpleasant aftereffect. (Dir: David Greene, 106 mins.)

Strange Affection (British, 1957)**½ Richard Attenborough, Colin Peterson. Boy is accused of murdering his father. Fairly good drama, nice performance by Peterson. (Dir: Wolf Rilla, 84 mins.)

Strange and Deadly Occurrence, The (1974)** Robert Stack, Vera Miles, L. Q. Jones, Herb Edelman. Home-owners, who think they have headaches, will shudder at the events which throw Robert Stack, Vera Miles and their family into a tailspin when they move into their new home. Fairly clever use of gimmicked suspense ploys. Made-for-

TV. (Dir: John L. Moxey, 72 mins.)

Strange Awakening (British, 1959)★ Lex Barker, Carole Mathews. Very contrived melodrama about an amnesia victim who is used in a swindling plot. Lex Barker (ex-Tarzan) is expressionless throughout the entire film. (Dir: Montgomery Tully, 75 mins.)

Strange Bedfellows (1964)★★½ Rock Hudson, Gina Lollobrigida, Gig Young. Wandering business executive tries to reconcile his wife to improve his corporate image. Fairly entertaining comedy based on the unlikely assumption that anyone would desert lovely Lollobrigida for any length of time. Some cute scenes. (Dir: Melvin Frank, 98 mins.)

Strange Cargo (1940)★★★ Clark Gable, Joan Crawford. Good exciting story of escape from a penal island in the tropics which almost loses itself in obscure symbolism. If you watch this try and figure out what kind of character Ian Hunter is playing. (Dir: Frank Borzage, 105 mins.)

Strange Case of Dr. Manning (British, 1958)★½ Ron Randell, Greta Gynt. Scotland Yard on the trail of kidnappers. Usual no-suspense story, as old as the Yard itself. (Dir: Arthur Crabtree, 75 mins.)

Strange Confession—See: **Impostor, The**

Strange Countess, The (German, 1961) ★½ Joachim Berger, Marianne Hoppe, Lil Dagover. Series of murders are connected to a countess and a woman released from prison. Confused Edgar Wallace mystery dubbed in English. (Dir: Josef Von Baky, 96 mins.)

Strange Death of Adolf Hitler (1943) ★★ Ludwig Donath, George Dolenz. Facial double for Hitler is forced by the Gestapo to pose as Der Fuhrer. Doesn't mean much now, but still an intriguing idea. (Dir: James Hogan, 72 mins.)

Strange Door, The (1952)★½ Charles Laughton, Boris Karloff, Sally Forrest. A horror tale that is intended to be chilling but is often laughable instead. Laughton and Karloff overact outrageously. Based on a Robert Louis Stevenson story. (Dir: Joseph Pevney, 81 mins.)

Strange Homecoming (1974)★★ Robert Culp, Barbara Anderson, Glen Campbell. Despite credibility gaps in the story line, star Robert Culp

682

manages to cover up the holes. He plays a murderer who pops up after a long absence and receives a hero's welcome from his sheriff-brother's family. Along with his looks and ready charm, Culp is also to convey tension as the villain, while the innocents around him slowly begin to catch on. Made-for-TV. (Dir: Lee H. Katzin, 72 mins.)

Strange Lady in Town (1955)★★½ Greer Garson, Dana Andrews, Cameron Mitchell, Lois Smith. Greer Garson seems out of place in this western. She plays a determined woman who disturbs Santa Fe's top figures upon her arrival. (Dir: Mervyn Le Roy, 112 mins.)

Strange New World (1975)★½ John Saxon, Kathleen Miller, Keene Curtis. "Made-for-TV" buffs (and they do exist) will be quick to recognize this as a further attempt to come up with a satisfactory pilot for a series based on the previous TV film, "Planet Earth"; it plays like a couple of episodes strung together. Saxon stars again, as one of a trio of survivors from an earlier time, brought back to earth. Strange, maybe—but not worth seeing. Made-for-TV. (Dir: Robert Butler, 100 mins.)

Strange One, The (1957)★★★½ Ben Gazzara, Mark Richman, George Peppard, Pat Hingle, Julie Wilson. Exciting screen version of Calder Willingham's play "End As A Man" about life in a Southern military academy as presided over by a sadistic upper classman. Superb performances by all, with Ben Gazzara a standout in his screen debut. (Dir: Jack Garfein, 100 mins.)

Strange Possession of Mrs. Oliver, The (1977)★★½ Karen Black, George Hamilton. Karen Black is a good actress, and she almost makes this contrived, obvious drama work—but only almost! She plays a housewife who suddenly takes on the personality of a woman who died five years earlier, and it's the split-personality theme which keeps your interest. George Hamilton plays her husband in such a wooden fashion that it makes his wife's search for a new life perfectly understandable. Made-for-TV. (Dir: Gordon Hessler, 76 mins.)

Strange World (1952)★★ Angelica Hauff, Alexander Carlos. Man returns to uncharted jungles to search for his father, finds a strange girl living there. Produced by Germans in Brazil, dubbed in English—quite a mixture, but this adventure story turns out fairly well, if a bit on the far-fetched side. Good jungle scenes.

Stranger, The (1946)***½ Edward G. Robinson, Orson Welles, Loretta Young. Professor in a small college town is respected by the citizens but in reality is a top-ranking Nazi. Suspenseful, gripping melodrama, directed with a fine flair by Welles. (95 mins.)

Stranger, The (1973)**½ Glenn Corbett. Old fugitive plot neatly wrapped up in semi-science-fiction trimmings. Astronaut Corbett crashes on an Earthlike planet known as Terra, and must keep on the run, since his ideas of freedom conflict with the autocratic society called the Perfect Order. Made-for-TV. (Dir: Lee H. Katzin.)

Stranger at My Door (1956)*** Macdonald Carey, Patricia Medina, Skip Homeier. Notorious outlaw takes refuge in a preacher's home, who tries to reform him. Offbeat western is well done. (Dir: William Witney, 85 mins.)

Stranger from Hong Kong (French, 1964)* Dalila, Chin Sing Long. Twin act becomes mixed up in intrigue in Hong Kong. Weird little adventure story dubbed in English; pretty weak.

Stranger in Between, The (British, 1952)*** Dirk Bogarde, Jon Whiteley, Elizabeth Sellars. Runaway finds a body and is taken captive by the murderer. Suspenseful, well acted melodrama. (Dir: Charles Crichton, 84 mins.)

Stranger in My Arms, A (1959)** June Allyson, Jeff Chandler, Sandra Dee. Widow defies her mother-in-law when she meets a man she wants to marry. Good production values, otherwise reminiscent of daytime serials. For the soap fans. (Dir: Helmut Kautner, 88 mins.)

Stranger in Town, A (Italian, 1966)*½ Tony Anthony, Frank Wolff. Mysterious gunslinger trots in and takes on a murderous bandito. The Italian view of U.S. westerns is strictly from pizza; might garner a few laughs, if nothing else. (Dir: Vance Lewis, 86 mins.)

Stranger Knocks, A (Danish, 1965)***½ Birgitte Federspiel, Preben Rye. A simple, honest, and ultimately extremely moving Danish film that was the subject of a Supreme Court decision in the U.S. The identity of a passing stranger is revealed to a young war widow in a final love scene that is both appropriate and explicit. Without this sequence, this straightforward Danish film is mutilated unfairly and the film is pointless. If your local TV station has the sense to show this film in an evening time slot without cutting it at all, this character study is well worth seeing.

Stranger on Horseback (1955)*** Joel McCrea, Miroslava, Kevin McCarthy. Fightin' judge cleans up a territory run by one man. Colorful, speedy western, well done. (Dir: Jacques Tourneur, 66 mins.)

Stranger on the Prowl (Italian, 1953)**½ Paul Muni, Joan Lorring. Fugitive from murder is joined by a small boy in his flight from the police. Grim drama, occasionally interesting. (Dir: Joseph Losey, 82 mins.)

Stranger on the Run (1968)**½ Henry Fonda, Anne Baxter, Michael Parks. This made-for-TV film is fortunate in having an expert cast to make the characters interesting even when the western drama is pushing to last out the two hours. Henry Fonda is being chased by a band of renegades who've been given badges by a railroad and a free hand to keep things going smoothly in the railroad's town. A first-rate contribution by Michael Parks as the head lawman. (Dir: Don Siegel, 97 mins.)

Stranger on the Third Floor (1940)*** Peter Lorre, John McGuire, Margaret Tallichet. Reporter is convinced a condemned man is innocent of murder, especially when the same pattern of crime reoccurs. Carefully produced, suspenseful thriller. (Dir: Boris Ingster, 64 mins.)

Stranger Returns, The (Italian, 1967)*½ Tony Anthony, Dan Vadis (Dan who????), Jill Banner. Once again the mysterious lone rider goes after stagecoach robbers. Mama mia, that'sa spicy meatball! This is a sequel to the rotten "A Stranger in Town." One of the spaghetti-westerns; dubbed-in English. (Dir: Vance Lewis, 90 mins.)

Stranger Within, The (1974)**½ Barbara Eden, George Grizzard. A bizarre tale in the tradition of "Rosemary's Baby." Barbara Eden is quite effective as a normal-appearing woman who finds herself pregnant, though husband George Grizzard has been certified impotent. Thus begins the nightmarish story leading to a suspenseful climax. Made-for-TV. (Dir: Lee Philips, 72 mins.)

Stranger Who Looks Like Me, The (1974)**½ Meredith Baxter, Beau Bridges, Whitney Blake. Thoughtful drama about a pair of young people who set out to find their real parents, knowing they are adopted. Whitney Blake, who is Miss Baxter's real-life mother, plays the girl's mother in this piece and their confrontation scene is well handled. Made-for-TV. (Dir: Larry Peerce.)

Strangers, The (Italian, 1954)**½ Ingrid Bergman, George Sanders. An English couple in Italy, rapidly approaching the point of divorce through incompatibility, experiences a miracle that brings them closer together. Despite the presence of the two stars, Rossellini direction, this drama remains vague, rather cold. (97 mins.)

Stranger's Hand (1955)***½ Trevor Howard, Richard Basehart, Alida Valli. An exciting and tense adventure drama of intrigue acted by an excellent cast. Trevor Howard stands out. (Dir: Mario Soldati, 86 mins.)

Strangers in 7A, The (1972)** Andy Griffith, Ida Lupino. One of those bank-robbery tales in which the young hoods show their muscle by slapping bystanders around. Griffith and Miss Lupino play the victims, an apartment-house super and his wife, who resist the robbers. Michael Brandon displays some flash as the chief villain, and Susanne Hildur uses her physical charms on the building's super. Made-for-TV. (Dir: Paul Wendkos, 73 mins.)

Strangers in the City (1962)**½ Robert Gentile, Rosita De Triana. Drama of a Puerto Rican family trying to adjust itself to the pattern of New York life, the resulting tragedy. Has an occasional ragged realism, but is often amateurish, uncertain.

Strangers on a Train (1951)***½ Robert Walker, Ruth Roman, Farley Granger. Taut and suspenseful psychological drama directed by the master of suspense Alfred Hitch-

cock. Walker and Granger meet on a train and form an unholy pact involving murder. Effective performance by the late Robert Walker. (101 mins.)

Strangers When We Meet (1960)**½ Kirk Douglas, Kim Novak, Barbara Rush. The attractiveness of the stars is the only factor of this screen translation of Evan Hunter's novel about extra-marital activities. The ladies who like their drama on a "soap opera" level will be in complete sympathy with Kim, who is married, as she falls hopelessly in love with an equally married architect (Kirk Douglas). (Dir: Richard Quine, 117 mins.)

Stranglehold (British, 1962)**½ Macdonald Carey, Barbara Shelley, Philip Friend. Temperamental movie actor nears the edge of madness when his gangster roles threaten to invade his private life. Well-acted suspense drama, especially by Carey.

Strangler, The (1964)**½ Victor Buono, David McLean, Diane Sayer. City is in terror and police work frantically to nab a psychotic strangler of women. Grim drama lent some distinction by Buono's fine performance, some good direction. Not for children. (Dir: Burt Topper, 89 mins.)

Strangler of Blackmoor Castle, The (German, 1960)*½ Karin Dor, Ingmar Zeisberg. Scotland Yard sleuth tracks down a murderer who's been bumping off people in an old English castle. Typically Germanic version of English creepy mystery, not much. Dubbed in English.

Stranglers of Bombay, The (British, 1960)*** Guy Rolfe, Allan Cuthbertson. Fascinating drama about a cult of evil worshippers in India during the 1800's and their effect on the British trading situation. The scenes of the cultist rites are not for the squeamish. (Dir: Terence Fisher, 81 mins.)

Strangler's Web (British, 1966)** Griffith Jones, John Stratton. Actor finds himself involved when a woman is found strangled. Routine mystery at least moves quickly.

Strategic Air Command (1955)**½ James Stewart, June Allyson. Somewhat interesting drama about the workings of the Strategic Air Command: the atom-carrying planes that help to maintain the peace, and the men who are involved. There's a romantic subplot which gives June Allyson a chance to shed a few tears but the highlights of the film are the aerial shots. (Dir: Anthony Mann, 114 mins.)

Strategy of Terror (1969)* Hugh O'Brian, Barbara Rush. Verbose, ponderous drama. Woman journalist discovers assassin's plot to subvert the United Nations. Originally seen as a two-parter on Kraft Suspense Theater called "In Darkness Waiting." Made-for-TV. (Dir: Jack Smight, 90 mins.)

Stratton Story, The (1949)*** James Stewart, June Allyson. This is the highly successful film biography based on the true story of baseball pitcher Monty Stratton who lost his leg in a hunting accident. The combination of Allyson and Stewart is used to good advantage in this sentimental comedy drama. (Dir: Sam Wood, 106 mins.)

Straw Dogs (1972)*** Dustin Hoffman, Susan George, David Warner. Controversial film because of a half-hour finale of unrivaled gruesome violence. Hoffman plays a young mathematician who has bought a house on the coast of England in the town where his wife grew up. His taunting and teasing wife (Miss George) is a sexual come-on to the men of the town, and after she has been raped, Hoffman is forced to act. Much of this premise is unbelievable, but the most interesting and effective sequence remains the charged ending where Hoffman gradually begins to enjoy the violence. (Dir: Sam Peckinpah, 113 mins.)

Strawberry Blonde (1941)*** Rita Hayworth, James Cagney, Olivia de Havilland. Cagney supports this little comedy about New York in the gay 90's. Jim's all over the picture so, in spite of a frail story, you may enjoy yourself. (Dir: Raoul Walsh, 97 mins.)

Strawberry Statement, The (1970)** Kim Darby, Bruce Davison. This tense drama about the college upheavals of the '60's doesn't pack a punch. Darby pushes too hard as the strong-willed girl who turns Davison from a mildly concerned college boy into a radical of sorts. (Dir: Stuart Hagmann, 103 mins.)

Street Is My Beat, The (1966)* Shary Marshall, Todd Lasswell. Young girl falls for high-class procurer, becomes involved in his line of work. Clumsy, distasteful. (Dir: Irvin Berwick, 93 mins.)

Street of Chance (1930)*** William Powell, Kay Francis, Jean Arthur. The life and loves of a notorious gambler who faces tragedy to protect his brother. Drama based vaguely on Arnold Rothstein's career stands the test of time remarkably well. Good performances. (Dir: John Cromwell)

Street of Chance (1942)*** Burgess Meredith, Claire Trevor. Amnesia victim regains his memory to find he is wanted for murder. Compact mystery melodrama boasts an excellent cast, good script. (Dir: Jack Hively, 74 mins.)

Street Scene (1931)***½ Elmer Rice's picture of life in the tenement district, adapted by King Vidor from the famous Broadway play, with Sylvia Sidney. Still a powerful finely made drama. (Dir: King Vidor, 90 mins.)

Street with No Name, The (1948) ***½ Mark Stevens, Richard Widmark, Lloyd Nolan. Another of those exciting semi-documentary films dealing with the FBI. Nothing unusual about the plot of an agent infiltrating the gang but beautifully done. (Dir: William Keighley, 91 mins.)

Streetcar Named Desire, A (1951) **** Vivien Leigh, Marlon Brando, Kim Hunter, Karl Malden. Superb adult drama. Well directed by Elia Kazan. The Tennessee Williams play about a neurotic woman who stays with her sister and her brute of a husband, the resulting tragedy. Explosively potent scenes, powerfully acted. Brando here sets a pattern for a host of poor actors without his prodigious talent. (122 mins.)

Streets of Laredo (1949)*** William Holden, Macdonald Carey, William Bendix. Two outlaws who have gone straight meet up with their former partner after many years, who is still on the wrong side of the law. Good western with more plot than usual. (Dir: Leslie Fenton, 92 mins.)

Strictly Dishonorable (1951)** Ezio Pinza, Janet Leigh. Noted opera singer takes steps to combat a newspaper's ire, finds himself in a compromising situation. An attempt to draw upon Pinza's "South Pacific" fame, but the comedy lacks punch.

(Dirs: Melvin Frank, Norman Panama, 86 mins.)

Strike (Russian, 1924)**** I. Kluvkin, Alexander Antonov, Grigori Alexandrov. One of the great achievements of the Russian directorial genius Sergei M. Eisenstein during the silent-film era. Story concerns a strike in tsarist Russia, spurred by the suicide of one of the workers after he is fired. When peaceful efforts to settle the strike fail, the state sends in cavalrymen who slaughter the strikers and their families. In this new recently released version an obtrusive soundtrack has been added. (82 mins.)

Strike Force (1975)* Cliff Gorman, Donald Blakely, Richard Gere. Pilot film about an anti-crime unit consisting of a New York City cop, a state trooper, and a Federal agent, hampered by a vague plot and funereal pacing. Gere is particularly wooden as the deer-stalking state trooper. Made-for-TV. (Dir: Barry Shear, 72 mins.)

Strike Me Deadly (1963)*½ Gary Clarke, Jeanine Riley. Ranger on his honeymoon witnesses a murder, tries to elude the killer in a raging fire. Weak melodrama gets no help from the production end.

Strike Me Pink (1935)***½ Eddie Cantor, Ethel Merman, Brian Donlevy. Very good Cantor film with songs by Harold Arlen as a bonus feature. Merman is around for songs and fun and Cantor is at his peak in this yarn set in an amusement park. (Dir: Norman Taurog, 110 mins.)

Strike Up the Band (1940)**½ Mickey Rooney, Judy Garland. All Rooney plus a dash of Garland in this overplotted musical which comes gloriously to life when the stars perform. (Dir: Busby Berkeley, 120 mins.)

Strip, The (1951)**½ Mickey Rooney, Sally Forrest, Vic Damone. Occasionally absorbing drama about an ex-soldier who tries to resume his career as a drummer after he gets out of the service but gets side tracked by a group of racketeers. Good musical numbers by many guest artists, including Vic Damone, Kay Brown, Louis Armstrong, Jack Teagarden, and Monica Lewis. (Dir: Leslie Kardos, 85 mins.)

Stripper, The (1963)**½ Joanne Woodward, Richard Beymer, Claire Trevor. Apart from a valiant try by Joanne Woodward in a role that required a Marilyn Monroe-type to carry it off successfully, this film is pure soap opera. Miss Woodward plays a girl working in a run-down road show, who decides to try for a new life and ends up falling for a young lad. Based on William Inge's play "Loss of Roses," which was a quick, deserved flop on Broadway. (Dir: Franklin Schaffner, 95 mins.)

Strongest Man in the World, The (1975)** Kurt Russell. Disney family fare. Simple-minded plot. Kurt Russell engagingly plays a college student who comes up with a vitamin formula that gives him superhuman strength. The villains of this piece are execs from a cereal company who try to get the secret formula. (Dir: Vincent McEveety, 92 mins.)

Student Prince, The (1954)** Ann Blyth, Edmund Purdom. Stuffy prince is sent to Heidelberg U. to learn how to unwind, and he does, falling for a winsome waitress. Corny operetta, with the voice of Mario Lanza on the soundtrack. (Dir: Richard Thorpe, 107 mins.)

Studs Lonigan (1960)** Christopher Knight, Frank Gorshin, Venetia Stevenson, Jack Nicholson. Rambling tale about the life and loves of a young drifter on Chicago's South Side in the 1920's, suffers from Knight's stiff acting in the lead role and a trite ending. Visually excellent, captures atmosphere of era. Nicholson has improved a lot! (Dir: Irving Lerner, 103 mins.)

Study in Terror, A (Great Britain-West Germany, 1965)**½ John Neville, Donald Houston, Anthony Quayle. Great detective Sherlock Holmes faces the villainous "Jack the Ripper" in this entertaining suspense tale buoyed by a flawless British cast. Action-packed, sly, and full of gore as a counterpoint to Holmes' staid sleuthing. (Dir: James Hill, 94 mins.)

Stump Run (1960)* Edgar Buchanan, Slim Pickens. Backwoods mountaineers' escapades involve moonshining, rival stills, and temperance vigilantes. Slim pickin's indeed! (Dir: Edward Dew, 78 mins.)

Stuntman (1959)** Gina Lollobrigida, Robert Viharo, Marisa Mell. Movie stunt man enticed to rob Indian statue by a pair of lovelies. If Miss Lollobrigida entices you, then steal a peek at this one. (Dir: Marcello Baldi, 95 mins.)

Subject Was Roses, The (1968)***½ Patricia Neal, Jack Albertson, Martin Sheen. Though Frank D. Gilroy's Pulitzer Prize-winning, intensely interesting three-character play is necessarily expanded in its transformation to the screen, it remains an appealing and provocative drama. It is the story of a young man who returns home from his Army duty after World War II, only to find his quarreling parents still engaged in battle. Sheen as the young man and Albertson as the father recreate their Broadway roles successfully. As for Miss Neal, this performance marked her return to acting after her near-fatal illness, playing the difficult role of the mother. (Dir: Ulu Grosbard, 107 mins.)

Submarine Command (1951)**½ William Holden, Nancy Olson, William Bendix. Moderately entertaining war drama (Korean) with good performances by the principals. Holden plays a sub commander who is plagued with self-doubt about his part in a past incident which cost some men their lives. The drama unfolds rather slowly but it should keep your interest. (Dir: John Farrow, 87 mins.)

Submarine Patrol (1938)***½ Richard Greene, Nancy Kelly, Preston Foster. Exciting tale of a World War I tub of a sub-chaser is good fare thanks to John Ford's direction. Nancy Kelly's screen debut, and she makes the most of her role. (Dir: John Ford, 95 mins.)

Submarine Raiders (1942)**½ John Howard, Marguerite Chapman. Exciting, above average "B," supposedly dramatizing some of the events that took place in the Pacific December 6-7, 1941.

Submarine X-1 (British, 1968)** James Caan, Rupert Davies. Scenic shenanigans as naval commander Caan trains three crews to man midget submarines and go against a huge German destroyer during WW I. Caan's acting is stoic, and the movie really becomes submerged by the scenes shot on sound stages. (Dir: William Graham, 89 mins.)

Subterfuge (U.S.-Great Britain, 1968)* Gene Barry, Joan Collins, Richard Todd, Suzanna Leigh. Barry plays an American agent forced to assist British intelligence in a manhunt for a defector. Slight suspense,

O.K. acting. (Dir: Peter Graham Scott, 92 mins.)

Subterraneans, The (1960)* Leslie Caron, George Peppard, Janice Rule, Nanette Fabray. Trashy, watered down version of Jack Kerouac's interesting novel, badly directed by Ranald MacDougall. Story about an ersatz-hip melange of beats, bores, bemused beauties and pre-hippie types in San Francisco. Tame stuff now, but it still cheapens and distorts the original material. (Dir: Ranald MacDougall, 89 mins.)

Subway in the Sky (British, 1959)** Van Johnson, Hildegarde Neff. Van Johnson stars in this somewhat muddled adventure about an American doctor in post-war Berlin who gets involved with murder, the black market and a glamorous nightclub entertainer. (Dir: Muriel Box, 85 mins.)

Success, The (Italian, 1965)***½ Vittorio Gassman, Anouk Aimee, Jean-Louis Trintignant. Real-estate man consumed with the desire for success despite the ordinary comforts sacrifices his happiness in his quest. Well-acted drama tells its story with the moral sharply outlined. Gassman is excellent and again shows that he's an actor with a truly staggering range. (Dir: Dino Risi, 103 mins.)

Such Good Friends (1971)*** Dyan Cannon, James Coco, Jennifer O'Neill, Ken Howard. Not an easy entry to rate or describe. About a sexually frustrated wife (Cannon) who discovers that her ailing husband has been philandering with most of their female friends, and then promptly sets out to make up for lost time by popping into bed with any willing male. Some of the scenes and dialogue are sardonic and funny, some witless and vulgar. (But it has one distinction no matter what—it's the only American film released by a major company that compares the relative merits of vaginal and anal intercourse.) Director Otto Preminger's penchant for vulgarity is evident throughout. Based on Lois Gould's titillating novel: the screen credit goes to a fictional name, but Elaine May and the husband-and-wife screenwriting team of John Dunne and Joan Didion all worked on the screenplay. (101 mins.)

Sudden Danger (1955)*** Bill Elliott,

Tom Drake, Beverly Garland. Detective helps a blind man, whose sight is restored after an operation, to track down his mother's murderer. Rates well above the usual Grade B run—exceptionally good direction, logical script, good performances. (Dir: Hubert Cornfield, 85 mins.)

Sudden Fear (1954)*** Joan Crawford, Jack Palance. Wealthy lady playwright marries a worthless actor who plans to murder her. Well acted, smoothly produced suspense thriller. (Dir: David Miller, 110 mins.)

Sudden Terror (Great Britain, 1970) **½ Lionel Jeffries, Susan George, Mark Lester. A fairly well done suspense thriller in the accepted vein. Mark Lester, an adorable child actor from "Oliver," is prone to telling tall tales. So you can't really blame his sister and grandfather when they reject his story about witnessing the assassination of a visiting African president on the island of Malta. It's not boring. (Dir: John Hough, 95 mins.)

Suddenly (1954)***½ Frank Sinatra, Sterling Hayden. A hired killer hits a small town bent on assassination. Sinatra's bravado performance as the cold-blooded thug, plus crisp direction, make this thriller above average. (Dir: Lewis Allen, 77 mins.)

Suddenly It's Spring (1947)*½ Fred MacMurray, Paulette Goddard. Forced, contrived comedy about a lawyer who wants to divorce his wife. She doesn't want to divorce him, and away we go. (Dir: Mitchell Leisen, 87 mins.)

Suddenly, Last Summer (1960)*** Elizabeth Taylor, Katharine Hepburn, Montgomery Clift. One of Tennessee Williams' macabre one-act plays has been watered down and transferred to the screen in an uneven but nevertheless effective drama. Miss Taylor is having a mental breakdown because of the events of last summer when she accompanied her homosexual cousin on his annual European jaunt and witnessed his death at the hands of starving young men. Dr. Clift is hired by Aunt Katharine to commit Miss Taylor to an asylum, but he wants to get to the bottom of the mystery, and this sets the stage for a long confession scene in which Miss Taylor overacts all over the place. (Dir: Joseph L. Mankiewicz, 114 mins.)

Suez (1938)*** Tyrone Power, Loretta Young, Annabella. Well photographed and lavish film which is supposed to tell the true story of how the Suez Canal was built. If it had done that, it might have been a great film instead of another contrived epic. (Dir: Allan Dwan, 104 mins.)

Sugarland Express, The (1974)***½ Goldie Hawn, William Atherton, Michael Sacks, Ben Johnson. Rewarding comedy-drama. Based on a 1969 true story, the film tells of a young Texas couple (Hawn and Atherton) running from the law, trying to regain custody of their baby, who has been farmed out to a foster family while they were in prison for some petty thefts. The chase becomes a circus as they cross the state in full view of TV cameras, stopping to sign autographs, trailed by a cavalcade of state troopers who hang back for fear of hurting the hostage—another state trooper. Goldie Hawn is terrific, as is everyone else, and the movie will have you alternately laughing and crying, but thoroughly entertained. On the strength of this, Spielberg was entrusted with "Jaws." Fine screenplay by Hal Barwood, Mathew Robbins. (Dir: Steven Spielberg, 110 mins.)

Suicide Run (1970)**½ Michael Caine, Cliff Robertson, Henry Fonda, Ian Bannen, Harry Andrews. Theatrically released as "Too Late the Hero," this war drama sports a thoroughly professional cast. The antique plot has British troops led by American Robertson on a suicide mission behind Japanese lines during WW II. Most of the movie concerns the troops escaping after the mission while being pursued by a Japanese officer who doesn't allow the men a moment's rest. Location filming in the Philippines. (Dir: Robert Aldrich, 133 mins.)

Suleiman the Conqueror (Italian, 1962)*½ Edmund Purdom, Giorgia Moll. Another of the Italian-made (English-dubbed) epics which should appeal to young adventure fans. This one deals with the beginnings of the Ottoman Empire, as seen through the eyes of an Italian quickie-movie mogul.

Sullivans, The (1944)**** Anne Baxter, Thomas Mitchell. The story of the five heroic brothers who died gallantly in Naval service during World War II. Well-made drama pulls the heartstrings in professional fashion. (Dir: Lloyd Bacon, 111 mins.)

Sullivan's Empire (1967)* Martin Milner, Clu Gulager. Three sons are reunited when they hear that their plantation-owner father has been kidnapped. The father is faced with headhunters, and you're faced with a boring picture. Originally made as a pilot for a TV series and shows it. (Dirs: Harvey Hart and Thomas Carr, 85 mins.)

Sullivan's Travels (1942)***½ Joel McCrea, Veronica Lake. Story of a movie director who wants to make a dramatic film so he sets out to learn about life. Preston Sturges makes this a fascinating adventure in off-beat screen entertainment. (91 mins.)

Summer and Smoke (1961)***½ Laurence Harvey, Geraldine Page, Rita Moreno. Plain, repressed girl secretly loves a dashing young medical student, but he prefers the wilder life, until it's too late. Somber, powerful Tennessee Williams drama receives superb performances, especially from Page who gives a haunting flawless portrayal, repeating her stage triumph. (Dir: Peter Glenville, 118 mins.)

Summer Holiday (1947)**½ Mickey Rooney, Gloria De Haven. Musical version of O'Neill's "Ah, Wilderness!" loses much of the original's quality and receives no aid trom a commonplace score. (Dir: Rouben Mamoulian, 92 mins.)

Summer Holiday (1963)*** Cliff Richards, Lauri Peters. A pleasant old-fashioned-plot musical. A group of young men travel across Europe in a double decker bus, and before too long they meet pretty young girls who join them. It's an innocent musical spree from then on, and fun for viewers.

Summer Love (1958)** John Saxon, Molly Bee, Judi Meredith. Teenage romance and complications when a musical combo lands a job at a co-ed summer camp. Okay for the younger set. (Dir: Charles Haas, 85 mins.)

Summer of '42 (1971)**** Jennifer O'Neill, Gary Grimes. A lovely nostalgic evocative film about a 15-year-old boy's coming of sexual age during the summer of 1942 in an island vacation community off New England. (Filmed on location on the Mendocino coast in northern California.) Some could label this simple tale about Hermie's (Grimes') adolescent crush on the beautiful 22-year-old war bride (O'Neill) corny and overly sentimental . . . but it works beautifully, I think, and that's its saving grace. The scene in which the war bride learns she has become a widow and subsequently goes to bed with the young boy is tasteful and moving. Screenplay by Herman Raucher is admittedly autobiographical. (Dir: Robert Mulligan, 102 mins.)

Summer Place, A (1959)*½ Richard Egan, Dorothy McGuire, Sandra Dee, Troy Donahue. A farrago of bad taste. Sleazy tale of a businessman who returns to his summer home, meets an old flame; love is rekindled, plus an affair begins between his daughter and her son. Rather sickening in its implications, made more so by the filmmakers' coating of pious sentiment. (Dir: Delmer Daves, 130 mins.)

Summer Soldiers (Japanese, 1971)*** Keith Sykes, Lee Reisen, Kazuo Kitamura. Interesting if partially unrealized story about an American GI stationed in Japan who deserts rather than go to Vietnam. Film is hampered by the unconvincing acting of the deserter (Sykes), but builds interest as we see Sykes and another GI aided by sympathetic Japanese civilians, who hide them from the American military establishment. It's worth noting that, whatever its shortcomings, this Japanese film asks more questions about the American presence in Vietnam than virtually any American feature film we can think of. (Dir: Hiroshi Teshigahara, 103 mins.)

Summer Stock (1950)**½ Judy Garland, Gene Kelly. Tuneful musical tailored for the talents of the stars. The plot concerns a farm, run by Judy, which is invaded by a group of show people who want to turn the barn into a summer theater. This sets the stage for many songs and dances including Judy's big number "Get Happy." (Dir: Charles Walters, 100 mins.)

Summer Storm (1944)*** Linda Darnell, George Sanders. A girl whose charm is fatal to men finally has it prove tragic to herself. Strong, well made drama. Good performances. (Dir: Douglas Sirk, 106 mins.)

Summer Wishes, Winter Dreams (1973)***½ Joanne Woodward, Martin Balsam, Sylvia Sidney. Poignant, often perceptive story written by Stewart Stern about a middle-aged New York couple who take a European trip to rekindle their flagging marriage. Miss Woodward deserved her Academy Award nomination for her luminous, deeply affecting portrayal of the housewife who clings to her memories of a childhood farm. They return to Bastogne and the sites of his World War II duty. Balsam and Sylvia Sidney (another Oscar nominee) are first-rate throughout. (Dir: Gilbert Cates, 93 mins.)

Summer Without Boys, A (1973)*** Barbara Bain, Kay Lenz, Michael Moriarty. Nostalgia runs high in this tale set on the home front during WW II. Drama about an attractive woman and her teen-aged daughter and the romantic confrontations they face during a summer stay at a resort. Both the dialogue and the physical production carefully evoke the tension and loneliness that pervaded the wartime atmosphere. Made-for-TV. (Dir: Jeannot Szwarc, 73 mins.)

Summertime (1955)***½ Katharine Hepburn, Rossano Brazzi. Romantic story, set in Venice, about an American schoolmarm and an Italian merchant. It's the kind of film you have to be in the mood for, but you'll seldom see as perceptive or touching a rendition of a spinster tentatively searching for affection as Hepburn here delivers. The scenes in color of Venice are lovely. (Dir: David Lean, 99 mins.)

Summertime Killer, The (French-Italian, 1972)** Karl Malden, Christopher Mitchum, Raf Vallone. Confusing revenge tale. Young man plans to punish the men who executed his father several years before. New York ex-cop (Malden) goes after him, providing several good chases, the picture's main asset. (Dir: Antonio Isasi, 109 mins.)

Summertree (1971)** Michael Douglas, Barbara Bel Geddes, Jack Warden, Brenda Vaccaro. A sensitive play mangled in its transfer to film. Douglas plays the young man torn by his parents' beliefs and his own convictions about the Vietnam War

and his life in general. Based on the hit off-Broadway play by Ron Cowen, but poorly adapted. Anthony Newley's direction doesn't help either. (88 mins.)

Sun Also Rises, The (1957)**½ Errol Flynn, Ava Gardner, Tyrone Power. Hemingway's sprawling novel about the drifters and dreamers known as the lost generation during the twenties is uneven in its transference to the screen, but contains some good on-location photography and a colorful performance by Flynn as a drunken bon vivant. (Dir: Henry King, 129 mins.)

Sun Comes Up, The (1948)** Jeanette MacDonald, Lloyd Nolan. Woman who loses her son falls in love with an orphan boy. Lassie is around to add an extra tear to your moist eyes. (Dir: Richard Thorpe, 93 mins.)

Sun Shines Bright (1953)***½ Charles Winninger, Arleen Whelan, John Russell. Small town judge has a hard time running for re-election. Superb piece of Americana directed by John Ford—one of his best films. (92 mins.)

Sun Valley Serenade (1941)*** Sonja Henie, John Payne. Pleasant, entertaining musical set in the fabulous Idaho resort. You'll see and hear the late great Glenn Miller's band and its manager in the film is Milton Berle. (Dir: H. Bruce Humberstone, 86 mins.)

Sunday Bloody Sunday (Great Britain, 1971)**** Glenda Jackson, Peter Finch, Peggy Ashcroft, Murray Head, Bessie Love, Vivian Pickles. A remarkably moving, graceful film about the absence of love, involving a bisexual triangle between Finch, Jackson and Head. This was John Schlesinger's first film since "Midnight Cowboy," and he chose an intelligent, altogether splendid screenplay by New Yorker magazine film critic and novelist Penelope Gilliatt. Concerns a young sculptor, Bob Elkin, played by Head, who is loved by both Finch and Jackson. In other hands this could be an exploitative theme, but as written by Gilliatt and brilliantly directed by Schlesinger, the roles are illumined by the wonderfully restrained and moving performances of Finch and Jackson. A triumph for all concerned. Based on an idea by Schlesinger. (110 mins.)

Sunday Encounter (French, 1959)** Bourvil, Danielle Darrieux, Arletty. An estranged couple find out that true love cannot be denied but not until they bore the audience with endless conversation.

Sunday in New York (1964)*** Jane Fonda, Rod Taylor, Cliff Robertson. A girl still pure meets a dashing young man and quite innocently has her brother thinking the wrong things. Comedy that can be called "cute," but pleasantly so—performances are refreshing, pace is smooth. (Dir: Peter Tewksbury, 105 mins.)

Sundays and Cybele (France, 1962)**** Hardy Kruger, Patricia Gozzi, Nicole Courcel. Touching, beautifully realized story about a troubled young man, an amnesiac who befriends an orphan girl, pretending to be her father and taking her on Sunday excursions in the park. Their relationship builds slowly. The man's psychotic tendencies are revealed as the story builds to a terrifying climax. The undertone of sexual attraction by both parties adds to the tension, and the actors are superb throughout. Don't miss it. (Dir: Serge Bourguignon, 110 mins.)

Sundown (1941)**½ Gene Tierney, Bruce Cabot, George Sanders. The British in Africa receive the aid of a jungle girl in defeating the attempts of the Nazis to take over. Well-produced but second-rate melodrama. (Dir: Henry Hathaway, 90 mins.)

Sundowners, The (1951)***½ Robert Preston, John Barrymore Jr. A renegade gunman rides in to cause trouble for a boy and his father. Topnotch western, well written, acted. (Dir: George Templeton, 83 mins.)

Sundowners, The (1960)**** Deborah Kerr, Robert Mitchum, Peter Ustinov. Excellent film about the people who earn their living in the sheep business in Australia. Director Fred Zinnemann gets beautiful performances from his cast and captures the scope of Australia in the superb on-location photography. A must for all ages. (133 mins.)

Sunrise at Campobello (1960)**** Ralph Bellamy, Greer Garson. Inspiring story of young FDR, his conquering of the crippling disease of polio enabling him to walk to the rostrum to nominate Al Smith at the Democratic Convention. Based on the stage play, with Bellamy repeating his fine performance as Roosevelt. Greer Garson is surprisingly effective as his wife. Heartwarming drama. Written by Dore Schary, (Dir: Vincent J. Donehue, 143 mins.)

Sunscorched (1964)*½ Mark Stevens, Mario Adorf, Marianne Koch. Would you believe a German-made western produced in Spain? Okay; it's about a group of outlaws who eventually get their just deserts. English-dubbed, thoroughly mediocre.

Sunset Boulevard (1950)**** Gloria Swanson, William Holden, Nancy Olson, Erich Von Stroheim. Magnificent Hollywood drama—rates with the great films of all time. Adult story of a down-and-out screenwriter who becomes the gigolo for a fading movie queen of the silent days who wishes to make a comeback. Fine performances, script, direction by Billy Wilder. Don't miss it. (110 mins.)

Sunshine (1973)*** Cristina Raines, Cliff De Young. An extraordinary tale about a free-spirited young woman, frenetically tied to life, destined to die of bone cancer at the age of 20. There are no overtones of the accommodating sweetness and resignation of Erich Segal's "Love Story." What is present is an adamant will to live and make every moment count, a wild cry that's more like a demand than a hope. Based on the true-life diary of a young woman, recorded on tape, it can't help but make you grit your teeth in sympathy. It's a bit overlong but the performances, particularly Raines as the girl, De Young as her devoted but agonized lover, and Vaccaro as her dedicated physician, are superb. The subsequent TV series was loosely based on this story. Made-for-TV. (Dir: Joseph Sargent, 130 mins.)

Sunshine Boys, The (1975)***½ George Burns, Walter Matthau, Richard Benjamin. Neil Simon's funny, touching play about two veteran vaudevillians who have shared a hate-love relationship for decades, works even better on the screen, thanks to Walter Matthau and George Burns' superb timing as the pair of disgruntled show-business codgers. Richard Benjamin also scores as Matthau's nephew who works valiantly to get the pair together for a TV reunion. The dialogue is delicious, and the stars know how to deliver it. George Burns won an Academy Award for this effort and he's wonderful. (Dir: Herbert Ross, 111 mins.)

Sunshine Patriot, The (1968)***½ Cliff Robertson, Dina Merrill. Under any conditions, this is a good spy story, but judged as a made-for-TV-film, it is an even more impressive achievement. The plot, a familiar one, has an experienced spy trapped behind the iron curtain, cleverly framing an American businessman and switching identities with him. What makes this so effective is that the characters are uniformly interesting, well played, and the story believable. Even the ending makes sense both dramatically and philosophically. The excellent cast is headed by Cliff Robertson in the dual role of spy and businessman, Dina Merrill as the latter's mistress, and Luther Adler is quite fascinating as the Communist security chief. (Dir: Joseph Sargent, 98 mins.)

Super Cops (1974)**½ Ron Leibman, David Selby. Leibman and Selby are much better than their material in this saga of two real-life New York cops (Greenberg and Hantz) who earned the nicknames of Batman and Robin because of their unorthodox methods in dealing with criminals. The twist here is that the two rookie cops actually work in the traffic division, but they wage their war on drug traffic during their own off-duty hours. Dedicated they certainly are, but the film makes them seem more comic-book heroic than documentary real-life cops. A poor man's version of "Serpico." (Dir: Gordon Parks Jr., 93 mins.)

Superdad (1974)* Bob Crane, Barbara Rush, Kathleen Cody, Kurt Russell, Joe Flynn. One of the more recent, most awful Disney efforts. Crane is a father trying to get closer to his teenaged daughter (Cody) by joining in on all her activities. The plotting is predictable, the script ludicrous, the actors struggle valiantly. Judith Lowry is effective as a college housemother. The kids should boycott this insensitive drivel. (Dir: Vincent McEveety, 95 mins.)

Support Your Local Gunfighter (1971) **½ James Garner, Suzanne Pleshette, Jack Elam, Joan Blondell, Harry Morgan. If you enjoyed

James Garner's breezy performance in the previous Western spoof, "Support Your Local Sheriff," you'll buy his equally casual playing in this broad tale of a gambler who runs away from a madam with marriage on her mind, and is mistaken for a gunfighter in the troubled town of Purgatory. The supporting cast, which aids and abets his antics, is uniformly hilarious. Garner is a charming farceur by now. (Dir: Burt Kennedy, 92 mins.)

Support Your Local Sheriff (1969) ***½ James Garner, Joan Hackett, Walter Brennan, Harry Morgan, Jack Elam. Droll western spoof with a funny turn by Garner as an adventurer who stumbles into a town which is feeling the bonanza of a gold rush and becomes its serious sheriff. The rowdy folks in town resent Garner's intrusion and their bouts with him supply many laughs. Miss Hackett impresses as a young miss who wants to be Garner's true love, and Brennan is wonderful as the head of the town's evil clan. If you liked "Cat Ballou" you'll enjoy "Sheriff." (Dir: Burt Kennedy, 93 mins.)

Suppose They Gave a War and Nobody Came (1970)** Brian Keith, Tony Curtis, Ernest Borgnine, Ivan Dixon. Deceptive title covers a mediocre service comedy about three old-time Army tankmen who have been stationed in a noncombatant base, and their war with the southern town in which it is located. The screenplay wavers from comedy to drama to satire, never maintaining a clear purpose. A recognizable supporting cast adds vitality. (Dir: Hy Averback, 113 mins.)

Surf Party (1964)* Bobby Vinton, Patricia Morrow. Youth will be surfed, and this time it's young love on the beach at Malibu! Vapid kids shaking their bottoms and jumping in and out of bed and onto surfboards. Don't bother crashing this waterlogged party.

Surgeon's Knife (British, 1957)** Donald Houston, Adrienne Corri. Confusing melodrama about a doctor who believes he has killed a patient through negligence and is being blackmailed for this act. Well acted but talky. (Dir: Gordon Parry, 75 mins.)

Surprise Package (1960)**½ Yul Brynner, Mitzi Gaynor, Noel Coward. Funny idea on paper, perhaps, but it doesn't smoothly transfer to the screen. Brynner plays a big-time gambler who is deported to his native Greece where he becomes involved with a phony King and some hot jewel dealings. Miss Gaynor hits the right note as a chorine who keeps Brynner company. (Dir: Stanley Donen, 100 mins.)

Surrender—Hell! (1959)*½ Keith Andes, Susan Cabot. Jumbled film about an American Colonel who forms a band of Filipino guerrillas to fight the Japanese during WW II. (Dir: John Barnwell, 85 mins.)

Survive! (Mexico, 1976)* Hugo Stiglitz, Norma Lazaren. Exploitative film based on the real-life incident about a group of air crash victims in 1972 in the Andes who resorted to cannibalism, feeding on the flesh of the dead passengers in order to survive. This is a trashy Mexican film produced in Latin America. The dubbing is poor. Some of the scenes may be too graphic for the squeamish! Banal American commentary added. (Dir: Rene Cardona, 86 mins.)

Susan and God (1940)**½ Joan Crawford, Fredric March, Ruth Hussey. Play which starred the great Gertrude Lawrence almost falls apart on the screen. Women will probably enjoy this story of a woman so wrapped up in religion she almost loses her family. (Dir: George Cukor, 115 mins.)

Susan Slade (1961)** Troy Donahue, Connie Stevens, Dorothy McGuire, Lloyd Nolan. Inexperienced girl is seduced, the guy gets himself killed, she finds she's pregnant, pop has a heart attack, the baby has an accident, but all's well as long as faithful stableboy Troy is around. For feminine masochists to take seriously, for others to have a good time keeping ahead of the plot. (Dir: Delmer Daves, 116 mins.)

Susan Slept Here (1954)*** Debbie Reynolds, Dick Powell, Anne Francis. Amusing comedy with Dick Powell, as a Hollywood writer, given custody of "Debbie" for a holiday period. Powell is good in a comedy performance and Debbie sparkles as usual. (Dir: Frank Tashlin, 98 mins.)

Suspect, The (1945)***½ Charles Laughton, Ella Raines. Middle-aged man married to a shrew falls in love with a younger woman and plans to do away with his wife. Superbly acted, suspenseful drama.

Suspended Alibi (British, 1957)* Patrick Holt, Honor Blackman. A wrong man is accused of murder and the action begins but never goes anywhere in this poor British "thriller." (Dir: Alfred Shaughnessy, 64 mins.)

Suspense (1946)*** Belita, Barry Sullivan, Albert Dekker. Small-time sharpie is hired by an ice palace, gets big ideas and plans to kill the owner to get his dough and his wife. Strong melodrama, a good job in all departments. (Dir: Frank Tuttle, 101 mins.)

Suspicion (1941)***½ Joan Fontaine, Cary Grant. Shy English girl marries a charming gentleman, then begins to suspect him of murderous intent. Thrilling Hitchcock melodrama, excellently acted, many suspenseful moments. (99 mins.)

Suzy (1936)** Jean Harlow, Cary Grant, Franchot Tone. Don't let the cast mislead you—this is an awful film in spite of them. Miss Harlow is pursuing Grant who wants other women and Franchot is her dead hubby who isn't dead. Set in France and England during 1914 so there's a few spies around too. (Dir: George Fitzmaurice, 90 mins.)

Svengali (British, 1955)** Hildegarde Neff, Donald Wolfit. The romantic and compelling drama of Trilby and Svengali is once more on the screen, this time not so successfully due to uneven performances and a mediocre script. (Dir: Noel Langley, 82 mins.)

Swamp of the Lost Monsters, The (Mexican, 1965)* Gaston Santos, Manola Savedra. Monster from a swamp throws the countryside into terror. Poor horror thriller dubbed in English.

Swamp Water (1941)**½ Walter Brennan, Walter Huston. Well acted drama of a fugitive hiding out in Georgia's Okefenokee Swamp. Acting does not make up for the confused script. (Dir: Jean Renoir, 90 mins.)

Swan, The (1956)**½ Grace Kelly, Alec Guinness, Louis Jourdan. A trio of attractive stars help to make this mild costume romance, based on Ference Molnar's play, entertaining. The plot revolves around Hungary's Crown Prince Albert's required selection of a wife and the intrigues surrounding his reluctant search.

This was Princess Grace's last film before she retired from the screen and the U.S.A. (Dir: Charles Vidor, 112 mins.)

Swashbuckler (1976)* Robert Shaw, James Earl Jones, Peter Boyle, Genevieve Bujold, Beau Bridges, Geoffrey Holder. Inept, embarrassing pirate film, circa 1718 in Jamaica. Plush production values and tongue-in-cheek tone don't hide the lack of plot and direction. Shaw grins enthusiastically throughout, Boyle wildly overacts as the villain of the piece, and Bujold is given a part so silly it can't be salvaged. Jamaica and the cast have never looked worse, thanks to bungling direction, among many other things. (Dir: James Goldstone, 101 mins.)

Sweet and Low Down (1944)*½ Benny Goodman, Lynn Bari, Jack Oakie. When the Goodman band plays this Grade B film is O. K. but unfortunately, there are many moments when they don't play. (Dir: Archie Mayo, 75 mins.)

Sweet Bird of Youth (1962)***½ Paul Newman, Geraldine Page, Ed Begley. No-goodnik causes more trouble when he returns to his home town accompanied by a neurotic, wasted in mind and body, suicidal actress. It's Tennessee Williams's absorbing play. Some fine performances, including an Academy Award one by Begley, keep things interesting. Page is simply fabulous, reason enough for tuning in, a truly virtuoso turn. (Dir: Richard Brooks, 120 mins.)

Sweet Charity (1969)*** Shirley MacLaine, John McMartin, Ricardo Montalban. An adaptation of Fellini's film "Nights of Cabiria." Musical saga of a dance-hall hostess with the proverbial heart of gold was a Broadway hit but the movie only partly duplicates its success. Miss MacLaine hits the right note as the pushed-around heroine but the production numbers are so overproduced that you soon lose sight of her splendid characterization. Bob Fosse directed with too much flash, as if he distrusted the impact of the material. Enough entertaining ingredients to sustain interest. (157 mins.)

Sweet Hostage (1975)**½ Martin Sheen, Linda Blair. A fine, colorful performance by Sheen as an escaped mental patient lifts this familiar kidnap yarn above the ordinary. He's an eccentric lunatic who spouts poetry, thinks fast on his feet and corrects the poor grammar of his uneducated teenage hostage, well played by Blair. Their scenes together in a remote mountain cabin hideout have an appealing simplicity which grows on you, until the inevitable tragic climax. One for the romanticists. Made-for-TV. (Dir: Lee Philips, 72 mins.)

Sweet Love, Bitter (1967)** Dick Gregory, Don Murray, Diane Varsi. Interracial friendships are unconvincingly explored in this tale about the downfall of a black jazz musician, partly based on the life of Charlie "Bird" Parker. Movie lacks depth, plausibility; actors flounder in their roles. Gregory, in his first film appearance, does as well as is possible. He's defiant, witty and self-assured in his role as the saxophonist. Based on the novel by John Alfred Williams, "Night Song." Danska co-authored the screenplay with Lewis Jacobs. (Dir: Herbert Danska, 92 mins.)

Sweet November (1968)*** Sandy Dennis, Anthony Newley, Theodore Bikel, Sandy Baron. A frequently touching, but maddening bittersweet comedy with a twist—this time she (Sandy Dennis) just wants to pop into bed with her various boyfriends without regret or apology, but he—or at least one of the he's—wants to get married. The reason for her hot pants in cool November is—well, Sandy is worth watching and finding out. Literate screenplay by Herman Raucher. (Dir: Robert Ellis Miller, 114 mins.)

Sweet Ride, The (1968)** Jacqueline Bisset, Tony Franciosa. The loves of a mod girl who hangs around with too many surfers and tennis bums for her own good. Sleazy tale made worth watching by the beauteous Jacqueline Bisset. With Michael Sarrazin, Bob Denver, Michael Wilding. (Dir: Harvey Hart, 110 mins.)

Sweet Rosie O'Grady (1943)*** Betty Grable, Robert Young. One of our World War II pin-up queens proves why in this foolish 1890s musical designed to show Betty's legs—which it does. (Dir: Irving Cummings, 74 mins.)

Sweet Saviour (1971)** Troy Donahue, Renay Granville. Distasteful exploitation of the Charles Manson killings. Donahue plays the leader of a "family" that takes over an orgy given by a pregnant actress in suburban New York. In the end, Donahue borrows a few forks and knives from the roast turkey and does in everyone. Makes you wish for Troy's "Hawaiian Eye" days. (Dir: Bob Roberts, 90 mins.)

Sweet Smell of Success (1957)******** Burt Lancaster, Tony Curtis. Biting, no-holds-barred look at the ruthless world of a powerful and evil New York columnist. Lancaster is miscast as the columnist. This is the film in which Tony Curtis emerged as a first rate actor and stopped being considered just another handsome Hollywood face. His slick, opportunistic press agent characterization is the backbone of this powerful drama. A much underrated film at the time of its initial release. (Dir: Alexander Mackendrick, 96 mins.)

Sweet Sweetback's Baadasssss Song (1971)******* Melvin Van Peebles, Simon Chuckster, Hubert Scales. A bitter black fairy tale, where all the blacks are potent studs and fine folks, and the whites are as evil as they are ignorant—and they are very stupid indeed. One of the black exploitation films of the period that tried to hit big at the box office by waging war on Whitey. Some effective, raunchy scenes, mostly those with Peebles himself, who plays Sweetback. You won't be seeing this angry entry unedited on commercial TV for a long while. Peebles plays a black, sexually inexhaustible ladykiller on the lam from the police. Written, directed and musical score by Melvin Van Peebles. (97 mins.)

Sweetheart of the Gods (German, 1959)****½** Peter Van Eyck, Ruth Leuwerik. Tragic drama of an actress who rises to fame during Hitler's time, finds the regime intolerable. Based on fact, this story moves slowly but has a good performance by Miss Leuwerik, realistic picture of the times. Dubbed in English.

Sweethearts (1938)******* Jeanette MacDonald, Nelson Eddy, Frank Morgan. Victor Herbert's music, MacDonald and Eddy in modern clothes for a change plus a fine supporting cast make this good musical entertainment. (Dir: W. S. Van Dyke, 120 mins.)

Sweethearts on Parade (1953)****** Ray Middleton, Lucille Norman. Proprietress of a music school sees her ex-husband return to town heading a carnival show. Leisurely turn of the century musical, might please the oldsters.

Swimmer, The (1968)*****½** Burt Lancaster, Janice Rule, Janet Landgard, Diana Muldaur, Kim Hunter. Absorbing story about a loser (wonderfully played by Lancaster) gradually flipping out of WASP society in suburban Connecticut, because he loathes the life style and mores of affluent executives. Underrated film that never got the attention it deserved because the releasing company —Columbia Pictures—didn't have the foggiest idea of how to handle this film which was kept lying around for a couple of years after it was finished by director Frank Perry, and then changed with the addition of several scenes directed by Sydney Pollack, notably Lancaster's major confrontation at the end of the film with Janice Rule. Lancaster does swim his way down various pools in Westport, Conn., but viewers who want something different will follow stroke by stroke. Screenwriter Eleanor Perry had an unusual film problem—expanding a very brief John Cheever short story into a full-length feature. She handled the task with enormous taste and skill. (94 mins.)

Swindle, The (Italian, 1955)****½** Broderick Crawford, Richard Basehart, Giulietta Masina. English-dubbed drama of three swindlers who con the poor people of Rome out of their money. Directed by Federico Fellini, one of his less successful efforts. Some good moments, mostly confused, wandering drama. (92 mins.)

Swing Time (1936)*****½** Fred Astaire, Ginger Rogers. Dancer with a yen for gambling has trouble saving money to marry, and when he does, he has fallen for another girl. Astaire-Rogers dancing is tops, and the slight story doesn't get in the way too much. (Dir: George Stevens, 120 mins.)

Swinger, The (1966)***** Ann-Margret, Tony Franciosa, Robert Coote. Authoress (A-M) writes a steaming sex novel and proceeds to live out her heroine's adventures. Leering farce, pretending to be a morality fable for addle-brained teenagers, with Ann-

Margret looking and acting incapable of reading, much less writing a book. It's films like this that give orgies a bad name! (Dir: George Sidney, 81 mins.)

Swinger's Paradise (1965)* Cliff Richards, Walter Slezak, Susan Hampshire. Supersenseless plot about boy, working as a stunt man in a movie, who simultaneously makes another movie because the leading girl isn't being used right. Treat this right and shut it off. (85 mins.)

Swingin' Along (1962)*½ Tommy Noonan, Peter L. Marshall, Barbara Eden, Ted Knight. Silly musical farce about an idiot who finally accomplishes something—a musical sonata—only to have it blown out the window. Some tempting musical tidbits were thrown in at the last minute by the producers, including a rare view of Ray Charles belting out his classic twist number, "What'd I Say?" Ted Knight plays the priest before his "Mary Tyler Moore Show" fame. (Dir: Charles Barton, 74 mins.)

Swingin' Summer, A (1965)*½ Raquel Welch, the Righteous Brothers, James Stacy. Romance, jealousy, and singing among a group of overdeveloped teen-agers. Plot is hardly the point, and the singing, which was good at the time, now seems dated. Miss Welch, early in her career, plays a bookworm with glasses who learns to "groove." (82 mins.)

Swingtime Johnny (1943)**½ Andrews Sisters, Harriet Hilliard, Peter Cookson. Sister act quit show biz and go to work in a defense plant during World War II. Sprightly little musical, better than the usual run of its kind. Some amusing sequences.

Swiss Family Robinson (1940)*** Thomas Mitchell, Freddie Bartholomew, Tim Holt. The classic of a family marooned on an uninhabited island who find a peaceful existence away from the troubles of the civilized world. Tastefully produced, well acted. (Dir: Edward Ludwig, 93 mins.)

Swiss Family Robinson (1964)*** John Mills, Dorothy McGuire. Living in a tree house with all the conveniences of home, riding ostriches, and playing with elephants on a flowered and fruited island—that's

the Robinson family after having left their Swiss home for New Guinea, and being shipwrecked along the way. In this Disney version of the Johann Wyss novel, everything is pleasing, and the rout of the invading pirates is cheered on by all. Fun for families and dreamers alike. (Dir: Ken Annakin, 126 mins.)

Swiss Family Robinson, The (1975) **½ Martin Milner, Pat Delany, Eric Olson, Michael-James Wixted. The family-fare adventure-epic which never looks tired, even though it has been done many times before. Irwin Allen (the disaster-film emperor) turned out this handsomely mounted version. Story of the shipwrecked Robinsons and their few friends, circa 19th century. Milner, Delany and youngsters Olson and Wixted go at it with energy. Special effects enhance the production. Made-for-TV. (Dir: Harry Harris, 100 mins.)

Switch (1975)** Robert Wagner, Eddie Albert, Charles Durning. Wagner and Albert team up as private eyes, playing the old con game to catch their mark, and they aren't hard to take as the smooth operator and the by-the-book ex-cop. With Durning as the chief law officer, the actors are superior to the material. Made-for-TV. (Dir: Robert Day, 72 mins.)

Sword and the Dragon, The (Russian, 1958)**½ Legendary hero Ilya Mourometz, armed with a magic sword, goes forth to fight the Mongol hordes. Generally entertaining English-dubbed fantasy, despite some naive scenes, hammy heroics. Lavish production, some good trick camerawork.

Sword in the Desert (1949)**½ Dana Andrews, Marta Toren, Stephen McNally. Moderately effective drama about the underground movement that smuggled refugees out of Europe to the Palestine coast. The actors play it straight and there's enough suspense to sustain action fans. (Dir: George Sherman, 100 mins.)

Sword of Alibaba (1965)*½ Peter Mann, Jocelyn Lane. Caliph's son thwarts the evil plans of a villainous Mongol. It's all been done before, in the Maria Montez era; in fact, this cheapie uses much footage from the original "Ali Baba and the 40 Thieves," which doesn't match the new footage. A costume clinker. (Dir: Virgil Vogel, 81 mins.)

Sword of Damascus (Italian, 1962)* Tony Russell, Gianni Solaro. Thief is sheltered from Roman soldiers, falls for the daughter of his protector. Weak costume adventure dubbed in English.

Sword of El Cid, The (Italian, 1962)* Roland Carey, Sandro Moretti. Two counts face stiff penalties for brutality to their wives, the daughters of the Cid. Laborious costume adventure dubbed in English. (Dir: Miguel Iglesias, 85 mins.)

Sword of Granada (Spanish, 1960)*½ Cesar Romero, Katy Jurado. Tired swashbuckler about a dashing adventurer who saves the day. Good photography, little else.

Sword of Islam, The (Italian, 1962)* Silvana Pampanini, Abed Elaziz. Princess struggles to save her people during the Islamic-Tartar invasions. Poor costume adventure dubbed in English.

Sword of Lancelot (1963)*** Cornel Wilde, Jean Wallace, Brian Aherne. The love story of Lancelot, Guinevere, and King Arthur, without the "Camelot" music but with an abundance of action, scope, and fidelity to the old English legend. Better than usual swashbuckling melodramatics, a credit to Wilde as both star and director. (Dir: Cornel Wilde, 116 mins.)

Sword of Sherwood Forest (British, 1961)**½ Richard Greene, Peter Cushing. Once again brave Robin Hood outwits the evil sheriff of Nottingham. Lively swashbuckler, not a compilation of the TV series but a completely original story. Fun for the kiddies. (Dir: Terence Fisher, 80 mins.)

Sword of the Conqueror (Italian, 1962)*½ Jack Palance, Eleonora Rossi-Drago. Leader of warlike empire covets a beauty of the opposition. Bad performances, big action, English-dubbing. (Dir: Carlo Campogalliani, 85 mins.)

Sword of the Empire (Italian, 1963)* Lang Jeffries, Enzo Tarasco. Roman consul infiltrates an enemy camp to check on reports of a barbarian invasion. Poorly done.

Sword Without a Country (Italian, 1965)*½ Jose Jaspe, Leonora Ruffo, Folco Lulli. Those peasants are rising again, this time led by a hero

who loves a nobleman's daughter. English-dubbed yawn.

Swordsman of Siena (France-Italy, 1962)*½ Stewart Granger, Sylva Koscina, Christine Kaufmann. MGM tried to imitate its golden days with this swashbuckler of a mercenary adventurer in the 16th century who finds his sense of moral duty while at the side of a princess, midway through the fighting. Alas, Granger is no Fairbanks or Flynn, and the plot shows its age. (Dir: Gus Agosta, 97 mins.)

Sylvia (1965)**½ Carroll Baker, George Maharis. An old-fashioned melodrama about a young lady who tries to better her poor lot but takes all the wrong steps. Good performances by the supporting cast, particularly Ann Sothern as a wisecracking ticket taker in a midway amusement gallery, spark this otherwise all too familiar story. (Dir: Gordon Douglas, 115 mins.)

Sylvia Scarlett (1936)*** Katharine Hepburn, Cary Grant, Brian Aherne. Young girl becomes involved with smugglers. Entertaining costume comedy-drama. (Dir: George Cukor, 100 mins.)

Symphony for a Massacre (France-Italy, 1963)**½ Claude Dauphin, Michael Auclair, Jean Rochefort. Excellent acting adds lustre to an interesting crime tale, as a member of a gang decides to go independent with his friends' money. Lack of pat moral ending, and an impassive emotionalism make this an offbeat entry. (Dir: Jacques Deray, 110 mins.)

Synanon (1965)**½ Chuck Connors, Alex Cord, Stella Stevens, Eartha Kitt. A bit of truth about drug addicts combined with Hollywood melodrama. This multiplotted story is set in Synanon, an actual rehabilitation community for drug addicts in California. Some very downbeat characters and situations are depicted, but the film ends on a hopeful note. Alex Cord registers in an overwritten role. (Dir: Richard Quine, 107 mins.)

Syncopation (1942)** Adolphe Menjou, Bonita Granville, Jackie Cooper. Story of the beginnings of jazz, and of a young trumpeter who wanted to make good. Good jazz music partially makes up for unsure story. (Dir: William Dieterle, 88 mins.)

System, The (1953)** Frank Lovejoy,

Joan Weldon, Bob Arthur. A young man discovers that his father is behind a big city's gambling combine. Overacted and clumsily written. (Dir: Lewis Seiler, 90 mins.)

T-Men (1947)***½ Dennis O'Keefe, Alfred Ryder. Documentary-type story of how Treasury agents broke up a gang of counterfeiters. Excellent; one of the best of its kind, with special mention for a tight script, Anthony Mann's lucid direction, John Alton's superb photography. (96 mins.)

Tabarin (French, 1958)** Sylvia Lopez, Michel Piccoli. The saga of a nightclub in Paris, its owners, stars, and patrons. Some music to brighten an otherwise dull film.

Take a Giant Step (1959)**** Estelle Hemsley, Ruby Dee, Frederick O'Neal, Ellen Holly, Johnny Nash. Poignant drama and an important one, because "Giant Step," at the time of its release, was the most forthright statement yet made by a major Hollywood film of what it felt like to be a Negro in a white-dominated Northern town. A Negro youth (Nash) enters adolescence, and discovers race prejudice. A box-office failure in the theaters at the time, but this beautifully acted drama is a winner on the home screen. Particularly moving scene between Beah Richards and her son (Nash).

Take a Letter, Darling (1942)**½ Rosalind Russell, Fred MacMurray. Miss Russell makes something out of nothing in this frail comedy about a lady executive who hires a male secretary-escort and, of course, they fall in love. (Dir: Mitchell Leisen, 93 mins.)

Take Her, She's Mine (1962)** James Stewart, Sandra Dee, Audrey Meadows. Once more Stewart appears in one of those father-is-an-idiot domestic comedies beneath his talents. This time concerns his efforts to prevent his daughter from leading a beatnik life, winding up in the soup himself. Some rare funny spots, the rest depressingly trite. (Dir: Henry Koster, 98 mins.)

Take It or Leave It (1944)*½ Phil Baker. Remember that popular quiz that gave away as much as 64 bucks? Well, this hodge-podge of old film clips is supposed to capitalize on the program's popularity. Definitely dated. (Dir: Benjamin Stoloff, 78 mins.)

Take Me Out to the Ball Game (1948) **½ Frank Sinatra, Esther Williams, Gene Kelly, Betty Garrett. Promising musical about the early days of baseball falters because of forced comedy and a weak script. Cast is also hampered by a commonplace score. Of course Miss Williams finds a pool where she can do a water ballet. (Dir: Busby Berkeley, 93 mins.)

Take Me to Town (1953)*** Ann Sheridan, Sterling Hayden. Good fun with Ann Sheridan at the peak of her comedy finesse as a dance hall girl by the name of Vermillion O'Toole (shades of Scarlett O'Hara). Sterling Hayden is equally effective as a preacher who doubles as a lumberjack. (Dir: Douglas Sirk, 81 mins.)

Take My Life (British, 1947)*** Hugh Williams, Greta Gynt. Opera star's husband is arrested for the murder of a former sweetheart; she sets out to prove his innocence. Well-made murder mystery is above average for this sort of thing.

Take One False Step (1949)**½ William Powell, Shelley Winters. Moderately absorbing drama about a college professor who innocently becomes entangled with the police after a blonde from his past runs into him on a business trip. (Dir: Chester Erskine, 94 mins.)

Take the High Ground (1953)*** Richard Widmark, Karl Malden, Elaine Stewart. Colorful and believable story about the tough sergeants who train raw recruits for the U.S. Infantry. Widmark and Malden are good foils for one another and their playing rings true. Elaine Stewart is called upon to look beautiful which she does beautifully. (Dir: Richard Brooks, 101 mins.)

Take the Money and Run (1969)**** Woody Allen, Janet Margolin, Lonny Chapman, Mark Gordon. Woody directed, starred in and co-authored this lunatic, gloriously funny farce—Allen's updated version of an ancient Biblical theme—the meek shall inherit the earth! Woody plays a timid, fumbling gangster. It turns out that he inherits more jail time than jewels. The plot doesn't matter—what does matter is that this is a fast-paced pot-pourri of frequently in-

698

spired sight gags and one-liners, and old and young will chuckle together over Woody's satirizing both "Bonnie and Clyde" and the 1930 and 1940 Hollywood gangster-prison films. Take the time to see this laughfest! (85 mins.)

Taking of Pelham One Two Three, The (1974)*** Walter Matthau, Robert Shaw, Martin Balsam, Hector Elizondo, and solid suspense yarn which holds up. Four men get on a New York subway, pull guns and hold a car full of passengers as hostages, demanding a million-dollar ransom from the mayor's office. Their plan is ingenious, and the efforts of the transit police and the New York police seem bumbling by comparison. The suspense reaches new highs every time you think the story may be bogging down, and the cast is excellent, including Matthau as the transit detective and Shaw as the cold-blooded leader of the unique heist. Screenplay by Peter Stone based on the novel by John Godey. (Dir: Joseph Sargent, 102 mins.)

Taking Off (1971)**½ Episodic adventures of Larry and Lynn Tyne (Buck Henry and Lynn Carlin), middle-class parents in pursuit of their off-to-the-Village daughter Jeanne (Linnea Heacock). Director and cowriter Milos Forman ("The Fireman's Ball") in his first American film treads along cliches so carefully that satire, comedy, and absurdity skillfully balance. Whether trying pot at a meeting of the Society for Parents of Fugitive Children or drunkenly undressing at a strip-poker game with his daughter a silent observer, Henry stands apart in his comic delivery. Uneven, but individual scenes really take off. (93 mins.)

Tale of Five Women (British, 1950) *** Bonar Colleano, Gina Lollobrigida, Eva Bartok. Magazine writer helps a man who has lost his memory regain his past by taking him to Europe. Interesting melodrama, well acted.

Tale of Two Cities (1936)**** Ronald Colman, Edna May Oliver. Dickens' novel of the French Revolution becomes a screen classic and a "must see" for all. It's true to the book and a fine cast brings the characters to life. Don't miss it. (Dir: Jack Conway, 130 mins.)

Tale of Two Cities (British, 1958) *** Dirk Bogarde, Cecil Parker. Dickens' story of the French Revolution and the bravery involved, not as good as previous version, but well made.

Talent for Loving, A (1969)**½ Richard Widmark, Genevieve Page, Topol, Cesar Romero. A lightweight comedy about the Old West which boasts star names in the leading roles and little else. Widmark is the man who comes to Mexico to claim his land and finds that Don Jose (Romero) has a claim on the same land. Disputes, arrangements, and slapstick comedy antics take over from there. There are some good scenes involving an ancient Aztec curse which dooms the Vicuna family regarding their arduous lovemaking. Didn't get much of a release in this country. (Dir: Richard Quine.)

Tales (1970)**½ Occasionally interesting but overlong low-budget independent film dealing with the sex fantasies of a group of New Yorkers who sit around a living room and discuss them with considerable frankness. (Dir: Cassandra Gerstein, 70 mins.)

Tales of Hoffmann, The (British, 1951)*** Robert Rounseville, Moira Shearer. The Offenbach opera is presented in its entirety; the story of the student who has strange adventures. Brilliant production and singers, but yet a highly stylized affair that is not for every taste. (Dirs: Michael Powell, Emeric Pressburger, 138 mins.)

Tales of Manhattan (1942)*** Charles Boyer, Ginger Rogers, Rita Hayworth, Henry Fonda. An all-star cast in a series of unrelated dramas around a dress shirt. Vignettes range from superb to mediocre. An interesting film. (Dir: Julien Duvivier, 118 mins.)

Talk of the Town (1942)***½ Cary Grant, Jean Arthur, Ronald Colman. Delightful comedy, loaded with social implications, about an outspoken man wrongly accused of murder. Excellent performances and direction. (Dir: George Stevens, 118 mins.)

Tall, Dark and Handsome (1941) ***½ Cesar Romero, Virginia Gilmore, Milton Berle. Highly amusing comedy about a soft-hearted gangster, the orphaned son of a deceased mobster and an assortment of crazy characters. Good fun. (Dir: H. Bruce Humberstone, 78 mins.)

Tall in the Saddle (1944)*** John Wayne, Ella Raines. Woman-hating cowboy takes over as ranch foreman only to find the new owners are a spinster and her young niece. Entertaining, fast paced western. (Dir: Edward L. Marin, 87 mins.)

Tall Lie, The (1952)***½ Paul Henreid, Kathleen Hughes. A college professor exposes the brutality and foul play behind the respected school fraternity. Hard-hitting melodrama, well directed (by Henreid), well acted. Strong stuff. (Dir: Paul Henreid, 93 mins.)

Tall Man Riding (1955)** Randolph Scott, Dorothy Malone. All the ingredients for a a predictable western —a crooked gambler, a pretty girl, two or three hired guns, another pretty girl and Randolph Scott. (Dir: Lesley Selander, 83 mins.)

Tall Men, The (1955)** Jane Russell, Clark Gable, Robert Ryan. Routine western fare with big production values and big names to bolster its appeal. Gable plays the granite-fisted cattle driver and Miss Russell decorates the wagon train. Action fans will enjoy the many hazards befalling the cattle drive. (Dir: Raoul Walsh, 122 mins.)

Tall Story (1960)*** Anthony Perkins, Jane Fonda. This tale of campus athletics and romance is enhanced greatly by the personal charm of the two stars. The plot concerns Tony as a basketball star and Jane's determination to win a degree and a husband. The fine supporting cast includes Ray Walston, Marc Connelly and Anne Jackson. (Dir: Joshua Logan, 91 mins.)

Tall Stranger (1957)*** Joel McCrea, Virginia Mayo. Good western, well-made. Joel joins a wagon train of settlers, helps them fight the bad guys. (Dir: Thomas Carr, 81 mins.)

Tall T, The (1957)**½ Randolph Scott, Richard Boone, Maureen O'Sullivan. Better than average Randolph Scott western tale. A good supporting cast keeps the action believable, as Randy battles Boone and his band of killers. (Dir: Budd Boetticher, 78 mins.)

Tall Target, The (1951)*** Dick Powell, Paula Raymond, Adolphe Menjou. Tense suspense yarn about a detective's efforts to thwart a plot to kill President Abraham Lincoln when he stops in Baltimore for a whistle stop speech. Most of the action is played on a train headed for Washington and the camera work in this confined area helps to heighten the gripping suspense. (Dir: Anthony Mann, 78 mins.)

Tall Texan, The (1953)*** Lloyd Bridges, Marie Windsor, Lee J. Cobb, Luther Adler. A group of assorted people band together on the desert to seek hidden gold which is cached in an Indian burial ground. Suspenseful western, off the beaten track.

Tam Lin (Great Britain, 1971)* Ava Gardner, Ian McShane, Cyril Cusack, Stephanie Beacham. Wretched jet-set tale of aging woman who surrounds herself with "beautiful people" in an attempt to stay young. When one of her young studs falls for the vicar's daughter, things get nasty. Roddy McDowall's first attempt at direction. He should stick to acting! McDowall says the film was re-edited by others without his approval. "Tam" never got a general release. (Dir: Roddy McDowall, 104 mins.)

Tamahine (Great Britain, 1963)** Nancy Kwan, John Fraser, Dennis Price. Rather foolish, fast-paced froth about lovely Polynesian girl who disrupts routine of a British boys' school. Naive, painless. Written by Dennis Cannan, from the book by Thelma Nicklaus. (Dir: Philip Leacock, 85 mins.)

Tamango (French, 1958)** Curt Jurgens, Dorothy Dandridge. Slaves revolt on a ship commanded by a brutal captain. Confused, unpleasant drama, not helped by dubbing of minor roles into English. (Dir: John Berry, 98 mins.)

Tamarind Seed, The (Great Britain, 1974)** Julie Andrews, Omar Sharif, Anthony Quayle. A lush bore. Confused, outdated story of a Cold War Romeo and Juliet. Andrews and Sharif are unconvincing as star-crossed lovers kept apart by international intrigue. On a Caribbean beach, Russian agent Sharif is anxious to bed Andrews. Hard to understand why! (Dir: Blake Edwards, 123 mins.)

Taming of the Shrew, The (U.S.-Italian, 1966)**** Elizabeth Taylor, Richard Burton, Cyril Cusack, Victor Spinetti. One of the rare occasions when Shakespeare really works on the screen. Credit director Franco Zeffirelli's exquisite mounting, and the spirited, thoughtful playing by stars Elizabeth Taylor and Richard Burton, for a wonderful romp. Burton seems to have been born to play the wily opportunist Petruchio who comes to Padua to woo and wed the man-hating Kate. His mellifluous voice and handsome bearing are a delight throughout. Miss Taylor is that rare combination of beauty, fire and luminous femininity as Kate. The extraordinary visual beauty of the film is due to cinematographers Oswald Morris and Luciano Trasatti. Don't miss this treat, and make sure to see it in color. (126 mins.)

Tammy and the Bachelor (1957)**½ Debbie Reynolds, Walter Brennan. Debbie Reynolds' energetic performance as a backwoods teenager who seems to have a knack for setting things straight is the bright spot of the film. More sophisticated tastes had better not bother but if you like your film comedy laced with corn and hokum, Miss Reynolds and company will oblige. (Dir: Joseph Pevney, 89 mins.)

Tammy and the Doctor (1963)** Sandra Dee, Peter Fonda, Macdonald Carey. Backwoods girl becomes a nurse's aide, finds romance with a young doctor. Sticky-sweet stuff for the femme-teen set. (Dir: Harry Keller, 88 mins.)

Tammy and the Millionaire (1967)* Debbie Watson, Frank McGrath, Denver Pyle. Fourth "Tammy" film is a composite made from four episodes of the '65-'66 TV series. Tammy gets ahead, with support from her backwoodsy relatives, despite uppity neighbors. Saccharine time-waster. (Dirs: Sidney Miller, Ezra Stone and Leslie Goodwins, 85 mins.)

Tammy Tell Me True (1961)**½ Sandra Dee, John Gavin, Beulah Bondi. The country girl decides it's time she got an education and packs off to college. Naive little romantic comedy isn't really as bad as it could have been. Girl teen-agers should take to it, while the rest should find it pleasant if unexceptional. (Dir: Harry Keller, 97 mins.)

Tampico (1944)** Edward G. Robinson, Victor McLaglen, Lynn Bari. Routine war drama about espionage in the merchant marine. Not too

much but almost passable, thanks to Robinson. (Dir: Lothar Mendes, 75 mins.)

Tanganyika (1954)** Van Heflin, Ruth Roman, Howard Duff. This jungle drama set in the early 1900's has all the plot ingredients usually found in similar adventure tales—natives, madmen, love, pestilence and massacre. Strictly for adventure fans. (Dir: Andre de Toth, 81 mins.)

Tank Force (British, 1958)** Victor Mature, Luciana Paluzzi, Leo Genn. Average war tale with Victor Mature playing a troubled American soldier who serves with the British in the African campaign. The usual battle scenes with time out for some romantic interludes. (Dir: Terence Young, 81 mins.)

Tany and the Jungle Hunter (1965) *½ Jacques Bergerac, Shary Marshall, Manuel Padilla. Hunter's son is afraid he'll lose his pet elephant so takes off with the beast in tow. For the kiddies who like jungle stuff, and for them exclusively.

Tap Roots (1948)**½ Susan Hayward, Van Heflin. The advent of the Civil War destroys plans for two people to marry, and enables the girl to find her true love. Lavish historical drama has some good moments, but generally the plot never seems to resolve itself; nor is the acting anything to rave about. (Dir: George Marshall, 109 mins.)

Tarantula (1956)**½ John Agar, Mara Corday, Leo G. Carroll. Giant spider escapes from the lab and begins terrorizing the territory. Well-done technically, this horror thriller carries its share of tense situations. Better than usual. (Dir: Jack Arnold, 80 mins.)

Taras Bulba (1962)**½ Yul Brynner, Tony Curtis, Christine Kaufmann. Strictly for the undiscriminating action fan. The plot is about the 16th Century Polish revolution which is on a comic book level but the production is lavish and eye-filling. Brynner has the title role of the famed Cossack and Curtis plays one of his sons, bent on revenge against the Poles. (Dir: J. Lee Thompson, 122 mins.)

Target Risk (1975)** Bo Svenson, Robert Coote, Meredith Baxter. Action piece on the problems of a bonded courier matching wits with jewel thieves who call the early shots.

Routine! Made-for-TV. (Dir: Robert Scheerer, 72 mins.)

Target, Sea of China (1954-66)* Harry Lauter, Lyle Talbot, Aline Towne. Feature version of serial "Trader Tom of the China Seas." Ragged action fare indicates how the once-mighty cliffhanger had fallen in latter days. (Dir: Franklin Andren, 100 mins.)

Target Zero (1955)*½ Richard Conte, Peggie Castle, Charles Bronson. An incredible war film. A group of infantry soldiers, led by a rugged lieutenant (Conte), run into a British tank unit and a female UN biochemist amid the war torn hills of Korea. (Dir: Harmon Jones, 92 mins.)

Targets (1968)***½ Tim O'Kelly, Boris Karloff. Offbeat, occasionally terrifying tale of a psychotic sniper (Tim O'Kelly) and an aging horror-movie star (Boris Karloff) whose paths cross during the most deadly play of all. Low-budget effort by Peter Bogdanovich shows an apt command of the film medium. He produced and directed this compelling meller at the ripe old age of 29. There's a brief clip from a terrible Karloff 1963 film, "The Terror," as well as a glimpse of Boris from the 1931 "The Criminal Code." (92 mins.)

Tarnished Angels, The (1958)**½ Rock Hudson, Robert Stack, Dorothy Malone. Fairly absorbing drama about flying daredevils during the thirties and their personal as well as professional problems. The cast is an attractive one and they all do well. Based on a Wm. Faulkner novel, "Pylon." (Dir: Douglas Sirk, 91 mins.)

Tarnished Heroes (British, 1961)** Dermot Walsh, Patrick McAlinney. Soldiers with questionable past records are sent on a dangerous mission. Average, familiar war story.

Tars and Spars (1946)**½ Sid Caesar, Alfred Drake, Janet Blair. In spite of Caesar and Drake, this is a bore. However, you will see one of Sid's funniest routines, and it almost makes the film worth sitting through.

Tartar Invasion (Italian, 1963)** Akim Tamiroff, Yoko Tani, Joe Robinson. Another Italian-made, English-dubbed, epic for action fans who don't care about accuracy or historical facts.

Tartars, The (Italian, 1960)* Victor Mature, Orson Welles. Big, boring. Vikings battle Tartars on the Asian steppes. Result is unrelenting gore, sadistic retaliations. Viking chieftain Mature and Tartar despot Welles trade off butcheries. Depressing to see Welles waste himself in rubbish like this. (Dir: Richard Thorpe, 83 mins.)

Tarzan and the Great River (1967)* Mike Henry, Rafer Johnson. Mike Henry takes a crack at the role of Tarzan, and he's no better or worse than many of his predecessors. Tarzan is up to his loincloth in trouble as he goes deep into the Amazon region. Hard to comment seriously in the 1970's on this kind of drivel. (Dir: Robert Day, 99 mins.)

Tarzan and the Jungle Boy (U.S.-Swiss, 1968)* Mike Henry, Rafer Johnson, Alizia Gur. Routine for the ape-man but, after 50 years, who cares any more! Tarzan, played by Mike Henry for the third time, goes into the jungle in search of a missing boy. (Film freaks, attention! Can you name the other 14 actors who played Tarzan in the films?) (Dir: Robert Day, 99 mins.)

Tarzan and the Lost Safari (British, 1957)** Gordon Scott, Betta St. John, Yolande Donlan. The jungle man has his work cut out for him when he tries to lead the party of a playboy crashed in the jungle to safety. Barely passable Tarzan thriller doesn't have the customary excitement. (Dir: H. Bruce Humberstone, 84 mins.)

Tarzan and the Trappers (1958)*½ Gordon Scott, Eve Brent, Ricky Sorensen. The jungle man frees the animals from some villainous trappers, who are also after the riches in a lost city. One of the weaker entries in this adventure series, made evidently with an eye on TV. (Dir: H. Bruce Humberstone, 74 mins.)

Tarzan and the Valley of Gold (U.S.-Switzerland, 1966)½ Mike Henry, Nancy Kovack. Tarzan jets into Mexico, exchanges his permanent-press for a loincloth, and is off to defend a lost Aztec city of gold from mercenary marauders. Inane update! Screenplay by Claire Huffaker. (Dir: Robert Day, 100 mins.)

Tarzan Goes to India (1962)**½ Jock Mahoney, Mark Dana, Jai. As these jungle epics starring Edgar Rice Burroughs' durable hero go, he.e's a pretty good one. The locale i. shifted from Africa to India. Tarzan does his best to create a sanctuary for elephants and other wild animals, whose existence is threatened by the construction of a dam. Mahoney is a convincing super Ape Man, and the actual Indian locations are impressively mounted. (Dir: Richard Thorpe, 86 mins.)

Tarzan, the Ape Man (1932)**½ Johnny Weissmuller, Maureen O'Sullivan. This was the daddy of all Tarzan pictures and, as such, is worth your attention. (Dir: W. S. Van Dyke, 100 mins.)

Tarzan, the Ape Man (1959)*½ Denny Miller, Joanna Barnes. Remake of the first Weissmuller Tarzan tale, or how Tarzan meets Jane. Also involves a search for the lost graveyard of the elephants. Pretty weak stuff; uses lots of leftover footage from the old film, and it doesn't match the new very well. (Dir: Joseph M. Newman, 82 mins.)

Tarzan the Magnificent (British, 1960)*** Gordon Scott, Betta St. John, Jock Mahoney. Tarzan captures the murderer of a policeman, but the criminal's family sets out to free him. Good entry in the Tarzan series doesn't let up the fast pace for a moment. Well-made and exciting. Filmed in Africa, which helps make it all believable. (Dir: Robert Day, 88 mins.)

Tarzan's Fight for Life (1958)** Gordon Scott, Eve Brent. The jungle man incurs the wrath of a tribal witch doctor when he becomes friendly with a doctor running a hospital in the jungle. Just fair Tarzan film, lacks the action and production of some of the better ones.

Tarzan's Greatest Adventure (British, 1959)*** Gordon Scott, Anthony Quayle, Sean Connery, Sara Shane. Tarzan on the trail of four men, including an old enemy, who don't stop at murder in seeking a diamond mine. One of the better jungle adventures—Tarzan speaks whole sentences, the African locations are beautiful, and the story's loaded with action, some of the more spectacular variety. Good fun. (Dir: John Guillermin, 88 mins.)

Tarzan's New York Adventure (1942) *** Johnny Weissmuller, Maureen O'Sullivan, Charles Bickford. Circus men kidnap Tarzan's boy, and the jungle man follows them to the big

city. Lively entrant in the series, with the change of locale amusing, exciting. (Dir: Richard Thorpe, 71 mins.)

Tarzan's Three Challenges (1963)*½ Jock Mahoney, Woody Strode. Fans of the Tarzan tales will no doubt be stirred by this Jock Mahoney starrer. Our hero is summoned to Southeast Asia on a special mission involving an heir to a kingdom whose throne and life are threatened. Sounds like John Wayne heroics, but it's only Tarzan in Asia. (Dir: Robert Day, 92 mins.)

Task Force (1949)*** Gary Cooper, Walter Brennan, Jane Wyatt. Story of development of naval aviation and aircraft carriers is too long but contains some interesting scenes and good acting. (Dir: Delmer Daves, 116 mins.)

Taste of Honey, A (British, 1962) **** Rita Tushingham, Murray Melvin. Warmly human, drama of an unlovely girl, her sudden entrance into womanhood. It's tops in acting, direction. Miss Tushingham's performance in this, her first film effort, is quite remarkable and deeply moving. Based on the fine British play which also was a hit on Broadway. Beautifully directed by Tony Richardson, this is a lovely often tender heartbreaking film. (Dir: Tony Richardson, 100 mins.)

Tattered Dress, The (1957)**½ Jeff Chandler, Jeanne Crain, Jack Carson. Somewhat muddled but moderately interesting murder drama with a large cast of stars who appear in brief roles. The production is slick and the courtroom scenes add a spark to the proceedings. (Dir: Jack Arnold, 93 mins.)

Taur the Mighty (Italian, 1961)* Joe Robinson, Bella Cortez. Lone hero fights mighty forces who have captured men in tribal wars. Ragged costume spectacle dubbed in English.

Taxi (1953)**½ Dan Dailey, Constance Smith. Cab driver helps an Irish immigrant girl with a baby to find her husband. Modest little comedy-drama manages to be quite entertaining; good performances by the leads, New York atmosphere. (Dir: Gregory Ratoff, 77 mins.)

Taxi Driver, The (Greek, 1958)* Mimis Fotopoulos. Paper-thin tale of a taxi driver who falls in love with a pedestrian, and almost runs her over while trying to meet her.

Bland dubbed comedy import. (Dir: George Tzavellas, 90 mins.)

Taxi Driver (1976)**** Robert De Niro, Cybill Shepherd, Jodie Foster, Peter Boyle, Leonard Harris, Harvey Keitel, Martin Scorsese. A lacerating, profoundly disturbing modern sociological horror story about urban alienation and, finally, madness. It builds carefully to a final terrifying, unforgettable scene of slaughter that has an undeniable orgasmic quality—the audience literally is left panting by the eruption and release, however loathsome, of such tension and energy. Robert De Niro's hypnotic portrait of Travis Bickle, the embittered, lonely Vietnam Marine Corps veteran who drives a taxi at night while turning into an urban guerrilla, is one of the most chilling, repellent characters in the history of modern films, as developed by writer Paul Schrader. Shepherd plays a well-bred young political campaign worker who meets and briefly dates Bickle. There are other splendid performances, including Jodie Foster playing Iris, a twelve-year-old prostitute, who works for a black pimp slain by the "Taxi Driver" in his frenzied rage. Scorsese establishes himself with "Taxi Driver" as one of the most gifted directors of his generation. This award-winning film, boasting a superlative musical score—his last—by Bernard Herrmann, is a haunting vision of the darkest side of the American dream in the mid-70's. (Dir: Martin Scorsese, 112 mins.)

Taxi for Tobruk (French, 1964)**½ Lino Ventura, Hardy Kruger, Charles Aznavour. Group of French soldiers stranded in the North African desert capture a German captain and some supplies, make their way toward safety. World War II drama with an ironic twist at the end; leisurely, but some good performances. Dubbed-in English. (Dir: Denys De La Patelliere, 90 mins.)

Taza, Son of Cochise (1954)** Rock Hudson, Barbara Rush. One of the many Western adventure films in which Rock Hudson served his apprenticeship under the Universal banner. The plot concerns the Indian's battle against the invading white man. Production is of high quality, but you've seen it all before. (Dir: Douglas Sirk, 79 mins.)

Tea and Sympathy (1952)***½ Deborah Kerr, John Kerr, Leif Erickson. The successful Broadway play by Robert Anderson is expanded and toned down somewhat in this film version and thereby loses some of its bite. Miss and Mr. Kerr (no relation) repeat their Broadway roles and manage to evoke the sympathy implied in the title. (Dir: Vincente Minnelli, 122 mins.)

Tea for Two (1950)**½ Doris Day, Gordon MacRae, Eve Arden. Mildly diverting musical comedy made long before Doris went dramatic. Based on the 20's play "No, No, Nanette." (Dir: David Bulter, 98 mins.)

Teacher and the Miracle, The (Italian, 1962)**½ Aldo Fabrizi, Eduardo Nevola. Teacher who has established an art school is crushed by the death of his son, but a miracle encourages him to carry on. Sensitive drama dubbed in English should please viewers who delight in a good cry. (Dir: Aldo Fabrizi, 88 mins.)

Teacher's Pet (1958)***½ Clark Gable, Doris Day, Mamie Van Doren, Gig Young. Rollicking comedy with Gable and Day at their respective best. He plays a hard-boiled city editor who becomes her star pupil in a journalism class. The laughs come often and the supporting cast is fine, especially Gig Young as a tipsy playboy. (Dir: George Stevens, 120 mins.)

Teahouse of the August Moon (1956)***½ Marlon Brando, Glenn Ford, Machiko Kyo. John Patrick's successful Broadway comedy about the rehabilitation of an Okinawan village by the U.S. Army is brought to the screen with most of the fun intact. Glenn Ford does fairly well as Capt. Fisby, the officer in charge of the military program, but Marlon Brando is miscast in the role of his unpredictable interpreter. (Dir: Daniel Mann, 123 mins.)

Teckman Mystery, The (British, 1954)*** Margaret Leighton, John Justin. Author writing a biography of an airman who crashed is convinced there is something mysterious about the death. Good mystery holds the attention. (Dir: Wendy Toye, 89 mins.)

Teenage Bad Girl (British, 1957)*** Anna Neagle, Sylvia Syms, Kenneth Haigh. Despite its bad title, this British movie about youth and their wild times is well acted and rewarding. (Dir: Herbert Wilcox, 100 mins.)

Teenage Caveman (1958)*½ Robert Vaughn, Darrah Marshall. A silly tale about "prehistoric times"— Robert Vaughn would probably like to forget this little opus made before his TV and film success.

Teenage Crime Wave (1955)*½ Tommy Cook, Mollie McCart. Inept juvenile delinquency pic with a collection of bad performances. A trigger-happy youth gets a young innocent girl involved in his criminal activities until the police intervene.

Teenage Millionaire (1961)*½ Jimmy Clanton, Rocky Graziano, Zasu Pitts. Teenager left a fortune becomes a recording star. One rock and roll number follows another in deadly procession in tepid comedy. (Dir: Lawrence Doheny, 84 mins.)

Teenage Monster—See: **Meteor Monster**

Teenage Rebel (1956)*½ Ginger Rogers, Michael Rennie, Betty Lou Keim. Glamorous mother has trouble with her daughter. Glug. (Dir: Edmund Goulding, 94 mins.)

Teenage Wolfpack (British, 1956) **½ Horst Buchholz, Karin Ball. Strong film about young kids seeking kicks. Acting better than the rest of the production.

Teenage Zombies (1960)* Don Sullivan, Katherine Victor, Steve Conte. Group of youngsters discover dirty work on an island inhabited by an evil woman doctor and some monsters. Nonsensical horror thriller; poor.

Teenagers from Outer Space (1959)* David Love, Dawn Anderson. The title tells the story. This isn't the worst film of its kind but it will do until another one comes along. (Dir: Tom Graeff, 86 mins.)

Tell It to the Judge (1949)**½ Rosalind Russell, Robert Cummings, Gig Young. The stars save this one from total disaster. Corny plot has Roz as a lady lawyer running away from her blonde-chasing husband for most of the film. (Dir: Norman Foster, 87 mins.)

Tell Me Lies (British, 1968)***½ Glenda Jackson, Peggy Ashcroft, Mark Jones, Robert Lloyd. Produced, directed and conceived by Peter Brook, who is undoubtedly the most brilliant director in the English-speaking theater, circa 1972. This is a fascinating, maddening, and notable film, not so much because of its special virtues as a piece of filmmaking, but because of its content. It is a savage, mocking, and frequently lacerating attack on the U.S. war policy in Indo-China, a subject rarely dealt with in American-produced films. Original footage, utilizing members of the Royal Shakespeare Company, is mixed with documentary footage of war violence and destruction in Vietnam. It's too bad the film isn't better on a technical level, but never mind. Your response to this angry, political essay will depend to a large degree on your attitude towards the Vietnam War itself, but "Tell Me Lies" is well worth seeing if your local TV station has the courage to broadcast it. (118 mins.)

Tell-Tale Heart, The (British, 1963) **½ Laurence Payne, Adrienne Corri, Dermot Walsh. Fair version of Poe's classic tale of horror, about a murderer who is haunted by the sound of his victim's beating heart. Some creepy sequences. (Dir: Ernest Morris, 81 mins.)

Tell Them Willie Boy Is Here (1969) ***½ Robert Redford, Robert Blake, Katharine Ross, Susan Clark, Barry Sullivan. Thanks to the thoughtful screenplay and excellent direction by Abraham Polonsky, "Willie Boy" is an exciting western chase story, but much more importantly, one of the few major Hollywood films that has ever dealt sensitively with the question of the American white man's treatment of the Indian. Story, set in 1909 during the Presidency of Taft, finds sheriff Redford hunting down a young Paiute Indian (well played by Robert Blake). Polonsky is a gifted film-maker who was blacklisted by Hollywood for nearly 20 years, and he has fashioned an absorbing drama in "Willie." (96 mins.)

Tempest (Italian, 1959)*** Van Heflin, Silvana Mangano, Viveca Lindfors, Geoffrey Horne. Impressively produced drama of old Russia, as a rebel leader sacrifices his life to protect a soldier who had once saved his own. Mammoth scenes of scope, excellent international cast. English dialogue. (Dir: Alberto Lattivado, 125 mins.)

Tempestuous Love (West German, 1957)** Lilli Palmer, Ivan Desny. Overdone soap opera, with Miss Palmer as the mistress of one of her husband's pupils. Waste of a talented actress. (Dir: Falk Harnack, 89 mins.)

Temple of the White Elephants (Italian, 1963)* Sean Flynn, Marie Versini. Viceroy's daughter and an officer in the Lancers are kidnaped by a jungle tribe in India. Errol's offspring in a poor adventure tale—pop would be ashamed. Dubbed in English.

Temptress, The (1926)*** Greta Garbo, Antonio Moreno. Silent melodrama with Greta playing, of course, the femme fatale, the action zipping back and forth between Europe and South America before Greta's fortune turns sour—she winds up as an impoverished Parisian prostitute. (Dirs: Mauritz Stiller and Fred Niblo, 117 mins.)

Ten Commandments, The (1956)*** Charlton Heston, Yul Brynner, Edward G. Robinson, Anne Baxter, Cedric Hardwicke. Cecil B. De Mille directed this spectacular film about the biblical epic of Moses, his people, and their exodus from Egypt. Combines a fine mixture of pageantry and drama, bolstered by an all-star cast led by Heston as Moses, Brynner as the Egyptian Pharaoh, plus a host of others. (221 mins.)

Ten Days' Wonder (French, 1972)* Orson Welles, Anthony Perkins, Michel Piccoli. Absurd mess about a boy (Perkins) who breaks one of the ten commandments every day. He falls in love with his stepmother, who is married to Welles, a rich eccentric who lives in a 1920's house. This travesty is based on an Ellery Queen story and the scenario was written by Eugene Archer. Direction was by Claude Chabrol. With all that talent, this is still a terrible film. (105 mins.)

Ten From Your Show of Shows (1973)***½ Sid Caesar, Imogene Coca, Carl Reiner, Howard Morris, Louis Nye. Ten classic sketches from the famed comedy series of the early 50's. The stars are marvelous in some of their best-remembered routines—including hilarious take-offs on "From Here to Eternity" and "This Is Your Life." Among the writers was the then unknown Mel Brooks. Kinescopes of the original black and white TV revue. Welcome reminder of Caesar's early, dazzling

brilliance. (Dir: Bill Hobin, 92 mins.)

Ten Gentlemen from West Point (1942)*** Laird Cregar, George Montgomery, Maureen O'Hara. Good juvenile drama of the beginning of the U.S.M.A. at West Point. Not true but an exciting adventure story in spite of itself. (Dir: Henry Hathaway, 102 mins.)

Ten Gladiators, The (Italian, 1961)* Roger Browne, Dan Vadis. Fighting the rule of the tyrant Nero, ten masked terrorists dare to help the oppressed. Slapdash costume spectacle, a bore despite all the action. Dubbed in English.

Ten Little Indians (British, 1966)**½ Hugh O'Brian, Shirley Eaton, Stanley Holloway, Dennis Price, Daliah Lavi. A new version of the marvelous 1945 film "And Then There Were None," but this second mounting of Agatha Christie's famed thriller is not as suspenseful. (And the director of this one, George Pollock, is not as talented as Rene Clair who helmed the first try.) A group is brought to an isolated spot and eliminated one by one. (Dir: George Pollack, 92 mins.)

Ten Little Indians (Italy-France-Spain-Germany, 1975)**½ Oliver Reed, Elke Sommer, Richard Attenborough, Gert Frobe, Herbert Lom, Stephane Audran, Charles Aznavour. Tediously acted, poorly directed disaster. Third remake of Agatha Christie's suspense classic features a bizarre change of location and a hodgepodge of international stars. Ten people are stranded in a hotel in the Iranian desert, while one is slowly doing away with his fellows. See the original "And Then There Were None," directed by Rene Clair, with Walter Huston and Barry Fitzgerald. Another awful film produced by Harry Alan Towers. (Dir: Peter Collinson, 98 mins.)

Ten Men Who Dared (1960)*½ Brian Keith, John Beal. Wish they hadn't! Ten men embark on an expedition to chart the Colorado River, an attempt that is wracked by disputes. Surprisingly weak Disney production: directionless, soapy. Acting is O.K., problems lie elsewhere. (Dir: William Beaudine, 92 mins.)

Ten North Frederick (1958)*** Gary Cooper, Diane Varsi, Suzy Parker, Geraldine Fitzgerald. A good cast overcomes many of the soap-opera tendencies of this script based on John O'Hara's novel about the politics, infidelity, and the ever present struggle between the weak and the strong. Cooper and Suzy Parker are believable in a May-December romantic subplot. (Dir: Philip Dunne, 102 mins.)

10 Rillington Place (1971)*** Richard Attenborough, Judy Geeson. Absorbing crime film brought to the screen with infinite care for detail and an absence of sensationalism, despite the macabre facts of the real-life multiple murder case on which it is based. Attenborough is superb as the mild-mannered man who is in reality a demented murderer of women and children, and the production is first-rate on all counts. (Dir: Richard Fleischer, 102 mins.)

Ten Seconds to Hell (1959)** Jack Palance, Jeff Chandler, Martine Carol. Slow moving adventure yarn about a couple of he-men who pit their strength against espionage agents at work in Europe. Palance and Chandler are victims of a weak script and appear more wooden than ever. (Dir: Robert Aldrich, 93 mins.)

Ten Tall Men (1951)***½ Burt Lancaster, Jody Lawrance, Gilbert Roland. A merry spoof on the Foreign Legionnaires and their escapades with harem girls, etc. Lots of fun—played in great tongue-in-cheek style. (Dir: Willis Goldbeck, 97 mins.)

Ten Thousand Bedrooms (1957)**½ Dean Martin, Anna Maria Alberghetti, Walter Slezak. One of those amiably empty musical confections Dino used to be caught in before producers discovered he could act. He's a hotel tycoon, Anna Maria's a stenographer, and after two hours of songs, comedy, and four writers trying to make a script out of nothing, all the right people get together. Harmless fun. (Dir: Richard Thorpe, 114 mins.)

Ten Wanted Men (1955)**½ Randolph Scott, Richard Boone, Jocelyn Brando. Randolph Scott is a cattle baron in Arizona who wants only peace but the desperadoes see it another way. (Dir: H. Bruce Humberstone, 80 mins.)

Tender Comrade (1944)**½ Ginger Rogers, Robert Ryan. Young wife carries on bravely while her husband goes off to war. Drama pushed the sticky sentiment too much. (Dir: Edward Dmytryk, 102 mins.)

Tender Is the Night ('62)**½ Jennifer Jones, Jason Robards Jr., Joan Fontaine, Tom Ewell. A lot of care has been lavished on this adaptation of F. Scott Fitzgerald's novel about a psychiatrist who marries one of his patients and enters into the mad whirl of the 20's, eventually finding the marriage will destroy them both. Robards is excellent, Miss Jones less so; and despite the meticulous production, the drama is overlong, superficial all too often. (Dir: Henry King, 146 mins.)

Tender Scoundrel (France-Italy, 1966)** Jean-Paul Belmondo, Nadja Tiller, Robert Morley, Stefania Sandrelli. Frenchman subsists on his attractiveness to women, is worn out by the "demands" of his vocation. Film wears out, too, despite the Belmondo charms. Location scenes in Tahiti. (Dir: Jean Becker, 94 mins.)

Tender Trap, The (1955)*** Frank Sinatra, Debbie Reynolds, David Wayne, Celeste Holm. The successful Broadway comedy is brought to the screen with a great deal of savoir-faire. Sinatra is perfect as the foot loose bachelor who avoids cute Debbie's inviting "trap" of marriage for most of the film's running time. David Wayne and Celeste Holm have some good, funny lines and they deliver them like the pros they are. (Dir: Charles Walters, 111 mins.)

Tennessee Champ (1954)**½ Shelley Winters, Dewey Martin. Entertaining tale about the fight game and the various people associated with it. Some nice touches, capable performances. (Dir: Fred M. Wilcox, 73 mins.)

Tennessee Johnson (1942)***½ Van Heflin, Lionel Barrymore, Ruth Hussey. Interesting biography of the man who became President when Lincoln was shot and missed being impeached by one vote. Van Heflin is superb in the title role.

Tennessee's Partner (1955)*** John Payne, Ronald Reagan, Rhonda Fleming. Stranger steps into the middle of an argument and becomes the friend of a gambler. Entertaining action drama with a good cast. (Dir: Allan Dwan, 87 mins.)

Tension (1949)**½ Richard Basehart, Audrey Totter, Cyd Charisse.

Well acted murder mystery thriller. Basehart plays the hen-pecked husband whose wife leaves him for another man. He quietly plans to get even with her but his scheme backfires. (Dir: John Berry, 95 mins.)

Tension at Table Rock (1956)**½ Richard Egan, Dorothy Malone. Another western dealing with personal problems rather than cattle stampedes. This time a man must prove he has been unjustly labeled a coward. Good performances. (Dir: Charles Marquis Warren, 93 mins.)

Tenth Avenue Angel (1948)* Margaret O'Brien, Angela Lansbury, George Murphy. Little girl plays Cupid to her aunt and an ex-convict. Poor slushy drama. (Dir: Roy Rowland, 74 mins.)

Tenth Victim, The (Italian, 1965) ***½ Marcello Mastroianni, Ursula Andress. Nightmarish tale of the next century, wherein trained men and women have a license to kill each other for sport. Fantasy is a mixture of suspense thriller and satire, frequently effective because of the unusual sets, photography. Macabre, disturbing compelling film. Dubbed in English. (Dir: Elio Petri, 92 mins.)

Teresa (1951)***½ Pier Angeli, Ralph Meeker, John Ericson. An exceptionally good film about a mixed-up lad (Ericson) who marries an Italian girl, Pier Angeli, during WW II and brings her home to New York City. The cast is fine, notably Patricia Collinge as the boy's jealous mother and Rod Steiger as a psychiatrist. Well written screenplay by Stewart Stern. (Dir: Fred Zinnemann, 102 mins.)

Term of Trial (1963)***½ Laurence Olivier, Simone Signoret. Just for Laurence Olivier's remarkable ability to submerge himself into a character, even so seedy a one as the schoolteacher he plays here, this film is worth your while. The cast of this downbeat tale about a British teacher in a slum school, victimized by a student (a 16-year-old girl), are all excellent. Simone Signoret plays his slovenly wife; a very young Sarah Miles plays the troublesome girl; and a youthful Terence Stamp plays another brash student. Written and directed by Peter Glenville. Olivier is the greatest actor of his time; he's worth 113 minutes of your time.

Terminal Man, The (1974)*½ George

Segal, Jill Clayburgh, Joan Hackett. There are two pluses in this otherwise muddled movie . . . George Segal's relish in portraying a modern-day, computerized Frankenstein monster, and a sequence which painstakingly details the steps of an operation in which a small computer is placed in the brain of Segal's paranoid psychotic. The rest is mush, with the operation going bad and Segal turning into a rampaging killer without rhyme or reason. Jill Clayburgh is also good in the film's most violent scene, playing a stripper who falls victim to "The Terminal Man." Based on the novel by Michael Crichton. Clumsily adapted and directed by Mike Hodges. (104 mins.)

Terraces (Made-for-TV—1977)** Lloyd Bochner, Julie Newmar. It was inevitable that someone would come up with a pilot for a series about tenants in a high-rise apartment building whose only connection is their "terraces" which touch. Vignettes about an ex-Vegas showgirl, a lawyer, a doctor and a bright-eyed newcomer to the building are familiar and hackneyed. Julie Newmar, who is always nice to look at, does what she can as the former chorine. (Dir: Lila Garrett, 72 mins.)

Terrible People, The (German, 1960) ** Joachim Berger, Karin Dor, Fritz Rasp. A condemned criminal promises to return from the grave, and the bloody aftermath makes it appear he has made good his threat. Well produced but involved, unsophisticated Edgar Wallace mystery. Dubbed in English. (Dir: Harold Reinl, 95 mins.)

Terrified (1963)* Rod Lauren, Steve Drexel. Some teen-agers try to solve the murder of a victim who was buried alive—which is what should have been done with the script of this unpleasant mélange of gruesomeness and wild youth.

Terror, The (1963)** Boris Karloff, Sandra Knight, Jack Nicholson. Young officer traces a lovely but mysterious girl to a castle inhabited by a madman. Standard horror thriller made quickly and cheaply, gives Boris another chance to say "Boo!" (Dir: Roger Corman, 81 mins.)

Terror After Midnight (German, 1960)** Christine Kaufmann, Martin Held. Teenage girl is kidnaped by a man seeking revenge on her family. Fairly suspenseful melodrama dubbed in English.

Terror at Black Falls (1963)* House Peters Jr., Sandra Knight, Peter Mamakos. Dull western tries for "High Noon" and gets low marks.

Terror from Year 5,000 (1956)** Ward Costello, Joyce Holden. Female monster comes from the past to kill. Farfetched horror tale has some scary scenes.

Terror in the City (1966)*½ Lee Grant, Richard Bray, Sylvia Miles. When a boy runs away from home, he befriends a prostitute, a gang of kids, and other colorful street people. Marred by episodic direction and self-conscious acting. Lee Grant wasted. (Dir: Allen Baron, 86 mins.)

Terror in the Crypt (1958)**½ Christopher Lee. Italian-made horror film that builds slowly and manages some suspense. A strange nobleman, fearing for his daughter's life according to an ancient legend, has a group of scientists come to his home to see what they can do to help.

Terror in the Haunted House (1958)** Gerald Mohr, Cathy O'Donnell. A house on a hill, a newlywed couple spending the night and lightning all over the place. That's the setting and you can take it from there.

Terror Is a Man (1960)**½ Francis Lederer, Greta Thyssen, Richard Derr. Above average horror film, mad doctor experiments on turning panthers into humans, is thwarted by a survivor of a shipwreck. Filmed in the Philippines. Good directorial touches, plenty of suspense. (Dir: Gerry DeLeon, 89 mins.)

Terror of Rome Against the Son of Hercules (Italian, 1963)* Mark Forrest, Marilu Tolo. Muscular hero battles a horde of gladiators, frees the Christians. Juvenile costume spectacle dubbed in English.

Terror of the Black Mask (Italian, 1960)*½ Pierre Brice, Helene Chanel. Masked cavalier defends the people against the evil of a Don. Limp swashbuckler dubbed in English.

Terror of the Bloodhunters (1962)* Robert Clarke, Steve Conte. Convicts try to escape Devil's Island through the jungle—which consists of some grainy stock footage. Producers should have saved their money.

Terror of the Red Mask *½ Lex Barker, Chelo Alonso. Italian-produced adventure epic dubbed in English. No better or worse than the other bores in this category. (Dir: Piero Pierotti, 90 mins.)

Terror of the Steppe (Italian, 1963)* Kirk Morris, Moria Orfei. Hero saves a princess held captive by descendants of Genghis Khan. They should have held the film, too—poor English-dubbed costume adventure.

Terror of the Tongs, The (British, 1961)** Christopher Lee, Yvonne Monlaur, Geoffrey Toone. Sea captain sets out to smash a terrorist Tong society when his daughter is killed. Average melodrama. (Dir: Anthony Bushell, 90 mins.)

Terror on a Train (1953)**½ Glenn Ford, Anne Vernon. The best feature of this film is that it is fast paced (a little over an hour and a quarter) and wastes no time on incidental plot. Ford plays an armament expert who is called upon to disarm a hidden bomb on a train carrying explosives. (Dir: Ted Tetzlaff, 78 mins.)

Terror on the Beach (1973)**½ Dennis Weaver, Estelle Parsons, Susan Dey. Hoodlums aboard dune buggies and an old fire truck terrorize a vacationing family camping on an isolated beach. The slow buildup of pranks produces the desired suspense, and the family differences contain the ring of honesty. Although the final plot twists stretch credibility, the cast keep things going smoothly. Made-for-TV. (Dir: Paul Wendkos, 73 mins.)

Terror on the 40th Floor (1974)*½ John Forsythe, Anjanette Comer, Joseph Campanella. When Hollywood moviemakers were on a disaster-theme kick, TV followed suit. In this effort, office workers, trapped by fire on a skyscraper's top floor, take turns at high-level histrionics. Result—low-level drama. Made-for-TV. (Dir: Jerry Jameson, 72 mins.)

Terrornauts, The (Great Britain, 1967)*½ Simon Oates, Zena Marshall, Max Adrian. Minor science-fiction chiller. Scientists, skeptical that there is life on other worlds, are sucked up by green savages from a distant planet. Serves them right. (Dir: Montgomery Tully, 75 mins.)

Tess of the Storm Country (1960)** Diane Baker, Lee Philips, Jack Ging. Young girl arrived from Scotland finds herself involved in a feud between the townspeople and a Mennonite family. Leisurely, pleasing costume drama on the old-fashioned side. (Dir: Paul Guilfoyle, 84 mins.)

Test Pilot (1937)*** Clark Gable, Myrna Loy, Spencer Tracy, Lionel Barrymore. Story of men who risk their lives testing aircraft should be remade today with jets. You'll find the planes funny but good acting makes this a pretty rousing drama. (Dir: Victor Fleming, 120 mins.)

Testament of Dr. Mabuse, The (German, 1960)** Gert Frobe, Alan Dijon. Notorious mad doctor-criminal hypnotizes the head of a sanitarium into carrying out his plans for crime. Remake of the famous old Fritz Lang thriller doesn't compare with the original, but manages to whip up some weird sequences. Dubbed in English. (Dir: Werner Klinger, 87 mins.)

Texans, The (1938)** Joan Bennett, Randolph Scott. Pretentious class "A" western has little more to offer than a low budget quickie except for a name cast. Story of Texas after the Civil War hasn't got too much action or entertainment value. (Dir: James Hogan, 100 mins.)

Texas (1941)*** William Holden, Glenn Ford, Claire Trevor. Two wandering cowpokes take different trails; one with a pretty ranch girl, the other with an outlaw band. Fine lusty western, with some hilarious comedy sequences, good actors. (Dir: George Marshall, 93 mins.)

Texas Across the River (1966)** Dean Martin, Alain Delon, Rosemary Forsyth. This western is geared for belly laughs, but only achieves grins and an occasional titter. Martin is a gun runner who befriends Delon, playing a Spanish nobleman who's having romantic problems. Just to make sure you know what you're to expect from this film, Joey Bishop plays Martin's wise-cracking Indian buddy. (Dir: Michael Gordon, 101 mins.)

Texas Carnival (1951)*** Red Skelton, Esther Williams, Howard Keel, Ann Miller. Carnival barker and a chorus girl become involved in mix-ups at a swank desert resort. Fast moving musical comedy has the usual funny Skelton clowning and a general air of merriment. (Dir: Charles Walters, 77 mins.)

Texas Lady (1955)** Claudette Colbert, Barry Sullivan. Claudette Colbert, always a lady to her fingertips on the screen, finds herself miscast as a crusading newspaper lady of the old west. (Dir: Tim Whelan, 86 mins.)

Texas Rangers, The (1951)**½ George Montgomery, Gale Storm, Jerome Courtland. A band of notorious outlaws get together to fight the Texas Rangers. Enough gunplay for a dozen westerns. (Dir: Phil Karlson, 68 mins.)

Texican, The (U.S.-Spain, 1966)*½ Audie Murphy, Broderick Crawford. Unjustly framed and hounded by a powerful frontier boss, Texan seeks revenge when his brother gets killed. O.K. western adventure. (Dir: Lesley Selander, 86 mins.)

Thank You All Very Much (British, 1969)*** Sandy Dennis, Eleanor Bron, Ian McKellen. Rosalind (Sandy Dennis), a Ph.D. candidate, finds herself pregnant after her first affair, and decides to have and keep her baby. Touching, unsentimental presentation of a "controversial" subject; the film does not moralize or patronize. It portrays Rosalind as vulnerable, while also capable of taking care of herself and succeeding as an independent person. Refreshing film, with moving performance from Miss Dennis. (Dir: Waris Hussein, 107 mins.)

Thank You, Jeeves (1936)**½ Arthur Treacher, David Niven. You'll love Mr. Treacher as P. G. Wodehouse's butler and David Niven as his tolerant employer. Plot of the film is horribly routine. (Dir: Arthur Greville, 60 mins.)

Thank Your Lucky Stars (1943)*** Eddie Cantor and All-Star Cast. Silly film containing all the Warner Bros. stars of 1943. A few good songs including "They're Either Too Young or Too Old." Recommended for star gazers. (Dir: David Bulter, 127 mins.)

Thanks a Million (1935)*** Fred Allen, Dick Powell, Ann Dvorak. Dated but often amusing musical about a crooner who runs for governor. Fred Allen steals the picture as the campaign manager. (Dir: Roy Del Ruth, 87 mins.)

Thanks for Everything (1938)*** Jack Haley, Jack Oakie, Adolphe Menjou. Very cute comedy about an advertising agency that discovers the perfect average American. Haley is perfect in the role. (Dir: William A. Seiter)

That Certain Feeling (1956)***½ Bob Hope, Eva Marie Saint, George Sanders. Artist is hired by a famous syndicated cartoonist to "ghost" a famous comic strip, falls for a secretary. In the better class of Hope comedies with bright lines, witty situations, delightful performances. (Dir: Norman Panama, 103 mins.)

That Certain Summer (1972)**** Hal Holbrook, Hope Lange. Sensitive treatment of controversial subject (for American TV) makes worthwhile drama. Holbrook gives a devastatingly touching performance as a homosexual who is confronted with the torment of discovering that his 14-year-old son has found out about him. Scott Jacoby, a talented young actor, brings a naturalness to the difficult role of Holbrook's son. Miss Lange as Holbrook's ex-wife, and Martin Sheen as the man he lives with, offer excellent support. Script is tasteful and honest. Made-for-TV. (Dir: Lamont Johnson, 73 mins.)

That Certain Woman (1937)** Bette Davis, Henry Fonda. Maudlin, sentimental drama of a woman trying desperately to live down her past. Too heavy for modern taste. (Dir: Edmund Goulding, 100 mins.)

That Cold Day in the Park (U.S.-Canada, 1969)* Sandy Dennis, Michael Burns, John Garfield, Jr. Early, distasteful Robert Altman film about a mature spinster who takes in a rain-soaked, silent boy from the street, becomes obsessed and possessive about him, while he milks her for material comforts and cavorts with an incestuous sister and her boyfriend on the sly. Acting is static. Based on this lurid claptrap, it's hard to believe Altman went on to become one of our most innovative, talented filmmakers. Screenplay by Gillian Freeman based on the novel by Gerald Perreau Saussine, alias Richard Miles. (Dir: Robert Altman, 112 mins.)

That Darn Cat (1965)**½ Dean Jones, Hayley Mills, Dorothy Provine. Jones, Mills and an independent Siamese cat romp through this amusing Disney opus. The plot is thin and convoluted—the cat stumbles on some bad guys—but fast-paced enough to keep the kids involved. The supporting cast includes

Elsa Lanchester, Roddy McDowall, William Demarest, Neville Brand, and Frank Gorshin. (Dir: Robert Stevenson, 116 mins.)

That Forsythe Woman (1949)**½ Greer Garson, Errol Flynn, Janet Leigh. Rather long and on the dull side. Greer Garson falls in love with the man who is engaged to her niece. Acting is good. Based on Galsworthy's "A Man of Property." (Dir: Compton Bennett, 114 mins.)

That Funny Feeling (1965)**½ Sandra Dee, Bobby Darin, Donald O'Connor. Girl who has been working as a maid meets a young executive, gives him her working address as a cover-up, and it's his apartment. Amusing comedy has occasional bright dialogue, pleasant performers. (Dir: Richard Thorpe, 93 mins.)

That Hagen Girl (1947)* Ronald Reagan, Shirley Temple. Pictures like this trash must be the reason Shirley is so happily retired. Here she's adopted, supposedly illegitimate, plagued by gossip but Ron comes to her rescue. Just in time for the obvious fade-out. (Dir: Peter Godfrey, 83 mins.)

That Hamilton Woman (1941)*** Vivien Leigh, Laurence Olivier. The romantic story of the love of Lord Nelson, British naval hero, for the beautiful Lady Hamilton, with its tragic outcome. Two fine stars in a long, but interesting costume drama. (Dir: Alexander Korda, 128 mins.)

That Kind of Woman (1959)** Sophia Loren, Tab Hunter, George Sanders. Fans of Sophia Loren will particularly appreciate this romantic yarn, which was among the first films made in this country by the glamorous Italian star. Despite some excellent New York location shots and the directorial talents of Sidney Lumet, the tale about a beautiful woman who makes an attempt to find true love with a young soldier (Tab Hunter) adds up to glossy soap opera for the ladies. (92 mins.)

That Lady (British, 1955)** Olivia de Havilland, Gilbert Roland, Paul Scofield. Love of a princess for a commoner is thwarted by the king's love for her and court intrigue. Stodgy costume drama moves slowly. Notable only for a small role well played by the brilliant Scofield. (Dir: Terence Young, 100 mins.)

That Lady in Ermine (1948)*** Betty

Grable, Cesar Romero, Douglas Fairbanks Jr. A mish-mash of dreams and ancestors stepping out of their portraits makes for an entertaining little sophisticated musical comedy. (Dir: Ernst Lubitsch, 89 mins.)

That Man from Rio (1964)*** Jean-Paul Belmondo, Francoise Dorleac. French director Philippe de Broca has fashioned a clever chase film, and he's been wise to cast Belmondo in the lead. Belmondo is all acrobatic energy and quizzical looks as the soldier on leave who finds himself in the middle of a treasure hunt led by international thieves . . . when all he wants to do is rescue his kidnapped fiancee, played by the late Miss Dorleac. The final scenes, set in Brasilia, are breathtakingly photographed. (114 mins.)

That Man George (French-Spanish-Italian, 1966)*½ George Hamilton, Claudine Auger, Daniel Invernal. Another perfect plan to snatch a gold bullion shipment goes awry. Lots of violence, little sense. (Dir: Jacques Deray, 90 mins.)

That Man in Istanbul (French-Spanish, 1965)*½ Horst Buchholz, Sylva Koscina, Klaus Kinsky. Straining for effects at all turns, this meandering espionage yarn runs out of steam long before it has run out of lovely shots of Istanbul. Buchholz makes an attractive playboy nightclub owner who is pressed into spy duty by a curvaceous Sylva Koscina, the Italian sexpot who mysteriously plays a U.S. agent in this dim-witted opus. (Dir: Anthony Isasi, 117 mins.)

That Midnight Kiss (1949)**½ Kathryn Grayson, Mario Lanza, Ethel Barrymore. Mario Lanza's debut film. Light and romantic story about a patroness of the arts (Ethel Barrymore) and her singing discoveries. Many songs by Lanza and Grayson. (Dir: Norman Taurog, 96 mins.)

That Night (1957)*** John Beal, Augusta Dabney. Dramatic tale of a man suffering a heart attack, the consequences of its aftermath. Well done artistically and technically. (Dir: John Newland, 88 mins.)

That Night in Rio (1941)**½ Alice Faye, Don Ameche, Carmen Miranda. Lavish but routine screen musical employing the old mistaken identity plot to no advantage. Carmen is great in her numbers but the film

isn't much. (Dir: Irving Cummings, 90 mins.)

That Touch of Mink (1962)***½ Cary Grant, Doris Day, Gig Young. All about how a business tycoon makes a play for an unemployed damsel, and vice versa, until the inevitable climax. Enjoyable comedy, lightly spicy, with some beautiful people romping in beautiful settings; just the thing for audience relaxation. (Dir: Delbert Mann, 99 mins.)

That Uncertain Feeling (1941)*** Merle Oberon, Melvyn Douglas, Burgess Meredith. When the wife falls for a screwball concert pianist, the husband decides it's high time he put his foot down. Delightful sophisticated comedy, directed by Ernst Lubitsch. Grand fun. (Dir: Ernst Lubitsch, 84 mins.)

That Way With Women (1947)** Dane Clark, Martha Vickers. Remake of Arliss' "The Millionaire" which has also been released for TV contains none of the flavor or charm of the original. (Dir: Frederick de Cordova, 84 mins.)

That Woman Opposite (British, 1957)** Phyllis Kirk, Dan O'Herlihy. Insurance investigator solves murder at a French resort. Slow mystery relies upon dialogue at the sacrifice of action.

That Wonderful Urge (1949)**½ Tyrone Power, Gene Tierney. Glamour girl has her revenge upon a reporter who's been writing nasty articles about her. Mildly pleasant romantic comedy. (Dir: Robert B. Sinclair, 82 mins.)

That's Entertainment (1974)**** Judy Garland, Fred Astaire, Frank Sinatra, Gene Kelly, Esther Williams. The title is right. It is marvelous entertainment. Scenes from some of the great MGM musicals released from 1929 to 1958 and most of them are still great entertainment. They won't be reproducing those lavish Esther Williams swimming scenes again, so tune in if you're nostalgic or in search of wonderful entertainers just struttin' their stuff. Written and directed by Jack Haley, Jr. (135 mins.)

That's Entertainment, Part 2 (1976)**** Fred Astaire, Gene Kelly, Judy Garland, Katharine Hepburn, Frank Sinatra, Spencer Tracy. Those believing that the cream of MGM's musical footage was exhausted by Part I are in for a pleasant surprise, as the studio's archives have delivered a spectacular sequel to the musical mélange that summed up a fair share of screen history. The 75 films culled are interwoven with new footage of Astaire and Kelly dancing together for the first time in 30 years. Virtually all of the stars are here, so whether your favorite is Garbo or Lassie, tune in for another marvelous, nostalgic orgy. Some of the fabulous goodies include the Judy Garland-Gene Kelly number "Be a Clown" from "The Pirate," ravishing Lena Horne singing "The Lady Is a Tramp," and Astaire and Cyd Charisse strutting through "All of You" from Cole Porter's "Silk Stockings." Gene Kelly directed the new sequences. (133 mins.)

That's My Boy (1951)** Dean Martin, Jerry Lewis, Eddie Mayehoff. Blustering former athletic hero wants his anemic son to follow in his footsteps. Early Martin & Lewis comedy suffers from hammering repetition of gags. Primarily for their fans. (Dir: Hal Walker, 98 mins.)

That's My Man (1947)**½ Don Ameche, Catherine McLeod. Gambler starts with a colt and a girl, becomes wealthy stable owner but a flop as a husband. Lengthy racing drama, heavy with sentiment, has good acting to see it through.

That's Right—You're Wrong (1939) **½ Kay Kyser, Lucille Ball, Dennis O'Keefe. Kyser's orchestra goes to Hollywood to make a picture, where the moguls try to change him. Amusing musical.

Theatre of Blood (British, 1973)*** Vincent Price, Diana Rigg, Robert Morley. Fine black comedy with Price as a Shakespearean actor seeking revenge on eight critics who he believes denied him a best-acting prize. Price is precious, and he is backed by an all-star supporting cast in the roles of the critics. (Dir: Douglas Hell, 104 mins.)

Theatre of Death (Great Britain, 1966)* Christopher Lee, Lelia Goldoni, Julian Glover. British-made thriller, not up to usual standards. Vampire-like killer stalks the stage of Parisian "Grand Guignol." (Dir: Samuel Gallu, 90 mins.)

Their Last Night (French, 1953)** Jean Gabin, Madeleine Robinson. Librarian who is really a notorious gang leader seeks the aid of a girl when the police begin to close in. Flat crime drama dubbed in English is reminiscent of prewar Gabin films, only not as good.

Them (1954)**½ James Whitmore, Edmund Gwenn, James Arness. Entertaining science fiction thriller about creatures from another age who appear suddenly near the Mojave Desert. Treated like a murder mystery rather than the shock approach usually employed in such SF films. (Dir: Gordon Douglas, 94 mins.)

Then Came Bronson (1969)** Michael Parks, Bonnie Bedelia, Akim Tamiroff. Another pilot film for a TV series! Michael Parks stars as Bronson, a young reporter who chucks it all when his friend commits suicide, leaving him his motorcycle. The film is slow moving and the dialogue, stilted. Parks, an exponent of the slouch and mumble school of acting, is well cast as the rebel searching for (as he puts it) "his piece of the world." Bonnie Bedelia is appealing as a runaway bride who latches on to Bronson and falls in love. (Dir: William Graham, 100 mins.)

Then There Were Three (1962)**½ Frank Latimore, Alex Nicol. German officer infiltrates the American lines to kill an Italian partisan. Neat little combination of WW II and mystery yarn, filmed in Italy. No epic, but well done. (Dir: Alex Nicol, 82 mins.)

Theodora, Slave Empress (Italian, 1954)** Irene Papas, Georges Marchal, Gianna Maria Canale. Lavish but dull epic film about the days of the Roman Empire. Acting is in exaggerated style of Grand Opera. (Dir: Riccardo Freda, 88 mins.)

There Goes Barder (French, 1955)*½ Eddie Constantine, May Britt. Soldier of fortune sees plenty of action when he is hired to deliver contraband machine guns. Weak imitation of American-style hard-boiled action tale. Dubbed in English.

There Goes My Girl (1937)*** Gene Raymond, Ann Sothern. Boy and girl reporters love each other, but are bitter rivals when a murder story breaks. Well done comedy, light and amusing. (Dir: Ben Holmes, 80 mins.)

There Goes My Heart (1939)**½ Fredric March, Virginia Bruce.

Spoiled heiress skips home and becomes a salesgirl, where a reporter discovers her secret. Pleasant, amusing comedy. (Dir: Norman Z. McLeod, 90 mins.)

There Goes the Groom (1937)**½ Burgess Meredith, Ann Sothern. Man blessed with sudden riches marries, and has in-law trouble. Diverting comedy. (Dir: Joseph Santley, 70 mins.)

There Was a Crooked Man (1970)*** Kirk Douglas, Henry Fonda, Hume Cronyn, Lee Grant, Burgess Meredith. Douglas, as a robber serving time in prison (circa 1880's), and Fonda, as a reform-oriented warden, spark this western tale. Although the script may get too talky at times, director Joseph L. Mankiewicz builds the action with a knowing hand, leading to the film's final confrontation between the two flinty leads. (118 mins.)

There Was an Old Couple (Russian, 1965)**** Ivan Marin, Vera Kuznetsova, Lyudmila Maximova. A gentle, touching and moving film about an aged Russian farm couple who go to live with one of their children after their home is destroyed. Sensitively directed by Grigory Choukhrai, who also directed the beautiful "Ballad of a Soldier." Uniformly well acted. English subtitles.

There's a Girl in My Soup (British, 1970)*** Peter Sellers, Goldie Hawn, Tony Britton. The delightful combination of confidant Sellers as a TV gourmet and scatterbrained Hawn as a girl who disrupts his freewheeling life-style adds up to fun. Based on the London and Broadway stage comedy, the screen version is better. It ambles along quite nicely, and some of the lines are very funny. (Dir: Roy Boulting, 96 mins.)

There's Always a Price Tag (French, 1957)** Michele Morgan, Daniel Gelin. Wicked wife draws her lover into a plot to get rid of her husband. Crime drama is bogged down in a welter of conversation. (Dir: Denys De La Patelliere, 102 mins.)

There's Always a Thursday (British, 1957)** Charles Victor, Frances Day. In this lightweight British comedy, a henpecked spouse blossoms into a full fledged louse. Some good acting.

There's Always a Woman (1938)*** Joan Blondell, Melvyn Douglas. Private eye returns to the D. A.'s

office and gives his agency to his wife; then they find themselves working on the same murder case. Entertaining comedy-mystery. (Dir: Alexander Hall, 80 mins.)

There's Always Tomorrow (1956)**½ Barbara Stanwyck, Fred MacMurray, Joan Bennett. A woman's picture about the noble sacrifice Miss Stanwyck makes when she realizes she's breaking up MacMurray and Miss Bennett's marriage of many years. Cliched and overacted, but the ladies will eat it up. (Dir: Douglas Sirk, 84 mins.)

There's No Business Like Show Business (1954)*** Ethel Merman, Marilyn Monroe, Donald O'Connor, Dan Dailey, Mitzi Gaynor, Johnny Ray. Over-produced show biz story about a trouping family and their plights on and off the stage. Many Irving Berlin songs make the film worthwhile. Some are "Remember," "Heat Wave," "Play a Simple Melody" and, of course, the title tune belted out by Miss Merman. (Dir: Walter Lang, 117 mins.)

Thérèse Etienne (French, 1957)** Francoise Arnoul, James Robertson-Justice, Pierre Vaneck. Old plot about the elderly farmer marrying the young servant girl, who is loved by the returning son. Dubbed in English.

These Are the Damned (British, 1963)** Oliver Reed, Viveca Lindfors, Alexander Knox, Shirley Ann Field. Choppy mixture of sci-fi and social commentary, as an American (Mcdonald Carey) comes upon some strange children while fleeing from a motorcycle gang. Drastically cut from the original length, which may explain the cloudiness of this film from fine director Joseph Losey. (77 mins.)

These Glamour Girls (1939)*** Lana Turner, Lew Ayres, Anita Louise. Good satirical comedy about college life although the film's social implications have lost their bite. You'll still enjoy seeing a sexy Lana make fools out of a pack of debutantes. (Dir: S. Sylvan Simon, 80 mins.)

These Thousand Hills (1959)**½ Don Murray, Richard Egan, Lee Remick, Patricia Owens, Stuart Whitman. Occasionally interesting, frequently meandering western about a young cowpoke who becomes prosperous in the Old West, and the troubles that beset him. Would have been better with more directness, less introspection. (Dir: Richard Fleischer, 96 mins.)

These Three (1936)***½ Merle Oberon, Joel McCrea, Miriam Hopkins. A watered-down version of Lillian Hellman's provocative play "The Children's Hour" about a scandal which ruins the lives of three people. Bonita Granville is excellent as a young school girl who sets the fuse of scandal about her two school teachers, the Misses Hopkins and Oberon. (Dir: William Wyler, 90 mins.)

These Wilder Years (1956)**½ James Cagney, Barbara Stanwyck, Walter Pidgeon. Steel magnate searches for his illegitimate son of 20, runs into unexpected opposition. Trouping by veterans saves this soap opera from becoming too much. (Dir: Roy Rowland, 91 mins.)

They All Kissed the Bride (1942)**½ Joan Crawford, Melvyn Douglas. Career girl learns the importance of love in this familiar, but mildly amusing film. (Dir: Alexander Hall, 85 mins.)

They Call It Murder (1971)** Jim Hutton, Lloyd Bochner, Jessica Walter. Average murder mystery, as the D.A. finds a corpse in a swimming pool and tries to link the victim to an insurance claim and a car crash. Based on an Erle Stanley Gardner novel. Made-for-TV. (Dir: Walter Grauman, 100 mins.)

They Call Me Mr. Tibbs (1970)** Sidney Poitier, Martin Landau, Barbara McNair, Juano Hernandez, Norma Crane. A sequel to the first-rate "In the Heat of the Night" but nowhere near as good. Sidney's playing Virgil Tibbs again, but this time the locale is not the Deep South but the Far West, and a lot's been lost in the trek to San Francisco. Absolutely routine homicide drama, with Poitier looking and acting, quite understandably, very bored. The fine Juano Hernandez is seen in his last film role, playing an intimidated building handyman. Actress Norma Crane, known to her intimate friends as "Tiger," does not claw anyone, but is effective in a supporting role. (Dir: Gordon Douglas, 108 mins.)

They Came to Cordura (1959)** Gary Cooper, Rita Hayworth, Van Heflin, Tab Hunter. Slow moving tale about six soldiers (circa 1916) and one woman who make an arduous trek across impossible terrain to reach Cordura, a military outpost. The personal feelings of the seven are bared during the interminable journey. Many big stars are wasted in this dry pic. (Dir: Robert Rossen, 123 mins.)

They Came to Rob Las Vegas (Spanish-French-West German-Italian, 1968)* Gary Lockwood, Elke Sommer, Lee J. Cobb, Jack Palance. Trivial crime drama in the Nevada desert as criminals rob an armored truck filled with gold. Shot in Spain. Burgled international junk. (Dir: Antonio Isasi, 130 mins.)

They Can't Hang Me (British, 1955)**½ Terence Morgan, Yolande Donlan. Condemned murderer bargains his freedom for information about a vital security leak. Unimportant but fast-moving mystery.

They Died with Their Boots On (1941)*** Errol Flynn, Olivia de Havilland. It's Custer and the famous battle of Little Big Horn with enough expense for every male extra in Hollywood to get shot. Not too accurate, of course, but a good western. (Dir: Raoul Walsh, 138 mins.)

They Drive by Night (1940)*** George Raft, Humphrey Bogart, Ann Sheridan, Ida Lupino. This story of the trucking business starts out in high but runs out of gas in the middle. Story of the competition in the trucking business is told with plenty of action and excitement but they had to bring in a silly murder trial and spoil the whole thing. (Dir: Raoul Walsh, 93 mins.)

They Gave Him a Gun (1937)*½ Spencer Tracy, Gladys George, Franchot Tone. Soldier likes guns so when he gets out he becomes a gangster. Silly, contrived, corny melodrama, unworthy of its cast. (Dir: W. S. Van Dyke, 100 mins.)

They Got Me Covered (1943)**½ Bob Hope, Dorothy Lamour, Otto Preminger. A typical Hope vs. the German enemy agents chase film, which means it's fun all the way. Hope's favorite brunette, Lamour, is around for the antics and director Otto Preminger is cast as a sinister enemy agent, a part he has played many times. (95 mins.)

They Knew What They Wanted (1940)***½ Charles Laughton, Carole Lombard. Italian grape-grower takes a lonely waitress as a bride, with tragedy following. Powerful, finely acted drama. (Dir: Garson Kanin, 96 mins.)

They Live By Night (1949)***½ Farley Granger, Cathy O'Donnell. Moving, occasionally lyrical story about two young doomed lovers during the depression in the 1930's based on the 1937 novel "Thieves Like Us," by Edward Anderson. An impressive directorial debut for Nicholas Ray. Interesting to compare Ray's handling of the novel with the 1974 "Thieves Like Us" directed by Robert Altman. (Dir: Nicholas Ray, 95 mins.)

They Made Me a Criminal (1939)*** John Garfield, Ann Sheridan, Dead End Kids. Mr. Garfield's dynamic, yet sensitive, portrayal of a fugitive boxer who thinks he has murdered a man is so stirring that it lifts this commonplace story to the level of entertainment. (Dir: Busby Berkeley, 110 mins.)

They Made Me a Killer (1946)**½ Robert Lowery, Barbara Britton. Young man is forced to join some bank robbers, but finally outwits them. Fast moving melodrama with plenty of action.

They Met In Bombay (1941)**½ Clark Gable, Rosalind Russell. Routine adventure story about a couple of jewel thieves who fall in love and in order to clear his name before the fadeout he joins forces with the English in a battle against the Japs. Confusing? Just another film. (Dir: Clarence Brown, 86 mins.)

They Might Be Giants (1971)*** George C. Scott, Joanne Woodward. Bizarre, sentimental fable displaying Scott as Justine Playfair, a retired judge who believes himself to be Sherlock Holmes. The judge's brother calls on a female Dr. Watson (Miss Woodward) to have Scott committed so he can inherit the family fortune. But Scott embraces a world too absurd to be touched by this ploy. Sometimes muddled, often appealing, and Scott and Woodward are splendid. Screenplay by James Goldman. (Dir: Anthony Harvey, 88 mins.)

They Only Come Out at Night (1975) *½ Jack Warden, Tim O'Connor, Madeline Sherwood, Joe Mantell. Jack Warden is better than his material in this routine police drama. He plays John St. John, an old member of the L.A.P.D. detective

716

division. Made-for-TV. (Dir: Daryl Duke, 72 mins.)

They Only Kill Their Masters (1972) **½ James Garner, June Allyson, Peter Lawford, Hal Holbrook. James Garner's casual approach to his role as a California town police chief is a diverting note in this offbeat murder mystery. A swinger is found dead on the beach. Prime suspects include June Allyson, as an aging woman with a key to the whole thing; Peter Lawford, as the victim's husband; and Hal Holbrook, as a veterinarian. Some nice moments in original screenplay by Lane Slate. (Dir: James Goldstone, 97 mins.)

They Ran for Their Lives (1965)* Boring chase film starring and directed by John Payne. He plays a man who helps a young woman evade her pursuers. The cliches are many and the characters one-dimensional. (Dir: John Payne, 92 mins.)

They Rode West (1954)*** Robert Francis, Donna Reed, May Wynn. Better than average western drama dealing with the efforts of a courageous young doctor to maintain peace with the Kiowa Indians. (Dir: Phil Karlson, 84 mins.)

They Shall Have Music (1939)**½ Joel McCrea, Walter Brennan, Marjorie Main. A moderately successful drama about an east side settlement house for young musicians. An attempt to duplicate the box-office success of the 1937 film "Dead End." The highlight of the film is the violin artistry of Jascha Heifetz. (Dir: Archie Mayo, 100 mins.)

They Shall Not Die—See: Serengeti

They Shoot Horses, Don't They? (1969)**** Jane Fonda, Michael Sarrazin, Gig Young. Excellent film depicting the madness and desperation of the depression era's marathon dance contests. Based on the 1935 novel by Horace McCoy. The cast is perfect . . . Jane Fonda's brittle, beaten Gloria; Gig Young's superbly seedy master-of-ceremonies; Susannah York's bewildered Hollywood starlet down on her luck; Michael Sarrazin's poetic young man; and Red Buttons' over-age sailor. The actual dance sessions, especially the "sprints," are magnificently staged by director Sydney Pollack. (121 mins.)

They Were Expendable (1945)***½ John Wayne, Robert Montgomery.

Good, exciting adventure story dedicated to the Navy men who fought Japanese vessels in small PT boats. A top drawer war picture if your taste still runs that way. (Dir: John Ford, 135 mins.)

They Were Sisters (British, 1946)*** James Mason, Phyllis Calvert. The love affairs and marital mishaps of three devoted sisters are related. Well acted drama. (Dir: Arthur Crabtree, 110 mins.)

They Were So Young (1955)*** Scott Brady, Johanna Matz. Innocent girls are sent to South America as entertainers and killed if they resist. Rather lurid but well-made melodrama with a good cast. Produced in Germany. (Dir: Kurt Neumann, 80 mins.)

They Who Dare (British, 1954)*** Dirk Bogarde, Akim Tamiroff. Six Englishmen and four Greek soldiers are assigned to blow up air fields in Rhodes when Allied communication lines are being hampered. Well made, frequently exciting drama of World War II. (Dir: Lewis Milestone, 101 mins.)

They Won't Believe Me (1947)***½ Robert Young, Susan Hayward. Man intending to kill his wife doesn't succeed, but through a quirk of fate goes on trial anyway. Absorbing ironic melodrama. (Dir: Irving Pichel, 95 mins.)

They Won't Forget (1937)**** Claude Rains, Allan Joslyn. An exceptional drama about a prosecutor in a southern town who turns a murder case into a political stepping stone. Good writing, superb acting and Mervyn Le Roy's expert direction make this a compelling film. (Dir: Mervyn Le Roy, 100 mins.)

Thief, The (1952)*** Ray Milland, Rita Gam. Story of how a Communist spy is forced to kill an FBI agent, and how his conscience causes him to give himself up. Unusual in that there is no dialogue; the only sounds are the musical score, and background noises. As such, a novelty; otherwise, the effect is forced, the melodrama routine. (Dir: Russell Rouse, 85 mins.)

Thief (1971)**½ Richard Crenna, Angie Dickinson, Cameron Mitchell, Hurd Hatfield. Writer John D. F. Black combines suspense with interesting character development as half-hero, half-heel Crenna is in a solid bind when he must rob to pay a gambling debt. Good support from Dickinson as a puzzled lady who wants to know her man better; Mitchell as a lawyer and Hatfield as a fence for jewelry. Made-for-TV. (Dir: William Graham, 72 mins.)

Thief of Bagdad, The (British, 1940)** Sabu, Conrad Veidt, June Duprez. The Arabian Nights tale about the wily thief who outwits the wicked Grand Visier of Bagdad with the aid of a powerful genii. All quite unbelievable, but entertaining if one goes for this sort of thing. (Dirs: Ludwig Berger, Tim Whelan, Michael Powell, 106 mins.)

Thief of Bagdad (Italian, 1962)** Muscle man Steve Reeves in the Arabian Nights adventure epic—colorful, but on a juvenile level. (Dir: Arthur Lubin, 90 mins.)

Thief Who Came to Dinner, The (1973)**½ Ryan O'Neal, Jacqueline Bisset, Warren Oates, Jill Clayburgh. If you are a Ryan O'Neal fan, you'll enjoy this ambling comedy crime film which casts the actor as a computer programmer who happens to be a cat burglar on the side. Some of the plot gets too involved, but you'll enjoy the characters, including beautiful Jacqueline Bisset and especially Jill Clayburgh, in the small role of Ryan's actress ex-wife who decides to look up her former husband again while passing through town with a touring company. (Dir: Bud Yorkin, 105 mins.)

Thieves' Highway (1949)*** Richard Conte, Valentino Cortesa, Lee J. Cobb. Action-melodrama concerning truckers, trollops and thugs, on the long haul delivering fresh vegetables to market. Italian actress Valentina Cortesa makes a fine American debut. (Dir: Jules Dassin, 94 mins.)

Thieves Like Us (1974)**** Keith Carradine, Shelley Duvall, John Schuck, Louise Fletcher, Joan Tewkesbury. A marvelous second screen version, directed by Robert Altman, of the 1937 novel by Edward Anderson and first filmed by Nicholas Ray in the 1949 entry "They Live By Night." Story, of a pair of doomed lovers during the Depression, is extremely skillfully adapted by Calder Willingham, Joan Tewkesbury and Altman himself. This was Altman's fifth film since "M*A*S*H" and it's a work

717

of great control, full of beautifully perceived, illuminating moments. The performances are uniformly excellent, especially Carradine and Duvall who give sensitive, touching performances as the doomed young lovers. (Dir: Robert Altman, 123 mins.)

Thin Air (U.S.-Great Britain, 1969)* George Sanders, Maurice Evans, Robert Flemyng. Parachutists vanish, extra-terrestrial beings are blamed. Unsteady sci-fi, liberally spiced with sexy attention-getters. Feeble script. (Dir: Gerry Levy, 91 mins.)

Thin Ice (1937)*** Sonja Henie, Tyrone Power. Fast moving, entertaining musical fantasy about the romance of a skating instructor and a prince. Plenty of Sonja's skating and generally a good film. (Dir: Sidney Lanfield, 78 mins.)

Thin Man, The (1933)***½ Myrna Loy, William Powell. Daddy of a long line of films concerning the adventures of the Dashiell Hammett character is fast, funny, well played and good entertainment. (Dir: W. S. Van Dyke, 100 mins.)

Thin Man Goes Home, The (1944)**½ William Powell, Myrna Loy. Series returns after a four-year hiatus and is way off standard. There's a murder, some good dialogue but it's sadly lacking in the usual fast paced witticisms. (Dir: Richard Thorpe, 100 mins.)

Thin Red Line, The (1964)**½ Keir Dullea, Jack Warden. James Jones' fine novel of the men who fought and died at Guadalcanal made into an uneven film with some fine rugged battle scenes, but a story treatment that never quite jells. (Dir: Andrew Marton, 99 mins.)

Thing, The (1951)*** Kenneth Tobey, Margaret Sheridan. Scientific research station in the Arctic comes across a monster from another world. Sufficiently thrilling fantastic melodrama. (Dir: Christian Nyby, 87 mins.)

Thing With Two Heads, The (1972)½ Ray Milland, Rosey Grier. Rubbish about grafted heads must have been made by people with a botched frontal lobotomy. Milland's head is grafted on to Grier's body and . . . (Dir: Lee Frost, 90 mins.)

Things to Come (British, 1936)*** Raymond Massey, Ralph Richardson. The H. G. Wells fantasy about

718

the destructive world war that wiped out life as we know it, but which paved the way for a better world. Imaginative, absorbing, elaborately produced. (Dr. William Cameron Menzies, 100 mins.)

Third Alibi, The (British, 1959)** Laurence Payne, Patricia Dainton, Jane Griffiths. Husband desiring to rid himself of his wife so he can marry her sister devises an elaborate murder plan. Average Grade B melodrama.

Third Day, The (1965)**½ George Peppard, Elizabeth Ashley, Roddy McDowall. Fairly engrossing tale about an amnesiac (George Peppard) who has to piece together many events in his past after an auto crash and a possible murder. Peppard looks bewildered enough to carry off his role but it's Roddy McDowall's performance as an oily relative ready to do him in at every turn which is the standout. The competent supporting cast includes Herbert Marshall, Arthur O'Connell and Arte Johnson in a serious role. (Dir: Jack Smight, 119 mins.)

Third Finger Left Hand (1940)** Melvyn Douglas, Myrna Loy. Not funny in spite of good acting is this sophisticated comedy about a cold cookie who falls for a guy but plays hard to get. (Dir: Robert Z. Leonard, 96 mins.)

Third Girl from the Left, The (1973)**½ Kim Novak, Tony Curtis, Michael Brandon. Miss Novak made her TV feature debut in this familiar story about an over-the-hill New York chorine who's reached the crossroads in her life—she loses her front-row spot in the chorus; terminates her 13-year engagement to her nightclub singer-comic boyfriend; and finds herself attracted to a very attentive and winning younger man. Dory Previn's script has flashes of truth and insight going for Miss Novak's character, but the men in her life fall into the cliche mold. (Dir: Peter Medak, 74 mins.)

Third Key (British, 1956)***½ Jack Hawkins, Dorothy Allison. Police search for a safecracker, and the chase leads them to murder. Exciting crime drama. (Dir: Charles Frend, 96 mins.)

Third Man, The (British, 1949)**** Joseph Cotten, Valli, Orson Welles, Trevor Howard. Masterpiece about an American writer in Vienna, who discovers his old friend may not be dead after all, but at the head of a vicious black market organization. One of the best post-war thrillers, written by Graham Greene, directed by Carol Reed. And that zither music! (104 mins.)

Third Secret, The (1964)*** Stephen Boyd, Pamela Franklin. Uneven but often interesting psychological drama. When a leading British psychiatrist dies and the coroner's verdict is suicide, his teen-age daughter convinces a TV commentator to investigate further. The film has a surprise ending. (Dir: Charles Crichton, 103 mins.)

Third Voice, The (1960)**** Edmond O'Brien, Laraine Day, Julie London. Fine suspense thriller made economically but excellently about an impostor hired to pose as a murdered financier by his private secretary. Particularly adept direction and script with top performances make this one a surprise hit. (Dir: Hubert Cornfeld, 79 mins.)

13 Frightened Girls (1963)½ Kathy Dunn, Murray Hamilton. Absurd, obvious, Cold War intrigues. Teen-ager capitalizes on her age to engage in some reckless spying, aiding her idol, a C.I.A. agent. Unintentionally funny. (Dir: William Castle, 89 mins.)

Thirteen Ghosts (1960)** Charles Herbert, Jo Morrow. A thoroughly gimmicked horror film. Mild entertainment, as a professor and family move into a haunted house. (Dir: William Castle, 88 mins.)

13 Rue Madeleine (1947)**½ James Cagney, Annabella. Fair semi-documentary spy story which gets confused in the middle and never seems to straighten out. If you'll accept American agent Cagney posing as a Frenchman, you may like this. (Dir: Henry Hathaway, 95 mins.)

13 West Street (1962)**½ Alan Ladd, Rod Steiger, Michael Callan, Dolores Dorn. Man beaten by a gang of teenagers refuses to cooperate with the police, seeks his own revenge. Tough little crime drama will generally have the viewer on its side; effective use of the it-could-happen-to-you idea. (Dir: Philip Leacock, 80 mins.)

13th Letter, The (1951)*** Charles Boyer, Linda Darnell, Constance Smith. Small town in Canada is in turmoil when a series of incriminating letters appear. Remake of French film "The Raven" carries suspense, fine performances, direction by Otto Preminger. Absorbing. (85 mins.)

—30— (1959)**½ Jack Webb, William Conrad. A night in the life of a powerful newspaper, Jack Webb-style. Okay, but not front page copy.

30 Foot Bride of Candy Rock, The (1959)*½ Lou Costello, Dorothy Provine. Corny, one joke idea that doesn't quite come off. Lou Costello falls in love with an out-sized beauty, Miss Provine blown up to 30 feet. (Dir: Sidney Miller, 75 mins.)

30 Is a Dangerous Age, Cynthia (British, 1968)***½ Suzy Kendall, Patricia Routledge, Eddie Foy, Jr., John Bird. All about the efforts of a piano player (Dudley Moore) to attain success and marriage by his 30th birthday—in six weeks' time. Moore is one of the English-speaking theater's most inventive comedy minds, and some of his virtuoso musical parodies give this uneven film moments of inspired lunacy. Kendall and Patricia Routledge are a great help, too. (Dir: Joseph McGrath, 98 mins.)

39 Steps, The (British, 1935)**** Robert Donat, Madeleine Carroll. A young man is accidentally thrown into a spy plot, races through England and Scotland with both the police and spies at his heels. A thriller classic! Excellent chase melodrama, one of Alfred Hitchcock's best. (Dir: Alfred Hitchcock, 80 mins.)

39 Steps, The (British, 1960)**½ Kenneth More, Taina Elg. This remake of the Alfred Hitchcock 1935 classic doesn't measure up to its predecessor, but suspense fans unfamiliar with the original will find enough here to sustain their interest. Mr. More and Miss Elg play a pair of innocent bystanders who become enmeshed in a tangle of murder and espionage. (Dir: Ralph Thomas, 95 mins.)

Thirty Seconds Over Tokyo (1944)*** Van Johnson, Spencer Tracy. An excellent war film which chronicles the story of our first raid on Japan. Slightly dated but still good entertainment. (Dir: Mervyn Le Roy, 138 mins.)

36 Hours (1964)*** James Garner, Rod Taylor, Eva Marie Saint. Army officer is abducted by the Nazis and made to believe the war has ended, so they can pry secrets from him. First half is excellent; as soon as the plot becomes clear, it gradually deteriorates into a routine World War II spy thriller. Performances quite good. (Dir: George Seaton, 115 mins.)

This Above All (1942)*** Tyrone Power, Joan Fontaine. Eric Knight's novel of the romance between a disillusioned British soldier and a patriotic girl is a powerful love story minus many of the book's values. Superbly directed, it is a bit too slow moving to hold sustained interest. Dated because of subject matter. (Dir: Anatole Litvak, 110 mins.)

This Angry Age (1958)*½ Anthony Perkins, Silvana Mangano, Jo Van Fleet, Richard Conte, Alida Valli. An attempt to make an American film with a foreign flavor by using an international cast and setting the action in Indo-China just doesn't come off. In fact, most of it is embarrassingly bad. Perkins and Mangano are brother and sister and they've just about had it with Mama Van Fleet's insane determination to make their poor rice plantation a going thing. The performances range from inept to awful. (Dir: Rene Clement, 111 mins.)

This Could Be the Night (1957)*** Jean Simmons, Anthony Franciosa, Paul Douglas. Entertaining comedy about a school teacher charmingly played by Jean Simmons, who takes a part-time job as a secretary to a night club owner, and ends up changing lives left and right. Franciosa comes on strong as the wolf who's tamed by Miss Simmons. (Dir: Robert Wise, 103 mins.)

This Earth Is Mine (1959)** Jean Simmons, Rock Hudson, Dorothy McGuire. Overdramatic tale about the internal problems of a neurotic family and the people who come in contact with them. Miss Simmons and Mr. Hudson make a very satisfactory love team and Miss McGuire does more than is required in an overwritten role. (Dir: Henry King, 125 mins.)

This Gun for Hire (1942)***½ Alan Ladd, Veronica Lake. Ladd's portrayal of a killer in this film made him a star. It's an exciting, tense tale of a hired killer who is double-crossed and seeks revenge. (Dir: Frank Tuttle, 80 mins.)

This Happy Breed (British, 1945) **** Robert Newton, Celia Johnson. Noel Coward's panoramic story of a family and of the house in which they live through two wars. Fine drama captures the spirit of England itself; exemplary in all departments. (Dir: David Lean, 110 mins.)

This Happy Feeling (1958)*** Debbie Reynolds, Curt Jurgens, John Saxon. Charming comedy about a young girl who fancies herself in love with a dashing older man. The complications are predictable but the cast plays it in the spirit in which it's intended. (Dir: Blake Edwards, 92 mins.)

This Is My Affair (1937)*** Robert Taylor, Barbara Stanwyck. Fairly colorful fiction about a secret service agent sent out by President McKinley to break up a gang of bank robbers. Well produced and exciting. (Dir: William A. Seiter, 99 mins.)

This Is Not a Test (1962)**½ Mary Morlas, Seamon Glass. Tough state trooper takes charge when word comes of an impending nuclear attack, joins a group held up by a roadblock. Grim little drama has the expected rough edges but occasionally whips up some powerful scenes.

This Is the West That Was (1974)*½ Ben Murphy, Kim Darby, Jane Alexander, Tony Franciosa, Matt Clark. Western comedies are often fragile vehicles, and this made-for-TV one just doesn't make it. Ben Murphy is Wild Bill Hickok, Kim Darby is Calamity Jane and Matt Clark is Buffalo Bill in this piece of nonsense which depicts Hickok as a hotshot gunfighter whose deeds of gunplay stem from the lively imagination of Calamity Jane. Made-for-TV. (Dir: Fielder Cook, 100 mins.)

This Island Earth (1955)**½ Faith Domergue, Jeff Morrow, Rex Reason. Scientists journey to a planet nearly destroyed by an interplanetary war. Some intriguing gadgetry for the sci-fi fans in this fanciful thriller. (Dir: Joseph M. Newman, 87 mins.)

This Land Is Mine (1943)***½ Charles Laughton, Maureen O'Hara, George Sanders. A timid schoolteacher becomes a hero when his country is overrun by Nazis. Fine performance by Laughton in this compelling drama. (Dir: Jean Renoir, 103 mins.)

This Love of Ours (1945)****½** Merle Oberon, Claude Rains, Charles Korvin. Maudlin soap opera about an unfaithful wife and mother who returns to her husband's home after 12 years to find resentment and finally love. Good performances by the cast. (Dir: William Dieterle, 90 mins.)

This Man Must Die (French, 1970) *****½** Michael Duchaussoy, Jean Yanne. Director Claude Chabrol has fashioned another fine crime tale. This time his main character is a man who vows to take revenge on the hit-and-run driver who killed his son. Duchaussoy plays the father, and Yanne plays the insidious and much-hated killer. The inevitability of their mutual destruction is beautifully played against the stunning backgrounds of France. (115 mins.)

This Man's Navy (1945)******* Wallace Beery, Tom Drake, Jan Clayton. Veteran officer in the balloon service "adopts" a lad and urges him to make good in the Navy. Familiar but well done melodrama. Good direction, performances. (Dir: William Wellman, 100 mins.)

This Property Is Condemned (1966) ****½** Natalie Wood, Robert Redford. The allure of stars Robert Redford and Natalie Wood, plus the characters created by Tennessee Williams in a one-act play, are the chief inducements in this Deep South soap opera about a free spirit of a girl (Miss Wood) longing for adventure and true love. The film begins interestingly enough, but it soon becomes as uneven as Natalie Wood's Southern accent. Redford manages to remain creditable as a railroad efficiency expert who comes to a small Mississippi town on business and remains for pleasure. Director Francis Ford Coppola and prize-winning producer Fred Coe had a hand in the screenplay. (Dir: Sydney Pollack, 110 mins.)

This Rebel Age—See: Beat Generation, The

This Rebel Breed (1960)****** Rita Moreno, Mark Damon, Gerald Mohr, Diane (later Dyan) Cannon. Undercover cops deal with narcotics and racial tensions in high school. We've seen it before, since and better! (Dir: Richard L. Bare, 90 mins.)

This Savage Land (1968)****** Barry Sullivan, Glenn Corbett, Kathryn Hayes, George C. Scott. Originally part of 1966 "The Road West" TV series, which starred Barry Sullivan as an Ohio widower heading out West with his family to start again in the 1800's. George C. Scott guest-starred in these two better than average episodes, as the Sullivan clan arrives in a town victimized by a group of vigilantes. Made-for-TV. (Dir: Vincent McEveety, 97 mins.)

This Side of the Law (1950)****** Viveca Lindfors, Kent Smith, Janis Paige. Contrived plot has Kent Smith hired by a shady lawyer to impersonate a missing wealthy man. The complications are as obvious as the outcome. (Dir: Richard L. Bare, 74 mins.)

This Sporting Life (British, 1963) ******** Richard Harris, Rachel Roberts. Earthy drama of an aggressive rugby player who lets nothing stand in the way of his success. Well acted in Brando style by Harris, with some explosively potent scenes, this should prove absorbing to the more discriminating viewer. Includes some of the best 'sporting' action ever captured on film. (Dir: Lindsay Anderson, 129 mins.)

This Thing Called Love (1941)******* Rosalind Russell, Melvyn Douglas. Newlyweds agree to a three-month platonic arrangement to test their marriage. Nicely played, amusing, adult comedy. (Dir: Alexander Hall, 98 mins.)

This Time for Keeps (1947)****½** Esther Williams, Jimmy Durante. Esther is always something in a bathing suit, add Lauritz Melchior, Durante and Johnny Johnston warbling a few tunes and you should have a good show. Unfortunately there's a pitiful plot and childish dialogue. Dir: Richard Thorpe, 105 mins.)

This Woman Is Dangerous (1952)****½** Joan Crawford, Dennis Morgan, David Brian. A must for Miss Crawford's legion of fans. She plays a typical Crawford role, that of a woman who finds love after she's been through the mill. Brian is quite good as a bigtime mobster who can't let Joan go. (Dir: Felix E. Feist, 100 mins.)

Thomas Crown Affair, The (1968) *****½** Steve McQueen, Faye Dunaway. Ingenious caper film with Steve

McQueen as the cool operator who masterminds a bank heist which is fascinating to follow. Miss Dunaway, gorgeously costumed, plays an efficient insurance company investigator who falls prey to McQueen's undeniable charm. Fun all the way, aided by sprightly directing of Norman Jewison. (102 mins.)

Thor and the Amazon Women (Italian, 1963)* Joe Robinson, Susy Andersen. Cult of ferocious women capture one man who, by overcoming them, will end their rule. Silly costume action drama dubbed in English.

Thoroughbreds Don't Cry (1937)**½ Mickey Rooney, Judy Garland, Sophie Tucker. Fairly good race track drama thanks to Rooney's expert playing of a jockey. Take a peek if you'd like to see some real early Judy Garland. Good for the kids. (Dir: Alfred E. Green, 80 mins.)

Thoroughly Modern Millie (1967)***½ Julie Andrews, James Fox, Mary Tyler Moore, Carol Channing. Entertaining musical extravaganza with songs, dances, and marvelous comedy sequences, with a 1920's setting. Julie Andrews, in the title role, is a delight as the heroine who finds true love in the person of James Fox, but not until she dances and warbles her way through many imaginative production numbers. Carol Channing and Beatrice Lillie are wonderful in the film's chief supporting roles. Fun for all! (Dir: George Roy Hill, 138 mins.)

Those Daring Young Men in Their Jaunty Jalopies (Italian-French-British, 1969)** Tony Curtis, Susan Hampshire, Peter Cook, Terry-Thomas. A lumbering, disappointing effort by director Ken Annakin to duplicate his triumphant "Those Magnificent Men in Their Flying Machines." About a 1500-mile endurance race in the 1920's, all heading for Monte Carlo but starting at five different locales. The big budget, lavish production doesn't turn up much besides a few pretty cars, familiar sight gags and auto crackups. (Dir: Ken Annakin, 93 mins.)

Those Magnificent Men in Their Flying Machines (1965)**** Stuart Whitman, Sarah Miles, Terry-Thomas. Just about as perfect as this kind of big-screen family entertainment picture can be. A lavish, wonderfully photographed comedy-adventure

about an air race from London to Paris during the early days of aviation. International cast finds Whitman as an American cowboy swapping his horse for an airplane, and Terry-Thomas is one of the most lovable villains movies have ever served up. There's tension concerning the race and some truly inventive hijinks in between. The whole family will get a kick out of this delicious romp. Another picture that is not seen to good advantage on TV, but it's so splendid to start with! (Dir: Ken Annakin, 113 mins.)

Those Redheads from Seattle (1953)** Rhonda Fleming, Gene Barry, Teresa Brewer, Guy Mitchell. Music and murder try but don't mix in this tale about the Gold Rush in Alaska. Teresa Brewer and Guy Mitchell sing pleasantly. (Dir: Lewis R. Foster, 90 mins.)

Those Were the Days (1940)**½ Bill Holden, Bonita Granville, Ezra Stone. Silly, but often amusing comedy about college back in the horse and buggy days. (Dir: Jay Reed, 76 mins.)

Thousand Clowns, A (1965)**** Jason Robards, Jr., Barbara Harris, Martin Balsam, Barry Gordon. A touching, wacky comedy based on the hit Broadway play by Herb Gardner. Jason Robards winningly recreates his role of the nonconformist writer, determined to make his teenage nephew charge wise before his time. The situation triggers some knowing dialogue, and the supporting characters are beautifully played by Barbara Harris as a social worker; Martin Balsam as the hero's successful businessman-brother; Barry Gordon as the lad growing up under his uncle's tutelage; and Gene Saks as a wild children's TV show host. (Dir: Fred Coe, 118 mins.)

Thousand Plane Raid, The (1969)* Christopher George, Laraine Stephens, J. D. Cannon. A dangerous mission, led by Christopher George, attempts to destroy Germany's main airplane factory. Boring World War II drama. (Dir: Boris Sagal, 100 mins.)

Thousands Cheer (1943)*** Kathryn Grayson, Gene Kelly, plus an all-star cast. Everybody who worked at MGM performs in this musical with an Army background. This is one of those rare occasions when a picture with an "all-star" cast really proves to be solid entertainment. It may strike you as dated because the whole film was aimed at a war-time audience. (Dir: George Sidney, 126 mins.)

Threat, The (1949)*** Charles Mc-Graw, Michael O'Shea, Virginia Grey. An escaped killer plans to avenge himself on those who sent him up. Fast, violent melodrama. (Dir: Charles R. Rondeau, 66 mins.)

Three and a Half Musketeers (Italian, 1961)** Tin Tan, Rosita Arenas. D'Artagnan strives to win full recognition as a King's Musketeer by protecting his Queen from scandal and saving the monarchy. Gagged up version of "The Three Musketeers."

Three Avengers, The (Italian, 1964)* Alan Steele, Rosalba Neri. Once again three fighters for freedom overcome a wicked ruler, with the same lack of finesse characterizing the other dubbed-English spectacles. (Dir: Gianfranco Parolini, 97 mins.)

Three Bad Sisters (1956)** Marla English, Kathleen Hughes, Sara Shane. Muddled story of three wealthy sisters and their attempts to get what they want. Suicides, accidents, and other mishaps abound in this weak melodrama. (Dir: Gilbert L. Kay, 76 mins.)

Three Bites of the Apple (1967)** David McCallum, Tammy Grimes, Sylva Koscina, Harvey Korman. Tammy Grimes looks tempting enough to peel and bite gently, but the rest of this "Apple" is mostly pits. Glorious location sequences photographed in Switzerland and Italy wasted on hokey story about tour guide (McCallum) winning a fortune at the gambling casino and becoming prey for an adventuress (Koscina). (Dir: Alvin Ganzer, 105 mins.)

Three Blind Mice (1938)**½ Loretta Young, Joel McCrea, David Niven. Pretty good comedy with the all too familiar plot about three girls who try to marry millionaires. (Dir: William A. Seiter, 75 mins.)

Three Blondes in His Life (1960)* Jock Mahoney, Greta Thyssen. Insurance investigator looks into a disappearance, uncovers murder and some sexy wenches. Poor mystery yarn never goes anywhere. (Dir: Leon Chooluck, 81 mins.)

Three Brave Men (1957)**½ Ray Milland, Ernest Borgnine, Frank Lovejoy, Nina Foch. A good story that could have been better pre-sented on the screen. Borgnine portrays a government employee who is asked to resign after years of loyal service because he has been labeled a "security risk." How this affects his life and family and the fight he puts up for reinstatement constitutes the bulk of the plot. (Dir: Philip Dunne, 88 mins.)

Three Came Home (1950)*** Claudette Colbert, Patric Knowles, Sessue Hayakawa. Good drama concerns the tortures undergone by captive women in a Japanese internment camp. Performances effective, particularly Hayakawa as the enemy commandant. (Dir: Jean Negulesco, 106 mins.)

Three Cases of Murder (British, 1954)***½ Orson Welles, Alan Badel, Elizabeth Sellars. A trio of separate tales: (1) Ghostly doings in an art gallery. (2) Two suspects when a girl is murdered. (3) A powerful lord is plagued by the memory of a House member he has publicly humiliated. The first and third are excellently done. The second, just an average murder mystery. All in all, above average. (Dir: Wendy Toye, 99 mins.)

Three Cheers for the Irish (1940)**½ Thomas Mitchell, Dennis Morgan. Entertaining little film about an Irish cop who is honored after his retirement from the force by being elected alderman. Hold on to your hats—Dennis Morgan plays a Scotsman. (Dir: Lloyd Bacon, 100 mins.)

Three Coins in the Fountain (1954)**½ Clifton Webb, Louis Jourdan, Dorothy McGuire, Jean Peters, Maggie McNamara. Romance is the keynote in this pleasant comedy drama about three American secretaries in the Eternal City, Rome. The gay action unfolds against the beautiful on-location splendor of Rome. (Dir: Jean Negulesco, 102 mins.)

Three Comrades (1938)***½ Robert Taylor, Robert Young, Margaret Sullavan, Franchot Tone. Erich Remarque's novel about post war (I) Germany is turned into a sensitive film. Not much on plot but deep in mood and character study. Margaret Sullavan is superb as a girl in love with an unsettled, sick veteran of the losing side. (Dir: Frank Borzage, 100 mins.)

Three Daring Daughters (1948)**½ Jeanette MacDonald, Jane Powell, Jose Iturbi, Edward Arnold. Daughters of a lady magazine editor have trouble adjusting themselves to her new husband. Long, mildly amusing musical. (Dir: Fred M. Wilcox, 115 mins.)

Three Days of the Condor (1975) ***½ Robert Redford, Faye Dunaway, Cliff Robertson, Max von Sydow. An intriguing, suspenseful spy story involving double agents, all of them, supposedly, working for the Central Intelligence Agency. Redford plays a C.I.A. agent paid to read books while working for a C.I.A. cover operation in New York. All Redford's colleagues are murdered one afternoon by von Sydow. Surprising plot twists along the way before "Condor" finds out who was trying to kill him and why. Based on the novel "Six Days of the Condor" by James Grady. Taut screenplay by Lorenzo Semple, Jr., and David Rayfiel. (Dir: Sidney Pollack, 118 mins.)

Three Desperate Men (1951) **½ Preston Foster, Jim Davis. Two deputies ride to save their brother from unjust punishment, but circumstances force all three outside the law. Above average western drama with good characterizations. (Dir: Sam Newfield, 71 mins.)

Three Etc's and the Colonel (Italian, 1962) *½ Anita Ekberg, Vittorio De Sica. Village council of a small town in Spain sees to it that the new governor gets everything he wishes, including feminine companionship. Costume comedy tries to be naughty, succeeds in being dull. Dubbed in English.

Three Faces of Eve, The (1957) *** Joanne Woodward, David Wayne, Lee J. Cobb. Psychiatrist helps a woman with three distinct personalities, helps her to lead a normal life. Oscar-winning performance by Woodward is the main attraction in this mildly interesting drama. (Dir: Nunnally Johnson, 91 mins.)

Three for Bedroom C (1952) ** Gloria Swanson, James Warren, Fred Clark. A glamorous screen star romances a scientist aboard a transcontinental train. Labored comedy never is as funny as it should be. (Dir: Milton Bren, 74 mins.)

Three for the Show (1955) ** Betty Grable, Jack Lemmon, Marge and Gower Champion. Downright foolish musical comedy about a Broadway star who believes her first husband

dead in the war and marries his best friend. Hubby No. 1 shows up intact and the mad whirl begins. Remake of "Too Many Husbands" with Jean Arthur. (Dir: H. C. Potter, 93 mins.)

Three Girls About Town (1941) **½ Joan Blondell, Binnie Barnes, Janet Blair. Three wise girls try to hide a body found in a hotel, to save the hotel's reputation. Senseless but amusing farce. (Dir: Leigh Jason, 73 mins.)

Three Godfathers (1948) *** John Wayne, Pedro Armendariz, Harry Carey, Jr. Remake of tale about western outlaws fleeing across the desert who find an abandoned child has the magic touch of John Ford's direction. Picture is entertaining, well acted and directed although not too expertly written.

Three Guns for Texas (1965) **½ Neville Brand, Peter Brown, Bill Smith. Three (3) episodes of the TV series "Laredo" have been strung together and the result is a fairly amusing Western-comedy. Shelley Morrison is very good as a homely Indian maiden who falls madly in love with Texas Ranger Bill Smith, and her devoted pursuit supplies laughs. (Dir: David Lowell Rich, 99 mins.)

Three Guys Named Mike (1951) **½ Jane Wyman, Van Johnson, Howard Keel, Barry Sullivan. Small town girl finds herself the object of assorted Romeos when she becomes an airline stewardess. Pleasing comedy keeps the chuckles coming fairly steadily. (Dir: Charles Walters, 90 mins.)

Three Hearts for Julia (1942) ** Ann Sothern, Melvyn Douglas. Well played, nonsensical farce about a man courting his wife while they're getting a divorce. Not too funny although the performers try hard. (Dir: Richard Thorpe, 89 mins.)

Three Hours to Kill (1954) *** Dana Andrews, Donna Reed. Dana Andrews rides into town to find the man who killed his former sweetheart's brother. He has three hours to do so. Tight and tense western with good performances. (Dir: Alfred L. Werker, 77 mins.)

300 Spartans, The (1962) ** Richard Egan, Diane Baker, Ralph Richardson. Relatively small band of soldiers stand against a mighty army of Persia in a fight for free Greece. Slightly better-than-usual production for a costume spectacle, but still stiff and stilted. Filmed in Greece. (Dir: Rudolph Mate, 114 mins.)

Three Husbands (1950)*** Emlyn Williams, Eve Arden, Vanessa Brown. A recently deceased playboy leaves a note saying he was intimate with one of three wives, and their husbands intend to find out which one. Bright, well acted sophisticated comedy. (Dir: Irving Reis, 78 mins.)

Three in the Attic (1969)* Christopher Jones, Yvette Mimieux, Nan Martin. A not uninteresting premise is given sleazy treatment here and is alternately tedious and disagreeable. Chris Jones as Paxton Quigley, bigtime college operator with the coeds, meets his waterloo in the person of 3 of his conquests who team up to teach him a lesson—they keep him prisoner in an attic offering him, in turn, all the lovemaking they can dish out. Yvette Mimieux does as well as possible considering the surrounding claptrap. (Dir: Richard Wilson, 92 mins.)

Three into Two Won't Go (British, 1969)*** Rod Steiger, Claire Bloom, Judy Geeson, Peggy Ashcraft. A British-made version of that familiar tale of the man approaching forty who finds his marriage difficult and seeks ego fulfillment with a cooperative young lady. If this one works better than most it's because Rod Steiger and Claire Bloom (they were Mr. & Mrs. at the time) play the couple, and adorable Judy Geeson as the object of Rod's affections will arouse much compassion for Steiger among male viewers. But Miss Geeson is a bad choice for a flirtation as Rod soon learns and therein hangs the picture. For TV, some scenes have been added about a social worker investigating Miss Geeson and it's a bit confusing. Directed by stage luminary Peter Hall. (93 mins.)

Three Is a Family (1944)*** Everything happens in the household of Fay Bainter and Charlie Ruggles, the home being a melange of married couples, babies, daughter Marjorie Reynolds, many laughs. (Dir: Edward Ludwig, 81 mins.)

Three Little Girls in Blue (1946)**½ June Haver, Vivian Blaine, Vera-Ellen. A tuneful score, attractive cast and a good production make up for the flimsy tale of the girls in search of millionaires. Celeste Holm makes her screen debut and walks off with the acting honors. (Dir: H. Bruce Humberstone, 90 mins.)

Three Little Words (1950)*** Fred Astaire, Debbie Reynolds, Red Skelton, Vera-Ellen, Arlene Dahl. If you like musicals with many production numbers, good dancing, pretty girls, and very little plot, this is right up your alley. The stars play tunesmiths Bert Kalmar and Harry Ruby and this is their story of how they made the big time. (Dir: Richard Thorpe, 102 mins.)

Three Lives of Thomasina, The (U.S.-Great Britain, 1963)**½ Patrick McGoohan, Susan Hampshire, Karen Dotrice. Disney story of a veterinarian's daughter who loses her will to live after her cat has been put to sleep, has a nice fairytale quality. Trying to bring the cat, Thomasina, back to life, the girl seeks out a mysterious healer living in the woods. The movie's first half has some bite; the ending is too saccharine. For the kiddies. Based on Paul Gallico's "Thomasina, The Cat Who Thought She Was God." (Dir: Don Chaffey, 97 mins.)

Three Loves Has Nancy (1938)**½ Janet Gaynor, Robert Montgomery, Franchot Tone. Two bachelor friends and a girl between them is the focal of this pleasant, well written and played little comedy. (Dir: Richard Thorpe, 70 mins.)

Three Men in a Boat (British, 1956)*** Laurence Harvey, Martita Hunt. Bright British comedy about three young men who have a field day on a gay excursion up the Thames. Martita Hunt is delicious and even Laurence Harvey isn't bad. (Dir: Ken Annakin, 84 mins.)

Three Men in White (1943)** Lionel Barrymore, Van Johnson, Ava Gardner. Routine Dr. Gillespie film with the old boy looking for an assistant and trying to decide between Key Luke and Van. (Dir: Willis Goldbeck, 85 mins.)

Three Men on a Horse (1936)***½ Sam Levene, Joan Blondell, Frank McHugh. One of our comedy classics. Story of the mild-mannered chap who can pick winners and the characters who try and use him is always good for laughs. Played to the hilt by an expert cast. Holds up very well. (Dir: Mervyn Le Roy, 90 mins.)

Three Murderesses (French, 1959)

**½ Alain Delon, Mylene Demongeot, Pascale Petit. Playboy spreads his affections among three beauties, they seek to get even with him. Lightweight amusing English-dubbed comedy with a misleading title. (Dir: Michael Boisrond, 96 mins.) Alternate title: Women Are Weak.

Three Musketeers (1935)*** Walter Abel, Paul Lukas. Dumas' classic of the dashing D'Artagnan who joins the King's Musketeers. Acceptable version of famous adventure tale. (Dir: Rowland V. Lee, 110 mins.)

Three Musketeers, The (1939)** Don Ameche, Ritz Brothers. Dumas' famous adventure novel, faithfully adapted except that the Ritzes appear in the title role. Mixture isn't good comedy or drama. (Dir: Allan Dwan, 73 mins.)

Three Musketeers, The (1948)*** Lana Turner, Gene Kelly, June Allyson. Dumas' classic as presented here is good juvenile action film set in France at the time of Louis XIII. (Dir: George Sidney, 125 mins.)

Three Musketeers, The (1973)**** Oliver Reed, Michael York, Raquel Welch, Richard Chamberlain, Faye Dunaway, Charlton Heston. A joyous whirlwind-paced remake (there may be as many as ten earlier cinema versions of the classic Dumas book) that is a rouser from start to finish. In between there are a whole slew of fabulous sight gags from inventive director Richard Lester and his international cast, with big name stars playing bit parts. Charlton Heston is Cardinal Richelieu, Michael York is D'Artagnan, who understandably wants to seduce the married neighborhood seamstress (Raquel Welch). Young and old will revel in this inspired lunacy. Gorgeous period costumes. (Dir: Richard Lester, 105 mins.)

3 on a Couch (1966)* Jerry Lewis, Janet Leigh, Mary Ann Mobley. Remember my witty quip to my psychiatrist "If I'm late start without me"? Well, Jerry started and finished this one without a script while trying to persuade his psychiatrist (Janet Leigh) to marry him. Stay on your couch and don't bother with Jerry's. (Dir: Jerry Lewis, 109 mins.)

Three on a Match (1932)**½ Joan Blondell, Bette Davis, Warren William, Ann Dvorak. Three schoolmates take different paths—one a chorine, one a stenographer, the

third a millionaire's wife. Interesting melodrama. (Dir: Mervyn Le Roy, 70 mins.)

Three on a Spree (British, 1961)*½ Jack Watling, Carole Lesley. Guy has to spend a large amount of money in 60 days if he is to inherit an even larger amount. Another version of "Brewster's Millions," with the plot showing its age, not helped by inept direction, performances. (Dir: Sidney J. Furie, 83 mins.)

Three Penny Opera (German, 1964) ****** Curt Jurgens, Hildegarde Neff, Gert Frobe. Draggy, uninspired version of the Kurt Weill-Bertolt Brecht satire about criminal Mack the Knife, who marries the daughter of the King of the Beggars, is trapped by the law, but escapes. Bumpy continuity, below-par performances; Sammy Davis Jr. occasionally appears as a sort of chorus, adding little. Dubbed in English. Too bad. (Dir: Wolfgang Staudte, 83 mins.)

Three Ring Circus (1954)** Dean Martin, Jerry Lewis, Zsa Zsa Gabor, Dean and Jerry join the circus for a mild amount of fun. Not their best, nor their worst. (Dir: Joseph Pevney, 103 mins.)

Three Sailors and a Girl (1953)** Jane Powell, Gordon MacRae, Gene Nelson. Not to be confused with "Two Girls and a Sailor," "Three Gobs and a Gal," or "Two Sailors and Two Girls," but if you do, it won't matter. It's all the same, anyway. (Dir: Roy Del Ruth, 95 mins.)

Three Secrets (1950)*** Eleanor Parker, Ruth Roman, Patricia Neal. Good drama for the gals. Through flashbacks it tells the story of the three women as they wait word of their loved ones involved in a fatal air crash on a mountain. (Dir: Robert Wise, 99 mins.)

Three Sisters, The (U.S.S.R., 1964) ****½** Lyubov Sokolova, Margarita Volodina. Disappointing Russian version of the great Chekhov play about the lives of the daughters of a late Russian officer living in rural Russia early in this century. Filmed in black and white with a couple of good performances. Adapted and directed by Samson Samsonov. Subtitles. (112 mins.)

Three Sisters, The (1965)***½ Kim Stanley, Geraldine Page, Sandy Dennis, Shelley Winters. A movie only by virtue of its being included in a film package, this is a taped version of Anton Chekhov's play as performed in cooperation with the Actors Studio. The Chekhovian drama of loneliness and frustration receives uneven treatment, with some brilliantly acted bits. Worth seeing. (Dir: Lee Strasberg, 168 mins.)

Three Smart Girls (1936)***½ Deanna Durbin, Ray Milland. Delightful comedy about three sisters trying to keep their father away from a scheming woman. Miss Durbin's voice is another asset. (Dir: Henry Koster, 90 mins.)

Three Smart Girls Grow Up (1939) *** Deanna Durbin, Robert Cummings, Charles Winninger. Light Deanna Durbin comedy about family involvements, notably the gay romances of three sisters. Charming Deanna is a delight. (Dir: Henry Koster, 100 mins.)

Three Steps North (Italian, 1951)*** Lloyd Bridges, Lea Padovani. Ex-GI returns to Italy to claim hidden loot. Well acted, interesting melodrama. English dialogue.

Three Stooges Go Around the World in a Daze, The (1963)* Three Stooges, Jay Sheffield, Joan Freeman. Conceived, no doubt, as a satire on "Around the World in 80 Days," but is more like "Boring Son of Around the World." Slapstick Stooges team up with Fogg's descendant for a modern-day attempt! (Dir: Norman Maurer, 94 mins.)

Three Stooges in Orbit, The (1962) ** Three Stooges, Carol Christensen. The boys run across a Martian agent after a professor's new invention. Wild slapstick for the kiddies. (Dir: Edward Bernds, 87 mins.)

Three Stooges Meet Hercules, The (1962)** Three Stooges, Vicki Trickett. The boys land in a time machine which takes them back to the days of kings and slaves. Amusing burlesque laced with slapstick. (Dir: Edward Bernds, 89 mins.)

Three Strangers (1946)*** Sydney Greenstreet, Geraldine Fitzgerald, Peter Lorre. Interesting, well played but contrived melodrama about three strangers who become partners on a sweepstake ticket and the intrigue of their individual lives. (Dir: Jean Negulesco, 92 mins.)

Three Stripes in the Sun (1955)**½ Aldo Ray, Dick York, Phil Carey. Formerly prejudiced against the Japanese, a G.I. Sgt. falls in love with a Japanese translator and is torn by his old beliefs. Reasonably interesting. (Dir: Richard Murphy, 93 mins.)

Three Swords of Zorro, The (Italian, 1964)*½ Guy Stockwell, Gloria Milland. Zorro's offspring battle a corrupt governor of California. Juvenile English-dubbed adventure tale.

3:10 to Yuma (1957)***½ Glenn Ford, Van Heflin, Felicia Farr. One of the best western dramas, almost in the league of "Shane" and "High Noon." A farmer takes the job of bringing a notorious killer into Yuma because he needs the money. They have to wait together in a hotel room until the train for Yuma arrives. Ford, in the role of the killer, is great as is Heflin as the farmer.

Three Violent People (1956)**½ Charlton Heston, Anne Baxter, Gilbert Roland. An action filled western yarn for horse opera fans. Heston is appropriately cast in the role of a rancher who puts up a valiant fight against the illegal land grabbers. Miss Baxter supplies the love interest. (Dir: Rudolph Mate, 100 mins.)

Three Women (1977)**** Shelley Duvall, Sissy Spacek, Janice Rule, John Cromwell, Robert Fortier. A fascinating, daring film written, produced and directed by Robert Altman. "Three Women" may have been inspired by a dream, but it owes most of its power to two extraordinarily varied and subtle performances by Duvall and Spacek, playing short-lived roommates in a Palm Springs, California motel. This is an audacious film in many ways, including the enormous challenge of trying to create a rich, textured film about two such vapid leading characters. But Duvall and Spacek are so revealing, seemingly improvising sometimes, that the slightest glances and nuances reveal more than most directors' major confrontation scenes. Duvall is a self-assured physical therapist modeling her life on the inspirations she finds in women's magazines like Good Housekeeping. There's one particularly poignant scene as Duvall prepares, with great joy, a really grotesque meal for two local police officers who are expected for dinner. Janice Rule has virtually no speaking part while playing the role of a spaced-out painter. Some critics have carped that "Three Women" is a "home movie." Maybe it is, whatever that means, but it's a remarkable work of art. (Dir: Robert Altman, 125 mins.)

Three Worlds of Gulliver, The (1960) *** Kerwin Mathews, Jo Morrow. Fast paced adventure fantasy aimed for the juvenile trade. Plenty of visual gimmicks. (Dir: Jack Sher, 100 mins.)

Three Young Texans (1954)** Mitzi Gaynor, Jeffrey Hunter, Keefe Brasselle. Cowboy tries to save his father, in the clutches of crooks, from robbing a train by doing it himself. Cast names can't help this from being anything but an ordinary western. (Dir: Henry Levin, 78 mins.)

Threepenny Opera, The (Germany-U.S., 1931) *** Lotte Lenya, Carola Neher. The by now famous musical play of Bertolt Brecht, with a glorious score by Kurt Weill, inspired by "The Beggar's Opera" by John Gay. Brecht's fantasy Soho, a coronation year in London during the 19th century. Lotte Lenya's portrait of Jenny, the prostitute, is reason enough to see this astonishing, complex film. (Pabst simultaneously shot a French version with a different cast, including Antonin Artaud.) (Dir: G. W. Pabst, 113 mins.)

Three's a Crowd (1969)**½ Larry Hagman, Jessica Walter, E. J. Peaker. An old bigamy plot, popular in the comedy films of the thirties and forties, is given an uninhibited modern touch in this made-for-TV movie. You'll probably stay with it to see whether husband Larry Hagman chooses wife #1 (E. J. Peaker) or wife #2 (Jessica Walter). The story is obvious, but the last few scenes played in a hotel during Hagman's two separate birthday celebrations provide some laughs. (Dir: Harry Falk, 75 mins.)

Thrill of a Romance (1945)** Van Johnson, Esther Williams. Air Corps hero romances a pretty swimming instructress at a mountain resort. Cloying, top-heavy musical comedy. (Dir: Richard Thorpe, 105 mins.)

Thrill of It All, The (1963) *** Doris Day, James Garner, Arlene Francis. Some bright moments in this amusing comedy about an obstetrician's wife who becomes a star of television commercials. Carl Reiner's script pokes fun at the TV huckstering business, while Day and Garner are capable funsters themselves. Nice entertainment. (Dir: Norman Jewison, 108 mins.)

Thunder Afloat (1939)**½ Wallace Beery, Chester Morris. Good comedy-drama about World War I campaign against subs by Naval Reserve. Basic plot is old-hat but Beery is fun to watch. (Dir: George B. Seitz, 100 mins.)

Thunder Alley (1967)* Annette Funicello, Fabian, Jan Murray. Fun on the beach is over. Fabian plays a murderous stock-car racer prone to blacking out behind the wheel, Annette's the nice kid who starts to nip at the whiskey. Unconvincing, woodenly acted. (Dir: Richard Rush, 90 mins.)

Thunder Bay (1953)**½ James Stewart, Joanne Dru, Dan Duryea. High spirited adventure yarn about oil prospectors and their run in with shrimp fishermen in Louisiana when an off-shore drilling operation interferes with the routine of a small fishing community. The cast is first rate. (Dir: Anthony Mann, 102 mins.)

Thunder in the East (1953)**½ Deborah Kerr, Alan Ladd, Charles Boyer, Corinne Calvet. Contrived but moderately entertaining film about a group of displaced persons and an American adventurer caught up in the new found independence fever in India. The heroics are heavy handed and Miss Kerr's love story with Alan Ladd may be hard to take. (Dir: Charles Vidor, 98 mins.)

Thunder in the Sun (1959)** Susan Hayward, Jeff Chandler. Wagon train of Basque settlers going to California to cultivate vineyards passes through hostile Indian territory. Triteness of the plot is saved at the last moment by a rousingly staged battle scene, giving this historical action drama the "fair" mark. (Dir: Russell Rouse, 81 mins.)

Thunder in the Valley (1947)**½ Lon McCallister, Edmund Gwenn, Peggy Ann Garner. Good juvenile drama about a boy's love for his dog. (Dir: Louis King, 103 mins.)

Thunder Island (1963)** Gene Nelson, Fay Spain, Brian Kelly. Low-budget suspense tale of assassination plot against an out-of-power South American dictator is told with gusto. Story and screenplay by Jack Nicholson and Don Devlin. (Dir: Jack Leewood, 65 mins.)

Thunder of Drums, A (1961)**½

Richard Boone, George Hamilton, Luana Patten, Richard Chamberlain. Newly commissioned lieutenant, son of a former general, is treated rough by the captain of a western fort until he can prove he's a soldier. Familiar Cavalry-vs.-Indians actioner benefits from good performances. (Dir: Joseph M. Newman, 97 mins.)

Thunder on the Hill (1951)*** Ann Blyth, Claudette Colbert, Robert Douglas. Mystery yarn set in a British convent during a rainstorm makes absorbing drama when handled as well as it is here. Miss Blyth plays a condemned murderess who is detained at the convent due to the storm and Miss Colbert plays a nun who sets out to prove Miss Blyth's innocence. (Dir: Douglas Sirk, 84 mins.)

Thunder Over Hawaii—See: Naked Paradise

Thunder Pass (1954)**½ Dane Clark, Dorothy Patrick. Cavalry captain attempts to lead settlers to safety before the Indians go on the warpath. Generally okay outdoor action melodrama keeps moving at a good rate. (Dir: Frank McDonald, 76 mins.)

Thunder Road (1958)** Robert Mitchum, Keeley Smith. Uneven drama about a group of people in the Kentucky hills who make moonshine whiskey and sell it. Odd little drama with good moments, some weak ones. (Dir: Arthur Ripley, 92 mins.)

Thunder Rock (British, 1942)**** Michael Redgrave, Lilli Palmer, James Mason. The keeper of an isolated lighthouse hates his fellow man, but is persuaded to return to society by spirits from the past. Thoughtful, excellently acted drama. (Dirs: John and Roy Boulting, 95 mins.)

Thunderball (Great Britain, 1965)***½ Sean Connery, Claudine Auger, Adolfo Celi, Bernard Lee, Luciana Paluzzi. An exciting James Bond adventure in which the villains are delightfully sinister and calculating and Sean Connery is at the top of his form as Agent 007. This time out, the ominous enemy organization, SPECTRE, is out to destroy the city of Miami if SPECTRE is not paid a ransom of 100 million pounds sterling—and super-hero Bond is not about to let all those tourists down. Adolfo Celi strikes the right pose as the arch-villain, and there are enough gorgeous ladies around to make Bond's task worthwhile. (Dir: Terence Young, 150 mins.)

Thunderbolt and Lightfoot (1974)*** Clint Eastwood, Jeff Bridges. The casting combination of Clint Eastwood and Jeff Bridges works to good advantage in this caper yarn set in the hill country of Montana. Clint is a Vietnam vet with a hankering to pull the big heist and retire forever. He teams up with young drifter Bridges. They take on two more guys in order to work out the armory robbery, and it takes almost half of the film before the well-executed theft sequence. Bridges is first-rate and this could have been an even better film with a little more care, but it works anyway. Promising directorial debut for Michael Cimino who also wrote the spirited screenplay. Cimino co-authored "Magnum Force." (115 mins.)

Thundercloud (formerly "Colt .45") (1950)**½ Randolph Scott, Ruth Roman, Zachary Scott. Fast paced western drama with the stress on action. Scott is a gun salesman whose merchandise (Colt .45's) is stolen and used to arm a band of outlaws. (Dir: Edward L. Marin, 74 mins.)

Thunderhead (1945)**½ Roddy McDowall, Preston Foster. Good juvenile film about a boy and a horse. A fair outdoor adventure with little of the fine qualities of "My Friend Flicka." (Dir: Louis King, 78 mins.)

Thursday's Game (1974)*** Gene Wilder, Bob Newhart, Ellen Burstyn, Cloris Leachman. A cast of top comedy actors adds spark to this tale about two friends (Wilder and Newhart) who decide to lie and continue their weekly night out after their poker game is disbanded. It's a satirical look at marriage and male friendships. Wilder is wonderful as a put-upon guy whose world is suddenly falling apart and Newhart underplays in his pleasing fashion as a successful businessman looking for an out from his marriage and finally finding one. Made-for-TV. (Dir: Robert Moore.)

THX 1138 (1971)*** Robert Duvall, Donald Pleasence. Opening sequence is a clip from a 1939 Buck Rogers serial, but the resemblance to such familiar, simple-minded sci-fi flicks ends there. A political science-fiction set in the 25th century, where life and love are dehumanized, and the totalitarian oppressors are more audible than visible. Directed, edited and partially written by a young film-maker George Lucas, who gets valuable assistance from the production designer whose white-on-white-antiseptic settings contribute to the clinical, eerie mood. A far cry from "2001," but more absorbing than most science-fiction films. (88 mins.)

Tiara Tahiti (British, 1963)**½ James Mason, John Mills, Claude Dauphin. Pompous former officer lands in Tahiti to build a modern hotel, but finds unexpected opposition in the form of an old army enemy, living a life of ease on the isle. Leisurely in pace as befits the climate, this tropical comedy gets its chief lift from the able performances of the leading players. (Dir: William Kotcheff, 100 mins.)

. . . tick . . . tick . . . tick (1970) **½ Jim Brown, Fredric March, George Kennedy. Fairly interesting drama about a southern town's sudden shift from a peaceful community to a veritable powder keg. The incident which sets off the situation is the election of the town's first black sheriff, played by Jim Brown. Fine supporting cast. (Dir: Ralph Nelson, 100 mins.)

Ticket to Tomahawk, A (1950)**½ Dan Dailey, Anne Baxter, Rory Calhoun. Small-time theatrical group invades the west. Marilyn Monroe has a bit role in this fairly amusing western spoof. (Dir: Richard Sale, 90 mins.)

Tickle Me (1965)** Elvis Presley, Jocelyn Lane, Julie Adams. Elvis as a rodeo star who winds up at a girls' health resort and helps uncover a hidden treasure. His fans won't mind, but he deserves better than this skimpy little nothing. (Dir: Norman Taurog, 90 mins.)

Ticklish Affair, A (1963)** Gig Young, Shirley Jones, Red Buttons, Carolyn Jones. Naval officer investigating an SOS encounters a widow and her children, and romance blossoms. Watery little comedy doesn't do right by the cast; weak script. (Dir: George Sidney, 89 mins.)

Tidal Wave (Japan, 1975)* Lorne Greene, Keiju Kobayashi, Rhonda Leigh Hopkins. Really two films in one—Roger Corman acquired some classy footage of Japan going under-

water done by a Japanese special effects team and intercut it with scenes of Lorne Greene as the U.S. Ambassador to the U.N., who tries to convince the Assembly to send aid to the stricken country. Miniature disasters are a relief after Irwin Allen's extravaganzas. (Dir: Andrew Meyer, 90 mins.)

Tiger and the Pussycat, The (1967) ** Ann-Margret, Vittorio Gassman, Eleanor Parker. This sex drama with comedy thrown in, also throws out the chance to make good use of Gassman's dazzling talent. Gassman is approaching middle age, and he is taken over the coals by Ann-Margret, who laughs at him behind his back. Eleanor Parker suffers quietly as Gassman's wife, and you'll suffer a little too as this soap opera plot offers few surprises. Filmed in Italy. (Dir: Dino Risi, 105 mins.)

Tiger Bay (British, 1958)**** Horst Buchholz, Hayley Mills, John Mills. Superb suspense yarn with a great plot twist. Hayley Mills is perfect in the role of a little girl who witnesses a murder and ends up protecting the young killer (effectively portrayed by Buchholz) from the authorities. This is the film which launched Miss Mills on her movie career. (Dir: J. Lee Thompson, 105 mins.)

Tiger by the Tail (British, 1958)** Larry Parks, Constance Smith. An American newspaperman goes to London on an assignment and gets involved with a gang of international thieves. Trite film, poorly acted, except by Parks.

Tiger Makes Out, The (1967)***½ Eli Wallach, Anne Jackson, Charles Nelson Reilly, Elizabeth Wilson. If you pay attention you'll catch Dustin Hoffman in a tiny part before he became a major world star in "The Graduate" released a few months after this Murray Schisgal comedy. But there are numerous other reasons for watching this wacky tale of a Greenwich Village bachelor who can't cope with the world and turns to kidnapping, the major one being the delicious performances of husband-and-wife team Eli Wallach and Anne Jackson. The Wallachs have never been seen together, before or since, to such good advantage in motion pictures. Based on Schisgal's one-act Broadway play "The Tiger." Later Arthur Hiller directed the much more conventional romance

"Love Story." (Dir: Arthur Hiller, 94 mins.)

Tiger of the Sea (Japanese, 1964)* Joe Shishido, Hideaki Nitani. Pirate finds he is accused of atrocities being committed by the same buccaneer who killed his father years ago. Childish adventure thriller dubbed in English.

Tight Little Island (British, 1949) **** Basil Radford, Joan Greenwood. Scottish islanders low on the spirits take drastic steps when a cargo of whisky is marooned off their shore. This British joy is one of the drollest consistently amusing films you can hope to see. A perennial delight, perfectly acted. (Dir: Alexander Mackendrick, 81 mins.)

Tight Shoes (1941)***½ Broderick Crawford, John Howard, Binnie Barnes. A gangster gets a shoe clerk started on his way in a political career. Surprisingly funny Damon Runyon comedy has a fast pace, good situations. (Dir: Albert S. Rogell, 68 mins.)

Tight Spot (1955)***½ Ginger Rogers, Edward G. Robinson, Brian Keith. Well acted crime drama about a girl set up by the police as a trap for a big time gang leader. Witty dialogue. (Dir: Phil Karlson, 97 mins.)

Tijuana Story, The (1957)** James Darren, Joy Stoner. A predictable drama about a youth's involvement with the "drug traffic" in the open city of Tijuana. Some action scenes break up the boredom. (Dir: Leslie Kardos, 72 mins.)

Tiko and the Shark (U.S.-France-Italy, 1962)** Al Kauwe, Marlene Among. Young Polynesian boy raises baby shark; friendship persists into adulthood despite threats from local fishing business. Sometimes trite plea for primitive ways, man and nature, over more "civilized," mechanized modes of life, but generally understated; a well-photographed, pleasant movie—antidote to irrational terror of the "killer" shark. (Dir: Folco Quilici, 88 mins.)

Till the Clouds Roll By (1946)*** June Allyson, Frank Sinatra, Judy Garland, Van Johnson. Fictionalized biography of composer Jerome Kern is a mushy mess but his delightful music makes most of the film a treat. (Dir: Richard Whorf, 120 mins.)

Till the End of Time (1946)***½ Dorothy McGuire, Guy Madison, Robert Mitchum, Bill Williams. Returned GI tries to readjust himself to civilian life, finds he has changed, falls for a flyer's widow. Potent, excellently produced drama. (Dir: Edward Dmytryk, 105 mins.)

Till We Meet Again (1940)*** Merle Oberon, George Brent. Remake of "One Way Passage." Story of the criminal and the dying girl is still passable if you like to cry. (Dir: Edmund Goulding, 99 mins.)

Time Bomb (1959)**½ Curt Jurgens, Mylene Demongeot. A French film with some suspense and good production values to recommend it. Curt Jurgens is the captain of a vessel which becomes an important part of a plot of intrigue. (Dir: Yves Ciampi, 92 mins.)

Time for Burning, A (1966)**** Rev. William Youngdahl, Ernie Chambers. An honest, extremely moving hour-long documentary about race relations in Omaha, Nebraska, conceived and directed by gifted filmmaker William Jersey, and first seen on the public television network. Nonprofessional actors in their real-life situation, as Jersey's camera crew records what happens when a white minister tries to integrate his lily-white congregation with a nearby Negro Lutheran church. One of the most thoughtful statements about deep-seated American racial prejudice ever captured on film.

Time for Killing, A—See: Long Ride Home, The

Time for Love, A (1973)**½ John Davidson, Chris Mitchum. Two introspective, visually handsome one-hour love stories for the young generation by the prolific writer Stirling Silliphant. Made-for-TV. Davidson's straight-arrow junior exec learns to trust his instincts and buck the patterned corporate-life groove from a questioning beauty (Lauren Hutton) in "No Promises, No Pledges," filmed on location at the Arizona Biltmore. Taking the other side of the coin in "Go Sing the Songs, Mark," Silliphant depicts a sad-faced rock singer who loves a teacher of deaf children, but won't relinquish his frenzied life-style. Robert Mitchum's son Christopher and comely Bonnie Bedelia search for answers against California coastline backgrounds. (Dirs: George Schaefer, Joseph Sargent, 99 mins.)

Time, Gentlemen, Please (British, 1953)**½ Eddie Byrne, Hermione Baddeley. The town loafer combats stuffy regulations in his own way, and winds up in clover. Pleasant comedy.

Time Is My Enemy (British, 1957) **½ Dennis Price, Renee Asherson. Criminal tries to blackmail his former wife, with murder the result. Interesting melodrama.

Time Limit (1957)***½ Richard Widmark, Richard Basehart, June Lockhart, Martin Balsam. The provocative war drama presented on B'way has been brought to the screen with taste and skill. Story concerns the issue of collaboration with enemy during the Korean campaign. Strong drama with excellent performances, notably by Basehart and Widmark. (Dir: Karl Malden, 96 mins.)

Time Lost and Time Remembered (1966)**½ Sarah Miles, Cyril Cusack. If the screenplay of this tale about a young girl's awakening to life and love matched its sensitive photography and splendid acting by Sarah Miles in the leading role, this would be a winner. But it turns out to be just an average tale, beautifully acted and photographed. (Dir: Desmond Davis, 91 mins.)

Time Machine, The (1960)***½ Rod Taylor, Yvette Mimieux, Alan Young. Imaginative tale based on the H. G. Wells story of a young inventor who constructs a machine enabling him to travel to the future, and the strange adventures he meets in doing so. Trick work is excellent, the story continually interesting and well acted. Superior fantasy fare. (Dir: George Pal, 103 mins.)

Time of Indifference (Italian, 1964)** Shelley Winters, Rod Steiger, Paulette Goddard, Claudia Cardinale. Grim, unpleasantly executed and played drama about the disintegration of a family in the late 20's. Air of unrelieved gloom with few compensating factors. (Dir: Francisco Maselli, 84 mins.)

Time of Their Lives, The (1946)*** Bud Abbott & Lou Costello, Marjorie Reynolds. A better than average Abbott & Costello comedy with less stress on slapstick and more on story. Good supporting performances. (Dir: Charles Barton, 82 mins.)

Time of Your Life, The (1949)**** James Cagney, Wayne Morris, Broderick Crawford. A little New York saloon, and the characters who frequent it. From William Saroyan's prize-winning play. Expertly handled. (Dir: H. C. Potter, 109 mins.)

Time Out for Love (French, 1962)*½ Jean Seberg, Maurice Ronet, Micheline Presle. American girl in France falls in with a trio of sophisticated modernists. Meandering romantic drama dubbed in English. (Dir: Philippe de Broca, 91 mins.)

Time Running Out (1959)** Dane Clark, Simone Signoret. Run-of the mill cops and robbers yarn set in France and starring American actor Dane Clark. Simone Signoret, as one of Clark's past mistresses, is totally wasted in a thankless role.

Time to Die, A—See: Amelie

Time to Kill (1942)** Lloyd Nolan, Heather Angel. Detective Michael Shayne on the trail of rare coin counterfeiters. Routine film is supported by Nolan's characterization.

Time to Love and a Time to Die, A (1958)*** John Gavin, Lilo Pulver. Erich Maria Remarque's novel about young romance during WW II in Nazi Germany comes off well in this screen adaptation. Although the film eventually becomes soap opera, it has some good moments in the earlier scenes. Gavin and Lilo Pulver do nicely in their starring assignments. (Dir: Douglas Sirk, 133 mins.)

Time to Remember (British, 1962)** Yvonne Monlaur, Harry H. Corbett. Real-estate agent searches for property which holds the key to treasure. Fair mystery based on an Edgar Wallace story.

Time Travelers, The (1964)**½ Preston Foster, Philip Carey, Merry Anders. Scientific team experimenting with time is projected into the future, don't exactly like what they find there. Intriguing scientific idea, handled with a fair amount of skill; some good special effects, capable cast. (Dir: Ib Melchior, 82 mins.)

Time Within Memory (Japanese, 1973) *** Takahiro Tamura, Atsuko Kaku. Visually stunning, told mostly in flashbacks. After a 30-year absence a man returns to a small island, the scene of his childhood. Directed and photographed by cinematographer Toichiro Narushima. (118 mins.)

Time Without Pity (British, 1958)** Michael Redgrave, Ann Todd, Joan Plowright. A father has 24 hours to save his son from the death sentence. Despite the fine cast, this suspense drama never quite clarifies itself. Some good moments, mostly drab boredom. (Dir: Joseph Losey, 88 mins.)

Timelock (British, 1957)**½ Robert Beatty, Betty McDowall. Tight British drama about a bank official who accidentally locks his son in the vault, which is set to open sixty-three hours later. The inevitable gimmick about the race against time is used to the breaking point.

Timetable (1956)*** Mark Stevens, Felicia Farr. A streamline train is robbed in a daringly intricate hold-up. Neat crime melodrama has many twists. (Dir: Mark Stevens, 79 mins.)

Tin Pan Alley (1940)***½ Alice Faye, Betty Grable, Jack Oakie. Tuneful, entertaining film musical following the adventures of song pluggers and composers in 1915-1918. Not a great film but good fun to watch. (Dir: Walter Lang, 95 mins.)

Tin Star, The (1957)***½ Henry Fonda, Anthony Perkins, Betsy Palmer. Expertly made western mixes humor with suspense, and a standout performance by Fonda as a wily bounty hunter who helps a young sheriff clean up a town. Superior of its type. (Dir: Anthony Mann, 93 mins.)

Tingler, The (1959)*** Vincent Price, Judith Evelyn. A gimmicked horror film that works. Vincent Price menaces everyone in sight and he's just the one who can do it effectively. Judith Evelyn is very fine as a frightened bystander. (Dir: William Castle, 80 mins.)

Tip on a Dead Jockey (1957)*** Robert Taylor, Dorothy Malone. Irwin Shaw's crime story makes a good film with Taylor giving one of his better screen portrayals as a pilot involved with smugglers. The action is fast and believable and the film seldom bogs down despite its length. (Dir: Richard Thorpe, 129 mins.)

Titanic (1953)*** Clifton Webb, Barbara Stanwyck, Robert Wagner, Thelma Ritter. Hollywood's version of the famous tragic event, the sinking of the sink-proof Titanic. Personal dramas are unfolded before the climax arrives when the ship hits the inevitable iceberg. Good performances keep the situation from becoming too maudlin. (Dir: Jean Negulesco, 98 mins.)

Titfield Thunderbolt, The (British, 1953)**** Stanley Holloway, George Relph. Villagers resent the closing of their railway line by the government, take over the train themselves. Rollicking, completely delightful comedy, great fun. (Dir: Charles Crichton, 84 mins.)

Titicut Follies (1967)**** An 85-minute documentary, photographed in 16-mm film, that is one of the most shattering films ever made about how the state brutalizes its citizens, and how we torture and dehumanize each other. The film about a state mental hospital in Massachusetts was altogether brilliantly produced, directed and edited by Frederick Wiseman, who may well be the most gifted documentary filmmaker recording the American scene in the late 1960's and the early 70's. (Wiseman's other films include "High School" "Hospital," and "Law & Order.") There is no commentary in this real-life chamber of horrors and none is needed. Unfortunately the State of Massachusetts, as of 1971, has prevented the public exhibition of this extraordinary film, which has cost filmmaker Wiseman over $100,-000 in legal fees. If you ever get a chance to see this detached, searing documentary, you'll never forget "Titicut Follies."

To All My Friends on Shore (1972)*** Bill Cosby, Gloria Foster. Strong performances and a believable script make this made-for-TV film about a hard-working black man, his sacrificing wife, and their doomed son worthwhile. Cosby completely immerses himself in the difficult role of a determined man with a dream . . . to get his family out of the small Connecticut ghetto and buy a modest home of their own. His good performance is matched by Miss Foster's commanding portrayal of his loyal, loving, but weary wife. Their plight is compounded by the nature of their son's illness, sickle-cell anemia. Strong drama. (Dir: Gilbert Cates, 74 mins.)

To Be or Not to Be (1942)***½ Jack Benny, Carole Lombard. A troupe of actors in Poland do their bit to outwit the Nazis when they march in. Excellent comedy-drama, skillful light handling of a difficult comedy theme. (Dir: Ernst Lubitsch, 100 mins.)

To Bed . . . or Not to Bed—See: **Devil, The**

To Catch a Spy (French, 1957)** Henri Vidal, Barbara Laage, Nicole Maurey. Secret-service man goes after stolen rocket plans. Routine espionage thriller with lots of action, girls, clichés. Dubbed in English.

To Catch a Thief (1955)*** Cary Grant, Grace Kelly. Ex-jewel thief on the Riviera romances an American girl while trying to prove he's innocent of a series of robberies. Hitchcock comedy thriller has spectacular scenery and popular players. However, the plot frequently dawdles, never proves really exciting. (Dir: Alfred Hitchcock, 97 mins.)

To Commit a Murder (France-Italy-West Germany, 1967)*½ Louis Jourdan, Edmond O'Brien, Senta Berger. Routine spy thriller! Louis Jourdan does what he can as a writer turned spy but the heavy plotting gets in his way. Edmond O'Brien playing a really evil villain gives the film's best performance. (Dir: Edouard Molinaro, 91 mins.)

To Die in Madrid (France, 1963)**** A superb documentary of the Spanish Civil War using newsreel footage from the archives of six different countries. Documents the beginning of the struggle in 1931 to Franco's assumption of complete power in 1939. Scenes of modern Spain skillfully juxtaposed and splendidly edited by Suzanne Baron. One of the best documentaries of its kind ever made. Narrated by John Gielgud, Irene Worth and others. (Dir: Frederic Rossif, 85 mins.)

To Die in Paris (1968)**½ Louis Jourdan, Kurt Krueger, Philippe Forquet, Robert Ellenstein. Fair suspense tale of French WW II Underground, casts Jourdan as Underground leader jailed by the Nazis, who faces two enemies after his escape: Nazi agents and the Underground itself. He's fearful he will be forced to disclose damning information once his identity is known by the Germans. Made-for-TV. (Dirs: Charles Dubin, Allen Reisner, 100 mins.)

To Each His Own (1946)*** Olivia de Havilland, John Lund. Splendidly acted tear-jerker about the unwed mother who watches her son grow up from afar. (Dir: Mitchell Leisen, 122 mins.)

To Find a Man (1972)*** Pamela Martin, Lloyd Bridges, Phyllis Newman, Darren O'Conner. Interesting and occasionally perceptive tale of a young girl in quest of an abortion and the young boy who matures by helping her. Newcomers Martin and O'Conner are excellent as the young couple, and help to overcome the sometimes thin premise. Screenplay by Arnold Schulman (who was the original director), based on the novel by S. J. Wilson. (Dir: Buzz Kulik, 94 mins.)

To Go and Come (Italian, 1972)**½ Laura Betti, Lucia Poli. Occasionally interesting short feature written and directed by Giuseppe Bertolucci and produced for RAI-TV. About a young couple who spend the night in a railway station and the fantasies that occur to the young man.

To Have and Have Not (1944)***½ Humphrey Bogart, Lauren Bacall. This is when the two lovebirds met and the picture has a good romance and plenty of intrigue to boot. Bogey is a fisherman in this one and between fishing for Nazis he manages to hook Lauren. Supposedly from a Hemingway story but not too accurately. (Dir: Howard Hawks, 100 mins.)

To Hell and Back (1955)*** Audie Murphy, Susan Kohner. Good screen adaptation of Audie Murphy's true heroic war adventures, which earned him the title of the most decorated soldier of World War II. The battle sequences are superior to the personal drama injected throughout the film, and Murphy plays himself with honesty and a surprising absence of arrogance. (Dir: Jesse Hibbs, 106 mins.)

To Kill a Dragon (1967)* Jack Palance assisted by buddy Aldo Ray, scuffles with Fernando Lamas. Oriental natives hire an adventurer to polish off a mystery man determined to walk off with a deadly cargo of nitro. Far Eastern hokum weighed down by heavy plot and dull actors.

To Kill a Mockingbird (1962)**** Gregory Peck, Mary Badham, Philip Alford, Brock Peters. Excellent production of Harper Lee's sensitive book about an Alabama lawyer bringing up his two motherless children. Peck was never better, and the two children are most affecting. Superb script (Horton Foote) and direction (Robert Mulligan), together with fine performances. Topnotch. In its own quiet way this is one of the best movies dealing with race relations that the American film industry has ever made. (Dir: Robert Mulligan, 129 mins.)

To Paris with Love (British, 1955) **½ Alec Guinness. Sometimes witty comedy about a father's lessons in love to his son. Alec Guinness scores again as the fun-loving father. The scenes shot in Paris itself are appealing. One of Guinness' minor films. (Dir: Robert Hamer, 78 mins.)

To Please a Lady (1950)**½ Clark Gable, Barbara Stanwyck. A romantic comedy-drama about a racing car enthusiast and his lady love, who objects to his risking his neck. Adolphe Menjou comes off better than the two stars. (Dir: Clarence Brown, 91 mins.)

To Sir, with Love (British, 1967)**** Sidney Poitier, Judy Geeson, Suzy Kendall, A good humored, touching story of an idealistic ex-engineer (Poitier, of course) and his experiences in teaching a group of rambunctious white high school students from the slum's of London's East End. Poitier is particularly appealing in this film based on the novel of E. R. Braithwaite and skillfully produced, adapted and directed by James Clavell. Judy Geeson is particularly affecting as a blonde toughie who comes to have a crush on her teacher. The almost-love scene between them is nicely handled. Implausible maybe. Appealing definitely! (105 mins.)

To the Ends of the Earth (1948) **** Dick Powell, Signe Hasso. Government agent chases a narcotic ring around the world. Intricate plotting keeps interest on high in this thrilling melodrama. Excellent. (Dir: Robert Stevenson, 109 mins.)

To the Shores of Hell (1965)* Marshall Thompson, Kiva Lawrence, Richard Arlen. Marine major struggles to rescue doctor brother from the Vietcong in a gawky awkward war saga that huffs and puffs through bazooka bursts. (Dir: Will Zens, 81 mins.)

To the Victor (1948)**½ Dennis Morgan, Viveca Lindfors. This film tries to say something but the message gets stuck in its throat. This romance of a black marketeer and a French girl collaborator in post-war Paris never gets off the ground. (Dir: Delmer Daves, 99 mins.)

To Trap a Spy (1966)* Robert Vaughn, Patricia Crowley, David McCallum. Pilot show for TV's "Man From U.N.C.L.E." lengthened by some added lovemaking footage, yielding an instant movie—uninspired and silly. Napoleon Solo must prevent a W.A.S.P. assassination while hanging from his thumbs in a steaming hot room (there's a beautiful girl in the same predicament). (Dir: Don Medford, 92 mins.)

Toast of New Orleans, The (1950)**½ Mario Lanza, Kathryn Grayson, David Niven. This was Mario Lanza's second film and the one in which he sang the popular "Be My Love." He plays a New Orleans fisherman who is converted into an opera star. The buxom Miss Grayson is vocally up to par and looks very attractive. Niven is wasted as a patron of the Arts who adores Miss Grayson. (Dir: Norman Taurog, 97 mins.)

Toast of New York (1937)*** Edward Arnold, Cary Grant, Frances Farmer. Story of Jim Fisk, who rose from peddler to a Wall Street tycoon. Interesting biographical drama, well made. (Dir: Rowland V. Lee, 120 mins.)

Tobacco Road (1941)**½ Charlie Grapewin, Marjorie Rambeau. Longrun Broadway play has been cleaned up for the screen and emerges as a fair tragi-comedy of moral depravity in the impoverished Georgia farmland. (Dir: John Ford, 84 mins.)

Tobruk (1967)** Rock Hudson, George Peppard. Routine World War II adventure with Rock Hudson and George Peppard cast as the ready heroes assigned to destroy Rommel's fuel supply at Tobruk. The production is well mounted but you've seen it dozens of times before.

Toby Tyler (1960)*** Kevin Corcoran, Henry Calvin, Bob Sweeney, Mr. Stubbs (the monkey). Popular kids' tale about a boy who runs away to join the circus and finds good pals—animal and people—and success there, is tailor-made for the Disney Studios. They've produced a touching, pleasant film, and young 'uns will adore it. (Dir: Charles Barton, 96 mins.)

Today We Live (1933)** Joan Crawford, Gary Cooper, Franchot Tone. This adaptation of a William Faulkner war story is so loaded with individual heroism and sacrifice that it will strike modern audiences as stupid. (Dir: Howard Hawks, 110 mins.)

Together Again (1944)*** Charles Boyer, Irene Dunne. Straitlaced lady mayor of a small Vermont town falls for a dashing New York sculptor. Amusing, well-acted romantic comedy. (Dir: Charles Vidor, 94 mins.)

Tokyo After Dark (1959)** Richard Long, Michi Kobi. Military policeman accidentally kills a Tokyo teenager, breaks jail when he learns he's to be tried in a Japanese court. Fair drama of postwar Japan. (Dir: Norman Herman, 80 mins.)

Tokyo File 212 (1951)*** Robert Peyton, Florence Marly. Army Intelligence officer mops up Communist sabotage in post-war Japan. Fast-moving melodrama aided by on-the-spot backgrounds.

Tokyo Joe (1949)** Humphrey Bogart, Florence Marly, Sessue Hayakawa. Not one of Bogart's better films. Slow moving story of adventure and intrigue in Japan. (Dir: Stuart Heisler, 88 mins.)

Tokyo Olympiad (Japan, 1965)*** The 1964 Olympics—beautifully, ambitiously recorded in one of the finest photographic monuments to athletics ever made. Though film was originally more comprehensive, a wide-ranging view of athletic endeavor and personal triumphs, picture has been edited by its American distributors to focus on events of interest in this country, making movie appear to be more newsreel reportage than a documentary overview. It is still a magnificent job, worthwhile, stirring. Included is the extraordinary women's volleyball final between Japan and the USSR. (Dir: Ken Ichikawa, 93 mins.)

Toll Gate, The (1920)*** William S. Hart. One of the best of Hart's films. Helps explain why he was the most popular of all the silent-film cowboy stars. Hart plays an outlaw (named with some flair and bravado, Black Deering) who risks capture to save a child from drowning. An appreciative sheriff lets Hart escape. (Dir: Lambert Hillyer, 59 mins.)

Tom Brown's School Days (British, 1953)***½ Robert Newton, Diana Wynyard. The adventures of a lad at an exclusive boys' school. Well-done version of classic story. (Dir: Gordon Parry, 93 mins.)

Tom, Dick and Harry (1941)**** Ginger Rogers, George Murphy, Burgess Meredith, Alan Marshall. Telephone operator dreams what life would be like with three eligible suitors. Completely charming, novel comedy, excellent. (Dir: Garson Kanin, 86 mins.)

Tom Jones (British, 1963)**** Albert Finney, Susannah York, Diane Cilento, Hugh Griffith, Dame Edith Evans. A fantastic, marvelous, hilarious film—one of the tiny number of films that it is hard to overpraise. The remarkable screenplay by John Osborne, based on Henry Fielding's now classic novel of life in 18th-century England, manages to pare down the lengthy Fielding novel without losing the spirit or infectious quality of the novel. Rollicking, bawdy, beautiful England of two centuries ago is brilliantly captured by director Tony Richardson who dwells fleetingly, or lovingly as the case may be, on the countryside or the fabulous cast he assembled. Finney, clearly one of the half-dozen greatest actors alive, portrays the rambunctious country boy wenching and winning his way through life, and he is spectacularly funny, whether courting a genteel lady or "dining" with Joyce Redman. This famous eating scene with the edible Miss Redman is, at one and the same time, one of the most riotous and one of the sexiest scenes ever filmed. Joan Greenwood is the epitome of elegant bitchery, and Hugh Griffith, playing the pixilated father of Finney's intended, deserved an Academy Award which he did not win. "Tom Jones" did win many awards, including the best picture of '63. In any year this is a joyous work of art. (131 mins.)

Tom Sawyer (1973)** Johnny Whitaker, Celeste Holm, Warren Oates, Jeff East, Jodie Foster. Strictly for the kids; the adults will be annoyed by this scrubbed-clean musical version of the Mark Twain classic. Shot entirely on location in Missouri (a plus), the film contains most of the familiar incidents, from the fence whitewashing to the scary chase through the caves. Whitaker

736

and East are too wholesome as Tom and Huck Finn, but Jodie Foster just about steals the movie as the perfect Becky Thatcher. Celeste Holm, as Aunt Polly, and Warren Oates, as Muff Potter, are the adults on hand. (Dir: Don Taylor, 100 mins.)

Tom Thumb (1958)*** Russ Tamblyn, Terry-Thomas, Peter Sellers. Grimm's fairy tale brought to life using real actors, puppets, and animation, all cleverly arranged together. Concerns tiny five-inch Tom who is forced to help robbers, and then later to capture them. Exemplary family fare. (Dir: George Pal, 98 mins.)

Toma (1973)**½ Tony Musante, Susan Strasberg. Good police story and pilot for the TV series. Musante is fine as Dave Toma, real-life Newark, N.J., police detective, whose unique approach to his work helped him to crack, almost single-handedly, a big numbers operation connected to the syndicate. The detailed detective work, piling clue upon clue, is interesting to follow, and the action is kept at a believable, exciting level, thanks to director Richard T. Heffron. (73 mins.)

Tomahawk (1951)** Van Heflin, Yvonne DeCarlo. Just another Indian and cowboy film. This time the plot is involved with Indian Affairs treaties and those who fight to protect the enforcement of said treaties. Some action during the proceedings. (Dir: George Sherman, 82 mins.)

Tombstone, the Town Too Tough to Die (1942)*** Richard Dix, Frances Gifford. Routine western rises way above the average thanks to slick production. Story of Wyatt Earp (again), and the infamous duel with the outlaws at Tombstone, Arizona.

Tommy (Great Britain, 1975)*** Ann-Margret, Oliver Reed, Jack Nicholson, Roger Daltrey, Elton John, Eric Clapton. A wildly uneven, often visually stunning musical of The Who's rock opera written by composer-guitarist Pete Townshend. Director Ken Russell wrote the screenplay, but the dialogue takes a back seat to the music, and some crazed, hallucinatory images that director Russell puts on the screen including an erupting TV set that you won't soon forget. Director Russell's flamboyant style is well-suited to this garish material, and there's a sur-

prisingly good performance in the lead role by Ann-Margret who received an Academy Award nomination for her all-out try. (Dir: Ken Russell, 110 mins.)

Tomorrow at 10 (British, 1963)**½ John Gregson, Robert Shaw, Helen Cherry. Kidnaper leaves his victim in a room with a time bomb, asks for ransom as the police race against time to nab him. Competent crime melodrama has quite a bit of suspense. (Dir: Lance Comfort, 80 mins.)

Tomorrow Is Another Day (1951)*** Ruth Roman, Steve Cochran. Fast paced action drama about hoodlums and their women. Ruth Roman tries to start a new life but her past proves too strong an obstacle. Good performances. (Dir: Felix E. Feist, 90 mins.)

Tomorrow Is Forever (1946)**½ Claudette Colbert, Orson Welles, George Brent. Twenty years after he supposedly was killed, a disfigured and crippled chemist comes back to his wife, who remarried. Well-produced but slow drama with an Enoch Arden theme. (Dir: Irving Pichel, 105 mins.)

Tomorrow Is My Turn (French, 1962)**½ Charles Aznavour, Georges Rivière. Long, grim saga of two French prisoners of war, their experiences on a farm in Germany. Superior direction, performances—and a wordy script, dubbed in English.

Tomorrow the World (1944)**** Fredric March, Betty Field. An American family adopts a German boy, discovers the Nazi influence has warped the child's mind. Excellent drama, thoughtful, gripping. (Dir: Leslie Fenton, 86 mins.)

Tonight and Every Night (1945)***½ Rita Hayworth, Lee Bowman, Janet Blair. London theatre keeps open and doesn't miss a performance even during the darkest days of World War II. Well made musical drama, with fine production numbers. (Dir: Victor Saville, 92 mins.)

Tonight at 8:30 (British, 1952)**** Valerie Hobson, Nigel Patrick, Stanley Holloway. Three of Noel Coward's short plays, all comic gems, sophisticated, worthwhile, stylishly performed for civilized viewers. (Dir: Anthony Pelissier, 81 mins.)

Tonight We Raid Calais (1943)**½ Annabella, John Sutton, Lee J. Cobb. Another of those wartime espionage films. This one is the well-acted, improbable tale of a British agent in France to find a factory the RAF wants to bomb. (Dir: John Brahm, 70 mins.)

Tonight We Sing (1953)******* David Wayne, Anne Bancroft, Ezio Pinza. Screen biography of impressario Sol Hurok features some superb classical music numbers, fine performance by Wayne in the role of Hurok. Class attraction, primarily for longhair audiences; but for them, very good. (Dir: Mitchell Leisen, 109 mins.)

Tonight's the Night (1955)******* David Niven, Yvonne DeCarlo. A whimsical comedy filmed in Ireland with authentic settings bolstering the film's appeal. David Niven is funny in his inimitable gentlemanly fashion. (Dir: Mario Zampi, 88 mins.)

Tonio Kroger (German-French, 1964)****½** Jean-Claude Brialy, Nadja Tiller, Gert Frobe. An academic, fairly literal version of Thomas Mann's autobiographical novella about growing up in Germany in the 19th century. If you haven't got the book handy, this might be a reasonable introduction to the story line, and provide a stimulus to reading the fine Mann work. As a film experience, it's stodgy, picturesque, with some lovely narration directly from the original. English subtitles.

Tonka (1959)******* Sal Mineo, Philip Carey. Disney's interpretation of Custer's Last Stand has heroes and villains on both sides. Mineo is quite good as an Indian youth. (Dir: Lewis R. Foster, 97 mins.)

Tony Draws a Horse (British, 1951)****½** Anne Crawford, Cecil Parker. A psychiatrist and his wife disagree over the treatment of their son, and as a result a happy marriage is nearly terminated. Mildly amusing comedy has some good moments. (Dir: John Paddy Carstairs, 90 mins.)

Tony Rome (1967)****** Frank Sinatra, Jill St. John, Richard Conte. Slick production values, tough dialogue, a parade of feminine pulchritude plus Sinatra as a private eye add up to not a hell of a lot, but with Miami Beach backgrounds, and the familiar plot Rome (Sinatra) is involved in a series of he-man confrontations with an assortment of sordid characters, as he tries to solve a jewel theft and murder. Frankie ain't Bogie! (Dir: Gordon Douglas, 110 mins.)

Too Bad She's Bad (Italian, 1955)****½** Sophia Loren, Vittorio De Sica, Marcello Mastroianni. Taxi driver gets involved with a band of crooks, but fails for one of the pretty ones. Mildly amusing English-dubbed comedy. (Dir: Alessandro Blasetti, 95 mins.)

Too Hot to Handle (1938)*****½** Clark Gable, Myrna Loy, Walter Pidgeon. Rival newsreel companies vie with each other for hot news. Big, exciting action melodrama, a most enjoyable show. (Dir: Jack Conway, 110 mins.)

Too Hot to Handle (British, 1960)***½** Jayne Mansfield, Leo Genn. Trashy crime melodrama about a nightclub entertainer trying to protect her boss from a murder frameup. Genn is wasted, Mansfield looks out of place. (Dir: Terence Young, 92 mins.)

Too Late Blues (1961)****** Bobby Darin, Stella Stevens. Glum, unpleasant story of a jazz musician who steals the affections of a blonde from his friend. Jazz atmosphere pervades, but it's pretty synthetic. However, Darin gives a good performance. (Dir: John Cassavetes, 100 mins.)

Too Late the Hero—See: **Suicide Run**

Too Late to Love (French, 1959)****½** Michele Morgan, Henri Vidal. Well acted poorly written drama about the alliance of a news photographer and a lady lawyer, for the purpose of proving a man's innocence.

Too Many Crooks (British, 1959)******* Terry-Thomas, George Cole. Thick-headed gang of crooks try to extort from a businessman. Amusingly daffy comedy. (Dir: Mario Zampi, 85 mins.)

Too Many Girls (1940)******* Lucille Ball, Richard Carlson, Ann Miller, Desi Arnaz, Eddie Bracken. Small college with ten co-eds to every boy wants badly to win a football game. Entertaining musical comedy. (Dir: George Abbott, 85 mins.)

Too Many Husbands (1940)******* Jean Arthur, Fred MacMurray, Melvyn Douglas. About to marry again, a woman finds her first husband, believed dead, has returned. Pleasing sophisticated comedy. (Dir: Wesley Ruggles, 84 mins.)

Too Many Lovers (French, 1957)****** Jeanmaire, Daniel Gelin, Henri Vidal. Lightweight French comedy dealing with a nightclub singer-dancer. The proceedings are en-

Too Many Thieves (1966)** Peter Falk. Moderately entertaining caper film with Falk playing an American lawyer who is hired by thieves who stole an art treasure from a Macedonian shrine. The character Falk plays is the same one he played in the short-lived TV series "The Trials of O'Brien." (Dir: Bob Hayes, 95 mins.)

Too Much, Too Soon (1958)** Dorothy Malone, Errol Flynn, Efrem Zimbalist, Jr. Depressing, maudlin drama of the late Diana Barrymore's life. No holds barred in the telling of Miss Barrymore's sordid, drunken years. Flynn plays John Barrymore, Diana's father, and the reason for her misfortune (according to this over-sensational screenplay). Miss Malone gives the part the old Academy-Award try but it's still too much, too late. (Dir: Art Napoleon, 121 mins.)

Too Young to Kiss (1951)*** Van Johnson, June Allyson, Gig Young. Young pianist can't get in to see a concert manager, so she poses as a 13-year-old. Bright comedy with plenty of laughs along the way. (Dir: Robert Z. Leonard, 91 mins.)

Too Young to Love (British, 1961)*½ Thomas Mitchell, Pauline Hahn. A judge hears the sad tale of a young girl who has turned to walking the streets. Tiresome juvenile-delinquency drama.

Top Banana (1954)***½ Phil Silvers, Rose Marie. A loud burlesque comic becomes a TV star and aids a young romance. From the Broadway stage hit, filmed as it was presented, this has nothing production-wise, but Silvers' yeoman service turns it into a funny show and you will see a couple of those wild sketches that made burlesque such a good training ground years ago for comedians. (Dir: Alfred E. Green, 100 mins.)

Top Floor Girl (British, 1957)** Kay Callard, Neil Hallett. Ruthless woman stops at nothing to get to the top of the business world. Mildly entertaining "female jungle" type of drama.

Top Hat (1935)**** Fred Astaire, Ginger Rogers. The best of the Astaire-Rogers films, and that's saying plenty. Fred plays a dancer who pursues the girl of his dreams from London to the Riviera. Irving Berlin tunes: "Cheek to Cheek," "Isn't This A Lovely Day." Isn't this a lovely show? It sure is! (Dir: Mark Sandrich, 110 mins.)

Top Man (1943)**½ Donald O'Connor, Richard Dix, Susanna Foster. Corny dated comedy about a young man's taking over as head of the family while his father goes to War (WW II). O'Connor is one of our favorites but he can't carry this one. (Dir: Charles Lamont, 74 mins.)

Top o' the Morning (1949)**½ Bing Crosby, Barry Fitzgerald, Ann Blyth. Bing on the Emerald Isle, as he plays an insurance agent out to find who stole the Blarney Stone. Lazily amusing comedy with Bing crooning the songs. (Dir: David Miller, 100 mins.)

Top of the Form (British, 1953)**½ Ronald Shiner, Jacqueline Pierreux. A race track tipster becomes the head of a boys' school by accident. Mildly amusing comedy.

Top of the World (1955)**½ Dale Robertson, Evelyn Keyes, Frank Lovejoy. Jet pilot is assigned to an Alaskan observation unit. Typical service melodrama, enlivened by some good scenes in the frozen North. (Dir: Lewis R. Foster, 90 mins.)

Top Secret (British, 1953)*** George Cole, Oscar Homolka. Sanitary engineer accidentally walks off with atomic secrets, is branded a traitor. Highly amusing topical comedy, good fun.

Top Secret Affair (1957)** Kirk Douglas, Susan Hayward. A tough Major General and a crusading lady publisher slug it out in a slight comedy about Washington politics and the diplomatic service. This could have been a funnier film but it never gets off the ground. (Dir: H. C. Potter, 99 mins.)

Topaz (1969)**½ John Forsythe, Frederic Stafford. An espionage tale which has agents and double agents jumping around the globe when it is discovered that the Russians have infiltrated into high French government positions. Although Alfred Hitchcock directed this tale, it doesn't have his usual stamp of excitement, but the narrative itself should keep spy fans intrigued. The cast has no real star names in the leads but John Vernon scores as a Castro-type revolutionary and Karin

Dor is beautiful and seductive as an undercover agent. (126 mins.)

Topaze (1933)***½ John Barrymore, Myrna Loy. Clever professor becomes a tycoon in business and romantic affairs. Literate superbly played comedy. One of Barrymore's best roles. (Dir: Harry D'Arrast, 80 mins.)

Topeka (1953)**½ Bill Elliott, Phyllis Coates. Outlaw is offered the job of sheriff, calls in his former gang members to help him clean up the territory. Lively western has plenty of action.

Topkapi (1964)**** Melina Mercouri, Maximilian Schell, Peter Ustinov. An exciting jewel of a film about an ingenious theft of a valuable jewel-encrusted dagger from the Topkapi Museum in Istanbul. The color photography is dazzling, whether showing the glories of Istanbul or the treasures of the museum. The big heist scene may strike you as a more elaborate re-shooting of the classic scene in "Rififi," and you'll be right, because they're both the work of ace director Jules Dassin. He has a flawless cast of charming rogues and charlatans assembled, and the film keeps bustling along at a seesaw pace. A delightful, droll adventure film. (120 mins.)

Topper (1937)***½ Cary Grant, Roland Young, Constance Bennett. Of how George and Marian Kirby became involved in their ghostly escapades. Grand fantastic comedy, the original in the "Topper" series. (Dir: Norman Z. McLeod, 100 mins.)

Topper Returns (1941)**** Roland Young, Joan Blondell, "Rochester," Dennis O'Keefe. Mr. Cosmo Topper and his ghostly friends are involved in a spooky murder mystery. The best of the Toppers. Hilarious, loaded with laughs, thrills, tip-top performers! (Dir: Roy Del Ruth, 85 mins.)

Topper Takes a Trip (1938)***½ Roland Young, Constance Bennett. Mr. Topper goes to the Riviera for a holiday, only to find the spirit of Marian Kirby in hot pursuit. Amusing comedy. (Dir: Norman Z. McLeod, 80 mins.)

Tora, Tora, Tora! (1970)*** Jason Robards, Martin Balsam, Joseph Cotten. From a production point of view, you'll seldom see a more detailed or expensively mounted bat-

tle sequence than the bombing of Pearl Harbor which takes up a good part of the last half of this WW II film. Reportedly costing close to $25 million, making it the second most expensive U.S. film ever after "Cleopatra," this re-creation of the events leading up to and just after that "day of infamy" has a cast of familiar faces, as well as many Japanese actors. However, they play second fiddle to the special-effects men who staged the massive Pearl Harbor attack. History in cinemascope and stereophonic terms, which suffer on the small home screen. (Dirs: Richard Fleischer, Toshio Masuda, and Kinji Fukasaku, 142 mins.)

Torch Song (1953)**½ Joan Crawford, Michael Wilding, Gig Young. This film marked Miss Crawford's return to a musical role after years of heavy-weight dramas. She wears tights, dances and sings (dubbed by India Adams) and, of course, cries once or twice. In the role of a Broadway musical comedy star whose personal life leaves much to be desired. Michael Wilding plays a blind pianist who is secretly in love with Miss Crawford. (Dir: Charles Walter, 90 mins.)

Tormented (1960)*½ Richard Carlson, Susan Gordon. Muddled melodrama about a nightclub singer and her strange boyfriend. It's like a detective TV show without series' regulars. (Dir: Bert I. Gordon, 75 mins.)

Torn Curtain (1966)** Paul Newman, Julie Andrews, Lila Kedrova. The only noteworthy thing about this chiller is that it's the 50th film directed by Alfred Hitchcock, the undisputed master of spy-chase films. This "Golden" Hitchcock 50th is badly tarnished and sub par for the master. Newman plays a science professor who gets involved in a fantastic espionage mission while attending a convention in Denmark. J. Andrews, in a sexy role for a change, is Newman's secretary-lover and she follows him to East Berlin. (128 mins.)

Torpedo Bay (Italian, 1963)**½ James Mason, Lilli Palmer, Gabriele Ferzetti. When an Italian sub surfaces in neutral waters, the crew of an antisub craft meets the crew in Tangiers, learn to like each other despite the enmity. Different sort of war drama, with English dialogue, moves leisurely but holds interest for the most part. (Dir: Charles Frend, 91 mins.)

Torpedo of Doom, The (1938-66)*** Lee Powell, Herman Brix, Eleanor Stewart. Feature version of serial "The Fighting Devil Dogs." Two Marines combat a mysterious hooded figure who wants to rule the world. As a serial, this rated with the best; excellently made for its type. Dated now but should still provide enough thrills for the kids, nostalgia for the elders. (Dirs: William Witney, John English, 100 mins.)

Torpedo Run (1958)**½ Glenn Ford, Ernest Borgnine, Dean Jones. Moderately interesting but slow moving submarine drama with some suspense. Glenn Ford plays the commander of the sub, whose mission is to sink a transport on which his family are passengers. (Dir: Joseph Pevney, 98 mins.)

Torrid Zone (1940)*** Pat O'Brien, Ann Sheridan, James Cagney. Good racy dialogue and the acting of the principals combine to make this a torrid picture. Jim is a no-good, Pat is his foreman and Ann gives out with plenty of oomph as a night club girl. (Dir: William Keighley, 88 mins.)

Tortilla Flat (1941)***½ Spencer Tracy, Hedy Lamarr, John Garfield. Steinbeck's delightful study about the tramps of unknown origin who populate sections of the California coast has been made into an intriguing though talky film. Definitely worth meeting these tramps. (Dir: Victor Fleming, 105 mins.)

Torture Garden (British, 1968)**½ Some eerie tales are spun by a sinister doctor (Burgess Meredith) at a sideshow. Best: the first one, about a cat's evil presence. Worst: the last, with a hammy Jack Palance performance. With Peter Cushing, Beverly Adams. (Dir: Freddie Francis, 93 mins.)

Touch and Go (British, 1956)*** Jack Hawkins, Margaret Johnson. Funny, sometimes hilarious comedy of a family's decision to pull up stakes and move to Australia. Jack Hawkins shines in the lead role. (Dir: Michael Truman, 84 mins.)

Touch of Class, A (Great Britain, 1972)**** Glenda Jackson, George Segal. A delightful romantic comedy about a pair of clandestine lovers in a London-Spain tryst. Their quarrelsome "brief encounter" in sunny Spain is quite deft, and Jackson and Segal are enormously charming together. The screenplay by Melvin Frank and Jack Rose is not invariably sophisticated, but it's great fun most of the way—and Hepburn and Tracy are not making romantic films any more. Overlook the dopey song at the end. "Class" is the best work from Melvin Frank in a good while. Glenda Jackson won an Academy Award for her enchanting performance. Also nominated for an Academy Award as best picture and for best screenplay. (Dir: Melvin Frank, 106 mins.)

Touch of Evil (1958)***½ Orson Welles, Charlton Heston, Janet Leigh. Absorbing weirdie in the Wellesian manner—he wrote, directed, plays a leading role as a gross copper investigating a murder, kidnapping and assorted felonies down Mexico way. Other bizarre characters include Marlene Dietrich and Joseph Cotten in bit roles, plus Mercedes McCambridge as a particularly sinister overaged delinquent. Good for those seeking the unusual. (Dir: Orson Welles, 95 mins.)

Touch of Larceny, A (British, 1960) *** James Mason, Vera Miles, George Sanders. Lothariolike military man dreams up a scheme to make it appear that he has defected to the Russians with secrets—so he can sell his memoirs and obtain money to marry. Mason is charming in this clever little comedy with a good portion of sly humor. (Dir: Guy Hamilton, 94 mins.)

Touch of the Sun, A (British, 1958) *½ Frankie Howerd, Dennis Price. Howerd is a comic appreciated in England—here he plays a stumbling hotel porter who inherits a fortune. If the situations seem labored and unfunny, remember Britain is our ally and we still need all the friends we can get.

Touch of Treason, A (French, 1962) *½ Roger Hanin, Dany Carrel, Claude Brasseur. Humdrum spy thriller, French and Soviet agents collaborating to find out who-stole-the-documents. Plenty of action, but not so well done. Dubbed in English.

Touchables, The (British, 1968)* Judy Huxtable, Esther Anderson, Marilyn Rickard, Kathy Simmonds, David Anthony. Not worth touching or seeing. Tasteless nonsense about four screwy London mods who kidnap a popular singing idol to satisfy their sexual appetites. Should be seen with a deodorizer handy, if you must. (Dir: Robert Freeman, 97 mins.)

Toughest Gun in Tombstone (1958) ** George Montgomery, Beverly Tyler. Dull sagebrush saga of a cowboy out to avenge the murder of his wife and bring to justice the villainous outlaw, Johnny Ringo. (Dir: Earl Bellamy, 72 mins.)

Toughest Man Alive (1955)**½ Dane Clark, Lita Milan. Government agent poses as a gun runner to break up a smuggling ring. Fast moving melodrama. (Dir: Sidney Salkow, 72 mins.)

Toughest Man in Tombstone (1958)** George Montgomery, Jim Davis, Beverly Tyler. Another horse opera with the clichés all in place. Montgomery and Davis are old hands at this sort of thing so even the performances fall into a pattern.

Tout Va Bien (France, 1971)** Jane Fonda, Yves Montand, Jean Pignol. More political agit-prop from Jean-Luc Godard, but this story about a workers' strike in a French sausage factory is one of his least interesting contributions. Fonda plays a correspondent-broadcaster and Montand plays He, her French husband. Godard is/was a great artist but the politics and the symbolism here are simple-minded. Written and directed by Godard and Jean-Pierre Gorin. (95 mins.)

Tovarich (1937) ***½ Claudette Colbert, Charles Boyer, Basil Rathbone. Top drawer comedy about two royal paupers who are carrying 40 billion francs for the czar but would rather starve than spend it. Translated from Jacques Deval's play by Robert E. Sherwood. (Dir: Anatole Litvak, 100 mins.)

Toward the Unknown (1956)**½ William Holden, Lloyd Nolan, Virginia Leith. Fairly interesting drama about the test jet-pilots and their personal involvements. Holden plays a nervous major whose past record makes him over-zealous in the performance of his duty.

Tower of London (1939)**½ Boris Karloff, Basil Rathbone, Nan Grey. History and horror are mixed in this costume drama about Queen Elizabeth and the exiled Henry Tudor. Karloff plays the menacing executioner of the Tower. (Dir: Rowland V. Lee, 100 mins.)

Town Like Alice, A (British, 1957) ***½ Virginia McKenna, Peter Finch. Powerful film about the tragedy of a group of women who miss being evacuated from Malaya at the outbreak of World War II and suffer many indignities in the hands of the conquering Japanese Army. The acting is first rate. (Dir: Jack Lee, 107 mins.)

Town on Trial (1957)*** John Mills, Charles Coburn. Well done tale of a murder investigation which leads a Scotland Yard man into a town loaded with secrets. The characters are well written and acted thus raising this above the commonplace. (Dir: John Guillermin, 94 mins.)

Town Tamer (1965)* Dana Andrews, Terry Moore, Pat O'Brien, Lon Chaney, Bruce Cabot, Jean Cagney, Barton MacLane. Lawyer, avenging his wife's death, corrals the lawless in Western towns. Full of vintage film characters, otherwise tiresome. (Dir: Lesley Selander, 89 mins.)

Town Without Pity (1961)** Kirk Douglas, E. G. Marshall, Christine Kaufmann. Army major in Germany is assigned to defend a quartet of GIs accused of attacking a young girl. Downbeat, grim drama moves stodgily, is obvious in its presentation. Filmed in Germany. (Dir: Gottfried Reinhardt, 105 mins.)

Toy Tiger (1956)**½ Jeff Chandler, Laraine Day. Pleasant comedy about a neglected child who plays cupid for his career Mom and selects her new husband, one of her staff commercial artists. The cast is attractive and the pace keeps things hopping. (Dir: Jerry Hopper, 88 mins.)

Toys in the Attic (1963)**½ Dean Martin, Geraldine Page, Wendy Hiller, Yvette Mimieux. A no-good rover returns to his New Orleans home with his childlike bride, brings trouble for his spinster sisters. Lillian Hellman's drama becomes commonplace when it should be provoking. Some capable performers, but the general result is disappointing. (Dir: George Roy Hill, 90 mins.)

Track of the Cat (1954)** Robert Mitchum, Teresa Wright, Diana Lynn, Tab Hunter. A cougar hunt amid family squabbles makes up the action of this otherwise slow-paced movie. Best feature is the fine photography. (Dir: William Wellman, 102 mins.)

Track of the Vampire (1966)*½ William Campbell, Sandra Knight. Mad artist-vampire paints beautiful girls, then does them in. Gruesome, badly-made horror thriller.

Track of Thunder (1968)* Feuding drivers going round and round the stock-car racing track. Plot does the same; needs a lubricating job. With Tom Kirk, Ray Stricklyn, H. M. Wynant, Brenda Benet (she's cute). (Dir: Joseph Kane, 83 mins.)

Trackers, The (1971)*½ Sammy Davis, Jr., Ernest Borgnine, Julie Adams. Sammy Davis, Jr., as a deputy marshal in this very mundane western. A few interesting characters along the way. Made-for-TV. (Dir: Earl Bellamy, 72 mins.)

Trade Winds (1938)*** Fredric March, Joan Bennett. Chasing a beautiful murder suspect around the globe, a detective falls in love with her. Entertaining. (Dir: Tay Garnett, 100 mins.)

Trader Horn (1931)**½ Harry Carey, Edwina Booth. This exciting jungle thriller scared the daylights out of 1931 audiences. You may find it funny but it was a step forward in realistic movie making. (Dir: W. S. Van Dyke, 130 mins.)

Traffic (France-Italy, 1970)*** Jacques Tati, Maria Kimberley. Not as inspired a bit of tomfoolery as "Mr. Hulot's Holiday," but there are some inventive scenes in this virtually plotless free-form series of running gags about Paris, its traffic and automobile drivers. Jacques Tati also wrote this slight satire about transporting a model camping car to an automobile show in Holland. "Traffic" is the fourth film Tati has made in a 25-year period. There are virtually no closeups in "Traffic" and we see more of Tati's back than his face, but there are other rewards to be found here. (Dir: Jacques Tati, 89 mins.)

Trail of the Vigilantes (1941)**** Franchot Tone, Broderick Crawford, Peggy Moran. Easterner is sent west to break up an outlaw gang. Excellent western, with emphasis on some hilarious comedy. (Dir: Allan Dwan, 78 mins.)

Train, The (1965)***½ Burt Lancaster, Paul Scofield. An exciting World War II drama set in Paris during the German occupation which builds scene by scene to a magnificently staged climax in a railroad yard. Burt Lancaster stars as a railroad boss who seeks the aid of the powerful French Resistance fighters when it becomes known that France's valuable art treasures are going to be transported by train to Germany. Suspense builds well under John Frankenheimer's direction. The cast is first-rate, particularly Paul Scofield as a German officer and marvelous French character actor Michel Simon as a bull-headed train engineer. (Dir: John Frankenheimer, 113 mins.)

Train of Events (British, 1949)**½ Valerie Hobson, John Clements, Joan Dowling. Various groups of persons aboard a train have their problems, which are resolved in one way or another when the train is involved in an accident. Episodic film manages to hold the attention, with one story line being extremely humorous, another intensely dramatic.

Train Ride to Hollywood (1975)*½ Guy Marks, Michael Payne. A silly film, but it is so good-natured that you might enjoy it if you're in the mood. A black rock singer dreams he's a porter on a train heading for Hollywood, on which many stars turn out to be traveling: Gable, Harlow, Bogart, W. C. Fields, Nelson Eddy and Jeanette MacDonald. The plot is dumb, and the writing and directing inept, but some of the characters are amusing—Marks as Bogart, Payne as a demented producer named Eric Van Johnson. (Dir: Charles Rondeau, 85 mins.)

Train Robbers, The (1973)*½ John Wayne, Ann-Margret. Dull western which finds Duke Wayne helping the helpless widow-lady Ann-Margret get her rightful share of the gold her thieving, dead husband stashed . . . or at the very least, a share of the reward money. It's as routine as it sounds and a scene in which Ann-Margret attempts to light a romantic fire under tired Wayne's hulking frame comes across ludicrously. Some action and a surprise plot twist at the end can't save this one. (Dir: Burt Kennedy, 92 mins.)

Train Robbery Confidential (Brazilian, 1959)** Eliezer Gomes, Grande Otelo. A novelty—the true story of six men who perpetrated a payroll robbery on a Brazilian railroad. Technically below par, but the locale, treatment are interesting. Dubbed in English. (Dir: Roberto Farias, 102 mins.)

Tramp, Tramp, Tramp (1942)*½ Jackie Gleason, Florence Rice. Wartime comedy about a pair of 4-F barbers is silly and forced. See Jackie though and satisfy your curiosity. (Dir: Charles Barton, 70 mins.)

Tramplers, The (1966)** Gordon Scott, Joseph Cotten, Jim Mitchum. Confederate soldier returns home to encounter trouble from his father and the problems left by war's aftermath. A Civil War western, but produced in Spain. Some good moments, some erratic ones. (Dir: Albert Band, 105 mins.)

Trap, The (1959)**½ Richard Widmark, Tina Louise, Lee J. Cobb. Head of a crime syndicate trying to flee the country isolates a small desert town. Fairly suspenseful crime melodrama. (Dir: Norman Panama, 84 mins.)

Trap, The (Great Britain-Canada, 1966)*** Rita Tushingham, Oliver Reed. A raw, tough, unusual movie; a fur trapper and the mute girl he has bartered for as wife struggle in the northern wilderness of 19th-century Canada. Authentic, exciting adventure tale, spiced by low-key humor and an off-beat romance. The performances are top-notch. Filmed on location in British Columbia. (Dir: Sidney Hayers, 106 mins.)

Trapeze (1956)**½ Burt Lancaster, Tony Curtis, Gina Lollobrigida. Corny but colorful drama played against a circus background. Lancaster plays a former aerialist who helps a young acrobat achieve fame under the big top. Good European locations, some exciting camera work and Gina Lollobrigida are added assets. (Dir: Carol Reed, 105 mins.)

Trapped (1949)***½ Barbara Payton, Lloyd Bridges, John Hoyt. T-men release a counterfeiter from jail, hoping he will lead them to a big money ring. Excellent documentary-type crime melodrama rates with the best of them. (Dir: Richard Fleischer, 78 mins.)

Trapped (1973)*½ James Brolin, Susan Clark, Earl Holliman, Robert Hooks. How far can a movie go with a story line that locks a victim of teenaged muggers in a department store men's room, and then confronts him with killer dogs? Brolin

struggles to stay alive and keep the movie rolling. Made-for-TV. (Dir: Frank De Felitta, 72 mins.)

Trapped Beneath the Sea (1974)**½ Lee J. Cobb, Martin Balsam. Wellmade drama about the rescue of an experimental submarine. Good performances and realistic underwater sequences lift this disaster film above the average. Most of the action is told in flashbacks during a Navy inquiry into the incident. The film mirrors a similar real-life story of four men who were trapped in a mini-sub. Made-for-TV. (Dir: William Graham, 72 mins.)

Trapped by Fear (French, 1960)** Jean-Paul Belmondo, Alexandra Stewart, Sylva Koscina. Ex-soldier becomes a hunted man when he kills a policeman despite efforts of his friend to help. Occasionally interesting, often routine "new-wavish" melodrama dubbed in English.

Trash (1970)**½ Joe Dallesandro, Holly Woodlawn, Geri Miller. You won't see an uncut version of this cinema garbage heap on your regular TV station, but those of you who've heard about it on the big screen may be able to see this during the 1970's via TV cartridges, cassettes or on a late night cable TV channel programmed by a fearless disciple of Andy Warhol. It's almost impossible to sensibly rate a movie like this, or avoid the temptation of agreeing with the title. It's a sleazy story, with some improvised dialogue, about various repellent, vapid-minded, foul-mouthed drug addicts. It will have a bizarre fascination for some of you, and there are critics who take this film, and its spiritual predecessor "Flesh," quite seriously.

Trauma (1962)* John Conte, Lynn Bari, Lorrie Richards. Muddled melodrama that drags along. Psychological gibberish about a girl who cracks after witnessing her aunt's murder. (Dir: Robert Malcolm Young, 92 mins.)

Traveling Saleswoman, The (1950) ** Joan Davis, Andy Devine. Strictly for slapstick and mugging fans. Joan Davis & Andy Devine vie for laughs in this cornball Western about a soap saleswoman and her rotund fiance. (Dir: Charles F. Reisner, 75 mins.)

Travels with My Aunt (1972)***½ Alec McCowen, Lou Gossett. Most of the time this is delightful, sophisticated fare, immeasurably aided by Maggie Smith's glowing, winning performance as Aunt Augusta out to ransom her old lover and, in the process, liberate her nephew Henry (McCowen). Screenwriter Jay Presson Allen has scaled down Graham Greene's best-selling novel and added a few not very felicitous plot twists. But the stylish Miss Smith and lively direction from veteran George Cukor keep things moving along briskly and divertingly. (109 mins.)

Traviata, La (Italy, 1966)*** Anna Moffo, Franco Bonisolli, Gino Bechi. Excellent screen production of Verdi's opera from Dumas' novel "The Lady of the Camellias." (The same story is behind the memorable Garbo movie, "Camille," about an Italian courtesan who tragically loves a man of modest, respectable means.) The singing and sets are marvelous; Ms. Moffo is outstanding—a delicate, matchless Italian beauty and a superb actress. Other acting is poor. (Dir: Mario Lanfranchi, 110 mins.)

Travis Logan, D.A. (1971)**½ Vic Morrow, Hal Holbrook, Brenda Vaccaro. Here's another law series pilot —this one from the Quinn Martin TV stable. Vic Morrow plays a low-keyed small-town district attorney who puzzles over an open killing by a stationer after finding his wife in his best friend's arms. Though a psychiatrist labels the man insane, D.A. Logan believes it is premeditated murder and he faces an uphill battle to prove it. Hal Holbrook plays the stationer, a man who must be clever enough to fool a psychiatrist, and his performance keys the ingenious story by Andy Lewis. (Dir: Paul Wendkos, 100 mins.)

Treasure Island (1934)*** Wallace Beery, Jackie Cooper. The kids will love this version of the Stevenson book and you will find a lot of nostalgia in it. Well acted and directed. (Dir: Victor Fleming, 110 mins.)

Treasure of Lost Canyon (1952)*½ William Powell, Julie Adams. Even William Powell can't make this western yarn any more than it is. A rather dull tale of buried treasure and how it changes many lives. (Dir: Ted Tetzlaff, 82 mins.)

Treasure of Pancho Villa, The (1955) ** Rory Calhoun, Shelley Winters, Gilbert Roland. American adventurer plots a train robbery with the inten-tion of delivering the gold to Villa's forces. Picturesque Mexican backgrounds support a routine plot; standard outdoor drama. (Dir: George Sherman, 96 mins.)

Treasure of Ruby Hill (1955)** Zachary Scott, Carole Mathews. Rancher steps in the middle of a fight to control range land. Undistinguished western. (Dir: Frank McDonald, 71 mins.)

Treasure of San Teresa (1951)** Dawn Addams, Eddie Constantine. A predictable espionage yarn with more narrow escapes than you can keep straight. This plot-boiler has all the clichés neatly intact, and the international cast breezes through the proceedings with professional ease.

Treasure of the Golden Condor (1953) ** Cornel Wilde, Constance Smith, Anne Bancroft. Predictable costume adventure film which traps its stars in an 18th century melodrama. Wilde plays the rightful heir to a noble fortune who is cheated and forced to live as a fugitive. Treasure hunting in Central America fills the better half of the movie. (Dir: Delmer Daves, 93 mins.)

Treasure of the Sierra Madre (1947) **** Humphrey Bogart, Walter Huston. Greed, one of man's basic emotions, is graphically portrayed in this magnificent film. Directed by John Huston, story of an unholy partnership of men in search of gold is a "must see" for everyone. Walter Huston's award winning performance is one of the best character or supporting performances ever turned in. Superbly written, this is a great movie in every respect! (126 mins.)

Tree Grows in Brooklyn, A (1945) ***½ Dorothy McGuire, Joan Blondell, James Dunn. Betty Smith's sensitive story of people brought up in Brooklyn is captured on the screen by fine performances and Elia Kazan's directorial skill. Tenement life in a big city has never been more convincingly done but, overall, it's a little too long and episodic. (128 mins.)

Tree Grows in Brooklyn, A (1974)** Cliff Robertson, Diane Baker, Nancy Malone. Labored remake of the marvelous earlier film version (1945) of Betty Smith's touching novel about life in the tenements of Brooklyn, circa 1912. Robertson, as the hard-drinking singing waiter and occasional breadwinner of the Nolan family, somehow slips into caricature rather than characterization. Miss Baker is more successful as the brave but stern Katie Nolan, but it's Pamela Ferdin, as the teen-age Francine, who delivers the film's best performance. Made-for-TV. (Dir: Joel Hardy.)

Trent's Last Case (British, 1953)** Michael Wilding, Margaret Lockwood, Orson Welles. Amateur sleuth investigates the mysterious killing of a financial tycoon. Film version of classic mystery novel is all talk, on the boring side. (Dir: Herbert Wilcox, 90 mins.)

Trial (1955)***½ Glenn Ford, Dorothy McGuire, Arthur Kennedy. Absorbing drama about the murder trial of a Mexican boy which is fantastically exploited by a Communist-backed organization for their own underhanded purposes. The cast is top notch with Arthur Kennedy the standout as a two-faced legal mind working for the organization. (Dir: Mark Robson, 105 mins.)

Trial, The (1963)***½ Anthony Perkins, Jeanne Moreau, Romy Schneider, Orson Welles. Kafka's frightening allegory of a nameless man accused of a crime without being informed of what it was. Orson Welles as producer and director gives it the Wellesian treatment, meaning some inspired scenes and good performances. This interesting try is certainly worth seeing for discriminating viewers. (118 mins.)

Trial and Error (British, 1962)**½ Peter Sellers, Beryl Reid, Richard Attenborough, David Lodge. A study in character acting from Peter Sellers and Attenborough, as a bungling barrister and an accused murderer. They're fine, but the film becomes a thespic exhibition at the expense of the narrative, which is thin indeed.

Trial at Kamplli (Japanese, 1963)** Minoru Ohki, Elice Richter. Japanese officer goes on trial before the War Crimes Commission, but his former prisoners come to his defense. Fairly interesting English-dubbed war drama.

Trial of Billy Jack, The (1974)½ Tom Laughlin, Delores Taylor, William Wellman, Jr., Scheen Littlefeather. A repellent bit of simple-minded neo-fascistic rubbish that extols violence while supposedly condemning it. Laughlin is again the crusading Indian half-breed fighting corruption in government, business, etc. (Movie-going halfwits made this pap a huge commercial success at the time of its release.) Feeble script belched out by Laughlin and his wife. Laughlin again directed, though he gives the formal screen credit to his 19-year-old son Frank. (Dir: Frank Laughlin, 170 mins.)

Trial of Chaplain Jensen, The (1975)**½ James Franciscus, Charles Durning, Joanna Miles, Lynda Day George, Harris Yulin. Offbeat theme, based on a real life incident, given a good mounting here. Franciscus is well cast as the handsome, devout Navy chaplain who is court-martialed when two Navy wives accuse him of adultery. Dialogue is fairly explicit, the story will hold you. Made-for-TV. (Dir: Robert Day, 72 mins.)

Trial of the Catonsville Nine, The (1972)***½ Ed Flanders, Richard Jordon, Peter Strauss, Douglas Watson, Nancy Malone. Flawed but often moving filmed record of a play by Daniel Berrigan about the trial of a group of anti-Vietnam war protesters, who raided the offices of the draft board in Catonsville, Maryland, and burned some of the files in May 1968. It's a pity that this isn't a great film, because it's one of the very few films that documents accurately the moral rage and commitment to peace of those who took part in this kind of Quaker-like "raid." (Film was financed and produced by Gregory Peck as an expression of his anti-war concerns.) Flanders plays Father Berrigan. There are many deeply moving statements in this static yet powerful drama. (Dir: Gordon Davidson, 85 mins.)

Trial Run (1968)**½ Leslie Nielsen, James Franciscus, Janice Rule, Diane Baker. Another slick made-for-TV feature film with the climaxes conveniently constructed to fit the commercial breaks. However, Leslie Nielsen's expert performance as a self-made successful attorney with a troubled personal life, makes this one better than most. As for the rest, it's familiar fare about the machinations of a young, eager and somewhat ruthless lawyer (Franciscus) who gets his big chance to shine when he's assigned by his boss

(Nielsen) to defend a man who murdered his unfaithful wife. (Dir: William Graham, 98 mins.)

Trials of Oscar Wilde, The (Great Britain, 1960)*** Peter Finch, Yvonne Mitchell, James Mason, John Fraser, Nigel Patrick. One of two concurrently-made British films about the playwright's libel trial and the scandals which sent him into self exile when he was accused of sodomy. Finch portrays Wilde sympathetically, playing up childlike attributes—petulance, susceptibility —to make him seem more victim than victimizer. (Dir: Ken Hughes, 123 mins.)

Trials of Private Schweik (German, 1964)*½ Peter Alexander, Rudolf Prack. Weak military comedy about a soldier who gets into hot water constantly, just like our "Hargrove." Germanic humor isn't improved by dubbing into English.

Tribe, The (1974)* Tale about a group of Cro-Magnon men and women might be subtitled "Cave Family Robinson," since it spends most of the time depicting the laborious everyday activities of the Cro-Magnon people. Their lives must have been more interesting than "Tribe" or we wouldn't be around. Made-for-TV. (Dir: Richard Colla, 72 mins.)

Tribe That Hides from Man, The (British, 1970)**** Extraordinary feature-length documentary made for British television. Focuses on the efforts of a dedicated anthropologist, Claudio Villas Boas, to establish contact with and help "save" a small band of tribal Indians, the Kreen-Akrore, in the jungles of northern Brazil. Color photography is extraordinary, penetrating areas never before seen by white men, to say nothing of cameramen. You'll discover, with misgivings and heartbreak, what the advent of "civilization" meant to these remote Indians —violent death thanks to bullets of white intruders, diseases to which they had no immunity or medicine, the destruction of their plant life and ecology, and the broken promises of the white settlers. (Dir: Adrian Cowell.)

Tribes (1970)*** Jan-Michael Vincent, Darren McGavin, Earl Holliman. Absorbing, well made TV feature film about a drafted hippie in Marine boot camp. Marine stories invariably pit a top drill sgt. against a recruit with Marine philosophy winning in the end, but not so here. The hippie (Jan-Michael Vincent) can't be broken, and his survival methods are adopted by his barracks mates to the consternation of the drill instructor (McGavin). Scenes of recruits sitting in the lotus position while meditating are a bit much. Competent direction and acting. The Marine Corps approved this story, for whatever that's worth—part of their new "lenient" image, no doubt! (Dir: Joseph Sargent, 74 mins.)

Tribute to a Bad Man (1956)*** James Cagney, Irene Papas, Don Dubbins. A powerful performance by James Cagney as a big horse breeder whose ruthless tactics alienate those closest to him as the bulwark of this under-rated western drama. Greek actress Irene Papas is impressive as the woman who loves him despite his obvious failings. (Dir: Robert Wise, 95 mins.)

Trick Baby—See: **Double Con, The**

Trilogy (1969)***½ Maureen Stapleton, Martin Balsam, Geraldine Page, Mildred Natwick. Three different short stories by Truman Capote, originally produced for TV, are combined in this rewarding, magnificently acted collection. All three stories were adapted by Capote and writer Eleanor Perry, and directed by Frank Perry. "Among the Paths to Eden" is set in a cemetery and features two lovely performances by Martin Balsam and Maureen Stapleton, who hauntingly plays a middle-aged spinster looking for a husband. The last story, "A Christmas Memory," is narrated by Capote and features a lovely performance by Geraldine Page preparing for the Christmas season. (Dir: Frank Perry, 110 mins.)

Trilogy of Terror (1975)**½ Karen Black, Robert Burton, John Karlin, George Gaynes. Karen Black, always an interesting actress, has a field day playing four tormented women in three bizarre, off-beat short stories by Richard Matheson. Miss Black's batting average here isn't bad—she's almost scary as the amoral bitch ready to murder her sister in the opener; then becomes more restrained, in a calculating way, as a teacher being blackmailed by a student in the second; and finally lets writer Matheson dominate in the weird finale about a fetish doll coming to life . . . the best of the trio. Made-for-TV. (Dir: Dan Curtis, 72 mins.)

Trio (British, 1950)***½ Jean Simmons, Nigel Patrick, James Hayter. Three Somerset Maugham tales—about a church verger ; an obnoxious shipboard passenger ; and romance in a sanatorium. Absorbing compilation, with the first two better than the last. (Dir: Ken Annakin, 91 mins.)

Triple Cross (French-British, 1967) **½ Christopher Plummer, Romy Schneider, Trevor Howard, Yul Brynner. A no-holds-barred WW II espionage yarn for those who like their escapes narrow, their double agents invincible, and their action pulsating. Christopher Plummer plays a double agent who pulls out all stops in his missions crossing from Germany to England with care and know-how, and meeting his attractive cast of co-stars playing various spy types. Based on the real WW II exploits of famed British double-spy Eddie Chapman. (Dir: Terence Young, 126 mins.)

Triple Deception (British, 1956)***½ Michael Craig, Brenda de Banzie. Sailor poses as a member of a gold smuggling gang to get the goods on them. Rattling good melodrama, heavy on suspense. (Dir: Guy Green, 85 mins.)

Triple Play (1971)** William Windom, Rosemary Forsyth, Larry Hagman. With hosting stints performed by Dan Rowan and Dick Martin, three situation comedy pilots comprise this made-for-TV triplet. The best of the three is the third, "Doctor in the House," starring William Windom playing a small-town New England doctor fencing with his new assistant, a big beautiful lady physician (Rosemary Forsyth). Patients are of secondary interest to the budding romance between the M.D.'s in this ingratiating pilot. The second, titled "The Good Life," stars Larry Hagman and Jane Miller. The opener is a slapstick "Mission: Impossible" spoof.

Tripoli (1950)** Maureen O'Hara, John Payne, Howard da Silva. The year is 1805 and the Marine Forces headed by John Payne defeat the Tripoli pirates but not until Countess Maureen O'Hara gets her man. Howard da Silva gives a very good per-

formance as a Greek captain. (Dir: Will Price, 95 mins.)

Tristana (Spanish-French, 1970)**** Catherine Deneuve, Fernando Rey, Franco Nero. Another chilling, surrealist psychological horror story from one of the acknowledged masters of world cinema, the great Spanish-born director Luis Bunuel. He made his first film dazzler, "Un Chien Andalou," in 1928, and this is another—a tale of a young virginal school girl (Deneuve) who goes to live with an aging, impoverished aristocrat and soon becomes his mistress. Bunuel artfully develops the demonic qualities in our heroine, and the film is full of stunning insights and visual splendors.

Triumph of Hercules, The (Italian, 1964)* Dan Vadis, Pierre Cressoy. Muscleman fights a wicked sorceress. (Dir: Alberto DeMartino, 90 mins.)

Triumph of Michael Strogoff (French, 1964)*½ Curt Jurgens, Capucine. Brave officer of the Czar aids a young prince against the Turks. Not a remake for a change, but another adventure of the Jules Verne-created character. But it's dull in action and acting. English dubbed.

Triumph of Robin Hood (Italian, 1962)*½ Don Burnett, Gia Scala. The famous archer of Sherwood Forest helps King Richard battle the Normans. Juvenile adventure dubbed in English.

Triumph of the Son of Hercules (Italian, 1963)* Kirk Morris, Cathia Caro. Muscleman leads a revolt against a wicked queen. English-dubbed action spectacle is revolting.

Triumph of the Ten Gladiators (Italian, 1964)* Dan Vadis. Heroes are sent to rescue a kidnaped queen. Seedy English-dubbed action spectacle. (Dir: Nick Nostro, 94 mins.)

Trog (1970)** Joan Crawford. The superstars of the '30's and '40's all seem to get around to making one of these sci-fi monster epics. In this outing, Joan Crawford gets her turn. She's an anthropologist who has come across what she believes to be the missing link. The only thing missing here is credibility. It's hard to evaluate Miss Crawford's performance since she has to play with an apelike creature, and you know how hard it is to follow an animal act. (Dir: Freddie Francis, 91 mins.)

Trooper Hook (1957)**½ Joel McCrea, Barbara Stanwyck. Good western drama bolstered by the stars. There are Indian raids and plenty of action sequences for adventure-seeking fans. (Dir: Charles Marquis Warren, 81 mins.)

Tropic Holiday (1938)** Dorothy Lamour, Ray Milland, Martha Raye. Romantic comedy set in Mexico is weak entertainment. Martha's fans may enjoy her bull fighting scenes. (Dir: Theodore Reed, 80 mins.)

Tropic of Cancer (1970)*** Rip Torn, Ginette Le Clerc, James Callahan, Phil Brown. A series of good-natured sexual vignettes and escapades photographed in Paris in the late 60's, but ostensibly taking place during the 1930's. Based on Henry Miller's celebrated underground classic, it features a miscast Rip Torn portraying Henry Miller during this guided tour of Miller's bawdy adventures, including the brothels themselves. Sequences showing some of the fat, over-the-hill whores may cause a momentary business decline for bordellos in countries where this film has been shown, but we'll all recover, and the birth rate will continue to climb! (Dir: Joseph Strick, 87 mins.)

Tropic Zone (1953)** Ronald Reagan, Rhonda Fleming. The independent banana plantation owners are plagued by a villainous shipping magnate who wants control of the whole works. Ronald Reagan changes horses in mid-stream to join Rhonda Fleming who looks worried but beautiful. You may not care much one way or the other. (Dir: Lewis R. Foster, 94 mins.)

Trouble Along the Way (1953)*½ John Wayne, Donna Reed. Wayne plays a football coach with a two-fisted approach to the game and life. Sentimental and sticky. (Dir: Michael Curtiz, 110 mins.)

Trouble at 16—See: Platinum High School

Trouble Comes to Town (1974)**½ Lloyd Bridges, Thomas Evans, Pat Hingle. The film tells the story of a black Chicago youngster who goes South to live with a white sheriff, and it's surprisingly effective at times. The three leads give the script a nice realistic touch by not pushing too hard. Young Evans as the gangly kid who enters the small town with a chip on his shoulder proves to be an interesting actor. Made-for-TV. (Dir: Daniel Petrie, 73 mins.)

Trouble for Father (Greek, 1958)* Basil Logothetidis. Weak story about a man who plans to take a trip after his son returns from college to handle the business. His trip is thwarted, and so is the film by the triteness of the plot. (Dir: A. Sakelarios, 100 mins.)

Trouble for Two (1936)*** Robert Montgomery, Rosalind Russell. Good exciting adventure tale loosely based on Robert Louis Stevenson's "Suicide Club." Scene about the club is as chilling a bit of business as you'll ever see and is not suggested for the youngsters. (Dir: J. Walker Reuben, 80 mins.)

Trouble in Paradise (1932)**** Miriam Hopkins, Kay Francis, Charles Ruggles, Herbert Marshall, Edward Everett Horton. One of the most delightful and sophisticated comedies directed by that German master Ernst Lubitsch. Marshall is a charming scoundrel and jewel thief, and the action moves from Venice to other European settings including Paris. Horton and Lubitsch combine to provide a running gag throughout the film that really works—Horton trying to remember where he has seen Miss Francis' secretary before. Incidentally, that first voice you hear while watching a scene of Venice is the legendary Enrico Caruso. (Dir: Ernst Lubitsch, 90 mins.)

Trouble in the Glen (British, 1954)** Orson Welles, Margaret Lockwood, Forrest Tucker. Scottish laird returns from South America to land in the middle of a feud over a closed road. Some good players here, but a draggy pace and a script that misfires undermines what was a promising comedy idea. (Dir: Herbert Wilcox, 91 mins.)

Trouble in the Sky (British, 1960)**½ Michael Craig, Bernard Lee, Peter Cushing, George Sanders, Elizabeth Seal. Efforts made to clear a pilot of negligence when his jet crashes. Okay English chins-up pluck!

Trouble with Angels, The (1966)** Rosalind Russell, Hayley Mills, June Harding. Unsophisticated comedy geared for family viewing. Two high-spirited young students at St. Francis Academy, played with super-abundant energy by Hayley Mills and June Harding, keep things hopping for the understanding Mother

Superior (Rosalind Russell) and her staff of bewildered Sisters. Episodic, and some of the intended comedy is strained, but the two teen-age girls and their pranks have a modest, mindless appeal. (Dir: Ida Lupino, 112 mins.)

Trouble with Girls, The (1969)**½ Elvis Presley in the roaring '20's, and believe it or not, this is a notch or two above most of his films of the '60's. Elvis heads a combination entertainment-education traveling show, and there's a good deal of plot for the cast to wade through, even including a murder. Don't fret, Elvis sings too. (Dir: Peter Tewksbury, 105 mins.)

Trouble with Harry, The (1955)*** John Forsythe, Shirley MacLaine, Edmund Gwenn. When a body is discovered in the Vermont woods, various people have a hard time disposing of it. Alfred Hitchcock's macabre comic touch deftly makes this kooky little comedy worthwhile. (99 mins.)

Trouble with Women, The (1947)** Ray Milland, Teresa Wright. Psychology professor has his theories on women tested by an enterprising female reporter in this mild comedy. (Dir: Sidney Lanfield, 80 mins.)

True Confession (1937)***½ Carole Lombard, Fred MacMurray, John Barrymore. Fast moving, superbly played farce about a girl on trial for murder. Some of it may strike you as dated, but the method has been borrowed for many of our modern film comedies. (Dir: Wesley Ruggles, 90 mins.)

True Grit (1969)**** John Wayne, Glen Campbell, Kim Darby, Robert Duvall, Dennis Hopper. John Wayne's Academy Award winning role as Rooster Cogburn, a one-eyed crotchety U.S. marshal who can still shoot straight. Old Duke's never been better, and he's been damn good several times before. A delightful western chase-down of the bad guys featuring an appealing performance from Kim Darby as a 14-year-old tomboy out to avenge her murdered father. Glen Campbell is dreary but that's about the only shortcoming of this Henry Hathaway-directed crowd pleaser. (128 mins.)

True Story of Jesse James, The (1957)**½ Robert Wagner, Jeffrey Hunter, Hope Lange, Agnes Moorehead. Director Nicholas Ray injects the vitality that is evident throughout this umpteenth rehashing of the legend of the James brothers. Bob Wagner as Jesse and Jeff Hunter as Frank offer good performances, and are ably assisted by Miss Moorehead as their mother and Hope Lange as Jesse's wife. (92 mins.)

True Story of Lynn Stuart, The (1958)*½ Betsy Palmer, Jack Lord. Good actors are wasted in this trite meller about a woman who works undercover for the cops.

True to Life (1943)**½ Mary Martin, Dick Powell, Victor Moore. Cute little comedy about a soap opera writer who goes to live with a nice family and uses their conversations and actions in his scripts. (Dir: George Marshall, 94 mins.)

Trunk to Cairo (Israel-West Germany, 1966)* Audie Murphy, George Sanders, Marianne Koch. Ludicrous spy chase, supposedly set in Egypt. German scientist's moon-rocket plans are sought by both Israelis and Egyptians intent on converting them into an imposing, earth-side weapon. A lot of dashing about, little entertainment! (Dir: Menahem Golem, 80 mins.)

Truth, The (France, 1960)**½ Brigitte Bardot, Charles Vanel, Paul Meurisse. An interesting film; an exploration of justice under France's outdated Napoleonic Code, using as vehicle and foil the uncontrollable sexuality of Miss Bardot, chronicling her trial for a murder which her defense claims was one of passion. We believe Brigitte is passionate and her performance has an unexpected range. Although there is very little here of director Henri-Georges Clouzot's earlier triumph, "Diabolique," the film features the Vanel-Meurisse combination, superb and fiercely combative as the opposing lawyers. (Dir: Henri-Georges Clouzot, 127 mins.)

Truth About Spring, The (1965)**½ Hayley Mills, John Mills, James MacArthur. Daughter of a rascally seaman experiences her first pangs of love when she meets a wealthy young man. Leisurely but entertaining romantic tale, aided by pretty tropic scenery, nice players. Harmless fun. (Dir: Richard Thorpe, 102 mins.)

Truth About Women, The (British, 1958)**½ Laurence Harvey, Julie Harris, Diane Cilento. A fine cast does what it can to make this somewhat contrived comedy romance workable. There are many voluptuous females in the cast and Laurence Harvey plays the roue with a flair. (Dir: Muriel Box, 98 mins.)

Try and Get Me (1950)***½ Frank Lovejoy, Lloyd Bridges. Two kidnapers murder their victim, and are themselves victimized by mob violence upon their capture. Dramatic thunderbolt pulls no punches, is morbidly gripping stuff. (Dir: Cyril Endfield, 85 mins.)

Trygon Factor, The (British, 1967) ** Stewart Granger, Susan Hampshire, Robert Morley. If you don't look for logic in this Scotland Yard mystery film, you may enjoy it. Granger is all British cool as the superintendent in charge of a murder investigation. (Dir: Cyril Frankel, 87 mins.)

Tugboat Annie (1933)*** Wallace Beery, Marie Dressler. Enjoy again the antics of Marie Dressler in the title role and Wallace Beery as her husband. It's an acting treat, filled with laughs and sentiment. (Dir: Mervyn Le Roy, 90 mins.)

Tulsa (1949)*** Susan Hayward, Robert Preston. A fiery redhead battles for an oil empire in the early thirties, only to lose it all and become poorer but wiser. Good melodrama of the oil fields, with plenty of action. (Dir: Stuart Heisler, 90 mins.)

Tunes of Glory (1960)**** John Mills, Alec Guinness. A beautiful English film, recommended particularly for the magnificent and memorable performances of its two stars. Story concerns the bitter struggle between a vicious, careless, goldbricking colonel (Guinness) and the intelligent, disciplined, civilized young officer (Mills) who supersedes him in command. "Tunes" has moments of cinema glory. (Dir: Ronald Neame, 106 mins.)

Tunnel of Love, The (1958)*** Richard Widmark, Doris Day, Gig Young, Gia Scala. Pleasantly performed comedy about a suburban couple who go through all sorts of red tape to adopt a child. Some bright lines of dialogue, fairly steady pace. (Dir: Gene Kelly, 98 mins.)

Turn the Key Softly (British, 1953) *** Yvonne Mitchell, Joan Collins, Terence Morgan. Concerning the adventure of three women recently released from prison, their attempts to adjust themselves to society. Excellent performances give this drama a lift. (Dir: Jack Lee, 83 mins.)

Turnabout (1940)**½ Adolphe Menjou, John Hubbard, Carole Landis. Through a mysterious power, husband and wife have a chance to change sexes, with the natural confusion resulting. Risque comedy has a fair share of laughs. (Dir: Hal Roach, 83 mins.)

Turning Point, The (1952)**½ William Holden, Alexis Smith, Edmond O'Brien. Reporter learns that the father of the chairman of a crime investigating committee is mixed up with the crooks himself. Familiar crime melodrama competently done. (Dir: William Dieterle, 85 mins.)

Turning Point of Jim Malloy, The (1975)** John Savage, Gig Young, Biff McGuire. John O'Hara's "Gibbsville" stories are the basis for this adaptation by Frank D. Gilroy, who also directed. The result is an ambling, "Peyton Place"-type of soap opera, with some serious overtones. A young man (unevenly played by John Savage) returns to his hometown in Pennsylvania after being expelled from Yale and gets a job on the local newspaper. Made-for-TV. (Dir: Frank D. Gilroy, 72 mins.)

Tuttles of Tahiti, The (1942)*** Charles Laughton, Jon Hall, Peggy Drake. The easy-going head of a large tropic family takes life as it comes, as long as it doesn't involve work. Pleasing story of the South Seas, pleasant entertainment. (Dir: Charles Vidor, 91 mins.)

Twelve Angry Men (1957)**** Henry Fonda, Lee J. Cobb, Ed Begley, E. G. Marshall. Engrossing drama about a jury of men who have to decide whether a young boy killed his father with a knife. The entire drama is played in the jury room and each juror shows his true colors. Suspenseful, brilliantly acted, and expertly directed by Sidney Lumet. Based on Reginald Rose's original TV drama presented on Studio One. The whole cast is near perfect but Jack Warden's performance deserves special recognition. (95 mins.)

Twelve Chairs, The (1970)*** Mel Brooks, Dom DeLuise, Frank Langella, Ron Moody. Remember the Fred Allen 1945 starrer "It's in the Bag"? Well, this romp, filmed in Yugoslavia, written and directed by Mel Brooks, is based on the same

Russian comedy-fable, and some of it is quite funny. Brooks plays a small part at the beginning of the film, and there's nothing in the rest of the film to match his high-intensity nuttiness, but there are a few good laughs strewn along the way as an impoverished nobleman (Moody) tries to track down some precious jewel-filled chairs. (94 mins.)

Twelve Hours to Kill (1960)*½ Nico Minardos, Barbara Eden. Greek engineer in New York witnesses a gangland killing and becomes a target for death as he flees. Mediocre melodrama with bad handling marring the suspense. (Dir: Edward L. Cahn, 83 mins.)

Twelve O'Clock High (1950)**** Gregory Peck, Dean Jagger, Hugh Marlowe. Powerful, perceptive psychological drama of WW II, dealing with the problems of an Air Force bomber-group commander who has to drive his men to the point of breaking. Dean Jagger copped an Oscar for his supporting role. Acting is top-notch throughout. (Dir: Henry King, 132 mins.)

Twelve to the Moon (1960)*½ Ken Clark, Michi Kobi. Space ship takes off for lunar territory and boredom. (Dir: David Bradley, 74 mins.)

20th Century (1934)*** John Barrymore, Carole Lombard. Zany play by Ben Hecht and Charles MacArthur is a romp for Barrymore. Story of an egotistical producer, a ride on the famous Chicago-New York City train and crazy incidents right and left. Dated by our standards—but fun. (Dir: Howard Hawks, 90 mins.)

25th Hour, The (French-Yugoslavian, 1967)*** Anthony Quinn, Virna Lisi, Michael Redgrave, Alexander Knox. Sometimes implausible but often affecting drama about Rumanian participation in WW II, and shortly thereafter. Tries to deal with the holocaust of the war in personal, human terms. (Dir: Henri Verneuil, 119 mins.)

24 Eyes (Japan, 1954)**½ Hideko Takamine. Heartwarming story about a young schoolteacher who sees her beloved pupils grow up and go off to war. It is 1928 as the film begins, and young Miss Hisako arrives in the Shodo Island's grammar school. Anti-war messages trotted out in the latter part of the film tend to bog it down a bit, but it's still

752

worthwhile. (Dir: Keisuke Kinoshita, 110 mins.)

24 Hours to Kill (1965)* Mickey Rooney, Lex Barker, Walter Slezak. Espionage, junior grade. Mickey Rooney is a purser on a plane which has a 24-hour layover in Beirut. Before too long, he's kidnapped and . . . his abductors should also have swiped this movie-to-sleep-by! (Dir: Peter Bezencenet, 92 mins.)

Twenty Million Miles to Earth (1957)*½ William Hopper, Joan Taylor. Science-fiction rides again! This opus has a "gelatinous mass" which duplicates its size overnight. (Where have we heard this before?) The army is called in and eventually destroys the "gook" atop the Colosseum in Rome (shades of King Kong and the Empire State). (Dir: Nathan Juran, 82 mins.)

21 Days (British, 1938)**½ Laurence Olivier, Vivien Leigh. Young lawyer has committed murder, finds he has three weeks with his love before justice intervenes. Lot of talent stuck in a drama that doesn't come off; moderate, at best. Film historians will value seeing one of Olivier's early films. (Dir: Basil Dean, 72 mins.)

Twenty-one Hours at Munich (1976) *** William Holden, Shirley Knight, Franco Nero. A fine recreation of the dramatic, unforgettable and terrifying slaughter of the Israeli athletes at the hands of Arab terrorists during the 1972 Olympics. The film has been impeccably produced using the actual Munich locations and the cast is very good, especially Franco Nero as the Arab guerrilla leader, Shirley Knight as the German member of the Olympic security police who served as an intermediary between the guerrillas and the Munich police, and William Holden as the Munich Police Chief. It's well done, from the devastating beginning, as the Arabs steal into the Olympic compound, to the exciting finale at an airstrip outside of Munich. Made-for-TV. (Dir: William A. Graham, 105 mins.)

Twenty Plus Two (1961)*½ David Janssen, Jeanne Crain, Dina Merrill. Murder of a crooked agent involves a man in blackmail, kidnaping and mayhem. Hopelessly confused mystery, good cast wasted. (Dir: Joseph M. Newman, 102 mins.)

27th Day, The (1957)**½ Gene

Barry, Valerie French. A science fiction tale with a few novel twists —at least there are no oversized prehistoric monsters in this one. A selected group of earth people are given capsules which can destroy mankind and our hero has to track them down. (Dir: William Asher, 75 mins.)

20,000 Eyes (1961)** Gene Nelson, Merry Anders. Investment counselor needing ready cash plots a perfect crime. Passable crime melodrama. (Dir: Jack Leewood, 60 mins.)

20,000 Leagues Across the Land (French, 1959)**½ Jean Gaven, Tatiana Samilova. Three Frenchmen seek an old war buddy in Russia. Interesting Franco-Soviet co-production, dubbed in English; plot is a bit ragged but the novelty makes it an unusual offering.

20,000 Leagues Under the Sea (1954) *** Kirk Douglas, Paul Lukas, James Mason, Peter Lorre. Walt Disney's epic version of Jules Verne's nautical tale. Douglas is the robust harpooner who, along with shipmates Lukas and Lorre, is plunged into a series of exciting events aboard Captain Nemo's (Mason's) cosmic-powered submarine, circa 1860s. It's well produced and entertaining from start to finish. (Dir: Richard Fleischer, 127 mins.)

20,000 Pound Kiss, The (British, 1962)** Dawn Addams, Michael Goodliffe. Extortion ring tries to blackmail a member of Parliament, which leads to murder. Fair Edgar Wallace mystery. (Dir: John Moxey, 57 mins.)

23 Paces to Baker Street (British, 1956)*** Van Johnson, Vera Miles. Neat mystery keeps the attention, as a blind man attempts to solve a murder. (Dir: Henry Hathaway, 103 mins.)

Twilight for the Gods (1958)** Rock Hudson, Cyd Charisse, Arthur Kennedy. Ernest Gann's novel is brought to the screen with a strange mixture of miscasting and overdrawn characterizations. The setting is a tramp steamer and the drama unfolds as the passengers begin to distrust each other's reasons for the voyage. (Dir: Joseph Pevney, 120 mins.)

Twilight of Honor (1963)** Richard Chamberlain, Claude Rains, Joey Heatherton. This film was designed to capitalize on TV's Dr. Kildare fame, but MGM didn't want to demand too much of Chamberlain his first time out on the big screen so they changed him from a sincere young doctor to a sincere young lawyer, defending a murder suspect. Should have been tightly knit, but isn't, except for Joey Heatherton's gowns. (Dir: Boris Sagal, 115 mins.)

Twilight's Last Gleaming (1977)**½ Burt Lancaster, Richard Widmark, Charles Durning, Melvyn Douglas. Director Robert Aldrich was, among other things, trying to make a major statement in 1977, condemning the horrors and immorality of the Vietnam War. Unfortunately, he got his Vietnam message mixed up with another theme set in 1981 about a former Army general and three other inmates of death row who escape from prison, take over a SAC missile silo, and threaten to launch bombs on Russia and start World War III if their political grievances are not settled. The two stories fundamentally are in conflict with one another in this flawed, off-beat political thriller. Based on the novel "Viper Three" by Walter Wager. Screenplay by Ronald M. Cohen and Edward Huebsch. Some suspense, considering that Hollywood has studiously avoided dealing with the Vietnam war. It's a pity Aldrich didn't focus on that untold story. (Dir: Robert Aldrich, 144 mins.)

Twin Detectives (1976)* Jim Hager, Jon Hager, Lillian Gish, Patrick O'Neal, David White. Identical-twin detectives fool the culprits by appearing to be in two places at once. Country and Western singers Jim and Jon Hager do the twin bit. Venerable Lillian Gish portrays a wealthy old lady hoping to get in touch with her late husband through the Psychic Institute. Only for those who remember Gish's first movie role. Made-for-TV. (Dir: Robert Day, 72 mins.)

Twinkle In God's Eye (1955)** Mickey Rooney, Coleen Gray, Hugh O'Brian. Parson arrives in a lawless frontier town to build a church. Offbeat role for Rooney, but still a maudlin drama. (Dir: George Blair, 73 mins.)

Twist All Night (1962)*½ Louis Prima, June Wilkinson. Low-budget musical exploiting the twist—and June's bust, which is much larger than her talent.

Twist Around the Clock (1962)**½

Chubby Checker, Dion, Clay Cole. Average musical about the origins of the revolutionary dance and chock-full of early rock standards like "The Wanderer" and "Runaround Sue." Chubby Checker and Dion appear as themselves, and there's a fairly credible story line holding the whole show together. (Dir: Oscar Rudolph, 86 mins.)

Twist of Fate (1954)** Ginger Rogers, Herbert Lom, Stanley Baker. Ex-actress on the Riviera learns her husband-to-be is a dangerous criminal. Overdone melodrama has Lom's good performance, little else of distinction. (Dir: David Miller, 89 mins.)

Two and Two Make Six (British, 1962)** George Chakiris, Janette Scott. American airman, a girl, and a motorbike encounter a similar trio and swap partners. Mild romantic comedy never really gets into gear. (Dir: Freddie Francis, 89 mins.)

Two Colonels, The (Italian, 1962)** Walter Pidgeon, Toto. Captured British officer strikes up a friendship with his enemy opposite member. Mild wartime comedy dubbed in English has good players but doesn't do right by them.

Two Daughters (Indian, 1961)***½ Anil Chatterjee. India's most famous film director, Satyajit Ray, created two gems, each a story about love as experienced by a young woman. The first, "The Postmaster," is a quiet but penetrating story about a young servant girl's devotion to her postmaster employer; the other, "The Conclusion," is a charming tale about a young bride who runs away from her forced marriage to a nice man, only to return to find love. (114 mins.)

Two English Girls (France, 1971)***½ Jean-Pierre Leaud, Kika Markham, Stacey Tendeter. Truffaut said he tried to make a physical film about love. He did that and much more in this graceful, tender tale which reverses the central story line of Truffaut's masterpiece, "Jules and Jim." In "Two English Girls," two English sisters are in love with the same young Frenchman (Leaud). Based on the second novel by Henri-Pierre Roche, who also wrote "Jules and Jim" when he was a ripe old 74. Once again, the setting is Paris before World War I, delicately captured by cinematographer Nestor Almendros. Elegant, tactful, sometimes witty, always involving. (Dir: Francois Truffaut, 130 mins.)

Two-Faced Woman (1941)*** Greta Garbo, Melvyn Douglas. Fairly amusing comedy with Garbo posing as her own twin sister to test husband Melvyn's love for her. (Dir: George Cukor, 94 mins.)

Two Faces of Dr. Jekyll, The (1961)** Paul Massie. Still another version of the Robert Louis Stevenson story about the tormented Dr. Jekyll whose split personality makes him lead a double life. Massie is the troubled scientist whose life is far from sunny even with Dawn Addams. (Dir: Terence Fisher, 103 mins.)

Two Flags West (1950)** Joseph Cotten, Linda Darnell, Jeff Chandler. Spectacular battle scenes make up most of the excitement in this Civil War Western. Inept performances slow down the action. (Dir: Robert Wise, 92 mins.)

Two for the Money (1972)**½ Robert Hooks, Stephen Brooks, Walter Brennan, Mercedes McCambridge. About ex-cops, one black (Hooks) and one white (Brooks), who open a private detective office. Case involves the search for a mass murderer, at large for over a decade. Good characterizations by competent pros Brennan, McCambridge, and Neville Brand supply substance for an offbeat tale. Made-for-TV. (Dir: Bernard L. Kowalski, 73 mins.)

Two for the Road (1967)**** Audrey Hepburn, Albert Finney. Refreshing, sophisticated comedy-drama about a marriage which isn't working out after a number of years. Audrey Hepburn is not merely a fashion plate in this outing—she gives a convincing portrayal of a woman who loves the man she married and hates what he has become. Albert Finney is great as the husband who has a roving eye but still wants his wife. The flashback technique is used effectively throughout. Directed with great flair by Stanley Donen, and the sprightly screenplay was authored by Frederic Raphael. (112 mins.)

Two for the Seesaw (1962)*** Shirley MacLaine, Robert Mitchum. Essentially a two-character comedy-drama about a disillusioned lawyer from Omaha who meets and loves a tough-tender New York girl. The superb intimacy of the Broadway stage production is negated somewhat by adding characters to the screen version, and rather questionable casting of the leading roles. Mitchum does quite well, Miss MacLaine somewhat less so; but it has its moments, both humorous and poignant. (Dir: Robert Wise, 120 mins.)

Two Girls and a Sailor (1943)***½ Van Johnson, June Allyson, Jimmy Durante, Gloria De Haven. One of those entertaining, first-rate musicals that MGM became famous for. June and Gloria both love Van and Jimmy is around for plenty of laughs. The music is good too and there's plenty of guest stars. (Dir: Richard Thorpe, 124 mins.)

Two Gladiators (Italian, 1962)*½ Richard Harrison. Hunt is on for the twin brother of an ineffectual ruler, to persuade him to take over. Usual sort of English-dubbed costume spectacle.

Two Guys from Texas (1948)**½ Jack Carson, Dennis Morgan, Dorothy Malone. Stranded vaudeville team outwits city thugs down in Texas. Mildly amusing musical comedy. (Dir: David Bulter, 86 mins.)

Two Headed Spy, The (British, 1959)*** Jack Hawkins, Gia Scala. Highly suspenseful spy yarn with good performances by Hawkins and Gia Scala as a couple of British agents working inside the German lines. Good climax with an exciting chase sequence.

200 Motels (British, 1971)*** Ringo Starr, Frank Zappa, Theodore Bikel. Mind trip for those who don't mind plotless films and especially for fans of the dynamic rock star Frank Zappa. Supposedly follows the exploits of Zappa's group, the Mothers of Invention, who are stranded in groupie-laden Centerville. When the Mothers play they resort to melting fingers and dissolving faces. Most important thing about the film is that it's the first to be made by the videotape 50 process. Many interesting visual techniques and montages, and Zappa fans will enjoy the rock score. (Dirs: Frank Zappa and Tony Palmer, 98 mins.)

Two Little Bears, The (1961)** Eddie Albert, Brenda Lee, Jane Wyatt. Grammar-school principal finds his children can turn themselves into bears. Mild fantasy should be enjoyed best by the younger set. (Dir: Randall Hood, 81 mins.)

Two Lost Worlds (1950)** Laura Elliott, Jim Arness. A colony from Australia lands on a mysterious isle where prehistoric monsters roam. Low grade thriller; if you're a TV movie fan, you'll spot stock footage from "Captain Fury," "One Million B.C." and "Captain Caution" used to stretch the budget. (Dir: Norman Dawn, 61 mins.)

Two Loves (1961)** Shirley Mac-Laine, Laurence Harvey, Jack Hawkins. Miscasting and mis-scripting combine to throw this drama for a loss. About a teacher in New Zealand and her problems with a mixed-up young fatalist who nevertheless brings love to her spinsterish life. Pretty drab going. (Dir: Charles Walters, 99 mins.)

Two Men of Karamoja (1974)**** Iain Ross, Paul Ssalli. Superb color documentary filmed on location in Kidepo Valley National park in Uganda. White game-park warden trains his black, native assistant to take over the full responsibilities for the park—including protecting the animals from human poachers. Director-producer Eugene S. Jones (who made "A Face of War") has captured some remarkable animal scenes, including a sequence showing the white warden trapped in a small jeep while besieged by an enraged elephant. Even more unusual and important is the way Jones honestly records the tensions and friendship that mark the relationship between the old and the new order, as the black man prepares to take over full responsibility for the land's animals and people entrusted to his care. (102 mins.)

Two Minute Warning (1976)* Charlton Heston, John Cassavetes, Martin Balsam, Gena Rowlands. A mindless piece of disagreeable claptrap about a mad sniper in a jammed football stadium. Charlton Heston playing a Los Angeles police captain is more wooden than usual, and his performance is matched perfectly by the terrible script by Edward Hume and the relentlessly heavy-handed direction of Larry Peerce. Be warned! This is a "disaster" film all right, but not what the producers had in mind. (Dir: Larry Peerce, 112 mins.)

Two Mrs. Carrolls (1947)** Humphrey Bogart, Barbara Stanwyck, Alexis Smith. Story of a nut who likes to bump off his wives after he paints their portraits is so melodramatic it may make you laugh. (Dir: Peter Godfrey, 99 mins.)

Two Mules for Sister Sara (1971)**½ Clint Eastwood and Shirley MacLaine. The two stars are so attractive you'll be able to overlook many of the weaknesses of the film and just enjoy them. Almost everything in this story, including Miss MacLaine dressed in a nun's habit, is not what it appears to be. The action of this western yarn is well paced by director Don Siegel, with good location scenes in Mexico. (104 mins.)

Two Nights with Cleopatra (Italian, 1953)*½ Sophia Loren, Ettore Manni, Alberto Sordi. Your editor would gladly settle for one night with Sophia. You'll have to settle here for a boring costume epic.

Two of Us, The (French, 1967)**** Michel Simon, Alain Cohen, Luce Fabiole. A beautiful, touching, moving film about racial prejudice and anti-semitism, featuring two near perfect performances from a crusty old bigot (Michel Simon) and the young Jewish boy (Cohen) who comes to board in rural France during the Nazi occupation of Paris during WW II. Wonderfully written and directed by Claude Berri, this wise and witty film should be seen and treasured by old and young alike. (Dir: Claude Berri, 86 mins.)

Two on a Guillotine (1965)* Connie Stevens, Dean Jones, Cesar Romero. Silly horror film about a haunted house, an heiress (Miss Stevens), a reporter (Jones) and a mad magician (Romero) whose big act was a guillotine bit which he plans to revive. No chills, thrills or much of anything. (Dir: William Conrad, 107 mins.)

Two Orphans, The (Italian, 1966)*½ Mike Marshall, Valeria Ciangottine. Classic tale of two sisters and their adventures in Paris prior to the French Revolution has been filmed many times before, including once with the Gish sisters. This one doesn't add anything. English dubbed.

Two People (1973)*½ Peter Fonda, Lindsay Wagner, Estelle Parsons. A sloppy, pretentious soap opera interesting only for the Paris, Marra-

kesh, and New York scenery and the supporting performance by Estelle Parsons. Fonda is a wandering Vietnam deserter on his way home to turn himself in. Wagner is a drifting high-fashion model going back to her illegitimate son. Naturally they find each other irresistible! A terribly old-fashioned film, written by Richard De Roy and directed in pedestrian form by Robert Wise. (100 mins.)

Two Rode Together (1961)**½ James Stewart, Richard Widmark, Shirley Jones. A Texas marshal and a cavalry lieutenant lead a wagon train into Comanche territory to rescue captives of the Indians. A John Ford western—not his best. (Dir: John Ford, 109 mins.)

Two Sisters from Boston (1945)*** Kathryn Grayson, June Allyson, Peter Lawford. A lot to like in this cute musical set at the turn of the century about two well-bred Boston girls who go to work in a joint on New York's Bowery. Jimmy Durante steals the show as owner of the tavern. (Dir: Henry Koster, 112 mins.)

Two Smart People (1946)*½ Lucille Ball, John Hodiak. Crime pays until just about the end of this miserable hokum about some thieves and a friendly detective. (Dir: Jules Dassin, 93 mins.)

2001: A Space Odyssey (1968)**** Keir Dullea, Gary Lockwood. Brilliant film; the plot and explanation exist on an almost subliminal level in this tracing of man's history and his contact with new life. In the beginning, the earth heated; the earth cooled; apes moved to man; man to superman and beyond; a space voyage to Jupiter manned by astronauts Bowman (Dullea) and Poole (Lockwood) and computer HAL. The intensity of the landing sequence is blindingly absorbing. This masterpiece by director and co-writer Stanley Kubrick defines film in terms of abstract communication. (138 mins.)

Two Thousand Women (British, 1943)***½ Phyllis Calvert, Flora Robson. Nazis interne British women, but they turn the tables and secretly help downed RAF fliers to escape occupied territory. Suspenseful melodrama, mixing humor and thrills in a skillful blend.

Two Tickets to Broadway (1951)**½

Janet Leigh, Tony Martin, Ann Miller, Eddie Bracken. Small-town girl and a singer arrange a hoax to get them on a TV show. Fairly pleasing musical comedy. (Dir: James V. Kern, 106 mins.)

Two Tickets to London (1943)** Michele Morgan, Alan Curtis, Barry Fitzgerald. Espionage and love don't mix as the hero finds out in this WW II tale of German U-Boats and Admiralty dragnets. But Morgan and Fitzgerald are customarily professional. (Dir: Edwin L. Martin, 79 mins.)

Two-Way Stretch (British, 1961)***½ Peter Sellers, Wilfrid Hyde-White, Lionel Jeffries. Prisoners plan to break out of jail, pull a robbery, and break back into prison again. Once again the British come up with a novel comedy idea. Sellers, and Jeffries as a brutal guard, are superb. Very amusing. (Dir: Robert Day, 78 mins.)

Two Weeks in Another Town (1952) **½ Kirk Douglas, Edward G. Robinson, Cyd Charisse, Claire Trevor, George Hamilton. The sensational best seller about American film makers loving and working in Rome makes a flashy but empty film. Kirk Douglas does what he can in the complex role of a has-been actor who attempts a comeback in the Roman film capital. (Dir: Vincente Minnelli, 107 mins.)

Two Weeks in September (1967)* Brigitte Bardot, Laurent Terzieff, Michael Sarne. Bardot and the Scottish moors in a tenuous tale of a model in love with two macho men. (Dir: Serge Bourguignon, 96 mins.)

Two Weeks with Love (1950)**½ Jane Powell, Ricardo Montalban, Debbie Reynolds. Daughter's growing up, parents refuse to realize it. She makes them see the light while on a Catskill vacation. Mildly amusing comedy of the early 1900s. Some enjoyable ricky-tick oldtime turns, cute performance by young Debbie Reynolds. (Dir: Roy Rowland, 92 mins.)

Two Wives at One Wedding (British, 1961)*½ Gordon Jackson, Christina Gregg, Lisa Daniely. About to be married, confused man discovers he may have been wed before. Comedy minus laughs. (Dir: Montgomery Tully, 66 mins.)

Two Women (1962)**** Sophia Loren, Raf Vallone. Miss Loren won many awards for her performance as an Italian mother who faces tragedy with her daughter during World War II. You can see she deserved the accolades. Deeply moving Italian entry, realistic, well directed. Loren's intensity and conviction was a revelation in this beautiful film. (Dir: Vittorio De Sica, 99 mins.)

Two Yanks in Trinidad (1942)*** Pat O'Brien, Brian Donlevy, Janet Blair. Two racketeers enlist in the Army, get patriotism when Pearl Harbor happens. Breezy comedy-drama has some bright dialogue, amusing situations. (Dir: Gregory Ratoff, 88 mins.)

Two Years Before the Mast (1946) **½ Alan Ladd, William Bendix, Brian Donlevy. A shanghaied crew on a trip around the Horn in the 1880's is the salty background for this famous tale of the sea. Although it has some fine scenes, it never comes close to joining the list of film classics set on the sea.

Tycoon (1947)*** John Wayne, Laraine Day. Young railroad builder meets with many obstructions before he achieves his goal. Way too long, otherwise nicely made, well acted melodrama. (Dir: Richard Wallace, 128 mins.)

Typhoon Over Nagasaki (French, 1959)** Danielle Darrieux, Jean Marais. Engineer in Japan falls for a local girl, then his sweetheart arrives from France. Watery romance not helped by English dubbing; some nice Japanese location scenes, not too much else.

Tyrant of Castile, The (Italian, 1964) * Mark Damon, Rada Rassimov. Ruler of Spain turns into a tyrant when his love falls for his stepbrother, or maybe he just had to watch this rubbish, and got mad.

Tyrant of Lydia Against the Son of Hercules (Italian, 1963)* Gordon Scott, Massimo Serato. Muscleman rescues a princess from a tyrant. English-dubbed spectacle has been done before—and no better.

UFO Target Earth (1974)* Nick Plakias, Cynthia Cline. Low-budget, sub-par science-fiction thriller. Two scientists and a psychic investigate alien invaders. (Dir: Michael A. deGaetano)

Ugetsu (Japanese, 1953)***½ Machiko Kyo. Beautifully photographed film set in 16th century Japan. The drama centers around two friends who go their separate ways in their search for fulfillment. Exciting scenes showing the barbarous armies attacking small villages. (Dir: Kenji Mizoguchi, 96 mins.)

Ugly American, The (1963)*** Marlon Brando, Eiji Okada, Arthur Hill. The many-faceted Mr. Brando tries the role of a distinguished American Ambassador to an Asian country whose failure to understand differences in policy brings personal and political disaster. He does well in the part, and while the script and direction override some salient story points, the result is a film drama endeavoring to make a serious comment about topical situations. (Dir: George H. Englund, 120 mins.)

Ulysses (Italian, 1955)** Kirk Douglas, Silvana Mangano, Anthony Quinn. Adventures of the King of Ithaca and his warriors during the Trojan wars, lavishly cast and produced, but somehow doesn't seem much better than the usual run of spectacles. English dialogue. (Dir: Mario Camerini, 104 mins.)

Ulysses Against the Son of Hercules (Italian, 1963)*½ Georges Marchal, Michael Lane. Two opposing musclemen join forces when they are captured by a strange people ruled by a wicked queen. Way-out action spectacle is so farfetched it might afford some amusement. Dubbed in English.

Ulzana's Raid (1972)*** Burt Lancaster, Bruce Davison. Deceptively ordinary Indian vs. cavalry yarn turns into a tense, well-acted, and ultimately absorbing film. Lancaster is cast as an Indian scout who assists an inexperienced cavalry officer (Davison) in trying to roust renegade Apache Ulzana and his band out on a rampage of murder, rape, and revenge against the white man. Taut western . . . and one that makes you think. (Dir: Robert Aldrich, 93 mins.)

Umberto D (1955)**** Carlo Battisti, Maria Pia Casilio. Italian director De Sica's masterpiece; shattering study of a lonely old man, succumbing to the ravages of age. Packs an uncompromising wallop. One of the remarkable European films of the decade. See it. (Dir: Vittorio De Sica, 89 mins.)

Umbrellas of Cherbourg, The (French, 1964)*** Catherine Deneuve, Nino Castelnuovo. Tender romantic tale of young lovers, their sad parting, his return to find her married to another. Told entirely in song, which is a novelty if not exactly conducive to complete absorption. Beautifully photographed; for those who desire something different. (Dir: Jacques Demy, 91 mins.)

UMC (1969)** James Daly, Richard Bradford, Maurice Evans. Good acting highlights this routine drama, which served as the pilot film for the TV series "Medical Center." Subplots include malpractice suits; supporting cast boasts Edward G. Robinson and Kim Stanley. Made-for-TV. (Dir: Boris Sagal, 100 mins.)

Uncertain Glory (1944) ** Errol Flynn, Paul Lukas. Errol is a French crook but he's willing to pretend to be a saboteur and die if it will help France. If that doesn't sound convincing it's because the picture is trite and hackneyed. Paul Lukas is superb as a detective. (Dir: Raoul Walsh, 102 mins.)

Unchained (1955)**** Elroy Hirsch, Chester Morris, Barbara Hale. Warden of an honor prison tames unruly convicts. Based on fact, this is one of the best prison films. Excellently made. Well acted. (Dir: Hall Bartlett, 75 mins.)

Uncle Harry (1945)*** George Sanders, Ella Raines. Henpecked by his two sisters, a man takes drastic steps when they begin to interfere with his romance. Excellent performances and a suspenseful atmosphere atone for the poor conclusion to this drama. (Dir: Robert Siodmak, 80 mins.)

Uncle Vanya (1958)**½ Franchot Tone, Dolores Dorn-Heft, George Voskovec, Peggy McCay. Chekhov's atmospheric play about an aging professor and his beautiful wife who visit their country estate is brought to film almost intact from its 1956 Broadway production. Acting is generally excellent, but it is never opened up to utilize the film medium. But Chekhov is a great writer. Adaptation by Stark Young. (Dirs: John Goetz, Franchot Tone, 98 mins.)

Uncle Was a Vampire (Italian, 1961) **½ Renato Rascel, Christopher Lee, Sylva Koscina. Former baron now working as a hotel porter has trouble on his hands when his uncle turns up in vampire form. Amusing spoof of horror films, dubbed in English. Rascel is a likable buffoon.

Unconquered (1947)**½ Gary Cooper, Paulette Goddard. White man vs. Indian in 1863, tons of action, plenty of movement, and nothing to say are the total assets of this mammoth De Mille production. (Dir: Cecil B. De Mille, 146 mins.)

Undefeated, The (1969)**½ John Wayne, Rock Hudson. Routine western, bolstered somewhat by the presence of Wayne and Hudson. Wayne is an ex-Union officer who is on his way to sell horses to Mexico's emperor and meets up with his former enemy, Confederate officer Hudson. The climax involves their joining forces against Juarez and his bandits. Football fans, note that handsome quarterback Roman Gabriel plays a supporting role in the flick. (Dir: Andrew V. McLaglen, 118 mins.)

Under Capricorn (1949)*** Ingrid Bergman, Joseph Cotten, Michael Wilding. Romantic drama set in Australia in 1831 boasts superb acting by Miss Bergman and a fine cast but the script is much too talky. (Dir: Alfred Hitchcock, 117 mins.)

Under My Skin (1950)** John Garfield, Micheline Presle, Luther Adler. An Ernest Hemingway yarn about the racing game and a one-time crooked jockey's efforts to go straight. Involved drama, spottily acted. (Dir: George Blair, 86 mins.)

Under Ten Flags (1960)** Van Heflin, Charles Laughton, Mylene Demongeot, John Ericson. German raider commanded by a humane captain cleverly thwarts British efforts to capture her. Italian-British coproduction makes one wonder who really should have won the war—all the sympathy is on the German side. Aside from this, it's well made. (Dir: Duillo Coletti, 92 mins.)

Under the Yum Yum Tree (1963)**½ Jack Lemmon, Carol Lynley, Dean Jones. Good fun, Broadway comedy transfers to the screen with ease, thanks to Jack Lemmon's energetic performance as an amorous landlord. Carol Lynley is cute as one of Lemmon's tenants who is trying to keep her boyfriend at bay. (Dir: David Swift, 110 mins.)

Under Two Flags (1936)**½ Ronald Colman, Claudette Colbert, Rosalind Russell, Victor McLaglen. Creaky, perennial story of love and adventure in the Foreign Legion gets new life in this film but still falls short of top notch entertainment. (Dir: Frank Lloyd, 105 mins.)

Undercover Maisie (1947)** Ann Sothern, Barry Nelson. Blonde chorus girl becomes an undercover investigator for the police. Average comedy in the series. (Dir: Harry Beaumont, 90 mins.)

Undercover Man, The (1949)*** Glenn Ford, Nina Foch, James Whitmore. Tax experts try to pin the goods on a notorious gangster by legal means. Different sort of G-Man melodrama with a nice style, some suspenseful moments. (Dir: Joseph H. Lewis, 85 mins.)

Undercurrent (1946)**½ Katharine Hepburn, Robert Taylor, Robert Mitchum. The acting is good but the story of a girl who slowly discovers she has married a villain is not new and, in this case, not too well told. (Dir: Vincente Minnelli, 116 mins.)

Underground (1941)*** Jeffrey Lynn, Phillip Dorn. Exciting melodrama about the underground in Nazi Germany. Not a Grade A film but all involved turn in "A" work in this story of people risking their lives to create secret broadcasts under the Germans' noses. (Dir: Vincent Sherman, 95 mins.)

Underground Commando (1966)* Jose Vergara, Henry Duval. Ridiculous tale of three men trying to infiltrate caves which the Nazis are using for gasoline dumps. (90 mins.)

Underground Man, The (1974)**½ Peter Graves, Jack Klugman, Sharon Farrell. Ross Macdonald's best seller is adapted with care and attention by producer Howard Koch. Graves makes a fairly convincing Lew Archer—Macdonald's laconic, compassionate sleuth—and there's a first-class supporting cast including Dame Judith Anderson, Jo Ann Pflug, and Celeste Holm. Archer's task is delving into the murder of a man investigating his father's disappearance. Made-for-TV. (Dir: Paul Wendkos.)

Undertow (1950)**½ Scott Brady, Peggy Dow, John Russell. Fast moving, routine chase melodrama about a man who is wrongly accused of murder and has to prove his innocence. Brady makes an effective temporary fugitive and Peggy Dow is lovely as a schoolmarm who aids him. (Dir: William Castle, 71 mins.)

Underwater (1955)**½ Jane Russell, Gilbert Roland, Richard Egan. Two skin-divers brave the perils of the deep to locate sunken treasure. Passable melodrama has good underwater photography. (Dir: John Sturges, 99 mins.)

Underwater City, The (1962)* William Lundigan, Julie Adams. A seaslug. Engineer designs a pre-fab submerged city in anticipation of atomic holocaust. Looks like soggy papier-mâché. (Dir: Frank McDonald, 78 mins.)

Underworld Story, The (1950)*** Dan Duryea, Gale Storm, Herbert Marshall. Reporter buys an interest in a small-town newspaper and starts things humming by exposing corruption in back of a murder case. Tightly knit drama with a hard-hitting script, capable performances by a good cast. (Dir: Cy Endfield, 90 mins.)

Underworld, USA (1961)*** Cliff Robertson, Dolores Dorn, Beatrice Kay. Kid who has had a hard road in life grows up determined to get the men who murdered his father in a gang slaying. Crime drama covers familiar ground, but does so expertly. Better than average for its type, good fare for action fans. (Dir: Samuel Fuller, 100 mins.)

Une Femme Douce (France, 1969)*** Dominique Sanda, Guy Frangin, Jane Lobre. The first color film made by the interesting French director Robert Bresson, and based on the story "A Gentle Soul," by Fyodor Dostoyevsky. A study of alienation and dryness in a man married to a cheerful, independent, spirited wife. Unfolds leisurely with great attention to detail as is always the case in Bresson's films, and Sanda is splendid. (Dir: Robert Bresson, 88 mins.)

Unearthly Stranger (British, 1964)**½ John Neville, Gabriella Licudi. Scientist working on a secret project learns other scientists have been killed, then suspects his wife of being not of this earth. Creepy sci-fi thriller handled with finesse. Good for the fans.

Unexpected Uncle (1941)**½ Charles Coburn, Anne Shirley, James Craig. Old reprobate aids a shopgirl in her romance with a rich man. Mildly amusing comedy.

Unfaithfully Yours (1948)*** Rex Harrison, Linda Darnell. Sophisticated comedy about a symphony conductor who suspects his wife's fidelity. Where the script falters Mr. Harrison jumps in and saves it. (Dir: Preston Sturges, 105 mins.)

Unfaithfuls, The (Italian, 1952)*½ May Britt, Gina Lollobrigida, Marina Vlady. Dubbed foreign films leave something to be desired even if they are good to begin with, which this one isn't. The best way to enjoy this film is without sound—with Gina, May Britt and Marina Vlady, who needs dialogue? (Dir: Stefano Steno, 90 mins.)

Unfinished Business (1941)** Irene Dunne, Robert Montgomery. Irene Dunne, a small town girl, goes to the big city to find adventure and love in this silly comedy romance. (Dir: Gregory La Cava, 96 mins.)

Unfinished Dance, The (1947)**½ Cyd Charisse, Danny Thomas, Margaret O'Brien. Some nice ballet sequences for fans of the dance but story of a little girl who worships a ballerina and tries to stop another dancer from taking her place is not convincingly played or written. (Dir: Henry Koster, 101 mins.)

Unforgiven, The (1960)*** Burt Lancaster, Audrey Hepburn, Audie Murphy, Lillian Gish, John Saxon, Charles Bickford. Director John Huston has assembled a good cast for this sprawling Western drama about a pioneer family who are faced with Indian hostility when it becomes known that their young daughter may be an Indian. There's a very exciting climactic sequence. (125 mins.)

Unguarded Moment (1957)** Esther Williams, John Saxon, George Nader. Esther Williams doesn't swim in this one—she plays a school teacher who's attacked by one of her pupils (high school boy) and thereby hangs the psychological yarn. Flimsy story (scripted by Rosalind Russell) and unconvincing performances. (Dir: Harry Keller, 95 mins.)

Unholy Garden, The (1931)** Ronald Colman, Fay Wray. Fair melodrama by Ben Hecht and Charles MacArthur which serves as a vehicle for Ronald Colman. The ladies will go for it.

Unholy Intruders, The (German, 1956)*½ Philip Dorn, Olga Tache. Mawkish English-dubbed drama about an ex-convict who helps a poor family find a place to live by moving them into an unoccupied cloister.

Unholy Partners (1941)**½ Edward G. Robinson, Edward Arnold. Well-acted, contrived drama of an editor who is in partnership with a racketeer and decides to expose him in their own paper. (Dir: Mervyn Le Roy, 94 mins.)

Unholy Wife (1957)** Diana Dors, Rod Steiger, Tom Tryon. Diana Dors is buxom and Rod Steiger proceeds to chew up the scenery in this muddled story of a wealthy wife's infidelity and plans for murder. (Dir: John Farrow, 95 mins.)

Uninhibited, The (Spain-France-Italy, 1965)** Melina Mercouri, James Mason, Hardy Kruger. Incoherent melodrama about a worldly-wise woman, a besotted novelist, and a searching youth in a small Spanish fishing village. Fine seaside atmosphere, but dramatic impact peters out early. (Dir: Juan Antonio Bardem, 104 mins.)

Uninvited, The (1944)*** Ray Milland, Ruth Hussey. Ghost fans will love this well told chiller about a young couple who buy a house in England that is haunted. (Dir: Lewis Allen, 98 mins.)

Union Pacific (1939)*** Joel McCrea, Barbara Stanwyck. Akim Tamiroff. Grandiose western directed by De Mille won't be as stupendous on a TV screen, but it's still good entertainment. Saga of linking the east and west by rails has no message, but is well-acted and loaded with action. (Dir: Cecil B. De Mille, 140 mins.)

Union Station (1950)*** William Holden, Barry Fitzgerald, Nancy Olson, Robert Preston. Police join in a manhunt for the kidnaper of a blind girl. Suspenseful crime drama holds the interest. (Dir: Rudolph Mate, 80 mins.)

Unknown Guest, The (1943)***½ Victor Jory, Pamela Blake. A stranger stops in a small village, and is suspected to be an escaped criminal. Tense, exciting melodrama, well acted, far above average. (Dir: Kurt Neumann, 64 mins.)

Unknown Man, The (1951)**½ Walter Pidgeon, Ann Harding, Keefe Brasselle. Honest lawyer defends a murder suspect, finds afterwards his client really was guilty, and finally

accomplishes his strange revenge. Involved crime melodrama, with the twists and turns of the plot sustaining interest most of the way. (Dir: Richard Thorpe, 86 mins.)

Unman, Wittering, and Zigo (British, 1971)**½ David Hemmings, Carolyn Seymour. Hemmings as a schoolteacher at a boys' school who takes over at midterm after his predecessor has taken a suspicious tumble on the stairs. Did the kids have anything to do with the nasty fall? This appears to be the answer. Handsomely mounted, but not terribly interesting. It very much resembles the better-made "Child's Play." (Dir: John MacKenzie, 100 mins.)

Unseen, The (1945)***½ Joel McCrea, Gail Russell. Exciting chiller-diller about a young girl who comes to a mysterious home to replace a governess who was murdered. Top drawer for fans of this type of fiction. (Dir: Lewis Allen, 81 mins.)

Unsinkable Molly Brown, The (1964) *** Debbie Reynolds, Harve Presnell. Rowdy, raucous Meredith Willson musical entertainment for the whole family. Debbie Reynolds is all hustle and bustle as Molly, the tough backwoods girl who goes after money, social position, and love with non-stop energy (she's still nowhere near as good as Tammy Grimes who created the Broadway role), and she's seldom been better. The musical numbers are deftly staged by Peter Gennaro, and Harve Presnell as Molly's gold-prospecting husband has a good strong voice, and cuts a romantic figure. Tuneful outing. (Dir: Charles Walters, 128 mins.)

Unstoppable Man, The (Great Britain, 1960)* Cameron Mitchell, Marius Goring. Businessman's professional wife succeeds at tracking down his kidnapped son when Scotland Yard fails to. Interest in film stops quickly. (Dir: Terry Bishop, 68 mins.)

Untamed (1955)** Tyrone Power, Susan Hayward. Overly romantic adventure yarn about the he-men who pioneered the Zulu territory of Africa. Plenty of action interspersed with a silly quadrangular love interest. The stars go through the paces in a satisfactory professional manner. (Dir: Henry King, 111 mins.)

Untamed Frontier (1952)**½ Joseph Cotten, Shelley Winters, Scott Brady. Sprawling western with a good cast to give the film some added appeal. Story concerns the Texas frontier when cattle barons ran things and range wars were commonplace. (Dir: Hugo Fregonese, 75 mins.)

Untamed Youth (1957)*½ Mamie Van Doren, Lori Nelson, John Russell. Lowgrade sex drama set on a correction farm with both male and female inmates. Amid the super charged events, there are many rock'n roll numbers thrown in although this is not supposed to be a musical. (Dir: Howard W. Koch, 80 mins.)

Until They Sail (1957)*** Paul Newman, Jean Simmons, Joan Fontaine, Piper Laurie, Sandra Dee. Soap opera made palatable by a good all star cast, Newman, Simmons, Fontaine, Laurie and Dee. Plot revolves around the events in the lives of four sisters living in New Zealand during World War II. Newman and Miss Simmons make an attractive pair of lovers and Miss Laurie handles the heavy dramatics of the story in a most competent fashion. (Dir: Robert Wise, 95 mins.)

Untouched (Mexican, 1956)**½ Ricardo Montalban, Ariadne Welter. Man encounters a recluse in the jungle, falls in love with his beautiful daughter, but has to return to his wife. Inferior English dubbing detracts from a colorful, interesting drama posing the problem of so-called civilized life vs. withdrawal from mankind. Off the beaten path, well directed.

Unvanquished, The—See: Aparajito

Unwed Father (1974)**½ Joseph Bottoms, Kay Lenz, Beverly Garland, Kim Hunter, Joseph Campanella. Despite the silly title, this TV feature has some credible and interesting moments. It tells the story of a principled young man who fights for the custody of his illegitimate child, going against the wishes of his girl friend who wants to put the baby up for adoption. A good cast and an intelligent script. (Dir: Jeremy Kagan.)

Unwed Mother (1958)** Norma Moore, Robert Vaughn, Diana Darrin. Attractive girl gets involved with a lady killer, finds herself pregnant, refuses to give her baby up for adoption. "True confessions" type drama on the sordid side; well acted. (Dir: Walter Doniger, 74 mins.)

Up from the Beach (1965)*** Cliff Robertson, Irina Demick. Interesting World War II story about a group of American soldiers who liberate a small French village on the day after D-Day. The group, headed by Cliff Robertson, take over a farmhouse where three German SS soldiers are holding hostages. The suspense builds satisfactorily. (Dir: Robert Parrish, 100 mins.)

Up Front (1951)*** David Wayne, Tom Ewell. Bill Mauldin's zany cartoon characters, Willie and Joe, are excellently brought to life by Wayne and Ewell in this amusing film about G.I.'s fighting in Italy during World War II. (Dir: Alexander Knox, 92 mins.)

Up in Arms (1944)*** Danny Kaye, Dinah Shore, Dana Andrews. The film that made Danny Kaye a star in movies. He plays a green recruit in the Army and he gets into more trouble than anybody since Harold Lloyd. Dinah Shore fans will be doubly pleased. (Dir: Elliott Nugent, 106 mins.)

Up in Central Park (1948)** Deanna Durbin, Dick Haymes, Vincent Price. Film version of stage musical with Deanna Durbin playing a young Irish colleen during the turn of the century. Strictly for the undiscriminating musical fans. (Dir: William A. Seiter, 88 mins.)

Up in Mabel's Room (1943)**½ Dennis O'Keefe, Marjorie Reynolds, Mischa Auer, Charlotte Greenwood. A flustered husband tries to retrieve a memento given innocently to his old flame. Farce gets pretty funny at times. (Dir: Allan Dwan, 76 mins.)

Up Periscope (1959)**½ James Garner, Edmond O'Brien. Routine submarine drama made by Warner Bros. at a time when Garner's TV popularity in "Maverick" was at its height. Garner deserved better material as his later film career proved. For action fans. (Dir: Gordon Douglas, 111 mins.)

Up the Creek (British, 1958)**½ Wilfrid Hyde-White, Peter Sellers, David Tomlinson. Not as funny as some other British naval comedies but many lively moments do come about due to the antics of David Tomlinson as an ingenious lieutenant. (Dir: Val Guest, 84 mins.)

Up the Down Staircase (1967)**** Sandy Dennis, Patrick Redford, Eileen Heckart, Jean Stapleton. Bel

Kaufman's perceptive best-selling novel about the experiences of a young teacher in a New York high school is transferred to the screen with taste and skill by director Robert Mulligan and screenwriter Tad Mosel. Sandy Dennis has never been better and she's very moving, indeed. She's the dedicated teacher who overcomes the bureaucracy of high school administrators, and a series of problems with her students. Thoughtful, literate drama, well played by all, including Jean Stapleton who achieved TV recognition in the TV series "All in the Family." The best film about American schools in years. (124 mins.)

Up the Sandbox (1972)***½ Barbra Streisand, David Selby, Ariane Heller. A funny, wry, and often genuinely touching story about a young New York housewife living on Riverside Drive. One of the very first American films to deal with the women's-rights movement. Benefits greatly, in this her sixth film, by one of Streisand's most observant, restrained performances—she sings nary a note and is delicious delivering various comic monologues or relating to her neighbors. Extremely well adapted by playwright Paul Zindel from the novel by Anne Richardson Roiphe. Nicely handled, except for a clumsy ending, by veteran director Irvin Kershner. (97 mins.)

Up to His Neck (British, 1954)** Ronald Shiner, Laya Raki. Wacky, mixed-up farce with only a few funny moments.

Upstairs and Downstairs (British, 1960)*** Michael Craig, Anne Heywood, Mylene Demongeot. Charming domestic comedy about a young married couple and their problems in obtaining the right servant girl. Nice chuckling narrative, delightful performance by Demongeot as a Swedish beauty. Good fun. (Dir: Ralph Thomas, 100 mins.)

Uptown Saturday Night (1974)*** Sidney Poitier, Bill Cosby, Harry Belafonte, Flip Wilson, Calvin Lockhart, Richard Pryor, Roscoe Lee Browne. High-spirited fun as Cosby and Poitier play a pair of innocents whose night on the town is interrupted when they're held up at an illegal after-hours nightclub. Funny screenplay by Richard Wesley. The plot's merely an excuse to have the duo run into some zany characters including Belafonte as a black godfather (made up in a perfect parody of Brando), Pryor as a frenetic private eye, Wilson as the Reverend whose sermon on loose lips sinking ships and marriages is a comic tour-de-force and Browne as a phony black-is-beautiful congressman. The vigorous humor is so good-natured, it'll make you smile even if you don't like the jokes. Black is beautiful becomes, here, black is fun, too. (Dir: Sidney Poitier, 104 mins.)

Urge to Kill (British, 1962)** Patrick Barr, Ruth Dunning. Police seem to be stymied when a series of girl killings occur. Fair Edgar Wallace mystery.

Utopia (French, 1950)*½ Stan Laurel, Oliver Hardy, Suzy Delair. Stan and Ollie inherit a Pacific island, where uranium is discovered. Last L&H effort, and a sad farewell it is. They speak English, the rest of the cast is dubbed, while the scriptwriters apparently spoke to no one. Aside from the comedy duo, nil.

U-238 and the Witch Doctor (1953-66) * Clay Moore, Phyllis Coates. Feature version of serial "Jungle Drums of Africa." Hero in Africa to develop mining properties runs afoul of a foreign agent after uranium. Dull cliffhanger stuff. (Dir: Fred C. Brannon, 99 mins.)

Vacation from Marriage (1945)*** Robert Donat, Deborah Kerr, Ann Todd. Cute little "sleeper" about a mild little English couple who go into service during the war and have their personalities overhauled. Donat and Kerr are a great help as the couple. (Dir: Alexander Korda, 110 mins.)

Vagabond King, The (1956)** Kathryn Grayson, Oreste, Rita Moreno. Operetta about François Villon, poet and vagabond, and the revolt in Paris. Pretty starchy; the tunes are still pleasant, but the treatment is strictly small-time. (Dir: Michael Curtiz, 86 mins.)

Valachi Papers, The (French-Italian, 1972)** Charles Bronson, Lino Ventura, Joseph Wiseman. Based on Peter Maas' best seller, this violent saga of the Cosa Nostra from the late '20's to the late '50's is strictly patented movie-gangster melodrama.

Bronson plays the dim-witted Joe Valachi, a Mafia soldier who turned informer for the McClellan Committee. The performances are exaggerated, to say the least, except for Ventura as Vito Genovese. Wiseman gives the worst performance of his career as a poetry-spouting Mafia leader . . . he reads his lines in an accent that might be described as Borscht Belt Italian. (Dir: Terence Young, 125 mins.)

Valentino (1951)** Anthony Dexter, Eleanor Parker, Richard Carlson. A romanticized version of the Valentino Legend; produced in elaborate style. Against a background of gaudy splendor of the early Hollywood days, the phenomenal career of Rudolph Valentino unfolds. Anthony Dexter bears a striking physical resemblance to the original "Sheik of the Silver Screen," but that's where the resemblance ends. (Dir: Lewis Allen, 102 mins.)

Valley of Decision, The (1944)*** Greer Garson, Gregory Peck. Story of a girl who became a servant in a Pittsburgh industrialist's home and spent the rest of her life there—as a maid and then married to the son. Not a great film but, thanks to cast and production, top screen entertainment. (Dir: Tay Garnett, 111 mins.)

Valley of Mystery (1967)* Richard Egan, Peter Graves. Cliched story of a group of airline passengers forced to land in a South American jungle, fighting for survival. Acting is wooden. (Dir: Joseph Leytes, 94 mins.)

Valley of the Dolls (1967)* Patty Duke, Barbara Parkins, Sharon Tate. The book by Jacqueline Susann was a piece of trash. So is the sanitized movie version directed by Mark Robson. Cheap, melodramatic mishmash chronicling the rise and fall of three young ladies in show business. Patty Duke is sorely miscast as a Judy Garland type of star; Barbara Parkins has little to do but look stunning in a series of wigs and gowns; and the late Sharon Tate is lovely to look at as the doomed starlet. You're doomed to a stupefying two hours if you watch. (123 mins.)

Valley of the Doomed (German, 1962) *½ Don Megowan, Hildegarde Neff. Two-fisted engineer battles to build a railroad across perilous territory.

764

Banal adventure drama dubbed in English—good scenery, silly plot.

Valley of the Eagles (British, 1951) **½ Jack Warner, John McCallum, Nadia Gray. Young scientist has his invention stolen, follows the culprits together with a police inspector to the wastes of Lapland. Up-to-par melodrama with some unusual Northern scenes.

Valley of the Gwangi (1969)*½ James Franciscus, Gila Golan, Richard Carlson. Hold on to your ray gun, pardner—this is a science-fiction western about a prehistoric world hidden in the Forbidden Valley, located in the Mexico of 1912. Visual effects OK, but short of logic. Not for kids unless they love dinosaurs. (Dir: James O'Connolly, 95 mins.)

Valley of the Kings (1954)**½ Robert Taylor, Eleanor Parker, Carlos Thompson. Passable adventure set in Egypt. Taylor plays an archeologist who accompanies Eleanor Parker and her villainous husband on an expedition to the tombs of Pharaoh Rahotep. Miss Parker's reasons for the trek are purely for the sake of historical fact while her husband has other ideas. (Dir: Robert Pirosh, 86 mins.)

Valley of the Lions (Italian, 1962) *½ Ed Fury. More adventures of mighty Ursus. They're mighty dreary. (Dir: George Marshall, 83 mins.)

Valley of the Sun (1942)*** Lucille Ball, James Craig, Dean Jagger. Frontiersman finally exposes a crooked Indian agent. Exciting, fast-moving western with a good cast.

Vampire, The—See: Mark of the Vampire (1957, John Beal)

Vampires (Italian, 1965)* Gordon Scott, Gianna Maria. Creature-feature as band of androids led by the Vampire (no relation to Bela) kidnap young women to sell them as slaves. Our hero's name is Goliath, but the only strength of this one is the harem of beauties. (91 mins.)

Vampire's Coffin, The (Mexican, 1959)* Abel Salazar, Ariadne Welter, Jermon Robles. Vampire is revived from the dead, menaces a young girl. Inept horror thriller dubbed in English.

Vanished (1971)*** Richard Widmark, James Farentino, Robert Young. The best-selling novel by Fletcher Knebel is turned to a full-length film-made-for-TV. The surprising thing is that it works out very nicely indeed. Richard Widmark is effective as the fictitious President of the United States who faces a major crisis when one of his top advisers is allegedly kidnapped by what appears to be a foreign power. The situation has built-in suspense, and fine production heightens it at every turn. The supporting cast is uniformly good, particularly James Farentino as an efficient and likable press secretary to the President; E. G. Marshall as an overly fastidious and dedicated CIA Director; and Robert Young as a colorful and shady old Senator. (Dir: Buzz Kulik, 200 mins.)

Vanishing Point (1971)*½ Barry Newman, Cleavon Little, Dean Jagger. An automobile is the real star as Newman gets involved in a personal race against time and then the police as he drives from Colorado to California. On the way he becomes a youth folk hero as a blind, black disk jockey named Super Soul broadcasts bulletins across the Far West. Silly stuff with excitement kept to a bare minimum. One long car chase if you're a devotee. (Dir: Richard Sarafian, 99 mins.)

Vanishing Virginian, The (1941)** Frank Morgan, Kathryn Grayson. Sentimental, sugary little story which is set back at the beginning of the fight for women's suffrage. (Dir: Frank Borzage, 97 mins.)

Varan, the Unbelievable (1962)* Myron Healey, Tsuruko Kobayashi. Japanese horror about a monster on the loose with some American footage tacked on—a cheapie-creepie.

Variety Girl (1947)**½ All-star cast. Big mass of stars show their mugs and make this thing passable. Crosby and Hope have the best lines. (Dir: George Marshall, 83 mins.)

Vatican Affair, The (1970)*½ Walter Pidgeon, Ira Furstenberg. Shoddy caper film involving the Vatican treasures. Pidgeon is a blind man with an obsessive interest in the Vatican's collection of jewels and artifacts, so he sets up a team to steal them. (Dir: Emilio Miraglia, 120 mins.)

Veils of Bagdad (1954)** Victor Mature, Mari Blanchard. Victor Mature seems very much at home in his 16th century costumes of a palace guard in Bagdad. Action fans will get more than their share in this typical Arabian Nights adventure. (Dir: George Sherman, 82 mins.)

Velvet Touch (1948)**½ Rosalind Russell, Leo Genn. Famous stage actress is involved in a murder case. Slick but conventional mystery drama gives Miss Russell a chance to emote in several big scenes. (Dir: John Gage, 98 mins.)

Vendetta (1966)* Alexander Gavrick, Helen Jovan. Confusing tale about envy among brothers in post-World War II Eastern Europe. Entire town is destroyed before the winners ride into the sunset, but what everyone was fighting over is anybody's guess, and who cares. (80 mins.)

Vendetta to a Saint (1968)** Roger Moore, Ian Hendrey, Rosemary Dixter. Remember Roger Moore's Simon Templar, alias the Saint, before he became agent 007 in those James Bond films? Well, here's an episode with added footage from the original series, with dashing Moore playing it cool under pressures coming from his "vendetta" against the syndicate bosses. Naturally, there are plenty of beauteous distractions for Simon along the way. (72 mins.)

Venetian Affair, The (1967)*½ Robert Vaughn, Boris Karloff, Elke Sommer, Felicia Farr. Reporter (Vaughn) works for the CIA and imperils his life. Tedious, jumbled. (Dir: Jerry Thorpe, 92 mins.)

Vengeance of Fu Manchu, The (British, 1967)* Christopher Lee, Douglas Wilmer, Tony Ferrer, Tsai Chin. The mad Oriental tyrant is out to set up an international crime syndicate. Farfetched melodramatics, for fanciers of the exotic of another day. You're mad if you waste your time on Fu! (Dir: Jeremy Summers, 91 mins.)

Vengeance of She, The (British, 1968) *½ Olinka Berova, John Richardson, Edward Judd, Colin Blakely. Young woman is thought to be the reincarnation of the queen of a lost city, which means danger for her. Wild adventure-fantasy has some thrills. (Dir: Cliff Owen, 100 mins.)

Vengeance of the Three Musketeers (French, 1963)*½ Gerard Barray, Mylene Demongeot. D'Artagnan and his cronies save a lady in distress from the evil plans of a nobleman. Hokey English-dubbed swashbuckler.

Vengeance Valley (1951)*** Burt Lancaster, Robert Walker, Joanne Dru. Two fisted western adventure with Burt Lancaster the tall man in the saddle. Robert Walker plays Burt's young brother with an eye for the ladies and a penchant for trouble. Good action, ruggedly presented. (Dir: Richard Thorpe, 83 mins.)

Venice, the Moon and You (Italian, 1959)*½ Alberto Sordi, Marisa Alasio. English-dubbed comedy about a gondolier who can't resist flirting with the pretty tourists. Overlong, not so funny.

Venus in Furs (Great Britain-Italy-West Germany, 1970)*½ James Darren, Barbara McNair, Maria Rohm, Dennis Price. Confusing tale of a young man haunted by the sadistic murder of his lover. Good footage of Istanbul and stock footage of the Rio carnival add flavor, but the plot can't be overcome. (Dir: Jess Franco, 86 mins.)

Venus Meets the Son of Hercules— See: Mars, God of War

Vera Cruz (1954)**½ Gary Cooper, Burt Lancaster. The often used western plot of two opportunistic adventurers is on hand once again. This time it's Mexico during the Revolution of 1866. Cooper and Lancaster play the gunmen who inevitably come to grips. Denise Darcel and Sarita Montiel are merely decorative in their brief roles. (Dir: Robert Aldrich, 94 mins.)

Verboten (1958)** James Best, Tom Pittman, Susan Cummings. GI in Berlin uncovers a secret organization of Nazi youths bent on restoring the old regime. Postwar drama of occupied German crams a bit of everything into its plot; some stirring moments, mostly overloaded. (Dir: Samuel Fuller, 93 mins.)

Verdict (1946)**½ Sydney Greenstreet, Peter Lorre. Everybody enjoys the antics of the two masters of intrigue but in this one they're saddled with an inconsequential whodunit and the verdict is guilty. (Dir: Don Siegel, 86 mins.)

Verdict, The (British, 1963)** Cec Linder, Nigel Davenport. International criminal fixes the jury of his murder trial. Fair crime melodrama.

Vertigo (1958)**** James Stewart, Kim Novak, Barbara Bel Geddes. An Alfred Hitchcock thriller that makes no sense whatsoever but is a dazzling display of directorial finesse, weird situations. A retired San Francisco detective is hired to shadow an old friend's wife, finds

himself falling for her—then tragedy occurs. Believable or not, it's excellently done. (120 mins.)

Very Missing Person (1972)** Eve Arden. It's good to have Miss Arden back. Eve plays Hildegarde Withers, spinster sleuth, a character Edna May Oliver played back in a few 1930's movies. Curious Hildegarde, wearing atrocious hats, picks locks with a hatpin and wards off assailants by swinging her handbag, while tracing a wealthy youngster. The story and supporting cast aren't up to the star's level. Made-for-TV. (Dir: Russell Mayberry, 73 mins.)

Very Private Affair, A (France-Italy, 1962)*½ Brigitte Bardot, Marcello Mastroianni, Louis Malle. Early film by Louis Malle details the thirst for privacy of a successful movie idol (Bardot). A merciless portrait of the misery, nonfulfillment of stardom is superficial and tedious. Obviously based partially on Bardot herself; Mastroianni wasted. (Dir: Louis Malle, 95 mins.)

Very Special Favor, A (1965)**½ Rock Hudson, Leslie Caron, Charles Boyer. French lawyer persuades Rock, as a favor, to romance his daughter to help her find herself as a woman. Glossy comedy with a pretty production and familiar players; sometimes the intent is funnier than the execution, but the laughs come with fair frequency. (Dir: Michael Gordon, 104 mins.)

Vice and Virtue (Italy-France, 1963) ** Annie Girardot, Robert Hossein, Catherine Deneuve. Misguided attempt to update two novels by de Sade ("Juliette," "Justine") and make a relevant comment about contemporary society. Two sisters, one virtuous, one decadent, cope with the Nazi occupation of France. Direction compromised by naive plotting, excessive symbolism. (Dir: Roger Vadim, 108 mins.)

Vice Raid (1960)* Mamie Van Doren, Richard Coogan, Brad Dexter. Sleazy crime drama of call-girl racket crackdown, uses TV cop techniques. (Dir: Edward L. Cahn, 71 mins.)

Vice Squad (1953)**½ Edward G. Robinson, Paulette Goddard. A day in the life of a cop, with more plot than you can count on your fingers and toes. Robinson is tough, Goddard is pseudo-sultry, and the result is haphazard. Strictly for the cops-

and-robbers crowd. (Dir: Arnold Laven, 87 mins.)

Vicious Circle (British, 1957)*** John Mills, Noelle Middleton. Surgeon is suspected of murder when a film star is found dead in his flat. Suspenseful, compact mystery with good performances. (Dir: Gerald Thomas, 84 mins.)

Vicki (1953)** Jeanne Crain, Richard Boone, Jean Peters. Dogged detective tries to pin murder of a local glamour girl on her suitor. This was better as "I Wake Up Screaming" with Grable and Mature. (Dir: Harry Horner, 85 mins.)

Victim (British, 1961)***½ Dirk Bogarde, Sylvia Syms, Dennis Price. Made by the same talented team of filmmakers responsible for the splendid entry "Sapphire." When a lawyer (Bogarde) becomes involved in a case with homosexual implications, his own past jeopardizes his career. Generally thoughtful effort, and one of the earliest movies, to deal with the heretofore forbidden screen subject of homosexuality. Makes an earnest plea for changing the antiquated law making homosexuality a crime. Bogarde is particularly effective. (Dir: Basil Dearden, 100 mins.)

Victim, The (1972)* Elizabeth Montgomery in a tepid thriller about a woman trapped in a remote house during a violent storm. Made-for-TV. (Dir: Herschel Daugherty, 73 mins.)

Victors, The (1963)***½ George Peppard, George Hamilton, Eli Wallach, Jeanne Moreau, Melina Mercouri, Vincent Edwards. Curious, sprawling saga of a squad of American soldiers, following them through Europe during World War II. Uneven results, but done on a broad canvas, commendable in intent. Some splendid sequences, always well acted by a large cast. (Dir: Carl Foreman, 175 mins.)

Victory (1940)*** Fredric March, Betty Field, Cedric Hardwicke. Tense dramatic tale of a recluse who seeks peace on a South Sea island which is invaded by a girl and a band of killers. Superbly acted but, unfortunately, the story disintegrates in the middle of the film. (Dir: John Cromwell, 78 mins.)

Victory at Sea (1959)**** Splendid documentary of the course of World War II at sea, adapted from the multi-award winning TV series. One of the best of its kind. Alexander Scourby, narrator. (108 mins.)

View from Pompey's Head, The (1955) **½ Richard Egan, Dana Wynter, Cameron Mitchell. Full blown soap opera played in the attractive trappings of the southern social set. Egan plays an executive of a publishing house who goes back home to investigate a claim of money due by an aging author who lives in an air of mystery. A bit slow moving and predictable. Based on Hamilton Basso's best seller. (Dir: Philip Dunne, 97 mins.)

View from the Bridge, A (1961)**** Raf Vallone, Maureen Stapleton, Carol Lawrence, Jean Sorel, Raymond Pellegrin. Excellent screen version of Arthur Miller's play about an Italian longshoreman and his eruptive relationships with his wife and niece. The performances are individually exciting and perfectly blended for full dramatic effect. The climactic scene, played in a wet Brooklyn street, is one of the most shattering few minutes ever put on film. Another fine directing job from Sidney Lumet. (110 mins.)

Vigil in the Night (1940)***½ Carole Lombard, Brian Aherne, Anne Shirley. A young nurse in an English hospital makes a fatal mistake, for which her sister takes the blame. Grim but excellently done drama. (Dir: George Stevens, 96 mins.)

Viking Queen, The (British, 1967)** Don Murray, Carita. Although made in England, this film very neatly fits the Hollywood adventure category. It is a costumed period piece about the Roman occupation of Britain, and the love that was not meant to be between the Roman military governor and the queen of the local tribe. (Dir: Don Chaffey, 91 mins.)

Vikings, The (1958)**½ Kirk Douglas, Janet Leigh, Tony Curtis. An all star cast enhances this elaborately mounted adventure epic which places the stress on action. The battle sequences are the highlights of the film which tells the story of the Vikings' invasion of England. On location photography in Norway is another plus factor. (Dir: Richard Fleischer, 114 mins.)

Villa Rides (1968)**½ Action-packed adventure stars Yul Brynner as the famed rebel leader Pancho Villa, and Robert Mitchum as a gun-running aviator who joins forces with Villa to further the revolution in Mexico. (Dir: Buzz Kulik, 100 mins.)

Village, The (Swiss, 1954)*** John Justin, Eva Dahlbeck. Two teachers at the Pestalozzi school for DP children fall in love, but she is from behind the Iron Curtain. Frequently touching drama, multi-lingual, with some fine performances from the children.

Village of Daughters (1958)** Eric Sykes, Scilla Gabel. A strained but somewhat funny comedy about a British traveling salesman who encounters hot-blooded Italians in their full passion while stranded in a small town.

Village of the Damned (British, 1960)**** George Sanders, Barbara Shelley, Martin Stephens. Outstanding low-budget, high-shudder shocker, based on the novel "The Midwich Cuckoos." Fine direction from Wolf Rilla in this chiller about strange kids trying to conquer a village. Reminds us that sometimes the eeriest thrills and chills are the quiet ones. (78 mins.)

Village of the Giants (1965)* Tommy Kirk, Johnny Crawford, Beau Bridges. Inept and tasteless fantasy about a group of teenagers out for kicks who stumble across a potion that will make them huge—they take over the town. Even the trick photography doesn't register. (Dir: Bert I. Gordon, 80 mins.)

Villain (1971)**½ Richard Burton, Ian McShane. Uneven crime melodrama with a heavy accent on violence. Burton gives a good account of himself in the offbeat role of a sadistic thief who stops at nothing to get his job done. Burton's character is also a jealous homosexual, which adds some bite to the already heavily plotted film. Lots of blood and gore, some of which will be edited for TV. (Dir: Michael Tuchner.)

Villain Still Pursued Her, The (1941)** Alan Mowbray, Buster Keaton, Anita Louise, Richard Cromwell, Billy Gilbert. Hiss the villain, cheer the hero, in a burlesque of old-time melodrama with everything from ham acting to custard pie throwing. (Dir: Edward Cline, 66 mins.)

Violent Men, The (1955)**½ Glenn Ford, Barbara Stanwyck, Edward

G. Robinson. A large sprawling Western drama about a ruthless land baron who loses his grip on things due to violent forces opposing him. Good performances by all. (Dir: Rudolph Mate, 96 mins.)

Violent Moment (British, 1962)** Lyndon Brook, Jane Hylton. Army deserter lives with a woman and her son, commits murder when she intends to place the boy up for adoption. Fairly interesting drama based on a story by Edgar Wallace.

Violent Ones (French, 1958)*** Paul Meurisse, Francoise Fabian. Suspenseful drama of a series of murders that sends a whole town into terror. Good acting and fine script.

Violent Ones, The (1967)* Fernando Lamas, Aldo Ray, David Carradine, Lisa Gaye. Sheriff (Lamas) tries to save murder suspects from a lynch mob. In the process he loses the picture, and because Fernando also directed, he takes a double rap for this junk. (84 mins.)

Violent Patriot, The (Italian, 1957)*½ Vittorio Gassman, Anna Maria Ferrero. John of the Medicis becomes a hero when he sets out to repel the Franco-German invaders. Stilted English-dubbed costume drama.

Violent Playground (British, 1958)*** Stanley Baker, Peter Cushing. Policeman tries to prevent crime in a tenement area of Liverpool. Gripping, well-acted drama of juvenile delinquents.

Violent Road (1958)** Brian Keith, Efrem Zimbalist, Jr. Average drama about the truck drivers who transport high explosive rocket fuel to a newly built missile base and the dangers they encounter. You can see this sort of thing done better on TV. (Dir: Howard W. Koch, 86 mins.)

Violent Saturday (1955)*** Victor Mature, Richard Egan, Sylvia Sidney, Ernest Borgnine, Stephen McNally, Lee Marvin. A good cast bolsters this episodic yarn about a planned bank robbery in a small town by a trio of hoods. Many of the townspeople's stories come into focus as the bank robbers stake out the town before the heist. (Dir: Richard Fleischer, 91 mins.)

Violent Summer (Italy, 1959)*** Eleonora Rossi-Drago, Jean-Louis Trintignant, Jacqueline Sassard. Quiet, perceptive film despite that title. About a frivolous romance solidifying into a passionate, mature affair, set against the upheaval of Mussolini's rotting fascist regime. Trintignant appears to advantage in this early film, his first non-Bardot vehicle, and his performance is complimented by Miss Rossi-Drago's compelling portrait of the older woman drawn to him. Film has delicacy, is well photographed. (Dir: Valero Zurlini, 95 mins.)

V.I.P.'s, The (1963)*** Elizabeth Taylor, Richard Burton, Louis Jourdan, Margaret Rutherford, Orson Welles. A sort of "Grand Hotel" localed at a London airport, as passengers waiting for a delayed flight intercross each other's lives. Practically an all-star cast lends credence to the multi-plots, with an award-winning performance by Margaret Rutherford and equally good ones by Rod Taylor and Maggie Smith standing out. Good show. (Dir: Anthony Asquith, 119 mins.)

Virgin Island (British, 1959)** John Cassavetes, Virginia Maskell, Sidney Poitier. Young writer and his bride buy an island in the Caribbean, live there with the help of a local fisherman. Romantic comedy is pleasant but moves leisurely, uneventfully. (Dir: Pat Jackson, 84 mins.)

Virgin Queen, The (1955)*** Bette Davis, Richard Todd, Joan Collins. Bette Davis fans will not want to miss their favorite in the flashy role of the aging Queen Elizabeth and her relationship with Sir Walter Raleigh, gallantly played by Richard Todd. Miss Davis gives a flamboyant performance as the British Queen and the supporting cast is more than competent. TV movie fans might find it interesting to compare this film with the 1939 "Private Lives of Elizabeth & Essex" in which Miss Davis played the same role opposite Errol Flynn. (Dir: Henry Koster, 92 mins.)

Virgin Spring, The (Sweden, 1960) **** Max von Sydow, Birgitta Valberg, Gunnel Lindblom, Birgitta Pettersson. Bergman's quietly chilling morality play, set in the Swedish countryside of the 14th century, about pagan lusts, Christian renewal. Based on a Swedish ballad and legend, a young virgin girl is brutally despoiled and murdered after her sister invokes a pagan curse. Bergman has captured the quality of ancient legends: their primitive passions; human sorrows; abrupt beauty, for one of his most powerful films. (Dir: Ingmar Bergman, 88 mins.)

Virginia City (1940)*** Errol Flynn, Miriam Hopkins, Randolph Scott, Humphrey Bogart. Just from the cast you know this is a virile, action-packed western and you're right the first time. Loaded with cliches and contrivances, it still comes out entertainment. Not as provocative as the later rage called "adult westerns" but still good. (Dir: Michael Curtiz, 121 mins.)

Virginia Hill Story, The (1974)** Dyan Cannon, Harvey Keitel. Dyan Cannon stars in this tale about a poor Southern girl who hits the big time as a gangster's moll, and she gives her all to the character of Virginia Hill, the girlfriend of Bugsy Siegel, who was ambushed in Beverly Hills back in 1947. Version, based on a true story, is a pale copy of the real thing. Made-for-TV. (Dir: Joel Schumacher, 72 mins.)

Virginian, The (1946)*** Joel McCrea, Brian Donlevy, Sonny Tufts. Not exactly powerful, but fairly interesting western about the age old "horse opera" struggle between ranchers and rustlers. (Dir: Stuart Gilmore, 90 mins.)

Virtuous Bigamist, The (French, 1956)**½ Fernandel, Guilia Rubini. Fernandel helps a mademoiselle in distress—she needs a husband because she is about to become a mother. Both funny and touching.

Viscount, The (France-Italy-Spain, 1967)½ Kerwin Mathews, Edmond O'Brien, Jane Fleming. Plodding crime tale about a "viscount"-investigator, drearily played by Mathews, who helps uncover an international drug ring. (Dir: Maurice Cloche, 98 mins.)

Visions (1972)** Monte Markham, Telly Savalas, Barbara Anderson. A good cast and Denver locations add substance to this action film. Clairvoyant professor warms police about impending bombing in Denver. When a building is dynamited, police first suspect the professor. Made-for-TV. (Dir: Lee Katzin, 73 mins.)

Visions of Eight (1973)***½ A documentary about the 1972 summer Olympics in Munich based on an imaginative idea. Give the opportunity to a number of the best directors in the world to each film their vision of one particular event. Inevitably, some of the sequences are more illuminating and work better than others, but there are insights into the philosophy, beauty and agonies of sports found in few other sports films, fiction or documentary. And the remarkable list of directors and the events they document includes Arthur Penn (pole-vaulters), Kon Ichikawa (100-meter dash), Claude Lelouch (the losers), John Schlesinger (marathon-runners), Milos Forman (decathlon), Judi Ozerov (the beginning), Michael Pfleghar (the women), Mai Zetterling (weight-lifting). Only Schlesinger's segment deals with the horrendous massacre of the Israeli athletes. Some lyrical (Penn), some ironic (Forman), this is a unique essay on the pressures and glories of the Olympics. Also released in a shortened version as "Olympic Visions." (110 mins.)

Visit, The (U.S.-West German-French-Italian)** Anthony Quinn, Ingrid Bergman. It took the combined efforts of four countries to help dilute the fascinating play by Swiss playwright Friedrich Durrenmatt. The story line remains intact, but the cynical, brittle cutting edge of the original has been lost in the trip over the Alps. Ingrid is a strong-willed woman who goes to great lengths to wreak vengeance on her former lover. Too bad it couldn't have been filmed with Alfred Lunt and Lynn Fontanne who were so superb on Broadway in the title roles. (Dir: Bernhard Wicki, 100 mins.)

Visit to a Small Planet (1960)** Jerry Lewis, Joan Blackman. Impish creature from outer space lands on earth to study the ways of us earthlings. Jerry as a spaceman might bring some laughs, but the satiric point of the original Broadway play by Gore Vidal is blunted with slapstick. (Dir: Norman Taurog, 85 mins.)

Vitelloni (Italian, 1953)**** Franco Interleghi, Franco Fabrizi. Young Lothario won't settle down, even after marriage. Penetrating portrait of youth in a small town in Italy. Well worthwhile. Directed by F. Fellini. See it.

Viva Las Vegas! (1964)**½ Elvis Presley, Ann-Margret. One of Elvis' better films. Musical set in the fun capital of the world—Las Vegas.

Presley is a hot-rod racer and Ann-Margret plays the sexy nightclub dancer who captures his attention amid the songs, dances, and exciting racing sequences of the film. (Dir: George Sidney, 86 mins.)

Viva Maria! (French, 1965)**½ Jeanne Moreau, Brigitte Bardot, George Hamilton. A good try at a turn-of-the-century revolution yarn. The place is Central America and the two gals, both named Maria, are dancers who become involved with the cause of the local revolutionaries when they fall for the charms of the leading revolutionary (Hamilton). Most of the comedy is tongue-in-cheek, and some of it works. (Dir: Louis Malle, 119 mins.)

Viva Max! (1969)**½ Peter Ustinov, Jonathan Winters, Pamela Tiffin, Keenan Wynn. A funny premise never quite takes hold in what promises to be a hilarious romp. In any case, there are plenty of laughs as Ustinov, playing a modern-day Mexican general with a thick accent, leads a scraggly group of men over the border and into the Alamo, reclaiming the tourist attraction for his homeland. The fine supporting cast is led by Winters as a National Guard officer, one of his brilliant bumbler characterizations. (Dir: Jerry Paris, 92 mins.)

Viva Portugal (West Germany-France, 1975)*** A technically crude but generally interesting documentary record of the first year of Portugal's shaky new democracy, which ended in 1974 Europe's longest-lived 20th-century dictatorship. Scenes in Lisbon and of factory workers and farmers who have just taken over land formerly ruled by absentee landlords. Also one remarkable scene about part of the brief fighting filmed by Portuguese TV. Filmed "collectively." (Dirs: Christiane Gerhards, Peer Oliphant, Samuel Schirmbeck, Malte Rauch, Serge July, 99 mins.)

Viva Revolution (Mexican, 1956)***½ Pedro Armendariz, Maria Felix. Well made film about the Mexican Revolution. Pedro Armendariz is superb in the leading role.

Viva Villa! (1933)*** Wallace Beery, Leo Carrillo, Fay Wray. Wild, rousing story of Pancho Villa is well written and exciting but a bit too episodic. Beery is fine as Mexico's renowned Robin Hood. (Dir: Jack Conway, 120 mins.)

Viva Zapata! (1952)**** Marlon Brando, Jean Peters, Anthony Quinn. Excellent historical drama of Mexican revolutionary leader Emiliano Zapata. Follows his rise from peon to the Presidency of Mexico. Brando is magnificent as Zapata. Anthony Quinn won an Oscar for his superb depiction of Zapata's brother. Kazan directed the John Steinbeck script. (113 mins.)

Vivacious Lady (1938)***½ Ginger Rogers, James Stewart. College professor marries a night club singer, then has difficulty having her accepted by his family. Sparkling comedy has many laughs.· (Dir: George Stevens, 90 mins.)

Voice in the Mirror (1958)*** Richard Egan, Julie London, Arthur O'Connell. With a little more work on the script, this drama about alcoholism and the long road back could have been a very good film. As it is, it's worth your attention. Egan has never been better and Julie London matches his restrained performance, with character actor Arthur O'Connell a standout.

Voice in the Wind (1943)*** Francis Lederer, Sigrid Gurie. Tragic drama of a mentally-shattered refugee pianist who finds his lost love on a tropical isle. Strange, moody, well-acted. Excellent piano interludes.

Voice of Silence, The (Italian, 1952)** Aldo Fabrizi, Jean Marais, Daniel Gelin, Rossana Podesta. Five men go into a religious retreat and try to face their personal problems. Grim, uneven drama, dubbed in English. Some okay performances, but the story drags.

Voice of the Turtle (1947)***½ Ronald Reagan, Eleanor Parker. Broadway play about a week-end romance in a New York apartment between a budding actress and a soldier on leave is throughout amusing. You'll like Eve Arden in a supporting role.

Volcano (Italian, 1953)** Anna Magnani, Rossano Brazzi. Women with a past returns to her home on a volcanic isle, finds her sister about to marry a rascally diver. Lumbering, cliche-ridden melodrama, and the English dubbing doesn't aid matters any.

Volcano (1969)** Maximilian Schell, Diane Baker, Brian Keith, Rossano Brazzi, Sal Mineo. Released under the title "Krakatoa, East of Java," this forerunner of the 70s disaster films doesn't measure up to, say, "The Towering Inferno," but it is passable entertainment for fans of the genre. There is the climactic volcanic eruption and tidal wave, but none of the characters evokes any sympathy. Cartographers in the audience take note that Krakatoa is really West of Java and there was a ghastly volcanic explosion there in August of 1883. (Dir: Bernard Kowalski, 135 mins.)

Von Ryan's Express (1965)*** Frank Sinatra, Trevor Howard. Exciting World War II adventure yarn with Frank Sinatra giving a fine performance as an American Army colonel who goes from heel to hero. Trevor Howard is also excellent as the British officer who is the prisoners' unofficial leader until Ryan takes over. The last quarter of the film follows the escaping prisoners as they commandeer a German train, and you can't ask for a more exciting sequence. (Dir: Mark Robson, 117 mins.)

Voodoo Island (1957)** Boris Karloff, Beverly Tyler, Murvyn Vye. Horror fans will be a bit disappointed by this slow moving tale of witchcraft and monsters. Even Karloff can't make it chilling.

Voyage of the Yes, The (1972)** Desi Arnaz, Jr., Mike Evans. Another opus about whites learning to live with blacks. It's a pedestrian drama about a rich California youngster who sails off to Hawaii with an inexperienced Chicago black on the lam. Storms, sharks, and the black youngster's inability as a seaman keep the action going as the kids work out their prejudices. Made-for-TV. (Dir: Lee Katzin.)

Voyage to Danger (German, 1962)*½ John Hansen, Karin Baal. A freighter makes a perilous run down the African coast. Dubbed-English adventure has little aboard but tedium.

Voyage to the Bottom of the Sea (1961)**½ Walter Pidgeon, Joan Fontaine, Barbara Eden, Frankie Avalon. Submarine speeds to explode a radiation belt threatening earth, is hampered by dirty work aboard. Sci-fi melodrama on the juvenile side, enhanced by superb trick photography and special effects.

Voyage to the End of the Universe (Czech, 1964)*½ Dennis Stephens,

Francis Smolen. Spaceship of the future has a terrifying time reaching a distant planet. Occasional good effects, mostly farfetched sci-fi, dubbed-in English.

Vulture, The (U.S.-British-Canadian, 1967)**½ Robert Hutton, Akim Tamiroff, Broderick Crawford. Effective spine-tingler. Atomic scientist uses nuclear energy to reincarnate rampaging composite of a sea captain and gigantic, vulturous bird, both buried alive a century earlier. Location scenes filmed in Cornwall, England. (Dir: Lawrence Huntington, 91 mins.)

Wabash Avenue (1950)*** Betty Grable, Victor Mature, Phil Harris. Typical Betty Grable musical set at the turn of the century. She sings, dances, throws vases at Victor Mature, sings some more, dances some more and ends up in Victor Mature's arms. The musical numbers are fun and Miss Grable, in her prime here, is an able performer. (Dir: Henry Koster, 92 mins.)

Wackiest Ship in the Army, The (1961)*** Jack Lemmon, Ricky Nelson, Chips Rafferty, John Lund. Slightly different mixture of war heroics and comedy blended into an entertaining film, about a sailing expert who's tricked into commanding an aged hulk disguised as a sailing vessel which will secretly land a scout in enemy territory. Some good suspense, effective lighter moments. (Dir: Richard Murphy, 99 mins.)

Waco (1966)* Howard Keel, Jane Russell, Brian Donlevy. Routine western with Howard Keel in the title role of a gunfighter who cleans up a small town steeped in corruption. Jane Russell plays a preacher's wife (how times have changed!). (Dir: R. G. Springsteen, 85 mins.)

Wages of Fear (French, 1953)**** Yves Montand, Charles Vanel. A convoy of trucks driven by derelicts transports dangerous nitro over bad roads to try and quell oil well fire. Grim, suspenseful drama, finely done, but for strong stomachs. A brilliant thrilling winner. (Dir: H. G. Clouzot, 105 mins.)

Wagonmaster (1950)*** Ben Johnson, Harry Carey Jr., Joanne Dru. Two wandering cowpokes join a wagon train of Mormons across frontier territory to Utah. Leisurely but pleasant John Ford western. (Dir: John Ford, 86 mins.)

Wagons Roll at Night (1941)**½ Eddie Albert, Joan Leslie, Anthony Quinn, Humphrey Bogart. Carnival comedy gets a big assist from Albert as a fledgling lion tamer but help from other sources, mainly script, never arrives. (Dir: Ray Enright, 84 mins.)

Waikiki Wedding (1937)*** Bing Crosby, Shirley Ross, Martha Raye. Pleasant musical about a pineapple queen's experiences in Hawaii. As Bing is the press agent for the pineapples, we get a nice mixture of romance and comedy. (Dir: Frank Tuttle, 90 mins.)

Wait for the Dawn (1960)**½ Leo Genn. One of director Roberto Rossellini's lesser efforts but worth watching. Genn plays an Englishman who keeps one step ahead of the Nazis in war-torn Italy. His escapes and encounters with a series of helpful strangers form the basis of this adventure drama.

Wait 'Til the Sun Shines, Nellie (1952)**** David Wayne, Jean Peters. Fine piece of Americana! Tender story of a small town barber, his hopes and disappointments through the early part of the 20th century. Wayne is superb, as is the rest of the cast. Catch this much underrated film. (Dir: Henry King, 108 mins.)

Wait Until Dark (1967)***½ Audrey Hepburn, Alan Arkin, Efrem Zimbalist, Jr. Tense suspense involving a blind woman (Hepburn) who has inadvertently obtained an antique doll full of heroin which Arkin must retrieve. The film is based on Frederick Knott's stage play, and one hardly notices that the action rarely moves from the interior of the house—especially when the lights go out and the pursuer becomes the blind. Arkin is genuinely devilish in his evilness and charm. Sit forward and get some scares. (Dir: Terence Young, 108 mins.)

Wake Island (1942)*** Brian Donlevy, William Bendix. Dramatic saga of the glorious but bitter defeat suffered by the Marines of Wake Island early in the war. (Dir: John Farrow, 78 mins.)

Wake Me When It's Over (1960)** Dick Shawn, Ernie Kovacs. Mildly amusing service comedy with Dick

Shawn working very hard as a WW II vet who gets drafted all over again due to an error. This premise should give you an idea of what to expect. Shawn and his blundering and thundering commanding officer, overplayed by Ernie Kovacs, set up a luxury spa in the middle of the Pacific island and the contrived complications mount up. (Dir: Mervyn Le Roy, 126 mins.)

Wake Me When the War Is Over (1969)*½ Ken Berry, Eva Gabor, Werner Klemperer. Inept, silly made-for-TV comedy about an American lieutenant who is kept prisoner in a lush mansion during WW II, not by the enemy but by Baroness Eva Gabor. The one-joke premise is milked to the point of tedium, and even the actors look tired of the whole affair before long. (Dir: Gene Nelson, 73 mins.)

Wake of the Red Witch (1946)**½ John Wayne, Gail Russell, Luther Adler. A few good action scenes in this confused sea story about a rivalry between a ship's owner and its captain over pearls and a gal. (Dir: Edward Ludwig, 106 mins.)

Wake Up and Live (1937)**½ Walter Winchell, Ben Bernie, Alice Faye. The mock feud of Winchell and Bernie died some years ago with the untimely death of the "old maestro." This film was made to exploit the feud but even now it's an O.K. musical film, with Jack Haley stealing the show as a crooner with mike fright. (Dir: Sidney Lanfield, 100 mins.)

Walk a Crooked Mile (1948)**½ Louis Hayward, Dennis O'Keefe. Fine, 100 percent pure American is stealing atomic secrets for the Russians. Routine FBI drama. (Dir: Gordon Douglas, 91 mins.)

Walk Don't Run (1966)**½ Cary Grant, Samantha Eggar, Jim Hutton. A remake of the 1943 comedy "The More The Merrier." Cary Grant doesn't play the lover in this one, but he's customarily charming as a matchmaking tycoon in Japan during the 1964 Olympics in Tokyo. Cary brings Miss Eggar and Jim Hutton together while the three of them are sharing one apartment in crowded Tokyo. It's a frothy tour and the kids—Samantha and Jim—are an attractive couple. (Dir: Charles Walters, 114 mins.)

Walk East on Beacon (1952)***

George Murphy, Virginia Gilmore. FBI cracks a Red spy ring. Documentary-style; earnest, but rather commonplace. (Dir: Alfred L. Werker, 98 mins.)

Walk in the Shadow (Great Britain, 1962)**½ Michael Craig, Patrick McGoohan, Janet Munro. Incisive, refined soap opera; a man who allows his daughter to die because of his inflexible religious beliefs begins to loosen up as grief and realities take hold. Understated, intelligent, well-acted; effectively shot in a bleak coastal setting in northern England. (Dir: Basil Dearden, 93 mins.)

Walk in the Sun (1945)***½ Dana Andrews, Richard Conte, John Ireland. War story of a platoon of Texas Division infantrymen in Italy, whose task it is to clear a farmhouse of Germans entrenched there. One of the best World War II dramas. Realistic, well acted. (Dir: Lewis Milestone, 117 mins.)

Walk Into Hell (Australian, 1956) *** Chips Rafferty, Francoise Christophe. New Guinea official and party, investigating oil deposits in the jungle, are captured by savages. Continually interesting, frequently exciting jungle drama. Fine location scenery. (Dir: Lee Robinson, 93 mins.)

Walk Like a Dragon (1960)**½ James Shigeta, Nobu McCarthy, Jack Lord, Mel Torme. Saving a Chinese girl from the San Francisco slave market, a man brings her to his home town, along with a young Chinese immigrant. There's soon plenty of trouble. Drama of racial problems in the early west has the advantage of a different sort of plot and sincere performances, helping it through some of the shaky sections. (Dir: James Clavell, 95 mins.)

Walk on the Wild Side (1962)** Laurence Harvey, Capucine, Jane Fonda, Barbara Stanwyck, Anne Baxter. A muddled, botched-up drama based on Nelson Algren's hard-hitting novel about the sinful side of life in New Orleans. Stanwyck plays a madame of a house in the Quarter where Fonda and Capucine toil. (Dir: Edward Dmytryk, 114 mins.)

Walk Softly, Stranger (1950)*** Joseph Cotten, Valli. A small-time crook is reformed by the love of a crippled girl. Well written, deftly acted melodrama. (Dir: Robert Stevenson, 81 mins.)

Walk Tall (1960)*½ Willard Parker, Joyce Meadows. Army captain searches for a renegade who has murdered innocent Indians. Mediocre western. (Dir: Maury Dexter, 60 mins.)

Walk the Proud Land (1956)*** Audie Murphy, Anne Bancroft, Pat Crowley. Better than average Audie Murphy western. He plays an Indian agent who wins the Apache's friendship and loses the white man's trust in the process. Anne Bancroft is wasted in the role of an Indian maiden. (Dir: Jesse Hibbs, 88 mins.)

Walk with Love and Death, A (1969)* Slumbering melodrama. Casting of Anjelica Huston and Assaf Dayan as the principals doesn't help. (Dir: John Huston, 90 mins.)

Walkabout (1971)***½ Jenny Agutter, Lucien John, David Gumpilil. Stimulating adventure story with disturbing social overtones. Two white Australian children are stranded in the Outback, and must negotiate their way across the desert. They adapt to the harsh conditions with the help of an aborigine familiar with the terrain. Edward Bond's screenplay and Nicolas Roeg's visually arresting direction provide nostalgia for innocence. Based on the novel by James Vance Marshall. The relationship between brother and sister and between sister and the young aborigine boy delicately handled. A moving journey indeed. Directed and photographed on location in Australia by Nicolas Roeg. (95 mins.)

Walking Dead, The (1936)** Boris Karloff, Ricardo Cortez. This was the height of the Karloff-horror era and in this one they resurrect the excellent actor from the dead. We know today that he outlived those roles. (Dir: Michael Curtiz, 70 mins.)

Walking Hills (1949)*** Randolph Scott, Ella Raines, John Ireland. Ill-assorted group of adventurers seek a lost gold mine. Better than average western with a good script. (Dir: John Sturges, 78 mins.)

Walking My Baby Back Home (1954)**½ Donald O'Connor, Janet Leigh, Buddy Hackett. If you forget the plot in this muddled musical comedy, you'll enjoy the musical numbers and Buddy Hackett's comedy routines.

O'Connor and Leigh make an attractive pair and their dancing is easy to take. (Dir: Lloyd Bacon, 95 mins.)

Walking Stick, The (Great Britain, 1970)**½ Samantha Eggar, David Hemmings, Emlyn Williams, Phyllis Calvert. An outstanding, finely etched performance by Samantha Eggar makes this otherwise predictable drama worthwhile. Eggar is a cripple, stricken by polio in childhood, who is befriended by artist-thief David Hemmings. Their developing relationship is sensitively handled. (Dir: Eric Till, 101 mins.)

Walking Tall (1973)**½ Joe Don Baker, Elizabeth Hartman. A sanitized version of a real Tennessee sheriff, Buford Pusser, is still filled with enormous violence. Pusser did take a stand against his hometown syndicate-owned gambling operations, and one brutal beating from the mobsters almost cost him his life—it took 192 stitches to put his face back together. But director Phil Karlson, who said he wanted to make a picture in which people will learn respect for a decent lawman, has made a film which glorifies brutal conduct on the part of lawman Pusser. In any event, "Walking" was a huge commercial bonanza, grossing over 40 million dollars domestically. Hartman plays Pusser's wife who gets killed by the local mobsters. Written by producer Mort Briskin, who got the idea of doing the film after seeing a CBS News feature about Pusser reported by Roger Mudd. (Dir: Phil Karlson, 125 mins.)

Walking Tall, Part II (1975)** Bo Svenson, Luke Askew, Noah Beery. Continuation of the "true" story of Tennessee sheriff Buford Pusser takes over precisely where part one left off. Lawman-extraordinaire Pusser, now played by Bo Svenson, attempts to track down the man who killed his wife in an ambush which left him severly wounded. Efforts to eradicate Pusser keep coming, but the clever sheriff always seems to avoid trouble. Bo Svenson is as convincing as possible under the circumstances. Not quite as violent as "Walking" #1. (Dir: Earl Bellamy, 109 mins.)

Wall of Death (British, 1951)** Laurence Harvey, Maxwell Reed. A motorcycle rider and a boxer are both in love with the same girl. Thin plot, some suspenseful motorcycle sequences.

Wall of Fury (German, 1962)*½ Tony Sailer, Richard Goodman. Jilted mountain climber causes plenty of trouble for his two companions during an attempt to climb the Alps. Some spectacular Alpine photography here, but a trite plot slows things up. Dubbed in English.

Wall of Noise (1963)**½ Suzanne Pleshette, Ty Hardin, Dorothy Provine. A tough look at horse racing and the people who are closely involved in that world. The story starts off promisingly, but unfortunately, it soon reverts to romantic soap opera with the two female leads vying for Hardin's masculine charms. (Dir: Richard Wilson, 112 mins.)

Wallflower (1948)*** Robert Hutton, Joyce Reynolds. Pleasant little comedy about a "wallflower" who blossoms out very neatly and gets involved in a scandal. Edward Arnold is particularly good in this one. (Dir: Frederick de Cordova, 77 mins.)

Walls Came Tumbling Down (1946)*** Lee Bowman, Marguerite Chapman. Columnist investigates the death of a priest, becomes involved in murder and stolen paintings. Well written, entertaining mystery. (Dir: Lothar Mendes, 82 mins.)

Walls of Fear (French, 1962)** Mouloudji, Louise Carletti, Francis Blanche. Partisan hiding from the Gestapo in an asylum has trouble proving he's not insane. Good idea for a suspense thriller dissipated in routine treatment; rates fair. Dubbed in English.

Waltz of the Toreadors (British, 1962)*** Peter Sellers, Margaret Leighton. Whimsical tale of a crusty retired general, and his ever-present, ever-elusive love. Not quite what it should be, but as a carryover from the original play, has a certain charm and the acting is first rate. Frequently intellectually stimulating. (Dir: John Guillermin, 105 mins.)

Wanted for Murder (British, 1946)**½ Eric Portman, Roland Culver, Dulcie Gray, Kieron Moore. While Scotland Yard searches for a demented strangler, a girl falls for him. Competent thriller with the music, Portman's acting being noteworthy. (Dir: Lawrence Huntington, 95 mins.)

Wanted: The Sundance Woman (1976)**½ Katharine Ross, Stella Stevens. Katharine Ross repeats her "Butch Cassidy and the Sundance Kid" role of Etta Place in this TV feature which picks up where the blockbuster movie left off. Ms. Ross is quite good as Sundance's woman, who has to revert to the life of a fugitive every time a Pinkerton detective gets wind of her trail. The film is bolstered by good location photography and a colorful supporting performance by Hector Elizondo as the charismatic Pancho Villa. Far better than a previous TV film entitled "Mrs. Sundance," which had Elizabeth Montgomery in the leading role. Made-for-TV. (Dir: Lee Philips, 105 mins.)

Wanton Contessa, The (Italian, 1954) ** Alida Valli, Farley Granger. Tragic drama of a noblewoman who sacrifices her marriage when she loves a handsome but cowardly young officer. Beautifully photographed, lavishly produced, otherwise murky, slow moving. Dubbed in English. Alternate title: "Senso." (Dir: Luchino Visconti, 90 mins.)

War and Peace (1956)*** Audrey Hepburn, Henry Fonda, Mel Ferrer. Tolstoy's classic tale is clumsily brought to the screen with the stress on spectacle and romance. The meat of Tolstoy's narrative about the Russian aristocracy during Napoleon's march on Europe is translated into Hollywood terms and the result is an over-long (3½ hrs.) ornate costume epic. Some of the performances, mostly by the supporting cast, come off better than the stars. If you don't mind all the icing, this may hold your interest. (Dir: King Vidor, 208 mins.)

War and Peace (Russian, 1968)***½ Ludmila Savelyeva, Sergei Bondarchuk. Here's the epic over-6-hour-long, multimillion-dollar Russian film adaptation of the great Tolstoy novel. It offers some of the grandest spectacle ever to be put on the screen. Compared to the U.S. version made some years ago with Henry Fonda and Audrey Hepburn in the leading roles, this film is vastly more faithful to the original and obviously more complete. Russia's most popular director, Sergei Bondarchuk, also plays one of the leading roles, that of Pierre, and Natasha Rostov is played by Ludmila Savelyeva. As an epic, few films can even touch it. (373 mins.)

War Arrow (1954)** Maureen O'Hara, Jeff Chandler. An action-filled western with a predictable plot. Chandler arrives at a Texas cavalry garrison to train Seminole Indians for the purpose of quieting a Kiowa uprising. In between drilling the Redskins, he falls for redheaded Miss O'Hara. (Dir: George Sherman, 78 mins.)

War Between the Tates, The (1977) Elizabeth Ashley, Richard Crenna, Annette O'Toole. Elizabeth Ashley is unquestionably the star of this film adaptation of Alison Lurie's novel about Mrs. Tate and her war with Mr. Tate over his ridiculous affair with Wendy, a cloying flower child of the 60s. Wendy is luminously played by Annette O'Toole. Uneven and tiresome as this film is, Elizabeth Ashley's Mrs. Tate is wonderfully appealing. Made-for-TV. (Dir: Lee Philips, 104 mins.)

War Drums (1957)** Lex Barker, Joan Taylor, Ben Johnson. Apache chief takes a Mexican girl for his wife, hopes against hope for peace among his brave brothers and the white man. Meandering western drama has a plot too big for the low budget. (Dir: Reginald Le Borg, 75 mins.)

War Game, The (Great Britain, 1965) **** Enormously powerful "staged" documentary about the horrors of nuclear war after a missile attack. Cleverly, perhaps manipulatively, combines simulated newsreels and various street interviews with a bland narrative. This disturbing, searing short film was made for BBC-TV but not shown by them on TV. A powerful anti-war statement. Written and directed by Peter Watkins. (50 mins.)

War Gods of Babylon (Italian, 1962) *½ Howard Duff, Jackie Lane. Tragedy when two brothers clash over a girl, defying the decree of the gods. Dull costume drama dubbed in English.

War Hunt (1962)***½ John Saxon, Robert Redford. An off-beat war film with good acting to recommend it. John Saxon does very well as a young soldier in the Korean war who loses his perspective and begins to enjoy killing. Robert Redford is also effective as a young private who sees

through Saxon's heroics. (Dir: Denis Sanders, 81 mins.)

War Is Hell (1964)**½ Tony Russell, Baynes Barron. Soldier on Korea patrol stops at nothing, including murder, to grab his share of glory. Grim and violent war drama packs a punch in its own small way. (Dir: Burt Topper, 81 mins.)

War Italian Style (Italian, 1965)*½ Buster Keaton, Martha Hyer. The great Keaton as a bumbling German general who allows two American marines to escape with secret battle plans. Keaton's genius wasted in this, his last film, though he does enliven the otherwise dreary proceedings. (Dir: Luigi Scattini, 74 mins.)

War Lord, The (1965)*** Charlton Heston, Richard Boone, Rosemary Forsyth, Maurice Evans. Governor of a coastal village in 11th-century England falls in love with a local girl, which starts many conflicts, leading to tragedy. Costume spectacle with some intelligence in production, direction, and script—for a change. Well done, with excellent performances. (Dir: Franklin Schaffner, 123 mins.)

War Lover, The (1962)**½ Steve McQueen, Robert Wagner, Shirley Ann Field. While it stays in the air, this story of a reckless and unlikable hotshot pilot is graphically absorbing. On the ground, the trite love story involving pilot, copilot, and an English girl is for the birds. Good performances by McQueen and Wagner. (Dir: Philip Leacock, 105 mins.)

War of Children, A (1972)*** Vivien Merchant, Jenny Agutter. Often poignant drama on the agonizing war between Catholics and Protestants in northern Ireland. James Costigan writes about the emergence of blind hate and the departure of all reason from a sweet Catholic Belfast housewife, after her husband is carted off to prison for a small act of friendship. Even the woman's pigeon-flying little son becomes infected by the ubiquitous hate, for author Costigan's plotting of a tricky situation spares no one. Made in Ireland. Made-for-TV. (Dir: George Schaefer, 73 mins.)

War of the Monsters (Japanese, 1968)* Kajiro Hongo, Kyoko Enami. Revel in camp as a stolen opal turns into Barugon, the 130-foot monster who is afraid of the water. Enter Gammera, just returned from Mars. Exit viewers, gone to sleep. (95 mins.)

War of the Wildcats (1943)*** John Wayne, Martha Scott. Ex-cowpuncher fights an oil tycoon for the rights to Indian oil lands. Good melodrama of the oil boom days; plenty of action. (Dir: Albert S. Rogell, 102 mins.)

War of the Worlds, The (1953)*** Gene Barry, Ann Robinson. Magnificent special effects make this sci-fi thriller fascinating. Simple plot about the earth battling an invasion from Mars, but the trickery's the thing. Meat for fantasy fans. (Dir: Byron Haskin, 85 mins.)

War Paint (1953)*** Robert Stack, Joan Taylor. Cavalry detachment experiences treachery and danger when they try to deliver a peace treaty to an Indian chief. Exciting outdoor drama has plenty of action, a good story. (Dir: Lesley Selander, 89 mins.)

War Wagon, The (1967)*** John Wayne, Kirk Douglas, Howard Keel. Good, action-filled western with John Wayne playing an ex-con who is bent on revenge for being framed and robbed of his gold-yielding land. The ingredients are familiar for western fans and they won't be disappointed when Wayne teams up with two-fisted Kirk Douglas to steal the gold shipment being transported in a specially armored stage known as the War Wagon. (Dir: Burt Kennedy, 101 mins.)

Warlock (1959)*** Richard Widmark, Henry Fonda, Anthony Quinn, Dorothy Malone. Gunfighter is hired by a town to wipe out outlaws; afterward his own rule is challenged by a cowboy who helped him clean up. Sprawling western has too many plot threads going at the same time, but good performances make it all interesting. (Dir: Edward Dmytryk, 121 mins.)

Warm December, A (Great Britain-U.S., 1972)*½ Sidney Poitier, Esther Anderson, Yvette Curtis. A black "Love Story," and the fatal illness is sickle-cell anemia. You may die of sugar overdose before this romantic tale is quite finished. Poitier, in his second directorial effort, fares better in front of the camera, and he's chosen a beautiful and evidently talented actress,

Esther Anderson, to play the object of his affections. Once again Poitier offers black protagonists who aren't full of rage against Whitey, snorting dope, or committing murder. He's proud of that and maybe it's almost enough for some audiences. Poitier plays an American doctor who visits London. Written by Lawrence Roman. (Dir: Sidney Poitier, 103 mins.)

Warning from Space (Japanese, 1963) *½ Creatures from space try to warn earth of a collision with another planet, but get a cold reception. Some clever effects in this English-dubbed sci-fi thriller, but the rest is rather childish.

Warning Shot (1967)**½ Tough, slick, hard-hitting detective yarn with a series of fine performances by a cast of pros—Lillian Gish, Eleanor Parker, Joan Collins, Walter Pidgeon, George Sanders, Ed Begley, George Grizzard—plus the able playing of star David Janssen. Janssen's a police detective who shoots a seemingly respectable doctor in the line of duty and finds himself in hot water up to his badge. (Dir: Buzz Kulik, 100 mins.)

Warpath (1951)** Edmond O'Brien, Polly Bergen, Dean Jagger. A routine western yarn with enough action to satisfy "cowboys and Indians" fans. The plot has Edmond O'Brien riding a trail of revenge for the murder of his fiancee. The big scene comes at the finale when the Sioux attack the fort. (Dir: Byron Haskin, 95 mins.)

Warrendale (Canadian, 1967)**** One of the most powerful and shattering documentaries ever made. A record of the unique treatment offered to emotionally disturbed teenagers at an innovative treatment center in Warrendale, Ontario. Produced and directed by Allan King, this early cinema verite entry is remarkable in many ways. King had to get to know the psychiatric staff and the committed children so they would trust him and, hopefully, come to ignore King and his ever-present camera crew. The treatment involves encouraging the disturbed children to honestly deal with and express all their emotions while the staff literally hugs and holds the youngsters during their fits of frenzy and abuse, the warmth and body contact being, ultimately, reassuring and comforting. You'll hear a lot of profanity from young children, but this is one of the most deeply human and compassionate films you'll ever see. Made for Canadian TV, which initially refused to telecast the film because of the profanity. Black and white. (100 mins.)

Warrior Empress, The (Italian, 1960) *½ Kerwin Mathews, Tina Louise. The beauteous Sappho falls in love with and aids a rebel leader, but both are victims of treachery. Lavish sets and a silly script. More sappy than Sappho. (Dir: Pietro Francisci, 87 mins.)

Warriors, The (1955)**½ Errol Flynn, Joanne Dru, Peter Finch. Flynn swashbuckles his way to lovely Joanne Dru's boudoir and kills many tyrants on the way. Lavish sets and costumes make things easier to watch. (Dir: Henry Levin, 85 mins.)

Warriors Five (Italian, 1962)**½ Jack Palance, Giovanna Ralli, Serge Reggiani. Four Italian liberated prisoners aid an American paratrooper in carrying out sabotage during World War II. Made in Italy and dubbed in English, this war story has several good suspenseful scenes, is well cast, has an ample share of action. (Dir: Leopoldo Savona, 85 mins.)

Washington Story (1952)** Van Johnson, Patricia Neal, Louis Calhern. Writer is assigned to do a hatchet-job on the capital and selects a sincere young Congressman as her target. Well-meant but mild, rather dry drama. (Dir: Robert Pirosh, 81 mins.)

Wasp Woman, The (1960)* Susan Cabot, Anthony Eisley. Ridiculous horror film about a cosmetic firm head who turns into the wasp woman. Grade "Z" film fare.

Wastrel, The (1962)*½ Van Heflin, Ellie Lambetti. Italian-Greek production with good acting but an inept script about the life of a man relived as he struggles for survival after a shipwreck.

Watch on the Rhine (1943)**** Paul Lukas, Bette Davis. A sensitive dramatic adaptation of Lillian Hellman's moving play. Although the war is over there's still a wealth of dramatic power in this story of a German underground leader who brings his family to the U. S. and finds himself almost helplessly trapped by the Nazis while in the U. S. (Dir: Herman Shumlin, 114 mins.)

Watch the Birdie (1951)**½ Red Skelton, Arlene Dahl, Ann Miller. Typical Red Skelton comedy. Red's fans will enjoy his crazy antics as a photographer who focuses on trouble. There's a wild chase sequence at the end that makes up for any shortcoming the film might have. (Dir: Jack Donohue, 70 mins.)

Watch Your Stern (Great Britain, 1960)*½ Kenneth Connor, Eric Barker. Farcical takeoff on the British Navy; two "limeys" become quick-change con artists when they bungle an official mission. Made by the "Carry On" farceurs, the film has some good lines, and the situations develop unrelentingly. But the comedy gets distended, the jokes corny. (Dir: Gerald Thomas, 88 mins.)

Waterhole No. 3 (1967)*** James Coburn, Carroll O'Connor, Joan Blondell. An attempt to make a zany western that succeeds more than half the time. Colburn is a roguish adventurer who is after a hidden cache of gold. He isn't the only one, as it turns out. Carroll O'Connor's performance is a help too, as is Joan Blondell's, playing the proprietress of a busy bordello. (Dir: William Graham, 95 mins.)

Waterloo (Italy-U.S.S.R., 1970)*½ Rod Steiger, Christopher Plummer, Jack Hawkins, Orson Welles, Virginia McKenna. Despite a lavish budget, the use of the Russian army (20,000 men and 3,000 horses), and the directorial talents of epic film-maker Sergei "War and Peace" Bondarchuk, this production of Napoleon's escape from exile, rise to power and subsequent defeat by the combined forces of England, Austria, Prussia and Russia is a Waterloo for everyone except Christopher Plummer. Steiger offers a ludicrous, overdrawn portrayal of the charismatic French general, while Plummer is Byronic as the victorious Wellington. If you're a devotee of huge, sprawling movie battle scenes, please watch the last hour or so if you're not aready asleep. It concentrates almost entirely on the historic battle of June 18, 1815. Banal screenplay by H. A. L. Craig and director Bondarchuk. A spectacle without a point of view toward anything. (Dir: Sergei Bondarchuk, 123 mins.)

Waterloo Bridge (1940)******* Vivien Leigh, Robert Taylor. The ladies will eat this one up. Miss Leigh is superb as the ballet dancer who falls in love with a soldier and turns to the primrose path when she believes him dead. Send the men out for this one. (Dir: Mervyn Le Roy, 103 mins.)

Waterloo Road (British, 1945)******* John Mills, Stewart Granger. An Army private leads everyone a merry chase when he goes AWOL after learning his wife has been seeing an oily rogue. Fast, suspenseful comedy-drama, good fun. (Dir: Sidney Gilliat, 77 mins.)

Watermelon Man (1970)****½** Godfrey Cambridge, Estelle Parsons, Howard Caine. When insurance salesman Jeff Gerber wakes up in his suburban home, he's startled to find he's turned black overnight! That's the intriguing premise of this uneven comedy which features Godfrey Cambridge as the average racist who must endure the indignities of being a black American. The laughs are broad, but the energies of Melvin Van Peebles, who not only directed but scored the music and produced the film, shine through. Thought-provoking satire that's not above using vaudeville jokes to entertain. Script by veteran author Herman Raucher ("Summer of '42"). (Dir: Melvin Van Peebles, 100 mins.)

Watusi (1959)****** George Montgomery, Taina Elg, David Farrar. Slightly altered remake of the highly successful African adventure "King Solomon's Mines." This attempt fails in comparison and offers no surprises in the routine trek through the jungle in search of cached treasure. (Dir: Kurt Neumann, 85 mins.)

Way Ahead, The (British, 1944)*****½** David Niven, Stanley Holloway. A group of civilians are drafted into the infantry during World War II, serve bravely in North Africa. Excellently acted, authentic war drama. (Dir: Carol Reed, 91 mins.)

Way of a Gaucho (1952)****** Rory Calhoun, Gene Tierney. A slow-moving tale of the people who live in the untamed Argentine territory during the end of the 19th century. There's love, jealousy and murder thrown into this melodrama. (Dir: Jacques Tourneur, 91 mins.)

Way of Youth, The (French, 1960)****½** Françoise Arnoul, Bourvil, Alain Delon. During the Occupation, a father finds his son has been having an affair with a woman whose husband is a prisoner of war. Slow, fairly interesting drama of wartime moral problems. Good performance by Bourvil as the father. Dubbed in English. (Dir: Michel Boisrond, 81 mins.)

Way Out West (1936)******** Stan Laurel, Oliver Hardy. This is the great slapstick pair's version of a western, as Stan and Ollie help a young girl who is being cheated out of her inheritance. Lots of funny gags, better direction than usual—all in all, perhaps their best film; and a must for Laurel and Hardy fans. (Dir: James W. Horne, 70 mins.)

Way to the Gold, The (1957)****** Barry Sullivan, Sheree North, Jeffrey Hunter. Moderately suspenseful chase drama concerning a young convict who is the only one who knows where a fortune in stolen gold is hidden. The supporting cast includes veteran Walter Brennan and he's better than the stars. (Dir: Robert D. Webb, 94 mins.)

Way We Were, The (1973)******** Barbra Streisand, Robert Redford, Bradford Dillman, Lois Chiles. The charismatic appeal of the two stars makes this film an appealing and occasionally touching love story, despite a lot of flaws in the script. Forget the over-simplified political content as Streisand chases, catches and loses her "gorgeous goyishe guy." Barbra's a college leftist in the late thirties and . . . never mind just sit back and enjoy the two of them together, drunk or sober in and out of bed. (Dir: Sydney Pollack, 118 mins.)

Way West, The (1967)****** Kirk Douglas, Robert Mitchum, Richard Widmark, Lola Albright. The fine novel by A. B. Guthrie, Jr., has been turned into a hackneyed, disappointing saga of a wagon train on the great trek to Oregon in the 1840's. Good cast helps a little but not enough. (Dir: Andrew V. McLaglen, 122 mins.)

Wayward Bus, The (1957)****½** Joan Collins, Jayne Mansfield, Dan Dailey, Rick Jason. John Steinbeck's novel about a group of people who take a short bus ride in California makes an occasionally interesting film. Miss Mansfield plays it straight for a change as a former bubble dancer who wants to go legit and she's not bad. Dan Dailey is ideally cast as the heavy-drinking travelling salesman with a gift of gab. Joan Collins and Rick Jason have some torrid love scenes. (Dir: Victor Vicas, 90 mins.)

Wayward Wife, The (Italian, 1952) *½ Gina Lollobrigida, Gabriele Ferzetti. Girl with a past finds her newly married life threatened by blackmail. Mediocre English-dubbed drama, except for the visual interest of Lollo's curves. (Dir: Mario Soldati, 91 mins.)

W. C. Fields and Me (1976) *** Rod Steiger, Valerie Perrine, John Marley, Milt Kamen, Jack Cassidy, Bernadette Peters. The "Me" in the title is Fields' mistress for the last fourteen years of his life, played by Valerie Perrine, and based upon a book by Carlotta Monti who did indeed live with the legendary comic for many years. Some of the film is maddening, some touching, funny and poignant. Rod Steiger is, for him, remarkably restrained, giving an interpretation of Fields rather than trying to imitate or mimic the master. Some detaiils are falsified to make Fields less repellent and cruel than he really was. There are some droll touches involving Fields' pals, including John Barrymore. As a Fields worshipper, I'd rather have this flawed tale of the surly genius than none at all. Uneven screenplay by Bob Merrill. (Dir: Arthur Hiller, 110 mins.)

We Are All Murderers (French, 1957) **** Raymond Pellegrin, Mouloudji. Youth with three strikes against him is tried and convicted for murder. Moving plea against capital punishment, extremely well directed. A disturbing and rewarding film. (Dir: Andre Cayette, 113 mins.)

We Are In the Navy Now (British, 1962) *** Kenneth More, Lloyd Nolan, Joan O'Brien. Whacky comedy about a naval officer who continually gets himself into hot water, is bounced from post to post, finally winds up hero of a revolution. Nicely played, some funny moments. (Dir: Wendy Toye, 102 mins.)

We Are Not Alone (1939) ***½ Paul

Muni, Jane Bryan. Beautiful, sensitive adaptation of the James Hilton novel superbly played by Paul Muni, Jane Bryan and Flora Robson. This story, because its prime interest is characters and their motivations, plays more like a fine teleplay than a movie. (Dir: Edmund Goulding, 120 mins.)

We Live Again (1934) **½ Fredric March, Anna Sten. Only fairly interesting drama based on Tolstoy's "Resurrection." A good deal of the blame for this film can be placed on director Rouben Mamoulian's shoulders—he manages to slow things down to a halt in many spots. (Dir: Rouben Mamoulian, 90 mins.)

We Shall Return (1963) * Cesar Romero, Linda Libera. Anti-Castro planter flees Cuba with his family, discovers one of his sons is pro-regime and ready to betray his brother. Sincere but inept topical drama.

We Were Dancing (1941) ** Norma Shearer, Melvyn Douglas. Contrived rehash of some Noel Coward one-act plays has flashes of wit, is well played but not entertaining. (Dir: Robert Z. Leonard, 94 mins.)

We Were Strangers (1949) **½ Jennifer Jones, John Garfield, Pedro Armendariz. Despite the powerhouse cast, this movie about political intrigue and revolution in Cuba during the 30's is a disappointment. (Dir: John Huston, 106 mins.)

Weapon, The (British, 1957) **½ Steve Cochran, Lizabeth Scott. Boy flees after accidentally shooting a playmate. Fairly suspenseful melodrama. (Dir: Hal E. Chester, 80 mins.)

Web, The (1947) *** Edmond O'Brien, Ella Raines, William Bendix. Tight and exciting melodrama about a bodyguard who kills his boss's arch enemy only to find himself involved in a double-cross. Good script and fine performances. (Dir: Michael Gordon, 87 mins.)

Web of Evidence (British, 1957) **½ Van Johnson, Vera Miles. A man's search to find out about his father. Good performances by the American stars and a competent supporting cast add to the film's interest. (Dir: Jack Cardiff, 88 mins.)

Web of Fear (French, 1964) ** Michele Morgan, Claude Rich, Dany Saval. Woman hides a murderer in her apartment, becomes a blackmail victim. Ordinary melodrama with a predictable plot. Dubbed in English. (Dir: Francois Villiers, 92 mins.)

Web of Passion (French, 1961)** Madeleine Robinson, Jean-Paul Belmondo, Antonella Lualdi. Mysterious girl next door threatens to disrupt an unhappy family until she's suddenly murdered. Intricate whodunit is visually dazzling, obscure in plot development, unsympathetic in characterization. Dubbed in English. Alternate title: "Leda." (Dir: Claude Chabrol, 101 mins.)

Web of Suspicion (British, 1957)** Susan Beaumont, Philip Friend. Man has to prove his innocence when all the evidence points to his guilt. Ordinary suspense drama.

Wedding Night, The (1935)*** Gary Cooper, Anna Sten, Ralph Bellamy. Tenderly played drama about a cosmopolitan gentleman who falls in love with a simple Connecticut farm girl, very well defined by Anna Sten. Film holds up well for today's audiences. (Dir: King Vidor, 90 mins.)

Wedding of Lili Marlene, The (British, 1955)* Lisa Daniely, Hugh McDermott. Talented entertainer finds a jealous leading lady trying to ruin her career. Poor romance, sequel to an equally weak film.

Weddings and Babies (1958)***½ Viveca Lindfors, John Myhers. Momentary, moody affair involving a photographer and a model, both past the age of tender young love. Filmed amid spontaneous New York City activity, this critically acclaimed but neglected feature is worth seeing. (Dir: Morris Engel, 81 mins.)

Wednesday's Child (Great Britain, 1971)***½ Sandy Ratcliff, Bill Dean, Grace Cave, Malcolm Tierney. A harrowing, deeply moving film that is directed like a documentary about a mentally disturbed young woman and her family, but is a fictional story based on a 1967 BBC teleplay by David Mercer called "In Two Minds." Director Ken Loach elicits remarkable performances from a non-professional cast. There are some real questions raised about the nature of the counseling and psychiatric help she gets but, leaving that and a few other captious quibbles aside, this is a riveting, rewarding low-budget entry, superbly directed by Ken Loach, remembered for his lovely "Kes." (108 mins.)

Wee Geordie (British, 1955)***½ Bill Travers. Charming comedy about a skinny Scottish boy who grows up into a big, brawny man after sending for a "British Charles Atlas" body building correspondence. Travers is perfect, and gets good support from a marvelous cast which includes Alastair Sim. (Dir: Frank Launder, 93 mins.)

Wee Willie Winkle (1937)*** Shirley Temple, Victor McLaglen. Shirley practically stops a war in India's Khyber Pass as part of the plot in this overly sentimental tale of garrison life in India. Shirley's fans will love it—others beware. (Dir: John Ford, 100 mins.)

Weed of Crime, The (Japanese, 1964)** Makoto Sato. Narcotics inspector goes after a dope syndicate. Routine crime drama, with its locale the main attraction. Dubbed in English.

Weekend (France-Italy, 1967)***½ Mireille Darc, Jean-Pierre Kalfon, Jean-Pierre Leaud, Jean Kanne. One of director Jean-Luc Godard's most daring and disturbing diatribes against the bourgeois, capitalist societies of the West, including his native France. "Weekend" starts out focusing on a car ride of a young couple heading for the countryside and the apathy, anger, and violence they see along the way. They eventually become political guerrilas. Some vignettes are ambitious and exploring, others heavy-handed and repetitive, but "Weekend" is an often astonishing tract about the malaise of modern industrial man. Written and directed by Jean-Luc Godard. (103 mins.)

Weekend at the Waldorf (1945)**½ Ginger Rogers, Lana Turner, Van Johnson, Walter Pidgeon. A lot of good talent in a contrived variation of Vicki Baum's "Grand Hotel" using New York's Waldorf as a setting. (Dir: Robert Z. Leonard, 130 mins.)

Weekend for Three (1941)*** Dennis O'Keefe, Jane Wyatt, Philip Reed. Newlyweds are troubled by a weekend guest who is attracted to the wife. Amusing comedy has good dialogue, pleasant players. (Dir: Irving Reis, 61 mins.)

Weekend in Havana (1941)**½ Alice Faye, Carmen Miranda, Cesar Romero. Another musical made at the time Latin American music was catching on. Routine, passable musical.

Weekend, Italian Style (1968)★★ Sandra Milo, Enrico Maria Salerno. Fair Italian feature about a marriage that has to test its durabiliy in order to survive. Bored housewife is off to an Adriatic resort for fun in the sun and her businessman husband shows up soon after, bringing along his jealousy.

Weekend Nun, The (1972)★★½ Joanna Pettet, Vic Morrow, Ann Sothern. Based on a true story about Joyce Duco, a former nun who served in an experimental program in which she donned civilian clothes and functioned as a juvenile probation officer by day, returning to the convent each night. Miss Pettet, in the difficult title role, manages to project a combination of naivete and a straightforward sense of duty to her new tasks. Miss Duco is no longer a nun. Made-for-TV. (Dir: Jeannot Szwarc, 78 mins.)

Weekend of Terror (1970)★★ Lee Majors, Robert Conrad, Lois Nettleton. A kidnap yarn with gimmicks to sustain interest. Robert Conrad and Lee Majors play a couple of desperate criminals whose kidnap victim accidentally dies, forcing them to snatch a substitute in order to collect the ransom. As it turns out, along come three nuns with auto trouble and the plot thickens. It's all a fairly predictable made-for-TV yarn but the cast is okay, particularly Lois Nettleton as a vacillating nun who figures most prominently in the scheme of the hoods. (Dir: Jud Taylor, 73 mins.)

Weekend with Father (1952)★★½ Van Heflin, Patricia Neal, Gigi Perreau. Well acted comedy about a widower and a widow who combine their families when they decide to marry and watch the strange reactions of their offspring. Fast paced and good dialogue. (Dir: Douglas Sirk, 83 mins.)

Weird Woman (1944)★★½ Lon Chaney, Evelyn Ankers. Chaney comes home with a tropic bride, raised in the South Seas, and finds himself in trouble with an old girl friend. Okay melodrama, helped by good production. (Dir: Reginald Le Borg, 64 mins.)

Welcome Home, Johnny Bristol (1972)★★½ Martin Landau, Jane Alexander. Perplexing drama that should pique your curiosity. Landau is very good as Johnny Bristol, an army captain who returns to the U.S. after having been a prisoner in Vietnam for two years, and discovers there's no trace of the town in Vermont where he grew up. Miss Alexander has the thankless role of the nurse who falls for Johnny ; and Forrest Tucker, in a well-written supporting role, is effective. Made-for-TV. (Dir: George McCowen, 99 mins.)

Welcome Stranger (1947)★★★½ Bing Crosby, Barry Fitzgerald. Young carefree doctor arrives to take over practice of conservative country doctor, and thereby hangs this flimsy story. Performances, however, make it a delightful entertainment. (Dir: Elliott Nugent, 107 mins.)

Welcome to Arrow Beach (1974)★ Laurence Harvey, Joanna Pettet, Stuart Whitman. The late Laurence Harvey's last film, which he also directed, is a ponderous melodrama with bad performances. Harvey is a weirdo who picks up a young girl and takes her to his beach home which he shares with his sister. The nightmare begins! Dull script by Wallace C. Bennett. (Dir: Laurence Harvey, 108 mins.)

Welcome to Hard Times (1967)★★½ Henry Fonda, Janice Rule, Aldo Ray. With a little more care and a better script this interesting western drama could have been a class film. However it gets bogged down in its effort to mix psychology and basic cowboy film ingredients. Henry Fonda plays a leading citizen of "Hard Times" who doesn't stand up to a crazed gunman, played with dripping evil by Aldo Ray. A better than average supporting cast helps things along. (Dir: Burt Kennedy, 104 mins.)

Welcome to L.A. (1976)★★★ Keith Carradine, Sally Kellerman, Geraldine Chaplin, Lauren Hutton, Sissy Spacek. A very promising debut from young (32) writer-director Alan Rudolph about "The City of One-Night Stands," which is the subtitle for the movie. This poetic vision of loneliness and disinterest is fragmented and flawed, but it emerges as one of the most illuminating films ever made about Hollywood and the mystique of movie-Lotus land. An innovative, ambitious film, produced by Robert Altman. A lot of Altman's movie stock company are in "Welcome." People tumble in and out of bed without really connecting in any meaningful way with their partners, but director Rudolph does often connect with his audience. (Dir: Alan Rudolph, 106 mins.)

Well, The (1951)**** Richard Rober, Barry Kelley. Mob violence flares when a child disappears; however, the town bands together when she is discovered trapped in a well. Breathless, gripping drama, excellent in all departments. (Dirs: Leo Popkin, Russell Rouse, 85 mins.)

We'll Bury You (1961)**½ Okay documentary tells of the rise of Communism. Contains little unfamiliar material. Should have been much better in all particulars.

Wells Fargo (1937)*** Joel McCrea, Bob Burns, Frances Dee. This is a "super" western about the beginnings of the famous company that transports money. Some good adventure but it's heavy with romance and plot. (Dir: Frank Lloyd, 120 mins.)

We're No Angels (1955)**½ Humphrey Bogart, Aldo Ray, Peter Ustinov, Joan Bennett. Three escaped convicts from Devil's Island take over the store of a French shopkeeper, right some wrongs. Comedy has its amusing scenes, but the stage origin is too evident in its talkiness, lack of movement. (Dir: Michael Curtiz, 106 mins.)

We're Not Married (1952)***½ Ginger Rogers, Fred Allen, Marilyn Monroe, Mitzi Gaynor, David Wayne. Five couples are informed that their marriages are not legal. Episodic comedy with some sequences better than others—but the Fred Allen-Ginger Rogers section is a comedy gem. All in all, superior fun. (Dir: Edmund Goulding, 85 mins.)

Werewolf in a Girls' Dormitory (European, 1963)* Barbara Lass, Carl Schell. Members of the staff of a school are suspected when a series of murders occur. English-dubbed horror flub. (Dir: Richard Benson, 84 mins.)

Werewolf of London (1935)**½ Henry Hull, Warner Oland. Leisurely but interesting chiller. A doctor, bitten by a werewolf, turns into a fiend. Good performances by Hull and Oland make this yarn worth staying with, despite the slow spots. (Dir: Stuart Walker, 75 mins.)

West of the Pecos (1945)**½ Robert Mitchum, Barbara Hale. Cowboy saves a meat packer's daughter, disguised as a boy, from bandits. Pleasing, well made western.

West Point Story, The (1950)** James Cagney, Doris Day, Gordon MacRae, Virginia Mayo. Corny musical comedy about a Broadway director who stages a big revue at West Point. It's a delight though to see James Cagney hoofing again. (Dir: Roy Del Ruth, 107 mins.)

West Point Widow (1941)**½ Anne Shirley, Richard Carlson. Nurse marries an Army football star, but the secret union is in jeopardy when she is about to become a mother. Slight romantic tale receives occasional witty dialogue, pleasing performers.

West Side Story (1961)**** Natalie Wood, Rita Moreno, Richard Beymer, George Chakiris, Russ Tamblyn. The celebrated Broadway musical masterpiece about rival white and Puerto Rican gangs in a New York ghetto becomes a spectacular movie musical. Jerome Robbins' brilliant choreography in this modern Romeo and Juliet story is enhanced greatly by the magnificent New York City location photography and the cast is very good. In addition, the familiar score by Leonard Bernstein and Stephen Sondheim hasn't diminished in quality or effectiveness since it was first introduced on the stage. (Dir: Robert Wise, 155 mins.)

Westbound (1959)** Randolph Scott, Virginia Mayo. For Randolph Scott fans only. The leather faced cowboy gives another tight lipped performance in this predictable western. Virginia Mayo is a notch above the usual Scott leading lady. (Dir: Budd Boetticher, 72 mins.)

Western Union (1941)*** Randolph Scott, Robert Young, Dean Jagger. A good western based on the laying of the first transcontinental Western Union wire in 1861. (Dir: Fritz Lang, 94 mins.)

Westerner, The (1940)*** Gary Cooper, Walter Brennan, Dana Andrews. Good cowboy epic which tells the story of a dispute over land rights and the action taken by those who considered themselves in the right. Brennan plays Judge Roy Bean, who ran things his way—(he won an Oscar for his performance), (Dir: William Wyler, 100 mins.)

Westward the Women (1951)**½
Robert Taylor, Denise Darcel, John
McIntire. Rancher and his trail boss
lead some women on a 1500-mile
trek from Chicago to California as
prospective brides for the settlers
there. "Wagon Train" in skirts, this
outdoor saga has some impressive
moments, along with some dull ones.
Fairly good entertainment. (Dir:
William Wellman, 118 mins.)

Westworld (1973)*** Richard Benjamin, Yul Brynner, James Brolin.
An original, offbeat sci-fi story which
is fun to watch. Will cinema and
televised violence eventually do us
all in? Benjamin and Brolin are two
friends who come to a vacation spot
which offers the ultimate fantasy—
playing in such settings as Medieval-
world, Romanworld and Westworld. Each resort is equipped with
robots programmed to do your bidding and help you play out your secret dreams. The two robust 21st-
century men choose the wild-West
life, where they keep running into
Brynner, a robot gunman. Suddenly,
the robots start disobeying orders!
Written and directed by Michael
Crichton. (88 mins.)

Wet Asphalt (German, 1961)**½
Horst Buchholz, Martin Held, Marina Perschy. Young idealist has his
illusions shattered when the journalist he idolizes engages in distorting
the truth. Wet asphalt becomes
soggy drama.

What! (Italian, 1963)** Daliah Lavi,
Christopher Lee, Tony Kendall.
Grisly murders commence when a
dastardly brother returns to his castle after a long absence. Gothic
horror thriller dubbed in English is
overdone but should satisfy the fans.
Some chilling moments.

What a Life (1939)*** Jackie Cooper, Betty Field. The original Henry
Aldrich story about the high-school
boy who can't stay out of trouble.
A chance for all of us to go back
nostalgically to our high-school
days. Good fun.

What a Way to Go (1963)** Shirley
MacLaine, Paul Newman, Dick Van
Dyke, Robert Mitchum, Gene Kelly,
Dean Martin, Bob Cummings. Fair
comedy with MacLaine that adds up
to very little. Shirley's a simple
country girl who marries a succession of wealthy men. (Dir: J. Lee
Thompson, 111 mins.)

What Are Best Friends For? (1973)**
Lee Grant, Larry Hagman, Ted Bessell, Barbara Feldon. Wacky, implausible comedy about an immature
cuckold (Bessell) who finds a sanctuary with his best friends during
his period of adjustment. Enter a
liberated divorcee who talks as if
she was weaned on TV situation
comedies, and love finds a way.
Thankless roles for the quartet of
actors. Made-for-TV. (Dir: Jay
Sandrich.)

What Did You Do in the War, Daddy?
(1966)* James Coburn, Dick Shawn,
Harry Morgan. Another Hollywood
reminder—and a vulgar, distasteful
one at that—that war, this time WW
II in Sicily, is just a hilarious bunch
of chuckles and good clean fun for
everyone concerned. (Dir: Blake
Edwards, 119 mins.)

What Next, Corporal Hargrove?
(1945)**½ Robert Walker, Keenan
Wynn. Weak follow-up to the original. This is pure slapstick with
Hargrove over in France romancing
some French cuties. (Dir: Richard
Thorpe, 95 mins.)

What Price Glory? (1926)**** Victor
McLaglen, Edmund Lowe, Dolores
Del Rio. Superb saga of men at war,
a classic of the silent film genre,
based on the play by Laurence Stal-
lings and Maxwell Anderson. Eloquent anti-war drama, remarkable
for the outstanding performances of
McLaglen and Lowe as two tough
but human Marines fighting in the
trenches of World War I, and Del
Rio as the French country girl who
sparks their intense rivalry. Full of
humor and despair, with the battle
scenes surreal, stark and used spar-
ingly. The film's strength is in its
emphasis on character. (Dir: Raoul
Walsh, 120 mins.)

What Price Glory (1952)**½ James
Cagney, Dan Dailey, Corinne Calvet.
Although not as successful as the
original film classic of the same
title, this remake is greatly aided by
the robust performances of James
Cagney and Dan Dailey as hard
drinking, two-fisted soldiers stationed in France during World War
I. John Ford directed. (Dir: John
Ford, 111 mins.)

What Price Murder (French, 1957)
*** Henri Vidal, Mylène Demongeot.
A French drama of suspense that
leads to an exciting climax. Added
attraction is provocative Mylene

Demongeot. (Dir: Henri Verneuil, 105 mins.)

Whatever Happened to Aunt Alice? (1969)**½ Geraldine Page, Ruth Gordon, Mildred Dunnock. Here's another in the line of Grand Guignol mellers starring veteran actresses who can chew up the scenery and what little there is of the script as well. Ruth Gordon, as dotty as ever, is the prime victim of crazy Geraldine Page. It's all about housekeepers who keep disappearing after they are hired by Miss Page . . . get the picture? Produced by Robert Aldrich, who directed the '62 entry, "Whatever Happened to Baby Jane?" that started this series of horror stories starring some of cinema's grand dames. (Dir: Lee H. Katzin, 101 mins.)

Whatever Happened to Baby Jane? (1962)*** Bette Davis, Joan Crawford. Grand Guignol in the grand manner, with a chilling performance by Bette Davis as a faded former child movie star who lives in seclusion and gets kicks by mentally torturing her crippled sister. This unpleasant tale grips the attention. Virtuoso direction by Robert Aldrich, the performances of its stars, and an admirably nasty acting job in a supporting role by Victor Buono. (Dir: Robert Aldrich, 132 mins.)

What's a Nice Girl Like You . . . ? ** Brenda Vaccaro, Jack Warden, Vincent Price, Roddy McDowall. Passable comedy about a Bronx girl who poses as a socialite in an elaborate extortion plot. Made-for-TV. (Dir: Jerry Paris, 72 mins.)

What's New, Pussycat? (U.S.-France, 1965)**½ Peter Sellers, Peter O'Toole, Woody Allen, Romy Schneider, Ursula Andress, Paula Prentiss, Capucine, Louise Lasser, Richard Burton. Before Woody Allen found his stride as a triple-threat movie magician, he wrote and co-starred in this occasionally funny comedy, which rambles all over the place but never really jells. Sellers is a wacky psychiatrist; O'Toole is a tireless ladies' man; Woody is O'Toole's bumbling and hapless buddy; and Romy Schneider, Ursula Andress, Paula Prentiss and Capucine are various sexy women popping in and out of the boudoir. A faint glimmer of the Woody Allen films to come. Song, "Here I Am," sung by Dionne

Warwick. (Dir: Clive Donner, 108 mins.)

What's So Bad About Feeling Good? (1968)** George Peppard, Mary Tyler Moore. Silly, harmless little comedy about a bird which spreads a strange virus resulting in "instant happiness." The possibilities are fairly obvious and the film touches on most of them. The attractive stars, Peppard and Mary Tyler Moore and the able supporting cast, are merely stooges for their infectious feathered friends. (Dir: George Seaton, 94 mins.)

What's the Matter with Helen? (1971)**½ Debbie Reynolds, Shelley Winters, Dennis Weaver, Agnes Moorehead. Another in the long line of grande-dame, Grand Guignol dramas, which rely on the talents of actresses who enjoy rolling their eyes and going through the entire film looking as if they're trying to be Bette Davis' "Baby Jane." In this outing, Helen is Shelley Winters, and she's a super-loony who, along with Debbie Reynolds, moves to Hollywood when their sons become involved in a Leopold-Loeb type of murder. It gets pretty hairy, and sometimes scary. Written by Henry Farrell, author of "What Ever Happened to Baby Jane?" (Dir: Curtis Harrington, 101 mins.)

What's Up, Doc? (1972)*** Barbra Streisand, Ryan O'Neal. Director Peter Bogdanovich was weaned on the screwball comedies of Howard Hawks and Ernst Lubitsch, and here is his valentine to the genre—not totally successful but often daffy fun. Streisand almost single-handedly manages to keep the outrageous plot bubbling along. She's a college coed and O'Neal, with glasses, is cast as the proverbial absent-minded professor (Cary Grant is sorely missed). They meet in a series of misadventures leading to the flagrantly outlandish, derivative car chase. (Dir: Peter Bogdanovich, 90 mins.)

What's Up, Tiger Lily? (1966)*** Woody Allen, Lovin' Spoonful. The background of this frequently funny and always wacky film is every bit as crazy as the film itself. The zany Mr. Allen wrote some incongruous English dialogue to accompany a magnificently photographed Japanese ('64) spy story which just happened to be a terrible film without any prospect of a profitable release in the U.S. This juxtaposition of original footage with a new soundtrack has been done before, but a lot of this is quite wild, if you're in the mood for this kind of a romp. (80 mins.)

Wheeler and Murdock (1972)*½ Jack Warden, Christopher Stone. An unsold pilot about private eyes which was no worse or better than many that made it as a series. Jack Warden is his usual solid, dependable presence as the older and firmer half of a detective partnership, and younger, swinging Christopher Stone fills the bill as the other half. The plot deals with some Mafia money. Predictable. Made-for-TV. (Dir: Joseph Sargent, 73 mins.)

Wheeler Dealers, The (1963)*** James Garner, Lee Remick. Zany comedy about an oil tycoon who comes to New York to raise money for some drilling, runs across a pretty stock analyst. Witty dialogue, performances by a cast filled with funsters like Jim Backus, Phil Harris, John Astin, Louis Nye. (Dir: Arthur Hiller, 106 mins.)

When a Woman Ascends the Stairs (Japan, 1960)*** Hideko Takamine. A contemporary story, circa 1960, about a Japanese bar girl of the Ginza district in Tokyo. There are subtle touches in the performance of Hideko Takamine as Keiko, a woman who has managed to earn a living as a bar hostess for many years without having to sleep with the customers . . . until she succumbs to one, and then another and another. The scenes in the bar are contrasted nicely with vignettes involving Keiko's friends. (Dir: Mikio Naruso, 150 mins.)

When Comedy Was King (1962)***½ Compilation of scenes from various comedy films featuring the great talents of Charlie Chaplin, Harry Langdon, Fatty Arbuckle, Gloria Swanson, etc. For the nostalgic and those who never have been exposed to the giant comedy stars of yesterday. Quite entertaining. (81 mins.)

When Eight Bells Toll (Great Britain, 1971)** Anthony Hopkins, Robert Morley, Jack Hawkins. Failed attempt to fashion a stylish action picture features a plodding script by Alistair MacLean, and the waste of a superb British cast. Clichés center on Hopkins' underwater search for

786

stolen bullion. (Dir: Etienne Perier, 94 mins.)

When Hell Broke Loose (1958)** Charles Bronson, Violet Rensing. Racketeer in the army has a rough time until the love of a German girl reforms him. Good performance by Bronson in an ordinary war drama. (Dir: Kenneth Crane, 78 mins.)

When I Grow Up (1951)***½ Robert Preston, Martha Scott, Bobby Driscoll. His parents fail to understand a mischievous youngster, until the grandfather takes a hand and straightens things out. Very good drama of a boy's problems, handled with insight and care. (Dir: Michael Kanin, 80 mins.)

When in Rome (1952)**½ Van Johnson, Paul Douglas. During the Holy Year 1950, a con man swipes a priest's clothes, finds the outfit beginning to get him. Dated but fairly amusing comedy-drama, aided by good performances. (Dir: Clarence Brown, 78 mins.)

When Ladies Meet (1940)** Joan Crawford, Robert Taylor. Talky bit of nothing which tries to say that you shouldn't steal another woman's husband. A boring film. (Dir: Robert Z. Leonard, 108 mins.)

When Michael Calls (1971)*½ Elizabeth Ashley, Ben Gazzara, Michael Douglas. Limp thriller which has Miss Ashley receiving phone calls from a child who is supposedly dead, but who insists on avenging the murder of his mother. Made-for-TV. (Dir: Philip Leacock, 73 mins.)

When My Baby Smiles at Me (1948)**½ Betty Grable, Dan Dailey. "Burlesque," the play about a comic and his wife, has been set to music for this routine film. Really not too bad, but so routine. (Dir: Walter Lang, 98 mins.)

When the Boys Meet the Girls (1965)** Connie Francis, Harve Presnell, Herman's Hermits. The best thing about this remake of the Judy Garland–Mickey Rooney musical "Girl Crazy" is the songs, such as "I Got Rhythm," "Bidin' My Time," and "Embraceable You." The thin plot about a ranch on the verge of bankruptcy which is turned into a dude ranch, serves as a stage wait between musical numbers. The stars are best when vocalizing, and there's a large group of guest stars including Liberace, Louis Armstrong, Sam the Sham and The Pharaohs. (Dir: Alvin Ganzer, 110 mins.)

When the Daltons Rode (1940)*** Randolph Scott, Kay Francis, Brian Donlevy. Good old-fashioned Western with plenty of action. Supporting players make it better than average. (Dir: George Marshall, 80 mins.)

When the Girls Take Over (1962)* Jackie Coogan, Robert Lowery, James Ellison. Unfunny farce about attempts to oust a bearded revolutionist from a Caribbean republic.

When the Legends Die (1972)**** Richard Widmark, Frederic Forrest, Luana Anders. Lovely, understated, perceptive story about a young Indian boy who leaves his reservation to try his luck on the rodeo circuit under the aegis of his hard-drinking guardian (Widmark). Old pro Widmark has never been better, playing the deteriorating con man who is genuinely fond of his maturing charge, Tom Black Bull, played well, if impassively, by newcomer Forrest. Special tribute must be paid to the tact and restraint of director Stuart Millar, who makes an impressive debut. From the lovely opening scenes of mountainous Colorado, there's hardly a false note in this poignant story, which features some quite marvelous shots, including slow-motion sequences, of rodeo riding. (105 mins.)

When the North Wind Blows (1974)** Dan Haggerty, Henry Brandon. Another in the line of nature dramas produced by the company which gave us "Grizzly Adams." This time, the plot centers around an old trapper who hides in the wilderness and befriends wild animals, after accidentally wounding a young boy. Dan Haggerty, TV's "Grizzly Adams," plays a villager who tries to convince him to come back. (Dir: Stewart Raffill, 108 mins.)

When Tomorrow Comes (1939)**½ Irene Dunne, Charles Boyer, Barbara O'Neil. A tear jerker for the women; Charles Boyer falls in love with Irene Dunne and understandably asks her to go to Paris with him despite the fact that he is already married. (Dir: John M. Stahl, 100 mins.)

When Willie Comes Marching Home (1950)*** Dan Dailey, Corinne Calvet. Delightful and somewhat touching film about a West Virginian lad

who goes into the Army (World War II) and has a series of adventures including an interlude with a beautiful French underground leader. (Dir: John Ford, 81 mins.)

When Worlds Collide (1951)** Barbara Rush, Richard Derr. The race is on to build a rocketship in order to leave earth when two astral bodies head in its direction. Trick work effective, in contrast to the routine plot. Okay for sci-fi fans. (Dir: Rudolph Mate, 81 mins.)

When You're Smiling (1950)**½ Frankie Laine, Jerome Courtland, Lola Albright. Fairly amusing musical comedy about the ups and downs of the record business. Frankie Laine gets a chance to sing several songs.

Where Angels Go—Trouble Follows! (1968)** Rosalind Russell, Stella Stevens. A sequel to Roz Russell's earlier tedious film "The Trouble With Angels," in which she played Mother Superior of St. Francis Academy for Girls. This second outing has Roz, representing the old line religious leadership, opposing new ideas in the person of young nun, Sister George (Stella Stevens). It's contrived and overly cute, but if this is what you're in the mood for, by all means tune in. (Dir: James Neilson, 95 mins.)

Where Do We Go from Here (1945) *** Fred MacMurray, June Haver. This fantasy deserves an "A" for effort but a "B" for performance. Fred takes us through a cavalcade of American history as a genie grants his request to be in the Army but puts him in the wrong one. Score by Kurt Weill and Ira Gershwin helps. (Dir: Gregory Ratoff, 77 mins.)

Where Eagles Dare (1969)**½ Richard Burton, Clint Eastwood. Supercharged superheroics are served up in this adventure yarn about a dangerous mission during World War II. Agents Burton and Eastwood are pawns in the tale; they take turns performing incredible feats against impossible odds, attempting to free an important American officer being held prisoner in one of those supposedly escape-proof prisons. A good round of cliff-hanging exploits. (Dir: Brian G. Hutton, 158 mins.)

Where Have All the People Gone? (1974)** Peter Graves, Verna Bloom, Michael-James Wixted. Another disaster movie, fairly well handled. Concerns a radioactive explosion and the virus it causes, decimating the population and leaving only a few survivors. Among the living are archeologist Steven Anders (Graves) and his children, who come down from the mountain and meet a disturbed woman (Bloom). Made-for-TV. (Dir: John L. Moxey, 72 mins.)

Where It's At (1969)****½** David Janssen, Robert Drivas, Rosemary Forsyth. Fairly entertaining comedy examining a father-son relationship which at best is offbeat. Dad is David Janssen who runs a Las Vegas casino-hotel and his son (Drivas) is a college student with a different set of moral and ethical standards. When they meet in Vegas, Garson Kanin's script has them clashing in their efforts to understand one another. A parade of Las Vegas types dots the scene, but Brenda Vaccaro's slightly dumb secretary is tops. Garson Kanin's first directorial effort since "Tom, Dick and Harry" in '41. (97 mins.)

Where Love Has Gone (1964)***½** Susan Hayward, Bette Davis, Mike Connors. An embarrassingly bad sex drama based on Harold Robbins' novel about a famous sculptress whose lover is stabbed to death. Bette Davis plays Miss Hayward's socially prominent mother, and Miss Davis and Miss Hayward seem to be engaged in a contest to see who can give the worst performance. (Dir: Edward Dmytryk, 114 mins.)

Where the Boys Are (1960)****½** Dolores Hart, George Hamilton, Yvette Mimieux, Connie Francis, Paula Prentiss. Or, what college boys and girls do in Fort Lauderdale while on vacation. Combination of songs, comedy, and drama will be best appreciated by the teenage set. (Dir: Henry Levin, 100 mins.)

Where the Bullets Fly (British, 1966)***½** Tom Adams, Dawn Addams. Inept spy spoof with Tom Adams playing a James Bond type of super agent who is so super cool in the face of every disaster—and one calamity crops up every five minutes. (Dir: John Gilling, 88 mins.)

Where the Hot Wind Blows (Italian, 1960)****** Melina Mercouri, Gina Lollobrigida, Marcello Mastroianni, Yves Montand. Gifted director Jules Dassin bombed with this one. A melodrama about the decadence of a small town from the peasants to the aristocracy. Good cast wasted in banal theatrics. English dubbed. (120 mins.)

Where the Lilies Bloom (1974)******** Julie Gholson, Jan Smithers, Harry Dean Stanton. A lovely, gentle, and altogether superior film for children and adults alike, produced by Robert B. Radnitz (who produced the memorable "Sounder"). Filmed on location in rural North Carolina, the touching story is about four children orphaned when their father dies. The plucky 14-year-old daughter (Gholson) assumes command of the household, which consists of an older sister and a younger brother and baby sister. She conspires to keep the news of her father's passing from her neighbors for months. Screenplay, without a false note, written by Earl Hamner, Jr., based on the prize-winning novel by Vera and Bill Cleaver. Uniformly fine acting and the sympathetic direction of William A. Graham make this one of the most rewarding family films in years. (97 mins.)

Where the Red Fern Grows (1974)****½** James Whitmore, Beverly Garland, Jack Ging, Stewart Petersen. Family fare that borrows liberally from Disney. Stewart Petersen is a young lad who wants nothing more than to own and train redbone hounds to be the best coon hunters in the county. He almost gets his wish. James Whitmore is quite good as the boy's philosophizing grandpa. (Dir: Norman Tokar, 108 mins.)

Where the Sidewalk Ends (1950)****** Dana Andrews, Gene Tierney. Melodrama about a police detective whose reputation for being rough with criminals backfires when he accidentally kills a murder suspect. The situation is complicated by the fact that the interest ends before either the film or the sidewalk. (Dir: Otto Preminger, 95 mins.)

Where the Spies Are (1965)******* David Niven, Francoise Dorleac. Diverting and frequently clever spy tale with a rather good performance by David Niven as a doctor recruited for espionage service. Although this is hardly a James Bond adventure, Niven manages to acquit himself admirably against all the contrived obstacles the writers have placed in his way. One obstacle, Francoise Dorleac, is as appealing as any of the advertised scenery. (Dir: Val Guest, 110 mins.)

Where There's Life (1947)*** Bob Hope, Signe Hasso, William Bendix. Disc jockey becomes ruler of foreign kingdom in this zany Hope film that will appeal mainly to Bob's most ardent fans, and the youngsters. (Dir: Sidney Lanfield, 75 mins.)

Where Were You When the Lights Went Out? (1968)* Doris Day, Robert Morse, Terry-Thomas, Steve Allen. Someone was bound to make a film based on the big Eastern Seaboard blackout of 1965, and it's been turned into another vapid Doris Day comedy. It's a bedroom farce with everyone running around and mugging outrageously. (Dir: Hy Averback, 95 mins.)

Where's Charley? (British, 1952)**** Ray Bolger, Allyn McLerie, Robert Shackleton. The musical version of the classic British farce "Charley's Aunt." Broadway hit boasts music and lyrics by Frank Loesser, and old and young alike will enjoy catching Ray Bolger in his show-stopper "Once in Love with Amy." (Dir: David Bulter.)

Where's Poppa? (1970)***½ George Segal, Ruth Gordon, Trish Van Devere, Ron Leibman. Wild, imaginative farce about a bachelor (Segal) scheming to eliminate his aging mother. Director Carl Reiner is a deft hand with sight gags, and there's one uproarious sequence where Leibman, playing Segal's brother, is "mugged" in Central Park, gets booked for assault, only to be released from the police station after getting a bunch of flowers from a grateful cop. It'll be a long time before the unexpurgated version of this bawdy romp ever shows up on home-screen TV. You may argue about whether or not "Poppa's?" all in good taste, but there's no denying that much of it is very funny indeed. Septuagenarian scene-stealer Ruth Gordon is a joy.

Wherever She Goes (Australian, 1951)**½ Muriel Steinbeck, Suzanne Parrett. This true story of famed pianist Eileen Joyce, who rose to recognition from a childhood filled with hardship. Production shortcomings, a sincere film with fine musical interludes played by Miss Joyce.

Which Way to the Front? (1970)**

Jerry Lewis grinds these slapstick efforts out like hamburger. The comedy was left in the trenches. (96 mins.)

Whirlpool (1949)*** Gene Tierney, Richard Conte, Jose Ferrer. Suspenseful drama dealing with blackmail, hypnosis, and murder. Jose Ferrer delivers a fine portrayal as a villainous charlatan. (Dir: Otto Preminger, 97 mins.)

Whirlpool (British, 1959)*½ Juliette Greco, O. W. Fischer. Shady lady fleeing from a murder charge finds refuge on a barge. Tedious melodrama, with only the Rhine locations of interest.

Whiskey and Sofa (German, 1961)** Maria Schell, Karl Michael. Pretty architect enters a competition, plans to beat out her rival, who is a notorious wolf. Thin romantic comedy, nothing unusual. Dubbed in English.

Whispering Footsteps (1943)***½ John Hubbard, Rita Quigley. A bank clerk fits the description of a mad killer, and his friends turn against him in fear and distrust. Excellent suspense melodrama deserves credit for such a neat job done on a small budget.

Whispering Ghosts (1942)** Milton Berle, Brenda Joyce. Milton gets a few laughs out of this film but not enough for success. He's out to solve a sea captain's murder and recover some buried treasure. (Dir: Alfred L. Werker, 75 mins.)

Whispering Smith (1949)*** Alan Ladd, Robert Preston, Brenda Marshall. Railroad detective finds his best friend is in with bandits. Good western is nicely made, actionful. (Dir: Leslie Fenton, 88 mins.)

Whistle at Eton Falls (1951)**½ Lloyd Bridges, Dorothy Gish. Union leader suddenly finds himself as manager of a plant, with the necessity of laying off men. Sincere but talky, rather slow drama. (Dir: Robert Siodmak, 96 mins.)

Whistle Down the Wind (British, 1962) **** Hayley Mills, Alan Bates. An almost perfect film about a trio of children who find an escaped criminal in their barn and mistake him to be Christ. Miss Mills and Alan Bates, as the convict, give excellent performances. Touching, honest, wonderfully directed and altogether recommended. (Dir: Bryan Forbes, 98 mins.)

Whistling in Brooklyn (1943)**½

Red Skelton, Ann Rutherford. Another in the fairly amusing comic detective series with Red again playing "The Fox." There's a lot of laughs in the scene where Red pitches against the Dodgers. (Dir: S. Sylvan Simon, 87 mins.)

Whistling in Dixie (1942)**½ Red Skelton, Ann Rutherford. Red's fans and the kids will like this mystery-comedy set in some old southern mansions and abandoned forts.

Whistling in the Dark (1940)*** Red Skelton, Ann Rutherford. Red's first starring film and his fans will have a lot of fun with it. He's in the hands of killers and imprisoned in one of those Hollywood houses complete with sliding doors and hidden passageways. (Dir: S. Sylvan Simon, 77 mins.)

White Banners (1938)*** Claude Raines, Fay Bainter, Jackie Cooper. Miss Bainter's magnificent acting makes something out of this Lloyd C. Douglas morality fable. Very talky. (Dir: Edmund Goulding, 100 mins.)

White Cargo (1942)** Hedy Lamarr, Walter Pidgeon. Boring tale of an Englishman who succumbs to a lovely native girl. Hedy is Tondelayo and she is gorgeous. (Dir: Richard Thorpe, 90 mins.)

White Christmas (1954)*** Bing Crosby, Danny Kaye, Rosemary Clooney, Vera-Ellen. Colorful package of holiday entertainment for the whole family—songs, dances, clowning, plus Irving Berlin's title tune. The cast fits perfectly into the lightweight story which merely serves as a framework for the 15 musical numbers. (Dir: Michael Curtiz, 120 mins.)

White Cliffs of Dover, The (1943)*** Irene Dunne, Van Johnson. Well acted, occasionally slow but moving story of an American girl who marries an English lord in 1914. He dies in 1918 and the story, based on Alice Duer Miller's poem "The White Cliffs," follows her life in England. (Dir: Clarence Brown, 126 mins.)

White Corridors (British, 1952)*** Googie Withers, James Donald. Researcher is accidentally infected with disease germs, asks a lady doctor to try a new test on him. Behind-the-scenes medical drama showing routine in a hospital is well done; good performances, subplots tied together nicely.

White Feather (1955)** Robert Wagner, Debra Paget, Jeffrey Hunter. Routine western with some action scenes for cowboys-and-Indians fans. Wagner plays a government man who tries to get a tribe of Cheyenne to move to a reservation. Debra Paget and blue-eyed Jeff Hunter play Indians. (Dir: Robert D. Webb, 102 mins.)

White Heat (1949)***½ James Cagney, Virginia Mayo, Edmond O'Brien. Exciting, taut, brutal gangster melodrama with Cagney reverting to type as a heartless killer. This is not for the squeamish for it is a realistic study of a hood. (Dir: Raoul Walsh, 114 mins.)

White Huntress (British, 1957)** Susan Stephen, Robert Urquhart. Good on-location photography in Kenya helps bolster this routine adventure about ivory hunters and their plans to cheat the natives.

White Lightning (1973)**½ Burt Reynolds, Jennifer Billingsley, Ned Beatty, Louise Latham. The whole is less than the sum of its parts, which offer some sparkling moments in this fast-paced melodrama about murder, revenge and moonshine in the new South. Reynolds is a convict who's released in order to help the Feds nail sadistic-sheriff Beatty. (Dir: Joseph Sargent, 101 mins.)

White Line Fever (1975)*** Jan-Michael Vincent, Kay Lenz, Slim Pickens, L. Q. Jones. Sensitive treatment of a young trucker's troubles at fighting corruption in his profession. Forced to smuggle contraband goods, Air Force vet-turned-independent-trucker Vincent rebels and is faced with an onslaught of reprisal against himself and his pregnant wife. Skillful direction makes the violence grimly realistic and Vincent's struggle credible. Imaginatively directed by Jonathan Kaplan. (89 mins.)

White Nights (Italian, 1959)** Maria Schell, Marcello Mastroianni, Jean Marais. Despite this stellar line-up, this turgid melodrama fails to generate any excitement. Miss Schell is cast as a very mixed-up creature who has two men's love. The photography strains for artistic effects and only adds to the confusion. (Dir: Luchino Visconti, 94 mins.)

White Slave Ship (Italian, 1962)**

Pier Angeli, Edmund Purdom. Mutiny on a prison ship carrying girls from London jails en route to the colonies. A young doctor, also a prisoner, aids the captain in quelling it. Passable costume adventure dubbed in English. (Dir: Silvio Amadio, 92 mins.)

White Spider, The (German, 1963)*½ Joachim Berger, Karin Dor, Horst Frank. Master sleuth tracks down a murder ring that leaves a spiderlike charm in the hands of its victims. It leaves nothing for the audience however.

White Sun of the Desert, The (Russian, 1972)* Clumsy old-fashioned nonsense about Russian peasant farmer returning to the land and his sturdy wife after years of the struggle for "liberation." The revolutionary platitudes seem particularly absurd in this dubbed version, as spoken by a born New Yorker. "Desert" is an arid film. (Dir: V. Motyl.)

White Tie and Tails (1946)**½ Dan Duryea, Ella Raines, William Bendix. A screwy comedy about a butler who takes charge of his employer's mansion when his employer goes on vacation. Deft performances. (Dir: Charles Barton, 81 mins.)

White Tower (1950)*** Glenn Ford, Valli, Claude Rains. Six people risk their lives to scale the Swiss Alps. Thrilling mountain climbing melodrama.

White Warrior, The (Italian, 1959)*½ Steve Reeves, Georgia Moll. Brave tribal chieftain fights against the Czar's troops and battles treachery within his own ranks—and a silly plot, bad English-dubbing, stilted acting, etc. (Dir: Riccardo Freda, 86 mins.)

White Witch Doctor (1953)**½ Robert Mitchum, Susan Hayward, Walter Slezak. Top Bwana (Mitchum) and his not so trusty second (Slezak) set out with titian-haired nurse (Hayward) into the darkest regions of Bakuba territory. Sweet Susan wants to bring the magic of modern medicine to the hostile savages, but Bad Bob and Wicked Walter are more interested in finding a hidden treasure of gold. The locale and action help some. (Dir: Henry Hathaway, 96 mins.)

Who Are You, Mr. Sorge? (French, 1960)***½ Jacques Berthier, Thomas Holtzman. Lengthy but frequently fascinating account of the master spy who played both ends against the middle in working for the Russians and the Germans and was involved in obtaining the secret of Japan's attack on Pearl Harbor. Real-life story is superior to most fictional ones. Dubbed in English.

Who Does She Think She Is? (1974)**½ "She" is Rosalyn Drexler, and to anyone unfamiliar with her novels, plays and paintings, this documentary's title may seem to be an appropriate question, given the evidence presented here. Drexler, seen improvising scenes for a low-budget movie, at home with her family, and singing at a small New York City nightclub, appears alternately petulant and serious. But, through the chaos, enough glimpses of wit and intelligence are seen to convince us that Newsweek editor Jack Kroll was right when he said: "Her essential insight is that people and things are completely insane, and she speaks from inside the whale." (Dirs: Patricia Lewis Jaffe, Gaby Rodgers, 60 mins.)

Who Done It? (1942)*½ Bud Abbott & Lou Costello, Don Porter. For Abbott & Costello fans only; trite murder mystery about a real murder occurring during a mystery show broadcast. (Dir: Erle C. Kenton, 75 mins.)

Who Is the Black Dahlia? (1975)**½ Lucie Arnaz, Efrem Zimbalist, Jr., Macdonald Carey, Donna Mills. Sensational 1947 Los Angeles murder is exhumed and receives fairly interesting treatment. Lucie Arnaz stars as the mixed-up, movie-struck girl who ends up a corpse in a vacant lot. Efrem Zimbalist, Jr., portrays detective Harry Hansen, a patient man who must check out every nut in Los Angeles, the many would-be confessors to the lurid crime. Made-for-TV. (Dir: Joseph Pevney, 100 mins.)

Who Killed Mary Whats'ername? (1971)** Red Buttons, Sylvia Miles, Alice Playten. The murder of a Greenwich Village prostitute leads former lightweight champion, now diabetic Red Buttons, out of the boredom of retirement to play amateur sleuth. Good cast is wasted on a screenplay whose main ingredient is plot loopholes. (Dir: Ernie Pintoff, 90 mins.)

Who Killed Teddy Bear? (1965)**

Sal Mineo, Juliet Prowse, Jan Murray, Elaine Stritch. Sexually psychotic busboy preys on disco dancer, as cop trails. Low-key direction creates a portrait of obsession, with some suspense. (Dir: Joseph Cates, 90 mins.)

Who Slew Auntie Roo? (U.S.-British, 1971)**½** Shelley Winters, Mark Lester, Ralph Richardson. Another in the line of "who" films casting flamboyant actresses as macabre, slightly mad ladies in gothic tales. It's Shelley Winters this time as an American widow living in a large house in England who takes her cue from the wicked witch in "Hansel and Gretel" and tries to lure young children into her lair. It gets pretty silly at times, but Miss Winters rolls her eyes and shrieks with the best of them, and young Lester ("Oliver") is an intelligent child actor, not prone to overplaying. (Dir: Curtis Harrington, 91 mins.)

Who Was Maddox? (British, 1964)** Bernard Lee, Jack Watling, Suzanne Lloyd. Executive rivalry at a publishing house leads to blackmail, murder, and robbery. Ordinary Edgar Wallace mystery.

Who Was That Lady? (1960)**½** Tony Curtis, Dean Martin, Janet Leigh. Fast-paced comedy romp that fizzles out before the finale. Tony Curtis and Dean Martin play men-about-town, one married and one not, and their adventures lead to complications found only in French farces—especially those based on bad Broadway musicals. (Dir: George Sidney, 115 mins.)

Whole Town's Talking, The (1935) *** Edward G. Robinson, Jean Arthur. Meek, white collar worker is mistaken for Public Enemy No. 1. Excellent 1935 comedy-drama is still fairly entertaining. (Dir: John Ford, 90 mins.)

Whole Truth, The (British, 1958)** Stewart Granger, Donna Reed, George Sanders. A who-dun-it with very little suspense. Plot concerns an actress' murder which is pinned on an American producer whose wife refuses to believe he did it. (Dir: John Guillermin, 84 mins.)

Whole Truth, The (German, 1961)** Peter Van Eyck. Prosecutor of a brutal murder case suddenly finds himself a defendant. Average drama dubbed in English.

Whole World Is Watching, The (1969)

** Burl Ives, Joseph Campanella, James Farentino, Hal Holbrook. Still another pilot film for a TV series. Ives, Campanella, and Farentino play a trio of lawyers, each with a different temperament and style. They take on the defense of a leader of a college student uprising arrested for the murder of a campus policeman. There are numerous scenes in which the students and the faculty get to air their views, but no sensible conclusions emerge. (Dir: Richard Colla, 97 mins.)

Who's Afraid of Virginia Woolf (1966) **** Elizabeth Taylor, Richard Burton, Sandy Dennis, George Segal. Edward Albee's brilliant, biting play about the love-hate relationship between a middle-aged, resigned college professor and his vitriolic, denigrating, yet seductive wife is turned into a movie experience to be cherished. It's a cinematic feast thanks to Mike Nichols' astute direction; Elizabeth Taylor's towering portrayal as the foul-mouthed Martha (the best performance of her career so far); Richard Burton's magnificent portrait of the tortured professor; Sandy Dennis' Oscar-winning performance as the nervous young bride; and to a lesser degree George Segal's playing of Sandy Dennis' teacher-husband. (Dir: Mike Nichols, 129 mins.)

Who's Been Sleeping in My Bed? (1963)**½** Dean Martin, Elizabeth Montgomery, Carol Burnett. The kind of movie that often looks better on TV than it did originally in theaters. It's about a TV idol whose fiancé wants to get him hitched before his affinity for the girls becomes too strong. Carol Burnett in her first movie role has an hilarious scene near the end. The dialogue and situations are frequently amusing, and the supporting cast includes some fine performers. (Dir: Daniel Mann, 103 mins.)

Who's Got the Action? (1963)**½** Dean Martin, Lana Turner, Walter Matthau. All the familiar jokes and characters involved in the world of a compulsive horseplayer are trotted out in this occasionally diverting comedy. Lana Turner and Dean Martin are around as attractive window dressing, but Walter Matthau steals the movie with his broad interpretation of an underworld biggie. The plot has Lana trying to curtail hubby Dean's out-of-hand betting habits by secretly joining forces with a bookie. (Dir: Daniel Mann, 93 mins.)

Who's Minding the Mint? (1967)*** Milton Berle, Joey Bishop, Jack Gilford, Walter Brennan, Dorothy Provine, Jim Hutton. One working comic named Howard Morris has directed a zany, spirited romp that capitalizes on the performing talents of a large bunch of his second banana pals. For those of you who care about the plot, Jim Hutton plays a charming young man who works in the U. S. Mint. When he accidentally burns a large batch of new bills, he sets up an operation to replace them. The kids will enjoy this farce and the grown-ups too, if you're in the mood for this kind of good clean fun. Jack Gilford, an extraordinarily funny man, too long wasted by Hollywood film makers, is marvelous playing a hard-of-hearing safecracker. (Dir: Howard Morris, 97 mins.)

Who's Minding the Store? (1963)*½ Jerry Lewis, Jill St. John, John McGiver. Jerry's uncritical fans will get a few forced laughs from his antics as a department store flunky who's in love with the boss' daughter (Jill St. John). It's all pretty labored, but there is one funny scene as Jerry sells some shoes to a muscular lady wrestler. (Dir: Frank Tashlin, 90 mins.)

Why Bother to Knock? (British, 1961) ** Elke Sommer, Richard Todd. Young man on the make indiscriminately gives out keys to his apartment, but all the girls show up at the same time. Lumbering comedy wastes the talents of a fine cast. Some amusing moments, but not enough. (Dir: Cyril Frankel, 88 mins.)

Why Must I Die? (1960)*½ Terry Moore, Debra Paget. Artificial plea for abolishment of capital punishment. Miss Moore plays an innocent victim who is sentenced to die for murder on flimsy evidence. The acting is absurd and detracts from seriousness of the film. (Dir: Roy Del Ruth, 86 mins.)

Wichita (1955)**½ Joel McCrea, Vera Miles, Lloyd Bridges. Wyatt Earp is once again the lawman who western town which is overrun with brings law and order to a small outlaws. The cast is good and action fans will not feel cheated. (Dir: Jacques Tourneur, 81 mins.)

Wicked Drama of Paula Schultz, The

(1968)* Elke Sommer, Bob Crane, Werner Klemperer. Tasteless, claptrap comedy in which Elke Sommer stars as an Olympic athlete who finds herself the object of a cold-war ploy. The double entendres are worthy of grade-school snickers, and the actors, including "Hogan's Heroes" stars Crane and Klemperer, all overplay shamefully. (Dir: George Marshall, 113 mins.)

Wicked Go to Hell, The (French, 1956)* Marina Vlady, Henri Vidal, Serge Reggiani. In a just world, the wicked producers of this tedious drama would also wind up in hell.

Wicked Lady, The (British, 1946) **½ Margaret Lockwood, James Mason. Scheming woman takes over all the men who cross her path, eventually joins a highwayman as his aide. Theatrical costume drama is lifted a bit by Mason's tongue-in-cheek portrayal of a bandit. (Dir: Leslie Arliss, 98 mins.)

Wicked Ones, The—See: Teenage Wolf Pack

Wide Blue Road, The (Italian, 1957) *½ Yves Montand, Alida Valli. Fisherman illegally dynamites for his catch, which proves to be his downfall. Wide road, thin drama. (Dir: Gillo Pontecorvo, 100 mins.)

Widow (1976)**½ Michael Learned, Bradford Dillman, Farley Granger, Robert Lansing. Moderately absorbing drama based on Lynn Caine's autobiographical best-seller. Michael Learned plays the withdrawn widow attempting to cope with two young children, a lack of money, and a new suitor. Made-for-TV. (Dir: J. Lee Thompson, 98 mins.)

Wife Versus Secretary (1935)** Clark Gable, Jean Harlow, Myrna Loy. Title tells the whole story and, if it wasn't for its big name stars, this would have been an ordinary second feature. (Dir: Clarence Brown, 85 mins.)

Wild Affair, The (Great Britain, 1965) * Nancy Kwan, Terry-Thomas, Victor Spinetti, Bud Flanagan. Secretary decides to take a last fling before her marriage, ends up soused, and all wet besides. An inane exercise clumsily written and directed by John Krish. (88 mins.)

Wild and the Innocent, The (1959) **½ Audie Murphy, Sandra Dee, Gilbert Roland, Joanne Dru. Slightly offbeat story of a fur trader, a wild mountain waif and their misadventures in town during a Fourth of July celebration. Never quite makes the top grade but rates credit for a good try. (Dir: Jack Sher, 84 mins.)

Wild and the Willing, The (Great Britain, 1962)*½ Virginia Maskell, Paul Rogers, Ian McShane, Samantha Eggar. Lethargic tanglings, sexual and otherwise, between students and teachers at a small English university. Young people are attractive, but the movie is a deadly bore. Mordecai Richler co-authored this drivel, based on the play "The Tinker." (Dir: Ralph Thomas, 123 mins.)

Wild and Wonderful (1964)** Tony Curtis, Christine Kaufmann, Larry Storch. When a French poodle with a thirst for liquor is found by an American in Europe, and the owner's pretty daughter goes looking for the pooch—you have a typically uninspired light comedy. The poodle is cute. (Dir: Michael Anderson, 88 mins.)

Wild Angels, The (1966)* Peter Fonda, Nancy Sinatra. It's Peter Fonda on a motorcycle, long before his "Easy Rider." But this is a sleazy, savage shallow look at the toughs who roam in motorcycle gangs through Southern California. More junk from Roger Corman's trunk. (Dir: Roger Corman, 93 mins.)

Wild Bunch, The (1969)***½ William Holden, Ernest Borgnine, Robert Ryan. Balletlike violence on the Texas-Mexican border in 1913 with cynical band of outlaws vs. law, order, and the Mexican Army. Motorcars and machine guns are used in symbolic elegance as director Sam Peckinpah delivers a cinematic coup by turning on the audience to blood-gushing death and destruction. Rousing ending where the "bunch" try for a redeeming good deed and take on the Mexican Army. (135 mins.)

Wild Child, The (France, 1969)**** Jean-Pierre Cargol, Jean Daste, Francois Truffaut. An absolutely beautiful essay on teaching, and the giving, and eventually receiving, of love. "The Wild Child" is quite literally that—a baby abandoned in the woods of France and discovered years later, around 1797, by a local farmer. It does not do either film justice to suggest that this is a Gallic "Miracle Worker," but Truffaut's glorious film is every bit as moving

in its own way. Truffaut himself portrays, and very gracefully too, the dedicated Dr. Jean Itard, a Frenchman who undertook the formidable task of training the brutish child and later wrote a memoir about the case, published in Paris in 1806. Truffaut's story, based on Itard's journal, documents the learning process for both child and teacher. (Dir: Francois Truffaut, 90 mins.)

Wild Geese Calling (1941)** Henry Fonda, Joan Bennett. Set in 1890, this story of a man with the wanderlust is sensitively told but is a dull film. Sleep may call before the geese. (Dir: John Brahm, 77 mins.)

Wild Guitar (1962)* Arch Hall Jr., Cash Flagg, William Walters. Young rock-and-roll singer wants to make it in the field of big-time music. Inept drama with plenty of songs, little talent.

Wild Heart (1952)** Jennifer Jones, David Farrar. Wealthy man falls in love with a gypsy girl. Uneventful, unconvincing, vague drama; it misses. (Dirs: Michael Powell, Emeric Pressburger, 82 mins.)

Wild Heritage (1958)**½ Will Rogers Jr., Maureen O'Sullivan, Troy Donahue. Two pioneer families trek west to make their home in a new land, meet with many adventures along the way. Refreshing change from ordinary western fare moves leisurely but pleasantly. (Dir: Charles Haas, 78 mins.)

Wild in the Country (1961)** Elvis Presley, Hope Lange, Tuesday Weld. Rural boy is saved from delinquency by a female social worker, who encourages him in his writing talent. Wild in the country is boring at home. (Dir: Philip Dunne, 114 mins.)

Wild in the Streets (1968)***½ Christopher Jones, Shelley Winters, Hal Holbrook. Inventive, intelligent screenplay by Robert Thom about the fictitious takeover of the U.S. by a young rock singer who becomes the nation's first hip President (Chris Jones). The new head of the country sends everyone over 30 to concentration-type camps, including Mom (Shelley Winters), and there are other equally way-out plot developments. Provocative, rewarding drama. (Dir: Barry Shear, 97 mins.)

Wild Is the Wind (1957)*** Anna Magnani, Anthony Quinn, Anthony Franciosa. The ladies will like this soap opera, marinara-style. The trio of explosive stars do what they can to make this tale of love, marriage, and infidelity work, and they succeed most of the time. Plot: Quinn brings Miss Magnani from Italy to become his wife but doesn't figure on the attraction between Anna and his ward, Anthony Franciosa. (Dir: George Cukor, 114 mins.)

Wild 90 (1969)*½ Norman Mailer, Buzz Farber, Mickey Knox. If the sight of Norman Mailer struggling hard in a new medium and falling flat on his talented face is your idea of a good time, you might have fun with this self-indulgent item. (Dir: Norman Mailer.)

Wild North, The (1952)** Stewart Granger, Cyd Charisse, Wendell Corey. He-man adventure drama about fur trappers and their many fights with nature. Cyd Charisse is wasted as the love interest in a very small role. (Dir: Andrew Marton, 97 mins.)

Wild Ones, The (1954)***½ Marlon Brando, Mary Murphy, Lee Marvin. Brando gives a powerful performance as Johnny, leader of a motorcycle gang that invades a small town and raises havoc. The actors contribute to a striking film. (Dir: Laslo Benedek, 79 mins.)

Wild Party, The (1957)** Anthony Quinn, Carol Ohmart, Kathryn Grant. Former football hero on the skids joins a group of beatniks and holds a couple captive. Way-out drama features some hipster dialogue that's practically unintelligible but has some suspense. (Dir: Harry Horner, 81 mins.)

Wild Party, The (1974)**½ James Coco, Raquel Welch, Perry King. Chalk this one up as a good try that just didn't work. James Coco stars as a silent-movie comedy star down on his luck, trying for a comeback by giving a big party at which he plans to show his latest movie. The party turns into a wild, sexual free-for-all, and Coco's desperate comic ends up killing his mistress, played by Raquel Welch, and her latest male companion (Perry King). Loosely based on the real-life Fatty Arbuckle scandal which ruined the silent-film star's career. There's good acting here, especially by James Coco, and Welch. Raquel's musical number, "Singapore Sally," is a dilly. Baruch Lumet, director Sidney Lumet's father, appears as a tailor. (Dir: James Ivory, 100 mins.)

Wild Ride, The (1960)* Jack Nicholson, Georgianna Carter. Rebellious hot-rodder tries to break up a romance and brings tragedy to all concerned. Nasty little low-budget melodrama not worth the ride.

Wild River (1960)***½ Montgomery Clift, Lee Remick, Jo Van Fleet. An excellent film about the dramatic conflicts surrounding the Tennessee Valley Authority's efforts to build dams during the tail end of the depression years. Director Elia Kazan and a superb cast bring this period of recent history graphically to life. A vastly underrated film when it was first released. (Dir: Elia Kazan, 110 mins.)

Wild Rovers (1971)*** William Holden, Ryan O'Neal, Karl Malden. Holden's crisp, strong performance as a cowboy on the shady side of 50 makes this unusual western drama interesting. He and O'Neal make an unlikely pair as they team up for a bank robbery and the inevitable getaway trek to Mexico. There's a smattering of the expected western ingredients throughout but it's basically a character study of the old and young cowboy, united in their plight. (Dir: Blake Edwards, 106 mins.)

Wild Seed, The (1965)** Michael Parks, Celia Kaye. Young drifter befriends a teen-age girl running away from her foster parents; together they seek happiness. Slow-moving drama uses younger players to advantage, but the story's no help. (Dir: Brian Hutton, 99 mins.)

Wild Stallion (1952)**½ Ben Johnson, Edgar Buchanan, Martha Hyer. Orphan grows up obsessed with the idea of recapturing a wild stallion he lost as a boy. Pleasant outdoor drama, a welcome relief from the usual run western. (Dir: Lewis D. Collins, 72 mins.)

Wild Stampede (Mexican, 1962)** Luis Aguilar, Christiane Martel. Outlaws and revolutionaries fight for a valuable herd of wild horses. Passable outdoor action drama helped by picturesque photography. Dubbed in English.

Wild, Wild Planet (Italian, 1965)**½ Tony Russell, Lisa Gastoni. Complicated science fiction about a mad scientist. The deranged man likes to spend his time kidnapping specimens from Earth and grafting and transplanting. . . . English dubbing better than usual. (Directors: Anthony Dawson and Antonio Margheriti, 93 mins.)

Wild Women (1970)*½ Hugh O'Brian, Anne Francis, Marilyn Maxwell. Brave Hugh O'Brian, women stockade prisoners, and U.S. Army Engineers fight off Indians and Mexicans in this made-for-TV western, which leans heavily on comedy. Silent Hugh hasn't much to say while his band of ladies (Anne Francis, Marilyn Maxwell, Marie Windsor, Sherry Jackson, Cynthia Hall) drink, shoot and wisecrack, overplaying at every turn. (Dir: Don Taylor, 73 mins.)

Wild Youth (1960)*½ Robert Hutton, Steve Rowland, Carol Ohmart. Escapees from a prison camp team up with a dope peddler and his moll, with the police in hot pursuit. Lurid juvenile delinquency drama on the trashy side.

Wildcats on the Beach (Italian, 1962) ** Alberto Sordi, Rita Gam, Elsa Martinelli, Georges Marchal. Four separate stories taking place on the Côte d'Azur, European playground. Some amusing moments thanks to Sordi, but the plots are insignificant, the pace slow. Dubbed in English.

Will Penny (1968)***½ Charlton Heston, Joan Hackett, Donald Pleasence. Memorable, a quiet Western with action, not for action's sake, but growing out of the character development. . . . Saga of a saddle-worn cowboy (Heston) who tries to stay uninvolved and peaceful despite interfering circumstances. Joan Hackett registers strongly as a young frontier woman who wants to build a new life for her son and herself. There's also excellent photographs throughout. Underrated film which never got the attention it deserved, written and directed by Tom Gries. (109 mins.)

Will Success Spoil Rock Hunter (1957)**½ Tony Randall, Jayne Mansfield. Tony Randall's performance as a wildly unpredictable publicity agent is the best thing about this disjointed comedy based on the Broadway farce which prominently placed Jayne Mansfield in the public eye. (Dir: Frank Tashlin, 95 mins.)

Willard (1971)**½ Bruce Davison, Ernest Borgnine, Elsa Lanchester. Silly but nevertheless engrossing horror film about a deeply disturbed lad in his 20's who turns to rats for companionship, and then sets out to train them to do his bidding in order to avenge those he hates. It's overdrawn in many departments, but the chills are there. Those who cringe at the sight of one rat—picture an army of them. Not for the squeamish. (Dir: Daniel Mann, 95 mins.)

Willy Wonka and the Chocolate Factory (1971)*** Gene Wilder, Jack Albertson. Charming for the moppets. Based on a children's story by Roald Dahl, with a musical score by Anthony Newley and Leslie Bricusse. Gene Wilder plays Willy, a world-famous candy-maker who offers a prize of a lifetime supply of candy and a tour of his factory to five lucky kids. The fantasy, particularly the candy factory sequences, should entertain the kids. (Dir: Mel Stuart, 110 mins.)

Wilson (1944)**** Alexander Knox, Geraldine Fitzgerald. Biography of our World War I President is a powerful story, superbly performed and graphically proving his great philosophy and foresight. Film begins with Wilson at Princeton and follows him all the way to his futile attempts to make us part of the League of Nations. A "must." (Dir: Henry King, 154 mins.)

Winchester 73 (1950)*** James Stewart, Shelley Winters, Dan Duryea. Better than average western drama about a man who trails a man and a gun through a series of adventures until an old score is settled. Good performances by the entire cast. (Dir: Anthony Mann, 92 mins.)

Winchester 73 (1967)** Tom Tryon, John Saxon, Dan Duryea, John Drew Barrymore. Remade, revised version of the exciting Jimmy Stewart western lacks the tautness of the original. Story of a renegade after a valuable rifle moves sluggishly, is just another routine western. Made-for-TV. (Dir: Herschel Daugherty, 97 mins.)

Wind Across the Everglades (1958) **½ Burl Ives, Christopher Plummer, Gypsy Rose Lee. Unusual film about a game warden's life in the Florida Everglades during the turn of the century. The trouble with this film is that it can't make up its mind whether it's a comedy, a drama, or a comedy-drama. Good cast. (Dir: Nicholas Ray, 93 mins.)

Wind and the Lion, The (1975)*** Brian Keith, Candice Bergen, Sean

Connery. Based on a true incident, this sweeping drama plays more like fiction, and you'll be swept up by the adventure and pageantry. In 1904, President Teddy Roosevelt (Brian Keith in an overstated performance) sends Marines to Morocco to rescue an American widow (Candice Bergen) and her two children who have been kidnapped by a desert chieftain, played with dash by Sean Connery. Photography is excellent, the script sometimes funny and campy. Written by John Milius who also makes an auspicious directorial debut. (119 mins.)

Wind Cannot Read, The (Great Britain, 1958)**½ Dirk Bogarde, Yoko Tani, Ronald Lewis. Far Eastern color highlights uneven tale of British pilot in WW II and his romance with a Japanese woman training him for language duty. Bogarde and Tani are charming as the lovers. Together with the sensitive direction, they avoid many sentimental pitfalls in the trite plot. (Dir: Ralph Thomas, 115 mins.)

Windom's Way (British, 1958)*** Peter Finch, Mary Ure. Doctor in a remote Malay village tries to prevent the oppressed natives from going Communist. Absorbing drama with some food for thought. (Dir: Ronald Neame, 108 mins.)

Window, The (1949)***½ Bobby Driscoll, Arthur Kennedy, Ruth Roman. Child witnesses a murder, but no one will believe him. Terrifically tense, suspenseful melodrama. (Dir: Ted Tetzlaff, 73 mins.)

Window to the Sky, A—See: Other Side of the Mountain, The

Wing and a Prayer (1944)*** Don Ameche, Dana Andrews. Story of Navy pilots aboard a carrier and their wartime heroism is a good action drama, well acted and directed. (Dir: Henry Hathaway, 97 mins.)

Winged Victory (1944)***½ Lon McCallister, Jeanne Crain, Edmond O'Brien. Moss Hart's stirring tribute to the Air Corps is a well done and entertaining film. You'll get a kick out of watching the all-airmen cast (except for the girls) in action. Watch for Peter Lind Hayes, Red Buttons, Gary Merrill, Barry Nelson and Lee J. Cobb. (Dir: George Cukor, 130 mins.)

Wings (1927)**** Clara Bow, Charles Rogers, Richard Arlen, Gary Cooper, Hedda Hopper. One of the most exciting silent dramas, featuring some of the best aerial photography and dogfighting to be seen in any film. About American pilots in World War I. Cooper is seen briefly but to good advantage, and Clara Bow gets to Europe as a driver to be near her boyfriend. Both director William A. Wellman and screenwriter John Monk Saunders were veterans of the Lafayette Escadrille unit which fought in Europe and their firsthand knowledge and concern for the courageous air pilots greatly aid this enduring entry. (Dir: William A. Wellman, 130 mins.)

Wings and the Woman (British, 1942)*** Anna Neagle, Robert Newton. Story of Jim and Amy Mollison, renowned airplane pilots. Good biographical drama.

Wings of Fire (1967)*½ Suzanne Pleshette, James Farentino, Ralph Bellamy, Lloyd Nolan, Juliet Mills. Hopelessly cluttered, pretentious drama of a lady pilot, the war hero with a hangup who married someone else, and assorted dull clichés peculiar to inferior magazine fiction. Some good aerial photography the sole asset. (Dir: David Lowell Rich, 100 mins.)

Wings of the Eagle (1957)**½ John Wayne, Dan Dailey, Maureen O'Hara. He-man Wayne brawls and grins his way through this robust comedy-drama about Commander "Spig" Wead, who started as a barnstormer and ended up a war hero. The first half of the film contains most of the comedy and is by far the best part. Dan Dailey and Wayne's favorite female co-star, Maureen O'Hara, are adequate in support. John Ford directed.

Wings of the Hawk (1953)** Van Heflin, Julia Adams, Abbe Lane. Predictable adventure set in Mexico involving renegades and their efforts to take over the government. Van Heflin is hardly the dashing hero type and seems rather uncomfortable in that pose. (Dir: Budd Boetticher, 80 mins.)

Wings of the Morning (British, 1936)**½ Henry Fonda, Annabella. Gypsies, romance and horsemanship in modern Ireland. Studied, often captivating romantic drama. Songs by the great tenor John McCormack. (Dir: Harold D. Schuster, 89 mins.)

Winner Take All (1975)**½ Shirley Jones, Laurence Luckinbill, Joan

797

Blondell. Director Paul Bogart deserves credit for his handling of this story about a compulsive gambler—a housewife this time, which manages to get some freshness out of essentially predictable material. Shirley Jones plays the addict, frantically attempting to raise the money she has gambled away out of her husband's savings. Made-for-TV. (Dir: Paul Bogart, 100 mins.)

Winning (1969)*** Paul Newman, Joanne Woodward, Robert Wagner, Richard Thomas. A credible drama played out against the exciting, pulsating world of professional car racing. Newman, a winner on the track, is less heroic in his personal life after he meets and weds divorcee Woodward. Wagner is the rival driver who vies for Miss Woodward's affection. The racing sequences leading to the Indianapolis 500 are superbly staged, and the cast is first-rate. Richard Thomas made his film debut as Miss Woodward's teen-age son and he's also quite good. The massive car crash is the real McCoy from the '68 smashup during the Indianapolis 500. (Dir: James Goldstone, 123 mins.)

Winning Team, The (1952)**½ Doris Day, Ronald Reagan, Frank Lovejoy. Baseball pitcher Grover Cleveland Alexander's biography. Both Doris Day and Ronald Reagan have trouble in this not too convincing film. (Dir: Lewis Seiler, 98 mins.)

Winslow Boy, The (British, 1949) **** Robert Donat, Margaret Leighton, Cedric Hardwicke. A noted lawyer is engaged to defend a boy accused of stealing at school. Literate, wonderfully well acted drama, excellent. Donat is superb. (Dir: Anthony Asquith, 97 mins.)

Winter Carnival (1939)**½ Ann Sheridan, Richard Carlson. An on-again-off-again romance between a professor and a glamor girl is played against the background of the famous winter carnival at Dartmouth University. Good skiing scenes, not much on story. (Dir: Charles F. Reisner, 100 mins.)

Winter Light (Sweden, 1963)***½ Ingrid Thulin, Gunnar Bjornstrand, Max von Sydow. Disillusioned pastor, doubting in God, love, hope, and most of the other basic tenets of Christianity, watches his congregation crumble along with his faith.

Bergman's chilling exploration of man's spiritual debasement, the poverty of human, Christian interdependence, and the relation of love to God. Stark, strikingly framed and flawlessly acted. A lean, powerful film. Second in the trilogy of which "Through A Glass Darkly" was first and "The Silence" the third. (Dir: Ingmar Bergman, 80 mins.)

Winter Meeting (1948)**½ Bette Davis. Bette is in love with a man who wants to be a priest but a terribly talky script bogs down a potentially dramatic situation. (Dir: Bretaigne Windust, 104 mins.)

Winter Soldier (1972)**** A searing "documentary" about the Vietnam war that, lamentably, never got the attention or exposure it deserved when this powerful anti-war statement was released. On January 3, 1971, in Detroit, the Vietnam Veterans Against the War started several days of hearings on the war. This lacerating reminder of the agonies of the war is largely a filmed record of the statements of 28 veterans between ages 20 and 27 who describe the unspeakable horrors they had seen and, in some cases, committed in Vietnam. These veterans, remember, all received honorable discharges and many were given medals for their heroism in combat. Through the anguished testimony you'll hear details of clear war crimes committed by American soldiers, which suggest that the events at My Lai were not a one-of-a-kind nightmare. Produced and directed collectively by concerned filmmakers. (99 mins.)

Winterkill (1974)**½ Andy Griffith, Sheree North, Joyce Van Patten. Andy Griffith as a chief of police in a mountain resort area. It's a pretty sound murder yarn with a killer on the loose and a guest star lineup of victims and suspects. Griffith is well cast as the friendly lawman who wants to crack the multiple murder case before big-time outside help is brought in. Made-for-TV. (Dir: Jud Taylor.)

Winterset (1936)**** Burgess Meredith, Margo. Twenty years after his father was executed for a crime he didn't commit, his son searches for the real criminal. Fine version of Maxwell Anderson's play; poetic, dramatic, powerful. (Dir: Alfred Santell, 80 mins.)

Wintertime (1943)**½ Sonja Henie, Jack Oakie. Sonja's fans may enjoy this musical about a skating star who saves a broken down hotel from bankruptcy. Not much here but Sonja's skating. (Dir: John Brahm, 82 mins.)

Wishing Well (British, 1954)**½ Brenda De Banzie, Donald Houston. Three women use a wishing well to make their dreams come true. Leisurely little comedy-drama, but well acted.

Wistful Widow of Wagon Gap, The (1947)** Bud Abbott & Lou Costello, Marjorie Main. Abbott & Costello on the range this time with Marjorie Main as the "wishful and willing widow." Not one of the comedy team's best. (Dir: Charles Barton, 78 mins.)

Witches of Salem—See: Crucible, The

Witch's Curse, The (Italian, 1961)*½ Kirk Morris. Legends and spectacle go together and this tale about Maciste and a curse which lasts for centuries takes full advantage of the two ingredients. This curse only seems like it lasts for centuries.

Witch's Mirror, The (Mexican, 1961) * Antonio Calve, Rosita Arenas. Powers of black magic cannot prevent a man from murdering his wife so he can marry another, but he suffers tragedy eventually. Muddled horror thriller, dubbed in English; poor.

With a Song in My Heart (1952)***½ Susan Hayward, David Wayne, Rory Calhoun, Thelma Ritter. A very entertaining film despite a bad script. The film biopic of singer Jane Froman and her comeback after a near fatal air crash which left her almost completely crippled. Miss Hayward gives a strong performance with a stress on the dramatics. Many songs are sung by Miss Froman with Susan doing an admirable miming job. (Dir: Walter Lang, 117 mins.)

With Fire and Sword (Italian, 1961) ** Jeanne Crain, John Drew Barrymore. Lavish but stale English-dubbed epic telling of the Cossacks' revolt against the Poles. Miss Crain looks lovely and is required to do no more than that. (Dir: Fernando Cerchio, 96 mins.)

With Six You Get Eggroll (1968)** Doris Day, Brian Keith. If you weren't positive this was a feature film, you'd swear you tuned in any of a dozen familiar TV situation comedy series. It's one of those bumbling affairs which casts Doris Day as a widow with three kids who teams up with widower Brian Keith who has only one daughter. Howard Morris has coaxed from Doris one of her better, less unctuous performances. (Dir: Howard Morris, 95 mins.)

Without Love (1944)*** Spencer Tracy, Katharine Hepburn. Talky, often amusing comedy about a scientist and a widow who get married just for convenience. You know what happens in the end but the Tracy-Hepburn antics should make the wait pleasant. (Dir: Harold S. Bucquet, 111 mins.)

Without Reservations (1946)**½ Claudette Colbert, John Wayne, Don DeFore. Couple of Marines out for fun and romance encounter a lady novelist on a Hollywood-bound train. Amusing romantic comedy has a couple of cute moments, some funny "guest" appearances. (Dir: Mervyn Le Roy, 107 mins.)

Without Warning (1952)***½ Adam Williams, Meg Randall. Police search for a mad killer who strangles blondes without reason. Sordid tale is surmounted by fine direction of Arnold Laven, giving this documentary-type melodrama a big lift.

Witness for the Prosecution (1958) **** Tyrone Power, Charles Laughton, Marlene Dietrich. Agatha Christie's clever and suspenseful play about a sensational London murder trial is excellently recreated on the screen. The cast is uniformly brilliant. Laughton, as an aging barrister, is a standout; Power gives one of his best performances. Even the usually decorative Miss Dietrich gets a chance to emote and is very effective. (Dir: Billy Wilder.)

Witness in the City (Franco-Italian, 1959)**½ Lino Ventura, Sandra Milo. When a cab driver is murdered, his buddies band together to trap the killer. Pretty fair mystery melodrama keeps a good pace, is well acted. Dubbed in English.

Witness to Murder (1954)*** Barbara Stanwyck, Gary Merrill, George Sanders. Well-acted, minor little suspense tale. Barbara sees the murder. George commits it and Gary is the cop. (Dir: Roy Rowland, 83 mins.)

Wives (Norway, 1975)***½ Anne Marie Ottersen, Froydis Armand. A perceptive, frequently droll, off-beat look at the by now familiar theme of the awakening woman and her flight from failing marriage. This low-budget, genial story is about three women who meet for the first time since high school and decide to leave their husbands briefly and go on a spree together. There are some lovely scenes as director Breien reverses the usual sex roles. The trio ogles and then tries to pick up men on a busy Oslo street corner. Very perceptive touches throughout. Written by Anja Breien with the help of the cast and charmingly directed by her. (84 mins.)

Wives and Lovers (1963)*** Van Johnson, Janet Leigh, Shelley Winters. A sparkling sophisticated comedy with brittle dialogue and stylish performances. It's all about a "nice-guy" writer whose sudden success changes him into a silly strutting egomaniac, and almost destroys his happy marriage. Credit director John Rich with fashioning a bright comedy about Hollywood and Broadway types. (103 mins.)

Wizard of Baghdad, The (1960)*½ Dick Shawn, Diane Baker. Genie without much talent is ordered to settle down in his work, is assigned to Baghdad. Arabian Nights fantasy tries for laughs, but Shawn can't supply these—silly and dull. (Dir: George Sherman, 92 mins.)

Wizard of Oz, The (1939)**** Judy Garland, Frank Morgan, Ray Bolger, Bert Lahr, Jack Haley. This musical fantasy about the farm girl whisked to the incredible land of Oz and her adventures with the scarecrow, the tin woodman, and the cowardly lion has become a TV classic over the years. Just to hear "Over the Rainbow" once again is worth tuning in for. (Dir: Victor Fleming, 100 mins.)

Wizards (1977)**½ A very uneven animated fable about good vs. evil, two brothers who grow up with different notions of ethics and morality. Not one of the best efforts from talented writer-director Ralph Bakshi. (80 mins.)

Wolf Larsen (1958)** Barry Sullivan, Peter Graves. Brutal sea captain meets his match. If this looks like "The Sea Wolf" it's a remake—in other words, warmed over. (Dir: Harmon Jones, 83 mins.)

Wolf Man, The (1941)*** Claude

Rains, Lon Chaney. Effective horror film. Whenever there is a full moon, mild-mannered Lon Chaney is transformed into a hairy, prowling night-creature. Good acting and direction heighten the suspense. (Dir: George Waggner, 71 mins.)

Wolves of the Deep (Italian, 1959)**½ Massimo Girotti, Jean-Marc Bory, Horst Frank. Sub crew is trapped on the bottom, with the escape hatch damaged and only one man able to get free. Interesting, frequently suspenseful drama of World War II; good performances. Dubbed in English.

Woman Bait—See: Inspector Maigret

Woman Chases Man (1937)*** Joel McCrea, Miriam Hopkins, Broderick Crawford. Vastly entertaining screwball comedy about love among the rich. Played in grand comedy style. (Dir: John G. Blystone, 71 mins.)

Woman in a Dressing Gown (British, 1957)***½ Yvonne Mitchell, Sylvia Syms, Anthony Quayle. Touching adult story about a married couple who get too used to one another and decide on a divorce. Quayle is wonderful as a man who looks for his lost youth by dating a young, beautiful woman. Extremely well directed by J. Lee Thompson. (93 mins.)

Woman in Hiding (1950)** Ida Lupino, Howard Duff, Peggy Dow. Contrived drama about a ruthless man who stops at nothing, from marriage to murder, to get control of a prosperous mill. Miss Lupino spends most of her time looking terrified and running and the rest of the cast gets caught up in the melodramatics of the piece. (Dir: Michael Gordon, 92 mins.)

Woman in Question, The (British, 1951)*** Jean Kent, Dirk Bogarde. A questionable fortune teller is found murdered, a police investigation reveals many sides of her character. Neat mystery, more of a character study than a whodunit, with a well-shaded performance by Miss Kent. (Dir: Anthony Asquith, 82 mins.)

Woman in the Dunes (Japan, 1964)**** Eiji Okada, Kyoko Kishida. A haunting, engrossing allegory about a man and a woman trapped in a shack at the bottom of a desolate sand pit amidst isolated dunes. Based on the critically acclaimed Japanese novel by Kobe Abe who also adapted for the screen. But the impact of the film is due principally to the camerawork of Hiroshi Segawa, and particularly to the extraordinary direction of Hiroshi Teshigahara. The man and woman bicker and, in time, make love. The love-making sequences are erotic, involving and deeply moving. A hypnotic, remarkable film. (Dir: Hiroshi Teshigahara, 123 mins.)

Woman in the Window, The (1944) ***½ Edward G. Robinson, Joan Bennett, Raymond Massey, Dan Duryea. His family on holiday, a professor makes a chance acquaintance with a beautiful woman, becomes involved in murder. Despite a weak, silly ending, this remains a superbly thrilling, tense melodrama. Fine Fritz Lang direction, good performances. (99 mins.)

Woman in White (1948)** Eleanor Parker, Alexis Smith, Sydney Greenstreet. If this one strikes you as a Victorian melodrama that's because it is. Story of a man who likes to drive innocent women to their end is so foolish it's almost comedy. (Dir: Peter Godfrey, 109 mins.)

Woman Obsessed (1959)** Susan Hayward, Stephen Boyd. Woman finds love again after her husband is accidentally killed. Soapy drama. (Dir: Henry Hathaway, 102 mins.)

Woman of Distinction, A (1950)**½ Ray Milland, Rosalind Russell. A woman Dean of a college finds that she must choose between her career and love. Old stuff nicely played. (Dir: Edward Buzzell, 85 mins.)

Woman of Dolwyn, The (British, 1949)***½ The story of the last days of a Welsh village, which is wiped away by flood at the conclusion. Fine cast includes Emlyn Williams (who also wrote and directed), Dame Edith Evans, Richard Burton. (Dir: Emlyn Williams, 90 mins.)

Woman of Rome (Italian, 1955)** Gina Lollobrigida, Daniel Gelin. Gina plays a down-trodden girl of easy virtue as she has many times before. Nothing new, plot-wise, but Gina is pleasant to watch. (Dir: Luigi Zampa, 93 mins.)

Woman of Straw (British, 1964)**½ Gina Lollobrigida, Sean Connery, Ralph Richardson. If you don't examine the plot too closely, you may enjoy this well-dressed murder mystery starring sex symbols Gina Lollobrigida and Sean Connery. However,

the two smoldering stars are completely upstaged by veteran pro Ralph Richardson, who plays the stuffings out of a wheelchair-bound millionaire with some eccentric views on life. (Dir: Basil Dearden, 117 mins.)

Woman of the Town, The (1943) ***½ Claire Trevor, Albert Dekker, Barry Sullivan. The saga of Bat Masterson, frontier marshal whose love for dance hall girl Dora Hand ended tragically when he cleaned up the town. Good western drama with an adult story; well acted. (Dir: George Archainbaud, 90 mins.)

Woman of the Year (1941)**** Spencer Tracy, Katharine Hepburn. Wonderful comedy about the marriage of a nonchalant sports writer and a charming international reporter. Funny, witty, brilliantly played and a "must" see. (Dir: George Stevens, 112 mins.)

Woman on the Beach (1947)*** Joan Bennett, Robert Ryan, Charles Bickford. Naval officer loves the wife of a blind painter, then believes the painter is faking blindness. Suspenseful, well acted melodrama. (Dir: Jean Renoir, 71 mins.)

Woman on the Run (1950)*** Ann Sheridan, Dennis O'Keefe. When her husband witnesses a murder and flees, his wife and the police try to catch up with him before the real killer does. Compact melodrama. suspenseful.

Woman Rebels, A (1936)**½ Katharine Hepburn, Herbert Marshall. Mid-Victorian girl wages a battle for feminine freedom. Mildly pleasing costume drama. (Dir: Mark Sandrich, 88 mins.)

Woman Times Seven (1967)**½ Shirley MacLaine, Michael Caine, Peter Sellers, Alan Arkin. Shirley MacLaine has an actress' dream in this uneven film—she plays seven different roles with seven different leading men in as many episodes. Miss MacLaine is at her best in the episode which has her playing an ordinary wife who reverts to hysteria in order to capture her novelist-husband's attention. (Dir: Vittorio De Sica)

Woman Under the Influence, A (1974)**** Gena Rowlands, Peter Falk, Matthew Cassel. An ambitious, harrowing drama focusing on a mad lower-middle-class housewife searching for her own identity and quite devastatingly acted my Gena Rowlands. This haunting performance earned Rowlands an Academy Award nomination, and her director-husband John Cassavetes was also nominated for his directorial efforts. The credits say written and directed by Cassavetes, but perhaps "observed and directed" would be more accurate. Cassavetes achieves a remarkable sense of improvisation with his acting troupe here, and "Woman" steadily builds audience concern and interest. (Dir: John Cassavetes, 155 mins.)

Woman Who Wouldn't Die, The (U.S.-Great Britain, 1965)* Gary Merrill, Georgina Cookson. There is, supposedly, a surprise ending to this tale of murder, but only the most naive viewer will be startled by it. Merrill is the husband of a rich, overbearing woman who makes his life and that of her male secretary unbearable. So, they conspire to do her in! (Dir: Gordon Hessler, 84 mins.)

Woman's Devotion, A (1965)** Ralph Meeker, Janice Rule, Paul Henreid. Artist and his wife in Mexico are implicated in murder. Uneven, confused mystery melodrama. (Dir: Paul Henreid, 88 mins.)

Woman's Face, A (1941)** Joan Crawford, Melvyn Douglas. Joan is a bum and potential killer until her scarred face is restored by plastic surgery. Then her personality changes and she saves the day. A clumsy, disjointed thriller. (Dir: George Cukor, 105 mins.)

Woman's Secret, A (1949)*** Maureen O'Hara, Melvyn Douglas, Gloria Grahame. Police investigate why a singer should be shot by the woman who made her a success. Interesting melodrama. (Dir: Nicholas Ray, 85 mins.)

Woman's Vengeance, A (1947)***½ Charles Boyer, Ann Blyth, Jessica Tandy. Married man having an affair with a younger woman is placed on trial when his wife is found to have been poisoned. Great performances in this absorbing drama written by Aldous Huxley. (Dir: Zoltan Korda, 96 mins.)

Woman's World, A (1954)**½ June Allyson, Lauren Bacall, Arlene Dahl. As the title suggests, this is strictly a woman's picture. This glossy and ultra-sophisticated glimpse into the leather-lined world

of big business may not be an accurate one, but it provides the background for some chic fashions worn by the trio of female stars, and some slick dialogue by the male contingent, Van Heflin, Fred MacMurray, Cornel Wilde, and Clifton Webb. (Dir: Jean Negulesco, 94 mins.)

Women, The (1939)***½ Norma Shearer, Joan Crawford, Rosalind Russell. Clare Boothe Luce's wonderful play about women is a delight on the screen. Comedy-drama with a load of plots, but for the most part a top female cast makes merry with Mrs. Luce's dialogue. (Dir: George Cukor, 140 mins.)

Women and War (French, 1962)** Bernard Blier, Lucille Saint-Simon. Experiences of a small French town under the yoke of the Germans during World War II, its eventual liberation. War drama tries for deep characterization, doesn't make it—some fair sequences. Dubbed in English.

Women Are Like That (French, 1960)*½ Eddie Constantine, Françoise Brion. Once again undercover operator Lemmy Caution finds plenty of trouble and plenty of pulchritude as he's seeking a missing agent. Humdrum dubbed-English melodrama, imitation-American style.

Women Are Weak—See: **Three Murderesses**

Women in Chains (1972)*½ Ida Lupino. You've seen all those prison shows about the sadistic guard playing games with inmates—well, here's the same plot in a women's institution with veteran film actress Ida Lupino cast as the sadistic matron. Movie pros can predict Miss Lupino's lines as well as the story's various turns. The ladies go all out in this one with a cast including Belinda Montgomery and Lois Nettleton. Made-for-TV. (Dir: Bernard Kowalski, 73 mins.)

Women of Devil's Island (Italian, 1962)* Guy Madison, Michele Mercier. Accomplice of pirates out to steal the gold of Devil's Island is baited by a countess to trap him. English-dubbed adventure drama is one big yawn.

Women of Pitcairn Island (1957)*½ James Craig, Lynn Bari. In case you didn't know, Gable and Laughton left some exciting gals on the island after the Bounty mutiny. This contrived mess tells all about them and their kids. (Dir: Jean Yarbrough, 72 mins.)

Women's Prison (1955)** Ida Lupino, Jan Sterling, Phyllis Thaxter. Unbelievable account of conditions in a women's prison presided over by a ruthless superintendent. Reminiscent of far superior film on same subject, "Caged." (Dir: Lewis Seiler, 80 mins.)

Won Ton Ton, The Dog Who Saved Hollywood (1976)* Madeline Kahn, Bruce Dern. Pics like this may kill Hollywood! Inane farce about a dog as the star of a silent film. The lengthy roster of Hollywood oldtimers, who make fleeting on-camera appearances, is more interesting than anything that happens in this witless movie, with the exception of Madeline Kahn's breezy efforts. If you don't blink you'll see Richard Arlen, Billy Barty, Jackie Coogan, Janet Blair, Edgar Bergen, Dennis Day, Andy Devine, Gloria De Haven, William Demarest, Huntz Hall, Dick Haymes, Keye Luke, Victor Mature, Carmel Meyers, Rudy Vallee, Doodles Weaver and other luminaries of yore. (Dir: Michael Winner, 92 mins.)

Wonder Man (1945)*** Danny Kaye, Virginia Mayo. One of Kaye's best performances—he plays a dual role as twins, one twin is the bookish type while the other is a fast-talking nightclub entertainer. When the gangsters bump off the wrong twin, the bookish Kaye steps into his brother's shoes and the fun begins. (Dir: H. Bruce Humberstone, 99 mins.)

Wonder Woman (1974)** Cathy Lee Crosby. For devotees of the comic-book adventures of Wonder Woman, here's a film with newcomer Crosby in the title role. Diana Prince, Wonder Woman's other name, leaves her island habitat to take a job as secretary to the Chief of Operations of an intelligence agency. Enter villains and Wonder Woman steps into action. Made-for-TV. (Dir: Vincent McEveety.)

Wonderful Country, The (1959)**½ Robert Mitchum, Julie London. Fast action western tale with Mitchum cast as a Texan who has a strange allegiance to the Mexicans and consents to buy arms to be used in the Revolution. Julie London supplies the love interest and Pedro Armendariz fares best in a large supporting cast. (Dir: Robert Parrish, 96 mins.)

Wonders of Aladdin (1962)** Donald O'Connor, Noelle Adam. Strictly for the youngsters—a comedy version of Arabian Nights' adventure complete with magic lamps, genies, and flying carpets. (Dir: Henry Levin, 93 mins)

Woodstock (1970)**** Definitive documentary record of the historic four-day celebration at Woodstock. The film shows instead of tells; and it successfully attaches the audience to the participants on screen. The rock stars, an incredible array, are moving in performance if not all technically brilliant. Jimi Hendrix's closing rendition of "The Star-spangled Banner" is an awesome redefinition of American ideals through the spirituality of the music. (Dir: Michael Wadleigh, 184 mins.)

Words and Music (1948)**½ Mickey Rooney, Judy Garland, Gene Kelly. Ridiculous biography of composers Rodgers & Hart is a tuneful delight thanks to a score of their wonderful tunes. (Dir: Norman Taurog, 119 mins.)

Work Is a Four-Letter Word (Great Britain, 1968)**½ David Warner, Cilla Black, Zia Mohyeddin. Even in a future world of utter automation, there is a place for artificial "high." Giant mushrooms make the characters euphoric in this film, based on Henry Livingston's play, "Eh?"—you will be less so. Mildly antic fun. Directed by the illustrious theater director Peter Hall, his first film effort. (87 mins.)

World for Ransom, The (1954)**½ Dan Duryea, Gene Lockhart. Adventurer matches wits with a gang of criminals. A few twists help this one. (Dir: Robert Aldrich, 82 mins.)

World in His Arms, The (1952)*** Gregory Peck, Ann Blyth, Anthony Quinn. Rugged romantic adventure with old fashioned escapes, rescues, brawls and love scenes set amid the raucous, lawless period when fur traders brought their cargoes to San Francisco. Peck makes a dashing hero and Ann Blyth is more animated than usual as a Russian countess. (Dir: Raoul Walsh, 104 mins.)

World in My Corner (1956)**½ Audie Murphy, Barbara Rush. Familiar boxing story about the kid from the slums who tastes luxury by fighting in the ring and becomes addicted

803

until it almost ruins his life. Audie Murphy, in a change-of-pace role from his usual western films, does fairly well as the boxer and a good supporting cast helps. (Dir: Jesse Hibbs, 82 mins.)

World in My Pocket (1961)** Rod Steiger, Nadja Tiller, Ian Bannen, Jean Servais. Another payroll robbery, masterminded by a dame (Tiller). Some suspense. Filmed in Europe.

World of Abbott and Costello (1965) **½ Bud Abbott, Lou Costello. A difficult film to rate, if not describe, because your enjoyment of this film will depend on how you already feel about Bud and Lou. Consists of a mélange of their highlights from many films, and includes their daffy goodie, "Who's On First?" Narration by comic Jack E. Leonard, and clips from such A & C flicks as "Buck Privates," "Hit the Ice," "In Society," "Comin' Round the Mountain" and "Abbott and Costello Meet the Keystone Kops." (Dir: Sidney Meyers, 75 mins.)

World of Apu, The (India, 1959)**** Magnificent conclusion to Indian director Satyajit Ray's trilogy of Bengali family life, portraying a young man's struggle for success against strong odds. Superbly acted by native cast, dubbed in English.

World of Henry Orient, The (1964) **** A rare combination of humor and sensitivity makes this comedy very special. It tells a wacky story about a madly egocentric and overly amorous concert pianist (Peter Sellers), who is hilariously pursued all around New York City by two teenage fans. The adoring girls are brilliantly and naturally portrayed by Tippy Walker and Merrie Spaeth, and they steal the picture right from under the talented noses of Peter Sellers and a fine company of actors including Angela Lansbury, Paula Prentiss, Tom Bosley, and Phyllis Thaxter. New York is photographed to good advantage, in this touching and gay charade, nice directorial touches by George Roy Hill. (106 mins.)

World of Suzie Wong, The (1961)** William Holden, Nancy Kwan. Unpleasant and tasteless drama of an American artist and his love for a girl of the streets in Hong Kong. Tries to be daring, succeeds in merely being soap opera. (Dir: Richard Quine, 129 mins.)

World of the Vampire, The (Mexican, 1961)* Mauricio Garces, Silvia Fournier. Vampire seeks revenge upon survivors of a family whose ancestors had given him a hard time. Poor horror thriller dubbed in English.

World Premiere (1941)*** John Barrymore, Frances Farmer. Daffy satire on Hollywood openings involves some Nazis assigned to see that producer Barrymore's film never opens. Silly, somewhat dated but fun. (Dir: Ted Tetzlaff, 70 mins.)

World, the Flesh and the Devil (1959) *** Harry Belafonte, Inger Stevens, Mel Ferrer. An excellent premise gets this tale off to a fascinating start, but it runs out of steam before it has run its course. Harry Belafonte spends the first part of the film all alone on screen, supposedly the last survivor on earth after poisonous gasses have destroyed humanity. These early scenes of Belafonte wandering around New York City without a trace of life are skillfully handled by writer-director Ranald MacDougall and should grip your attention. Enter Inger Stevens and Mel Ferrer and conflicts begin, most of which are obvious and pat. Despite the flaws in the latter half and the ending, the film remains fairly provocative fare. (Dir: Ranald MacDougall, 95 mins.)

World Without End (1956)** Hugh Marlowe, Nancy Gates. An interesting premise makes this sci-fi tale a bit more absorbing than some comparable films. A space flight intended for Mars goes through the time barrier and ends up on Earth during the 26th century. (Dir: Edward Bernds, 80 mins.)

World Without Sun (1964)**** Excellent French documentary, showing the experiments of Jacques Ives Cousteau and his men under the Red Sea. Eerily fascinating scenes of underwater life, both human and aquatic, should absorb all viewers.

World's Greatest Athletes, The (1973) * Jan-Michael Vincent, Tim Conway, John Amos, Howard Cosell. Embarrassing witless drivel from the Disney Studios about a white youth, raised in Africa Tarzan-style, who is brought to America and . . . Only interesting sequence is a technical trick which finds a whimpering assistant coach shrunk to miniature proportions and fighting some Paul Bunyan-sized props. Even the kids will find this one of the world's greatest bores. (Dir: Robert Scheerer, 92 mins.)

Worm's Eye View (British, 1951) **½ Ronald Shiner, Diana Dors. Comic complications when five RAF men are billeted in a suburban villa during World War II. Helter-skelter, rather likeable comedy.

Wrath of God, The (1972)*½ Robert Mitchum, Frank Langella, Rita Hayworth. Robert Mitchum walks through this puzzling yarn about a defrocked Boston priest-adventurer who finds himself in an unspecified Latin American country in the throes of revolution during the 1920's. The supporting cast consists of stereotypes, but good actors try to instill them with life. For the record they include Frank Langella as a young, hot-headed rebel; Rita Hayworth as a long-suffering mother; Ken Hutchinson as an Irish adventurer; and Victor Buono as a sleazy soldier of fortune. (Dir: Ralph Nelson, 111 mins.)

Wreck of the Mary Deare, The (1959) **½ Charlton Heston, Gary Cooper. Rather slow-moving mystery-adventure yarn with good performances by the two stars and an excellent British supporting cast including Emlyn Williams, Michael Redgrave and Virginia McKenna. The plot concerns the strange circumstances surrounding the wreck of the freighter called the Mary Deare. (Dir: Michael Anderson, 105 mins.)

Wrecking Crew, The (1969)** Dean Martin, Elke Sommer, Nancy Kwan, Sharon Tate. Dean plays super, swinging sleuth Matt Helm once again, and it's a tedious carbon copy of his other not very exhilarating espionage yarns. This time, Matt has to almost single-handedly save the American and British economies by making certain a gold shipment, en route to London via Denmark, arrives safely. He's beaten, bitten, bombed, broken, and generally stomped on throughout, but Matt never says die. Despite all this, Martin plays Helm like he does everything else—relaxed! (Dir: Phil Karlson, 104 mins.)

Wrestling Women Vs. the Aztec Mummy (Mexican, 1965)* Lorena Velasquez, Armand Sylvestre. Outlandish horror thriller about a mummy, returned from the dead, who goes after a lady wrestler. Dubbed in English.

Written on the Wind (1957)*** Rock Hudson, Lauren Bacall, Dorothy Malone, Robert Stack. Melodrama with a capital M but well mounted and convincingly acted. Dorothy Malone won a best supporting actress Academy Award for her portrayal of a sexy, spoiled rich girl who almost manages to destroy her brother (Robert Stack) and the man she covets (Hudson). (Dir: Douglas Sirk, 100 mins.)

Wrong Arm of the Law (British, 1962)***½ Peter Sellers, Bernard Cribbins, Lionel Jeffries. Another British spoof of crime films, with Sellers the Brain planning a very elaborate robbery. It's very funny. (Dir: Cliff Owen, 90 mins.)

Wrong Box, The (Great Britain, 1966)**** John Mills, Ralph Richardson, Michael Caine, Peter Cook, Dudley Moore, Peter Sellers. Many, nimble farce, based on a tale coauthored by Robert Louis Stevenson, about Victorian inheritance intrigues and a migratory body, which tumbles between slapstick, black humor and beguiling absurdity, and is played with vigor by an incomparable cast. Utter nonsense, done superbly. Screenplay by Larry Gelbart and Burt Shevelove. (Dir: Bryan Forbes, 105 mins.)

Wrong Kind of Girl, The (1956)*** Marilyn Monroe, Don Murray, Arthur O'Connell. Naive cowhand meets a sexy entertainer at a bus stop, falls hard for her despite warnings from his pal. Good drama based on the Broadway stage success by William Inge presents Monroe in a good role. Some tender dramatic moments, some funny ones. Good entertainment. Alternate title: "Bus Stop." (Dir: Joshua Logan, 96 mins.)

Wrong Man, The (1957)***½ Henry Fonda, Vera Miles, Anthony Quayle. Frightening account of what happens to a man and his wife when he is wrongly accused of being the man who has performed a series of holdups. This story is based on real-life facts. Directed with his customary skill by Alfred Hitchcock. (105 mins.)

Wrong Number (British, 1959)** Lisa Gastoni, Peter Elliot. Crooks plan a big mail truck robbery, supposedly a "perfect" crime. That it doesn't come off is no news to crime melodrama devotees.

WUSA (1970)* Paul Newman, Joanne Woodward, Laurence Harvey, Anthony Perkins. A pretentious film with unfulfilled aspirations to dissect the Southern right-wing politics once and for all. Paul Newman, miscast, plays an ex-drunk who gets a job as a disc jockey on WUSA, an all-the-way-to-the-right radio station in New Orleans. The supporting cast includes Woodward as a loser who hooks up with Newman; Harvey as a bogus evangelist; and Perkins as a left-wing radical with assassination on his sick mind. Sophomoric screenplay by Robert Stone based on his critically acclaimed "A Hall of Mirrors." (Dir: Stuart Rosenberg, 115 mins.)

Wuthering Heights (1939)**** Laurence Olivier, Merle Oberon, David Niven. Emily Bronte's hypnotic, romantic novel is tastefully brought to the screen with the perfect cast. Laurence Olivier is the epitome of the mysterious, dashing Heathcliff and Merle Oberon registers in the role of his love, Cathy. William Wyler directed with his usual sure hand. (Dir: William Wyler, 110 mins.)

Wuthering Heights (1970)**½ This remake of the Bronte classic about the epic romance between the wild, dashing, uncontrolled spirit named Heathcliff and his lovely ladylove Catherine falls short of its brilliant predecessor. However, Timothy Dalton as Heathcliff manages better than his lackluster costar Anna Calder-Marshall. Also the physical production is handsome, and the tale remains interesting. (Dir: Robert Fuest, 105 mins.)

W.W. and the Dixie Dancekings 1975)*** Burt Reynolds, Art Carney, Jerry Reed, Ned Beatty, Conny Van Dyke. Fast-paced down-home story of a 1950's con man (Burt Reynolds) who becomes the manager of a third-rate country and western group called "The Dixie Dancekings." Through a series of comical "hustles" he guides them to stardom and the Grand Ole Opry. W.W. (Reynolds), playing a hillbilly Robin Hood, raises money by ripping-off gas stations that are part of a big oil company that once did him wrong. An engaging, off-beat com-

806

edy. (Dir: John G. Avildsen, 100 mins.)

Wyoming (1940)** Wallace Beery, Ann Rutherford. Typical Beery western which will appeal to his legions of fans. They'll particularly like his "Aw, shucks" romance with Marjorie Main. (Dir: Richard Thorpe, 89 mins.)

Wyoming Kid, The (1947)** Dennis Morgan, Jane Wyman, Janis Paige, Arthur Kennedy. Gambler is hired to capture a notorious stagecoach robber, falls for the outlaw's wife. Bigger cast than usual in this routine western; few of them look at home in the wide-open spaces. Alternate title: "Cheyenne." (Dir: Raoul Walsh, 100 mins.)

X—15 (1961)** Charles Bronson, Kenneth Tobey, Mary Tyler Moore. Stilted semi-documentary about test pilots on the X-15 missile project. This one is Grade B movie fare with all the cliches, including the patient wives who wait for their husbands while they serve science. (Dir: Richard Donner, 105 mins.)

X from Outer Space, The (Japanese, 1964)* Eiji Okada, Toshiya Wazaki. FAFC (Fupi-Astro Flying Center) launches a spaceship to Mars which returns with a slimy spore which grows into the devastating Guilula monster. (85 mins.)

X-Ray of a Killer (French, 1963)** Jean Servais, Dany Robin, Maurice Teynac. Police inspector suspects a famous surgeon of being a notorious spy, sets a trap for him. Standard espionage melodrama dubbed in English.

"X"—The Man with the X-Ray Eyes (1963)**½ Ray Milland, Diana Van Der Vlis, Harold J. Stone. Doctor experimenting with a new serum discovers he can see through objects, which eventually leads to a life of terror for him. Interesting type of sci-fi melodrama with Milland's customary sturdy performance, a plot that keeps moving and holds the attention. (Dir: Roger Corman, 80 mins.)

X—The Unknown (British, 1957)*½ Dean Jagger, Edward Chapman. This science fiction tale centers around a creature or thing that cannot be defined—well, neither can this plot. (Dir: Leslie Norman, 80 mins.)

X, Y and ZEE (British, 1972)*½ Elizabeth Taylor, Michael Caine, Susannah York. Trash. Good cast is caught up in a jet-set melodrama. Liz is married to Caine, but he is dissatisfied and finds a mistress in the person of Miss York. Liz does well as the boozing, vengeful shrew out to keep her husband, but the script turns the character into a caricature. The film never fails to be inane, overblown, and generally unbelievable. (Dir: Brian G. Hutton, 110 mins.)

Yank at Eton, A (1942)** Mickey Rooney, Peter Lawford. Brash Mickey goes to school in England and the result is forced, not too funny, comedy. (Dir: Norman Taurog, 88 mins.)

Yank at Oxford, A (1937)*** Robert Taylor, Maureen O'Sullivan, Vivien Leigh. Entertaining film which is perfectly described in the title. The English cast which supports the American stars is uncommonly good and you'll undoubtedly enjoy it in spite of an oft-used plot. (Dir: Jack Conway, 110 mins.)

Yank in the R.A.F., A (1941)*** Tyrone Power, Betty Grable. Dated but still exciting story of a Yank who joins the R.A.F. just to be near an old girl friend and has some of the cockiness knocked out of him by the R.A.F. spirit. (Dir: Henry King, 100 mins.)

Yank in Viet-Nam, A (1964)** Marshall Thompson, Enrique Magalona. Marine officer is freed from the Red forces and joins with a soldier to free a kidnaped doctor. Standard war story has the advantage of Vietnam locations, adding to the believability. (Dir: Marshall Thompson, 80 mins.)

Yankee Buccaneer (1952)** Jeff Chandler, Scott Brady, Suzan Ball. Strictly for action fans who like swashbuckling yarns. Chandler climbs the mast and commands a decoy U. S. naval ship which is rigged as a pirate vessel in order to dupe the thieves of the high seas. (Dir: Frederick de Cordova, 86 mins.)

Yankee Doodle Dandy (1942)**** James Cagney, Joan Leslie, Walter Huston. Irresistible screen biog of song-and-dance man George M. Cohan and family. Cagney's award-winning performance is a real achievement, there's songs, dances, and funny sayings for all, plus the necessary patriotism, all done up in a big musical package. Fine entertainment. (Dir: Michael Curtiz, 126 mins.)

Yankee Pasha (1954)**½ Jeff Chandler, Rhonda Fleming. Edison Marshall's best selling novel about a man who fights pirates, sultans, harem girls and other obstacles in order to win his lady fair, is elaborately brought to the screen. Action is plentiful and Miss Fleming is lovely to look at. (Dir: Joseph Pevney, 84 mins.)

Yearling, The (1946)**** Gregory Peck, Jane Wyman, Claude Jarman, Jr. For presenting a simple story of a boy's love for a pet fawn which his father must destroy this is one of the finest films of all time. The emotions involved are complex and real, yet this picture has captured all the feelings and depth of the best selling novel without even employing Hollywood tricks. A "must" for the whole family. (Dir: Clarence Brown, 134 mins.)

Years Between, The (British, 1946)**½ Michael Redgrave, Valerie Hobson. Believed dead, a prisoner of war returns to find his wife remarried. Occasionally interesting drama, despite some lags. (Dir: Compton Bennett, 90 mins.)

Yellow Balloon (British, 1953)*** Andrew Ray, Kenneth More, William Sylvester. Small boy is shocked by the accidental death of a playmate, is used for evil purposes by a petty crook. Gripping suspense melodrama, well done. (Dir: J. Lee Thompson, 80 mins.)

Yellow Cab Man, The (1950)**½ Red Skelton, Gloria De Haven, Walter Slezak. Fast and funny frolic for Red Skelton fans. Red's a cab driver who goes out of his way to pick up pretty girls and trouble. Hilarious, slapstick chase is the climax. (Dir: Jack Donohue, 85 mins.)

Yellow Canary (British, 1944)**½ Anna Neagle, Richard Greene. English girl poses as a Nazi sympathizer to track down spies. Fairly good espionage melodrama. (Dir: Herbert Wilcox, 84 mins.)

Yellow Canary, The (1963)**½ Pat Boone, Barbara Eden, Steve Forrest, Jack Klugman. Dramatically tight mystery-suspense tale, scripted by Rod Serling, about a singer whose infant son is kidnapped, falls short on characterization. Jack Klugman stands out in supporting role as the frustrated cop. Based on the novel "Evil Come, Evil Go," by Whit Masterson. (Dir: Buzz Kulik, 93 mins.)

Yellow Fin (1951)*** Wayne Morris, Adrian Booth. Young owner of tuna fishing boat is beset by troubles in the form of a rascally rival and a grasping dame. Good action melodrama.

Yellow Jack (1938)***½ Robert Montgomery, Virginia Bruce. Sidney Howard's award winning play is converted into a compelling film. Story of the men who risked their lives to determine the cause of yellow fever is a monument to courage minus the usual phony Hollywood heroics. (Dir: George B. Seitz, 80 mins.)

Yellow Mountain (1955)*½ Lex Barker, Mala Powers, Howard Duff. Dull western about a couple of two-fisted men who take on all comers in their efforts to strike it rich in gold. Lex Barker is wooden and looks uncomfortable in western garb. (Dir: Jesse Hibbs, 78 mins.)

Yellow Rolls Royce, The (1964)**** Rex Harrison, Ingrid Bergman, Shirley MacLaine, Omar Sharif, George C. Scott, Alain Delon. Most audiences will enjoy the star-studded cast in this film about the adventures of a fancy Rolls-Royce and the various people who own it. With so much talent before and behind the cameras, it should have been far better than it is. (Dir: Anthony Asquith, 122 mins.)

Yellow Sky (1948)*** Gregory Peck, Anne Baxter, Richard Widmark. Top Western drama pitting Gregory Peck against Richard Widmark for a prize of stolen gold and Anne Baxter. Widmark stands out with an exciting performance. (Dir: William Wellman, 98 mins.)

Yellow Submarine (1968)**** A film treat which shouldn't be missed. It's the delightful, engaging animated fantasy in which the Beatles fight off the Blue Meanies, who have the audacity to disrupt the tranquil amiability of the mythical kingdom of Pepperland of Sgt. Pepper's Lonely Hearts Club Band fame. There are many songs in the film (written and performed by the Beatles), including "All You Need Is Love," "Eleanor Rigby," "A Little Help from My Friends," "Lucy in the Sky with Diamonds," and the title tune, of course. (Dir: George Dunning, 85 mins.)

Yellowneck (1955)*** Lin McCarthy, Stephen Courtleigh. Civil War deserters try to make their way through the Florida Everglades to freedom. Strong drama made in Florida, heavy on the violence, deserves credit as an attempt to be different.

Yellowstone Kelly (1959)**½ Clint Walker, John Russell. Routine western, with most of the Warner Bros. stable of TV western stars. The plot offers nothing new and the cast is very much at home in the saddle and on the trail. (Dir: Gordon Douglas, 90 mins.)

Yes Sir, That's My Baby (1949)**½ Donald O'Connor, Gloria De Haven, Charles Coburn. Silly but entertaining comedy-musical about the campus life of ex-G.I.'s going to college on the G.I. Bill of Rights. A mixture of football, baby feedings, marital misunderstandings, and nick-of-time victories. (Dir: George Sherman, 80 mins.)

Yesterday, Today and Tomorrow (Italian, 1964)***½ Sophia Loren, Marcello Mastroianni. Three spicy stories tailored for the talents of the two stars, especially Loren; in one, she's a black marketeer who takes an unusual method of avoiding the law; in another, she's the flirtatious wife of an industrialist; in the last, she's a call girl whom a seminary student tries to reform. Funny adult fare. Dubbed in English. (Dir: Vittorio De Sica, 120 mins.)

Yesterday's Child (1977)**½ Shirley Jones, Geraldine Fitzgerald. Shirley Jones and Geraldine Fitzgerald, two good actresses, give this drama its validity. A 17-year-old girl is brought to her wealthy mother and grandmother's house claiming to be the little girl who was kidnapped and believed killed many years before. The device may be slightly old-hat, but the cast, particularly the ladies, keep it from going overboard. Stephanie Zimbalist, Efrem's daughter, plays the young girl who returns from the past. Made-for-TV. (Dir: Jerry Thorpe, 106 mins.)

Yesterday's Enemy (British, 1959) **½ Stanley Baker, Guy Rolfe. Moderately interesting British war film about a small group of soldiers who take over a Burmese jungle village. The action is believable and the performances above average. (Dir: Val Guest, 95 mins.)

Yojimbo (Japanese, 1962) **** Toshiro Mifune, Eijiro Tono. Superior samurai film with a large twist of black humor. The great Japanese actor Mifune is magnificent in the title role of a wandering samurai. Yojimbo swaggers into a town that is in the midst of a fighting feud between two corrupt factions—he hires himself out to both sides and proceeds to help them destroy most of the town. The action is fast, bloody, and plentiful and the attitude of the film is justly cynical. Directed by Akira Kurosawa with a good deal of style and authority. (112 mins.)

Yokel Boy (1942) *** Albert Dekker, Joan Davis, Eddie Foy Jr. A hick idea man for a Hollywood studio suggests the life of a notorious gangster—with the gangster himself in the lead. Highly amusing comedy. (Dir: Joseph Santley, 69 mins.)

Yolanda and the Thief (1945) ** Fred Astaire, Lucille Bremer. The dancing is good but the story of a con man and an innocent girl is too much weight for even Astaire to carry. (Dir: Vincente Minnelli, 110 mins.)

You Are What You Eat (1969) ** Tiny Tim, Peter Yarrow. An ancestor of the rock concert film, this sleazy-type job gets a number of big names together to do their thing in a rather unimaginative way. The film is interesting for one number only—"The Greta Garbo Home for Homeless Boys and Girls"—it's a knock-out! (Dir: Barry Feinstein, 75 mins.)

You Can't Cheat an Honest Man (1939) *** W. C. Fields, Edgar Bergen. Fields runs a traveling show, can't make a buck or stay ahead of the sheriff. Deft performances make this nonsense entertaining. (Dir: George Marshall, 80 mins.)

You Can't Get Away with Murder (1939) *** Humphrey Bogart, Gale Page. This was made while Bogey was playing crooks and his performance as a killer is so good that it's no wonder he was typed. It's a familiar death-house drama but engrossing and well acted. (Dir: Lewis Seiler, 80 mins.)

You Can't Have Everything (1937) *** Alice Faye, Don Ameche, Ritz Brothers. The Ritz Brothers supply the comedy and almost succeed in supporting the frail backstage plot. Alice sings well and it's fairly good screen entertainment—if you like the Ritz Brothers. (Dir: Norman Taurog, 100 mins.)

You Can't Run Away from It (1956) ** June Allyson, Jack Lemmon. Bad re-make of Clark Gable—Claudette Colbert classic "It Happened One Night" with music, no less. Dick Powell produced and directed this so-called comedy about a runaway heiress and a newspaper man. (Dir: Dick Powell, 95 mins.)

You Can't Take It with You (1938) *** James Stewart, Jean Arthur, Lionel Barrymore. The classic comedy about a devil-may-care family has lost a lot of its charm but still a treat. (Dir: Frank Capra, 130 mins.)

You Can't Win 'Em All (1970) *½ Tony Curtis, Charles Bronson, Michele Mercier. Feebleminded adventure. Curtis and Bronson play two-fisted (or should that be four-fisted) WW I adventurers out to make a big financial killing as the Ottoman Empire is collapsing all around them. Before long, the plot collapses too. (Dir: Peter Collinson, 97 mins.)

You for Me (1952) **½ Peter Lawford, Jane Greer, Gig Young. Two of Hollywood's most suave leading men, Lawford & Young, save this otherwise lightweight romantic comedy from total boredom. The object of their affection is pretty nurse Jane Greer. (Dir: Don Weis, 70 mins.)

You Gotta Stay Happy (1948) **½ James Stewart, Joan Fontaine, Eddie Albert. This could easily be called "The Flyer Takes A Lady"; Joan Fontaine and the flyer, none other than James Stewart. Fast but disappointing comedy. (Dir: H. C. Potter, 99 mins.)

You Live So Deep, My Love (1975) * Don Galloway, Barbara Anderson, Angel Tompkins, Walter Pidgeon. Flimsy little suspense thriller, short on both suspense and thrills. Made-for-TV. (Dir: David Lowell Rich, 72 mins.)

You Must Be Joking! (Great Britain, 1965) **½ Michael Callan, Lionel

Jeffries, Terry-Thomas, Denholm Elliott. Script has problems, but there's Terry-Thomas as a wacky Army psychiatrist who drafts five equally zany officers to perform a 48-hour "initiative test." Some chuckles. (Dir: Michael Winner, 100 mins.)

You Never Can Tell (1951)*** Dick Powell, Peggy Dow, Joyce Holden. Delightfully wacky film about the reincarnation of a dog and a horse into a private detective (Dick Powell) and a blonde secretary (Joyce Holden) respectively who come to earth to settle an old score concerning murder. Very amusing idea carried off with style. (Dir: Lou Breslow, 80 mins.)

You Only Live Once (1937)***½ Henry Fonda, Sylvia Sidney. Circumstances cause an innocent man to be sent to prison, there to be turned into a killer. Gripping drama, excellently directed by Fritz Lang. (Dir: Fritz Lang, 90 mins.)

You Only Live Twice (1967)*** Sean Connery, Donald Pleasence, Bernard Lee. Sean Connery as James Bond guarantees a good time for fans of the genre in this, the fifth Bond movie! Agent 007 facing the villains of SPECTRE in some of the most elaborate settings ever devised for a Bond film . . . with Japan as the backdrop for most of the action. Naturally, there are voluptuous girls hanging on Bond. Donald Pleasence makes a good German villain, and there's a spectacular finale in which gigantic explosions supply the excitement. Screenplay by Roald Dahl. (Dir: Lewis Gilbert, 116 mins.)

You Were Meant for Me (1948)*** Jeanne Crain, Dan Dailey. A nice score of popular standards, pleasing performances and a routine story of a girl who marries a bandleader she has known one day and then must learn to travel with him and love him. (Dir: Lloyd Bacon, 92 mins.)

You Were Never Lovelier (1942)*** Rita Hayworth, Fred Astaire. Jerome Kern's music, Fred's dancing and Rita's figure combine with some awful dialogue and plot. Result: entertaining but below expectations. (Dir: William A. Seiter, 97 mins.)

You'll Like My Mother (1972)**½ Patty Duke, Rosemary Murphy, Sian Barbara Allen, Richard Thomas. What saves this thriller from the

limitations of an awkward screenplay is the performances of its talented cast. Miss Duke, pregnant with her dead husband's child, comes to stay with her cold mother-in-law (Murphy) and retarded sister-in-law (Allen), with an evil villain lurking about. (Dir: Lamont Johnson, 105 mins.)

You'll Never Get Rich (1941)***½ Fred Astaire, Rita Hayworth. Theatrical producer is drafted, still manages to put on his big show. Sprightly musical comedy, with some fine dancing. (Dir: Sidney Lanfield, 88 mins.)

You'll Never See Me Again (1973)** David Hartman. Suspense thriller. When a couple of newlyweds quarrel, the bride bounces out of the house to visit her mom. Bridegroom Hartman conducts a panicky search, only to wind up as the prime murder suspect. Made-for-TV. (Dir: Jeannot Szwarc, 73 mins.)

Young and Willing (1942)** William Holden, Eddie Bracken, Susan Hayward. Some struggling young actors try to interest a big theatrical producer. Mildly amusing madcap comedy. (Dir: Edward Griffith, 82 mins.)

Young and Willing (1962)—See: **Wild and the Willing, The**

Young at Heart (1954)*** Frank Sinatra, Doris Day, Ethel Barrymore. Good drama about a shiftless piano player and his young wife. Both Frank & Doris have a chance to sing and really have a go at acting. The supporting cast is fine, notably Ethel Barrymore. Based on John Garfield movie "Four Daughters." (Dir: Gordon Douglas, 117 mins.)

Young Bess (1953)***½ Jean Simmons, Charles Laughton, Deborah Kerr, Stewart Granger. Handsomely mounted historical drama with two excellent performances by Jean Simmons as the high spirited Bess, and Charles Laughton as her father, Henry VIII. History students may find objections to various aspects of the film but it's entertaining and absorbing. (Dir: George Sidney, 112 mins.)

Young Billy Young (1969)* Robert Mitchum, Angie Dickinson, Robert Walker. A dull western from fade-in to fade-out. Mitchum is the stone-faced lawman who tries to bring young Billy Young (R. Walker) to justice but finds a hostile town standing in his way. (Dir: Burt Kennedy, 90 mins.)

Young Captives, The (1959)**½ Steven Marlo, Luana Patten, Ed Nelson. Teenage couple eloping to Mexico run afoul of a crazed killer who holds them captive. Tight little suspense drama made on a small budget, makes its point quickly and excitingly. (Dir: Irvin Kershner, 61 mins.)

Young Cassidy (1965)***½ Rod Taylor, Maggie Smith, Julie Christie. Interesting, if uneven, biographical drama about the early life of playwright Sean O'Casey, depicting his rise from the Dublin slums to the celebrated openings of his early plays. Rod Taylor does well in the central role, and the good cast includes: Flora Robson, Maggie Smith, Michael Redgrave, Edith Evans, and a brief but telling part by Julie Christie. (Dirs: John Ford, Jack Cardiff, 110 mins.)

Young Country, The (1970)**½ Roger Davis, Joan Hackett. If you like your western tales with a broad serving of comedy, this made-for-TV feature about a bumbler of a gambler and his adventures in the West will give you a few laughs. Roger Davis is a bewildered hero who gets into trouble trying to earn his keep playing cards. The supporting cast is very good, especially Walter Brennan as a veteran sheriff, and Joan Hackett and Peter Duel as a pair of shady characters. (Dir: Roy Huggins, 73 mins.)

Young Dillinger (1965)*½ Nick Adams, Robert Conrad, Mary Ann Mobley. A highly fictionalized account of the life of criminal John Dillinger and his cohorts. The action is kept at a fast clip but you'll still be able to spot the flaws in plot and performances, particularly a strutting one by Nick Adams in the title role. (Dir: Terry D. Morse, 102 mins.)

Young Doctors, The (1961)*** Fredric March, Ben Gazzara, Ina Balin, Dick Clark. Routine hospital soap opera elevated to good drama by the earnest playing of a fine cast. March is particularly good as a pathologist of the old school who clashes with the modern approach represented by Gazzara. Many sub-plots are well integrated into the drama. (Dir: Phil Karlson, 100 mins.)

Young Don't Cry, The (1957)** Sal Mineo, James Whitmore. Confused melodrama about a badly run Georgia orphanage and one teen-ager in particular who gets involved with an escaped convict. Over-acted. (Dir: Alfred L. Werker, 89 mins.)

Young Dr. Kildare (1938)*** Lew Ayres, Lionel Barrymore. Good, sensitive story of a young interne's problems in a big city hospital. First of the MGM series and well played by Ayres and Barrymore. (Dir: Harold S. Bucquet, 80 mins.)

Young Frankenstein (1974)**** Gene Wilder, Peter Boyle, Marty Feldman, Madeline Kahn, Gene Hackman, Cloris Leachman. Inspired lunacy dreamed up and written by guffaw wizards Mel Brooks and Gene Wilder, based on the characters from our old pal "Frankenstein," courtesy of Mary Shelley. Wilder plays the role of the grandson of the nefarious Baron Frankenstein who visits the old family homestead in Transylvania and decides, after proper meditation, to make a living creature himself. Marty Feldman is hilarious playing a hunchbacked assistant, and Kahn is absolutely delicious having a roll in a hay wagon with the lucky grandson. There are some incredibly funny sight gags strewn along the way by the maniacal madcap Mel. (Dir: Mel Brooks, 98 mins.)

Young Fury (1965)*½ Rory Calhoun, Virginia Mayo, Lon Chaney, Richard Arlen, John Agar, Jody McCrea, William Bendix. Top cast of old-time western stars aids floundering plot about a weary gunslinger returning home to find his son is leader of a terrorist band of young gunmen. (Dir: Christian Nyby, 80 mins.)

Young Girls of Good Families (French, 1963)*½ Marie-France Pisier, Ziva Rodann. Cover girl and her sisters get into complicated mixups with robbery while vacationing on the Riviera. Slow, silly romantic comedy. English-dubbed.

Young Girls of Rochefort, The (1967)** Catherine Deneuve, Gene Kelly. A charming score by Michel Legrand and the lovely Miss Deneuve and her late sister, Francoise Dorleac, are the best things about this overly sweet musical. It's a tale about a fair in the quaint French village of Rochefort-sur-Mer where the girls, Gene Kelly, George Chakiris, and a large cast fall in and out of love at the drop of a song cue. (Dir: Jacques Demy, 126 mins.)

Young Guns, The (1956)**½ Russ Tamblyn, Gloria Talbott, Scott Marlowe. A cast of exciting young acting talents make this western yarn seem better than it is. The plot is the familiar one about the boy who has to make a choice becoming a gunslinger or a law abiding citizen. (Dir: Albert Band, 84 mins.)

Young Guns of Texas (1962)** James Mitchum, Alana Ladd, Jody McCrea, Chill Wills. The chase is on after a group of Confederates as the Civil War ends, with Apaches on the warpath complicating matters. So-so western whose only novelty is the offspring of famous actors in leading roles. (Dir: Maury Dexter, 78 mins.)

Young Hellions—See: **High School Confidential**

Young in Heart, The (1938)***½ A dizzy family of cardsharps and fortune hunters is reformed by the kindness of a sweet old lady, whom they vow to help by leading better lives. Douglas Fairbanks Jr., Janet Gaynor, Paulette Goddard, and a fine supporting cast. Delightful comedy. (Dir: Richard Wallace, 100 mins.)

Young Jesse James (1960)** Ray Stricklyn, Robert Dix, Willard Parker. Still another version of how Jesse went bad—this time he joined Quantrill's raiders because Union soldiers killed his father. All adds up to just another western. (Dir: William Claxton, 73 mins.)

Young Land, The (1959)** Pat Wayne, Yvonne Craig. In early California, an American is placed on trial for killing a Mexican. Racial problems in the Old West—film tries a plea for tolerance but becomes a western minus much action. (Dir: Ted Tetzlaff, 89 mins.)

Young Lawyers, The (1969)*** Jason Evers, Keenan Wynn, Michael Parks. Taking into consideration that this film was a pilot for a projected series, it's a well-produced, well-acted and overall interesting entry. The action revolves around the activities of a new organization, known as the Boston Neighborhood Law Office, which gives student lawyers the opportunity to try cases in court. Three bright young actors, Zalman King, Judy Pace and Tom Fielding, play the fledgling advocates, and Jason Evers is their new director who puts

things into shape. The focus is on a case which pits cab-driver Keenan Wynn against two black musicians accused of assault and theft. Another plus is the excellent on-location photography of Boston. (Dir: Harvey Hart, 74 mins.)

Young Lions, The (1958)***½ Marlon Brando, Dean Martin, Montgomery Clift, Barbara Rush. Epic drama of three men in war—a blasé sophisticate, a tragic Jew, and a realistic German—and their eventual fates. Large-scale production holds the attention despite the length, many plots. Generally well acted. (Dir: Edward Dmytryk, 167 mins.)

Young Lovers, The (1949)***½ Sally Forrest, Keefe Brasselle. The ravages of polio cause a young dancer to readjust herself both physically and mentally. Gripping drama, sensitively directed by Ida Lupino, well acted.

Young Lovers, The (British, 1954)**½ Theodore Bikel, Odile Versois. A rather dull British movie proving once more that love can always find a way, even through the "iron curtain." Bikel turns in another affecting performance.

Young Lovers, The (1964)* Peter Fonda, Sharon Hugueny, Nick Adams, Deborah Walley. The pangs of first love, Hollywood-style. As usual, the principals act more dopey than romantic. (Dir: Samuel Goldwyn, Jr., 105 mins.)

Young Man with a Horn (1950)***½ Kirk Douglas, Lauren Bacall, Doris Day. Kirk Douglas gives an excellent performance in this yarn about a dedicated trumpet player who lived exclusively by his music until it was almost too late. Bacall plays a well written character who helps Douglas destroy himself in a hurry. Doris Day acts (not too well) and sings (very well). (Dir: Michael Curtiz, 112 mins.)

Young Man with Ideas (1952)**½ Glenn Ford, Ruth Roman, Denise Darcel. Lawyer moves his family to California and gets a job as a bill collector, which leads to complications. Story never hits any great heights, but the players are pleasant. (Dir: Mitchell Leisen, 84 mins.)

Young Mr. Lincoln (1939)*** Henry Fonda, Alice Brady, Marjorie Weaver. Story of young Abe as a lawyer is not the greatest of Lincoln stories but John Ford's direction and fine acting by Fonda and Alice Brady make it good entertainment. (Dir: John Ford, 100 mins.)

Young One, The (1960)** Zachary Scott, Bernie Hamilton, Kay Meersman. Negro musician fleeing the law is drawn into a web of danger when he lands on an island inhabited by a young girl and a lecherous older man. Unpleasant mixture of racial theme, "Lolita," and assorted violence. Well acted. Mexican-made. English dialogue.

Young Philadelphians, The (1959)*** Paul Newman, Barbara Rush, Alexis Smith. Rather long film based on the best seller about people from different levels of Philadelphia society. The performances are better than the screen play, with Robert Vaughn delivering the best one as a rich young man who is framed on a murder charge. (Dir: Vincent Sherman, 136 mins.)

Young Pioneers, The (1976)**½ Linda Purl, Roger Kern. Quality on-location production and two appealing young stars bolster this tale about two young newlyweds who trek to the wilds of Dakota to homestead land given to settlers in the 1870's. The hardships they endure are almost insurmountable. Talented and attractive leads are fresh and believable. Made-for-TV. (Dir: Michael O'Herlihy, 98 mins.)

Young Racers, The (1963)** Mark Damon, William Campbell, Luana Anders. Former racer turned writer intends to expose a reckless road ace in a book but grows to like him. Plenty of careening autos for the sports fans, all looking pretty much alike; story is slight but holds the interest. Fair result. (Dir: Roger Corman, 87 mins.)

Young Runaways, The (1968)** Brooke Bundy, Kevin Coughlin, Lloyd Bochner, Patty McCormack. Predictable, if earnest, attempt to focus on the kids who run away to Chicago's hippie section, in order to find themselves, circa 1968. Best performance is by lovely Brooke Bundy, a frequent guest star on TV series, and keen film fans will recognize Richard Dreyfuss ("The Apprenticeship of Duddy Kravitz") in a small role. (Dir: Arthur Dreifuss, 91 mins.)

Young Savages, The (1961)*** Burt Lancaster, Dina Merrill, Shelley Winters. Evan (Blackboard Jungle) Hunter's novel "A Matter of Conviction" makes for a hard-hitting crime drama with Burt Lancaster playing a determined assistant D A engaged in the battle against juvenile delinquency. There are many tough and brutally realistic scenes. (Dir: John Frankenheimer, 110 mins.)

Young Sinner, The (1965)*½ Tom Laughlin, Stefanie Powers. Tale about a young carouser whose only hope is to get a college football scholarship. After blowing his opportunity, he repents and goes to confession. Film dwells on the boy's malicious acts, but the moralizing ending is a bit much. (Dir: Tom Laughlin, 82 mins.)

Young Stranger (1957)*** James MacArthur, James Daly, Kim Hunter. A moving story of a boy and his relationship with his father, who doesn't take time from his busy schedule to try and understand his son. Based on a TV play directed by ace TV director John Frankenheimer. (84 mins.)

Young, the Evil and the Savage, The (Italy, 1968)** Michael Rennie, Mark Damon, Eleanor Brown. English girls' school provides setting for an unoriginal but painless murder mystery. Fair suspense! (Dir: Antonio Margheriti, 82 mins.)

Young Toerless (1968)***½ Matthieu Carriere. Barbara Steele. A very good film, based on the novel by Robert Musil. Beautifully photographed and lovingly written and acted, it is worth seeing for its poetry and dedication. (Dir: Volker Schlondorff.)

Young Tom Edison (1939)*** Mickey Rooney, Fay Bainter. Good biography of the youth of the great inventive genius. Mickey is in rare form and the whole family will enjoy this. (Dir: Norman Taurog, 82 mins.)

Young Warriors, The (1967)** James Drury, Steve Carlson. An average WW II tale which tries to analyze the effect killing has on a professional soldier and a young newcomer. It begins with some promise but the cliches soon take over. James Drury, of "The Virginian" TV series, handles the role of the tough sergeant with authority. (Dir: John Peyser, 93 mins.)

Young Winston (British, 1972)*** Simon Ward, Anne Bancroft, Robert Shaw. Interesting, highly enjoyable

813

biography of Winston Churchill as a young man. His lonely childhood, school days, fights in India, and exploits in the Boer War are all rousingly recalled. Battle sequences are particularly stunning. Ward plays Churchill with power, and Bancroft and Shaw are moving as Churchill's inattentive parents. (Dir: Richard Attenborough, 157 mins.)

Youngblood Hawke (1964)*½ James Franciscus, Suzanne Pleshette, Genevieve Page. Inept screen treatment of Herman Wouk's bestseller about a young author caught in the web of the big city's publishing world. Genevieve Page overacts to the point of distraction and James Franciscus is wooden throughout. (Dir: Delmer Daves, 137 mins.)

Youngest Spy, The (Russian, 1962) *** Story of a Russian lad whose parents were killed by the Nazis and became a spy behind the enemy lines. Good observation of child's thoughts, some poetic sequences. English dubbed. Alternate title: **My Name Is Ivan.** (Dir: Andrei Tarkovsky, 94 mins.)

Your Cheatin' Heart (1964)*** George Hamilton, Susan Oliver, Red Buttons. George Hamilton manages to overcome his handsome playboy image to create a solid characterization of the ill-fated country-western singer Hank Williams. Does a straightforward job of telling the public and private story of the country boy who rose to stardom, suffered career setbacks, and died before he was thirty. Tunes associated with the singer are mouthed by Hamilton in excellent fashion, and recorded for the soundtrack by Hank Williams, Jr. (Dir: Gene Nelson, 100 mins.)

Your Money or Your Wife (1972)*½ Ted Bessell, Elizabeth Ashley, Jack Cassidy. Out-of-work TV writer concocts a kidnapping plot and is talked into using his game plan on a nasty TV performer. Credibility takes a beating and so will you. Made-for-TV. (Dir: Allen Reisner, 73 mins.)

Your Past Is Showing (British, 1958) ***½ Terry-Thomas, Peter Sellers. Victims of a hated gossip writer band together to eliminate him, but their plans misfire. Often hilariously funny farce, contains many laughs. (Dir: Mario Zampi, 87 mins.)

Your Shadow Is Mine (Franco-Ital-

ian, 1962)*½ Jill Haworth, Michel Ruhl. Orphan girl raised by a family in a Cambodian village has her peaceful life shattered when she is found by her family after a long search. Mawkish, slow-moving drama dubbed in English.

Your Turn, Darling (French, 1963) *½ Eddie Constantine. Eddie Constantine, once again portraying F.B.I. agent Lemmy Caution, two-fists his way through another fast-paced Grade B crime film with all the predictable plot twists. This time, he cracks a kidnaping ring. English-dubbed. (Dir: Bernard Borderie, 93 mins.)

You're a Big Boy Now (1967)*** Peter Kastner, Elizabeth Hartman, Geraldine Page, Julie Harris. A fast-paced, often inventive comedy about a contemporary youth (Kastner) who is on the brink of becoming an adult. His escapade with a man-hating go-go dancer, well played by Elizabeth Hartman, leads to some wildly funny scenes, and a better-than-average supporting cast offers larger-than-life portraits of zany characters. It's not all flawless but it's high-spirited and imaginative. Impressive directorial debut for young (twenty-seven) Francis Ford Coppola, who also wrote this screenplay. (96 mins.)

You're in the Army Now (1941)**½ Jimmy Durante, Phil Silvers, Jane Wyman. You'll watch it anyway just to see Phil and Jimmy but don't expect miracles from this frail comedy about two vacuum cleaner salesmen who get into the Army by mistake. (Dir: Lewis Seiler, 79 mins.)

You're in the Navy Now (1951)** Gary Cooper, Jane Greer, Eddie Albert. Another awkward attempt at trying to make the war funny. A group of misfits led by Cooper (a green officer) are chosen to experiment with a craft outfitted with a steam turbine instead of the conventional diesel engine. The results are supposed to be uproariously funny. (Dir: Henry Hathaway, 93 mins.)

You're My Everything (1949)*** Dan Dailey, Anne Baxter, Shari Robinson. When this film is poking fun at the Hollywood heyday of the 30's, it borders on being great, but when it reverts to the cornball sentiment of the tragic backstage life of the stars, it is only average entertainment. Plenty of songs and dances by Dailey and a Shirley Temple-type moppet, Shari Robinson. (Dir: Walter Lang, 94 mins.)

You're Never Too Young (1955)** Dean Martin, Jerry Lewis, Diana Lynn, Raymond Burr. Jerry as a whacky barber who is forced to pose as a child, with a thief and murderer on his trail. Reworking of "The Major and the Minor" to suit the talents of Martin & Lewis furnishes some laughs but is stretched out; not one of the team's better comedies. (Dir: Norman Taurog, 102 mins.)

You're Only Young Once (1937)**½ Lewis Stone, Mickey Rooney. First in the Stone-Rooney group and a good example of wholesome family comedy which made the Hardy series so popular. (Dir: George B. Seitz, 80 mins.)

You're Telling Me (1934)**** W. C. Fields. The "master" appears in almost every hilarious scene of this film and he, and you, have a field day. He's an inventor and you'll hurt your sides laughing at the inventions. (Dir: Erle C. Kenton, 70 mins.)

Yours, Mine and Ours (1968)** Henry Fonda, Lucille Ball. You have to love Lucille Ball and Henry Fonda in order to tolerate this farce which has Lucy playing a widow with 8 kids who marries widower Fonda, who has 10 offspring. The result—bedlam, TV-series-style. If your kids aren't very sophisticated they may enjoy this sugar-coated candy. (Dir: Melville Shavelson, 111 mins.)

Yuma (1971)*½ Clint Walker, Barry Sullivan. That tree of a man, Clint Walker, rides again in a western packed with traditional ingredients. Walker is a cool, unflustered new sheriff who tames a wild town. Filmed in Arizona and Mexico, the backgrounds offer a picturesque outdoor setting for big wooden Clint. More TV pap. (Dir: Ted Post, 73 mins.)

Z (French-Algerian, 1968)**** Yves Montand, Irene Papas, Jean-Louis Trintignant. Marvelous political film. Based on the killing of a peace movement leader in Greece in 1963, the subsequent investigation which uncovered a right-wing terrorist organization with government connections, and the final military coup which destroyed democracy. Put in the frame of a thriller, this is not only fine social protest, but exciting moviemaking as well. Acting is fine, especially the subdued performance of Trintignant as the government investigator. (Dir: Costa-Gavras, 127 mins.)

Zabriskie Point (1970)* Mark Frechette, Daria Halprin, Rod Taylor, Kathleen Cleaver. A jumbled disaster from the hugely talented Antonioni. Another essay about desolation and alienation, and it's entirely appropriate that one of the locations used, in this, Antonioni's first feature shot in America, is Death Valley. One of the many mistakes made by Antonioni was the casting of a non-professional actor, Frechette, to play the role of Mark, a young radical. Frechette is so embarrassingly wooden and inept that the audience, after a while, simply doesn't care about an occasionally stunning image or moment elsewhere in the picture. Some extraordinary photography by Alfio Contini. Many writers worked on the screenplay, inspired by an Arizona newspaper story, including Antonioni himself and playwright Sam Shepard. (Dir: Michelangelo Antonioni, 110 mins.)

Zarak (1957)** Victor Mature, Michael Wilding, Anita Ekberg. Vic becomes an outlaw leader when he's driven from his village, with the British on his trail. Standard adventure opus, with Ekberg looking dazzling but adding little to the plot. (Dir: Terence Young, 100 mins.)

Zebra in the Kitchen (1965)**½ Jay North, Marshall Thompson. If this title intrigues you, you'll find out how it was derived in the final half of this Ivan Tors family movie about an animal-loving lad and his adventures. Jay North stars as the boy who causes an uproar when he frees all the animals from a zoo, including his recently captured pet mountain lion. The animals are the scene stealers here and the kids will enjoy their antics. (Dir: Ivan Tors, 93 mins.)

Zeppelin (Great Britain, 1971)** Michael York, Elke Sommer. A rather ridiculous World War I adventure-spy epic which relies on super heroics and a big dirigible which is used in a mission to obtain valuable English documents and thereby destroy

British morale. Michael York is surprisingly stiff and Elke Sommer is merely decorative. Good aerial sequences. Okay for kids. (Dir: Etienne Perier, 101 mins.)

Zero Hour (1957)** Dana Andrews, Linda Darnell, Sterling Hayden. Predictable tale about a man who was a fighter pilot (World War II). Dana Andrews strikes the right note as the troubled ex-pilot. (Dir: Hall Bartlett, 81 mins.)

Ziegfeld Follies (1945)***½ Fred Astaire, Lucille Ball, Lucille Bremer. You'll miss movie screen scope but this Follies imitation has a specialty number by everyone at MGM and is certainly better than most TV spectaculars. (Dir: Vincente Minnelli, 110 mins.)

Ziegfeld Girl (1940)**½ James Stewart, Judy Garland, Hedy Lamarr, Lana Turner. Lavish musical about the girls who were glorified by Ziegfeld is generally routine musical entertainment boasting a lot of attractive stars. (Dir: Robert Z. Leonard, 131 mins.)

Zigzag (1970)**½ George Kennedy, Anne Jackson, Eli Wallach. Another variation on a murder-for-insurance theme has Kennedy as a terminally ill man who frames himself for a murder to get insurance for his wife. Performances are fine, and especially good is Wallach playing Kennedy's Italian defense lawyer who knows it's a frame, but can't figure out who's doing it and why. (Dir: Richard J. Colla, 104 mins.)

Zita (France, 1968)*** Joanna Shimkus, Katina Paxinou, Jose Maria Flotats. Unusual, appealing film, about a young girl maturing after the double experiences of a loved aunt's death and her own first tastes of love and different sorts of living. Masterfully photographed, with some intriguing scenes of Paris after dark. Well-acted, though the pace slackens at times. (Dir: Robert Enrico, 92 mins.)

Zombies of Mora Tau (1957)*½ Gregg Palmer, Allison Hayes. Another inept horror film with the actors taking the whole thing very seriously. A small group starts on an expedition for sunken treasure but are thwarted by legends of zombies coupled with some strange occur-

rences. (Dir: Edward L. Cahn, 70 mins.)

Zorba the Greek (1965)**** Anthony Quinn, Irene Papas, Alan Bates. A marvelous rousing drama set in Crete about a lusty individualist determined to give his own life, free of any restrictions imposed upon him by an unyielding and unchanging Greek society. Boasts a particularly noteworthy performance from Quinn, whose magnetism and vitality are perfectly suited to portray this full-blooded, passionate Greek prototype. Miss Papas is memorable playing a young widow in a tiny Greek village, and director Michael Cacoyannis captures the mood and brooding spirit of the peasants and villagers in such communities. Lila Kedrova won an Oscar for her supporting performance of a pitiful, aging courtesan who dwells in the past. (Dir: Michael Cacoyannis, 146 mins.)

Zorikan the Barbarian (Italian, 1960) * Dan Vadis, Walter Brandi. Barbarian hordes attack Christians at the time of the Crusades, but a fighting soldier of fortune turns the tide. Poor costume action drama. Dubbed in English.

Zorro, the Avenger (Spanish, 1963) *½ Frank Latimore, Maria Luz Galicia. The masked avenger rides to save the innocent from injustice. Low-grade dubbed-English swashbuckling on horseback.

Zotz! (1962)** Tom Poston, Julia Meade, Jim Backus, Fred Clark. Professor finds an old coin with the magical power to make people move in slow motion, becomes a target for spies after the coin. Moderate comedy doesn't have the sparkle necessary to bring it off. (Dir: William Castle, 87 mins.)

Zulu (British, 1964)*** Stanley Baker, Jack Hawkins, James Booth, Michael Caine. An exciting adventure based on a real-life incident in African history, the massacre in 1879 of a British mission by Zulu warriors. The events leading to the epic battle are depicted in personal terms involving a missionary, his daughter, the mission's commander and his men. The cast is excellent, but the battle sequence is the real star of the film. (Dir. and co-author: Cy Endfield, 138 mins.)

ABOUT THE AUTHOR

Steven H. Scheuer is the editor and publisher of TV KEY, the most widely syndicated TV service in America, appearing daily in over 200 newspapers. Mr. Scheuer, who conceived the idea of previewing television shows, is the author of several critically acclaimed books, **Movies on TV,** and **The Movie Book,** a pictorial history of world cinema.

He is the executive producer and moderator of the weekly award-winning series carried on public television stations, "All About TV," the only TV program which candidly discusses television itself. Mr. Scheuer also broadcasts daily TV previews and commentary on commercial radio stations throughout the country, including WQXR in New York City.

The fifty-one-year-old Mr. Scheuer is a native New Yorker and a graduate of the Ethical Culture Schools in New York City. During the Second World War, Mr. Scheuer served as a supply officer in the U.S. Navy, serving in the Orient. Mr. Scheuer graduated from Yale University in 1948, and has done graduate work at the London School of Economics and Political Science, Columbia University, and New York University.

Mr. Scheuer is widely considered by many people in the TV industry to be the most knowledgeable TV critic in America. **Time** magazine called Mr. Scheuer "the most influential TV critic." **Access Magazine,** published by the National Citizens Committee for Broadcasting, called Mr. Scheuer the best TV critic in the country reporting on questions of television and the public interest.

He is on the faculty of the New School for Social Research where he teaches a course in the history of American television. Mr. Scheuer is a member of the Communications Media Committee of the American Civil Liberties Union, and lectures regularly for college audiences and women's clubs throughout the country on all phases of American television. He has served as a trustee of International Film Seminars.

Mr. Scheuer participates in many sports, and is a nationally ranked squash tennis player.

Facts at Your Fingertips!

☐ MOVIES ON TV (1978-79 Revised Ed.)	11451	$2.95
☐ THE BANTAM BOOK OF CORRECT LETTER WRITING	11229	$1.95
☐ THE COMMON SENSE BOOK OF KITTEN AND CAT CARE	11226	$1.95
☐ AMY VANDERBILT'S EVERYDAY ETIQUETTE	11025	$2.25
☐ SOULE'S DICTIONARY OF ENGLISH SYNONYMS	11011	$1.75
☐ DICTIONARY OF CLASSICAL MYTHOLOGY	10960	$1.95
☐ THE BETTER HOMES AND GARDENS HANDYMAN BOOK	10852	$1.95
☐ THE BANTAM NEW COLLEGE SPANISH & ENGLISH DICTIONARY	10746	$1.75
☐ THE GUINNESS BOOK OF WORLD RECORDS 15th Ed.	10166	$2.25
☐ THE PLANT DOCTOR	7902	$1.75
☐ IT PAYS TO INCREASE YOUR WORD POWER	2991	$1.50
☐ THE MOTHER EARTH NEWS ALMANAC	2927	$2.25
☐ THE BANTAM NEW COLLEGE FRENCH & ENGLISH DICTIONARY	11692	$1.95
☐ THE COMMON SENSE BOOK OF PUPPY AND DOG CARE	2658	$1.50
☐ SEARCHING FOR YOUR ANCESTORS	7890	$1.95
☐ WRITING AND RESEARCHING TERM PAPERS	11529	$1.95

Ask for them at your local bookseller or use this handy coupon:

Bantam Books, Inc., Dept. RB, 414 East Golf Road, Des Plaines, Ill. 60016

Please send me the books I have checked above. I am enclosing $_____ (please add 50¢ to cover postage and handling). Send check or money order —no cash or C.O.D.'s please.

Mr/Mrs/Miss_____

Address_____

City _____ State/Zip_____

RB—12/77

Please allow four weeks for delivery. This offer expires 6/78.